Eighth International Joint Conference on Natural Language Processing (IJCNLP 2017)

Long Papers

Taipei, Taiwan
1 December 2017

Volume 1 of 2

ISBN: 978-1-5108-5292-1

Eighth International Joint Conference on Natural Language Processing (IJCNLP 2017)

Long Papers

Taipei, Taiwan
1 December 2017

Volume 1 of 2

IJCNLP 2017

The Eighth International Joint Conference on Natural Language Processing

Proceedings of the Conference, Vol. 1 (Long Papers)

November 27 - December 1, 2017
Taipei, Taiwan

Gold Sponsors:

TOP
邁向頂尖大學計畫
Aim for the Top University Project

元智大學
大數據與數位匯流創新中心
Innovation Center for Big Data and Digital Convergence

Silver Sponsors:

AIP
Center for
Advanced Intelligence Project

Cyberon

Wisers 慧科
Advantage through Intelligence

TenMax
騰 學 廣 告 科 技

htc

Bronze Sponsors:

中華電信研究院
Chunghwa Telecom Laboratories

小牛翻译
NiuTrans

Supporters:

科 技 部
Ministry of Science and Technology

BUREAU OF FOREIGN TRADE

TAIPEI
觀光傳播局
Department of Information and Tourism

YUAN ZE UNIVERSITY 1989

Preface

Welcome to the 8th International Joint Conference on Natural Language Processing (IJCNLP). IJCNLP was initiated in 2004 by the Asian Federation of Natural Language Processing (AFNLP) with the major goal to provide a platform for researchers and professionals around the world to share their experiences related to natural language processing and computational linguistics. In the past years, IJCNLPs were held in 7 different places: Hainan Island (2004), Jeju Island (2005), Hyderabad (2008), Singapore (2009), Chiang Mai (2011), Nagoya (2013) and Beijing (2015). This year the 8th IJCNLP is held in Taipei Nangang Exhibition Hall on November 27-December 1, 2017.

We are confident that you will find IJCNLP 2017 to be technically stimulating. The conference covers a broad spectrum of technical areas related to natural language processing and computation. Besides main conference, the program includes 3 keynote speeches, 6 tutorials, 17 demonstrations, 5 workshops, and 5 shared tasks (new event).

Before closing this brief welcome, we would like to thank the entire organizing committee for their long efforts to create and event that we hope will be memorable for you. Program chairs Greg Kondrak and Taro Watanabe coordinate the review process allowing for top quality papers to be presented at the conference. Workshop chairs Min Zhang and Yue Zhang organize 5 nice pre-conference and post-conference workshops. Tutorial chairs Sadao Kurohashi and Michael Strube select 6 very good tutorials. Demo chairs Seong-Bae Park and Thepchai Supnithi recommend 17 demonstrations. Shared Task chairs Chao-Hong Liu, Preslav Nakov and Nianwen Xue choose 5 interesting shared tasks. Sponsorship chairs Youngkil Kim, Tong Xiao, Kazuhide Yamamoto and Jui-Feng Yeh design sponsor packages and find financial supports. We thank all the sponsors. Publicity chairs Pushpak Bhattacharya, Xuanjing Huang, Gina-Anne Levow, Chi Mai Loung and Sebastian Stüker help circulate the conference information and promote the conference. We would like to express our special thanks to publication chairs Lung-Hao Lee and Derek F. Wong. After the hard work, they deliver an excellent proceeding to the participants.

Finally, we would like to thank all authors for submitting high quality research this year. We hope all of you enjoy the conference program, and your stay at this beautiful city of Taipei.

General Chair

Chengqing Zong, Institute of Automation, Chinese Academy of Sciences, China

Organization Co-Chairs

Hsin-Hsi Chen, National Taiwan University, Taiwan
Yuen-Hsien Tseng, National Taiwan Normal University, Taiwan
Chung-Hsien Wu, National Cheng Kung University, Taiwan
Liang-Chih Yu, Yuan Ze University, Taiwan

Message from the Program Co-Chairs

Welcome to the 8th International Joint Conference on Natural Language Processing (IJCNLP 2017) organized by National Taiwan Normal University and the Association for Computational Linguistics and Chinese Language Processing (ACLCLP) and hosted by The Asian Federation of Natural Language Processing (AFNLP).

Since the first meeting in 2004, IJCNLP has established itself as a major NLP conference. This year, we received 580 submissions (337 long and 243 short), which is by far the largest number ever for a stand-alone IJCNLP conference. From these, 179 papers (103 long and 76 short) were accepted to appear at the conference, which represents an acceptance rate of 31%. In particular, approximately 46% of the accepted papers are from Asia Pacific, 30% from North America, and 20% from Europe.

Our objective is to keep the conference to three parallel sessions at any one time. 86 long papers and 21 short papers are scheduled as oral presentations, while 17 long papers and 55 short papers will be presented as posters.

We are also very pleased to announce three exciting keynote talks by the renowned NLP researchers: Rada Mihalcea (University of Michigan), Trevor Cohn (University of Melbourne) and Jason Eisner (Johns Hopkins University).

The conference will conclude with the award presentation ceremony. The Best Paper Award goes to Nikolaos Pappas and Andrei Popescu-Belis for their paper "Multilingual Hierarchical Attention Networks for Document Classification." The Best Student Paper award goes to "Roles and Success in Wikipedia Talk Pages: Identifying Latent Patterns of Behavior" by Keith Maki, Michael Yoder, Yohan Jo and Carolyn Rosé.

We would like to thank everyone who has helped make IJCNLP 2017 a success. In particular, the area chairs (who are listed in the Program Committee section) worked hard on recruiting reviewers, managing reviews, leading discussions, and making recommendations. The quality of the technical program reflects the expertise of our 536 reviewers. All submissions were reviewed by at least three reviewers. The review process for the conference was double-blind, and included an author response period, as well as subsequent discussions.

We would like to acknowledge the help and advice from the General Chair Chengqing Zong, and the Local Arrangements Committee headed by Liang-Chih Yu. We thank the Publication Chairs Lung-Hao Lee and Derek F. Wong for putting together the conference proceedings and handbook, and all the other committee chairs for their great work.

We hope you will enjoy IJCNLP 2017!

IJCNLP 2017 Program Co-Chairs

Greg Kondrak, University of Alberta
Taro Watanabe, Google

Organizing Committee

Conference Chair

Chengqing Zong, Institute of Automation, Chinese Academy of Sciences

Program Committee Co-Chairs

Greg Kondrak, University of Alberta
Taro Watanabe, Google

Workshop Co-Chairs

Min Zhang, Soochow University
Yue Zhang, Singapore University of Technology and Design

Tutorial Co-Chairs

Sadao Kurohashi, Kyoto University
Michael Strube, Heidelberg Institute for Theoretical Studies

Demo Co-Chairs

Seong-Bae Park, Kyungpook National University
Thepchai Supnithi, National Electronics and Computer Technology Center (NECTEC) of Thailand

Shared Task Workshop Co-Chairs

Chao-Hong Liu, ADAPT Centre, Dublin City University
Preslav Nakov, Qatar Computing Research Institute
Nianwen Xue, Brandies University

Publication Co-Chairs

Lung-Hao Lee, National Taiwan Normal University
Derek F. Wong, University of Macau

Sponsorship Co-Chairs

Youngkil Kim, ETRI
Tong Xiao, Northeast University
Kazuhide Yamamoto, Nagaoka University of Technology
Jui-Feng Yeh, National Chiayi University

Publicity Co-Chairs

Pushpak Bhattacharya, IITB
Xuanjing Huang, Fudan University
Gina-Anne Levow, University of Washington
Chi Mai Loung, Institute of Information Technology
Sebastian Stüker, Karlsruhe Institute of Technology

Financial Chair

Lun-Wei Ku, Institute of Information Sciences, Academia Sinica

Local Co-Chairs

Hsin-Hsi Chen, National Taiwan University
Yuen-Hsien Tseng, National Taiwan Normal University
Chung-Hsien Wu, National Cheng Kung University
Liang-Chih Yu, Yuan Ze University

Program Committee

Program Committee Co-Chairs

Greg Kondrak, University of Alberta
Taro Watanabe, Google

Area Chairs

Mausam (Information Extraction and Text Mining Area)
Asli Celikyilmaz (Semantics Area)
Wenliang Chen (Syntax and Parsing Area)
Colin Cherry (Machine Translation Area)
Jackie Chi Kit Cheung (Summarization and Generation Area)
Monojit Choudhury (Resources and Tools Area)
Kevin Duh (Semantics Area)
Micha Elsner (Discourse, Dialogue, Pragmatics Area)
Manaal Faruqui (Machine Learning Area)
Jianfeng Gao (Information Retrieval and Question Answering Area)
Yvette Graham (Machine Translation Area)
Gholamreza Haffari (Machine Learning Area)
Liang Huang (Syntax and Parsing Area)
Minlie Huang (Sentiment Analysis and Opinion Mining Area)
Mans Hulden (Morphology, Segmentation and Tagging Area)
Nancy Ide (Resources and Tools Area)
Jing Jiang (Sentiment Analysis and Opinion Mining Area)
Daisuke Kawahara (Semantics Area)
Mamoru Komachi (NLP Applications Area)
Fei Liu (Web and Social Media Area)
Zhiyuan Liu (Web and Social Media Area)
Wei Lu (Information Extraction and Text Mining Area)
Ryo Nagata (NLP Applications Area) Mikio Nakano (Discourse, Dialogue, Pragmatics Area)
Jong-Hoon Oh (Information Retrieval and Question Answering Area)
Thamar Solorio (Sentiment Analysis and Opinion Mining Area)
Xu Sun (Morphology, Segmentation and Tagging Area)
Jun Suzuki (Machine Learning Area)
Xiaojun Wan (Summarization and Generation Area)
Tiejun Zhao (Machine Translation Area)

Reviewers

Ahmed Abbasi, Željko Agić, Alan Akbik, Chris Alberti, Enrique Alfonseca, David Alvarez-Melis, Silvio Amir, Daniel Andrade, Marianna Apidianaki, Jun Araki, Yuki Arase, Yoav Artzi, Kristjan Arumae, Wilker Aziz

Alexandra Balahur, Niranjan Balasubramanian, Timothy Baldwin, Kalika Bali, Miguel Ballesteros, Rafael E. Banchs, Srinivas Bangalore, Clayton Barham, Roberto Basili, Timo Baumann, Kedar Bellare, Anja Belz, Steven Bethard, Chandra Bhagavatula, Suma Bhat, Joachim Bingel, Or Biran, Yonatan Bisk, Johannes Bjerva, Frédéric Blain, Dasha Bogdanova, Bernd Bohnet, Danushka Bollegala, Antoine Bosselut, Florian Boudin, Pavel Braslavski, Chris Brockett, Julian Brooke, William Bryce, Paul Buitelaar, Jill Burstein, Stephan Busemann, Miriam Butt

José G. C. de Souza, Deng Cai, Burcu Can, Ziqiang Cao, Yuan Cao, Vittorio Castelli, Daniel Cer,

Mauro Cettolo, Ming-Wei Chang, Baobao Chang, Kai-Wei Chang, Wanxiang Che, Xinchi Chen, Tao Chen, John Chen, Danqi Chen, Boxing Chen, Kuang-hua Chen, Colin Cherry, David Chiang, Hai Leong Chieu, laura chiticariu, KEY-SUN CHOI, Shamil Chollampatt, Monojit Choudhury, Christos Christodoulopoulos, Jennifer Chu-Carroll, Miriam Connor, John Conroy, Matthieu Constant, Danish Contractor, Anna Corazza, Mark Core, Benoit Crabbé, Danilo Croce, Paul Crook, Heriberto Cuayahuitl

bharath dandala, Kareem Darwish, Gerard de Melo, Luciano Del Corro, Leon Derczynski, Nina Dethlefs, Lipika Dey, Bhuwan Dhingra, Giuseppe Di Fabbrizio, Marco Dinarelli, Daxiang Dong, Li Dong, Doug Downey, Lan Du, Xiangyu Duan, Nadir Durrani

Richard Eckart de Castilho, Steffen Eger, Yo Ehara, Patrick Ehlen, Vladimir Eidelman, Akiko Eriguchi, Tomaž Erjavec, Ramy Eskander, Miquel Esplà-Gomis

Licheng Fang, Atefeh Farzindar, Geli Fei, Anna Feldman, Chong Feng, Oliver Ferschke, Andrew Finch, Orhan Firat, Margaret Fleck, Markus Forsberg, George Foster, Dayne Freitag, Atsushi Fujii, Fumiyo Fukumoto, Kotaro Funakoshi

Björn Gambäck, Michael Gamon, Matt Gardner, Tao Ge, Kallirroi Georgila, Pablo Gervás, Saptarshi Ghosh, Alfio Gliozzo, Dan Goldwasser, Carlos Gómez-Rodríguez, Kyle Gorman, Isao Goto, Yvette Graham, Spence Green, Jiatao Gu, Camille Guinaudeau

Thanh-Le Ha, Barry Haddow, Christian Hadiwinoto, Masato Hagiwara, Dilek Hakkani-Tur, Keith Hall, William L. Hamilton, Xianpei Han, Chung-Wei Hang, Kazi Saidul Hasan, Sadid A. Hasan, Kazuma Hashimoto, Eva Hasler, Matthew Hatem, Luheng He, John Henderson, Matthew Henderson, Aurélie Herbelot, Daniel Hershcovich, Ryuichiro Higashinaka, Cong Duy Vu Hoang, Chris Hokamp, Yu Hong, Kai Hong, Ales Horak, Baotian Hu, Ruihong Huang, Po-Sen Huang, Jen-Wei Huang, Zhongqiang Huang

Kenji Imamura, Michimasa Inaba, Kentaro Inui, Hitoshi Isahara

Donghong JI, Yangfeng Ji, Sittichai Jiampojamarn, Wenbin Jiang, Zhanming Jie, Melvin Johnson Premkumar

Nobuhiro Kaji, Tomoyuki Kajiwara, Hidetaka Kamigaito, Hung-Yu Kao, Arzoo Katiyar, David Kauchak, Anna Kazantseva, Hideto Kazawa, Casey Kennington, Jung-Jae Kim, Sunghwan Mac Kim, Norihide Kitaoka, Julien Kloetzer, Philipp Koehn, Mamoru Komachi, Kazunori Komatani, Parisa Kordjamshidi, Zornitsa Kozareva, Julia Kreutzer, Jayant Krishnamurthy, Lun-Wei Ku, Shankar Kumar, Jonathan K. Kummerfeld, Tsung-Ting Kuo

Sobha Lalitha Devi, Wai Lam, Man Lan, Ni Lao, Guy Lapalme, Carolin Lawrence, Joseph Le Roux, Logan Lebanoff, Kenton Lee, Hung-yi Lee, Sungjin Lee, John Lee, Lung-Hao Lee, Els Lefever, Gina-Anne Levow, Binyang Li, Junhui Li, Shaohua Li, Haibo Li, Yaliang Li, Lishuang Li, Zhenghua Li, Hang Li, Sujian Li, Qing Li, Haizhou Li, Sheng Li, Cheng-Te Li, Chenliang Li, Kexin Liao, Shou-de Lin, Xiao Ling, Pierre Lison, Xiaodong Liu, Shujie Liu, Pengfei Liu, Shulin Liu, Yang Liu, Qun Liu, Jiangming Liu, Yang Liu, Lemao Liu, Nikola Ljubešić, Chi-kiu Lo, Oier Lopez de Lacalle, Annie Louis, Wen-Hsiang Lu, Stephanie Lukin, Jiaming Luo, Franco M. Luque, Anh Tuan Luu

Wei-Yun Ma, Ji Ma, Xuezhe Ma, Wolfgang Macherey, Suraj Maharjan, Andreas Maletti, Benjamin Marie, Héctor Martínez Alonso, Yuichiroh Matsubayashi, Yuji Matsumoto, Takuya Matsuzaki, Diana McCarthy, Tara McIntosh, Susan McRoy, Sameep Mehta, Edgar Meij, Arul Menezes, Helen Meng, Adam Meyers, Bonan Min, Koji Mineshima, Amita Misra, Teruhisa Misu, Makoto Miwa, Daichi Mochihashi, Marie-Francine Moens, Samaneh Moghaddam, Karo Moilanen, Luis Gerardo Mojica de la Vega, Manuel Montes, Taesun Moon, Glyn Morrill, Alessandro Moschitti, Lili Mou, Aldrian Obaja Muis, Yugo Murawaki

Seung-Hoon Na, Tetsuji Nakagawa, Preslav Nakov, Courtney Napoles, Jason Naradowsky, Shashi Narayan, Alexis Nasr, Mark-Jan Nederhof, Graham Neubig, Guenter Neumann, Vincent Ng, Dong Nguyen, Jian-Yun NIE, Hiroshi Noji, Scott Nowson

Diarmuid Ó Séaghdha, Yusuke Oda, Stephan Oepen, Tim O'Gorman, Jong-Hoon Oh, Kiyonori Ohtake, Hidekazu Oiwa, Naoaki Okazaki, Manabu Okumura, Naho Orita, Petya Osenova, Hiroki

Ouchi

Inkit Padhi, Sebastian Padó, Hamid Palangi, Aasish Pappu, Peyman Passban, Adam Pease, Nanyun Peng, Gerald Penn, Juan Antonio Pérez-Ortiz, Verónica Pérez-Rosas, Karl Pichotta, Massimo Poesio, Octavian Popescu, Maja Popović, Daniel Preoţiuc-Pietro, Matthew Purver

Ashequl Qadir, Haoliang Qi, Xian Qian

Afshin Rahimi, Altaf Rahman, A Ramanathan, Sudha Rao, Pushpendre Rastogi, Georg Rehm, Martin Riedl, German Rigau, Brian Roark, Michael Roth, Alla Rozovskaya, Rachel Rudinger, Delia Rusu, Attapol Rutherford

Ashish Sabharwal, Kugatsu Sadamitsu, Markus Saers, Kenji Sagae, Rishiraj Saha Roy, Saurav Sahay, Keisuke Sakaguchi, Germán Sanchis-Trilles, Ryohei Sasano, Carolina Scarton, David Schlangen, Eva Schlinger, Allen Schmaltz, Sebastian Schuster, Djamé Seddah, Satoshi Sekine, Lei Sha, Kashif Shah, Rajiv Shah, Ehsan Shareghi, Shiqi Shen, Shuming Shi, Tomohide Shibata, Prasha Shrestha, Maryam Siahbani, Miikka Silfverberg, Patrick Simianer, Sameer Singh, Sunayana Sitaram, Pavel Smrz, Jan Šnajder, Yang Song, Wei Song, Hyun-Je Song, Sa-kwang Song, Matthias Sperber, Caroline Sporleder, Vivek Srikumar, Gabriel Stanovsky, Manfred Stede, Mark Steedman, Pontus Stenetorp, Svetlana Stoyanchev, Karl Stratos, Kristina Striegnitz, jinsong su, L V Subramaniam, Katsuhito Sudoh, Hiroaki Sugiyama, Md Arafat Sultan, Weiwei Sun, Huan Sun, Yui Suzuki

Sho Takase, David Talbot, Aleš Tamchyna, Liling Tan, Niket Tandon, Jiliang Tang, Duyu Tang, Takehiro Tazoe, Christoph Teichmann, Joel Tetreault, Ran Tian, Takenobu Tokunaga, Gaurav Singh Tomar, Sara Tonelli, Fatemeh Torabi Asr, Ming-Feng Tsai, Richard Tzong-Han Tsai, Masashi Tsubaki, Jun'ichi Tsujii, Yulia Tsvetkov, Zhaopeng Tu, Cunchao Tu, Gokhan Tur, Francis Tyers

Kiyotaka Uchimoto, Masao Utiyama

Tim Van de Cruys, Keith VanderLinden, Lucy Vanderwende, Vasudeva Varma, Eva Maria Vecchi, sriram venkatapathy, Marc Verhagen, David Vilar, David Vilares, Martin Villalba, Esau Villatoro-Tello, Svitlana Volkova, Ivan Vulić

Rui Wang, Baoxun Wang, Shuohang Wang, Xuancong Wang, Longyue Wang, Pidong Wang, Hsin-Min Wang, suge wang, Dingquan Wang, Wei Wang, Mingxuan Wang, William Yang Wang, Leo Wanner, Bonnie Webber, Ingmar Weber, Julie Weeds, Furu Wei, Aaron Steven White, Jason D Williams, Tak-Lam Wong, Kam-Fai Wong, Derek F. Wong, Dekai Wu, Fangzhao Wu, Shih-Hung Wu, Joern Wuebker

Fei Xia, Xinyan Xiao, Tong Xiao, Deyi Xiong, Wenduan Xu, Ying Xu, Feiyu Xu, Ruifeng Xu

Yi Yang, Cheng Yang, Bishan Yang, Helen Yannakoudakis, Jin-ge Yao, Wenpeng Yin, Anssi Yli-Jyrä, Naoki Yoshinaga, Koichiro Yoshino, Bei Yu, Dianhai Yu, Mo Yu, Jianfei Yu, Frances Yung

Fabio Massimo Zanzotto, Sina Zarrieß, Xiaodong Zeng, Feifei Zhai, Min Zhang, Sheng Zhang, Jian ZHANG, Jiajun Zhang, Chengzhi Zhang, Meishan Zhang, Zhisong Zhang, Longtu Zhang, Meishan Zhang, Jian Zhang, Zhe Zhang, Wei-Nan Zhang, Qi Zhang, Hao Zhang, Yu Zhang, Dongdong Zhang, Lei Zhang, Dongyan Zhao, Jun Zhao, Hai Zhao, Li Zhao, Alisa Zhila, Guangyou Zhou, Xiaoning Zhu, Muhua Zhu, Heike Zinsmeister, Pierre Zweigenbaum

Invited Talk: Words and People

Rada Mihalcea

University of Michigan

Abstract

What do the words we use say about us and about how we view the world surrounding us? And what do we - as speakers of those words with our own defining attributes, imply about the words we utter? In this talk, I will explore the relation between words and people and show how we can develop cross-cultural word models to identify words with cultural bias – i.e., words that are used in significantly different ways by speakers from different cultures. Further, I will also show how we can effectively use information about the speakers of a word (i.e., their gender, culture) to build better word models.

Biography

Rada Mihalcea is a Professor in the Computer Science and Engineering department at the University of Michigan. Her research interests are in computational linguistics, with a focus on lexical semantics, multilingual natural language processing, and computational social sciences. She serves or has served on the editorial boards of the Journals of Computational Linguistics, Language Resources and Evaluations, Natural Language Engineering, Research in Language in Computation, IEEE Transactions on Affective Computing, and Transactions of the Association for Computational Linguistics. She was a program co-chair for the Conference of the Association for Computational Linguistics (2011) and the Conference on Empirical Methods in Natural Language Processing (2009), and a general chair for the Conference of the North American Chapter of the Association for Computational Linguistics (2015). She is the recipient of a National Science Foundation CAREER award (2008) and a Presidential Early Career Award for Scientists and Engineers awarded by President Obama (2009). In 2013, she was made an honorary citizen of her hometown of Cluj-Napoca, Romania.

Invited Talk: Learning Large and Small: How to Transfer NLP Successes to Low-resource Languages

Trevor Cohn

University of Melbourne

Abstract

Recent advances in NLP have predominantly been based upon supervised learning over large corpora, where rich expressive models, such as deep learning methods, can perform exceptionally well. However, these state of the art approaches tend to be very data hungry, and consequently do not elegantly scale down to smaller corpora, which are more typical in many NLP applications.

In this talk, I will describe the importance of small data in our field, drawing particular attention to so-called "low-" or "under-resourced" languages, for which corpora are scarce, and linguistic annotations scarcer yet. One of the key problems for our field is how to translate successes on the few high-resource languages to practical technologies for the remaining majority of the world's languages. I will cover several research problems in this space, including transfer learning between high- and low-resource languages, active learning for selecting text for annotation, and speech processing in a low-resource setting, namely learning to translate audio inputs without transcriptions. I will finish by discussing open problems in natural language processing that will be critical in porting highly successful NLP work to the myriad of less-well-studied languages.

Biography

Trevor Cohn is an Associate Professor and ARC Future Fellow at the University of Melbourne, in the School of Computing and Information Systems. He received Bachelor degrees in Software Engineering and Commerce, and a PhD degree in Engineering from the University of Melbourne. He was previously based at the University of Sheffield, and before this worked as a Research Fellow at the University of Edinburgh. His research interests focus on probabilistic and statistical machine learning for natural language processing, with applications in several areas including machine translation, parsing and grammar induction. Current projects include translating diverse and noisy text sources, deep learning of semantics in translation, rumour diffusion over social media, and algorithmic approaches for scaling to massive corpora. Dr. Cohn's research has been recognised by several best paper awards, including best short paper at EMNLP in 2016. He will be jointly organising ACL 2018 in Melbourne.

Invited Talk: Strategies for Discovering Underlying Linguistic Structure

Jason Eisner

Johns Hopkins University

Abstract

A goal of computational linguistics is to automate the kind of reasoning that linguists do. Given text in a new language, can we determine the underlying morphemes and the grammar rules that arrange and modify them?

The Bayesian strategy is to devise a joint probabilistic model that is capable of generating the descriptions of new languages. Given data from a particular new language, we can then seek explanatory descriptions that have high prior probability. This strategy leads to fascinating and successful algorithms in the case of morphology.

Yet the Bayesian approach has been less successful for syntax. It is limited in practice by our ability to (1) design accurate models and (2) solve the computational problem of posterior inference. I will demonstrate some remedies: build only a partial (conditional) model, and use synthetic data to train a neural network that simulates correct posterior inference.

Biography

Jason Eisner is Professor of Computer Science at Johns Hopkins University, where he is also affiliated with the Center for Language and Speech Processing, the Machine Learning Group, the Cognitive Science Department, and the national Center of Excellence in Human Language Technology. His goal is to develop the probabilistic modeling, inference, and learning techniques needed for a unified model of all kinds of linguistic structure. His 100+ papers have presented various algorithms for parsing, machine translation, and weighted finite-state machines; formalizations, algorithms, theorems, and empirical results in computational phonology; and unsupervised or semi-supervised learning methods for syntax, morphology, and word-sense disambiguation. He is also the lead designer of Dyna, a new declarative programming language that provides an infrastructure for AI research. He has received two school-wide awards for excellence in teaching.

Table of Contents

Evaluating Layers of Representation in Neural Machine Translation on Part-of-Speech and Semantic Tagging Tasks
Yonatan Belinkov, Lluís Màrquez, Hassan Sajjad, Nadir Durrani, Fahim Dalvi and James Glass . . 1

Context-Aware Smoothing for Neural Machine Translation
Kehai Chen, Rui Wang, Masao Utiyama, Eiichiro Sumita and Tiejun Zhao 11

Improving Sequence to Sequence Neural Machine Translation by Utilizing Syntactic Dependency Information
An Nguyen Le, Ander Martinez, Akifumi Yoshimoto and Yuji Matsumoto 21

What does Attention in Neural Machine Translation Pay Attention to?
Hamidreza Ghader and Christof Monz 30

Grammatical Error Detection Using Error- and Grammaticality-Specific Word Embeddings
Masahiro Kaneko, Yuya Sakaizawa and Mamoru Komachi 40

Dependency Parsing with Partial Annotations: An Empirical Comparison
Yue Zhang, Zhenghua Li, Jun Lang, Qingrong Xia and Min Zhang 49

Neural Probabilistic Model for Non-projective MST Parsing
Xuezhe Ma and Eduard Hovy 59

Word Ordering as Unsupervised Learning Towards Syntactically Plausible Word Representations
Noriki Nishida and Hideki Nakayama 70

MIPA: Mutual Information Based Paraphrase Acquisition via Bilingual Pivoting
Tomoyuki Kajiwara, Mamoru Komachi and Daichi Mochihashi 80

Improving Implicit Semantic Role Labeling by Predicting Semantic Frame Arguments
Quynh Ngoc Thi Do, Steven Bethard and Marie-Francine Moens 90

Natural Language Inference from Multiple Premises
Alice Lai, Yonatan Bisk and Julia Hockenmaier 100

Enabling Transitivity for Lexical Inference on Chinese Verbs Using Probabilistic Soft Logic
Wei-Chung Wang and Lun-Wei Ku 110

An Exploration of Neural Sequence-to-Sequence Architectures for Automatic Post-Editing
Marcin Junczys-Dowmunt and Roman Grundkiewicz 120

Imagination Improves Multimodal Translation
Desmond Elliott and Ákos Kádár 130

Understanding and Improving Morphological Learning in the Neural Machine Translation Decoder
Fahim Dalvi, Nadir Durrani, Hassan Sajjad, Yonatan Belinkov and Stephan Vogel 142

Improving Neural Machine Translation through Phrase-based Forced Decoding
Jingyi Zhang, Masao Utiyama, Eiichro Sumita, Graham Neubig and Satoshi Nakamura 152

Convolutional Neural Network with Word Embeddings for Chinese Word Segmentation
Chunqi Wang and Bo Xu 163

Character-based Joint Segmentation and POS Tagging for Chinese using Bidirectional RNN-CRF
Yan Shao, Christian Hardmeier, Jörg Tiedemann and Joakim Nivre 173

Addressing Domain Adaptation for Chinese Word Segmentation with Global Recurrent Structure
Shen Huang, Xu Sun and Houfeng Wang 184

Information Bottleneck Inspired Method For Chat Text Segmentation
S Vishal, Mohit Yadav, Lovekesh Vig and Gautam Shroff 194

Distributional Modeling on a Diet: One-shot Word Learning from Text Only
Su Wang, Stephen Roller and Katrin Erk 204

A Computational Study on Word Meanings and Their Distributed Representations via Polymodal Embedding
Joohee Park and Sung-Hyon Myaeng 214

Geographical Evaluation of Word Embeddings
Michal Konkol, Tomáš Brychcín, Michal Nykl and Tomáš Hercig 224

On Modeling Sense Relatedness in Multi-prototype Word Embedding
Yixin Cao, Jiaxin Shi, Juanzi Li, Zhiyuan Liu and Chengjiang Li 233

Unsupervised Segmentation of Phoneme Sequences based on Pitman-Yor Semi-Markov Model using Phoneme Length Context
Ryu Takeda and Kazunori Komatani 243

A Sensitivity Analysis of (and Practitioners' Guide to) Convolutional Neural Networks for Sentence Classification
Ye Zhang and Byron Wallace 253

Coordination Boundary Identification with Similarity and Replaceability
Hiroki Teranishi, Hiroyuki Shindo and Yuji Matsumoto 264

Turning Distributional Thesauri into Word Vectors for Synonym Extraction and Expansion
Olivier Ferret 273

Training Word Sense Embeddings With Lexicon-based Regularization
Luis Nieto Piña and Richard Johansson 284

Learning How to Simplify From Explicit Labeling of Complex-Simplified Text Pairs
Fernando Alva-Manchego, Joachim Bingel, Gustavo Paetzold, Carolina Scarton and Lucia Specia
295

Domain-Adaptable Hybrid Generation of RDF Entity Descriptions
Or Biran and Kathleen McKeown 306

ES-LDA: Entity Summarization using Knowledge-based Topic Modeling
Seyedamin Pouriyeh, Mehdi Allahyari, Krzysztof Kochut, Gong Cheng and Hamid Reza Arabnia
316

Procedural Text Generation from an Execution Video
Atsushi Ushiku, Hayato Hashimoto, Atsushi Hashimoto and Shinsuke Mori 326

Text Sentiment Analysis based on Fusion of Structural Information and Serialization Information
Ling Gan and Houyu Gong 336

Length, Interchangeability, and External Knowledge: Observations from Predicting Argument Convincingness
Peter Potash, Robin Bhattacharya and Anna Rumshisky 342

Exploiting Document Level Information to Improve Event Detection via Recurrent Neural Networks
Shaoyang Duan, Ruifang He and Wenli Zhao 352

Embracing Non-Traditional Linguistic Resources for Low-resource Language Name Tagging
Boliang Zhang, Di Lu, Xiaoman Pan, Ying Lin, Halidanmu Abudukelimu, Heng Ji and Kevin
Knight 362

NMT or SMT: Case Study of a Narrow-domain English-Latvian Post-editing Project
Inguna Skadiņa and Mārcis Pinnis 373

Towards Neural Machine Translation with Partially Aligned Corpora
Yining Wang, Yang Zhao, Jiajun Zhang, Chengqing Zong and Zhengshan Xue 384

Identifying Usage Expression Sentences in Consumer Product Reviews
Shibamouli Lahiri, V.G.Vinod Vydiswaran and Rada Mihalcea 394

Between Reading Time and Syntactic/Semantic Categories
Masayuki Asahara and Sachi Kato 404

WiNER: A Wikipedia Annotated Corpus for Named Entity Recognition
Abbas Ghaddar and Phillippe Langlais 413

Reusing Neural Speech Representations for Auditory Emotion Recognition
Egor Lakomkin, Cornelius Weber, Sven Magg and Stefan Wermter 423

Local Monotonic Attention Mechanism for End-to-End Speech And Language Processing
Andros Tjandra, Sakriani Sakti and Satoshi Nakamura 431

Attentive Language Models
Giancarlo Salton, Robert Ross and John Kelleher 441

Diachrony-aware Induction of Binary Latent Representations from Typological Features
Yugo Murawaki 451

Image-Grounded Conversations: Multimodal Context for Natural Question and Response Generation
Nasrin Mostafazadeh, Chris Brockett, Bill Dolan, Michel Galley, Jianfeng Gao, Georgios Spithourakis and Lucy Vanderwende 462

A Neural Language Model for Dynamically Representing the Meanings of Unknown Words and Entities in a Discourse
Sosuke Kobayashi, Naoaki Okazaki and Kentaro Inui 473

Using Explicit Discourse Connectives in Translation for Implicit Discourse Relation Classification
Wei Shi, Frances Yung, Raphael Rubino and Vera Demberg 484

Tag-Enhanced Tree-Structured Neural Networks for Implicit Discourse Relation Classification
Yizhong Wang, Sujian Li, Jingfeng Yang, Xu Sun and Houfeng Wang 496

Cross-Lingual Sentiment Analysis Without (Good) Translation
Mohamed Abdalla and Graeme Hirst 506

Implicit Syntactic Features for Target-dependent Sentiment Analysis
Yuze Gao, Yue Zhang and Tong Xiao 516

Graph Based Sentiment Aggregation using ConceptNet Ontology
Srikanth Tamilselvam, Seema Nagar, Abhijit Mishra and Kuntal Dey 525

Sentence Modeling with Deep Neural Architecture using Lexicon and Character Attention Mechanism for Sentiment Classification
Huy-Thanh Nguyen and Minh-Le Nguyen 536

Combining Lightly-Supervised Text Classification Models for Accurate Contextual Advertising
Yiping Jin, Dittaya Wanvarie and Phu Le 545

Capturing Long-range Contextual Dependencies with Memory-enhanced Conditional Random Fields
Fei Liu, Timothy Baldwin and Trevor Cohn 555

Named Entity Recognition with Stack Residual LSTM and Trainable Bias Decoding
Quan Tran, Andrew MacKinlay and Antonio Jimeno Yepes 566

Neuramanteau: A Neural Network Ensemble Model for Lexical Blends
Kollol Das and Shaona Ghosh 576

Leveraging Discourse Information Effectively for Authorship Attribution
Elisa Ferracane, Su Wang and Raymond Mooney 584

Lightly-Supervised Modeling of Argument Persuasiveness
Isaac Persing and Vincent Ng 594

Multi-Task Learning for Speaker-Role Adaptation in Neural Conversation Models
Yi Luan, Chris Brockett, Bill Dolan, Jianfeng Gao and Michel Galley .605

Chat Disentanglement: Identifying Semantic Reply Relationships with Random Forests and Recurrent Neural Networks
Shikib Mehri and Giuseppe Carenini 615

Towards Bootstrapping a Polarity Shifter Lexicon using Linguistic Features
Marc Schulder, Michael Wiegand, Josef Ruppenhofer and Benjamin Roth 624

Cascading Multiway Attentions for Document-level Sentiment Classification
Dehong Ma, Sujian Li, Xiaodong Zhang, Houfeng Wang and Xu Sun .634

An Ensemble Method with Sentiment Features and Clustering Support
Nguyen Huy Tien and Nguyen Minh Le 644

Leveraging Auxiliary Tasks for Document-Level Cross-Domain Sentiment Classification
Jianfei Yu and Jing Jiang 654

Measuring Semantic Relations between Human Activities
Steven Wilson and Rada Mihalcea 664

Learning Transferable Representation for Bilingual Relation Extraction via Convolutional Neural Networks
Bonan Min, Zhuolin Jiang, Marjorie Freedman and Ralph Weischedel .674

Bilingual Word Embeddings for Bilingual Terminology Extraction from Specialized Comparable Corpora
Amir Hazem and Emmanuel Morin 685

A Bambara Tonalization System for Word Sense Disambiguation Using Differential Coding, Segmentation and Edit Operation Filtering
Luigi (Yu-Cheng) Liu and Damien Nouvel 694

Joint Learning of Dialog Act Segmentation and Recognition in Spoken Dialog Using Neural Networks
Tianyu Zhao and Tatsuya Kawahara 704

Predicting Users' Negative Feedbacks in Multi-Turn Human-Computer Dialogues
Xin Wang, Jianan Wang, Yuanchao Liu, Xiaolong Wang, Zhuoran Wang and Baoxun Wang ...713

Finding Dominant User Utterances And System Responses in Conversations
Dhiraj Madan and Sachindra Joshi 723

End-to-End Task-Completion Neural Dialogue Systems
Xiujun Li, Yun-Nung Chen, Lihong Li, Jianfeng Gao and Asli Celikyilmaz 733

End-to-end Network for Twitter Geolocation Prediction and Hashing
Jey Han Lau, Lianhua Chi, Khoi-Nguyen Tran and Trevor Cohn 744

Assessing the Verifiability of Attributions in News Text
Edward Newell, Ariane Schang, Drew Margolin and Derek Ruths 754

Domain Adaptation from User-level Facebook Models to County-level Twitter Predictions
Daniel Rieman, Kokil Jaidka, H. Andrew Schwartz and Lyle Ungar 764

Recognizing Explicit and Implicit Hate Speech Using a Weakly Supervised Two-path Bootstrapping Approach
Lei Gao, Alexis Kuppersmith and Ruihong Huang 774

Estimating Reactions and Recommending Products with Generative Models of Reviews
Jianmo Ni, Zachary C. Lipton, Sharad Vikram and Julian McAuley 783

Summarizing Lengthy Questions
Tatsuya Ishigaki, Hiroya Takamura and Manabu Okumura 792

Concept-Map-Based Multi-Document Summarization using Concept Coreference Resolution and Global Importance Optimization
Tobias Falke, Christian M. Meyer and Iryna Gurevych 801

Abstractive Multi-document Summarization by Partial Tree Extraction, Recombination and Linearization
Litton J Kurisinkel, Yue Zhang and Vasudeva Varma 812

Event Argument Identification on Dependency Graphs with Bidirectional LSTMs
Alex Judea and Michael Strube 822

Selective Decoding for Cross-lingual Open Information Extraction
Sheng Zhang, Kevin Duh and Benjamin Van Durme 832

Event Ordering with a Generalized Model for Sieve Prediction Ranking
Bill McDowell, Nathanael Chambers, Alexander Ororbia II and David Reitter 843

Open Relation Extraction and Grounding
Dian Yu, Lifu Huang and Heng Ji 854

Extraction of Gene-Environment Interaction from the Biomedical Literature
Jinseon You, Jin-Woo Chung, Wonsuk Yang and Jong C. Park 865

Course Concept Extraction in MOOCs via Embedding-Based Graph Propagation
Liangming Pan, Xiaochen Wang, Chengjiang Li, Juanzi Li and Jie Tang 875

Identity Deception Detection
Verónica Pérez-Rosas, Quincy Davenport, Anna Mengdan Dai, Mohamed Abouelenien and Rada
Mihalcea 885

Learning to Diagnose: Assimilating Clinical Narratives using Deep Reinforcement Learning
Yuan Ling, Sadid A. Hasan, Vivek Datla, Ashequl Qadir, Kathy Lee, Joey Liu and Oladimeji Farri
895

Dataset for a Neural Natural Language Interface for Databases (NNLIDB)
Florin Brad, Radu Cristian Alexandru Iacob, Ionel Alexandru Hosu and Traian Rebedea 906

*Acquisition and Assessment of Semantic Content for the Generation of Elaborateness and Indirectness
in Spoken Dialogue Systems*
Louisa Pragst, Koichiro Yoshino, Wolfgang Minker, Satoshi Nakamura and Stefan Ultes 915

Demographic Word Embeddings for Racism Detection on Twitter
Mohammed Hasanuzzaman, Gaël Dias and Andy Way 926

Automatically Extracting Variant-Normalization Pairs for Japanese Text Normalization
Itsumi Saito, Kyosuke Nishida, Kugatsu Sadamitsu, Kuniko Saito and Junji Tomita 937

Semantic Document Distance Measures and Unsupervised Document Revision Detection
Xiaofeng Zhu, Diego Klabjan and Patrick Bless 947

An Empirical Analysis of Multiple-Turn Reasoning Strategies in Reading Comprehension Tasks
Yelong Shen, Xiaodong Liu, Kevin Duh and Jianfeng Gao 957

Automated Historical Fact-Checking by Passage Retrieval, Word Statistics, and Virtual Question-Answering
Mio Kobayashi, Ai Ishii, Chikara Hoshino, Hiroshi Miyashita and Takuya Matsuzaki 967

*Integrating Subject, Type, and Property Identification for Simple Question Answering over Knowledge
Base*
Wei-Chuan Hsiao, Hen-Hsen Huang and Hsin-Hsi Chen 976

DailyDialog: A Manually Labelled Multi-turn Dialogue Dataset
Yanran Li, Hui Su, Xiaoyu Shen, Wenjie Li, Ziqiang Cao and Shuzi Niu 986

Inference is Everything: Recasting Semantic Resources into a Unified Evaluation Framework
Aaron Steven White, Pushpendre Rastogi, Kevin Duh and Benjamin Van Durme 996

Generating a Training Corpus for OCR Post-Correction Using Encoder-Decoder Model
Eva D'hondt, Cyril Grouin and Brigitte Grau 1006

Multilingual Hierarchical Attention Networks for Document Classification
Nikolaos Pappas and Andrei Popescu-Belis 1015

Roles and Success in Wikipedia Talk Pages: Identifying Latent Patterns of Behavior
Keith Maki, Michael Yoder, Yohan Jo and Carolyn Rosé..................................1026

Conference Program

Tuesday, November 28, 2017

10:30–11:50   **Machine Translation 1**

10:30–10:50   *Evaluating Layers of Representation in Neural Machine Translation on Part-of-Speech and Semantic Tagging Tasks*
Yonatan Belinkov, Lluís Màrquez, Hassan Sajjad, Nadir Durrani, Fahim Dalvi and James Glass

10:50–11:10   *Context-Aware Smoothing for Neural Machine Translation*
Kehai Chen, Rui Wang, Masao Utiyama, Eiichiro Sumita and Tiejun Zhao

11:10–11:30   *Improving Sequence to Sequence Neural Machine Translation by Utilizing Syntactic Dependency Information*
An Nguyen Le, Ander Martinez, Akifumi Yoshimoto and Yuji Matsumoto

11:30–11:50   *What does Attention in Neural Machine Translation Pay Attention to?*
Hamidreza Ghader and Christof Monz

Tuesday, November 28, 2017

10:30–11:50   **Syntax and Parsing**

10:30–10:50   *Grammatical Error Detection Using Error- and Grammaticality-Specific Word Embeddings*
Masahiro Kaneko, Yuya Sakaizawa and Mamoru Komachi

10:50–11:10   *Dependency Parsing with Partial Annotations: An Empirical Comparison*
Yue Zhang, Zhenghua Li, Jun Lang, Qingrong Xia and Min Zhang

11:10–11:30   *Neural Probabilistic Model for Non-projective MST Parsing*
Xuezhe Ma and Eduard Hovy

11:30–11:50   *Word Ordering as Unsupervised Learning Towards Syntactically Plausible Word Representations*
Noriki Nishida and Hideki Nakayama

Tuesday, November 28, 2017

<table>
<tr><td>10:30–11:50</td><td colspan="2">Semantics 1</td></tr>
</table>

10:30–11:50   **Semantics 1**

10:30–10:50   *MIPA: Mutual Information Based Paraphrase Acquisition via Bilingual Pivoting*
Tomoyuki Kajiwara, Mamoru Komachi and Daichi Mochihashi

10:50–11:10   *Improving Implicit Semantic Role Labeling by Predicting Semantic Frame Arguments*
Quynh Ngoc Thi Do, Steven Bethard and Marie-Francine Moens

11:10–11:30   *Natural Language Inference from Multiple Premises*
Alice Lai, Yonatan Bisk and Julia Hockenmaier

11:30–11:50   *Enabling Transitivity for Lexical Inference on Chinese Verbs Using Probabilistic Soft Logic*
Wei-Chung Wang and Lun-Wei Ku

Tuesday, November 28, 2017

13:30–14:50   **Machine Translation 2**

13:30–13:50   *An Exploration of Neural Sequence-to-Sequence Architectures for Automatic Post-Editing*
Marcin Junczys-Dowmunt and Roman Grundkiewicz

13:50–14:10   *Imagination Improves Multimodal Translation*
Desmond Elliott and Ákos Kádár

14:10–14:30   *Understanding and Improving Morphological Learning in the Neural Machine Translation Decoder*
Fahim Dalvi, Nadir Durrani, Hassan Sajjad, Yonatan Belinkov and Stephan Vogel

14:30–14:50   *Improving Neural Machine Translation through Phrase-based Forced Decoding*
Jingyi Zhang, Masao Utiyama, Eiichro Sumita, Graham Neubig and Satoshi Nakamura

Tuesday, November 28, 2017

13:30–14:50   Segmentation and Tagging

13:30–13:50   *Convolutional Neural Network with Word Embeddings for Chinese Word Segmentation*
Chunqi Wang and Bo Xu

13:50–14:10   *Character-based Joint Segmentation and POS Tagging for Chinese using Bidirectional RNN-CRF*
Yan Shao, Christian Hardmeier, Jörg Tiedemann and Joakim Nivre

14:10–14:30   *Addressing Domain Adaptation for Chinese Word Segmentation with Global Recurrent Structure*
Shen Huang, Xu Sun and Houfeng Wang

14:30–14:50   *Information Bottleneck Inspired Method For Chat Text Segmentation*
S Vishal, Mohit Yadav, Lovekesh Vig and Gautam Shroff

Tuesday, November 28, 2017

13:30–14:50   Semantics 2

13:30–13:50   *Distributional Modeling on a Diet: One-shot Word Learning from Text Only*
Su Wang, Stephen Roller and Katrin Erk

13:50–14:10   *A Computational Study on Word Meanings and Their Distributed Representations via Polymodal Embedding*
Joohee Park and Sung-Hyon Myaeng

14:10–14:30   *Geographical Evaluation of Word Embeddings*
Michal Konkol, Tomáš Brychcín, Michal Nykl and Tomáš Hercig

14:30–14:50   *On Modeling Sense Relatedness in Multi-prototype Word Embedding*
Yixin Cao, Jiaxin Shi, Juanzi Li, Zhiyuan Liu and Chengjiang Li

15:30–17:30   **Poster and Demo**

Unsupervised Segmentation of Phoneme Sequences based on Pitman-Yor Semi-Markov Model using Phoneme Length Context
Ryu Takeda and Kazunori Komatani

A Sensitivity Analysis of (and Practitioners' Guide to) Convolutional Neural Networks for Sentence Classification
Ye Zhang and Byron Wallace

Coordination Boundary Identification with Similarity and Replaceability
Hiroki Teranishi, Hiroyuki Shindo and Yuji Matsumoto

Turning Distributional Thesauri into Word Vectors for Synonym Extraction and Expansion
Olivier Ferret

Training Word Sense Embeddings With Lexicon-based Regularization
Luis Nieto Piña and Richard Johansson

Learning How to Simplify From Explicit Labeling of Complex-Simplified Text Pairs
Fernando Alva-Manchego, Joachim Bingel, Gustavo Paetzold, Carolina Scarton and Lucia Specia

Domain-Adaptable Hybrid Generation of RDF Entity Descriptions
Or Biran and Kathleen McKeown

ES-LDA: Entity Summarization using Knowledge-based Topic Modeling
Seyedamin Pouriyeh, Mehdi Allahyari, Krzysztof Kochut, Gong Cheng and Hamid Reza Arabnia

Procedural Text Generation from an Execution Video
Atsushi Ushiku, Hayato Hashimoto, Atsushi Hashimoto and Shinsuke Mori

Text Sentiment Analysis based on Fusion of Structural Information and Serialization Information
Ling Gan and Houyu Gong

Length, Interchangeability, and External Knowledge: Observations from Predicting Argument Convincingness
Peter Potash, Robin Bhattacharya and Anna Rumshisky

Exploiting Document Level Information to Improve Event Detection via Recurrent Neural Networks
Shaoyang Duan, Ruifang He and Wenli Zhao

Embracing Non-Traditional Linguistic Resources for Low-resource Language Name Tagging
Boliang Zhang, Di Lu, Xiaoman Pan, Ying Lin, Halidanmu Abudukelimu, Heng Ji and Kevin Knight

NMT or SMT: Case Study of a Narrow-domain English-Latvian Post-editing Project
Inguna Skadina and Mārcis Pinnis

Towards Neural Machine Translation with Partially Aligned Corpora
Yining Wang, Yang Zhao, Jiajun Zhang, Chengqing Zong and Zhengshan Xue

Identifying Usage Expression Sentences in Consumer Product Reviews
Shibamouli Lahiri, V.G.Vinod Vydiswaran and Rada Mihalcea

Between Reading Time and Syntactic/Semantic Categories
Masayuki Asahara and Sachi Kato

WiNER: A Wikipedia Annotated Corpus for Named Entity Recognition
Abbas Ghaddar and Phillippe Langlais

Wednesday, November 29, 2017

10:30–11:50   Machine Learning 1

10:30–10:50   *Reusing Neural Speech Representations for Auditory Emotion Recognition*
Egor Lakomkin, Cornelius Weber, Sven Magg and Stefan Wermter

10:50–11:10   *Local Monotonic Attention Mechanism for End-to-End Speech And Language Processing*
Andros Tjandra, Sakriani Sakti and Satoshi Nakamura

11:10–11:30   *Attentive Language Models*
Giancarlo Salton, Robert Ross and John Kelleher

11:30–11:50   *Diachrony-aware Induction of Binary Latent Representations from Typological Features*
Yugo Murawaki

Wednesday, November 29, 2017

10:30–11:50   Discourse 1

10:30–10:50   *Image-Grounded Conversations: Multimodal Context for Natural Question and Response Generation*
Nasrin Mostafazadeh, Chris Brockett, Bill Dolan, Michel Galley, Jianfeng Gao, Georgios Spithourakis and Lucy Vanderwende

10:50–11:10   *A Neural Language Model for Dynamically Representing the Meanings of Unknown Words and Entities in a Discourse*
Sosuke Kobayashi, Naoaki Okazaki and Kentaro Inui

11:10–11:30   *Using Explicit Discourse Connectives in Translation for Implicit Discourse Relation Classification*
Wei Shi, Frances Yung, Raphael Rubino and Vera Demberg

11:30–11:50   *Tag-Enhanced Tree-Structured Neural Networks for Implicit Discourse Relation Classification*
Yizhong Wang, Sujian Li, Jingfeng Yang, Xu Sun and Houfeng Wang

Wednesday, November 29, 2017

10:30–11:50   **Sentiment and Opinion 1**

10:30–10:50   *Cross-Lingual Sentiment Analysis Without (Good) Translation*
Mohamed Abdalla and Graeme Hirst

10:50–11:10   *Implicit Syntactic Features for Target-dependent Sentiment Analysis*
Yuze Gao, Yue Zhang and Tong Xiao

11:10–11:30   *Graph Based Sentiment Aggregation using ConceptNet Ontology*
Srikanth Tamilselvam, Seema Nagar, Abhijit Mishra and Kuntal Dey

11:30–11:50   *Sentence Modeling with Deep Neural Architecture using Lexicon and Character Attention Mechanism for Sentiment Classification*
Huy-Thanh Nguyen and Minh-Le Nguyen

Wednesday, November 29, 2017

13:30–14:50   **Machine Learning 2**

13:30–13:50   *Combining Lightly-Supervised Text Classification Models for Accurate Contextual Advertising*
Yiping Jin, Dittaya Wanvarie and Phu Le

13:50–14:10   *Capturing Long-range Contextual Dependencies with Memory-enhanced Conditional Random Fields*
Fei Liu, Timothy Baldwin and Trevor Cohn

14:10–14:30   *Named Entity Recognition with Stack Residual LSTM and Trainable Bias Decoding*
Quan Tran, Andrew MacKinlay and Antonio Jimeno Yepes

14:30–14:50   *Neuramanteau: A Neural Network Ensemble Model for Lexical Blends*
Kollol Das and Shaona Ghosh

13:30–14:50   **Discourse 2**

13:30–13:50   *Leveraging Discourse Information Effectively for Authorship Attribution*
Elisa Ferracane, Su Wang and Raymond Mooney

13:50–14:10   *Lightly-Supervised Modeling of Argument Persuasiveness*
Isaac Persing and Vincent Ng

14:10–14:30   *Multi-Task Learning for Speaker-Role Adaptation in Neural Conversation Models*
Yi Luan, Chris Brockett, Bill Dolan, Jianfeng Gao and Michel Galley

14:30–14:50   *Chat Disentanglement: Identifying Semantic Reply Relationships with Random Forests and Recurrent Neural Networks*
Shikib Mehri and Giuseppe Carenini

Wednesday, November 29, 2017

13:30–14:50   **Sentiment and Opinion 2**

13:30–13:50   *Towards Bootstrapping a Polarity Shifter Lexicon using Linguistic Features*
Marc Schulder, Michael Wiegand, Josef Ruppenhofer and Benjamin Roth

13:50–14:10   *Cascading Multiway Attentions for Document-level Sentiment Classification*
Dehong Ma, Sujian Li, Xiaodong Zhang, Houfeng Wang and Xu Sun

14:10–14:30   *An Ensemble Method with Sentiment Features and Clustering Support*
Nguyen Huy Tien and Nguyen Minh Le

14:30–14:50   *Leveraging Auxiliary Tasks for Document-Level Cross-Domain Sentiment Classification*
Jianfei Yu and Jing Jiang

Wednesday, November 29, 2017

15:30–16:50   Word

15:30–15:50   *Measuring Semantic Relations between Human Activities*
Steven Wilson and Rada Mihalcea

15:50–16:10   *Learning Transferable Representation for Bilingual Relation Extraction via Convolutional Neural Networks*
Bonan Min, Zhuolin Jiang, Marjorie Freedman and Ralph Weischedel

16:10–16:30   *Bilingual Word Embeddings for Bilingual Terminology Extraction from Specialized Comparable Corpora*
Amir Hazem and Emmanuel Morin

16:30–16:50   *A Bambara Tonalization System for Word Sense Disambiguation Using Differential Coding, Segmentation and Edit Operation Filtering*
Luigi (Yu-Cheng) Liu and Damien Nouvel

Wednesday, November 29, 2017

15:30–16:50   Dialogue

15:30–15:50   *Joint Learning of Dialog Act Segmentation and Recognition in Spoken Dialog Using Neural Networks*
Tianyu Zhao and Tatsuya Kawahara

15:50–16:10   *Predicting Users' Negative Feedbacks in Multi-Turn Human-Computer Dialogues*
Xin Wang, Jianan Wang, Yuanchao Liu, Xiaolong Wang, Zhuoran Wang and Baoxun Wang

16:10–16:30   *Finding Dominant User Utterances And System Responses in Conversations*
Dhiraj Madan and Sachindra Joshi

16:30–16:50   *End-to-End Task-Completion Neural Dialogue Systems*
Xiujun Li, Yun-Nung Chen, Lihong Li, Jianfeng Gao and Asli Celikyilmaz

Wednesday, November 29, 2017

15:30–16:50   Web and Social Media

15:30–15:50   *End-to-end Network for Twitter Geolocation Prediction and Hashing*
Jey Han Lau, Lianhua Chi, Khoi-Nguyen Tran and Trevor Cohn

15:50–16:10   *Assessing the Verifiability of Attributions in News Text*
Edward Newell, Ariane Schang, Drew Margolin and Derek Ruths

16:10–16:30   *Domain Adaptation from User-level Facebook Models to County-level Twitter Predictions*
Daniel Rieman, Kokil Jaidka, H. Andrew Schwartz and Lyle Ungar

16:30–16:50   *Recognizing Explicit and Implicit Hate Speech Using a Weakly Supervised Two-path Bootstrapping Approach*
Lei Gao, Alexis Kuppersmith and Ruihong Huang

Thursday, November 30, 2017

10:30–11:50   Summarization

10:30–10:50   *Estimating Reactions and Recommending Products with Generative Models of Reviews*
Jianmo Ni, Zachary C. Lipton, Sharad Vikram and Julian McAuley

10:50–11:10   *Summarizing Lengthy Questions*
Tatsuya Ishigaki, Hiroya Takamura and Manabu Okumura

11:10–11:30   *Concept-Map-Based Multi-Document Summarization using Concept Coreference Resolution and Global Importance Optimization*
Tobias Falke, Christian M. Meyer and Iryna Gurevych

11:30–11:50   *Abstractive Multi-document Summarization by Partial Tree Extraction, Recombination and Linearization*
Litton J Kurisinkel, Yue Zhang and Vasudeva Varma

Thursday, November 30, 2017

10:30–11:50   Information Extraction

10:30–10:50   *Event Argument Identification on Dependency Graphs with Bidirectional LSTMs*
Alex Judea and Michael Strube

10:50–11:10   *Selective Decoding for Cross-lingual Open Information Extraction*
Sheng Zhang, Kevin Duh and Benjamin Van Durme

11:10–11:30   *Event Ordering with a Generalized Model for Sieve Prediction Ranking*
Bill McDowell, Nathanael Chambers, Alexander Ororbia II and David Reitter

11:30–11:50   *Open Relation Extraction and Grounding*
Dian Yu, Lifu Huang and Heng Ji

Thursday, November 30, 2017

10:30–11:50   NLP Application

10:30–10:50   *Extraction of Gene-Environment Interaction from the Biomedical Literature*
Jinseon You, Jin-Woo Chung, Wonsuk Yang and Jong C. Park

10:50–11:10   *Course Concept Extraction in MOOCs via Embedding-Based Graph Propagation*
Liangming Pan, Xiaochen Wang, Chengjiang Li, Juanzi Li and Jie Tang

11:10–11:30   *Identity Deception Detection*
Verónica Pérez-Rosas, Quincy Davenport, Anna Mengdan Dai, Mohamed Abouelenien and Rada Mihalcea

11:30–11:50   *Learning to Diagnose: Assimilating Clinical Narratives using Deep Reinforcement
Learning*
Yuan Ling, Sadid A. Hasan, Vivek Datla, Ashequl Qadir, Kathy Lee, Joey Liu and
Oladimeji Farri

Thursday, November 30, 2017

13:30–14:50   Generation

13:30–13:50   *Dataset for a Neural Natural Language Interface for Databases (NNLIDB)*
Florin Brad, Radu Cristian Alexandru Iacob, Ionel Alexandru Hosu and Traian Rebedea

13:50–14:10   *Acquisition and Assessment of Semantic Content for the Generation of Elaborateness and Indirectness in Spoken Dialogue Systems*
Louisa Pragst, Koichiro Yoshino, Wolfgang Minker, Satoshi Nakamura and Stefan Ultes

14:10–14:30   *Demographic Word Embeddings for Racism Detection on Twitter*
Mohammed Hasanuzzaman, Gaël Dias and Andy Way

14:30–14:50   *Automatically Extracting Variant-Normalization Pairs for Japanese Text Normalization*
Itsumi Saito, Kyosuke Nishida, Kugatsu Sadamitsu, Kuniko Saito and Junji Tomita

Thursday, November 30, 2017

13:30–14:50   Documents and Questions

13:30–13:50   *Semantic Document Distance Measures and Unsupervised Document Revision Detection*
Xiaofeng Zhu, Diego Klabjan and Patrick Bless

13:50–14:10   *An Empirical Analysis of Multiple-Turn Reasoning Strategies in Reading Comprehension Tasks*
Yelong Shen, Xiaodong Liu, Kevin Duh and Jianfeng Gao

14:10–14:30   *Automated Historical Fact-Checking by Passage Retrieval, Word Statistics, and Virtual Question-Answering*
Mio Kobayashi, Ai Ishii, Chikara Hoshino, Hiroshi Miyashita and Takuya Matsuzaki

14:30–14:50   *Integrating Subject, Type, and Property Identification for Simple Question Answering over Knowledge Base*
Wei-Chuan Hsiao, Hen-Hsen Huang and Hsin-Hsi Chen

Thursday, November 30, 2017

13:30–14:30   **Resources and Tools**

13:30–13:50   *DailyDialog: A Manually Labelled Multi-turn Dialogue Dataset*
Yanran Li, Hui Su, Xiaoyu Shen, Wenjie Li, Ziqiang Cao and Shuzi Niu

13:50–14:10   *Inference is Everything: Recasting Semantic Resources into a Unified Evaluation
Framework*
Aaron Steven White, Pushpendre Rastogi, Kevin Duh and Benjamin Van Durme

14:10–14:30   *Generating a Training Corpus for OCR Post-Correction Using Encoder-Decoder
Model*
Eva D'hondt, Cyril Grouin and Brigitte Grau

Thursday, November 30, 2017

15:30–16:20   **Best Paper Session**

15:30–15:55   *Multilingual Hierarchical Attention Networks for Document Classification*
Nikolaos Pappas and Andrei Popescu-Belis

15:55–16:20   *Roles and Success in Wikipedia Talk Pages: Identifying Latent Patterns of Behavior*
Keith Maki, Michael Yoder, Yohan Jo and Carolyn Rosé

Evaluating Layers of Representation in Neural Machine Translation on Part-of-Speech and Semantic Tagging Tasks

Yonatan Belinkov[1]   Lluís Màrquez[2]   Hassan Sajjad[2]
Nadir Durrani[2]   Fahim Dalvi[2]   James Glass[1]

[1]MIT Computer Science and Artificial Intelligence Laboratory, Cambridge, MA 02139, USA
`{belinkov, glass}@mit.edu`
[2]Qatar Computing Research Institute, HBKU, Doha, Qatar
`{lmarquez, hsajjad, ndurrani, faimaduddin}@qf.org.qa`

Abstract

While neural machine translation (NMT) models provide improved translation quality in an elegant framework, it is less clear what they learn about language. Recent work has started evaluating the quality of vector representations learned by NMT models on morphological and syntactic tasks. In this paper, we investigate the representations learned at different layers of NMT encoders. We train NMT systems on parallel data and use the models to extract features for training a classifier on two tasks: part-of-speech and semantic tagging. We then measure the performance of the classifier as a proxy to the quality of the original NMT model for the given task. Our quantitative analysis yields interesting insights regarding representation learning in NMT models. For instance, we find that higher layers are better at learning semantics while lower layers tend to be better for part-of-speech tagging. We also observe little effect of the target language on source-side representations, especially in higher quality models.[1]

1 Introduction

Neural machine translation (NMT) offers an elegant end-to-end architecture, while at the same time improving translation quality. However, little is known about the inner workings of these models and their interpretability is limited. Recent work has started exploring what kind of linguistic information such models learn on morphological (Vylomova et al., 2016; Belinkov et al., 2017; Dalvi et al., 2017) and syntactic levels (Shi et al., 2016; Sennrich, 2017).

One observation that has been made is that lower layers in the neural MT network learn different kinds of information than higher layers. For example, Shi et al. (2016) and Belinkov et al. (2017) found that representations from lower layers of the NMT encoder are more predictive of word-level linguistic properties like part-of-speech (POS) and morphological tags, whereas higher layer representations are more predictive of more global syntactic information. In this work, we take a first step towards understanding what NMT models learn about semantics. We evaluate NMT representations from different layers on a semantic tagging task and compare to the results on a POS tagging task. We believe that understanding the semantics learned in NMT can facilitate using semantic information for improving NMT systems, as previously shown for non-neural MT (Chan et al., 2007; Liu and Gildea, 2010; Gao and Vogel, 2011; Wu et al., 2011; Jones et al., 2012; Bazrafshan and Gildea, 2013, 2014).

For the semantic (SEM) tagging task, we use the dataset recently introduced by Bjerva et al. (2016). This is a lexical semantics task: given a sentence, the goal is to assign to each word a tag representing a semantic class. The classes capture nuanced meanings that are ignored in most POS tag schemes. For instance, proximal and distal demonstratives (e.g., *this* and *that*) are typically assigned the same POS tag (DT) but receive different SEM tags (PRX and DST, respectively), and proper nouns are assigned different SEM tags depending on their type (e.g., geopolitical entity, organization, person, and location). As another example, consider pronouns like *myself*, *yourself*, and *herself*. They may have reflexive or emphasizing functions, as in (1) and (2), respectively:

(1) Sarah bought herself a book

(2) Sarah herself bought a book

Proceedings of the The 8th International Joint Conference on Natural Language Processing, pages 1–10,
Taipei, Taiwan, November 27 – December 1, 2017 ©2017 AFNLP

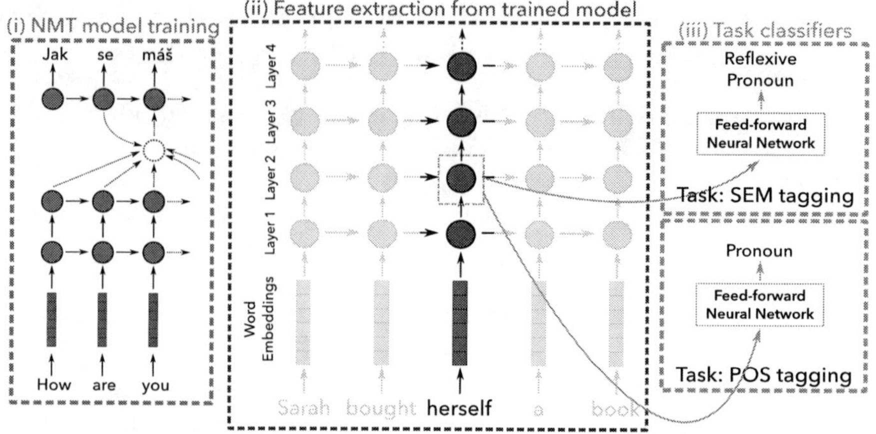

Figure 1: Illustration of our approach, after (Belinkov et al., 2017): (i) NMT system trained on parallel data; (ii) features extracted from pre-trained model; (iii) classifier trained using the extracted features. We train classifiers on either SEM or POS tagging using features from different layers (here: layer 2).

In these examples, *herself* has the same POS tag (PRP) but different SEM tags: REF for a reflexive function and EMP for an emphasizing function.

Capturing semantic distinctions of this sort can be important for producing accurate translations. For instance, example (1) would be translated to Spanish with the reflexive pronoun *se*, whereas (2) would be translated with the intensifier *misma*. Thus, a translation system needs to learn different representations of *herself* in the two sentences.

In order to assess the quality of the representations learned by NMT models, we adopt the following methodology from Shi et al. (2016) and Belinkov et al. (2017). We first train an NMT system on parallel data. Given a sentence, we extract representations from the pre-trained NMT model and train a word-level classifier to predict a tag for each word. Our assumption is that the performance of the classifier reflects the quality of the representation for the given task.

We compare POS and SEM tagging quality with representations from different layers or from models trained on different target languages, while keeping the English source fixed. Our results yield useful insights on representation learning in NMT:

- Consistent with previous work, we find that lower layer representations are usually better for POS tagging. However, we also find that representations from higher layers are better at capturing semantics, even though these are word-level labels. This is especially true with tags that are more semantic in nature such as discourse functions or noun concepts.

- In contrast to previous work, we observe little effect of the target language on source-side representation. We find that the effect of target language diminishes as the size of data used to train the NMT model increases.

2 Methodology

Given a parallel corpus of source and target sentence pairs, we train an NMT system with a standard sequence-to-sequence model with attention (Bahdanau et al., 2014; Sutskever et al., 2014). After training the NMT system, we fix its parameters and treat it as a feature generator for our classification task. Let $\mathbf{h}_j^k$ denote the output of the k-th layer of the encoder at the j-th word. Given another corpus of sentences, where each word is annotated with a label, we train a classifier that takes $\mathbf{h}_j^k$ as input features and maps words to labels. We then measure the performance of the classifier as a way to evaluate the quality of the representations generated by the NMT system. By extracting different NMT features we can obtain a quantitative comparison of representation learning quality in the NMT model for the given task. For instance, we may vary k in order to evaluate representations learned at different encoding layers.

In our case, we first train NMT systems on parallel corpora of an English source and several target languages. Then we train separate classifiers for predicting POS and SEM tags using the features $\mathbf{h}_j^k$ that are obtained from the English encoder and evaluate their accuracies. Figure 1 illustrates the process.

3 Data and Experimental Setup

3.1 Data

MT We use the fully-aligned United Nations corpus (Ziemski et al., 2016) for training NMT models, which includes 11 million multi-parallel sentences in six languages: Arabic (Ar), Chinese (Zh), English (En), French (Fr), Spanish (Es), and Russian (Ru). We train En-to-* models on the first 2 million sentences of the train set, using the official train/dev/test split. This dataset has the benefit of multiple alignment of the six languages, which allows for comparable cross-linguistic analysis.

Note that the parallel dataset is only used for training the NMT model. The classifier is then trained on the supervised data (described next) and all accuracies are reported on the English test sets.

Semantic tagging Bjerva et al. (2016) introduced a new sequence labeling task, for tagging words with semantic (SEM) tags in context. This is a good task to use as a starting point for investigating semantics because: *i)* tagging words with semantic labels is very simple, compared to building complex relational semantic structures; *ii)* it provides a large supervised dataset to train on, in contrast to most available datasets on word sense disambiguation, lexical substitution, and lexical similarity; and *iii)* the proposed SEM tagging task is an abstraction over POS tagging aimed at being language-neutral, and oriented to multi-lingual semantic parsing, all relevant aspects to MT. We provide here a brief overview of the task and its associated dataset, and refer to (Bjerva et al., 2016; Abzianidze et al., 2017) for more details.

The semantic classes abstract over redundant POS distinctions and disambiguate useful cases inside a given POS tag. Examples (1-2) above illustrate how fine-grained semantic distinctions may be important for generating accurate translations. Other examples of SEM tag distinctions include determiners like *every*, *no*, and *some* that are typically assigned a single POS tag (e.g., DT in the Penn Treebank), but have different SEM tags, reflecting universal quantification (AND), negation (NOT), and existential quantification (DIS), respectively. The comma, whose POS tag is a punctuation mark, is assigned different SEM tags representing conjunction, disjunction, or apposition, according to its discourse function. Proximal and distant demonstratives (*this* vs. *that*) have different SEM tags but the same POS tag. Named-entities,

		Train	Dev	Test
POS	Sentences	38K	1.7K	2.3K
	Tokens	908K	40K	54K
SEM	Sentences	42.5K	6.1K	12.2K
	Tokens	937K	132K	266K

Table 1: Statistics of the part-of-speech and semantic tagging datasets.

whose POS tag is usually a single tag for proper nouns, are disambiguated into several classes such as geo-political entity, location, organization, person, and artifact. Other nouns are divided into "role" entities (e.g., *boxer*) and "concepts" (e.g., *wheel*), a distinction reflecting existential consistency: an entity can have multiple roles but cannot be two different concepts.

The dataset annotation scheme includes 66 fine-grained tags grouped in 13 coarse categories. We use the silver part of the dataset; see Table 1 for some statistics.

Part-of-speech tagging For POS tagging, we simply use the Penn Treebank with the standard split (parts 2-21/22/23 for train/dev/test); see Table 1 for statistics. There are 34 POS tags.

3.2 Experimental Setup

Neural MT We use the seq2seq-attn toolkit (Kim, 2016) to train 4-layered long short-term memory (LSTM) (Hochreiter and Schmidhuber, 1997) attentional encoder-decoder NMT systems with 500 dimensions for both word embeddings and LSTM states. We compare both unidirectional and bidirectional encoders and experiment with different numbers of layers. Each system is trained with SGD for 20 epochs and the model with the best loss on the development set is used for generating features for the classifier.

Classifier The classifier is modeled as a feedforward neural network with one hidden layer, dropout (ratio of 0.5), a ReLU activation function, and a softmax layer onto the label set size.[2] The hidden layer is of the same size as the input coming from the NMT system (i.e., 500 dimensions). The classifier has no explicit access to context other than the hidden representation gen-

---

[2]We use a non-linear classifier because previous work found that it outperforms a linear classifier, while showing very similar trends (Qian et al., 2016b; Belinkov et al., 2017).

	MFT	UnsupEmb	Word2Tag
POS	91.95	87.06	95.55
SEM	82.00	81.11	91.41

Table 2: POS and SEM tagging accuracy with baselines and an upper bound. MFT: most frequent tag; UnsupEmb: classifier using unsupervised word embeddings; Word2Tag: upper bound encoder-decoder.

erated by the NMT system, which allows us to focus on the quality of the representation. We chose this simple formulation as our goal is not to improve the state-of-the-art on the supervised task, but rather to analyze the quality of the NMT representation for the task. We train the classifier for 30 epochs by minimizing the cross-entropy loss using Adam (Kingma and Ba, 2014) with default settings. Again, we use the model with the best loss on the development set for evaluation.

Baselines and an upper bound we consider two baselines: assigning to each word the most frequent tag (MFT) according to the training set (with the global majority tag for unseen words); and training with unsupervised word embeddings (UnsupEmb) as features for the classifier, which shows what a simple task-independent distributed representation can achieve. For the unsupervised word embeddings, we train a Skip-gram negative sampling model (Mikolov et al., 2013) with 500 dimensional vectors on the English side of the parallel data, to mirror the NMT word embedding size. We also report an upper bound of directly training an encoder-decoder on word-tag sequences (Word2Tag), simulating what an NMT-style model can achieve by directly optimizing for the tagging tasks.

4 Results

Table 2 shows baseline and upper bound results. The UnsupEmb baseline performs rather poorly on both POS and SEM tagging. In comparison, NMT word embeddings (Table 3, rows with $k = 0$) perform slightly better, suggesting that word embeddings learned as part of the NMT model are better syntactic and semantic representations. However, the results are still below the most frequent tag baseline (MFT), indicating that non-contextual word embeddings are poor representations for POS and SEM tags.

k	Ar	Es	Fr	Ru	Zh	En
	POS Tagging Accuracy					
0	88.0*	87.9*	87.9*	87.8*	87.7*	87.4*
1	92.4	91.9	92.1	92.1	91.5	89.4
2	91.9*	91.8	91.8	91.8*	91.3	88.3
3	92.0*	92.3*	92.1	91.6**	91.2*	87.9*
4	92.1*	92.4*	92.5*	92.0	90.5*	86.9*
	SEM Tagging Accuracy					
0	81.9*	81.9*	81.8*	81.8*	81.8*	81.2*
1	87.9	87.7	87.8	87.9	87.7	84.5
2	87.4*	87.5*	87.4*	87.3*	87.2*	83.2*
3	87.8	87.9*	87.9**	87.3*	87.3*	82.9*
4	88.3*	88.6*	88.4*	88.1*	87.7*	82.1*
	BLEU					
	32.7	49.1	38.5	34.2	32.1	96.6

Table 3: SEM and POS tagging accuracy using features from the k-th encoding layer of 4-layered NMT models trained with different target languages. "En" column is an English autoencoder. BLEU scores are given for reference. Statistically significant differences from layer 1 are shown at $p < 0.001^{(*)}$ and $p < 0.01^{(**)}$. See text for details.

4.1 Effect of network depth

Table 3 summarizes the results of training classifiers to predict POS and SEM tags using features extracted from different encoding layers of 4-layered NMT systems.[3] In the POS tagging results (first block), as the representations move above layer 0, performance jumps to around 91–92%. This is above the UnsupEmb baseline but only on par with the MFT baseline (Table 2). We note that previous work reported performance above a majority baseline for POS tagging (Shi et al., 2016; Belinkov et al., 2017), but used a weak global majority baseline (all words are assigned a single tag) whereas here we compare with a stronger baseline that assigns to each word the most frequent tag according to the training data. The results are also far below the Word2Tag upper bound (Table 2).

Comparing layers 1 through 4, we see that in 3/5 target languages (Ar, Ru, Zh), POS tagging accuracy peaks at layer 1 and does not improve

---

[3]The results given are with a unidirectional encoder; in section 4.5 we compare with a bidirectional encoder and observe similar trends.

at higher layers, with some drops at layers 2 and 3. In 2/5 cases (Es, Fr) the performance is higher at layer 4. This result is partially consistent with previous findings regarding the quality of lower layer representations for the POS tagging task (Shi et al., 2016; Belinkov et al., 2017). One possible explanation for the discrepancy when using different target languages is that French and Spanish are typologically closer to English compared to the other languages. It is possible that when the source and target languages are more similar, they share similar POS characteristics, leading to more benefit in using upper layers for POS tagging.

Turning to SEM tagging (Table 3, second block), representations from layers 1 through 4 boost the performance to around 87-88%, far above the UnsupEmb and MFT baselines. While these results are below the Word2Tag upper bound (Table 2), they indicate that NMT representations contain useful information for SEM tagging.

Going beyond the 1st encoding layer, representations from the 2nd and 3rd layers do not consistently improve semantic tagging performance. However, representations from the 4th layer lead to significant improvement with all target languages except for Chinese. Note that there is a statistically significant difference ($p < 0.001$) between layers 0 and 1 for all target languages, and between layers 1 and 4 for all languages except for Chinese, according to the approximate randomization test (Padó, 2006).

Intuitively, higher layers have a more global perspective because they have access to higher representations of the word and its context, while lower layers have a more local perspective. Layer 1 has access to context but only through one hidden layer which may not be sufficient for capturing semantics. It appears that higher representations are necessary for learning even relatively simple lexical semantics.

Finally, we found that En-En encoder-decoders (that is, English autoencoders) produce poor representations for POS and SEM tagging (last column in Table 3). This is especially true with higher layer representations (e.g., around 5% below the MT models using representations from layer 4). In contrast, the autoencoder has excellent sentence recreation capabilities (96.6 BLEU). This indicates that learning to translate (to any foreign language) is important for obtaining useful representations for both tagging tasks.

	Ar	Es	Fr	Ru	Zh	En
POS	88.7	90.0	89.6	88.6	87.4	85.2
SEM	85.3	86.1	85.8	85.2	85.0	80.7

Table 4: SEM and POS tagging accuracy using features extracted from the 4th NMT encoding layer, trained with different target languages on a smaller parallel corpus (200K sentences).

4.2 Effect of target language

Does translating into different languages make the NMT system learn different source-side representations? In previous work (Belinkov et al., 2017), we found a fairly consistent effect of the target language on the quality of encoder representations for POS and morphological tagging, with differences of ~2-3% in accuracy. Here we examine if such an effect exists in both POS and SEM tagging.

Table 3 also shows results using features obtained by training NMT systems on different target languages (the English source remains fixed). In both POS and SEM tagging, there are very small differences with different target languages (~0.5%), except for Chinese which leads to slightly worse representations. While the differences are small, they are mostly statistically significant. For example, at layer 4, all the pairwise comparisons with different target languages are statistically significant ($p < 0.001$) in SEM tagging, and all except for two comparisons (Ar vs. Ru and Es vs. Fr) are significant in POS tagging.

The effect of target language is much smaller than that reported in (Belinkov et al., 2017) for POS and morphological tagging. This discrepancy can be attributed to the fact that our NMT systems in the present work are trained on much larger corpora (10x), so it is possible that some of the differences disappear when the NMT model is of better quality. To verify this, we trained systems using a smaller data size (200K sentences), comparable to the size used in (Belinkov et al., 2017). The results are shown in Table 4. In this case, we observe a variance in classifier accuracy of 1-2%, based on target language, which is consistent with our earlier findings. This is true for both POS and SEM tagging. The differences in POS tagging accuracy are statistically significant ($p < 0.001$) for all pairwise comparisons except for Ar vs. Ru; the differences in SEM tagging accuracy are significant for all comparisons except for Ru vs. Zh.

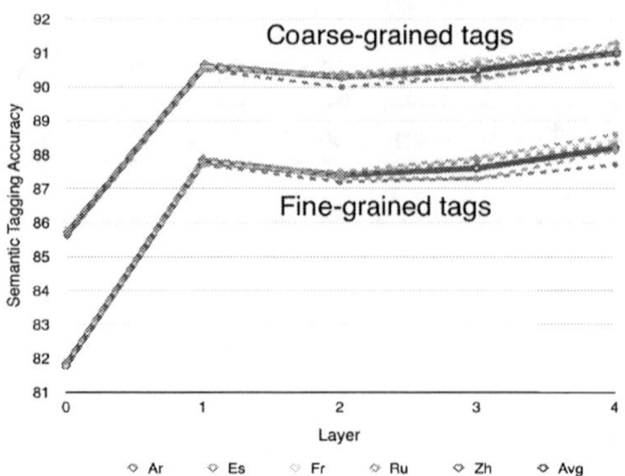

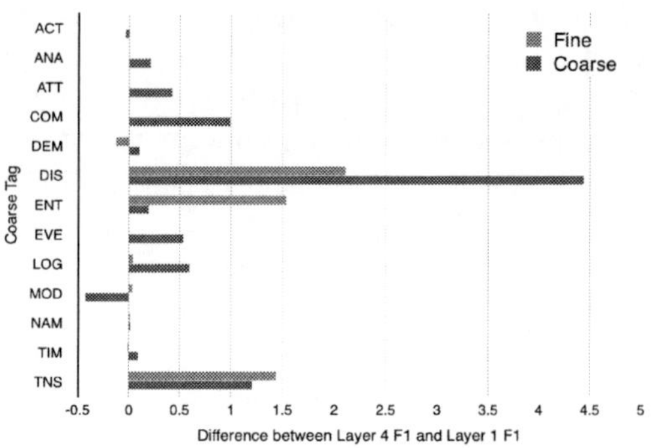

Figure 2: SEM tagging accuracy with fine/coarse-grained tags using features extracted from different encoding layers of 4-layered NMT models trained with different target languages.

Figure 3: Difference in F_1 when using representations from layer 4 compared to layer 1, showing F_1 when directly predicting coarse tags (blue) and when predicting fine-grained tags and averaging inside each coarse tag (red).

Finally, we note that training an English autoencoder on the smaller dataset results in much worse representations compared to MT models, for both POS and SEM tagging (Table 4, last column), consistent with the behavior we observed on the larger data (Table 3, last column).

4.3 Analysis at the semantic tag level

The SEM tags are grouped in coarse-grained categories such as events, names, time, and logical expressions (Bjerva et al., 2016). In Figure 2 (top lines), we show the results of training and testing classifiers on coarse tags. Similar trends to the fine-grained case arise, with higher absolute scores: significant improvement using the 1st encoding layer and some additional improvement using the 4th layer, both statistically significant ($p < 0.001$). Again, there is a small effect of the target language.

Figure 3 shows the change in F_1 score (averaged over target languages) when moving from layer 1 to layer 4 representations. The blue bars describe the differences per coarse tag when directly predicting coarse tags. The red bars show the same differences when predicting fine-grained tags and micro-averaging inside each coarse tag. The former shows the differences between the two layers at distinguishing among coarse tags. The latter gives an idea of the differences when distinguishing between fine-grained tags within a coarse category. The first observation is that in the majority of cases there is an advantage for classifiers trained with layer 4 representations, i.e., higher layer representations are better suited for learning the SEM tags, at both coarse and fine-grained levels.

Considering specific tags, higher layers of the NMT model are especially better at capturing semantic information such as *discourse relations* (DIS tag: subordinate vs. coordinate vs. apposition relations), semantic properties of nouns (*roles* vs. *concepts*, within the ENT tag), *events* and *predicate tense* (EVE and TNS tags), *logic relations* and *quantifiers* (LOG tag: disjunction, conjunction, implication, existential, universal, etc.), and *comparative constructions* (COM tag: equatives, comparatives, and superlatives). These examples represent semantic concepts and relations that require a level of abstraction going beyond the lexeme or word form, and thus might be better represented in higher layers in the deep network.

One negative example that stands out in Figure 3 is the prediction of the MOD tag, corresponding to *modality* (necessity, possibility, and negation). It seems that such semantic concepts should be better represented in higher layers following our previous hypothesis. Still, layer 1 is better than layer 4 in this case. One possible explanation is that words tagged as MOD form a closed class, with only a few and mostly unambiguous words ("no", "not", "should", "must", "may", "can", "might", etc.). It is enough for the classifier to memorize these words in order to predict this class with high F_1, and this is something that occurs better in lower layers. One final case worth mentioning is the NAM category, which stands for different types of named entities (person, location, organization, artifact, etc.). In principle, this seems a clear case of semantic abstractions suited for higher layers,

	L1	L4	
1	REL	*SUB*	Zimbabwe 's President Robert Mugabe has freed three men who were jailed for murder and sabotage <u>*as*</u> they battled South Africa 's anti-apartheid African National Congress in 1988 .
2	REL	*SUB*	The military says the battle erupted <u>*after*</u> gunmen fired on U.S. troops and Afghan police investigating a reported beating of a villager .
3	IST	*SUB*	Election authorities had previously told Haitian-born Dumarsais Simeus that he was not eligible to run <u>*because*</u> he holds U.S. citizenship .
4	AND	*COO*	Fifty people representing 26 countries took the Oath of Allegiance this week (Thursday) <u>*and*</u> became U.S. citizens in a special ceremony at the Newseum in Washington , D.C.
5	AND	*COO*	But rebel groups said on Sunday they would not sign <u>*and*</u> insisted on changes .
6	AND	*COO*	A Fox asked him , " How can you pretend to prescribe for others , when you are unable to heal your own lame gait <u>*and*</u> wrinkled skin ? "
7	NIL	*APP*	But Syria 's president <u>,</u> Bashar al-Assad , has already rejected the commission 's request [...]
8	NIL	*APP*	Hassan Halemi <u>,</u> head of the pathology department at Kabul University where the autopsies were carried out , said hours of testing Saturday confirmed [...]
9	NIL	*APP*	Mr. Hu made the comments Tuesday during a meeting with Ichiro Ozawa <u>,</u> the leader of Japan 's main opposition party .
10	*AND*	COO	[...] abortion opponents will march past the U.S. Capitol <u>*and*</u> end outside the Supreme Court .
11	*AND*	COO	Van Schalkwyk said no new coal-fired power stations would be approved unless they use technology that captures <u>*and*</u> stores carbon emissions .
12	*AND*	COO	A MEMBER of the Kansas Legislature meeting a Cake of Soap was passing it by without recognition , but the Cake of Soap insisted on stopping <u>*and*</u> shaking hands .

Figure 4: Examples of cases of disagreement between layer 1 (L1) and layer 4 (L4) representations when predicting SEM tags. The correct tag is *italicized* and the relevant word is <u>underlined</u>.

but the results from layer 4 are not significantly better than those from layer 1. This might be signaling a limitation of the NMT system at learning this type of semantic classes. Another factor might be the fact that many named entities are out of vocabulary words for the NMT system.

4.4 Analyzing discourse relations

In this section, we analyze specific cases of disagreement between predictions using representations from layer 1 and layer 4. We focus on discourse relations, as they show the largest improvement when going from layer 1 to layer 4 representations (DIS category in Figure 3). Intuitively, identifying discourse relations requires a relatively large context so it is expected that higher layers would perform better in this case.

There are three discourse relations in the SEM tags annotation scheme: subordinate (SUB), coordinate (COO), and apposition (APP) relations. For each of those, Figure 4 (examples 1-9) shows the first three cases in the test set where layer 4 representations correctly predicted the tag but layer 1 representations were wrong. Examples 1-3 have subordinate conjunctions (*as*, *after*, *because*) connecting a main and an embedded clause, which layer 4 is able to correctly predict. Layer 1 mistakes these as attribute tags (REL, IST) that are usually used for prepositions. In examples 4-5,

the coordinate conjunction *and* is used to connect sentences/clauses, which layer 4 correctly tags as COO. Layer 1 wrongly predicts the tag AND, which is used for conjunctions connecting shorter expressions like words (e.g., "murder *and* sabotage" in example 1). Example 6 is probably an annotation error, as *and* connects the phrases "lame gait" and "wrinkled skin" and should be tagged as AND. In this case, layer 1 is actually correct. In examples 7-9, layer 4 correctly identifies the comma as introducing an apposition, while layer 1 predicts NIL, a tag for punctuation marks without semantic content (e.g., end-of-sentence period). As expected, in most of these cases identifying the discourse function requires a fairly large context.

Finally, we show in examples 10-12 the first three occurrences of AND in the test set, where layer 1 was correct and layer 4 was wrong. Interestingly, two of these (10-11) are clear cases of *and* connecting clauses or sentences, which should have been annotated as COO, and the last (12) is a conjunction of two gerunds. The predictions from layer 4 in these cases thus appear justifiable.

4.5 Other architectural variants

Here we consider two architectural variants that have been shown to benefit NMT systems: bidirectional encoder and residual connections. We also experiment with NMT systems trained with different depths. Our motivation in this section is to see if the patterns we observed thus far hold in different NMT architectures.

Bidirectional encoder Bidirectional LSTMs have become ubiquitous in NLP and also give some improvement as NMT encoders (Britz et al., 2017). We confirm these results and note improvements in both translation (+1-2 BLEU) and SEM tagging quality (+3-4% accuracy), across the board, when using a bidirectional encoder. Some of our bidirectional models obtain 92-93% accuracy, which is close to the state-of-the-art on this task (Bjerva et al., 2016). We observed similar improvements on POS tagging. Comparing POS and SEM tagging (Table 5), we note that higher layer representations improve SEM tagging, while POS tagging peaks at layer 1, in line with our previous observations.

Residual connections Deep networks can sometimes be trained better if residual connections are introduced between layers. Such connections were also found useful for SEM tagging (Bjerva et al., 2016). Indeed, we noticed small but consistent improvements in both translation (+0.9 BLEU) and POS and SEM tagging (up to +0.6% accuracy) when using features extracted from an NMT model trained with residual connections (Table 5). We also observe similar trends as before: POS tagging does not benefit from features from the upper layers, while SEM tagging improves with layer 4 representations.

Shallower MT models In comparing network depth in NMT, Britz et al. (2017) found that encoders with 2 to 4 layers performed the best. For completeness, we report here results using features extracted from models trained originally with 2 and 3 layers, in addition to our basic setting of 4 layers. Table 6 shows consistent trends with our previous observations: POS tagging does not benefit from upper layers, while SEM tagging does, although the improvement is rather small in the shallower models.

5 Related Work

Techniques for analyzing neural network models include visualization of hidden units (Elman, 1991; Karpathy et al., 2015; Kádár et al., 2016; Qian et al., 2016a), which provide illuminating, but often anecdotal information on how the network works. A number of studies aim to ob-

		0	1	2	3	4
Uni	POS	87.9	92.0	91.7	91.8	91.9
	SEM	81.8	87.8	87.4	87.6	88.2
Bi	POS	87.9	93.3	92.9	93.2	92.8
	SEM	81.9	91.3	90.8	91.9	91.9
Res	POS	87.9	92.5	91.9	92.0	92.4
	SEM	81.9	88.2	87.5	87.6	88.5

Table 5: POS and SEM tagging accuracy with features from different layers of 4-layer Uni/Bidirectional/Residual NMT encoders, averaged over all non-English target languages.

		0	1	2	3	4
4	POS	87.9	92.0	91.7	91.8	91.9
	SEM	81.8	87.8	87.4	87.6	88.2
3	POS	87.9	92.5	92.3	92.4	–
	SEM	81.9	88.2	88.0	88.4	–
2	POS	87.9	92.7	92.7	–	–
	SEM	82.0	88.5	88.7	–	–

Table 6: POS and SEM tagging accuracy with features from different layers of 2/3/4-layer encoders, averaged over all non-English target languages.

tain quantitative correlations between parts of the neural network and linguistic properties, in both speech (Wu and King, 2016; Alishahi et al., 2017; Belinkov and Glass, 2017; Wang et al., 2017) and language processing models (Köhn, 2015; Qian et al., 2016a; Adi et al., 2016; Linzen et al., 2016; Qian et al., 2016b). Methodologically, our work is most similar to Shi et al. (2016) and Belinkov et al. (2017), who also used hidden vectors from neural MT models to predict linguistic properties. However, they focused on relatively low-level tasks (syntax and morphology, respectively), while we apply the approach to a semantic task and compare the results with a POS tagging task.

Our methodology is reminiscent of the approach taken by Pérez-Ortiz and Forcada (2001), who trained a recurrent neural network POS tagger in two steps. However, their goal was to improve POS tagging while we use it as a task to evaluate neural MT models.

6 Conclusion

While neural network models have improved the state-of-the-art in machine translation, it is difficult to interpret what they learn about language. In this work, we explore what kind of linguistic information such models learn at different layers. Our experimental evaluation leads to interesting insights about the hidden representations in NMT models such as the effect of layer depth and target language on part-of-speech and semantic tagging.

In the future, we would like to extend this work to other syntactic and semantic tasks that require building relations such as dependency relations and predicate-argument structure or to evaluate semantic representations of multi-word expressions. We believe that understanding how semantic properties are learned in NMT is a key step for creating better machine translation systems.

Acknowledgments

This research was carried out in collaboration between the HBKU Qatar Computing Research Institute (QCRI) and the MIT Computer Science and Artificial Intelligence Laboratory (CSAIL).

References

Lasha Abzianidze, Johannes Bjerva, Kilian Evang, Hessel Haagsma, Rik van Noord, Pierre Ludmann, Duc-Duy Nguyen, and Johan Bos. 2017. The Parallel Meaning Bank: Towards a Multilingual Corpus of Translations Annotated with Compositional Meaning Representations. In *Proceedings of the 15th Conference of the European Chapter of the Association for Computational Linguistics: Volume 2, Short Papers*, pages 242–247. Association for Computational Linguistics.

Yossi Adi, Einat Kermany, Yonatan Belinkov, Ofer Lavi, and Yoav Goldberg. 2016. Fine-grained Analysis of Sentence Embeddings Using Auxiliary Prediction Tasks. *arXiv preprint arXiv:1608.04207*.

Afra Alishahi, Marie Barking, and Grzegorz Chrupała. 2017. Encoding of phonology in a recurrent neural model of grounded speech. In *Proceedings of the SIGNLL Conference on Computational Natural Language Learning*, Vancouver, Canada. Association for Computational Linguistics.

Dzmitry Bahdanau, Kyunghyun Cho, and Yoshua Bengio. 2014. Neural Machine Translation by Jointly Learning to Align and Translate. *arXiv preprint arXiv:1409.0473*.

Marzieh Bazrafshan and Daniel Gildea. 2013. Semantic Roles for String to Tree Machine Translation. In *Proceedings of the 51st Annual Meeting of the Association for Computational Linguistics (Volume 2: Short Papers)*, pages 419–423, Sofia, Bulgaria. Association for Computational Linguistics.

Marzieh Bazrafshan and Daniel Gildea. 2014. Comparing Representations of Semantic Roles for String-To-Tree Decoding. In *Proceedings of the 2014 Conference on Empirical Methods in Natural Language Processing (EMNLP)*, pages 1786–1791, Doha, Qatar. Association for Computational Linguistics.

Yonatan Belinkov, Nadir Durrani, Fahim Dalvi, Hassan Sajjad, and James Glass. 2017. What do Neural Machine Translation Models Learn about Morphology? In *Proceedings of the 55th Annual Meeting of the Association for Computational Linguistics (Volume 1: Long Papers)*, pages 861–872. Association for Computational Linguistics.

Yonatan Belinkov and James Glass. 2017. Analyzing Hidden Representations in End-to-End Automatic Speech Recognition Systems. In *Advances in Neural Information Processing Systems (NIPS)*.

Johannes Bjerva, Barbara Plank, and Johan Bos. 2016. Semantic Tagging with Deep Residual Networks. In *Proceedings of COLING 2016, the 26th International Conference on Computational Linguistics: Technical Papers*, pages 3531–3541, Osaka, Japan. The COLING 2016 Organizing Committee.

Denny Britz, Anna Goldie, Thang Luong, and Quoc Le. 2017. Massive Exploration of Neural Machine Translation Architectures. *ArXiv e-prints*.

Seng Yee Chan, Tou Hwee Ng, and David Chiang. 2007. Word Sense Disambiguation Improves Statistical Machine Translation. In *Proceedings of the 45th Annual Meeting of the Association of Computational Linguistics*, pages 33–40. Association for Computational Linguistics.

Fahim Dalvi, Nadir Durrani, Hassan Sajjad, Yonatan Belinkov, and Stephan Vogel. 2017. Understanding and Improving Morphological Learning in the Neural Machine Translation Decoder. In *Proceedings of the 8th International Joint Conference on Natural Language Processing (Volume 1: Long Papers)*, Taipei, Taiwan. Association for Computational Linguistics.

Jeffrey L Elman. 1991. Distributed representations, simple recurrent networks, and grammatical structure. *Machine learning*, 7(2-3):195–225.

Qin Gao and Stephan Vogel. 2011. Utilizing Target-Side Semantic Role Labels to Assist Hierarchical Phrase-based Machine Translation. In *Proceedings of Fifth Workshop on Syntax, Semantics and Structure in Statistical Translation*, pages 107–115. Association for Computational Linguistics.

Sepp Hochreiter and Jürgen Schmidhuber. 1997. Long short-term memory. *Neural Computation*, 9(8):1735–1780.

Bevan Jones, Jacob Andreas, Daniel Bauer, Moritz Karl Hermann, and Kevin Knight. 2012. Semantics-Based Machine Translation with Hyperedge Replacement Grammars. In *Proceedings of COLING 2012*, pages 1359–1376. The COLING 2012 Organizing Committee.

Ákos Kádár, Grzegorz Chrupała, and Afra Alishahi. 2016. Representation of linguistic form and function in recurrent neural networks. *arXiv preprint arXiv:1602.08952*.

Andrej Karpathy, Justin Johnson, and Fei-Fei Li. 2015. Visualizing and Understanding Recurrent Networks. *arXiv preprint arXiv:1506.02078*.

Yoon Kim. 2016. Seq2seq-attn. `https://github.com/harvardnlp/seq2seq-attn`.

Diederik Kingma and Jimmy Ba. 2014. Adam: A Method for Stochastic Optimization. *arXiv preprint arXiv:1412.6980*.

Arne Köhn. 2015. What's in an Embedding? Analyzing Word Embeddings through Multilingual Evaluation. In *Proceedings of the 2015 Conference on Empirical Methods in Natural Language Processing*, pages 2067–2073, Lisbon, Portugal. Association for Computational Linguistics.

Tal Linzen, Emmanuel Dupoux, and Yoav Goldberg. 2016. Assessing the Ability of LSTMs to Learn Syntax-Sensitive Dependencies. *Transactions of the Association for Computational Linguistics*, 4:521–535.

Ding Liu and Daniel Gildea. 2010. Semantic Role Features for Machine Translation. In *Proceedings of the 23rd International Conference on Computational Linguistics (Coling 2010)*, pages 716–724. Coling 2010 Organizing Committee.

Tomas Mikolov, Ilya Sutskever, Kai Chen, Greg S Corrado, and Jeff Dean. 2013. Distributed Representations of Words and Phrases and their Compositionality. In *Advances in Neural Information Processing Systems*, pages 3111–3119.

Sebastian Padó. 2006. *User's guide to `sigf`: Significance testing by approximate randomisation.* `https://www.nlpado.de/~sebastian/software/sigf.shtml`.

Juan Antonio Pérez-Ortiz and Mikel L. Forcada. 2001. Part-of-Speech Tagging with Recurrent Neural Networks. In *Neural Networks, 2001. Proceedings. IJCNN '01. International Joint Conference on*, volume 3, pages 1588–1592.

Peng Qian, Xipeng Qiu, and Xuanjing Huang. 2016a. Analyzing Linguistic Knowledge in Sequential Model of Sentence. In *Proceedings of the 2016 Conference on Empirical Methods in Natural Language Processing*, pages 826–835, Austin, Texas. Association for Computational Linguistics.

Peng Qian, Xipeng Qiu, and Xuanjing Huang. 2016b. Investigating Language Universal and Specific Properties in Word Embeddings. In *Proceedings of the 54th Annual Meeting of the Association for Computational Linguistics (Volume 1: Long Papers)*, pages 1478–1488, Berlin, Germany. Association for Computational Linguistics.

Rico Sennrich. 2017. How Grammatical is Character-level Neural Machine Translation? Assessing MT Quality with Contrastive Translation Pairs. In *Proceedings of the 15th Conference of the European Chapter of the Association for Computational Linguistics: Volume 2, Short Papers*, pages 376–382. Association for Computational Linguistics.

Xing Shi, Inkit Padhi, and Kevin Knight. 2016. Does String-Based Neural MT Learn Source Syntax? In *Proceedings of the 2016 Conference on Empirical Methods in Natural Language Processing*, pages 1526–1534, Austin, Texas. Association for Computational Linguistics.

Ilya Sutskever, Oriol Vinyals, and Quoc VV Le. 2014. Sequence to Sequence Learning with Neural Networks. In *Advances in Neural Information Processing Systems*, pages 3104–3112.

Ekaterina Vylomova, Trevor Cohn, Xuanli He, and Gholamreza Haffari. 2016. Word Representation Models for Morphologically Rich Languages in Neural Machine Translation. *arXiv preprint arXiv:1606.04217*.

Yu-Hsuan Wang, Cheng-Tao Chung, and Hung-yi Lee. 2017. Gate Activation Signal Analysis for Gated Recurrent Neural Networks and Its Correlation with Phoneme Boundaries. *arXiv preprint arXiv:1703.07588*.

Dekai Wu, Pascale N Fung, Marine Carpuat, Chi-kiu Lo, Yongsheng Yang, and Zhaojun Wu. 2011. Lexical Semantics for Statistical Machine Translation. In *Handbook of Natural Language Processing and Machine Translation: DARPA Global Autonomous Language Exploitation*.

Zhizheng Wu and Simon King. 2016. Investigating Gated Recurrent Networks for Speech Synthesis. In *Acoustics, Speech and Signal Processing (ICASSP), 2016 IEEE International Conference on*, pages 5140–5144. IEEE.

Micha Ziemski, Marcin Junczys-Dowmunt, and Bruno Pouliquen. 2016. The United Nations Parallel Corpus v1.0. In *Proceedings of the Tenth International Conference on Language Resources and Evaluation (LREC 2016)*, Paris, France. European Language Resources Association (ELRA).

Context-Aware Smoothing for Neural Machine Translation

Kehai Chen[1]*, **Rui Wang**[2]†, **Masao Utiyama**[2], **Eiichiro Sumita**[2] and **Tiejun Zhao**[1]

[1]Machine Intelligence & Translation Laboratory, Harbin Institute of Technology
[2]ASTREC, National Institute of Information and Communications Technology (NICT)
{khchen and tjzhao}@hit.edu.cn
{wangrui, mutiyama and eiichiro.sumita}@nict.go.jp

Abstract

In Neural Machine Translation (**NMT**), each word is represented as a low-dimension, real-value vector for encoding its syntax and semantic information. This means that even if the word is in a different sentence context, it is represented as the fixed vector to learn source representation. Moreover, a large number of Out-Of-Vocabulary (**OOV**) words, which have different syntax and semantic information, are represented as the same vector representation of *unk*. To alleviate this problem, we propose a novel context-aware smoothing method to dynamically learn a sentence-specific vector for each word (including OOV words) depending on its local context words in a sentence. The learned context-aware representation is integrated into the NMT to improve the translation performance. Empirical results on NIST Chinese-to-English translation task show that the proposed approach achieves 1.78 BLEU improvements on average over a strong attentional NMT, and outperforms some existing systems.

1 Introduction

Neural Machine Translation (**NMT**) (Kalchbrenner and Blunsom, 2013; Sutskever et al., 2014; Bahdanau et al., 2015), has shown prominent performances in comparison with the conventional Phrase Based Statistical Machine Translation (**PBSMT**) (Koehn et al., 2003). In NMT, a source sentence is converted into a vector representation by an RNN called *encoder*, then another RNN called *decoder* generates target sentence word by word based on the source representation with attention information and target history.

One advantage of NMT systems is that each word is represented as a low-dimension, real-valued vector, instead of storing statistical rules as in PBSMT. This means that even if the word is in a different sentence context, it is represented as the fixed vector to learn source representation. Figure 1 (a) shows two pair of Chinese-to-English parallel sentences in which two Chinese sentences contain the same word *"da"*. Intuitively, the *"da"* denotes "beating" in the first Chinese sentence while the *"da"* denotes "playing" in the second Chinese sentence. It is obvious that the *"da"* which denotes different meanings in a specific sentence is represented as the same word vector in the encoder of NMT, as show in Figure 1 (b). Although the RNN-based encoder can capture the sentence context for each word, we believe that offering better word vector with context-aware representation might help improve translation quality of NMT.

Moreover, a large number of Out-Of-Vocabulary (**OOV**) words which have different syntax and semantic information are represented as the same vector representation of *unk*. Actually, this kind of simple approach may cause ambiguity of the sentences since the single *unk* breaks the structure of sentences, thus hurts representation learning of source sentence and translation prediction of the target word. For example, the *unk* firstly affects source representation learning in *encoder*; then the negative effect would be further transformed to the *decoder*, which generates the poverty context vector and hidden layer state for translation prediction, as shown in the gray parts of Figure 1 (c). Besides, when the generated target word may also be *unk*, the negative effect of *unk* will become more severe.

---

*Kehai Chen was an internship research fellow at NICT when conducting this work.
†Corresponding author.

Proceedings of the The 8th International Joint Conference on Natural Language Processing, pages 11–20,
Taipei, Taiwan, November 27 – December 1, 2017 ©2017 AFNLP

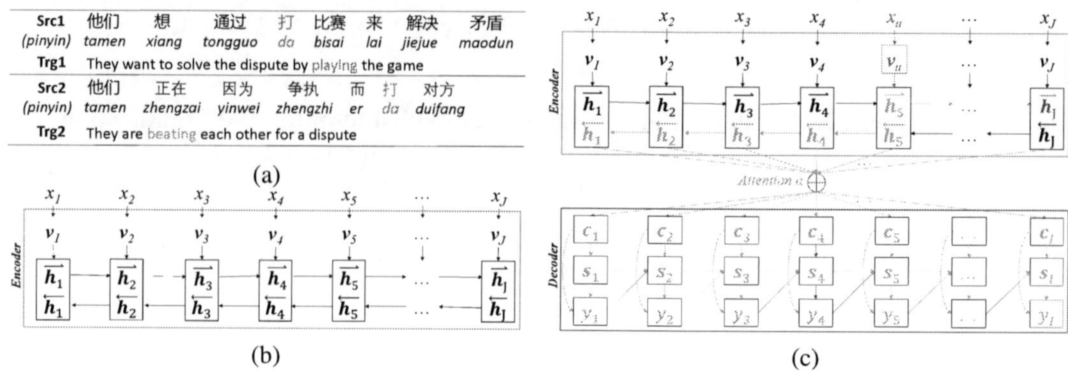

Figure 1: (a) Two parallel Chinese-to-English sentence pair; (b) The encoder of NMT; (c) The NMT with OOV, these gray parts indicate the parameters of NMT which are affected by the OOV x_u.

In this paper, we propose a novel context-aware smoothing method to dynamically learn a Context-Aware Representation (**CAR**) for each word (including OOV words) depending on its local context words in a sentence. We then use the learned CAR to extend word vector in a sentence, thus enhancing source representation for improving the translation performance of NMT. First, compared with the single *unk* vector, we encode the context words of each OOV as a Context-Aware Representation (**CAR**), which has the potential to capture the *OOV*'s semantic information. Second, we also extend the context-aware smoothing method to in-vocabulary words, which enhances *encoder* and *decoder* of NMT by more effectively utilizing context information by the learned CAR. To this end, we proposed two unique neural networks to learn the context-aware representation for each word depending on its context words in a fixed-size window. We then design four NMT models with CAR to improve translation performance by smoothing the encoder and decoder.

The remainder of the paper is organized as follows. Section 2 introduces the related work in the NMT. Section 3 presents two novel neural models to learn the CAR for each word. Section 4 integrates the CAR into the NMT by using smoothing strategies. Section 5 reports the experimental results obtained in the Chinese-to-English task. Finally, we conclude the contributions of the paper and discuss the further work in Section 6.

2 Related Work

In traditional SMT, there are many research works to improve the translations of OOVs. Fung and Cheung (2004) and Shao and Ng (2004) adopte comparable corpora and web resources to extract translations for each unknown word. Marton et al. (2009) and Mirkin et al. (2009) applied paraphrase model and entailment rules to replace unknown words with in-vocabulary synonyms before translation. A series of works (Knight and Graehl, 1997; Jiang et al., 2007; Al-Onaizan and Knight, 2002) utilized transliteration and web mining techniques with external monolingual/bilingual corpora, comparable data and the web resource to find the translation of the unknown words. Nearly most of the related PBSMT researches focused on finding the correct translation of the unknown words with external resources and ignored the negative effect for other words.

Compared with PBSMT, due to high computational cost, NMT has a more limited vocabulary size and severe OOV phenomenon. The existing PBSMT methods that used external resources to translate unknown words for SMT are hard to be directly introduced into NMT, because of NMT's *soft*-alignment mechanism (Bahdanau et al., 2015). To relieve the negative effect of unknown words for NMT, Luong et al. (2015) proposed a word alignment algorithm, allowing the NMT system to emit, for each OOV word in the target sentence, the position of its corresponding word in the source sentence, and to translate every OOV in a post-processing step using a external bilingual dictionary. Although these methods improved the translation of OOV, they must learn external bilingual dictionary information in advance.

From the point of vocabulary size, many works tried to use a large vocabulary size, thus covering more words. Jean et al. (2015) proposed a method based on importance sampling that allowed NMT model to use a very large target vocabulary for relieving the OOV phenomenon in NMT, which are only designed to reduce the computational complexity in training, not for decoding. Arthur et al. (2016) introduced discrete translation lexicons into NMT to imrpove the translations of these low-frequency words. Mi et al. (2016) proposed a vocabulary manipulation approach by limiting the number of vocabulary being predicted by each batch or sentence, to reduce both the training and the decoding complexity. These methods focused on the translation of OOV itself and ignored the other negative effect caused by the OOV, such as the translations of the words around the OOV.

Recently, many works exploited the granularity translation unit from words to smaller subwords or characters. Sennrich et al. (2016) introduced a simpler and more effective approach to encode rare and unknown words as sequences of subword units by Byte Pair Encoding (Gage, 1994). This is based on the intuition that various word classes are translatable via smaller units than words. Luong and Manning (2016) segmented the known words into character sequence, and learned the unknown word representation by character-level recurrent neural networks, thus achieving open vocabulary NMT. Li et al. (2016) replaced OOVs with in-vocabulary words by semantic similarity to reduce the negative effect for words around the OOVs. Costa-jussà and Fonollosa (2016) presented a character-based NMT, in which character-level embeddings were in combination with convolutional and highway layers to replace the standard lookup-based word representations. These methods extended the vocabulary to a larger or unlimited vocabulary and improved the performance of NMT tasks, especially in the morphological rich language pairs.

Instead of utilizing larger vocabulary or sub-unit information, we exploit to relieve more translation performance for NMT from the negative effect of OOVs by learning context-aware representations for OOVs. As a result, the proposed method can smooth the representation of word and reduce the *unk*'s negative effect in attention model, context annotations and decoding hidden states, thus improving the performance of NMT.

3 Context-Aware Representation

Intuitively, when one understands natural language sentence, especially including polysemy words or OOVs, one often inferences the meaning of these words depending on its context words. Context plays an important role in learning distributed representation of word (Mikolov et al., 2013a,b). Motivated by this, we propose two neural network methods, including Feedforward Context-of-Word Model (**FCWM**) and Convolutional Context-of-Words Model (**CCWM**), to learn a Context-Aware Representation (**CAR**) for each word.

3.1 Feedforward Context-of-Words Model

Inspired by the representation learning of word (Bengio et al., 2003), the proposed FCWM includes an input layer, a projection layer, and a non-linear output layer, as shown in Figure 2 (a).

Specifically, suppose there is a source language sentence, $\{x_1, x_2, \ldots, x_j, \ldots, x_J\}$. If the context window is set as $2n$ ($n = 2$), the context of each word x_i is defined as its historical n words and future n words:

$$L_j = x_{j-n}, \ldots, x_{j-1}, x_{j+1}, \ldots, x_{j+n}. \quad (1)$$

In the input layer, each word in L_j is transformed into one-hot representation. [1] The projection layer concatenates one-hot representations in L_j to a $(2nm)$-dimension vector $\boldsymbol{L}_j$,[2]

$$\boldsymbol{L}_j = [v_{j-n} : \ldots, v_{j-1} : v_{j+1} : \cdots : v_{j+n}], \quad (2)$$

where ":" denotes the concatenation operation of word vectors.

We then approximate to learn its semantic representation $\boldsymbol{V}_{L_j} \in R^m$ by a non-linear output layer instead of softmax layer:

$$\boldsymbol{V}_{L_j} = \sigma(\boldsymbol{W}_1 \boldsymbol{L}_j + \boldsymbol{b}_1)^T, \quad (3)$$

---

[1]If the L_j includes OOV, we use original *unk* vector to represent it. Besides, we also try the average vector of the current sentence word to represent it, but gain the similar translation performance.

[2]In this paper, the bold variable denotes a continuous space vector.

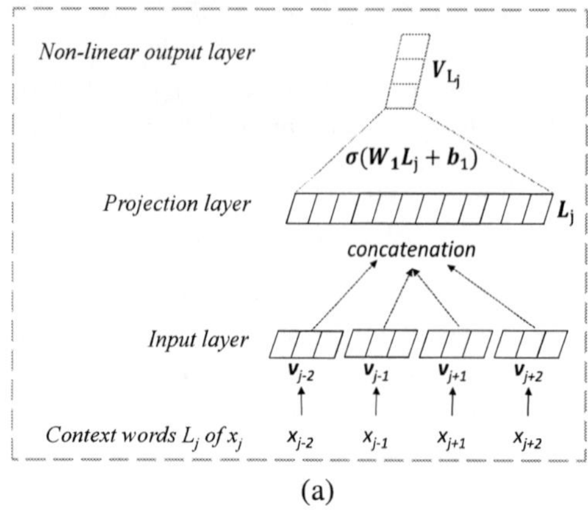
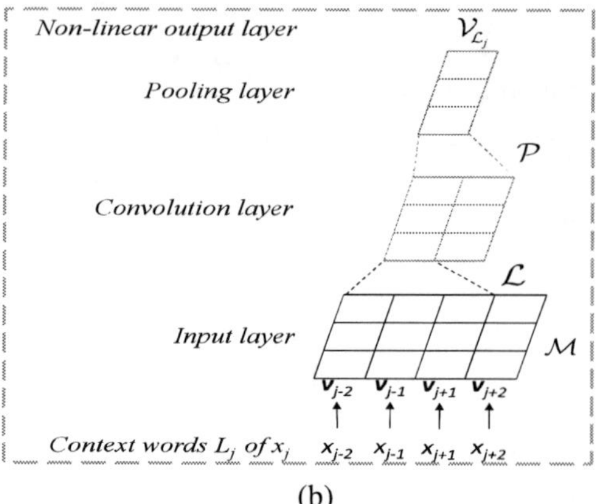

(a)   (b)

Figure 2: (a) Feedforward Context-of-Word Model; (b) Convolution Context-of-Word Model.

where σ is a non-linear activation function (e.g., *Tanh*), T represents matrix transpose, and W_1 is a weight matrix and b_1 is a bias term.

Finally, we extend each word with the learned CAR vector V_{L_j}, thus feeding into the NMT to enhance source representation for improving target word prediction. Therefore, the proposed FCWM plays the role of the function φ parameterized by θ_1, which maps the context L_j of each word into vector V_{L_j} as follows:

$$V_{L_j} = \varphi(L_j; \theta_1). \qquad (4)$$

3.2 Convolutional Context-of-Words Model

Compared with the FCWM, the proposed CCWM indirectly encodes the context words of each word as a compositional semantic representation to represent the OOV. Specifically, the proposed CCWM is a novel variant of the standard convolutional neural network (Collobert et al., 2011), including an input layer, a convolution layer, a pooling layer and a non-linear output layer, as shown in Figure 2 (b).

Input Layer: When the dimension of word vector is m and the context window is set to $2n$, the input layer is denoted as one vector matrix $\mathcal{M} \in R^{m \times 2n}$. In $\mathcal{M}$, each column denotes context words of word x_j, that is, $\mathcal{M}$ is $[v_{j-n}, \cdots, v_{j-1}, v_{j+1}, \cdots, v_{j+n}]$ for the context $\{x_{j-n}, \cdots, x_{j-1}, x_{j+1}, \cdots, x_{j+n}\}$ of x_j.

Convolutional Layer: In the convolutional layer, let the filter window size be $m \times k$ ($2 \leq k \leq 2n$), where the k is set to 3 in our experiments, thus generating feature map $\mathcal{L}_j$ as follows:

$$\mathcal{L}_j = \psi(W_2[v_j : v_{j+1} : \cdots : v_{j+k}] + b_2), \qquad (5)$$

where ψ is a non-linear activation function,[3] $W_2 \in R^{m \times k \cdot m}$ is the weight matrix and $b_2 \in R^m$ is a bias term. After the filter traverses the input matrix, the output of the feature map $\mathcal{L}$ is:

$$\mathcal{L} = [\mathcal{L}_1, \ldots, \mathcal{L}_{2n-k+1}]. \qquad (6)$$

Pooling Layer: The pooling operation (e.g., *max*, *average*) is commonly used to extract robust features from convolution. For the output feature map of the convolution layers, a column-wise *max* is performed over the consecutive columns of window size 2 as follows:

$$\mathcal{P}_l = max[\mathcal{L}_{2l-1}, \mathcal{L}_{2l}], \qquad (7)$$

where $1 \leq l \leq \frac{2n-k+1}{2}$. After the *max* pooling, the output of the feature map $\mathcal{P}$ is:

$$\mathcal{P} = [\mathcal{P}_1, \ldots, \mathcal{P}_{\frac{2n-k+1}{2}}]. \qquad (8)$$

Non-linear Output Layer: The output layer is typically a fully connected layer multiplied by a matrix. In this paper, first row-wise averaging from the pooling layers is performed without any parameters, and gain CAR of each word by non-linear active function σ (e.g., *Tanh*); hence, the CAR $V_{\mathcal{L}_j}$ of word x_j is obtained by

$$V_{\mathcal{L}_j} = \sigma(W_3(average(\sum_{l=1}^{\frac{2n-k+1}{2}} \mathcal{P}_l)) + b_3). \qquad (9)$$

Therefore, the above CCWM plays the role of the function φ parameterized by θ_2, which maps

---

[3] We used a ReLU activation function.

the context $\mathcal{L}_j$ of word x_j into vector $\mathcal{V}_{\mathcal{L}_j}$ as follows:

$$\mathcal{V}_{\mathcal{L}_j} = \varphi(\mathcal{L}_j; \theta_2) \tag{10}$$

In this case, the word x_j is represented as a CAR $\mathcal{V}_{\mathcal{L}_j}$.

4 NMT with Context-Aware Smoothing

4.1 NMT Background

An NMT model consists of an *encoder* process and a *decoder* process, and hence it is often called *encoder-decoder* model (Kalchbrenner and Blunsom, 2013; Sutskever et al., 2014; Bahdanau et al., 2015), as shown in Figure 1. Typically, each unit of source input $(x_1, \ldots, x_J)$ is firstly embedded as a vector $\boldsymbol{v}_{x_j}$, and then represented as annotation vector $\boldsymbol{h}_j$ by

$$\boldsymbol{h}_j = f_{enc}(\boldsymbol{v}_{x_j}, \boldsymbol{h}_{j-1}), \tag{11}$$

where f_{enc} is a bidirectional Recurrent Neural Network (**RNN**) (Bahdanau et al., 2015). These annotation vectors $\{\boldsymbol{h}_1, \ldots, \boldsymbol{h}_J\}$ are used to generate target word in *decoder*.

An RNN *decoder* is used to compute the target word y_i probability by a softmax layer g:

$$P(y_i|y_{<i}, x) = g(\boldsymbol{v}_{y_{i-1}}, \boldsymbol{s}_i, \boldsymbol{c}_i), \tag{12}$$

where $\boldsymbol{v}_{y_{i-1}}$ is vector representation of the previously emitted word y_{i-1}, $\boldsymbol{s}_i$ is an RNN hidden state for the current time step and the $\boldsymbol{c}_i$ is the current context vector.

4.2 Smoothing Strategy

In this subsection, we will introduce NMT with the learned CAR. This would relieve the translation performance of NMT from source representation. To this end, we use OOV as an example to integrate FCWM or CCWM into NMT; and then extend them to in-vocabulary words.

To learn the representation of source sentence, the proposed FCWM or CCWM are integrated into the *encoder* of NMT. If the source word x_j is in-vocabulary, its annotation vector $\boldsymbol{h}_j$ is learned by the traditional *encoder*; if the source word x_j is not in-vocabulary (OOV x_u), the FCWM or CCWM proposed in section 3 are used to learn its CAR instead of single *unk* vector, and further learn its annotation vector $\boldsymbol{h}_j$. According to the eq.(11), the *encoder* with CAR learns the annotation vector

$\boldsymbol{h}_j$ by the eq.(13):

$$\boldsymbol{h}_j = \begin{cases} f_{enc}(\boldsymbol{h}_{x_j}, \boldsymbol{h}_{j-1}), & x_j \in V_s \\ f_{enc}(\varphi_e(\boldsymbol{V}_{L_{x_j}}), \boldsymbol{h}_{j-1}), & x_j \notin V_s, \end{cases} \tag{13}$$

where V_s is source-side vocabulary table in NMT, φ_e is the proposed FCWM or CCWM integrated into the *encoder* according to eq.(4) or eq.(10), and $\boldsymbol{V}_{L_j}$ is the learned CAR over the source-side L_j from eq.(1):

$$L_j = x_{j-n}, \ldots, x_{j-1}, x_{j+1}, \ldots, x_{j+n}.^4 \tag{14}$$

Similarly, the proposed FCWM or CCWM are also integrated into the *decoder* in NMT. Compared with the *encoder* with CAR, the target-side OOV's context words of training processing is different from that of the decoding in which target-side OOV's future context is unknowable. That is, only the historical n words of y_{i-1} are used to learn the CAR of $\boldsymbol{V}_{L'_{i-1}}$. To be consistent with the decoding process, the previous $2n$ words of OOV are regarded as its context L'_{i-1} instead of the previous n words and future n words. Therefore, the *decoder* with CAR predicts the next target word by the eq.(15):

$$P(y_i|y_{<i}, x) = \begin{cases} g(\boldsymbol{v}_{y_{i-1}}, \boldsymbol{s}_i, \boldsymbol{c}_i), & y_{i-1} \in V_t \\ g(\varphi_d(L'_{i-1}), \boldsymbol{s}_i, \boldsymbol{c}_i), & y_{i-1} \notin V_t, \end{cases} \tag{15}$$

where V_t is target-side vocabulary table in NMT, φ_d denotes the proposed FCWM or CCWM integrated into the *decoder* according to eq.(4) or eq.(10), and $\boldsymbol{V}_{L'_{i-1}}$ is the learned CAR over the target-side context L'_{i-1} from eq.(1):

$$L'_{i-1} = y_{i-2n}, \ldots, y_{i-n}, \ldots, y_{i-1}.^5 \tag{16}$$

4.3 Models

Based on the above smoothing strategy, we design four novel NMT models: **CARNMT**-Encoder, **CARNMT**-Decoder, **CARNMT**-Both and an **ALLSmooth**, all of which can make use of CAR to enhance *encoder* or *decoder* of NMT for improving the translation performance:

- **CARNMT**-Encoder: Only smoothing source-side unk to relieve the influence in the *encoder*, as shown in Figure 3 (a).

---

[4]If the number of previous context or future context words is less n, we pads a sentence start symbol *BEG* or sentence end symbol *EOS*.

[5]If the number of previous context words is less $2n$, we pads L_{i-1} using a sentence start symbol *BEG*.

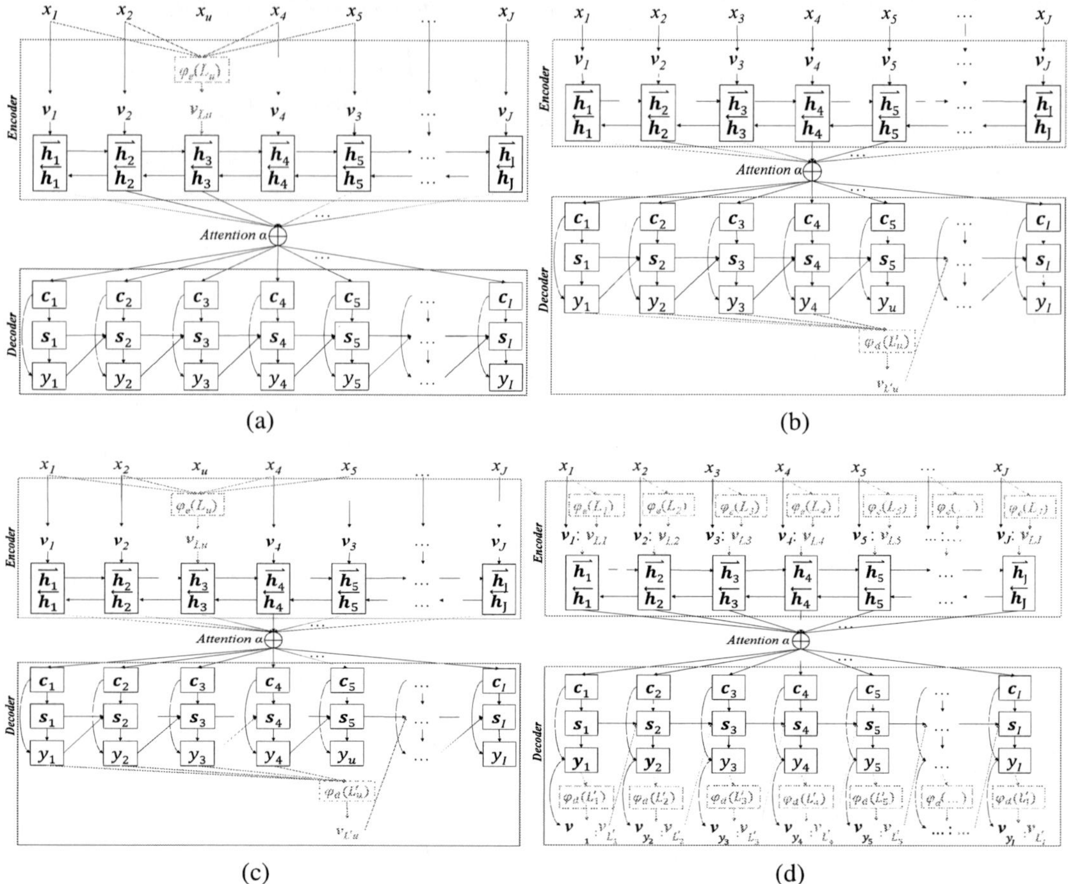

Figure 3: (a) **CARNMT**-Encoder; (b) **CARNMT**-Decoder; (c) **CARNMT**-Both; (d) **ALLSmooth**, in which the red dotted arrows obtain the context words of each word according to eq.(14) or eq.(16). The blue dotted boxes denote FCWM or CCWM proposed in section 2.

- **CARNMT**-Decoder: Only smoothing target-side unk in the *decoder*, as shown in Figure 3 (b).

- **CARNMT**-Both: Both smoothing the unks of source-side and target-side in the NMT, as shown in Figure 3 (c).

- **ALLSmooth**: this model smooths not only the *unk* words, but also all source-and target-side in-vocabulary words by the learned CARs, as shown in Figure 3 (d). Meanwhile, the vector of in-vocabularys word and its CARs are concatenated as a novel vector to represent the semantic information of the word instead of replacing the word vector with its CAR.

In our experiments, each model has two variants according to the integrated FCWM or CCWM.

For example, "CARNMT-encoder (CCWM)" indicates that the CAR for OOV is learned by the CCWM proposed in the section 3. In Figure 3, we take FCWM to learn the CAR for each word (including OOV). Therefore, there is easy to use the proposed CCWM instead of the FCWM.

Moreover, the proposed NMT models with CAR are an integrative architecture without any external information. Especially, the NMT and FCWM or CCWM, which are not isolated from each other, are trained by optimizing their parameters jointly. In other words, the θ_1 or θ_2 and the parameters of NMT are optimized jointly.

5 Experiments

5.1 Setting up

We carry out experiments on the Chinese-to-English translation task. The training dataset

System	Dev (MT02)	MT03	MT04	MT05	MT06	MT08	AVG
Moses	33.15	31.02	33.78	30.33	29.62	23.53	29.66
Bahdanau et al. (2015)	36.42	34.22	37.11	33.02	32.69	25.38	32.48
Sennrich et al. (2016)	36.89	35.39	38.24	33.73	32.74	26.22	33.26
Costa-jussà and Fonollosa (2016)	35.98	34.93	37.56	33.24	32.32	26.02	32.81
Li et al. (2016)	36.96	35.78	38.42	34.02	33.14	26.36	33.54
CARNMT-Encoder (FCWM)	36.78	35.56**	38.14*	33.69	33.13	26.16*	33.34
CARNMT-Decoder (FCWM)	36.67	34.65	37.60	33.26	33.01	26.15*	32.93
CARNMT-Both (FCWM)	37.36	35.43**	38.34**	33.43	**33.47**	**26.86****	**33.50**
ALLSmooth (FCWM)	37.71	35.73**	**38.53****	33.91*	**33.53***	**27.18****	**33.78**
CARNMT-Encoder (CCWM)	37.12	35.64**	38.14*	33.49	33.26*	26.57**	33.42
CARNMT-Decoder (CCWM)	36.33	34.56	37.43	33.24	32.96	25.86	32.81
CARNMT-Both (CCWM)	37.56	**35.83****	**38.52****	33.73	**33.37****	**27.06****	**33.70**
ALLSmooth (CCWM)	37.69	**36.23****	**38.89****	**34.69****	**33.83****	**27.94‡**	**34.32**

Table 1: Results on NIST Chinese-to-English Translation Task. "*" indicates statistically significant better than Bahdanau et al. (2015) at p-value < 0.05 and "**" at p-value < 0.01. "†" indicate statistically significant difference (p-value < 0.05) from the Li et al. (2016) which performed the best among baselines and "‡" at p-value < 0.01. **AVG** is average BLEU scores for MT03-MT08 test sets. The bold denotes the proposed model is superior to the Li et al. (2016) over the same test set.

consists of 1.42M sentence pairs extracted from LDC corpora.[6] We choose the NIST 2002 (MT02) and the NIST 2003-2008 (MT03-08) datasets as validation set and test sets, respectively. Case-insensitive *4*-gram NIST BLEU score (Papineni et al., 2002) is as evaluation metric, and the signtest (Collins et al., 2005) was as statistical significance test.

The baseline systems included the standard PB-SMT implemented in Moses (Koehn et al., 2007) and the standard attentional NMT (Bahdanau et al., 2015) . We also compared with state-of-the-art enhanced NMT methods for OOV: subword-based NMT (Sennrich et al., 2016), character-based NMT (Costa-jussà and Fonollosa, 2016), and replacing *unk* with similarity semantic in-vocabulary words (Li et al., 2016). All of these baselines and the proposed method are implemented in Nematus [7] (Sennrich et al., 2017).

For all NMT systems, we limit the source and target vocabularies to 30K, and the maximum sentence length is 80. We shuffle training set before training and the mini-batch size is 80. The word embedding dimension is 620-dimensions [8], the hidden layer dimension is 1000, and the default dropout technique (Hinton et al., 2012) in Nematus is used on the all the layers. Training is conducted on a single Tesla P100 GPU. All NMT models trained for 15 epochs[9] using ADADELTA

optimizer (Zeiler, 2012), and our training time is only about 10% slower than the standard attentional NMT.

5.2 Results and Analyses

Table 1 shows the translation performances on test sets measured in BLEU score. The standard attentional NMT (Bahdanau et al., 2015) outperforms Moses by 2.78 BLEU points on average, indicating that it is a strong baseline NMT system. All the comparison methods, including Sennrich et al. (2016), Costa-jussà and Fonollosa (2016), and Li et al. (2016), outperform the standard attentional NMT.

1) Over the standard attentional NMT, CARNMT-Encoder (FCWM/CCWM) gain improvements of 0.86/0.94 BLEU points on average, and CARNMT-Decoder (FCWM/CCWM) gain improvements of 0.45/0.33 BLEU points on average. CARNMT-Both (FCWM/CCWM) gain improvements of 1.02/1.30 BLEU points on average, which indicates that improvement in encoder and decoder are essentially orthogonal.

2) ALLSmooth (FCWM/CCWM) surpass CARNMT-Both (FCWM/CCWM) by 0.28/0.62 BLEU points on average. This indicates that the proposed context-aware smoothing method not only helps relieve the OOV affect, but also enhances representations of in-vocabulary words.

3) ALLSmooth (FCWM/CCWM) also outper-forms the best performed baseline Li et al. (2016), which replaces the *unk* words by using external lexicon similarity, by 0.24/0.78 BLEU points on

---

[6] LDC2002E18, LDC2003E07, LDC2003E14, Hansards portion of LDC2004T07, LDC2004T08, and LDC2005T06.

[7] https://github.com/EdinburghNLP/nematus

[8] For the ALLSmooth, the 360 dimensions are from V_{x_j} or V_{y_i} and the 260 dimensions were from the learned CAR

[9] All NMT models are convergent in the 15 epochs.

SRC: 用好 这个 战略 机遇期 (OOV), 力争 有所 作为 , 必须 把 发展 科学 技术 放在 更加 重要 , 更加 突出 的 位置
(pinyin) yonghao zhege zhanlue jiyuqi , lizheng yousuo zuowei , bixu ba fazhan kexue jishu fangzai gengjia zhongyao , gengjia tuchu de wiezhi

Bahdanau et al.(2015) : to make good use of this strategy , we should strive for the development of science and technology , and must put the development of science and technology into an even more important and prominent position

This work: in making good use of this strategic plan and striving to accomplish something , it is necessary to place the development of science and technology in a more important and more prominent position

Ref: to well use this strategic period of opportunity and strive to accomplish some achievments , the development of science and technology should be placed in a more prior and prominent position

Figure 4: Translation sample for source sentence with one OOV. The English phrases in color indicate they are translations from the corresponding Chinese phrase with the same color.

average.

4) The CCWM performs slightly better than FCWM. The reason may be that the convolution neural network can summarize the contextual information better than the feedforward neural network.

5.3 Translation Qualities for Sentences with Different Numbers of OOV

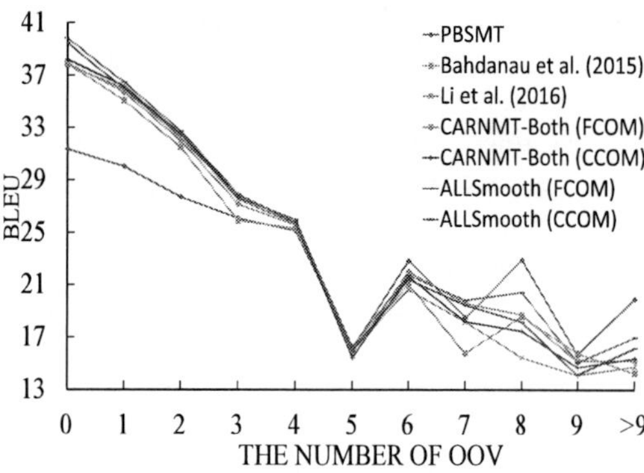

Figure 5: Translation qualities for sentences with different numbers of OOV.

To further verify our methods, we group sentences of same number OOVs all the test sets (MT03-08), for example, "5" indicates that all the source sentences include five OOV words in the group, and compute a BLEU score per group.

1) In Figure 5, we observe that when the number of OOVs is zero (no OOV), ALLSmooth (FCWM/CCWM) outperform other baseline systems, and the performances of CARNMT-Both (FCWM/CCWM) are similar to standard attentional NMT. This means that CARNMT-Both (FCWM/CCWM) degrade into standard attentional NMT because of these sentences not include

OOV, but our context-aware smoothing method enhances the representation of in-vocabulary words in the ALLSmooth (FCWM/CCWM).

2) With the increasing in the number of OOVs (especially when more than five), the gap between our methods and other methods (except PBSMT) become larger. This indicates that our methods are especially good at dealing with multi-OOV situation, in comparison with other NMT methods.

5.4 Samples Analysis

This subsection shows one translation sample for source sentence with one OOV, as shown in Figure 4. We compare our method ALLSmooth (CCWM) with Bahdanau et al. (2015) on the translation of a source sentence with the OOV "*jiyuqi*" ("*period of opportunity*" in English).

1) For both of Bahdanau et al. (2015)'s method and the proposed method, the OOV "*jiyuqi*" itself is not translated.

2) For Bahdanau et al. (2015)'s method, the phrase "*lizheng yousuo zuowei*" ("*strive to accomplish some achievments*" in English) after "*jiyuqi*" is not translated. The purple part of source sentence are translated twice in (Bahdanau et al., 2015)'s method. This is in consistent with our hypothesis in Section 1: the OOV which makes the structure of source sentence discontinuous affects source representation learning in encoder; then the negative effect would be further transformed to the decoder by the source annotation vectors, thus generating the poverty context vector and hidden layer state for translation prediction.

3) In comparison, the proposed method translates it into "*striving to accomplish something*", which is quite close to the reference. This indicates that our proposed context-aware smoothing method can relieve more translation

performance for NMT from the OOV's negative effect shown in Section 1.

6 Conclusion

In this paper, we explored the context information to smooth source representation with OOVs, and integrate the learned CAR into the Encoder and Decoder of NMT to improve the translation performance. Especially, we extended the method to smooth each word in-vocabulary, and further gained improvements over the proposed models for the NMT.

In the future, we will exploit richer context information, such as pos-tagger and named entity, to enhance the semantic representation of vocabulary in NMT.

Acknowledgments

We are grateful to the anonymous reviewers for their insightful comments and suggestions. This work was partially supported by the program "Promotion of Global Communications Plan: Research, Development, and Social Demonstration of Multilingual Speech Translation Technology" of MIC, Japan. Tiejun Zhao is supported by the National Natural Science Foundation of China (NSFC) via grant 91520204 and National High Technology Research & Development Program of China (863 program) via grant 2015AA015405.

References

Yaser Al-Onaizan and Kevin Knight. 2002. Translating named entities using monolingual and bilingual resources. In *Proceedings of 40th Annual Meeting of the Association for Computational Linguistics*, pages 400–408, Philadelphia, Pennsylvania, USA. Association for Computational Linguistics.

Philip Arthur, Graham Neubig, and Satoshi Nakamura. 2016. Incorporating discrete translation lexicons into neural machine translation. In *Proceedings of the 2016 Conference on Empirical Methods in Natural Language Processing*, pages 1557–1567, Austin, Texas. Association for Computational Linguistics.

Dzmitry Bahdanau, Kyunghyun Cho, and Yoshua Bengio. 2015. Neural machine translation by jointly learning to align and translate. In *Proceedings of the 3rd International Conference on Learning Representations*, San Diego, CA.

Yoshua Bengio, Réjean Ducharme, Pascal Vincent, and Christian Janvin. 2003. A neural probabilistic language model. *Journal of Machine Learning Research*, 3:1137–1155.

Michael Collins, Philipp Koehn, and Ivona Kucerova. 2005. Clause restructuring for statistical machine translation. In *Proceedings of the 43rd Annual Meeting of the Association for Computational Linguistics*, pages 531–540, Ann Arbor, Michigan. Association for Computational Linguistics.

Ronan Collobert, Jason Weston, Léon Bottou, Michael Karlen, Koray Kavukcuoglu, and Pavel Kuksa. 2011. Natural language processing (almost) from scratch. *Journal of Machine Learning Research*, 12:2493–2537.

Marta R. Costa-jussà and José A. R. Fonollosa. 2016. Character-based neural machine translation. In *Proceedings of the 54th Annual Meeting of the Association for Computational Linguistics*, pages 357–361, Berlin, Germany. Association for Computational Linguistics.

Pascale Fung and Percy Cheung. 2004. Mining very-non-parallel corpora: Parallel sentence and lexicon extraction via bootstrapping and em. In *Proceedings of the 2004 Conference on Empirical Methods in Natural Language Processing*, pages 57–63, Barcelona, Spain. Association for Computational Linguistics.

Philip Gage. 1994. A new algorithm for data compression. *C Users Journal*, 12(2):23–38.

Geoffrey E. Hinton, Nitish Srivastava, Alex Krizhevsky, Ilya Sutskever, and Ruslan Salakhutdinov. 2012. Improving neural networks by preventing co-adaptation of feature detectors. *CoRR*, abs/1207.0580.

Sébastien Jean, Kyunghyun Cho, Roland Memisevic, and Yoshua Bengio. 2015. On using very large target vocabulary for neural machine translation. In *Proceedings of the 53rd Annual Meeting of the Association for Computational Linguistics and the 7th International Joint Conference on Natural Language Processing*, pages 1–10, Beijing, China. Association for Computational Linguistics.

Long Jiang, Ming Zhou, Lee-Feng Chien, and Cheng Niu. 2007. Named entity translation with web mining and transliteration. In *Proceedings of the 20th International Joint Conference on Artifical Intelligence*, pages 1629–1634, San Francisco, CA, USA. Morgan Kaufmann Publishers Inc.

Nal Kalchbrenner and Phil Blunsom. 2013. Recurrent continuous translation models. In *Proceedings of the 2013 Conference on Empirical Methods in Natural Language Processing*, pages 1700–1709, Seattle, Washington, USA. Association for Computational Linguistics.

Kevin Knight and Jonathan Graehl. 1997. Machine transliteration. In *Proceedings of the 35th Annual Meeting of the Association for Computational Linguistics*, pages 128–135, Madrid, Spain. Association for Computational Linguistics.

Philipp Koehn, Hieu Hoang, Alexandra Birch, Chris Callison-Burch, Marcello Federico, Nicola Bertoldi, Brooke Cowan, Wade Shen, Christine Moran, Richard Zens, Chris Dyer, Ondrej Bojar, Alexandra Constantin, and Evan Herbst. 2007. Moses: Open source toolkit for statistical machine translation. In *Proceedings of the 45th Annual Meeting of the Association for Computational Linguistics Companion Volume Proceedings of the Demo and Poster Sessions*, pages 177–180, Prague, Czech Republic. Association for Computational Linguistics.

Philipp Koehn, Franz Josef Och, and Daniel Marcu. 2003. Statistical phrase-based translation. In *Proceedings of the 2003 Conference of the North American Chapter of the Association for Computational Linguistics on Human Language Technology*, pages 48–54, Stroudsburg, PA, USA. Association for Computational Linguistics.

Xiaoqing Li, Jiajun Zhang, and Chengqing Zong. 2016. Towards zero unknown word in neural machine translation. In *Proceedings of the Twenty-Fifth International Joint Conference on Artificial Intelligence*, pages 2852–2858.

Minh-Thang Luong and Christopher D. Manning. 2016. Achieving open vocabulary neural machine translation with hybrid word-character models. In *Proceedings of the 54th Annual Meeting of the Association for Computational Linguistics*, pages 1054–1063, Berlin, Germany. Association for Computational Linguistics.

Thang Luong, Ilya Sutskever, Quoc Le, Oriol Vinyals, and Wojciech Zaremba. 2015. Addressing the rare word problem in neural machine translation. In *Proceedings of the 53rd Annual Meeting of the Association for Computational Linguistics and the 7th International Joint Conference on Natural Language Processing*, pages 11–19, Beijing, China. Association for Computational Linguistics.

Yuval Marton, Chris Callison-Burch, and Philip Resnik. 2009. Improved statistical machine translation using monolingually-derived paraphrases. In *Proceedings of the 2009 Conference on Empirical Methods in Natural Language Processing*, pages 381–390, Singapore. Association for Computational Linguistics.

Haitao Mi, Zhiguo Wang, and Abe Ittycheriah. 2016. Vocabulary manipulation for neural machine translation. In *Proceedings of the 54th Annual Meeting of the Association for Computational Linguistics*, pages 124–129, Berlin, Germany. Association for Computational Linguistics.

Tomas Mikolov, Kai Chen, Greg Corrado, and Jeffrey Dean. 2013a. Efficient estimation of word representations in vector space. *arXiv preprint arXiv:1301.3781*.

Tomas Mikolov, Ilya Sutskever, Kai Chen, Greg S Corrado, and Jeff Dean. 2013b. Distributed representations of words and phrases and their compositionality. In *Advances in neural information processing systems*, pages 3111–3119.

Shachar Mirkin, Lucia Specia, Nicola Cancedda, Ido Dagan, Marc Dymetman, and Idan Szpektor. 2009. Source-language entailment modeling for translating unknown terms. In *Proceedings of the Joint Conference of the 47th Annual Meeting of the ACL and the 4th International Joint Conference on Natural Language Processing of the AFNLP*, pages 791–799, Suntec, Singapore. Association for Computational Linguistics.

Kishore Papineni, Salim Roukos, Todd Ward, and Wei-Jing Zhu. 2002. Bleu: a method for automatic evaluation of machine translation. In *Proceedings of 40th Annual Meeting of the Association for Computational Linguistics*, pages 311–318, Philadelphia, Pennsylvania, USA. Association for Computational Linguistics.

Rico Sennrich, Orhan Firat, Kyunghyun Cho, Alexandra Birch, Barry Haddow, Julian Hitschler, Marcin Junczys-Dowmunt, Samuel Läubli, Antonio Valerio Miceli Barone, Jozef Mokry, and Maria Nadejde. 2017. Nematus: a toolkit for neural machine translation. In *Proceedings of the Software Demonstrations of the 15th Conference of the European Chapter of the Association for Computational Linguistics*, pages 65–68, Valencia, Spain. Association for Computational Linguistics.

Rico Sennrich, Barry Haddow, and Alexandra Birch. 2016. Neural machine translation of rare words with subword units. In *Proceedings of the 54th Annual Meeting of the Association for Computational Linguistics*, pages 1715–1725, Berlin, Germany. Association for Computational Linguistics.

Li Shao and Hwee Tou Ng. 2004. Mining new word translations from comparable corpora. In *Proceedings of COLING 2004, the 20th International Conference on Computational Linguistics*, pages 618–624, Geneva, Switzerland. COLING.

Ilya Sutskever, Oriol Vinyals, and Quoc V Le. 2014. Sequence to sequence learning with neural networks. In *Advances in neural information processing systems*, pages 3104–3112.

Matthew D. Zeiler. 2012. ADADELTA: an adaptive learning rate method. *CoRR*, abs/1212.5701.

Improving Sequence to Sequence Neural Machine Translation by Utilizing Syntactic Dependency Information

An Nguyen Le, Ander Martinez, Akifumi Yoshimoto* and Yuji Matsumoto

Graduate School of Information Science, Nara Institute of Science and Technology,
8916-5, Takayama, Ikoma, Nara 630-0192, Japan

`{nguyen.an.mr9,ander.martinez.zy4,akifumi-y,matsu}@is.naist.jp`

Abstract

Sequence to Sequence Neural Machine Translation has achieved significant performance in recent years. Yet, there are some existing issues that Neural Machine Translation still does not solve completely. Two of them are translation of long sentences and "over-translation". To address these two problems, we propose an approach that utilize more grammatical information such as syntactic dependencies, so that the output can be generated based on more abundant information. In addition, the output of the model is presented not as a simple sequence of tokens but as a linearized tree construction. Experiments on the Europarl-v7 dataset of French-to-English translation demonstrate that our proposed method improves BLEU scores by 1.57 and 2.40 on datasets consisting of sentences with up to 50 and 80 tokens, respectively. Furthermore, the proposed method also solved the two existing problems, ineffective translation of long sentences and over-translation in Neural Machine Translation.

1 Introduction

Our task is to construct a model which learns input in sequence form and decodes output as a linearized dependency tree. In this work, we propose an approach in which dependency labels are incorporated into the model to represent more grammatical information in the output sequence. As we know, the Sequence to Sequence (`Seq2Seq`) Learning model (Sutskever et al., 2014; Aharoni et al., 2016) is extremely effective on a va-

riety of tasks that require a mapping between a sequence to sequence. Therefore, it is used to solve many tasks in natural language processing. The `Seq2Seq` model consists of an encoder-decoder neural network which encodes a variable-length input sequence into a vector and decodes it into a variable-length output. Since the model uses the information of the source representation and the previously generated words to produce the next-word token, this distributed representation allows the `Seq2Seq` model to generate appropriate mapping between the input and the output (Li et al., 2016). For specific tasks, Neural Machine Translation (NMT) model, which is based on the Seq2Seq learning, has achieved excellent translation performance in recent years (Sutskever et al., 2014; Bahdanau et al., 2015; Luong et al., 2015; Firat et al., 2016). In particular, the NMT model which is built upon an encoder-decoder framework with attention mechanism (Bahdanau et al., 2015) can also pay attention and its decoder knows which part of the input is relevant for the word that is currently being translated. Therefore, it has shown competitive results and outperformed conventional statistical methods (Bentivogli et al., 2016). Despite of these advantages, NMT model still has a couple particular issues to be solved such as dealing with fixed vocabulary, not applicable to small-data, additional phrases, wrong lexical choice errors, long sentence translation, over and under translation, etc. In this paper, we touch upon the following two major problems:

- Translation of long sentences

- Over-translation

Since the decoder of the `Seq2Seq` model produces the target language word by word simply based on the previous target words and the source-side representation vector until it reaches the spe-

---

This author's present affiliation is CyberAgent, Inc., Tokyo, Japan, yoshimoto_akifumi_xa@cyberagent.co.jp

Proceedings of the The 8th International Joint Conference on Natural Language Processing, pages 21–29,
Taipei, Taiwan, November 27 – December 1, 2017 ©2017 AFNLP

cial end token, it is incapable in capturing long-distance dependencies in history, so ineffective for long sentences translation (Zhang et al., 2016; Toral and Sánchez-Cartagena, 2017). Even with an attention mechanism, the `Seq2Seq` model just pays attention to the current alignment information between the inputs and the output at the current position but ignores past alignments information. Therefore, it cannot keep track of the attention history when it updates information at each current time step, leading to the over-production (Tu et al., 2016a,c; Mi et al., 2016; Tu et al., 2016b).

In order to address the above two issues, it is worth considering that using syntactic dependency information and representing the output as a tree structure would be effective. This approach allows the next tokens to be output based on not only the previous tokens but also the syntactic dependencies so far, thereby conditioning them on more abundant information so it has the ability to make smarter predictions. Basically, in this paper, we train the model with an encoder-decoder neural network and using dependencies in which the input of the source language is in sequence form and the output of the target language will be generated in a linearized dependency-based tree structure. That is, instead of predicting only words at each time step, the model trains the network to predict both words and their grammatical dependencies as a dependency tree at each time step. Therefore, it is hoped that the accuracy of output will be improved.

The major contributions of this work are as follows:

1. To utilize the information of both "head" words and syntactic dependencies between them to produce better output.

2. To settle the problems in the NMT task. In this paper, we desire to solve two tasks. First is the ineffective translation for long sentences. Second is the over-translation in NMT task.

Empirically, to assess the performance of the proposed method, we used Conditional Gated Recurrent Unit with Attention mechanism model of Bahdanau (2015) on the French-English portions of the Europarl-v7 dataset. As a result, the BLEU score is improved by 1.57 and 2.40 points for sentences of length up to 50 and 80 tokens, respec-

tively. Also, we compare and analyze the results of attention-based `Seq2Seq` model and the proposed approach.

2 Related Work

In fact, the effectiveness of using dependency information of words has been reported in some previous NLP tasks, for example, in dependency-based word embeddings, relation classification and sentence classification tasks (Liu et al., 2015; Socher et al., 2014; Levy and Goldberg, 2014; Komnios, 2016; Ono and Hatano, 2014). It has been shown that the combination of words and their dependency information can boost performance. Besides, in the work of Vinyals et al. (Vinyals et al., 2014), they also represent output as a linearized tree structure, but their work showed that generic sequence-to-sequence approaches can achieve excellent results on syntactic constituency parsing. At a glance, our proposed method is a little similar to the works of Dyer et al., Aharoni et al., Eriguchi et al., Wu et al. (Dyer et al., 2016; Aharoni and Goldberg, 2017; Eriguchi et al., 2017; Wu et al., 2017) in use of parse tree and generation. However, Dyer et al. and Aharoni et al.'s works concern predicting constituent trees. Eriguchi et al.'s model employs syntactic dependency parsing but their model is hybridized the decoder of NMT and the Recurrent Neural Network Grammars, and the target sentences are parsed in transition-based parsing. Wu et al.'s model also employs dependency parsing but their model separately predicts the target translation sequence and parsing action sequence which maps to translation. On the other hand, our proposed model's decoder directly predicts the linearized dependency tree itself in a single neural network in *Depth-first pre-order* order so that the next-word token is generated based on syntactic relations and tree construction itself. In other words, our model is able to learn and produce a tree of words and their dependency relations by itself.

3 Sequence-to-Dependency Model

In our proposed approach, the neural network model is trained to map the target-side output in a linearized dependency tree construction from the source-side input in a sequence. Thus, we call this model Sequence-to-Dependency (`Seq2Dep`) model. The problem is defined as follows: Given a source sequence $X = (x_1, x_2, \ldots, x_N)$ of length

N, we want the model to encode the input sequence X and decode it to a tree structure with both words and dependency information conditioned on the encoded vector. Therefore, the output will be represented in the form $(LY) = (\mathbf{ly}_1, \mathbf{ly}_2, \ldots, \mathbf{ly}_M)$. The conditional probability $p(ly|x)$ is decomposed as:

$$p(\mathbf{ly}|x) = \prod_{i=1}^{\infty} p(\mathbf{ly}_i|\mathbf{ly}_{<i}, x), \qquad (1)$$

in which $(\mathbf{ly}_1, \mathbf{ly}_2, ..., \mathbf{ly}_M)$ are words or dependency labels.

Therefore, the hidden state $\mathbf{s}_j$ at time step j is computed as follows:

$$\mathbf{s}_j = \mathrm{cGRU_{att}}\left(\mathbf{s}_{j-1}, \mathbf{ly}_{j-1}, \mathbf{C}_j\right), \qquad (2)$$

and the next token $\mathbf{ly}_j$, which may be a word or dependency label, will be generated as follows:

$$\mathbf{ly}_j = f\left(\mathbf{s}_j, \mathbf{ly}_{j-1}, \mathbf{C}_j\right), \qquad (3)$$

In this paper, dependencies are defined as the dependency labels which are achieved from the Stanford Dependency Parser (Chen and Manning, 2014). The decoder will decode the next output based on relations between governors and dependents in a linearized tree structure. In regards to the order of generating the dependency labels and the words, the decoder will produce these symbols in a manner called *Depth-first pre-order* traversal. In this section, we will describe the model step-by-step as follows:

3.1 Processing Data

Since there is no parallel corpus in which the source-side is represented in sequence and target-side is represented in linearized dependency tree, we have to prepare data for training by doing dependency parsing for the target-side language.

3.1.1 Dependency Parsing

In this paper, we do experiments on a French-English language pair so we use the Stanford Dependency Parser to obtain dependency parsing results for English. The Stanford Dependency Parser produces results in the form of a tree structure in which each word of the sentence is the dependent of exactly one token, either another word in the sentence or the distinguished "ROOT-0" token. The parsing result is represented in the format "*abbreviated relation name(governor, depen-*

dent)" in which a governor is a head word and dependency is a syntactic relation between a governor and a dependent. The governor and the dependent are words in the sentence. This dependency parsing result will be transformed in another step for traversing the tree, which will be described in the next section to create a dependency tree. The dependency tree represents the target language as an ordered tree structure which is necessary for training. The reason we chose the Stanford Dependency Parser for the parsing portion of this method is because it can represent the order of words in sentence. This information of the order is useful to traverse tree in the following step.

3.1.2 Transformation and Tree Traversal

In this section, we describe the Tree Transform and Tree Traversal process in which output in a linearized dependency tree form is created from the Stanford Dependency Parsing tree. For example, given a sentence *"She ate an apple today ."*, after obtaining dependency parsing tree from the above dependency parsing phase, we move the rooted *"ate"* and *"apple"* headwords to the same layers of their *dependents* which are directly connected to the headwords. We also concurrently make consideration to their positions in order while shifting headwords. The headwords are shifted in such a manner that the word order of sentence can be preserved, so we can evaluate the translated output afterwards. Next, the tree structure obtained in the fist step will be transformed into another tree structure for the next tree traversal step. Then we traverse this tree in a *Depth-first pre-order* traversal, which is the search tree in which tree is traversed from its left subtree to right subtree recursively until current node is empty, to create output with a linearized tree structure to train the model. That is, for each rooted subtree, governors and dependency labels of the sentence are predicted first, and their information will be used to predict the next dependent words. In other words, the model can capture the dependency information between label-word and word-word pairs to predict the next tokens. This means that the model is capable of modeling grammatical dependencies in the output symbols. Also, in `Seq2Dep` model, we define the *Nonterminal* "{*DEPENDENCY LABEL*", and *Node-closing* "}" tokens. *Nonterminal* indicates subtree (Dong and Lapata, 2016), which means open subtree to visit its children nodes. *Node-closing* indicates end-of-

Algorithm 1 Tree Transform

```
 1: procedure TRANSFORM TREE
 2:    Transform(T,Labels):
 3:        for label in Labels do
 4:            if label.children.size! = 0 then
 5:                Recur Transform(T,Labels)
 6:            else
 7:                Compare the order of current
 8:                    label's parent & children
 9:                if (label's children order is larger
                        than label's parent order) then
10:                    INSERT label's parent first
11:                else
12:                    INSERT label's children
```

Algorithm 2 Tree *Depth-first pre-order* traversal

```
Input: Sentence
Output: Linearized Dependency Tree
 1: Stanford Dependency Parsing
 2: Make Tree from Dependency Parsing Result
 3: Tree transform
 4: procedure TRAVERSE TREE
 5:    Traverse(T,N):
 6:        N as discovered
 7:        for all Node not in N do
 8:            if Node.children.size! = 0 then
 9:                Recursively call Traverse(T,N)
10:                    in pre-order traverse
11:            else
12:                if Node is Nonterminal then
13:                    OUTPUT Node-opening
14:                    VISIT children
15:                    OUTPUT Node-closing
16:                else
17:                    OUTPUT Node
```

subtree, that means finishing subtree traversal and returning to the upper layer to continue the next subtree traversal. And these defined tokens do not appear in original source and target datasets. Algorithms 1 and 2 show the definition of transformation and tree traversal in more detail respectively. The purpose of using *Depth-first pre-order* traversal is as follows:

1. To keep the words of the target language sequence in order when they are generated. With this generating order, the word order of the sentence is preserved, thus, we do not have to do any post-processing subsequently.

2. To utilize both information of the words and the dependency labels generated in the previous rooted subtree to predict the tokens of the next rooted subtree.

Figures 1, 2 and 3 show the Stanford dependency parsing tree, tree structure after the positions of "*head*" words are shifted and *Depth-first pre-order* Tree Traversal.

3.2 Sequence-to-Dependency Model

The proposed (Seq2Dep) model consists of an encoder which is a bidirectional GRU layer as in Bahdanau's model (2015)[1]. The input embeddings of the source sentences are shared by the forward and backward GRU, and the hidden states of the corresponding forward and backward GRU are added to obtain the hidden representation for that time step. The decoder of the model will decode the output as words and dependency labels in a linearized dependency tree structure in

a *Depth-first pre-order* traversal. Figure 4 shows the decoder which generates both dependency labels and words in the `Seq2Dep` model. In Figure 4, the previous token and context vector feeding are omitted for simplicity.

4 Experiments

4.1 Dataset

In our experiment, the proposed model was trained on the French-English parallel corpus of the *Europarl-v7* dataset. We used *newstest2011* and *newstest2012* of WMT16 as development and test data respectively. To confirm translation for long sentences, the whole test set was used without removing any sentences with a maximum length of 50 or 80. We performed experiment on the following two datasets:

- Europarl-v7 dataset consisting of sentences with a maximum length of 50.

- Europarl-v7 dataset consisting of sentences with a maximum length of 80.

For preprocessing data, we filtered out sentences which were longer than the above maximum lengths and cleaned the special symbols or characters which were not strings. We also omitted sentences which had multiple sentences in one line. The reason is that the parsing results obtained from the Stanford Dependency Parser in parsing

---

[1] https://github.com/nyu-dl/dl4mt-tutorial

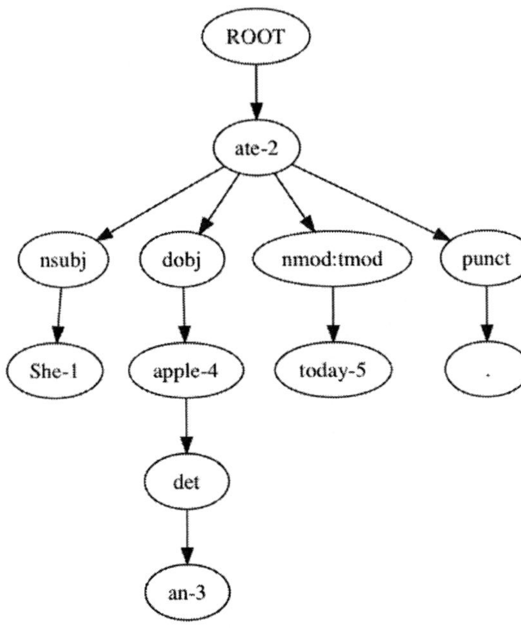

Figure 1: Stanford Dependency Parsing Tree

step would contain multi "{ROOT" tokens for sentences which have multiple sentences in one line, while it is necessary to generate the next child nodes starting from just one top {*ROOT* of a tree. Next, we tokenize and lowercase this dataset and perform dependency parsing. After that, we traverse the tree in a *Depth-first pre-order* to create the parallel corpus for the training model in which the source language, French is in sequence form, and the target language, English is in a linearized dependency tree structure form. The longer sentences are(particularly sentences with a maximum length of 80 tokens), the more CPU's memory and time cost for this processing data step.

In addition, we built a dictionary of the target language (English) that consists of both words and dependency labels. In this dictionary, we define 74 dependency labels based on the current representation of grammatical relations of the Stanford Dependency Parser.

4.2 Settings

In order to evaluate the performance of the proposed method, we set the same hyperparameters as the attention-based cGRU model in DL4MT-Tutorial and compare the obtained results of both Seq2Seq and Seq2Dep models.

The recurrent transformation weights for gates and hidden state proposal matrices were initialized as random orthogonal matrices. Weights were optimized using the Adadelta algorithm and were updated with a mini-batch size of 32 sentences. The vocabulary sizes of both source and target languages were set at 30k words, the beam size was set to 5, dropout was not applied and the gradients were clipped at 1.0. Morever, because the generated tokens are not only words but also dependency labels in Seq2Dep model, the maxlen parameter was set up so that dependency labels are not counted, therefore long sentences will not be removed in training.

4.3 Model Training

In the experiments, we trained the following 2 models on 1.65M sentences with a maximum length of 50 and 1.89M sentences with a maximum length of 80 from the Europarl-v7 French-English bitext.

Baseline Model
    This model is a Seq2Seq model with attention mechanism as in Firat (2016) that consists of an encoder that encodes the source language input in sequence form and a decoder that decodes target language output in sequence form.

Seq2Dep Model The proposed method. In this model, the model architecture is the same as the attention-based Seq2Seq model but the input is in sequence form and the output is in linearized dependency tree structure.

5 Results

In the Seq2Dep model, because the output consists of both words and dependency labels, we evaluated the result with post-processing, which is the process that removes the dependency labels from the translated result. From this section onwards, we will refer to the Seq2Seq and Seq2Dep models with sentences of maximum length 50 and 80 tokens as Seq2Seq-50, Seq2Dep-50, Seq2Seq-80 and Seq2Dep-80. As a result, the BLEU score of Seq2Dep-50 with post-processing was 20.88, which is higher than the BLEU score of 19.31 obtained by the attention-based Seq2Seq-50 model with a gain of up to 1.57 points. Similarly, the BLEU score improved by 2.40 points for datasets with maximum sentence lengths of 80.

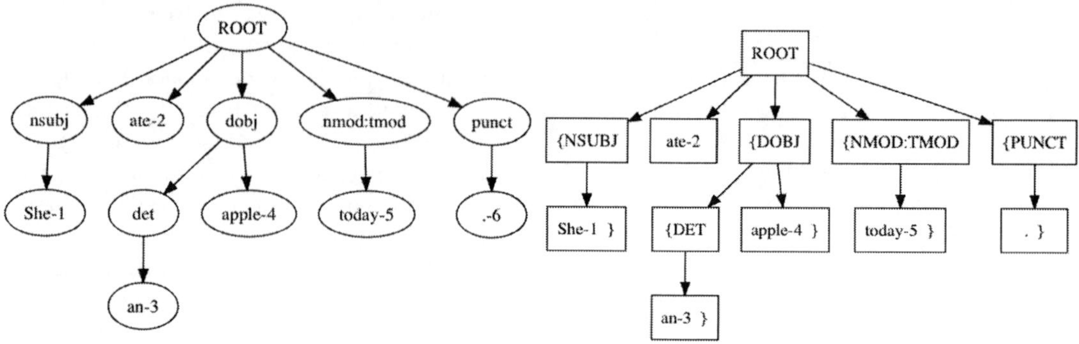

Figure 2: Dependency tree after shifting the positions of "*head*" words

Figure 3: *Depth-first pre-order* Tree Traversal

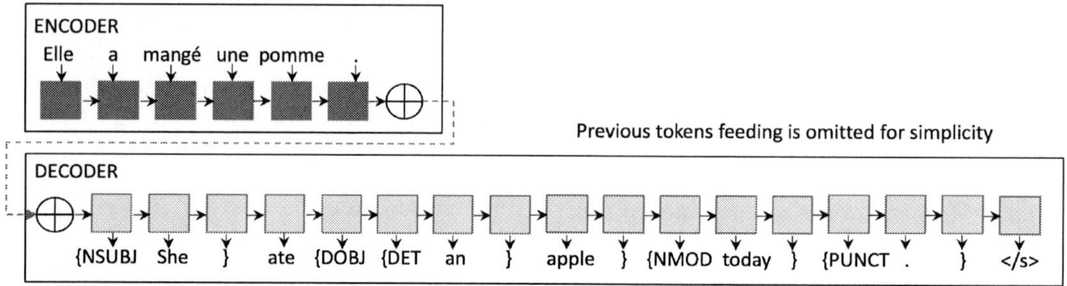

Figure 4: Encoder and decoder of `Seq2Dep` model

Table 1 shows BLEU and METEOR scores and TER error of the attention-based `Seq2Seq` and `Seq2Dep` models. Figure 5 shows the relation between BLEU score and the length of sentence.

Moreover, when we made a trial to evaluate the translation results without post-processing, the BLEU scores without post-processing were 42.76 and 43.41 for both datasets. From these scores, it is thought that the model can predict not only word-based tokens but also dependency labels well.

6   Additional Experiments

In order to verify the ability of the proposed approach to solve the repetition problem of NMT, over-translation, we measured the repetition of words in the translation results of attention-based `Seq2Seq` and `Seq2Dep` learnings in this section. The repetition rate is measured by the following formula:

$$rep\_rat = \sum_{i=1}^{T(\mathbf{y})} \frac{1 + r(\widetilde{y}_i)}{1 + r(Y)}, \qquad (4)$$

in which $\widetilde{y}_i$ and Y_i are the ith hypothesis sentence and i^{th} reference sentence respectively, and r is the number of the repeated words and is computed by:

$$r(X) = len(X) - len(set(X)) \qquad (5)$$

in which len(X) is the length of the sentence X and len(set(X)) is the number of words that are not repeated in sentence X. For example, given the sentence X=*"The big fish ate the smaller fish"*, in this case, set(X)={The, big, fish, ate, smaller}, len(X)=7, len(set(X))=5. Figure 6 shows the comparison of repetition rate in both models in which the horizontal axis is the length of sentences, vertical axis is the repetition rate respectively. In Figure 6, the repetition rate in both `Seq2Seq` and `Seq2Dep` learnings decreases as the length of the sentences increases. From Figure 6, we can see that the more tokens the model learns, the more the repetition rate decreases. Also, the repetition rate is reduced in the `Seq2Dep` model compared to the attention-based Seq2Seq model.

Table 1: Translation quality as measured by different metrics.

Model	Post-processing		
	BLEU	**METEOR**	**TER**
Seq2Seq-50	19.31	26.3	66.1
Seq2Dep-50	**20.88**	**27.0**	**62.5**
Seq2Seq-80	16.97	25.5	78.5
Seq2Dep-80	**19.37**	**25.6**	**65.6**

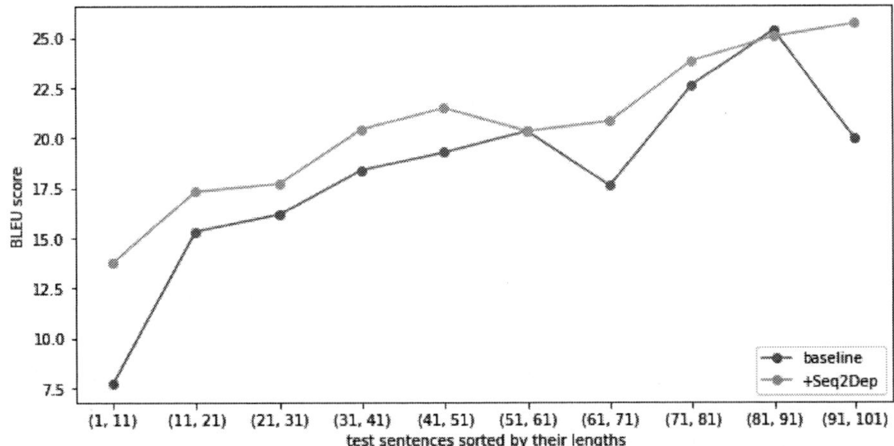

Figure 5: Comparison of BLEU score with respect to the length of sentences

7   Analysis and Discussion

In figure 5, except the span in which the sentence length is between 41 and 51 words, the BLEU score of the `Seq2Dep` model goes up gradually and almost overcomes that of the attention-based `Seq2Seq` model. The BLEU score falls from 19.31 to 16.97 with a 2.34 points difference for the attention-based `Seq2Seq` model while the point difference is 1.51 in the `Seq2Dep` model. From the experiments, we confirm that by using the syntactic dependency information, the `Seq2Dep` model can learn well and reduce the drop in BLEU score compared to the baseline model even if the sentence is very long. Besides, we can see the BLEU score is low for short sentences which have a length of 10 words or less. This is because of the brevity penalty on short sentences in BLEU (Papineni et al., 2002).

With regards to the BLEU score without post-processing, we see that the score of the `Seq2Dep-80` model is higher than that of the `Seq2Dep-50` model. The reason could be: The longer the sentences are, the more syntactic de-

pendencies the models require for generating better outputs.

Also, in terms of the over-translation problem, Figure 6 shows that the repetition rates of the two models decrease gradually with respect to the length of the sentences and the `Seq2Dep` model has a lower repetition rate. When we checked the translation results, we saw that *Node-closing* token "}" was almost generated after each subtree. Moreover, we saw that there were some very long sentences which the over-generation of *"UNK"*s occurred in the translation result of `Seq2Seq` model while that did not occur in translation results of `Seq2Deq` model. Our assumption is that after generating subtree, the `Seq2Dep` model can learn that it should generate the *Node-closing* token "}" next, instead of a chain of words. In other words, as mentioned in Kuncoro et al.'s work (Kuncoro et al., 2016) in which modeling of composition can achieve better performance, the `Seq2Dep` model which learns about the syntactic dependencies and tree structure performance is probably able to learn the blocks of the form *"Non-terminal* word }" like a phrase-structure in sen-

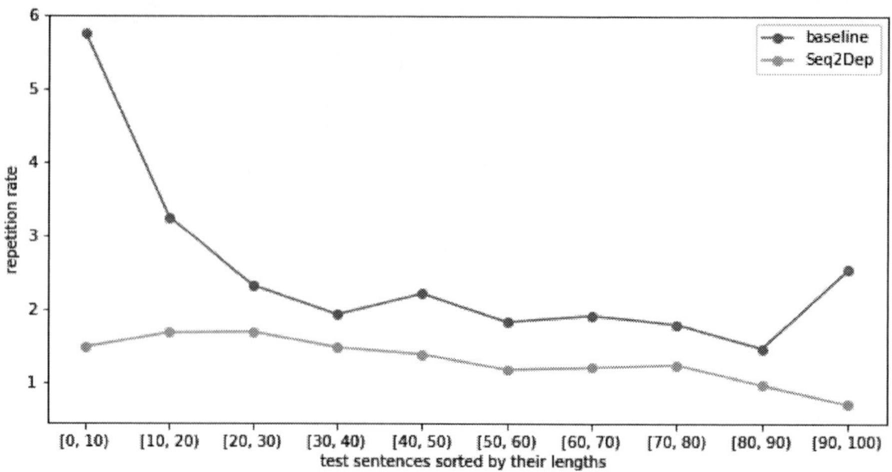

Figure 6: Comparison of the repetition rate of the baseline and Seq2Dep models

tences, so it is unlikely to generate the same word repeatedly. Therefore, it is possible to prevent the long repeated words in long sentences. Usually, because the block of the form "*Nonterminal* word }" is seen as a phrase in sentence or a subtree in tree structure, and it is rare for a phrase to occur repeatedly in sentence or for a subtree to repeat in a tree structure, so it is assumed that repetition of the blocks of form "*Nonterminal* word }" are also rare.

8   Conclusion

In this work, we proposed a method in which the Seq2Dep NMT model is trained by utilizing syntactic dependencies to provide the model more abundant information. In other words, Seq2Dep model learns the potential internal relative connections among tokens and their long term syntactic dependencies to predict the next-word tokens. Furthermore, the Seq2Dep model can also generate output as a linearized dependency tree structure in a *Depth-first pre-order* tree traversal over words and dependencies. The purpose of this work is to alleviate issues of translating long sentences and repetitive translation. We conduct experiments on the French-English parallel corpus of the Europarl-v7 dataset to compare the performance of the proposed method with the attention-based Seq2Seq model. The results demonstrated that the proposed model achieved a 1.57 and 2.40 points BLEU score improvement for sentences of length at most 50 and 80 tokens re-

spectively. Moreover, experiments verify that the proposed model also reduces the over-translation, particularly long sentences with over-generation of "*UNK*"s.

9   Future work

- Confirm how accurate the Seq2Dep model generates the dependency labels and the whole tree structure as well.

- In this paper, to compare performance of the proposed method with the baseline model, we set the same hyperparameters as the attention-based cGRU model in dl4mt-tutorial and trained the Seq2Dep model on only Europarl-v7 dataset. Since experiments were done on small vocabulary size and dataset, we plan to train the model on larger vocabulary and datasets with subword units segmentation.

- For future work, we plan to train models on datasets which consist of only long sentences with more than 50 or 80 tokens to compare the performance of long-sentences translation of the approach and baseline model.

Acknowledgments

We thank Assistant Professor Shindo Hiroyuki, Ouchi Hiroki, Michael Wentao Li of the NAIST Computational Linguistics Laboratory, and the reviewers for their valuable and constructive comments. Part of this work was supported by JSPS KAKENHI Grant Number JP17H06101.

References

Roee Aharoni and Yoav Goldberg. 2017. Towards string-to-tree neural machine translation. *CoRR*, abs/1704.04743.

Roee Aharoni, Yoav Goldberg, and Yonatan Belinkov. 2016. Improving sequence to sequence learning for morphological inflection generation: The biumit systems for the sigmorphon 2016 shared task for morphological reinflection. In *Proceedings of the 14th Annual SIGMORPHON Workshop on Computational Research in Phonetics, Phonology, and Morphology*, pages 41–48.

Dzmitry Bahdanau, Kyunghyun Cho, and Yoshua Bengio. 2015. Neural machine translation by jointly learning to align and translate. In *Proceedings of ICLR 2015*.

Luisa Bentivogli, Arianna Bisazza, Mauro Cettolo, and Marcello Federico. 2016. Neural versus phrase-based machine translation quality: a case study. *CoRR*, abs/1608.04631.

Danqi Chen and Christoher D. Manning. 2014. A fast and accurate dependency parser using neural networks. In *Proceedings of EMNLP 2014*.

Li Dong and Mirella Lapata. 2016. Language to logical form with neural attention. *Proceedings of ACL 2016*, pages 33–43.

Chris Dyer, Adhiguna Kuncoro, Miguel Ballesteros, and Noah A. Smith. 2016. Recurrent neural network grammars. *CoRR*, abs/1602.07776.

Akiko Eriguchi, Yoshimasa Tsuruoka, and Kyunghyun Cho. 2017. Learning to parse and translate improves neural machine translation. *CoRR*, abs/1702.03525.

Orhan Firat, Kyunghyun Cho, and Yoshua Bengio. 2016. Multi-way, multilingual neural machine translation with a shared attention mechanism. *arXiv.org1601.01073*.

Alexandros Komnios. 2016. Dependency based embeddings for sentence classification tasks. In *Proceedings of NAACL-HLT 2016*, pages 1490–1500.

Adhiguna Kuncoro, Miguel Ballesteros, Lingpeng Kong, Chris Dyer, Graham Neubig, and Noah A. Smith. 2016. What do recurrent neural network grammars learn about syntax? *CoRR*, abs/1611.05774.

Omer Levy and Yoav Goldberg. 2014. Dependency-based word embeddings. In *Proceedings of ACL 2014*, pages 302–308.

Xiaoqing Li, Jiajun Zhang, and Chengqing Zong. 2016. Towards zero unknown word in neural machine translation. In *Proceedings of IJCAI 2016*.

Yang Liu, Furu Wei, Sujian Li, Heng Ji, Ming Zhou, and Houfeng Wang. 2015. A dependency-based neural network for relation classification. In *Proceedings of ACL 2015*, pages 285–290.

Thang Luong, Hieu Pham, and Christopher D. Manning. 2015. Effective approaches to attention-based neural machine translation. In *Proceedings of EMNLP 2015*, pages 1412–1421.

Haitao Mi, Baskaran Sankaran, Zhiguo Wang, and Abe Ittycheriah. 2016. Coverage embedding models for neural machine translation. In *Proceedings of EMNLP 2016*, pages 955–960.

Kazuki Ono and Kenji Hatano. 2014. Dependency parsing and its application using hierarchical structure in japanese language. *International Journal on Advances in Internet Technology*, vol 7 no 3, 4.

Kishore Papineni, Salim Roukos, Todd Ward, and Wei-Jing Zhu. 2002. Bleu: a method for automatic evaluation of machine translation. *Proceedings of ACL 2002*, pages 311–318.

Richard Socher, Andrej Karpathy, Quoc V. Le, Christopher D. Manning, and Andrew Y. Ng. 2014. Grounded compositional semantics for finding and describing images with sentences. In *Transactions of the Association for Computational Linguistics*, pages 2: 207–218.

Ilya Sutskever, Oriol Vinyals, and Quoc V. Le. 2014. Sequence to sequence learning with neural networks. *Proceedings of NIPS 2014*.

Antonio Toral and Víctor M. Sánchez-Cartagena. 2017. A multifaceted evaluation of neural versus phrase-based machine translation for 9 language directions. *CoRR*, abs/1701.02901.

Zhaopeng Tu, Yang Liu, Lifeng Shang, Xiaohua Liu, and Hang Li. 2016a. Neural machine translation with reconstruction. In *Proceedings of Association for the Advancement of Artificial Intelligence 2016*.

Zhaopeng Tu, Zhengdong Lu, Yang Liu, Xiaohua Liu, and Hang Li. 2016b. Coverage-based neural machine translation. *CoRR*, abs/1601.04811.

Zhaopeng Tu, Zhengdong Lu, Yang Liu, Xiaohua Liu, and Hang Li. 2016c. Modeling coverage for neural machine translation. In *Proceedings of ACL 2016*, pages 76–85.

Oriol Vinyals, Lukasz Kaiser, Terry Koo, Slav Petrov, Ilya Sutskever, and Geoffrey E. Hinton. 2014. Grammar as a foreign language. *CoRR*, abs/1412.7449.

Shuangzhi Wu, Dongdong Zhang, Nan Yang, Mu Li, and Ming Zhou. 2017. Sequence-to-dependency neural machine translation. *Proceedings of ACL 2017*, pages 698–707.

Biao Zhang, Deyi Xiong, and Jinsong Su. 2016. Recurrent neural machine translation. *CoRR*, abs/1607.08725.

What does Attention in Neural Machine Translation Pay Attention to?

Hamidreza Ghader and **Christof Monz**

Informatics Institute, University of Amsterdam, The Netherlands

`h.ghader, c.monz@uva.nl`

Abstract

Attention in neural machine translation provides the possibility to encode relevant parts of the source sentence at each translation step. As a result, attention is considered to be an alignment model as well. However, there is no work that specifically studies attention and provides analysis of what is being learned by attention models. Thus, the question still remains that how attention is similar or different from the traditional alignment. In this paper, we provide detailed analysis of attention and compare it to traditional alignment. We answer the question of whether attention is only capable of modelling translational equivalent or it captures more information. We show that attention is different from alignment in some cases and is capturing useful information other than alignments.

1 Introduction

Neural machine translation (NMT) has gained a lot of attention recently due to its substantial improvements in machine translation quality achieving state-of-the-art performance for several languages (Luong et al., 2015b; Jean et al., 2015; Wu et al., 2016). The core architecture of neural machine translation models is based on the general encoder-decoder approach (Sutskever et al., 2014). Neural machine translation is an end-to-end approach that learns to encode source sentences into distributed representations and decode these representations into sentences in the target language. Among the different neural MT models, attentional NMT (Bahdanau et al., 2015; Luong et al., 2015a) has become popular due to its capability to use the most relevant parts of the source sentence at each translation step. This capability also makes the attentional model superior in translating longer sentences (Bahdanau et al., 2015; Luong et al., 2015a).

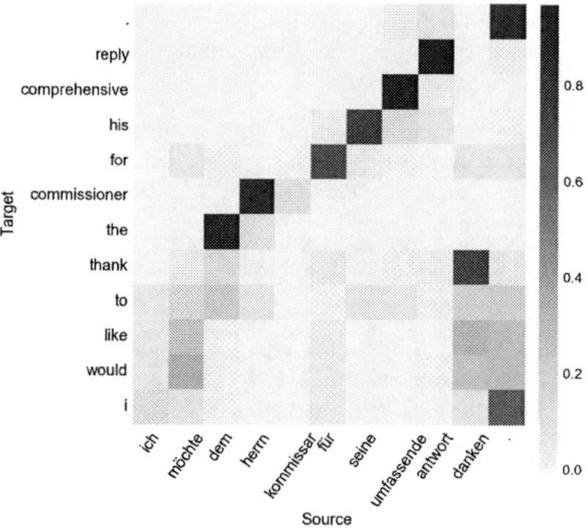

Figure 1: Visualization of the attention paid to the relevant parts of the source sentence for each generated word of a translation example. See how the attention is 'smeared out' over multiple source words in the case of "would" and "like".

Figure 1 shows an example of how attention uses the most relevant source words to generate a target word at each step of the translation. In this paper we focus on studying the relevance of the attended parts, especially cases where attention is 'smeared out' over multiple source words where their relevance is not entirely obvious, see, e.g., "would" and "like" in Figure 1. Here, we ask whether these are due to errors of the attention mechanism or are a desired behavior of the model.

Since the introduction of attention models in neural machine translation (Bahdanau et al., 2015) various modifications have been proposed (Luong et al., 2015a; Cohn et al., 2016; Liu et al., 2016). However, to the best of our knowledge

Proceedings of the The 8th International Joint Conference on Natural Language Processing, pages 30–39,
Taipei, Taiwan, November 27 – December 1, 2017 ©2017 AFNLP

there is no study that provides an analysis of what kind of phenomena is being captured by attention. There are some works that have looked to attention as being similar to traditional word alignment (Alkhouli et al., 2016; Cohn et al., 2016; Liu et al., 2016; Chen et al., 2016). Some of these approaches also experimented with training the attention model using traditional alignments (Alkhouli et al., 2016; Liu et al., 2016; Chen et al., 2016). Liu et al. (2016) have shown that attention could be seen as a reordering model as well as an alignment model.

In this paper, we focus on investigating the differences between attention and alignment and what is being captured by the attention mechanism in general. The questions that we are aiming to answer include: Is the attention model only capable of modelling alignment? And how similar is attention to alignment in different syntactic phenomena?

Our analysis shows that attention models traditional alignment in some cases more closely while it captures information beyond alignment in others. For instance, attention agrees with traditional alignments to a high degree in the case of nouns. However, it captures other information rather than only the translational equivalent in the case of verbs.

This paper makes the following contributions: 1) We provide a detailed comparison of attention in NMT and word alignment. 2) We show that while different attention mechanisms can lead to different degrees of compliance with respect to word alignments, global compliance is not always helpful for word prediction. 3) We show that attention follows different patterns depending on the type of the word being generated. 4) We demonstrate that attention does not always comply with alignment. We provide evidence showing that the difference between attention and alignment is due to attention model capability to attend the context words influencing the current word translation.

2 Related Work

Liu et al. (2016) investigate how training the attention model in a supervised manner can benefit machine translation quality. To this end they use traditional alignments obtained by running automatic alignment tools (GIZA++ (Och and Ney, 2003) and fast_align (Dyer et al., 2013)) on the training data and feed it as ground truth to the

attention network. They report some improvements in translation quality arguing that the attention model has learned to better align source and target words. The approach of training attention using traditional alignments has also been proposed by others (Chen et al., 2016; Alkhouli et al., 2016). Chen et al. (2016) show that guided attention with traditional alignment helps in the domain of e-commerce data which includes lots of out of vocabulary (OOV) product names and placeholders, but not much in the other domains. Alkhouli et al. (2016) have separated the alignment model and translation model, reasoning that this avoids propagation of errors from one model to the other as well as providing more flexibility in the model types and training of the models. They use a feed-forward neural network as their alignment model that learns to model jumps in the source side using HMM/IBM alignments obtained by using GIZA++.

Shi et al. (2016) show that various kinds of syntactic information are being learned and encoded in the output hidden states of the encoder. The neural system for their experimental analysis is not an attentional model and they argue that attention does not have any impact for learning syntactic information. However, performing the same analysis for morphological information, Belinkov et al. (2017) show that attention has also some effect on the information that the encoder of neural machine translation system encodes in its output hidden states. As part of their analysis they show that a neural machine translation system that has an attention model can learn the POS tags of the source side more efficiently than a system without attention.

Recently, Koehn and Knowles (2017) carried out a brief analysis of how much attention and alignment match in different languages by measuring the probability mass that attention gives to alignments obtained from an automatic alignment tool. They also report differences based on the most attended words.

The mixed results reported by Chen et al. (2016); Alkhouli et al. (2016); Liu et al. (2016) on optimizing attention with respect to alignments motivates a more thorough analysis of attention models in NMT.

3 Attention Models

This section provides a short background on attention and discusses two most popular attention models which are also used in this paper. The first model is a non-recurrent attention model which is equivalent to the "global attention" method proposed by Luong et al. (2015a). The second attention model that we use in our investigation is an input-feeding model similar to the attention model first proposed by Bahdanau et al. (2015) and turned to a more general one and called *input-feeding* by Luong et al. (2015a). Below we describe the details of both models.

Both non-recurrent and input-feeding models compute a context vector c_i at each time step. Subsequently, they concatenate the context vector to the hidden state of decoder and pass it through a non-linearity before it is fed into the softmax output layer of the translation network.

$$\tilde{h}_t = tanh(W_c[c_t; h'_t]) \qquad (1)$$

The difference of the two models lays in the way they compute the context vector. In the non-recurrent model, the hidden state of the decoder is compared to each hidden state of the encoder. Often, this comparison is realized as the dot product of vectors. Then the comparison result is fed to a softmax layer to compute the attention weight.

$$e_{t,i} = h_i^T h'_t \qquad (2)$$

$$\alpha_{t,i} = \frac{\exp(e_{t,i})}{\sum_{j=1}^{|x|} \exp(e_{t,j})} \qquad (3)$$

Here h'_t is the hidden state of the decoder at time t, h_i is ith hidden state of the encoder and $|x|$ is the length of the source sentence. Then the computed alignment weights are used to compute a weighted sum over the encoder hidden states which results in the context vector mentioned above:

$$c_i = \sum_{i=1}^{|x|} \alpha_{t,i} h_i \qquad (4)$$

The input-feeding model changes the context vector computation in a way that at each step t the context vector is aware of the previously computed context c_{t-1}. To this end, the input-feeding model feeds back its own $\tilde{h}_{t-1}$ to the network and uses the resulting hidden state instead of the context-independent h'_t, to compare to the hidden states of

	RWTH data
# of sentences	508
# of alignments	10534
% of sure alignments	91%
% of possible alignments	9%

Table 1: Statistics of manual alignments provided by RWTH German-English data.

the encoder. This is defined in the following equations:

$$h''_t = f(W[\tilde{h}_{t-1}; y_{t-1}]) \qquad (5)$$

$$e_{t,i} = h_i^T h''_t \qquad (6)$$

Here, f is the function that the stacked LSTM applies to the input, y_{t-1} is the last generated target word, and $\tilde{h}_{t-1}$ is the output of previous time step of the input-feeding network itself, meaning the output of Equation 1 in the case that context vector has been computed using $e_{t,i}$ from Equation 6.

4 Comparing Attention with Alignment

As mentioned above, it is a commonly held assumption that attention corresponds to word alignments. To verify this, we investigate whether higher consistency between attention and alignment leads to better translations.

4.1 Measuring Attention-Alignment Accuracy

In order to compare attentions of multiple systems as well as to measure the difference between attention and word alignment, we convert the hard word alignments into soft ones and use cross entropy between attention and soft alignment as a loss function. For this purpose, we use manual alignments provided by RWTH German-English dataset as the hard alignments. The statistics of the data are given in Table 1. We convert the hard alignments to soft alignments using Equation 7. For unaligned words, we first assume that they have been aligned to all the words in the source side and then do the conversion.

$$Al(x_i, y_t) = \begin{cases} \frac{1}{|A_{y_t}|} & \text{if } x_i \in A_{y_t} \\ 0 & \text{otherwise} \end{cases} \qquad (7)$$

Here A_{y_t} is the set of source words aligned to target word y_t and $|A_{y_t}|$ is the number of source words in the set.

After conversion of the hard alignments to soft ones, we compute the *attention loss* as follows:

$$L_{At}(y_t) = -\sum_{i=1}^{|x|} Al(x_i, y_t) \log(At(x_i, y_t)) \quad (8)$$

Here x is the source sentence and $Al(x_i, y_t)$ is the weight of the alignment link between source word x_i and the target word (see Equation 7). $At(x_i, y_t)$ is the attention weight $\alpha_{t,i}$ (see Equation 3) of the source word x_i, when generating the target word y_t.

In our analysis, we also look into the relation between translation quality and the quality of the attention with respect to the alignments. For measuring the quality of attention, we use the attention loss defined in Equation 8. As a measure of translation quality, we choose the loss between the output of our NMT system and the reference translation at each translation step, which we call *word prediction loss*. The word prediction loss for word y_t is logarithm of the probability given in Equation 9.

$$p_{nmt}(y_t \mid y_{<t}, x) = softmax(W_o \tilde{h}_t) \quad (9)$$

Here x is the source sentence, y_t is target word at time step t, $y_{<t}$ is the target history given by the reference translation and $\tilde{h}_t$ is given by Equation 1 for either non-recurrent or input-feeding attention models.

Spearman's rank correlation is used to compute the correlation between attention loss and word prediction loss:

$$\rho = \frac{\mathrm{Cov}(R_{L_{At}}, R_{L_{WP}})}{\sigma_{R_{L_{At}}} \sigma_{R_{L_{WP}}}} \quad (10)$$

where $R_{L_{At}}$ and $R_{L_{WP}}$ are the ranks of the attention losses and word prediction losses, respectively, Cov is the covariance between two input variables, and $\sigma_{R_{L_{At}}}$ and $\sigma_{R_{L_{WP}}}$ are the standard deviations of $R_{L_{At}}$ and $R_{L_{WP}}$.

If there is a close relationship between word prediction quality and consistency of attention versus alignment, then there should be high correlation between word prediction loss and attention loss. Figure 2 shows an example with different levels of consistency between attention and word alignments. For the target words "will" and "come" the attention is not focused on the

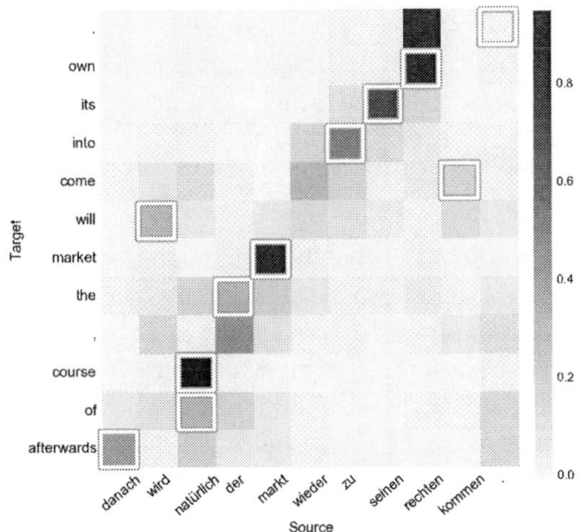

Figure 2: An example of inconsistent attention and alignment. The outlined cells show the manual alignments from the RWTH dataset (see Table 1). See how attention is deviated from alignment points in the case of "will" and "come".

manually aligned word but distributed between the aligned word and other words. The focus of this paper is examining cases where attention does not follow alignment, answering the questions whether those cases represent errors or desirable behavior of the attention model.

4.2 Measuring Attention Concentration

As another informative variable in our analysis, we look into the attention concentration. While most word alignments only involve one or a few words, attention can be distributed more freely. We measure the concentration of attention by computing the entropy of the attention distribution:

$$E_{At}(y_t) = -\sum_{i=1}^{|x|} At(x_i, y_t) \log(At(x_i, y_t))$$
$$(11)$$

5 Empirical Analysis of Attention Behaviour

We conduct our analysis using the two different attention models described in Section 3. Our first attention model is the global model without input-feeding as introduced by Luong et al. (2015a). The second model is the input-feeding model (Luong et al., 2015a), which uses recurrent attention. Our

System	test2014	test2015	test2016	RWTH
Non-recurrent	17.80	18.89	22.25	23.85
Input-feeding	19.93	21.41	25.83	27.18

Table 2: Performance of our experimental system in BLEU on different standard WMT test sets.

NMT system is a unidirectional encoder-decoder system as described in (Luong et al., 2015a), using 4 recurrent layers.

We trained the systems with dimension size of 1,000 and batch size of 80 for 20 epochs. The vocabulary for both source and target side is set to be the 30K most common words. The learning rate is set to be 1 and a maximum gradient norm of 5 has been used. We also use a dropout rate of 0.3 to avoid overfitting.

Data	# of Sent	Min Len	Max Len	Average Len
WMT15	4,240,727	1	100	24.7

Table 3: Statistics for the parallel corpus used to train our models. The length statistics are based on the source side.

5.1 Impact of Attention Mechanism

We train both of the systems on the WMT15 German-to-English training data, see Table 3 for some statistics. Table 2 shows the BLEU scores (Papineni et al., 2002) for both systems on different test sets.

Since we use POS tags and dependency roles in our analysis, both of which are based on words, we chose not to use BPE (Sennrich et al., 2016) which operates at the sub-word level.

	non-recurrent	input-feeding	GIZA++
AER	0.60	0.37	0.31

Table 4: Alignment error rate (AER) of the hard alignments produced from the output attentions of the systems with input-feeding and non-recurrent attention models. We use the most attended source word for each target word as the aligned word. The last column shows the AER for the alignment generated by GIZA++.

We report alignment error rate (AER) (Och and Ney, 2000), which is commonly used to measure alignment quality, in Table 4 to show the difference between attentions and human alignments provided by RWTH German-English dataset. To compute AER over attentions, we follow Luong

	non-recurrent	input-feeding
Attention loss	0.46	0.25

Table 5: Average loss between attention generated by input-feeding and non-recurrent systems and the manual alignment over RWTH German-English data.

et al. (2015a) to produce hard alignments from attentions by choosing the most attended source word for each target word. We also use GIZA++ (Och and Ney, 2003) to produce automatic alignments over the data set to allow for a comparison between automatically generated alignments and the attentions generated by our systems. GIZA++ is run in both directions and alignments are symmetrized using the grow-diag-final-and refined alignment heuristic.

As shown in Table 4, the input-feeding system not only achieves a higher BLEU score, but also uses attentions that are closer to the human alignments.

Table 5 compares input-feeding and non-recurrent attention in terms of attention loss computed using Equation 8. Here the losses between the attention produced by each system and the human alignments is reported. As expected, the difference in attention losses are in line with AER.

The difference between these comparisons is that AER only takes the most attended word into account while attention loss considers the entire attention distribution.

5.2 Alignment Quality Impact on Translation

Based on the results in Section 5.1, one might be inclined to conclude that the closer the attention is to the word alignments the better the translation. However, Chen et al. (2016); Liu et al. (2016); Alkhouli et al. (2016) report mixed results by optimizing their NMT system with respect to word prediction and alignment quality. These findings warrant a more fine-grained analysis of attention. To this end, we include POS tags in our analysis and study the patterns of attention based on POS tags of the target words. We choose POS tags be-

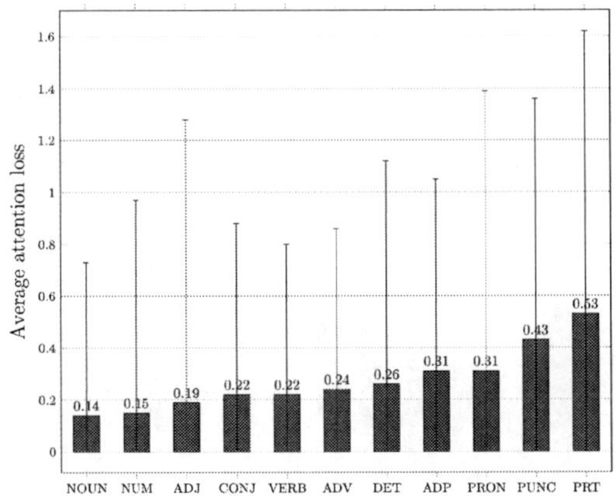
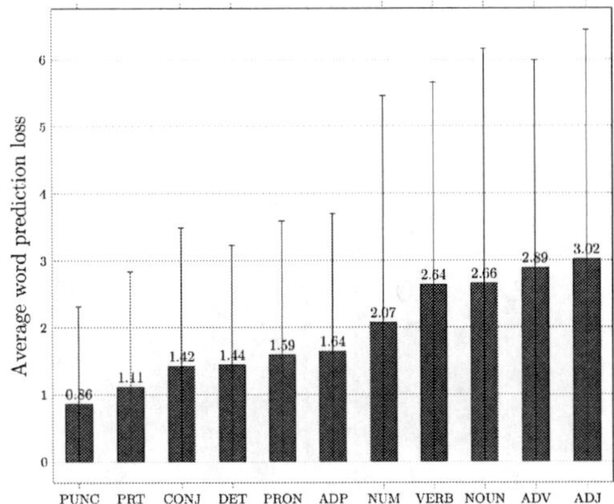

(a) Average attention loss based on the POS tags of the target side.

(b) Average word prediction loss based on the POS tags of the target side.

Figure 3: Average attention losses and word prediction losses from the input-feeding system.

Tag	Meaning	Example
ADJ	Adjective	large, latest
ADP	Adposition	in, on, of
ADV	Adverb	only, whenever
CONJ	Conjunction	and, or
DET	Determiner	the, a
NOUN	Noun	market, system
NUM	Numeral	2, two
PRT	Particle	's, off, up
PRON	Pronoun	she, they
PUNC	Punctuation	;, .
VERB	Verb	come, including

Table 6: List of the universal POS tags used in our analysis.

cause they exhibit some simple syntactic characteristics. We use the coarse grained universal POS tags (Petrov et al., 2012) given in Table 6.

To better understand how attention accuracy affects translation quality, we analyse the relationship between attention loss and word prediction loss for individual part-of-speech classes. Figure 3a shows how attention loss differs when generating different POS tags. One can see that attention loss varies substantially across different POS tags. In particular, we focus on the cases of NOUN and VERB which are the most frequent POS tags in the dataset. As shown, the attention of NOUN is the closest to alignments on average. But the average attention loss for VERB is almost two times larger than the loss for NOUN.

Considering this difference and the observations in Section 5.1, a natural follow-up would be to focus on getting the attention of verbs to be closer

to alignments. However, Figure 3b shows that the average word prediction loss for verbs is actually smaller compared to the loss for nouns. In other words, although the attention for verbs is substantially more inconsistent with the word alignments than for nouns, the NMT system translates verbs more accurately than nouns on average.

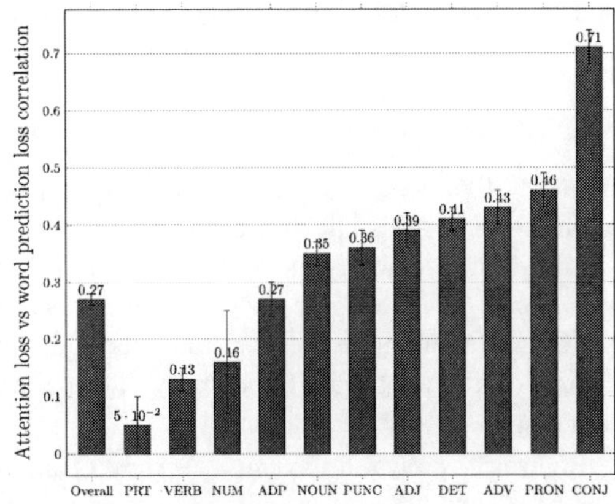

Figure 4: Correlation between word prediction loss and attention loss for the input-feeding model.

To formalize this relationship we compute Spearman's rank correlation between word prediction loss and attention loss, based on the POS tags of the target side, for the input-feeding model, see Figure 4.

The low correlation for verbs confirms that attention to other parts of source sentence rather than the aligned word is necessary for translating verbs and that attention does not necessarily have to follow alignments. However, the higher correla-

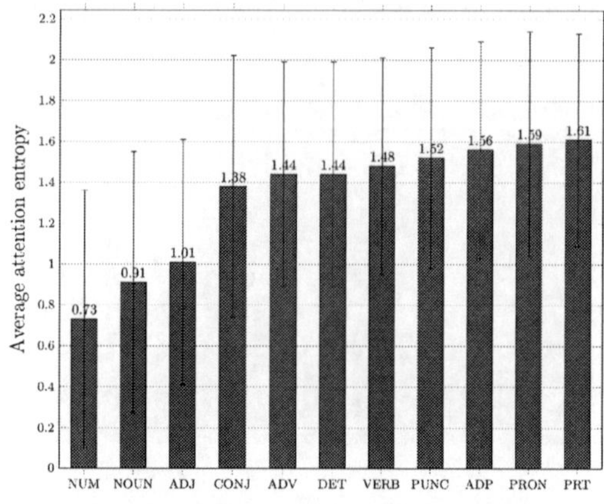

(a) Average attention entropy based on the POS tags.

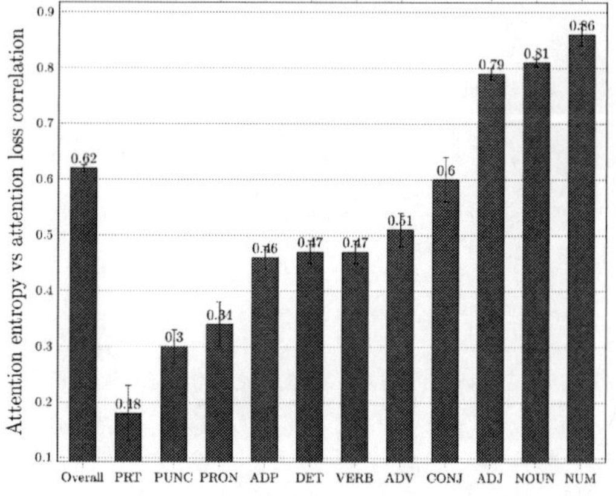

(b) Correlation between attention entropy and attention loss.

Figure 5: Attention entropy and its correlation with attention loss for the input-feeding system.

tion for nouns means that consistency of attention with alignments is more desirable. This could, in a way, explain the mixed result reported for training attention using alignments (Chen et al., 2016; Liu et al., 2016; Alkhouli et al., 2016). Especially the results by Chen et al. (2016) in which large improvements are achieved for the e-commerce domain which contains many OOV product names and placeholders, but no or very weak improvements were achieved over common domains.

5.3 Attention Concentration

In word alignment, most target words are aligned to one source word. The average number of source words aligned to nouns and verbs is 1.1 and 1.2 respectively. To investigate to what extent this also holds for attention we measure the attention concentration by computing the entropy of the attention distribution, see Equation 11.

Figure 5a shows the average entropy of attention based on POS tags. As shown, nouns have one of the lowest entropies meaning that on average the attention for nouns tends to be concentrated. This also explains the closeness of the attention to alignments for nouns. In addition, the correlation between attention entropy and attention loss in case of nouns is high as shown in Figure 5b. This means that attention entropy can be used as a measure of closeness of attention to alignment in the case of nouns.

The higher attention entropy for verbs, in Figure 5a, shows that the attention is more distributed compared to nouns. The low correlation between attention entropy and word prediction loss (see

Figure 6) shows that attention concentration is not required when translating into verbs. This also confirms that the correct translation of verbs requires the systems to pay attention to different parts of the source sentence.

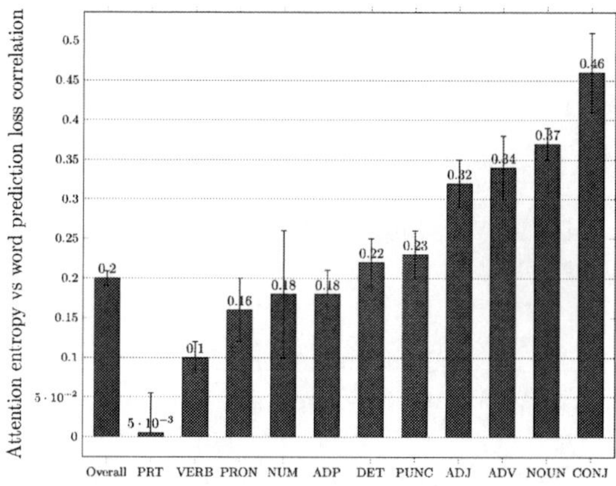

Figure 6: Correlation of attention entropy and word prediction loss for the input-feeding system.

Another interesting observation here is the low correlation for pronouns (PRON) and particles (PRT), see Figure 6. As can be seen in Figure 5a, these tags have more distributed attention comparing to nouns, for example. This could either mean that the attention model does not know where to focus or it deliberately pays attention to multiple, somehow relevant, places to be able to produce a better translation. The latter is supported by the relatively low word prediction losses, shown in the Figure 3b.

POS tag	roles(attention %)	description
NOUN	punc(16%)	Punctuations[1]
	pn(12%)	Prepositional complements
	attr(10%)	Attributive adjectives or numbers
	det(10%)	Determiners
VERB	adv(16%)	Adverbial functions including negation
	punc(14%)	Punctuations
	aux(9%)	Auxiliary verbs
	obj(9%)	Objects[2]
	subj(9%)	Subjects
CONJ	punc(28%)	Punctuations
	adv(11%)	Adverbial functions including negation
	conj(10%)	All members in a coordination[3]

Table 7: The most attended dependency roles with their received attention percentage from the attention probability mass paid to the words other than the alignment points. Here, we focus on the POS tags discussed earlier.

5.4 Attention Distribution

To further understand under which conditions attention is paid to words other than the aligned words, we study the distribution of attention over the source words. First, we measure how much attention is paid to the aligned words for each POS tag, on average. To this end, we compute the percentage of the probability mass that the attention model has assigned to aligned words for each POS tag, see Table 8.

POS tag	attention to alignment points %	attention to other words %
NUM	73	27
NOUN	68	32
ADJ	66	34
PUNC	55	45
ADV	50	50
CONJ	50	50
VERB	49	51
ADP	47	53
DET	45	55
PRON	45	55
PRT	36	64
Overall	54	46

Table 8: Distribution of attention probability mass (in %) over alignment points and the rest of the words for each POS tag.

One can notice that less than half of the attention is paid to alignment points for most of

the POS tags. To examine how the rest of attention in each case has been distributed over the source sentence we measure the attention distribution over dependency roles in the source side. We first parse the source side of RWTH data using the ParZu parser (Sennrich et al., 2013). Then we compute how the attention probability mass given to the words other than the alignment points, is distributed over dependency roles. Table 7 gives the most attended roles for each POS tag. Here, we focus on POS tags discussed earlier. One can see that the most attended roles when translating to nouns include adjectives and determiners and in the case of translating to verbs, it includes auxiliary verbs, adverbs (including negation), subjects, and objects.

6 Conclusion

In this paper, we have studied attention in neural machine translation and provided an analysis of the relation between attention and word alignment. We have shown that attention agrees with traditional alignment to a certain extent. However, this differs substantially by attention mechanism and the type of the word being generated. We have shown that attention has different patterns based on the POS tag of the target word. The concentrated pattern of attention and the relatively high correlations for nouns show that training the attention with explicit alignment labels is useful for generating nouns. However, this is not the case for verbs, since the large portion of attention being paid to words other than alignment points, is already capturing other relevant information. Training attention with alignments in this

---

[1]Punctuations have the role "root" in the parse generated using ParZu. However, we use the pos tag to discriminate them from tokens having the role "root".

[2]Attention mass for all different objects are summed up.

[3]Includes all different types of conjunctions and conjoined elements.

case will force the attention model to forget these useful information. This explains the mixed results reported when guiding attention to comply with alignments (Chen et al., 2016; Liu et al., 2016; Alkhouli et al., 2016).

Acknowledgments

This research was funded in part by the Netherlands Organization for Scientific Research (NWO) under project numbers 639.022.213 and 612.001.218.

References

Tamer Alkhouli, Gabriel Bretschner, Jan-Thorsten Peter, Mohammed Hethnawi, Andreas Guta, and Hermann Ney. 2016. Alignment-based neural machine translation. In *Proceedings of the First Conference on Machine Translation*, pages 54–65, Berlin, Germany. Association for Computational Linguistics.

Dzmitry Bahdanau, Kyunghyun Cho, and Yoshua Bengio. 2015. Neural machine translation by jointly learning to align and translate. In *International Conference on Learning Representations*, San Diego, California, USA.

Yonatan Belinkov, Nadir Durrani, Fahim Dalvi, Hassan Sajjad, and James Glass. 2017. What do neural machine translation models learn about morphology? *arXiv preprint arXiv:1704.03471*.

Wenhu Chen, Evgeny Matusov, Shahram Khadivi, and Jan-Thorsten Peter. 2016. Guided alignment training for topic-aware neural machine translation. *AMTA 2016, Vol.*, page 121.

Trevor Cohn, Cong Duy Vu Hoang, Ekaterina Vymolova, Kaisheng Yao, Chris Dyer, and Gholamreza Haffari. 2016. Incorporating structural alignment biases into an attentional neural translation model. In *Proceedings of the 2016 Conference of the North American Chapter of the Association for Computational Linguistics: Human Language Technologies*, pages 876–885, San Diego, California. Association for Computational Linguistics.

Chris Dyer, Victor Chahuneau, and Noah A. Smith. 2013. A simple, fast, and effective reparameterization of ibm model 2. In *Proceedings of the 2013 Conference of the North American Chapter of the Association for Computational Linguistics: Human Language Technologies*, pages 644–648, Atlanta, Georgia. Association for Computational Linguistics.

Sébastien Jean, Kyunghyun Cho, Roland Memisevic, and Yoshua Bengio. 2015. On using very large target vocabulary for neural machine translation. In *Proceedings of the 53rd Annual Meeting of the Association for Computational Linguistics and the 7th International Joint Conference on Natural Language Processing (Volume 1: Long Papers)*, pages 1–10, Beijing, China. Association for Computational Linguistics.

Philipp Koehn and Rebecca Knowles. 2017. Six challenges for neural machine translation. *arXiv preprint arXiv:1706.03872*.

Lemao Liu, Masao Utiyama, Andrew Finch, and Eiichiro Sumita. 2016. Neural machine translation with supervised attention. In *Proceedings of COLING 2016, the 26th International Conference on Computational Linguistics: Technical Papers*, pages 3093–3102, Osaka, Japan. The COLING 2016 Organizing Committee.

Thang Luong, Hieu Pham, and Christopher D. Manning. 2015a. Effective approaches to attention-based neural machine translation. pages 1412–1421.

Thang Luong, Ilya Sutskever, Quoc Le, Oriol Vinyals, and Wojciech Zaremba. 2015b. Addressing the rare word problem in neural machine translation. In *Proceedings of the 53rd Annual Meeting of the Association for Computational Linguistics and the 7th International Joint Conference on Natural Language Processing (Volume 1: Long Papers)*, pages 11–19, Beijing, China. Association for Computational Linguistics.

Franz Josef Och and Hermann Ney. 2000. Improved statistical alignment models. In *38th Annual Meeting of the Association for Computational Linguistics, Hong Kong, China, October 1-8, 2000*.

Franz Josef Och and Hermann Ney. 2003. A systematic comparison of various statistical alignment models. *Computational Linguistics*, 29(1):19–51.

Kishore Papineni, Salim Roukos, Todd Ward, and Wei-Jing Zhu. 2002. BLEU: a method for automatic evaluation of machine translation. In *Proceedings of the 40th Annual Meeting of the Association for Computational Linguistics*, pages 311–318.

Slav Petrov, Dipanjan Das, and Ryan Mcdonald. 2012. A universal part-of-speech tagset. In *Proceedings of the Language Resources and Evaluation Conference*.

Rico Sennrich, Barry Haddow, and Alexandra Birch. 2016. Neural machine translation of rare words with subword units. In *Proceedings of the 54th Annual Meeting of the Association for Computational Linguistics (Volume 1: Long Papers)*, pages 1715–1725. Association for Computational Linguistics.

Rico Sennrich, Martin Volk, and Gerold Schneider. 2013. Exploiting synergies between open resources for german dependency parsing, pos-tagging, and morphological analysis. In *Proceedings of the International Conference Recent Advances in Natural Language Processing RANLP 2013*, pages 601–609, Hissar, Bulgaria. INCOMA Ltd. Shoumen, BULGARIA.

Xing Shi, Inkit Padhi, and Kevin Knight. 2016. Does string-based neural mt learn source syntax? In *Proceedings of the 2016 Conference on Empirical Methods in Natural Language Processing*, pages 1526–1534, Austin, Texas. Association for Computational Linguistics.

Ilya Sutskever, Oriol Vinyals, and Quoc V Le. 2014. Sequence to sequence learning with neural networks. In *Advances in neural information processing systems (NIPS)*, pages 3104–3112.

Yonghui Wu, Mike Schuster, Zhifeng Chen, Quoc V Le, Mohammad Norouzi, Wolfgang Macherey, Maxim Krikun, Yuan Cao, Qin Gao, Klaus Macherey, et al. 2016. Google's neural machine translation system: Bridging the gap between human and machine translation. *arXiv preprint arXiv:1609.08144*.

Grammatical Error Detection Using Error- and Grammaticality-Specific Word Embeddings

Masahiro Kaneko, Yuya Sakaizawa and **Mamoru Komachi**
Tokyo Metropolitan University
{kaneko-masahiro@ed, sakaizawa-yuya@ed, komachi@}.tmu.ac.jp

Abstract

In this study, we improve grammatical error detection by learning word embeddings that consider grammaticality and error patterns. Most existing algorithms for learning word embeddings usually model only the syntactic context of words so that classifiers treat erroneous and correct words as similar inputs. We address the problem of contextual information by considering learner errors. Specifically, we propose two models: one model that employs grammatical error patterns and another model that considers grammaticality of the target word. We determine grammaticality of n-gram sequence from the annotated error tags and extract grammatical error patterns for word embeddings from large-scale learner corpora. Experimental results show that a bidirectional long-short term memory model initialized by our word embeddings achieved the state-of-the-art accuracy by a large margin in an English grammatical error detection task on the First Certificate in English dataset.

1 Introduction

Grammatical error detection that can identify the location of errors is useful for second language learners and teachers. It can be seen as a sequence labeling task, which is typically solved by a supervised approach. For example, Rei and Yannakoudakis (2016) achieved the state-of-the-art accuracy in English grammatical error detection using a bidirectional long-short term memory

Phrase pair	W2V	C&W	EWE	GWE	E&GWE
in summer & on summer	0.84	0.75	0.64	0.58	0.54
in summer & in spring	0.84	0.77	0.90	0.80	0.88
in summer & in English	0.40	0.46	0.36	0.25	0.30
on summer & on spring	0.85	0.71	0.82	0.76	0.80

Table 1: Cosine similarity of phrase pairs for each word embedding method.

(Bi-LSTM) neural network. Their approach uses word embeddings learned from a large-scale native corpus to address the data sparseness problem of learner corpora.

However, most of the word embeddings, including the one used by Rei and Yannakoudakis (2016), model only the context of the words from a raw corpus written by native speakers, and do not consider specific grammatical errors of language learners. This leads to the problem wherein the word embeddings of correct and incorrect expressions tend to be similar (Table 1, columns W2V and C&W) so that the classifier must decide grammaticality of a word from contextual information with a similar input vector.

To address this problem, we introduce two methods: 1) error-specific word embeddings (EWE), which employ grammatical error patterns, that is to say the word pairs that learners tend to easily confuse; 2) grammaticality-specific word embeddings (GWE), which consider grammatical correctness of n-grams. In this paper, we use the term grammaticality to refer to the correct or incorrect label of the target word given its surrounding context. We also combine these methods, which we will refer to as error-and grammaticality-specific word embeddings (E&GWE).

Table 1 shows the cosine similarity of phrase

Proceedings of the The 8th International Joint Conference on Natural Language Processing, pages 40–48,
Taipei, Taiwan, November 27 – December 1, 2017 ©2017 AFNLP

pairs using word2vec (W2V), C&W embeddings (Collobert and Weston, 2008), EWE, GWE, and E&GWE[1]. It illustrates that EWE, GWE, and E&GWE are able to distinguish between correct and incorrect phrase pairs while maintaining the contextual relation.

Furthermore, we conducted experiments using the large-scale Lang-8[2] English learner corpus. The results demonstrated that representation learning is crucial for exploiting a noisy learner corpus for grammatical error detection.

The main contributions of this study are summarized as follows:

- We achieve the state-of-the-art accuracy in grammatical error detection on the First Certificate in English dataset (FCE-public) using a Bi-LSTM model initialized using our word embeddings that consider grammaticality and error patterns extracted from the FCE-public corpora.
- We demonstrate that updating word embeddings using error patterns extracted from the Lang-8 (Mizumoto et al., 2011) in addition to FCE-public corpora greatly improves grammatical error detection.
- The proposed word embeddings can distinguish between correct and incorrect phrase pairs.
- We have released our code and learned word embeddings[3].

The rest of this paper is organized as follows: in Section 2, we first give a brief overview of English grammatical error detection; Section 3 describes our grammatical error detection model using error- and grammaticality-specific word embeddings; Section 4 evaluates this model on the FCE-public dataset, and Section 5 presents an analysis of the grammatical error detection model and learned word embeddings; and Section 6 concludes this paper.

2 Related Works

Many studies on grammatical error detection try to address specific types of grammatical errors (Tetreault and Chodorow, 2008; Han et al., 2006; Kochmar and Briscoe, 2014). In contrast, Rei and Yannakoudakis (2016) target all errors using a Bi-

LSTM, whose embedding layer is initialized with word2vec. We also address unrestricted grammatical error detection; however, we focus on learning word embeddings that consider a learner's error pattern and grammaticality of the target word. In this paper, subsequently, our word embeddings give statistically significant improvements over their method using exactly the same training data.

Several studies considering grammatical error patterns in language learning have been performed. For example, Sawai et al. (2013) suggest correction candidates for verbs using the learner error pattern, and Liu et al. (2010) automatically correct verb selection errors in English essays written by Chinese students learning English, based on the error patterns created from a synonym dictionary and an English-Chinese bilingual dictionary. The main difference between these previous studies and ours is that the previous studies focused only on verb selection errors.

As an example of research on learning word embeddings that consider grammaticality, Alikaniotis et al. (2016) proposed a model for constructing word embeddings by considering the importance of each word in predicting a quality score for an English learner's essay. Their approach learns word embedding from a document-level score using the mean square error whereas we learn word embeddings from a word-level binary error information using the hinge loss.

The use of a large-scale learner corpus on grammatical error correction is described in works such as Xie et al. (2016) and Chollampatt et al. (2016a,b). These studies used the Lang-8 corpus as training data for phrase-based machine translation (Xie et al., 2016) and neural network joint models (Chollampatt et al., 2016a,b). In our study, Lang-8 was used to extract error patterns that were then utilized to learn word embeddings. Our experiments show that Lang-8 cannot be used as a reliable annotation for LSTM-based classifiers. Instead, we need to extract useful information as error patterns to improve the performance of error detection.

3 Grammatical Error Detection Using Error- and Grammaticality-Specific Word Embeddings

In this section, we describe the details of the proposed word embeddings: EWE, GWE, and E&GWE. These models extend an existing word

---

[1] The similarity of the phrase pairs was calculated based on the similarity of the mean vector of the word vectors.

[2] http://lang-8.com/

[3] https://github.com/kanekomasahiro/grammatical-error-detection

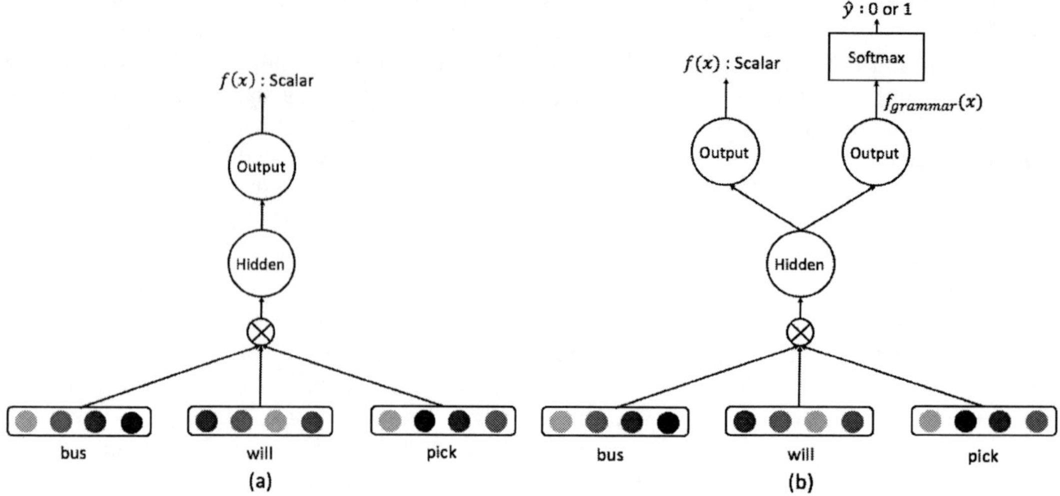

Figure 1: Architecture of our learning methods for word embeddings (a) EWE and (b) GWE. Both models concatenate the word vectors of a sequence for window size and feed them into the hidden layer. Then, EWE outputs a scalar value, and GWE outputs a prediction of the scalar value and the label of the word in the middle of the sequence.

embedding learning algorithm called C&W Embeddings (Collobert and Weston, 2008) and learn word embeddings that consider grammatical error patterns and grammaticality of the target word. We first describe the well-known C&W embeddings, and then explain our extensions. Finally, we introduce how we incorporate the learned word embeddings to the grammatical error detection task using a Bi-LSTM.

3.1 C&W Embeddings

Collobert and Weston (2008; 2011) proposed a window-based neural network model that learns distributed representations of target words based on the local context.

Here, target word w_t is the central word in the window sized sequence of words $S = (w_1, \ldots, w_t, \ldots, w_n)$. The representation of the target word w_t is compared with the representations of other words that appear in the same sequence ($\forall w_i \in S | w_i \neq w_t$). A negative sample $S' = (w_1, ..., w_c, ..., w_n | w_c \sim V)$ is created by replacing the target word w_t with a randomly selected word from the vocabulary V to distinguish between the negative sample S' and the original word sequence S. In their method, the word sequence S and the negative sample S' are converted into vectors in the embedding layer, which are fed as embeddings. They concatenate each converted

vector and treat it as input vector $x \in \mathbb{R}^{n \times D}$, where D is the dimension of the embedding layer. The input vector x is then subjected to a linear transformation (Eq. (1)) to calculate the vector i of the hidden layer. Then, the resulting vector is subjected to another linear transformation (Eq. (2)) to obtain the output $f(x)$.

$$i = \sigma(W_{hx}x + b_h) \tag{1}$$
$$f(x) = W_{oh}i + b_o \tag{2}$$

Here, W_{hx} is the weight matrix between the input vector and the hidden layer, W_{oh} is the weight matrix between the hidden layer and the output layer, b_o and b_h are biases, and σ is an element-wise nonlinear function tanh.

This model for word representation learns distributed representations by making the ranking of the original word sequence S higher than that of the negative samples S', which includes noise due to replaced words. The difference between the original word sequence and the word sequence including noise is optimized to be at least 1.

$$loss_c(S, S') = \max(0, 1 - f(x) + f(x')) \tag{3}$$

Here, x' is a transformed vector at the embedding layer obtained by converting the word w_c of the negative sample S'.

Our proposed models learn distributed representations using the same hinge loss (Eq. (3)) so the model could distinguish between correct and incorrect phrase pairs.

3.2 Error-Specific Word Embeddings (EWE)

EWE learns word embeddings using the same model as C&W embeddings. However, rather than creating negative samples randomly, we created them by replacing the target word w_t with words w_c that learners tend to easily confuse with the target word w_t. In such a case, w_c is sampled by the conditional probability:

$$P(w_c|w_t) = \frac{|w_c, w_t|}{\sum_{w_{c\prime}} |w_{c\prime}, w_t|} \qquad (4)$$

where, w_t is a target word, $w_{c\prime}$ is a set of w_c regarding w_t.

This model learns to distinguish between a correct and an incorrect word by considering error patterns. Replacement candidates, treated as error patterns, are extracted from a learner corpus annotated with correction. Figure 1a represents architecture of EWE.

*The bus will pick you up right at your hotel **entery/*entrance**.*

The above sentence is a simple example from the test data of FCE-public corpus. In this sentence, the word "entery" is incorrect and the "entrance" is the correct word. In this case, w_t is "entrance" and w_c is "entery". Note that we use only one-to-one (substitution) error patterns.

Due to the data sparseness problem, the context of infrequent words cannot be properly learned. This problem is solved by using a large corpus to pre-train word2vec. By fine-tuning vectors whose contexts have already been learned, it is possible to learn word embeddings with no or few replacement candidates in a learner corpus.

3.3 Grammaticality-Specific Word Embeddings (GWE)

Similar to the approach of Alikaniotis et al. (2016) for essay score prediction, we extend C&W embeddings to distinguish between correct words and incorrect words by including grammaticality in distributed representations (Figure 1b). For that purpose, we add an additional output layer to predict grammaticality of word sequences, and extend Equation (3) to calculate following two error func-

tions.

$$f_{grammar}(x) = W_{gh}i + b_g \qquad (5)$$
$$\hat{y} = softmax(f_{grammar}(x)) \qquad (6)$$
$$loss_p(S) = -\sum y \cdot \log(\hat{y}) \qquad (7)$$
$$loss(S, S') = \\ \alpha \cdot loss_c(S, S') + (1 - \alpha) \cdot loss_p(S) \qquad (8)$$

In Equation (5), $f_{grammar}$ is the predicted label of the original word sequence S. W_{gh} is the weight matrix and b_g is the bias. In Equation (6), the prediction probability $\hat{y}$ is computed using the softmax function for $f_{grammar}$. The error $loss_p$ is computed using the cross-entropy function using the gold label's vector y of the target word (Eq. (7)). Finally, two errors are combined to calculate $loss$ (Eq. (8)). Here, α is a hyperparameter that determines the weight of the two error functions.

We use the original tag label (0/1) of the FCE-public data as the grammaticality of word sequences for learning. Note that we do not use label information from Lang-8, because the error annotation of Lang-8 error annotations are too noisy to train an error detection model directly from the corpus. Negative examples of GWE are created randomly, that are similar to the case with C&W.

3.4 Error- and Grammaticality-Specific Word Embeddings (E&GWE)

E&GWE is a model that combines EWE and GWE. In particular, E&GWE model creates negative examples using an error pattern as in EWE and outputs score and predicts grammaticality as in GWE.

3.5 Bidirectional LSTM (Bi-LSTM)

We use bidirectional LSTM (Bi-LSTM) (Graves and Schmidhuber, 2005) as a classifier for all our experiments for English grammatical error detection, because Bi-LSTM demonstrates the state-of-the-art accuracy for this task compared to other architectures such as CRF and CNNs (Rei and Yannakoudakis, 2016).

The LSTM calculation is expressed as follows:

$$i_t = \\ \sigma(W_{ie}e_t + W_{ih}h_{t-1} + W_{ic}c_{t-1} + b_i) \qquad (9)$$
$$f_t = \\ \sigma(W_{fe}e_t + W_{fh}h_{t-1} + W_{fc}c_{t-1} + b_f) \qquad (10)$$

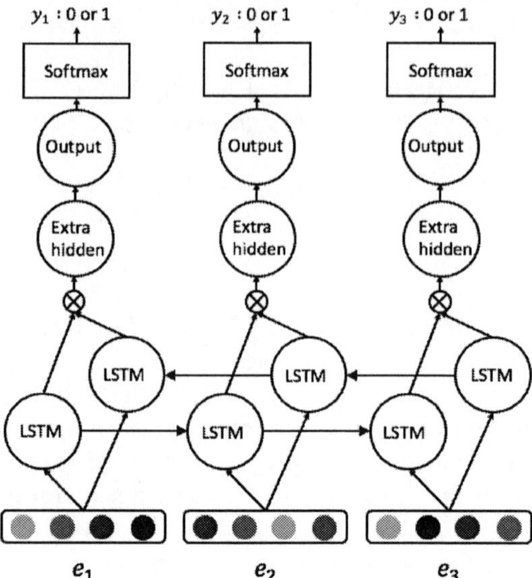

Figure 2: A bidirectional LSTM network. The word vectors e_i enter the hidden layer to predict the labels of each word.

$$c_t = i_t \odot g(W_{ce}e_t + W_{ch}h_{t-1} + b_c) + f_t \odot c_{t-1} \quad (11)$$

$$o_t = \sigma(W_{oe}e_t + W_{oh}h_{t-1} + W_{oc}c_t + b_o) \quad (12)$$

$$h_t = o_t \odot h(c_t) \quad (13)$$

Here, e_t is the word embedding of word w_t, and W_{ie}, W_{fe}, W_{ce} and W_{oe} are weight matrices. Each b_i, b_f, b_c and b_o are biases. An LSTM cell block has an input gate i_t, a memory cell c_t, a forget gate f_t and an output gate o_t to control information flow. In addition, g and h are the sigmoid function and σ is the tanh. $\odot$ is the pointwise multiplication.

We apply a bidirectional extension of LSTM, as shown in Figure 2, to encode the word embedding e_i from both left-to-right and right-to-left directions.

$$y_t = W_{yh}(h_t^L \otimes h_t^R) + b_y \quad (14)$$

The Bi-LSTM model maps each word w_t to a pair of hidden vectors h_t^L and h_t^R, i.e., the hidden vector of the left-to-right LSTM and right-to-left LSTM, respectively. $\otimes$ is the concatenation. W_{yh} is a weight matrix and b_y is a bias. We also added an extra hidden layer for linear transformation between each of the composition function and the output layer, as discussed in the previous study.

4 Experiments

4.1 Settings

We used the FCE-public dataset and the Lang-8 English learner corpus to train classifiers and word embeddings. For this evaluation, we used the test set from the FCE-public dataset (Yannakoudakis et al., 2011) for all experiments.

FCE-public dataset. First, we compared the proposed methods (EWE, GWE, and E&GWE) to previous methods (W2V and C&W) relative to training word embeddings (see Table 2a). For this purpose, we trained our word embeddings and a classifier, which were initialized using pre-trained word embeddings, with the training set from the FCE-public dataset.

This dataset is one of the most famous English learner corpus in grammatical error correction. It contains essays written by English learners. It is annotated with grammatical errors along with error classification. We followed the official split of the data: $30,953$ sentences as a training set, $2,720$ sentences as a test set, and $2,222$ sentences as a development set. In the FCE-public dataset, the number of target words of error patterns is 4,184, the number of tokens of the replacement candidates is 9,834, and the number of types is 6,420. All manually labeled words in the FCE-public dataset were set as the gold target to train the GWE. For a missing word error, an error label is assigned to the word immediately after the missing word (see Table 4 (c)). To prevent overfitting, singleton words in the training data were taken as unknown words.

Lang-8 corpus. Furthermore, we added the large-scale Lang-8 English learner corpus to the FCE-public dataset to train word embeddings (FCE+EWE-L8 and FCE+E&GWE-L8) to explore the effect of a large data on the proposed methods. We used a classifier trained using only the FCE-public dataset whose word embeddings were initialized with the large-scale pre-trained word embeddings to compare the results with those of a classifier trained directly using a noisy large-scale data whose word embeddings were initialized using word2vec (FCE&L8+W2V, see Table 2b).

Lang-8 learner corpus has over 1 million manually annotated English sentences written by ESL learners. Extraction of error patterns from Lang-8 in the process of creating negative samples to train word embeddings was performed as follows:

1. Extract word pairs using the dynamic programming from a correct sentence and an incorrect sentence.

2. If the learner's word of the extracted word pair is included in the vocabulary created from FCE-public, include it to the error patterns.

In the Lang-8 dataset the number of types of target words of the replacement candidates is 10,372, the number of tokens of the replacement candidates is 272,561, and the number of types is 61,950.

Our experiments on FCE+EWE-L8 and FCE+E&GWE-L8 were conducted by combining error patterns from all of Lang-8 corpus and the training part of FCE-public corpus to train word embeddings. However, since the number of error patterns of Lang-8 is larger than that of FCE-public, we normalized each frequency so that the ratio was 1:1.

We use $F_{0.5}$ as the main evaluation measure, following a previous study (Rei and Yannakoudakis, 2016). This measure was also adopted in the CoNLL-14 shared task on error correction task (Ng et al., 2014). It combines both precision and recall, while assigning twice as much weight to precision because accurate feedback is often more important than coverage in error detection applications (Nagata and Nakatani, 2010). Nagata and Nakatani (2010) presented a precision-oriented error detection system for articles and numbers that demonstrated precision of 0.72 and a recall of 0.25 and achieved a learning effect that is comparable to that of a human tutor.

4.2 Word Embeddings

We set parameters for word embeddings according to the previous study (Rei and Yannakoudakis, 2016). The dimension of the embedding layer of C&W, GWE, EWE and E&GWE is 300 and the dimension of the hidden layer is 200. We used a publicly released word2vec vectors (Chelba et al., 2013) trained on the News crawl from Google news[4] as pre-trained word embeddings. We set other parameters in our model by running a preliminary experiment in which the window size is 3, the number of negative samples is 600, the linear interpolation α is 0.03, and the optimizer is the ADAM algorithm (Kingma and Ba, 2015)

---

[4]https://github.com/mmihaltz/word2vec-GoogleNews-vectors

with the initial learning rate of 0.001. GWE is initialized randomly and EWE is initialized using pre-trained word2vec.

4.3 Classifier

We use EWE, GWE, and E&GWE word embeddings to initialize the Bi-LSTM neural network, and predict the correctness of the target word in the input sentence. We update initialized weights of embedding layer while training classifiers, since it showed better results. The parameters and settings of the network are the same as in a previous study (Rei and Yannakoudakis, 2016). Specifically, in Bi-LSTM the dimensions of the embedding layer, the first hidden layer, and the second hidden layer are 300, 200, and 50, respectively. The Bi-LSTM model was optimized using the ADAM algorithm (Kingma and Ba, 2015) with an initial learning rate of 0.001, and a batch size of 64 sentences.

4.4 Results

Table 2a shows experimental results comparing Bi-LSTM models trained on FCE-public dataset initialized with two baselines (FCE+W2V and FCE+C&W) and the proposed word embeddings (FCE+EWE, FCE+GWE and FCE+E&GWE) in the error detection task. We used two models for FCE+W2V: FCE+W2V (R&Y 2016) is the experimental result reported in a previous study (Rei and Yannakoudakis, 2016), and FCE+W2V (our reimplementation of (R&Y, 2016)) is the experimental result of our reimplementation of Rei and Yannakoudakis (2016). FCE+E&GWE is a model combining FCE+EWE and FCE+GWE. We conducted Wilcoxon signed rank test (p $\leq$ 0.05) 5 times.

Table 2b shows the result of using additional large-scale Lang-8 corpus. Compared to FCE&L8+W2V, FCE+EWE-L8 has better results within the three evaluation metrics. From this result, it can be seen that it is better to extract and use error patterns than simply using Lang-8 corpus as a training data to train a classifier, as it contains noise in the correct sentences. Furthermore, by combining with GWE method, accuracy was improved as in the above experiment.

In terms of precision, recall, and $F_{0.5}$, the methods in our study were ranked as FCE+E&GWE-L8 > FCE+EWE-L8 > FCE+E&GWE > FCE+GWE > FCE+EWE > FCE+W2V > FCE+C&W. Error patterns and grammaticality

Bi-LSTM + embeddings	P	R	$F_{0.5}$
FCE + W2V (R&Y, 2016)	46.1	28.5	41.1
FCE + W2V (our reimplementation of (R&Y, 2016))	45.8±0.1	27.8±0.4	40.5±0.3
FCE + C&W	45.1±0.3	26.7±0.4	39.6±0.3
FCE + EWE	46.1±0.1⋆	28.0±0.1⋆	40.8±0.1⋆
FCE + GWE	46.5±0.1⋆	28.3±0.4⋆	41.2±0.2⋆
FCE + E&GWE	**46.7**±0.1⋆	**28.6**±0.1⋆	**41.4**±0.1⋆

(a) LSTM and word embeddings are trained only using FCE-public.

Bi-LSTM + embeddings	P	R	$F_{0.5}$
FCE&L8 + W2V	12.3±2.6	32.8±2.2	14.0±2.6
FCE + EWE-L8	50.5±3.4⋆	**30.1**±1.2⋆	44.4±2.7⋆
FCE + E&GWE-L8	**50.8**±3.6⋆	30.0±1.2⋆	**44.6**±2.8⋆

(b) Either FCE-public and a large-scale Lang-8 corpus are used to train LSTM or word embeddings.

Table 2: Results of grammatical error detection by Bi-LSTM. Asterisks indicate that there is a significant difference for the confidence interval 0.95 for the P, R and $F_{0.5}$ against FCE + W2V (our reimplementation of (R&Y, 2016)).

	Error type	Verb	Missing-article	Noun	Noun type
(a)	FCE + W2V	56	**48**	26	9
	FCE + C&W	53	46	24	7
(b)	FCE + EWE	60	37	29	12
	FCE + GWE	62	43	29	11
	FCE + E&GWE	64	40	31	14
(c)	FCE + EWE-L8	66	36	37	**19**
	FCE + E&GWE-L8	**67**	40	**39**	18
	Total number of errors	131	112	77	32

Table 3: Numbers of correct instances for typical error types.

consistently improved the accuracy of grammatical error detection, showing that the proposed methods are effective. Also, our proposed method has a statistically significant difference compared with previous research even without using large-scale Lang-8 corpus. It outperformed the preceding state-of-the-art (Rei and Yannakoudakis, 2016) in all evaluation metrics.

5 Discussion

Table 3 shows the number of correct answers of each model for some typical errors. Error types are taken from the gold label of the FCE-public dataset.

First, we analyze verb errors and missing articles, which have the largest differences between the numbers of correct answers of baselines and the proposed methods (see Table 3 (a) and (b)). The proposed methods gave more correct answers for verb errors, whereas FCE+W2V and FCE+C&W gave more correct answers for missing article errors. A possible explanation is that unigram-based error patterns are too powerful for word embeddings to learn other errors that can be learned from the contextual clues.

Second, we examine the difference made by adding the error patterns extracted from Lang-8 (see Table 3 (b) and (c)): FCE+EWE and FCE+EWE-L8 have the greatest difference in the number of correct answers in noun and noun type errors. FCE+EWE-L8 has more correct answers for noun errors such as *suggestion* and *advice* and noun type errors such as *time* and *times*. The reason is that Lang-8 includes a wide variety of lexical choice errors of nouns while FCE-public covers only a limited number of error variations.

Table 4 demonstrates the examples of error detection of the baseline FCE+W2V and the best proposed method FCE+E&GWE-L8 on the test data. Table 4(a) shows an example of a noun error,

	Bi-LSTM + embeddings	Detection result
(a)	Gold	The bus will pick you up right at your hotel *entrance*.
	FCE + W2V	The bus will pick you up right at your hotel entery.
	FCE + E&GWE-L8	The bus will pick you up right at your hotel **entery**.
(b)	Gold	There are shops which *sell clothes*, *food*, and books ···
	FCE + W2V	There are shops which sales cloths, foods, and books ···
	FCE + E&GWE-L8	There are shops which sales cloths, **foods**, and books ···
(c)	Gold	All the buses and *the MTR* have air-condition.
	FCE + W2V	All the buses and **MTR** have air-condition.
	FCE + E&GWE-L8	All the buses and MTR have air-condition.

Table 4: Examples of error detection by FCE+W2V and FCE+E&GWE-L8. Gold corrections in *italic*, and detected errors in **bold**.

and as it can be seen, FCE+E&GWE-L8 detected the error in contrast to FCE+W2V. Noun type errors are presented in Table 4(b). Here, FCE+W2V did not detect any error, while FCE+E&GWE-L8 could detect the mass noun error, frequently found in a learner corpus. Detection of "sale" and "cloths" was failed in both models, but they are hard to detect since the former requires syntactic information and the latter involves common knowledge. In Table 4(c), FCE+W2V succeeded in detection of a missing article error, but FCE+E&GWE-L8 did not. Even though proposed word embeddings learn substitution errors effectively, they cannot properly learn insertion and deletion errors. It is our future work to extend word embeddings to include these types of errors and focus on contextual errors that are difficult to deal with the model, for example, missing articles.

Figure 3 visualizes word embeddings (FCE+W2V and FCE+E&GWE-L8) of frequently occurring errors in learning data using t-SNE. We plot prepositions and some typical verbs[5], where FCE+E&GWE-L8 showed better results compared to FCE+W2V. Proportional to the frequency of errors, the position of the word embeddings of FCE+E&GWE-L8 changes in comparison with that of FCE+W2V. For example, FCE+E&GWE-L8 learned the embeddings of high-frequency words such as *was* and *could* differently from FCE+W2V. On the other hand, low-frequency words such as *under* and *walk* were learned similarly. Also, almost all words shown in this figure move to the upper right. These visualization can be used to analyze errors made by learners.

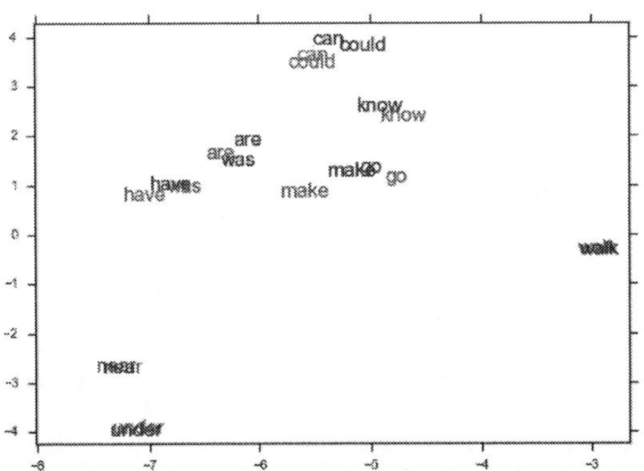

Figure 3: Visualization of word embeddings by FCE+W2V and FCE+E&GWE-L8. The red color represents the word of FCE+W2V and the blue represents FCE+E&GWE-L8.

6 Conclusion

In this study, we proposed word embeddings that can improve grammatical error detection accuracy by considering grammaticality and error patterns. We achieved the state-of-the-art accuracy on the FCE-public dataset using a Bi-LSTM model initialized with the proposed word embeddings. The word embeddings trained on a learner corpus can distinguish between correct and incorrect phrase pairs. In addition, we conducted experiments using a large-scale Lang-8 corpus. As a result, we showed that it is better to extract error patterns from such a corpus to train word embeddings than simply add Lang-8 corpus as a training data to train a classifier. We analyzed the detection results for some typical error types and showed the characteristics of learned word representations. We hope that the learned word embeddings are general enough to be of use to help NLP applications

---

[5] This dataset includes modal verbs as verb errors.

to language learning.

7 Acknowledgments

We thank Yangyang Xi of Lang-8, Inc. for kindly allowing us to use the Lang-8 learner corpus. We also thank the anonymous reviewers for their insightful comments. This work was partially supported by JSPS Grant-in-Aid for Young Scientists (B) Grant Number JP16K16117.

References

Dimitrios Alikaniotis, Helen Yannakoudakis, and Marek Rei. 2016. Automatic text scoring using neural networks. In *ACL*. pages 715–725.

Ciprian Chelba, Tomas Mikolov, Mike Schuster, Qi Ge, Thorsten Brants, Phillipp Koehn, and Tony Robinson. 2013. One billion word benchmark for measuring progress in statistical language modeling. *arXiv preprint arXiv:1312.3005* .

Shamil Chollampatt, Duc Tam Hoang, and Hwee Tou Ng. 2016a. Adapting grammatical error correction based on the native language of writers with neural network joint models. In *EMNLP*. pages 1901–1911.

Shamil Chollampatt, Kaveh Taghipour, and Hwee Tou Ng. 2016b. Neural network translation models for grammatical error correction. *arXiv preprint arXiv:1606.00189* .

Ronan Collobert and Jason Weston. 2008. A unified architecture for natural language processing: Deep neural networks with multitask learning. In *ICML*. pages 160–167.

Ronan Collobert, Jason Weston, Léon Bottou, Michael Karlen, Koray Kavukcuoglu, and Pavel Kuksa. 2011. Natural language processing (almost) from scratch. *Journal of Machine Learning Research* 12:2493–2537.

Alex Graves and Jürgen Schmidhuber. 2005. Framewise phoneme classification with bidirectional LSTM and other neural network architectures. *Neural Networks* 18(5):602–610.

Na-Rae Han, Martin Chodorow, and Claudia Leacock. 2006. Detecting errors in English article usage by non-native speakers. *Natural Language Engineering*. pages 115–129.

Diederik Kingma and Jimmy Ba. 2015. Adam: A method for stochastic optimization. In *ICLR*.

Ekaterina Kochmar and Ted Briscoe. 2014. Detecting learner errors in the choice of content words using compositional distributional semantics. In *COLING*. pages 1740–1751.

Xiaohua Liu, Bo Han, Kuan Li, Stephan Hyeonjun Stiller, and Ming Zhou. 2010. SRL-based verb selection for ESL. In *EMNLP*. pages 1068–1076.

Tomoya Mizumoto, Mamoru Komachi, Masaaki Nagata, and Yuji Matsumoto. 2011. Mining revision log of language learning SNS for automated Japanese error correction of second language learners. In *IJCNLP*. pages 147–155.

Ryo Nagata and Kazuhide Nakatani. 2010. Evaluating performance of grammatical error detection to maximize learning effect. In *COLING*. pages 894–900.

Hwee Tou Ng, Siew Mei Wu, Ted Briscoe, Christian Hadiwinoto, Raymond Hendy Susanto, and Christopher Bryant. 2014. The CoNLL-2014 shared task on grammatical error correction. In *CoNLL Shared Task*. pages 1–14.

Marek Rei and Helen Yannakoudakis. 2016. Compositional sequence labeling models for error detection in learner writing. In *ACL*. pages 1181–1191.

Yu Sawai, Mamoru Komachi, and Yuji Matsumoto. 2013. A learner corpus-based approach to verb suggestion for ESL. In *ACL*. pages 708–713.

Joel R Tetreault and Martin Chodorow. 2008. The ups and downs of preposition error detection in ESL writing. In *COLING*. pages 865–872.

Ziang Xie, Anand Avati, Naveen Arivazhagan, Dan Jurafsky, and Andrew Y Ng. 2016. Neural language correction with character-based attention. *arXiv preprint arXiv:1603.09727* .

Helen Yannakoudakis, Ted Briscoe, and Ben Medlock. 2011. A new dataset and method for automatically grading ESOL texts. In *ACL-HLT*. pages 180–189.

Dependency Parsing with Partial Annotations: An Empirical Comparison

Yue Zhang[†], Zhenghua Li[†,*], Jun Lang[‡], Qingrong Xia[†], Min Zhang[†]

[†]Soochow University, Suzhou, China

{yzhang1107,qrxia}@stu.suda.edu.cn, {zhli13,minzhang}@suda.edu.cn

[‡]Alibaba Group, Hangzhou, China

langjun.lj@alibaba-inc.com

Abstract

This paper describes and compares two straightforward approaches for dependency parsing with partial annotations (PA). The first approach is based on a forest-based training objective for two CRF parsers, i.e., a biaffine neural network graph-based parser (Biaffine) and a traditional log-linear graph-based parser (LLGPar). The second approach is based on the idea of constrained decoding for three parsers, i.e., a traditional linear graph-based parser (LGPar), a globally normalized neural network transition-based parser (GN3Par) and a traditional linear transition-based parser (LTPar). For the test phase, constrained decoding is also used for completing partial trees. We conduct experiments on Penn Treebank under three different settings for simulating PA, i.e., random, most uncertain, and divergent outputs from the five parsers. The results show that LLGPar is most effective in directly learning from PA, and other parsers can achieve best performance when PAs are completed into full trees by LLGPar.

1 Introduction

Traditional supervised approaches for structural classification assume full annotation (FA), meaning that the training instances have complete manually-labeled structures. In the case of dependency parsing, FA means a complete parse tree is provided for each training sentence. However, recent studies suggest that it is more economic and effective to construct labeled data with partial annotation (PA). A lot of research effort has been attracted to obtain partially-labeled data for different

---

*Correspondence author

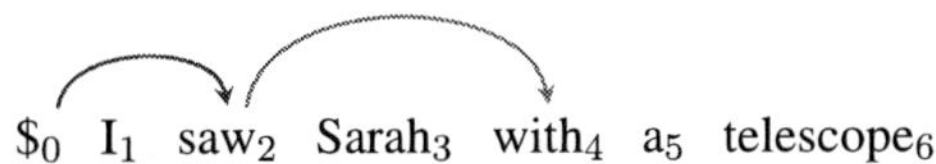

Figure 1: An example partial tree, where only the heads of "*saw*" and "*with*" are given.

tasks via active learning (Sassano and Kurohashi, 2010; Mirroshandel and Nasr, 2011; Li et al., 2012; Marcheggiani and Artières, 2014; Flannery and Mori, 2015; Li et al., 2016), cross-lingual syntax projection (Spreyer and Kuhn, 2009; Ganchev et al., 2009; Jiang et al., 2010; Li et al., 2014), or mining natural annotation implicitly encoded in web pages (Jiang et al., 2013; Liu et al., 2014; Nivre et al., 2014; Yang and Vozila, 2014). Figure 1) gives an example sentence partially annotated with two dependencies. However, there still lacks systematic study on how to build dependency parsers with PA. Most previous works listed above rely on ad-hoc strategies designed for only basic dependency parsers. One exception is that Li et al. (2014) convert partial trees into forests and train a traditional log-linear graph-based dependency parser (LLGPar) with PA based on a forest-based objective, showing promising results. Meanwhile, it is still unclear how PAs can be used by other main-stream dependency parsers, such as the traditional linear graph-based parser (LGPar) and transition-based parser (LTPar), and the newly proposed biaffine neural network graph-based parser (Biaffine) (Dozat and Manning, 2017) and globally normalized neural network transition-based parser (GN3Par) (Andor et al., 2016).

This paper aims to thoroughly study this issue and make systematic comparison on different approaches for dependency parsing with PA. In sum-

49

Proceedings of the The 8th International Joint Conference on Natural Language Processing, pages 49–58,
Taipei, Taiwan, November 27 – December 1, 2017 ©2017 AFNLP

mary, we make the following contributions.

- We present a general framework for directly training GN3Par, LGPar and LTPar with PA based on *constrained decoding*. The basic idea is to use the current feature weights to parse the sentence under the PA-constrained search space, and use the best parse as a pseudo gold-standard reference for feature weight update during perceptron training.

- We also implement the forest-objective based approach of Li et al. (2014) for the two CRF parsers, i.e., LLGPar and Biaffine.

- We have made thorough comparison among different *directly-train* approaches under three different settings for simulating PA, i.e., random dependencies, most uncertain dependencies, and dependencies with divergent outputs from the five parsers. We have also compared the proposed directly-train approaches with the straightforward *complete-then-train* approach.

- Extensive experiments lead to several interesting and clear findings.

2 Dependency Parsing

Given an input sentence $\mathbf{x} = w_0 w_1 ... w_n$, a dependency tree comprises a set of dependencies, namely $\mathbf{d} = \{i \curvearrowright j : 0 \leq i \leq n, 1 \leq j \leq n\}$, where $i \curvearrowright j$ is a dependency from a *head* word i to a *modifier* word j. A complete dependency tree contains n dependencies, namely $|\mathbf{d}| = n$, whereas a partial dependency tree contains less than n dependencies, namely $|\mathbf{d}| < n$. Alternatively, FA can be understood as a special form of PA. For clarity, we denote a complete tree as $\mathbf{d}$ and a partial tree as $\mathbf{d}^p$.

The decoding procedure aims to find an optimal complete tree $\mathbf{d}^*$:

$$\mathbf{d}^* = \arg\max_{\mathbf{d} \in \mathcal{Y}(\mathbf{x})} Score(\mathbf{x}, \mathbf{d}; \mathbf{w}) \qquad (1)$$

where $\mathcal{Y}(\mathbf{x})$ defines the search space containing all legal trees for $\mathbf{x}$ and $\mathbf{w}$ is the model parameters.

2.1 Graph-based Approach

The graph-based method factorizes the score of a dependency tree into those of small subtrees $\mathbf{p}$:

$$Score(\mathbf{x}, \mathbf{d}; \mathbf{w}) = \sum_{\mathbf{p} \subseteq \mathbf{d}} Score(\mathbf{x}, \mathbf{p}; \mathbf{w}) \qquad (2)$$

Dynamic programming based *exact search* are usually applied to find the optimal tree (McDonald et al., 2005; McDonald and Pereira, 2006; Carreras, 2007; Koo and Collins, 2010).

Biaffine belongs to the first-order model and only incorporates scores of single dependencies. In contrast, for LLGPar and LGPar, we follow Li et al. (2014) and adopt the second-order model of McDonald and Pereira (2006) considering scores of single dependencies and adjacent siblings. Biaffine and LLGPar both belong to CRF parser. Please note that the original Biaffine is locally trained on each word. In this work, we follow Ma and Hovy (2017) and add a global CRF loss in the projective case, in order to directly use the proposed approach of Li et al. (2014). In other words, we extend the original Biaffine Parser described in Dozat and Manning (2017) by adding a CRF layer. Under the CRF model, the conditional probability of $\mathbf{d}$ given $\mathbf{x}$ is:

$$p(\mathbf{d}|\mathbf{x}; \mathbf{w}) = \frac{e^{Score(\mathbf{x}, \mathbf{d}; \mathbf{w})}}{\sum_{\mathbf{d}' \in \mathcal{Y}(\mathbf{x})} e^{Score(\mathbf{x}, \mathbf{d}'; \mathbf{w})}} \qquad (3)$$

For training, $\mathbf{w}$ is optimized using gradient descent to maximize the likelihood of the training data.

Biaffine uses a neural network to compute the score of each dependency. First, the input word and POS tag sequence are fully encoded with two BiLSTM layers. Then, two MLPs are applied to each word position i to obtain two word representations, i.e., $\mathbf{r}_i^h$ (w_i as head) $\mathbf{r}_i^m$ (w_i as modifier). Finally, a biaffine classifier predicts the score of an arbitary dependency $i \curvearrowright j$.

$$score(i \curvearrowright j) = \mathbf{r}_i^h \cdot W \cdot \mathbf{r}_j^m + \mathbf{r}_i^h \cdot V \qquad (4)$$

where W (matrix) and V (vector) are the biaffine parameters.

LLGPar is a traditional discrete feature based model, which defines the score of a tree as

$$Score(\mathbf{x}, \mathbf{d}; \mathbf{w}) = \mathbf{w} \cdot \mathbf{f}(\mathbf{x}, \mathbf{d}) \qquad (5)$$

$\mathbf{f}(\mathbf{x}, \mathbf{d})$ is a sparse accumulated feature vector corresponding to $\mathbf{d}$.

LGPar uses perceptron-like online training to directly learn $\mathbf{w}$. The workflow is similar to Algorithm 1, except that the gold-standard reference $\mathbf{d}^+$ is directly provided in the training data without the need of constrained decoding in line 7.

Algorithm 1 Perceptron training based on constrained decoding.

1: **Input:** Partially labeled data $\mathcal{D} = \{(\mathbf{x}_j, \mathbf{d}_j^p)\}_{j=1}^N$; **Output: w**;
2: **Initialization:** $\mathbf{w}^{(0)} = \mathbf{0}$, $k = 0$
3: **for** $i = 1$ **to** I **do** // iterations
4:   **for** $(\mathbf{x}_j, \mathbf{d}_j^p) \in \mathcal{D}$ **do** // traverse
5:     $\mathbf{d}^- = \arg\max_{\mathbf{d} \in \mathcal{Y}(\mathbf{x}_j)} Score(\mathbf{x}_j, \mathbf{d}; \mathbf{w})$ // Unconstrained decoding: LGPar
6:     $\mathbf{a}^- = \arg\max_{\mathbf{a} \to \mathbf{d} \in \mathcal{Y}(\mathbf{x}_j)} Score(\mathbf{x}_j, \mathbf{a} \to \mathbf{d}; \mathbf{w})$ // Unconstrained decoding: LTPar
7:     $\mathbf{d}^+ = \arg\max_{\mathbf{d} \in \mathcal{Y}(\mathbf{x}_j, \mathbf{d}_j^p)} Score(\mathbf{x}_j, \mathbf{d}; \mathbf{w})$ // Constrained decoding: LGPar
8:     $\mathbf{a}^+ = \arg\max_{\mathbf{a} \to \mathbf{d} \in \mathcal{Y}(\mathbf{x}_j, \mathbf{d}_j^p)} Score(\mathbf{x}_j, \mathbf{a} \to \mathbf{d}; \mathbf{w})$ // Constrained decoding: LTPar
9:     $\mathbf{w}_{k+1} = \mathbf{w}_k + \mathbf{f}(\mathbf{x}, \mathbf{d}^+) - \mathbf{f}(\mathbf{x}, \mathbf{d}^-)$ // Update: LGPar
10:    $\mathbf{w}_{k+1} = \mathbf{w}_k + \mathbf{f}(\mathbf{x}, \mathbf{a}^+) - \mathbf{f}(\mathbf{x}, \mathbf{a}^-)$ // Update: LTPar
11:    $k = k + 1$
12:   **end for**
13: **end for**

2.2 Transition-based Approach

The transition-based method builds a dependency by applying sequence of shift/reduce actions $\mathbf{a}$, and factorizes the score of a tree into the sum of scores of each action in $\mathbf{a}$ (Yamada and Matsumoto, 2003; Nivre, 2003; Zhang and Nivre, 2011):

$$Score(\mathbf{x}, \mathbf{d}; \mathbf{w}) = Score(\mathbf{x}, \mathbf{a} \to \mathbf{d}; \mathbf{w})$$
$$= \sum_{i=1}^{|\mathbf{a}|} Score(\mathbf{x}, c_i, a_i; \mathbf{w}) \tag{6}$$

where $\mathbf{a}_i$ is the action taken at step i and c_i is the configuration status after taking action $a_1...a_{i-1}$. Transition-based methods use inexact beam search to find a highest-scoring action sequence.

GN3Par uses a neural network to predict scores of different actions given a state (Chen and Manning, 2014; Andor et al., 2016). First, 48 atomic features are embedded and concatenated as the input layer. Then, two hidden layers are applied to get the scores of all feasible actions. Unlike the traditional perceptron-like training, which only considers the best action sequence in the beam and the gold-standard sequence, their idea of global normalization is to approximately compute the probabilities of all the sequences in the beam to obtain a global CRF-like loss.

LTPar is a traditional discrete feature based model like LLGPar and LGPar, and adopts global perceptron-like training to learn the feature weights $\mathbf{w}$. We build an arc-eager transition-based dependency parser and features described in Zhang and Nivre (2011).

3 Directly training parsers with PA

As described in Li et al. (2014), CRF parsers such as **LLGPar** and **Biaffine** can naturally learn

from PA based on the idea of ambiguous labeling, which allows a sentence to have multiple parse trees (forest) as its gold-standard reference (Riezler et al., 2002; Dredze et al., 2009; Täckström et al., 2013). First, a partial tree $\mathbf{d}^p$ is converted into a forest by adding all possible dependencies pointing to remaining words without heads, with the constraint that a newly added dependency does not violate existing ones in $\mathbf{d}^p$. The forest can be formally defined as $\mathcal{F}(\mathbf{x}, \mathbf{d}^p) = \{\mathbf{d} : \mathbf{d} \in \mathcal{Y}(\mathbf{x}), \mathbf{d}^p \subseteq \mathbf{d}\}$, whose conditional probability is the sum of probabilities of all trees that it contains:

$$p(\mathbf{d}^p|\mathbf{x}; \mathbf{w}) = \sum_{\mathbf{d} \in \mathcal{F}(\mathbf{x}, \mathbf{d}^p)} p(\mathbf{d}|\mathbf{x}; \mathbf{w}) \tag{7}$$

Then, we can define a forest-based training objective function to maximize the likelihood of training data as described in Li et al. (2014).

LGPar can be extended to directly learn from PA based on the idea of constrained decoding, as shown in Algorithm 1, which has been previously applied to Chinese word segmentation with partially labeled sequences (Jiang et al., 2010). The idea is using the best tree $\mathbf{d}^+$ in the constrained search space $\mathcal{Y}(\mathbf{x}_j, \mathbf{d}_j^p)$ (line 7) as a pseudo gold-standard reference for weight update. In traditional perceptron training, $\mathbf{d}^+$ would be a complete parse tree provided in the training data. It is trivial to implement constrained decoding for graph-based parsers, and we only need to disable some illegal combination operations during dynamic programming.

LTPar can also directly learn from PA in a similar way, as shown in Algorithm 1. Constrained decoding is performed to find a pseudo gold-standard reference (line 8). It is more complicate to design constrained decoding for transition-based parsing

	train-1K	train-39K	dev	test
#Sentence	1,000	38,832	1,700	2,416
#Token	24,358	925,670	40,117	56,684

Table 1: Data Statistics. FA is always used for train-1K, whereas PA is simulated for train-39K.

than graph-based parsing. Fortunately, Nivre et al. (2014) propose a constrained decoding procedure for the arc-eager parsing system. We ignore the details due to the space limitation.

GN3Par learns from PA in a similar manner with LTPar. The difference is that for each sentence, all the sequences in beam are used as negative examples in Line 6, and $\mathbf{a}^+$ obtained in Line 8 as gold-standard. Then, the global loss is computed in the same way with the case of FA.[1] Meanwhile, since GN3Par uses the arc-standard transition system, we also develop a constrained decoding procedure for the arc-standard system, which will be released as supporting documents.

4 Experiments

Data. We conduct experiments on Penn Treebank (PTB), and follow the standard data splitting (sec 2-21 as training, sec 22 as development, and sec 23 as test). Original bracketed structures are converted into dependency structures using Penn2Malt with default head-finding rules. We build a CRF-based bigram part-of-speech (POS) tagger to produce automatic POS tags for all train/dev/test data (10-way jackknifing on training data), with tagging accuracy 97.3% on test data. As suggested by an earlier anonymous reviewer, we further split the training data into two parts. We assume that the first $1K$ training sentences are provided as a small-scale data with FA, which can be obtained by a small amount of manual annotation or through cross-lingual projection methods. We simulate PA for the remaining $39K$ sentences. Table 1 shows the data statistics.

Parameter settings. We implement all five parsers from scratch using C++, which will be released publicly in the future. For those who are immediately interested, please contact us. We train LLGPar with stochastic gradient descent (Finkel et al., 2008). For LTPar and GN3Par,

the beam size is 64 and the standard early update is adopted during training (Collins, 2002). For LGPar and LTPar, averaged perceptron is adopted (Collins, 2002).

For Biaffine, we directly adopt most hyperparameters of the released code of Dozat and Manning (2017), only removing the components related with dependency labels, since we focus on unlabeled dependency parsing in this work. The LSTM (two forward plus two backward) layers all use 300-dimension hidden cells. Dropout with ratio of 0.75 is applied to most layers before output. The two MLPs both have 100-dimension outputs without hidden layer. Adam optimization is adopted with $\alpha_1 = \alpha_2 = 0.9$.

For GN3Par, we follow Daniel et al. (2016), and use two 1024×1024 hidden layers, and adopt momentum (ratio of 0.9) Adam optimization.

For both Biaffine and GN3Par, we set the embedding dimension of both word/tag to 100, and use the GloVe pretrained word embedding for initialization[2], and randomly initialize embeddings of POS tags.

Since we have two sets of training data, we adopt the simple corpus-weighting strategy of Li et al. (2014). In each iteration, we merge train-1K and a subset of random $10K$ sentences from train-$39K$, shuffle them, and then use them for training. For all parsers, training terminates when the peak parsing accuracy on dev data does not improve in 30 consecutive iterations.

For **evaluation metrics**, we use the standard unlabeled attachment score (UAS) excluding punctuation marks.

4.1 Three settings for simulating PA on train-39K

In order to simulate PA for each sentence in train-$39K$, we only keep α% gold-standard dependencies (not considering punctuation marks), and remove all other dependencies. We experiment with three simulation settings to fully investigate the capability of different approaches in learning from PA.

Random (30% or 15%):[3] For each sentence in train-39K, we randomly select α% words, and only keep dependencies linking to these words.

---

[1] We have also tried to use all sequences in the beam in Line 8 as gold-standard, instead of the best $\mathbf{a}^+$, considering that there may be many gold-standard references in the case of PA. However, the accuracies become lower.

[2] https://nlp.stanford.edu/projects/glove/

[3] We choose 15% since the parsers achieve about 85% UAS when trained on train-1K (see Table 4). Then 30% aim to find the effect of different levels of supervision.

	Biaffine	LLGPar	LGPar	GN3Par	LTPar	Berkeley	Turbo	Mate-tool	ZPar
on Dev	**94.37**	93.16	93.00	93.32	92.77	92.84	92.86	92.58	92.42
on Test	**94.18**	92.42	92.43	93.26	92.01	92.85	92.63	92.48	92.12

Table 2: UAS of different parsers trained on all training data ($40K$)

	FA(random)			PA(random)		PA(uncertain)		PA(divergence)
	100%	30%	15%	30%	15%	30%	15%	21.33%
Biaffine	**94.37**	93.06 (-1.31)	**92.10** (-2.27)	**92.84** (-1.53)	**91.92** (-2.45)	**93.63** (-0.74)	**92.83** (-1.54)	**93.58** (-0.79)
LLGPar	93.16	91.93 (**-1.23**)	91.15 (**-2.01**)	92.39 (**-0.77**)	91.66 (**-1.50**)	93.02 (**-0.14**)	92.44 (**-0.72**)	92.83 (**-0.33**)
LGPar	93.00	91.76 (-1.24)	90.80 (-2.20)	91.63 (-1.37)	90.62 (-2.38)	92.46 (-0.54)	91.64 (-1.36)	92.42 (-0.58)
GN3Par	93.32	91.99 (-1.33)	91.17 (-2.15)	91.43 (-1.89)	90.34 (-2.98)	92.40 (-0.92)	91.80 (-1.52)	92.60 (-0.72)
LTPar	92.77	91.22 (-1.55)	90.35 (-2.42)	91.12 (-1.65)	90.12 (-2.65)	91.35 (-1.42)	90.99 (-1.78)	91.04 (-1.73)

Table 3: UAS on dev data: parsers are directly trained on train-$1K$ with FA and train-$39K$ with PA. "FA (random) α%" means randomly selecting α% sentences with FA from train-$39K$ for training. Numbers in parenthesis are the accuracy gap from the second column "FA (100%)".

With this setting, we aim to purely study the issue without biasing to certain structures. This setting may be best fit the scenario automatic syntax projection based on bitext, where the projected dependencies tend to be arbitrary (and noisy) due to the errors in automatic source-language parses and word alignments and non-isomorphism syntax between languages.

Uncertain (30% or 15%): In their work of active learning with PA, Li et al. (2016) show that the marginal probabilities from LLGPar is the most effective uncertainty measurement for selecting the most informative words to be annotated. Following their work, we first train LLGPar on train-$1K$ with FA, and then use LLGPar to parse train-$39K$ and select α% most uncertain words. We use the gold-standard heads of the selected words as PAs for model training.

Following Li et al. (2016), we measure the uncertainty of a word w_i according to the *marginal probability gap* between its two most likely heads h_i^0 and h_i^1.

$$Uncertainty(\mathbf{x}, i) = p(h_i^0 \curvearrowright i | \mathbf{x}) - p(h_i^1 \curvearrowright i | \mathbf{x}) \quad (8)$$

This setting fits the scenario of active learning, which aims to save annotation effort by only annotating the most useful structures.

Divergence (21.33%): We train all five parsers on train-$1K$, and use them to parse train-$39K$. If their output trees do not assign the same head to a word, then we keep the gold-standard dependency pointing to the word, leading to 21.33% remaining dependencies. This setting fits to the tri-training scenario investigated in Li et al. (2014).

4.2 Results of different parsers trained on FA

We train the five parsers on all the training data with FA. We also employ four publicly available parsers with their default settings. BerkeleyParser (v1.7) is a constituent-structure parser, whose results are converted into dependency structures (Petrov and Klein, 2007). TurboParser (v2.1.0) is a linear graph-based dependency parser using linear programming for inference (Martins et al., 2013). Mate-tool (v3.3) is a linear graph-based dependency parser very similar to our implemented LGPar (Bohnet, 2010). ZPar (v0.6) is a linear transition-based dependency parser very similar to our implemented LTPar (Zhang and Clark, 2011). The results are shown in Table 2.

We can see that the five parsers that we adopt achieve competitive parsing accuracy and serve as strong baselines. Especially, the recently proposed neural network Biaffine outperforms other parser by more than 1%.

4.3 Results of the directly-train approaches

The five parsers are directly trained on train-$1K$ with FA and train-$39K$ with PA based on the methods described in Section 3. Table 3 shows the results.

Comparing the five parsers, we have several clear findings. (1) LLGPar is the most effective in directly learning from PA since its accuracy drop is the smallest over all PA settings compared with FA (100%). (2) Although Biaffine achieves best

Parser for completion	No constraints	PA (random)		PA (uncertain)		PA (divergence)
	0%	30%	15%	30%	15%	21.33%
Biaffine-$1K$	**87.08**	92.10 (+5.02)	89.79 (+2.71)	96.78 (+9.70)	93.47 (+6.39)	96.76 (+9.68)
LLGPar-$1K$	86.67	**92.65** (+5.98)	**90.02** (+3.35)	**97.43** (+10.76)	**94.43** (+7.76)	**97.07** (+10.40)
LGPar-$1K$	86.05	92.16 (+6.11)	89.48 (+3.43)	97.30 (+11.25)	94.11 (**+8.06**)	96.99 (+10.94)
GN3Par-$1K$	85.86	92.34 (**+6.48**)	89.54 (**+3.68**)	97.02 (+11.16)	93.69 (+7.83)	96.56 (+10.70)
LTPar-$1K$	85.38	91.76 (+6.38)	88.89 (+3.51)	96.90 (**+11.52**)	93.35 (+7.97)	96.72 (**+11.34**)
LLGPar-$1K$+$39K$	–	95.55	93.37	**98.30**	**96.22**	97.69
Biaffine-$1K$+$39K$	–	**95.77**	**93.52**	98.27	96.17	**97.73**

Table 4: UAS of full trees in train-$39K$ completed via constrained decoding.

accuracy over all settings, thanks to its strong performance under the basic FA setting, we find that the accuracy gap between LLGPar and Biaffine becomes much smaller with PA than with FA. This also indicates that LLGPar is more effective in directly learning from PA. (3) LTPar achieves the lowest accuracy over all settings, especially on PA under uncertain (30%, 15%) and divergence. It is also clear that the accuracy declines the largest on these three settings, compared with FA (100%).

FA (random) vs. PA (random):[4] from the results in the two major columns, we can see that LLGPar achieves higher accuracy by about 0.5% when trained on sentences with $\alpha\%$ random dependencies than when trained on $\alpha\%$ random sentences with FA. This is reasonable and can be explained under the assumption that LLGPar can make full use of PA in model training. In fact, in both cases, the training data contains approximately the same number of annotated dependencies. However, from the perspective of model training, given some dependencies in the case of PA, more information about the syntactic structure can be derived.[5]

Taking Figure 1 as an example, "I_1" can only modify "saw_2" due to the single-root and single-head constraints; similarly, "$Sarah_3$" can only modify either "saw_2" or "$with_2$"; and so on. More-

over, since LLGPar is a second-order model, the presence of certain dependencies can directly affect the choice of other dependencies through the scores of adjacent siblings. Therefore, given the same amount of annotated dependencies, random PA contains more syntactic information than random FA, which explains why LLGPar performs better with PA than FA.

In contrast, all other four parsers achieve lower accuracy with PA than with FA. Biaffine differs from LLGPar in being a first-order model, and thus cannot fully utilize PA by considering sibling scores. The problem of LGPar may lie in the perceptron training with constrained decoding, which only considers a single best tree that complies with the given PA as gold-standard (Line 7 in Algorithm 1), unlike the forest-based objective of LLGPar that consider all trees weighted with probabilities. Both GN3Par and LTPar suffer from the inexact search problem. In other words, the approximate beam search can cause the correct tree drops off the beam too soon due to lower scores for earlier actions, and thus return a bad $\mathbf{a}^+$ that causes the model be updated to bias to wrong structures (Line 8 in Algorithm 1).

PA (random) vs. PA (uncertain):[6] we can see that all five parsers achieve much higher accuracy in the latter case.[7] The annotated dependencies in PA (uncertain) are most uncertain ones for current statistical parser (i.e., LLGPar), and thus are more helpful for training the models than those in PA (random). Another phenomenon is that, in the case of PA (uncertain), increasing $\alpha\% = 15\%$ to

---

[4] These two settings should give the clearest evidence whether a parser can effectively learn from PAs. Under the same $\alpha\%$, although containing approximately the same number of dependencies, PA certainly provide more syntactic information than FA, since 1) it is more expensive to annotate PA than FA in the terms of annotation time per dependency; 2) in PA, partially annotated dependencies can provide strong constraints on the remaining undecided dependencies. Therefore, we assume that a parser is effectively in learning from PA if it can achieve at least higher accuracy under PA.

[5] Also, as suggested in the work of Li et al. (2016), annotating PA is more time-consuming than annotating FA in terms of averaged time for each dependency, since dependencies in the same sentence are correlated and earlier annotated dependencies usually make later annotation easier.

[6] From the idea of active learning, we know that annotating the most informative dependencies as more training data can help models best. So, we select the most uncertain dependencies and compare the result on the setting with randomly-selected dependencies.

[7] The only exception is LTPar with 30% PA, the accuracy increases by only $91.35 - 91.12 = 0.23\%$, which may be caused by the ineffectiveness of LTPar in learning from PA.

30% actually doubles the number of annotated dependencies, but only boost accuracy of LLGPar by $93.02 - 92.44 = 0.58\%$, which indicates that newly added 15% dependencies are much less useful since the model can already well handle these low-uncertainty dependencies.

PA (uncertain, 30%) vs. PA (divergence):[8] we can see that the all five parsers achieve similar parsing accuracies under the two settings. This indicates that the divergence strategy can find very useful dependencies for all parsers, whereas uncertainty measurement based on LLGPar might be biased towards itself to a certain extent.

In summary, we can conclude from the results that *LLGPar is the most effective in directly learning from PA among all five parsers, due to both the second-order modeling and the forest-based training objective.*

4.4 Results of the complete-then-train methods

The most straight-forward method for learning from PA is the complete-then-learn method (Mirroshandel and Nasr, 2011). The idea is first using an existing parser to complete partial trees in train-$39K$ into full trees based on constrained decoding, and then training the target parser on train-$1K$ with FA and train-$39K$ with completed FA.

Results of completing via constrained decoding: Table 4 reports UAS of the completed trees on train-$39K$ using two different strategies for completion. "No constraints (0%)" means that train-$39K$ has no annotated dependencies and normal decoding without constraints is used. In the remaining columns, each parser performs constrained decoding on PA where $\alpha\%$ dependencies are provided in each sentence.

- **Coarsely-trained-self for completion**: We complete PA into FA using corresponding parsers coarsely trained on only train-$1K$ with FA. We call these parsers *Biaffine-$1K$, LLGPar-$1K$, LGPar-$1K$, GN3Par-$1K$, LTPar-$1K$* respectively.

- **Fine-trained-LLGPar for completion**: We complete PA into FA using LLGPar fine trained on both train-$1K$ with FA and train-$39K$ with PA. We call this LLGPar

---

[8]Selecting uncertain dependencies according to LLGPar may cause the resulting data to be biased to LLGPar. Therefore, we consider the divergence among all parsers for selection.

as *LLGPar-$1K$+$39K$*. Please note that *LLGPar-$1K$+$39K$* actually performs *closed test* in this setting, meaning that it parses its training data. For example, *LLGPar-$1K$+$39K$* trained on random (30%) is employed to complete the same data by filling the remaining 70% dependencies.

- **Fine-trained-Biaffine for completion**: This is the same with the case of "Fine-trained-LLGPar", except that we replace LLGParser with Biaffine. We call the resulting parser as *Biaffine-$1K$+$39K$*.

Comparing the five parsers trained on train-$1K$, we can see that constrained decoding has similar effects on all five parsers, and is able to return much more accurate trees. Numbers in parenthesis show the accuracy gap between unconstrained 0% and constrained decoding. This suggests that constrained decoding itself is not responsible for the ineffectiveness of Algorithm 1 for other parsers, especially LTPar.

Comparing the results of LLGPar-$1K$ and LLGPar-$1K$+$39K$, it is obvious that the latter produces much better full trees since the fine-trained LLGPar can make extra use of PA in train-$39K$ during training.

LLGPar-$1K$+$39K$ and Biaffine-$1K$+$39K$ achieve similar accuracies. We choose to use the former for completion since LLGPar is the most effective in both learning from PA and completing PA, as indicated by the results in Table 3 and 4.

Results of training on completed FA: Table 5 compares performance of the five parsers trained on train-$1K$ with FA and train-$39K$ with completed FA, from which we can draw several clear and interesting findings. First, different from the case of directly training on PA, the accuracy gaps among the five parsers become much more stable when trained on data with completed FA in both completion settings. Second, *using parsers coarsely-trained on train-$1K$ for completion leads to very bad performance*, which is even much worse than those of the directly-train method in Table 3 except for LTPar with uncertain (30%) and divergence. Third, *using the fine-trained LLGPar-$1K$+$39K$ for completion makes LGPar and LTPar achieve nearly the same accuracies with LLGPar,* which may be because LLGPar provides complementary effects during completion, analogous to the scenario of co-training.

	Completed by self-$1K$					Completed by LLGPar-$1K$+$39K$				
	PA (random)		PA (uncertain)		PA (divergence)	PA (random)		PA (uncertain)		PA (divergence)
	30%	15%	30%	15%	21.33%	30%	15%	30%	15%	21.33%
Biaffine	**90.88**	**89.77**	**92.91**	**91.55**	**92.83**	**93.13**	**92.46**	**93.52**	**93.02**	**93.48**
LLGPar	89.91	88.69	92.05	90.77	92.28	92.29	91.54	92.86	92.33	92.76
LGPar	89.42	88.32	91.85	90.66	92.07	92.17	91.59	92.84	92.21	92.79
GN3Par	89.77	88.38	92.07	90.71	92.07	92.43	91.83	92.82	92.45	92.66
LTPar	89.17	87.72	91.59	90.12	91.67	92.05	91.37	92.42	92.10	92.40

Table 5: UAS on dev data: parsers trained on train-$1K$ with FA and train-$39K$ with completed FA.

	Directly train on train-$39K$ with PA					Train-$39K$ with FA completed by LLGPar-$1K$+$39K$				
	PA (random)		PA (uncertain)		PA (divergence)	PA (random)		PA (uncertain)		PA (divergence)
	30%	15%	30%	15%	21.33%	30%	15%	30%	15%	21.33%
Biaffine	**92.76**	**91.66**	**93.44**	**92.82**	**93.43**	**92.82**	**92.00**	**93.20**	**92.88**	**93.30**
LLGPar	91.73	91.02	92.34	91.83	92.34	91.46	90.99	92.20	91.59	92.18
LGPar	91.17	90.36	91.99	91.28	91.74	91.55	90.96	91.98	91.57	92.01
GN3Par	91.15	89.86	92.12	91.91	92.50	92.12	91.44	92.65	92.27	92.56
LTPar	90.79	89.89	90.47	90.37	90.75	91.48	90.78	91.80	91.45	91.87

Table 6: UAS on test data: comparison of the directly-train and complete-then-train methods.

4.5 Results on test data: directly-train vs. complete-then-train

Table 6 reports UAS on the test data of parsers directly trained on train-$1K$ with FA and train-$39K$ with PA, and of those trained on train-$1K$ with FA and train-$39K$ with FA completed by fine-trained LLGPar-$1K$+$39K$. The results are consistent with the those on dev data in Table 3 and 5. Comparing the two settings, we can draw two interesting findings. First, LLGPar performs slightly better with the directly-train method. Second, the two settings lead to very similar performance on Biaffine, without a clear trend. Third, LGPar performs slightly better with the complete-then-train method in most cases except for uncertain (30%). Four, GN3Par and LTPar perform much better with the complete-then-train method.

5 Related work

In parsing community, most previous works adopt ad-hoc methods to learn from PA. Sassano and Kurohashi (2010), Jiang et al. (2010), and Flannery and Mori (2015) convert partially annotated instances into local dependency/non-dependency classification instances, which may suffer from the lack of non-local correlation between dependencies in a tree.

Mirroshandel and Nasr (2011) and Majidi and Crane (2013) adopt the complete-then-learn method. They use parsers coarsely trained on existing data with FA for completion via constrained decoding. However, our experiments show that this leads to dramatic decrease in parsing accuracy.

Nivre et al. (2014) present a constrained decoding procedure for arc-eager transition-based parsers. However, their work focuses on allowing their parser to effectively exploit external constraints during the evaluation phase. In this work, we directly employ their method and show that constrained decoding is effective for LTPar and thus irresponsible for its ineffectiveness in learning PA.

Directly learning from PA based on constrained decoding is previously proposed by Jiang et al. (2013) for Chinese word segmentation, which is treated as a character-level sequence labeling problem. In this work, we first apply the idea to LGPar and LTPar for directly learning from PA.

Directly learning from PA based on a forest-based objective in LLGPar is first proposed by Li et al. (2014), inspired by the idea of *ambiguous labeling*. Similar ideas have been extensively explored recently in sequence labeling tasks (Liu et al., 2014; Yang and Vozila, 2014; Marcheggiani and Artières, 2014).

Hwa (1999) pioneers the idea of exploring PA for constituent grammar induction based on a variant Inside-Outside re-estimation algorithm (Pereira and Schabes, 1992). Clark and Curran (2006) propose to train a Combinatorial Categorial Grammar parser using partially labeled data only containing predicate-argument dependencies. Mielens et al. (2015) propose to impute missing dependencies based on Gibbs sampling in order to enable traditional parsers to learn from partial trees.

6 Conclusions

This paper investigates the problem of dependency parsing with partially labeled data. Particularly, we focus on the realistic scenario where we have a small-scale training dataset with FA and a large-scale training dataset with PA. We experiment with three settings for simulating PA and compare several directly-train and complete-then-train approaches with five mainstream parsers, i.e., Biaffine, LLGPar, LGPar, GN3Par and LTPar.

Based on this work, we may draw the following conclusions.

- For the complete-then-train approach, using parsers coarsely trained on small-scale data with FA for completion leads to unsatisfactory results.

- LLGPar is the most effective in directly learning from PA due to both its second-order modeling and probabilistic forest-based training objective.

- All other four parsers are less effective in directly learning from PA, but can achieve their best performance with the complete-then-train approach where PAs are completed into FAs by LLGPar fine-trained on all FA+PA data.

However, as our reviewers kindly point out, more extensive experiments and systematic analysis are needed to really understand this interesting issue and provide stronger findings, which we leave for future work.

Acknowledgments

The authors would like to thank the anonymous reviewers for the helpful comments. We are greatly grateful to Jiayuan Chao for her earlier-stage experiments on this work, and to Wenliang Chen for the helpful discussions. This work was supported by National Natural Science Foundation of China (Grant No. 61525205, 61373095, 61502325).

References

Daniel Andor, Chris Alberti, David Weiss, Aliaksei Severyn, Alessandro Presta, Kuzman Ganchev, Slav Petrov, and Michael Collins. 2016. Globally normalized transition-based neural networks. In *Proceedings of ACL*, pages 2442–2452.

Bernd Bohnet. 2010. Top accuracy and fast dependency parsing is not a contradiction. In *Proceedings of COLING*, pages 89–97.

Xavier Carreras. 2007. Experiments with a higher-order projective dependency parser. In *Proceedings of EMNLP/CoNLL*, pages 141–150.

Danqi Chen and Christopher Manning. 2014. A fast and accurate dependency parser using neural networks. In *Conference on Empirical Methods in Natural Language Processing*, pages 740–750.

Stephen Clark and James Curran. 2006. Partial training for a lexicalized-grammar parser. In *Proceedings of the Human Language Technology Conference of the NAACL*, pages 144–151.

Michael Collins. 2002. Discriminative training methods for hidden markov models: Theory and experiments with perceptron algorithms. In *Proceedings of EMNLP 2002*, pages 1–8.

Timothy Dozat and Christopher D. Manning. 2017. Deep biaffine attention for neural dependecy parsing. In *ICLR*.

Mark Dredze, Partha Pratim Talukdar, and Koby Crammer. 2009. Sequence learning from data with multiple labels. In *ECML/PKDD Workshop on Learning from Multi-Label Data*.

Jenny Rose Finkel, Alex Kleeman, and Christopher D. Manning. 2008. Efficient, feature-based, conditional random field parsing. In *Proceedings of ACL*, pages 959–967.

Daniel Flannery and Shinsuke Mori. 2015. Combining active learning and partial annotation for domain adaptation of a japanese dependency parser. In *Proceedings of the 14th International Conference on Parsing Technologies*, pages 11–19.

Kuzman Ganchev, Jennifer Gillenwater, and Ben Taskar. 2009. Dependency grammar induction via bitext projection constraints. In *Proceedings of ACL-IJCNLP 2009*, pages 369–377.

Rebecca Hwa. 1999. Supervised grammar induction using training data with limited constituent information. In *Proceedings of ACL*, pages 73–79.

Wenbin Jiang, , and Qun Liu. 2010. Dependency parsing and projection based on word-pair classification. In *ACL*, pages 897–904.

Wenbin Jiang, Meng Sun, Yajuan Lü, Yating Yang, and Qun Liu. 2013. Discriminative learning with natural annotations: Word segmentation as a case study. In *Proceedings of ACL*, pages 761–769.

Terry Koo and Michael Collins. 2010. Efficient third-order dependency parsers. In *ACL*, pages 1–11.

Shoushan Li, Guodong Zhou, and Chu-Ren Huang. 2012. Active learning for Chinese word segmentation. In *Proceedings of COLING 2012: Posters*, pages 683–692.

Zhenghua Li, Min Zhang, and Wenliang Chen. 2014. Soft cross-lingual syntax projection for dependency parsing. In *COLING*, pages 783–793.

Zhenghua Li, Min Zhang, Yue Zhang, Zhanyi Liu, Wenliang Chen, Hua Wu, and Haifeng Wang. 2016. Active learning for dependency parsing with partial annotation. In *ACL*.

Yijia Liu, Yue Zhang, Wanxiang Che, Ting Liu, and Fan Wu. 2014. Domain adaptation for CRF-based Chinese word segmentation using free annotations. In *Proceedings of EMNLP*, pages 864–874.

Xuezhe Ma and Eduard Hovy. 2017. Neural probabilistic model for non-projective mst parsing. In *arxiv:https://arxiv.org/abs/1701.00874*.

Saeed Majidi and Gregory Crane. 2013. Active learning for dependency parsing by a committee of parsers. In *Proceedings of IWPT*, pages 98–105.

Diego Marcheggiani and Thierry Artières. 2014. An experimental comparison of active learning strategies for partially labeled sequences. In *Proceedings of EMNLP*, pages 898–906.

Andre Martins, Miguel Almeida, and Noah A. Smith. 2013. Turning on the turbo: Fast third-order non-projective turbo parsers. In *Proceedings of ACL*, pages 617–622.

Ryan McDonald, Koby Crammer, and Fernando Pereira. 2005. Online large-margin training of dependency parsers. In *Proceedings of ACL*, pages 91–98.

Ryan McDonald and Fernando Pereira. 2006. Online learning of approximate dependency parsing algorithms. In *Proceedings of EACL*, pages 81–88.

Jason Mielens, Liang Sun, and Jason Baldridge. 2015. Parse imputation for dependency annotations. In *Proceedings of ACL-IJCNLP*, pages 1385–1394.

Seyed Abolghasem Mirroshandel and Alexis Nasr. 2011. Active learning for dependency parsing using partially annotated sentences. In *Proceedings of the 12th International Conference on Parsing Technologies*, pages 140–149.

Joakim Nivre. 2003. An efficient algorithm for projective dependency parsing. In *Proceedings of IWPT*, pages 149–160.

Joakim Nivre, Yoav Goldberg, and Ryan McDonald. 2014. Constrained arc-eager dependency parsing. In *Computational Linguistics*, volume 40, pages 249–258.

Fernando Pereira and Yves Schabes. 1992. Inside-outside reestimation from partially bracketed corpora. In *Proceedings of the Workshop on Speech and Natural Language (HLT)*, pages 122–127.

Slav Petrov and Dan Klein. 2007. Improved inference for unlexicalized parsing. In *Proceedings of NAACL*.

Stefan Riezler, Tracy H. King, Ronald M. Kaplan, Richard Crouch, John T. III Maxwell, and Mark Johnson. 2002. Parsing the wall street journal using a lexical-functional grammar and discriminative estimation techniques. In *Proceedings of ACL*, pages 271–278.

Manabu Sassano and Sadao Kurohashi. 2010. Using smaller constituents rather than sentences in active learning for japanese dependency parsing. In *Proceedings of ACL*, pages 356–365.

Kathrin Spreyer and Jonas Kuhn. 2009. Data-driven dependency parsing of new languages using incomplete and noisy training data. In *CoNLL*, pages 12–20.

Oscar Täckström, Ryan McDonald, and Joakim Nivre. 2013. Target language adaptation of discriminative transfer parsers. In *Proceedings of NAACL*, pages 1061–1071.

Hiroyasu Yamada and Yuji Matsumoto. 2003. Statistical dependency analysis with support vector machines. In *Proceedings of IWPT*, pages 195–206.

Fan Yang and Paul Vozila. 2014. Semi-supervised Chinese word segmentation using partial-label learning with conditional random fields. In *Proceedings of EMNLP*, pages 90–98.

Yue Zhang and Stephen Clark. 2011. Syntactic processing using the generalized perceptron and beam search. *Computational Linguistics*, 37(1):105–151.

Yue Zhang and Joakim Nivre. 2011. Transition-based dependency parsing with rich non-local features. In *Proceedings of ACL*, pages 188–193.

Neural Probabilistic Model for Non-projective MST Parsing

Xuezhe Ma and **Eduard Hovy**
Language Technologies Institute
Carnegie Mellon University
Pittsburgh, PA 15213, USA
xuezhem@cs.cmu.edu, hovy@cmu.edu

Abstract

In this paper, we propose a probabilistic parsing model that defines a proper conditional probability distribution over non-projective dependency trees for a given sentence, using neural representations as inputs. The neural network architecture is based on bi-directional LSTM-CNNs, which automatically benefits from both word- and character-level representations, by using a combination of bidirectional LSTMs and CNNs. On top of the neural network, we introduce a probabilistic structured layer, defining a conditional log-linear model over non-projective trees. By exploiting Kirchhoff's Matrix-Tree Theorem (Tutte, 1984), the partition functions and marginals can be computed efficiently, leading to a straightforward end-to-end model training procedure via back-propagation. We evaluate our model on 17 different datasets, across 14 different languages. Our parser achieves state-of-the-art parsing performance on nine datasets.

1 Introduction

Dependency parsing is one of the first stages in deep language understanding and has gained interest in the natural language processing (NLP) community, due to its usefulness in a wide range of applications. Many NLP systems, such as machine translation (Xie et al., 2011), entity coreference resolution (Ng, 2010; Durrett and Klein, 2013; Ma et al., 2016), low-resource languages processing (McDonald et al., 2013; Ma and Xia, 2014), and word sense disambiguation (Fauceglia et al., 2015), are becoming more sophisticated, in part because of utilizing syntactic knowledge such as dependency parsing trees.

Dependency trees represent syntactic relationships through labeled directed edges between heads and their dependents (modifiers). In the past few years, several dependency parsing algorithms (Nivre and Scholz, 2004; McDonald et al., 2005b; Koo and Collins, 2010; Ma and Zhao, 2012a,b) have been proposed, whose high performance heavily rely on hand-crafted features and task-specific resources that are costly to develop, making dependency parsing models difficult to adapt to new languages or new domains.

Recently, non-linear neural networks, such as recurrent neural networks (RNNs) with long-short term memory (LSTM) and convolution neural networks (CNNs), with as input distributed word representations, also known as word embeddings, have been broadly applied, with great success, to NLP problems like part-of-speech (POS) tagging (Collobert et al., 2011) and named entity recognition (NER) (Chiu and Nichols, 2016). By utilizing distributed representations as inputs, these systems are capable of learning hidden information representations directly from data instead of manually designing hand-crafted features, yielding end-to-end models (Ma and Hovy, 2016). Previous studies explored the applicability of neural representations to traditional graph-based parsing models. Some work (Kiperwasser and Goldberg, 2016; Wang and Chang, 2016) replaced the linear scoring function of each arc in traditional models with neural networks and used a margin-based objective (McDonald et al., 2005a) for model training. Other work (Zhang et al., 2016; Dozat and Manning, 2016) formalized dependency parsing as independently selecting the head of each word with cross-entropy objective, without the guarantee of a general non-projective tree structure output. Moreover, there have yet been no previous work on deriving a neural prob-

Proceedings of the The 8th International Joint Conference on Natural Language Processing, pages 59–69,
Taipei, Taiwan, November 27 – December 1, 2017 ©2017 AFNLP

abilistic parsing model to define a proper conditional distribution over non-projective trees for a given sentence.

In this paper, we propose a probabilistic neural network-based model for non-projective dependency parsing. This parsing model uses bi-directional LSTM-CNNs (BLSTM-CNNs) as backbone to learn neural information representations, on top of which a probabilistic structured layer is constructed with a conditional log-linear model, defining a conditional distribution over all non-projective dependency trees. The architecture of BLSTM-CNNs is similar to the one used for sequence labeling tasks (Ma and Hovy, 2016), where CNNs encode character-level information of a word into its character-level representation and BLSTM models context information of each word. Due to the probabilistic structured output layer, we can use negative log-likelihood as the training objective, where the partition function and marginals can be computed via Kirchhoff's Matrix-Tree Theorem (Tutte, 1984) to process the optimization efficiently by back-propagation. At test time, parsing trees can be decoded with the maximum spanning tree (MST) algorithm (Mc-Donald et al., 2005b). We evaluate our model on 17 treebanks across 14 different languages, achieving state-of-the-art performance on 9 treebanks. The contributions of this work are summarized as: (i) proposing a neural probabilistic model for non-projective dependency parsing. (ii) giving empirical evaluations of this model on benchmark data sets over 14 languages. (iii) achieving state-of-the-art performance with this parser on nine different treebanks.

2 Neural Probabilistic Parsing Model

In this section, we describe the components (layers) of our neural parsing model. We introduce the neural layers in our neural network one-by-one from top to bottom.

2.1 Edge-Factored Parsing Layer

In this paper, we will use the following notation: $\mathbf{x} = \{x_1, \ldots, x_n\}$ represents a generic input sentence, where x_i is the ith word. $\mathbf{y}$ represents a generic (possibly non-projective) dependency tree, which represents syntactic relationships through labeled directed edges between heads and their dependents. For example, Figure 1 shows a dependency tree for the sentence, "Economic news had

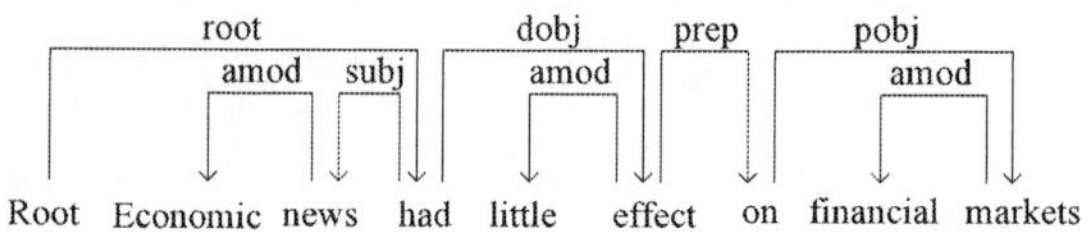

Figure 1: An example labeled dependency tree.

little effect on financial markets", with the sentences root-symbol as its root. $T(\mathbf{x})$ is used to denote the set of possible dependency trees for sentence $\mathbf{x}$.

The probabilistic model for dependency parsing defines a family of conditional probability $p(\mathbf{y}|\mathbf{x}; \Theta)$ over all $\mathbf{y}$ given sentence $\mathbf{x}$, with a log-linear form:

$$P(\mathbf{y}|\mathbf{x}; \Theta) = \frac{\exp\left(\sum_{(x_h, x_m) \in \mathbf{y}} \phi(x_h, x_m; \Theta)\right)}{Z(\mathbf{x}; \Theta)}$$

where Θ is the parameter of this model, $s_{hm} = \phi(x_h, x_m; \Theta)$ is the score function of edge from x_h to x_m, and

$$Z(\mathbf{x}; \Theta) = \sum_{\mathbf{y} \in T(\mathbf{x})} \exp\left(\sum_{(x_h, x_m) \in \mathbf{y}} s_{hm}\right)$$

is the partition function.

Bi-Linear Score Function. In our model, we adopt a bi-linear form score function:

$$\phi(x_h, x_m; \Theta) = \varphi(x_h)^T \mathbf{W} \varphi(x_m) + \mathbf{U}^T \varphi(x_h) + \mathbf{V}^T \varphi(x_m) + \mathbf{b}$$

where $\Theta = \{\mathbf{W}, \mathbf{U}, \mathbf{V}, \mathbf{b}\}$, $\varphi(x_i)$ is the representation vector of x_i, $\mathbf{W}, \mathbf{U}, \mathbf{V}$ denote the weight matrix of the bi-linear term and the two weight vectors of the linear terms in ϕ, and $\mathbf{b}$ denotes the bias vector.

As discussed in Dozat and Manning (2016), the bi-linear form of score function is related to the bi-linear attention mechanism (Luong et al., 2015). The bi-linear score function differs from the traditional score function proposed in Kiperwasser and Goldberg (2016) by adding the bi-linear term. A similar score function is proposed in Dozat and Manning (2016). The difference between their and our score function is that they only used the linear term for head words ($\mathbf{U}^T \varphi(x_h)$) while use them for both heads and modifiers.

Matrix-Tree Theorem. In order to train the probabilistic parsing model, as discussed in Koo et al. (2007), we have to compute the *partition function* and the *marginals*, requiring summation over the set $T(\mathbf{x})$:

$$Z(\mathbf{x}; \Theta) = \sum_{\mathbf{y} \in T(\mathbf{x})} \prod_{(x_h, x_m) \in \mathbf{y}} \psi(x_h, x_m; \Theta)$$
$$\mu_{h,m}(\mathbf{x}; \Theta) = \sum_{\mathbf{y} \in T(\mathbf{x}):(x_h, x_m) \in \mathbf{y}} P(\mathbf{y}|\mathbf{x}; \Theta)$$

where $\psi(x_h, x_m; \Theta)$ is the potential function:

$$\psi(x_h, x_m; \Theta) = \exp\left(\phi(x_h, x_m; \Theta)\right)$$

and $\mu_{h,m}(\mathbf{x}; \Theta)$ is the marginal for edge from hth word to mth word for $\mathbf{x}$.

Previous studies (Koo et al., 2007; Smith and Smith, 2007) have presented how a variant of Kirchhoff's Matrix-Tree Theorem (Tutte, 1984) can be used to evaluate the partition function and marginals efficiently. In this section, we briefly revisit this method.

For a sentence $\mathbf{x}$ with n words, we denote $\mathbf{x} = \{x_0, x_1, \ldots, x_n\}$, where x_0 is the root-symbol. We define a complete graph G on $n + 1$ nodes (including the root-symbol x_0), where each node corresponds to a word in $\mathbf{x}$ and each edge corresponds to a dependency arc between two words. Then, we assign non-negative weights to the edges of this complete graph with $n + 1$ nodes, yielding the weighted adjacency matrix $\mathbf{A}(\Theta) \in \mathbb{R}^{n+1 \times n+1}$, for $h, m = 0, \ldots, n$:

$$\mathbf{A}_{h,m}(\Theta) = \psi(x_h, x_m; \Theta)$$

Based on the adjacency matrix $\mathbf{A}(\Theta)$, we have the Laplacian matrix:

$$\mathbf{L}(\Theta) = \mathbf{D}(\Theta) - \mathbf{A}(\Theta)$$

where $\mathbf{D}(\Theta)$ is the weighted degree matrix:

$$\mathbf{D}_{h,m}(\Theta) = \begin{cases} \sum\limits_{h'=0}^{n} \mathbf{A}_{h',m}(\Theta) & \text{if } h = m \\ 0 & \text{otherwise} \end{cases}$$

Then, according to Theorem 1 in Koo et al. (2007), the partition function is equal to the minor of $\mathbf{L}(\Theta)$ w.r.t row 0 and column 0:

$$Z(\mathbf{x}; \Theta) = \mathbf{L}^{(0,0)}(\Theta)$$

where for a matrix $\mathbf{A}$, $\mathbf{A}^{(h,m)}$ denotes the *minor of* $\mathbf{A}$ w.r.t row h and column m; i.e., the determinant of the submatrix formed by deleting the hth row and mth column.

The marginals can be computed by calculating the matrix inversion of the matrix corresponding to $\mathbf{L}^{(0,0)}(\Theta)$. The time complexity of computing the partition function and marginals is $O(n^3)$.

Labeled Parsing Model. Though it is originally designed for unlabeled parsing, our probabilistic parsing model is easily extended to include dependency labels.

In labeled dependency trees, each edge is represented by a tuple (x_h, x_m, l), where x_h and x_m are the head word and modifier, respectively, and l is the label of dependency type of this edge. Then we can extend the original model for labeled dependency parsing by extending the score function to include dependency labels:

$$\begin{aligned} \phi(x_h, x_m, l; \Theta) &= \varphi(x_h)^T \mathbf{W}_l \varphi(x_m) \\ &+ \mathbf{U}_l^T \varphi(x_h) + \mathbf{V}_l^T \varphi(x_m) \\ &+ \mathbf{b}_l \end{aligned}$$

where $\mathbf{W}_l, \mathbf{U}_l, \mathbf{V}_l, \mathbf{b}_l$ are the weights and bias corresponding to dependency label l. Suppose that there are L different dependency labels, it suffices to define the new adjacency matrix by assigning the weight of an edge with the sum of weights over different dependency labels:

$$\mathbf{A}'_{h,m}(\Theta) = \sum_{l=1}^{L} \psi(x_h, x_m, l; \Theta)$$

The partition function and marginals over labeled dependency trees are obtained by operating on the new adjacency matrix $\mathbf{A}'(\Theta)$. The time complexity becomes $O(n^3 + Ln^2)$. In practice, L is probably large. For English, the number of edge labels in Stanford Basic Dependencies (De Marneffe et al., 2006) is 45, and the number in the treebank of CoNLL-2008 shared task (Surdeanu et al., 2008) is 70. While, the average length of sentences in English Penn Treebank (Marcus et al., 1993) is around 23. Thus, L is not negligible comparing to n.

It should be noticed that in our labeled model, for different dependency label l we use the same vector representation $\varphi(x_i)$ for each word x_i. The dependency labels are distinguished (only) by the parameters (weights and bias) corresponding to each of them. One advantage of this is that it significantly reduces the memory requirement comparing to the model in Dozat and Manning (2016) which distinguishes $\varphi_l(x_i)$ for different label l.

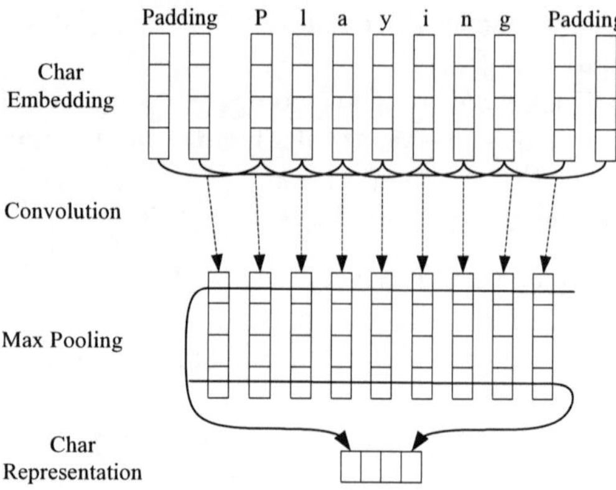

Figure 2: The convolution neural network for extracting character-level representations of words. Dashed arrows indicate a dropout layer applied before character embeddings are input to CNN.

Maximum Spanning Tree Decoding. The decoding problem of this parsing model can be formulated as:

$$\mathbf{y}^* = \operatorname*{argmax}_{\mathbf{y} \in T(\mathbf{x})} P(\mathbf{y}|\mathbf{x}; \Theta)$$
$$= \operatorname*{argmax}_{\mathbf{y} \in T(\mathbf{x})} \sum_{(x_h, x_m) \in \mathbf{y}} \phi(x_h, x_m; \Theta)$$

which can be solved by using the Maximum Spanning Tree (MST) algorithm described in McDonald et al. (2005b).

2.2 Neural Network for Representation Learning

Now, the remaining question is how to obtain the vector representation of each word with a neural network. In the following subsections, we will describe the architecture of our neural network model for representation learning.

2.2.1 CNNs

Previous work (Santos and Zadrozny, 2014) have shown that CNNs are an effective approach to extract morphological information (like the prefix or suffix of a word) from characters of words and encode it into neural representations, which has been proven particularly useful on Out-of-Vocabulary words (OOV). The CNN architecture our model uses to extract character-level representation of a given word is the same as the one used in Ma and Hovy (2016). The CNN architecture is shown in Figure 2. Following Ma and Hovy (2016), a dropout layer (Srivastava et al., 2014) is applied before character embeddings are input to CNN.

2.2.2 Bi-directional LSTM

LSTM Unit. Recurrent neural networks (RNNs) are a powerful family of connectionist models that have been widely applied in NLP tasks, such as language modeling (Mikolov et al., 2010), sequence labeling (Ma and Hovy, 2016) and machine translation (Cho et al., 2014), to capture context information in languages. Though, in theory, RNNs are able to learn long-distance dependencies, in practice, they fail due to the gradient vanishing/exploding problems (Bengio et al., 1994; Pascanu et al., 2013).

LSTMs (Hochreiter and Schmidhuber, 1997) are variants of RNNs designed to cope with these gradient vanishing problems. Basically, a LSTM unit is composed of three multiplicative gates which control the proportions of information to pass and to forget on to the next time step.

BLSTM. Many linguistic structure prediction tasks can benefit from having access to both past (left) and future (right) contexts, while the LSTM's hidden state $\mathbf{h}_t$ takes information only from past, knowing nothing about the future. An elegant solution whose effectiveness has been proven by previous work (Dyer et al., 2015; Ma and Hovy, 2016) is bi-directional LSTM (BLSTM). The basic idea is to present each sequence forwards and backwards to two separate hidden states to capture past and future information, respectively. Then the two hidden states are concatenated to form the final output. As discussed in Dozat and Manning (2016), there are more than one advantages to apply a multilayer perceptron (MLP) to the output vectors of BLSTM before the score function, eg. reducing the dimensionality and overfitting of the model. We follow this work by using a one-layer perceptron with elu (Clevert et al., 2015) as activation function.

2.3 BLSTM-CNNs

Finally, we construct our neural network model by feeding the output vectors of BLSTM (after MLP) into the parsing layer. Figure 3 illustrates the architecture of our network in detail.

For each word, the CNN in Figure 2, with character embeddings as inputs, encodes the character-level representation. Then the character-level representation vector is concatenated with the word embedding vector to feed into the BLSTM network. To enrich word-level information, we also use POS embeddings. Finally, the output vec-

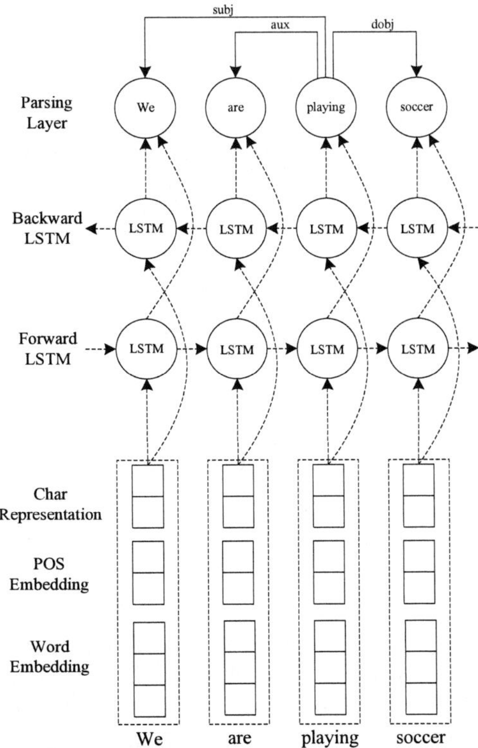

Figure 3: The main architecture of our parsing model. The character representation for each word is computed by the CNN in Figure 2. Then the character representation vector is concatenated with the word and pos embedding before feeding into the BLSTM network. Dashed arrows indicate dropout layers applied on the input, hidden and output vectors of BLSTM.

Layer	Hyper-parameter	Value
CNN	window size	3
	number of filters	50
LSTM	number of layers	2
	state size	256
	initial state	0.0
	peepholes	Hadamard
MLP	number of layers	1
	dimension	100
Dropout	embeddings	0.15
	LSTM hidden states	0.25
	LSTM layers	0.33
Learning	optimizer	Adam
	initial learning rate	0.002
	decay rate	0.5
	gradient clipping	5.0

Table 1: Hyper-parameters for all experiments.

tors of the neural netwok are fed to the parsing layer to jointly parse the best (labeled) dependency tree. As shown in Figure 3, dropout layers are applied on the input, hidden and output vectors of BLSTM, using the form of recurrent dropout proposed in Gal and Ghahramani (2016).

3 Network Training

In this section, we provide details about implementing and training the neural parsing model, including parameter initialization, model optimization and hyper parameter selection.

3.1 Parameter Initialization

Word Embeddings. For all the parsing models on different languages, we initialize word vectors with pretrained word embeddings. For Chi-

nese, Dutch, English, German and Spanish, we use the structured-skipgram (Ling et al., 2015) embeddings, and for other languages we use the Polyglot (Al-Rfou et al., 2013) embeddings. The dimensions of embeddings are 100 for English, 50 for Chinese and 64 for other languages.

Character Embeddings. Following Ma and Hovy (2016), character embeddings are initialized with uniform samples from $[-\sqrt{\frac{3}{dim}}, +\sqrt{\frac{3}{dim}}]$, where we set $dim = 50$.

POS Embedding. Our model also includes POS embeddings. The same as character embeddings, POS embeddings are also 50-dimensional, initialized uniformly from $[-\sqrt{\frac{3}{dim}}, +\sqrt{\frac{3}{dim}}]$.

Weights Matrices and Bias Vectors. Matrix parameters are randomly initialized with uniform samples from $[-\sqrt{\frac{6}{r+c}}, +\sqrt{\frac{6}{r+c}}]$, where r and c are the number of of rows and columns in the structure (Glorot and Bengio, 2010). Bias vectors are initialized to zero, except the bias $\mathbf{b}_f$ for the forget gate in LSTM , which is initialized to 1.0 (Jozefowicz et al., 2015).

3.2 Optimization Algorithm

Parameter optimization is performed with the Adam optimizer (Kingma and Ba, 2014) with $\beta 1 = \beta 2 = 0.9$. We choose an initial learning rate of $\eta_0 = 0.002$. The learning rate η was adapted using a schedule $S = [e_1, e_2, \ldots, e_s]$, in which the learning rate η is annealed by

Model	English				Chinese				German			
	Dev		Test		Dev		Test		Dev		Test	
	UAS	LAS	UAS	LAS	UAS	LAS	UAS	LAS	UAS	LAS	UAS	LAS
Basic	94.51	92.23	94.62	92.54	84.33	81.65	84.35	81.63	90.46	87.77	90.69	88.42
+Char	94.74	92.55	94.73	92.75	85.07	82.63	85.24	82.46	92.16	89.82	92.24	90.18
+POS	94.71	92.60	94.83	92.96	88.98	87.55	89.05	87.74	91.94	89.51	92.19	90.05
Full	94.77	92.66	94.88	92.98	88.51	87.16	88.79	87.47	92.37	90.09	92.58	90.54

Table 2: Parsing performance (UAS and LAS) of different versions of our model on both the development and test sets for three languages.

multiplying a fixed decay rate $\rho = 0.5$ after $e_i \in S$ epochs respectively. We used $S = [10, 30, 50, 70, 100]$ and trained all networks for a total of 120 epochs. While the Adam optimizer automatically adjusts the global learning rate according to past gradient magnitudes, we find that this additional decay consistently improves model performance across all settings and languages. To reduce the effects of "gradient exploding", we use a gradient clipping of 5.0 (Pascanu et al., 2013). We explored other optimization algorithms such as stochastic gradient descent (SGD) with momentum, AdaDelta (Zeiler, 2012), or RMSProp (Dauphin et al., 2015), but none of them meaningfully improve upon Adam with learning rate annealing in our preliminary experiments.

Dropout Training. To mitigate overfitting, we apply the dropout method (Srivastava et al., 2014; Ma et al., 2017) to regularize our model. As shown in Figure 2 and 3, we apply dropout on character embeddings before inputting to CNN, and on the input, hidden and output vectors of BLSTM. We apply dropout rate of 0.15 to all the embeddings. For BLSTM, we use the recurrent dropout (Gal and Ghahramani, 2016) with 0.25 dropout rate between hidden states and 0.33 between layers. We found that the model using the new recurrent dropout converged much faster than standard dropout, while achiving similar performance.

3.3 Hyper-Parameter Selection

Table 1 summarizes the chosen hyper-parameters for all experiments. We tune the hyper-parameters on the development sets by random search. We use the same hyper-parameters across the models on different treebanks and languages, due to time constrains. Note that we use 2-layer BLSTM followed with 1-layer MLP. We set the state size of LSTM to 256 and the dimension of MLP to 100. Tuning these two parameters did not significantly impact the performance of our model.

	Dev		Test	
	UAS	LAS	UAS	LAS
cross-entropy	94.10	91.52	93.77	91.57
global-likelihood	94.77	92.66	94.88	92.98

Table 3: Parsing performance on PTB with different training objective functions.

4 Experiments

4.1 Setup

We evaluate our neural probabilistic parser on the same data setup as Kuncoro et al. (2016), namely the English Penn Treebank (PTB version 3.0) (Marcus et al., 1993), the Penn Chinese Treebank (CTB version 5.1) (Xue et al., 2002), and the German CoNLL 2009 corpus (Hajič et al., 2009). Following previous work, all experiments are evaluated on the metrics of unlabeled attachment score (UAS) and Labeled attachment score (LAS).

4.2 Main Results

We first construct experiments to dissect the effectiveness of each input information (embeddings) of our neural network architecture by ablation studies. We compare the performance of four versions of our model with different inputs — Basic, +POS, +Char and Full — where the Basic model utilizes only the pretrained word embeddings as inputs, while the +POS and +Char models augments the basic one with POS embedding and character information, respectively. According to the results shown in Table 2, +Char model obtains better performance than the Basic model on all the three languages, showing that character-level representations are important for dependency parsing. Second, on English and German, +Char and +POS achieves comparable performance, while on Chinese +POS significantly outperforms +Char model. Finally, the Full model achieves the best accuracy on English and German, but on Chinese +POS obtains the best. Thus, we guess that the POS information is more useful

System	English		Chinese		German	
	UAS	LAS	UAS	LAS	UAS	LAS
Bohnet and Nivre (2012)	–	–	87.3	85.9	91.4	89.4
Chen and Manning (2014)	91.8	89.6	83.9	82.4	–	–
Ballesteros et al. (2015)	91.6	89.4	85.3	83.7	88.8	86.1
Dyer et al. (2015)	93.1	90.9	87.2	85.7	–	–
Kiperwasser and Goldberg (2016): graph	93.1	91.0	86.6	85.1	–	–
Ballesteros et al. (2016)	93.6	91.4	87.7	86.2	–	–
Wang and Chang (2016)	94.1	91.8	87.6	86.2	–	–
Zhang et al. (2016)	94.1	91.9	87.8	86.2	–	–
Cheng et al. (2016)	94.1	91.5	88.1	85.7	–	–
Andor et al. (2016)	94.6	92.8	–	–	90.9	89.2
Kuncoro et al. (2016)	94.3	92.1	88.9	87.3	91.6	89.2
Dozat and Manning (2016)	**95.7**	**94.1**	**89.3**	**88.2**	**93.5**	**91.4**
This work: Basic	94.6	92.5	84.4	81.6	90.7	88.4
This work: +Char	94.7	92.8	85.2	82.5	92.2	90.2
This work: +POS	94.8	93.0	89.1	87.7	92.2	90.1
This work: Full	94.9	93.0	88.8	87.5	92.6	90.5

Table 4: UAS and LAS of four versions of our model on test sets for three languages, together with top-performance parsing systems.

for Chinese than English and German.

Table 3 gives the performance on PTB of the parsers trained with two different objective functions — the cross-entropy objective of each word, and our objective based on likelihood for an entire tree. The parser with global likelihood objective outperforms the one with simple cross-entropy objective, demonstrating the effectiveness of the global structured objective.

4.3 Comparison with Previous Work

Table 4 illustrates the results of the four versions of our model on the three languages, together with twelve previous top-performance systems for comparison. Our Full model significantly outperforms the graph-based parser proposed in Kiperwasser and Goldberg (2016) which used similar neural network architecture for representation learning (detailed discussion in Section 5). Moreover, our model achieves better results than the parser distillation method (Kuncoro et al., 2016) on all the three languages. The results of our parser are slightly worse than the scores reported in Dozat and Manning (2016). One possible reason is that, as mentioned in Section 2.1, for labeled dependency parsing Dozat and Manning (2016) used different vectors for different dependency labels to represent each word, making their model require much more memory than ours.

4.4 Experiments on CoNLL Treebanks

Datasets. To make a thorough empirical comparison with previous studies, we also evaluate our system on treebanks from CoNLL shared task on dependency parsing — the English treebank from CoNLL-2008 shared task (Surdeanu et al., 2008) and all 13 treebanks from CoNLL-2006 shared task (Buchholz and Marsi, 2006). For the treebanks from CoNLL-2006 shared task, following Cheng et al. (2016), we randomly select 5% of the training data as the development set. UAS and LAS are evaluated using the official scorer[1] of CoNLL-2006 shared task.

Baselines. We compare our model with the third-order Turbo parser (Martins et al., 2013), the low-rank tensor based model (Tensor) (Lei et al., 2014), the randomized greedy inference based (RGB) model (Zhang et al., 2014), the labeled dependency parser with inner-to-outer greedy decoding algorithm (In-Out) (Ma and Hovy, 2015), and the bi-direction attention based parser (Bi-Att) (Cheng et al., 2016). We also compare our parser against the best published results for individual languages. This comparison includes four additional systems: Koo et al. (2010), Martins et al. (2011), Zhang and McDonald (2014) and Pitler and McDonald (2015).

---

[1] http://ilk.uvt.nl/conll/software.html

	Turbo	Tensor	RGB	In-Out	Bi-Att	+POS	Full	Best Published	
	UAS	UAS	UAS	UAS [LAS]	UAS [LAS]	UAS [LAS]	UAS [LAS]	UAS	LAS
ar	79.64	79.95	80.24	79.60 [67.09]	80.34 [68.58]	80.05 [67.80]	80.80 [**69.40**]	**81.12**	–
bg	93.10	93.50	93.72	92.68 [87.79]	93.96 [89.55]	93.66 [89.79]	**94.28** [**90.60**]	94.02	–
zh	89.98	92.68	93.04	92.58 [88.51]	–	**93.44** [90.04]	93.40 [**90.10**]	93.04	–
cs	90.32	90.50	90.77	88.01 [79.31]	91.16 [85.14]	91.04 [85.82]	**91.18** [**85.92**]	91.16	85.14
da	91.48	91.39	91.86	91.44 [85.55]	91.56 [85.53]	91.52 [86.57]	91.86 [**87.07**]	**92.00**	–
nl	86.19	86.41	87.39	84.45 [80.31]	87.15 [82.41]	87.41 [84.17]	**87.85** [**84.82**]	87.39	–
en	93.22	93.02	93.25	92.45 [89.43]	–	94.43 [92.31]	**94.66** [**92.52**]	93.25	–
de	92.41	91.97	92.67	90.79 [87.74]	92.71 [89.80]	93.53 [91.55]	**93.62** [**91.90**]	92.71	89.80
ja	93.52	93.71	93.56	93.54 [91.80]	93.44 [90.67]	93.82 [92.34]	**94.02** [**92.60**]	93.80	–
pt	92.69	91.92	92.36	91.54 [87.68]	92.77 [88.44]	92.59 [**89.12**]	92.71 [88.92]	**93.03**	–
sl	86.01	86.24	86.72	84.39 [73.74]	86.01 [75.90]	85.73 [76.48]	86.73 [**77.56**]	**87.06**	–
es	85.59	88.00	88.75	86.44 [83.29]	88.74 [84.03]	88.58 [85.03]	**89.20** [**85.77**]	88.75	84.03
sv	91.14	91.00	91.08	89.94 [83.09]	90.50 [84.05]	90.89 [86.58]	91.22 [**86.92**]	**91.85**	85.26
tr	76.90	76.84	76.68	75.32 [60.39]	**78.43** [**66.16**]	75.88 [61.72]	77.71 [65.81]	78.43	66.16
av	88.73	89.08	89.44	88.08 [81.84]	–	89.47 [84.24]	89.95 [84.99]	89.83	–

Table 5: UAS and LAS on 14 treebanks from CoNLL shared tasks, together with several state-of-the-art parsers. "Best Published" includes the most accurate parsers in term of UAS among Koo et al. (2010), Martins et al. (2011), Martins et al. (2013), Lei et al. (2014), Zhang et al. (2014), Zhang and McDonald (2014), Pitler and McDonald (2015), Ma and Hovy (2015), and Cheng et al. (2016).

Results. Table 5 summarizes the results of our model, along with the state-of-the-art baselines. On average across 14 languages, our approach significantly outperforms all the baseline systems. It should be noted that the average UAS of our parser over the 14 languages is better than that of the "best published", which are from different systems that achieved best results for different languages.

For individual languages, our parser achieves state-of-the-art performance on both UAS and LAS on 8 languages — Bulgarian, Chinese, Czech, Dutch, English, German, Japanese and Spanish. On Arabic, Danish, Portuguese, Slovene and Swedish, our parser obtains the best LAS. Another interesting observation is that the Full model outperforms the +POS model on 13 languages. The only exception is Chinese, which matches the observation in Section 4.2.

5 Related Work

In recent years, several different neural network based models have been proposed and successfully applied to dependency parsing. Among these neural models, there are three approaches most similar to our model — the two graph-based parsers with BLSTM feature representation (Kiperwasser and Goldberg, 2016; Wang and Chang, 2016), and the neural bi-affine attention parser (Dozat and Manning, 2016).

Kiperwasser and Goldberg (2016) proposed a graph-based dependency parser which uses BLSTM for word-level representations. Wang and Chang (2016) used a similar model with a way to learn sentence segment embedding based on an extra forward LSTM network. Both of these two parsers trained the parsing models by optimizing margin-based objectives. There are three main differences between their models and ours. First, they only used linear form score function, instead of using the bi-linear term between the vectors of heads and modifiers. Second, They did not employ CNNs to model character-level information. Third, we proposed a probabilistic model over non-projective trees on the top of neural representations, while they trained their models with a margin-based objective. Dozat and Manning (2016) proposed neural parsing model using bi-affine score function, which is similar to the bi-linear form score function in our model. Our model mainly differ from this model by using CNN to model character-level information. Moreover, their model formalized dependency parsing as independently selecting the head of each word with cross-entropy objective, while our probabilistic parsing model jointly encodes and decodes parsing trees for given sentences.

6 Conclusion

In this paper, we proposed a neural probabilistic model for non-projective dependency parsing, using the BLSTM-CNNs architecture for representation learning. Experimental results on 17 treebanks across 14 languages show that our parser significantly improves the accuracy of both dependency structures (UAS) and edge labels (LAS), over several previously state-of-the-art systems.

Acknowledgements

This research was supported in part by DARPA grant FA8750-12-2-0342 funded under the DEFT program. Any opinions, findings, and conclusions or recommendations expressed in this material are those of the authors and do not necessarily reflect the views of DARPA.

References

Rami Al-Rfou, Bryan Perozzi, and Steven Skiena. 2013. Polyglot: Distributed word representations for multilingual nlp. In *Proceedings of CoNLL-2013*. Sofia, Bulgaria, pages 183–192.

Daniel Andor, Chris Alberti, David Weiss, Aliaksei Severyn, Alessandro Presta, Kuzman Ganchev, Slav Petrov, and Michael Collins. 2016. Globally normalized transition-based neural networks. In *Proceedings of ACL-2016 (Volume 1: Long Papers)*. Berlin, Germany, pages 2442–2452.

Miguel Ballesteros, Chris Dyer, and Noah A. Smith. 2015. Improved transition-based parsing by modeling characters instead of words with lstms. In *Proceedings of EMNLP-2015*. Lisbon, Portugal, pages 349–359.

Miguel Ballesteros, Yoav Goldberg, Chris Dyer, and Noah A. Smith. 2016. Training with exploration improves a greedy stack lstm parser. In *Proceedings of EMNLP-2016*. Austin, Texas, pages 2005–2010.

Yoshua Bengio, Patrice Simard, and Paolo Frasconi. 1994. Learning long-term dependencies with gradient descent is difficult. *Neural Networks, IEEE Transactions on* 5(2):157–166.

Bernd Bohnet and Joakim Nivre. 2012. A transition-based system for joint part-of-speech tagging and labeled non-projective dependency parsing. In *Proceedings of EMNLP-2012*. Jeju Island, Korea, pages 1455–1465.

Sabine Buchholz and Erwin Marsi. 2006. CoNLL-X shared task on multilingual dependency parsing. In *Proceeding of CoNLL-2006*. New York, NY, pages 149–164.

Danqi Chen and Christopher Manning. 2014. A fast and accurate dependency parser using neural networks. In *Proceedings of EMNLP-2014*. Doha, Qatar, pages 740–750.

Hao Cheng, Hao Fang, Xiaodong He, Jianfeng Gao, and Li Deng. 2016. Bi-directional attention with agreement for dependency parsing. In *Proceedings of EMNLP-2016*. Austin, Texas, pages 2204–2214.

Jason Chiu and Eric Nichols. 2016. Named entity recognition with bidirectional lstm-cnns. *Transactions of the Association for Computational Linguistics* 4:357–370.

Kyunghyun Cho, Bart Van Merriënboer, Dzmitry Bahdanau, and Yoshua Bengio. 2014. On the properties of neural machine translation: Encoder-decoder approaches. *arXiv preprint arXiv:1409.1259* .

Djork-Arné Clevert, Thomas Unterthiner, and Sepp Hochreiter. 2015. Fast and accurate deep network learning by exponential linear units (elus). *arXiv preprint arXiv:1511.07289* .

Ronan Collobert, Jason Weston, Léon Bottou, Michael Karlen, Koray Kavukcuoglu, and Pavel Kuksa. 2011. Natural language processing (almost) from scratch. *The Journal of Machine Learning Research* 12:2493–2537.

Yann N Dauphin, Harm de Vries, Junyoung Chung, and Yoshua Bengio. 2015. Rmsprop and equilibrated adaptive learning rates for non-convex optimization. *arXiv preprint arXiv:1502.04390* .

Marie-Catherine De Marneffe, Bill MacCartney, Christopher D. Manning, et al. 2006. Generating typed dependency parses from phrase structure parses. In *Proceedings of LREC-2006*. pages 449–454.

Timothy Dozat and Christopher D. Manning. 2016. Deep biaffine attention for neural dependency parsing. *arXiv preprint arXiv:1611.01734* .

Greg Durrett and Dan Klein. 2013. Easy victories and uphill battles in coreference resolution. In *Proceedings of EMNLP-2013*. Seattle, Washington, USA, pages 1971–1982.

Chris Dyer, Miguel Ballesteros, Wang Ling, Austin Matthews, and Noah A. Smith. 2015. Transition-based dependency parsing with stack long short-term memory. In *Proceedings of ACL-2015 (Volume 1: Long Papers)*. Beijing, China, pages 334–343.

Nicolas R Fauceglia, Yiu-Chang Lin, Xuezhe Ma, and Eduard Hovy. 2015. Word sense disambiguation via propstore and ontonotes for event mention detection. In *Proceedings of the The 3rd Workshop on EVENTS: Definition, Detection, Coreference, and Representation*. Denver, Colorado, pages 11–15.

Yarin Gal and Zoubin Ghahramani. 2016. A theoretically grounded application of dropout in recurrent neural networks. In *Advances in Neural Information Processing Systems*.

Xavier Glorot and Yoshua Bengio. 2010. Understanding the difficulty of training deep feedforward neural networks. In *International conference on artificial intelligence and statistics*. pages 249–256.

Jan Hajič, Massimiliano Ciaramita, Richard Johansson, Daisuke Kawahara, Maria Antònia Martí, Lluís Màrquez, Adam Meyers, Joakim Nivre, Sebastian Padó, Jan Štěpánek, et al. 2009. The conll-2009 shared task: Syntactic and semantic dependencies in multiple languages. In *Proceedings of CoNLL-2009: Shared Task*. pages 1–18.

Sepp Hochreiter and Jürgen Schmidhuber. 1997. Long short-term memory. *Neural computation* 9(8):1735–1780.

Rafal Jozefowicz, Wojciech Zaremba, and Ilya Sutskever. 2015. An empirical exploration of recurrent network architectures. In *Proceedings of the 32nd International Conference on Machine Learning (ICML-15)*. pages 2342–2350.

Diederik Kingma and Jimmy Ba. 2014. Adam: A method for stochastic optimization. *arXiv preprint arXiv:1412.6980* .

Eliyahu Kiperwasser and Yoav Goldberg. 2016. Simple and accurate dependency parsing using bidirectional lstm feature representations. *Transactions of the Association for Computational Linguistics* 4:313–327.

Terry Koo and Michael Collins. 2010. Efficient third-order dependency parsers. In *Proceedings of ACL-2010*. Uppsala, Sweden, pages 1–11.

Terry Koo, Amir Globerson, Xavier Carreras, and Michael Collins. 2007. Structured prediction models via the matrix-tree theorem. In *Proceedings of EMNLP-2007*. Prague, Czech Republic, pages 141–150.

Terry Koo, Alexander M. Rush, Michael Collins, Tommi Jaakkola, and David Sontag. 2010. Dual decomposition for parsing with non-projective head automata. In *Proceedings of EMNLP-2010*. Cambridge, MA, pages 1288–1298.

Adhiguna Kuncoro, Miguel Ballesteros, Lingpeng Kong, Chris Dyer, and Noah A. Smith. 2016. Distilling an ensemble of greedy dependency parsers into one mst parser. In *Proceedings of EMNLP-2016*. Austin, Texas, pages 1744–1753.

Tao Lei, Yu Xin, Yuan Zhang, Regina Barzilay, and Tommi Jaakkola. 2014. Low-rank tensors for scoring dependency structures. In *Proceedings of ACL-2014 (Volume 1: Long Papers)*. Baltimore, Maryland, pages 1381–1391.

Wang Ling, Chris Dyer, Alan W Black, and Isabel Trancoso. 2015. Two/too simple adaptations of word2vec for syntax problems. In *Proceedings of NAACL-2015*. Denver, Colorado, pages 1299–1304.

Thang Luong, Hieu Pham, and Christopher D. Manning. 2015. Effective approaches to attention-based neural machine translation. In *Proceedings of EMNLP-2015*. Lisbon, Portugal, pages 1412–1421.

Xuezhe Ma, Yingkai Gao, Zhiting Hu, Yaoliang Yu, Yuntian Deng, and Eduard Hovy. 2017. Dropout with expectation-linear regularization. In *Proceedings of the 5th International Conference on Learning Representations (ICLR-2017)*. Toulon, France.

Xuezhe Ma and Eduard Hovy. 2015. Efficient inner-to-outer greedy algorithm for higher-order labeled dependency parsing. In *Proceedings of EMNLP-2015*. Lisbon, Portugal, pages 1322–1328.

Xuezhe Ma and Eduard Hovy. 2016. End-to-end sequence labeling via bi-directional lstm-cnns-crf. In *Proceedings of ACL-2016 (Volume 1: Long Papers)*. Berlin, Germany, pages 1064–1074.

Xuezhe Ma, Zhengzhong Liu, and Eduard Hovy. 2016. Unsupervised ranking model for entity coreference resolution. In *Proceedings of NAACL-2016*. San Diego, California, USA.

Xuezhe Ma and Fei Xia. 2014. Unsupervised dependency parsing with transferring distribution via parallel guidance and entropy regularization. In *Proceedings of ACL-2014*. Baltimore, Maryland, pages 1337–1348.

Xuezhe Ma and Hai Zhao. 2012a. Fourth-order dependency parsing. In *Proceedings of COLING 2012: Posters*. Mumbai, India, pages 785–796.

Xuezhe Ma and Hai Zhao. 2012b. Probabilistic models for high-order projective dependency parsing. *Technical Report, arXiv:1502.04174* .

Mitchell Marcus, Beatrice Santorini, and Mary Ann Marcinkiewicz. 1993. Building a large annotated corpus of English: the Penn Treebank. *Computational Linguistics* 19(2):313–330.

Andre Martins, Miguel Almeida, and Noah A. Smith. 2013. Turning on the turbo: Fast third-order non-projective turbo parsers. In *Proceedings of ACL-2013 (Volume 2: Short Papers)*. Sofia, Bulgaria, pages 617–622.

Andre Martins, Noah Smith, Mario Figueiredo, and Pedro Aguiar. 2011. Dual decomposition with many overlapping components. In *Proceedings of EMNLP-2011*. Edinburgh, Scotland, UK., pages 238–249.

Ryan McDonald, Koby Crammer, and Fernando Pereira. 2005a. Online large-margin training of dependency parsers. In *Proceedings of ACL-2005*. Ann Arbor, Michigan, USA, pages 91–98.

Ryan McDonald, Joakim Nivre, Yvonne Quirmbach-Brundage, Yoav Goldberg, Dipanjan Das, Kuzman Ganchev, Keith Hall, Slav Petrov, Hao Zhang, Oscar Täckström, Claudia Bedini, Núria Bertomeu Castelló, and Jungmee Lee. 2013. Universal dependency annotation for multilingual parsing. In *Proceedings of ACL-2013*. Sofia, Bulgaria, pages 92–97.

Ryan McDonald, Fernando Pereira, Kiril Ribarov, and Jan Hajic. 2005b. Non-projective dependency parsing using spanning tree algorithms. In *Proceedings of HLT/EMNLP-2005*. Vancouver, Canada, pages 523–530.

Tomas Mikolov, Martin Karafiát, Lukas Burget, Jan Cernocký, and Sanjeev Khudanpur. 2010. Recurrent neural network based language model. In *Interspeech*. volume 2, page 3.

Vincent Ng. 2010. Supervised noun phrase coreference research: The first fifteen years. In *Proceedings of ACL-2010*. Association for Computational Linguistics, Uppsala, Sweden, pages 1396–1411.

Joakim Nivre and Mario Scholz. 2004. Deterministic dependency parsing of English text. In *Proceedings of COLING-2004*. Geneva, Switzerland, pages 64–70.

Razvan Pascanu, Tomas Mikolov, and Yoshua Bengio. 2013. On the difficulty of training recurrent neural networks. In *Proceedings of ICML-2013*. pages 1310–1318.

Emily Pitler and Ryan McDonald. 2015. A linear-time transition system for crossing interval trees. In *Proceedings of NAACL-2015*. Denver, Colorado, pages 662–671.

Cicero D Santos and Bianca Zadrozny. 2014. Learning character-level representations for part-of-speech tagging. In *Proceedings of ICML-2014*. pages 1818–1826.

David A. Smith and Noah A. Smith. 2007. Probabilistic models of nonprojective dependency trees. In *Proceedings of EMNLP-2007*. Prague, Czech Republic, pages 132–140.

Nitish Srivastava, Geoffrey Hinton, Alex Krizhevsky, Ilya Sutskever, and Ruslan Salakhutdinov. 2014. Dropout: A simple way to prevent neural networks from overfitting. *The Journal of Machine Learning Research* 15(1):1929–1958.

Mihai Surdeanu, Richard Johansson, Adam Meyers, Lluís Màrquez, and Joakim Nivre. 2008. The conll-2008 shared task on joint parsing of syntactic and semantic dependencies. In *Proceedings of CoNLL-2008*. pages 159–177.

William Thomas Tutte. 1984. *Graph theory*, volume 11. Addison-Wesley Menlo Park.

Wenhui Wang and Baobao Chang. 2016. Graph-based dependency parsing with bidirectional lstm. In *Proceedings of ACL-2016 (Volume 1: Long Papers)*. Berlin, Germany, pages 2306–2315.

Jun Xie, Haitao Mi, and Qun Liu. 2011. A novel dependency-to-string model for statistical machine translation. In *Proceedings of EMNLP-2011*. Edinburgh, Scotland, UK., pages 216–226.

Nianwen Xue, Fu-Dong Chiou, and Martha Palmer. 2002. Building a large-scale annotated chinese corpus. In *Proceedings of COLING-2002*. pages 1–8.

Matthew D Zeiler. 2012. Adadelta: an adaptive learning rate method. *arXiv preprint arXiv:1212.5701* .

Hao Zhang and Ryan McDonald. 2014. Enforcing structural diversity in cube-pruned dependency parsing. In *Proceedings of ACL-2014 (Volume 2: Short Papers)*. Baltimore, Maryland, pages 656–661.

Xingxing Zhang, Jianpeng Cheng, and Mirella Lapata. 2016. Dependency parsing as head selection. *arXiv preprint arXiv:1606.01280* .

Yuan Zhang, Tao Lei, Regina Barzilay, and Tommi Jaakkola. 2014. Greed is good if randomized: New inference for dependency parsing. In *Proceedings of EMNLP-2014*. Doha, Qatar, pages 1013–1024.

Word Ordering as Unsupervised Learning
Towards Syntactically Plausible Word Representations

Noriki Nishida and **Hideki Nakayama**
Graduate School of Information Science and Technology
The University of Tokyo
`{nishida,nakayama}@nlab.ci.i.u-tokyo.ac.jp`

Abstract

The research question we explore in this study is how to obtain syntactically plausible word representations without using human annotations. Our underlying hypothesis is that word ordering tests, or linearizations, is suitable for learning syntactic knowledge about words. To verify this hypothesis, we develop a differentiable model called Word Ordering Network (WON) that explicitly learns to recover correct word order while implicitly acquiring word embeddings representing syntactic knowledge. We evaluate the word embeddings produced by the proposed method on downstream syntax-related tasks such as part-of-speech tagging and dependency parsing. The experimental results demonstrate that the WON consistently outperforms both order-insensitive and order-sensitive baselines on these tasks.

1 Introduction

Distributed word representations have been successfully utilized to transfer lexical knowledge to downstream tasks in a semi-supervised manner, and well known to benefit various applications (Turian et al., 2010; Collobert et al., 2011; Socher et al., 2011). As different applications generally require different features, it is crucial to choose representations suitable for target downstream tasks.

The research question we want to explore in this study is how to obtain *syntactically plausible word representations* without human annotations, with a focus on syntax-related tasks (parsing, etc.). Whereas a variety of approaches related to *semantic* word embeddings have been pro-

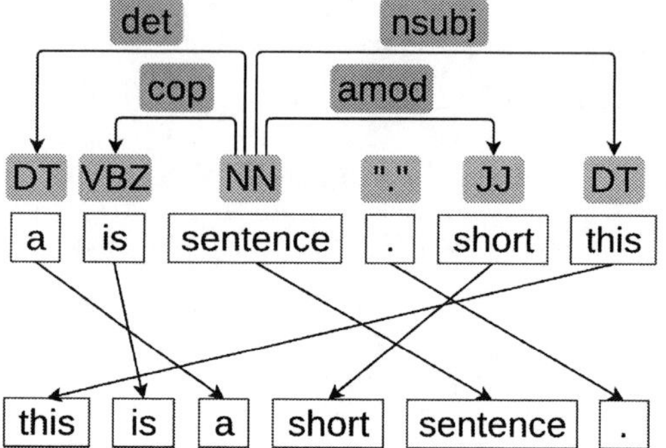

Figure 1: Illustration of the word ordering task. The goal of the word ordering task is to recover an original order given a set of shuffled tokens. The figure shows an example where original sentence is *"this is a short sentence."* To correctly reorder the tokens, syntactic knowledge about words (e.g. grammatical classes of words and their possible relations) is indispensable. In this study, we explore how well the word ordering task can be an objective to obtain syntactic word representations.

posed (Mikolov et al., 2013a,b; Pennington et al., 2014), it still remains unclear how we should obtain *syntactic* word embeddings from unannotated corpora.

Word ordering tests, or linearizations, are commonly used to evaluate students' language proficiency. Suppose that we are given a set of randomly shuffled tokens {*"a"*, *"is,"* *"sentence,"* *"short,"* *"this,"* *"."*}. In this case we can easily recover the original order: *"this is a short sentence."* We consider this doable thanks to our knowledge about grammatical classes (e.g., part-of-speech (POS) tags) of words and their possible relations. We depict the above explanation in Figure 1. Of course, it might not be necessary for machines to mimic exactly the same reasoning pro-

Proceedings of the The 8th International Joint Conference on Natural Language Processing, pages 70–79,
Taipei, Taiwan, November 27 – December 1, 2017 ©2017 AFNLP

cess in humans. However, syntactic knowledge about words is crucial for both humans and machines to solve the word ordering task.

Inspired by this observation, in this study, we develop an end-to-end model called the Word Ordering Network (WON) that explicitly learns to recover correct word orders while implicitly acquiring word embeddings representing syntactic information. Our underlying hypothesis is that the word ordering task can be an objective for learning syntactic knowledge about words. The WON receives a set of shuffled tokens and first transforms them independently to low-dimensional continuous vectors, which are then aggregated to produce a single summarization vector. We formalize the word ordering task as a sequential prediction problem of a permutation matrix. We use a recurrent neural network (RNN) (Elman, 1990) with long short-term memory (LSTM) units (Hochreiter and Schmidhuber, 1997) and a soft attention mechanism (Bahdanau et al., 2014; Luong et al., 2015) that constructs rows of permutation matrices sequentially conditioned on summarization vectors.

We evaluate the proposed word embeddings on downstream syntax-related tasks such as POS tagging and dependency parsing. The experimental results demonstrate that the WON outperforms both order-insensitive and order-sensitive baselines, and successfully yields the highest performance. In addition, we also evaluate the WON on traditional word-level benchmarks, such as word analogy and word similarity tasks. Combined with semantics-oriented embeddings by a simple fine-tuning technique, the WON gives competitive or better performances than the other baselines. Interestingly, we find that the WON has a potential to refine and improve semantic features. Moreover, we qualitatively analyze the feature space produced by the WON and find that the WON tends to capture not only syntactic but also semantic regularities between words. The source code of this work is available online. [1]

2 The Proposed Method

In this section, we formulate the WON which implicitly acquires syntactic word embeddings through learning to solve word ordering problems.

---

[1] https://github.com/norikinishida/won

2.1 Embedding Layer

Given a set of shuffled tokens $\mathcal{X} = \{w_1, \ldots, w_N\}$, the WON first transforms every single symbol w_c into a low-dimensional continuous vector, i.e.,

$$\boldsymbol{e}_c = F(w_c) \in \mathbb{R}^D, \tag{1}$$

where F is a learnable function. Please note that the number of tokens N in the input $\mathcal{X}$ can vary in the word ordering task.

2.2 Aggregation

To perform reordering on a set of shuffled embeddings $\{\boldsymbol{e}_1, \ldots, \boldsymbol{e}_N\}$, we aggregate the embeddings and compute a single summarization vector. The aggregation function is a sum of word embeddings followed by a non-linear transformation:

$$\tilde{\boldsymbol{e}} = \tanh(\boldsymbol{W}_\mathrm{a} \sum_{c=1}^{N} \boldsymbol{e}_c + \boldsymbol{b}_\mathrm{a}) \in \mathbb{R}^D, \tag{2}$$

where $\boldsymbol{W}_a \in \mathbb{R}^{D \times D}$ and $\boldsymbol{b}_a \in \mathbb{R}^D$ are a projection matrix and bias vector, respectively.

2.3 Prediction of a Permutation Matrix

We formalize a reordering problem as a prediction task of a permutation matrix.

A permutation matrix is a square binary matrix and every row and column contains exactly one entry of 1 and 0s elsewhere. The left-multiplication of a matrix $\boldsymbol{E} \in \mathbb{R}^{N \times D}$ by a permutation matrix $\boldsymbol{P} \in \mathbb{R}^{N \times N}$ rearranges the rows of the matrix $\boldsymbol{E}$, e.g.

$$\begin{pmatrix} \boldsymbol{e}_1^\top \\ \boldsymbol{e}_2^\top \\ \boldsymbol{e}_3^\top \\ \boldsymbol{e}_4^\top \end{pmatrix} = \boldsymbol{P}\boldsymbol{E} \tag{3}$$

$$= \begin{pmatrix} 0 & 1 & 0 & 0 \\ 0 & 0 & 0 & 1 \\ 1 & 0 & 0 & 0 \\ 0 & 0 & 1 & 0 \end{pmatrix} \begin{pmatrix} \boldsymbol{e}_3^\top \\ \boldsymbol{e}_1^\top \\ \boldsymbol{e}_4^\top \\ \boldsymbol{e}_2^\top \end{pmatrix}. \tag{4}$$

Equation 4 gives an example where $\boldsymbol{E} = (\boldsymbol{e}_3, \boldsymbol{e}_1, \boldsymbol{e}_4, \boldsymbol{e}_2)^\top$, and the original sentence (correct order) is w_1, w_2, w_3, w_4.

In the word ordering task, one of the issues in predicting permutation matrices is that the number of tokens N changes according to the variable lengths of input sentences. Therefore, it is impossible to define and train learning models that have fixed-dimensional outputs such as multi-layer perceptrons.

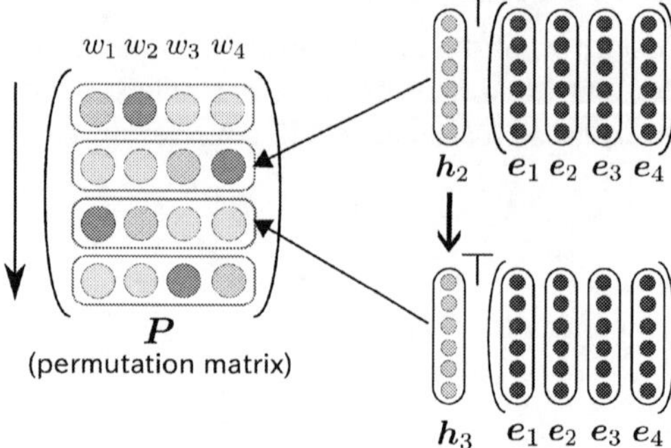

Figure 2: Visualization of our approach to sequentially predict a permutation matrix $\boldsymbol{P} \in \mathbb{R}^{N \times N}$. In this case, we are given $N = 4$ shuffled tokens (w_1, w_2, w_3, w_4). We first independently embeds each symbol to dense vectors (e_1, e_2, e_3, e_4). Then, by using an RNN and a soft attention mechanism, we sequentially constructs the rows of the permutation matrix $\boldsymbol{P} = (\boldsymbol{p}_1, \boldsymbol{p}_2, \boldsymbol{p}_3, \boldsymbol{p}_4)^\top$ for N steps through a scoring function. The vector $\boldsymbol{h}_r \in \mathbb{R}^D$ denotes the r-th hidden state of the RNN. One can interpret $\boldsymbol{p}_r$ as a selective probability distribution over the input tokens. For simplicity, in this figure, we ignore the projection matrix in the scoring function (Eq. 8).

Recently, Vinyals et al. (2015) proposed the *Pointer Networks* (PtrNets) that were successfully applied to geometric sorting problems. Inspired by the PtrNet, we develop an LSTM (Hochreiter and Schmidhuber, 1997) with a soft attention mechanism (Bahdanau et al., 2014; Luong et al., 2015). The LSTM constructs rows of a permutation matrix $\boldsymbol{P} = (\boldsymbol{p}_1, \dots, \boldsymbol{p}_N)^\top$ conditioned on a set of word embeddings $\{e_1, \dots, e_m\}$ calculated by Equation 1. If $\sum_{c=1}^N p_{r,c} = 1$ holds, one can interpret $p_{r,c}$ as the probability of the token w_c to be placed at r-th position. In Figure 2, we show a visualization of our approach to predict a permutation matrix with the LSTM.

The LSTM's r-th hidden state $\boldsymbol{h}_r \in \mathbb{R}^D$ and memory cells $\boldsymbol{c}_r \in \mathbb{R}^D$ are computed as follows:

$$\boldsymbol{h}_r, \boldsymbol{c}_r = \begin{cases} \tilde{\boldsymbol{e}}, \boldsymbol{0} & (r = 0) \\ F_{\text{LSTM}}(\boldsymbol{e}_{i_{r-1}}, \boldsymbol{h}_{r-1}, \boldsymbol{c}_{r-1}) & (1 \leq r \leq N) \end{cases} \tag{5}$$

where the function F_{LSTM} is a state-update function and $i_{r-1} \in \{1, \dots, N\}$ denotes the index of the token $w_{i_{r-1}}$ that is placed at the previous posi-

tion, i.e.,

$$i_{r-1} = \operatorname*{argmax}_{c \in \{1, \dots, N\}} p_{r-1,c}. \tag{6}$$

Subsequently, we predict a selective distribution over the input tokens:

$$p_{r,c} = \frac{\exp(\text{score}(\boldsymbol{h}_r, \boldsymbol{e}_c))}{\sum_{k=1}^N \exp(\text{score}(\boldsymbol{h}_r, \boldsymbol{e}_k))}, \tag{7}$$

where the scoring function score computes the confidence of placing the token w_c at r-th position. We define the scoring function as a bilinear model as follows

$$\text{score}(\boldsymbol{u}, \boldsymbol{v}) = \boldsymbol{u}^\top \boldsymbol{W}_s \boldsymbol{v} \in \mathbb{R}. \tag{8}$$

where $\boldsymbol{W}_s \in \mathbb{R}^{D \times D}$ denotes a learnable matrix.

2.4 Objective Function

As the WON is designed to be fully differentiable, it can be trained with any gradient descent algorithms, such as RMSProp (Tieleman and Hinton, 2012). Given a set of shuffled tokens $\mathcal{X} = \{w_1, \dots, w_N\}$, we define a loss function as the following negative log likelihood:

$$\mathcal{L}(\mathcal{X}) = \sum_{r=1}^N -\log p_{r,t_r} \tag{9}$$

where $t_r \in \{1, \dots, N\}$ denotes the index of the ground-truth token that appears at r-th position in the original sentence. In other words, an ordered sequence $w_{t_1}, w_{t_2}, \dots, w_{t_N}$ forms the original sentence.

3 Related Work

Among the most popular methods for learning word embeddings are the *skip-gram* (SG) model and the *continuous bag-of-words* (CBOW) of Mikolov et al. (2013a,b), or the GloVe introduced by Pennington et al. (2014). These are formalized as simple log-bilinear models based on the inner product between two word vectors. The core idea is based on the *distributional hypothesis* (Harris, 1954; Firth, 1957), stating that words appearing in similar contexts tend to have similar meanings. For example, SG and CBOW are trained by making predictions of bag-of-words contexts appearing in a fixed-size window around target words, and vice versa. Although word embeddings produced by these models have been shown to give improvements in a variety of downstream tasks, it still remains difficult for these models to learn syntactic word representations owing to their insensitivity to word order. As a consequence, word embeddings produced by these order-insensitive models are thus suboptimal for syntax-related tasks such as parsing (Andreas and Klein, 2014). In contrast, our method mainly focuses on word order information and utilize it in the learning process.

Ling et al. (2015b) introduced the *structured skip-gram* (SSG) model and the *continuous window* (CWindow) that extend SG and CBOW respectively. Let c be the window size. These models learn $2c$ context-embedding matrices to be aware of relative positions of context words in a window. The recent work of Trask et al. (2015) is also based on the same idea as SSG and CWindow. Ling et al. (2015a) proposed an approach to integrating an order-sensitive attention mechanism into CBOW, which allows for consideration of the contexts of words, and where the context words appear in a window. Bengio et al. (2003) presented a neural network language model (NNLM) where word embeddings are simultaneously learned along with a language model. One of the major shortcomings of these window-based approaches is that it is almost impossible to learn longer dependencies between words than the pre-fixed window size c. In contrast, the recurrent architecture allows the WON to take into account dependencies over an entire sentence.

Mikolov et al. (2010) applied an RNN for language modeling (RNNLM), and demonstrated that the word embeddings learned by the RNNLM capture both syntactic and semantic regularities. The main shortcoming of the RNNLM is that it is very slow to train unfortunately. This is a consequence of having to predict the probability distribution over an entire vocabulary V, which is generally very large in the real world. In contrast, the WON predicts the probability distribution over entire sentences, whose length N is usually less than $50 \ll |V|$. In our preliminary experiments, we found that the computation time for one iteration (= `forward` + `backward` + `parameter update`) of the WON is about 4 times faster than that of the RNNLM (LSTMLM).

Levy and Goldberg (2014) introduced dependency-based word embeddings. The method applies the *skip-gram with negative sampling* (SGNS) model (Mikolov et al., 2013b) to *syntactic contexts* derived from dependency parse-trees. Their method heavily relies on pre-trained dependency parsers to produce words' relations for each sentence in training corpora, thus encountering error propagation problems. In contrast, our method only requires raw corpora, and our aim is to produce word embeddings that improve syntax-related tasks, such as parsing, without using any human annotations.

The WON can be interpreted as a simplification of the recently proposed pointer network (PtrNet) (Vinyals et al., 2015). The main difference between the WON and the PtrNet is the *encoder* part. The PtrNet uses an RNN to encode an unordered set $\mathcal{X} = \{w_1, \ldots, w_N\}$ sequentially, i.e.,

$$e_i = \text{RNN}_{\text{enc}}(w_i, e_{i-1}). \qquad (10)$$

In contrast, the WON treats each symbol independently (Eq. 1) and aggregates them with a simpler function (Eq. 2). In the word ordering task, the order of $\mathcal{X} = (w_1, \ldots, w_N)$ is meaningless because $\mathcal{X}$ is an out-of-order set. Nonetheless, according to Equation 10, the vector e_i depends on the input order of $w_1, \ldots, w_{i-1}$. Vinyals et al. (2015) evaluated the PtrNet on geometric sorting tasks (e.g., Travelling Salesman Problem) where each input w_i forms a continuous vector that represents the cartesian coordinate of the point (e.g., a city). However, in the word ordering task, Equation 10 suffers from the data sparseness problem, as each input w_i forms a high-dimensional discrete symbol.

4 Experimental Setting

4.1 Dataset and Preprocessing

We used the English Wikipedia corpus as the training corpus. We lowercased and tokenized all tokens, and then replaced all digits with "7" (e.g., "ABC2017"→"ABC7777"). We built a vocabulary of the most frequent 300K words and replaced out-of-vocabulary tokens with a special "⟨UNK⟩" symbol. Subsequently, we appended special "⟨EOS⟩" symbols to the end of each sentence. The resulting corpus contains about 97 million sentences with about 2 billion tokens. We randomly extracted $5K$ sentences as the validation set.

4.2 Hyper Parameters

We set the dimensionality of word embeddings to 300. The dimensionality of the hidden states of the LSTM was 512. The $L2$ regularization term (called weight decay) was set to 4×10^{-6}. For the stochastic gradient descent algorithm, we used the SMORMS3 (Func, 2015), and the mini-batch size was set to 180.

4.3 Baselines

For a fair comparison, we trained the following order-insensitive/sensitive baselines on exactly the same pre-processed corpus described in Section 4.1.

- **SGNS** (Mikolov et al., 2013b): We used the `word2vec` implementation in Gensim[2] to train the Skip-Gram with Negative Sampling (SGNS). We set the window size to 5, and the number of negative samples to 5.

- **GloVe** (Pennington et al., 2014): GloVe's embeddings are trained by using the original implementation[3] provided by the authors. We set the window size to 15. In our preliminary experiments, we found that GloVe with a window size of 15 yields higher performances than that with a window size of 5.

- **SSG, CWindow** (Ling et al., 2015b): We built word embeddings by using the structured skip-gram (SSG) and the continuous window (CWindow). We used the original implementation[4] developed by the authors. The window size was 5, and the number of negative samples was 5.

- **LSTMLM**: We also compared the proposed method with the RNNLM (Mikolov et al., 2010) with LSTM units (LSTMLM). The hyper parameters were the same with that of the WON except for the mini-batch size. We used a mini-batch size of 100 for the LSTMLM.

5 Evaluation on Part-of-Speech Tagging

In this experiment, we evaluated the learned word embeddings by using them as pre-trained features in supervised POS tagging.

	Test Acc. (%)
SGNS (Mikolov et al., 2013b)	96.76
GloVe (Pennington et al., 2014)	96.31
SSG (Ling et al., 2015b)	96.94
CWindow (Ling et al., 2015b)	96.78
LSTMLM	96.92
WON	**97.04**

Table 1: Comparison results on part-of-speech tagging with different word embeddings. The dataset is the Wall Street Journal (WSJ) portion of the Penn Treebank (PTB) corpus. The evaluation metric is accuracy (%).

5.1 Supervised POS Tagger

In POS tagging, every token in a sentence is classified into its POS tag (NN for nouns, VBD for past tense verbs, JJ for adjectives, etc.). We first used the learned word embeddings to project three successive tokens (w_{i-1}, w_i, w_{i+1}) in an input sentence to feature vectors (e_{i-1}, e_i, e_{i+1}) that are then concatenated and fed to a two-layer perceptron followed by a softmax function:

$$P(c|w_{i-1}, w_i, w_{i+1}) = \text{MLP}([e_{i-1}; e_i; e_{i+1}]), \tag{11}$$

where $[\cdot\,;\,\cdot\,;\,\cdot]$ denotes vector concatenation. The classifier MLP predicts the probability distribution over POS tags of the center token w_i. We put special padding symbols at the beginning and end of each sentence. The dimensionality of the hidden layer of the MLP was 300. The MLP classifier was trained via the SMORMS3 optimizer (Func, 2015) without updating the word embedding layer.

We used the Wall Street Journal (WSJ) portion of the Penn Treebank (PTB) corpus[5] (Marcus et al., 1993). We followed the standard section partition, which is to use sections 0-18 for training, sections 19-21 for validation, and sections 22-24 for testing. The dataset contains 45 tags. The evaluation metric was the word-level accuracy.

5.2 Results & Discussion

Table 1 presents the comparison of the WON to the other baselines on the test split. The results demonstrate that the WON gives the highest performance, which supports our hypothesis that the word ordering task is effective for acquiring syntactic knowledge about words. We also

	Dev		Test	
	UAS	LAS	UAS	LAS
SGNS	91.56	90.09	91.11	89.89
GloVe	88.87	87.09	88.28	86.61
SSG	91.11	89.60	90.93	89.43
CWindow	91.23	89.69	91.16	89.67
LSTMLM	91.83	90.34	91.49	90.08
WON	**91.92**	**90.49**	**91.82**	**90.38**

Table 2: Results on dependency parsing with different word embeddings. The dataset was the WSJ portion of the PTB corpus. The evaluation metrics were Unlabeled Attachment Score (UAS) and Labeled Attachment Score (LAS).

observe that the order-sensitive methods (WON, LSTMLM, and SSG) tend to outperform the order-insensitive methods (SGNS and GloVe), which indicates that, as we expect, word order information is crucial for learning syntactic word embeddings.

6 Evaluation on Dependency Parsing

In this experiment, as in Section 5, we evaluated the learned word embeddings on supervised dependency parsing.

6.1 Supervised Dependency Parser

Dependency parsing aims to identify syntactic relations between token pairs in a sentence. We used Stanford's neural network dependency parser (Chen and Manning, 2014)[6], whose word embeddings were initialized with the learned word embeddings. We followed all the default settings except for the word embedding size (`embeddingSize = 300`) and the number of training iterations (`maxIter = 6000`).

We used the WSJ portion of the PTB corpus and followed the standard splits of sections 2-21 for training, 22 for validation, and 23 for testing. We converted the treebank corpus to Stanford style dependencies using the Stanford converter. The parsing performances were evaluated in terms of Unlabeled Attachment Score (UAS) and Labeled Attachment Score (LAS).

6.2 Results & Discussion

Table 2 shows the results of the different word embeddings on dependency parsing. First we observe that the WON consistently outperforms

---

[6]http://nlp.stanford.edu/software/nndep.shtml

the baselines on both UAS and LAS. Next, by comparing the unlimited-context models (WON and LSTMLM) with the limited-context models (SGNS, GloVe, SSG, CWindow), we can notice that the former give higher parsing scores than the latter. These results are reasonable because the former can learn arbitrary-length syntactic dependencies between words without constraints from the fixed-size window size based on which the limited-window models are trained.

7 Fusion with Semantic Features

In various NLP tasks, both syntactic and semantic features can benefit performances. To enrich our syntax-oriented word embeddings with semantic information, in this section, we adopt a simple fine-tuning technique and verify its effectiveness. More precisely, we first initialize the word embeddings W with pre-trained parameters W_{sem} produced by a semantics-oriented model such as the SGNS. Subsequently we add the following penalty term to the loss function in Equation 9:

$$\lambda \|W - W_{\text{sem}}\|_{\mathcal{F}}^2, \qquad (12)$$

where $\lambda \in \mathbb{R}$ is a hyper parameter to control the intensity of the penalty term in the learning process, and $\|\cdot\|_{\mathcal{F}}^2$ is the Frobenius norm. This term attempts to keep the word embeddings W close to the semantic representations W_{sem} while minimizing the syntax-oriented objective on the word ordering task. In our experiments, we used the SGNS's embeddings as W_{sem} and set λ to 1. The SGNS was trained as explained in Section 4.3.

In this section, we quantitatively evaluated the WON with the above fine-tuning technique on two major benchmarks: (1) word analogy task, and (2) word similarity task.

7.1 Word Analogy

The word analogy task has been used in previous work to evaluate the ability of word embeddings to represent semantic and syntactic regularities. In this experiment, we used the word analogy dataset produced by Mikolov et al. (2013a). The dataset consists of questions like "A is to B what C is to ?." denoted as "A : B :: C : ?." The dataset contains about 20K such questions, divided into a *syntactic subset* and a *semantic subset*. The syntactic subset contains nine question types, such as `adjective-to-adverb` and `opposite`, while the semantic subset contains five question

Question Types	SGNS	GloVe	SSG	CWindow	LSTMLM	WON
adjective-to-adverb	24.1	23.3	**29.9**	12.1	4.3	**29.9**
opposite	36.2	29.9	37.0	11.7	15.0	**37.8**
comparative	85.7	79.5	88.5	73.5	55.3	**88.7**
superlative	59.3	49.1	**68.7**	43.8	22.4	62.8
present-participle	64.9	61.0	**73.6**	57.4	27.1	71.8
nationality-adjective	89.4	**92.2**	89.7	87.3	30.5	90.8
past-tense	58.0	52.2	59.0	54.0	33.1	**61.4**
plural	75.2	**83.0**	75.2	70.4	26.4	75.4
plural-verbs	78.9	56.0	**84.6**	64.6	61.0	82.9
capital-common	94.5	95.3	92.5	93.1	53.8	**95.5**
captal-world	87.8	**94.5**	84.0	66.6	22.1	82.6
currency	12.8	8.7	**14.0**	3.7	1.9	10.7
city	66.0	60.7	56.9	61.9	13.6	**67.4**
family	**84.2**	77.9	81.8	59.1	62.9	**84.2**
Total	69.9	68.3	69.7	58.2	27.0	**70.6**

Table 3: Results on the word analogy task (Mikolov et al., 2013a) with different word embeddings. The first upper block presents the results on nine syntactic question types. In the lower block we show the results on five semantic question types. The last row presents the total score. The evaluation metric is accuracy (%).

types such as `city-in-state` and `family`. Suppose that a vector e_w is a representation of a word w, and is normalized to unit norm. Following a previous work (Mikolov et al., 2013a), we answer an analogy question "A : B :: C : ?" by finding a word w^* that has the closest representation to $(e_B - e_A + e_C)$ in terms of cosine similarity, i.e.,

$$w^* = \operatorname*{argmax}_{w \in V \setminus \{A,B,C\}} \frac{(e_B - e_A + e_C)^\top e_w}{\|e_B - e_A + e_C\|}, \quad (13)$$

where V denotes the vocabulary. The evaluation was performed using accuracy, which denotes the percentage of words predicted correctly.

In Table 3, we report the results of the different word embeddings on this task. As can be seen in the Table 3, the WON outperforms the baselines on four out of nine syntactic question types, and tends to yield higher accuracies by a large margin than the baselines except for the SSG. Our method and the SSG totally give the best performances on seven of nine syntactic question types. This tendency, as in Section 5.2, indicates that word order information is crucial to learn syntactic word embeddings. In regard to semantics, the WON achieves the best scores on three out of five semantic question types. Interestingly, on two semantic question types (`capital-common` and `city`), the WON outperforms the SGNS that was used to

	WS-353	MC	RG
SGNS	71.26	81.96	78.86
GloVe	62.54	71.57	75.54
SSG	**73.08**	81.78	**80.37**
CWindow	70.31	80.92	77.80
LSTMLM	53.34	66.76	63.23
WON	70.97	**82.43**	77.64

Table 4: Results on the word similarity task with different word embeddings. Spearman's rank correlation coefficents (%) are computed on three datasets: WS-353, MC, and RG.

initialize our word embeddings. This result implies that the word ordering task has the potential to improve not only syntactic but also semantic features. Our method achieves the highest accuracy on the overall score.

7.2 Word Similarity

The word similarity benchmark is commonly used to evaluate word embeddings in terms of distributional semantic similarity. The word similarity datasets consist of triplets like (w_1, w_2, s), where $s \in \mathbb{R}$ is a human-annotated similarity score between two words (w_1, w_2). In this task, we compute cosine similarity between two word embeddings. The evaluation is performed with the Spearman's rank correlation coefficient between

Query	The 3 most similar words		
he	she	they	we
him	them	us	me
his	their	our	your
boy	kid	creature	girl
boys	ladies	guys	folks
dragon	werewolf	dwarf	vamp
dragons	robots	giants	spiders
city	village	library	palace
cities	countries	kingdoms	neighborhoods
drive	ride	walk	hike
drives	draws	pisses	causes
drove	rode	marched	strode
driving	traveling	walking	riding
driven	flown	propelled	shaken
happy	pleased	unhappy	thrilled
happier	crazier	prettier	tougher
happiest	hottest	toughest	coolest
good	nice	bad	decent
better	easier	worse	safer
best	worst	hardest	biggest
in	on	into	under

Table 5: Query words and their most similar words. Cosine similarities are computed between their embeddings produced by the WON.

the human-annotated similarities and the computed similarities.

Table 4 presents the results on three datasets: WordSim-353 (Finkelstein et al., 2001), MC (Miller and Charles, 1991), and RG (Rubenstein and Goodenough, 1965). we observe that the WON gives a slightly higher performance than the baselines on the MC dataset. On the other datasets, the SSG yields the best performances. These results are interesting because the two models rely on word order information while the word similarity task originally focuses on topical semantic similarities between words.

Further investigation into the interaction between syntactic and semantic representations would be interesting and needs to be explored.

8 Qualitative Analysis

In this section, we inspect the learned vector space by computing the similarities between word embeddings.

In this experiment we trained the WON on the BookCorpus (Zhu et al., 2015) that is preprocessed in the same way described in Section 4.1. The BookCorpus consists of a large collection of nov-

els, which results in a grammatically sophisticated text corpus that would be suitable for qualitative analysis. Note that to clearly investigate the word embeddings produced by the WON we neither initialize our word embeddings with other models nor use fine-tuning techniques, as in experiments on downstream syntax-related tasks (Section 5 and Section 6). We choose queries focusing on (1) declension of personal pronouns, (2) singular and plural forms of nouns, (3) verb conjugation, (4) comparative/superlative forms of adjectives, and (5) prepositions.

Table 5 presents some representative queries for (1)-(5) and their respective most similar words in the learned vector space. First we can observe that our word embeddings produce a continuous vector space that successfully captures syntactic regularities. In addition to the syntactic regularities, interestingly, we found that the WON prefers to gather words in terms of those meanings or semantic categories.

9 Conclusion and Future Work

The research question we explored in this study was how to learn *syntactic word embeddings* without using any human annotations. Our underlying hypothesis is that the word odering task is suitable for obtaining syntactic knowledge about words. To verify this idea, we developed the WON, which implicitly learns syntactic word representations through learning to explicitly solve the word ordering task. The experimental results demonstrate that the WON gives improvements over baselines particularly on syntax-related tasks, such as part-of-speech tagging and dependency parsing. We can also observe that the WON, by combined with a simple fine-tuning technique, has the potential to refine not only syntactic but also semantic features.

It remains unclear how well order-sensitive models like the WON can learn syntactic knowledge about words in languages other than English. Especially, it is interesting to investigate cases on languages with richer morphology and freer word order. We leave this to future work.

Acknowledgements

The authors would like to thank the anonymous reviewers for their constructive and helpful suggestions on this work. We also thank Makoto Miwa and Naoaki Okazaki for valuable comments and discussion. This work was supported by JSPS KAKENHI Grant Number 16H05872 and JST CREST JPMJCR1304.

References

Jacob Andreas and Dan Klein. 2014. How much do word embeddings encode about syntax? In *Proceedings of the 52nd Annual Meeting of the Association for Computational Linguistics*.

Dzmitry Bahdanau, Kyunghyun Cho, and Yoshua Bengio. 2014. Neural machine translation by jointly learning to align and translate. *arXiv preprint arXiv:1409.0473*.

Yoshua Bengio, Réjean Ducharme, Pascal Vincent, and Christian Jauvin. 2003. A neural probabilistic language model. *Journal of Machine Learning Research*, 3(Feb):1137–1155.

Danqi Chen and Christopher D. Manning. 2014. A fast and accurate dependency parser using neural networks. In *Proceedings of the 2014 Conference on Empirical Methods in Natural Language Processing*.

Ronan Collobert, Jason Weston, Léon Bottou, Michael Karlen, Koray Kavukcuoglu, and Pavel Kuksa. 2011. Natural language processing (almost) from scratch. *Journal of Machine Learning Research*, 12:2493–2537.

Jeffrey L. Elman. 1990. Finding structure in time. *Cognitive Science*, 14(2):179–211.

Lev Finkelstein, Evgeniy Gabrilovich, Yossi Matias, Ehud Rivlin, Zach Solan, Gadi Wolfman, and Eytan Ruppin. 2001. Placing search in context: The concept revisited. In *Proceedings of the 10th International Conference on World Wide Web*.

John R. Firth. 1957. *A synopsis of linguistic theory, 1930-1955*. Blackwell.

Simon Func. 2015. Smorms3 - blog entry: Rmsprop loses to smorms3 - beware the epsilon! *http://sifter.org/ simon/journal/20150420.html*.

Zellig S. Harris. 1954. Distributional structure. *Word*, 10(2-3):146–162.

Sepp Hochreiter and Jürgen Schmidhuber. 1997. Long short-term memory. *Neural Computation*, 9(8):1735–1780.

Over Levy and Yoav Goldberg. 2014. Dependency-based word embeddings. In *Proceedings of the 52nd Annual Meeting of the Association for Computational Linguistics*.

Wang Ling, Lin Chu-Cheng, Yulia Tsvetkov, and Silvio Amir. 2015a. Not all contexts are created equal: Better word representations with variable attention. In *Proceedings of the 2015 Conference of Empirical Methods in Natural Language Processing*.

Wang Ling, Chris Dyer, Alan Black, and Isabel Trancoso. 2015b. Two/too simple adaptation of word2vec for syntax problems. In *Proceedings of the 2015 Conference of the North American Chapter of the Association for Computational Linguistics: Human Language Technologies*.

Minh-Thang Luong, Hieu Pham, and Christopher D. Manning. 2015. Effective approaches to attention-based neural machine translation. In *Proceedings of the 2015 Conference on Empirical Methods in Natural Language Processing*.

Mitchell P. Marcus, Mary Ann Marcinkiewicz, and Beatrice Santorini. 1993. Building a large annotated corpus of english: The penn treebank. *Computational Linguistics*, 19(2):313–330.

Tomas Mikolov, Kai Chen, Greg S. Corrado, and Jeffrey Dean. 2013a. Efficient estimation of word representations in vector space. *arXiv preprint arXiv:1301.3781*.

Tomas Mikolov, Martin Karafiát, Lukas Burget, Jan Cernocký, and Sanjeev Khudanpur. 2010. Recurrent neural network based language model. In *Proceedings of INTERSPEECH*.

Tomas Mikolov, Ilya Sutskever, Kai Chen, Greg S. Corrado, and Jeff Dean. 2013b. Distributed representations of words and phrases and their compositionality. In *Advances in Neural Information Processing Systems*.

George A. Miller and Walter G. Charles. 1991. Contextual correlates of semantic similarity. *Language and Cognitive Processes*, 6(1):1–28.

Jeffrey Pennington, Richard Socher, and Christopher D. Manning. 2014. Glove: Global vectors for word representations. In *Proceedings of the 2014 Conference on Empirical Methods in Natural Language Processing*.

Herbert Rubenstein and John B. Goodenough. 1965. Contextual correlates of synonymy. *Communications of the ACM*, 8(10):627–633.

Richard Socher, Jeffrey Pennington, Eric H Huang, Andrew Y Ng, and Christopher D Manning. 2011. Semi-supervised recursive autoencoders for predicting sentiment distributions. In *Proceedings of the conference on empirical methods in natural language processing*.

Tijmen Tieleman and Geoffrey Hinton. 2012. Lecture 6.5-rmsprop: Divide the gradient by a running average of its recent magnitude. *COURSERA: Neural networks for machine learning*, 4(2).

Andrew Trask, David Gilmore, and Matthew Russell. 2015. Modeling order in neuralword embeddings at scale. In *Proceedings of The 32nd International Conference on Machine Learning*.

Joseph Turian, Lev Ratinov, and Yoshua Bengio. 2010. Word representations: A simple and general method for semi-supervised learning. In *Proceedings of the 48th Annual Meeting of the Association for Computational Linguistics.*

Oriol Vinyals, Meire Fortunato, and Navdeep Jaitly. 2015. Pointer networks. In *Advances in Neural Information Processing Systems.*

Yukun Zhu, Ryan Kiros, Richard Zemel, Ruslan Salakhutdinov, Raquel Urtasun, Antonio Torralba, and Sanja Fidler. 2015. Aligning books and movies: Towards story-like visual explanations by watching movies and reading books. *arXiv preprint arXiv:1506.06724.*

MIPA: Mutual Information Based
Paraphrase Acquisition via Bilingual Pivoting

Tomoyuki Kajiwara[*]   **Mamoru Komachi**[†]   **Daichi Mochihashi**[‡]

[*]Tokyo Metropolitan University, Tokyo, Japan, `kajiwara-tomoyuki@ed.tmu.ac.jp`
[†]Tokyo Metropolitan University, Tokyo, Japan, `komachi@tmu.ac.jp`
[‡]The Institute of Statistical Mathematics, Tokyo, Japan, `daichi@ism.ac.jp`

Abstract

We present a pointwise mutual information (PMI) based approach for formalizing paraphrasability and propose a variant of PMI, called mutual information based paraphrase acquisition (MIPA), for paraphrase acquisition. Our paraphrase acquisition method first acquires lexical paraphrase pairs by bilingual pivoting and then reranks them by PMI and distributional similarity. The complementary nature of information from bilingual corpora and from monolingual corpora renders the proposed method robust. Experimental results show that the proposed method substantially outperforms bilingual pivoting and distributional similarity themselves in terms of metrics such as mean reciprocal rank, mean average precision, coverage, and Spearman's correlation.

1 Introduction

Paraphrases are useful for flexible language understanding in many NLP applications. For example, the usefulness of the paraphrase database PPDB (Ganitkevitch et al., 2013; Pavlick et al., 2015), a publicly available large-scale resource for lexical paraphrasing, has been reported for tasks such as learning word embeddings (Yu and Dredze, 2014) and semantic textual similarity (Sultan et al., 2015). In PPDB, paraphrase pairs are acquired via word alignment on a bilingual corpus by a process called bilingual pivoting (Bannard and Callison-Burch, 2005). Figure 1 shows an example of English language paraphrase acquisition using the German language as a pivot.

Although bilingual pivoting is widely used for paraphrase acquisition, it always includes noise

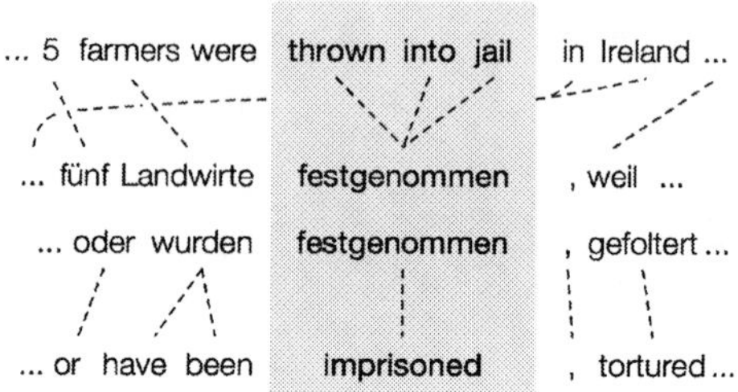

Figure 1: Paraphrase acquisition via bilingual pivoting (Ganitkevitch et al., 2013).

due to unrelated word pairs caused by word alignment errors on the bilingual corpus. Distributional similarity, another well-known method for paraphrase acquisition, is free of alignment errors, but includes noise due to antonym pairs that share the same contexts on the monolingual corpus (Mohammad et al., 2013).

In this study, we formalize the paraphrasability of paraphrase pairs acquired via bilingual pivoting using pointwise mutual information (PMI) and reduce the noise by reranking the pairs using distributional similarity. The proposed method extends Local PMI (Evert, 2005), which is a variant of weighted PMI that aims to avoid low-frequency bias in PMI, for paraphrase acquisition. Since bilingual pivoting and distributional similarity have different advantages and disadvantages, we combine them to construct a complementary paraphrase acquisition method, called mutual information based paraphrase acquisition (MIPA). Experimental results show that MIPA outperforms bilingual pivoting and distributional similarity themselves in terms of metrics such as mean reciprocal rank (MRR), mean average precision (MAP), coverage, and Spearman's correlation.

The contributions of our study are as follows.

Proceedings of the The 8th International Joint Conference on Natural Language Processing, pages 80–89,
Taipei, Taiwan, November 27 – December 1, 2017 ©2017 AFNLP

- Bilingual pivoting-based lexical paraphrase acquisition is generalized using PMI.

- Lexical paraphrases are acquired robustly using both bilingual and monolingual corpora.

- We release our lexical paraphrase pairs[1].

2 Bilingual Pivoting

Bilingual pivoting (Bannard and Callison-Burch, 2005) is a method used to acquire large-scale lexical paraphrases by two-level word alignment on a bilingual corpus. Bilingual pivoting employs a conditional paraphrase probability $p(e_2|e_1)$ as a paraphrasability measure, when word alignments exist between an English phrase e_1 and a foreign language phrase f, and between the foreign language phrase f and another English phrase e_2 on a bilingual corpus. It calculates the probability from an English phrase e_1 to another English phrase e_2 using word alignment probabilities $p(f|e_1)$ and $p(e_2|f)$; here, the foreign language phrase f is used as the pivot.

$$p(e_2|e_1) = \sum_f p(e_2|f,e_1)\, p(f|e_1)$$
$$\approx \sum_f p(e_2|f)\, p(f|e_1) \quad (1)$$

It assumes conditional independence of e_1 and e_2 given f, so that the equation above can be estimated easily using phrase-based statistical machine translation models. One of its advantages is that it requires only two translation models to acquire paraphrases on a large scale. However, since the conditional probability is asymmetric, it may introduce irrelevant paraphrases that do not hold the same meaning as the original one. In addition, owing to the data sparseness problem in the bilingual corpus, paraphrase probabilities may be overestimated for low-frequency word pairs.

To mitigate this, PPDB (Ganitkevitch et al., 2013) defined the symmetric paraphrase score $s_{bp}(e_1, e_2)$ using bi-directional bilingual pivoting.

$$s_{bp}(e_1, e_2) = -\lambda_1 \log p(e_2|e_1) - \lambda_2 \log p(e_1|e_2) \quad (2)$$

Unlike Equation (1), s_{bp} enforces mutual paraphrasability of e_1 and e_2. As discussed later, this does not necessarily increase the performance of paraphrase acquisition, because the symmetric constraint may be too strict to allow the extraction of broad-coverage paraphrases. In this study,

without loss of generality, we set[2] $\lambda_1 = \lambda_2 = -1$.

$$s_{bp}(e_1, e_2) = \log p(e_2|e_1) + \log p(e_1|e_2) \quad (3)$$

Although these paraphrase acquisition methods can extract large-scale paraphrase knowledge, the results may contain many fragments caused by word alignment error.

3 MIPA: Mutual Information Based Paraphrase Acquisition

To mitigate overestimation, we acquire lexical paraphrases with the conditional paraphrase probability by using Kneser-Ney smoothing (Kneser and Ney, 1995) and reranking them using information theoretic measure from a bilingual corpus and distributional similarity calculated from a large-scale monolingual corpus.

3.1 Smoothing of Bilingual Pivoting

Since bilingual pivoting adopts the conditional probability $p(e_2|e_1)$ as paraphrasability, we can mitigate the problem of overestimation by applying a smoothing method.

In the hierarchical Bayesian model, the conditional probability $p(y|x)$ is expressed using the Dirichlet distribution with parameter α_y and maximum likelihood estimation $\hat{p}_{y|x}$ as follows.

$$
\begin{aligned}
p(y|x) &= \frac{n(y|x) + \alpha_y}{\sum_y (n(y|x) + \alpha_y)} \\
&\simeq \frac{n(y|x)}{n(x) + \sum_y \alpha_y} \quad \because \alpha_y \ll 1 \\
&= \frac{n(x)}{n(x) + \sum_y \alpha_y} \cdot \frac{n(y|x)}{n(x)} \\
&= \frac{n(x)}{n(x) + \sum_y \alpha_y} \cdot \hat{p}_{y|x}
\end{aligned}
\quad (4)
$$

Here, $n(x)$ indicates the frequency of a word x and $n(y|x)$ indicates the co-occurrence frequency of word y following x. As $\sum_y \alpha_y$ is too large to be ignored, especially when the frequency $n(x)$ is small, Equation (4) shows that the maximum likelihood estimation $\hat{p}_{y|x}$ estimates the probability to be excessively large.

Therefore, we propose using Kneser-Ney smoothing (Kneser and Ney, 1995), which is considered to be an extension of the Dirichlet smoothing above, to mitigate overestimation of paraphrase probability in bilingual pivoting.

[1]https://github.com/tmu-nlp/pmi-ppdb

[2]PPDB[3]: $\lambda_1 = \lambda_2 = 1$
[3]http://www.cis.upenn.edu/~ccb/ppdb/

$$p_{\text{KN}}(e_2 \mid e_1) = \frac{n(e_2 \mid e_1) - \delta}{n(e_1)} + \gamma(e_1) p_{\text{KN}}(e_2)$$

$$\delta = \frac{N_1}{N_1 + 2N_2}$$

$$\gamma(e_1) = \frac{\delta}{n(e_1)} N(e_1) \qquad (5)$$

$$p_{\text{KN}}(e_2) = \frac{N(e_2)}{\sum_i N(e_i)}$$

Here, N_n indicates the number of types of word pairs of frequency n and $N(e_1)$ indicates the number of types of paraphrase candidates of word e_1.

3.2 Generalization of Bilingual Pivoting using Mutual Information

The bi-directional bilingual pivoting of PPDB (Ganitkevitch et al., 2013) constrains paraphrase acquisition to be strictly symmetric. However, although it is extremely effective for extracting synonymous expressions, it tends to give high scores to frequent but irrelevant phrases, since bilingual pivoting itself contains noisy phrase pairs because of word alignment errors.

To address the problem of frequent phrases, we smooth paraphrasability by bilingual pivoting in Equation (3) using word probabilities $p(e_1)$ and $p(e_2)$ from a monolingual corpus that is sufficiently larger than the bilingual corpus.

$$s_{pmi}(e_1, e_2) = \log p(e_2 \mid e_1) + \log p(e_1 \mid e_2) \\ - \log p(e_1) - \log p(e_2) \qquad (6)$$

Thus, we can interpret the bi-directional bilingual pivoting as an unsmoothed version of PMI. Since the difference in the logarithms of the numerator and denominator is equal to the logarithm of the quotient, we can transform Equation (6) as

$$s_{pmi}(e_1, e_2) = \log \frac{p(e_2 \mid e_1)}{p(e_2)} + \log \frac{p(e_1 \mid e_2)}{p(e_1)} \\ = 2\text{PMI}(e_1, e_2) \qquad (7)$$

since we can transform PMI into the following forms using Bayes' theorem.

$$\text{PMI}(x, y) = \log \frac{p(x, y)}{p(x)p(y)} \qquad (8)$$

$$= \log \frac{p(y \mid x)p(x)}{p(x)p(y)} = \log \frac{p(y \mid x)}{p(y)}$$

$$= \log \frac{p(x \mid y)p(y)}{p(x)p(y)} = \log \frac{p(x \mid y)}{p(x)}$$

Plugging Equation (8) into Equation (7), we can interpret PMI as a geometric mean of two models.

$$\text{PMI}(x, y) = \frac{1}{2}\text{PMI}(x, y) + \frac{1}{2}\text{PMI}(x, y) \qquad (9)$$

$$= \frac{1}{2} \log \frac{p(y \mid x)}{p(y)} + \frac{1}{2} \log \frac{p(x \mid y)}{p(x)}$$

$$= \log \left[\left\{ \frac{p(y \mid x)}{p(y)} \right\}^{\frac{1}{2}} \cdot \left\{ \frac{p(x \mid y)}{p(x)} \right\}^{\frac{1}{2}} \right]$$

Bilingual pivoting in Equation (1) can be regarded as a mixture model that considers only the $e_1 \rightarrow e_2$ direction. However, as shown in Equation (9), our proposed method can be regarded as a product model (Hinton, 2002) that considers both directions. PPDB (Pavlick et al., 2015) also considers the paraphrase probability in both directions, but the authors did not regard it as a product model; instead the paraphrase probability in each direction is treated as one of the features of supervised learning.

3.3 Incorporating Distributional Similarity

In low-frequency word pairs, it is well-known that PMI becomes unreasonably large because of coincidental co-occurrence. In order to avoid this problem, Evert (2005) proposed Local PMI, which assigns weights to PMI depending on the co-occurrence frequency of word pairs.

$$\text{LocalPMI}(x, y) = n(x, y) \cdot \text{PMI}(x, y) \qquad (10)$$

In this study, however, it was difficult to directly calculate the weight corresponding to $n(x, y)$ in Equation (10) on the bilingual corpus. Furthermore, our aim was to calculate not the strength of co-occurrence (relation) between words, but the paraphrasability. Therefore, it is not appropriate to count the co-occurrence frequency on a monolingual corpus such as Local PMI.

Alternatively, we use as a weight the distributional similarity, which is frequently used for paraphrase acquisition from a monolingual corpus (Chan et al., 2011; Glavaš and Štajner, 2015).

$$s_{lpmi}(e_1, e_2) = cos(e_1, e_2) \cdot s_{pmi}(e_1, e_2) \\ = cos(e_1, e_2) \cdot 2\text{PMI}(e_1, e_2) \qquad (11)$$

Here, $cos(e_1, e_2)$ indicates cosine similarity between vector representations of word e_1 and word e_2. Equation (11) simultaneously considers paraphrasability based on the monolingual corpus (distributional similarity) and on the bilingual corpus

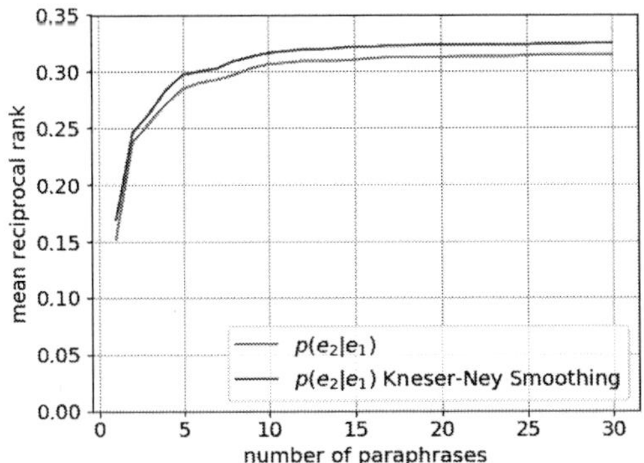
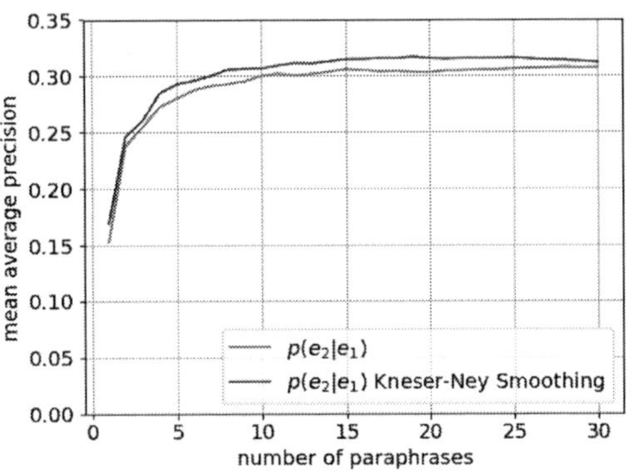

Figure 2: Effectiveness of smoothing of bilingual pivoting evaluated by paraphrase ranking in MRR.

Figure 3: Effectiveness of smoothing of bilingual pivoting evaluated by paraphrase ranking in MAP.

(bilingual pivoting). Distributional similarity, as opposed to bilingual pivoting, is robust against noise associated with unrelated word pairs. Bilingual pivoting is robust against noise arising from antonym pairs, unlike distributional similarity. Therefore, $s_{lpmi}(e_1, e_2)$ can perform paraphrase acquisition robustly by compensating the disadvantages. Hereinafter, we refer to $s_{lpmi}(e_1, e_2)$ as MIPA, mutual information based paraphrase acquisition via bilingual pivoting.

4 Experiments

4.1 Settings

We used French-English parallel data[4] from Europarl-v7 (Koehn, 2005) and GIZA++ (Och and Ney, 2003) (IBM model 4) to calculate the conditional paraphrase probability $p(e_2|e_1)$ and $p(e_1|e_2)$. We also used the English Gigaword 5th Edition[5] and KenLM (Heafield, 2011) to calculate the word probability $p(e_1)$ and $p(e_2)$. For $cos(e_1, e_2)$, we used the CBOW model[6] of word2vec (Mikolov et al., 2013a). Finally, we acquired paraphrase candidates of 170,682,871 word pairs, excepting the paraphrase of itself ($e_1 = e_2$).

We employed the conditional paraphrase probability of bilingual pivoting given in Equation (1), the symmetric paraphrase score of PPDB given by Equation (3), and distributional similarity as baselines, and compared them with PMI shown in Equation (7) and the MIPA score given in Equation (11). Note that distributional similarity im-

plies that the paraphrase pairs acquired via bilingual pivoting were reranked by distributional similarity rather than by using the top-k distributionally similar words among all the vocabularies.

4.2 Evaluation Datasets and Metrics

For evaluation, we used two datasets included in Human Paraphrase Judgments[7] published by Pavlick et al. (2015); hereafter, we call these datasets HPJ-Wikipedia and HPJ-PPDB, respectively.

First, Human Paraphrase Judgments includes a paraphrase list of 100 words or phrases randomly extracted from Wikipedia and processed using a five-step manual evaluation for each paraphrase pair (HPJ-Wikipedia). A correct paraphrase is a word that gained three or more evaluations in manual evaluation. We used this dataset to evaluate the acquired paraphrase pairs by MRR and MAP, following Pavlick et al. (2015). Furthermore, we evaluated the coverage of the top-k paraphrase pairs. Function words such as "as" have more than 50,000 types of paraphrase candidates, because they are sensitive to word alignment errors in bilingual pivoting. However, since many of these paraphrase candidates are word pairs that are not in fact paraphrases, we evaluated the coverage in terms of the extent to which they can reduce unnecessary candidates while preserving the correct paraphrases.

Second, Human Paraphrase Judgments also includes a five-step manual evaluation of 26,456 word pairs sampled from PPDB (Ganitkevitch et al., 2013) (HPJ-PPDB)

---

[4] http://www.statmt.org/europarl/
[5] https://catalog.ldc.upenn.edu/LDC2011T07
[6] https://code.google.com/archive/p/word2vec/

[7] http://www.seas.upenn.edu/~epavlick/data.html

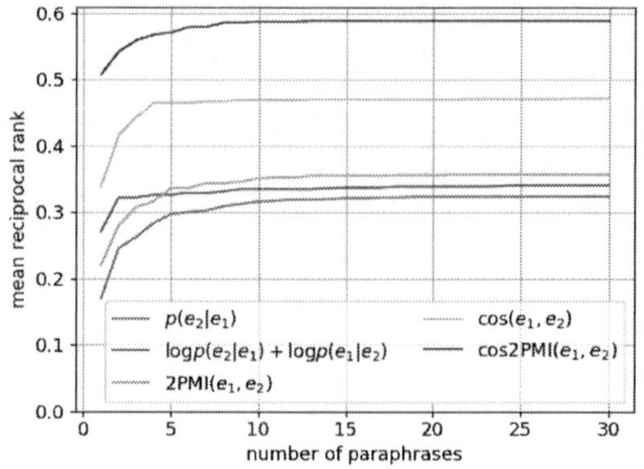

Figure 4: Paraphrase ranking in MRR.

Figure 5: Paraphrase ranking in MAP.

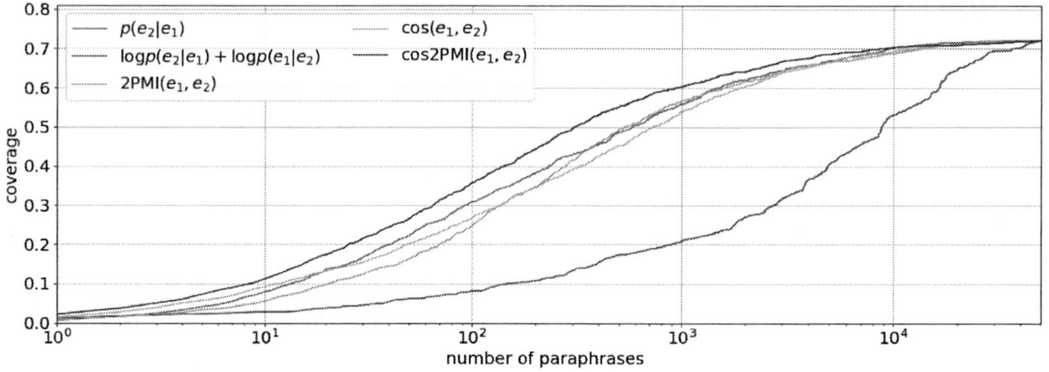

Figure 6: Coverage of the top-k paraphrase pairs.

together with the paraphrase list of 100 words. We used this dataset to evaluate the overall paraphrase ranking based on Spearman's correlation coefficient, as in Pavlick et al. (2015).

4.3 Results

Figures 2 and 3 show the effectiveness of adopting Kneser-Ney smoothing for bilingual pivoting in terms of MRR and MAP on HPJ-Wikipedia. The horizontal axis of each graph represents the evaluation of the paraphrase up to the top-k of the paraphrase score. The results confirm that the ranking of paraphrases acquired via bilingual pivoting was improved by applying Kneser-Ney smoothing. In the rest of this study, we always applied Kneser-Ney smoothing to conditional paraphrase probability.

Figures 4 and 5 show the comparison of paraphrase rankings in MRR and MAP on HPJ-Wikipedia. The evaluation by MRR, shown in Figure 4, demonstrates that the ranking performance of paraphrase pairs is improved by making bilingual pivoting symmetric. PMI slightly outperforms the baselines of bilingual pivoting below the top five. Furthermore, MIPA shows the highest performance, because reranking by distributional similarity greatly improves bilingual pivoting.

The evaluation using MAP, shown in Figure 5, also reinforced the same result, i.e., reranking by distribution similarity improved bilingual pivoting, and MIPA showed the highest performance.

Figure 6 shows the coverage of the top-ranked paraphrases on HPJ-Wikipedia. Despite the fact that the symmetric paraphrase score is better than the conditional paraphrase probability in the ranking performance of the top three in MRR and MAP, it shows a poor performance in terms of coverage. Although there is not a significant difference between MIPA and the other methods, MIPA was shown to outperform them.

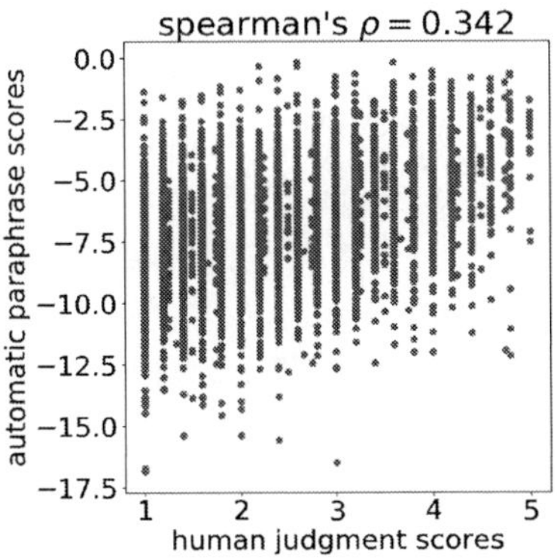

Figure 7: $\rho : \log p(e_2|e_1)$.

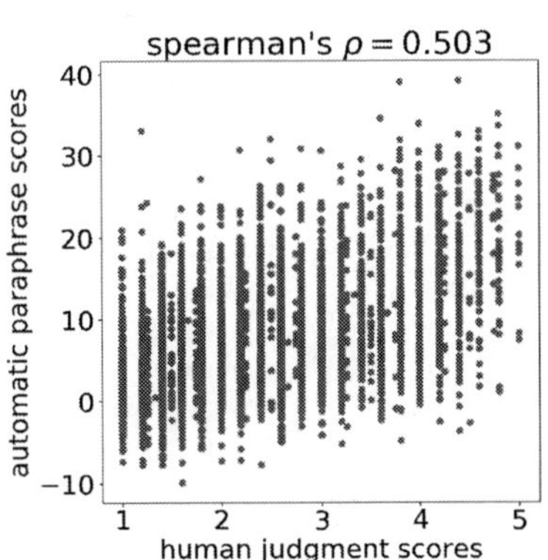

Figure 8: $\rho : \mathrm{MIPA}(e_1, e_2)$.

	$p(e_2|e_1)$	$\log p(e_2|e_1) + \log p(e_1|e_2)$	$2\mathrm{PMI}(e_1, e_2)$	$\cos(e_1, e_2)$	$\cos(e_1, e_2)2\mathrm{PMI}(e_1, e_2)$
1.	diverse	*culturally*	culturally-based	historical	*socio-cultural*
2.	harvests	*culture*	culturaldevelopment	*culture*	*culture*
3.	firstly	151	cultural-social	educational	*multicultural*
4.	understand	charter	economic-cultural	linguistic	*intercultural*
5.	flowering	monuments	culture-	*multicultural*	educational
6.	trying	art	cultural-educational	*cross-cultural*	intellectual
7.	structure	casal	kulturkampf	diversity	*culturally*
8.	january	kahn	cultural-political	technological	*sociocultural*
9.	*culture*	13	multiculture	intellectual	*heritage*
10.	*culturally*	caning	*culturally*	preservation	architectural

Table 1: Paraphrase examples of *cultural*. Italicized words are the correct paraphrases.

Figures 7 and 8 show the scatter plots and Spearman's correlation coefficient of each paraphrase score and manual evaluation (average value of five evaluators) on HPJ-PPDB. As in the previous experimental results, MIPA showed a high correlation. In particular, the noise generated by false positives at the upper left of the scatter plot can be reduced by combining PMI and distributional similarity.

5 Discussion

5.1 Qualitative Analysis

Table 1 shows examples of the top 10 in paraphrase rankings. In the paraphrase examples of *cultural*, conditional paraphrase probability does not score the correct paraphrase as top-ranked words. Although the symmetric paraphrase score ranked the correct paraphrase at the top, words other than the top words are less reliable, as shown by the previous experimental results. PMI is strongly influenced by low-frequency words, and many of the top-ranked words are singleton words in the bilingual corpus. MIPA, in contrast, mitigates the problem of low-frequency bias, and many of the top-ranked words are correct paraphrases. Distributional similarity-based methods include relatively numerous correct paraphrases at the top, and the other top-ranked words are also strongly related to *cultural*. From the viewpoint of paraphrases, 3 of the top 10 words of the proposed method are incorrect, but these words may also be useful for applications such as learning word embeddings (Yu and Dredze, 2014) and semantic textual similarity (Sultan et al., 2015).

Table 2 shows correct examples of the paraphrase rankings. In the paraphrase examples of *labourers*, there were 20 correct paraphrases that received a rating of 3 or higher in manual evaluation. With respect to the conditional paraphrase probability and PMI, it is necessary to consider up to the 400th place to cover all correct paraphrases. However, distributional similarity-based methods have correct paraphrases of higher rank. In particular, MIPA was able to include 10 words of correct paraphrases in the top 20 words; that is, our method can obtain paraphrases with high coverage by using only the highly ranked paraphrases.

$p(e_2 \mid e_1)$		$\log p(e_2 \mid e_1) + \log p(e_1 \mid e_2)$		$2\mathrm{PMI}(e_1, e_2)$		$\cos(e_1, e_2)$		$\cos(e_1, e_2)2\mathrm{PMI}(e_1, e_2)$	
1.	workers	9.	gardeners	10.	workmen	2.	workers	2.	workers
2.	employees	42.	harvesters	11.	wage-earners	8.	people	4.	workmen
9.	farmers	62.	workers	16.	earners	10.	persons	5.	craftsmen
13.	labour	71.	seafarers	19.	workers	11.	farmers	6.	wage-earners
16.	gardeners	73.	unions	21.	craftsmen	15.	craftsmen	9.	persons
17.	people	99.	homeworkers	22.	workforces	26.	wage-earners	12.	employees
28.	workmen	283.	works	26.	employed	27.	workmen	13.	earners
30.	employed	394.	workmen	27.	employees	29.	harvesters	15.	farmers
33.	craftsmen	395.	employees	50.	labour	31.	seafarers	18.	people
59.	harvesters	412.	wage-earners	55.	persons	32.	employees	19.	workforces
80.	work	415.	craftsmen	75.	farmers	42.	gardeners	37.	harvesters
88.	earners	417.	earners	103.	homeworkers	47.	earners	42.	individuals
90.	wage-earners	419.	labour	105.	individuals	55.	workforces	53.	labour
106.	persons	420.	employed	112.	work	57.	individuals	55.	seafarers
109.	individuals	431.	people	135.	people	79.	unions	65.	gardeners
114.	seafarers	433.	farmers	187.	harvesters	103.	labour	88.	employed
115.	unions	446.	workforces	273.	gardeners	140.	homeworkers	100.	homeworkers
131.	workforces	451.	work	317.	seafarers	144.	work	105.	work
166.	homeworkers	453.	persons	456.	unions	170.	employed	149.	unions
401.	works	474.	individuals	469.	works	222.	works	254.	works

Table 2: Correct paraphrase examples of *labourers*.

	$p(e_2 \mid e_1)$	$\log p(e_2 \mid e_1) + \log p(e_1 \mid e_2)$	$2\mathrm{PMI}(e_1, e_2)$	$\cos(e_1, e_2)$	$\cos(e_1, e_2)2\mathrm{PMI}(e_1, e_2)$
STS-2012	**0.539**	0.466	0.383	0.363	0.442
STS-2013	0.489	0.469	0.463	0.483	**0.499**
STS-2014	0.464	0.460	0.471	0.453	**0.475**
STS-2015	0.611	0.655	0.660	0.642	**0.671**
STS-2016	0.444	0.518	**0.550**	0.518	0.542
ALL	0.536	0.543	0.534	0.523	**0.555**

Table 3: Evaluation by Pearson's correlation coefficient in semantic textual similarity task.

5.2 Quantitative Analysis

Next, we applied the acquired paraphrase pairs to the semantic textual similarity task and evaluated the extent to which the acquired paraphrases improve downstream applications. The semantic textual similarity task deals with calculating the semantic similarity between two sentences. In this study, we conducted the evaluation by applying Pearson's correlation coefficient with a five-step manual evaluation using five datasets constructed by SemEval (Agirre et al., 2012, 2013, 2014, 2015, 2016). We applied the acquired paraphrase pairs to the unsupervised method of DLC@CU (Sultan et al., 2015), which achieved excellent results using PPDB in the semantic textual similarity task of SemEval-2015 (Agirre et al., 2015). DLS@CU performs word alignment (Sultan et al., 2014) using PPDB, and calculates sentence similarity according to the ratio of aligned words:

$$sts(s_1, s_2) = \frac{n_a(s_1) + n_a(s_2)}{n(s_1) + n(s_2)} \qquad (12)$$

Here, $n(s)$ indicates the number of words in sentence s and $n_a(s)$ indicates the number of aligned words. Although DLS@CU targets all the paraphrases of PPDB, we used only the top 10 words of the paraphrase score for each target word and compared the performance of the paraphrase scores.

Table 3 shows the experimental results of the semantic textual similarity task. "ALL" is the weighted mean value of the Pearson's correlation coefficient over the five datasets. MIPA achieved the highest performance on three out of the five datasets. In other words, the proposed method extracted paraphrase pairs useful for calculating sentence similarity at the top-rank.

5.3 Reranking PPDB 2.0

Finally, we reranked paraphrase pairs from a publicly available state-of-the-art paraphrase database.[8] PPDB 2.0 (Pavlick et al., 2015) scores paraphrase pairs using supervised learning with

---

[8]http://paraphrase.org/

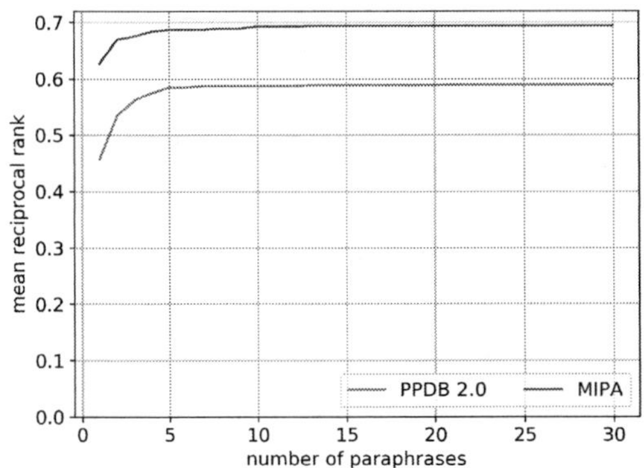

Figure 9: Reranking PPDB 2.0 in MRR.

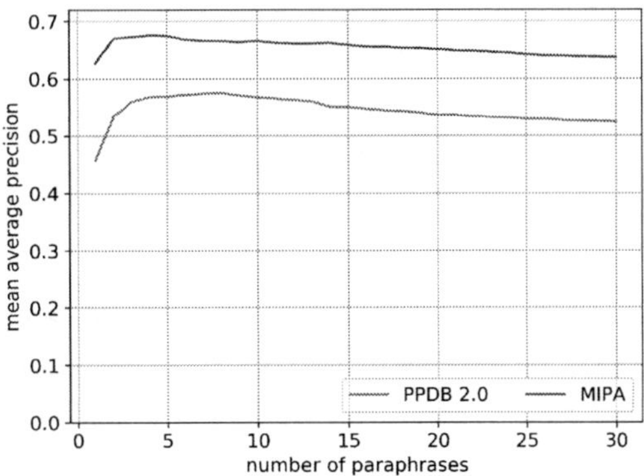

Figure 10: Reranking PPDB 2.0 in MAP.

26,455 labeled data and 209 features. We sorted the paraphrase pairs from PPDB 2.0 using the MIPA instead of the PPDB 2.0 score and used the same evaluation means as described in Section 4. Surprisingly, our unsupervised approach outperformed the paraphrase ranking performance of PPDB 2.0's supervised approach in terms of MRR (Figure 9) and MAP (Figure 10).

6 Related Work

Levy and Goldberg (2014) explained a well-known representation learning method for word embeddings, the skip-gram with negative-sampling (SGNS) (Mikolov et al., 2013a,b), as a matrix factorization of a word-context co-occurrence matrix with shifted positive PMI. In this paper, we explained a well-known method for paraphrase acquisition, bilingual pivoting (Bannard and Callison-Burch, 2005; Ganitkevitch et al., 2013), as a (weighted) PMI.

Chan et al. (2011) reranked paraphrase pairs acquired via bilingual pivoting using distributional similarity. The main idea of reranking paraphrase pairs using information from a monolingual corpus is similar to ours, but Chan et al.'s method failed to acquire semantically similar paraphrases. We succeeded in acquiring semantically similar paraphrases because we effectively combined information from a bilingual corpus and a monolingual corpus by using weighted PMI.

In addition to English, paraphrase databases are constructed in many languages using bilingual pivoting (Bannard and Callison-Burch, 2005). Ganitkevitch and Callison-Burch (2014) constructed paraphrase databases[8] in 23 languages, including European languages and Chinese.

Furthermore, Mizukami et al. (2014) constructed the Japanese version[9]. In this study, we improved bilingual pivoting using a monolingual corpus. Since large-scale monolingual corpora are easily available for many languages, our proposed method may improve paraphrase databases in each of these languages.

PPDB (Ganitkevitch et al., 2013) constructed by bilingual pivoting is used in many NLP applications, such as learning word embeddings (Yu and Dredze, 2014), semantic textual similarity (Sultan et al., 2015), machine translation (Mehdizadeh Seraj et al., 2015), sentence compression (Napoles et al., 2016), question answering (Sultan et al., 2016), and text simplification (Xu et al., 2016). Our proposed method may improve the performance of many of these NLP applications supported by PPDB.

7 Conclusion

We proposed a new approach for formalizing lexical paraphrasability based on weighted PMI and acquired paraphrase pairs using information from both a bilingual corpus and a monolingual corpus. Our proposed method, MIPA, uses bilingual pivoting weighted by distributional similarity to acquire paraphrase pairs robustly, as each of the methods complements the other. Experimental results using manually annotated datasets for lexical paraphrase showed that the proposed method outperformed bilingual pivoting and distributional similarity in terms of metrics such as MRR, MAP, coverage, and Spearman's correlation. We also confirmed the effectiveness of the proposed method

---

[9]http://ahclab.naist.jp/resource/jppdb/

by conducting an extrinsic evaluation on a semantic textual similarity task. In addition to the semantic textual similarity task, we hope to improve the performance of many NLP applications based on the results of this study.

Acknowledgements

This research was (partly) supported by Grant-in-Aid for Research on Priority Areas, Tokyo Metropolitan University, "Research on social big-data."

References

Eneko Agirre, Carmen Banea, Claire Cardie, Daniel Cer, Mona Diab, Aitor Gonzalez-Agirre, Weiwei Guo, Inigo Lopez-Gazpio, Montse Maritxalar, Rada Mihalcea, German Rigau, Larraitz Uria, and Janyce Wiebe. 2015. SemEval-2015 Task 2: Semantic Textual Similarity, English, Spanish and Pilot on Interpretability. In *Proceedings of the 9th International Workshop on Semantic Evaluation*. pages 252–263.

Eneko Agirre, Carmen Banea, Claire Cardie, Daniel Cer, Mona Diab, Aitor Gonzalez-Agirre, Weiwei Guo, Rada Mihalcea, German Rigau, and Janyce Wiebe. 2014. SemEval-2014 Task 10: Multilingual Semantic Textual Similarity. In *Proceedings of the 8th International Workshop on Semantic Evaluation*. pages 81–91.

Eneko Agirre, Carmen Banea, Daniel Cer, Mona Diab, Aitor Gonzalez-Agirre, Rada Mihalcea, German Rigau, and Janyce Wiebe. 2016. SemEval-2016 Task 1: Semantic Textual Similarity, Monolingual and Cross-Lingual Evaluation. In *Proceedings of the 10th International Workshop on Semantic Evaluation*. pages 497–511.

Eneko Agirre, Daniel Cer, Mona Diab, and Aitor Gonzalez-Agirre. 2012. SemEval-2012 Task 6: A Pilot on Semantic Textual Similarity. In **SEM 2012: The First Joint Conference on Lexical and Computational Semantics*. pages 385–393.

Eneko Agirre, Daniel Cer, Mona Diab, Aitor Gonzalez-Agirre, and Weiwei Guo. 2013. *SEM 2013 shared task: Semantic Textual Similarity. In *Second Joint Conference on Lexical and Computational Semantics*. pages 32–43.

Colin Bannard and Chris Callison-Burch. 2005. Paraphrasing with Bilingual Parallel Corpora. In *Proceedings of the 43rd Annual Meeting of the Association for Computational Linguistics*. pages 597–604.

Tsz Ping Chan, Chris Callison-Burch, and Benjamin Van Durme. 2011. Reranking Bilingually Extracted Paraphrases Using Monolingual Distributional Similarity. In *Proceedings of the GEMS 2011 Workshop on GEometrical Models of Natural Language Semantics*. pages 33–42.

Stefan Evert. 2005. *The Statistics of Word Cooccurrences: Word Pairs and Collocations*. Ph.D. thesis, University of Stuttgart.

Juri Ganitkevitch and Chris Callison-Burch. 2014. The Multilingual Paraphrase Database. In *Proceedings of the Ninth International Conference on Language Resources and Evaluation*. pages 4276–4283.

Juri Ganitkevitch, Benjamin Van Durme, and Chris Callison-Burch. 2013. PPDB: The Paraphrase Database. In *Proceedings of the 2013 Conference of the North American Chapter of the Association for Computational Linguistics: Human Language Technologies*. pages 758–764.

Goran Glavaš and Sanja Štajner. 2015. Simplifying Lexical Simplification: Do We Need Simplified Corpora? In *Proceedings of the 53rd Annual Meeting of the Association for Computational Linguistics and the 7th International Joint Conference on Natural Language Processing*. pages 63–68.

Kenneth Heafield. 2011. KenLM: Faster and Smaller Language Model Queries. In *Proceedings of the Sixth Workshop on Statistical Machine Translation*. pages 187–197.

Geoffrey E. Hinton. 2002. Training Products of Experts by Minimizing Contrastive Divergence. *Neural Computation* 14(8):1771–1800.

Reinhard Kneser and Hermann Ney. 1995. Improved Backing-off for M-gram Language Modeling. In *Proceedings of the IEEE International Conference on Acoustics, Speech and Signal Processing*. volume 1, pages 181–184.

Philipp Koehn. 2005. Europarl: A Parallel Corpus for Statistical Machine Translation. In *Proceedings of the Machine Translation Summit*. pages 79–86.

Omer Levy and Yoav Goldberg. 2014. Neural Word Embedding as Implicit Matrix Factorization. In *Advances in Neural Information Processing Systems*. pages 2177–2185.

Ramtin Mehdizadeh Seraj, Maryam Siahbani, and Anoop Sarkar. 2015. Improving Statistical Machine Translation with a Multilingual Paraphrase Database. In *Proceedings of the 2015 Conference on Empirical Methods in Natural Language Processing*. pages 1379–1390.

Tomas Mikolov, Kai Chen, Greg S Corrado, and Jeff Dean. 2013a. Efficient Estimation of Word Representations in Vector Space. In *Proceedings of Workshop at the International Conference on Learning Representations*. pages 1–12.

Tomas Mikolov, Ilya Sutskever, Kai Chen, Greg S Corrado, and Jeff Dean. 2013b. Distributed Representations of Words and Phrases and Their Compositionality. In *Advances in Neural Information Processing Systems*. pages 3111–3119.

Masahiro Mizukami, Graham Neubig, Sakriani Sakti, Tomoki Toda, and Satoshi Nakamura. 2014. Building a Free, General-Domain Paraphrase Database for Japanese. In *Proceedings of the 17th Oriental COCOSDA Conference*. pages 129 – 133.

Saif M. Mohammad, Bonnie J. Dorr, Graeme Hirst, and Peter D. Turney. 2013. Computing Lexical Contrast. *Computational Linguistics* 39(3):555–590.

Courtney Napoles, Chris Callison-Burch, and Matt Post. 2016. Sentential Paraphrasing as Black-Box Machine Translation. In *Proceedings of the 2016 Conference of the North American Chapter of the Association for Computational Linguistics*. pages 62–66.

Franz Josef Och and Hermann Ney. 2003. A Systematic Comparison of Various Statistical Alignment Models. *Computational Linguistics* 29(1):19–51.

Ellie Pavlick, Pushpendre Rastogi, Juri Ganitkevitch, Benjamin Van Durme, and Chris Callison-Burch. 2015. PPDB 2.0: Better paraphrase ranking, fine-grained entailment relations, word embeddings, and style classification. In *Proceedings of the 53rd Annual Meeting of the Association for Computational Linguistics and the 7th International Joint Conference on Natural Language Processing*. pages 425–430.

Md Arafat Sultan, Steven Bethard, and Tamara Sumner. 2014. Back to Basics for Monolingual Alignment: Exploiting Word Similarity and Contextual Evidence. *Transactions of the Association for Computational Linguistics* 2:219–230.

Md Arafat Sultan, Steven Bethard, and Tamara Sumner. 2015. DLS@CU: Sentence Similarity from Word Alignment and Semantic Vector Composition. In *Proceedings of the 9th International Workshop on Semantic Evaluation*. pages 148–153.

Md Arafat Sultan, Vittorio Castelli, and Radu Florian. 2016. A Joint Model for Answer Sentence Ranking and Answer Extraction. *Transactions of the Association for Computational Linguistics* 4:113–125.

Wei Xu, Courtney Napoles, Ellie Pavlick, Quanze Chen, and Chris Callison-Burch. 2016. Optimizing Statistical Machine Translation for Text Simplification. *Transactions of the Association for Computational Linguistics* 4:401–415.

Mo Yu and Mark Dredze. 2014. Improving Lexical Embeddings with Semantic Knowledge. In *Proceedings of the 52nd Annual Meeting of the Association for Computational Linguistics*. pages 545–550.

Improving Implicit Semantic Role Labeling
by Predicting Semantic Frame Arguments

Quynh Ngoc Thi Do[1], Steven Bethard[2], Marie-Francine Moens[1]
[1]Katholieke Universiteit Leuven, Belgium
[2]University of Arizona, United States
quynhngocthi.do@cs.kuleuven.be
bethard@email.arizona.edu
sien.moens@cs.kuleuven.be

Abstract

Implicit semantic role labeling (iSRL) is
the task of predicting the semantic roles of
a predicate that do not appear as explicit arguments, but rather regard common sense
knowledge or are mentioned earlier in the
discourse. We introduce an approach to
iSRL based on a predictive recurrent neural semantic frame model (PRNSFM) that
uses a large unannotated corpus to learn
the probability of a sequence of semantic
arguments given a predicate. We leverage the sequence probabilities predicted
by the PRNSFM to estimate selectional
preferences for predicates and their arguments. On the NomBank iSRL test set, our
approach improves state-of-the-art performance on implicit semantic role labeling
with less reliance than prior work on manually constructed language resources.

1 Introduction

Semantic role labeling (SRL) has traditionally focused on semantic frames consisting of verbal or
nominal predicates and *explicit arguments* that occur *within* the clause or sentence that contains the
predicate. However, many predicates, especially
nominal ones, may bear arguments that are left
implicit because they regard common sense knowledge or because they are mentioned earlier in a
discourse (Ruppenhofer et al., 2010; Gerber et al.,
2009). These arguments, called *implicit arguments*,
are resolved by another semantic task, implicit semantic role labeling (iSRL). Consider a NomBank
(Meyers et al., 2004) annotation example:

> [*A0* The network] had been expected to
> have [*NP* losses] [*A1* of \$20 million]
> ... Those [*NP* losses] may widen because
> of the short Series.

The predicate *loss* in the first sentence has two arguments annotated explicitly: A0, *the entity losing
something*, and A1, *the thing lost*. Meanwhile, the
other instance of the same predicate in the second
sentence has no associated arguments. However,
for a good reader, a reasonable interpretation of the
second *loss* should be that it receives the same A0
and A1 as the first instance. These arguments are
implicit to the second *loss*.

As an emerging task, implicit semantic role labeling faces a lack of resources. First, hand-crafted
implicit role annotations for use as training data are
seriously limited: SemEval 2010 Task 10 (Baker
et al., 1998) provided FrameNet-style (Baker et al.,
1998) annotations for a fairly large number of predicates but with few annotations per predicate, while
Gerber and Chai (2010) provided PropBank-style
(Palmer et al., 2005) data with many more annotations per predicate but covering just 10 predicates. Second, most existing iSRL systems depend
on other systems (explicit semantic role labelers,
named entity taggers, lexical resources, etc.), and
as a result not only need iSRL annotations to train
the iSRL system, but annotations or manually built
resources for all of their sub-systems as well.

We propose an iSRL approach that addresses
these challenges, requiring no manually annotated
iSRL data and only a single sub-system, an explicit
semantic role labeler. We introduce a predictive
recurrent neural semantic frame model (PRNSFM),
which can estimate the probability of a sequence
of semantic arguments given a predicate, and can
be trained on unannotated data drawn from the
Wikipedia, Reuters, and Brown corpora, coupled
with the predictions of the MATE (Björkelund et al.,
2010) explicit semantic role labeler on these texts.
The PRNSFM forms the foundation for our iSRL
system, where we use its probability estimates over
sequences of semantic arguments to predict *selectional preferences* for associating predicates with

Proceedings of the The 8th International Joint Conference on Natural Language Processing, pages 90–99,
Taipei, Taiwan, November 27 – December 1, 2017 ©2017 AFNLP

their implicit semantic roles. Our PRNSFM-based iSRL model improves state-of-the-art performance, outperforming the only other system that depends on just an explicit semantic role labeler by 10 % F1, and achieving equal or better F1 score than several other models that require many more lexical resources.

Our work fits today's interest in natural language understanding, which is hampered by the fact that content in a discourse is often not expressed explicitly because it was mentioned earlier or because it regards common sense or world knowledge that resides in the mind of the communicator or the audience. In contrast, humans easily combine relevant evidence to infer meaning, determine hidden meanings and make explicit what was left implicit in the text, using the *anticipatory power* of the brain that predicts or "imagines" circumstantial situations and outcomes of actions (Friston, 2010; Vernon, 2014) which makes language processing extremely effective and fast (Kurby and Zacks, 2015; Schacter and Madore, 2016). The neural semantic frame representations inferred by our PRNSFM take a first step towards encoding something like anticipatory power for natural language understanding systems.

The remainder of the paper is organized as follows: First, section 2 describes the related work. Second, section 3 proposes the predictive recurrent neural semantic frame model including the formal definition, architecture, and an algorithm to extract selectional preferences from the trained model. Third, in section 4, we introduce the application of our PRNSFM in implicit semantic role labeling. Fourth, the experimental results and discussions are presented in section 5. Finally, we conclude our work and suggest some future work in section 6.

2   Related work

Language Modeling   Language models, from n-gram models to continuous space language models (Mikolov et al., 2013; Pennington et al., 2014), provide probability distributions over sequences of words and have shown their usefulness in many natural language processing tasks. However, to our knowledge, they have not yet been used to model semantic frames. Recently, Peng and Roth (2016) developed two distinct models that capture semantic frame chains and discourse information while abstracting over the specific mentions of predicates and entities, but these models focus on discourse processing tasks, not semantic frame processing.

Semantic Role Labeling   In unsupervised SRL, Woodsend and Lapata (2015) and Titov and Khoddam (2015) induce embeddings to represent a predicate and its arguments from unannotated texts, but in their approaches, the arguments are words only, not the semantic role labels, while in our models, both are considered.

Low-resource Implicit Semantic Role Labeling Several approaches have attempted to address the lack of resources for training iSRL systems. Laparra and Rigau (2013) proposed an approach based on exploiting argument coherence over different instances of a predicate, which did not require any manual iSRL annotations but did require many other manually-constructed resources: an explicit SRL system, WordNet super-senses, a named entity tagger, and a manual categorization of Super-SenseTagger semantic classes. Roth and Frank (2015) generated additional training data for iSRL through comparable texts, but the resulting model performed below the previous state-of-the-art of Laparra and Rigau (2013). Schenk and Chiarcos (2016) proposed an approach to induce prototypical roles using distributed word representations, which required only an explicit SRL system and a large unannotated corpus, but their model performance was almost 10 points lower than the state-of-the-art of Laparra and Rigau (2013). Similar to Schenk and Chiarcos (2016), our model requires only an explicit SRL system and a large unannotated corpus, but we take a very different approach to leveraging these, and as a result improve state-of-the-art performance.

3   Predictive Recurrent Neural Semantic Frame Model

Our goal is to use unlabeled data to acquire selectional preferences that characterize how likely a phrase is to be an argument of a semantic frame. We rely on the fact that current explicit SRL systems achieve high performance on verbal predicates, and run a state-of-the-art explicit SRL system on unlabeled data. We then construct a predictive recurrent neural semantic frame model (PRNSFM) from these explicit frames and roles.

Our PRNSFM views semantic frames as a *sequence*: a predicate, followed by the arguments in their textual order, and terminated by a special EOS symbol. We draw predicates from PropBank verbal semantic frames, and represent arguments with their nominal/pronominal heads. For example, *Michael Phelps swam at the Olympics* is represented as [*swam*:PRED, *Phelps*:A0, *Olympics*:AM-LOC, EOS], where the predicate is labeled PRED and the arguments *Phelps* and *Olympics* are labeled A0 and AM-LOC, respectively. Our PRNSFM's task is thus to take a predicate and zero or more arguments, and predict the next argument in the sequence, or EOS if no more arguments will follow.

We choose to model semantic frames as a sequence (rather than, say, a bag of arguments) because in English, there are often fairly strict constraints on the order in which arguments of a verb may appear. A sequential model should thus be able to capture these constraints and use them to improve its probability estimates. Moreover, a sequential model has the ability to learn the interaction between arguments in the same semantic frame. For example, considering a swimming event, if *Phelps* is A0, then *Olympics* is more likely to be the AM-LOC than *lake*.

Formally, for each tth argument of a semantic frame f, we denote its word (e.g., *Phelps*) as $w_{f,t}$, its semantic label (e.g., A0) as $l_{f,t}$, where $w \in \mathbf{V}$, the word vocabulary, and $l \in \mathbf{L} \cup [\text{PRED}]$, the set of semantic labels. We denote the predicate word and label, which are always at the 0th position in the sequence, in the same way as arguments: $w_{f,0}$ and $l_{f,0}$. We denote the sequence $[w_{f,0}, w_{f,1}, \ldots, w_{f,t-1}]$ as $w_{f,<t}$, and the sequence $[l_{f,0}, l_{f,1}, \ldots, l_{f,t-1}]$ as $l_{f,<t}$. Our model aims to estimate the conditional probability of the occurrence of $w_{f,t}$ as semantic role $l_{f,t}$ given the preceding words and their labels:

$$P(w_{f,t}{:}l_{f,t}|w_{f,<t}{:}l_{f,<t})$$

We use a recurrent neural network to learn this probability distribution over sequences of semantic frame arguments. For a semantic frame f with N arguments, at each time step $0 \leq t \leq N$, given the input $w_{f,t}{:}l_{f,t}$, the model computes the distribution $P(w_{f,t+1}{:}l_{f,t+1}|w_{f,<t+1}{:}l_{f,<t+1})$ and predicts the next most likely argument (or EOS). During training, model parameters are optimized by minimizing prediction errors over all time steps.

We consider two versions of this model that differ in input ($\mathbf{V_{in}}$) and output ($\mathbf{V_{out}}$) vocabularies.

3.1 Model 1: Joint Embedding LSTM

We adopt the standard recurrent neural network language model (Mikolov et al., 2010), which is a natural architecture to deal with a sequence prediction problem.

Model 1 consists of three layers (see Figure 1): an embedding layer that learns vector representations for input values; a long short-term memory (LSTM) layer that controls the sequential information receiving the vector representation as input; and a softmax layer to predict the next argument using the output of the LSTM layer as input.

This model treats the word and semantic label as a single unit in both input and output layers. The model, therefore, learns joint embeddings for the word and its corresponding semantic label. For example, if we take "Michael Phelps swam at the Olympics" as training data, the three input values would be *swam*:PRED, *Phelps*:A0 and *Olympics*:AM-LOC, and the three expected outputs would be *Phelps*:A0, *Olympics*:AM-LOC, EOS. Since each word:label is considered as a single unit, the embedding layer will learn three vector representations, one for *swam*:PRED, one for *Phelps*:A0, and one for *Olympics*:AM-LOC. As can be seen, an important difference between our problem and the traditional language model is that we have to deal with two different types of information – word and label. By concatenating word and label, the standard recurrent neural network model can be applied directly to our data.

The detail of Model 1 is as following:

Embedding Layer is a matrix of size $|\mathbf{V_{in}}| \times d$ that maps each unit of input into an d-dimensional vector. The matrix is initialized randomly and updated during network training.

LSTM Layer consists of m standard LSTM units which take as input the output of the embedding layer, x_t, and produce an output h_t by updating at every time step $0 \leq t \leq T$:

$$i_t = sigmoid(W_i x_t + U_i h_{t-1} + b_i)$$
$$\hat{C}_t = tanh(W_c x_t + U_c h_{t-1} + b_c)$$
$$f_t = sigmoid(W_f x_t + U_f h_{t-1} + b_f)$$
$$C_t = i_t * \hat{C}_t + f_t * C_{t-1}$$
$$o_t = sigmoid(W_o x_t + U_o h_{t-1} + b_o)$$
$$h_t = o_t * tanh(C_t)$$

where W_i, W_c, W_f, W_o are weight matrices of size $d \times m$; U_i, U_c, U_f, U_o are weight matrices of size $m \times m$; b_i, b_c, b_f, b_o are bias vectors of size m; and $*$ is element-wise multiplication. As per the standard LSTM formulation, $i_t, \hat{C}_t, f_t, C_t, o_t$ represent

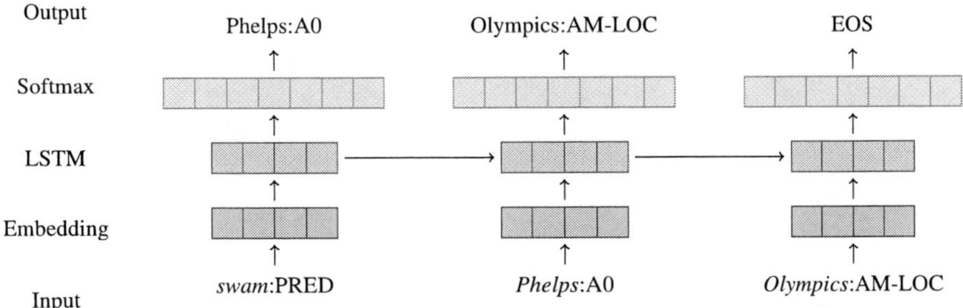

Figure 1: Model 1 – Joint Embedding LSTM

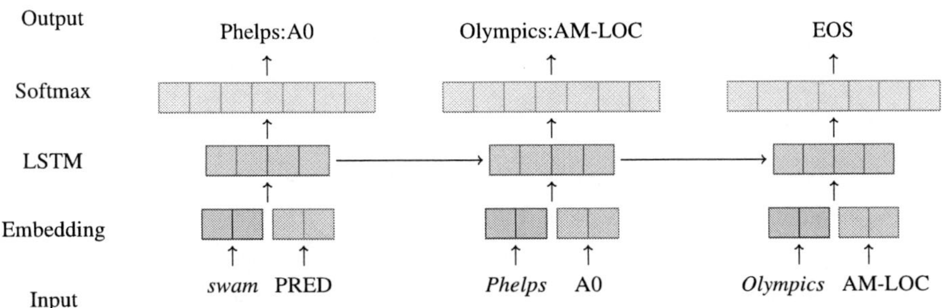

Figure 2: Model 2 – Separate Embedding LSTM

the input gate, states of the memory cells, activation of the memory cells' forget gates, memory cells' new state, and output gates' values, respectively.

Softmax Layer computes the probability distribution of the next argument given the preceding arguments at time step t:

$$P(w_{f,t+1}{:}l_{f,t+1}|w_{f,<t+1}{:}l_{f,<t+1}) =$$
$$softmax(h_t W + b) \quad (1)$$

where W is a weight matrix of size $m \times |\mathbf{V_{out}}|$, and b is a bias vector of size $|\mathbf{V_{out}}|$. The predicted next argument is:

$$\underset{w_{f,t+1}{:}l_{f,t+1}}{\operatorname{argmax}} \quad P(w_{f,t+1}{:}l_{f,t+1}|w_{f,<t+1}{:}l_{f,<t+1})$$

The network is trained using the negative log-likelihood loss function.

3.2 Model 2: Separate Embedding LSTM

Model 2 shares the same basic structure as Model 1, but considers the word and the semantic label as two different units in the input layer. As shown in Figure 2, we use two different embedding layers, one for word values and one for semantic labels, and the two embedding vectors are concatenated before being passed to the LSTM layer. The LSTM

and softmax layers are then the same as in Model 1. For example, if we take "Michael Phelps swam at the Olympics" as training data, the three input words would be *swam*, *Phelps*, and *Olympics*, the three input roles would be PRED, A0 and AM-LOC, and the three expected outputs would be *Phelps*:A0, *Olympics*:AM-LOC, EOS. A total of six different vector representations will be learned: a word embedding for each of *swam*, *Phelps*, and *Olympics*, and a label embedding for each of PRED, A0 and AM-LOC.

In this model, the embedding layer for labels is initialized randomly (as in Model 1), but the embedding layer for word values is initialized with publicly available word embeddings that have been trained on a large dataset (Mikolov et al., 2013).

As compared to the joint-embedding Model 1, the separate-embedding Model 2 gives up a little power to represent the interaction between words and labels, but has a less sparse input vocabulary and gains the ability to incorporate pre-trained word embeddings.

3.3 Selectional Preferences

While the PRNSFM can predict the probability of an argument given the predicate and the preceding arguments, $P(w_{f,t}{:}l_{f,t}|w_{f,<t}{:}l_{f,<t})$, an iSRL

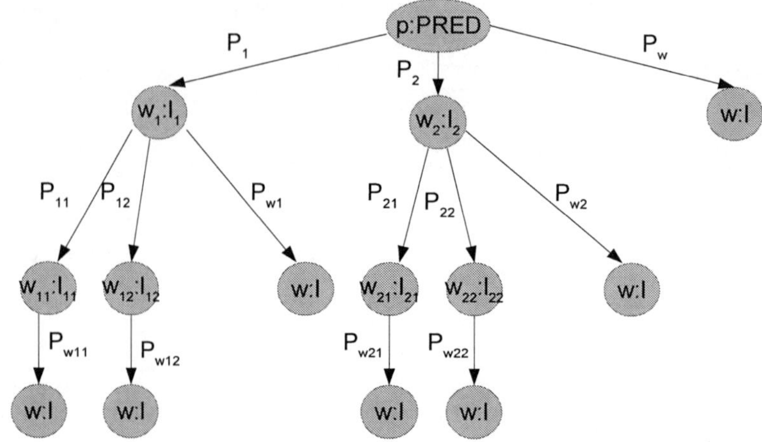

Time 0: S_0 = [[p:PRED]]

Time 1: S_1 = [[p:PRED,w_1:l_1], [p:PRED,w_2:l_2]]

Time 2: S_2 = [[p:PRED,w_1:l_1,w_{11}:l_{11}], [[p:PRED,w_1:l_1,w_{12}:l_{12}], [p:PRED,w_2:l_2,w_{21}:l_{21}], [p:PRED,w_2:l_2,w_{22}:l_{22}]]

$P(w{:}l|p) \sim P_w + P_{w1}P_1 + P_{w2}P_2 + P_{w11}P_{11}P_1 + P_{w12}P_{12}P_1 + P_{w21}P_{21}P_2 + P_{w22}P_{22}P_2$

Figure 3: Selectional Preference Inference example: k=2, T=3. The possible sequences are represented as a tree. Each arrow label is the probability of the target node to be predicted given the path from the tree root to the parent of the target node.

system needs a *selectional preference* score representing the probability of a word w being the l argument of predicate p, $P(w{:}l|p{:}PRED)$. Thus, to convert our PRNSFM probabilities to selectional preferences, we need to marginalize over the possible argument sequences.

We approximate this marginalization by constructing a tree where the root is the predicate, p, the branches are likely sequences of arguments, and the leaves are the word and label for which we need to estimate a probability, $w{:}l$. Formally, we define this tree of possible sequences as:

$$\mathbf{S_t} = \begin{cases} \{[p{:}PRED]\} & \text{if } t = 0 \\ \{[q, w_t{:}l_t]: q \in \mathbf{S_{t-1}}, & \text{if } 0 < t < T \\ \quad w_t{:}l_t \in \mathbf{argmax}^k(q)\} \\ \{[q, w{:}l]: q \in \mathbf{S_{t-1}}\} & \text{if } t = T \end{cases}$$

where $w_{f,0}{:}l_{f:0} = p{:}PRED$; k and T are thresholds; and $\mathbf{argmax}^k(q)$ is the k word:label pairs that have the highest probability of being the next argument given the sequence q according to the PRNSFM.

We then estimate $P(w{:}l|p{:}PRED)$ as the sum of the probabilities of all the sequences encoded in the tree. Formally:

$$P(w{:}l|p{:}PRED) \approx \sum_{0 \leq t \leq T} P(w{:}l|w_{f,<t+1}{:}l_{f,<t+1})$$

$$\approx \sum_{0 \leq t \leq T} \sum_{q \in \mathbf{S_t}} P(w{:}l|q) \times P(q)$$

where the probability of an argument sequence q is the product of the PRNSFM's estimates for each step in the sequence:

$$P(q) = P(w_t{:}l_t|w_{t-1}{:}l_{t-1}, \dots, p{:}PRED)$$
$$\times\ P(w_{t-1}{:}l_{t-1}|w_{t-2}{:}l_{t-2}, \dots, p{:}PRED)$$
$$\times\ \dots \times P(w_1{:}l_1|p{:}PRED) \quad (2)$$

An example of the calculation of $P(w{:}l|p{:}PRED)$ is shown in Figure 3.

Intuitively, the tree enumerates all possible argument sequences that start with the predicate, have zero or more intervening arguments, and end with the word and label of interest, $w{:}l$. The probability of $w{:}l$ given the predicate is the sum of the probabilities of all branches in this tree, i.e., of all possible sequences that end with $w{:}l$. In reality, we do not have the computational power to explore all possible sequences, so we must limit the tree somehow. Thus, we only ask the PRNSFM for its top k predictions at each branch point, and we only explore sequences with a maximum length of T.

4 Implicit Semantic Role Labeling

As you will recall from previous sections, implicit semantic role labeling is the task of identifying discourse-level arguments of a semantic frame, which are missed by standard semantic role labeling, which operates on individual sentences. For instance, in "This house has a new owner. The sale was finalized 10 days ago.", the semantic frame evoked by "sale" in the second sentence should receive "the house" as an implicit A1 semantic role. Humans easily resolve the object of the sale given the candidates (in our example: "house" and "owner"), but for a machine this is more difficult unless it has knowledge on what the likely objects of a sale are. This kind of knowledge of selectional preferences can be extracted from our trained PRNSFM.

The previous section described how to extract selectional preferences from our PRNSFM. However, that model is trained on verbal predicates, and the test data that we use (Gerber and Chai, 2010) contains nominal predicates. Thus, for each triple of a nominal predicate np, a word candidate w, and a label l, we approximate the selectional preference score of w being the implicit argument role l of np as:

$$P(w{:}l|np) = max_{p \in V(np)} P(w{:}l|p{:}\text{PRED})$$

where $P(w{:}l|p)$ is the selectional preference score described in Section 3.3, and $V(np)$ is set of verbal forms of np. Here, we use the NomBank lexicon to get verbs associated with each nominal predicate, and then find instances of those verbs in the explicit SRL training data. For example, for the noun *funds*, $V(funds) = \{funds, fund, funding, funded\}$.

We apply selectional preferences to iSRL following (Laparra and Rigau, 2013). For each nominal predicate np and implicit label l, the current and previous two sentences are designated the *context window*. Each sentence in the context window is annotated with the explicit SRL system. If any instances of np or $V(np)$ in the text have an explicit argument of type l, we deterministically predict the closest such argument as the implicit l argument of np. Otherwise, we run the PRNSFM over each word in the context window, and select the

word with the highest selectional preference score above a threshold s. If all the candidates' scores are less than s, the system leaves the missing argument unfilled. We optimized this threshold on the development data, resulting in $s = 0.0003$.

As in Laparra and Rigau (2013), we apply a *sentence recency factor* to emphasize recent candidates. The selectional preference score x is updated as $x' = x - z + z \times \alpha^d$ where d is the sentence distance, and α and z are parameters. We set $z = 0.00005$ based on the development set and set $\alpha = 0.5$ as in (Laparra and Rigau, 2013).

5 Experiments

We evaluate the two PRNSFM models on the iSRL task. The tools, resources, and settings we used are as follows:

Semantic Role Labeling We used the full pipeline from MATE (https://code.google.com/archive/p/mate-tools/) (Björkelund et al., 2010) as the explicit SRL system, retraining it on just the CoNLL 2009 training portion.

Unannotated Data The unannotated data used in the experiments was drawn from Wikipedia (http://corpus.byu.edu/wiki/), Reuters (http://about.reuters.com/researchandstandards/corpus/), and Brown (https://catalog.ldc.upenn.edu/ldc99t42).

Dataset for PRNSFM The first 15 milion short and medium (less than 100 words) sentences from the unannotated data (described above) were annotated automatically by the explicit SRL system. The obtained annotations were then used together with the gold standard CoNLL 2009 SRL training data to train the PRNSFM.

Neural network training and inference Parameters were selected using the CoNLL 2009 development set. We set the dimensions of word and label embeddings in the PRNSFM to 50 and 16, respectively. The hidden sizes of LSTM layers are the same as their input sizes. Word embedding layers are initialized by Skip-gram embeddings learned by training the word2vec tool (Mikolov et al., 2013) on the unannotated data. Our models were trained for 120 epochs using the AdaDelta optimization algorithm (Zeiler, 2012). For fast selectional preference computing, we set $k = 1$ and $T = 4^1$.

---

[1]We selected relatively small values for the parameters to reduce the training and prediction time. We tried some larger values of the parameters on a small dataset, but found that the

Evaluation We follow the evaluation setting in Gerber and Chai (2010); Laparra and Rigau (2013); Schenk and Chiarcos (2016)[2]: the method is evaluated on the evaluation portion of the nominal iSRL data by Dice coefficient metrics. For each missing argument position of a predicate instance, the system is required to either (1) identify a single constituent that fills the missing argument position or (2) make no prediction and leave the missing argument position unfilled. To give partial credit for inexact argument boundaries, predictions are scored by using the Dice coefficient, which is defined as follows:

$$Dice(predicted, true) = \frac{2\,|predicted \cap true|}{|predicted| + |true|}$$

Predicted contains the tokens that the model has identified as the filler of the implicit argument position. *True* is the set of tokens from a single annotated constituent that truely fill the missing argument position. The model's prediction receives a score equal to the maximum Dice overlap across any of the annotated fillers (AF)[3]:

$$Score(predicted) = \max_{true \in AF} Dice(predicted, true)$$

Precision is equal to the summed prediction scores divided by the number of argument positions filled by the model. Recall is equal to the summed prediction scores divided by the number of argument positions filled in the annotated data.

5.1 Experimental Setup

In the **baseline mode**, instead of using the PRNSFM, we only use the deterministic prediction by the explicit SRL system. We refer to this mode as *Baseline* in Table 1.

In the **main mode**, the joint embedding LSTM model (Model 1) and the separate embedding LSTM model (Model 2) were trained on the same dataset which is a combination of the automatic SRL annotations and the gold standard CoNLL

2009 training data as described in the previous section. We denote this mode as *gold CoNLL 2009 + unlabeled* in Table 1.

To evaluate how well the system acquires knowledge from unlabeled data, we also train the PRNSFM only on the gold standard CoNLL 2009 training data. We denote this mode as *CoNLL 2009* in Table 1.

In order to compare the performance of our sequential model to a non-sequential model, we train a skip-gram neural language model on the same unlabeled and labeled data as the PRNSFM in the main mode. The skip-gram model treats the predicates and arguments as a bag of labeled words rather than a sequence. The $P(w{:}l|p)$ is computed at the output layer of the skip-gram model by considering $w{:}l$ as the context of p. We denote this mode as *Skip-gram* in Table 1.

5.2 Results and Discussion

Table 1 shows the prior state-of-the-art and the performance of the baseline, skip-gram and our PRNSFM-based methods.

Our Model 2 achieves the highest precision and F1 score. This is notable because the first two models require many more language resources than just an explicit SRL system: Gerber and Chai (2010) use WordNet and manually annotated iSRL data, while Laparra and Rigau (2013) use WordNet, named entity annotations, and manual semantic category mappings. Schenk and Chiarcos (2016), like our approach, use only an explicit SRL system, but both our models strongly outperform their results. We assume that the difference here is caused by our proposed neural semantic frame model (PRNSFM). Schenk and Chiarcos (2016) measure the selectional preference of a predicate and a role as a cosine between a standard word2vec embedding for the candidate word, and the average of all word2vec embeddings for all words that appear in that role. Our algorithms are very different: we take a language modeling approach and leverage the sequence of semantic roles, we learn custom word/role embeddings tuned for SRL, and then marginalize over many possible argument sequences. We assume that the learned PRNSFM representations are better informed about semantic frames than simple word embeddings, which only capture knowledge of contextual words.

Table 1 also shows that training on large unlabeled data results in a marked improvement com-

---

small values reported in the article achieved similar results with faster processing times.

[2] Following Schenk and Chiarcos (2016), we do not perform the alternative evaluation of Gerber and Chai (2012) that evaluates systems on the iSRL training set, since the iSRL training set overlaps with the CoNLL 2009 explicit semantic role training set on which MATE is trained.

[3] For iSRL, one implicit role may receive more than one annotated filler across a coreference chain in the discourse.

Method	PRNSFM training data	iSRL data	SRL system	WordNet	NER system	P	R	F1
Gerber and Chai (2010)		✓	✓	✓		44.5	40.4	42.3
Laparra and Rigau (2013)			✓	✓	✓	47.9	43.8	45.8
Schenk and Chiarcos (2016)			✓			33.5	39.2	36.1
Baseline			✓			75.3	17.2	28.0
Skip-gram	gold CoNLL 2009 + unlabeled		✓			26.3	32.3	29.0
Model 1: Joint Embedding	gold CoNLL 2009 + unlabeled		✓			48.0	38.2	42.6
Model 2: Separate Embedding	gold CoNLL 2009 + unlabeled		✓			52.6	41.0	**46.1**
Model 1: Joint Embedding	gold CoNLL 2009		✓			39.2	34.1	36.5
Model 2: Separate Embedding	gold CoNLL 2009		✓			40.2	36.0	38.0

Table 1: Implicit role labeling evaluation.

pared to training on only the CoNLL 2009 labeled data, providing evidence that the models have acquired linguistic knowledge from the unlabeled data. Although the automatically annotated data used to train the PRNSFM can be noisy, using a large amount of data has smoothed out the noise.

Moreover, the better performance of our models over the standard skip-gram neural language model proves the effectiveness of modeling semantic frames as sequential data. The intuition here is that explicit semantic arguments have typical orderings in which they occur, so a sequential model should be a good fit for this problem. Modeling this sequential aspect of the problem is effective, but requires us to marginalize out positional information to compute selectional preferences, since implicit semantic arguments can occur anywhere in the discourse and do not have a typical position.

Among our two models, Model 2, which learns separate vector representations for words and semantic roles, is better than Model 1, which learns a single vector representation of each (word, semantic role) pair. The separate representation of words and roles means that Model 2 can share information across multiple occurrences of a word even if the semantic roles of that word are different, and this model can use publicly available embeddings pre-trained from even larger unannotated corpora when initializing its embeddings.

Gerber and Chai (2012) report an inter-annotator agreement of 64.3% using Cohen's kappa measure on the annotated NomBank-based iSRL data. This value is borderline between low and moderate agreement indicating the sheer complexity of the

Predicate	Baseline	2010	2013	2016	2017
sale	36.2	44.2	40.3	37.2	**52.8**
price	15.4	34.2	**53.3**	27.3	29.0
investor	9.8	38.4	41.2	33.9	**43.1**
bid	32.3	21.3	**52.0**	40.7	35.5
plan	38.5	64.7	40.7	47.4	**76.8**
cost	34.8	**62.9**	53.0	36.9	44.4
loss	52.6	**83.3**	65.8	58.9	72.8
loan	18.2	37.5	22.2	37.9	**38.6**
investment	0.0	30.8	**40.8**	36.6	23.5
fund	0.0	15.4	**44.4**	37.5	42.8

Table 2: A comparison on F1 scores (%). 2010: (Gerber and Chai, 2010), 2013: (Laparra and Rigau, 2013), 2016: Best model from (Schenk and Chiarcos, 2016), 2017: Our best model (Model 2).

annotation task, and explaining the relatively low performance of the iSRL systems.

In Table 2, we compare the F1 scores over all the ten predicates of our Model 2 to other state-of-the-art systems [4]. Our system obtains relatively high scores ($> 50\%$) on three predicates including "sale", "plan" and "loss". These three are the most frequent predicates (among the 10 defined in the nominal iSRL dataset) in the CoNLL 2009 training data – they occur 1016, 318 and 275 times in verbal forms, respectively. In contrast, irregular predicates such as "bid" or "loan" usually have low performance. This is possibly caused by the de-

---

[4] As an overly conservative estimate, we take a t-test over the 10 predicate-level F1 scores as can be seen in Table 2. Comparing against Model 2, this yields p=0.28 for Gerber and Chai (2010), p=0.46 for Laparra and Rigau (2013), and most importantly p=0.058 for Schenk and Chiarcos (2016).

pendence of our PRNSFM on the performance of the explicit semantic role labeling system on verbal predicates.

It is important to consider how iSRL can be extended beyond the 10 annotated predicates of Gerber and Chai (2010). Our models do not require any handcrafted iSRL annotations for training, and thus can be applied to all predicates observed in large unannotated data on which they are trained.

However, as other work in iSRL, our approach still relies on a resource-heavy SRL system to learn selectional preferences. It would be interesting to investigate in further studies whether this SRL system can be replaced by a low-resource system (Collobert et al., 2011; Connor et al., 2012).

6 Conclusion and Future Work

We have presented recurrent neural semantic frame models for learning probability distributions over semantic argument sequences. By modeling selectional preferences from these probability distributions, we have improved state-of-the-art performance on the NomBank iSRL task while using fewer language resources. In the future, we believe that our semantic frame models are valuable in many language processing tasks that require discourse-level understanding of language, such as summarization, question answering and machine translation.

Acknowledgment

This work is carried out in the frame of the EU CHIST-ERA project "MUltimodal processing of Spatial and TEmporal expRessions" (MUSTER), and the "MAchine Reading of patient recordS" project (MARS, KU Leuven, C22/015/016).

References

Collin F. Baker, Charles J. Fillmore, and John B. Lowe. 1998. The berkeley framenet project. In *Proceedings of the 36th Annual Meeting of the Association for Computational Linguistics and 17th International Conference on Computational Linguistics - Volume 1*. Association for Computational Linguistics, Stroudsburg, PA, USA, ACL '98, pages 86–90. https://doi.org/10.3115/980845.980860.

Anders Björkelund, Bernd Bohnet, Love Hafdell, and Pierre Nugues. 2010. A high-performance syntactic and semantic dependency parser. In *Coling 2010: Demonstrations*. Coling 2010 Organizing Committee, Beijing, China, pages 33–36. http://www.aclweb.org/anthology/C10-3009.

Ronan Collobert, Jason Weston, Léon Bottou, Michael Karlen, Koray Kavukcuoglu, and Pavel Kuksa. 2011. Natural language processing (almost) from scratch. *J. Mach. Learn. Res.* 12:2493–2537. http://dl.acm.org/citation.cfm?id=1953048.2078186.

M. Connor, C. Fisher, and D. Roth. 2012. Starting from Scratch in Semantic Role Labeling: Early Indirect Supervision. *Cognitive Aspects of Computational Language Acquisition* .

Karl Friston. 2010. The free-energy principle: a unified brain theory? *Nature Reviews Neuroscience* 11(2):127–138. https://doi.org/10.1038/nrn2787.

Matt Gerber, Joyce Y. Chai, and Adam Meyers. 2009. The role of implicit argumentation in nominal srl. In *Proceedings of Human Language Technologies: The 2009 Annual Conference of the North American Chapter of the Association for Computational Linguistics*. Association for Computational Linguistics, Stroudsburg, PA, USA, NAACL '09, pages 146–154. http://dl.acm.org/citation.cfm?id=1620754.1620776.

Matthew Gerber and Joyce Chai. 2010. Beyond NomBank: A Study of Implicit Arguments for Nominal Predicates. In *Proceedings of the 48th Annual Meeting of the Association for Computational Linguistics*. Association for Computational Linguistics, Uppsala, Sweden, pages 1583–1592. http://www.aclweb.org/anthology-new/P/P10/P10-1160.bib.

Matthew Gerber and Joyce Y. Chai. 2012. Semantic role labeling of implicit arguments for nominal predicates. *Computational Linguistics* 38(4):755–798.

C.A. Kurby and J.M. Zacks. 2015. *Situation Models in Naturalistic Comprehension*, Cambridge University Press, pages 59–76.

Egoitz Laparra and German Rigau. 2013. Impar: A deterministic algorithm for implicit semantic role labelling. In *Proceedings of the 51st Annual Meeting of the Association for Computational Linguistics, ACL 2013, 4-9 August 2013, Sofia, Bulgaria, Volume 1: Long Papers*. pages 1180–1189. http://aclweb.org/anthology/P/P13/P13-1116.pdf.

A. Meyers, R. Reeves, C. Macleod, R. Szekely, V. Zielinska, B. Young, and R. Grishman. 2004. The nombank project: An interim report. In A. Meyers, editor, *HLT-NAACL 2004 Workshop: Frontiers in Corpus Annotation*. Association for Computational Linguistics, Boston, Massachusetts, USA, pages 24–31.

Tomas Mikolov, Kai Chen, Greg Corrado, and Jeffrey Dean. 2013. Efficient estimation of word representations in vector space. *CoRR* abs/1301.3781. http://arxiv.org/abs/1301.3781.

Tomas Mikolov, Martin Karafit, Lukas Burget, Jan Cernock, and Sanjeev Khudanpur. 2010. Recurrent neural network based language model. In Takao Kobayashi, Keikichi Hirose, and Satoshi Nakamura, editors, *INTERSPEECH*. ISCA, pages 1045–1048.

Martha Palmer, Daniel Gildea, and Paul Kingsbury. 2005. The Proposition Bank: An annotated corpus of semantic roles. *Computational Linguistics* 31(1):71–106. http://www.cs.rochester.edu/ gildea/palmer-propbank-cl.pdf.

Haoruo Peng and Dan Roth. 2016. Two discourse driven language models for semantics. In *Proceedings of the 54th Annual Meeting of the Association for Computational Linguistics, ACL 2016, August 7-12, 2016, Berlin, Germany, Volume 1: Long Papers.* http://aclweb.org/anthology/P/P16/P16-1028.pdf.

Jeffrey Pennington, Richard Socher, and Christopher D. Manning. 2014. Glove: Global vectors for word representation. In *Empirical Methods in Natural Language Processing (EMNLP).* pages 1532–1543. http://www.aclweb.org/anthology/D14-1162.

Michael Roth and Anette Frank. 2015. Inducing Implicit Arguments from Comparable Texts: A Framework and its Applications. *Computational Linguistics* 41:625–664.

Josef Ruppenhofer, Caroline Sporleder, Roser Morante, Collin Baker, and Martha Palmer. 2010. Semeval-2010 task 10: Linking events and their participants in discourse. In *Proceedings of the 5th International Workshop on Semantic Evaluation.* Association for Computational Linguistics, Stroudsburg, PA, USA, SemEval '10, pages 45–50. http://dl.acm.org/citation.cfm?id=1859664.1859672.

D.L. Schacter and K.P. Madore. 2016. Remembering the past and imagining the future: Identifying and enhancing the contribution of episodic memory. *Memory Studies* 9(3):245–255.

Niko Schenk and Christian Chiarcos. 2016. Unsupervised learning of prototypical fillers for implicit semantic role labeling. In *NAACL HLT 2016, The 2016 Conference of the North American Chapter of the Association for Computational Linguistics: Human Language Technologies, San Diego California, USA, June 12-17, 2016.* pages 1473–1479. http://aclweb.org/anthology/N/N16/N16-1173.pdf.

Ivan Titov and Ehsan Khoddam. 2015. Unsupervised induction of semantic roles within a reconstruction-error minimization framework. In *Proceedings of the North American chapter of the Association for Computational Linguistics (NAACL).*

David Vernon. 2014. *Artificial Cognitive Systems: A Primer.* The MIT Press.

Kristian Woodsend and Mirella Lapata. 2015. Distributed representations for unsupervised semantic role labeling. In *Proceedings of the 2015 Conference on Empirical Methods in Natural Language Processing.* Association for Computational Linguistics, Lisbon, Portugal, pages 2482–2491. http://aclweb.org/anthology/D15-1295.

Matthew D. Zeiler. 2012. ADADELTA: an adaptive learning rate method. *CoRR* abs/1212.5701. http://arxiv.org/abs/1212.5701.

Natural Language Inference from Multiple Premises

Alice Lai[1] **Yonatan Bisk**[2] **Julia Hockenmaier**[1]

[1]Department of Computer Science, University of Illinois at Urbana-Champaign
[2]Paul G. Allen School of Computer Science & Engineering, Univ. of Washington

aylai2@illinois.edu, ybisk@cs.washington.edu, juliahmr@illinois.edu

Abstract

We define a novel textual entailment task that requires inference over multiple premise sentences. We present a new dataset for this task that minimizes trivial lexical inferences, emphasizes knowledge of everyday events, and presents a more challenging setting for textual entailment. We evaluate several strong neural baselines and analyze how the multiple premise task differs from standard textual entailment.

1 Introduction

Standard textual entailment recognition is concerned with deciding whether one statement (the hypothesis) follows from another statement (the premise). However, in some situations, multiple independent descriptions of the same event are available, e.g. multiple news articles describing the same story, social media posts by different people about a single event, or multiple witness reports for a crime. In these cases, we want to use multiple independent reports to infer what really happened.

We therefore introduce a variant of the standard textual entailment task in which the premise text consists of multiple independently written sentences, all describing the same scene (see examples in Figure 1). The task is to decide whether the hypothesis sentence 1) can be used to describe the same scene (entailment), 2) cannot be used to describe the same scene (contradiction), or 3) may or may not describe the same scene (neutral). The main challenge is to infer what happened in the scene from the multiple premise statements, in some cases aggregating information across multiple sentences into a coherent whole.

Premises:
1. Two girls sitting down and looking at a book.
2. A couple laughs together as they read a book on a train.
3. Two travelers on a train or bus reading a book together.
4. A woman wearing glasses and a brown beanie next to a girl with long brown hair holding a book.

Hypothesis:
Women smiling.   ⇒ENTAILMENT

Premises:
1. Three men are working construction on top of a building.
2. Three male construction workers on a roof working in the sun.
3. One man is shirtless while the other two men work on construction.
4. Two construction workers working on infrastructure, while one worker takes a break.

Hypothesis:
A man smoking a cigarette.   ⇒NEUTRAL

Premises:
1. A group of individuals performed in front of a seated crowd.
2. Woman standing in front of group with black folders in hand.
3. A group of women with black binders stand in front of a group of people.
4. A group of people are standing at the front of the room, preparing to sing.

Hypothesis:
A group having a meeting.   ⇒CONTRADICTION

Figure 1: The Multiple Premise Entailment Task

Similar to the SICK and SNLI datasets (Marelli et al., 2014; Bowman et al., 2015), each premise sentence in our data is a single sentence describing everyday events, rather than news paragraphs as in the RTE datasets (Dagan et al., 2006), which require named entity recognition and coreference resolution. Instead of soliciting humans to write new hypotheses, as SNLI did, we use simplified versions of existing image captions, and use a word overlap filter and the structure of the denotation graph of Young et al. (2014) to minimize the presence of trivial lexical relationships.

2 Related Standard Entailment Tasks

In the following datasets, premises are single sentences drawn from image or video caption data

Proceedings of the The 8th International Joint Conference on Natural Language Processing, pages 100–109,
Taipei, Taiwan, November 27 – December 1, 2017 ©2017 AFNLP

that describe concrete, everyday activities.

The **SICK** dataset (Marelli et al., 2014) consists of 10K sentence pairs. The premise sentences come from the FLICKR8K image caption corpus (Rashtchian et al., 2010) and the MSR Video Paraphrase Corpus (Agirre et al., 2012), while the hypotheses were automatically generated. This process introduced some errors (e.g. "A motorcycle is riding standing up on the seat of the vehicle") and an uneven distribution of phenomena across entailment classes that is easy to exploit (e.g. negation (Lai and Hockenmaier, 2014)).

The **SNLI** dataset (Bowman et al., 2015) contains over 570K sentence pairs. The premises come from the FLICKR30K image caption corpus (Young et al., 2014) and VisualGenome (Krishna et al., 2016). The hypotheses were written by Mechanical Turk workers who were given the premise and asked to write one definitely true sentence, one possibly true sentence, and one definitely false sentence. The task design prompted workers to write hypotheses that frequently parallel the premise in structure and vocabulary, and therefore the semantic relationships between premise and hypothesis are often limited to synonym/hyponym lexical substitution, replacement of short phrases, or exact word matching.

3   The Multiple Premise Entailment Task

In this paper, we propose a variant of entailment where each hypothesis sentence is paired with an unordered set of independently written premise sentences that describe the same event. The premises may contain overlapping information, but are typically not paraphrases. The majority of our dataset requires consideration of multiple premises, including aggregation of information from multiple sentences.

This Multiple Premise Entailment (MPE) task is inspired by the Approximate Textual Entailment (ATE) task of Young et al. (2014). Each item in the ATE dataset consists of a premise set of four captions from FLICKR30K, and a short phrase as the hypothesis. The ATE data was created automatically, under the assumption that items are positive (approximately entailing) if the hypothesis comes from the same image as the four premises, and negative otherwise. However, Young et al. found that this assumption was only true for just over half of the positive items. For MPE, we also start with four FLICKR30K captions as the premises and a

related/unrelated sentence as the hypothesis, but we restrict the hypothesis to have low word overlap with the premises, and we collect human judgments to label the items as entailing, contradictory, or neutral.

4   The MPE Dataset

The MPE dataset (Figure 1) contains 10,000 items (8,000 training, 1,000 development and 1,000 test), each consisting of four premise sentences (captions from the same FLICKR30K image), one hypothesis sentence (a simplified FLICKR30K caption), and one label (entailment, neutral, or contradiction) that indicates the relationship between the set of four premises and the hypothesis. This label is based on a consensus of five crowdsourced judgments. To analyze the difference between multiple premise and single premise entailment (Section 5.2), we also collected pair label annotations for each individual premise-hypothesis pair in the development data. This section describes how we selected the premise and hypothesis sentences, and how we labeled the items via crowdsourcing.

4.1   Generating the Items

Hypothesis simplification   The four premise sentences of each MPE item consist of four original FLICKR30K captions from the same image. Since complete captions are too specific and are likely to introduce new details that are not entailed by the premises, the hypotheses sentences are simplified versions of FLICKR30K captions. Each hypothesis sentence is either a simplified variant of the fifth caption of the same image as the premises, or a simplified variant of one of the captions of a random, unrelated image.

Our simplification process relies on the denotation graph of Young et al. (2014), a subsumption hierarchy over phrases, constructed from the captions in FLICKR30K. They define a set of normalization and reduction rules (e.g. lemmatization, dropping modifiers and prepositional phrases, replacing nouns with their hypernyms, extracting noun phrases) to transform the original captions into shorter, more generic phrases that are still true descriptions of the original image.

To simplify a hypothesis caption, we consider all sentence nodes in the denotation graph that are ancestors (more generic versions) of this caption, but exclude nodes that are also ancestors of any of the premises. This ensures that the simplified hypothesis cannot be trivially obtained from a premise via the same automatic simplification procedure. Therefore, we avoid some obvious semantic relationships between premises and hypothesis, such as hypernym replacement, dropping modifiers or PPs, etc.

Limiting lexical overlap Given the set of simplified, restricted hypotheses, we further restrict the pool of potential items to contain only pairings where the hypothesis has a word overlap $\leq$ 0.5 with the premise set. We compute word overlap as the fraction of hypothesis tokens that appear in at least one premise (after stopword removal). This eliminates trivial cases of entailment where the hypothesis is simply a subset of the premise text. Table 1 shows that the mean word overlap for our training data is much lower than SNLI.

| | SNLI | | MPE | |
Data	full	lemma	full	lemma
All	0.44 ± 0.29	0.48 ± 0.29	0.28 ± 0.22	0.33 ± 0.20
E	0.59 ± 0.31	0.64 ± 0.30	0.34 ± 0.21	0.38 ± 0.19
N	0.41 ± 0.24	0.45 ± 0.24	0.28 ± 0.21	0.33 ± 0.19
C	0.33 ± 0.25	0.36 ± 0.25	0.23 ± 0.22	0.30 ± 0.21

Table 1: Mean word overlap for full training data and each label, original and lemmatized sentences. MPE has much lower word overlap than SNLI.

Data selection From this constrained pool of premises-hypothesis pairings, we randomly sampled 8000 items from the FLICKR30K training split for our training data. For test and development data, we sample 1000 items from FLICKR30K test and 1000 from dev. The hypotheses in the training data must be associated with at least two captions in the FLICKR30K train split, while the hypotheses in dev/test must be associated with at least two captions in the union of the training and dev/test, and with at least one caption in dev/test alone. Since the test and dev splits of FLICKR30K are smaller than the training split, this threshold selects hypotheses that are rare enough to be interesting and frequent enough to be reasonable sentences.

4.2 Assigning Entailment Labels

Crowdsourcing procedure For each item, we solicited five responses from Crowdflower and Amazon Mechanical Turk as to whether the hypothesis was *entailed*, *contradictory*, or *neither*

given a set of four premises. Instructions are shown in Table 2. We provided labeled examples to illustrate the kinds of assumptions we expected.

Entailment labels We assume three labels (entailment, neutral, contradiction). For entailment, we deliberately asked annotators to judge whether the hypothesis could *very probably* describe the same scene as the premises, rather than specifying that the hypothesis must *definitely* be true, as Bowman et al. (2015) did for SNLI. Our instructions align with the standard definition of textual entailment: "T entails H if humans reading T would typically infer that H is most likely true" (Dagan et al., 2013). We are not only interested in what is logically required for a hypothesis to be true, but also in what human readers assume is true, given their own world knowledge.

Final label assignment Of the 10,000 items for which we collected full label annotations, 90% had a majority label based on the five judgments, including 16% with a 3-2 split between entailment and contradiction. The remaining 10% had a 2-2-1 split across the three classes. We manually adjudicated the latter two cases. As a result, 82% of the final labels in the dataset correspond to a majority vote over the judgments (the remaining 18% differ due to our manual correction). The released dataset contains both our final labels and the crowdsourced judgments for all items.

Image IDs Premises in the our dataset have corresponding image IDs from FLICKR30K. We are interested in the information present in linguistic descriptions of a scene, so our labels reflect the textual entailment relationship between the premise text and the hypothesis. Future work could apply multi-modal representations to this task, with the caveat that the image would likely resolve many neutral items to either entailment or contradiction.

5 Data Analysis

5.1 Statistics

The dataset contains 8000 training items, 1000 development items, and 1000 test items. Table 3 shows overall type and token counts and sentence lengths as well as the label distribution.

The mean annotator agreement, i.e. the fraction of annotators who agreed with the final label, is 0.70 for the full dataset, or 0.82 for the entailment

Table 2: The annotation instructions we provided to Crowdflower and Mechanical Turk annotators.

	SNLI	MPE
#Lexical types	36,616	9,254
#Lexical tokens	12 million	468,524
Mean premise length	14.0 ± 6.0	53.2 ± 12.8
Mean hypothesis length	8.3 ± 3.2	5.3 ± 1.8
Label distribution		
Entailment	33.3%	32.3%
Neutral	33.3%	26.3%
Contradiction	33.3%	41.6%

Table 3: Type and token counts, sentence lengths, and label distributions for training data.

class, 0.42 for neutral, and 0.78 for contradiction. That is, on average, four of the five crowdsourced judgments agree with the final label for the entailment and contradiction items, whereas for the neutral items, only an average of two of the five original annotators assigned the neutral label, and the other three were split between contradiction and entailment.

5.2 MPE vs. Standard Entailment

Multiple premise entailment (MPE) differs from standard single premise entailment (SPE) in that each premise consists of four independently written sentences about the same scene. To understand how MPE differs from SPE, we used crowdsourcing to collect pairwise single-premise entailment labels for each individual premise-hypothesis pair in the development data. Each consensus label is based on three judgments.

In Table 4, we compare the full MPE entailment labels (bold $\Rightarrow$**E**, $\Rightarrow$**N**, $\Rightarrow$**C**), to the four pair SPE labels (E, N, C). The number of SPE labels that agree with the MPE label yields the five categories in Table 4, ranging from the most difficult case where none of the SPE labels agree with the MPE label (21.8% of the data) to the simplest case where all four SPE labels agree with the MPE label (9.8% of the data).

We observe that a simple majority voting scheme over the gold standard SPE labels would not be sufficient, since it assigns the correct MPE label to only 34.6% of the development items (i.e. those cases where three or four SPE pairs agree with the MPE label). We also evaluate a slightly more sophisticated voting scheme that applies the following heuristic (here, E, N, C are the number of SPE labels of each class):

> If $E > C$, predict entailment.
> Else if $C > E$, predict contradiction.
> Otherwise, predict neutral.

This baseline achieves an accuracy of 41.7%. These results indicate that MPE cannot be trivially reduced to SPE. That is, even if a model had access to the correct SPE label for each individual premise (an unrealistic assumption), it would require more than simple voting heuristics to obtain the correct MPE label from these pairwise labels. Table 4 illustrates that the majority of MPE items require aggregation of information about the described entities and events across multiple premises. In the first example, the first premise is consistent with a scene that involves a team of football players, while only the last premise indi-

# pairs agree	% of data	Pair Label	Example **Hypothesis** and Four Premises
0	21.8	N	A football player in a red uniform is standing in front of other football players in a stadium.
		N	A football player facing off against two others.
		N	A football player wearing a red shirt.
		N	Defensive player waiting for the snap.
		⇒E	**The team waiting.**
1	26.9	N	A person is half submerged in water in their yellow kayak.
		C	A woman has positioned her kayak nose down in the water.
		N	A person in a canoe is rafting in wild waters.
		N	A kayaker plunges into the river.
		⇒C	**A man in a boat paddling through waters.**
2	16.7	E	A batter playing cricket missed the ball and the person behind him is catching it.
		E	A cricket player misses the pitch.
		N	The three men are playing cricket.
		N	A man struck out playing cricket.
		⇒E	**A man swings a bat.**
3	24.8	N	A young gymnast, jumps high in the air, while performing on a balance beam.
		N	A gymnast performing on the balance beam in front of an audience.
		E	The young gymnast's supple body soars above the balance beam.
		N	A gymnast is performing on the balance beam.
		⇒N	**A woman doing gymnastics.**
4	9.8	C	A man with a cowboy hat is riding a horse that is jumping.
		C	A cowboy riding on his horse that is jumping in the air.
		C	A cowboy balances on his horse in a rodeo.
		C	Man wearing a cowboy hat riding a horse.
		⇒C	**Men pulled by animals.**

Table 4: MPE examples that illustrate the difference between pair labels and the full label. We include one example for each category, based on the number of pair labels that agree with the full label, and indicate the size of each category as a percentage of the development data.

cates that the team may be waiting. Moreover, the simple majority voting would work on the fourth example but fail on the second example, while the more sophisticated voting scheme would work on the second example and fail on the fourth.

5.3 Semantic Phenomena

We used a random sample of 100 development items to examine the types of semantic phenomena that are useful for inference in this dataset. We categorized each item by type of knowledge or reasoning necessary to predict the correct label for the hypothesis given the premises. An item belongs to a category if at least one premise in that item exhibits that semantic phenomenon in relation to the hypothesis, and an item may belong to multiple categories. For each category, Table 5 contains its frequency, an illustrative example containing the relevant premise, and the distribution over entailment labels. We did our analysis on full items (four premises and the corresponding hypothesis), but the examples in Table 5 have been simplified to a single premise for simplicity.

Word equivalence Items in this category contain a pair of equivalent words (synonyms or paraphrases). The word in the hypothesis can be exchanged for the word in the premise without significantly changing the meaning of the hypothesis.

Word hypernymy These items involve lexical hypernyms: someone who is a man is also a person (entailment), but a person may or may not be a man (neutral), and somebody who is a man is not a child (contradiction).

Phrase equivalence These items involve equivalent phrases, i.e. synonyms or paraphrases. The phrase in the hypothesis can be replaced by the phrase in the premise without significantly changing the meaning of the hypothesis.

Phrase hypernymy Items in this category involve a specific phrase and a general phrase: the more general phrase "doing exercises" can refer to multiple types of exercises in addition to "stretching their legs."

Mutual exclusion Distinguishing between contradiction and neutral items involves identifying

	#	E	N	C	Example Premise and **Hypothesis** Pair
Total	100	31	29	40	
Word equivalence	16	12	4	0	*A person climbing a rock face.* **A rock climber scales a cliff.** ⇒**E**
Word hypernymy	19	6	6	7	*Girl in a blue sweater painting while looking at a bird in a book.* **A child painting a picture.** ⇒**E**
Phrase equivalence	7	6	1	0	*A couple in their wedding attire stand behind a table with a wedding cake and flowers.* **Newlyweds standing.** ⇒**E**
Phrase hypernymy	8	6	2	0	A group of young boys wearing track jackets *stretch their legs* on a gym floor as they sit in a circle. **A group doing exercises.** ⇒**E**
Mutual exclusion	25	0	0	25	A woman in a red vest *working at a computer.* **Lady doing yoga.** ⇒**C**
Compatibility	18	0	18	0	*Onlookers watch.* **A girl at bat in a softball game.** ⇒**N**
World knowledge	35	14	9	12	A young woman gives directions to an older woman outside a subway station. **Women standing.** ⇒**E**

Table 5: Analysis of 100 random dev items. For each phenomenon, we show the distribution over labels and an example. The label is indicated with E, N, C. We use color and underlining to indicate the relevant comparisons. The indicated span of text is part of the necessary information to predict the correct label, but may not be sufficient on its own.

actions that are mutually exclusive, i.e. cannot be performed simultaneously by the same agent ("Two doctors perform surgery" vs. "Two surgeons are having lunch").

Compatibility The opposite of mutual exclusion is compatibility: two actions that can be performed simultaneously by the same agent (e.g. "A boy flying a red and white kite" vs. "A boy is smiling").

World knowledge These items require extra-linguistic knowledge about the relative frequency and co-occurrence of events in the world (not overlapping with the mutual exclusion or compatibility phenomena). A human reader can infer that children in a potato sack race are having fun (while a marathon runner competing in a race might not be described as having fun).

5.4 Combining Information Across Premises

In addition to the semantic phenomena we have just discussed, the data presents the challenge of how to combine information across multiple premises. We examined examples from the development data to analyze the different types of information aggregation present in our dataset.

Coreference resolution This case requires cross-caption coreference resolution of entity mentions from multiple premises and the hypothesis. In this example, a human reader can recognize that "two men" and "two senior citizens" refer to the same entities, i.e. the "two older men" in the hypothesis. Given that information, the reader can additionally infer that the two older men on the street are likely to be standing.

1. Two men in tan coats exchange looks on the city sidewalk.
2. Two senior citizens talking on a public street.
3. Two men in brown coats on the street.
4. Two men in beige coats, talking.

Two older men stand. ⇒**ENTAILMENT**

Event resolution This case requires resolving various event descriptions from multiple premises and the hypothesis. In the following example, a human reader recognizes that the man is sitting on scaffolding so that he can repair the building, and therefore he is doing construction work.

1. A man is sitting on a scaffolding in front a white building.
2. A man is sitting on a platform next to a building ledge.
3. A man looks down from his balcony from a stone building.
4. Repairing the front of an old building.

A man doing construction work. ⇒**ENTAILMENT**

Visual ambiguity resolution This case involves reconciling apparently contradictory information across premises. These discrepancies are largely due to the fact that the premise captions were written to describe an image. Sometimes the image contained visually ambiguous entities or events that are then described by different caption writers. In this example, in order to resolve the discrepancy, the reader must recognize from context that "woman" and "young child" (also "person") refer to the same entity.

1. A person in a green jacket and pants appears to be digging in a wooded field with several cars in the background.
2. A young child in a green jacket rakes leaves.
3. A young child rakes leaves in a wooded area.
4. A woman cleaning up a park.

A woman standing in the forest.　　　⇒**ENTAILMENT**

Scene resolution These examples require the reader to build a mental representation of the scene from the premises in order to assess the probability that the hypothesis is true. In the first example, specific descriptions – a jumping horse, a cowboy balancing, a rodeo – combine to assign a high probability that the specific event described by the hypothesis is true.

1. A man with a cowboy hat is riding a horse that is jumping.
2. A cowboy riding on his horse that is jumping in the air.
3. A cowboy balances on his horse in a rodeo.
4. Man wearing a cowboy hat riding a horse.

An animal bucking a man.　　　⇒**ENTAILMENT**

In the next example, the hypothesis does not contradict any individual premise sentence. However, a reader who understands the generic scene described knows that the very specific hypothesis description is unlikely to go unmentioned. Shirtlessness would be a salient detail in the this scene, so the fact that none of the premises mention it means that the hypothesis is likely to be false.

1. A young couple sits in a park eating ice cream as children play and other people enjoy themselves around them.
2. Couple in park eating ice cream cones with three other adults and two children in background.
3. A couple enjoying ice cream outside on a nice day.
4. A couple eats ice cream in the park.

A shirtless man sitting.　　　⇒**CONTRADICTION**

In the final example, the premises present a somewhat generic description of the scene. While some premises lean towards entailment (a woman and a man in *discussion* could be having a work meeting) and others lean towards contradiction (two people conversing outdoors at a restaurant are probably not working), none of them contain overwhelming evidence that the scene entails or contradicts the hypothesis. Therefore, the hypothesis is neutral given the premises.

1. A blond woman wearing a gray jacket converses with an older man in a green shirt and glasses while sitting on a restaurant patio.
2. A blond pony-tailed woman and a gray-haired man converse while seated at a restaurant's outdoor area.
3. A woman with blond hair is sitting at a table and talking to a man with glasses.
4. A woman discusses something with an older man at a table outside a restaurant.

A woman doing work.　　　⇒**NEUTRAL**

6 Models

We apply several neural models from the entailment literature to our data. We also present a model designed to handle multiple premises, as this is unique to our dataset.

LSTM In our experiments, we found that the conditional LSTM (Hochreiter and Schmidhuber, 1997) model of Rocktäschel et al. (2016) outperformed a Siamese LSTM network (e.g. Bowman et al. (2015)), so we report results using the conditional LSTM. This model consists of two LSTMs that process the hypothesis conditioned on the premise. The first LSTM reads the premise. Its final cell state is used to initialize the cell state of the second LSTM, which reads the hypothesis. The resulting premise vector and hypothesis vector are concatenated and passed through a hidden layer and a softmax prediction layer. When handling four MPE premise sentences, we concatenate them into a single sequence (in the order of the caption IDs) that we pass to the first LSTM. When we only have a single premise sentence, we simply pass it to the first LSTM.

Word-to-word attention Neural attention models have shown a lot of success on SNLI. We evaluate the word-to-word attention model of Rocktäschel et al. (2016).[1] This model learns a soft alignment of words in the premise and hypothesis. One LSTM reads the premise and produces an output vector after each word. A second LSTM, initialized by the final cell state of the first, reads the hypothesis one word at a time. For each word w_t in the hypothesis, the model produces attention weights α_t over the premise output vectors. The final sentence pair representation is a nonlinear combination of the attention-weighted representation of the premise and the final output vector from the hypothesis LSTM. This final sentence pair representation is passed through a softmax layer to compute the cross-entropy loss. Again, when training on MPE, we concatenate premise sentences into a single sequence as input to the premise LSTM.

Premise-wise sum of experts (SE) The previous models all assume that the premise is a single sentence, so in order to apply them naively to our dataset, we have to concatenate the four premises.

---

[1]Our experiments use a reimplementation of their model https://github.com/junfenglx/reasoning_attention

106

Training	Class	LSTM	SE	Attention
SNLI only		52.6	**55.9**	55.0
	E	85.8	71.5	81.7
	N	8.4	21.6	16.4
	C	55.7	62.0	54.5
MPE only		53.5	**56.3**	53.9
	E	63.1	61.3	48.3
	N	39.2	30.2	30.6
	C	53.5	66.5	71.2
SNLI+MPE		60.4	60.0	**64.0**
	E	65.1	65.4	75.9
	N	40.9	42.7	32.8
	C	67.2	65.1	71.5

Table 6: Entailment accuracy on MPE (test). SE is best when training only on SNLI or MPE. Attention is best when training on SNLI+MPE.

To capture what distinguishes our task from standard entailment, we also consider a premise-wise sum of experts (SE) model that makes four independent decisions for each premise paired with the hypothesis. This model can adjust how it processes each premise based on the relative predictions of the other premises.

We apply the conditional LSTM repeatedly to read each premise and the hypothesis, producing four premise vectors $p_1 ... p_4$ and four hypothesis vectors $h_1 ... h_4$ (conditioned on each premise). Each premise vector p_i is concatenated with its hypothesis vector h_i and passed through a feed-forward layer to produce logit prediction l_i. We sum $l_1 ... l_4$ to obtain the final prediction, which we use to compute the cross-entropy loss.

When training on SNLI, we apply the conditional LSTM only once to read the premise and hypothesis and produce p_1 and h_1. We pass the concatenation of p_1 and h_1 through the feedforward layer to produce l_1, which we use to compute the cross-entropy loss.

7   Training Details

For the LSTM and SE models, we use 300d GloVe vectors (Pennington et al., 2014) trained on 840B tokens as the input. The attention model uses word2vec vectors (Mikolov et al., 2013) (replacing with GloVe had almost no effect on performance). We use the Adam optimizer (Kingma and Ba, 2014) with the default configuration. We train each model for 10 epochs based on convergence on dev. For joint SNLI+MPE training, we use the same parameters and pretrain for 10 epochs on SNLI, then train for 10 epochs on MPE. This was the best joint training approach we found.

When training on SNLI, we use the best parameters reported for the word-to-word attention model.[2] When training on MPE only, we set dropout, learning rate, and LSTM dimensionality as the result of a grid search on dev.[3]

8   Experimental Results

8.1   Overall Performance

Table 6 contains the test accuracies of the models from Section 6: LSTM, sum of experts (SE), and word-to-word attention under three training regimes: SNLI only, MPE only, and SNLI+MPE.

We train only on SNLI to see whether models can generalize from one entailment task to the other. Interestingly, the attention model's accuracy on MPE is higher after training only on SNLI than training on MPE, perhaps because it requires much more data to learn reasonable attention weighting parameters.

When training on SNLI or MPE alone, the best model is SE, the only model that handles the four premises. It is not surprising that the LSTM model performs poorly, as it is forced to reduce a very long sequence of words to a single vector. The LSTM performs on par with SE when training on SNLI+MPE, but our analysis (Section 5.3) shows that their errors are quite different.

The attention model trained on SNLI+MPE has the highest accuracy overall. We reason that pretraining on SNLI is necessary to learn reasonable parameters for the attention weights before training on MPE, a smaller dataset where word-to-word inferences may be less obvious. When trained only on MPE, the attention model performs much worse than SE, with particularly low accuracy on entailing items.

We implemented a model that adds attention to the SE model, but it overfit on SNLI and could not match other models' accuracy, reaching only about 58% on dev compared to 59-63%. Future work will investigate other approaches to combining the benefits of the SE and attention models.

8.2   Performance by Pair Agreement

To get a better understanding of how our task differs from standard entailment, we analyze how

---

[2]Dropout: 0.8, learning rate: 0.001, vector dim: 100, batch size: 32

[3]LSTM: dropout: 0.8, vector dim: 75. SE: dropout: 0.8, vector dim: 100. Attention: dropout: 0.6, vector dim: 100. Learning rate: 0.001 for all models

Accuracy on SPE-MPE agreement subsets					
# pairs agree	0	1	2	3	4
% of data	21.8	26.9	16.7	24.8	9.8
LSTM	57.3	57.6	60.5	67.1	63.3
SE	59.6	**58.0**	63.3	62.9	66.3
Attention	**65.6**	57.6	62.9	**68.3**	**70.4**

Table 7: Accuracy for each model (trained on SNLI+MPE) on the dev data subsets that have 0–4 SPE labels that match the MPE label (Table 4).

performance is affected by the number of premises whose SPE label agrees with the MPE label. Table 7 shows the accuracy of each SNLI+MPE-trained model on the dev data grouped by SPE-MPE label agreement (as in Table 4).

The attention model has the highest accuracy on three of five categories, including the most difficult category where none of the SPE labels match the MPE label. SE has the highest accuracy in the remaining two categories. The attention model demonstrates large gains in the easiest categories, perhaps because there is less advantage to aggregating individual premise predictions (as SE does) and more cases where attention weighting of individual words is useful. On the other hand, the attention model also does well on the most difficult category, indicating that it may be able to partially aggregate premises by increasing attention weights on phrases from multiple sentences. Attention and SE exhibit complementary strengths that we hope to combine in future work.

8.3 Performance by Semantic Phenomenon

Table 8 shows the performance of the three SNLI+MPE-trained models over semantic phenomena, based on the 100 annotated dev items (see Section 5.3 and Table 5). It may not be informative to analyze performance on smaller classes (e.g. phrase equivalence and phrase hypernymy), but we can still look at other noticeable differences between models.

Although the attention model outperformed both LSTM and SE models in overall accuracy, it is not the best in every category. Both SE and attention have access to the same information, but the attention model does better on items that contain relationships like hypernyms and synonyms for both words and short phrases. The SE model is best at mutual exclusion, compatibility, and world knowledge categories, e.g. knowing that a man who is *resting* is not *kayaking*, and a *bride* is not also a *cheerleader*. In cases that require analy-

	Accuracy			
Phenomenon	LSTM	SE	Att	#
Word equivalence	50.0	56.2	**68.8**	16
Word hypernymy	**52.6**	47.4	**52.6**	19
Phrase equivalence	57.1	57.1	**85.7**	7
Phrase hypernymy	50.0	50.0	**62.5**	8
Mutual exclusion	68.0	**72.0**	60.0	25
Compatibility	50.0	**61.1**	50.0	18
World knowledge	57.1	**62.9**	45.7	35

Table 8: Accuracy for each semantic phenomenon on 100 dev items. While attention was the best model overall, it does not have the highest accuracy for all phenomena.

sis of mutually exclusive or compatible events, a model like SE has an advantage since it can reinforce its weighted combination prediction by examining each premise separately.

9   Conclusion

We presented a novel textual entailment task that involves inference over longer premise texts and aggregation of information from multiple independent premise sentences. This task is an important step towards a system that can create a coherent scene representation from longer texts, such as multiple independent reports. We introduced a dataset for this task (`http://nlp.cs.illinois.edu/ HockenmaierGroup/data.html`) which presents a more challenging, realistic entailment problem and cannot be solved by majority voting or related heuristics. We presented the results of several strong neural entailment baselines on this dataset, including one model that aggregates information from the predictions of separate premise sentences. Future work will investigate aggregating information at earlier stages to address the cases that require explicit reasoning about the interaction of multiple premises.

Acknowledgments

This project is supported by NSF grants 1053856, 1205627, 1405883 and 1563727, a Google Research Award, and Contract W911NF-15-1-0461 with the US Defense Advanced Research Projects Agency (DARPA) and the Army Research Office (ARO). Approved for Public Release, Distribution Unlimited. The views expressed are those of the authors and do not reflect the official policy or position of the Department of Defense or the U.S. Government.

References

Eneko Agirre, Mona Diab, Daniel Cer, and Aitor Gonzalez-Agirre. 2012. Semeval-2012 task 6: A pilot on semantic textual similarity. In *Proceedings of the First Joint Conference on Lexical and Computational Semantics-Volume 1: Proceedings of the main conference and the shared task, and Volume 2: Proceedings of the Sixth International Workshop on Semantic Evaluation*, pages 385–393. Association for Computational Linguistics.

Samuel R. Bowman, Gabor Angeli, Christopher Potts, and Christopher D. Manning. 2015. A large annotated corpus for learning natural language inference. In *Proceedings of the 2015 Conference on Empirical Methods in Natural Language Processing*, pages 632–642.

Ido Dagan, Oren Glickman, and Bernardo Magnini. 2006. The PASCAL recognising textual entailment challenge. In *Proceedings of the First International Conference on Machine Learning Challenges: Evaluating Predictive Uncertainty Visual Object Classification, and Recognizing Textual Entailment*, MLCW'05, pages 177–190, Berlin, Heidelberg. Springer-Verlag.

Ido Dagan, Dan Roth, Mark Sammons, and Fabio Massimo Zanzotto. 2013. Recognizing textual entailment: Models and applications. *Synthesis Lectures on Human Language Technologies*, 6(4):1–220.

Sepp Hochreiter and Jürgen Schmidhuber. 1997. Long short-term memory. *Neural Comput.*, 9(8):1735–1780.

Diederik P. Kingma and Jimmy Ba. 2014. Adam: A method for stochastic optimization. In *International Conference on Learning Representations (ICLR)*.

Ranjay Krishna, Yuke Zhu, Oliver Groth, Justin Johnson, Kenji Hata, Joshua Kravitz, Stephanie Chen, Yannis Kalantidis, Li-Jia Li, David A Shamma, Michael Bernstein, and Li Fei-Fei. 2016. Visual genome: Connecting language and vision using crowdsourced dense image annotations.

Alice Lai and Julia Hockenmaier. 2014. Illinois-LH: A denotational and distributional approach to semantics. In *Proceedings of the 8th International Workshop on Semantic Evaluation (SemEval 2014)*, pages 329–334.

Marco Marelli, Stefano Menini, Marco Baroni, Luisa Bentivogli, Raffaella Bernardi, and Roberto Zamparelli. 2014. A SICK cure for the evaluation of compositional distributional semantic models. In *Proceedings of the Ninth International Conference on Language Resources and Evaluation (LREC-2014)*.

Tomas Mikolov, Ilya Sutskever, Kai Chen, Greg S Corrado, and Jeff Dean. 2013. Distributed representations of words and phrases and their compositionality. In *Advances in neural information processing systems*, pages 3111–3119.

Jeffrey Pennington, Richard Socher, and Christopher D. Manning. 2014. GloVe: Global vectors for word representation. In *Empirical Methods in Natural Language Processing (EMNLP)*, pages 1532–1543.

Cyrus Rashtchian, Peter Young, Micah Hodosh, and Julia Hockenmaier. 2010. Collecting image annotations using Amazon's Mechanical Turk. In *Proceedings of the NAACL HLT 2010 Workshop on Creating Speech and Language Data with Amazon's Mechanical Turk*, pages 139–147. Association for Computational Linguistics.

Tim Rocktäschel, Edward Grefenstette, Karl Moritz Hermann, Tomas Kocisky, and Phil Blunsom. 2016. Reasoning about entailment with neural attention. In *International Conference on Learning Representations (ICLR)*.

Peter Young, Alice Lai, Micah Hodosh, and Julia Hockenmaier. 2014. From image descriptions to visual denotations. *Transactions of the Association of Computational Linguistics – Volume 2, Issue 1*, pages 67–78.

Enabling Transitivity for Lexical Inference on Chinese Verbs Using Probabilistic Soft Logic

Wei-Chung Wang, Lun-Wei Ku
Academia Sinica
128 Academia Road, Section2
Nankang, Taipei 11529, Taiwan
{anthonywang, lwku}@iis.sinica.edu.tw

Abstract

To learn more knowledge, enabling transitivity is a vital step for lexical inference. However, most of the lexical inference models with good performance are for nouns or noun phrases, which cannot be directly applied to the inference on events or states. In this paper, we construct the largest Chinese verb lexical inference dataset containing 18,029 verb pairs, where for each pair one of four inference relations are annotated. We further build a probabilistic soft logic (PSL) model to infer verb lexicons using the logic language. With PSL, we easily enable transitivity in two layers, the observed layer and the feature layer, which are included in the knowledge base. We further discuss the effect of transitives within and between these layers. Results show the performance of the proposed PSL model can be improved at least 3.5% (relative) when the transitivity is enabled. Furthermore, experiments show that enabling transitivity in the observed layer benefits the most.

1 Introduction

Lexical inference is an important component of natural language understanding for NLP tasks such as textual entailment (Garrette et al., 2011), metaphor detection (Mohler et al., 2013), and text generation (Biran and McKeown, 2013) to acquire implications not explicitly written in context. Given two words, the goal of lexical inferences is to detect whether there is an inference relation between the lexicon pair. For example, the word 'buy' entails the word 'have'. With the help of lexical inference system, we can know "Mom has ap-

ples" from the ground truth "Mom buys apples" to answer the question "Who has apples?" without explicitly mentioning it.

An intuitive solution to this problem is to first represent the sense of words in the lexicon to calculate the confidence of inferences from one sense to another, or to build a classifier to distinguish inference relations from other relations. Most related research is of one of these two types (Szpektor and Dagan, 2008a; Kiela et al., 2015). However, for this problem it is difficult for these models to take into account transitivity. In the framework of a lexical inference system, transitivity can be included in three layers: the observed layer, the feature layer, and the prediction layer. Figure 1 illustrates these layers and the corresponding transitives. The observed layer includes inference relations we already know, e.g., true inferences from the gold labels or ontologies; the feature layer includes the observed features for all lexicon pairs to be predicted, i.e., features for the testing data, and the predicted layer saves the predicted inference pairs, i.e., the relations of pairs in the testing data, predicted by the model. As inference usually involves available knowledge, the knowledge base (KB) is shown in Figure 1 as well. KB contains known information for the models. Therefore, in this system, it includes the observed layer and the feature layer which contain gold relations and the features for the testing data respectively.

There has been several new rising research directions involving lexical inference. The most representative ones are the automatic problem solvers and the open-domain question answering systems, where inferring between events or states like *Some animals grow thick fur* effecting *Some animals stay warm* is critical (Clark et al., 2016). However, many recent works of lexical inference are only designed for or being tested on nouns or noun phrases (Jiang and Conrath, 1997; Kiela et al.,

Proceedings of the The 8th International Joint Conference on Natural Language Processing, pages 110–119,
Taipei, Taiwan, November 27 – December 1, 2017 ©2017 AFNLP

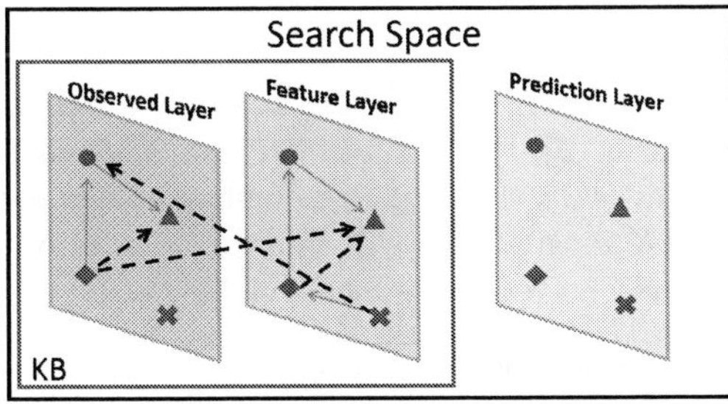

Figure 1: Three-layer lexical inference system. Points of the same shape in each layer are the same verbs; the solid arrow indicates the known inference relation; the dotted arrow indicates the hidden inference relation which can be inferred by the known inference relations.

2015; Shwartz et al., 2016), which makes them limited or not capable for these newly proposed research problems.

In this paper, we adopt the probabilistic soft logic (PSL) model to find lexical inference on Chinese verbs toward the math word problem solver. The contributions of this paper are listed as follows: (1) We build the largest Chinese verb lexical inference dataset with four types of inference relations as a potential testbed in the future. (2) We show that in the proposed PSL model the transitivity is easy to enabled and can benefit the lexical inference on Chinese verbs. (3) We implement and discuss the transitivity inter- and intra- layers and conclude the transitivity within the observed layer brings the most performance gain.

2 Related Work

One mainstream lexical inference extracts either explicit or implicit features from the manually constructed lexical knowledge. Szpektor (2009) constructs a WordNet inference chain through substitution relations (synonyms and hypernyms) defined in WordNet. Aharon (2010) proposed a FrameNet Entailment-rule Derivation (FRED) algorithm to inference on the framework of FrameNet. FrameNet models the semantic argument structure of predicates in terms of prototypical situation, which is called *frames*. Predicates belong to the same *frames* are highly related to a specific situation defined for the frame. Therefore, it is intuitive to acquire lexical inference pairs from predicates in the same frame. However, no matter WordNet or FrameNet was used, the cov-

erage problem was always an issue when leveraging handcraft resources. Moreover, the relations of verbs in WordNet are rather flat compared to nouns, which brings problems when directly adopting approaches utilizing WordNet to detect the inference between verbs.

An unsupervised concept, distributional similarity, for measuring relations between words was proposed to overcome the coverage problem. Distributional similarity related algorithms utilized a large, unstructured corpus to learn lexical entailment relations by assuming that semantically similar lexicons appear with similar context (Harris, 1954). Various implementations were proposed to assess contextual similarity between two lexicons, including (Berant et al., 2010; Lin and Pantel, 2001; Weeds et al., 2004). Lin Similarity, or known as DIRT, is one commonly adopted method to measure the lexical context similarity (Lin and Pantel, 2001). Instead of applying the Distributional Hypothesis to verbs, Lin applied this hypothesis to the paths in dependency trees. They hypothesize that the meaning of two phrases is similar, if their paths tend to link the same sets of words in a dependency tree. Later, Weeds and Weir (2004) proposed a general framework for directional similarity measurement. The measurement examined the coverage of word w_l's features against those of w_r's, and more coverage indicated more similarity.

Lin Similarity generates errors as its symmetric structure cannot tell the difference between $w_l \rightarrow w_r$ and $w_r \rightarrow w_l$. That is, it makes errors on non-symmetric examples, like *buy* $\rightarrow$ *take*. Moreover, Weeds' method generates high score when an infrequent lexicon has features similar to those of another lexicon, which harms the performance as it happens a lot for non-entailed lexicons. Therefore, Szpektor and Dagan (2008a) proposed a hybrid method **Balanced-Inclusion, BInc**, and it was proved to outperform methods proposed prior to it. In this paper, we adopt BInc measurement and complement with lexical resource method to construct a hybrid model, which was proved to outperform both methods separately on our dataset.

Recent research is exploiting the effect of transitivity during model training. The intuition is that some implicit entailment relation is difficult to be identified when there is no direct features supporting it. Sometimes previous work could find the entailment pairs $w_1 \rightarrow w_2$ and $w_2 \rightarrow w_3$, but failed to answer distant entailment relation like $w_1 \rightarrow w_3$. Skeptor and Dagan (2009) first applied transitive chaining in the knowledge provided by the lexical ontology Wordnet (Miller, 1995) in the feature layer. Berant et al. (2011) built a lexical entailment knowledge graph given the predicted results from the base classifier. They used integer linear programming (ILP) to find the latent entailment in the prediction cascade, which transits in the prediction layer. Kloetzer et al. (2015), whose system outperformed Berant et al.'s on their own corpus, further use cascade entailment inference in the feature layer. They applied short transitivity optimization by a two-layered SVM classifier (Kloetzer et al., 2015). A set of candidate transitivity paths were created by concatenating two identified inference pairs from the first SVM classifier, e.g., $w_1 \rightarrow w_2$ and $w_2 \rightarrow w_3$ result in a candidate path $w_1 \rightarrow w_2 \rightarrow w_3$. Then the two-layered SVM classifier re-predicted whether there was an inference relation for the lexical pair $w_1 \rightarrow w_3$. However, none of these models takes into account transitivity in the observed layer or transitivity between two layers.

We select probabilistic soft logic (PSL) to model the lexical inference problem. PSL is a recently proposed alternative framework for probabilistic logic (Bach et al., 2015). It was first applied to the category prediction and similarity propagation on Wikipedia documents to align ontologies on a standard corpus of bibliographic ontology (Brocheler et al., 2012). It has been adopted in social network analysis, including social group modeling (Huang et al., 2012) and social trust analysis (Huang et al., 2013). For natural language processing, recently, Dhanya Sridhar (2014) applied the PSL model to stance classification of on-line debates. Islam Beltagy (2014) approached the textual problem by transforming sentences into their logic representations and applying a PSL model to analyze word-to-word semantic coverage between the hypothesis and the premise. All these show that PSL is good at capturing relations. However, PSL has not been utilized yet in the lexical inference problem, and its power to provide lexical transitivity has not been tested, either. Thus in this paper, we explore its ability on detecting verb lexical inference and on enabling the transitivity.

3 Approach

We start from describing the features for each lexicon pair. To use PSL, we define atoms and design rules to enable the inter- and intra-layer transitives. Finally, PSL will automatically learn the rule weights by MLE to yield the best results.

3.1 Lexicon Pair Features

3.1.1 Lexical ontology features

E-HowNet is a large Chinese lexical resource extended from HowNet (Dong and Dong, 2006). Manually constructed by several linguistic experts, it contains 93,953 Chinese words and 9,197 semantic types (concepts; some are sememes). It was designed as an ontology of semantic types, each is listed in both Chinese and in English. For example, one semantic type is ($Give$|給). Each semantic type has some instances which inherit the concept of it. Lexical relations are also defined. In addition to hypernym-hyponym pairs, E-Hownet contains conflation pairs, including preconditions like ($Divorce$|離婚) is to ($GetMarried$|結婚), consequences like ($Labor$|臨產) is to ($Pregnant$|懷孕), and same-events like ($Sell$|賣) is to (Buy|買). The hypernym-hyponym relation and the conflation relation are two features that we use to represent a lexicon pair.

3.1.2 Cohesion path score

Given two semantically related words, a key aspect of detecting lexical inference is the generality of the hypothesis compared to the premise. Though we have a lexical ontology to tell us explicitly the hypernym-hyponym relations, a score to estimate the degree of this compared generality is still necessary for model learning. Therefore, We define the cohesion score of a semantic type with E-Hownet to model the generality. For each semantic type $s_i \in S$ which has a set of instantiate words V_{si}, the cohesion score of s_i is calculated as

$$Coh\,(s_i) = \frac{1}{N} \sum_{v_1 \neq v_2} sim\,(v_1, v_2)\,; \quad v_1, v_2 \in V_{s_i} \tag{1}$$

where $sim(v_1, v_2)$ is the word-embedding cosine similarity of words v_1 and v_2.

We construct a graph by considering hypernym, hyponym, and conflation relations in E-HowNet where nodes are semantic types and instantiate words, and where edges are relations. Given a word pair (v_l, v_r), a set of paths P from v_l to

v_r can be found by traversing this graph, each of which is denoted as p with edges in the edge set E. Each of these edges in E is represented by the triple $e(n_1, n_2, type_e)$, where node n_2 is of type $type_e$ to node n_1. Nodes here can be a word or a semantic type. The $PathScore(p)$ is defined as:

$$PathScore(p) = \prod_{e \in E_p} \begin{cases} coh(s_e), type_e = \text{Hyponym} \\ 1, \text{otherwise} \end{cases} \quad (2)$$

The idea of $PathScore(p)$ is to calculate the generality lost, which is caused by hyponym relations, of each step of inference. The hypernym or conflation relation does not lose generality, so the $PathScore(p)$ is always 1.

Empirically, those path p whose length exceed 10 are dropped as the inference chain is too long. Finally, the cohesion path score of word pair (v_1, v_2) is defined as:

$$CohPathScore(v_1, v_2) = \frac{\ln(\max_{p \in P} PathScore(p)) - \ln(m)}{\ln(M) - \ln(m)} \quad (3)$$

while M and m are the Maximum and Minimum PathScore respectively. The cohesion path score also serves as a feature to build the PSL model.

3.1.3 Distributional similarity

Distributional semantics has been used to exploit the semantic similarities of the linguistic items through large language data.

We applied the CKIP parser [1], a well-known Chinese text parser, to raw sentences. Context of words are extracted as features fs of words, according to parsed sentence trees.

Some pre-prosessing steps are performed. Words appearing only once in the corpus are dropped to reduce Chinese segmentation error. For each Word v, we retrieve all the words that share at least one feature with w and call them candidate words. Drop the candidate word if it shares less than 1 percent features, counted by frequency, with word w. We then calculate the distributional similarity score between w and its candidate words.

Balanced-inclusion (BInc, (Szpektor and Dagan, 2008a)) is a well-known scoring function for determining lexical entailment. It contains two parts, one is semantic similarity measurement, and one is semantic coverage direction measurement. Given two words w_l, w_r and their feature sets F_l, F_r, the semantic similarity between w_l and w_r is calculated by Lin similarity (Lin and Pantel, 2001):

$$Lin(v_l, v_r) = \frac{\sum_{f \in F_l \cap F_r} [w_{vl}(f) + w_{vr}(f)]}{\sum_{f \in F_l} w_{vl}(f) + \sum_{f \in F_r} w_{vr}(f)} \quad (4)$$

The coverage direction measurement, which provides clues of direction of entailment relation, is calculated by Weed's (Weeds et al., 2004) coverage measurement:

$$weed(v_l, v_r) = \frac{\sum_{f \in F_l \cap F_r} w_{vl}(f)}{\sum_{f \in F_l} w_{vl}(f)} \quad (5)$$

The weight of each feature $w(f)$ is the Pointwise Mutual Information (PMI) between the word v and the feature f:

$$w_v(f) = \log[\frac{pr(f|v)}{pr(f)}] \quad (6)$$

where $pr(f)$ is probability of feature f. BInc is defined as geometric mean of the above two:

$$BInc(v_l, v_r) = \sqrt{Lin(v_l, v_r) \cdot Weed(v_l, v_r)} \quad (7)$$

To compare BInc's performance to the proposed PSL model and utilize it as a feature, we implemented it on the Chinese experimental dataset to calculate the BInc score of each lexicon pair.

3.1.4 Word Embeddings

Previous work has shown that word embeddings work well on entailment relation recognition of noun-noun pairs and (adj+noun)-noun pairs (Baroni et al., 2012; Roller et al., 2014). We choose glove (Pennington et al., 2014) to train embeddings of each word, and concatenate the embedding of two words to create the embedding for each word pair. This embedding then serves as the feature in the rbf-kernel SVM classifier to predict the entailment relation of the corresponding word pair.

3.2 Probabilistic Soft Logic (PSL)

We use the PSL model to find the latent inference relations by enabling the transitivity of lex-

---

[1]CKIP parser : http://parser.iis.sinica.edu.tw/

ical relations. The lexical relations include features described in Section 3.1, and the known inference relations in the observed layer. In PSL, each relation of the lexicon pair v_l, v_r is written as a (ground) atom $a(v_l, v_r)$ in the logic language. The description of the transitivity of atoms $a_i(v_1, v_2)$, $a_j(v_2, v_3)$ and its latent inference relation, $Etl(v_1, v_3)$ is written as a rule in the logic language:

$$a_i(v_1, v_2) \wedge a_j(v_2, v_3) \rightarrow Etl(v_1, v_3) \qquad (8)$$

Each rule is assigned a weight to denote the reliability of the hypothesis that given $a_i(v_1, v_2)$, $a_j(v_2, v_3)$ are true, $Etl(v_1, v_3)$ is also true. The PSL model learns the rule weights by the training set. We encode the transitivity inter-($i = j$) and intra-($i \neq j$) different types of relations and their resulting latent inference relation to construct the experimental rule set.

Given a set of (ground) atoms $a = \{a_1, ..., a_n\}$, we denote an *interpretation* the mapping $I : a \rightarrow [0, 1]^n$ from ground atoms to soft truth value. The *distance to satisfaction* of each ground rule is defined as:

$$d(r, I) = \max\{0, I(r_{antecedent}) - I(r_{consequent})\} \qquad (9)$$

The PSL model learns the weights λ_r of these rules and optimizes the most probable *interpretation* of entailment relations, through the probability density function f over I:

$$f(I) = \frac{1}{Z} \exp[-\sum_{r \in R} \lambda_r (d(r, I))^p]; \qquad (10)$$

where Z is the normalization term, λ_r is the weight of rule r, R is the set of all ground rules, and $p \in \{1, 2\}$. In this paper, we set p to 2, indicating a squared function.

In the following section, we are going to describe the atoms defined in our lexical inference model in Section 3.2.1. Then rules are defined in Section 3.2.2. Last, weight learning is described in Section 3.2.3

3.2.1 Atoms for PSL

Atoms are types of information provided in Knowledge base in PSL model, Table 1 lists all atoms defined in our lexical inference model. Etl denotes the entailment relation serving as the prediction target. It is the only unknown atom. In PSL model the number of prediction target grows quadratically with the number of the entities (verbs), if no limitation is provided, which is not desired and is time consuming. Thus Cdd indicates canopies (McCallum et al., 2000) over the prediction target. $Hypr$, Con, Coh, and $BInc$ are the hypernym, conflation, cohesion path score, and distributional similarity score BInc features described in Section 3.1. Svm is the prediction of SVM classifier which takes concatenation of word embeddings as feature. Obv represents the knowledge of observed entailment lexical pairs for the training phase. Note that the set of pairs with $Obv = true$ must not overlap with the testing set.

3.2.2 Inference rules for PSL

Having defined the atoms, the five features $Hypr$, Con, $BInc$, Coh, and Svm are used in the design of five basic rules in Eq. 11. We further apply the inference chain by concatenating two atoms to create 25 rules shown as Eq.12 for feature-layer transitivity. For transitivity in the observed layer, we concatenate Obv atoms as shown in Eq.13. Then we concatenate Obv with other features and vice versa to add 10 additional rules shown as in Eq.14,15 for bidirectional transitives between the feature and the observed layers. Finally, the rule $\neg Etl(v_1, v_2)$ states that v_1 does not entail v_2 if the previous rules are not applicable.

$$\begin{aligned} &Rel(v_1, v_2) \rightarrow Etl(v_1, v_2); \\ &Rel \in \{Hypr, Con, BInc, Coh, Svm\} \end{aligned} \qquad (11)$$

$$Rel(v_1, v_2) \wedge Rel(v_2, v_3) \rightarrow Etl(v_1, v_3) \qquad (12)$$

$$Obv(v_1, v_2) \wedge Obv(v_2, v_3) \rightarrow Etl(v_1, v_3) \qquad (13)$$

$$Obv(v_1, v_2) \wedge Rel(v_2, v_3) \rightarrow Etl(v_1, v_3) \qquad (14)$$

$$Rel(v_1, v_2) \wedge Obv(v_2, v_3) \rightarrow Etl(v_1, v_3) \qquad (15)$$

3.2.3 Learning inference rule weights

The rule weights(λ_r) are determined using maximum-likelihood estimation.

$$\frac{\partial}{\partial \lambda_r} \log p(I) = \\ -\sum_{r \in R_i} (d(r, I)) + E\left[\sum_{r \in R_i} (d(r, I))\right] \qquad (16)$$

Atom Name	Description
Cdd(v_1,v_2)	Canopies over prediction target. Return 1 if (v_1,v_2) is the prediction target in the task
Etl(v_1,v_2)	Entail statement which is the prediction target.
Hypr(s_1,s_2)	Hypernym relation between two semantic concept: s_1 is hypernym of s_2.
Con(s_1,s_2)	Conflation relation between two semantic types.
Ehow(v_1, v_2)	E-HowNet algorithm.
Dis(v_1,v_2)	BInc between v_1 and v_2.
Svm(v_1,v_2)	Svm prediction featured by word embeddings
Obv(v_1,v_2)	Observed entail statement.

Table 1: List of atoms in lexical inference model

The expected value $E\left[\sum_{r \in R_i} (d(r, I))\right]$ is intractable. Thus it is approximated via $\sum_{r \in R_i} d_r(I^*)$, where I^* is the most probable interpretation given the current weight (Kimmig et al., 2012).

4 Evaluation

4.1 Experiment Dataset

There are some of entailment dataset open to research utility, but the Chinese Verb entailment dataset (CVED) is special in some way. First, most of the open entailment dataset include the entailment between noun-noun pairs, adjective_noun-noun pairs, and quantity_noun-quantity_noun pairs, but none of them consider the entailment between verb-verb pairs like CVED. Second, in my knowledge, our CVED is the largest Chinese entailment dataset.

To get more verb lexical inference pairs for our experiments, we collected verb pairs from math application problems, which usually contain logical relations in the descriptions for each problem. A total of 995 verbs and 18,029 verb pairs were extracted from 20,000 Chinese elementary math problems, where the verbs in each pair are from the same problem. Few types of verb are discarded, including **V_1**, **V_2**, **VH**, **VI**, **VJ**, **VK** and **VL** ,which are adjective[2] and statement associated verbs defined in CKIP[3].

Given a set of verbs extracted from a math problem, every possible directed verb pair was labeled. If there were n verbs, $n \times (n-1)$ directed verb pairs ($v_i \rightarrow v_j$) were collected, where v_i is the premise and v_j is the hypothesis. For example, if we extracted "sell", "buy", and

"pay" from the descriptions of the problem, we added six directed verb pairs to the annotation set: $\{(sell, buy), (sell, pay), (buy, pay), (buy, sell), (pay, sell), (pay, buy)\}$ We provide four types of entailment label in CVED. One is commonly seen hypernym relation. The same-event relations are verb pairs related to same thing but in different point of view Some examples are (sell, buy) and (give, got). These are used by most earlier research or in small-scale experiments (Szpektor and Dagan, 2008b; Kiela et al., 2015). Another two are casual relations, as premises in the *precondition* and *consequence* relations are likely to be true given their hypothesis in our daily life, and because these relations are more useful in real applications, we further consider these relations as entailment relations. These relations are usually selected for web-scale experiments (Aharon et al., 2010; Berant et al., 2011; Kloetzer et al., 2015). Among all experimental verb pairs, 10% were used for testing, 10% were used for developing and the remaining dataset was for training. A five-fold training process was performed to learn the best parameters for the testing model.

4.2 Experiment Setting

To achieve better performance, weights are randomly initialized and retrained 10 times for each fold. The best combination is derived by averaging the five best weight sets obtained in the five-fold cross-validation process. Two baselines are provided for the evaluation of the models with transitivity disabled. Hyper+Conf is the ontology-based baseline. In this setting, verb pairs with hypernym and conflation relations found in E-Hownet are reported as entailment pairs. BInc is the distributional similarity baseline, where we set a best threshold for the development set and apply it

---

[2] Adjective words are seen as kind of verbs in CKIP
[3] http://rocling.iis.sinica.edu.tw/CKIP/tr/ 9305_2013%20revision.pdf

115

	Precision	Recall	F1
Hyper+Conf	**0.547**	0.189	0.281
BInc	0.150	0.098	0.119
PSL	0.270	**0.474**	**0.344**

Table 2: Model performance: transitivity disabled.

to the testing set to identify the entailment relation. The 20,000 elementary math problems together with 61,777 sentences from Sinica Treebank[4] are utilized to calculate the BInc score of each verb pair. A set of 300 dimensional word embedding representation is trained by a hybrid of Sinica Treebank, elementary math problems and Chinese Wikipedia.

To discuss the effect of transitivity within (intra-) and between (inter-) different layers, we build three additional models for PSL. PSL_TrFeat allows transitivity within the feature layer, PSL_TrObv allows transitivity within the observed layer on top of PSL_TrFeat, and PSL_TrFeatObv allows transitivity betwen the observed layer and the feature layer on top of PSL_TrObv. Here we set the degree of transitivity to 2, and leave the determination of the best transitivity degree as future work. For comparison, we implement a SVM baseline ,the state-of-the-art entailment classifier (Kloetzer(base)), and its transitivity framework (Kloetzer(TrFeatPred)) (Kloetzer et al., 2015). We use rbf-kernel SVM and the other hyper-parameters are selected from the 5-fold training.

4.3 Results and Discussion

Table 2 shows the performance of the proposed PSL model when transitivity is disabled (PSL). Unsurprisingly, Hyper+Conf achieves the highest precision as the relations found in E-Hownet are built manually. False alarms come from pairs that contain various unknown Chinese compound words that E-Hownet does not include, e.g., 分給(distribute to) is composed of 分(issue) and 給(give). We attempt to find its head to determine its sense, which sometimes causes errors. Compared to BInc, though in general distributional approaches may outperform ontology-based approaches at least in recall, Hyper+Conf still performs much better. We think the reason is that E-Hownet already contains a large number of words

[4]sinica treeback: http://rocling.iis.sinica.edu.tw/CKIP/engversion/treebank.htm

and adopting the heuristic of finding the head for compound words which could mitigates the coverage problem.

Table 3 shows the performance of various PSL models when transitivity is enabled. We conduct a SVM baseline, SVM(w2v), by concatenating the word embeddings of two verbs as the features of the verb pair and it performs comparably well, indicating word embeddings are strong features. Therefore, we discuss the effect of the strong and the weak base settings here. The strong base setting involves the prediction of SVM by word embeddings (relation *SVM*), while the weak base setting involves the rest relations *Hypr*, *Con*, *BInc* and *Coh*. The SVM model from Kloetzer serves as the second baseline. It involves more than 100 features but does not include word embeddings, and hence we compare it with the PSL models of the weak base setting. For the weak base setting, the performance of PSL cannot beat that of Kloetzer's SVM in the very beginning, as SVM is generally considered a more powerful classifier and the Kloetzer's SVM model involves comparably more features. Surprisingly, this state-of-the-art model from Kloetzer does not improve its F1 score after enabling the transitivity in the feature layer by their transitivity framework. (Kloetzer(TrFeatPred) vs. Kloetzer(base): they report a 2% improvement in average precision in their paper.) For the proposed PSL models, enabling transitivity in the feature layer (PSL(TrFeat) vs. PSL(base)) does improve the F1 score from the gain of recall. The reason for this could be that the transitivities of Kloetzer's features depend on the transitivities of the prediction results. If the predictions don't indicate a path to transit, their features will not be combined together for the next prediction. Therefore, their transitivity framework may involve the noise from the first prediction. On the contrary, in our PSL models, all possible feature-layered transitivities between pairs are explored. Hence, our feature-layered transitivity models have the capabilities to improve the recall.

A significant improvement comes from enabling transitivity in the observed layer, that is, if we know $w_1 \rightarrow w_2$ and $w_2 \rightarrow w_3$, we add $w_1 \rightarrow w_3$ to the gold labels. As the relations in the observed layer constitute prior knowledge (known from the training data and saved in the PSL knowledge base), inferring from one relation to the other involves less uncertainty. Therefore, compared to

	Precision	Recall	F1
SVM(w2v)	0.850	0.500	0.630
PSL(WeakBase)	0.314	0.570	0.405
PSL(WeakBase_TrFeat)	0.348	0.645	0.452
PSL(WeakBase_TrObv)	0.675	0.577	0.622
PSL(WeakBase_TrFeatObv)	0.544	0.613	0.577
Kloetzer(base)	0.390	0.590	0.469
Kloetzer(TrFeatPred)	0.385	0.604	0.470
PSL(StrongBase)	0.670	0.649	0.660
PSL(StrongBase_TrFeat)	0.667	0.649	0.658
PSL(StrongBase_TrObv)	0.624	0.757	**0.684**
PSL(StrongBase_TrFeatObv)	0.612	**0.764**	0.680

Table 3: Model performance: transitivity enabled. PSL(StrongBase_TrObv) is significantly better than all the other models with p-value < 0.001.

PSL(WeakBase_TrFeat), PSL(WeakBase_TrObv) shows a great improvement in both precision and F1. For recall, the feature-layer transitivity (PSL(WeakBase_TrFeat)) enables the model to reach more words for a better recall, while the enrichment of the prior knowledge in PSL(WeakBase_TrObv) helps to eliminate uncertainty but decreases recall. If we go further to enable transitivity between the observed layer and the feature layer using model PSL(WeakBase_TrFeatObV), it begins to suffer from the lower precision caused by longer transitivity. Overall, PSL(WeakBase_TrObV) achieves best among all PSL(WeakBase) models, with improvements of 21.7% over the transitivity-disabled PSL model.

Compared to the models of the weak base setting, the PSL model of the strong base setting without transitivity enabled has achieved good performance in the very beginning (F1=0.66). Its performance is better than 3 baselines, SVM(w2v), Kloetzer(base) and Kloetzer(TrFeatPred). It also performs better than the best PSL model of the weak base setting, PSL(WeakBase_TrObv). The great thing is, enabling transitivity achieves even better performance in PSL(StrongBase_TrObv) and PSL(StrongBase_TrFeatObv). For all models of the strong base settings, only enabling the transitivity in the feature layer does not benefit the performance as this decreases the precision.

From all the experiment results, we can conclude the followings. First, enabling transitivities help to find more inference pairs no matter the initial model is strong or weak. Second, for a general model, transitivities inter- or intra- layers both help it become stronger; however, for a strong model, only the transitivities intra- or inter the observed layer, i.e., involving the gold labels, contribute to the performance gain. In other words, only solid knowledge can make a strong model even stronger through transitivities.

5 Conclusion

We have proposed a PSL model to explore the power of transitivity. In this process, the easy and straightforward nature of PSL in considering transitives for lexical inference is demonstrated. Results show that the best PSL model achieves the F1 score 0.684. Moreover, the proposed base PSL model has already achieved well and models with transitivity enabled achieve even better, which confirms the power of transitivity for solving the lexical inference problem on verbs. We will release the current experimental dataset. Future goals include enlarging our dataset by including web word pairs and applied the predicted results in textual entailment tasks. The constructed CVED dataset can be found in the NLPSA lab webpage[5].

Acknowledgments

Research of this paper was partially supported by Ministry of Science and Technology, Taiwan, under the contract 105-2221-E-001-007-MY3.

---

[5]http://academiasinicanlplab.github.io/

References

Roni Ben Aharon, Idan Szpektor, and Ido Dagan. 2010. Generating entailment rules from framenet. In *Proceedings of the ACL 2010 Conference Short Papers*. Association for Computational Linguistics, pages 241–246.

Stephen H Bach, Matthias Broecheler, Bert Huang, and Lise Getoor. 2015. Hinge-loss markov random fields and probabilistic soft logic. *arXiv preprint arXiv:1505.04406* .

Marco Baroni, Raffaella Bernardi, Ngoc-Quynh Do, and Chung-chieh Shan. 2012. Entailment above the word level in distributional semantics. In *Proceedings of the 13th Conference of the European Chapter of the Association for Computational Linguistics*. Association for Computational Linguistics, pages 23–32.

Islam Beltagy, Katrin Erk, and Raymond J Mooney. 2014. Probabilistic soft logic for semantic textual similarity. In *ACL (1)*. pages 1210–1219.

Jonathan Berant, Ido Dagan, and Jacob Goldberger. 2010. Global learning of focused entailment graphs. In *Proceedings of the 48th Annual Meeting of the Association for Computational Linguistics*. Association for Computational Linguistics, pages 1220–1229.

Jonathan Berant, Ido Dagan, and Jacob Goldberger. 2011. Global learning of typed entailment rules. In *Proceedings of the 49th Annual Meeting of the Association for Computational Linguistics: Human Language Technologies-Volume 1*. Association for Computational Linguistics, pages 610–619.

Rahul Bhagat, Patrick Pantel, Eduard H Hovy, and Marina Rey. 2007. Ledir: An unsupervised algorithm for learning directionality of inference rules. In *EMNLP-CoNLL*. pages 161–170.

Or Biran and Kathleen McKeown. 2013. Classifying taxonomic relations between pairs of wikipedia articles. In *IJCNLP*. pages 788–794.

Matthias Brocheler, Lilyana Mihalkova, and Lise Getoor. 2012. Probabilistic similarity logic. *arXiv preprint arXiv:1203.3469* .

Peter Clark, Oren Etzioni, Tushar Khot, Ashish Sabharwal, Oyvind Tafjord, Peter Turney, and Daniel Khashabi. 2016. Combining retrieval, statistics, and inference to answer elementary science questions .

Zhendong Dong and Qiang Dong. 2006. *HowNet and the Computation of Meaning*. World Scientific.

Dan Garrette, Katrin Erk, and Raymond Mooney. 2011. Integrating logical representations with probabilistic information using markov logic. In *Proceedings of the Ninth International Conference on Computational Semantics*. Association for Computational Linguistics, pages 105–114.

Klir George J and Yuan Bo. 2008. Fuzzy sets and fuzzy logic, theory and applications. - .

Zellig S Harris. 1954. Distributional structure. *Word* 10(2-3):146–162.

Bert Huang, Stephen H Bach, Eric Norris, Jay Pujara, and Lise Getoor. 2012. Social group modeling with probabilistic soft logic. In *NIPS Workshop on Social Network and Social Media Analysis: Methods, Models, and Applications*. volume 7.

Bert Huang, Angelika Kimmig, Lise Getoor, and Jennifer Golbeck. 2013. A flexible framework for probabilistic models of social trust. In *Social Computing, Behavioral-Cultural Modeling and Prediction*, Springer, pages 265–273.

Jay J Jiang and David W Conrath. 1997. Semantic similarity based on corpus statistics and lexical taxonomy. *arXiv preprint cmp-lg/9709008* .

Douwe Kiela, Laura Rimell, Ivan Vulic, and Stephen Clark. 2015. Exploiting image generality for lexical entailment detection. In *Proceedings of the 53rd Annual Meeting of the Association for Computational Linguistics (ACL 2015)*. ACL.

Angelika Kimmig, Stephen Bach, Matthias Broecheler, Bert Huang, and Lise Getoor. 2012. A short introduction to probabilistic soft logic. In *Proceedings of the NIPS Workshop on Probabilistic Programming: Foundations and Applications*. pages 1–4.

Julien Kloetzer, Kentaro Torisawa, Chikara Hashimoto, and Jong-hoon Oh. 2013. Large-scale acquisition of entailment pattern pairs. In *In Information Processing Society of Japan (IPSJ) Kansai-Branch Convention*. Citeseer.

Julien Kloetzer, Kentaro Torisawa, Chikara Hashimoto, and Jong-Hoon Oh. 2015. Large-scale acquisition of entailment pattern pairs by exploiting transitivity .

Dekang Lin and Patrick Pantel. 2001. Discovery of inference rules for question-answering. *Natural Language Engineering* 7(04):343–360.

Andrew McCallum, Kamal Nigam, and Lyle H Ungar. 2000. Efficient clustering of high-dimensional data sets with application to reference matching. In *Proceedings of the sixth ACM SIGKDD international conference on Knowledge discovery and data mining*. ACM, pages 169–178.

Tomas Mikolov, Kai Chen, Greg Corrado, and Jeffrey Dean. 2013. Efficient estimation of word representations in vector space. *arXiv preprint arXiv:1301.3781* .

George A Miller. 1995. Wordnet: a lexical database for english. *Communications of the ACM* 38(11):39–41.

Michael Mohler, David Bracewell, David Hinote, and Marc Tomlinson. 2013. Semantic signatures for example-based linguistic metaphor detection. In *Proceedings of the First Workshop on Metaphor in NLP*. pages 27–35.

Jeffrey Pennington, Richard Socher, and Christopher D Manning. 2014. Glove: Global vectors for word representation. In *EMNLP*. volume 14, pages 1532–43.

Stephen Roller, Katrin Erk, and Gemma Boleda. 2014. Inclusive yet selective: Supervised distributional hypernymy detection. In *COLING*. pages 1025–1036.

Vered Shwartz, Yoav Goldberg, and Ido Dagan. 2016. Improving hypernymy detection with an integrated path-based and distributional method. *arXiv preprint arXiv:1603.06076* .

Dhanya Sridhar, Lise Getoor, and Marilyn Walker. 2014. Collective stance classification of posts in online debate forums. *ACL 2014* page 109.

Idan Szpektor and Ido Dagan. 2008a. Learning entailment rules for unary templates. In *Proceedings of the 22nd International Conference on Computational Linguistics-Volume 1*. Association for Computational Linguistics, pages 849–856.

Idan Szpektor and Ido Dagan. 2008b. Learning entailment rules for unary templates. In *Proceedings of the 22nd International Conference on Computational Linguistics-Volume 1*. Association for Computational Linguistics, pages 849–856.

Idan Szpektor and Ido Dagan. 2009. Augmenting wordnet-based inference with argument mapping. In *Proceedings of the 2009 Workshop on Applied Textual Inference*. Association for Computational Linguistics, pages 27–35.

Julie Weeds, David Weir, and Diana McCarthy. 2004. Characterising measures of lexical distributional similarity. In *Proceedings of the 20th international conference on Computational Linguistics*. Association for Computational Linguistics, page 1015.

An Exploration of Neural Sequence-to-Sequence Architectures for Automatic Post-Editing

Marcin Junczys-Dowmunt
Department for Natural Language Processing
Adam Mickiewicz University in Poznań
junczys@amu.edu.pl

Roman Grundkiewicz
School of Informatics
University of Edinburgh
rgrundki@inf.ed.ac.uk

Abstract

In this work, we explore multiple neural architectures adapted for the task of automatic post-editing of machine translation output. We focus on neural end-to-end models that combine both inputs mt (raw MT output) and src (source language input) in a single neural architecture, modeling $\{mt, src\} \rightarrow pe$ directly. Apart from that, we investigate the influence of hard-attention models which seem to be well-suited for monolingual tasks, as well as combinations of both ideas. We report results on data sets provided during the WMT-2016 shared task on automatic post-editing and can demonstrate that dual-attention models that incorporate all available data in the APE scenario in a single model improve on the best shared task system and on all other published results after the shared task. Dual-attention models that are combined with hard attention remain competitive despite applying fewer changes to the input.

1 Introduction

Given the raw output of a (possibly unknown) machine translation system from language src to language mt, Automatic Post-Editing (APE) is the process of automatic correction of raw MT output (mt), so that a closer resemblance to human post-edited MT output (pe) is achieved. While APE systems that only model $mt \rightarrow pe$ yield good results, the field has always strived towards methods that also integrate src in various forms.

With neural encoder-decoder models, and multi-source models in particular, this can be now achieved in more natural ways than for previously popular phrase-based statistical machine transla-

tion (PB-SMT) systems. Despite this, previously reported results for multi-source or dual-source models in APE scenarios are unsatisfying in terms of performance.

In this work, we explore a number of single-source and dual-source neural architectures which we believe to be better fits to the APE task than vanilla encoder-decoder models with soft attention. We focus on neural end-to-end models that combine both inputs mt and src in a single neural architecture, modeling $\{mt, src\} \rightarrow pe$ directly. Apart from that, we investigate the influence of hard-attention models, which seem to be well-suited for monolingual tasks. Finally, we create combinations of both architectures.

We report results on data sets provided during the WMT-2016 shared task on automatic post-editing (Bojar et al., 2016) and compare our performance against the shared task winner, the system submitted by the Adam Mickiewicz University (AMU) team (Junczys-Dowmunt and Grundkiewicz, 2016), and a more recent system by Pal et al. (2017) with the previously best published results on the same test set.

Our main contributions are: (1) we perform a thorough comparison of end-to-end neural approaches to APE during which (2) we demonstrate that dual-attention models that incorporate all available data in the APE scenario in a single model achieve the best reported results for the WMT-2016 APE task, and (3) show that models with a hard-attention mechanism reach competitive results although they execute fewer edits than models relying only on soft attention.

The remainder of the paper is organized as follows: Previous relevant work is described in Section 2. Section 3 summarizes the basic encoder-decoder with attention architecture that is further extended with multiple non-standard attention mechanisms in Section 4. These attention mecha-

Proceedings of the The 8th International Joint Conference on Natural Language Processing, pages 120–129,
Taipei, Taiwan, November 27 – December 1, 2017 ©2017 AFNLP

nisms are: hard-attention in Section 4.1, a combination of hard attention and soft attention in Section 4.2, dual soft attention in Section 4.3 and a combination of hard attention and dual soft attention in Section 4.4. We describe experiments and results in Section 5 and conclude in Section 7.

2   Previous work

Before the application of neural sequence-to-sequence models to APE, most APE systems would rely on phrase-based SMT following a monolingual approach first introduced by Simard et al. (2007). Béchara et al. (2011) proposed a "source-context aware" variant of this approach where automatically created word alignments were used to create a new source language which consisted of joined MT output and source token pairs. The inclusion of source-language information in that form was shown to improve the automatic post-editing results (Béchara et al., 2012; Chatterjee et al., 2015). The quality of the used word alignments plays an important role for this methods, as demonstrated for instance by Pal et al. (2015).

During the WMT-2016 APE shared task two systems relied on neural models, the CUNI system (Libovický et al., 2016) and the shared task winner, the system submitted by the AMU team (Junczys-Dowmunt and Grundkiewicz, 2016). This submission explored the application of neural translation models to the APE problem and achieved good results by treating different models as components in a log-linear model, allowing for multiple inputs (the source src and the translated sentence mt) that were decoded to the same target language (post-edited translation pe). Two systems were considered, one using src as the input ($src \rightarrow pe$) and another using mt as the input ($mt \rightarrow pe$). A simple string-matching penalty integrated within the log-linear model was used to control for higher faithfulness with regard to the raw MT output. The penalty fired if the APE system proposed a word in its output that had not been seen in mt. The influence of the components on the final result was tuned with Minimum Error Rate Training (Och, 2003) with regard to the task metric TER.

Following the WMT-2016 APE shared task, Pal et al. (2017) published work on another neural APE system that integrated precomputed word-alignment features into the neural structure and en-

forced symmetric attention during the neural training process. The result was the best reported single neural model for the WMT-2016 APE test set prior to this work. With n-best list re-ranking and combination with phrase-based post-editing systems, the authors improved their results even further. None of their systems, however, integrated information from src, all modeled $mt \rightarrow pe$.

3   Attentional Encoder-Decoder

Implementations of all models explored in this paper are available in the Marian[1] toolkit (Junczys-Dowmunt et al., 2016). The attentional encoder-decoder model in Marian is a re-implementation of the NMT model in Nematus (Sennrich et al., 2017). The model differs from the standard model introduced by Bahdanau et al. (2015) by several aspects, the most important being the conditional GRU with attention. The summary provided in this section is based on the description in Sennrich et al. (2017).

Given the raw MT output sequence $(x_1, \dots, x_{T_x})$ of length T_x and its manually post-edited equivalent $(y_1, \dots, y_{T_y})$ of length T_y, we construct the encoder-decoder model using the following formulations.

Encoder context   A single forward encoder state $\overrightarrow{\mathbf{h}}_i$ is calculated as:

$$\overrightarrow{\mathbf{h}}_i = \text{GRU}(\overrightarrow{\mathbf{h}}_{i-1}, \mathbf{F}[x_i]),$$

where $\mathbf{F}$ is the encoder embeddings matrix. The GRU RNN cell (Cho et al., 2014) is defined as:

$$\text{GRU}(\mathbf{s}, \mathbf{x}) = (1 - \mathbf{z}) \odot \underline{\mathbf{s}} + \mathbf{z} \odot \mathbf{s}, \qquad (1)$$
$$\underline{\mathbf{s}} = \tanh\left(\mathbf{W}\mathbf{x} + \mathbf{r} \odot \mathbf{U}\mathbf{s}\right),$$
$$\mathbf{r} = \sigma\left(\mathbf{W}_r\mathbf{x} + \mathbf{U}_r\mathbf{s}\right),$$
$$\mathbf{z} = \sigma\left(\mathbf{W}_z\mathbf{x} + \mathbf{U}_z\mathbf{s}\right),$$

where $\mathbf{x}$ is the cell input; $\mathbf{s}$ is the previous recurrent state; $\mathbf{W}, \mathbf{U}, \mathbf{W}_r, \mathbf{U}_r, \mathbf{W}_z, \mathbf{U}_z$ are trained model parameters[2]; σ is the logistic sigmoid activation function. The backward encoder state is calculated analogously over a reversed input sequence with its own set of trained parameters.

Let $\mathbf{h}_i$ be the annotation of the source symbol at position i, obtained by concatenating the forward and backward encoder RNN hidden states, $\mathbf{h}_i = [\overrightarrow{\mathbf{h}}_i; \overleftarrow{\mathbf{h}}_i]$, the set of encoder states $C = \{\mathbf{h}_1, \dots, \mathbf{h}_{T_x}\}$ then forms the encoder context.

---

[1] https://github.com/marian-nmt/marian
[2] Biases have been omitted.

Decoder initialization The decoder is initialized with start state s_0, computed as the average over all encoder states:

$$\mathbf{s}_0 = \tanh\left(\mathbf{W}_{init}\frac{\sum_{i=1}^{T_x}\mathbf{h}_i}{T_x}\right).$$

Conditional GRU with attention We follow the Nematus implementation of the conditional GRU with attention, cGRU$_{att}$:

$$\mathbf{s}_j = \text{cGRU}_{att}\left(\mathbf{s}_{j-1}, \mathbf{E}[y_{j-1}], \mathbf{C}\right), \qquad (2)$$

where $\mathbf{s}_j$ is the newly computed hidden state, $\mathbf{s}_{j-1}$ is the previous hidden state, C the source context and $\mathbf{E}[y_{j-1}]$ is the embedding of the previously decoded symbol y_{i-1}.

The conditional GRU cell with attention, cGRU$_{att}$, has a complex internal structure, consisting of three parts: two GRU layers and an intermediate attention mechanism ATT.

Layer GRU$_1$ generates an intermediate representation $\mathbf{s}_j'$ from the previous hidden state $\mathbf{s}_{j-1}$ and the embedding of the previous decoded symbol $\mathbf{E}[y_{j-1}]$:

$$\mathbf{s}_j' = \text{GRU}_1\left(\mathbf{s}_{j-1}, \mathbf{E}[y_{j-1}]\right).$$

The attention mechanism, ATT, inputs the entire context set C along with intermediate hidden state $\mathbf{s}_j'$ in order to compute the context vector $\mathbf{c}_j$ as follows:

$$\mathbf{c}_j = \text{ATT}\left(\mathbf{C}, \mathbf{s}_j'\right) = \sum_i \alpha_{ij}\mathbf{h}_i,$$

$$\alpha_{ij} = \frac{\exp(e_{ij})}{\sum_{k=1}^{T_x}\exp(e_{kj})},$$

$$e_{ij} = \mathbf{v}_a^\mathsf{T}\tanh\left(\mathbf{U}_a\mathbf{s}_j' + \mathbf{W}_a\mathbf{h}_i\right),$$

where α_{ij} is the normalized alignment weight between source symbol at position i and target symbol at position j, and $\mathbf{v}_a, \mathbf{U}_a, \mathbf{W}_a$ are trained model parameters.

Layer GRU$_2$ generates $\mathbf{s}_j$, the hidden state of the cGRU$_{att}$, from the intermediate representation $\mathbf{s}_j'$ and context vector $\mathbf{c}_j$:

$$\mathbf{s}_j = \text{GRU}_2\left(\mathbf{s}_j', \mathbf{c}_j\right).$$

Deep output Finally, given $\mathbf{s}_j$, y_{j-1}, and $\mathbf{c}_j$, the output probability $p(y_j|\mathbf{s}_j, y_{j-1}, \mathbf{c}_j)$ is computed by a softmax activation as follows:

$$p(y_j|\mathbf{s}_j, y_{j-1}, \mathbf{c}_j) = \text{softmax}\left(\mathbf{t}_j\mathbf{W}_o\right),$$
$$\mathbf{t}_j = \tanh\left(\mathbf{s}_j\mathbf{W}_{t_1} + \mathbf{E}[y_{j-1}]\mathbf{W}_{t_2} + \mathbf{c}_j\mathbf{W}_{t_3}\right).$$

$\mathbf{W}_{t_1}, \mathbf{W}_{t_2}, \mathbf{W}_{t_3}, \mathbf{W}_o$ are the trained model parameters.

This rather standard encoder-decoder model with attention is our baseline and denoted as CGRU.

4 Encoder-Decoder Models with APE-specific Attention Models

The following models reuse most parts of the architecture described above wherever possible, most differences occur in the decoder RNN cell and the attention mechanism. The encoders are identical, so are the deep output layers.

4.1 Hard Monotonic Attention

Aharoni and Goldberg (2016) introduce a simple model for monolingual morphological re-inflection with hard monotonic attention. This model looks at one encoder state at a time, starting with the left-most encoder state and progressing to the right until all encoder states have been processed.

The target word vocabulary V_y is extended with a special step symbol ($V_y' = V_y \cup \{\langle\text{STEP}\rangle\}$) and whenever $\langle\text{STEP}\rangle$ is predicted as the output symbol, the hard attention is moved to the next encoder state. Formally, the hard attention mechanism is represented as a precomputed monotonic sequence $(a_1, \ldots, a_{T_y})$ which can be inferred from the target sequence $(y_1, \ldots, y_{T_y})$ (containing original target symbols and T_x step symbols) as follows:

$$a_1 = 1,$$
$$a_j = \begin{cases} a_{j-1} + 1 & \text{if } y_{j-1} = \langle\text{STEP}\rangle \\ a_{j-1} & \text{otherwise.} \end{cases}$$

For a given context $\mathbf{C} = \{\mathbf{h}_1, \ldots, \mathbf{h}_{T_x}\}$, the attended context vector at time step j is simply h_{a_j}.

Following the description by Aharoni and Goldberg (2016) for their LSTM-based model, we adapt the previously described encoder-decoder model to incorporate hard attention. Given the sequence of attention indices $(a_1, \ldots, a_{T_y})$, the conditional GRU cell (Eq. 2) used for hidden state updates of the decoder is replaced with a simple GRU cell (Eq. 1) (thus removing the soft-attention mechanism):

$$\mathbf{s}_j = \text{GRU}\left(\mathbf{s}_{j-1}, \left[\mathbf{E}[y_{j-1}]; \mathbf{h}_{a_j}\right]\right), \qquad (3)$$

where the cell input is now a concatenation of the embedding of the previous target symbol $\mathbf{E}[y_{j-1}]$

and the currently attended encoder state $\mathbf{h}_{a_j}$. This model is labeled GRU-HARD.

We find this architecture compelling for monolingual tasks that might require higher faithfulness with regard to the input. With hard monotonic attention, the translation algorithm can enforce certain constraints:

1. The end-of-sentence symbol can only be generated if the hard attention mechanism has reached the end of the input sequence, enforcing full coverage;

2. The ⟨STEP⟩ symbol cannot be generated once the end-of-sentence position in the source has been reached. It is however still possible to generate content tokens.

This model requires a target sequence with correctly inserted ⟨STEP⟩ symbols. For the described APE task, using the Longest Common Subsequence algorithm (Hirschberg, 1977), we first generate a sequence of match, delete and insert operations which transform the raw MT output $(x_1, \cdots x_{T_x})$ into the corrected post-edited sequence $(y_1, \cdots y_{T_y})$[3]. Next, we map these operations to the final sequence of steps and target tokens according to the following rules:

- For each matched pair of tokens x, y we produce symbols: ⟨STEP⟩ y;

- For each inserted target token y we produce the same token y;

- For each deleted source token x we produce ⟨STEP⟩;

- Since at initialization of the model $a_1 = 1$, i.e. the first encoder state is already attended to, we discard the first symbol in the new sequence if it is a ⟨STEP⟩ symbol.

4.2 Hard and Soft Attention

While the hard attention model can be used to enforce faithfulness to the original input, we would also like the model to be able to look at information anywhere in the source sequence which is a property of the soft attention model.

By re-introducing the conditional GRU cell with soft attention into the GRU-HARD model while also inputting the hard-attended encoder

---

[3]Similar to GNU `wdiff`.

state h_{a_j}, we can try to take advantage of both attention mechanisms. Combining Eq. 2 and Eq. 3, we get:

$$\mathbf{s}_j = \text{cGRU}_{\text{att}}\left(\mathbf{s}_{j-1}, \left[\mathbf{E}[y_{j-1}]; \mathbf{h}_{a_j}\right], \mathbf{C}\right). \quad (4)$$

The rest of the model is unchanged; the translation process is the same as before and we use the same target step/token sequence for training. This model is called CGRU-HARD.

4.3 Soft Dual-Attention

Neural multi-source models (Zoph and Knight, 2016) seem to be a natural fit for the APE task as raw MT output and original source language input are available. Although applications to the APE problem have been reported (Libovický and Helcl, 2017), state-of-the-art results seem to be missing.

In this section we give details about our dual-source model implementation. We rename the existing encoder C to $\mathbf{C}^{mt}$ to signal that the first encoder consumes the raw MT output and introduce a structurally identical second encoder $C^{src} = \{\mathbf{h}_1^{src}, \ldots, \mathbf{h}_{T_{src}}^{src}\}$ over the source language. To compute the decoder start state s_0 for the multi-encoder model we concatenate the averaged encoder contexts before mapping them into the decoder state space:

$$\mathbf{s}_0 = \tanh\left(\mathbf{W}_{init}\left[\frac{\sum_{i=1}^{T_{mt}} \mathbf{h}_i^{mt}}{T_{mt}}; \frac{\sum_{i=1}^{T_{src}} \mathbf{h}_i^{src}}{T_{src}}\right]\right).$$

In the decoder, we replace the conditional GRU with attention, with a doubly-attentive cGRU cell (Calixto et al., 2017) over contexts $\mathbf{C}^{mt}$ and $\mathbf{C}^{src}$:

$$\mathbf{s}_j = \text{cGRU}_{\text{2-att}}\left(\mathbf{s}_{j-1}, \mathbf{E}[y_{j-1}], \mathbf{C}^{mt}, \mathbf{C}^{src}\right). \quad (5)$$

The procedure is similar to the original cGRU, differing only in that in order to compute the context vector $\mathbf{c}_j$, we first calculate contexts vectors $\mathbf{c}_j^{mt}$ and $\mathbf{c}_j^{src}$ for each context and then concatenate[4] the results:

---

[4]Calixto et al. (2017) combine their two attention models by modifying their GRU cell to include another set of parameters that is multiplied with the additional context vector and summed in the GRU-components. Formally, both approaches give identical results, as for concatenation the original parameters have to grow in size to match the now longer input vector dimensions. The GRU cell itself does not need to be modified.

$$\mathbf{s}'_j = \text{GRU}_1\left(\mathbf{s}_{j-1}, \mathbf{E}[y_{j-1}]\right),$$

$$\mathbf{c}^{mt}_j = \text{ATT}\left(\mathbf{C}^{mt}, \mathbf{s}'_j\right) = \sum_i^{T_{mt}} \alpha_{ij}\mathbf{h}^{mt}_i,$$

$$\mathbf{c}^{src}_j = \text{ATT}\left(\mathbf{C}^{src}, \mathbf{s}'_j\right) = \sum_i^{T_{src}} \alpha_{ij}\mathbf{h}^{src}_i,$$

$$\mathbf{c}_j = \left[\mathbf{c}^{mt}_j; \mathbf{c}^{src}_j\right],$$

$$\mathbf{s}_j = \text{GRU}_2\left(\mathbf{s}'_j, \mathbf{c}_j\right).$$

This could be easily extended to an arbitrary number of encoders with different architectures. During training, this model is fed with a tri-parallel corpus, and during translation both input sequences are processed simultaneously to produce the corrected output. This model is denoted as M-CGRU.

4.4 Hard Attention with Soft Dual-Attention

Analogously to the procedure described in section 4.2, we can extend the doubly-attentive cGRU to take the hard-attended encoder context as additional input:

$$\mathbf{s}_j = \text{cGRU}_{2\text{-att}}\left(\mathbf{s}_{j-1}, \left[\mathbf{E}[y_{j-1}]; \mathbf{h}^{mt}_{a_j}\right], \mathbf{C}^{mt}, \mathbf{C}^{src}\right).$$

In this formulation, only the first encoder context $\mathbf{C}^{mt}$ is attended to by the hard monotonic attention mechanism. The target training data consists of the step/token sequences used for all previous hard-attention models. We call this model M-CGRU-HARD.

5 Experiments and Results

5.1 Training, Development, and Test Data

We perform all our experiments[5] with the official WMT-2016 (Bojar et al., 2016) automatic post-editing data and the respective development and test sets. The training data consists of a small set of 12,000 post-editing triplets (src, mt, pe), where src is the original English text, mt is the raw MT output generated by an English-to-German system, and pe is the human post-edited MT output. The MT system used to produce the raw MT output is unknown, so is the original training data. The task consists of automatically correcting the MT output so that it resembles human

Data set	Sentences	TER
training set	12,000	26.22
development set	1,000	24.81
test set	2,000	–
artificial-large	4,335,715	36.63
artificial-small	531,839	25.28

Table 1: Statistics for artificial data sets in comparison to official training and development data. Adapted from Junczys-Dowmunt and Grundkiewicz (2016).

post-edited data. The main task metric is TER (Snover et al., 2006) — the lower the better — with BLEU (Papineni et al., 2002) as a secondary metric.

To overcome the problem of too little training data, Junczys-Dowmunt and Grundkiewicz (2016) — the authors of the best WMT-2016 APE shared task system — generated large amounts of artificial data via round-trip translations. The artificial data has been filtered to match the HTER statistics of the training and development data for the shared task and was made available for download[6]. Table 1 summarizes the data sets used in this work.

To produce our final training data set we over-sample the original training data 20 times and add both artificial data sets. This results in a total of slightly more than 5M training triplets. We validate on the development set for early stopping and report results on the WMT-2016 test set. The data is already tokenized. Additionally we true-case all files and apply segmentation into BPE sub-word units (Sennrich et al., 2016). We reuse the subword units distributed with the artificial data set. For the hard-attention models, we create target training and development files following the LCS-based procedure outlined in section 4.1.

5.2 Training parameters

All models are trained on the same training data. Models with single input encoders take only the raw MT output (mt) as input, dual-encoder models use raw MT output (mt) and the original source (pe). The training procedures and model settings are the same whenever possible:

---

[5]All experiments in this sections can be reproduced following the instructions on `https://marian-nmt.github.io/examples/exploration/`.

[6]The artificial filtered data has been made available at `https://github.com/emjotde/amunmt/wiki/AmuNMT-for-Automatic-Post-Editing`.

Model	dev 2016		test 2016	
	TER↓	BLEU↑	**TER**↓	BLEU↑
WMT-2016 BASELINE-1 (Bojar et al., 2016)	25.14	62.92	24.76	62.11
WMT-2016 BASELINE-2 (Bojar et al., 2016)	–	–	24.64	63.47
Junczys-Dowmunt and Grundkiewicz (2016)	21.46	68.94	21.52	67.65
Pal et al. (2017) SYMMETRIC	–	–	21.07	67.87
Pal et al. (2017) RERANKING	–	–	20.70	**69.90**

Table 2: Results from the literature for the WMT-2016 APE development and test set.

Model	dev 2016		test 2016	
	TER↓	BLEU↑	**TER**↓	BLEU↑
CGRU	22.01	68.11	22.27	66.90
GRU-HARD	22.72	66.82	22.72	65.86
CGRU-HARD	22.11	67.82	22.10	67.15
M-CGRU	20.79	69.28	20.69	68.56
M-CGRU × 4	20.10	**70.24**	**19.92**	69.40
M-CGRU-HARD	20.83	69.02	20.87	68.14
M-CGRU-HARD × 4	**20.08**	70.05	20.34	68.96

Table 3: Results for models explored in this work. Models with × 4 are ensembles of four models. The main WMT 2016 APE shared task metric was TER (the lower the better).

- All embedding vectors consist of 512 units; the RNN states use 1024 units. We choose a vocabulary size of 40,000 for all inputs and outputs. When hard attention models are trained the maximum sentence length is 100 to accommodate the additional step symbols, otherwise 50.

- To avoid overfitting, we use pervasive dropout (Gal and Ghahramani, 2016) over GRU steps and input embeddings, with dropout probabilities 0.2, and over source and target words with probabilities 0.2.

- We use Adam (Kingma and Ba, 2014) as our optimizer, with a mini-batch size of 64. All models are trained with Asynchronous SGD (Adam) on three to four GPUs.

- We train all models until convergence (early-stopping with a patience of 10 based on development set cross-entropy cost), saving model checkpoints every 10,000 mini-batches. For different models we observed early stopping to be triggered between 600,000 and 900,000 mini-batch updates or between 8 and 11 epochs.

- The best eight model checkpoints w.r.t. development set cross-entropy of each training run are averaged element-wise (Junczys-Dowmunt et al., 2016) resulting in new single models with generally improved performance.

- For the multi-source models we repeat the mentioned procedure four times with different randomly initialized weights.

Training time for one model on four NVIDIA GTX 1080 GPUs or NVIDIA TITAN X (Pascal) GPUs is between one and two days, depending on model complexity. The M-CGRU-HARD model is the most complex and trains longest.

5.3 Evaluation

Table 2 contains relevant results for the WMT-2016 APE shared task — during the task and afterwards. WMT-2016 BASELINE-1 is the raw uncorrected MT output. BASELINE-2 is the result of a vanilla phrase-based Moses system (Koehn et al., 2007) trained only on the official 12,000 sentences. Junczys-Dowmunt and Grundkiewicz (2016) is the best system at the shared task. Pal

Model	TER-pe	TER-mt
CGRU	22.27	12.01
GRU-HARD	22.72	9.48
CGRU-HARD	22.10	11.57
M-CGRU	20.69	15.98
M-CGRU $\times$ 4	19.92	15.41
M-CGRU-HARD	20.87	13.62
M-CGRU-HARD $\times$ 4	20.34	13.34

Table 4: TER w.r.t. the reference compared to TER w.r.t. the input on test 2016. Lower results for TER-mt indicate greater similarity to the input.

Model	Mod.	Imp.	Det.
CGRU	1575	871	399
GRU-HARD	1479	783	362
CGRU-HARD	1564	897	371
M-CGRU	1668	1020	379
M-CGRU $\times$ 4	1612	1037	322
M-CGRU-HARD	1688	1044	388
M-CGRU-HARD $\times$ 4	1672	1074	341

Table 5: Number of test set sentences modified, improved and deteriorated by each model.

et al. (2017) SYMMETRIC is the currently best reported result on the WMT-2016 APE test set for a single neural model (single source), whereas Pal et al. (2017) RERANKING — the overall best reported result on the test set — is a system combination of Pal et al. (2017) SYMMETRIC with phrase-based models via n-best list re-ranking.

In Table 3 we present the results for the models discussed in this work. Unsurprisingly, none of the single attention models can compete with the better systems reported in the literature. The encoder-decoder model with only hard monotonic attention (GRU-HARD) is the clear loser, while the comparison between CGRU and CGRU-HARD remains inconclusive. CGRU-HARD seems to generalize slightly better, but would not have been chosen based on the development set performance.

The dual-attention models each outperform the best WMT-2016 system and the currently reported best single-model Pal et al. (2017) SYMMETRIC. The ensembles also beat the system combination Pal et al. (2017) RERANKING in terms of TER (not in terms of BLEU though). The simpler dual-attention model with no hard-attention M-CGRU reaches slightly better results on the test set than its counterpart with added hard attention M-CGRU-HARD, but the situation would have been less clear if only the development set were used to determine the best model. The hard-attention model with dual soft-attention benefits less from ensembling.

6 Analysis

6.1 Faithfulness and Errors

We postulated that the hard-attention models might have a potential for higher faithfulness. Since the APE task is a mostly monolingual task,

we can verify this by comparing TER scores with regard to the reference post-edition (TER-pe) and TER scores with regard to the raw MT output (TER-mt). The lower the TER-mt score the fewer changes have been made to the input to arrive at the output, thus resulting in higher faithfulness. Table 4 contains this comparison for the WMT-2016 APE test set. The hard-attention models indeed make fewer changes than their soft-attention counterparts. This difference is especially dramatic for M-CGRU and M-CGRU-HARD, where only small differences in TER-pe occur, but a gap of more than two TER points for TER-mt. This shows that hard-attention models can reach similar TER scores to soft-attention models while performing fewer changes. It might also explain why ensembling has a lower impact on the hard-attention models: higher faithfulness means less variety which results in smaller benefits from ensembles.

Table 5 compares the number of modified, improved and deteriorated test set sentences (2000 in total) for all models. The majority of sentences is being modified. While the number of deteriorated sentences is comparable between models, the number of improved sentences increases for the dual-source architectures. Ensembles lower the number of deteriorated sentences rather than increasing the number of improved sentences.

6.2 Visualization of Attention Types

Figures 1 and 2 visualize the behavior of the presented attention variants examined in this work for the example sentences in Table 6.

For this sentence, the unseen MT system mistranslated the word "Set" as "festlegen". The monolingual $mt \rightarrow pe$ systems cannot easily correct the error as the original meaning is lost, but

mt	Wählen Sie einen Tastaturbefehlssatz im Menü festlegen .
src	Select a shortcut set in the Set menu .
CGRU	Wählen Sie einen Tastaturbefehlssatz im Menü aus .
GRU-HARD	Wählen Sie einen Tastaturbefehlssatz im Menü aus .
CGRU-HARD	Wählen Sie einen Tastaturbefehlssatz im Menü aus .
M-CGRU	Wählen Sie einen Tastaturbefehlssatz im Menü " Satz " aus .
M-CGRU-HARD	Wählen Sie einen Tastaturbefehlssatz im Menü " Satz . "
pe	Wählen Sie einen Tastaturbefehlssatz im Menü " Satz . "

Table 6: Example corrections for different models. Only the multi-source models manage to restore the missing translation for "Set" and insert quotes. The added particle "aus" does not appear in the reference, but is grammatically correct as well.

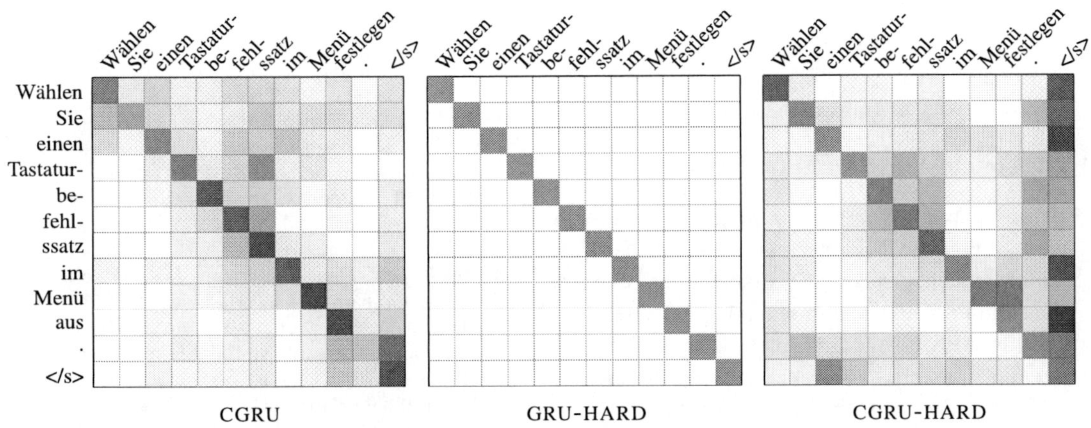

Figure 1: Behavior of different monolingual attention models (best viewed in color).

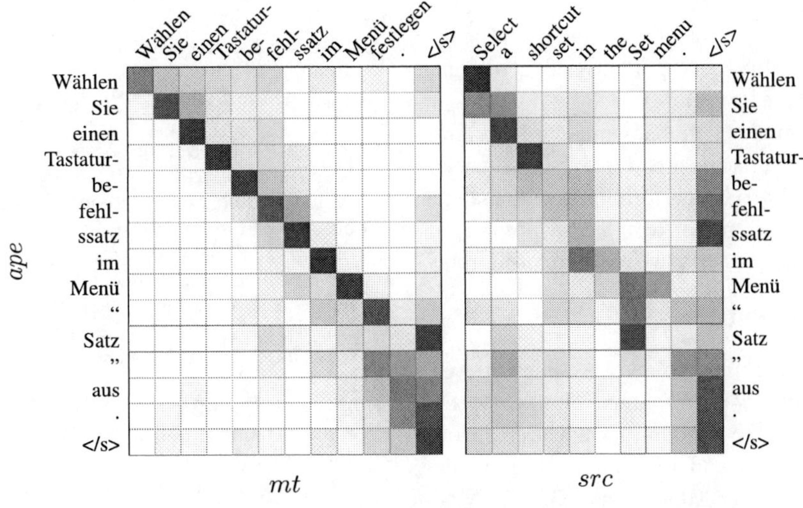

Figure 2: Attention matrices for dual-soft-attention model M-CGRU (best viewed in color).

they improve grammaticality. In Figure 1, we see how the soft attention model (CGRU) follows the input roughly monotonically. The monotonic hard attention model (GRU-HARD) does this naturally. For CGRU-HARD, it is interesting to see how the monotonic attention now allows the soft attention mechanism to look around the input sentence more freely or to remain inactive instead of following the monotonic path.

Both $\{mt, src\} \rightarrow pe$ systems take advantage of the src information and improve the input. The proposed modifications could be accepted as correct; one matches the reference. The highlighted rows and columns in Figure 2 show how the original source was used to reconstruct the missing word "Satz" and how both attention mechanisms interact. The attention over src seems to spend most time in a "parking" position at the sentence end unless it can provide useful information; the attention over mt follows the input closely.

7 Conclusions and Future Work

In this paper we presented several neural APE models that are equipped with non-standard attention mechanisms and combinations thereof. Among these, hard attention models have been applied to APE for the first time, whereas dual-soft attention models have been proposed before for APE tasks, but with non-conclusive results.

This is the first work to report state-of-the-art results for dual-attention models that integrate full post-edition triplets into a single end-to-end model. The ensembles of dual-attention models provide more than 1.52 TER points improvement over the best WMT-2016 system and 0.7 TER improvement over the best reported system combination for the same test set.

We also demonstrated that while hard-attention models yield similar results to pure soft-attention models, they do so by performing fewer changes to the input. This might be a useful property in scenarios where conservative edits are preferred.

Acknowledgments

This research was funded by the Amazon Academic Research Awards program. This project has received funding from the European Union's Horizon 2020 research and innovation program under grant 644333 (TraMOOC) and 645487 (ModernMT). This work was partially funded by Facebook. The views and conclusions contained herein are those of the authors and should not be interpreted as necessarily representing the official policies or endorsements, either expressed or implied, of Facebook.

References

Roee Aharoni and Yoav Goldberg. 2016. Sequence to sequence transduction with hard monotonic attention. *arXiv preprint arXiv:1611.01487*.

Dzmitry Bahdanau, Kyunghyun Cho, and Yoshua Bengio. 2015. Neural machine translation by jointly learning to align and translate. In *Proceedings of the International Conference on Learning Representations*, San Diego, CA.

Hanna Béchara, Yanjun Ma, and Josef van Genabith. 2011. Statistical post-editing for a statistical MT system. In *Proceedings of the 13th Machine Translation Summit*, pages 308–315, Xiamen, China.

Hanna Béchara, Raphaël Rubino, Yifan He, Yanjun Ma, and Josef van Genabith. 2012. An evaluation of statistical post-editing systems applied to RBMT and SMT systems. In *Proceedings of COLING 2012*, pages 215–230, Mumbai, India.

Ondrej Bojar, Rajen Chatterjee, Christian Federmann, Yvette Graham, Barry Haddow, Matthias Huck, Antonio Jimeno Yepes, Philipp Koehn, Varvara Logacheva, Christof Monz, Matteo Negri, Aurelie Neveol, Mariana Neves, Martin Popel, Matt Post, Raphael Rubino, Carolina Scarton, Lucia Specia, Marco Turchi, Karin Verspoor, and Marcos Zampieri. 2016. Findings of the 2016 conference on machine translation. In *Proceedings of the First Conference on Machine Translation*, pages 131–198, Berlin, Germany. Association for Computational Linguistics.

Iacer Calixto, Qun Liu, and Nick Campbell. 2017. Doubly-attentive decoder for multi-modal neural machine translation. *CoRR*, abs/1702.01287.

Rajen Chatterjee, Marion Weller, Matteo Negri, and Marco Turchi. 2015. Exploring the planet of the APEs: a comparative study of state-of-the-art methods for MT automatic post-editing. In *Proceedings of the 53rd Annual Meeting of the Association for Computational Linguistics and the 7th International Joint Conference on Natural Language Processing*, pages 156–161, Beijing, China. Association for Computational Linguistics.

Kyunghyun Cho, Bart Van Merriënboer, Caglar Gulcehre, Dzmitry Bahdanau, Fethi Bougares, Holger Schwenk, and Yoshua Bengio. 2014. Learning Phrase Representations Using RNN Encoder-Decoder for Statistical Machine Translation. In *Proc. of Empirical Methods in Natural Language Processing*.

Yarin Gal and Zoubin Ghahramani. 2016. A theoretically grounded application of dropout in recurrent neural networks. In *Advances in Neural Information Processing Systems 29 (NIPS)*.

Daniel S. Hirschberg. 1977. Algorithms for the longest common subsequence problem. *J. ACM*, 24(4):664–675.

Marcin Junczys-Dowmunt, Tomasz Dwojak, and Hieu Hoang. 2016. Is neural machine translation ready for deployment? A case study on 30 translation directions. In *Proceedings of the 9th International Workshop on Spoken Language Translation (IWSLT)*, Seattle, WA.

Marcin Junczys-Dowmunt and Roman Grundkiewicz. 2016. Log-linear combinations of monolingual and bilingual neural machine translation models for automatic post-editing. In *Proceedings of the First Conference on Machine Translation*, pages 751–758.

Diederik P. Kingma and Jimmy Ba. 2014. Adam: A method for stochastic optimization. In *Proceedings of the 3rd International Conference on Learning Representations (ICLR)*.

Philipp Koehn, Hieu Hoang, Alexandra Birch, Chris Callison-Burch, Marcello Federico, Nicola Bertoldi, Brooke Cowan, Wade Shen, Christine Moran, Richard Zens, et al. 2007. Moses: Open source toolkit for statistical machine translation. In *Proceedings of the 45th Annual Meeting of the Association for Computational Linguistics*, pages 177–180. Association for Computational Linguistics.

Jindrich Libovický and Jindrich Helcl. 2017. Attention strategies for multi-source sequence-to-sequence learning. *CoRR*, abs/1704.06567.

Jindrich Libovický, Jindrich Helcl, Marek Tlustý, Ondrej Bojar, and Pavel Pecina. 2016. CUNI system for WMT16 automatic post-editing and multimodal translation tasks. In *Proceedings of the First Conference on Machine Translation*, pages 646–654, Berlin, Germany. Association for Computational Linguistics.

Franz Josef Och. 2003. Minimum error rate training in statistical machine translation. In *Proceedings of the 41st Annual Meeting of the Association for Computational Linguistics*, pages 160–167, Sapporo, Japan. Association for Computational Linguistics.

Santanu Pal, Sudip Kumar Naskar, Mihaela Vela, Qun Liu, and Josef van Genabith. 2017. Neural automatic post-editing using prior alignment and reranking. In *Proceedings of the European Chapter of the Association for Computational Linguistics*, pages 349–355.

Santanu Pal, Mihaela Vela, Sudip Kumar Naskar, and Josef van Genabith. 2015. USAAR-SAPE: An English–Spanish statistical automatic post-editing system. In *Proceedings of the Tenth Workshop on Statistical Machine Translation*, pages 216–221, Lisbon, Portugal. Association for Computational Linguistics.

Kishore Papineni, Salim Roukos, Todd Ward, and Wei-Jing Zhu. 2002. BLEU: A method for automatic evaluation of machine translation. In *Proceedings of the 40th Annual Meeting on Association for Computational Linguistics*, ACL '02, pages 311–318, Stroudsburg, PA, USA. Association for Computational Linguistics.

Rico Sennrich, Orhan Firat, Kyunghyun Cho, Alexandra Birch, Barry Haddow, Julian Hitschler, Marcin Junczys-Dowmunt, Samuel Läubli, Antonio Valerio Miceli Barone, Jozef Mokry, and Maria Nadejde. 2017. Nematus: a toolkit for neural machine translation. In *Proceedings of the Software Demonstrations of the 15th Conference of the European Chapter of the Association for Computational Linguistics*, pages 65–68, Valencia, Spain. Association for Computational Linguistics.

Rico Sennrich, Barry Haddow, and Alexandra Birch. 2016. Neural machine translation of rare words with subword units. In *Proceedings of the 54th Annual Meeting of the Association for Computational Linguistics*, pages 1715–1725, Berlin, Germany. Association for Computational Linguistics.

Michel Simard, Cyril Goutte, and Pierre Isabelle. 2007. Statistical phrase-based post-editing. In *Proceedings of the Conference of the North American Chapter of the Association for Computational Linguistics*, pages 508–515, Rochester, New York. Association for Computational Linguistics.

Matthew Snover, Bonnie Dorr, Richard Schwartz, Linnea Micciulla, and John Makhoul. 2006. A study of translation edit rate with targeted human annotation. In *Proceedings of Association for Machine Translation in the Americas*.

Barret Zoph and Kevin Knight. 2016. Multi-source neural translation. In *Proceedings of the 2016 Conference of the North American Chapter of the Association for Computational Linguistics: Human Language Technologies*, pages 30–34, San Diego, California. Association for Computational Linguistics.

Imagination Improves Multimodal Translation

Desmond Elliott[*◇] and **Ákos Kádár**[†]
*ILLC, University of Amsterdam
◇School of Informatics, University of Edinburgh
†TiCC, Tilburg University
d.elliott@ed.ac.uk, a.kadar@uvt.nl

Abstract

We decompose multimodal translation into two sub-tasks: learning to translate and learning visually grounded representations. In a multitask learning framework, translations are learned in an attention-based encoder-decoder, and grounded representations are learned through image representation prediction. Our approach improves translation performance compared to the state of the art on the Multi30K dataset. Furthermore, it is equally effective if we train the image prediction task on the external MS COCO dataset, and we find improvements if we train the translation model on the external News Commentary parallel text.

1 Introduction

Multimodal machine translation is the task of translating sentences in context, such as images paired with a parallel text (Specia et al., 2016). This is an emerging task in the area of multilingual multimodal natural language processing. Progress on this task may prove useful for translating the captions of the images illustrating online news articles, and for multilingual closed captioning in international television and cinema.

Initial efforts have not convincingly demonstrated that visual context can improve translation quality. In the results of the First Multimodal Translation Shared Task, only three systems outperformed an off-the-shelf text-only phrase-based machine translation model, and the best performing system was equally effective with or without the visual features (Specia et al., 2016). There remains an open question about how translation models should take advantage of visual context.

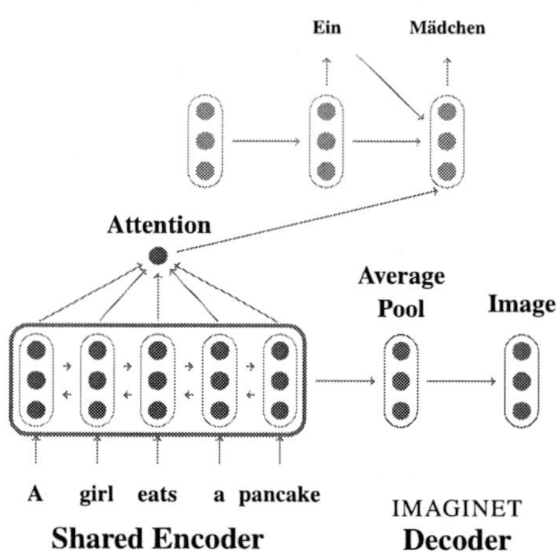

Figure 1: The Imagination model learns visually-grounded representations by sharing the encoder network between the Translation Decoder with image prediction in the IMAGINET Decoder.

We present a multitask learning model that decomposes multimodal translation into learning a translation model and learning visually grounded representations. This decomposition means that our model can be trained over external datasets of parallel text or described images, making it possible to take advantage of existing resources. Figure 1 presents an overview of our model, Imagination, in which source language representations are shared between tasks through the Shared Encoder. The translation decoder is an attention-based neural machine translation model (Bahdanau et al., 2015), and the image prediction decoder is trained to predict a global feature vector of an image that is associated with a sentence (Chrupała et al., 2015, IMAGINET). This decomposition encourages grounded learning in the shared encoder because the IMAGINET decoder is trained to imagine

Proceedings of the The 8th International Joint Conference on Natural Language Processing, pages 130–141,
Taipei, Taiwan, November 27 – December 1, 2017 ©2017 AFNLP

the image associated with a sentence. It has been shown that grounded representations are qualitatively different from their text-only counterparts (Kádár et al., 2016) and correlate better with human similarity judgements (Chrupała et al., 2015). We assess the success of the grounded learning by evaluating the image prediction model on an image–sentence ranking task to determine if the shared representations are useful for image retrieval (Hodosh et al., 2013). In contrast with most previous work, our model does not take images as input at translation time, rather it learns grounded representations in the shared encoder.

We evaluate Imagination on the Multi30K dataset (Elliott et al., 2016) using a combination of in-domain and out-of-domain data. In the in-domain experiments, we find that multitasking translation with image prediction is competitive with the state of the art. Our model achieves 55.8 Meteor as a single model trained on multimodal in-domain data, and 57.6 Meteor as an ensemble.

In the experiments with out-of-domain resources, we find that the improvement in translation quality holds when training the IMAGINET decoder on the MS COCO dataset of described images (Chen et al., 2015). Furthermore, if we significantly improve our text-only baseline using out-of-domain parallel text from the News Commentary corpus (Tiedemann, 2012), we still find improvements in translation quality from the auxiliary image prediction task. Finally, we report a state-of-the-art result of 59.3 Meteor on the Multi30K corpus when ensembling models trained on in- and out-of-domain resources.

The main contributions of this paper are:

- We show how to apply multitask learning to multimodal translation. This makes it possible to train models for this task using external resources alongside the expensive triple-aligned source-target-image data.

- We decompose multimodal translation into two tasks: learning to translate and learning grounded representations. We show that each task can be trained on large-scale external resources, e.g. parallel news text or images described in a single language.

- We present a model that achieves state of the art results without using images as an input. Instead, our model learns visually grounded source language representations using an auxiliary image prediction objective. Our model does not need any additional parameters to translate unseen sentences.

2 Problem Formulation

Multimodal translation is the task of producing target language translation y, given the source language sentence x and additional context, such as an image v (Specia et al., 2016). Let x be a source language sentence consisting of N tokens: x_1, x_2, ..., x_n and let y be a target language sentence consisting of M tokens: y_1, y_2, ..., y_m. The training data consists of tuples $\mathcal{D} \in (x, y, v)$, where x is a description of image v, and y is a translation of x.

Multimodal translation has previously been framed as minimising the negative log-likelihood of a translation model that is additionally conditioned on the image, i.e. $J(\theta) = -\sum_j \log \mathrm{p}(y_j | y_{<j}, x, v)$. Here, we decompose the problem into learning to translate and learning visually grounded representations. The decomposition is based on sharing parameters θ between these two tasks, and learning task-specific parameters ϕ. We learn the parameters in a multitask model with shared parameters in the source language encoder. The translation model has task-specific parameters ϕ^t in the attention-based decoder, which are optimized through the translation loss $J_T(\theta, \phi^t)$. Grounded representations are learned through an image prediction model with task-specific parameters ϕ^g in the image-prediction decoder by minimizing $J_G(\theta, \phi^g)$. The joint objective is given by mixing the translation and image prediction tasks with the parameter w:

$$J(\theta, \phi) = w J_T(\theta, \phi^t) + (1 - w) J_G(\theta, \phi^g) \quad (1)$$

Our decomposition of the problem makes it straightforward to optimise this objective without paired tuples, e.g. where we have an external dataset of described images $\mathcal{D}_{image} \in (x, v)$ or an external parallel corpus $\mathcal{D}_{text} \in (x, y)$.

We train our multitask model following the approach of Luong et al. (2016). We define a primary task and an auxiliary task, and a set of parameters θ to be shared between the tasks. A minibatch of updates is performed for the primary task with probability w, and for the auxiliary task with $1 - w$. The primary task is trained until convergence and weight w determines the frequency of parameter updates for the auxiliary task.

3 Imagination Model

3.1 Shared Encoder

The encoder network of our model learns a representation of a sequence of N tokens $x_{1\ldots n}$ in the source language with a bidirectional recurrent neural network (Schuster and Paliwal, 1997). This representation is shared between the different tasks. Each token is represented by a one-hot vector $\mathbf{x_i}$, which is mapped into an embedding $\mathbf{e_i}$ through a learned matrix $\mathbf{E}$:

$$\mathbf{e_i} = \mathbf{x_i} \cdot \mathbf{E} \tag{2}$$

A sentence is processed by a pair of recurrent neural networks, where one captures the sequence left-to-right (forward), and the other captures the sequence right-to-left (backward). The initial state of the encoder $\mathbf{h_{-1}}$ is a learned parameter:

$$\overrightarrow{\mathbf{h_i}} = \overrightarrow{\mathrm{RNN}}(\overrightarrow{\mathbf{h_{i-1}}}, \mathbf{e_i}) \tag{3}$$

$$\overleftarrow{\mathbf{h_i}} = \overleftarrow{\mathrm{RNN}}(\overleftarrow{\mathbf{h_{i-1}}}, \mathbf{e_i}) \tag{4}$$

Each token in the source language input sequence is represented by a concatenation of the forward and backward hidden state vectors:

$$\mathbf{h_i} = [\overrightarrow{\mathbf{h_i}}; \overleftarrow{\mathbf{h_i}}] \tag{5}$$

3.2 Neural Machine Translation Decoder

The translation model decoder is an attention-based recurrent neural network (Bahdanau et al., 2015). Tokens in the decoder are represented by a one-hot vector $\mathbf{y_j}$, which is mapped into an embedding $\mathbf{e_j}$ through a learned matrix $\mathbf{E_y}$:

$$\mathbf{e_j} = \mathbf{y_j} \cdot \mathbf{E_y} \tag{6}$$

The inputs to the decoder are the previously predicted token $\mathbf{y_{j-1}}$, the previous decoder state $\mathbf{d_{j-1}}$, and a timestep-dependent context vector $\mathbf{c_j}$ calculated over the encoder hidden states:

$$\mathbf{d_j} = \mathrm{RNN}(\mathbf{d_{j-1}}, \mathbf{y_{j-1}}, \mathbf{e_j}) \tag{7}$$

The initial state of the decoder $\mathbf{d_{-1}}$ is a nonlinear transform of the mean of the encoder states, where $\mathbf{W}_{init}$ is a learned parameter:

$$\mathbf{d_{-1}} = \tanh(\mathbf{W}_{init} \cdot \frac{1}{N} \sum_i^N \mathbf{h_i}) \tag{8}$$

The context vector c_j is a weighted sum over the encoder hidden states, where N denotes the length of the source sentence:

$$\mathbf{c_j} = \sum_{i=1}^{N} \alpha_{ji} \mathbf{h_i} \tag{9}$$

The α_{ji} values are the proportion of which the encoder hidden state vectors $\mathbf{h_{1\ldots n}}$ contribute to the decoder hidden state when producing the jth token in the translation. They are computed by a feed-forward neural network, where $\mathbf{v_a}$, $\mathbf{W_a}$ and $\mathbf{U_a}$ are learned parameters:

$$\alpha_{ji} = \frac{\exp(e_{ji})}{\sum_{l=1}^{N} \exp(e_{li})} \tag{10}$$

$$e_{ji} = \mathbf{v_a} \cdot \tanh(\mathbf{W_a} \cdot \mathbf{d_{j-1}} + \mathbf{U_a} \cdot \mathbf{h_i}) \tag{11}$$

From the hidden state $\mathbf{d_j}$ the network predicts the conditional distribution of the next token y_j, given a target language embedding $\mathbf{e_{j-1}}$ of the previous token, the current hidden state $\mathbf{d_j}$, and the calculated context vector $\mathbf{c_j}$. Note that at training time, y_{j-1} is the true observed token; whereas for unseen data we use the inferred token $\hat{y}_{j-1}$ sampled from the output of the softmax:

$$p(y_j|y_{<j}, c) = \mathrm{softmax}(\tanh(\mathbf{e_{j-1}} + \mathbf{d_j} + \mathbf{c_j})) \tag{12}$$

The translation model is trained to minimise the negative log likelihood of predicting the target language output:

$$J_{NLL}(\theta, \phi^t) = -\sum_j \log \mathrm{p}(y_j|y_{<j}, x) \tag{13}$$

3.3 Imaginet Decoder

The image prediction decoder is trained to predict the visual feature vector of the image associated with a sentence (Chrupała et al., 2015). It encourages the shared encoder to learn grounded representations for the source language.

A source language sentence is encoded using the Shared Encoder, as described in Section 3.1. Then we transform the shared encoder representation into a single vector by taking the mean pool over the hidden state annotations, the same way we initialise the hidden state of the translation decoder (Eqn. 8). This sentence representation is the input to a feed-forward neural network that predicts the visual feature vector $\hat{\mathbf{v}}$ associated with a

	Size	Tokens	Types	Images
Multi30K: parallel text with images				
En	31K	377K	10K	31K
De		368K	16K	
MS COCO: external described images				
En	414K	4.3M	24K	83K
News Commentary: external parallel text				
En	240K	8.31M	17K	–
De		8.95M		–

Table 1: The datasets used in our experiments.

sentence with parameters $\mathbf{W_{vis}}$:

$$\hat{\mathbf{v}} = \tanh(\mathbf{W_{vis}} \cdot \frac{1}{N} \sum_{i}^{N} \mathbf{h_i}) \tag{14}$$

This decoder is trained to predict the true image vector $\mathbf{v}$ with a margin-based objective, parameterised by the minimum margin α, and the cosine distance $d(\cdot, \cdot)$. A margin-based objective has previously been used in grounded representation learning (Vendrov et al., 2016; Chrupała et al., 2017). The contrastive examples $\mathbf{v}'$ are drawn from the other instances in a minibatch:

$$J_{MAR}(\theta, \phi^t) = \sum_{\mathbf{v}' \neq \mathbf{v}} \max\{0, \alpha - d(\hat{\mathbf{v}}, \mathbf{v}) + d(\hat{\mathbf{v}}, \mathbf{v}')\} \tag{15}$$

4 Data

We evaluate our model using the benchmark Multi30K dataset (Elliott et al., 2016), which is the largest collection of images paired with sentences in multiple languages. This dataset contains 31,014 images paired with an English language sentence and a German language translation: 29,000 instances are reserved for training, 1,014 for development, and 1,000 for evaluation.[1]

The English and German sentences are preprocessed by normalising the punctuation, lowercasing and tokenizing the text using the Moses toolkit. We additionally decompound the German text using Zmorge (Sennrich and Kunz, 2014).

This results in vocabulary sizes of 10,214 types for English and 16,022 for German.

We also use two external datasets to evaluate our model: the MS COCO dataset of English described images (Chen et al., 2015), and the English-German News Commentary parallel corpus (Tiedemann, 2012). When we perform experiments with the News Commentary corpus, we first calculate a 17,597 sub-word vocabulary using SentencePiece (Schuster and Nakajima, 2012) over the concatenation of the Multi30K and News Commentary datasets. This gives us a shared vocabulary for the external data that reduces the number of out-of-vocabulary tokens.

Images are represented by 2048D vectors extracted from the 'pool5/7x7_s1' layer of the GoogLeNet v3 CNN (Szegedy et al., 2015).

5 Experiments

We evaluate our multitasking approach with in- and out-of-domain resources. We start by reporting results of models trained using only the Multi30K dataset. We also report the results of training the IMAGINET decoder with the COCO dataset. Finally, we report results on incorporating the external News Commentary parallel text into our model. Throughout, we report performance of the En→De translation using Meteor (Denkowski and Lavie, 2014) and BLEU (Papineni et al., 2002) against lowercased tokenized references.

5.1 Hyperparameters

The encoder is a 1000D Gated Recurrent Unit bidirectional recurrent neural network (Cho et al., 2014, GRU) with 620D embeddings. We share all of the encoder parameters between the primary and auxiliary task. The translation decoder is a 1000D GRU recurrent neural network, with a 2000D context vector over the encoder states, and 620D word embeddings (Sennrich et al., 2017). The Imaginet decoder is a single-layer feed-forward network, where we learn the parameters $\mathbf{W_{vis}} \in \mathbb{R}^{2048 \times 2000}$ to predict the true image vector with $\alpha = 0.1$ for the Imaginet objective (Equation 15). The models are trained using the Adam optimiser with the default hyperparameters (Kingma and Ba, 2015) in minibatches of 80 instances. The translation task is defined as the primary task and convergence is reached when BLEU has not increased for five epochs on the validation data. Gradients are clipped when their norm ex-

---

[1] The Multi30K dataset also contains 155K independently collected descriptions in German and English. In order to make our experiments more comparable with previous work, we do not make use of this data.

	Meteor	BLEU
NMT	54.0 ± 0.6	35.5 ± 0.8
Calixto et al. (2017)	55.0	36.5
Calixto and Liu (2017)	55.1	37.3
Imagination	55.8 ± 0.4	36.8 ± 0.8
Toyama et al. (2016)	56.0	36.5
Hitschler et al. (2016)	56.1	34.3
Moses	56.9	36.9

Table 2: En→De translation results on the Multi30K dataset. Our Imagination model is competitive with the state of the art when it is trained on in-domain data. We report the mean and standard deviation of three random initialisations.

ceeds 1.0. Dropout is set to 0.2 for the embeddings and the recurrent connections in both tasks (Gal and Ghahramani, 2016). Translations are decoded using beam search with 12 hypotheses.

5.2 In-domain experiments

We start by presenting the results of our multitask model trained using only the Multi30K dataset. We compare against state-of-the-art approaches and text-only baselines. Moses is the phrase-based machine translation model (Koehn et al., 2007) reported in (Specia et al., 2016). NMT is a text-only neural machine translation model. Calixto et al. (2017) is a double-attention model over the source language and the image. Calixto and Liu (2017) is a multimodal translation model that conditions the decoder on semantic image vector extracted from the VGG-19 CNN. Hitschler et al. (2016) uses visual features in a target-side retrieval model for translation. Toyama et al. (2016) is most comparable to our approach: it is a multimodal variational NMT model that infers latent variables to represent the source language semantics from the image and linguistic data.

Table 2 shows the results of this experiment. We can see that the combination of the attention-based translation model and the image prediction model is a 1.8 Meteor point improvement over the NMT baseline, but it is 1.1 Meteor points worse than the strong Moses baseline. Our approach is competitive with previous approaches that use visual features as inputs to the decoder and the target-side reranking model. It also competitive with

	Meteor	BLEU
Imagination	55.8 ± 0.4	36.8 ± 0.8
Imagination (COCO)	55.6 ± 0.5	36.4 ± 1.2

Table 3: Translation results when using out-of-domain described images. Our approach is still effective when the image prediction model is trained over the COCO dataset.

	Meteor	BLEU
NMT	52.8 ± 0.6	33.4 ± 0.6
+ NC	56.7 ± 0.3	37.2 ± 0.7
+ Imagination	56.7 ± 0.1	37.4 ± 0.3
+ Imagination (COCO)	57.1 ± 0.2	37.8 ± 0.7
Calixto et al. (2017)	56.8	39.0

Table 4: Translation results with out-of-domain parallel text and described images. We find further improvements when we multitask with the News Commentary (NC) and COCO datasets.

Toyama et al. (2016), which also only uses images for training. These results confirm that our multitasking approach uses the image prediction task to improve the encoder of the translation model.

5.3 External described image data

Recall from Section 2 that we are interested in scenarios where x, y, and v are drawn from different sources. We now experiment with separating the translation data from the described image data using $\mathcal{D}_{image}$: MS COCO dataset of 83K described images[2] and $\mathcal{D}_{text}$: Multi30K parallel text.

Table 3 shows the results of this experiment. We find that there is no significant difference between training the IMAGINET decoder on in-domain (Multi30K) or out-of-domain data (COCO). This result confirms that we can separate the parallel text from the described images.

5.4 External parallel text data

We now experiment with training our model on a combination of the Multi30K and the News Commentary English-German data. In these experiments, we concatenate the Multi30K and News

---

[2]Due to differences in the vocabularies of the respective datasets, we do not train on examples where more than 10% of the tokens are out-of-vocabulary in the Multi30K dataset.

	Parallel text		Described images			
	Multi30K	News Commentary	Multi30K	COCO	Meteor	BLEU
Zmorge	✓				56.2	37.8
	✓		✓		57.6	39.0
Sub-word	✓				54.4	35.0
	✓	✓			58.6	39.4
	✓	✓	✓		59.0	39.5
	✓	✓		✓	**59.3**	**40.2**

Table 5: Ensemble decoding results. Zmorge denotes models trained with decompounded German words; Sub-word denotes joint SentencePiece word splitting (see Section 4 for more details).

Commentary datasets into a single $\mathcal{D}_{text}$ training dataset, similar to Freitag and Al-Onaizan (2016). We compare our model against Calixto et al. (2017), who pre-train their model on the WMT'15 English-German parallel text and back-translate (Sennrich et al., 2016) additional sentences from the bilingual independent descriptions in the Multi30K dataset (Footnote 2).

Table 4 presents the results. The text-only NMT model using sub-words is 1.2 Meteor points lower than decompounding the German text. Nevertheless, the model trained over a concatenation of the parallel texts is a 2.7 Meteor point improvement over this baseline (+ NC) and matches the performance of our Multitasking model that uses only in-domain data (Section 5.2). We do not see an additive improvement for the multitasking model with the concatenated parallel text and the in-domain data (+ Imagination) using a training objective interpolation of $w = 0.89$ (the ratio of the training dataset sizes). This may be because we are essentially learning a translation model and the updates from the IMAGINET decoder are forgotten. Therefore, we experiment with multitasking the concatenated parallel text and the COCO dataset ($w = 0.5$). We find that balancing the datasets improves over the concatenated text model by 0.4 Meteor (+ Imagination (COCO)). Our multitasking approach improves upon Calixto et al. by 0.3 Meteor points. Our model can be trained in 48 hours using 240K parallel sentences and 414K described images from out-of-domain datasets. Furthermore, recall that our model does not use images as an input for translating unseen data, which results in 6.2% fewer parameters compared to using the 2048D Inception-V3 visual features to initialise the hidden state of the decoder.

5.5 Ensemble results

Table 5 presents the results of ensembling different randomly initialised models. We achieve a start-of-the-art result of 57.6 Meteor for a model trained on only in-domain data. The improvements are more pronounced for the models trained using sub-words and out-of-domain data. An ensemble of baselines trained on sub-words is initially worse than an ensemble trained on Zmorge decompounded words. However, we always see an improvement from ensembling models trained on in- and out-of-domain data. Our best ensemble is trained on Multi30K parallel text, the News Commentary parallel text, and the COCO descriptions to set a new state-of-the-art result of 59.3 Meteor.

5.6 Multi30K 2017 results

We also evaluate our approach against 16 submissions to the WMT Shared Task on Multimodal Translation and Multilingual Image Description (Elliott et al., 2017). This shared task features a new evaluation dataset: Multi30K Test 2017 (Elliott et al., 2017), which contains 1,000 new evaluation images. The shared task submissions are evaluated with Meteor and human direct assessment (Graham et al., 2017). We submitted two systems, based on whether they used only the Multi30K dataset (constrained) or used additional external resources (unconstrained). Our constrained submission is an ensemble of three Imagination models trained over only the Multi30K training data. This achieves a Meteor score of 51.2, and a joint 3rd place ranking according to human assessment. Our unconstrained submission is an ensemble of three Imagination models trained with the Multi30K, News Commentary, and MS COCO datasets. It achieves a Meteor score of

Source:	two children on their stomachs lay on the ground under a pipe	
NMT:	zwei kinder auf ihren gesichtern liegen unter dem boden auf dem boden	
Ours:	zwei kinder liegen bäuchlings auf dem boden unter einer schaukel	
Source:	small dog in costume stands on hind legs to reach dangling flowers	
NMT:	ein kleiner hund steht auf dem hinterbeinen und läuft , nach links von blumen zu sehen	
Ours:	ein kleiner hund in einem kostüm steht auf den hinterbeinen , um die blumen zu erreichen	
Source:	a bird flies across the water	
NMT:	ein vogel fliegt über das wasser	
Ours:	ein vogel fliegt durch das wasser	

Table 6: Examples where our model improves or worsens the translation compared to the NMT baseline. Top: NMT translates the wrong body part; both models skip "pipe". Middle: NMT incorrectly translates the verb and misses several nouns. Bottom: Our model incorrectly translates the preposition.

53.5, and 2nd place in the human assessment.

5.7 Qualitative examples

Table 6 shows examples of where the multitasking model improves or worsens translation performance compared to the baseline model[3]. The first example shows that the baseline model makes a significant error in translating the pose of the children, translating "on their stomachs" as "on their faces"). The middle example demonstrates that the baseline model translates the dog as walking ("läuft") and then makes grammatical and sense errors after the clause marker. Both models neglect to translate the word "dangling", which is a low-frequency word in the training data. There are instances where the baseline produces better translations than the multitask model: In the bottom example, our model translates a bird flying through the water ("durch") instead of "over" the water.

6 Discussion

6.1 Does the model learn grounded representations?

A natural question to ask if whether the multitask model is actually learning representations that are relevant for the images. We answer this question by evaluating the Imaginet decoder in an image–sentence ranking task. Here the input is a source language sentence, from which we predict its im-

age vector $\hat{\mathbf{v}}$. The predicted vector $\hat{\mathbf{v}}$ can be compared against the true image vectors $\mathbf{v}$ in the evaluation data using the cosine distance to produce a ranked order of the images. Our model returns a median rank of 11.0 for the true image compared to the predicted image vector. Figure 2 shows examples of the nearest neighbours of the images predicted by our multitask model. We can see that the combination of the multitask source language representations and IMAGINET decoder leads to the prediction of relevant images. This confirms that the shared encoder is indeed learning visually grounded representations.

6.2 The effect of visual feature vectors

We now study the effect of varying the Convolutional Neural Network used to extract the visual features used in the Imaginet decoder. It has previously been shown that the choice of visual features can affect the performance of vision and language models (Jabri et al., 2016; Kiela et al., 2016). We compare the effect of training the IMAGINET decoder to predict different types of image features, namely: 4096D features extracted from the 'fc7'' layer of the VGG-19 model (Simonyan and Zisserman, 2015), 2048D features extracted from the 'pool5/7x7_s1' layer of InceptionNet V3 (Szegedy et al., 2015), and 2048D features extracted from 'avg_pool' layer of ResNet-50 (He et al., 2016). Table 7 shows the results of this experiment. There is a clear difference between predicting the 2048D

(a) Nearest neighbours for "a native woman is working on a craft project ."

(b) Nearest neighbours for "there is a cafe on the street corner with an oval painting on the side of the building ."

Figure 2: We can interpret the IMAGINET Decoder by visualising the predictions made by our model.

	Meteor	Median Rank
Inception-V3	56.0 ± 0.1	11.0 ± 0.0
Resnet-50	54.7 ± 0.4	11.7 ± 0.5
VGG-19	53.6 ± 1.8	13.0 ± 0.0

Table 7: The type of visual features predicted by the IMAGINET Decoder has a strong impact on the Multitask model performance.

vectors (Inception-V3 and ResNet-50) compared to the 4096D vector from VGG-19). This difference is reflected in both the translation Meteor score and the Median rank of the images in the validation dataset. This is likely because it is easier to learn the parameters of the image prediction model that has fewer parameters (8.192 million for VGG-19 vs. 4.096 million for Inception-V3 and ResNet-50). However, it is not clear why there is such a pronounced difference between the Inception-V3 and ResNet-50 models[4].

7 Related work

Initial work on multimodal translation used semantic or spatially-preserving image features as inputs to a translation model. Semantic image features are typically extracted from the final layer of a pre-trained object recognition CNN, e.g. 'pool5/7x7_s1' in GoogLeNet (Szegedy et al., 2015). This type of vector has been used as input to the encoder (Elliott et al., 2015; Huang et al., 2016), the decoder (Libovický et al., 2016), or as features in a phrase-based translation model (Shah et al., 2016; Hitschler et al., 2016). Spatially-preserving image features are extracted from deeper inside a CNN, where the position of a feature is related to its position in the image. These features have been used in "double-attention models", which calculate independent context vectors for the source language and a convolutional image features (Calixto et al., 2016; Caglayan et al., 2016; Calixto et al., 2017). We use an attention-based translation model but our multitask model does not use images for translation.

More related to our work is an extension of Variational Neural Machine Translation to infer latent variables to *explicitly* model the semantics of source sentences from visual and linguistic information (Toyama et al., 2016). They report improvements on the Multi30K data set but their model needs additional parameters in the "neural inferrer" modules. In our model, the grounded semantics are represented *implicitly* in the shared encoder. They assume Source-Target-Image training data, whereas our approach achieves equally good results if we train on separate Source-Image and Source-Target datasets. Saha et al. (2016) study cross-lingual image description where the task is to generate a sentence in language L_1 given the image, using only Image-L_2 and L_1-L_2 training corpora. They propose a Correlational Encoder-Decoder to model the Image-L_2 and L_1-L_2 data, which learns correlated representations for paired Image-L_2 data and decodes L_1 from the joint representation. Similar to our work, the encoder is trained by minimizing two loss functions: the Image-L_2 correlation loss, and the L_1 decoding

---

[4]We used pre-trained CNNs (https://github.com/fchollet/deep-learning-models), which claim equal ILSVRC object recognition performance for both models: 7.8% top-5 error with a single-model and single-crop.

cross-entropy loss. Nakayama and Nishida (2017) consider a zero-resource problem, where the task is to translate from L_1 to L_2 with only Image-L_1 and Image-L_2 corpora. Their model embeds the image, L_1, and L_2 in a joint multimodal space learned by minimizing a multi-task ranking loss between both pairs of examples. In this paper, we focus on *enriching* source language representations with visual information instead of zero-resource learning.

Multitask Learning improves the generalisability of a model by requiring it to be useful for more than one task (Caruana, 1997). This approach has recently been used to improve the performance of sentence compression using eye gaze as an auxiliary task (Klerke et al., 2016), and to improve shallow parsing accuracy through the auxiliary task of predicting keystrokes in an out-of-domain corpus (Plank, 2016). More recently, Bingel and Søgaard (2017) analysed the beneficial relationships between primary and auxiliary sequential prediction tasks. In the translation literature, multitask learning has been used to learn a one-to-many languages translation model (Dong et al., 2015), a multi-lingual translation model with a single attention mechanism shared across multiple languages (Firat et al., 2016), and in multitask sequence-to-sequence learning without an attention-based decoder (Luong et al., 2016). We explore the benefits of grounded learning in the specific case of multimodal translation. We combine sequence prediction with continuous (image) vector prediction, compared to previous work which multitasks different sequence prediction tasks.

Visual representation prediction has been studied using static images or videos. Lin and Parikh (2015) use a conditional random field to imagine the composition of a clip-art scene for visual paraphrasing and fill-in-the-blank tasks. Chrupała et al. (2015) predict the image vector associated with a sentence using an L2 loss; they found this improves multi-modal word similarity compared to text-only baselines. Gelderloos and Chrupała (2016) predict the image vector associated with a sequence of phonemes using a max-margin loss, similar to our image prediction objective. Collell et al. (2017) learn to predict the visual feature vector associated with a word for word similarity and relatedness tasks. As a video reconstruction problem, Srivastava et al. (2015) propose an LSTM Autoencoder to predict video frames as a reconstruction task or as a future prediction task. Pasunuru and Bansal (2017) propose a multitask model for video description that combines unsupervised video reconstruction, lexical entailment, and video description. They find improvements from using out-of-domain resources for entailment and video prediction, similar to the improvements we find from using out-of-domain parallel text and described images.

8   Conclusion

We decompose multimodal translation into two sub-problems: learning to translate and learning visually grounded representations. In a multitask learning framework, we show how these sub-problems can be addressed by sharing an encoder between a translation model and an image prediction model[5]. Our approach achieves state-of-the-art results on the Multi30K dataset without using images for translation. We show that training on separate parallel text and described image datasets does not hurt performance, encouraging future research on multitasking with diverse sources of data. Furthermore, we still find improvements from image prediction when we improve our text-only baseline with the out-of-domain parallel text. Future work includes adapting our decomposition to other NLP tasks that may benefit from out-of-domain resources, such as semantic role labelling, dependency parsing, and question-answering; exploring methods for inputting the (predicted) image into the translation model; experimenting with different image prediction architectures; multitasking different translation languages into a single shared encoder; and multitasking in both the encoder and decoder(s).

Acknowledgments

We are grateful to the anonymous reviewers for their feedback. We thank Joost Bastings for sharing his multitasking Nematus model, Wilker Aziz for discussions about formulating the problem, Stella Frank for finding and explaining the qualitative examples to us, and Afra Alishahi, Grzegorz Chrupała, and Philip Schulz for feedback on earlier drafts of the paper. DE acknowledges the support of an Amazon Research Award, NWO Vici grant nr. 277-89-002 awarded to K. Sima'an, and a hardware grant from the NVIDIA Corporation.

---

[5]Code: http://github.com/elliottd/imagination

References

Dzmitry Bahdanau, Kyunghyun Cho, and Yoshua Bengio. 2015. Neural machine translation by jointly learning to align and translate. In *International Conference on Learning Representations*.

J. Bingel and A. Søgaard. 2017. Identifying beneficial task relations for multi-task learning in deep neural networks. In *Proceedings of the 15th Conference of the European Chapter of the Association for Computational Linguistics*, pages 164–169.

Ozan Caglayan, Loïc Barrault, and Fethi Bougares. 2016. Multimodal attention for neural machine translation. *CoRR*, abs/1609.03976.

Iacer Calixto, Desmond Elliott, and Stella Frank. 2016. DCU-UvA Multimodal MT System Report. In *Proceedings of the First Conference on Machine Translation*, pages 634–638.

Iacer Calixto and Qun Liu. 2017. Incorporating global visual features into attention-based neural machine translation. In *Proceedings of the 2017 Conference on Empirical Methods in Natural Language Processing*, pages 1003–1014.

Iacer Calixto, Qun Liu, and Nick Campbell. 2017. Doubly-Attentive Decoder for Multi-modal Neural Machine Translation. In *Proceedings of the 55th Annual Meeting of the Association for Computational Linguistics (Volume 1: Long Papers)*, pages 1913–1924.

Rich Caruana. 1997. Multitask learning. *Machine Learning*, 28(1):41–75.

Xinlei Chen, Hao Fang, Tsung-Yi Lin, Ramakrishna Vedantam, Saurabh Gupta, Piotr Dollár, and C. Lawrence Zitnick. 2015. Microsoft COCO captions: Data collection and evaluation server. *CoRR*, abs/1504.00325.

K. Cho, B. Van Merriënboer, C. Gulcehre, D. Bahdanau, F. Bougares, H. Schwenk, and Y. Bengio. 2014. Learning phrase representations using RNN encoder-decoder for statistical machine translation. pages 1724–1734.

Grzegorz Chrupała, Lieke Gelderloos, and Afra Alishahi. 2017. Representations of language in a model of visually grounded speech signal. In *Proceedings of the 55th Annual Meeting of the Association for Computational Linguistics (Volume 1: Long Papers)*, pages 613–622.

Grzegorz Chrupała, Ákos Kádár, and Afra Alishahi. 2015. Learning language through pictures. In *Proceedings of the 53rd Annual Meeting of the Association for Computational Linguistics and the 7th International Joint Conference on Natural Language Processing*, pages 112–118.

Guillem Collell, Teddy Zhang, and Marie-Francine Moens. 2017. Imagined visual representations as multimodal embeddings. In *Proceedings of the Thirty-First AAAI Conference on Artificial Intelligence (AAAI-17)*, pages 4378–4384.

Michael Denkowski and Alon Lavie. 2014. Meteor universal: Language specific translation evaluation for any target language. In *Proceedings of the EACL 2014 Workshop on Statistical Machine Translation*.

D. Dong, H. Wu, W. He, D. Yu, and H. Wang. 2015. Multi-task learning for multiple language translation. In *Proceedings of the 53rd Annual Meeting of the Association for Computational Linguistics and the 7th International Joint Conference on Natural Language Processing*, pages 1723–1732.

Desmond Elliott, Stella Frank, Loïc Barrault, Fethi Bougares, and Lucia Specia. 2017. Findings of the second shared task on multimodal machine translation and multilingual image description. In *Proceedings of the Second Conference on Machine Translation, Volume 2: Shared Task Papers*, pages 215–233, Copenhagen, Denmark. Association for Computational Linguistics.

Desmond Elliott, Stella Frank, and Eva Hasler. 2015. Multi-language image description with neural sequence models. *CoRR*, abs/1510.04709.

Desmond Elliott, Stella Frank, Khalil. Sima'an, and Lucia Specia. 2016. Multi30K: Multilingual English-German Image Descriptions. In *Proceedings of the 5th Workshop on Vision and Language*.

O. Firat, K. Cho, and Y. Bengio. 2016. Multi-way, multilingual neural machine translation with a shared attention mechanism. In *Proceedings of the 2016 Conference of the North American Chapter of the Association for Computational Linguistics: Human Language Technologies*, pages 866–875.

Markus Freitag and Yaser Al-Onaizan. 2016. Fast domain adaptation for neural machine translation. *CoRR*, abs/1612.06897.

Yarin Gal and Zoubin Ghahramani. 2016. A theoretically grounded application of dropout in recurrent neural networks. In *Advances in Neural Information Processing Systems 29*, pages 1019–1027.

Lieke Gelderloos and Grzegorz Chrupała. 2016. From phonemes to images: levels of representation in a recurrent neural model of visually-grounded language learning. In *Proceedings of COLING 2016, the 26th International Conference on Computational Linguistics*, pages 1309–1319.

Yvette Graham, Timothy Baldwin, Alistair Moffat, and Justin Zobel. 2017. Can machine translation systems be evaluated by the crowd alone. *Natural Language Engineering*, 23(1):3–30.

Kaiming He, Xiangyu Zhang, Shaoqing Ren, and Jian Sun. 2016. Deep residual learning for image recognition. In *The IEEE Conference on Computer Vision and Pattern Recognition (CVPR)*, pages 770–778.

Julian Hitschler, Shigehiko Schamoni, and Stefan Riezler. 2016. Multimodal Pivots for Image Caption Translation. In *Proceedings of the 54th Annual Meeting of the Association for Computational Linguistics*, pages 2399–2409.

Micah Hodosh, Peter Young, and Julia Hockenmaier. 2013. Framing image description as a ranking task: Data, models and evaluation metrics. *Journal of Artificial Intelligence Research*, 47:853–899.

Po-Yao Huang, Frederick Liu, Sz-Rung Shiang, Jean Oh, and Chris Dyer. 2016. Attention-based multimodal neural machine translation. In *Proceedings of the First Conference on Machine Translation*, pages 639–645.

Allan Jabri, Armand Joulin, and Laurens van der Maaten. 2016. Revisiting visual question answering baselines. In *European conference on computer vision*, pages 727–739.

Akos Kádár, Grzegorz Chrupała, and Afra Alishahi. 2016. Representation of linguistic form and function in recurrent neural networks. *arXiv preprint arXiv:1602.08952*.

Douwe Kiela, Anita L. Verő, and Stephen Clark. 2016. Comparing Data Sources and Architectures for Deep Visual Representation Learning in Semantics. In *Proceedings of the Conference on Empirical Methods in Natural Language Processing (EMNLP-16)*, pages 447–456.

Diederik P. Kingma and Jimmy Ba. 2015. Adam: A method for stochastic optimization. *International Conference on Learning Representations*.

Ondřej Klejch, Eleftherios Avramidis, Aljoscha Burchardt, and Martin Popel. 2015. Mt-compareval: Graphical evaluation interface for machine translation development. *The Prague Bulletin of Mathematical Linguistics*, 104(1):63–74.

Sigrid Klerke, Yoav Goldberg, and Anders Søgaard. 2016. Improving sentence compression by learning to predict gaze. In *Proceedings of the 2016 Conference of the North American Chapter of the Association for Computational Linguistics: Human Language Technologies*, pages 1528–1533.

Philipp Koehn, Hieu Hoang, Alexandra Birch, Chris Callison-Burch, Marcello Federico, Nicola Bertoldi, Brooke Cowan, Wade Shen, Christine Moran, Richard Zens, et al. 2007. Moses: Open source toolkit for statistical machine translation. In *Proceedings of the 45th Annual meeting of Association for Computational Linguistics*, pages 177–180.

Jindřich Libovický, Jindřich Helcl, Marek Tlustý, Ondřej Bojar, and Pavel Pecina. 2016. Cuni system for wmt16 automatic post-editing and multimodal translation tasks. In *Proceedings of the First Conference on Machine Translation*, pages 646–654.

Xiao Lin and Devi Parikh. 2015. Don't just listen, use your imagination: Leveraging visual common sense for non-visual tasks. In *Proceedings of the IEEE Conference on Computer Vision and Pattern Recognition*, pages 2984–2993.

Minh-Thang Luong, Quoc V. Le, Ilya Sutskever, Oriol Vinyals, and Lukasz Kaiser. 2016. Multi-task sequence to sequence learning. In *ICLR*.

Hideki Nakayama and Noriki Nishida. 2017. Zero-resource machine translation by multimodal encoder-decoder network with multimedia pivot. *Machine Translation*, 31(1-2):49–64.

Kishore Papineni, Salim Roukos, Todd Ward, and Wei-Jing Zhu. 2002. Bleu: A method for automatic evaluation of machine translation. In *Proceedings of the 40th Annual Meeting on Association for Computational Linguistics*, pages 311–318.

R. Pasunuru and M. Bansal. 2017. Multi-Task Video Captioning with Video and Entailment Generation. In *Proceedings of the 55th Annual Meeting of the Association for Computational Linguistics (Volume 1: Long Papers)*, pages 1273–1283.

Barbara Plank. 2016. Keystroke dynamics as signal for shallow syntactic parsing. In *26th International Conference on Computational Linguistics*, pages 609–619.

Amrita Saha, Mitesh M. Khapra, Sarath Chandar, Janarthanan Rajendran, and Kyunghyun Cho. 2016. A correlational encoder decoder architecture for pivot based sequence generation. In *26th International Conference on Computational Linguistics: Technical Papers*, pages 109–118.

Mike Schuster and Kaisuke Nakajima. 2012. Japanese and korean voice search. In *2012 IEEE International Conference on Acoustics, Speech and Signal Processing (ICASSP)*, pages 5149–5152.

Mike Schuster and Kuldip K Paliwal. 1997. Bidirectional recurrent neural networks. *IEEE Transactions on Signal Processing*, 45(11):2673–2681.

R. Sennrich, O. Firat, K. Cho, A. Birch, B. Haddow, J. Hitschler, M. Junczys-Dowmunt, S. Läubli, A. Valerio Miceli Barone, J. Mokry, and M. Nădejde. 2017. Nematus: a Toolkit for Neural Machine Translation. pages 65–68.

Rico Sennrich, Barry Haddow, and Alexandra Birch. 2016. Improving neural machine translation models with monolingual data. In *Proceedings of the 54th Annual Meeting of the Association for Computational Linguistics*, pages 86–96.

Rico Sennrich and Beat Kunz. 2014. Zmorge: A german morphological lexicon extracted from wiktionary. In *Language Resources and Evaluation Conference*, pages 1063–1067.

Kashif Shah, Josiah Wang, and Lucia Specia. 2016. Shef-multimodal: Grounding machine translation on images. In *Proceedings of the First Conference on Machine Translation*, pages 660–665.

Karen Simonyan and Andrew Zisserman. 2015. Very deep convolutional networks for large-scale image recognition. In *Proceedings of the International Conference on Learning Representations*.

Lucia Specia, Stella Frank, Khalil Sima'an, and Desmond Elliott. 2016. A shared task on multimodal machine translation and crosslingual image description. In *Proceedings of the First Conference on Machine Translation*, pages 543–553.

Nitish Srivastava, Elman Mansimov, and Ruslan Salakhudinov. 2015. Unsupervised learning of video representations using LSTMs. In *International Conference on Machine Learning*, pages 843–852.

Christian Szegedy, Vincent Vanhoucke, Sergey Ioffe, Jonathon Shlens, and Zbigniew Wojna. 2015. Rethinking the inception architecture for computer vision. *CoRR*, abs/1512.00567.

Jörg Tiedemann. 2012. Parallel data, tools and interfaces in opus. In *Eight International Conference on Language Resources and Evaluation (LREC'12)*.

Joji Toyama, Masanori Misono, Masahiro Suzuki, Kotaro Nakayama, and Yutaka Matsuo. 2016. Neural machine translation with latent semantic of image and text. *CoRR*, abs/1611.08459.

Ivan Vendrov, Ryan Kiros, Sanja Fidler, and Raquel Urtasun. 2016. Order-embeddings of images and language. *ICLR*.

Understanding and Improving Morphological Learning in the Neural Machine Translation Decoder

Fahim Dalvi   Nadir Durrani   Hassan Sajjad
Yonatan Belinkov*   Stephan Vogel

Qatar Computing Research Institute – HBKU, Doha, Qatar
{faimaduddin, ndurrani, hsajjad, svogel}@qf.org.qa

*MIT Computer Science and Artificial Intelligence Laboratory, Cambridge, MA 02139, USA
belinkov@mit.edu

Abstract

End-to-end training makes the neural machine translation (NMT) architecture simpler, yet elegant compared to traditional statistical machine translation (SMT). However, little is known about linguistic patterns of morphology, syntax and semantics learned during the training of NMT systems, and more importantly, which parts of the architecture are responsible for learning each of these phenomena. In this paper we i) analyze how much morphology an NMT decoder learns, and ii) investigate whether injecting target morphology into the decoder helps it produce better translations. To this end we present three methods: i) joint generation, ii) joint-data learning, and iii) multi-task learning. Our results show that explicit morphological information helps the decoder learn target language morphology and improves the translation quality by 0.2–0.6 BLEU points.

1 Introduction

Neural machine translation (NMT) offers an elegant end-to-end architecture, improving translation quality compared to traditional phrase-based machine translation. These improvements are attributed to more fluent output (Toral and Sánchez-Cartagena, 2017) and better handling of morphology and long-range dependencies (Bentivogli et al., 2016). However, systematic studies are required to understand what kinds of linguistic phenomena (morphology, syntax, semantics, etc.) are learned by these models and more importantly, which of the components is responsible for each phenomenon.

A few attempts have been made to understand what NMT models learn about morphology (Belinkov et al., 2017a), syntax (Shi et al., 2016) and semantics (Belinkov et al., 2017b). Shi et al. (2016) used activations at various layers from the NMT encoder to predict syntactic properties on the source-side, while Belinkov et al. (2017a) and Belinkov et al. (2017b) used a similar approach to investigate the quality of word representations on the task of morphological and semantic tagging.

Belinkov et al. (2017a) found that word representations learned from the encoder are rich in morphological information, while representations learned from the decoder are significantly poorer. However, the paper does not present a convincing explanation for this finding. Our first contribution in this work is to provide a more comprehensive analysis of morphological learning on the decoder side. We hypothesize that other components of the NMT architecture – specifically the encoder and the attention mechanism, learn enough information about the target language morphology for the decoder to perform reasonably well, without incorporating high levels of morphological knowledge into the decoder. To probe this hypothesis, we investigate the following questions:

- What is the effect of attention on the performance of the decoder?

- How much does the encoder help the decoder in predicting the correct morphological variant of the word it generates?

To answer these questions, we train NMT models for different language pairs, involving morphologically rich languages such as German and Czech. We then use the trained models to extract features from the decoder for words in the language of interest. Finally we train a classifier using the extracted features to predict the morphological tag of the words. The accuracy of this ex-

Proceedings of the The 8th International Joint Conference on Natural Language Processing, pages 142–151,
Taipei, Taiwan, November 27 – December 1, 2017 ©2017 AFNLP

ternal classifier gives us a quantitative measure of how well the NMT model learned features that are relevant to morphology. Our results indicate that both the encoder and the attention mechanism aid the decoder in generating correct morphological forms, and thus limit the need of the decoder to learn target morphology.

Motivated by these findings, we hypothesize that it may be possible to force the decoder to learn more about morphology by injecting the morphological information during training which can in turn improve the overall translation quality. In order to test this hypothesis, we experiment with three possible solutions:

1. *Joint Generation*: An NMT model is trained on the concatenation of words and morphological tags on the target side.

2. *Joint-data learning*: An NMT model is trained where each source sequence is used twice with an artificial token to either predict target words or morphological tags.

3. *Multi-task learning*: A multi-task NMT system with two objective functions is trained to jointly learn translation and morphological tagging.

Our experiments show that word representations learned after explicitly injecting target morphology improve morphological tagging accuracy of the decoder by 3% and also improves the translation quality by up to 0.6 BLEU points.

The remainder of this paper is organized as follows. Section 2 describes our experimental setup. Section 3 shows an analysis of the decoder. Section 4 describes the three proposed methods to integrate morphology into the decoder. Section 5 presents the results. Section 6 gives an account of related work and Section 7 concludes the paper.

2 Experimental Design

Parallel Data

We used the German-English and Czech-English datasets from the WIT[3] TED corpus (Cettolo, 2016) made available for IWSLT 2016. We used the official training sets to analyze and evaluate the proposed methods for integrating morphology. The corpus also provides four test sets, test-11 through test-14. We used test-11 for tuning, and the other test sets for evaluation. The statistics for the sets are provided in Table 1.

Language-pair	Sentences	$\text{tok}_{de/cz}$	tok_{en}
De↔En	210K	4M	4.2M
Cz↔En	122K	2.1M	2.5M

Table 1: Statistics for the data used for training, tuning and testing

Morphological Annotations

In order to train and evaluate the external classifier on the extracted features, we required data annotated with morphological tags. We used the following tools recommended on the Moses website[1] to annotate the data: LoPar (Schmid, 2000) for German, Tree-tagger (Schmid, 1994) for Czech and MXPOST (Ratnaparkhi, 1998) for English. The number of tags produced by these taggers is 214 for German and 368 for Czech.

Data preprocessing

We used the standard MT pre-processing pipeline of tokenizing and truecasing the data using Moses (Koehn et al., 2007) scripts. We did not apply byte-pair encoding (BPE) (Sennrich et al., 2016b), which has recently become a common part of the NMT pipeline, because both our analysis and the annotation tools are word level.[2] However, experimenting with BPE and other representations such as character-based models (Kim et al., 2015) would be interesting.[3]

NMT Systems

We used the `seq2seq-attn` implementation (Kim, 2016) with the following default settings: word embeddings and LSTM states with 500 dimensions, SGD with an initial learning rate of 1.0 and decay rate of 0.5 (after the 9th epoch), and dropout rate of 0.3. We use two uni-directional hidden layers for both the encoder and the decoder.

---

[1]These have been used frequently to annotate data in the previous evaluation campaigns (Birch et al., 2014; Durrani et al., 2014a).

[2]The difficulty with using these is that it is not straightforward to derive word representations out of a decoder that processes BPE-ed text, because the original words are split into subwords. We considered aggregating the representations of BPE subword units, but the choice of aggregation strategy may have an undesired impact on the analysis. For this reason we decided to leave exploration of BPE for future work.

[3]Character-based models are becoming increasingly popular in Neural MT, for addressing the rare word problem – and they have been used previously also to benefit MT for morphologically rich (Luong et al., 2010; Belinkov and Glass, 2016; Costa-jussà and Fonollosa, 2016) and closely related languages (Durrani et al., 2010; Sajjad et al., 2013).

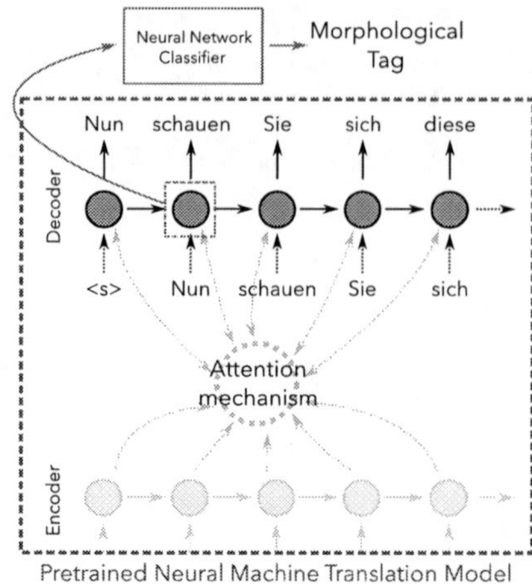

Figure 1: Features for the word *Nun* (DEC_{t_1}) are extracted from the decoder of a pre-trained NMT system and provided to the classifier for training

The NMT system is trained for 13 epochs, and the model with the best validation loss is used for extracting features for the external classifier. We use a vocabulary size of 50000 on both the source and target side.

Classifier Settings

For the classification task, we used a feed-forward network with one hidden layer, dropout ($\rho = 0.5$), a ReLU non-linearity, and an output layer mapping to the tag set (followed by a Softmax). The size of the hidden layer is set to be identical to the size of the NMT decoder's hidden state (500 dimensions). The classifier has no explicit access to context other than the hidden representation generated by the NMT system, which allows us to focus on the quality of the representation. We use Adam (Kingma and Ba, 2014) with default parameters to minimize the cross-entropy objective.

3   Decoder Analysis

3.1   Methodology

We follow a process similar to Shi et al. (2016) and Belinkov et al. (2017a) to analyze the NMT systems but with a focus on the decoder component of the architecture. Formally, given a source sentence $s = \{s_1, s_2, ..., s_N\}$ and a target sentence $t = \{t_1, t_2, ..., t_M\}$, we first use the encoder (Equation 1) to compute a set of hidden states $h = \{h_1, h_2, ..., h_N\}$. We then use an attention mechanism (Bahdanau et al., 2014) to compute a

weighted average of these hidden states from the previous decoder state (d_{i-1}), known as the context vector c_i (Equation 2). The context vector is a real valued vector of k dimensions, which is set to be the same as the hidden states in our case. The attention model computes a weight w_{h_i} for each hidden state of the encoder, thus giving soft alignment for each target word. The context vector is then used by the decoder (Equation 3) to generate the next word in the target sequence:

$$\text{ENC} : s = \{s_1, ..., s_N\} \mapsto h = \{h_1, ..., h_N\} \quad (1)$$
$$\text{ATTN}_i : h, d_{i-1}, t_{i-1} \mapsto c_i \in \mathbb{R}^k (1 \leq i \leq M) \quad (2)$$
$$\text{DEC} : \{c_1, ..., c_M\} \mapsto t = \{t_1, t_2, ..., t_M\} \quad (3)$$

After training the NMT system, we freeze the parameters of the network and use the encoder or the decoder as a feature extractor to generate vectors representing words in the sentence. Let ENC_{s_i} denote the representation of a source word s_i. We use ENC_{s_i} to train the external classifier that for predicting the morphological tag for s_i and evaluate the quality of the representation based on our ability to train a good classifier. For word representations on the target side, we feed our word of interest t_i as the previously predicted word, and extract the representation DEC_{t_i} from the higher layers (See Figure 1 for illustration).

Note that in the decoder, the target word representations DEC_{t_i} are not learned for predicting the word t_i, but the next word (t_{i+1}). Hence, it is arguable that DEC_{t_i} actually captures morphological information about t_{i+1} rather than t_i, which can also explain the poorer decoder accuracies. To test this argument, we also trained our systems assuming that DEC_{t_i} encodes morphological information about the next word t_{i+1}. In this case, the decoder performance dropped by almost 15%. DEC_{t_i} probably encodes morphological information about both the current word (t_i) and the next word (t_{i+1}). However, we leave this exploration for future work, and work with the assumption that DEC_{t_i} encodes information about word t_i.

3.2   Analysis

Before diving into the decoder's performance, we first compare the performance of encoder versus decoder by training De↔En[4] and Cz↔En NMT models. We use the De→En/Cz→En models to extract encoder representations, and the

---

[4]By De↔En, we mean independently trained German-to-English and English-to-German models.

Baseline	ENC$_{s_i}$	DEC$_{t_i}$
De↔En	89.5	44.55
Cz↔En	77.0	36.35

Table 2: Comparison of morphological accuracy for the encoder and decoder representations

	DEC$_{t_i}$	w/o-ATTN	DEC$_{t_i}$+ENC$_{t_i}$	ENC$_{t_i}$
En→De	44.55	50.26	60.34	43.43
En→Cz	36.35	42.09	48.64	36.36

Table 3: Morphological Tagging accuracy of the Decoder with and without attention, and effect of considering the most attended source word (ENC$_{t_i}$)

En→De/En→Cz models to extract decoder representations. We then feed these representations to our classifier to predict morphological tags for German and Czech words. Table 2 shows that German and Czech representations learned on the encoder-side (using the De→En/Cz→En models) give much better accuracy compared to the ones learned on the decoder-side (using the En→De/En→Cz models).

Given this difference in performance between the two components in our NMT system, we analyze the decoder further in various settings: comparing the performance i) with and without the attention mechanism, and ii) augmenting the decoder representation with the representation of the most attended source word. The baseline NMT models were trained with an attention mechanism. In an attempt to probe what effect the attention mechanism has on the decoder's performance in the context of learning target language morphology, we trained NMT models without attention. Next we tried to take our baseline model (with attention) and augment its decoder representations with the encoder hidden state corresponding to the maximum attention (hereby denoted as ENC$_{t_i}$). Our hypothesis is that since the decoder focuses on this hidden state to output the next target word, it may also encode some useful information about target morphology. Lastly, we also train a classifier on ENC$_{t_i}$ alone in order to compare the ability of the encoder and decoder in learning *target* language morphology.

Table 3 summarizes the results of these experiments. Comparing systems with (DEC$_{t_i}$) and without attention (w/o-ATTN), we see that the accuracy on the morphological tagging task goes up when no attention is used. This can be explained by the fact that in the case of no attention, the decoder only receives a single context vector from the encoder and it has to learn more information about each target word to make accurate predictions. It is difficult for the encoder to transfer information about each target word using the same context vector cleanly, causing the decoder

to learn more, resulting in better decoder performance in regards to the morphological information learned.

The second part of the table presents results involving encoder representations to aid morphological analysis of target words. There is a significant boost in the classifier's performance when the decoder representation for a target word t_i is concatenated with the encoder representation of the most attended source word (DEC$_{t_i}$+ENC$_{t_i}$). This hints towards several hypotheses: i) because the source and target words are translations, they share some morphological properties (e.g. nouns get translated to nouns, etc.), ii) the encoder also learns and stores information about the target language, so that the attention mechanism can make use of this information while deciding which word to focus on next. To ensure that the encoder and decoder indeed learn different information, we also tried to classify the morphological tag of a given word t_i based on the encoder representation of the most attended source word alone (ENC$_{t_i}$). We see a drop in accuracy, showing that both encoder and decoder learned different things about the same target word and are complementary representations. We can also see that the accuracy of the combined representation (DEC$_{t_i}$+ENC$_{t_i}$) still lags behind the encoder's performance in predicting source morphology (Table 2). This indicates that there is still room for improvement in the NMT model's ability to learn target side morphology.

In this section, we showed that the encoder and decoder learn different amounts of morphology due to the varying nature of their tasks within NMT architecture. The decoder depends on the encoder and attention mechanism to generate the correct morphological variant of a target word.

4 Morphology-aware Decoder

Motivated by the result that the decoder learns considerably less amount of morphology than the

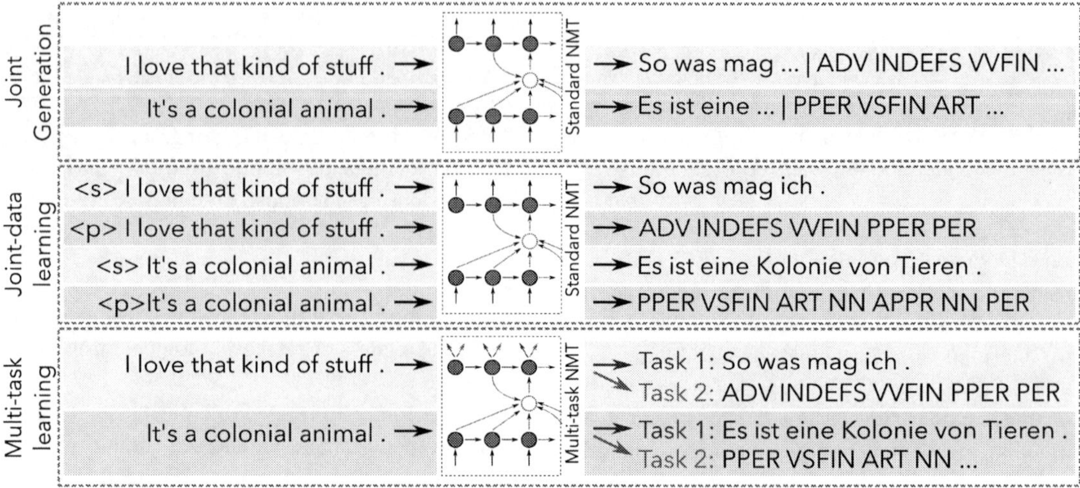

Figure 2: Various approaches to inject morphological knowledge into the decoder

encoder (Table 2) and the overall system does not learn as much about target morphology as source morphology, we investigated three ways to directly inject target morphology into the decoder, namely: i) Joint Generation, ii) Joint-data Learning, iii) Multi-task Learning. Figure 2 illustrates the approaches.

4.1 Joint Generation

As our first approach, we considered a solution that uses the standard NMT architecture, but is trained on a modified dataset. To incorporate morphological information, we modify the target sentence by appending the morphological tag sequence to it. The NMT system trained on this data learns to produce both words and morphological tags simultaneously. Formally, given a source sentence $s = \{s_1, ..., s_N\}$, target sentence $t = \{t_1, ..., t_M\}$ and its morphological sequence $m = \{m_1, ..., m_M\}$, we train an NMT system on (s', t') pairs, where $s' = s$ and $t' = t + m$. Although this model is quite weak and the (word and morphological) bases are quite far away, we posit that the attention mechanism might be able to attend to the same source word twice. Given this, the decoder gets a similar representation from which it has to predict a word in the first instance, and a tag in the second - thus helping in common learning for the two tasks.

4.2 Joint-data Learning

Given the drawbacks of the first approach, we considered another data augmentation technique

inspired by multilingual NMT systems (Johnson et al., 2016). Instead of having multiple source and target languages, we used one source language and two target language variations. The training data consists of sequences of source→target words and source→target morphological tags. We added an artificial token in the beginning of each source sentence indicating whether we want to generate target words or morphological tags. Using an artificial token in the source sentence has been explored and shown to work well to control the style of the target language (Sennrich et al., 2016a). The objective function is the same as the one in usual sequence-to-sequence models, and is hence shared to minimize both morphological and translation error given the mixed data.

4.3 Multi-task Learning

In this final method, we decided to follow a more principled approach and modified the standard sequence-to-sequence for multi-task learning. The goal in multi-task training is to learn several tasks simultaneously such that each task can benefit from the mutual information learned (Collobert and Weston, 2008). [5] With this motivation, we modified the NMT decoder to predict not only a word but also its corresponding tag. All of the layers below the output layers are shared. We have two output layers in parallel – the first to predict the target word, and the second to predict the morphological tag of the target word. Both ouput lay-

---

[5]For example, Eriguchi et al. (2017) jointly learned the tasks of parsing and translation.

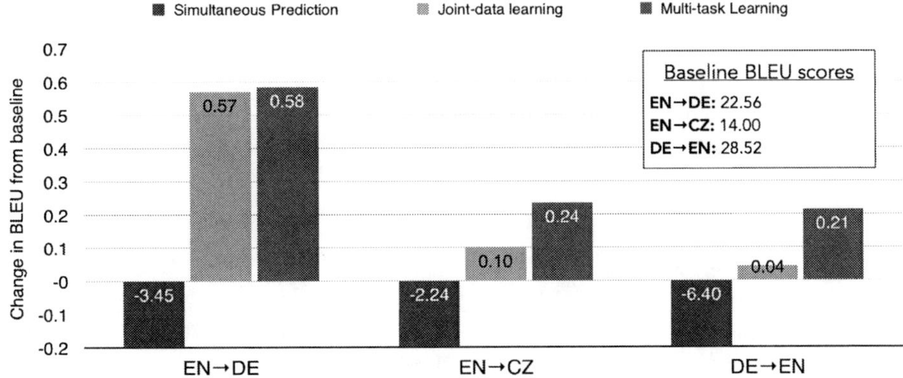

Figure 3: Improvements from adding morphology. A y-value of zero represents the baseline

ers have their own separate loss function. While training, we combine the losses from both output layers to jointly train the system. This is different from the Joint-data learning technique, where we predict entire sequences of words or tags without any dependence on each other.

Formally, given a set of N tasks, sequence-to-sequence multi-task learning involves an objective function minimizing the overall loss, which is a weighted combination of the N individual task losses. In our scenario, the training corpus consisted of a multi-target corpus: source→target words and source→target morphological tags, i.e $N = 2$. Hence, given a set of training examples $D = \{\langle s^{(n)}, t^{(n)}, m^{(n)} \rangle\}_{n=1}^{N}$, where s is the source sentence, t is the target sentence and m is the target morphological tag sequence, the new objective function to maximize is as follows:

$$\mathcal{L} = (1 - \lambda) \sum_{n=1}^{N} \log P(t^{(n)} | s^{(n)}; \theta)$$

$$+ \lambda \sum_{n=1}^{N} \log P(m^{(n)} | s^{(n)}; \theta)$$

Where λ is a hyper-parameter used to shift focus towards translation or the morphological tagging.[6]

5 Results and Discussion

Our results show that the multi-task learning approach performed the best among the three approaches, while the Joint Generation method has the poorest performance. Figure 3 summarizes the results for different language pairs. The joint generation method degrades overall translation performance, as expected, given its weakness from

a modeling perspective. It is possible that even though the attention mechanism is able to focus on the source sequence in two passes, the parts of the network that predict words and tags are not tightly coupled enough to learn from each other.

The BLEU scores improved when using the other two methods. We achieved an improvement of up to 0.6 BLEU points and 3% (in tagging accuracy). The best improvements were obtained in the En→De direction, while we observed lesser gains in the De→En. This is perhaps because English is morphologically poorer, and the baseline system was able to learn the required amount of morphological information from the text itself. Improvements were also obtained for the En→Cz direction, although not as much as in German. This could be due to data sparsity: Czech is much richer in morphology,[7] and the available TED En↔Cz data was 40% less than the En↔De data.

Joint-data vs. Multi-task Learning

Both Joint-data learning and Multi-task learning improved overall translation performance. In the case of En→De, the performance of both approaches is very similar. However, each has its own pros and cons. While the joint-data learning method is a simple approach that allows to add morphology and other linguistic information without needing to change the architecture, the multi-task learning approach is a more principled and powerful way of integrating the same information into the decoder. Having separate objective functions in multi-task learning also allows us to adjust the balance between the two tasks, which can

---

[6]We tuned the weight parameter on held-out data.

[7]The number of morphological tags in Czech are 368 versus 214 in German.

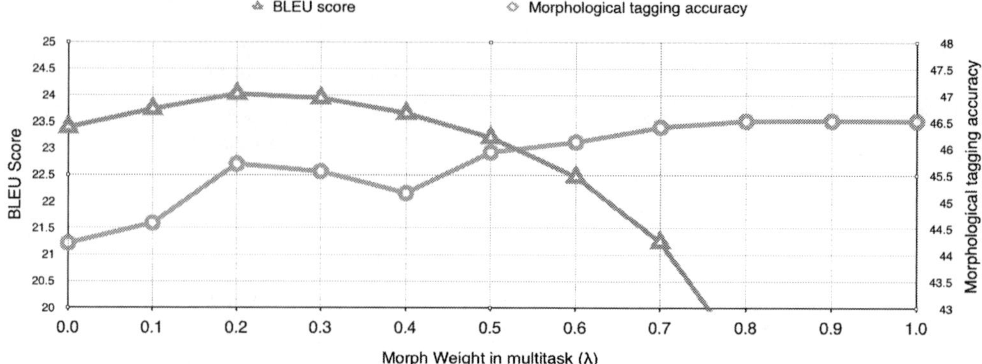

Figure 4: Multi-task learning: Translation vs. Morphological Tagging weight for En→De model

be handy if the morphological information quality is not very high. On the flip side, this additional explicit weight adjustment can also be viewed as a potential constraint that is not present in the joint-data learning approach.

Multi-task Weight Hyper-Parameter

As discussed, the multi-task learning approach has an additional weight hyper-parameter λ that adjusts the balance between word and tag prediction. Figure 4 shows the result of varying λ from no morphological information ($\lambda = 0$) to only morphological information ($\lambda = 1$) on test-11 set. The left y-axis presents the BLEU score and the right y-axis presents the morphological accuracy. The best morphological accuracy is achieved at $\lambda = 1$ which does not correspond to best translation quality since at that point the model is only minimizing the tag objective function. Similarly at $\lambda = 0$, the model falls back to the baseline model with a single objective function minimizing translation error. For all language pairs, we consistently achieved the best BLEU score at $\lambda = 0.2$. The parameter was tuned on a separate held out development set (test-11), and the results shown in Figure 3 are on blind test sets (test-12,13). Averages are reported in the figure.

6   Related Work

The related work to this paper can be broken into two groups:

Analysis   Several approaches have been devised to analyze MT models and the linguistic properties that are learned during training. A common approach has been to use activations from a trained model to train an external classifier to predict some

relevant information about the input. Köhn (2015) and Qian et al. (2016b) analyzed linguistic information learned in word embeddings, while Qian et al. (2016a) went further and analyzed linguistic properties in the hidden states of a recurrent neural network. Adi et al. (2016) looked at the overall information learned in a sentence summary vector generated by an RNN using a similar approach. Our approach closely aligns with that of Shi et al. (2016) and Belinkov et al. (2017a), where the activations from various layers in a trained NMT system are used to predict linguistic properties.

Integrating Morphology   Some work has also been done in injecting morphological or more general linguistic knowledge into an NMT system. Sennrich and Haddow (2016) proposed a factored model that incorporates linguistic features on the source side as additional factors. An embedding is learned for each factor, just like a source word, and then the word and factor embeddings are combined before being passed on to the encoder. Aharoni and Goldberg (2017) proposed a method to predict the target sentence along with its syntactic tree. They linearize the tree in order to use the existing sequence-to-sequence model. Nadejde et al. (2017) also evaluated several methods of incorporating syntactic knowledge on both the source and target. While they used factors on the source side, their best method for the target side was to linearize the information and interleave it between the target words. García-Martínez et al. (2016) used a neural MT model with multiple outputs, like in our case of *Multi-task learning*. Their model predicts two properties at every step, the lemma of the target word and its morphological information. They then use an external tool to use this information to generate the actual target word. Dong et al. (2015) presented multi-task learning to translate a language into multiple target languages, and Luong et al. (2015) did experiments involving several levels of source and target language information. There have been previous efforts to integrate morphology into MT systems by learning factored models (Koehn and Hoang, 2007; Durrani et al., 2014b) over POS and morphological tags.

7 Conclusion

In this paper we analyzed and investigated ways to improve morphological learning in the NMT decoder. We carried a series of experiments to understand why the decoder learns considerably less morphology than the encoder in the NMT architecture. We found that the decoder needs assistance from the encoder and the attention mechanism to generate correct target morphology. Additionally we explored three ways to explicitly inject morphology in the decoder: joint generation, joint-data learning, and multi-task learning. We found multi-task learning to outperform the other two methods. The simpler joint-data learning method also gave decent improvements. The code for the experiments and the modified framework is available at `https://github.com/fdalvi/seq2seq-attn-multitask`.

References

Yossi Adi, Einat Kermany, Yonatan Belinkov, Ofer Lavi, and Yoav Goldberg. 2016. Fine-grained Analysis of Sentence Embeddings Using Auxiliary Prediction Tasks. *arXiv preprint arXiv:1608.04207*.

Roee Aharoni and Yoav Goldberg. 2017. Towards String-To-Tree Neural Machine Translation. In *Proceedings of the 55th Annual Meeting of the Association for Computational Linguistics (Volume 2: Short Papers)*, pages 132–140. Association for Computational Linguistics.

Dzmitry Bahdanau, Kyunghyun Cho, and Yoshua Bengio. 2014. Neural Machine Translation by Jointly Learning to Align and Translate. *arXiv preprint arXiv:1409.0473*.

Yonatan Belinkov, Nadir Durrani, Fahim Dalvi, Hassan Sajjad, and James Glass. 2017a. What do Neural Machine Translation Models Learn about Morphology? In *Proceedings of the 55th Annual Meeting of the Association for Computational Linguistics (Volume 1: Long Papers)*, pages 861–872. Association for Computational Linguistics.

Yonatan Belinkov and James Glass. 2016. Large-Scale Machine Translation between Arabic and Hebrew: Available Corpora and Initial Results. In *Proceedings of the Workshop on Semitic Machine Translation*, pages 7–12, Austin, Texas. Association for Computational Linguistics.

Yonatan Belinkov, Lluis Marquez, Hassan Sajjad, Nadir Durrani, Fahim Dalvi, and James Glass. 2017b. Evaluating layers of representation in neural machine translation on parts-of-speech and semantic tagging task. In *Proceedings of the 8th International Joint Conference on Natural Language Processing (Volume 1: Long Papers)*, Taipei, Taiwan. Association for Computational Linguistics.

Luisa Bentivogli, Arianna Bisazza, Mauro Cettolo, and Marcello Federico. 2016. Neural versus Phrase-Based Machine Translation Quality: a Case Study. In *Proceedings of the 2016 Conference on Empirical Methods in Natural Language Processing*, pages 257–267, Austin, Texas. Association for Computational Linguistics.

Alexandra Birch, Matthias Huck, Nadir Durrani, Nikolay Bogoychev, and Philipp Koehn. 2014. Edinburgh SLT and MT system description for the IWSLT 2014 evaluation. In *Proceedings of the 11th International Workshop on Spoken Language Translation*, IWSLT '14, Lake Tahoe, CA, USA.

Mauro Cettolo. 2016. An Arabic-Hebrew parallel corpus of TED talks. In *Proceedings of the AMTA Workshop on Semitic Machine Translation (SeMaT)*, Austin, US-TX.

Ronan Collobert and Jason Weston. 2008. A unified architecture for natural language processing: Deep neural networks with multitask learning. In *Proceedings of the 25th International Conference on Machine Learning*, ICML '08, pages 160–167, New York, NY, USA. ACM.

Marta R. Costa-jussà and José A. R. Fonollosa. 2016. Character-based Neural Machine Translation. In *Proceedings of the 54th Annual Meeting of the Association for Computational Linguistics (Volume 2: Short Papers)*, pages 357–361, Berlin, Germany. Association for Computational Linguistics.

Daxiang Dong, Hua Wu, Wei He, Dianhai Yu, and Haifeng Wang. 2015. Multi-Task Learning for Multiple Language Translation. In *ACL (1)*.

Nadir Durrani, Barry Haddow, Philipp Koehn, and Kenneth Heafield. 2014a. Edinburgh's phrase-based machine translation systems for WMT-14. In *Proceedings of the ACL 2014 Ninth Workshop on Statistical Machine Translation*, pages 97–104, Baltimore, MD, USA.

Nadir Durrani, Philipp Koehn, Helmut Schmid, and Alexander Fraser. 2014b. Investigating the Usefulness of Generalized Word Representations in SMT. In *Proceedings of COLING 2014, the 25th International Conference on Computational Linguistics:*

Technical Papers, pages 421–432, Dublin, Ireland. Dublin City University and Association for Computational Linguistics.

Nadir Durrani, Hassan Sajjad, Alexander Fraser, and Helmut Schmid. 2010. Hindi-to-Urdu Machine Translation through Transliteration. In *Proceedings of the 48th Annual Meeting of the Association for Computational Linguistics*, pages 465–474, Uppsala, Sweden. Association for Computational Linguistics.

Akiko Eriguchi, Yoshimasa Tsuruoka, and Kyunghyun Cho. 2017. Learning to parse and translate improves neural machine translation. In *Proceedings of the 55th Annual Meeting of the Association for Computational Linguistics (Volume 2: Short Papers)*, pages 72–78. Association for Computational Linguistics.

Mercedes García-Martínez, Loïc Barrault, and Fethi Bougares. 2016. Factored neural machine translation. *CoRR*, abs/1609.04621.

Melvin Johnson, Mike Schuster, Quoc V. Le, Maxim Krikun, Yonghui Wu, Zhifeng Chen, Nikhil Thorat, Fernanda B. Viégas, Martin Wattenberg, Greg Corrado, Macduff Hughes, and Jeffrey Dean. 2016. Google's multilingual neural machine translation system: Enabling zero-shot translation. *CoRR*, abs/1611.04558.

Yoon Kim. 2016. Seq2seq-attn. https://github.com/harvardnlp/seq2seq-attn.

Yoon Kim, Yacine Jernite, David Sontag, and Alexander M Rush. 2015. Character-aware Neural Language Models. *arXiv preprint arXiv:1508.06615*.

Diederik Kingma and Jimmy Ba. 2014. Adam: A Method for Stochastic Optimization. *arXiv preprint arXiv:1412.6980*.

Philipp Koehn and Hieu Hoang. 2007. Factored Translation Models. In *Proceedings of the 2007 Joint Conference on Empirical Methods in Natural Language Processing and Computational Natural Language Learning (EMNLP-CoNLL)*, pages 868–876, Prague, Czech Republic. Association for Computational Linguistics.

Philipp Koehn, Hieu Hoang, Alexandra Birch, Chris Callison-Burch, Marcello Federico, Nicola Bertoldi, Brooke Cowan, Wade Shen, Christine Moran, Richard Zens, Chris Dyer, Ondrej Bojar, Alexandra Constantin, and Evan Herbst. 2007. Moses: Open source toolkit for statistical machine translation. In *Proceedings of the Association for Computational Linguistics (ACL'07)*, Prague, Czech Republic.

Arne Köhn. 2015. What's in an Embedding? Analyzing Word Embeddings through Multilingual Evaluation. In *Proceedings of the 2015 Conference on Empirical Methods in Natural Language Processing*, pages 2067–2073, Lisbon, Portugal. Association for Computational Linguistics.

Minh-Thang Luong, Quoc V. Le, Ilya Sutskever, Oriol Vinyals, and Lukasz Kaiser. 2015. Multitask sequence to sequence learning. *CoRR*, abs/1511.06114.

Minh-Thang Luong, Preslav Nakov, and Min-Yen Kan. 2010. A Hybrid Morpheme-Word Representation for Machine Translation of Morphologically Rich Languages. In *Proceedings of the 2010 Conference on Empirical Methods in Natural Language Processing*, pages 148–157. Association for Computational Linguistics.

Maria Nadejde, Siva Reddy, Rico Sennrich, Tomasz Dwojak, Marcin Junczys-Dowmunt, Philipp Koehn, and Alexandra Birch. 2017. Syntax-aware neural machine translation using CCG. *CoRR*, abs/1702.01147.

Peng Qian, Xipeng Qiu, and Xuanjing Huang. 2016a. Analyzing Linguistic Knowledge in Sequential Model of Sentence. In *Proceedings of the 2016 Conference on Empirical Methods in Natural Language Processing*, pages 826–835, Austin, Texas. Association for Computational Linguistics.

Peng Qian, Xipeng Qiu, and Xuanjing Huang. 2016b. Investigating Language Universal and Specific Properties in Word Embeddings. In *Proceedings of the 54th Annual Meeting of the Association for Computational Linguistics (Volume 1: Long Papers)*, pages 1478–1488, Berlin, Germany. Association for Computational Linguistics.

Adwait Ratnaparkhi. 1998. *Maximum Entropy Models for Natural Language Ambiguity Resolution*. Ph.D. thesis, University of Pennsylvania, Philadelphia, PA.

Hassan Sajjad, Kareem Darwish, and Yonatan Belinkov. 2013. Translating Dialectal Arabic to English. In *Proceedings of the 51st Conference of the Association for Computational Linguistics (ACL)*.

Helmut Schmid. 1994. Part-of-Speech Tagging with Neural Networks. In *Proceedings of the 15th International Conference on Computational Linguistics (Coling 1994)*, pages 172–176, Kyoto, Japan. Coling 1994 Organizing Committee.

Helmut Schmid. 2000. LoPar: Design and Implementation. Bericht des Sonderforschungsbereiches "Sprachtheoretische Grundlagen fr die Computerlinguistik" 149, Institute for Computational Linguistics, University of Stuttgart.

Rico Sennrich and Barry Haddow. 2016. Linguistic input features improve neural machine translation. In *Proceedings of the First Conference on Machine Translation*, pages 83–91, Berlin, Germany. Association for Computational Linguistics.

Rico Sennrich, Barry Haddow, and Alexandra Birch. 2016a. Controlling Politeness in Neural Machine Translation via Side Constraints. In *Proceedings of the 2016 Conference of the North American Chapter of the Association for Computational Linguistics:*

Human Language Technologies, San Diego, California.

Rico Sennrich, Barry Haddow, and Alexandra Birch. 2016b. Neural Machine Translation of Rare Words with Subword Units. In *Proceedings of the 54th Annual Meeting of the Association for Computational Linguistics (Volume 1: Long Papers)*, pages 1715–1725, Berlin, Germany. Association for Computational Linguistics.

Xing Shi, Inkit Padhi, and Kevin Knight. 2016. Does String-Based Neural MT Learn Source Syntax? In *Proceedings of the 2016 Conference on Empirical Methods in Natural Language Processing*, pages 1526–1534, Austin, Texas. Association for Computational Linguistics.

Antonio Toral and Víctor M. Sánchez-Cartagena. 2017. A Multifaceted Evaluation of Neural versus Phrase-Based Machine Translation for 9 Language Directions. In *Proceedings of the 15th Conference of the European Chapter of the Association for Computational Linguistics: Volume 1, Long Papers*, pages 1063–1073, Valencia, Spain. Association for Computational Linguistics.

Improving Neural Machine Translation
through Phrase-based Forced Decoding

Jingyi Zhang[1,2], **Masao Utiyama**[1], **Eiichro Sumita**[1]
Graham Neubig[3,2], **Satoshi Nakamura**[2]
[1]National Institute of Information and Communications Technology, Japan
[2]Graduate School of Information Science, Nara Institute of Science and Technology, Japan
[3]Language Technologies Institute, Carnegie Mellon University, USA
`jingyizhang/mutiyama/eiichiro.sumita@nict.go.jp`
`gneubig@cs.cmu.edu, s-nakamura@is.naist.jp`

Abstract

Compared to traditional statistical machine translation (SMT), neural machine translation (NMT) often sacrifices adequacy for the sake of fluency. We propose a method to combine the advantages of traditional SMT and NMT by exploiting an existing phrase-based SMT model to compute the phrase-based decoding cost for an NMT output and then using this cost to rerank the n-best NMT outputs. The main challenge in implementing this approach is that NMT outputs may not be in the search space of the standard phrase-based decoding algorithm, because the search space of phrase-based SMT is limited by the phrase-based translation rule table. We propose a soft forced decoding algorithm, which can always successfully find a decoding path for any NMT output. We show that using the forced decoding cost to rerank the NMT outputs can successfully improve translation quality on four different language pairs.

1 Introduction

Neural machine translation (NMT), which uses a single large neural network to model the entire translation process, has recently been shown to outperform traditional statistical machine translation (SMT) such as phrase-based machine translation (PBMT) on several translation tasks (Koehn et al., 2003; Bahdanau et al., 2015; Sennrich et al., 2016a). Compared to traditional SMT, NMT generally produces more fluent translations, but often sacrifices adequacy, such as translating source words into completely unrelated target words, over-translation or under-translation (Koehn and Knowles, 2017).

There are a number of methods that combine the two paradigms to address their respective weaknesses. For example, it is possible to incorporate neural features into traditional SMT models to disambiguate hypotheses (Neubig et al., 2015; Stahlberg et al., 2016). However, the search space of traditional SMT is usually limited by translation rule tables, reducing the ability of these models to generate hypotheses on the same level of fluency as NMT, even after reranking. There are also methods that incorporate knowledge from traditional SMT into NMT, such as lexical translation probabilities (Arthur et al., 2016; He et al., 2016), phrase memory (Tang et al., 2016; Zhang et al., 2017), and n-gram posterior probabilities based on traditional SMT translation lattices (Stahlberg et al., 2017). These improve the adequacy of NMT outputs, but do not impose hard alignment constraints like traditional SMT systems and therefore cannot effectively solve all over-translation or under-translation problems.

In this paper, we propose a method that exploits an existing phrase-based translation model to compute the phrase-based decoding cost for a given NMT translation.[1] That is, we force a phrase-based translation system to take in the source sentence and generate an NMT translation. Then we use the cost of this phrase-based forced decoding to rerank the NMT outputs. The phrase-based decoding cost will heavily punish completely unrelated translations, over-translations, and under-translations, as they will not be able to be found in the translation phrase table.

One challenge in implementing this method is that the NMT output may not be in the search space of the phrase-based translation model, which is limited by the phrase-based translation

---

[1]In fact, our method can take in the output of *any* upstream system, but we experiment exclusively with using it to rerank NMT output.

152

Proceedings of the The 8th International Joint Conference on Natural Language Processing, pages 152–162,
Taipei, Taiwan, November 27 – December 1, 2017 ©2017 AFNLP

rule table. To solve this problem, we propose a soft forced decoding algorithm, which is based on the standard phrase-based decoding algorithm and integrates new types of translation rules (deleting a source word or inserting a target word). The proposed forced decoding algorithm can always successfully find a decoding path and compute a phrase-based decoding cost for any NMT output. Another challenge is that we need a diverse NMT n-best list for reranking. Because beam search for NMT often lacks diversity in the beam – candidates only have slight differences, with most of the words overlapping – we use a random sampling method to obtain a more diverse n-best list.

We test the proposed method on English-to-Chinese, English-to-Japanese, English-to-German and English-to-French translation tasks, obtaining large improvements over a strong NMT baseline that already incorporates discrete lexicon features.

2 Attentional NMT

Our baseline NMT model is similar to the attentional model of Bahdanau et al. (2015), which includes an encoder, a decoder and an attention (alignment) model. Given a source sentence $F = \{f_1, ..., f_J\}$, the encoder learns an annotation $h_j = \left[\vec{h}_j; \overleftarrow{h}_j\right]$ for f_j using a bi-directional recurrent neural network.

The decoder generates the target translation from left to right. The probability of generating next word e_i is,[2]

$$P_{NMT}\left(e_i | e_1^{i-1}, F\right) = softmax\left(g\left(e_{i-1}, t_i, s_i\right)\right) \tag{1}$$

where t_i is a decoding state for time step i, computed by,

$$t_i = f\left(t_{i-1}, e_{i-1}, s_i\right) \tag{2}$$

s_i is a source representation for time i, calculated as,

$$s_i = \sum_{j=1}^{J} \alpha_{i,j} \cdot h_j \tag{3}$$

where $\alpha_{i,j}$ scores how well the inputs around position j and the output at position i match, computed as,

$$\alpha_{i,j} = \frac{\exp\left(a\left(t_{i-1}, h_j\right)\right)}{\sum_{k=1}^{J} \exp\left(a\left(t_{i-1}, h_k\right)\right)} \tag{4}$$

As we can see, NMT only learns an attention (alignment) distribution for each target word over all source words and does not provides exact mutually-exclusive word or phrase level alignments. As a result, it is known that attentional NMT systems make mistakes in over- or undertranslation (Cohn et al., 2016; Mi et al., 2016).

3 Phrase-based Forced Decoding for NMT

3.1 Phrase-based SMT

In phrase-based SMT (Koehn et al., 2003), a phrase-based translation rule r includes a source phrase, a target phrase and a translation score $S(r)$. Phrase-based translation rules can be extracted from the word-aligned training set and then used to translate new sentences. Word alignments for the training set can be obtained by IBM models (Brown et al., 1993).

Phrase-based decoding uses a list of translation rules to translate source phrases in the input sentence and generate target phrases from left to right. A basic concept in phrase-based decoding is hypotheses. As shown in Figure 1, the hypothesis H_1 consists of two rules r_1 and r_2. The score of a hypothesis $S(H)$ can be calculated as the product of the scores of all applied rules.[3] An existing hypothesis can be expanded into a new hypothesis by applying a new rule. As shown in Figure 1, H_1 can be expanded into H_2, H_3 and H_4. H_2 cannot be further expanded, because it covers all source words, while H_3 and H_4 can (and must) be further expanded. The decoder starts with an initial empty hypothesis H_0 and selects the hypothesis with the highest score from all completed hypotheses.

During decoding, hypotheses are stored in stacks. For a source sentence with J words, the decoder builds J stacks. The hypotheses that cover j source words are stored in stack s_j. The decoder expands hypotheses in $s_1, s_2, ..., s_J$ in turn as shown in Algorithm 1. Here, EXPAND(H) is expanding H to get new hypotheses and putting the new hypotheses into corresponding stacks. For each stack, a beam of the best n hypotheses is kept to speed up the decoding process.

---

[2]g, f and a in Equation 1, 2 and 4 are nonlinear, potentially multi-layered, functions.

[3]In actual phrase-based decoding it is common to integrate reordering probabilities in the forced decoding score defined in Equation 9. However, because NMT generally produces more properly ordered sentences than traditional SMT, in this work we do not consider reordering probabilities in our forced decoding algorithm.

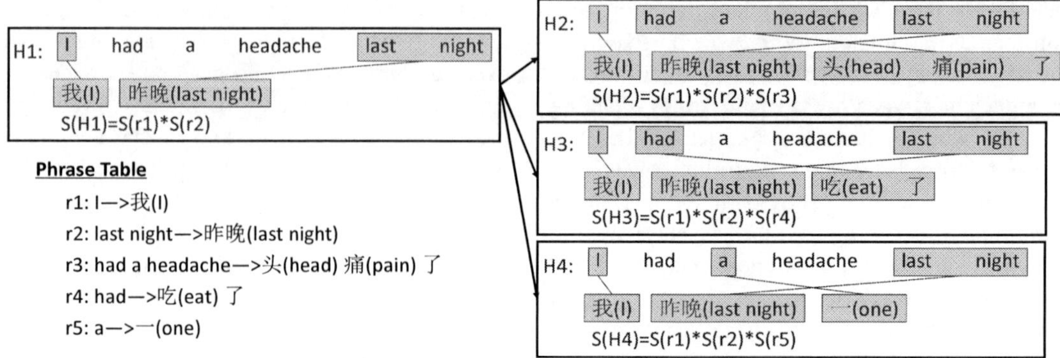

Figure 1: An example of phrase-based decoding.

Algorithm 1 Standard phrase-based decoding.

Require: Source sentence F with length J
Ensure: Translation E and decoding path D
  initialize H_0 and $s_1, s_2, ..., s_J$
  EXPAND(H_0)
  for $j = 1$ to $J - 1$ **do**
    for each hypothesis H_{jk} in s_j **do**
      EXPAND(H_{jk})
  select best hypothesis in s_J

3.2 Forced Decoding for NMT

As stated in the introduction, our goal is not to generate new hypotheses with phrase-based SMT, but instead use the phrase-based model to calculate scores for NMT output. In order to do so, we can perform *forced decoding*, which is very similar to the algorithm in the previous section but discards all partial hypotheses that do not match the NMT output. However, the NMT output is not limited by the phrase-based rule table, so there may be no decoding path that completely matches the NMT output when using only the phrase-based rules.

To remedy this problem, inspired by previous work in forced decoding for training phrase-based SMT systems (Wuebker et al., 2010, 2012) we propose a soft forced decoding algorithm that can always successfully find a decoding path for a source sentence F and an NMT translation E.

First, we introduce two new types of rules R_1 and R_2.

R_1 A source word f can be translated into a special word `null`. This corresponds to deleting f during translation. The score of deleting f is cal-

culated as,

$$s(f \rightarrow \texttt{null}) = \frac{\text{unalign}(f)}{|\mathcal{T}|} \qquad (5)$$

where unalign (f) is how many times f is unaligned in the word-aligned training set $\mathcal{T}$ and $|\mathcal{T}|$ is the number of sentence pairs in $\mathcal{T}$.

R_2 A target word e can be translated from a special word `null`, which corresponds to inserting e during translation. The score of inserting e is calculated as,

$$s(\texttt{null} \rightarrow e) = \frac{\text{unalign}(e)}{|\mathcal{T}|} \qquad (6)$$

where unalign (e) is how many times e is unaligned in $\mathcal{T}$.

One motivation for Equations 5 and 6 is that function words usually have high frequencies, but do not have as clear a correspondence with a word in the other language as content words. As a result, in the training set function words are more often unaligned than content words. As an example, Table 1 and Table 2 show how many times different words occur and how many times they are unaligned in the word-aligned training set of English-to-Chinese and English-to-French tasks in our experiments. As we can see, generally there are less unaligned words in the English-to-French task, however, function words are more likely to be unaligned in both tasks. Based on Equation 5 and Equation 6, the scores of deleting or inserting "of" and "a" will be higher.

In our forced decoding, we choose to model the score of each translation rule that exists in the phrase table as the product of direct and inverse phrase translation probabilities. To make sure that

154

Words	of	a	practice	water
Occur	1.3M	1.0M	2.2K	29K
Unaligned	0.51M	0.41M	0.25K	3.5K

Table 1: The number of times that words occur in the English-to-Chinese training corpus and the number of times that they are unaligned.

Words	of	a	practice	water
Occur	1.7M	0.83M	8.8K	7.4K
Unaligned	0.16M	0.12M	0.38K	0.19K

Table 2: The number of times that words occur in the English-to-French training corpus and the number of times that they are unaligned.

the scale of the scores for R_1 and R_2 match the other phrase (which are the product of two probabilities), we use the square of the score in Equation 5/6 as the rule score for R_1/R_2.

Algorithm 2 shows the forced decoding algorithm that integrates the new rules. Because the translation E is given for the forced decoding algorithm, the proposed forced decoding algorithm keeps I stacks, where I is the length of E. In other words, the stack size is corresponding to the target word size during forced decoding while the stack size is corresponding to the source word size during standard phrase-based decoding. The stack s_i' in Algorithm 2 contains all hypotheses in which the first i target words have been generated. We expand hypotheses in $s_1', s_2', ..., s_I'$ in turn. When expanding a hypothesis H_{old} in s_i', besides expanding it using the original rule table $\text{EXPAND}(H_{old})$,[4] we also expand H_{old} by inserting the next target word e_{i+1} at the end of H_{old} to get an additional hypothesis H_{new} and put H_{new} into s_{i+1}'. For a final hypothesis in stack s_I', it may not cover all source words. We update its score by translating uncovered words into `null`.

Because different decoding paths can generate the same final translation, there can be different decoding paths that fit the NMT translation E. We use the score of the single decoding path with the highest decoding score as the forced decoding score for E.

<hr>

[4]The new introduced word inserting/deleting rules are not used when performing $\text{EXPAND}(H_{old})$.

Algorithm 2 Forced phrase-based decoding.

Require: Source sentence F with length J and translation E with length I

Ensure: Decoding path D

   initialize H_0 and $s_1', s_2', ..., s_I'$

   $\text{EXPAND}(H_0)$

   expand H_0 with rule $\texttt{null} \to e_1$

   for $i = 1$ to $I - 1$ **do**

      for each hypothesis H_{ik} in s_i' **do**

         $\text{EXPAND}(H_{ik})$

         expand H_{ik} with rule $\texttt{null} \to e_{i+1}$

   for each hypothesis H_{Ik} in s_I' **do**

      update $S(H_{Ik})$ for uncovered source words

   select best hypothesis in s_I'

---

4 Reranking NMT Outputs with Phrase-based Decoding Score

We rerank the n-best NMT outputs using the phrase-based forced decoding score according to Equation 7.

$$\log P\left(E|F\right) = w_1 \cdot \log P_n\left(E|F\right) + w_2 \cdot \log S_d\left(E|F\right) \quad (7)$$

where $P_n\left(E|F\right)$ is the original NMT translation probability as calculated by Equation 1;

$$P_n\left(E|F\right) = \prod_{i=1}^{I} P_{NMT}\left(e_i|e_1^{i-1}, F\right) \quad (8)$$

$S_d\left(E|F\right)$ is the forced decoding score, which is the score of the decoding path $\hat{D}$ with the highest decoding score as described above;

$$S_d\left(E|F\right) = \prod_{r \in \hat{D}} S\left(r\right) \quad (9)$$

w_1 and w_2 are weights that can be tuned on the n-best list of the development set.

The easiest way to get an n-best list for NMT is by using the n-best translations from beam search, which is the standard decoding algorithm for NMT. While beam search is likely to find the highest-scoring hypothesis, it often lacks diversity in the beam: candidates only have slight differences, with most of the words overlapping. In order to obtain a more diverse list of hypotheses for reranking, we additionally augment the 1-best hypothesis discovered by beam search with translations sampled from the NMT conditional probability distribution.

The standard method for sampling hypotheses in NMT is ancestral sampling, where we randomly select a word from the vocabulary according to

$P_{NMT}\left(e_i|e_1^{i-1}, F\right)$ (Shen et al., 2016). This will make a diverse list of hypotheses, but may reduce the probability of selecting a highly scoring hypothesis, and the whole n-best list may not contain any candidate with better translation quality than the standard beam search output.

Instead, we take an alternative approach that proved empirically better in our experiments: at each time step i, we use sampling to randomly select the next word from e' and e'' according to Equation 10. Here, e' and e'' are the two target words with the highest probability according to Equation 1.

$$P_{rdm}\left(e'\right) = \frac{P_{NMT}\left(e'|e_1^{i-1}, F\right)}{P_{NMT}\left(e'|e_1^{i-1}, F\right) + P_{NMT}\left(e''|e_1^{i-1}, F\right)}$$
$$P_{rdm}\left(e''\right) = \frac{P_{NMT}\left(e''|e_1^{i-1}, F\right)}{P_{NMT}\left(e'|e_1^{i-1}, F\right) + P_{NMT}\left(e''|e_1^{i-1}, F\right)}$$
$$(10)$$

The sampling process ends when $\langle/s\rangle$ is selected as the next word.

We repeat the decoding process $1,000$ times to sample $1,000$ outputs for each source sentence. We additionally add the 1-best output of standard beam search, making the size of the list used for reranking to be $1,001$.

5 Experiments

5.1 Settings

We evaluated the proposed approach for English-to-Chinese (en-zh), English-to-Japanese (en-ja), English-to-German (en-de) and English-to-French (en-fr) translation tasks. For the en-zh and en-ja tasks, we used datasets provided for the patent machine translation task at NTCIR-9 (Goto et al., 2011).[5] For the en-de and en-fr tasks, we used version 7 of the Europarl corpus as training data, WMT 2014 test sets as our development sets and WMT 2015 test sets as our test sets. The detailed statistics for training, development and test sets are given in Table 3. The word segmentation was done by BaseSeg (Zhao et al., 2006) for Chinese and Mecab[6] for Japanese.

We built attentional NMT systems with Lamtram[7]. Word embedding size and hidden layer size

---

[5]Note that NTCIR-9 only contained a Chinese-to-English translation task, we used English as the source language in our experiments. In NTCIR-9, the development and test sets were both provided for the zh-en task while only the test set was provided for the en-ja task. We used the sentences from the NTCIR-8 en-ja and ja-en test sets as the development set in our experiments.

[6]http://sourceforge.net/projects/mecab/files/

[7]https://github.com/neubig/lamtram

			SOURCE	TARGET
en-de	TRAIN	#Sents	1.90M	
		#Words	52.2M	49.7M
		#Vocab	113K	376K
	DEV	#Sents	3,003	
		#Words	67.6K	63.0K
	TEST	#Sents	2,169	
		#Words	46.8K	44.0K
en-fr	TRAIN	#Sents	1.99M	
		#Words	54.4M	60.4M
		#Vocab	114K	137K
	DEV	#Sents	3,003	
		#Words	71.1K	81.1K
	TEST	#Sents	1.5K	
		#Words	27.1K	29.8K
en-zh	TRAIN	#Sents	954K	
		#Words	40.4M	37.2M
		#Vocab	504K	288K
	DEV	#Sents	2K	
		#Words	77.5K	75.4K
	TEST	#Sents	2K	
		#Words	58.1K	55.5K
en-ja	TRAIN	#Sents	3.14M	
		#Words	104M	118M
		#Vocab	273K	150K
	DEV	#Sents	2K	
		#Words	66.5K	74.6K
	TEST	#Sents	2K	
		#Words	70.6K	78.5K

Table 3: Data sets.

are both 512. We used Byte-pair encoding (BPE) (Sennrich et al., 2016b) and set the vocabulary size to be 50K. We used the Adam algorithm for optimization.

To obtain a phrase-based translation rule table for our forced decoding algorithm, we used GIZA++ (Och and Ney, 2003) and *grow-diag-final-and* heuristic to obtain symmetric word alignments for the training set. Then we extracted the rule table using Moses (Koehn et al., 2007).

5.2 Results and Analysis

Table 4 shows results of the phrase-based SMT system[8], the baseline NMT system, the lexicon integration method (Arthur et al., 2016) and the proposed reranking method. We tested three features for reranking: the NMT score P_n, the forced decoding score S_d and a word penalty (WP) feature, which is the length of the translation. The best NMT system and the systems that have no significant difference from the best NMT system at the $p < 0.05$ level using bootstrap resampling (Koehn, 2004) are shown in bold font.

As we can see, integrating lexical translation probabilities improved the baseline NMT system

---

[8]We used the default Moses settings for phrase-based SMT.

	en-zh		en-ja		en-de		en-fr	
	dev	test	dev	test	dev	test	dev	test
PBMT	30.73	27.72	35.67	33.46	12.37	13.95	25.96	27.50
NMT	34.60	32.71	41.67	39.00	12.52	14.05	23.63	23.99
NMT+lex	36.06	34.80	44.47	41.09	13.36	15.60	24.00	24.91
NMT+lex+rerank(P_n)	34.38	33.23	38.92	34.18	12.34	13.59	23.13	23.61
NMT+lex+rerank(S_d)	36.17	34.09	42.91	40.16	13.08	15.29	24.28	25.71
NMT+lex+rerank(P_n+S_d)	37.94	**35.59**	45.34	41.75	**14.56**	**16.61**	**25.96**	**27.12**
NMT+lex+rerank(P_n+WP)	37.44	34.93	45.81	41.90	13.75	15.46	24.47	25.09
NMT+lex+rerank(S_d+WP)	36.44	33.73	43.52	40.49	13.39	15.71	24.74	26.25
NMT+lex+rerank(P_n+S_d+WP)	**38.69**	**35.75**	**46.92**	**43.17**	**14.61**	**16.65**	**25.98**	**27.15**

Table 4: Translation results (BLEU). NMT+lex: (Arthur et al., 2016); NMT+lex+rerank: we rerank the n-best outputs of NMT+lex using different features (P_n, S_d and WP).

	en-zh		en-ja		en-de		en-fr	
	METEOR	chrF	METEOR	chrF	METEOR	chrF	METEOR	chrF
PBMT	34.70	37.87	35.22	39.45	26.66	50.02	32.33	56.36
NMT	34.51	39.91	35.07	42.02	24.91	44.50	29.58	49.99
NMT+lex	35.56	42.22	36.48	44.34	25.49	45.67	30.10	50.89
NMT+lex+rerank(P_n)	34.56	40.80	32.63	38.57	23.57	40.35	29.15	48.64
NMT+lex+rerank(S_d)	36.02	42.65	36.87	44.85	**26.48**	**48.73**	**31.56**	**54.42**
NMT+lex+rerank(P_n+S_d)	36.40	43.73	37.22	45.69	26.26	47.27	**31.62**	53.99
NMT+lex+rerank(P_n+WP)	36.04	42.86	36.90	44.93	25.03	44.05	30.21	50.78
NMT+lex+rerank(S_d+WP)	36.34	42.78	37.05	45.03	26.16	47.82	31.32	53.75
NMT+lex+rerank(P_n+S_d+WP)	**36.88**	**44.09**	**37.94**	**46.66**	**26.20**	47.12	**31.61**	53.98

Table 5: METEOR and chrF scores on the test sets for different system outputs in Table 4.

	en-zh		en-ja		en-de		en-fr	
	dev	test	dev	test	dev	test	dev	test
PBMT	1.008	1.018	1.005	0.998	1.077	1.069	0.986	1.004
NMT	0.953	0.954	0.960	0.961	1.059	1.038	0.985	0.977
NMT+lex	0.936	0.966	0.955	0.963	1.054	1.019	1.030	0.977
NMT+lex+rerank(P_n)	0.875	0.898	0.814	0.775	0.874	0.854	0.904	0.900
NMT+lex+rerank(S_d)	0.973	0.989	0.985	0.981	1.062	1.060	1.030	1.031
NMT+lex+rerank(P_n+S_d)	0.949	0.965	0.945	0.936	1.000	0.992	0.999	0.992
NMT+lex+rerank(P_n+WP)	0.996	1.019	0.999	0.983	1.000	0.975	0.998	1.001
NMT+lex+rerank(S_d+WP)	1.000	1.024	1.001	1.001	1.011	1.007	0.999	0.989
NMT+lex+rerank(P_n+S_d+WP)	0.990	1.014	1.000	0.986	1.000	0.989	1.000	0.992

Table 6: Ratio of translation length to reference length for different system outputs in Table 4.

and reranking with the three features all together achieved further improvements for all four language pairs. Even on English-to-Chinese and English-to-Japanese tasks, where the NMT system outperformed the phrase-based SMT system by 7-8 BLEU scores, using the forced decoding score for reranking NMT outputs can still achieve significant improvements. With or without the word penalty feature, using both P_n and S_d for reranking gave better results than only using P_n or S_d alone. We also show METEOR and chrF scores on the test sets in Table 5. Our reranking method improved both METEOR and chrF significantly.

The Word Penalty Feature The word penalty feature generally improved the reranking results, especially when only the NMT score P_n was used for reranking. As we can see, using only P_n for reranking decreased the translation quality compared to the standard beam search result of NMT. Because the search spaces of beam search and random sampling are quite different, the best beam search output does not necessarily have the highest NMT score compared to random sampling outputs. Therefore, even the P_n reranking results do have higher NMT scores, but have lower BLEU scores according to Table 4. To explain why this happened, we show the ratio of translation length to reference length in Table 6. As we can see, the P_n reranking outputs are much shorter. This is because NMT generally prefers shorter translations, since Equation 8 multiplies all target word probabilities together. So the word penalty feature can improve the P_n reranking results considerably, by preferring longer sentences. Because the forced decoding score S_d as shown in Equation 9 does not obviously prefer shorter or longer sentences, when S_d was used for reranking, the word penalty

Source	for hypophysectomized (hypop hy sec to mized) rats , the drinking water additionally contains 5 % glucose .
Reference	对于(for) 去(remove) 垂体(hypophysis) 大(big) 鼠(rat) ，饮用水(drinking water) 中(in) 另外(also) 含有(contain) 5 % 葡萄糖(glucose) 。
PBMT	用于(for) 大(big) 鼠(rat) 垂体(hypophysis) HySecto, (Hy Sec to ,) 饮用水(drinking water) 另外(also) 含有(contain) 5 % 葡萄糖(glucose) 。
NMT	对于(for) 过(pass) 盲肠(cecum) 的(of) 大(big) 鼠(rat) ，饮用水(drinking water) 另外(also) 含有(contain) 5 % 葡萄糖(glucose) 。
NMT+lex NMT+lex+P_n NMT+lex+P_n+WP	对于(for) 低(low) 酪(cheese) 蛋白(protein) 切除(remove) 的(of) 大(big) 鼠(rat) ，饮用水(drinking water) 另外(also) 含有(contain) 5 % 葡萄糖(glucose) 。
NMT+lex+S_d NMT+lex+S_d+WP	对于(for) 垂体(hypophysis) 在(is) 切除(remove) 大(big) 鼠(rat) 中(in) ，饮用水(drinking water) 另外(also) 含有(contain) 5 % 葡萄糖(glucose) 。
NMT+lex+P_n+S_d NMT+lex+P_n+S_d+WP	对于(for) 垂体(hypophysis) 在(is) 切除(remove) 的(of) 大(big) 鼠(rat) 中(in) ，饮用水(drinking water) 另外(also) 含有(contain) 5 % 葡萄糖(glucose) 。

Table 7: An example of improving inaccurate rare word translation by using S_d for reranking.

feature became less helpful. When both P_n and S_d were used for reranking, the word penalty feature only achieved further significant improvement on the English-to-Japanese task.

T_1 (NMT+lex):	
for →对于(for)	-3.04
r_a: hy →低(low)	-12.19
r_b: null→酪(cheese)	-21.99
r_c: null→蛋白(protein)	-13.83
to mized →切除(remove)	-6.22
null→的(of)	-1.53
rats →大(big) 鼠(rat)	-1.52
, the drinking water →， 饮用水(drinking water)	-1.38
additionally contains →另外(also) 含有(contain)	-3.68
5 % →5 %	-0.51
glucose . →葡萄糖(glucose) 。	-0.60
r_d: hypop→null	-25.33
sec→null	-20.66
T_2 (NMT+lex+P_n+S_d):	
for →对于(for)	-3.04
hypop hy →垂体(hypophysis)	-5.09
the →在(is)	-5.32
to mized →切除(remove)	-6.22
null→的(of)	-1.53
rats →大(big) 鼠(rat)	-1.52
, →中(in) ,	-4.11
drinking water →饮用水(drinking water)	-1.03
additionally contains →另外(also) 含有(contain)	-3.68
5 % →5 %	-0.51
glucose . →葡萄糖(glucose) 。	-0.60
sec→null	-20.66

Table 9: Forced decoding paths for T_1 and T_2: used rules and log scores. The translation rules with shade are used only for T_1 or T_2.

Table 7 gives translation examples of our reranking method from the English-to-Chinese task. The source English word "hypophysectomized" is an unknown word which does not occur in the training set. By employing BPE, this word is split into "hypop", "hy", "sec", "to" and "mized". The correct translation for "hypophysectomized" is "去(remove) 垂体(hypophysis)" as shown in the reference sentence. The original attentional NMT translated it into incorrect translation "过(pass) 盲肠(cecum)". After integrating lexicons, the NMT system translated it into "低(low) 酪(cheese) 蛋白(protein) 切除(remove)". The last word "切除(remove)" is correct, but the rest of the translation is still wrong. Only by using the forced decoding score S_d for reranking, we get the more accurate translation "垂体(hypophysis) 在(is) 切除(remove)".

To further demonstrate how the reranking method works, Table 9 shows translation rules and their log-scores contained in the forced decoding paths found for T_1, the NMT translation without reranking and T_2, the NMT translation using both P_n and S_d for reranking. As we can see, the four rules r_a, r_b, r_c and r_d used for T_1 have low scores. r_a is an unlikely translation. In r_b, r_c and r_d, "酪(cheese)", "蛋白(protein)" and "hypop" are content words, which are unlikely to be deleted or inserted during translation. Table 9 also shows that the translation of function words is very flexible. The score of inserting a function word "的(of)" is very high. The translation rule "the →在(is)" used for T_2 is incorrect, but its score is relatively high, because function words are often

Source	such changes in reaction conditions include , but are not limited to , an increase in temperature or change in ph .
Reference	所(such) 述(said) 反应(reaction) 条件(condition) 的(of) 改变(change) 包括(include) 但(but) 不(not) 限于(limit) 温度(temperature) 的(of) 增加(increase) 或(or) pH 值(value) 的(of) 改变(change) 。
PBMT	中(in) 的(of) 这种(such) 变化(change) 的(of) 反应(reaction) 条件(condition) 包括(include) , 但(but) 不(not) 限于(limit) , 增加(increase) 的(of) 温度(temperature) 或(or) pH 变化(change) 。
NMT	这种(such) 反应(reaction) 条件(condition) 的(of) 变化(change) 包括(include) 但(but) 不(not) 限于(limit) pH 或(or) pH 的(of) 变化(change) 。
NMT+lex NMT+lex+P_n	这种(such) 反应(reaction) 条件(condition) 的(of) 变化(change) 包括(include) , 但(but) 不(not) 限于(limit) , pH 的(of) 升高(increase) 或(or) pH 变化(change) 。
NMT+lex+S_d	这种(such) 反应(reaction) 条件(condition) 的(of) 变化(change) 包括(include) 但(but) 不(not) 限于(limit) , 温度(temperature) 的(of) 升高(increase) 或(or) 改变(change) pH 值(value) 。
NMT+lex+P_n+S_d	这种(such) 反应(reaction) 条件(condition) 的(of) 变化(change) 包括(include) , 但(but) 不(not) 限于(limit) , 温度(temperature) 的(of) 升高(increase) 或(or) 改变(change) pH 值(value) 。
NMT+lex+P_n+WP	这种(such) 反应(reaction) 条件(condition) 的(of) 变化(change) 包括(include) , 但(but) 不(not) 限于(limit) , pH 的(of) 升高(increase) 或(or) 改变(change) pH 值(value) 。
NMT+lex+S_d+WP NMT+lex+P_n+S_d+WP	这种(such) 反应(reaction) 条件(condition) 的(of) 变化(change) 包括(include) , 但(but) 不(not) 限于(limit) , 温度(temperature) 的(of) 升高(increase) 或(or) 改变(change) pH 值(value) 。

Table 8: An example of improving under-translation and over-translation by using S_d for reranking.

incorrectly aligned in the training set. The reason why function words are more likely to be incorrectly aligned to each other is that they usually have high frequencies and do not have clear correspondences between different languages.

In T_1, "hypophysectomized (hypop hy sec to mized)" is incorrectly translated into "低(low) 酪(cheese) 蛋白(protein) 切除(remove)". However, from Table 9, we can see that the forced decoding algorithm learns it as unlikely translation (hy→低(low)), over-translation (null→酪(cheese), null→蛋白(protein)) and under-translation (hypop→null, sec→null), because there is no translation rule between "hypop" "sec" and "酪(cheese)" "蛋白(protein)". Because content words are unlikely to be deleted or inserted during translation, they have low forced decoding scores. So using the forced decoding score for reranking NMT outputs can naturally improve over-translation or under-translation as shown in Table 8. As we can see, without using S_d for reranking, NMT under-translated "temperature" and over-translated "ph" twice, which will be assigned low scores by forced decoding. By using S_d for reranking, the correct translation was selected.

We did human evaluation on 100 sentences randomly selected from the English-to-Chinese test set to test the effectiveness of our forced decoding method. We compared the outputs of two systems:

- NMT+lex+rerank(P_n+WP)

- NMT+lex+rerank(P_n+S_d+WP)

For each source sentence, we compared the two system outputs. Table 10 shows the numbers of sentences that our forced decoding feature helped to reduce completely unrelated translation, over-translation and under-translation. The last line of Table 10 means that for 73 source sentences, our forced decoding feature neither reduced nor caused more unrelated/over/under translation. That is our forced decoding feature never caused more unrelated/over/under translation for the sampled 100 sentences, which shows that our method is very robust for improving unrelated/over/under translation.

	both under- and over- translation	2
Reduce	under-translation	11
	over-translation	10
	unrelated translation	4
No difference		73

Table 10: Human evaluation results.

Reranking PBMT Outputs with NMT We also did experiments that use the NMT score as an additional feature to rerank PBMT outputs (unique $1,000$-best list). The results are shown in Table 11. We also copy results of baseline PBMT and NMT from Table 4 for direct comparison. As we can see, using NMT to rerank PBMT outputs achieved improvements over the baseline PBMT system. However, when the baseline NMT system is significantly better than the baseline PBMT system (en-zh, en-ja), even using NMT to rerank PBMT outputs still achieved lower translation quality compared to the baseline NMT system.

		en-zh	en-ja	en-de	en-fr
PBMT+rerank		32.77	37.68	**14.23**	**28.86**
PBMT	dev	30.73	35.67	12.37	25.96
NMT		**34.60**	**41.67**	12.52	23.63
PBMT+rerank		30.04	35.14	**15.89**	**29.77**
PBMT	test	27.72	33.46	13.95	27.50
NMT		**32.71**	**39.00**	14.05	23.99

Table 11: Results of using NMT for reranking PBMT outputs.

6 Related Work

Wuebker et al. (2010, 2012) applied forced decoding on the training set to improve the training process of phrase-based SMT and prune the phrase-based rule table. They also used word insertions and deletions for forced decoding, but they used a high penalty for all insertions and deletions. In contrast, our soft forced decoding algorithm for NMT outputs uses a small penalty for function words and a high penalty for content words, because function words are usually translated very flexibly and more likely to be inserted or deleted compared to content words. For example, the under-translation of a content word can hurt the adequacy of the translation heavily. But function words may naturally disappear during translation (e.g. the English word "the" disappears in Chinese). By assigning a high penalty to words that should not be deleted or inserted during translation, our soft forced decoding method aims to improve the adequacy of NMT, which is very different from previous forced decoding methods that are used to improve general SMT training (Yu et al., 2013; Xiao et al., 2016).

A major difference of traditional SMT and NMT is that the alignment model in traditional SMT provides exact word or phrase level alignments between the source and target sentences while the attention model in NMT only computes an alignment probability distribution for each target word over all source words, which is the main reason why NMT is more likely to produce completely unrelated translations, over-translation or under-translation compared to traditional SMT. To relieve NMT of these problems, there are methods that modify the NMT neural network structure (Tu et al., 2016; Meng et al., 2016; Alkhouli et al., 2016) while we rerank NMT outputs by exploiting knowledge from traditional SMT.

There are also existing methods that rerank NMT outputs by using target-bidirectional NMT models (Liu et al., 2016; Sennrich et al., 2016a). Their reranking method aims to overcome the issue of unbalanced accuracy in NMT outputs while our reranking method aims to solve the inadequacy problem of NMT.

7 Conclusion

In this paper, we propose to exploit an existing phrase-based SMT model to compute the phrase-based decoding cost for NMT outputs and then use the phrase-based decoding cost to rerank the n-best NMT outputs, so we can combine the advantages of both PBMT and NMT. Because an NMT output may not be in the search space of standard phrase-based SMT, we propose a forced decoding algorithm, which can always successfully find a decoding path for any NMT output by deleting source words and inserting target words. Results show that using the forced decoding cost to rerank NMT outputs improved translation accuracy on four different language pairs.

References

Tamer Alkhouli, Gabriel Bretschner, Jan-Thorsten Peter, Mohammed Hethnawi, Andreas Guta, and Hermann Ney. 2016. Alignment-based neural machine translation. In *Proceedings of the First Conference on Machine Translation*, pages 54–65.

Philip Arthur, Graham Neubig, and Satoshi Nakamura. 2016. Incorporating discrete translation lexicons into neural machine translation. In *Proceedings of the 2016 Conference on Empirical Methods in Natural Language Processing*, pages 1557–1567.

Dzmitry Bahdanau, Kyunghyun Cho, and Yoshua Bengio. 2015. Neural machine translation by jointly learning to align and translate. In *International Conference on Learning Representations*.

Peter F Brown, Vincent J Della Pietra, Stephen A Della Pietra, and Robert L Mercer. 1993. The mathematics of statistical machine translation: Parameter estimation. *Computational Linguistics*, 19(2):263–311.

Trevor Cohn, Cong Duy Vu Hoang, Ekaterina Vymolova, Kaisheng Yao, Chris Dyer, and Gholamreza Haffari. 2016. Incorporating structural alignment biases into an attentional neural translation model. In *Proceedings of the 2016 Conference of the North American Chapter of the Association for Computational Linguistics: Human Language Technologies*, pages 876–885.

Isao Goto, Bin Lu, Ka Po Chow, Eiichiro Sumita, and Benjamin K Tsou. 2011. Overview of the patent machine translation task at the NTCIR-9 workshop. In *Proc. NTCIR-9*, pages 559–578.

Wei He, Zhongjun He, Hua Wu, and Haifeng Wang. 2016. Improved neural machine translation with SMT features. In *Thirtieth AAAI conference on artificial intelligence*.

Philipp Koehn. 2004. Statistical significance tests for machine translation evaluation. In *Proceedings of the 2004 Conference on Empirical Methods in Natural Language Processing*, pages 388–395.

Philipp Koehn, Hieu Hoang, Alexandra Birch, Chris Callison-Burch, Marcello Federico, Nicola Bertoldi, Brooke Cowan, Wade Shen, Christine Moran, Richard Zens, Chris Dyer, Ondrej Bojar, Alexandra Constantin, and Evan Herbst. 2007. Moses: Open source toolkit for statistical machine translation. In *Proceedings of the 45th Annual Meeting of the Association for Computational Linguistics Companion Volume Proceedings of the Demo and Poster Sessions*, pages 177–180.

Philipp Koehn and Rebecca Knowles. 2017. Six challenges for neural machine translation. In *Proceedings of the First Workshop on Neural Machine Translation*, pages 28–39.

Philipp Koehn, Franz Josef Och, and Daniel Marcu. 2003. Statistical phrase-based translation. In *Proceedings of the 2003 Conference of the North American Chapter of the Association for Computational Linguistics on Human Language Technology-Volume 1*, pages 48–54.

Lemao Liu, Masao Utiyama, Andrew Finch, and Eiichiro Sumita. 2016. Agreement on target-bidirectional neural machine translation. In *Proceedings of the 2016 Conference of the North American Chapter of the Association for Computational Linguistics: Human Language Technologies*, pages 411–416.

Fandong Meng, Zhengdong Lu, Hang Li, and Qun Liu. 2016. Interactive attention for neural machine translation. In *Proceedings of COLING 2016, the 26th International Conference on Computational Linguistics: Technical Papers*, pages 2174–2185.

Haitao Mi, Baskaran Sankaran, Zhiguo Wang, and Abe Ittycheriah. 2016. Coverage embedding models for neural machine translation. In *Proceedings of the 2016 Conference on Empirical Methods in Natural Language Processing*, pages 955–960.

Graham Neubig, Makoto Morishita, and Satoshi Nakamura. 2015. Neural reranking improves subjective quality of machine translation: NAIST at WAT2015. In *Proceedings of the 2nd Workshop on Asian Translation (WAT2015)*.

Franz Josef Och and Hermann Ney. 2003. A systematic comparison of various statistical alignment models. *Computational Linguistics*, 29(1):19–51.

Rico Sennrich, Barry Haddow, and Alexandra Birch. 2016a. Edinburgh neural machine translation systems for WMT 16. In *Proceedings of the First Conference on Machine Translation*, pages 371–376.

Rico Sennrich, Barry Haddow, and Alexandra Birch. 2016b. Neural machine translation of rare words with subword units. In *Proceedings of the 54th Annual Meeting of the Association for Computational Linguistics (Volume 1: Long Papers)*, pages 1715–1725.

Shiqi Shen, Yong Cheng, Zhongjun He, Wei He, Hua Wu, Maosong Sun, and Yang Liu. 2016. Minimum risk training for neural machine translation. In *Proceedings of the 54th Annual Meeting of the Association for Computational Linguistics (Volume 1: Long Papers)*, pages 1683–1692.

Felix Stahlberg, Adrià de Gispert, Eva Hasler, and Bill Byrne. 2017. Neural machine translation by minimising the Bayes-risk with respect to syntactic translation lattices. In *Proceedings of the 15th Conference of the European Chapter of the Association for Computational Linguistics: Volume 2, Short Papers*, pages 362–368.

Felix Stahlberg, Eva Hasler, Aurelien Waite, and Bill Byrne. 2016. Syntactically guided neural machine translation. In *Proceedings of the 54th Annual Meeting of the Association for Computational Linguistics (Volume 2: Short Papers)*, pages 299–305.

Yaohua Tang, Fandong Meng, Zhengdong Lu, Hang Li, and Philip LH Yu. 2016. Neural machine translation with external phrase memory. *arXiv preprint arXiv:1606.01792*.

Zhaopeng Tu, Zhengdong Lu, Yang Liu, Xiaohua Liu, and Hang Li. 2016. Modeling coverage for neural machine translation. In *Proceedings of the 54th Annual Meeting of the Association for Computational Linguistics (Volume 1: Long Papers)*, pages 76–85.

Joern Wuebker, Mei-Yuh Hwang, and Chris Quirk. 2012. Leave-one-out phrase model training for large-scale deployment. In *Proceedings of the Seventh Workshop on Statistical Machine Translation*, pages 460–467.

Joern Wuebker, Arne Mauser, and Hermann Ney. 2010. Training phrase translation models with leaving-one-out. In *Proceedings of the 48th Annual Meeting of the Association for Computational Linguistics*, pages 475–484.

Tong Xiao, Derek F Wong, and Jingbo Zhu. 2016. A loss-augmented approach to training syntactic machine translation systems. *IEEE/ACM Transactions on Audio, Speech, and Language Processing*, 24(11):2069–2083.

Heng Yu, Liang Huang, Haitao Mi, and Kai Zhao. 2013. Max-violation perceptron and forced decoding for scalable MT training. In *Proceedings of the 2013 Conference on Empirical Methods in Natural Language Processing*, pages 1112–1123.

Jiacheng Zhang, Yang Liu, Huanbo Luan, Jingfang Xu, and Maosong Sun. 2017. Prior knowledge integration for neural machine translation using posterior regularization. In *Proceedings of the 55th Annual Meeting of the Association for Computational Linguistics (Volume 1: Long Papers)*, pages 1514–1523.

Hai Zhao, Chang-Ning Huang, Mu Li, et al. 2006. An improved chinese word segmentation system with conditional random field. In *Proceedings of the Fifth SIGHAN Workshop on Chinese Language Processing*, pages 162–165.

Convolutional Neural Network with Word Embeddings for Chinese Word Segmentation

Chunqi Wang[1,2] and **Bo Xu**[1]

[1]Institute of Automation, Chinese Academy of Sciences
[2]University of Chinese Academy of Sciences
`chqiwang@126.com, xubo@ia.ac.cn`

Abstract

Character-based sequence labeling framework is flexible and efficient for Chinese word segmentation (CWS). Recently, many character-based neural models have been applied to CWS. While they obtain good performance, they have two obvious weaknesses. The first is that they heavily rely on manually designed bigram feature, i.e. they are not good at capturing n-gram features automatically. The second is that they make no use of full word information. For the first weakness, we propose a convolutional neural model, which is able to capture rich n-gram features without any feature engineering. For the second one, we propose an effective approach to integrate the proposed model with word embeddings. We evaluate the model on two benchmark datasets: PKU and MSR. Without any feature engineering, the model obtains competitive performance — 95.7% on PKU and 97.3% on MSR. Armed with word embeddings, the model achieves state-of-the-art performance on both datasets — 96.5% on PKU and 98.0% on MSR, without using any external labeled resource.

1 Introduction

Unlike English and other western languages, most east Asian languages, including Chinese, are written without explicit word delimiters. However, most natural language processing (NLP) applications are word-based. Therefore, word segmentation is an essential step for processing those languages. CWS is often treated as a character-based sequence labeling task (Xue et al., 2003; Peng et al., 2004). Figure 1 gives an intuitive

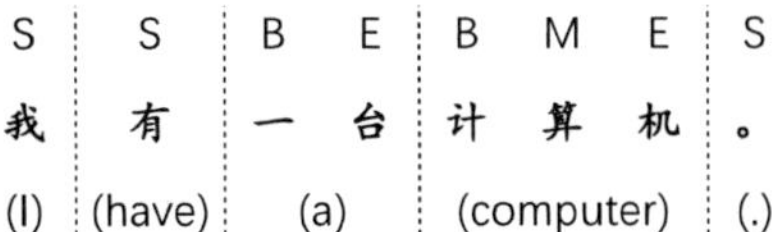

Figure 1: Chinese word segmentation as a sequence labeling task. This figure presents the common *BMES* (Begining, Middle, End, Singleton) tagging scheme.

explaination. Linear models, such as Maximum Entropy (ME) (Berger et al., 1996) and Conditional Random Fields (CRF) (Lafferty et al., 2001), have been widely used for sequence labeling tasks. However, they often depend heavily on well-designed hand-crafted features.

Recently, neural networks have been widely used for NLP tasks. Collobert et al. (2011) proposed a unified neural architecture for various sequence labeling tasks. Instead of exploiting hand-crafted input features carefully optimized for each task, their system learns internal representations automatically. As for CWS, there are a series of works, which share the main idea with Collobert et al. (2011) but vary in the network architecture. In particular, feed-forward neural network (Zheng et al., 2013), tensor neural network (Pei et al., 2014), recursive neural network (Chen et al., 2015a), long-short term memory (LSTM) (Chen et al., 2015b), as well as the combination of LSTM and recursive neural network (Xu and Sun, 2016) have been used to derive contextual representations from input character sequences, which are then fed to a prediction layer.

Despite of the great success of above models, they have two weaknesses. The first is that they are not good at capturing n-gram features automatically. Experimental results show that their models perform badly when no bigram feature is explicitly used. One of the strengths of neural networks is the ability to learn features automatically. However, this strength has not been well exploited in

Proceedings of the The 8th International Joint Conference on Natural Language Processing, pages 163–172,
Taipei, Taiwan, November 27 – December 1, 2017 ©2017 AFNLP

their works. The second is that they make no use of full word information. Full word information has shown its effectiveness in word-based CWS systems (Andrew, 2006; Zhang and Clark, 2007; Sun et al., 2009). Recently, Liu et al. (2016); Zhang et al. (2016) utilized word embeddings to boost performance of word-based CWS models. However, for character-based CWS models, word information is not easy to be integrated.

For the first weakness, we propose a convolutional neural model, which is also character-based. Previous works have shown that convolutional layers have the ablity to capture rich n-gram features (Kim et al., 2016). We use stacked convolutional layers to derive contextual representations from input sequence, which are then fed into a CRF layer for sequence-level prediction. For the second weakness, we propose an effective approach to incorporate word embeddings into the proposed model. The word embeddings are learned from large auto-segmented data. Hence, this approach belongs to the category of semi-supervised learning.

We evaluate our model on two benchmark datasets: PKU and MSR. Experimental results show that even without the help of explicit n-gram feature, our model is capable of capturing rich n-gram information automatically, and obtains competitive performance — 95.7% on PKU and 97.3% on MSR (F score). Furthermore, armed with word embeddings, our model achieves state-of-the-art performance on both datasets — 96.5% on PKU and 98.0% on MSR, without using any external labeled resource. [1]

2 Architecture

In this section, we introduce the architecture from bottom to top.

2.1 Lookup Table

The first step to process a sentence by deep neural networks is often to transform words or characters into embeddings (Bengio et al., 2003; Collobert et al., 2011). This transformation is done by lookup table operation. A character lookup table $M_{char} \in \mathbb{R}^{|V_{char}| \times d}$ (where $|V_{char}|$ denotes the size of the character vocabulary and d denotes the dimension of embeddings) is associated with all

---

[1]The tensorflow (Abadi et al., 2016) implementation and related resources can be found at `https://github.com/chqiwang/convseg`.

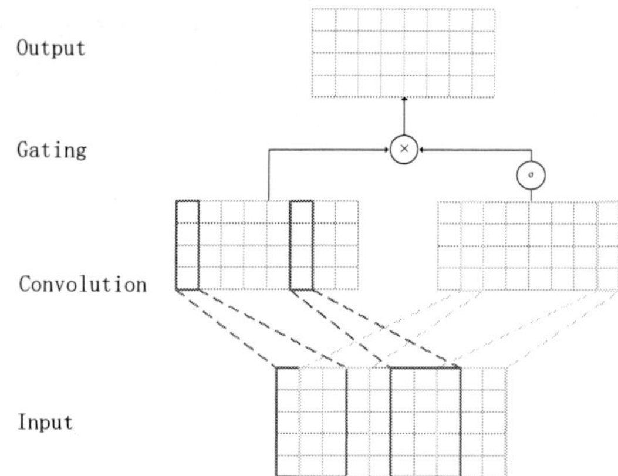

Figure 2: Structure of a convolutional layer with GLU. There are five input channels and four output channels in this figure.

characters. Given a sentence $\mathcal{S} = (c_1, c_2, ..., c_L)$, after the lookup table operation, we obtain a matrix $X \in \mathbb{R}^{L \times d}$ where the i'th row is the character embedding of c_i.

Besides the character, other features can be easily incorporated into the model (we shall see word feature in section 3). We associate to each feature a lookup table (some features may share the same lookup table) and the final representation is calculated as the concatenation of all corresponding feature embeddings.

2.2 Convolutional Layer

Many neural network models have been explored for CWS. However, experimental results show that they are not able to capure n-gram information automatically (Pei et al., 2014; Chen et al., 2015a,b). To achieve good performance, n-gram feature must be used explicitly. To overcome this weakness, we use convolutional layers (Waibel et al., 1989) to encode contextual information. Convolutional neural networks (CNNs) have shown its great effectiveness in computer vision tasks (Krizhevsky et al., 2012; Simonyan and Zisserman, 2014; He et al., 2016). Recently, Zhang et al. (2015) applied character-level CNNs to text classification task. They showed that CNNs tend to outpeform traditional n-gram models as the dataset goes larger. Kim et al. (2016) also observed that character-level CNN learns to differentiate between different types of n-grams — prefixes, suffixes and others, automatically.

Our network is quite simple — only convolutional layers is used (no pooling layer). Gated lin-

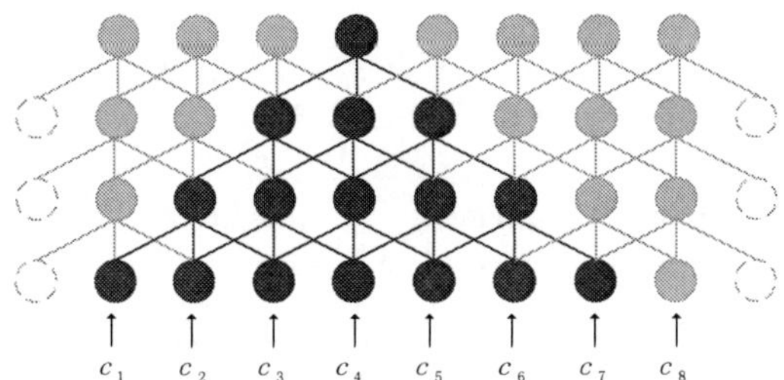

Figure 3: Stacked convolutional layers. There is one input layer on the bottom and three convolutional layers on the top. Dashed white circles denote paddings. Black circles and lines mark the pyramid in the perspective of c_4.

ear unit (GLU) (Dauphin et al., 2016) is used as the non-linear unit in our convolutional layer, which has been shown to surpass rectified linear unit (ReLU) on the language modeling task. For simplicity, GLU can also be easily replaced by ReLU with performance slightly hurt (with roughly the same number of network parameters). Figure 2 shows the structure of a convolutional layer with GLU. Formally, we define the number of input channels as N, the number of output channels as M, the length of input as L and kernel width as k. The convolutional layer can be written as

$$F(X) = (X * W + b) \otimes \sigma(X * V + c)$$

where $*$ denotes one dimensional convolution operation, $X \in \mathbb{R}^{L \times N}$ is the input of this layer, $W \in \mathbb{R}^{k \times N \times M}$, $b \in \mathbb{R}^M$, $V \in \mathbb{R}^{k \times N \times M}$, $c \in \mathbb{R}^M$ are parameters to be learned, σ is the sigmoid function and $\otimes$ represents element-wise product. We make $F(X) \in \mathbb{R}^{L \times M}$ by augmenting the input X with paddings.

A succession of convolutional layers are stacked to capture long distance information. From the perspective of each character, information flows in a pyramid. Figure 3 shows a network with three convolutional layers stacked. On the topmost layer, a linear transformation is used to transform the output of this layer to unnormalized label scores $E \in \mathbb{R}^{L \times C}$, where C is the number of label types.

2.3 CRF Layer

For sequence labeling tasks, it is often beneficial to explicitly consider the correlations between adjacent labels (Collobert et al., 2011).

Correlations between adjacent labels can be modeled as a transition matrix $T \in \mathbb{R}^{C \times C}$. Given a sentence $\mathcal{S} = (c_1, c_2, ..., c_L)$, we have corresponding scores $E \in \mathbb{R}^{L \times C}$ given by the convolutional layers. For a label sequence $y = (y_1, y_2, ..., y_L)$, we define its unnormalized score to be

$$s(\mathcal{S}, y) = \sum_{i=1}^{L} E_{i,y_i} + \sum_{i=1}^{L-1} T_{y_i, y_{i+1}}.$$

then the probability of the label sequence is defined as

$$P(y|\mathcal{S}) = \frac{e^{s(\mathcal{S}, y)}}{\sum_{y' \in \mathcal{Y}} e^{s(\mathcal{S}, y')}}$$

where $\mathcal{Y}$ is the set of all valid label sequences. This actually takes the form of linear chain CRF (Lafferty et al., 2001). Then the final loss of the proposed model is defined as the negative log-likelihood of the ground-truth label sequence y^*

$$\mathcal{L}(\mathcal{S}, y^\star) = -log P(y^\star | \mathcal{S}).$$

During training, the loss function is minimized by back propagation. During test, Veterbi algorithm is applied to quickly find the label sequence with maximum probability.

3 Integration with Word Embeddings

Character-based CWS models have the superiority of being flexible and efficient. However, full word information is not easy to be incorporated. There is another type of CWS models: the word-based models. Models belong to this category utilize not only character-level information, but also word-level (Zhang and Clark, 2007; Andrew, 2006; Sun et al., 2009). Recent works have shown that word embeddings learned from large auto-segmented data lead to great improvements in word-based CWS systems (Liu et al., 2016; Zhang et al., 2016). We propose an effective approach to integrate word embeddings with our character-based model. The integration brings two benefits. On the one hand, full word information can be used. On the other hand, large unlabeled data can be better exploited.

To use word embeddings, we design a set of word features, which are listed in Table 1. We associate to the word features a lookup table M_{word}. Then the final representation of c_i is defined as

$$R(c_i) = M_{char}[c_i] \oplus$$
$$M_{word}[c_i] \oplus M_{word}[c_{i-1}c_i] \oplus \cdots \oplus$$
$$M_{word}[c_i c_{i+1} c_{i+2} c_{i+3}]$$

Length	Features
1	$\underline{c_i}$
2	$c_{i-1}\underline{c_i}$ $\underline{c_i}c_{i+1}$
3	$c_{i-2}c_{i-1}\underline{c_i}$ $c_{i-1}\underline{c_i}c_{i+1}$ $\underline{c_i}c_{i+1}c_{i+2}$
4	$c_{i-3}c_{i-2}c_{i-1}\underline{c_i}$ $c_{i-2}c_{i-1}\underline{c_i}c_{i+1}$ $c_{i-1}\underline{c_i}c_{i+1}c_{i+2}$ $\underline{c_i}c_{i+1}c_{i+2}c_{i+3}$

Table 1: Word features at position i given a sentence $S = (c_1, c_2, ..., c_L)$. Only the words that include the current character c_i (marked with underline) are considered as word feature. Hence, the number of features can be controlled in a reasonable range. We also restrict the max length of words to 4 since few words contain more than 4 characters in Chinese. Note that the feature space is still tremendous ($O(N^4)$), where N is the number of characters).

Hyper-parameters	Value
dimension of character embedding	200
dimension of word embedding	50
number of conv layers	5
number of channels per conv layer	200
kernel width of filters	3
dropout rate	0.2

Table 2: Hyper-parameters we choose for our model.

where $\oplus$ denotes the concatenation operation. Note that the max length of word features is set to 4, therefore the feature space is extremely large ($O(N^4)$). A key step is to shrink the feature space so that the memory cost can be confined within a feasible scope. In the meanwhile, the problem of data sparsity can be eased. The solution is as following. Given the unlabeled data $\mathcal{D}_{un}$ and a teacher CWS model, we segment $\mathcal{D}_{un}$ with the teacher model and get the auto-segmented data $\mathcal{D}'_{un}$. A vocabulary V_{word} is generated from $\mathcal{D}'_{un}$ where low frequency words are discarded [2]. We replace $M_{word}[*]$ with $M_{word}[UNK]$ if $* \notin V_{word}$ (UNK denotes the unknown words).

To better exploit the auto-segmented data $\mathcal{D}'_{un}$, we adopt an off-the-self tool $word2vec$[3] (Mikolov et al., 2013) to pretrain the word embeddings. The whole procedure is summarized as following setps:

1. Train a *teacher* model that does not rely on word feature.

2. Segment unlabeled data $\mathcal{D}$ with the *teacher* model and get the auto-segmented data $\mathcal{D}'$.

3. Build a vocabulary V_{word} from $\mathcal{D}'$. Replace all words not appear in V_{word} with UNK.

4. Pretrain word embeddings on $\mathcal{D}'$ using *word2vec*.

5. Train the *student* model with word feature using the pretrained word embeddings.

Note that no external labeled data is used in this procedure.

4 Experiments

4.1 Settings

Datasets We evaluate our model on two benchmark datasets, PKU and MSR, from the second International Chinese Word Segmentation Bakeoff (Emerson, 2005). Both datasets are commonly used by previous state-of-the-art models. For both datasets, last 10% of the training data are used as development set. The unlabeled data used in this work is news data collected by *Sogou* [4].

We do not perform any preprocessing for these datasets, such as replacing continuous digits and English characters with a single token.

Dropout Dropout (Srivastava et al., 2014) is a very efficient method for preventing overfit, especially when the dataset is small. We apply dropout to our model on all convolutional layers and embedding layers. The dropout rate is fixed to 0.2.

Hyper-parameters For both datasets, we use the same set of hyper-parameters, which are presented in Table 2. For all convolutional layers, we just use the same number of channels. Following the practice of designing very deep CNN in computer vision (Simonyan and Zisserman, 2014), we use a small kernal width, i.e. 3, for all convolutional layers. To avoid computational inefficiency, we use a relatively small dimension, i.e. 50, for word embeddings.

Pretraining Character embeddings and word embeddings are pretrained on unlabeled or auto-segmented data by *word2vec*. Since the pretrained embeddings are not task-oriented, they are fine-tuned during supervised training by normal back-propagation.[5]

Optimization Adam algorithm (Kingma and Ba, 2014) is applied to optimize our model. We use default parameters given in the original paper

---

[2] The threshold of frequency is set to 5, which is the default setting of *word2vec*.
[3] https://code.google.com/p/word2vec

[4] http://www.sogou.com/labs/resource/ca.php
[5] We also try to use fixed word embeddings as Zhang et al. (2016) do but no significant difference is observed.

Models	PKU			MSR		
	P	R	F	P	R	F
(Tseng, 2005)	94.6	95.4	95.0	96.2	96.6	96.4
(Zhang and Clark, 2007)	-	-	94.5	-	-	97.2
(Zhao and Kit, 2011)	-	-	95.40	-	-	97.58
(Sun et al., 2012)	95.8	94.9	95.4	97.6	97.2	97.4
(Zhang et al., 2013)	96.5	95.8	96.1	-	-	97.45
(Pei et al., 2014)	-	-	95.2	-	-	97.2
(Chen et al., 2015a)*◇	96.5	**96.3**	96.4	97.4	97.8	97.6
(Chen et al., 2015b)*◇	96.6	**96.4**	**96.5**	97.5	97.3	97.4
(Cai and Zhao, 2016)◇	95.8	95.2	95.5	96.3	96.8	96.5
(Liu et al., 2016)	-	-	95.67	-	-	97.58
(Zhang et al., 2016)	-	-	95.7	-	-	97.7
(Xu and Sun, 2016)*◇	-	-	96.1	-	-	96.3
CONV-SEG	96.1	95.2	95.7	97.4	97.3	97.3
WE-CONV-SEG (+ word embeddings)	**96.8**	96.1	**96.5**	**97.9**	**98.1**	**98.0**

Table 3: Performance of our models and previous state-of-the-art models. Note that (Chen et al., 2015a,b; Xu and Sun, 2016) used a external Chinese idiom dictionary. To make the comparison fair, we mark them with *. Chen et al. (2015a,b); Cai and Zhao (2016); Xu and Sun (2016) also preprocessed the datasets by replacing the conitinous English character and digits with a unique token. We mark them with ◇.

and we set batch size to 100. For both datasets, we train no more than 100 epochs. The final models are chosen by their performance on the development set.

Weight normalization (Salimans and Kingma, 2016) is applied for all convolutional layers to accelerate the training procedure and obvious acceleration is observed.

4.2 Main Results

Table 3 gives the performances of our models, as well as previous state-of-the-art models. Two proposed models are shown in the table:

- **CONV-SEG** It is our preliminary model without word embeddings. Character embeddings are pretrained on large unlabeled data.
- **WE-CONV-SEG** On the basis of CONV-SEG, word embeddings are used. We use CONV-SEG as the teacher model (see section 3).

Our preliminary model CONV-SEG achieves competitive performance without any feature engineering. Armed with word embeddings, WE-CONV-SEG obtains state-of-the-art performance on both PKU and MSR datasets without using any external labeled data. WE-CONV-SEG outperforms state-of-the-art neural model (Zhang et al., 2016) in a large margin (+0.8 on PKU and +0.3 in MSR). Chen et al. (2015b) preprocessed all datasets by replacing Chinese idioms with a sin-

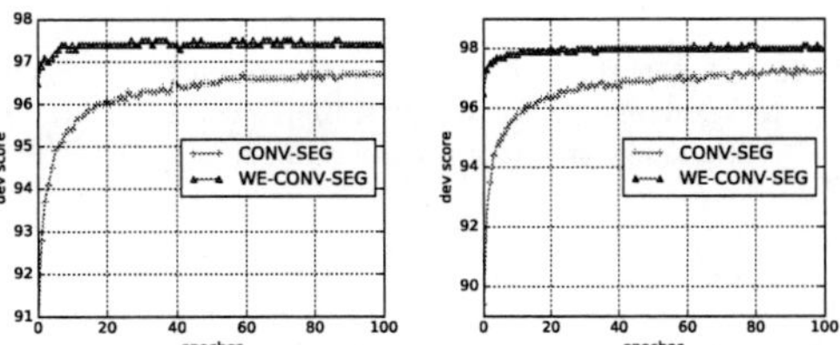

Figure 4: Learning curves (dev scores) of our models on PKU (left) and MSR (right).

gle token and thus their model obtains excellent score on PKU dataset. However, WE-CONV-SEG achieves the same performance on PKU and outperforms their model on MSR, without any data preprocessing.

We also observe that WE-CONV-SEG converges much faster compared to CONV-SEG. Figure 4 presents the learning curves of the two models. It takes 10 to 20 epochs for WE-CONV-SEG to converge while it takes more than 60 epochs for CONV-SEG to converge.

4.3 Network Depth

Network depth shows great influence on the performance of deep neural networks. A too shallow network may not fit the training data very well while a too deep network may overfit or is hard to train. We evaluate the performance of the proposed model with varying depth. Figure 5 shows

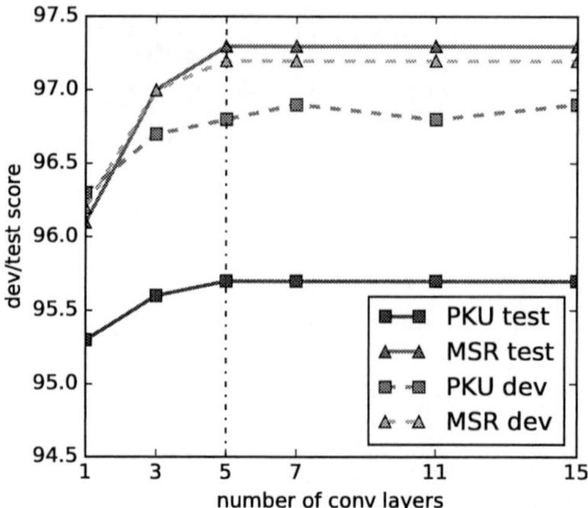

Figure 5: Scores on dev set and test set with respect to the number of convolutional layers. The vertical dashed line marks the depth we choose.

Model Options	PKU	MSR
without pretraining	94.7	96.7
with pretraining	**95.7**	**97.3**

Table 4: Test performances with or without pretraining character embeddings. "without pretraining" means that the character embeddings are randomly initialized.

the results. It is obvious that five convolutional layers is a good choise for both datasets. When we increase the depth from 1 to 5, the performance is improved significantly. However, when we increase depth from 5 to 7, even to 11 and 15, the performance is almost unchanged. This phenomenon implies that CWS rarely relies on context larger than 11 [6]. With more training data, deeper networks may perform better.

4.4 Pretraining Character Embeddings

Previous works have shown that pretraining character embeddings boost the performance of neural CWS models significantly (Pei et al., 2014; Chen et al., 2015a,b; Cai and Zhao, 2016). We verify this and get a consistent conclusion. Table 4 shows the performances with or without pretraining. Our model obtains significant improvements (+1.0 on PKU and +0.6 on MSR) with pretrained character embeddings.

Models	PKU	MSR	PKU	MSR
(Cai and Zhao, 2016)$^{\diamond}$	95.5	96.5	-	-
(Zheng et al., 2013)	92.8‡	93.9‡	-	-
(Pei et al., 2014)	94.0	94.9	-	-
(Chen et al., 2015a)	94.5†	95.4†	96.1*	96.2*
(Chen et al., 2015b)	94.8†	95.6†	96.0*	96.6*
(Xu and Sun, 2016)	-	-	96.1*	96.3*
CONV-SEG	95.7	97.3	-	-
(Pei et al., 2014)	95.2 (+1.2)	97.2 (+2.3)	-	-
(Chen et al., 2015a)	-	-	96.4* (+0.3)	97.6* (+1.4)
(Chen et al., 2015b)	-	-	96.5* (+0.5)	97.3* (+0.7)
AVEBE-CONV-SEG	95.4 (-0.3)	97.1 (-0.2)	-	-
W2VBE-CONV-SEG	95.9 (+0.2)	97.5 (+0.2)	-	-

Table 5: The first/second group summarize results of models without/with bigram feature. The number in the parentheses is the absolute improvement given by explicit bigram feature. Results with * used external dictionary. Results with † come from Cai and Zhao (2016). Results with ‡ come from Pei et al. (2014). $^{\diamond}$ marks word-based models.

4.5 N-gram Features

In this section, we test the ability of our model in capturing n-gram features. Since unigram is indispensable and trigram is beyond memory limit, we only consider bigram.

Bigram feature has shown to play a vital role in character-based neural CWS models (Pei et al., 2014; Chen et al., 2015a,b). Without bigram feature, previous models perform badly. Table 5 gives a summarization. Without bigram feature, our model outperforms previous character-based models in a large margin (+0.9 on PKU and +1.7 on MSR). Compared with word-based model (Cai and Zhao, 2016), the improvements are also significant (+0.2 on PKU and +0.8 on MSR).

Then we arm our model with bigram feature. The bigram feature we use is the same with Pei et al. (2014); Chen et al. (2015a,b). The dimension of bigram embedding is set to 50. Following Pei et al. (2014); Chen et al. (2015a,b), the bigram embeddings are initialized by the average of corresponding pretrained character embeddings. The result model is named AVEBE-CONV-SEG and the performance is shown in Table 5. Unexpectedly, the performance of AVEBE-CONV-SEG is worse than the preliminary model CONV-SEG that uses no bigram feature (-0.3 on PKU and -0.2

---

[6]Context size is calculated by $(k - 1) \times d + 1$, where k and d denotes the kernel size and the number of convolutional layers, respectively.

on MSR). This result is dramatically inconsistent with previous works, in which the performance is significantly improved by the method. We also observe that the training cost of AVEBE-CONV-SEG is much lower than CONV-SEG. Hence we can conclude that the inconsistency is casued by overfitting. A reasonable conjecture is that the model CONV-SEG already capture abundant bigram feature automatically, therefore the model is tend to overfit when bigram feature is explicitly added.

A practicable way to overcome overfitting is to introduce priori knowledge. We introduce priori knowledge by using bigram embeddings directly pretrained on large unlabeled data, which is simmillar with (Mansur et al., 2013). We convert the unlabeled text to bigram sequence and then apply *word2vec* to pretrain the bigram embeddings directly. The result model is named W2VBE-CONV-SEG, and the performance is also shown in Table 5. This method leads to substantial improvements (+0.5 on PKU and +0.4 MSR) over AVEBE-CONV-SEG. However, compared to CONV-SEG, there are only slight gains (+0.2 on PKU and MSR).

All above observations verify that our proposed network has considerable superiority in capturing n-gram, at least bigram features automatically.

4.6 Word Embeddings

Word embeddings lead to significant improvements over the strong baseline model CONV-SEG. The improvements come from the teacher model and the large unlabeled data. A natural question is how much unlabeled data can lead to significant improvements. We study this by halving the unlabeled data. Figure 6 presents the results. As the unlabeled data becomes smaller, the performance remains unchanged at the beginning and then becomes worse. This demonstrates that the mass of unlabeled data is a key factor to achieve high performance. However, even with only 68MB unlabeled data, we can still observe remarkable improvements (+0.4 on PKU and MSR). We also observe that MSR dataset is more robust to the size of unlabeled data than PKU dataset. We conjecture that this is because MSR training set is larger than PKU training set[7].

We also study how the teacher's performance influence the student. We train other two mod-

---

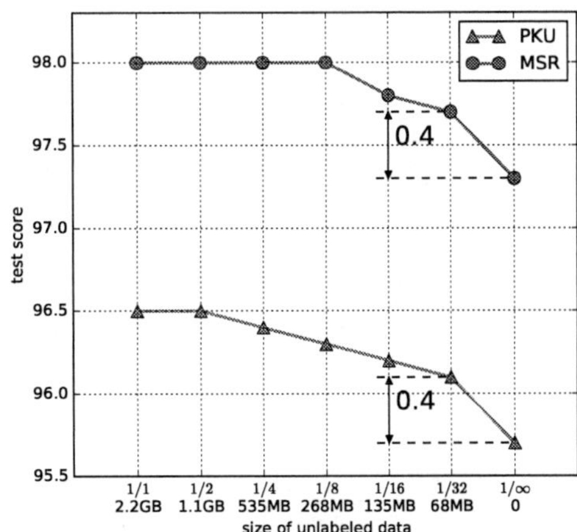

Figure 6: Test performances with varying size of unlabeled data for pretraining word embeddings. With full size, the model is WE-CONV-SEG. With the 0 size, the model degenerates to CONV-SEG.

Models	teacher		student	
	PKU	MSR	PKU	MSR
WE-CONV-SEG	95.7	97.4	96.5	98.0
worse teacher	95.4	97.1	96.4	97.9
better teacher	96.5	98.0	96.5	98.0

Table 6: Performances of student models and teacher models. A previous trained model maybe reused in following so that there are some

els that use different teacher models. One of them uses a worse teacher and the other uses a better teacher. The results are shown in Table 6. As expected, the worse teacher indeed creates a worse student, but the effect is marginal (-0.1 on PKU and MSR). And the better teacher brings no improvements. These facts demonstrate that the student's performance is relatively insensitive to the teacher's ability as long as the teacher is not too weak.

Not only the pretrained word embeddings, we also build a vocabulary V_{word} from the large auto-segmented data. Both of them should have positive impacts on the improvements. To figure out their contributions quantitatively, we train a contrast model, where the pretrained word embeddings are not used but the word features and the vocabulary are persisted, i.e. the word embeddings are randomly initialized. The results are shown in Table 7. According to the results, we conclude that the pretrained word embeddings and the vocabulary have roughly equal contributions to the final

---

[7]There are 2M words in MSR training set but only 1M words in PKU training set.

Models	PKU	MSR
WE-CONV-SEG	**96.5**	**98.0**
-word emb	96.1	97.6
-word feature	95.7	97.3

Table 7: Performances of our models with different word feature options. "-word emb" denotes the model in which word features and the vocabulary are used but the pretrained word embeddings are not. "-word feature" denotes the model that uses no word feature, i.e. CONV-SEG.

improvements.

5   Related Work

CWS has been studied with considerable efforts in NLP commutinity. Xue et al. (2003) firstly modeled CWS as a character-based sequence labeling problem. They used a sliding-window maximum entropy classifier to tag Chinese characters into one of four position tags, and then coverted these tags into a segmentation using rules. Following their work, Peng et al. (2004) applied CRF to the problem for sequence-level prediction. Recently, under the sequence labeling framework, various neural models have been explored for CWS. Zheng et al. (2013) firstly applied a feed-forward neural network for CWS. Pei et al. (2014) improved upon Zheng et al. (2013) by explicitly modeling the interactions between local context and previous tag. Chen et al. (2015a) proposed a gated recursive neural network (GRNN) to model the combinations of context characters. Chen et al. (2015b) utilized Long short-term memory (LSTM) to capture long distant dependencies. Xu and Sun (2016) combined LSTM and GRNN to efficiently integrate local and long-distance features.

Our proposed model is also a neural sequence labeling model. The difference from above models lies in that CNN is used to encode contextual information. CNNs have been successfully applied in many NLP tasks, such as text classification (Kalchbrenner et al., 2014; Kim, 2014; Zhang et al., 2015; Conneau et al., 2016), language modeling (Kim et al., 2016; Pham et al., 2016; Dauphin et al., 2016), machine translation (Meng et al., 2015; Kalchbrenner et al., 2016; Gehring et al., 2016). Experimental results show that the convolutional layers are capable to capture more n-gram features than previous introduced networks. Collobert et al. (2011) also proposed a CNN based seuqence labeling model. However, our model

is significantly different from theirs since theirs adopt max-pooling to encode the whole sentence into a fixed size vector and use position embeddings to demonstrate which word to be tagged while ours does not. Our model is more efficient due to the sharing structure in lower layers. Contemporary to this work, Strubell et al. (2017) applied dilated CNN to named entity recognition.

The integration with word embeddings is inspired by word-based CWS models (Andrew, 2006; Zhang and Clark, 2007; Sun et al., 2009). Most recently, Zhang et al. (2016); Liu et al. (2016); Cai and Zhao (2016) proposed word-based neural models for CWS. Particularly, Zhang et al. (2016); Liu et al. (2016) utilized word embeddings learned from large auto-segmented data, which leads to significant improvements. Different from their word-based models, we integrate word embeddings with the proposed character-based model.

Simillar to this work, Wang et al. (2011) and Zhang et al. (2013) also enhanced character-based CWS systems by utilizing auto-segmented data. However, they didn't use word embeddings, but only used statistics features. Sun (2010) and Wang et al. (2014) combined character-based and word-based CWS model via bagging and dual decomposition respectively and achieved better performance than single model.

6   Conclusion

In this paper, we address the weaknesses of character-based CWS models. We propose a novel neural model for CWS. The model utilizes stacked convolutional layers to derive contextual representations from input sequence, which are then fed to a CRF layer for prediction. The model is capable to capture rich n-gram features automatically. Furthermore, we propose an effective approach to integrate the proposed model with word embeddings, which are pretrained on large auto-segmented data. Evaluation on two benchmark datasets shows that without any feature engineering, much better performance than previous models (also without feature engineering) is obtained. Armed with word embeddings, our model achieves state-of-the-art performance on both datasets, without using any external labeled data.

Acknowledgements

This work is supported by the National Key Research & Development Plan of China (No.2013CB329302). Thanks anonymous reviewers for their valuable suggestions. Thanks Wang Geng, Zhen Yang and Yuanyuan Zhao for their useful discussions.

References

Martín Abadi, Ashish Agarwal, Paul Barham, Eugene Brevdo, Zhifeng Chen, Craig Citro, Greg S Corrado, Andy Davis, Jeffrey Dean, Matthieu Devin, et al. 2016. Tensorflow: Large-scale machine learning on heterogeneous distributed systems. *arXiv preprint arXiv:1603.04467*.

Galen Andrew. 2006. A hybrid markov/semi-markov conditional random field for sequence segmentation. In *Conference on Empirical Methods in Natural Language Processing*, pages 465–472.

Yoshua Bengio, R Ducharme, jean, Pascal Vincent, and Christian Janvin. 2003. A neural probabilistic language model. *Journal of Machine Learning Research*, 3(6):1137–1155.

Adam L Berger, Vincent J. Della Pietra, and Stephen A. Della Pietra. 1996. A maximum entropy approach to natural language processing. *Computational Linguistics*, 22(1):39–71.

Deng Cai and Hai Zhao. 2016. Neural word segmentation learning for chinese. In *Meeting of the Association for Computational Linguistics*, pages 409–420.

Xinchi Chen, Xipeng Qiu, Chenxi Zhu, and Xuanjing Huang. 2015a. Gated recursive neural network for chinese word segmentation. In *ACL (1)*, pages 1744–1753.

Xinchi Chen, Xipeng Qiu, Chenxi Zhu, Pengfei Liu, and Xuanjing Huang. 2015b. Long short-term memory neural networks for chinese word segmentation. In *Conference on Empirical Methods in Natural Language Processing*, pages 1197–1206.

Ronan Collobert, Jason Weston, L Bottou, Michael Karlen, Koray Kavukcuoglu, and Pavel Kuksa. 2011. Natural language processing (almost) from scratch. *Journal of Machine Learning Research*, 12(1):2493–2537.

Alexis Conneau, Holger Schwenk, Loïc Barrault, and Yann Lecun. 2016. Very deep convolutional networks for natural language processing. *arXiv preprint arXiv:1606.01781*.

Yann N. Dauphin, Angela Fan, Michael Auli, and David Grangier. 2016. Language modeling with gated convolutional networks.

Thomas Emerson. 2005. The second international chinese word segmentation bakeoff. In *Proceedings of the fourth SIGHAN workshop on Chinese language Processing*, volume 133.

Jonas Gehring, Michael Auli, David Grangier, and Yann N. Dauphin. 2016. A convolutional encoder model for neural machine translation.

Kaiming He, Xiangyu Zhang, Shaoqing Ren, and Jian Sun. 2016. Deep residual learning for image recognition. In *The IEEE Conference on Computer Vision and Pattern Recognition (CVPR)*.

Nal Kalchbrenner, Lasse Espeholt, Karen Simonyan, Aaron Van Den Oord, Alex Graves, and Koray Kavukcuoglu. 2016. Neural machine translation in linear time.

Nal Kalchbrenner, Edward Grefenstette, and Phil Blunsom. 2014. A convolutional neural network for modelling sentences. In *Proceedings of the 52nd Annual Meeting of the Association for Computational Linguistics (Volume 1: Long Papers)*, pages 655–665, Baltimore, Maryland. Association for Computational Linguistics.

Yoon Kim. 2014. Convolutional neural networks for sentence classification. In *Proceedings of the 2014 Conference on Empirical Methods in Natural Language Processing (EMNLP)*, pages 1746–1751, Doha, Qatar. Association for Computational Linguistics.

Yoon Kim, Yacine Jernite, David Sontag, and Alexander M. Rush. 2016. Character-aware neural language models. In *Proceedings of the Thirtieth AAAI Conference on Artificial Intelligence*, AAAI'16, pages 2741–2749. AAAI Press.

Diederik Kingma and Jimmy Ba. 2014. Adam: A method for stochastic optimization. *arXiv preprint arXiv:1412.6980*.

Alex Krizhevsky, Ilya Sutskever, and Geoffrey E Hinton. 2012. Imagenet classification with deep convolutional neural networks. pages 1097–1105.

John D. Lafferty, Andrew Mccallum, and Fernando C. N. Pereira. 2001. Conditional random fields: Probabilistic models for segmenting and labeling sequence data. pages 282–289.

Yijia Liu, Wanxiang Che, Jiang Guo, Bing Qin, and Ting Liu. 2016. Exploring segment representations for neural segmentation models.

Mairgup Mansur, Wenzhe Pei, and Baobao Chang. 2013. Feature-based neural language model and chinese word segmentation. In *IJCNLP*, pages 1271–1277.

Fandong Meng, Zhengdong Lu, Mingxuan Wang, Hang Li, Wenbin Jiang, and Qun Liu. 2015. Encoding source language with convolutional neural network for machine translation. *arXiv preprint arXiv:1503.01838*.

Tomas Mikolov, Kai Chen, Greg Corrado, and Jeffrey Dean. 2013. Efficient estimation of word representations in vector space. *arXiv preprint arXiv:1301.3781*.

Wenzhe Pei, Tao Ge, and Baobao Chang. 2014. Max-margin tensor neural network for chinese word segmentation. In *Meeting of the Association for Computational Linguistics*, pages 293–303.

Fuchun Peng, Fangfang Feng, and Andrew McCallum. 2004. Chinese segmentation and new word detection using conditional random fields. In *Proceedings of the 20th international conference on Computational Linguistics*, page 562. Association for Computational Linguistics.

Ngoc Quan Pham, Germn Kruszewski, and Gemma Boleda. 2016. Convolutional neural network language models. In *Conference on Empirical Methods in Natural Language Processing*, pages 1153–1162.

Tim Salimans and Diederik P. Kingma. 2016. Weight normalization: A simple reparameterization to accelerate training of deep neural networks.

Karen Simonyan and Andrew Zisserman. 2014. Very deep convolutional networks for large-scale image recognition. *arXiv preprint arXiv:1409.1556*.

Nitish Srivastava, Geoffrey E Hinton, Alex Krizhevsky, Ilya Sutskever, and Ruslan Salakhutdinov. 2014. Dropout: a simple way to prevent neural networks from overfitting. *Journal of Machine Learning Research*, 15(1):1929–1958.

Emma Strubell, Patrick Verga, David Belanger, and Andrew Mccallum. 2017. Fast and accurate sequence labeling with iterated dilated convolutions.

Weiwei Sun. 2010. Word-based and character-based word segmentation models: Comparison and combination. In *Proceedings of the 23rd International Conference on Computational Linguistics: Posters*, pages 1211–1219. Association for Computational Linguistics.

Xu Sun, Houfeng Wang, and Wenjie Li. 2012. Fast online training with frequency-adaptive learning rates for chinese word segmentation and new word detection.

Xu Sun, Yaozhong Zhang, Takuya Matsuzaki, Yoshimasa Tsuruoka, and Jun'Ichi Tsujii. 2009. A discriminative latent variable chinese segmenter with hybrid word/character information. In *Human Language Technologies: the 2009 Conference of the North American Chapter of the Association for Computational Linguistics*, pages 56–64.

Huihsin Tseng. 2005. A conditional random field word segmenter. In *In Fourth SIGHAN Workshop on Chinese Language Processing*.

Alex Waibel, Toshiyuki Hanazawa, Geoffrey Hinton, Kiyohiro Shikano, and Kevin J Lang. 1989. Phoneme recognition using time-delay neural networks. *IEEE transactions on acoustics, speech, and signal processing*, 37(3):328–339.

Mengqiu Wang, Rob Voigt, and Christopher D Manning. 2014. Two knives cut better than one: Chinese word segmentation with dual decomposition. In *Meeting of the Association for Computational Linguistics*, pages 193–198.

Yiou Wang, Jun ' Ichi Kazama, Yoshimasa Tsuruoka, Wenliang Chen, Yujie Zhang, and Kentaro Torisawa. 2011. Improving chinese word segmentation and pos tagging with semi-supervised methods using large auto-analyzed data. In *International Joint Conference on Natural Language Processing*.

Jingjing Xu and Xu Sun. 2016. Dependency-based gated recursive neural network for chinese word segmentation. In *The 54th Annual Meeting of the Association for Computational Linguistics*, page 567.

Nianwen Xue et al. 2003. Chinese word segmentation as character tagging. *Computational Linguistics and Chinese Language Processing*, 8(1):29–48.

Longkai Zhang, Houfeng Wang, Xu Sun, and Mairgup Mansur. 2013. Exploring representations from unlabeled data with co-training for chinese word segmentation.

Meishan Zhang, Yue Zhang, and Guohong Fu. 2016. Transition-based neural word segmentation. In *Meeting of the Association for Computational Linguistics*, pages 421–431.

Xiang Zhang, Junbo Zhao, and Yann LeCun. 2015. Character-level convolutional networks for text classification. In *Advances in neural information processing systems*, pages 649–657.

Yue Zhang and Stephen Clark. 2007. Chinese segmentation with a word-based perceptron algorithm. In *ACL 2007, Proceedings of the Meeting of the Association for Computational Linguistics, June 23-30, 2007, Prague, Czech Republic*.

Hai Zhao and Chunyu Kit. 2011. Integrating unsupervised and supervised word segmentation: The role of goodness measures. *Information Sciences*, 181(1):163–183.

Xiaoqing Zheng, Hanyang Chen, and Tianyu Xu. 2013. Deep learning for chinese word segmentation and pos tagging. In *Conference on Empirical Methods in Natural Language Processing*.

Character-based Joint Segmentation and POS Tagging for Chinese using Bidirectional RNN-CRF

Yan Shao and **Christian Hardmeier** and **Jörg Tiedemann*** and **Joakim Nivre**
Department of Linguistics and Philology, Uppsala University
*Department of Modern Languages, University of Helsinki
{yan.shao, christian.hardmeier, joakim.nivre}@lingfil.uu.se
jorg.tiedemann@helsinki.fi

Abstract

We present a character-based model for joint segmentation and POS tagging for Chinese. The bidirectional RNN-CRF architecture for general sequence tagging is adapted and applied with novel vector representations of Chinese characters that capture rich contextual information and sub-character level features. The proposed model is extensively evaluated and compared with a state-of-the-art tagger respectively on CTB5, CTB9 and UD Chinese. The experimental results indicate that our model is accurate and robust across datasets in different sizes, genres and annotation schemes. We obtain state-of-the-art performance on CTB5, achieving 94.38 F1-score for joint segmentation and POS tagging.

1 Introduction

Word segmentation and part-of-speech (POS) tagging are core steps for higher-level natural language processing (NLP) tasks. Given the raw text, segmentation is applied at the very first step and POS tagging is performed on top afterwards. As by convention the words in Chinese are not delimited by spaces, segmentation is non-trivial, but its accuracy has a significant impact on POS tagging. Moreover, POS tags provide useful information for word segmentation. Thus, modelling word segmentation and POS tagging jointly can outperform the pipeline models (Ng and Low, 2004; Zhang and Clark, 2008).

POS tagging is a typical sequence tagging problem over segmented words, while segmentation also can be modelled as a character-level tagging problem via predicting the labels that identify the word boundaries. Ng and Low (2004) propose a joint model which predicts the combinatory labels of segmentation boundaries and POS tags at the character level. Joint segmentation and POS tagging becomes a standard character-based sequence tagging problem and therefore the general machine learning algorithms for structured prediction can be applied.

The bidirectional recurrent neural network (RNN) using conditional random fields (CRF) (Lafferty et al., 2001) as the output interface for sentence-level optimisation (BiRNN-CRF) achieves state-of-the-art accuracies on various sequence tagging tasks (Huang et al., 2015; Ma and Hovy, 2016) and outperforms the traditional linear statistical models. RNNs with gated recurrent cells, such as long-short term memory (LSTM) (Hochreiter and Schmidhuber, 1997) and gated recurrent units (GRU) (Cho et al., 2014) are capable of capturing long dependencies and retrieving rich global information. The sequential CRF on top of the recurrent layers ensures that the optimal sequence of tags over the entire sentence is obtained.

In this paper, we model joint segmentation and POS tagging as a fully character-based sequence tagging problem via predicting the combinatory labels. The BiRNN-CRF architecture is adapted and applied. The Chinese characters are fed into the neural networks as vector representations. In addition to utilising the pre-trained character embeddings, we propose a concatenated n-gram-representation of the characters. Furthermore, sub-character level information, namely radicals and orthographical features extracted by convolutional neural networks (CNNs), are also incorporated and tested. Three datasets of different sizes, genres and with different annotation schemes are employed for evaluation. Our model is thoroughly evaluated and compared with the joint segmentation and POS tagging model in ZPar

Proceedings of the The 8th International Joint Conference on Natural Language Processing, pages 173–183,
Taipei, Taiwan, November 27 – December 1, 2017 ©2017 AFNLP

(Zhang and Clark, 2010), which is a state-of-the-art joint tagger using structured perceptron and beam decoding. According to the experimental results, our proposed model outperforms ZPar on all the datasets in terms of accuracy.

The main contributions of this work include: 1. We apply the BiRNN-CRF model for general sequence tagging to joint segmentation and POS tagging for Chinese and achieve state-of-the-art accuracy. The experimental results show that our tagger is robust and accurate across datasets of different sizes, genres and annotation schemes. 2. We propose a novel approach for vector representations of characters that leads to substantial improvements over the baseline model. 3. Additional improvements are obtained via exploring the feasibility of utilising sub-character level information. 4. We provide an open-source implementation of our method along with pre-trained character embeddings.[1]

2 Model

2.1 Neural Network Architecture

Our baseline model is an adaptation of BiRNN-CRF. As illustrated in Figure 1, the Chinese characters are represented as vectors and fed into the bidirectional recurrent layers. The character representations will be described in detail in the following sections. For the recurrent layer, we employ GRU as the basic recurrent unit as it has similar functionalities but fewer parameters compared to LSTM (Chung et al., 2014). Dropout (Srivastava et al., 2014) is applied to the outputs of the bidirectional recurrent layers. The outputs are concatenated and passed to the first-order chain CRF layer. The optimal sequence of the combinatory labels is predicted at the end. There is a post processing step to retrieve both segmentation and POS tags from the combinatory tags.

2.2 Tagging Scheme

Following the work of Kruengkrai et al. (2009a), the employed tags indicating the word boundaries are B, I, E, S representing a character at the beginning, inside, end of a word or as a single-character word. The CRF layer models conditional scores over all possible combinatory labels given the input characters. Incorporating the transition scores between the successive labels, the op-

---

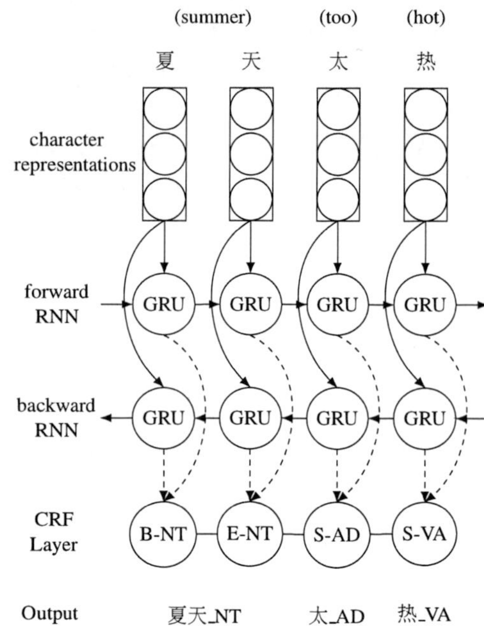

Figure 1: The BiRNN-CRF model for joint Chinese segmentation and POS tagging. The dashed arrows indicate that dropout layers are applied to the outputs of the recurrent layers.

timal sequence can be obtained efficiently via the Viterbi algorithm both for training and decoding.

The time complexity for the Viterbi algorithm is linear with respect to the sentence length n as $\mathcal{O}(k^2 n)$, where k is constant and equals to the total number of combinatory labels. The efficiency can be improved if we reduce k. For some POS tags, combining them with the full boundary tags is redundant. For instance, only the functional word 的 can be tagged as DEG in Chinese Treebank (Xue et al., 2005). Since it is a single-character word, combinatory tags of B-DEG, I-DEG, and E-DEG never occur in the experimental data and should therefore be pruned to reduce the search space. Similarly, if the maximum length of words under a given POS tag is two in the training data, we prune the corresponding label.

2.3 Character Representations

We propose three different approaches to effectively represent Chinese characters as vectors for the neural network.

2.3.1 Concatenated N-gram

The prevalent character-based neural models assume that larger spans of text, such as words and

---

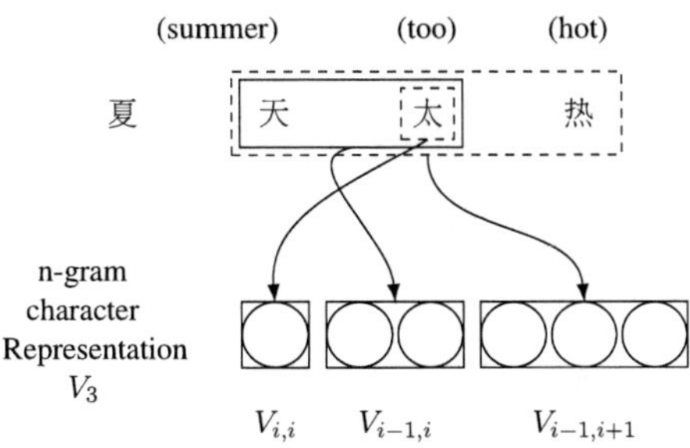

Figure 2: Vector representations of the Chinese characters as incrementally concatenated n-gram vectors in a given context.

n-grams, can be represented by the sequence of characters that they consist of. For example, the vector representation $V_{m,n}$ of a span $c_{m,n}$ is obtained by passing the vector representations v_i of the characters c_i to a functions f as:

$$V_{m,n} = f(v_m, v_{m+1}, ..., v_n) \qquad (1)$$

where f is usually an RNN (Ling et al., 2015) or a CNN (dos Santos and Zadrozny, 2014).

In this paper, instead of completely relying on the BiRNN to extract contextual features from context-free character representations, we encode rich local information in the character vectors via employing the incrementally concatenated n-gram representation as demonstrated in Figure 2. In the example, the vector representation of the pivot character 太 in the given context is the concatenation of the context-free vector representation $V_{i,i}$ of 太 itself along with $V_{i-1,i}$ of the bigram 天太 as well as $V_{i-1,i+1}$ of the trigram 天太热.

Instead of constructing the vector representation $V_{m,n}$ of an n-gram $c_{m,n}$ from the character representations as in Equation 1, $V_{m,n}$ in different orders, such as $V_{i,i}$, $V_{i-1,i}$, and $V_{i-1,i+1}$, are randomly initialised separately. We use a single special vector to represent all the unknown n-grams per order. The n-grams in different orders are then concatenated incrementally to form up the vector representations of a Chinese character in the given context, which is passed further to the recurrent layers. As shown in Figure 2, the neighbouring characters on both sides of the pivot character are taken into account.

2.3.2 Radicals and Orthographical Features

Chinese characters are logograms. As opposed to alphabetical languages, there is rich information

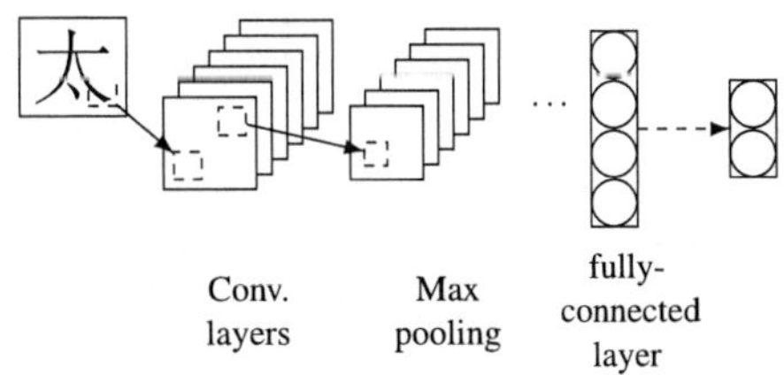

Figure 3: Convolutional Neural Networks for orthographical feature extraction. Only the first convolutional layer and its following max-pooling layer are presented.

encrypted in the graphical components. For instance, the Chinese characters that share the same part 钅 (gold) are all somewhat related to metals, such as 银 (silver), 铁 (iron), 针 (needle) and so on. The shared part 钅 is known as the radical, which functions as a semantic indicator. Hence, we investigate the effectiveness of using the information below the character level for our task.

Radicals are first represented as randomly initialised vectors and concatenated as parts of the character representations. Radicals are traditionally used as indices in Chinese dictionaries. In our approach, they are retrieved via the unicode representation of Chinese characters as the characters that share the same radical are grouped together. They are organised in consistent with the categorisation in Kangxi Dictionary (康熙字典), in which all the Chinese characters are grouped under 214 different radicals. We only employ the radicals of the common characters in the unicode range of (U+4E00, U+9FFF). For the characters out of the range and the non-Chinese characters, we use a single special vector as their radical representations.

Additionally, instead of presuming that only radicals encode sub-character level information, we use convolutional neural networks (CNNs) to extract graphical features from scratch by regarding the Chinese characters as pictures and feed their pixels as the input. As illustrated in Figure 3, there are two convolutional layers, both followed by a max-pooling layer. The output of the second max-pooling layer is reshaped and passed to a regular fully-connected layer. Dropout is applied to the output of the fully-connected layer. The output is then concatenated as parts of the character representation. The CNNs are trained jointly with the main network.

2.3.3 Pre-trained Character Embeddings

The context-free vector representations of single characters introduced in section 2.3.1 can be replaced by pre-trained character embeddings retrieved from large corpora. We employ GloVe (Pennington et al., 2014) to train our character embeddings on Wikipedia[2] and the freely available Sogou News Corpora (SogouCS).[3] We use randomly initialised vectors as the representations of the characters that are not in the embedding vocabulary. Pre-trained embeddings for higher-order n-grams are not employed in this paper.

2.4 Ensemble Decoding

At the final decoding phase, we use ensemble decoding, a simple averaging technique, to mitigate the deviations led by random weight initialisation of the neural network. For the chain CRF decoder, the final sequence of the combinatory tags y is obtained via the conditional scores $S(y_i|x_i)$ and the transition scores $T(y_i, y_j)$ given the input sequence x. Instead of computing the optimal sequence with respect to the scores returned by a single model, both the conditional scores and transition scores are averaged over four models with identical parameter settings that are trained independently:

$$y^* = \underset{y \in L(x)}{\mathrm{argmax}}\, p(y|x; \{\bar{S}\}, \{\bar{T}\}) \qquad (2)$$

Ensemble decoding is only applied to the best performing model according to the feature experiments at the final testing phase in this paper.

3 Implementation

Our neural networks are implemented using the TensorFlow 1.2.0 library (Abadi et al., 2016). We group the sentences with similar lengths into the same buckets and the sentences in the same bucket are padded to the same length accordingly. We construct sub-computational graphs respectively for each bucket. The training and tagging speed of our neural network on GPU devices can be drastically improved thanks to the bucket model. The training time is proportional to both the size of the training set and the number of POS tags.

Table 1 shows the adopted hyper-parameters. We use one set of parameters for all the experiments on different datasets. The weights of the

[2]https://dumps.wikimedia.org/
[3]http://www.sogou.com/labs/resource/cs.php

Char. embedding size	64
n-gram embedding size	64
Radical embedding size	30
Character font	simsun (宋体)
Character size	30×30
GRU state size	200
Conv. filter size	5×5
Conv. filter number	32
Max pooling size	2×2
Fully-connected size	100
Optimiser	Adagrad
Initial learning rate	0.1
Decay rate	0.05
Gradient Clipping	5.0
Dropout rate	0.5
Batch size	10

Table 1: Hyper-parameters.

neural networks, including the randomly intialised embeddings, are initialised using the scheme introduced in Glorot and Bengio (2010). The network is trained with the error back-propagation algorithm. All the embeddings are fine-tuned during training by back-propagating gradients. Adagrad (Duchi et al., 2011) with mini-batches is employed for optimisation with the initial learning rate $\eta_0 = 0.1$, which is updated with a decay rate $\rho = 0.05$ as $\eta_t = \frac{\eta_0}{\rho(t-1)+1}$, where t is the index of the current epoch.

The model is optimised with respect to the performance on the development sets. F1-scores of both segmentation ($F1_{Seg}$) and joint POS tagging ($F1_{Seg\&Tag}$) are employed as $F1_{Seg} * F1_{Seg\&Tag}$ to measure the performance of the model after each epoch during training. In our experiments, the models are trained for 30 epochs. To ensure that the weights are well optimised, we only adopt the best epoch after the model is trained at least for 5 epochs.

4 Experiments

4.1 Datasets

We employ three different datasets for our experiments, namely Chinese Treebank (Xue et al., 2005) 5.0 (CTB5) and 9.0 (CTB9) along with the Chinese section in Universal Dependencies (UD Chinese) (Nivre et al., 2016) of version 1.4.

CTB5 is the most employed dataset for joint segmentation and POS tagging in previous research. It is composed of newswire data. We follow the conventional split of the dataset as in Jiang et al. (2008); Kruengkrai et al. (2009a);

Zhang and Clark (2010). CTB9 consists of source texts in various genres, CTB5 is a subset of it. We split CTB9 by referring to the partition of CTB7 in Wang et al. (2011). We extend the training, development and test sets from CTB5 by adding 80% of the new data in CTB9 to training and 10% each to development and test. The double-checked files are all placed in the test set. The detailed splitting information can be found in Table 10 in Appendix. UD Chinese has both universal and language-specific POS tags. They are not predicted jointly in this paper. For the sake of convenience, we refer the universal tags as UD1 and the language-specific ones as UD2 in the following sessions. To make the model benefit from the pre-trained character embeddings, we convert the texts in UD Chinese from traditional Chinese into simplified Chinese.

Table 2 shows brief statistics of the employed datasets in numbers of words. The out-of-vocabulary (OOV) words are counted regardless of the POS tags. We can see that the size of UD Chinese is much smaller and it has a notably higher OOV rate than the two CTB datasets.

	CTB5	CTB9	UD Chinese
Train	493,935	1,696,322	98,608
Dev	6,821	136,468	12,663
Test	8,008	242,317	12,012
OOV rate (dev)	8.11	2.93	12.13
OOV rate (test)	3.47	3.13	12.46

Table 2: Statistics of the employed datasets in numbers of words.

4.2 Experimental Results

Both segmentation (Seg) and joint segmentation and POS tagging (Seg&Tag) are evaluated in our experiments.[4] We employ word-level recall (R), precision (P) and F1-score (F) as the evaluation metrics. A series of feature experiments are carried out on the development sets to evaluate the effectiveness of the proposed approaches for vector representations of the characters. Finally, the best performing model according to the feature experiment is applied to the test sets in the forms of single as well as ensemble and compared with ZPar.

---

[4]The evaluation script is downloaded from:
http://people.sutd.edu.sg/ yue_zhang/doc/doc/joint_files /evaluate.py

4.2.1 Feature Experiments

Table 3 shows the evaluation results of using concatenated n-grams up to different orders as the character representations. By introducing 2-grams, we can obtain vast improvements over solely using the conventional character embeddings, which indicates that not all the local information can be effectively captured by the BiRNN using context-free character representations. Utilising the concatenated n-grams ensures that the same character has different but yet closely related representations in different contexts, which is an effective way to encode contextual features.

From the table, we see that notable improvements can be achieved further via employing 3-grams. 4-grams still help but only to CTB9 while adding 5-grams achieves almost no improvement on any of the datasets. The results imply that concatenating higher-order n-grams can be detrimental, especially on datasets in smaller sizes due to the fact that higher-order n-grams are more sparse in the training data and their vector representations cannot be trained well enough. Besides, adopting higher-order n-grams also substantially increases the numbers of weights and therefore both training and decoding become less efficient. Under the circumstances, we consider that 3-gram model is optimal for our task and it is employed in the following experiments for all the datasets.

The concatenated n-grams have a bigger size compared to the basic character representation. We conduct one additional experiment using a basic 1-gram character model with a larger character vector size of 300. The evaluation scores are similar to the basic character model with the size of 64, which shows that the improvements obtained by the n-gram model are not matched by enlarging the size of the vector representation.

The evaluation scores of the sub-character level features are reported in Table 4. The relevant features are added on top of the 3-gram model. Employing radicals and graphical features achieves similar improvements for segmentation while utilising radicals obtains better results for joint POS tagging on CTB5. However, radicals are not a very effective feature on CTB9, UD1 and UD2 whereas a notable enhancement is observed when employing graphical features on UD1. Using CNNs to extract graphical features is computationally much more expensive than simply adopting radicals via a lookup table, especially when GPU is not avail-

	CTB5		CTB9		UD1		UD2	
	Seg	Seg&Tag	Seg	Seg&Tag	Seg	Seg&Tag	Seg	Seg&Tag
size = 300	95.22	91.71	95.53	90.89	91.84	85.43	92.40	85.63
1-gram	95.14	91.52	95.25	90.43	91.74	85.07	91.83	84.93
2-gram	97.08	93.72	96.30	91.66	**94.50**	88.36	94.42	88.14
3-gram	**97.14**	94.01	96.47	91.75	94.36	88.27	**94.43**	**88.32**
4-gram	97.13	**94.02**	96.48	**91.89**	94.25	88.37	94.16	88.24
5-gram	96.94	93.84	**96.50**	91.88	94.40	**88.47**	94.25	88.03

Table 3: Evaluation of concatenated n-gram representations on the development sets in F1-scores

	CTB5		CTB9		UD1		UD2	
	Seg	Seg&Tag	Seg	Seg&Tag	Seg	Seg&Tag	Seg	Seg&Tag
3-gram	97.14	94.01	96.47	91.75	94.36	88.27	**94.43**	88.32
+radicals	**97.26**	**94.42**	96.42	91.74	94.37	88.21	94.39	**88.36**
+graphical	97.25	94.08	**96.50**	**91.78**	**94.50**	**88.59**	94.23	87.95

Table 4: Evaluation of sub-character level features on the development sets in F1-scores.

	CTB5		CTB9		UD1		UD2	
	Seg	Seg&Tag	Seg	Seg&Tag	Seg	Seg&Tag	Seg	Seg&Tag
1-gram	95.14	91.52	95.25	90.43	91.74	85.07	91.83	84.93
+GloVe	95.82	92.45	95.44	90.57	92.77	86.48	93.01	86.48
3-gram, radicals	97.26	94.42	96.42	91.74	94.37	88.21	94.39	88.36
+GloVe	**97.42**	**94.58**	**96.56**	**91.96**	**95.12**	**89.69**	**95.02**	**89.20**

Table 5: Evaluation of the pre-trained character embeddings on the development sets in F1-scores.

able.

From Table 5, we can learn that employing pre-trained embeddings as initial vector representations for the characters achieves improvements in general, whereas the improvements are comparatively smaller if the the concatenated n-gram representations and the radicals are added. Additionally, the improvements obtained on UD Chinese are more significant than on CTBs, which indicates that the pre-trained character embeddings are more beneficial to the datasets in smaller sizes.

In general, the feature experiments indicate that the proposed Chinese character representations are all sensitive to dataset size. Using higher-order n-grams requires more data for training. On the other hand, the pre-trained embeddings are more vital if the dataset is small. In addition, the different representations are sensitive to tagging schemes as the evaluation results on UD1 and UD2 are quite diverse. Taking both robustness and efficiency into consideration, we select 3-grams along with radicals and pre-trained character embeddings as the best setting for final evaluation.

4.2.2 Final Results

Table 6 shows the final scores on the test sets. The complete evaluation results in precision, re-

call and F1-scores are contained in Table 11 and Table 12 in Appendix. Our system is compared with ZPar. We retrained a ZPar model on CTB5 that reproduces the evaluation scores reported in Zhang and Clark (2010). We also modified the source code so that it is applicable to CTB9 and UD Chinese. In addition, we perform the mid-p McNemar's test (Fagerland et al., 2013) to examine the statistical significances.

As shown in Table 6, the single model is worse than the ensemble model but still outperforms ZPar on all the tested datasets. ZPar incorporates discrete local features at both character and word levels and employs structured perceptron for global optimisation, whereas we encode rich local information in the character representations and employ BiRNN to effectively extract global features and capture long term dependencies. The chain CRF layer is used for sentence-level optimisation, which functions similarly to structured perceptron. As opposed to the taggers built with traditional machine learning algorithms, our model avoids heavy feature engineering and benefits from large plain texts via utilising pre-trained character embeddings. It is also very flexible to add sub-character level features as parts of the character representations. The model

		CTB5		CTB9		UD1		UD2	
		Seg	Seg&Tag	Seg	Seg&Tag	Seg	Seg&Tag	Seg	Seg&Tag
	ZPar	97.77	93.82	96.28	91.62	93.75	88.11	93.98	88.16
	Single (3-gram, rad., GloVe)	97.89	94.07**	96.47**	91.89**	94.85**	89.41**	94.93**	89.00**
	Ensemble (4 models)	**98.02***	**94.38***	**96.67***	**92.34***	**95.16***	**89.75***	**95.09***	**89.42***
OOV recall	ZPar	76.98	68.34	**75.83**	63.71	78.69	64.40	79.56	64.86
	Single	**78.78**	69.78	74.16	62.58	81.36	67.40	81.16	66.73
	Ensemble	77.34	**70.50**	75.52	**64.14**	**82.16**	**68.14**	**81.56**	**68.00**

Table 6: Evaluations of the best model on the final test sets in F1-scores as well as the recalls of out-of-vocabulary words. Significance tests for Single are in comparison to ZPar, while tests for Ensemble are in comparison to Single ($^{**}p < 0.01$, $^{*}p < 0.05$)

performs very well despite being fully character based. Moreover, it has clear advantages when applied to smaller datasets like UD Chinese, while the prevalence is much smaller on CTB5.

Both our model and ZPar segment OOV words in UD Chinese with higher accuracies than the ones in CTBs despite that UD Chinese is notably smaller and the overall OOV rate is higher. Compared to CTB, the words in UD Chinese are more fine-grained and the average word length is shorter, which makes it easier for the tagger to correctly segment the OOV words as Zhang et al. (2016) show that the longer words are more difficult to be segmented correctly. For joint POS tagging for OOV words, the two systems both perform significantly better on CTB5 as it is only composed of news text.

In general, our model is more robust to OOV words than ZPar, except that ZPar yields better result for segmentation by a small margin on CTB9. ZPar also obtains higher accuracy for joint POS tagging than the single model on CTB9. The differences between ZPar and our model for both segmentation and POS tagging are more substantial on UD Chinese, which indicates that our model is relatively more advantageous for handling OOV words when the training sets are small, whereas ZPar is able to perform equally well when substantial amount of training data is available as they achieve similar results on the CTB sets.

The single model is further improved by ensemble-averaging four independently trained models. The improvements are not drastic but they are observed systematically across all the datasets. In general, ensemble decoding is beneficial to handling OOV words as well except that a small drop for segmentation on CTB5 is observed.

Table 7 displays the evaluation of the ensemble model and ZPar on the decomposed test sets

	Ensemble		ZPar	
	Seg	Seg&Tag	Seg	Seg&Tag
BN	**97.89***	**94.48***	97.68	94.22
CS	**96.67***	**91.78***	95.61	90.15
FM	**96.54***	**91.92***	96.30	91.51
MG	**94.54***	**89.23***	94.22	88.60
NS	97.56	**93.92***	97.49	93.70
SM	**96.43***	**91.78***	96.13	90.32
SP	**97.29***	**93.93***	96.69	93.35
WB	**94.27***	**88.44***	93.38	86.88

Table 7: Evaluation on Broadcast News (BN), Conversations (CS), Forum (FM), Magazine (MG), News (NS), Short Messages (SM), Speech (SP) and Weblogs (WB) in CTB9. ($^{**}p < 0.01$, $^{*}p < 0.05$)

of CTB9 in different genres. Our model surpasses ZPar on all the genres in both segmentation and joint POS tagging. The differences are subtle on the genres in which the texts are normalised, such as News and Broadcast News. This, to a very large extent, explains why our model is only marginally better than ZPar on CTB5, whereas the experimental results reveal that our model is substantially better at processing non-standard text as it yields significantly higher scores on Conversations, Short Messages and Weblogs. The evaluation results of both our model and ZPar vary substantially across different genres as some genres are fundamentally more challenging to process.

Our models are compared with the previous best-performing systems on CTB5 in Table 8. Our models are not optimised particularly with respect to CTB5 but still yield competitive results, especially for joint POS tagging. We are the first to report evaluation scores on CTB9 and UD Chinese.

4.3 Tagging Speed

Our joint segmentation and POS tagger is very efficient with GPU devices and can be practically

	Seg	Seg&Tag
Kruengkrai et al. (2009b)	97.98	94.00
Zhang and Clark (2010)	97.78	93.67
Sun (2011)	**98.17**	94.02
Wang et al. (2011)	98.11	94.18
Shen et al. (2014)	98.02	93.80
Single	97.89	94.07
Ensemble	98.02	**94.38**

Table 8: Result comparisions on CTB5 in F1-scores.

used for processing very large files. The memory demand of decoding is drastically milder compared to training, a large batch size therefore can be employed. The tagger takes constant time to build the sub-computational graphs and load the weights.

With bucket size of 10 and batch size of 500, Table 9 shows the tagging speed of the tagger using a single Tesla K80 GPU card and the pre-trained model on CTB5. The tagging speed of ZPar is also presented for comparison. GPU devices are not supported by ZPar and therefore the tagging speed is calculated using an Intel Core i7 CPU.

	Init. Time (s)	Sentence/s	Chars/s
Single	20	299.40	40,188.17
Ensemble	23	230.41	30,928.22
ZPar	4	134.59	18,090.09

Table 9: Tagging speed in numbers of sentences and characters per second

5   Related Work

The fundamental BiRNN-CRF architecture is task-independent and has been applied to many sequence tagging problems on Chinese. Peng and Dredze (2016) adopt the model for Chinese segmentation and named entity recognition in the context of multi-task and multi-domain learning. Dong et al. (2016) employ a character level BiLSTM-CRF model that utilises radical-level information for Chinese named entity recognition. Ma and Sun (2016) use a similar architecture but feed the Chinese characters pairwise as edge embeddings instead. Their model is applied respectively to chunking, segmentation and POS tagging.

Zheng et al. (2013) model joint Chinese segmentation and POS tagging via predicting the combinatory segmentation and POS tags. They

employ the adaptation of the feed forward neural network introduced in Collobert et al. (2011) that only extracts local features in a context window. A perceptron-style training algorithm is employed for sentence level optimisation, which is the same as the training algorithm of the BiRNN-CRF model. Their proposed model is not evaluated on CTB5 and therefore difficult to be compared with our system. Kong et al. (2015) apply segmental recurrent neural networks to joint segmentation and POS tagging but the evaluation results are substantially below the state-of-the-art on CTB5.

Bojanowski et al. (2016) retrieve word embeddings via representing words as a bag of character n-grams for morphologically rich languages. A similar character n-gram model is proposed by Wieting et al. (2016). Sun et al. (2014) attempt to encode radical information into the conventional character embeddings. The radical-enhanced embeddings are employed and evaluated for Chinese segmentation. The results show that radical-enhanced embeddings outperform both skip-ngram and continues bag-of-word (Mikolov et al., 2013) in word2vec.

6   Conclusion

We adapt and apply the BiRNN-CRF model for sequence tagging in NLP to joint Chinese segmentation and POS tagging via predicting the combinatory tags of word boundaries and POS tags. Concatenated n-grams as well as sub-character features are employed along with the conventional pre-trained character embeddings as the vector representations for Chinese characters. The feature experiments indicate that concatenated n-grams contribute substantially. However, both radicals and graphical features as sub-character level information are less effective. How to incorporate the sub-character level information more effectively will be further explored in the future.

The proposed model is extensively evaluated on CTB5, CTB9 and UD Chinese. Despite the fact that different character representation approaches are sensitive to data size and tagging schemes, we use one set of hyper-parameters and universal feature settings so that the model is robust across datasets. The experimental results on the test sets show that our model outperforms ZPar which is built on structured perceptron on all the datasets. We obtain state-of-the-art performances on CTB5.

The results on UD Chinese and CTB9 also reveal that our model has great advantages in processing non-standard text, such as weblogs, forum text and short messages. Moreover, the implemented tagger is very efficient with GPU devices and therefore can be applied to tagging very large files.

Acknowledgments

We acknowledge the computational resources provided by CSC in Helsinki and Sigma2 in Oslo through NeIC-NLPL (www.nlpl.eu). This work is supported by the Chinese Scholarship Council (CSC) (No. 201407930015).

References

Martín Abadi, Paul Barham, Jianmin Chen, Zhifeng Chen, Andy Davis, Jeffrey Dean, Matthieu Devin, Sanjay Ghemawat, Geoffrey Irving, Michael Isard, et al. 2016. TensorFlow: A system for large-scale machine learning. In *Proceedings of the 12th USENIX Symposium on Operating Systems Design and Implementation (OSDI)*. Savannah, Georgia, USA.

Piotr Bojanowski, Edouard Grave, Armand Joulin, and Tomas Mikolov. 2016. Enriching word vectors with subword information. *arXiv preprint arXiv:1607.04606*.

Kyunghyun Cho, Bart Van Merriënboer, Dzmitry Bahdanau, and Yoshua Bengio. 2014. On the properties of neural machine translation: Encoder-decoder approaches. *arXiv preprint arXiv:1409.1259*.

Junyoung Chung, Caglar Gulcehre, KyungHyun Cho, and Yoshua Bengio. 2014. Empirical evaluation of gated recurrent neural networks on sequence modeling. *arXiv preprint arXiv:1412.3555*.

Ronan Collobert, Jason Weston, Léon Bottou, Michael Karlen, Koray Kavukcuoglu, and Pavel Kuksa. 2011. Natural language processing (almost) from scratch. *Journal of Machine Learning Research* 12(August):2493–2537.

Chuanhai Dong, Jiajun Zhang, Chengqing Zong, Masanori Hattori, and Hui Di. 2016. Character-based LSTM-CRF with radical-level features for Chinese named entity recognition. In *International Conference on Computer Processing of Oriental Languages*. Springer, pages 239–250.

Cícero Nogueira dos Santos and Bianca Zadrozny. 2014. Learning character-level representations for part-of-speech tagging. In *Proceedings of The 31st International Conference on Machine Learning*. pages 1818–1826.

John Duchi, Elad Hazan, and Yoram Singer. 2011. Adaptive subgradient methods for online learning and stochastic optimization. *Journal of Machine Learning Research* 12(Jul):2121–2159.

Morten W Fagerland, Stian Lydersen, and Petter Laake. 2013. The McNemar test for binary matched-pairs data: mid-p and asymptotic are better than exact conditional. *BMC medical research methodology* 13(1):91.

Xavier Glorot and Yoshua Bengio. 2010. Understanding the difficulty of training deep feedforward neural networks. In *Aistats*. pages 249–256.

Sepp Hochreiter and Jürgen Schmidhuber. 1997. Long short-term memory. *Neural computation* 9(8):1735–1780.

Zhiheng Huang, Wei Xu, and Kai Yu. 2015. Bidirectional LSTM-CRF models for sequence tagging. *arXiv preprint arXiv:1508.01991*.

Wenbin Jiang, Liang Huang, Qun Liu, and Yajuan Lü. 2008. A cascaded linear model for joint Chinese word segmentation and part-of-speech tagging. In *In Proceedings of the 46th Annual Meeting of the Association for Computational Linguistics*. Citeseer.

Lingpeng Kong, Chris Dyer, and Noah A Smith. 2015. Segmental recurrent neural networks. *arXiv preprint arXiv:1511.06018*.

Canasai Kruengkrai, Kiyotaka Uchimoto, Jun'ichi Kazama, Yiou Wang, Kentaro Torisawa, and Hitoshi Isahara. 2009a. An error-driven word-character hybrid model for joint Chinese word segmentation and POS tagging. In *Proceedings of the Joint Conference of the 47th Annual Meeting of the ACL and the 4th International Joint Conference on Natural Language Processing of the AFNLP: Volume 1-Volume 1*. Association for Computational Linguistics, Singapore, pages 513–521.

Canasai Kruengkrai, Kiyotaka Uchimoto, Jun'ichi Kazama, WANG Yiou, Kentaro Torisawa, and Hitoshi Isahara. 2009b. Joint Chinese word segmentation and POS tagging using an error-driven word-character hybrid model. *IEICE transactions on information and systems* 92(12):2298–2305.

John Lafferty, Andrew McCallum, Fernando Pereira, et al. 2001. Conditional random fields: Probabilistic models for segmenting and labeling sequence data. In *Proceedings of the eighteenth international conference on machine learning, ICML*. volume 1, pages 282–289.

Wang Ling, Chris Dyer, W. Alan Black, Isabel Trancoso, Ramon Fermandez, Silvio Amir, Luis Marujo, and Tiago Luis. 2015. Finding function in form: Compositional character models for open vocabulary word representation. In *Proceedings of the 2015 Conference on Empirical Methods in Natural Language Processing*. Association for Computational Linguistics, pages 1520–1530.

Shuming Ma and Xu Sun. 2016. A new recurrent neural CRF for learning non-linear edge features. *arXiv preprint arXiv:1611.04233* .

Xuezhe Ma and Eduard Hovy. 2016. End-to-end sequence labeling via bi-directional LSTM-CNNs-CRF. In *Proceedings of the 54th Annual Meeting of the Association for Computational Linguistics*. Berlin, Germany, page 10641074.

Tomas Mikolov, Kai Chen, Greg Corrado, and Jeffrey Dean. 2013. Efficient estimation of word representations in vector space. *arXiv preprint arXiv:1301.3781* .

Hwee Tou Ng and Jin Kiat Low. 2004. Chinese part-of-speech tagging: One-at-a-time or all-at-once? word-based or character-based? In *Proceedings of the 2004 Conference on Empirical Methods in Natural Language Processing*. Barcelona, Spain, pages 277–284.

Joakim Nivre, Marie-Catherine de Marneffe, Filip Ginter, Yoav Goldberg, Jan Hajic, Christopher D. Manning, Ryan McDonald, Slav Petrov, Sampo Pyysalo, Natalia Silveira, Reut Tsarfaty, and Daniel Zeman. 2016. Universal dependencies v1: A multilingual treebank collection. In *Proceedings of the 10th International Conference on Language Resources and Evaluation (LREC 2016)*. pages 1659–1666.

Nanyun Peng and Mark Dredze. 2016. Multi-task multi-domain representation learning for sequence tagging. *arXiv preprint arXiv:1608.02689* .

Jeffrey Pennington, Richard Socher, and Christopher D. Manning. 2014. GloVe: Global vectors for word representation. In *Empirical Methods in Natural Language Processing (EMNLP)*. Doha, Qatar, pages 1532–1543.

Mo Shen, Hongxiao Liu, Daisuke Kawahara, and Sadao Kurohashi. 2014. Chinese morphological analysis with character-level POS tagging. In *Proceedings of the 52nd Annual Meeting of the Association for Computational Linguistics (Volume 2: Short Papers)*. Association for Computational Linguistics, Baltimore, Maryland, pages 253–258.

Nitish Srivastava, Geoffrey E Hinton, Alex Krizhevsky, Ilya Sutskever, and Ruslan Salakhutdinov. 2014. Dropout: a simple way to prevent neural networks from overfitting. *Journal of Machine Learning Research* 15(1):1929–1958.

Weiwei Sun. 2011. A stacked sub-word model for joint Chinese word segmentation and part-of-speech tagging. In *Proceedings of the 49th Annual Meeting of the Association for Computational Linguistics: Human Language Technologies-Volume 1*. Association for Computational Linguistics, Portland, Oregon, USA, pages 1385–1394.

Yaming Sun, Lei Lin, Nan Yang, Zhenzhou Ji, and Xiaolong Wang. 2014. Radical-enhanced Chinese character embedding. In *International Conference on Neural Information Processing*. Springer, pages 279–286.

Yiou Wang, Jun'ichi Kazama, Yoshimasa Tsuruoka, Wenliang Chen, Yujie Zhang, and Kentaro Torisawa. 2011. Improving Chinese word segmentation and POS tagging with semi-supervised methods using large auto-analyzed data. In *Proceedings of 5th International Joint Conference on Natural Language Processing*. Asian Federation of Natural Language Processing, pages 309–317.

John Wieting, Mohit Bansal, Kevin Gimpel, and Karen Livescu. 2016. CHARAGRAM: Embedding words and sentences via character n-grams. *arXiv preprint arXiv:1607.02789* .

Naiwen Xue, Fei Xia, Fu-Dong Chiou, and Marta Palmer. 2005. The Penn Chinese treebank: Phrase structure annotation of a large corpus. *Natural language engineering* 11(02):207–238.

Meishan Zhang, Yue Zhang, and Guohong Fu. 2016. Transition-based neural word segmentation. In *Proceedings of the 54th Annual Meeting of the Association for Computational Linguistics (Volume 1: Long Papers)*. Association for Computational Linguistics, pages 421–431.

Yue Zhang and Stephen Clark. 2008. Joint word segmentation and POS tagging using a single perceptron. In *Proceedings of the 46th Annual Meeting of the Association for Computational Linguistics*. Columbus, Ohio, pages 888–896.

Yue Zhang and Stephen Clark. 2010. A fast decoder for joint word segmentation and POS-tagging using a single discriminative model. In *Proceedings of the 2010 Conference on Empirical Methods in Natural Language Processing*. Association for Computational Linguistics, Massachusetts, USA, pages 843–852.

Xiaoqing Zheng, Hanyang Chen, and Tianyu Xu. 2013. Deep learning for Chinese word segmentation and POS tagging. In *Proceedings of the 2013 Conference on Empirical Methods in Natural Language Processing*. Seattle, USA, pages 647–657.

Appendix

Dataset	CTB chapter IDs
Train	0044-0143, 0170-0270, 0400-0899, 1001-1017, 1019, 1021-1035, 1037-1043, 1045-1059, 1062-1071, 1073-1117, 1120-1131, 1133-1140, 1143-1147, 1149-1151, 2000-2915, 4051-4099, 4112-4180, 4198-4368, 5000-5446, 6000-6560, 7000-7013
Dev	0301-0326, 2916-3030, 4100-4106, 4181-4189, 4369-4390, 5447-5492, 6561-6630, 7013-7014
Test	0001-0043, 0144-0169, 0271-0301, 0900-0931, 1018, 1020, 1036, 1044, 1060, 1061, 1072, 1118, 1119, 1132, 1141, 1142, 1148, 3031-3145, 4107-4111, 4190-4197, 4391-4411, 5493-5558, 6631-6700, 7015-7017

Table 10: The split of Chinese Treebank 9.0

		P	R	F
CTB5	Single	97.49	98.30	97.89
	Ensemble	97.57	98.47	98.02
CTB9	Single	96.38	96.55	96.47
	Ensemble	96.61	96.74	96.67
UD1	Single	94.71	94.99	94.85
	Ensemble	95.07	95.27	95.17
UD2	Single	94.98	94.93	94.93
	Ensemble	95.00	95.22	95.11

Table 11: Evaluation of segmentations in precision, recall and F1-scores

		P	R	F
CTB5	Single	93.68	94.47	94.07
	Ensemble	93.95	94.81	94.38
CTB9	Single	91.81	91.97	91.89
	Ensemble	92.28	92.40	92.34
UD1	Single	89.28	89.54	89.41
	Ensemble	89.67	89.86	89.77
UD2	Single	88.95	89.04	89.00
	Ensemble	89.33	89.54	89.43

Table 12: Evaluation of joint segmentations and POS tagging in precision, recall and F1-scores

Addressing Domain Adaptation for Chinese Word Segmentation with Global Recurrent Structure

Shen Huang and **Xu Sun** and **Houfeng Wang**[*]

Key Laboratory of Computational Linguistics, Ministry of Education
School of Electronics Engineering and Computer Science, Peking University
Beijing, P.R.China, 100871
`huangshenno1,xusun,wanghf@pku.edu.cn`

Abstract

Boundary features are widely used in traditional Chinese Word Segmentation (CWS) methods as they can utilize un-labeled data to help improve the Out-of-Vocabulary (OOV) word recognition performance. Although various neural network methods for CWS have achieved performance competitive with state-of-the-art systems, these methods, constrained by the domain and size of the training corpus, do not work well in domain adaptation. In this paper, we propose a novel BLSTM-based neural network model which incorporates a global recurrent structure designed for modeling boundary features dynamically. Experiments show that the proposed structure can effectively boost the performance of Chinese Word Segmentation, especially OOV-Recall, which brings benefits to domain adaptation. We achieved state-of-the-art results on 6 domains of CNKI articles, and competitive results to the best reported on the 4 domains of SIGHAN Bakeoff 2010 data.

1 Introduction

Since Chinese writing system does not have explicit word delimiters, word segmentation becomes an essential first step for further Chinese language processing. In recent years, Chinese Word Segmentation (CWS) has experienced great advancement. One mainstream method is to regard word segmentation task as a sequence labeling problem (Xue, 2003; Peng et al., 2004) where each character is assigned a tag indicating its position in the word. This method has been proved

effective as it turns word segmentation into a structured discriminative learning task which can be handled by supervised learning algorithms such as Maximum Entropy (ME) (Berger et al., 1996) and Conditional Random Fields (CRF) (Lafferty et al., 2001). Furthermore, rich features can be incorporated into these systems to improve their performances and most state-of-the-art systems are still based on feature-based models.

Recently, neural network models are drawing increasing attention in Natural Language Processing (NLP) tasks. They significantly reduced feature engineering effort and achieved competitive or state-of-the-art results in many NLP tasks. Collobert et al. (2011) developed a general neural network architecture for sequence labeling tasks. Following this work, many neural network models (Zheng et al., 2013; Pei et al., 2014; Chen et al., 2015a,b) have been applied to CWS and some approached state-of-the-art performance.

However, these neural network models, as well as other supervised methods, do not work well in domain adaptation. In recent years, manually annotated training corpus mostly come from the news domain. When it shifts to other domains such as literature or medicine, where there are many domain-related words that rarely appear in other domains, Out-of-Vocabulary (OOV) word recognition becomes an important problem. Moreover, different domains means different language usages and contexts. Therefore, the In-Vocabulary (IV) word segmentation performance is also affected. As a result, CWS accuracies can drop gravely on cross-domain corpora. For example, consider a sentence "三聚氰胺(melamine) / 致(lead to) / 婴幼儿(baby) / 泌尿系(urinary tract) / 结石(stones)". Here the word "三聚氰胺(melamine)" is a chemical that often appears in medicine-related domains while seldom appears in other domains. It is a four-Chinese-character word

---

[*]Corresponding author

Proceedings of the The 8th International Joint Conference on Natural Language Processing, pages 184–193,
Taipei, Taiwan, November 27 – December 1, 2017 ©2017 AFNLP

where each character stands for 'three', 'gather', 'cyanide' and 'amine'. The four characters are totally irrelevant. A supervised CWS system trained on news domain corpus would face great challenges on segmenting this word correctly

Several approaches have been proposed to address the domain adaption problem for CWS. One major family proposed to compose boundary features by fitting the relevance of consecutive characters using Accessor Variety (AV) (Feng et al., 2004a,b), or Chi-square Statistics (Chi2) (Chang and Han, 2010). Combining the boundary features with other hand-crafted features, these methods were shown to achieve better performance on OOV words.

Inspired by these models, we propose a novel BLSTM-based neural network model which incorporates a global recurrent structure designed to model boundary features dynamically. This structure can learn to utilize the target domain corpus and extract the correlation or irrelevance between characters, which is a reminiscence of the discrete boundary features such as Accessor Variety (AV).

The contributions of this paper are two folds:

- First, we propose a global recurrent structure and incorporate it in the BLSTM-based neural network model for CWS. The structure can capture correlations between characters, and thus is especially efficient for segmenting OOV words and enhancing the performance of CWS on non-news domains.

- We obtain competitive results comparing to the best reported in the literature on the SIGHAN Bakeoff 2010 data, which is a benchmark dataset for cross-domain CWS.

2 BLSTM Architecture for Chinese Word Segmentation

We regard Chinese word segmentation task as a character-based sequence labeling problem, by labeling each character a tag from $\{S, B, E, M\}$. These tags indicate the position of the character in the segmented word. B, E, M represents *Begin, Middle, End* of a multi-character segmentation respectively, while S represents a single-character segmentation.

Figure 1 illustrates the general BLSTM architecture for Chinese word segmentation.

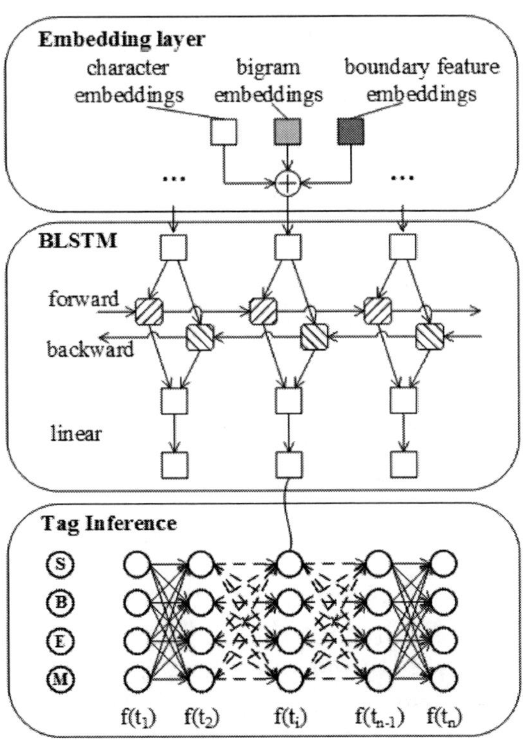

Figure 1: General architecture for Chinese word segmentation.

2.1 Embeddings

The outputs of the embedding layer is a concatenation of three parts: character embeddings, bigram embeddings and boundary feature embeddings.

We adopt the the local window approach which assumes that the tag of a character largely depends on its neighboring characters. For each character c_i in a given input sentence $c_{[1:n]}$, the context characters $c_{[i-w/2:i+w/2]}$ and their corresponding bigrams are chosen to be fed into the networks, where w is the context window size. As most CWS methods do, we will set $w = 5$ in our experiments.

Given a character set V of size $|V|$, each character $c \in V$ will be mapped into a d-dimensional embedding space as $Emb_c(c) \in \mathbb{R}^d$ by a lookup table $\mathbf{M_c} \in \mathbb{R}^{d \times |V|}$. Similarly, each bigram $b \in \{c_1 c_2 | c_1 \in V, c_2 \in V\}$ will be mapped into a d-dimensional embedding space as $Emb_b(b) \in \mathbb{R}^d$ by a lookup table $\mathbf{M_b} \in \mathbb{R}^{d \times |V| \times |V|}$.

The boundary feature embeddings are hidden vectors computed from the current bigrams and the whole bigarm history, which will be explained in detail in Section 3.

Three kinds of embeddings of the context characters $c_{[i-2:i+2]}$ and their corresponding bigrams are then concatenated into a single vector $x_i \in \mathbb{R}^{H_1}$, where $H_1 = 5d + 4d + 4d_{bf}$. d_{bf} is the number of hidden units output by the boundary feature embeddings. Then, this vector x_i is fed into the BLSTM layer.

2.2 Bidirectional LSTM Network

Following the embedding layer is an one-layer BLSTM network (Graves and Schmidhuber, 2005). By combining hidden states from two separate LSTM layers, it can incorporate long periods of contextual information from both directions. The LSTM cell is implemented as follows (Graves et al., 2013):

$$
\begin{aligned}
i_t &= \sigma(W_{xi}x_t + W_{hi}h_{t-1} + W_{ci}c_{t-1} + b_i) \\
f_t &= \sigma(W_{xf}x_t + W_{hf}h_{t-1} + W_{cf}c_{t-1} + b_f) \\
c_t &= f_t c_{t-1} + i_t tanh(W_{xc}x_t + W_{hc}h_{t-1} + b_c) \\
o_t &= \sigma(W_{xo}x_t + W_{ho}h_{t-1} + W_{co}c_t + b_o) \\
h_t &= o_t tanh(c_t)
\end{aligned}
\tag{1}
$$

where σ is the logistic sigmoid function, and i, f, o and c are the input gate, forget gate, output gate and the cell respectively, all of which are the same dimension as the hidden output h. The subscripts of the weight matrix describe the meaning as the name suggests. For instance, W_{xi} is the input gate weight matrix for input x.

The outputs of the BLSTM layer are the concatenation of a forward hidden sequence $\overrightarrow{h}$ and a backward hidden sequence $\overleftarrow{h}$ which will be fed to the decoding layer that contains a linear transformation with no non-linear function:

$$
f(t_i|c_{[i-w/2:i+w/2]}) = W_d(\overrightarrow{h_i} \oplus \overleftarrow{h_i}) + b_d \tag{2}
$$

where $W_d \in \mathbb{R}^{|T| \times H_2}$, $b_d \in \mathbb{R}^{|T|}$. H_2 is the number of hidden units of the outputs for the BLSTM layer. $f(t_i|c_{[i-w/2:i+w/2]}) \in \mathbb{R}^{|T|}$ is the score vector for each possible tag. Here in Chinese word segmentation, we set $T = \{S, B, E, M\}$.

2.3 Tag Inference

To model the correlations between tags in neighborhoods and jointly decode the best chain of tags for a given sentence, a transition score A_{ij} is introduced to measure the probability of jumping from tag $i \in T$ to tag $j \in T$ (Collobert et al., 2011). For an input sentence $c_{[1:n]}$ with a tag sequence $t_{[1:n]}$, a sentence-level score can be formulated as follows:

$$
s(c_{[1:n]}, t_{[1:n]}, \theta) = \sum_{i=1}^{n}(A_{t_{i-1}t_i} + f_\theta(t_i|c_{[i-2:i+2]})) \tag{3}
$$

where $f_\theta(t_i|c_{[i-2:i+2]})$ indicates the score output for the ith tag computed by the neural network described above with parameters θ.

3 Global Recurrent Structure

Chinese word segmentation is essentially a task of resolving the relevance of consecutive characters. Lacking knowledge of such relevance, recognizing out-of-domain words has been the bottleneck of domain adaption in CWS. However, Boundary features such as Accessor Variety (AV) (Feng et al., 2004a,b), Mutual Information (Sun and Xu, 2011) and Chi-square Statistics (Chi2) (Chang and Han, 2010) are features designed to fit such relevance. A significant advantage of boundary features is that they can compute the correlation of characters from a large scale corpora, annotated or not, to boost the OOV word recognition performance. As a result, they are especially effective for cross-domain CWS.

In this paper, we propose 5 novel global recurrent structures to generate embeddings that mimic the boundary features for further computing, which needs minimal pre-processing and feature engineering. The structures are designed to capture the intuition that nearby sentences in a single-domain corpus often share certain words. Thus the correlation of characters within or across certain words can be learned, and those involving OOV words notably enhance domain adaption for CWS.

GRS-1 The basic structure(GRS-1) is illustrated in Figure 2. It looks like LSTM-2 (Chen et al., 2015b) when incorporated into the BLSTM model. However, the difference is that common recurrent networks will reset the hidden states every time they process a new sentence in NLP problems while the hidden states in our structure are never reset.

$$
h_{k+1,0}, c_{k+1,0} = h_{k,n_k}, c_{k,n_k} \tag{4}
$$

where $h_{k,i}$ and $c_{k,i}$ are the hidden state and cell vector of the kth sentence at the ith step, n_k is the

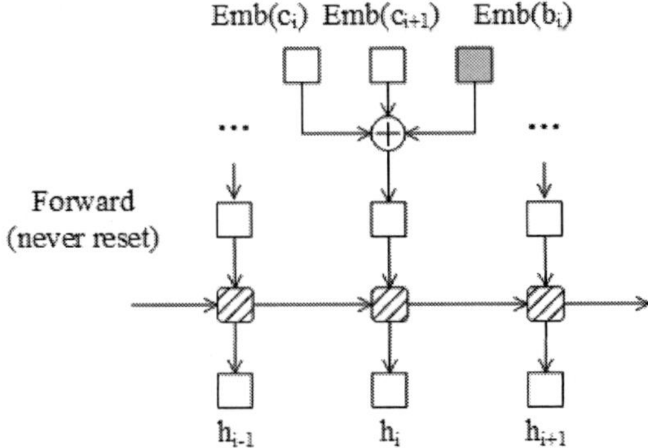

Figure 2: Global recurrent structure.

length of the kth sentence. For simplicity, in the following part we will ignore the subscript k and always indicate the current sentence.

As a result of such warm start mechanism, our structure can to some extent record the history information in recent sentences. And some information may last long in the structure.

Here we choose the LSTM cell as it can learn to keep relatively long term memory. We follow the equations (1) to implement it and directly take h_i as the boundary feature embeddings for the bigram $b_i = c_i c_{i+1}$ in the basic structure, where the input is the concatenation of embeddings of a bigram and its corresponding characters $Emb_b(b_i) \oplus Emb_c(c_i) \oplus Emb_c(c_{i+1})$.

$$Emb_{bf}(b_i) = h_i \qquad (5)$$

where h_i is the output of the recurrent network at the ith step.

We also propose four more variants of the structure that are shown in Figure 3.

GRS-2 To better fit the boundary features, we add a full-connection hidden layer following the recurrent network. The boundary feature embeddings are calculated as follows:

$$Emb_{bf}(b_i) = \sigma(W_{bf} h_i + b_{bf}) \qquad (6)$$

where σ is the logistic sigmoid function.

GRS-3 Considering the hidden states are noisy and contains much information of other words, we want the hidden values more relevant to the current bigram, so a gate is introduced to the structure. The boundary feature embeddings are calculated

as follows:

$$E_i = Emb_c(c_i) \oplus Emb_c(c_{i+1}) \oplus Emb_b(b_i)$$
$$g(b_i) = \sigma(W_g E_i + b_g) \qquad (7)$$
$$Emb_{bf}(b_i) = g(b_i) h_i$$

where $\oplus$ is the symbol for concatenation.

GRS-4 GRS-4 is a combination version of GRS-2 and GRS-3 by adding a full-connection hidden layer following the gated output.

GRS-5 GRS-5 is a more complicated version which tries to mimic the **Accessor Variety(AV)** criterion. AV criterion is a feature describing the number of distinct characters that precede or succeed a certain string s. For simplicity, we only focus on strings with $length = 2$, in other words, bigrams. Therefore, we substitute the input of GRS-4 with a bigarm and its preceding character to fit its left AV and similarly with a bigram and its succeeding character to fit its right AV. At last, we simply concatenate the two embeddings as the final boundary feature embeddings (Actually they are trigram boundary feature embeddings):

$$E_i^L = Emb_c(c_{i-1}) \oplus Emb_b(b_i)$$
$$E_i^R = Emb_c(c_{i+1}) \oplus Emb_b(b_{i-1})$$
$$g^L(tri_i) = \sigma(W_g^L E_i^L + b_g^L)$$
$$g^R(tri_i) = \sigma(W_g^R E_i^R + b_g^R)$$
$$Emb_{bf}^L(tri_i) = \sigma(W_{bf}^L g^L(tri_i) h_i^L + b_{bf}^L)$$
$$Emb_{bf}^R(tri_i) = \sigma(W_{bf}^R g^R(tri_i) h_i^R + b_{bf}^R)$$
$$Emb_{bf}(tri_i) = Emb_{bf}^L(tri_i) \oplus Emb_{bf}^R(tri_i)$$
$$(8)$$

where $tri_i = c_{i-1} c_i c_{i+1}$ and other values have the same meanings as above.

4 Training

Instead of using the Max-Margin criterion (Taskar et al., 2005) adopted by previous neural network models for CWS (Zheng et al., 2013; Pei et al., 2014; Chen et al., 2015a,b), we try to directly maximize the log-probability of the correct tag sequence following Lample et al. (2016):

$$log(p(y|X)) = s(X, y) - log(\sum_{\tilde{y} \in Y_X} e^{s(X, \tilde{y})})$$
$$= s(X, y) - \underset{\tilde{y} \in Y_X}{logadd}\, s(X, \tilde{y}) \qquad (9)$$

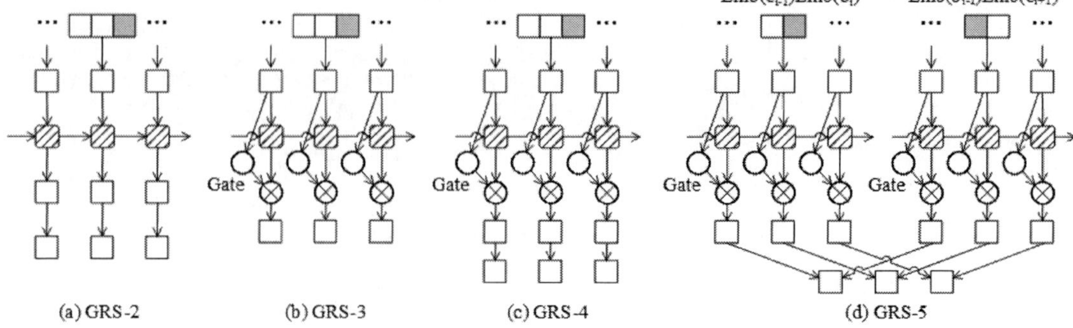

Figure 3: Four variants of the global recurrent structure.

where Y_X represents all possible tag sequences for a sentence X. While decoding, we predict the output sequence which obtains the maximum score as follows:

$$y^* = \underset{\tilde{y} \in Y_X}{\arg\max}\, s(X, \tilde{y}) \qquad (10)$$

The optimal sequence can be computed using dynamic programming. We use Adam (Kingma and Ba, 2014) to maximize the objective function.

5 Experiments

5.1 Experimental Setup

Data. We use the PKU corpus drawn from news domain for the source-domain training. The PKU dataset is provided by SIGHAN Bakeoff 2005 (Emerson, 2005). We regard the random 90% sentences of the training data as training set and the rest 10% sentences as development set. We also use the test part of the PKU dataset to measure the in-domain segmentation ability of our models. Following Liu et al. (2014)'s settings, our domain adaption experiments are performed on the four testing sets from the SIGHAN Bakeoff 2010 (Zhao and Liu, 2010) whose domains cover finance, computer, medicine and literature. In addition, we manually annotate six more corpora from non-news domains as testing sets, including finance, medicine, geology, agriculture, material and weather domains, which are extracted from abstracts of papers in **CNKI**[1]. These data are annotated following the guideline proposed by Yu et al. (2001). The OOV rate of these data are relatively high because they are more academic. Statistics

<hr>

[1]http://www.cnki.net/

of the training and testing data are shown in the Table 1.

All datasets are pre-processed by replacing the Chinese idioms and the continuous English letters and digits with a unique token.

Embeddings. We use *word2vec*[2] to pre-train character embeddings on the training corpus. The bigram embeddings are initialized with the average of the corresponding two characters' embeddings.

Discrete Boundary Features. The discrete boundary features which will be used in Section 5.3 are extracted from the datasets mentioned above and the Chinese Gigaword corpus[3], following methods in Sun and Xu (2011)'s paper.

Hyper-parameters. The hyper-parameters are tuned according to the experimental results. The detailed values are shown in Table 2.

Character & bigram embedding size	100
Boundary feature embedding size	100
Hidden unit number(cell in GRS)	300
Hidden unit number(cell in BLSTM)	300
Batch size	10
Early stop	5
Initial learning rate	0.02
Dropout rate on input layer	0.2
Regularization	10^{-4}

Table 2: Settings of the hyper-parameters.

5.2 Model Selection

We evaluate the baseline BLSTM model and our five proposed structures with the parameter settings in Table 2 on the PKU test data and six do-

<hr>

[2] http://word2vec.googlecode.com/
[3]https://catalog.ldc.upenn.edu/LDC2003T05

Dataset	Train	Test	Test-Bakeoff2010			
	PKU		Finance	Computer	Medicine	Literature
# of Sent.	19056	1945	561	1330	1309	671
# of Words	1109947	104372	33035	35319	31499	35735
OOV Rate		0.0575	0.0874	0.1522	0.1102	0.0694

Dataset	Test-CNKI					
	Finance	Medicine	Geology	Agriculture	Material	Weather
# of Sent.	100	100	100	100	100	100
# of Words	27549	37803	29251	28780	26778	27228
OOV Rate	0.0437	0.2247	0.1910	0.1689	0.2224	0.1449

Table 1: Statistics of datasets used in this paper.

mains from the **CNKI** dataset. The results are shown in Table 3. The BLSTM+GRS-4 model with a gate and an additional full-connection hidden layer achieves the best performances among all domains. Surprisingly, the most delicate structure GRS-5 seems to be of no help to the CWS task.

To examine whether OOV recognition can benefit from GRS, we also look into the IV and OOV recalls of the PKU dataset respectively. Table 4 and Table 5 show that the proposed GRS can effectively improve the segmentation performance on OOV words, which empirically proves its domain adaption ability. BSLTM-2, similar to LSTM-2 (Chen et al., 2015b), is an architecture comprised of two stacking bidirectional LSTM hidden layers. GRS-4 is short for BLSTM+GRS-4 model.

Methods	IV Recall	OOV Recall
BLSTM	**97.12**	83.01
BLSTM-2	96.89	82.59
GRS-4	96.91	**83.78**

Table 4: IV and OOV recalls on the PKU development data.

Methods	IV Recall	OOV Recall
BLSTM	**96.35**	82.67
BLSTM-2	96.11	82.01
GRS-4	96.25	**83.96**

Table 5: IV and OOV recalls on the PKU test data.

5.3 Final Results

In this section, We compare our BLSTM+GRS-4 model with previous state-of-the-art methods.

Experimental results on the four test domains from SIGHAN Bakeoff 2010 are shown in Ta-

ble 6. We also attempt to integrate discrete boundary features into the models. In our experiments, we choose the **Accessor Variety(AV)** (Feng et al., 2004a,b) which is a feature widely used in traditional Chinese word segmentation. Our F-scores and OOV recalls are competitive to those reported by Liu et al. (2014) and Jiang et al. (2013). However, following Liu et al. (2014)'s setting, we choose the PKU dataset as the training corpus while Jiang et al. (2013)'s model is trained on a different corpus. The results are not directly comparable. The results prove the incredible effectiveness of the global recurrent structure on OOV recognition and overall segmentation, comparable to the BLSTM model that directly incorporates discrete AV features. Adding discrete AV features into our model seem not to be a notable improvement, which also confirms that our model already has certain domain adaption ability.

Models	PKU	MSRA
(Zheng et al., 2013)	92.8	93.9
(Pei et al., 2014)	95.2	97.2
(Chen et al., 2015a)	96.4	97.6
(Chen et al., 2015b)	**96.5**	97.4
(Chen et al., 2015a)*	94.5	95.4
(Chen et al., 2015b)*	94.8	95.6
(Cai and Zhao, 2016)	95.5	96.5
(Zhang et al., 2016)	95.7	**97.7**
BLSTM	95.9	97.0
This work	95.9	97.1

Table 7: Comparison of our model with previous neural models on the PKU and MSRA datasets. Results with * are from runs on their released implementation (Cai and Zhao, 2016).

We compare the in-domain experimental results on the PKU and MSRA datasets with previ-

189

Dataset	Baseline(F%)	GRS-1(F%)	GRS-2(F%)	GRS-3(F%)	GRS-4(F%)	GRS-5(F%)
PKU	95.91	95.17	95.90	95.35	**95.92**	94.81
Out-of-Domain						
Finance	96.87	**97.15**	96.78	96.68	**97.15**	96.09
Medicine	85.01	86.24	85.98	85.83	**87.13**	85.97
Geology	87.59	88.52	88.90	88.38	**89.22**	86.90
Agriculture	89.51	90.54	91.16	90.90	**91.18**	90.08
Material	87.29	88.84	89.04	88.28	**89.62**	87.79
Weather	90.62	92.21	92.70	92.21	**93.21**	91.15

Table 3: Experimental results of the baseline BLSTM model and our proposed structures on the PKU test data and six domains from the **CNKI** dataset.

Method	Finance		Computer		Medicine		Literature		Avg-F	Avg-Roov
	F	Roov	F	Roov	F	Roov	F	Roov		
BLSTM	94.70	86.02	92.17	81.84	91.34	73.51	92.51	73.80	92.68	78.79
BLSTM+AV	95.77	90.91	93.57	82.82	92.50	83.12	93.79	**84.60**	93.91	**85.36**
GRS-4	**95.81**	**91.21**	**93.99**	83.81	92.26	**83.27**	**94.33**	81.30	**94.10**	84.90
GRS-4+AV	95.77	91.02	93.20	83.97	91.80	82.17	93.50	82.01	93.57	84.77
Liu2014	95.54	88.53	93.93	**87.53**	92.47	78.28	92.49	76.84	93.61	82.80
Jiang2013	93.16		91.19		**93.34**		93.53		92.80	

Table 6: Experimental results of the baseline BLSTM model, best-performance BLSTM+GRS-4 model, models with discrete AV features and models proposed by others on the SIGHAN Bakeoff2010 data.

ous neural models, which is shown in Table 7. The baseline BLSTM model with no modification or augmentation can achieve comparative results while the GRS does little help to the in-domain Chinese word segmentation task.

5.4 Error Analysis

We collect and analyze the errors on the Medicine corpus from Sighan Bakeoff 2010 in light of the fact that the results are the worst among the four domains. We calculate accuracies of individual OOV words, where accuracies are simply treated as 0 or 1 for further counting, and categorize them according to their frequencies in the testing corpus. Statistics are shown in Figure 4. From the trendlines we can infer that in our proposed GRS more occurrences yield higher accuracy while common BLSTM models can rarely benefit from this. That conforms to the intuition of our model that can utilize correlation information of testing corpora. Our model thereupon performs better with the increase of the size of testing corpus as long as the OOV words appear more.

Although the trendline of our model is promising, there are some OOV words that occurs frequently but are wrongly segmented. Some examples are listed in Table 8. Errors involving

"肾脏"(kidney) and "维生素C"(vitamin C) are typical examples of the Combination Ambiguity, where there are some words containing "肾脏" such as "肾脏病学"(nephrology). Likewise, "维生素"(vitamin) is a frequent word that confuses our model. "甲型H1N1流感"(influenza A(H1N1)) reveals another severe problem that most CWS systems confront when processing the mix of Chinese characters and digits, punctuations or letters from other languages. The commonly used methods by treating consecutive digits or letters as one indeed boost the performance on corpora where most characters are Chinese. However, with the increase of characters other than Chinese, it is becoming a problem that should be reconsidered carefully.

OOV Word	English	Correct	Total
肾脏	kidney	15	39
甲型H1N1流感	influenza A (H1N1)	0	30
维生素C	vitamin C	2	23

Table 8: Some examples of wrongly segmented OOV words with high frequency.

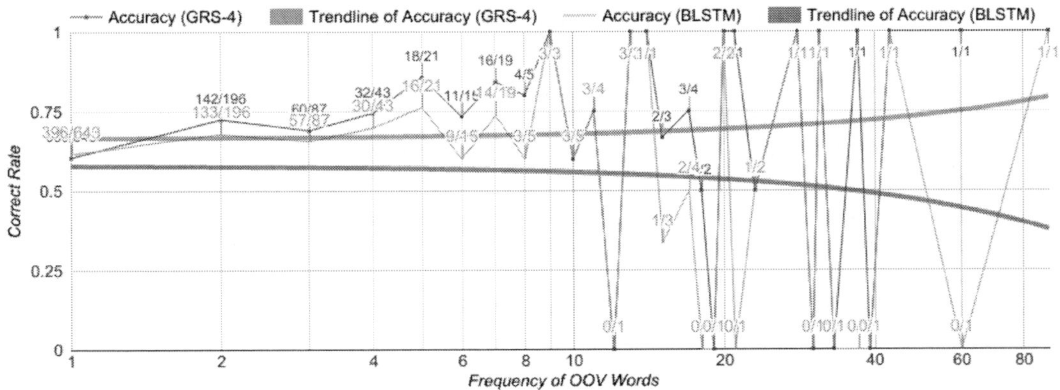

Figure 4: OOV word recognition accuracies on the Medicine corpus.

6 Related Work

Word segmentation has been pursued with considerable efforts in the Chinese NLP community. One mainstream method is regarding word segmentation task as a sequence labeling problem (Xue, 2003; Peng et al., 2004). Recently, researchers have tended to explore neural network based approaches (Collobert et al., 2011; Zheng et al., 2013; Qi et al., 2014) to reduce efforts of feature engineering. Pei et al. (2014) used a neural tensor model to capture the complicated interactions between tags and context characters. Experiments in his paper also show that bigram embeddings are of great benefit. To incorporate complicated combinations and long-term dependency information of the context characters, gated recursive model (Chen et al., 2015a) and LSTM model (Chen et al., 2015b) were used respectively. Moreover, Xu and Sun (2016) proposed a dependency-based gated recursive model which merges the benefits of the two models above. Coincidentally, Cai and Zhao (2016) and Zhang et al. (2016) both addressed the problem of lacking word-based features that previous neural CWS models have. Cai and Zhao (2016) proposed a novel gated combination neural network which thoroughly eliminates context windows and can utilize complete segmentation history. Zhang et al. (2016) proposed a transition-based neural model which replaces manually designed discrete features with neural features.

Domain adaption for Chinese word segmentation has been widely exploited before neural CWS models are proposed. Jiang et al. (2013) utilized the web text(160K Wikipedia) to improves seg-mentation accuracies on several domains. Zhang et al. (2014) studied type-supervised domain adaptation for Chinese segmentation by making use of domain-specific tag dictionaries and only unlabeled target domain data. Liu et al. (2014) proposed a variant CRF model to leverage both fully and partially annotated data transformed from different sources of free annotations consistently.

Some researches which focus on making use of unlabeled data for word segmentation also do help to domain adaption. Zhao and Kit (2008) and Zhang et al. (2013a) improved segmentation performance by mutual information between characters, collected from large unlabeled data. Li and Sun (2009) used punctuation information in a large raw corpus to learn a segmentation model, and achieve better recognition of OOV words. Sun and Xu (2011) explored several statistical features derived from both unlabeled data to help improve character-based word segmentation. Zhang et al. (2013b) proposed a semi-supervised approach that dynamically extracts representations of label distributions from both in-domain corpora and out-of-domain corpora.

7 Conclusion and Perspectives

In this paper, we propose a novel global recurrent structure to model dynamic boundary features and incorporate it in the BLSTM-based neural network model for Chinese Word Segmentation. The structure can capture correlations between characters, and thus is especially effective for segmenting OOV words and enhancing the performance of CWS on non-news domains.

The proposed global recurrent structure is not limited to the Chinese word segmentation task. It can be easily adapted to other sequence labeling problems that may benefit from the history information carried in the structure.

Although the structure is effective in this task, it's admittedly hard to train a stable model. As our future work, we would like to try some pretraining methods to handle this problem. And we plan to apply our method to other natural language processing tasks, such as Name Entity Recognition (NER). Also, the hybrid model is a great idea to try and we will do it later.

Acknowledgments

Our work is supported by National Natural Science Foundation of China (No.61370117 & No.61433015). The corresponding author of this paper is Houfeng Wang.

References

Adam L. Berger, Vincent J. Della Pietra, and Stephen A. Della Pietra. 1996. A maximum entropy approach to natural language processing. *Computational Linguistics* 22(1):39–71.

Deng Cai and Hai Zhao. 2016. Neural word segmentation learning for chinese. *CoRR* abs/1606.04300.

Baobao Chang and Dongxu Han. 2010. Enhancing domain portability of chinese segmentation model using chi-square statistics and bootstrapping. In *Proceedings of the 2010 Conference on Empirical Methods in Natural Language Processing*. Association for Computational Linguistics, pages 789–798.

Xinchi Chen, Xipeng Qiu, Chenxi Zhu, and Xuanjing Huang. 2015a. Gated recursive neural network for chinese word segmentation. In *Proceedings of the 53rd Annual Meeting of the Association for Computational Linguistics and the 7th International Joint Conference on Natural Language Processing (Volume 1: Long Papers)*. Association for Computational Linguistics, Beijing, China, pages 1744–1753.

Xinchi Chen, Xipeng Qiu, Chenxi Zhu, Shiyu Wu, and Xuanjing Huang. 2015b. Sentence modeling with gated recursive neural network. In *Proceedings of the 2015 Conference on Empirical Methods in Natural Language Processing*. Association for Computational Linguistics, Lisbon, Portugal, pages 793–798.

Ronan Collobert, Jason Weston, Léon Bottou, Michael Karlen, Koray Kavukcuoglu, and Pavel Kuksa. 2011. Natural language processing (almost) from scratch. *The Journal of Machine Learning Research* 999888:2493–2537.

Thomas Emerson. 2005. The second international chinese word segmentation bakeoff. In *Proceedings of the Second SIGHAN Workshop on Chinese Language Processing*. pages 123–133.

Haodi Feng, Kang Chen, Xiaotie Deng, and Weimin Zheng. 2004a. Accessor variety criteria for chinese word extraction. *Computational Linguistics, Volume 30, Number 1, March 2004* .

Haodi Feng, Kang Chen, Chunyu Kit, and Xiaotie Deng. 2004b. Unsupervised segmentation of chinese corpus using accessor variety. In *Natural Language Processing - IJCNLP 2004, First International JointConference, Hainan Island, China, March 22-24, 2004, Revised Selected Papers*. pages 694–703.

Alex Graves, Abdel rahman Mohamed, and Geoffrey E. Hinton. 2013. Speech recognition with deep recurrent neural networks. *CoRR* abs/1303.5778.

Alex Graves and Jürgen Schmidhuber. 2005. Framewise phoneme classification with bidirectional lstm and other neural network architectures. *Neural Networks* 18:602–610.

Wenbin Jiang, Meng Sun, Yajuan Lü, Yating Yang, and Qun Liu. 2013. Discriminative learning with natural annotations: Word segmentation as a case study. In *ACL*.

Diederik P. Kingma and Jimmy Ba. 2014. Adam: A method for stochastic optimization. *CoRR* abs/1412.6980.

John D. Lafferty, Andrew McCallum, and Fernando C. N. Pereira. 2001. Conditional random fields: Probabilistic models for segmenting and labeling sequence data. In *Proceedings of the Eighteenth International Conference on Machine Learning*. ICML '01, pages 282–289.

Guillaume Lample, Miguel Ballesteros, Sandeep Subramanian, Kazuya Kawakami, and Chris Dyer. 2016. Neural architectures for named entity recognition. In *HLT-NAACL*.

Zhongguo Li and Maosong Sun. 2009. Punctuation as implicit annotations for chinese word segmentation. *Computational Linguistics* 35:505–512.

Yijia Liu, Yue Zhang, Wanxiang Che, Ting Liu, and Fan Wu. 2014. Domain adaptation for crf-based chinese word segmentation using free annotations. In *EMNLP*.

Wenzhe Pei, Tao Ge, and Baobao Chang. 2014. Max-margin tensor neural network for chinese word segmentation. In *Proceedings of the 52nd Annual Meeting of the Association for Computational Linguistics (Volume 1: Long Papers)*. Association for Computational Linguistics, Baltimore, Maryland, pages 293–303.

Fuchun Peng, Fangfang Feng, and Andrew Mccallum. 2004. Chinese Segmentation and New Word Detection using Conditional Random Fields. In *Proceedings of COLING*. pages 562–571.

Yanjun Qi, Sujatha G. Das, Ronan Collobert, and Jason Weston. 2014. Deep learning for character-based information extraction. In *ECIR*.

Weiwei Sun and Jia Xu. 2011. Enhancing chinese word segmentation using unlabeled data. In *EMNLP*.

Ben Taskar, Vassil Chatalbashev, Daphne Koller, and Carlos Guestrin. 2005. Learning structured prediction models: a large margin approach. In *ICML*.

Jingjing Xu and Xu Sun. 2016. Dependency-based gated recursive neural network for chinese word segmentation. In *ACL*.

Nianwen Xue. 2003. Chinese Word Segmentation as Character Tagging. *Computational Linguistics* 8(1):29–48.

Shiwen Yu, Jianming Lu, Xuefeng Zhu, Huiming Duan, Shiyong Kang, Honglin Sun, Hui Wang, Qiang Zhao, and Weidong Zhan. 2001. Processing norms of modern chinese corpus. *Technical report* .

Longkai Zhang, Li Li, Zhengyan He, Houfeng Wang, and Ni Sun. 2013a. Improving chinese word segmentation on micro-blog using rich punctuations. In *ACL*.

Longkai Zhang, Houfeng Wang, Xu Sun, and Mairgup Mansur. 2013b. Exploring representations from unlabeled data with co-training for chinese word segmentation. In *EMNLP*.

Meishan Zhang, Yue Zhang, Wanxiang Che, and Ting Liu. 2014. Type-supervised domain adaptation for joint segmentation and pos-tagging. In *EACL*.

Meishan Zhang, Yue Zhang, and Guohong Fu. 2016. Transition-based neural word segmentation. In *ACL*.

Hai Zhao and Chunyu Kit. 2008. An empirical comparison of goodness measures for unsupervised chinese word segmentation with a unified framework. In *IJCNLP*.

Hongmei Zhao and Qiu Liu. 2010. The cips-sighan clp2010 chinese word segmentation backoff.

Xiaoqing Zheng, Hanyang Chen, and Tianyu Xu. 2013. Deep learning for Chinese word segmentation and POS tagging. In *Proceedings of the 2013 Conference on Empirical Methods in Natural Language Processing*. Association for Computational Linguistics, Seattle, Washington, USA, pages 647–657.

Information Bottleneck Inspired Method For Chat Text Segmentation

S Vishal[1,*], **Mohit Yadav**[2,*,$], **Lovekesh Vig**[1] and **Gautam Shroff**[1]
[1]TCS Research New Delhi, India
[2]University of Massachusetts, Amherst
s.vishal3@tcs.com, ymohit@cs.umass.edu, lovekesh.vig@tcs.com, gautam.shroff@tcs.com

Abstract

We present a novel technique for segmenting chat conversations using the information bottleneck method (Tishby et al., 2000), augmented with sequential continuity constraints. Furthermore, we utilize critical non-textual clues such as time between two consecutive posts and people mentions within the posts. To ascertain the effectiveness of the proposed method, we have collected data from public Slack conversations and Fresco, a proprietary platform deployed inside our organization. Experiments demonstrate that the proposed method yields an absolute (relative) improvement of as high as 3.23% (11.25%). To facilitate future research, we are releasing manual annotations for segmentation on public Slack conversations.

1 Introduction

The prolific upsurge in the amount of chat conversations has notably influenced the way people wield languages for conversations. Moreover, conversation platforms have now become prevalent for both personal and professional usage. For instance, in a large enterprise scenario, project managers can utilize these platforms for various tasks such as decision auditing and dynamic responsibility allocation (Joty et al., 2013). Logs of such conversations offer potentially valuable information for various other applications such as automatic assessment of possible collaborative work among people (Rebedea et al., 2011).

It is thus vital to invent effective segmentation methods that can seperate discussions into small granules of independent conversational snippets. By 'independent', we meant a segment should as much as possible be self-contained and discussing the same topic, such that a segment can be suggested if any similar conversation occurs again. As an outcome of this, various short text similarity methods can be employed directly. Segmentation can also potentially act as an empowering preprocessing step for various down-streaming tasks such as automatic summarization (Dias et al., 2007), text generation (Barzilay and Lee, 2004), information extraction (Allan, 2012), and conversation visualization (Liu et al., 2012). It is worth noting that chat segmentation presents a number of gruelling challenges such as, the informal nature of the text, the frequently short length of the posts and a significant proportion of irrelevant interspersed text (Schmidt and Stone).

Research in text segmentation has a long history going back to the earliest attempt of Kozima (1993). Since then many methods, including but not limited to, Texttiling (Hearst, 1997), Choi's segmentation (Choi, 2000), representation learning based on semantic embeddings (Alemi and Ginsparg, 2015), and topic models (Du et al., 2015a) have been presented. Albeit, very little research effort has been proposed for segmenting informal chat text. For instance, Schmidt and Stone have attempted to highlight the challenges with chat text segmentation, though they have not presented any algorithm specific to chat text.

The Information Bottleneck (IB) method has been successfully applied to clustering in the NLP domain (Slonim and Tishby, 2000). Specifically, IB attempts to balance the trade-off between accuracy and compression (or complexity) while clustering the target variable, given a joint probability distribution between the target variable and an ob-

---

* indicates that both authors contributed equally. $ indicates that the author was at TCS Research New-Delhi during the course of this work.

Proceedings of the The 8th International Joint Conference on Natural Language Processing, pages 194–203,
Taipei, Taiwan, November 27 – December 1, 2017 ©2017 AFNLP

served relevant variable. Similar to clustering, this paper interprets the task of text segmentation as a compression task with a constraint that allows only contiguous text snippets to be in a group.

The focus of this paper is to develop text segmentation methods for chat text utilizing the IB framework. In the process, this paper makes the following major contributions:

(i) We introduce an IB inspired objective function for the task of text segmentation.

(ii) We develop an agglomerative algorithm to optimize the proposed objective function that also respects the necessary sequential continuity constraint for text segmentation.

(iii) To the best of our knowledge, this paper is a first attempt that addresses segmentation for chat text and incorporates non-textual clues.

(iv) We have created a chat text segmentation dataset and releasing it for future research.

The remainder of this paper is organized as follows: we present a review of related literature in Section 2. Then, we formulate the text segmentation problem and define necessary notations in Section 3. Following this, we explain the proposed methodology in Section 4. Section 5 presents experiments and provides details on the dataset, experimental set-up, baselines, results, and effect of parameters. Finally, conclusions and potential directions for future work are outlined in Section 6.

2   Related Work

The IB method (Tishby et al., 2000) was originally introduced as a generalization of rate distortion theory which balances the tradeoff between the preservation of information about a relevance variable and the distortion of the target variable. Later on, similar to this work, a greedy bottom-up (agglomerative) IB based approach (Slonim and Tishby, 1999, 2000) has been successfully applied to NLP tasks such as document clustering.

Furthermore, the IB method has been widely studied for multiple machine learning tasks, including but not limited to, speech diarization (Vijayasenan et al., 2009), image segmentation (Bardera et al., 2009), image clustering (Gordon et al., 2003), and visualization (Kamimura, 2010). Particularly, similar to this paper, image segmentation has considered segmentation as the compression part of the IB based method. But, image segmentation does not involve continuity constraints as their application can abolish the exploitation of similarity within the image. Yet another similar attempt that utilizes information theoretic terms as an objective (only the first term of the IB approach) has been made for the task of text segmentation and alignment (Sun et al., 2006).

Broadly stating, a typical text segmentation method comprises of a method that: (a) consumes text representations for every independent text snippet, and (b) applies a search procedure for segmentation boundaries while optimizing objectives for segmentation. Here, we review literature of text segmentation by organizing them into 3 categories based on their focus: *Category1* - (a), *Category2* - (b), and *Category3* - both (a) and (b).

Category1 approaches utilize or benefit from a great amount of effort put in developing robust topic models that can model discourse in natural language texts (Brants et al., 2002). Recently, Du et al. (2013, 2015b) have proposed a hierarchical Bayesian model for unsupervised topic segmentation that integrates a point-wise boundary sampling algorithm used in Bayesian segmentation into a structured (ordering-based) topic model. For a more comprehensive view of classical work on topic models for text segmentation, we refer to Misra et al. (2009); Riedl and Biemann (2012). This work does not explore topic models and is left as a direction for future research.

Category2 approaches comprise of different search procedures proposed for the task of text segmentation, including but not limited to, divisive hierarchical clustering (Choi, 2000), dynamic programming (Kehagias et al., 2003), and graph based clustering (Pourvali and Abadeh, 2012; Glavas et al., 2016; Utiyama and Isahara, 2001). This work proposes an agglomerative IB based hierarchical clustering algorithm - an addition to the arsenal of the approaches that falls in this category.

Similar to the proposed method, *Category3* cuts across both of the above introduced dimensions of segmentation. Alemi and Ginsparg (2015) have proposed the use of semantic word embeddings and a relaxed dynamic programming procedure. We have also argued to utilize chat clues and introduced an IB based approach augmented with sequential continuity constraints. Yet another similar attempt has been made by Joty et al. (2013) in which they use topical and conversational clues and introduce an unsupervised random walk model for the task of text segmentation.

Beyond the above mentioned categorization, a significant amount of research effort has been put up in studying the evaluation metric for text segmentation (Pevzner and Hearst, 2002; Scaiano and Inkpen, 2012). Here, we make use of the classical and most widely utilized metric introduced by Beeferman et al. (1999). Also, there have been attempts to track topic boundaries for thread discussions (Zhu et al., 2008; Wang et al., 2008). While these methods look similar to the proposed method, they differ as they attempt to recover thread structure with respect to the topic level view of the discussions within a thread community.

The most similar direction of research to this work is on conversation trees (Louis and Cohen, 2015) and disentangling chat conversations (Elsner and Charniak, 2010). Both of these directions cluster independent posts leading to topic labelling and segmentation of these posts simultaneously. It is important to note that these methods do not have a sequential continuity constraint and consider lexical similarity even between long distant posts (Elsner and Charniak, 2011). Moreover, if these methods are applied only for segmentation then they are very likely to produce segments with relatively very smaller durations; as reflected in the ground truth annotations of correspondingly released dataset (Elsner and Charniak, 2008). It is worth noting that Elsner and Charniak (2010) have also advocated to utilize time gap and people mentions similar to the proposed method of this work.

3 Problem Description And Notations

Let C be an input chat text sequence $C = \{c_1, ..., c_i, ..., c_{|t|}\}$ of length $|C|$, where c_i is a text snippet such as a sentence or a post from chat text. In a chat scenario, text post c_i will have a corresponding time-stamp c_i^t. A segment or a subsequence can be represented as $C_{a:b} = \{c_a, ..., c_b\}$. A segmentation of C is defined as a segment sequence $S = \{s_1, ..., s_p\}$, where $s_j = C_{a_j:b_j}$ and $b_j + 1 = a_{j+1}$. Given an input text sequence C, the segmentation is defined as the task of finding the most probable segment sequence S.

4 Proposed Methodology

This section firstly presents the proposed IB inspired method for text segmentation that conforms to the necessary constraint of sequential continu-ity, in Section 4.1. Next, in Section 4.2, the proposed IB inspired method is augmented to incorporate important non-textual clues that arise in a chat scenario. More specifically, the time between two consecutive posts and people mentions within the posts are integrated into the proposed IB inspired approach for the text segmentation task.

4.1 IB Inspired Text Segmentation Algorithm

The IB introduces a set of relevance variables R which encapsulate meaningful information about C while compressing the data points (Slonim and Tishby, 2000). Similarly, we propose that a segment sequence S should also contain as much information as possible about R (i.e., maximize $I(R, S)$), constrained by mutual information between S and C (i.e., minimize $I(S, C)$). Here, C is a chat text sequence, following the notation introduced in the previous section. The IB objective can be achieved by maximizing the following:

$$F = I(R, S) - \frac{1}{\beta} \times I(S, C) \tag{1}$$

In other words, the above IB objective function attempts to balance a trade-off between the most informative segmentation of R and the most compact representation of C; where β is a constant parameter to control the relative importance.

Similar to Tishby et al. (2000), we model R as word clusters and optimize F in an agglomerative fashion, as explained in Algorithm 1. In simple words, the maximization of F boils down to agglomeratively merging an adjacent pair of posts that correspond to least value of d. In Algorithm 1, $p(\overline{s})$ is equal to $p(s_i) + p(s_{i+1})$ and $d(s_i, s_{i+1})$ is computed using the following definition:

$$d(s_i, s_{i+1}) = JSD[p(R|s_i), p(R|s_{i+1})] - \frac{1}{\beta} \times JSD[p(C|s_i), p(C|s_{i+1})] \tag{2}$$

Here, JSD indicates Jensen-Shannon-Divergence. The computation of R and $p(R, C)$ is explained later in Section 5.2. Stopping criterion for Algorithm 1 is $SC > \theta$, where SC is computed as follows:

$$SC = \frac{I(R, S)}{I(R, C)} \tag{3}$$

The value of SC is expected to decrease due to a relatively large dip in the value of $I(R, S)$ when

---

Algorithm 1: IB inspired text segmentation

Input	: Joint distribution: $p(R, C)$,
	Tradeoff parameter: β
Output	: Segmentation sequence: S

Initialization: $S \leftarrow C$

Calculate $\Delta F(s_i, s_{i+1}) = p(\overline{s}) \times d(s_i, s_{i+1}) \ \forall \ s_i \in S$

1 **while** *Stopping criterion is false* **do**
2     $\{i\} = argmin_{i'} \Delta F(s_{i'}, s_{i'+1})$;
3   Merge $\{s_i, s_{i+1}\} \Rightarrow \overline{s} \in S$;
4   Update $\Delta F(\overline{s}, s_{i-1})$ and $\Delta F(\overline{s}, s_{i+2})$;
5 **end**

---

more dissimilar clusters are merged. Therefore, SC provides strong clues to terminate the proposed IB approach. The inspiration behind this specific computation of SC has come from the fact that it has produced stable results when experimented with a similar task of speaker diarization (Vijayasenan et al., 2009). The value of θ is tuned by optimizing the performance over a validation dataset just like other hyper-parameters.

The IB inspired text segmentation algorithm (Algorithm 1) respects the sequential continuity constraint, as it considers merging only adjacent pairs (see step 2, 3, and 4 of Algorithm 1) while optimizing F; unlike the agglomerative IB clustering (Slonim and Tishby, 2000). As a result of this, the proposed IB based approach requires a limited number of involved computations, more precisely, linear in terms of number of text snippets.

4.2 Incorporating Non-Textual Clues

As mentioned above, we submit that non-textual clues (such as time between two consecutive posts and people mentions within the posts) are critical for segmenting chat text. To incorporate these two important clues, we augment Algorithm 1, developed in the previous section. More precisely, we modify d of Equation 2 to $\overline{d}$ as follows:

$$\overline{d}(s_i, s_{i+1}) = w_1 \times d(s_i, s_{i+1}) + w_2 \times (c_{a_{i+1}}^t - c_{b_i}^t) + w_3 \times ||s_i^p - s_{i+1}^p|| \tag{4}$$

Here, $c_{a_{i+1}}^t$, $c_{b_i}^t$ and s_i^p represent time-stamp of the first post of segment s_{i+1}, time-stamp of last post of segment s_i, and representation for poster information embedded in segment s_i, respectively. The s_i^p representation is computed as a bag of posters counting all the people mentioned in the

posts and posters themselves in a segment. w_1, w_2, w_3 are weights indicating the relative importance of distance terms computed for all three different clues. $||.||$ in Equation 4 indicates euclidean norm.

It is important to note that Algorithm 1 utilizes d of Equation 2 to represent textual dissimilarity between a pair of posts in order to achieve the optimal segment sequence S. Following the same intuition, $\overline{d}$ in Equation 4 measures weighted distances based not only on textual similarity but also based on information in time-stamps, posters and people mentioned. The intuition behind the second distance term in $\overline{d}$ is that if the time difference between two posts is small then they are likely to be in the same segment. Additionally, the third distance term in $\overline{d}$ is intended to merge segments that involve a higher number of common posters and people mentions. Following the same intuition, in addition to the changes in $\overline{d}$, we modify the stopping criterion as well while the rest stays the same as in Algorithm 1. The stopping criterion is defined as $SC > \theta$, where SC is as follows:

$$SC = w_1 \times \frac{I(R, S)}{I(R, C)} + w_2 \times \\ (1 - \frac{G(S)}{G_{max}}) + w_3 \times \frac{H(S)}{H_{max}} \tag{5}$$

Here, the $G(S)$ and $H(S)$ mentioned in Equation 5 are computed as follows:

$$G(S) = \sum_{s_i \in S} c_{b_i}^t - c_{a_i}^t \tag{6}$$

$$H(S) = \sum_{i=1}^{|S|} ||s_i^p - s_{i+1}^p|| \tag{7}$$

The first term in SC in Equation 5 is taken from the stopping criterion of Algorithm 1 and the remaining second and third terms are similarly derived. Both the second and third terms decrease as the cardinality of S is decreased and reflect analogous behaviour to the two introduced important clues. The first term computes the fraction of information contained in S about R, normalized by the information contained in C about R; similarly, the second term computes the fraction of time duration between segments normalized by total duration of chat text sequence (i.e. 1 - fraction of durations of all segments normalized by total duration), and the third term computes the sum of

	Slack	*Fresco*
# Threads	4	46
# Posts	9000	5000
# Segments	900	800
# Documents	73	73

Table 1: Statistics of the chat datasets.

inter segment distances in terms of poster information normalized by the maximum distance of similar terms (i.e. when each post is a segment).

5 Experiments

This section starts with a description of the datasets collected from the real world conversation platforms in Subsection 5.1. Later in Subsection 5.2, we explain the evaluation metric utilized in our experiments. Subsection 5.3 describes the meaningful baselines developed for a fair comparison with the proposed IB approach. Next in Subsections 5.4 and 5.5, we discuss the performance accomplished by the proposed approach on both of the collected datasets. Lastly, we analyse the stability of the proposed IB approach with respect to parameters β and θ in Subsection 5.6.

5.1 Dataset Description

We have collected chat text datasets, namely, *Slack* and *Fresco*, respectively from http://slackarchive.io/ and http://talk.fresco.me/. After that, we have manually annotated them for the text segmentation task. We have utilized the annotations done by 3 workers with problematic cases resolved by consensus. Datasets' statistics is mentioned in Table 1. The collected raw data was in the form of threads, which was later divided into segments. Further, we have created multiple documents where each document contains N continuous segments from the original threads. N was selected randomly between 5 and 15. 60% of these documents were used for tuning hyperparameters which include weights (w_1, w_2, w_3), θ, and β; and the remaining were used for testing.

A small portion of one of the documents from the *Slack* dataset is depicted in Figure 1(a). Here, manual annotations are marked by a bold black horizontal line, and also enumerated as 1), 2), and 3). Every text line is a post made by one of the users on the *Slack* platform during conversations. As mentioned above, in a chat scenario, every post has following three integral components:

1) poster (indicated by corresponding identity in Figure 1, from beginning till '-=[*says*'),
2) time-stamp (between '-=[*' and '*]=-)', and
3) textual content (after '*]=-:::* 'till end).
One must also notice that some of the posts also have people mentions within the posts (indicated as '<@USERID>' in Figure 1).

To validate the differences between the collected chat datasets and traditional datasets such as Choi's dataset (Choi, 2000), we computed the fraction of words occurring with a frequency less than a given word frequency, as shown in Figure 2. It is clearly evident from the Figure 2 that chat segmentation datasets have a significantly high proportion of less frequent words in comparison to the traditional text segmentation datasets. The presence of large infrequent words makes it hard for textual similarity methods to succeed as it will increase the proportion of out of vocabulary words (Gulcehre et al., 2016). Therefore, it becomes even more critical to utilize the non-textual clues while processing chat text.

5.2 Evaluation and Setup

For performance evaluation, we have employed P_k metric (Beeferman et al., 1999) which is widely utilized for evaluating the text segmentation task. A sliding window of fixed size k (usually half of the average of length of all the segments in the document) slides over the entire document from top to bottom. Both inter and intra segment errors for all posts k apart is calculated by comparing inferred and annotated boundaries.

We model the set of relevance variables R as word clusters estimated by utilizing agglomerative IB based document clustering (Slonim and Tishby, 2000) where posts are treated as relevance variables. Consequently, R comprises of informative word clusters about posts. Thus, each entry $p(r_i, c_j)$ in matrix $p(R, C)$ represents the joint probability of getting a word cluster r_i in post c_j. We calculate $p(r_i, c_j)$ simply by counting the common words in r_i and c_j and then normalizing.

5.3 Baseline Approaches

For comparisons, we have developed multiple baselines. In *Random*, 5 to 15 boundaries are inserted randomly. In case of *No Boundary*, the entire document is labelled as one segment. Next, we implemented *C-99* and *Dynamic Programming*, which are classical benchmarks for the text segmentation task. Another very simple and yet effec-

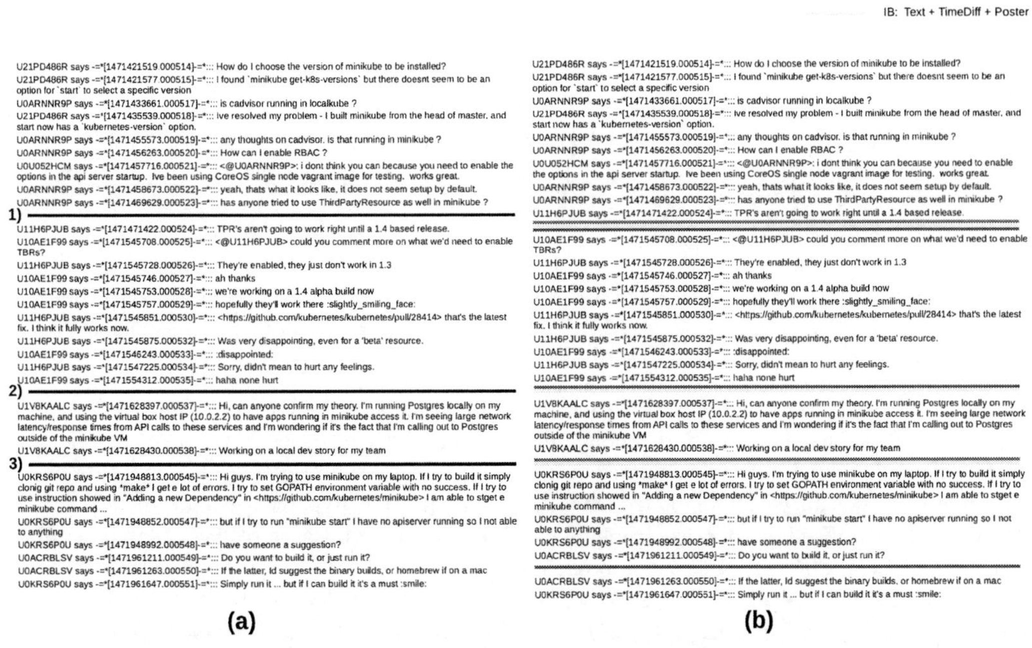

Figure 1: (a) Manually created ground truth for *Slack* public conversations. Black color lines represents segmentation boundaries. (b) Results obtained for multiple approaches. Text best read magnified.

Methods	Span of Weights	*Slack*	*Fresco*
Random	−	60.6	54
No Boundary	−	36.76	45
Average Time	−	32	35
C-99	−	35.18	37.75
Dynamic Programming	−	28.7	35
Encoder-Decoder Distance	−	29	38
LDA Distance	−	36	44
IB Variants:			
Text	$w_1 = 1, w_2 = 0, w_3 = 0$	33	42
TimeDiff	$w_1 = 0, w_2 = 1, w_3 = 0$	**26.75**	**34.25**
Poster	$w_1 = 0, w_2 = 0, w_3 = 1$	34.52	41.50
Text + TimeDiff	$\forall w \in \{w_1, w_2\}, w \in (0,1); w_3 = 0; w_1 + w_2 = 1$	**26.47**	**34.68**
Text + Poster	$\forall w \in \{w_1, w_3\}, w \in (0,1); w_2 = 0; w_1 + w_3 = 1$	**28.57**	38.21
Text+TimeDiff+Poster	$\forall w \in \{w_1, w_2, w_3\}, w \in (0,1); w_1 + w_2 + w_3 = 1$	**25.47**	**34.80**

Table 2: Performance evaluation: P_k metric [in terms of % error] for various methods. Lower is better.

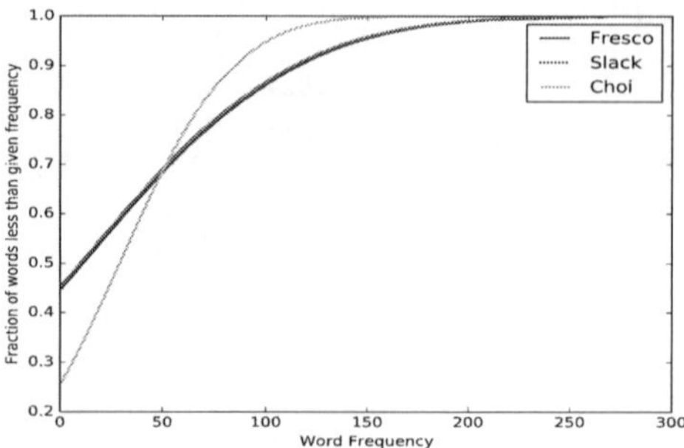

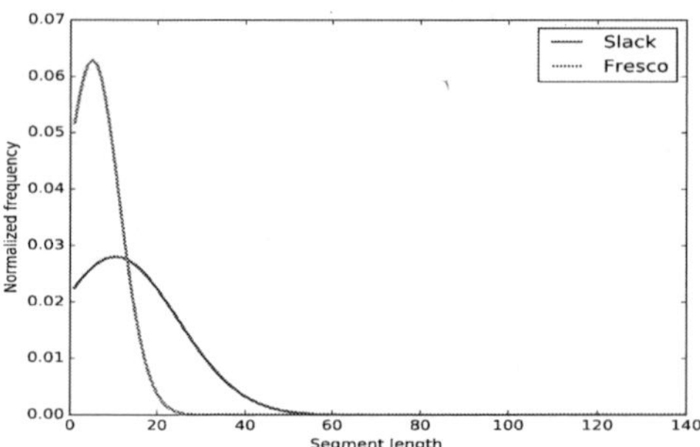

Figure 2: Fraction of words less than a given word frequency.

Figure 3: Normalized frequency distribution of segment length for both the collected chat datasets.

tive baseline *Average Time* is prepared, in which boundaries are inserted after a fixed amount of time has elapsed. Fixed time is calculated from a certain separate portion of our annotated dataset.

Next baseline utilized in our experiments is *Encoder-Decoder Distance*. In this approach, we have trained a sequence to sequence RNN encoder-decoder (Sutskever et al., 2014) utilizing 1.5 million posts from the publicly available *Slack* dataset excluding the labelled portion. The network comprises of 2 hidden layers and the hidden state dimension was set to 256 for each. The encoded representation was utilized and greedily merged in an agglomerative fashion using Euclidean distance. The stopping criterion for this approach was similar to the third term in Equation 5 corresponding to poster information. The optimization of hidden state dimension was computationally demanding hence left for further exploration in future. Similar to *Encoder-Decoder Distance*, we have developed *LDA Distance* where representations have come from a topic model (Blei et al., 2003) having 100 topics.

5.4 Quantitative Results

The results for all prepared baselines and variants of IB on both *Slack* and *Fresco* datasets are mentioned in Table 2. For both *Slack* and *Fresco* datasets, multiple variants of IB yield superior performance when compared against all the developed baselines. More precisely, for *Slack* dataset, 4 different variants of the proposed IB based method achieve higher performance with an absolute improvement of as high as **3.23%** and a relative improvement of **11.25%**, when compared against the baselines. In case of *Fresco* dataset, 3

different variants of the proposed method achieve superior performance but not as significantly in terms of absolute P_k value, as they do for the *Slack* dataset. We hypothesize that such a behaviour is potentially because of the lesser value of posts per segment for *Fresco* (5000/800=6.25) in comparison to *Slack* (9000/900=10). Also, note that just the time clue in IB framework performs best on *Fresco* dataset indicating that the relative importance of time clue will be higher for a dataset with smaller lengths of segments (i.e. low value of posts per segment). To validate our hypothesize further, we estimate the normalized frequency distribution of segment length (number of posts per segment) for both datasets, as shown in Figure 3.

It is worth noting that the obtained empirical results support the major hypothesis of this work. As variants of IB yield superior performance on both the datasets. Also, on incorporation of individual non-textual clues, superior improvements of 3.23% and 7.32% are observed from *Text* to *Text+TimeDiff* for *Slack* and *Fresco*, respectively; similarly, from *Text* to *Text+Poster* improvements of 4.43% and 3.79% are observed for *Slack* and *Fresco*, respectively. Further, the best performance is achieved for both the datasets on fusing both the non-textual clues indicating that clues are complementary as well.

5.5 Qualitative Results

Results obtained for multiple approaches, namely, *Average Time*, *IB:TimeDiff*, and *IB:Text+TimeDiff+Poster*, corresponding to a small portion of chat text placed in part (a) of Figure 1 are presented in part (b) of Figure 1. *Average Time* baseline (indicated by purple) managed to find three boundaries, albeit one of the boundary is significantly off, potentially due to the constraint of fixed time duration.

Similarly, the next *IB:TimeDiff* approach also manages to find first two boundaries correctly but fails to recover the third boundary. Results seem to indicate that the time clue is not very effective to reconstruct segmentation boundaries when segment length varies a lot within the document. Interestingly, the combination of all three clues as happens in the *IB:Text+TimeDiff+Poster* approach, yielded the best results as all of three segmentation boundaries in ground truth are recovered with high precision. Therefore, we submit that the incorporation of non-textual clues is critical to achieve superior results to segment chat text.

5.6 Effect Of Parameters

To analyse the behaviour of the proposed IB based methods, we compute the average performance metric P_k of *IB:Text* with respect to β and θ, over the test set of *Slack* dataset. Also, to facilitate the reproduction of results, we mention optimal values of all the parameters for all the variants of the proposed IB approach in Table 5.5.

Figure 4 shows the behaviour of the average of performance evaluation metric P_k over the test set of *Slack* dataset with respect to hyper-parameter β. As mentioned above also, the parameter β represents a trade-off between the preserved amount of information and the level of compression. It is clearly observable that the optimal value of β does not lie on extremes indicating the importance of both the terms (as in Equation 1) of the proposed IB method. The coefficient of the second term (i.e. $\frac{1}{\beta}$ equals to 10^{-3}) is smaller. One could interpret the behaviour of thr second term as a regularization term because $\frac{1}{\beta}$ controls the complexity of the learnt segment sequence S. Furthermore, optimal values in Table 5.5 for variants with fusion of two or more clues indicate complementary and relative importance of the studied non-textual clues.

The average performance evaluation metric P_k over test set of the *Slack* dataset with respect to hyper-parameter θ is depicted in Figure 5. Figure 5 makes the appropriateness of the stopping criterion clearly evident. Initially, the average of P_k value decreases as more coherent posts are merged and continues to decrease till it is less than a particular value of θ. After that, the average of P_k value starts increasing potentially due to the merging of

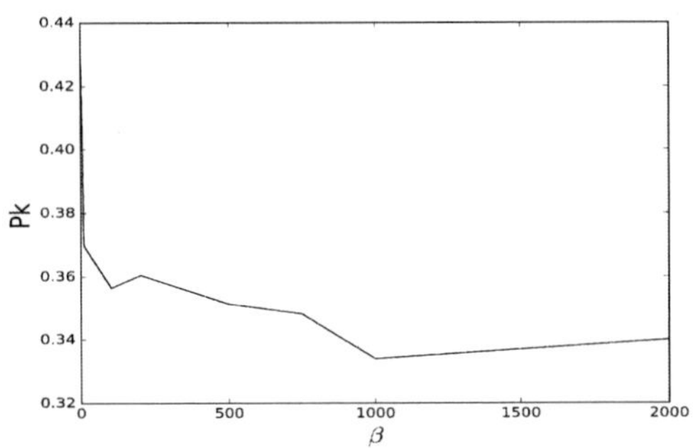

Figure 4: Average evaluation metric P_k over *Slack* dataset with respect to hyper-parameter β.

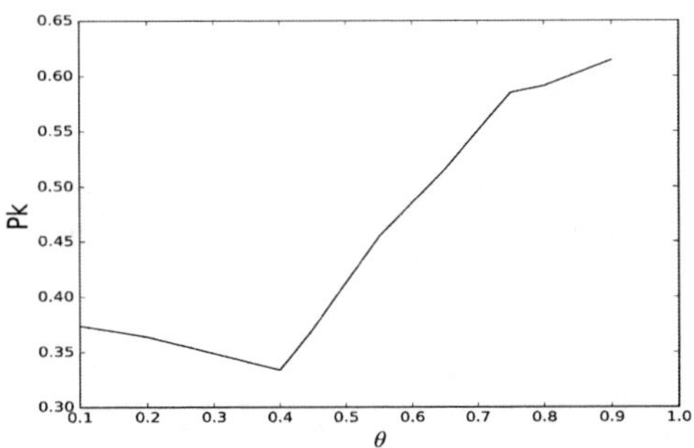

Figure 5: Average evaluation metric P_k over *Slack* dataset with respect to hyper-parameter θ.

more dissimilar segments. The optimal values of θ varies significantly from one variant to another requiring a mandatory tuning over the validation dataset, as mentioned in Table 5.5, for all *IB* variants proposed in this work.

6 Discussion And Future Work

We started by highlighting the increasing importance of efficient methods to process chat text, in particular for text segmentation. We have collected and introduced datasets for the same. Our introduction of chat text datasets has enabled us to explore segmentation approaches that are specific to chat text. Further, our results demonstrate that the proposed IB method yields an absolute improvement of as high as **3.23%**. Also, a significant boost (**3.79%-7.32%**) in performance is observed on incorporation of non-textual clues indicating their criticality. In future, it will be interesting to investigate the possibility of incorporat-

IB Variants:	Slack			Fresco		
	β	(w_1, w_2, w_3)	θ	β	(w_1, w_2, w_3)	θ
Text	1000	(1,0,0)	0.4	1000	(1,0,0)	0.5
TimeDiff	750	(0,1,0)	0.9	750	(0,1,0)	0.9
Poster	750	(0,0,1)	0.09	750	(0,0,1)	0.1
Text+TimeDiff	750	(0.3,0.7,0)	0.75	750	(0.3,0.7,0)	0.75
Text+Poster	750	(0.1,0,0.9)	0.2	∞	(0.3,0,0.7)	0.2
Text+TimeDiff+Poster	750	(0.24,0.58,0.18)	0.65	750	(0.10,0.63,0.27)	0.65

Table 3: Optimal values of parameters corresponding to results obtained by IB variants in Table 2.

ing semantic word embeddings in the proposed IB method (Alemi and Ginsparg, 2015).

References

Alexander A Alemi and Paul Ginsparg. 2015. Text segmentation based on semantic word embeddings. *arXiv preprint arXiv:1503.05543*.

James Allan. 2012. *Topic detection and tracking: event-based information organization*, volume 12. Springer Science & Business Media.

Anton Bardera, Jaume Rigau, Imma Boada, Miquel Feixas, and Mateu Sbert. 2009. Image segmentation using information bottleneck method. *IEEE Transactions on Image Processing*, 18(7):1601–1612.

Regina Barzilay and Lillian Lee. 2004. Catching the drift: Probabilistic content models, with applications to generation and summarization. *arXiv preprint arXiv: 0405039*.

Doug Beeferman, Adam Berger, and John Lafferty. 1999. Statistical models for text segmentation. *Machine Learning*, 34(1-3):177–210.

David M Blei, Andrew Y Ng, and Michael I Jordan. 2003. Latent dirichlet allocation. *Journal of machine Learning research*, 3(Jan):993–1022.

Thorsten Brants, Francine Chen, and Ioannis Tsochantaridis. 2002. Topic-based document segmentation with probabilistic latent semantic analysis. In *Proceedings of the Eleventh International Conference on Information and Knowledge Management*, CIKM '02, pages 211–218.

Freddy Y. Y. Choi. 2000. Advances in domain independent linear text segmentation. In *Proceedings of the 1st North American Chapter of the Association for Computational Linguistics Conference*, pages 26–33.

Gaël Dias, Elsa Alves, and José Gabriel Pereira Lopes. 2007. Topic segmentation algorithms for text summarization and passage retrieval: An exhaustive evaluation. In *Proceedings of the 22Nd National Conference on Artificial Intelligence - Volume 2*, AAAI'07, pages 1334–1339. AAAI Press.

Lan Du, Wray L. Buntine, and Mark Johnson. 2015a. Topic segmentation with a structured topic model. In *HLT-NAACL*. The Association for Computational Linguistics.

Lan Du, John K Pate, and Mark Johnson. 2013. Topic segmentation with a structured topic model. In *Proceedings of the North American Chapter of the Association for Computational Linguistics Conference*, pages 190–200.

Lan Du, John K Pate, and Mark Johnson. 2015b. Topic segmentation with an ordering-based topic model. In *Proceedings of the Twenty-Ninth AAAI Conference on Artificial Intelligence*, pages 2232–2238.

Micha Elsner and Eugene Charniak. 2008. You talking to me? a corpus and algorithm for conversation disentanglement. pages 834–842.

Micha Elsner and Eugene Charniak. 2010. Disentangling chat. *Computation Linguistics*, 36:389–409.

Micha Elsner and Eugene Charniak. 2011. Disentangling chat with local coherence models. In *Proceedings of the 49th Annual Meeting of the Association for Computational Linguistics: Human Language Technologies - Volume 1*, pages 1179–1189.

Goran Glavas, Federico Nanni, and Simone Paolo Ponzetto. 2016. Unsupervised text segmentation using semantic relatedness graphs. In *Proceedings of the Fifth Joint Conference on Lexical and Computational Semantics (*SEM 2016)*, pages 125–130.

Shiri Gordon, Hayit Greenspan, and Jacob Goldberger. 2003. Applying the information bottleneck principle to unsupervised clustering of discrete and continuous image representations. In *Proceedings of the Ninth IEEE International Conference on Computer Vision - Volume 2*, ICCV '03, pages 370–, Washington, DC, USA. IEEE Computer Society.

Caglar Gulcehre, Sungjin Ahn, Ramesh Nallapati, Bowen Zhou, and Yoshua Bengio. 2016. Pointing the unknown words. *arXiv preprint arXiv:1603.08148*.

Marti A Hearst. 1997. Texttiling: Segmenting text into multi-paragraph subtopic passages. *Computational linguistics*, 23(1):33–64.

Shafiq Joty, Giuseppe Carenini, and Raymond T Ng. 2013. Topic segmentation and labeling in asynchronous conversations. *Journal of Artificial Intelligence Research*, 47:521–573.

Ryotaro Kamimura. 2010. Information-theoretic enhancement learning and its application to visualization of self-organizing maps. *Neurocomputing*, 73(13):2642–2664.

Athanasios Kehagias, Fragkou Pavlina, and Vassilios Petridis. 2003. Linear text segmentation using a dynamic programming algorithm. In *Proceedings of the tenth conference on European chapter of the Association for Computational Linguistics-Volume 1*, pages 171–178. Association for Computational Linguistics.

Hideki Kozima. 1993. Text segmentation based on similarity between words. In *Proceedings of the 31st Annual Meeting on Association for Computational Linguistics*, ACL '93, pages 286–288.

Shixia Liu, Michelle X Zhou, Shimei Pan, Yangqiu Song, Weihong Qian, Weijia Cai, and Xiaoxiao Lian. 2012. Tiara: Interactive, topic-based visual text summarization and analysis. *ACM Transactions on Intelligent Systems and Technology (TIST)*, 3(2):25.

Annie Louis and Shay B. Cohen. 2015. Conversation trees: A grammar model for topic structure in forums. In *Proceedings of the Empirical Methods on Natural Language Processing*, pages 1543–1553. The Association for Computational Linguistics.

Hemant Misra, François Yvon, Joemon M. Jose, and Olivier Cappe. 2009. Text segmentation via topic modeling: An analytical study. In *Proceedings of the 18th ACM Conference on Information and Knowledge Management*, CIKM '09, pages 1553–1556.

Lev Pevzner and Marti A Hearst. 2002. A critique and improvement of an evaluation metric for text segmentation. *Computational Linguistics*, 28:19–36.

Mohsen Pourvali and Ph D Mohammad Saniee Abadeh. 2012. A new graph based text segmentation using wikipedia for automatic text summarization. *Editorial Preface*, 3(1).

Traian Rebedea, Mihai Dascalu, Stefan Trausan-Matu, Gillian Armitt, and Costin Chiru. 2011. Automatic assessment of collaborative chat conversations with polycafe. In *European Conference on Technology Enhanced Learning*, pages 299–312. Springer.

Martin Riedl and Chris Biemann. 2012. Text segmentation with topic models. In *Journal for Language Technology and Computational Linguistics*, volume 27.1, pages 47–69.

Martin Scaiano and Diana Inkpen. 2012. Getting more from segmentation evaluation. In *Proceedings of the 2012 conference of the North American Chapter of the Association for Computational Linguistics: Human Language Technologies*, pages 362–366. Association for Computational Linguistics.

Alan P Schmidt and Trevor KM Stone. . Detection of topic change in irc chat logs. *http://www.trevorstone.org/school/ircsegmentation.pdf*.

Noam Slonim and Naftali Tishby. 1999. Agglomerative information bottleneck. In *Advances in Neural Information Processing Systems*, pages 617–623.

Noam Slonim and Naftali Tishby. 2000. Document clustering using word clusters via the information bottleneck method. In *Proceedings of the 23rd annual international ACM SIGIR conference on Research and development in information retrieval*, pages 208–215. ACM.

Bingjun Sun, Ding Zhou, Hongyuan Zha, and John Yen. 2006. Multi-task text segmentation and alignment based on weighted mutual information. In *Proceedings of the 15th ACM International Conference on Information and Knowledge Management*, CIKM '06, pages 846–847.

Ilya Sutskever, Oriol Vinyals, and Quoc V Le. 2014. Sequence to sequence learning with neural networks. In *Advances in neural information processing systems*, pages 3104–3112.

Naftali Tishby, Fernando C. N. Pereira, and William Bialek. 2000. The information bottleneck method. *arXiv preprint arXiv: 0004057*.

Masao Utiyama and Hitoshi Isahara. 2001. A statistical model for domain-independent text segmentation. In *Proceedings of the 39th Annual Meeting on Association for Computational Linguistics*, ACL '01, pages 499–506.

Deepu Vijayasenan, Fabio Valente, and Hervé Bourlard. 2009. An information theoretic approach to speaker diarization of meeting data. *IEEE Transactions on Audio, Speech, and Language Processing*, 17(7):1382–1393.

Yi-Chia Wang, Mahesh Joshi, William W. Cohen, and Carolyn Penstein Ros. 2008. Recovering implicit thread structure in newsgroup style conversations. In *Proceedings of The International Conference on Weblogs and Social Media*, pages 152–160. The AAAI Press.

Mingliang Zhu, Weiming Hu, and Ou Wu. 2008. Topic detection and tracking for threaded discussion communities. In *Web Intelligence and Intelligent Agent Technology, 2008. WI-IAT'08. IEEE/WIC/ACM International Conference on*, volume 1, pages 77–83. IEEE.

Distributional Modeling on a Diet:
One-shot Word Learning from Text Only

Su Wang♠   **Stephen Roller♣**   **Katrin Erk♠**
♠Department of Linguistics, ♣Department of Computer Science
The University of Texas at Austin
shrekwang@utexas.edu
roller@cs.utexas.edu, katrin.erk@mail.utexas.edu

Abstract

We test whether distributional models can do one-shot learning of definitional properties from text only. Using Bayesian models, we find that first learning overarching structure in the known data, regularities in textual contexts and in properties, helps one-shot learning, and that individual context items can be highly informative. Our experiments show that our model can learn properties from a single exposure when given an informative utterance.

1 Introduction

When humans encounter an unknown word in text, even with a single instance, they can often infer approximately what it means, as in this example from Lazaridou et al. (2014):

> We found a cute, hairy *wampimuk* sleeping behind the tree.

People who hear this sentence typically guess that a wampimuk is an animal, or even that it is a mammal. Distributional models, which describe the meaning of a word in terms of its observed contexts (Turney and Pantel, 2010), have been suggested as a model for how humans learn word meanings (Landauer and Dumais, 1997). However, distributional models typically need hundreds of instances of a word to derive a high-quality representation for it, while humans can often infer a passable meaning approximation from one sentence only (as in the above example). This phenomenon is known as *fast mapping* (Carey and Bartlett, 1978), Our primary modeling objective in this paper is to explore a plausible model for fast-mapping learning from textual context.

While there is preliminary evidence that fast mapping can be modeled distributionally (Lazaridou et al., 2016), it is unclear what enables it.

How do humans infer word meanings from so little data? This question has been studied for *grounded* word learning, when the learner perceives an object in non-linguistic context that corresponds to the unknown word. The literature emphasizes the importance of learning general knowledge or overarching structure, which we define as the information that is learned by accumulation across concepts (e.g. regularities in property co-occurrence), across all concepts (Kemp et al., 2007), In grounded word learning, overarching structure that has been proposed includes knowledge about which properties. For example knowledge about which properties are most important to object naming (Smith et al., 2002; Colunga and Smith, 2005), or a taxonomy of concepts (Xu and Tenenbaum, 2007).

In this paper we study models for fast mapping in word learning[1] from textual context alone, using probabilistic distributional models. Our task differs from the grounded case in that we do not perceive any object labeled by the unknown word. In that context, learning *word meaning* means learning the associated definitional properties and their weights (see Section 3). For the sake of interpretability, we focus on learning definitional properties We ask what kinds of overarching structure in distributional contexts and in properties will be helpful for one-shot word learning.

We focus on learning from syntactic context. Distributional representations of syntactic context are directly interpretable as selectional constraints, which in manually created resources are typically characterized through high-level taxonomy classes (Kipper-Schuler, 2005; Fillmore et al., 2003). So they should provide good evidence for

---

[1]In this paper, we interchangeably use the terms *unknown word* and *unknown concept*, as we learn properties, and properties belong to concepts rather than words, and we learn them from text, where we observe words rather than concepts.

Proceedings of the The 8th International Joint Conference on Natural Language Processing, pages 204–213,
Taipei, Taiwan, November 27 – December 1, 2017 ©2017 AFNLP

the meaning of role fillers. Also, it has been shown that selectional constraints can be learned distributionally (Erk et al., 2010; Ó Séaghdha and Korhonen, 2014; Ritter et al., 2010). However, our point will not be that syntax is needed for fast word learning, but that it helps to observe overarching structure, with syntactic context providing a clear test bed.

We test two types of overarching structure for their usefulness in fast mapping. First, we hypothesize that it is helpful to learn about commonalities among context items, which enables mapping from contexts to properties. For example the syntactic contexts *eat-dobj* and *cook-dobj* should prefer similar targets: things that are cooked are also things that are eaten (Hypothesis **H1**).

The second hypothesis is that it will be useful to learn co-occurrence patterns between properties. That is, we hypothesize that in learning an entity is a `mammal`, we may also infer it is `four-legged` (Hypothesis **H2**).

We do not intent to make *strong* cognitive claims, for which additional experimentation will be in order, and we leave this for future work. This work sets its goal on building a plausible computational model that models human fast-mapping in learning (i) well from limited grounded data, (ii) effectively from only one instance.

2 Background

Fast mapping and textual context. Fast mapping (Carey and Bartlett, 1978) is the human ability to construct provisional word meaning representations after one or few exposures. An important reason for why humans can do fast mapping is that they acquire overarching structure that constrains learning (Smith et al., 2002; Colunga and Smith, 2005; Kemp et al., 2007; Xu and Tenenbaum, 2007; Maas and Kemp, 2009). In this paper, we ask what forms of overarching structure will be useful for text-based word learning.

Lazaridou et al. (2014) consider fast mapping for grounded word learning, mapping image data to distributional representations, which is in a way the mirror image of our task. Lazaridou et al. (2016) were the first to explore fast mapping for text-based word learning, using an extension to word2vec with both textual and visual features. However, they model the unknown word simply by averaging the vectors of known words in the sentence, and do not explore what types of knowl-

edge enable fast mapping.

Definitional properties. Feature norms are definitional properties collected from human participants. Feature norm datasets are available from McRae et al. (2005) and Vigliocco et al. (2004). In this paper we use feature norms as our target representations of word meaning. There are several recent approaches that learn to map distributional representations to feature norms (Johns and Jones, 2012; Rubinstein et al., 2015; Făgărăşan et al., 2015; Herbelot and Vecchi, 2015a). We also map distributional information to feature norms, but we do it based on a single textual instance (one-shot learning).

In the current paper we use the **Quantified McRae (QMR)** dataset (Herbelot and Vecchi, 2015b), which extends the McRae et al. (2005) feature norms by ratings on the proportion of category members that have a property, and the **Animal** dataset (Herbelot, 2013), which is smaller but has the same shape. For example, *most* alligators are dangerous. The quantifiers are given probabilistic interpretations, so if *most* alligators are dangerous, the probability for a random alligator to be dangerous would be 0.95. This makes this dataset a good fit for our probabilistic distributional model. We discuss QMR and the Animal data further in Section 4.

Bayesian models in lexical semantics. We use Bayesian models for the sake of interpretability and because the existing definitional property datasets are small. The Bayesian models in lexical semantics that are most related to our approach are Dinu and Lapata (2010), who represent word meanings as distributions over latent topics that approximate senses, and Andrews et al. (2009) and Roller and Schulte im Walde (2013), who use multi-modal extensions of Latent Dirichlet Allocation (LDA) models (Blei et al., 2003) to represent co-occurrences of textual context and definitional features. Ó Séaghdha (2010) and Ritter et al. (2010) use Bayesian approaches to model selectional preferences.

3 Models

In this section we develop a series of models to test our hypothesis that acquiring general knowledge is helpful to word learning, in particular knowledge about similarities between context items (H1) and co-occurrences between properties (H2). The count-based model will implement neither hypothesis, while the bimodal topic model will implement both. To test the hypotheses separately, we employ two clustering approaches via Bernoulli Mixtures, which we use as extensions to the count-based model and bimodal topic model.

3.1 The Count-based Model

Independent Bernoulli condition. Let Q be a set of definitional properties, C a set of concepts that the learner knows about, and V a vocabulary of context items. For most of our models, context items $w \in V$ will be predicate-role pairs such as *eat-dobj*. The task is determine properties that apply to an unknown concept $u \notin C$. Any concept $c \in C$ is associated with a vector $\mathbf{c}_{\text{Ind}}$ (where "Ind" stands for "independent Bernoulli probabilities") of $|Q|$ probabilities, where the i-th entry of $\mathbf{c}_{\text{Ind}}$ is the probability that an instance of concept c would have property q_i. These probabilities are independent Bernoulli probabilities. For instance, $\mathbf{alligator}_{\text{Ind}}$ would have an entry of 0.95 for `dangerous`. An *instance* $\underline{\mathbf{c}} \in \{0,1\}^{|Q|}$ of a concept $c \in C$ is a vector of zeros and ones drawn from $\mathbf{c}_{\text{Ind}}$, where an entry of 1 at position i means that this instance has the property q_i.

The model proceeds in two steps. First it learns property probabilities for context items $w \in V$. The model observes instances $\underline{\mathbf{c}}$ occurring textually with context item w, and learns property probabilities for w, where the probability that w has for a property q indicates the probability that w would appear as a context item with an instance that has property q. In the second step the model uses the acquired context item representations to learn property probabilities for an unknown concept u. When u appears with w, the context item w "imagines" an instance (samples it from its property probabilities), and uses this instance to update the property probabilities of u. Instead of making point estimates, the model represents its uncertainty about the probability of a property through a Beta distribution, a distribution over Bernoulli probabilities. As a Beta distribution is characterized by two parameters α and β, we associate each context item $w \in V$ with vectors $\mathbf{w}^\alpha \in \mathbb{R}^{|Q|}$ and $\mathbf{w}^\beta \in \mathbb{R}^{|Q|}$, where the i-th α and β values are the parameters of the Beta distribution for property q_i. When an instance $\underline{\mathbf{c}}$ is observed with context item w, we do a Bayesian update on w simply as

$$\begin{aligned}\mathbf{w}^\alpha &= \mathbf{w}^\alpha + \underline{\mathbf{c}} \\ \mathbf{w}^\beta &= \mathbf{w}^\beta + (1 - \underline{\mathbf{c}})\end{aligned} \qquad (1)$$

because the Beta distribution is the conjugate prior of the Bernoulli. To draw an instance from w, we draw it from the predictive posterior probabilities of its Beta distributions, $\mathbf{w}_{\text{Ind}} = \mathbf{w}^\alpha / (\mathbf{w}^\alpha + \mathbf{w}^\beta)$.

Likewise, we associate an unknown concept u with vectors $\mathbf{u}^\alpha$ and $\mathbf{u}^\beta$. When the model observes u in the context of w, it draws an instance from $\mathbf{w}_{\text{Ind}}$, and performs a Bayesian update as in (1) on the vectors associated with u. After training, the property probabilities for u are again the posterior predictive probabilities $\mathbf{u}_{\text{Ind}} = \mathbf{u}^\alpha / (\mathbf{u}^\alpha + \mathbf{u}^\beta)$. The model can be used for multi-shot learning and one-shot learning in the same way.

Multinomial condition. We also test a multinomial variant of the count-based model, for greater comparability with the LDA model below. Here, the concept representation $\mathbf{c}_{\text{Mult}}$ is a multinomial distribution over the properties in Q. (That is, all the properties compete in this model.) An instance of concept c is now a single property, drawn from c's multinomial. The representation of a context item w, and also the representation of the unknown concept u, is a Dirichlet distribution with $|Q|$ parameters. Bayesian update of the representation of w based on an occurrence with c, and likewise Bayesian update of the representation of u based on an occurrence with w, is straightforward again, as the Dirichlet distribution is the conjugate prior of the multinomial.

The two count-based models do not implement either of our two hypotheses. They compute separate selectional constraints for each context item, and do not attend to co-occurrences between properties. In the experiments below, the count-based models will be listed as **Count Independent** and **Count Multinomial**.

3.2 The Bimodal Topic Model

We use an extension of LDA (Blei et al., 2003) to implement our hypotheses on the usefulness of overarching structure, both commonalities in selectional constraints across predicates, and co-occurrence of properties across concepts. In particular, we build on Andrews et al. (2009) in using a *bimodal topic model*, in which a single topic simultaneously generates both a context item and a property. We further build on Dinu and Lapata (2010) in having a "pseudo-document" for each concept c to represent its observed occurrences. In our case, this pseudo-document contains pairs of a context item $w \in V$ and a property $q \in Q$,

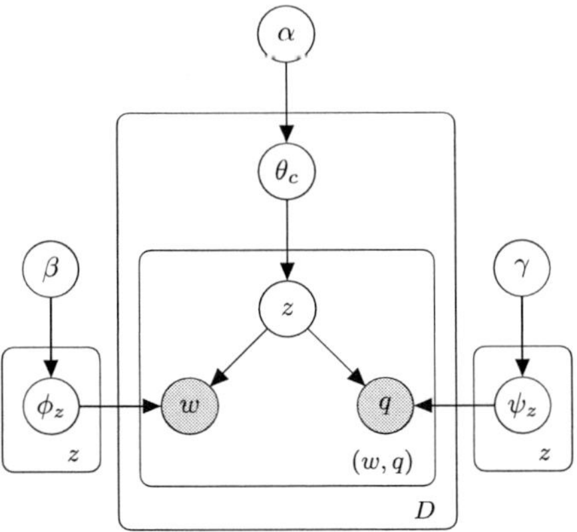

Figure 1: Plate diagram for the Bimodal Topic Model (bi-TM)

meaning that w has been observed to occur with an instance of c that had q.

The generative story is as follows. For each known concept c, draw a multinomial θ_c over topics. For each topic z, draw a multinomial ϕ_z over context items $w \in V$, and a multinomial ψ_z over properties $q \in Q$. To generate an entry for c's pseudo-document, draw a topic $z \sim Mult(\theta_c)$. Then, from z, simultaneously draw a context item from ϕ_z and a property from ψ_z. Figure 1 shows the plate diagram for this model.

To infer properties for an unknown concept u, we create a pseudo-document for u containing just the observed context items, no properties, as those are not observed. From this pseudo-document d_u we infer the topic distribution θ_u. Then the probability of a property q given d_u is

$$P(q|d_u) = \sum_z P(z|\theta_u)P(q|\psi_z) \qquad (2)$$

For the one-shot condition, where we only observe a single context item w with u, this simplifies to

$$P(q|w) = \sum_z P(z|w)P(q|\psi_z) \qquad (3)$$

We refer to this model as **bi-TM** below. The topics of this model implement our hypothesis H1 by grouping context items that tend to occur with the same concepts and the same properties. The topics also implement our hypothesis H2 by grouping properties that tend to occur with the same concepts and the same context items. By using multinomials ψ_z it makes the simplifying assumption that all properties compete, like the Count Multinomial model above.

3.3 Bernoulli Mixtures

With the Count models, we investigate word learning without any overarching structures. With the bi-TMs, we investigate word learning with both types of overarching structures at once. In order to evaluate each of the two hypotheses separately, we use clustering with Bernoulli Mixture models of either the context items or the properties.

A Bernoulli Mixture model (Juan and Vidal, 2004) assumes that a population of m-dimensional binary vectors $\mathbf{x}$ has been generated by a set of mixture components K, each of which is a vector of m Bernoulli probabilities:

$$p(\mathbf{x}) = \sum_{k=1}^{|K|} p(k)p(\mathbf{x}|k) \qquad (4)$$

A Bernoulli Mixture can represent co-occurrence patterns between the m random variables it models without assuming competition between them.

To test the effect of modeling *cross-predicate selectional constraints*, we estimate a Bernoulli Mixture model from n instances $\underline{\mathbf{w}}$ for each $w \in V$, sampled from $\mathbf{w}_{\text{Ind}}$ (which is learned as in the Count Independent model). Given a Bernoulli Mixture model of $|K|$ components, we then assign each context item w to its closest mixture component as follows. Say the instances of w used to estimate the Bernoulli Mixture were $\{\underline{\mathbf{w}}_1, \ldots, \underline{\mathbf{w}}_n\}$, then we assign w to the component

$$k_w = \text{argmax}_k \sum_{j=1}^{n} p(k|\underline{\mathbf{w}}_j) \qquad (5)$$

We then re-train the representations of context items in the Count Multinomial condition, treating each occurrence of c with context w as an occurrence of c with k_w. This yields a Count Multinomial model called **Count BernMix H1**.

To test the effect of modeling *property co-occurrences*, we estimate a $|K|$-component Bernoulli Mixture model from n instances of each known concept $c \in C$, sampled from $\mathbf{c}_{\text{Ind}}$. We then represent each concept c by a vector $\mathbf{c}_{\text{Mult}}$, a multinomial with $|K|$ parameters, as follows. Say the instances of c used to estimate the Bernoulli Mixture were $\{\underline{\mathbf{c}}_1, \ldots, \underline{\mathbf{c}}_n\}$, then the k-th entry in $\mathbf{c}_{\text{Mult}}$ is the average probability, over all $\underline{\mathbf{c}}_i$, of being generated by component k:

$$\mathbf{c}_k = \frac{1}{n} \sum_{j=1}^{n} p(k|\underline{\mathbf{c}}_j) \qquad (6)$$

This can be used as a Count Multinomial model where the entries in $\mathbf{c}_{\text{Mult}}$ stand for Bernoulli Mixture components rather than individual properties. We refer to it as **Count BernMix H2**.[2]

Finally, we extend the bi-TM with the H2 Bernoulli Mixture in the same way as a Count Multinomial model, and list this extension as **bi-TM BernMix H2**. While the bi-TM already implements both H1 and H2, its assumption of competition between all properties is simplistic, and bi-TM BernMix H2 tests whether lifting this assumption will yield a better model. We do not extend the bi-TM with the H1 Bernoulli Mixture, as the assumption of competition between context items that the bi-TM makes is appropriate.

4 Data and Experimental Setup

Definitional properties. As we use probabilistic models, we need probabilities of properties applying to concept instances. So the QMR dataset (Herbelot and Vecchi, 2015b) is ideally suited. QMR has 532 concrete noun concepts, each associated with a set of quantified properties. The quantifiers have been given probabilistic interpretations, mapping `all`→1, `most`→0.95, `some`→0.35, `few`→0.05, `none`→0.[3] Each concept/property pair was judged by 3 raters. We choose the majority rating when it exists, and otherwise the minimum proposed rating. To address sparseness, especially for the one-shot learning setting, we omit properties that are named for fewer than 5 concepts. This leaves us with 503 concepts and 220 properties We intentionally choose this small dataset: One of our main objectives is to explore the possibility of learning effectively from very limited training data. In addition, while the feature norm dataset is small, our distributional dataset (the BNC, see below) is not. The latter essentially serves as a pivot for us to propagate the knowledge from the feature norm data to the wider semantic space.

It is a problem of both the original McRae et al. (2005) data and QMR that if a property is not named by participants, it is not listed, even if it applies. For example, the property `four-legged`

is missing for *alligator* in QMR. So we additionally use the **Animal** dataset of Herbelot (2013), where every property has a rating for every concept. The dataset comprises 72 animal concepts with quantification information for 54 properties.

Distributional data. We use the British National Corpus (BNC) (The BNC Consortium, 2007), with dependency parses from Spacy. [4] As context items, we use pairs ⟨pred, dep⟩ of predicates pred that are content words (nouns, verbs, adjectives, adverbs) but not stopwords, where a concept from the respective dataset (QMR, Animal) is a dependency child of pred via dep. In total we obtain a vocabulary of 500 QMR concepts and 72 Animal concepts that appear in the BNC, and 29,124 context items. We refer to this syntactic context as **Syn**. For comparison, we also use a baseline model with a bag-of-words (**BOW**) context window of 2 or 5 words, with stopwords removed.

Models. We test our probabilistic models as defined in the previous section. While our focus is on one-shot learning, we also evaluate a multi-shot setting where we learn from the whole BNC, as a sanity check on our models. (We do not test our models in an incremental learning setting that adds one occurrence at a time. While this is possible in principle, the computational cost is prohibitive for the bi-TM.) We compare to the Partial Least Squares (**PLS**) model of Herbelot and Vecchi (2015a)[5] to see whether our models perform at state of the art levels. We also compare to a baseline that always predicts the probability of a property to be its relative frequency in the set C of known concepts (**Baseline**).

We can directly use the property probabilities in QMR and the Animal data as concept representations $\mathbf{c}_{\text{Ind}}$ for the Count Independent model. For the Count Multinomial model, we never explicitly compute $\mathbf{c}_{\text{Mult}}$. To sample from it, we first sample an instance $\underline{\mathbf{c}} \in \{0,1\}^{|Q|}$ from the independent Bernoulli vector of c, $\mathbf{c}_{\text{Ind}}$. From the properties that apply to $\underline{\mathbf{c}}$, we sample one (with equal probabilities) as the observed property. All priors for the count-based models (Beta priors or Dirichlet priors, respectively) are set to 1.

For the bi-TM, a pseudo-document for a known

---

[2]We use the H2 Bernoulli Mixture as a soft clustering because it is straightforward to do this through concept representations. For the H1 mixture, we did not see an obvious soft clustering, so we use it as a hard clustering.

[3]The dataset also contains `KIND` properties that do not have probabilistic interpretations. Following Herbelot and Vecchi (2015a) we omit these properties.

[4]https://spacy.io

[5]Herbelot and Vecchi (2015a) is the only directly relevant previous work on the subject. Further, to the best of our knowledge, for one-shot property learning from text (only), our work has been the first attempt.

Models		QMR		Animal
		BOW5	Syn	Syn
Baseline		0.12	0.16	0.63
PLS		**0.24**	0.35	0.71
Count	Mult.	0.13	0.25	0.64
	Ind.	0.11	0.23	0.64
	BernMix H1	0.11	0.17	0.65
	BernMix H2	0.10	0.18	0.63
bi-TM	plain	0.23	**0.36**	0.80
	BernMix H2	0.20	0.34	**0.81**

Table 1: MAP scores, multi-shot learning on the QMR and Animal datasets

concept c is generated as follows: Given an occurrence of known concept c with context item w in the BNC, we sample a property q from c (in the same way as for the Count Multinomial model), and add $\langle w, q \rangle$ to the pseudo-document for c. For training the bi-TM, we use collapsed Gibbs sampling (Steyvers and Griffiths, 2007) with 500 iterations for burn-in. The Dirichlet priors are uniformly set to 0.1 following Roller and Schulte im Walde (2013). We use 50 topics throughout.

For all our models, we report the average performance from 5 runs. For the PLS benchmark, we use 50 components with otherwise default settings, following Herbelot and Vecchi (2015a).

Evaluation. We test all models using 5-fold cross validation and report average performance across the 5 folds. We evaluate performance using *Mean Average Precision* (MAP) , which tests to what extent a model ranks definitional properties in the same order as the gold data. Assume a system that predicts a ranking of n datapoints, where 1 is the highest-ranked, and assume that each datapoint i has a gold rating of $I(i) \in \{0, 1\}$. This system obtains an Average Precision (AP) of

$$AP = \frac{1}{\sum_{i=1}^{n} I(i)} \sum_{i=1}^{n} \text{Prec}_i \cdot I(i)$$

where Prec_i is precision at a cutoff of i. Mean Average Precision is the mean over multiple AP values. In our case, $n = |Q|$, and we compare a model-predicted ranking of property probabilities with a binary gold rating of whether the property applies to any instances of the given concept. For the one-shot evaluation, we make a separate prediction for each occurrence of an unknown concept u in the BNC, and report MAP by averaging over the AP values for all occurrences of u.

5 Results and Discussion

Multi-shot learning. While our focus in this paper is on one-shot learning, we first test all models in a multi-shot setting. The aim is to see how well they perform when given ample amounts of training data, and to be able to compare their performance to an existing multi-shot model (as we will not have any related work to compare to for the one-shot setting.) The results are shown in Table 1, where *Syn* shows results that use syntactic context (encoding selectional constraints) and *BOW5* is a bag-of-words context with a window size of 5. We only compare our models to the baseline and benchmark for now, and do an in-depth comparison of our models when we get to the one-shot task, which is our main focus.

Across all models, the syntactic context outperforms the bag-of-words context. We also tested a bag-of-words context with window size 2 and found it to have a performance halfway between *Syn* and *BOW5* throughout. This confirms our assumption that it is reasonable to focus on syntactic context, and for the rest of this paper, we test models with syntactic context only.

Focusing on *Syn* conditions now, we see that almost all models outperform the property frequency baseline, though the MAP scores for the baseline do not fall far behind those of the weakest count-based models.[6] The best of our models perform on par with the PLS benchmark of Herbelot and Vecchi (2015a) on QMR, and on the Animal dataset they outperform the benchmark. Comparing the two datasets, we see that all models show better performance on the cleaner (and smaller) *Animal* dataset than on QMR. This is probably because QMR suffers from many false negatives (properties that apply but were not mentioned), while Animal does not. The Count Independent model shows similar performance here and throughout all later experiments to the Count Multinomial (even though it matches the construction of the QMR and Animal datasets better), so to avoid clutter we do not report on it further below.

One-shot learning. Table 2 shows the perfor-

---

[6]This is because MAP gives equal credit for all properties correctly predicted as non-zero. When we evaluate with Generalized Average Precision (GAP) (Kishida, 2005), which takes gold weights into account, the baseline model is roughly 10 points below other models. This indicates our models learn approximate property distributions. We omit GAP scores because they correlate strongly with MAP for non-baseline models.

Models			all	oracle top20	AvgCos top20
QMR	Count	Mult.	0.16	0.37	0.28
		BernMix H1	0.14	0.33	0.21
		BernMix H2	0.15	0.31	0.22
	bi-TM	plain	**0.21**	**0.47**	**0.35**
		BernMix H2	0.18	0.45	0.34
Animal	Count	Mult.	0.58	0.77	0.61
		BernMix H1	0.60	0.80	0.57
		BernMix H2	0.59	0.81	0.59
	bi-TM	plain	0.64	0.88	0.63
		BernMix H2	**0.65**	**0.89**	**0.66**

Table 2: MAP scores, one-shot learning on the QMR and Animal datasets

Count Mult.	`clothing, made_of_metal, different_colours, an_animal, is_long`
bi-TM	`clothing, made_of_material, has_sleeves,    different_colours, worn_by_women`
bi-TM one-shot	`clothing,    is_long,    made_of_material,    different_colours, has_sleeves`

Table 3: QMR: top 5 properties of *gown*. Top 2 entries: multi-shot. Last entry: one-shot, context *undo-dobj*

Top	*undo-dobj* (0.70), *nylon-nmod* (0.66), *pink-amod* (0.65), *retie-dobj* (0.64), *silk-amod* (0.64)
Bottom	*sport-nsubj* (0.01), *contemplate-dobj* (0.01), *comic-amod* (0.01), *wait-nsubj* (0.01), *fibrous-amod* (0.01)

Table 4: QMR one-shot: AP for top and bottom 5 context items of *gown*

mance of our models on the one-shot learning task. We cannot evaluate the benchmark PLS as it is not suitable for one-shot learning. The baseline is the same as in Table 1. The numbers shown are Average Precision (AP) values for learning from a single occurrence. Column *all* averages over all occurrences of a target in the BNC (using only context items that appeared at least 5 times in the BNC), and column *oracle top-20* averages over the 20 context items that have the highest AP for the given target. As can be seen, AP varies widely across sentences: When we average over all occurrences of a target in the BNC, performance is close to baseline level.[7] But the most *informative* instances yield excellent information about an unknown concept, and lead to MAP values that are much higher than those achieved in multi-shot learning (Table 1). We explore this more below.

Comparing our models, we see that the bi-TM does much better throughout than any of the count-based models. Since the bi-TM model implements both cross-predicate selectional constraints (H1) and property co-occurrence (H2), we find both of our hypotheses confirmed by these results. The Bernoulli mixtures improved performance on the Animal dataset, with no clear pattern of which one improved performance more. On QMR, adding a Bernoulli mixture model harms performance across both the count-based and bi-TM models. We suspect that this is because of the false negative entries in QMR; an inspection of Bernoulli mixture H2 components supports this intuition, as the QMR ones were found to be of poorer quality than those for the Animal data.

Comparing Tables 1 and 2 we see that they show

---

[7] Context items with few occurrences in the corpus perform considerably worse than baseline, as their property distributions are dominated by the small number of concepts with which they appear.

the same patterns of performance: Models that do better on the multi-shot task also do better on the one-shot task. This is encouraging in that it suggests that it should be possible to build incremental models that do well both in a low-data and an abundant-data setting.

Table 3 looks in more detail at what it is that the models are learning by showing the five highest-probability properties they are predicting for the concept *gown*. The top two entries are multi-shot models, the third shows the one-shot result from the context item with the highest AP. The bi-TM results are very good in both the multi-shot and the one-shot setting, giving high probability to some quite specific properties like `has_sleeves`. The count-based model shows a clear frequency bias in erroneously giving high probabilities to the two overall most frequent properties, `made_of_metal` and `an_animal`. This is due to the additive nature of the Count model: In updating unknown concepts from context items, frequent properties are more likely to be sampled, and their effect accumulates as the model does not take into account interactions among context items. The bi-TM, which models these interactions, is much more robust to the effect of property frequency.

Informativity. In Table 2 we saw that one-shot performance averaged over all context items in the whole corpus was quite bad, but that good, *informative* context items can yield high-quality property information. Table 4 illustrates this point fur-

	Model		Freq.	Entropy	AvgCos
QMR	Count	Mult.	0.09	-0.12	0.18
	Count	BernMix H1	0.07	-0.10	0.17
	Count	BernMix H2	0.10	-0.09	0.17
	bi-TM	plain	0.15	-0.09	0.41·
	bi-TM	BernMix H2	0.16	-0.10	0.39·
Ani.	bi-TM	plain	0.25	-0.40	0.49*
	bi-TM	BernMix H2	0.23·	-0.37·	0.52*

Table 5: Correlation of informativity with AP, Spearman's ρ. * and · indicate significance at $p < 0.05$ and $p < 0.1$

Type	MAP
Function	0.45
Taxonomic	**0.62**
Visual	0.34
Encyclopaedic	0.35
Perc	0.40

Table 6: QMR, bi-TM, one-shot: MAP by property type over (oracle) top 20 context items

ther. For the concept *gown*, it shows the five context items that yielded the highest AP values, at the top *undo-obj*, with an AP as high as 0.7.

This raises the question of whether we can predict the informativity of a context item.[8] We test three measures of informativity. The first is simply the **frequency** of the context item, with the rationale that more frequent context items should have more stable representations. Our second measure is based on **entropy**. For each context item w, we compute a distribution over properties as in the count-independent model, and measure the entropy of this distribution. If the distribution has few properties account for a majority of the probability mass, then w will have a low entropy, and would be expected to be more informative. Our third measure is based on the same intuition, that items with more "concentrated" selectional constraints should be more informative. If a context item w has been observed to occur with known concepts $c_1, \ldots, c_n$, then this measure is the average cosine (**AvgCos**) of the property distributions (viewed as vectors) of any pair of $c_i, c_j \in \{c_1, \ldots, c_n\}$.

We evaluate the three informativity measures using Spearman's rho to determine the correlation of the informativity of a context item with the AP it produces for each unknown concept. We expect frequency and AvgCos to be positively correlated with AP, and entropy to be negatively correlated with AP. The result is shown in Table 5. Again, all measures work better on the Animal data than on QMR, where they at best approach significance. The correlation is much better on the bi-TM models than on the count-based models, which is probably due to their higher-quality predictions. Overall, AvgCos emerges as the most robust indicator

for informativity.[9] We now test AvgCos, as our best informativity measure, on its ability to select good context items. The last column of Table 2 shows MAP results for the top 20 context items based on their AvgCos values. The results are much below the oracle MAP (unsurprisingly, given the correlations in Table 5), but for QMR they are at the level of the multi-shot results of Table 1, showing that it is possible to some extent to automatically choose informative examples for one-shot learning.

Properties by type. McRae et al. (2005) classify properties based on the brain region taxonomy of Cree and McRae (2003). This enables us to test what types of properties are learned most easily in our fast-mapping setup by computing average AP separately by property type. To combat sparseness, we group property types into five groups, *function* (the function or use of an entity), *taxonomic*, *visual*, *encyclopaedic*, and *other perceptual* (e.g., sound). Intuitively, we would expect our contexts to best reflect *taxonomic* and *function* properties: Predicates that apply to noun target concepts often express functions of those targets, and manually specified selectional constraints are often characterized in terms of taxonomic classes. Table 6 confirms this intuition. Taxonomic properties achieve the highest MAP by a large margin, followed by functional properties. Visual properties score the lowest.

6 Conclusion

We have developed several models for one-shot learning word meanings from single textual contexts. Our models were designed learn word properties using distributional contexts (H1) or about co-occurrences of properties (H2). We find evidence that both kinds of general knowledge are

---

[8]Lazaridou et al. (2016), who use a bag-of-words context in one-shot experiments, propose an informativity measure based on the number of contexst that constitute properties. we cannot do that with our syntactic context.

[9]We also tested a binned variant of the frequency measure, on the intuition that medium-frequency context items should be more informative than either highly frequent or rare ones. However, this measure did not show better performance than the non-binned frequency measure.

helpful, especially when combined (in the bi-TM), or when used on clean property data (in the Animal dataset). We further saw that some contexts are highly informative, and preliminary expirements in informativity measures found that average pairwise similarity of seen role fillers (Avg-Cos) achieves some success in predicting which contexts are most useful.

In the future, we hope to test with other types of general knowledge, including a taxonomy of known concepts (Xu and Tenenbaum, 2007); wider-coverage property data (Baroni and Lenci, 2010, Type-DM); and alternative modalities (Lazaridou et al., 2016, image features as "properties"). We expect our model will scale to these larger problems easily.

We would also like to explore better informativity measures and improvements for AvgCos. Knowledge about informative examples can be useful in human-in-the-loop settings, for example a user aiming to illustrate classes in an ontology with a few typical corpus examples. We also note that the bi-TM cannot be used in for truly incremental learning, as the cost of global re-computation after each seen example is prohibitive. We would like to explore probabilistic models that support incremental word learning, which would be interesting to integrate with an overall probabilistic model of semantics (Goodman and Lassiter, 2014).

Acknowledgments

This research was supported by the DARPA DEFT program under AFRL grant FA8750-13-2-0026 and by the NSF CAREER grant IIS 0845925. Any opinions, findings, and conclusions or recommendations expressed in this material are those of the author and do not necessarily reflect the view of DARPA, DoD or the US government. We acknowledge the Texas Advanced Computing Center for providing grid resources that contributed to these results.

References

Mark Andrews, Gabriella Vigliocco, and David Vinson. 2009. Integrating experiential and distributional data to learn semantic representations. *Psychological Review*, 116(3):463–498.

Marco Baroni and Alexandero Lenci. 2010. Distributional memory: a general framework for corpus-based semantics. *Computational Linguistics*, 36(4):673–721.

David Blei, Andrew Ng, and Michael Jordan. 2003. Latent Dirichlet Allocation. *Journal of Machine Learning Research*, 3(4-5):993–1022.

Susan Carey and Elsa Bartlett. 1978. Acquiring a single new word. *Papers and Reports on Child Language Development*, 15:17–29.

Eliana Colunga and Linda B. Smith. 2005. From the lexicon to expectations about kinds: A role for associative learning. *Psychological Review*, 112(2):347–382.

George S. Cree and Ken McRae. 2003. Analyzing the factors underlying the structure and computation of the meaning of chipmunk, cherry, chisel, cheese, and cello (and many other such concrete nouns). *Journal of Experimental Psychology: General*, 132:163–201.

Georgiana Dinu and Mirella Lapata. 2010. Measuring distributional similarity in context. In *Proceedings of EMNLP*, Cambridge, MA.

Katrin Erk, Sebastian Padó, and Ulrike Padó. 2010. A flexible, corpus-driven model of regular and inverse selectional preferences. *Computational Linguistics*, 36(4).

Luana Făgărăşan, Eva Maria Vecchi, and Stephen Clark. 2015. From distributional semantics to feature norms: Grounding semantic models in human perceptual data. In *Proceedings of IWCS*, London, Great Britain.

C. J. Fillmore, C. R. Johnson, and M. Petruck. 2003. Background to FrameNet. *International Journal of Lexicography*, 16:235–250.

Noah D. Goodman and Daniel Lassiter. 2014. Probabilistic semantics and pragmatics: Uncertainty in language and thought. In Shalom Lappin and Chris Fox, editors, *Handbook of Contemporary Semantics*. Wiley-Blackwell.

Aurélie Herbelot. 2013. What is in a text, what isn't and what this has to do with lexical semantics. *Proceedings of IWCS*.

Aurélie Herbelot and Eva Vecchi. 2015a. Building a shared world:mapping distributional to model-theoretic semantic spaces. In *Proceedings of EMNLP*.

Aurélie Herbelot and Eva Maria Vecchi. 2015b. Many speakers, many worlds. *Linguistic Issues in Language Technology*, 12(4):1–20.

Brendan T Johns and Michael N Jones. 2012. Perceptual inference through global lexical similarity. *Topics in Cognitive Science*, 4(1):103–120.

Alfons Juan and Enrique Vidal. 2004. Bernoulli mixture models for binary images. In *Proceedings of ICPR*.

Charles Kemp, Amy Perfors, and Joshua B. Tenenbaum. 2007. Learning overhypotheses with hierarchical Bayesian models. *Developmental Science*, 10(3):307–321.

Karin Kipper-Schuler. 2005. *VerbNet: A broad-coverage, comprehensive verb lexicon*. Ph.D. thesis, Computer and Information Science Dept., University of Pennsylvania, Philadelphia, PA.

Kazuaki Kishida. 2005. Property of average precision and its generalization: An examination of evaluation indicator for information retrieval experiments. *NII Technical Reports*, 2005(14):1–19.

Thomas Landauer and Susan Dumais. 1997. A solution to Plato's problem: The latent semantic analysis theory of acquisition, induction, and representation of knowledge. *Psychological Review*, pages 211–240.

Angeliki Lazaridou, Elia Bruni, and Marco Baroni. 2014. Is this a wampimuk? Cross-modal mapping between distributional semantics and the visual world. In *Proceedings of ACL*.

Angeliki Lazaridou, Marco Marelli, and Marco Baroni. 2016. Multimodal word meaning induction from minimal exposure to natural text. *Cognitive Science*, pages 1–30.

Andrew L. Maas and Charles Kemp. 2009. One-shot learning with Bayesian networks. In *Proceedings of the 31st Annual Conference of the Cognitive Science Society*, Amsterdam, The Netherlands.

Ken McRae, George S. Cree, Mark S. Seidenberg, and Chris McNorgan. 2005. Semantic feature production norms for a large set of living and nonliving things. *Behavior Research Methods*, 37(4):547–559.

Diarmuid Ó Séaghdha. 2010. Latent variable models of selectional preference. In *Proceedings of ACL*.

Diarmuid Ó Séaghdha and Anna Korhonen. 2014. Probabilistic distributional semantics with latent variable models. *Computational Linguistics*, 40(3):587–631.

Alan Ritter, Mausam, and Oren Etzioni. 2010. A Latent Dirichlet Allocation method for selectional preferences. In *Proceedings of ACL*.

Stephen Roller and Sabine Schulte im Walde. 2013. A multimodal lda model integrating textual, cognitive and visual modalities. In *Proceedings of EMNLP*.

Dana Rubinstein, Effi Levi, Roy Schwartz, and Ari Rappoport. 2015. How well do distributional models capture different types of semantic knowledge? In *Proceedings of ACL*, volume 2, pages 726–730.

Linda B. Smith, Susan S. Jones, Barbara Landau, Lisa Gershkoff-Stowe, and Larissa Samuelson. 2002. Object name learning provides on-the-job training for attention. *Psychological Science*, 13(1):13–19.

Mark Steyvers and Tom Griffiths. 2007. Probabilistic topic models. *In T. Landauer, D.S. McNamara, S. Dennis, and W. Kintsch, eds., Handbook of Latent Semantic Analysis*.

The BNC Consortium. 2007. *The British National Corpus, version 3 (BNC XML Edition)*. Oxford University Computing Services, URL: http://www.natcorp.ox.ac.uk/.

Peter Turney and Patrick Pantel. 2010. From frequency to meaning: Vector space models of semantics. *Journal of Artificial Intelligence Research*, 37:141–188.

Gabriella Vigliocco, David Vinson, William Lewis, and Merrill Garrett. 2004. Representing the meanings of object and action words: The featural and unitary semantic space hypothesis. *Cognitive Psychology*, 48:422–488.

Fei Xu and Joshua B. Tenenbaum. 2007. Word learning as Bayesian inference. *Psychological Review*, 114(2):245–272.

A Computational Study on Word Meanings and Their Distributed Representations via Polymodal Embedding

Joohee Park[*]
Korea Advanced Institute
of Science and Technology
`james.joohee.park@navercorp.com`

Sung-hyon Myaeng
Korea Advanced Institute
of Science and Technology
`myaeng@kaist.ac.kr`

Abstract

A distributed representation has become a popular approach to capturing a word meaning. Besides its success and practical value, however, questions arise about the relationships between a true word meaning and its distributed representation. In this paper, we examine such a relationship via polymodal embedding approach inspired by the theory that humans tend to use diverse sources in developing a word meaning. The result suggests that the existing embeddings lack in capturing certain aspects of word meanings which can be significantly improved by the polymodal approach. Also, we show distinct characteristics of different types of words (e.g. concreteness) via computational studies. Finally, we show our proposed embedding method outperforms the baselines in the word similarity measure tasks and the hypernym prediction tasks.

1 Introduction

Word representations based on the distributional hypothesis of Harris (1954) have become a dominant approach including word2vec (Mikolov et al., 2013) and GloVe (Pennington et al., 2014), which show remarkable performances in a wide spectrum of natural language processing. However, a question arises about a relationship between a true word meaning and its distributed representation. While the context-driven word representations seem to be able to capture word-to-word relations, for example, *men* is to *women* as *king* is to *queen*, it still remains unclear what aspects of

word meaning they capture and miss. For example, a word, *coffee*, can be understood from multiple perspectives. It may be associated with a ceramic cup filled with dark brown liquid from the perceptual perspective or an emotion such as happiness or tranquility. It may provoke other related concepts like *bagel* or *awakening*. We raise the question of how well the current distributed representation captures such aspects of word meanings.

In order to help answering this question, we propose a polymodal word representation based on the theory that humans tend to use diverse sources in developing a word meaning. In particular, we construct six modules for polymodality including linear context, syntactic context, visual perception, cognition, emotion, and sentiments based on the human cognitive model proposed by Maruish and Moses (2013). They are combined to build a single word representation.

We conduct a series of experiments to examine the relationships between word meanings and their distributed representations and compare the results with other representations such as word2vec, GloVe, and meta-embedding (Yin and Schütze, 2015). We attempt to understand how well the model capture the diverse aspects of word meanings via two experiments: the property norms analysis and the sentiment polarity analysis. The result suggests that the existing embedding methods lack in capturing visual properties and sentiment polarities and show that they can be much improved by adopting polymodal approaches.

Finally, we examine distinct characteristics of different types of words via computational studies, focusing along the dimension of concept concreteness and similarity. We find that the importance of a certain module (e.g. visual perception or lexical relations) varies depending on the word properties. Our study provides some computational evidence for the heterogeneous nature of word meanings,

---

[*] Currently at Search Solutions Inc., Seongnam, 13561, Korea

Proceedings of the The 8th International Joint Conference on Natural Language Processing, pages 214–223,
Taipei, Taiwan, November 27 – December 1, 2017 ©2017 AFNLP

which has been extensively studied in the field of psycholinguistics. We briefly introduce it in the following subsection.

2 Related Work

2.1 Theoretical works

Word meanings are thought to have diverse aspects. Steels (2008) address that languages are inherently built upon our cognitive system to fulfill the purpose of communication between mutually unobservable internal representations. So many psycholinguistic theories have attempted to understand the diverse nature of word meanings by human minds. Barsalou (1999) claims that many human modalities such as conceptual/perceptual systems cooperate with each other in a complex way and influence word meanings, while Pulvermüller (1999) argues that concepts are grounded in complex simulations of physical and introspective events, activating the frontal region of the brain that coordinates the multimodal information. Studies on semantic priming (Plaut and Booth, 2000) also supports them that words can be similar to each other in various ways to foster the priming effect. The experiments in this paper are designed to provide some computational evidence on such studies on the multifaceted nature of word meanings.

2.2 Multimodal approaches

From a computational point of view, there exist a number of bimodal approaches that extend the semantic representation to include perceptual information or understandings of the world around us. Bruni et al. (2014) and Kiros et al. (2014a) propose a way to augment text-based word embeddings using public image datasets while Roller and Im Walde (2013) integrate visual features into LDA models. A recent study on Image caption generation (Xu et al., 2015) suggests an interesting way to align word embeddings and image features. Moreover, Kiros et al. (2014b) jointly trains the image abstraction network and sentence abstraction network altogether, making the visual features naturally combined into word embeddings. Similar attempts have been made not only for visual perception but also auditory (Kiela and Clark, 2015) and olfactory (Kiela et al., 2015) perception. On the other hand, Henriksson (2015) demonstrates that semantic space ensemble models created by exploiting various corpora are

able to outperform any single constituent model. Yin and Schütze (2015) propose meta-Embedding that ensembles multiple semantic spaces trained by different methods with different tasks such as word2vec, GloVe, HLBL (Luong et al., 2013) and C&W (Collobert and Weston, 2008). Above works succeed to improve word embedding quality by extending the semantic representation, but it still remains unclear how those improvements are related to the word meanings.

3 Polymodal word embedding

To embrace the multifaceted nature of word meanings, we propose a polymodal word embedding. More specifically, we take into account perception, sentiment, emotion, and cognition (lexical relation) derived from diverse sources, in addition to linear context and syntactic context obtained from the corpus. Note that the term *polymodal* is used to distinguish it from *bimodal* (Kiela, 2017). In bimodal approach, a single cognitive modality is used whereas more than one modalities are used in polymodal.

3.1 Modules

We describe each of the modules in detail.

Linear context refers to linear embeddings (Mikolov et al., 2013) comprising 300-dimensional vectors trained over 100 billion words from the Google News dataset using skip-gram and negative sampling.

Syntactic context takes a similar skip-gram approach as in linear context but defines the context window differently using a dependency parsing result (Levy and Goldberg, 2014). While the linear skip-gram defines the contexts of a target word w as $w_{-k}, w_{-k+1}, ..., w_{k-1}, w_k$ where k is a size of the window, syntactic context defines them as $(m_1, lbl_1), (m_2, lbl_2), ..., (m_k, lbl_k), (m_{-1}, lbl_{-1})$ where m is the modifiers of word w and lbl is the type of dependency relation.

Both linear and syntactic contexts are similar in the sense that they capture word characteristics from the corpus. However, the different definitions of the contexts make the model focus on the different aspects of word meanings. Levy and Goldberg (2014) report that linear context tends to capture topical similarity whereas syntactic context captures functional similarity. For example, the word *Florida* is close to *Miami* in linear context but close to *California* in syntactic context.

We harness both types of contexts to take into account functional and syntactic similarities.

Cognition (Lexical relation) encompasses all the relations between words, which are captured in the form of a lexicon or ontology in a cognitive system. In this paper, we mainly focus on synonym, hypernym and hyponym relations in WordNet (Miller, 1995) which contains 149k words and 935k relations between them. We train lexical-relation-specific word embedding using retro-fitting (Faruqui et al., 2015).

Specifically, let $V = \{w_1, ..., w_n\}$ be a vocabulary and Ω be an ontology that encodes semantic relations between words in V. Ω can be represented as a set of edges of undirected graph where $(w_i, w_j) \in \Omega$ if w_i and w_j holds semantic relationship of interest. The matrix $\hat{Q}$ is the collection of the vector representation of $\hat{q}_i \in \mathbb{R}^d$ for each word $w_i \in V$ where d is the length of pre-trained word vectors. In this experiment, we use GloVe as such vectors. The objective of learning is to train the matrix $Q = (q_1, ..., q_n)$ so as to make q_i close to its counterpart $\hat{q}_i$ and also to its adjacent vertices in Ω. Thus the objective function to be minimized can be written as

$$\Psi(Q) = \sum_{i=1}^{n} \left[\alpha_i ||q_i - \hat{q}_i||^2 + \sum_{(i,j) \in \Omega} \beta_{ij} ||q_i - q_j||^2 \right]$$

where α_i and β_{ij} are hyperparameters. This procedure of training transforms the manifold of semantic space to make words in relations located more closer in Euclidean distance.

Perception is a vital component for human cognition and has a significant influence on word meanings. In this paper, we only consider visual perception. We jointly train the embeddings of images and sentences together into the multi-modal vector space to build vision-specific word embeddings (Kiros et al., 2014b).

In particular, let T be the training dataset where one image I_i is associated with a corresponding caption sentence S_i, i.e., $(I_i, S_i) \in T$. An embedding of image I_i, $x_i \in \mathbb{R}^d$, can be obtained through convolutional neural networks, in this case, 19-layer OxfordNet (Simonyan and Zisserman, 2014), where d is the size of the dimension of multimodal space. Similarly, an embedding of sentence S_i, $x_s \in \mathbb{R}^d$, can be composed through one of the sentence modeling networks, in this case, LSTM (Hochreiter and Schmidhuber, 1997). These two image and sentence modeling networks are jointly trained together to minimize the pairwise ranking loss function

$$L = \sum_{x_i} \sum_{x_{\hat{s}}} max(0, \alpha - x_i \cdot x_s + x_i \cdot x_{\hat{s}}) +$$

$$\sum_{x_s} \sum_{x_{\hat{i}}} max(0, \alpha - x_s \cdot x_i + x_s \cdot x_{\hat{i}})$$

to place correct samples closer while separating negative samples farther in the joint space. α is a hyperparameter and $x_{\hat{s}}$ and $x_{\hat{i}}$ are incorrect image and sentence pair obtained through negative sampling. We use MS COCO dataset (Lin et al., 2014) to train the network which contains 300k images and 5 captions per image. Final perception embeddings of dimension 1024 are sampled from the joint space regarding one word as a sentence.

Sentiment, either positive or negative, is determined for words that have sentiment orientations depending on their inherent meanings, usages, backgrounds etc. To capture the sentiment polarity of words (positive and negative), we use SentiWordNet3.0 (Baccianella et al., 2010), a lexical resource that automatically annotates the degree of positivity, negativity, and neutrality of English words. It is a one-dimensional value and if a word has multiple senses, we take the difference between the maximum positivity and the minimum negativity.

Emotion are considered by using NRC Emotion Lexicon (Mohammad and Turney, 2013) to reflect the emotional characteristics of words. It contains 15k words that are annotated with 10 emotion categories: anger, anticipation, disgust, fear, joy, sadness, surprise, trust, negative and positive. We built 10-dimensional one-hot emotion vectors based on this dataset.

Note that some embedding sets may not cover every word in our set of test vocabulary. In that case, out-of-vocabulary (OOV) words are initialized to zero for the missing modules. All embeddings are L2-normalized.

3.2 Ensemble methods

While the most rudimentary way for the amalgamation of several vectors is a concatenation with weights, other ensemble methods are expected to produce the vectors with improved quality (Henriksson, 2015). Faruqui and Dyer (2015) suggest that singular value decomposition (SVD) can be a promising way to merge the information by approximating the original matrix. Motivated by their work, we examine two matrix factorization techniques, SVD and non-negative matrix factorization (NMF). In addition, we explore an unsupervised ensemble method via autoencoder (AE) networks. The details of these methods are illustrated below. Hyperparameters such as dimension d are selected to obtain the highest Spearmans correlation score in the RG-65 dataset (Rubenstein and Goodenough, 1965), which is used as a development set to minimize the interference on the test set. Note that before applying SVD, NMF, and AE, embeddings from different modules are concatenated with weights.

Concatenation (CONC) is used as the first step for ensembling multiple vectors of different dimensions. That is, let S be a set of n semantic spaces and s_i be a single vector space in S. $e_{id} \in s_i$ is a representation of word w_d in the semantic space $s_i \in S$. Then the resulting concatenated embedding e_d of word w_d is

$$e_d = \alpha_1 e_{d1} \oplus ... \oplus \alpha_i e_{di} \oplus ... \oplus \alpha_n e_{dn}$$

where $\oplus$ is the concatenation operator and $\sum_i \alpha_i = 1$. RG-65 is used as a development set to tune the weights α_i of particular embedding e_{di}.

Singular Value Decomposition (SVD) is a generalization of eigenvalue decomposition to any $m \times n$ matrix where it is reported to be effective in signal processing (Sahidullah and Kinnunen, 2016). Let V be the set of m words and k is the dimension of word embedding e_i for word $w_i \in V$. The dictionary matrix M is a $m \times k$ matrix where each row vector m_i of M is an embedding vector of e_i of word w_i. Then this matrix M is decomposed into $M = U\Sigma V^T$ where U and V are $m \times m$ and $n \times n$ real unitary matrices respectively, and Σ is a $m \times n$ non-negative real rectangular diagonal matrix. u_{id} is the first d dimension of i-th row vector u_i of U and we use it as a representation of word w_i. d is 230 for SVD. The size of vocabulary m is 20150.

Non-negative matrix factorization (NMF) has been reported to be effective method in various research areas including bioinformatics (Taslaman and Nilsson, 2012), signal denoising (Schmidt et al., 2007), and topic modeling (Arora et al., 2013). Two non-negative matrix W and H are optimized to approximate the dictionary matrix $M^T \approx WH$ by minimizing the frobenius norm $||M^T - WH||_F$ where $W, H \geq 0$. NMF has an inherent property of clustering the column vectors of the target matrix. To make M^T non-negative, we normalize the values of each embedding into the [0,1]. Let s_{id} be the first d dimension of i-th column vector s_i of W. Then we use s_{id} as a representation of word w_i. d is 200 for NMF.

Autoencoder (AE) is a neural network used for unsupervised learning of efficient coding for data compression or dimensionality reduction (Hinton and Sejnowski, 1986). Previous work suggests that an autoencoder may be able to learn relationships between the modules and result in higher-level embeddings (Silberer and Lapata, 2014). Our autoencoder consists of simple feedforward network. We trained two matrices W_{enc} of size $k \times d$ and W_{dec} of size $d \times k$ to learn efficient coding of word representation where k is the dimension of original word embedding and d is the dimension of compressed representation. Parameters are optimized to minimize cosine proximity loss:

$$L = \sum_{x \in T} 1 - \frac{\tilde{x} \cdot x}{||\tilde{x}|| \cdot ||x||}$$

where x is a k-dimensional word embedding, T is a training data set of size 20150 words, $\tilde{x} = f(W_{dec}f(W_{enc}x + b_{enc}) + b_{dec})$ and f is a ReLU non-linear activation function. We set $d = 900$.

4   Experiments

We introduce the experiments taken to examine how well the representations embed word meanings incorporating distinct properties. First, we apply our proposed embedding method to a word similarity measure task and a hypernym prediction task to measure its overall quality. Then we conducted a series of experiments for analyzing the characteristics of word meanings.

4.1   Word Similarity Measure and Hypernym Prediction

To assess the overall quality of proposed embedding method, we examined its performance via the word similarity task on SimLex-999 (Hill et al., 2016), WordSim-353 (Agirre et al., 2009), and MEN (Bruni et al., 2014) datasets. The similarity of each word pair is computed through cosine proximity, and we use Spearman's rank correlation as an evaluation metric. We also measure the performance of the different ensemble methods described in subsection 3.2. The result is compared with three baselines: Word2Vec, GloVe, and

Meta-embedding(1toN) (Yin and Schütze, 2015). The result is shown on table 1.

Baseline	SL	WS	MEN
Word2Vec	.442	.698	.782
GLoVe	.453	.754	.816
MetaEmb	.464	.745	.816
Polymodal (CONC)	**.533**	.622	.778
Polymodal (SVD)	**.580**	**.775**	**.838**
Polymodal (AE)	**.507**	.599	.751
Polymodal (NMF)	.414	.509	.589
Avg. Human	.780	.791	.840

Table 1: Spearman's correlation score on SimLex-999 (SL), WordSim-353 (WS), and MEN datasets. "Avg. Human" score is an inter-agreement between human annotators.

Our proposed method clearly outperforms the baselines in all the datasets, with near-human performance in WordSim-353 and MEN. Among the ensemble methods, SVD gave the best result showing its strong capability of combining information from different modules for this task.

We also conducted a hypernym prediction experiment using HyperLex dataset (Vulić et al., 2016) to analyze the quality of proposed embedding from a different perspective. Given a pair of two words, the task is to predict the degree of the first word being a type of the second word, for example "To what degree is *chemistry* a type of *science?*". We build a 2-layer feedforward network of dimensions 1000 and 500 respectively with a ReLU activation function to predict the hypernyms. Then the network is trained to predict the degree of hypernymity of the scale from 0.0 to 10.0 to minimize categorial cross-entropy loss using AdaGrad optimizer on the training set. The final evaluation metrics are obtained by calculating Spearman's correlation between the predicted degrees and the test set.

As in Table 2, the proposed method shows the highest correlation to the test set among all the cases including the baselines. Among the ensemble method, SVD again shows the highest performance. For the hypernym prediction, NMF gives a slightly better result than the simple weighted concatenation.

4.2 Property Norms Analysis

While the corpus-driven word representations such as Word2vec and GLoVe have been shown to

	Test correlation (ρ)
Word2Vec	.319
GloVe	.391
MetaEmb	.400
Polymodal (CONC)	.445
Polymodal (SVD)	**.463**
Polymodal (NMF)	.454
Polymodal (AE)	.434

Table 2: Spearman's correlation score of Hyper-Lex test dataset and predictions. The proposed method shows the highest correlation with the test dataset.

embed some word-to-word relations such as *men* is to *women* as *king* is to *queen*, but it is still uncertain that they are also able to capture the properties like *has_ four_ legs* or *is_ delicious*. To see how well the models capture such properties of words, we perform the property norms analysis. We utilize the CSLB concept property norms dataset (Devereux et al., 2014) which annotates the normalized feature labels to the set of concepts. This dataset provides the normalized features of five categories: visual perceptual, other perceptual, taxonomic, encyclopedic, and functional. C is the set of all concepts and F is the set of all normalized features in CSLB dataset where $|C| = 638$ and $|F| = 5929$. For $f \in F$ and $c \in C$, $c \in C_f$ if and only if c has the feature f where $C_f \subset C$. The valid feature set F_v is a subset of F such that $f \in F_v$ only if there exist more than three concepts that have f, or equivalently, $|C_f| > 3$. Then the $|F_v| = 1053$.

To examine how well each representation captures the normalized feature $f_i \in F_v$, we calculate the cosine similarity between $R(c)$ for $c \in C_{f_i}$ and $R(\overline{C_{f_i}})$ where $R(\cdot)$ is a mapping from concept to its distributed representation and $\overline{C_{f_i}}$ is a centroid of all concepts in C_{f_i} or

$$\overline{C_{f_i}} = \frac{1}{|C_{f_i}|} \sum_{c \in C_{f_i}} R(c)$$

In other words, $\overline{C_{f_i}}$ is a centroid of concepts that share the feature f_i. We define the *feature density* as the cosine similarity between the concept and the centroid. That is,

$$\textit{feature density}(c, f) = R(c) \cdot \overline{C_f}$$

We calculate the feature density of all target concept-feature pairs assuming vectors that share

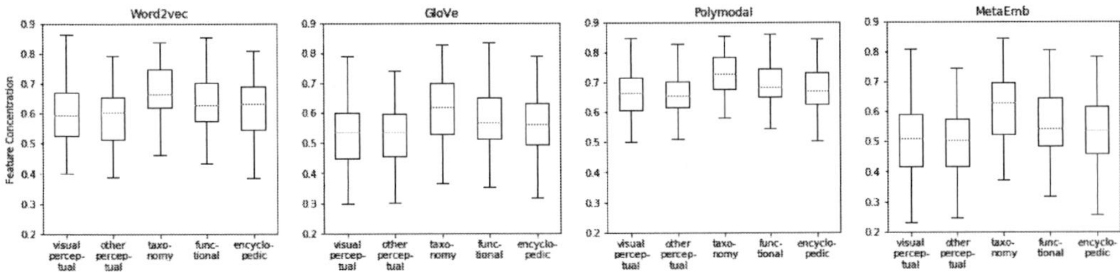

Figure 1: The feature density of different types of embedding on CSLB Concept Property Norms dataset.

	Word2Vec	GloVe	MetaEmb	Proposed
All features	.308	.262	.283	.343
Visual Perceptual	.204	.162	.188	.241
Other Perceptual	.122	.143	.148	.148
Taxonomic	.271	.236	.244	.263
Encyclopedic	.138	.129	.145	.136
Functional	.314	.288	.280	.310

Table 3: Spearman's correlation between the CSLB normalized feature representation and the target distributed representation.

the same features will also be distributionally similar (Erk, 2016).

In Figure 1 that summarizes the result, the proposed embedding method shows higher averages and lower deviations of feature densities across all the categories. It shows that our proposed embedding method is more capable of capturing normalized features than the baselines.

To further cement the observations, we calculate Spearman's correlation of word similarity measures between the normalized feature representation and the target distributed representation. The normalized feature representation of a concept is constructed as an one-hot vector which assigns 1 if the concept has the feature and 0 otherwise, and then L2-normalized to have length 1. Then we calculate the correlations of similarity measures by the feature categories. The results are shown in Table 3. While the proposed embedding method shows the highest correlation to the case of using all normalized features, it also shows a noticeable improvement in the visual perceptual category.

4.3 Positive vs Negative

One of the critical weakness of context-based word representation is that it cannot differentiate the sentiment polarity correctly. So we examine the ratio of neighbors that have same/opposite/neutral sentiment polarities with a

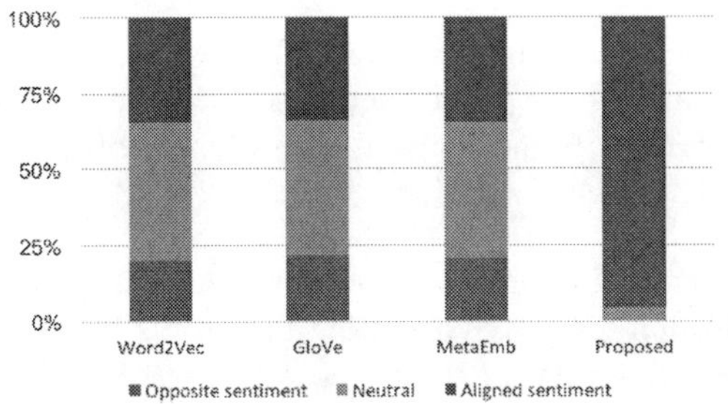

Figure 2: The ratio of 10 nearest neighbors that have same/opposite/neutral sentiment polarities of 15010 words.

target word among 15010 words and see how this problem can be mitigated. Figure 2 illustrates the result. The three context-based approaches show roughly 20% of incorrect sentiment differentiation. This can be benefited greatly from the sentiment module of the proposed approach as this issue is almost perfectly resolved by simply attaching sentiment values to the embedding. The result might be straightforward but this can improve the quality of embedding greatly.

4.4 Concrete vs Abstract

We hypothesize that the role of a certain module would be different depending on word characteristics such as the degree of concreteness. To validate this idea, we divided the Simlex-999 dataset into two groups for different degrees of concept concreteness. This corresponds to 500 pairs of concrete words vs. 499 pairs of abstract words. Then we examine the relative importance of the different modules to each group via an ablation test. The result is reported in Table 4.

Modules	All	Concrete	Abstract
L (linear)	.442	.462	.449
T (syntactic)	.446	.439	.459
C (cognition)	.464	.451	.456
P (perception)	.157	.355	.010
S (sentiment)	.221	-.100	.293
E (emotion)	.376	.350	.385
All-but-L	.527▽	.464▽	.538▽
All-but-T	.524▽	.478▽	.501▽
All-but-C	.514▽	.466▽	.492▽
All-but-P	.531▽	.476▽	.570▲
All-but-S	.503▽	.491▲	.484▽
All-but-E	.526▽	.488▲	.540▽
All	.533	.483	.545

Table 4: Ablation tests for different word groups in Simlex-999. The metric is Spearman's correlation. Embeddings here are ensembled via weighted concatenation.

Interesting properties are revealed through the ablation test. By comparing the results between the different word groups, we can observe that the importance of a certain word aspect varies depending on the word characteristics. While concrete words profit from perception embeddings, the sentiment and emotion aspects are somewhat disturbing. We can observe an opposite result for abstract words. This result is quite intuitive since we can easily imagine the perceptual image from a concrete concept but not from an abstract one like *love*.

For a deeper analysis, we further investigate the role of each module in different word groups. For instance, since concrete concepts are perception-revealing, they would benefit from a strong emphasis on the perception embedding. On the other hand, emotion-revealing word groups such as abstract concepts would be opposite. Noting that the different types of words may have different sensitivity toward the modules, we adjusted the relative weights for a particular aspect of interest to be from 0.1 to 3.5 while maintaining others to 1.0. Then we observed the changes of the performance in word similarity task. The result is shown in Figure 3.

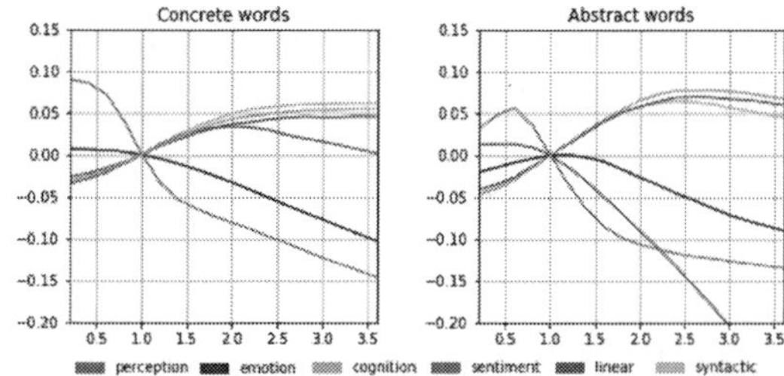

Figure 3: The result of sensitivity analysis. The weight of aspect-of-interest is adjusted while others are fixed to 1. These graphs reveal the distinct profiles of different word groups. Gradual patterns of emotion and perception are opposite for the concrete and abstract word groups.

The result of sensitivity analysis supports the idea that different word groups are influenced by each module with varying degrees. The x-axis refers to the relative weight of a particular aspect while setting the others to 1.0. The y-axis indicates the changes of Spearman's correlation score ρ on Simlex-999. The results in Figure 3 illustrate the different preferences among different word groups, which show the distinct nature between the two groups. In particular, the gradual patterns revealed by increasing relative weights of perception and emotion are contrary to concrete and abstract words. Increasing the weight of perception is beneficial for concrete word groups but detrimental to abstract word groups. However an exactly reverse pattern can be observed for the emotion. Increasing the weight of emotion is advantageous for abstract words but adverse for concrete words.

4.5 Similarity vs Relatedness

The "similarity" between two words is more strict term than the "relatedness". While the relatedness measures how much the two words are related to each other in some senses, the similarity measures how much the two words can be regarded as "similar" than just simply related. For example, consider the three word pairs: (bread, butter), (bread, toast), and (bread, stale). All of them can be regarded as "related" but only the (bread, toast) pairs can be regarded as "similar" because the other two words (butter and stale) are related but not similar to the "bread".

The two data sets SimLex-999 and WordSim-

353 capture this difference of similarity and relatedness. While the scores of WordSim-353 focus on the relatedness, those of the Simlex-999 deliberately try to distinguish between them. For example, a word pair (cloth, closet) is scored 8.00 in WordSim-353 dataset whereas 1.96 in the SimLex-999 dataset. To capture the difference between relatedness and similarity and see what modules contributes most to capture the similarity or the relatedness, we conduct a sensitivity analysis on WordSim-353 and SimLex-999 dataset.

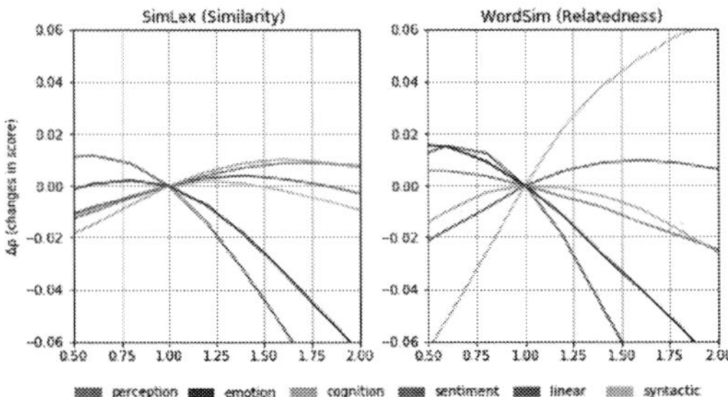

Figure 4: The result of sensitivity analysis on word similarity and word relatedness. While context information is important to the relatedness, sentiment polarity and lexical relations are important to the similarity.

Figure 4 shows the result of sensitivity analysis. In the SimLex-999 dataset which focuses on the word similarity, the cognition (lexical relation) and the sentiment modules turned out to be important. On the other hand, in the WordSim-353 dataset which focuses on the word relatedness, both linear context and syntactic context are turned out to be critical. This difference can be interpreted that the word properties extracted from the contexts are of the word relatedness, and in order to differentiate the similarity from the relatedness, additional properties such as lexical relations and sentiment polarities need to be introduced.

5 Conclusion

In this paper, we raise a question if the current distributed word representations sufficiently capture different aspects of word meanings. To address the question, we proposed a novel method for composing word embeddings, inspired by a human cognitive model. We compared our proposed embedding to the current state-of-the-art distributed word embedding methods such as Word2Vec, GloVe, and Meta-embedding from the perspective of capturing diverse aspects of word meanings.

Our proposed embedding performs better in the word similarity and hypernym prediction tasks than the baselines. We further conducted a series of experiments to study how well the word meanings are reflected by the representations and analyze the relationships between the modules and the word properties. From the property norms analysis, our findings show that the proposed method can capture the visual properties of words better than the baselines. Also, harnessing sentiment values helps the embedding greatly to resolve the sentiment polarity issue which is a limitation of current context-driven approaches. Based on the experimental results, we can conclude that some aspects of word meanings are not captured enough from the corpus and we can further improve the word embedding by referring to additional data related to a human mind model.

Finally, using our proposed method we show the different characteristics of concrete and abstract word groups and the difference between the concept relatedness and the concept similarity. We observe that emotional information is more important than the perceptual information for the abstract words whereas the opposite result is observed for the concrete words. Also, we see that the context-driven embeddings mostly capture the word relatedness and therefore lexical relation and sentiment polarities would be beneficial when considering the word similarity.

In conclusion, we concentrate on analyzing the relationships between the diverse aspects of word meanings and their distributed representations and propose a way to improve them by harnessing additional information based on the human cognitive model. Since our proposed method largely relies on the labeled extra data, this work has a limitation in terms of the scalability. For future research, we need to explore unsupervised ways of introducing perceptual properties and lexical relationships of words and annotating their sentiment and emotional properties. It will make our method more scalable.

Acknowledgements

This work was supported by Institute for Information communications Technology Promotion (IITP) grant funded by the Korea government (MSIP) (No. 2013-0-00179, Development of Core Technology for Context-aware Deep-

Symbolic Hybrid Learning and Construction of Language Resources)

References

Eneko Agirre, Enrique Alfonseca, Keith Hall, Jana Kravalova, Marius Paşca, and Aitor Soroa. A study on similarity and relatedness using distributional and WordNet-based approaches. In *Proceedings of Human Language Technologies: The 2009 Annual Conference of the North American Chapter of the Association for Computational Linguistics*, pages 19–27. Association for Computational Linguistics, 2009.

Sanjeev Arora, Rong Ge, Yonatan Halpern, David M Mimno, Ankur Moitra, David Sontag, Yichen Wu, and Michael Zhu. A practical algorithm for topic modeling with provable guarantees. In *ICML (2)*, pages 280–288, 2013.

Stefano Baccianella, Andrea Esuli, and Fabrizio Sebastiani. Sentiwordnet 3.0: An enhanced lexical resource for sentiment analysis and opinion mining. In *LREC*, volume 10, pages 2200–2204, 2010.

LW Barsalou. Perceptual symbol system. *Behavioral and Brain Science*, 22(4):577–609, 1999.

Elia Bruni, Nam-Khanh Tran, and Marco Baroni. Multimodal distributional semantics. *J. Artif. Intell. Res.(JAIR)*, 49(1-47), 2014.

Ronan Collobert and Jason Weston. A unified architecture for natural language processing: Deep neural networks with multitask learning. In *Proceedings of the 25th international conference on Machine learning*, pages 160–167. ACM, 2008.

Barry J Devereux, Lorraine K Tyler, Jeroen Geertzen, and Billi Randall. The centre for speech, language and the brain (CSLB) concept property norms. *Behavior research methods*, 46(4):1119, 2014.

Katrin Erk. What do you know about an alligator when you know the company it keeps? *Semantics and Pragmatics*, 9:17–1, 2016.

Manaal Faruqui and Chris Dyer. Non-distributional word vector representations. *arXiv preprint arXiv:1506.05230*, 2015.

Manaal Faruqui, Jesse Dodge, Sujay K. Jauhar, Chris Dyer, Eduard Hovy, and Noah A. Smith. Retrofitting word vectors to semantic lexicons. In *Proceedings of NAACL*, 2015.

Zellig S Harris. Distributional structure. *Word*, 10(2-3):146–162, 1954.

Aron Henriksson. *Ensembles of semantic spaces: On combining models of distributional semantics with applications in healthcare*. PhD thesis, Department of Computer and Systems Sciences, Stockholm University, 2015.

Felix Hill, Roi Reichart, and Anna Korhonen. Simlex-999: Evaluating semantic models with (genuine) similarity estimation. *Computational Linguistics*, 2016.

Geoffrey E Hinton and Terrence J Sejnowski. Learning and releaming in Boltzmann machines. *Parallel Distrilmted Processing*, 1, 1986.

Sepp Hochreiter and Jürgen Schmidhuber. Long short-term memory. *Neural computation*, 9(8):1735–1780, 1997.

Douwe Kiela. Deep embodiment: grounding semantics in perceptual modalities. Technical report, University of Cambridge, Computer Laboratory, 2017.

Douwe Kiela and Stephen Clark. Multi- and cross-modal semantics beyond vision: Grounding in auditory perception. In *Proceedings of the 2015 Conference on Empirical Methods in Natural Language Processing*, pages 2461–2470, Lisbon, Portugal, September 2015. Association for Computational Linguistics.

Douwe Kiela, Luana Bulat, and Stephen Clark. Grounding semantics in olfactory perception. In *ACL (2)*, pages 231–236, 2015.

Ryan Kiros, Ruslan Salakhutdinov, and Richard S Zemel. Multimodal neural language models. In *Icml*, volume 14, pages 595–603, 2014a.

Ryan Kiros, Ruslan Salakhutdinov, and Richard S Zemel. Unifying visual-semantic embeddings with multimodal neural language models. *arXiv preprint arXiv:1411.2539*, 2014b.

Omer Levy and Yoav Goldberg. Dependency-based word embeddings. In *ACL 2014*, 2014.

Tsung-Yi Lin, Michael Maire, Serge Belongie, James Hays, Pietro Perona, Deva Ramanan, Piotr Dollár, and C Lawrence Zitnick. Microsoft COCO: Common objects in context. In *European Conference on Computer Vision*, pages 740–755. Springer, 2014.

Thang Luong, Richard Socher, and Christopher D Manning. Better word representations with recursive neural networks for morphology. In *CoNLL*, pages 104–113, 2013.

Mark E Maruish and James A Moses. *Clinical neuropsychology: Theoretical foundations for practitioners*. Psychology Press, 2013.

Tomas Mikolov, Ilya Sutskever, Kai Chen, Greg S Corrado, and Jeff Dean. Distributed representations of words and phrases and their compositionality. In *Advances in neural information processing systems*, pages 3111–3119, 2013.

George A Miller. Wordnet: a lexical database for english. *Communications of the ACM*, 38(11):39–41, 1995.

Saif M Mohammad and Peter D Turney. Crowdsourcing a word–emotion association lexicon. *Computational Intelligence*, 29(3):436–465, 2013.

Jeffrey Pennington, Richard Socher, and Christopher D Manning. Glove: Global vectors for word representation. In *EMNLP*, volume 14, pages 1532–1543, 2014.

David C Plaut and James R Booth. Individual and developmental differences in semantic priming: Empirical and computational support for a single-mechanism account of lexical processing. *Psychological review*, 107(4):786, 2000.

Friedemann Pulvermüller. Words in the brain's language. *Behavioral and brain sciences*, 22(02):253–279, 1999.

Stephen Roller and Sabine Schulte Im Walde. A multimodal LDA model integrating textual, cognitive and visual modalities. In *Proceedings of the 2013 Conference on Empirical Methods in Natural Language Processing*, pages 1146–1157, 2013.

Herbert Rubenstein and John B Goodenough. Contextual correlates of synonymy. *Communications of the ACM*, 8(10):627–633, 1965.

Md Sahidullah and Tomi Kinnunen. Local spectral variability features for speaker verification. *Digital Signal Processing*, 50:1–11, 2016.

Mikkel N Schmidt, Jan Larsen, and Fu-Tien Hsiao. Wind noise reduction using non-negative sparse coding. In *Machine Learning for Signal Processing, 2007 IEEE Workshop on*, pages 431–436. IEEE, 2007.

Carina Silberer and Mirella Lapata. Learning grounded meaning representations with autoencoders. In *ACL (1)*, pages 721–732, 2014.

Karen Simonyan and Andrew Zisserman. Very deep convolutional networks for large-scale image recognition. *arXiv preprint arXiv:1409.1556*, 2014.

Luc Steels. The symbol grounding problem has been solved. so whats next. *Symbols and embodiment: Debates on meaning and cognition*, pages 223–244, 2008.

Leo Taslaman and Björn Nilsson. A framework for regularized non-negative matrix factorization, with application to the analysis of gene expression data. *PloS one*, 7(11):e46331, 2012.

Ivan Vulić, Daniela Gerz, Douwe Kiela, Felix Hill, and Anna Korhonen. Hyperlex: A large-scale evaluation of graded lexical entailment. *arXiv preprint arXiv:1608.02117*, 2016.

Kelvin Xu, Jimmy Ba, Ryan Kiros, Kyunghyun Cho, Aaron C Courville, Ruslan Salakhutdinov, Richard S Zemel, and Yoshua Bengio. Show, attend and tell: Neural image caption generation with visual attention. In *ICML*, volume 14, pages 77–81, 2015.

Wenpeng Yin and Hinrich Schütze. Learning meta-embeddings by using ensembles of embedding sets. *arXiv preprint arXiv:1508.04257*, 2015.

Geographical Evaluation of Word Embeddings

Michal Konkol[1], **Tomáš Brychcín**[1], **Michal Nykl**[1], and **Tomáš Hercig**[1,2]

[1]NTIS – New Technologies for the Information Society,
Faculty of Applied Sciences, University of West Bohemia, Czech Republic
[2]Department of Computer Science and Engineering,
Faculty of Applied Sciences, University of West Bohemia, Czech Republic
`{konkol,brychcin,nyklm,hercig}@kiv.zcu.cz`

Abstract

Word embeddings are commonly compared either with human-annotated word similarities or through improvements in natural language processing tasks. We propose a novel principle which compares the information from word embeddings with reality. We implement this principle by comparing the information in the word embeddings with geographical positions of cities. Our evaluation linearly transforms the semantic space to optimally fit the real positions of cities and measures the deviation between the position given by word embeddings and the real position. A set of well-known word embeddings with state-of-the-art results were evaluated. We also introduce a visualization that helps with error analysis.

1 Introduction

In recent years the improvements in quality of word embeddings led to significant improvements in many natural language processing (NLP) tasks, e.g. sentiment analysis (Maas et al., 2011), named entity recognition (Lample et al., 2016), or machine translation (Zou et al., 2013). New models for word embeddings and improvements to the old ones are introduced rapidly (Bojanowski et al., 2017; Salle et al., 2016; Yin and Schütze, 2016). As the number of various word embeddings increases, it becomes very time consuming to choose word embeddings for a particular task (Nayak et al., 2016).

To mitigate the problem, it is necessary to provide appropriate evaluation together with the word embeddings. The evaluation should cover multiple properties of word embeddings in order to allow the user to choose the model directly based on

the results (Nayak et al., 2016). Many evaluation approaches have already been proposed and they can be roughly divided to intrinsic and extrinsic (Schnabel et al., 2015).

The intrinsic evaluation measures the quality of the model directly by comparison with human-annotated data that capture semantic information. The advantage of this approach is that it is fast, simple, and easy to reproduce and analyze (Schnabel et al., 2015; Nayak et al., 2016). The main issue is that the evaluation score often does not correlate with improvements in NLP tasks (Chiu et al., 2016).

The extrinsic evaluation is indirect and measures the improvements through other tasks – currently mainly through NLP tasks. The advantage of this approach is that for each task we know which model to choose. The disadvantage is the computational complexity (Nayak et al., 2016). For each new word embeddings we need to train models for several approaches to several tasks and find the optimal hyperparameters of the models. Moreover, the same data and implementations should be used by all researchers for the evaluation.

We propose a new evaluation paradigm that is in between the intrinsic and extrinsic evaluation (actually, half the people believe its intrinsic and the other half believe its extrinsic). We measure neither the semantic word similarity as in intrinsic evaluation nor improvements in a particular task that uses word embeddings. We compare the information encoded in word embeddings directly with real-world data. We implement the paradigm with geographical data. We take GPS coordinates of cities and measure to what degree is the information encoded in the word embeddings.

The paper is organized as follows. In Section 2 we describe commonly used evaluation approaches for word embeddings and discuss their

Proceedings of the The 8th International Joint Conference on Natural Language Processing, pages 224–232,
Taipei, Taiwan, November 27 – December 1, 2017 ©2017 AFNLP

strengths and weaknesses. Our evaluation metric is introduced in Section 3. In Section 4 we provide various experiments with our evaluation metric, including evaluation of state-of-the-art word embeddings. Finally, we conclude in Section 5.

2 Related Work

There are two common tasks which fall under intrinsic evaluation: word similarity and word analogy tasks.

In the word similarity task, the evaluation data consist of pairs of words and their similarity annotated by humans. The word embeddings are compared with the evaluation data usually by Spearman rank correlation. The word similarity task has a long tradition in the semantics research (Rubenstein and Goodenough, 1965). Currently there are multiple corpora created to test different properties of the word embeddings (Finkelstein et al., 2001; Agirre et al., 2009; Luong et al., 2013; Hill et al., 2015).

The word analogy task evaluates the ability of the word embeddings to capture relations between words consistently. The evaluation data consists of questions (with answers) in the form: if word a is related to word b the same way as word c is related to word d, what word is d given a, b, and c? The word embeddings are compared based on their accuracy. The Google Word Analogy corpus is usually used for evaluation (Mikolov et al., 2013a). The word analogy task is closest to our evaluation because some of the questions are also based on real-world data, e.g. countries and their capital cities. Unlike our evaluation, they handle city names as common words, use the global semantic space, and compare them using cosine similarity.

The extrinsic evaluation uses other NLP tasks for comparison of word embeddings. Many tasks are used for extrinsic evaluation, e.g. sentiment analysis (Schnabel et al., 2015), named entity recognition (Konkol et al., 2015), or parsing (Bansal et al., 2014). Word embeddings are compared based on the improvements measured with standard evaluation metrics for the given task.

Both intrinsic and extrinsic evaluations have their advantages and disadvantages. The word similarity task was analysed and criticized by multiple authors (Faruqui et al., 2016; Chiu et al., 2016; Batchkarov et al., 2016; Gladkova and Drozd, 2016). The advantages of word similar-

ity evaluation are that it is very fast and can be easily interpreted from the linguistic point of view (or generally by human). The corpora often suffer from a subset of the following disadvantages: low correlation with extrinsic evaluation (applications), polysemy is not supported, subjectivity of single value similarity, overfitting (no training, heldout, test sets), significance tests are not common for word similarity, and the data are often small.

The word analogy task has the same disadvantages as the word similarity task; moreover the evaluation is quite slow, because it is necessary to sort all words based on their similarity with the question. Linzen (2016) provides a detailed analysis of the word analogy task and shows that results in this evaluation are to a large extent based on proximity in the semantic space rather than consistent offsets between the word pairs.

The main advantage of the extrinsic evaluation is that it directly measures application improvements. The main disadvantage is computational complexity. There exist many tasks that could be used for evaluation, but it is intractable to use all of them (Nayak et al., 2016). Moreover, there exist many approaches to all the tasks and some embeddings might be good for one approach and bad for the others. Choosing a single approach as a general benchmark could lead to incorrect conclusions. If we still want to choose a single model, then which one? On one hand, the state-of-the-art approaches of the tasks evolve in time – state-of-the-art method may well become a baseline in a few years. On the other hand, using baseline approaches loses the ability to measure application improvements. Word embeddings may have a high score with the baseline approach, but may contain the same information that is already present in the state-of-the-art approach. Other embeddings may have low score with the baseline approach, but the information may be usable in the state-of-the-art approach.

Many disadvantages of intrinsic evaluation are also related to particular tasks in extrinsic evaluation, e.g. named entity recognition or sentiment analysis usually do not use significance tests, are subjective, or use small data sets.

Nayak et al. (2016) propose a system for standard automatic extrinsic evaluation. They selected a representative subset of tasks for the evaluation and chose a single approach for each task (based on standard neural network architectures) in order to achieve reasonable evaluation times (4-5 hours). Even though this approach has the disadvantages presented in the previous two paragraphs, it is definitely a step forward to a standardized evaluation.

3 Proposed Evaluation

The evaluation data set consists of a list of n names of cities and their GPS coordinates stored in matrix $\mathbf{G} \in \mathbb{R}^{n \times 2}$. We assume that Earth is perfectly spherical and its radius is 6,371. Given the assumption, the GPS coordinates in matrix $\mathbf{G}$ can be transformed to Euclidean coordinates in matrix $\mathbf{Y} \in \mathbb{R}^{n \times 3}$ and back. The word embeddings of cities are in matrix $\mathbf{X} \in \mathbb{R}^{n \times d}$ with a d-dimensional vector for each city name. We normalize rows of $\mathbf{X}$ and $\mathbf{Y}$, because it is helpful for stability of the optimization and we need only the cosine similarity between the rows.

The first step of our evaluation is to find a subspace of the original d-dimensional word embeddings space that contains the information about city locations. The word embeddings transformed to the subspace are represented by matrix $\mathbf{W} \in \mathbb{R}^{n \times 3}$. The matrices $\mathbf{W}$ and $\mathbf{Y}$ have to share the same dimensions because we want to compare the distances between their rows (cities). We are looking for a linear transformation $\mathbf{W} = \mathbf{XT}$ parametrized by transformation matrix $\mathbf{T} \in \mathbb{R}^{d \times 3}$. We use the least squares cost function, the optimal transformation matrix $\mathbf{T}^*$ is defined as a transformation matrix that minimizes squared distances between real and approximate city positions $\|\mathbf{W} - \mathbf{Y}\|_2$. This optimization problem is highly prone to overfitting as $n \approx d$; moreover the row rank of $\mathbf{X}$ is likely lower than n, because the embeddings for cities are highly correlated and thus they are likely linearly dependent. Thus we employ L_2 regularization. The final optimization problem is given by Equation (1), where α is the regularization weight.

$$\mathbf{T}^* = \arg\min_{\mathbf{T}}(\|\mathbf{XT} - \mathbf{Y}\|_2 + \alpha \|\mathbf{T}\|_2) \qquad (1)$$

Finally, we can compare $\mathbf{W}$ and $\mathbf{Y}$. The primary metric for the evaluation is mean geographic distance, i.e. the distance between two points on a globe measured on the surface. We firstly need to normalize rows of $\mathbf{W}$ because the vectors can be above or below the surface. The geographic distance can be measured using Equation (2), where

g is the geographic distance, $\mathbf{w}_i$ and $\mathbf{y}_i$ denote the i-th row of $\mathbf{W}$ and $\mathbf{Y}$ respectively, and r is the radius of Earth.

$$g = r \cdot \arccos(\mathbf{w}_i \cdot \mathbf{y}_i) \qquad (2)$$

While the mean geographic distance is a good metric for a global view, it does not take the local structure into account, i.e. a random model moves the cities in all directions and breaks the local structure (nearest neighbors), but other model (with the same mean geographic distance) can move the cities in one direction and preserve local structure. We measure the ability of the embeddings to capture local structure by Precision at K (Prec@K). This metric creates two sets of K nearest neighbors for each city, one for the evaluation data $\mathbf{Y}$ and one for the transformed word embeddings $\mathbf{W}$. The precision between these two sets is averaged over all cities.

We also provide more statistics that help with understanding of the primary score. Median geographic distance gives a better idea about common distances, because it is not affected by extreme values. Sometimes, we found it easier to think about the errors in angles rather than distances, mainly because angles are independent of the size of the globe.

4 Experiments

In this section we firstly describe the data used for the proposed evaluation. Then we briefly introduce the word embeddings used to demonstrate the proposed evaluation. Finally, we follow with experiments that show some properties of the evaluation.

4.1 Data

We downloaded the list of 640 known cities from `https://www.timeanddate.com/worldclock/full.html` and further adjusted it. We removed cities that consist of multiple words from the list, because the evaluated models were trained only on single word expressions. It has lead to a reduction of the set to 540 cities. Then we created a dictionary of the top 10,000 words from Wikipedia and filtered out cities not present in the models, which resulted into a set of 483 cities. Finally we removed cities with ambiguous names and inconsistent use of diacritics, leaving us with 440 cities.

Model	Data	Dimension	Mean distance	Median distance	Mean angle	Prec@10	Prec@20
Random placement	—	—	10007	10007	90°	0.03	0.06
Random embeddings	—	300	10040	10422	90.3°	0.031	0.065
GloVe	6B	50	3776	3086	34.0°	0.144	0.236
GloVe	6B	100	3177	2565	28.6°	0.150	0.258
GloVe	6B	200	2756	2158	24.8°	0.210	0.336
GloVe	6B	300	2604	2116	23.4°	0.218	0.339
GloVe	42B	300	2504	1948	22.5°	0.192	0.313
GloVe	840B	300	2044	1681	18.4°	0.260	0.408
LexVec – cc	58B	300	1992	1662	17.9°	0.267	0.414
LexVec – w + nc	7B	300	1908	1508	17.2°	0.304	0.439
MetaEmbeddings	—	200	3322	2845	29.9°	0.129	0.237
SkipGram – BoW2	1-5B	300	2279	1762	20.5°	0.278	0.407
SkipGram – BoW5	1-5B	300	1985	1642	17.9°	0.273	0.422
SkipGram – Dep	1-5B	300	3240	2464	29.1°	0.176	0.265
FastText	1-5B	300	1686	1429	15.2°	0.338	0.482
WoRel	2.5B	300	1921	1487	17.3°	0.284	0.446
LSA	1-5B	300	1437	1159	12.9°	0.423	0.563
PPMI-SVD	2.5B	300	1869	1487	16.8°	0.331	0.466

Table 1: Results of the selected set of word embeddings.

The data needed to be split into the training and test set. The training set is used to find optimal transformation matrix $\mathbf{T}^*$ and optimal regularization weight α. The test set is used for the evaluation.

We manually selected the train set from the cities to evenly cover geographical area by the cities with the highest Wikipedia term frequency. The final train set contains 124 cities and the final test set contains 316 cities.

4.2 Word Embeddings

We chose a set of well-known word embeddings to show their differences using the proposed evaluation. In the following paragraphs we briefly introduce the chosen word embeddings.

SkipGram is a neural network based model (Mikolov et al., 2013b). Levy and Goldberg (2014) provide trained SkipGram models with two sizes of the context window (2, 5) and their own model that uses dependency-based context, denoted by SkipGram - BoW2, SkipGram - BoW5, and SkipGram - Dep, respectively.

GloVe is a log-bilinear model that tries to find word embeddings that are good at predicting global word co-occurence statistics (Pennington et al., 2014). We use embeddings provided by authors of the model trained on various corpus sizes (6, 42, and 840 billions words) and with various vector dimensions (50, 100, 200, 300).

FastText is an extension to SkipGram, where the word is represented as character n-grams (Bojanowski et al., 2017). We use embeddings provided by authors of the model trained on Wikipedia.

LexVec is based on factorization of positive point-wise mutual information matrix using proven strategies from GloVe, SkipGram, and methods based on singular value decomposition (Salle et al., 2016). We use two models provided by the authors of the model trained on Wikipedia and News Crawl (LexVec - w + nc), and Common Crawl (LexVec - cc).

MetaEmbeddings is an ensemble method that combines several embeddings (Yin and Schütze, 2016). We use the embeddings provided by the authors of the model.

WoRel is an extension of SkipGram, where a phrase (instead of a word) is used to guess the context words (Konkol, 2017). We use the model provided by the authors trained on Wikipedia and Gigaword corpus.

LSA is a count based method that creates a word-document co-occurrence matrix and reduces its dimension by singular value decomposition (SVD) (Landauer et al., 1998). We trained the models on Wikipedia.

PPMI-SVD creates word co-occurrence matrix where the co-ocurence is measured by positive pointwise mutual information. The dimension of the matrix is then reduced by SVD. We used the hyperwords package (Levy et al., 2015) and trained it on Wikipedia and Gigaword corpus.

4.3 Evaluation

In our first experiment we evaluate the selected set of embeddings with the proposed evaluation metric. The results are shown in Table 1.

We provide results for two baselines. The first baseline (random placement) places cities randomly on the globe. The results for this baseline are computed analytically. The second baseline generates random embeddings, each value is selected randomly from uniform distribution between -1 and 1. The random embeddings are then evaluated in the same way as normal embeddings. The results show average results for five random embeddings. The comparison of the baselines show that the evaluation works as expected: random embeddings produce randomly placed cities.

The results show that all the evaluated word embeddings are significantly better than the baselines. This proves that the embeddings do not capture only the similarity between words but also nontrivial knowledge about the world.

Most geographic information was clearly captured by LSA, followed by FastText. A group of models, namely WoRel, SkipGram – BoW5, PPMI-SVD, and LexVec, achieved similar results and are only slightly worse than FastText. Surprisingly, GloVe (trained with similar amount of data) performed significantly worse. MetaEmbeddings achieved the worst results, probably because the ensemble was optimized for other purposes.

There is a high correlation between the performance in the mean geographic distance and Prec@10 measures. Models that are good at capturing global structure tend to be good at capturing local structure.

The type of the training data is probably more important than the size of the data. This can be seen on the LexVec models, where the model trained on Wikipedia and news articles outperforms the other model trained on significantly more data. Still, an extreme amount of data leads to good results as seen on the results of GloVe trained on various corpus sizes.

Recently, most of the NLP tasks use word embeddings based on local (window-based) context. Surprisingly, our evaluation shows that LSA, a

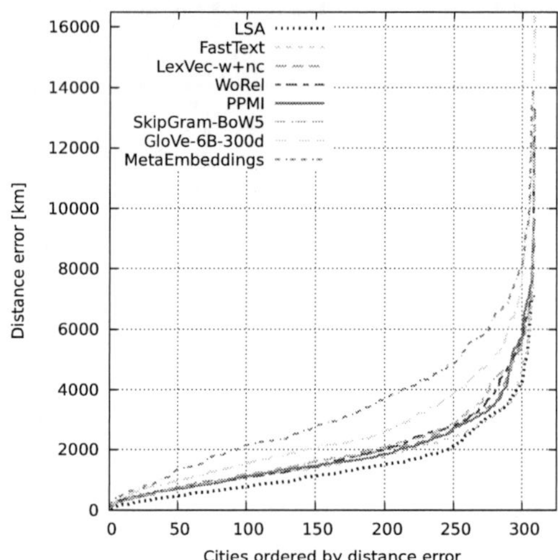

Figure 1: Distribution of distance errors.

method based on global (document-wide) context, outperforms all the other models in the proposed evaluation. The comparison of count based (PPMI-SVD) and predictive models (e.g. Skip-Gram, FastText) shows no significant differences between these two approaches.

Our evaluation shows that the mainstream models such as SkipGram and GloVe that perform similarly in intrinsic word similarity and extrinsic task based evaluations may have very different results in other types of evaluation.

4.4 Error Analysis

Figure 1 shows the distribution of geographic distance errors for individual cities. The distance error is reasonable ($\leq$ 2500 km) for approximately 90% of the cities for most of the word embeddings. Unfortunately, the rest of the cities has significantly larger error. In this section, we try to identify the source of the extreme errors.

Firstly, we suspected that the reason is sparseness and the extreme errors are caused by underrepresented words. In Figure 2 we show a relation between the number of occurrences of the city name in Wikipedia (training data for most of the methods) and the mean distance error. The word occurrences are equidistantly grouped into ten bins. We concluded that there is no clear relation between the number of occurrences of a city name and the distance error.

We also suspected ambiguity with common words. To check this hypothesis, we counted how

228

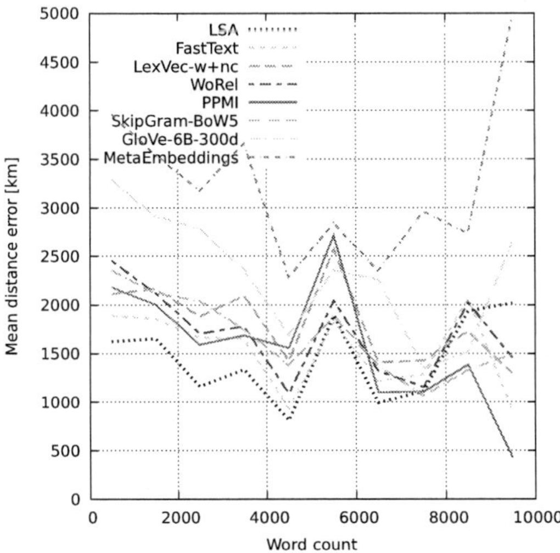

Figure 2: Relation between the number of occurrences of the city name and the distance error for LSA.

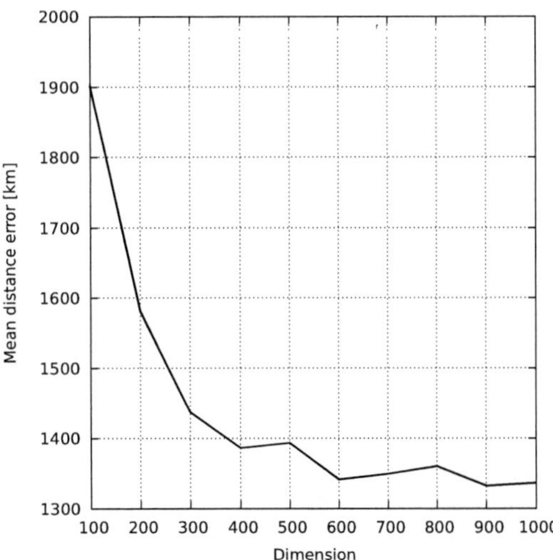

Figure 3: The relation between dimension of the vector space and the mean distance error for LSA.

many times the city name appears as lowercase and how many times with a capital letter. We found out that most of the words does not appear at all in lowercase version. A small portion of words has significant number of occurrences of the lowercase version (e.g. Phoenix), but they do not correlate with the distance error.

Lastly, we manually checked all the cities with extreme distance errors. We found out that the main problem is ambiguity with other named entities that are more famous than the city, e.g. the city Kobe is overshadowed by Kobe Bryant, Bismarck by Otto von Bismarck, Montgomery by the common first name. A special case of this problem is multiple cities with the same name. This is not a problem if there is large difference between the fame of the cities (e.g. London), but it is a problem for cities that are similar in size and fame (e.g. Midland, Kingstown, Bridgetown).

4.5 Embeddings Dimension

The dimension of the word embeddings obviously affects their results (Table 1). In this experiment we explore the effect of higher dimensions on the results. This should provide a hint to the authors of the semantic spaces how to choose the appropriate dimension.

In Figure 3, we show the results of LSA with dimension ranging from 100 to 1000. The performance degrades quickly as we decrease the dimen-

sion under 300. The results slightly improve as we increase the dimension from 300 to 600. There are no significant improvements as the dimension is increased over 600.

4.6 Regularization

The proposed evaluation uses regularization and requires the regularization weight α. Setting optimal regularization weight is difficult for some algorithms. We conducted an experiment to prove that the regularization weight does not play an important role in the evaluation, i.e. the scores of the embeddings are not heavily affected by our inability to find optimal regularization weights.

We performed randomized 10-fold cross-validation to find optimal regularization weight multiple times. The variance of the found regularization weights and also the impact of this variance were very small for a particular word embeddings method. Moreover, the optimal regularization weight is very similar for all the word embeddings. Figure 4 shows the mean geographic distance as a function of the regularization weight and suggests that the function can be easily optimized.

4.7 Noise Sensitivity

Given a set of models, the evaluation metric should be able to rank them reliably based on their quality. Batchkarov et al. (2016) propose a test of the reliability. They incrementally add noise to

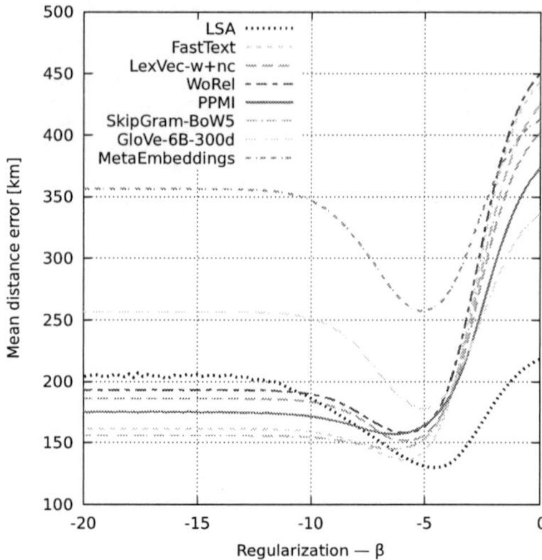

Figure 4: Influence of the regularization weight $\alpha = e^\beta$ on the mean geographic distance. The values are computed using 10 fold cross-validation on the training data.

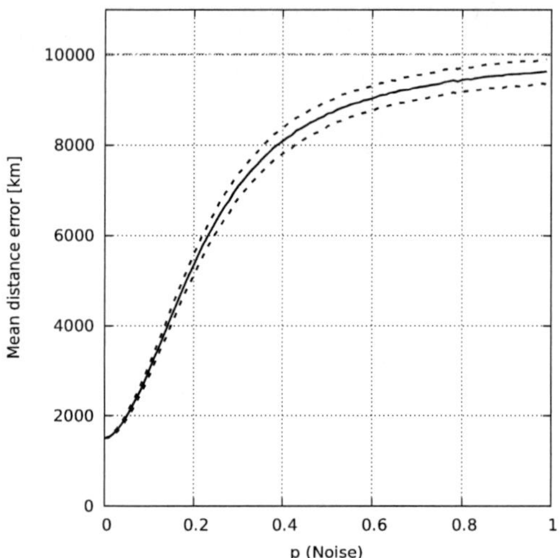

Figure 5: The effect of noise added to LSA embeddings. The figure shows mean value and standard deviation of 1000 runs. The red line on the top represents random city placement.

word embeddings and assume that word embeddings with more noise have lower quality. The metric should be able to capture the differences of the quality and smoothly and monotonically go from good results to results of random embeddings.

In Figure 5 we show the behavior of the proposed metric. We use the best embeddings (LSA) as a starting point. Then we add noise uniformly sampled from interval $[0, p]$ to each value in the embeddings. The parameter p is incrementally increased with step 0.01 from 0 to 1. For each value of p we repeat the evaluation 1000 times. The proposed metric works as expected. Firstly, the mean distance error almost linearly increases. As the embeddings become more random the increases slow down until they converge to the results of random embeddings.

4.8 Visualization

As a side effect, our evaluation approach also produces a natural visualization presented in Figure 6. The visualization can be used for comparison of methods, error analysis, or demonstration of semantics and unsupervised learning. The transformation also allows us to visualize common words on the map, not only city names.

5 Conclusion

We have proposed a new evaluation method for word embeddings. It measures how much information about geographic location of cities is contained in word embeddings. This type of evaluation differs from previously presented evaluations and forms a new word embeddings evaluation paradigm. The new paradigm does not evaluate the embeddings from the natural language processing view, but rather from the artificial intelligence view, where the algorithm tries to capture some information about the world.

We have analyzed both the evaluation metric and commonly used embeddings. We have shown that the metric is stable and can reliably distinguish between good and poor models.

LSA achieved the best results with mean geographic distance error of 1437 kilometers. Surprisingly, it outperformed mainstream models such as SkipGram. GloVe, with state-of-the-art results from other evaluations, performed rather poorly in the proposed evaluation.

In the future, we would like to implement the proposed paradigm with other similar evaluations, where we try to find out if the model is able to capture a specific real-world information.

The dataset and the evaluation software can be

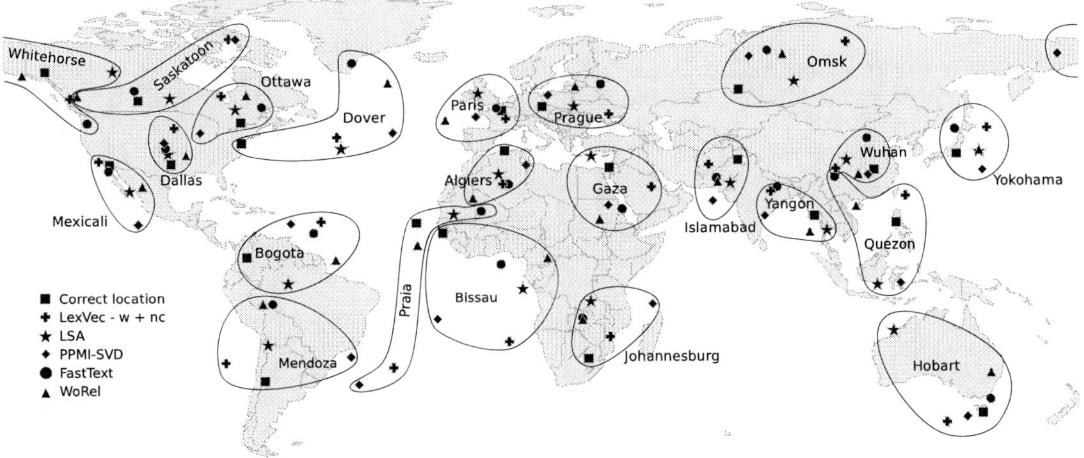

Figure 6: A visualization of selected cities placed on the map based on various word embeddings. Each circle denotes one city.

downloaded from the authors' websites[1].

Acknowledgments

This publication was supported by the project LO1506 of the Czech Ministry of Education, Youth and Sports under the program NPU I and by the university specific research project SGS-2016-018 Data and Software Engineering for Advanced Applications.

References

Eneko Agirre, Enrique Alfonseca, Keith Hall, Jana Kravalova, Marius Paşca, and Aitor Soroa. 2009. A study on similarity and relatedness using distributional and wordnet-based approaches. In *Proceedings of Human Language Technologies: The 2009 Annual Conference of the North American Chapter of the Association for Computational Linguistics*, NAACL '09, pages 19–27, Stroudsburg, PA, USA. Association for Computational Linguistics.

Mohit Bansal, Kevin Gimpel, and Karen Livescu. 2014. Tailoring continuous word representations for dependency parsing. In *Proceedings of the 52nd Annual Meeting of the Association for Computational Linguistics (Volume 2: Short Papers)*, pages 809–815, Baltimore, Maryland. Association for Computational Linguistics.

Miroslav Batchkarov, Thomas Kober, Jeremy Reffin, Julie Weeds, and David Weir. 2016. A critique of word similarity as a method for evaluating distributional semantic models. In *Proceedings of the 1st Workshop on Evaluating Vector-Space Representations for NLP*, pages 7–12, Berlin, Germany. Association for Computational Linguistics.

Piotr Bojanowski, Edouard Grave, Armand Joulin, and Tomas Mikolov. 2017. Enriching word vectors with subword information. *Transactions of the Association for Computational Linguistics*, 5:135–146.

Billy Chiu, Anna Korhonen, and Sampo Pyysalo. 2016. Intrinsic evaluation of word vectors fails to predict extrinsic performance. In *The First Workshop on Evaluating Vector Space Representations for NLP*. Association for Computational Linguistics.

Manaal Faruqui, Yulia Tsvetkov, Pushpendre Rastogi, and Chris Dyer. 2016. Problems with evaluation of word embeddings using word similarity tasks. In *Proceedings of the 1st Workshop on Evaluating Vector-Space Representations for NLP*, pages 30–35, Berlin, Germany. Association for Computational Linguistics.

Lev Finkelstein, Evgeniy Gabrilovich, Yossi Matias, Ehud Rivlin, Zach Solan, Gadi Wolfman, and Eytan Ruppin. 2001. Placing search in context: The concept revisited. In *Proceedings of the 10th International Conference on World Wide Web*, WWW '01, pages 406–414, New York, NY, USA. ACM.

Anna Gladkova and Aleksandr Drozd. 2016. Intrinsic evaluations of word embeddings: What can we do

---

[1]Currently at `konkol.me` and `nlp.kiv.zcu.cz`

better? In *Proceedings of the 1st Workshop on Evaluating Vector-Space Representations for NLP*, pages 36–42, Berlin, Germany. Association for Computational Linguistics.

Felix Hill, Roi Reichart, and Anna Korhonen. 2015. Simlex-999: Evaluating semantic models with genuine similarity estimation. *Comput. Linguist.*, 41(4):665–695.

Michal Konkol. 2017. Joint Unsupervised Learning of Semantic Representation of Words and Roles in Dependency Trees. In *RANLP 2017 – Recent Advances in Natural Language Processing*.

Michal Konkol, Tomáš Brychcín, and Miloslav Konopík. 2015. Latent semantics in named entity recognition. *Expert Systems with Applications*, 42(7):3470 – 3479.

Guillaume Lample, Miguel Ballesteros, Sandeep Subramanian, Kazuya Kawakami, and Chris Dyer. 2016. Neural architectures for named entity recognition. In *Proceedings of the 2016 Conference of the North American Chapter of the Association for Computational Linguistics: Human Language Technologies*, pages 260–270, San Diego, California. Association for Computational Linguistics.

Thomas K Landauer, Peter W Foltz, and Darrell Laham. 1998. An introduction to latent semantic analysis. *Discourse processes*, 25(2-3):259–284.

Omer Levy and Yoav Goldberg. 2014. Dependency-based word embeddings. In *Proceedings of the 52nd Annual Meeting of the Association for Computational Linguistics (Volume 2: Short Papers)*, pages 302–308, Baltimore, Maryland. Association for Computational Linguistics.

Omer Levy, Yoav Goldberg, and Ido Dagan. 2015. Improving distributional similarity with lessons learned from word embeddings. *TACL*, 3:211–225.

Tal Linzen. 2016. Issues in evaluating semantic spaces using word analogies. In *Proceedings of the 1st Workshop on Evaluating Vector-Space Representations for NLP*, pages 13–18, Berlin, Germany. Association for Computational Linguistics.

Thang Luong, Richard Socher, and Christopher D. Manning. 2013. Better word representations with recursive neural networks for morphology. In *Proceedings of the Seventeenth Conference on Computational Natural Language Learning, CoNLL 2013, Sofia, Bulgaria, August 8-9, 2013*, pages 104–113.

Andrew L. Maas, Raymond E. Daly, Peter T. Pham, Dan Huang, Andrew Y. Ng, and Christopher Potts. 2011. Learning word vectors for sentiment analysis. In *Proceedings of the 49th Annual Meeting of the Association for Computational Linguistics: Human Language Technologies - Volume 1*, HLT '11, pages 142–150, Stroudsburg, PA, USA. Association for Computational Linguistics.

Tomas Mikolov, Kai Chen, Greg Corrado, and Jeffrey Dean. 2013a. Efficient estimation of word representations in vector space. *CoRR*, abs/1301.3781.

Tomas Mikolov, Kai Chen, Greg Corrado, and Jeffrey Dean. 2013b. Efficient estimation of word representations in vector space. *CoRR*, abs/1301.3781.

Neha Nayak, Gabor Angeli, and Christopher D Manning. 2016. Evaluating word embeddings using a representative suite of practical tasks. In *The First Workshop on Evaluating Vector Space Representations for NLP*. Association for Computational Linguistics.

Jeffrey Pennington, Richard Socher, and Christopher D. Manning. 2014. Glove: Global vectors for word representation. In *Empirical Methods in Natural Language Processing (EMNLP)*, pages 1532–1543.

Herbert Rubenstein and John B. Goodenough. 1965. Contextual correlates of synonymy. *Commun. ACM*, 8(10):627–633.

Alexandre Salle, Aline Villavicencio, and Marco Idiart. 2016. Matrix factorization using window sampling and negative sampling for improved word representations. In *Proceedings of the 54th Annual Meeting of the Association for Computational Linguistics (Volume 2: Short Papers)*, pages 419–424, Berlin, Germany. Association for Computational Linguistics.

Tobias Schnabel, Igor Labutov, David Mimno, and Thorsten Joachims. 2015. Evaluation methods for unsupervised word embeddings. In *Proceedings of the 2015 Conference on Empirical Methods in Natural Language Processing*, pages 298–307, Lisbon, Portugal. Association for Computational Linguistics.

Wenpeng Yin and Hinrich Schütze. 2016. Learning word meta-embeddings. In *Proceedings of the 54th Annual Meeting of the Association for Computational Linguistics (Volume 1: Long Papers)*, pages 1351–1360, Berlin, Germany. Association for Computational Linguistics.

Will Y. Zou, Richard Socher, Daniel M. Cer, and Christopher D. Manning. 2013. Bilingual word embeddings for phrase-based machine translation. In *EMNLP*, pages 1393–1398. ACL.

On Modeling Sense Relatedness in Multi-prototype Word Embedding

Yixin Cao and **Juanzi Li**[*] and **Jiaxin Shi** and **Zhiyuan Liu** and **Chengjiang Li**
Dept. of Computer Science and Technology, Tsinghua University, China 100084
{cao-yx13,ljz,shi-jx,liuzy,licj17}@mail.tsinghua.edu.cn

Abstract

To enhance the expression ability of distributional word representation learning model, many researchers tend to induce word senses through clustering, and learn multiple embedding vectors for each word, namely multi-prototype word embedding model. However, most related work ignores the relatedness among word senses which actually plays an important role. In this paper, we propose a novel approach to capture word sense relatedness in multi-prototype word embedding model. Particularly, we differentiate the original sense and extended senses of a word by introducing their global occurrence information and model their relatedness through the local textual context information. Based on the idea of fuzzy clustering, we introduce a random process to integrate these two types of senses and design two non-parametric methods for word sense induction. To make our model more scalable and efficient, we use an online joint learning framework extended from the Skip-gram model. The experimental results demonstrate that our model outperforms both conventional single-prototype embedding models and other multi-prototype embedding models, and achieves more stable performance when trained on smaller data.

1 Introduction

Word embedding, representing words in a low dimentional vector space, plays an increasing important role in various IR and NLP related tasks, such as language modeling (Bengio et al., 2006;

Mnih and Hinton, 2009), named entity recognition and disambiguation (Turian et al., 2010; Collobert et al., 2011), and syntactic parsing (Socher et al., 2011, 2013). This trend has been accelerated by the CBOW and the Skip-gram models of (Mikolov et al., 2013b,a) due to its efficiency and remarkable semantic compositionality of embedding vectors (e.g. *vec(king)-vec(queen)=vec(man)-vec(woman)*). However, the assumption that each word is represented by only one single vector is problematic when dealing with the polysemous words.

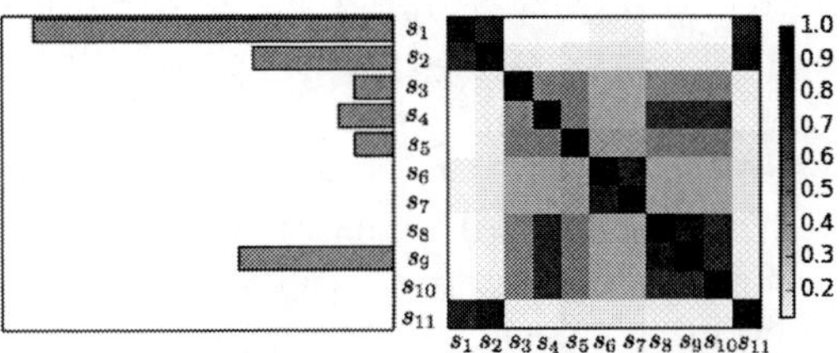

Figure 1: Relatedness among senses of the word "*book*".

To enhance the expression ability of the embedding model, recent research has a rising enthusiasm for representing words at sense level. That is, an individual word is represented as multiple vectors, where each vector corresponds to one of its meanings. Pervious work mostly focus on using clustering to induce word senses (each cluster refers to one of the senses) and then learn the word sense representations respectively (Reisinger and Mooney, 2010; Huang et al., 2012; Tian et al., 2014; Neelakantan et al., 2014; Li and Jurafsky, 2015). However, the above approaches ignore the relatedness among the word senses. Hence the following limitations arise in the usage of hard clustering. First of all, many clustering errors will be caused by using hard clustering based method because the senses of the polysemous word actu-

233

Proceedings of the The 8th International Joint Conference on Natural Language Processing, pages 233–242,
Taipei, Taiwan, November 27 – December 1, 2017 ©2017 AFNLP

---

[*] Corresponding author.

ally have no distinct semantic boundary (Liu et al., 2015). Secondly, due to dividing the occurrences of a word into separate clusters, the embedding model will suffer from more data sparsity issue as compared to the Skip-gram model. Thirdly, the embedding quality is considerably sensitive to the clustering results due to the isolation of different sense clusters.

To address this problem, we learn the embedding vectors of the word senses with some common features if the senses are related. Instead of clearly cutting the sense cluster boundaries, one occurrence of the word will be assigned into multiple sense clusters with different probabilities, which agrees with a classic task of word sense annotation, Graded Word Sense Assignment (Erk and McCarthy, 2009; Jurgens and Klapaftis, 2013).

Actually, the senses of a polysemous word are related not only by the contiguity of meaning within a semantic field[1], but also by the extended relationship between the original meaning and the extended meaning (Von Engelhardt and Zimmermann, 1988). We investigate the relatedness of the synsets (word senses) in WordNet (Miller, 1995) through the Wu & Palmer measure[2] (Wu and Palmer, 1994), and present an interesting example of the word "*book*" in Figure 1. The right side is the similarity matrix of its 11 nominal synsets, where s_i denotes the ith synset. Each tile represents a similarity value between two synsets whose color deepens as the value increases. The left side is their frequencies in WordNet. On one hand, we can see apparent correlations among these senses in different levels. Note that (s_1, s_2, s_{11}) are strongly related, and so are (s_6, s_7) and (s_8, s_9, s_{10}). This is because of their extended relationship. Take (s_1, s_2, s_{11}) for example, s_1 refers to the sense of "*the written work printed on pages bound together*", s_2 refers to "*physical objects consisting of a number of pages bound together*" and s_3 refers to "*a number of sheets (or stamps, etc.) bound together*". Obviously, s_1 is the original meaning, s_2 and s_{11} are the extended meanings. Moreover, the relatedness suggests that the senses share some common textual features in the contexts. On the other hand, the frequency of the original meaning s_1 is much

higher than that of the extended meanings s_2 and s_{11}, which suggests that the word sense distribution in corpus should be taken into account when modeling word sense relatedness.

In this paper, we propose a novel method, namely FCSE (Fuzzy Clustering-based multi-Sense Embedding model), that models the relatedness among word senses by using the fuzzy clustering based method for word sense induction, and then learns sense embeddings via a variant of Skip-gram model. The basic idea behind fuzzy clustering is that the senses may be related and share common features through the overlaps of the sense clusters. Based on our observations of the original meaning and the extended meaning, we further design two non-parametric methods, FCSE-1 and FCSE-2, to model the local textual context information of senses as well as their global occurrence distribution by incorporating the Generalized Polya Urn (GPU) model. For efficiency and scalability, our proposed model also adopts an online joint learning procedure.

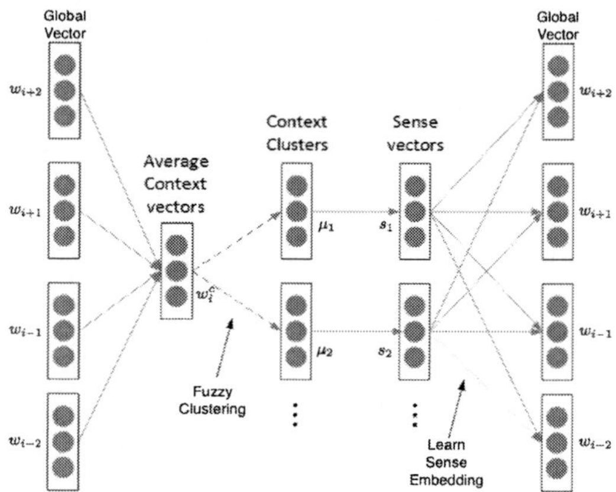

Figure 2: Framework of FCSE

2 The Framework of FCSE

FCSE adopts an online procedure that induces the word sense and learns the sense embeddings jointly. Given a word sequence $D = \{w_1, w_2, \ldots, w_M\}$, we obtain the input of our model, the word and its context words, by sliding a window with the length of $2k + 1$. The output is also the context words. During the learning process, two types of vectors are maintained for each word, the global vector w_i and its sense vectors[3]

---

[1] According to https://en.wikipedia.org/wiki/Polysemy.

[2] The Wu & Palmer measure is an edge based approach that is tied to the structure of WordNet. Also, one can try different relatedness approaches and will find similar results.

[3] All the vectors are randomly initialized.

$w_i^{s_i}$. Note that the number of senses $|S_i|$ is varying because the cluster method is non-parametric.

As shown in Figure 2, there are mainly two steps: the clustering step and the embedding learning step. The former step incrementally clusters all the occurrences of one word according to its context vectors by computing the average sum of the global vectors of the context words: $\mathbf{w_i^c} = \frac{1}{2k}\sum_{-k\leq j\leq k}\mathbf{w_{i+j}}$. Each cluster refers to one word sense, thus each occurrence will be annotated with at least one sense.

In the second step, we update the sense embeddings via a variant of the Skip-gram model (Mikolov et al., 2013b). The main difference between our model and Skip-gram is that we aim to predict the context words given the exact sense of the target word instead of the word itself. Moreover, because several senses are assigned to the current word with probabilities, we leverage all the related senses to predict the context words. The intuition is that the related senses tend to have common context words as mentioned in Section 1. Thus, all the assigned sense vectors will be updated with weights simultaneously as follows:

$$\mathcal{L}(D) = \frac{1}{M}\sum_{i=1}^{M}\sum_{-k\leq j\leq k}\sum_{s_i}^{|S_i|}\lambda_{s_i}\log p(w_{i+j}|w_i^{s_i})$$

$$(1)$$

where the probability of $p(w_{i+j}|w_i^{s_i})$ is defined using softmax function, and s_i denotes the sense index of word w_i. S_i is the set of existing senses, λ_{s_i} is the update weight of sense s_i. We set the weights proportional to the probabilities of the current word being annotated with sense s_i, which is equivalent to the results of fuzzy clustering, the likelihood of the context w_i^c assigned into the sense cluster s_i:

$$\lambda_{s_i} \propto \begin{cases} p(s_i|w_i^c) & s_i \ is \ sampled \\ 0 & otherwise \end{cases} \quad (2)$$

Finally, we use negative sampling technique [4] for efficient learning.

3 Word Sense Induction

Section 2 describes the framework of our model including how to obtain the input features of clustering and to use the cluster results for the sense

---

[4]More detailed information can be found in (Mikolov et al., 2013b).

embedding learning. In this section, we present two fuzzy clustering based methods for clustering-based word sense induction, FCSE-1 and FCSE-2. Both of them are non-parametric and conduct online procedures.

Based on our observations in Section 1, the occurrence of word senses is usually distinguishing between the original meaning and the extended meaning, while the original meaning and its extended meanings are semantically related with some common textual contexts. Considering both of the two aspects, in FCSE-1, we induce the word sense according to the cluster probability proportional to the distance of its centroid to the current word's contexts; and FCSE-2 utilizes a random process, the Generalized Polya Urn (GPU) model, to further incorporate the senses' global occurrence distribution.

3.1 FCSE-1

Adopting an online procedure, FCSE-1 clusters the contexts of one word incrementally. When first meet one word, we create a cluster with the centroid of its context vector. Then, for each occurrence of the word, several existing clusters are sampled following a probability distribution; or a new cluster is created only if all the probabilities of the context belonging to the clusters equal to zero. Finally, all the sampled clusters will be updated by adding the current context vector into them.

Remember that each word w_i is associated with a global vector, varying number of clusters, and the corresponding sense vectors. FCSE-1 measures the semantic distance of the context vector to its cluster centers, and aims to sample the nearest ones (maybe multiple related senses). Given the context vector w_i^c, the probability of the word belonging to the existing lth sense is:

$$p(s_i = l|w_i^c) = \begin{cases} \frac{1}{Z}Sim(\mu_i^l, w_i^c) \\ 0 \ if \ Sim(\mu_i^l, w_i^c) < \epsilon_{under} \end{cases}$$

$$(3)$$

where μ_i^l denotes the centroid of the lth sense cluster, Z is the normalization term and $Sim(\cdot,\cdot)$ can be any similarity measurement. In the experiments we use cosine similarity as the semantic distance measurement. ϵ_{under} is a pre-defined threshold that indicates how easily we create a new sense cluster. Similarly, we use another threshold ϵ_{upper} for deciding the number of sampled clusters. Suppose that the probabilities $\{p_{n_i}|n_i \in S_i\}$ is ranked in descending order, then we pick up the clusters with top n_i probabilities until $p_{n_i} - p_{n_i+1} > \epsilon_{upper}$. Note that the hyper-parameters meet $0 \leq \epsilon_{under}, \epsilon_{upper} \leq 1$.

3.2 FCSE-2

Since FCSE-1 uses two hyper-parameters to respectively control a new cluster initialization and the number of clusters sampled, which is difficult to set manually. So, instead of the fixed thresholds, we make a further randomization by introducing a random process, GPU, in FCSE-2. Besides, more inherit properties of the word senses can be taken into account, including not only the local information of the semantic distance from the context to the cluster centers, but also the frequency, which is related to how likely the current sense is an original meaning or an extended meanings.

In this section, we will firstly give a brief summarization of the GPU model, and then introduce how to incorporate it into our model.

3.2.1 Generalized Polya Urn model

Polya urn model is a type of random process that draws balls from an urn and replaces it along with extra balls. Suppose that there are some balls of colors in the urn at the beginning. For each draw, the ball of the ith color is selected followed by the distribution:

$$p(color = i) = \frac{m_i}{m}$$

where m is the total number of balls, and m_i is the number of balls of the ith color. A standard urn model returns the ball back along with an extra ball of the same color, which can be seen as a reinforcement and sometimes expressed as the richer gets richer. More detailed information can be found in the survey paper (Pemantle et al., 2007). Polya urn model can be used for non-parametric clustering, where each data point refers to a ball in the urn, and its cluster label is denoted by the ball's color.

Since the fixed replacement lacks of flexibility, the GPU model conducts the reinforcement process following another distribution over the colors. That is, when a ball of color i is drawn, another A_{ij} balls of color j will be put back. Then, for each draw, we replace the ball with different number of balls of various colors according to the distribution matrix A. As repeating this process, the

drawing probability will be altered if the number of extra balls are nonzero.

3.2.2 Incorporating GPU into Embedding model

The induction process of the word senses can be regarded as a GPU model. The original meaning is sampled firstly, and then the extended meanings are sampled through the reinforcement. That is, we sample an extended meaning according to a conditional probability given the original meaning. The basic idea is that knowing the original meaning is necessary for understanding the target word annotated with an extended meaning in a document. For example, the extended meaning of the word "milk" when used in the terms "glacier milk" won't be well understood unless we know the original meaning of "milk".

Correspondingly, in the GPU model, a urn denotes a word, the ball and the color refers to the occurrence and the sense, respectively. Note that each ball has an index that distinguishes different occurrences. Thus, the balls of the same color correspond to a sense cluster.

We sample the related senses in two stages. In the first stage, for the occurrence of the word w_i, we sample a sense $s_{io} = l$ considering the global distribution of the word senses as well as the semantic distance from the context features to the cluster center. In the second stage, several senses are sampled conditioned on the previous result: $p(s_{ie} = l'|s_{io} = l)$.

In this way, we find the original meaning and the extended meanings separately following different distributions. Considering the observation that the original meaning occurs more frequently (as described in Section 1), we define the probability distribution of the original meaning as follows:

$$p(s_{io} = l|w_i^c) \propto \begin{cases} \frac{m_{il}}{\gamma + m_i} \cdot Sim(\mu_i^l, w_i^c) & l \in S_i \\ \frac{\gamma}{\gamma + m_i} & l \ is \ new \end{cases} \tag{4}$$

where m_i is the total number of occurrences of the target word w_i, m_{il} is the number of the lth cluster and we have $\sum_l^{S_i} m_{il} = m_i$. Note that γ is a hyper-parameter that indicates how likely a new cluster will be created, and its impact decreases as the size of training data m_i increases.

The probability of sampling an extended meaning is proportional to the semantic distance of the corresponding cluster center to the context features as well as the cluster center sampled in the first stage, which is defined as follows:

$$p(s_{ie} = l'|s_{io} = l, w_i^c) \propto \epsilon_e \cdot Sim(w_i^{s_{ie}}, \frac{w_i^{s_{io}} + w_i^c}{2}) \tag{5}$$

where ϵ_e varies from 0 to 1 and controls the strength of the reinforcement. We will talk about it in the next subsection.

Sampling separately, the relatedness of the original meaning and the extended meanings are modeled and each occurrence of the word has been annotated with one original sense and several extended senses (or there is no additional extended meanings). Note that the likelihood of the occurrence of the word annotated with an extended meaning is $p(s_{ie} = l'|s_{io} = l, w_i^c)p(s_{io} = l|w_i^c)$. Clearly, the probabilities of sampling the extended meanings are always lower than that of the original meaning.

3.3 Relationship with State-of-the-art Methods

FCSE-1 The hyper-parameters meet $0 \leq \epsilon_{under}, \epsilon_{upper} \leq 1$. ϵ_{upper} is used to control the number of clusters assigned to the current word, and FCSE-1 will degrade to hard assignment if we set $\epsilon_{upper} = 0$, which is similar with the NP-MSSG model in (Neelakantan et al., 2014). We can use ϵ_{under} to control the sense number of each word, and an extreme case of $\epsilon_{under} = 0$ denotes that we create only a sense cluster for each word, then the model is equivalent to the Skip-gram.

FCSE-2 The number of the extended meanings $|S_{ie}|$ varies from 0 to $|S_i^{-l}|$, where S_i^{-l} denotes the set excluding the original meaning s_i^l. The hyper-parameter $0 \leq \epsilon_e \leq 1$ is used to control the strength of the GPU reinforcement as well as the number of the extended meanings. Particularly, if we set $\epsilon_e = 0$, the second sample for the extended meanings has been turned off, and then FCSE-2 degrades to the SG+ model in (Li and Jurafsky, 2015), which is another state-of-the-art method for multi-prototype word embedding model based on hard clustering. By setting $\gamma = 0$ in Equation 4, which is used to control the probability of creating a new sense, FCSE-2 won't create new senses. Learning a single sense for each word makes the step of sense sampling becomes meaningless. Thus, FCSE-2 uses the only embedding of the current word to predict its context words, which is equivalent to the Skip-gram.

4 Empirical Evaluation

In this section, we demonstrate the effectiveness of our model from two aspects, qualitative and quantitative analysis. For qualitative analysis, we presents nearest 10 neighbors for each word sense to give an intuitive impression. For quantitative analysis, we conduct a series of experiments on the NLP task of word similarity using two benchmark datasets, and explore the influence of the size of training corpus.

4.1 Data Preparation

We train our model on Wikipedia, the April 2010 dump also used by (Huang et al., 2012; Liu et al., 2015; Neelakantan et al., 2014). Before training, we have conducted a series of preprocessing steps. At first, the articles have been splitted into sentences, following by stemming and lemmatization using the python package of NLTK[5]. Then, we rank the vocabulary according to their frequencies, and only learn the embeddings of the top 200,000 words. The other words out of the vocabulary are replaced by a pre-defined mark "UNK". Note that FCSE is slower than word2vec[6], but the efficiency is far away from being an obstacle on training.

Below we describe three baseline methods and parameter settings, followed by qualitative analysis of nearest neighbors of each word sense. Then, quantitative performance will be presented via experiments on two benchmark word similarity tasks.

4.2 Baseline Methods

Word Embedding model can be roughly divided into two types: single vector embedding model and multi-prototype embedding model. To validate the performance, we compare our model with three models of both the two types: Skip-gram, NP-MSSG and SG+. The reason why we select them as the baseline methods is because: (i) they are the state-of-the-art methods of word embedding model; (ii) NP-MSSG and SG+ adopts the similar learning framework to our model.

- **Skip-gram*** aims to leverage the current word to predict the context words and learn

---

[5]http://www.nltk.org/
[6]https://code.google.com/archive/p/word2vec/.

<table>
<tr><td colspan="2">Apple</td></tr>
<tr><td>Skip-gram*</td><td>iigs, boysenberry, apricot, nectarine, ibook, ipad, blackberry, blackcurrants, loganberry, macintosh</td></tr>
<tr><td rowspan="2">NP-MSSG*</td><td>nectarine, boysenberry, peach, blackcurrants, pear, passionfruit, feijoa, loganberry, elderflower, apricot</td></tr>
<tr><td>macintosh, mac, iigs, macworks, macwrite, bundled, compatible, laserwriter, ibook, ipod</td></tr>
<tr><td rowspan="2">FCSE-1</td><td>nectarine, blackcurrants, loganberry, pear, boysenberry, strawberry, apricot, plum, cherry, blueberry</td></tr>
<tr><td>macintosh, imac, iigs, ibook, ipod, pcpaint, iphone, booter, ipad, macbook</td></tr>
<tr><td colspan="2">Berry</td></tr>
<tr><td>Skip-gram*</td><td>greengage, thimbleberry, loganberry, dewberry, boysenberry, pome, passionfruit, acai, maybellene, blackcurrant</td></tr>
<tr><td>NP-MSSG*</td><td>thimbleberry, pome, nectarine, greengage, fruit, boysenberry, dewberry, acai, loganberry, ripe</td></tr>
<tr><td rowspan="2">FCSE-1</td><td>nectarine, thimbleberry, blueberry, fruit, pome, loganberry, apple, elderberry, passionfruit, litchi</td></tr>
<tr><td>gordy, taylor, lambert, osborne, satchell, earland, thornton, fullwood, allen, sherrell</td></tr>
</table>

Table 1: Nearest 10 neighbors of each sense of the words *"apple"* and *"berry"*, computed by cosine similarity, for different models.

the embeddings within a two-layer neural network.

- **NP-MSSG*** measures the distance of the current word to each sense, picks up the nearest one and learning its embedding via a standard Skip-gram model.

- **SG+*** improves the NP-MSSG model by introducing a random process that induces the word sense with probabilities.

The symbol $*$ denotes that we, instead of using their released codes, carefully reimplement these models for the sake of making the comparisons as fairly as possible. Thus, all the models share the same program switched by the correspondingly parameters (as described in Section 3.3). Note that there may be some minor differences such as optimizing tricks between our program and that of their released.

4.3 Parameter Setting

As discussed in Section 3.3, our model can degrade to the baseline methods by switching different parameters: the threshold ϵ_{upper}, ϵ_e and the max number of word senses N_{MAX}. All the meth-

ods are implemented on the same java program[7], and use, at the greatest extent, the same settings including the training corpus, shared parameters and the program code, etc.

Switching parameters For FCSE-1 and NP-MSSG, ϵ_{upper} is set 0.05 and 0, respectively. Similarly, We set $\epsilon_e = 1$ for FCSE-2, and $\epsilon_e = 0$ for SG+. When setting $N_{MAX} = 1$, all the multi-prototype word embedding models degrade to single vector embedding model, that is, the Skip-gram model.

Shared parameters Following the original papers of NP-MSSG and SG+, the threshold ϵ_{under} in FCSE-1 is also set with -0.5, and $\gamma = 0.01$ is used in both FCSE-2 and SG+. The initial learning rate $\alpha = 0.015$ is used for parameter estimation. We pick up 5 words as the context window, and 400 dimensional vectors to learn sense embeddings of the top 200,000 frequent words. Note that all the parameters including the embedding vectors are initialized randomly.

---

[7]We will publish the code if accepted, which is based on the published project of SG+ in https://github.com/jiweil/mutli-sense-embedding.

4.4 Qualitative Analysis

Before conducting the experiments on word similarity task, we first give qualitative analysis of our model as well as two baseline models[8] by representing the word sense with its nearest neighbors, which are computed through cosine similarity of the embeddings between each of the word senses and the senses of the other words.

Table 1 presents the nearest 10 neighbors of each sense of two words ranked through the similarity. Skip-gram shows a mixed result of different senses, while the other two models produce a reasonable number of word sense, and their neighbors are indeed semantically correlated. For the word "*Apple*", there are two meanings of the fruit and technology company. NP-MSSG and FCSE-1 can differentiate the two senses, but FCSE-1 clearly achieves a more coherent ranking results. For the word "*Berry*", FCSE-1 outperforms NP-MSSG for it successfully identifies another sense of person's name except the dominant sense of fruit. This is because "*Berry*" is used as a person's name much less frequently than a fruit. Thus, it may cause the data sparsity issue, while our model is capable of addressing this problem by improving the usage of training corpus, which will be further discussed in Section 4.5.3.

4.5 Word Similarity

In this subsection, we evaluate our embeddings on two classic tasks of measuring word similarity: word similarity and contextual word similarity. To better test the ability of our model to address the problem of data sparsity, we train it using only 30% of the training corpus (sampled randomly). Also, we give comparisons with the performance using all the training data.

WordSim353 (Finkelstein et al., 2001) is a benchmark dataset for word similarity. It contains 353 word pairs and their similarity scores assessed by 16 subjects. SCWS, released by (Huang et al., 2012), is a benchmark dataset for contextual word similarity, which computes the semantic relatedness between two words conditioned on the specific context. It consists 2,003 pairs of words and their sentential contexts. WordSim353 focuses on the ambiguity among similar words, and SCWS is for the ambiguity of word senses in different con-

texts.

4.5.1 Evaluation Metrics

To evaluate the performance of our model, we compute the similarity between each word pair through some measurement, and then use the spearman correlation between our results and the human judgments to evaluate the performance of the model.

Working on WordSim353, we compute the average similarity between the word pairs the same as(Reisinger and Mooney, 2010; Neelakantan et al., 2014). And working on SCWS, we use two similarity measurements, avgSimC and maxSimC, proposed by (Neelakantan et al., 2014; Liu et al., 2015). avgSimC focuses on evaluating the average similarity between all the senses of the two words, and maxSimC evaluates the similarity between the senses with max probability for the current word.

4.5.2 Results and Analysis

Table 2 and 3 shows the overall performance of our proposed model as well as the baseline methods on WordSim353 and SCWS datasets. We only obtain lower performance numbers for SG+, which suggests that they may be more susceptible to noise and worse generalization ability. However, this is a fair comparison because all the methods share the same parameter settings and the code. The following is indicated in the results:

Model	$\rho \times 100$
NP-MSSG*	67.3
SG+*	66.9
Skip-gram*	66.7
FCSE-1	68.8
FCSE-2	**69.5**

Table 2: Results on the wordsim353 dataset. The table presents spearman correlation ρ between each model's similarity rank results and the human judgement.

- Both of FCSE-1 and FCSE-2 outperform all of the baseline methods, because it models the relatedness among word senses through the common features, which inherits the advantages of multi-prototype model and ensures adequate training data as compared to single vector model.

---

[8]To be fair, we only show the comparisons among FCSE-1, NP-MSSG and Skip-gram, since the paper of SG+ (Li and Jurafsky, 2015) didn't give the qualitative results.

Model	avg	max
NP-MSSG*	64.0	65.2
SG+*	64.4	65.6
Skip-gram*	64.1	65.5
FCSE-1	**67.1**	67.1
FCSE-2	66.3	**67.5**

Table 3: Results on the SCWS dataset. "avg" and "max" respectively denotes the similarity measurements of avgSimC and maxSimC.

- The skip-gram model achieves rather comparative performance due to its good generalization ability, especially in a smaller training set as compared to hard-cluster based multi-prototype word embedding models.

- FCSE-2 achieves the best performance due to the separately sample for the original meaning and the extended meanings, which follows different distributions incorporating both the global and local information.

We also investigate the ability of our method that helps address the data sparsity issue by training on different size of data.

4.5.3 Training on Different Size Data

Generally speaking, the embedding model performs better when trained on a larger corpus. The multi-prototype embedding model suffers more data sparsity issue than single prototype embedding due to its further partition on the set of words' contexts by clustering, and then performs even worse using a smaller training corpus. In this subsection, we study the capability of FCSE to helps address this problem by testing the performance when training on different size corpus.

Figure 3 shows the comparison between the performance of all the models trained on 30% data and on 100% data. As the training data decreases, all the models perform worse especially the hard clustering based method. Compared to full corpus, we can see more apparent gap between NP-MSSG and FCSE-1 (from 2.6% to 3.1%), SG+ and FCSE-2 (from 0.1% to 1.9%). That is, the gap between FCSE and other methods gets closer when there are adequate training corpus, which is in accordance with the intuition. The data sparsity issue gradually vanishes along with the growth of training data. Besides, the performance of the single-prototype word embedding model increases

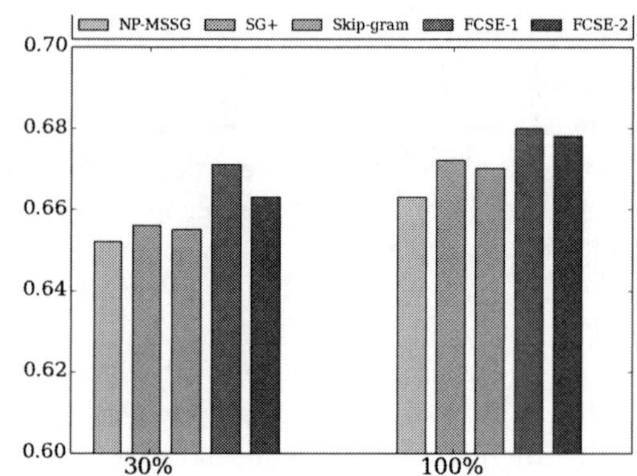

Figure 3: The performance of each model when training on different size of data

only 1.6%. Our proposed model, both FCSE-1 and FCSE-2, achieves more stable performance (0.2% and 0.6% changes).

5 Related Work

Multi-prototype word embedding has been extensively studied in the literature (Chen et al., 2014; Cao et al., 2017; Liu et al., 2015; Reisinger and Mooney, 2010; Huang et al., 2012; Tian et al., 2014; Neelakantan et al., 2014; Li and Jurafsky, 2015). They can be roughly divided into three groups. The first group is clustering based methods. As described in Section 1, (Reisinger and Mooney, 2010; Huang et al., 2012; Tian et al., 2014; Neelakantan et al., 2014; Li and Jurafsky, 2015) use clustering to induce word sense and then learn sense embeddings via Skip-gram model. The second group is to introduce topics to represent different word senses, such as (Liu et al., 2015) considers that a word under different topics leads to different meanings, so it embeds both word and topic simultaneously and combines them as the word sense. However, it is difficult to determine the number of topics. The third group incorporates external knowledge (i.e. knowledge bases) to induce word/phrase senses. (Chen et al., 2014) jointly represents and disambiguates the word sense on the basis of the synsets in WordNet. (Cao et al., 2017) regards entities in KBs as word/phrase senses, and first learn word/phrase and sense embeddings separately, then align them via Wikipedia anchors. However, it fails to deal with the words that are not included in knowledge bases.

6 Conclusion

In this paper, we propose a novel method that models the word sense relatedness in multi-prototype word embedding model. It considers the difference and relatedness between the original meanings and the extended meanings. Our proposed method adopts an online framework to induce the word sense and learn sense embeddings jointly, which makes our model more scalable and efficient. Two non-parametric methods for fuzzy clustering produce flexible number of word senses. Particularly, FCSE-2 introduces the Generalized Polya Urn process to integrate both the global occurrence information and local textual context information. The qualitative and quantitative results demonstrate the stable and higher performance of our model.

In the future, we are interested in incorporating external knowledge, such as WordNet, to supervise the clustering results, and in extending our model to learn more precise sentence and document embeddings.

7 Acknowledgments

The work is supported by 973 Program (No. 2014CB340504), NSFC key project (No. 6153301861661146007), Fund of Online Education Research Center, Ministry of Education (No. 2016ZD102), and THUNUS NExT Co-Lab.

References

Yoshua Bengio, Holger Schwenk, Jean-Sébastien Senécal, Fréderic Morin, and Jean-Luc Gauvain. 2006. Neural probabilistic language models. In *Innovations in Machine Learning*, pages 137–186. Springer.

Yixin Cao, Lifu Huang, Heng Ji, Xu Chen, and Juanzi Li. 2017. Bridge text and knowledge by learning multi-prototype entity mention embedding. In *Proceedings of the 55th annual meeting of the association for computational linguistics*. Association for Computational Linguistics.

Xinxiong Chen, Zhiyuan Liu, and Maosong Sun. 2014. A unified model for word sense representation and disambiguation. In *Proceedings of the 2014 Conference on Empirical Methods in Natural Language Processing (EMNLP)*, pages 1025–1035.

Ronan Collobert, Jason Weston, Léon Bottou, Michael Karlen, Koray Kavukcuoglu, and Pavel Kuksa. 2011. Natural language processing (almost) from scratch. *The Journal of Machine Learning Research*, 12:2493–2537.

Katrin Erk and Diana McCarthy. 2009. Graded word sense assignment. In *Proceedings of the 2009 Conference on Empirical Methods in Natural Language Processing: Volume 1-Volume 1*, pages 440–449. Association for Computational Linguistics.

Lev Finkelstein, Evgeniy Gabrilovich, Yossi Matias, Ehud Rivlin, Zach Solan, Gadi Wolfman, and Eytan Ruppin. 2001. Placing search in context: The concept revisited. In *Proceedings of the 10th international conference on World Wide Web*, pages 406–414. ACM.

Eric H Huang, Richard Socher, Christopher D Manning, and Andrew Y Ng. 2012. Improving word representations via global context and multiple word prototypes. In *Proceedings of the 50th Annual Meeting of the Association for Computational Linguistics: Long Papers-Volume 1*, pages 873–882. Association for Computational Linguistics.

David Jurgens and Ioannis Klapaftis. 2013. Semeval-2013 task 13: Word sense induction for graded and non-graded senses. In *Second joint conference on lexical and computational semantics (* SEM)*, volume 2, pages 290–299.

Jiwei Li and Dan Jurafsky. 2015. Do multi-sense embeddings improve natural language understanding? In *Proceedings of the 2015 Conference on Empirical Methods in Natural Language Processing, EMNLP 2015, Lisbon, Portugal, September 17-21, 2015*, pages 1722–1732.

Yang Liu, Zhiyuan Liu, Tat-Seng Chua, and Maosong Sun. 2015. Topical word embeddings. In *Twenty-Ninth AAAI Conference on Artificial Intelligence*.

Tomas Mikolov, Kai Chen, Greg Corrado, and Jeffrey Dean. 2013a. Efficient estimation of word representations in vector space. *CoRR*, abs/1301.3781.

Tomas Mikolov, Ilya Sutskever, Kai Chen, Greg S Corrado, and Jeff Dean. 2013b. Distributed representations of words and phrases and their compositionality. In *Advances in neural information processing systems*, pages 3111–3119.

George A Miller. 1995. Wordnet: a lexical database for english. *Communications of the ACM*, 38(11):39–41.

Andriy Mnih and Geoffrey E Hinton. 2009. A scalable hierarchical distributed language model. In *Advances in neural information processing systems*, pages 1081–1088.

Arvind Neelakantan, Jeevan Shankar, Alexandre Passos, and Andrew McCallum. 2014. Efficient non-parametric estimation of multiple embeddings per word in vector space. In *Proceedings of the 2014 Conference on Empirical Methods in Natural Language Processing, EMNLP 2014, October 25-29, 2014, Doha, Qatar, A meeting of SIGDAT, a Special Interest Group of the ACL*, pages 1059–1069.

Robin Pemantle et al. 2007. A survey of random processes with reinforcement. *Probab. Surv*, 4(0):1–79.

Joseph Reisinger and Raymond J Mooney. 2010. Multi-prototype vector-space models of word meaning. In *Human Language Technologies: The 2010 Annual Conference of the North American Chapter of the Association for Computational Linguistics*, pages 109–117. Association for Computational Linguistics.

Richard Socher, John Bauer, Christopher D Manning, and Andrew Y Ng. 2013. Parsing with compositional vector grammars. In *In Proceedings of the ACL conference*. Citeseer.

Richard Socher, Cliff C Lin, Chris Manning, and Andrew Y Ng. 2011. Parsing natural scenes and natural language with recursive neural networks. In *Proceedings of the 28th international conference on machine learning (ICML-11)*, pages 129–136.

Fei Tian, Hanjun Dai, Jiang Bian, Bin Gao, Rui Zhang, Enhong Chen, and Tie-Yan Liu. 2014. A probabilistic model for learning multi-prototype word embeddings. In *Proceedings of COLING*, pages 151–160.

Joseph Turian, Lev Ratinov, and Yoshua Bengio. 2010. Word representations: a simple and general method for semi-supervised learning. In *Proceedings of the 48th annual meeting of the association for computational linguistics*, pages 384–394. Association for Computational Linguistics.

Wolf Von Engelhardt and Jörg Zimmermann. 1988. *Theory of earth science*. CUP Archive.

Zhibiao Wu and Martha Palmer. 1994. Verbs semantics and lexical selection. In *Proceedings of the 32nd annual meeting on Association for Computational Linguistics*, pages 133–138. Association for Computational Linguistics.

Unsupervised Segmentation of Phoneme Sequences based on Pitman-Yor Semi-Markov Model using Phoneme Length Context

Ryu Takeda and **Kazunori Komatani**

The Institute of Scientific and Industrial Research, Osaka University

8-1, Mihogaoka, Ibaraki, Osaka 567-0047, Japan

{rtakeda, komatani}@sanken.osaka-u.ac.jp

Abstract

Unsupervised segmentation of phoneme sequences is an essential process to obtain unknown words during spoken dialogues. In this segmentation, an input phoneme sequence without delimiters is converted into segmented sub-sequences corresponding to words. The Pitman-Yor semi-Markov model (PYSMM) is promising for this problem, but its performance degrades when it is applied to phoneme-level word segmentation. This is because of insufficient cues for the segmentation, e.g., homophones are improperly treated as single entries and their different contexts are also confused. We propose a phoneme-length context model for PYSMM to give a helpful cue at the phoneme-level and to predict succeeding segments more accurately. Our experiments showed that the peak performance with our context model outperformed those without such a context model by 0.045 at most in terms of F-measures of estimated segmentation.

1 Introduction

1.1 Motivation

The final goal of our current project is to achieve the development of robots or systems that acquire knowledge during spoken interactions between them and human beings in the open world. Unknown or new words appear frequently in our daily lives, and because their meanings may be different for the systems deployed in different areas, automatic lexicon acquisition is a useful function for maintenance-free spoken dialogue systems.

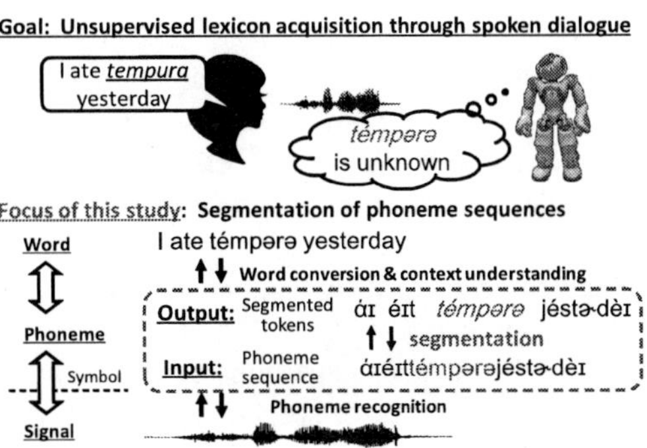

Figure 1: Our target problem

In this paper, we focus on the phoneme-level representation of utterance – not in the signal-level – to relax the problem, which results in an issue with phoneme sequence segmentation. The *segmentation* converts an input phoneme sequence into segmented sub-sequences corresponding to individual words. The focus of our study is illustrated in Figure 1. When the robot listens to a human utterance that includes an unknown word like "tempura," the robot will estimate the unknown segment "tempura" by the iterative search based on trial-and-error of many hypotheses among different layers. Here, the phoneme sequence of an unknown word is necessary as an intermediate representation between signals and lexicon because we cannot directly obtain the spelling of an unknown word just from sound information. Note that our assumption of a phoneme sequence given is partly supported by the high accuracy of state-of-the-art speech and phoneme recognition (Dahl et al., 2012; Hinton et al., 2012; Seide et al., 2011a,b).

Approaches based on Bayesian nonparametrics are promising methods to achieve lexical acquisition from unsegmented characters or phonemes. These methods estimate the *segmentation labels* of

Proceedings of the The 8th International Joint Conference on Natural Language Processing, pages 243–252,
Taipei, Taiwan, November 27 – December 1, 2017 ©2017 AFNLP

Word (character)	Phoneme	Phoneme length		Word	I	see	him	[EOS]
I	ɑ́ɪ	2		Phoneme	ɑ́ɪ	si:	hím	[EOS]
ate	éɪt	3		Length	0 2	2	3	0
yesterday	jéstə-dèɪ	8		Context (Bi-gram)	(2,0) (2,2)	(3,2)	(0,3)	
see	si:	2						
sea	si:	2		**Our idea**				

Figure 2: Example of phoneme-length and its context

phonemes corresponding to words with an unsupervised manner. The label represents the boundary of each *word*. Mochihashi *et al.* proposed the nested Pitman-Yor language model (NPYLM) (Mochihashi et al., 2009), or Pitman-Yor semi-Markov model (PYSMM) in other words. The model achieved high computational efficiency and high segmentation accuracy compared with a previous method based on the hierarchical Dirichlet process using simple Gibbs sampling (Goldwater et al., 2006). Uchiumi *et al.* also proposed a method that estimates the segmentation labels and part-of-speech tagging of words at the same time based on Pitman-Yor hidden semi-Markov models (PYHSMM) for character-level segmentation (Murphy, 2002; Uchiumi et al., 2015). PYHSMM has not been applied to the segmentation of phoneme sequences.

The difficulty with phoneme sequence segmentation is insufficient cues to distinguish or predict the context and segmentation labels. For example, the homophones are improperly treated as single entry and their different contexts are also confused in phoneme-level segmentation. This is a similar situation with the homographs in character-level segmentation, but it occurs much more frequently in phoneme-level segmentation, resulting in more serious problem. Although NPYLM and PYHSMM have been applied to character-level segmentation, they do not utilize cues useful for phoneme-level segmentation. We need to determine such useful cues to achieve accurate segmentation of phoneme sequences. Note that the performance comparison of NPYLM and PYHSMM methods in phoneme-level segmentation have not been conducted. We believe that comparing these methods on the basis of phoneme sequences is also useful for further improvement of the model.

We propose a *phoneme-length* context model for segmentation, which was not used in the NPYLM and PYHSMM. Note that the *length* is not the *duration* of a phoneme (the phoneme 'a' continues for three frames in the time axis, for example), which is used in signal-level segmentation (Lee and Glass, 2012). Figure 2 illustrates phoneme length and its contexts in the case of bi-grams. The phoneme sequence of 'see' and 'sea' is same and both lengths are two as shown in the left side of Fig. 2. The context of phoneme length is the sequence of these lengths. For example, if 'him' succeeds to 'see', the bi-gram of phoneme length is the pair of 3 and 2 where 3 is the length of phonemes 'him' and 2 is the length of phonemes 'si:'. We denote the pair as (3, 2) as shown in the right side of Fig. 2. Since the length of each segmented phoneme also depends on the previously segmented phonemes, this context represents one aspect of parts of speech. For example, the phoneme-length context captures the tendency that the length of the adposition is usually short and the length of the succeeding segment will be relatively long. We expect the phoneme-length context to be another cue for segmentation because the phoneme-length context is more abstract than word-level context. This phoneme-length model is expected to capture a rhythmic aspect of language.

We model the phoneme-length context as a prior probability distribution of sequential segmentation labels. This is because the probability distribution is expected to control how long each segmented phoneme becomes. Since the joint prior probability distribution of sequential segmentation labels were decomposed into factorized probabilities like N-gram, the phoneme-length model follows the Markov process and has a transition probability. The transition probability is also modeled and smoothed by using the Pitman-Yor N-gram model as other language models did. Our method, using NPYLM and PYHSMM, is evaluated by using a conversational corpus in English and Japanese in terms of the F-measures of the estimated segmentation labels. Because the corpus contains fillers and hesitations, the property of utterance used for evaluation matches our research purpose.

1.2 Related Work

There are several approaches based on Bayesian nonparametrics to achieve lexical acquisition from raw audio signals (Neubig et al., 2010; Lee and Glass, 2012; Kamper et al., 2016; Taniguchi et al., 2016), unsegmented phonemes, or words (Mochihashi et al., 2009;

Index	1 2 3 ...				L_c
c	ɑɪ	éɪt	témpərə	jéstɚ	dèɪ
z	0 1	0 0 1	0 0 0 0 0 0 1	0 0 0 0 1	0 0 1
Segmented phoneme seq.	ɑ́ɪ	éɪt	témpərə	jéstɚ	dèɪ

Figure 3: Word segmentation

Goldwater et al., 2009; Elsner et al., 2013; Uchiumi et al., 2015). The lexical acquisition technique is necessary in other areas, such as dialogue system that acquires knowledge through dialogue (Ono et al., 2016).

The advantages of Bayesian approach compared with other approaches (Kuo et al., 2007; Räsänen et al., 2015) are that a) the number of words in the system's vocabulary can be increased automatically in accordance with the amount of data and b) the semi-supervised learning of segmentation labels is easy to apply to utilize our knowledge of language. A typical estimation procedure is a Gibbs-sampling-based iteration of 1) the estimation of borders (segmentation labels) given a temporal N-gram language model (Goodman, 2001) and 2) the estimation of an N-gram language model given the temporal segmentation labels.

2   Unsupervised Segmentation and Baselines

We explain the overview and segmentation algorithm of NPYLM and PYHSMM as baseline methods. PYHSMM is an extended model of NPYLM to estimate the part-of-speech tagging of segmented words at the same time.

2.1   Overview

The unsupervised segmentation problem is defined finding the latent segmentation labels $\mathbf{z} = [z_1, ..., z_{L_c}]^T$ that correspond to each phoneme in the phoneme sequence $\mathbf{c} = [c_1, ..., c_{L_c}]^T$ with length L_c. If the binary label $z_i = 1$, the phoneme sequence is separated after the phoneme c_i. Figure 3 illustrates the role of $\mathbf{z}$. Other latent parameters $\mathbf{m} = [m_1, ..., m_{L_m}]$ with length L_m are also introduced to represent part of speech labels for each segmented phoneme sequences if necessary. The number of classes of part of speech label, M, is defined in advance of this study. The latent parameters are estimated by maximizing the follow-

ing probabilities:

$$\arg\max_{\mathbf{z}} p(\mathbf{z}|\mathbf{c}) \propto p(\mathbf{c}|\mathbf{z}) \quad \text{or} \tag{1}$$

$$\arg\max_{\mathbf{z},\mathbf{m}} p(\mathbf{z}, \mathbf{m}|\mathbf{c}) \propto p(\mathbf{c}|\mathbf{z}, \mathbf{m})p(\mathbf{m}), \tag{2}$$

where NPYLM uses Eq. (1) and PYHSMM uses Eq. (2). The definition of each likelihood, such as $p(\mathbf{c}|\mathbf{z})$ and $p(\mathbf{c}|\mathbf{z}, \mathbf{m})$, is important. Because the border of phonemes $\mathbf{z}$ is given in these models, the likelihood can be factorized like N-gram probability. For example, the likelihood can be factorized as $p(c_{i+1}, ..., c_N|c_1, ..., c_i, \mathbf{z})p(c_1, ..., c_i|\mathbf{z})$, where the phoneme segments are considered to be two *word* segments $w_1 = c_1...c_i$ and $w_2 = c_{i+1}...c_{L_c}$. This N-gram modeling is also adopted to decompose the part-of-speech label $\mathbf{m}$, and this controls the grammar and the number of words.

The nested hierarchical Pitman-Yor language model (NPYLM) is used to represent the factorized N-gram probability (Mochihashi et al., 2009). Here, we represent the context of N-gram as $\vec{h}$ and the depth of the hierarchical context tree of $\vec{h}$ as $|\vec{h}|$. Given the seating arrangement of customers that are represented by hidden variables $\vec{s}$ in the hierarchical Chinese restaurant process (CRP), the conditional probability of a word segment w with the context $\vec{h}$ is defined as follows:

$$p(w|\vec{s}, \vec{h}) =$$
$$\frac{c_{\vec{h}w} - d_{|\vec{h}|}t_{\vec{h}w}}{c_{\vec{h}*} + \theta_{|\vec{h}|}} + \frac{\theta_{\vec{h}} + d_{|\vec{h}|}t_{\vec{h}*}}{c_{\vec{h}*} + \theta_{|\vec{h}|}}p(w|\vec{s}, \vec{h}'), \tag{3}$$

where $c_{\vec{h}w}$ is the count of word w at context $\vec{h}$, and $c_{\vec{h}*} = \sum_w c_{\vec{h}w}$ is its sum. $\vec{h}'$ is the reduced context of $\vec{h}$, in which the relationship $|\vec{h}'| = |\vec{h}| - 1$ exists. $t_{\vec{h}w}$ is the number of tables at context $\vec{h}$, and $t_{\vec{h}*}$ is its sum. $\theta_{|\vec{h}|}$ and $d_{|\vec{h}|}$ are the common parameters of $\vec{h}$ with the same depth $|\vec{h}|$. Here, the uni-gram segment probability $p(w = c_i...c_j)$ is smoothed by the phoneme-level N-gram probability $p(c_i, ..., c_j) = p(c_j|c_i, ..., c_{j-1})p(c_i, ..., c_{j-1})$. Please see the work of Teh (2006) for the sampling algorithm of seating arrangement.

The segmentation labels $\mathbf{z}$ and other parameters such as the N-gram language model are updated iteratively. If the segmentation labels are given, we can calculate the statistics of the N-gram model. If the N-gram model is given, we can estimate the probability of the segmentation labels. Because the update of the N-gram model is well known, we explain the update of the estimation of the segmentation labels in the latter parts of this section.

Algorithm 1 Backward sampling: Θ represents parameter set

Require: $t \leftarrow N, i \leftarrow 0, w_0 \leftarrow \mathbb{E}$
  while $t > 0$ **do**
    Draw $k \propto p(w_i | c_{t-k+1}^t, \Theta)\alpha[t][k]$
    Set $w_i \leftarrow c_{t-k+1}^t$
    Set $t \leftarrow t - k, i \leftarrow i + 1$
  end while

2.2 Inference for NPYLM

Mochihashi *et al.* (2009) proposed introducing the forward-backward inference to estimate the segmentation labels efficiently. This method uses a semi-Markov model, and it considers the problem as a sequential estimation of the hidden labels. The procedure consists of two steps: forward filtering and backward sampling.

The forward filtering calculates the forward probability that is used for the Bayesian learning of the hidden Markov model (HMM) (Scott, 2002). The following equation denotes $\alpha[t][k]$ as the probability of generating the partial phonemes $c_1, ..., c_t$ of **c** using the last k phonemes in the case of bi-grams.

$$\alpha[t][k] = \sum_{j=1}^{t-k} p(c_{t-k+1}^t | c_{t-k-j+1}^{t-k})\alpha[t-k][j], \quad (4)$$

where $\alpha[0][0] = 1$ and $c_n, ..., c_m = c_n^m$.

Backward sampling is achieved by drawing a phoneme segment w from the end of a sentence by using forward probability $\alpha[t][k]$. Because the end of sentence is represented by the special symbol $\mathbb{E}$, we can start sampling a word with the probability proportional to $p(\mathbb{E}|c_{N-k}^N)$. The algorithm is summarized in Alg. 1.

Note that we do not use the correction of phoneme-level N-gram probability based on the phoneme length using the Poisson distribution in the NPYLM. This is because the length property is embedded into our model naturally.

2.3 Inference for PYHSMM

The PYHSMM, which is an extended model of NPYLM, estimates the parts of speech of each segmented phoneme. We expect that the performance of PYHSMM is better than that of NPYLM. The forward probability, $\alpha[t][k][m]$, is newly introduced in the case of bi-grams, and the following equation denotes it as the probability of generating the partial phonemes $c_1, ..., c_t$ with

part-of-speech m from the last k phonemes.

$$\alpha[t][k][m] = \sum_{j=1}^{t-k} \sum_{r=0}^{M} p(c_{t-k+1}^t | c_{t-k-j+1}^{t-k}, m)$$
$$p(m|r)\alpha[t-k][j][r] \quad (5)$$

where $p(m|r)$ is the transition probability of the latent parts of speech and assumed the hierarchical Pitman-Yor language model.

The algorithm of the backward sampling is similar to that of NPYLM. The parts of speech are sampled as well as the segmentation label. Because the end of the sentence and its parts of speech are represented using the special symbol $\mathbb{E}$, we can start sampling a word with the probability proportional to $p(\mathbb{E}|c_{N-k}^N, \mathbb{E})p(\mathbb{E}|m)$ like NPYLM. Note that *the computational cost of PYHSMM is larger than that of NPYLM* due to the search part-of-speech labels.

3 Analysis and Our Approach

We focus on the distribution of phoneme length to distinguish the confused contexts. If we have two different words with the same pronunciation, we can sometimes distinguish the phoneme representations of them on the basis of the lenght of the preceding or succeeding phoneme segments. The phoneme-length context will capture the tendency that the length of the adposition is usually short and the length of the succeeding segment will be relatively long.

Figure 4 illustrates the real phoneme-length distribution in the English and Japanese spoken-dialogue transcriptions used in our evaluation (Sec. 5.2). Given that the function $len(w)$ returns the phoneme length of word w, the matrices represent the bi-gram length probability $p(len(w_n)|len(w_{n-1}))$, and the horizontal axis is $len(w_{n-1})$ and the vertical axis is $len(w_n)$. w_n represents the n-th word in each sentences. The line graphs represent the uni-gram length probability $p(len(w_n))$. These probabilities were calculated on the basis of maximum likelihood estimation. *Verb* and *Noun* represent the phoneme-length probability of verbs and nouns in Japanese data, respectively. The definitions of bi-gram and uni-gram probability for *Verb* and *Noun* are $p(len(w_n)|len(w_{n-1}), pos(w_n))$ and $p(len(w_n|pos(w_n))$, where $pos(w)$ is a function that returns a part-of-speech tag of the word w.

We determined that the phoneme-length probability depends on 1) language, 2) context, and

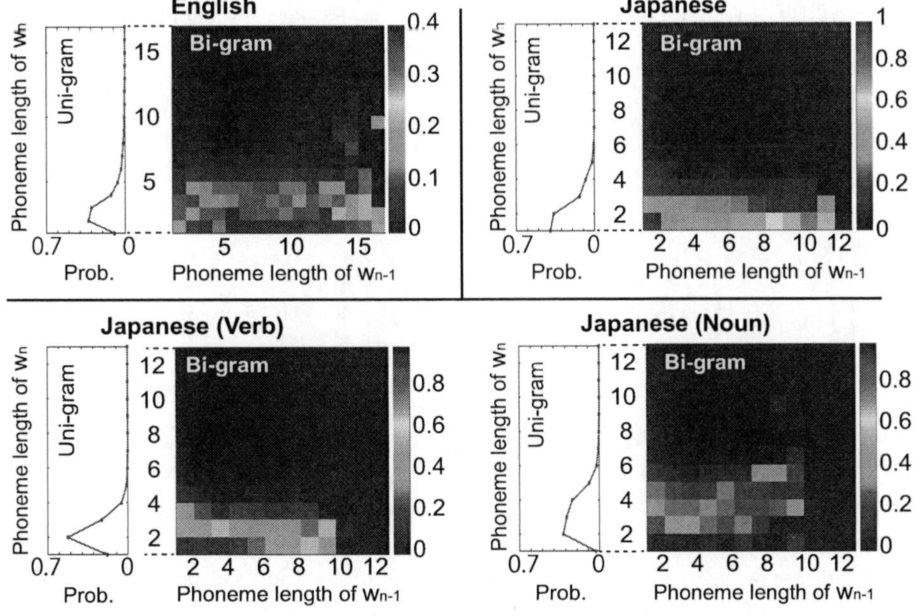

Figure 4: Real phoneme-length distribution

3) parts of speech. The bi-gram phoneme-length probabilities in English are relatively similar to each other but different from those in Japanese. Some bi-gram probabilities have several peaks, and they vary in accordance with parts of speech. If we utilize this information, we will achieve an accurate segmentation.

The straightforward approach to exploit phoneme-length information is to utilize the prior distribution of the segmentation labels $\mathbf{z}$ that is not used in either NPYLM and PYSHMM. Because the prior probability is considered to be the source that determines the length of each phoneme segment, embedding this prior into a model is expected to improve the segmentation performance. Therefore, we need to construct a model that considers the prior of the segmentation labels and should also reveal the performance of these models for phoneme-level word segmentation.

4 Phoneme-Length Context Model for Pitman-Yor Semi-Markov Models

We extend the NPYLM and PYHSMM to exploit the phoneme-length patterns of each phoneme segment. First, we explain our problem statement for unsupervised segmentation of phoneme sequences. Next, we derive the context model of the phoneme length and show the forward-backward algorithms for our extended NPYLM

and PYHSMM.

4.1 Problem Statement and Model

We exploit the probability of phoneme length in estimating latent segmentation labels $\mathbf{z}$ and latent part-of-speech labels $\mathbf{m}$. The parameters are estimated by maximizing the following probabilities:

$$\arg\max_{\mathbf{z}} p(\mathbf{z}|\mathbf{c}) \propto p(\mathbf{c}|\mathbf{z})p(\mathbf{z}) \quad \text{or} \tag{6}$$

$$\arg\max_{\mathbf{z},\mathbf{m}} p(\mathbf{z},\mathbf{m}|\mathbf{c}) \propto p(\mathbf{c}|\mathbf{z},\mathbf{m})p(\mathbf{z}|\mathbf{m})p(\mathbf{m}). \tag{7}$$

The former objective function is for NPYLM, and the latter is for PYHSMM. The probabilities of segmentation labels $p(\mathbf{z})$ in Eq. (6) and $p(\mathbf{z}|\mathbf{m})$ in Eq. (7) are used in our objective functions. $p(\mathbf{z})$ is a prior probability distribution of segmentation labels $\mathbf{z}$ in Eq. (6).

We decompose each joint probability into N-gram probabilities. For an easy explanation of this decomposition, here we use the length of part-of-speech labels L_m and the correct segmentation labels as if these are given, which are actually searched for during training. The non-zero indices of segmentation labels $\mathbf{z}$ are represented by $\mathbf{g} = [g_1, ..., g_W]$, where W is the number of "true" phoneme segments. W equals L_m in the case of part-of-speech estimation. We also define $g_i' = g_i + 1$. The factorized models in the case of bi-grams for NPYLM and PYHSMM are represented as follows:

$$p(\mathbf{c}|\mathbf{z}) = \prod_i p(c_{g'_{i-1}}^{g_i} | c_{g'_{i-2}}^{g_{i-1}}, z_{g'_{i-1}}^{g_i}, z_{g'_{i-2}}^{g_{i-1}}), \qquad (8)$$

$$p(\mathbf{z}) = \prod_i p(z_{g'_{i-1}}^{g_i} | z_{g'_{i-2}}^{g_{i-1}}), \qquad (9)$$

$$p(\mathbf{c}|\mathbf{z}, \mathbf{m}) = \prod_i p(c_{g'_{i-1}}^{g_i} | c_{g'_{i-2}}^{g_{i-1}}, z_{g'_{i-1}}^{g_i}, z_{g'_{i-2}}^{g_{i-1}}, m_i), (10)$$

$$p(\mathbf{z}|\mathbf{m}) = \prod_i p(z_{g'_{i-1}}^{g_i} | z_{g'_{i-2}}^{g_{i-1}}, m_i), \qquad (11)$$

$$p(\mathbf{m}) = \prod_i p(m_i | m_{i-1}), \qquad (12)$$

where $p(m_i | m_{i-1})$ is a transition probability of latent part-of-speech labels, $z_{g'_{i-1}}^{g_i} = z_{g_{i-1}+1}, ..., z_{g_i}$ and $p(z_{g'_{i-1}}^{g_i} | z_{g'_{i-2}}^{g_{i-1}})$ and $p(z_{g'_{i-1}}^{g_i} | z_{g'_{i-2}}^{g_{i-1}}, m_i)$ are transition probabilities of the segmentation labels. The transition probability of segmentation labels is derived naturally. The latent variables for the seating arrangement of N-gram probability in Eq. (3) are omitted in these equations.

We design the transition probability of segmentation labels, such as $p(z_{g'_{i-1}}^{g_i} | z_{g'_{i-2}}^{g_{i-1}})$, to depend on the length of each phoneme segment. Because the length of each segment can be represented using the non-zero indices $\mathbf{g}$, the bi-gram transition probability is rewritten as

$$p(z_{g'_{i-1}}^{g_i} | z_{g'_{i-2}}^{g_{i-1}}) = p(g_i - g_{i-1} | g_{i-1} - g_{i-2}) \quad (13)$$

where m_{g_i} is omitted in the case of PYHSMM, and each integer, such as $g_i - g_{i-1}$, is considered as a symbol or label. This transition probability is the phoneme-length bi-gram probability as mentioned in Sec. 3, and it is also modeled by the hierarchical Pitman-Yor language model (HPYLM) not by a Poisson distribution (Mochihashi et al., 2009) because HPYLM is a count-based representation, which is appropriate for multimodal distribution. Such probability for duration modeling is also seen in (Kuo et al., 2007).

4.2 Inference

We derived the forward-backward algorithms to estimate the segmentation labels and part-of-speech labels. The inference for NPYLM is introduced first; then, the inference of PYHSMM is explained. Note that the segmentation label $\mathbf{z}$ and part-of-speech labels $\mathbf{m}$ are estimated simultaneously.

The forward probability $\alpha[t][k]$ of NPYLM with phoneme-length context is modified as follows.

$$\alpha[t][k] = \sum_{j=1}^{t-k} p(c_{t-k+1}^t | c_{t-k-j+1}^{t-k}, k, j)$$
$$p(k|j)\alpha[t-k][j] \qquad (14)$$

where $p(k|j)$ is a transition probability of the length of each phoneme segment. The forward probability is modified by the bi-gram probability of lengths. We can use $p(c_{t-k+1}^t | c_{t-k-j+1}^{t-k}, k)$ instead of $p(c_{t-k+1}^t | c_{t-k-j+1}^{t-k}, k, j)$ because information of length j is included in the phoneme sequence representation, $c_{t-k-j+1}^{t-k}$.

As with NPYLM, the context of phoneme lengths can be embedded into PYHSMM. The forward probability is also represented as

$$\alpha[t][k][m] = \sum_{j=1}^{t-k} \sum_{r=0}^{M} p(c_{t-k+1}^t | c_{t-k-j+1}^{t-k}, k, j, m)$$
$$p(k|j, m)p(m|r)\alpha[t-k][j][r] \qquad (15)$$

where m represents a part of speech. The forward probability is also biased by a transition probability of the length of each phoneme segment $p(k|j, m)$. We can also use $p(c_{t-k+1}^t | c_{t-k-j+1}^{t-k}, k, m)$. Because the number of parameters is large in this case of latent parts of speech, the convergence speed will degrade compared with NPYLM. Backward sampling of both cases is achieved in the same way as in NPYLM. The details are omitted due to space limitation.

4.3 Substitution

We substitute the conditional probability into simpler one by ignoring the dependency on length k in this work as follows:

$$p(c_{t-k+1}^t | c_{t-k-j+1}^{t-k}, k) := p(c_{t-k+1}^t | c_{t-k-j+1}^{t-k}). (16)$$

The probability should be ideally normalized only on the tokens that have length k, and this substitution makes a double count of the length information of token c_{t-k+1}^t. On the other hand, the difference between NPYLM and our proposed model in the inference is clear. The transition probability $p(k|j)$ is added in our model, and its implementation becomes simple. Our strict model will be evaluated in the future work.

We also use $p(c_{t-k+1}^{t}|c_{t-k-j+1}^{t-k}, m)$ instead of $p(c_{t-k+1}^{t}|c_{t-k-j+1}^{t-k}, k, m)$.

Note that there are several options on the back-off structure of the conditional probability $p(c_{t-k+1}^{t}|c_{t-k-j+1}^{t-k}, k)$. For example, the word uni-gram $p(c_{t-k+1}^{t}|k)$ might be smoothed by un-conditioned word uni-gram or by the k-conditioned character N-gram. If the amount of data is limited, the parameter estimation of the conditional character N-gram may fail. We adopt the existing model, NPYLM, as the structure in this work. The optimal structure should also be investigated in the future work.

5 Experiments

5.1 Evaluation Procedure

We evaluated each model by comparing the estimated segmented labels with the correct segmented original phoneme text (transcription of speech corpus). Utterances in the corpus were divided manually, and each utterance was treated as one sentence. The unsegmented phoneme text is generated by replacing the word-segmented transcription text into phoneme text with a dictionary and by removing whitespaces.

The criteria for the evaluations were the F-measures of the estimated lexicon set and segmentation label set. These F-measures are the harmonic mean of recall and precision; therefore, we could consider the recall and precision at the same time. The lexicon set after unsupervised segmentation was compared with that of the original segmented phoneme text. The estimated set of segmentation labels was also compared with that of the original phoneme text.

We used a development set to monitor the maximum performance of segmentation methods. The 1% data set was randomly selected from each test set, and its F-measure of segmentation labels was used to determine the epochs for calculating F-measures. Since we can obtain some correctly-transcribed text in a real situation, this evaluation process is reasonable. First, we ran each method over a sufficient number of epochs. Next, we calculated the F-measure of each development set's segmentation label and identified the 20-epoch section where the averaged F-measure was the highest. We calculated the F-measures of test sets that averaged over 20 epochs corresponding to the identified 20-epoch section. Note that each method is based on sampling and the max-

Table 1: Parameters of experiment

	English	Japanese
Target text	SwitchBoard	CSJ
# of sentences	5,239	17,493
# of segments	88,127	132,900
# of phonemes	276,329	264,544
Vocab. size (word)	6,203	8,325
Vocab. size (phoneme)	5,422	6,589
Phoneme set	43	79

imum likelihood estimation sometimes does not match the segmentation on the basis of linguistic definitions.

5.2 Data

We used two types of speech transcription in English and Japanese for evaluation. This is because the distribution of phoneme length also differs in languages as mentioned in Sec. 3.

We used the Switchboard-1 Telephone Speech Corpus (Godfrey et al., 1992) for the English set, which includes the transcription of conversational dialogue speech[1]. We selected 5,239 sentences from the session "ID 20," which included 88,127 word segments with 6,203 unique words. These words were converted into phonemes, totaling 276,329 phoneme characters. The vocabulary size in terms of phoneme representation was 5,422, and this was a unique number of phoneme sequences of words. For example, because the pronunciation of the words "see" and "sea" is the same "si:", the phoneme sequence "si:" is considered to be a unique vocabulary item. The phoneme set used in the English corpus included 43 phonemes in total including end-of-sentence symbols. The properties of the corpus are summarized in Table 1.

We used the Corpus of Spontaneous Japanese (CSJ) for the Japanese set, which is a collection of spoken dialogue recordings and their transcriptions (Maekawa, 2003). We used 17,493 sentences, including 132,900 word segments with 8,325 of them being unique words. The phoneme set for Japanese includes the combination of consonants and vowels and almost completely corresponds to *"katakana"* in Japanese to remove redundancy. The words were also transformed into phonemes (*"katakana"*), resulting in 264,544 of them. The vocabulary size in terms of phoneme representation was 6,589, and this was the unique number of phoneme sequences of words. The phoneme set used in the Japanese corpus included

---

[1]http://www.isip.msstate.edu/projects/switchboard/releases/

79 phonemes in total including end-of-sentence symbols. The properties of the corpus are also summarized in Table 1.

5.3 Parameter Settings

The parameters of NPYLM were the same for all models. The hyper parameters of the word language model were initialized as $\theta_{|h|} = 2.0$, $d_{|h|} = 0.5$, and the other parameters of prior probability distribution were all set to 1.0, such as the parameters of the beta distribution in NPYLM.

The hyper parameters of the phoneme (character) language, part-of-speech model and length model were the same as those in the language model. We set the maximum length of the phoneme sequence L_c to 10 due to the computational complexity. The number of classes of part of speech label, M, was set to 4 due to the small corpus size and computational cost. The initial labels of parts of speech were initialized randomly within the number of classes.

5.4 Results

The maximum F-measures of the lexicon and segmentation are listed in Tables 2 and 3 for the English and Japanese test sets. The notations *Lex.* and *Seg.* represent the F-measures of the lexicon and segmentation, respectively. *NPYLM-D* denotes the proposed NPYLM with our phoneme-length context model in Table 2, and *PYHSMM-D* denotes the proposed PYHSMM with our context model in Table 3.

The F-measures of the proposed NPYLM-D outperformed the NPYLM for both the English and Japanese test sets as shown in Table 2. The improvements in the Japanese corpus, 0.067 (Lex.) and 0.045 (Seg.), were larger than those in the English corpus, 0.003 (Lex.) and 0.01 (Seg.). This is because the bi-gram probability of phoneme length varies more in Japanese than in English, and the NPYLM-D could capture such tendencies. The NPYLM does not use any information other than the context of a segmented phoneme sequence. Therefore, the length model is useful to model the phoneme-level features. The lower performance of NPYLM-D after convergence might be caused by the conditional probability substitution and its double-count of length information.

The F-measures of the proposed PYHSMM-D were worse than those of PYHSMM for both the English and Japanese test sets as shown in Table 3. The performances of these methods were

Table 2: F-measures of segmentation by NPYLM and NPYLM-D

		NPYLM (baseline)	NPYLM-D (proposed)
English	Lex.	0.602	**0.605**
	Seg.	0.897	**0.907**
Japanese	Lex.	0.344	**0.411**
	Seg.	0.748	**0.793**

Table 3: F-measures of segmentation by PYHSMM and PYHSMM-D

		PYHSMM (baseline)	PYHSMM-D (proposed)
English	Lex.	0.528	0.471
	Seg.	0.825	0.788
Japanese	Lex.	0.202	0.158
	Seg.	0.499	0.437

worse than those of NPYLM and NPYLM-D. The reasons for this are due to 1) the smaller amount of data to treat latent context variable m and 2) the overlap of *contextual information* between the phoneme length and the latent variable m. Since the latent variable m represents the class of context, a sufficient amount of data will be required for achieving stable performance compared with NPYLM. Moreover, the context information represented by the latent variable m possibly includes our phoneme length context. Thus, it might be difficult for the PYHSMM-D to separate these two contexts in the case of completely unsupervised training. These problems may be solved in the *semi-supervised* case where we exploit pre-labeled data with already segmented words and their tagged parts of speech.

The F-measures of segmentation during training for the English and Japanese test sets are shown in Figures 5 and 6, respectively. The horizontal axis represents the epoch of Gibbs sampling, and the vertical axis represents the F-measures for the segmentation label set. The Gibbs sampling was stopped after at least ten days. Note that the F-measure of segmentation does not necessarily correlate with the likelihood and all methods were based on stochastic segmentation.

The F-measures of NPYLM and PYHSMM for the English and Japanese corpora improved in proportion to the number of epochs, and those of PYHSMM and PYHSMM-D did not converge as shown in Figures 5 and 6. Because the number of hidden parameters of PYHSMM and PYHSMM-D was large, their convergence speeds were slow.

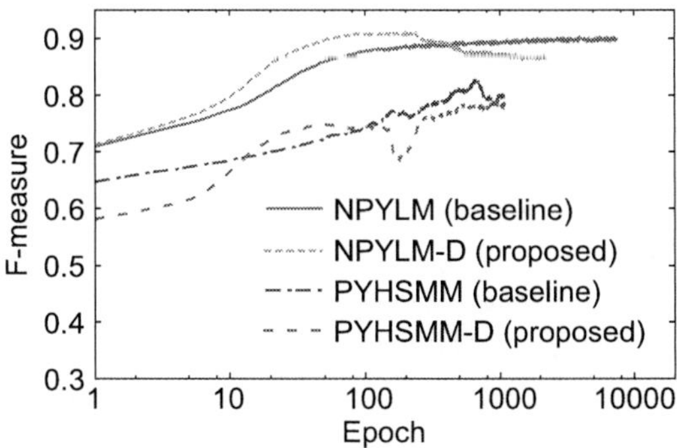

Figure 5: F-measures of segmentation for English test set

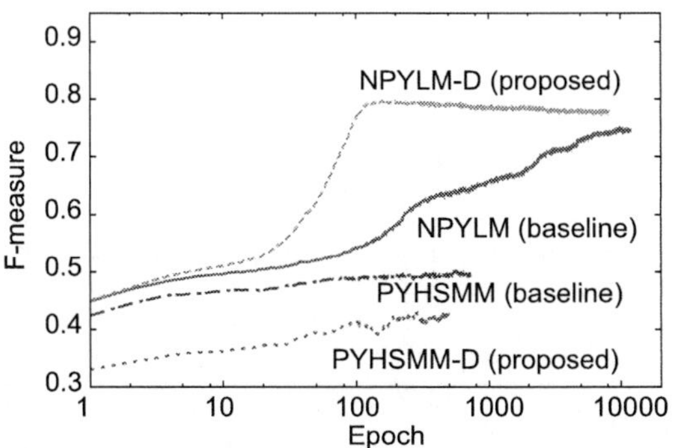

Figure 6: F-measures of segmentation for Japanese test set

The proposed NPYLM-D had peak F-measures at 100–200 epochs, and they went down and converged as the number of epochs increased. This was mainly because the phoneme-length context model accelerated the segmentation in the early epochs, and the small number of observations and un-supervised condition caused over-fitting. Therefore, the performance of the NPYLM-D is expected to be improved by using a larger corpus or by optimizing hyper parameters to match the actual prior probability of phoneme length.

The semi-supervised training would be effective for segmentation in practical use because it matches the actual use case. Evaluating the performance under such a condition is planned for future work. We expect the PYHSMM-D to work well more after 1000 epochs, but it requires a large computational cost. Its results could also be improved with a larger corpus and semi-supervised condition.

6   Conclusions

Unsupervised segmentation of phoneme sequences is an essential process to obtain unknown words during spoken dialogues with users. The PYSMM is a promising model to achieve unsupervised segmentation, but its performance degrades when it is applied to phoneme-level word segmentation. We proposed a phoneme-length context model for PYSMM to give a helpful cue at the phoneme-level and to predict succeeding phoneme segmentation more accurately. Our experiments showed that the peak performances with our context model outperformed those without such a context model by 0.045 at most in terms of F-measures of estimated segmentation labels.

There are the several future works on 1) optimization of parameters, 2) evaluation of semi-supervised training and other languages, and 3) improvement of our model and inference method. To further improve our method, we must investigate the hyper parameters setting for the estimation of segmentation labels to operate efficiently. The semi-supervised training will also improve the performance of our method. We will evaluate our method not only for English and Japanese but also other languages, such as African languages because the rhythmic information might be vivid. The performance of our strict model and the optimal back-off structure should be investigated to reveal the limitation of our model. The modification of inference algorithm will be required due to the computational efficiency when we use longer context information more than tri-gram. Since the rhythm information of latent segmentation might not be captured well by bi-grams, the challenge of using longer context is one of the important issues for our purpose.

Acknowledgments

We thank anonymous reviewers for their insightful comments. This work was supported partly by JSPS KAKENHI Grant Number JP16H02869.

References

George E Dahl, Dong Yu, Li Deng, and Alex Acero. 2012. Context-dependent pre-trained deep neural networks for large-vocabulary speech recognition. *IEEE Transactions on Audio, Speech, and Language Processing*, 20(1):30–42.

Micha Elsner, Sharon Goldwater, Naomi Feldman, and Frank Wood. 2013. A joint learning model of word segmentation, lexical acquisition, and phonetic variability. In *Proceedings of the Conference on Empirical Methods on Natural Language Processing*, pages 42–54.

John J Godfrey, Edward C Holliman, and Jane McDaniel. 1992. Switchboard: Telephone speech corpus for research and development. In *Proceesings of IEEE International Conference on Acoustics, Speech, and Signal Processing*, volume 1, pages 517–520.

Sharon Goldwater, Thomas L Griffiths, and Mark Johnson. 2006. Contextual dependencies in unsupervised word segmentation. In *Proceedings of the 21st International Conference on Computational Linguistics and the 44th annual meeting of the Association for Computational Linguistics*, pages 673–680.

Sharon Goldwater, Thomas L Griffiths, and Mark Johnson. 2009. A bayesian framework for word segmentation: Exploring the effects of context. *Cognition*, 112(1):21–54.

Joshua T. Goodman. 2001. A bit of progress in language modeling. *Computer Speech & Language*, 15(4):403–434.

Geoffrey Hinton, Li Deng, Dong Yu, George E Dahl, Abdel-rahman Mohamed, Navdeep Jaitly, Andrew Senior, Vincent Vanhoucke, Patrick Nguyen, Tara N Sainath, et al. 2012. Deep neural networks for acoustic modeling in speech recognition: The shared views of four research groups. *Signal Processing Magazine*, 29(6):82–97.

Herman Kamper, Aren Jansen, and Sharon Goldwater. 2016. Unsupervised word segmentation and lexicon discovery using acoustic word embeddings. *IEEE/ACM Trans. on Audio, Speech, and Language Processing*, 24(4):669–679.

Jen-Wei Kuo, Hung-Yi Lo, and Hsin-Min Wang. 2007. Improved HMM/SVM methods for automatic phoneme segmentation. In *Proceedings of Interspeech*, pages 2057–2060.

Chia-ying Lee and James Glass. 2012. A nonparametric bayesian approach to acoustic model discovery. In *Proceedings of the 50th Annual Meeting of the Association for Computational Linguistics: Long Papers-Volume 1*, pages 40–49. Association for Computational Linguistics.

Kikuo Maekawa. 2003. Corpus of spontaneous Japanese: Its design and evaluation. In *Inproceedings of the ISCA & IEEE Workshop on Spontaneous Speech Processing and Recognition*.

Daichi Mochihashi, Takeshi Yamada, and Naonori Ueda. 2009. Bayesian unsupervised word segmentation with nested Pitman-Yor language modeling. In *Proceedings of the Joint Conference of the 47th Annual Meeting of the ACL and the 4th International Joint Conference on Natural Language Processing of the AFNLP: Volume 1-Volume 1*, pages 100–108.

Kevin P Murphy. 2002. Hidden semi-Markov models.

Graham Neubig, Masato Mimura, Shinsuke Mori, and Tatsuya Kawahara. 2010. Learning a language model from continuous speech. In *Proceesings of Interspeech*, pages 1053–1056.

Kohei Ono, Ryu Takeda, Eric Nichols, Mikio Nakano, and Kazunori Komatani. 2016. Toward lexical acquisition during dialogues through implicit confirmation for closed-domain chatbots. In *Second Workshop on Chatbots and Conversational Agent Technologies*.

Okko Räsänen, Gabriel Doyle, and Michael C Frank. 2015. Unsupervised word discovery from speech using automatic segmentation into syllable-like units. In *Proceedings of Interspeech*, pages 3204–3208.

Steven L Scott. 2002. Bayesian methods for hidden markov models: Recursive computing in the 21st century. *Journal of the American Statistical Association*, 97(457):337–351.

Frank Seide, Gang Li, Xie Chen, and Dong Yu. 2011a. Feature engineering in context-dependent deep neural networks for conversational speech transaction. In *Proceedings of the IEEE Workshop on Automatic Speech Recognition and Understanding*, pages 24–29.

Frank Seide, Gang Li, and Dong Yu. 2011b. Conversational speech transcription using context-dependent deep neural network. In *Proceedings of Interspeech*, pages 437–440.

Tadahiro Taniguchi, Shogo Nagasaka, and Ryo Nakashima. 2016. Nonparametric bayesian double articulation analyzer for direct language acquisition from continuous speech signals. *IEEE Transactions on Cognitive and Developmental Systems*, 8(3):171–185.

Yee Whey Teh. 2006. A bayesian interpretation of interpolated kneser-ney. *Technical Report TRA2/06, School of Computing, NUS*.

Kei Uchiumi, Hiroshi Tsukahara, and Daichi Mochihashi. 2015. Inducing word and part-of-speech with Pitman-Yor hidden semi-Markov models. In *Proceedings of the 53rd Annual Meeting of the Association for Computational Linguistics and the 7th International Joint Conference on Natural Language Processing*, volume 1, pages 1774–1782.

A Sensitivity Analysis of (and Practitioners' Guide to) Convolutional Neural Networks for Sentence Classification

Ye Zhang
Dept. of Computer Science
University of Texas at Austin
yezhang@utexas.edu

Byron C. Wallace
College of Computer and Information Science
Northeastern University
byron@ccs.neu.edu

Abstract

Convolutional Neural Networks (CNNs) have recently achieved remarkably strong performance on the practically important task of sentence classification (Kim, 2014; Kalchbrenner et al., 2014; Johnson and Zhang, 2014; Zhang et al., 2016). However, these models require practitioners to specify an exact model architecture and set accompanying hyperparameters, including the filter region size, regularization parameters, and so on. It is currently unknown how sensitive model performance is to changes in these configurations for the task of sentence classification. We thus conduct a sensitivity analysis of one-layer CNNs to explore the effect of architecture components on model performance; our aim is to distinguish between important and comparatively inconsequential design decisions for sentence classification. We focus on one-layer CNNs (to the exclusion of more complex models) due to their comparative simplicity and strong empirical performance, which makes it a modern standard baseline method akin to Support Vector Machine (SVMs) and logistic regression. We derive practical advice from our extensive empirical results for those interested in getting the most out of CNNs for sentence classification in real world settings.

1 Introduction

Convolutional Neural Networks (CNNs) have recently been shown to achieve impressive results on the practically important task of sentence categorization (Kim, 2014; Kalchbrenner et al., 2014; Wang et al., 2015; Goldberg, 2015; Iyyer et al., 2015; Zhang et al., 2016, 2017). CNNs can capitalize on distributed representations of words by first converting the tokens comprising each sentence into a vector, forming a matrix to be used as input (e.g., see Fig. 1). The models need not be complex to realize strong results: Kim (2014), for example, proposed a simple one-layer CNN that achieved state-of-the-art (or comparable) results across several datasets. The very strong results achieved with this comparatively simple CNN architecture suggest that it may serve as a drop-in replacement for well-established baseline models, such as SVM (Joachims, 1998) or logistic regression. While more complex deep learning models for text classification will undoubtedly continue to be developed, those deploying such technologies in practice will likely be attracted to simpler variants, which afford fast training and prediction times.

Unfortunately, a downside to CNN-based models – even simple ones – is that they require practitioners to specify the exact model architecture to be used and to set the accompanying hyperparameters. In practice, tuning all of these hyperparameters is simply not feasible, especially because parameter estimation is computationally intensive. Emerging research has begun to explore hyperparameter optimization methods, including random search (Bengio, 2012), and Bayesian optimization (Yogatama and Smith, 2015; Bergstra et al., 2013). However, these sophisticated search methods still require knowing which hyperparameters are worth exploring to begin with (and reasonable ranges for each).

In this work our aim is to identify empirically the settings that practitioners should expend effort tuning, and those that are either inconsequential with respect to performance or that seem to have a 'best' setting independent of the specific dataset, and provide a reasonable range for each hyperpa-

Proceedings of the The 8th International Joint Conference on Natural Language Processing, pages 253–263,
Taipei, Taiwan, November 27 – December 1, 2017 ©2017 AFNLP

rameter. We take inspiration from previous empirical analyses of neural models due to Coates et al. (2011) and Breuel (2015), which investigated factors in unsupervised feature learning and hyperparameter settings for Stochastic Gradient Descent (SGD), respectively. Here we report the results of a large number of experiments exploring different configurations of CNNs run over nine sentence classification datasets. Most previous work in this area reports only mean accuracies calculated via cross-validation. But there is substantial variance in the performance of CNNs, even on the *same folds* and with model configuration held constant. Therefore, in our experiments we perform replications of cross-validation and report accuracy/Area Under Curve (AUC) score means and ranges over these.

2 Background and Preliminaries

Deep and neural learning methods are now well established in machine learning (LeCun et al., 2015; Bengio, 2009). They have been especially successful for image and speech processing tasks. More recently, such methods have begun to overtake traditional sparse, linear models for NLP (Goldberg, 2015; Bengio et al., 2003; Mikolov et al., 2013; Collobert and Weston, 2008; Collobert et al., 2011; Kalchbrenner et al., 2014; Socher et al., 2013).

Recently, word embeddings have been exploited for sentence classification using CNN architectures. Kalchbrenner (2014) proposed a CNN architecture with multiple convolution layers, positing latent, dense and low-dimensional word vectors (initialized to random values) as inputs. Kim (2014) defined a one-layer CNN architecture that performed comparably. This model uses pre-trained word vectors as inputs, which may be treated as *static* or *non-static*. In the former approach, word vectors are treated as fixed inputs, while in the latter they are 'tuned' for a specific task. Elsewhere, Johnson and Zhang (2014) proposed a similar model, but swapped in high dimensional 'one-hot' vector representations of words as CNN inputs. Their focus was on classification of longer texts, rather than sentences (but of course the model can be used for sentence classification).

The relative simplicity of Kim's architecture – which is largely the same as that proposed by Johnson and Zhang (2014), modulo the word vec-

tors – coupled with observed strong empirical performance makes this a strong contender to supplant existing text classification baselines such as SVM and logistic regression. But in practice one is faced with making several model architecture decisions and setting various hyperparameters. At present, very little empirical data is available to guide such decisions; addressing this gap is our aim here.

2.1 CNN Architecture

We begin with a tokenized sentence which we then convert to a *sentence matrix*, the rows of which are word vector representations of each token. These might be, e.g., outputs from trained word2vec (Mikolov et al., 2013) or GloVe (Pennington et al., 2014) models. We denote the dimensionality of the word vectors by d. If the length of a given sentence is s, then the dimensionality of the sentence matrix is $s \times d$. Suppose that there is a filter matrix w with region size h; $\mathbf{w}$ will contain $h \cdot d$ parameters to be estimated. We denote the sentence matrix by $\mathbf{A} \in \mathbb{R}^{s \times d}$, and use $\mathbf{A}[i : j]$ to represent the sub-matrix of $\mathbf{A}$ from row i to row j. The output sequence $\mathbf{o} \in \mathbb{R}^{s-h+1}$ of the convolution operator is obtained by repeatedly applying the filter on sub-matrices of $\mathbf{A}$:

$$o_i = \mathbf{w} \cdot \mathbf{A}[i : i + h - 1], \tag{1}$$

where $i = 1 \ldots s - h + 1$, and $\cdot$ is the dot product between the sub-matrix and the filter (a sum over element-wise multiplications). We add a bias term $b \in \mathbb{R}$ and an activation function f to each o_i, inducing the *feature map* $\mathbf{c} \in \mathbb{R}^{s-h+1}$ for this filter:

$$c_i = f(o_i + b). \tag{2}$$

One may use multiple filters for the same region size to learn complementary features from the same regions. One may also specify multiple kinds of filters with different region sizes (i.e., 'heights'). The dimensionality of the feature map generated by each filter will vary as a function of the sentence length and the filter region size. A pooling function is thus applied to each feature map to induce a fixed-length vector. A common strategy is *1-max pooling* (Boureau et al., 2010b), which extracts a scalar from each feature map. Together, the outputs generated from each filter map can be concatenated into a fixed-length, 'top-level' feature vector, which is then fed through a softmax function to generate the final classification. At this softmax layer, one may apply 'dropout' (Hinton et al., 2012) as a means of regularization. This entails randomly setting values in the weight vector to 0. One may also impose an $l2$ norm constraint, i.e., linearly scale the $l2$ norm of the vector to a pre-specified threshold when it exceeds this. Fig. 1 provides a schematic illustrating the model architecture just described. The training objective to be minimized is the categorical cross-entropy loss. The parameters to be estimated include the weight vector(s) of the filter(s), the bias term in the activation function, and the weight vector of the softmax function. In the 'non-static' approach, one also tunes the word vectors. Optimization is performed using SGD and back-propagation (Rumelhart et al., 1988).

3 Datasets

We use nine sentence classification datasets in all; seven of which were also used by Kim (2014). Briefly, these are summarized as follows. (1) **MR**: sentence polarity dataset from (Pang and Lee, 2005). (2) **SST-1**: Stanford Sentiment Treebank (Socher et al., 2013). To make input representations consistent across tasks, we only train and test on sentences, in contrast to the use in (Kim, 2014), wherein models were trained on both phrases and sentences. (3) **SST-2**: Derived from SST-1, but pared to only two classes. We again only train and test models on sentences, excluding phrases. (4) **Subj**: Subjectivity dataset (Pang and Lee, 2005). (5) **TREC**: Question classification dataset (Li and Roth, 2002). (6) **CR**: Customer review dataset (Hu and Liu, 2004). (7) **MPQA**: Opinion polarity dataset (Wiebe et al., 2005). Additionally, we use (8) **Opi**: Opinosis Dataset, which comprises sentences extracted from user reviews on a given topic, e.g. "sound quality of ipod nano". There are 51 such topics and each topic contains approximately 100 sentences (Ganesan et al., 2010). (9) **Irony** (Wallace et al., 2014): this contains 16,006 sentences from *reddit* labeled as ironic (or not). The dataset is imbalanced (relatively few sentences are ironic). Thus before training, we under-sampled negative instances to make classes sizes equal.[1] For this dataset we report the Area Under Curve (AUC), rather than accuracy, because it is imbalanced.

---

[1]Empirically, under-sampling outperformed over-sampling in mitigating imbalance, see also Wallace (2011).

4 Baseline Models

4.1 Baseline Configuration

We give a baseline CNN configuration described in Table 1. We argue that it is critical to assess the variance due strictly to the parameter estimation procedure. Most prior work, unfortunately, has not reported such variance, despite a highly stochastic learning procedure. This variance is attributable to estimation via SGD, random dropout, and random weight parameter initialization.

Description	Values
input word vectors	Google word2vec
filter region size	(3,4,5)
feature maps	100
activation function	ReLU
pooling	1-max pooling
dropout rate	0.5
$l2$ norm constraint	3

Table 1: Baseline configuration. 'feature maps' refers to the number of feature maps for each filter region size. 'ReLU' refers to *rectified linear unit* (Maas et al., 2013), a commonly used activation function in CNNs.

Then we consider the effect of different architecture decisions and hyperparameter settings. To this end, we hold all other settings constant (as per Table 1) and vary only the component of interest. For every configuration that we consider, we replicate the experiment 10 times, where each replication constitutes a run of 10-fold CV. We report average CV means and associated ranges achieved over the replicated CV runs.

4.2 Effect of input word vectors

A nice property of sentence classification models that start with distributed representations of words as inputs is the flexibility such architectures afford to swap in different pre-trained word vectors during model initialization. Therefore, we first explore the sensitivity of CNNs for sentence classification with respect to the input representations used. Specifically, we replaced word2vec with GloVe representations. Google word2vec uses a local context window model trained on 100 billion words from Google News (Mikolov et al., 2013), while GloVe is a model based on global word-word co-occurrence statistics (Pennington et al., 2014). We used a GloVe model trained on a cor-

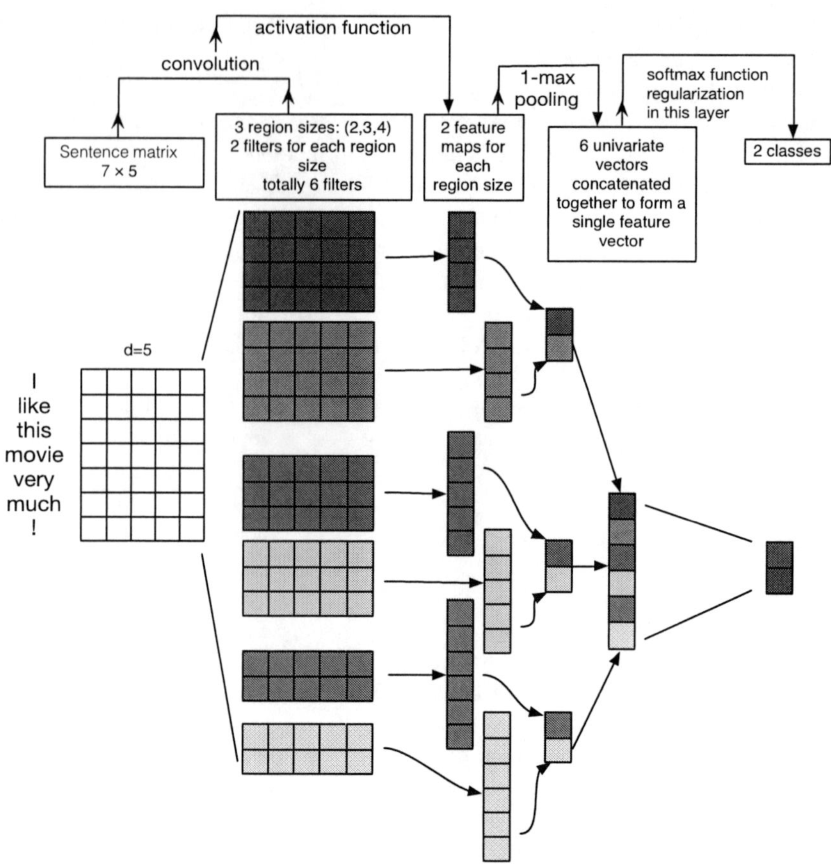

Figure 1: Illustration of a CNN architecture for sentence classification. We depict three filter region sizes: 2, 3 and 4, each of which has 2 filters. Filters perform convolutions on the sentence matrix and generate (variable-length) feature maps; 1-max pooling is performed over each map, i.e., the largest number from each feature map is recorded. Thus a univariate feature vector is generated from all six maps, and these 6 features are concatenated to form a feature vector for the penultimate layer. The final softmax layer then receives this feature vector as input and uses it to classify the sentence; here we assume binary classification and hence depict two possible output states.

pus of 840 billion tokens of web data. For both word2vec and GloVe we induce 300-dimensional word vectors. We report results achieved using GloVe representations in Table 2. Here we only report non-static GloVe results (which uniformely outperformed the static variant).

We also experimented with concatenating word2vec and GloVe representations, thus creating 600-dimensional word vectors to be used as input to the CNN. Pre-trained vectors may not always be available for specific words (either in word2vec or GloVe, or both); in such cases, we randomly initialized the corresponding sub-vectors. Results are reported in the final column of Table 2. The relative performance

achieved using GloVe versus word2vec depends on the dataset, and, unfortunately, simply concatenating these representations does necessarily seem helpful. For how to better utilize multiple sets of embeddings, we refer to (Zhang et al., 2016).

We also experimented with using long, sparse one-hot vectors as input word representations, in the spirit of Johnson and Zhang (2014). In this strategy, each word is encoded as a one-hot vector, with dimensionality equal to the vocabulary size. Though this representation combined with one-layer CNN achieves good results on document classification, it is still unknown whether this is useful for sentence classification. We keep the other settings the same as in the basic con-

Dataset	Non-static word2vec-CNN	Non-static GloVe-CNN	Non-static GloVe+word2vec CNN
MR	81.24 (80.69, 81.56)	81.03 (80.68,81.48)	81.02 (80.75,81.32)
SST-1	47.08 (46.42,48.01)	45.65 (45.09,45.94)	45.98 (45.49,46.65)
SST-2	85.49 (85.03, 85.90)	85.22 (85.04,85.48)	85.45 (85.03,85.82)
Subj	93.20 (92.97, 93.45)	93.64 (93.51,93.77)	93.66 (93.39,93.87)
TREC	91.54 (91.15, 91.92)	90.38 (90.19,90.59)	91.37 (91.13,91.62)
CR	83.92 (82.95, 84.56)	84.33 (84.00,84.67)	84.65 (84.21,84.96)
MPQA	89.32 (88.84, 89.73)	89.57 (89.31,89.78)	89.55 (89.22,89.88)
Opi	64.93 (64.23,65.58)	65.68 (65.29,66.19)	65.65 (65.15,65.98)
Irony	67.07 (65.60,69.00)	67.20 (66.45,67.96)	67.11 (66.66,68.50)

Table 2: Performance using non-static word2vec-CNN, non-static GloVe-CNN, and non-static GloVe+word2vec CNN, respectively. Each cell reports the mean (min, max) of summary performance measures calculated over multiple runs of 10-fold cross-validation. We will use this format for all tables involving replications

figuration, and the one-hot vector is fixed during training. Compared to using embeddings as input to the CNN, we found the one-hot approach to perform poorly for sentence classification tasks. We believe that one-hot CNN may not be suitable for sentence classification, likely due to sparsity: the sentences are perhaps too brief to provide enough information for this high-dimensional encoding. Alternative one-hot architectures (Johnson and Zhang, 2015) might be more appropriate for this scenario.

4.3 Effect of filter region size

Region size	MR
1	77.85 (77.47,77.97)
3	80.48 (80.26,80.65)
5	81.13 (80.96,81.32)
7	**81.65 (81.45,81.85)**
10	81.43 (81.28,81.75)
15	81.26 (81.01,81.43)
20	81.06 (80.87,81.30)
25	80.91 (80.73,81.10)
30	80.91 (80.72,81.05)

Table 3: Effect of single filter region size. Due to space constraints, we report results for only one dataset here, but these are generally illustrative.

We first explore the effect of filter region size when using only one region size, and we set the number of feature maps for this region size to 100 (as in the baseline configuration). We consider region sizes of 1, 3, 5, 7, 10, 15, 20, 25 and 30, and record the means and ranges over 10 replications of 10-fold CV for each. We report results in Table 3 and Fig. 2. Because we are only interested in the trend of the accuracy as we alter the region size (rather than the absolute performance on each

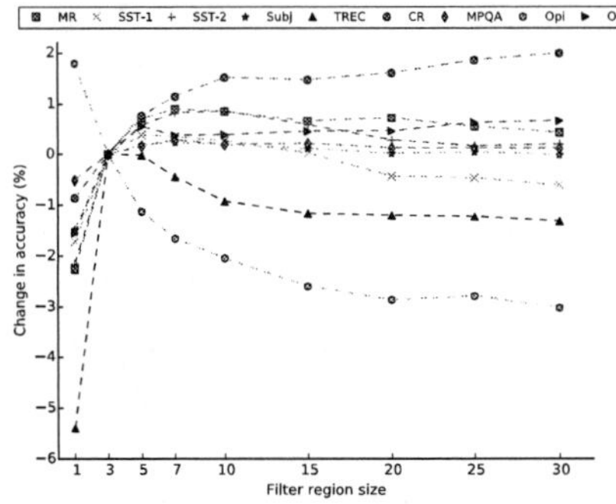

Figure 2: Effect of the region size (using only one).

task), we show only the percent change in accuracy (AUC for Irony) from an arbitrary baseline point (here, a region size of 3).

From the results, one can see that each dataset has its own optimal filter region size. Practically, this suggests performing a coarse grid search over a range of region sizes; the figure here suggests that a reasonable range for sentence classification might be from 1 to 10. However, for datasets comprising longer sentences, such as CR (maximum sentence length is 105, whereas it ranges from 36-56 on the other sentiment datasets used here), the optimal region size may be larger. We also explored the effect of combining different filter region sizes, while keeping the number of feature maps for each region size fixed at 100. We found that combining several filters with region sizes close to the optimal single region size can improve performance, but adding region sizes far from the optimal range may hurt performance. For example, when using a single filter size, one can observe that the optimal single region size for the MR dataset is 7. We therefore combined several different filter region sizes close to this optimal range, and compared this to approaches that use region sizes outside of this range. From Table 5, one can see that using (5,6,7),and (7,8,9) and (6,7,8,9) – sets near the best single region size – produce the best results. The difference is especially pronounced when comparing to the baseline setting of (3,4,5). Note that even only using a single good filter region size (here, 7) results in better performance than combining different sizes (3,4,5). The best performing strategy is to simply use many feature maps (here, 400) all with region size equal to 7, i.e., the single best region size. However, we note that in some cases (e.g., for the TREC dataset), using multiple different, but near-optimal, region sizes performs best. We report its results in table 4.

Multiple region size	Accuracy (%)
(3)	91.21 (90.88,91.52)
(5)	91.20 (90.96,91.43)
(2,3,4)	91.48 (90.96,91.70)
(3,4,5)	91.56 (91.24,91.81)
(4,5,6)	91.48 (91.17,91.68)
(7,8,9)	90.79 (90.57,91.26)
(14,15,16)	90.23 (89.81,90.51)
(2,3,4,5)	**91.57 (91.25,91.94)**
(3,3,3)	91.42 (91.11,91.65)
(3,3,3,3)	91.32 (90.53,91.55)

Table 4: Effect of filter region size with several region sizes using non-static word2vec-CNN on TREC dataset

In light of these observations, we believe it advisable to first perform a coarse line-search over a single filter region size to find the 'best' size for the dataset under consideration, and then explore

Multiple region size	Accuracy (%)
(7)	81.65 (81.45,81.85)
(3,4,5)	81.24 (80.69, 81.56)
(4,5,6)	81.28 (81.07,81.56)
(10,11,12)	81.52 (81.27,81.87)
(11,12,13)	81.53 (81.35,81.76)
(3,4,5,6)	81.43 (81.10,81.61)
(6,7,8,9)	81.62 (81.38,81.72)
(7,7,7)	81.63 (81.33,82.08)
(7,7,7,7)	**81.73 (81.33,81.94)**

Table 5: Effect of filter region size with several region sizes on the MR dataset.

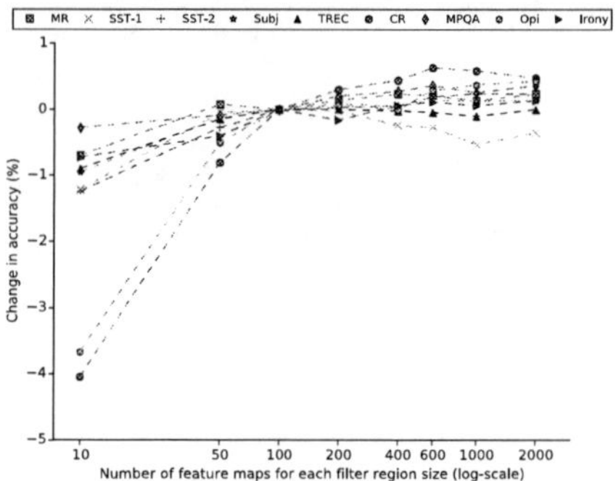

Figure 3: Effect of the number of feature maps.

the combination of several region sizes nearby this single best size, including combining both different region sizes and copies of the optimal sizes.

4.4 Effect of number of feature maps for each filter region size

We again hold other configurations constant, and thus have three filter region sizes: 3, 4 and 5. We change only the number of feature maps for each of these relative to the baseline of 100; we consider values $\in \{10, 50, 100, 200, 400, 600, 1000, 2000\}$. We report results in Fig. 3.

The 'best' number of feature maps for each filter region size depends on the dataset. However, it would seem that increasing the number of maps beyond 600 yields at best very marginal returns, and often hurts performance (likely due to overfitting). Another salient practical point is that it takes a longer time to train the model when the number of feature maps is increased.

In practice, the evidence here suggests perhaps searching over a range of 100 to 600. Note that this range is only provided as a possible standard trick when one is faced with a new similar sentence classification problem; it is of course possible that in some cases more than 600 feature maps will be beneficial, but the evidence here suggests expending the effort to explore this is probably not worth it. In practice, one should consider whether the best observed value falls near the border of the range searched over; if so, it is probably worth exploring beyond that border, as suggested in (Bengio, 2012).

4.5 Effect of activation function

We consider seven different activation functions in the convolution layer, including: ReLU (as per the baseline configuration), hyperbolic tangent (tanh),

Sigmoid function (Maas et al., 2013), SoftPlus function (Dugas et al., 2001), Cube function (Chen and Manning, 2014), and tanh cube function (Pei et al., 2015). We use 'Iden' to denote the identity function, which means not using any activation function.

We show the numerical results of tanh, Softplus, Iden and ReLU in table 6. For 8 out of 9 datasets, the best activation function is one of Iden, ReLU and tanh. The SoftPlus function outperform these on only one dataset (MPQA). Sigmoid, Cube, and tanh cube all consistently performed worse than alternative activation functions. The performance of the tanh function may be due to its zero centering property (compared to Sigmoid). ReLU has the merits of a non-saturating form compared to Sigmoid, and it has been observed to accelerate the convergence of SGD (Krizhevsky et al., 2012). One interesting result is that not applying any activation function (Iden) sometimes helps. This indicates that on some datasets, a linear transformation is enough to capture the correlation between the word embedding and the output label. However, if there are multiple hidden layers, Iden may be less suitable than non-linear activation functions. Practically, with respect to the choice of the activation function in one-layer CNNs, our results suggest experimenting with ReLU and tanh, and perhaps also Iden.

4.6   Effect of pooling strategy

We next investigated the effect of the pooling strategy and the pooling region size. We fixed the filter region sizes and the number of feature maps as in the baseline configuration, thus changing only the pooling strategy or pooling region size.

In the baseline configuration, we performed 1-max pooling globally over feature maps, inducing a feature vector of length 1 for each filter. However, pooling may also be performed over small equal sized local regions rather than over the entire feature map (Boureau et al., 2011). Each small local region on the feature map will generate a single number from pooling, and these numbers can be concatenated to form a feature vector for one feature map. The following step is the same as 1-max pooling: we concatenate all the feature vectors together to form a single feature vector for the classification layer. We experimented with local region sizes of 3, 10, 20, and 30, and found that 1-max pooling outperformed all local max pooling

configurations. This result held across all datasets.

We also considered a k-max pooling strategy similar to (Kalchbrenner et al., 2014), in which the maximum k values are extracted from the entire feature map, and the relative order of these values is preserved. We explored the $k \in \{5, 10, 15, 20\}$, and again found 1-max pooling fared best, consistently outperforming k-max pooling.

Next, we considered taking an average, rather than the max, over regions (Boureau et al., 2010a). We experimented with local average pooling region sizes $\{3, 10, 20, 30\}$. We found that average pooling uniformly performed (much) worse than max pooling, at least on the CR and TREC datasets.

Our analysis of pooling strategies shows that 1-max pooling consistently performs better than alternative strategies for the task of sentence classification. This may be because the location of predictive contexts does not matter, and certain n-grams in the sentence can be more predictive on their own than the entire sentence considered jointly.

4.7   Effect of regularization

Two common regularization strategies for CNNs are dropout and $l2$ norm constraints; we explore the effect of these here. 'Dropout' is applied to the input to the penultimate layer. We experimented with varying the dropout rate from 0.0 to 0.9, fixing the $l2$ norm constraint to 3, as per the baseline configuration. The results for non-static CNN are shown in in Fig. 4, with 0.5 designated as the baseline. We also report the accuracy achieved when we remove both dropout and the $l2$ norm constraint (i.e., when no regularization is performed), denoted by 'None'.

Separately, we considered the effect of the $l2$ norm imposed on the weight vectors that parametrize the softmax function. Recall that the $l2$ norm of a weight vector is linearly scaled to a constraint c when it exceeds this threshold, so a smaller c implies stronger regularization. (Like dropout, this strategy is applied only to the penultimate layer.) We show the relative effect of varying c on non-static CNN in Figure 5, where we have fixed the dropout rate to 0.5; 3 is the baseline here (again, arbitrarily).

From Figures 4 and 5, one can see that non-zero dropout rates can help (though very little) at some points from 0.1 to 0.5, depending on datasets. But

Dataset	tanh	Softplus	Iden	ReLU
MR	81.28 (81.07, 81.52)	80.58 (80.17, 81.12)	**81.30 (81.09, 81.52)**	81.16 (80.81, 83.38)
SST-1	47.02 (46.31, 47.73)	46.95 (46.43, 47.45)	46.73 (46.24,47.18)	**47.13 (46.39, 47.56)**
SST-2	**85.43 (85.10, 85.85)**	84.61 (84.19, 84.94)	85.26 (85.11, 85.45)	85.31 (85.93, 85.66)
Subj	**93.15 (92.93, 93.34)**	92.43 (92.21, 92.61)	93.11 (92.92, 93.22)	93.13 (92.93, 93.23)
TREC	91.18 (90.91, 91.47)	91.05 (90.82, 91.29)	91.11 (90.82, 91.34)	**91.54 (91.17, 91.84)**
CR	84.28 (83.90, 85.11)	83.67 (83.16, 84.26)	**84.55 (84.21, 84.69)**	83.83 (83.18, 84.21)
MPQA	89.48 (89.16, 89.84)	**89.62 (89.45, 89.77)**	89.57 (89.31, 89.88)	89.35 (88.88, 89.58)
Opi	**65.69 (65.16,66.40)**	64.77 (64.25,65.28)	65.32 (64.78,66.09)	65.02 (64.53,65.45)
Irony	**67.62 (67.18,68.27)**	66.20 (65.38,67.20)	66.77 (65.90,67.47)	66.46 (65.99,67.17)

Table 6: Performance of different activation functions

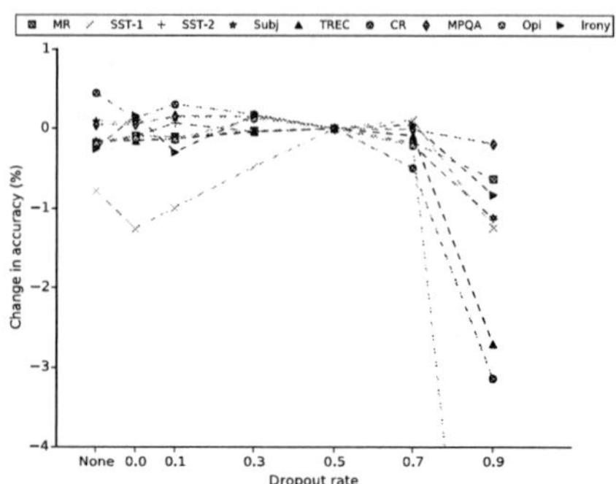

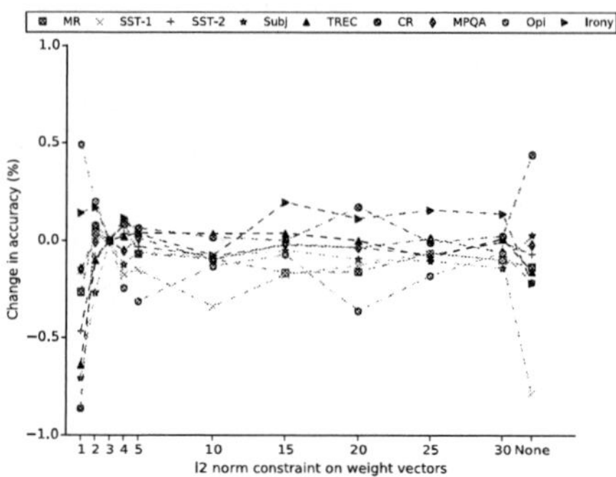

Figure 4: Effect of dropout rate. The accuracy when the dropout rate is 0.9 on the Opi dataset is about 10% worse than baseline, and thus is not visible on the figure at this point.

Figure 5: Effect of the $l2$ norm constraint on weight vectors.

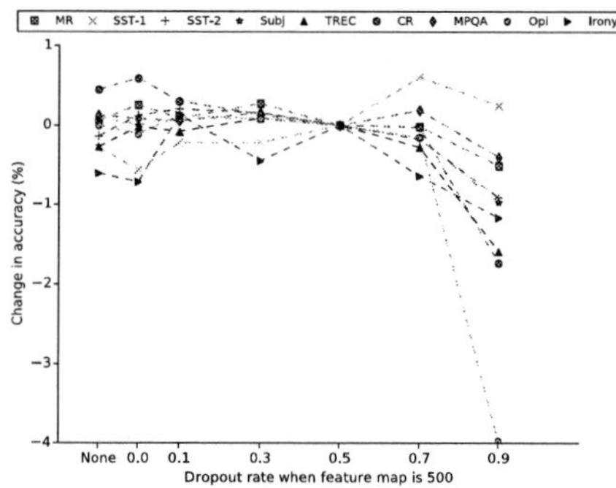

imposing an $l2$ norm constraint generally does not improve performance much (except on Opi), and even adversely effects performance on at least one dataset (CR).

We then also explored dropout rate effect when increasing the number of feature maps. We increase the number of feature maps for each filter size from 100 to 500, and set max $l2$ norm constraint as 3. The effect of dropout rate is shown in Fig. 6. We see that the effect of dropout rate is almost the same as when the number of feature maps is 100, and it does not help much. But we observe that for the dataset SST-1, dropout rate actually helps when it is 0.7. Referring to Fig. 3, we can see that when the number of feature maps is larger than 100, it hurts the performance possibly due to overfitting, so it is reasonable that in this case dropout would mitigate this effect.

We also experimented with applying dropout only to the convolution layer, but still setting the max norm constraint on the classification layer to 3, keeping all other settings exactly the same. This means we randomly set elements of the sentence matrix to 0 during training with probability p, and

Figure 6: Effect of dropout rate when using 500 feature maps.

then multiplied p with the sentence matrix at test time. The effect of dropout rate on the convolution layer is shown in Fig. 7. Again we see that dropout on the convolution layer helps little, and large dropout rate dramatically hurts performance.

To summarize, contrary to some of the existing literature (Srivastava et al., 2014), we found that dropout had little beneficial effect on CNN performance. We attribute this observation to the fact that one-layer CNN has a smaller number parameters than multi-layer deep learning models. Another possible explanation is that using word em-

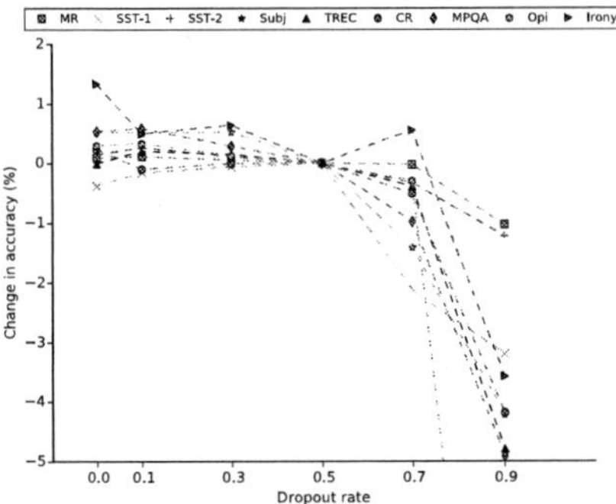

Figure 7: Effect of dropout rate on the convolution layer (The accuracy when the dropout rate is 0.9 on the Opi dataset is not visible on the figure at this point, as in Fig. 4)

beddings helps to prevent overfitting (compared to bag of words based encodings). However, we are not advocating completely foregoing regularization. Practically, we suggest setting the dropout rate to a small value (0.0-0.5) and using a relatively large max norm constraint, while increasing the number of feature maps to see whether more features might help. When further increasing the number of feature maps seems to degrade performance, it is probably worth increasing the dropout rate.

5 Conclusions

We have conducted an extensive experimental analysis of CNNs for sentence classification. We conclude here by summarizing our main findings and deriving from these practical guidance for researchers and practitioners looking to use and deploy CNNs in real-world sentence classification scenarios.

From our experimental analysis we draw several conclusions that we hope will guide future work and be useful for researchers new to using CNNs for sentence classification.

- We find that, even when tuning them to the task at hand, the choice of input word vector representation (e.g., between word2vec and GloVe) has an impact on performance, however different representations perform better for different tasks. At least for sentence classification, both seem to perform better than using one-hot vectors directly. Consider starting with the basic configuration described in Table 1 and using non-static word2vec or GloVe.

- The filter region size can have a large effect on performance, and should be tuned. Line-search over the single filter region size to find the 'best' single region size. A reasonable range might be 1∼10. However, for datasets with very long sentences like CR, it may be worth exploring larger filter region sizes. Once this 'best' region size is identified, it may be worth exploring combining multiple filters using regions sizes near this single best size, given that empirically multiple 'good' region sizes always outperformed using only the single best region size.

- 1-max pooling uniformly outperforms other pooling strategies.

- Consider different activation functions if possible: ReLU and tanh are the best overall candidates.

- Alter the number of feature maps for each filter region size from 100 to 600, and when this is being explored, use a small dropout rate (0.0-0.5) and a large max norm constraint. Pay attention whether the best value found is near the border of the range (Bengio, 2012). If the best value is near 600, it may be worth trying larger values.

- When assessing the performance of a model (or a particular configuration thereof), it is imperative to consider variance. Therefore, replications of the cross-fold validation procedure should be performed and variances and ranges should be considered.

Of course, the above suggestions are applicable only to datasets comprising sentences with similar properties to the those considered in this work. And there may be examples that run counter to our findings here. Nonetheless, we believe these suggestions are likely to provide a reasonable starting point for researchers or practitioners looking to apply a simple one-layer CNN to real world sentence classification tasks.

We recognize that manual and grid search over hyperparameters is sub-optimal, and note that our suggestions here may also inform hyperparameter ranges to explore in random search or Bayesian optimization frameworks.

References

Yoshua Bengio. 2009. Learning deep architectures for ai. *Foundations and trends in Machine Learning*, 2(1):1–127.

Yoshua Bengio. 2012. Practical recommendations for gradient-based training of deep architectures. In *Neural Networks: Tricks of the Trade*, pages 437–478. Springer.

Yoshua Bengio, Réjean Ducharme, Pascal Vincent, and Christian Janvin. 2003. A neural probabilistic language model. *The Journal of Machine Learning Research*, 3:1137–1155.

James Bergstra, Daniel Yamins, and David Daniel Cox. 2013. Making a science of model search: Hyperparameter optimization in hundreds of dimensions for vision architectures.

Y-Lan Boureau, Francis Bach, Yann LeCun, and Jean Ponce. 2010a. Learning mid-level features for recognition. In *Computer Vision and Pattern Recognition (CVPR), 2010 IEEE Conference on*, pages 2559–2566. IEEE.

Y-Lan Boureau, Jean Ponce, and Yann LeCun. 2010b. A theoretical analysis of feature pooling in visual recognition. In *Proceedings of the 27th International Conference on Machine Learning (ICML-10)*, pages 111–118.

Y-Lan Boureau, Nicolas Le Roux, Francis Bach, Jean Ponce, and Yann LeCun. 2011. Ask the locals: multi-way local pooling for image recognition. In *Computer Vision (ICCV), 2011 IEEE International Conference on*, pages 2651–2658. IEEE.

Thomas M Breuel. 2015. The effects of hyperparameters on sgd training of neural networks. *arXiv preprint arXiv:1508.02788*.

Danqi Chen and Christopher D Manning. 2014. A fast and accurate dependency parser using neural networks. In *Proceedings of the 2014 Conference on Empirical Methods in Natural Language Processing (EMNLP)*, volume 1, pages 740–750.

Adam Coates, Andrew Y Ng, and Honglak Lee. 2011. An analysis of single-layer networks in unsupervised feature learning. In *International conference on artificial intelligence and statistics*, pages 215–223.

Ronan Collobert and Jason Weston. 2008. A unified architecture for natural language processing: Deep neural networks with multitask learning. In *Proceedings of the 25th international conference on Machine learning*, pages 160–167. ACM.

Ronan Collobert, Jason Weston, Léon Bottou, Michael Karlen, Koray Kavukcuoglu, and Pavel Kuksa. 2011. Natural language processing (almost) from scratch. *The Journal of Machine Learning Research*, 12:2493–2537.

Charles Dugas, Yoshua Bengio, François Bélisle, Claude Nadeau, and René Garcia. 2001. Incorporating second-order functional knowledge for better option pricing. *Advances in Neural Information Processing Systems*, pages 472–478.

Kavita Ganesan, ChengXiang Zhai, and Jiawei Han. 2010. Opinosis: a graph-based approach to abstractive summarization of highly redundant opinions. In *Proceedings of the 23rd International Conference on Computational Linguistics*, pages 340–348. Association for Computational Linguistics.

Yoav Goldberg. 2015. A primer on neural network models for natural language processing. *arXiv preprint arXiv:1510.00726*.

Geoffrey E Hinton, Nitish Srivastava, Alex Krizhevsky, Ilya Sutskever, and Ruslan R Salakhutdinov. 2012. Improving neural networks by preventing co-adaptation of feature detectors. *arXiv preprint arXiv:1207.0580*.

Minqing Hu and Bing Liu. 2004. Mining and summarizing customer reviews. In *Proceedings of the tenth ACM SIGKDD international conference on Knowledge discovery and data mining*, pages 168–177. ACM.

Mohit Iyyer, Varun Manjunatha, Jordan Boyd-Graber, and Hal Daumé III. 2015. Deep unordered composition rivals syntactic methods for text classification.

Thorsten Joachims. 1998. *Text categorization with support vector machines: Learning with many relevant features*. Springer.

Rie Johnson and Tong Zhang. 2014. Effective use of word order for text categorization with convolutional neural networks. *arXiv preprint arXiv:1412.1058*.

Rie Johnson and Tong Zhang. 2015. Semi-supervised convolutional neural networks for text categorization via region embedding. In *Advances in neural information processing systems*, pages 919–927.

Nal Kalchbrenner, Edward Grefenstette, and Phil Blunsom. 2014. A convolutional neural network for modelling sentences. In *Proceedings of the 52nd Annual Meeting of the Association for Computational Linguistics (Volume 1: Long Papers)*, pages 655–665, Baltimore, Maryland. Association for Computational Linguistics.

Yoon Kim. 2014. Convolutional neural networks for sentence classification. *arXiv preprint arXiv:1408.5882*.

Alex Krizhevsky, Ilya Sutskever, and Geoffrey E Hinton. 2012. Imagenet classification with deep convolutional neural networks. In *Advances in neural information processing systems*, pages 1097–1105.

Yann LeCun, Yoshua Bengio, and Geoffrey Hinton. 2015. Deep learning. *Nature*, 521(7553):436–444.

Xin Li and Dan Roth. 2002. Learning question classifiers. In *Proceedings of the 19th international conference on Computational linguistics-Volume 1*, pages 1–7. Association for Computational Linguistics.

Andrew L Maas, Awni Y Hannun, and Andrew Y Ng. 2013. Rectifier nonlinearities improve neural network acoustic models. In *Proc. ICML*, volume 30.

Tomas Mikolov, Ilya Sutskever, Kai Chen, Greg S Corrado, and Jeff Dean. 2013. Distributed representations of words and phrases and their compositionality. In *Advances in neural information processing systems*, pages 3111–3119.

Bo Pang and Lillian Lee. 2005. Seeing stars: Exploiting class relationships for sentiment categorization with respect to rating scales. In *Proceedings of the ACL*.

Wenzhe Pei, Tao Ge, and Baobao Chang. 2015. An effective neural network model for graph-based dependency parsing. In *Proc. of ACL*.

Jeffrey Pennington, Richard Socher, and Christopher D Manning. 2014. Glove: Global vectors for word representation. *Proceedings of the Empiricial Methods in Natural Language Processing (EMNLP 2014)*, 12:1532–1543.

David E Rumelhart, Geoffrey E Hinton, and Ronald J Williams. 1988. Learning representations by back-propagating errors. *Cognitive modeling*, 5:3.

Richard Socher, Alex Perelygin, Jean Y Wu, Jason Chuang, Christopher D Manning, Andrew Y Ng, and Christopher Potts. 2013. Recursive deep models for semantic compositionality over a sentiment treebank. In *Proceedings of the conference on empirical methods in natural language processing (EMNLP)*, volume 1631, page 1642. Citeseer.

Nitish Srivastava, Geoffrey Hinton, Alex Krizhevsky, Ilya Sutskever, and Ruslan Salakhutdinov. 2014. Dropout: A simple way to prevent neural networks from overfitting. *The Journal of Machine Learning Research*, 15(1):1929–1958.

Byron C Wallace, Laura Kertz Do Kook Choe, and Eugene Charniak. 2014. Humans require context to infer ironic intent (so computers probably do, too). In *Proceedings of the Annual Meeting of the Association for Computational Linguistics (ACL)*, pages 512–516.

Byron C Wallace, Kevin Small, Carla E Brodley, and Thomas A Trikalinos. 2011. Class imbalance, redux. In *Data Mining (ICDM), 2011 IEEE 11th International Conference on*, pages 754–763. IEEE.

Peng Wang, Jiaming Xu, Bo Xu, Chenglin Liu, Heng Zhang, Fangyuan Wang, and Hongwei Hao. 2015. Semantic clustering and convolutional neural network for short text categorization. In *Proceedings of the 53rd Annual Meeting of the Association for Computational Linguistics and the 7th International Joint Conference on Natural Language Processing (Volume 2: Short Papers)*, pages 352–357, Beijing, China. Association for Computational Linguistics.

Janyce Wiebe, Theresa Wilson, and Claire Cardie. 2005. Annotating expressions of opinions and emotions in language. *Language resources and evaluation*, 39(2-3):165–210.

Dani Yogatama and Noah A Smith. 2015. Bayesian optimization of text representations. *arXiv preprint arXiv:1503.00693*.

Ye Zhang, Matthew Lease, and Byron C Wallace. 2017. Exploiting domain knowledge via grouped weight sharing with application to text categorization. *arXiv preprint arXiv:1702.02535*.

Ye Zhang, Stephen Roller, and Byron Wallace. 2016. Mgnc-cnn: A simple approach to exploiting multiple word embeddings for sentence classification. *arXiv preprint arXiv:1603.00968*.

Coordination Boundary Identification with Similarity and Replaceability

Hiroki Teranishi   **Hiroyuki Shindo**   **Yuji Matsumoto**
Nara Institute of Science and Technology
{teranishi.hiroki.sw5, shindo, matsu}@is.naist.jp

Abstract

We propose a neural network model for coordination boundary detection. Our method relies on two common properties — similarity and replaceability in conjuncts — in order to detect both similar and dissimilar pairs of conjuncts. The model improves the identification of clause-level coordination using bidirectional recurrent neural networks incorporating two properties as features. We show that our model outperforms existing state-of-the-art methods for the coordination annotated Penn Treebank and Genia corpus without any syntactic information from parsers.

1 Introduction

Coordination is a common structure and one of major ambiguities in human languages. Although coordination gives a large amount of syntactic or semantic information of coordinated phrases, disambiguating coordination still remains one of the difficult problems that state-of-the-art parsers cannot cope with.

Given a coordinator word, how can we find conjuncts? Coordinate structures are characterized by two properties: (1) similar structures often appear in conjuncts, and (2) one conjunct can be replaced with another conjunct without losing sentence consistency in syntax or semantics. However, many previous studies of coordination disambiguation rely only on the similarities between conjuncts, despite the fact that similarities are not always helpful (Shimbo and Hara, 2007; Hara et al., 2009; Hanamoto, 2012). For example, the sentence *"[at least two commercial versions have been put on the U.S. market], and [an estimated 500 have been sold]."* does not have sim-

ilar phrases around the coordinating conjunction *"and."* Thus, existing methods sometimes fail to capture coordination. In addition to the case where there is a lack of similarities, many similarity-based methods use handcrafted features, heuristic rules, or external resources such as thesauri.

To overcome these problems, Ficler and Goldberg (2016) proposed a neural network model with the replaceability feature as well as the similarity feature. Their model produces candidate pairs of conjuncts using probabilities assigned by the Berkeley Parser. All candidate pairs are scored on the basis of the similarity, replaceability and parser-derived features, and then the best scored pair is picked. Their approach outperforms existing constituent parsers for the Penn Treebank and similarity-based coordination disambiguation methods such as those by Shimbo and Hara (2007) and Hara et al. (2009) for the Genia treebank. Although Ficler and Goldberg's (2016) method improves performance significantly, it heavily depends on the syntactic parser. They use the outputs from the parser not only for candidates generation and the feature for scoring, but also for computation of the similarities. The problems of propagated errors from the parser and dependencies on external resources still remain in their work.

In this work, we propose a neural network model for coordination disambiguation that does not require any external syntactic parser. Our model exploits both the similarity and replaceability properties to avoid suffering from an absence of these properties (Section 2). We use bidirectional recurrent neural networks (RNNs) to obtain the contextual information of candidate conjuncts and then compute similarity and replaceability features without syntactic information (Section 3). We show that our model performs well for both types of coordination: NP coordination (whose conjuncts tend to be similar) and S coordination

Proceedings of the The 8th International Joint Conference on Natural Language Processing, pages 264–272,
Taipei, Taiwan, November 27 – December 1, 2017 ©2017 AFNLP

(whose conjuncts make sense individually) and outperforms the methods by Ficler and Goldberg (2016) and Hara et al. (2009) in Section 4.

The contributions of our work include the following:

(i) Our model can capture dissimilar conjuncts as well as similar ones using the similarity and replaceability features.

(ii) Our model performs better than others without any thesauri, feature engineering, or syntactic parsers to extract conjunct features.

2 Coordinate Structure Analysis

2.1 Task Description

Coordination is a frequently occurring syntactic structure along with several phrases, known as conjuncts. The task of coordination disambiguation is identifying the boundaries of each conjunct with a single coordinator word as one coordinate structure instance. Given a coordinator word (e.g., "and," "or," or "but"), a system must return each conjunct span if the word actually plays the role of a coordinator; otherwise, NONE is output for the absence of coordination. The task sounds simple, yet is difficult because two complex phenomena appear in coordination.

1. A coordinator does not always connect two conjuncts. Sometimes, a coordinate structure consists of three or more consecutive conjuncts. For example[1],

   "It was not an unpleasant evening, certainly, thanks to [the high level of performance], [the compositional talents of Mr. Douglas], and$_{25}$ [the obvious sincerity with which Mr. Stoltzman chooses his selection]."

2. Two or more coordinate structures can be found in the same sentence. In addition, one coordinate structure can be nested inside another. For example,

   "Aside from [the Soviet economic plight] and$_7$ [talks on cutting (strategic) and$_{12}$ (chemical) arms], one other issue the Soviets are likely to want to raise is naval force reduction."

Input Sentence:
But$_1$ it said Charles Johnston, ISI chairman and$_9$ president, agreed to sell his 60% stake in ISI to Memotec upon completion of the tender offer for a combination of cash, Memotec stock and$_{37}$ debentures.

Expected Output:
[Original Task]
    but$_1$: NONE
    and$_9$: (8, 8) chairman ; (10, 10) president
    and$_{37}$: (33, 33) cash ; (35, 36) Memotec stock ;
           (38, 38) debentures

[Our Subtask]:
    but$_1$: NONE
    and$_9$: (8, 10) chairman and president
    and$_{37}$: (33, 38) cash, Memotec stock and debentures

Figure 1: The coordination identification task and our subtask.

In this work, we solve this task by focusing on identifying the beginning and end of an entire coordinate structure. Figure 1 shows our task. We attempt to identify two conjuncts to the left and right sides of a conjunction. We call these conjuncts the *preconjunct* and *post-conjunct*, respectively[2]. In addition, we assume that the end of the preconjunct and the beginning of the post-conjunct adjoin a coordinator word; thus it appears that we work on the subtask of coordinate structure span identification. After identifying a coordination span, we recover individual conjuncts within the span.

2.2 Conjunct Properties

Coordination has many unique traits other than its structure. We focus on the key properties between conjuncts that can be helpful to disambiguate a coordination boundary.

(a) **Similarity**: Conjuncts in a coordination have a similar structure or meaning.

(b) **Replaceability**: A conjunct can be replaced with another conjunct in the same coordination.

Conjuncts tend to have similar semantic or syntactic constituents. For example, the three conjuncts *"the high level of performance," "the compositional talents of MR. Douglas,"* and *"the obvious sincerity with which Mr. Stolzman chooses his selection"* have part-of-speech (POS) tag sequences starting with *"DT JJ NN(S) IN NN(P)*

---

[1]We write coordinator words with their position in a sentence in the form of $word_{position}$ to distinguish them.

[2]If two or more conjuncts appear before a conjunction, we regard them as one conjunct.

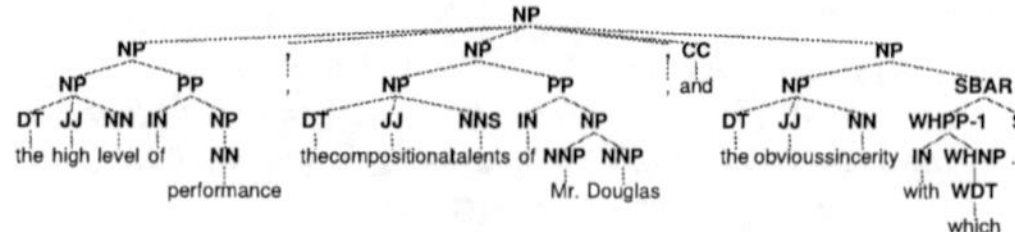

(a) Similar structures between conjuncts

1. Aside from [the Soviet economic plight], one other ...

2. Aside from [talks on cutting (strategic) arms], one other ...

3. Aside from [talks on cutting (chemical) arms], one other ...

(b) Replaceability

Figure 2: Characteristic of conjuncts

... " in common. At a phrase level, they all are categorized as NP and have identical tree structures (Figure 2 (a)). Many previous works exploit this characteristic to detect conjuncts (Shimbo and Hara, 2007; Hara et al., 2009).

The replaceability of conjuncts is also often observed. A sentence is still consistent even if one conjunct is replaced with another one. For example, the coordination *"Aside from [the Soviet economic plight] and [talks on cutting (strategic) and (chemical) arms]"* can be transformed into *"Aside from [talks on cutting (chemical) and (strategic) arms] and [the Soviet economic plight]"* by exchanging conjuncts. Using this property, we can expand a coordinate structure as one sentence by one conjunct (Figure 2 (b)). Replaceability has recently been used to capture conjuncts (Ficler and Goldberg, 2016).

The two properties described above are essential clues to identify conjunct spans; however, they are not always available. Coordination sometimes has different types of conjuncts or an ellipsis in conjuncts. For similarity, when conjuncts belong to the S type or are different types of syntactic categories, their semantic and syntactic structures can be apart from each other (e.g., *"[We turned the trading system on]s, and [it did whatever it was programmed to do]s."* ; *"Bill is [in trouble]PP and [trying to come up with an excuse]VP."*). For replaceability, when words are omitted in a latter conjunct, we cannot replace one conjunct with another unless we supplement omitted words (e.g., *"[Honeywell's contract totaled $69.7 million], and [IBM's $68.8 million]."*). To cope with the case where there is a lack of similarity or replaceability, our proposed method incorporates both features.

3 Proposed Method

Our proposed model calculates the scores of all possible preconjunct and post-conjunct pairs. Given a sentence $x = \{x_1, x_2, x_3, \ldots, x_N\}$ and coordinator word x_k, the preconjunct and post-conjunct can be written as $s_1 = \{x_i, \ldots, x_{k-1}\}$ $(1 \leq i \leq k - 1)$ and $s_2 = \{x_{k+1}, \ldots, x_j\}$ $(k + 1 \leq j \leq N)$, respectively. As we mentioned in Section 2, we fix the end of the preconjunct at $k - 1$ and the beginning of the post-conjunct at $k + 1$. Thus, our model learns and predicts a set of spans (i, j), which indicate the two positions of the beginning and end of a coordination. We identify preconjuncts and post-conjuncts by picking the highest scoring pairs as predicted conjunct spans.

Figure 3 shows an overview of our neural network architecture. This model consists of four components.

Input Layer: Map a sequence of one-hot words and POS tags onto their representations from embeddings.

RNN Layer: Produce a sequence of sentence-level representations based on contexts using a bidirectional RNN.

Feature Extractor: Generate the conjunct phrase representations and feature vectors of possible pairs of conjuncts.

Output Layer: Calculate the scores of pairs of conjuncts using MLP.

In the following subsections, we describe these components in detail.

3.1 Input Layer

The first step of our neural network model is to represent a sequence of words and POS tags in distributed vectors, known as embeddings (Bengio et al., 2003). Our model receives a sequence of one-hot encoded words and POS tags $\{x_n^{word}\}_{n=1}^{N}$, $\{x_n^{tag}\}_{n=1}^{N}$ and then looks them up in the matrices $E^{word} \in \mathbb{R}^{d_{word} \times |v_{word}|}$, $E^{tag} \in \mathbb{R}^{d_{tag} \times |v_{tag}|}$, resulting in a sequence of real-valued vectors $\mathbf{h}_n^{word} \in \mathbb{R}^d$, $\mathbf{h}_n^{tag} \in \mathbb{R}^d$, respectively. These real-valued vectors are concatenated as the input of the

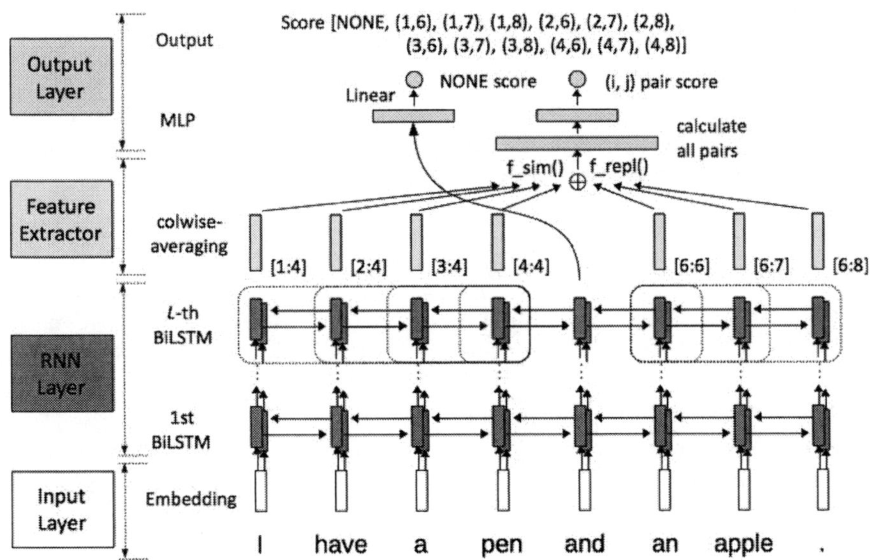

Figure 3: Overview of the architecture for coordination analysis.

next layer.

$$\mathbf{h}_t^{word} = W^{word} x_t^{word}$$
$$\mathbf{h}_t^{tag} = W^{tag} x_t^{tag}$$
$$\mathbf{h}_t^{(0)} = [\mathbf{h}_t^{word}; \mathbf{h}_t^{tag}] \tag{1}$$
$$\mathbf{h}^{(0)} = \{\mathbf{h}_1^{(0)}, \ldots, \mathbf{h}_N^{(0)}\}$$

3.2 RNN Layer

A sequence of distributed vectors is transformed into hidden state vectors using stacked bidirectional RNNs. Bidirectional RNNs process a time series of inputs from the past to a future direction and from the future to a past direction. We can make use of left-to-right (forward) and right-to-left (backward) contexts using these networks. The output of the ℓ-th layer of stacked bidirectional RNNs at a time step t in the forward direction, which is denoted as $\mathbf{h}_{\ell,t}^f$, is computed as

$$\mathbf{h}_{\ell,t}^f = f(\mathbf{h}_{\ell,t-1}^f, \mathbf{h}_{\ell-1,t}) \tag{2}$$

where $\mathbf{h}_{\ell,t-1}^f$ is the hidden state vector of the same layer at the previous time step $t-1$ in the same direction and $\mathbf{h}_{\ell-1,t}$ is the hidden state vector of the previous bidirectional layer at the same time step t. The hidden vector of the ℓ-th layer of stacked bidirectional RNNs at a time step t in the backward direction is also computed in the same way. The stacked bidirectional RNNs that we use in this work output hidden state vectors by concatenating

the vectors $\{\mathbf{h}_{\ell,t}^f\}_{t=1}^T$ from the forward direction and $\{\mathbf{h}_{\ell,t}^b\}_{t=1}^T$ from the backward direction at each time step t in every layer.

In general, an RNN has a function $f(\cdot)$ expressed as

$$f(\mathbf{x}_t, \mathbf{h}_{t-1}) = g(W\mathbf{x}_t + U\mathbf{h}_{t-1})$$

where $g(\cdot)$ is an arbitrary nonlinear function such as the hyperbolic tangent $tanh(\cdot)$ or rectified linear unit (ReLU). We use the long short term memory (LSTM) (Hochreiter and Schmidhuber, 1997) as the function $f(\cdot)$ to prevent backpropagated errors from vanishing or exploding, which arise in RNNs (Pascanu et al., 2013).

3.3 Feature Extractor

This component produces a feature vector based on a representation of a preconjunct and postconjunct and a series of vectors $\{\mathbf{h}_t\}_{t=1}^T$ from bidirectional RNNs. We compute the preconjunct representation $\mathbf{v}_i^{pre}$ and post-conjunct $\mathbf{v}_j^{post}$ using the function $g(\cdot)$. In this work, we define element-wise averaging as the function $g(\cdot)$.

$$g(\mathbf{h}_{l:m}) = \text{average}(\mathbf{h}_l, \mathbf{h}_{l+1}, \ldots, \mathbf{h}_{m-1}, \mathbf{h}_m) \tag{3}$$

Thus, $\mathbf{v}_i^{pre}$ and $\mathbf{v}_j^{post}$ are expressed as

$$\mathbf{v}_i^{pre} = g(\mathbf{h}_{i:k-1}) \ (1 \leq i \leq k-1)$$
$$\mathbf{v}_j^{post} = g(\mathbf{h}_{k+1:j}) \ (k+1 \leq j \leq N) \tag{4}$$

Then $\mathbf{v}_i^{pre}$ and $\mathbf{v}_j^{post}$ are fed into the following two feature extraction functions.

Similarity feature vector

In order to capture the similarity between the pre-conjunct and the post-conjunct, the feature vector is computed as follows:

$$f_{sim}(\mathbf{v}_i^{pre}, \mathbf{v}_j^{post}) = \left[|\mathbf{v}_i^{pre} - \mathbf{v}_j^{post}|; \mathbf{v}_i^{pre} \odot \mathbf{v}_j^{post}\right] \tag{5}$$

where $|\mathbf{v}_i^{pre} - \mathbf{v}_j^{post}|$ is the absolute value of element-wise subtraction, and $\mathbf{v}_i^{pre} \odot \mathbf{v}_j^{post}$ is element-wise multiplication. These subtraction and multiplication operations are intended to model the semantic distance and relatedness (Ji and Eisenstein, 2013; Tai et al., 2015; Hashimoto et al., 2016).

Replaceability feature vector

We define a feature vector based on the conjunct replaceability as follows.

$$f_{repl}(\mathbf{h}_{1:N}, i, j, k) =$$
$$\left[|\mathbf{h}_{i-1} \odot \mathbf{h}_i - \mathbf{h}_{i-1} \odot \mathbf{h}_{k+1}|; \right. \tag{6}$$
$$\left. |\mathbf{h}_j \odot \mathbf{h}_{j+1} - \mathbf{h}_{k-1} \odot \mathbf{h}_{j+1}|\right]$$

where $\mathbf{h}_{i-1}$ is the context vector that is linked to the heads of conjuncts and $\mathbf{h}_{j+1}$ is the context vector that is linked to the tails of conjuncts. The first subtraction $|\mathbf{h}_{i-1} \odot \mathbf{h}_i - \mathbf{h}_{i-1} \odot \mathbf{h}_{k+1}|$ is the difference between two context-conjunct connections at the beginning of coordination. The second subtraction $|\mathbf{h}_j \odot \mathbf{h}_{j+1} - \mathbf{h}_{k-1} \odot \mathbf{h}_{j+1}|$ is the difference between two context-conjunct connections at the end of coordination. These distance measures can be interpreted as difficulty in replacing conjuncts. Note that the function $f_{repl}(\mathbf{h}_{1:N}, i, j, k)$ returns a zero vector when $i = 0$ or $j = N$.

3.4 Output Layer

This layer computes the scores of pairs of conjuncts based on the similarity feature vectors and the replaceability feature vectors. The network is a multilayered perceptron (MLP) that consists of multiple layers of computational units interconnected in a feed-forward way. The score of a pre-conjunct $(i, k - 1)$ and post-conjunct $(k + 1, j)$ candidate pair is calculated as

$$\text{Score}(i, j) =$$
$$\text{MLP}\left(\left[f_{sim}(\mathbf{v}_i^{pre}, \mathbf{v}_j^{post}); \right.\right. \tag{7}$$
$$\left.\left. f_{repl}(\mathbf{h}_{1:N}, i, j, k)\right]\right)$$

To cope with the absence of coordination against a coordinator, we also calculate the score for a candidate of NONE. The score NONE is simply computed as the product of a weight vector and the sentence-level representation of the coordinator from the RNN layer.

$$\text{Score}(\text{NONE}) = w \cdot \mathbf{h}_k + b \tag{8}$$

Using these scoring functions, we assign scores to all possible pairs of conjuncts. Thus, when the length of a sentence is N and a coordinator appears as the k-th word, we obtain $(k - 1) \times (N - k) + 1$ candidates and choose the pair with the best score as the predicted conjuncts with the softmax function.

$$\mathbf{s} = [\text{Score}(\text{NONE}); \text{Score}(1, k + 1); \ldots;$$
$$\text{Score}(1, N); \ldots; \text{Score}(k - 1, N)]$$
$$\hat{p}_\theta(y|x) = \text{softmax}(\mathbf{s})$$
$$\hat{y} = \underset{y}{\arg\max}\left(\hat{p}_\theta(y|x)\right)$$
$$\tag{9}$$

3.5 Learning

The loss function is the negative log-likelihood of the true pair of conjuncts $y^{(k)}$:

$$J(\theta) = -\sum_{d=1}^{D} \log \hat{p}_\theta(y^{(d)}|x^{(d)}) + \frac{\lambda}{2}\|\theta\|^2 \tag{10}$$

where D is the number of occurrences of coordinator words in a training dataset, θ is a set of model parameters, and the hyperparameter λ adjusts the regularization strength. The model parameters are optimized by minimizing the loss using the stochastic gradient descent (SGD).

4 Experiments

We evaluate our proposed model using the coordination annotated Penn Treebank (Ficler, 2016) and the Genia treebank beta (Kim et al., 2003). We present the number of occurrences of coordinator words and the number of sentences with coordination in Table 1[3].

---

[3] We consider "and," "or," "but," "nor," and "and/or" in the PTB and "and," "or," and "but" in the Genia as coordinator words following Ficler and Goldberg (2016) and Hara et al. (2009).

	# Coordinators	# Sentences
Penn Treebank	27903 (24450)	21314 (19095)
Training	22670 (17893)	17282 (13932)
Development	953 (848)	742 (673)
Testing	1282 (1099)	985 (873)
Genia	3598 (3598)	2508 (2508)

Table 1: The number of coordinators in the datasets. (#count) indicates the number of actual presences of coordination.

4.1 Evaluation Using the Penn Treebank

4.1.1 Experimental Setup

We use the coordination annotated Penn Treebank and divide it into wsj 2-21 as the training set, wsj 22 as the development set, and wsj 23 as the testing set. We use pretrained 200-dimensional word embeddings from the New York Times section in English Gigaword (fifth edition) (Parker et al., 2011) using Word2Vec[4] with its default parameter. For the POS tags, we use 10-way jackknifing using the Stanford POS Tagger (Toutanova et al., 2003) and initialize the 50-dimensional embeddings with the uniform distribution within $[-1, 1]$. We use three-layer bidirectional LSTMs as an RNN layer. The dimensionality of the LSTM hidden vectors in each direction is selected from $\{400, 600\}$. Our MLP consists of one hidden layer with ReLU activation, and an output layer. The number of the hidden layer units is selected from $\{1200, 2400\}$. The model parameters are optimized by the mini-batched SGD with a batch size of 20. The learning rate is automatically tuned by Adam (Kingma and Ba, 2014). When training, we apply dropout (Srivastava et al., 2014) to the embeddings, input vectors of each LSTM in bidirectional LSTMs (except the first layer), and the hidden layer of the MLP. Dropout ratio is selected from $\{0.33, 0.50\}$. We choose the regularization strength λ from $\{0.0001, 0.0005, 0.001\}$. We train our model for 50 iterations and choose the model that achieves the best F1 score[5] on the development set and evaluate it with the testing set. We present the final hyperparameters choice in Table 2.

4.1.2 Evaluation Metrics

We evaluate our model on the basis of the ability to predict the beginning and end of each co-

Parameter	Value
Dimension of the LSTM hidden vector	600
MLP units in the hidden layer	2400
Dropout ratio (all)	0.50
Regularization term λ	0.0001

Table 2: The final hyperparameters in the experiment for the Penn Treebank.

ordination (*whole*) with the precision, recall, and F1 measures. In another setup, we focus on NP coordination[6]. To compare the performance with Ficler and Goldberg (2016), we also evaluate our model with two conjunct spans that are adjacent to the coordinator (*inner*), the first and last conjuncts (*outer*), and all complete conjuncts (*exact*). Furthermore, in order to investigate the effectiveness of our proposed features, we perform the experiment with a simple baseline model that uses two averaged vectors as features (Eq. 3) and feeds them into the MLP instead of the similarity and replaceability features (Eq. 7).

Note that our proposed model learns and predicts the coordinate structure boundaries and not each conjunct; thus, when evaluating the inner, outer, and exact metrics, we simply divide the pre-conjuncts into subconjuncts using the character "," as the divider.

4.1.3 Results

We present the results in Table 3. For all metrics, the recall values are low compared with the precision values. Our model is likely to produce NONE for some coordinators by mistake. The proposed model suffers from a worse outer metric than the inner metric. Intuitively, this is because the pre-conjunct for the inner prediction is placed next to a coordinator and it is easier to identify its span, while outer conjuncts occur apart from the coordinators.

Table 4 summarizes the performance of different uses of features. The similarity and replaceability features work better than the baseline independently. However, the joint model performs the best by exploiting both features.

Table 5 presents a comparison with existing methods. For all coordination, our proposed method outperforms the state-of-the-art models with a test set F1 score of 72.81 (0.11 better than

---

[4]https://code.google.com/archive/p/word2vec/

[5]This F1 score is measured for the *whole* criterion, which is mentioned later.

[6]We consider that NP and NX are NP coordination as in Ficler and Goldberg (2016).

	All			NP		
	P	R	F	P	R	F
whole	75.92	72.87	74.36	77.90	75.05	76.45
outer	72.48	69.57	70.99	76.24	73.45	74.82
inner	74.07	71.10	72.56	77.43	74.59	75.99
exact	72.11	69.22	70.63	75.77	72.99	74.35

Table 3: Performance difference by the metrics for the PTB development set.

	All			NP		
	P	R	F	P	R	F
Baseline	70.83	68.75	69.77	74.27	72.87	73.57
f_{sim}	71.79	69.92	70.84	74.76	73.22	73.98
f_{repl}	74.29	71.58	72.91	76.12	73.68	74.88
Both	75.92	72.87	74.36	77.90	75.05	76.45

Table 4: Performance of different sets of features for the PTB development set for the outer metric. "f_{sim}," "f_{repl}," and "Both" indicate the use of similarity feature vectors, replaceability feature vectors, and both feature vectors, respectively.

the previously reported result). For NP coordination, our model achieves competitive results, despite the rough extraction of conjuncts from pre-conjuncts, even for inner-conjunct prediction.

4.2 Evaluation Using Genia

4.2.1 Experimental Setup

We also evaluate our model with the Genia treebank beta to compare with the previous work of Hara et al. (2009) and Ficler and Goldberg (2016). The settings of this experiment are based on those presented in Section 4.1.1, except for the following hyperparameters: Word embeddings are initialized by the pretrained 200-dimensional representation that BioASQ (Tsatsaronis et al., 2012) provides. These embeddings are trained from biomedical abstracts by using Word2Vec. We use gold POS as in Hara et al. (2009), and the dimension of the POS embeddings is 50. For regularization, we set $\lambda = 0.0005$ and train our model for 20 iterations.

4.2.2 Evaluation Metrics

As in Hara et al. (2009), we measure the recall values of coordinate structure boundary prediction, disregarding individual conjunct spans[7]. Thus, we do not decode conjuncts because our model can be compared directly. Coordination phrases in the

---

[7]In the Genia corpus, all coordinator words are associated with conjuncts; thus, there is no absence of coordination, as described in Table 1.

	Dev			Test		
	P	R	F	P	R	F
	All Coordination					
Berkeley	70.14	70.72	70.42	68.52	69.33	68.92
Zpar	72.21	72.72	72.46	68.24	69.42	68.82
Ficler16	72.34	72.25	72.29	72.81	72.61	72.7
Ours	74.07	71.10	**72.56**	73.46	72.16	**72.81**
	NP Coordination					
Berkeley	67.53	70.93	69.18	69.51	72.61	71.02
Zpar	69.14	72.31	70.68	69.81	72.92	71.33
Ficler16	75.17	74.82	74.99	76.91	75.31	**76.1**
Ours	77.43	74.59	**75.99**	75.87	74.76	75.31

Table 5: Performance of inner-conjunct prediction on all coordination and on NP coordination for the PTB. The results for the three methods other than our method are reported in Ficler16 : (Ficler and Goldberg, 2016).

COOD	#	Ours	Ficler16	Hara09
Overall	3598	**65.98**	64.14	61.5
NP	2317	**66.59**	65.08	64.2
VP	465	63.87	**71.82**	54.2
ADJP	321	78.50	74.76	**80.4**
S	188	**52.65**	17.02	22.9
PP	167	53.89	56.28	**59.9**
UCP	60	50.00	**51.66**	36.7
SBAR	56	78.57	**91.07**	51.8
ADVP	21	**85.71**	80.95	85.7
Others	3	33.33	33.33	**66.7**

Table 6: Recall with Genia treebank beta. The numbers in the columns "Ficler16" and "Hara09" are taken from their papers; Ficler16 : (Ficler and Goldberg, 2016) ; Hara09 : (Hara et al., 2009).

Genia treebank are explicitly annotated with a special label (COOD). Making use of this label, we also measure the performance for each type of coordination, as reported in previous work. We evaluate our model by five-fold cross-validation, as in Hara et al. (2009).

4.2.3 Results

We present the results in Table 6. For all coordination, our model outperforms the scores reported by Hara et al. (2009) and Ficler and Goldberg (2016). In the evaluation of each type, our method greatly improves the performance for VP, SBAR, and especially the S type of coordination compared with the similarity-based method of Hara et al. (2009). Regarding the S type, our results are considerably better than those of Ficler and Goldberg (2016). As presented in Table 4, our proposed replaceability feature significantly contributes to the detection of this type of coordination, where only the similarity feature does not work because of a collapse of similarity between conjuncts. The results for NP coordination, which accounts for nearly 65% of all coordination, are fairly good for the Genia corpus; however, the model proposed by Ficler and Goldberg (2016) exhibits better performance than ours for the PTB for the inner metric.

5   Related Works

Approaches using the similarity property between conjuncts have been developed in previous works. Regarding the task of coordination identification in Japanese, Kurohashi and Nagao (1994) used a chart to compute the similarity between conjuncts and identify conjunct spans with a dynamic programming technique. Shimbo and Hara (2007) proposed a sequence alignment model with dynamic programming to capture locally similar structures in two conjuncts on the basis of the set of features including word surfaces, POS tags, and morphological characteristics. The similarity score in their work is computed by a weighted linear combination (perceptron) of manually designed features assigned to edges and nodes in graphs, while the score in the work of Kurohashi and Nagao (1994) is calculated from a score function that uses some rules based on the observation of coordination. Although the method of Shimbo and Hara (2007) could not handle nested coordinate structures, Hara et al. (2009) extended their work to cope with nested coordination as well as three or more than consecutive conjuncts. Their proposed method defined several production rules to build consistent coordination trees with discriminative functions based on the similarity score. Hanamoto (2012) used dual decomposition to combine an HPSG parser with the model of Hara et al. (2009).

The method of use of the replaceability property has recently been adopted by Ficler and Goldberg (2016). They incorporated the replaceability property between conjuncts into the feature representations, as well as the similarity property. They made use of these properties to assign scores to candidate pairs of conjuncts. Their method consists of three components: a binary classifier to detect the presence of coordination, the parser extended from the Berkeley Parser (Petrov et al., 2006) to generate candidate pairs, and a discriminative neural network to identify conjuncts. As similarity features, they compute the Euclidean distance between the two representations of conjuncts, which are computed from syntactic trees generated by the parser, and this is more efficient with respect to the time complexity compared with the methods with graphs. The replaceability feature vectors are produced from bidirectional LSTMs by processing two sentences that are produced by leaving out one of two conjuncts. Their model then scores all candidate pairs of conjuncts from feature vectors including similarities, replaceabilities, and additional three values derived from the probabilities assigned by the parser. The best scored pair is selected as the most probable conjuncts. For the Genia corpus, their model outperformed the method of Hara et al. (2009) which only relied on the similarity property. Using neural networks, they overcame the problems of manually elaborated features and of access to external sources such as thesauri. However, their method heavily depends on their extension of the Berkeley Parser. Therefore, the problem of error propagation between components and the parser still remains.

Kawahara and Kurohashi (2008) tried to resolve coordination disambiguation without any similarities on the basis of the dependency relations and generative probabilities of phrases including conjuncts. Yoshimoto et al. (2015) extended the graph-based dependency parsing algorithm to handle coordinations.

6   Conclusions

We propose a neural network model to disambiguate coordinate structure boundaries. Our method relies on two properties: (i) conjuncts tend to have a similar structure in syntax or semantics and (ii) conjuncts can be replaced with each other, maintaining sentence consistency. On the basis of these observations, we compute two feature vectors from a sequence of vectors produced by bidirectional RNNs. Our model can capture the connections between conjuncts and other parts of sentences and sentence-level coordination. As a result, our model outperforms existing methods and achieves state-of-the-art performance. The biggest contribution of our work is resolving dependency on information from syntactic parsers.

We plan to improve our model to handle three or more conjuncts in future work. In addition, since our method treats nested coordinate structures individually, we expect to create constraints to build non-overlapping coordination spans.

Acknowledgments

This work was partly supported by JST CREST Grant Number JPMJCR1513, Japan. We are grateful to our colleagues in the NAIST Computational Linguistics Laboratory and the anonymous reviewers for their helpful insights and comments.

References

Yoshua Bengio, Réjean Ducharme, Pascal Vincent, and Christian Jauvin. 2003. A neural probabilistic language model. *Journal of machine learning research*, 3(Feb):1137–1155.

Jessica Ficler. 2016. Coordination Annotation Extension in the Penn Tree Bank. *Proceedings of the 54th Annual Meeting of the Association for Computational Linguistics (ACL 2016)*, pages 834–842.

Jessica Ficler and Yoav Goldberg. 2016. A neural network for coordination boundary prediction. *arXiv preprint arXiv:1610.03946*.

Atsushi Hanamoto. 2012. Coordination Structure Analysis using Dual Decomposition. pages 430–438.

Kazuo Hara, Masashi Shimbo, Hideharu Okuma, and Yuji Matsumoto. 2009. Coordinate Structure Analysis with Global Structural Constraints and Alignment-Based Local Features. 1(August):967–975.

Kazuma Hashimoto, Caiming Xiong, Yoshimasa Tsuruoka, and Richard Socher. 2016. A joint many-task model: Growing a neural network for multiple nlp tasks. *arXiv preprint arXiv:1611.01587*.

Sepp Hochreiter and Jürgen Schmidhuber. 1997. Long short-term memory. *Neural computation*, 9(8):1735–1780.

Yangfeng Ji and Jacob Eisenstein. 2013. Discriminative improvements to distributional sentence similarity. In *EMNLP*, pages 891–896.

Daisuke Kawahara and Sadao Kurohashi. 2008. Coordination disambiguation without any similarities. In *Proceedings of the 22nd International Conference on Computational Linguistics-Volume 1*, pages 425–432. Association for Computational Linguistics.

J-D Kim, Tomoko Ohta, Yuka Tateisi, and Junichi Tsujii. 2003. Genia corpusa semantically annotated corpus for bio-textmining. *Bioinformatics*, 19(suppl 1):i180–i182.

Diederik Kingma and Jimmy Ba. 2014. Adam: A method for stochastic optimization. *arXiv preprint arXiv:1412.6980*.

Sadao Kurohashi and Makoto Nagao. 1994. A syntactic analysis method of long japanese sentences based on the detection of conjunctive structures. *Computational Linguistics*, 20(4):507–534.

Robert Parker, David Graff, Junbo Kong, Ke Chen, and Kazuaki Maeda. 2011. English gigaword fifth edition. LDC2011T07.

Razvan Pascanu, Tomas Mikolov, and Yoshua Bengio. 2013. On the difficulty of training recurrent neural networks. In *International Conference on Machine Learning*, pages 1310–1318.

Slav Petrov, Leon Barrett, Romain Thibaux, and Dan Klein. 2006. Learning accurate, compact, and interpretable tree annotation. In *Proceedings of the 21st International Conference on Computational Linguistics and the 44th annual meeting of the Association for Computational Linguistics*, pages 433–440. Association for Computational Linguistics.

Masashi Shimbo and Kazuo Hara. 2007. A Discriminative Learning Model for Coordinate Conjunctions. (June):610–619.

Nitish Srivastava, Geoffrey E Hinton, Alex Krizhevsky, Ilya Sutskever, and Ruslan Salakhutdinov. 2014. Dropout: a simple way to prevent neural networks from overfitting. *Journal of Machine Learning Research*, 15(1):1929–1958.

Kai Sheng Tai, Richard Socher, and Christopher D Manning. 2015. Improved semantic representations from tree-structured long short-term memory networks. *arXiv preprint arXiv:1503.00075*.

Kristina Toutanova, Dan Klein, Christopher D Manning, and Yoram Singer. 2003. Feature-rich part-of-speech tagging with a cyclic dependency network. In *Proceedings of the 2003 Conference of the North American Chapter of the Association for Computational Linguistics on Human Language Technology-Volume 1*, pages 173–180. Association for Computational Linguistics.

George Tsatsaronis, Michael Schroeder, Georgios Paliouras, Yannis Almirantis, Ion Androutsopoulos, Eric Gaussier, Patrick Gallinari, Thierry Artieres, Michael R Alvers, Matthias Zschunke, et al. 2012. Bioasq: A challenge on large-scale biomedical semantic indexing and question answering. In *AAAI fall symposium: Information retrieval and knowledge discovery in biomedical text*.

Akifumi Yoshimoto, Kazuo Hara, Masashi Shimbo, and Yuji Matsumoto. 2015. Coordination-aware dependency parsing (preliminary report). *IWPT 2015*, page 66.

Turning Distributional Thesauri into Word Vectors for Synonym Extraction and Expansion

Olivier Ferret

CEA, LIST, Vision and Content Engineering Laboratory,
Gif-sur-Yvette, F-91191 France.
`olivier.ferret@cea.fr`

Abstract

In this article, we propose to investigate a new problem consisting in turning a distributional thesaurus into dense word vectors. We propose more precisely a method for performing such task by associating graph embedding and distributed representation adaptation. We have applied and evaluated it for English nouns at a large scale about its ability to retrieve synonyms. In this context, we have also illustrated the interest of the developed method for three different tasks: the improvement of already existing word embeddings, the fusion of heterogeneous representations and the expansion of synsets.

1 Introduction

Early work about distributional semantics (Grefenstette, 1994; Lin, 1998; Curran and Moens, 2002) was strongly focused on the notion of distributional thesaurus. Recent work in this domain has been more concerned by the notions of semantic similarity and relatedness (Budanitsky and Hirst, 2006) and by the representation of distributional data. This trend has been strengthened even more recently with all work about distributed word representations and embeddings, whether they are built by neural networks (Mikolov et al., 2013) or not (Pennington et al., 2014).

From a more global perspective, distributional thesauri and distributional data, *i.e.* distributional contexts of words, can be considered as dual representations of the same semantic similarity information. Distributional data are an intensional form of this information that can take an extensional form as distributional thesauri by applying a similarity measure to them. Going from an intensional to an extensional representation corresponds to the

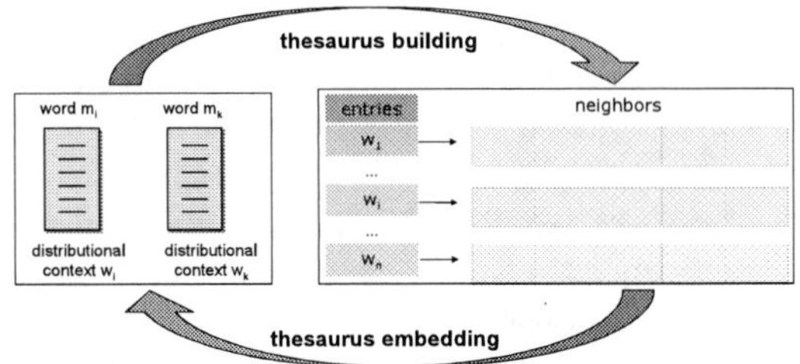

Figure 1: Duality of semantic information

rather classical process underlying the building of distributional thesauri. In the context of word embeddings, Perozzi et al. (2014a) extend this process to the building of lexical networks.

Going to the other way, from an extensional to an intensional representation, is, as far as we know, a new problem in the context of distributional semantics. The interest of this transformation is twofold. First, whatever the initial form of the semantic knowledge, it can be turned into the most suitable form for a particular use. For instance, thesauri are more suitable for tasks like query expansion while word embeddings are more adapted as features for statistical classifiers. Second, each form is also associated with specific methods of improvement. A lot of work has been done for improving distributional contexts by studying various parameters, which has led to an important improvement of distributional thesauri. Conversely, work such as (Claveau et al., 2014) has focused on methods for improving thesauri themselves. It would clearly be interesting to transpose the improvements obtained in such a way to distributional contexts, as illustrated by Figure 1.

Hence, we propose in this article to investigate the problem of turning a distributional thesaurus into word embeddings, that is to say embedding a thesaurus. We will show that such process can

Proceedings of the The 8th International Joint Conference on Natural Language Processing, pages 273–283,
Taipei, Taiwan, November 27 – December 1, 2017 ©2017 AFNLP

be achieved without losing too much information and moreover, that its underlying principles can be used for improving already existing word embeddings. Finally, we will illustrate the interest of such process for building word embeddings integrating external knowledge more efficiently and extending this knowledge.

2 Embedding Distributional Thesauri

A distributional thesaurus is generally viewed as a set of entries with, for each entry, a list of semantic neighbors ranked in descending order of semantic similarity with this entry. Since the neighbors of an entry are also entries of the thesaurus, such thesaurus can be considered as a graph in which vertices are words and edges are the semantic neighborhood relations between them, weighted according to their semantic similarity. The resulting graph is undirected if the semantic similarity measure between words is symmetric, which is the most common case. Such representation was already adopted for improving distributional thesauri by reranking the neighbors of their entries (Claveau et al., 2014) for instance.

One specificity of distributional thesauri from that perspective is that although the weight between two words is representative of their semantic similarity, we know from work such as (Ferret, 2010; Claveau et al., 2014) that the relevance of the semantic neighbors based on this weight strongly decreases as the rank of the neighbors increases. Consequently, our strategy for embedding distributional thesauri is two-fold: first, we build an embedding by relying on methods for embedding graphs, either by exploiting directly their structure or from their representation as matrices; second, we adapt the embedding resulting from the first step according to the specificities of distributional thesauri. We detail these two steps in the next two sections.

2.1 Graph Embedding

The problem of embedding graphs in the perspective of dimension reduction is not new and was already tackled by much work (Yan et al., 2007), going from spectral methods (Belkin and Niyogi, 2001) to more recently neural methods (Perozzi et al., 2014b; Cao et al., 2016). As graphs can be represented by their adjacency matrix, this problem is also strongly linked to the matrix factorization problem. The basic strategy is to perform the eigendecomposition of the matrix as for instance in the case of Latent Semantic Analysis (LSA) (Landauer and Dumais, 1997). However, such decomposition is computationally expensive and for large matrices, as in the context of Collaborative Filtering (Koren, 2008), less constrained matrix factorization techniques are used.

For turning a distributional thesaurus into word embeddings, we tested three different methods:

- the LINE algorithm (Tang et al., 2015), a recent method for embedding weighted graphs;
- the application of Singular Value Decomposition (SVD) to the adjacency matrix of the thesaurus;
- the matrix factorization approach proposed by Hu et al. (2008), also applied to the adjacency matrix of the thesaurus.

LINE defines a probabilistic model over the space $V \times V$, with V, the set of vertices of the considered graph. This probabilistic model is based on the representation of each vertex as a low-dimensional vector. This vector results from the minimization of an objective function based on the Kullback-Leibler divergence between the probabilistic model and the empirical distribution of the considered graph. This minimization is performed by the Stochastic Gradient Descent (SGD) method. Tang et al. (2015) propose more precisely two probabilistic models: one is based on the direct relation between two vertices while the second defines the proximity of two vertices according to the number of neighbors they share. We adopted the second model, which globally gives better results on several benchmarks.

In our second option, SVD factorizes T, the adjacency matrix of the thesaurus to embed, into the product $U \cdot \Sigma \cdot V^\mathsf{T}$. U and V are orthonormal and Σ is a diagonal matrix of eigenvalues. We classically adopted the truncated version of SVD by keeping only the first d elements of Σ, which finally leads to $T_d = U_d \cdot \Sigma_d \cdot V_d^\mathsf{T}$. Levy et al. (2015) investigated in the context of word co-occurrence matrices the best option for the low-dimensional representation of words as the usual setting was $U_d \cdot \Sigma_d$ while Caron (2001) suggested that $U_d \cdot \Sigma_d^P$ with $P < 1$ would be a better option. They found that $P = 0$ or $P = 0.5$ are clearly better than $P = 1$, with a slight superiority for $P = 0$. Similarly, we found $P = 0$ to be the best option.

Our last choice is based on a less constrained form of matrix factorization where T is decomposed into two matrices in such a way that $U \cdot V = \hat{T} \approx T$, with $T \in \mathbb{R}^{m \cdot n}$, $U \in \mathbb{R}^{m \cdot d}$, $V \in \mathbb{R}^{d \cdot n}$ and $d \ll m, n$. U and V are obtained by minimizing the following expression:

$$\sum_{i,j}(t_{ij} - u_i^\intercal v_j)^2 + \lambda(\|u_i\|^2 + \|v_j\|^2) \quad (1)$$

where the first term minimizes the reconstruction error of T by the product $U \cdot V$ while the second term is a regularization term, controlled by the parameter λ for avoiding overfitting. We used U as embedding of the initial thesaurus. (Hu et al., 2008) is a slight variation of this approach where t_{ij} is turned into a confidence score and the minimization of equation 1 is performed by the Alternating Least Squares method. One of the interests of this matrix factorization approach is its ability to deal with undefined values, which implements an implicit feedback in the context of recommender systems and can deal in our context with the fact that the input graph is generally sparse and does not include the furthest semantic neighbors of an entry.

2.2 From Graph to Thesaurus Embeddings

As mentioned previously, all the graph embedding methods of the previous section exploit the semantic similarity between words but for an entry, this similarity is not linearly correlated with the rank of its relevant neighbors in the thesaurus. In other words, the relevance of the semantic neighbors of an entry strongly decreases as their rank increases and the first neighbors are particularly important.

For taking into account this observation, we have adopted a strategy consisting in using the first neighbors of each entry of the initial thesaurus as constraints for adapting the embeddings built from this thesaurus by the graph embedding methods we consider. Such adaptation has already been tackled by some work in the context of the injection of external knowledge made of semantic relations into embeddings built mainly by neural methods such as the Skip-Gram model (Mikolov et al., 2013). Methods for performing such injection can roughly be divided into two categories: those operating during the building of the embeddings, generally by modifying the objective function supporting this building (Yih et al., 2012; Zhang et al., 2014), and those applied after the building of the embeddings (Yu and Dredze, 2014; Xu et al., 2014). We have more particularly used or adapted two methods from the second category

and transposed one method from the first category for implementing our endogenous strategy.

The first method we have considered is the *retrofitting* method from Faruqui et al. (2015). This method performs the adaptation of a set of word vectors q_i by minimizing the following objective function through a label propagation algorithm (Bengio et al., 2006):

$$\sum_{i=1}^{n} \left[\|q_i - \hat{q}_i\|^2 + \sum_{(i,j) \in E} \|q_i - q_j\|^2 \right] \quad (2)$$

where $\hat{q}_i$ are the q_i vectors after their adaptation. The first term is a stability term ensuring that the adapted vectors do not diverge too much from the initial vectors while the second term represents an adaptation term, tending to bring closer the vectors associated with words that are part of a relation from an external knowledge source E. In our case, this knowledge corresponds to the relations between each entry of the initial thesaurus and its first neighbors.

The second method, *counter-fitting* (Mrkšić et al., 2016), is close to *retrofitting* and mainly differentiates from it by adding to the objective function a repelling term for pushing vectors corresponding to antonymous words away from each other. However, a distributional thesaurus does not contain identified antonymous words[1]. Hence, we discarded this term and used the following objective function, minimized by SGD:

$$\sum_{i=1}^{N} \sum_{j \in N(i)} \tau(dist(\hat{q}_i, \hat{q}_j) - dist(q_i, q_j))$$
$$+ \sum_{(i,j) \in E} \tau(dist(\hat{q}_i, \hat{q}_j)) \quad (3)$$

with $dist(x, y) = 1 - \cos(x, y)$ and $\tau(x) = \max(0, x)$. As in equation 2, the first term tends to preserve the initial vectors. In this case, this preservation does not focus on the vectors themselves but on the pairwise distances between a vector and its nearest neighbors ($N(i)$). The second term is quite similar to the second term of equation 2 with the use of a distance derived from the Cosine similarity instead of the Euclidean distance[2].

---

[1] We tried to exploit semantic neighbors that are not very close to their entry as antonyms but results were globally better without them.

[2] Since the Cosine similarity is used as similarity measure between words through their vectors, this distance should be more adapted in this context than the Euclidean distance.

The last method we have used for improving the embeddings built from the initial thesaurus, called *rank-fitting* hereafter, is a transposition of the method proposed by Liu et al. (2015). The objective of this method is to integrate into embeddings order constraints coming from external knowledge with the following form: similarity$(w_i, w_j) >$ similarity(w_i, w_k), abbreviated $s_{ij} > s_{ik}$ in what follows. This kind of constraints particularly fits our context as the semantic neighbors of an entry in a distributional thesaurus are ranked and can be viewed as a set of such constraints. More precisely, i corresponds in this case to an entry and j and k to two of its neighbors such that *rank(j) > rank(k)*. However, the method of Liu et al. (2015) is linked to the Skip-Gram model and was defined as a modification of the objective function underlying this model. We have transposed this approach for its application to the adaptation of embeddings after their building, without a specific link to the Skip-Gram model.

The general idea is to adapt vectors to minimize $s_{ij} - s_{ik}$ $\forall (i, j, k) \in E$. The objective to minimize takes more specifically the following form:

$$\sum_{(i,j,k) \in E} f(s_{ik} - s_{ij}) \qquad (4)$$

where $f(s_{ik} - s_{ij}) = \max(0, s_{ik} - s_{ij})$ corresponds to a kind of hinge loss function and the similarity between words i and j, s_{ij}, is given by the Cosine measure between their associated vectors. The minimization of this objective is performed as for *counter-fitting* by SGD.

Finally, we have also defined a mixed *counter-rank-fitting* method that associates constraints about the proximity of word vectors and their relative ranking. This association was done by mixing the objective functions of *counter-fitting* and *rank-fitting* through the addition of the second term of equation 3, *i.e.* its adaptation term, and equation 4. In this configuration, the first term of the *counter-fitting* function, that preserves the initial embeddings, was not found useful anymore in preliminary experiments.

3   Evaluation of Thesaurus Embedding

3.1   Experimental Framework

For testing and evaluating the proposed approach, we needed first to choose a reference corpus and to build a distributional thesaurus from it. We chose the AQUAINT-2 corpus, already used for various evaluations, a middle-size corpus of around 380 million words made of news articles in English. The main preprocessing of the corpus was the application of lemmatization and the removal of function words. According to (Bullinaria and Levy, 2012), the lemmatization of words leads to only a small improvement in terms of results but it is also a way to obtain the same results with a smaller corpus.

The building of our reference distributional thesaurus, T_{cnt}, was achieved by relying on a classical count-based approach with a set of parameters that were found relevant by several systematic studies (Baroni et al., 2014; Kiela and Clark, 2014; Levy et al., 2015):

- distributional contexts: co-occurrents restricted to nouns, verbs and adjectives having at least 10 occurrences in the corpus, collected in a 3 word window, *i.e.* +/-1 word around the target word;
- directional co-occurrents, which were found having a good performance by Bullinaria and Levy (2012);
- weighting function of co-occurrents in contexts = *Positive Pointwise Mutual Information* (PPMI) with the *context distribution smoothing* factor proposed by (Levy et al., 2015), equal to 0.75;
- similarity measure between contexts, for evaluating the semantic similarity of two words = *Cosine* measure;
- filtering of contexts: removal of co-occurrents with only one occurrence.

The building of the thesaurus from the distributional data was performed as in (Lin, 1998) or (Curran and Moens, 2002) by extracting the closest semantic neighbors of each of its entries. More precisely, the similarity measure was computed between each entry and its possible neighbors. Both the entries of the thesaurus and their possible neighbors were nouns with at least 10 occurrences in the corpus. These neighbors were then ranked in the decreasing order of the values of this measure.

The evaluation of distributional objects such as thesauri or word embeddings is currently a subject of research as both intrinsic (Faruqui et al., 2016; Batchkarov et al., 2016) and extrinsic (Schnabel et al., 2015) evaluations exhibit insufficiencies that question their reliability. In our case, we per-

Method	#eval. words	#syn./ word	R@100	R_{prec}	MAP	P@1	P@2	P@5
T_{cnt}			29.0	11.3	13.1	15.7	11.4	6.6
GloVe	10,544	2.9	21.3	6.7	8.0	9.8	7.4	4.5
SGNS			22.4	8.7	10.3	12.3	8.8	5.2

Table 1: Evaluation of the initial thesaurus and two reference models of embeddings (values x 100)

formed an intrinsic evaluation relying on the synonyms of WordNet 3.0 (Miller, 1990) as Gold Standard. This choice was first justified by our overall long-term perspective, illustrated in Section 5, which is the extraction of synonyms from documents and the expansion of already existing sets of synonyms. However, it is also likely to alleviate some evaluation problems as it narrows the scope of the evaluation, by restricting to a specific type of semantic relations, but performs it at a large scale, the combination of which making its results more reliable. For focusing on the evaluation of the extracted semantic neighbors, the WordNet 3.0's synonyms were filtered to discard entries and synonyms that were not part of the AQUAINT-2 vocabulary. The number of evaluated words and the average number of synonyms in our Gold Standard for each entry are given by the second and the third columns of Table 1.

In terms of methodology, the kind of evaluation we have performed follows (Curran and Moens, 2002; Ferret, 2010) by adopting an Information Retrieval point of view in which each entry is considered as a query and its neighbors are viewed as retrieved synonyms. Hence, we adopted the classical evaluation measures in the field: the R-precision (R_{prec}) is the precision after the first R neighbors were retrieved, R being the number of Gold Standard synonyms; the Mean Average Precision (MAP) is the mean of the precision values each time a Gold Standard synonym is found; precision at different cut-offs is given for the 1, 2, 5 first neighbors. We also give the global recall for the first 100 neighbors.

Table 1 shows the evaluation according to these measures of our initial distributional thesaurus T_{cnt} along with the evaluation in the same framework of two reference models for building word embeddings from texts: GloVe from Pennington et al. (2014) and Skip-Gram with negative sampling (SGNS) from Mikolov et al. (2013)[3]. The input of these two models was the lemmatized version of the AQUAINT-2 corpus as for T_{cnt} but with all its words. Each model was built with the best parameters found from previous work and tested on this corpus. For GloVe: vectors of 300 dimensions, window size = 10, addition of word and context vectors and 100 iterations; for SGNS: vectors of 400 dimensions, window size = 5, 10 negative examples and default value for downsampling of highly frequent words.

Two main trends can be drawn from this evaluation. First, T_{cnt} significantly outperforms GloVe and SGNS for all measures[4]. This superiority of a count-based approach over two predict-based approaches can be seen as contradictory with the findings of Levy et al. (2015). Our analysis is that the use of directional co-occurrences, a rarely tested parameter, explains a large part of this superiority. The second conclusion is that SGNS significantly outperforms GloVe for all measures. Hence, we will report results hereafter only for SGNS as a reference word embedding model.

3.2 Graph Embedding Evaluation

We have evaluated the three methods presented in Section 2.1 for embedding our initial thesaurus T_{cnt} according to the evaluation framework presented in the previous section. For all methods, the main parameters were the number of neighbors taken into account and the number of dimensions of the final vectors. In all cases, the number of neighbors was equal to 5,000, LINE being not very affected by this parameter, and the size of the vectors was 600[5]. For LINE, 10 billion samplings of the similarity values were done and for the matrix factorization (MF) approach, we used $\lambda = 0.075$.

According to Table 2, SVD significantly appears as the best method even if LINE is a competitive alternative. SVD outperforms GloVe while

---

[3]Following (Levy et al., 2015), SGNS was preferred to the Continuous Bag-Of-Word (CBOW) model.

[4]The statistical significance of differences were judged according to a paired Wilcoxon test with p-value < 0.05. The same test was applied for results reported hereafter.

[5]The values of these parameters were optimized on another thesaurus, coming from (Ferret, 2010).

Method	R_{prec}	MAP	P@1	P@2	P@5
T_{cnt}	11.3	13.1	15.7	11.4	6.6
SGNS	8.7	10.3	12.3	8.8	5.2
SVD	**7.8**	**9.5**	**11.3**	**8.1**	**5.0**
LINE	6.8	8.3	9.7	7.1	4.4
MF	4.0	4.9	5.9	4.4	2.7

Table 2: Evaluation of the embedding of a thesaurus as a graph

Method	R_{prec}	MAP	P@1	P@2	P@5
T_{cnt}	11.3	13.1	15.7	11.4	6.6
SGNS	8.7	10.3	12.3	8.8	5.2
SVD	7.8	9.5	11.3	8.1	5.0
Retrofit	**10.9**	**12.9**	**15.2**	11.4	6.8
Counterfit	10.6	12.8	14.0	**11.9**	**7.3**
Rankfit	9.0	10.5	12.6	9.0	5.3
Counter-rankfit	10.7	12.4	**15.2**	11.0	6.3

Table 3: Evaluation of the global thesaurus embedding process

LINE is equivalent to it, which is a first interesting result: this first embedding step of a distributional thesaurus is already able to produce better word representations than a state-of-the-art method, even if it does not reach the level of the best one (SGNS). However, Table 2 also shows that there is still room for improvement for reaching the level of the initial thesaurus T_{cnt}. Finally, the matrix factorization approach is obviously a bad option, at least under the tested form.

3.3 Thesaurus Embedding Evaluation

Table 3 shows the results of the evaluation of the word embedding adaptation methods of Section 2.2, which is also the evaluation of the global thesaurus embedding process. For all methods, the input embeddings were produced by applying SVD to the initial thesaurus T_{cnt}, which was shown as the best option by Table 2. For *retrofitting* (Retrofit) and *counter-fitting* (Counterfit), only the relations between each entry of the thesaurus and its first and second neighbors were considered. For *rank-fitting* (Rankfit), the neighborhood was extended to the first 50 neighbors. For the optimization processes, we used the default settings of the methods: 10 iterations for *retrofitting* and 20 iterations for *counter-fitting*. We also used 20 iterations for *rank-fitting* and *counter-rank-fitting* (Counter-rankfit). For all optimizations by SGD, the learning rate was 0.01.

Several observations can be done. First, all the tested methods significantly improve the initial embeddings. Second, the results of the different methods are quite close for all measures. *retrofitting* outperforms *counter-fitting* but not significantly for R_{prec}. *rank-fitting* is significantly the worst method and its association with *counter-fitting* is better than *retrofitting* for P@1 only, but not significantly. However, we can globally note that the association of SVD and the best adapta-

tion methods obtains results close to the results of the initial T_{cnt} (the difference is even not significant for R_{prec} and P@5). As a consequence, we can conclude, in connection with our initial objective, that embedding a distributional thesaurus while preserving its information in terms of semantic similarity is possible.

4 Applications of Thesaurus Embedding

4.1 Improvement of Existing Embeddings

In the previous section, we have shown that the strongest relations of a distributional thesaurus can be used for improving word vectors built from the embedding of this thesaurus. Since this adaptation is performed after the building of the vectors, it can actually be applied to all kinds of embeddings elaborated from the corpus used for building the distributional thesaurus. As for the process of the previous section, this is a kind of bootstrapping approach in which the knowledge extracted from a corpus is used for improving the word representations elaborated from this corpus. Moreover, as GloVe and most word embedding models, SGNS relies on first-order co-occurrences between words. From that perspective, adapting SGNS embeddings with relations coming from a distributional thesaurus built from the same corpus as these embeddings is a way to incorporate second-order co-occurrence relations into them.

Method	R_{prec}	MAP	P@1	P@2	P@5
(S)GNS	8.7	10.3	12.3	8.8	5.2
$Emb_{retrof}(T_{cnt})$	10.9	12.9	15.2	11.4	6.8
S+Counter-rankfit	**9.5**	**11.1**	**13.8**	**9.9**	**5.6**
S+Retrofit	9.3	10.6	13.2	9.6	5.5

Table 4: Evaluation of the adaptation of SGNS embeddings with thesaurus relations

For this experiment, we applied both *retrofitting* and *counter-rank-fitting* with exactly the same parameters as in Section 3.3. The results of Table 4 clearly validate the benefit of the technique: both *retrofitting* and *counter-rank-fitting* significantly improve SGNS embeddings. As in Section 3.3, the results of *retrofitting* and *counter-rank-fitting* are rather close, with a global advantage for *counter-rank-fitting*. We can also note that the improved versions of SGNS embeddings are still far from the best results of our thesaurus embedding method (*SVD + Retrofit*).

4.2 Fusion of Heterogeneous Representations

Being able to turn a distributional thesaurus into word embeddings also makes it possible to fusion different types of distributional data. In the case of thesaurus, fusion processes were early proposed by Curran (2002) and more recently by Ferret (2015). In the case of word embeddings, the recent work of Yin and Schütze (2016) applied ensemble methods to several word embeddings. By exploiting the possibility to change from one type of representation to another, we propose a new kind of fusion, performed between a thesaurus and word embeddings and leading to improve both the input thesaurus and the embeddings.

The first step of this fusion process consists in turning the input word embeddings into a distributional thesaurus. Then, the resulting thesaurus is merged with the input thesaurus, which consists in merging two lists of ranked neighbors for each of their entries. We followed (Ferret, 2015) and applied for this fusion the CombSum strategy to the similarity values between entries and their neighbors, normalized with the Zero-one method (Wu et al., 2006). Finally, we applied the method of Section 2 for turning the thesaurus resulting from this fusion into word embeddings.

Method	R_{prec}	MAP	P@1	P@2	P@5
$(T)_{cnt}$	11.3	13.1	15.7	11.4	6.6
$(S)GNS$	8.7	10.3	12.3	8.8	5.2
Fusion T-S	12.5	14.8	17.2	12.8	7.5
$Emb_{retrof}($ fusion T-S$)$	11.8	13.8	16.7	12.4	7.0

Table 5: Evaluation of the fusion of a distributional thesaurus T and word embeddings S

The evaluation of this fusion process, performed in a shared context as the considered thesaurus and word embeddings are built from the same corpus, is given in Table 5. The *Fusion T-S* line corresponds to the evaluation of the thesaurus resulting from the second step of the fusion process. The significant difference with the results of T_{cnt} and SGNS confirms the conclusions of Ferret (2015) about the interest of merging thesauri built differently. The *Emb_{retrof}(fusion T-S)* line shows the evaluation of the word embeddings produced by the global fusion process. In a similar way to the findings of Section 3.3, the embeddings built from the *Fusion T-S* thesaurus are less effective than the thesaurus itself but the difference is small here too. Moreover, we can note that these embeddings have significantly higher results than SGNS, the input embeddings, but also higher results than the input thesaurus T_{cnt}, once again without any external knowledge.

5 Knowledge Injection and Synset Expansion

In this section, we will illustrate how the improvement of a distributional thesaurus, obtained in our case by the injection of external knowledge, can be transposed to word embeddings. Moreover, we will show that the thesaurus embedding process achieving this transposition obtains better results for taking into account external knowledge than methods, such as *retrofitting*, that are applied to embeddings built directly from texts (SGNS in our case). We will demonstrate this superiority more precisely in the context of synset expansion.

The overall principle is quite straightforward: first, the external knowledge is integrated into a distributional thesaurus built from the source corpus (T_{cnt} in our experiments). Then, the resulting thesaurus is embedded following the method of Section 2. This external knowledge is supposed to be made of semantic similarity relations. We have considered more particularly pairs of synonyms (E, K) such that E is an entry of T_{cnt} and K is a synonym of E randomly selected from the WordNet 3.0's synsets E is part of. Each E is part of only one pair (E, K).

5.1 Injecting External Knowledge into a Thesaurus

The integration of the semantic relations into a distributional thesaurus is done for each entry E by reranking the neighbor K of the (E, K) pair at the highest rank with the highest similarity. The line $T_{cnt}+K$ of Table 6 gives the evaluation of this integration for 10,544 pairs (E, K) of synonyms, which means one synonym by entry.

	Evaluation of memorization					Global evaluation				
Method	R_{prec}	MAP	P@1	P@2	P@5	R_{prec}	MAP	P@1	P@2	P@5
SGNS	6.5	9.7	6.5	4.6	2.6	8.7	10.3	12.3	8.8	5.2
SGNS+retrof(K)	82.4	90.3	82.4	47.8	19.9	80.1	82.0	98.1	72.3	36.9
T_{cnt}	8.5	12.4	8.5	5.9	3.2	11.3	13.1	15.7	11.4	6.6
svd(T_{cnt})	5.8	9.0	5.8	4.0	2.3	7.8	9.5	11.3	8.1	5.0
svd(T_{cnt})+retrof(K)	86.6	92.8	86.6	48.8	20.0	81.5	83.5	98.8	72.6	37.4
T_{cnt}+K	100	100	100	50.0	20.0	62.7	63.8	100	54.0	23.1
svd(T_{cnt}+K)	12.0	18.0	12.0	8.3	4.7	13.8	17.1	19.0	13.7	8.1
svd(T_{cnt}+K)+retrof(K)	**88.3**	**93.9**	**88.3**	**49.2**	**20.0**	**82.6**	**84.5**	**99.5**	**73.2**	**38.2**

Table 6: Evaluation of the injection of external knowledge into word embeddings for synset expansion

As our evaluation methodology is based on the synonyms of WordNet, we have split our evaluation in two parts. One part takes as Gold Standard the synonyms used for the knowledge injection (see the *Evaluation of memorization* columns in Table 6) and evaluates to what extent the injected knowledge has been memorized. The second part (see the *Global evaluation* columns in Table 6) considers all the synonyms used for the evaluations in the previous sections as Gold Standard for evaluating the ability of models not only to memorize the injected knowledge but also to retrieve new synonyms, *i.e.* synonyms that are not part of the injected knowledge. In the context of our evaluation, which is based on synonym retrieval, this kind of generalization can also be viewed as a form of synset expansion. This is another way to extract synonyms from texts compared to work such as (Leeuwenberg et al., 2016; Minkov and Cohen, 2014; van der Plas and Tiedemann, 2006).

In the case of T_{cnt}+K, we can note that the memorization is perfect, which is not a surprise since the injection of knowledge into the thesaurus corresponds to a kind of memorization. No specific generalization effect beyond the synonyms already present in the thesaurus is observed for the same reason.

5.2 From a Knowledge-Boosted Thesaurus to Word Embeddings

The result of the process described in the previous section is what we could call a knowledge-boosted distributional thesaurus. However, its form is not different from a classical distributional thesaurus and it can be embedded similarly by applying the method of Section 2. The only difference with this method concerns its second step: instead of leveraging the first n neighbors of each entry for improving the embeddings obtained by SVD, we ex-

ploited the set of relations used for "boosting" the initial thesaurus.

The evaluation of the new method we propose for building word embeddings integrating external knowledge is presented in Table 6. More precisely, three different methods are compared: a state-of-the-art method, *SGNS+retrof(K)*, consisting in applying *retrofitting* to SGNS embeddings. *retrofitting* was chosen as it is quick and gives good results. The second method, *svd(T_{cnt})+retrof(K)*, applies *retrofitting* to the embeddings built from T_{cnt} by SVD. The last method, *svd(T_{cnt}+K)+retrof(K)*, corresponds to the full process we have presented, where the external knowledge is first injected into the initial thesaurus T_{cnt} before its embedding.

First, we can note that all the methods considered for producing word embeddings by taking into account external knowledge leads to a very strong improvement of results compared to their starting point. This is true both for the memorization and global evaluations. From the memorization viewpoint, all the injected synonyms can be found among the first five neighbors returned by the three methods as illustrated by their P@5 and even at the first rank in nearly nine times out of ten for the best method, which is clearly our thesaurus embedding process (except the pure memorization performed by T_{cnt}+K).

We can also observe that the method used for knowledge injection can reverse initial differences. For instance, the application of SVD to a thesaurus built from a corpus, *svd(T_{cnt})*, obtains lower results than the application of SGNS to the same corpus. After the injection of external knowledge, this ranking is reversed: the values of the evaluation measures are higher for *svd(T_{cnt})+retrof(K)* than for *SGNS+retrofit(K)*.

More importantly, Table 6 shows that the inte-

Entries	K	Synonyms in neighbors of T_{cnt}+K	Synonyms in neighbors of svd(T_{cnt}+K)+retrof(K)
richness	fullness	fullness [1] 1.0, affluence [1,665] 0.06, profusion [1,950] 0.06, fertility [2,000] 0.06, cornucopia [2,919] 0.06	fullness [1] 0.80, affluence [2] 0.71, cornucopia [3] 0.71, fertility [5] 0.66, profusion [6] 0.44
butchery	abattoir	abattoir [1] 1.0, slaughterhouse [2] 0.05, carnage [65] 0.03, slaughter [90] 0.03, massacre [132] 0.03, shambles [3,735] 0.02	abattoir [1] 0.64, massacre [2] 0.62, carnage [3] 0.61, slaughterhouse [4] 0.53, shambles [5] 0.45, slaughter [11] 0.21
idiom	dialect	dialect [1] 1.0, phrase [16] 0.09, accent [62] 0.09, parlance [2,971] 0.07	dialect [1] 0.80, phrase [2] 0.75, accent [3] 0.71, parlance [4] 0.71
spectator	witness	witness [1] 1.0, viewer [28] 0.14, watcher [519] 0.12	watcher [1] 0.59, witness [2] 0.56, viewer [3] 0.51, looker [10] 0.30

Table 7: Examples of the interest of thesaurus embedding for synset expansion. Each synonym is given with its [rank] among the neighbors of the entry and its similarity value with the entry

gration of external knowledge into the thesaurus before its embedding is clearly effective as illustrated by the significant differences between *SGNS+retrofit(K)* and *svd(T_{cnt}+K)+retrof(K)*. Finally, from the synset expansion viewpoint, it is worth adding that the P@2 value of our best method means that the first synonym proposed by the expansion in addition to the injected synonyms is correct with a precision equal to 46.9, which represents 4,945 new synonyms and illustrates the generalization capabilities of the method.

Table 7 illustrates more qualitatively for some words the interest of the thesaurus embedding method we propose for the expansion of existing synsets. In accordance with the findings of Table 6, it first shows that the method has a good memorization capability of the injected knowledge (K) in the initial thesaurus since in the resulting embeddings (*svd(T_{cnt}+K)+retrof(K)*), the synonym provided for each entry appears as the first or the second neighbor.

Table 7 also illustrates the good capabilities of the method observed in Table 6 in terms of generalization as the rank of synonyms of an entry not provided as initial knowledge tend to decrease strongly. For instance, for the entry *idiom*, the rank of the synonym *parlance* is equal to 2,971 in the initial thesaurus with the injected knowledge (T_{cnt}+K) while it is only equal to 4 after the embedding of the thesaurus. Interestingly, this improvement in terms of rank comes from a change in the distributional representation of words that also impacts the evaluation of the semantic similarity between words. While the similarity between the word *richness* and its synonym *profusion* was initially very low (0.06), its value after the embedding process is very much higher (0.66)

and more representative of the relation between the two words.

6   Conclusion and Perspectives

In this article, we presented a method for building word embeddings from distributional thesauri with a limited loss of semantic similarity information. The resulting embeddings outperforms state-of-the-art embeddings built from the same corpus. We also showed that this method can improve already existing word representations and the injection of external knowledge into word embeddings.

A first extension to this work would be to better leverage the ranking of neighbors in a thesaurus and to integrate more tightly the two steps of our embedding method. We also would like to define a more elaborated method for injecting external knowledge into a distributional thesaurus, more precisely by exploiting the injected knowledge to rerank its semantic neighbors. Finally, we would be interested in testing further the capabilities of the embeddings with injected knowledge for extending resources such as WordNet.

References

Marco Baroni, Georgiana Dinu, and Germán Kruszewski. 2014. Don't count, predict! A systematic comparison of context-counting vs. context-predicting semantic vectors. In *52nd Annual Meeting of the Association for Computational Linguistics (ACL 2014)*, pages 238–247, Baltimore, Maryland.

Miroslav Batchkarov, Thomas Kober, Jeremy Reffin, Julie Weeds, and David Weir. 2016. A critique of word similarity as a method for evaluating distributional semantic models. In *1st Workshop on Evalu-*

ating Vector-Space Representations for NLP, pages 7–12, Berlin, Germany.

Mikhail Belkin and Partha Niyogi. 2001. Laplacian Eigenmaps and Spectral Techniques for Embedding and Clustering. In *Advances in Neural Information Processing Systems 14*, pages 585–591.

Yoshua Bengio, Olivier Delalleau, and Nicolas Le Roux. 2006. Label Propagation And Quadratic Criterion. In *Semi-Supervised Learning*, pages 193–216. MIT Press.

Alexander Budanitsky and Graeme Hirst. 2006. Evaluating WordNet-based Measures of Lexical Semantic Relatedness. *Computational Linguistics*, 32(1):13–47.

John A Bullinaria and Joseph P Levy. 2012. Extracting semantic representations from word co-occurrence statistics: stop-lists, stemming, and SVD. *Behavior research methods*, 44(3):890–907.

Shaosheng Cao, Wei Lu, and Qiongkai Xu. 2016. Deep Neural Networks for Learning Graph Representations. In *Thirtieth AAAI Conference on Artificial Intelligence (AAAI 2016)*, pages 1145–1152. AAAI Press.

John Caron. 2001. Computational Information Retrieval. chapter Experiments with LSA Scoring: Optimal Rank and Basis, pages 157–169. Society for Industrial and Applied Mathematics, Philadelphia, PA, USA.

Vincent Claveau, Ewa Kijak, and Olivier Ferret. 2014. Improving distributional thesauri by exploring the graph of neighbors. In 25th *International Conference on Computational Linguistics (COLING 2014)*, pages 709–720, Dublin, Ireland.

James Curran. 2002. Ensemble Methods for Automatic Thesaurus Extraction. In *2002 Conference on Empirical Methods in Natural Language Processing (EMNLP 2002)*, pages 222–229.

James R. Curran and Marc Moens. 2002. Improvements in automatic thesaurus extraction. In *Workshop of the ACL Special Interest Group on the Lexicon (SIGLEX)*, pages 59–66, Philadelphia, USA.

Manaal Faruqui, Jesse Dodge, Sujay Kumar Jauhar, Chris Dyer, Eduard Hovy, and Noah A. Smith. 2015. Retrofitting Word Vectors to Semantic Lexicons. In *2015 Conference of the North American Chapter of the Association for Computational Linguistics: Human Language Technologies (NAACL HLT 2015)*, pages 1606–1615, Denver, Colorado.

Manaal Faruqui, Yulia Tsvetkov, Pushpendre Rastogi, and Chris Dyer. 2016. Problems With Evaluation of Word Embeddings Using Word Similarity Tasks. In *1st Workshop on Evaluating Vector-Space Representations for NLP*, pages 30–35, Berlin, Germany.

Olivier Ferret. 2010. Testing Semantic Similarity Measures for Extracting Synonyms from a Corpus. In 7th *International Conference on Language Resources and Evaluation (LREC'10)*, pages 3338–3343, Valletta, Malta.

Olivier Ferret. 2015. Early and Late Combinations of Criteria for Reranking Distributional Thesauri. In 53rd *Annual Meeting of the Association for Computational Linguistics and 7th International Joint Conference on Natural Language Processing (ACL-IJCNLP 2015)*, pages 470–476, Beijing, China.

Gregory Grefenstette. 1994. *Explorations in automatic thesaurus discovery*. Kluwer Academic Publishers.

Y. Hu, Y. Koren, and C. Volinsky. 2008. Collaborative Filtering for Implicit Feedback Datasets. In *2008 Eighth IEEE International Conference on Data Mining (ICDM'08)*, pages 263–272.

Douwe Kiela and Stephen Clark. 2014. A Systematic Study of Semantic Vector Space Model Parameters. In 2nd *Workshop on Continuous Vector Space Models and their Compositionality (CVSC)*, pages 21–30, Gothenburg, Sweden.

Yehuda Koren. 2008. Factorization Meets the Neighborhood: A Multifaceted Collaborative Filtering Model. In *14th ACM SIGKDD International Conference on Knowledge Discovery and Data Mining (KDD 2008)*, pages 426–434.

Thomas K. Landauer and Susan T. Dumais. 1997. A solution to Plato's problem: the latent semantic analysis theory of acquisition, induction, and representation of knowledge. *Psychological review*, 104(2):211–240.

Artuur Leeuwenberg, Mihaela Vela, Jon Dehdari, and Josef van Genabith. 2016. A Minimally Supervised Approach for Synonym Extraction with Word Embeddings. *The Prague Bulletin of Mathematical Linguistics*, (105):111–142.

Omer Levy, Yoav Goldberg, and Ido Dagan. 2015. Improving Distributional Similarity with Lessons Learned from Word Embeddings. *Transactions of the Association for Computational Linguistics (TALC)*, 3:211–225.

Dekang Lin. 1998. Automatic retrieval and clustering of similar words. In 17th *International Conference on Computational Linguistics and 36th Annual Meeting of the Association for Computational Linguistics (ACL-COLING'98)*, pages 768–774, Montral, Canada.

Quan Liu, Hui Jiang, Si Wei, Zhen-Hua Ling, and Yu Hu. 2015. Learning Semantic Word Embeddings based on Ordinal Knowledge Constraints. In *53rd Annual Meeting of the Association for Computational Linguistics and the 7th International Joint Conference on Natural Language Processing (ACL-IJCNLP 2015)*, pages 1501–1511, Beijing, China.

Tomas Mikolov, Kai Chen, Greg Corrado, and Jeffrey Dean. 2013. Efficient estimation of word representations in vector space. In *International Conference on Learning Representations 2013 (ICLR 2013), workshop track.*

George A. Miller. 1990. WordNet: An On-Line Lexical Database. *International Journal of Lexicography*, 3(4).

Einat Minkov and William W. Cohen. 2014. Adaptive graph walk-based similarity measures for parsed text. *Natural Language Engineering*, 20(3):361397.

Nikola Mrkšić, Diarmuid Ó Séaghdha, Blaise Thomson, Milica Gašić, Lina M. Rojas-Barahona, Pei-Hao Su, David Vandyke, Tsung-Hsien Wen, and Steve Young. 2016. Counter-fitting Word Vectors to Linguistic Constraints. In *2016 Conference of the North American Chapter of the Association for Computational Linguistics: Human Language Technologies (NAACL HLT 2016)*, pages 142–148, San Diego, California.

Jeffrey Pennington, Richard Socher, and Christopher D. Manning. 2014. GloVe: Global Vectors for Word Representation. In *2014 Conference on Empirical Methods in Natural Language Processing (EMNLP 2014)*, pages 1532–1543, Doha, Qatar.

Bryan Perozzi, Rami Al-Rfou, Vivek Kulkarni, and Steven Skiena. 2014a. *Inducing Language Networks from Continuous Space Word Representations*. Springer International Publishing, Bologna, Italy.

Bryan Perozzi, Rami Al-Rfou, and Steven Skiena. 2014b. DeepWalk: Online Learning of Social Representations. In *20th ACM SIGKDD International Conference on Knowledge Discovery and Data Mining (KDD 2014)*, pages 701–710.

Lonneke van der Plas and Jörg Tiedemann. 2006. Finding Synonyms Using Automatic Word Alignment and Measures of Distributional Similarity. In *21st International Conference on Computational Linguistics and 44th Annual Meeting of the Association for Computational Linguistics (COLING-ACL 2006)*, pages 866–873, Sydney, Australia.

Tobias Schnabel, Igor Labutov, David Mimno, and Thorsten Joachims. 2015. Evaluation methods for unsupervised word embeddings. In *2015 Conference on Empirical Methods in Natural Language Processing (EMNLP 2015)*, pages 298–307, Lisbon, Portugal.

Jian Tang, Meng Qu, Mingzhe Wang, Ming Zhang, Jun Yan, and Qiaozhu Mei. 2015. LINE: Large-scale Information Network Embedding. In *24th International Conference on World Wide Web (WWW 2015)*, WWW '15, pages 1067–1077.

Shengli Wu, Fabio Crestani, and Yaxin Bi. 2006. Evaluating Score Normalization Methods in Data Fusion. In *Third Asia Conference on Information Retrieval Technology (AIRS'06)*, pages 642–648. Springer-Verlag.

Chang Xu, Yalong Bai, Jiang Bian, Bin Gao, Gang Wang, Xiaoguang Liu, and Tie-Yan Liu. 2014. RC-NET: A General Framework for Incorporating Knowledge into Word Representations. In *23rd ACM International Conference on Conference on Information and Knowledge Management (CIKM 2014)*, pages 1219–1228.

S. Yan, D. Xu, B. Zhang, H. j. Zhang, Q. Yang, and S. Lin. 2007. Graph Embedding and Extensions: A General Framework for Dimensionality Reduction. *IEEE Transactions on Pattern Analysis and Machine Intelligence*, 29(1):40–51.

Wen-tau Yih, Geoffrey Zweig, and John Platt. 2012. Polarity Inducing Latent Semantic Analysis. In *2012 Joint Conference on Empirical Methods in Natural Language Processing and Computational Natural Language Learning (EMNLP-CoNLL 2012)*, pages 1212–1222, Jeju Island, Korea.

Wenpeng Yin and Hinrich Schütze. 2016. Learning Word Meta-Embeddings. In *54th Annual Meeting of the Association for Computational Linguistics (ACL 2016)*, pages 1351–1360, Berlin, Germany.

Mo Yu and Mark Dredze. 2014. Improving Lexical Embeddings with Semantic Knowledge. In *52nd Annual Meeting of the Association for Computational Linguistics (ACL 2014)*, pages 545–550, Baltimore, Maryland.

Jingwei Zhang, Jeremy Salwen, Michael Glass, and Alfio Gliozzo. 2014. Word Semantic Representations using Bayesian Probabilistic Tensor Factorization. In *2014 Conference on Empirical Methods in Natural Language Processing (EMNLP 2014)*, pages 1522–1531, Doha, Qatar.

Training Word Sense Embeddings With Lexicon-based Regularization

Luis Nieto-Piña and **Richard Johansson**
University of Gothenburg
{luis.nieto.pina, richard.johansson}@gu.se

Abstract

We propose to improve word sense embeddings by enriching an automatic corpus-based method with lexicographic data. Information from a lexicon is introduced into the learning algorithm's objective function through a regularizer. The incorporation of lexicographic data yields embeddings that are able to reflect expert-defined word senses, while retaining the robustness, high quality, and coverage of automatic corpus-based methods. These properties are observed in a manual inspection of the semantic clusters that different degrees of regularizer strength create in the vector space. Moreover, we evaluate the sense embeddings in two downstream applications: word sense disambiguation and semantic frame prediction, where they outperform simpler approaches. Our results show that a corpus-based model balanced with lexicographic data learns better representations and improve their performance in downstream tasks.

1 Introduction

Word embeddings, as a tool for representing the meaning of words based on the context in which they appear, have had a considerable impact on many of the traditional Natural Language Processing tasks in recent years. (Turian et al., 2010; Collobert et al., 2011; Socher et al., 2011; Glorot et al., 2011) This form of semantic representation has come to replace in many instances traditional count-based vectors (Baroni et al., 2014), as they yield high-quality semantic representations in a computationally efficient manner, which allows them to leverage information from large corpora.

Due to this success, some attention has been devoted to the question of whether their representational power can be refined to further advance the state of the art in those tasks that can benefit from semantic representations. One instance in which this could be realized concerns polysemous words, which has led to several attempts at representing word senses instead of simple word forms. Doing so would help avoid the situation in which several meanings of a word have to be conflated into just one embedding, typical of simple word embeddings.

Among the different approaches to learning word sense embeddings, a distinction can be made between those that make use of a semantic network (SN) and those that do not. Approaches in the latter group usually apply an unsupervised strategy for clustering instances of words based on the context formed by surrounding words. The resulting clusters are then used to represent the different meanings of a word. These representations characterize word usage in the training corpus rather than lexicographic senses, and run the risk of marginalizing under-represented word senses. Nonetheless, for well represented word senses, this strategy proves to be effective and adaptable to changes.

The alternative is to integrate an SN in the learning process. This kind of resource encodes a lexicon of word senses, connecting lexically and semantically related concepts, usually in the form of a graph. Methods that take this approach are able to work with lexicographic word senses as defined by experts, usually integrating them in different ways with corpus-learned embeddings. However, their completeness depends on the quality of the underlying SN.

In this paper, we present an approach that tries to achieve a balance between these two variants. We propose to make use of an SN for learn-

Proceedings of the The 8th International Joint Conference on Natural Language Processing, pages 284–294,
Taipei, Taiwan, November 27 – December 1, 2017 ©2017 AFNLP

ing word sense embeddings by leveraging its signal through a regularizer function that is applied on top of a traditional objective function used to learn embeddings from corpora. In this manner, our model is able to merge these two opposed sources of data with the expectation that each one will balance the limitations of the other: flexible, high-quality embeddings learned from a corpus, with well defined separation between the expert-defined senses of any given polysemic word. The influence of each source of information can be regulated through a mix parameter.

As the corpus-based part of our model, we use a version of the Skip-gram (Mikolov et al., 2013) model that is modified so that it is able to learn two distinct vocabularies: word senses and word forms as introduced by Nieto-Piña and Johansson (2015). Regarding the SN data, we focus our attention on its underlying graph. We assume that neighboring nodes in such a graph correspond to semantically related concepts. Thus, given a word sense, a sequence of related word senses can be generated from its neighbors. A regularizer function can then be used to update their corresponding embeddings so that they become closer in the vector space. This has the benefit of creating clear separations between the different senses of polysemic words, precisely as they are described in the SN, even in the cases where this separation would not be clear from the data in a corpus.

We give an overview of related work in Section 2, and our model is described in detail in Section 3. The resulting word sense embeddings are evaluated in Section 4 on two separate automated tasks: word sense disambiguation (WSD) and lexical frame prediction (LFP). The experiments used for evaluation allow us to investigate the influence of the lexicographic data on the embeddings by comparing different model parameterizations. We conclude with a discussion of our results in Section 5.

2   Related Work

The recent success of word embeddings as effective semantic representations across the broad spectrum of NLP tasks has led to an increased interest in developing embedding methods further in order to acquire finer-grained representations able to handle polysemy and homonymy. This effort can be divided into two approaches: those that tackle the problem as an unsupervised task, aiming to discover different usages of words in corpora, and those that make use of knowledge resources as a way of injecting linguistic knowledge into the models.

Among the earliest efforts in the former group is the work of Reisinger and Mooney (2010) and Huang et al. (2012), who propose to cluster occurrences of words based on their contexts to account for different meanings. With the advent of the Skip-gram model (Mikolov et al., 2013) as an efficient way of training prediction-based word embedding models, much of the research into obtaining word sense representations revolved around it. Neelakantan et al. (2014) and Nieto-Piña and Johansson (2015) make use of context-based word sense disambiguation (WSD) during corpus training to allow on-line learning of multiple senses of a word with modified versions of Skip-gram. Li and Jurafsky (2015) and Bartunov et al. (2016) apply stochastic processes to allow for representations of a variable number of senses per word to be learnt in unsupervised fashion from corpora.

The embeddings obtained using this approach tend to be word-usage oriented, rather than represent formally defined word senses. While this is descriptive of the texts in the corpus at hand, it can be problematic for generalization. For instance, word senses that are underrepresented or absent in the training corpus will not be assigned a functional embedding. On the other hand, due to the ability of these models to process large amounts of data, well-represented word senses will acquire meaningful representations.

The alternative approach to unsupervised methods is to include data from knowledge resources, usually graph-encoded semantic networks (SN) such as WordNet (Miller, 1995). Chen et al. (2014) and Iacobacci et al. (2015) propose to make use of knowledge resources to produce a sense-annotated corpus, on which known techniques can then be applied to generate word sense embeddings. A usual way of circumventing the lack of sense-annotated corpora is to apply post-processing techniques onto pre-trained word embeddings as a way of leveraging lexical information to produce word sense embeddings. The following models share this method: Johansson and Nieto-Piña (2015) formulate an optimization problem to derive multiple word sense representations from word embeddings, while Pilehvar and Collier (2016) and one of the models proposed by Jauhar et al. (2015) use graph learning techniques to do so.

A characteristic of this approach is that these models can generate embeddings for a complete inventory of word senses. However, the dependence on manually crafted resources can potentially lead to incompleteness, in case of unlisted word senses, or to inflexibility in the face of changes in meaning, failing to account for new meanings of a word.

The model that we present in this article tries to preserve desirable characteristics from both approaches. On one side, the model learns word sense embeddings from a corpus using a predictive learning algorithm that is efficient, streamlined, and flexible with respect to being able to discriminate between different usages of a word from running text. This learning algorithm is based on the idea of adding an extra latent variable to the Skip-gram objective function to account for different senses of a word, that has been explored in previous work by Jauhar et al. (2015) and Nieto-Piña and Johansson (2015). On the other side, the learning process is guided by a regularizer function that introduces information from an SN, in an attempt to achieve a clear, complete, and fair division between the different senses of a word. Furthermore, from a technical point of view, the effect of the regularizer function is applied in parallel to the embedding learning process. This eliminates the need for a two-step training process or pretrained word embeddings, and makes it possible to regulate the influence that each source of data (corpus and SN) has on the learning process.

3 Model Description

3.1 Learning Word Sense Embeddings

The Skip-gram word embedding model (Mikolov et al., 2013) works on the premise of training the vector for a word w to be able to predict those context words c_i with which it appears often together in a large training corpus, according to the following objective function:

$$\sum_{i=1}^{n} \log p(c_i|w)$$

where $p(c_i|w)$ can be approximated using the softmax function, The model, thus, works by maintaining two separate vocabularies which represent word forms in their roles as *target* and *context*

words. The resulting word embeddings (usually those vectors trained for the target word vocabulary) are able to store meaningful semantic information about the words they represent.

The original Skip-gram model is, however, limited to word forms in both its vocabularies. Nieto-Piña and Johansson (2015) introduced a modification of this model in which the target vocabulary holds a variable number of vectors for each word form, intended to represent its different senses. The training objective of such a model now has the following shape:

$$\log p(s|w) + \sum_{i=1}^{n} \log p(c_i|s) \qquad (1)$$

Thus the word sense embeddings are trained to maximize the log-probability of context words c_i given a word's sense s plus the log-probability of that sense given the word w. For our purposes, this prior is a constant, $p(s|w) = \frac{1}{n}$, as we do not have information on the probability of each sense of a given word.

This formulation requires a sense s of word w to be selected for each instance in which the objective function above is applied. This word sense disambiguation is applied on-line at training time and based on the target word's context: The sense s chosen to disambiguate an instance of w is the one whose embedding maximizes the dot product with the sum of the context words' embeddings.

$$\arg\max_{s} \frac{e^{s\sum_i c_i}}{\sum_s e^{s\sum_i c_i}} \qquad (2)$$

This unsupervised model learns different usages of a word with minimal overhead computation on top of the original, word-based Skip-gram. The number of senses per word can be obtained from a lexicon or set to a fixed number.

3.2 Embedding a Lexicon

In order to adapt the graph-structured nature of the data in an SN to be used in continuous representations, we propose to introduce it through a regularizer that can act upon the same embeddings trained by the unsupervised model described above.

Any given node s in a graph will have a set of neighbors n_i directly connected to it. In the graph underlying an SN, we assume n_i to be lexically or semantically similar to s. In this setting, a collection of sequences composed of word senses s

and n_i can be collected by visiting all nodes in the SN's graph and collecting its immediate neighbors. Note that extracting such a collection of sequences from a semantic graph follows quite naturally, but in fact it could be generated from any other resource that relates concepts, such as a thesaurus, even if it is not encoded in a graph, as long as the relations it contains are relevant to the model being trained.

We propose to use a collection of sequences of related word senses to update their corresponding word sense vectors by pulling any two vectors closer together in their geometric space whenever they are encountered in a sequence. This action can be easily modeled by minimizing the following expression:

$$\sum_{i=1}^{k} ||s - n_i||^2 \qquad (3)$$

for each sequence of word senses $(s, n_1, n_2, \ldots, n_k)$. By minimizing the distance in the vector space between vectors representing interconnected concepts according to the SN's organization, the vector model is effectively representing that organization in a way that geometrical distance correlates with lexical or semantical relatedness, a central concept in the word embedding literature.

3.3 Combined Model

The two preceding sections describe the two parts of a combined model that is able to learn simultaneously from a corpus and an SN. This is achieved by training embeddings from a corpus with the objective described in Equation 1, and complementing this procedure with lexicographic data by means of using Equation 3 as a regularizer. The extent of the regularizer's influence on the model is adapted by a mix parameter $\rho \in [0, 1]$: the higher the value of ρ, the more influence the SN data has on the model, and vice versa.

Thus, the objective function of our model is as follows:

$$\log p(s|w) + (1-\rho) \sum_{i=1}^{n} \log p(c_i|s) - \rho \sum_{j=1}^{m} ||s - n_j||^2$$

In practice, this objective is realized by alternating updates through each of the model's parts, the number of which is regulated by ρ. Updates on the corpus-based part are executed with Skip-gram

with negative sampling (Mikolov et al., 2013), adapted to work with a vocabulary of word senses as explained in §3.1.

On top of the formulation of the lexicon-based part of the model given in the previous section we propose two variations on this model in order to explore the extent to which the SN data can be used to influence the combined model explained in the following section. The initial formulation of the model will be referenced as V0 in this paper.

In the first variation (henceforth V1) we propose to only apply Equation 3 on word senses pertaining to polysemous words. If by using the SN we intend to learn clear separations between different senses of a word, it attends to reason to limit its application to those cases, while monosemous words can be sufficiently well trained by the usual corpus-based approach, and act as semantic anchors in the broader vector space.

The second variation (henceforth V2) deals with the specific architecture of the corpus-based training algorithm. As mentioned in the previous section, this model trains a target and a context vocabulary. We propose to use the regularizer to act not only on word sense vectors, but also on context (word form) vectors. By doing this we expect the context vocabulary to be ready for instances of different senses of a word, training context vectors to be potentially more effective in the disambiguation scheme introduced in Equation 2. This variation introduces an extra term into Equation 3,

$$\sum_{i=0}^{n} ||w(s) - w(n_i)||^2$$

where $w(x)$ is a mapping from a given sense x to its corresponding word form.

4 Experiments

4.1 Experimental Setting

We trained the three variants of our model using different parameterizations of $\rho \in (0, 1)$. Each of these instances learned target and context embeddings of 50 dimensions, using a window of size 5 on the corpus-based part of the training algorithm, for a total number of 5 iterations over a number of updates equal to the size of the training corpus.

Below we describe the lexicon and corpus used to train the sense embeddings.

4.1.1 SALDO: a Semantic Network of Swedish Word Senses

SALDO (Borin et al., 2013) is the largest graph-structured semantic lexicon available for Swedish. The version used here contains roughly 125,000 concepts (word senses) organized into a single semantic network.

The sense nodes in the SALDO network are connected by edges that are defined in terms of semantic *descriptors*. A descriptor of a sense is another sense used to define its meaning. The most important descriptor is called the *primary* descriptor (PD), and since every sense in SALDO (except an abstract root sense) has a single unique PD, the PD subgraph of SALDO forms a tree. In most cases, the PD of a sense s is a hypernym or a synonym of s, but other types of semantic relations are also possible.

To exemplify, Figure 1 shows a fragment of the PD tree. In the example, there are some cases where the PD edges correspond to hypernymy, such as *hard rock* being a type of *rock music*, which in turn is a type of *music*, but there are also other types of relations, such as *music* being defined in terms of *to sound*.

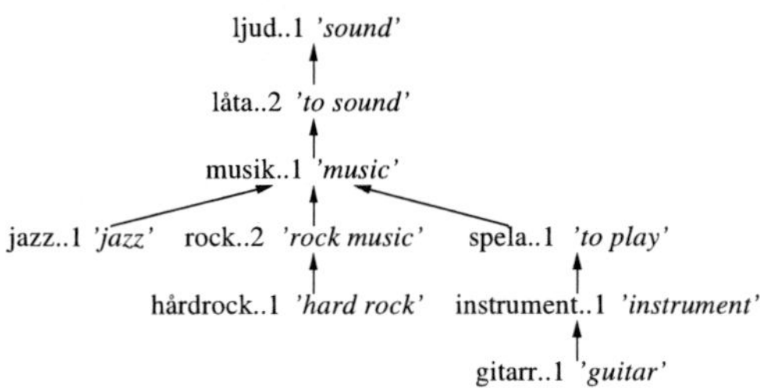

Figure 1: A fragment of the network in SALDO.

4.1.2 Training Corpus

For training the embedding models, we created a mixed-genre corpus of approximately 1 billion words downloaded from Språkbanken, the Swedish language bank.[1] The texts were tokenized, part-of-speech-tagged and lemmatized. Compounds were segmented automatically and when a compound-word lemma was not listed as an entry in the SALDO lexicon, we used the compound parts instead. For instance, *hårdrock* 'hard rock' would occur as a single token in the corpus, while *rockstjärna* 'rock star' would be split into two separate tokens.

---

[1] http://spraakbanken.gu.se

4.2 Qualitative Inspection of Word Senses

By inspecting lists of nearest neighbors to a given embedding, some insight can be gained into how a model represents the meaning of the concept it represents. It is especially interesting in the case of polysemous words, where the neighbors of each of its senses can help judging how well it manages to separate their different meanings.

In Table 1 we list nearest neighbors for each of the two senses of the Swedish word *rock*: 'coat' and 'rock music'. The neighboring concepts in the table are extracted from two separate vector models trained with different parameterizations for the mix parameter ρ: The first, $\rho = 0.01$, has little influence from the lexicon and thus is similar to a corpus-only approach; the second, $\rho = 0.5$, allows for more information from the lexicon to influence the embeddings. In our corpus, the music sense is overrepresented; this can be seen in the table, where both senses trained with $\rho = 0.01$ have most of their nearest neighbors semantically related to music. The model that is more influenced by the lexicon with $\rho = 0.5$ is, however, able to learn two distinct senses. Note how the music sense is not negatively affected by this change: many of its nearest neighbors are the same in both models, and all of them keep the music-related topic in common.

It is also interesting to filter these lists of nearest neighbors to limit them to unlisted words; i.e., words that are not present in the lexicon and appear only in the corpus. This provides an observation of how well those embeddings that are trained by both parts of the model are integrated with those others whose training is based only on the corpus. Table 2 contains such lists of unlisted items for the two senses of *rock* on two models with different parameterization. It presents a similar behavior to the previous experiment: In a model with low influence from the lexicon, the representations of both senses tend towards that of the overrepresented one; when more influence from the lexicon is allowed, a clear separation of the two senses into their expected meanings is observed.

4.3 Word Sense Disambiguation

We trained and evaluated several parameterizations of our model on a Swedish language word sense disambiguation (WSD) task. The aim of this task is to select a sense of an instance of a polyse-

rock-1 'coat'		rock-2 'rock music'	
$\rho = 0.01$	$\rho = 0.5$	$\rho = 0.01$	$\rho = 0.5$
syrtut 'frock coat'	*syrtut* 'frock coat'	*hårdrock* 'hard rock music'	*punk* 'punk music'
Rhythm 'rhythm music'	*kappa* 'coat'	*pop* 'pop music'	*rappa* 'to rap'
rockband 'rock band'	*kåpa* 'cowl'	*punk* 'punk music'	*rap* 'rap music'
Peepshows 'peep shows'	*päls* 'fur coat'	*jazza* 'to jazz'	*pop* 'pop music'
skaband 'ska band'	*mudd* 'cuff'	*dödsmetall* 'death metal music'	*jam* 'music jam'

Table 1: Nearest neighbors for the two senses of *rock* 'coat' and ' rock music' for different ρ.

rock-1 'coat'		rock-2 'rock music'	
$\rho = 0.01$	$\rho = 0.5$	$\rho = 0.01$	$\rho = 0.5$
Rhythm 'rhythm music'	*jesussandaler* 'Jesus sandals'	*nu-metal* 'nu metal'	*metal* 'metal music'
Peepshows 'peep shows'	*tubsockar* 'tube socks'	*goth* ' goth music'	*rnb* 'RnB music'
skabandk 'ska band'	*blåjeans* 'blue jeans'	*psytrance* ' psytrance music'	*indie* 'indie music'
Punkrock 'punk rock'	*snowjoggers* 'snow joggers'	*boogierock* 'boogie rock'	*dubstep* 'dubstep music'
sleaze 'to sleaze'	*midjekort* 'doublet jacket'	*synthband* 'synth music band'	*goth* 'goth music'

Table 2: Nearest unlisted neighbors for the two senses of *rock* 'coat' and 'rock music' for different ρ.

mous word in context. For this purpose, we use a disambiguation mechanism similar to the one introduced in §3.1. Given an ambiguous word in context, a score is calculated for each of its possible senses by applying the expression in Equation 2; however, to correct for skewed sense distributions, we replaced the uniform prior with a power-law prior $P(s_k|w) \propto k^{-2}$, where k is the numerical identifier of the sense. The highest scoring sense is then selected to disambiguate that instance of the word.

As baselines for this experiment, we used random sense and first sense[2] selection. Additionally, we show the results achieved by a disambiguation system, UKB, based on Personalized PageRank (Agirre and Soroa, 2009), and which was trained on the PD tree from SALDO. The implementation of this model makes no assumptions on the underlying graph and thus it is easily adaptable to work with any kind of SN. Our models were all parameterized with $\rho = 0.9$ based on the results obtained on the SweFN dataset. All evaluated systems including the baselines are unsupervised: none of them has used a sense-annotated corpus during training.

4.3.1 Sense-annotated Datasets

We evaluated the WSD systems on eleven different datasets, which to our knowledge are all sense-annotated datasets that exist for Swedish. The datasets consist of instances, where each instance is a sentence where a single target word has been selected for disambiguation.

Two datasets consist of *lexicographical examples* (Lex-Ex): the *SALDO examples* (SALDO-ex) and *Swedish FrameNet examples* (SweFN-ex). The latter of these is annotated in terms of semantic frames, but there is a deterministic mapping from frames to SALDO senses.

Two additional datasets are taken from the Senseval-2 Swedish lexical sample task (Kokkinakis et al., 2001). It uses a different sense inventory, which we mapped manually to SALDO senses. The lexical sample originally consisted of instances for 40 lemmas, out of which we removed 7 lemmas because they were unambiguous in SALDO. Since we are using an unsupervised experimental setup, we report results not only on the designated test set but also on the training set.

The other datasets come from the *Koala* annotation project (Johansson et al., 2016). The latest version consists of seven different corpora, each sampled from text in a separate domain: blogs, novels, Wikipedia, European Parliament proceedings, political news, newsletters from a government agency, and government press releases. Unlike the two lexicographical example sets and the Senseval-2 lexical sample, in which the instances have been selected by lexicographers to be prototypical and to have a good coverage of the sense variation, the instances in the Koala corpora are annotated 'as is' in running text.

The sentences in all datasets were tokenized, compound-split, and lemmatized, and for each target word we automatically determined the set of possible senses, given its context and inflec-

---

[2]No frequency information is available for SALDO's sense inventory and the senses are not ordered by frequency. The senses are ordered by lexicographers so that the lower-numbered senses are more "central" or "primitive", which often but not always correlates with the sense frequency.

Test set	Subset	Size	RND	S1	UKB	V0	V1	V2
Lex-Ex	Average	2,365	39.86	53.90	54.76	61.23	**61.26**	58.34
	SweFN-Ex	1,197	40.43	54.80	54.64	60.90	**61.90**	59.06
	SALDO-Ex	1,168	39.29	53.00	54.88	**61.56**	60.62	57.62
Senseval	Average	8,237	35.90	50.36	44.37	**54.29**	52.95	53.61
	Train	6,995	35.98	50.48	45.43	**54.40**	53.57	53.11
	Test	1,242	35.83	50.24	43.32	**54.19**	52.33	54.11
Koala	Average	11,167	41.83	69.50	67.17	65.17	**73.49**	68.59
	Blogs	2,222	41.86	**71.02**	66.70	60.98	67.78	64.27
	Europarl	1,838	41.80	66.16	65.61	61.26	**71.60**	68.28
	Novels	2,446	41.04	72.85	67.46	67.95	**73.47**	71.30
	Wikipedia	2,444	42.50	75.98	67.59	73.65	**76.68**	73.98
	Political news	1,082	40.60	69.41	69.04	67.47	**75.69**	69.59
	Newsletters	280	42.04	63.57	65.00	58.93	**73.21**	64.29
	Press releases	855	42.99	67.49	68.77	65.96	**76.02**	68.42
Total		21,769	40.40	63.18	60.77	62.48	**67.53**	64.00

Table 3: WSD accuracy on baselines, UKB, and the three variants of our model ($\rho = 0.9$) on all test sets.

tion. We only considered senses of content words: nouns, verbs, adjectives, and adverbs. Multi-word targets were not included, and we removed all instances where only one sense was available.[3]

4.3.2 Disambiguation Results

Table 3 shows disambiguation accuracies for our models on the datasets described above, along with the scores achieved by our baselines and the UKB model. The results of each variant of our model were obtained with a parameterization of $\rho = 0.9$, which was chosen as the best scoring value on the Swe-FN subset used as validation set. The model which only applies the regularizer to polysemous words (V1) dominates most highest scores, overtaken in some instances by V0 and in one by the first sense baseline. Note how the general magnitudes of the scores within each type of dataset underline their different characteristics explained above.

Additionally, for the sake of making a more detailed analysis of the influence of the parameter ρ that dominates the extent of the lexicon's influence on the model, Figure 2 shows the average performance of our models on each dataset for a wide range of values for ρ. There is a clear pattern across all models and datasets by which a greater input from the SN translates into a better performance in WSD. These figures also confirm the superior performance of the variant V1 of our model seen in Table 3.

---

[3]In addition, to facilitate a comparison to the UKB system as a baseline, we removed a small number of instances that could not be lemmatized unambiguously.

4.4 Frame Prediction

In our second evaluation, we investigated how well the sense vector models learned by the different training algorithms correspond to semantic classes defined by the Swedish FrameNet (Friberg Heppin and Toporowska Gronostaj, 2012). In a frame-semantic model of lexical meaning (Fillmore and Baker, 2009), the meaning of words is defined by associating them with broad semantic classes called *frames*; for instance, the word *falafel* would belong to the frame FOOD. Important classes of frames include those corresponding to objects and people, mainly populated by nouns, such as FOOD or PEOPLE_BY_AGE; verb-dominated frames corresponding to events, such as IMPACT, STATEMENT, or INGESTION; and frames dominated by adjectives, often referring to relations, qualities, and states, e.g. ORIGIN or EMOTION_DIRECTED.

In case a word has more than one sense, it may belong to more than one frame. In the Swedish FrameNet, unlike its English counterpart, these senses are explicitly defined using SALDO (see §4.1.1): for instance, for the highly polysemous noun *slag*, its first sense ('type') belongs to the frame TYPE, the second ('hit') to IMPACT, the third ('battle') to HOSTILE_ENCOUNTER, etc.

In the evaluation, we trained classifiers to determine whether a SALDO sense, represented as a sense vector, belongs to a given frame or not. To train the classifiers, we selected the 546 frames from the Swedish FrameNet for which at least 5 entries were available. In total we had 28,842 verb, noun, adjective, and adverb entries, which we split into training (67% of the entries in each

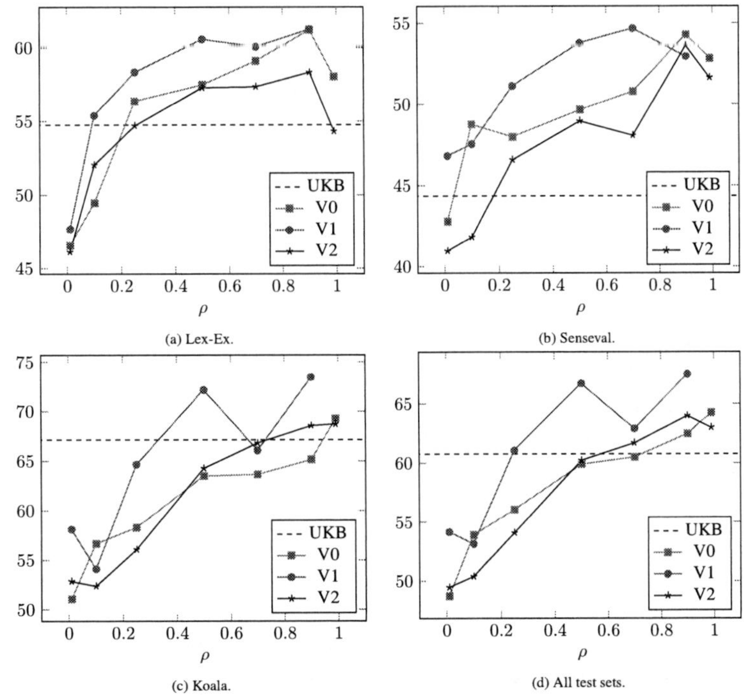

Figure 2: Average WSD accuracies on all instances of each dataset for different values of ρ on the three variants of our model.

frame) and test sets (33%). For each frame, we used LIBLINEAR (Fan et al., 2008) to train a linear support vector machine, using the vectors of the senses associated with that frame as positive training instances, and all other senses listed in FrameNet as negative instances.

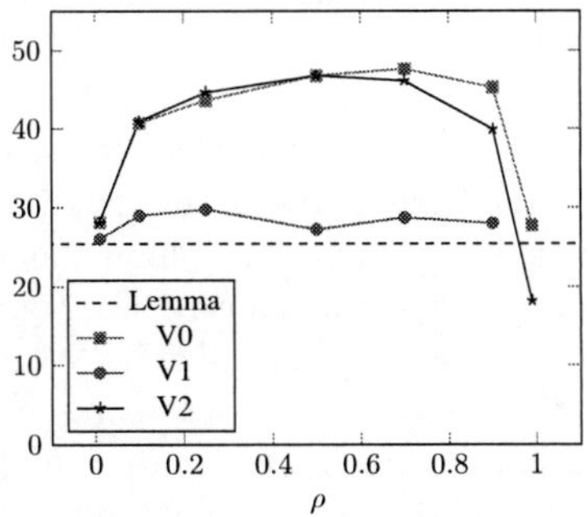

Figure 3: MAP scores for the frame prediction classifiers for the different types of models.

4.4.1 Evaluation Results

At test time, for each frame we applied the SVM scoring function of its classifier to each sense in the test set. The ranking induced by this score was evaluated using the Average Precision (AP) metric commonly used to evaluate rankers; the goal of this ranking step is to score the senses belonging to the frame higher than those that do not. We computed the Mean Averaged Precision (MAP) score by macro-averaging the AP scores over the set of frames.

Figure 3 shows the MAP scores of frame predictors based on different sense vector models. We compared the three training algorithms described in Section 3 for different values of the regularization strength parameter ρ. As a baseline, we included a model that does not distinguish between different senses: it represents a SALDO sense with the word vector of its lemma.

As the figure shows, almost all sense-aware vector models outperformed the model that just used lemma vectors. The result shows tendencies that are different from what we saw in the WSD experiments. The best MAP scores were achieved with mid-range values of ρ, so it seems that this task requires embeddings that strike a balance between representing the lexicon structure faithfully and representing the cooccurrence patterns in the corpus. An model with very light influence of the lexicon was hardly better than just using lemma embeddings, and unlike what we saw for the WSD task we see a strong dropoff when increasing ρ.

In addition, the tendencies here differ from the WSD results in that the training algorithm that only applies the lexicon-based regularizer to polysemous words (V1) gives lower scores than the other two approaches. We believe that this is because it is crucial in this task that sense vectors are clustered into coherent groups, which makes it more useful to move sense vectors closer to their neighbors even when they are monosemous; this as opposed to the WSD task, where it is more useful to leave the monosemous sense vectors in place as "anchors" for the senses of polysemous words. The context-regularized training algorithm (V2) gives no improvement over the original approach (V0), which is expected since context vectors are not used in this task.

Frame	Lemma	V0	V1
ANIMALS	0.73	**0.86**	0.76
FOOD	0.72	**0.84**	0.77
REMOVING	0.20	**0.50**	0.22
MAKE_NOISE	0.40	**0.62**	0.46
ORIGIN	0.90	**0.90**	0.89
COLOR	0.73	**0.88**	0.80
FREQUENCY	0.40	**0.43**	0.35
TIME_VECTOR	0.40	**0.52**	0.27

Table 4: Frame prediction AP scores for selected frames dominated by nouns, verbs, adjectives, and adverbs respectively.

To get a more detailed picture of the strengths and weaknesses of the models in this task, we selected eight frames: two frames dominated by nouns, two for verbs, two for adjectives, two for adverbs. Table 4 shows the AP scores for these frames of the lemma-vector baseline, the initial approach (V0), and the version that only regularizes senses of polysemous words (V1). All lexicon-aware models used a ρ value of 0.7. Almost across the board, the V0 method gives very strong improvements. The exception is the frame ORIGIN, which contains adjectives of ethnicity and nationality (*Mexican, African,* etc); this set of adjectives is already quite coherently clustered by a simple word vector model and is not substantially improved by any lexicon-based approach.

5 Conclusion

In this article we have introduced a family of word sense embedding models that are able to leverage information from two concurrent sources of information: a semantic network and a corpus. Our hypothesis was that by combining them, the robustness and coverage of embeddings trained on a large corpus could achieve a more balanced and linguistically informed representation of the senses of polysemic words. This point has been proved in the evaluation of our models on Swedish language tasks.

A manual inspection of the word sense representation through their nearest neighbors exemplified it in §4.2. Indeed, an increased influence from the SN causes a clearer distinction between different senses of a word, even in the case where one of them is underrepresented in the corpus.

A WSD experiment was carried out on a variety of sense-annotated datasets. Our model consistently outperformed random and first sense baselines, as well as a comparable graph-based WSD system trained on a Swedish SN, which underlines the fact that the strength of our model resides in a combination of lexicon- and corpus-learning.

This is further confirmed in the evaluation of our model on a frame prediction task: A well balanced combination of lexicon and corpus data produces word sense embeddings that outperform common word embeddings when used to predict their semantic frame membership. Furthermore, this superiority is uniform across common frames dominated by different parts of speech.

An analysis of different values of our model's mix parameter ρ showed the value of using lexicographic information in conjunction with corpus data. Especially on WSD, larger values of ρ (i.e., more influence from the SN) generally lead to improved results.

In conclusion, we have shown that automatic word sense representation benefits greatly from using a semantic network in addition to the usual corpus-learning. The combination of these sources of information yields robust, high-quality, and balanced embeddings that excel in downstream tasks where accurate representation of word meaning is crucial. Given these findings, we intend to continue exploring more refined ways in which data from a semantic network can be leveraged to increase sense-awareness in embedding models.

Acknowledgments

This research was funded by the Swedish Research Council under grant 2013–4944. The Koala corpus was developed in a project funded by Riksbankens Jubilemsfond, grant number In13-0320:1.

References

Eneko Agirre and Aitor Soroa. 2009. Personalizing PageRank for word sense disambiguation. In *Proceedings of the 12th Conference of the European Chapter of the Association for Computational Linguistics*, pages 33–41. Association for Computational Linguistics.

Marco Baroni, Georgiana Dinu, and Germán Kruszewski. 2014. Don't count, predict! A systematic comparison of context-counting vs. context-predicting semantic vectors. In *Proceedings of the 52nd Annual Meeting of the Association for Computational Linguistics*, volume 1.

Sergey Bartunov, Dmitry Kondrashkin, Anton Osokin, and Dmitry Vetrov. 2016. Breaking sticks and ambiguities with adaptive skip-gram. In *Artificial Intelligence and Statistics*, pages 130–138.

Lars Borin, Markus Forsberg, and Lennart Lönngren. 2013. SALDO: a touch of yin to WordNet's yang. *Language Resources and Evaluation*, 47:1191–1211.

Xinxiong Chen, Zhiyuan Liu, and Maosong Sun. 2014. A unified model for word sense representation and disambiguation. In *Proceedings of the 2014 Conference on Empirical Methods in Natural Language Processing (EMNLP)*, pages 1025–1035.

Ronan Collobert, Jason Weston, Léon Bottou, Michael Karlen, Koray Kavukcuoglu, and Pavel Kuksa. 2011. Natural language processing (almost) from scratch. *The Journal of Machine Learning Research*, 12:2493–2537.

Rong-En Fan, Kai-Wei Chang, Cho-Jui Hsieh, Xiang-Rui Wang, and Chih-Jen Lin. 2008. LIBLINEAR: A library for large linear classification. *Journal of Machine Learning Research*, 9:1871–1874.

Charles J. Fillmore and Collin Baker. 2009. A frames approach to semantic analysis. In B. Heine and H. Narrog, editors, *The Oxford Handbook of Linguistic Analysis*, pages 313–340. Oxford: OUP.

Karin Friberg Heppin and Maria Toporowska Gronostaj. 2012. The rocky road towards a Swedish FrameNet – creating SweFN. In *Proceedings of the Eighth conference on International Language Resources and Evaluation (LREC-2012)*, pages 256–261, Istanbul, Turkey.

Xavier Glorot, Antoine Bordes, and Yoshua Bengio. 2011. Domain adaptation for large-scale sentiment classification: A deep learning approach. In *Proceedings of the 28th International Conference on Machine Learning (ICML-11)*, pages 513–520.

Eric H Huang, Richard Socher, Christopher D Manning, and Andrew Y Ng. 2012. Improving word representations via global context and multiple word prototypes. In *Proceedings of the 50th Annual Meeting of the Association for Computational Linguistics: Long Papers-Volume 1*, pages 873–882. Association for Computational Linguistics.

Ignacio Iacobacci, Mohammad Taher Pilehvar, and Roberto Navigli. 2015. Sensembed: Learning sense embeddings forword and relational similarity. In *53rd Annual Meeting of the Association for Computational Linguistics and the 7th International Joint Conference on Natural Language Processing of the Asian Federation of Natural Language Processing, ACL-IJCNLP 2015*. Association for Computational Linguistics (ACL).

Sujay Kumar Jauhar, Chris Dyer, and Eduard Hovy. 2015. Ontologically grounded multi-sense representation learning for semantic vector space models. In *Proc. NAACL*, volume 1.

Richard Johansson, Yvonne Adesam, Gerlof Bouma, and Karin Hedberg. 2016. A multi-domain corpus of Swedish word sense annotation. In *Proceedings of the Language Resources and Evaluation Conference (LREC)*, pages 3019–3022, Portorož, Slovenia.

Richard Johansson and Luis Nieto-Piña. 2015. Embedding a semantic network in a word space. In *Proceedings of the 2015 Conference of the North American Chapter of the Association for Computational Linguistics: Human Language Technologies*, pages 1428–1433, Denver, Colorado. Association for Computational Linguistics.

Dimitrios Kokkinakis, Jerker Järborg, and Yvonne Cederholm. 2001. SENSEVAL-2: The Swedish framework. In *Proceedings of SENSEVAL-2 Second International Workshop on Evaluating Word Sense Disambiguation Systems*, pages 45–48, Toulouse, France.

Jiwei Li and Dan Jurafsky. 2015. Do multi-sense embeddings improve natural language understanding? In *Empirical Methods in Natural Language Processing (EMNLP)*.

Tomas Mikolov, Ilya Sutskever, Kai Chen, Greg S Corrado, and Jeff Dean. 2013. Distributed representations of words and phrases and their compositionality. In *Advances in Neural Information Processing Systems*, pages 3111–3119.

George A Miller. 1995. WordNet: a lexical database for English. *Communications of the ACM*, 38(11):39–41.

Arvind Neelakantan, Jeevan Shankar, Alexandre Passos, and Andrew McCallum. 2014. Efficient non-parametric estimation of multiple embeddings per word in vector space. In *Proceedings of the 2014 Conference on Empirical Methods in Natural Language Processing (EMNLP)*, pages 1059–1069, Doha, Qatar. Association for Computational Linguistics.

Luis Nieto-Piña and Richard Johansson. 2015. A simple and efficient method to generate word sense representations. In *Proceedings of the International Conference Recent Advances in Natural Language Processing*, pages 465–472, Hissar, Bulgaria.

Mohammad Taher Pilehvar and Nigel Collier. 2016. De-conflated semantic representations. In *Proceedings of the 2016 Conference on Empirical Methods in Natural Language Processing*, pages 1680–1690, Austin, Texas. Association for Computational Linguistics.

Joseph Reisinger and Raymond J Mooney. 2010. Multi-prototype vector-space models of word meaning. In *Human Language Technologies: The 2010 Annual Conference of the North American Chapter of the Association for Computational Linguistics*, pages 109–117. Association for Computational Linguistics.

Richard Socher, Eric H Huang, Jeffrey Pennin, Christopher D Manning, and Andrew Y Ng. 2011. Dynamic pooling and unfolding recursive autoencoders for paraphrase detection. In *Advances in Neural Information Processing Systems*, pages 801–809.

Joseph Turian, Lev Ratinov, and Yoshua Bengio. 2010. Word representations: a simple and general method for semi-supervised learning. In *Proceedings of the 48th Annual Meeting of the Association for Computational Linguistics*, pages 384–394. Association for Computational Linguistics.

Learning How to Simplify From Explicit Labeling of Complex-Simplified Text Pairs

Fernando Alva-Manchego[1] and **Joachim Bingel**[2] and **Gustavo H. Paetzold**[1]
Carolina Scarton[1] and **Lucia Specia**[1]
[1]Department of Computer Science, University of Sheffield, UK
[2]Department of Computer Science, University of Copenhagen, Denmark
`{f.alva,g.h.paetzold,c.scarton,l.specia}@sheffield.ac.uk`
`bingel@di.ku.dk`

Abstract

Current research in text simplification has been hampered by two central problems: (i) the small amount of high-quality parallel simplification data available, and (ii) the lack of explicit annotations of simplification operations, such as deletions or substitutions, on existing data. While the recently introduced Newsela corpus has alleviated the first problem, simplifications still need to be learned directly from parallel text using black-box, end-to-end approaches rather than from explicit annotations. These complex-simple parallel sentence pairs often differ to such a high degree that generalization becomes difficult. End-to-end models also make it hard to interpret what is actually learned from data. We propose a method that decomposes the task of TS into its sub-problems. We devise a way to automatically identify operations in a parallel corpus and introduce a sequence-labeling approach based on these annotations. Finally, we provide insights on the types of transformations that different approaches can model.

1 Introduction

Text Simplification (TS) is the task of reducing the complexity of a text without changing its meaning. Simplification can be applied at various linguistic levels, from lexical substitution to more global operations such as sentence splitting, paraphrasing or the deletion or reordering of entire clauses.

Existing corpora for TS generally come in one of two variants. The first focuses on very specific sub-problems, such as sentence compression

---

FA and JB contributed equally to this paper.

(Bingel and Søgaard, 2016) or the identification of difficult words (Paetzold and Specia, 2016a), and typically encodes relevant simplification operations as discrete labels on tokens. The other variant includes more general, higher-level types of simplifications that often entail the rephrasing or re-structuring of sentences, with content added or removed. These "natural" simplifications are often created for end-users rather than for research purposes. Examples of the latter simplification resources include the Newsela (Xu et al., 2015) and Simple English Wikipedia corpora (Zhu et al., 2010; Coster and Kauchak, 2011b). These resources generally encode interdependencies between different types of simplification better than single-purpose resources and may thus seem favorable for learning simplifications. However, the freedom given to editors and lack of explicit labels on the modifications performed makes generalization much more difficult, especially when existing resources are relatively small in comparison to corpora for other text-to-text problems like machine translation (MT). Nevertheless, these corpora have been extensively used to learn phrase-based statistical and neural models for end-to-end TS systems that bear resemblance to MT models (Specia, 2010; Zhu et al., 2010; Coster and Kauchak, 2011b; Wubben et al., 2012; Narayan and Gardent, 2014; Xu et al., 2016; Zhang and Lapata, 2017; Zhang et al., 2017; Nisioi et al., 2017).

Adaptability and interpretability MT-style models are essentially black boxes that offer little or no control over the way in which a given input is modified. Additionally, in most cases the types of modifications that are actually learned are limited to paraphrasing of short sequences of words. We believe a middle ground is missing in terms of resources and approaches for TS, where models are learned from a more informed labeled

Proceedings of the The 8th International Joint Conference on Natural Language Processing, pages 295–305,
Taipei, Taiwan, November 27 – December 1, 2017 ©2017 AFNLP

dataset of natural simplifications, and can then be applied in a controlled way, e.g., in adaptive simplification scenarios that prioritize different ways of simplifying (e.g. compression or sentence splitting) depending on a particular user's needs.

The only previous work on TS via explicitly predicting simplification operations is that by Bingel and Søgaard (2016), who create training data from comparable text to label entire syntactic units and train a sequence labeling model to predict deletions and phrase substitutions in a complex sentence. Our approach is different in that it captures a larger variety of operations in a more global fashion, by using sentence-wide word alignments rather than surface heuristics. Furthermore, we use a more reliable (professionally created) corpus and our approach is more flexible as we do not rely on syntactic parse trees at test time.

Contributions This paper introduces the following main contributions: **(1)** We provide an in-depth analysis on the potential and limitations of the dominant approach to TS: end-to-end MT-style models; **(2)** We devise a method to automatically identify specific simplification operations in aligned sentences from complex-to-simple simplification corpora. This results in a corpus that can be used to study how human experts perform simplification tasks, as well as to train simplification models to address specific problems; and **(3)** We propose a sequence labeling model built from such a corpus to predict which simplification operations should be performed as a first step for a complete simplification pipeline. This approach is highly modular: once operations are identified, different methods can be applied to cover each simplification operation. We show that this operation-based TS approach is able to produce simpler texts than end-to-end models. The code for extracting the simplification operations is available at `https://github.com/ghpaetzold/massalign`, while our sequence labeling model is released at `https://github.com/jbingel/ijcnlp2017_simplification`.

2 Related Work

In what follows we give a brief description of previous work on statistical and neural models for TS. We first compare methods using versions of Simple English Wikipedia data (Zhu et al., 2010; Coster and Kauchak, 2011b), before considering recent work that relies on the professionally edited Newsela corpus (Xu et al., 2015).

Simple English Wikipedia Zhu et al. (2010) propose a syntax-based translation model for TS that learns operations over the parse trees of the complex sentences. They outperform several baselines in terms of Flesch index. Coster and Kauchak (2011b) train a phrase-based machine translation (PBMT) system and obtain significant improvements in terms of BLEU (Papineni et al., 2002) over a baseline. Coster and Kauchak (2011a) extend a PBMT model to include phrase deletion and outperform Coster and Kauchak (2011b). Wubben et al. (2012) also train a PBMT system for TS with a dissimilarity-based re-ranking heuristic, outperforming Zhu et al. (2010) in terms of BLEU. Narayan and Gardent (2014) built TS systems by combining discourse representation structures with a PBMT model, which outperforms previous approaches. Xu et al. (2016) modify a syntax-based MT system in order to use a new metric – SARI – for optimization and to include special rules for paraphrasing. Although their system does not outperform previous work in terms of BLEU, it achieves the best results according to SARI and human evaluation. Zhang et al. (2017) train a lexically constrained sequence-to-sequence neural network model for TS, based on the encoder-decoder architecture for MT. The system outperforms baseline systems (including a PBMT system) in terms of BLEU. Finally, Nisioi et al. (2017) propose a model for TS that is able to perform lexical replacements and content reduction. They use a neural encoder-decoder approach where they combine pre-trained (general domain and in-domain) word embeddings for the source and target sentences. They also perform beam search, finding the best beam size using either BLEU or SARI. Their best model outperforms previous PBMT-based approaches in terms of BLEU.

Newsela corpus To the best of our knowledge, Zhang and Lapata (2017) is the only work that explores MT-based approaches on the Newsela corpus. They train an attention-based encoder-decoder model (Bahdanau et al., 2014) and use reinforcement learning with a reward policy combining SARI, BLEU and cosine similarity (to measure meaning preservation). Their approach shows improvements over a PBMT system in terms of

BLEU and SARI, but no insights are given with respect to the transformations that are actually learned or how distant from the original sentences the simplifications are. They also experiment with the Simple Wikipedia corpus, yet do not outperform Narayan and Gardent (2014) on this data.

The neural end-to-end model we implement as a baseline in this paper is equivalent to that in Zhang et al. (2017) without the lexical constraints, while the statistical model is equivalent to the one in Coster and Kauchak (2011b).

3 Simplification via End-to-End Models

In addition to requiring large amounts of training data, MT-based approaches to TS are limited because of their black-box way of addressing the problem. As we are going to show in this section, standard end-to-end systems without special adaptation to TS do not succeed in learning alternative formulations of the original text. With a few exceptions (by the neural model), they tend to repeat the original text. We conjecture that this is because, for most original-side material, TS corpora do not consistently enough offer alternative simplified formulations: in the majority of instances, most words are kept as in the original.

To study the potential and limitations of end-to-end translation models for TS, we build models using state-of-the-art MT-based approaches and the Newsela corpus, arguably the most reliable (professionally created) and realistic (aimed at a target audience rather than research) resource to date.

The Newsela Corpus.[1] Newsela is a multi-comparable corpus where each document comes in up to six levels of simplicity, from 0 (original) to 5 (simplest). In our experiments, we only use sentence pairs stemming from adjacent levels of simplicity within the same document.[2]

Translation approaches require data aligned at the sentence level. Given the original Newsela corpus, which only aligns different versions of the same document, we first align sentences using the algorithms described in (Paetzold and Specia, 2016b). Their algorithms search for the best alignment path between the paragraphs and sentences of parallel documents based on TF-IDF cosine similarity and an incremental vicinity search range. They address limitations of previous strategies (Barzilay and Elhadad, 2003; Coster and Kauchak, 2011b; Smith et al., 2010; Xu et al., 2015; Bott and Saggion, 2011) by disregarding the need for (semi-) supervised training, allowing long-distance alignment skips, and capturing N-to-N alignments. The alignments produced are categorized as:

- **Identical:** The alignment is one-to-one and the sentences are exactly the same (96,909 pairs across all adjacent levels).
- **1-to-1:** The alignment is one-to-one and the original-simplified sentences are different (130,790 pairs across all adjacent levels).
- **Split:** The alignment is 1-to-N (42,545 pairs across all adjacent levels).
- **Join:** The alignment is N-to-1 (7,962 pairs across all adjacent levels).

Translation Models. We built two types of models using state-of-the-art MT-based approaches: a phrase-based statistical MT model using Moses (Koehn et al., 2007),[3] and a neural MT model using Nematus (Sennrich et al., 2017).[4] The Neural Text Simplification tool (NTS) made available by Nisioi et al. (2017) was also used for comparison.[5]

For our translation-based experiments, we consider two combinations of sentence alignments, using (i) only one-to-one alignments (**1-to-1**) (130,970 sentence pairs), and (ii) all alignments (**all**), i.e., the entire sentence-aligned corpus with identical, 1-to-1, split and join alignments (278,206 sentence pairs). The first type of data (1-to-1) is the focus of this paper (see §4). The latter variant is included in the experiments for comparison, in particular to address the question whether more (but not necessarily better) data can aid data-intensive translation-based approaches. For all

---

[1] The Newsela Article Corpus was downloaded from https://newsela.com/data, version 2016-01-29.

[2] The motivations for only using adjacent levels are (i) that we assume that these are not "naturally" created (i.e. an expert would not start from an original text and directly generate a level 5 text, but rather go from 0 to 1, 1 to 2, ..., 4 to 5), and (ii) that the high degree of linguistic and stylistic differences between non-adjacent levels makes learning even more complex. For example, the average edit distance for sentences in the 0-1 group is 0.19, while for sentences in the 0-5 group, it is 0.65. As far as the first reason is concerned, note that we could not find any publicly available simplification guidelines for the Newsela corpus.

[3] We follow instructions from http://www.statmt.org/moses/?n=Moses.Baseline

[4] We use a vocabulary size of $30,000$ and the same parameters as in Sennrich et al. (2016).

[5] We use the same configurations as Nisioi et al. (2017).

System	Hyp vs. Ref		Hyp vs. Orig			
	BLEU↑	**TER↓**	**BLEU**	**TER**	**%Same↓**	**SARI↑**
Moses (all)	69.64	30.20	98.77	0.41	93.03	27.45
Nematus (all)	36.46	52.66	45.40	42.30	21.60	22.91
NTS (all)	68.35	31.37	90.52	7.19	72.91	27.36
Moses (1-to-1)	57.79	40.19	98.30	0.86	89.50	24.58
Nematus (1-to-1)	46.90	52.84	76.29	20.10	30.45	29.89
NTS (1-to-1)	53.79	45.24	77.63	16.70	42.76	30.44
Silver operations (1-to-1)	67.33	22.66	61.63	26.01	10.83	61.71
Predicted operations (1-to-1)	41.37	48.72	59.71	25.24	14.06	31.29

Table 1: Performance of translation-based and operation-based TS models (using silver or predicted operation labels, with only DELETION and REPLACE applied). Metrics are BLEU and TER between simplified version (Hyp) and reference (Ref) or original version (Orig), the percentage of sentences copied from the input (%Same), and SARI for the simplifications.

experiments, the respectively used data was first randomly split into training (80%), development (10%) and test (10%) sets and normalized for entities (incl. names, locations, numbers).

Simplification Quality. The first and second sections of Table 1 show the results of translation-based systems according to several metrics: similarity metrics commonly used in MT, comprising BLEU (Papineni et al., 2002) and TER (Snover et al., 2006, minimum edit distance), as well a specific text simplification metric, SARI (Xu et al., 2016). SARI measures how good the words added, deleted and kept by a simplification system are, after comparing the produced output to the original sentence and the simplification reference(s). It is similar to BLEU but rewards copying words from the original sentence. According to experiments performed by Xu et al. (2016), SARI is the metric that best correlates with human judgments of simplicity.

For both "all" and "1-to-1" variants, the BLEU and TER scores between hypotheses and references are worse for Nematus, showing that a baseline neural model tends to be more aggressive and potentially generate noisier modifications than Moses equivalents. To measure how strongly the various approaches modify the input sentences, these scores are also reported between the generated simplifications and the original inputs. Again, these metrics are worse for Nematus-based models, showing that they indeed perform more modifications on the sentences. Moses in turn is very conservative, keeping 90-93% of the test sentences

exactly in their original version. SARI shows low scores for all systems. NTS is also conservative in the "all" variant (attested by the high BLEU score between hypotheses and original sentences). For "1-to-1", NTS produces more simplifications, diverging more from the original sentences.

Sentence-level Operations. Interestingly, even though Moses and Nematus are trained on the same data, they differ substantially with respect to what they can learn. This is demonstrated by an automatic inspection we conducted on the simplifications produced by both systems trained over all types of sentence alignments, i.e. including sentence splits and joins.

Table 2 reports the count and proportion of instances in the test set representing types of sentence-level transformation between the original and simplified sentence. It can be noted that Moses is much more conservative than Nematus and simply tends to copy the original as the output ("Identical" cases). However, as the majority (57%) of aligned sentences in the professional Newsela simplifications are edited, we do not consider copying a valid "simplification" in most cases. Note also that Moses displays an excessively high BLEU score between the *original* and hypothesis sentences (98.77), while the similarity between the original and reference sentences is much lower (71.57).

Manually inspecting some of the simplifications made, we find that when it comes to sentence splits, both MT-based simplifiers seem to be able to perform this type of transformation in an accu-

	Moses		Nematus	
Operation	Count	%	Count	%
Identical	25,882	93.03	10,906	39.20
1-to-1	1,920	6.90	15,428	55.45
Split	14	0.05	354	1.27
Join	4	0.01	1,132	4.07

Table 2: Count and proportion of instances affected by each type of simplification transformation performed by Moses and Nematus.

rate way. However, the proportion of such cases is very low (0.05% and 1.27% for Moses and Nematus, respectively) compared to the proportion in the gold data (13.5%) of the sentence pairs contain at least one split.

Moses only joins sentences in four cases, but these are all spurious instances where a period is incorrectly removed. Nematus is more successful at learning this type of operation. In most cases, it discards entire clauses that contain less relevant content. For example, it simplifies the sentence *"Lincoln often cried in public and recited sad poetry, according to Joshusa Wolf Shenk, who wrote a book called Lincoln's Melancholy"* to *"Lincoln often cried in public and recited sad poetry"*. We also find a few examples where the content that is not discarded is rewritten to some extent, mostly for grammaticality. The Nematus simplification of *"Frank was what the instructors called a 'rock star'; he emerged as a leader who worked hard to keep the group together"* onto *"Frank was a leader who worked hard to keep the group together "* is a good example of that.

When it comes to 1-to-1 transformations, which can include a number of different operations (see §4), most transformations made by Nematus consist of segment deletions, some of which are paired with localized segment rewritings. As for Moses, most 1-to-1 outputs are identical to the original except for a few spurious typographic and punctuation changes. Because of that, Nematus simplifications are in average four tokens shorter than both complex originals and Moses simplifications.

A strong limitation of both models is their inability to address lexical complexity, performing very few lexical replacements. Most of the sentences that are lexically simplified have only one word replaced by another that does not preserve its original meaning. Take, for example, the word *clears* in the sentence *"It clears the way for troops on the ground with its huge bullets"*, which was replaced by *gathers* by Nematus, and the word *agribusiness*, which was replaced by *offering* by Moses in sentence *"Older brother Nate has taken college courses on livestock raising and agribusiness"*. Some of these issues become more evident in the human evaluation we performed comparing both end-to-end systems to our proposed approach (§5.2).

4 Simplification via Sequence Labeling

Our approach to TS differs from translation-based models by explicitly predicting a set of operations to be applied at different positions in a complex sentence. Concretely, we tackle simplification as a sequence labeling problem, predicting operations at the token level and applying them downstream. As there are no high-quality and large-scale resources from which such operation sequences could be learned, we first generate training data as explained below.[6]

4.1 Generating Training Data

Given 1-to-1 sentence pairs, our method for data generation identifies deletions, additions, substitutions, rewrites (replacing or adding non-content words), and reorderings performed between sentences pairs.

Automatic operation annotation. The annotation process uses the following set of operation labels: DELETE (D), REPLACE (R), and MOVE (M) in the original (source) sentence; ADD (A) in the simplified sentence; and REWRITE (RW) in both.[7]

We first generate word alignments between the original and simplified sentences using the aligner by Sultan et al. (2014). Based on these alignments, we perform a word-level annotation for labels DELETE and REPLACE. Our heuristics are that if two words are aligned and are not an exact match, then the corresponding label is REPLACE. If a word in the original sentence is not aligned, it

---

[6]For the experiments with the proposed TS approach, only 1-to-1 alignments are suitable. It is indeed not realistic to expect that complex operations that involve significant structural changes (e.g., splitting or joining sentences) could be modeled using sequence labeling approaches. For such complex operations, we believe explicitly representing the sentences' syntactic structures and learning abstract syntactic transformation rules (e.g. as in Woodsend and Lapata (2011) or Feblowitz and Kauchak (2013)) would be more advisable. However, we note that, as previously shown, translation-based end-to-end approaches also fail to learn such complex operations.

[7]Target-side annotations serve for analysis; they are ignored in our experiments as they are unavailable at test time.

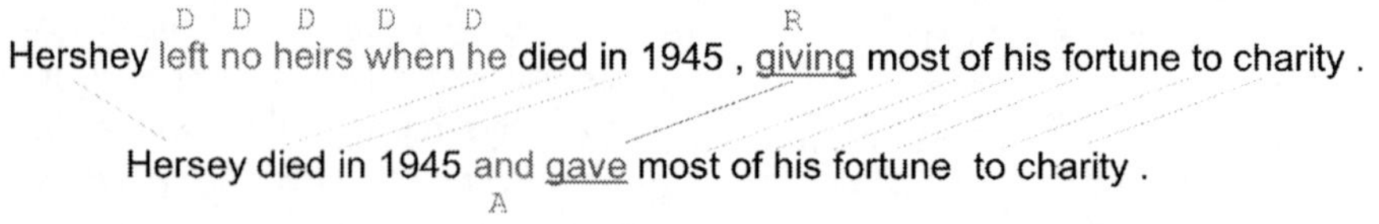

Figure 1: Example of automatic labeling based on word alignments between an original (top) and a simplified (bottom) sentence in the Newsela corpus. Unaligned words on the original side receive label 'D' (DELETE), while words that are aligned to a different form receive 'R' (REPLACE). Aligned words without an explicit label receive a 'C' label (COPY). Sentences are from the Newsela Article Corpus.

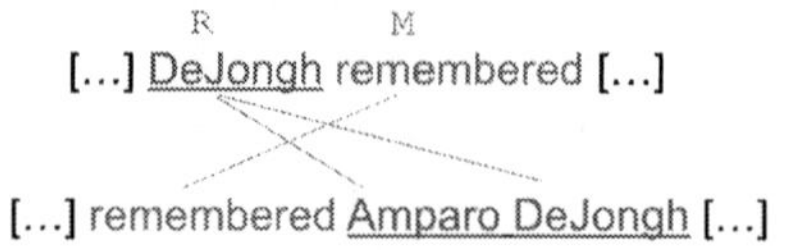

Figure 2: Example of automatic annotation for label MOVE ('M'). Sentences are from the Newsela Article Corpus.

must be a DELETE, and if a word in the simplified sentence is not aligned, it is an ADD. In any other case, the word receives label C (COPY) or O (not part of a simplification operation) in the original or simplified sentence, respectively. For details, see Algorithm 1 in the supplementary material. Figure 1 presents an example for our automatic labeling approach. We consider REWRITE labels as special cases of REPLACE where the words involved are isolated (not in a group of same operation labels) and belong to a list of non-content words.

Finally, we label reorderings (MOVE) by determining if the relative index of a word (considering preceding or following deletions and additions) in the original sentence changes in the simplified one (Algorithm 2). See Figure 2 for an example. Words or phrases that are kept, replaced or rewritten, may be subject to reorderings, such that a token may have more than one label (e.g. REPLACE and MOVE). For that, we extend the set of operations by the compound operations REPLACE+MOVE (RM) and REWRITE+MOVE (RWM).

Evaluation of automatic labels. To test our algorithms, we compare their output to manual annotations for 100 sentences from level pair 0-1 of the Newsela corpus. The manual annotations were performed by four proficient English speakers. For 30 of those sentences, we calculated the pairwise inter-annotator agreement between annotators, yielding an average kappa value

of 0.57. We obtain an accuracy of 0.92 for all labels, and a micro-averaged F_1 score of 0.70 for all positive labels (i.e. excluding 'C' and 'O'). Table 3 presents details on the performance of our annotation algorithms over the identified operations. Of the positive labels, the algorithms annotate most accurately additions and deletions. According to the confusion matrix in Table 4, the relatively low ability of capturing replacements is due to labeling them as deletions. This is mainly caused by word miss-alignments and by parser errors that our heuristics cannot recover from. The same logic applies for labels REPLACE+MOVE and REWRITE+MOVE. We are also able to capture most MOVEments (high recall), but our reordering heuristic still requires improvement.

Label	Prec.	Rec.	F_1	Support
A	0.66	0.92	0.77	261
D	0.76	0.90	0.82	371
M	0.17	0.92	0.28	24
R	0.70	0.39	0.50	71
RM	0.22	0.33	0.27	12
RW	0.24	0.07	0.11	57
RWM	0.00	0.00	0.00	6
C	0.99	0.94	0.96	1932
O	0.99	0.95	0.97	2112
avg / total	0.92	0.92	0.92	4846

Table 3: Per-label performance of automatic annotation of operations.

We refer to these automatically generated labels as **silver labels**. As we describe in the next sections, the corpus annotated with these labels will be used to train our sequence labeling approach, eliminating the need for costly human-annotated data (i.e. gold labels). As a second way of evaluating the quality of our automatic labeling, we use these silver labels in a semi-oracle trial where we apply the actual simplification operations as given in the annotated corpus. In other words, we simply take the automatic labels as true and use the

	Automatically Annotated								
	A	D	M	R	RM	RW	RWM	C	O
A	240	0	0	0	0	2	0	0	19
D	15	333	8	4	5	1	1	4	0
M	0	1	22	0	0	0	0	1	0
R	0	33	0	28	6	0	0	4	0
RM	0	8	0	0	4	0	0	0	0
RW	3	31	4	7	2	4	0	6	0
RWM	0	6	0	0	0	0	0	0	0
C	0	24	98	1	1	1	0	1807	0
O	105	0	0	0	0	9	0	0	1998

Table 4: Confusion matrix of true (rows) and automatically annotated (columns) operations on the manually annotated data.

alignments between original and simplified words to apply the actual operations. This is what we refer to as **silver operations** in Table 1. Using the automatic labeling would lead to much more accurate and less conservative simplifications than all translation-based approaches: it achieves the highest SARI and BLEU scores, and the lowest rate of copied input sentences among all systems tested using the 1-to-1 alignments. Therefore, the challenges now are (i) to predict such labels (§5.1), and (ii) to devise high-performing TS modules to apply simplification operations for each type of label (§4.2).

4.2 Application of Operations

For our experiments (§5), we consider two of the operations that our algorithms can identify with high precision: DELETE and REPLACE.[8] Applying deletions is straightforward and amounts to simply omitting the respective token when generating the hypothesis sentence. For the REPLACE operation, we use the supervised Lexical Simplification approach of Paetzold and Specia (2017). Their simplifier generates candidate substitutions for target words using parallel complex-to-simple corpora and retrofitted context-aware word embedding models, selects the ones that fit the context of the target word through the unsupervised boundary ranking approach, then ranks candidates using a supervised neural ranking model trained

over manually annotated simplifications. It also performs a final confidence check step: the target is only replaced by the highest ranking candidate if the trigram probability of two words preceding the target is higher for the candidate.

5 Experiments

Based on the automatic annotation procedure outlined above, we generate sequence annotations of 1-to-1 simplification operations in the Newsela corpus. On this data, we explore the questions (i) whether we can predict simplification operations to be performed on unseen data, and (ii) to what degree the prediction of these operations allows us to generate good simplifications.

5.1 Prediction of Simplification Operations

To predict simplification operations for each input word, we train a bidirectional recurrent neural network, with an initial embedding layer of size 300 and two hidden LSTM (Long-Short Term Memory) layers of size 100. The training is done using Keras (Chollet, 2015), with a batch size of 64, categorical cross-entropy loss and a dropout rate of 0.2 after the hidden layers. We optimize the model with Adagrad (Duchi et al., 2011). We monitor the tagging accuracy on held-out development data and employ early stopping when the development loss increases. We repeat this process ten times with random initializations and select the best model based on development set accuracy.

Table 5 shows that the LSTM model does not predict the silver labels very well. In particular, the model is relatively conservative with respect to the prediction of simplification operations, and tends to overpredict the majority class (i.e., to copy a token).[9] DELETE is the operation that our model predicts best. Table 6 shows the relative confusion of predicted operations versus the silver labels, and confirms that the main error type of our system is to keep a token rather than performing some simplification operation on it. We also see a tendency for other operations to be predicted as deletions.

The results in the lower part of Table 1 ("Predicted operations (1-to-1)"), however, show that even though the operation predictions are far from the silver labels, our system is able to generate simple output by only applying the DELETE and

---

[8]We focus on this subset of operations since we currently lack good models to apply to the remaining operations. ADD, for example, would presume access to an external resource such as a knowledge base that would serve as a basis for inferring added content (which is oftentimes background information, for example an explanation that a certain person has a certain function). The results we obtain can thus be viewed as a lower bound on the simplification quality that can be expected from a model that integrates other operations.

[9]By weighting the loss function by the ground truth class support at each timestep, we were able to alleviate the effect of a predominant majority class to some degree.

Label	Prec.	Rec.	F_1	Support
D	.30	.49	.37	58,692
M	.21	.16	.18	29,719
R	.13	.34	.19	7,208
RM	.00	.00	.00	2,817
RW	.14	.07	.10	646
RWM	.00	.00	.00	141
C	.68	.51	.58	154,481
avg / total	.51	.45	.47	253,704

Table 5: Per-label performance of automatic operation prediction with the LSTM model.

			Predicted			
	D	M	R	RM	RW	RWM	C
D	.49	.06	.07	.00	.00	.00	.38
M	.41	.16	.05	.00	.00	.00	.38
R	.23	.05	.34	.00	.00	.00	.38
RM	.32	.09	.21	.00	.00	.00	.38
RW	.38	.00	.00	.00	.07	.00	.54
RWM	.62	.03	.00	.00	.04	.00	.32
C	.33	.09	.06	.00	.00	.00	.51

Table 6: Confusion matrix of true (rows) and predicted (columns) operations on the test data.

REPLACE operations. In particular, our method achieves a better SARI score than all the baseline systems on the 1-to-1 alignments. As we consider the extrinsic evaluation of the final TS results to be more indicative of the quality of our model than its intrinsic evaluation in the sequence labeling task, we view this as a positive result.

5.2 Human Evaluation

We finally conduct a human evaluation of 100 simplifications produced by five simplifiers:

- The experts' **Reference** simplification.

- The **Moses** simplifier (1-to-1).

- The **Nematus** simplifier (1-to-1).

- The **NTS** simplifier (1-to-1).

- Our **Sequence Labeling (SL)** simplifier.

Human evaluators (four NLP experts) are given the original sentence and the simplification in each of the above versions, and are asked to judge each of them with respect to their grammaticality (G), meaning preservation (M) and simplicity (S), using a Likert scale between 1 (worst) and 5 (best) for each aspect. We define "simplicity" as the extent to which the sentence was simpler than the original and thus easier to understand. A control set of 20 sentences is evaluated by all annotators in order to compute inter-annotator agreement.

	G	M	S
Reference	5.00±0.0	4.45±0.9	2.70±1.3
SL	4.16±1.0	3.91±1.1	1.66±0.9
Nematus	4.49±0.9	3.99±1.2	1.46±0.9
Moses	4.98±0.2	4.99±0.1	1.14±0.4
NTS	4.75±0.6	4.08±1.26	1.53±1.0
Fleiss' Kappa	0.372	0.457	0.342

Table 7: Average scores and standard deviation for grammaticality (G), meaning preservation (M) and simplicity (S) for the systems evaluated. The last row shows the inter-annotator agreement scores in terms of Fleiss' Kappa.

Table 7 illustrates the average scores and standard deviations obtained by each system according to each criterion. As expected, the Moses simplifier obtains the highest grammaticality and meaning preservation scores, but the lowest simplicity scores, given that it tends to merely reproduce the input. Although Nematus and NTS manage to obtain slightly higher simplification scores, they still average very close to the lower end of the simplicity scale. Our SL approach, in turn, shows significantly higher simplicity scores than the other systems (according to a t-test with $p < 0.05$). Its less conservative edits, however, may in some cases come at the cost of lower scores for grammaticality and meaning preservation. The last row in Table 7 shows the values of inter-annotator agreement in terms of Fleiss' Kappa for each evaluation aspect. Table 8 exemplifies some of the sentences for which our system was rated better and worse than the baselines. It is important to mention that, although the first two reference simplifications in Table 8 feature only minor punctuation changes, only 2,538 references (0.8%) in the dataset are of this type.

6 Conclusions and Further Work

We presented a novel approach to sentence simplification that uses automatically labeled training data from a large simplification corpus. Based on this annotated corpus, we devise a sequence labeling approach to text simplification that predicts simplification operations for individual words in the original sentence. Specific modules are then triggered to deal with each predicted operation.

SL better than other Moses, Nematus and NTS

O	Kyarra Garrett has learned how to take blood pressure and perform CPR – and she is not even out of high school yet.
R	Kyarra Garrett has learned how to take blood pressure and perform CPR, and she is not even out of high school yet.
M	*Kyarra Garrett has learned how to take blood pressure and perform CPR – and she is not even out of high school yet.*
N	*UNK Garrett loves out to take blood pressure and perform, and she is not even out of high school yet.*
T	*Chance Garrett has learned how to take blood pressure.*
L	*Kyarra Garrett has learned how to take blood pressure and perform CPR.*

O	in her mind she stops at particular locations to pick up the correct cookie crumbs.
R	in her mind, she stops at particular locations to pick up the correct cookie crumbs.
M	*in her mind she stops at particular locations to pick up the correct cookie crumbs.*
N	*she stops at particular locations to pick up the correct cookie UNK.*
T	*in her mind she stops at particular locations to pick up the correct cookie momentum.*
L	*in her mind she stops at particular areas to pick up cookie crumbs.*

SL worse than Moses, Nematus or NTS

O	despite the limitations, Palestinian cooking is not without its fans.
R	despite the limitations, Palestinian cooking has its fans.
M	*despite the limitations, Palestinian cooking is not without its fans.*
N	*Palestinian cooking is not without its fans.*
T	*even Palestinian cooking is not without its fans.*
L	*despite the limitations, Palestinian cooking is not without its fans.*

O	"we always thought there has to be a more efficient way of doing this," Zach Fiene said.
R	he said he always thought there had to be a better way of doing it.
M	*"we always thought there has to be a more efficient way of doing this," Zach Fiene said.*
N	*"we always thought there has to be a more efficient way of doing this," said Zach Ghani, who is the 18-year-old said.*
T	*Zach Fiene said there has to be a more efficient way of doing this.*
L	*"we always thought there has to be more efficient way doing this said.*

Table 8: Example including original (O) and reference (R) sentences from the Newsela Article Corpus, and outputs generated by Moses (M), Nematus (N), NTS (T) and our sequence labeling approach (**L**).

The experiments reported here cover only deletions and lexical substitutions as operations.

Our approach has several theoretical advantages over end-to-end translation models, including easier interpretability of the types of simplification learned, as well as the possibility for late decoding for adaptive simplification. In practical terms, we showed that our system outperforms translation-based approaches on a number of metrics and overcomes the problems of excessive repetition of the original content.

According to human evaluation, our system achieves higher simplicity scores than the baseline systems, although this comes at the cost of slightly lower meaning preservation and grammaticality. We hypothesize that some of the problematic cases stem from not realizing the addition operation. In general, our approach will likely profit from good models for the remaining operations, especially those that can also operate on spans of several tokens, making research on such models a natural direction for further work.

Acknowledgements

This work was partly supported by the EC project SIMPATICO (H2020-EURO-6-2015, grant number 692819).

References

Dzmitry Bahdanau, Kyunghyun Cho, and Yoshua Bengio. 2014. Neural machine translation by jointly learning to align and translate. *CoRR*, abs/1409.0473.

Regina Barzilay and Noemie Elhadad. 2003. Sentence alignment for monolingual comparable corpora. In *Proceedings of EMNLP*, pages 25–32.

Joachim Bingel and Anders Søgaard. 2016. Text Simplification as Tree Labeling. In *Proceedings of ACL*, pages 337–343.

Stefan Bott and Horacio Saggion. 2011. An unsupervised alignment algorithm for text simplification corpus construction. In *Proceedings of MTTG*, pages 20–26.

François Chollet. 2015. Keras. `https://github.com/fchollet/keras`.

William Coster and David Kauchak. 2011a. Learning to simplify sentences using wikipedia. In *Proceedings of the Workshop on Monolingual Text-To-Text Generation*, pages 1–9.

William Coster and David Kauchak. 2011b. Simple English Wikipedia: a new text simplification task. In *Proceedings of ACL*, pages 665–669.

John Duchi, Elad Hazan, and Yoram Singer. 2011. Adaptive subgradient methods for online learning and stochastic optimization. *Journal of Machine Learning Research*, 12:2121–2159.

Dan Feblowitz and David Kauchak. 2013. Sentence simplification as tree transduction. In *Proceedings of the PITR Workshop*, pages 1–10.

Philipp Koehn, Hieu Hoang, Alexandra Birch, Chris Callison-Burch, Marcello Federico, Nicola Bertoldi, Brooke Cowan, Wade Shen, Christine Moran, Richard Zens, Chris Dyer, Ondřej Bojar, Alexandra Constantin, and Evan Herbst. 2007. Moses: Open source toolkit for statistical machine translation. In *Proceedings of ACL - Demonstration Session*, pages 177–180.

Shashi Narayan and Claire Gardent. 2014. Hybrid simplification using deep semantics and machine translation. In *Proceedings of ACL*, pages 435–445.

Sergiu Nisioi, Sanja Štajner, Simone Paolo Ponzetto, and Liviu P. Dinu. 2017. Exploring neural text simplification models. In *Proceedings of ACL*, pages 85–91.

Gustavo H. Paetzold and Lucia Specia. 2016a. Semeval 2016 task 11: Complex word identification. In *Proceedings of the 10th SemEval*, pages 560–569.

Gustavo Henrique Paetzold and Lucia Specia. 2016b. Vicinity-driven paragraph and sentence alignment for comparable corpora. *CoRR*, abs/1612.04113.

Gustavo Henrique Paetzold and Lucia Specia. 2017. Lexical simplification with neural ranking. *Proceedings of EACL*, pages 34–40.

Kishore Papineni, Salim Roukos, Todd Ward, and Wei-Jing Zhu. 2002. BLEU: a method for automatic evaluation of machine translation. In *Proceedings of ACL*, pages 311–318.

Rico Sennrich, Orhan Firat, Kyunghyun Cho, Alexandra Birch, Barry Haddow, Julian Hitschler, Marcin Junczys-Dowmunt, Samuel Läubli, Antonio Valerio Miceli Barone, Jozef Mokry, and Maria Nadejde. 2017. Nematus: a toolkit for neural machine translation. In *Proceedings of the Software Demonstrations of EACL*, pages 65–68, Valencia, Spain. ACL.

Rico Sennrich, Barry Haddow, and Alexandra Birch. 2016. Edinburgh neural machine translation systems for wmt 16. In *Proceedings of WMT*, pages 371–376.

Jason R Smith, Chris Quirk, and Kristina Toutanova. 2010. Extracting parallel sentences from comparable corpora using document level alignment. In *Proceedings of NAACL*, pages 403–411.

Matthew Snover, Bonnie Dorr, Richard Schwartz, Linnea Micciulla, and John Makhoul. 2006. A study of translation edit rate with targeted human annotation. In *Proceedings of AMTA*, pages 223–231.

Lucia Specia. 2010. Translating from complex to simplified sentences. In *Computational Processing of the Portuguese Language*, pages 30–39. Springer.

Md Sultan, Steven Bethard, and Tamara Sumner. 2014. Back to basics for monolingual alignment: Exploiting word similarity and contextual evidence. *TACL*, 2:219–230.

Kristian Woodsend and Mirella Lapata. 2011. Learning to simplify sentences with quasi-synchronous grammar and integer programming. In *Proceedings of EMNLP*, pages 409–420.

Sander Wubben, Antal van den Bosch, and Emiel Krahmer. 2012. Sentence simplification by monolingual machine translation. In *Proceedings of ACL*, pages 1015–1024.

Wei Xu, Chris Callison-Burch, and Courtney Napoles. 2015. Problems in current text simplification research: New data can help. *TACL*, 3:283–297.

Wei Xu, Courtney Napoles, Ellie Pavlick, Quanze Chen, and Chris Callison-Burch. 2016. Optimizing statistical machine translation for text simplification. *TACL*, 4:401–415.

Xingxing Zhang and Mirella Lapata. 2017. Sentence simplification with deep reinforcement learning. In *Proceedings of EMNLP*, pages 595–605.

Yaoyuan Zhang, Zhenxu Ye, Yansong Feng, Dongyan Zhao, and Rui Yan. 2017. A constrained sequence-to-sequence neural model for sentence simplification. *CoRR*, abs/1704.02312.

Zhemin Zhu, Delphine Bernhard, and Iryna Gurevych. 2010. A monolingual tree-based translation model for sentence simplification. In *Proceedings of COLING*, pages 1353–1361.

Domain-Adaptable Hybrid Generation of RDF Entity Descriptions

Or Biran[*]
n-Join
or@n-join.com

Kathleen McKeown
Columbia University
kathy@cs.columbia.edu

Abstract

RDF ontologies provide structured data on entities in many domains and continue to grow in size and diversity. While they can be useful as a starting point for generating descriptions of entities, they often miss important information about an entity that cannot be captured as simple relations. In addition, generic approaches to generation from RDF cannot capture the unique style and content of specific domains. We describe a framework for hybrid generation of entity descriptions, which combines generation from RDF data with text extracted from a corpus, and extracts unique aspects of the domain from the corpus to create domain-specific generation systems. We show that each component of our approach significantly increases the satisfaction of readers with the text across multiple applications and domains.

1   Introduction

RDF ontologies are a wonderful source for generation: they feature standardized structure, are constantly expending and span many interesting domains. However, generation from RDF introduces two major difficulties. First, RDF contains relationships between entities but often lacks other important information about an entity (e.g., historical background and context) which is hard to capture with simple relations. Second, RDF data spans many domains, and presents the difficulty of handling specific domains in generation.

Generally speaking, there are three approaches: domain-specific approaches (with hand-written or other rules relevant to each domain), which are not scalable; generic approaches (generating in

exactly the same way for all domains) which result in unnatural text and miss important content; and domain adaptation, which attempts to automatically transfer an approach from one domain to another.

Our approach aims to leverage the advantages of all three. We present a generic framework of generation *meta-systems* for RDF applications, which uses domain adaptation to create domain-specific systems. Biography and Company Description are examples of applications (an application is the description of RDF entities of a particular type), while Politician and Model are examples of domains within the Biography application.

The reason our framework is able to adapt to new domains automatically is that it relies on hybrid concept-to-text (C2T) and text-to-text (T2T) generation: part of the generated text consists of messages that are created from structured data according to a generic recipe, while another part comes from messages extracted from a domain corpus. In addition, we use existing methods to extract paraphrases and discourse models from the domain corpus, which further refines how text is generated differently for each domain.

2   Related Work

Generation from RDF data is not a new topic. Duboue and McKeown (2003) described a content selection approach for generation from RDF data. Sun and Mellish (2006) present a domain-independent approach for sentence generation from RDF triples. Duma and Klein (2013) propose an architecture for learning end-to-end generation systems from aligned RDF data and sampled generated text. End-to-end concept-to-text systems were proposed by Galanis et al. (2009), Androutsopoulos et al. (2013) and Cimiano et al. (2013), among others. For a survey of the

---

[*] Work done while at Columbia University

Proceedings of the The 8th International Joint Conference on Natural Language Processing, pages 306–315,
Taipei, Taiwan, November 27 – December 1, 2017 ©2017 AFNLP

history of generation from semantic web data and its difficulties, see (Bouayad-Agha et al., 2014).

Generation *meta-systems* which can be automatically adapted to a new domain have been explored in recent years. Angeli et al. (2010) learn to make decisions about content selection and (separately) template selection from an aligned corpus of database records and text describing them. Kondadadi et al. (2013) describe a framework that learns domain-specific templates, content selection, ordering and template selection from an aligned corpus. Both approaches rely on supervised learning from an aligned corpus of data and sample texts generated from the data, which is a rare resource that does not exist for most domains.

Other recent work has focused on domain adaptation for existing generation systems (as opposed to creating adaptable meta-systems). There has been work on adapting generated text for different user groups (Janarthanam and Lemon, 2010; Gkatzia et al., 2014); adapting summarization systems to new genres (Lloret and Boldrini, 2015); adapting dialog generation systems to new applications (Rieser and Lemon, 2011) and domains (Walker et al., 2007); and parameterizing existing hand-crafted systems to increase the range of domains they can handle (Lukin et al., 2015).

In comparison, hybrid C2T-T2T generation is fairly unexplored territory. One recent example is Saldanha et al. (2016), which evaluated two approaches to generating company descriptions - one with Wikipedia structured data, the other utilizing web search results - and determined that the best results were achieved by combining the two. However, the hybrid system in this case was only a concatenation of two independent approaches.

3 Framework Overview

Our approach is a *framework* for creating generation *meta-systems* for specific applications of RDF entity description, such as *biography* and *company description* generation. Each meta-system, in turn, can be automatically adapted to a new *domain* within the application (e.g., the *politician* domain within the *biography* application) with only a simple text corpus, resulting in a *concrete generation system* that is specifically adapted to the domain. The generation system uses hybrid generation, building core messages from RDF data (C2T) and adding domain-specific secondary messages from the text corpus (T2T).

3.1 Semantic Data Structures

Our main data structure is the *Semantic Typed Template (STT)*. An STT is a tuple $\langle V, R, L \rangle$ consisting of a set of vertices labeled with entity types $V = \{v_1, \ldots, v_n\}$, a set of edges labeled with relations among the vertices $R = \{r_1, \ldots, r_m\}$ and a set of lexical templates $L = \{l_1, \ldots, l_k\}$. The lexical templates L are all assumed to be lexicalizations of the semantics of the STT and paraphrases of each other, and must be phrases or sentences (that is, multiple-sentence lexicalizations are not allowed). The STT represents both the meaning and possible realizations of a sentence-level unit of semantics, without directly modeling the meaning in any way other than through the graph embodied in V and R. Instead, the meaning is grounded in the lexical template set.

A *message* is an instance of an STT τ with a concrete set of entities E. The set of types $V(\tau)$ constrains the number and types of entities that are allowed to participate in E, and the set of relations $R(\tau)$ constrains them further (the entities must have the proper relations among them).

3.2 Application Definition

RDF is a framework for organizing data using *triples*. Each triple contains a subject, a predicate and an object. In this paper, we use DBPedia (Auer et al., 2007) as our source of RDF data.

Each RDF application defines a single entity type η: each instance of the application is an entity belonging to this type (that is, there exists a triple such that the subject is the instance entity, the predicate is typeOf and the object is η). In Biography, $\eta =$ Person, while in Company Description $\eta =$ Company. In addition, each application defines a domain-differentiating predicate π: in Biography, $\pi =$ Occupation, while in Company Description $\pi =$ Industry. π must be chosen so that for each instance of the application, there exists an RDF triple where the subject is the instance entity and the predicate is π.

4 Domain Preparation

Our framework defines each application as a generation *meta-system*: a generic system from which concrete, domain-adapted systems can be created using a text corpus. This section describes the process of domain adaptation.

In this paper, we use Wikipedia as our source for domain corpora (each corpus is the set of Wikipedia articles for all entities of the domain). While it is convenient to select the corpus in this way, there is nothing in the framework that requires the domain corpus to come from Wikipedia.

4.1 Extracting Domain STTs and Messages

Given a new domain corpus, we first extract *definitional sentences*: sentences in the corpus which contain an entity which is an instance of the domain. For example, in the Company Description application, in the Computer Hardware domain, definitional sentences for the entity *Apple* may include "Apple is an American multinational technology company" and "In 1984, Apple launched the Macintosh, the first computer to be sold without a programming language at all".

To templatize the sentence and find its paraphrases, we use the approach of (Biran et al., 2016). Each definitional sentence is parsed, and NNPs that match an entity in DBPedia become typed slots, resulting in a template and a set of entities that match the slot types. The slot types are determined in two stages - sense disambiguation and hierarchical positioning - both achieved by leveraging the DBPedia ontology in combination with vector representations. We then use the templated paraphrase detection method described in (Biran et al., 2016) to compare the template with existing STTs that match the entities' types and relations (all of which are known from the RDF ontology). The paraphrasing approach uses sentence-level vector representations to calculate the similarity of the template to all of the existing lexicalizations of an STT. If the template is determined to be a paraphrase for an existing STT, it is added as a new lexicalization; otherwise it is treated as a new STT. This new STT (or the old STT with a new lexicalization) can be used for any entity sets that have the appropriate types and relations.

In addition, we create a domain message from the STT and the entities found in the definitional sentence (effectively making the definitional sentence itself a possible lexicalization of this message, along with any alternative lexicalizations if the STT contains any). This gives us the set of potential secodary messages which we will use in the generation pipeline.

Figure 1 shows an example of this process. Two definitional sentences for the entity are found and templatized, and the first is matched to an existing STT (STT_1) as a paraphrase. The first two lexica-

lizations of this STT are the default ones, created for all RDF triples as explained in Section 5.1; the third is the template of the definitional sentence. The STT can be used with any matching entity set, but in particular, it is matched to the entity set of the definitional sentence to create domain message 1. The second template cannot be matched to an existing STT, so a new one is created, along with domain message 2.

Entity: Candice Bergen (a model)

Definitional sentences (found in Wikipedia):
- "Candice Bergen was born and raised in Beverly Hills, California"
- "Bergen began her career as a fashion model and appeared on the front cover of Vogue magazine"

Templates:
- [Person] was born and raised in [City]
- [Model] began her career as a fashion model and appeared on the front cover of [Fashion Magazine]

STT_1 (matched through paraphrasing):
$V = \{\text{Person}, \text{City}\}$
$R = \{v_2 \text{ birthPlace } v_1\}$
$L = \{$
"The birth place of $[v_1]$ is $[v_2]$",
"$[v_1]$'s birth place is $[v_2]$",
"$[v_1]$ was born and raised in $[v_2]$",
$\ldots\}$

Domain message 1:
$STT = STT_1$
$E = \{\text{Candice Bergen}, \text{Beverly Hills}\}$

STT_2 (new, no RDF relation):
$V = \{\text{Model}, \text{Fashion Magazine}\}$
$R = \{\emptyset\}$
$L = \{$ "$[v_1]$ began her career as a fashion model and appeared on the front cover of $[v_2]$" $\}$

Domain message 2:
$STT = STT_2$
$E = \{\text{Candice Bergen}, \text{Vogue Magazine}\}$

Figure 1: An example of the domain STT and message extraction process.

4.2 Extracting the Discourse Planning Model

A discourse planning model is extracted from the domain corpus as described in (Biran and McKeown, 2015). The model provides prior and transition probabilities for the four top-level Penn Discourse TreeBank (PDTB) (Prasad et al., 2008) discourse relations: *expansion*, *comparison*, *contingency* and *temporal*. These probabilities reflect the discourse style that characterizes the domain, and will be used in Section 5 to determine the ordering of, and relations between, generated messages.

4.3 Extracting the Language Model

The language model used in the realization component of the pipeline is not a typical n-gram model. We are not trying to generate words within a sentence. Instead, we have a set of templates for each message to generate (which corresponds to a sentence or phrase in the final text) and we want to choose one that best fits the context. For this purpose, we define and extract three cross-sentence language models.

The first language model is a cross-sentence model for pairs of words that appear in adjacent sentences. The probability that a word w appears in a sentence if word v appears in the previous sentence, independently of everything else, is

$$P(w|v) = \frac{Count(v, w)}{Count(v)}$$

For the probability of a particular template $\mathcal{T}$ given a selected previous sentence $\mathcal{S}$, we take the average over all word pairs:

$$P_{LM_1}(\mathcal{T}|\mathcal{S}) = \frac{\sum_{(w,v)\in\{\mathcal{T}\times\mathcal{S}\}} P(w|v)}{|\{\mathcal{T}\times\mathcal{S}\}|}$$

The second language model is a POS bigram pair model. It treats POS bigrams as individual words in the first model; in other words, $P_{LM_2}(\mathcal{T}|\mathcal{S})$ is defined in the same way as $P_{LM_1}(\mathcal{T}|\mathcal{S})$, except that w and v stand for POS bigrams (instead of words) in the candidate template and the selected previous sentence, respectively.

The third is a sentence length model. Here we compute the expected length of a sentence $\mathcal{T}$ given the length of the previous sentence $\mathcal{S}$ as

$$E[\#\mathcal{T}|\#\mathcal{S}] = \frac{\sum_{\{\sigma_i:\#\sigma_{i-1}=\#\mathcal{S}\}} \#\sigma_i}{|\{\sigma_i : \#\sigma_{i-1} = \#\mathcal{S}\}|}$$

where $\#\mathcal{S}$ is the length of sentence $\mathcal{S}$ in words. We then smooth this expectation estimate using the estimates of nearby lengths:

$$\tilde{E}[\#\mathcal{T}|\#\mathcal{S}] = \frac{\sum_{i=\#\mathcal{S}-3}^{\#\mathcal{S}+3} E[\#\mathcal{T}|i]}{7}$$

Based on this smoothed expectation, we define the probability of a template $\mathcal{T}$ given a selected previous sentence $\mathcal{S}$:

$$P_{LM_3}(\mathcal{T}|\mathcal{S}) \triangleq \frac{1}{(\#\mathcal{T} - \tilde{E}[\#\mathcal{T}|\#\mathcal{S}])^2}$$

This definition is not intended to have a true probabilistic interpretation, but it preserves an order of likelihood since it increases monotonically as the length of $\mathcal{T}$ approaches the expected values.

These models are used in Section 5 to rank possible templates for a message being generated.

5 Generation

Once a domain has been prepared, we can generate text for any instance in that domain. The generation pipeline contains four components: *core message selection, domain message selection, discourse planning* and *realization*.

5.1 Core Message Selection

For each instance, we produce one core message from each RDF triple that has the instance's entity as the subject. To create a message from a triple, we first match it to an STT based on the predicate. Each predicate becomes an STT with two entity types (the type of the subject, which is the instance entity, and the type of the object) in V; a single relation between the two types (the predicate) in R; and two simple initial templates in L:

- The (PREDICATE) of $[v_1]$ is $[v_2]$

- $[v_1]$'s (PREDICATE) is $[v_2]$

where (PREDICATE) is replaced with the relevant predicate. Additional templates are then found using paraphrasal template mining as described in the previous section. We also create plural versions for cases where v_2 is a list of entities.

For example, in the biography domain, we create an STT for the *birthDate* predicate with $V = \{person, date\}$; $R = \{v_1 \text{ birthDate } v_2\}$; and an initial template set $L = \{$"The birth date of $[v_1]$ is $[v_2]$", "$[v_1]$'s birth date is $[v_2]$"$\}$. In the preparation stage described in Section 4, L may be expanded with paraphrasal templates found in the corpus, for example "$[v_1]$ was born in $[v_2]$" (see Figure 1 for an example).

We then create a message that contains the relevant STT and the entities in the triple. In case there are multiple triples with the same subject and predicate but different objects, we create a single message with a plural version of the STT and define the second entity as the list of all objects. We shall refer to the set of core messages as C.

In this paper we separate the content selection problem into two parts. The first (this component) is application-dependent and domain-agnostic, and handles the skeleton or core structure of the generated text; the next component handles additional domain-specific content.

5.2 Domain Message Selection

The set of core messages gives us the core entities which participate in the core messages.

We also have the set of domain messages for the domain which are prepared (extracted from the domain corpus) ahead of time as described in Section 4. The set P of *potential domain messages* for generation is the subset of domain messages which contain the instance entity. In this stage of the pipeline, we select a subset of these potential domain messages to include in the generated text.

To select domain messages, we utilize the energy minimization framework described by Barzilay and Lapata (2005). They describe a formulation that allows efficient optimization of what they call *independent scores* of content units and *link scores* among them through the energy minimization framework. The function to minimize is:

$$\sum_{p \in S} ind_N(p) + \sum_{p \in N} ind_S(p) + \sum_{\substack{p_i \in S \\ p_j \in N}} link(p_i, p_j)$$

where S is the subset of P selected for generation, N is the subset not selected ($P - S = N$), $ind_S(p)$ is p's intrinsic tendency to be selected, $ind_N(p)$ is p's intrinsic tendency to not be selected and $link(p_i, p_j)$ is the dependency score for the link between p_i and p_j. A globally optimal partition of P to S and N can be found in polynomial time by constructing a particular kind of graph and finding a minimal cut partition (Greig et al., 1989).

The base preference of a message p is defined

$$Bp(p) = \begin{cases} |R(\tau(p))| & \text{if } M(p) = E(p) \\ -|E(p) \setminus M(p)| \frac{\#L(\tau(p))}{10} & \text{otherwise} \end{cases}$$

where $M(p)$ is the subset of $E(p)$ - the entities of message p - which contains only entities that participate in at least one relation in $R(\tau(p))$, and $\#L(\tau(p))$ is the average length in words of the templates of the STT $\tau(p)$. This definition results in a positive score for a message where all entities participate in a relation, whose weight is the number of relations it covers; conversely, messages which have entities that do not participate in a relation (*unaccounted entities*), have a negative score which increases in magnitude with the number of unaccounted entities and with the length of the templates realizing them. The intuition is that a long message containing many entities that match no triples is unlikely to be relevant.

Then, we define the individual preference scores $ind(p)$ as an average of the similarity of p to each of the core messages using the Jaccard coefficient as a similarity score:

$$ind(p) = \frac{\sum_{m \in C} J(p, m)}{|C|}$$

Finally, we define $ind_S(p)$ and $ind_N(p)$ as

$$ind_S(p) = \begin{cases} Bp(p) \times ind(p) & \text{if } Bp(p) \geq 0 \\ 0 & \text{otherwise} \end{cases}$$

$$ind_N(p) = \begin{cases} \frac{Bp(p)}{ind(p)} & \text{if } Bp(p) < 0 \\ 0 & \text{otherwise} \end{cases}$$

The link scores $link(p_i, p_j)$ are defined using a type similarity score. In contrast to the individual preference scores, where we maximize the entity overlap with core messages (to avoid including messages with no connection to the core of the text), we should not encourage the domain messages to all share the exact same set of entities. Instead, we focus on a softer semantic similarity: shared entity types. This score enhances the coherence of the generated text (for example, by encouraging a focus on the executives of a company in a particular instance, and on its products in another) but allows a flexible range of messages to be selected. The link score definition is

$$link(p_i, p_j) = \frac{\sum_{(e_i, e_j) \in \{E(p_i) \times E(p_j)\}} typsim(e_i, e_j)}{|\{E(p_i) \times E(p_j)\}|}$$

where

$$typsim(e_i, e_j) = \begin{cases} 1 & \text{if } type(e_i) = type(e_j) \\ 0 & \text{otherwise} \end{cases}$$

Denoting the subset of P selected by this process as $selected(P)$, at the end of this process, we have $M = C \cup selected(P)$ - the full set of messages to be generated.

5.3 Discourse Planning

The discourse planning component transforms the unordered set of messages M into an ordered sequence of paragraphs $\mathcal{P} = (p_1, \ldots, p_k)$ where each paragraph p_i is an ordered discourse sequence $p_i = (m_1, r_1, m_2, r_2, \ldots, r_{n-1}, m_n)$, where the alternating m_i and r_i are messages and discourse relations, respectively.

First, we calculate the semantic similarity of each pair of messages in M as follows:

$$sim(m_i, m_j) = \cos(\mathcal{V}_{\psi_{m_i}}, \mathcal{V}_{\psi_{m_j}})link(m_i, m_j)$$

where ψ_{m_i} is the pseudo-sentence of message m_i, constructed by concatenating all of its templates; $\mathcal{V}_{\psi_{m_i}}$ is the vector representing ψ_{m_i}, defined as the geometric mean of the vectors of all words participating in ψ_{m_i} (the word vectors are traditional context vectors extracted from Gigaword with a window of 5 words); and $link(m_i, m_j)$ is defined as above. Essentially, this is a combination of the entity type-based semantic similarity and the distributional similarity of the lexicalizations.

We use single-linkage agglomerative clustering (with a stopping criteria of $sim(m_i, m_j) \leq 0.05$) to group the messages into semantic groups of messages that are similar in topic. Then, within each semantic group, we find potential discourse relations for each pair of messages:

1. If the STTs of m_i and m_j are the same but they have no entities in common then there is a potential *comparison* relation between them

2. If $J(m_i, m_j) \geq 0.5$ then there is a potential *expansion* relation between them

3. Manually annotated relations for 20 specific pairs of RDF predicates, e.g. *birthPlace* and *residence* may have a temporal or a comparison relation between them

4. All message pairs can have a *norel* relation

Next, we use the discourse model extracted from the domain corpus to generate a discourse sequence. In order to make sure entity coherence is taken into account when choosing the ordering in addition to discourse coherence, we augment

the probabilities coming from the discourse model $P_\mathcal{D}(r_i|R_{i-1})$, where R_{i-1} is the sequence of relations chosen so far, with the entity coherence score $J(m_i, m_{i-1})$, so that the probability of a relation between two messages is given by

$$P(r_i|R_{i-1}, m_i, m_{i-1}) = P_\mathcal{D}(r_i|R_{i-1})J(m_i, m_{i-1})$$

The discourse sequence is created stochastically using these probabilities as described in (Biran and McKeown, 2015). Then, we break the discourse sequence into paragraphs that do not contain *norel* relations. Concatenating all of the paragraphs built from the discourse sequences of all semantic groups, we have an unordered set of paragraphs $\mathcal{P}$, where each p_i is an ordered discourse sequence of messages and relations.

To order the paragraphs, we use the following importance score:

$$imp(p_i) = \frac{\sum_{m \in p_i} |\{e|e \in E(m)\}||Bp(m)}{|p_i|}$$

which is the average number of entities in a message of p_i, weighted by the base preference score $Bp(m)$. The paragraphs are then sorted in decreasing order using this score, so that the paragraphs containing the most important messages tend to appear earlier in the text.

5.4 Realization

At this stage, we have the ordered set of paragraphs $\mathcal{P}$ to be realized. To generate a paragraph, we select a template for each message and then select a discourse connective, or choose not to use one, for each discourse relation.

Selecting a template is done using the three language models prepared ahead of time, as described in Section 4. We build a ranker from each model, and choose the template from $\{l \in L(\tau(m))\}$ that maximizes the the sum of ranks given the previously realized sentence (in the paragraph) s:

$$\hat{l} = \underset{l \in L(\tau(m))}{\operatorname{argmax}} \sum_{i=1}^{3} rank\big(P_{LM_i}(l|s)\big)$$

Once the template is chosen, we fill the slots with the entities $E(m)$ to make it a sentence.

At this point we have the final lexical form of the message, and the last task is to link it with the previous sentence. We have a small set of discourse connective templates for each one of the 4 class-level PDTB relations (for example, "m_i. However, m_j" is one of the templates for the *comparison* relation), and we know the relation between the message and the previous message. We randomly select a connective, with a 50% chance of having no connective and a uniform distribution among the connectives for the relation, but avoid using connectives for sentence pairs that are together larger than 40 words.

At the end of this step, all paragraphs are generated with lexicalized sentences and connectives.

6   Evaluation

To evaluate our RDF applications we conducted a crowd-sourced human experiment using texts generated from four domains in two applications: Biographies of *Politicians* and *Models*, and Company Descriptions of *Automobile Manufacturers* and *Video Game Developers*. We picked 100 instances from each domain of each application, for a total of 400 (we picked the instances that had the most RDF triples in each domain). Then, we generated 4 versions for each instance:

1. A full-system version

2. A version that excludes paraphrase detection (so core messages only had the two manually-created templates, and domain messages only had a single template each)

3. A version that excludes the discourse model (so discourse planning was done using only entity coherence scores)

4. A baseline version that has no domain adaptation at all and is fully C2T instead of hybrid (i.e., only core messages were generated, without any extracted domain messages)

Using these 4 versions, we devised 3 questions for each instance. In each question, the annotator saw two texts about the same entity - the full system version, and one of the other three versions - and was asked which is better (with an option of saying they are equal), along several criteria. The questions were presented in random order and the systems were anonymized. We showed each question to three annotators and used the majority vote, throwing out results where there was total disagreement between the annotators, which happened 12% of the time for the baseline version and $17 - 21\%$ of the time for the other variants.

The questions included four criteria: the *content* of the text (information relevance); the *ordering* of the sentences and paragraphs; the *style* of the text (how human-like it is); and the *overall* satisfiability of the text as a description of the person/company in question.

We show the results of the experiment in Table 1. The results in this table are for both applications and all four domains. Each comparison (e.g., "No Hybrid VS Full System" shows the breakdown of preference by annotators when they were shown texts generated by the two variants: how many (in percentage) preferred the baseline system (e.g. No Hybrid), how many preferred the full system, and how many thought they were equal. We also show the *winning difference* between the two systems, i.e. those who thought that the full system was better than the baseline minus those who thought the opposite, and we measure statistical significance on these differences. Statistically significant results are marked with a dagger.

6.1   Discussion

The most striking result of Table 1 is that the full system is overwhelmingly favored by annotators over the non-hybrid baseline, with a $32\% - 46\%$ lead in all categories. This result, more than anything, shows the value of our framework and the hybrid approach. The full system was particularly better than this baseline in *content*, which is generally expected since it by definition contains less content than the full system (it only generates the core messages); note, however, that this result suggests that the extracted and selected messages are *relevant* and enhance the reader's satisfaction with the text. The baseline (which, in addition to not using extracted domain messages, also does not use the extracted paraphrasal templates and discourse model) also loses heavily to the full system in *ordering* and *style*, as well as overall. In all criteria, the percentage of annotators who thought the texts were equally good was low ($11\% - 20\%$), suggesting that the difference was very visible.

While the effect of removing a single component is not as dramatic as removing both in addition to the domain messages, it is clearly visible in the preferences of Table 1. Both reduced versions (*No Paraphrases* and *No Discourse Model*) lose to the full system in every criteria, often in double digits. The more meaningful component

	Preference	Content	Ordering	Style	Overall
No Hybrid VS Full System	No Hybrid	20%	27%	24%	22%
	Equal	14%	11%	20%	14%
	Full System	66%	62%	56%	64%
	Full - baseline win diff.	**46%** †	**35%** †	**32%** †	**42%** †
No Paraphrases VS Full System	No Paraphrases	29%	33%	29%	30%
	Equal	31%	26%	28%	27%
	Full System	40%	41%	43%	43%
	Full - baseline win diff.	**11%** †	**8%** †	**14%** †	**13%** †
No Discourse Model VS Full System	No Discourse Model	33%	34%	32%	34%
	Equal	30%	22%	26%	23%
	Full System	37%	44%	42%	43%
	Full - baseline win diff.	**4%**	**10%** †	**10%**	**9%** †

Table 1: Preferences, with different criteria, given by the human annotators when presented with two versions - the full system VS each of the baseline versions. Statistically significant winning differences are marked with a dagger.

appears to be the paraphrases: the *No Paraphrases* version loses to the full system more heavily than *No Discourse* in *content*, *style* and *overall*. This result is not surprising since paraphrases have a dramatic effect on the text itself (they change the templates that are used to convey information, enhance the diversity of the text and may merge messages that are duplicates), and it suggests that the paraphrases we find are generally more satisfying than the default. It is also not surprising that the *No Discourse Model* variant loses most on ordering. While the difference is not as dramatic here, it is statistically significant and shows that our extracted domain-specific discourse model produces a more satisfying ordering of the text.

6.2 Examples

Figure 2 shows the output of the biography for politician *Marine Le Pen* of the full system and the non-hybrid baseline. To show the contributions of different components, we mark sentences generated from extracted domain messages in **bold**, and sentences generated from core messages using an extracted paraphrase in *italics*. Sentences in unmarked typeface are those that were generated from core messages using a default template.

The two variants make clear the main advantage of the full system: it simply has more content. The full output contains six sentences (messages) more than the baseline, which are clearly relevant to the biography. The entire last paragraph, concerned with Le Pen's policies and positions - an important part of a politician's biography - is missing

from the baseline. These messages were extracted from the corpus and show the power of the hybrid approach. In addition to the final paragraph, two extracted messages are included which are concerned with Le Pen's controversial history, and together with the RDF-derived message about her offices, they comprise a paragraph generally about her political background. This is typical of the way that extracted messages contribute to the organization of the text in addition to the content: in the baseline version, the offices message is lumped together with messages about her background in general (alma mater, birth date, religion, partner etc). It demonstrates how the full system consistently outperforms the baseline in the *ordering* and *style* criteria, in addition to *content* and *overall*.

Figure 3 shows the output of the company description for video game developer *Taito Corporation* of the full system and the no-paraphrases variant. In this case the two outputs contain exactly the same information and have almost the same organization of the text. The way in which the text is realized, however, is very different in the last paragraph. The full system realizes four of the six messages in that paragraph using extracted templates, and merges two messages into a single template in one case ("Taito Corporation was founded in 1953 by Michael Kogan", instead of the two sentences in the no-paraphrases baseline). The single-sentence messages also look better, e.g. "Taito Corporation has around 662 employees" instead of the awkward-sounding "Taito

Full system output:	Baseline output:
Marine Le Pen's birth places are Neuilly-sur-Seine and France. Marine Le Pen's residences are Millas, Hénin-Beaumont and Saint-Cloud. The birth name of Marine Le Pen is Marion Anne Perrine Le Pen. Marine Le Pen's offices are Leader of the National Front, Municipal Councillor, Member of the European Parliament and Regional Councillor. **Marine Le Pen's ups and downs in the political arena follow those of the National Front at the time. Marine Le Pen stirred up controversy during the internal campaign.** The homepage of Marine Le Pen is http://www.marinelepen.fr/. The alma mater of Marine Le Pen is Panthéon-Assas University. Marine Le Pen's birth date was 1968-08-05. Marine Le Pen's religion is Catholic Church. Marine Le Pen's occupation is Politician. Marine Le Pen's partner is Louis Aliot. **Marine Le Pen regularly denounces sharp rises in energy prices which has "harmful consequences on the purchasing power of the working and middle-class families". Marine Le Pen denounces the current corporate tax as "a crying injustice". Marine Le Pen advocates to "vote for the abolition of the law enabling the regularization of the illegal immigrants". Marine Le Pen seeks to establish a moratorium on legal immigration.**	Marine Le Pen's party is National Front. Marine Le Pen's occupation is Politician. Marine Le Pen's homepage is http://www.marinelepen.fr/. Marine Le Pen's offices are Leader of the National Front, Municipal Councillor, Member of the European Parliament and Regional Councillor. Marine Le Pen's birth name is Marion Anne Perrine Le Pen. Marine Le Pen's religion is Catholic Church. Marine Le Pen's alma mater is Panthéon-Assas University. Marine Le Pen's birth date was 1968-08-05. Marine Le Pen's partner is Louis Aliot. The birth places of Marine Le Pen are Neuilly-sur-Seine and France. Marine Le Pen's residences are Millas, H'enin-Beaumont and Saint-Cloud.

Figure 2: Output for *Marine Le Pen*.

Full system output:	No-paraphrases output:
The homepage of Taito Corporation is http://www.taito.com. The products of Taito Corporation are Lufia, Bubble Bobble, Cooking Mama, Space Invaders, Chase H.Q., Gun Fight and Puzzle Bobble. *Taito Corporation was founded in 1953 by Michael Kogan. Taito Corporation has around 662 employees.* Taito Corporation's location is Shibuya, Tokyo, Japan. **Taito Corporation currently has a subsidiary in Beijing, China.** *Taito Corporation was merged with "Square Enix".*	Taito Corporation's homepage is http://www.taito.com. The products of Taito Corporation are Lufia, Bubble Bobble, Cooking Mama, Space Invaders, Chase H.Q., Gun Fight and Puzzle Bobble. Taito Corporation's founding year is 1953. The founder of Taito Corporation is Michael Kogan. Taito Corporation's owner is Square Enix. **Taito Corporation currently has a subsidiary in Beijing, China.** Taito Corporation's location is Shibuya, Tokyo, Japan. Taito Corporation's number of employees is 662.

Figure 3: Output for *Taito Corporation*.

Corporation's number of employees is 662".

7 Conclusion

We introduced a framework for creating hybrid concept-to-text and text-to-text generation systems that produce descriptions of RDF entities, and can be automatically adapted to a new domain with only a simple text corpus. We showed through a human evaluation that both the hybrid approach and domain adaptation result in significantly more satisfying descriptions, and that individual methods of domain adaptation help with the criteria we expect them to (i.e., finding paraphrases helps with content and style while an extracted discourse model helps with ordering). The code for this framework is available at `www.cs.columbia.edu/~orb/hygen/`.

References

Ion Androutsopoulos, Gerasimos Lampouras, and Dimitrios Galanis. 2013. Generating natural language descriptions from owl ontologies: the naturalowl system. *Journal of Artificial Intelligence Research*, pages 671–715.

Gabor Angeli, Percy Liang, and Dan Klein. 2010. A simple domain-independent probabilistic approach to generation. In *Proceedings of the 2010 Conference on Empirical Methods in Natural Language Processing*, EMNLP '10, pages 502–512, Stroudsburg, PA, USA. Association for Computational Linguistics.

Sören Auer, Christian Bizer, Georgi Kobilarov, Jens Lehmann, Richard Cyganiak, and Zachary Ives. 2007. Dbpedia: a nucleus for a web of open data. In *Proceedings of the 6th international The semantic web and 2nd Asian conference on Asian semantic web conference*, ISWC'07/ASWC'07, pages 722–735, Berlin, Heidelberg. Springer-Verlag.

Regina Barzilay and Mirella Lapata. 2005. Collective content selection for concept-to-text generation. In *Proceedings of the HLT/EMNLP*, pages 331–338, Vancouver.

Or Biran, Terra Blevins, and Kathleen McKeown. 2016. Mining paraphrasal typed templates from a plain text corpus. In *Proceedings of the Association for Computational Linguistics (ACL)*. Association for Computational Linguistics.

Or Biran and Kathleen McKeown. 2015. Discourse planning with an n-gram model of relations. In *Proceedings of the 2015 Conference on Empirical Methods in Natural Language Processing*, pages 1973–1977, Lisbon, Portugal. Association for Computational Linguistics.

Nadjet Bouayad-Agha, Gerard Casamayor, and Leo Wanner. 2014. Natural language generation in the context of the semantic web. *Semantic Web*, 5(6):493–513.

Philipp Cimiano, Janna Lüker, David Nagel, and Christina Unger. 2013. Exploiting ontology lexica for generating natural language texts from rdf data. In *Proceedings of the 14th European Workshop on Natural Language Generation*, pages 10–19, Sofia, Bulgaria. Association for Computational Linguistics.

Pablo A. Duboue and Kathleen R. McKeown. 2003. Statistical acquisition of content selection rules for natural language generation. In *Proceedings of the 2003 Conference on Empirical Methods in Natural Language Processing*, EMNLP '03, pages 121–128, Stroudsburg, PA, USA. Association for Computational Linguistics.

Daniel Duma and Ewan Klein. 2013. Generating natural language from linked data: Unsupervised template extraction. In *Proceedings of the 10th International Conference on Computational Semantics (IWCS 2013) – Long Papers*, pages 83–94. ASSOC COMPUTATIONAL LINGUISTICS-ACL.

Dimitrios Galanis, George Karakatsiotis, Gerasimos Lampouras, and Ion Androutsopoulos. 2009. An open-source natural language generator for owl ontologies and its use in protÉgÉ and second life. In *Proceedings of the 12th Conference of the European Chapter of the Association for Computational Linguistics: Demonstrations Session*, EACL '09, pages 17–20, Stroudsburg, PA, USA. Association for Computational Linguistics.

Dimitra Gkatzia, Helen Hastie, and Oliver Lemon. 2014. Multi-adaptive natural language generation using principal component regression. In *Proceedings of the International Natural Language Generation (INLG)*.

D. M. Greig, B. T. Porteous, and A. H. Seheult. 1989. Exact maximum a posteriori estimation for binary images. *Journal of the Royal Statistical Society. Series B (Methodological)*, 51(2):271–279.

Srinivasan Janarthanam and Oliver Lemon. 2010. Adaptive referring expression generation in spoken dialogue systems: Evaluation with real users. In *Proceedings of the 11th Annual Meeting of the Special Interest Group on Discourse and Dialogue*, SIGDIAL '10, pages 124–131, Stroudsburg, PA, USA. Association for Computational Linguistics.

Ravi Kondadadi, Blake Howald, and Frank Schilder. 2013. A statistical NLG framework for aggregated planning and realization. In *ACL*, pages 1406–1415. The Association for Computer Linguistics.

E. Lloret and E. Boldrini. 2015. Multi-genre summarization: Approach, potentials and challenges. In *eChallenges e-2015 Conference*, pages 1–9.

Stephanie Lukin, Lena Reed, and Marilyn Walker. 2015. Generating sentence planning variations for story telling. In *Proceedings of the 16th Annual Meeting of the Special Interest Group on Discourse and Dialogue*, pages 188–197, Prague, Czech Republic. Association for Computational Linguistics.

Rashmi Prasad, Nikhil Dinesh, Alan Lee, Eleni Miltsakaki, Livio Robaldo, Aravind Joshi, and Bonnie Webber. 2008. The penn discourse treebank 2.0. In *In Proceedings of LREC*.

Verena Rieser and Oliver Lemon. 2011. Learning and evaluation of dialogue strategies for new applications: Empirical methods for optimization from small data sets. *Comput. Linguist.*, 37(1):153–196.

Gavin Saldanha, Or Biran, Kathleen McKeown, and Alfio Gliozzo. 2016. An entity-focused approach to generating company descriptions. In *Proceedings of the Association for Computational Linguistics (ACL)*, Stroudsburg, PA, USA. Association for Computational Linguistics.

Xiantang Sun and Chris Mellish. 2006. Domain independent sentence generation from rdf representations for the semantic web. In *Combined Workshop on Language-Enabled Educational Technology and Development and Evaluation of Robust Spoken Dialogue Systems, European Conference on AI*.

Marilyn Walker, Amanda Stent, François Mairesse, and Rashmi Prasad. 2007. Individual and domain adaptation in sentence planning for dialogue. *J. Artif. Int. Res.*, 30(1):413–456.

ES-LDA: Entity Summarization using Knowledge-based Topic Modeling

Seyedamin Pouriyeh[1], Mehdi Allahyari[*2], Krys Kochut[1], Gong Cheng[3], and Hamid Reza Arabnia[1]

[1]Computer Science Department, University of Georgia, Athens, GA, USA
{pouriyeh,kkochut,hra@uga.edu}
[2]Department of Computer Science, Georgia Sothern University, Statesboro, USA
{mallahyari@georgiasouthern.edu}
[3]National Key Laboratory for Novel Software Technology, Nanjing University, Nanjing, China
{gcheng@nju.edu.cn}

Abstract

With the advent of the Internet, the amount of Semantic Web documents that describe real-world entities and their inter-links as a set of statements have grown considerably. These descriptions are usually lengthy, which makes the utilization of the underlying entities a difficult task. Entity summarization, which aims to create summaries for real world entities, has gained increasing attention in recent years. In this paper, we propose a probabilistic topic model, ES-LDA, that combines prior knowledge with statistical learning techniques within a single framework to create more reliable and representative summaries for entities. We demonstrate the effectiveness of our approach by conducting extensive experiments and show that our model outperforms the state-of-the-art techniques and enhances the quality of the entity summaries.

1 Introduction

With the emergence of Linked Open Data (LOD)[1] as a way of publishing and interacting with the information, many datasets such as DBpedia (Bizer et al., 2009) and YAGO (Hoffart et al., 2013) have been created and are publicly available on the Web. For example, DBpedia as part of LOD is a knowledge base extracted from Wikipedia that consists of Wikipedia resources (entities) described as RDF statements (i.e., RDF triples). The Resource Description Framework (RDF) is the Semantic Web standard data model used for representing information on the Web. An RDF triple is represented in the form of

---
[*]Equal contribution
[1]http://linkeddata.org

$< subject, predicate, object >$. The latest English version of DBpedia contains over 4.5 million entities collectively described by over 1.6 billion triples. This means that each entity description has an average of 355 RDF triples. Human users and computer applications need to consider these lengthy descriptions while performing various semantic tasks. Thus, *entity summarization*, a task of producing more concise, but still sufficient entity description, has garnered a significant amount of attention.

Recently, with the huge growth of information, summarization techniques are becoming some of the main approaches to making the information more readily available. In fact, summarization techniques aim to facilitate the identification of structure and meaning in data. Researchers in different communities have taken a strong interest in this task and, accordingly, have proposed various methods for a wide variety of summarization techniques in multiple areas. Document summarization (Nenkova and McKeown, 2012), database summarization (Bu et al., 2005), and graph summarization (Navlakha et al., 2008) are just a few examples that have been studied by different communities. RDF data summarization and in particular entity summarization, has attracted considerable attentions in recent years as it can benefit many other tasks in the natural language processing area, including entity recognition (Zhao and Kit, 2008), entity disambiguation (Dai et al., 2011), and many others. Several approaches have been developed to summarize RDF data with respect to entities, including RELIN (Cheng et al., 2011), FACES (Gunaratna et al., 2015), and LinkSUM (Thalhammer et al., 2016). RDF summarization differs from document summarization in the sense that RDF triples are structured and do not have many frequently used words to help the summarization task, which makes RDF

Proceedings of the The 8th International Joint Conference on Natural Language Processing, pages 316–325,
Taipei, Taiwan, November 27 – December 1, 2017 ©2017 AFNLP

summarization more challenging.

Topic modeling has become a popular method for uncovering the hidden themes from text corpora. Topic models usually consider each document as a mixture of topics, where a topic is a probability distribution over words. When the topic proportions of documents are estimated, they can be used as the themes (high-level semantics) of the documents. Topic models have been widely used for various text mining tasks, such as machine translation (Su et al., 2015), word embedding (Batmanghelich et al., 2016; Das et al., 2015), automatic topic labeling (Wan and Wang, 2016; Allahyari and Kochut, 2015; Allahyari et al., 2017b), and others(Allahyari et al., 2017a).

In this paper, we propose a novel topic model, called ES-LDA, that integrates prior knowledge with the topic modeling within a single framework for RDF entity summarization. In our approach, each entity, which is considered as a document, is a multinomial distribution over the predicates (properties), where each predicate is a probability distribution over the subjects and objects of the triples in the RDF data. We rank the triples based on their probability distributions and choose the top-k triples that best describe the underlying entity as its summary. We evaluated our approach against state-of-the-art techniques and our experiments indicate that our approach outperforms other methods in terms of the quality of summarization.

The rest of the paper is organized as follows: Section 2 presents an overview of related work. Section 3 introduces the baseline for this paper. In Section 4, we define the main problem and propose our model in detail and afterwards, in Section 5, we explain the configurations of our model and describe the experiments. Finally, in Sections 6 and Section 7, we discuss the results and conclude the paper, respectively.

2 Related Work

Summarization methods can be divided into two main categories, which are called extractive and none-extractive (abstractive) summarization. In extractive approaches, which are usually applicable in text and ontology summarization (Jones, 2007) (Zhang et al., 2007), a set of features is extracted directly from the input data. On the other hand, in non-extractive methods, which generally are employed in graph (Navlakha et al., 2008) and database (Bu et al., 2005) summarization, new sentences from the input data are generated (Hahn and Mani, 2000) to form a summary. In this research, we focus on extractive summarization. The concept of entity summarization in the form of RDF graph data has attracted more attention in recent years. Cheng et al. (Cheng et al., 2011) proposed entity summarization method, called RELIN, based on the PageRank algorithm to extract representative triples, called representative features for RDF graph entities. Because of the centrality based ranking issue, RELIN highlights the most similar and central triples, while in summarization, the diversity of summarized triples is the key point.

SUMMARUM (Thalhammer and Rettinger, 2014) is a system for a better navigation within Linked Data through the ranking of triples. This system also uses the PageRank algorithm to rank triples according to the popularity of resources with the help of Wikipedia pages. Two aforementioned approaches could not meet the diversity requirement in the summarization process. FACES (Gunaratna et al., 2015), on the other hand, tries to keep a balance between the centrality and diversity of the selected triples for each entity. It utilizes a clustering algorithm, called Cobweb (Fisher, 1987), to cluster related triples before ranking them to keep the diversity in the summarization. The recent version of SUMMARUM, which is called LinkSUM (Thalhammer et al., 2016), focused more on the objects instead of the diversity of properties for entities and showed a better result on the same dataset, in comparison with FACES. Beside the aforementioned techniques dedicated to entity summarization, there are various ranking models and tools, including TripleRank (Franz et al., 2009) and TRank (Tonon et al., 2013) that rank triples and concepts, respectively, incorporating ranking algorithms. However, Cheng et al. (2011) indicated that these methods are not appropriate for the entity summarization problem, which needs ranking of feature sets based on their importance to identify the underlying entity.

3 Preliminaries

An RDF data graph is a collection of nodes and edges that connect the nodes together. Nodes are usually recognized by unique IDs which are called *Uniform Resource Identifiers (URIs)* or exact values (i.e. numbers, dates, etc) namely *Lit-*

Table 1: J.C.Penny entity predicates and corresponding objects with the top-5 ES-LDA summary.

Predicate	Object	Top-5
http://dbpedia.org/property/areaServed	http://dbpedia.org/resource/United_States	✗
http://dbpedia.org/ontology/foundedBy	http://dbpedia.org/resource/James_Cash_Penney	✓
http://dbpedia.org/property/founder	http://dbpedia.org/resource/James_Cash_Penney	✗
http://dbpedia.org/ontology/industry	http://dbpedia.org/resource/Retail	✓
http://dbpedia.org/property/keyPerson	http://dbpedia.org/resource/Ron_Johnson	✓
http://dbpedia.org/property/homepage	http://www.jcpenney.com/	✗
http://dbpedia.org/ontology/location	http://dbpedia.org/resource/Plano,_Texas	✓
http://dbpedia.org/ontology/regionServed	http://dbpedia.org/resource/United_States	✗
http://dbpedia.org/property/tradedAs	http://dbpedia.org/resource/S&P_500	✗
http://dbpedia.org/ontology/type	http://dbpedia.org/resource/Public_company	✓

erals. An RDF graph is represented in a form of a collection of triples, each including a *Subject, Predicate, and Object*. In an RDF graph, an entity is defined as a subject with all predicates and corresponding objects to those predicates, collectively forming the entity's description. As Table 1 shows, the *J.C.Penny* entity is represented by its predicates (properties) and the corresponding objects in the triple format. For example, the triple $< J.C.Penny, industry, Retail >$ introduces *J.C.Penny*'s industry as *Retail* (due to space limitations we have dropped the first part of the *URIs*).

Definition 1 (Entity summary): Given an entity e and a positive integer k, a summary of the entity e, denoted *Sum(e, k)*, is the top-k subset of all predicates and corresponding objects that are most relevant to that entity. As Table1 shows the top-5 summary for *J.C.Penny* entity, which is represented through *foundedBy, industry, keyPerson, location, and type*.

3.1 Latent Dirichlet Allocation (LDA)

The Latent Dirichlet Allocation (LDA) is a generative probabilistic model for extracting thematic information (topics) from a collection of documents. LDA assumes that each document is made up of various topics, where each topic is a probability distribution over words.

Let $\mathcal{D} = \{d_1, d_2, \ldots, d_{|\mathcal{D}|}\}$ be a corpus of documents and $\mathcal{V} = \{w_1, w_2, \ldots, w_{|\mathcal{V}|}\}$ a vocabulary (words) of the corpus. A topic $z_j, 1 \leq j \leq K$ is represented as a multinomial probability distribution over the $|\mathcal{V}|$ words, $p(w_i|z_j), \sum_i^{|\mathcal{V}|} p(w_i|z_j) = 1$. LDA generates the words in a two-stage process: words are gener-

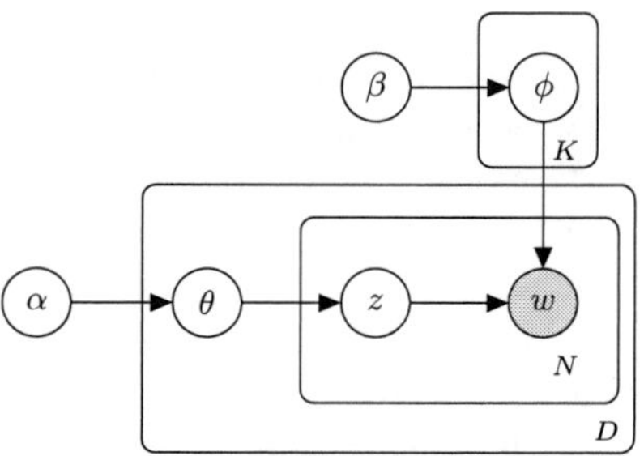

Figure 1: LDA Graphical Representation

ated from topics and topics are generated by documents. More formally, the distribution of words, given the document, is calculated as follows:

$$p(w_i|d) = \sum_{j=1}^{K} p(w_i|z_j)p(z_j|d) \qquad (1)$$

The graphical model of LDA is shown in Figure 1 and the generative process for the corpus $\mathcal{D}$ is:

1. For each topic $k \in \{1, 2, \ldots, K\}$, sample a word distribution $\phi_k \sim \text{Dir}(\beta)$

2. For each document $d \in \{1, 2, \ldots, \mathcal{D}\}$,

   (a) Sample a topic distribution $\theta_d \sim \text{Dir}(\alpha)$
   (b) For each word w_n, where $n \in \{1, 2, \ldots, N\}$, in document d,
       i. Sample a topic $z_i \sim \text{Mult}(\theta_d)$
       ii. Sample a word $w_n \sim \text{Mult}(\phi_{z_i})$

In the LDA model, the word-topic distribution $p(w|z)$ and topic-document distribution $p(z|d)$ are learned entirely in an unsupervised manner, without any prior knowledge about what words are related to the topics and what topics are related to individual documents.

4 Problem Statement

In this section, we first describe the problem and then define how to utilize topic models for RDF graphs. Then, we formally introduce our ES-LDA model and explain how to integrate prior knowledge from RDF data graph within a topic model for entity summarization.

4.1 Problem Definition

Generating summaries for voluminous Semantic Web data, and in particular RDF data, for quick identification of entities has gained considerable attention as a challenging problem in the Semantic Web community. In the literature, *Entity Summarization* is defined as selecting a small but representative subset of the original triples associated with an entity. In this context, given an RDF data set comprising a collection of entities, where each entity is described by a set of its properties (i.e., all triples with the entity as the subject), our goal is to choose *top-k* representative triples for each entity. In other words, since all triples associated with an entity (as its description) share the same subject, our objective is to select *top-k* predicates and their corresponding objects among these triples that best summarize the entity's description.

4.2 Topic Models for RDF Graphs

Topic models were originally introduced for text documents, however, they have been applied to other types of data, such as images (Blei and Jordan, 2003), and recently (Sleeman et al., 2015) used topic modeling for RDF graphs. The first step in applying topic models is to define documents and word-like elements as the basic building blocks of documents. Since an RDF graph is usually represented as a set of triples, where each triple t consists of a subject s, predicate p, and an object o, in the form of $<s, p, o>$, we can consider a collection of such triples as a "document".

Definition 2 (document): A document d is defined as a set of triples, $d = \{t_1, t_2, \cdots, t_n\}$, that describe a single entity e. In other words, all triples of a document d have the same subject.

"Words" of a document can be extracted from different parts of its triples. We define a "**word**" w as the subject or object of a triple t in document d. Therefore, each document is represented by a "bag of words" including all the subjects and objects of its triples. In this paper, all subjects in the triples of a document are the same, because each document corresponds to a single entity, hence, in practice each document is a "bag of objects"[2]

Topic models usually utilize some data pre-processing, such as punctuation removal, downcasting, and abbreviation expansion, etc., to enhance the final performance. We also performed preprocessing on the RDF data and filtered out the schema and dataset dependent predicates, such as *sameAs, wikiPageExternalLink, subject, wikiPageWikiLink*, in addition to *literals*. Since we work with RDF graphs that differ from typical text documents in the sense that RDF data are represented as triples, we need to address several challenges mentioned in (Sleeman et al., 2015) to be able to run topic models on RDF data. These challenges include sparseness, use of unnatural language, and the lack of context. RDF data can be affected by **Sparseness**. We consider documents as sets of triples associated with a single entity. Such a set can be very large, leading to a large bag of words with a semantic theme, or small (sparse), resulting in a poor bag of words with less contextual information. It is also possible that a document with a high number of triples ends up having a small bag of words after pre-processing; for example based on Table 1, *J.C.Penny* entity comes with *United_States, James_Cash_Penney, Retail, Ron_Johnson, Plano,_Texas, United_States, S&P_500 and Public_company* as a bag of words for *J.C.Penny* entity, which shows sparseness in this document. **Unnatural Language** can be problematic for RDF data. A typical text document contains sentences where each sentence has a natural structure. These extra components of a sentence usually provide a further "**context**" for understanding words that are ambiguous or have multiple meanings, such as polysemous or homonymous ones. The aforementioned example for the *J.C.Penny* entity also confirms the unnatural language problem. The "**lack of context**" can further impact RDF data because they are potentially sparse, described by unnatural language, and often using words that have multiple meanings, difficult to differentiate (*J.C.Penny* bag of words example). Additionally, triples are more prone to pre-processing, because it is not uncom-

---

[2]"bag of words" and "bag of objects" are interchangeably used.

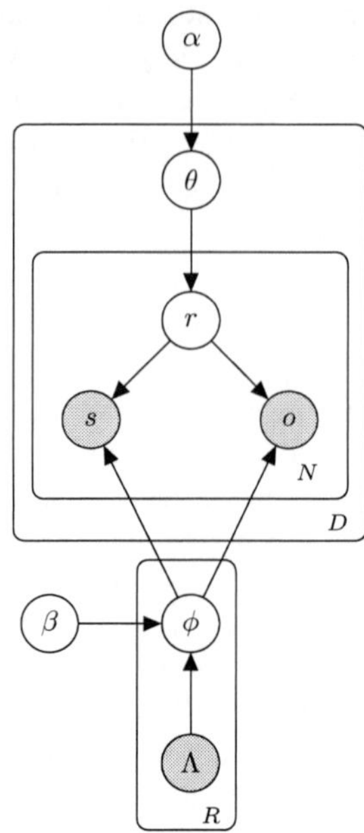

Figure 2: Entity Summarization Model

Algorithm 1: ES-LDA Model

1 **foreach** predicate $r \in \{1, 2, \ldots, R\}$ **do**
2   Draw an object distribution $\phi_r \sim$ $\mathrm{Dir}(\beta_r \times \Lambda_r)$
3 **end**
4 **foreach** document $d \in \{1, 2, \ldots, D\}$ **do**
5   Draw a predicate distribution $\theta_d \sim$ $\mathrm{Dir}(\alpha_d)$
6   **foreach** subject s and object o of document d **do**
7   Draw a predicate $r \sim \mathrm{Mult}(\theta_d)$
8   Draw a subject s from predicate $r, s \sim \mathrm{Mult}(\phi_r)$
9   Draw an object o from predicate $r, o \sim \mathrm{Mult}(\phi_r)$
10   **end**
11 **end**

---

mon for triples to contain unexpected characters. RDF data resemble short texts in terms of the aforementioned challenges. Sparseness in a short text causes the model to be less discriminative to recognize how words are related and the limited context makes it hard for the model to identify the meanings of the words in such short text documents (Yan et al., 2013). In order to alleviate these issues, researchers usually take two approaches. They either augment the short text or design custom versions of the LDA model that address their specific problems. In this paper, we have used both approaches. We describe how to supplement the RDF data in the following section and describe the details of our model in section 4.4.

4.3 Supplementing RDF Data

As topic modeling is based on statistics of the co-occurrence of terms (Sleeman et al., 2015), when we are dealing with short texts with a very limited number of repetitions, which is the case with RDF data, we need to find a way to supplement the data to elevate the performance of the topic modeling approach. We augment the documents using two different methods. In the first method, we increase the frequency of the words in each document. But the question is *"How many times each word of a document should be repeated?"*.

Entities in DBpedia have been organized into a category network, therefore, every entity has a number of categories associated with it. The relationship between an entity and a category is defined by the *"http://purl.org/dc/terms/subject"* predicate. Since each word of a document is an object of a triple, and accordingly, an entity in DBpedia, it is related to several categories. We assume that objects (words) of a document that have more categories are likely more important. Thus, We expand each document by increasing the frequency of each object by the number of its categories. In the second method, instead of repeating each object a certain number of times, we enlarge each document by adding categories of the objects as extra words, directly to the document. There are multiple advantages of supplementing each document by adding object categories: (i) the sparseness in the document, related to each entity, is lowered as we are adding a number of related words to it; (ii) we reduce the ambiguity in the document, because adding extra categories alleviates the lack of context and helps distinguish the appropriate meanings of the words with multiple connotations; and lastly (iii), adding object categories makes the documents semantically more relevant to their topical themes. We evaluated our model using both methods and the results demonstrate that the first method gives significantly better summaries than the second method.

4.4 Proposed Model

ES-LDA is a probabilistic generative model for modeling entities in RDF graphs. The key idea behind our model is twofold: (1) we exploit statistical topic models as the underlying quantitative framework for entity summarization; and (2) ES-LDA incorporates the prior knowledge from the RDF knowledge base directly into the topic model. The plate notation is shown in Figure 2.

In our model, each document is a multinomial distribution over the predicates. If we consider predicates as topics, at the document level, our model is the same as standard LDA. However, we set the number of topics in ES-LDA to be the number of unique predicates in the corpus. Unlike the standard LDA, where each topic is a multinomial distribution over the vocabulary from the Dirichlet prior β, in our model each predicate is a multinomial distribution over all the subjects and objects of the RDF graph. In our approach, a document consists of a set of triples describing a single entity, i.e. all these triples share the same subject. Thus, we constrain the documents to only have the objects of related triples and also restrict the predicates to be defined only over the objects. In addition, for each predicate r, we further smooth its distribution by Λ_r. Λ is a matrix that has encoded the background knowledge about predicate-object values from DBpedia. Section 4.5 explains how Λ is constructed. The generative process of ES-LDA is shown in Algorithm 1.

Following this process, the joint probability of generating a corpus $D = \{d_1, d_2, \ldots, d_{|D|}\}$, the predicate assignments $\mathbf{r}$ given the hyperparameters α, β and the prior matrix Λ is:

$$P(\mathbf{o}, \mathbf{s}, \mathbf{r}|\alpha, \beta, \Lambda)$$

$$= \int_\phi P(\phi|\beta; \Lambda) \prod_d \sum_{r_d} P(\mathbf{o_d}|r_d, \phi) P(\mathbf{s_d}|r_d, \phi)$$

$$\times \int_\theta P(\theta|\alpha) P(\mathbf{r_d}|\theta, \phi) d\theta d\phi \quad (2)$$

4.5 Constructing Predicate-Object Prior Matrix Λ

In the ES-LDA model, each predicate has a probability distribution over the objects of the RDF graph. Entity summarization is the task of choosing the top-k predicate-object pairs that best describe an entity. Presumably, if an object is associated with more categories in DBpedia, it is likely more important. We create the the Λ matrix to encode the prior weight of the predicate-object pairs

and utilize it to smooth the predicate-object distributions ϕ by incorporating this domain knowledge into the topic model. We build the Λ matrix of size $R \times O$, where R is the number of predicates and O is the number of objects in the RDF graph. Let f be an indicator function where $f(i, j) = 1$ if there is a triple in RDF graph with predicate i and object j, and 1 otherwise, for $1 \leq i \leq R$ and $1 \leq j \leq O$. Additionally, let c be the number of categories assigned to object j. Then, we define Λ_{ij} as follows:

$$\Lambda_{ij} = \begin{cases} c & \text{if } f(i, j) = 1 \\ 1 & \text{otherwise.} \end{cases} \quad (3)$$

For example, the "*Barack_Obama*" entity has multiple predicate-object pairs in DBpedia, including "*profession-author*", "*profession-lawyer*" and "*profession-professor*" pairs. According to DBpedia, $c_{author} = 2$, $c_{lawyer} = 4$ and $c_{professor} = 2$. It is reasonable to expect a higher probability for the "*profession-lawyer*" pair as it seems to be slightly more important than the other two pairs for "*Barack_Obama*". As a result, $\Lambda_{profession-lawyer} = 4$, which promotes "*profession-lawyer*" in Eq. 5.

4.6 Inference using Gibbs Sampling

Since the posterior inference of the LDA is intractable, we need to find an algorithm for estimating the posterior inference. A variety of algorithms have been used to estimate the parameters of topic models, such as variational EM (Blei et al., 2003) and Gibbs sampling (Griffiths and Steyvers, 2004). In this paper we use the collapsed Gibbs sampling procedure for our ES-LDA topic model. Collapsed Gibbs sampling (Griffiths and Steyvers, 2004) is a Markov Chain Monte Carlo (MCMC) (Robert and Casella, 2004) algorithm, which constructs a Markov chain over the latent variables in the model and converges to the posterior distribution, after a number of iterations. In our case, we aim to construct a Markov chain that converges to the posterior distribution over $\mathbf{r}$ conditioned on observed subjects $\mathbf{s}$, objects $\mathbf{o}$, hyperparameters α, β, and the prior matrix Λ.

In our modified version of the learning algorithm to infer $p(o_i|r_j)$ and $p(r_j|d)$, we (1) constrain the objects that are not paired with a predicate to have 0 probability, i.e. $p(o_i|r_j) = 0$, if $(r_i, o_j) \notin$ RDF graph, and (2) $P(s|r_j) = 1$, since all the triples of a document have the same subject s. We derive the posterior inference from Eq. 2 as follows:

$$P(\mathbf{r}|\mathbf{o}, \mathbf{s}, \alpha, \beta, \Lambda) = \frac{P(\mathbf{r}, \mathbf{o}, \mathbf{s}|\alpha, \beta, \Lambda)}{P(\mathbf{o}|\alpha, \beta, \Lambda)} \tag{4}$$

$$\propto P(\mathbf{r}, \mathbf{o}|\alpha, \beta, \Lambda) \propto P(\mathbf{r})P(\mathbf{o}|\mathbf{r})P(\mathbf{s}|\mathbf{r})$$

$$P(r_i = r|o_i = o, \mathbf{r}_{-i}, \mathbf{o}_{-i}, \alpha, \beta, \Lambda) \propto$$

$$\frac{n^{(d)}_{r,-i} + \alpha_r}{\sum_{r'} (n^{(d)}_{r',-i} + \alpha_{r'})} \times \frac{n^{(r)}_{o,-i} + \Lambda_{ro}\beta_o}{\sum_{o'} (n^{(r)}_{o',-i} + \Lambda_{ro}\beta_o)} \tag{5}$$

where $n^{(r)}_o$ is the number of times object o is assigned to predicate r. $n^{(d)}_r$ denotes the number of times predicate r is associated with document d. The subscript $-i$ indicates that the contribution of the current object o_i being sampled is removed from the counts. After Gibbs sampling, we can use the sampled predicate to estimate the probability of a predicate, given a document, θ_{dr} and the probability of an object, given a predicate, ϕ_{ro}:

$$\theta_{dr} = \frac{n^{(d)}_r + \alpha_r}{\sum_{r'} (n^{(d)}_{r'} + \alpha_{r'})} \tag{6}$$

$$\phi_{ro} = \frac{n^{(r)}_o + \Lambda_{ro}\beta_o}{\sum_{o'} (n^{(r)}_{o'} + \Lambda_{ro}\beta_o)} \tag{7}$$

5 Experiments

We evaluated our ES-LDA model against the state-of-the-art LinkSUM (Thalhammer et al., 2016) and FACES (Gunaratna et al., 2015) systems. Our goal was to show that the ES-LDA model produces results that are closer to human judgment, in comparison with the other approaches. We used the same dataset[3] that was used in the experiments conducted with FACES, as well as LinkSUM models. The dataset contained 50 entities randomly selected from DBpedia (English version 3.9) in domains including *politician, actors, scientist, song, film, country, city, river, company, game, etc.*. 15 people in the field of Semantic Web were selected as reviewers and each entity was evaluated by at least 7 reviewers to produce the top-5 and top-10 summaries. The average number of properties for each entity was 44.

Based on the two types of RDF supplement methods we discussed in 4.3, we applied two different configurations for the proposed model. In

[3]http://wiki.knoesis.org/index.php/FACES

the first experiment, ES-LDA @config-1, we configured the system to supplement each entity (document) by repeating each object based on the *number of categories* that the object has in the DBpedia knowledge base. For example, for the triple $< J.C.Penney, industry, Retail >$ we repeated *Retail* object, 5 times in that document, as *Retail* has five different categories in DBpedia (i.e. "*Retailers, Retailing, French words and phrases, Merchandising, Marketing*")

In the second experiment, ES-LDA @config-2, we configured the system to supplement each entity (document) by adding the corresponding category(ies) of each object into the document. In this case, each entity is defined as a bag of words including objects and categories of each object. For example, for the aforementioned triple, in addition to the *Retail* we included "*Retailers, Retailing, French words and phrases, Merchandising, Marketing*" as the corresponding categories to the *Retail* object.

For the other parameters, we assumed a symmetric Dirichlet prior and set $\beta = 0.01$ and $\alpha = 50/R$, where R is the total number of unique predicates. We ran the Gibbs sampling algorithm for 1000 iterations and computed the posterior inference after the last sampling iteration. We selected the top-5 and top-10 most probable properties for each entity and calculate the quality of the summary for each entity through equation 8.

$$Quality(Sum(e)) = \frac{1}{n} \sum_{i=1}^{n} |Sum(e) \cap Sum_i^I(e)| \tag{8}$$

In our experiments, we used the quality of the summary proposed in (Cheng et al., 2011), in which n ideal summaries $Sum_i^I(e)$ generated by expert users for $i = 1, ..., n$ and the summaries generated by the system $Sum(e)$ were compared. The average of the overlap between an ideal summary and a summary generated by the system is denoted as the quality of the summary, which is $0 \le Quality(Sum(e)) \le k$ in the top-k settings.

5.1 Experiment Results

The summary in our model is defined as sets of representative triples that can summarize each entity (sets of triples with the same subject) in a way close to a human-created summary. We decided to use the last part of a *URI* to compare the generated summaries with the expert summaries and produce

Table 2: Overall quality results of different models. Best result are bold.

Model	Top-5	Top-10
ES-LDA @ config-1	**1.20**	**3.50**
ES-LDA @ config-2	1.10	3.26
LinkSUM@ config-1	1.20	3.15
LinkSUM@ config-2	1.20	3.20
FACES	0.93	2.92

the Summary Quality for each entity and average them. As (Thalhammer et al., 2016) reproduced the FACES overall Summary Quality based on this criteria and also applied it to their model, we decided to use their result as it was completely aligned with our summary definition.

In Table 2, we compare the quality of the results from LinkSUM, FACES, and ES-LDA with two distinct configurations (supplementing by object reputation and object categories). As Table 2 shows, the quality of our model outperforms the FACES approach, in both cases. The ES-LDA @ config-2 demonstrates a comparable result with the two configurations of LinkSUM, while ES-LDA @ config-1 outperforms LinkSUM. For some of the entities, the predicates that ES-LDA selected as top-5 most probable did not exist in the FACES dataset. It forced us to calculate the quality of summary for some of the entities with just 4 predicates instead of 5. We believe to be the only reason why top-5 Quality of Summary was lower than or equal to LinkSUM. Although, we had the same issue for the top-10 results, overall, ES-LDA shows a better performance in two configurations.

6 Discussion

We evaluated our approach against the state-of-the-art summarization techniques, including LinkSUM and FACES. LinkSUM primarily focuses on the most relevant facts for each entity, while FACES tries to keep a balance between diversity and relevancy in entity summarization. There is usually a trade-off between diversity and relevancy of the selected predicates. Our ES-LDA model maintains both diversity and relevancy, while representing each entity through *top-k* predicates. As shown in Table 2, our model outperforms the state-of-the-art approaches.

Table 3 illustrates a sample of entities from the dataset along with their top-10 predicates, for all approaches. As Table 3 shows, the LinkSUM model is focusing more on the *objects*, while predicate repetition is permitted. For example, *<Marie_Curie, birthPlace, Warsaw>*, *<Marie_Curie, birthPlace, Russian_Empire>*, and *<Marie_Curie, birthPlace, Congress_Polandare>* are representing *Marie_Curie*'s birth place. Although, they differ in terms of objects, it is arguable that referring to the same predicate with multiple objects that are more likely relevant reduces the chance of other important triples that could potentially appear in the summary. It should be noted that in the current ES-LDA configuration, we have not considered predicate repetition, thus, all the predicates of the triples appearing in the resultant summary are unique. FACES on the other hand, considers predicate diversity and tries to keep a balance between the diversity and relevancy but the overall quality of the FACES model is lower than LinkSUM and ES-LDA. In the FACES model, there are selected predicates which seems to be less informative in the sense to be top-10 representative for a particular entity. For example, *<Marie_Curie, thumbnail, 200px-Marie_Curie_c1920.png>*, which is referring to a *png* file, could be replaced with more descriptive one. Additionally, our proposed technique features several unique characteristics: (1) the ES-LDA is a *knowledge-based probabilistic* model that combines prior knowledge with statistical learning technique into a unified framework for entity summarization; (2) for each entity, it ranks all predicates based on their importance by computing marginal probabilities for the predicates. Table 4 illustrates the top-5 predicates for a sample of two entities; and finally (3), each predicate can be represented as a probability distribution over objects in the ES-LDA model, which allows us to describe the relations (predicates) of the RDF graph based on its nodes as shown in Table 5.

7 Conclusions

We have proposed a knowledge-based probabilistic topic model, called ES-LDA, based on the RDF entity representation for entity summarization. In our experiments, we have applied two different configurations: one based on object repetitions and the other based on adding object's categories, to alleviate common RDF data problems including

Table 3: Top-10 predicates for three randomly selected entities after applying three different models.

MARIE CURIE			REIGN OF FIRE			SEYCHELLES		
ES-LDA	LinkSUM	FACES	ES-LDA	LinkSUM	FACES	ES-LDA	LinkSUM	FACES
doctoralStudents	birthPlace	spouse	starring	country	starring	leaderName	largestCity	leaderName
doctoralAdvisor	birthPlace	field	producer	starring	country	governmentType	governmentType	governmentType
deathPlace	field	workInstitutions	music	starring	distributor	leaderTitle	governmentType	largestCity
children	field	birthPlace	director	starring	musicComposer	officialLanguage	governmentType	sovereigntyType
knownFor	knownFor	deathPlace	cinematography	studio	director	capital	governmentType	source
spouse	almaMater	doctoralAdvisor	country	producer	editing	currency	sovereigntyType	capital
almaMater	birthPlace	knownFor	distributor	producer	studio	timeZone	source	leaderTitle
birthPlace	knownFor	almaMater	studio	director	music	legislature	capital	language
field	doctoralAdvisor	doctoralStudents	editing	artist	producer	anthem	language	languages
establishedEvent	knownFor	thumbnail	screenplay	producer	thumbnail	callingCode	timeZone	legislature

Table 4: Probabilities of top-5 predicates for two randomly selected entities.

LEXUS		MORTAL KOMBAT TRILOGY	
Predicate	Probability	Predicate	Probability
foundedBy	0.21	platforms	0.30
owner	0.17	publisher	0.18
location	0.15	developer	0.17
keyPerson	0.06	computingMedia	0.07
service	0.04	designer	0.05

Table 5: Distributions of two randomly selected predicates over top-5 objects.

PARTY		STARRING	
Object	Probability	Object	Probability
Democratic Party (United States)	0.36	Arnold Schwarzenegger	0.05
Republican Party (United States)	0.17	Angelina Jolie	0.04
Democratic-Republican Party	0.12	Raven Symone	0.03
Communist Party of the Soviet Union	0.08	Matthew McConaughey	0.02
Independent(politician)	0.08	Alan Arkin	0.02

sparseness, unnatural language, and lack of context. We conducted extensive experiments, which show the quality of the top-10 triples in both configurations outperforms the state-of-the-art techniques, LinkSUM and FACES, while for the top-5 quality we surpassed FACES and equaled the LinkSUM results.

There are many interesting future research directions of this work. It would be interesting to investigate how this model and a much richer set of topic models that combine prior knowledge with statistical learning techniques could be used for various tasks in the Semantic Web domain, such as ontology summarization, ontology tagging, and finding similar ontologies.

Acknowledgments

Gong Cheng was partially funded by the NSFC under Grant 61572247.

References

Mehdi Allahyari and Krys Kochut. 2015. Automatic topic labeling using ontology-based topic models. In *14th International Conference on Machine Learning and Applications (ICMLA), 2015*. IEEE.

Mehdi Allahyari, Seyedamin Pouriyeh, Mehdi Assefi, Saied Safaei, Elizabeth D Trippe, Juan B Gutierrez, and Krys Kochut. 2017a. A brief survey of text mining: Classification, clustering and extraction techniques. *arXiv preprint arXiv:1707.02919* .

Mehdi Allahyari, Seyedamin Pouriyeh, Krys Kochut, and Hamid R Arabnia. 2017b. A knowledge-based topic modeling approach for automatic topic labeling. *INTERNATIONAL JOURNAL OF ADVANCED COMPUTER SCIENCE AND APPLICATIONS* 8(9):335–349.

Kayhan Batmanghelich, Ardavan Saeedi, Karthik Narasimhan, and Sam Gershman. 2016. Nonparametric spherical topic modeling with word embeddings. *arXiv preprint arXiv:1604.00126* .

Christian Bizer, Jens Lehmann, Georgi Kobilarov, Sören Auer, Christian Becker, Richard Cyganiak, and Sebastian Hellmann. 2009. Dbpedia-a crystallization point for the web of data. *Web Semantics: science, services and agents on the world wide web* 7(3):154–165.

David M Blei and Michael I Jordan. 2003. Modeling annotated data. In *Proceedings of the 26th annual international ACM SIGIR conference on Research and development in informaion retrieval*. ACM, pages 127–134.

David M Blei, Andrew Y Ng, and Michael I Jordan. 2003. Latent dirichlet allocation. *the Journal of machine Learning research* 3:993–1022.

Shaofeng Bu, Laks VS Lakshmanan, and Raymond T Ng. 2005. Mdl summarization with holes. In *Proceedings of the 31st international conference on Very large data bases*. VLDB Endowment, pages 433–444.

Gong Cheng, Thanh Tran, and Yuzhong Qu. 2011. Relin: relatedness and informativeness-based centrality for entity summarization. *The Semantic Web–ISWC 2011* pages 114–129.

Hong-Jie Dai, Richard Tzong-Han Tsai, Wen-Lian Hsu, et al. 2011. Entity disambiguation using a markov-logic network. In *IJCNLP*. pages 846–855.

Rajarshi Das, Manzil Zaheer, and Chris Dyer. 2015. Gaussian lda for topic models with word embeddings. In *ACL (1)*. pages 795–804.

Douglas H Fisher. 1987. Knowledge acquisition via incremental conceptual clustering. *Machine learning* 2(2):139–172.

Thomas Franz, Antje Schultz, Sergej Sizov, and Steffen Staab. 2009. Triplerank: Ranking semantic web data by tensor decomposition. *The Semantic Web-ISWC 2009* pages 213–228.

Thomas L Griffiths and Mark Steyvers. 2004. Finding scientific topics. *Proceedings of the National academy of Sciences of the United States of America* 101(Suppl 1):5228–5235.

Kalpa Gunaratna, Krishnaprasad Thirunarayan, and Amit P Sheth. 2015. Faces: diversity-aware entity summarization using incremental hierarchical conceptual clustering .

Udo Hahn and Inderjeet Mani. 2000. The challenges of automatic summarization. *Computer* 33(11):29–36.

Johannes Hoffart, Fabian M Suchanek, Klaus Berberich, and Gerhard Weikum. 2013. Yago2: A spatially and temporally enhanced knowledge base from wikipedia. *Artificial Intelligence* 194:28–61.

Karen Spärck Jones. 2007. Automatic summarising: The state of the art. *Information Processing & Management* 43(6):1449–1481.

Saket Navlakha, Rajeev Rastogi, and Nisheeth Shrivastava. 2008. Graph summarization with bounded error. In *Proceedings of the 2008 ACM SIGMOD international conference on Management of data*. ACM, pages 419–432.

Ani Nenkova and Kathleen McKeown. 2012. A survey of text summarization techniques. In *Mining text data*, Springer, pages 43–76.

Christian P Robert and George Casella. 2004. *Monte Carlo statistical methods*, volume 319. Citeseer.

Jennifer Sleeman, Tim Finin, and Anupam Joshi. 2015. Topic modeling for rdf graphs. In *LD4IE@ ISWC*. pages 48–62.

Jinsong Su, Deyi Xiong, Yang Liu, Xianpei Han, Hongyu Lin, Junfeng Yao, and Min Zhang. 2015. A context-aware topic model for statistical machine translation. In *ACL (1)*. pages 229–238.

Andreas Thalhammer, Nelia Lasierra, and Achim Rettinger. 2016. Linksum: using link analysis to summarize entity data. In *International Conference on Web Engineering*. Springer, pages 244–261.

Andreas Thalhammer and Achim Rettinger. 2014. Browsing dbpedia entities with summaries. In *European Semantic Web Conference*. Springer, pages 511–515.

Alberto Tonon, Michele Catasta, Gianluca Demartini, Philippe Cudré-Mauroux, and Karl Aberer. 2013. Trank: Ranking entity types using the web of data. In *International Semantic Web Conference*. Springer, pages 640–656.

Xiaojun Wan and Tianming Wang. 2016. Automatic labeling of topic models using text summaries. In *ACL (1)*.

Xiaohui Yan, Jiafeng Guo, Yanyan Lan, and Xueqi Cheng. 2013. A biterm topic model for short texts. In *Proceedings of the 22nd international conference on World Wide Web*. ACM, pages 1445–1456.

Xiang Zhang, Gong Cheng, and Yuzhong Qu. 2007. Ontology summarization based on rdf sentence graph. In *Proceedings of the 16th international conference on World Wide Web*. ACM, pages 707–716.

Hai Zhao and Chunyu Kit. 2008. Unsupervised segmentation helps supervised learning of character tagging for word segmentation and named entity recognition. In *IJCNLP*. pages 106–111.

Procedural Text Generation from an Execution Video

Atsushi Ushiku   Hayato Hashimoto   Atsushi Hashimoto   Shinsuke Mori
Yoshida-honmachi, Sakyo-ku,
Kyoto University, Kyoto, Japan
`d460655046504@gmail.com hashimoto.hayato.73e@st.kyoto-u.ac.jp`
`ahasimoto@mm.media.kyoto-u.ac.jp forest@i.kyoto-u.ac.jp`

Abstract

In recent years, there has been a surge of interest in automatically describing images or videos in a natural language. These descriptions are useful for image/video search, etc. In this paper, we focus on procedure execution videos, in which a human makes or repairs something and propose a method for generating procedural texts from them. Since available video/text pairs are limited in size, the direct application of end-to-end deep learning is not feasible. Thus we propose to train Faster R-CNN network for object recognition and LSTM for text generation and combine them at run time. We took pairs of recipe and cooking video as an example, generated a recipe from a video, and compared it with the original recipe. The experimental results showed that our method can produce a recipe as accurate as the state-of-the-art scene descriptions.

1   Introduction

Massive effort has been done to develop a method for generating text from vision in the field of natural language processing and computer vision. More specifically, there are number of studies on generating captions for given images or videos (Yang et al., 2011; Rohrbach et al., 2013; Li et al., 2015; Donahue et al., 2015; Karpathy and Fei-Fei, 2015; Shetty and Laaksonen, 2016; Johnson et al., 2016). Most of the existing researches for video captioning, however, deal with simple and short videos (Li et al., 2015; Donahue et al., 2015; Shetty and Laaksonen, 2016) such as a ten second video in which a man playing guitar in a park.

In this paper, we propose a new problem in this field: generating a procedural text from an execu-tion video such as cooking or machine assembly. The goal is to develop a method that takes video of a chef cooking a dish from ingredients or a me-chanic assembling a machine from parts as the in-put, and outputs a procedural text that helps an-other person reproduce the same product.

We also give an initial solution to the problem, taking cooking recipe generation as an example. Because no large scale corpus consisting of re-lated execution video and procedural text is avail-able for now, we divide the problem into two sub-problems, object recognition and text generation, and train two modules independently using differ-ent resources as their training set. Then we com-bine them and search for the best text. The object recognition module is designed to spot the changes in state of progress of the procedure from video and texts are generated at each time. Finally, some of the generated sentences are selected to cover the entire procedure with discarding redundant sen-tences.

In the experiments, we use KUSK Dataset (Hashimoto et al., 2014), which consists of pairs of recipes submitted by users to a recipe hosting service Cookpad and video of cooking according to that recipe in a laboratory. The experimental results showed that our method is capable of pro-ducing a recipe of reasonable quality.

2   Related Work

Recent studies on automatic caption generation have reported great results both in images (Xu et al., 2015; Karpathy and Fei-Fei, 2015; Johnson et al., 2016) and short video clips (Li et al., 2015; Donahue et al., 2015; Shetty and Laaksonen, 2016) by using convolutional neural network (CNN), re-current neural network, and LSTM. (Venugopalan et al., 2015) improved the accuracy with a sequence to sequence model (Sutskever et al., 2014). In addi-

Proceedings of the The 8th International Joint Conference on Natural Language Processing, pages 326–335,
Taipei, Taiwan, November 27 – December 1, 2017 ©2017 AFNLP

tion, (Laokulrat et al., 2016; Guo et al., 2016) also improved the accuracy of automatic caption generation by introducing an LSTM equipped with an attention mechanism. One of the features of these end-to-end models is that they directly generate sentences from videos without determining content words such as subjects and predicates. Common datasets (Lin et al., 2014; Chen and Dolan, 2011; Torabi et al., 2015; Rohrbach et al., 2015) made research on automatic caption generation popular.

Before the above end-to-end models succeeded, many researchers concentrated models generating sentences via content words or intermediate states (Guadarrama et al., 2013; Rohrbach et al., 2013). As an advantage of the technique of using intermediate states, object recognition or motion recognition model can be diverted as it is. Thus data of pairs of a medium and a caption have not been particularly required. These methods with intermediate states are inferior in accuracy to the end-to-end models using CNN and LSTM in case that enough size of training data are available. On the other hand, since creation of medium-caption pairs is expensive, methods using intermediate states are also considered to be sufficiently practical for a problem where we have insufficient size of data available for model training.

Unlike conventional methods using intermediate states such as subjects, objects, and predicates, for procedure execution videos, there is a problem that the use of recognition results of general actions is not appropriate because of the abstraction level. It is considered preparing tailored data for motion recognition for each kind of procedure execution videos have high cost because it is often vague even for human annotators to assign every concrete motions into text-level motion categories. In contrast, objects directly appear in texts and there is much less ambiguity than motions. Therefore, it is reasonable for the procedural text generation to focus more on object recognition than motion recognition. In addition, the procedure execution videos generally show works performed by one person, thus subject recognition is not necessary. It is preferable to set the object recognition results as an intermediate state and generate sentences from it. Since predicates are not easy to be recognized, they are estimated or supplemented from recognized objects using language knowledge.

Many studies generate a caption consisting of one sentence for a video clip. Studies on the automatic caption generation of documents consisting of multiple sentences like procedural text do not attract much attention as far as we know. One similar study is done by (Kaufman et al., 2016), which gives captions for a movie that is divided into scenes beforehand.

3 Task Definition

In this section, we describe our novel task in detail. Then we present prerequisites of our solution.

3.1 Procedural Text Generation from Video

We propose a task of generating a procedural text from an execution video. Figure 1 shows the overview of the task. In general, an execution video records a sequence of activities to make or repair something from the beginning to the end. As the first trial, we deal with cooking videos in which only one person appears (mainly the hands only). In the beginning, there are some ingredients and tools on the cooking table and some appear in the video later. Then it finishes with a completed dish. This is the input of the task.

The output of our task is a procedural text, consisting of some sentences in a natural language, which explains procedures to be conducted by workers to make or repair something. The counterpart of cooking videos of the first trial is recipes. A recipe describes how to cook a certain dish. In general, a recipe includes the dish name and an ingredient list in addition to the instruction text part. In our task, however, we focus on generating the text part only. Thus, this is the output of the task. In the subsequent sections, we refer to that text part by the term recipe.

As an evaluation metrics, it is preferable to measure how much the output text helps another chef produce the same dish. Thus, the ideal may be

Table 1: Definition of r-NE tags.

r-NE tag	meaning
F	Food
T	Tool
D	Duration
Q	Quantity
Ac	Action by the chef
Af	Action by foods
Sf	State of foods
St	State of tools

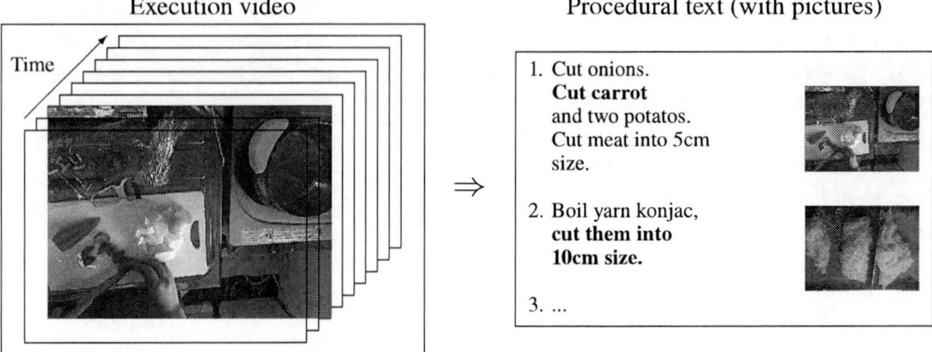

Figure 1: Task overview.

objective evaluation over the dishes produced by chefs reading the generated recipes. We propose, however, to adopt BLEU score as a metric of procedural text for the convenience of automated evaluation.

One of the advantages to choose the cooking domain as a benchmark of procedural text generation from video is that there are a huge number of recipes available on the Web. Therefore it is easy to develop a generative model of recipes for the task. In addition, there are recipe/video pairs available for various researches. For example, the KUSK Dataset (Hashimoto et al., 2014), which we use in the experiments, contains recipes and their cooking videos. Note that the lengths of these cooking videos are about 20 minutes or more, which are much longer than video clips used in automatic video captioning researches. And also note that the texts are kinds of summaries mentioning only the necessary objects and actions to complete a certain mission. Such texts are intrinsically different from scene descriptions in automatic video (or image) captioning researches.

3.2 Prerequisites

To solve the problem above, we enumerate the preconditions necessary for our method in the recipe generation case.

3.2.1 Domain Specific Named Entity

First we assume a set of terms (word sequences) called named entities (x-**NEs**) representing important object names in the target domain x. They are the objects to be recognized by computer vision (CV).

In the recipe case, noun phrases for ingredients and tools are important object names. In this paper, we adopt the recipe named entities (**r-NEs**) defined in (Mori et al., 2014), whose types are listed in Table 1. There are eight r-NE tag types, but our CV part recognizes only foods (F) and tools (T). We use the notation "チンゲン 菜/F" ("qing-geng-cai/F") to indicate that "チンゲン 菜" is an r-NE and its type is food (F)[1].

3.2.2 Named Entity Recognizer

In order to develop a useful generative model we must locate x-NEs in given sentences. So-called named entity recognizer (**NER**) is suitable for this task. In this paper, we adopt NERs based on sequence labeling techniques that can be trained by an annotated corpus.

3.2.3 Object Recognition

Our method requires the module that can detect the appearance and the disappearance of materials and tools involved in the procedure. In the cooking video case, we use Faster R-CNN model (Ren et al., 2015) fine-tuned with relatively small set of images of foods and cooking tools.

3.2.4 Procedural Text Examples

As we mentioned in Section 1, there is no large amount of video/sentence pairs available for our problem. But instead, in some cases, large text-only corpus is available in the domain. The corpus will allow us to train a generative model of the instruction sentences.

4 Proposed Method

In this section, we explain the proposed method for recipe generation from cooking videos. The out-

---

[1] The language resources used in our experiments are in Japanese. Thus our system outputs recipes in Japanese. However, our method can generate recipes in another language by preparing the prerequisites in that language.

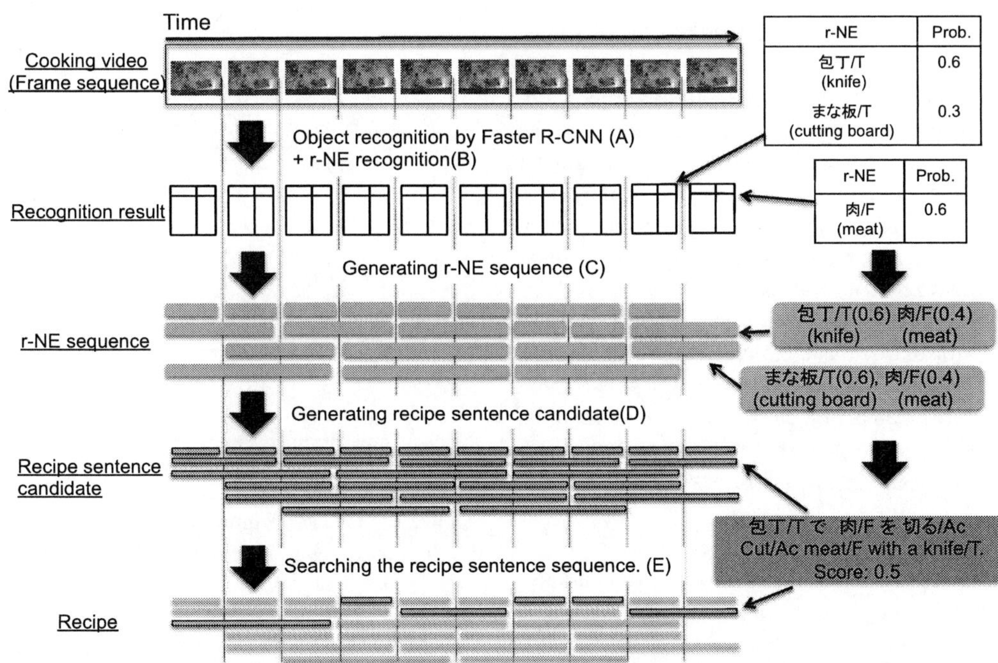

Figure 2: Overview of the proposed method.

line of this method is shown in Figure 2. First, we recognize objects in the video as a sequence of frames with a CNN and give an r-NE tag to each object (Figure 2 A, B). Next, we create an r-NE sequence from each partial frame sequence (Figure 2 C) and generate a candidate recipe sentence for each corresponding r-NE sequence (Figure 2 D). Each candidate recipe sentence is the one which maximizes the score indicating the likelihood of a sentence as a procedural text within the partial frame sequence. Finally, we select the sequence of recipe candidate sequences that maximizes the total score through the entire video based on Viterbi search. We output that sentence sequence as the procedural text for the input procedure execution video (Figure 2 E).

4.1 Object Recognition

Object recognition is performed only on the frames at which the chef picks up an object or places it, that is provided in KUSK Object Dataset (Hashimoto et al., 2016) with the object regions. Note that the provided frames and regions can contain plural objects because the method used in (Hashimoto et al., 2016) is based on background subtraction. To divide the detected region into object-wise regions, we adopted Faster R-CNN

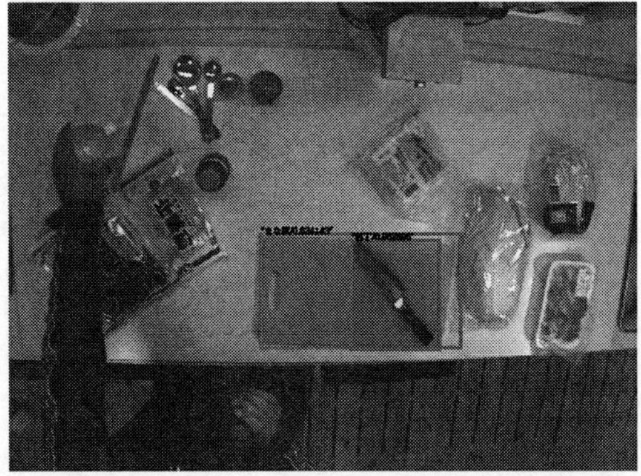

Figure 3: An example of object recognition by Faster R-CNN.

(Ren et al., 2015). This neural network outputs identified object region as a rectangular area while recognizing its category (Figure 2 A). It also provides confidence as a probability. An example of visualization of object recognition is shown in Figure 3, where a cutting board and a knife are in the region detected by (Hashimoto et al., 2016) .

We utilized Faster R-CNN's ability of object region identification to suppress another type of false detection. The regions provided in (Hashimoto et al., 2016) contains objects that are moved only slightly by coming in contact with the hands. Such objects should not be related to the procedure. To suppress such detection but spot only objects obviously related to the procedure, we compare the location of object-wise regions before and after the contact, and ignore object regions if they have the same object name and have a certain score in Jaccard index, which is general method to measure the size of intersection of two regions. After the test of region intersection, only the objects with an obvious location change are regarded as procedure-related. This module passes only procedure-related objects to the second module. Note also that we discarded objects whose name is not listed in x-NEs before passing them to the second module.

Hereafter, we only focus the frames with the procedure-related objects listed in x-NEs, and describe the sequence of such frames as follows:

$$\boldsymbol{f} = f_1,\ f_2,\ \ldots,\ f_{|\boldsymbol{f}|}, \tag{1}$$

where f_i is the i-th frame and $|\boldsymbol{f}|$ is the length of the sequence.

4.2 Recipe Named Entity Recognition

We use the named entity recognizer (Sasada et al., 2015) to the object in the i-th frame f_i (Figure 2 B). Let $\mathcal{E}_i$ be the object set whose tags are F or T in f_i. Then, we denote the number of elements in this set as $|\mathcal{E}_i|$. The j-th r-NE of $\mathcal{E}_i$ is denoted as e_i^j. Then $P(e_i^j|f_i)$ denotes the conditional probability in which the element e_i^j (a food or a tool) is estimated to exist in the frame f_i.

4.3 Recipe Named Entity Sequence

Let $\boldsymbol{f}_i^{i+(l-1)} = f_i, f_{i+1}, ..., f_{i+(l-1)}$ be a substring, of length l, of $\boldsymbol{f}$ that corresponds to a single recipe sentence. A frame f_i may contain some r-NEs $\mathcal{E}_i$. Then a sequence of r-NEs contained in $\boldsymbol{f}_i^{i+(l-1)}$ can be expressed by $e \in \mathcal{E}_i \times \mathcal{E}_{i+1} \times \ldots \times \mathcal{E}_{i+(l-1)}$. Note that the number of all the possible sequences is $\prod_{k=i}^{i+(l-1)} |\mathcal{E}_k|$. For example in Figure 2, e is (cutting board/T, meat/F) or (knife/T, meat/F).

In addition, in order to treat a sequence as a set, we introduce the following notation:

$$\{e\} = \{e_k^{j_k} | i \le k \le i + (l - 1)\}. \tag{2}$$

Note that j_k depends on k.

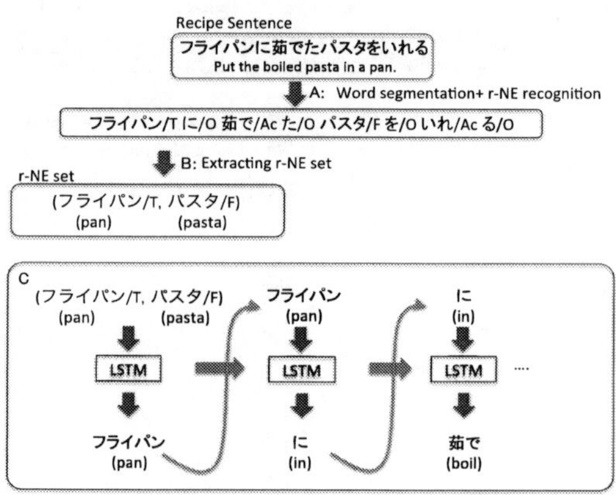

Figure 4: LSTM language model training. This model generates a sentence given an r-NE set.

Considering the likelihood of object recognition and the likelihood of a combination of r-NEs included in the sequence, we set the likelihood $P(e)$ that e appears as follows:

$$P(e) = \overline{P}(e) \times P(\{e\})^{-l}, \tag{3}$$

where $\overline{P}(e)$ is the average of the probability of the result of object recognition:

$$\overline{P}(e) = \frac{1}{l} \sum_{k=i}^{i+(l-1)} P(e_k^{j_k}|f_k). \tag{4}$$

This value indicates the likelihood of object recognition. Also $P(\{e\})^{-l}$ is the likelihood of a combination of r-NEs determined from the frequency of a sentence in which all the elements of $\{e\}$ appear in the corpus.

$$P(\{e\}) = \left(\frac{count(\{e\})}{C}\right), \tag{5}$$

where C is the number of sentences in the recipe corpus and $count(\{e\})$ is the frequency of sentences in which all the elements of $\{e\}$ appear at the same time. Thus, this value indicates the likelihood of the r-NE combination. In addition as the number of elements in the r-NE set increases, the frequency decreases. This is the reason why we introduce $P(\{e\})^{-l}$ considering the sequence length l.

4.4 Recipe Sentence Candidate Generation

For each partial frame sequence, we generate the most likely sentence and its score without referring to the neighboring sentences. Some of these sentences may, however, be discarded in the next step. Thus we call it a recipe sentence candidate. The input to this process is the r-NE sequence and the scores of the r-NEs. And the output is the recipe sentence candidate that maximizes the score for the given partial frame sequence (Figure 2 D).

For the sentence candidate generation we use an LSTM language model. It outputs a sentence and its likelihood. Different from the ordinary LSTM, it takes a set of r-NEs as the input, but not a sequence. In addition, it is trained on the corpus in which r-NEs are recognized and replaced with r-NE tags as summarized in Figure 4. The first step of its training is preprocessing, in which we conduct word segmentation (Neubig et al., 2011) (not necessary for English or some other languages) and r-NE recognition (Sasada et al., 2015) for each recipe sentence in the recipe corpus (Figure 4 A). Then we filter out sentences containing r-NEs other than Ac, F and T and delete Ac tags for the reasons below:

- We cannot get information about r-NEs other than F and T by the object recognition module.

- A predicate denoting an action (Ac) is necessary for a complete sentence.

Putting it in another way, our method guesses a suitable predicate (verb) from the objects (foods and/or tools) and the corpus. From each of the resultant sentences, we generate a sentence in which F and T are replaced with tags and the set of the r-NEs contained in it (Figure 4 B). Finally we train the LSTM language model on the corpus. The LSTM can map a set of r-NEs to a recipe sentence with its likelihood (Figure 4 C).

As the likelihood of this module, our method returns the following score:

$$Score(e) = P_{\text{LSTM}}(r_{max}(e)|e) \times P(e),$$

where $r(e)$ is the sentence generated by the LSTM language model given e as the input. $P_{\text{LSTM}}(r(e)|e)$ is the generation probability of $r(e)$. $r_{max}(e)$ is the sentence that maximizes $P_{\text{LSTM}}(r(e)|e)$ with the beam search decoder given e.

$$r_{max}(e) = \underset{r(e) \in \mathcal{R}(e)}{\text{argmax}} \; P_{\text{LSTM}}(r(e)|e),$$

where $\mathcal{R}(e)$ is a set of sentences that can be generated by beam search when e is the input and $r(e)$

is the sentence corresponding to it. The generation probability of a sentence is calculated by the following formula:

$$P_{\text{LSTM}}(r(e)|e) = \prod_{k=1}^{N_d} P(d_k|d_1, d_2, ..., d_{k-1}; e),$$

where $r(e) = d_1, d_2, ..., d_{N_d}$ is a word string and N_d is the length of the word string. And $P(d_k|d_1, d_2, ..., d_{k-1}; e)$ denotes the generation probability of the k-th word d_k, when the input is e. The sentence is generated by the LSTM language model by beam search. The sentence is, however, aborted when the word length exceeds 20 or the terminal symbol appears. $P(e)$ is introduced to reflect the likelihood that the r-NE sequences e appear (see Equation (3)).

Calculating the above scores for all the possible e of a partial frame sequence, we define e_{max} as the r-NE sequences which maximize the score. At this stage, the generated sentence is no more than a recipe sentence candidate $r_{max}(e_{max})$, whose score is $Score(e_{max})$. When the scores earned by partial frame sequences are all 0, no recipe sentence candidate is generated.

4.5 Generating Recipe

As we see above, a set of recipe sentence candidates is generated from the partial frame sequences. The frame sequence is divided into partial sequences so that the overall score of the division, which is the sum of the $Score(e)$ in each partial sequence, is maximized (Figure 2 E). The partial sequences cover the entire video, thus the corresponding sentences, sequences of $r(e)$, form a complete recipe.

Since it is almost impossible for one chef to perform two operations in parallel, the corresponding partial frame sequences of the recipe sentence candidates must not overlap. In addition, in order to prevent the same recipe sentence from appearing more than once, the score of the recipe sentence candidate which has appeared once in the recipe is set to be 0. Under this condition, the score of a recipe sentence candidate can change. Although it should be totally searched for score maximization, we use the Viterbi algorithm for the calculation, because the change of the score is limited at the time of generation of the same sentence and it is considered that it does not occur so much.

By calculating the path of the recipe sentence candidate sequence for increasing the score, the

Table 2: The BLEU scores.

Configuration	BLEU			
	$N=1$	$N=2$	$N=3$	$N=4$
w/o $P(\{e\})^{-l}$	22.73	13.13	7.48	4.11
with $P(\{e\})^{-l}$	26.73	15.42	9.09	**5.50**

generated recipe sentence sequence is output as a recipe. The higher the score, the more recipe-like the sentences are.

5 Experiments and Evaluation

In this section we evaluate our method experimentally. We first describe the settings of the experiments, then report the experimental results, and finally evaluate our method. [2]

5.1 Experimental Setting

We used the following dataset to train and evaluate our model.

5.1.1 Test Dataset

KUSK Dataset   This dataset contains 20 recipes and corresponding cooking videos.

5.1.2 Train Dataset

KUSK Object Dataset   This dataset contains 180 categories of objects in total, which comprise ingredients, cooking tools, and others (bottle cap, dish cloth, and so on), observed in cooking videos in KUSK Dataset. Since all videos are recorded at the same kitchen, exactly the same cooking tools appear through all videos, including ones in the test set. More detailed information and examples are available in (Hashimoto et al., 2016).

Cookpad NII corpus   This corpus contains 1720000 recipes collected from cookpad website. 187700 sentences are extracted for training.

Flow Graph Corpus   This corpus contains randomly chosen 208 recipes (867 sentences) from Cookpad NII corpus. The text is annotated with the r-NE tags. (Mori et al., 2014).

5.1.3 Training Faster-RNN and Named Entity Recognizer

As the first module, an object recognizer for frames, we use Faster R-CNN(Ren et al., 2015).

We fine-tuned Faster R-CNN with KUSK Object Dataset. The dataset contains 180 categories in total, but some categories, for example dish clothes or bottle caps, will not appear in recipe texts. Thus we ignored such categories and used 95 categories to fine-tune the Faster R-CNN model, which is done in the manner of leave-one-video-out.

Because this module is a pre-process of the second module, to achieve higher recall rather than a higher precision, we used any detection proposals from Faster R-CNN with more than 0.01% in confidence score, and set the intersection threshold of Jaccard Index 0.5. This setting earned 78.8% of recall and 22.3% of the precision on average through the 95 categories.

For the second module we trained an NE recognizer PWNER (Sasada et al., 2015), which is based on support vector machines and Viterbi best path search, with Flow Graph Corpus. Its accuracy is about 90% in F-measure (Mori et al., 2014).

5.1.4 Recipe Named Entity Sequence and Recipe Sentence Candidate Generation

When generating the r-NE sequences, we should specify the sequence length l. Most of the sentences in our recipe corpus contain no more than three r-NEs of F or T[3]. So we set the length of frame sequences as $l = 1 \sim 3$.

The training data of the LSTM language model consists of 11,705 sentences and the number of r-NE tokens is 4,025. These training data are a set of recipe sentences extracted so as to satisfy the following conditions:

- The total number of F and T is between 1 and 3,

- Each sentence does not contain any r-NE other than Ac, F, and T (see Section 4.4).

As a result the LSTM language model has a tendency not to generate sentences containing 4 or more r-NEs.

The setting of the LSTM language model training is as follows. The epoch number is 100, the batch size is 100, and the number of units of LSTM is 1,000. The objective function is the softmax cross entropy and the optimization algorithm is Adam (Kingma and Ba, 2014). The beam width for recipe sentence candidate generation is set to be 1.

[2]The code used in our experiment is available on our website. http://www.ar. media.kyoto-u.ac.jp/member/hayato/ procedural-text-generation/

[3]The percentage is slightly less than 75%.

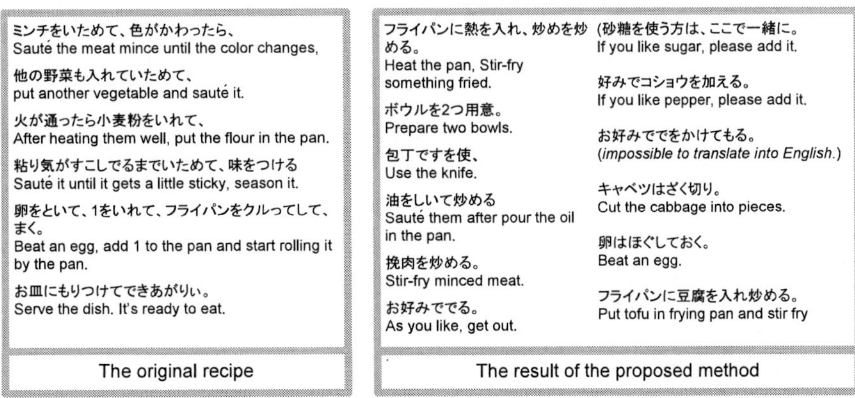

Figure 5: The original recipe for a cooking video and the generated recipe by the proposed method.

5.1.5 Evaluation Metrics

We generated a recipe for each of 16 cooking videos corresponding to seven recipes in KUSK Dataset. As we mentioned in Section 3 they are excluded from the training data. In order to investigate the effectiveness of $P(\{e\})^{-l}$, we compared the results of the models with and without it.

The evaluation metrics is BLEU ($N = 1 \sim 4$) (Papineni et al., 2002) taking the original human-written recipes as the reference. The cooking actions in the KUSK Dataset video part were performed with following these recipes. Unlike BLEU calculation in MT, we treat the entire recipe, a sequence of sentences, as the unit instead of a single sentence. This is because one can describe the same actions in various ways with different number of sentences. An example pair is "cut onions and potatoes." and "cut onions. then cut potatoes."

5.2 Results and Discussion

Since our task is quite novel and existing end-to-end video captioning methods do not obviously work because of lack of large training data, there is no direct baseline. Thus we discuss absolute BLEU scores of some settings and examples of generated sentences.

Table 2 shows the BLEU scores. The absolute BLEU values (ex. 5.50 for $N = 4$) are much higher than the results of cinema caption generation (Kaufman et al., 2016) (0.8 for $N = 4$), which is regarded as one of the state-of-the-arts of text generation for videos longer than video clips. This result is worth noting considering that cooking videos are raw recording of execution and not edited nor divided into scenes, while input of cinema caption generation is an *edited* video and scene segmentation is available. Our higher accuracy may be due to a large amount of text data in the target domain.

We then examined generated recipes and the original recipes. Figure 5 presents a recipe example actually generated by the proposed method and its original recipe used in the cooking video recording. We see that there are suitable sentences such as "挽肉を炒める。" ("Stir-fry minced meat."), "卵はほぐしておく。" ("Beat an egg.") in the result. These sentences correspond to "ミンチをいためて、色がかわったら、" ("Saute the meat mince until the color changes") and "卵をといて、" ("Beat an egg,") in the original recipe. On the other hand, the result contains some unnecessary sentences. For example, in the third line of the generation result, "包丁ですを使" ("Use the knife is."). The sentence itself is semantically correct, but is not suitable for a recipe (and grammatically wrong). This is actually the difference from the existing video clip description research.

Even if the object recognition functions perfectly, the sentence generation part has to ignore some objects focusing only on the actions to be taken. Such errors can be alleviated by considering the recipe structure such as relations of r-NEs. There are also ungrammatical sentences such as "お好みででを" ("pour over it that if if you like and serve") in the result. This sort of errors are caused by the LSTM language model. We may need a language model incorporating grammatical structures (Chelba and Jelinek, 2000).

Despite the errors mentioned above, our method

solves the novel problem, procedural text generation from execution video in a certain accuracy. As it is clear from the explanation of our method, it has the correspondence between the sentence and the video frame region. Thus one can use our method for various practical multimedia applications, such as multimedia document generation from an execution video.

6 Conclusion

In this paper, we have proposed a novel task of procedural text generation from an execution video and the first attempt at solving it. Contrary to the ordinary video captioning task, it requires some kind of abstraction, that is, selecting objects to be mentioned. In addition, no existing end-to-end method is applicable due to the limited amount of video/text pairs for training. Instead, our method decomposes the problem into object recognition and sentence generation. Then we train the models for them independently with maximum available resources for each one. Finally we search for the best procedural text referring to them at once. For evaluation, we conduct recipe generation from cooking videos as an example case. The quality was as good as or better than the state-of-the-art scenario description for cinemas. Thus we can say that our method is promising to solve this novel task. We also gave some error analyses to allow further improvements in solutions of this difficult but interesting task.

Acknowledgement

In this paper, we used recipe data provided by Cookpad and the National Institute of Informatics. The work is supported by JSPS Grants-in-Aid for Scientific Research Grant Number 26280084.

References

Ciprian Chelba and Frederick Jelinek. 2000. Structured language modeling. *Computer Speech and Language* 14:283–332.

David L Chen and William B Dolan. 2011. Collecting highly parallel data for paraphrase evaluation. In *Proceedings of the 49th Annual Meeting of the Association for Computational Linguistics: Human Language Technologies-Volume 1*. Association for Computational Linguistics, pages 190–200.

Jeffrey Donahue, Lisa Anne Hendricks, Sergio Guadarrama, Marcus Rohrbach, Subhashini Venugopalan, Kate Saenko, and Trevor Darrell. 2015. Long-term recurrent convolutional networks for visual recognition and description. In *Proceedings of the IEEE conference on computer vision and pattern recognition*. pages 2625–2634.

Sergio Guadarrama, Niveda Krishnamoorthy, Girish Malkarnenkar, Subhashini Venugopalan, Raymond Mooney, Trevor Darrell, and Kate Saenko. 2013. Youtube2text: Recognizing and describing arbitrary activities using semantic hierarchies and zero-shot recognition. In *Proceedings of the 14th International Conference on Computer Vision*. Sydney, Australia, pages 2712–2719.

Zhao Guo, Lianli Gao, Jingkuan Song, Xing Xu, Jie Shao, and Heng Tao Shen. 2016. Attention-based lstm with semantic consistency for videos captioning. In *Proceedings of the 2016 ACM on Multimedia Conference*. ACM, pages 357–361.

Atsushi Hashimoto, Shinsuke Mori, Masaaki Iiyama, and Michihiko Minoh. 2016. Kusk object dataset: Recording access to objects in food preparation. In *Proc. of IEEE International Conference on Multimedia and Expo Workshops*. IEEE.

Atsushi Hashimoto, Sasada Tetsuro, Yoko Yamakata, Shinsuke Mori, and Michihiko Minoh. 2014. KUSK Dataset: Toward a direct understanding of recipe text and human cooking activity. In *Workshop on Smart Technology for Cooking and Eating Activities*. pages 583–588.

Justin Johnson, Andrej Karpathy, and Li Fei-Fei. 2016. Densecap: Fully convolutional localization networks for dense captioning. In *Proceedings of the IEEE Conference on Computer Vision and Pattern Recognition*. pages 4565–4574.

Andrej Karpathy and Li Fei-Fei. 2015. Deep visual-semantic alignments for generating image descriptions. In *Proceedings of the IEEE Conference on Computer Vision and Pattern Recognition*. pages 3128–3137.

Dotan Kaufman, Gil Levi, Tal Hassner, and Lior Wolf. 2016. Temporal tessellation for video annotation and summarization. *arXiv preprint arXiv:1612.06950*.

Diederik Kingma and Jimmy Ba. 2014. Adam: A method for stochastic optimization. *arXiv preprint arXiv:1412.6980*.

Natsuda Laokulrat, Sang Phan, Noriki Nishida, Raphael Shu, Yo Ehara, Naoaki Okazaki, Yusuke Miyao, and Hideki Nakayama. 2016. Generating video description using sequence-to-sequence model with temporal attention.

Guang Li, Shubo Ma, and Yahong Han. 2015. Summarization-based video caption via deep neural networks. In *Proceedings of the 23rd ACM international conference on Multimedia*. ACM, pages 1191–1194.

Tsung-Yi Lin, Michael Maire, Serge Belongie, James Hays, Pietro Perona, Deva Ramanan, Piotr Dollár, and C Lawrence Zitnick. 2014. Microsoft coco: Common objects in context. In *European Conference on Computer Vision*. Springer, pages 740–755.

Shinsuke Mori, Hirokuni Maeta, Yoko Yamakata, and Tetsuro Sasada. 2014. Flow graph corpus from recipe texts. In *Proceedings of the Ninth International Conference on Language Resources and Evaluation*.

Graham Neubig, Yosuke Nakata, and Shinsuke Mori. 2011. Pointwise prediction for robust, adaptable japanese morphological analysis. pages 529–533.

Kishore Papineni, Salim Roukos, Todd Ward, and Wei-Jing Zhu. 2002. Bleu: a method for automatic evaluation of machine translation. In *Proceedings of the 40th annual meeting on association for computational linguistics*. Association for Computational Linguistics, pages 311–318.

Shaoqing Ren, Kaiming He, Ross Girshick, and Jian Sun. 2015. Faster r-cnn: Towards real-time object detection with region proposal networks. In *Advances in neural information processing systems*. pages 91–99.

Anna Rohrbach, Marcus Rohrbach, Niket Tandon, and Bernt Schiele. 2015. A dataset for movie description. In *Proceedings of the IEEE Conference on Computer Vision and Pattern Recognition*.

Marcus Rohrbach, Wei Qiu, Ivan Titov, Stefan Thater, Manfred Pinkal, and Bernt Schiele. 2013. Translating video content to natural language descriptions. In *Proceedings of the IEEE International Conference on Computer Vision*. pages 433–440.

Tetsuro Sasada, Shinsuke Mori, Tatsuya Kawahara, and Yoko Yamakata. 2015. Named entity recognizer trainable from partially annotated data. In *Proceedings of the Eleventh International Conference Pacific Association for Computational Linguistics. 2015.*. ACM, pages 10–17.

Rakshith Shetty and Jorma Laaksonen. 2016. Frame- and segment-level features and candidate pool evaluation for video caption generation. In *Proceedings of the 2016 ACM on Multimedia Conference*. ACM, pages 1073–1076.

Ilya Sutskever, Oriol Vinyals, and Quoc V Le. 2014. Sequence to sequence learning with neural networks. In *Advances in neural information processing systems*. pages 3104–3112.

Atousa Torabi, Christopher Pal, Hugo Larochelle, and Aaron Courville. 2015. Using descriptive video services to create a large data source for video annotation research. *arXiv preprint arXiv:1503.01070*.

Subhashini Venugopalan, Marcus Rohrbach, Jeffrey Donahue, Raymond Mooney, Trevor Darrell, and Kate Saenko. 2015. Sequence to sequence-video to text. In *Proceedings of the IEEE International Conference on Computer Vision*. pages 4534–4542.

Kelvin Xu, Jimmy Ba, Ryan Kiros, Kyunghyun Cho, Aaron C Courville, Ruslan Salakhutdinov, Richard S Zemel, and Yoshua Bengio. 2015. Show, attend and tell: Neural image caption generation with visual attention. In *ICML*. volume 14, pages 77–81.

Yezhou Yang, Ching Lik Teo, Hal Daumé III, and Yiannis Aloimonos. 2011. Corpus-guided sentence generation of natural images. In *Proceedings of the Conference on Empirical Methods in Natural Language Processing*. Association for Computational Linguistics, pages 444–454.

Text Sentiment Analysis based on Fusion of Structural Information and Serialization Information

Ling Gan and **Houyu Gong**

College of Computer Science and Tecnology

Chongqing University of Posts and Telecommunications

Chongqing 400065, China

`ganling@cqupt.edu.cn,gonghouyu_b103@163.com`

Abstract

Tree-structured Long Short-Term Memory (Tree-LSTM) has been proved to be an effective method in the sentiment analysis task. It extracts structural information on text, and uses Long Short-Term Memory (LSTM) cell to prevent gradient vanish. However, though combining the LSTM cell, it is still a kind of model that extracts the structural information and almost not extracts serialization information. In this paper, we propose three new models in order to combine those two kinds of information: the structural information generated by the Constituency Tree-LSTM and the serialization information generated by Long-Short Term Memory neural network. Our experiments show that combining those two kinds of information can give contributes to the performance of the sentiment analysis task compared with the single Constituency Tree-LSTM model and the LSTM model.

1 Introduction

Text sentiment analysis, namely Opinion mining, is an important research direction in the field of Natural Language Processing (NLP). It aims to extract the author's subjective information from text and provide useful values for us. In recent years, there were more and more researchers paying attention to the study of text sentiment analysis.

Up to date, a variety of methods have been developed for improving the performance of sentiment analysis models. The distributed representation for words has been proposed in 2003 (Bengio et al., 2003). This model trained by two kinds of three-layer neural networks generates vectors to represent words. Glove, which is

the improvement of the model mentioned above, has been proposed in 2014 (Pennington et al., 2014). The improved representation of words gives contribution to the research of NLP tasks including sentiment analysis, and are used as the input of sentiment analysis models. There are several kinds of deep learning methods to extract text features. Sequential models such as Recurrent Neural Network (Schmidhuber, 1990), Bidirectional Recurrent Neural Networks (Member et al., 1997), Long Short-Term Memory (Hochreiter and Schmidhuber, 2012) and Gated Recurrent Unit (Cho et al., 2014) mainly extract serialization information of text. Multi-layer sequential models have also been proposed for sentiment analysis (Wang et al., 2016)(Tang et al., 2015)(He et al., 2016)(Yang et al., 2016). Tree-structured models extract structural information. The first tree-structured model named Recursive Neural Network has been proposed in 2012 (Socher et al., 2012b), followed by more models such as Matrix-Vector Recursive Neural Network (Socher et al., 2012a) and Recursive Neural Tensor Network (Socher et al., 2013). In 2015, Tree-structured Long Short-Term Memory Neural Network (Tree-LSTM), which combines the LSTM cell and tree-structured models, has been proposed and it outperforms the traditional LSTM and tree-structured neural networks (Le and Zuidema, 2015)(Tai et al., 2015)(Zhu et al., 2015). Different from the traditional tree-structured model, Tree-LSTM uses the LSTM cell to control the information from bottom to top so that it can effectively prevent the vanishing gradient problem.

As mentioned above, though combining the LSTM cell, Tree-LSTM does not really combine the structural information and serialization information. In this paper, we introduce three models: Tree-Composition LSTM (TC-LSTM), Leaf-Tree LSTM (LT-LSTM) and Leaf-Composition-Tree L-

Proceedings of the The 8th International Joint Conference on Natural Language Processing, pages 336–341,
Taipei, Taiwan, November 27 – December 1, 2017 ©2017 AFNLP

STM (LCT-LSTM). Those models combine those two kinds of information and experiments show that they perform better than the traditional LSTM and the Constituency Tree-LSTM model.

The remainder of this paper is organized as follows: Section 2 introduces the LSTM and Tree-LSTM model which are related to our work. Section 3 introduces the models proposed in this paper. Experimental results are shown in Section 4 and in Section 5 we give the conclusions and future work.

2 Background

2.1 Long Short-Term Memory

Recurrent Neural Network (RNN) (Schmidhuber, 1990) encodes text information according to time. Giving a sentence, its words are encoded by the model in chronological order. For example, x_t represents the vector of input word at time step t, the hidden unit of time step t can be calculated as follows:

$$h_t = tanh(Wx_t + Uh_{t-1} + b). \qquad (1)$$

h_t represents the hidden layer at time step t, h_{t-1} represents the hidden state at time step $t - 1$, W is the weight matrix of the input layer, U is the weight matrix between h_{t-1} and h_t, b represents the bias and $tanh$ is the activation function which can normalize output information:

$$tanh(x) = \frac{sinh(x)}{cosh(x)} = \frac{e^x - e^{-x}}{e^x + e^{-x}}. \qquad (2)$$

At each time step, the hidden layer produces an output layer:

$$o_t = softmax(Vh_t + b). \qquad (3)$$

Usually, the output of the final time step can be used to represent the feature of a sentence. Then, after forward propagation, the weights of model are trained by the backward propagation. Traditional RNN model has the problem of gradient vanish. Long Short-Term Memory (LSTM) (Hochreiter and Schmidhuber, 2012) Neural Network has effectively solved the problem. The model has four gates which help to selectively forget or remember information. A memory cell has also been added to memory information transmitted over time steps. The information calculated by an LSTM unit can be shown as follows (Tai et al., 2015):

$$i_t = \sigma(W^{(i)}x_t + U^i h_{t-1} + b^i), \qquad (4)$$

$$f_t = \sigma(W^{(f)}x_t + U^f h_{t-1} + b^f), \qquad (5)$$

$$o_t = \sigma(W^{(o)}x_t + U^o h_{t-1} + b^o), \qquad (6)$$

$$u_t = tanh(W^{(u)}x_t + U^u h_{t-1} + b^u), \qquad (7)$$

$$c_t = i_t * u_t + f_t * c_{t-1}, \qquad (8)$$

$$h_t = o_t * tanh(c_t). \qquad (9)$$

Here, i_t, f_t, u_t, o_t denote the four gates, c_t is the memory cell, $*$ represents element-wise multiplication. Intuitively, input gate (i_t) and update gate (u_t) denote how much the memory cell update information, forget gate (f_t) determines how much the memory cell forget history information and output gate (o_t) controls how much the hidden unit get information from the cell. σ represents the sigmoid function. The weights of different layers are different but they are shared at each time step in the same layer.

2.2 Tree-LSTM

Dependency Tree-LSTM and Constituency Tree-LSTM are two types of Tree-LSTM structures. We discuss the latter because it achieves a better performance in the sentiment analysis task (Tai et al., 2015). Constituency Tree-LSTM includes three types of layers. Input layer includes the leaf nodes, it consists of the words in the sentence, each word is represented by a vector. Composition layer acts as the hidden layer which composes the information flowing from the leaf nodes to the root node. Each composition unit can be seen as the structural feature of its leaf nodes. The final composition node (root node) represents the structural feature of the whole sentence, it is the input of output layer. LSTM cell is used to control the information flowed bottom-up. Different from the cell in sequential models, the hidden information of a composition node comes from their two child nodes:

$$i_j = \sigma(W^{(i)}x_j + \sum_{l=1}^{N} U_l^{(i)} h_{jl} + b^{(i)}), \qquad (10)$$

$$f_{jk} = \sigma(W^{(f)}x_j + \sum_{l=1}^{N} U_{kl}^{(f)} h_{jl} + b^{(f)}), \qquad (11)$$

$$o_j = \sigma(W^{(o)}x_j + \sum_{l=1}^{N} U_l^{(o)} h_{jl} + b^{(o)}), \qquad (12)$$

$$u_j = tanh(W^{(u)}x_j + \sum_{l=1}^{N} U_l^{(u)}h_{jl} + b^{(u)}), \quad (13)$$

$$c_j = i_j * u_j + \sum_{l=1}^{N} f_{jl} * c_{jl}, \quad (14)$$

$$h_j = o_j * tanh(c_j). \quad (15)$$

It is worth noting that, in the input layer, the information composing the gates only include the input words (x_j) but do not have hidden information (h_{jl}). In the composition layer and output layer, only hidden information from two sub nodes participates in the construction of gates. The structure of Constituency Tree-LSTM model is shown in Figure 1.

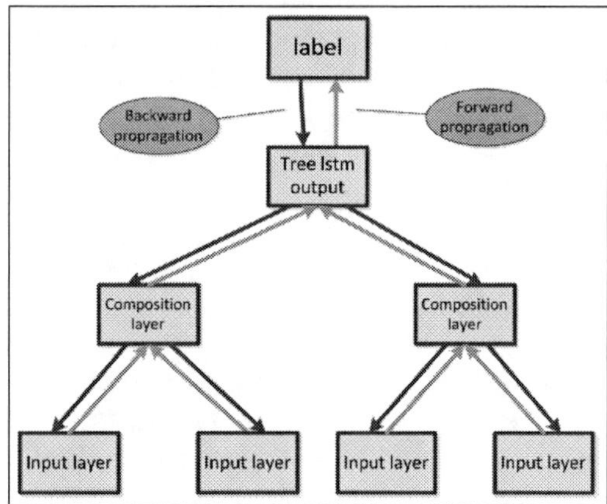

Figure 1: Constituency Tree-LSTM model. The upward arrows represent the direction of forward propagation, the downward arrows represent the direction of the backward propagation.

3 Our model

In this section, we discuss three new models which combine the structural information generated by tree-structured model (Constituency Tree-LSTM) and serialization information generated by sequential model (LSTM).

3.1 TC-LSTM

Constituency Tree-LSTM uses composition node at the root of the tree to represent the feature of sentence. We propose a new model named Tree-Composition LSTM (TC-LSTM) which generates a new feature taking all the leaf nodes, composition nodes and their sequential information into account. Firstly, we use postorder traversal to get all the nodes in the tree, and those nodes are treated as a sequence. The sequence contains not only the words in the sentence, but also the structural information in their parent composition nodes. Then we put the sequence into LSTM model for training, thus obtaining the serialization information of those hidden nodes with structural information. It is worth noting that, though sharing the same hidden nodes, in our first proposed model, the weights of the original Tree-LSTM module and the new added LSTM module are trained independently. The input word vectors firstly perform forward propagation on the Tree-LSTM, and then, the sequence mentioned above is obtained. Then the forward propagation of the sequence is performed on the LSTM model. The output error and gradient of the two modules are obtained through the training label separately. Finally, the backward propagation performs independently of each other. The gradients of back propagation updating the word vectors of input layer only flows from Tree-LSTM module.

TC-LSTM model is shown in Figure 2. After training, we only use the output of LSTM module to test on test data in order to verify the performance of sequential information extracted from tree-structured model.

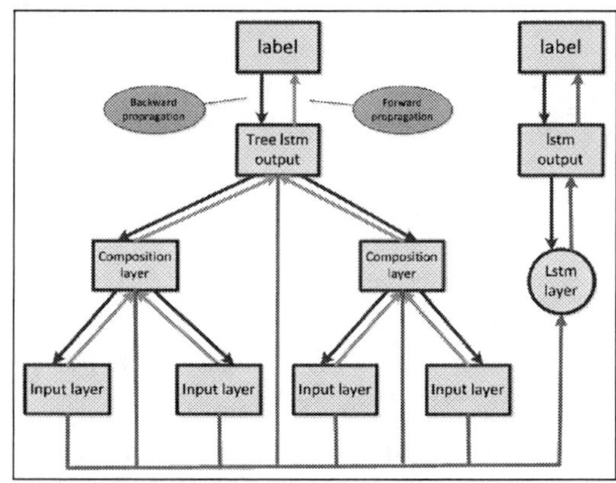

Figure 2: TC-LSTM model. New LSTM module is added to the original Tree-LSTM model. They shared the same hidden nodes but trained separately. Only the output of LSTM module is used to do the prediction.

3.2 LT-LSTM

We propose the Leaf-Tree LSTM (LT-LSTM) model to give a combination of the structural information and sequential information of a sentence. Similar to TC-LSTM, this model has two modules but it only has one output. The first module is the same to Tree-LSTM, and the second module is the LSTM module which takes the leaf nodes of the tree, namely only the words of a sentence as input. During the forward propagation, we add the output of two modules and take the result as the output of the whole model. Gradient of the whole model is generated by the output, and then, assigned to the output of two modules for their backward propagation. Figure 3 shows the structure of the LT-LSTM model.

The output represents the combination of those two kinds of information: structural information and serialization information. Correspondingly, The gradient of the output layer contains the error information of the Tree-LSTM module and LSTM module. Letting the gradient propagate top-down through those two modules can make them learn from each other, thus having the chance to make the comprehensive performance of the whole model better.

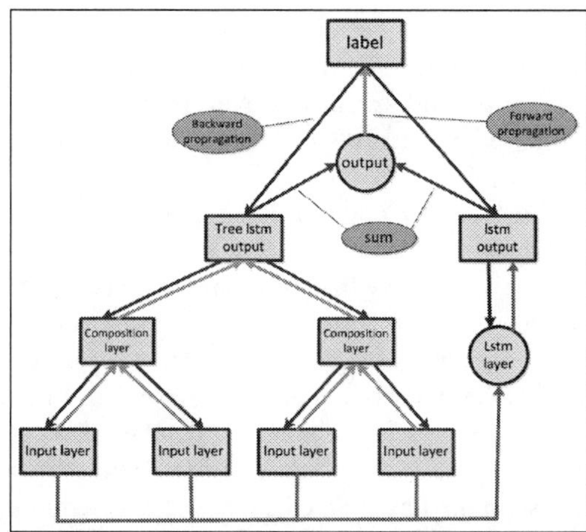

Figure 3: LT-LSTM model. The new added LSTM model only takes the leaf nodes as input. The output represent the fusion of two kinds of information, and its gradient trains the whole model.

3.3 LCT-LSTM

The third model proposed by us is Leaf-Composition-Tree LSTM (LCT-LSTM).Different from the LT-LSTM and TC-LSTM, this model not only takes the composition nodes into consideration when building the LSTM layer, but also makes sum of the outputs of two modules mentioned above. That is, LCT-LSTM can be seen as the composition of TC-LSTM and LT-LSTM for

the reason of not only building the sequential feature for the composition nodes which contain the structural information, but also combining the sequential feature and the structural feature of the input sentence. The structure of LCT-LSTM is shown in Figure 4.

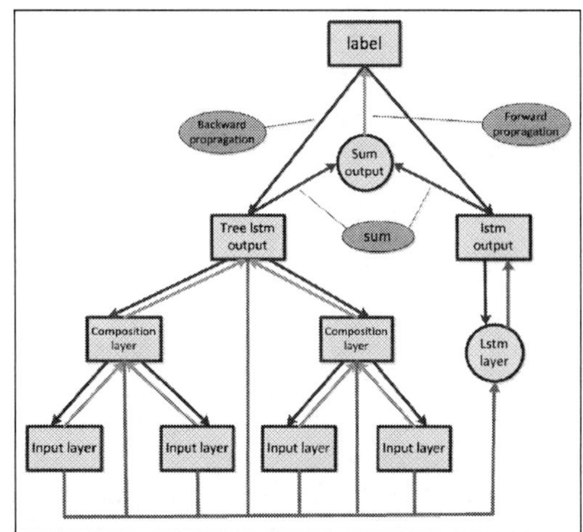

Figure 4: LCT-LSTM model.

4 Experiment

4.1 Dataset

We evaluate our proposed models on the Stanford Sentiment Tree Bank (SST) dataset, which contains sentences collected from movie reviews. The sentences in the dataset are split into three parts: 8544 for training, 1101 for development and 2210 for test. SST dataset has two classification tasks, one for fine-grained classification (five categories: very negative, negative, neutral, positive, and very positive) and the other for binary classification (two categories: negative and positive). The fine-grained subtask is evaluated on 8544/1101/2210 splits, and the binary classification is evaluated on 6920/872/1821 splits (there are fewer sentences because the neutral examples are excluded). Every sentence in the dataset is processed into tree structure, and every phrase (corresponding to the nodes in the tree) in the sentence is also labeled.

4.2 Hyperparameters and Training Details

We use the Glove vectors of 300 dimension (Pennington et al., 2014) to represent the input words. Word embeddings are fine-tuned during training and the learning rate used for the input layer is 0.1, for the other layers is 0.05. Adagrad

| | $\theta - all$ | | |
Models	F	B	$\theta - com$
LSTM	271955	271653	271200
Tree-LSTM	317555	317253	316800
TC-LSTM	499510	498906	498755
LT-LSTM	499510	498906	498755
LCT-LSTM	499510	498906	498755

Table 1: Parameters of models. $\theta - all$ represents the number of all the parameters in a model for F (fine-grained) tasks and B (binary tasks). $\theta - com$ represents parameters of composition layer. TC-LSTM, LT-LSTM and LCT-LSTM have the same number of parameters but they are trained in different ways.

Models	Fine-grained	Binary
LSTM (Tai et al., 2015)	46.4	84.9
Bi-LSTM (Tai et al., 2015)	49.1	87.5
RNN (Socher et al., 2013)	43.2	82.4
MV-RNN (Socher et al., 2013)	44.4	82.9
RNTN (Socher et al., 2013)	45.7	85.4
Constituency Tree-LSTM	50.7	88.0
TC-LSTM	49.6	88.2
LT-LSTM	**51.0**	88.5
LCT-LSTM	50.9	**88.7**

Table 2: The result of accuracy on the test set. Fine-grained represents the five-category classification and the Binary represents the positive/negative classification.

algorithm is used for training, the minibatch size set by us is 25, L2-regularization is used for each batch using the value of 1e-4, and the dropout for the output layer is 0.5.

The dimension of the input layer is the same as the word vector, and the hidden layer consisted of tree nodes has the dimension of 150. For the sequential module, both of the inputs and the hidden layer have the dimension of 150, the vectors of leaf nodes are projected into the 150 dimension when put into the sequential part. The numbers of parameters for all the models are shown in Table 1.

Every model is trained on the training set for 20 epochs, and tested on the development set for validation after finishing every epoch. We choose the parameters performing best among them to do the evaluation on the test set. For every model, we repeat experiments for 8 times and take the average of their results as the final performance of the model.

4.3 Baseline

The models proposed by us fuse the structural information and serialization information, so we compare those models with other models which do not combine those two kinds of information. We choose the Constituency Tree-LSTM, LSTM and BiLSTM mentioned in 2015 (Tai et al., 2015) as the baseline models, other tree-structure models such as RNN, MV-RNN and RNTN are also used for comparison.

4.4 Result

The results of experiment are shown in Table 2. We use accuracy to measure the performance of models.

From Table 2, we can see that on the whole, the models fusing structural and serialization information outperform other models which do not combine those two kinds of information. LT-LSTM achieves the best performance among our compared models in the fine-grained subtask and LCT-LSTM has the best performance in the binary subtask. TC-LSTM performs slightly better than Constituency Tree-LSTM in the binary subtask but worse than fine-grained subtask, but it still performs better than other single sequential models and tree-structured models.

We find that building the serialization feature for the nodes in tree-structure (TC-LSTM) does not really help the tree-structural models, but fusing the structural information and serialization information gives help to it. While fusing, adding the hidden nodes containing the structural information to the sequential model (LCT-LSTM) performs better in the binary subtask, but slightly worse in the fine-grained subtask compared to the model does not do so (LT-LSTM).

5 Conclusion

In this paper, we propose three new models in order to explore the effect of fusing the structural and sequential information. We evaluate our models on the Stanford Sentiment Tree Bank (SST). Experiments show that fusing the structural information and sequential information is an effective way to improve the performance of models proposed before. Future work can be focused on finding better ways to fusing those two features. Other models, such as the Bidirectional Long Short-Term Memory (BiLSTM), Bidirectional Tree-LSTM (Teng and Zhang, 2016) and TreeGRU (Kokkinos and Potamianos, 2017) can be used in place of the tree-structured model and the sequential model used in our models. Attention mechanism (Luong et al., 2015) can also be used to do some improvement.

References

Yoshua Bengio, Rjean Ducharme, Pascal Vincent, Christian Jauvin, K Jaz, Thomas Hofmann, Tomaso Poggio, and John Shawe-Taylor. 2003. Journal of machine learning research 3 (2003) 1137–1155 submitted 4/02; published 2/03 a neural probabilistic language model .

Kyunghyun Cho, Bart Van Merrienboer, Caglar Gulcehre, Dzmitry Bahdanau, Fethi Bougares, Holger Schwenk, and Yoshua Bengio. 2014. Learning phrase representations using rnn encoder-decoder for statistical machine translation. *Computer Science* .

Yunchao He, Liang Chih Yu, Chin Sheng Yang, K. Robert Lai, and Weiyi Liu. 2016. Yzu-nlp team at semeval-2016 task 4: Ordinal sentiment classification using a recurrent convolutional network. In *International Workshop on Semantic Evaluation*. pages 251–255.

Sepp Hochreiter and Schmidhuber. 2012. Long short-term memory. *Neural Computation* 9(8):1735–1780.

Filippos Kokkinos and Alexandros Potamianos. 2017. Structural attention neural networks for improved sentiment analysis .

Phong Le and Willem Zuidema. 2015. Compositional distributional semantics with long short term memory. *Computer Science* .

Minh Thang Luong, Hieu Pham, and Christopher D. Manning. 2015. Effective approaches to attention-based neural machine translation. *Computer Science* .

Member, IEEE, Mike Schuster, and Kuldip K. Paliwal. 1997. Bidirectional recurrent neural networks. *IEEE Transactions on Signal Processing* 45(11):2673–2681.

Jeffrey Pennington, Richard Socher, and Christopher Manning. 2014. Glove: Global vectors for word representation. In *Conference on Empirical Methods in Natural Language Processing*. pages 1532–1543.

Schmidhuber. 1990. Recurrent networks adjusted by adaptive critics .

R. Socher, A. Perelygin, J. Y. Wu, J. Chuang, C. D. Manning, A. Y. Ng, and C. Potts. 2013. Recursive deep models for semantic compositionality over a sentiment treebank .

Richard Socher, Brody Huval, Christopher D Manning, and Andrew Y Ng. 2012a. Semantic compositionality through recursive matrix-vector spaces. In *Joint Conference on Empirical Methods in Natural Language Processing and Computational Natural Language Learning*. pages 1201–1211.

Richard Socher, Chiung Yu Lin, Andrew Y. Ng, and Christopher D. Manning. 2012b. Parsing natural scenes and natural language with recursive neural networks. In *International Conference on Machine Learning, ICML 2011, Bellevue, Washington, Usa, June 28 - July*. pages 129–136.

Kai Sheng Tai, Richard Socher, and Christopher D. Manning. 2015. Improved semantic representations from tree-structured long short-term memory networks. *Computer Science* 5(1):: 36.

Duyu Tang, Bing Qin, and Ting Liu. 2015. Document modeling with gated recurrent neural network for sentiment classification. In *Conference on Empirical Methods in Natural Language Processing*. pages 1422–1432.

Zhiyang Teng and Yue Zhang. 2016. Bidirectional tree-structured lstm with head lexicalization .

Jin Wang, Liang Chih Yu, K. Robert Lai, and Xuejie Zhang. 2016. Dimensional sentiment analysis using a regional cnn-lstm model. In *Meeting of the Association for Computational Linguistics*. pages 225–230.

Zichao Yang, Diyi Yang, Chris Dyer, Xiaodong He, Alex Smola, and Eduard Hovy. 2016. Hierarchical attention networks for document classification. In *Conference of the North American Chapter of the Association for Computational Linguistics: Human Language Technologies*. pages 1480–1489.

Xiaodan Zhu, Parinaz Sobhani, and Hongyu Guo. 2015. Long short-term memory over tree structures .

Length, Interchangeability, and External Knowledge:
Observations from Predicting Argument Convincingness

Peter Potash, Robin Bhattacharya, Anna Rumshisky
Department of Computer Science
University of Massachusetts Lowell
{ppotash, rbhattac, arum}@cs.uml.edu

Abstract

In this work, we provide insight into three key aspects related to predicting argument convincingness. First, we explicitly display the power that text length possesses for predicting convincingness in an unsupervised setting. Second, we show that a bag-of-words embedding model posts state-of-the-art on a dataset of arguments annotated for convincingness, outperforming an SVM with numerous hand-crafted features as well as recurrent neural network models that attempt to capture semantic composition. Finally, we assess the feasibility of integrating external knowledge when predicting convincingness, as arguments are often more convincing when they contain abundant information and facts. We finish by analyzing the correlations between the various models we propose.

1 Introduction

Predicting argument convincingness has mostly been studied in relation to the overall quality of a persuasive essay (Attali and Burstein, 2004; Landauer, 2003; Shermis et al., 2010), with a recent focus specifically on predicting argument strength (Persing and Ng, 2015; Wachsmuth et al., 2016). Zhang et al. (2016) have also attempted to predict argument convincingness, in the form of predicting debate winners. Unfortunately, these are very rare argumentative formats that are seldom encountered in everyday life. In practice, at least at the moment, we tend to digest a large quantity of our information from social media and engage in a tremendous amount of interpersonal communication using it. Since, in social media, communications are roughly a single paragraph, analyzing

arguments in a persuasive essay or oxford-style debate is not applicable to our primary means of community engagement. Presenting an entire convincing argument within a single paragraph can be an invaluable skill in the modern world. This paper seeks to improve upon previous methodology for predicting argument convincingness.

Prompt: Is it better to have a lousy father or to be fatherless? **Stance:** It is better to have a lousy father.

Argument 1	Argument 2
It is better to have a lousy father because researchers at the McGill University have warned that growing up without a father can permanently change the structure of a child's brain and make him/her more aggressive and angry.	Having a lousy father is better because when a child does not have a father, it causes him/her to look for a father figure. During such searches, a child may end up getting sexual harassed or being emotionally exploited to various degrees.

Table 1: Example of an argument pair where Argument 1 is more convincing.

Habernal and Gurevych (2016b) have recently released a dataset of short, single-paragraph arguments annotated for convincingness, which we will refer to as UKPConvArg. For 16 issues, arguments with the *same* stance are compared with each other to determine, given a pair of arguments, which one is more convincing. Table 1 provides an example of an argument pair with arguments from the prompt 'Is it better to have a lousy father or to be fatherless'; and the stance: 'It is better to have a lousy father'. In this pair Argument 1 is chosen to be more convincing. Other such issues include: 'Does India have the potential to

Proceedings of the The 8th International Joint Conference on Natural Language Processing, pages 342–351,
Taipei, Taiwan, November 27 – December 1, 2017 ©2017 AFNLP

lead the world?', 'Which web browser is better, Internet Explorer or Mozilla Firefox?', and 'Should physical education be mandatory in schools'. In follow-up work, Habernal and Gurevych (2016a) examined the *reasoning* behind the annotations in their original corpus. That is, why arguments were selected as more convincing. Overwhelmingly, the reasons could be expressed by the following statement "Argument X has more details, information, facts or examples / more reasons / better reasoning / goes deeper / is more specific". Although Habernal and Gurevych (2016b) experimented with two promising models, the models were not intended to directly take into account the reasons why an argument could be more convincing, as expressed in the previous quotation. The primary task of the dataset is, given two arguments with the same stance toward a topic, determine which argument is more convincing – this corresponds to outputting a binary label. Most of our experiments focus on this task, as it was the annotation directive for annotating convincingness in Habernal and Gurevych (2016b). From the pairwise annotation, they also derived convincingness scores for individual arguments, which is posed as a regression task. We evaluate on this task in Section 3.1.

In our work, we improve upon the initial experiments of Habernal and Gurevych in 3 ways: (1) we offer heuristic-based methods that requiring no training or fitting of a model to data; (2) we explore modifications of the initial 'deep' model used by Habernal and Gurevych (2016a), which was a Bidirectional Long Short-Term Memory (BLSTM) network; (3) we test the feasibility of offering factually relevant knowledge in the form of Wikipedia articles related to the argument topics.

In terms of heuristics, we examine the effectiveness of Metric Entropy (ME) of text to predict convincingness, which is inspired by the notion that written English language is well-formed, as opposed to random. Specifically, high ME corresponds to high randomness. The second heuristic uses a similarity to Wikipedia articles, with the hypothesis that the Wikipedia articles can act as a factual support reference for the arguments. We also hypothesize that Wikipedia articles have the potential to grade the quality of the writing in the arguments, on the assumption that arguments that better match the writing in Wikipedia articles are more likely to exhibit the qualities that make an argument convincing. For all methods that use the presence of Wikipedia articles, we use several variations of a corpus to determine how well the methods leverage topic-specific articles, as opposed to randomly selected articles.

In terms of supervised techniques, we first follow previous approaches to classifying paired data that create separate learned representations of elements in a pair that are then concatenated for the final predictive model (Bowman et al., 2015; Mueller and Thyagarajan, 2016; Potash et al., 2016b). Specifically, we experiment with creating separate representations using either a BLSTM or summing individual token embeddings. We then propose modifications of the supervised models to leverage external data. The models grow with increasing complexity, approaching a form of Memory Network (Sukhbaatar et al., 2015) that computes a weighted sum of representations of Wikipedia articles.

Our experimental results reveal several important insights into how to approach predicting convincingness. We summarize our findings as follows: 1) Unsupervised text length is an extremely competitive baseline that performs on par with highly-engineered classifiers and deep learning models; 2) The current state-of-the-art approach treats tokens as interchangeable, bypassing the need to model compositionality; 3) Wikipedia articles can provide meaningful external knowledge, though, naive models have trouble dealing with the noise in a large corpus of documents, whereas a model that attends to the Wikipedia corpus is better equipped to handle the noise.

2   Related Work

Habernal and Gurevych (2016b) present two methods in their dataset paper: (1) an SVM with numerous hand-crafted features; (2) a BLSTM that only uses word embeddings as input. Aside from the original corpus authors, only one other work has tested on the UKPConvArg dataset. Chalaguine and Schulz (2017) use a feature-selection method to determine the raw feature representation that serves as input into a feed-forward neural network. The authors conduct a thorough ablation study of the performance of individual feature types. The authors' best model records an accuracy of .766, compared to .781 and .757 of Habernal and Gurevych's SVM and BLSTM, respectively. Although the authors make an effort to determine the influence of individual feature type, their work continues to use supervised methods, which obscures the pure predictive power of individual features/metrics.

There are few datasets annotated for the convincingness of arguments. Zhang et al. (2016) published a dataset of debate transcripts, annotated with audience polling that occurs before and after the debate. In terms of argumentation, the key distinction between this dataset and that of Habernal and Gurevych (2016b) is that in the debate dataset, the debate teams have *opposing* stances on a topic, whereas Habernal and Gurevych's dataset has labels for arguments with the same stance towards a topic. Persing and Ng (2015) constructed a corpus of persuasive essays annotated for the essays' argument strength, which is slightly different to other annotated persuasive essay corpora, which have more of a focus on overall writing quality.

NLP datasets involving the processing of text pairs have become more prevalent. Examples include predicting textual entailment (Marelli et al., 2014; Bowman et al., 2015), predicting semantic relatedness/similarity (Marelli et al., 2014; Agirre et al., 2016), and predicting humor (Potash et al., 2016b; Shahaf et al., 2015). These tasks present interesting challenges from a modeling perspective, as methods must allow for semantic comparison between the texts.

Although relatively rare in the argument mining community, leveraging external knowledge sources is ubiquitous for the task of question-answering (Kolomiyets and Moens, 2011), using information retrieval techniques to mine the available documents for answers. Work such as Berant et al. (2013) forms a knowledge base from external documents, and maps queries to knowledge-base entries. Weston et al. (2014) have proposed a neural network-based approach for large-scale question-answering. In the argument mining community, Rinott et al. (2015) created a dataset for predicting potential support clauses for argumentative topics, while Braunstain et al. (2016) rank Wikipedia sentences for supporting answers made by online user answers. Conversely, Wachsmuth et al. (2017) approach the problem of measuring relevance amongst arguments themselves, proposing a methodology based on PageRank (Page et al., 1999).

3 Heuristic Methods

As Habernal and Gurevych (2016b) note in their paper, comparing the SVM and BLSTM systems, it is desirable for methodologies to require minimal preprocessing of text. Along those lines, methods that use heuristics can circumvent the need for supervised training. We refer to the models in this section as heuristic models, as opposed to unsupervised models, because they do not fit themselves to data – they merely compare various metric values to determine convincingness. We experiment with two types of heuristics: ME and Wikipedia similarity. The motivation of these heuristics is as follows: Metric Entropy has previously been applied to the task of predicting tweet deletion (Potash et al., 2016a), with the idea that tweets with high ME are likely to be spam. Moreover, ME conveys how well-formed the language is in a piece of text, since higher ME means a higher randomness in the language. Conversely, Wikipedia similarity attempts to use external knowledge to measure the factual validity of the arguments, but also potentially measuring the writing quality of the arguments.

3.1 Metric Entropy

The Shannon Entropy of a text T containing a set of characters C is defined as:

$$H(T) = -\sum_{c \in C} P(c) \log_2 P(c) \qquad (1)$$

where

$$P(c) = \frac{freq(c)}{len(T)} \qquad (2)$$

and $freq(c)$ is the number of times c appears in T. Consequently, ME is the Shannon entropy divided by the text length, $len(T)$. Since ME produces a continuous output, it is sensible to evaluate it using the regression task from Habernal and Gurevych (2016b). Because ME is a combination of Shannon Entropy and text length, we also evaluate their effectiveness separately as well. We admit, however, that our initial experiments only included ME and Shannon Entropy, but given the vastly different performance of the two metrics, we decided to test length on its own as well.

3.2 Wikipedia Similarity

Suppose we have vector representations of an argument a and a Wikipedia article w. The similarity score, $sim(a, w)$ is simply the dot product of the two representations, aw^{T}. Therefore, given a corpus of Wikipedia articles W, we define the Wikipedia Similarity Score, WSS of an argument a as:

$$WSS(a) = \sum_{w \in W} aw^{\mathsf{T}} \tag{3}$$

For pairwise prediction, we predict the argument with the higher score as the more convincing argument.

We consider two possible representations for texts: 1) term-frequency (TF) count, and 2) Summing the embeddings of all the tokens in the text. For the TF representation, we use the `CountVectorizer` class from Scikit-learn (Pedregosa et al., 2011) to process the text and create the appropriate representation. For the embedding representation, we use GloVe (Pennington et al., 2014) 300 dimensions learned from the Common Crawl corpus with 840 billion tokens.

Our Wikipedia data is from the May 20th, 2017 dump[1]. We clean the raw Wikipedia data using *gensim* (Řehůřek and Sojka, 2010). We experiment with three different Wikipedia corpora. The first corpus has a set of 30 hand-picked Wikipedia articles, chosen to be of the same subject matter of the various topics in the argument convincingness corpora. We refer to this corpus as Wiki hand-picked (hp). The second corpus contains 38k random Wikipedia articles, chosen to be approximately the length of the hand-picked articles. The motivation behind the second corpus is to determine how valuable the topic-specific information is for assessing the validity of the arguments. The second corpus also simulates a situation where a model accesses an arbitrary knowledge base, as opposed to one that is hand-selected. We refer this corpus as Wiki random (ran). The third corpus combines the first two corpora, with the goal of determining how well the heuristic method can deal with the potential 'noise' of randomly chosen Wikipedia articles. We refer to this corpus as Wiki hp+ran.

4   Supervised Methods

Habernal and Gurevych (2016b) propose two supervised experiments for predicting argument convincingness: an SVM with numerous hand-crafted features, and a BLSTM that only uses word embeddings as input. While our heuristic methods

Model	Pearson	Spearman
SVM	0.351	0.402
BLSTM	0.270	0.354
SE	0.097	0.227
LEN	0.353	**0.425**
ME	**0.358**	0.422

Table 2: Results of the Metric Entropy experiments on the regression task. SE = Shannon Entropy, LEN = 1/text length, ME = Metric Entropy.

show promising results, they do not yet achieve state-of-the-art on the argument convincingness dataset. In this section, we motivate our supervised experiments with a combination of results from Section 3.2 and Habernal and Gurevych. All models have the same cost function, which is the binary cross-entropy of the training set, based on the sigmoid activation of a continuous value from a 1-dimensional dense layer.

4.1   Siamese BLSTM

The BSLTM model that Habernal and Gurevych (2016b) propose concatenates the text of the argument pairs, separated by a special delimiter. This single sequence is then run over by forward and backward LSTMs to produce the BLSTM embedding that is then used for logistic regression. We propose to model each argument in the argument pair separately, creating a representation for each argument pair that is then concatenated together for logistic regression output. The term 'Siamese' refers to the fact that the representations are created separately (we adopt the terminology from Mueller and Thyagarajan (2016)). Each argument goes through a BLSTM to produce its individual representation, using GloVe vectors as input to the BLSTM.

4.2   Siamese BOW Embedding

While a BLSTM model is very logical for most language tasks, given its sequential nature, work such as Joulin et al. (2016) shows that simply summing individual token embeddings can be extremely competitive for the task of text classification. Furthermore, in the current climate of increasingly complex deep learning models, it is important to continue to compare to simpler models. For this method, we represent an argument in an argument pair as the sum of its tokens' embeddings. Given the TF representation of a set of texts

---

[1] `https://dumps.wikimedia.org/enwiki/20170520/`

	Topic (Wiki corpus)	WS-TF hp	WS-TF ran	WS-TF hp+ran	WS-E hp	WS-E ran	WS-E hp+ran
Should physical edu.	No	0.792	**0.825***	**0.825***	0.783	0.783	0.783
be mandatory?	Yes	0.711	0.736	0.736	0.778	**0.784**	**0.784**
Ban Plastic	No	0.826	0.840	0.840	**0.851**	0.847	0.847
Water Bottles?	Yes	**0.905**	0.838	0.838	0.833	0.835	0.835
Christianity or Atheism	Atheism	0.713	0.777	0.777	**0.801**	**0.801**	**0.801**
	Christianity	**0.736**	0.716	0.716	0.697	0.705	0.705
Evolution vs. Creation	Creation	0.772	0.817	0.817	0.848	**0.846**	**0.846**
	Evolution	**0.678**	0.634	0.634	0.596	0.603	0.603
Firefox vs. Internet Exp	IE	0.785	0.668	0.668	**0.796**	0.792	0.792
	Firefox	0.774	0.768	0.768	**0.797**	0.793	0.793
Gay marriage -	Right	**0.802**	0.703	0.703	0.762	0.765	0.765
right or wrong?	Wrong	0.774	**0.841**	**0.841**	0.828	0.830	0.830
Should parents	No	0.766	0.796	0.796	**0.829**	0.821	0.821
use spanking?	Yes	0.648	0.672	0.672	0.808	**0.814***	**0.814***
If your spouse	No	**0.689**	0.601	0.604	0.683	0.677	0.677
committed murder [...]	Yes	0.682	0.673	0.673	0.795	**0.798***	**0.798***
India has the potential	No	0.784	0.776	0.776	**0.792**	**0.792**	**0.792**
to lead the world	Yes	**0.749**	0.714	0.714	0.685	0.687	0.687
Lousy father	Fatherless	0.707	0.711	0.711	**0.760**	**0.760**	**0.760**
or fatherless?	Lousy father	**0.675**	0.663	0.663	0.666	0.663	0.663
Is porn wrong?	No	**0.761**	0.703	0.703	0.746	0.749	0.749
	Yes	0.789	**0.838**	**0.838**	0.820	0.829	0.829
Is the school uniform	Bad	**0.706**	0.702	0.702	0.699	0.695	0.695
a good or bad idea?	Good	0.722	0.711	0.711	0.825	**0.827**	**0.827**
Pro choice vs. Pro life	Choice	0.681	0.678	0.678	**0.728**	**0.728**	**0.728**
	Life	0.807	0.726	0.726	0.807	**0.809**	**0.809**
TV is better than books	No	**0.747**	0.736	0.736	0.721	0.721	0.721
	Yes	0.774	0.770	0.770	**0.789**	0.780	0.780
Personal pursuit or	Common	0.728	**0.768**	**0.768**	0.720	0.718	0.718
common good?	Personal	**0.653**	0.610	0.610	0.641	0.650	0.650
Farquhar as the	No	**0.743**	0.682	0.682	0.714	0.723	0.723
founder of Singapore	Yes	0.660	0.702	0.702	**0.828**	0.820	0.820
AVERAGE		0.742	0.731	0.731	0.763	**0.764**	**0.764**

Table 3: Results of Wikipedia similarity experiments, using either a term-frequency representation (TF) or a sum of word embeddings (E). We experiment with three types of Wikipedia corpora: 30 hand-picked articles chosen to been highly relevant to the argument topics (hp); roughly 38k randomly chosen articles (ran); a combination of the first two corpora (hp+ran).

T in matrix format A and a corresponding embedding matrix E, the BOW Embedding, $BOWE$, representation is equivalent to:

$$BOWE(T) = AE \qquad (4)$$

For our application, our input will have two matrices, T_l and T_r, representing the left and right arguments in the pair. Once the individual representations are created, as with the Siamese BLSTM, we concatenate them together as the input for lo-

gistic regression. Lastly, instead of continuing to train the initialized embedding matrix E, we fix E, calling it E_{fixed}, and pass it through a fully-connected layer, W_{emb},

$$E_{learned} = E_{fixed}W_{emb} \qquad (5)$$

Thus, $E_{learned}$ replaces E in Equation 4. Because we are summing embedding vectors to create the representation, the values of representations' dimensions could become large, causing a dramatically increased loss. While such methods as gradient clipping and gradient normalization could be used, we found it simple enough to divide the representation by 100.

4.3 Supervised Wikipedia Similarity

We now begin to modify the methodology described in Section 3.2 to add an increasing amount of complexity to better integrate the Wikipedia articles. The first model we propose uses the representations from Equation 4 to represent the arguments and Wikipedia articles, however, it is computed slightly differently for the arguments and wikipedia articles. While the argument representations use $E_{learned}$, the Wikipedia articles use E_{fixed}, and then the result of $BOWE(T)$ passes through a fully-connected layer, W_{wiki}. Just as we artificially normalized the argument representations, we divide the Wikipedia representations by 10,000, due to their greatly increased length compared to the argument text. Once we have the individual representations, we compute a similarity score as done in Equation 3. The one difference, though, is that we apply tanh to the result of the dot product to keep the summation in a manageable range, which aids training. The resulting similarity scores, one for each argument in the pair, become the features for a 2-dimensional logistic regression model. This model does not use dropout at the fully-connected layer.

4.4 Memory Network with Wikipedia

The model from Section 4.3 gives equal importance to the similarity scores from all Wikipedia articles. However, it's more intuitive for more relevant articles to have more importance. Therefore, we construct a model similar to the end-to-end Memory Network from Sukhbaatar et al. (2015). We create a weight for each score (also interpretable as a probability score P^j) for each Wikipedia article, w_i, and argument, a_j, as[2]:

$$P^j(w_i) = \text{softmax}(a_j w_i^\mathsf{T}) \qquad (6)$$

which is used to create a weighted sum of the Wikipedia articles, s_j, for each argument j:

$$s_j = \sum_i^{|W|} P^j(w_i)w_i \qquad (7)$$

---

[2]We note that we also experimented with an attention mechanism more akin that of Bahdanau et al. (2014), which uses a latent vector v to dot product with the sum $a_j + w_i$. However, this yielded the same results as the currently presented model.

We create the final representation, o_j, for argument j as follows:

$$o_j = a_j + s_j \qquad (8)$$

which is the representation that is the input to the logistic regression layer (one for each argument in the pair).

5 Results

In each table that presents results, bold face indicates that a given system performed highest on a given topic within that table. An asterisk indicates that a given system performed highest on a given topic across *all* tables.

5.1 Heuristic Methods

Results of our ME experiments are shown in Table 2. We present the results on the regression task. The results of the Wikipedia similarity experiments are shown in Table 3.

5.2 Supervised Methods

Results of our supervised experiments are shown in Tables 4 and 5. We present the results of the Siamese BLSTM (SBLSTM), Siamese BOW Embeddings (SBOWE), Supervised Wikipedia similarity (SWS), and Memory Network with Wikipedia (MNW). Each model that uses Wikipedia articles is run with Wiki hp, Wiki ran, and Wiki hp+ran, as described in Section 3.2. All reported results are the average of three different runs. We report the accuracy on each topic, as well as the macro average across all topics. We compare our results with the SVM and BLSTM models from Habernal and Gurevych (2016b) in Table 4.

All models have dropout (Srivastava et al., 2014) of 0.5 at the dense layer (except for the model described in Section 4.3) and use a batch size of 32, as done by Habernal and Gurevych (2016b) in their BLSTM model. All models are implemented in TensorFLow (Abadi et al., 2016) and train for four epochs. The entire dataset has 11,650 argument pairs across all 32 topics. Since one topic is held-out for testing at a time, there is on average an 11,286/364 train/test split.

6 Discussion

6.1 Heuristic Methods

First, it is rather remarkable that text length alone, as a stand-alone metric, is able to record state-of-

	Topic	SVM	BLSTM	SBOWE	SBLSTM
Should physical edu. be mandatory?	No	0.79	**0.8**	0.788	0.750
	Yes	0.79	0.78	**0.879***	0.801
Ban Plastic Water Bottles?	No	0.85	0.76	**0.861**	0.760
	Yes	0.9	0.83	**0.910***	0.798
Christianity or Atheism	Atheism	0.81	0.8	**0.832**	0.771
	Christianity	0.68	0.75	0.747	**0.770**
Evolution vs. Creation	Creation	0.84	0.88	**0.893**	0.809
	Evolution	0.66	0.77	**0.809**	0.796
Firefox vs. Internet Explorer	IE	0.84	0.81	**0.931***	0.774
	Firefox	0.82	0.78	**0.893***	0.814
Gay marriage - right or wrong?	Right	0.76	0.74	**0.797**	0.735
	Wrong	0.82	0.87	**0.902**	0.799
Should parents use spanking?	No	0.84	0.78	**0.861***	0.745
	Yes	**0.79**	0.68	0.765	0.648
If your spouse committed murder [...]	No	0.71	0.64	**0.757**	0.633
	Yes	0.79	0.72	**0.795**	0.720
India has the potential to lead the world	No	0.82	0.77	**0.843**	0.747
	Yes	0.69	0.79	**0.874**	0.817
Is it better to have a lousy father	Fatherless	**0.77**	0.69	0.765	0.638
or to be fatherless?	Lousy father	0.67	0.6	**0.731**	0.584
Is porn wrong?	No	0.82	0.79	**0.835**	0.790
	Yes	0.85	0.85	**0.886**	0.785
Is the school uniform a good or bad idea?	Bad	0.75	0.78	**0.839**	0.829
	Good	**0.83***	0.74	0.795	0.681
Pro choice vs. Pro life	Choice	0.71	0.68	**0.741**	0.730
	Life	0.79	0.8	**0.862**	0.709
TV is better than books	No	0.78	0.73	**0.857**	0.740
	Yes	0.78	0.75	**0.860***	0.799
Personal pursuit or common good?	Common	0.72	**0.78***	0.773	0.712
	Personal	0.67	0.68	**0.696***	0.661
Farquhar as the founder of Singapore	No	0.79	0.63	**0.824**	0.736
	Yes	**0.85***	0.76	0.806	0.651
AVERAGE		0.781	0.757	**0.825***	0.742

Table 4: Results of supervised models that do not use Wikipedia. SVM and BLSTM results are reported from Habernal and Gurevych (2016b).

the-art results on the regression task. Although Chalaguine and Schulz (2017) directly showed the power of text length in a supervised setting, our results show an even simpler method for producing predictions on par with the previous state-of-the-art. There is intuitive reasoning for this result, since, as mentioned in Section 1, arguments are predominantly more convincing when they provide *more*; more facts, more information, more depth, etc. When evaluated on the pairwise binary prediction task, Metric Entropy and text length record 77.2% and 77.3% accuracy, respectively.

Reviewing the Wikipedia similarity results, it is evident that the BOW embedding representation does offer greater predictive power when compared to the term-frequency representation. This unsupervised method even outperforms the supervised methods BLSTM and SBLSTM. Furthermore, compared to other methods that use Wikipedia articles, this method is more insensitive to the content of the articles, as it actually shows a very slight improvement when the hand-picked articles are not present, which is the opposite of all the other Wikipedia-based methods.

Topic (Wiki corpus)		SWS hp	SWS ran	SWS hp+ran	MNW hp	MNW ran	MNW hp+ran
Should physical edu.	No	0.797	**0.819**	0.794	0.802	0.792	0.775
be mandatory?	Yes	0.880	0.846	0.851	**0.877**	0.878	0.868
Ban Plastic Water Bottles?	No	0.821	0.844	0.811	0.829	0.852	**0.862***
	Yes	0.894	0.893	0.901	0.899	**0.906**	**0.906**
Christianity or Atheism	Atheism	0.822	0.804	0.821	0.800	0.838	**0.844***
	Christianity	**0.777***	0.727	0.747	0.765	0.756	0.743
Evolution vs. Creation	Creation	**0.904***	0.834	0.872	0.883	0.886	0.892
	Evolution	0.813	0.802	0.783	**0.832***	0.795	0.800
Firefox vs. Internet Exp	IE	0.901	0.888	0.889	**0.925**	0.903	0.906
	Firefox	0.876	0.884	0.876	**0.880**	0.840	0.856
Gay marriage -	Right	**0.815***	0.771	0.762	0.814	0.787	0.786
right or wrong?	Wrong	0.903	0.889	0.885	**0.908***	0.891	0.901
Should parents	No	0.813	0.816	0.840	0.835	**0.857**	0.853
use spanking?	Yes	0.773	0.748	0.735	0.773	0.782	**0.786**
If your spouse	No	**0.761***	0.733	0.728	0.760	0.732	0.748
committed murder [...]	Yes	0.779	0.780	0.761	0.789	**0.798***	0.750
India has the potential	No	0.833	0.824	0.820	0.842	0.847	**0.848***
to lead the world	Yes	0.861	0.869	**0.880***	0.867	0.870	0.856
Lousy father	Fatherless	**0.780***	0.760	0.751	**0.780**	0.746	0.753
or fatherless?	Lousy father	0.704	0.678	0.711	0.725	0.724	**0.732***
Is porn wrong?	No	0.791	0.836	0.834	0.824	**0.839***	0.816
	Yes	0.883	0.861	0.879	**0.892***	**0.892***	**0.892***
Is the school uniform	Bad	0.840	0.837	0.831	**0.851***	0.815	0.843
a good or bad idea?	Good	0.771	0.752	0.762	0.771	**0.792**	**0.792**
Pro choice vs. Pro life	Choice	**0.746***	0.721	0.723	0.733	0.716	0.722
	Life	0.856	0.834	**0.866***	0.852	0.854	0.850
TV is better than books	No	0.856	0.861	0.834	**0.864***	0.846	0.846
	Yes	0.837	0.849	**0.853**	0.835	0.847	0.849
Personal pursuit	Common	0.760	0.727	0.714	0.763	**0.766**	0.719
or common good?	Personal	0.682	0.669	0.686	0.680	0.687	**0.691**
Farquhar as the	No	0.794	0.783	0.799	0.820	**0.831***	0.823
founder of Singapore	Yes	0.820	0.776	0.794	0.806	0.814	**0.821**
AVERAGE		0.817	0.804	0.806	**0.821**	0.818	0.817

Table 5: We experiment with three types of Wikipedia corpora: 30 hand-picked articles chosen to been highly relevant to the argument topics (hp); roughly 38k randomly chosen articles (ran); a combining the first two corpora (hp+ran).

6.2 Supervised Methods

The first result to note is that the BOW Embedding model posts a new state-of-the-art on the dataset. This shows that the current best approach to predicting argument convincingness treats word order as interchangeable. Although, it is reasonable to surmise that facts and information are dependent on local compositionality, current methods to model such linguistic phenomena under-perform.

When comparing supervised models that integrate Wikipedia articles, we see that the MNW model is better equipped to handle the noise from a large corpus of documents, when compared to the SWS results, which shows roughly a 1% drop in accuracy when the *ran* corpus is added to the *hp* corpus.

6.3 Model Correlations

Table 6 presents correlations between various models when comparing the accuracies of the individual topics. First, text length has a .96 correlation with the SVM model. This means that

	BLSTM	LEN	MNW	SBLSTM	SBOWE	SVM	SWS	WS-E	WS-TF
BLSTM	1.000	0.508	0.739	0.733	0.740	0.534	**0.785**	0.519	0.585
LEN	0.508	1.000	0.574	0.202	0.647	**0.964**	0.585	0.915	0.530
MNW	0.739	0.574	1.000	0.726	0.969	0.608	**0.975**	0.465	0.651
SBLSTM	**0.733**	0.202	0.726	1.000	0.722	0.277	0.723	0.173	0.528
SBOWE	0.740	0.647	**0.969**	0.722	1.000	0.681	0.948	0.552	0.683
SVM	0.534	**0.964**	0.608	0.277	0.681	1.000	0.615	0.904	0.584
SWS	0.785	0.585	**0.975**	0.723	0.948	0.615	1.000	0.528	0.630
WS-E	0.519	**0.915**	0.465	0.173	0.552	0.904	0.528	1.000	0.505
WS-TF	0.585	0.530	0.651	0.528	**0.683**	0.584	0.630	0.505	1.000

Table 6: Correlations between systems. Bold indicates the highest correlation for a given row.

the main predictive power of the SVM model can be distilled into using the text length to predict argument convincingness. What is perhaps more surprising is how high LEN correlates with WS-E. This could potentially be explained by the fact that articles with more words will sum together more embeddings, resulting in vectors with larger norms, which create larger dot-products when taken with the argument representations. However, the same argument can be made for the TF representation, so a more valid reason remains to be seen (note though that SBOWE and WS-TF have a low correlation with LEN). Secondly, we see that all models based on BOW embeddings have a very high correlation with each other, which is an intuitive finding.

7   Conclusion

In this work we have shown three key insights into the task of predicting argument convincingness: 1) Heuristic text length is an extremely competitive baseline that performs on par with highly-engineered classifiers and deep learning models; 2) The current state-of-the-art approach treats tokens as interchangeable, bypassing the need to model compositionality; 3) Wikipedia articles can provide meaningful external knowledge, though, naive models have trouble dealing with the noise in a large corpus of document, whereas a model that attends to the Wikipedia corpus is better equipped to handle the noise. Future work can focus on models that better handle compositionality, as well as integration of external knowledge, with an aim to surpass our new state-of-the-art on the corpus. One simple way to potentially enhance our MNW model is to perform multiple hops, a technique shown to greatly increase performance when using Memory Networks for other applications (Sukhbaatar et al., 2015).

Acknowledgments

This work was supported in part by the U.S. Army Research Office under Grant No. W911NF-16-1-0174.

References

Martín Abadi, Ashish Agarwal, Paul Barham, Eugene Brevdo, Zhifeng Chen, Craig Citro, Greg S Corrado, Andy Davis, Jeffrey Dean, Matthieu Devin, et al. 2016. Tensorflow: Large-scale machine learning on heterogeneous distributed systems. *arXiv preprint arXiv:1603.04467*.

Eneko Agirre, Carmen Banea, Daniel M Cer, Mona T Diab, Aitor Gonzalez-Agirre, Rada Mihalcea, German Rigau, and Janyce Wiebe. 2016. Semeval-2016 task 1: Semantic textual similarity, monolingual and cross-lingual evaluation. In *SemEval@ NAACL-HLT*, pages 497–511.

Yigal Attali and Jill Burstein. 2004. Automated essay scoring with e-rater® v. 2.0. *ETS Research Report Series*, 2004(2).

Dzmitry Bahdanau, Kyunghyun Cho, and Yoshua Bengio. 2014. Neural machine translation by jointly learning to align and translate. *arXiv preprint arXiv:1409.0473*.

Jonathan Berant, Andrew Chou, Roy Frostig, and Percy Liang. 2013. Semantic parsing on freebase from question-answer pairs. In *EMNLP*, volume 2, page 6.

Samuel R Bowman, Gabor Angeli, Christopher Potts, and Christopher D Manning. 2015. A large annotated corpus for learning natural language inference. *arXiv preprint arXiv:1508.05326*.

Liora Braunstain, Oren Kurland, David Carmel, Idan Szpektor, and Anna Shtok. 2016. Supporting human answers for advice-seeking questions in cqa sites. In *European Conference on Information Retrieval*, pages 129–141. Springer, Cham.

Lisa Andreevna Chalaguine and Claudia Schulz. 2017. Assessing convincingness of arguments in online debates with limited number of features. In *Proceedings of the Student Research Workshop at the 15th Conference of the European Chapter of the Association for Computational Linguistics*.

Ivan Habernal and Iryna Gurevych. 2016a. What makes a convincing argument? empirical analysis and detecting attributes of convincingness in web argumentation. In *EMNLP*, pages 1214–1223.

Ivan Habernal and Iryna Gurevych. 2016b. Which argument is more convincing? analyzing and predicting convincingness of web arguments using bidirectional lstm. In *ACL (1)*.

Armand Joulin, Edouard Grave, Piotr Bojanowski, and Tomas Mikolov. 2016. Bag of tricks for efficient text classification. *arXiv preprint arXiv:1607.01759*.

Oleksandr Kolomiyets and Marie-Francine Moens. 2011. A survey on question answering technology from an information retrieval perspective. *Information Sciences*, 181(24):5412–5434.

Thomas K Landauer. 2003. Automated scoring and annotation of essays with the intelligent essay assessor. *Automated essay scoring: A crossdisciplinary perspective*.

Marco Marelli, Stefano Menini, Marco Baroni, Luisa Bentivogli, Raffaella Bernardi, and Roberto Zamparelli. 2014. A sick cure for the evaluation of compositional distributional semantic models. In *LREC*, pages 216–223.

Jonas Mueller and Aditya Thyagarajan. 2016. Siamese recurrent architectures for learning sentence similarity. In *AAAI*, pages 2786–2792.

Lawrence Page, Sergey Brin, Rajeev Motwani, and Terry Winograd. 1999. The pagerank citation ranking: Bringing order to the web. Technical report, Stanford InfoLab.

Fabian Pedregosa, Gaël Varoquaux, Alexandre Gramfort, Vincent Michel, Bertrand Thirion, Olivier Grisel, Mathieu Blondel, Peter Prettenhofer, Ron Weiss, Vincent Dubourg, et al. 2011. Scikit-learn: Machine learning in python. *Journal of Machine Learning Research*, 12(Oct):2825–2830.

Jeffrey Pennington, Richard Socher, and Christopher D Manning. 2014. Glove: Global vectors for word representation. In *EMNLP*, volume 14, pages 1532–1543.

Isaac Persing and Vincent Ng. 2015. Modeling argument strength in student essays.

Peter Potash, Eric Bell, and Joshua Harrison. 2016a. Using topic modeling and text embeddings to predict deleted tweets. *Proceedings of AAAI WIT-EC*.

Peter Potash, Alexey Romanov, and Anna Rumshisky. 2016b. # hashtagwars: Learning a sense of humor. *arXiv preprint arXiv:1612.03216*.

Radim Řehůřek and Petr Sojka. 2010. Software Framework for Topic Modelling with Large Corpora. In *Proceedings of the LREC 2010 Workshop on New Challenges for NLP Frameworks*, pages 45–50, Valletta, Malta. ELRA. `http://is.muni.cz/publication/884893/en`.

Ruty Rinott, Lena Dankin, Carlos Alzate Perez, Mitesh M Khapra, Ehud Aharoni, and Noam Slonim. 2015. Show me your evidence-an automatic method for context dependent evidence detection. In *EMNLP*, pages 440–450.

Dafna Shahaf, Eric Horvitz, and Robert Mankoff. 2015. Inside jokes: Identifying humorous cartoon captions. In *Proceedings of the 21th ACM SIGKDD International Conference on Knowledge Discovery and Data Mining*, pages 1065–1074. ACM.

Mark D Shermis, Jill Burstein, Derrick Higgins, and Klaus Zechner. 2010. Automated essay scoring: Writing assessment and instruction. *International encyclopedia of education*, 4(1):20–26.

Nitish Srivastava, Geoffrey E Hinton, Alex Krizhevsky, Ilya Sutskever, and Ruslan Salakhutdinov. 2014. Dropout: a simple way to prevent neural networks from overfitting. *Journal of Machine Learning Research*, 15(1):1929–1958.

Sainbayar Sukhbaatar, Jason Weston, Rob Fergus, et al. 2015. End-to-end memory networks. In *Advances in neural information processing systems*, pages 2440–2448.

Henning Wachsmuth, Khalid Al Khatib, and Benno Stein. 2016. Using argument mining to assess the argumentation quality of essays. In *COLING*, pages 1680–1691.

Henning Wachsmuth, Benno Stein, and Yamen Ajjour. 2017. pagerank for argument relevance. In *Proceedings of the 15th Conference of the European Chapter of the Association for Computational Linguistics*, volume 1, pages 1117–1127.

Jason Weston, Sumit Chopra, and Antoine Bordes. 2014. Memory networks. *arXiv preprint arXiv:1410.3916*.

Justine Zhang, Ravi Kumar, Sujith Ravi, and Cristian Danescu-Niculescu-Mizil. 2016. Conversational flow in oxford-style debates. *arXiv preprint arXiv:1604.03114*.

Exploiting Document Level Information to Improve Event Detection via Recurrent Neural Networks

Shaoyang Duan[1,2] and **Ruifang He**[1,2] and **Wenli Zhao**[1,2]

[1]School of Computer Science and Technology, Tianjin University, Tianjin, China

[2]Tianjin Key Laboratory of Cognitive Computing and Applications, Tianjin, China

{syduan,rfhe}@tju.edu.cn, wlzhao@gmail.com

Abstract

This paper tackles the task of event detection, which involves identifying and categorizing events. The previous work mainly exists two problems: (1) the traditional feature-based methods apply cross-sentence information, yet need taking a large amount of human effort to design complicated feature sets and inference rules; (2) the representation-based methods though overcome the problem of manually extracting features, while just depend on local sentence representation. Considering local sentence context is insufficient to resolve ambiguities in identifying particular event types, therefore, we propose a novel document level Recurrent Neural Networks (DLRNN) model, which can automatically extract cross-sentence clues to improve sentence level event detection without designing complex reasoning rules. Experiment results show that our approach outperforms other state-of-the-art methods on ACE 2005 dataset neither the external knowledge base nor the event arguments are used explicitly.

1 Introduction

Event detection is a crucial subtask of event extraction, which aims to extract event triggers (most often a single verb or noun) and classify them into specific types in text. For instance, according to the ACE 2005 annotation guideline[1], in the sentence "central command says **troops** were involved in a **gun battle yesterday**", an event detection system should be able to detect an **Attack** event with the trigger word "battle". However, this task is very challenging, as the same event might appear with various trigger words and a trigger expression might evoke different event types in different context.

Most of the existing methods either employed feature-based models with cross-sentence level information (Ji and Grishman, 2008)(Liao and Grishman, 2010)(Hong et al., 2011)(Huang and Riloff, 2012) or followed representation-based architectures with sentence level context (Chen et al., 2015)(Nguyen and Grishman, 2015)(Liu et al., 2016)(Nguyen and Grishman, 2016)(Nguyen et al., 2016)(Liu et al., 2017)(Chen et al., 2017). Both models have some inherent flaws: (1) feature-based approaches not only need to elaborately design rich features and often suffer error propagation from the existing natural language processing tools (i.e part of speech tags and dependency), but also the cross-sentence clues are embodied by devising complex inference rules, which is difficult to cover all the semantic laws; (2) though representation-based models can effectively alleviate the problem of manually extract features, local sentence context information may be insufficient for event detection models or even humans to classify events from isolated sentences. For example, consider the following sentences from ACE2005 dataset:

S1: Saba hasn't delivered yet.[2]

S2: I knew it was time to leave.[3]

It is very difficult to identify S1 as a Be-Born event with the trigger "delivered", which means that a person entity is given birth to. Similarly, we have low confidence to tag "leave" as a trigger for End-Position event in the S2, which means that a person entity stops working for an organization. However, the wider context that "She wants to cal-

---

[1]https://www.ldc.upenn.edu/sites/www.ldc.upenn.edu/files/english-events-guidelines-v5.4.3.pdf.

[2]Selected from the file "CNN_IP_20030414.1600.04".

[3]Selected from the file "CNN_CF_20030303.1900.05".

Proceedings of the The 8th International Joint Conference on Natural Language Processing, pages 352–361,
Taipei, Taiwan, November 27 – December 1, 2017 ©2017 AFNLP

l her pregnant daughter Saba in Sweden to see if she has delivered." would give us more confidence to tag "delivered" as a Be-Born event in the S1. It is easy to identify the "leave" as a trigger for End-Position event in the S2, if we know the previous information that " this is when you were in the Senate – less and less information was new, fewer and fewer arguments were fresh, and the repetitiveness of the old arguments became tiresome. I was becoming almost as cynical as my constituents".

In fact, each document often has a main content in ACE 2005 English corpus. For example, if the content of a document is about terrorist attack, the document is more likely to contain Injure events, Die events, Attack events, and is unlikely to describe Be-Born events. In other words, there is a strong association between events appearing in a document. In addition, event types contained in documents with the related topics are also consistent. Therefore how to use intra and inter document information becomes particularly important. Although there have been already some work to capture the clues beyond sentence to improve sentence level event detection (Ji and Grishman, 2008)(Liao and Grishman, 2010)(Hong et al., 2011), they still exist the following disadvantages: (1) inherent defects in feature-based models; (2) document level information was used by a large number of inference rules, this is not only complicated and time-consuming, but also difficult to cover all of the semantic laws.

In this paper, we propose a document level recurrent neural networks (**DLRNN**) model for event detection to solve the above problems. Firstly, to capture lexical-level clues and minimize the dependence on supervised tools and resources for features, we introduce a distributed word representation model (Mikolov et al., 2013a), which has been proved very effective for event detection (Chen et al., 2015)(Nguyen and Grishman, 2015)(Nguyen and Grishman, 2016). Secondly, we employ bidirectional recurrent networks to encode sentence level clues, which can effectively reserve the history clues and the following information of the current word. Thirdly, to capture document level and cross-document level clues without complicated inference rules. We introduce a document representation, which uses a distributed vector to represent a document and has been showed to be able to get better performance on text classification and sentiment analysis tasks (Le and Mikolov, 2014). Finally, we use BILOU labeling method to solve the problem that a trigger contains multiple words.

In summary, our main contributions are as follows: (1) we prove the importance of document level information for event detection. (2) to capture document level clues, we devise a document level Recurrent Neural Networks (DLRNN) model for event detection, which can automatically learn features beyond sentence. (3) moreover, to solve the problem that a trigger word contains multiple words, we introduce BILOU labeling method. (4) finally, we improve the performance and achieve the best performance on ACE 2005 dataset neither the external knowledge base nor the event arguments are used explicitly.

2   Task Description

This paper focuses on addressing event detection task, which is a crucial subtask of event extraction. According to Automatic Context Extraction (ACE) evaluation[4], which annotates 8 types and 33 subtypes for event mention. An event is defined as a specific occurrence involving one or more participants. Firstly, we introduce some ACE terminologies to facilitate the understanding of event extraction task:

Entity: an object or a set of objects in one of the semantic categories of interests.

Entity mention: a reference to an entity (typically, a noun phrase).

Event trigger: the main word that most clearly expresses an event occurrence.

Event arguments: the mentions that are involved in an event (participants).

Event mention: a phrase or sentence within which an event is described, including the trigger and arguments.

Given an English document, an event extraction system should identify event triggers and their corresponding arguments with specific subtypes or the roles for each sentence, but an event detection system only needs to identify event trigger and their subtype. For instance, for the sentence "central command says **troops** were involved in a **gun battle yesterday**", an event extraction system is supposed to detect the word "battle" as the event trigger of **Attack** event and identify the word

---

[4] `https://project.ldc.upenn.edu/ace`

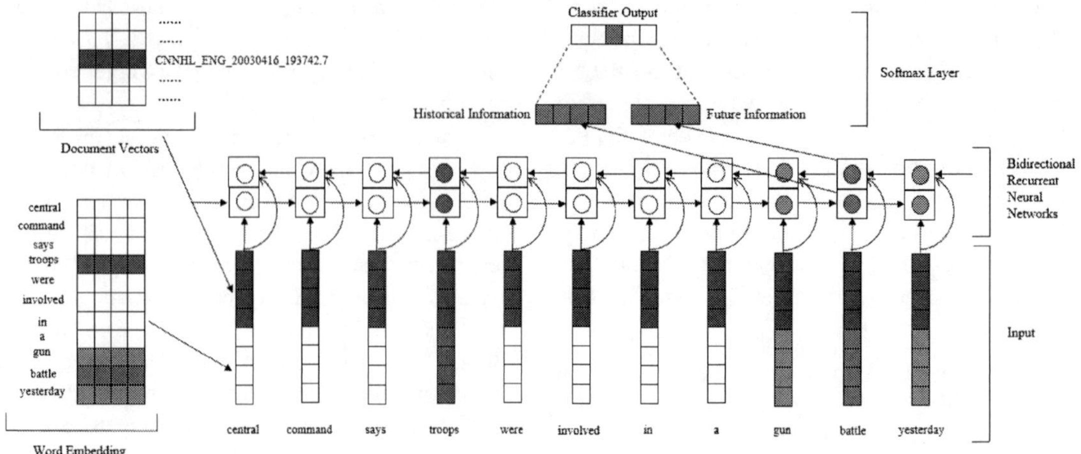

Figure 1: An illustration of our DLRNN model for detecting the trigger word "battle" in the input sentence "central command says troops were involved in a gun battle yesterday".

"troops", "gun" and "yesterday" as event argument whose roles are **Attacker**, **Instrument** and **Time-Within**. However, for an event detection system, identifying the word "troops", "gun" and "yesterday" as event argument whose roles are **Attacker**, **Instrument** and **Time-Within** is not involved. Following previous work, we treat these simply as 33 separate event types and ignore the hierarchical structure among them.

3 Model

In this section, we give the details for the DLRNN model (show in Figure 1). First of all, we formalize the event detection task as a multi-classes classification problem following previous work. More precisely, for each word in a sentence, our goal is to classify them into one of 34 classes (33 trigger types and None class).

Our DLRNN model primarily includes four parts: (i) word embedding, which contains lexical information for each word and is trained from external corpus in an unsupervised manner; (ii) document vector, which reveals the topic of a document is trained in an unsupervised mechanism; (iii) bidirectional recurrent neural networks encoding, which can learn the historical and future abstractive representation of a candidate trigger; (iv) trigger prediction, which calculates a confidence score for each event subtype candidate.

3.1 Word Embedding

The representation of the words as continuous vectors (word embedding) are proved more powerful than discrete representation (Bengio et al., 2003)(Mikolov et al., 2013b). Word embedding not only addresses the problem of dimension disaster, but also makes the word vector contain richer semantic information. The closer the vector space, the closer the semantic. In addition, word embedding can automatically learn lexical-level clues in the process of pre-training. Not only does not require human ingenuity, but also effectively alleviates the error propagation brought by other NLP lexical analysis toolkits. Recent work has demonstrated that using word embedding can enhance the robustness of event detection model (Nguyen and Grishman, 2015)(Chen et al., 2015)(Nguyen and Grishman, 2016).

In this paper, we pre-trained word embedding via skip-gram model (Mikolov et al., 2013b) and New York Times corpus[5]. Given a sequence of training words $w_1, w_2, w_3, ..., w_T$, the skip-gram model trains the embedding by maximizing the average log probability:

$$\frac{1}{T} \sum_{t=k}^{T-k} \log p(w_{t-k}, ..., w_{t+k} | w_t) \qquad (1)$$

where $w_{t-k}, ..., w_{t+k}$ is the context of w_t and the window size is k, usually it is expressed by the concatenation or sum of all word vectors in the

[5] https://catalog.ldc.upenn.edu/LDC2008T19

context; $p(w_{t-k},...,w_{t+k}|w_t)$ is calculated via soft-max. There, we have:

$$p(w_{t-k}, ..., w_{t+k}|w_t) = \frac{e^{y_{w_{t-k},...,w_{t+k}}}}{\sum_i e^{y_i}} \quad (2)$$

where each of y_i is un-normalized log-probability for each output context of the word i, computed as

$$y = b + U w_t \quad (3)$$

where U,b are the sofmax parameters.

3.2 Document Vector

In order to illustrate the importance of the document vector for event detection in terms of disambiguity. we propose three hypotheses from intra and inter document context perspectives.

H1: As we all know, the same word in different context often has different meanings. For instance, the word "delivered" in S1 can mean that someone is born or bring something to a destination, when given different context.

H2: Events in a document exist consistency. For example, Die events and Marry events almost never appear in the same document, but Die events often occur with Attack events and Injure events in a document.

H3: The event types in documents with the related topics exist consistency. For instance, if the document that describing a financial crisis contains End-Position events and End-Org events, and then another document related to the financial crisis topic is more likely to happen End-Position events and End-Org events.

Based on the above three assumptions, we introduced an advanced document representation method. Documents are represented by the distributed vector like word embedding, which not only contains the main content of a document, but also the more relevant documents, the closer the document vector. For all the words in a document, the document vector is shared and is concatenated with word embedding, serving as the semantic representation of a word, as shown in Figure 1. Concatenating the document vector to word embedding has the following advantages: (i) a word is no longer represented by a unique word vector, but expressed by different vector in different documents. This can help event detection model to disambiguate event type; (ii) the consistency of events in a document is guaranteed. Since all the words in a document share a document vector,

which passes the identified event subtype information. For example, if some candidate triggers containing a particular document vector are mostly identified as Attack events, Die events, and Injuries events, and then the other candidate triggers that containing the document vector will be less likely to be identified as Marry events or Be-Born events. (iii) documents with related topic almost contain the same event types. Due to the fact that the more relevant topic of the documents, the closer document vectors, the model will be given high confidence to label candidate trigger in a document as the types that appearing in the relevant topic of the documents.

In this paper, we trained document vectors by using the PV-DM model (Le and Mikolov, 2014), which is very similar to the CBOW model that is another word embedding model (Mikolov et al., 2013a). Unlike the skip-gram model, given a document that contains training words $w_1,w_2,w_3,...,w_T$, document vector is trained by maximizing the average log probability:

$$\frac{1}{T} \sum_{t=k}^{T-k} \log p(w_t|w_{t-k}, ..., w_{t+k}, doc) \quad (4)$$

where $w_{t-k},...,w_{t+k}$ is the context of w_t and the window size is k; doc is the document vector containing the training words, which can be randomly initialized to a fixed dimension of vector like word embedding, see (Le and Mikolov, 2014) for details.

3.3 Bidirectional Recurrent Neural Networks Encoding

Recurrent neural networks (RNN) has been shown to perform considerably better than standard feed-forward architecture (Hammerton, 2003)(Sutskever et al., 2011)(Liu et al., 2014)(Sundermeyer et al., 2014). In this paper, we used RNN to encode word level information and document level clues. In the following, we describe our encoding model in detail.

The traditional RNN predicts the current tag with the consideration of the current input and history information before the current input. It loses the following information after the current input. In order to address this problem, we ran two RNNs, one of the RNNs is responsible for encoding the history information, and the other one is responsible for encoding the future information. In addition, the standard RNN often suffers from gradient vanishing or gradient exploding problems during training via backpropagation (Bengio et al., 1994). To remedy this problem, we used long short-term memory (LSTM) (Hochreiter and Schmidhuber, 1997) that is a variant of RNN to replace the standard RNN.

Formally, given candidate input sequence $X = \{x_1, x_2, ..., x_n\}$. We run LSTM1 to get the hidden representation $\{h_{f_1}, h_{f_2}, ..., h_{f_n}\}$ and run LSTM2 to get the hidden representation $\{h_{b_1}, h_{b_2}, ..., h_{b_n}\}$. Each h_{f_i} and h_{b_i} are computed by:

$$h_{f_i} = \overrightarrow{LSTM}(x_i, h_{f_{i-1}}) \qquad (5)$$

$$h_{b_i} = \overleftarrow{LSTM}(x_i, h_{b_{i+1}}) \qquad (6)$$

where x_i is the concatenation of the word embedding of token i in candidate sentence and document vector that contains token i, as shown in Figure 1; $h_{f_{i-1}}$ contains the historical information before x_i; $h_{b_{i+1}}$ contains the future clues after x_i. Eventually, we obtain the context information over the whole sentence $\{h_1, h_2, ..., h_n\}$ with a greater focus on the position i by concentrating $\{h_{f_1}, h_{f_2}, ..., h_{f_n}\}$ and $\{h_{b_1}, h_{b_2}, ..., h_{b_n}\}$, where $h_i = [h_{f_i}, h_{b_i}]$.

3.4 Trigger Prediction

In the actual situation, due to the fact that a trigger may contain multiple words, we introduce the BILOU labeling method, which has been shown to be able to achieve better results than BIO labeling in entity recognition tasks (Gupta et al., 2016). In the BILOU labeling method, B represents the beginning of a trigger word, I indicates that the word is inside a trigger word, L represents that the word is the last word for a trigger word, O signifies that the word is not a trigger word, U denotes the trigger word contains unique word.

After bidirectional long short-term memory (BiLSTM) encoding, we get the global abstract representation h_i that encapsulates all context of the input sentence (see in section 3.3). And then, we feed h_i into a feed-forward neural network with a softmax layer (as shown in Figure 1). In the end, we get a 34 dimensions vector [6], where the k-th term o_k is the probability value for classifying x_i to the k-th event type.

Given all of our (suppose T) training samples $(x^{(i)}; y^{(i)})$, we can then define the loss function as

the average negative log-likelihood:

$$J(\theta) = -\frac{1}{T} \sum_{i=1}^{T} \log p(y^{(i)} | x^{(i)}, \theta) \qquad (7)$$

In order to compute the network parameter θ, we minimize the average negative log-likelihood $J(\theta)$ via stochastic gradient descent (SGD) over shuffled mimi-batches with Adam update rule (Kingma and Ba, 2014) and the dropout regularization (Zaremba et al., 2014).

4 Experiments

4.1 Dataset and Experimental Setup

We evaluate our DLRNN model on the ACE2005 English corpus. For fair comparisons, the same with (Ji and Grishman, 2008)(Liao and Grishman, 2010)(Hong et al., 2011)(Liu et al., 2017)(Chen et al., 2017), we select the same 40 newswire documents as the test set, the same 30 documents from different genres as development set and the remaining 529 documents are used as training set. Furthermore, we also follow the criteria of the previous work (Ji and Grishman, 2008)(Liao and Grishman, 2010)(Hong et al., 2011)(Li et al., 2013)(Liu et al., 2017)(Chen et al., 2017) to judge the correctness of the predicted event mentions and use *Precision* (P), *Recall* (R), *F-measure* (F_1) as the evaluation metrics.

We set the the dimension of word embedding to 200, the dimension of document vectors to 100, the size of hidden layer to 300, the size of mini-batch to 100, the dropout rate to 0.5, the learning rate to 0.002. All of the above hyper-parameter are adjusted on the development set.

4.2 Baseline Methods

In order to validate our DLRNN model, we choose the following models as our baselines, which are the state-of-the-art methods in sentence level and cross-sentence level event detection models.
Cross-Sentence Level Baselines:

1) **Cross-Document Inference:** It is the feature-based model proposed by (Ji and Grishman, 2008), which is the first time to use document information to assist in sentence level event detection. They employed document theme clustering and designed a lot of reasoning rules to ensure event consistency within the scope of the document and clustering.

2) **Cross-Event Inference:** This is the feature-based method proposed by (Liao and Grishman,

---

[6] As a result of the BILOU tag, the actual dimension is more than 34 dimensions, but it is described as 34 dimensions for ease of understanding.

Methods	P	R	F_1
Ji's cross-document†	60.2	76.4	67.3
Liao's cross-event†	68.7	68.9	68.8
Hong's cross-entity†	72.9	64.3	68.3
Li's joint model	73.7	62.3	67.5
Ngyuen's JRNN	66.0	73.0	69.3
Chen's DMCNN	75.6	63.6	69.1
Chen's DMCNN+DS	75.7	66.0	70.5
Liu's ANN	79.5	60.7	68.8
Liu's ANN+Attention	78.0	66.3	71.7
Our DLRNN†	77.2	64.9	70.5

Table 1: Overall Performance on Blind Test Data. "†" designates the model that employs the evidences beyond sentence level. The boldface indicates that the model is representation-based model.

2010), which not only used the consistency information of the same type events in a document, but also explored the clues from the co-occurrence of different event types in the same document.

3) **Cross-Entity Inference:** It is the feature-based approach proposed by (Hong et al., 2011), which used the entity co-occurrence as a key feature to predict event mention.

Sentence Level Baselines:

4) **Joint Model:** It is the feature-based model proposed by (Li et al., 2013), which exploited argument information implicitly and captured the dependencies between two triggers within the same sentence.

5) **Joint RNN:** It is the representation-based method proposed by (Gupta et al., 2016), which exploited the inter-dependence of event trigger and event argument.

6) **DMCNN + Distant Supervision:** It is the representation-based method proposed by (Chen et al., 2017), which used the Freebase and FrameNet to extend the training corpus through distant supervision.

7) **ANN + Attention:** It is the representation-based approach proposed by (Liu et al., 2017), which exploited argument information explicitly for event detection via supervised attention mechanisms.

4.3 Performance Comparison

Table 1 are the comparisons of experimental results of our method with the baseline methods on the same blind test dataset. Seen from Table 1, we make the following observations:

1) The performance of representation-based models is better than that of feature-based models. It indicates the artificially well-designed features are not sufficient for event detection, and automatically extracting features based on neural networks can capture richer semantic clues. In detail, the F_1 score of our DLRNN model is higher than state-of-the-arts feature-based model (Liao's cross-event) by 1.7%; the other three representation-based models achieved better experimental results than that of Liao's cross-event model, which gain 0.5%,1.7% and 2.9% improvement, respectively.

2) The feature-based models that using cross-sentence information is more advantageous than the sentence level model. More accurately, in the cross-sentence models, only the performance of the Ji's cross-document method is slightly lower than Li's joint model (-0.2%), but the performance of the remaining models is better than Li's joint model (an improvement of 0.8% and 1.3% in F_1 score). It proves the clues beyond sentence are very important for event detection.

3) Our DLRNN method outperforms all cross-sentence level feature-based event detection models. In detail, DLRNN gains 3.2% improvement on F_1 score than Ji's cross-document, gains 1.7% improvement on F_1 score than Liao's cross-event and gains 2.2% improvement on F_1 score than Hong's cross-entity. The reasons are as follows: on the one hand, artificially constructed inference rules are difficult to cover all semantic laws; on the other hand, our DLRNN is better able to capture document level clues (including intra and inter-document context).

4) In spite that the performance of our DLRNN model does not improve the F_1 score compared with Chen's DMCNN+DS model, even the performance is not as good as Liu's ANN+Attention model. However, our method neither explicitly utilized event argument information, nor extended training data through using world knowledge (Freebase) and linguistic knowledge (FrameNet). If removed the event argument information and the knowledge base (Chen's DMCNN and Liu's ANN), the F_1 score of our DLRNN model is superior to the DMCNN and ANN methods, which are -1.4% and -1.7% lower, respectively. This not only illustrates that document level clues are very effective for the representation-based model, but

also prove that the effectiveness of the proposed method.

4.4 The Effectiveness of Document Vector

In order to verify the effectiveness of the document vector trained by PV-DM model for event detection, we design four experiments as baselines for comparison with our DLRNN (as shown in Table 2): BiLSTM, BiLSTM+TF-IDF, BiLSTM+AVE and BiLSTM+LDA.

1) **BiLSTM:** BiLSTM is similar to DLRNN except for removing the document vectors, only uses word embedding as the input of model.

2) **BiLSTM+TF-IDF:** Selected the word vector of the most important word for each document as the document vector for the document.

3) **BiLSTM+AVE:** The document vector is obtained by averaging the vector of each word in the document.

4) **BiLSTM+LDA:** The probability that each document corresponds to each topic is the document vector of the document.

5) **DLRNN:** DLRNN model uses the document vector, which is trained by PV-DM approach instead of averaging the word vector in the document[7].

Methods	P	R	F_1
BiLSTM	76.1	63.5	69.3
BiLSTM+TF-IDF†	74.2	64.6	69.1
BiLSTM+AVE†	75.4	64.7	69.6
BiLSTM+LDA†	74.3	66.1	70.0
DLRNN†	77.2	64.9	70.5

Table 2: Overall Performance on Blind Test Data. "†" designates the model that employs the evidences beyond sentence level."+TF-IDF" represents the document vector was obtained by TF-IDF."+LDA" represents the document vector was obtained by LDA."+AVE" represents the document vector was obtained by averaging the word vector in the document.

Seen from Table 2, we get the following observations: 1) in addition to BiLSTM+TF-IDF, the event detection models with the document vector can achieve better experimental results. In detail, BiLSTM+AVE, BiLSTM+LDA and DLRNN are 0.3%, 0.7% as well as 1.2% better than

BiLSTM on F_1 score, respectively. This indicates that document level clues can contribute to sentence level event detection model. 2) compared to BiLSTM+TF-IDF, BiLSTM+AVE, BiLSTM+LDA, DLRNN gains 1.4%, 0.9%, 0.5% on F_1 score. This illustrates PV-DM model is able to capture richer semantic information.

In addition, in order to illustrate the documents that their vectors are similar contain the consistent event types. We visualize the document vectors. In detail, we randomly selected a document containing the events from ACE2005 English corpus, and found a document that is most similar to the selected document by calculating the cosine similarity of document vectors. Finally, we systematically compared the events contained in the two documents.

We randomly selected the document CNNHL_ENG_20030624_133331.33 as a source document, and found the document CNNHL_ENG_20030624_230338.34 is most similar to it by computing the cosine similarity of document vectors[8]. Seen from Figure 2, we observe that the two documents contain the same event types, except that the document CNNHL_ENG_20030624_133331.33 does not contain Attack event. Event type overlapping rate is up to 80%. This proves that there is correlation between the documents of similar document vectors.

Selected document	Most similar document
CNNHL_ENG_20030624_133331.33	CNNHL_ENG_20030624_230338.34
SUBTYPE="Transport"	SUBTYPE="Transport"
SUBTYPE="Transport"	SUBTYPE="Transport"
SUBTYPE="Transport"	SUBTYPE="Transport"
SUBTYPE="Transport"	SUBTYPE="Transport"
SUBTYPE="Die"	SUBTYPE="Die"
SUBTYPE="Die"	SUBTYPE="Attack"
SUBTYPE="Die"	N/A
SUBTYPE="Charge-Indict"	SUBTYPE="Charge-Indict"
SUBTYPE="Phone-Write"	SUBTYPE="Phone-Write"
SUBTYPE="Injure"	SUBTYPE="Injure"

Figure 2: The comparison of event types on the most similar documents.

4.5 The Event Consistency in a Document

Seen from the Table 3, we observe that the Injure event often appears along with the Attack events, the Die events, and the Transport events

---

[7]we clean the documents up by converting everything to lower case and removing punctuation and the stop words.

[8]The cosine similarity is 0.992

Event Subtype	Conditional Probability
Attack	0.4399
Die	0.2018
Transport	0.1555
Meet	0.0287
Demonstrate	0.0221
......	......
Nominate	0.0
Elect	0.0

Table 3: The ranking probability of events co-occurrence with Injure events.

in the same document. The total probability of the above three types of events concurrence with Injure event is about 0.797. Furthermore, the Nominate events, the Elect events, and so on, have never been appeared in the same document containing the Injure events. This indicates that only certain types of events can occur in the same document, therefore the introduction of the document vector will help to predict event types in a document. Thus, the inter-document information reflected in document vector is useful to event detection.

4.6 The Effectiveness of BILOU Labeling

According to statistics, ACE2005 English corpus contains 235 trigger words, which are composed of multiple words, about 4.39% of the total trigger words. It is not appropriate to treat identifying the triggers that contains multiple words as a word classification task, because most of the triggers of multiple words contain prepositions. However, the prepositions in such triggers do not trigger event independently. Therefore, using BILOU encoding helps to treat the multiple words trigger as a whole. Table 3 demonstrates the effectiveness of the BILOU encoding (an improvement of 0.2% on F_1 score).

Methods	P	R	F_1
DLRNN-BILOU	78.8	63.5	70.3
DLRNN	77.2	64.9	70.5

Table 4: Overall Performance on Blind Test Data. "-BILOU" indicates that the model has not the BILOU labeling.

5 Related Work

Event detection is a challenging task in the field of natural language processing, which has attracted more and more researchers' attention in recent years. The current event detection models can roughly be divided into: (1) the sentence level event detection models and (2) the cross-sentence level event detection models.

(1) The sentence level event detection models: they are designed to use the sentence information for event classification. According to the differences in how to use sentence information, they can be divided into two categories: the feature-based models and the representation-based models. The early event detection models are almost all feature-based models, which transformed lexical features, syntactic features and semantic features into one-hot vectors by other natural language processing toolkits, and then sended these well-designed features into the classifiers (eg: structure perceptron or support vector machine) and eventually completed the event classification (Ahn, 2006)(Li et al., 2013). With the success of deep learning in entity identification and relationship classification (Collobert and Weston, 2008)(Zeng et al., 2014), many event detection researchers turned to focus on the representation-based models. This kind of models do not need to extract the features manually. They used the distributed word vector as the input and encoded the word vector into low-dimensional abstractive representation by the neural network to complete event detection (Nguyen and Grishman, 2015)(Chen et al., 2015)(Nguyen et al., 2016)(Nguyen and Grishman, 2016)(Liu et al., 2016)(Liu et al., 2017)(Chen et al., 2017).

(2) The cross-sentence level event detection models: they aim to explore the clues beyond sentence to improve sentence level event detection. Remarkable researches are cross-document inference (Ji and Grishman, 2008), cross-event inference (Liao and Grishman, 2010), cross-entity inference (Hong et al., 2011) and modeling textual cohesion (Huang and Riloff, 2012). There mainly have two disadvantages: 1) The existing cross-sentence event detection models are feature-based models, which not only need to construct complex manual features and lack generalization ability; 2) utilizing the clues beyond sentence through designing complex and numerous reasoning rules, is not only complex, but also can not cover all semantic phenomenon. Different from the above methods, our approach makes the machine automatically learn the document level information by the representation based way to improve the per-

formance of event detection.

6 Conclusion

In this paper, we propose a novel model (DLRN-N) to automatically extract cross-sentence level clues for event detection by concatenating word vector and document vector. Moreover, we use BILOU encoding to solve the problem that contains multiple words in a trigger word. In order to prove the effectiveness of the proposed method, we systematically conduct a series of experiments on ACE2005 dataset. Experimental results show that the proposed method is better than state-of-the-arts cross-sentence level feature-based models and the sentence level representation-based models without using argument information and external corpus, such as Freebase and FrameNet (Liu et al., 2017)(Chen et al., 2017), which demonstrates that intra and inter-document context is effective for event detection.

Acknowledgments

This work was supported by the National Science Foundation of China (No. 61472277), the National Key Basic Research and Development Program of China (973 Program, No. 2013CB329301).

References

David Ahn. 2006. The stages of event extraction. *In Proceedings of ACL*, pages 1–8.

Yoshua Bengio, Rejean Ducharme, Pascal Vincent, and Christian Jauvin. 2003. A neural probabilistic language model. *The Journal of Machine Learning Research* 3(6):1137–1155.

Yoshua Bengio, Patrice Simard, and Paolo Frasconi. 1994. Learning long-term dependencies with gradient descent is difficult. *The Journal of IEEE transactions on neural networks* 5(2):157–166.

Yubo Chen, Shulin Liu, Xiang Zhang, Kang Liu, and Jun Zhao. 2017. Automatically labeled data generation for large scale event extraction. *In Proceedings of ACL* .

Yubo Chen, Liheng Xu, Kang Liu, Daojian Zeng, and Jun Zhao. 2015. Event extraction via dynamic multi-pooling convolutional neural networks. *In Proceedings of IJCNLP*, pages 167–176.

Ronan Collobert and Jason Weston. 2008. A unified architecture for natural language processing:deep neural networks with multitask learning. *In Proceedings of ICML*, pages 160–167.

Pankaj Gupta, Hinrich Schtze, and Bernt Andrassy. 2016. Table filling multi-task recurrent neural network for joint entity and relation extraction. *In Proceedings of COLING*, pages 2537–2547.

James Hammerton. 2003. Named entity recognition with long short-term memory. *In Proceedings of NAACL*, pages 172–175.

Sepp Hochreiter and Jurgen Schmidhuber. 1997. Long short-term memory. *The Journal of Neural Computation*, 9(8):1735–1780.

Yu Hong, Jianfeng Zhang, Bin Ma, Jianmin Yao, Guodong Zhou, and Qiaoming Zhu. 2011. Using cross-entity inference to improve event extraction. *In Proceedings of ACL*, pages 1127–1136.

Ruihong Huang and Ellen Riloff. 2012. Modeling textual cohesion for event extracion. *In Proceedings of AAAI*, pages 1664–1670.

Heng Ji and Ralph Grishman. 2008. Refining event extraction through cross-document inference. *In Proceedings of ACL*, pages 254–262.

Diederik Kingma and Jimmy Ba. 2014. Adam: A method for stochastic optimization. *arXiv preprint arXiv:1412.6980* .

Quoc Le and Tomas Mikolov. 2014. Distributed representations of sentences and documents. *In Proceedings of ICML*, pages 1188–1196.

Qi Li, Heng Ji, and Liang Huang. 2013. Joint event extraction via structured prediction with global features. *In Proceedings of ACL*, pages 73–82.

Shasha Liao and Ralph Grishman. 2010. Using document level cross-event inference to improve event extraction. *In Proceedings of ACL*, pages 789–797.

Shujie Liu, Nan Yang, Mu Li, and Ming Zhou. 2014. A recursive recurrent neural network for statistical machine translation. *In Proceedings of ACL*, pages 1491–1500.

Shulin Liu, Yubo Chen, Shizhu He, Kang Liu, and Jun Zhao. 2016. Leveraging framenet to improve automatic event detection. *In Proceedings of ACL* pages 2134–2143.

Shulin Liu, Yubo Chen, Kang Liu, and Jun Zhao. 2017. Exploiting argument information to improve event detection via supervised attention mechanisms. *In Proceedings of ACL* .

Tomas Mikolov, Kai Chen, Greg Corrado, and Jeffrey Dean. 2013a. Efficient estimation of word representations in vector space. *arXiv preprint arXiv:1301.3781* .

Tomas Mikolov, Ilya Sutskever, Kai Chen, Greg Corrado, and Jeffrey Dean. 2013b. Distributed representations of words and phrases and their compositionality. *In Proceedings of Advances in Neural Information Processing Systems*, pages 3111–3119.

Thien Huu Nguyen, Kyunghyun Cho, and Ralph Grishman. 2016. Joint event extraction via recurrent neural networks. *In Proceedings of NAACL,* pages 300–309.

Thien Huu Nguyen and Ralph Grishman. 2015. Event detection and domain adaptation with convolution neural networks. *In Proceedings of IJCNLP,* pages 365–371.

Thien Huu Nguyen and Ralph Grishman. 2016. Modeling skip-grams for event detection with convolution neural networks. *In Proceedings of EMNLP,* pages 886–891.

Martin Sundermeyer, Tamer Alkhouli, Joern Wuebker, and Hermann Ney. 2014. Translation modeling with bidirectional recurrent neural networks. *In Proceedings of EMNLP,* pages 14–25.

Ilya Sutskever, James Martens, and Geoffrey Hinton. 2011. Generating text with recurrent neural networks. *In Proceedings of ICML,* pages 1017–1024.

Wojciech Zaremba, Ilya Sutskever, and Oriol Vinyals. 2014. Recurrent neural network regularization. *arXiv preprint arXiv:1409.2329 .*

Daojian Zeng, Kang Liu, Siwei Lai, Guangyou Zhou, and Jun Zhao. 2014. Relation classification via convolutional deep neural network. *In Proceedings of COLING,* pages 2335–2344.

Embracing Non-Traditional Linguistic Resources for Low-resource Language Name Tagging

Boliang Zhang[1], Di Lu[1], Xiaoman Pan[1], Ying Lin[1],
Halidanmu Abudukelimu[2], Heng Ji[1], Kevin Knight[3]

[1] Computer Science Department, Rensselaer Polytechnic Institute
{zhangb8,lud2,panx2,liny9,jih}@rpi.edu
[2] Computer Science Department, Tsinghua University
abdklmhldm@gmail.com
[3] Information Sciences Institute, University of Southern California
knight@isi.edu

Abstract

Current supervised name tagging approaches are inadequate for most low-resource languages due to the lack of annotated data and actionable linguistic knowledge. All supervised learning methods (including deep neural networks (DNN)) are sensitive to noise and thus they are not quite portable without massive clean annotations. We found that the F-scores of DNN-based name taggers drop rapidly (20%-30%) when we replace clean manual annotations with noisy annotations in the training data. We propose a new solution to incorporate many *non-traditional* language universal resources that are readily available but rarely explored in the Natural Language Processing (NLP) community, such as the World Atlas of Linguistic Structure, CIA names, PanLex and survival guides. We acquire and encode various types of non-traditional linguistic resources into a DNN name tagger. Experiments on three low-resource languages show that feeding linguistic knowledge can make DNN significantly more robust to noise, achieving 8%-22% absolute F-score gains on name tagging without using any human annotation [1].

1 Introduction

There is a general agreement that Deep Neural Networks provides a general, powerful underlying model for Information Extraction (IE), confirmed by improved state-of-the-art performance on many tasks such as name tagging (Chiu and Nichols, 2016; Lample et al., 2016), relation classification (Zeng et al., 2014; Liu et al., 2015; Nguyen

and Grishman, 2015b; Yang et al., 2016) and event detection (Nguyen and Grishman, 2015b; Chen et al., 2015; Nguyen and Grishman, 2015a, 2016; Feng et al., 2016). For example, our experiments on several languages show that a DNN-based name tagger generally outperforms (up to 6% F-score gain) a Conditional Random Fields (CRFs) model trained from the same labeled data and feature set. DNN architecture is attractive to couple with character/word embeddings for IE tasks because it is easy to learn and usually effective enough to eliminate the need of explicit linguistic feature design.

However, training general models like DNN usually requires a massive amount of clean annotated data, which is often not available for low-resource languages and difficult to obtain during emergent settings (Zhang et al., 2016a). In order to compensate this data requirement, various automatic annotation generation methods have been proposed, including knowledge base driven distant supervision (An et al., 2003; Mintz et al., 2009; Ren et al., 2015), cross-lingual projection (Li et al., 2012; Kim et al., 2012; Che et al., 2013; Wang et al., 2013; Wang and Manning, 2014; Zhang et al., 2016b), and leveraging naturally existing noisy annotations such as Wikipedia markups (Nothman et al., 2008; Dakka and Cucerzan, 2008; Ringland et al., 2009; Alotaibi and Lee, 2012; Nothman et al., 2012; Althobaiti et al., 2014; Pan et al., 2017). Annotations produced from these methods are usually very noisy, while DNN is sensitive to noise just like many other machine learning methods. Our name tagging experiment shows that the F-score of the same DNN model learned from noisy training data is 20-30% lower than that trained from clean data. One major reason is that most of these methods solely rely on implicit embedding features in order to be (almost) language-independent.

Moreover, certain types of linguistic properties

Proceedings of the The 8th International Joint Conference on Natural Language Processing, pages 362–372,
Taipei, Taiwan, November 27 – December 1, 2017 ©2017 AFNLP

are difficult to be captured by embeddings, such as: (1) language-specific structures. For example, the Subject (S), Verb (V) and Object (O) orders in Tagalog are VS, VO, and VSO, which indicates that the word at the beginning of a sentence is usually a verb and thus unlikely to be a name. (2) culture-specific knowledge. For example, a Uyghur person's last name is the same as his/her father's first name.

On an almost parallel research avenue, linguists and domain experts have created a wide variety of multi-lingual resources, such as World Atlas of Linguistic Structure (WALS) (Dryer and Haspelmath, 2013b), Central Intelligence Agency (CIA) Names, grammar books, and survival guides. Such resources have been largely ignored by the mainstream statistical NLP research, because they were not specifically designed for NLP purpose at the first place and they are often far from complete. Thus they are not immediately actionable - converted into features, rules or patterns for a target NLP application. In this paper we design various methods to convert them into machine readable features for a new DNN architecture. Very little work has used non-traditional resources mentioned in this paper for practical downstream NLP applications. Limited work only used them for resource building (e.g., (Sarma et al., 2012)) or studying word order typology (Ostling, 2015). To the best of our knowledge, our work is the first to encode them as actionable knowledge for IE.

We aim to answer the following research questions: How to effectively acquire linguistic knowledge from non-traditional resources, and represent them for computational models? How much further gain can be obtained in addition to traditional resources?

2 Approach Overview

2.1 A Typical Baseline DNN Model

A typical supervised name tagger is presented in (Lample et al., 2016), consisted of Bi-directional Long Short-Term Memory networks (Bi-LSTM) and CRFs. We can consider name tagging as a sequence labeling problem, to tag each token in a sentence as the Beginning (B), Inside (I) or Outside (O) of a name mention with a certain type. In this paper we classify names into three types: person (PER), organization (ORG) and location (LOC). Predicting the tag for each token needs evidence from both of its previous context and future context

Languages	# of Documents		# of Names		# of Sentences	
	Train	Test	Train	Test	Train	Test
Hausa	137	100	3,414	1,320	3,156	1,130
Turkish	128	100	2,341	2,173	1,973	2,119
Uzbek	127	100	3,577	3,137	3,588	3,037

Table 1: Data Statistics.

in the entire sentence. Bi-LSTM networks (Graves et al., 2013) meet this need by processing each sequence in both directions with two separate hidden layers, which are then fed into the same output layer. Moreover, there are strong classification dependencies among name tags in a sequence. For example, "I-LOC" cannot follow "B-ORG". CRFs model, which is particularly good at jointly modeling tagging decisions, can be built on top of the Bi-LSTM networks.

2.2 Baseline's Sensitiveness to Noise

In low-resource settings where few clean annotations are available, we could try to automatically generate some annotations to train the above model. For instance, we can project automatic annotations from a high-resource language (HL) to a low-resource language (LL) through parallel data. Figure 1 shows an example of projecting English automatic name annotations to Hausa through a parallel sentence pair.

We are interested in studying how sensitive DNN is to noise in such automatically generated training data. For our experiments we use English as the HL and use three LLs with different linguistic properties: Turkish, Uzbek and Hausa. We evaluate our approaches using the ground-truth name tagging annotations from the DARPA LORELEI program [2]. For fair comparison with previous LORELEI work (Tsai et al., 2016; Zhang et al., 2016a; Pan et al., 2017), we use the same 100 test documents. Table 1 shows detailed data statistics.

We use 80% of the name annotated LL documents for training and 20% for development, and parallel sentences to artificially create noisy training data as follows. We use S to denote the sentences in LL and T to denote the sentences in HL. We apply Stanford English name tagger (Manning et al., 2014) on T and project English names onto S, using the following measurements to determine whether a candidate LL name string n_l matches an expected English name n_e: (1) If the edit distance

---

[2] http://www.darpa.mil/program/low-resource-languages-for-emergent-incidents

English While speaking on the launch, the [AU]ORG president, [Nkosazana Dlamini-Zuma]PER expressed her joy over the assistance coming from different parts of [Africa]LOC for the fight against Ebola virus in [West Africa]LOC.

Hausa Da take jawabi albarkacin bikin kaddamarwa, shugabar kungiyar [AU]ORG , [Nkosazana Dlamini-Zuma]PER , ta bayyana jin dadinta kan wannan tallafi dake fitowa daga yankunan [Afrika]LOC daban daban domin yaki da annobar cutar Ebola a [yammacin Afrika]LOC.

* Projection 1 is incorrect and results in a noisy instance in the automatically generated Hausa annotations. The correct name mention is "kungiyar AU (Africa Union)" instead of "AU".

Figure 1: Noisy Training Data Generation by Projecting English Automatic Name Annotations to Hausa.

between n_e and n_l is not greater than two. (2) We check the pronunciations of n_e and n_l based on Soundex (Odell, 1956), Metaphone (Philips, 1990) and NYSIIS (Taft, 1970) algorithms. We consider two codes match if their edit distance is not greater than two. (3) If n_e and n_l are aligned in the parallel data by running GIZA++ word alignment tool (Och and Ney, 2003).

In this way we obtain an automatically generated noisy training data set $Train_{noise}$. We denote $Train_{clean}$ as the ground truth which is manually created by human annotators on set S. We mix $Train_{noise}$ and $Train_{clean}$ in different proportions to obtain a training set $Train_{mix}$ on various noise levels. We define *noise level* as $1 - fscore(Train_{mix})$ where the f-score of $Train_{mix}$ is computed against $Train_{clean}$. For example, when $Train_{mix}$ is full of manually created clean data, the noise level is 0; when we mix half $Train_{noise}$ and half $Train_{clean}$ of the Hausa data, the f-score of $Train_{mix}$ is 80.1%, and the noise level is 19.9%.

To learn embeddings, we use 12,624 Hausa documents from the LORELEI program, and use 288,444 Turkish documents and 128,763 Uzbek documents from a June 2015 Wikipedia dump. Figure 2 shows the performance of the baseline tagger trained from $Train_{mix}$ for three languages. We can clearly see that the performance drops rapidly as the training data includes more noise.

2.3 A New Improved Model

We propose to acquire non-traditional linguistic resources and encode them as new actionable features (Section 3). In Figure 3, we design three integration methods to incorporate explicit linguistic features into Bi-LSTM networks: (1) concatenate the linguistic features and word embeddings at the input level, (2) concatenate the linguistic features and the bidirectional encodings of each token before feeding them into the output layer that computes the tag probability, and (3) use an additional Bi-LSTM to consume the feature embeddings of

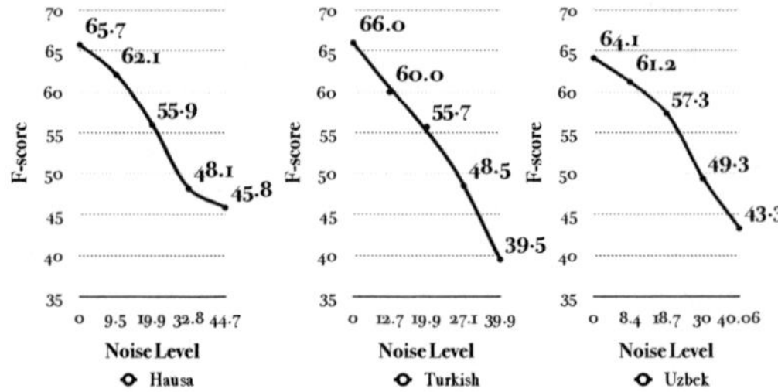

Figure 2: Performance of baseline DNN Name Taggers Trained from Data with Various Noise Levels (The noise level is created by assigning the proportion of $Train_{noise}$ in $Train_{mix}$ as 0%, 25%, 50%, 75% and 100% respectively.)

each token and concatenate both Bi-LSTM encodings of feature embeddings and word embeddings before the output layer. We set the word input dimension to 100, word LSTM hidden layer dimension to 100, character input dimension to 50, character LSTM hidden layer dimension to 25, input dropout rate to 0.5, and use stochastic gradient descent with learning rate 0.01 for optimization.

3 Incorporating Non-traditional Linguistic Knowledge

In this section we will describe the detailed methods to acquire and encode various types of non-traditional resources. We call them as *non-traditional* because they have been rarely used in previous NLP research.

3.1 Basic Knowledge about the Language

Wikipedia Description. An English Wikipedia page about a language usually provides us general descriptions of the language. In particular, the list of usable characters, gender indicators, capitalization information, transliteration and number spelling rules are most useful for name tagging. The list of usable characters for regular words in a particular language can help us detect foreign borrow words, which are likely to be names. For example, "*th*" usually does not appear at the begin-

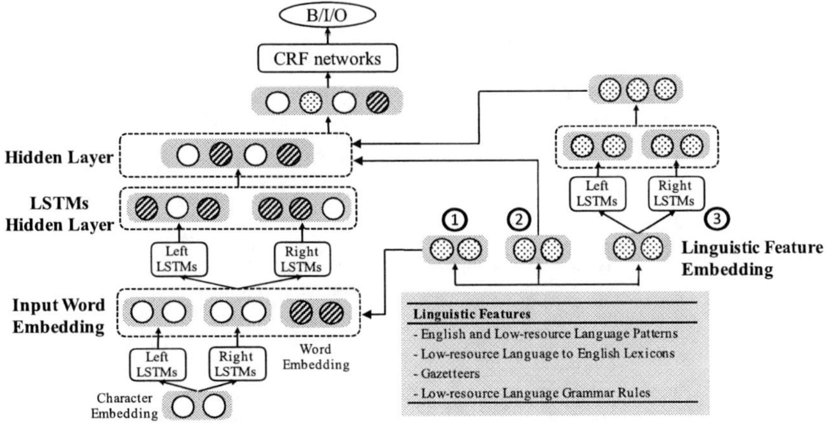

Figure 3: Three Integration Methods to Incorporate Explicit Linguistic Features into DNN.

ning of a Turkish word. Thus "*Thomas Marek*" is likely to be a foreign name.

Grammar Book. From grammar books we can also extract more language-specific contextual words, prefixes, suffixes and stemming rules. Name related lists contain: case suffix, preposition, postposition, ordinal number, definite article, negation, conjunction, pronoun, quantifier, numeral, time, locative, question particle, demonstrative, degree word, plural prefix/suffix, subordinator, reduplication, possessive, situational and epistemic markers. Table 2 shows some examples of name related suffix features.

3.2 Linguistic Structure

Recently linguists have made great efforts at building linguistic knowledge bases for thousands of languages in the world. Two such examples are WALS database (Dryer and Haspelmath, 2013a) and Syntactic Structures of the World's Languages [3]. These databases classify languages according to a large number of topological properties (phonological, lexical and grammatical). For example, WALS consists of 141 maps with accompanying text on diverse properties, gathered from descriptive materials (such as reference grammars). Altogether there are 2,676 languages and more than 58,000 data points; each data point is a (language, feature, feature value) tuple that specifies the value of the feature in a particular language. (e.g., (English, canonical word order, SVO)). In total we extract 188 linguistic properties related to name tagging, belonging to 20 Phonology, 13 Lexicon, 12 Morphology, 29 Nominal, 8 Nominal Syntax, 17 Verbal Categories, 56 Word Order,

26 Simple Clauses, and 7 Complex Sentences categories respectively. Table 3 shows some examples.

3.3 Multi-lingual Dictionaries

CIA Names. We utilize the CIA Name Files [4], which include biographical sketches, memorandums, telegrams, legislative records, legal documents, statements, and other records. We used the version cleaned up by Lawson et al. [5] that includes documents about names in 41 languages. Besides, person names in certain regions often include some common syllable patterns. Table 4 presents some examples. In languages such as Turkish, Uzbek and Uyghur, a person's last name inherits from his or her father's first name. In Uyghur, there are no additional suffixes. In Uzbek, additional suffixes include "*-ov*", "*-ev*", "*-yev*", "*-eva*" and "*-yeva*". In Turkish, a male's first name often ends with a consonant, and his last name consists of his father's first name and a suffix "*-oğlu* (son of)". We exploit this kind of knowledge to improve gazetteer match and name boundary identification.

Unicode CLDR. Unicode Common Locale Data Repository (CLDR) [6] is a data collection for 194 languages, maintained by the Unicode Consortium to support software internationalization and localization. We extract bi-lingual location gazetteers, and exploit patterns and lists of currencies, months, weekdays, day periods and time units to remove them from name candidates because they share some features with names (e.g., capitalization, "*Ocak*" in Turkish means "*January*").

---

[3] http://sswl.railsplayground.net/

[4] https://www.archives.gov/iwg/declassified-records/rg-263-cia-records
[5] https://www.researchgate.net/profile/Edwin_Lawson
[6] http://cldr.unicode.org/

Languages	Features	Description	Examples
Uzbek	Name	**-ni** (accusative), **-ning** (possessive), **-da** (locative), **-dan** (ablative)	**Turkiyaning** (of Turkey), **Turkiyada** (in Turkey), **Turkiyaga** (to Turkey), **Turkiyadan** (from Turkey).
	Non-Name	Suffix **-roq** indicates adjectives	**qoraroq** (darker)
		Suffixes **-lar/-ler** indicate plurals	**qizlar** (daughters)
Hungarian	Name	Foreign name with >1 tokens and an adjective marker	New York-**i** (from New York)
		Most names with adjective or verbal suffix are lowercased	Balzac + **-os** ⇒ **balzacos**
		Possession relation	Péter-**ék** (Peter and his group), Péter-**é** (that of Peter)
		Affixes associated with names	Sartre-**nak** (to Sartre), Bordeaux-**ban** (in Bordeaux), Smith-**ért** (for Smith)
	Non-Name	Non-Name POS tag	adjectives (**-tlen**: "**-less**"), verbs tense (**meg-**:"completed"), conjunctions (**-ért**: "because of")
		Complete inflectional for nominals	karoknak (for arms) → karok (arms) → kar (arm)
Uyghur	Name	Animacy suffixes	**ning**, **ni**, **luq**, and **lik**
		Geopolitical or location suffixes	**ke**, **ge**, **qa**, **gha**, **te**, **de**, **ta**, **da**, **tin**, **din**, **tiki**, **diki**, **kiche**, **giche**, **qiche**, and **ghiche**.
Turkish	Name	Postpositions	karaköy**de** (in Karaköy)

Table 2: Name-related Knowledge Summarized from Grammar Books.

Languages	Categories	Description	Name Related Characteristics
Tagalog	Subject, Verb, Object Order	VS, VO, VSO	the word at the beginning of a sentence is unlikely to be a name
Turkish	Negation	Suffix -me at the root of a verb indicates negations	not a name
Bengali	Animacy	-ta is a case that indicates inanimacy	
Thai	Nested Name Structure	Delimiter between modifier and head, [ORG กระทรวงต่างประเทศ] **ของ**[LOC อินโดนีเซีย] ([ORG Foreign Ministry] of [LOC Indonesia])	Name boundary
Tamil	Conjunction Structure	Name1-**yum** Name2-**yum** (Name1 and Name2)	Name type consistency

Table 3: Name-related Knowledge Extracted from WALS.

Languages	Frequent Syllable Patterns	Examples
Slavic	Suffixes: -ov, -ev -ova, -eva; -ovich, -ich, -enko, -ko, -chuk, -yuk, -ak, -chenko, -skiy, -ski, -vych, -vich	Karim<u>ov</u>, Yuriy Yar<u>ov</u>, Abdulaziz Komil<u>ov</u>, Yamonkul<u>ov</u> Yaxshiboyev<u>ich</u>, Shevch<u>enko</u>
Arabic	Prefixes: al-, Ahl, Abdul-, Abdu-	<u>Abdul</u> Khaliq, <u>Abdul</u> Latif, <u>Abdul</u> Maajid
	Suffixes: -allah, -ullah	Daifa<u>llah</u>, Dhikru<u>llah</u>, Faizu<u>llah</u>, Fatha<u>llah</u>
Uzbek	Suffixes: -ov, -ova, -ev -yev, -eva, -yeva; -ovich, -evich, -ich	Karim Ahmed<u>ov</u>, Ahmed Ali<u>ev</u>, Zulfiya Karim<u>ova</u>, Karmm Sharafovich Rashid<u>ov</u>

Table 4: Common Syllable Patterns Extracted from CIA Names.

Wiktionary. Wiktionary [7] is a web-based collaborative project to create an English content dictionary of all words in many languages. We collected dictionaries in 1,247 languages.

Panlex. Panlex [8] (Baldwin et al., 2010; Kamholz et al., 2014) database contains 1.1 billion pairwise translations among 21 million expressions in about 10,000 language varieties.

Multilingual WordNet. We leverage three versions of multi-lingual WordNet: (1) Open Multilingual WordNet (Bond and Paik, 2012) which links words in many languages to English WordNet based on Wiktionary and CLDR; (2) Universal WordNet (de Melo and Weikum, 2019) which automatically extends English WordNet with around 1.5 million meaning links for 800,000 words in over 200 languages, based on WordNets, translation dictionaries and parallel corpora; and (3) Etymological WordNet (de Melo and Weikum, 2010; de Melo, 2014) that provides information about how words in various languages are etymologically related based on Wiktionary.

Phrase Pairs Mined from Wikipedia. From Wikipedia we extracted all pairs of titles that are connected by cross-lingual links. And we extracted more phrase translation pairs using parenthesis patterns from the beginning sentences of Wikipedia pages. For example, from the first sentence of the English Wikipedia page about Ürümqi: "*Ürümqi (ئۈرۈمچى) is the capital of the*

[7]https://en.wiktionary.org
[8]http://panlex.org/

Xinjiang Uyghur Autonomous Region of the People's Republic of China in Northwest China," we can extract an Uyghur-English name translation pair of "ئۈرۈمچى" and "*Ürümqi*". Moreover, we retrieved related Wikipedia articles, and mined common names in many languages and regions.

GeoNames. We exploit the geo-political and location entities in multilingual GeoNames database [9]. It contains over 10 million geographical names and over 9 million unique features of the following properties: id, name, asciiname, alternate names, latitude, longitude, feature class, feature code, country code, administrative code, population, elevation and time zone.

JRC Names. Finally we include the JRC Names (Steinberger et al., 20011), a large list of person and organization names (about 205,000 entries) in over 20 different scripts. Some entries include additional information such as frequency, title and date ranges.

Grounding to KB and Typing. For names that we are able to acquire English translations, we further ground ("wikify") them to an external knowledge base (KB, DBpedia in our work) if they are linkable. We use two measures (Pan et al., 2015) for linking: (1) Popularity: we prefer popular entities in the KB; (2) Coherence: we link a pair of a foreign name and its English translation simultaneously and favor their candidate entities that are also strongly connected in the KB through a direct cross-lingual page link, a common neighbor, or sharing similar properties. After linking, we assign an entity type to each pair based on their properties in the KB (e.g., an entity with a birth-date and a death-date is likely to be a person). The typing component is a Maximum Entropy model learned from the Abstract Meaning Representation (Banarescu et al., 2013) corpus that includes both entity type and Wikipedia link for each entity mention, using KB properties as features.

3.4 Phrase Books

Finally we exploit phrase books that include phrase translations between many languages and English.

Language Survival Kits. FAMiliarization [10] offers language survival kits (LSKs) for 100 languages, each of which has up to 10 kits of different topics. LSK encodes phrases, translations, and romanizations and is available for 55 languages. FAMiliarization also provides translations of name-

Language	Gazetteer			Title	Non-Name	Suffix
	PER	LOC	ORG			
Hausa	1,174	5,123	199	42	391	21
Turkish	2,819	7,271	262	231	411	181
Uzbek	1,771	5,331	103	178	271	209

Table 5: Name Related List Statistics (# of entries).

related words and phrases.

For each language, we first extracted $2,000$ to $3,000$ parallel sentence/phrase pairs. Then we ran GIZA++ over these pairs and combined structure rules from WALS to obtain word translation pairs. We also extracted translations of the following English lists: cardinal number, currency, disease, location affixes, title, nationalities, topical keywords, organization suffixes, temporal words, locations and people, and stop words which are unlikely to be names.

Elicitation Corpus. An elicitation corpus is a controlled corpus translated by a bilingual consultant in order to produce high quality word aligned sentence pairs. During the elicitation process, the user will translate a subset of these sentences that is dynamically determined to be sufficient for learning the desired grammar rules. We extracted word and phrase translation pairs from the Elicitation corpus developed by CMU (Probst et al., 2001; Alvarez et al., 2005) [11] for the DARPA LORELEI which contains pairs of sentences in a low-resource language and English.

3.5 Encoding Linguistic Features

We merged the linguistic resources collected above into three types of features: (1) name gazetteers; (2) list of suffixes and contextual words (e.g., titles) that indicate names; and (3) list of words that indicate non-names (e.g., time expressions). Ultimately we obtained 30 explicit linguistic feature categories. Table 5 shows the statistics of the encoded features.

For each token w_i in a sentence, we check whether w_i, its previous token w_{i-1} and its next token w_{i+1} exist in these lists, and concatenate them into an initial feature vector for w_i. For any resources (e.g., lexicons and phrase books) that contain English translations, we also use them to translate each w_i, and check whether its translation is capitalized or exists in English name tagging resources (contextual words, gazetteers), whether its contexts match any English patterns as described

---

[9]http://www.geonames.org/
[10]http://fieldsupport.dliflc.edu/

[11]http://www.cs.cmu.edu/afs/cs.cmu.edu/project/cmt-40/Nice/Elicitation/Elicitation_Corpus-LDC/

in (Zhang et al., 2016a).

4 Experiments

Using the data sets mentioned in Section 2.2, we conduct experiments for three languages: Hausa, Turkish and Uzbek.

4.1 Overall Performance

Table 6 compares the results of three feature integration methods described in Section 2.3 and Figure 3. We can see that the third integration method (Integration 3) consistently outperforms the others for all three languages.

Models	Hausa	Turkish	Uzbek
Bi-LSTMs	65.7	65.9	64.1
+ Integration 1	71.1	71.8	67.4
+ Integration 2	71.5	73.1	67.2
+ Integration 3	**72.2**	**74.3**	**68.4**

Table 6: Feature Integration Methods Comparison.

We compare the following models: a baseline model that uses only character and word embedding features, a model adding traditional linguistic features as described in (Zhang et al., 2016a), and a model further adding non-traditional linguistic features using the third integration method. Figure 4 presents the results. Clearly models trained with linguistic features substantially outperform the baseline models on all noise levels for all languages. As the noise level increases, the performance of the baseline model drops drastically while the model trained with linguistic features successfully curbs the downward trend and forms a relatively flat curve at last. Adding non-traditional linguistic features provides further gains in almost all settings. Notably for Turkish, adding linguistic features and using 100% automatically generated noisy training data, our approach achieves the same performance as the baseline model using 75% manually created clean data and 25% automatically created noisy data. In other words, explicit linguistic knowledge has significantly saved annotation cost (2,367 sentences). Our results without using any manually labeled training data are much better than state-of-the-art reported in our previous work (Zhang et al., 2016a) which used most traditional resources mentioned in this paper and (Pan et al., 2017) which derived noisy training data from Wikipedia markups. On the same test sets we achieved 5.5% higher F-score for Hausa than (Zhang et al., 2016a), 27.7% higher F-score

Category	Hausa	Turkish	Uzbek
A Embedding feature	45.8	39.5	43.3
B (A)+Pattern mining and projection	46.7	40.9	45.4
C (B)+Basic knowledge and linguistic structure	50.4	53.3	52.4
D (C)+Dictionaries	52.0	57.7	56.1
E (D)+Phrase books	53.8	60.0	57.8

Table 7: Contributions of Various Categories of Linguistic Knowledge (F-score (%)).

for Turkish and 13.6% higher F-score for Uzbek than (Pan et al., 2017).

4.2 Detailed Analysis

Table 7 presents the contribution of each linguistic feature category when using 100% automatically created training data. Figure 5 shows some examples of errors corrected by each category. Some remaining challenges pertain to the lack of contextual clues for identifying the boundaries of long organizations, especially when they include nested or conjunction structures (e.g., "*Uluslararası ve Stratejik Araştırmalar Merkezi'nde (International and Strategic Research Center)*" in Turkish). The performance of organization tagging is 16%-31% lower than that of persons and locations. We also observe a "*popularity bias*" challenge, especially because we don't have enough resources and tools to perform a deep understanding of the contexts. For example, when a journal name "*New England*" appears in Hausa texts, all of its mentions are mistakenly labeled as location instead of organization, because the dominant type label of "*New England*" is location in all of our resources.

5 Related Work

The major novel contribution of this paper is to systematically explore many non-traditional linguistic resources which have been largely neglected by the mainstream NLP community. Some previous efforts used WALS to study the typological relations across languages (Rama and Prasanth, 2012; O'Horan et al., 2016; Yamauchi and Murawaki, 2016) but very little work used it for practical NLP applications. Most DNN methods solely relied on character embeddings and word embeddings as features for name tagging (e.g., (Huang et al., 2015; Lample et al., 2016; Chiu and Nichols, 2016)). (Shimaoka et al., 2017) used hand-crafted features to improve the performance of DNN on fine-grained entity typing. (Chiu and Nichols, 2016) attempted to incorporate gazetteers as ex-

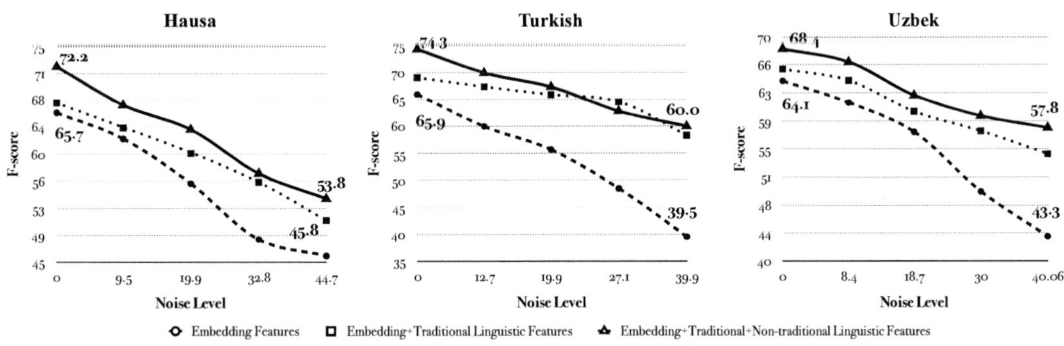

Figure 4: Name Tagging Performance.

Pattern mining and projection

Turkish	Quinnipiac Üniversitesi, CBS haber kanalı ve New York Times gazetesi tarafından yapılan seçim anketlerinde…
Model A	
Model B	*Model B corrects the boundary of "CBS harber kanalı" by using the pattern:* [<Name> …], <Name_{n-i}> <single term> <Name_n>, where all names have the same type.
Translation	Polls of Quinnipiac University, CBS news channel, and the New York Times …

Basic knowledge and linguistic structure

Turkish	Ankara , ve muğladan yüzyüze satılacaktır …
Model B	
Model C	*Model C uses morphological suffix "-dan" (from/via) to identify the name.*
Translation	It would be sold personally from Ankara and Muğla...

Dictionaries

Hausa	An samu dukkan gawawwakin wadanda suka mutu sakamakon bala'in zabtarewar kasa a lardin Yunnan.
Model C	
Model D	*Model D identifies the location with location designator "lardin (province)" in the dictionary*
Translation	It is found all the bodies of those who died in the disastrous landslides in Yunnan Province.

Phrase books

Uzbek	AQShning Xonobod bazasi uchun to'lov masalasi tortishuvga sabab bo'lmoqda.
Model D	
Model E	*Model E correctly classifies the mention as ORG since "Xonobod bazasi (Khanabad base)" is in the phrase book.*
Translation	US-Khanabad base to debate the issue of payment.

ORG   LOC   Missing

Figure 5: Examples of Corrections Made by Each Category of Linguistic Knowledge.

plicit linguistic features, and found that gazetteers are not very effective when they have a low coverage of name variants or when they contain many ambiguous entries. We addressed this challenge by integrating gazetteers gathered from a much wider range of sources.

Some recent studies (Zhang et al., 2016a; Littell et al., 2016a; Tsai et al., 2016; Pan et al., 2017) under the DARPA LORELEI program focused on name tagging for low-resource languages. Most noise tolerant supervised learning algorithms (Bylander, 1994; Dredze et al., 2008; Crammer et al., 2009; Kalapanidas et al., 2003; Scott et al., 2013) have been applied for improving image classification (Mnih and Hinton, 2012; Natarajan et al., 2013; Sukhbaatar et al., 2014; Xiao et al., 2015). Coupling our idea with these algorithms is also likely to yield further improvement.

6 Conclusions and Future Work

Using name tagging as a case study, we demonstrated the power of acquiring and encoding non-traditional linguistic resources. Experiments showed that they can significantly improve the quality of supervised models like DNNs and make them much more robust to noise in automatically created training data. Recent trend of DNN research in the NLP community boasts getting rid of explicit feature design. Our work argues that data-driven implicit knowledge like word embeddings cannot cover all linguistic phenomena in low-resource settings. We propose to embrace the readily available universal resources for many languages, and proved this process of making them actionable is not costly and does not require a system developer to "know" the language. Many more non-traditional linguistic resources remain to explore in the future, including Lexvo (de Melo, 2015), Multilingual Entity Taxonomy (de Melo and Weikum, 2010), EZGlot, URIEL knowledge base (Littell et al., 2016b), travel phrase books and yellow phone books. We will also investigate whether these linguistic resources can make DNN more robust to other factors such as data size and topical relatedness.

Acknowledgments

This work was supported by the U.S. DARPA LORELEI Program No. HR0011-15-C-0115. The views and conclusions contained in this document are those of the authors and should not be interpreted as representing the official policies, either expressed or implied, of the U.S. Government. The U.S. Government is authorized to reproduce and distribute reprints for Government purposes notwithstanding any copyright notation here on.

References

Fahd Alotaibi and Mark Lee. 2012. Mapping arabic wikipedia into the named entities taxonomy. In *Proceedings of the International Conference on Computational Linguistics*.

Maha Althobaiti, Udo Kruschwitz, and Massimo Poesio. 2014. Automatic creation of arabic named entity annotated corpus using wikipedia. In *Proceedings of the Student Research Workshop at the 14th Conference of the European Chapter of the Association for Computational Linguistics*.

Alison Alvarez, Lori Levin, Robert Frederking, Jeff Good, and Erik Peterson. 2005. Semi-automated elicitation corpus generation. In *Proceedings of MT Summit X*.

Joohui An, Seungwoo Lee, and Gary Geunbae Lee. 2003. Automatic acquisition of named entity tagged corpus from world wide web. In *Proceedings of the 41st Annual Meeting on Association for Computational Linguistics*.

Timothy Baldwin, Jonathan Pool, and Susan Colowick. 2010. Panlex and lextract: Translating all words of all languages of the world. In *Proceedings of the 23rd International Conference on Computational Linguistics*.

Laura Banarescu, Claire Bonial, Shu Cai, Madalina Georgescu, Kira Griffitt, Ulf Hermjakob, Kevin Knight, Philipp Koehn, Martha Palmer, and Nathan Schneider. 2013. Abstract meaning representation for sembanking. In *ACL Workshop on Linguistic Annotation and Interoperability with Discourse*.

Francis Bond and Kyonghee Paik. 2012. A survey of wordnets and their licenses. In *Proceedings of the 6th Global WordNet Conference*.

Tom Bylander. 1994. Learning linear threshold functions in the presence of classification noise. In *Proceedings of the seventh annual conference on Computational learning theory*.

Wanxiang Che, Mengqiu Wang, Christopher D Manning, and Ting Liu. 2013. Named entity recognition with bilingual constraints. In *Proceedings of the 2013 Conference of the North American Chapter of the Association for Computational Linguistics*.

Yubo Chen, Liheng Xu, Kang Liu, Daojian Zeng, and Jun Zhao. 2015. Event extraction via dynamic multi-pooling convolutional neural networks. In *Proceedings of the 53rd Annual Meeting of the Association for Computational Linguistics and the 7th International Joint Conference on Natural Language Processing*.

Jason P.C. Chiu and Eric Nichols. 2016. Named entity recognition with bidirectional lstm-cnns. In *Transaction of Association for Computational Linguistics*.

Koby Crammer, Alex Kulesza, and Mark Dredze. 2009. Adaptive regularization of weight vectors. In *Advances in neural information processing systems*.

Wisam Dakka and Silviu Cucerzan. 2008. Augmenting wikipedia with named entity tags. In *Proceedings of the International Joint Conference on Natural Language Processing*.

Gerard de Melo. 2014. Etymological wordnet: Tracing the history of words. In *Proceeddings of the Conference on Language Resources*.

Gerard de Melo. 2015. Lexvo.org: Language-related information for the linguistic linked data cloud. *Semantic Web* 6:4.

Gerard de Melo and Gerhard Weikum. 2010. Towards universal multilingual knowledge bases. In *Proceedings of the 5th Global Wordnet Conference*.

Gerard de Melo and Gerhard Weikum. 2019. Towards a universal wordnet by learning from combined evidence. In *Proceeddings of The Conference on Information and Knowledge Management*.

Mark Dredze, Koby Crammer, and Fernando Pereira. 2008. Confidence-weighted linear classification. In *Proceedings of the 25th international conference on Machine learning*.

Matthew S. Dryer and Martin Haspelmath, editors. 2013a. *WALS Online*.

Matthew S. Dryer and Martin Haspelmath. 2013b. The world atlas of language structures online. In *Leipzig: Max Planck Institute for Evolutionary Anthropology*.

Xiaocheng Feng, Heng Ji, Duyu Tang, Bing Qin, and Ting Liu. 2016. A language-independent neural network for event detection. In *Proceeddings of the 54th Annual Meeting of the Association for Computational Linguistics*.

Alan Graves, Navdeep Jaitly, and Abdel-rahman Mohamed. 2013. Hybrid speech recognition with deep bidirectional lstm. In *Automatic Speech Recognition and Understanding, 2013 IEEE Workshop on.*

Zhiheng Huang, Wei Xu, and Kai Yu. 2015. Bidirectional lstm-crf models for sequence tagging. *arXiv preprint arXiv:1508.01991* .

Elias Kalapanidas, Nikolaos Avouris, Marian Craciun, and Daniel Neagu. 2003. Machine learning algorithms: A study on noise sensitivity. In *Proceeddings of 1st Balcan Conference in Informatics.*

David Kamholz, Jonathan Pool, and Susan Colowick. 2014. Panlex: Building a resource for panlingual lexical translation. In *Proceedings of the Ninth International Conference on Language Resources and Evaluation.*

Sungchul Kim, Kristina Toutanova, and Hwanjo Yu. 2012. Multilingual named entity recognition using parallel data and metadata from wikipedia. In *Proceedings of the 50th Annual Meeting of the Association for Computational Linguistics.*

Guillaume Lample, Miguel Ballesteros, Kazuya Kawakami, Sandeep Subramanian, and Chris Dyer. 2016. Neural architectures for named entity recognition. In *Proceeddings of the 2016 Conference of the North American Chapter of the Association for Computational Linguistics – Human Language Technologies.*

Qi Li, Haibo Li, Heng Ji, Wen Wang, Jing Zheng, and Fei Huang. 2012. Joint bilingual name tagging for parallel corpora. In *Proceedings of The Conference on Information and Knowledge Management.*

Patrick Littell, Kartik Goyal, David Mortensen, Alexa Little, Chris Dyer, and Lori Levin. 2016a. Named entity recognition for linguistic rapid response in low-resource languages: Sorani kurdish and tajik. In *Proceedings of the Conference on Computational Linguistics.*

Patrick Littell, David Mortensen, and Lori Levin (eds.). 2016b. Uriel typological database. *Pittsburgh: Carnegie Mellon University (Available online at http://www.cs.cmu.edu/ dmortens/uriel.html)* .

Yang Liu, Furu Wei, Sujian Li, Heng Ji, and Ming Zhou. 2015. A dependency-based neural network for relation classification. In *Proceeddings of the 53rd Annual Meeting of the Association for Computational Linguistics.*

Christopher D. Manning, Mihai Surdeanu, John Bauer, Jenny Finkel, Steven J. Bethard, and David McClosky. 2014. The stanford corenlp natural language processing toolkit. In *Proceedings of 52nd Annual Meeting of the Association for Computational Linguistics.*

Mike Mintz, Steven Bills, Rion Snow, and Dan Jurafsky. 2009. Distant supervision for relation extraction without labeled data. In *Proceeddings of the conference of the Association for Computational Linguistics.*

Volodymyr Mnih and Geoffrey E Hinton. 2012. Learning to label aerial images from noisy data. In *Proceedings of the 29th International Conference on Machine Learning.*

Nagarajan Natarajan, Inderjit S Dhillon, Pradeep K Ravikumar, and Ambuj Tewari. 2013. Learning with noisy labels. In *Advances in neural information processing systems.*

Thien Huu Nguyen and Ralph Grishman. 2015a. Event detection and domain adaptation with convolutional neural networks. In *Proceedings of the 53rd Annual Meeting of the Association for Computational Linguistics and the 7th International Joint Conference on Natural Language Processing.*

Thien Huu Nguyen and Ralph Grishman. 2015b. Relation extraction: Perspective from convolutional neural networks. In *Proceedings of NAACL Workshop on Vector Space Modeling for NLP.*

Thien Huu Nguyen and Ralph Grishman. 2016. Joint event extraction via recurrent neural networks. In *Proceedings of the 53rd Annual Meeting of the Association for Computational Linguistics.*

Joel Nothman, James R. Curran, and Tara Murphy. 2008. Transforming wikipedia into named entity training data. In *Proceedings of the Australasian Language Technology Association Workshop 2008.*

Joel Nothman, Nicky Ringland, Will Radford, Tara Murphy, and James R. Curran. 2012. Learning multilingual named entity recognition from Wikipedia. *Artificial Intelligence* .

Franz Josef Och and Hermann Ney. 2003. A systematic comparison of various statistical alignment models. *Computational Linguistics* .

Margaret King Odell. 1956. *The Profit in Records Management.* Systems (New York).

Helen O'Horan, Yevgeni Berzak, Ivan Vulić, Roi Reichart, and Anna Korhonen. 2016. Survey on the use of typological information in natural language processing. In *Proceedings of the International Conference on Computational Linguistics.*

Robert Ostling. 2015. Word order typology through multilingual word alignment. In *Proceedings of the 53rd Annual Meeting of the Association for Computational Linguistics.*

Xiaoman Pan, Taylor Cassidy, Ulf Hermjakob, Heng Ji, and Kevin Knight. 2015. Unsupervised entity linking with abstract meaning representation. In *Proceedings of the 2015 Conference of the North American Chapter of the Association for Computational Linguistics – Human Language Technologies.*

Xiaoman Pan, Boliang Zhang, Jonathan May, Joel Nothman, Kevin Knight, and Heng Ji. 2017. Cross-lingual name tagging and linking for 282 languages. In *Proc. the 55th Annual Meeting of the Association for Computational Linguistics*.

Lawrence Philips. 1990. Hanging on the metaphone. *Computer Language* 7(12).

Katharina Probst, Ralf D. Brown, Jaime G. Carbonell, Alon Lavie, and Lori Levin. 2001. Design and implementation of controlled elicitation for machine translation of low-density languages. In *Proceedings of Workshop MT2010 at Machine Translation Summit VIII*.

Taraka Rama and Kolachina Prasanth. 2012. How good are typological distances for determining genealogical relationships among languages? In *Proceedings of the International Conference on Computational Linguistics*.

Xiang Ren, Ahmed El-Kishky, Chi Wang, Fangbo Tao, Clare R. Voss, Heng Ji, and Jiawei Han. 2015. Clustype: Effective entity recognition and typing by relation phrase-based clustering. In *Proceeddings of the 21st ACM SIGKDD Conference on Knowledge Discovery and Data Mining*.

Nicky Ringland, Joel Nothman, Tara Murphy, and James R Curran. 2009. Classifying articles in english and german wikipedia. In *Proceedings of Australasian Language Technology Association Workshop 2009*.

Shikhar Kr. Sarma, Dibyajyoti Sarmah, Biswajit Brahma, Mayashree Mahanta, Himadri Bharali, and Utpal Saikia. 2012. Building multilingual lexical resources using wordnets: Structure, design and implementation. In *Proceedings of the 3rd Workshop on Cognitive Aspects of the Lexicon*.

Clayton Scott, Gilles Blanchard, and Gregory Handy. 2013. Classification with asymmetric label noise: Consistency and maximal denoising. In *the Conference On Learning Theory*.

Sonse Shimaoka, Pontus Stenetorp, Kentaro Inui, and Sebastian Riedel. 2017. Neural architectures for fine-grained entity type classfication. In *Proceedings of the European Chapter of the Association for Computational Linguistics*.

Ralf Steinberger, Bruno Pouliquen, Mijail Kabadjov, and Erik van der Goot. 20011. Jrc-names: A freely available, highly multilingual named entity resource. In *Proceeddings of the 8th International Conference on Recent Advances in Natural Language Processing*.

Sainbayar Sukhbaatar, Joan Bruna, Manohar Paluri, Lubomir Bourdev, and Rob Fergus. 2014. Training convolutional networks with noisy labels. *arXiv preprint arXiv:1406.2080* .

Robert L Taft. 1970. *Name Search Techniques*. New York State Identification and Intelligence System, Albany, New York, US.

Chen-Tse Tsai, Stephen Mayhew, and Dan Roth. 2016. Cross-lingual named entity recognition via wikification. In *Proceedings of the Conference on Natural Language Learning*.

Mengqiu Wang, Wanxiang Che, and Christopher D Manning. 2013. Joint word alignment and bilingual named entity recognition using dual decomposition. In *Proceedings of the Association for Computational Linguistics*.

Mengqiu Wang and Christopher Manning. 2014. Cross-lingual projected expectation regularization for weakly supervised learning. In *Transactions of the Association of Computational Linguistics*.

Tong Xiao, Tian Xia, Yi Yang, Chang Huang, and Xiaogang Wang. 2015. Learning from massive noisy labeled data for image classification. In *Proceedings of the IEEE Conference on Computer Vision and Pattern Recognition*.

Kenji Yamauchi and Yugo Murawaki. 2016. Contrasting vertical and horizontal transmission of typological features. In *Proceedings of the International Conference on Computational Linguistics*.

Yunlun Yang, Yunhai Tong, Shulei Ma, and Zhi-Hong Deng. 2016. A position encoding convolutional neural network based on dependency tree for relation classification. In *Proceedings of the Empirical Methods on Natural Language Processing*.

Daojian Zeng, Kang Liu, Siwei Lai, Guangyou Zhou, and Jun Zhao. 2014. Relation classification via convolutional deep neural network. In *Proceeddings of the 25th International Conference on Computational Linguistics*.

Boliang Zhang, Xiaoman Pan, Tianlu Wang, Ashish Vaswani, Heng Ji, Kevin Knight, and Daniel Marcu. 2016a. Name tagging for low-resource incident languages based on expectation-driven learning. In *Proceeddings of the 2016 Conference of the North American Chapter of the Association for Computational Linguistics – Human Language Technologies*.

Dongxu Zhang, Boliang Zhang, Xiaoman Pan, and Heng Ji. 2016b. Bitext name tagging for annotation projection. In *Proceedings of the 26th International Conference on Computational Linguistics*.

NMT or SMT: Case Study of a Narrow-domain English-Latvian Post-editing Project

Inguna Skadiņa and **Mārcis Pinnis**
Tilde, Vienibas gatve 75A, Riga, Latvia
{inguna.skadina,marcis.pinnis}@tilde.lv

Abstract

The recent technological shift in machine translation from statistical machine translation (SMT) to neural machine translation (NMT) raises the question of the strengths and weaknesses of NMT. In this paper, we present an analysis of NMT and SMT systems' outputs from narrow domain English-Latvian MT systems that were trained on a rather small amount of data. We analyze post-edits produced by professional translators and manually annotated errors in these outputs. Analysis of post-edits allowed us to conclude that both approaches are comparably successful, allowing for an increase in translators' productivity, with the NMT system showing slightly worse results. Through the analysis of annotated errors, we found that NMT translations are more fluent than SMT translations. However, errors related to accuracy, especially, mistranslation and omission errors, occur more often in NMT outputs. The word form errors, that characterize the morphological richness of Latvian, are frequent for both systems, but slightly fewer in NMT outputs.

1 Introduction

For many years, the central problem in machine translation (MT) has been the quality. MT quality has been recognized as a complicated research question when translation is performed into a morphologically rich (and also under-resourced) language with a relatively free word order, e.g., Bulgarian, Croatian, Estonian, Finnish, Greek or Latvian. Possible solutions for widely used statistical machine translation have been studied for many years (e.g., Koehn and Hoang 2007; Tamchyna

and Bojar 2013; Burlot and Yvon 2015).

Today machine translation is experiencing a paradigm shift from (phrase-based) statistical machine translation (SMT) to neural machine translation (NMT). The first results obtained in recent years are promising, as it can be seen from the results of WMT 2016 (Bojar et al., 2016) and WMT 2017 (Bojar et al., 2017).

As NMT becomes more and more popular, the question of what can we expect from NMT in terms of quality becomes very important. Recent analysis of English to German SMT and NMT outputs of manual transcripts of short speeches showed that NMT can decrease the post-editing effort (Bentivogli et al., 2016). A comparison of NMT and SMT systems for nine language directions (English to and from Czech, German, Romanian, Russian, and English to Finnish) on news stories made by Toral and Sánchez-Cartagena (2017) showed that translations produced by NMT systems are more fluent and more accurate in terms of word order compared to translations produced by SMT systems. By analyzing of manually error-annotated outputs of generic English-Croatian MT systems, Klubička et al. (2017) found that NMT handles all types of agreement better than SMT (including factored models).

In this paper, we delve further into analyzing the strengths and weaknesses of NMT from the perspective of translation quality and the needs of the localization industry. We analyze translations of good quality domain-specific (medicine related) English-Latvian SMT and NMT systems that were trained on a rather small (ca. 325K sentences) data set. The target language - Latvian - is a morphologically rich under-resourced language (about 1.5 million speakers). As it is a synthetically inflected language, words change their form according to their grammatical function. In Latvian only half of the word endings are unambiguous, while for

Proceedings of the The 8th International Joint Conference on Natural Language Processing, pages 373–383,
Taipei, Taiwan, November 27 – December 1, 2017 ©2017 AFNLP

the rest, multiple base forms may be derived from the inflected form (Skadiņa et al., 2012).

We analyze outputs of NMT and SMT systems in a post-editing (PE) scenario. Data on PE time, keystrokes, and typical operations were collected during the PE process. Analysis of these data allowed us to conclude that both approaches (SMT and NMT) are comparably successful allowing to increase translator productivity, with the NMT system showing slightly worse results. We believe that the reason translations from the SMT system are better in our case, is that from the small amount of data, SMT learns better terminology and phrases which are specific for the particular narrow domain. The situation could be different for broad domain MT systems, as it can be seen from recent WMT 2017 English-Latvian news domain results, where NMT and hybrid approaches were better (Bojar et al., 2017; Pinnis et al., 2017).

In addition, for a small sub-set of the MT system translations, manual error annotation was performed. This allowed us to identify the main error categories for each MT system. Through analysis of annotated errors, we found that NMT translations are more fluent than SMT translations, NMT produces significantly fewer typography errors than SMT. At the same time errors related to accuracy, especially, mistranslation and omission errors, occur more often in NMT outputs. The word form errors, which characterize the morphological richness of Latvian, are slightly fewer in NMT outputs.

2   Related work

Questions on how to evaluate the quality and usefulness of machine translation have been studied for several decades. For localization industry needs, MT quality and PE productivity have been analyzed by Flournoy and Duran (2009); Groves and Schmidtke (2009); Plitt and Masselot (2010); Skadiņš et al. (2011); Pinnis et al. (2016) and others. These studies report significant productivity increase when good quality SMT systems are used. Recently, for English-Spanish Sanchez-Torron and Koehn (2016) reported that "for 1-point increase in BLEU, there is a PE time decrease of 0.16 seconds per word, about 3-4%".

Several studies have recently compared SMT and NMT systems. Bentivogli et al. (2016) conducted a detailed analysis of SMT and NMT output for the English-German language pair on

translations of manual transcripts of TED talks [1]. They found that NMT decreases post-editing effort, but degrades faster than SMT for longer sentences. They also found that NMT output contains fewer morphology errors, lexical errors and substantially fewer word order errors. Toral and Sánchez-Cartagena (2017) compared NMT and SMT systems submitted to WMT16 news translation task for nine translation directions (English to and from Czech, German, Romanian, Russian, and English to Finnish). The authors found that the translations produced by NMT systems were more fluent and more accurate in terms of word order compared to translations produced by SMT systems. They observed that NMT systems are also more accurate at producing inflected forms, but they perform poorly when translating very long sentences.

However, when Farajian et al. (2017) compared the performance of generic English-French NMT and SMT systems, that were trained on a generic parallel corpus composed of data from different domains, they found that on such multi-domain data SMT outperforms its neural counterpart. Moreover, Castilho et al. (2017) in their study, in which human evaluators compared NMT and SMT output for a range of language pairs, reported mixed results from the human evaluation. Similarly to the previous authors, they reported an increase in fluency, but inconsistent results for adequacy (the neural model showed a greater number of errors of omission, addition, and mistranslation) for NMT when compared to SMT. They argue that, although "NMT shows significant improvements for some language pairs and specific domains, there is still much room for research and improvement before broad generalizations can be made."

Analysis of NMT and SMT errors was recently made by Klubička et al. (2017) for English-Croatian MT systems. The authors analyzed manual error annotations of SMT and NMT system translations in the news domain and concluded that the NMT system reduces the errors produced by the SMT system by 54%.

3   Data and MT Systems

The SMT and NMT systems were trained on the parallel corpus from the European Medicines Agency (EMEA), which is a part of the OPUS cor-

---

[1] http://www.ted.com/

Corpus	Sentences before filtering	Sentences after filtering
Parallel	378,869	325,332
Monolingual	378,869	332,652

Table 1: Statistics of the training corpora

pus (Tiedemann, 2009), and the latest documents from the EMEA website (years 2009-2014)[2].

Prior to the training of the MT systems, we pre-processed the training data using tools for corpora cleaning, filtering, non-translatable token (e.g., URL, e-mail address, different code, etc.) identification, tokenization, and true-casing. The statistics of the training corpora before and after pre-processing are given in Table 1.

3.1 Statistical Machine Translation System

The SMT system is a standard phrase-based system that was trained on the Tilde MT platform (Vasiļjevs et al., 2012) with Moses (Koehn et al., 2007). The system features a 7-gram translation model and a 5-gram language model. The language model was trained with KenLM (Heafield, 2011). The system was tuned with MERT (Bertoldi et al., 2009) using a held-out set of 2,000 sentence pairs.

3.2 Neural Machine Translation System

We used the sub-word neural machine translation toolkit Nematus (Sennrich et al., 2017) for training the NMT system. The toolkit allows training attention-based encoder-decoder models with gated recurrent units in the recurrent layers. For word splitting in sub-word units, we use the byte pair encoding tools from the subword-nmt toolkit (Sennrich et al., 2015). The NMT system was trained using a vocabulary of 40,000 word parts (39,500 for byte pair encoding), a projection (embedding) layer of 500 dimensions, recurrent units of 1024 dimensions, a batch size of 20 and dropout enabled. All other parameters were set to the default parameters as used by the developers of Nematus for their WMT 2016 submissions (Sennrich et al., 2016).

3.3 MT System Evaluation

SMT and NMT systems were evaluated on a held-out set of 1000 randomly selected sentence pairs.

System	BLEU	NIST	ChrF2
SMT	46.57±1.46	9.45±0.18	0.7586
NMT	38.44±1.62	8.63±0.15	0.7065

Table 2: Automatic evaluation results

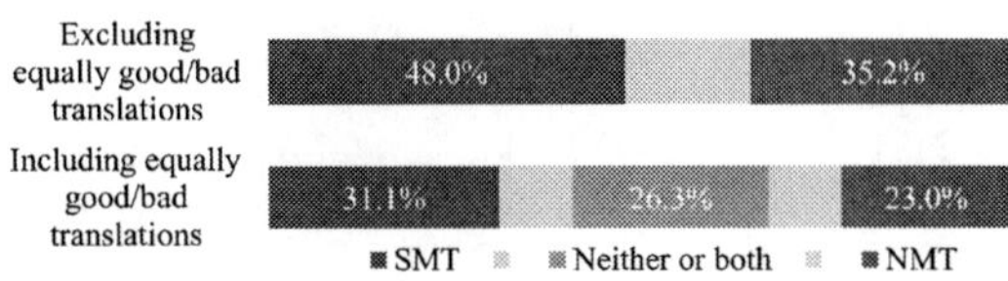

Figure 1: Human comparative evaluation results for SMT and NMT systems

The automatic evaluation results are given in Table 2. The results show that the SMT system achieves better results than the NMT system. This could be explained by the relatively small size of the parallel corpus and a very narrow domain, i.e., from the small amount of data, SMT learns better terminology and phrases which are specific for the particular narrow domain.

When translation is performed into a morphologically rich language, such as Latvian, automatic metrics (e.g. BLEU score) are not always good indicators of translation quality. Table 3 illustrates a case, where both translations have the same quality, but because of different word order the SMT translation received 41.38 BLEU points, while the NMT translation - only 24.42 points. To validate the automatic evaluation results, we performed a small blind comparative evaluation task. The task was performed by 5 professional translators who evaluated 198 segments in total. The results of the comparative evaluation show that the translations of the SMT system are preferred more often by evaluators than the translations of the NMT system (see Figure 1). However, the difference is not statistically significant according to the methodology by Skadiņš et al. (2010). Therefore, both systems were further used in the post-editing and error annotation experiments.

4 What Can Be Learned from Post-edits?

4.1 Post-editing process

For post-editing, we compiled a list of 22,500 segments (360,000 words) from EMEA documents. Then, we split the list into documents consisting of 100 segments so that the original sequence of sentences is preserved, and translated the documents

---

[2]http://www.ema.europa.eu/

Sentence	BLEU	Text
Source	-	Seek medical advice straight away if you develop a severe rash, itching or shortness of breath or difficulty breathing.
Human	100.00	Nekavējoties meklējiet medicīnisku palīdzību , ja Jums parādās izsitumi , rodas nieze vai elpas trūkums , vai apgrūtināta elpošana .
SMT	41.38	Nekavējoties meklējiet medicīnisko palīdzību , ja Jums rodas smagi izsitumi , nieze vai elpas trūkums vai apgrūtināta elpošana .
NMT	24.42	Ja Jums rodas smagi izsitumi, nieze vai elpas trūkums vai apgrūtināta elpošana , nekavējoties meklējiet medicīnisko palīdzību .

Table 3: Influence of word order on BLEU score for similar translations by SMT and NMT systems

with both MT systems.

At first, translators were asked to post-edit SMT translations. Then, three months later, they were asked to post-edit NMT translations. For the NMT post-editing task, the documents were redistributed to translators, to ensure that each translator has different set of documents in SMT and NMT post-editing tasks.

We asked translators to post-edit translated segments with the post-editing tool PET (Aziz et al. 2012). It allowed us to track the time spent on each segment and to log all keystrokes that the translator performed while post-editing each segment. Translators were asked not to spend excessive amounts of time on each segment because the quality expectations were not "human translation quality", but rather "post-editing quality".

To assist post-editing, translators were provided with an automatically extracted in-domain term collection that was integrated into PET and provided translation suggestions for known terms.

After post-editing each segment, translators were asked to evaluate the quality of the MT translation, marking it as one of the following: *"near perfect"*, *"very good"*, *"poor"*, and *"very poor"*. If the translator did not apply any changes, the system automatically assigned the highest quality rating - *"Unchanged"*.

Five professional translators were involved in the SMT post-editing task and seven in the NMT post-editing task. Finally, we asked the translators who participated in both tasks (4 in total) to translate two documents without pre-translated segments in order to measure each translator's pure translation productivity.

4.2 Post-editing Results

Most of the translators involved in this experiment post-edited 20 documents (in each post-editing

	Doc.	Segments	Tokens
Translation	8	797	14,924
SMT	80	5,280	99,375
NMT	80	4,688	86,651
Total	**168**	**10,765**	**200,950**

Table 4: Statistics of post-edited data

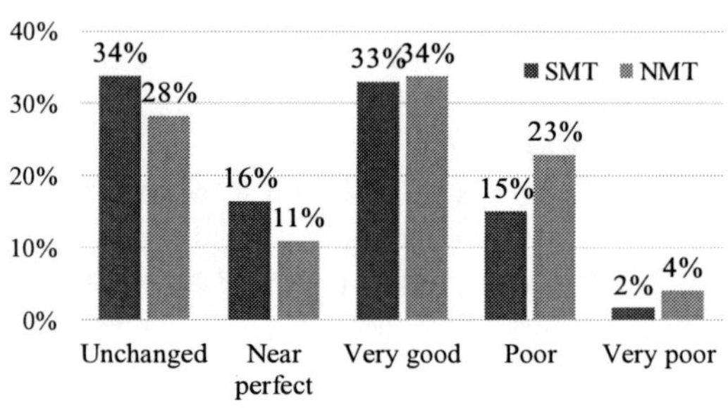

Figure 2: Distribution of rankings for MT segments

task). To perform a fair comparison between SMT and NMT post-editing tasks, we limit our analysis to the first 20 documents post-edited by each translator participating in both post-editing tasks. We perform the analysis only on segments that were not found in the MT system training data (approximately 36% of segments were discarded). The statistics of the post-edited data that are used for the further analysis is given in Table 4.

We start the analysis by examining the MT quality assessments produced by translators during post-editing. The Figure 2 summarizes the distribution of rankings showing that the SMT system produced a larger proportion of near perfect and perfect translations than the NMT system - 50.2% compared to just 39.3%.

The detailed logs of each translators work allowed to measure the time spent on post-editing

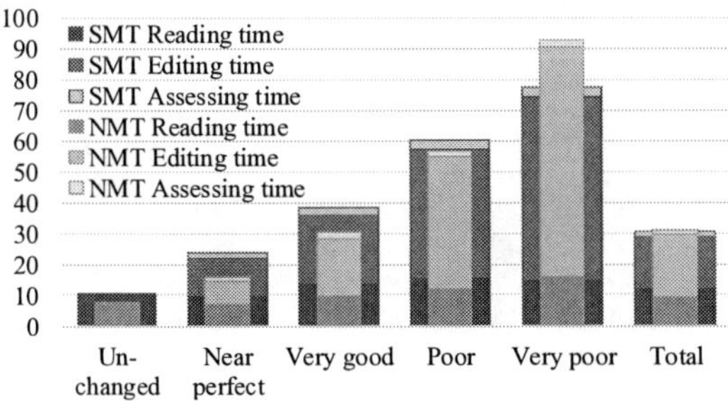

Figure 3: Average time in seconds spent on a segment

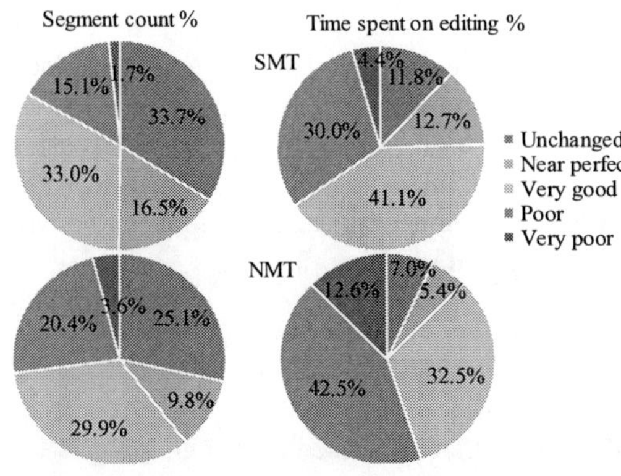

Figure 4: Segment count and editing time distribution for different quality MT segments

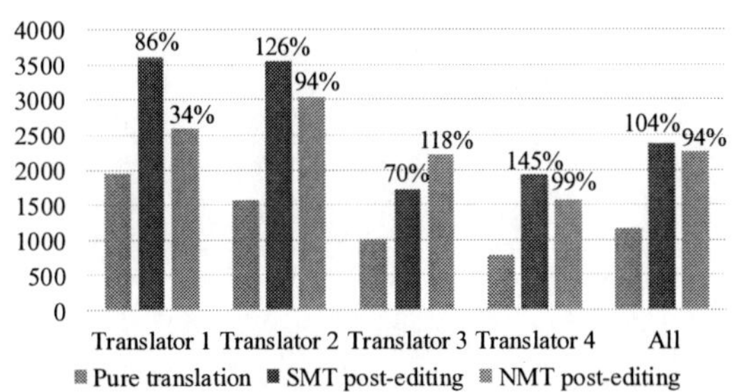

Figure 5: Individual translator productivity (tokens translated/post-edited per hour) based on actually measured numbers

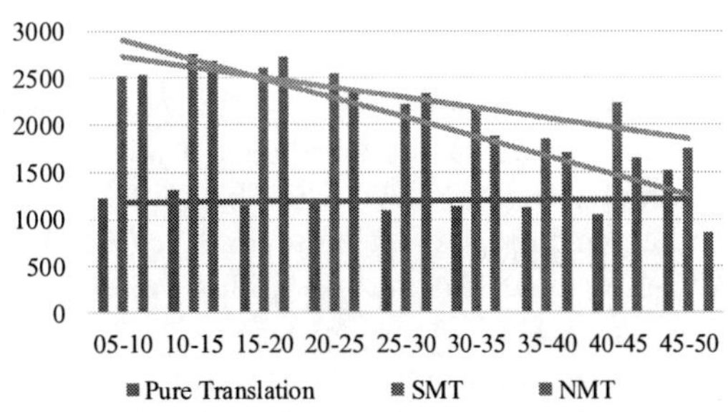

Figure 6: Translation and post-editing productivity (tokens translated/post-edited per hour) for segments with different length with linear trendlines

in three distinct intervals: the amount of time that elapsed between the appearance of an MT segment and the first click, or *"reading time"*; the amount of time between the first edit and approval of the segment, or *"editing time"*; and the amount of time spent between approval of the segment and completion of the quality assessment, referred to as *"assessment time"*. The results of the log data analysis in Figure 3 show that on average it takes 30% more time for translators to start editing SMT translations. It is also obvious that editing of good, very good and near perfect SMT translations requires 16-62% more time than for NMT translations. However, the situation is opposite for poor and very poor translations - it requires 3-25% more time to post-edit NMT translations. This difference is more noticeable in Figure 4, which shows that post-editing poor and very poor NMT translations (24% of all post-edited NMT translations) required more than half of the editing time (55.1%). In comparison post-editing of poor SMT translations (16.8% of all post-edited SMT translations) required just 34.4% of time.

In terms of productivity (see Figure 5), it is evident that both tasks (SMT and NMT post-editing) obtain higher productivity than pure translation. However, the productivity is higher for post-editing SMT translations (104% compared to 94%).

When analyzing the effect of the length of segments on productivity (tokens translated/post-edited per hour), the results in Figure 6 showed that there is an obvious decrease in post-editing productivity for longer segments, with the NMT post-editing productivity decreasing faster than for SMT post-editing. It is interesting that there is almost no change in productivity when translating without MT support.

The information on the time spent on each segment allows us to analyze the relationship between the post-editing productivity and the post-editing effort that is expressed with the help of the Human-targeted Translation Edit Rate (HTER; Snover et al. 2006). Figure 7 depicts the aver-

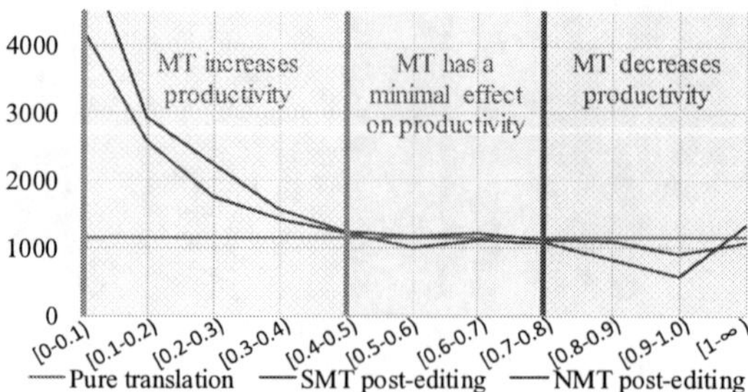

Figure 7: Average productivity (tokens translated/post-edited per hour; y axis) at different MT suggestion quality thresholds (HTER; x axis)

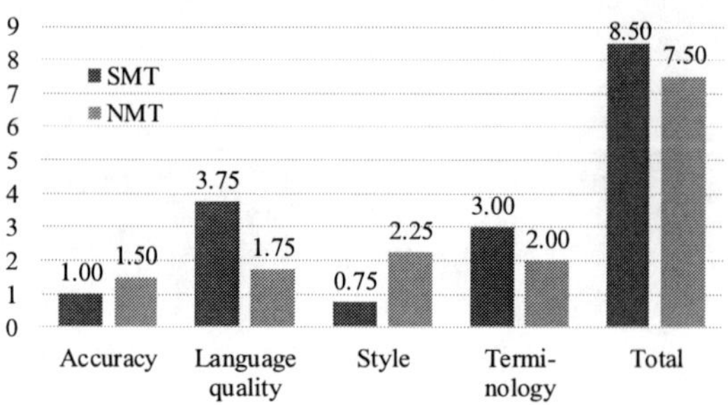

Figure 8: Average error score (per 1000 words)

age productivity for different MT translation quality intervals. It shows that we can identify average MT system quality thresholds, at which post-editing becomes productive (HTER of 0.4 or less) and at which it stops being productive (HTER of 0.7 or higher). The average HTER scores of the SMT and NMT systems are 0.22 and 0.31 respectively. The figure also shows that there is little difference between SMT and NMT post-editing, with the NMT post-editing being faster at individual quality levels. Still, because the NMT system produced more poor translations, the overall post-editing productivity is higher for the SMT post-editing task.

To validate, whether the post-edits are of good quality, we performed quality assessment of the post-edits according to the LISA Quality Assurance model[3]. The quality assessment was performed by professional editors from our localization department. The results in Figure 8 show that even though the task for translators was to perform light post-editing, the quality of the post-edited translations is rated as excellent (i.e., the average error score for both SMT and NMT post-edits is below 10 per 1000 words).

5 MT Error Annotation

The aim of the error annotation task was to identify common and specific errors for both MT architectures and their influence on the overall quality of MT output.

5.1 Error Annotation Task

For error annotation (EA), 1800 English segments and their translations into Latvian by SMT and

NMT systems were selected. Only translations that were marked as "Very good" during post-editing for both MT systems were included. The main reason for including only segments that have good translations was the necessity to avoid wrong annotations due to very bad input.

The error classification used, in this task, is based on Multidimensional Quality Metrics (MQM; Lommel et al. 2014). More specifically, the subset that is defined by Burchardt and Lommel (2014) was used. In this classification, errors are divided into three top categories: accuracy, fluency, and terminology. These top level categories then include more detailed categories from the MQM issue type hierarchy.

The EA was performed four months after finishing both post-editing tasks. Two translators, who participated in both post-editing tasks, were involved to ensure consistency between post-editing and error annotation tasks and to avoid a situation when translators annotate errors, which were not requested to be corrected during post-editing.

The error annotation was performed in the Translate5[4] platform. Before translators started the error annotation, they were introduced to a video tutorial, written guidelines, and the decision process. During annotation, translators saw the source segment, MT output, and post-edited MT output.

Each translator annotated 1000 segments translated by the SMT system and the same 1000 segments translated by the NMT system. Although inter-annotator agreement was not our main interest, 200 translations from each system were annotated by both translators.

---

[3]LISA QA model: http://web.archive.org/web/20080124014404/http://www.lisa.org/products/qamodel/

Error type	SMT error annotation			NMT error annotation		
	Count	Total	%	Count	Total	%
Accuracy	**39**	**1078**	**28%**	**50**	**1634**	**44%**
Addition	282	282	7%	271	271	7%
Mistranslation	275	275	7%	683	683	19%
Omission	402	402	10%	568	568	15%
Untranslated	80	80	2%	62	62	2%
Fluency	**234**	**2734**	**71%**	**213**	**2023**	**55%**
Grammar	11	1329	35%	2	1006	27%
Function words	0	171	4%	0	136	4%
Extraneous	49	49	1%	49	49	1%
Incorrect	56	56	1%	55	55	1%
Missing	66	66	2%	32	32	1%
Word form	282	809	21%	266	714	19%
Part of speech	38	38	1%	35	35	1%
Agreement	429	429	11%	367	367	10%
Tense/aspect/mood	60	60	2%	46	46	1%
Word order	338	338	9%	154	154	4%
Spelling	326	326	8%	394	394	11%
Typography	835	835	22%	396	396	11%
Unintelligible	10	10	0%	14	14	0%
Terminology	**35**	**35**	**1%**	**31**	**31**	**1%**
All types		**3847**	**100%**		**3688**	**100%**

Table 5: Summary of error annotation task (count - number of errors for particular category; total - sum of errors, including subcategories)

5.2 Observations from the Error Annotation Task

The overall results of the error annotation task are summarized in Table 5. Results show that although the segments were ranked as good, most of them contain more than one error per segment. The total number of errors is higher for SMT. There are twice as many errors related to fluency (77%) as to accuracy (28%) for SMT, while for NMT the fluency errors comprise 55% of errors, but accuracy errors - 44%.

The complexity of Latvian morphology is a reason why more than 1/4 of errors are grammar errors (35% for SMT and 27% for NMT), from which almost 1/5 of errors are word form errors (SMT 21%, NMT - 19%). For instance, both MT systems generate the wrong form for the word *"aerosols (spray)"* when translating the sentence *"How to use the nasal spray"*: the SMT system generates the singular nominative form *aerosols (spray)*, while the NMT system generates singular genitive form *aerosola (spray)*.

A significant difference between SMT and NMT outputs has been observed for three error subcategories - typography (the subcategory of fluency), mistranslation (the subcategory of accuracy) and omission (the subcategory of accuracy).

Typography errors are much more widespread in SMT (21.70%) than in NMT (11%). Usually these are cases where spaces are wrongly used (e.g. *"beta - 2 - agonisti"* instead of *"beta-2-agonisti"* (beta-2-agonists), or wrong separators appear in numbers (e.g. *"3,644"* instead of *"3644"*, or *"0.5"* instead of *"0,5"*). These errors, especially wrong separators, are not frequent in NMT translations.

The Latvian language has a very rich, morphology-based word-building potential (words are usually built by adding affixes to the stem). This feature resulted in a high number (19%) of mistranslations from the NMT system. Typical cases of mistranslation from the NMT system include the incorrect translation of numbers (e.g., *30 July 2012* is translated as *2008. gada 30. jūlijs*), terms (e.g., *drop (piliens)* is translated as *injekcija (injection)*) and named entities (e.g., *Naglazyme (Naglazyme)* is translated

[4] http://translate5-metashare.dfki.de

as *MabCampath*).

Latvian also has a relatively free word order. In the case of a formal, narrow domain, where usually the word order is strict, it has a rather small influence even for the SMT system (9% of errors), while in the case of more general systems this could have much greater impact.

Errors of omission are much more frequent for NMT (15%) than for SMT outputs (10%). NMT also produces fewer (4%) word order errors than SMT (9%), while SMT has fewer (8%) spelling errors than NMT (11%).

5.3 Inter-annotator Agreement

Although the aim of this research was not to study consistency between annotations, but to identify and analyze the main error categories, 200 segments translated by SMT and NMT systems were annotated by two translators. The reason for having only two annotators was seriously debated in the consortium of the QT21 project [5] by a number of leading MT researchers. It was agreed that, to show inconsistencies/issues, common understanding of the annotation task, it is enough to have two annotators. The inter-annotator agreement is more like a sanity check for the fine-grained annotation levels (whether annotators have common understanding or not). Table 6 presents the summary on errors annotated in these segments.

Similarly to the whole error annotation task, slightly more errors are found in the SMT system's output. Table 6 also confirms the finding from the overall error annotation task, that NMT produces less typography and word order errors than SMT, but it produces more mistranslation and omission errors.

There are several error categories where translators have different opinions about the applicability of the particular categories. The table clearly demonstrates that the most complicated case was the identification of a correct subcategory for wrong word form errors. The annotator A1 mostly assigned the top category "word form" for such errors, while the annotator A2 marked them as agreement errors.

Another case of significant disagreement between annotators can be observed for fluency errors in the NMT post-editing task. As there was no consistent correspondence between an error category assigned by annotator A2 for cases where an-

[5]http://www.qt21.eu/

Error type	SMT		NMT	
	A1	A2	A1	A2
Accuracy	2	0	0	10
Addition	42	37	32	23
Mistranslation	11	16	17	24
Omission	32	26	37	22
Untranslated	8	10	8	10
Fluency	3	0	33	4
Grammar	6	0	0	0
Function words	0	0	0	0
Extraneous	1	2	0	7
Incorrect	0	3	0	4
Missing	1	3	0	12
Word form	43	0	41	1
Part of speech	0	5	0	2
Agreement	4	41	8	46
Tense/aspect/mood	3	8	0	8
Word order	18	16	6	4
Spelling	43	44	58	56
Typography	84	71	43	42
Unintelligible	3	1	1	1
Terminology	3	0	0	5
All categories	307	283	284	281

Table 6: Error annotation summary for 200 segments annotated by 2 translators (A1 and A2)

notator A1 marked fluency errors, we asked annotator A1 to explain her reasoning. She told us that she marked fluency errors where a post-editor during post-editing applied just stylistic corrections. After inspecting these cases, we agreed with her explanation.

For inter-annotator agreement, we calculated free-marginal kappa under three different conditions (see Table 7): perfect match analysis (i.e., by taking the precise positions and (sub)categories of errors into account), error count analysis (i.e., by ignoring error positions), and error presence analysis (i.e., by just looking at whether both annotators identified that a segment contains a certain (sub)category of errors)[6]. The results show that when taking positions into account, there is just slight agreement between the annotators. This is explained by the different understanding of where errors need to be marked: one translator annotated errors at the character level, while the other - at the token level. For instance, in the case of wrong

[6]Free-marginal kappa is interpreted as: 0.01-0.20 = slight agreement, 0.21-0.40 = fair agreement, 0.41-0.60 = moderate agreement, 0.61-0.80 = substantial agreement, 0.81-1.00 = almost perfect agreement (Landis and Koch, 1977)

	SMT	NMT	Both
Perfect match analysis			
Instances	493	446	939
Agreed inst.	54	54	108
Kappa	0.065	0.077	0.071
Agreement %	11%	12%	12%
Error count analysis			
Instances	401	418	819
Agreed inst.	189	147	336
Kappa	0.445	0.319	0.381
Agreement %	47%	35%	41%
Error presence analysis			
Instances	355	388	743
Agreed inst.	172	133	305
Kappa	0.459	0.310	0.381
Agreement %	48%	34%	41%

Table 7: Inter-annotator agreement (free-marginal kappa) on the 200 segment data sets

separators in numbers (e.g. 7.5), one annotator marked only the punctuation mark, while the other - the whole number. If we analyze the agreement on just error count and error presence levels, we see that the annotators reached moderate agreement for the annotation of errors for the SMT system's translations, but only fair agreement for the NMT system's translations. This is mainly due to the disagreement on how to annotate fluency errors.

The inter-annotator agreement scores highlight the necessity for improvements in the general guidelines to mitigate the potential for disagreement. That being said, the inter-annotator agreement in the higher error levels (i.e., if we do not split errors up in 4 levels of sub-categories, but analyze only the top 2 levels) is good (over 0.6) for SMT and moderate (over 0.4) for NMT.

6 Conclusion

In this paper, we presented an analysis of narrow domain English-Latvian SMT and NMT systems, that were trained on a rather small in-domain corpus.

Translations of both systems were post-edited by professional translators and ranked depending on the complexity of editing. 83% of SMT translations and 73% of NMT translations were ranked as perfect, near perfect or very good, thus confirming the fact that in-domain MT systems can produce good quality translations even when the amount of training data is limited. The analysis of post-edited data allowed us to conclude that both approaches allow for an increase in translator productivity, with the NMT system showing slightly worse results in general, but better for good quality MT output. We believe that the lower results for the NMT system are linked to the relatively small size of the parallel corpus and the narrow domain.

By analysis of the manually annotated errors, we found that the SMT system produced twice as many errors related to fluency (77%) in comparison to those related to accuracy (28%), while for the NMT system the fluency errors comprise 55% of all errors, but accuracy errors - 44%. In terms of error subcategories, widespread errors for both systems are grammar errors (35% for SMT and 27% for NMT), especially wrong word form errors (21% for SMT and 19% for NMT), indicating that morphologically rich languages, e.g., Latvian, are problematic for both MT systems, while improving with NMT. A significant difference between SMT and NMT outputs has been observed for three error subcategories - typography (22% for SMT and 11% for NMT), mistranslation (7% for SMT and 19% for NMT) and omission (10% for SMT and 15% for NMT).

The obtained results show that in the case of a narrow domain, if MT systems are trained on a small amount of data, the SMT system performs better than the NMT system. The reason why the SMT system in our case is better, is that from the small amount of data, SMT learns better terminology and phrases which are specific for the particular narrow domain. The situation differs for broad domain MT systems, as it has been demonstrated by recent WMT 2017 English-Latvian news domain results, where NMT and hybrid approaches were better.

Acknowledgments

We would like to thank Tilde's Localization Department for the hard work they did to prepare material for the analysis presented in this paper. The work within the QT21 project has received funding from the European Union under grant agreement n° 645452. The research has been supported by the ICT Competence Centre (www.itkc.lv) within the project "2.2. Prototype of a Software and Hardware Platform for Integration of Machine Translation in Corporate Infrastructure" of EU Structural funds, ID n° 1.2.1.1/16/A/007.

References

Wilker Aziz, Sheila CM De Sousa, and Lucia Specia. 2012. Pet: a tool for post-editing and assessing machine translation. In *In Proceedings of the Eight International Conference on Language Resources and Evaluation (LREC12)*, pages 3982–3987.

Luisa Bentivogli, Arianna Bisazza, Mauro Cettolo, and Marcello Federico. 2016. Neural versus phrase-based machine translation quality: a case study. In *Proceedings of the 2016 Conference on Empirical Methods in Natural Language Processing, EMNLP 2016, Austin, Texas, USA, November 1-4, 2016*, pages 257–267.

Nicola Bertoldi, Barry Haddow, and Jean-Baptiste Fouet. 2009. Improved Minimum Error Rate Training in Moses. *The Prague Bulletin of Mathematical Linguistics*, 91(1):7–16.

Ondrej Bojar, Rajen Chatterjee, Christian Federmann, Yvette Graham, Barry Haddow, Matthias Huck, Antonio Jimeno Yepes, Philipp Koehn, Varvara Logacheva, Christof Monz, et al. 2016. Findings of the 2016 conference on machine translation (wmt16). *Proceedings of WMT*.

Ondřej Bojar, Rajen Chatterjee, Christian Federmann, Yvette Graham, Barry Haddow, Shujian Huang, Matthias Huck, Philipp Koehn, Qun Liu, Varvara Logacheva, Christof Monz, Matteo Negri, Matt Post, Raphael Rubino, Lucia Specia, and Marco Turchi. 2017. Findings of the 2017 conference on machine translation (wmt17). In *Proceedings of the Second Conference on Machine Translation, Volume 2: Shared Task Papers*, pages 169–214, Copenhagen, Denmark. Association for Computational Linguistics.

Aljoscha Burchardt and Arle Lommel. 2014. Practical guidelines for the use of mqm in scientific research on translation quality. *Preparation and Launch of a Large-scale Action for Quality Translation Technology, report*, page 19.

Franck Burlot and François Yvon. 2015. Morphology-aware alignments for translation to and from a synthetic language. In *Proc. IWSLT*, pages 188–195.

Sheila Castilho, Joss Moorkens, Federico Gaspari, Iacer Calixto, John Tinsley, and Andy Way. 2017. Is neural machine translation the new state of the art? *The Prague Bulletin of Mathematical Linguistics*, 108(1):109–120.

M Amin Farajian, Marco Turchi, Matteo Negri, Nicola Bertoldi, and Marcello Federico. 2017. Neural vs. phrase-based machine translation in a multi-domain scenario. *EACL 2017*, page 280.

Raymond Flournoy and Christine Duran. 2009. Machine translation and document localization at adobe: From pilot to production. *MT Summit XII: proceedings of the twelfth Machine Translation Summit*, pages 425–428.

Declan Groves and Dag Schmidtke. 2009. Identification and analysis of post-editing patterns for mt. In *Proceedings of MT Summit*, volume 12, pages 429–436.

Kenneth Heafield. 2011. KenLM : Faster and Smaller Language Model Queries. In *Proceedings of the Sixth Workshop on Statistical Machine Translation*, 2009, pages 187–197. Association for Computational Linguistics.

Filip Klubička, Antonio Toral, and Víctor M Sánchez-Cartagena. 2017. Fine-grained human evaluation of neural versus phrase-based machine translation. *The Prague Bulletin of Mathematical Linguistics*, 108(1):121–132.

Philipp Koehn and Hieu Hoang. 2007. Factored translation models. In *EMNLP-CoNLL*, pages 868–876.

Philipp Koehn, Hieu Hoang, Alexandra Birch, Chris Callison-Burch, Marcello Federico, Nicola Bertoldi, Brooke Cowan, Wade Shen, Christine Moran, Richard Zens, Chris Dyer, Ond\vrej Bojar, Alexandra Constantin, and Evan Herbst. 2007. Moses: Open Source Toolkit for Statistical Machine Translation. In *Proceedings of the 45th Annual Meeting of the ACL on Interactive Poster and Demonstration Sessions*, ACL '07, pages 177–180, Stroudsburg, PA, USA. Association for Computational Linguistics.

J Richard Landis and Gary G Koch. 1977. The measurement of observer agreement for categorical data. *Biometrics*, pages 159–174.

Arle Richard Lommel, Aljoscha Burchardt, and Hans Uszkoreit. 2014. Multidimensional quality metrics (MQM): A framework for declaring and describing translation quality metrics. *Tradumtica: tecnologies de la traducci*, 0(12):455–463.

Mārcis Pinnis, Rihards Kalniņš, Raivis Skadiņš, and Inguna Skadiņa. 2016. What Can We Really Learn from Post-editing? In *Proceedings of the 12th Conference of the Association for Machine Translation in the Americas (AMTA 2016), vol. 2: MT Users*, pages 86–91, Austin, USA. Association for Machine Translation in the Americas.

Mārcis Pinnis, Rihards Krišlauks, Toms Miks, Daiga Deksne, and Valters Šics. 2017. Tilde's machine translation systems for wmt 2017. In *Proceedings of the Second Conference on Machine Translation*, pages 374–381.

Mirko Plitt and François Masselot. 2010. A productivity test of statistical machine translation post-editing in a typical localisation context. *The Prague bulletin of mathematical linguistics*, 93:7–16.

Marina Sanchez-Torron and Philipp Koehn. 2016. Machine translation quality and post-editor productivity. *AMTA 2016, Vol.*, page 16.

Rico Sennrich, Orhan Firat, Kyunghyun Cho, Alexandra Birch, Barry Haddow, Julian Hitschler, Marcin Junczys-Dowmunt, Samuel Läubli, Antonio Valerio Miceli Barone, Jozef Mokry, et al. 2017. Nematus: a toolkit for neural machine translation. *arXiv preprint arXiv:1703.04357*.

Rico Sennrich, Barry Haddow, and Alexandra Birch. 2015. Neural Machine Translation of Rare Words with Subword Units. In *Proceedings of the 54th Annual Meeting of the Association for Computational Linguistics (ACL 2015)*, Berlin, Germany. Association for Computational Linguistics.

Rico Sennrich, Barry Haddow, and Alexandra Birch. 2016. Edinburgh Neural Machine Translation Systems for WMT 16. In *Proceedings of the First Conference on Machine Translation (WMT 2016), Volume 2: Shared Task Papers*.

Raivis Skadiņš, Kārlis Goba, and Valters Šics. 2010. Improving SMT for Baltic Languages with Factored Models. In *Human Language Technologies: The Baltic Perspective: Proceedings of the Fourth International Conference, Baltic HLT 2010*, volume 219, pages 125–132. IOS Press.

Inguna Skadiņa, Andrejs Veisbergs, Andrejs Vasiļjevs, Tatjana Gornostaja, Iveta Keiša, and Alda Rudzīte. 2012. *The Latvian language in the digital age.* Springer.

Raivis Skadiņš, Māris Puriņš, Inguna Skadiņa, and Andrejs Vasiļjevs. 2011. Evaluation of SMT in Localization to Under-Resourced Inflected Language. In *Proceedings of the 15th International Conference of the European Association for Machine Translation (EAMT 2011)*, May, pages 35–40, Leuven, Belgium. European Association for Machine Translation.

Matthew Snover, Bonnie Dorr, Richard Schwartz, Linnea Micciulla, and John Makhoul. 2006. A Study of Translation Edit Rate with Targeted Human Annotation. In *Proceedings of the 7th biennial conference of the Association for Machine Translation in the Americas*, August, pages 223–231, Cambridge, MA, USA.

Aleš Tamchyna and Ondřej Bojar. 2013. No Free Lunch in Factored Phrase-Based Machine Translation. In *Proc. of CICLing 2013*, volume 7817 of *LNCS*, pages 210–223, Samos, Greece. Springer-Verlag.

Jörg Tiedemann. 2009. News from OPUS - A Collection of Multilingual Parallel Corpora with Tools and Interfaces. In *Recent advances in natural language processing*, volume 5, pages 237–248.

Antonio Toral and Víctor M. Sánchez-Cartagena. 2017. A multifaceted evaluation of neural versus phrase-based machine translation for 9 language directions. In *Proceedings of the 15th Conference of the European Chapter of the Association for Computational Linguistics: Volume 1, Long Papers*, pages 1063–1073, Valencia, Spain. Association for Computational Linguistics.

Andrejs Vasiļjevs, Raivis Skadiņš, and Jörg Tiedemann. 2012. Letsmt!: a cloud-based platform for do-it-yourself machine translation. In *Proceedings of the ACL 2012 System Demonstrations*, pages 43–48. Association for Computational Linguistics.

Towards Neural Machine Translation with Partially Aligned Corpora

Yining Wang[†‡], **Yang Zhao**[†‡], **Jiajun Zhang**[†‡], **Chengqing Zong**[†‡*] and **Zhengshan Xue**[#]

[†]National Laboratory of Pattern Recognition, CASIA, Beijing, China
[‡]University of Chinese Academy of Sciences, Beijing, China
[*]CAS Center for Excellence in Brain Science and Intelligence Technology, Shanghai, China
[#]Toshiba (China) Co.,Ltd.
{yining.wang, yang.zhao, jjzhang, cqzong}@nlpr.ia.ac.cn
xuezhengshan2@toshiba.com.cn

Abstract

While neural machine translation (NMT) has become the new paradigm, the parameter optimization requires large-scale parallel data which is scarce in many domains and language pairs. In this paper, we address a new translation scenario in which there only exists monolingual corpora and phrase pairs. We propose a new method towards translation with partially aligned sentence pairs which are derived from the phrase pairs and monolingual corpora. To make full use of the partially aligned corpora, we adapt the conventional NMT training method in two aspects. On one hand, different generation strategies are designed for aligned and unaligned target words. On the other hand, a different objective function is designed to model the partially aligned parts. The experiments demonstrate that our method can achieve a relatively good result in such a translation scenario, and tiny bitexts can boost translation quality to a large extent.

1 Introduction

Neural machine translation (NMT) proposed by Kalchbrenner et al.(2013), Sutskever et al.(2014) and Cho et al.(2014) has achieved significant progress in recent years. Different from traditional statistical machine translation(SMT) (Koehn et al., 2003; Chiang, 2005; Liu et al., 2006; Zhai et al., 2012) which contains multiple separately tuned components, NMT builds an end-to-end framework to model the whole translation process. For several language pairs, NMT is reaching significantly better translation performance than SMT (Luong et al., 2015b; Wu et al., 2016).

In general, in order to obtain an NMT model

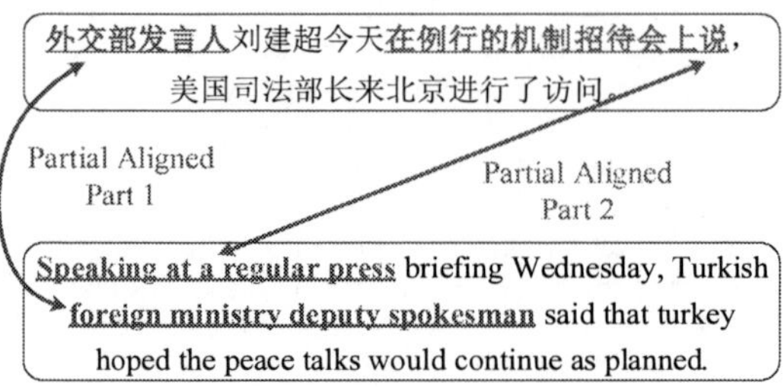

Figure 1: An example of our partially aligned training data, in which the source sentence and target sentence are not parallel but they include two parallel parts (highlight in blue and red respectively).

of great translation quality, we usually need large-scale parallel data. Unfortunately, the large-scale parallel data is always insufficient in many domains and language pairs. Without sufficient parallel sentence pairs, NMT tends to learn poor estimates on low-count events.

Actually, there have been some effective methods to deal with the situation of translating language pairs with limited resource under different scenarios (Johnson et al., 2016; Cheng et al., 2017; Sennrich et al., 2016a; Zhang and Zong, 2016). In this paper, we address a new translation scenario in which we do not have any parallel sentences but have massive monolingual corpora and phrase pairs. The previous methods are hard to be used to learn an NMT model under this situation. In this paper, we propose a novel method to learn an NMT model using only monolingual data and phrase pairs.

Our main idea is that although there does not exist the parallel sentences, we can derive the sentence pairs which are non-parallel but contain the parallel parts (in this paper, we call these sentences as **partially aligned sentences**) with the

Proceedings of the The 8th International Joint Conference on Natural Language Processing, pages 384–393,
Taipei, Taiwan, November 27 – December 1, 2017 ©2017 AFNLP

monolingual data and phrase pairs. Then we can utilize these partially aligned sentences to train an NMT model. Figure 1 shows an example of our data. Source sentence and target sentence are not fully aligned but contain two translation fragments: ("外交部发言人", "foreign ministry deputy") and ("在例行的记者招待会上说", "speaking at a regular press"). Intuitively, these kinds of sentence pairs are useful in building an NMT model.

To use these partially aligned sentences, the training method should be different from the original methods which are designed for parallel corpora. In this work, we adapt the conventional NMT training method mainly from two perspectives. On one hand, different generation strategies are designed for aligned and unaligned target words. For aligned words, our method guides the translation process based on both the context of source side and previously predicted words. When generating the unaligned target words , our model only depends on the words previously generated without considering the context of source side. On the other hand, we redesign the objective function so as to emphasize the partially aligned parts in addition to maximizing the log-likelihood of the target sentence.

The contributions of our paper are twofold:

1) Our approach addresses a new translation scenario, where there only exists monolingual data and phrase pairs. We propose a method to train an NMT model under this scenario. The method is simple and easy to implement, which can be used in arbitrary attention-based NMT framework.

2) Empirical experiments on the Chinese-English translation tasks under this scenario show that our method can achieve a relatively good result. Moreover, if we only add a tiny parallel corpus, the method can obtain significant improvements in terms of translation quality.

2 Review of Neural Machine Translation

Our approach can be easily applied to any end-to-end attention-based NMT framework. In this work, we follow the neural machine translation architecture by Bahdanau et al. (2015), which we will summarize in this section.

Given the source sentence $X = \{x_1, x_2, ..., x_{Tx}\}$ and the target sentence $Y = \{y_1, y_2, ..., y_{Ty}\}$. The goal of machine translation is to transform source sentence into the target sentence. The end-to-end NMT framework consists of two recurrent neural networks, which are respectively called encoder and decoder. First, the encoder network encodes the X into context vectors C. Then, the decoder network generates the target translation sentences one word each time based on the context vectors C and target words previously generated. More specifically, that is $p(y_i|y_{<i}, C)$.

In encoding stage, it transforms X into a sequence of vectors $h_{enc} = \{h_1^k, h_2^k, h_3^k, ..., h_T^k\}$ using m stacked LSTM (Hochreiter and Schmidhuber, 1997) layers. Finally, the encoder chooses the hidden states of the top encoder layer as $h_{top} = \{h_1^m, h_2^m, h_3^m, ..., h_T^m\}$ that we will use in attention mechanism to calculate context vector later.

In decoding stage, it generates one target word at a time from conditional probability $p(y_i|y_{<i}, C; \theta)$ also via m stacked LSTM layers parameterized by θ. Supposing we have obtained the context vector, the conditional probability $p(y_i|y_{<i}, C; \theta)$ is calculated as follows:

$$p(y_i|y_{<i}, C; \theta) = p(y_i|y_{<i}, c_i) \\ = softmax(g(W_{y_i}, z_i^m, c_i)) \tag{1}$$

Where W_{y_i} is embedding of the target word, z_i^m is current hidden states of top layer in decoder network. Note that the first hidden states of decoder z_0^k are set to the last hidden states of encoder as follows:

$$z_0^k = h_T^k \tag{2}$$

c_i can be computed as a weighted sum of the source-side h_s as follows:

$$c_i = \sum_{j=1}^{T_x} a_{ij} h_i^m \tag{3}$$

Where a_{ij} is alignment probability, which can be calculated in multiple ways (Luong et al., 2015a). In our method, we use a simple single-layer feed forward network. This alignment probability measures how relevant i-th context vector of source sentence is in deciding the current symbol in translation. The probability will be further normalized:

$$a_{ij} = \frac{exp(e_{ij})}{\sum_{k=1}^{Tx} exp(e_{ik}))} \tag{4}$$

A detailed introduction of the encoder-decoder framework is described in Bahdanau et al. (2015). In order to train NMT system, we use parallel data to optimize the network parameters by maximizing the conditional log-likelihood:

$$L(\theta, D) = \frac{1}{N} \sum_{n=1}^{N} \sum_{i}^{T_y} log(p(y_i^{(n)}|p(y_{<i}^{(n)}, X^{(n)}, \theta))$$

(5)

3 NMT with Partially Aligned Data

In §2 we gave a brief description of the attention-based NMT models whose network parameters are trained using parallel sentence pairs. However, in the translation scenario where there only exists monolingual corpora and phrase pairs, the conventional NMT framework is hard to be used in training a model. In this section, we first explain how we actually obtain the partially aligned corpora with aligned positions using phrase pairs and monolingual corpora, then introduce our method to train the NMT models using the partially aligned sentences according to the particular properties of the corpora.

3.1 Constructing partially Aligned Corpora

Assuming there exists abundant phrase pairs and monolingual sentences in source and target languages, we define our approach to extract partially aligned sentence pairs for training.

Given a phrase pair (ph_s, ph_t), ph_s may appear in a source-side monolingual sentence X, and ph_t may appear in a target-side monolingual sentence Y. Then, X and Y are non-parallel but contain the parallel part. We call these kinds of data the partially aligned sentences. In this work, we collect the partially aligned sentences by searching the phrase pairs in both of the source and target monolingual data simultaneously. In order to reduce the time of the searching process, the monolingual training corpora are first split into many parts. Then, we retrieve the source phrase in each part to restrict the source range of partially aligned corpus. With the retrieved results, we can search the final results of the partially aligned sentences pairs easily. In this way we can construct our corpora, in which only one or more phrases are aligned in every sentence pairs. We denote a partially aligned sentence $(X = x_1, x_2, ...x_{Tx}, Y = y_1, y_2, ..., y_{Ty})$, in which a set of the phrase pairs

aligned with each other. We call these pairs partially aligned part:

$$P_x^{(k)} = x_{k1}, ..., x_{kp}$$
$$P_y^{(k)} = y_{k1}, ..., x_{kq}$$

(6)

$P_x^{(k)}$ and $P_y^{(k)}$ are the phrases in the source and target sentences respectively, and they are translation equivalents.

3.2 Model Descriptions

In §3.1, we acquired the partially aligned corpora with the phrase pairs and monolingual sentences. Now, we need to use them to train the NMT model. As the traditional NMT model is designed for the parallel sentences, it is not suitable for partially aligned sentences. Thus we redesign the traditional NMT model as follows. Figure 2 shows the basic framework of our training method. Our model has 4 different parts from conventional NMT model, including initial states, generation process, objective functions and vocabulary size.

3.2.1 Initial States

The first difference is the initial hidden states of decoder. In the conventional NMT model, the initial hidden states of decoder z_0^k is set to the last hidden state in encoder h_{Tx}^k, including initial states, generation process, objective functions and vocabulary size. shown in Eq. (2). For parallel sentences, this setting is reasonable, while for partially aligned sentence, this initial method is inappropriate. The reason is that the hidden state of last word in source sentence is irrelevant to the target sentence, considering the fact that under our scenario, the target side sentences may entirely uncorrelated to the source sentences. Thus, in our model, z_0^k is set to a zero vector as follows:

$$Z_0^k = \mathbf{0}$$

(7)

In Figure 2, the hidden state of "<start>" symbol is set to zero vector when y_1 does not belong to parallel part of the sentence pair.

3.2.2 Generation Process

The second difference is the generation process. In the conventional NMT system, the model generates each target word based on the context vector c_i and previously predicted words $y_{<i}$ as shown in Eq. (1). This generation strategy is unsuitable for the partially aligned corpora, since there exists many unaligned target words. Intuitively,

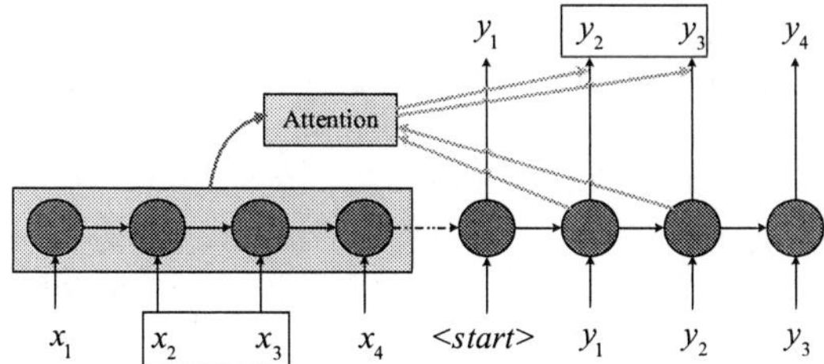

Figure 2: The framework of our training method for partially aligned sentence, in which (x_2,x_3) and (y_2,y_3) are parallel parts.

when the model generates the non-parallel parts, it is unnecessary to take the context vector c_i into consideration. As Figure 2 illustrated, (x_2,x_3) and (y_2,y_3) are parallel parts in this partially aligned sentence pair, and we use context vector which is generated by attention mechanism only when the decoder outputs y_2 and y_3. Therefore, the decoder in our model can be described as follows:

$$c_i = \begin{cases} \sum_j^{Tx} a_{ij}h_i & if\ y_i \in P_y^{(k)} \\ 0 & if\ y_i \notin P_y^{(k)} \end{cases} \quad (8)$$

where a_{ij} is calculated as Eq. (2), $P_y^{(k)}$ is the target partial part, as shown in Eq. (5). In Eq. (8), our model generates the aligned target words based on the context vector c_i and previously predicted words $y_{<i}$. When generating the unaligned target words, the model sets the context vector c_i to zero, indicating that the model generates these words only based on the LSTM-based RNN language model.

3.2.3 Objective Function

Third, we redesign the objective function. Given the parallel data, the objective function is to maximize the log-likelihood of each target word as shown in Eq. (5). For the partially aligned sentence, besides the source and target sentence, we know the phrase alignment information. Hence, apart from maximizing the log-likelihood of each target word, we also hope to make the source and target words in partially aligned part align to each other. As shown in Figure 2, when predicting the words y_2 and y_3, we want to attend more information of corresponding words x_2 and x_3. Thus, we inject an auxiliary object function to achieve it. More specifically, our objective function is de-

signed as follows:

$$L_P(\theta, D) =$$

$$\frac{1}{N}\sum_{n=1}^{N}\{\sum_{i}^{T_y} log(p(y_i^{(n)}|p(y_{<i}^{(n)}, X^{(n)}; \theta)) \quad (9)$$

$$+ \lambda \times \triangle(a^{(n)}, \widehat{a}^{(n)}); \theta)\}$$

Where $a^{(n)}$ is defined in Eq. (4), $\triangle$ is a loss function that encourages the agreement between $a^{(n)}$ and $\widehat{a}^{(n)}$. $\widehat{a}^{(n)}$ is the supervised attention determined by alignment relationship between P_X and P_Y, and can be calculated as follows:

$$\widehat{a}_{i,j}^{(n)} = \begin{cases} 1 & if\ x_j \in P_X\ and\ y_i \in P_Y \\ 0 & others \end{cases} \quad (10)$$

$\lambda > 0$ is a hyper-parameter that balances the preference between likelihood and agreement. In this paper, it is set to 0.3.

As shown in Eq. (8), our objective function does not only consider to maximize the log-likelihood of the target sentence, but also encourages the alignment a_{ij} produced by NMT to have a larger agreement with the prior alignment information. This objective function is similar to that used by the supervised attention method (Mi et al., 2016a; Liu et al., 2016). Inspired by Liu et al. (2016), the agreement between $a^{(n)}$ and $\widehat{a}^{(n)}$ can be defined in different ways:

- Multiplication (MUL)

$$\triangle(a^{(n)}, \widehat{a}_{i,j}^{(n)}; \theta)$$

$$= -\sum_{i=0}^{T_y}\sum_{j=0}^{T_x} a(\theta)_{i,j}^{(n)} \times \widehat{a}_{i,j}^{(n)} \quad (11)$$

where $\widehat{a}_{i,j}^{(n)}$ is computed by Eq. (10)

- Mean Squared Error (MSE)

$$\triangle(a^{(n)}, \widehat{a}_{i,j}^{(n)}; \theta)$$

$$= -\sum_{i=0}^{T_y}\sum_{j=0}^{T_x} \frac{1}{2}(a(\theta)_{i,j}^{(n)} - \widehat{a}_{i,j}^{(n)})^2 \quad (12)$$

3.2.4 Limited Vocabulary

The last difference is the vocabulary size during decoding. To make use of phrase pairs as much as possible, we extract a number of special phrase pairs whose source and target are both one word.

In decoding phase, as what Mi et al. (2016b) have done, we can use these special phrase pairs to reduce the vocabulary size when computing the final score distribution. In this way, we can not only acquire more accurate translation of each word, but also accelerate the decoding speed. The vocabulary size can be reduced as follows:

$$V = V_1 \cup V_2 \qquad (13)$$

Where V_1 contains the most frequently target words and V_2 is a target words set. This set V_2 is made up of all the target words of the special phrase pairs whose corresponding source words belong to the source sentence.

4 Experiment

In this section, we perform the experiment on Chinese-English translation tasks to test our method.

4.1 Dataset

We evaluate our approach on large-scale monolingual data set from LDC corpus, which includes 13M Chinese sentences and 10M English sentences. Table 1 shows the detailed statistics of our training data. To test our model, we use NIST 2003(MT03) as development set, and NIST 2004-2006(MT04-06) as test set. The evaluation metric is case-insensitive BLEU (Papineni et al., 2002) as calculated by the $multi\text{-}bleu.perl$.

Corpus		Chinese	English
	#Sent.	13.33M	10.03M
monolingual	#Word	327.10M	276.07M
	Vocab	1.83M	1.07M

Table 1: The statistics of monolingual dataset on the LDC corpus.

4.2 Data Preparing and Preprocessing

Considering the fact that the amount of manually annotated phrase pairs is not enough, in order to imitate the environment of experiment, we extract phrase pairs from parallel corpora automatically to make up for the shortage of quantity. To do this, we use Moses (Koehn et al., 2007) in its training step to learn a phrase table from LDC corpus, which includes 0.63M sentence pairs. In order to simulate the experiment as far as possible, we adopt three strategies to filter low quality phrase pairs: 1) the phrases containing the punctuation should be filtered out. (The special phrase parirs introduced in §3.2.4 should be retain) 2) the length of source phrase and target phrase should be greater than 3. 3) only the phrase pairs whose translation probability exceed 0.5 should be retain. In this way, we can get 3M phrase pairs in our experiment. According to our analysis, the average length of phrases are 4.15 and 4.70 on source and target side respectively.

When we search the phrase pairs in monolingual sentences, an obstacle is that one phrase pair will get different source sentences with same target sentence or same source sentence with different target sentences. Therefore, for one phrase pair, we have to restrict the number n of both source sentences and target sentences. To balance the search speed of the phrase pairs in monolingual corpora and the amount of partially aligned sentences, we set the hyper-parameter n to 7. We can search for 5M partially aligned sentences in our experiment. We also calculate the average length ratio of aligned phrases against the whole sentence, which is only 21% and 23% respectively on source and target side.

To ensure the quality of the partially aligned corpora, we also set the number of phrases that aligned to each other in one sentence pair must be greater than a threshold. Here, the threshold is set to 2. That is to say the partially aligned sentence pair should contain at least two aligned phrase pairs.

4.3 Training Details

We build our described method based on the Zoph_RNN toolkit[1] written in C++/CUDA. Both encoder and decoder consist of two stacked LSTM layers. We set minibatch size to 128. The word embedding dimension of both source and target sides is 1000, and the dimensions of hidden layers unit is set to 1000. In our baseline model, we limit the vocabulary of both source and target languages to 30K most frequent words, and other words are replaced by a special symbol "UNK". We run our model on the training corpus 20 iterations in total with stochastic gradient decent algorithm. We set learning rate to 0.1 at the beginning and halve the threshold while the perplexity increases on the development set. Dropout is applied to our model, and the rate is set to 0.2. For

---

[1] https://github.com/isi-nlp/ZophRNN

#	System	MT03	MT04	MT05	MT06	Ave
1	Phrase NMT Model	3.64	4.25	3.55	3.77	3.80
2	Partially Aligned Model(MUL)	3.80	4.37	3.75	4.24	4.04
3	Partially Aligned Model(MSE)	5.11	5.04	4.26	4.95	4.84
4	Partially Aligned Model(MSE) + LimitedVocab	**6.63**	**6.81**	**5.59**	**5.77**	**6.20**
5	Phrase NMT model + LimitedVocab	3.78	4.33	3.63	3.94	3.92

Table 2: Translation results (BLEU score) for different translation methods.

testing, we employ beam search algorithm, and the beam size is 12.

4.4 Training Methods

We conduct our experiment on the dataset mentioned above, and we list the training methods used as follows:

1) **Phrase NMT Model:** As mentioned above, the only parallel resource is phrase pairs. We use attention-based NMT system to train only on the 3M phrase pairs to get our baseline result.

2) **Partially Aligned Model(MUL):** We train our NMT model using the objective function of multiplication method on the partially aligned sentences.

3) **Partially Aligned Model(MSE):** We train our NMT model using the objective function of Mean Squared Error(MSE) method.

4) **Partially Aligned Model(MSE) + Limited-Vocab:** It is similar to Partially Aligned Model(MSE) and the only difference is that we restrict the final score distribution on a limited target vocabulary, which is described in §3.2.4.

5) **Phrase NMT Model + LimitedVocab:** It is the method that LimitedVocab is used in Phrase NMT model.

5 Results and Analysis

5.1 Phrase NMT Model vs. Partially Aligned Method

We present the translation results in BLEU scores of different systems in Table 2. Our first concern is whether the proposed model can actually improve the translation quality. As Table 2 shows, we find that our partially aligned model (both MUL supervised method and MSE supervised method) is superior to the Phrase NMT Model, which indicates that our Partially Aligned method is effective in improving the translation quality.

Source sentence:	布什说：“此项计划将对劳动大众提供减税优惠。”
Phrase NMT model:	The bush says the <UNK> tax concessions be made a possible member
Our model:	Bush said, the scheme will provide tax concessions to the community.

Figure 3: A translation example comparing between phrase NMT model and our partially aligned method.

Figure 3 lists a comparison example of Phrase NMT model and our model. Obviously, our model can achieve the correct translation while the Phrase NMT model generates the unfaithful result. It demonstrates that our model is actually having the ability to learn translation adequacy from aligned parts and fluency from both aligned and unaligned parts.

In §3.2, we described two objective functions in our model. We focus on the difference of these two approaches. As a comparison, MSE method (Row 3) outperforms the MUL method (Row 2) with an average improvement of 0.8 BLEU points, indicating that MSE method is more effective as an object function for our partially aligned model. In the following experiment, we adopt the MSE method as the new objective function used in our model.

5.2 Effect of Limited Vocabulary

In Table 2, an interesting result is that using a reduced vocabulary can significantly improve the performance (+1.36 BLEU points), but it can only achieve 0.12 BLEU points improvement for Phrase NMT model. According to Mi et al. (2016b), this approach is useful in conventional

NMT model. Our result is in agreement with their findings, and the improvement is more prominent in our partially aligned model. Under our scenario, compared to the parallel corpora, fewer parallel parts appear in sentence pairs. The faithfulness of our translation result is relatively poor while the fluency is relatively good. With the limited relevant vocabulary, the faithfulness of the translation results is much improved.

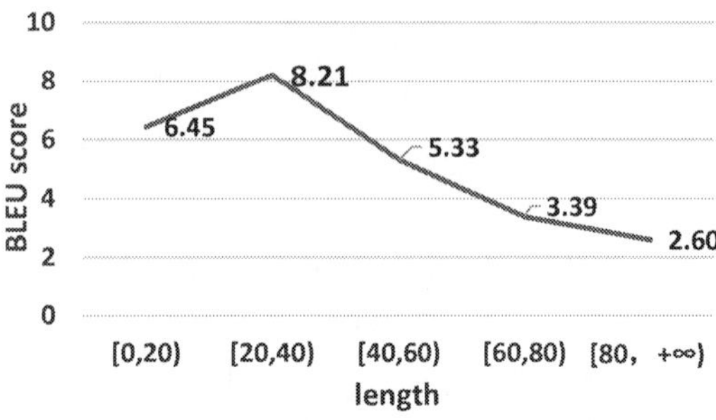

Figure 4: Translation results (BLEU score) of different lengths.

5.3 Result of Different Sentence Lengths

The performance of our partially aligned model with different lengths is another problem we care about. We randomly select 1000 sentences from translation results of test set (MT03-08), which are trained by the Partially Aligned Model(MSE)+ReduceDict method. We classify them into five categories according to the length. Figure 4 shows the results of the experiment.

We find that the sentences with shorter length (lower than 40) yield better results than the long sentences. When the length of sentences exceeds 80, the quality of translation is rather poor. The reason is that we mainly use phrase pairs in our method, and the length of phrase is relative short compared to whole sentence. So our model is more suitable for the translation of short sentences. When we translate long sentences, the parameters in our model are not adjusted for tuning, and our approach can not produce translation of high quality.

5.4 Effect of Adding Small Parallel Corpus

We concern that when we have a tiny parallel corpus, whether the small scale parallel corpus can boost the translation performance of the partially aligned method. Here, we fine-tune the partially aligned translation model on these corpora. The details of these corpora are introduced in Table 3.

Corpus			Chinese	English
parallel	#Sent.		0.1M	
	#Word		3.00M	3.86M
	Vocab		0.07M	0.04M

Table 3: The statistics of small-scale parallel datasets.

The result is presented in Table 4. We can observe that the translation result tends to be poor by only using a small-scale parallel corpora. It indicates that conventional NMT system cannot learn a good model on the small-scale datasets. However, when fine-tuning our partially aligned model with this small parallel corpus, we can get a surprising improvement. The results suggest that when under a scenario in which we only have monolingual corpora and phrase pairs, even a few bitexts can boost translation quality to a large extent.

We investigate the effect of the different corpora size on the final translation results. According to Table 4, when the number of parallel sentences is quite small (lower than 60K), we can acquire a measurable improvement (more than 10 BLEU) compared to the conventional NMT system result. Especially, when the size of sentence pairs is 40K and 60K, our method obtains the enormous improvement over the NMT model by +13.82 BLEU points and +13.21 BLEU points respectively. When using more than 60K sentence pairs, we still get a relatively high promotion of translation quality. However, the promotion is not very remarkable as Row1-3 reveal in Table 4. We can see when the number of parallel corpora is 100K(Row 5), the improvement over NMT Model is +3.95 BLEU points, which indicates that as the size of parallel corpora increases, the improvement of fine-tuning model is decreasing.

6 Related Work

Most of existing work in neural machine translation focus on integrating SMT strategies (He et al., 2016; Zhou et al., 2017; Wang et al., 2017; Shen et al., 2015), handling rare words (Li et al., 2016; Sennrich et al., 2016b; Luong et al., 2015b) and designing the better framework (Tu et al., 2016; Luong et al., 2015a; Meng et al., 2016). As for translation scenarios, training NMT model under

#Sent.	Method	MT03	MT04	MT05	MT06	Ave
20K	**NMT Model**	1.60	1.22	1.05	1.70	1.39
	Partially Aligned Model(MSE) + Para	12.36	15.07	11.64	14.61	13.42
40K	**NMT Model**	1.87	2.00	1.47	2.24	1.90
	Partially Aligned Model(MSE) + Para	14.12	17.84	13.66	17.26	15.72
60K	**NMT Model**	3.72	5.04	3.49	4.47	4.18
	Partially Aligned Model(MSE) + Para	15.54	19.62	15.16	19.25	17.39
80K	**NMT Model**	7.96	11.85	8.16	10.53	9.63
	Partially Aligned Model(MSE) + Para	17.16	21.18	16.65	20.61	18.90
100K	**NMT Model**	14.50	18.21	14.29	17.49	16.12
	Partially Aligned(MSE) Model + Para	18.30	22.50	17.92	21.55	20.07

Table 4: Effect of different data size of parallel corpus. Method NMT Model means the result of conventional NMT system trained on these low-count parallel sentences. Partially Aligned Model(MSE) + Para means the result of our model fine-tuned by these parallel sentences.

different scenarios has drawn intensive attention in recent years. Actually, there have been some effective methods to deal with them. We divide the related work into three categories:

6.1 Pivot-based Scenario

Pivot-based scenario assumes that there only exists source-pivot and pivot-target parallel corpora, which can be used to train source-to-pivot and pivot-to-target translation models. Cheng et al. (2017) propose to translate source language into pivot language, and then the pivot language will be translated into target language. According to the fact that parallel sentences should have close probabilities of generating a sentence in a third language, Chen et al. (2017) construct a Teacher-Student framework, in which existing pivot-target NMT model guides the learning process of the source-target model.

6.2 Multilingual Scenario

In multilingual scenario, there exists multiple language pairs but no source-target sentence pairs. Johnson et al. (2016) use parallel corpora of multiple languages to train a universal NMT model. This universal model learns translation knowledge from multiple different languages, which makes zero-shot translation feasible. Firat et al. (2016) present a multi-way, multilingual model to resolve the zero-resource translation. They use other language to train a multi-way NMT model. The model generates pseudo parallel corpora to fine-tune attention mechanism, so as to achieve better translation.

6.3 Monolingual Data Scenario

In this scenario, an NMT model of good quality has been trained on existing parallel corpora, but a preferable translation result is still in need by incorporating additional data resource. Gülçehre et al. (2015) propose to incorporate target-side corpora as a language model. Sennrich et al. (2016a) attempt to enhance the decoder network model of NMT by incorporating the target-side monolingual data. Luong et at. (2016) explore the sequence autoencoders and skip-thought vectors method to exploit the monolingual data of source language. Zhang and Zong (2016) propose two approaches, self-training algorithm and multi-task learning framework, to incorporate source-side monolingual data. Besides that, Cheng et al. (2016) have explored the usage of both source and target monolingual data using a semi-supervised method to reconstruct both source and target side monolingual language, where two NMT frameworks will be used.

Above methods are designed for different scenarios, and their work can achieve great results on these scenarios. However, when in the scenario we propose in this work, that is we only have monolingual sentences and some phrase pairs, their methods are hard to be utilized to train an NMT model. Under this scenario, monolingual data can be acquired easily, and high quality phrase pairs can be obtained using some effective methods (Zhang et al., 2014). To learn a good NMT model in our translation scenario, we adapt the conventional training procedure by designing a different generation mechanism and a different objective function.

7 Conclusion

In this paper, we have presented a new translation scenario for NMT in which we have only monolingual data and bilingual phrase pairs. We obtain large-scale partially aligned sentence pairs from the monolingual data and phrase pairs by an information retrieval algorithm. The generation process and objective function are specially designed in NMT training to take full advantage of the partially aligned corpora. The empirical experiments show that the proposed method is capable to achieve a relatively good result. We further find that only a little amount of parallel sentences can significantly boost the translation quality.

We also notice that the proposed approach with only partially aligned data cannot obtain high translation quality. In the future, we plan to design better approaches to model the partially aligned corpus. We also attempt to evaluate our approach on other language pairs, especially low-resource language pairs.

Acknowledgments

The research work has been funded by the Natural Science Foundation of China under Grant No. 61333018 and No. 61402478, and it is also supported by the Strategic Priority Research Program of the CAS under Grant No. XDB02070007

References

Dzmitry Bahdanau, Kyunghyun Cho, and Yoshua Bengio. 2015. Neural machine translation by jointly learning to align and translate. *In Proceedings of ICLR 2015*.

Yun Chen, Yong Cheng, Yang Liu, and Li Victor, O.K. 2017. A teacher-student framework for zero-resource neural machine translation. *In Proceedings of ACL 2017*.

Yong Cheng, Yang Liu, Qian Yang, Maosong Sun, and Wei Xu. 2017. Joint training for pivot-based neural machine translation. *In Proceedings of IJCAI 2017*.

Yong Cheng, Wei Xu, Zhongjun He, Wei He, Hua Wu, Maosong Sun, and Yang Liu. 2016. Semi-supervised learning for neural machine translation. *In Proceedings of ACL 2016*.

David Chiang. 2005. A hierarchical phrase-based model for statistical machine translation. *In Proceedings of ACL 2005*.

Kyunghyun Cho, Bart van Merriënboer Caglar Gulcehre, Dzmitry Bahdanau, Fethi Bougares Holger Schwenk, and Yoshua Bengio. 2014. Learning phrase representations using rnn encoder–decoder for statistical machine translation. *In Proceedings of EMNLP 2014*.

Orhan Firat, Baskaran Sankaran, Yaser Alonaizan, Fatos T. Yarman Vural, and Kyunghyun Cho. 2016. Zero-resource translation with multi-lingual neural machine translation. *In Proceedings of EMNLP 2016*.

Caglar Gülçehre, Orhan Firat, Kelvin Xu, Kyunghyun Cho, Loıc Barrault, Huei-Chi Lin, Fethi Bougares, Holger Schwenk, and Yoshua Bengio. 2015. On using monolingual corpora in neural machine translation. *CoRR, abs/1503.03535*.

Wei He, Zhongjun He, Hua Wu, and Haifeng Wang. 2016. Improved neural machine translation with smt features. *In Proceedings of AAAI 2016*.

Sepp Hochreiter and Jürgen Schmidhuber. 1997. Long short-term memory. *Neural computation*, 9(8):1735–1780.

Melvin Johnson, Mike Schuster, Quoc V Le, Maxim Krikun, Yonghui Wu, Zhifeng Chen, Nikhil Thorat, Fernanda Vié gas, Martin Wattenberg, and Greg Corrado. 2016. Google's multilingual neural machine translation system: Enabling zero-shot translation. *arXiv preprint arXiv:1611.04558*.

Nal Kalchbrenner and Phil Blunsom. 2013. Recurrent continuous translation models. *In Proceedings of EMNLP 2013*.

Philipp Koehn, Hieu Hoang, Alexandra Birch, Chris Callison-Burch, Marcello Federico, Nicola Bertoldi, Brooke Cowan, Wade Shen, Christine Moran, Richard Zens, et al. 2007. Moses: Open source toolkit for statistical machine translation. *In Proceedings of ACL 2007*, pages 177–180.

Philipp Koehn, Franz J. Och, and Daniel Marcu. 2003. Statistical phrase-based translation. *In Proceedings of ACL-NAACL 2013*.

Xiaoqing Li, Jiajun Zhang, and Chengqing Zong. 2016. Towards zero unknown word in neural machine translation. *In Proceedings of IJCAI 2016*.

Lemao Liu, Masao Utiyama, Andrew Finch, and Eiichiro Sumita. 2016. Neural machine translation with supervised attention. *In Proceedings of COLING 2016*.

Yang Liu, Qun Liu, and Shouxun Lin. 2006. Tree-to-string alignment template for statistical machine translation. *In Proceedings of ACL 2006*.

Minh-Thang Luong, Quoc V Le, Ilya Sutskever, Oriol Vinyals, and Lukasz Kaiser. 2016. Multi-task sequence to sequence learning. *In Proceedings of ICLR 2016*.

Minh-Thang Luong, Hieu Pham, and Christopher D Manning. 2015a. Effective approaches to attention-based neural machine translation. *In Proceedings of EMNLP 2015*.

Minh-Thang Luong, Ilya Sutskever, Quoc V Le, Oriol Vinyals, and Wojciech Zaremba. 2015b. Addressing the rare word problem in neural machine translation. *In Proceedings of ACL 2015*.

Fandong Meng, Zhengdong Lu, Hang Li, and Qun Liu. 2016. Interactive attention for neural machine translation. In *In Proceedings of COLING 2016*.

Haitao Mi, Zhiguo Wang, and Abe Ittycheriah. 2016a. Supervised attentions for neural machine translation. *In Proceedings of EMNLP 2016*.

Haitao Mi, Zhiguo Wang, and Abe Ittycheriah. 2016b. Vocabulary manipulation for neural machine translation. *In Proceedings of ACL 2016*.

Kishore Papineni, Salim Roukos, Todd Ward, and Wei-Jing Zhu. 2002. Bleu: a method for automatic evaluation of machine translation. *In Proceedings of ACL 2002*, pages 311–318.

Rico Sennrich, Barry Haddow, and Alexandra Birch. 2016a. Improving neural machine translation models with monolingual data. *In Proceedings of ACL 2016*.

Rico Sennrich, Barry Haddow, and Alexandra Birch. 2016b. Neural machine translation of rare words with subword units. *In Proceedings of ACL 2016*.

Shiqi Shen, Yong Cheng, Zhongjun He, Wei He, Hua Wu, Maosong Sun, and Yang Liu. 2015. Minimum risk training for neural machine translation. *In Proceedings of ACL 2015*.

Ilya Sutskever, Oriol Vinyals, and Quoc V Le. 2014. Sequence to sequence learning with neural networks. *In Proceedings of NIPS 2014*.

Zhaopeng Tu, Zhengdong Lu, Yang Liu, Xiaohua Liu, and Hang Li. 2016. Coverage-based neural machine translation. *In Proceedings of ACL 2016*.

Xing Wang, Zhengdong Lu, Zhaopeng Tu, Hang Li, Deyi Xiong, and Min Zhang. 2017. Neural machine translation advised by statistical machine translation. *In Proceedings of AAAI 2017*.

Yonghui Wu, Mike Schuster, Zhifeng Chen, Quoc V Le, Mohammad Norouzi, Wolfgang Macherey, Maxim Krikun, Yuan Cao, Qin Gao, Klaus Macherey, et al. 2016. Google's neural machine translation system: Bridging the gap between human and machine translation. *arXiv preprint arXiv:1609.08144*.

Feifei Zhai, Jiajun Zhang, Yu Zhou, Chengqing Zong, et al. 2012. Tree-based translation without using parse trees. *In Proceedings of COLING 2012*.

Jiajun Zhang, Shujie Liu, Mu Li, Ming Zhou, and Chengqing Zong. 2014. Bilingually-constrained phrase embeddings for machine translation. *In Proceedings of ACL 2014*.

Jiajun Zhang and Chengqing Zong. 2016. Exploiting source-side monolingual data in neural machine translation. *In Proceedings of EMNLP 2016*.

Long Zhou, Wenpeng Hu, Jiajun Zhang, and Chengqing Zong. 2017. Neural system combination for machine translation. *In Proceedings of ACL 2017*.

Identifying Usage Expression Sentences in Consumer Product Reviews

Shibamouli Lahiri and **V. G. Vinod Vydiswaran** and **Rada Mihalcea**
University of Michigan
{lahiri, vgvinodv, mihalcea}@umich.edu

Abstract

In this paper we introduce the problem of identifying usage expression sentences in a consumer product review. We create a human-annotated gold standard dataset of 565 reviews spanning five distinct product categories. Our dataset consists of more than 3,000 annotated sentences. We further introduce a classification system to label sentences according to whether or not they describe some "usage." The system combines lexical, syntactic, and semantic features in a product-agnostic fashion to yield good classification performance. We show the effectiveness of our approach using importance ranking of features, error analysis, and cross-product classification experiments.

1 Introduction

Identification of *usage expressions* — phrases or sentence snippets describing product use in reviews — is an important problem in mining consumer product reviews. Identifying such usage expressions accurately allows us to view the relationship between consumers and products more clearly (e.g., by indicating how frequently a consumer uses a product). Further, the language and style employed in describing product use bring relevant and unseen aspects of the products to the fore (e.g., describing usage of a product in non-traditional and unique ways).

Usage expressions can take several forms, such as which aspects of the product are used, why the product is used, where it is used, how it is used, when it is used, and so forth (c.f. Section 3 for specific examples). The product could be used by a consumer in a number of ways, sometimes in unique ways not intended for originally. Hence

enumerating all possible uses of a product is computationally intractable. In this paper, therefore, we focus on four specific cases of product usage: why the product is used, where it is used, how it is used, and if there are any non-standard or non-traditional use (cf. Section 3).

While the relationship between product usage and consumer behavior has mostly been discussed by marketing researchers and psychologists, the question of whether the phenomenon of *usage* has any detectable signature in terms of the *language* used by consumers has not been addressed thus far. In this paper, we introduce the task of identifying usage expressions from consumer product reviews. In particular, we focus on classifying review sentences as to whether they contain a *usage expression* or not. We create our own human-annotated corpus of 565 reviews on five distinct product categories containing more than 3000 sentences. We introduce a system that classifies sentences according to whether they contain a usage expression or not with 87.2% accuracy. We also show that an appropriate combination of lexical, syntactic, and semantic features performs better than individual feature categories.

2 Related Work

Existing research could be organized into six self-consistent psycho-sociological theories, namely psycho-analysis, social theories, stimulus-response theories, trait and factor theories, self-theories, and life style theories. Kassarjian (1971) offers a comprehensive review of the literature on consumer behavior and psychological traits. Robertson and Myers (1969) found weak relationships between opinion leadership and innovative buying behavior, but observed that the relationship *strength* varied by product category. Tucker and Painter (1961), and Sparks and Tucker

Proceedings of the The 8th International Joint Conference on Natural Language Processing, pages 394–403,
Taipei, Taiwan, November 27 – December 1, 2017 ©2017 AFNLP

(1971) showed that there were correlations between personality traits and the *types* of products used. Dolich (1969) posited that products as *symbols* were organized into congruent relationships with the consumer's *self-image*. More recently, Govers and Schoormans (2005) found that people preferred products with a *product personality* that matched their self-image, and the positive effect of product-personality congruence was independent of user-image congruence.

In natural language processing research, the closest problem to usage expressions is perhaps that of opinion mining from product reviews and product aspects. Dave et al. (2003) classified reviews as expressing positive or negative sentiment. They identified four problems with review classification, including rating inconsistency, ambivalence, data sparseness, and skewed distribution. Hu and Liu (2004) extracted product features from the reviews of a single product, taking user opinion into account. Opinion/product features were mined if a reviewer had commented on them. Popescu and Etzioni (2005) presented OPINE, an unsupervised information extraction system that mined reviews in order to build a model of important product features, their evaluation by reviewers, and their relative quality across products. OPINE's use of *relaxation labeling* led to strong performance on the tasks of finding opinion phrases and their polarity. Ding et al. (2008) presented a *"holistic lexicon-based approach"* for mining *context-dependent* opinion words. The proposed method used an aggregating function for multiple conflicting opinion words in a sentence. The authors further implemented a system called "Opinion Observer" based on their method. Lastly, Wu et al. (2009) implemented a special dependency parser for opinion mining that used phrases (rather than words) as the primitive building blocks. Since many product features are in fact phrases, this approach led to good results for extracting relations between product features and opinion expressions.

Yet another related task is that of mining *semantic affordances* (Chao et al., 2015). In this task, "usage" of a product can be viewed as an *action* performed on an *object* with the help of the *product*. Relationships between such actions and objects are known as "semantic affordances". As Chao et al. showed, text mining can be very effective at ascertaining affordance relationships between verb and noun classes. Similar verb-noun relationships have also been formulated in the problem of learning *selectional preferences* from text (Resnik, 1997; Brockmann and Lapata, 2003; Erk, 2007; Pantel et al., 2007; Bergsma et al., 2008; Van de Cruys, 2014), and more generally, in the problem of *probabilistic frame induction* (Chambers and Jurafsky, 2011; Cheung et al., 2013; Chen et al., 2013).

Another topic of research related to our work is the problem of *research idea extraction* from academic papers. Gupta and Manning (2011) took the first stab at this problem by implementing a bootstrapping algorithm on dependency tree kernels. Gupta and Manning's method was later refined by Tsai et al. (2013) who worked with a more crisp set of *idea categories*. We view this problem as conceptually parallel to ours; however, a key difference is that usage expressions are typically more obscure in text as compared to research ideas.

3 Building a Usage Expression Dataset

Product reviews often contain usage information. Specifically, in addition to opinions on product quality, reviewers often share how, where, or why they use the product. We therefore build our dataset of product usage expressions starting with a collection of product reviews.

We collect Amazon product reviews for five different product categories, as shown in Table 1. The particular product lines we use are: a *laundry product:* specifically, Downy Unstopables In Wash Fresh Scent Booster 13.2 Oz; two kinds of *cooking agents*, namely, *Olive oil:* Baja Precious Extra Virgin Olive Oil from Baja California (750ml Bottle) and *Vinegar:* Raw Organic Apple Cider Vinegar by Bragg (1 gallon); a *Medicine:* Kirkland Signature Low Dose Aspirin, 2 bottles – 365-Count Enteric Coated Tablets each; and a *household item*, namely *Toothpaste:* Colgate Optic White Toothpaste, 4 Ounce (Pack of 2). The reviews are split into sentences, with the total number of sentences and average number of sentences per review as shown in Table 1. In all, there are 3020 sentences in 565 reviews, with an average of 5.34 sentences per review.

With the help of three linguistics undergraduate students, each sentence in the dataset was annotated as containing a usage expression or not. Initially, as an early trial, we asked the annota-

Product category	Product	# Reviews	# Sentences	Avg # Sentences per Review
Laundry product	Scent booster	125	695	5.56
Cooking agent	Olive oil	110	588	5.35
Cooking agent	Vinegar	110	623	5.66
Medicine	Aspirin	110	463	4.21
Household item	Toothpaste	110	651	5.92
Total	–	565	3020	5.34

Table 1: Product categories in our dataset.

tors to indicate if a sentence contained a usage expression. This approach led to low inter-annotator agreement, so we refined the annotation process to a two-step process as follows.

In the first step, we instructed the annotators to read each product review carefully, identify all usage expressions in the review (examples below), and write them in a given textbox, one usage expression per line. Annotators were requested to write the usage expressions in their own words. This component was employed to make sure annotators carefully read and understood the review.

The second step involved answering the following four questions on usage types:

(A) Does the sentence describe <u>why</u> the product was being used? (usage reason/purpose) E.g., *"I used unstopables to <u>freshen my room</u>."*

(B) Does the sentence describe <u>where</u> the product was used? E.g., *"I used unstopables <u>with my cat litter</u>."*

(C) Does the sentence describe <u>how</u> the product was used? E.g., *"I use <u>three cups</u> of Downy Unstopables <u>in every wash</u>."*

(D) Does the sentence describe any <u>non-traditional</u> or <u>non-standard</u> usage of the product? E.g., *"I always love to <u>add some hot water to unstopables and make my own DIY air freshener</u> !"*

If a sentence had a positive answer to one or more of these four questions, then it was labeled as containing a usage expression.[1]

Additionally, several specific instructions were added to deal with potentially difficult or complex cases, by asking annotators to (1) consider the context (one sentence before and after the target sentence) before deciding whether to mark a

sentence or not. (2) determine if a sentence contains an opinion (*"Love it"*, *"Hate it"*, etc.) or a recommendation (*"I'd recommend this product to all aspiring gardeners"*), and if so, pairing it with an explicit usage expression in some form. (3) determine if a sentence talks about usage of another product that is not the primary focus of the review (i.e., a secondary product), then mark the sentence only if the primary product is being used in addition to the secondary product. (4) determine if the secondary product is used instead of the primary product: *"Unstopables were not good, so I used sheets instead."*, or if only the secondary product was used: *"I used sheets, they are better."* then do not label the sentence. (5) focus only on products, and ignore other (named) entities like persons, organizations, locations, and dates.

Table 2 shows an example product review, and sentences that were agreed upon by all annotators to contain, or not, a usage expression. We also show sentences on which there was no consensus. Note that such sentences have a fair amount of ambiguity. For example, the sentence *"I do recommend this for times when you may want extra freshness for your clothes or towels."* does not seem to contain an explicit usage expression, but it does indicate that the consumer used the product to obtain extra freshness for clothes or towels. Sentences like this demonstrate the difficulty of identifying usage expressions in product reviews.

Inter-annotator agreement values, shown in Table 3, indicate that the task is moderately difficult. We can see that different products have different difficulty levels, with Vinegar being the least difficult (highest A_3 agreement as well as highest κ), while for the other four products, κ was between 0.43 and 0.48. This is presumably owing to the fact that Vinegar is a cooking agent and used in many different ways, thus providing more opportunity to find a usage sentence (by several people) in a product review.

To construct a gold standard, we took the majority of the three votes assigned by the three anno-

---

[1]Note that in this paper, we ignore the different ways of product usage (why, where, how, non-traditional), but we plan to utilize the detailed annotations in future work.

Sample Review
I used this recently when I washed my blankets and towels, and I was definitely impressed. Just a small amount (half a capful) was necessary to give my blankets and towels an extra burst of freshness. The scent is a little bit floral and lasts for a few days. I put the Downy booster directly into the washer. (Instructions say NOT to put in your dispenser) And it does work fine with high efficiency washers. I do recommend this for times when you may want extra freshness for your clothes or towels.
Usage annotations (agreed by all)
I used this recently when I washed my blankets and towels, and I was definitely impressed.
Just a small amount (half a capful) was necessary to give my blankets and towels an extra burst of freshness.
Non-usage annotations (agreed by all)
The scent is a little bit floral and lasts for a few days.
Mixed usage/non-usage annotations
I put the Downy booster directly into the washer. (Instructions say NOT to put in your dispenser) And it does work fine with high efficiency washers. I do recommend this for times when you may want extra freshness for your clothes or towels.

Table 2: An example review and its annotations.

tators to each sentence. There were 36 sentences (1.19% of all sentences) that did not have a majority. One of the authors manually arbitrated these sentences into "usage" ($n = 22$) and "not usage" ($n = 14$) classes.

4 Finding Usage Expression Sentences

Once the annotated dataset was finalized, our primary goal was to build a classifier to predict if a given sentence contains usage expressions or not. We learn the classifier over five categories of features extracted from the sentence and neighboring context. In this paper, we show the performance using a logistic regression classifier, chosen based on its performance on a small development dataset of usage-annotated sentences drawn from 20 product reviews. The following features are included:

(A) Lexical features: As n-grams are usually very helpful in document classification, we explore their utility on the task of usage expression sentence classification. We use word unigrams and bigrams, part-of-speech (POS) bigrams, and character trigrams. We use the CRFTagger (Phan, 2006) for POS tagging.

(B) Embeddings: Embeddings encode *latent semantics* and could reflect usage patterns. We train a word embedding using word2vec (Mikolov et al., 2013) over a large corpus of $55,463$ product reviews. This corpus is constructed from all Amazon reviews associated with any product that

has "Unstopables", "Olive oil", "Vinegar", "Aspirin", or "Toothpaste" in its title. Once the word embedding is trained, a sentence is represented by the weighted average of the embeddings of all the unique words in it.

(C) Syntax: We use bags of constituency and dependency production rules, obtained from the output of the Stanford parser (Klein and Manning, 2003; Chen and Manning, 2014). For constituency grammar, we use terminal and non-terminal rules separately as well as together. For the dependency grammar, we use the (collapsed) dependency types (*amod*, *nsubj*, etc.), and the lexicalized dependencies (e.g., *(nsubj, Kirkland, seems)*) as separate features.

(D) Style: We extract thirteen shallow surface-level and style features to encode the stylistic properties of a sentence, in the hope that they would be predictive of whether the sentence contains a usage expression. These features are: sentence position, average word length (in chars), sentence length (in words and characters), type-token ratio, Flesch Reading Ease (Flesch, 1948; Farr et al., 1951), Automated Readability Index (Senter and Smith, 1967), Flesch-Kincaid Grade Level (Kincaid et al., 1975), Coleman-Liau Index (Coleman and Liau, 1975), Gunning Fog Index (Gunning, 1968), SMOG Score (McLaughlin, 1969), Formality (Heylighen and Dewaele, 1999), and Lexical Density (Ure, 1971).

(E) Semantics: Since *usage* is above all a semantic phenomenon, a *semantic space* should be able to capture the dominant properties of the usage expression. We use the following feature sets to capture a semantic space for a sentence. Each feature set effectively describes a *lexicon*, and we turn "on" the features in the lexicon that are present in the target sentence.

1. **Product categories:** This feature set consists of the list of product categories obtained from the Walmart API.[2] We use both main categories and sub-categories.

2. **Concreteness:** The set of words, along with their concreteness scores, available as part of the Free Association Norms Database (Nelson et al., 1998). There are more than 3,000 words available as part of the database.

3. **Levin classes:** The set of coarse and fine-grained variations of Levin verb classes and

---

[2]`https://developer.walmartlabs.com/`

Product type	Majority Yes	Majority No	Majority Not Sure	All Yes	All No	A_3	κ
Scent booster	201	494	0	80	385	66.91	0.46
Olive oil	91	493	4	40	395	73.98	0.43
Vinegar	190	430	3	139	369	81.54	0.71
Aspirin	94	366	3	47	282	71.06	0.48
Toothpaste	137	514	0	56	411	71.74	0.46
Overall	713	2297	10	362	1842	72.98	0.52

Table 3: Majority label statistics, and three-way inter-annotator agreement. A_3 is the % of sentences where all three annotators agreed. κ is the Fleiss' kappa among three annotators (Fleiss, 1971).

verb alternations, leading to four types of features (Levin, 1993).

4. **LIWC:** Like Levin classes, we included another set of features derived from the LIWC dictionary of psychological word categories (Tausczik and Pennebaker, 2010).

5. **Semantic lexicons:** Like Levin classes, we use the Roget thesaurus and WordNet Affect word categories, with a binary feature representation. If a word falls under any of the Roget word categories, the corresponding feature is set.

6. **Named Entities:** We use the Stanford NER (Finkel et al., 2005) to identify named entities in our corpus, and then use these entities as bag-of-features. We use the terms, the entity types, and the lexicalized entity types (terms + entities) as our bags. Standard tf, tfidf, and binary representations are used. We use the seven-class typology of named entities (Location, Person, Organization, Money, Percent, Date, Time).

7. **Spatial Prepositions:** Recent studies have shown prepositions to be a precious source of semantic information (Srikumar and Roth, 2013; Schneider et al., 2015, 2016). We use a lexicon of *spatial prepositions*[3] as a bag-of-words feature. The rationale was to observe if spatial properties of usage of objects ("use olive oil **with** celery", "put detergent **in** washer") can be captured in terms of prepositions such as *on, in, by, with*, etc.

8. **Semantic Distance:** Finally, we added the

(weighted) WordNet distance[4] between all words and the verb *use*, where weights are set as binary, tf, and tfidf, as before. The rationale behind this feature is that it captures words similar to the verb *use* in the sentence, and their relative importance.

5 Evaluation

We use the dataset introduced in Section 3 to evaluate the accuracy of the usage detection classifier. 20% of the data for each product is held out as test data, and the remaining 80% is used for training.

We start by evaluating each individual feature using a ten-fold cross-validation on the training data. We then explore three combination methods, applied on a subset of seven feature sets, selected based on their performance and diversity: word unigrams, POS bigrams, character trigrams, embeddings, constituency rules, product categories, and concreteness. We combine these features through: classifier voting, where we assign the class predicted by the majority of the classifiers; feature fusion, where we join all the individual features into one feature vector used in the classification; and meta-learning, where we use the output of the individual classifiers as input into another classifier (again using logistic regression for the meta-learner). Table 4 shows the results of these evaluations. As seen in the table, while simple features, such as word n-grams and character trigrams, lead to the best performance among the individual features, better performance is obtained when they are combined with other features (bottom rows of Table 4).

The meta-learner based combination strategy resulted in the best performing classifier during the cross-validation experiments on training data. We next evaluate this classifier on the test data consisting of 20% reviews of all five products. Table 5 shows the results obtained on the test data. For

---

[3]Obtained by combining the two lists at `https://owl.english.purdue.edu/owl/resource/594/04/` and `http://www.firstschoolyears.com/literacy/sentence/grammar/prepositions/resources/Spatial%20Prepositions%20word%20bank.pdf`.

[4]We use the Wu-Palmer similarity (Wu and Palmer, 1994).

Feature Type	Prec.	Rec.	F-score	Accu.
Word unigrams	71.56	54.94	62.16	**83.88**
Word bigrams	**77.06**	30.85	44.06	81.13
Character trigrams	70.06	**57.19**	**62.98**	83.80
POS bigrams	55.72	39.69	46.36	77.87
Embeddings	71.92	47.49	57.20	82.88
Constituency	70.49	52.17	59.96	83.22
Dependency	57.53	33.10	42.02	78.00
Style	54.17	11.27	18.65	76.33
Product categories	67.19	44.37	53.44	81.38
Concreteness	59.61	53.21	56.23	80.04
Levin classes	59.72	37.26	45.89	78.83
LIWC	57.14	38.13	45.74	78.20
Semantic lexicons	56.02	50.78	53.27	78.54
Spatial prepositions	41.67	3.47	6.40	75.57
Semantic distance	66.29	20.45	31.26	78.33
Classifier voting	66.84	**67.76**	**67.30**	84.13
Feature fusion	63.92	60.49	62.15	82.25
Meta learner	**73.61**	59.45	65.77	**85.09**

Table 4: Micro-averaged sentence-level results (%) under 10-fold cross-validation on the training data. Maximum value in each column (within each section) is boldfaced.

Feature Type	Prec.	Rec.	F-score	Accu.
Majority	0.00	0.00	0.00	76.13
Word unigrams	71.82	58.09	64.23	85.92
Meta learner	**76.92**	**58.82**	**66.67**	**87.20**

Table 5: Micro-averaged sentence-level results (%) on the **test set** (20% of all products). Maximum value in each column is boldfaced.

comparison, the table also shows the performance of the word unigram classifier, as well as a majority class baseline that labels every sentence as "non-usage." As before, the meta-learner significantly improves over the unigram classifier,[5] and also over the majority class baseline.[6]

We also report the performance of the meta-learner classifier on individual products in Table 6. Across all the products, vinegar appears to have the highest F-score. This can be partly explained by the high inter-annotator agreement: the same product had the highest three-way agreement in the manual annotations, as shown in Table 3, likely an indication of a less difficult dataset.

6 Additional Analyses

To gain further insights, we perform several additional analyses, to determine: the role played by different features; the relation between classifier performance and amount of training data; the role of in-domain vs. cross-domain classification; and

<hr>

[5]Paired t-test, p-value=0.07
[6]Paired t-test, p-value < 0.0001

Product	Prec.	Rec.	F-score	Accu.
Scent booster	78.57	68.75	73.33	87.69
Olive oil	50.00	25.00	33.33	89.26
Vinegar	81.58	79.49	80.52	88.37
Aspirin	70.00	36.84	48.28	84.54
Toothpaste	80.00	53.33	64.00	85.00

Table 6: Micro-averaged sentence-level results (%) *per product* using the meta learner.

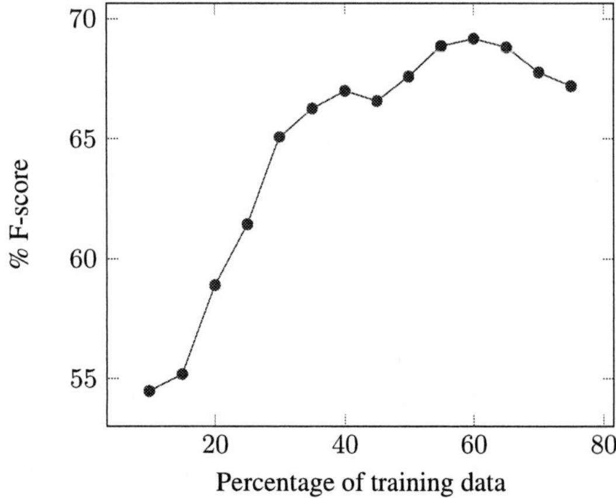

Figure 1: Learning curve using micro-averaged sentence-level results for the meta-learner classifier.

finally the types of errors produced by the system.

6.1 Feature Importance Ranking

Table 7 shows the top features (ranked by their Gini importance (Breiman et al., 1984)) for three prominent individual feature-based classifiers — viz. word unigrams, category words, and concreteness — and the meta-learner. Note that top-ranking words include product properties (*smell*), secondary objects on which the product was used (*clothes*), how the product was used (*day, daily, drink, water*), usage verbs (*use*), prepositions and conjunctions (*and, for, with*), pronouns (*i, it, this*), and articles (*a, the*). For the meta learner, lexical features (character trigrams and word unigrams) and embedding features (Word2vec) are among the top-ranked feature classes.

6.2 Learning Curve

Next, we experiment with varying the size of the training data to understand the learning curve. We gradually increased the amount of training data from 10% to 80%, in steps of 5%; and evaluated on the full test data. Figure 1 shows the variation of F-score achieved by the meta-learner as

Word unigrams		Category words		Concreteness		Meta learner	
and	0.023	the	0.040	smell	0.025	Character trigrams	0.309
my	0.019	my	0.036	use	0.024	Word2vec	0.236
smell	0.014	smell	0.029	day	0.023	Word unigrams	0.171
day	0.014	a	0.028	for	0.019	Constituency	0.119
use	0.014	use	0.025	clothes	0.017	Concreteness	0.077
it	0.011	day	0.023	i	0.016	Category words	0.053
clothes	0.010	this	0.020	with	0.014	POS bigrams	0.035
a	0.010	clothes	0.018	drink	0.014		
bought	0.009	daily	0.015	water	0.013		
drink	0.009	drink	0.013	daily	0.013		

Table 7: Feature importance ranking for four feature types. We show ten top-ranked features along with their importance scores. For the meta-learner, we show the ranking over the subset of seven feature sets used in this classifier.

Feature Type	Prec.	Rec.	F-score	Accu.
Baseline	0.00	0.00	0.00	76.39
Word unigrams	69.15	35.20	46.65	80.99
Meta-learner	70.62	38.43	**49.77**	**81.69**

Table 8: Cross-domain classification: Micro-averaged sentence-level results (%), where test set is an individual product, and training set is four other products. Maximum value in each column is boldfaced.

Feature Type	Prec.	Rec.	F-score	Accu.
Baseline	0.00	0.00	0.00	78.24
Word unigrams	74.19	50.74	60.26	85.44
Meta-learner	76.53	55.15	**64.10**	**86.56**

Table 9: In-domain classification: Micro-averaged sentence-level results (%), where test set is 20% of an individual product, and training set is 80% of the same product. Maximum value in each column is boldfaced.

the training data is increased, smoothed over three consecutive data points. The test performance was the highest when trained on 60% of training data and then decreased gradually, which suggests that the system might not benefit from additional training data.

6.3 The Role of In-Domain Data

To understand the role played by in-domain data, we further experiment with two different configurations of training and test sets.

In one configuration, we train on four products, and test on the remaining product (*cross-domain training*). As can be seen from Table 8, this results in lower F-scores than Table 5. This suggests that identifying usage expressions of a product is intimately related to the identity of the product, echoing the findings by Govers and Schoormans (2005).

In the second configuration, we train on 80% of a product, and test on 20% of the same product (*in-domain training*). The results, averaged over the five products, are shown in Table 9. Note that the F-score values are much improved compared to the previous configuration, and are comparable to the results shown in Table 5. This suggests that when storage/memory might be a concern, we could simply use training data from *within the do-*

main to achieve comparable performance. This strategy also results in a faster training time and a smaller model, similar to the findings in (Bucilǎ et al., 2006).

6.4 Error Analysis

Finally, we also conducted a manual inspection of two broad categories of errors – **false positives**, i.e. "not usage" sentences marked as "usage" ($n = 25$), and **false negatives**, i.e. "usage" sentences marked as "not usage" ($n = 56$). This analysis revealed the following sub-categories for the false positives:

- **Number expressions:** Seven instances (29.17%) of errors can be attributed to numeric expressions occurring within sentences ("two years", "3am", "third bottle", etc.).

- **Erroneous gold labels:** Six instances (25%) were actually correctly labeled as "usage" by the system, whereas the gold label was wrong (*"I really love the smell of fresh laundry, and the smell of Downy."*).

- **Shortcomings:** Six examples (25%) talk about actual or perceived shortcoming(s) of a product. *"Olive oil used for healthy properties doesn't keep well in plastic.[sic]"*

- **Others:** Five instances (20.83%) were not
  captured by the above categories: *"I used to
  drink a small shot each day, but haven't for a
  while."*

False negatives have the following sub-categories:

- **Positive adjectives and adverbs:** 21 instances (37.5%) can be attributed to positive adjectives ("good", "great", "excellent"),
  and/or positive adverbs ("really", "impres-
  sively", "well"). *"It smells amazing and lasts
  forever."*

- **Use-related verb in primary clause:** Eleven
  examples (19.64%) contain a use-related
  verb ("use", "help", "need") in the primary
  clause: *"I use this to eat, not to cook with."*

- **Erroneous gold labels:** Nine instances
  (16.07%) are actually correctly labeled as
  "not usage" by the system, but the gold
  label was wrong (*"When I have to hang
  dry clothes, they get this horrible egg water
  odor."*).

- **Non-traditional usage:** There are three
  instances (5.36%) that talk about non-
  traditional or innovative usage of a product:
  *"I have since made small sachet bags for my
  closets, car and as gifts."*

- **Others:** Twelve instances (21.43%) were not
  captured by the above categories: *"I actually
  saw results after the first use."*

7   Conclusion

In this paper, we introduced the task of identifying
usage expression sentences in consumer product
reviews. A dataset comprising more than $3,000$
annotated sentences was created from reviews of
five products. We also trained a binary classifier
to identify sentences that talk about the usage of a
product. Extensive feature tuning and fusion experiments resulted in performance values comparable to the inter-annotator agreement. Detailed
feature ranking, error analysis, and per-product
performance numbers have been reported. Directions for future research include: experiments
on a larger dataset of reviews with more diverse
product types, expanding to other genres of reviews such as product blogs, and identifying types
of usage expressions (how, where, why, and non-
traditional uses). The work can also be extended
to model the "personality" of a product with the
"personality" of users – perhaps measured by the
average personality of all people using the target
product.

The annotated dataset is publicly available
for research use from `http://lit.eecs.umich.edu/downloads.html`.

Acknowledgments

We thank Charles Welch, Aparna Garimella, Erin
Donahue, Katie Cox, and Michelle Huang for
their help with the annotations; Srayan Datta and
Soumik Mandal for many helpful discussions and
ideas. This material is based in part upon work
supported by the Michigan Institute for Data Science. Any opinions, findings, and conclusions or
recommendations expressed in this material are
those of the author and do not necessarily reflect
the views of the Michigan Institute for Data Science.

References

Shane Bergsma, Dekang Lin, and Randy Goebel. 2008.
Discriminative Learning of Selectional Preference
from Unlabeled Text. In *Proceedings of the 2008
Conference on Empirical Methods in Natural Lan-
guage Processing*, pages 59–68, Honolulu, Hawaii.
Association for Computational Linguistics.

Leo Breiman, Jerome H. Friedman, Richard A. Olshen,
and Charles J. Stone. 1984. *Classification and Regression Trees*. Wadsworth and Brooks, Monterey,
CA.

Carsten Brockmann and Mirella Lapata. 2003. Evaluating and Combining Approaches to Selectional
Preference Acquisition. In *Proceedings of the Tenth
Conference on European Chapter of the Association
for Computational Linguistics - Volume 1*, EACL
'03, pages 27–34, Stroudsburg, PA, USA. Association for Computational Linguistics.

Cristian Buciluǎ, Rich Caruana, and Alexandru
Niculescu-Mizil. 2006. Model Compression. In
*Proceedings of the 12th ACM SIGKDD Interna-
tional Conference on Knowledge Discovery and
Data Mining*, KDD '06, pages 535–541, New York,
NY, USA. ACM.

Nathanael Chambers and Dan Jurafsky. 2011.
Template-Based Information Extraction without
the Templates. In *Proceedings of the 49th Annual
Meeting of the Association for Computational
Linguistics: Human Language Technologies*, pages
976–986, Portland, Oregon, USA. Association for
Computational Linguistics.

Yu-Wei Chao, Zhan Wang, Rada Mihalcea, and Jia Deng. 2015. Mining Semantic Affordances of Visual Object Categories. In *IEEE Conference on Computer Vision and Pattern Recognition, CVPR 2015, Boston, MA, USA, June 7-12, 2015*, pages 4259–4267.

Danqi Chen and Christopher Manning. 2014. A Fast and Accurate Dependency Parser using Neural Networks. In *Proceedings of the 2014 Conference on Empirical Methods in Natural Language Processing (EMNLP)*, pages 740–750, Doha, Qatar. Association for Computational Linguistics.

Yun-Nung Chen, William Yang Wang, and Alexander I. Rudnicky. 2013. Unsupervised induction and filling of semantic slots for spoken dialogue systems using frame-semantic parsing. In *2013 IEEE Workshop on Automatic Speech Recognition and Understanding, Olomouc, Czech Republic, December 8-12, 2013*, pages 120–125.

Jackie Chi Kit Cheung, Hoifung Poon, and Lucy Vanderwende. 2013. Probabilistic Frame Induction. In *Proceedings of the 2013 Conference of the North American Chapter of the Association for Computational Linguistics: Human Language Technologies*, pages 837–846, Atlanta, Georgia. Association for Computational Linguistics.

Meri Coleman and T. L. Liau. 1975. A computer readability formula designed for machine scoring. *Journal of Applied Psychology*, 60(2):283.

Tim Van de Cruys. 2014. A Neural Network Approach to Selectional Preference Acquisition. In *Proceedings of the 2014 Conference on Empirical Methods in Natural Language Processing (EMNLP)*, pages 26–35, Doha, Qatar. Association for Computational Linguistics.

Kushal Dave, Steve Lawrence, and David M. Pennock. 2003. Mining the Peanut Gallery: Opinion Extraction and Semantic Classification of Product Reviews. In *Proceedings of the Twelfth International World Wide Web Conference, WWW 2003, Budapest, Hungary, May 20-24, 2003*, pages 519–528.

Xiaowen Ding, Bing Liu, and Philip S. Yu. 2008. A Holistic Lexicon-Based Approach to Opinion Mining. In *Proceedings of the 2008 International Conference on Web Search and Data Mining*, WSDM '08, pages 231–240, New York, NY, USA. ACM.

Ira J. Dolich. 1969. Congruence Relationships Between Self Images and Product Brands. *Journal of Marketing Research*, 6(1):80–84.

Katrin Erk. 2007. A Simple, Similarity-based Model for Selectional Preferences. In *Proceedings of the 45th Annual Meeting of the Association of Computational Linguistics*, pages 216–223, Prague, Czech Republic. Association for Computational Linguistics.

James N. Farr, James J. Jenkins, and Donald G. Paterson. 1951. Simplification of Flesch Reading Ease Formula. *Journal of applied psychology*, 35(5):333.

Jenny Rose Finkel, Trond Grenager, and Christopher Manning. 2005. Incorporating Non-local Information into Information Extraction Systems by Gibbs Sampling. In *Proceedings of the 43rd Annual Meeting on Association for Computational Linguistics*, ACL '05, pages 363–370, Stroudsburg, PA, USA. Association for Computational Linguistics.

Joseph L. Fleiss. 1971. Measuring Nominal Scale Agreement Among Many Raters. *Psychological Bulletin*, 76(5):378–382.

Rudolph Flesch. 1948. A new readability yardstick. *Journal of applied psychology*, 32(3):221.

P. C. M. Govers and J. P. L. Schoormans. 2005. Product personality and its influence on consumer preference. *Journal of Consumer Marketing*, 22(4):189–197.

Robert Gunning. 1968. *The technique of clear writing*. McGraw-Hill New York.

Sonal Gupta and Christopher Manning. 2011. Analyzing the Dynamics of Research by Extracting Key Aspects of Scientific Papers. In *Proceedings of 5th International Joint Conference on Natural Language Processing*, pages 1–9, Chiang Mai, Thailand. Asian Federation of Natural Language Processing.

Francis Heylighen and Jean-Marc Dewaele. 1999. Formality of Language: definition, measurement and behavioral determinants. *Interner Bericht, Center "Leo Apostel", Vrije Universiteit Brüssel*.

Minqing Hu and Bing Liu. 2004. Mining Opinion Features in Customer Reviews. In *Proceedings of the Nineteenth National Conference on Artificial Intelligence, Sixteenth Conference on Innovative Applications of Artificial Intelligence, July 25-29, 2004, San Jose, California, USA*, pages 755–760.

Harold H. Kassarjian. 1971. Personality and Consumer Behavior: A Review. *Journal of marketing Research*, pages 409–418.

J. Peter Kincaid, Robert P. Fishburne Jr., Richard L. Rogers, and Brad S. Chissom. 1975. Derivation of new readability formulas (automated readability index, fog count and flesch reading ease formula) for navy enlisted personnel. Technical report, DTIC Document.

Dan Klein and Christopher D. Manning. 2003. Accurate Unlexicalized Parsing. In *Proceedings of the 41st Annual Meeting of the Association for Computational Linguistics*, pages 423–430, Sapporo, Japan. Association for Computational Linguistics.

Beth Levin. 1993. *English Verb Classes And Alternations: A Preliminary Investigation*. The University of Chicago Press.

G. Harry McLaughlin. 1969. SMOG grading: A new readability formula. *Journal of reading*, 12(8):639–646.

Tomas Mikolov, Ilya Sutskever, Kai Chen, Gregory S. Corrado, and Jeffrey Dean. 2013. Distributed Representations of Words and Phrases and their Compositionality. In *Advances in Neural Information Processing Systems 26: 27th Annual Conference on Neural Information Processing Systems 2013. Proceedings of a meeting held December 5-8, 2013, Lake Tahoe, Nevada, United States.*, pages 3111–3119.

D. L. Nelson, C. L. McEvoy, and T. A. Schreiber. 1998. The University of South Florida word association, rhyme, and word fragment norms.

Patrick Pantel, Rahul Bhagat, Bonaventura Coppola, Timothy Chklovski, and Eduard Hovy. 2007. ISP: Learning Inferential Selectional Preferences. In *Human Language Technologies 2007: The Conference of the North American Chapter of the Association for Computational Linguistics; Proceedings of the Main Conference*, pages 564–571, Rochester, New York. Association for Computational Linguistics.

Xuan-Hieu Phan. 2006. CRFTagger: CRF English POS Tagger.

Ana-Maria Popescu and Oren Etzioni. 2005. Extracting Product Features and Opinions from Reviews. In *Proceedings of the Conference on Human Language Technology and Empirical Methods in Natural Language Processing*, HLT '05, pages 339–346, Stroudsburg, PA, USA. Association for Computational Linguistics.

Philip Resnik. 1997. Selectional Preference and Sense Disambiguation. In *Proceedings of the ACL SIGLEX Workshop on Tagging Text with Lexical Semantics: Why, What, and How*, pages 52–57. Washington, DC.

Thomas S. Robertson and James H. Myers. 1969. Personality Correlates of Opinion Leadership and Innovative Buying Behavior. *Journal of Marketing Research*, pages 164–168.

Nathan Schneider, Jena D. Hwang, Vivek Srikumar, Meredith Green, Abhijit Suresh, Kathryn Conger, Tim O'Gorman, and Martha Palmer. 2016. A Corpus of Preposition Supersenses. In *Proceedings of the 10th Linguistic Annotation Workshop*, Berlin, Germany. Association for Computational Linguistics.

Nathan Schneider, Vivek Srikumar, Jena D. Hwang, and Martha Palmer. 2015. A Hierarchy with, of, and for Preposition Supersenses. In *Proceedings of The 9th Linguistic Annotation Workshop*, pages 112–123.

R. J. Senter and E. A. Smith. 1967. Automated readability index. Technical report, DTIC Document.

David L. Sparks and William T. Tucker. 1971. A Multivariate Analysis of Personality and Product Use. *Journal of Marketing Research*, 8(1):67–70.

Vivek Srikumar and Dan Roth. 2013. Modeling Semantic Relations Expressed by Prepositions. 1:231–242.

Yla R. Tausczik and James W. Pennebaker. 2010. The Psychological Meaning of Words: LIWC and Computerized Text Analysis Methods.

Chen-Tse Tsai, Gourab Kundu, and Dan Roth. 2013. Concept-Based Analysis of Scientific Literature. In *Proceedings of the 22nd ACM international conference on Conference on information & knowledge management*, CIKM '13, pages 1733–1738, New York, NY, USA. ACM.

William T. Tucker and John J. Painter. 1961. Personality and product use. *Journal of Applied Psychology*, 45(5):325.

Jean Ure. 1971. Lexical density and register differentiation. *Applications of Linguistics*, pages 443–452.

Yuanbin Wu, Qi Zhang, Xuangjing Huang, and Lide Wu. 2009. Phrase Dependency Parsing for Opinion Mining. In *Proceedings of the 2009 Conference on Empirical Methods in Natural Language Processing*, pages 1533–1541, Singapore. Association for Computational Linguistics.

Zhibiao Wu and Martha Palmer. 1994. Verb Semantics and Lexical Selection. In *Proceedings of the 32Nd Annual Meeting on Association for Computational Linguistics*, ACL '94, pages 133–138, Stroudsburg, PA, USA. Association for Computational Linguistics.

Between Reading Time and Syntactic/Semantic Categories

Masayuki Asahara † and **Sachi Kato** ‡

National Institute for Japanese Language and Linguistics, Japan †, ‡

`masayu-a@ninjal.ac.jp` †

Abstract

This article presents a contrastive analysis between reading time and syntactic/semantic categories in Japanese. We overlaid the reading time annotation of BCCWJ-EyeTrack and a syntactic/semantic category information annotation on the 'Balanced Corpus of Contemporary Written Japanese'. Statistical analysis based on a mixed linear model showed that verbal phrases tend to have shorter reading times than adjectives, adverbial phrases, or nominal phrases. The results suggest that the preceding phrases associated with the presenting phrases promote the reading process to shorten the gazing time.

1 Introduction

Most of the studies on sentence processing by humans are based on confirmatory data analysis. The methodology involves developing a hypothesis, constructing sample sentences, including the target language phenomena, and performing a psycholinguistic experiment, such as recording reading time or event-related potentials. In recent times, the 'Balanced Corpus of Contemporary Written Japanese' (hereafter 'BCCWJ') (Maekawa et al., 2014) was compiled and published. The reading time annotation on BCCWJ: BCCWJ-EyeTrack (Asahara et al., 2016) is available for the linguistic research community. The data in the BCCWJ enable us to perform exploratory data analysis in fair and reproducible environments.

We measured the readability of humans. More concretely, we performed a contrast comparison between reading time and syntactic/semantic categories of words. We prepared the annotation of word senses on BCCWJ based on 'Word List by Semantic Principles' (国立国語研究所, 1964, 2004). The original WLSP label annotation is on both short unit words and long unit words in the BCCWJ. We then mapped these annotations into *Bunsetsu*(base phrase)-units.

The statistical analysis using a mixed linear model shows that verbal phrases tend to have shorter reading times than adjective/adverbial phrases or nominal phrases.

Section 2 presents the related research. Section 3 shows the data and methods. Section 4 presents the results, and Section 5 is the discussion. Section 6 concludes this article and presents the implications of our current work and the future work we plan to conduct.

2 Related Work

First, we present related work on eye tracking. The Dundee Eyetracking Corpus (Kennedy and Pynte, 2005) contains reading times for English and French newspaper editorials from 10 native speakers of each language that were recorded using eye-tracking equipment. The corpus does not target a specific set of linguistic phenomena but instead provides naturally occurring texts for testing diverse hypotheses. For example, (Demberg and Keller, 2008) used the corpus to test Gibson's dependency locality theory (DLT) (Gibson, 2008) and Hale's surprisal theory (Hale, 2001). The corpus also allows for replications to be conducted; for example, (Roland et al., 2012) concluded that previous analyses (Demberg and Keller, 2007) had been distorted by the presence of a few outlier data points.

Second, we present language analyses or models with reading time or eye tracking gaze information. (Barrett et al., 2016) presented a POS tagging model with gaze patterns. (Klerke et al.,

Proceedings of the The 8th International Joint Conference on Natural Language Processing, pages 404–412,
Taipei, Taiwan, November 27 – December 1, 2017 ©2017 AFNLP

Table 1: Data format of BCCWJ-EyeTrack

name	type	decription
surface	factor	surface form
time	int	reading time
logtime	num	reading time (log)
measure	factor	reading time type
sample	factor	sample name
article	factor	article information
metadata_orig	factor	document structure tag
metadata	factor	metadata
length	int	number of characters
space	factor	segment boundary with space or not
subj	factor	participant ID
setorder	factor	presentation order
dependent	int	syntactic dependency
sessionN	int	session order
articleN	int	article display order
screenN	int	screen display order
lineN	int	line display order
segmentN	int	segmentation display
is_first	factor	the left most
is_last	factor	the right most
is_second_last	factor	the second right most
WLSPLUWFALSE	factor	unknown word in WLSP
WLSPLUWA	factor	semantic category in WLSP
WLSPLUWB	factor	syntactic category in WLSP

2015) presented a grammaticality detection model for machine-processed sentences. (Iida et al., 2013) presented an analysis of eye-tracking data for the annotation of predicate–argument relations.

Our paper is slightly different from these preceding papers. We present a corpus-based psycholinguistic research on the relationship between reading time and syntactic/semantic categories.

3 Data and Method

We used the overlaid data of BCCWJ-EyeTrack and syntactic/semantic categories, as given in Table 1. We present the data below in detail.

3.1 BCCWJ and its annotation

We used BCCWJ (Maekawa et al., 2014) and its annotation data. BCCWJ is a balanced corpus of Japanese. We used newspaper articles from the core data. The data were sampled by their production. The sentences were segmented into word unit boundaries of short unit words, long unit words, and *bunsetsu*. The morphological information for the short unit words and long unit words was annotated by human annotators.

We also used *bunsetsu*-based syntactic dependency annotation(Asahara and Matsumoto, 2016) for the data to investigate the correlation between syntactic dependency attachments and reading time.

3.2 Reading Time Data: BCCWJ-EyeTrack

We now explain the two methods used for measuring the reading time: eye tracking and self-paced reading. The order of tasks was fixed with eye tracking in the first session and self-paced reading in the second session. Each participant saw each text once with the task and segmentation of the texts counterbalanced across participants.

Eye tracking was recorded with a tower-mounted EyeLink 1000 (SR Research Ltd). The view was binocular, but data were collected from each participant's right eye at a resolution of 1000 Hz. Participants looked at the display using a half-mirror; their heads were fixed with their chins on a chin rest. Unlike self-paced reading, during eye tracking all segments were shown simultaneously. This allowed more natural reading because each participant could freely return and reread earlier parts of the text on the same screen. However, participants were not allowed to return to previous screens. Stimulus texts were shown in a fixed full-width font (MS Mincho 24 point) and displayed horizontally as is customary with computer displays for Japanese; there were five lines per screen on a 21.5-in display.[1] Under the segmented condition, a half-width space was used to indicate the boundary between segments. In order to improve vertical tracking accuracy, three empty lines were placed between the lines of text. A line break was inserted at the end of a sentence or when the maximum 53 full-width characters per line was attained. Moreover, line breaks were inserted at the same points in the segmented and unsegmented conditions to guarantee that the same number of non-space characters was shown under both conditions.

The same procedure was adopted for the self-paced reading presentation except that the chin rest was not used, and participants could move their heads freely while looking directly at the display. Doug Rohde's Linger program Version 2.94[2] was used to record keyboard-press latencies while sentences were shown using a non-cumulative self-paced moving-window presenta-

---

[1] EIZO FlexScan EV2116W (resolution: 1920×1080 pixels) set at 50 cm from the chin rest.

[2] http://tedlab.mit.edu/~dr/Linger/

tion. This had the best correlation with eye-tracking data when different styles of presentation were compared for English (Just et al., 1982). Sentence segments were initially shown masked with dashes. Participants pressed the space key of the keyboard to reveal each subsequent segment of the sentence, while all other segments reverted to dashes. Participants were not allowed to go back and reread earlier segments.

Twenty-four native Japanese speakers, who were 18 years or older at the time, participated in the experiment with due financial compensation. The experiments were conducted from September to December 2015. The collected profile data included the age (in 5-year brackets), gender, educational background, eyesight (all participants had uncorrected vision or vision corrected with soft contact lenses or prescription glasses), geographical linguistic background (i.e., the prefecture within Japan where they lived until the age of 15), and parents' place of birth. The vocabulary size of the participants was measured using a Japanese language vocabulary evaluation test (Amano and Kondo, 1998). Participants indicated words they knew from a list of 50 words, and scores were calculated by taking word-familiarity estimates into consideration. As a measure of the working memory capacity, the Japanese version of a reading span test was conducted (Osaka and Osaka, 1994). Each participant read sentences aloud, each of which contained an underlined content word. After each set of sentences, the participants recalled the underlined words. If they successfully recalled all the words, the set size was increased by one sentence (sets of two to five sentences were used). The final score was the largest set for which all words were correctly recalled; a half point was added if half the number of words were recalled in the last trial.

Reading times were collected for a subset of the core data of the BCCWJ (Maekawa et al., 2014), which consisted of newspaper article (PN: published newspaper) samples. Articles were chosen if they were annotated with information such as syntactic dependencies, predicative clausal structures, co-references, focus of negation, and similar details following the list of articles that were given annotation priority in the BCCWJ.

The 21 newspaper articles[3] chosen were divided into four data sets containing five articles each: A, B, C, and D. Table 2 presents the numbers of words, sentences, and screens (i.e., pages) for each data set. Each article was presented starting on a new screen.

Table 2: Data set sizes

Data set	Segments	Sentences	Screens
A	470	66	19
B	455	67	21
C	355	44	16
D	363	41	15

Articles were shown segmented or unsegmented (i.e., with or without a half-width space to mark the boundary between segments). Segments conformed to the definition for *bunsetsu* units (a content word followed by functional morphology, e.g., a noun with a case marker) in the BCCWJ as prescribed by the National Institute for Japanese Language and Linguistics. Each participant was assigned to one of eight groups of three participants each. Each group was subjected to one of the eight experimental conditions with varying combinations of measurement methods, and boundary marking for different data sets was presented in different orders.

During the self-paced reading session, each segment was displayed separately, and participants could not return to reread earlier parts of the text. Therefore, the latencies for the button presses are straightforward measures of the time spent on each segment.

With regard to data from eye tracking, five types of measurements were used: first fixation time (FFT), first pass time (FPT), regression path time (RPT), second pass time (SPT), and total time (TOTAL). These are explained in Figure 1.

The FFT is the duration of fixation measured when the gaze first enters the area of interest. In the figure, the FFT for "the first fiscal year settling of accounts also" (hereafter "the area of interest") is the duration of fixation 5.

The FPT is the total duration of fixation from the moment the gaze first stops within the area of interest until it leaves the focus area by moving to the right or left of this area. In the figure, the FPT

---

[3]The original BCCWJ-EyeTrack paper (Asahara et al., 2016) presented 20 articles. However, there were two consecutive articles in data set C. These two articles were presented on separate screens. Thus, we split them into two for statistical analysis.

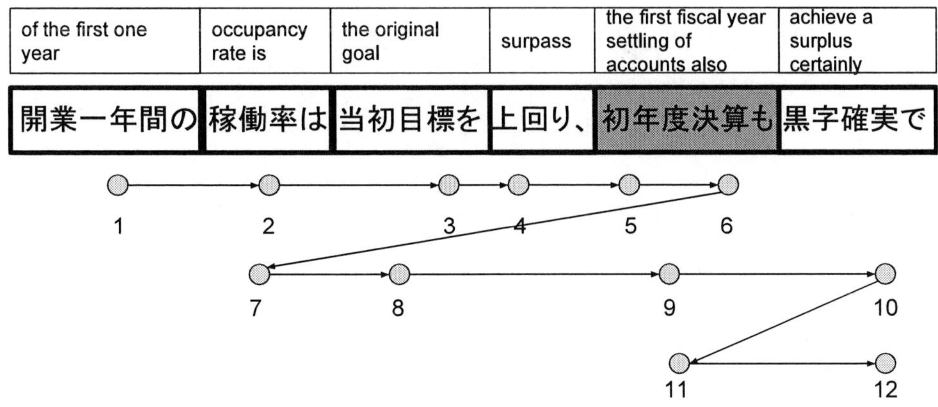

Figure 1: Example of fixations

is the sum of the durations of fixations 5 and 6.

The RPT is the total span of time from the moment the gaze enters the area of interest until it crosses the right boundary of this area for the first time. In the figure, the RPT is the sum of the durations for fixations 5–9. The RPT can include fixations to the left of the left boundary (e.g., 7 and 8) and the durations of fixations when the gaze returns to the area of interest (e.g., 9).

The SPT is the total span of time the gaze rests in the area of interest excluding the FPT. In the figure, the SPT is the sum of the durations of fixations 9 and 11.

The TOTAL is the total duration the gaze rests within the area of interest. In other words, it is the sum of SPT and FPT. In the figure, TOTAL is the sum of the durations of fixations 5, 6, 9, and 11.

Table 1 presents the data. `surface` is the surface form of the word. The reading time (i.e., `time`) is converted into log scale (i.e., `logtime`). `measure` is the reading type {SELF, FFT, FPT, RPT, SPT, TOTAL}. `sample, article, metadata_orig, metadata` are information related to the article. `length` is the number of characters in the surface form. `space` denotes spaces, if they are present between segments. `subj` is the participant ID, which is used as a random effect for the statistical analysis. `dependent` is the number of dependents for the segments. The dependency relation is annotated by humans (Asahara and Matsumoto, 2016). `sessionN, articleN, screenN, lineN, segmentN` are the display order of the elements. `is_first, is_last, is_second_first`

are the layout features on the screen. `WLSPLUWFALSE, WLSPLUWA, WLSPLUWB` are described in the next subsection.

3.3 WLSP and annotation

'Word List by Semantic Principles' (*Bunrui Goihyo*) (国立国語研究所, 1964) is 'a A collection of words classified and arranged by their meanings'. The first published version of WLSP in 1964 includes around 33,000 words. The revised and enlarged version of WLSP (国立国語研究所, 2004) was published in 2004. The data include around 79,000 word tokens with 100,000 word sense tokens.

Table 3 shows an example entry 'この (*kono*: this)' in WLSP. The article number '3.1010' identifies a word belonging to the syntactic/semantic category. The first digit of the article number refers to 'class', which is a syntactic category of the entry: class '1' represents a '体' nominal entry; class '2' represents a '用' verbal entry; class '3' is an '相' adjective entry; and class '4' is a '他' other entry including conjunctive and interjection. This category classification is originally from the 'Awakening of Faith in the Mahayana' (大乗起信論; 大乗起信論) in Mahayana Buddhism.

The digits to the right of a period identify the semantic category. The first decimal digit represents a 'division', which is a major semantic category: division '.1' is a '抽象的関係 (関係)' relation entry; division '.2' is a '人間活動の主体 (主体)' subject entry; division '.3' is a '精神および行為 (活動)' action entry; division '.4' is a '生産物および用具 (生産物)' product entry; and division '.5' is a '自然物および自然現象 (自然)' nature entry. The

Table 3: WLSP example entry 'この (*kono*)' (article number 3.1010)

class	devision	section	article
相 (3)	関係 (.1)	真偽 (.10)	こそあど (.1010)
Adj/adv	Relation	Boolean	Demonstrative

first two decimal digits refer to the 'section'. Four decimal digits refer to the 'article', which is article number 895, of the finest semantic categories.

We annotated the words from these WLSP article numbers based on the BCCWJ core samples. The annotation was carried out for content words for short unit words and long unit words of BCCWJ. Functional words were not annotated in the WLSP category. Now, the samples of BCCWJ-EyeTrack have already been annotated. We defined the set of right-most long unit words as the category of the *bunsetsu*. The semantic category (class) and syntactic category (division) were reassigned on segments. We called them WLSPLUWA and WLSPLUWB, respectively. We note that, there are still unassigned entries for the segment even if all the words have been manually checked. We assigned the boolean value of WLSPLUWFALSE for the unassigned words.

3.4 Statistical Analysis

We investigated the reading time (logtime) of NPs that were annotated with the WLSP labels. Whereas Asahara et al.'s paper was based on time, ours was based on logtime to reduce the outliers in the model. During the preprocessing, we excluded data {authorsData, caption, listItem, profile, titleBlock} of metadata. We also excluded zero-millisecond data points from the eye tracking data. The number of data points were 17,628 for SELF (100.0%); 13,232 for FFT, FPT, RPT, and TOTAL (75.0%); and 4,769 for SPT (27.0%). After model-based trimming was used to eliminate points beyond 3.0 standard deviations, the model was rebuilt (Baayen, 2008). subj and article were considered as random effects, as expressed in the formula in Figure 2. We used the lme4 package on R.

4 Results

Table 4 shows the results. Each number shows the coefficient with the standard error in brackets. A negative value of the coefficient indicates that the factor shortens the reading time. A positive value of the coefficient indicates that the factor lengthens the reading time. The base fixed effect of the syntactic category is the nominal phrase(WLSPLUWA1), and the base fixed effect of the semantic category is the relation (WLSPLUWB1). Note that the time is based on logarithm.

First, we confirm the results of the non-WLSP related terms. The presentation with spaces between segments makes the reading time of FPT, RPT, SPT, and TOTAL faster than the one without spaces for eye tracking methods. To improve the readability of texts, one should simply introduce spaces at *Bunsetsu* boundaries. The longer length of the segment makes reading times long except for FFT, because the gazing area in this case is correlated to the probability of the fixation. More dependency arcs make shorter reading times for the segment. This fact supports *Anti-locality* (Konieczny, 2000). The layout information (is_first, is_last, is_second_last) is for the eye movement at the text wrap. All reading times other than SPT is longer at the left most segment (is_first). The reading time of FPT, RPT, and Total is longer at the right most and the second right most segments (is_last, is_second_last). With regard to the presentation order (sessionN, articleN, screenN, lineN, segmentN), As the experiment progressed, the reading time became shorter. This means that the subject participants become more familiar with the experiment.

Next, we confirm the results related to the WLSP syntactic categories. For all types of reading times, the verbal segments (WLSPLUWA2) had significantly shorter reading times than the nominal segments (WLSPLUWA1). For reading time types other than FFT, the adjective/adverbial segments (WLSPLUWA3) had significantly shorter reading times than the nominal segments (WLSPLUWA1). For reading time types other than SPT, the adjective/adverbial segments (WLSPLUWA3) had significantly longer reading times than the verbal segments (WLSPLUWA1).

```
logtime ~ space * sessionN  + length + dependent
  + is_first + is_last + is_second_last
  + articleN + screenN + lineN + segmentN
  + WLSPLUWFALSE + WLSPLUWA + WLSPLUWB
  + (1 | subj) + (1 | article)
```

Figure 2: Lmer formula for the statistical analysis

Table 4: The results of statistical analysis

| | *Dependent variable:* | | | | | |
| | logtime | | | | | |
	SELF	FFT	FPT	SPT	RPT	TOTAL
space=True	−0.001	−0.006	−0.017***	−0.039***	−0.018***	−0.029***
	(0.002)	(0.004)	(0.005)	(0.009)	(0.006)	(0.005)
length	0.086***	−0.003	0.135***	0.022***	0.115***	0.130***
	(0.001)	(0.002)	(0.003)	(0.005)	(0.003)	(0.003)
dependent	−0.008***	−0.003	−0.016***	−0.016***	−0.012***	−0.018***
	(0.002)	(0.002)	(0.003)	(0.006)	(0.004)	(0.003)
is_first	0.052***	0.019***	0.090***	−0.027**	0.030***	0.069***
	(0.004)	(0.006)	(0.008)	(0.013)	(0.009)	(0.008)
is_last	0.033***	−0.009	0.014*	−0.052***	0.088***	−0.007
	(0.004)	(0.006)	(0.008)	(0.016)	(0.010)	(0.008)
is_second_last	−0.010***	−0.001	0.034***	−0.005	0.045***	0.034***
	(0.004)	(0.006)	(0.007)	(0.012)	(0.008)	(0.007)
sessionN	−0.022	−0.022	−0.041*	−0.036**	−0.049*	−0.047*
	(0.021)	(0.016)	(0.024)	(0.018)	(0.025)	(0.024)
articleN	−0.028***	−0.004	−0.005	−0.002	−0.007	−0.001
	(0.005)	(0.004)	(0.007)	(0.007)	(0.007)	(0.008)
screenN	−0.029***	−0.004	−0.018***	−0.015***	−0.017***	−0.025***
	(0.002)	(0.003)	(0.003)	(0.006)	(0.004)	(0.003)
lineN	−0.010***	−0.010***	−0.018***	−0.018***	−0.007**	−0.018***
	(0.001)	(0.002)	(0.003)	(0.005)	(0.003)	(0.003)
segmentN	−0.004***	0.003***	−0.005***	−0.009***	−0.013***	−0.012***
	(0.001)	(0.001)	(0.001)	(0.002)	(0.002)	(0.001)
WLSPLUWFALSE (unassigned word)	−0.030	0.020	−0.075	−0.031	−0.109	−0.160**
	(0.019)	(0.061)	(0.076)	(0.299)	(0.092)	(0.079)
WLSPLUWA2 (verb)	−0.047***	−0.038***	−0.096***	−0.029**	−0.088***	−0.101***
	(0.004)	(0.006)	(0.007)	(0.014)	(0.009)	(0.008)
WLSPLUWA3 (adj/adv)	−0.036***	−0.003	−0.056***	−0.034*	−0.054***	−0.071***
	(0.005)	(0.008)	(0.010)	(0.020)	(0.012)	(0.010)
WLSPLUWA4 (other)	−0.031*	−0.020	−0.127***	−0.238**	−0.137***	−0.189***
	(0.018)	(0.033)	(0.040)	(0.100)	(0.049)	(0.042)
WLSPLUWB.2 (subject)	0.001	0.014**	0.018**	0.011	0.005	0.018**
	(0.004)	(0.006)	(0.007)	(0.013)	(0.009)	(0.008)
WLSPLUWB.3 (action)	−0.007**	0.015***	0.024***	0.012	0.021***	0.023***
	(0.003)	(0.005)	(0.006)	(0.011)	(0.007)	(0.006)
WLSPLUWB.4 (product)	0.017***	0.005	0.022*	0.009	0.018	0.037***
	(0.007)	(0.010)	(0.013)	(0.021)	(0.015)	(0.013)
WLSPLUWB.5 (nature)	0.014	0.034**	0.017	0.054	0.024	0.040**
	(0.010)	(0.015)	(0.019)	(0.034)	(0.023)	(0.020)
space1:sessionN	−0.016	0.044	0.059	0.060*	0.061	0.061
	(0.042)	(0.031)	(0.049)	(0.035)	(0.050)	(0.048)
Constant	2.790***	2.299***	2.532***	2.456***	2.603***	2.672***
	(0.022)	(0.017)	(0.026)	(0.023)	(0.027)	(0.026)
Observations	17,628	13,232	13,232	4,769	13,232	13,232

Note: *p<0.1; **p<0.05; ***p<0.01

Finally, we confirm the result related to WLSP semantic categories. The abstract relation (WLSPLUWB.1) shows significantly longer reading times of FFT and TOTAL than of others such as subject (WLSPLUWB.2), action (WLSPLUWB.3), and product (WLSPLUWB.4).

5 Discussions

In this section, we discuss why reading time varies in syntactic and semantic categories.

Anti-locality is the term used to describe the phenomenon in which segments with more dependents in their preceding context have shorter reading times (Konieczny, 2000). This phenomenon was reported for German double objects (Konieczny and Döring, 2003). It was then investigated for Japanese double objects (Uchida et al., 2014). These shortened reading times cannot be explained by the predictions of the working memory models, in which segments with more dependents load for the reading (Gibson, 2008), or in which the number of dependents do not affect the reading time of the succeeding segments.

This phenomenon is compatible with surprisal theory (Hale, 2001; Levy and Gibson, 2013). It explains how double objects of head final languages, in which the predicate has both a direct and an indirect object tend to have shorter reading times than one that has only a direct object. Asahara et al. (2016) investigated the *anti-locality* phenomenon in more general settings with the `dependency` from BCCWJ-DepPara (Asahara and Matsumoto, 2016). The results show that the segment with higher dependency has a shorter reading time than a segment with a lower dependency.

In this research, the reading time tends to be shorter in the order of Noun (体, `WLSPLUWA1`) > Adjective/Adverb (相, `WLSPLUWA3`) > Verb (用, `WLSPLUWA2`) in the syntactic categories. The noun (`WLSPLUWA1`) tends to indicate the object and to become the argument of a predicate such as a verb or an adjective. Although the noun can also become a predicate with a copula verb, the modifier or argument for the noun is limited. The category (`WLSPLUWA3`) includes a predicative adjective with arguments. The verb (`WLSPLUWA2`) tends to be a predicate with arguments at the clause end. The tendency is reliable because the standard errors of the coefficients are very small. Though we included `dependency` as a fixed factor, we observed these tendencies for the reading time, in which the syntactic category with more argument tends to have a shorter reading time than the others. It indicates that arguments of a predicate in Japanese tend not to be overtly Appearing in the context. The omitted arguments may help predict the upcoming predicate, although the arguments tend to be omitted in the context. Therefore, the results do not support the working memory model, in which the load to memorize the preceding contexts interferes with the reading. The prediction model is a more plausible hypothesis than the working memory model.

In the semantic category, the abstract relation has a shorter reading time than others. The relation has at least two arguments. The existence of the arguments helps to promote the reading time.

6 Conclusions

This article explores the correlation between reading time and the syntactic/semantic category of the text. The reading time tends to be shorter in the order of Noun (1) > Adjective/Adverb (3) > Verb (2) in the syntactic categories. The relation (WLSPLUWB.1) tends to be the shortest in the semantic categories. The results show that the *bunsetsu* with arguments tend to have shorter reading times than the ones without arguments. This fact supports the *anti-locality* (Konieczny and Döring, 2003) and Hale's surprisal theory (Hale, 2001).

Our current work comprises two analyses. The first one is a contrastive analysis between reading time and information structure annotation. We overlaid the annotation of information structures (Miyauchi et al., 2017) on the reading time data. The result showed that reading time can reveal the difference in whether the target nominal phrase is hearer-new or bridging (Asahara, 2017). The second one is contrastive analysis between reading time and the clause boundary category annotation. The result shows that the clause end segments tend to have shorter reading times. Furthermore, the reading time of clause boundaries vary according to the classification of the clauses.

In our future work, we plan to introduce Bayesian linear mixed model (Sorensen et al., 2016) for the statistical modelling. We also hope to investigate the correlation between reading time and word familiarity rate. Word familiarity rate is the fundamental data to estimate Japanese language vocabulary evaluation test (Amano and Kondo, 1998). However, word-familiarity-rate data were constructed around 20 years ago. We now plan to reconstruct word-familiarity-rate data on WLSP entries by crowd sourcing using a Bayesian linear mixed model.

Acknowledgments

The work reported in this article was supported by the NINJAL research project of the Center for Corpus Development. This work was also supported by JSPS KAKENHI Grant Number JP25284083 and JP17H00917.

References

S. Amano and T. Kondo. 1998. Estimation of mental lexicon size with word familiarity database. In *Proceedings of International Conference on Spoken Language Processing*. volume 5, pages 2119–2122.

M. Asahara. 2017. Between reading time and information structure. In *Proceedings of the 31st Pacific Asia Conference on Language, Information and Computation (PACLIC 31)*. page (to appear).

M. Asahara and Y. Matsumoto. 2016. BCCWJ-DepPara: A Syntactic Annotation Treebank on the 'Balanced Corpus of Contemporary Written Japanese'. In *Proceedings of the 12th Workshop on Asian Langauge Resources (ALR12)*. pages 49–58.

M. Asahara, H. Ono, and E. T. Miyamoto. 2016. Reading-Time Annotations for 'Balanced Corpus of Contemporary Written Japanese'. In *Proceedings of COLING 2016, the 26th International Conference on Computational Linguistics: Technical Papers*. pages 684–694.

R. H. Baayen. 2008. *Analyzing Linguistic Data: A practical Introduction to Statistics using R*. Cambridge University Press.

M. Barrett, J. Bingel, F. Keller, and A. Søgaard. 2016. Weakly supervised part-of-speech tagging using eye-tracking data. In *Proceedings of the 54th Annual Meeting of the Association for Computational Linguistics (Volume 2: Short Papers)*. pages 579–584.

V. Demberg and F. Keller. 2007. Eye-tracking evidence for integration cost effects in corpus data. In *Proceedings of the 29th Meeting of the Cognitive Science Society (CogSci-07)*. pages 947–952.

V. Demberg and F. Keller. 2008. Data from eye-tracking corpora as evidence for theories of syntactic processing complexity. *Cognition* 109(2):193–210.

E. Gibson. 2008. Linguistic complexity: Locality of syntactic dependencies. *Cognition* 68:1–76.

J. Hale. 2001. A probabilistic earley parser as a psycholinguistic model. In *Proceedings of the second conference of the North American chapter of the association for computational linguistics*. volume 2, pages 159–166.

R. Iida, K. Mitsuda, and T. Tokunaga. 2013. Investigation of annotator's behaviour using eye-tracking data. In *Proceedings of the 7th Linguistic Annotation Workshop and Interoperability with Discourse*. pages 214–222.

M. A. Just, P. A. Carpenter, and J. D. Woolley. 1982. Paradigms and processes in reading comprehension. *Journal of Experimental Psychology: General* 3:228–238.

A. Kennedy and J. Pynte. 2005. Parafoveal-on-foveal effects in normal reading. *Vision Research* 45:153–168.

Sigrid Klerke, Héctor Martínez Alonso, and Anders Søgaard. 2015. Looking hard: Eye tracking for detecting grammaticality of automatically compressed sentences. In *Proceedings of the 20th Nordic Conference of Computational Linguistics (NODALIDA 2015)*. pages 97–105.

L. Konieczny. 2000. Locality and parsing complexity. *Journal of Psycholinguistic Research* 29(6).

L. Konieczny and P. Döring. 2003. Anticipation of clause-final heads. evidence from eye-tracking and srns. In *Proceedings of the 4th International Conference on Cognitive Science*.

R. Levy and E. Gibson. 2013. Surprisal, the pdc, and the primary locus of processing difficulty in relative clauses. *Frontiers in Psychology* 4(229).

K. Maekawa, M. Yamazaki, T. Ogiso, T. Maruyama, H. Ogura, W. Kashino, H. Koiso, M. Yamaguchi, M. Tanaka, and Y. Den. 2014. Balanced Corpus of Contemporary Written Japanese. *Language Resources and Evaluation* 48:345–371.

T. Miyauchi, M. Asahara, N. Nakagawa, and S. Kato. 2017. Annotation of Information Structure on 'The Balanced Corpus of Contemporary Written Japanese'. In *Proceedings of PACLING 2017*. pages 166–175.

M. Osaka and N. Osaka. 1994. [working memory capacity related to reading: measurement with the japanese version of reading span test] (in japanese). *Shinrigaku Kenkyu: The Japanese Journal of Psychology* 65(5):339–345.

D. Roland, G. Mauner, C. O'Meara, and H. Yun. 2012. Discourse expectations and relative clause processing. *Journal of Memory and Language* 66(3):479–508.

T. Sorensen, S. Hohenstein, and S. Vasishth. 2016. Bayesian linear mixed models using stan: A tutorial for psychologists, linguists, and cognitive scientists. *Quantitative Methods for Psychology* 12:175–200.

S. Uchida, E. T. Miyamoto, Y. Hirose, Y. Kobayashi, and T. Ito. 2014. An erp study of parsing and memory load in japanese sentence processing – a comparison between left-corner parsing and the dependency locality theory –. In *Proceedings of the Thought and Language/the Mental Architecture of Processing and Learning of Language 2014.*

国立国語研究所, editor. 1964. **分類語彙表**. 秀英出版.

国立国語研究所, editor. 2004. **分類語彙表** –増補改訂版–. 大日本図書.

WiNER: A Wikipedia Annotated Corpus for Named Entity Recognition

Abbas Ghaddar
RALI-DIRO
Université de Montréal
Montréal, Canada
abbas.ghaddar@umontreal.ca

Philippe Langlais
RALI-DIRO
Université de Montréal
Montréal, Canada
felipe@iro.umontreal.ca

Abstract

We revisit the idea of mining Wikipedia in order to generate named-entity annotations. We propose a new methodology that we applied to the English Wikipedia to build WiNER, a large, high quality, annotated corpus. We evaluate its usefulness on 6 NER tasks, comparing 4 popular state-of-the art approaches. We show that `LSTM-CRF` is the approach that benefits the most from our corpus. We report impressive gains with this model when using a small portion of WiNER on top of the CONLL training material. Last, we propose a simple but efficient method for exploiting the full range of WiNER, leading to further improvements.

1 Introduction

Named-Entity Recognition (NER) is the task of identifying textual mentions and classifying them into a predefined set of types. It is an important pre-processing step in NLP and Information Extraction. Various approaches have been proposed to tackle the task, including conditional random fields (Finkel et al., 2005), perceptrons (Ratinov and Roth, 2009), and neural network approaches (Collobert et al., 2011; Lample et al., 2016; Chiu and Nichols, 2016).

One issue with NER is the small amount of annotated data available for training, and their limited scope (see Section 4.1). Furthermore, some studies (Onal and Karagoz, 2015; Augenstein et al., 2017) have demonstrated that named-entity systems trained on news-wire data perform poorly when tested on other text genres. This motivated some researchers to create a named-entity labelled corpus from Wikipedia. This was notably attempted by Nothman et al. (2008) and more re-

cently revisited by Al-Rfou et al. (2015) in a multilingual context. Both studies leverage the link structure of Wikipedia to generate named-entity annotations. Because only a tiny portion of texts in Wikipedia are anchored, some strategies are typically needed to infer more annotations (Ghaddar and Langlais, 2016b). Such a process typically yields a noisy corpus for which filtering is required.

In this paper, we revisit the idea of automatically extracting named-entity annotations out of Wikipedia. Similarly to the aforementioned works, we gather anchored strings in a page as well as their type according to Freebase (Bollacker et al., 2008) but, more importantly, we also generate annotations for texts not anchored in Wikipedia. We do this by considering coreference mentions of anchored strings as candidate annotations, and by exploiting the out-link structure of Wikipedia. We applied our methodology on a 2013 English Wikipedia dump, leading to a large annotated corpus called WiNER, which contains more annotations than similar corpora and, as we shall see, is more useful for training NER systems.

We discuss related work in Section 2 and present the methodology we used to automatically extract annotations from Wikipedia in Section 3. The remainder of the article describes the experiment we conducted to measure the impact of WiNER for training NER systems. We describe the datasets and the different NER systems we trained in Section 4. We report the experiments we conducted in Section 5. We propose a simple but efficient two stage strategy we designed in order to benefit the full WiNER corpus in Section 6. We report error analysis in Section 7 and conclude in Section 8.

Proceedings of the The 8th International Joint Conference on Natural Language Processing, pages 413–422,
Taipei, Taiwan, November 27 – December 1, 2017 ©2017 AFNLP

2   Related Work

Turning Wikipedia into a corpus of named entities annotated with types is a task that received some attention in a monolingual setting (Toral and Munoz, 2006; Nothman et al., 2008), as well as in a multilingual one (Richman and Schone, 2004; Al-Rfou et al., 2015).

In (Nothman et al., 2008) the authors describe an approach that exploits links between articles in Wikipedia in order to detect entity mentions. They describe a pipeline able to detect their types (ORG, PER, LOC, MISC), making use of hand-crafted rules specific to Wikipedia, and a boot-strapping approach for identifying a subset of Wikipedia articles where the type of the entity can be predicted with confidence. Since anchored strings in Wikipedia lack coverage (in part because Wikipedia rules recommend that only the first mention of a given concept be anchored in a page), the authors also describe heuristics based on redirects to identify more named-entity mentions. They tested several variants of their corpus on three NER benchmarks and showed that systems trained on Wikipedia data may perform better than domain-specific systems in an out-domain setting.

Al-Rfou et al. (2015), follow a similar path albeit in a multilingual setting. They use Freebase to identify categories (PER, LOC, ORG), and trained a neural network on the annotations extracted. In order to deal with non-anchored mentions in Wikipedia, they propose a first-order coreference resolution algorithm where they link mentions in a text using exact string matching (thus *Obama* will be linked to the concept *Barack Obama* and labelled PER). They still had to perform some sentence selection, based on an oversampling strategy, in order to construct a subset of the original training data.

Our work revisits the idea developed in these two studies. Our main contribution consists in dealing specifically with non anchored strings in Wikipedia pages. We do this by analyzing the out-link structure in Wikipedia, coupled to the information of all the surface forms that have been used in a Wikipedia article to mention the main concept being described by this article. This process, detailed in the next section, leads to a much larger set of annotations, whose quality obviates the need for ad-hoc filtering or oversampling strategies.

3   WiNER

We applied the pipeline described hereafter to a dump of English Wikipedia from 2013, and obtained WiNER, a resource built out of 3.2M Wikipedia articles, comprising more than 1.3G tokens accounting for 54M sentences, 41M of which contain at least one named-entity annotation. We generated a total of 106M annotations (an average of 2 entities per sentence).

3.1   Annotation Pipeline

The pipeline used to extract named-entity annotations from Wikipedia is illustrated in Figure 1, for an excerpt of the Wikipedia article *Chilly_Gonzales*, hereafter named the target article. Similarly to (Nothman et al., 2008; Al-Rfou et al., 2015), the anchored strings of out-links in the target article are elected mentions of named entities. For instance, we identify *Warner Bros. Records* and *Paris* as mentions in our target article. In general, a Wikipedia article has an equivalent page in Freebase. We remove mentions that do not have such a page. This way, we filter out anchored strings that are not named entities (such as *List of Presidents of the United States*). We associate a category with each mention by a simple strategy, similar to (Al-Rfou et al., 2015), which consists in mapping Freebase attributes to entity types. For instance, we map `organization/organization`, `location/location` and `people/person` attributes to ORG, LOC and PER, respectively. If an entry does not belong to any of the previous classes, we tag it as MISC.

Because the number of anchored strings in Wikipedia is rather small — less than 3% of the text tokens according to (Al-Rfou et al., 2015) — we propose to leverage: (1) the out-link structure of Wikipedia, (2) the information of all the surface strings used to describe the main concept of a Wikipedia article. For the latter, we rely on the resource[1] described in (Ghaddar and Langlais, 2016a) that lists, for all the articles in Wikipedia (those that have a Freebase counterpart), all the text mentions that are coreferring to the main concept of an article. For instance, for the article *Chilly_Gonzales*, the resource lists proper names (e.g. Gonzales, Beck), nominal (e.g. the per-

---

[1] `http://rali.iro.umontreal.ca/rali/en/wikipedia-main-concept`

[Chilly Gonzales]$_{\text{PER}}$ (born [Jason Charles Beck]$_{\text{PER}}$; 20 March 1972) is a [Canadian]$_{\text{MISC}}$ musician who resided in [Paris]$_{\text{LOC}}$, [France]$_{\text{LOC}}$ for several years, and now lives in [Cologne]$_{\text{LOC}}$, [Germany]$_{\text{LOC}}$. Though best known for his first MC [...], he is a pianist, producer, and songwriter. He was signed to a three-album deal with Warner Music Canada in 1995, a subsidiary of [Warner Bros. Records]$_{\text{ORG}}$ ... While the album's production values were limited [Warner Bros.]$_{\text{ORG}}$ simply ...

Paris LOC	
↪ Europe, France, Napoleon, ...	
Cologne LOC	
↪ Germany, Alsace, ...	**OLT**

Warner Bros. Records ORG	
↪ Warner, Warner Bros., ...	
France LOC	**CT**
↪ French Republic, Kingdom...	

Figure 1: Illustration of the process with which we gather annotations into WiNER for the target page `https://en.wikipedia.org/wiki/Chilly_Gonzales`. Bracketed segments are the annotations, underlined text are anchored strings in the corresponding Wikipedia page. OLT represents the out-link table (which is compiled from the Wikipedia out-link graph structure), and CT represents the coreference table we gathered from the resource.

former) and pronominal (e.g. he) mentions that refer to Chilly Gonzales. From this resource, we consider proper name mentions, along with their Freebase type.

Our strategy for collecting extra annotations is a 3-step process, where:

1. We consider direct out-links of the target article. We search in its text the titles of the articles we reach that way. We also search for their coreferences as listed in the aforementioned resource. For instance, we search (exact match) *Warner Bros. Records* and its coreferences (e.g. *Warner, Warner Bros.*) in the target article. Each match is labelled with the type associated (in Freebase) with the out-linked article (in our example, ORG).

2. We follow out-links of out-links, and search in the target article (by an exact string match) the titles of the articles reached. For instance, we search for the strings *Europe, France, Napoleon*, as well as other article titles from the out-link list of the article *Paris*. The matched strings are elected named entities and are labeled with their Freebase type.

3. For the titles matched at step 2, we also match their coreferent mentions. For instance, because we matched *France*, we also search its coreferences as listed in the coreference table (CT).

During this process, some collisions may occur. We solve the issue of overlapping annotations by applying the steps exactly in the order presented above. Our steps have been ordered in such a

way that the earlier the step, the more confidence we have in the strings matched at that step. It may also happen that two out-link articles contain the same mention (for instance *Washington_State* and *George_Washington* both contain the mention *Washington*), in which case we annotate this ambiguous mention with the type of the closest[2] unambiguous mention.

Step 1 of our pipeline raises the coverage[3] from less than 3% to 9.5%, while step 2 and 3 increase it to 11.3% and 15% respectively. This is actually very close to the coverage of the manually annotated CONLL-2003 dataset, which is 17%. Considering that we do not apply any specific filtering, as is done for instance in (Nothman et al., 2008), our corpus contains many more annotations than existing Wikipedia-based named-entity annotated corpora.

3.2 Manual Evaluation

We assessed the annotation quality of a random subset of 1000 mentions. While we measure an accuracy of 92% for mentions detected during step 1, the accuracy decreases to 88% and 77% during step 2 and 3 respectively. We identified two main sources for errors in the coreferent mentions detection procedure. One source of error comes from the resource used to identify the mentions of the main concept. We measured in a previous work (Ghaddar and Langlais, 2016a), that the process we rely on for this (a binary classifier) has an accuracy of 89%. Example (a) of Figure 2 illus-

---

[2]Before or after the named-entity.

[3]Ratio of annotated tokens.

trates such a mistake where the family name *Pope* is wrongly assumed coreferent to the brewery *Eldridge Pope*. We also found that our 3-step process and the disambiguation rule fails in 15% of the cases. Figure 2 illustrates an example where we erroneously recognize the mention *Toronto* (referring to the town) as a coreferent of the (non ambiguous mention) *Toronto FC*, simply because the latter is close to the former.

a) *[Eldridge Pope]*ORG was a traditional brewery.....Sixteen years later the *[Pope]*ORG⋆ brothers floated the business...

b) Montreal Impact's biggest rival is *[Toronto FC]*ORG because Canada's two largest cities have rivalries in and out of sport. Montreal and *[Toronto]*ORG⋆ professional soccer teams have competed against each other for over 40 years.

c) I didn't want to open up my *[Rolodex]*ORG⋆ and get everyone to sing for me.

Figure 2: Examples of errors in our annotation pipeline. Faulty annotations are marked with a star.

Table 1 shows the counts of token strings annotated with at least two types. For instance, there are 230k entities that are annotated in WiNER as PER and LOC. It is reassuring that different mentions with the same string are labelled differently. The cells on the diagonal indicate the number of mentions labelled with a given tag.

	PER	LOC	ORG	MISC
PER	28M	230k	80k	250k
LOC	-	29M	120k	190k
ORG	-	-	13M	206k
MISC	-	-	-	36M

Table 1: Number of times a text string (mention) is labelled with (at least) two types in WiNER. The cells on the diagonal indicate the number of annotations.

We further examined a random subset of 100 strings that were annotated differently (in different contexts) and found that 89% of the time, the correct type was identified. For instance, in example Figure 2c) — a sentence of the *Chilly_Gonzales* article — the mention *Rolodex* is labelled as ORG, while the correct type is MISC. Our pipeline fails to disambiguate the company from its product.

4 Protocol

4.1 Data Sets

We used a number of datasets in our experiments. For CONLL, MUC and ONTO, that are often used to benchmark NER, we used the test sets distributed in official splits. For the other test sets, that are typically smaller, we used the full dataset as a test material.

CONLL the CONLL-2003 NER Shared Task dataset (Tjong Kim Sang and De Meulder, 2003) is a well known collection of Reuters newswire articles that contains a large portion of sports news. It is annotated with four entity types (PER, LOC, ORG and MISC).

MUC the MUC-6 (Chinchor and Sundheim, 2003) dataset consists of newswire articles from the Wall Street Journal annotated with PER, LOC, ORG, as well as a number of temporal and numerical entities that we excluded from our evaluation for the sake of homogeneity.

ONTO the OntoNotes 5.0 dataset (Pradhan et al., 2012) includes texts from five different text genres: broadcast conversation (200k), broadcast news (200k), magazine (120k), newswire (625k), and web data (300k). This dataset is annotated with 18 fine grained NE categories. Following (Nothman, 2008), we applied the procedure for mapping annotations to the CONLL tag set. We used the CONLL 2012 (Pradhan et al., 2013) standard test set for evaluation.

WGOLD WikiGold (Balasuriya et al., 2009) is a set of Wikipedia articles (40k tokens) manually annotated with CONLL-2003 NE classes. The articles were randomly selected from a 2008 English dump and cover a number of topics.

WEB Ratinov and Roth (2009) annotated 20 web pages (8k tokens) on different topics with the CONLL-2003 tag set.

TWEET Ritter et al. (2011) annotated 2400 tweets (comprising 34k tokens) with 10 named-entity classes, which we mapped to the CONLL-2003 NE classes.

4.2 Metrics

Since we use many test sets in this work, we are confronted with a number of inconsistencies. One is the definition of the MISC class, which differs from a dataset to another, in addition to not being annotated in MUC. This led us to report token-level F1 score for 3 classes only (LOC, ORG and PER). We computed this metric with the `conlleval` script.[4]

We further report OD_{F1}, a score that measures how well a named-entity recognizer performs on out-domain material. We compute it by randomly sampling 500 sentences[5] for each out-domain test set, on which we measure the token-level F1. Sampling the same number of sentences per test set allows to weight each corpus equally. This process is repeated 10 times, and we report the average over those 10 folds. On average, the newly assembled test set contains 50k tokens and roughly 3.5k entity mentions. We excluded the CONLL-2003 test set from the computation since this corpus is in-domain[6] (see section 5.2).

4.3 Reference systems

We chose two feature-based models: the `StanfordNER` (Finkel et al., 2005) CRF classifier, and the perceptron-based `Illinois` NE Tagger (Ratinov and Roth, 2009). Those systems have been shown to yield good performance overall. Both systems use handcrafted features; the latter includes gazetteer features as well.

We also deployed two neural network systems: the one of (Collobert et al., 2011), as implemented by Attardi (2015), and the `LSTM-CRF` system of Lample et al. (2016). Both systems capitalize on representations learnt from large quantities of unlabeled text[7]. We use the default configuration for each system.

5 Evaluation of WiNER

5.1 Other Wikipedia-based corpora

We compare WiNER to existing Wikipedia-based annotated corpora. Nothman et al. (2008) released two versions of their corpus, WP2 and WP3, each containing 3.5 million tokens. Both versions enrich the annotations deduced from anchored strings in Wikipedia by identifying coreferences among NE mentions. They differ by the rules used to conduct coreference resolution. We randomly generated 10 equally-sized subsets of WiNER (of 3.5 million tokens each). On each subset, we trained the `Illinois` NER tagger and compared the performances obtained on the CONLL test set by the resulting models, compared to those trained on WP2 and WP3. Phrase-level F1 score are reported in Table 2. We also report the results published in (Al-Rfou et al., 2015) with the Polyglot corpus, which is unfortunately not available.

	with MISC	w/o MISC
WP2	68.2	72.8
WP3	68.3	72.9
Polyglot	-	71.3
WiNER	**71.2** [70.3,71.6]	**74.5** [73.4,75.2]

Table 2: Performance of the `Illinois` toolkit on CONLL, as a function of the Wikipedia-based training material used. The figures on the last line are averaged over the 10 subsets of WiNER we randomly sampled. Bracketed figures indicate the minimum and maximum values.

Using WiNER as a source of annotations systematically leads to better performance, which validates the approach we described in Section 3. Note that in order to generate WP2 and WP3, the authors applied filtering rules that are responsible for the loss of 60% of the annotations. Al-Rfou et al. (2015) also perform sentence selection. We have no such heuristics here, but we still observe a competitive performance. This is a satisfactory result considering that WiNER is much larger.

5.2 Cross-domain evaluation

In this experiment, we conduct a cross-domain evaluation of the reference systems described in Section 4.3 on the six different test sets presented in Section 4.1. Following a common trend in the field, we evaluate the performance of those systems when they are trained on the CONLL material. We also consider systems trained on CONLL plus a subset of WiNER. We report results obtained with a subset of randomly chosen sentences summing up to 3 million tokens, as well as a variant where we use as much as possible of the training material available in WiNER. Larger datasets

---

[4] `http://www.cnts.ua.ac.be/conll2000/chunking/conlleval.txt`

[5] The smallest test set has 617 sentences.

[6] Figures including this test set do not change drastically from what we observe hereafter.

[7] We use the pre-trained representations.

	CONLL	ONTO	MUC	TWEET	WEB	WGOLD	OD$_{F1}$
CRF							
CONLL	91.6	70.2	80.3	38.7	61.9	68.4	67.0
+WiNER(3M)	-	-	-	-	-	-	-
+WiNER(1M)	89.3 (-2.4)	71.8 (+1.7)	78.6 (-1.8)	49.2 (+10.5)	63.0 (+1.1)	69.1 (+0.8)	69.2(+2.2)
Illinois							
CONLL	**92.6**	71.9	84.1	44.9	57.0	71.4	68.3
+WiNER(3M)	85.5 (-6.9)	71.4 (-0.5)	76.2 (-7.9)	51.1 (+6.2)	**65.5 (+8.5)**	71.8 (+0.4)	69.5(+1.2)
+WiNER(30M)	82.0 (-10.6)	71.6 (-0.3)	75.6 (-8.5)	**52.2 (+7.3)**	63.3 (+6.3)	71.6 (+0.3)	69.0(+0.7)
Senna							
CONLL	90.3	68.8	73.2	36.7	58.6	70.0	64.3
+WiNER(3M)	86.6 (-3.7)	70.1 (+1.3)	73.9 (+0.7)	43.2 (+6.4)	62.6 (+4.0)	69.9 (-0.1)	67.0(+2.7)
+WiNER(7M)	86.8 (-3.5)	70.0 (+1.2)	72.9 (-0.4)	44.8 (+8.1)	61.5 (+2.9)	69.3 (-0.7)	66.2(+1.9)
LSTM-CRF							
CONLL	92.3	71.3	76.6	36.7	57.4	68.0	65.0
+WiNER(3M)	91.5 (-0.8)	74.7 (+3.4)	**84.7 (+8.1)**	48.1 (+11.4)	62.7 (+5.2)	73.2 (+5.2)	72.0 (+7.0)
+WiNER(5M)	91.1 (-1.2)	**76.6 (+5.3)**	84.0 (+7.4)	48.4 (+11.7)	64.4 (+7.0)	**74.3 (+6.4)**	**73.0 (+8.0)**

Table 3: Cross-domain evaluation of NER systems trained on different mixes of CONLL and WiNER. Figures are token-level F1 score on 3 classes, while figures in parentheses indicate absolute gains over the configuration using only the CONLL training material. Bold figures highlight column-wise best results.

were created by randomly appending material to smaller ones. Datasets were chosen once (no cross-validation, as that would have required too much time for some models). Moreover, for the comparison to be meaningful, each model was trained on the same 3M dataset. The results are reported in Table 3.

First, we observe the best overall performance with the LSTM-CRF system (73% OD$_{F1}$), the second best system being a variant of the Illinois system (69.5% OD$_{F1}$). We also observe that the former system is the one that benefits the most from WiNER (an absolute gain of 8% in OD$_{F1}$). This may be attributed to the fact that this model can explore the context on both sides of a word with (at least in theory) no limit on the context size considered. Still, it is outperformed by the Illinois system on the WEB and the TWEET test sets. Arguably, those two test sets have a NE distribution which differs greatly from the training material.

Second, on the CONLL setting, our results are satisfyingly similar to those reported in (Ratinov and Roth, 2009) and (Lample et al., 2016). The former reports 91.06 phrasal-level F1 score on 4 classes, while our score is 90.8 .The latter reports an F1 score of 90.94 while we have 90.76. The best results reported far on the CONLL setting are those of (Chiu and Nichols, 2016) with a BiLSTM-CNN model, and a phrasal-level F1 score of 91.62 on 4 classes. So while the models

we tested are slightly behind on CONLL, they definitely are competitive. For other tasks, the comparison with other studies is difficult since the performance is typically reported with the full tagset.

Third, the best performances are obtained by configurations that use WiNER, with the exception of CONLL. That this does not carry over to CONLL confirms the observations made by several authors (Finkel et al., 2005; Al-Rfou et al., 2015), who highlight the specificity of CONLL's annotation guidelines as well as the very nature of the annotated text, where sport teams are overrepresented. These teams add to the confusion because they are often referred to with a city name. We observe that, on CONLL, the LSTM-CRF model is the one that registers the lowest drop in performance. The drop is also modest for the CRF model. The WiNER's impact is particularly observable on TWEET (an absolute gain of 8.8 points) and WEB (a gain of 5.5), again two very different test sets. This suggests that WiNER helps models to generalize.

Last, we observe that systems differ in their ability to exploit large training sets. For the two feature-based models we tested, the bottleneck is memory. We did train models with less features, but with a significantly lower performance. With the CRF model, we could only digest a subset of WiNER of 1 million tokens, while Illinois could handle 30 times more. As far as neural network systems are concerned, the issue is training time. On the computer we used for this work — a Linux cluster equipped with a GPU — training `Senna` and `LSTM-CRF` required over a month each for 7 and 5 millions WiNER tokens respectively. This prevents us from measuring the benefit of the complete WiNER resource.

6 Scaling up to WiNER

6.1 Our 2-stage approach

Because we were not able to employ the full WiNER corpus with the NER systems mentioned above, we resorted to a simple method to leverage all the annotations available in the corpus. It consists in decoupling the segmentation of NEs in a sentence — we leave this to a reference NER system — from their labelling, for which we train a local classifier based on contextual features computed from WiNER. Decoupling the two decision processes is not exactly satisfying, but allows us to scale very efficiently to the full size of WiNER, our main motivation here.

6.1.1 Contextual representations

Our classifier exploits a small number of features computed from two representations of WiNER. In one of them, each named-entity is bounded by a beginning and end token tags — both encoding its type — as illustrated on line MIX of Figure 3. In the second representation, the words of the named-entity are replaced with its type, as illustrated on line CONT. The former representation encodes information from both the context and the the words of the segment we wish to label while the second one only encodes the context of a segment.

WiNER [Gonzales]$_{PER}$ will be featured on [Daft Punk]$_{MISC}$.

MIX $\langle$B-PER$\rangle$ Gonzales $\langle$L-PER$\rangle$ will be featured on $\langle$B-MISC$\rangle$ Daft Punk $\langle$L-MISC$\rangle$

CONT $\langle$PER$\rangle$ will be featured on $\langle$MISC$\rangle$.

Figure 3: Two representations of WiNER's annotation used for feature extraction.

With each representation, we train a 6-gram backoff language model using `kenLM` (Heafield et al., 2013). For the MIX one, we also train word embeddings of dimension 50 using `Glove` (Pennington et al., 2014).[8] Thus, we have the embed-

---

[8]We used a window size of 5 in this work.

dings of plain words, as well as those of token tags. The language and embedding models are used to provide features to our classifier.

6.1.2 Features

Given a sentence and its hypothesized segmentation into named-entities (as provided by another NER system), we compute with the Viterbi algorithm the sequence of token tags that leads to the smallest perplexity according to each language model. Given this sequence, we modify the tagging of each segment in turn, leading to a total of 4 perplexity values per segment and per language model. We normalize those perplexity values so as to interpret them as probabilities. Table 4 shows the probability given by both language models to the segment *Gonzales* of the sentence of our running example. We observe that both models agree that the segment should be labelled PER. We also generate features thanks to the embedding model. This time, however, this is done without considering the context: we represent a segment as the sum of the representation of its words. We then compute the cosine similarity between this segment representation and that of each of the 4 possible tag pairs (the sum of the representation of the begin and end tags); leading to 4 similarity scores per segment. Those similarities are reported on line EMB in Table 4.

	LOC	MISC	ORG	PER
CONT	0.11	0.35	0.06	**0.48**
MIX	0.26	0.19	0.18	**0.37**
EMB	0.39	0.23	0.258	**0.46**

Table 4: Features for the segment *Gonzales* in the sentence *Gonzales will be featured on Daft Punk*.

To these 4 scores provided by each model, we add 16 binary features that encode the rank of each token tag according to one model (does $\langle$tag$\rangle$ have rank $\langle$i$\rangle$?). We also compute the score difference given by a model to any two possible tag pairs, leading to 6 more scores. Since we have 3 models, we end up with 78 features.

6.1.3 Training

We use `scikit-learn` (Pedregosa et al., 2011) to train a Random Forest classifier[9] on the 29k mentions of the CONLL training data. We

---

[9]We tried other algorithms provided by the platform with less success.

adopted this training material to ensure a fair comparison with other systems that are typically trained on this dataset. Another possibility would be to split WiNER into two parts, one for computing features, and the other for training the classifier. We leave this investigation as future work. Because of the small feature set we have, training such a classifier is very fast.

6.2 Results

We measure the usefulness of the complete WiNER resource by varying the size of the training material of both language models and word embeddings, from 5M tokens (the maximum size the `LSTM-CRF` mode could process) to the full WiNER resource size.

	Co	On	Mu	Tw	We	Wg	OD$_{F1}$
5M	84.3	72.0	78.7	39.8	61.9	70.2	68.1
50M	86.8	75.6	82.3	44.9	64.7	73.8	71.7
500M	88.9	76.2	84.8	45.8	**66.6**	75.5	74.1
All	90.5	**76.9**	**85.9**	**46.6**	65.3	**77.0**	74.7

Table 5: Influence of the portion of WiNER used in our 2-stage approach for the CONLL test set, using the segmentation produced by `LSTM-CRF`+WiNER(5M). These results have to be contrasted with the last line of Table 3.

To this end, we provide the performance of our 2-stage approach on CONLL, using the segmentation output by `LSTM-CRF`+WiNER(5M) [10]. Results are reported in Table 5. As expected, we observe that computing features on the same WiNER(5M) dataset exploited by `LSTM-CRF` leads to a notable loss overall (OD$_{F1}$ of 68.1 versus 73.0), while still outperforming `LSTM-CRF` trained on CONLL only (OD$_{F1}$ of 65.0). More interestingly, we observe that for all test sets, using more of WiNER leads to better performance, even if a plateau effect emerges. Our approach does improve systematically across all test sets by considering 100 times more WiNER data than what `LSTM-CRF` can handle in our case. Using all of WiNER leads to an OD$_{F1}$ score of 74.7, an increase of 1.7 absolute points over `LSTM-CRF`+WiNER(5M).

Table 6 reports the improvements in OD$_{F1}$ of our 2-stage approach (RF), which uses all of

---

	Native	RF
CRF		
CONLL	67.0	73.6 (+6.6)
+WiNER(3M)	-	-
+WiNER(1M)	69.2	73.0 (+2.8)
Illinois		
CONLL	68.3	74.4 (+6.1)
+WiNER(3M)	69.5	74.2 (+4.7)
+WiNER(30M)	69.0	74.3 (+4.3)
Senna		
CONLL	64.3	70.1 (+5.8)
+WiNER(3M)	67.0	70.8 (+3.8)
+WiNER(7M)	66.2	72.0 (+5.8)
LSTM-CRF		
CONLL	65.0	69.7 (+4.7)
+WiNER(3M)	72.0	**74.8 (+2.8)**
+WiNER(5M)	73.0	74.7 (+1.7)

Table 6: OD$_{F1}$ score of native configurations, and of our two-stage approach (RF) which exploits the full WiNER corpus. Figures in parenthesis indicate absolute gains over the native configuration.

the WiNER material and the segmentation produced by several native systems. Applying our 2-stage approach systematically improves the performance of the native configuration. Gains are larger for native configurations that cannot exploit a large quantity of WiNER. We also observe that the 2-stage approach delivers roughly the same level of performance (OD$_{F1} \simeq 74$) when using the segmentation produced by the `Illinois` or the `LSTM-CRF` systems.

7 Error Analysis

Table 7 indicates the number of disagreements between the `LSTM-CRF`+WiNER(5M) system (columns) and the 2-stage approach (rows). The table also shows the percentage of times the latter system was correct. For instance, the bottom left cell indicates that, on 38 distinct occasions, the classifier changed the tag PER proposed by the native system to ORG and that is was right in 85% of these occasions. We exclude errors made by both systems, which explains the low counts observed (1.7% is the absolute difference between the two approaches).

We observe that in most cases the classifier makes the right decision when an entity tag is changed from PER to either LOC or ORG (86% and

	PER	LOC	ORG
PER	-	50% [12]	25% [12]
LOC	86% [20]	-	21% [28]
ORG	85% [38]	81% [19]	-

Table 7: Percentage of correctness of the 2-stage system (rows) when tagging a named-entity differently than the LSTM-CRF+WiNER(5M) (columns). Bracketed figures indicate the average number of differences over the out-domain test sets.

85% respectively). Most often, re-classified entities are ambiguous ones. Our approach chooses correctly mostly by examining the context of the mention. For instance, the entity *Olin* in example (a) of Figure 4 is commonly known as a last name. It was correctly re-classified as ORG thanks to its surrounding context. Replacing *its* by *his* in the sentence makes the classifier tag the entity as PER. Similarly, the entity *Piedmont* in example (b) was re-classified as ORG, although it is mostly used as the region name (even in Wikipedia), thanks to the context-based CONT and MIX features that identify the entity as ORG (0.61 and 0.63 respectively).

(a) ... would give [Olin]$_{\text{PER}\rightarrow\text{ORG}}$ access to its production processes ...

(b) Wall Street traders said [Piedmont]$_{\text{LOC}\rightarrow\text{ORG}}$ shares fell partly ...

(c) ⋆ ... performed as a tenor at New York City 's [Carnegie Hall]$_{\text{ORG}\rightarrow\text{LOC}}$.

Figure 4: Example of entities re-classified by our 2-stage approach.

Misclassification errors do occur, especially when the native system tagged an entity as ORG. In such cases, the classifier is often misled by a strong signal emerging from one family of features. For instance, in example (c) of Figure 4, both MIX — $p(\text{ORG}) = 0.39$ vs. $p(\text{LOC}) = 0.33$ — and EMB — $p(\text{ORG}) = 0.39$ vs. $p(\text{LOC}) = 0.38$ — features are suggesting that the entity should be tagged as LOC, but the CONT signal — $p(\text{LOC}) = 0.63$ vs. $p(\text{ORG}) = 0.1$ — strongly impacts the final decision. This was to be expected considering the simplicity of our classifier, and leaves room for further improvements.

8 Conclusion and Future Work

We revisited the task of using Wikipedia for generating annotated data suitable for training NER systems. We significantly extended the number of annotations of non anchored strings, thanks to coreference information and an analysis of the Wikipedia's link structure. We applied our approach to a dump of English Wikipedia from 2013, leading to WiNER, a corpus which surpasses other similar corpora, both in terms of quantity and of annotation quality. We evaluated the impact of our corpus on 4 reference NER systems with 6 different NER benchmarks. The LTSM-CRF system of (Lample et al., 2016) seems to be the one that benefits the most from WiNER overall. Still, shortage of memory or lengthy training times prevent us from measuring the full potential of our corpus. Thus, we proposed an entity-type classifier that exploits a set of features computed over an arbitrary large part of WiNER. Using this classifier for labelling the types of segments identified by a reference NER system yields a 2-stage process that further improves overall performance. WiNER and the classifier we trained are available at `http://rali.iro.umontreal.ca/rali/en/winer-wikipedia-for-ner`. As future work, we want to study the usefulness of WiNER on a fine-grained entity type task, possibly revisiting the simple classifier we resorted to in this work, and testing its benefits for other currently successful models.

Acknowledgments

This work has been partly funded by the TRIBE Natural Sciences and Engineering Research Council of Canada CREATE program and Nuance Foundation. We are grateful to the reviewers for their helpful comments.

References

Rami Al-Rfou, Vivek Kulkarni, Bryan Perozzi, and Steven Skiena. 2015. Polyglot-NER: Massive multilingual named entity recognition. In *Proceedings of the 2015 SIAM International Conference on Data Mining, Vancouver, British Columbia, Canada*. SIAM.

Giuseppe Attardi. 2015. Deepnl: A Deep Learning NLP Pipeline. In *Proceedings of Workshop on Vector Space Modeling for NLP, NAACL-HLT*, pages 109–115.

Isabelle Augenstein, Leon Derczynski, and Kalina Bontcheva. 2017. Generalisation in named entity recognition: A quantitative analysis. *Computer Speech & Language*, 44:61–83.

Dominic Balasuriya, Nicky Ringland, Joel Nothman, Tara Murphy, and James R Curran. 2009. Named Entity Recognition in Wikipedia. In *Proceedings of the 2009 Workshop on The People's Web Meets NLP: Collaboratively Constructed Semantic Resources*, pages 10–18. Association for Computational Linguistics.

Kurt Bollacker, Colin Evans, Praveen Paritosh, Tim Sturge, and Jamie Taylor. 2008. Freebase: A Collaboratively Created Graph Database for Structuring Human Knowledge. In *Proceedings of the 2008 ACM SIGMOD International Conference on Management of Data*, SIGMOD '08, pages 1247–1250.

Nancy Chinchor and Beth Sundheim. 2003. Message understanding conference (MUC) 6. *LDC2003T13*.

Jason PC Chiu and Eric Nichols. 2016. Named entity recognition with bidirectional LSTM-CNNs. In *Proceedings of the 54st Annual Meeting of the Association for Computational Linguistics*.

Ronan Collobert, Jason Weston, Léon Bottou, Michael Karlen, Koray Kavukcuoglu, and Pavel Kuksa. 2011. Natural language processing (almost) from scratch. *Journal of Machine Learning Research*, 12(Aug):2493–2537.

Jenny Rose Finkel, Trond Grenager, and Christopher Manning. 2005. Incorporating Non-local Information into Information Extraction Systems by Gibbs Sampling. In *Proceedings of the 43rd Annual Meeting on Association for Computational Linguistics*, pages 363–370. Association for Computational Linguistics.

Abbas Ghaddar and Philippe Langlais. 2016a. Coreference in Wikipedia: Main Concept Resolution. In *CoNLL*, pages 229–238.

Abbas Ghaddar and Philippe Langlais. 2016b. WikiCoref: An English Coreference-annotated Corpus of Wikipedia Articles. In *Proceedings of the Tenth International Conference on Language Resources and Evaluation (LREC 2016)*, Portorož, Slovenia.

Kenneth Heafield, Ivan Pouzyrevsky, Jonathan H. Clark, and Philipp Koehn. 2013. Scalable Modified Kneser-Ney Language Model Estimation. In *Proceedings of the 51st Annual Meeting of the Association for Computational Linguistics*, pages 690–696, Sofia, Bulgaria.

Guillaume Lample, Miguel Ballesteros, Sandeep Subramanian, Kazuya Kawakami, and Chris Dyer. 2016. Neural architectures for Named Entity Recognition. *arXiv preprint arXiv:1603.01360*.

Joel Nothman. 2008. *Learning named entity recognition from Wikipedia*. Ph.D. thesis, The University of Sydney Australia 7.

Joel Nothman, James R Curran, and Tara Murphy. 2008. Transforming Wikipedia into named entity training data. In *Proceedings of the Australian Language Technology Workshop*, pages 124–132.

Kezban Dilek Onal and Pinar Karagoz. 2015. Named entity recognition from scratch on social media. In *ECML-PKDD, MUSE Workshop*.

F. Pedregosa, G. Varoquaux, A. Gramfort, V. Michel, B. Thirion, O. Grisel, M. Blondel, P. Prettenhofer, R. Weiss, V. Dubourg, J. Vanderplas, A. Passos, D. Cournapeau, M. Brucher, M. Perrot, and E. Duchesnay. 2011. Scikit-learn: Machine learning in Python. *Journal of Machine Learning Research*, 12:2825–2830.

Jeffrey Pennington, Richard Socher, and Christopher D Manning. 2014. Glove: Global Vectors for Word Representation. In *EMNLP*, volume 14, pages 1532–1543.

Sameer Pradhan, Alessandro Moschitti, Nianwen Xue, Hwee Tou Ng, Anders Björkelund, Olga Uryupina, Yuchen Zhang, and Zhi Zhong. 2013. Towards Robust Linguistic Analysis using OntoNotes. In *CoNLL*, pages 143–152.

Sameer Pradhan, Alessandro Moschitti, Nianwen Xue, Olga Uryupina, and Yuchen Zhang. 2012. CoNLL-2012 shared task: Modeling multilingual unrestricted coreference in OntoNotes. In *Joint Conference on EMNLP and CoNLL-Shared Task*, pages 1–40.

Lev Ratinov and Dan Roth. 2009. Design challenges and misconceptions in named entity recognition. In *Proceedings of the Thirteenth Conference on Computational Natural Language Learning*, pages 147–155. Association for Computational Linguistics.

Alexander E. Richman and Patrick Schone. 2004. Mining Wiki Resources for Multilingual Named Entity Recognition In proceedings. In *Proceedings of the 46th Annual Meeting of the Association for Computational Linguistics*, pages 1–9.

Alan Ritter, Sam Clark, Mausam, and Oren Etzioni. 2011. Named Entity Recognition in Tweets: An Experimental Study. In *EMNLP*.

Erik F Tjong Kim Sang and Fien De Meulder. 2003. Introduction to the CoNLL-2003 shared task: Language-independent named entity recognition. In *Proceedings of the seventh conference on Natural language learning at HLT-NAACL 2003-Volume 4*, pages 142–147. Association for Computational Linguistics.

A. Toral and R. Munoz. 2006. A proposal to automatically build and maintain gazetteers for Named Entity Recognition by using Wikipedia. In *Proceedings of the EACL-2006 Workshop on New Text: Wikis and blogs and other dynamic text sourcesEACL Workhop on NEW TEXT-Wikis and blogs and ther dynamic text sources*, pages 56–61.

Reusing Neural Speech Representations for Auditory Emotion Recognition

Egor Lakomkin   **Cornelius Weber**   **Sven Magg**   **Stefan Wermter**

Department of Informatics, Knowledge Technology
University of Hamburg
Vogt-Koelln Str. 30, 22527 Hamburg, Germany
{lakomkin, weber, magg, wermter}@informatik.uni-hamburg.de

Abstract

Acoustic emotion recognition aims to categorize the affective state of the speaker and is still a difficult task for machine learning models. The difficulties come from the scarcity of training data, general subjectivity in emotion perception resulting in low annotator agreement, and the uncertainty about which features are the most relevant and robust ones for classification. In this paper, we will tackle the latter problem. Inspired by the recent success of transfer learning methods we propose a set of architectures which utilize neural representations inferred by training on large speech databases for the acoustic emotion recognition task. Our experiments on the IEMOCAP dataset show 10% relative improvements in the accuracy and F1-score over the baseline recurrent neural network which is trained end-to-end for emotion recognition.

1 Introduction

Speech emotion recognition (SER) has received growing interest and attention in recent years. Being able to predict the affective state of a person gives valuable information which could improve dialog systems in human-computer interaction. To fully understand a current emotion expressed by a person, also knowledge of the context is required, like facial expressions, the semantics of a spoken text, gestures and body language, and cultural peculiarities. This makes it challenging even for people that have all this information to accurately predict the affective state. In this work, we are focusing solely on inferring the speaker's emotional state by analysing acoustic signals which are also the only source of information in situations when

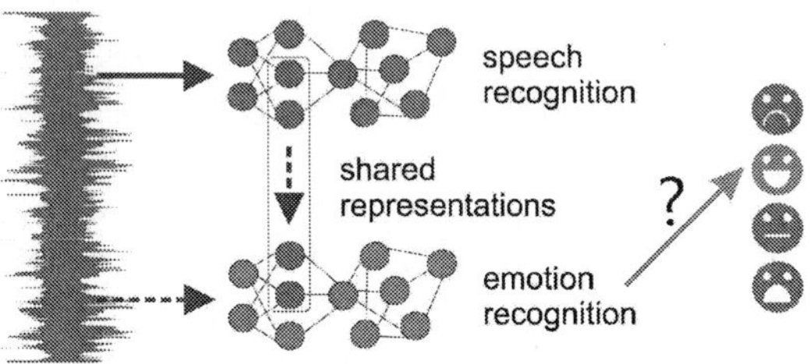

Figure 1: High-level system architecture. Acoustic emotion recognition system uses neural speech representations for affective state classification.

the speaker is not directly observable.

With recent advances in deep learning, which made it possible to train large end-to-end models for image classification (Simonyan and Zisserman, 2014), speech recognition (Hannun et al., 2014) and natural language understanding (Sutskever et al., 2014), the majority of the current work in the area of acoustic emotion recognition is neural network-based. Diverse neural architectures were investigated based on convolutional and recurrent neural networks (Fayek et al., 2017; Trigeorgis et al., 2016). Alternatively, methods based on linear models, like SVM with careful feature engineering, still show competitive performance on the benchmark datasets (Schuller et al., 2013, 2009). Such methods were popular in computer vision until the AlexNet approach (Krizhevsky et al., 2012) made automatic feature learning more wide-spread. The low availability of annotated auditory emotion data is probably one of the main reasons for traditional methods being competitive. The appealing property of neural networks compared to SVM-like methods is their ability to identify automatically useful patterns in the data and to scale linearly with the number of training samples. These properties drive the research community to investigate different neural architectures.

Proceedings of the The 8th International Joint Conference on Natural Language Processing, pages 423–430,
Taipei, Taiwan, November 27 – December 1, 2017 ©2017 AFNLP

In this paper, we present a model that neither solely learns feature representations from scratch nor uses complex feature engineering but uses the features learned by a speech recognition network.

Even though the automatic speech recognition (ASR) task is agnostic to the speaker's emotion and focuses only on the accuracy of the language transcription, low-level neural network layers trained for ASR might still extract useful information for the task of SER. Given that the size of the data suitable for training ASR systems is significantly larger than SER data, we can expect that trained ASR systems are more robust to speaker and condition variations. Recently, a method of transferring knowledge learned by the neural network from one task to another has been proposed (Rusu et al., 2016; Anderson et al., 2016). This strategy also potentially prevents a neural network from overfitting to the smaller of the two datasets and could work as an additional regularizer. Moreover, in many applications, such as dialog systems, we would need to transcribe spoken text and identify its emotion jointly.

In this paper, we evaluate several dual architectures which integrate representations of the ASR network: a fine-tuning and a progressive network. The fine-tuning architecture reuses features learnt by the recurrent layers of a speech recognition network and can use them directly for emotion classification by feeding them to a softmax classifier or can add additional hidden SER layers to tune ASR representations. Additionally, the ASR layers can be static for the whole training process or can be updated as well by allowing to backpropagate through them. The progressive architecture complements information from the ASR network with SER representations trained end-to-end. Therefore, in contrast to the fine-tuning model, a progressive network allows learning such low-level emotion-relevant features which the ASR network never learns since they are irrelevant to the speech recognition task. Our contribution in this paper is two-fold: 1) we propose several neural architectures allowing to model speech and emotion recognition jointly, and 2) we present a simple variant of a fine-tuning and a progressive network which improves the performance of the existing end-to-end models.

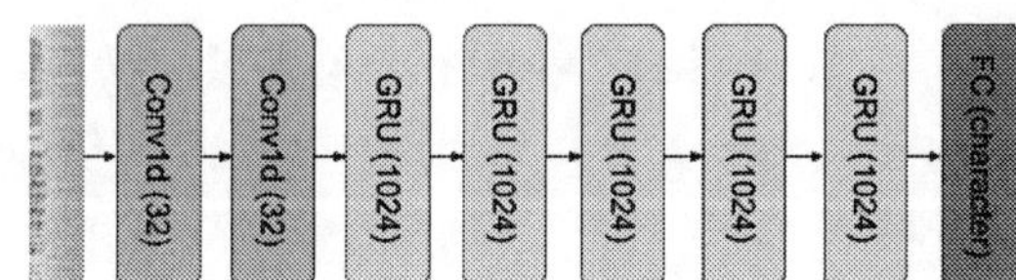

Figure 2: Architecture of the ASR model used in this work, following the DeepSpeech 2 architecture.

2 Related work

The majority of recent research is aimed at searching for optimal neural architectures that learn emotion-specific features from little or not processed data. An autoencoder network (Ghosh et al., 2016) was demonstrated to learn to compress the speech frames before the emotion classification. An attention mechanism (Huang and Narayanan, 2016) was proposed to adjust weights for each of the speech frames depending on their importance. As there are many speech frames that are not relevant to an expressed emotion, such as silence, the attention mechanism allows focusing only on the significant part of the acoustic signal. Another approach probabilistically labeling each speech frame as emotional and non-emotional was proposed by (Chernykh et al., 2017). A combination of convolutional and recurrent neural networks was demonstrated by (Trigeorgis et al., 2016) by training a model directly from the raw, unprocessed waveform, significantly outperforming manual feature engineering methods.

One of the first examples of the knowledge transfer among neural networks was demonstrated by (Bengio, 2012) and (Yosinski et al., 2014). Eventually, fine-tuning became the de-facto standard for computer vision tasks that have a small number of annotated samples, leveraging the ability of trained convolutional filters to be applicable to different tasks. Our work is mainly inspired by recently introduced architectures with an ability to transfer knowledge between recurrent neural networks in a domain different from computer vision (Rusu et al., 2016; Anderson et al., 2016).

Previously, to our knowledge, there was only one attempt to analyze the correlation between automatic speech and emotion recognition (Fayek et al., 2016). This approach showed the possibility of knowledge transfer from the convolutional neural acoustic model trained on the TIMIT corpus (Garofolo et al., 1993) for the emotion recognition task. The authors proposed several variants of fine-tuning. They reported a significant drop in the performance by using the ASR network as a feature extractor and training only the output softmax layer, compared to an end-to-end convolution neural network model. Gradual improvements were observed by allowing more ASR layers to be updated during back-propagation but, overall, using ASR for feature extraction affected the performance negatively.

3 Models and experiment setup

3.1 Models

We introduce two models that use a pre-trained ASR network for acoustic emotion recognition. The first one is the fine-tuning model which only takes representations of the ASR network and learns how to combine them to predict an emotion category. We compare two variants of tuning ASR representations: simply feeding them into a softmax classifier or adding a new Gated Recurrent Units (GRU) layer trained on top of the ASR features. The second is the progressive network which allows us to train a neural network branch parallel to the ASR network which can capture additional emotion-specific information. We present all SER models used in this work in Figure 3.

3.1.1 ASR model

Our ASR model (see Figure 2) is a combination of convolutional and recurrent layers inspired by the DeepSpeech (Hannun et al., 2014) architecture for speech recognition. Our model contains two convolutional layers for feature extraction from power FFT spectrograms, followed by five recurrent bi-directional GRU layers with the softmax layer on top, predicting the character distribution for each speech frame (ASR network in all our experiments, left branch of the network in the Figures 3b, 3c and 3d). The ASR network is trained on pairs of utterances and the corresponding transcribed texts (see 3.2.2 "Speech data" section for details). Connectionist Temporal classification (CTC) loss (Graves et al., 2006) was used as a metric to measure how good the alignment produced by the network is compared to the ground truth transcription. Power spectrograms were extracted using a Hamming window of 20ms width and 10 ms stride, resulting in 161 features for each speech frame. We trained the ASR network with Stochastic Gradient Descent with a learning rate of

0.0003 divided by 1.1 after every epoch until the character error rate stopped improving on the validation set (resulting in 35 epochs overall). In all our experiments we keep the ASR network static by freezing its weights during training for SER.

3.1.2 Baseline

As a baseline (see Figure 3a), we used a two-layer bi-directional GRU neural network. Utterances were represented by averaging hidden vector representations obtained on the second GRU layer and fed to a softmax layer for emotion classification. Dropout with the probability of 0.25 was applied to the utterance representation during training to prevent overfitting. We evaluate this architecture as a baseline as it was proven to yield strong results on the acoustic emotion recognition task (Huang and Narayanan, 2016). As there are significantly less emotion-annotated samples available the SER-specific network is limited to two layers compared to the ASR network.

3.1.3 Fine-tuning model

We propose several variants of reusing speech representations: 1) By averaging hidden memory representations of the layer number x of the ASR network (*Fine-tuning MP-x* later in the text where MP stands for *Mean Pooling*), we train only the output softmax layer to predict an emotion class. (2) We feed hidden memory representations as input to a new GRU network (emotion-specific) initialized randomly and trained for emotion classification (*Fine-tuning RNN-x*). The intuition is that bottom layers of the ASR network can be used as feature extractors and the top level GRU can combine them to predict the emotion class. Similar to the *Fine-tuning MP-x* setup we average representations of the newly attached GRU layer and feed them to the classifier. In both experiments, dropout with the rate of 0.25 was applied to averaged representations. Figure 3b shows the *Fine-tuning MP-1* model pooling ASR representation of the first ASR layer, and Figure 3c shows the *Fine-tuning RNN-1* setup.

3.1.4 Progressive neural network

The progressive network combines fine-tuning with end-to-end training. The scheme of the model is presented in Figure 3d. It contains two branches: first, a speech recognition branch (left in Figure 3d and identical to Figure 2) which is static and not updated, and second, an emotion recogni-

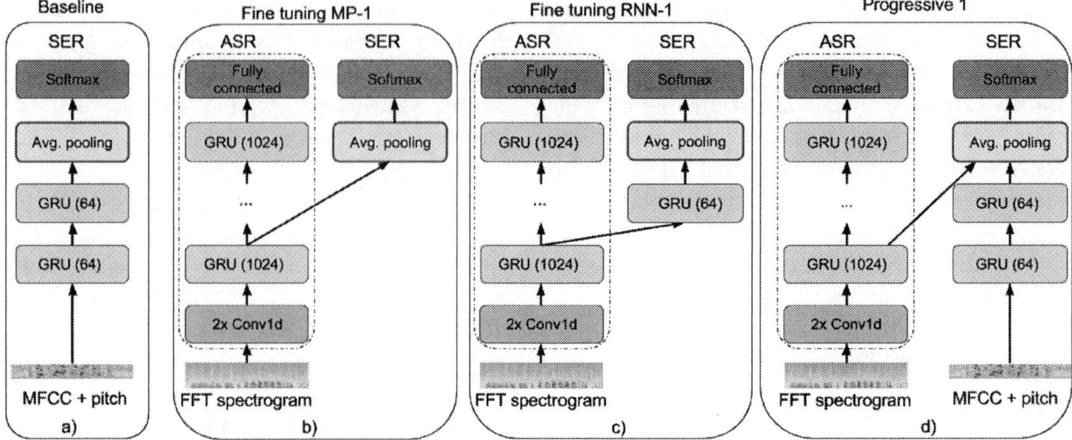

Figure 3: (a) Baseline speech emotion recognition (SER) model, containing two bi-directional GRU layers (b) A variant of the fine-tuning network (Fine-tuning MP-1) which uses the temporal pooled representations of the first recurrent layer of the ASR network. (c) A variant of the fine-tuning network (Fine-tuning RNN-1) which uses hidden memory representations of the first recurrent layer of the ASR network as input to a new emotion-specific GRU layer. (d) The progressive network combines representations from the emotion recognition path with the temporal pooled first layer representations of the ASR network (here Progressive net 1). A concatenated vector is fed into the softmax layer for the final emotion classification. The ASR branch of the network remains static and is not tuned during backpropagation in (b), (c) and (d).

tion branch (right), with the same architecture as the baseline model which we initialized randomly and trained from scratch. We feed the same features to the emotion recognition branch as to the baseline model for a fair comparison. Theoretically, a network of such type can learn task specific features while incorporating knowledge already utilized in the ASR network if it contributes positively to the prediction.

3.2 Data

3.2.1 Emotion data

The Interactive Emotional Dyadic Motion Capture dataset IEMOCAP (Busso et al., 2008) contains five recorded sessions of conversations between two actors, one from each gender. The total amount of data is 12 hours of audio-visual information from ten speakers annotated with categorical emotion labels (Anger, Happiness, Sadness, Neutral, Surprise, Fear, Frustration and Excited), and dimensional labels (values of the activation and valence from 1 to 5). Similarly as in previous work (Huang and Narayanan, 2016), we merged the *Excited* class with *Happiness*. We performed several data filtering steps: we kept samples where at least two annotators agreed on the emotion la-

bel, discarded samples where an utterance was annotated with 3 different emotions and used samples annotated with neutral, angry, happy and sad, resulting in 6,416 samples (1,104 of Anger, 2,496 of Happiness, 1,752 of Neutral and 1,064 of Sadness). We use 4 out of 5 sessions for training and the remaining one for validation and testing (as there are two speakers in the session, one was used for validation and the other for testing).

3.2.2 Speech data

We concatenated three datasets to train the ASR model: LibriSpeech, TED-LIUM v2, and Vox-Forge. LibriSpeech (Panayotov et al., 2015) contains around 1,000 hours of English-read speech from audiobooks. TED-LIUM v2 (Rousseau et al., 2014) is a dataset composed of transcribed TED talks, containing 200 hours of speech and 1495 speakers. VoxForge is an open-source collection of transcribed recordings collected using crowd-sourcing. We downloaded all English recordings[1], which is around 100 hours of speech. Overall, 384,547 utterances containing 1,300 hours of speech from more than 3,000 speakers were used

---

[1] `http://www.repository.voxforge1.org/downloads/SpeechCorpus/Trunk/Audio/Original/48kHz_16bit/`

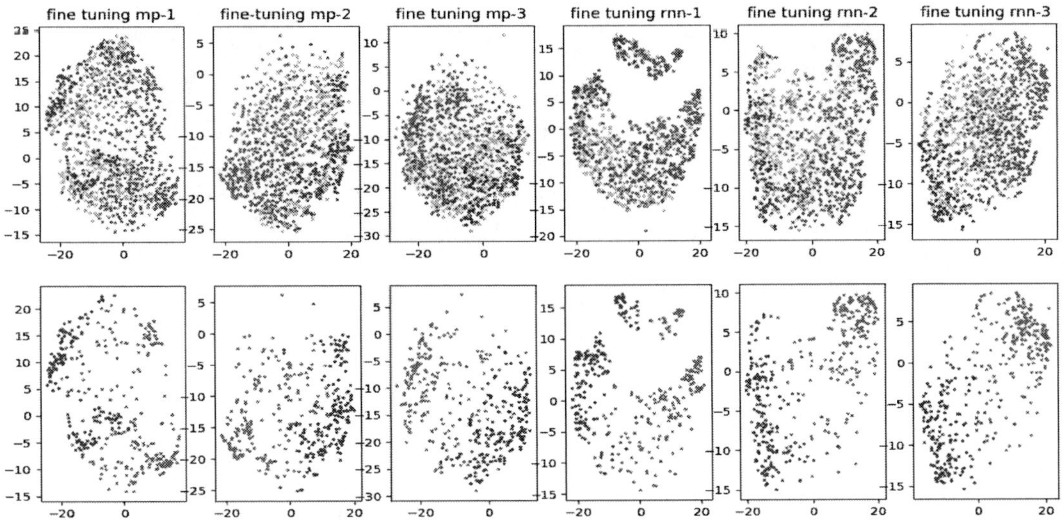

Figure 4: Representations of the IEMOCAP utterances generated by the *Fine-tuning MP-x* and *Fine-tuning RNN-x* networks (*x* stands for the ASR layer number of which the representation is used) projected into 2-dimensional space using the t-SNE technique. Top: all four classes, bottom: only *Sadness* and *Anger*. Color mapping: *Anger* - red, *Sadness* - blue, *Neutral* - cyan, *Happiness* - green. We can observe that *Fine-tuning MP-2 and MP-3* networks can separate *Anger* and *Sadness* classes even though these representations are directly computed from the ASR network without any emotion-specific training. *Fine-tuning RNN* networks benefit from being trained directly for emotion recognition and form visually distinguishable clusters.

to train the ASR model. We conducted no preprocessing other than the conversion of recordings to WAV format with single channel 32-bit format and a sampling rate of 16,000. Utterances longer than 15 seconds were filtered out due to GPU memory constraints.

3.3 Extracted features

The ASR network was trained on power spectrograms with filter banks computed over windows of 20ms width and 10ms stride. For the progressive network, we used the same features as for the ASR branch, and for the SER-specific branch, we used 13 MFCC coefficients and their deltas extracted over windows of 20ms width and 10ms stride. We have extracted pitch values smoothed with moving average with a window size of 15 using the OpenSMILE toolkit (Eyben et al., 2013). The reason for the choice of high-level features like MFCC and pitch for the SER-branch was the limited size of emotion annotated data, as learning efficient emotion representation from low-level features like raw waveform or power-spectrograms might be difficult on the dataset of a size of IEMO-

CAP. In addition, such feature set showed state-of-the-art results (Huang and Narayanan, 2016). In both cases, we normalized each feature by subtracting the mean and dividing by standard deviation per utterance.

3.3.1 Training

The Adam optimizer (Kingma and Ba, 2014) was used in all experiments with a learning rate of 0.0001, clipping the norm of the gradient at the level of 15 with a batch size of 64. During the training, we applied learning rate annealing if the results on the validation set did not improve for two epochs and stopped it when the learning rate reaches the value of 1e-6. We applied the Sorta-Grad algorithm (Amodei et al., 2015) during the first epoch by sorting utterances by the duration (Hannun et al., 2014). We performed data augmentation during the training phase by randomly changing tempo and gain of the utterance within the range of 0.85 to 1.15 and -3 to +6 dB respectively. The model with the lowest cross-entropy loss on the validation set was picked to evaluate the test set performance.

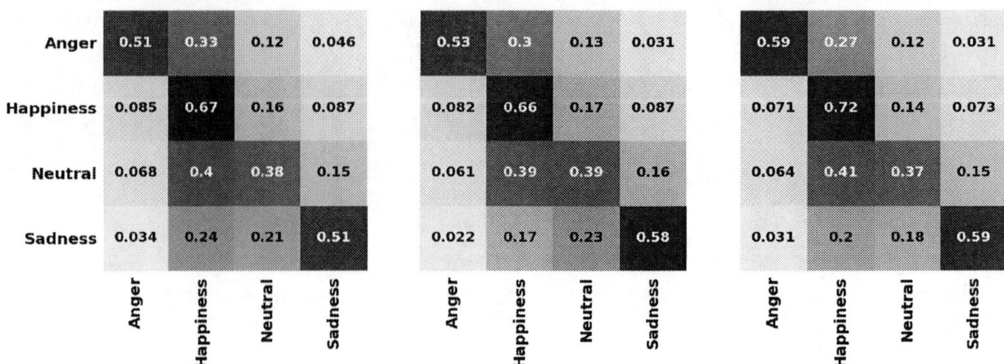

Figure 5: Confusion matrices for our best baseline, *Fine-tuning MP* and *Progressive* models averaged over 10-folds on the IEMOCAP dataset.

Table 1: Utterance-level emotion 4-way classification performance (unweighted and weighted accuracy and f1-score). Several variants of fine-tuning and progressive networks are evaluated: using first, second or third ASR layers as input for Fine-tuning MP, Fine-tuning RNN, and progressive networks.

Model	U-Acc	W-acc	F1-score
Most frequent class	0.39 ± 0.04	0.33 ± 0.2	NaN
Random prediction	0.25 ± 0.02	0.25 ± 0.02	0.24 ± 0.02
Baseline 64 units	0.52 ± 0.04	0.54 ± 0.06	0.48 ± 0.05
Baseline 96 units	$\mathbf{0.53} \pm 0.01$	$\mathbf{0.55} \pm 0.03$	$\mathbf{0.51} \pm 0.02$
Baseline 128 units	0.50 ± 0.04	0.51 ± 0.06	0.47 ± 0.05
Fine-tuning MP-1	0.46 ± 0.05	0.52 ± 0.07	0.31 ± 0.11
Fine-tuning MP-2	0.54 ± 0.04	0.54 ± 0.06	0.52 ± 0.04
Fine-tuning MP-3	$\mathbf{0.55} \pm 0.02$	$\mathbf{0.56} \pm 0.03$	$\mathbf{0.53} \pm 0.03$
Fine-tuning RNN-1	0.53 ± 0.04	0.57 ± 0.04	0.48 ± 0.08
Fine-tuning RNN-2	$\mathbf{0.57} \pm 0.03$	$\mathbf{0.59} \pm 0.05$	$\mathbf{0.56} \pm 0.03$
Fine-tuning RNN-3	0.56 ± 0.02	0.57 ± 0.04	0.55 ± 0.03
Progressive net-1	0.56 ± 0.02	0.57 ± 0.04	0.55 ± 0.03
Progressive net-2	$\mathbf{0.58} \pm 0.03$	$\mathbf{0.61} \pm 0.04$	$\mathbf{0.57} \pm 0.03$
Progressive net-3	0.57 ± 0.03	0.59 ± 0.03	0.56 ± 0.04

4 Results

Table 1 summarizes the results obtained from ASR-SER transfer learning. We evaluate several baseline models by varying the number of GRU units in a network, and three variants for *Fine-tuning MP-x*, *Fine-tuning RNN-x* and *Progressive net-x* by utilizing representations of layer x of the ASR network. We report weighted and unweighted accuracy and f1-score to reflect imbalanced classes. These metrics were averaged over ten runs of a ten-fold leave-one-speaker-out cross-validation to monitor an effect of random initialization of a neural network. Also, our results reveal the difficulty of separating *Anger* and *Happiness* classes, and *Neutral* and *Happiness* (see

Figure 5). Our best *Fine-tuning MP-3* model achieved 55% unweighted and 56% weighted accuracy, which significantly outperforms the baseline (p-value $\leq$ 0.03) end-to-end 2-layer GRU neural network similar to (Huang and Narayanan, 2016) and (Ghosh et al., 2016). The fine-tuning model has around 30 times less trainable parameters (as only the softmax layer is trained) and achieves significantly better performance than the baseline. These results show that putting an additional GRU layer on top of ASR representations affects the performance positively and shows significantly better results than the baseline (p-value $\leq$ 0.0007). Results prove our hypothesis that intermediate features extracted by the ASR network contain useful information for emotion classification.

The progressive network consistently outperforms baseline end-to-end models, reaching 58% unweighted and 61% weighted accuracy. In all variants, the addition of the second recurrent layer representations of the ASR's network contributes positively to the performance compared to the baseline. Our results support the hypothesis that the progressive architecture of the network allows to combine the ASR low-level representations with the SER-specific ones and achieve the best accuracy result.

In addition to the quantitative results, we tried to analyze the reason of such effectiveness of the ASR representations, by visualizing the representations of the utterances by *Fine-tuning MP-x* and *Fine-tuning RNN-x* networks (see Figure 4). We observe that a prior ASR-trained network can separate *Sadness* and *Anger* samples even by pooling representations of the first ASR layer. On the 3rd layer, *Anger*, *Sadness* and *Happiness* form visually distinguishable clusters which could explain the surprising effectiveness of *Fine-tuning MP-2/3* models. *Fine-tuning RNN-x* networks can separate four classes better due to an additional trained GRU network on top of the ASR representations. Also, we found that activations of some neurons in the ASR network correlate significantly with the well-known prosodic features like loudness. Figure 6 shows the activation of the neuron number 840 of the second GRU layer of the ASR network and the loudness value of the speech frame for two audio files. We found that, on average, the Pearson's correlation between loudness and activation of the 840th neuron calculated on the IEMOCAP dataset is greater than 0.64 which is an indicator that the ASR network is capable of learning prosodic features which is useful for emotion classification.

5   Discussion and conclusion

In this paper, various neural architectures were proposed utilizing speech recognition representations. Fine-tuning provides an ability to use the ASR network for the emotion recognition task quickly. A progressive network allows to combine speech and emotion representations and train them in parallel. Our experimental results confirm that trained speech representations, even though expected to be agnostic to a speaker's emotion,

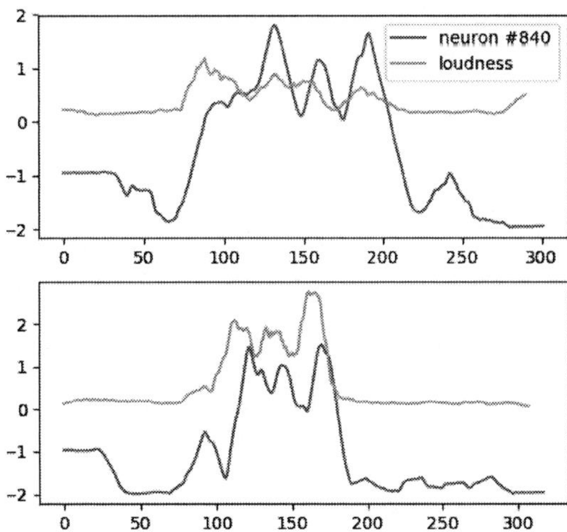

Figure 6: Activations of the neuron number 840 of the second GRU layer of the ASR model (blue) and loudness of two utterances selected randomly from IEMOCAP dataset (orange).

contain useful information for affective state predictions.

A possible future research direction would be to investigate the influence of linguistic knowledge on the speech representations and how it affects the system performance. Additionally, the ASR system can be fine-tuned in parallel with the emotion branch by updating the layers of the ASR network. Potentially, this could help the system to adapt better to the particular speakers and their emotion expression style. Furthermore, analyzing linguistic information of the spoken text produced by the ASR network could possibly alleviate the difficulty of separating *Anger* and *Happiness* classes, and *Neutral* and *Happiness*.

Acknowledgments

This project has received funding from the European Union's Horizon 2020 research and innovation programme under the Marie Sklodowska-Curie grant agreement No 642667 (SECURE) and partial support from the German Research Foundation DFG under project CML (TRR 169).

References

Dario Amodei, Rishita Anubhai, Eric Battenberg, Carl Case, Jared Casper, and et al. 2015. Deep speech 2: End-to-end speech recognition in English and Mandarin. *CoRR*, abs/1512.02595.

Ark Anderson, Kyle Shaffer, Artem Yankov, Court Corley, and Nathan Hodas. 2016. Beyond Fine Tuning: A Modular Approach to Learning on Small Data. *CoRR*, abs/1611.01714.

Yoshua Bengio. 2012. Deep learning of representations for unsupervised and transfer learning. *ICML Unsupervised and Transfer Learning*, 27:17–36.

Carlos Busso, Murtaza Bulut, Chi-Chun Lee, Abe Kazemzadeh, Emily Mower, Samuel Kim, Jeannette N. Chang, Sungbok Lee, and Shrikanth S. Narayanan. 2008. IEMOCAP: interactive emotional dyadic motion capture database. *Language Resources and Evaluation*, 42(4):335.

Vladimir Chernykh, Grigoriy Sterling, and Pavel Prihodko. 2017. Emotion recognition from speech with recurrent neural networks. *CoRR*, abs/1701.08071.

Florian Eyben, Felix Weninger, Florian Gross, and Björn Schuller. 2013. Recent developments in opensmile, the munich open-source multimedia feature extractor. In *Proceedings of the 21st ACM International Conference on Multimedia*, pages 835–838. ACM.

Haytham M. Fayek, Margaret Lech, and Lawrence Cavedon. 2016. On the Correlation and Transferability of Features Between Automatic Speech Recognition and Speech Emotion Recognition. pages 3618–3622.

Haytham M. Fayek, Margaret Lech, and Lawrence Cavedon. 2017. Evaluating deep learning architectures for Speech Emotion Recognition. *Neural Networks*, vol. 92:60–68.

J. S. Garofolo, L. F. Lamel, W. M. Fisher, J. G. Fiscus, and D. S. Pallett. 1993. DARPA TIMIT acoustic-phonetic continuous speech corpus CD-ROM. NIST speech disc 1-1.1. *NASA STI/Recon Technical Report N*, 93.

Sayan Ghosh, Eugene Laksana, Louis-Philippe Morency, and Stefan Scherer. 2016. Representation Learning for Speech Emotion Recognition. *INTERSPEECH*, pages 3603–3607.

Alex Graves, Santiago Fernandez, Faustino Gomez, and Jrgen Schmidhuber. 2006. Connectionist temporal classification: labelling unsegmented sequence data with recurrent neural networks. In *Proceedings of the 23rd International Conference on Machine Learning*, pages 369–376. ACM.

Awni Hannun, Carl Case, Jared Casper, Bryan Catanzaro, and et al. 2014. Deep Speech: Scaling up end-to-end speech recognition. *CoRR*, abs/1412.5567.

Che-Wei Huang and Shrikanth S. Narayanan. 2016. Attention Assisted Discovery of Sub-Utterance Structure in Speech Emotion Recognition. In *Proceedings of Interspeech*, pages 1387–1391.

Diederik P. Kingma and Jimmy Ba. 2014. Adam: A Method for Stochastic Optimization. *arXiv:1412.6980 [cs]*. ArXiv: 1412.6980.

Alex Krizhevsky, Ilya Sutskever, and Geoffrey E Hinton. 2012. ImageNet Classification with Deep Convolutional Neural Networks. In F. Pereira, C. J. C. Burges, L. Bottou, and K. Q. Weinberger, editors, *Advances in Neural Information Processing Systems 25*, pages 1097–1105. Curran Associates, Inc.

Vassil Panayotov, Guoguo Chen, Daniel Povey, and Sanjeev Khudanpur. 2015. Librispeech: an ASR corpus based on public domain audio books. In *Acoustics, Speech and Signal Processing (ICASSP), 2015 IEEE International Conference on*, pages 5206–5210. IEEE.

Anthony Rousseau, Paul Deléglise, and Yannick Estève. 2014. Enhancing the ted-lium corpus with selected data for language modeling and more ted talks. In *LREC*, pages 3935–3939.

Andrei A. Rusu, Neil C. Rabinowitz, Guillaume Desjardins, Hubert Soyer, James Kirkpatrick, Koray Kavukcuoglu, Razvan Pascanu, and Raia Hadsell. 2016. Progressive Neural Networks. *arXiv:1606.04671 [cs]*. ArXiv: 1606.04671.

Björn Schuller, Stefan Steidl, Anton Batliner, Alessandro Vinciarelli, Klaus Scherer, Fabien Ringeval, Mohamed Chetouani, Felix Weninger, Florian Eyben, Erik Marchi, et al. 2013. The interspeech 2013 computational paralinguistics challenge: social signals, conflict, emotion, autism.

Björn Schuller, Bogdan Vlasenko, Florian Eyben, Gerhard Rigoll, and Andreas Wendemuth. 2009. Acoustic emotion recognition: A benchmark comparison of performances. In *Automatic Speech Recognition & Understanding*, pages 552–557. IEEE.

Karen Simonyan and Andrew Zisserman. 2014. Very deep convolutional networks for large-scale image recognition. *CoRR*, abs/1409.1556.

Ilya Sutskever, Oriol Vinyals, and Quoc V. Le. 2014. Sequence to sequence learning with neural networks. In *Advances in neural information processing systems*, pages 3104–3112.

George Trigeorgis, Fabien Ringeval, Raymond Brueckner, Erik Marchi, Mihalis A. Nicolaou, Bjrn Schuller, and Stefanos Zafeiriou. 2016. Adieu features? End-to-end speech emotion recognition using a deep convolutional recurrent network. In *Acoustics, Speech and Signal Processing (ICASSP), 2016 IEEE International Conference on*, pages 5200–5204. IEEE.

Jason Yosinski, Jeff Clune, Yoshua Bengio, and Hod Lipson. 2014. How transferable are features in deep neural networks? In *Advances in neural information processing systems*, pages 3320–3328.

Local Monotonic Attention Mechanism
for End-to-End Speech and Language Processing

Andros Tjandra, Sakriani Sakti, and **Satoshi Nakamura**
Graduate School of Information Science
Nara Institute of Science and Technology, Japan
{andros.tjandra.ai6, ssakti, s-nakamura}@is.naist.jp

Abstract

Recently, encoder-decoder neural networks have shown impressive performance on many sequence-related tasks. The architecture commonly uses an attentional mechanism which allows the model to learn alignments between the source and the target sequence. Most attentional mechanisms used today is based on a global attention property which requires a computation of a weighted summarization of the whole input sequence generated by encoder states. However, it is computationally expensive and often produces misalignment on the longer input sequence. Furthermore, it does not fit with monotonous or left-to-right nature in several tasks, such as automatic speech recognition (ASR), grapheme-to-phoneme (G2P), etc. In this paper, we propose a novel attention mechanism that has local and monotonic properties. Various ways to control those properties are also explored. Experimental results on ASR, G2P and machine translation between two languages with similar sentence structures, demonstrate that the proposed encoder-decoder model with local monotonic attention could achieve significant performance improvements and reduce the computational complexity in comparison with the one that used the standard global attention architecture.

1 Introduction

End-to-end training is a newly emerging approach to sequence-to-sequence mapping tasks, that allows the model to directly learn the mapping between variable-length representation of different modalities (i.e., text-to-text sequence (Bahdanau et al., 2014; Sutskever et al., 2014), speech-to-text sequence (Chorowski et al., 2014; Chan et al., 2016), image-to-text sequence (Xu et al., 2015), etc).

One popular approaches in the end-to-end mapping tasks of different modalities is based on encoder-decoder architecture. The earlier version of an encoder-decoder model is built with only two different components (Sutskever et al., 2014; Cho et al., 2014b): (1) an encoder that processes the source sequence and encodes them into a fixed-length vector; and (2) a decoder that produces the target sequence based on information from fixed-length vector given by encoder. Both the encoder and decoder are jointly trained to maximize the probability of a correct target sequence given a source sequence. This architecture has been applied in many applications such as machine translation (Sutskever et al., 2014; Cho et al., 2014b), image captioning (Karpathy and Fei-Fei, 2015), and so on.

However, such architecture encounters difficulties, especially for coping with long sequences. Because in order to generate the correct target sequence, the decoder solely depends only on the last hidden state of the encoder. In other words, the network needs to compress all of the information contained in the source sequence into a single fixed-length vector. (Cho et al., 2014a) demonstrated a decrease in the performance of the encoder-decoder model associated with an increase in the length of the input sentence sequence. Therefore, (Bahdanau et al., 2014) introduced attention mechanism to address these issues. Instead of relying on a fixed-length vector, the decoder is assisted by the attention module to get the related context from the encoder sides, depends on the current decoder states.

Most attention-based encoder-decoder model

Proceedings of the The 8th International Joint Conference on Natural Language Processing, pages 431–440,
Taipei, Taiwan, November 27 – December 1, 2017 ©2017 AFNLP

used today has a "global" property (Bahdanau et al., 2014; Luong et al., 2015). Every time the decoder needs to predict the output given the previous output, it must compute a weighted summarization of the whole input sequence generated by the encoder states. This global property allows the decoder to address any parts of the source sequence at each step of the output generation and provides advantages in some cases like machine translation tasks. Specifically, when the source and the target languages have different sentence structures and the last part of the target sequence may depend on the first part of the source sequence. However, although the global attention mechanism has often improved performance in some tasks, it is very computationally expensive. For a case that requires mapping between long sequences, misalignments might happen in standard attention mechanism (Kim et al., 2017). Furthermore, it does not fit with monotonous or left-to-right natures in several tasks, such as ASR, G2P, etc.

In this paper, we propose a novel attention module that has two important characteristics to address those problems: local and monotonicity properties. The local property helps our attention module focus on certain parts from the source sequence that the decoder wants to transcribe, and the monotonicity property strictly generates alignment left-to-right from beginning to the end of the source sequence. In case of speech recognition task that need to produces a transcription given the speech signal, the attention module is now able to focus on the audio's specific timing and always move in one direction from the start to the end of the audio. Similar way can be applied also for G2P or machine translation (MT) between two languages with similar sentences structure, i.e., Subject-Verb-Object (SVO) word order in English and French languages. Experimental results demonstrate that the proposed encoder-decoder model with local monotonic attention could achieve significant performance improvements and reduce the computational complexity in comparison with the one that used the standard global attention architecture.

2   Attention-based Encoder Decoder Neural Network

The encoder-decoder model is a neural network that directly models conditional probability

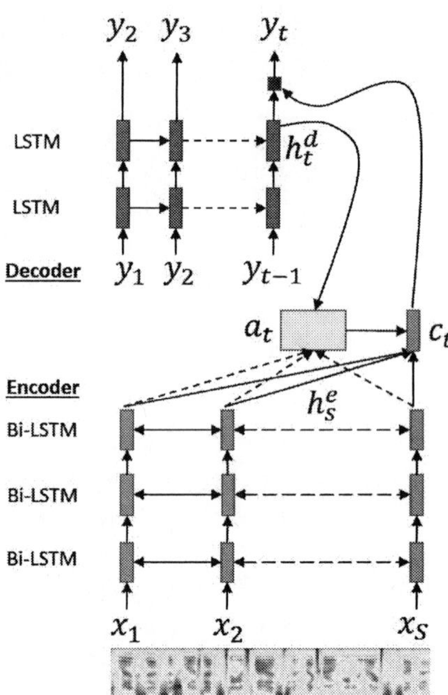

Figure 1: Attention-based encoder-decoder architecture.

$p(\mathbf{y}|\mathbf{x})$, where $\mathbf{x} = [x_1, ..., x_S]$ is the source sequence with length S and $\mathbf{y} = [y_1, ..., y_T]$ is the target sequence with length T. Figure 1 shows the overall structure of the attention-based encoder-decoder model that consists of encoder, decoder and attention modules.

The encoder task processes input sequence $\mathbf{x}$ and outputs representative information $\mathbf{h}^e = [h_1^e, ..., h_S^e]$ for the decoder. The attention module is an extension scheme for assisting the decoder to find relevant information on the encoder side based on the current decoder hidden states (Bahdanau et al., 2014; Luong et al., 2015). Usually, attention modules produces context information c_t at the time t based on the encoder and decoder hidden states:

$$c_t = \sum_{s=1}^{S} a_t(s) * h_s^e \tag{1}$$

$$a_t(s) = \text{Align}(h_s^e, h_t^d)$$
$$= \frac{\exp(\text{Score}(h_s^e, h_t^d))}{\sum_{s=1}^{S} \exp(\text{Score}(h_s^e, h_t^d))} \tag{2}$$

There are several variations for score functions:

$$\text{Score}(h_s^e, h_t^d) = \begin{cases} \langle h_s^e, h_t^d \rangle, & \text{dot product} \\ h_s^{e\mathsf{T}} W_s h_t^d, & \text{bilinear} \\ V_s^\mathsf{T} \tanh(W_s[h_s^e, h_t^d]), & \text{MLP} \end{cases} \quad (3)$$

where $\text{Score} : (\mathbb{R}^M \times \mathbb{R}^N) \to \mathbb{R}$, M is the number of hidden units for encoder and N is the number of hidden units for decoder. Finally, the decoder task, which predicts the target sequence probability at time t based on previous output and context information c_t can be formulated:

$$\log p(\mathbf{y}|\mathbf{x}) = \sum_{t=1}^{T} \log p(y_t|y_{<t}, c_t) \quad (4)$$

For speech recognition task, most common input $\mathbf{x}$ is a sequence of feature vectors like Mel-spectral filterbank and/or MFCC. Therefore, $\mathbf{x} \in \mathbb{R}^{S \times D}$ where D is the number of features and S is the total frame length for an utterance. Output $\mathbf{y}$, which is a speech transcription sequence, can be either phoneme or grapheme (character) sequence. In text-related task such as machine translation, $\mathbf{x}$ and $\mathbf{y}$ are a sequence of word or character indexes.

3 Locality and Monotonicity Properties

In the previous section, we explained the standard global attention-based encoder-decoder model. However, in order to control the area and focus attention given previous information, such mechanism requires to apply the scoring function into all the encoder states and normalizes them with a softmax function. Another problem is we cannot explicitly enforce the probability mass generated by the current attention modules that are always moving incrementally to the end of the source sequence. In this section, we discuss and explain how to model the locality and monotonicity properties on the attention module. This way, we could improve the sensitivity of capturing regularities and ensure to focus only an important subset instead of whole sequence.

Figure 2 illustrates the overall mechanism of our proposed local monotonic attention, and details are described blow.

1. **Monotonicity-based Prediction of Central Position**

   First, we define how to predict the next central position of the alignment illustrated in

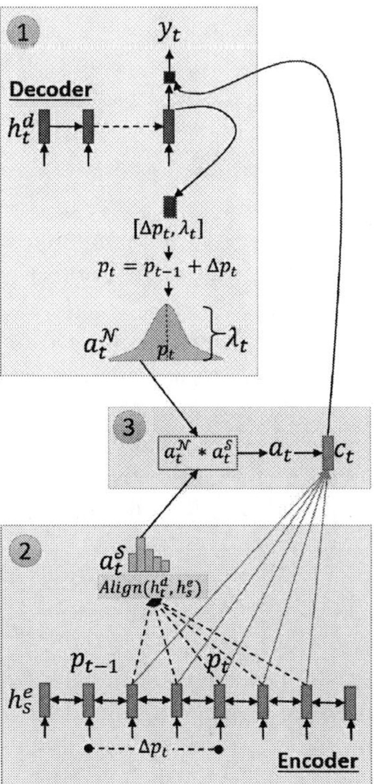

Figure 2: Local monotonic attention.

Part (1) of Figure 2. Assume we have source sequence with length S, which is encoded by the stack of Bi-LSTM (see Figure 1) into S encoded states $\mathbf{h^e} = [h_1^e, ..., h_S^e]$. At time t, we want to decode the t-th target output given the source sequence, previous output y_{t-1}, and current decoder hidden states $h_t^d \in \mathbb{R}^N$. In standard approaches, we use hidden states h_t^d to predict the position difference Δp_t with a multilayer perceptron (MLP). We use variable Δp_t to determine how far we should move the center of the alignment compared to previous center p_{t-1}.

In this paper, we propose two different formulations for estimating Δp_t to ensure a forward or monotonicity movement:

- **Constrained position prediction:**
  We limit maximum range from Δp_t with hyperparameter C_{max} with the following equation:

  $$\Delta p_t = C_{max} * \text{sigmoid}(V_p^\mathsf{T} \tanh(W_p h_t^d)) \quad (5)$$

  Here we can control how far our next center of alignment position p_t

433

relies on our datasets and guarantee $0 \leq \Delta p_t \leq C_{max}$. However, it requires us to handle hyperparameter C_{max}.

- **Unconstrained position prediction:** Compared to a previous formulation, since we do not limit the maximum range of Δp_t, here we can ignore hyperparameter C_{max} and use exponential (exp) function instead of sigmoid. We can also use another function (e.g softplus) as long as the function satisfy $f : \mathbb{R} \to \mathbb{R}_0^+$ and the result of $\Delta p_t \geq 0$. We formulate unconstrained position prediction with following equation:

$$\Delta p_t = \exp(V_p^\mathsf{T} \tanh(W_p h_t^d)) \quad (6)$$

Here $V_p \in \mathbb{R}^{K \times 1}$, $W_p \in \mathbb{R}^{K \times N}$, N is the number of decoder hidden units and K is the number of hidden projection layer units. We omit the bias for simplicity. Both equations guarantee monotonicity properties since $\forall t \in [1..T], p_t \geq (p_{t-1} + \Delta p_t)$.

Additionally, we also used scaling variable λ_t to scale the unnormalized Gaussian distribution that depends on h_t. We calculated λ_t with following equation:

$$\lambda_t = \exp(V_\lambda^\mathsf{T} \tanh(W_p h_t^d)) \quad (7)$$

where $V_\lambda \in \mathbb{R}^{K \times 1}$. In our initial experiments, we discovered that we improved our model performance by scaling with λ_t for each time-step. The main objective of this step is to generate a scaled Gaussian distribution $a_t^{\mathcal{N}}$:

$$a_t^{\mathcal{N}}(s) = \lambda_t * \exp\left(-\frac{(s - p_t)^2}{2\sigma^2}\right). \quad (8)$$

where p_t is the mean and σ is the standard deviation, both of which are used to calculate the weighted sum from the encoder states to generate context vector c_t later. In this paper, we treat σ as a hyperparameter.

2. **Locality-based Alignment Generation**
After calculating new position p_t, we generate locality-based alignment, as shown in Part (2) of Figure 2. Based on predicted position p_t, we follow (Luong et al., 2015) to generate

alignment $a_t^{\mathcal{S}}$ only within $[p_t - 2\sigma, p_t + 2\sigma]$:

$$a_t^{\mathcal{S}}(s) = \text{Align}(h_s^e, h_t^d), \quad (9)$$
$$\forall s \in [p_t - 2\sigma, p_t + 2\sigma].$$

Since p_t is a real number and the indexes for the encoder states are integers, we convert p_t into an integer with floor operation. After we know the center of the position p_t, we only need to calculate the scores (Eq. 3) for each encoder states in $[p_t - 2\sigma, .., p_t + 2\sigma]$ then calculate the context alignment scores (Eq. 2).

Compared to the standard global attention, we can reduce the decoding computational complexity $O(T * S)$ into $O(T * \sigma)$ where $\sigma \ll S$ and σ is constant, T is total decoding step, S is the length of the encoder states.

3. **Context Calculation**
In the last step, we calculate context c_t with alignments $a_t^{\mathcal{N}}$ and $a_t^{\mathcal{S}}$, as shown in Part (3) of Figure 2:

$$c_t = \sum_{s=(p_t - 2\sigma)}^{(p_t + 2\sigma)} \left(a_t^{\mathcal{N}}(s) * a_t^{\mathcal{S}}(s)\right) * h_s^e \quad (10)$$

Context c_t and current hidden state h_t^d will later be utilized for calculating current output y_t.

Overall, we can rephrase the first step as generating "prior" probabilities $a_t^{\mathcal{N}}$ based on the previous p_{t-1} position and the current decoder states. Then the second step task generates "likelihood" probabilities $a_t^{\mathcal{S}}$ by measuring the relevance of our encoder states with the current decoder states. In the third step, we combine our "prior" and "likelihood" probability into an unnormalized "posterior" probability a_t and calculate expected context c_t.

4 Experiment on Speech Recognition

We applied our proposed architecture on ASR task. The local property helps our attention module focus on certain parts from the speech that the decoder wants to transcribe, and the monotonicity property strictly generates alignment left-to-right from beginning to the end of the speech.

4.1 Speech Data

We conducted our experiments on the TIMIT [1] (Garofolo et al., 1993) dataset with the same set-

---

[1] https://catalog.ldc.upenn.edu/ldc93s1

up for training, development, and test sets as defined in the Kaldi s5 recipe (Povey et al., 2011). The training set contains 3696 sentences from 462 speakers. We also used another sets of 50 speakers for the development set and the test set contains 192 utterances, 8 each from 24 speakers. For every experiment, we used 40-dimensional fbank with delta and acceleration (total 120-dimension feature vector) extracted from the Kaldi toolkit. The input features were normalized by subtracting the mean and divided by the standard deviation from the training set. For our decoder target, we re-mapped the original target phoneme set from 61 into 39 phoneme class plus the end of sequence mark (eos).

4.2 Model Architectures

On the encoder sides, we projected our input features with a linear layer with 512 hidden units followed by tanh activation function. We used three bidirectional LSTMs (Bi-LSTM) for our encoder with 256 hidden units for each LSTM (total 512 hidden units for Bi-LSTM). To reduce the computational time, we used hierarchical subsampling (Graves, 2012; Bahdanau et al., 2016), applied it to the top two Bi-LSTM layers, and reduced their length by a factor of 4.

On the decoder sides, we used a 64-dimensional embedding matrix to transform the input phonemes into a continuous vector, followed by two unidirectional LSTMs with 512 hidden units. For every local monotonic model, we used an MLP with 256 hidden units to generate Δp_t and λ_t. Hyperparameter 2σ was set to 3, and C_{max} for constrained position prediction (see Eq. 5) was set to 5. Both hyperparameters were empirically selected and generally gave consistent results across various settings in our proposed model. For our scorer module, we used bilinear and MLP scorers (see Eq 3) with 256 hidden units. We used an Adam (Kingma and Ba, 2014) optimizer with a learning rate of $5e - 4$.

In the recognition phase, we generated transcriptions with best-1 (greedy) search from the decoder. We did not use any language model in this work. All of our models were implemented on the Chainer framework (Tokui et al., 2015).

For comparison, we evaluated our proposed model with the standard global attention-based encoder-decoder model and *local-m* attention (Luong et al., 2015) as the baseline. Most of the con-figurations follow the above descriptions, except the baseline model that does not have an MLP for generating Δp_t and λ_t.

5 Result and Discussion for Speech Recognition

Table 1 summarizes our experiments on our proposed local attention models and compares them to the baseline model using several possible scenarios.

5.1 Constrained vs Unconstrained Position Prediction

Considering the use of constrained and unconstrained position prediction Δp_t, our results show that the model with the unconstrained position prediction (exp) model gives better results than one based on the constrained position prediction (sigmoid) model on both MLP and bilinear scorers. We conclude that it is more beneficial to use the unconstrained position prediction formulation since it gives better performance and we do not need to handle the additional hyperparameter C_{max}.

5.2 Alignment Scorer vs Non-Scorer

Next we investigate the importance of the scorer module by comparing the results between a model with and without it. Our results reveal that, by only relying on Gaussian alignment $a_t^{\mathcal{N}}$ and set $a_t^{\mathcal{S}} = 1$, our model performance's was worse than one that used both the scorer and Gaussian alignment. This might be because the scorer modules are able to correct the details from the Gaussian alignment based on the relevance of the encoder states in the current decoder states. Thus, we conclude that alignment with the scorer is essential for our proposed models.

5.3 Overall comparison to the baseline

Overall, our proposed encoder-decoder model with local monotonic attention significantly improved the performance and reduced the computational complexity in comparison with one that used standard global attention mechanism (we cannot compare directly with (Chorowski et al., 2014) since its pretrained with HMM state alignment). We also tried *local-m* attention from (Luong et al., 2015), however our model cannot converge and we hypothesize the reason is because ratio length between the speech and their corresponding text is larger than 1, therefore the

Table 1: Results from baseline and proposed models on ASR task with TIMIT test set.

Model	Test PER (%)
Global Attention Model (Baseline)	
Att Enc-Dec (pretrained with HMM align) (Chorowski et al., 2014)	18.6
Att Enc-Dec (Pereyra et al., 2017)	23.2
Att Enc-Dec (Luo et al., 2016)	24.5
Att Enc-Dec with MLP Scorer (ours)	23.8
Att Enc-Dec with *local-m* (ours) (Luong et al., 2015)	-

| **Local Attention Model (Proposed)** | | | |
| **Monotonicity** | **Locality** | | |
Pos Prediction Δp_t	**Alignment** **Score**(h_s^e, h_t^d)	**Func. Type**	**Test PER (%)**
Const (*sigmoid*)	No	-	23.2
Const (*sigmoid*)	Yes	Bilinear	21.9
Const (*sigmoid*)	Yes	MLP	21.7
Unconst (*exp*)	No	-	23.1
Unconst (*exp*)	Yes	Bilinear	**20.9**
Unconst (*exp*)	Yes	MLP	21.4

Δp_t cannot be represented by fixed value. The best performance achieved by our proposed model with unconstrained position prediction and bilinear scorer, and provided 12.2% relative error rate reduction to our baseline.

6 Experiment on Grapheme-to-Phoneme

We also investigated our proposed architecture on G2P conversion task. Here, the model need to generate corresponding phoneme given small segment of characters and its always moving from left to right. The local property helps our attention module focus on certain parts from the grapheme source sequence that the decoder wants to convert into phoneme, and the monotonicity property strictly generates alignment left-to-right from beginning to the end of the grapheme source sequence.

6.1 Dataset

Here, we used the CMUDict dataset[2]. It contains 113438 words for training and 12753 for testing (12000 unique words). For validation, we randomly select 3000 sentences from the training set. The evaluation metrics for this task are phoneme error rate (PER) and word error rate (WER). In the evaluation process, there are some words has multiple references (pronunciations). Therefore, we

---

[2]CMUdict: `https://sourceforge.net/ projects/cmusphinx/files/G2P%20Models/ phonetisaurus-cmudict-split.tar.gz`

select one of the references that has lowest PER between compared to our hypothesis, and if the hypothesis completely match with one of those references, then the WER is not increasing. For our encoder input, we used 26 letter (A-Z) + single quotes ('). For our decoder target, we used 39 phonemes plus the end of sequence mark (eos).

6.2 Model Architectures

On the encoder sides, the characters input were projected into 256 dims using embedding matrix. We used two bidirectional LSTMs (Bi-LSTM) for our encoder with 512 hidden units for each LSTM (total 1024 hidden units for Bi-LSTM). On the decoder sides, the phonemes input were projected into 256 dims using embedding matrix, followed by two unidirectional LSTMs with 512 hidden units. For local monotonic model, we used an MLP with 256 hidden units to generate Δp_t and λ_t. For this task, we only used the unconstrained formulation because based on previous sections, we able to achieved better performance and we didn't need to find optimal hyperparameter for C_{max}. For our scorer module, we used MLP scorer with 256 hidden units.

In the decoding phase, we used beam search strategy with beam size 3 to generate the phonemes given the character sequences. For comparison, we evaluated our model with standard global attention and *local-m* attention model (Luong et al., 2015) as the baseline.

6.3 Result Discussion

Table 2 summarizes our experiment on proposed local attention models. We compared our proposed models with several baselines from other algorithm as well. Our model significantly improving the PER and WER compared to encoder-decoder, attention-based global softmax and *local-m* attention (fixed-step size). Compared to Bi-LSTM model which was trained with explicit alignment, we achieve slightly better PER and WER with larger window size ($2\sigma = 3$).

7 Experiment on Machine Translation

We also conducted experiment on machine translation task, specifically between two languages with similar sentences structure. By using our proposed method, we able to focus only to a small related segment on the source side and the target

Table 2: Results from baseline and proposed method on G2P task with CMUDict test set

Model	PER (%)	WER (%)
Baseline		
Enc-Dec LSTM (2 lyr) (Yao and Zweig, 2015)	7.63	28.61
Bi-LSTM (3 lyr) (Yao and Zweig, 2015)	5.45	23.55
Att Enc-Dec with Global MLP Scorer (ours)	5.96	25.55
Att Enc-Dec with *local-m* (ours) (Luong et al., 2015)	5.64	24.32
Proposed		
Att Enc-Dec + Unconst (exp) ($2\sigma = 2$)	5.45	**23.15**
Att Enc-Dec + Unconst (exp) ($2\sigma = 3$)	**5.43**	23.19

generation process usually follows the source sentence structure without many reordering process.

7.1 Dataset

We used BTEC dataset (Kikui et al., 2003) and chose English-to-France and Indonesian-to-English parallel corpus. From BTEC dataset, we extracted 162318 sentences for training and 510 sentences for test data. Because there are no default development set, we randomly sampled 1000 sentences from training data for validation set. For all language pairs, we preprocessed our dataset using Moses (Koehn et al., 2007) tokenizer. For training, we replaced any word that appear less then twice with unknown (unk) symbol. In details, we keep 10105 words for French corpus, 8265 words for English corpus and 9577 words for Indonesian corpus. We only used sentence pairs where the source is no longer than 60 words in training phase.

7.2 Model Architecture

On both encoder and decoder sides, the input words were projected into 256 dims using embedding matrix. We used three Bi-LSTM for our encoder with 512 hidden units for each LSTM (total 1024 hidden unit for Bi-LSTM). For our decoder, we used three LSTM with 512 hidden units. For local monotonic model, we used an MLP with 256 hidden units to generate Δp_t and λ_t. Same as previous section, we only used the unconstrained for-

mulation for local monotonic experiment. For our scorer module, we used MLP scorer with 256 hidden units. In the decoding phase, we used beam search strategy with beam size 5 and normalized length penalty with $\alpha = 1$ (Wu et al., 2016). For comparison, we evaluate our model with standard global attention and *local-m* attention model (Luo et al., 2016) as the baseline.

Table 3: Results from baseline and proposed method on English-to-France and Indonesian-to-English translation tasks.

Model	BLEU
BTEC English to France	
Baseline	
Att Enc-Dec with Global MLP Scorer	49.0
Att Enc-Dec with *local-m* (ours) (Luong et al., 2015)	50.4
Proposed	
Att Enc-Dec + Unconst (exp) ($2\sigma = 4$)	**51.2**
Att Enc-Dec + Unconst (exp) ($2\sigma = 6$)	51.1
BTEC Indonesian to English	
Baseline	
Att Enc-Dec with Global MLP Scorer	38.2
Att Enc-Dec with *local-m* (ours) (Luong et al., 2015)	39.8
Proposed	
Att Enc-Dec + Unconst (exp) ($2\sigma = 4$)	40.9
Att Enc-Dec + Unconst (exp) ($2\sigma = 6$)	**41.8**

7.3 Result Discussion

Table 3 summarizes our experiment on proposed local attention models compared to baseline global attention model and *local-m* attention model (Luong et al., 2015). Generally, local monotonic attention had better result compared to global attention on both English-to-France and Indonesian-to-English translation task. Our proposed model were able to improve the BLEU up to 2.2 points on English-to-France and 3.6 points on Indonesian-to-English translation task compared to standard global attention. Compared to *local-m* attention with fixed step size, our proposed model able to improve the performance up to 0.8 BLEU on

English-to-France and 2.0 BLEU on Indonesian-to-English translation task.

8 Related Work

Humans do not generally process all of the information that they encounter at once. Selective attention, which is a critical property in human perception, allows attention to be focused on particular information while filtering out a range of other information. The biological structure of the eye and the eye movement mechanism is one part of visual selective attention that provides the ability to focus attention selectively on parts of the visual space to acquire information when and where it is needed (Rensink, 2000). In the case of the cocktail party effect, humans can selectively focus their attentive hearing on a single speaker among various conversation and background noise sources (Cherry, 1953).

The attention mechanism in deep learning has been studied for many years. But, only recently have attention mechanisms made their way into the sequence-to-sequence deep learning architectures that were proposed to solve machine translation tasks. Such mechanisms provide a model with the ability to jointly align and translate (Bahdanau et al., 2014). With the attention-based model, the encoder-decoder model significantly improved the performance on machine translation (Bahdanau et al., 2014; Luong et al., 2015) and has successfully been applied to ASR tasks (Chorowski et al., 2014; Chan et al., 2016).

However, as we mentioned earlier, most of those attention mechanism are based on "global" property, where the attention module tries to match the current hidden states with all the states from the encoder sides. This approach is inefficient and computationally expensive on longer source sequences. A "local attention" was recently introduced by (Luong et al., 2015) which provided the capability to only focus small subset of the encoder sides. They also proposed monotonic attention but limited to fixed step-size and not suitable for a task where the length ratio between source and target sequence is vastly different. Our proposed method are able to elevated this problem by predicting the step size dynamically instead of using fixed step size. After we constructed our proposed framework, we found work by (Raffel et al., 2017) recently that also proposed a method for producing monotonic alignment by using Bernoulli random variable to control when the alignment should stop and generate output. However, it cannot attend the source sequence outside the range between previous and current position. In contrast with our approach, we are able to control how large the area we want to attend based on the window size.

(Chorowski et al., 2014) also proposed a soft constraint to encourage monotonicity by invoking a penalty based on the current alignment and previous alignments. However, the methods still did not guarantee a monotonicity movement of the attention.

To the best of our knowledge, only few studies have explored about local and monotonicity properties on an attention-based model. This work presents a novel attention module with locality and monotonicity properties. Our proposed mechanism strictly enforces monotonicity and locality properties in their alignment by explicitly modeling them in mathematical equations. The observation on our proposed model can also possibly act as regularizer by only observed a subset of encoder states. Here, we also explore various ways to control both properties and evaluate the impact of each variations on our proposed model. Experimental results also demonstrate that the proposed encoder-decoder model with local monotonic attention could provide a better performances in comparison with the standard global attention architecture and *local-m* attention model (Luong et al., 2015).

9 Conclusion

This paper demonstrated a novel attention mechanism for encoder decoder model that ensures monotonicity and locality properties. We explored various ways to control these properties, including dynamic monotonicity-based position prediction and locality-based alignment generation. The results reveal our proposed encoder-decoder model with local monotonic attention significantly improved the performance on three different tasks and able to reduced the computational complexity more than one that used standard global attention architecture.

10 Acknowledgement

Part of this work was supported by JSPS KAKENHI Grant Numbers JP17H06101 and JP17K00237.

References

Dzmitry Bahdanau, Kyunghyun Cho, and Yoshua Bengio. 2014. Neural machine translation by jointly learning to align and translate. *arXiv preprint arXiv:1409.0473*.

Dzmitry Bahdanau, Jan Chorowski, Dmitriy Serdyuk, Philemon Brakel, and Yoshua Bengio. 2016. End-to-end attention-based large vocabulary speech recognition. In *Acoustics, Speech and Signal Processing (ICASSP), 2016 IEEE International Conference on*, pages 4945–4949. IEEE.

William Chan, Navdeep Jaitly, Quoc Le, and Oriol Vinyals. 2016. Listen, attend and spell: A neural network for large vocabulary conversational speech recognition. In *Acoustics, Speech and Signal Processing (ICASSP), 2016 IEEE International Conference on*, pages 4960–4964. IEEE.

E Colin Cherry. 1953. Some experiments on the recognition of speech, with one and with two ears. *The Journal of the acoustical society of America*, 25(5):975–979.

Kyunghyun Cho, Bart van Merriënboer, Dzmitry Bahdanau, and Yoshua Bengio. 2014a. On the properties of neural machine translation: Encoder–decoder approaches. *Syntax, Semantics and Structure in Statistical Translation*, page 103.

Kyunghyun Cho, Bart Van Merriënboer, Caglar Gulcehre, Dzmitry Bahdanau, Fethi Bougares, Holger Schwenk, and Yoshua Bengio. 2014b. Learning phrase representations using RNN encoder-decoder for statistical machine translation. *arXiv preprint arXiv:1406.1078*.

Jan Chorowski, Dzmitry Bahdanau, Kyunghyun Cho, and Yoshua Bengio. 2014. End-to-end continuous speech recognition using attention-based recurrent NN: First results. *arXiv preprint arXiv:1412.1602*.

John S Garofolo, Lori F Lamel, William M Fisher, Jonathon G Fiscus, and David S Pallett. 1993. Darpa TIMIT acoustic-phonetic continous speech corpus cd-rom. NIST speech disc 1-1.1. *NASA STI/Recon technical report n*, 93.

Alex Graves. 2012. Supervised sequence labelling. In *Supervised Sequence Labelling with Recurrent Neural Networks*, pages 5–13. Springer.

Andrej Karpathy and Li Fei-Fei. 2015. Deep visual-semantic alignments for generating image descriptions. In *Proceedings of the IEEE Conference on Computer Vision and Pattern Recognition*, pages 3128–3137.

Genichiro Kikui, Eiichiro Sumita, Toshiyuki Takezawa, and Seiichi Yamamoto. 2003. Creating corpora for speech-to-speech translation. In *Eighth European Conference on Speech Communication and Technology*.

Suyoun Kim, Takaaki Hori, and Shinji Watanabe. 2017. Joint ctc-attention based end-to-end speech recognition using multi-task learning. In *Acoustics, Speech and Signal Processing (ICASSP), 2017 IEEE International Conference on*, pages 4835–4839. IEEE.

Diederik Kingma and Jimmy Ba. 2014. Adam: A method for stochastic optimization. *arXiv preprint arXiv:1412.6980*.

Philipp Koehn, Hieu Hoang, Alexandra Birch, Chris Callison-Burch, Marcello Federico, Nicola Bertoldi, Brooke Cowan, Wade Shen, Christine Moran, Richard Zens, et al. 2007. Moses: Open source toolkit for statistical machine translation. In *Proceedings of the 45th annual meeting of the ACL on interactive poster and demonstration sessions*, pages 177–180. Association for Computational Linguistics.

Yuping Luo, Chung-Cheng Chiu, Navdeep Jaitly, and Ilya Sutskever. 2016. Learning online alignments with continuous rewards policy gradient. *arXiv preprint arXiv:1608.01281*.

Minh-Thang Luong, Hieu Pham, and Christopher D Manning. 2015. Effective approaches to attention-based neural machine translation. *arXiv preprint arXiv:1508.04025*.

Gabriel Pereyra, George Tucker, Jan Chorowski, Łukasz Kaiser, and Geoffrey Hinton. 2017. Regularizing neural networks by penalizing confident output distributions. *arXiv preprint arXiv:1701.06548*.

Daniel Povey, Arnab Ghoshal, Gilles Boulianne, Lukas Burget, Ondrej Glembek, Nagendra Goel, Mirko Hannemann, Petr Motlicek, Yanmin Qian, Petr Schwarz, Jan Silovsky, Georg Stemmer, and Karel Vesely. 2011. The Kaldi speech recognition toolkit. In *IEEE 2011 Workshop on Automatic Speech Recognition and Understanding*. IEEE Signal Processing Society. IEEE Catalog No.: CFP11SRW-USB.

Colin Raffel, Thang Luong, Peter J Liu, Ron J Weiss, and Douglas Eck. 2017. Online and linear-time attention by enforcing monotonic alignments. *arXiv preprint arXiv:1704.00784*.

Ronald A Rensink. 2000. The dynamic representation of scenes. *Visual cognition*, 7(1-3):17–42.

Ilya Sutskever, Oriol Vinyals, and Quoc V Le. 2014. Sequence-to-Sequence learning with neural networks. In *Advances in neural information processing systems*, pages 3104–3112.

Seiya Tokui, Kenta Oono, Shohei Hido, and Justin Clayton. 2015. Chainer: a next-generation open source framework for deep learning. In *Proceedings of Workshop on Machine Learning Systems (LearningSys) in The Twenty-ninth Annual Conference on Neural Information Processing Systems (NIPS)*.

Yonghui Wu, Mike Schuster, Zhifeng Chen, Quoc V Le, Mohammad Norouzi, Wolfgang Macherey, Maxim Krikun, Yuan Cao, Qin Gao, Klaus Macherey, et al. 2016. Google's neural machine translation system: Bridging the gap between human and machine translation. *arXiv preprint arXiv:1609.08144*.

Kelvin Xu, Jimmy Ba, Ryan Kiros, Kyunghyun Cho, Aaron C. Courville, Ruslan Salakhutdinov, Richard S. Zemel, and Yoshua Bengio. 2015. Show, attend and tell: Neural image caption generation with visual attention. In *Proceedings of the 32nd International Conference on Machine Learning, ICML 2015, Lille, France, 6-11 July 2015*, pages 2048–2057.

Kaisheng Yao and Geoffrey Zweig. 2015. Sequence-to-sequence neural net models for grapheme-to-phoneme conversion. In *Sixteenth Annual Conference of the International Speech Communication Association*.

Attentive Language Models

Giancarlo D. Salton and **Robert J. Ross** and **John D. Kelleher**

Applied Intelligence Research Centre
School of Computing
Dublin Institute of Technology
Ireland
`giancarlo.salton@mydit.ie` `{robert.ross,john.d.kelleher}@dit.ie`

Abstract

In this paper, we extend Recurrent Neural Network Language Models (RNN-LMs) with an attention mechanism. We show that an *Attentive* RNN-LM (with 14.5M parameters) achieves a better perplexity than larger RNN-LMs (with 66M parameters) and achieves performance comparable to an ensemble of 10 similar sized RNN-LMs. We also show that an *Attentive* RNN-LM needs less contextual information to achieve similar results to the state-of-the-art on the wikitext2 dataset.

1 Introduction

Language Models (LMs) are an essential component in a range of Natural Language Processing applications, such as Statistical Machine Translation and Speech Recognition (Schwenk et al., 2012). An LM provides a probability for a sequence of words in a given language, reflecting fluency and the likelihood of that word sequence occurring in that language.

In recent years Recurrent Neural Networks (RNNs) have improved the state-of-the-art in LM research (Józefowicz et al., 2016). Sequential data prediction, however, is still considered a challenge in Artificial Intelligence (Mikolov et al., 2010) given that, in general, prediction accuracy degrades as the size of sequences increase.

RNN-LMs sequentially propagate forward a context vector by integrating the information generated by each prediction step into the context used for the next prediction. One consequence of this forward propagation of information is that older information tends to fade from the context as new information is integrated into the context. As a result, RNN-LMs struggle in situations where there is a long-distance dependency because the relevant

information from the start of the dependency has faded by the time the model has spanned the dependency. A second problem is that the context can be dominated by the more recent information so when an RNN-LM does make an error this error can be propagated forward resulting in a cascade of errors through the rest of the sequence.

In recent sequence-to-sequence research the concept of "attention" has been developed to enable RNNs to align different parts of the input and output sequences. Examples of attention based architectures include Neural Machine Translation (NMT) (Bahdanau et al., 2015; Luong et al., 2015) and image captioning (Xu et al., 2015).

In this paper we extend the RNN-LM context mechanism with an attention mechanism that enables the model to bring forward context information from different points in the context sequence history. We hypothesis that this attention mechanism enables RNN-LMs to: (a) bridge long-distance dependencies, thereby avoiding errors; and, (b) to overlook recent errors by choosing to focus on contextual information preceding the error, thereby avoiding error propagation.

We show that a medium sized[1] *Attentive* RNN-LM[2] achieves better performance than larger "standard" models and performance comparable to an ensemble of 10 "medium" sized LSTM RNN-LMs on the PTB. We also show that an *Attentive* RNN-LM needs less contextual information in order to achieve similar results to state-of-the-art results over the wikitext2 dataset.

Outline: §2 introduces RNN-LMs and related research, §3 outlines our approach, §4 describes our experiments, §5 presents our analysis of the models' performance and §6 our conclusions.

---

[1]We adopt the terminology of Zaremba et al. (2015) and Press and Wolf (2016) when referring to the size of the RNNs.
[2]Code available at `https://github.com/giancds/attentive_lm`

Proceedings of the The 8th International Joint Conference on Natural Language Processing, pages 441–450,
Taipei, Taiwan, November 27 – December 1, 2017 ©2017 AFNLP

2 RNN-Language Models

RNN-LMs model the probability of a sequence of words by modelling the joint probability of the words in the sequence using the chain rule:

$$p(w_1, \ldots, w_N) = \prod_{t=1}^{N} p(w_n | w_1, \ldots, w_{n-1}) \quad (1)$$

where N is the number of words in the sequence. The context of the word sequence is modelled by an RNN and for each position in the sequence the probability distribution over the vocabulary is calculated using a softmax on the output related to that position of the RNN's last layer (i.e., the last layer's hidden state) (Józefowicz et al., 2016). Examples of such models include Zaremba et al. (2015) and Press and Wolf (2016). These models are composed of LSTM units (Hochreiter and Schmidhuber, 1997) and apply regularization to improve the RNN performance. In addition, Press and Wolf (2016) also uses the same embedding matrix that is used to transform the input words to transform the output of the last RNN layer to feed it to the softmax layer to make the next prediction.

Attention mechanisms were first proposed in "encoder-decoder" architectures for NMT systems. Bahdanau et al. (2015) proposed a model that stores all the encoder RNN's outputs and uses them together with the decoder RNN's state h_{t-1} to compute a context vector that, in turn, is used to compute the state h_t. In Luong et al. (2015) a generalization of the model of Bahdanau et al. (2015) is presented which uses the decoder RNN's state, in this instance h_t rather than h_{t-1}, along with the outputs of the encoder RNN to compute a context vector that it then concatenated with h_t before making the next prediction. Both models have similar performance and achieve state-of-the-art performance for some language pairs; however, they suffer from repeating words or dropping translations at the output (Mi et al., 2016).

There is previous work on using past information to improve RNN-LMs. Tran et al. (2016) propose an extension to LSTM cells to include memory areas, which depend on input words, at the output of every hidden layer. The model produces good results but the dependency on input words expands the number of parameters in each LSTM cell in proportion to the vocabulary size in use.

Similarly, Cheng et al. (2016) propose storing the LSTM's memory cells of every layer at each timestep and draw a context vector for each memory cell for each new input to attend to previous content and compute its output. Although their model requires fewer parameters than the model of Tran et al. (2016), the performance of the model is worse than regularized "standard" RNN-LM as in Zaremba et al. (2015) and Press and Wolf (2016).

Daniluk et al. (2017) propose an augmented version of the attention mechanism proposed by Bahdanau et al. (2015) on which their model outputs 3 vectors called *key-value-predict*. The *key* (a vector of real numbers) is used to retrieve a single hidden state from the past. Grave et al. (2017) propose an LM augmented with a "memory cache" that stores tuples of hidden-states plus word embeddings (for the word predicted from that hidden state). The memory cache is used to help the current prediction by retrieving the word embedding associated with the hidden state in the memory most similar to the current hidden state. Merity et al. (2017) proposed a mixture model that includes an RNN and a pointer network. This model computes one distribution for the softmax component and one distribution for the pointer network, using a sentinel gating function to combine both distributions. In spite of the fact that their model is similar to the model of Grave et al. (2017), their model requires an extra transformation between the current state of the RNN and those stored in the memory.

These recent models have a number of drawbacks. The systems that extend the architecture of LSTM units struggle to process large vocabularies because the system memory expands to the size of the vocabulary. For systems that retrieve a single hidden-state or word from memory, if the prediction is not correct, the RNN-LM will not receive the correct past information. Finally, the models of Merity et al. (2017) and Grave et al. (2017) use a fixed-length memory of L previous hidden states to store and retrieve information from the past (100 states in the case of Merity et al. (2017) and 2,000 states in the case of Grave et al. (2017)). As we shall explain in §3 our "attentive" RNN-LMs have a memory of dynamic-length that grows with the length of the input and therefore, in general, are computationally cheaper.

We see our "attentive" RNN-LM (see §3) as a generalized version of these models as we rely on the encoded information in the hidden state of the

RNN-LM to represent previous input words and we use a set of attention weights (instead of a *key*) to retrieve information from the past inputs. The main advantages of our approach are: (a) our model does not need vocabulary sized matrices in the computations of the attention mechanism and therefore has a reduced number of parameters; and (b) as we use all previous hidden states of the RNN-LM in the computation for the attention weights, all of those states will influence the next prediction based on the weights calculated.

3   Attentive Language Models

In this work we extend RNN-LMs to include an attention mechanism over previous inputs. We employ a multi-layered RNN to encode the input and, at each timestep, we store the output of the last recurrent layer (i.e., its hidden state $\mathbf{h}_t$) into a memory buffer. We compute a score for each hidden state $\mathbf{h}_i$ ($\forall\, i \in \{1,\ldots,t-1\}$) stored in memory and use these scores to weight each $\mathbf{h}_i$. From these weighted hidden states we generate a context vector $\mathbf{c}_t$ that is concatenated with the current hidden state $\mathbf{h}_t$ to predict the next word in the sequence. Figure 1 illustrates a step of our model when predicting the fourth word in a sequence.

We propose two different attention score functions that can be used to compute the context vector $\mathbf{c}_t$. One calculates the attention score of each $\mathbf{h}_i$ using just the information in the state (the $single(\mathbf{h}_i)$ score introduced below). The other calculates the attention scores for each $\mathbf{h}_i$ by combining the information from that state with the information from the current state $\mathbf{h}_t$ (the $combined(\mathbf{h}_i, \mathbf{h}_t)$ score described below). Each of these mechanisms defines a separate *Attentive* RNN-LMs and we report results for each of these LMs in our experiments.

More formally, each $\mathbf{h}_t$ is computed as follows, where $\mathbf{x}_t$ is the input at timestep t:

$$\mathbf{h}_t = RNN(\mathbf{x}_t, \mathbf{h}_{t-1}) \qquad (2)$$

The context vector $\mathbf{c}_t$ is then generated using Eq. (3) where each scalar weight a_i is a softmax (Eq. (4)) and the score for each hidden state ($\mathbf{h}_i$) in the memory buffer is one of Eq. (5) or Eq. (6).

$$\mathbf{c}_t = \sum_{i=1}^{t-1} a_i \mathbf{h}_i \qquad (3)$$

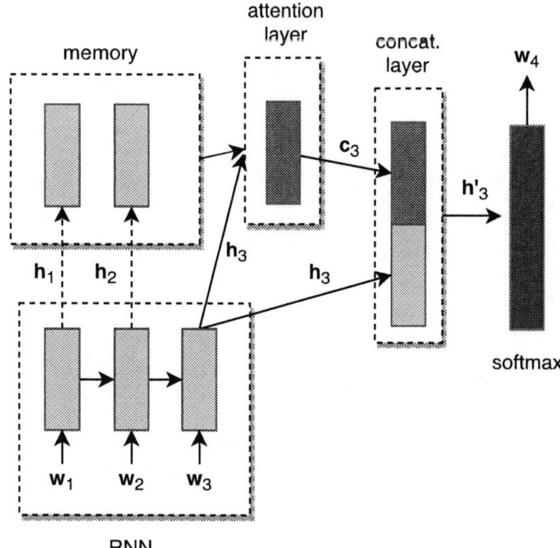

Figure 1: Illustration of a step of the *Attentive* RNN-LM with *combined* score. In this example, the model receives the third word as input ($\mathbf{w}_3$) after storing the previous states ($\mathbf{h}_1$ and $\mathbf{h}_2$) in memory. After producing $\mathbf{h}_3$, the model computes the context vector (in this case $\mathbf{c}_3$) that will be concatenated to $\mathbf{h}_3$ before the softmax layer for the prediction of the fourth word $\mathbf{w}_4$. Note that if the *single* score is in use (Eq. (9)), the arrow from the RNN output for $\mathbf{h}_3$ to the attention layer is dropped. Also note that $\mathbf{h}_3$ is stored in memory only at the end of this process.

$$a_i = \frac{exp(score(\mathbf{h}_i, \mathbf{h}_t))}{\sum_{j=1}^{t-1} exp(score(\mathbf{h}_j, \mathbf{h}_t))} \qquad (4)$$

$$score(\mathbf{h}_i, \mathbf{h}_t) = \begin{cases} single(\mathbf{h}_i) & (5) \\ combined(\mathbf{h}_i, \mathbf{h}_t) & (6) \end{cases}$$

We then merge $\mathbf{c}_t$ with the current state $\mathbf{h}_t$ using a concatenation layer[3], where $\mathbf{W}_c$ is a matrix of parameters and $\mathbf{b}_t$ is a bias vector.

$$\mathbf{h}'_t = tanh(\mathbf{W}_c[\mathbf{h}_t; \mathbf{c}_t] + \mathbf{b}_t) \qquad (7)$$

We compute the next word probability using Eq.8 where $\mathbf{W}$ is a matrix of parameters and $\mathbf{b}$ is a bias vector.

---

[3]We also have experimented with using a dot product and a feedforward layer to combine $\mathbf{h}_t$ and $\mathbf{c}_t$ and also using only $\mathbf{c}_t$, but those results were far below previous work in RNN-LM so we do not report them here.

$$p(w_t|w_{<t}, x) = softmax(\mathbf{W}\mathbf{h}'_t + \mathbf{b}) \quad (8)$$

Single score. This score is calculated for each $\mathbf{h}_i$ using just the information stored the state in itself. The score $single(\mathbf{h}_i)$ is defined as

$$single(\mathbf{h}_i) = \mathbf{v}_s \odot tanh(\mathbf{W}_s\mathbf{h}_i) \quad (9)$$

where the parameter matrix $\mathbf{W}_s$ and vector $\mathbf{v}_s$ are both learned by the attention mechanism and $\odot$ represents the dot product.

When applying the $single(\mathbf{h}_i)$ score, we can think of the score a_i as a scalar summary of the "absolute relevance" of the state $\mathbf{h}_i$. When a new state $\mathbf{h}_t$ is added to the buffer its scalar summary a_i is calculated by first using Eq.9 to get the score for the state and then applying a softmax function over the set of state scores including the score for the new state. Although the scores for each state do not change from one timestep to the next, applying the softmax results in recalculation of the distribution of the scalar summaries for all the states $\mathbf{h}_0, \ldots, \mathbf{h}_t$. As a result the a_i's for each state in Eq.3 changes from one prediction to the next as new states are added and the weight mass is distributed across more states.

Combined score. This score is calculated for each $\mathbf{h}_i$ by combining the information from that state with the information from the current state $\mathbf{h}_t$. The score $combined(\mathbf{h}_i, \mathbf{h}_t)$ is defined as

$$combined(\mathbf{h}_i, \mathbf{h}_t) = \mathbf{v}_s \odot tanh(\mathbf{W}_s\mathbf{h}_i + \mathbf{W}_q\mathbf{h}_t) \quad (10)$$

where the parameter matrices $\mathbf{W}_s$ and $\mathbf{W}_q$ and vector $\mathbf{v}_s$ are learned by the attention mechanism, and $\odot$ is the same as in Eq. 9. Notice that because $\mathbf{W}_q\mathbf{h}_t$ does not depend on any other state and is used in the computations with all other h_i, we can efficiently compute it once and use the results in Eq. 10, thus reducing computation time.

The score a_i defined by $combined(\mathbf{h}_i, \mathbf{h}_t)$, can be understood as the "relative relevance" of state $\mathbf{h}_i$ to the current state $\mathbf{h}_t$. Using this attention mechanism the score for each $\mathbf{h}_i$ is different for each timestep according to its relevance to the current hidden state $\mathbf{h}_t$ of the RNN. Consequently, the

scores for each $\mathbf{h}_i$ and the distribution over these scores changes from one timestep to the next. Using this scoring, the model can decide whether it should pay more attention to the current state, to a previous state or use past states to "supplement" the information for the next prediction. In §5 we present and analysis of how the model attends to different parts of its history as it generates a sequence of predictions.

4 Experiments

To evaluate our *Attentive* RNN-LMs we conducted experiments over the PTB (Marcus et al., 1994) and wikitext2 (Merity et al., 2017) datasets. We first describe the setup of our *Attentive* RNN-LM for the PTB (§4.1) and wikitext2 (§4.2) datasets and then discuss the results (§4.3). We compare our results on PTB to Zaremba et al. (2015) and Press and Wolf (2016) the best performing LSTM-LMs on the PTB, two memory augmented networks (Grave et al. (2017) and Merity et al. (2017)) and PTB state-of-the-art ensemble models of Zaremba et al. (2015). On wikitext2 we take (Merity et al., 2017), the creators of the dataset, and (Grave et al., 2017), the current state-of-the-art, as our baselines.

4.1 PTB Setup

We evaluate our *Attentive* RNN-LM over the PTB dataset using the standard split which consists of 887K, 70K and 78K tokens on the training, validation and test sets respectively.

We follow, in part, the parameterization used by Zaremba et al. (2015) and Press and Wolf (2016) with some changes. We trained an *Attentive* RNN-LM with 2 layers of 650 LSTM units using Stochastic Gradient Descent (SGD) with an initial learning rate of 1.0, halving the learning rate at each epoch after 12 epochs, to minimize the average negative log probability of the target words.

We train the models until we do not get any perplexity improvements over the validation set with an early stop counter of 10 epochs (i.e., patience of 10 epochs). Once the model runs out of patience, we rollback its parameters and use the model that achieved the best validation perplexity to calculate the perplexity over the test set. We initialize the weight matrices of the network uniformly in $[-0.05, 0.05]$ while all biases are initialized to a constant value at 0.0. We also apply 50% dropout (Srivastava et al., 2014) to the non-recurrent connections and clip the norm of the gradients, normalized by mini-batch size, at 5.0. In all our experiments, we follow Press and Wolf (2016) and tie the matrix $\mathbf{W}$ in Eq. (8) to be the embedding matrix (which also has 650 dimensions) used to represent the input words.

Contrary to Zaremba et al. (2015) and Press and Wolf (2016), we do not allow successive mini-batches to sequentially traverse the dataset. In other words, we follow the standard practice to reinitialize the hidden state of the network at the beginning of each mini-batch, by setting it to all zeros. This way, we do not allow the attention window to span across sentence boundaries[4]. We use all sentences in the training set, we truncate all sentences longer than 35 words and pad all sentences shorter than 35 words with a special symbol so all sentences are the same size. We use a vocabulary size of 10K words and a batch size of 32. All UNK words (following the pre-processing of (2015)) were kept during the training, validation and testing phases.

4.2 wikitext2 Setup

We also evaluate our *Attentive* RNN-LM over the wikitext2 dataset (Merity et al., 2017). We use the standard train, validation and test splits which consists of around 2M, 217K tokens and 245k tokens respectively. This dataset is composed of "Good" and "Featured" articles on Wikipedia.

There is an important difference between how we trained and tested our models on the wikitext2 dataset and how the baseline systems were trained and tested. Both Merity et al. (2017) and Grave et al. (2017) permitted the memory buffers of their systems to span sentence boundaries (and, indeed, they also did mini-batch traversal which allowed the memory buffers to traverse mini-batch boundaries) whereas we reset our systems memory at each sentence boundary. This difference is important because in the wikitext2 dataset the sentences are not shuffled and, therefore, are sequentially related to each other. As a result, systems that carry sequential information from previous sentences into the current sentence have an advantage in that they utilise contextual cues from the preceding sentence to inform the predictions at the start of the new sentence. By compari-

son, systems that reset their memory at the start of each sentence must reconstruct their context models from scratch and face a "cold-start" problem for the early predictions in the sentence.

The core reason why (Merity et al., 2017) and (Grave et al., 2017) did not reset their memories across sentence boundaries and we do is that these baseline systems use a fixed length memory whereas our "attention" mechanism has a variable length memory. A variable length memory has benefits in terms of both computational cost and the fact that the memory size is dynamically fitted to the context. However, just as the system designer for a fixed length memory LM must fix the memory size hyper-parameter in some fashion, so to the designer of a variable length memory LM must decide when the memory buffer is reset. For our work, we have decided to reset our memory buffer at sentence boundaries because many of the tasks for which LMs are used (e.g. NMT) work on a sentence by sentence basis. If required it would be possible for us to extend the memory buffer to the start of the preceding sentence (or some other landmark is the sequence history). However, this would incur extra computational cost, and as we shall see our *Attentive* RNN-LMs are still competitive on the wikitext2 dataset despite the fact that the baselines systems are given access to longer context sequences.

We trained an *Attentive* RNN-LM with 2 layers of 1000 LSTM units using Stochastic Gradient Descent (SGD) with an initial learning rate of 1.0, decaying the learning rate by a factor of 1.15 at each epoch after 14 epochs, to minimize the average negative log probability of the target words.

Similarly to the PTB model we also train this model with an early stop counter of 10 epochs and we initialize the weight matrices of the network uniformly in $[-0.05, 0.05]$ while all biases are initialized to a constant value at 0.0. We apply 65% dropout to the non-recurrent connections and clip the norm of the gradients, normalized by mini-batch size, at 5.0. In all our experiments, we also follow Press and Wolf (2016) and tie the matrix $\mathbf{W}$ in Eq. (8) to be the embedding matrix (which has 1000 dimensions for this model) used to represent the input words. We use all sentences in the training set, we truncate all sentences longer than 35 words and pad all sentences shorter than 35 words with a special symbol so all sentences are the same length. We use a vocabulary size of

---

[4]We also experimented to with successive mini-batches to sequentially traverse the dataset as in Zaremba et al. (2015) but the performance of the model dropped considerably so we do not report those results here.

33,278 and a batch size of 32. All UNK words (following the pre-processing of (2017)) were kept during the training, validation and testing phases.

4.3 Results

In Table 1 we report the results of our experiments on the PTB dataset. As we can see in this table, the *Attentive* RNN-LMs outperforms all other single models on the PTB dataset. Although *Attentive* RNN-LMs have less parameters (10M) than the large "regularized" LSTM-LMs (66M parameters), they were capable of reducing the perplexity over both validation and test sets. This result shows that using an *Attentive* RNN-LM it is possible to achieve better perplexity scores with far fewer model parameters. Furthermore, *Attentive* RNN-LMs are able to achieve roughly the same results as the averaging of 10 RNN-LM models (with no attention) of the same size.

In addition, there is little difference between the results of the *Attentive* RNN-LM with *single* score (Eq.9) and the *Attentive* RNN-LM with *combined* score (Eq.10) with the *single* score slightly outperforming the the *combined* score. We believe this is because the model using the $combined(\mathbf{h}_i, \mathbf{h}_t)$ score has more parameters to optimize and, thus, more difficulties in settling to a good local optima.

In Table 2 we report the results on the wikitext2 dataset. Despite the fact that we reset the memory for the *Attentive* RNN-LM at each sentence boundary whereas the caches for the baseline systems span sentence boundaries, our best *Attentive* RNN-LM is within 1 perplexity point of the system of (2017) (which is allowed to cache 2,000 previous hidden states), and has a lower perplexity than all of the other baselines.

5 Analysis of the Models

The purpose of our attention mechanism is to enable an RNN-LM to bridge long distance dependencies in language. Therefore, we expect the attention mechanism to select previous hidden states that are relevant to the current predictions. To analyse whether the attention mechanism is functioning as intend we analysed the evolution of attention weights in our *Attentive* RNN-LM as we calculated the perplexity for samples sentences using the models trained over the wikitext2[5].

---

[5]The behaviour of the models on wikitext2 is similar to that of the models trained and evaluated on the PTB dataset, so for space reasons we only present the wikitext2 analysis here.

Figure 2 show the evolution of attention weights, using both single and combined scoring, when calculating perplexities for 2 sentences containing nominal modifiers. In addition, Figure 3 show the evolution of attention weights for two sentences containing relative clauses, once again using both single and combined scoring. The words in the X-axis (horizontal) are the inputs at each timestep and the words in the Y-axis (vertical) are the next (or predicted) words. We suppressed weights that either equal to 1.0 (black squares) or 0.0 (white squares). Note that given the rounding to 4 decimal places, weights in some rows of the matrices may not sum to 1.0.

None of the attention mechanisms worked as a proper attention mechanism. In other words, none of the mechanisms generated larger weights for specific words in the sentence, in comparison to the other words in the same sentence. Comparing the attention weights generated by both *combined* score and *single* score for both sentences, it is striking that the distribution of attention weights is very similar. For both *Attentive* RNN-LM models the attention spreads out across the history in a relatively equal fashion.

Indeed, both models seem to take into consideration all previous states, creating a *smoothing effect* for the hidden states in the buffer. Therefore, no single state dominates the context vector by receiving a much larger attention weight than the others. We believe that this behaviour enables the models to bring forward information from the beginning of the sentence at the time it is making a prediction. This way, the models do not let information fade away from the context as it progresses to subsequent steps in a sequence and all previous information about the words that preceded the current timestep is available to the classifier in a manner that disregards recency.

As a consequence of the *smoothing effect*, the model does not necessarily need to store information about the context of the sequence in the recurrent connections of the RNN. This behaviour enable the model to retrieve information from the buffer to remember past words without relying solely on the RNN's internal "memory". Therefore, the model can maximize the features extracted about an input word, creating an advantage over other RNN-LMs that need to both extract features and keep context regarding the sequence in its connections.

Model	Params	Valid. Set	Test Set
Single Models			
Medium Regularized LSTM (Zaremba et al., 2015)	20M	86.2	82.7
Large Regularized LSTM (Zaremba et al., 2015)	66M	82.2	78.4
Large + BD + WT (Press and Wolf, 2016)	51M	75.8	73.2
Neural cache model (size = 500) (Grave et al., 2017)	-	-	72.1
Medium Pointer Sentinel-LSTM (Merity et al., 2017)	21M	72.4	70.9
Attentive LM w/ *combined* score function	14.5M	72.6	70.7
Attentive LM w/ *single* score function	14.5M	71.7	**70.1**
Model Averaging			
2 Medium regularized LSTMs (Zaremba et al., 2015)	40M	80.6	77.0
5 Medium regularized LSTMs (Zaremba et al., 2015)	100M	76.7	73.3
10 Medium regularized LSTMs (Zaremba et al., 2015)	200M	75.2	72.0
2 Large regularized LSTMs (Zaremba et al., 2015)	122M	76.9	73.6
10 Large regularized LSTMs (Zaremba et al., 2015)	660M	72.8	69.5
38 Large regularized LSTMs (Zaremba et al., 2015)	2508M	71.9	**68.7**

Table 1: Perplexity results over the PTB. Symbols: WT = weight tying (Press and Wolf, 2016); WD = weight decay and BD = Bayesian Dropout, both suggested by Gal and Ghahramani (2015).

Model	Params	Valid. Set	Test Set
Zoneout + Variational LSTM (Merity et al., 2017)	20M	108.7	100.9
LSTM-LM (Grave et al., 2017)	-	-	99.3
Variational LSTM (Merity et al., 2017)	20M	101.7	96.3
Neural cache model (size = 100) (Grave et al., 2017)	-	-	81.6
Pointer LSTM (window = 100) (Merity et al., 2017)	21M	84.8	80.8
Attentive LM w/ *combined* score function	50M	74.3	70.8
Attentive LM w/ *single* score function	50M	73.7	69.7
Neural cache model (size = 2000) (Grave et al., 2017)	-	-	**68.9**

Table 2: Perplexity results over the wikitext2.

Another interpretation of the *smoothing effect* is that it "reinforces" the signal in a similar fashion to residual connections in other RNNs and Deep Neural Networks architectures. Other RNN architectures use these residual connections as a shortcut to "reinforce" the signal of the current input and, thus, it still considers the current input only. The *Attentive* RNN-LM, however, uses all the previous hidden states to achieve a similar effect and create a stronger signal to the softmax classifier.

6   Conclusions

This paper proposes the use of attention mechanisms in RNN-LMs. These attention mechanisms enable an RNN-LM to consider information from its past when it is predicting the next word. We believe that this can help the LM to overcome the fading of relevant information as it traverses a long-distance dependency within a sequence and also to recover from a mistaken prediction by focusing on the context preceding the error.

Our results show that an *Attentive* RNN-LM outperforms both RNN-LM models that use and that do not use past information to predict the next word in a sequence when trained on the PTB dataset. Furthermore, our *Attentive* RNN-LM achieves this performance using far fewer units than the "standard" RNN-LM and, therefore, less model parameters. Our results also show that our *Attentive* RNN-LM achieves similar results to an ensemble that averages over 10 similar sized (in terms of number of LSTM units) RNN-LMs.

In addition, our results demonstrate that our *Attentive* RNN-LM achieves similar to state-of-the-art results over the wikitext2 dataset. It is an interesting result given that we do not allow our model to look beyond the boundaries of the current sequence it is processing, whilst the state-of-the-art model is allowed to store 2,000 previous states in its cache.

In future work we plan to (a) test the performance of ensembles of *Attentive* RNN-LMs and (b) to study the use of the *Attentive* RNN-LM as the decoder within an NMT system.

Acknowledgments

This research was partly funded by the ADAPT Centre. The ADAPT Centre is funded under the SFI Research Centres Programme (Grant 13/RC/2106) and is co-funded under the European Regional Development Fund. Giancarlo D. Salton would like to thank CAPES ("Coordenação de Aperfeiçoamento de Pessoal de Nível Superior") for his Science Without Borders scholarship, proc n. 9050-13-2.

References

Dzmitry Bahdanau, Kyunghyun Cho, and Yoshua Bengio. 2015. Neural machine translation by jointly learning to align and translate. In *International Conference on Learning Representations*, volume abs/1409.0473v6.

Jianpeng Cheng, Li Dong, and Mirella Lapata. 2016. Long short-term memory-networks for machine reading. In *Proceedings of the 2016 Conference on Empirical Methods in Natural Language Processing*, pages 551–561, Austin, Texas. Association for Computational Linguistics.

Michal Daniluk, Tim Rocktäschel, Johannes Welbl, and Sebastian Riedel. 2017. Frustratingly Short Attention Spans in Neural Language Modeling. *5th International Conference on Learning Representations (ICLR'2017)*.

Yarin Gal and Zoubin Ghahramani. 2015. A theoretically grounded application of dropout in recurrent neural networks.

Edouard Grave, Armand Joulin, and Nicolas Usunier. 2017. Improving neural language models with a continuous cache. *5th International Conference on Learning Representations (ICLR'2017)*.

Sepp Hochreiter and Jürgen Schmidhuber. 1997. Long short-term memory. volume 9, pages 1735–1780.

Rafal Józefowicz, Oriol Vinyals, Mike Schuster, Noam Shazeer, and Yonghui Wu. 2016. Exploring the limits of language modeling.

Minh-Thang Luong, Hieu Pham, and Christopher D. Manning. 2015. Effective approaches to attention-based neural machine translation. In *Proceedings of the 2015 Conference on Empirical Methods in Natural Language Processing*, pages 1412–1421.

Mitchell Marcus, Grace Kim, Mary Ann Marcinkiewicz, Robert MacIntyre, Ann Bies, Mark Ferguson, Karen Katz, and Britta Schasberger. 1994. The penn treebank: Annotating predicate argument structure. In *Proceedings of the Workshop on Human Language Technology*, pages 114–119.

Stephen Merity, Caiming Xiong, James Bradbury, and Richard Socher. 2017. Pointer sentinel mixture models. *5th International Conference on Learning Representations (ICLR'2017)*.

Haitao Mi, Baskaran Sankaran, Zhiguo Wang, and Abe Ittycheriah. 2016. Coverage embedding models for neural machine translation. In *Proceedings of the 2016 Conference on Empirical Methods in Natural Language Processing*, pages 955–960, Austin, Texas. Association for Computational Linguistics.

Tomas Mikolov, Martin Karafiát, Lukás Burget, Jan Cernocký, and Sanjeev Khudanpur. 2010. Recurrent neural network based language model. In *INTERSPEECH 2010, 11th Annual Conference of the International Speech Communication Association, Makuhari, Chiba, Japan, September 26-30, 2010*, pages 1045–1048.

Ofir Press and Lior Wolf. 2016. Using the output embedding to improve language models. volume abs/1608.05859.

Holger Schwenk, Anthony Rousseau, and Mohammed Attik. 2012. Large, pruned or continuous space language models on a gpu for statistical machine translation. In *Proceedings of the NAACL-HLT 2012 Workshop: Will We Ever Really Replace the N-gram Model? On the Future of Language Modeling for HLT*, pages 11–19.

Nitish Srivastava, Geoffrey Hinton, Alex Krizhevsky, Ilya Sutskever, and Ruslan Salakhutdinov. 2014. Dropout: A simple way to prevent neural networks from overfitting. *Journal of Machine Learning Research*, 15:1929–1958.

Ke M. Tran, Arianna Bisazza, and Christof Monz. 2016. Recurrent memory network for language modeling. *arXiv*, abs/1601.01272.

Kelvin Xu, Jimmy Ba, Ryan Kiros, Kyunghyun Cho, Aaron Courville, Ruslan Salakhudinov, Rich Zemel, and Yoshua Bengio. 2015. Show, attend and tell: Neural image caption generation with visual attention. In *Proceedings of the 32nd International Conference on Machine Learning (ICML-15)*, pages 2048–2057.

Wojciech Zaremba, Ilya Sutskever, and Oriol Vinyals. 2015. Recurrent neural network regularization. volume abs/1409.2329.

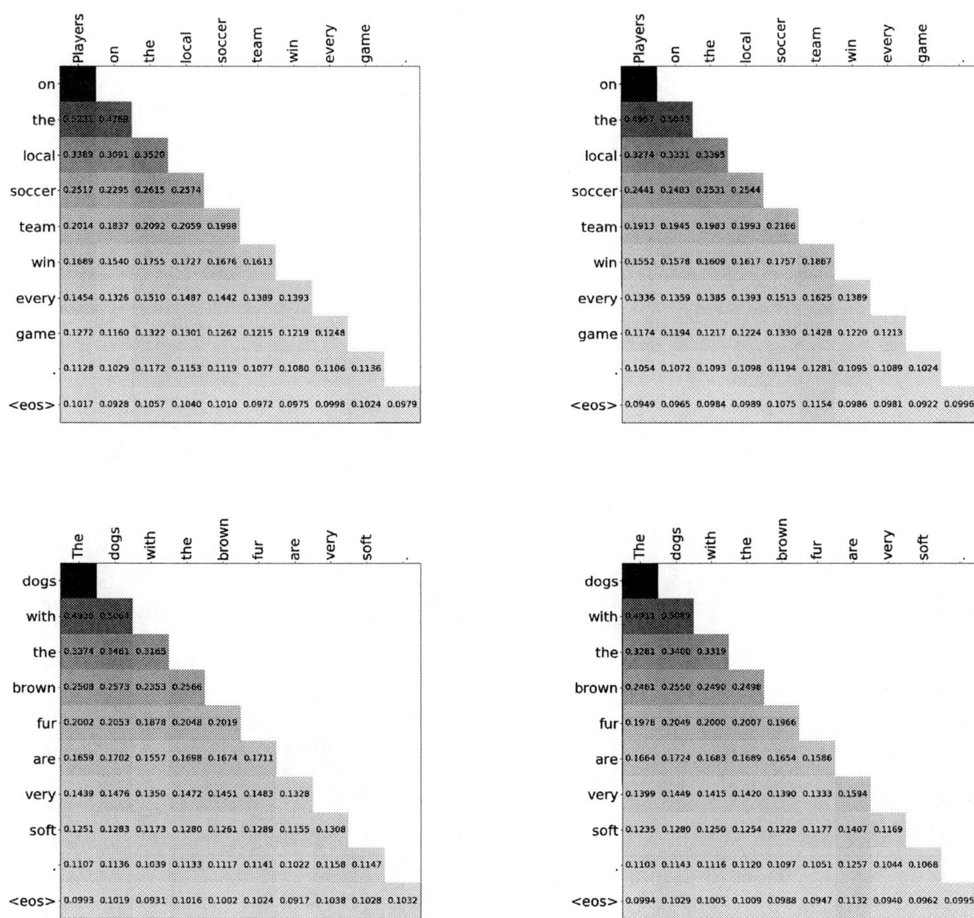

Figure 2: Plot of attention weights for two sentences containing nominal modifiers. On the left column are the attention weights calculated by the *combined* score. On the right column are the attention weights calculated by the *single* score. The words in the X-axis (horizontal) are the inputs at each timestep and the words in the Y-axis (vertical) are the next (or predicted) words. We suppressed weights that either equal to 1.0 (black squares) or 0.0 (white squares). Note that given the rounding to 4 decimal places, weights in some rows of the matrices may not sum to 1.0.

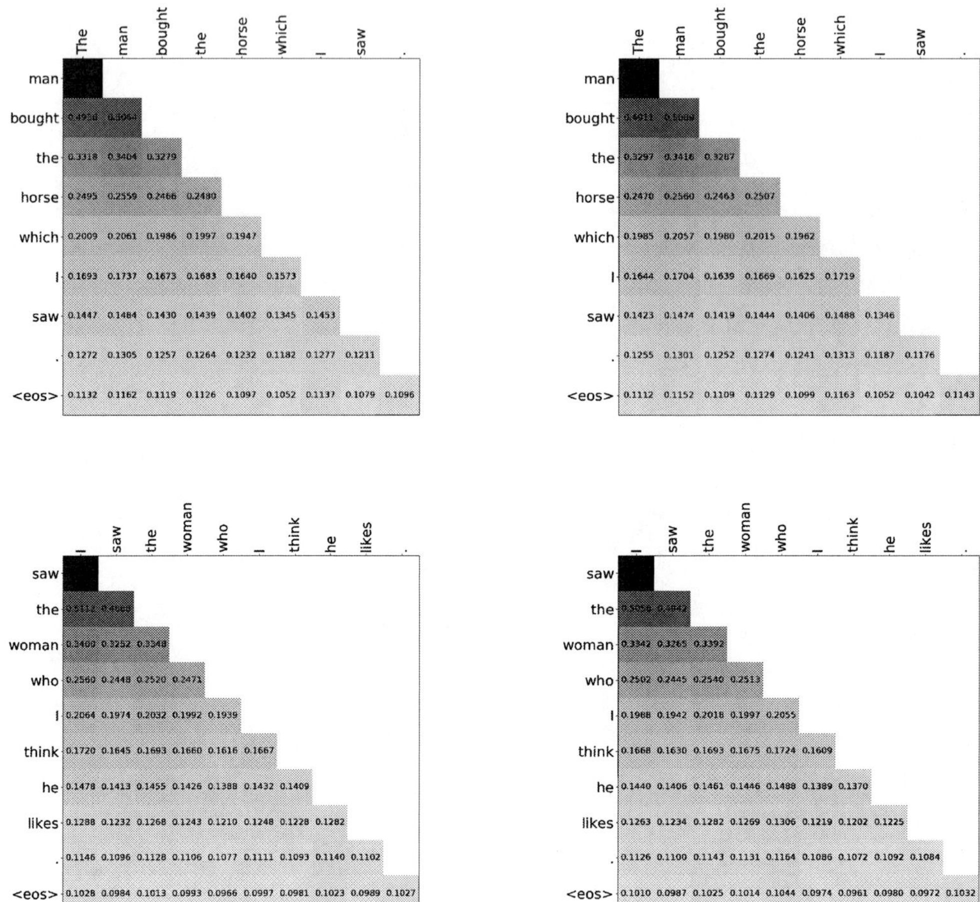

Figure 3: Plot of attention weights for two sentences containing relative clauses. On the left column are the attention weights calculated by the *combined* score. On the right column are the attention weights calculated by the *single* score. The words in the X-axis (horizontal) are the inputs at each timestep and the words in the Y-axis (vertical) are the next (or predicted) words. We suppressed weights that either equal to 1.0 (black squares) or 0.0 (white squares). Note that given the rounding to 4 decimal places, weights in some rows of the matrices may not sum to 1.0.

Diachrony-aware Induction of Binary Latent Representations
from Typological Features

Yugo Murawaki

Graduate School of Informatics, Kyoto University

Yoshida-honmachi, Sakyo-ku, Kyoto, 606-8501, Japan

`murawaki@i.kyoto-u.ac.jp`

Abstract

Although features of linguistic typology are a promising alternative to lexical evidence for tracing evolutionary history of languages, a large number of missing values in the dataset pose serious difficulties for statistical modeling. In this paper, we combine two existing approaches to the problem: (1) the synchronic approach that focuses on interdependencies between features and (2) the diachronic approach that exploits phylogenetically- and/or spatially-related languages. Specifically, we propose a Bayesian model that (1) represents each language as a sequence of binary latent *parameters* encoding inter-feature dependencies and (2) relates a language's parameters to those of its phylogenetic and spatial neighbors. Experiments show that the proposed model recovers missing values more accurately than others and that induced representations retain phylogenetic and spatial signals observed for surface features.

1 Introduction

Features of linguistic typology such as basic word order (examples are SVO and SOV) and the presence or absence of tone constitute a promising resource that can potentially be used to uncover the evolutionary history of languages. It has been argued that in exceptional cases, typological features can reflect a time span of 10,000 years or more (Nichols, 1994). Since typological features, by definition, allow us to compare an arbitrary pair of languages, they can be seen as the last hope for language isolates and tiny language families such as Ainu, Basque, and Japanese, for which lexicon-based historical-comparative lin-

guistics[1] has failed to identify genetic relatives. Fortunately, the publication of a large typology database (Haspelmath et al., 2005) made it possible to take computational approaches to this area of study (Daumé III and Campbell, 2007).

Murawaki (2015) pursued a pipeline approach to utilizing typological features for phylogenetic inference. Exploiting interdependencies found among features, Murawaki (2015) first mapped each language, represented as a sequence of surface features, into a sequence of continuous latent components. It was in this continuous space that phylogenetic relations among languages were subsequently inferred. Murawaki (2015) argued that since the conversion and the resulting latent representations were designed to reflect typological naturalness, reconstructed ancestral languages were also likely to be typologically natural.

In this paper, however, we show that Murawaki (2015) rests on fragile underpinnings so that they need to be rebuilt. One of the most important problems underestimated by Murawaki (2015) is an alarmingly large number of missing values. The dataset is a matrix where languages are represented as rows and features as columns, but only less than 30% of the items are present after a modest preprocessing. What is worse, the situation is unlikely to change in the foreseeable future because of the thousands of languages in the world, there is ample documentation for only a handful. These missing values pose serious difficulties for statistical modeling. Ignoring uncertainty in data, however, Murawaki (2015) relied on point estimates of missing values provided by an existing method of imputation when inducing latent representations. In this paper, we take a Bayesian approach because it is known for its robustness in

---

[1] By lexicon-based historical-comparative linguistics, we mean broad topics including sound laws, cognates, and historical changes in inflectional paradigms.

451

Proceedings of the The 8th International Joint Conference on Natural Language Processing, pages 451–461,
Taipei, Taiwan, November 27 – December 1, 2017 ©2017 AFNLP

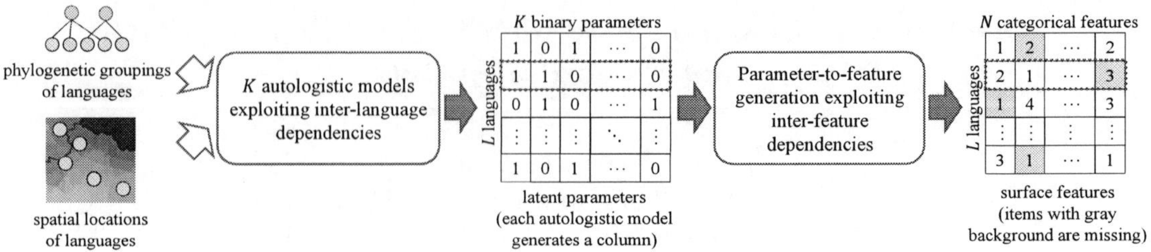

Figure 1: Overview of the proposed Bayesian generative model. Dotted boxes indicate the latent and surface representations of a language. Solid arrows show the direction of stochastic generation.

modeling uncertainties. We demonstrate that we can jointly infer missing values and latent representations.

Another question left unanswered is how good the induced representations are. In this paper, we present two quantitative analyses of the induced representations. The first one is rather indirect: we measure how well a model recovers missing values, with the assumption that good representations must capture regularity in surface features. We show that the proposed method outperformed the pipelined imputation method of Murawaki (2015) among others.

The second analysis involves geography. It is well known that the values of a surface feature do not distribute randomly in the world but reflect vertical (phylogenetic) transmissions from parents to children and horizontal (spatial or areal) transmissions between populations (Nichols, 1992). For example, languages of Mainland Southeast Asia are known for having similar tone systems even though they belong to different language families. To measure the degrees of the two modes of transmissions, we use an autologistic model that investigates dependencies among languages (Towner et al., 2012; Yamauchi and Murawaki, 2016). Since it requires the input to be discrete, we evaluate a new model that focuses on inter-feature dependencies in the same way as Murawaki (2015) but induces *binary* latent representations. We show that vertical and horizontal signals observed for surface features largely vanish from latent representations when only inter-feature dependencies are exploited. Although not directly applicable to the model of Murawaki (2015), our results suggest that the pipeline approach suffers from noise during phylogenetic inference. To address this problem, we extend the induction model to incorporate the autologistic model at the level of latent representations, rather

than surface features. With this integrated model, we manage to let induced representations retain surface signals.

In the end, the Bayesian generative model we propose induces binary latent representations by combining inter-feature dependencies and inter-language dependencies, with primacy given to the former (Figure 1). Whereas inter-feature dependencies are synchronic in nature, inter-language dependencies reflect diachrony. Thus we call the integrated model diachrony-aware induction.

Due to space limitation, we had to put technical details into the supplementary material. However, we would like to stress that the proposed model works only if it is armed with statistical techniques rarely found in the NLP literature. Together with missing values and binary representations, a large number of continuous variables that connect binary representations to surface features need to be inferred. Unfortunately, a naïve Metropolis-Hastings algorithm does not converge within realistic time scales. We solve this problem by adopting Hamiltonian Monte Carlo (Neal, 2011) since it enables us to efficiently sample a large number of continuous variables at once. Likewise, the autologistic model contains an intractable normalization term, which prevents the application of the standard Metropolis-Hastings sampler. We use an approximate sampler instead (Liang, 2010).

2 Related Work

2.1 Inter-feature Dependencies

Interdependencies among features have long been observed across the world's languages. For example, OV (object-verb) languages tend to be AN for the order of adjective and noun. Greenberg (1963) proposed dozens of such patterns known as *linguistic universals*. A statistical model for discovering Greenbergian universals was presented by Daumé III and Campbell (2007). Itoh and Ueda (2004) used the Ising model to model the interaction between features. Although these studies entirely focused on surface patterns, they imply the presence of some latent structure behind these surface features.

Some generative linguists argue for the existence of binary latent *parameters* behind surface features although they are controversial even among generative linguists (Boeckx, 2014). We borrow the term *parameter* from generative linguistics because the name of *feature* is reserved for surface variables.

Parameters are part of the *principles and parameters* (P&P) framework (Chomsky and Lasnik, 1993), where, the structure of a language is explained by (1) a set of universal principles that are common to all languages and (2) a set of parameters whose values vary among languages. Here we skip the former since our focus is on structural variability. According to P&P, if we set specific values to all the parameters, then we obtain a specific language. Each parameter is binary and, in general, sets the values of multiple surface features in a deterministic manner. For example, the head directionality parameter is either `head-initial` or `head-final`. If `head-initial` is chosen, then surface features are set to `VO`, `NA` and `Prepositions`; otherwise the language in question becomes `OV`, `AN` and `Postpositions` (Baker, 2002). Baker (2002) discussed a number of parameters such as head directionality, polysynthesis, and topic prominent parameters.

Partly inspired by the P&P framework, we use a sequence of binary variables as the latent representation of a language. However, there are non-negligible differences between P&P and ours, which are discussed in Section S.2 of the supplementary material.

What the structure behind surface features looks like is almost exclusively discussed by generative linguists, but it should be noted that they are not the only group who attempts to explain surface patterns. Roughly speaking, generative linguists are part of the *synchronist* camp, as contrasted with *diachronists*, who consider that at least some patterns observed in surface features arise from common paths of diachronic development (Anderson, 2016). An important factor of diachronic development is grammaticalization, by which content words change into function words (Heine and Kuteva, 2007). For example, the correlation between the order of adposition and noun and the order of genitive and noun might be explained by the fact that adpositions often derive from nouns.

2.2 Inter-language Dependencies

The standard model for phylogenetic inference is the tree model, where a trait is passed on from a parent to a child with occasional modifications. In fact, the recent success in the applications of statistical models to historical linguistic problems is largely attributed to the tree model (Gray and Atkinson, 2003; Bouckaert et al., 2012). In linguistic typology, however, a non-tree-like mode of evolution has emerged as one of the central topics (Trubetzkoy, 1928; Campbell, 2006). Typological features, like loanwords, can be borrowed from one language to another, and as a result, vertical (phylogenetic) signals are obscured by horizontal (spatial) transmission.

The task of incorporating both vertical and horizontal transmissions within a statistical model of evolution is notoriously challenging because of the excessive flexibility of horizontal transmissions. This is the reason why previously proposed models are coupled with some very strong assumptions, for example, that a reference tree is given a priori (Nelson-Sathi et al., 2010), and that horizontal transmissions can be modeled through time-invariant areal clusters (Daumé III, 2009).

Consequently, we pursue a line of research in linguistic typology that draws on information on the current distribution of typological features without explicitly requiring the reconstruction of previous states (Nichols, 1992, 1995; Parkvall, 2008; Wichmann and Holman, 2009). The basic assumption is that if the feature in question is vertically stable, then a phylogenetically defined group of languages will tend to share the same value. Similarly, if the feature in question is horizontally diffusible, then spatially close languages would be expected to frequently share the same feature value. Since the current distribution of typological features is more or less affected by these factors, we need to disentangle the effects of each of these factors. To do this, Yamauchi and Murawaki (2016) adopted a variant of the autologistic model, which had been widely used to model the spatial distribution of a feature (Besag, 1974; Towner et al., 2012). The model was also used to impute missing values because the phylogenetic and spatial neighbors of a language had some predictive power over its feature values.

3 Data and Preprocessing

The dataset we used in the present study is the online edition[2] of the *World Atlas of Language Structures* (WALS) (Haspelmath et al., 2005). While Greenberg (1963) and generative linguists have manually induced patterns and parameters, WALS makes it possible to take computational approaches to modeling features (Daumé III and Campbell, 2007; Daumé III, 2009; Murawaki, 2015; Takamura et al., 2016; Murawaki, 2016).

WALS is essentially a matrix where languages are represented as rows and features as columns. As of 2017, it contained 2,679 languages and 192 surface features. It covered less than 15% of items in the matrix, however.

We removed sign languages, pidgins and creoles from the matrix. We imputed some missing values that could trivially be inferred from other features. We then removed features that covered less than 10% of the languages. After the preprocessing, the number of languages L was 2,607 while the number of features N was reduced to 104. The coverage went up to 26.9%, but the rate was still alarmingly low.

In WALS, languages are accompanied by additional information. We used the following fields to model inter-language dependencies. (1) genera, the lower of the two-level phylogenetic groupings, and (2) single-point geographical coordinates (longitude and latitude). By connecting every pair of languages within a genus, we constructed a phylogenetic neighbor graph. A spatial neighbor graph was constructed by linking all language pairs that were located within a distance of $R = 1000$ km. On average, each language had 30.8 and 89.1 neighbors, respectively.

The features in WALS are categorical. For example, Feature 81A, "Order of Subject, Object and Verb" has seven possible values: SOV, SVO, VSO, VOS, OVS, OSV and No dominant order, and each language incorporates one of these seven values. For each language, we arranged its features into a sequence. A sequence of categorical features can alternatively be represented as a binary sequence using the 1-of-F_i coding scheme: Feature i with F_i possible values was converted into F_i binary items among which only one item takes 1. The number of binarized features M was 723.

[2]http://wals.info/

L	# of languages
K	# of parameters
M	# of binarized features
N	# of categorical features
$Z \in \{0,1\}^{L \times K}$	Binary parameter matrix
$W \in \mathbb{R}^{K \times M}$	Weight matrix
$\tilde{\Theta} \in \mathbb{R}^{L \times M}$	Feature score matrix
$\Theta \in [0,1]^{L \times M}$	Feature probability matrix
$X \in \mathbb{N}^{L \times N}$	Categorical feature matrix

Table 1: Notations.

4 Proposed Method

Since the proposed model is rather complicated, we present two key components before going into the integrated model. Table 1 shows notations used in this paper. Surface features have two ways of indexing. First, feature values are serialized as $(1,1), \cdots, (1, F_1), (2,1), \cdots, (i,j), \cdots, (N, F_N)$, where (i,j) points to feature i's j-th value. Then they are given the flat index $1, \cdots, m, \cdots, M$ $(M = \sum_{i=1}^{N} F_i)$. Two indices are mapped by the function $f(i,j) = m$. We need the flat representation because that is what latent parameters work on. A parameter is expected to capture the relation between one feature's particular value (e.g., VO for the order of object and verb) and another feature's particular value (NA for the order of adjective and noun).

4.1 Inter-feature Dependencies

Figure 2 illustrates how surface features are generated from binary latent parameters. We use matrix factorization (Srebro et al., 2005; Griffiths and Ghahramani, 2011) to capture inter-feature dependencies. Since categorical feature matrix X cannot directly be decomposed into two, we first construct (unnormalized) feature score matrix $\tilde{\Theta}$ and then stochastically generate X using $\tilde{\Theta}$.

$\tilde{\Theta}$ is a product of binary parameter matrix Z and weight matrix W. The generation of Z will be described in Section 4.2.[3] Each item of $\tilde{\Theta}$, $\tilde{\theta}_{l,m}$, is a score for language l's m-th binarized feature. It is affected only by parameters with $z_{l,k} = 1$ because

$$\tilde{\theta}_{l,m} = \sum_{k=1}^{K} z_{l,k} w_{k,m}. \tag{1}$$

---

[3] Although the natural choice for modeling binary latent matrices is an Indian buffet process (IBP) (Griffiths and Ghahramani, 2011), we do not take this approach for reasons we explain in Section S.1 of the supplementary material.

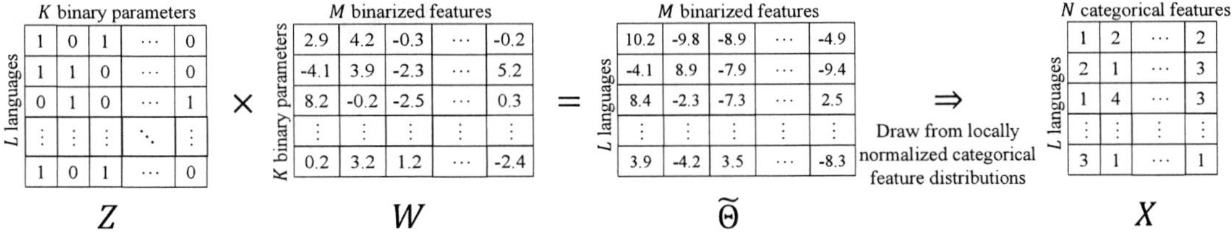

Figure 2: Stochastic parameter-to-feature generation. $\tilde{\Theta} = ZW$ encodes inter-feature dependencies.

We locally apply normalization to $\tilde{\Theta}$ to obtain Θ, in which $\theta_{l,i,j}$ is the probability of language l taking value j for categorical feature i

$$\theta_{l,i,j} = \frac{\exp(\tilde{\theta}_{l,f(i,j)})}{\sum_{j'} \exp(\tilde{\theta}_{l,f(i,j')})}. \tag{2}$$

Finally, language l's i-th categorical feature, $x_{l,i}$, is generated from this distribution.

$$P(x_{l,i} \mid z_{l,*}, W) = \theta_{l,i,x_{l,i}}, \tag{3}$$

where $z_{l,*} = (z_{l,1}, \cdots, z_{l,K})$.

Combining Eqs. (1) and (2), we obtain

$$\theta_{l,i,j} \propto \exp(\sum_{k=1}^{K} z_{l,k} w_{k,f(i,j)})$$

$$= \prod_{k=1}^{K} \exp(z_{l,k} w_{k,f(i,j)}). \tag{4}$$

We can see from Eq. (4) that this is a product-of-experts model (Hinton, 2002). If $z_{l,k} = 0$, parameter k has no effect on $\theta_{l,i,j}$ because $\exp(z_{l,k} w_{k,f(i,j)}) = 1$. Otherwise, if $w_{k,f(i,j)} > 0$, it makes $\theta_{l,i,j}$ larger, and if $w_{k,f(i,j)} < 0$, it lowers $\theta_{l,i,j}$.

Suppose that for parameter k, a certain group of languages takes $z_{l,k} = 1$. If two categorical feature values (i_1, j_1) and (i_2, j_2) have positive weights (i.e., $w_{k,f(i_1,j_1)} > 0$ and $w_{k,f(i_2,j_2)} > 0$), the pair must often co-occur in these languages. Likewise, the fact that two feature values do not co-occur can be encoded as a positive weight for one value and a negative weight for the other.

4.2 Inter-language Dependencies

The autologistic model is used to generate each column of Z, $z_{*,k} = (z_{1,k}, \cdots, z_{L,k})$. To construct the model, we use two neighbor graphs and the corresponding three counting functions, as illustrated in Figure 3. $V(z_{*,k})$ returns the number

of pairs sharing the same value in the phylogenetic neighbor graph, and $H(z_{*,k})$ is the spatial equivalent of $V(z_{*,k})$. $U(z_{*,k})$ gives the number of languages that take the value 1.

We now introduce the following variables: vertical stability $v_k > 0$, horizontal diffusibility $h_k > 0$, and universality $-\infty < u_k < \infty$ for each feature k. Then the probability of $z_{*,k}$ conditioned on v_k, h_k and u_k is given as

$$P(z_{*,k} \mid v_k, h_k, u_k) =$$

$$\frac{\exp\left(v_k V(z_{*,k}) + h_k H(z_{*,k}) + u_k U(z_{*,k})\right)}{\sum_{z'_{*,k}} \exp\left(v_k V(z'_{*,k}) + h_k H(z'_{*,k}) + u_k U(z'_{*,k})\right)}.$$

The denominator is a normalization term, ensuring that the sum of the distribution equals one.

The autologistic model can be interpreted in terms of the competition associated with possible assignments of $z_{*,k}$ for the probability mass 1. If a given value, $z_{*,k}$, has a relatively large $V(z_{*,k})$, then setting a large value for v_k enables it to appropriate fractions of the mass from its weaker rivals. However, if too large a value is set for v_k, then it will be overwhelmed by its stronger rivals.

To acquire further insights into the model, let us consider the probability of language l taking value $b \in \{0, 1\}$, conditioned on the rest of the languages, $z_{-l,k}$:

$$P(z_{l,k} = b \mid z_{-l,k}, v_k, h_k, u_k) \propto$$
$$\exp\left(v_k V_{l,k,b} + h_k H_{l,k,b} + u_k b\right), \tag{5}$$

where $V_{l,k,b}$ is the number of language l's phylogenetic neighbors that assume value b, and $H_{l,k,b}$ is its spatial counterpart. $P(z_{l,k} = b \mid z_{-l,k}, v_k, h_k, u_k)$ is expressed by the weighted linear combination of the three factors in the log-space. It will increase with a rise in the number of phylogenetic neighbors that assume value b. However, this probability depends not only on the phy-

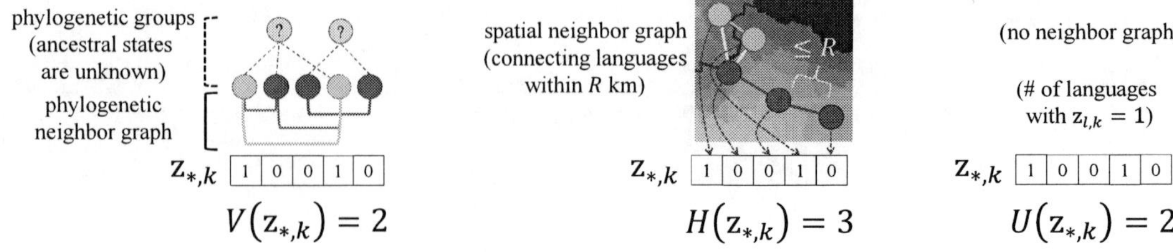

Figure 3: Neighbor graphs and counting functions used to encode inter-language dependencies.

logenetic neighbors of language l, but it also depends on its spatial neighbors and on universality. How strongly these factors affect the stochastic selection is controlled by v_k, h_k, and u_k.

4.3 Integrated Model

Now we complete the generative model by integrating the two types of dependencies. The joint distribution is defined as

$$P(A, Z, W, X) = P(A)P(Z|A)P(W)P(X|Z, W),$$

where hyperparameters are omitted for brevity and A is a set of latent variables that control the generation of Z:

$$P(A) = \prod_{k=1}^{K} P(v_k)P(h_k)P(u_k).$$

Their prior distributions are: $v_k \sim \mathrm{Gamma}(\kappa, \theta)$, $h_k \sim \mathrm{Gamma}(\kappa, \theta)$, and $u_k \sim \mathcal{N}(0, \sigma^2)$.[4]

Next, $\mathbf{z}_{*,k}$'s are generated as described in Section 4.2:

$$P(Z \mid A) = \prod_{k=1}^{K} P(\mathbf{z}_{*,k} \mid v_k, h_k, u_k).$$

The generation of Z is followed by that of the corresponding weight matrix $W \in \mathbb{R}^{K \times M}$, and then we obtain the feature score matrix $\tilde{\Theta} = ZW$. Each item of W, $w_{k,m}$, is generated from Student's t-distribution with 1 degree of freedom. We choose this distribution for two reasons. First, it has heavier tails than the Gaussian distribution and allows some weights to fall far from 0. Second, our inference algorithm demands that the negative logarithm of the probability density function be differentiable (see Section S.4 for details).

The t-distribution satisfies the condition while the Laplace distribution does not.

Finally, X is generated using $\tilde{\Theta} = ZW$, as described in Section 4.1:

$$P(X \mid Z, W) = \prod_{l=1}^{L} \prod_{i=1}^{N} P(x_{l,i} \mid \mathbf{z}_{l,*}, W).$$

4.4 Inference

As usual, we use Gibbs sampling to perform posterior inference. Given observed values $x_{l,i}$, we iteratively update $z_{l,k}$, v_k, h_k, u_k, and $\mathbf{w}_{k,*}$ as well as missing values $x_{l,i}$.

Update $x_{l,i}$. $x_{l,i}$ is sampled from Eq. (3).

Update $z_{l,k}$. The posterior probability $P(z_{l,k} \mid -)$ is proportional to Eq. (5) times the product of Eq. (3) for all feature i's of language l.

Update v_k, h_k and u_k. We want to sample v_k (and h_k and u_k) from $P(v_k \mid -) \propto P(v_k)P(\mathbf{z}_{*,k} \mid v_k, h_k, u_k)$. This belongs to a class of problems known as sampling from doubly-intractable distributions (Møller et al., 2006; Murray et al., 2006). While it remains a challenging problem in statistics, it is not difficult to approximately sample the variables if we give up theoretical rigorousness (Liang, 2010). The details of the algorithm we use can be found in Section S.3 of the supplementary material.

Update $\mathbf{w}_{k,*}$. The remaining problem is how to update $w_{k,m}$. Since the number of weights is very large ($K \times M$), the simple Metropolis-Hastings algorithm (Görür et al., 2006; Doyle et al., 2014) is not a workable option. To address this problem, we block-sample $\mathbf{w}_{k,*} = (w_{k,1}, \cdots, w_{k,M})$ using Hamiltonian Monte Carlo (HMC) (Neal, 2011). A sketch of the algorithm can be found in Section S.4 of the supplementary material.

---

[4] In the experiments, we set shape $\kappa = 1$, scale $\theta = 1$, and standard deviation $\sigma = 10$. These priors were not noninformative, but they were sufficiently gentle in the regions where these parameters typically resided.

5 Experiments

5.1 Missing Value Imputation

We indirectly evaluated the proposed model, called SYNDIA, by means of missing value imputation. If it predicts missing feature values better than reasonable baselines, we can say that the induced parameters are justified. Although no ground truth exists for the missing portion of the dataset, missing value imputation can be evaluated by hiding some observed values and verifying the effectiveness of their recovery. We conducted a 10-fold cross-validation.

We ran SYNDIA with two different settings: $K = 50$ and 100. We performed posterior inference for 500 iterations. After that, we collected 100 samples of $x_{l,i}$ for each language, one per iteration. For each missing value $x_{l,i}$, we output the most frequent value among the 100 samples. The HMC parameters ϵ and S were set to 0.05 and 10, respectively.

We applied simulated annealing to the sampling of $z_{l,k}$. For the first 100 iterations, the inverse temperature was increased from 0.1 to 1.0.

We compared SYNDIA with several baselines.

MFV For each categorical feature i, always output the most frequent value among observed $x_{l,i}$.

Surface-DIA An autologistic model applied to surface features (Yamauchi and Murawaki, 2016). The details of the model are presented in Section S.5 of the supplementary material.

DPMPM A Dirichlet process mixture of multinomial distributions with a truncated stick-breaking construction (Si and Reiter, 2013) used by Blasi et al. (2017). It assigns a single categorical latent variable to each language. As an implementation, we used the R package *NPBayesImpute*.

MCA A variant of multiple correspondence analysis (Josse et al., 2012) used by Murawaki (2015). We used the `imputeMCA` function of the R package *missMDA*.

SYN A simplified version of SYNDIA, with v_k and h_k removed from the model. See Section S.6 of the supplementary material for details.

MFV and Surface-DIA can be seen as the models of inter-language dependencies while DPMPM, MCA and SYN are these of inter-feature dependencies.

Table 2 shows the result. We can see that SYNDIA with $K = 50$ performed the best.

Type	Model	Accuracy
Lang.	MFV	60.95%
	Surface-DIA	66.22%
Feat.	DPMPM ($K^* = 50$)	69.08%
	MCA	69.88%
	SYN ($K = 50$)	73.83%
	SYN ($K = 100$)	72.87%
Both	SYNDIA ($K = 50$)	**74.46%**
	SYNDIA ($K = 100$)	74.00%

Table 2: Accuracy of missing value imputation. The first column indicates the types of dependencies the models exploit: inter-language dependencies, inter-feature dependencies and both.

Model	Accuracy
Full model (SYNDIA)	74.46%
-vertical	73.89%
-horizontal	**74.47%**
-vertical -horizontal (SYN)	73.83%

Table 3: Ablation experiments for missing value imputation. $K = 50$.

Smaller K yielded higher accuracy although the likelihood $P(X \mid Z, W)$ went up as K increased. Due to the high ratio of missing values, the model might have overfitted the data with larger K.

The fact that SYN outperformed Surface-DIA suggests that inter-feature dependencies have more predictive power than inter-language dependencies in the dataset. However, they are complimentary in nature as SYNDIA outperformed SYN.

We can confirm the limited expressive power of single categorical latent variables because DPMPM performed poorly even if a small value was set to the truncation level K^* to avoid overfitting. MCA employs more expressive representations of a sequence of continuous variables for each language. It slightly outperformed DPMPM but was beaten by SYN by a large margin. We conjecture that MCA was more sensitive to initialization than the Bayesian model armed with MCMC sampling. In any case, this result indicates that the latent representations Murawaki (2015) obtained were of poorer quality than those of SYN, not to mention those of SYNDIA.

We also conducted ablation experiments by removing either v_k or h_k from the model. The result is shown in Table 3. It turned out that the horizontal factor had stronger predictive power than the vertical factor, which has a negative implication on typology-based phylogenetic inference.

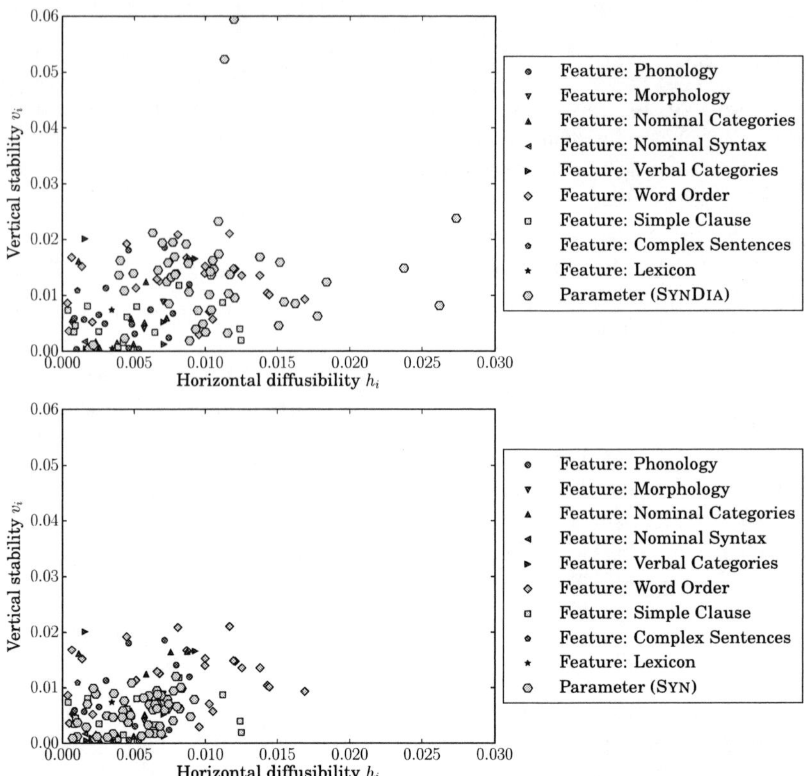

Figure 4: Scatter plots of surface features and induced parameters, with vertical stability v_i (v_k) as the y-axis and horizontal diffusibility h_i (h_k) as the x-axis. Larger v_i (h_i) indicates that feature i is more stable (diffusible). Comparing the absolute values of a v_i and an h_i makes no sense because they are tied with different neighbor graphs. Features are classified into 9 broad categories (called *Area* in WALS). v_k (and h_k) is the geometric mean of the 100 samples. The induction models are SYNDIA (Top) and SYN (Bottom). For both models, $K = 50$.

5.2 Vertical and Horizontal Signals

Hereafter we use all observed features to perform posterior inference. We examined how vertically stable and horizontally diffusible the induced parameters were. For SYNDIA, we simply extracted v_k and h_k from posterior samples. For comparison, we used Surface-DIA to estimate vertical stability and horizontal diffusibility of surface features. The same autologistic model was used to estimate v_k and h_k of SYN *after* the posterior inference. For details, see Sections S.5 and S.6.2 of the supplementary material.

Figure 4 summarizes the results. We can see that the most vertically stable latent parameters of SYNDIA are comparable to the most vertically stable surface features. The same holds for the most horizontally diffusible ones. Thus we can conclude that the induced representations retain vertical and horizontal signals observed for surface features.

On the other hand, SYN halved vertical stability and horizontal diffusibility when transforming surface features into latent parameters. A plausible explanation of this failure is that for many scarcely documented languages, we simply did not have enough observed surface features to determine their latent representations only from inter-feature dependencies. Due to the inherent uncertainty, $z_{l,k}$ swung between 0 and 1 during posterior inference, regardless of the states of their neighbors. As a result, these languages seem to have blocked vertical and horizontal signals. By contrast, SYNDIA appears to have flipped $z_{l,k}$ without disrupting inter-language dependencies when there were.

In summary, the experimental results have neg-

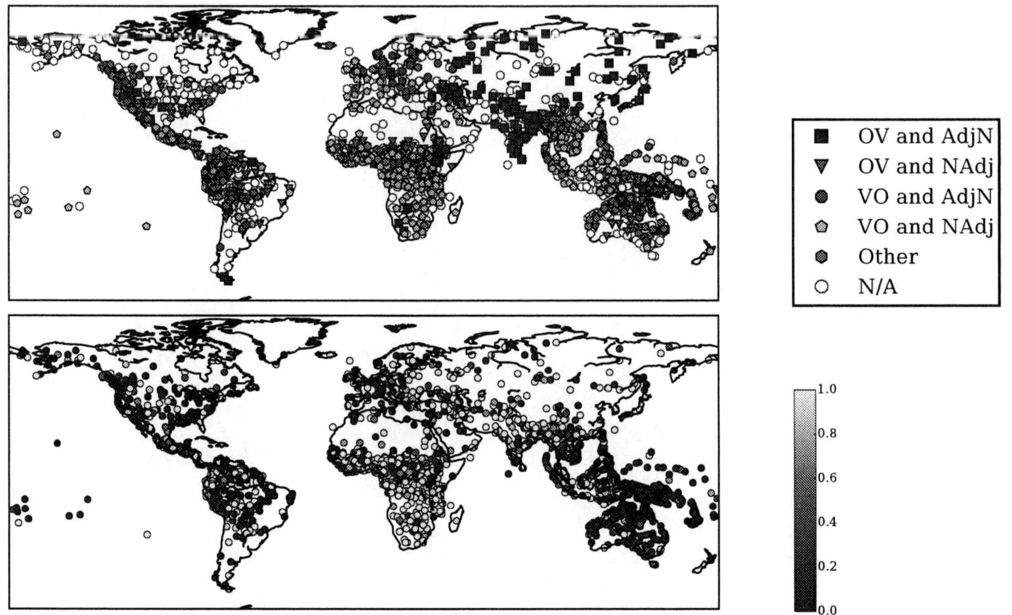

Figure 5: A comparison of a surface feature and a latent parameter in terms of geographical distribution. Each point denotes a language. (Top) Feature 97A, "Relationship between the Order of Object and Verb and the Order of Adjective and Noun." Missing values are denoted as N/A. (Bottom) A parameter of SYNDIA with $K_0 = 50$. Lighter nodes indicate higher frequencies of $z_{l,k} = 1$ among 100 samples.

ative implications for the pipeline approach pursued by Murawaki (2015), where the inter-feature dependency-based induction of latent representations is followed by phylogenetic inference. Fortunately, evidence presented up to this point suggests that it can be readily replaced with the proposed model.

5.3 Discussion

Figure 5 compares a latent parameter of SYNDIA with a surface feature on the world map. Some surface features show several geographic clusters of large size, telling something about the evolutionary history of languages. Even with a large number of missing values, SYNDIA yielded comparable geographic clusters for some parameters. Some geographic clusters were also produced by SYN, especially when the estimation of $z_{l,k}$ was stable. In our subjective evaluation, SYNDIA appeared to show clearer patterns than SYN. Needless to say, not all surface features were associated with clear geographic patterns, and not all latent parameters were. Overall, the results shed a positive light on the applicability of the induced representations to phylogenetic inference.

We also checked the weight matrix W (Fig-

ure S.2). It is not easy to analyze qualitatively but it deserves future investigation.

6 Conclusion

In this paper, we presented a Bayesian model that induces binary latent parameters from surface features of linguistic typology. We combined inter-language dependencies with inter-feature dependencies to obtain the latent representations of better quality. Gathering various statistical techniques, we managed to create the complex but workable model. The source code is publicly available at `https://github.com/murawaki/latent-typology`.

We pointed out that typology-based phylogenetic inference proposed by Murawaki (2015) had weak foundations, and we rebuilt them from scratch. The whole long paper was needed to do so, but our ultimate goal is the same as the one stated by Murawaki (2015). In the future, we would like to utilize the new latent representations to uncover the evolutionary history of languages.

Acknowledgments

This work was partly supported by JSPS KAKENHI Grant Number 26730122.

References

Stephen R. Anderson. 2016. Synchronic versus diachronic explanation and the nature of the language faculty. *Annual Review of Linguistics*, 2:1–425.

Mark C. Baker. 2002. *The Atoms of Language: The Mind's Hidden Rules of Grammar*. Basic Books.

Julian Besag. 1974. Spatial interaction and the statistical analysis of lattice systems. *Journal of the Royal Statistical Society. Series B (Methodological)*, pages 192–236.

Damián E. Blasi, Susanne Maria Michaelis, and Martin Haspelmath. 2017. Grammars are robustly transmitted even during the emergence of creole languages. *Nature Human Behaviour*.

Cedric Boeckx. 2014. What principles and parameters got wrong. In M. Carme Picallo, editor, *Treebanks: Building and Using Parsed Corpora*, pages 155–178. Oxford University Press.

Remco Bouckaert, Philippe Lemey, Michael Dunn, Simon J. Greenhill, Alexander V. Alekseyenko, Alexei J. Drummond, Russell D. Gray, Marc A. Suchard, and Quentin D. Atkinson. 2012. Mapping the origins and expansion of the Indo-European language family. *Science*, 337(6097):957–960.

Lyle Campbell. 2006. Areal linguistics. In *Encyclopedia of Language and Linguistics, Second Edition*, pages 454–460. Elsevier.

Noam Chomsky and Howard Lasnik. 1993. The theory of principles and parameters. In Joachim Jacobs, Arnim von Stechow, Wolfgang Sternefeld, and Theo Vennemann, editors, *Syntax: An International Handbook of Contemporary Research*, volume 1, pages 506–569. De Gruyter.

Hal Daumé III. 2009. Non-parametric Bayesian areal linguistics. In *Proceedings of Human Language Technologies: The 2009 Annual Conference of the North American Chapter of the Association for Computational Linguistics*, pages 593–601.

Hal Daumé III and Lyle Campbell. 2007. A Bayesian model for discovering typological implications. In *Proceedings of the 45th Annual Meeting of the Association of Computational Linguistics*, pages 65–72.

Gabriel Doyle, Klinton Bicknell, and Roger Levy. 2014. Nonparametric learning of phonological constraints in optimality theory. In *Proceedings of the 52nd Annual Meeting of the Association for Computational Linguistics (Volume 1: Long Papers)*, pages 1094–1103.

Dilan Görür, Frank Jäkel, and Carl Edward Rasmussen. 2006. A choice model with infinitely many latent features. In *Proceedings of the 23rd International Conference on Machine Learning*, pages 361–368.

Russell D. Gray and Quentin D. Atkinson. 2003. Language-tree divergence times support the Anatolian theory of Indo-European origin. *Nature*, 426(6965):435–439.

Joseph H. Greenberg, editor. 1963. *Universals of language*. MIT Press.

Thomas L. Griffiths and Zoubin Ghahramani. 2011. The Indian buffet process: An introduction and review. *Journal of Machine Learning Research*, 12:1185–1224.

Martin Haspelmath, Matthew Dryer, David Gil, and Bernard Comrie, editors. 2005. *The World Atlas of Language Structures*. Oxford University Press.

Bernd Heine and Tania Kuteva. 2007. *The Genesis of Grammar: A Reconstruction*. Oxford University Press.

Geoffrey E. Hinton. 2002. Training products of experts by minimizing contrastive divergence. *Neural Computation*, 14(8):1771–1800.

Yoshiaki Itoh and Sumie Ueda. 2004. The ising model for changes in word ordering rules in natural languages. *Physica D: Nonlinear Phenomena*, 198(3):333–339.

Julie Josse, Marie Chavent, Benot Liquet, and François Husson. 2012. Handling missing values with regularized iterative multiple correspondence analysis. *Journal of Classification*, 29(1):91–116.

Faming Liang. 2010. A double Metropolis–Hastings sampler for spatial models with intractable normalizing constants. *Journal of Statistical Computation and Simulation*, 80(9):1007–1022.

Jesper Møller, Anthony N. Pettitt, R. Reeves, and Kasper K. Berthelsen. 2006. An efficient Markov chain Monte Carlo method for distributions with intractable normalising constants. *Biometrika*, 93(2):451–458.

Yugo Murawaki. 2015. Continuous space representations of linguistic typology and their application to phylogenetic inference. In *Proceedings of the 2015 Conference of the North American Chapter of the Association for Computational Linguistics: Human Language Technologies*, pages 324–334.

Yugo Murawaki. 2016. Statistical modeling of creole genesis. In *Proceedings of the 2016 Conference of the North American Chapter of the Association for Computational Linguistics: Human Language Technologies*.

Iain Murray, Zoubin Ghahramani, and David J. C. MacKay. 2006. MCMC for doubly-intractable distributions. In *Proceedings of the Twenty-Second Conference on Uncertainty in Artificial Intelligence*, pages 359–366.

Radford M. Neal. 2011. MCMC using Hamiltonian dynamics. In Steve Brooks, Andrew Gelman, Galin L. Jones, and Xiao-Li Meng, editors, *Handbook of Markov Chain Monte Carlo*, pages 113–162. CRC Press.

Shijulal Nelson-Sathi, Johann-Mattis List, Hans Geisler, Heiner Fangerau, Russell D. Gray, William Martin, and Tal Dagan. 2010. Networks uncover hidden lexical borrowing in Indo-European language evolution. *Proceedings of the Royal Society B: Biological Sciences*.

Johanna Nichols. 1992. *Linguistic Diversity in Space and Time*. University of Chicago Press.

Johanna Nichols. 1994. The spread of language around the Pacific rim. *Evolutionary Anthropology: Issues, News, and Reviews*, 3(6):206–215.

Johanna Nichols. 1995. Diachronically stable structural features. In Henning Andersen, editor, *Historical Linguistics 1993. Selected Papers from the 11th International Conference on Historical Linguistics, Los Angeles 16–20 August 1993*. John Benjamins Publishing Company.

Mikael Parkvall. 2008. Which parts of language are the most stable? *STUF-Language Typology and Universals Sprachtypologie und Universalienforschung*, 61(3):234–250.

Yajuan Si and Jerome P. Reiter. 2013. Nonparametric Bayesian multiple imputation for incomplete categorical variables in large-scale assessment surveys. *Journal of Educational and Behavioral Statistics*, 38(5):499–521.

Nathan Srebro, Jason D. M. Rennie, and Tommi S. Jaakkola. 2005. Maximum-margin matrix factorization. In *Proceedings of the 17th International Conference on Neural Information Processing Systems*, pages 1329–1336.

Hiroya Takamura, Ryo Nagata, and Yoshifumi Kawasaki. 2016. Discriminative analysis of linguistic features for typological study. In *Proceedings of the Tenth International Conference on Language Resources and Evaluation (LREC 2016)*, pages 69–76.

Mary C. Towner, Mark N. Grote, Jay Venti, and Monique Borgerhoff Mulder. 2012. Cultural macroevolution on neighbor graphs: Vertical and horizontal transmission among western north American Indian societies. *Human Nature*, 23(3):283–305.

Nikolai Sergeevich Trubetzkoy. 1928. Proposition 16. In *Acts of the First International Congress of Linguists*, pages 17–18.

Søren Wichmann and Eric W. Holman. 2009. *Temporal Stability of Linguistic Typological Features*. Lincom Europa.

Kenji Yamauchi and Yugo Murawaki. 2016. Contrasting vertical and horizontal transmission of typological features. In *Proceedings of COLING 2016, the 26th International Conference on Computational Linguistics: Technical Papers*, pages 836–846.

Image-Grounded Conversations:
Multimodal Context for Natural Question and Response Generation

Nasrin Mostafazadeh[1*]**, Chris Brockett**[2]**, Bill Dolan**[2]**, Michel Galley**[2]**, Jianfeng Gao**[2]**,**
Georgios P. Spithourakis[3*]**, Lucy Vanderwende**[2]

1 BenevolentAI,   2 Microsoft Research,

3 University College London

nasrin.m@benevolent.ai,   chrisbkt@microsoft.com

Abstract

The popularity of image sharing on social media and the engagement it creates between users reflect the important role that visual context plays in everyday conversations. We present a novel task, Image-Grounded Conversations (IGC), in which natural-sounding conversations are generated about a shared image. To benchmark progress, we introduce a new multiple-reference dataset of crowd-sourced, event-centric conversations on images. IGC falls on the continuum between chit-chat and goal-directed conversation models, where visual grounding constrains the topic of conversation to event-driven utterances. Experiments with models trained on social media data show that the combination of visual and textual context enhances the quality of generated conversational turns. In human evaluation, the gap between human performance and that of both neural and retrieval architectures suggests that multi-modal IGC presents an interesting challenge for dialog research.

1 Introduction

Bringing together vision & language in one intelligent conversational system has been one of the longest running goals in AI (Winograd, 1972). Advances in image captioning (Fang et al., 2014; Chen et al., 2015; Donahue et al., 2015) have enabled much interdisciplinary research in vision and language, from video transcription (Rohrbach et al., 2012; Venugopalan et al., 2015), to answering questions about images (Antol et al., 2015; Malinowski and Fritz, 2014), to storytelling around series of photographs (Huang et al., 2016).

Figure 1: A naturally-occurring Image-Grounded Conversation.

Most recent work on vision & language focuses on either describing (captioning) the image or answering questions about their visible content. Observing how people naturally engage with one another around images in social media, it is evident that it is often in the form of conversational threads. On Twitter, for example, uploading a photo with an accompanying tweet has become increasingly popular: in June 2015, 28% of tweets reportedly contained an image (Morris et al., 2016). Moreover, across social media, the conversations around shared images range beyond what is explicitly visible in the image. Figure 1 illustrates such a conversation. As this example shows, the conversation is grounded not only in the visible objects (e.g., the boys, the bikes) but more importantly, in the events and actions (e.g., the race, winning) implicit in the image that is accompanied by the textual utterance. To humans, it is these latter aspects that are likely to be the most interesting and most meaningful components of a natural conversation, and to the systems, inferring such implicit aspects can be the most challenging.

In this paper we shift the focus from image as an artifact (as is in the existing vision & language work, to be described in Section 2), to image as the context for interaction: we introduce the task of Image-Grounded Conversation (IGC) in which a system must generate conversational turns to proactively drive the interaction forward. IGC thus falls on a continuum between chit-chat

---

* This work was performed at Microsoft.

Proceedings of the The 8th International Joint Conference on Natural Language Processing, pages 462–472,
Taipei, Taiwan, November 27 – December 1, 2017 ©2017 AFNLP

(open-ended) and goal-oriented task-completion dialog systems, where the visual context in IGC naturally serves as a detailed topic for a conversation. As conversational agents gain increasing ground in commercial settings (e.g., Siri and Alexa), they will increasingly need to engage humans in ways that seem intelligent and anticipatory of future needs. For example, a conversational agent might engage in a conversation with a user about a camera-roll image in order to elicit background information from the user (e.g., special celebrations, favorite food, the name of the friends and family, etc.).

This paper draws together two threads of investigation that have hitherto remained largely unrelated: vision & language and data-driven conversation modeling. Its contributions are threefold: (1) we introduce multimodal conversational context for formulating questions and responses around images, and support benchmarking with a publicly-released, high-quality, crowd-sourced dataset of 4,222 multi-turn, multi-reference conversations grounded on event-centric images. We analyze various characteristics of this IGC dataset in Section 3.1. (2) We investigate the application of deep neural generation and retrieval approaches for question and response generation tasks (Section 5), trained on 250K 3-turn naturally-occurring image-grounded conversations found on Twitter. (3) Our experiments suggest that the combination of visual and textual context improves the quality of generated conversational turns (Section 6-7). We hope that this novel task will spark new interest in multimodal conversation modeling.

2   Related Work

2.1   Vision and Language

Visual features combined with language modeling have shown good performance both in image captioning (Devlin et al., 2015; Xu et al., 2015; Fang et al., 2014; Donahue et al., 2015) and in question answering on images (Antol et al., 2015; Ray et al., 2016; Malinowski and Fritz, 2014), when trained on large datasets, such as the COCO dataset (Lin et al., 2014). In Visual Question Answering (VQA) (Antol et al., 2015), a system is tasked with answering a question about a given image, where the questions are constrained to be answerable directly from the image. In other words, the VQA task primarily serves to evaluate the extent to which the system has recognized the explicit content of the image.

Figure 2: Typical crowdsourced conversations in IGC (left) and VisDial (right).

Das et al. (2017a) extend the VQA scenario by collecting sequential questions from people who are shown only an automatically generated caption, not the image itself. The utterances in this dataset, called 'Visual Dialog' (VisDial), are best viewed as simple one-sided QA exchanges in which humans ask questions and the system provides answers. Figure 2 contrasts an example ICG conversation with the VisDial dataset. As this example shows, IGC involves natural conversations with the image as the grounding, where the literal objects (e.g., the pumpkins) may not even be mentioned in the conversation at all, whereas VisDial targets explicit image understanding. More recently, Das et al. (2017b) have explored the VisDial dataset with richer models that incorporate deep-reinforcement learning.

Mostafazadeh et al. (2016b) introduce the task of visual question generation (VQG), in which the system itself outputs questions about a given image. Questions are required to be 'natural and engaging', i.e. a person would find them interesting to answer, but need not be answerable from the image alone. In this work, we introduce multimodal context, recognizing that images commonly come associated with a verbal commentary that can affect the interpretation. This is thus a broader, more complex task that involves implicit commonsense reasoning around both image and text.

2.2 Data-Driven Conversational Modeling

This work is also closely linked to research on data-driven conversation modeling. Ritter et al. (2011) posed response generation as a machine translation task, learning conversations from parallel message-response pairs found on social media. Their work has been successfully extended with the use of deep neural models (Sordoni et al., 2015; Shang et al., 2015; Serban et al., 2015a; Vinyals and Le, 2015; Li et al., 2016a,b). Sordoni et al. (2015) introduce a context-sensitive neural language model that selects the most probable response conditioned on the conversation history (i.e., a text-only context). In this paper, we extend the contextual approach with multimodal features to build models that are capable of asking questions on topics of interest to a human that might allow a conversational agent to proactively drive a conversation forward.

3 Image-Grounded Conversations

3.1 Task Definition

We define the current scope of IGC as the following two consecutive conversational steps:

• **Question Generation:** Given a visual context I and a textual context T (e.g., the first statement in Figure 1), generate a coherent, natural question Q about the image as the second utterance in the conversation. It has been shown that humans achieve greater consensus on what constitutes a natural question to ask given an image (the task of VQG) than on captioning or asking a visually verifiable question (VQA) (Mostafazadeh et al., 2016b). As seen in Figure 1, the question is not directly answerable from the image. Here we emphasize on questions as a way of potentially engaging a human in continuing the conversation.

• **Response Generation:** Given a visual context I, a textual context T, and a question Q, generate a coherent, natural, response R to the question as the third utterance in the conversation. In the interests of feasible multi-reference evaluation, we pose question and response generation as two separate tasks. However, all the models presented in this paper can be fed with their own generated question to generate a response.

3.2 The ICG Dataset

The majority of the available corpora for developing data-driven dialogue systems contain task-oriented and goal-driven conversational data (Serban et al., 2015b). For instance, the Ubuntu dia-

logue corpus (Lowe et al., 2015) is the largest corpus of dialogues (almost 1 million mainly 3-turn dialogues) for the specific topic of troubleshooting Ubuntu problems. On the other hand, for open-ended conversation modeling (chitchat), now a high demand application in AI, shared datasets with which to track progress are severely lacking. The ICG task presented here lies nicely in the continuum between the two, where the visual grounding of event-centric images constrains the topic of conversation to contentful utterances.

To enable benchmarking of progress in the IGC task, we constructed the IGC_{Crowd} dataset for validation and testing purposes. We first sampled eventful images from the VQG dataset (Mostafazadeh et al., 2016b) which has been extracted by querying a search engine using event-centric query terms. These were then served in a photo gallery of a crowd-sourcing platform we developed using the Turkserver toolkit (Mao et al., 2012), which enables synchronous and real-time interactions between crowd workers on Amazon Mechanical Turk. Multiple workers wait in a virtual lobby to be paired with a conversation partner. After being paired, one of the workers selects an image from the large photo gallery, after which the two workers enter a chat window in which they conduct a short conversation about the selected image. We prompted the workers to naturally drive the conversation forward without using informal/IM language. To enable multi-reference evaluation (Section 6), we crowd-sourced five additional questions and responses for the IGC_{Crowd} contexts and initial questions.

Table 1 shows three full conversations found in the IGC_{Crowd} dataset. These examples show show that eventful images lead to conversations that are semantically rich and appear to involve commonsense reasoning. Table 2 summarizes basic dataset statistics. The IGC_{Crowd} dataset has been released as the Microsoft Research Image-Grounded Conversation dataset (https://www.microsoft.com/en-us/download/details.aspx?id=55324&751be11f-ede8).

4 Task Characteristics

In this Section, we analyze the IGC dataset to highlight a range of phenomena specific to this task. (Additional material pertaining to the lexical distributions of this dataset can be found in the Supplementary Material.)

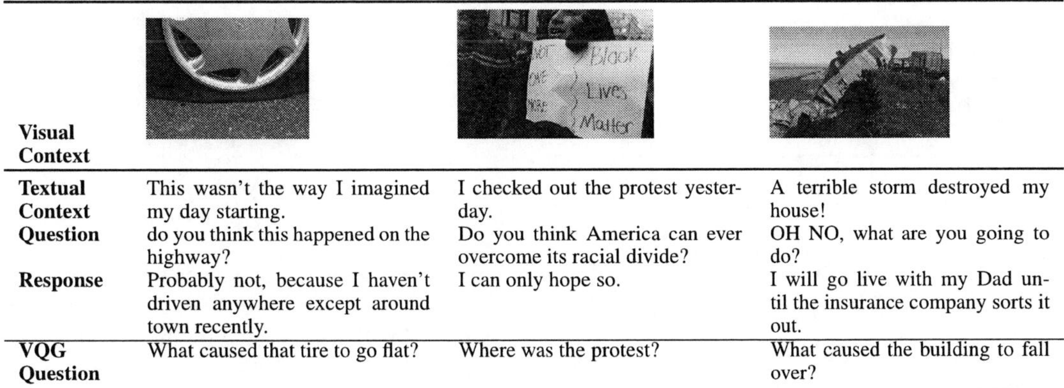

Visual Context			
Textual Context	This wasn't the way I imagined my day starting.	I checked out the protest yesterday.	A terrible storm destroyed my house!
Question	do you think this happened on the highway?	Do you think America can ever overcome its racial divide?	OH NO, what are you going to do?
Response	Probably not, because I haven't driven anywhere except around town recently.	I can only hope so.	I will go live with my Dad until the insurance company sorts it out.
VQG Question	What caused that tire to go flat?	Where was the protest?	What caused the building to fall over?

Table 1: Example full conversations in our IGC$_{\text{Crowd}}$ dataset. For comparison, we also include VQG questions in which the image is the only context.

IGC$_{\text{Crowd}}$ (val and test sets, split: 40% and 60%)	
# conversations = # images	**4,222**
total # utterances	**25,332**
# all workers participated	308
Max # conversations by one worker	20
Average payment per worker (min)	1.8 dollars
Median work time per worker (min)	10.0
IGC$_{\text{Crowd}-multiref}$ (val and test sets, split: 40% and 60%)	
# additional references per question/response	5
total # multi-reference utterances	**42,220**

Table 2: Basic Dataset Statistics.

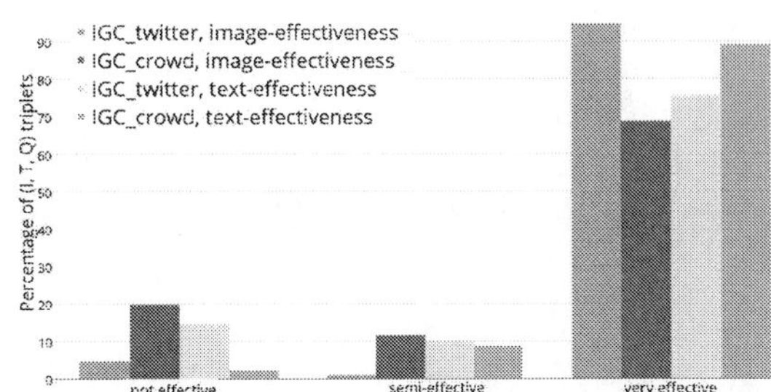

Figure 3: The effectiveness of textual and visual context for asking questions.

4.1 The Effectiveness of Multimodal Context

The task of IGC emphasizes modeling of not only visual but also textual context. We presented human judges with a random sample of 600 triplets of image, textual context, and question (I, T, Q) from each IGC$_{\text{Twitter}}$ and IGC$_{\text{Crowd}}$ datasets and asked them to rate the effectiveness of the visual and the textual context. We define 'effectiveness' to be "the degree to which the image or text is required in order for the given question to sound natural". The workers were prompted to make this judgment based on whether or not the question already makes sense without either the image or the text. As Figure 3 demonstrates, both visual and textual contexts are generally highly effective, and understanding of both would be required for the question that was asked. By way of comparison, Figure 3 also shows the effectiveness of image and text for a sample taken from Twitter data presented in Section 4.4. We note that the crowd-sourced dataset is more heavily reliant on understanding the textual context than is the Twitter set.

4.2 Frame Semantic Analysis of Questions

The grounded conversations starting with questions contain a considerable amount stereotypical commonsense knowledge. To get a better sense of the richness of our IGC$_{\text{Crowd}}$ dataset, we manually annotated a random sample of 330 (I, T, Q) triplets in terms of Minsky's Frames: Minsky defines 'frame' as follows: *"When one encounters a new situation, one selects from memory a structure called a Frame" (Minsky, 1974)*. A frame is thus a commonsense knowledge representation data-structure for representing stereotypical situations, such as a wedding ceremony. Minsky further connects frames to the nature of questions: *"[A Frame] is a collection of questions to be asked about a situation"*. These questions can ask about the cause, intention, or side-effects of a presented situation.

We annotated[1] the FrameNet (Baker et al., 1998) frame evoked by the image I, to be called (I_{FN}), and the textual context T, (T_{FN}). Then, for the question asked, we annotated the frame

---

[1] These annotations can be accessed through `https://goo.gl/MVyGzP`

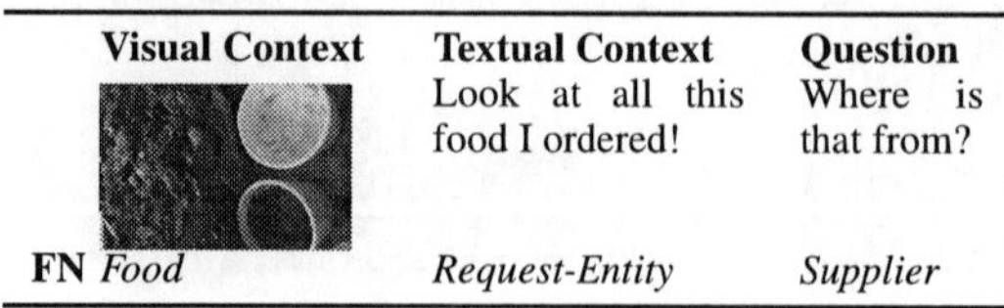

Visual Context	Textual Context	Question
	Look at all this food I ordered!	Where is that from?
FN *Food*	*Request-Entity*	*Supplier*

Table 3: FrameNet (FN) annotation of an example.

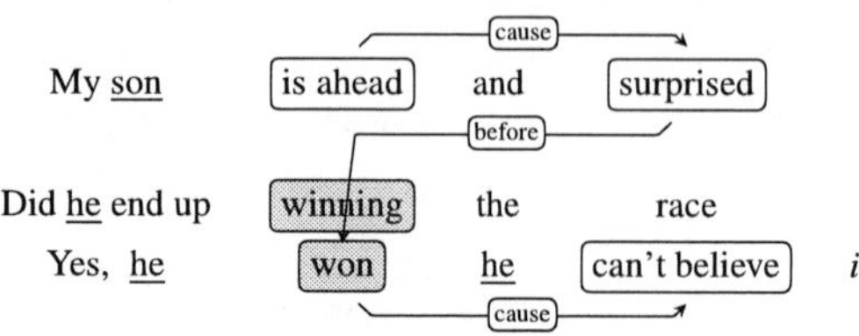

Figure 4: An example causal and temporal (CaTeRS) annotation on the conversation presented in Figure 1. The rectangular nodes show the event entities and the edges are the semantic links. For simplicity, we show the 'identity' relation between events using gray nodes. The coreference chain is depicted by the underlined words.

slot ($Q_{FN-slot}$) associated with a context frame (Q_{FN}). For 17% of cases, we were unable to identify a corresponding $Q_{FN-slot}$ in FrameNet. As the example in Table 3 shows, the image in isolation often does not evoke any uniquely contentful frame, whereas the textual context frequently does. In only 14% of cases does $I_{FN}=T_{FN}$, which further supports the complementary effect of our multimodal contexts. Moreover, $Q_{FN}=I_{FN}$ for 32% our annotations, whereas $Q_{FN}=T_{FN}$ for 47% of the triplets, again, showing the effectiveness of textual context in determining the question.

4.3 Event Analysis of Conversations

To further investigate the representation of events and any stereotypical causal and temporal relations between them in the IGC$_{Crowd}$ dataset, we manually annotated a sample of 20 conversations with their causal and temporal event structures. Here, we followed the Causal and Temporal Relation Scheme (CaTeRS) (Mostafazadeh et al., 2016a) for event entity and event-event semantic relation annotations. Our analysis shows that the IGC utterances are indeed rich in events. On average, each utterance in IGC has 0.71 event entity mentions, such as 'win' or 'remodel'. The semantic link annotation reflects commonsense relation between event mentions in the context of the ongoing conversation. Figure 4 shows an example CaTeRS annotation. The distribution of semantic

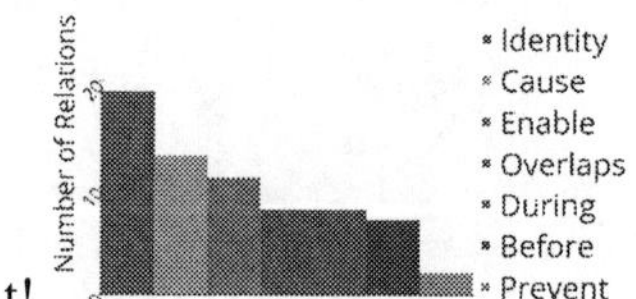

Figure 5: The frequency of event-event semantic links in a random sample of 20 IGC conversations.

links in the annotated sample can be found in Figure 5. These numbers further suggest that in addition to jointly understanding the visual and textual context (including multimodal anaphora resolution, among other challenges), capturing causal and temporal relations between events will likely be necessary for a system to perform the IGC task.

4.4 IGC$_{Twitter}$ Training Dataset

Previous work in neural conversation modeling (Ritter et al., 2011; Sordoni et al., 2015) has successfully used Twitter as the source of natural conversations. As training data, we sampled 250K quadruples of {visual context, textual context, question, response} tweet threads from a larger dataset of 1.4 million, extracted from the Twitter Firehose over a 3-year period beginning in May 2013 and filtered to select just those conversations in which the initial turn was associated with an image and the second turn was a question.

Regular expressions were used to detect questions. To improve the likelihood that the authors are experienced Twitter conversationalists, we further limited extraction to those exchanges where users had actively engaged in at least 30 conversational exchanges during a 3-month period.

Twitter data is noisy: we performed simple normalizations, and filtered out tweets that contained mid-tweet hashtags, were longer than 80 characters[2] or contained URLs not linking to the image. (Sample conversations from this dataset can be found in the Supplementary Material.) A random sample of tweets suggests that about 46% of the Twitter conversations is affected by prior history between users, making response generation particularly difficult. In addition, the abundance of screenshots and non-photograph graphics is potentially a major source of noise in extracting features for neural generation, though we did not attempt to exclude these from the training set.

---

[2]Pilot studies showed that 80 character limit more effectively retains one-sentence utterances that are to the point.

5 Models

5.1 Generation Models

Figure 6 overviews our three generation models. Across all the models, we use the VGGNet architecture (Simonyan and Zisserman, 2015) for computing deep convolutional image features. We use the 4096-dimensional output of the last fully connected layer ($fc7$) as the input to all the models sensitive to visual context.

Visual Context Sensitive Model *(V-Gen).* Similar to Recurrent Neural Network (RNN) models for image captioning (Devlin et al., 2015; Vinyals et al., 2015), *(V-Gen)* transforms the image feature vector to a 500-dimensional vector that serves as the initial recurrent state to a 500-dimensional one-layer Gated Recurrent Unit (GRU) which is the decoder module. The output sentence is generated one word at a time until the <EOS> (end-of-sentence) token is generated. We set the vocabulary size to 6000 which yielded the best results on the validation set. For this model, we got better results by greedy decoding. Unknown words are mapped to an <UNK> token during training, which is not allowed to be generated at decoding time.

Textual Context Sensitive Model *(T-Gen).* This is a neural Machine Translation-like model that maps an input sequence to an output sequence (Seq2Seq model (Cho et al., 2014; Sutskever et al., 2014)) using an encoder and a decoder RNN. The decoder module is like the model described above, in this case the initial recurrent state being the 500-dimensional encoding of the textual context. For consistency, we use the same vocab size and number of layers as in the *(V-Gen)* model.

Visual & Textual Context Sensitive Model *(V&T-Gen).* This model fully leverages both textual and visual contexts. The vision feature is transformed to a 500-dimensional vector, and the textual context is likewise encoded into a 500-dimensional vector. The textual feature vector can be obtained using either a bag-of-words *(V&T.BOW-Gen)* representation, or an RNN *(V&T.RNN-Gen)*, as depicted in Figure 7. The textual feature vector is then concatenated to the vision vector and fed into a fully connected (FC) feed forward neural network. As a result, we obtain a single 500-dimensional vector encoding both visual and textual context, which then serves as the initial recurrent state of the decoder RNN.

In order to generate the response (the third utterance in the conversation), we need to represent the conversational turns in the textual context input. There are various ways to represent conversational history, including a bag of words model, or a concatenation of all textual utterances into one sentence (Sordoni et al., 2015). For response generation, we implement a more complex treatment in which utterances are fed into an RNN one word at a time (Figure 7) following their temporal order in the conversation. An <UTT> marker designates the boundary between successive utterances.

Decoding and Reranking. For all generation models, at decoding time we generate the N-best lists using left-to-right beam search with *beam-size* 25. We set the maximum number of tokens to 13 for the generated partial hypotheses. Any partial hypothesis that reaches <EOS> token becomes a viable full hypothesis for reranking. The first few hypotheses on top of the N-best lists generated by Seq2Seq models tend to be very generic,[3] disregarding the input context. In order to address this issue we rerank the N-best list using the following score function:

$$log\ p(h|C) + \lambda\ idf(h,D) + \mu|h| + \kappa\ V(h) \quad (1)$$

where $p(h|C)$ is the probability of the generated hypothesis h given the context C. The function V counts the number of verbs in the hypothesis and $|h|$ denotes the number of tokens in the hypothesis. The function *idf* is the inverse document frequency, computing how common a hypothesis is across all the generated N-best lists. Here D is the set of all N-best lists and d is a specific N-best list. We define $idf(h, D) = log \frac{|D|}{|\{d \in D : h \in d\}|}$, where we set N=10 to cut short each N-best list. These parameters were selected following reranking experiments on the validation set. We optimize all the parameters of the scoring function towards maximizing the smoothed-BLEU score (Lin and Och, 2004) using the Pairwise Ranking Optimization algorithm (Hopkins and May, 2011).

5.2 Retrieval Models

In addition to generation, we implemented two retrieval models customized for the tasks of question and response generation. Work in vision and language has demonstrated the effectiveness of retrieval models, where one uses the annotation (e.g., caption) of a nearest neighbor in the training image set to annotate a given test image (Mostafazadeh et al., 2016b; Devlin et al., 2015;

---

[3] An example generic question is *where is this?* and a generic response is *I don't know.*

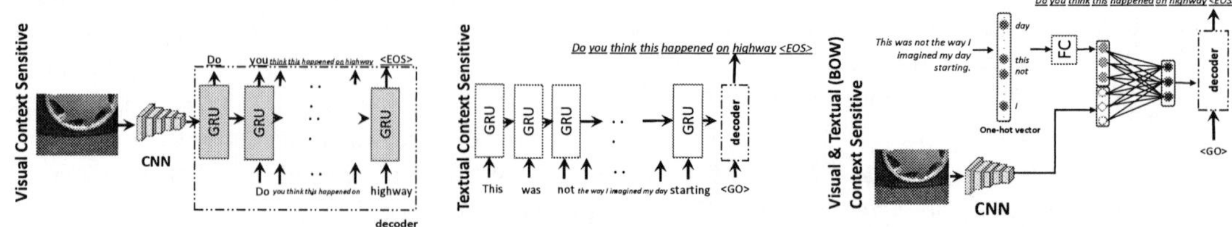

Figure 6: Question generation using the Visual Context Sensitive Model *(V-Gen)*, Textual Context Sensitive Model *(T-Gen)*, and the Visual & Textual Context Sensitive Model *(V&T.BOW-Gen)*, respectively.

	Visual Context			
Question Generation	**Textual Context**	The weather was amazing at this baseball game.	I got in a car wreck today!	My cousins at the family re-union.
	Gold Question	Nice, which team won?	Did you get hurt?	What is the name of your cousin in the blue shirt?
	V&T-Ret	U at the game? or did someone take that pic for you?	**You driving that today?**	**U had fun?**
	V-Gen	Where are you?	Who's is that?	Who's that guy?
	V&T-Gen	**Who's winning?**	**What happened?**	**Where's my invite?**
Response Generation	**Textual Context**	The weather was amazing at this baseball game. <UTT> Nice, which team won?	I got in a car wreck today! <UTT> Did you get hurt?	My cousins at the family re-union. <UTT> What is the name of your cousin in the blue shirt?
	Gold Response	My team won this game.	No it wasn't too bad of a bang up.	His name is Eric.
	V&T-Ret	10 for me and 28 for my dad.	**Yes.**	lords cricket ground . beautiful.
	V&T-Gen	ding ding ding!	**Nah, I'm at home now.**	**He's not mine!**

Table 4: Example question and response generations on $\text{IGC}_{\text{Crowd}}$ test set. All the generation models use beam search with reranking. In the textual context, <UTT> separates different utterances. The generations in bold are acceptable utterances given the underlying context.

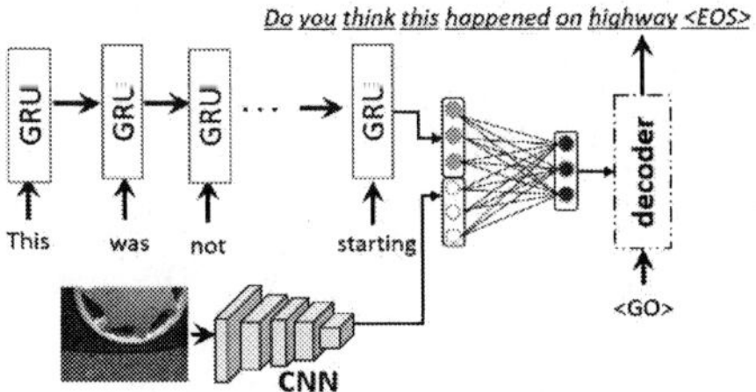

Figure 7: The visual & textual context sensitive model with RNN encoding (*V&T.RNN-Gen*).

Hodosh et al., 2013; Ordonez et al., 2011; Farhadi et al., 2010).

Visual Context Sensitive Model (*V-Ret*). This model uses only the provided image for retrieval. First, we find a set of K nearest training images for the given test image based on cosine similarity of the $fc7$ vision feature vectors. Then we retrieve those K annotations as our pool of K candidates. Finally, we compute the textual similarity among the questions in the pool according to a Smoothed-BLEU (Lin and Och, 2004) similarity score, then emit the sentence that has the highest similarity to the rest of the pool.

Visual & Textual Context Sensitive Model (*V&T-Ret*). This model uses a linear combination of $fc7$ and word2vec feature vectors for retrieving similar training instances.

6 Evaluation Setup

We provide both human (Table 5) and automatic (Table 6) evaluations for our question and response generation tasks on the IGC$_{Crowd}$ test set. We crowdsourced our human evaluation on an AMT-like crowdsourcing system, asking seven crowd workers to each rate the quality of candidate questions or responses on a three-point Likert-like scale, ranging from 1 to 3 (the highest). To ensure a calibrated rating, we showed the human judges all system hypotheses for a particular test case at the same time. System outputs were randomly ordered to prevent judges from guessing which systems were which on the basis of position. After collecting judgments, we averaged the scores throughout the test set for each model. We discarded any annotators whose ratings varied from the mean by more than 2 standard deviations.

Although human evaluation is to be preferred, and currently essential in open-domain generation tasks involving intrinsically diverse outputs, it is useful to have an automatic metric for day-to-day

evaluation. For ease of replicability, we use the standard Machine Translation metric, BLEU (Papineni et al., 2002), which captures n-gram overlap between hypotheses and multiple references. Results reported in Table 6 employ BLEU with equal weights up to 4-grams at corpus-level on the multi-reference IGC$_{Crowd}$ test set. Although Liu et al. (2016) suggest that BLEU fails to correlate with human judgment at the sentence level, correlation increases when BLEU is applied at the document or corpus level (Galley et al., 2015; Przybocki et al., 2008).

7 Experimental Results

We experimented with all the models presented in Section 5. For question generation, we used a visual & textual sensitive model that uses bag-of-words (*V&T.BOW-Gen*) to represent the textual context, which achieved better results. Earlier vision & language work such as VQA (Antol et al., 2015) has shown that a bag-of-words baseline outperforms LSTM-based models for representing textual input when visual features are available (Zhou et al., 2015). In response generation, which needs to account for textual input consisting of two turns, we used the *V&T.RNN-Gen* model as the visual & textual-sensitive model for the response rows of tables 5 and 6. Since generating a response solely from visual context is unlikely to be successful, we did not use the *V-Gen* model in response generation. All models are trained on IGC$_{Twitter}$ dataset, except for VQG, which shares the same architecture as with the (*V-Gen*) model, but is trained on 7,500 questions from the VQG dataset (Mostafazadeh et al., 2016b) as a point of reference. We also include the gold human references from the IGC$_{Crowd}$ dataset in the human evaluation to set a bound on human performance.

Table 4 presents example generations by our best performing systems. In human evaluation shown in Tables 5, the model that encodes both visual and textual context outperforms others. We note that human judges preferred the top generation in the n-best list over the reranked best, likely owing to the tradeoff between a safe and generic utterance and a riskier but contentful one. The human gold references are consistently favored throughout the table. We take this as evidence that IGC$_{Crowd}$ test set provides a robust and challenging test set for benchmarking progress.

As shown in Table 6, BLEU scores are low, as is characteristic for language tasks with intrin-

	Human	**Generation** (Greedy)			**Generation** (Beam, best)				**Generation** (Reranked, best)			**Retrieval**	
	Gold	Textual	Visual	V & T	Textual	Visual	V & T	VQG	Textual	Visual	V & T	Visual	V & T
Question	<u>2.68</u>	1.46	1.58	1.86	1.07	1.86	**2.28**	2.24	1.03	2.06	2.13	1.59	1.54
Response	<u>2.75</u>	1.24	–	1.40	1.12	–	**1.49**	–	1.04	–	1.44	–	1.48

Table 5: Human judgment results on the IGC_{Crowd} test set. The maximum score is 3. Per model, the human score is computed by averaging across multiple images. The boldfaced numbers show the highest score among the systems. The overall highest scores (underlined) are the human gold standards.

		Generation			**Retrieval**	
	Textual	Visual	V & T	VQG	Visual	V & T
Question	1.71	3.23	4.41	**8.61**	0.76	1.16
Response	1.34	–	**1.57**	–	–	0.66

Table 6: Results of evaluating using multi-reference BLEU.

sically diverse outputs (Li et al., 2016b,a). On BLEU, the multimodal *V&T* model outperforms all the other models across test sets, except for the VQG model which does significantly better. We attribute this to two issues: (1) the VQG training dataset contains event-centric images similar to the IGC_{Crowd} test set, (2) Training on a high-quality crowd-sourced dataset with controlled parameters can, to a significant extent, produce better results on similarly crowd-sourced test data than training on data found "in the wild" such as Twitter. However, crowd-sourcing multi-turn conversations between paired workers at large scale is prohibitively expensive, a factor that favors the use of readily available naturally-occurring but noisier data.

Overall, in both automatic and human evaluation, the question generation models are more successful than response generation. This disparity might be overcome by (1) implementation of more sophisticated systems for richer modeling of long contexts across multiple conversational turns, (2) training on larger, higher-quality datasets.

8 Conclusions

We have introduced a new task of multimodal image-grounded conversation, in which, given an image and a natural language text, the system must generate meaningful conversational turns, the second turn being a question. We are releasing to the research community a crowd-sourced dataset of 4,222 high-quality, multiple-turn, multiple-reference conversations about eventful images. Inasmuch as this dataset is not tied to the characteristics of any specific social media resource, e.g., Twitter or Reddit, we expect it to remain sta-ble over time, as it is less susceptible to attrition in the form of deleted posts or accounts.

Our experiments provide evidence that capturing multimodal context improves the quality of question and response generation. Nonetheless, the performance gap between our best models and humans opens opportunities further research in the continuum from casual chit-chat conversation to more topic-oriented dialog. We expect that addition of other forms of grounding, such as temporal and geolocation information, often embedded in images, will further improve performance.

In this paper, we illustrated the application of this dataset using simple models trained on conversations on Twitter. In the future, we expect that more complex models and richer datasets will permit emergence of intelligent human-like agent behavior that can engage in implicit commonsense reasoning around images and proactively drive the interaction forward.

Acknowledgments

We are grateful to Piali Choudhury, Rebecca Hanson, Ece Kamar, and Andrew Mao for their assistance with crowd-sourcing. We would also like to thank our reviewers for their helpful comments.

References

Stanislaw Antol, Aishwarya Agrawal, Jiasen Lu, Margaret Mitchell, Dhruv Batra, C. Lawrence Zitnick, and Devi Parikh. 2015. VQA: Visual question answering. In *Proc. ICCV*.

Collin F. Baker, Charles J. Fillmore, and John B. Lowe. 1998. The Berkeley FrameNet Project. In *Proc. COLING*.

Jianfu Chen, Polina Kuznetsova, David Warren, and Yejin Choi. 2015. Déjà image-captions: A corpus of expressive descriptions in repetition. In *Proc. NAACL-HLT*.

Kyunghyun Cho, Bart Van Merriënboer, Caglar Gulcehre, Dzmitry Bahdanau, Fethi Bougares, Holger Schwenk, and Yoshua Bengio. 2014. Learning phrase representations using rnn encoder-decoder for statistical machine translation. In *Proc. EMNLP*.

Abhishek Das, Satwik Kottur, Khushi Gupta, Avi Singh, Deshraj Yadav, José M. F. Moura, Devi Parikh, and Dhruv Batra. 2017a. Visual dialog. In *Proc. CVPR*.

Abhishek Das, Satwik Kottur, José M. F. Moura, Stefan Lee, and Dhruv Batra. 2017b. Learning cooperative visual dialog agents with deep reinforcement learning. In *Proc. ICVV*.

Jacob Devlin, Hao Cheng, Hao Fang, Saurabh Gupta, Li Deng, Xiaodong He, Geoffrey Zweig, and Margaret Mitchell. 2015. Language models for image captioning: The quirks and what works. In *Proc. ACL-IJCNLP*.

Jeff Donahue, Lisa Anne Hendricks, Sergio Guadarrama, Marcus Rohrbach, Subhashini Venugopalan, Kate Saenko, and Trevor Darrell. 2015. Long-term recurrent convolutional networks for visual recognition and description. In *Proc. CVPR*.

Hao Fang, Saurabh Gupta, Forrest N. Iandola, Rupesh Srivastava, Li Deng, Piotr Dollár, Jianfeng Gao, Xiaodong He, Margaret Mitchell, John C. Platt, C. Lawrence Zitnick, and Geoffrey Zweig. 2014. From captions to visual concepts and back. In *Proc. CVPR*.

Ali Farhadi, Mohsen Hejrati, Mohammad Amin Sadeghi, Peter Young, Cyrus Rashtchian, Julia Hockenmaier, and David Forsyth. 2010. Every picture tells a story: Generating sentences from images. In *Proc. ECCV*.

Michel Galley, Chris Brockett, Alessandro Sordoni, Yangfeng Ji, Michael Auli, Chris Quirk, Margaret Mitchell, Jianfeng Gao, and Bill Dolan. 2015. deltaBLEU: A discriminative metric for generation tasks with intrinsically diverse targets. In *Proc. ACL-IJCNLP*.

Micah Hodosh, Peter Young, and Julia Hockenmaier. 2013. Framing image description as a ranking task: Data, models and evaluation metrics. *J. Artif. Int. Res.*, 47(1):853–899.

Mark Hopkins and Jonathan May. 2011. Tuning as ranking. In *Proc. EMNLP*.

Ting-Hao (Kenneth) Huang, Francis Ferraro, Nasrin Mostafazadeh, Ishan Misra, Aishwarya Agrawal, Jacob Devlin, Ross Girshick, Xiaodong He, Pushmeet Kohli, Dhruv Batra, C. Lawrence Zitnick, Devi Parikh, Lucy Vanderwende, Michel Galley, and Margaret Mitchell. 2016. Visual storytelling. In *Proc. NAACL-HLT*.

Jiwei Li, Michel Galley, Chris Brockett, Jianfeng Gao, and Bill Dolan. 2016a. A diversity-promoting objective function for neural conversation models. In *Proc. NAACL-HLT*.

Jiwei Li, Michel Galley, Chris Brockett, Jianfeng Gao, and Bill Dolan. 2016b. A persona-based neural conversation model. In *Proc. ACL*.

Chin-Yew Lin and Franz Josef Och. 2004. Automatic evaluation of machine translation quality using longest common subsequence and skip-bigram statistics. In *Proc. ACL*.

Tsung-Yi Lin, Michael Maire, Serge Belongie, James Hays, Pietro Perona, Deva Ramanan, Piotr Dollr, and C. Lawrence Zitnick. 2014. Microsoft coco: Common objects in context. In *Proc. ECCV*.

Chia-Wei Liu, Ryan Lowe, Iulian Serban, Mike Noseworthy, Laurent Charlin, and Joelle Pineau. 2016. How NOT to evaluate your dialogue system: An empirical study of unsupervised evaluation metrics for dialogue response generation. In *Proc. EMNLP*.

Ryan Lowe, Nissan Pow, Iulian Serban, and Joelle Pineau. 2015. The ubuntu dialogue corpus: A large dataset for research in unstructured multi-turn dialogue systems. In *Proc. SIGDIAL*.

Mateusz Malinowski and Mario Fritz. 2014. A multiworld approach to question answering about realworld scenes based on uncertain input. In *NIPS*.

Andrew Mao, David Parkes, Yiling Chen, Ariel D. Procaccia, Krzysztof Z. Gajos, and Haoqi Zhang. 2012. Turkserver: Enabling synchronous and longitudinal online experiments. In *Workshop on Human Computation (HCOMP)*.

Marvin Minsky. 1974. A framework for representing knowledge. Technical report, Cambridge, MA, USA.

Meredith Ringel Morris, Annuska Zolyomi, Catherine Yao, Sina Bahram, Jeffrey P. Bigham, and Shaun K. Kane. 2016. "with most of it being pictures now, I rarely use it": Understanding twitter's evolving accessibility to blind users. In *Proc. CHI*.

Nasrin Mostafazadeh, Alyson Grealish, Nathanael Chambers, James F. Allen, and Lucy Vanderwende. 2016a. Caters: Causal and temporal relation scheme for semantic annotation of event structures. In *Proceedings of the The 4th Workshop on EVENTS: Definition, Detection, Coreference, and Representation*.

Nasrin Mostafazadeh, Ishan Misra, Jacob Devlin, Margaret Mitchell, Xiaodong He, and Lucy Vanderwende. 2016b. Generating natural questions about an image. In *Proc. ACL*.

Vicente Ordonez, Girish Kulkarni, and Tamara L. Berg. 2011. Im2text: Describing images using 1 million captioned photographs. In *Proc. NIPS*.

Kishore Papineni, Salim Roukos, Todd Ward, and Wei-Jing Zhu. 2002. BLEU: A method for automatic evaluation of machine translation. In *Proc. ACL*.

M. Przybocki, K. Peterson, and S. Bronsart. 2008. Official results of the NIST 2008 metrics for machine translation challenge. In *Proc. MetricsMATR08 workshop*.

Arijit Ray, Gordon Christie, Mohit Bansal, Dhruv Batra, and Devi Parikh. 2016. Question relevance in VQA: identifying non-visual and false-premise questions. In *Proc. EMNLP*.

Alan Ritter, Colin Cherry, and William B Dolan. 2011. Data-driven response generation in social media. In *Proc. EMNLP*.

Marcus Rohrbach, Sikandar Amin, Mykhaylo Andriluka, and Bernt Schiele. 2012. A database for fine grained activity detection of cooking activities. In *Proc. CVPR*.

Iulian V Serban, Alessandro Sordoni, Yoshua Bengio, Aaron Courville, and Joelle Pineau. 2015a. Hierarchical neural network generative models for movie dialogues. *arXiv preprint arXiv:1507.04808*.

Iulian Vlad Serban, Ryan Lowe, Laurent Charlin, and Joelle Pineau. 2015b. A survey of available corpora for building data-driven dialogue systems. *CoRR*, abs/1512.05742.

Lifeng Shang, Zhengdong Lu, and Hang Li. 2015. Neural responding machine for short-text conversation. In *Proc. ACL-IJCNLP*.

K. Simonyan and A. Zisserman. 2015. Very deep convolutional networks for large-scale image recognition. In *Proc. ICLR*.

Alessandro Sordoni, Michel Galley, Michael Auli, Chris Brockett, Yangfeng Ji, Margaret Mitchell, Jian-Yun Nie, Jianfeng Gao, and Bill Dolan. 2015. A neural network approach to context-sensitive generation of conversational responses. In *Proc. NAACL-HLT*.

Ilya Sutskever, Oriol Vinyals, and Quoc V. Le. 2014. Sequence to sequence learning with neural networks. In *NIPS*.

Subhashini Venugopalan, Huijuan Xu, Jeff Donahue, Marcus Rohrbach, Raymond Mooney, and Kate Saenko. 2015. Translating videos to natural language using deep recurrent neural networks. In *Proc. NAACL-HLT*.

Oriol Vinyals and Quoc Le. 2015. A neural conversational model. In *Proc. Deep Learning Workshop, ICML*.

Oriol Vinyals, Alexander Toshev, Samy Bengio, and Dumitru Erhan. 2015. Show and tell: A neural image caption generator. In *Proc. CVPR*.

Terry Winograd. 1972. *Understanding Natural Language*. Academic Press, New York.

Kelvin Xu, Jimmy Ba, Ryan Kiros, Kyunghyun Cho, Aaron C. Courville, Ruslan Salakhutdinov, Richard S. Zemel, and Yoshua Bengio. 2015. Show, attend and tell: Neural image caption generation with visual attention. In *Proc. ICML*.

Bolei Zhou, Yuandong Tian, Sainbayar Sukhbaatar, Arthur Szlam, and Rob Fergus. 2015. Simple baseline for visual question answering. *CoRR*, abs/1512.02167.

A Neural Language Model for Dynamically Representing the Meanings of Unknown Words and Entities in a Discourse

Sosuke Kobayashi

Preferred Networks, Inc., Japan

`sosk@preferred.jp`

Naoaki Okazaki

Tokyo Institute of Technology, Japan

`okazaki@c.titech.ac.jp`

Kentaro Inui

Tohoku University / RIKEN, Japan

`inui@ecei.tohoku.ac.jp`

Abstract

This study addresses the problem of identifying the meaning of unknown words or entities in a discourse with respect to the word embedding approaches used in neural language models. We proposed a method for on-the-fly construction and exploitation of word embeddings in both the input and output layers of a neural model by tracking contexts. This extends the dynamic entity representation used in Kobayashi et al. (2016) and incorporates a copy mechanism proposed independently by Gu et al. (2016) and Gulcehre et al. (2016). In addition, we construct a new task and dataset called *Anonymized Language Modeling* for evaluating the ability to capture word meanings while reading. Experiments conducted using our novel dataset show that the proposed variant of RNN language model outperformed the baseline model. Furthermore, the experiments also demonstrate that dynamic updates of an output layer help a model predict reappearing entities, whereas those of an input layer are effective to predict words following reappearing entities.

1 Introduction

Language models that use probability distributions over sequences of words are found in many natural language processing applications, including speech recognition, machine translation, text summarization, and dialogue utterance generation. Recent studies have demonstrated that language models trained using neural network (Bengio et al., 2003; Mikolov et al., 2010) such as recurrent neural network (RNN) (Jozefowicz et al., 2016) and convolutional neural network (Dauphin

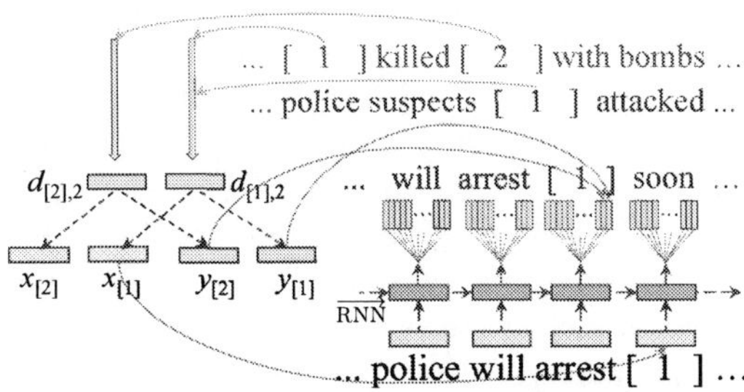

Figure 1: Dynamic Neural Text Modeling: the embeddings of unknown words, denoted by coreference indexes "[k]" are dynamically computed and used in both the input and output layers ($x_{[k]}$ and $y_{[k]}$) of a RNN language model. These are constructed from contextual information ($d_{[k],i}$) preceding the current $(i + 1)$-th sentence.

et al., 2016) achieve the best performance across a range of corpora (Mikolov et al., 2010; Chelba et al., 2014; Merity et al., 2017; Grave et al., 2017).

However, current neural language models have a major drawback: the language model works only when applied to a closed vocabulary of fixed size (usually comprising high-frequency words from the given training corpus). All occurrences of out-of-vocabulary words are replaced with a single dummy token "<unk>", showing that the word is unknown. For example, the word sequence, *Pikotaro sings PPAP on YouTube* is treated as *<unk> sings <unk> on <unk>* assuming that the words *Pikotaro*, *PPAP*, and *YouTube* are out of the vocabulary. The model therefore assumes that these words have the same meaning, which is clearly incorrect. The derivation of *meanings of unknown words* remains a persistent and nontrivial challenge when using word embeddings.

In addition, existing language models further assume that the meaning of a word is the same and universal across different documents. Neural

473

Proceedings of the The 8th International Joint Conference on Natural Language Processing, pages 473–483,
Taipei, Taiwan, November 27 – December 1, 2017 ©2017 AFNLP

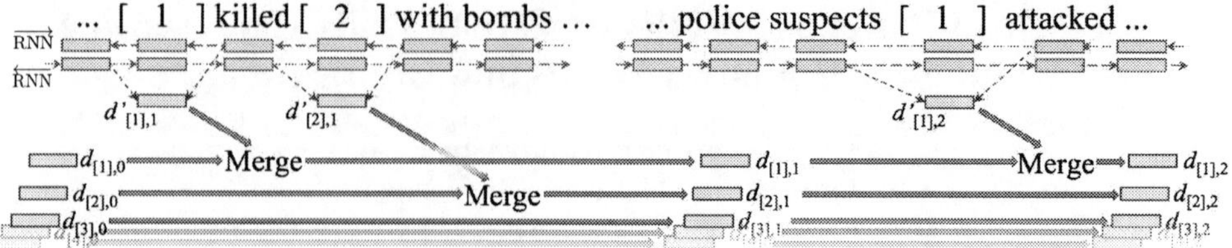

Figure 2: Dynamic Neural Text Modeling: the meaning representation of each unknown word, denoted by a coreference index "[k]", is inferred from the local contexts in which it occurs.

language models also make this assumption and represent all occurrences of a word with a single word vector across all documents. However, the assumption of a universal meaning is also unlikely correct. For example, the name *John* is likely to refer to different individuals in different documents. In one story, *John* may be a pianist while another *John* denoted in a second story may be an infant. A model that represents all occurrences of *John* with the same vector fails to capture the very different behavior expected from *John* as a pianist and *John* as an infant.

In this study, we address these issues and propose a novel neural language model that can build and dynamically change distributed representations of words based on the multi-sentential discourse. The idea of incorporating dynamic meaning representations into neural networks is not new. In the context of reading comprehension, Kobayashi et al. (2016) proposed a model that dynamically computes the representation of a named entity mention from the local context given by its prior occurrences in the text. In neural machine translation, the *copy mechanism* was proposed as a way of improving the handling of out-of-vocabulary words (e.g., named entities) in a source sentence (Gu et al., 2016; Gulcehre et al., 2016). We use a variant of recurrent neural language model (RNLM), that combines dynamic representation and the copy mechanism. The resulting novel model, *Dynamic Neural Text Model*, uses the dynamic word embeddings that are constructed from the context in the output and input layers of an RNLM, as shown in Figures 1 and 2.

The contributions of this paper are three-fold. First, we propose a novel neural language model, which we named the *Dynamic Neural Text Model*. Second, we introduce a new evaluation task and dataset called *Anonymized Language Modeling*. This dataset can be used to evaluate the ability of a language model to capture word meanings from contextual information (Figure 3). This task involves a kind of one-shot learning tasks, in which the meanings of entities are inferred from their limited prior occurrences. Third, our experimental results indicate that the proposed model outperforms baseline models that use only global and static word embeddings in the input and/or output layers of an RNLM. Dynamic updates of the output layer helps the RNLM predict reappearing entities, whereas those of the input layer are effective to predict words following reappearing entities. A more detailed analysis showed that the method was able to successfully capture the meanings of words across large contexts, and to accumulate multiple context information.

2 Background

2.1 RNN Language Model

Given a sequence of N tokens of a document $D = (w_1, w_2, ..., w_N)$, an RNN language model computes the probability $p(D) = \prod_{t=1}^{N} p(w_t|w_1, ..., w_{t-1})$. The computation of each factorized probability $p(w_t|w_1, ..., w_{t-1})$ can also be viewed as the task of predicting a following word w_t from the preceding words $(w_1, ..., w_{t-1})$. Typically, RNNs recurrently compute the probability of the following word w_t by using a hidden state $\boldsymbol{h}_{t-1}$ at time step $t-1$,

$$p(w_t|w_1, ..., w_{t-1}) = \frac{\exp(\vec{\boldsymbol{h}}_{t-1}^{\mathsf{T}} \boldsymbol{y}_{w_t} + b_{w_t})}{\sum_{w \in V} \exp(\vec{\boldsymbol{h}}_{t-1}^{\mathsf{T}} \boldsymbol{y}_w + b_w)}, \quad (1)$$

$$\vec{\boldsymbol{h}}_t = \overrightarrow{\mathrm{RNN}}(\boldsymbol{x}_{w_t}, \vec{\boldsymbol{h}}_{t-1}). \quad (2)$$

Here, $\boldsymbol{x}_{w_t}$ and $\boldsymbol{y}_{w_t}$ denote the input and output word embeddings of w_t respectively, V represents the set of words in the vocabulary, and b_w is a bias value applied when predicting the word w. The function $\overrightarrow{\mathrm{RNN}}$ is often replaced with

LSTM (Hochreiter and Schmidhuber, 1997) or GRU (Cho et al., 2014) to improve performance.

2.2 Dynamic Entity Representation

RNN-based models have been reported to achieve better results on the CNN QA reading comprehension dataset (Hermann et al., 2015; Kobayashi et al., 2016). In the CNN QA dataset, every named entity in each document is anonymized. This is done to allow the ability to comprehend a document using neither prior nor external knowledge to be evaluated. To capture the meanings of such anonymized entities, Kobayashi et al. (2016) proposed a new model that they named *dynamic entity representation*. This encodes the local contexts of an entity and uses the resulting context vector as the word embedding of a subsequent occurrence of that entity in the input layer of the RNN. This model: (1) constructs context vectors $d'_{e,i}$ from the local contexts of an entity e at the i-th sentence; (2) merges multiple contexts of the entity e through max pooling and produces the dynamic representation $d_{e,i}$; and (3) replaces the embedding of the entity e in the $(i+1)$-th sentence with the dynamic embedding $x_{e,i+1}$ produced from $d_{e,i}$. More formally,

$$x_{e,i+1} = W_{dc}d_{e,i} + b_e, \tag{3}$$
$$d_{e,i} = \text{maxpooling}(d'_{e,i}, d_{e,i-1}), \tag{4}$$
$$d'_{e,i} = \text{ContextEncoder}(e, i). \tag{5}$$

Here, b_e denotes a bias vector, maxpooling is a function that yields the largest value from the elementwise inputs, and ContextEncoder is an encoding function. Figure 2 gives an example of the process of encoding and merging contexts from sentences. An arbitrary encoder can be used for ContextEncoder; Kobayashi et al. (2016) used bidirectional RNNs, encoding the words surrounding the entity e of a sentence in both directions. If the entity e fails to appear in the i-th sentence, the embedding is not updated, i.e., $d_{e,i} = d_{e,i-1}$.

3 Proposed Method: Dynamic Neural Text Modeling

In this section, we introduce the extension of dynamic entity representation to language modeling. From Equations 1 and 2, RNLM uses a set of word embeddings in the input layer to encode the preceding contextual words, and another set of word embeddings in the output layer to predict a word from the encoded context. Therefore, we consider incorporating the idea of dynamic representation into the word embeddings in the output layer (y_w in Equation 1) as well as in the input layer (x_w in Equation 2; refer to Figure 1). The novel extension of dynamic representation to the output layer affects predictions made for entities that appear repeatedly, whereas that in the input layer is expected to affect the prediction of words that follow the entities.

The procedure for constructing dynamic representations of e, $d_{e,i}$ is the same as that introduced in Section 2.2. Before reading the $(i+1)$-th sentence, the model constructs the context vectors $[d'_{e,1}, ..., d'_{e,i}]$ from the local contexts of e in every preceding sentence. Here, $d'_{e,j}$ denotes the context vector of e in the j-th sentence. ContextEncoder in the model produces a context vector d'_e for e at the t-th position in a sentence, using a bidirectional RNN[1] as follows:

$$d'_e = \text{ReLU}(W_{hd}[\vec{h}_{t-1}, \overleftarrow{h}_{t+1}] + b_d), \tag{6}$$
$$\vec{h}_t = \overrightarrow{\text{RNN}}(x_{w_t}, \vec{h}_{t-1}), \tag{7}$$
$$\overleftarrow{h}_t = \overleftarrow{\text{RNN}}(x_{w_t}, \overleftarrow{h}_{t+1}). \tag{8}$$

Here, ReLU denotes the ReLU activation function (Nair and Hinton, 2010), while W_{dc} and W_{hd} correspond to learnable matrices; b_d is a bias vector. As in the RNN language model, $\vec{h}_{t-1}$ and $\overleftarrow{h}_{t+1}$ as well as their composition d'_e can capture information necessary to predict the features of the target e at the t-th word.

Following context encoding, the model merges the multiple context vectors, $[d'_{e,1}, ..., d'_{e,i}]$, into the dynamic representation $d_{e,i}$ using a merging function. A range of functions are abailable for merging multiple vectors, while Kobayashi et al. (2016) used only max pooling (Equation 4). In this study, we explored three further functions: GRU, GRU followed by ReLU ($d_{e,i} = \text{ReLU}(\text{GRU}(d'_{e,i}, d_{e,i-1}))$) and a function that selects only the latest context, i.e., $d_{e,i} = d'_{e,i}$. This comparison clarifies the effect of the accumulation of contexts as the experiments proceeded[2].

---

[1] Equations 2 and 7 are identical but do not share internal parameters.

[2] Note that merging functions are not restricted to considering two arguments (a new context and a merged past context) recurrently but can consider all vectors over the whole history $[d'_{e,1}, ..., d'_{e,i}]$ (e.g., by using attention mechanism (Bahdanau et al., 2015)). However, for simplicity, this research focuses only on the case of a function with two arguments.

Original Version

The hottest gift *this Christmas* could be *Sony's new PlayStation 2*, but good luck finding one. As *Greg Lefevre* reports, many stores have sold out of *the game* even ...

Anonymized Version

the hottest gift [1] could be [2] , but good luck finding one . as [3] reports , many stores have sold out of [2] even ...

Figure 3: An example document for Anonymized Language Modeling. Token "[k]" is an anonymized token that appears k-th in the entities in a document. Language models predict the next word from the preceding words, and calculate probabilities for whole word sequences.

The merging function produces the dynamic representation $\boldsymbol{d}_{e,i}$ of e. In language modeling, to read the $(i+1)$-th sentence, the model uses two dynamic word embeddings of e in the input and output layers. The input embedding $\boldsymbol{x}_e$, used to encode contexts (Equation 2), and the output embedding $\boldsymbol{y}_e$, used to predict the occurrence of e (Equation 1), are replaced with dynamic versions:

$$\boldsymbol{x}_e = W_{dx}\boldsymbol{d}_{e,i} + \boldsymbol{b}_e^x, \quad (9)$$

$$\boldsymbol{y}_e = W_{dy}\boldsymbol{d}_{e,i} + \boldsymbol{b}_e^y, \quad (10)$$

where W_{dx} and W_{dy} denote learnable matrices, and $\boldsymbol{b}_e^x$ and $\boldsymbol{b}_e^y$ denote learnable vectors tied to e. We can observe that a conventional RNN language model is a variant that removes the dynamic terms ($W_{dx}\boldsymbol{d}_{e,i}$ and $W_{dy}\boldsymbol{d}_{e,i}$) using only the static terms ($\boldsymbol{b}_e^x$ and $\boldsymbol{b}_e^y$) to represent e. The initial dynamic representation $\boldsymbol{d}_{e,0}$ is defined as a zero vector, so that the initial word embeddings ($\boldsymbol{x}_e$ and $\boldsymbol{y}_e$) are identical to the static terms ($\boldsymbol{b}_e^x$ and $\boldsymbol{b}_e^y$) until the point at which the first context of the target word e is observed. All parameters in the end-to-end model are learned entirely by backpropagation, maximizing the log-likelihood in the same way as a conventional RNN language model.

We can view the approach in Kobayashi et al. (2016) as a variant on the proposed method, but using the dynamic terms only in the input layer (for $\boldsymbol{x}_e$). We can also view the copy mechanism (Gu et al., 2016; Gulcehre et al., 2016) as a variant on the proposed method, in which specific embeddings in the output layer are replaced with special dynamic vectors.

4 Anonymized Language Modeling

This study explores methods for on-the-fly capture and exploitation of the meanings of unknown words or entities in a discourse. To do this, we introduce a novel evaluation task and dataset that we called *Anonymized Language Modeling*. Figure 3 gives an example from the dataset. Briefly, the dataset anonymizes certain noun phrases, treating them as unknown words and retaining their coreference relations. This allows a language model to track the context of every noun phrase in the discourse. Other words are left unchanged, allowing the language model to preserve the context of the anonymized (unknown) words, and to infer their meanings from the known words. The process was inspired by Hermann et al. (2015), whose approach has been explored by the research on reading comprehension.

More precisely, we used the OntoNotes (Pradhan et al., 2012) corpus, which includes documents with coreferences and named entity tags manually annotated. We assigned an anonymous identifier to every coreference chain in the corpus[3] in order of first appearance[4], and replaced mentions of a coreference chain with its identifier. In our experiments, each coreference chain was given a dynamic representation. Following Mikolov et al. (2010), we limited the vocabulary to 10,000 words appearing frequently in the corpus. Finally, we inserted "<bos>" and "<eos>" tokens to mark the beginning and end of each sentence.

An important difference between this dataset and the one presented in Hermann et al. (2015) is in the way that coreferences are treated. Hermann et al. (2015) used automatic resolusion of coreferences, whereas our study made use of the manual annotations in the OntoNotes. Thus, the process of Hermann et al. (2015) introduced (intentional and unintentional) errors into the dataset. Additionally, the dataset did not assign an entity iden-

[3] We used documents with no more than 50 clusters, which covered more than 97% of the corpus.

[4] Following the study of Luong et al. (2015), we assigned "<unk1>", "<unk2>", ... to coreference clusters in order of first appearance.

Split	Train	Valid	Test
# of documents	2725	335	336
Avg. # of sentences	25.7	27.2	26.4
Avg. # of unique entities	15.6	16.8	15.8
Avg. # of unique entities occurring more than once	9.3	9.9	9.5
Avg. # of occurrences of an entity	3.2	3.2	3.1

Table 1: Statistics of Anonymized Language Modeling dataset.

tifier to a pronoun. In contrast, as our dataset has access to the manual annotations of coreferences, we are able to investigate the ability of the language model to capture meanings from contexts.

Dynamic updating could be applied to words in all lexical categories, including verbs, adjectives, and nouns without requiring additional extensions. However, verbs and adjectives were excluded from targets of dynamic updates in the experiments, for two reasons. First, proper nouns and nouns accounted for the majority (70%) of the low-frequency (unknown) words, followed by verbs (10%) and adjectives (9%). Second, we assumed that the meaning of a verb or adjective would shift less over the course of a discourse than that of a noun. When semantic information of unknown verbs and adjectives is required, their embeddings may be extracted from ad-hoc training on a different larger corpus. This, however, was beyond the scope of this study.

5 Experiments

5.1 Setting

An experiment was conducted to investigate the effect of *Dynamic Neural Text Model* on the *Anonymized Language Modeling* dataset. The split of dataset followed that of the original corpus (Pradhan et al., 2012). Table 1 summarizes the statistics of the dataset.

The baseline model was a typical LSTM RNN language model with 512 units. We compared three variants of the proposed model, using different applications of dynamic embedding: in the input layer only (as in Kobayashi et al. (2016)), in the output layer only, and in both the input and output layers. The context encoders were bidirectional LSTMs with 512 units, the parameters of which were not the same as those in the LSTM RNN language models. All models were trained by maximizing the likelihood of correct tokens, to

achieve best perplexity on the validation dataset[5]. Most hyper-parameters were tuned and fixed by the baseline model on the validation dataset[6].

It is difficult to adequately train the all parts of a model using only the small dataset of Anonymized Language Modeling. We therefore pretrained word embeddings and ContextEncoder (the bidirectional RNNs and matrices in Equations 6–8) on a sentence completion task in which clozes were predicted from the surrounding words in a large corpus (Melamud et al., 2016)[7]. We used the objective function with negative sampling (Mikolov et al., 2013): $\sum_e (\log \sigma(\hat{x}_e^\mathsf{T} x_e) + \sum_{v \in Neg} (\log \sigma(-\hat{x}_e^\mathsf{T} x_v)))$. Here, $\hat{x}_e$ is a context vector predicted by ContextEncoder, x_e denotes the word embedding of a target word e appearing in the corpus, and Neg represents randomly sampled words. These pretrained parameters of ContextEncoder were fixed when the whole language model was trained on the Anonymized Language Modeling dataset. We implemented models in Python using the `Chainer` neural network library (Tokui et al., 2015). The code and the constructed dataset are publicly available[8].

5.2 Results and Analysis

5.2.1 Perplexity

Table 2 shows performance of the baseline model and the three variants of the proposed method in terms of perplexity. The table reports the mean and standard error of three perplexity values after training using three different randomly chosen initializations (we used the same convention

---

[5] We performed a validation at the end of every half epoch out of five epochs.

[6] Batchsize was 8. Adam (Kingma and Ba, 2015) with learning rate 10^{-3}. Gradients were normalized so that their norm was smaller than 1. Truncation of backpropagation and updating was performed after every 20 sentences and at the end of document.

[7] We pretrained a model on the Gigaword Corpus, excluding sentences with more than 32 tokens. We performed training for 50000 iterations with a batch size of 128 and five negative samples. Only words that occurred no fewer than 500 times are used; other words were treated as unknown tokens. Melamud et al. (2016) used three different sets of word embeddings for the two inputs with respect to the encoders ($\overrightarrow{RNN}$ and $\overleftarrow{RNN}$) and the output (target). However, we forced the sets of word embeddings to share a single set of word embeddings in pretraining. We initialized the word embeddings in both the input layer (x_w) and the output layer (y_w) of the novel models, including the baseline model, with this single set. The word embeddings of all anonymized tokens were initialized as unknown words with the word embedding of "<unk>".

[8] `https://github.com/soskek/dynamic_neural_text_model`

Models	(1) All	(2) Reappearing entities	(3) Following entities	(4) Non-entities
LSTM LM (Baseline) (A)	64.8±0.6	48.0±2.6	128.6±2.0	68.5±0.2
With only dynamic input (B)	62.8±0.3	42.4±1.1	109.5±1.4	**66.4±0.3**
With only dynamic output (C)	62.5±0.3	35.9±3.7	129.0±0.7	69.5±0.3
With dynamic input & output (D)	**60.7±0.2**	**34.0±1.3**	**106.8±0.6**	67.6±0.04

Table 2: Perplexities for each token group of models on the test set of Anonymized Language Modeling dataset. All values are averages with standard errors, calculated respectively by three models (trained with different random numbers). Dynamic models used GRU followed by ReLU as the merging function.

throughout this paper). Here, we discuss the proposed method using GRU followed by ReLU as the merging function, as this achieved the best perplexity (see Section 5.2.2 for a comparison of functions). We also show perplexitiy values when evaluating words of specific categories: (1) all words; (2) reappearing entity words; (3) words following entities; and (4) non-entity words.

All variants of the proposed method outperformed the baseline model. Focusing on the categories (2) and (3) highlights the roles of dynamic updates of the input and output layers. Dynamic updates of the input layer (B) had a larger improvement for predicting words following entities (3) than those of the output layer (C). In contrast, dynamic updates of the output layer (C) were quite effective for predicting reappearing entities (2) whereas those of the input layer (B) were not. These facts confirm that: dynamic updates of the input layer help a model predict words following entities by supplying on-the-fly context information; and those of the output layer are effective to predict entity words appearing multiple times.

In addition, dynamic updates of both the input and output layers (D) further improved the performance from those of either the output (C) or input (B) layer. Thus, the proposed dynamic output was shown to be compatible with dynamic input, and *vice versa*. These results demonstrated the positive effect of capturing and exploiting the context-sensitive meanings of entities.

In order to examine whether dynamic updates of the input and output embeddings capture context-sensitive meanings of entities, we present Figures 4, 5 and 6. Figure 4 depicts the perplexity of words with different positions in a document[9]. The figure confirms that the advantage of the proposed method over the baseline is more evident

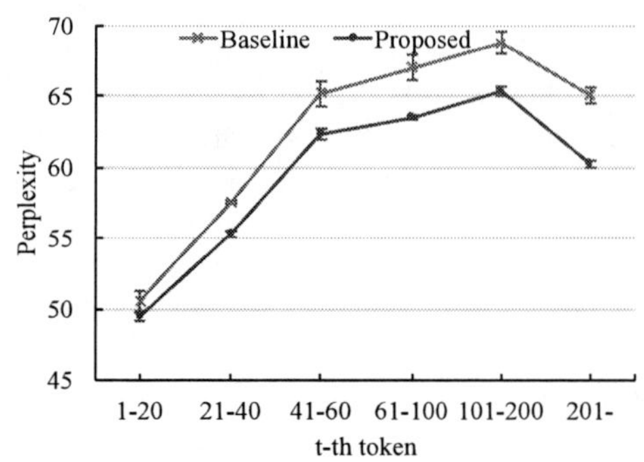

Figure 4: Perplexity of all tokens relative to the time at which they appear in the document.

especially in the latter part of documents, where repeated words are more likely to occur.

Figure 5 shows the perplexity with respect to the frequency of words t within documents. Note that the word embedding at the first occurrence of an entity is static. This figure indicates that entities appearing many times enjoy the benefit of the dynamic language model. Figure 6 visualizes the perplexity of entities with respect to the numbers of their antecedent candidates. It is clear from this figure that the proposed method is better at memorizing the semantic information of entities appearing repeatedly in documents than the baseline. These results also demonstrated the contribution of dynamic updates of word embeddings.

5.2.2 Comparison of Merging functions

Table 3 compares models with different merging functions; GRU-ReLU, GRU, max pooling, and the use of the latest context. The use of the latest context had the worst performance for all variants of the proposed method. Thus, a proper accumulation of multiple contexts is indispensable for dynamic updates of word embeddings. Although Kobayashi et al. (2016) used only max pooling as the merging function, GRU and GRU-ReLU were

---

[9]It is more difficult to predict tokens appearing latter in a document because the number of new (unknown) tokens increases as a model reads the document.

Models	Merging function	# of parameters (to be finetuned)	(1) All	(2) Reappearing entities	(3) Following entities	(4) Non-entities
Only	GRU-ReLU	18.9M (14.2M)	**62.8±0.3**	**42.4±1.1**	**109.5±1.4**	**66.4±0.3**
dynamic input	GRU	18.9M (14.2M)	63.2±0.4	43.3±2.7	111.2±0.7	66.8±0.4
	Max pool.	17.3M (12.6M)	63.6±0.4	45.0±2.6	116.0±1.0	67.0±0.2
	Only latest	17.3M (12.6M)	64.0±0.4	44.1±1.6	127.6±0.7	67.5±0.2
Only	GRU-ReLU	18.9M (14.2M)	62.5±0.3	**35.9±3.7**	129.0±0.7	69.5±0.3
dynamic output	GRU	18.9M (14.2M)	62.6±0.2	39.0±2.0	**121.1±8.3**	69.1±0.2
	Max pool.	17.3M (12.6M)	**62.2±0.4**	41.1±1.9	126.9±1.5	**68.4±0.6**
	Only latest	17.3M (12.6M)	64.9±0.1	49.8±1.8	129.1±1.6	70.6±0.2
Dynamic	GRU-ReLU	19.2M (14.4M)	**60.7±0.2**	**34.0±1.3**	**106.8±0.6**	67.6±0.04
input & output	GRU	19.2M (14.4M)	60.9±0.3	37.5±0.3	108.9±0.8	67.2±0.4
	Max pool.	17.6M (12.9M)	**60.7±0.3**	39.5±3.4	107.5±1.3	**66.8±0.8**
	Only latest	17.6M (12.9M)	63.4±0.2	47.9±4.2	116.4±0.4	68.9±0.1
Baseline		12.3M (12.3M)	64.8±0.6	48.0±2.6	128.6±2.0	68.5±0.2

Table 3: Results for models with different merging functions on the test set of the Anonymized Language Modeling dataset, as same as in Table 2.

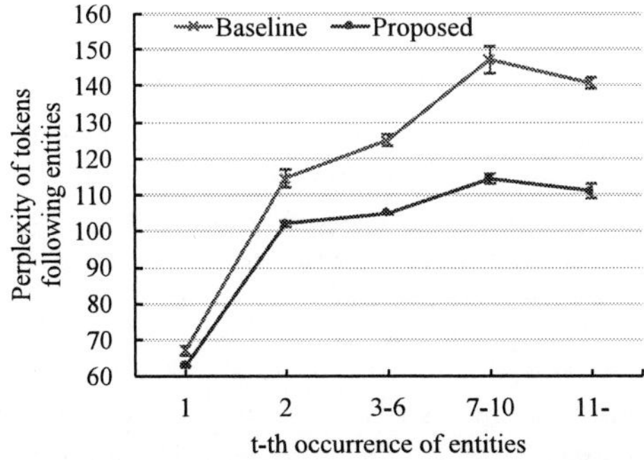

Figure 5: Perplexity of tokens following the entities relative to the time at which the entity occurs.

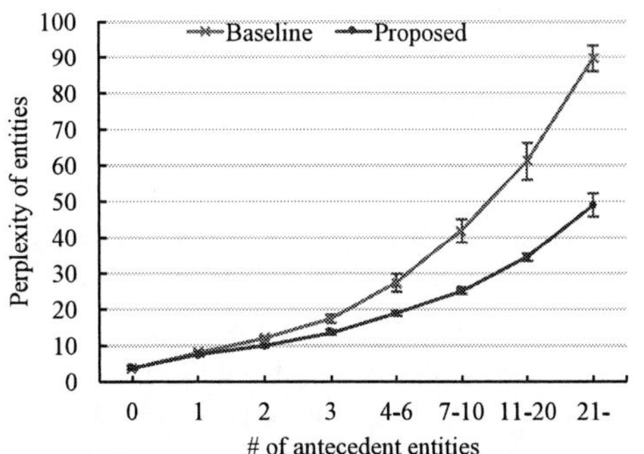

Figure 6: Perplexity of entities relative to the number of antecedent entities.

shown to be comparable in performance and superior to max pooling when predicting tokens related to entities (2) and (3).

5.2.3 Predicting Entities by Likelihood of a Sentence

In order to examine contribution of the dynamic language models on a downstream task, we conducted cloze tests for comprehension of a sentence with reappearing entities in a discourse. Given multiple preceding entities $E = \{e^+, e^1, e^2, ...\}$ followed by a cloze sentence, the models were required to predict the true antecedent e^+ which allowed the cloze to be correctly filled, among the other alternatives $E^- = \{e^1, e^2, ...\}$.

Language models solve this task by comparing the likelihoods of sentences filled with antecedent candidates in E and returning the entity with the highest likelihood of the sentence. In this experiment, the performance of a model was represented by the *Mean Quantile* (MQ) (Guu et al., 2015).

The MQ computes the mean ratio at which the model predicts a correct antecedent e^+ more likely than negative antecedents in E^-,

$$ \mathrm{MQ} = \frac{|\{e^- \in E^- : p(e^-) < p(e^+)\}|}{|E^-|}. \quad (11) $$

Here, $p(e)$ denotes the likelihood of a sentence whose cloze is filled with e. If the correct antecedent e^+ yields highest likelihood, MQ gets 1.

Table 4 reports MQs for the three variants and merging functions. Dynamic updates of the input layer greatly boosted the performance by approximately 10%, while using both dynamic input and output improved it further. In this experiment, the merging functions with GRUs outperform the others. These results demonstrated that Dynamic Neural Text Models can accumulate a new information in word embeddings and contribute to modeling the semantic changes of entities in a discourse.

Models	Merging func.	MQ
Baseline		.525±.001
Only dynamic input	GRU-ReLU	.630±.005
	GRU	.633±.005
	Max pool.	.617±.002
	Only latest	.600±.004
Only dynamic output	GRU-ReLU	.519±.001
	GRU	.522±.000
	Max pool.	.519±.001
	Only latest	.519±.003
Dynamic input & output	GRU-ReLU	**.642±.004**
	GRU	.637±.005
	Max pool.	.620±.002
	Only latest	.613±.002

Table 4: Mean Quantile of a true coreferent entity among antecedent entities.

6 Related Work

An approach to addressing the unknown word problem used in recent studies (Kim et al., 2016; Sennrich et al., 2016; Luong and Manning, 2016; Schuster and Nakajima, 2012) comprises the embeddings of unknown words from character embeddings or subword embeddings. Li and Jurafsky (2015) applied word disambiguation and use a sense embedding to the target word. Choi et al. (2017) captured the context-sensitive meanings of common words using word embeddings, applied through a gating function controlled by history words, in the context of machine translation. In future work, we will explore a wider range of models, to integrate our dynamic text modeling with methods that estimate the meaning of unknown words or entities from their constituents. When addressing well-known entities such as *Obama* and *Trump*, it makes sense to learn their embeddings from external resources, as well as dynamically from the preceding context in a given discourse (as in our Dynamic Neural Text Model). The integration of these two sources of information is an intriguing challenge in language modeling.

A key aspect of our model is its incorporation of the copy mechanism (Gu et al., 2016; Gulcehre et al., 2016), using dynamic word embeddings in the output layer. Independently of this study, several research groups have explored the use of variants of the copy mechanisms in language modeling (Merity et al., 2017; Grave et al., 2017; Peng and Roth, 2016). These studies, however, did not incorporate dynamic representations in the input layer. In contrast, our proposal incorporates the copy mechanism through the use of dynamic representations in the output layer, integrating them with dynamic mechanisms in both the input and output layers by applying dynamic entity-wise representation. Our experiments have demonstrated the benefits of such integration.

Another related trend in recent studies is the use of neural network to capture the information flow of a discourse. One approach has been to link RNNs across sentences (Wang and Cho, 2016; Serban et al., 2016), while a second approach has exploited a type of memory space to store contextual information (Sukhbaatar et al., 2015; Tran et al., 2016; Merity et al., 2017). Research on reading comprehension (Kobayashi et al., 2016; Henaff et al., 2017) and coreference resolution (Wiseman et al., 2016; Clark and Manning, 2016b,a) has shown the salience of entity-wise context information. Our model could be located within such approaches, but is distinct in being the first model to make use of entity-wise context information in both the input and output layers for sentence generation.

We summarize and compare works for entity-centric neural networks that read a document. Kobayashi et al. (2016) pioneered entity-centric neural models tracking states in a discourse. They proposed *Dynamic Entity Representation*, which encodes contexts of entities and updates the states using entity-wise memories. Wiseman et al. (2016) also proposed a method for managing similar entity-wise features on neural networks and improved a coreference resolution model. Clark and Manning (2016b,a) incorporated such entity-wise representations in mention-ranking coreference models. Our paper follows Kobayashi et al. (2016) and exploits dynamic entity reprensetions in a neural language model, where dynamic reporesentations are used not only in the neural encoder but also in the decoder, applicable to various sequence generation tasks, e.g., machine translation and dialog response generation. Simultaneously with our paper, Ji et al. (2017) use dynamic entity representation in a neural language model for reranking outputs of a coreference resolution system. Yang et al. (2017) experiment language modeling with referring to internal contexts or external data. Henaff et al. (2017) focus on neural networks tracking contexts of entities, achieving the state-of-the-art result in bAbI (Weston et al., 2015), a reading comprehension task. They encode the contexts of each entity by an attention-like gated RNN instead of using coreference links directly. Dhingra et al. (2017) also try to improve a reading comprehension model using coreference links. Similarly to our dynamic entity representation, Bahdanau et al. (2017) construct on-the-fly word embeddings of rare words from dictionary definitions.

The fisrt key component of dynamic entity representation is a function to merge more than one contexts about an entity into a consistent representation of the entity. Various choices for the function exist, e.g., max or average-pooling (Kobayashi et al., 2016; Clark and Manning, 2016b), RNN (GRU, LSTM (Wiseman et al., 2016; Yang et al., 2017) or other gated RNNs (Henaff et al., 2017; Ji et al., 2017)), or using the latest context only (without any merging) (Yang et al., 2017). This paper is the first work comparing the effects of those choices (see Section 5.2.2).

The second component is a function to encode local contexts from a given text, e.g., bidirectional RNN encoding (Kobayashi et al., 2016), unidirectional RNN used in a language model (Ji et al., 2017; Yang et al., 2017), feedforward neural network with a sentence vector and an entity's word vector (Henaff et al., 2017) or hand-crafted features with word embeddings (Wiseman et al., 2016; Clark and Manning, 2016b). This study employs bi-RNN analogously to Kobayashi et al. (2016), which can access full context with powerful learnable units.

In the task setting proposed in this study, a model must capture the meaning of a given specific word from a small number of its contexts in a given discourse. The task could also be seen as novel one-shot learning (Fei-Fei et al., 2006) of word meanings. One-shot learning for NLP like this has been little studied, with the exception of the study by Vinyals et al. (2016), which used a task in which the context of a target word is matched with a different context of the same word.

7   Conclusion

This study addressed the problem of identifying the meaning of unknown words or entities in a discourse with respect to the word embedding approaches used in neural language models. We proposed a method for on-the-fly construction and exploitation of word embeddings in both the input layer and output layer of a neural model by tracking contexts. This extended the dynamic entity representation presented in Kobayashi et al. (2016), and incorporated a copy mechanism proposed independently by Gu et al. (2016) and Gulcehre et al. (2016). In the course of the study, we also constructed a new task and dataset, called *Anonymized Language Modeling*, for evaluating the ability of a model to capture word meanings while reading. Experiments conducted using our novel dataset demonstrated that the RNN language model variants proposed in this study outperformed the baseline model. More detailed analysis indicated that the proposed method was particularly successful in capturing the meaning of an unknown words from texts containing few instances.

Acknowledgments

This work was supported by JSPS KAKENHI Grant Number 15H01702 and JSPS KAKENHI Grant Number 15H05318. We thank members of Preferred Networks, Inc., Makoto Miwa and Daichi Mochihashi for suggestive discussions.

References

Dzmitry Bahdanau, Tom Bosc, Stanisław Jastrzębski, Edward Grefenstette, Pascal Vincent, and Yoshua Bengio. 2017. Learning to compute word embeddings on the fly. *arXiv preprint arXiv:1706.00286*.

Dzmitry Bahdanau, Kyunghyun Cho, and Yoshua Bengio. 2015. Neural machine translation by jointly learning to align and translate. In *Proceedings of ICLR*.

Yoshua Bengio, Réjean Ducharme, Pascal Vincent, and Christian Jauvin. 2003. A neural probabilistic language model. *JOURNAL OF MACHINE LEARNING RESEARCH*, 3:1137–1155.

Ciprian Chelba, Tomas Mikolov, Mike Schuster, Qi Ge, Thorsten Brants, Phillipp Koehn, and Tony Robinson. 2014. One billion word benchmark for measuring progress in statistical language modeling. In *Proceedings of INTERSPEECH*, pages 2635–2639.

Kyunghyun Cho, Bart van Merrienboer, Çaglar Gülçehre, Dzmitry Bahdanau, Fethi Bougares, Holger Schwenk, and Yoshua Bengio. 2014. Learning phrase representations using RNN encoder-decoder for statistical machine translation. In *Proceedings of EMNLP*.

Heeyoul Choi, Kyunghyun Cho, and Yoshua Bengio. 2017. Context-dependent word representation for neural machine translation. *Computer Speech & Language*, 45:149–160.

Kevin Clark and Christopher D. Manning. 2016a. Deep reinforcement learning for mention-ranking coreference models. In *Proceedings of EMNLP*, pages 2256–2262.

Kevin Clark and Christopher D. Manning. 2016b. Improving coreference resolution by learning entity-level distributed representations. In *Proceedings of ACL*, pages 643–653.

Yann N. Dauphin, Angela Fan, Michael Auli, and David Grangier. 2016. Language Modeling with Gated Convolutional Networks. *arXiv preprint arXiv:1612.08083*.

Bhuwan Dhingra, Zhilin Yang, William W Cohen, and Ruslan Salakhutdinov. 2017. Linguistic knowledge as memory for recurrent neural networks. *arXiv preprint arXiv:1703.02620*.

Li Fei-Fei, Rob Fergus, and Pietro Perona. 2006. One-shot learning of object categories. *IEEE transactions on TPAMI*, 28(4):594–611.

Edouard Grave, Armand Joulin, and Nicolas Usunier. 2017. Improving neural language models with a continuous cache. In *Proceedings of ICLR*.

Jiatao Gu, Zhengdong Lu, Hang Li, and O.K. Victor Li. 2016. Incorporating copying mechanism in sequence-to-sequence learning. In *Proceedings of ACL*, pages 1631–1640.

Caglar Gulcehre, Sungjin Ahn, Ramesh Nallapati, Bowen Zhou, and Yoshua Bengio. 2016. Pointing the unknown words. In *Proceedings of ACL*, pages 140–149.

Kelvin Guu, John Miller, and Percy Liang. 2015. Traversing knowledge graphs in vector space. In *Proceedings of EMNLP*, pages 318–327.

Mikael Henaff, Jason Weston, Arthur Szlam, Antoine Bordes, and Yann LeCun. 2017. Tracking the world state with recurrent entity networks. In *Proceedings of ICLR*.

Karl Moritz Hermann, Tomas Kocisky, Edward Grefenstette, Lasse Espeholt, Will Kay, Mustafa Suleyman, and Phil Blunsom. 2015. Teaching machines to read and comprehend. In *Proceedings of NIPS*, pages 1684–1692.

Sepp Hochreiter and Jürgen Schmidhuber. 1997. Long short-term memory. *Neural computation*, 9(8):1735–1780.

Yangfeng Ji, Chenhao Tan, Sebastian Martschat, Yejin Choi, and Noah A. Smith. 2017. Dynamic entity representations in neural language models. In *Proceedings of EMNLP*.

Rafal Jozefowicz, Oriol Vinyals, Mike Schuster, Noam Shazeer, and Yonghui Wu. 2016. Exploring the limits of language modeling. *arXiv preprint arXiv:1602.02410*.

Yoon Kim, Yacine Jernite, David Sontag, and Alexander M. Rush. 2016. Character-aware neural language models. In *Proceedings of AAAI*, pages 2741–2749.

Diederik Kingma and Jimmy Ba. 2015. Adam: A method for stochastic optimization. In *Proceedings of ICLR*.

Sosuke Kobayashi, Ran Tian, Naoaki Okazaki, and Kentaro Inui. 2016. Dynamic entity representation with max-pooling improves machine reading. In *Proceedings of NAACL-HLT*, pages 850–855.

Jiwei Li and Dan Jurafsky. 2015. Do multi-sense embeddings improve natural language understanding? In *Proceedings of EMNLP*, pages 1722–1732.

Minh-Thang Luong and D. Christopher Manning. 2016. Achieving open vocabulary neural machine translation with hybrid word-character models. In *Proceedings of ACL*, pages 1054–1063.

Thang Luong, Ilya Sutskever, Quoc Le, Oriol Vinyals, and Wojciech Zaremba. 2015. Addressing the rare word problem in neural machine translation. In *Proceedings of ACL*, pages 11–19.

Oren Melamud, Jacob Goldberger, and Ido Dagan. 2016. context2vec: Learning generic context embedding with bidirectional lstm. In *Proceedings of CoNLL*, pages 51–61.

Stephen Merity, Caiming Xiong, James Bradbury, and Richard Socher. 2017. Pointer sentinel mixture models. In *Proceedings of ICLR*.

Tomáš Mikolov, Martin Karafiát, Lukáš Burget, Jan Černocký, and Sanjeev Khudanpur. 2010. Recurrent neural network based language model. In *Proceedings of INTERSPEECH*, pages 1045–1048.

Tomas Mikolov, Ilya Sutskever, Kai Chen, Gregory S. Corrado, and Jeffrey Dean. 2013. Distributed representations of words and phrases and their compositionality. In *Proceedings of NIPS*, pages 3111–3119.

Vinod Nair and Geoffrey E. Hinton. 2010. Rectified linear units improve restricted boltzmann machines. In *Proceedings of ICML*, pages 807–814. Omnipress.

Haoruo Peng and Dan Roth. 2016. Two discourse driven language models for semantics. In *Proceedings of ACL*, pages 290–300.

Sameer Pradhan, Alessandro Moschitti, Nianwen Xue, Olga Uryupina, and Yuchen Zhang. 2012. CoNLL-2012 shared task: Modeling multilingual unrestricted coreference in OntoNotes. In *Proceedings of CoNLL*.

Mike Schuster and Kaisuke Nakajima. 2012. Japanese and korean voice search. In *Proceedings of ICASSP*, pages 5149–5152.

Rico Sennrich, Barry Haddow, and Alexandra Birch. 2016. Neural machine translation of rare words with subword units. In *Proceedings of ACL*, pages 1715–1725.

Iulian V. Serban, Alessandro Sordoni, Yoshua Bengio, Aaron Courville, and Joelle Pineau. 2016. Building end-to-end dialogue systems using generative hierarchical neural network models. In *Proceedings of AAAI*, pages 3776–3783.

Sainbayar Sukhbaatar, Arthur Szlam, Jason Weston, and Rob Fergus. 2015. End-to-end memory networks. In *Proceedings of NIPS*, pages 2440–2448.

Seiya Tokui, Kenta Oono, Shohei Hido, and Justin Clayton. 2015. Chainer: a next-generation open source framework for deep learning. In *Proceedings of Workshop on LearningSys in NIPS 28*.

Ke Tran, Arianna Bisazza, and Christof Monz. 2016. Recurrent memory networks for language modeling. In *Proceedings of NAACL-HLT*, pages 321–331.

Oriol Vinyals, Charles Blundell, Tim Lillicrap, koray kavukcuoglu, and Daan Wierstra. 2016. Matching networks for one shot learning. In *Proceedings of NIPS*, pages 3630–3638.

Tian Wang and Kyunghyun Cho. 2016. Larger-context language modelling with recurrent neural network. In *Proceedings of ACL*, pages 1319–1329.

Jason Weston, Antoine Bordes, Sumit Chopra, and Tomas Mikolov. 2015. Towards ai-complete question answering: A set of prerequisite toy tasks. *arXiv preprint arXiv:1502.05698*.

Sam Wiseman, Alexander M. Rush, and Stuart M. Shieber. 2016. Learning global features for coreference resolution. In *Proceedings of NAACL-HLT*, pages 994–1004.

Zichao Yang, Phil Blunsom, Chris Dyer, and Wang Ling. 2017. Reference-aware language models. In *Proceedings of EMNLP*.

Using Explicit Discourse Connectives in Translation for Implicit Discourse Relation Classification

Wei Shi[1], Frances Yung[1], Raphael Rubino[1,3] and Vera Demberg[1,2]

[1]Dept. of Language Science and Technology
[2]Dept. of Mathematics and Computer Science, Saarland University
[3]German Research Center for Artificial Intelligence (DFKI)
Saarland Informatic Campus, 66123 Saarbrücken, Germany
{w.shi, frances, vera}@coli.uni-saarland.de
raphael.rubino@dfki.de

Abstract

Implicit discourse relation recognition is an extremely challenging task due to the lack of indicative connectives. Various neural network architectures have been proposed for this task recently, but most of them suffer from the shortage of labeled data. In this paper, we address this problem by procuring additional training data from parallel corpora: When humans translate a text, they sometimes add connectives (a process known as *explicitation*). We automatically back-translate it into an English connective, and use it to infer a label with high confidence. We show that a training set several times larger than the original training set can be generated this way. With the extra labeled instances, we show that even a simple bidirectional Long Short-Term Memory Network can outperform the current state-of-the-art.

1 Introduction

When humans comprehend language, their interpretation consists of more than just the sum of the content of the sentences. Additional semantic relations (known as coherence relations or discourse relations) are inferred between sentences in the text. Identification of discourse relations is useful for various NLP applications such as question answering (Jansen et al., 2014; Liakata et al., 2013), summarization (Maskey and Hirschberg, 2005; Yoshida et al., 2014; Gerani et al., 2014), machine translation (Guzmán et al., 2014; Meyer et al., 2015) and information extraction (Cimiano et al., 2005). Recently, the task has drawn increasing attention, including two CoNLL shared tasks (Xue et al., 2015, 2016).

Discourse relations are sometimes expressed with an *explicit* discourse connective (DC), such as "because", "but", "if". Example 1 shows an explicit discourse relation marked by "because"; the text spans between which the relation holds are marked as *Arg1* and *Arg2*. DCs serve as strong cues and allow us to classify discourse relations with high accuracy (Pitler et al., 2008, 2009; Lin et al., 2014).

However, more than half of the discourse relations in a text are not signalled by a connective. See for example 2: a contrastive relation can be inferred between the text spans marked as *Arg1* and *Arg2*. Implicit relation classification is very challenging and represents a bottleneck of the entire discourse parsing system.

1. *[The city's Campaign Finance Board has refused to pay Mr Dinkins $95,142 in matching funds]$_{Arg1}$* **because** *[his campaign records are incomplete.]$_{Arg2}$*

   — Explicit, Contingency.Cause

2. *[They desperately needed somebody who showed they cared for them, who loved them.]$_{Arg1}$ [The last thing they needed was another drag-down blow.]$_{Arg2}$*

   —Implicit, Comparison.Contrast

In order to classify an implicit discourse relation, it is necessary to represent the semantic content of the relational arguments, which may give a cue to the coherence relation, e.g. "care" – "drag-down blow" in 2. Early methods have focused on designing various features to overcome data sparsity and more effectively identify relevant concepts in the two discourse relational arguments. (Lin et al., 2009; Zhou et al., 2010; Biran and McKeown, 2013; Park and Cardie, 2012; Rutherford and Xue, 2014), while recent efforts use distributed representations with neural network architectures (Zhang et al., 2015; Ji and Eisenstein,

Proceedings of the The 8th International Joint Conference on Natural Language Processing, pages 484–495,
Taipei, Taiwan, November 27 – December 1, 2017 ©2017 AFNLP

2015; Ji et al., 2016; Chen et al., 2016; Qin et al., 2016, 2017). Both streams of methods suffer from insufficient annotated data (Wang et al., 2015), since the Penn Discourse Treebank (PDTB) (Prasad et al., 2008), which is the discourse annotated resource mostly used by the community, consists of just 12763 implicit instances in the usual training set and 761 relations in the test set. Some second-level relations only have about a dozen instances. It is therefore crucial to obtain extra data for machine learning.

In this paper, we propose a simple approach to automatically extract samples of implicit discourse relations from parallel corpus via back-translation: Our approach is motivated by the fact that humans sometimes omit connectives during translation (*implicitation*), or insert connectives not originally present in the source text (*explicitation*) (Laali and Kosseim, 2014; Koppel and Ordan, 2011; Cartoni et al., 2011; Hoek and Zufferey, 2015; Zufferey, 2016). When explicitating an implicit relation, the human translator is, in other words, disambiguating the source implicit relation with an explicit DC in the target language.

Our contribution is twofold: Firstly, we propose a pipeline to automatically label English implicit discourse relation samples based on explicitation of DCs in human translation, which is the target side of a parallel corpus. Secondly, we show that the extra instances mined by the proposed method improve the performance of a standard neural classifier by a large margin, when evaluated on the PDTB 2.0 benchmark test set as well as by cross-validation (Shi and Demberg, 2017).

2 Related Work

Early works addressing discourse relation parsing were trying to classify unmarked discourse relations by training on explicit discourse relations with the marker been removed (Marcu and Echihabi, 2002). While this method promised to provide almost unlimited training data, it was shown that explicit relations differ in systematic ways from implicit relations (Asr and Demberg, 2012), so that performance on implicits is very poor when learning on explicits only (Sporleder and Lascarides, 2008).

The release of PDTB (Prasad et al., 2008), the largest available corpus which annotates implicit examples, lead to substantial improvements in classification of implicit relations, and spurred a variety of approaches to the task, including feature-based methods (Pitler et al., 2009; Lin et al., 2009; Park and Cardie, 2012; Biran and McKeown, 2013; Rutherford and Xue, 2014) and neural network models (Zhang et al., 2015; Ji and Eisenstein, 2015; Ji et al., 2016; Chen et al., 2016; Qin et al., 2016, 2017). However, the limited size of the annotated corpus, in combination with the difficulty of the task of inferring the type of relation between given text spans, presents a problem both in training (Rutherford et al. (2017) find that a simple feed-forward architecture can outperform more complex architectures, and argues that the larger number of parameters can not be estimated adequately on the small amount of training data) and testing (Shi and Demberg (2017) report experiments showing that results on the standard test set are not reliable due to the small set of just 761 relations).

Data extension has therefore been a longstanding goal in discourse relation classification. The main idea has been to select explicit discourse instances that are similar to implicit ones to add to the training set. Wang et al. (2012) proposed to differentiate typical and atypical examples for each discourse relation, and augment training data for implicits only by typical explicits. In a similar vein, Rutherford and Xue (2015) proposed criteria for selecting among explicitly marked relations ones that contain discourse connectives which can be omitted without changing the interpretation of the discourse. These relations are then added to the implicit instances in training.

On the other hand, Lan et al. (2013) presented multi-task learning based systems, which in addition to the main implicit relation classification task, contain the task of predicting previously removed connectives for explicit relations, and profit from shared representations between the tasks. Similarly, Hernault et al. (2010) observes features that occur in both implicit and explicit discourse relations, and exploit such feature co-occurrence to extend the features for classifying implicits using explicitly marked relations. Mihăilă and Ananiadou (2014) and Hidey and McKeown (2016) proposed semi-supervised learning and self-learning methods to improve recognition of patterns that typically signal causal discourse relations.

The approach proposed here differs from previous approaches, because we extend our training data only by originally implicit relations, and obtain the label through the disambiguation that sometimes happens in human translation.

Parallel corpora have been exploited as a resource of discourse relation data in previous work but have mostly been used with goals different from ours: Cartoni et al. (2013) and Meyer et al. (2015) use parallel corpora to label and disambiguate discourse connectives in the target language based on explicitly marked English relations, in order to help machine translation. A second application has been to project discourse annotation from English onto other languages through parallel corpora, in order to construct discourse annotated resources for the target language (Versley, 2010; Zhou et al., 2012; Laali and Kosseim, 2014).

The approach that is in spirit most similar to ours is by Wu et al. (2016), who extracted bilingual-constrained synthetic implicit data from a sentence-aligned English-Chinese corpus and got improvements by incorporating these data via a multi-task neural network on the 4-way classification.

3 Method

Our proposed method aims at sentence pairs in the parallel corpora where an *implicit* discourse relations on the source English side has been translated by human translators into an explicitly marked relation on the target side. The inserted connective hence disambiguates the originally implicit relation, and the discourse relation can be classified with confidence (under the assumption that the same discourse relation holds in the original source text).

The pipeline of our approach is detailed in below steps.

1. The target side of a sentence-aligned parallel corpus, with English as the source text, is back-translated to English using a pre-trained machine translation system.

2. An end-to-end discourse relation parser for English is run on both the source side and the back-translated target side. The parser will output a list of explicit and implicit relations, including the relation sense and argument spans of each relation.

3. Implicit-to-explicit discourse relation alignments are identified according to the output

of the end-to-end parser. Implicit relations in the PDTB are only ever annotated between consecutive sentences. Therefore, we specifically extract pairs of consecutive sentences on the source English side:

- that are identified as the *Arg1* and *Arg2* of an *implicit* discourse relation[1];
- whose corresponding back-translated target sentences are identified as the *Arg1* and *Arg2* of an *explicit* relation;
- that are not part of the *Arg1* or *Arg2* of any other discourse relations[2].

4. Label the source English implicit relation with the relation class of the explicit relation in back-translated target text. The two consecutive sentences are marked as *Arg1* and *Arg2* respectively.

Figure 1 illustrates the pipeline of our approach, which takes an English-to-French parallel corpus as input and outputs a list of implicit discourse relations, each containing two arguments from the source English text and a relation class according to the back-translated French DC.

We then compare the performance of a neural implicit discourse relation classifier trained with the annotated implicit relation samples in PDTB alone and also with the extra training samples mined from the parallel corpus. The classifier performance is evaluated on the standard PDTB implicit relation test set and by cross-validation.

3.1 Advantages of using back-translation

In the proposed method, we disambiguate implicit relations according to the explicitated translation. Instead of directly classifying the explicit relation in the target language, we back-translate the target text to the source language by machine translation (MT) because:

- Discourse parsers on low-resource languages do not perform well, or are even not available.

- Different languages have different sets of discourse relation classes defined. By the means of back-translation, we can use an English discourse parser on the target text, and thus

---

[1] Relations signaled by *Alternative Lexicalization* are counted as implicit relations and extracted as samples. However, *NoRel* and *EntRel* are excluded.

[2] This restriction avoids mis-alignment of relations between source and target texts.

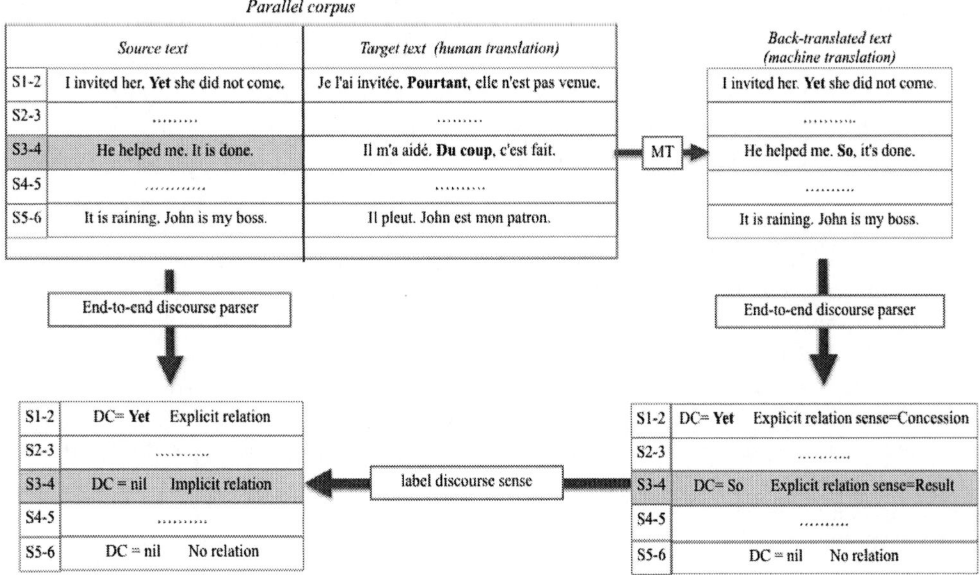

Figure 1: Pipeline showing how an implicit discourse relation sample, sentence pair 3-4, is extracted and labeled using a parallel corpus.

label the implicit relations with the same set of relation labels defined for English.

- The quality of the MT system has limited impact on our approach. Since the DC tokens are powerful features to disambiguate an explicit relation, limited contextual features are required. We just need correct translation of the explicit DC tokens, irrespective of word order and the rest of the translation.

3.2 Inter-sentential and intra-sentential relations

Only inter-sentential implicit relations are annotated in the PDTB, due to time and resource constraints (Prasad et al., 2008). However, this does not mean that implicit relations only hold between consecutive sentences.

We decided to extract intra-sentential relation samples from the parallel corpus based on two motivations: Firstly, we hypothesize that intra-sentential implicit relations share similar features as inter-sentential ones. Including both types may hence increase dataset size. In fact, we will see in the experiment results that intra-sentential training samples largely improve classification of implicit relations, even though the test data from PDTB contains inter-sentential samples only. An analysis on what we learn from the intra-sentential samples is presented in Section 6.1.

Secondly, intra-sentential relations can potentially be identified with higher reliability: Parallel corpora are typically sentence-aligned. This makes it a lot easier to extract sentences that are detected by the end-to-end discourse relation parser as explicit in the (back-)translation target side but not on the original source side, without needing to worry about whether any sentences in the dataset were removed or the order changed during preprocessing (which would be detrimental for detecting intra-sentential relations).

3.3 Argument spans

It is possible but not entirely trivial to determine the argument spans of the discourse relations labeled with the back-translation method. In this paper, we chose a neural network model that concatenates the *Arg1* and *Arg2* representations (see Section 4.4), so that determining exact text spans of Arg1 and Arg2 was not necessary. We are not the first one to do like this, in the work by Rönnqvist et al. (2017), they modeled the *Arg1-Arg2* pairs as a joint sequence and did not compute intermediate representations of arguments separately, to make it more generally flexible in modeling discourse units and easily extend to additional contexts.

4 Experiment

4.1 Data

Parallel Corpora The corpora used for the extraction of implicit discourse relation samples are publicly available bilingual English-French parallel datasets compiled by Rabinovich et al. (2015).[3] They consist of European parliamentary proceedings, literary works and the Hansard corpus – genres that are different from the PDTB, because we want to expand the diversity of discourse relation samples available in the PDTB. These corpora contain a total of $\sim$ 1.9M sentence pairs with an average of 22.7 words per English sentence. Each corpus contains an originally written part in English (used as target for the MT system) and its corresponding human translation in French (used as source). We use the same corpora to train the French–English MT system (Section 4.2), to back-translate the French side into English and to extract additional discourse training data.

The Penn Discourse Treebank (PDTB) We use the Penn Discourse Treebank 2.0 (Prasad et al., 2008) for the training and testing of the implicit discourse relation classifier. PDTB is the largest available manually annotated corpus of explicit and implicit discourse relations based on one million word tokens from the Wall Street Journal. Each discourse relation is annotated with at most two senses from a three-level hierarchy of discourse relations. The first level roughly categorizes the relations into four major classes, each of which is further categorized in to more distinct relation types. Conventionally, discourse relation classifiers are either evaluated by the accuracy of the first-level 4-way classification(Pitler et al., 2009; Rutherford and Xue, 2014; Chen et al., 2016), or the second-level 11-way classification (Lin et al., 2009; Ji and Eisenstein, 2015; Qin et al., 2016, 2017).

4.2 Machine Translation System

We train an MT system to back-translate the target side of the parallel corpus to English. To produce the highest-quality back-translation, we use a neural MT system trained on the same parallel corpus. The system is implemented by Open-source Neural Machine Translation (OpenNMT) (Klein et al., 2017). Source words are first mapped to word vectors and then fed into a recurrent neural network.

At each target time step, *attention* is applied over the source RNN and combined with the current hidden state to produce a prediction of the next word, and this prediction would be fed back into the target RNN.

We evaluate the MT system on *newstest2014* and *newsdiscusstest2015*, reaching 24.63 and 22.58 BLEU respectively. The French side of the training data back-translated into English is evaluated against the originally written English source, leading to a BLEU score of 34.17.[4] The evaluation of the back-translated corpus indicates that the source text is not exactly reproduced. Critically, we assume that the MT system preserves the explicitness of the target DCs, instead of expliciting or implicitating DCs as in the human translation.

4.3 End-to-end discourse parser

We employ the PDTB-style End-to-End Discourse Parser (Lin et al., 2014) to identify and classify the explicit instances from the back-translated English sentences. It achieved about 87% F1 score for explicit relations on level-2 types, even higher than human agreement of 84%. The accuracy on explicit DC identification is 96%.

On the source side, the end-to-end parser is applied to pick implicit relations from other types of relations, i.e. explicit relations or *no relation*, in order to extract implicit-to-explicit DC translation from the parallel corpus[5]. On the back-translation, the end-to-end parser is applied to identify only explicitly marked discourse relations.

4.4 Implicit relation classification model

We use a Bidirectional Long Short-Term Memory (LSTM) network as the implicit relation classification model to evaluate the samples extracted by the proposed method. This architecture inspects both left and right contextual information and has been proven effective in relation classification (Zhou et al., 2016; Rönnqvist et al., 2017).

The model is illustrated in Figure 2, where each word from the two discourse relational arguments is represented as a vector, which is found through a look-up word embedding. Given the word representations $[\mathbf{w}_1,\mathbf{w}_2,...,\mathbf{w}_n]$ as the input sequence, an

---

[3]All corpora are available at http://cl.haifa.ac.il/projects/translationese/

[4]Case sensitive BLEU implemented in *mteval-v13a.pl*. Test sets available at http://www.statmt.org/wmt15/translation-task.html

[5] The non-explicit sense classification module of this parser is thus not used in the proposed method.

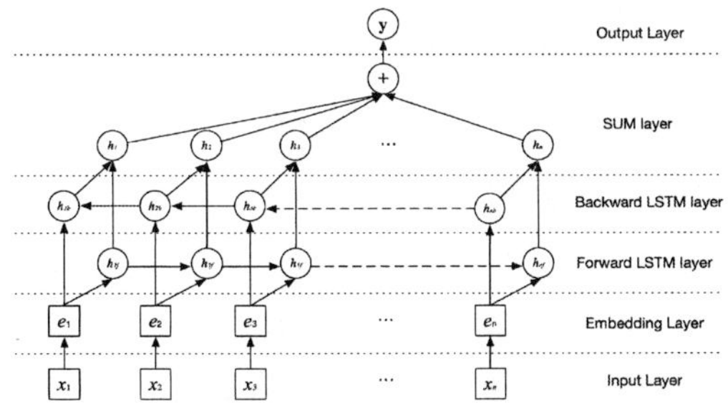

Figure 2: The bidirectional LSTM Network for the task of implicit discourse relation classification.

LSTM computes the state sequence $[\mathbf{h}_1, \mathbf{h}_2, ..., \mathbf{h}_n]$ with the following equations:

$$\mathbf{i}_t = \sigma(\mathbf{W}_w^i \mathbf{w}_t + \mathbf{W}_h^i \mathbf{h}_{t-1} + \mathbf{W}_c^i \mathbf{w}_{t-1} + \mathbf{b}_i)$$

$$\mathbf{f}_t = \sigma(\mathbf{W}_w^f \mathbf{w}_t + \mathbf{W}_h^f \mathbf{h}_{t-1} + \mathbf{W}_c^f \mathbf{w}_{t-1} + \mathbf{b}_f)$$

$$\mathbf{g}_t = tanh(\mathbf{W}_w^c \mathbf{w}_t + \mathbf{W}_h^c \mathbf{h}_{t-1} + \mathbf{b}_c)$$

$$\mathbf{c}_t = \mathbf{f}_t \odot \mathbf{c}_{t-1} + \mathbf{i}_t \odot \mathbf{g}_t$$

$$\mathbf{o}_t = \sigma(\mathbf{W}_w^o \mathbf{w}_t + \mathbf{W}_h^o \mathbf{h}_{t-1} + \mathbf{b}_o)$$

$$\mathbf{h}_t = tanh(\mathbf{c}_t) \odot \mathbf{o}_t$$

The forward and backward LSTM layers traverse the sequence $\boldsymbol{e}_i$, producing sequences of vectors $\boldsymbol{h}_{if}$ and $\boldsymbol{h}_{ib}$ respectively, which are summed together in the coming sum layer.

Following the preprocessing method in (Lin et al., 2009), relations with too few instances (*Contingency.Condition, Pragmatic Condition; Comparison.Pragmatic Contrast, Pragmatic Concession; Expansion.Exception*) are removed during training and evaluation, resulting in 11 types of relations. Among instances annotated with two relation senses, we only use the first sense.

The model is implemented in Keras[6], which is capable of running on top of Theano. We use word embeddings of 300 dimensions, which are trained on the original English side of the parallel corpora as well as PDTB with the Skip-gram architecture in *Word2Vec* (Mikolov et al., 2013). We initial-

[6]https://keras.io/

Relation	intra-	inter-	Total
explicit → explicit	199,047	111,090	310,137
explicit → implicit	101,381	29,964	131,345
implicit → explicit	77,228	25,086	102,314

[1] "→" means from source to target side.

Table 1: Numbers of intra/inter-sentence samples extracted from parallel corpora.

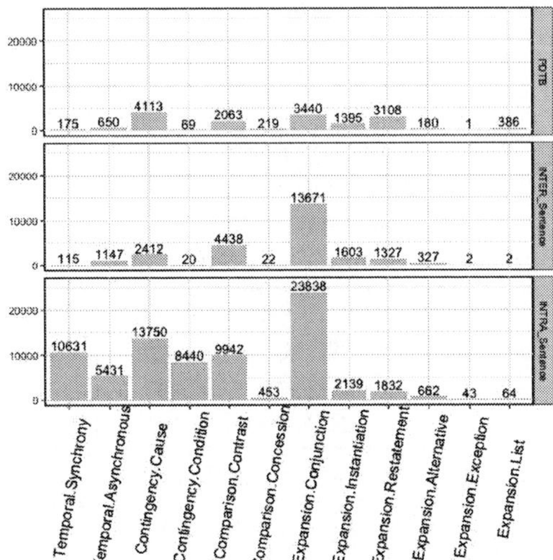

Figure 3: Relation sense distribution of implicit relations in PDTB and the extra intra- and inter-sentence samples

ize the weights with uniform random; use standard cross-entropy as our loss function; employ Adagrad as the optimization algorithm of choice and set dropout layers after the embedding layer and output layer with a drop rate of 0.2 and 0.5 respectively. Each LSTM has a vector dimension of 300, matching the embedding size.

We split the PDTB data and evaluate the classifier in two settings. Firstly, we adopt the standard PDTB splitting convention, where section 2-21, 22, and 23 are used as train, validation and test sets respectively (Lin et al., 2009). Secondly, we conduct 10-fold cross validation on the whole corpus including sections 0-24, as advocated in (Shi and Demberg, 2017). And extra samples are only added into training folds in the CV setting, which means that testing fold consists of instances from PDTB only. Models trained with and without extra samples we extracted, on top of the PDTB data, are compared.

5   Distribution of additional instances

In total, $102,314$ implicit discourse relation samples are extracted, of which $25,086$ are inter-sentential relations and $77,228$ are intra-sentential[7]. Inter-sentential relations are much less abundant because stricter screening strategy is applied (the end of point 3 in Section 3). From Table 1 we can also see that majority of DCs in the

[7]A dataset containing these additional instances will be made available to researchers upon publication of the paper.

Models		PDTB Test Set	Cross Validation
Most common class		25.36	25.59
Lin et al. (2009)		40.20	-
Qin et al. (2016)		43.81	-
Qin et al. (2017)		44.65	-
Rutherford et al. (2017)		39.56	-
Shi and Demberg (2017) (no surface features)		37.68	34.44
Ours	PDTB only	34.32	30.01
	PDTB + inter-sentential samples	42.29	34.14
	PDTB + intra-sentential samples	44.29	35.08
	PDTB + all samples	**45.50**	**37.84**

[1] "-" means no result currently.

Table 2: Accuracy of 11-way classification of implicit discourse relations on PDTB test set and by cross validation.

source side have been translated into the target side explicitly.

Figure 3 compares the distribution of relation senses among the annotated implicit relations in the PDTB and our extracted samples. The relation distribution generally corresponds to the distribution in PDTB, but some relations, such as *Temporal* and *Contingency.Condition*, are particularly numerous in the intra-sentential samples.

6 Results

We compare our model with current state-of-the-art models that were evaluated under the same setting (11-way classification, PDTB section 23 as test set) (Qin et al., 2016, 2017; Rutherford et al., 2017), as well as a model based on linguistic features (Lin et al., 2009) that uses this setting for evaluation.

Qin et al. (2017) developed an adversarial model, which consists of two CNNs in which arguments are represented separately, a four-layer Perceptron and a dense layer for classification, to enable an adaptive imitation scheme through competition between the implicit network and a rival feature discriminator. Our model substantially differs from that setup, as it uses a much simpler network architecture and represents the two discourse relation arguments jointly, i.e. without knowledge of the arguments' spans. We can see that our baseline model performs substantially less well than the state of the art, and also less well than (Shi and Demberg, 2017), who also use an LSTM but represent discourse relational arguments separately. As adding training data can be expected to

be largely orthogonal to the choice of classification model, we are here most interested in seeing whether adding the new instances improves over the baseline model with identical architecture.

Table 2 shows that including the extra inter- and intra-sentential instances leads to very substantial improvements in classification accuracy. Using the additional data, our method not only improves performance by 11%-points on the PDTB test set compared to training on the PDTB implicit relations only, but also outperforms much more complex neural network models (Qin et al., 2016, 2017) on this task.

The evaluation using cross-validation (around 8% point improvement over the baseline) furthermore shows that the obtained improvements do not only hold for the PDTB standard test set but also are stable across the whole PDTB data. These results strongly support the effectiveness of the implicit relation samples mined from parallel texts.

The accuracies reported for our models are based on 10 repeat-runs with different initializations of the network. This allows us to show the amount of variance in results we obtained in Figure 4. We found that results sometimes varied a lot between different runs, and would therefore like to encourage others in the field to also report variability due to initialization or other random factors. For instance, our best run achieved 49.84% accuracy on the PDTB test set trained with all additional instances, while mean performance for that setting is 45.50% accuracy. Variances were substantially smaller for the cross-validation setting, as the number of overall instances going into the

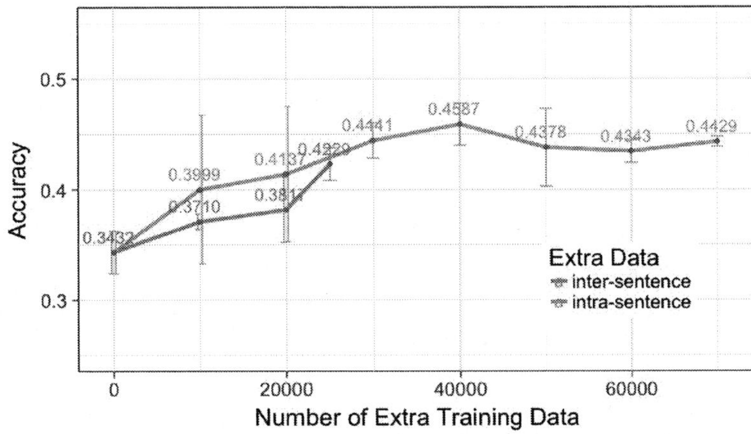

Figure 4: Average and variance of classification accuracy evaluated on the PDTB test set with different sample size.

evaluation is a lot larger in this setting, and hence yields more stable performance estimates.

6.1 Qualitative Analysis

In order to illustrate what kinds of instances our method extracts, we show an instances below. The underlined DC is the explicit DC identified in the back-translated target text; the discourse relation is automatically classified based on the back-translation.

3. *[Justice demands it.]*$_{Arg1}$ **_but_** *[The minister refuses.]*$_{Arg2}$
— *Comparison.Contrast*

One strength of the proposed method is that it can mine and label discourse relations that are not commonly regarded as discourse relations and hence not annotated in PDTB. Below are some examples where the bold DC was identified in the (back-)translation:

4. *A conservative member was kicked out of his caucus for defending Nova Scotians.*
— **because**, Contingency.Cause

5. *A failure to do so would affect our attitude to their eventual accession.*
—**if**, Contingency.Condition

These extra samples are in fact an invaluable resource of discourse-informative patterns, which are not available to discourse relation parsers that are trained only on the PDTB dataset. These cases provide evidence that our proposed method can not only provide instances that are similar to implicit labelled instances, but detect additional patterns, as attempted in (Mihăilă and Ananiadou, 2014; Hidey and McKeown, 2016) for causal relations, and generalize from the semantic content observed in such relations to actual implicit discourse relations.

For example, as reported in Section 5, numerous *Temporal* relations are mined from the parallel corpus. These include cases where the original text contained a verbal construction which expresses the temporal relation, which through back-translation gets expressed as a discourse relation, or where explicit relations include gerunds in the Arg2, e.g.

"any plan takes time to have the effect required" → *"before getting the effect required"*

"how much longer do women have to wait for fairness?" → *"before women have fairness."*

"having gone over the estimates" → *"after going over the estimates."*

(source text followed by (back-)translation, where the explicitated DC is underlined).

In this work, we only extracted inter- and intra-sentential discourse relations, but the method can be in principle extended to other discourse relations that are not annotated in the PDTB, such as implicit relation between non-consecutive sentences. Discourse parsers that identify a larger range of relations are more useful in end applications. More importantly, identification of discourse-informative linguistic patterns by the proposed method opens the opportunity to mine extra samples under a monolingual setting and further improve classification performance.

6.2 Quantitative Analysis

In order to get detailed insights on how much extra data is most beneficial to the task, we also trained our classifier with different numbers of additional extracted samples. Figure 4 compares the classification accuracy when training on incremental number of extra instances. We find that the performance increases with samples size, but plateaus after $40,000$ intra-sentential samples.

In fact, this sample size produces the highest averaged classification accuracy of 45.87%, which is even higher than our model which includes all extracted samples. A possible reason for not seeing further improvement in adding more intra-sentential examples is the difference in distribution and properties of these extra samples compared to the PDTB data. We also experimented with training on the parallel-text samples only (i.e., without any PDTB training samples), but the result was worse than using PDTB only. Adding more *inter-sentential* samples might further improve the performance, as these instances are closer to the PDTB data.

6.3 Methodological Discussion

Our proposed method uses back-translated target DCs to label implicit relations. The quality of the relation label is intrinsically subject to the translation policy of the parallel corpora and also extrinsically subject to the accuracy of explicit DC classification by the end-to-end parser and the quality of the MT system. For example, a particularly high proportion of *Contingency.Condition* relations is found in the intra-sentential samples. Analyzing these samples, we found numerous instances where the word 'if' is wrongly identified as a DC (e.g. *He asked if it was correct.*). It is not surprising to have noisy samples extracted because limited screening strategy is applied in the current method.

As a reference for the quality of the relation label produced, we analysed the intra-sentential relations in the parallel corpus that are explicit on the source side and also in the (back-)translation. We found that 68% of the originally explicit DCs are (back-)translated to the same explicit DCs and 75% to DCs of the same level-2 sense, according to automatic explicit DC classification of the end-to-end parser.

7 Conclusion and Future work

We showed that explicitation during human translation can provide a valuable signal for expanding datasets for implicit discourse relations. As the expansion of training instances is orthogonal to the mechanism of DR classification, this method can be applied to improve any methods of implicit DR classification.

We see plenty of room for further improvement by controlling the sample quality, such as selection based on explicit discourse connective identification confidence, restraining the discourse relation structure, identifying Arg1 and Arg2 such that approaches which use two separate representations for arguments instead of a single concatenated vector become possible, reducing language-specific bias by mining from parallel corpora of other language pairs, and fine-tuning the MT system for discourse connective translation. We leave the exploration of these areas to future work.

Acknowledgments

We would like to thank the anonymous reviewers for their careful reading, valuable and insightful comments. This work was funded by the German Research Foundation (DFG) as part of SFB 1102 "Information Density and Linguistic Encoding".

References

Fatemeh Torabi Asr and Vera Demberg. 2012. Implicitness of discourse relations. In *Proceedings of COLING 2012*. The COLING 2012 Organizing Committee, Mumbai, India, pages 2669–2684.

Or Biran and Kathleen McKeown. 2013. Aggregated word pair features for implicit discourse relation disambiguation. In *Proceedings of the 51st Annual Meeting of the Association for Computational Linguistics*. Association for Computational Linguistics, Sofia, Bulgaria, pages 69–73.

Bruno Cartoni, Sandrine Zufferey, and Thomas Meyer. 2013. Annotating the meaning of discourse connectives by looking at their translation: The translation-spotting technique. *D&D* 4(2):65–86.

Bruno Cartoni, Sandrine Zufferey, Thomas Meyer, and Andrei Popescu-Belis. 2011. How comparable are parallel corpora? measuring the distribution of general vocabulary and connectives. In *Proceedings of the 4th Workshop on Building and Using Comparable Corpora: Comparable Corpora and the Web*. Association for Computational Linguistics, pages 78–86.

Jifan Chen, Qi Zhang, Pengfei Liu, Xipeng Qiu, and Xuanjing Huang. 2016. Implicit discourse relation detection via a deep architecture with gated relevance network. In *Proceedings of the 54th Annual Meeting of the Association for Computational Linguistics*. Association for Computational Linguistics, pages 1726–1735.

Philipp Cimiano, Uwe Reyle, and Jasmin Šarić. 2005. Ontology-driven discourse analysis for information extraction. *Data & Knowledge Engineering* 55(1):59–83.

Shima Gerani, Yashar Mehdad, Giuseppe Carenini, Raymond T. Ng, and Bita Nejat. 2014. Abstractive summarization of product reviews using discourse structure. In *Proceedings of the 2014 Conference on Empirical Methods in Natural Language Processing*. Association for Computational Linguistics, pages 1602–1613.

Francisco Guzmán, Shafiq R. Joty, Lluís Màrquez, and Preslav Nakov. 2014. Using discourse structure improves machine translation evaluation. In *Proceedings of the 52nd Annual Meeting of the Association for Computational Linguistics*. Association for Computational Linguistics, pages 687–698.

Hugo Hernault, Danushka Bollegala, and Mitsuru Ishizuka. 2010. A semi-supervised approach to improve classification of infrequent discourse relations using feature vector extension. In *Proceedings of the 2010 Conference on Empirical Methods in Natural Language Processing*. Association for Computational Linguistics, pages 399–409.

Christopher Hidey and Kathleen McKeown. 2016. Identifying causal relation using parallel wikipedia articles. In *Proceedings of the 54th Annual Meeting of the Association for Computational Linguistics*. Association for Computational Linguistics, pages 1424–1433.

Jet Hoek and Sandrine Zufferey. 2015. Factors influencing the implicitation of discourse relations across languages. In *Proceedings 11th Joint ACL-ISO Workshop on Interoperable Semantic Annotation (isa-11)*. TiCC, Tilburg center for Cognition and Communication, pages 39–45.

Peter Jansen, Mihai Surdeanu, and Peter Clark. 2014. Discourse complements lexical semantics for nonfactoid answer reranking. In *Proceedings of the 52nd Annual Meeting of the Association for Computational Linguistics*. Association for Computational Linguistics, pages 977–986.

Yangfeng Ji and Jacob Eisenstein. 2015. One vector is not enough: Entity-augmented distributed semantics for discourse relations. *Transactions of the Association for Computational Linguistics* 3:329–344.

Yangfeng Ji, Gholamreza Haffari, and Jacob Eisenstein. 2016. A latent variable recurrent neural network for discourse relation language models. In *Proceedings of the 2016 Conference of the North American Chapter of the Association for Computational Linguistics on Human Language Technology*. Association for Computational Linguistics, pages 332–342.

Guillaume Klein, Yoon Kim, Yuntian Deng, Jean Senellart, and Alexander M. Rush. 2017. Opennmt: Open-source toolkit for neural machine translation. *arXiv preprint arXiv:1701.02810* .

Moshe Koppel and Noam Ordan. 2011. Translationese and its dialects. In *Proceedings of the 49th Annual Meeting of the Association for Computational Linguistics*. Association for Computational Linguistics, pages 1318–1326.

Majid Laali and Leila Kosseim. 2014. Inducing discourse connectives from parallel texts. In *Proceedings of the 25th International Conference on Computational Linguistics (COLING-2014)*. pages 610–619.

Man Lan, Yu Xu, Zheng-Yu Niu, et al. 2013. Leveraging synthetic discourse data via multi-task learning for implicit discourse relation recognition. In *Proceedings of the 51st Annual Meeting of the Association for Computational Linguistics*. Association for Computational Linguistics, pages 476–485.

Maria Liakata, Simon Dobnik, Shyamasree Saha, Colin R. Batchelor, and Dietrich Rebholz-Schuhmann. 2013. A discourse-driven content model for summarising scientific articles evaluated in a complex question answering task. In *Proceedings of the 2013 Conference on Empirical Methods in Natural Language Processing*. Association for Computational Linguistics, pages 747–757.

Ziheng Lin, Min-Yen Kan, and Hwee Tou Ng. 2009. Recognizing implicit discourse relations in the penn discourse treebank. In *Proceedings of the 2009 Conference on Empirical Methods in Natural Language Processing*. Association for Computational Linguistics, Singapore, pages 343–351.

Ziheng Lin, Hwee Tou Ng, and Min-Yen Kan. 2014. A pdtb-styled end-to-end discourse parser. *Natural Language Engineering* 20(02):151–184.

Daniel Marcu and Abdessamad Echihabi. 2002. An unsupervised approach to recognizing discourse relations. In *Proceedings of the 40th Annual Meeting on Association for Computational Linguistics*. Association for Computational Linguistics, pages 368–375.

Sameer Maskey and Julia Hirschberg. 2005. Comparing lexical, acoustic/prosodic, structural and discourse features for speech summarization. In *Ninth European Conference on Speech Communication and Technology*.

Thomas Meyer, Najeh Hajlaoui, and Andrei Popescu-Belis. 2015. Disambiguating discourse connectives for statistical machine translation. *Transactions on Audio, Speech, and Language Processing* 23(7):1184–1197.

Claudiu Mihăilă and Sophia Ananiadou. 2014. Semi-supervised learning of causal relations in biomedical scientific discourse. *Biomedical engineering online* 13(2):1.

Tomas Mikolov, Ilya Sutskever, Kai Chen, Greg S. Corrado, and Jeff Dean. 2013. Distributed representations of words and phrases and their compositionality. In *Advances in neural information processing systems*. pages 3111–3119.

Joonsuk Park and Claire Cardie. 2012. Improving implicit discourse relation recognition through feature set optimization. In *Proceedings of the 13th Annual Meeting of the Special Interest Group on Discourse and Dialogue*. Association for Computational Linguistics, pages 108–112.

Emily Pitler, Annie Louis, and Ani Nenkova. 2009. Automatic sense prediction for implicit discourse relations in text. In *Proceedings of the 47th Annual Meeting of the Association for Computational Linguistics*. Association for Computational Linguistics, Suntec, Singapore, pages 683–691.

Emily Pitler, Mridhula Raghupathy, Hena Mehta, Ani Nenkova, Alan Lee, and Aravind K. Joshi. 2008. Easily identifiable discourse relations. In *Proceedings of the 22nd International Conference on Computational Linguistics (COLING-2008)*. Manchester, UK, pages 85–88.

Rashmi Prasad, Nikhil Dinesh, Alan Lee, Eleni Miltsakaki, Livio Robaldo, Aravind K. Joshi, and Bonnie L. Webber. 2008. The penn discourse treebank 2.0. In *LREC*. European Language Resources Association, Marrakech, Morocco.

Lianhui Qin, Zhisong Zhang, and Hai Zhao. 2016. Implicit discourse relation recognition with context-aware character-enhanced embeddings. In *Proceedings of COLING 2016, the 26th International Conference on Computational Linguistics*.

Lianhui Qin, Zhisong Zhang, Hai Zhao, Zhiting Hu, and Eric P. Xing. 2017. Adversarial connective-exploiting networks for implicit discourse relation classification. In *Proceedings of the 55th Annual Meeting of the Association for Computational Linguistics (Volume 1: Long Papers)*. Association for Computational Linguistics, Vancouver, Canada, pages 1006–1017.

Ella Rabinovich, Shuly Wintner, and Ofek Luis Lewinsohn. 2015. The haifa corpus of translationese. *arXiv preprint arXiv:1509.03611*.

Samuel Rönnqvist, Niko Schenk, and Christian Chiarcos. 2017. A recurrent neural model with attention for the recognition of chinese implicit discourse relations. In *Proceedings of the 55th Annual Meeting of the Association for Computational Linguistics (Volume 2: Short Papers)*. Association for Computational Linguistics, Vancouver, Canada, pages 256–262.

Attapol Rutherford, Vera Demberg, and Nianwen Xue. 2017. A systematic study of neural discourse models for implicit discourse relation. In *Proceedings of the 15th Conference of the European Chapter of the Association for Computational Linguistics*. Association for Computational Linguistics, pages 281–291.

Attapol Rutherford and Nianwen Xue. 2014. Discovering implicit discourse relations through brown cluster pair representation and coreference patterns. In *Proceedings of the 14th Conference of the European Chapter of the Association for Computational Linguistics*. Association for Computational Linguistics, pages 645–654.

Attapol Rutherford and Nianwen Xue. 2015. Improving the inference of implicit discourse relations via classifying explicit discourse connectives. In *Proceedings of the 2015 Conference of the North American Chapter of the Association for Computational Linguistics on Human Language Technology*. Association for Computational Linguistics, pages 799–808.

Wei Shi and Vera Demberg. 2017. On the need of cross validation for discourse relation classification. In *Proceedings of the 15th Conference of the European Chapter of the Association for Computational Linguistics*. Association for Computational Linguistics, pages 150–156.

Caroline Sporleder and Alex Lascarides. 2008. Using automatically labelled examples to classify rhetorical relations: An assessment. *Natural Language Engineering* 14(3):369–416.

Yannick Versley. 2010. Discovery of ambiguous and unambiguous discourse connectives via annotation projection. In *AEPC*. pages 83–82.

Peilu Wang, Yao Qian, Frank K Soong, Lei He, and Hai Zhao. 2015. Word embedding for recurrent neural network based tts synthesis. In *Acoustics, Speech and Signal Processing (ICASSP), 2015 IEEE International Conference on*. IEEE, pages 4879–4883.

Xun Wang, Sujian Li, Jiwei Li, and Wenjie Li. 2012. Implicit discourse relation recognition by selecting typical training examples. In *Proceedings of the 24th International Conference on Computational Linguistics (COLING-2012)*. pages 2757–2772.

Changxing Wu, Xiaodong Shi, Yidong Chen, Yanzhou Huang, and Jinsong Su. 2016. Bilingually-constrained synthetic data for implicit discourse relation recognition. In *Proceedings of the 2016 Conference on Empirical Methods in Natural Language Processing*. Association for Computational Linguistics, pages 2306–2312.

Nianwen Xue, Hwee Tou Ng, Sameer Pradhan, Rashmi Prasad, Christopher Bryant, and Attapol Rutherford. 2015. The conll-2015 shared task on shallow discourse parsing. In *Proceedings of the CoNLL-15 Shared Task*. Association for Computational Linguistics, pages 1–16.

Nianwen Xue, Hwee Tou Ng, Attapol Rutherford, Bonnie Webber, Chuan Wang, and Hongmin Wang. 2016. Conll 2016 shared task on multilingual shallow discourse parsing. In *Proceedings of the CoNLL-16 shared task*. Association for Computational Linguistics, pages 1–19.

Yasuhisa Yoshida, Jun Suzuki, Tsutomu Hirao, and Masaaki Nagata. 2014. Dependency-based discourse parser for single-document summarization. In *Proceedings of the 2014 Conference on Empirical Methods in Natural Language Processing*. Association for Computational Linguistics, pages 1834–1839.

Biao Zhang, Jinsong Su, Deyi Xiong, Yaojie Lu, Hong Duan, and Junfeng Yao. 2015. Shallow convolutional neural network for implicit discourse relation recognition. In *Proceedings of the 2015 Conference on Empirical Methods in Natural Language Processing*. Association for Computational Linguistics, pages 2230–2235.

Lanjun Zhou, Wei Gao, Bin Li, Zhong Wei, and Kam-Fai Wong. 2012. Cross-lingual identification of ambiguous discourse connectives for resource-poor language. In *Proceedings of COLING 2012: Posters*. The COLING 2012 Organizing Committee, pages 1409–1418.

Peng Zhou, Wei Shi, Jun Tian, Zhenyu Qi, Bingchen Li, Hongwei Hao, and Bo Xu. 2016. Attention-based bidirectional long short-term memory networks for relation classification. In *Proceedings of the 54th Annual Meeting of the Association for Computational Linguistics*. Association for Computational Linguistics, pages 207–212.

Zhi-Min Zhou, Yu Xu, Zheng-Yu Niu, Man Lan, Jian Su, and Chew Lim Tan. 2010. Predicting discourse connectives for implicit discourse relation recognition. In *Proceedings of the 23rd International Conference on Computational Linguistics (COLING 2010)*. Association for Computational Linguistics, Beijing, China, pages 1507–1514.

Sandrine Zufferey. 2016. Discourse connectives across languages. *Languages in Contrast* 16(2):264–279.

Tag-Enhanced Tree-Structured Neural Networks for Implicit Discourse Relation Classification

Yizhong Wang[1] **Sujian Li**[1,2] **Jingfeng Yang**[1] **Xu Sun**[1] **Houfeng Wang**[1,2]

[1]Key Laboratory of Computational Linguistics, Peking University, MOE, China
[2]Collaborative Innovation Center for Language Ability, Xuzhou, Jiangsu, China
`{yizhong, lisujian, yjfllpyym, xusun, wanghf}@pku.edu.cn`

Abstract

Identifying implicit discourse relations between text spans is a challenging task because it requires understanding the meaning of the text. To tackle this task, recent studies have tried several deep learning methods but few of them exploited the syntactic information. In this work, we explore the idea of incorporating syntactic parse tree into neural networks. Specifically, we employ the Tree-LSTM model and Tree-GRU model, which are based on the tree structure, to encode the arguments in a relation. Moreover, we further leverage the constituent tags to control the semantic composition process in these tree-structured neural networks. Experimental results show that our method achieves state-of-the-art performance on PDTB corpus.

1 Introduction

It is widely agreed that text units such as clauses or sentences are usually not isolated. Instead, they correlate with each other to form coherent and meaningful discourse together. To analyze how text is organized, discourse parsing has gained much attention from both the linguistic (Weiss and Wodak, 2007; Tannen, 2012) and computational (Marcu, 1997; Soricut and Marcu, 2003) communities, but the current performance is far from satisfactory. The most challenging part is to identify the discourse relations between text spans, especially when the discourse connectives (e.g., "because" and "but") are not explicitly shown in the text. Due to the absence of such evident linguistic clues, trying to model and understand the meaning of the text becomes the key point in identifying such implicit relations.

Arg1: The index is intended to measure future economic performance

Arg2: A figure above 50 indicates the economy is likely to expand

(Expansion.Restatement.Specification, wsj_0233)

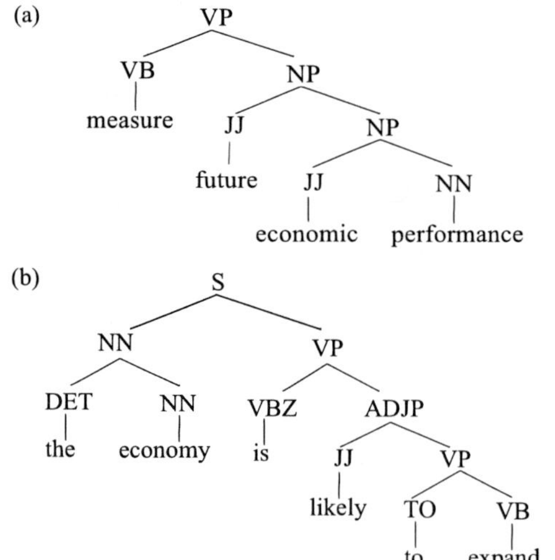

Figure 1: An example of two sentences with their discourse relation as *Expansion.Restatement.Specification*. Subfigure (a) and (b) are partial parse trees of the two important phrases with yellow background.

Previous studies in this field treat the task of recognizing implicit discourse relations as a classification problem and various techniques in semantic modeling have been adopted to encode the arguments in each relation, ranging from tradional feature-based models (Lin et al., 2009; Pitler et al., 2009) to the currently prevailing deep learning methods (Ji and Eisenstein, 2014; Liu and Li, 2016; Qin et al., 2017). Despite of the superior ability of the deep learning models, the syntactic

Proceedings of the The 8th International Joint Conference on Natural Language Processing, pages 496–505,
Taipei, Taiwan, November 27 – December 1, 2017 ©2017 AFNLP

information, which proves to be helpful for identifying discourse relations in many early studies (Subba and Di Eugenio, 2009; Lin et al., 2009), is seldom employed by recent work. Therefore we are curious to explore whether such missing syntactic information can be leveraged in deep learning methods to further improve the semantic modeling for implicit discourse relation classification.

Tree-structured neural networks, which recursively compose the representation of smaller text units into larger text spans along the syntactic parse tree, can tactfully combine syntatic tree structure with neural network models and recently achieve great success in several semantic modeling tasks (Eriguchi et al., 2016; Kokkinos and Potamianos, 2017; Chen et al., 2017). One useful property of these models is that the representation of phrases can be naturally captured while computing the representations from bottom up. Taking Figure 1 for an example, those highlighted phrases could provide important signals for classifying the discourse relation. Therefore, we will employ two latest tree-structuerd models, i.e. the Tree-LSTM model (Tai et al., 2015; Zhu et al., 2015) and the Tree-GRU model (Kokkinos and Potamianos, 2017), in our work. Hopefully, these models can learn to preserve or highlight such helpful phrasal information while encoding the arguments.

Another important syntactic signal comes from the constituent tags on the tree nodes (e.g., NP, VP, ADJP). Those tags, derived from the production rules, describe the generative process of text and therefore could indicate which part is more important in each constituent. For example, considering a node tagged with NP, its child node tagged with DT is usually neglectable. Thus we propose to incorporate this tag information into the tree-structured neural networks, where those constituent tags can be used to control the semantic compostion process.

Therefore, in this paper, we will approach the discourse relation classification task with two tree-structured neural networks proposed recently (Tree-LSTM and Tree-GRU). To our knowledge, this is the first time these models are applied to discourse relation classification. Moreover, we further enhance these models by leveraging the constituent tags to compute the gates in these models. Experiments on PDTB 2.0 (Prasad et al., 2008) show that the models we propose can achieve state-of-the-art results.

2 Related Work

2.1 Implicit Discourse Relation Classication

Discourse relation identification is an important but difficult sub-component of discourse analysis. One fundamental step forward recently is the release of the large-scale Penn Discourse TreeBank (PDTB) (Prasad et al., 2008), which annotates discourse relations with their two textual arguments over the 1 million word Wall Street Journal corpus. The discourse relations in PDTB are broadly categorized as either "Explicit" or "Implicit" according to whether there are connectives in the original text that can indicate the sense of the relations. In the absence of explicit connectives, identifying the sense of the relations has proved to be much more difficult (Park and Cardie, 2012; Rutherford and Xue, 2014) since the inferring is solely based on the arguments.

Prior work usually tackles this task of implicit discourse relation identification as a classification problem with the classes defined in PDTB corpus. Early attempts use traditional various feature-based methods and the work inspiring us most is Lin et al. (2009), in which they show that the syntactic parse structure can provide useful signals for discourse relation classification. More specifically they employ the production rules with constituent tags (e.g., SBJ) as features and get competitive performance. Recently, with the popularity of deep learning methods, many cutting-edge models are also applied to our task of implicit discourse relation classification. Qin et al. (2016) tries to model the sentences with Convolutional Neural Networks. Liu and Li (2016) encodes the text with Long Short Term Memory model and employ multi-level attention mechanism to capture important signals. Qin et al. (2017) proposes a framework based on adversarial network to incorporate the connective information. To be noted, Ji and Eisenstein (2014) adopts Recursive Neural Network to exploit the representation of sentences and entities, which is the first yet simple tree-structured neural network applied in this task.

2.2 Tree-Structured Neural Networks

Tree-structured neural networks are one of the most widely-used deep learning models in natural language processing. Such neural networks usually recursively computes the representation of larger text spans from its constituent units according to the syntactic parse tree. Thanks to this compositional nature of text, tree-structured neural network models show superior ability in a variety of semantic modeling tasks, such as sentiment classification (Kokkinos and Potamianos, 2017), natural language inference (Chen et al., 2017) and machine translation (Eriguchi et al., 2016).

The earliest and simplest tree-structure neural network is the Recursive Neural Network proposed by Socher et al. (2011), in which a global matrix is learned to linearly combine the constituent vectors. This work is further extended by replacing the global matrix with a global tensor to form the Recursive Neural Tensor Network (Socher et al., 2013). Based on them, Qian et al. (2015) first proposes to incorporate tag information, which is very similar as our idea described in Section 3.2, by either choosing a composition function according to the tag of a phrase (Tag-Guided RNN/RNTN) or combining the tag embeddings with word embeddings (Tag-Embedded RNN/RNTN). Our method of incorporating tag information improves from theirs and somewhat combines these two methods by using the tag embedding to dynamically determine the composition function via the gates in LSTM or GRU.

One fatal weakness of vanilla RNN/RNTN is the well-known gradient exploding or vanishing problem due to the multiple computation steps in the vertical direction. Therefore Tai et al. (2015) and Zhu et al. (2015) propose to import the Long Short Term Memory into tree structured neural networks and design a novel network architecture called Tree-LSTM. The adoption of the memory cell enables the Tree-LSTM model to preserve information even though the tree becomes very high. Similar to Tree-LSTM, Kokkinos and Potamianos (2017) introduces the so-called Tree-GRU network, which replace the LSTM unit with Gated Recurrent Unit (GRU). With less parameters to train, Tree-GRU achieves better performance on the sentiment analysis task. In this work, we will experiment with these Tree-LSTM and Tree-GRU models for the semantic modeling in implicit relation classification.

3 Our Method

This section details the models we use for implicit discourse relation classification. Given two textual arguments without explicit connectives, our task is to classify the discourse relation between them. It can be viewed as two parts: 1) modeling the semantics of the two arguments; 2) classifying the relations based on the semantics. Our main contribution concentrates on the semantic modeling part with two types of tree-structured neural networks described in Section 3.1 and we further illustrate how to leverage the constituent tags to enhance these two models in Section 3.2. In Section 3.3, we will shortly introduce the relation classifier and the training procedure of our model. The architecture of our system is illustrated in Figure 2.

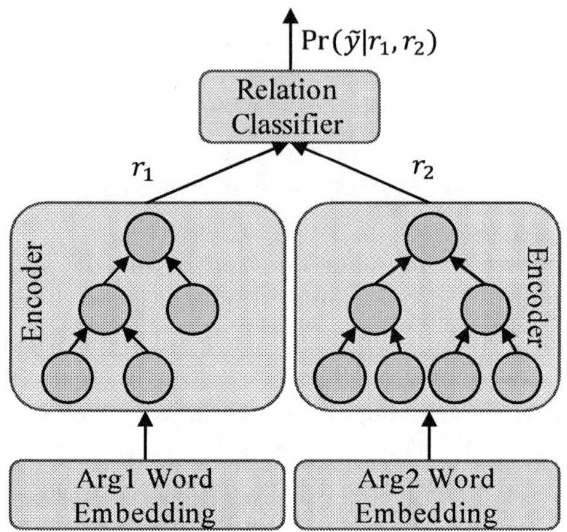

Figure 2: Architecture of our discourse relation classification model. Layers with the same color share the same parameters.

3.1 Modeling the Arguments with Tree-Structured Neural Networks

In a typical tree-structured neural network, given a parse tree of the text, the semantic representations of smaller text units are recursively composed to compute the representation of larger text spans and finally compute the representation for the whole text (e.g., sentence). In this work, we will construct our models based on the constituency parse tree, as is shown in Figure 1. Following previous convention (Eriguchi et al., 2016; Zhao et al., 2017), we convert the general parse tree, where the branching factor may be arbitrary, into a binary tree so that we only need to consider the left and right children at each step. Then the following Tree-LSTM and Tree-GRU models can be used to obtain a vector representation of each argument.

Tree-LSTM Model. In a standard sequential LSTM model, the LSTM unit is repeated at each step to take the word at current step and previous output as its input, update its memory cell and output a new hidden vector. In the Tree-LSTM model, a similar LSTM unit is applied to each node in the tree in a bottom-up manner. Since each internal node in the binary parse tree has two children, the Tree-LSTM unit has to consider information from two preceding nodes, as opposed to the single preceding node in the sequential LSTM model. Each Tree-LSTM unit (indexed by j) contains an input gate i_j, a forget gate f_j [1] and an output gate o_j. The computation equations at node j are as follows:

$$i_j = \sigma\left(W^{(i)}x_j + U^{(i)}\left[h_j^L, h_j^R\right]\right) \quad (1)$$

$$f_j = \sigma\left(W^{(f)}x_j + U^{(f)}\left[h_j^L, h_j^R\right]\right) \quad (2)$$

$$o_j = \sigma\left(W^{(o)}x_j + U^{(o)}\left[h_j^L, h_j^R\right]\right) \quad (3)$$

$$u_j = \tanh\left(W^{(u)}x_j + U^{(u)}\left[h_j^L, h_j^R\right]\right) \quad (4)$$

$$c_j = i_j \odot u_j + f_j \odot c_j^L + f_j \odot c_j^R \quad (5)$$

$$h_j = o_j \odot \tanh\left(c_j\right) \quad (6)$$

where x_j is the embedded word input at current node j, σ denotes the logistic sigmoid function and $\odot$ denotes element-wise multiplication. h_j^L, h_j^R are the output hidden vectors of the left and right children, and c_j^L, c_j^R are the memory cell states from them, respectively. To save space, we leave out all the bias terms in affine transformations and the same is true for other affine transformations in this paper.

Intuitively, u_j can be regarded as a summary of the inputs at current node, which is then filtered by i_j. The memory from left and right children are forgotten by f_j and then we compose them together with the new inputs to form the the new memory c_j. At last, part of the information in memory c_j is exposed by o_j to generate the output vector h_j for current step. Another thing to note is that only leaf nodes in the constituency tree have words as its input, so x_j is set to a zero vector in other cases.

Tree-GRU Model. Similar to Tree-LSTM, the Tree-GRU model extends the sequential GRU model to tree structures. The only difference between Tree-GRU and Tree-LSTM is how they

modulate the flow of information inside the unit. Specifically, Tree-GRU unit removes the separate memory cell and only uses two gates to simulate the reset and update procedure in information gathering. The computation equations in each Tree-GRU unit are the following:

$$r_j = \sigma\left(W^{(r)}x_j + U^{(r)}\left[h_j^L, h_j^R\right]\right) \quad (7)$$

$$z_j = \sigma\left(W^{(z)}x_j + U^{(z)}\left[h_j^L, h_j^R\right]\right) \quad (8)$$

$$\tilde{h}_j = \tanh\left(W^{(h)}x_j + U^{(h)}\left[h_j^L \odot r_j, h_j^R \odot r_j\right]\right) \quad (9)$$

$$h_j = z_j \odot \tilde{h}_j + (1 - z_j) \odot \left(h_j^L + h_j^R\right) \quad (10)$$

where r_j is the reset gate and z_j is the update gate. The reset gate allows the network to forget previous computed representations, while the update gate decides the degree of update to the hidden state. There is no memory cell in Tree-GRU, with only h_j^L and h_j^R as the hidden states from the left and right children.

3.2 Controlling the Semantic Composition with Constituent Tags

The constituent tag in a parse tree describes the grammatical role of its corresponding constituent in the context. Bies et al. (1995) defines several types of constituent tags, including clause-level tags (e.g., SBAR, SINV, SQ), phrase-level tags (e.g., NP, VP, PP) and word-level tags (e.g., NN, VP, JJ). These constituent tags greatly interleave with the semantics and in some ways can provide determinant signals for the importance of a constituent. For example, for most of the time, constituents with PP (prepositional phrase) tag are less important than those with VP (verb phrase) tag. Therefore we argue that these tags are worth considering when we compose the semantics in the tree-structured neural networks.

One way to leverage such tags is using tag-specific composition functions but that would lead to large number of parameters and some tags are very sparse so it's very hard to train their corresponding parameters sufficiently. To solve this problem, we propose to use tag embeddings and dynamically control the composition process via the gates in our model.

Gates in Tree-LSTM and Tree-GRU units control the flow of information and thus determine how the semantics from child nodes are composed

---

[1] The original Binary Tree-LSTM in (Tai et al., 2015) contains separate forget gates for different child nodes but we find single forget gate performs better in our task.

to a new representation. Furthermore, these gates are computed dynamically according to the inputs at a certain step. Therefore, it's natural to incorporate the tag embeddings in the computation of these gates. Based on this idea, we propose the Tag-Enhanced Tree-LSTM model, where the input, forget and output gates in each unit are calculated as follows:

$$i_j = \sigma \left(W^{(i)} x_j + M^{(i)} t_j + U^{(i)} \left[h_j^L, h_j^R \right] \right) \tag{11}$$

$$f_j = \sigma \left(W^{(f)} x_j + M^{(f)} t_j + U^{(f)} \left[h_j^L, h_j^R \right] \right) \tag{12}$$

$$o_j = \sigma \left(W^{(o)} x_j + M^{(o)} t_j + U^{(o)} \left[h_j^L, h_j^R \right] \right) \tag{13}$$

Similarly, we can have the Tag-Enhanced Tree-GRU model with new reset and update gates:

$$r_j = \sigma \left(W^{(r)} x_j + M^{(r)} t_j + U^{(r)} \left[h_j^L, h_j^R \right] \right) \tag{14}$$

$$z_j = \sigma \left(W^{(z)} x_j + M^{(z)} t_j + U^{(z)} \left[h_j^L, h_j^R \right] \right) \tag{15}$$

where t_j is the embedding of the tag at current node (indexed by j).

3.3 Relation Classification and Training

In our work, the two arguments are encoded with the same network in order to reduce the number of parameters. After that we get a vector representation for each argument, which can be denoted as r_1 for argument 1 and r_2 for argument 2. Supposing that there are totally n relation types, the predicted probability distribution $\hat{y} \in \mathbb{R}^n$ is calculated as:

$$\hat{y} = softmax \left(W^{(\hat{y})} \left[r_1, r_2 \right] + b^{(\hat{y})} \right) \tag{16}$$

To train our model, the training objective J is dened as the cross-entropy loss with $L2$ regularization:

$$E \left(\hat{y}, y \right) = - \sum_{j=1}^{n} y_j \times \log \hat{y}_j \tag{17}$$

$$J \left(\theta \right) = \frac{1}{N} \sum_{k=1}^{N} E \left(\hat{y}, y \right) + \frac{\lambda}{2} \|\theta\|^2 \tag{18}$$

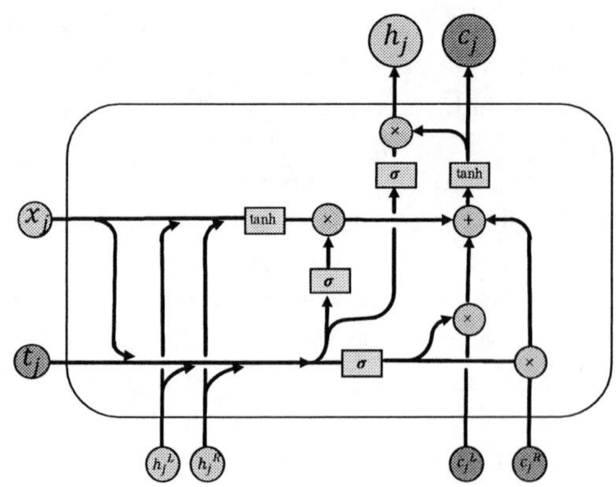

Figure 3: Flow of Information in Tag-Enhanced Tree-LSTM unit.

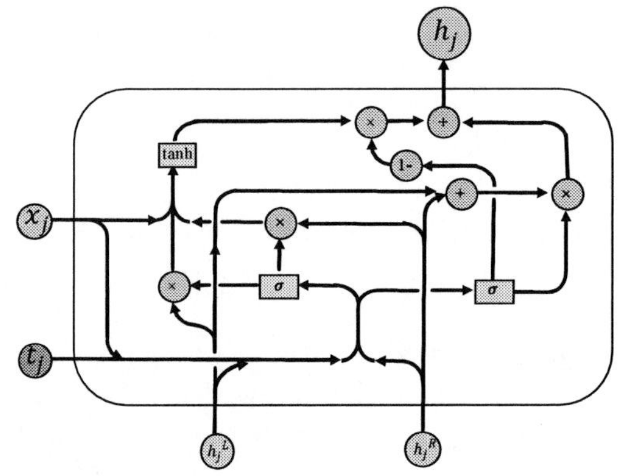

Figure 4: Flow of Information in Tag-Enhanced Tree-GRU unit.

where $\hat{y}$ is the predicted probability distribution, y is the one-hot representation of the gold label and N is the number of training samples.

4 Experiments

4.1 Experiment Setup

Corpus. We evaluate our method on the Penn Discourse Treebank (PDTB) (Prasad et al., 2008), which provides annotations of discourse relations over the Wall Street Journal corpus. Each relation instance consists of two arguments, typically adjacent pairs of sentences in a text. As is mentioned in Section 2.1, the relations in PDTB are generally categorized into either explicit or implicit and our work focuses on the more challenging implicit relation classification task. Totally, there are 16,224 implicit relation instances in PDTB dataset, with a three-level hierarchy. The first level is defined as 4 major classes of the relation, including: *Tem-*

Models	Level-1 Classification		Level-2 Classification	
	Dev	Test	Dev	Test
Bi-LSTM	55.10	56.88	35.02	42.44
Bi-GRU	55.21	57.01	35.34	42.46
Tree-LSTM	56.04	58.89	35.76	43.02
Tree-GRU	55.36	58.98	36.09	43.78
Tag-Enhanced Tree-LSTM	**56.97**	**59.85**	35.92	**45.21**
Tag-Enhanced Tree-GRU	56.63	59.75	**36.93**	44.55

Table 1: The accuracy score of multi-class classification

poral, *Contingency*, *Comparison* and *Expansion*. Then for each class, it is further divided into different types, which is supposed to provide finer pragmatic distinctions. This totally yields 16 relation types at the second level. At last, a third level of subtypes is defined for some types according to the semantic contribution of each argument.

Preprocesssing. Following the common setup convention (Rutherford and Xue, 2014; Ji and Eisenstein, 2014; Liu and Li, 2016), we split the dataset into training set (Sections 2-20), development set (Sections 0-1), and test set (Section 21-22). For preprocessing, we employ the Stanford CoreNLP toolkit (Manning et al., 2014) to lemmatize all the words and get the constituency parse tree for each sentence. Then we convert the parse tree into binary with right branching and we remove the internal nodes that have only one child so that our binary tree-structured models can be applied. Small portion of the arguments in PDTB are composed of multiple sentences. In such cases, we add a new "Root" node and link the original root nodes of those sentences to this shared "Root" before converting the tree into binary.

Multi-Class Classification There are mainly two ways to set up the classification tasks in previous work. Early studies (Pitler et al., 2009; Park and Cardie, 2012) train and evaluate separate "one-versus-all" classifiers for each discourse relation since the classes are extremely imbalanced in PDTB. However, recent work put more emphasis on the multi-class classification, where the goal is to identify a discourse relation from all possible choices. According to Rutherford and Xue (2014), the multi-class classification setting is more natural and realistic. Moreover, the multi-class classifier can directly serve as one building block of a complete discourse parser (Qin et al., 2017). Therefore, in this work, we will focus on the multi-

class classification task. Moreover, we will experiment on the classification of both the Level-1 classes and the Level-2 types, so that we can compare with most of previous systems and thoroughly analyze the performance of our method.

It should be noted that roughly 2% of the implicit relation instances are annotated with more than one types. Following Ji and Eisenstein (2014), we treat these different types as multiple instances while training our model. During testing, if the classifier hits either of the annotated types, we consider it to be correct. We also follow previous studies (Lin et al., 2009; Ji and Eisenstein, 2014) to remove the instances of 5 very rare relation types in the second level. Therefore we have totally 11 types to classify for Level-2 classification and 4 classes for Level-1 classification.

4.2 Model Settings

We tune the hyper-parameters of our Tag-Enhanced Tree-LSTM model based on the development set and other models share the same set of hyper-parameters. The best-validated hyper-parameters, including the size of the word embeddings ω, the size of the tag embeddings τ, the dimension of the Tree-LSTM or Tree-GRU hidden state d, the learning rate η, the weight of L2 regularization term λ and the batch size b are shown in Table 2.

ω	τ	d	η	λ	b
50	50	250	0.01	0.0001	10

Table 2: Hyper-parameters of our model

The Pre-trained 50-dimentional Glove Vectors (Pennington et al., 2014), which is case-insensitive, are used for initializing the word embeddings and they are tuned together with other parameters in the same learning rate during training.

We adopt the AdaGrad optimizer (Duchi et al., 2011) for training our model and we validate the performance every epoch. It takes around 5 hours (5 epochs) for the Tag-Enhanced Tree-LSTM and 4 hours (6 epochs) for the Tag-Enhanced Tree-GRU model to converge to the best performance, using one INTEL(R) Core(TM) I7 3.4GHz CPU and one NVIDIA GeForce GTX 1080 GPU.

4.3 Results

The evaluation results of our models on both the Level-1 classification and the Level-2 classification are reported in Table 1. Accuracy score is used to measure the overall performance and we present our performance on both the development set and the test set. In addition to the four tree-structured neural networks described in Section 3, we also implement two baseline models: the bi-directional LSTM model and the bi-directional GRU model. The hyper-parameters of these two models are tuned separately from other models. Due to the space limitation, we don't present the details here. Comparison of these sequential models with the tree-structured models are expected to show the effects of tree structures.

From Table 1, we can see that the sequential Bi-LSTM model and Bi-GRU model perform worst for our task, which confirms our hypothesis that the tree-structured neural networks can really capture some important signals that are missing in the sequential models.

Furthermore, if we add the tag information to tree-structured models, both the Tag-Enhanced Tree-LSTM model and the Tag-Enhanced Tree-GRU model provide conspicuous improvement (around 1%) compared with the no-tag version. This demonstrates the usefulness of those constituent tags and the effectiveness of our method to incorporate this important feature. Especially, since both the Tree-LSTM model and Tree-GRU model rely on the gating machanism to control the flow of information, this double confirms that the tag information can help with the computation of such gates and therefore can be leveraged to control the semantic composition process.

Another discovery from our results is that the GRU models performs similarly as its corresponding variant of LSTM model. This conforms to previous empirical observation in sequential models that LSTM and GRU have comparable capability (Chung et al., 2014). However, the Tree-GRU

Systems	Accuracy
Zhang et al. (2015)	55.39
Rutherford and Xue (2014)	55.50
Rutherford and Xue (2015)	57.10
Liu et al. (2016)	57.27
Liu and Li (2016)	57.57
Ji et al. (2016)	59.50
Tag-Enhanced Tree-LSTM	**59.85**
Tag-Enhanced Tree-GRU	59.75

Table 3: Accuracy (%) for Level-1 multi-class classification on the test set, compared with other state-of-the-art systems.

Systems	Accuracy
Lin et al. (2009)	40.66
Ji and Eisenstein (2014)	44.59
Qin et al. (2016)	45.04
Qin et al. (2017)	**46.23**
Tag-Enhanced Tree-LSTM	45.21
Tag-Enhanced Tree-GRU	44.55

Table 4: Accuracy (%) for Level-2 multi-class classification on the test set, compared with other state-of-the-art systems.

model have less parameters to train which could alleviate the problem of overfitting and also cost less training time.

4.4 Comparison with Other Systems

For a comprehensive study, we compare our models with other state-of-the-art systems. The systems that conduct Level-1 classification are reported in Table 3, including:

- Zhang et al. (2015) proposes to use convolutional neural networks to encode the arguments.

- Rutherford and Xue (2014) manually extracts features to represent the arguments and use a maximum entropy classifier for classification. Rutherford and Xue (2015) further exploits discourse connectives to enrich the training data.

- Liu et al. (2016) employs a multi-task framework that can leverage other discourse-related data to help with the training of discourse relation classifier.

- Liu and Li (2016) represents arguments with LSTM and introduces a multi-level attention mechanism to model the interaction between the two arguments.

- Ji et al. (2016) treats the discourse relation as latent variable and proposes to model them jointly with the sequences of words using a latent variable recurrent neural network architecture.

And in Table 4, we present the following systems, which focus on Level-2 classification:

- Lin et al. (2009) uses traditional feature-based model to classify relations. Especially, constituent and dependency parse trees are exploited.

- Ji and Eisenstein (2014) models both the semantics of argument and the meaning of entity mention with two recursive neural networks, which are then combined to classify relations.

- Qin et al. (2016) utilize convolutional neural network for argument modeling and a collaborative gated neural network to model their interaction.

- Qin et al. (2017) proposes to incorporate the connective information via a novel pipelined adversarial framework.

The comparison with these latest work shows that our system achieves currently best performance for the Level-1 classification and ranks second for the Level-2. With the state-of-the-art performance on both levels, we can verify the effectiveness of our method.

4.5 Qualitative Analysis

To get a deeper insight into the proposed tag-enhanced models, we project the constituent tag embeddings learned in our Tag-Enhanced Tree-LSTM model into two dimensions using the t-SNE method (Maaten and Hinton, 2008) and normalize the values in each dimension. The projected embeddings are visualized in Figure 5 and we highlight some representative tags that may share some kind of commonality in their functions.

According to the definition in Bies et al. (1995), the tags with red color are all verb-related, while those with blue color describes noun-related syntax. Despite of some noisy points, we can see that they are roughly separated into two groups.

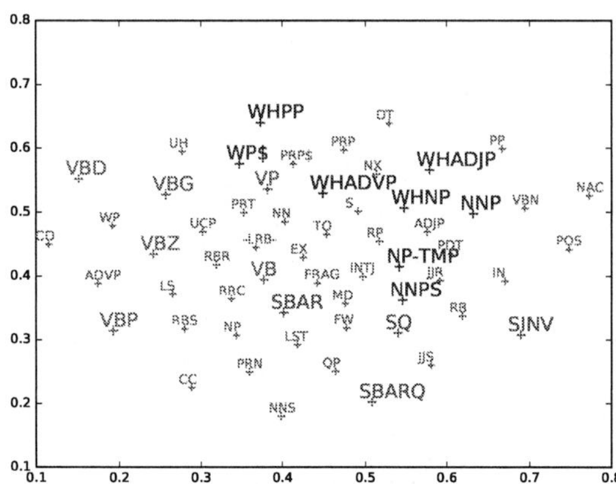

Figure 5: t-SNE Visualization (Maaten and Hinton, 2008) of the constituent tag embeddings

In addition, the purple tags correspond to words or phrase that are wh-related (e.g., what, when, where, which) and we can see they are distributed similarly. Moreover, the green tags are, which are located in the right-bottom corner, all describe the clause-level constituents.

Therefore, from this visualization, we can conclude that the tag embeddings we learned are somewhat meaningful and really capture some functionalities of these tags. Since these embeddings are used to compute the gates and the gates further determine the flow of information, we argue that these tags can indeed help to control the semantic composition process in our tree-structured networks.

5 Conclusion

In this work, we propose to use two latest tree-structured neural networks to model the arguments for discourse relation classification. The syntactic parse tree are exploited from two aspects: first, we leverage the tree structure to recursively compose semantics in a bottom-up manner; second, the constituent tags are used to control the semantic composition process at each step via gating mechanism. Comprehensive experiments show the effectiveness of our proposed method and our system achieves state-of-the-art performance for the challenging task of implicit discourse relation classification. For future work, we will try other types of syntax embeddings and we are also working on incorporating structural attention mechanism into our tree-based models.

Acknowledgments

We thank all the anonymous reviewers for their insightful comments on this paper. This work was partially supported by National Natural Science Foundation of China (61572049 and 61333018). The correspondence author of this paper is Sujian Li.

References

Ann Bies, Mark Ferguson, Karen Katz, Robert MacIntyre, Victoria Tredinnick, Grace Kim, Mary Ann Marcinkiewicz, and Britta Schasberger. 1995. Bracketing guidelines for treebank ii style penn treebank project. *University of Pennsylvania*, 97:100.

Qian Chen, Xiaodan Zhu, Zhen-Hua Ling, Si Wei, Hui Jiang, and Diana Inkpen. 2017. Enhanced lstm for natural language inference. In *Proc. ACL*.

Junyoung Chung, Çaglar Gülçehre, KyungHyun Cho, and Yoshua Bengio. 2014. Empirical evaluation of gated recurrent neural networks on sequence modeling. *CoRR*, abs/1412.3555.

John Duchi, Elad Hazan, and Yoram Singer. 2011. Adaptive subgradient methods for online learning and stochastic optimization. *Journal of Machine Learning Research*, 12(Jul):2121–2159.

Akiko Eriguchi, Kazuma Hashimoto, and Yoshimasa Tsuruoka. 2016. Tree-to-sequence attentional neural machine translation. *arXiv preprint arXiv:1603.06075*.

Yangfeng Ji and Jacob Eisenstein. 2014. One vector is not enough: Entity-augmented distributional semantics for discourse relations. *arXiv preprint arXiv:1411.6699*.

Yangfeng Ji, Gholamreza Haffari, and Jacob Eisenstein. 2016. A latent variable recurrent neural network for discourse relation language models. *arXiv preprint arXiv:1603.01913*.

Filippos Kokkinos and Alexandros Potamianos. 2017. Structural attention neural networks for improved sentiment analysis. *arXiv preprint arXiv:1701.01811*.

Ziheng Lin, Min-Yen Kan, and Hwee Tou Ng. 2009. Recognizing implicit discourse relations in the penn discourse treebank. In *Proceedings of the 2009 Conference on Empirical Methods in Natural Language Processing: Volume 1-Volume 1*, pages 343–351. Association for Computational Linguistics.

Yang Liu and Sujian Li. 2016. Recognizing implicit discourse relations via repeated reading: Neural networks with multi-level attention. *arXiv preprint arXiv:1609.06380*.

Yang Liu, Sujian Li, Xiaodong Zhang, and Zhifang Sui. 2016. Implicit discourse relation classification via multi-task neural networks. In *AAAI*, pages 2750–2756.

Laurens van der Maaten and Geoffrey Hinton. 2008. Visualizing data using t-sne. *Journal of Machine Learning Research*, 9(Nov):2579–2605.

Christopher D. Manning, Mihai Surdeanu, John Bauer, Jenny Finkel, Steven J. Bethard, and David McClosky. 2014. The stanford corenlp natural language processing toolkit. In *Association for Computational Linguistics (ACL) System Demonstrations*, pages 55–60.

Daniel Marcu. 1997. The rhetorical parsing of natural language texts. In *Proceedings of the 35th Annual Meeting of the Association for Computational Linguistics and Eighth Conference of the European Chapter of the Association for Computational Linguistics*, pages 96–103. Association for Computational Linguistics.

Joonsuk Park and Claire Cardie. 2012. Improving implicit discourse relation recognition through feature set optimization. In *Proceedings of the SIGDIAL 2012 Conference, The 13th Annual Meeting of the Special Interest Group on Discourse and Dialogue*, pages 108–112.

Jeffrey Pennington, Richard Socher, and Christopher D. Manning. 2014. Glove: Global vectors for word representation. In *Empirical Methods in Natural Language Processing (EMNLP)*, pages 1532–1543.

Emily Pitler, Annie Louis, and Ani Nenkova. 2009. Automatic sense prediction for implicit discourse relations in text. In *Proceedings of the Joint Conference of the 47th Annual Meeting of the ACL and the 4th International Joint Conference on Natural Language Processing of the AFNLP: Volume 2-Volume 2*, pages 683–691. Association for Computational Linguistics.

Rashmi Prasad, Nikhil Dinesh, Alan Lee, Eleni Miltsakaki, Livio Robaldo, Aravind K. Joshi, and Bonnie L. Webber. 2008. The penn discourse treebank 2.0. In *Proceedings of the International Conference on Language Resources and Evaluation, LREC 2008, 26 May - 1 June 2008, Marrakech, Morocco*.

Qiao Qian, Bo Tian, Minlie Huang, Yang Liu, Xuan Zhu, and Xiaoyan Zhu. 2015. Learning tag embeddings and tag-specific composition functions in recursive neural network. In *ACL (1)*, pages 1365–1374.

Lianhui Qin, Zhisong Zhang, and Hai Zhao. 2016. A stacking gated neural architecture for implicit discourse relation classification. In *EMNLP*, pages 2263–2270.

Lianhui Qin, Zhisong Zhang, Hai Zhao, Zhiting Hu, and Eric P Xing. 2017. Adversarial connective-exploiting networks for implicit discourse relation classification. *arXiv preprint arXiv:1704.00217*.

Attapol Rutherford and Nianwen Xue. 2014. Discovering implicit discourse relations through brown cluster pair representation and coreference patterns. In *Proceedings of the 14th Conference of the European Chapter of the Association for Computational Linguistics, 2014*, pages 645–654.

Attapol Rutherford and Nianwen Xue. 2015. Improving the inference of implicit discourse relations via classifying explicit discourse connectives. In *The 2015 Conference of the North American Chapter of the Association for Computational Linguistics: Human Language Technologies*, pages 799–808.

Richard Socher, Cliff C Lin, Chris Manning, and Andrew Y Ng. 2011. Parsing natural scenes and natural language with recursive neural networks. In *Proceedings of the 28th international conference on machine learning (ICML-11)*, pages 129–136.

Richard Socher, Alex Perelygin, Jean Y Wu, Jason Chuang, Christopher D Manning, Andrew Y Ng, Christopher Potts, et al. 2013. Recursive deep models for semantic compositionality over a sentiment treebank. In *Proceedings of the conference on empirical methods in natural language processing (EMNLP)*, volume 1631, page 1642.

Radu Soricut and Daniel Marcu. 2003. Sentence level discourse parsing using syntactic and lexical information. In *Proceedings of the 2003 Conference of the North American Chapter of the Association for Computational Linguistics on Human Language Technology-Volume 1*, pages 149–156. Association for Computational Linguistics.

Rajen Subba and Barbara Di Eugenio. 2009. An effective discourse parser that uses rich linguistic information. In *Proceedings of Human Language Technologies: The 2009 Annual Conference of the North American Chapter of the Association for Computational Linguistics*, pages 566–574. Association for Computational Linguistics.

Kai Sheng Tai, Richard Socher, and Christopher D Manning. 2015. Improved semantic representations from tree-structured long short-term memory networks. *arXiv preprint arXiv:1503.00075*.

Deborah Tannen. 2012. Discourse analysis–what speakers do in conversation. *Linguistic Society of America*.

Gilbert Weiss and Ruth Wodak. 2007. *Critical discourse analysis*. Springer.

Biao Zhang, Jinsong Su, Deyi Xiong, Yaojie Lu, Hong Duan, and Junfeng Yao. 2015. Shallow convolutional neural network for implicit discourse relation recognition. In *Proceedings of the 2015 Conference on Empirical Methods in Natural Language Processing*, pages 2230–2235.

Kai Zhao, Liang Huang, and Mingbo Ma. 2017. Textual entailment with structured attentions and composition. *CoRR*, abs/1701.01126.

Xiaodan Zhu, Parinaz Sobihani, and Hongyu Guo. 2015. Long short-term memory over recursive structures. In *International Conference on Machine Learning*, pages 1604–1612.

Cross-Lingual Sentiment Analysis Without (Good) Translation

Mohamed Abdalla and **Graeme Hirst**

`msa@` and `gh@cs.toronto.edu`

Department of Computer Science, University of Toronto

Toronto, Canada

Abstract

Current approaches to cross-lingual sentiment analysis try to leverage the wealth of labeled English data using bilingual lexicons, bilingual vector space embeddings, or machine translation systems. Here we show that it is possible to use a single linear transformation, with as few as 2000 word pairs, to capture fine-grained sentiment relationships between words in a cross-lingual setting. We apply these cross-lingual sentiment models to a diverse set of tasks to demonstrate their functionality in a non-English context. By effectively leveraging English sentiment knowledge without the need for accurate translation, we can analyze and extract features from other languages with scarce data at a very low cost, thus making sentiment and related analyses for many languages inexpensive.

1 Introduction

Methods for sentiment analysis and classification have largely been limited to English, making use of large amounts of labeled data to produce sentiment classification. As a consequence, many developed approaches cannot be readily applied to other languages, which usually do not have the wealth of labeled data that is exclusive to English. Therefore many approaches which deal with other languages often: i) experiment with small datasets that are limited in domain or size of training and testing sets (Lee and Renganathan, 2011; Tan and Zhang, 2008), or ii) attempt to elucidate sentiment lexicons for their respective languages (Mohammad et al., 2016).

A growing number of publications attempt to leverage labeled English data to compensate for the relative lack of training material in the other languages. This is usually done through the use of either bilingual lexicons (Balamurali et al., 2012), machine translation (MT) systems (Salameh et al., 2015; Zhou et al., 2016), or more recently, through the use of bilingual vector space embeddings (Chen et al., 2016).

Unfortunately, in some cases such data is still expensive to obtain. Many languages do not have good, or sometimes any, MT systems, and the cost of producing word alignments or sentence alignments for training bilingual word embeddings (BWE) (Zou et al., 2013; Bengio and Corrado, 2015) or similar techniques (Jain and Batra, 2015) is prohibitive for data-poor languages.

Here we introduce a high-performance, low-cost approach to cross-lingual sentiment classification, which can be used to benchmark more expensive methods. We demonstrate the utility of this approach by highlighting how very limited training data suffices for effective cross-lingual sentiment analysis in various contexts (both at the word and sentence/document level). Our approach relies on the simple vector space translation matrix method (Mikolov et al., 2013a), which computes a matrix to convert from the vector space of one language to that of another. It hinges on the observation that sentiment is highly "preserved" even in the face of poor translation accuracy. We observed that a sentiment classifier trained only with word vectors from English (hereafter referred to as the target language) performs well on unseen words from other unseen languages (referred to as the source languages) that are translated into the English vector space through the simple matrix method, even with very poor translation scores.[1]

---

[1] This work involves transfers in both directions between English and other languages. We will take the perspective of the translation matrix (section 3.2) and refer to English as the target language and the others as source languages.

Proceedings of the The 8th International Joint Conference on Natural Language Processing, pages 506–515,
Taipei, Taiwan, November 27 – December 1, 2017 ©2017 AFNLP

We quantitatively evaluate our methods by training on English and testing on words from Spanish and Chinese. We chose these languages in order to show: i) the robustness of the technique irrespective of the grammar of the source and target languages and, ii) the ability to validate the technique (*i.e.,* as baselines for experiments). We emphasize that, regardless of the source languages used, we treated them as if they had no MT systems. We made use of only 2000, 4500, or 8500 word pairs – a task easily accomplished by a human translator on a data-poor language. We experiment with differing amounts of data during training to show the robustness of our observation. We then apply the fine-grained sentiment regressor to the task of review classification as done by Chen et al. (2016), and show that our naïve algorithm achieves results similar to their benchmark but at a much lower cost.

2 Previous Work

2.1 Cross-Lingual Word Embeddings

Monolingual word embedding algorithms use large unlabeled datasets to learn useful features about the given language (Pennington et al., 2014; Mikolov et al., 2013b). These algorithms learn vector representations for the words of the language — an encoding that has proven utility in a variety of NLP tasks including sentiment analysis (Maas et al., 2011) and machine translation (Mikolov et al., 2013a).

When working with more than one language, we seek to satisfy two objectives: i) monolingually, similar words of the same language have similar embeddings; and ii) cross-lingually, similar words across languages also have similar embeddings. Satisfying these two criteria would allow us to use algorithms trained for the embeddings of a single language (such as English, with a wealth of labeled data) for other languages as well. Below we discuss algorithms to achieve the cross-lingual objective, their costs, performance, and the rationale underlying our algorithm design.

2.1.1 Offline Alignment

The simplest approach to achieving the cross-lingual objective is to train each monolingual objective separately (create a model for each language), and then learn a transformation to enforce the second objective. This approach uses a dictionary of paired words in order to learn a trans-

formation or 'alignment' from the vector space of one language to that of another.

First introduced by Mikolov et al. (2013a), and later extended by Faruqui and Dyer (2014), this offline alignment is fast and low cost, but does not achieve a high translation accuracy. A big drawback of these approaches is that using a dictionary ignores the polysemic nature of languages. It is also not clear or proven that a single transformation would be able to capture the relationship between all the words in a cross-lingual setting.

We opt to use offline alignment to show that such a low-cost approach does, in fact, capture a significant part of the relationship between words of different languages when it comes to sentiment. That is, a single transformation (linear in the case of our work) is sufficient to learn a projection which allows one to use labeled English data to aid in sentiment analysis.

2.1.2 Parallel-Only

An alternative approach to offline alignment is the parallel-only approach. Approaches which fall into this group, such as BiCVM (Hermann and Blunsom, 2013) and bilingual auto-encoder (BAE) (Sarath Chandar et al., 2014), rely exclusively on sentence-aligned parallel data to train a model with similar representations. Such approaches can be effective, but require extremely expensive data. Another drawback is that these approaches can be affected by the writing style of the parallel text (Bengio and Corrado, 2015).

2.1.3 Jointly-Trained Model

Combining the offline alignment and parallel-only algorithms is a third class of jointly-trained approaches. These approaches jointly optimize the monolingual objective at the same time as the cross-lingual objective, making use of both monolingual and parallel data. Approaches like those of Klementiev et al. (2012) and Zou et al. (2013) use word-aligned data in order to learn the fine-grained cross-lingual features and tend to be quite slow. Other approaches (including that of Bengio and Corrado (2015)) rely on sentence-aligned data and are faster than those using word-aligned data. While these models are more cost-efficient than parallel-only approaches, it remains expensive and sometimes prohibitive to obtain sentence alignments for many languages (a problem that we seek to avoid).

A lower-cost alternative to these expensive

jointly trained models was proposed by Duong et al. (2016) and later used to project multiple languages in the same vector space (Duong et al., 2017). The model involved creating and making use of translations produced using a bilingual dictionary during training. Using expectation–maximization–inspired training, sentence translations were produced by selecting translations of words based on context to deal with polysemy, and this approach demonstrated improvements on the simple linear transformation method. However, even this model uses a significantly larger amount of data than the methods used in this work, with its smallest dictionary being composed of 35,000 word pairs compared to our approach, which can use as little as 2000 words for both translation and sentiment regression.

2.2 Cross-Lingual Sentiment Analysis

Previous approaches to cross-lingual sentiment analysis can be classified into two main categories: i) those that rely on parallel corpora to train BWE's (*i.e.,* they use pre-trained embeddings) (Chen et al., 2016; Sarath Chandar et al., 2014; Tang and Wan, 2014), and ii) those that use translation systems (Zhou et al., 2015, 2016) in order to obtain aligned inputs to learn to extract features which work on both languages. Both approaches allow the sentiment portion of training and testing data to be in the same vector space. However, many languages have no MT system, and it is extremely expensive to create one on a language-by-language basis.

Our proposed approach is simpler in that it requires only a small word-list to learn both the embedding and the sentiment classification, the duality of which cannot be claimed by previous approaches.

3 Methods and Data

3.1 Data

3.1.1 Vector Space Data

English Vector Space Model For English we used a model pre-trained on part of the Google News dataset (which is composed of approximately 100 billion words).[2] The words are represented by 300-dimensional vectors.

Spanish Vector Space Model For the Spanish word embeddings we opted to use a model pre-trained on the Spanish Billion Word Corpus (Cardellino, 2016). It consists of just under 1.5 billion words compiled from a variety of Spanish resources. As with the English model, the words are represented by 300-dimensional vectors.

Chinese Vector Space Model For Chinese word embeddings we learned our own vector representations using a Wikimedia dump[3] composed of around 150 million words from 250,000 articles in both simplified and traditional Chinese. We used OpenCC[4] to translate the articles in simplified Chinese to traditional. To segment the text into tokens we used Jieba[5]. Finally, to create the actual word embedding model, we used Gensim (Řehůřek and Sojka, 2011) with the minimum count set to 1, using continuous bag of words (CBOW), a window of 8, and vector dimension set to 300.

3.1.2 Word Lists

Translation Word List For the process of learning a translation matrix from one language to the other, a lexicon of approximately 10,000 English words was obtained online by scraping the most commonly used words as determined by n-gram frequency analysis in Google's "Trillion Word Corpus"[6]. The lexicon was then translated using Google Translate[7] in order to obtain corresponding words in Spanish and Chinese. For alignment lists of smaller sizes during experimentation, a random subset of the larger list was selected. During the randomized selection, we discarded any words which were not in the target language vector space and whose translation was not in the source language(s) vector space(s).

Binary Sentiment Word List For the task of binary sentiment classification we used a list[8] curated by Hu and Liu (2004) containing both positive and negative English opinion words (or sentiment words). Google Translate was used to translate the list into the other languages to obtain cross-lingual word pairs. During training and testing we made sure to balance the dataset and to discard words that were not in the vector space of the target language or whose translation was not in the vector space of the source language(s).

---

[2]https://code.google.com/archive/p/word2vec/

[3]https://dumps.wikimedia.org/zhwiki/latest/
[4]https://github.com/BYVoid/OpenCC
[5]https://github.com/fxsjy/Jieba
[6]https://github.com/first20hours/google-10000-english
[7]https://translate.google.com/
[8] https://github.com/williamgunn/SciSentiment

	Low Stimulus	**High Stimulus**
Arousal	*relaxed* (2.39)	*infatuation* (7.02)
Dominance	*victim* (2.69)	*confident* (7.68)
Valence	*death* (1.61)	*beauty* (7.82)

Table 1: Examples of words on each end of the spectrum for each of the three dimensions of ANEW. Numeric stimulus value is shown in parentheses.

3.1.3 Fine-Grained Data

For fine-grained sentiment regression, we used Affective Norms for English Words (ANEW) (Bradley and Lang, 1999). The creators of ANEW sought to provide emotional ratings for a large number of words in the English language.

ANEW proposes that all human emotion can be organized in a vector space with three basic underlying dimensions (or axes). The first dimension, *valence*, ranges from *pleasant* to *unpleasant*; the second dimension, *arousal*, ranges from *calm* to *excited*; and the third dimension, *dominance*, ranges from *in-control* to *out-of-control*. Examples are shown in Table 1.

Bradley and Lang (1999) used a nonverbal pictographic measure, the Self-Assessment Manikin (SAM) (Bradley and Lang, 1994), to measure stimuli across these three dimensions. The figures in the SAM consist of bipolar scales depicting different values along each of the three emotional dimensions. For example, when considering valence, SAM ranges from a frowning unhappy figure to a smiling happy figure. Similar ranges are extended across the two other dimensions. Using this test, Bradley and Lang were able to arrive at a numerical value representing a word's stimulus for each dimension ranging from 1 to 9; where 1 is the low value (*unpleasant, calm, in-control*) and 9 is the high value (*pleasant, excited, out-of-control*).

3.1.4 Review Data

In this subsection, we discuss the data used to replicate the review classification task done by Chen et al. (2016) as a means of validating the utility of our model. This experiment was done using only English and Chinese because there was no Spanish data for this task and the Arabic review data-set that Chen et al. (2016) used was not freely available.

Labeled English Reviews Following Chen et al. (2016), we obtained a balanced dataset of 700,000 reviews of businesses on Yelp from Zhang et al.

(2015) with their sentiment ratings as labels ranging from 1 for very negative to 5 for very positive.

Labeled Chinese Reviews Here we use a dataset from Lin et al. (2015). Their work provides hotel reviews, with labels ranging from 1 for very negative to 5 for very positive. In order to fairly compare our work with that of Chen et al. (2016), we use 10,000 reviews for model selection, and another unseen 10,000 as our test set.

3.2 Translation Matrix Technique

As described by Mikolov et al. (2013a), the translation matrix technique assumes that we are given a set of word pairs and their associated vector space representations. More specifically, we are given j word pairs, $\{x_i, z_i\}_{i=1}^{j}$ where $x_i \in \mathbb{R}^n$ is a vector from the source language of word i and $z_i \in \mathbb{R}^m$ is the vector representation of the corresponding translated word in the target language.

We then want to find a transformation matrix W such that Wx_i approximates z_i. We learn this by solving the following optimization problem:

$$\min_{W} \sum_{i=1}^{j} ||Wx_i - z_i||^2$$

Instead of solving with stochastic gradient descent, we instead opt to use the closed-form solution.

To translate a word from source language to target language, we can map it using $z = Wx$, and then find the closest word in that language space using cosine similarity as the measure of distance. The method of testing was Monte Carlo cross-validation run 10 times with a split of 90% training data and 10% test data.

3.3 Models

3.3.1 Binary Sentiment Analysis Model

The sentiment analysis model, Figure 1(a), is a simple linear support vector machine (SVM) classifier. Implemented using Sci-kit Learn's *SGD-Classifier* function (Pedregosa et al., 2011), this model takes a word represented as a vector with dimension of 300 and outputs a prediction of either -1 or $+1$ (for negative and positive respectively). The classifier itself performs stochastic gradient descent (SGD) with $l2$ regularization to arrive at the best classification.

The training procedure of this model is quite simple and involves only the target language. The model is trained only on word embeddings from

Translation	1000 WORDS		4500 WORDS		8500 WORDS	
	P@1	P@5	P@1	P@5	P@1	P@5
EN → ES	20.3	34.6	33.42	46.13	34.79	47.79
EN → CN	2.4	11.6	7.60	20.29	8.87	23.01

Table 2: Accuracy of the word translation method. P@1 and P@5 represent Top-1 and Top-5 accuracy respectively.

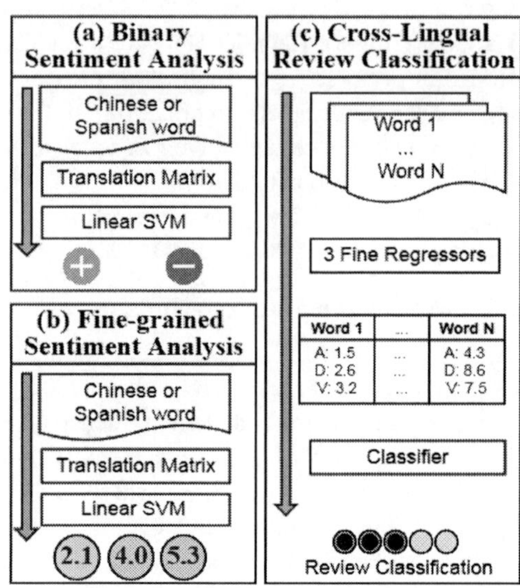

Figure 1: The three models used in the experiments.

the target language but tested on embeddings returned by the translation of words originally from the source language(s). We made sure that the English translation of the test words had not been seen before in training. The training/testing split was changed to 80% and 20% from the previous 90%/10% to account for the smaller number of examples in the dataset (and the fact that we wanted to test on a representative sample of the data).

3.3.2 Fine-Grained Sentiment Analysis Model

The fine-grained sentiment analysis model in Figure 1(b) is a regression model to predict the ANEW values for each of the three dimensions. For this task, we built a regressor for each of the three dimensions whose input is a 300-dimension vector and whose output is a real number from 1 to 9. The regressor used was a Bayesian Ridge regressor, which estimates a probabilistic model of the regression problem. The prior for the parameter w is given by a spherical Gaussian:

$$p(w|\lambda) = \mathcal{N}(w|0, \lambda^{-1}I_p).$$

The model is similar to that of the Ridge regression. The model was implemented using Sci-kit Learn's with hyperparameters alpha_1 and alpha_2 set to 1.

The training procedure of this model is quite simple and similar to that of the previous model.

Again, it only trains on the vector of the target language, and is tested purely on words from the source language whose translation into the target language was not seen in the training of the regressor (so that there may be no chance of skewing the results). The training/testing split here was 75%/25%.

3.3.3 Review Classification Model

For the task of review classification, another model Figure 1(c), was built to make use of the previously described fine-grained sentiment analysis model. The classifier used for this task is a logistic regression classifier. For a given review r_i in the target language, composed of n words, we construct a $1 \times Max\_length$ sentiment vector (where Max_length is the number of words of the longest target review). We construct this vector by passing in the word embedding for every word into the sentiment analysis model and placing the resulting values (of 1 to 9) into the constructed array. The array is then padded with 0's in order to make it of length Max_length.

For reviews in the source language, the process is similar, with the only change being that the words are first translated from their original vector space to that of the target language before being passed into the sentiment classifier. Once the review vector has been constructed, it is passed to the classifier to produce a classification of 1 to 5.

As with the previous classifier, the training procedure is quite simple and involves only the target language (*i.e.*, the classifier is trained only on reviews which are originally from the target language, but it is tested on reviews only from the source language).

4 Results

4.1 Translation Accuracy

We first measure the accuracy of the matrix translation method using the same test described by Mikolov et al. (2013a). The purpose of these tests is two-fold: i) verifying that the data used and implementation of the technique reproduces what is

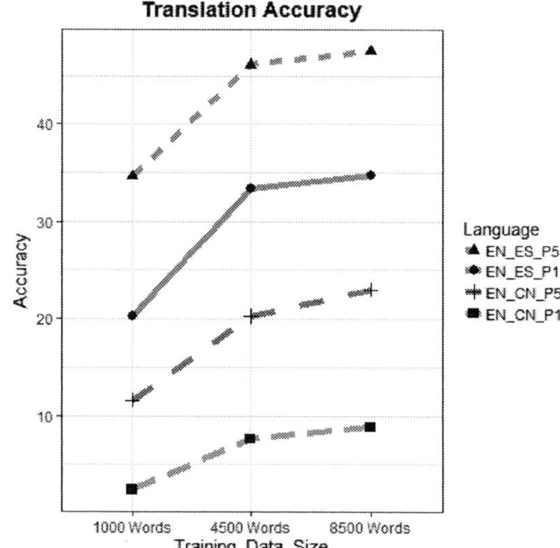

Figure 2: Top-1 and Top-5 accuracy for Spanish and Chinese using various amounts of training data.

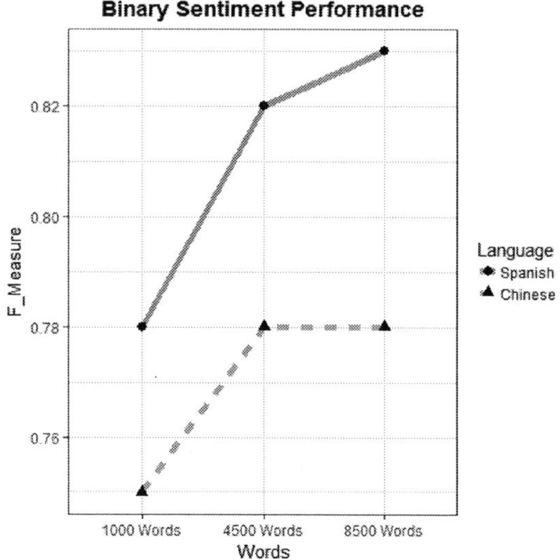

Figure 3: F-measure of binary sentiment classifier with varying amounts of training data for both Spanish and Chinese.

expected, and ii) quantifying how much sentiment is preserved with low translation accuracy (by explicitly noting the poor accuracy of the translation). The data used is described in section 2.1. Table 2 shows the effect of training size (number of words) on the accuracy of the translation matrix method. As expected (and previously shown by Mikolov et al. (2013a)), the translation accuracy increases with more training examples, as shown in Figure 2. The data and methods used in this work are further validated as the translation accuracy results closely approximate those of Mikolov et al. (2013a), with English-Spanish translational accuracy achieving 35% and 48% accuracy for P@1 and P@5 respectively when compared to the original 33% and 51%. This concordance is further validation of the method. It is also interesting to note that Chinese, which is less like English than Spanish is, also suffers a lower translation score across both categories. However, we see that this large drop is not represented significantly in later portions.

4.2 Binary Word Sentiment Classification

The second experiment tested the binary cross-lingual sentiment classification capabilities of the matrix translation method, *i.e.*, how well can we differentiate between positive and negative words of a language we have not seen before using a model trained only on English words? Here we used the binary sentiment word list described in section 2.1.2 in order to assess whether or not the translation matrix would preserve sentiment even with poor translation accuracy scores. Given that the classifier is trained only on the target language vectors, we used the translation matrices produced previously to translate a word from source to target language embedding space.

As we can see in Table 3 and Figure 3, even with low translation accuracy, such as the 1000-word Chinese translation matrix, we are able to achieve good binary sentiment classification. We also noted that a significant drop in translation accuracy results in only a relatively small drop in sentiment classification performance.

4.3 Fine-Grained Sentiment Analysis

In the third experiment, we tested the accuracy of cross-lingual regression when it comes to predicting a word's value in any of the three ANEW dimensions of *valence*, *arousal*, and *dominance*. We attempted to predict the *valence*, *arousal*, and *dominance* of words in source language, having only trained on target language. As we saw in the last experiment, massive drop-off in translation accuracy need not result in a massive drop-off in sentiment analysis. As this is a regression problem, Table 4 presents both the r^2 and the mean squared error (MSE) as measurements of model performance. The MSE per dimension is visual-

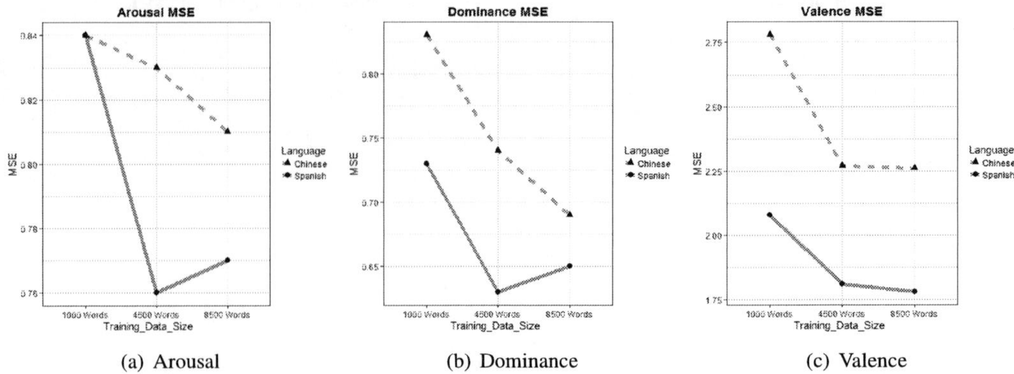

(a) Arousal   (b) Dominance   (c) Valence

Figure 4: Mean squared error for each regression problem with varying amounts of training data for all three of the ANEW dimensions. (Lower is better).

	Spanish	Chinese
1000 Words		
Precision	0.77	0.76
Recall	0.79	0.74
F-measure	0.78	0.75
4500 Words		
Precision	0.82	0.79
Recall	0.82	0.77
F-measure	0.82	0.78
8500 Words		
Precision	0.83	0.80
Recall	0.83	0.77
F-measure	0.83	0.78

Table 3: Results of the binary sentiment classification task for each language with each translation matrix.

	Spanish	Chinese
1000 Words		
Arousal	0.24 (0.84)	0.24 (0.84)
Dominance	0.31 (0.73)	0.23 (0.83)
Valence	0.48 (2.08)	0.32 (2.78)
4500 Words		
Arousal	0.33 (0.76)	0.28 (0.83)
Dominance	0.39 (0.63)	0.28 (0.74)
Valence	0.54 (1.81)	0.44 (2.27)
8500 Words		
Arousal	0.33 (0.77)	0.29 (0.81)
Dominance	0.38 (0.65)	0.31 (0.69)
Valence	0.54 (1.78)	0.43 (2.26)

Table 4: Results of the fine-grained sentiment regression task for each language with each translation matrix, in the form of $r^2(MSE)$.

ized in Figure 4. Given the data's scale from 1 to 9 with an average standard deviation among participants for each word of 2.02, an average mean squared error of approximately 1 shows that our model has high predictive power.

4.4 Sentiment Classification of Reviews

In the fourth experiment, we sought to show that the regressor developed in section 3.3.2 could be used as a feature extractor in performing other tasks. To this end, we replicated the experiment by Chen et al. (2016), who predicted hotel ratings from Chinese reviews using a model trained only on English restaurant reviews.

Chen et al. (2016) had two baseline models which they beat with their new model: i) a lo-gistic regression classifier (line 1 in Table 5), and ii) a non-adversarial variation of adversarial deep averaging network (ADAN) (line 2), referred to as DAN (deep averaging network), which is one of the state-of-the-art neural models for sentiment classification. These were the only two models which did not make use of either labeled Chinese examples or an MT system, and therefore were chosen to serve as a fair comparison to our method. Both models use bilingual word embeddings as an input representation to map words from both languages into the same vector space. Our own model (line 3 in Table 5) uses logistic regression on sentence arrays created by predicting their ANEW values for each dimension to predict review scores.

Approach	Accuracy
Logistic regression (BWE)	30.58%
Deep averaging network (DAN)	29.11%
Logistic regression (ANEW)	28.05%

Table 5: Model performance on sentiment extracted vectors versus previous approaches. Logistic regression on predicted sentiment (ANEW) values preformed similariy to both regression and DAN on BWEs.

Table 5 shows that we were able to closely match the accuracy of the baseline systems implemented by Chen et al. (2016) for Chinese reviews. These results demonstrate that our sentiment regressors encoded enough information into the sentence vectors to achieve similar results to the baseline models which took bilingual word embedding as input, and that the fine-grained sentiment model can be used to extract sentiment-based features for other tasks in languages where aligned data might be expensive to obtain.

5 Discussion and Future Work

We have shown that the matrix translation method can be used to infer and predict cross-lingual sentiment. More notably we observed that: i) sentiment is preserved accurately even with sub-par translations, and ii) this low-cost approach also maintained fine-grained sentiment information between languages.

We further cemented these observations through a variety of experiments. The first experiment preformed was testing the translation accuracy of the method presented to verify validity of the algorithm. The second experiment, was binary word classification into either positive and negative for words in Chinese or Spanish, given a model that was trained only with English. With a translation P@5 as low as 11%, our linear classifier was still able to predict with 75% precision and recall the polarity of a word's sentiment. The third experiment, in which we were able to predict a word's position on the three-dimensional ANEW 9-point scale with an error margin of 1 (per dimension), lent further credibility to the validity and data-efficiency of our approach. Our fine-grained sentiment analysis with the ANEW scale is notable as it demonstrates how the algorithm works at the word level — useful in building sentiment lexicons in an automated fashion at a very low cost and with little manual effort. Our last experiment, Chinese review classification, further highlighted the robustness of our model, by showing that vectors created using the regressor encoded enough sentiment information to match the baseline methods of passing in bilingual word embeddings to a trained model. We showed how competitive the proposed approach is when compared to much more expensive methods and that it can directly be applied to sentiment classification tasks for data-poor languages.

Throughout the experiments, we saw the general trend of reduced error and increased accuracy with more training data. However the increase in accuracy starts to diminish with around 8500 words. The root of this leveling of accuracy could be the inherent limitation of either the translation technique used or the classification or regression algorithms used or both.

A surprising finding was how well sentence vectors composed of ANEW values for each word performed when compared to the baselines of Chen et al. (2016), Table 5. Achieving similar results to the previous baseline using the same classification algorithm (logistic regression) means that the sentence vectors composed of ANEW values encode enough (and as much) information as the BWE, or that the classification algorithm used on the BWEs isn't strong enough to extract more meaningful relationships between the values. The truth is probably a mixture of both reasons.

By choosing the number and type of languages selected we have shown that this observation holds across languages with different roots and different grammar systems, which is further re-affirmed by the fact that we train our models only on English data, but test purely on Chinese and Spanish.

We explore the effect of poor translation on fine-grained sentiment analysis by taking a look at a few concrete examples of poor translations (Table 6). Table 6 presents four different Chinese words with predicted valence of varying accuracy. We can see that even with poor translation (*i.e.*, the closest five words are all completely unrelated, as is the case with *hungry*), sentiment is still accurately predicted. On the other hand we also show that it is possible to have related words but have poor prediction, as is the case with *misery*, because the base sentiment predictor itself is not perfectly accurate. This suggests that the sentiment vector space, a hypothetical space produced by finding the sentiment value of each point in the original

Chinese Word (English)	Computed English Translation	True Valence (Predicted Valence)
飢餓 (Hungry)	Mugabe misrule	3.58 (2.85)
	Boo hoo	
	Quagmire	
	Chikwanine	
	Sylvain Angerlotte	
街 (Incentive)	Circumstances dictate	7.00 (6.17)
	Selfless sacrifices	
	Humilty	
	President Obama	
	EquityMarketReport	
善良 (Kindness)	Really hateful lemmings	7.81 (6.84)
	Loving	
	Dad	
	Flowering orchids	
	Dear robin	
苦難 (Misery)	Violence begets violence	1.93 (3.91)
	Indignations	
	Sufferings	
	Sincerely	
	Unconfessed sin	

Table 6: Four poorly translated Chinese words, their accompanying true English translation, the five nearest English words to the translated vector, and the true (English) valence with the accompanying predicted valence of the translated vector.

embedding space, which we term topological sentiment map, has two properties: i) it is maintained through linear transformation, and ii) it is "flat" enough that highly accurate mapping (read: translation) between languages is not required to arrive at usable sentiment classification. This second property allows for the sentiment analysis of languages where a large amount of labeled material is not available at an extremely low cost, and can also be used to aid in many cross-lingual sentiment related tasks.

In the future we hope to extend both the analysis and experiments discussed here to other languages and applications. For example the cross-lingual fine-grained sentiment analysis techniques could possibly be used to study the change in sentiment of words in a single language over time, leading to new insights or re-affirming old ones. Future analysis could compare different transformations and their effect on sentiment analysis. The ability to produce a "stable" topographic sentiment map could also be used to evaluate algorithms which create the vector spaces as well.

Lastly, future work will focus on developing other low-cost approaches, possibly by implementing Duong et al. (2016)'s technique to improve the accuracy and precision of sentiment regression. This would serve to demonstrate the (expected) limits of the linear transformation model's

in handling polysemy and subsequently its impact on the topological mapping of sentiment in vector space.

Acknowledgements

We would like to thank Moustafa Abdalla for his help and discussions. The work was financially supported by the Natural Sciences and Engineering Research Council of Canada.

References

AR Balamurali, Aditya Joshi, and Pushpak Bhattacharyya. 2012. Cross-lingual sentiment analysis for Indian languages using linked WordNets. In *Proceedings of the International Conference on Computational Linguistics (COLING)*, pages 73–82. Association for Computational Linguistics.

Yoshua Bengio and Greg Corrado. 2015. BilBOWA: Fast bilingual distributed representations without word alignments. *arXiv:1410.2455*.

Margaret M Bradley and Peter J Lang. 1994. Measuring emotion: The self-assessment manikin and the semantic differential. *Journal of Behavior Therapy and Experimental Psychiatry*, 25(1):49–59.

Margaret M Bradley and Peter J Lang. 1999. Affective norms for English words (ANEW): Instruction manual and affective ratings. Technical report, Center for Research in Psychophysiology, University of Florida.

Cristian Cardellino. 2016. Spanish Billion Words Corpus and Embeddings.

Xilun Chen, Ben Athiwaratkun, Yu Sun, Kilian Q Weinberger, and Claire Cardie. 2016. Adversarial deep averaging networks for cross-lingual sentiment classification. *arXiv:1606.01614*.

Long Duong, Hiroshi Kanayama, Tengfei Ma, Steven Bird, and Trevor Cohn. 2016. Learning crosslingual word embeddings without bilingual corpora. In *Proceedings of the 2016 Conference on Empirical Methods in Natural Language Processing (EMNLP)*, pages 1285–1295.

Long Duong, Hiroshi Kanayama, Tengfei Ma, Steven Bird, and Trevor Cohn. 2017. Multilingual training of crosslingual word embeddings. In *Proceedings of the 15th Conference of the European Chapter of the Association for Computational Linguistics (EACL)*, pages 893–903.

Manaal Faruqui and Chris Dyer. 2014. Improving vector space word representations using multilingual correlation. In *Proceedings of the 14th Conference of the European Chapter of the Association for Computational Linguistics (EACL)*, pages 462–471.

Karl Moritz Hermann and Phil Blunsom. 2013. Multilingual distributed representations without word alignment. *arXiv:1312.6173*.

Minqing Hu and Bing Liu. 2004. Mining and summarizing customer reviews. In *Proceedings of the ACM SIGKDD International Conference on Knowledge Discovery and Data Mining* (KDD-2004), pages 168–177. ACM.

Sarthak Jain and Shashank Batra. 2015. Cross-lingual sentiment analysis using modified BRAE. In *Proceedings of the 2015 Conference on Empirical Methods in Natural Language Processing* (EMNLP), pages 159–168.

Alexandre Klementiev, Ivan Titov, and Binod Bhattarai. 2012. Inducing crosslingual distributed representations of words. In *Proceedings of the 24th International Conference on Computational Linguistics* (COLING), pages 1459–1474.

Huey Yee Lee and Hemnaath Renganathan. 2011. Chinese sentiment analysis using maximum entropy. In *Proceedings of the Workshop on Sentiment Analysis where AI meets Psychology* (SAAIP), page 89.

Yiou Lin, Hang Lei, Jia Wu, and Xiaoyu Li. 2015. An empirical study on sentiment classification of Chinese review using word embedding. *arXiv:1511.01665*.

Andrew L Maas, Raymond E Daly, Peter T Pham, Dan Huang, Andrew Y Ng, and Christopher Potts. 2011. Learning word vectors for sentiment analysis. In *Proceedings of the 49th Annual Meeting of the Association for Computational Linguistics: Human Language Technologies* (ACL-HLT), pages 142–150.

Tomas Mikolov, Quoc V Le, and Ilya Stuskever. 2013a. Exploiting similarities among languages for machine translation. *arXiv:1309.4168*.

Tomas Mikolov, Ilya Sutskever, Kai Chen, Greg S Corrado, and Jeff Dean. 2013b. Distributed representations of words and phrases and their compositionality. In *Advances in Neural Information Processing Systems* (NIPS), pages 3111–3119.

Saif M Mohammad, Mohammad Salameh, and Svetlana Kiritchenko. 2016. Sentiment lexicons for Arabic social media. In *Proceedings of the International Conference on Language Resources and Evaluation* (LREC), pages 33–37.

F Pedregosa, G Varoquaux, A Gramfort, V Michel, B Thirion, O Grisel, M Blondel, P Prettenhofer, R Weiss, V Dubourg, J Vanderplas, A Passos, D Cournapeau, M Brucher, M Perrot, and E Duchesnay. 2011. Scikit-learn: Machine learning in Python. *Journal of Machine Learning Research*, 12:2825–2830.

Jeffrey Pennington, Richard Socher, and Christopher D Manning. 2014. GloVe: Global vectors for word representation. In *Proceedings of the 2014 Conference on Empirical Methods on Natural Language Processing* (EMNLP), volume 14, pages 1532–1543.

R Řehůřek and P Sojka. 2011. Gensim - Python framework for vector space modelling. Technical report, NLP Centre, Faculty of Informatics, Masaryk University, Brno, Czech Republic.

Mohammad Salameh, Saif M Mohammad, and Svetlana Kiritchenko. 2015. Sentiment after translation: A case-study on Arabic social media posts. In *Proceedings of the 2015 Conference of the North American Chapter of the Association for Computational Linguistics: Human Language Technologies* (NAACL—HLT).

AP Sarath Chandar, Stanislas Lauly, Hugo Larochelle, Mitesh Khapra, Balaraman Ravindran, Vikas C Raykar, and Amrita Saha. 2014. An autoencoder approach to learning bilingual word representations. In *Advances in Neural Information Processing Systems* (NIPS).

Songbo Tan and Jin Zhang. 2008. An empirical study of sentiment analysis for Chinese documents. *Expert Systems with Applications*, 34(4):2622–2629.

Xuewei Tang and Xiaojun Wan. 2014. Learning bilingual embedding model for cross-language sentiment classification. In *Proceedings of the 2014 IEEE/WIC/ACM International Joint Conferences on Web Intelligence (WI) and Intelligent Agent Technologies (IAT)-Volume 02*, pages 134–141. IEEE Computer Society.

Xiang Zhang, Junbo Zhao, and Yann LeCun. 2015. Character-level convolutional networks for text classification. In *Advances in Neural Information Processing Systems* (NIPS), pages 649–657.

Huiwei Zhou, Long Chen, Fulin Shi, and Degen Huang. 2015. Learning bilingual sentiment word embeddings for cross-language sentiment classification. In *Proceedings of the 53rd Annual Meeting of the Association for Computational Linguistics* (ACL), pages 430–440.

Xinjie Zhou, Xianjun Wan, and Jianguo Xiao. 2016. Cross-lingual sentiment classification with bilingual document representation learning. In *Proceedings of the 54th Annual Meeting of the Association for Computational Linguistics* (ACL), pages 1403–1412.

Will Y. Zou, Richard Socher, Daniel Cer, and Christopher D. Manning. 2013. Bilingual word embeddings for phrase-based machine translation. In *Proceedings of the 2013 Conference on Empirical Methods in Natural Language Processing* (EMNLP), pages 1393–1398.

Author Index

Abdalla, Mohamed, 506
Abouelenien, Mohamed, 885
Abudukelimu, Halidanmu, 362
Allahyari, Mehdi, 316
Alva-Manchego, Fernando, 295
Arabnia, Hamid Reza, 316
Asahara, Masayuki, 404

Baldwin, Timothy, 555
Belinkov, Yonatan, 1, 142
Bethard, Steven, 90
Bhattacharya, Robin, 342
Bingel, Joachim, 295
Biran, Or, 306
Bisk, Yonatan, 100
Bless, Patrick, 947
Brad, Florin, 906
Brockett, Chris, 462, 605
Brychcín, Tomáš, 224

Cao, Yixin, 233
Cao, Ziqiang, 986
Carenini, Giuseppe, 615
Celikyilmaz, Asli, 733
Chambers, Nathanael, 843
Chen, Hsin-Hsi, 976
Chen, Kehai, 11
Chen, Yun-Nung, 733
Cheng, Gong, 316
Chi, Lianhua, 744
Chung, Jin-Woo, 865
Cohn, Trevor, 555, 744

D'hondt, Eva, 1006
Dai, Anna Mengdan, 885
Dalvi, Fahim, 1, 142
Das, Kollol, 576
Datla, Vivek, 895
Davenport, Quincy, 885
Demberg, Vera, 484
Dey, Kuntal, 525
Dias, Gaël, 926
Do, Quynh Ngoc Thi, 90
Dolan, Bill, 462, 605
Duan, Shaoyang, 352

Duh, Kevin, 832, 957, 996
Durrani, Nadir, 1, 142

Elliott, Desmond, 130
Erk, Katrin, 204

Falke, Tobias, 801
Farri, Oladimeji, 895
Ferracane, Elisa, 584
Ferret, Olivier, 273
Freedman, Marjorie, 674

Galley, Michel, 462, 605
Gan, Ling, 336
Gao, Jianfeng, 462, 605, 733, 957
Gao, Lei, 774
Gao, Yuze, 516
Ghaddar, Abbas, 413
Ghader, Hamidreza, 30
Ghosh, Shaona, 576
Glass, James, 1
Gong, Houyu, 336
Grau, Brigitte, 1006
Grouin, Cyril, 1006
Grundkiewicz, Roman, 120
Gurevych, Iryna, 801

Hardmeier, Christian, 173
Hasan, Sadid A., 895
Hasanuzzaman, Mohammed, 926
Hashimoto, Atsushi, 326
Hashimoto, Hayato, 326
Hazem, Amir, 685
He, Ruifang, 352
Hercig, Tomáš, 224
Hirst, Graeme, 506
Hockenmaier, Julia, 100
Hoshino, Chikara, 967
Hosu, Ionel Alexandru, 906
Hovy, Eduard, 59
Hsiao, Wei-Chuan, 976
Huang, Hen-Hsen, 976
Huang, Lifu, 854
Huang, Ruihong, 774
Huang, Shen, 184

Huy Tien, Nguyen, 644

Iacob, Radu Cristian Alexandru, 906
Inui, Kentaro, 473
Ishigaki, Tatsuya, 792
Ishii, Ai, 967

J Kurisinkel, Litton, 812
Jaidka, Kokil, 764
Ji, Heng, 362, 854
Jiang, Jing, 654
Jiang, Zhuolin, 674
Jimeno Yepes, Antonio, 566
Jin, Yiping, 545
Jo, Yohan, 1026
Johansson, Richard, 284
Joshi, Sachindra, 723
Judea, Alex, 822
Junczys-Dowmunt, Marcin, 120

Kádár, Ákos, 130
Kajiwara, Tomoyuki, 80
Kaneko, Masahiro, 40
Kato, Sachi, 404
Kawahara, Tatsuya, 704
Kelleher, John, 441
Klabjan, Diego, 947
Knight, Kevin, 362
Kobayashi, Mio, 967
Kobayashi, Sosuke, 473
Kochut, Krzysztof, 316
Komachi, Mamoru, 40, 80
Komatani, Kazunori, 243
Konkol, Michal, 224
Ku, Lun-Wei, 110
Kuppersmith, Alexis, 774

Lahiri, Shibamouli, 394
Lai, Alice, 100
Lakomkin, Egor, 423
Lang, Jun, 49
Langlais, Phillippe, 413
Lau, Jey Han, 744
Le, Phu, 545
Lee, Kathy, 895
Li, Chengjiang, 233, 875
Li, Juanzi, 233, 875
Li, Lihong, 733
Li, Sujian, 496, 634
Li, Wenjie, 986
Li, Xiujun, 733
Li, Yanran, 986
Li, Zhenghua, 49

Lin, Ying, 362
Ling, Yuan, 895
Lipton, Zachary C., 783
Liu, Fei, 555
Liu, Joey, 895
Liu, Luigi (Yu-Cheng), 694
Liu, Xiaodong, 957
Liu, Yuanchao, 713
Liu, Zhiyuan, 233
Lu, Di, 362
Luan, Yi, 605

Ma, Dehong, 634
Ma, Xuezhe, 59
MacKinlay, Andrew, 566
Madan, Dhiraj, 723
Magg, Sven, 423
Maki, Keith, 1026
Margolin, Drew, 754
Màrquez, Lluís, 1
Martinez, Ander, 21
Matsumoto, Yuji, 21, 264
Matsuzaki, Takuya, 967
McAuley, Julian, 783
McDowell, Bill, 843
McKeown, Kathleen, 306
Mehri, Shikib, 615
Meyer, Christian M., 801
Mihalcea, Rada, 394, 664, 885
Min, Bonan, 674
Minh Le, Nguyen, 644
Minker, Wolfgang, 915
Mishra, Abhijit, 525
Miyashita, Hiroshi, 967
Mochihashi, Daichi, 80
Moens, Marie-Francine, 90
Monz, Christof, 30
Mooney, Raymond, 584
Mori, Shinsuke, 326
Morin, Emmanuel, 685
Mostafazadeh, Nasrin, 462
Murawaki, Yugo, 451
Myaeng, Sung-Hyon, 214

Nagar, Seema, 525
Nakamura, Satoshi, 152, 431, 915
Nakayama, Hideki, 70
Neubig, Graham, 152
Newell, Edward, 754
Ng, Vincent, 594
Nguyen Le, An, 21
Nguyen, Huy-Thanh, 536

Nguyen, Minh-Le, 536
Ni, Jianmo, 783
Nieto Piña, Luis, 284
Nishida, Kyosuke, 937
Nishida, Noriki, 70
Niu, Shuzi, 986
Nivre, Joakim, 173
Nouvel, Damien, 694
Nykl, Michal, 224

Okazaki, Naoaki, 473
Okumura, Manabu, 792
Ororbia II, Alexander, 843

Paetzold, Gustavo, 295
Pan, Liangming, 875
Pan, Xiaoman, 362
Pappas, Nikolaos, 1015
Park, Jong C., 865
Park, Joohee, 214
Pérez-Rosas, Verónica, 885
Persing, Isaac, 594
Pinnis, Mārcis, 373
Popescu-Belis, Andrei, 1015
Potash, Peter, 342
Pouriyeh, Seyedamin, 316
Pragst, Louisa, 915

Qadir, Ashequl, 895

Rastogi, Pushpendre, 996
Rebedea, Traian, 906
Reitter, David, 843
Rieman, Daniel, 764
Roller, Stephen, 204
Rosé, Carolyn, 1026
Ross, Robert, 441
Roth, Benjamin, 624
Rubino, Raphael, 484
Rumshisky, Anna, 342
Ruppenhofer, Josef, 624
Ruths, Derek, 754

Sadamitsu, Kugatsu, 937
Saito, Itsumi, 937
Saito, Kuniko, 937
Sajjad, Hassan, 1, 142
Sakaizawa, Yuya, 40
Sakti, Sakriani, 431
Salton, Giancarlo, 441
Scarton, Carolina, 295
Schang, Ariane, 754
Schulder, Marc, 624

Schwartz, H. Andrew, 764
Shao, Yan, 173
Shen, Xiaoyu, 986
Shen, Yelong, 957
Shi, Jiaxin, 233
Shi, Wei, 484
Shindo, Hiroyuki, 264
Shroff, Gautam, 194
Skadina, Inguna, 373
Specia, Lucia, 295
Spithourakis, Georgios, 462
Strube, Michael, 822
Su, Hui, 986
Sumita, Eiichiro, 11
Sumita, Eiichro, 152
Sun, Xu, 184, 496, 634

Takamura, Hiroya, 792
Takeda, Ryu, 243
Tamilselvam, Srikanth, 525
Tang, Jie, 875
Teranishi, Hiroki, 264
Tiedemann, Jörg, 173
Tjandra, Andros, 431
Tomita, Junji, 937
Tran, Khoi-Nguyen, 744
Tran, Quan, 566

Ultes, Stefan, 915
Ungar, Lyle, 764
Ushiku, Atsushi, 326
Utiyama, Masao, 11, 152

Van Durme, Benjamin, 832, 996
Vanderwende, Lucy, 462
Varma, Vasudeva, 812
Vig, Lovekesh, 194
Vikram, Sharad, 783
Vishal, S, 194
Vogel, Stephan, 142
Vydiswaran, V.G.Vinod, 394

Wallace, Byron, 253
Wang, Baoxun, 713
Wang, Chunqi, 163
Wang, Houfeng, 184, 496, 634
Wang, Jianan, 713
Wang, Rui, 11
Wang, Su, 204, 584
Wang, Wei-Chung, 110
Wang, Xiaochen, 875
Wang, Xiaolong, 713
Wang, Xin, 713

Wang, Yining, 384
Wang, Yizhong, 496
Wang, Zhuoran, 713
Wanvarie, Dittaya, 545
Way, Andy, 926
Weber, Cornelius, 423
Weischedel, Ralph, 674
Wermter, Stefan, 423
White, Aaron Steven, 996
Wiegand, Michael, 624
Wilson, Steven, 664

Xia, Qingrong, 49
Xiao, Tong, 516
Xu, Bo, 163
Xue, Zhengshan, 384

Yadav, Mohit, 194
Yang, Jingfeng, 496
Yang, Wonsuk, 865
Yoder, Michael, 1026
Yoshimoto, Akifumi, 21
Yoshino, Koichiro, 915
You, Jinseon, 865
Yu, Dian, 854
Yu, Jianfei, 654
Yung, Frances, 484

Zhang, Boliang, 362
Zhang, Jiajun, 384
Zhang, Jingyi, 152
Zhang, Min, 49
Zhang, Sheng, 832
Zhang, Xiaodong, 634
Zhang, Ye, 253
Zhang, Yue, 49, 516, 812
Zhao, Tianyu, 704
Zhao, Tiejun, 11
Zhao, Wenli, 352
Zhao, Yang, 384
Zhu, Xiaofeng, 947
Zong, Chengqing, 384

Association for Computational Linguistics
209 N. Eighth Street
Stroudsburg, Pennsylvania 18360

Eighth International Joint Conference on Natural Language Processing (IJCNLP 2017)

Long Papers

Taipei, Taiwan
1 December 2017

Volume 2 of 2

Eighth International Joint Conference on Natural Language Processing (IJCNLP 2017)

Long Papers

Taipei, Taiwan
1 December 2017

Volume 2 of 2

ISBN: 978-1-5108-5292-1

IJCNLP 2017

The Eighth International Joint Conference on Natural Language Processing

Proceedings of the Conference, Vol. 1 (Long Papers)

November 27 - December 1, 2017
Taipei, Taiwan

Gold Sponsors:

Silver Sponsors:

Bronze Sponsors:

Supporters:

Preface

Welcome to the 8th International Joint Conference on Natural Language Processing (IJCNLP). IJCNLP was initiated in 2004 by the Asian Federation of Natural Language Processing (AFNLP) with the major goal to provide a platform for researchers and professionals around the world to share their experiences related to natural language processing and computational linguistics. In the past years, IJCNLPs were held in 7 different places: Hainan Island (2004), Jeju Island (2005), Hyderabad (2008), Singapore (2009), Chiang Mai (2011), Nagoya (2013) and Beijing (2015). This year the 8th IJCNLP is held in Taipei Nangang Exhibition Hall on November 27-December 1, 2017.

We are confident that you will find IJCNLP 2017 to be technically stimulating. The conference covers a broad spectrum of technical areas related to natural language processing and computation. Besides main conference, the program includes 3 keynote speeches, 6 tutorials, 17 demonstrations, 5 workshops, and 5 shared tasks (new event).

Before closing this brief welcome, we would like to thank the entire organizing committee for their long efforts to create and event that we hope will be memorable for you. Program chairs Greg Kondrak and Taro Watanabe coordinate the review process allowing for top quality papers to be presented at the conference. Workshop chairs Min Zhang and Yue Zhang organize 5 nice pre-conference and post-conference workshops. Tutorial chairs Sadao Kurohashi and Michael Strube select 6 very good tutorials. Demo chairs Seong-Bae Park and Thepchai Supnithi recommend 17 demonstrations. Shared Task chairs Chao-Hong Liu, Preslav Nakov and Nianwen Xue choose 5 interesting shared tasks. Sponsorship chairs Youngkil Kim, Tong Xiao, Kazuhide Yamamoto and Jui-Feng Yeh design sponsor packages and find financial supports. We thank all the sponsors. Publicity chairs Pushpak Bhattacharya, Xuanjing Huang, Gina-Anne Levow, Chi Mai Loung and Sebastian Stüker help circulate the conference information and promote the conference. We would like to express our special thanks to publication chairs Lung-Hao Lee and Derek F. Wong. After the hard work, they deliver an excellent proceeding to the participants.

Finally, we would like to thank all authors for submitting high quality research this year. We hope all of you enjoy the conference program, and your stay at this beautiful city of Taipei.

General Chair

Chengqing Zong, Institute of Automation, Chinese Academy of Sciences, China

Organization Co-Chairs

Hsin-Hsi Chen, National Taiwan University, Taiwan
Yuen-Hsien Tseng, National Taiwan Normal University, Taiwan
Chung-Hsien Wu, National Cheng Kung University, Taiwan
Liang-Chih Yu, Yuan Ze University, Taiwan

Message from the Program Co-Chairs

Welcome to the 8th International Joint Conference on Natural Language Processing (IJCNLP 2017) organized by National Taiwan Normal University and the Association for Computational Linguistics and Chinese Language Processing (ACLCLP) and hosted by The Asian Federation of Natural Language Processing (AFNLP).

Since the first meeting in 2004, IJCNLP has established itself as a major NLP conference. This year, we received 580 submissions (337 long and 243 short), which is by far the largest number ever for a stand-alone IJCNLP conference. From these, 179 papers (103 long and 76 short) were accepted to appear at the conference, which represents an acceptance rate of 31%. In particular, approximately 46% of the accepted papers are from Asia Pacific, 30% from North America, and 20% from Europe.

Our objective is to keep the conference to three parallel sessions at any one time. 86 long papers and 21 short papers are scheduled as oral presentations, while 17 long papers and 55 short papers will be presented as posters.

We are also very pleased to announce three exciting keynote talks by the renowned NLP researchers: Rada Mihalcea (University of Michigan), Trevor Cohn (University of Melbourne) and Jason Eisner (Johns Hopkins University).

The conference will conclude with the award presentation ceremony. The Best Paper Award goes to Nikolaos Pappas and Andrei Popescu-Belis for their paper "Multilingual Hierarchical Attention Networks for Document Classification." The Best Student Paper award goes to "Roles and Success in Wikipedia Talk Pages: Identifying Latent Patterns of Behavior" by Keith Maki, Michael Yoder, Yohan Jo and Carolyn Rosé.

We would like to thank everyone who has helped make IJCNLP 2017 a success. In particular, the area chairs (who are listed in the Program Committee section) worked hard on recruiting reviewers, managing reviews, leading discussions, and making recommendations. The quality of the technical program reflects the expertise of our 536 reviewers. All submissions were reviewed by at least three reviewers. The review process for the conference was double-blind, and included an author response period, as well as subsequent discussions.

We would like to acknowledge the help and advice from the General Chair Chengqing Zong, and the Local Arrangements Committee headed by Liang-Chih Yu. We thank the Publication Chairs Lung-Hao Lee and Derek F. Wong for putting together the conference proceedings and handbook, and all the other committee chairs for their great work.

We hope you will enjoy IJCNLP 2017!

IJCNLP 2017 Program Co-Chairs

Greg Kondrak, University of Alberta
Taro Watanabe, Google

Organizing Committee

Conference Chair

Chengqing Zong, Institute of Automation, Chinese Academy of Sciences

Program Committee Co-Chairs

Greg Kondrak, University of Alberta
Taro Watanabe, Google

Workshop Co-Chairs

Min Zhang, Soochow University
Yue Zhang, Singapore University of Technology and Design

Tutorial Co-Chairs

Sadao Kurohashi, Kyoto University
Michael Strube, Heidelberg Institute for Theoretical Studies

Demo Co-Chairs

Seong-Bae Park, Kyungpook National University
Thepchai Supnithi, National Electronics and Computer Technology Center (NECTEC) of Thailand

Shared Task Workshop Co-Chairs

Chao-Hong Liu, ADAPT Centre, Dublin City University
Preslav Nakov, Qatar Computing Research Institute
Nianwen Xue, Brandies University

Publication Co-Chairs

Lung-Hao Lee, National Taiwan Normal University
Derek F. Wong, University of Macau

Sponsorship Co-Chairs

Youngkil Kim, ETRI
Tong Xiao, Northeast University
Kazuhide Yamamoto, Nagaoka University of Technology
Jui-Feng Yeh, National Chiayi University

Publicity Co-Chairs

Pushpak Bhattacharya, IITB
Xuanjing Huang, Fudan University
Gina-Anne Levow, University of Washington
Chi Mai Loung, Institute of Information Technology
Sebastian Stüker, Karlsruhe Institute of Technology

Financial Chair

Lun-Wei Ku, Institute of Information Sciences, Academia Sinica

Local Co-Chairs

Hsin-Hsi Chen, National Taiwan University
Yuen-Hsien Tseng, National Taiwan Normal University
Chung-Hsien Wu, National Cheng Kung University
Liang-Chih Yu, Yuan Ze University

Program Committee

Program Committee Co-Chairs

Greg Kondrak, University of Alberta
Taro Watanabe, Google

Area Chairs

Mausam (Information Extraction and Text Mining Area)
Asli Celikyilmaz (Semantics Area)
Wenliang Chen (Syntax and Parsing Area)
Colin Cherry (Machine Translation Area)
Jackie Chi Kit Cheung (Summarization and Generation Area)
Monojit Choudhury (Resources and Tools Area)
Kevin Duh (Semantics Area)
Micha Elsner (Discourse, Dialogue, Pragmatics Area)
Manaal Faruqui (Machine Learning Area)
Jianfeng Gao (Information Retrieval and Question Answering Area)
Yvette Graham (Machine Translation Area)
Gholamreza Haffari (Machine Learning Area)
Liang Huang (Syntax and Parsing Area)
Minlie Huang (Sentiment Analysis and Opinion Mining Area)
Mans Hulden (Morphology, Segmentation and Tagging Area)
Nancy Ide (Resources and Tools Area)
Jing Jiang (Sentiment Analysis and Opinion Mining Area)
Daisuke Kawahara (Semantics Area)
Mamoru Komachi (NLP Applications Area)
Fei Liu (Web and Social Media Area)
Zhiyuan Liu (Web and Social Media Area)
Wei Lu (Information Extraction and Text Mining Area)
Ryo Nagata (NLP Applications Area) Mikio Nakano (Discourse, Dialogue, Pragmatics Area)
Jong-Hoon Oh (Information Retrieval and Question Answering Area)
Thamar Solorio (Sentiment Analysis and Opinion Mining Area)
Xu Sun (Morphology, Segmentation and Tagging Area)
Jun Suzuki (Machine Learning Area)
Xiaojun Wan (Summarization and Generation Area)
Tiejun Zhao (Machine Translation Area)

Reviewers

Ahmed Abbasi, Željko Agić, Alan Akbik, Chris Alberti, Enrique Alfonseca, David Alvarez-Melis, Silvio Amir, Daniel Andrade, Marianna Apidianaki, Jun Araki, Yuki Arase, Yoav Artzi, Kristjan Arumae, Wilker Aziz

Alexandra Balahur, Niranjan Balasubramanian, Timothy Baldwin, Kalika Bali, Miguel Ballesteros, Rafael E. Banchs, Srinivas Bangalore, Clayton Barham, Roberto Basili, Timo Baumann, Kedar Bellare, Anja Belz, Steven Bethard, Chandra Bhagavatula, Suma Bhat, Joachim Bingel, Or Biran, Yonatan Bisk, Johannes Bjerva, Frédéric Blain, Dasha Bogdanova, Bernd Bohnet, Danushka Bollegala, Antoine Bosselut, Florian Boudin, Pavel Braslavski, Chris Brockett, Julian Brooke, William Bryce, Paul Buitelaar, Jill Burstein, Stephan Busemann, Miriam Butt

José G. C. de Souza, Deng Cai, Burcu Can, Ziqiang Cao, Yuan Cao, Vittorio Castelli, Daniel Cer,

Mauro Cettolo, Ming-Wei Chang, Baobao Chang, Kai-Wei Chang, Wanxiang Che, Xinchi Chen, Tao Chen, John Chen, Danqi Chen, Boxing Chen, Kuang-hua Chen, Colin Cherry, David Chiang, Hai Leong Chieu, laura chiticariu, KEY-SUN CHOI, Shamil Chollampatt, Monojit Choudhury, Christos Christodoulopoulos, Jennifer Chu-Carroll, Miriam Connor, John Conroy, Matthieu Constant, Danish Contractor, Anna Corazza, Mark Core, Benoit Crabbé, Danilo Croce, Paul Crook, Heriberto Cuayahuitl

bharath dandala, Kareem Darwish, Gerard de Melo, Luciano Del Corro, Leon Derczynski, Nina Dethlefs, Lipika Dey, Bhuwan Dhingra, Giuseppe Di Fabbrizio, Marco Dinarelli, Daxiang Dong, Li Dong, Doug Downey, Lan Du, Xiangyu Duan, Nadir Durrani

Richard Eckart de Castilho, Steffen Eger, Yo Ehara, Patrick Ehlen, Vladimir Eidelman, Akiko Eriguchi, Tomaž Erjavec, Ramy Eskander, Miquel Esplà-Gomis

Licheng Fang, Atefeh Farzindar, Geli Fei, Anna Feldman, Chong Feng, Oliver Ferschke, Andrew Finch, Orhan Firat, Margaret Fleck, Markus Forsberg, George Foster, Dayne Freitag, Atsushi Fujii, Fumiyo Fukumoto, Kotaro Funakoshi

Björn Gambäck, Michael Gamon, Matt Gardner, Tao Ge, Kallirroi Georgila, Pablo Gervás, Saptarshi Ghosh, Alfio Gliozzo, Dan Goldwasser, Carlos Gómez-Rodríguez, Kyle Gorman, Isao Goto, Yvette Graham, Spence Green, Jiatao Gu, Camille Guinaudeau

Thanh-Le Ha, Barry Haddow, Christian Hadiwinoto, Masato Hagiwara, Dilek Hakkani-Tur, Keith Hall, William L. Hamilton, Xianpei Han, Chung-Wei Hang, Kazi Saidul Hasan, Sadid A. Hasan, Kazuma Hashimoto, Eva Hasler, Matthew Hatem, Luheng He, John Henderson, Matthew Henderson, Aurélie Herbelot, Daniel Hershcovich, Ryuichiro Higashinaka, Cong Duy Vu Hoang, Chris Hokamp, Yu Hong, Kai Hong, Ales Horak, Baotian Hu, Ruihong Huang, Po-Sen Huang, Jen-Wei Huang, Zhongqiang Huang

Kenji Imamura, Michimasa Inaba, Kentaro Inui, Hitoshi Isahara

Donghong JI, Yangfeng Ji, Sittichai Jiampojamarn, Wenbin Jiang, Zhanming Jie, Melvin Johnson Premkumar

Nobuhiro Kaji, Tomoyuki Kajiwara, Hidetaka Kamigaito, Hung-Yu Kao, Arzoo Katiyar, David Kauchak, Anna Kazantseva, Hideto Kazawa, Casey Kennington, Jung-Jae Kim, Sunghwan Mac Kim, Norihide Kitaoka, Julien Kloetzer, Philipp Koehn, Mamoru Komachi, Kazunori Komatani, Parisa Kordjamshidi, Zornitsa Kozareva, Julia Kreutzer, Jayant Krishnamurthy, Lun-Wei Ku, Shankar Kumar, Jonathan K. Kummerfeld, Tsung-Ting Kuo

Sobha Lalitha Devi, Wai Lam, Man Lan, Ni Lao, Guy Lapalme, Carolin Lawrence, Joseph Le Roux, Logan Lebanoff, Kenton Lee, Hung-yi Lee, Sungjin Lee, John Lee, Lung-Hao Lee, Els Lefever, Gina-Anne Levow, Binyang Li, Junhui Li, Shaohua Li, Haibo Li, Yaliang Li, Lishuang Li, Zhenghua Li, Hang Li, Sujian Li, Qing Li, Haizhou Li, Sheng Li, Cheng-Te Li, Chenliang Li, Kexin Liao, Shou-de Lin, Xiao Ling, Pierre Lison, Xiaodong Liu, Shujie Liu, Pengfei Liu, Shulin Liu, Yang Liu, Qun Liu, Jiangming Liu, Yang Liu, Lemao Liu, Nikola Ljubešić, Chi-kiu Lo, Oier Lopez de Lacalle, Annie Louis, Wen-Hsiang Lu, Stephanie Lukin, Jiaming Luo, Franco M. Luque, Anh Tuan Luu

Wei-Yun Ma, Ji Ma, Xuezhe Ma, Wolfgang Macherey, Suraj Maharjan, Andreas Maletti, Benjamin Marie, Héctor Martínez Alonso, Yuichiroh Matsubayashi, Yuji Matsumoto, Takuya Matsuzaki, Diana McCarthy, Tara McIntosh, Susan McRoy, Sameep Mehta, Edgar Meij, Arul Menezes, Helen Meng, Adam Meyers, Bonan Min, Koji Mineshima, Amita Misra, Teruhisa Misu, Makoto Miwa, Daichi Mochihashi, Marie-Francine Moens, Samaneh Moghaddam, Karo Moilanen, Luis Gerardo Mojica de la Vega, Manuel Montes, Taesun Moon, Glyn Morrill, Alessandro Moschitti, Lili Mou, Aldrian Obaja Muis, Yugo Murawaki

Seung-Hoon Na, Tetsuji Nakagawa, Preslav Nakov, Courtney Napoles, Jason Naradowsky, Shashi Narayan, Alexis Nasr, Mark-Jan Nederhof, Graham Neubig, Guenter Neumann, Vincent Ng, Dong Nguyen, Jian-Yun NIE, Hiroshi Noji, Scott Nowson

Diarmuid Ó Séaghdha, Yusuke Oda, Stephan Oepen, Tim O'Gorman, Jong-Hoon Oh, Kiyonori Ohtake, Hidekazu Oiwa, Naoaki Okazaki, Manabu Okumura, Naho Orita, Petya Osenova, Hiroki

Ouchi

Inkit Padhi, Sebastian Padó, Hamid Palangi, Aasish Pappu, Peyman Passban, Adam Pease, Nanyun Peng, Gerald Penn, Juan Antonio Pérez-Ortiz, Verónica Pérez-Rosas, Karl Pichotta, Massimo Poesio, Octavian Popescu, Maja Popović, Daniel Preoţiuc-Pietro, Matthew Purver

Ashequl Qadir, Haoliang Qi, Xian Qian

Afshin Rahimi, Altaf Rahman, A Ramanathan, Sudha Rao, Pushpendre Rastogi, Georg Rehm, Martin Riedl, German Rigau, Brian Roark, Michael Roth, Alla Rozovskaya, Rachel Rudinger, Delia Rusu, Attapol Rutherford

Ashish Sabharwal, Kugatsu Sadamitsu, Markus Saers, Kenji Sagae, Rishiraj Saha Roy, Saurav Sahay, Keisuke Sakaguchi, Germán Sanchis-Trilles, Ryohei Sasano, Carolina Scarton, David Schlangen, Eva Schlinger, Allen Schmaltz, Sebastian Schuster, Djamé Seddah, Satoshi Sekine, Lei Sha, Kashif Shah, Rajiv Shah, Ehsan Shareghi, Shiqi Shen, Shuming Shi, Tomohide Shibata, Prasha Shrestha, Maryam Siahbani, Miikka Silfverberg, Patrick Simianer, Sameer Singh, Sunayana Sitaram, Pavel Smrz, Jan Šnajder, Yang Song, Wei Song, Hyun-Je Song, Sa-kwang Song, Matthias Sperber, Caroline Sporleder, Vivek Srikumar, Gabriel Stanovsky, Manfred Stede, Mark Steedman, Pontus Stenetorp, Svetlana Stoyanchev, Karl Stratos, Kristina Striegnitz, jinsong su, L V Subramaniam, Katsuhito Sudoh, Hiroaki Sugiyama, Md Arafat Sultan, Weiwei Sun, Huan Sun, Yui Suzuki

Sho Takase, David Talbot, Aleš Tamchyna, Liling Tan, Niket Tandon, Jiliang Tang, Duyu Tang, Takehiro Tazoe, Christoph Teichmann, Joel Tetreault, Ran Tian, Takenobu Tokunaga, Gaurav Singh Tomar, Sara Tonelli, Fatemeh Torabi Asr, Ming-Feng Tsai, Richard Tzong-Han Tsai, Masashi Tsubaki, Jun'ichi Tsujii, Yulia Tsvetkov, Zhaopeng Tu, Cunchao Tu, Gokhan Tur, Francis Tyers

Kiyotaka Uchimoto, Masao Utiyama

Tim Van de Cruys, Keith VanderLinden, Lucy Vanderwende, Vasudeva Varma, Eva Maria Vecchi, sriram venkatapathy, Marc Verhagen, David Vilar, David Vilares, Martin Villalba, Esau Villatoro-Tello, Svitlana Volkova, Ivan Vulić

Rui Wang, Baoxun Wang, Shuohang Wang, Xuancong Wang, Longyue Wang, Pidong Wang, Hsin-Min Wang, suge wang, Dingquan Wang, Wei Wang, Mingxuan Wang, William Yang Wang, Leo Wanner, Bonnie Webber, Ingmar Weber, Julie Weeds, Furu Wei, Aaron Steven White, Jason D Williams, Tak-Lam Wong, Kam-Fai Wong, Derek F. Wong, Dekai Wu, Fangzhao Wu, Shih-Hung Wu, Joern Wuebker

Fei Xia, Xinyan Xiao, Tong Xiao, Deyi Xiong, Wenduan Xu, Ying Xu, Feiyu Xu, Ruifeng Xu

Yi Yang, Cheng Yang, Bishan Yang, Helen Yannakoudakis, Jin-ge Yao, Wenpeng Yin, Anssi Yli-Jyrä, Naoki Yoshinaga, Koichiro Yoshino, Bei Yu, Dianhai Yu, Mo Yu, Jianfei Yu, Frances Yung

Fabio Massimo Zanzotto, Sina Zarrieß, Xiaodong Zeng, Feifei Zhai, Min Zhang, Sheng Zhang, Jian ZHANG, Jiajun Zhang, Chengzhi Zhang, Meishan Zhang, Zhisong Zhang, Longtu Zhang, Meishan Zhang, Jian Zhang, Zhe Zhang, Wei-Nan Zhang, Qi Zhang, Hao Zhang, Yu Zhang, Dongdong Zhang, Lei Zhang, Dongyan Zhao, Jun Zhao, Hai Zhao, Li Zhao, Alisa Zhila, Guangyou Zhou, Xiaoning Zhu, Muhua Zhu, Heike Zinsmeister, Pierre Zweigenbaum

Invited Talk: Words and People

Rada Mihalcea

University of Michigan

Abstract

What do the words we use say about us and about how we view the world surrounding us? And what do we - as speakers of those words with our own defining attributes, imply about the words we utter? In this talk, I will explore the relation between words and people and show how we can develop cross-cultural word models to identify words with cultural bias – i.e., words that are used in significantly different ways by speakers from different cultures. Further, I will also show how we can effectively use information about the speakers of a word (i.e., their gender, culture) to build better word models.

Biography

Rada Mihalcea is a Professor in the Computer Science and Engineering department at the University of Michigan. Her research interests are in computational linguistics, with a focus on lexical semantics, multilingual natural language processing, and computational social sciences. She serves or has served on the editorial boards of the Journals of Computational Linguistics, Language Resources and Evaluations, Natural Language Engineering, Research in Language in Computation, IEEE Transactions on Affective Computing, and Transactions of the Association for Computational Linguistics. She was a program co-chair for the Conference of the Association for Computational Linguistics (2011) and the Conference on Empirical Methods in Natural Language Processing (2009), and a general chair for the Conference of the North American Chapter of the Association for Computational Linguistics (2015). She is the recipient of a National Science Foundation CAREER award (2008) and a Presidential Early Career Award for Scientists and Engineers awarded by President Obama (2009). In 2013, she was made an honorary citizen of her hometown of Cluj-Napoca, Romania.

Invited Talk: Learning Large and Small: How to Transfer NLP Successes to Low-resource Languages

Trevor Cohn

University of Melbourne

Abstract

Recent advances in NLP have predominantly been based upon supervised learning over large corpora, where rich expressive models, such as deep learning methods, can perform exceptionally well. However, these state of the art approaches tend to be very data hungry, and consequently do not elegantly scale down to smaller corpora, which are more typical in many NLP applications.

In this talk, I will describe the importance of small data in our field, drawing particular attention to so-called "low-" or "under-resourced" languages, for which corpora are scarce, and linguistic annotations scarcer yet. One of the key problems for our field is how to translate successes on the few high-resource languages to practical technologies for the remaining majority of the world's languages. I will cover several research problems in this space, including transfer learning between high- and low-resource languages, active learning for selecting text for annotation, and speech processing in a low-resource setting, namely learning to translate audio inputs without transcriptions. I will finish by discussing open problems in natural language processing that will be critical in porting highly successful NLP work to the myriad of less-well-studied languages.

Biography

Trevor Cohn is an Associate Professor and ARC Future Fellow at the University of Melbourne, in the School of Computing and Information Systems. He received Bachelor degrees in Software Engineering and Commerce, and a PhD degree in Engineering from the University of Melbourne. He was previously based at the University of Sheffield, and before this worked as a Research Fellow at the University of Edinburgh. His research interests focus on probabilistic and statistical machine learning for natural language processing, with applications in several areas including machine translation, parsing and grammar induction. Current projects include translating diverse and noisy text sources, deep learning of semantics in translation, rumour diffusion over social media, and algorithmic approaches for scaling to massive corpora. Dr. Cohn's research has been recognised by several best paper awards, including best short paper at EMNLP in 2016. He will be jointly organising ACL 2018 in Melbourne.

Invited Talk: Strategies for Discovering Underlying Linguistic Structure

Jason Eisner

Johns Hopkins University

Abstract

A goal of computational linguistics is to automate the kind of reasoning that linguists do. Given text in a new language, can we determine the underlying morphemes and the grammar rules that arrange and modify them?

The Bayesian strategy is to devise a joint probabilistic model that is capable of generating the descriptions of new languages. Given data from a particular new language, we can then seek explanatory descriptions that have high prior probability. This strategy leads to fascinating and successful algorithms in the case of morphology.

Yet the Bayesian approach has been less successful for syntax. It is limited in practice by our ability to (1) design accurate models and (2) solve the computational problem of posterior inference. I will demonstrate some remedies: build only a partial (conditional) model, and use synthetic data to train a neural network that simulates correct posterior inference.

Biography

Jason Eisner is Professor of Computer Science at Johns Hopkins University, where he is also affiliated with the Center for Language and Speech Processing, the Machine Learning Group, the Cognitive Science Department, and the national Center of Excellence in Human Language Technology. His goal is to develop the probabilistic modeling, inference, and learning techniques needed for a unified model of all kinds of linguistic structure. His 100+ papers have presented various algorithms for parsing, machine translation, and weighted finite-state machines; formalizations, algorithms, theorems, and empirical results in computational phonology; and unsupervised or semi-supervised learning methods for syntax, morphology, and word-sense disambiguation. He is also the lead designer of Dyna, a new declarative programming language that provides an infrastructure for AI research. He has received two school-wide awards for excellence in teaching.

Table of Contents

Evaluating Layers of Representation in Neural Machine Translation on Part-of-Speech and Semantic Tagging Tasks
Yonatan Belinkov, Lluís Màrquez, Hassan Sajjad, Nadir Durrani, Fahim Dalvi and James Glass . . 1

Context-Aware Smoothing for Neural Machine Translation
Kehai Chen, Rui Wang, Masao Utiyama, Eiichiro Sumita and Tiejun Zhao 11

Improving Sequence to Sequence Neural Machine Translation by Utilizing Syntactic Dependency Information
An Nguyen Le, Ander Martinez, Akifumi Yoshimoto and Yuji Matsumoto 21

What does Attention in Neural Machine Translation Pay Attention to?
Hamidreza Ghader and Christof Monz 30

Grammatical Error Detection Using Error- and Grammaticality-Specific Word Embeddings
Masahiro Kaneko, Yuya Sakaizawa and Mamoru Komachi 40

Dependency Parsing with Partial Annotations: An Empirical Comparison
Yue Zhang, Zhenghua Li, Jun Lang, Qingrong Xia and Min Zhang 49

Neural Probabilistic Model for Non-projective MST Parsing
Xuezhe Ma and Eduard Hovy 59

Word Ordering as Unsupervised Learning Towards Syntactically Plausible Word Representations
Noriki Nishida and Hideki Nakayama 70

MIPA: Mutual Information Based Paraphrase Acquisition via Bilingual Pivoting
Tomoyuki Kajiwara, Mamoru Komachi and Daichi Mochihashi 80

Improving Implicit Semantic Role Labeling by Predicting Semantic Frame Arguments
Quynh Ngoc Thi Do, Steven Bethard and Marie-Francine Moens 90

Natural Language Inference from Multiple Premises
Alice Lai, Yonatan Bisk and Julia Hockenmaier 100

Enabling Transitivity for Lexical Inference on Chinese Verbs Using Probabilistic Soft Logic
Wei-Chung Wang and Lun-Wei Ku 110

An Exploration of Neural Sequence-to-Sequence Architectures for Automatic Post-Editing
Marcin Junczys-Dowmunt and Roman Grundkiewicz 120

Imagination Improves Multimodal Translation
Desmond Elliott and Ákos Kádár 130

Understanding and Improving Morphological Learning in the Neural Machine Translation Decoder
Fahim Dalvi, Nadir Durrani, Hassan Sajjad, Yonatan Belinkov and Stephan Vogel 142

Improving Neural Machine Translation through Phrase-based Forced Decoding
Jingyi Zhang, Masao Utiyama, Eiichro Sumita, Graham Neubig and Satoshi Nakamura 152

Convolutional Neural Network with Word Embeddings for Chinese Word Segmentation
Chunqi Wang and Bo Xu 163

Character-based Joint Segmentation and POS Tagging for Chinese using Bidirectional RNN-CRF
Yan Shao, Christian Hardmeier, Jörg Tiedemann and Joakim Nivre 173

Addressing Domain Adaptation for Chinese Word Segmentation with Global Recurrent Structure
Shen Huang, Xu Sun and Houfeng Wang 184

Information Bottleneck Inspired Method For Chat Text Segmentation
S Vishal, Mohit Yadav, Lovekesh Vig and Gautam Shroff 194

Distributional Modeling on a Diet: One-shot Word Learning from Text Only
Su Wang, Stephen Roller and Katrin Erk 204

A Computational Study on Word Meanings and Their Distributed Representations via Polymodal Embedding
Joohee Park and Sung-Hyon Myaeng 214

Geographical Evaluation of Word Embeddings
Michal Konkol, Tomáš Brychcín, Michal Nykl and Tomáš Hercig 224

On Modeling Sense Relatedness in Multi-prototype Word Embedding
Yixin Cao, Jiaxin Shi, Juanzi Li, Zhiyuan Liu and Chengjiang Li 233

Unsupervised Segmentation of Phoneme Sequences based on Pitman-Yor Semi-Markov Model using Phoneme Length Context
Ryu Takeda and Kazunori Komatani 243

A Sensitivity Analysis of (and Practitioners' Guide to) Convolutional Neural Networks for Sentence Classification
Ye Zhang and Byron Wallace 253

Coordination Boundary Identification with Similarity and Replaceability
Hiroki Teranishi, Hiroyuki Shindo and Yuji Matsumoto 264

Turning Distributional Thesauri into Word Vectors for Synonym Extraction and Expansion
Olivier Ferret 273

Training Word Sense Embeddings With Lexicon-based Regularization
Luis Nieto Piña and Richard Johansson 284

Learning How to Simplify From Explicit Labeling of Complex-Simplified Text Pairs
Fernando Alva-Manchego, Joachim Bingel, Gustavo Paetzold, Carolina Scarton and Lucia Specia
295

Domain-Adaptable Hybrid Generation of RDF Entity Descriptions
Or Biran and Kathleen McKeown 306

ES-LDA: Entity Summarization using Knowledge-based Topic Modeling
Seyedamin Pouriyeh, Mehdi Allahyari, Krzysztof Kochut, Gong Cheng and Hamid Reza Arabnia
316

Procedural Text Generation from an Execution Video
Atsushi Ushiku, Hayato Hashimoto, Atsushi Hashimoto and Shinsuke Mori 326

Text Sentiment Analysis based on Fusion of Structural Information and Serialization Information
Ling Gan and Houyu Gong 336

Length, Interchangeability, and External Knowledge: Observations from Predicting Argument Convincingness
Peter Potash, Robin Bhattacharya and Anna Rumshisky 342

Exploiting Document Level Information to Improve Event Detection via Recurrent Neural Networks
Shaoyang Duan, Ruifang He and Wenli Zhao 352

Embracing Non-Traditional Linguistic Resources for Low-resource Language Name Tagging
Boliang Zhang, Di Lu, Xiaoman Pan, Ying Lin, Halidanmu Abudukelimu, Heng Ji and Kevin Knight 362

NMT or SMT: Case Study of a Narrow-domain English-Latvian Post-editing Project
Inguna Skadiņa and Mārcis Pinnis 373

Towards Neural Machine Translation with Partially Aligned Corpora
Yining Wang, Yang Zhao, Jiajun Zhang, Chengqing Zong and Zhengshan Xue 384

Identifying Usage Expression Sentences in Consumer Product Reviews
Shibamouli Lahiri, V.G.Vinod Vydiswaran and Rada Mihalcea 394

Between Reading Time and Syntactic/Semantic Categories
Masayuki Asahara and Sachi Kato 404

WiNER: A Wikipedia Annotated Corpus for Named Entity Recognition
Abbas Ghaddar and Phillippe Langlais 413

Reusing Neural Speech Representations for Auditory Emotion Recognition
Egor Lakomkin, Cornelius Weber, Sven Magg and Stefan Wermter 423

Local Monotonic Attention Mechanism for End-to-End Speech And Language Processing
Andros Tjandra, Sakriani Sakti and Satoshi Nakamura 431

Attentive Language Models
Giancarlo Salton, Robert Ross and John Kelleher 441

Diachrony-aware Induction of Binary Latent Representations from Typological Features
Yugo Murawaki 451

Image-Grounded Conversations: Multimodal Context for Natural Question and Response Generation
Nasrin Mostafazadeh, Chris Brockett, Bill Dolan, Michel Galley, Jianfeng Gao, Georgios Spithourakis and Lucy Vanderwende 462

A Neural Language Model for Dynamically Representing the Meanings of Unknown Words and Entities in a Discourse
Sosuke Kobayashi, Naoaki Okazaki and Kentaro Inui 473

Using Explicit Discourse Connectives in Translation for Implicit Discourse Relation Classification
Wei Shi, Frances Yung, Raphael Rubino and Vera Demberg 484

Tag-Enhanced Tree-Structured Neural Networks for Implicit Discourse Relation Classification
Yizhong Wang, Sujian Li, Jingfeng Yang, Xu Sun and Houfeng Wang 496

Cross-Lingual Sentiment Analysis Without (Good) Translation
Mohamed Abdalla and Graeme Hirst 506

Implicit Syntactic Features for Target-dependent Sentiment Analysis
Yuze Gao, Yue Zhang and Tong Xiao 516

Graph Based Sentiment Aggregation using ConceptNet Ontology
Srikanth Tamilselvam, Seema Nagar, Abhijit Mishra and Kuntal Dey 525

Sentence Modeling with Deep Neural Architecture using Lexicon and Character Attention Mechanism for Sentiment Classification
Huy-Thanh Nguyen and Minh-Le Nguyen 536

Combining Lightly-Supervised Text Classification Models for Accurate Contextual Advertising
Yiping Jin, Dittaya Wanvarie and Phu Le 545

Capturing Long-range Contextual Dependencies with Memory-enhanced Conditional Random Fields
Fei Liu, Timothy Baldwin and Trevor Cohn 555

Named Entity Recognition with Stack Residual LSTM and Trainable Bias Decoding
Quan Tran, Andrew MacKinlay and Antonio Jimeno Yepes 566

Neuramanteau: A Neural Network Ensemble Model for Lexical Blends
Kollol Das and Shaona Ghosh 576

Leveraging Discourse Information Effectively for Authorship Attribution
Elisa Ferracane, Su Wang and Raymond Mooney 584

Lightly-Supervised Modeling of Argument Persuasiveness
Isaac Persing and Vincent Ng 594

Multi-Task Learning for Speaker-Role Adaptation in Neural Conversation Models
Yi Luan, Chris Brockett, Bill Dolan, Jianfeng Gao and Michel Galley 605

Chat Disentanglement: Identifying Semantic Reply Relationships with Random Forests and Recurrent Neural Networks
Shikib Mehri and Giuseppe Carenini 615

Towards Bootstrapping a Polarity Shifter Lexicon using Linguistic Features
Marc Schulder, Michael Wiegand, Josef Ruppenhofer and Benjamin Roth 624

Cascading Multiway Attentions for Document-level Sentiment Classification
Dehong Ma, Sujian Li, Xiaodong Zhang, Houfeng Wang and Xu Sun 634

An Ensemble Method with Sentiment Features and Clustering Support
Nguyen Huy Tien and Nguyen Minh Le 644

Leveraging Auxiliary Tasks for Document-Level Cross-Domain Sentiment Classification
Jianfei Yu and Jing Jiang 654

Measuring Semantic Relations between Human Activities
Steven Wilson and Rada Mihalcea 664

Learning Transferable Representation for Bilingual Relation Extraction via Convolutional Neural Networks
Bonan Min, Zhuolin Jiang, Marjorie Freedman and Ralph Weischedel 674

Bilingual Word Embeddings for Bilingual Terminology Extraction from Specialized Comparable Corpora
Amir Hazem and Emmanuel Morin..685

A Bambara Tonalization System for Word Sense Disambiguation Using Differential Coding, Segmentation and Edit Operation Filtering
Luigi (Yu-Cheng) Liu and Damien Nouvel 694

Joint Learning of Dialog Act Segmentation and Recognition in Spoken Dialog Using Neural Networks
Tianyu Zhao and Tatsuya Kawahara 704

Predicting Users' Negative Feedbacks in Multi-Turn Human-Computer Dialogues
Xin Wang, Jianan Wang, Yuanchao Liu, Xiaolong Wang, Zhuoran Wang and Baoxun Wang...713

Finding Dominant User Utterances And System Responses in Conversations
Dhiraj Madan and Sachindra Joshi 723

End-to-End Task-Completion Neural Dialogue Systems
Xiujun Li, Yun-Nung Chen, Lihong Li, Jianfeng Gao and Asli Celikyilmaz..................733

End-to-end Network for Twitter Geolocation Prediction and Hashing
Jey Han Lau, Lianhua Chi, Khoi-Nguyen Tran and Trevor Cohn.......................744

Assessing the Verifiability of Attributions in News Text
Edward Newell, Ariane Schang, Drew Margolin and Derek Ruths 754

Domain Adaptation from User-level Facebook Models to County-level Twitter Predictions
Daniel Rieman, Kokil Jaidka, H. Andrew Schwartz and Lyle Ungar.........................764

Recognizing Explicit and Implicit Hate Speech Using a Weakly Supervised Two-path Bootstrapping Approach
Lei Gao, Alexis Kuppersmith and Ruihong Huang 774

Estimating Reactions and Recommending Products with Generative Models of Reviews
Jianmo Ni, Zachary C. Lipton, Sharad Vikram and Julian McAuley.......................783

Summarizing Lengthy Questions
Tatsuya Ishigaki, Hiroya Takamura and Manabu Okumura 792

Concept-Map-Based Multi-Document Summarization using Concept Coreference Resolution and Global Importance Optimization
Tobias Falke, Christian M. Meyer and Iryna Gurevych...............................801

Abstractive Multi-document Summarization by Partial Tree Extraction, Recombination and Linearization
Litton J Kurisinkel, Yue Zhang and Vasudeva Varma 812

Event Argument Identification on Dependency Graphs with Bidirectional LSTMs
Alex Judea and Michael Strube 822

Selective Decoding for Cross-lingual Open Information Extraction
Sheng Zhang, Kevin Duh and Benjamin Van Durme.................................832

Event Ordering with a Generalized Model for Sieve Prediction Ranking
Bill McDowell, Nathanael Chambers, Alexander Ororbia II and David Reitter 843

Open Relation Extraction and Grounding
Dian Yu, Lifu Huang and Heng Ji 854

Extraction of Gene-Environment Interaction from the Biomedical Literature
Jinseon You, Jin-Woo Chung, Wonsuk Yang and Jong C. Park 865

Course Concept Extraction in MOOCs via Embedding-Based Graph Propagation
Liangming Pan, Xiaochen Wang, Chengjiang Li, Juanzi Li and Jie Tang 875

Identity Deception Detection
Verónica Pérez-Rosas, Quincy Davenport, Anna Mengdan Dai, Mohamed Abouelenien and Rada
Mihalcea 885

Learning to Diagnose: Assimilating Clinical Narratives using Deep Reinforcement Learning
Yuan Ling, Sadid A. Hasan, Vivek Datla, Ashequl Qadir, Kathy Lee, Joey Liu and Oladimeji Farri
895

Dataset for a Neural Natural Language Interface for Databases (NNLIDB)
Florin Brad, Radu Cristian Alexandru Iacob, Ionel Alexandru Hosu and Traian Rebedea 906

*Acquisition and Assessment of Semantic Content for the Generation of Elaborateness and Indirectness
in Spoken Dialogue Systems*
Louisa Pragst, Koichiro Yoshino, Wolfgang Minker, Satoshi Nakamura and Stefan Ultes 915

Demographic Word Embeddings for Racism Detection on Twitter
Mohammed Hasanuzzaman, Gaël Dias and Andy Way 926

Automatically Extracting Variant-Normalization Pairs for Japanese Text Normalization
Itsumi Saito, Kyosuke Nishida, Kugatsu Sadamitsu, Kuniko Saito and Junji Tomita 937

Semantic Document Distance Measures and Unsupervised Document Revision Detection
Xiaofeng Zhu, Diego Klabjan and Patrick Bless 947

An Empirical Analysis of Multiple-Turn Reasoning Strategies in Reading Comprehension Tasks
Yelong Shen, Xiaodong Liu, Kevin Duh and Jianfeng Gao 957

Automated Historical Fact-Checking by Passage Retrieval, Word Statistics, and Virtual Question-Answering
Mio Kobayashi, Ai Ishii, Chikara Hoshino, Hiroshi Miyashita and Takuya Matsuzaki 967

*Integrating Subject, Type, and Property Identification for Simple Question Answering over Knowledge
Base*
Wei-Chuan Hsiao, Hen-Hsen Huang and Hsin-Hsi Chen 976

DailyDialog: A Manually Labelled Multi-turn Dialogue Dataset
Yanran Li, Hui Su, Xiaoyu Shen, Wenjie Li, Ziqiang Cao and Shuzi Niu 986

Inference is Everything: Recasting Semantic Resources into a Unified Evaluation Framework
Aaron Steven White, Pushpendre Rastogi, Kevin Duh and Benjamin Van Durme 996

Generating a Training Corpus for OCR Post-Correction Using Encoder-Decoder Model
Eva D'hondt, Cyril Grouin and Brigitte Grau 1006

Multilingual Hierarchical Attention Networks for Document Classification
Nikolaos Pappas and Andrei Popescu-Belis 1015

Roles and Success in Wikipedia Talk Pages: Identifying Latent Patterns of Behavior
Keith Maki, Michael Yoder, Yohan Jo and Carolyn Rosé..................................1026

Conference Program

Tuesday, November 28, 2017

10:30–11:50   Machine Translation 1

10:30–10:50   *Evaluating Layers of Representation in Neural Machine Translation on Part-of-Speech and Semantic Tagging Tasks*
Yonatan Belinkov, Lluís Màrquez, Hassan Sajjad, Nadir Durrani, Fahim Dalvi and James Glass

10:50–11:10   *Context-Aware Smoothing for Neural Machine Translation*
Kehai Chen, Rui Wang, Masao Utiyama, Eiichiro Sumita and Tiejun Zhao

11:10–11:30   *Improving Sequence to Sequence Neural Machine Translation by Utilizing Syntactic Dependency Information*
An Nguyen Le, Ander Martinez, Akifumi Yoshimoto and Yuji Matsumoto

11:30–11:50   *What does Attention in Neural Machine Translation Pay Attention to?*
Hamidreza Ghader and Christof Monz

Tuesday, November 28, 2017

10:30–11:50   Syntax and Parsing

10:30–10:50   *Grammatical Error Detection Using Error- and Grammaticality-Specific Word Embeddings*
Masahiro Kaneko, Yuya Sakaizawa and Mamoru Komachi

10:50–11:10   *Dependency Parsing with Partial Annotations: An Empirical Comparison*
Yue Zhang, Zhenghua Li, Jun Lang, Qingrong Xia and Min Zhang

11:10–11:30   *Neural Probabilistic Model for Non-projective MST Parsing*
Xuezhe Ma and Eduard Hovy

11:30–11:50   *Word Ordering as Unsupervised Learning Towards Syntactically Plausible Word Representations*
Noriki Nishida and Hideki Nakayama

Tuesday, November 28, 2017

10:30–11:50	**Semantics 1**

10:30–10:50   *MIPA: Mutual Information Based Paraphrase Acquisition via Bilingual Pivoting*
Tomoyuki Kajiwara, Mamoru Komachi and Daichi Mochihashi

10:50–11:10   *Improving Implicit Semantic Role Labeling by Predicting Semantic Frame Arguments*
Quynh Ngoc Thi Do, Steven Bethard and Marie-Francine Moens

11:10–11:30   *Natural Language Inference from Multiple Premises*
Alice Lai, Yonatan Bisk and Julia Hockenmaier

11:30–11:50   *Enabling Transitivity for Lexical Inference on Chinese Verbs Using Probabilistic Soft Logic*
Wei-Chung Wang and Lun-Wei Ku

Tuesday, November 28, 2017

13:30–14:50	**Machine Translation 2**

13:30–13:50   *An Exploration of Neural Sequence-to-Sequence Architectures for Automatic Post-Editing*
Marcin Junczys-Dowmunt and Roman Grundkiewicz

13:50–14:10   *Imagination Improves Multimodal Translation*
Desmond Elliott and Ákos Kádár

14:10–14:30   *Understanding and Improving Morphological Learning in the Neural Machine Translation Decoder*
Fahim Dalvi, Nadir Durrani, Hassan Sajjad, Yonatan Belinkov and Stephan Vogel

14:30–14:50   *Improving Neural Machine Translation through Phrase-based Forced Decoding*
Jingyi Zhang, Masao Utiyama, Eiichro Sumita, Graham Neubig and Satoshi Nakamura

Tuesday, November 28, 2017

13:30–14:50   **Segmentation and Tagging**

13:30–13:50   *Convolutional Neural Network with Word Embeddings for Chinese Word Segmentation*
Chunqi Wang and Bo Xu

13:50–14:10   *Character-based Joint Segmentation and POS Tagging for Chinese using Bidirectional RNN-CRF*
Yan Shao, Christian Hardmeier, Jörg Tiedemann and Joakim Nivre

14:10–14:30   *Addressing Domain Adaptation for Chinese Word Segmentation with Global Recurrent Structure*
Shen Huang, Xu Sun and Houfeng Wang

14:30–14:50   *Information Bottleneck Inspired Method For Chat Text Segmentation*
S Vishal, Mohit Yadav, Lovekesh Vig and Gautam Shroff

Tuesday, November 28, 2017

13:30–14:50   **Semantics 2**

13:30–13:50   *Distributional Modeling on a Diet: One-shot Word Learning from Text Only*
Su Wang, Stephen Roller and Katrin Erk

13:50–14:10   *A Computational Study on Word Meanings and Their Distributed Representations via Polymodal Embedding*
Joohee Park and Sung-Hyon Myaeng

14:10–14:30   *Geographical Evaluation of Word Embeddings*
Michal Konkol, Tomáš Brychcín, Michal Nykl and Tomáš Hercig

14:30–14:50   *On Modeling Sense Relatedness in Multi-prototype Word Embedding*
Yixin Cao, Jiaxin Shi, Juanzi Li, Zhiyuan Liu and Chengjiang Li

15:30–17:30   Poster and Demo

Unsupervised Segmentation of Phoneme Sequences based on Pitman-Yor Semi-Markov Model using Phoneme Length Context
Ryu Takeda and Kazunori Komatani

A Sensitivity Analysis of (and Practitioners' Guide to) Convolutional Neural Networks for Sentence Classification
Ye Zhang and Byron Wallace

Coordination Boundary Identification with Similarity and Replaceability
Hiroki Teranishi, Hiroyuki Shindo and Yuji Matsumoto

Turning Distributional Thesauri into Word Vectors for Synonym Extraction and Expansion
Olivier Ferret

Training Word Sense Embeddings With Lexicon-based Regularization
Luis Nieto Piña and Richard Johansson

Learning How to Simplify From Explicit Labeling of Complex-Simplified Text Pairs
Fernando Alva-Manchego, Joachim Bingel, Gustavo Paetzold, Carolina Scarton and Lucia Specia

Domain-Adaptable Hybrid Generation of RDF Entity Descriptions
Or Biran and Kathleen McKeown

ES-LDA: Entity Summarization using Knowledge-based Topic Modeling
Seyedamin Pouriyeh, Mehdi Allahyari, Krzysztof Kochut, Gong Cheng and Hamid Reza Arabnia

Procedural Text Generation from an Execution Video
Atsushi Ushiku, Hayato Hashimoto, Atsushi Hashimoto and Shinsuke Mori

Text Sentiment Analysis based on Fusion of Structural Information and Serialization Information
Ling Gan and Houyu Gong

Length, Interchangeability, and External Knowledge: Observations from Predicting Argument Convincingness
Peter Potash, Robin Bhattacharya and Anna Rumshisky

Exploiting Document Level Information to Improve Event Detection via Recurrent Neural Networks
Shaoyang Duan, Ruifang He and Wenli Zhao

Embracing Non-Traditional Linguistic Resources for Low-resource Language Name Tagging
Boliang Zhang, Di Lu, Xiaoman Pan, Ying Lin, Halidanmu Abudukelimu, Heng Ji and Kevin Knight

NMT or SMT: Case Study of a Narrow-domain English-Latvian Post-editing Project
Inguna Skadina and Mārcis Pinnis

Towards Neural Machine Translation with Partially Aligned Corpora
Yining Wang, Yang Zhao, Jiajun Zhang, Chengqing Zong and Zhengshan Xue

Identifying Usage Expression Sentences in Consumer Product Reviews
Shibamouli Lahiri, V.G. Vinod Vydiswaran and Rada Mihalcea

Between Reading Time and Syntactic/Semantic Categories
Masayuki Asahara and Sachi Kato

WiNER: A Wikipedia Annotated Corpus for Named Entity Recognition
Abbas Ghaddar and Phillippe Langlais

Wednesday, November 29, 2017

10:30–11:50   Machine Learning 1

10:30–10:50   *Reusing Neural Speech Representations for Auditory Emotion Recognition*
Egor Lakomkin, Cornelius Weber, Sven Magg and Stefan Wermter

10:50–11:10   *Local Monotonic Attention Mechanism for End-to-End Speech And Language Processing*
Andros Tjandra, Sakriani Sakti and Satoshi Nakamura

11:10–11:30   *Attentive Language Models*
Giancarlo Salton, Robert Ross and John Kelleher

11:30–11:50   *Diachrony-aware Induction of Binary Latent Representations from Typological Features*
Yugo Murawaki

Wednesday, November 29, 2017

10:30–11:50   Discourse 1

10:30–10:50   *Image-Grounded Conversations: Multimodal Context for Natural Question and Response Generation*
Nasrin Mostafazadeh, Chris Brockett, Bill Dolan, Michel Galley, Jianfeng Gao, Georgios Spithourakis and Lucy Vanderwende

10:50–11:10   *A Neural Language Model for Dynamically Representing the Meanings of Unknown Words and Entities in a Discourse*
Sosuke Kobayashi, Naoaki Okazaki and Kentaro Inui

11:10–11:30   *Using Explicit Discourse Connectives in Translation for Implicit Discourse Relation Classification*
Wei Shi, Frances Yung, Raphael Rubino and Vera Demberg

11:30–11:50   *Tag-Enhanced Tree-Structured Neural Networks for Implicit Discourse Relation Classification*
Yizhong Wang, Sujian Li, Jingfeng Yang, Xu Sun and Houfeng Wang

10:30–11:50   Sentiment and Opinion 1

10:30–10:50   *Cross-Lingual Sentiment Analysis Without (Good) Translation*
Mohamed Abdalla and Graeme Hirst

10:50–11:10   *Implicit Syntactic Features for Target-dependent Sentiment Analysis*
Yuze Gao, Yue Zhang and Tong Xiao

11:10–11:30   *Graph Based Sentiment Aggregation using ConceptNet Ontology*
Srikanth Tamilselvam, Seema Nagar, Abhijit Mishra and Kuntal Dey

11:30–11:50   *Sentence Modeling with Deep Neural Architecture using Lexicon and Character Attention Mechanism for Sentiment Classification*
Huy-Thanh Nguyen and Minh-Le Nguyen

Wednesday, November 29, 2017

13:30–14:50   Machine Learning 2

13:30–13:50   *Combining Lightly-Supervised Text Classification Models for Accurate Contextual Advertising*
Yiping Jin, Dittaya Wanvarie and Phu Le

13:50–14:10   *Capturing Long-range Contextual Dependencies with Memory-enhanced Conditional Random Fields*
Fei Liu, Timothy Baldwin and Trevor Cohn

14:10–14:30   *Named Entity Recognition with Stack Residual LSTM and Trainable Bias Decoding*
Quan Tran, Andrew MacKinlay and Antonio Jimeno Yepes

14:30–14:50   *Neuramanteau: A Neural Network Ensemble Model for Lexical Blends*
Kollol Das and Shaona Ghosh

Wednesday, November 29, 2017

13:30–14:50   Discourse 2

13:30–13:50   *Leveraging Discourse Information Effectively for Authorship Attribution*
Elisa Ferracane, Su Wang and Raymond Mooney

13:50–14:10   *Lightly-Supervised Modeling of Argument Persuasiveness*
Isaac Persing and Vincent Ng

14:10–14:30   *Multi-Task Learning for Speaker-Role Adaptation in Neural Conversation Models*
Yi Luan, Chris Brockett, Bill Dolan, Jianfeng Gao and Michel Galley

14:30–14:50   *Chat Disentanglement: Identifying Semantic Reply Relationships with Random Forests and Recurrent Neural Networks*
Shikib Mehri and Giuseppe Carenini

Wednesday, November 29, 2017

13:30–14:50   Sentiment and Opinion 2

13:30–13:50   *Towards Bootstrapping a Polarity Shifter Lexicon using Linguistic Features*
Marc Schulder, Michael Wiegand, Josef Ruppenhofer and Benjamin Roth

13:50–14:10   *Cascading Multiway Attentions for Document-level Sentiment Classification*
Dehong Ma, Sujian Li, Xiaodong Zhang, Houfeng Wang and Xu Sun

14:10–14:30   *An Ensemble Method with Sentiment Features and Clustering Support*
Nguyen Huy Tien and Nguyen Minh Le

14:30–14:50   *Leveraging Auxiliary Tasks for Document-Level Cross-Domain Sentiment Classification*
Jianfei Yu and Jing Jiang

Wednesday, November 29, 2017

15:30–16:50   Word

15:30–15:50   *Measuring Semantic Relations between Human Activities*
Steven Wilson and Rada Mihalcea

15:50–16:10   *Learning Transferable Representation for Bilingual Relation Extraction via Convolutional Neural Networks*
Bonan Min, Zhuolin Jiang, Marjorie Freedman and Ralph Weischedel

16:10–16:30   *Bilingual Word Embeddings for Bilingual Terminology Extraction from Specialized Comparable Corpora*
Amir Hazem and Emmanuel Morin

16:30–16:50   *A Bambara Tonalization System for Word Sense Disambiguation Using Differential Coding, Segmentation and Edit Operation Filtering*
Luigi (Yu-Cheng) Liu and Damien Nouvel

Wednesday, November 29, 2017

15:30–16:50   Dialogue

15:30–15:50   *Joint Learning of Dialog Act Segmentation and Recognition in Spoken Dialog Using Neural Networks*
Tianyu Zhao and Tatsuya Kawahara

15:50–16:10   *Predicting Users' Negative Feedbacks in Multi-Turn Human-Computer Dialogues*
Xin Wang, Jianan Wang, Yuanchao Liu, Xiaolong Wang, Zhuoran Wang and Baoxun Wang

16:10–16:30   *Finding Dominant User Utterances And System Responses in Conversations*
Dhiraj Madan and Sachindra Joshi

16:30–16:50   *End-to-End Task-Completion Neural Dialogue Systems*
Xiujun Li, Yun-Nung Chen, Lihong Li, Jianfeng Gao and Asli Celikyilmaz

Wednesday, November 29, 2017

15:30–16:50   **Web and Social Media**

15:30–15:50   *End-to-end Network for Twitter Geolocation Prediction and Hashing*
Jey Han Lau, Lianhua Chi, Khoi-Nguyen Tran and Trevor Cohn

15:50–16:10   *Assessing the Verifiability of Attributions in News Text*
Edward Newell, Ariane Schang, Drew Margolin and Derek Ruths

16:10–16:30   *Domain Adaptation from User-level Facebook Models to County-level Twitter Predictions*
Daniel Rieman, Kokil Jaidka, H. Andrew Schwartz and Lyle Ungar

16:30–16:50   *Recognizing Explicit and Implicit Hate Speech Using a Weakly Supervised Two-path Bootstrapping Approach*
Lei Gao, Alexis Kuppersmith and Ruihong Huang

Thursday, November 30, 2017

10:30–11:50   **Summarization**

10:30–10:50   *Estimating Reactions and Recommending Products with Generative Models of Reviews*
Jianmo Ni, Zachary C. Lipton, Sharad Vikram and Julian McAuley

10:50–11:10   *Summarizing Lengthy Questions*
Tatsuya Ishigaki, Hiroya Takamura and Manabu Okumura

11:10–11:30   *Concept-Map-Based Multi-Document Summarization using Concept Coreference Resolution and Global Importance Optimization*
Tobias Falke, Christian M. Meyer and Iryna Gurevych

11:30–11:50   *Abstractive Multi-document Summarization by Partial Tree Extraction, Recombination and Linearization*
Litton J Kurisinkel, Yue Zhang and Vasudeva Varma

Thursday, November 30, 2017

10:30–11:50   Information Extraction

10:30–10:50   *Event Argument Identification on Dependency Graphs with Bidirectional LSTMs*
Alex Judea and Michael Strube

10:50–11:10   *Selective Decoding for Cross-lingual Open Information Extraction*
Sheng Zhang, Kevin Duh and Benjamin Van Durme

11:10–11:30   *Event Ordering with a Generalized Model for Sieve Prediction Ranking*
Bill McDowell, Nathanael Chambers, Alexander Ororbia II and David Reitter

11:30–11:50   *Open Relation Extraction and Grounding*
Dian Yu, Lifu Huang and Heng Ji

Thursday, November 30, 2017

10:30–11:50   NLP Application

10:30–10:50   *Extraction of Gene-Environment Interaction from the Biomedical Literature*
Jinseon You, Jin-Woo Chung, Wonsuk Yang and Jong C. Park

10:50–11:10   *Course Concept Extraction in MOOCs via Embedding-Based Graph Propagation*
Liangming Pan, Xiaochen Wang, Chengjiang Li, Juanzi Li and Jie Tang

11:10–11:30   *Identity Deception Detection*
Verónica Pérez-Rosas, Quincy Davenport, Anna Mengdan Dai, Mohamed Abouelenien and Rada Mihalcea

11:30–11:50   *Learning to Diagnose: Assimilating Clinical Narratives using Deep Reinforcement Learning*
Yuan Ling, Sadid A. Hasan, Vivek Datla, Ashequl Qadir, Kathy Lee, Joey Liu and Oladimeji Farri

13:30–14:50   **Generation**

13:30–13:50   *Dataset for a Neural Natural Language Interface for Databases (NNLIDB)*
Florin Brad, Radu Cristian Alexandru Iacob, Ionel Alexandru Hosu and Traian Rebedea

13:50–14:10   *Acquisition and Assessment of Semantic Content for the Generation of Elaborateness and Indirectness in Spoken Dialogue Systems*
Louisa Pragst, Koichiro Yoshino, Wolfgang Minker, Satoshi Nakamura and Stefan Ultes

14:10–14:30   *Demographic Word Embeddings for Racism Detection on Twitter*
Mohammed Hasanuzzaman, Gaël Dias and Andy Way

14:30–14:50   *Automatically Extracting Variant-Normalization Pairs for Japanese Text Normalization*
Itsumi Saito, Kyosuke Nishida, Kugatsu Sadamitsu, Kuniko Saito and Junji Tomita

13:30–14:50   **Documents and Questions**

13:30–13:50   *Semantic Document Distance Measures and Unsupervised Document Revision Detection*
Xiaofeng Zhu, Diego Klabjan and Patrick Bless

13:50–14:10   *An Empirical Analysis of Multiple-Turn Reasoning Strategies in Reading Comprehension Tasks*
Yelong Shen, Xiaodong Liu, Kevin Duh and Jianfeng Gao

14:10–14:30   *Automated Historical Fact-Checking by Passage Retrieval, Word Statistics, and Virtual Question-Answering*
Mio Kobayashi, Ai Ishii, Chikara Hoshino, Hiroshi Miyashita and Takuya Matsuzaki

14:30–14:50   *Integrating Subject, Type, and Property Identification for Simple Question Answering over Knowledge Base*
Wei-Chuan Hsiao, Hen-Hsen Huang and Hsin-Hsi Chen

Thursday, November 30, 2017

13:30–14:30   **Resources and Tools**

13:30–13:50   *DailyDialog: A Manually Labelled Multi-turn Dialogue Dataset*
Yanran Li, Hui Su, Xiaoyu Shen, Wenjie Li, Ziqiang Cao and Shuzi Niu

13:50–14:10   *Inference is Everything: Recasting Semantic Resources into a Unified Evaluation Framework*
Aaron Steven White, Pushpendre Rastogi, Kevin Duh and Benjamin Van Durme

14:10–14:30   *Generating a Training Corpus for OCR Post-Correction Using Encoder-Decoder Model*
Eva D'hondt, Cyril Grouin and Brigitte Grau

Thursday, November 30, 2017

15:30–16:20   **Best Paper Session**

15:30–15:55   *Multilingual Hierarchical Attention Networks for Document Classification*
Nikolaos Pappas and Andrei Popescu-Belis

15:55–16:20   *Roles and Success in Wikipedia Talk Pages: Identifying Latent Patterns of Behavior*
Keith Maki, Michael Yoder, Yohan Jo and Carolyn Rosé

Implicit Syntactic Features for Targeted Sentiment Analysis

Yuze Gao[†], Yue Zhang[†] and Tong Xiao[‡]
Singapore University of Technology and Design[†]
Northeastern University[‡]
`yuze_gao,yue_zhang@sutd.edu.sg`
`xiaotong@mail.neu.edu.cn`

Abstract

Target-dependent sentiment analysis investigates the sentiment polarities on given target mentions from input texts. Different from sentence-level sentiment, it offers more fine-grained knowledge on each entity mention. While early work leveraged syntactic information, recent research has used neural representation learning to induce features automatically, thereby avoiding error propagation of syntactic parsers, which are particularly severe on social media texts.

We study a method to leverage syntactic information without explicitly building parser outputs, by training an encoder-decoder structure parser model on standard syntactic treebanks, and then leveraging its hidden encoder layers when analysing tweets. Such hidden vectors do not contain explicit syntactic outputs, yet encode rich syntactic features. We use them to augment the inputs to a baseline state-of-the-art target-dependent sentiment classifier, observing significant improvements on various benchmark datasets. We obtain the best accuracies on two different test sets for targeted sentiment.

1 Introduction

Target-dependent sentiment analysis investigates the problem of assigning sentiment polarity labels to a set of given target mentions in input sentences. Some example are shown in Table 1. For instance, given a sentence "I like [*Twitter*] better than [*Facebook*]", a target-specific sentiment model is expected to assign a positive (+) sentiment label on

"I like [***Twitter***]$_+$ better than *Facebook*"
"I like *Twitter* better than [***Facebook***]$_-$"
[***lindsay lohan***]$_0$ goes on yet another emo rant on her twitter.
Choose [***NBI***]$_+$ for insulation, home energy audits, housing repairing, air sealing, windows and doors,furnaces, air conditioners and en energy efficient appliances.

Table 1: Target-dependent sentiment analysis

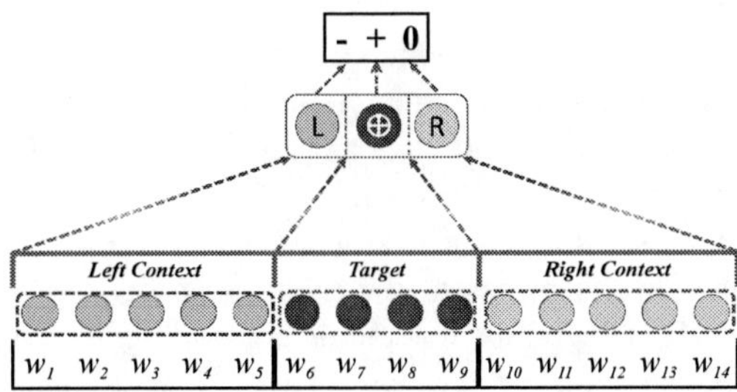

Figure 1: Sentence level context

the target *Twitter* and a negative ($-$) sentiment label on the target *Facebook*.

The task has been addressed using neural network models, which learn target-specific representations of the input sentence. These representations are then used for predicting target-dependent sentiment polarities. In particular, Dong et al. (2014) derive the syntactic structure of input sentence using a dependency grammar, before transforming the tree structure to a target-centered form. A recursive neural network is used to transform the dependency syntax of a sentence into a target-specific vector for sentiment classification. More recently Vo and Zhang (2015) split the input sentence into three segments, with the target entity mention being in the center, and its left and right contexts surrounding it, as shown in Figure 1.

516

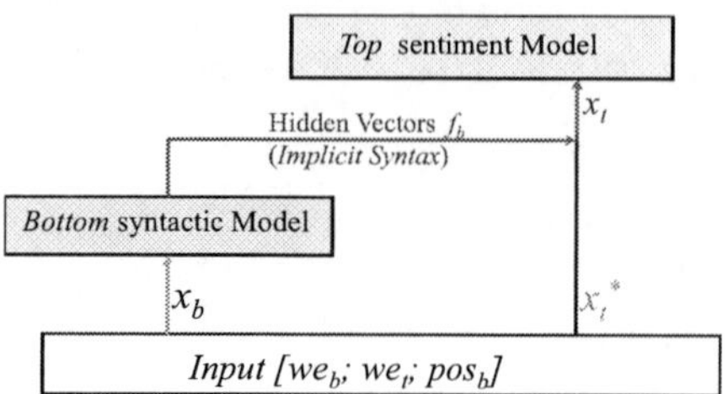

Figure 2: Model structure

Rich word embedding features are extracted from the target entity mention and its contexts, which are then used for classification by a linear SVM model. Without using syntactic information, this model gives better accuracies compared with the method of Dong et al. (2014).

Since syntactic parsing of tweets can be inaccurate due to intrinsic noise in their writing style, most subsequent work followed Vo and Zhang (2015), avoiding the use of syntactic information explicitly. Zhang et al. (2016) applied a bidirectional Gated RNN to learn a dense representation of the input sentence, and then use a three-way gated network structure to integrate target entity mention and its left and right contexts. The final resulting representation is used for softmax classification. Tang et al. (2015) also use a RNN (LSTM) to represent the input sentence, yet directly integrating the target embedding to each hidden state for deriving a target-specific vector, which is used for sentiment classification. Liu and Zhang (2017) extended both Zhang et al. (2016) and Tang et al. (2015) by introducing the attention mechanism, obtaining the best accuracies on both datasets so far.

Intuitively, syntactic information should be useful for sentiment analysis given a target, since target-related semantic information such as predicate-argument structure information is contained in syntactic structures. The main issue of Dong et al. (2014)'s method is that *explicit* syntactic structures are inaccurate and noisy. We try to avoid this issue by using *implicit* syntactic information, by integrating the hidden feature layers of a state-of-the-art neural dependency parsing as features to the state-of-the-art targeted sentiment classification models of Liu and Zhang (2017), using neural stacking (Zhang and Weiss 2016; Chen et al. 2016). The main structure of our model is shown in Figure 2.

We choose the parser of Dozat and Manning (2016) as our syntactic model, which gives the best results on a WSJ benchmark by using multilayer LSTMs to encode rich input information. The structure of the model is shown in Figure 4, which first learns a vector form of each input word (**W** and **T**), and then uses a simple bi-affine attention mechanism to find word-word relations. The feature vectors (**A** and **D**) thus contain rich syntactic information about each word, yet do not explicitly specify the syntactic structure of the sentence. Hence, using them as features gives our model more syntactic background of the sentence, yet without suffering from error propagation.

Results on both the dataset of Zhang et al. (2016) and the dataset of Tang et al. (2015) show that syntactic information is highly useful for improving the accuracies of target-dependent sentiment analysis. Our final models give the best reported results on both datasets. The source code is released at https://github.com/CooDL/TSSSF.

2 Model

As shown in Figure 2, our neural stacking model consists of two brief components: a bottom level syntactic model for obtaining the syntactic information and a top level sentiment model for target-dependent sentiment classification.

2.1 Input representation

Given an input sentence, we first obtain its word representations. In particular, we train two separate word embedding sets for the bottom level syntactic model and top level sentiment model, respectively, denoted as we_b and we_t, respectively. This is because our syntactic parser is trained on news data, while our sentiment classification is trained on Twitter data.

In addition, for the bottom syntactic model, we also use optionally part-of-speech tag embeddings pos_b, which are randomly initialised and learned during the training of the model. Formally, given a word w, the representation for the bottom level model is:

$$x_b = we_b \oplus pos_b,$$

and the input form of the top level model is

$$x_t = x_t^* \oplus f_b = we_t \oplus Bottom(x_b)$$

Here we use $Bottom(x_b)$ indicate the bottom level syntax model.

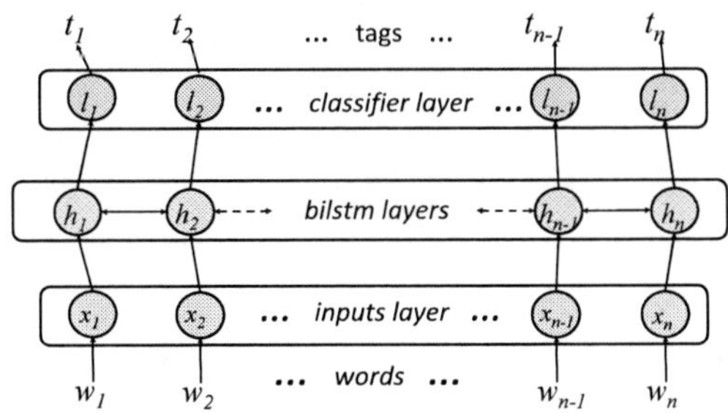

Figure 3: POS-tagging model

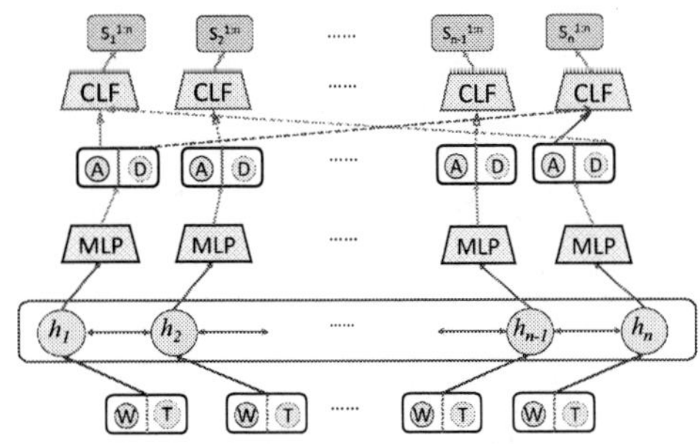

Figure 4: Dependency parsing model

2.2 Syntactic Sub Models

The twitter data suffer poor accuracies by syntax parsers in contrast with news data such as PTB. Directly using explicit twitter syntax features has an error propagation problem. We use a pre-trained syntax model to turn raw word embeddings into implicit syntactic features. Both a POS model and a dependency model are used to utilize syntax features.

2.2.1 POS Model

We employ a simplified bi-directional LSTM (BiLSTM) POS-tagging model (see Figure 3), trained on PTB3 (Toutanova et al. 2003; Labeau et al. 2015). As for every sentence sequence $w_1, w_2, ..., w_n$, its corresponding word embedding sequence $x_1, x_2, ..., x_n$, we integrate its word embedding into a k_1-layer BiLSTM:

$$\begin{aligned} S' &= [h_1, h_2, ..., h_n] \\ &= \text{BiLSTM}([x_1, x_2, ..., x_n])^{k_1}, \end{aligned} \quad (1)$$

where S' is the k_1-layer BiLSTM hidden state output. A classifier is then used to weight the hidden state of each word in S' and derive the label. Here W_1 is the weight matrix and b is the bias:

$$Labels = \text{Classifier}(W_1 S' + b), \quad (2)$$

The BiLSTM hidden layer $h_1, h_2, ..., h_n$ and the result of $W_1 S' + b$ (the labels' logits) will act as our implicit syntactic features.

2.2.2 Dependency Model

In this model, we use a dependency parser to replace the POS-tagging model in Section 2.2.1. In particular, the model of Dozat and Manning (2016) is used, which fuses several BiLSTM layers to encode the input sentence before doing bi-affine attention to learn dependency arcs betwtween different words.

Two different dependency models are trained: one being a POS$\oplus$ dependency with bottom input $we_b \oplus pos_b$, one being no-POS dependency model with just word embedding we_b. , given a sentence sequence $w_1, w_2, ..., w_n$, it integrates the word embedding $we_b(\boldsymbol{W})$ and POS-tag embedding $pos_b(\boldsymbol{T})$ into a k_2-layer BiLSTM and generate the LSTM states S' of the words in sentence $\boldsymbol{S}$, here $x_i = we_b^i \oplus pos_b^i$, $h_i = \overleftarrow{h_i} \oplus \overrightarrow{h_i}$,

$$\begin{aligned} S' &= [h_1, h_2, ..., h_n] \\ &= \text{BiLSTM}([x_1, x_2, ..., x_n])^{k_2}, \end{aligned} \quad (3)$$

MLP (Multilayer Perceptron) layers are used to reduce the dimension size and build features from the BiLSTM state output S'. Here it gives four kind features: $head_{arc}, head_{dep}, rel_{arc}, rel_{dep}$:

$$\begin{aligned} head_{arc}, head_{dep}, rel_{arc}, rel_{dep} \\ = \text{MLP}([h_1, h_2, ..., h_n])^{k_3}, \end{aligned} \quad (4)$$

Based on the features, a bi-affine classifier gives every word in the sentence S a corresponding dependency $head$ using the feature $head_{arc}(\mathbf{A})$ and $head_{dep}(\mathbf{D})$. We obtain the $head$ relation set $S'_{head} = \{head_i^j, i, j \in [1, n]\}$:

$$head_i^j = \text{Classifier}(head_{arc}^i, head_{dep}^j) \quad (5)$$

Another bi-affine classifier is used to classify the dependency relation based on the feature $head_{arc}(\mathbf{A})$, $head_{dep}(\mathbf{D})$ and $head_i^j$, and we obtain the rel relation label set $S'_{rel} = \{rel_i^j, i, j \in [1, n]\}$:

$$rel_i^j = \text{Classifier}(head_{arc}^i, head_{dep}^j, head_i^j), (6)$$

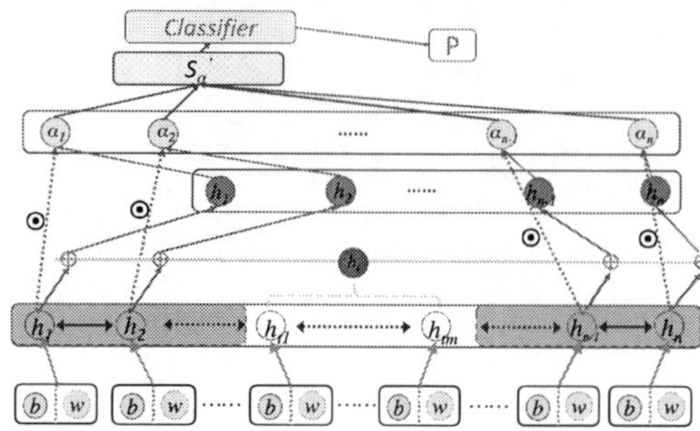

Figure 5: Target-dependent sentiment analysis with attention, shadow parts donate the attention part in a sentence

Using the two classifiers, we obtain the dependency root and relation between every two words in the sentence S. We pre-train the dependency parser model with 4 bi-directional LSTM layers and 2 layers of MLP, and use its intermediate output (the MLP output vector) as implicit syntactic feature inputs to the top sentiment model.

The normal dependency syntax model shares the same network frame with the no-POS dependency model. They have slight differences in the classifier. Both models are end-to-end denpendency parsers with different initial inputs. We choose the same output (Bi-LSTM hidden vector and MLP vector) of the two models as implicit syntactic features.

2.3 Target-dependent Sentiment Model

We use the attention-based model of Liu and Zhang (2017) as our top level model. The overall structure is shown in Figure 5. Given a sentence, it first uses several BiLSTM layers to learn its syntactic features, and then an attention layer is used to select the relative weghits of the words according to the target entity over the untargeted words in the whole sentence (Bahdanau et al. 2014; Yang et al. 2016). In particular, for a target word, it applies the target word hidden vector to find a weight forevery word (except the target words) in the sentence (see Figure 5). The model also uses a BiLSTM to represent the feature layer from bottom syntactic model $f_b(\boldsymbol{b})$ and the word embedding $we_t(\boldsymbol{w})$ of a word sequence $w_1, w_2, ..., w_n$ as the hidden vector of each word.

$$[h_1, h_2, ..., h_n] = \text{BiLSTM}([r_1, r_2, ..., r_n])^{k_4}, \quad (7)$$

where $r_i = f_b^i \oplus we_t^i$ and k_4 is the BiLSTM

layer number.

The target phrase words $h_{t_1}, h_{t_2}, ..., h_{t_m}$ are represented as one vector h_t($h_t \notin [h_1, h_n]$). It is the average of the target phrase words hidden vectors, $h_t = \frac{1}{m} \sum_{i=1}^{m} h_{t_i}$.

We build a vanilla attention model by calculating a weight value α_i for each word in the sentence. The sentence S then can be represented as follows:

$$\begin{aligned} S'_\alpha &= \text{Attention}([h_1, h_2, ..., h_n], h_t) \\ &= \sum_{i=1}^{n} \alpha_i h_i, \end{aligned} \quad (8)$$

where $\alpha_i = \exp(\beta_i) / \sum_{j=1}^{n} exp(\beta_j)$.
The weight scores β_i are calculated by using target representation h_t and each word hidden vector representation in the sentence,

$$\beta_i = U^T \tanh(W_2 \cdot [h_i : h_t] + b_1), \quad (9)$$

The sentence representation S'_α is used to predict the probability vector P sentiment labels on target by:

$$P = \text{Classifier}(W_3 \cdot S'_\alpha + b_2), \quad (10)$$

2.4 Training

Our training procedure consists of two steps, one being to pre-train the bottom syntactic models, the other being to apply the pre-trained bottom syntactic model and train the top sentiment analysis model.

All models are trained by minimizing the sum of cross-entropy loss and a $L2$ regularization loss of all trainable weights ΔW.

$$loss = \frac{1}{n} \sum_{i}^{n} \sigma(y_i, y'_i) + \frac{\lambda}{2} ||\Delta W||^2, \quad (11)$$

The model feature inputs (word embeddings, POS-tag embeddings) are the sum of a trainable embedding and a pre-trained (or learned) embedding. All the weight matrix will be initialized with an orthogonal loss less than $1e^{-6}$.

We choose different intermediate outputs of different bottom level syntax models. For POS-tagging model, we use the BiLSTM hidden output (lm_{pos}) and POS-tags vector before softmax (lt_{pos}). For the dependency sub model, we utilize

Bottom Syntactic Model	
LSTM Size(d_{blstm})	300
MLP Size (d_{mlp})	100
LSTM Layers(POS Model) (k_1)	2
LSTM Layers(Dep. Model) (k_2)	4
LSTM Dropout Rate (dr_{blstm})	0.6
MLP Layers (k_3)	2
MLP Dropout Rate (dr_{mlp})	0.67
Batch Size(b_b)	1000
Word Embeddings (d_{bw})	100
POS Embeddings (d_{pos})	100
Top Sentiment Model	
LSTM Size(d_{tlstm})	200
LSTM Layers(k_4)	1
Word Embedding(d_{tw})	200
Batch Size(b_t)	200
LSTM Dropout Rate(dr_{tlstm})	0.5
Same Parameters	
Word Minimum Occurance	3
Learning Rate(lr)	0.02
Learning Rate Decay Rate(lr_{speed})	0.75
Decay Steps($lr_{distance}$)	1500
Random Seed	1314
Train Iterations	30000

Table 2: Hyper-parameters values

		Total	Pos	Neg	Neu
T-set	Train	6248	1561	1560	3127
	Test	692	173	173	346
Z-set	Train	9489	2416	2384	4689
	Dev	1036	255	272	509
	Test	1170	294	295	581

Table 3: Sentiment Distribution

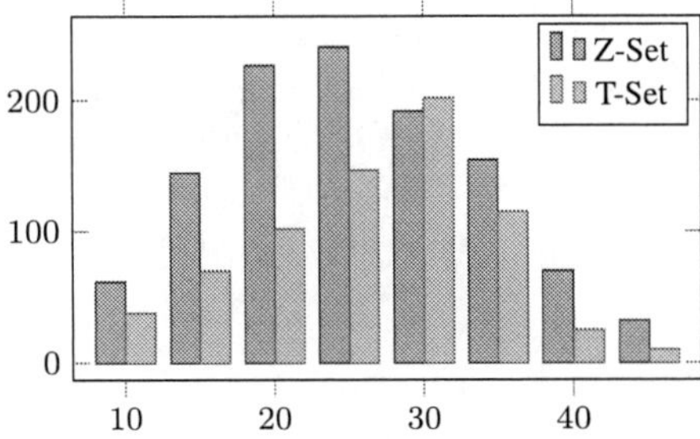

Figure 6: Test-set length distribution

the last BiLSTM layer hidden feature(lm_{dep}) and the MLP layer output (mlp_{dep}) optionally.

3 Experiments

We evaluate the performances of our model and compare them with state-of-the-art results using two standard datasets for target-dependent sentiment (Zhang et al., 2016; Tang et al., 2015). The PTB3 dataset is used to pre-train our bottom level syntax models.

3.1 Data

We conduct experiments on two datasets, one being the training/dev/test dataset of Zhang et al. (2016) (Z-Set), which consists of the MPQA corpus[1] and Mitchell et al. (2013)'s corpus[2], the other being the dataset of the benchmark training/test dataset of ? (T-Set), we label these datasets' POS-tags with the open parser tools ZPar (Zhang and Clark, 2011). Two sets of word embedding are used in this experiment: The GloVe[3] (Pennington et al., 2014) twitter embedding (100 dimensions) for the bottom model, and the GloVe twit-

ter word embedding (200 dimensions) for the top target-dependent sentiment analysis model. Also, due to lack of syntactically labelled twitter data, we used the PTB3 dataset to pre-train our bottom models. We follow the standard splits of PTB3, using 2-21 as the bottom model training data, section 22 for the development set and 23 as the test set.

We calculate statistics on sentiment polorities and lengths for both datasets. Table 3 shows the same percentage of three sentiment labels and Figure 6 shows length distribution on the test sets.

3.2 Trainning Settings

First, we use the PTB3 dataset with the standard split method pre-train the POS syntax model and dependency syntax model with the hyper-parameters listed in Table 2. A best model on the devset is saved for the neural stacking bottom syntax model.

Once obtaining the pre-trained bottom syntax model, we build the top sentiment model based on intermediate output syntax model features f_b and top word embedding we_t.

3.3 Hyper-parameters

Embedding Size: Our embedding is a superposition of a trainable and a pre-trained word embedding. We fixed the word embedding dimension of we_b and we_t to 100 and 200, respectively to match two pre-trained GloVe word embeddings set from Pennington et al. (2014).

[1]http://mpqa.cs.pitt.edu/corpora/mpqa corpus/
[2]http://www.m-mitchell.com/code/index.html
[3]https://nlp.stanford.edu/projects/glove/

Models	Acc.(%)	F1(%)	UAS	LAS
POS-tagging	92.4	91.6	/	/
Normal Dep.	/	/	95.6	93.8
No-POS Dep.	/	/	94.3	92.7

Table 4: Results for Syntactic Sub Model on PTB3 development set.

Dropout Rate: Dropout wrappers are applied to both the bottom level syntax model and top level sentiment model to avoid overfitting and learn better features. For the bottom syntax model, we use the PTB3 dataset to pre-train and tune hyper-parameters. A dropout rate of $\xi = 0.6$ for the BiLSTM layer and a softmax classifier layer to classify the learned features from hidden BiLSTM vector are used, respectively. Dropout rates of $\xi = 0.6$ and $\xi = 0.67$ are applied to every second BiLSTM layer and MLP layer, respectively, in the dependency model. We gain the best results (see Table 4) of different bottom syntax models on the PTB3 dataset.

For the top sentiment model, we use the model with only top word embedding inputs as our baseline. Here, the bottom syntactic features f_b are pre-processed with a dropout wrapper of $\phi = 0.5$ before being concatenated to the top model word embedding we_t, which is also wrapped with a dropout of $\varphi = 0.8$ for training models.

Training: We tune the hyper-parameters of the bottom syntax model on the PTB3 development set and top sentiment on the Z-Set development set. Words that occur less than a minimum amount of 3 times are treated as unknown words. Standard SGD with a decaying learning rate $(2e^{-2})$ is used for optimization, where the decay rate (0.75) is used to reduce the learning rate after each training iteration step $(lr_{distance})$.

$$lr_{new} = lr \cdot (lr_{speed})^{total_{steps}/lr_{distance}}, \quad (12)$$

There are several hyper-parameters in our models. We tune all the model hyper-parameters on the dev set with grid-search. With a learning rate of $\varphi = 2e^{-2}$, we did a large parameter iteration on learning rate decay steps $lr_{distance}$, decay rate lr_{speed}, batch size $(b_b\&b_t)$ and dropout. The batch size $(b_b\&b_t)$ has a great impact on model weights gradient and training speeds, and we choose a balanced point of 200 and 1000 for top and bottom model respectively. The decaying learning rate can also help in avoiding early overfitting and

Models	Acc.(%)
Baseline	73.24
$+lm_{pos}$	73.53
$+lt_{pos}$	73.34
$+lm_{pos}\<pos$	73.81
$+mlp_{dep}$	74.23
$+lm_{dep}$	73.96
$+lm_{dep}\&mlp_{dep}$	74.59

Table 5: Dev set accuracies for sentiment sub model

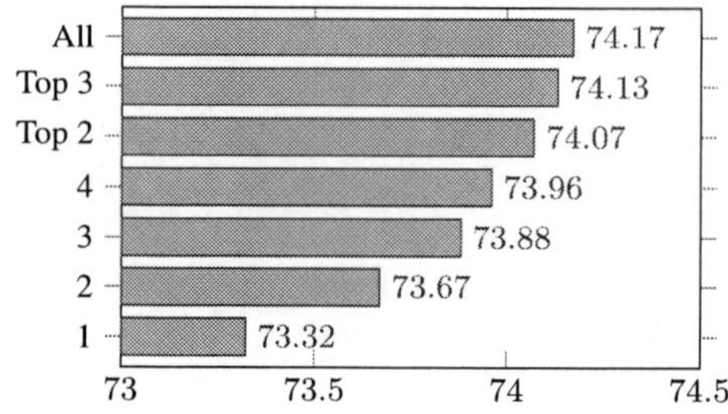

Table 6: Dev Results on BiLSTM feature layers

large weights optimization. The details of other hyper-parameters are listed in Table 2.

3.4 Development Experiments

Syntactic features: We measure the efficience of different syntax features; the results are listed in Table 5. Within syntactic features, the baseline system (our implementation of Liu and Zhang (2017)) gives an accuracy of 73.24%. With only POS features, the accuracies can reach 74.23%, which is significantly ($p < 0.01$ by T-test) higher. With dependency information, the accuracy further rises to 74.59%, which is significant improved by 1.4 points to the baseline. This shows that syntactic information is indeed useful for target-dependent sentiment classification.

BiLSTM Layers: We also concatenate the hidden BiLSTM vector from different layers to construct a fast forword feature network to build feature from the dependency model.

$$lm_{dep} = \mathrm{MLP}(\mathrm{CONCAT}(lm_{dep}[1:n])), \quad (13)$$

here, MLP is used to reduce the concatenated lm_{dep} dimensions and ($1 <= n <= 4$). A dropout wrapper of $\phi = 0.6$ is applied for the concatenated LSTM vectors $lm_{dep}[1:n]$.

The results of fast forwards features from different LSTM layer are shown in Tabel 6. Here

Models	Acc.(%)		F1(%)	
	Z_{set}	T_{set}	Z_{set}	T_{set}
Jiang et al. (2011)	/	63.4	/	63.3
Dong et al. (2014)	/	66.3	/	65.9
Vo and Zhang (2015)	69.6	71.1	65.6	69.9
Tang et al. (2015)	/	71.5	/	69.5
Zhang et al. (2016)	71.9	72.0	69.6	70.9
Liu and Zhang (2017)	73.5	72.4	70.6	70.5
Baseline	*73.0*	*71.7*	*70.2*	*70.1*
+ lm_{pos} [a]	73.5	72.4	71.2	70.4
+ lt_{pos} [b]	73.2	72.0	70.8	70.2
+ lm_{pos}&lt_{pos} [c]	**73.9**	**72.5**	**71.4**	**70.7**
+ lm_{dep}	73.5	72.2	70.7	70.6
+ mlp_{dep}	74.0	72.6	71.3	70.9
+ lm_{dep}&mlp_{dep}	**74.1**	**72.7**	**71.7**	**71.3**
+ lm^*_{dep} [d]	73.3	72.4	70.9	70.5
+ mlp^*_{dep} [e]	74.2	72.8	71.3	70.5
+ lm^*_{dep}&mlp^*_{dep} [f]	**74.3**	**72.8**	**71.8**	**71.4**

Table 7: Test set results with different syntactic features, the features with * means they are built from the no-POS dependency syntax model

		Pos	Neg	Neu
Z-Set	Baseline	61.64	69.83	78.67
	$POS_{[c]}$	61.43	70.17	78.97
	$DEP_{[f]}$	61.14	71.14	79.63
T-Set	Baseline	62.57	69.36	75.70
	$POS_{[c]}$	61.84	69.41	77.62
	$DEP_{[f]}$	62.74	70.31	78.42

Table 8: F1 values(%) of each polarity on test set of Z-Set, T-Set, the $POS_{[c]}$ and $DEP_{[f]}$ indicate the features listed in Table 7

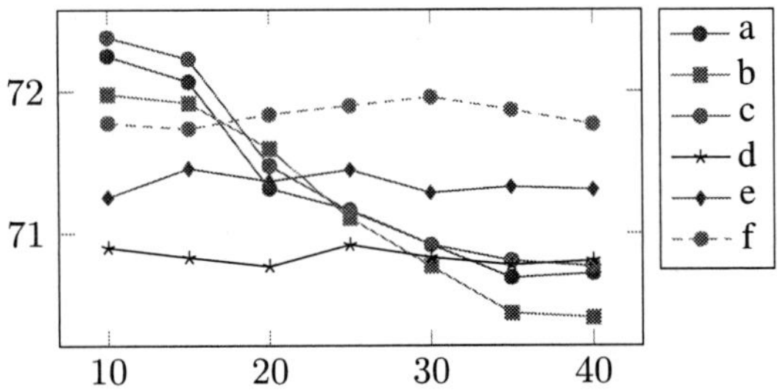

Figure 7: Test-set Accuracy against sentence length (Z-Set), a,b,c,d,e,f indicate the features listed in Table 7, respectively

we refer to the *first* BiLSTM layer as 1, and the *last* BiLSTM layer as 4. *Top 2* indicates the *layer3 & layer4*. Without fast forward connections, the results are 73.24%. With setting 1 to 4, the accuracies increase from 73.24% to 73.32%, 73.67%, 73.88% and 73.96%, respectively. Finally, the best results are obtained with 74.17%. We thus use the settings *layer4* for final tests, for a nice balance of efficiency and accuracy.

3.5 Results

We conduct final tests on the test set of Z-Set and T-Set, respectively investigating two questions. First, we verify whether this kind implicit features enhance the accuracy of twitter target-dependent sentiment analysis. Second, we measure how syntax affect target-dependent sentiment analysis results.

First, we compare the effects of different features on target target-dependent sentiment analysis. We take the top model with only word embedding inputs as our baseline system. The results are listed in Table 7. We can see that the syntactic features contribute to enhancing the accuracy of target-dependent sentiment analysis. Compared with our baseline on both test-set, we obtain an increase of Acc. by 1.3 points ($p < 0.01$) on Z-Set and 1 point ($p < 0.05$) on T-Set. For the POS-tagging model, the lm_{pos} feature provides more information than the lt_{pos} feature, and the lt_{pos} has

little impact in their combination case.

The dependency model features work better than the POS-tag features. lm_{dep} is weaker than the mlp_{dep} feature, since mlp_{dep} feature contains more learned and special features, which provide the model with sentence level dependency structure.

Second, we separately test the effect of features made with respect to different sentence lengths and sentiment polarities. As two datasets have different max sentence lengths (Z-set 84 words, T-set 44 words), we focus on the length range [10,40] and treat the sentence with length 10- and 40+ as 10 and 40, respectively. The results are listed in Table 8, Figure 7 (Here we use the test set of Zhang et al. (2016)). The POS-tags features (a,b,c in Table 7) have advantages in short sentence (10-15 words), it gains a significant higher than the dependency features. In contrast, the dependency features (d,e,f in Table 7) show larger contribution on longer sentence (30-40 words).

Finally, our model gives a F1 score of 71.8% and 71.4% on both test sets, respectively, which are the best reported results so far.

3.6 Analysis

The results show that features have different contributions to enhance the accuracy of targeted sentiment classification. The bottom syntax model output contains different syntactic information. Using them as features do contribution to the top model gain the information about sentence structure or word interrelation.

The POS-tagging model features perform well on short sentences. We believe that a POS-tagging model feature vector contains relation between a present word and its POS context words. This matches its adjacent words, helping model gain local phrase-level structure information. For example, if a word has a VB tag and its adjacent words are RB and NN, a tighter relation will be generated between VB and NN.

Phrase-level structure contributes to short sentences, but can be ambiguous for long sentence. Even though a RNN can learn some sentence-level information, with the increasing of the sentence length, this local benefit can decrease gradually. This can be the reason of the result in Figure 7 where the F1 value of the POS-tagging model drops as the sentence length increase.

The stable performance of the dependency model in Figure 7 suggests that the overall sentence structure and local phrase-level structure can be both provided by the dependency model features. The more nonlocal sentence structure can help the model grasp the sentence sentiment easier. It has a slightly weakened in the overall structures of longer sentence.

The benefits from semantic features is structural and non-sentiment related. Though POS-tag information can generate dependency relations, we use the PTB3 data to pre-train the bottom level models, where noise may weaken the advantages. In contrast, the dependency model contains more detailed information, and is useful for PTB-like formal data. The effect can be discounted on twitter data. The results from Table 8 show that the F1 values show no significant variation on different sentiment polarities.

3.7 Attention values

We compared both types of features with the baseline on the attention values and structural relation between words (Figure 8). The relation is computed by the top model LSTM hidden vector under feature $[f]$ in Table 7. The grey level cor-

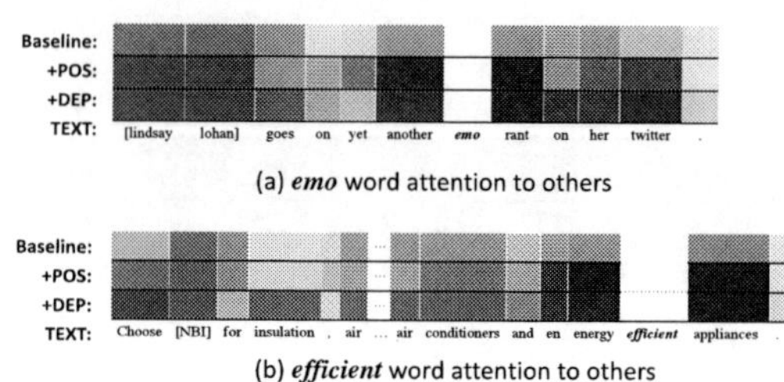

Figure 8: Word attention under implicit syntactic features, darker grayscale means closer attention

responds to their attention values. Darker colors mean closer attention. Here the baseline is the top model with only word embedding inputs. Figure 8(a) is a short sentence (12 words). We can see that the different features do not affect the sentence structure significantly. The POS-tagging model features focus on its adjacent and related words, such as the word '*emo*', which has a tight relation with the adjacent word '*rant*' and its adjunct word '*another*'. When the sentence length increases, the difference between POS and DEP becomes obvious. In Figure 8(b), the DEP has more related darker grey words attention compared to a normal word in the sentence (20+ words, we here hide some words due to limited space). For the phrase '*en engery efficient appliances*', for example, the POS features give shallow local relations, but deep remote semantic relations are given by the DEP features, such as the nominal modifier word '*Choose*' and its paralleling structure word '*insulation*'.

4 Conclusion

We investigated the use of implicit syntactic features for improving target-dependent sentiment analysis, by using hidden word representations of a state-of-the-art parsing to augment the input of a state-of-the-art target-dependent sentiment classifier. Neural stacking is used, where the parser is first trained using news article data, and then fine-tuned during the training of the sentiment classification system. In this way, our method leverages syntactic information, which is intuitively useful for target-dependent sentiment analysis, yet does not suffer from error propagations of using explicit syntactic parsing output features. Results on two target-dependent sentiment datasets show that our use of syntax can significantly enhance the accuracies of the baseline model, and our final model outperforms existing methods that use explicit syntactic features and without syntactic features, giving the best accuracies on both datasets.

Acknowledgement

We thank the anonymous reviewers for their detailed and constructive comments. Yue Zhang is the corresponding author.

References

Dzmitry Bahdanau, Kyunghyun Cho, and Yoshua Bengio. 2014. Neural machine translation by jointly learning to align and translate. *arXiv preprint arXiv:1409.0473* .

Hongshen Chen, Yue Zhang, and Qun Liu. 2016. Neural network for heterogeneous annotations pages 731–741. https://www.aclweb.org/anthology/D/D16/D16-1070.pdf.

Li Dong, Furu Wei, Chuanqi Tan, Duyu Tang, Ming Zhou, and Ke Xu. 2014. Adaptive recursive neural network for target-dependent twitter sentiment classification. In *ACL (2)*. pages 49–54.

Timothy Dozat and Christopher D Manning. 2016. Deep biaffine attention for neural dependency parsing. *arXiv preprint arXiv:1611.01734* .

Long Jiang, Mo Yu, Ming Zhou, Xiaohua Liu, and Tiejun Zhao. 2011. Target-dependent twitter sentiment classification. In *Proceedings of the 49th Annual Meeting of the Association for Computational Linguistics: Human Language Technologies-Volume 1*. Association for Computational Linguistics, pages 151–160.

Matthieu Labeau, Kevin Löser, Alexandre Allauzen, and Rue John von Neumann. 2015. Non-lexical neural architecture for fine-grained pos tagging. In *EMNLP*. pages 232–237.

Jiangming Liu and Yue Zhang. 2017. Attention modeling for targeted sentiment. *EACL 2017* page 572.

Margaret Mitchell, Jacqueline Aguilar, Theresa Wilson, and Benjamin Van Durme. 2013. Open domain targeted sentiment. In *EMNLP 2013*. pages 1643–1654.

Jeffrey Pennington, Richard Socher, and Christopher D Manning. 2014. Glove: Global vectors for word representation. In *EMNLP*. volume 14, pages 1532–1543.

Duyu Tang, Bing Qin, Xiaocheng Feng, and Ting Liu. 2015. Effective lstms for target-dependent sentiment classification. In *COLING*. pages 3298–3307.

Kristina Toutanova, Mark Mitchell, and Christopher D Manning. 2003. Optimizing local probability models for statistical parsing. *Lecture notes in computer science* pages 409–420.

Duy-Tin Vo and Yue Zhang. 2015. Target-dependent twitter sentiment classification with rich automatic features. In *IJCAI*. pages 1347–1353.

Zichao Yang, Diyi Yang, Chris Dyer, Xiaodong He, Alex Smola, and Eduard Hovy. 2016. Hierarchical attention networks for document classification. In *NAACL-HLT*. pages 1480–1489.

Meishan Zhang, Yue Zhang, and Duy-Tin Vo. 2016. Gated neural networks for targeted sentiment analysis. In *AAAI*. pages 3087–3093.

Yuan Zhang and David Weiss. 2016. Stack-propagation: Improved representation learning for syntax. *arXiv preprint arXiv:1603.06598* .

Yue Zhang and Stephen Clark. 2011. Syntactic processing using the generalized perceptron and beam search. *Computational linguistics* 37(1):105–151.

Graph Based Sentiment Aggregation using ConceptNet Ontology

Srikanth G Tamilselvam and **Seema Nagar** and **Abhijit Mishra** and **Kuntal Dey**
IBM Research, Bangalore and New Delhi, India
{srikanth.tamilselvam, senagar3, abhijimi, kuntadey}@in.ibm.com

Abstract

The *sentiment aggregation problem* accounts for analyzing the sentiment of a user towards various aspects/features of a product, and meaningfully assimilating the pragmatic significance of these features/aspects from an opinionated text. The current paper addresses the sentiment aggregation problem, by assigning weights to each aspect appearing in the user-generated content, that are proportionate to the strategic importance of the aspect in the pragmatic domain. The novelty of this paper is in computing the pragmatic significance (weight) of each aspect, using graph centrality measures (applied on domain specific ontology-graphs extracted from *ConceptNet*), and deeply ingraining these weights while aggregating the sentiments from opinionated text. We experiment over multiple real-life product review data. Our system consistently outperforms the state of the art - by as much as a F-score of 20.39% in one case.

1 Introduction

User-generated content accounts for a large fraction of the online content that is available today. The advent of web-platforms such as on online social networks (*e.g., Facebook, Twitter etc.*), blogs, discussion forums and product portals (*e.g.,* Amazon) has resulted in creation of a plethora of user-generated opinionated-content. The task of sentiment analysis focuses on analyzing such text, and deciphering user sentiment towards given products or their features, often referred to as *aspects*.

The task of sentiment aggregation builds upon sentiment analysis processes in general. While sentiment analysis (SA) aims to classify an opinion into positive or negative or neutral categories (in case of coarse-grained SA) or into more intricate categories (in case of fine-grained/dimensional SA), often enough, it considers the opinion in its entirety, and is agnostic of the aspect-specific sentiments expressed. However, in practical settings, opinions expressed by users (such as product reviews) often tend to focus on multiple aspects, not just one. The diversity of the aspects, does not allow the aspect-specific sentiment-polarity values to be just naively summed up for the purpose of obtaining an overall aggregated sentiment of a given user towards a given product.

As an example, let us consider the following text regarding a software application: *This app has a beautiful interface. It is not bug free though.* The first sentence here is a positive feel to it from the *interface* feature (aspect). The second sentence has a negative feel to it from the *accuracy (bug)* feature (aspect). Thus, a simple linear aggregation (sum of the individual polarities) of the features, will yield a overall neutral review polarity score. This is not necessarily accurate. While an interface is a necessary enabler for users to use a software, it is of imperative necessity that the software runs accurately, without posing problems of bugs. Perhaps, a reasonable interface with an error-free running platform, is more necessary for an application software, than to just have a beautiful interface and erroneous execution. So the overall polarity of this review should be negative.

Let us flip the above example to the following: *This app has a bad and unfriendly interface. The software is, however, stellar in terms of execution.* This time, the first sentence shows a negative intent, while the second shows positive. Again, clearly, the overall sentiment can be deemed positive, although a simple-minded sum of the individual aspects would yield a neutral value.

Proceedings of the The 8th International Joint Conference on Natural Language Processing, pages 525–535,
Taipei, Taiwan, November 27 – December 1, 2017 ©2017 AFNLP

While in the previous examples the words such as *however* and *though* could potentially appear to act as discourse markers, such discourse markers will not appear in most of the cases. For instance, consider the following review example: *I hated the little hints they gave us hardcore NDers on the Dare to Play message board. I had extremely high hopes for this game–I adored Last Train to Blue Moon Canyon and waited AGES for this game. Now, besides the absurd level of difficulty in this game [it was seemingly VERY hard in my eyes–I could not make it the first time through without the assistance of a walkthrough], I LOVED it.* Clearly, while there are both positive and negative aspects in the review, the aggregate sentiment of the review is overall positive. And there is no discourse marker to simplify detecting the aggregated sentiment.

Assigning an overall review polarity requires a deeper aggregation of the sentiment polarity of each aspect. This involves not only understanding the sentiment purely from a natural language processing (NLP) standpoint, but also needs to account for the domain, and the pragmatic significance of the feature in the given domain.

Multiple works in the literature, such as (Hatzivassiloglou and Wiebe, 2000), (Turney, 2002), (Wu et al., 2009) and (Chen and Yao, 2010) have attempted to perform sentiment aggregation. One promising line of work explores usage of *domain ontologies* in order to factor for the *pragmatic value* of each aspect of the product. A recent work by (Mukherjee and Joshi, 2013) attempted to use *ConceptNet* (Liu and Singh, 2004), to learn the product attribute-hierarchy over *attributes*, *synonyms*, *essential components* and *functionalities*, and create a domain-specific ontology tree, using ConceptNet relationships across concepts. They subsequently map the sentiments associated with each feature of each given product to this ontology tree, and determine the overall aggregated sentiment as a weighted sum of these features, where the weights are computed as a function of proximity of the concept to the root node of the ontology.

Our work also uses domain ontologies for sentiment aggregation; however, we do not use the concept of ontology trees that has been used in the literature (Mukherjee and Joshi, 2013). We propose a novel approach, that extracts ontology-graphs from ConceptNet, around given themes, *e.g.*, *software*. The extracted concepts are assigned weights using a measure of their *centrality* to the theme under consideration (*e.g.*, the centrality of *bug* given the theme *software*). Akin to Mukherjee and Joshi (2013), these weights are combined with the associated feature sentiments, and a weighted aggregation is carried out to obtain the final sentiment aggregation scores for each user review.

For experiments, we use the same datasets as used by (Mukherjee and Joshi, 2013). Our system is more effective compared to the rest of the literature: it outperforms the state of the art for all the domains, including a large F-score margin of 20.39% in one case. Amongst the four datasets we experiment with, *closeness centrality* often outperforms the other graph centrality measures we use, namely *betweenness centrality* and *PageRank*; however, *betweenness centrality* outperforms the rest in a few cases. These centrality measures are explained in Section 3.1.

Overall, we provide a novel graph-driven baseline over domain ontologies, for deeply ingraining pragmatic information of various aspects of product reviews. Experiments indicate that the performance of our system is consistent across datasets, and also it consistently outperforms the state of the art. The system is expected to provide insights to organizations in understanding overall user sentiments towards products, by analyzing user-generated natural language text content.

2 Related Work

Sentiment analysis (SA) has been an area of long-standing area of research. A seminal work was carried out by Hatzivassiloglou and McKeown (1997), attempting to identify the sentiment polarity orientation of adjectives, using conjunction constraints, using a four-step supervised learning algorithm. One school of research has conducted significant exploration towards SA from user generated content, and a large fraction of these works look at the social media such as Twitter. This includes works by Agarwal et al. (2011), Barbosa and Feng (2010) and Kouloumpis et al. (2011), and Opinion Finder at University of Pittsburgh (Wilson et al., 2005). Many recent works, such as Khan et al. (2015), Kolchyna et al. (2015), Le and Nguyen (2015), Severyn and Moschitti (2015), and Zimbra et al. (2016), have also investigated the sentiment analysis problem on user generated content. Recent systems are based on variants of deep neural network built on top of embeddings. A few representative works in this direction for sentiment analysis are based on Convolutional Neural Networks (CNNs) (dos Santos and Gatti, 2014; Kim, 2014; Tang et al., 2014), Recurrent Neural Networks (RNNs) (Dong et al., 2014; Liu et al., 2015) and combined architecture (Wang et al., 2016). A few works exist on using deep neural networks for sarcasm detection, such as by Ghosh and Veale (2016) that uses a combination of RNNs and CNNs.

Sentiment analysis for product reviews has been investigated since a long time, in the literature. An early work attempting to classify reviews into positive vs. negative was conducted by Tong (2001), generating sentiment timelines. This was followed by several works, that attempted to replace the bag-of-words based early models by more sophisticated feature driven models (such as lexical, syntactic and semantic features). Some noteworthy works in this space include Hatzivassiloglou and Wiebe (2000), Kamps et al. (2001), Turney (2002) and Turney and Littman (2003). However, neither did these works consider domain-specific information, nor did they account for users' views on the different aspects (features) of a given product - all of which are central to comprehend the overall aggregate sentiment of a user towards a product.

Subsequent works attempted to incorporate user sentiments towards specific product aspects (product features); few of these incorporated deeper NLP techniques, such as dependency parsing (Wu et al., 2009; Chen and Yao, 2010; Mukherjee and Bhattacharyya, 2012) and joint sentiment topic models using LDA (Lin and He, 2009). These works, however, do not provide methodical or robust approaches to combine the feature-specific sentiments, to form the aggregate review polarity of a given user towards a given product.

Mukherjee and Joshi (2013), which happens to be the work closest to ours, attempt to overcome this shortcoming, extending over Wei and Gulla (2010) and Sureka et al. (2010). Wei and Gulla (2010) propose a hierarchical learning method for labeling product attributes and the associated sentiments in product reviews, using a Sentiment Ontology Tree (HL SOT) with a supervised learning technique. However, the work requires feature-specific labeling, which is not practicable in real-life applications, as well as, falls short of proposing any elegant aggregation mechanism for integrating feature-specific sentiments. Sureka et al.

(2010) were among the first ones to use ConceptNet (Liu and Singh, 2004) in sentiment analysis. Mukherjee and Joshi (2013) borrow from the concept of sentiment ontology tree, extract feature-specific ontology using ConceptNet, and finally present an Expected Sentiment Weight based combination of the feature-specific polarities, relying upon (a) the feature-specific sentiment polarity and strength, and (b) the weight of the sentiment derived as a function of the distance of the concept phrase (feature) from the root of the ontology tree. Their system also accounts for noisy and one-to-many relations in ConceptNet, and topic drift.

We notice that, there is scope in research, to fully exploit the intricate inter-relationship of the non-independent concepts that are practically bound to arise in a real-life setting. For example, in a world of *camera*, the concepts of *lens* and *flash* cannot be completely independent. And yet, in the ontology-tree based approach, such interdependencies go uncaptured. Such examples are clearly seen in Figure 1 in Mukherjee and Joshi (2013). This motivates the need to better capture the intricate interdependencies of such concepts, in terms of interdependencies as well as the significance of such dependencies. We hence propose a graph-based approach, where graph vertex properties, including weights, derived from the connectivity structures, can accommodate for such factors. Our approach is weakly supervised, unlike most of the recent SA systems mentioned above, including the conceptually similar but supervised approach of Socher et al. (2013) who model RNN on sentiment treebank for sentiment aggregation. The system is easy to implement and deploy, and consistently outperforms the literature for all the sentiment aggregation benchmark datasets.

3 Why Graph based Solutions?

As discussed earlier, a sentiment aggregator should leverage an ontology structure to alleviate the lack of awareness of the inter-relationships between aspects. It is, however, essential for ontology-driven sentiment aggregators to be aware of all possible inter-relationships between the aspects appearing in the opinionated text. The problem with the existing method of *transforming the ontology into a tree structure and aggregation of sentiment in a bottom-up manner* (Mukherjee and Joshi, 2013) is that it assumes the relationships between aspects (which are essentially mapped to concepts present in the ontology) to be hierarchical, thereby straight-away eliminating non-hierarchical relationships (like *metonymy*). As discussed earlier, concepts like "lens" and "flash" in camera domain do not share a parent-child relationship; it is thus impossible to find a connection between these two nodes in the ontology-tree. Moreover, as per Mukherjee and Joshi (2013), the intensity of sentiment expressed are aggregated from the leaf node towards the root. This does not allow sharing of sentiment related information between nodes at same levels (like "lens" and "flash"). Our proposed systems overcomes this problem by using the ontology-graph structure as it is, without performing any lossy transformation, unlike Mukherjee and Joshi (2013). We measure the pragmatic importance of the nodes of the ontology-graph through various centrality measures (discussed in Section 3.1), which helps our system decide how much sentiment-information can be shared across nodes during sentiment aggregation. We believe, a graph-based sentiment aggregation technique like ours offers a more natural way of sentiment aggregation that preserves all possible interrelationships amongst aspects.

3.1 Graph Centrality: Definitions

The centrality measures, the key constituents our approach, are explained below. The definitions are borrowed from the domain of graph theory.

Closeness Centrality: The closeness centrality (Bavelas, 1950) of a vertex in a connected graph indicates how central the vertex is to the overall graph structure. This is defined as the average length of the shortest paths between the given vertex and all other vertices in the given graph. If a given connected graph G comprises n vertices, then, the closeness centrality $C(v)$ of a vertex $v \in G$ is computed as

$$C(v) = \frac{n-1}{\sum_u d(u,v)} \approx \frac{n}{\sum_u d(u,v)}, \text{if } (n \gg 1)$$

where $d(u,v)$ represents the shortest path distance between the vertices u and v.

Betweenness Centrality: For each pair of vertices in any connected graph, there exists at least one shortest path between the pair of vertices, such that, the number of edges constructing the path is minimized (in case of unweighted graphs), or, the total weight of the edges constructed is minimized (weighted graphs). The betweenness cen-

trality (Freeman, 1977) of a given vertex of a graph is defined as the number of such shortest paths passing through the vertex. For a given vertex v, this is computed as

$$g(v) = \sum_{s \neq v \neq t} \frac{\sigma_{st}(v)}{\sigma_{st}}$$

where σ_{st} is the total number of shortest paths from vertex s to vertex t and $\sigma_{st}(v)$ of these pass through vertex v.

PageRank: The PageRank (Brin and Page, 1998) of a given vertex in a graph denotes the stationary probability of a random walk with restarts to arrive on the given vertex. For a given vertex v_i on a given graph G constituting of n vertices, the PageRank of the vertex $P(v_i)$ is computed as

$$P(v_i) = \alpha \sum_j u_{ji} \frac{v_j}{L_j} + \frac{1-\alpha}{n}$$

where $L_j = \sum_i u_{ji}$ is the number of neighbors of vertex j, and α, the damping factor, represents the probability of the random walk to continue.

4 Our Approach: Sentiment Aggregation using Graph Centrality

Our approach consists of two steps for assigning an overall polarity to a review for a product, based on the polarities expressed for individual aspects.

- The first step computes the *pragmatic significance* score for each aspect of a product, based on the graph centrality metrics obtained from domain specific ontology-graphs constructed from ConceptNet.

- The second step aggregates the polarities of different aspects to get one overall polarity for a review text, based on the scores from the earlier step and the polarities expressed for each aspect.

We provide the details of our approach below.

4.1 Ontology Graph Construction

We first construct the *ontology graph*, for each given concept/domain. Domain ontology captures intricate relationships and dependencies among different aspects of a product. We exploit the domain ontology in constructing a rich graph where nodes represent aspects and edges connecting them represent relationships among them. The graph representation rightly captures all the dependencies among the aspects as well as the complicated relationships among them.

The graph is constructed as follows. The concept/domain is identified by a *seed word* such as, *camera, automobile, etc.*. A vertex is constructed for the seed word, and is marked as *unexplored* in the set of graph vertices. This is added to $\mathcal{V}$, the set of vertices in the ontology graph $\mathcal{G} = (\mathcal{V}, \mathcal{E})$. For each *unexplored* vertex v in the graph, each concept in ConceptNet that has at least one relationship with v, a vertex u is added to the vertex set $\mathcal{V}$ and is marked as *unexplored*, as well as, an edge (u, v) is added to $\mathcal{E}$. At this stage, the vertex v is marked as *explored*. The ontology graph creation algorithm completes, when all vertices in $\mathcal{V}$ are marked as *explored*. We provide a maximum graph distance cut-off of n (a given number), where n is number of edges on the minimum-length path to reach from the concept to the seed word in the graph. Algorithm 1 provides the details of the ontology graph creation algorithm.

Hierarchical	LocatedNear, HasA, PartOf, MadeOf, IsA, InheritsFrom
Synonymous	Synonym, ConceptuallyRelatedTo
Functional	UsedFor, CapableOf, DefinedAs, HasProperty

Table 1: Categorization of ConceptNet Relationship Types

Three types of ConceptNet relationships are used to form the edges, shown in Table 1. *Hierarchical* relationships represent parent-child relationships of concepts. *Synonymous* relationships are used to identify related concepts. *Functional* relationships are used to identify the purpose or property of interest of the given concept.

4.2 Graph Centrality Computation

This step computes the centrality of each concept appearing in the domain ontology graph constructed in the earlier step. For computing pragmatic significance score for each aspect, we employ graph centrality measures. Specifically, we propose to use centrality metrics such as closeness centrality, betweenness centrality and page rank, since these centrality measures captures significance of a node from different perspectives. In

Algorithm 1 ONTOLOGY GRAPH CREATION

1: *function* **OntologyGraphCreate():**
2: $\mathcal{V} \leftarrow$ domain seed word as vertex s
3: **REM** *E.g.*: kitchen, automobile, software, camera *etc.*
4: mark s as *unexplored*
5: $\mathcal{E} \leftarrow \phi$
6: **while** there exists at least one *unexplored* vertex $v \in \mathcal{V}$ **do**
7:     **for** $u \in neighbors(v)$ **do**
8:         (**REM** neighbors(e) includes all vertices that have Hierarchical, Synonymous and Functional relationships with vertex e)
9:         **if** graph_distance(s,u) $\leq n$ **then**
10:             $\mathcal{V} \leftarrow \mathcal{V} \cup u$
11:             mark u as *unexplored* if not already explored previously
12:             $\mathcal{E} \leftarrow \mathcal{E} \cup (u, v)$
13:         **end if**
14:         mark v as *explored*
15:     **end for**
16: **end while**
17: **Output:** $\mathcal{G} \leftarrow (V, E)$

computation of the different centrality metrics we do not consider the type of relationship on an edge. An example of a closeness centrality graph, has been provided in Figure 1, for the domain *camera*.

4.3 Feature/Aspect-Specific Sentiment Computation

A user's opinion (review) could constitute of multiple aspects (features) of a given product, and different sentiment (opinion) polarities with respect to each aspect. The process of overall user sentiment analysis, mandates understanding the user's sentiment towards each of these aspects. To determine the sentiment polarity expressed by a user towards each aspect (feature), we perform *dependency parsing* of each review, to associate a given aspect of the review, with the opinion of the user towards the given feature, expressed in the text.

Let R be a user review towards a product. Let W be the words constituting the review R. Following the approach of (Mukherjee and Bhattacharyya, 2012), we perform dependency parsing, and obtain D, the set of significant dependency relations in the corpus (*e.g.*, *nsubj, amod, dobj, etc*). For each dependency D_l where $D_l(d_i, d_j) \in D$, a graph $G(W, E)$ is constructed

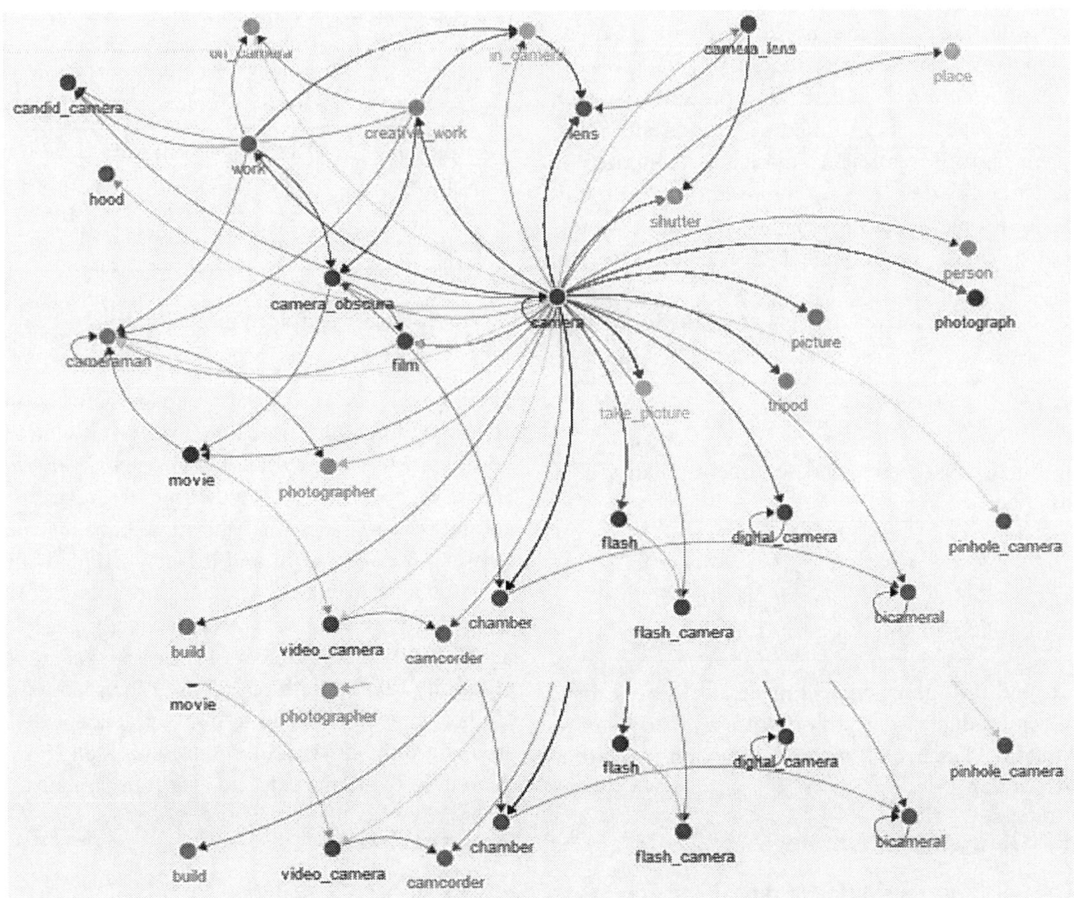

Figure 1: Depiction of closeness centrality measure for Camera Ontology

s.t. all $(w_i, w_j) \in W$ are connected by edge $e_k \in E$.

A PoS tagger is used to extract the entities (nouns). These entities are used as the initial feature (aspect) set $f_i \in F$. For each feature f_i, a cluster C_i is initiated, where f_i acts as the cluster head of C_i. Each word $w \in W$ occurring in review R, is assigned to the cluster having closest cluster head. The "closest" distance is measured, using the number of edges in the shortest path, that connects the word to the closest cluster head. Two clusters are merged, if the distance between the two cluster heads are less than a given threshold.

The set of words W_i belonging to each cluster C_i, are used to determine the user's opinion about feature f_i. This is attained by conducting a simple *majority voting* of the sentiment values of the individual words $w_i \in W_i$, using sentiment lexicons. A final aspect-specific sentiment score is produced, as -1 for negative, 0 for neutral and $+1$ for positive.

Also note that, we use the simple negation handling framework that was also adopted by (Mukherjee and Joshi, 2013). We reverse the sentiment polarities of all the words appearing within a window of size 5 (Hu and Liu, 2004), starting from any of the negation operators *not, nor, neither* and *no*.

4.4 Sentiment Polarity Aggregation

In this step, we aggregate polarities across all the aspects, to assign overall polarity to a review text. We define the overall polarity of a text as a weighted sum of (a) the sentiment polarity expressed by the user towards each aspect (feature) of the product the review text, and (b) the pragmatic significance of the aspect in the given domain, reflected in the graph centrality measures. These two factors ensure that the final polarity value for a given review text aggregates polarity values across different aspects, with adequate weightage that the aspect requires.

Let R be a review text, for a product P which has M aspects. Let m_i and $m_i{}^p$ represent i^{th} aspect, and it's sentiment polarity as computed as described earlier. Let c_{m_i} represent the centrality score for an aspect m_i computed using the ontology graph for the domain which P belongs to. The polarity value $p(sum)$ for a review text R is found by computing the polarity value, as the following:

$$p(sum) = \sum_{i=1}^{M} m_i{}^p \times c_{m_i}$$

Finally, the aggregated sentiment polarity S is assigned as:

$$\begin{cases} S = Positve & if\, p(sum) > 0 \\ S = Negative & if\, p(sum) < 0 \\ S = Neutral & if\, p(sum) = 0 \end{cases}$$

To find the aggregate sentiment of all users for a given product, we again opt for a *majority-voting* strategy. The overall methodology is presented in Algorithm 2.

5 Datasets and Ontologies

Dataset from four different domains corresponding to *automobile*, *camera*, *kitchen* and *software* are used for experiments. The camera reviews are collected from Mukherjee and Joshi (2013). The automobile, kitchen and software reviews are taken from Blitzer et al. (2007). Table 2 shows the dataset statistics.

	Positive	Negative	Total
Domain	Reviews	Reviews	Reviews
Automobile	584	152	736
Camera	986	210	1196
Kitchen	1001	1000	2001
Software	1000	915	1915

Table 2: Dataset Statistics

Note that, akin to Mukherjee and Joshi (2013), all the words have been lemmatized in the reviews, which ensures that all the terms such as *camera* and *cameras* are treated as the root word *camera*. Further, words such as *hvnt*, *dnt* have been replaced to their original forms.

In the ontology graph construction process, we keep adding *unexplored* vertices to the vertex set,

Domain	Corpus Frequent Features	Ontology Nodes	Ontology Edges
Automobile	132	114	778
Camera	986	979	1280
Kitchen	767	670	10629
Software	150	135	842

Table 3: Ontology-graph Statistics

as long as, there is at least one edge between the corresponding concept to an existing vertex in the vertex-set, of one of the types *functional, hierarchical* or *synonymous*. However, we restrict to adding vertices such that the maximum distance between the *seed word* and the newly added concept remains less than a given threshold n. We empirically fix $n = 4$, which practically provides a sufficiently large number of concepts that are realistically related to the concept of the seed word. Higher values of n lead to domain concept delusion and topic drift. Table 3 presents statistics of the ontology graphs extracted for four domains.

6 Experiments

6.1 Tools and Resources

We use several well-known tools and resources.

- For PoS tagging, we use Stanford NLP Toolkit[1]. PoS tagging is carried out to tag the user reviews, which in turn is used to identify the entities (noun concepts) in the reviews.

- For ontology construction for the domains, we use ConceptNet 5[2].

- To compute centrality measures of the ontology graphs, we use the graph tool $\mathbf{R}$[3].

- For dependency parsing of the user reviews, we use Stanford Dependency Parser[4].

- For sentiment lexicons, we experiment with SentiWordNet (Baccianella et al., 2010) and Bing Liu sentiment dictionary (Hu and Liu, 2004). Although we report our results only for the Bing Liu sentiment dictionary for the

---

[1]http://nlp.stanford.edu/software/tagger.shtml
[2]http://conceptnet5.media.mit.edu
[3]https://www.r-project.org
[4]http://nlp.stanford.edu/software/lex-parser.shtml

Algorithm 2 THE OVERALL APPROACH

1: $\mathcal{G}(\mathcal{V}, \mathcal{E}) \leftarrow$ OntologyGraphCreate()

2: **for** each vertex $v \in \mathcal{G}$ **do**
3:      centrality(v) $\leftarrow$ centrality measure value of vertex v in graph $\mathcal{G}$
4: **end for**

5: $total\_senti \leftarrow 0$
6: **for** each user review $\mathcal{R}$ **do**
7:      extract entities $\mathcal{T}$ from $\mathcal{R}$
8:      perform dependency parsing of $\mathcal{R}$
9:      $user\_senti \leftarrow 0$
10:     **for** each dependency $\mathcal{D}$ where $f = headword(\mathcal{D}) \in$ the full feature/aspect set $\mathcal{F}$ **do**
11:         (**REM** Each headword represents an aspect of the review)
12:         $dep\_senti(f) \leftarrow 0$
13:         **for** each word-concept $w \in \mathcal{D}$ **do**
14:             $dep\_senti(f) \leftarrow dep\_senti(f) + Sentiment(w)$
15:         **end for**
16:         **if** $f \in \mathcal{V}$ **then**
17:             $user\_senti \leftarrow user\_senti + dep\_senti(f) \times centrality(f)$
18:         **end if**
19:     **end for**
20:     $user\_senti\_set \leftarrow user\_senti\_set \cup < \mathcal{R}, user\_senti >$
21:     $total\_senti \leftarrow total\_senti + user\_senti$
22: **end for**
23: **Output:** $total\_senti, user\_senti\_set$

24: *function* **Sentiment(Word Concept** w**):**
25: return Sentiment_Dictionary_Lookup(w) (**REM** SentiWordNet, Bing Liu *etc.*)

---

sake of brevity, we observe similar performances using SentiWordNet also.

6.2 Results

We establish the first baseline of our work, using the *lexical classification* based approach of (Taboada et al., 2011). In this approach, a sentiment lexicon is used as a reference, that consists of words having positive and negative sentiment polarities. In a given review, if the total number of positive terms is higher compared to the total number of negative terms, the review is considered positive, and is considered negative if the opposite holds true. The baseline does not incorporate the feature (aspect) specific approach. We modify the approach to associate the lexical terms with the aspects (features), and thus obtain a feature-specific lexical sentiment. We subsequently aggregate these sentiments, to obtain improved baseline results. For sentiment lexicon, we empirically explore with SentiWordNet and Bing Liu sentiment dictionary.

We further compare our work against the reported approach for the same task by (Mukherjee and Joshi, 2013) which also uses ConceptNet, and has an approach similar to ours. However, as mentioned earlier, they consider ontology as a *tree* while we construct a *graph*. Also, they assign pragmatic weights to each aspect present in the review, using the height (distance) of the aspect from the root (*seed word*) of the ontology tree they construct, while we use graph centrality measures.

Table 4 illustrates the results we obtain with different approaches. The performance of the systems are reported in terms of accuracy (to ensure direct comparison with previous work) and **weighted F1-score** (to tackle class-imbalances). We report the results of the lexical baseline by (Taboada et al., 2011) using Bing Liu sentiment dictionary baseline, the results of Mukherjee and

Models	Automobile		Camera		Kitchen		Software	
	F1	Acc.	F1	Acc.	F1	Acc.	F1	Acc.
Lexical Baseline (Bing Liu)	73.45	64.43	79.74	63.65	66.77	67.11	66.04	69.38
Hierarchical Aggr. (Mukherjee et al., 2013)	71.48	70.23	81.22	70.38	67.28	67.62	70.19	70.28
Aggr. *Closeness* (Our approach)	75.93	**73.85**	**84.68**	**74.00**	85.66	**72.96**	**70.87**	**70.52**
Aggr. *Betweenness* (Our approach)	**76.47**	72.91	82.68	73.16	**87.67**	71.61	68.79	69.10
Aggr. *PageRank* (Our approach)	75.96	73.68	82.99	71.56	85.2	71.31	68.87	69.60
McNemar Significance Test (p)	< 0.0001		< 0.0001		< 0.0001		< 0.0001	

Table 4: Overall F1 score and accuracy (in %) of all models across all domains. For all domains, the performance improvements obtained using *Closeness* centrality measure over that reported in the literature (Mukherjee et al., 2013) are statistically significant (with $p \ll 0.05$), as confirmed by McNemar test.

Joshi (2013), and our results, using the three different graph centrality measures. As observed, all our proposed centrality based approaches outperform the baseline. The *closeness* centrality measure performs the best, with statistically significant improvement ($p \ll 0.05$) observed over the system reported by Mukherjee and Joshi (2013). Other graph based approaches also show improvement, except for the *software* domain.

7   Conclusion and Future Work

In this paper, we performed sentiment aggregation as a combination of user sentiments, analyzed towards multiple aspects/features of a product, from user-generated content. The novelty of this work was in deeply ingraining the sentiment weight of each entity derived from the user generated content, and pragmatic significance of the entity in the domains that was obtained by using a graph-structured ontology. We observe a consistently high performance of our system across all the keywords that we experiment with. We outperform the state of the art by a F-score of 3.02%, 3.46%, 20.39% and 0.68%, for *automobile, camera, kitchen* and *software* respectively. Further, the effectiveness of our system often increases by using *closeness centrality* over the other graph centrality measures such as *betweenness centrality* and *PageRank*, although *betweenness centrality* does outperform the rest of the methods in some cases. In future, we would like to improve the current technique to include the intensity of sentiment bearing words appearing in the reviews. Integrating lexico-semantic knowledge acquired through concept-embeddings learned from ontology structures in the aggregation step is also a future work. Our system will have significant real-life impact in helping organizations understand overall user sentiment towards products, on e-commerce sites (*e.g.,* Amazon) as well as online social networks, discussion forums and blogs.

Acknowledgments

We gratefully acknowledge the encouragement and existing intellectual assets we received from Sachindra Joshi, IBM Research India, and Subhabrata Mukherjee, Max Planck Institute Germany, towards our work, and sincerely thank them.

References

Apoorv Agarwal, Boyi Xie, Ilia Vovsha, Owen Rambow, and Rebecca Passonneau. 2011. Sentiment analysis of twitter data. In *Proceedings of the Workshop on Languages in Social Media*. Association for Computational Linguistics, pages 30–38.

Stefano Baccianella, Andrea Esuli, and Fabrizio Sebastiani. 2010. Sentiwordnet 3.0: An enhanced lexical resource for sentiment analysis and opinion mining. In *LREC*. volume 10, pages 2200–2204.

Luciano Barbosa and Junlan Feng. 2010. Robust sentiment detection on twitter from biased and noisy data. In *Proceedings of the 23rd International Conference on Computational Linguistics: Posters*. Association for Computational Linguistics, pages 36–44.

Alex Bavelas. 1950. Communication patterns in task-oriented groups. *The Journal of the Acoustical Society of America* 22(6):725–730.

John Blitzer, Mark Dredze, Fernando Pereira, et al. 2007. Biographies, bollywood, boom-boxes and blenders: Domain adaptation for sentiment classification. In *ACL*. volume 7, pages 440–447.

Sergey Brin and Lawrence Page. 1998. The anatomy of a large-scale hypertextual web search engine. *Computer networks and ISDN systems* 30(1):107–117.

Mosha Chen and Tianfang Yao. 2010. Combining dependency parsing with shallow semantic analysis for chinese opinion-element relation identification. In *Universal Communication Symposium (IUCS), 2010 4th International*. IEEE, pages 299–305.

Li Dong, Furu Wei, Chuanqi Tan, Duyu Tang, Ming Zhou, and Ke Xu. 2014. Adaptive recursive neural network for target-dependent twitter sentiment classification. In *ACL (2)*. pages 49–54.

Cícero Nogueira dos Santos and Maira Gatti. 2014. Deep convolutional neural networks for sentiment analysis of short texts. In *Proceedings of COLING*.

Linton C Freeman. 1977. A set of measures of centrality based on betweenness. *Sociometry* pages 35–41.

Aniruddha Ghosh and Tony Veale. 2016. Fracking sarcasm using neural network. In *Proceedings of NAACL-HLT*. pages 161–169.

Vasileios Hatzivassiloglou and Kathleen R McKeown. 1997. Predicting the semantic orientation of adjectives. In *Proceedings of the eighth conference on European chapter of the Association for Computational Linguistics*. Association for Computational Linguistics, pages 174–181.

Vasileios Hatzivassiloglou and Janyce M Wiebe. 2000. Effects of adjective orientation and gradability on sentence subjectivity. In *Proceedings of the 18th conference on Computational linguistics-Volume 1*. Association for Computational Linguistics, pages 299–305.

Minqing Hu and Bing Liu. 2004. Mining and summarizing customer reviews. In *Proceedings of the tenth ACM SIGKDD international conference on Knowledge discovery and data mining*. ACM, pages 168–177.

Jaap Kamps, Maarten Marx, Robert J Mokken, and Marten de Rijke. 2001. *Words with attitude*. Citeseer.

Aamera ZH Khan, Mohammad Atique, and VM Thakare. 2015. Combining lexicon-based and learning-based methods for twitter sentiment analysis. *International Journal of Electronics, Communication and Soft Computing Science & Engineering (IJECSCSE)* page 89.

Yoon Kim. 2014. Convolutional neural networks for sentence classification. In *Proceedings of the 2014 Conference on Empirical Methods in Natural Language Processing (EMNLP)*. Association for Computational Linguistics, Doha, Qatar, pages 1746–1751.

Olga Kolchyna, Thársis TP Souza, Philip Treleaven, and Tomaso Aste. 2015. Twitter sentiment analysis. *arXiv preprint arXiv:1507.00955* .

Efthymios Kouloumpis, Theresa Wilson, and Johanna Moore. 2011. Twitter sentiment analysis: The good the bad and the omg! *ICWSM* 11:538–541.

Bac Le and Huy Nguyen. 2015. Twitter sentiment analysis using machine learning techniques. In *Advanced Computational Methods for Knowledge Engineering*, Springer, pages 279–289.

Chenghua Lin and Yulan He. 2009. Joint sentiment/topic model for sentiment analysis. In *Proceedings of the 18th ACM conference on Information and knowledge management*. ACM, pages 375–384.

Hugo Liu and Push Singh. 2004. Conceptneta practical commonsense reasoning tool-kit. *BT technology journal* 22(4):211–226.

Pengfei Liu, Shafiq R Joty, and Helen M Meng. 2015. Fine-grained opinion mining with recurrent neural networks and word embeddings. In *EMNLP*. pages 1433–1443.

Subhabrata Mukherjee and Pushpak Bhattacharyya. 2012. Feature specific sentiment analysis for product reviews. *Computational Linguistics and Intelligent Text Processing* pages 475–487.

Subhabrata Mukherjee and Sachindra Joshi. 2013. Sentiment aggregation using conceptnet ontology. In *IJCNLP*. pages 570–578.

Aliaksei Severyn and Alessandro Moschitti. 2015. Twitter sentiment analysis with deep convolutional neural networks. In *Proceedings of the 38th International ACM SIGIR Conference on Research and Development in Information Retrieval*. ACM, pages 959–962.

Richard Socher, Alex Perelygin, Jean Y Wu, Jason Chuang, Christopher D Manning, Andrew Y Ng, Christopher Potts, et al. 2013. Recursive deep models for semantic compositionality over a sentiment treebank. In *Proceedings of the conference on empirical methods in natural language processing (EMNLP)*. volume 1631, page 1642.

Ashish Sureka, Vikram Goyal, Denzil Correa, and Anirban Mondal. 2010. Generating domain-specific ontology from common-sense semantic network for target specific sentiment analysis. In *Proceedings of the fifth international conference of the Global WordNet Association. Mumbai, India*. pages 1–8.

Maite Taboada, Julian Brooke, Milan Tofiloski, Kimberly Voll, and Manfred Stede. 2011. Lexicon-based methods for sentiment analysis. *Computational linguistics* 37(2):267–307.

Duyu Tang, Furu Wei, Bing Qin, Ting Liu, and Ming Zhou. 2014. Coooolll: A deep learning system for twitter sentiment classification. In *Proceedings of the 8th International Workshop on Semantic Evaluation (SemEval 2014)*. pages 208–212.

Richard M Tong. 2001. An operational system for detecting and tracking opinions in on-line discussion. In *Working Notes of the ACM SIGIR 2001 Workshop on Operational Text Classification*. volume 1, page 6.

Peter D Turney. 2002. Thumbs up or thumbs down?: semantic orientation applied to unsupervised classification of reviews. In *Proceedings of the 40th annual meeting on association for computational linguistics*. Association for Computational Linguistics, pages 417–424.

Peter D Turney and Michael L Littman. 2003. Measuring praise and criticism: Inference of semantic orientation from association. *ACM Transactions on Information Systems (TOIS)* 21(4):315–346.

Jin Wang, Liang-Chih Yu, K. Robert Lai, and Xuejie Zhang. 2016. Dimensional sentiment analysis using a regional cnn-lstm model. In *Proceedings of the 54th Annual Meeting of the Association for Computational Linguistics (Volume 2: Short Papers)*. Association for Computational Linguistics, Berlin, Germany, pages 225–230.

Wei Wei and Jon Atle Gulla. 2010. Sentiment learning on product reviews via sentiment ontology tree. In *Proceedings of the 48th Annual Meeting of the Association for Computational Linguistics*. Association for Computational Linguistics, pages 404–413.

Theresa Wilson, Paul Hoffmann, Swapna Somasundaran, Jason Kessler, Janyce Wiebe, Yejin Choi, Claire Cardie, Ellen Riloff, and Siddharth Patwardhan. 2005. Opinionfinder: A system for subjectivity analysis. In *Proceedings of hlt/emnlp on interactive demonstrations*. Association for Computational Linguistics, pages 34–35.

Yuanbin Wu, Qi Zhang, Xuanjing Huang, and Lide Wu. 2009. Phrase dependency parsing for opinion mining. In *Proceedings of the 2009 Conference on Empirical Methods in Natural Language Processing: Volume 3-Volume 3*. Association for Computational Linguistics, pages 1533–1541.

David Zimbra, M Ghiassi, and Sean Lee. 2016. Brand-related twitter sentiment analysis using feature engineering and the dynamic architecture for artificial neural networks. In *2016 49th Hawaii International Conference on System Sciences (HICSS)*. IEEE, pages 1930–1938.

Sentence Modeling with Deep Neural Architecture using Lexicon and Character Attention Mechanism for Sentiment Classification

Huy Thanh Nguyen and **Minh Le Nguyen**

Japan Advanced Institute of Science and Technology
Ishikawa, Japan
{huy.nguyen, nguyenml}@jaist.ac.jp

Abstract

Tweet-level sentiment classification in Twitter social networking has many challenges: exploiting syntax, semantic, sentiment and context in tweets. To address these problems, we propose a novel approach to sentiment analysis that uses lexicon features for building lexicon embeddings (LexW2Vs) and generates character attention vectors (CharAVs) by using a Deep Convolutional Neural Network (DeepCNN). Our approach integrates LexW2Vs and CharAVs with continuous word embeddings (ContinuousW2Vs) and dependency-based word embeddings (DependencyW2Vs) simultaneously in order to increase information for each word into a Bidirectional Contextual Gated Recurrent Neural Network (Bi-CGRNN). We evaluate our model on two Twitter sentiment classification datasets. Experimental results show that our model can improve the classification accuracy of sentence-level sentiment analysis in Twitter social networking.

1 Introduction

Tweet-level sentiment classification is a fundamental task of sentiment analysis in Twitter social networking and is essential to understand user generated contents in social networking. Twitter sentiment classification have intensively researched in recent years (Go et al., 2009) (Nakov et al., 2016). There are many works related to deep learning methods involved learning word representation (Socher et al., 2011). Word representation is central to deep learning and essential feature extractor that encode different features of words in their dimensions. The combination of word representation and deep learning achieved impressive results because word embeddings enable efficient computation of word similarities through low-dimensional matrix operations (Kim, 2014). In addition, deep learning models achieved remarkable performance. Some researchers use Convolution Neural Network (CNN) for sentiment classification. CNN utilizes convolution filters applied to local features. CNN models has been shown to be effective for NLP. For example, the model of (Dos Santos and Gatti, 2014) used CNN to form a sentence-level representation for sentiment classification. In addition, Bidirectional Gated Recurrent Neural Network (Bi-GRNN) is another deep learning model that has achieved an excellent result for sentiment analysis and other traditional tasks (Chung et al., 2014).

Inspired by the models above, the goal of this research is to build a model for exploiting syntax, semantic, sentiment and context of tweets by constructing four kinds of embeddings: CharAVs, LexW2Vs, ContinuousW2Vs and DependencyW2Vs. On the other hand, we modify Bi-GRNN of (Chung et al., 2014) into Bi-CGRNN to take word embeddings in order to produce a sentence-wide representation from sentence compositions. Our paper makes the following contributions:

- We construct a tweet processor which standardizes tweets by using pre-processing steps and a semantic rule-based approach. We construct four kinds of embeddings: CharAvs, LexW2Vs, ContinuousW2Vs and DependencyW2Vs. A DeepCNN is used for training CharAVs by producing fixed-size feature vectors and attending on the best feature vectors. CharAVs can capture the morphology and shape of a word. The morphological and shape information illustrate how words are

Proceedings of the The 8th International Joint Conference on Natural Language Processing, pages 536–544,
Taipei, Taiwan, November 27 – December 1, 2017 ©2017 AFNLP

formed, and their relationship to other words.

- We create an integration of CharAVs and LexW2Vs with ContinuousW2Vs and DependencyW2Vs. Such embeddings are advanced continuous word embeddings and advanced dependency-based word embeddings.

- We modify a standard Bi-GRNN to be a Bi-CGRNN by incorporating contextual features (e.g., Syntactic contexts) in order to take both advanced word embeddings. The output of Bi-CGRNN is sentence compositions that are formed into a sentence-wide representation. The purpose of Bi-CGRNN is to connect the information of words in a sequence and maintain the order of words for a sentence-level representation.

The organization of the paper is as follows: Section 2 describes the model architecture which introduces the structure of the model. We explain the basic idea of the model and the way of constructing the model. Section 3 shows results and analysis and Section 4 summarizes this paper.

2 Model architecture

2.1 Basic Idea

Our proposed model consists of a tweet processor and a deep learning module that are treated as two distinct components. The tweet processor standardizes tweets, applies semantic rules and then generates embeddings. The deep learning module is a combination of Bi-CGRNN and Deep-CNN. To formulate our challenges in increasing the classification accuracy, we illustrate the basic idea of our model in Figure 1 as follows: Tweets are firstly considered by the tweet processor based on pre-processing steps of (Go et al., 2009) and the semantic rule-based approach from (Appel et al., 2016). Then, we construct four kinds of embeddings in the representation-level step: ContinuousW2Vs, CharAVs, LexW2Vs and DependencyW2Vs, where CharAVs are generated from a DeepCNN. The DeepCNN is constructed from two wide convolutions which can learn to recognize specific n-grams at every position in a word and allow features to be extracted independently of these positions in the word. These features maintain the order and relative positions of characters and are formed at a higher abstract level. In those embeddings, ContinuousW2Vs take the syntax and semantic of words (Mikolov et al., 2013)

while the LexW2Vs can capture the sentiment of words (Shin et al., 2016). DependencyW2Vs derive the syntactic relations of words and exhibit more functional similarity than the original skip-gram embeddings led to form global syntactic contexts of words (Levy and Goldberg, 2014). Twitter sentiment label belongs to global sentence level while traditional word embeddings capture local contexts only. Therefore, DependencyW2Vs are useful in capturing global context of tweets. On the other hand, we create two advanced embeddings by integrating LexW2Vs and CharAVs with ContinuousW2Vs and DependencyW2Vs for Bi-CGRNN. A Bi-CGRNN is enhanced from a standard Bi-GRNN of (Chung et al., 2014) by incorporating contextual features (e.g., dependency-based contexts) into the model. The Bi-CGRNN produces a sentence-level representation from sentence compositions in order to maintain the order of word and capture syntax, semantic, sentiment and context of a sentence based on these embeddings.

2.2 Data Preparation

- *Stanford - Twitter Sentiment Corpus (STS Corpus):* STS Corpus contains 1,600K training tweets collected by a crawler from (Go et al., 2009). (Go et al., 2009) constructed a test set manually with 177 negative and 182 positive tweets. The Stanford test set is small. However, it has been widely used in different evaluation tasks (Go et al., 2009) (Dos Santos and Gatti, 2014).

- *Health Care Reform (HCR):* This dataset was constructed by crawling tweets containing the hashtag *#hcr* (Speriosu et al., 2011). The task of this paper is to predict positive/negative tweets.

2.3 Tweet Processor

We first take the unique properties of Twitter to reduce the feature space such as *Username, Usage of links, None, URLs* and *Repeated Letters*. We then process *retweets, stop words, links, URLs, mentions, punctuation* and *accentuation*. For emoticons in the dataset, we consider them as words in order that deep learning classifiers can capture information from emoticons. Because the test set contains emoticons, they do not influence classifiers if emoticons do not contain in its training data. Therefore, the emoticons would be useful

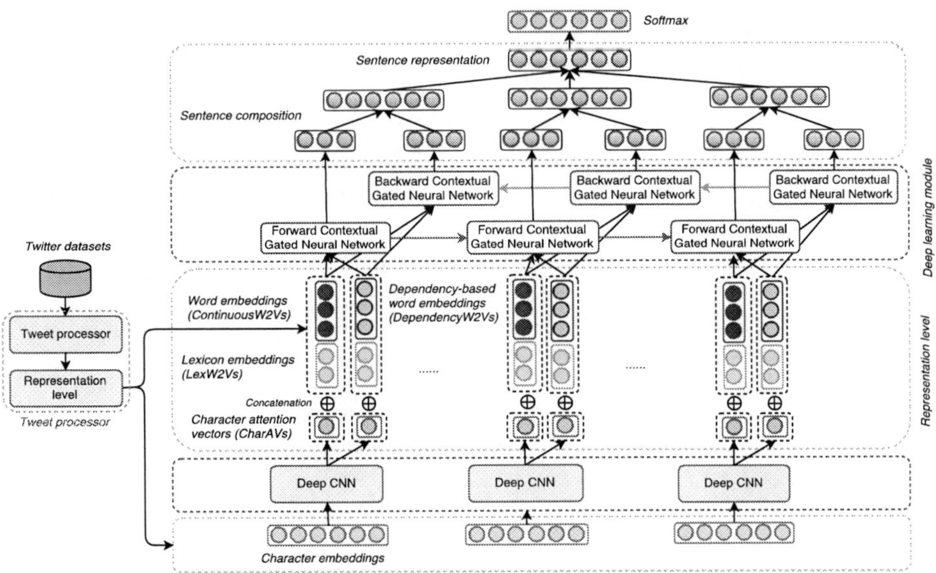

Figure 1: The overview of a deep learning system.

when classifying test data by using deep learning model. However, our preprocessing steps are different from (Go et al., 2009), they remove the emoticons out from their training datasets because they revealed that the training process makes the usage of emoticons as noisy labels and if they consider the emoticons, there is a negative impact on classification accuracy. In addition, traditional classifiers can not focus on non-emoticons (e.g., unigrams and bi-grams) to predict exactly the sentiment of tweets. After the pre-processing steps, we apply the semantic rules based on the idea of (Appel et al., 2016) and use a tweet processor from our previous work (Nguyen and Nguyen, 2017) to remove unnecessary sub-sentences from tweets in order that the deep learning model learns essential features from tweets. The semantic rule-based approach can handles negation and shows advances led to effectively affect the output of classifiers.

2.4 Representation Level

In this section, we describe how the kinds of embeddings are constructed by the representation module. To construct embedding inputs for our model, we use a fixed-sized word vocabulary V^{word} and a fixed-sized character vocabulary V^{char}. Given a word w_i is composed from characters $\{c_1, c_2, ..., c_M\}$, the character-level embeddings are encoded by column vectors u_i in the embedding matrix $W^{char} \in R^{d^{char} \times |V^{char}|}$, where V^{char} is the size of the character vocabulary. For

continuous word-level embedding r_{word}, we use a pre-trained word-level. We build every word w_i into two advanced word embeddings:

- Advanced continuous word embeddings $v_i = [r_i; e_i; l_i]$ is constructed by three sub-vectors: the pre-trained word-level embedding $r_i \in R^{d^{word}}$, the character attention vector $e_i \in R^l$ of w_i where l is the length of the filter of wide convolutions, the lexicon embedding $l_i \in R^{d^{score}}$ where d^{score} is list of sentiment scores for that word in lexicon datasets.

- Advanced dependency-based word embeddings $d_i = [de_i, e_i; l_i]$ is also built by three sub-vectors: the dependency-based word embedding $de_i \in R^{d^{word}}$, the character attention vector e_i and the lexicon embedding l_i. The advanced dependency-based word embeddings contain syntactic contexts and is increased information from LexW2Vs and CharAVs.

This deals with three main problems: (i) Sentences have any different size; (ii) Important information of characters that can appear at any position in a word are extracted; (iii) The syntax, semantic, sentiment, context and the morphology of words in a sentence are captured by concatenating two advanced embeddings via Bi-CGRNN in order to produce sentence representation.

We have N fixed-size CharAVs corresponding to word-level embeddings in a sentence. In subsection 2.5, 2.6 and 2.7, we illustrate the methods of constructing LexW2Vs, CharAVs using Deep-CNN and DependencyW2Vs.

2.5 Lexicon Embeddings (LexW2Vs)

The LexW2Vs are constructed by taking scores from various lexicon datasets. In lexicon datasets, each word contains key-value pairs in which the key is a word and the value is a list of sentiment scores for that word. These scores range from -1 to 1, where -1 is most negative and 1 is most positive, respectively.

For each word $w_i \in V^{word}$, where V^{word} is a fixed-sized word vocabulary, a lexicon embedding is constructed by concatenating all of the scores among lexicon datasets with respect to w_i. If w_i does not exist in a certain dataset, 0 value is substituted. The lexicon embedding is a form of a vector $l_i \in R^{d^{score}}$, where d^{score} is the total number of scores across all lexicon datasets. We use seven lexicon datasets for building LexW2Vs:

- Bing Liu Opinion Lexicon (Hu and Liu, 2004).

- NRC Hashtag Sentiment Lexicon (Mohammad et al., 2013).

- Sentiment140 Lexicon (Mohammad et al., 2013).

- NRC Sentiment140 Lexicon (Kiritchenko et al., 2014).

- MaxDiff Twitter Sentiment Lexicon (Kiritchenko et al., 2014).

- National Research Council Canada (NRC) Hashtag Affirmative and Negated Context Sentiment Lexicon (Kiritchenko et al., 2014).

- Large-Scale Twitter-Specific Sentiment Lexicon (Tang et al., 2014).

The purpose of building LexW2Vs is to take the different kinds of words for capturing the different sentiments of words. Table 1 illustrates the type of words for each dataset. We share idea with (Shin et al., 2016). However, our LexW2Vs are distinguished their approaches in the aspect: We cover the colloquial expressions and colloquial emoticons in tweets by using Large-scale Twitter-Specific Sentiment Lexicon.

Lexicon dataset	The type of words
Bing Liu Opinion Lexicon	Sentiment adjective words
NRC Hashtag Sentiment Lexicon	Hashtag emotion words & Hashtag topic words
Sentiment140 Lexicon	Emoticons & Sentiment words
NRC Sentiment140 Lexicon	Affirmative context words & Sentiment140 Negated Context words
MaxDiff Twitter Sentiment Lexicon	Twitter sentiment words
Hashtag Affirmative and Negated Context Sentiment Lexicon	Hashtag affirmative words & Negated contextual words
Large-Scale Twitter-Specific Sentiment Lexicon	Colloquial words & Emoticons

Table 1: The types of words in lexicon dataset.

We call such lexicon-based features as lexicon embeddings because embeddings are a feature input of deep learning model and describe the properties of a word or a phrase. Each word in each lexicon datasets actually has many values that can be built by training a neural network. The deep learning model uses this input for calculating a computational graph (weight matrix) that describe relatedness among words (n-gram order).

2.6 Character Attention Vectors (CharAVs)

Figure 2 describes the way of forming a character attention vector. We use a DeepCNN with two wide convolutions. The first convolution produces a fixed-size character feature vector named *m-gram* features by extracting local features around each character window of the given word and using a max pooling over vertical character windows. The second convolution retrieves the fixed-size character feature and transforms the representation to yield a character attention vector by performing max pooling on each row of matrix instead of each column. The purpose of this method is to attend on the highest *n-gram* feature in order to transform these *m-gram* features at previous level into a representation at a more focused abstract level and produces an attention over only the best feature vector. Character attention vectors has two advantages: One is that this model could adaptively assign an importance score to each piece of word embedding according to its semantic relatedness with characters of each word. Another advantage is that this attention model is differentiable, so that it could be easily trained together with other components in an end-to-end fashion. In the next sub-section, we introduce the structure of CNN with wide convolution.

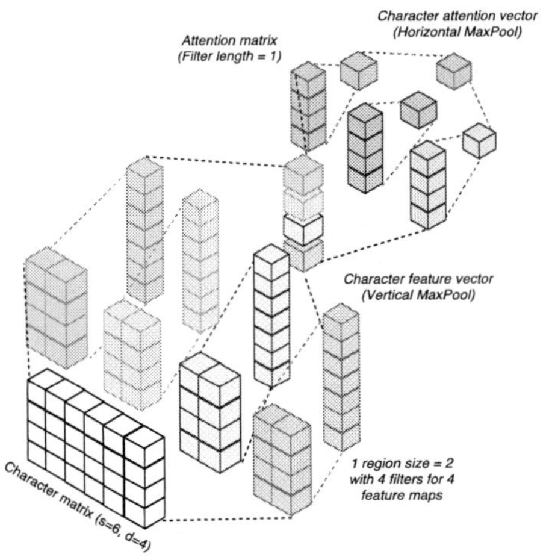

Figure 2: DeepCNN for the sequence of character embeddings of a word. For example with 1 region size is 2 and 4 feature maps in the first convolution and 1 region size is 3 with 3 feature maps in the second convolution. The CharAVs is then created by performing max pooling on each row of the attention matrix.

Convolutional Neural Network: The convolution has a filter vector m and take the dot product of filter m with each *m-grams* in the sequence of characters $s_i \in R$ of a word in order to obtain a sequence c:

$$c_j = m^T s_{j-m+1:j} \qquad (1)$$

Based on Equation 1, we have two types of convolutions that depend on the range of the index j. The narrow type requires that $s \geq m$ and produce a sequence $c \in R^{s-m+1}$. The wide type does not require on s or m and produce a sequence $c \in R^{s+m-1}$. Out-of-range input values s_i where $i < 1$ or $i > s$ are taken to be zero.

Wide Convolution: Given a word w_i composed of M characters $\{c_1, c_2, ..., c_M\}$, we take a character embedding $u_i \in R^{d^{char}}$ for each character c_i and construct a character matrix $W^{char} \in R^{d^{char}} \times |V^{char}|$. The values of the embeddings u_i are parameters that are optimized during training. The trained weights in the filter m correspond to a feature detector which learns to recognize a specific class of *n-grams*. The use of a wide convolution has some advantages more than a narrow convolution because a wide convolution ensures that all weights of filter reach the whole characters of

a word at the margins. The resulting matrix has dimension $d \times (s + m - 1)$.

2.7 Dependency-based Word Vectors (DependencyW2Vs)

To construct context embeddings, we use the idea of (Levy and Goldberg, 2014) to derive syntactic contexts based on the syntactic relations of a word. Most previous works on neural word embeddings take the contexts of a word by computing *linear-context* words that precede and follow the target word. However, these contexts can be exploited similar by generalizing the *SKIP-GRAM* model. The model for learning Dependency-based Word Vectors is improved from *SKIP-GRAM* model in which the linear bag of words contexts are replaced with arbitrary word contexts from dependency tree. Syntactic contexts are derived from produced dependency parse-trees. Specifically, the bag-of-words in the *SKIP-GRAM* model yield *broad topical similarities*, while the dependency-based contexts yield more *functional similarities* of a *cohyponym nature*. In the *SKIP-GRAM* model, the contexts of a word are the words surrounding it in the text. However, there is a limitation of *SKIP-GRAM* word embeddings: Contexts need not correspond to all of the words and the number of context-types maybe larger than the number of word-types. Therefore, dependency-based contexts capture more information than bag-of-words contexts. In Figure 3, the contexts are extracted for each word in the sentence and the contexts of a word are derived from syntactic relations of a word in the sentence. For parsing syntactic dependencies, we use a parser from (Goldberg and Nivre, 2013) for Stanford dependencies and the corpus are tagged with parts-of-speech using Stanford parser [1].

After parsing each sentence, we consider word context as Figure 3: For a target word w with modifiers $m_1, m_2, ..., m_n$ and a head h, we form the contexts as $(m_1, lbl_1), ..., (m_n, lbl_n), (h, lbl_h^{-1})$, where lbl is the type of the dependency relation between the head and the modifier, lbl^{-1} is used to mark the inverse-relation. The advantages of syntactic dependencies are inclusive and more focused than bag-of-words. In addition, they can capture relations that out-of-reach with small windows and filter out contexts that are not directly related to the target word. For example, *Australian*

---

[1] https://nlp.stanford.edu/software/lex-parser.shtml

is not used as the context for *discovers*. Therefore, we have more focused embeddings that capture more functional and less topical similarity.

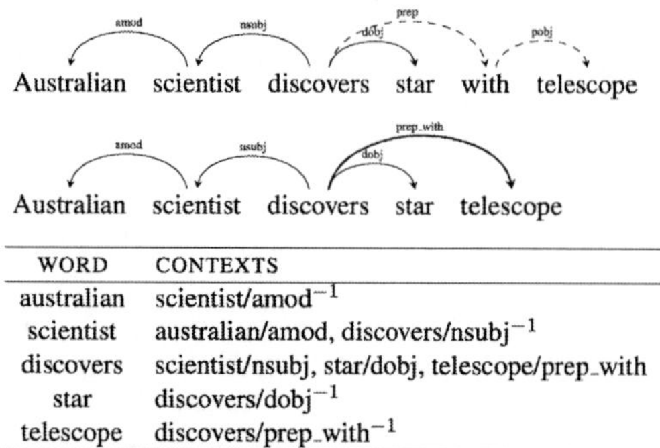

WORD	CONTEXTS
australian	scientist/amod^{-1}
scientist	australian/amod, discovers/nsubj^{-1}
discovers	scientist/nsubj, star/dobj, telescope/prep_with
star	discovers/dobj^{-1}
telescope	discovers/prep_with^{-1}

Figure 3: Dependency-based context extraction
example (Levy and Goldberg, 2014)

2.8 Contextual Gated Recurrent Neural Network (CGRNN)

Gated Recurrent Neural Network: The Bi-
GRNN is a version of (Chung et al., 2014) in
which a Gated Recurrent Unit (GRU) has two
gates, a reset gate r_t and a update gate z_t. Intuitively, the reset gate determines how to combine the new input with the previous memory, and
the update gate defines how much of the previous memory to keep around. We use GRUs for
our model because GRUs are quite new and their
tradeoffs have not been fully explored yet. On the
other hand, GRUs have fewer parameters (U and
W are smaller) and thus may train a bit faster or
need less data to generalize. The equation 2 illustrates the construction of a GRU cell:

$$r_t = \sigma(W_{xr}x_t + W_{hr}h_{t-1} + b_r)$$
$$z_t = \sigma(W_{xz}x_t + W_{hz}h_{t-1} + b_z)$$
$$\hat{h}_t = g(x_t W_{xh} + (r_t \odot h_{t-1})W_{hh} + b_h)$$
$$h_t = (1 - z_t) \odot h_{t-1} + z_t \odot \hat{h}_t. \quad (2)$$

Contextual Gated Recurrent Neural Network:
Based on the idea of GRNN model, we build a
power of syntactic contexts into a standard Bi-
GRNN model which adapt GRNN cell to take both
words and syntactic contexts by modifying the
equations representing operations of the GRNN
cell. A GRNN cell is added dependency-based
word vector T to reset gate, update gate and hidden state. In the Equation 3, the term in bold is the
modification made to the original GRNN equation.

Based on these equations, adding dependency-
based word vector T is corresponding to considering a composite input $[x_i, T]$ to the GRNN cell that
concatenates the advanced continuous word embeddings and advanced dependency-based word
embeddings.

$$r_t = \sigma(W_{xr}x_t + W_{hr}h_{t-1} + \mathbf{W_{Ti}T} + b_r)$$
$$z_t = \sigma(W_{xz}x_t + W_{hz}h_{t-1} + \mathbf{W_{Ti}T} + b_z)$$
$$\hat{h}_t = g(x_t W_{xh} + (r_t \odot h_{t-1})W_{hh} + \mathbf{W_{Ti}T} + b_h)$$
$$h_t = (1 - z_t) \odot h_{t-1} + z_t \odot \hat{h}_t.$$
$$(3)$$

This approach of concatenating syntactic contexts and word embeddings works better in practice and deal with the context challenge in sentiment analysis.

3 Results and Analysis

3.1 Experimental setups

For the Stanford Twitter Sentiment Corpus (STS
Corpus), we use the number of samples as
(Dos Santos and Gatti, 2014). The training data
is selected 80K tweets for a training data and 16K
tweets for the development set randomly from the
training data of (Go et al., 2009). We conduct a
binary prediction for STS Corpus.

In Health Care Reform Corpus (HCR Corpus),
we also select 10% randomly for the development
set in a training set and construct as (Da Silva
et al., 2014) for comparison. We describe the summary of datasets in Table 2.

Data	**Set**	N	c	l_w	l_c	$|V_w|$	$|V_c|$
	Train	80K		33	110		
STS	Dev	16K	2	28	48	67083	134
	Test	359		21	16		
	Train	621		25	70		
HCR	Dev	636	2	26	16	3100	60
	Test	665		20	16		

Table 2: Summary statistics for the datasets after
using semantic rules. c: the number of classes.
N: The number of tweets. l_w: Maximum sen-
tence length. l_c: Maximum character length. $|V_w|$:
Word alphabet size. $|V_c|$: Character alphabet size.

Hyperparameters: For all datasets, the filter window size (h) is 7 with 6 feature maps each for the
first wide convolution layer, the second wide convolution layer has a filter window size of 1 with 14
feature maps each. Dropout rate (p) is 0.5, l_2 constraint, learning rate is 0.1 and momentum of 0.9.

Mini-batch size for STS Corpus is 100 and HCR corpus is 4. Training is done through stochastic gradient descent over shuffled mini-batches with Adadelta update rule (Zeiler, 2012).

Pre-trained Word Vectors: We use the publicly available *Word2Vec* [2] trained from 100 billion words from Google and *TwitterGlove* [3] of Stanford is performed on aggregated global word-word co-occurrence statistics from a corpus. *Word2Vec* has dimensionality of 300 and *Twitter Glove* have dimensionality of 200. Words that do not present in the set of pre-train words are initialized randomly.

3.2 Experimental results

Table 3 shows the results of our model for sentiment analysis against other models. The different kinds of models are constructed to evaluate the impacts of embeddings on classification accuracy. We build the Bi-CGRNN enhanced CharAVs and LexW2Vs. In addition, we evaluate separately the effectiveness of CharAVs and LexW2Vs on Twitter datasets by incorporating with standard Bi-GRNN.

We compare our model performance with the approaches of (Go et al., 2009) and (Dos Santos and Gatti, 2014). The model of (Go et al., 2009) displays the good results in the previous time and the model of (Dos Santos and Gatti, 2014) reported the state-of-the-art so far by using a charSCNN. Our model shows the result of *88.57* is the best prediction accuracy for STS Corpus.

For HCR Corpus, we compare the performance with the results of (Da Silva et al., 2014) that used an ensemble of multiple base classifiers (ENS) such as Naive Bayes (NB), Random Forest (RF), SVM and Logistic Regression (LR). The ENS model is combined with bag-of-words (BoW), feature hashing (FH) and lexicons (lex). Our model outperforms the model of (Da Silva et al., 2014) with result of *80* so far.

3.3 Analysis

The model with CharAVs and LexW2Vs built on top of $GoogleW2V$ vectors and DependencyW2Vs is effective in order to increase classification accuracy. These experiments show that CharAVs and LexW2Vs achieve good performances and contribute in enhancing information for words. However, the experiments indicate that

[2]code.google.com/p/word2vec/
[3]https://nlp.stanford.edu/projects/glove/

Model	STS	HCR
CharSCNN/Pre-trained (Dos Santos and Gatti, 2014)	86.4	-
CharSCNN/Random (Dos Santos and Gatti, 2014)	81.9	-
SCNN/Pre-trained (Dos Santos and Gatti, 2014)	85.2	-
SCNN/Random (Dos Santos and Gatti, 2014)	82.2	-
MaxEnt (Go et al., 2009)	83.0	-
NB (Go et al., 2009)	82.7	-
SVM (Go et al., 2009)	82.2	-
SVM-BoW	-	73.99
SVM-BoW + lex	-	75.94
RF-BoW	-	70.83
RF-BoW + lex	-	72.93
LR-BoW	-	73.83
LR-BoW + lex	-	74.73
MNB-BoW	-	72.48
MNB-BoW + lex	-	75.33
ENS (RF + MNB + LR) - BoW	-	75.19
ENS (SVM + RF + MNB + LR) - BoW + lex	-	**76.99**
Bi-CGRNN + CharAVs + LexW2Vs + GoogleW2Vs	**88.5**	78.47
Bi-CGRNN + CharAVs + LexW2Vs + GloveW2Vs	86.9	**80.0**
Bi-CGRNN + GoogleW2Vs	85.7	77.74
Bi-GRNN + CharAVs + GoogleW2Vs	86.0	79.09
Bi-GRNN + LexW2Vs + GoogleW2Vs	88.0	78.79

Table 3: Accuracy of different models for binary classification.

CharAVs are more effective in small dataset than LexW2Vs. In addition, the Bi-CGRNN enhanced CharAVs and LexW2Vs have a great impact on Twitter datasets. Table 4 displays the effectiveness of our model in predicting the tweets. In the table 4, the Bi-GRNN using LexW2Vs captures the positive words (green words) and negative words (red words) for computing scores and predicts wrong labels because of the contexts of tweets while the Bi-CGRNN enhanced CharAVs and LexW2Vs recognizes contexts for true prediction. For example, the model using LexW2Vs predicts the last tweet to be positive because 'strong' word has sentiment stronger than 'no' word, however, the context of this tweet is negative. The pre-train word vectors are good, universal feature extractors. The syntactic contexts support in dealing context problems in tweets and the lexicons support word embeddings in dealing the sentiment of tweets. The difference between our model and other approaches is the ability of our model to capture enough features and combine these features at high level. In addition, the usage of DeepCNN for characters can learns a structure of words in higher abstract level. LexW2Vs and syntactic contexts

Model	Input from HCR Corpus	Gold Label	Prediction
Bi-CGRNN + CharAVs + LexW2Vs	@seanbaran74 well that's what's next. after #hcr they'll save the environment, give us CFLs and take away our TVs.	Negative	True
Bi-GRNN + LexW2Vs			False
Bi-CGRNN + CharAVs + LexW2Vs	All of us fighting for #HCR ask ourselves who #imherefor. Who are you fighting for? http://bit.ly/9-st	Positive	True
Bi-GRNN + LexW2Vs			False
Bi-CGRNN + CharAVs + LexW2Vs	Stephen Lynch strong 'no' on health bill despite talk with President obama http://bit.ly/cQIujP #hcr #tcot #tlot	Negative	True
Bi-GRNN + LexW2Vs			False

Table 4: The label prediction between the Bi-GRNN model using LexW2Vs and the Bi-CGRNN model using CharAVs and LexW2Vs (The red words are negative and the green words are positive).

contribute in supporting information for word embeddings. This helps the model not only learns to recognize single n-grams of a word, negation, but also patterns in n-grams led to form a structure significance of a sentence.

4 Conclusions

In the present work, we build a model that solves four challenges in Twitter: syntax, semantic, sentiment and context. Our results show the well-establish evidence that CharAVs, LexW2Vs and DependencyW2Vs are important ingredients for ContinuousW2Vs in increasing classification accuracy for sentiment analysis. Our source and processed data are available at Github[4].

Acknowledgments

This work was supported by JSPS KAKENHI Grant number JP15K16048 and CREST, JST.

References

Orestes Appel, Francisco Chiclana, Jenny Carter, and Hamido Fujita. 2016. A hybrid approach to the sentiment analysis problem at the sentence level. *Knowledge-Based Systems*, 108:110–124.

Junyoung Chung, Çaglar Gülçehre, KyungHyun Cho, and Yoshua Bengio. 2014. Empirical evaluation of gated recurrent neural networks on sequence modeling. *CoRR*, abs/1412.3555.

Nadia F. F. Da Silva, Eduardo R. Hruschka, and Estevam R. Hruschka. 2014. Tweet sentiment analysis with classifier ensembles. *Decision Support Systems*, 66:170–179.

C'icero N. Dos Santos and Maira Gatti. 2014. Deep convolutional neural networks for sentiment analysis of short texts. In *COLING*, pages 69–78.

Alec Go, Richa Bhayani, and Lei Huang. 2009. Twitter sentiment classification using distant supervision. *CS224N Project Report, Stanford*, 1(12).

Yoav Goldberg and Joakim Nivre. 2013. Training deterministic parsers with non-deterministic oracles. *Transactions of the association for Computational Linguistics*, 1:403–414.

Minqing Hu and Bing Liu. 2004. Mining and summarizing customer reviews. In *Proceedings of the tenth ACM SIGKDD international conference on Knowledge discovery and data mining*, pages 168–177. ACM.

Yoon Kim. 2014. Convolutional neural networks for sentence classification. *CoRR*, abs/1408.5882.

Svetlana Kiritchenko, Xiaodan Zhu, and Saif M Mohammad. 2014. Sentiment analysis of short informal texts. *Journal of Artificial Intelligence Research*, 50:723–762.

Omer Levy and Yoav Goldberg. 2014. Dependency-based word embeddings. In *Proceedings of the 52nd Annual Meeting of the Association for Computational Linguistics, ACL 2014, June 22-27, 2014, Baltimore, MD, USA, Volume 2: Short Papers*, pages 302–308.

Tomas Mikolov, Ilya Sutskever, Kai Chen, Greg S. Corrado, and Jeff Dean. 2013. Distributed representations of words and phrases and their compositionality. In *Advances in Neural Information Processing Systems 26*, pages 3111–3119. Curran Associates, Inc.

Saif M. Mohammad, Svetlana Kiritchenko, and Xiaodan Zhu. 2013. Nrc-canada: Building the state-of-the-art in sentiment analysis of tweets. *CoRR*, abs/1308.6242.

Preslav Nakov, Alan Ritter, Sara Rosenthal, Fabrizio Sebastiani, and Veselin Stoyanov. 2016. SemEval-2016 task 4: Sentiment analysis in twitter. *Proceedings of SemEval*, pages 1–18.

Huy Nguyen and Minh-Le Nguyen. 2017. A deep neural architecture for sentence-level sentiment classification in twitter social networking. *PACLING 2017*.

---

[4]https://github.com/titanbt/contextualGRU-attention-lexicon

Bonggun Shin, Timothy Lee, and Jinho D. Choi. 2016. Lexicon integrated CNN models with attention for sentiment analysis. *CoRR*, abs/1610.06272.

Richard Socher, Jeffrey Pennington, Eric H. Huang, Andrew Y. Ng, and Christopher D. Manning. 2011. Semi-supervised recursive autoencoders for predicting sentiment distributions. In *Proceedings of the conference on empirical methods in natural language processing*, pages 151–161. Association for Computational Linguistics.

Michael Speriosu, Nikita Sudan, Sid Upadhyay, and Jason Baldridge. 2011. Twitter polarity classification with label propagation over lexical links and the follower graph. In *Proceedings of the First workshop on Unsupervised Learning in NLP*, pages 53–63. Association for Computational Linguistics.

Duyu Tang, Furu Wei, Bing Qin, Ming Zhou, and Ting Liu. 2014. Building large-scale twitter-specific sentiment lexicon : A representation learning approach. In *Proceedings of COLING 2014, the 25th International Conference on Computational Linguistics: Technical Papers*, pages 172–182, Dublin, Ireland.

Matthew D. Zeiler. 2012. ADADELTA: an adaptive learning rate method. *arXiv preprint arXiv:1212.5701*.

Combining Lightly-Supervised Text Classification Models
for Accurate Contextual Advertising

Yiping Jin
Dept. of Mathematics &
Computer Science
Chulalongkorn university
Thailand 10300
`Yiping.Ji@student`
`.chula.ac.th`

Dittaya Wanvarie
Dept. of Mathematics &
Computer Science
Chulalongkorn university
Thailand 10300
`Dittaya.W@chula.ac.th`

Phu T. V. Le
Knorex Pte. Ltd.
2 Science Park Drive,
Singapore 118222
`le_phu@knorex.com`

Abstract

In this paper we propose a lightly-supervised framework to rapidly build text classifiers for contextual advertising. In contextual advertising, advertisers often want to target to a specific class of webpages most relevant to their product, which may not be covered by a pre-trained classifier. Moreover, the advertisers are only interested in the target class. Therefore, it is more suitable to model as a one-class classification problem, in contrast to traditional classification problems where disjoint classes are defined a priori.

We first apply two state-of-the-art lightly-supervised classification models, generalized expectation (GE) criteria (Druck et al., 2008) and multinomial naïve Bayes (MNB) with priors (Settles, 2011) to one-class classification where the user only provides a small list of labeled words for the target class. We fuse the two models together by using MNB to automatically enrich the constraints for GE training. We also explore ensemble method to further improve the accuracy. On a corpus of real-time bidding requests, the proposed model achieves the highest average F_1 of 0.69 and closes half of the gap between previous state-of-the-art lightly-supervised models to a fully-supervised MaxEnt model.

1 Introduction

Contextual advertising (or contextual targeting) is a technique to maximize the relevance of online advertisements by performing page analysis of the webpages. Contextual advertising is closely related to text classification problem, which is well-known to the NLP community. Underlying, the system classifies webpages into predefined Ads verticals (categories). Based on the classification result, the real-time bidding (RTB) system will decide whether to bid for a particular page to display their Ads. Successful contextual advertising leads to lower advertising cost and higher click-through and conversion rate (Chatterjee et al., 2003; Broder et al., 2007).

Contextual targeting differs from traditional text classification in three ways. Firstly, with thousands of vastly different products coming to market every day, there are large number of categories (usually thousands of categories). Secondly, the advertisers often want to customize an existing category or create new categories to target a set of more relevant webpages. I.e. the classes are not static but evolving. It is therefore unrealistic to ask the advertisers to provide labeled webpages for each new or modified category they want to target. Lastly, while the advertisers can provide prior knowledge for the class they want to target, they cannot accurately specify the irrelevant (or negative) category because it likely covers broad topics in the wild. However, to train a classifier, usually labeled instances for each class are required. Because of these constraints, prominent service providers such as Peer39 [1] and Grapeshot [2] build their contextual targeting systems mainly using hand-crafted keywords instead of learning based approaches.

In this work, we model contextual targeting as lightly-supervised one-class classification problem. The algorithm takes unlabelled documents [3] DOC_U and the user provided keywords S_c for the

---

[1] https://www.sizmek.com/peer39/

[2] https://www.grapeshot.com/

[3] We classify only based on the text in the webpages. Henceforth we use "document" to refer to "webpage", conforming to the terminology commonly used in NLP.

545

Proceedings of the The 8th International Joint Conference on Natural Language Processing, pages 545–554,
Taipei, Taiwan, November 27 – December 1, 2017 ©2017 AFNLP

target class c as input and returns a classifier M_c that can classify documents belonging to class c. It is lightly-supervised because we do not use any document labels , but labeled keywords instead. It is one-class classification because the users need to provide labeled keywords only for the class they want to target, not the negative class.

We apply two state-of-the-art lightly-supervised classification models, generalized expectation (GE) criteria (Druck et al., 2008) and multinomial naïve Bayes (MNB) with priors (Settles, 2011) in the one-class classification setting. Inspired by the relative strength and weakness of the two models, we propose a novel approach to fuse them together where MNB is trained first. The salient words are read off from the posterior class-word distributions and automatically added to form additional constraints for GE. We also employ ensemble method to produce a final classifier that closed more than half of the gap between previous state-of-the-art lightly-supervised models to a fully-supervised MaxEnt model.

The contributions of this paper are:

1. Extended state-of-the-art semi-supervised classifiers for one-class classification problem.

2. Enriched expectation constraints for GE using a MNB model trained using EM algorithm.

3. Successfully employed ensemble method to produce a final classifier that closed more than half of the gap between previous state-of-the-art semi-supervised models to a fully-supervised MaxEnt model.

The paper is organized as follows: Section 2 presents previous works in two related fields: semi-supervised classification and one-class classification. We review the two previous state-of-the-art models we depend heavily on, generalized expectation (GE) criteria and multinomial naïve Bayes (MNB) with priors in Section 3 and 4, followed by applying them to one-class classification problem (Section 5). Section 6 describes two distinct approaches to combine these two models together. In section 7, we present our experimental results. Lastly, we present conclusions and suggest future directions.

2 Related Work

2.1 Semi-Supervised Text Classification

Supervised text classification methods were successfully applied to various tasks, such as sentiment analysis (Pang et al., 2002; Wang and Manning, 2012), information extraction (Jin et al., 2013) and stance recognition (Hasan and Ng, 2014). The main problem of supervised classification technique is that it requires sizeable set of labeled training documents for each predefined class.

Various semi-supervised classification methods have been proposed to address the lack of training documents. We are particularly interested in *lightly-supervised* methods that exploit prior knowledge (usually in the form of labeled words for each class) and eliminate the need of any labeled documents. Two main categories of approaches are often employed to exploit the word labels. The first one is to build an initial weak classifier to obtain soft labels of the documents and then apply expectation maximization (EM) algorithm (Liu et al., 2004; Schapire et al., 2002). More recently, there is growing interest in methods that incorporate labeled word features directly into the classification model, either as constraints in an objective function (Druck et al., 2008; Zhao et al., 2016) or as priors on model parameters (Settles, 2011; Lucas and Downey, 2013).

Liu at al. (2004) proposed to label a set of representative words for each class, which is used to extract a set of documents as the initial training set. EM algorithm was then applied to iteratively refine the labels of the documents and to improve the accuracy of the classifier. Schapire et al. (2002) used hand-crafted rules based on keywords to label documents, and modified AdaBoost to fit both the labeled training data and the soft-labeled data.

The methods above convert domain knowledge into labeled documents. An alternative approach is to use the domain knowledge to provide model constraints. Druck at al. (2008; 2011) proposed generalized expectation (GE) criteria, which use labeled words to constrain the model's predictions on unlabeled data. GE has been successfully applied on different tasks, such as text categorization (Druck et al., 2008), semantic tagging (Druck et al., 2009), information structure analysis of scientific documents (Guo et al., 2015) and language identification in mixed-language documents (King and Abney, 2013). Similarly, Zhao et al. (2016)

made use of word-level statistical constraints to preserve the class distribution on words, so that the classifier will not drift due to the extra (noisy) labels introduced by EM algorithm.

Labeled words can also provide priors for generative models. Settles (2011) extended multinomial naïve Bayes model to allow labels for words by increasing their Dirichlet prior. His method consists of three steps: firstly to estimate the initial parameters using only the priors; secondly to apply the induced classifier on unlabeled documents; lastly to re-estimate the model parameters using both labeled and probabilistically-labeled documents. Using an interactive approach to query document and word labels from the user, the system can achieve 90% of state-of-the-art performance after a few minutes of annotation.

Dermouche et al. (2013) also exploited prior knowledge in a multinomial naïve Bayes model. Instead of modifying the priors, their method artificially modifies the occurrences of the terms in the right and wrong class. This method uses the full set of document labels and a large sentiment lexicon consisting of around eight thousand terms, making it less suitable for the lightly-supervised setting for contextual targeting.

2.2 One-Class Classification

Another area related to our work is one-class classification problem (Moya and Hush, 1996), where no labeled negative instance is available. One-class SVM (Schölkopf et al., 2001) learns only from positive examples. The model classifies new instances as similar or different to the training set. Lee at al. (2003) observed that this approach is highly sensitive to the input representation and it did not perform well for text classification.

We highlight that one-class classification problem is not restricted to using only positive labeled instances. When positive and *unlabelled* data are available, a popular approach is to randomly assign the negative class to unlabelled instances in the beginning and iteratively refine the labels using EM-like algorithms (Yu et al., 2002; Liu et al., 2003; Li et al., 2009).

Our task lies in the intersection of semi-supervised classification and one-class classification, yet it differs from both tasks in principled ways. Aforementioned semi-supervised classification algorithms were applied on corpora with predefined (two or more) classes. When the ir-relevant (or negative) class refers to "everything else", we cannot accurately provide prior knowledge for the irrelevant class using expert domain knowledge. On the other hand, previous one-class classification problems assumed the presence of labeled instances of the positive class, without which neither the similarity-based nor the EM-like algorithms can be applied directly.

3 Generalized Expectation (GE) Criteria

Generalized expectation (GE) criteria (Mann and McCallum, 2008) are constraint terms used to train discriminative linear models. GE provides a flexible framework for encoding prior knowledge to provide training signals for parameter estimation. When applied to text classification, constraint functions G_k are expressed as the reference distribution of the feature labels. [4] For example $puck \rightarrow \{baseball : 0.1, hockey : 0.9\}$ means 90% of documents containing the word "puck" should be labeled the class "hockey". Each constraint is translated into a term to add to the objective function to encourage parameters that yield predictions conforming to the reference distribution on unlabeled documents. Formally, the combined objective function can be written as:

$$C = - \sum_{k \in K} D(\hat{p}(y|x_k > 0)\|\tilde{p}(y|x_k > 0)) - \Delta$$

where $\hat{p}(y|x_k > 0)$ is the reference distribution, $\tilde{p}(y|x_k > 0)$ is the empirical distribution and D is a distance function. Δ is shorthand for a zero-mean σ^2-variance Gaussian prior on parameters.

GE does not require one-to-one correspondence between constraint functions G_k and model feature functions. The optimization problem for GE is always under-constrained, meaning the number of parameters to be estimated far exceeds the number of constraints the user provides. To make the optimization tractable, the model updates the gradient for an unlabeled feature j based on how often j co-occurs with a labeled feature k. [5] Hence Druck et al. (2009) commented that GE can also be interpreted as a bootstrapping method that estimates parameters using limited training signals.

---

[4]The features consist of word unigrams in both Druck et al. (2008) and in this paper.

[5]Please refer to Druck et al. (2008) for the derivation.

4 Multinomial Naïve Bayes (MNB) with Priors

Multinomial Naïve Bayes is a generative classification algorithm making a strong assumption that each word w_k occurs independent of each other when conditioned on the class label c_j. Hence,

$$\hat{y} = \operatorname*{argmax}_{j \in \{1,...,J\}} P(c_j) \prod_{k=1}^{n_d} P(w_k|c_j)$$

where $P(c_j)$ is the probability of class c_j and $P(w_k|c_j)$ is the probability of generating word w_k given class c_j. $P(w_k|c_j)$ is estimated using:

$$P(w_k|c_j) = \frac{m_{jk} + \sum_i P(c_j|x^{(i)})f_k(x^{(i)})}{Z(f_k)}$$

where $f_k(x^{(i)})$ is the count of word w_k in the ith document in the training set and $Z(f_k)$ is a normalization constant summing over all words in the vocabulary. Typically, a uniform Laplacian prior is used (all m_{jk} have the same value 1). To incorporate the word labels, Settles (2011) increased the prior m_{jk} by α if word w_k is labeled with class c_j. To exploit unlabeled documents, Settles (2011) used an initial model estimated with only the priors to probabilistically label the unlabeled documents. The probabilistically labeled documents are combined with the labeled words and documents to estimate the parameters for the final model using a single-iteration EM algorithm.

5 Applying GE and MNB to One-Class Classification

In Druck et al. (2009) and Settles (2011), the authors ran their models using human labeled keywords for each predefined class. Analogous to one-class classification, where the system takes only positive (and unlabelled) documents as input, We now try to train GE and MNB with priors using only *user-provided* positive keywords and unlabelled documents as input. [6]

GE cannot cope with one-class classification by nature. If we only provide labeled words for the "+" class, the "+" label will be "propagated" to all the word features co-occurring with a labeled word. The trained classifier will predict "+" for

all the unseen documents. In contrary, MNB with priors can be trained using only the "+" keywords. When we increase the prior for labeled words in class c_+, it decreases $P(w_k'|c_+)$ with respect to $P(w_k'|c_-)$ for an unlabeled feature w_k' (the normalization constant Z_+ is greater that Z_- due to the increased priors in the "+" class). This is desirable because if a document only contains random unlabeled words, the model will predict "-".

5.1 Labeling Words for the Target Class

Liu et al. (2004) observed that it is difficult for the user to come up with a set of representative words for each class independently because they usually can only provide a few words, which are insufficient to train an accurate classifier. Therefore, it is critical that the system can assist the user by suggesting a good set of candidate words to label instead of asking them to come up with all the words by themselves. We use a hybrid candidate word suggestion method that asks the user to input a seed keyword (in most cases, it is merely the class name they want to target) and the system will suggest other words that are closely related to it. We make use of word vectors (Mikolov et al., 2013), pointwise mutual information (PMI) (Church and Hanks, 1990) and Wikipedia.

Word vectors have been widely used to measure word similarities (Tang et al., 2014; Levy et al., 2015). We calculate cosine similarity using pretrained GloVe word vectors [7] (Pennington et al., 2014) to find similar words to the seed word. Word vectors can identify linguistically or semantically related words. E.g. "luxurious" and "lavish" are the nearest neighbours of "luxury".

We use PMI to mine the words that tend to co-occur with the seed word. For example, "resort", "BMW", "Gucci" all receive high PMI scores with "luxury" while none of them are near the word "luxury" in the word vector space.

Lastly, we automatically extract the keywords and keyphrases from the Wikipedia page of the seed word (if the page exists). This method is aimed to cover the technical terms that are confident indicators but are rarely observed in the corpus. E.g. "Somniloquy" is a synonym of "sleeptalking" but it is thirty time less frequent than the latter.

We show the top 50 candidate words suggested by each of the three methods to the user, who will

---

[6] We use positive/+ to denote the target class and negative/- to denote the irrelevant class.

[7] http://nlp.stanford.edu/projects/glove/

select relevant words to add to the keyword list. Based on user study reported in Settles (2011), labeling words takes on average 3.2 seconds. This suggests the total time for the user to complete labeling is within 10 minutes.

5.2 Special Treatment for GE

As mentioned above, GE also requires labeled words for the "-" class to train. However, it is impractical and time-consuming to ask the users to label a list of words irrelevant to the target class. We form the keyword list for the "-" class by simply performing a multinomial sampling from the vocabulary, where each word is weighted by its log count in the unlabeled corpus. This assumes that a randomly sampled word is unlikely to be a keyword for the target class. Additionally, we use L_2-based penalty instead of the default KL divergence because previous work showed that it is more robust to label noises (Druck, 2011).

The labeled words are translated into GE constraints using Schapire-distributions (Schapire et al., 2002). For the user labeled "+" keywords, We assign $P_+ = 0.9$ and $P_- = 0.1$. I.e. if "puck" is a labeled word for the class "hockey", the corresponding constraint will be $puck \rightarrow \{hockey : 0.9, others : 0.1\}$. For the "-" class, we randomly sample 20 times more keywords than the "+" class but use a more even distribution, where we set $P_+ = 0.25$ and $P_- = 0.75$. This is in the same spirit with *biased sparsity* in Wang et al. (2016), which says the word distribution of the targeted topic only focuses on a small number of representative words and the word distribution of non-targeted topics contain almost all possible words. We do not use too many negative keywords (constraints) because it significantly increases the computational cost to train GE.

We refer to this system as $GE/Random$ because it uses randomly sampled "-" keywords.

6 Combining GE and MNB

6.1 Using MNB to Enrich GE Constraints

Settles (2011) observed that MNB outperformed GE when the number of labeled words were between five to 20. When the number of labeled keywords increased (with more prior knowledge), GE usually performed better. This inspired us to fuse the two models together, in which MNB's role is to bootstrap more labeled words to train a more accurate GE classifier.

We first use the user labeled "+" words and unlabeled documents to train an MNB model. Then we obtain a list of salient words for the "+" class which are not already covered in the user labeled words. We use a simple rule that word w_k will be added to the set S_{MNB} if $\frac{P(w_k|c_+)}{P(w_k|c_-)} > 10$ (w_k appears 10 times more likely given the "+" class than given the "-" class) . [8] In this way, we exploit the strength of a generative model (MNB) to discover latent structure and topics from unlabeled data to augment a discriminative model (GE), which usually achieves higher accuracy for classification tasks.

Algorithm 1 summarizes the training procedure for the combined model GE/MNB. Line 2-4 are the procedure to train a MNB with priors model with EM algorithm. We obtain the list of salient words for the target class in line 5. All the words in S_{user}, S_{MNB} and S_{rand} are translated into GE constraints to train the final GE/MNB model.

Algorithm 1: Train GE/MNB Classifier

1   train classifier (S_{user},DOC$_U$);
    Input   : User labeled features S_{user} and unlabeled corpus DOC$_U$
    Output: Trained GE/MNB classifier
2   $M_{MNB/Priors}$ = train(S_{user});
3   DOC$_{prob}$ = $M_{MNB/Priors}$.classify(DOC$_U$);
4   $M_{MNB/Priors+EM_1}$ = train(S_{user}, DOC$_{prob}$);
5   S_{MNB} = $M_{MNB/Priors+EM_1}$.getSalientWords();
6   S_{rand} = randomlySampleWords();
7   $M_{GE/MNB}$ = train([S_{user}, S_{MNB}, S_{rand}], DOC$_U$);
8   return $M_{GE/MNB}$;

6.2 Using Ensemble Approach

Another intuitive way to combine GE and MNB is to train the two classifiers independently and use ensemble approach (Dietterich, 2000) to combine the prediction results of the two classifiers. GE and MNB behave quite differently although they make use of the same labeled keywords. The variety they introduce is a critical condition for the success of ensemble approach (Dietterich, 2000).

We first group the aforementioned classifiers into two families based on the algorithm to train their final classifier. The GE family includes GE/Random and GE/MNB. The MNB family includes MNB/Priors and MNB/Priors+EM$_1$. We used a simple ensemble rule: the classifier ensemble outputs "+" if and only if at least one GE **and**

---

[8] We also tried to replace the randomly sampled "-" keywords with words that have high $\frac{P(w_k|c_-)}{P(w_k|c_+)}$. However, the result was worse in general.

one MNB classifier output "+". We denote this classifier ensemble as $GE_1 \land MNB_1$. We used this heuristic rule instead of stacking or other more sophisticated techniques because it does not require any labeled documents to train the ensemble.

7 Evaluation

7.1 Baselines and Datasets

We compared the proposed GE/MNB and $GE_1 \land MNB_1$ with various baselines. For GE, we experimented with GE/Random, which uses user provided keywords for the target class and randomly sampled negative keywords to train. For MNB with priors, we ran two configurations following Settles (2011), $MNB/Priors+EM_1$, the full model using EM algorithm and MNB/Priors, the initial model using only user labeled priors. We also compared with a keyword voting baseline and a fully-supervised MaxEnt model trained using labeled documents. The results of the MaxEnt model is for reference purpose, as our goal is not to beat a supervised model, but to improve from previous lightly-supervised models.

We use the GE implementation in the MALLET toolkit [9] and the implementation of MNB with priors provided by Settles (2011) [10], which also extends from MALLET. All the classifiers share the same standard preprocessing pipeline.

We made use of two datasets for evaluation. The first dataset is sampled from the actual real-time bidding (RTB) requests. The second one is the well-known 20 Newsgroups corpus (Lang, 1995). The results on the first corpus is more relevant and indicative while the results on the 20 Newsgroups allows to benchmark the models beyond the application of RTB.

7.2 Evaluations on RTB Dataset

We created the real-time bidding (RTB) dataset from a database of 30 million historical requests. We used open-source Boilerpipe library (Kohlschütter et al., 2010) to extract the textual content from the webpages and we obtained the category labels for the webpages from a leading Ad Exchange platform (in total 2,200 categories). [11]

---

[9]http://mallet.cs.umass.edu

[10]https://github.com/burrsettles/dualist

[11]The dataset is available at https://sites.google.com/site/jinyipingnus/research for future works to reproduce our results.

Class	Docs	+/- Ratio
Cold & Flu	1,363	1:50
Cancer	3,234	1:20
Diabetes	1,394	1:50
Sleep Disorder	2,592	1:25
Nutrition	22,176	1:3
Sampled "-" docs	68,626	

Table 1: Number of documents for each class and relevant/irrelevant class ratio.

We randomly selected five categories in the "Health" domain to carry out evaluation. For each experiment, the documents labeled with one of the selected categories were assigned to be the "+" class. We uniformly sampled from all other categories to use as the "-" class. We hide the document labels during training for all models except for MaxEnt.

Table 1 shows the number of documents for each class and the rounded +/- ratio. We can see that the +/- classes are very imbalanced, which is to be expected in real-world RTB requests. In practice, we cannot simply perform up- or down-sampling without the labels of the documents. Therefore, we did not try to modify the class ratio to make it more balanced. For each set of experiment, we used the same 9:1 split of training and testing set.

One author of this paper composed the labeled keywords with the assistance of the hybrid keyword suggestion method described in Section 5.1. The keywords for each class were composed independently. He was not allowed to add words not suggested by the system so that we can validate the utility of the keyword suggestion method. Table 2 shows the keywords for each category he composed. The labeling stopped when either he finished reviewing all the suggested words or the time reached 10 minutes.

Table 3 shows the $P/R/F_1$ scores of each classifier for each class. We did not use the accuracy measure because the ratio of +/- classes is strongly imbalanced. We used the same set of user labeled keywords for system 0-5. For GE and MNB with priors, we used the parameter setting proposed in the original papers (GE: Gaussian Prior=1; MNB: α=50).

We can make some interesting observations from the result. Firstly, the keyword voting approach lagged behind all of the lightly-supervised models. This shows that learning based approaches improved from a simple rule-based sys-

550

Cold & Flu	*cough, flu, throat, nasal, sinus, congestion, respiratory, sneezing, influenza, mucus, runny, stuffy, decongestant, phlegm, pandemic, epidemic, measles, typhoid, diphtheria, antihistamines*
Cancer	*cancer, tumor, chemotherapy, radiation, melanoma, leukemia, lymph, malignant, oncology, chemo, biopsy, oncologist, carcinoma, neoplasm, benign, colonoscopy, fibroid, invasive,lumpectomy, nonmelanoma, metastasis, palliative, adjuvant, neoadjuvant, polyp, smear, pathologist, prognosis, colposcopy*
Diab.	*diabetes, insulin, glucose, mellitus, diabetic, ketoacidosis, ketosis, dka, hyperosmolar, hyperglycemic, nonketotic, niddm, polydipsia, polyphagia, polyuria, glucagon, metformin*
Sleep Dis.	*sleep, asleep, awake, bedtime, sleepy, dream, snoring, snooze, nap, pillow, melatonin, circadian, apnoea, somnipathy, polysomnography, actigraphy, dyssomnias, parasomnias, apnea, sleepwalking, catathrenia, hypopnea, hypersomnia, narcolepsy, cataplexy, nocturia, enuresis, somniphobia*
Nutri.	*nutrition, protein, nutrients, livestrong, vitamin, intake, carbohydrates, fiber, myplate, minerals, carb, grain, metabolism, dietary, antioxidants, calcium, nutritional, nutritious, nutritionist*

Table 2: Labeled words for each class

tem using the same prior knowledge.

Secondly, GE/Random and MNB/Priors+EM$_1$ performed comparably, with GE/Random performing slightly better.

The combined GE/MNB classifier improved recall by 4% from GE/Random. This is mainly due to the additional keywords we obtained from the MNB model. On average, 53 new keywords were added for each classifier, doubling the number of the original user labeled words.

The average precision dropped slightly due to the decreased precision of "ColdFlu" and "Cancer" class. After error analysis, we identified that for these two classes, some common words frequently co-occurring with user labeled keywords were introduced by MNB as new constraints. E.g. for "ColdFlu": cold, congestion, swine; for "cancer": breast, prostate. Such words are not real indicators of the target class and likely cause the precision to drop. Table 4 shows the top 10 automatically added keywords for each class.

The performance of the classifier ensemble GE$_1\wedge$ MNB$_1$ was impressive, improving a further 4% from GE/MNB and reaching macro average F_1 score of 0.69. The system achieved the highest or close to the highest F_1 for all the classes among the lightly-supervised models. Its F_1 score

is only 3% lower than the fully-supervised MaxEnt model. This is particularly encouraging because the MaxEnt model was trained using many thousands of labeled training documents.

7.3 Evaluations on 20 Newsgroups Corpus

We also applied the systems on the well-known 20 Newsgroups corpus (Lang, 1995) to facilitate future comparisons. The corpus contains 20 different newsgroups having 1,000 documents each. We used the documents with file name ending with "0" for testing (roughly 10% of the corpus) and the rest for training.

Following Druck at al. (2008), we used mutual information of the candidate words with the oracle document labels to mine the keywords for each class. This simulates the scenario where a domain expert can suggest and label relevant keywords. We further removed the keywords that appear in more than two classes. While keywords that appear in many classes can be "balanced out" in multi-class classification setting. We find that including them will usually harm the performance for one-class classification. We used in total 262 keywords (on average 13.1 per class).

We ran 20 experiments using each newsgroup as the target class at a time. We differentiate from Druck at al. (2008) and Settles (2011) mainly in that for each experiment, we only take the keywords for the target class as input, but not the keywords for other classes. We made this decision in order to be consistent with the one-class classification problem. We can think of this experiment as more lightly-supervised than Druck at al. (2008) and Settles (2011). Table 5 shows the performance of various systems.

We were not surprised that GE performed worse that the MNB counterpart given the small list of labeled words. By bootstrapping labeled words using MNB, the GE/MNB model improved recall by 3% at the sacrifice of 2% precision, which is similar to the result on the RTB dataset.

The classifier ensemble GE$_1\wedge$ MNB$_1$ still managed to achieve the highest precision and F_1 score (tie with MNB/Priors+EM$_1$), showing its robustness despite the lackluster performance of individual classifiers.

We also experimented with MaxEnt varying the amount of the training data. MaxEnt (γ=0.1) used 10% of the corpus (2,000 labelled documents) for training. Its average F_1 score is similar to the

System	Cold Flu	Cancer	Diabetes	Sleep Dis.	Nutrition	Macro Avg.
0: keyword voting	.44/.63/.52	.60/.59/.60	.65/.61/.63	.53/.65/.58	.64/.44/.52	.57/.59/.58
1: GE/Random	.56/.63/.59	**.78**/.56/.65	.77/.56/.65	.72/.65/.68	.78/.45/.57	**.72**/.57/.64
2: MNB/Priors +EM$_1$	**.59**/.56/.57	.66/.53/.59	.62/.56/.59	.72/.60/.66	.58/**.86**/**.67**	.63/.62/.63
3: MNB/Priors	.37/**.81**/.50	.51/**.76**/.61	.56/**.84**/.67	.33/**.79**/.47	.62/.70/.66	.48/**.78**/.59
4: GE/MNB	.50/.65/.57	.67/.67/.67	**.80**/.59/.68	.73/.62/.67	.80/.53/.63	.70/.61/.65
5: GE$_1 \wedge$ MNB$_1$	.54/.72/**.62**	.71/.66/**.68**	.73/.77/**.75**	**.74**/.64/**.69**	**.84**/.55/.66	.71/.67/**.69**
MaxEnt	.75/.65/.70	.71/.66/.68	.70/.70/.70	.76/.71/.73	.83/.76/.79	.75/.69/.72

Table 3: Precision/Recall/F_1 scores on RTB dataset. The best score for each measure is bolded. The last line shows the performance of a fully-supervised MaxEnt model for reference purpose.

Cold & Flu	*lisinopril, colds, congestion, neti, vaporub, sinusitis, swine, nostril, throat, runny*
Cancer	*lymphoma, metastatic, colorectal, humira, cancerous, ovarian, prostate, hpv, metastases, xeloda*
Diab.	*hypoglycemia, diabetics, prediabetes, lisinopril, glycemic, hyperglycemia, ckd, pancreas, catspyjamas, retinopathy*
Sleep Dis.	*zaps, ryu, insomnia, cpap, urara, rem, naps, toranosuke, rls, lucid*
Nutri.	*carbs, ldl, whey, folate, amino, creatine, niacin, potassium, fats, antioxidant*

Table 4: Top 10 automatically added constraints in GE/MNB for each class

System	Macro Avg.
0: keyword voting	.62/.43/.50
1: GE/Random	.62/.50/.55
2: MNB/Priors+EM$_1$	.63/.64/**.63**
3: MNB/Priors	.39/**.69**/.50
4: GE/MNB	.60/.53/.56
5: GE$_1 \wedge$ MNB$_1$	**.67**/.60/**.63**
MaxEnt ($\gamma = 0.1$)	.86/.42/.57
MaxEnt	.88/.72/.79

Table 5: Macro average Precision/Recall/F$_1$ scores for each classifier on 20 Newsgroups corpus.

lightly-supervised models. Based on the user experiments in Settles (2011), annotating documents takes 10.8s on average. Therefore the estimated time to annotate the training data for this model is 6 hours, roughly 25 times the time needed to label 262 keywords. The last line shows the result of the MaxEnt model using the full training set. Its average F$_1$ score is 16% higher than GE$_1 \wedge$ MNB$_1$.

The larger gap is likely because the keywords used on the 20 Newsgroups Corpus are automatically extracted from the corpus, while the keywords used on the RTB dataset exploited external resources (pre-trained word vectors and Wikipedia) and they are curated by a human annotator. In the real-world scenario, the keywords will be composed by non-technical users, instead of researchers in NLP who are familiar with the algorithm. Therefore, we cannot make assumptions of the quality of the keywords the user composes. However, this further confirms the importance of a good keyword suggestion method to assist the user to compose high-quality keywords.

8 Conclusions and Future Works

This paper proposed a framework to build lightly-supervised one-class text classifiers by applying generalized expectation (GE) criteria (Druck et al., 2008) and multinomial naïve Bayes (MNB) with priors (Settles, 2011). The classification methods make use of user-labeled words for the target class as the form of supervision and do not require any labeled documents. Motivated by the relative strengths of the two models, we merged them by using MNB to enrich the set of GE constraints.

We further improved the classification accuracy by combining the output of two families of classifiers through ensemble method. This resulted in a classifier ensemble which achieved an average of 0.69 F_1 score on a dataset of webpages from real-time bidding requests. It is 5% or 6% higher than previous state-of-the-art lightly-supervised models and 3% lower than a supervised MaxEnt model.

The framework has been deployed into an online advertising platform where advertisers can build customized classifiers to target their Ads to the most relevant webpages.

A direction for future work is to further improve the classification accuracy and to match the performance of not just a MaxEnt model, but a more recent fully-supervised deep neural network models such as Lai et al. (2015). This would likely require a more complex non-linear model and a novel method to train such model in a lightly-supervised manner.

In ongoing research, we are exploring to build multi-modal classifiers by exploiting information in the webpages beyond the textual content, such as URLs and images. We are also exploring transfer learning methods which can use the predictions for existing classes to improve the accuracy for new classes.

References

Andrei Broder, Marcus Fontoura, Vanja Josifovski, and Lance Riedel. 2007. A semantic approach to contextual advertising. In *Proceedings of the 30th annual international ACM SIGIR conference on Research and development in information retrieval*, pages 559–566. ACM.

Patrali Chatterjee, Donna L Hoffman, and Thomas P Novak. 2003. Modeling the clickstream: Implications for web-based advertising efforts. *Marketing Science*, 22(4):520–541.

Kenneth Ward Church and Patrick Hanks. 1990. Word association norms, mutual information, and lexicography. *Computational linguistics*, 16(1):22–29.

Mohamed Dermouche, Leila Khouas, Julien Velcin, and Sabine Loudcher. 2013. Ami&eric: How to learn with naive bayes and prior knowledge: an application to sentiment analysis. *Atlanta, Georgia, USA*, page 364.

Thomas G. Dietterich. 2000. Ensemble Methods in Machine Learning. *Multiple Classifier Systems*, 1857:1–15.

Gregory Druck. 2011. *Generalized expectation criteria for lightly supervised learning*. Ph.D. thesis, University of Massachusetts Amherst.

Gregory Druck, Gideon Mann, and Andrew McCallum. 2008. Learning from labeled features using generalized expectation criteria. In *Proceedings of the 31st annual international ACM SIGIR conference on Research and development in information retrieval*, pages 595–602. ACM.

Gregory Druck, Burr Settles, and Andrew McCallum. 2009. Active learning by labeling features. In *Proceedings of the 2009 Conference on Empirical Methods in Natural Language Processing: Volume 1-Volume 1*, pages 81–90. Association for Computational Linguistics.

Yufan Guo, Roi Reichart, and Anna Korhonen. 2015. Unsupervised declarative knowledge induction for constraint-based learning of information structure in scientific documents. *Transactions of the Association for Computational Linguistics*, 3:131–143.

Kazi Saidul Hasan and Vincent Ng. 2014. Why are you taking this stance? identifying and classifying reasons in ideological debates. In *EMNLP*, pages 751–762.

Yiping Jin, Min-Yen Kan, Jun-Ping Ng, and Xiangnan He. 2013. Mining scientific terms and their definitions: A study of the acl anthology. In *Proceedings of the 2013 Conference on Empirical Methods in Natural Language Processing*, pages 780–790.

Ben King and Steven P Abney. 2013. Labeling the languages of words in mixed-language documents using weakly supervised methods. In *HLT-NAACL*, pages 1110–1119.

Christian Kohlschütter, Peter Fankhauser, and Wolfgang Nejdl. 2010. Boilerplate detection using shallow text features. In *Proceedings of the third ACM international conference on Web search and data mining*, pages 441–450. ACM.

Siwei Lai, Liheng Xu, Kang Liu, and Jun Zhao. 2015. Recurrent Convolutional Neural Networks for Text Classification. *Twenty-Ninth AAAI Conference on Artificial Intelligence*, pages 2267–2273.

Ken Lang. 1995. Newsweeder: Learning to filter netnews. In *Proceedings of the 12th international conference on machine learning*, pages 331–339.

Wee Sun Lee and Bing Liu. 2003. Learning with Positive and Unlabeled Examples Using Weighted Logistic Regression. *Algorithmic Learning Theory*, 348(1):71–85.

Omer Levy, Yoav Goldberg, and Ido Dagan. 2015. Improving distributional similarity with lessons learned from word embeddings. *Transactions of the Association for Computational Linguistics*, 3:211–225.

Xiaoli Li, S Yu Philip, Bing Liu, and See-Kiong Ng. 2009. Positive unlabeled learning for data stream classification. In *SDM*, volume 9, pages 257–268. SIAM.

Bing Liu, Yang Dai, Xiaoli Li, Wee Sun Lee, and Philip S Yu. 2003. Building text classifiers using positive and unlabeled examples. In *Data Mining, 2003. ICDM 2003. Third IEEE International Conference on*, pages 179–186. IEEE.

Bing Liu, Xiaoli Li, Wee Sun Lee, and Philip S Yu. 2004. Text classification by labeling words. In *AAAI*, volume 4, pages 425–430.

Michael Lucas and Doug Downey. 2013. Scaling semi-supervised naive bayes with feature marginals. In *Proceedings of the 51st Annual Meeting of the Association for Computational Linguistics*, pages 343–351.

Gideon S Mann and Andrew McCallum. 2008. Generalized expectation criteria for semi-supervised learning of conditional random fields.

Tomas Mikolov, Ilya Sutskever, Kai Chen, Greg S Corrado, and Jeff Dean. 2013. Distributed representations of words and phrases and their compositionality. In *Advances in neural information processing systems*, pages 3111–3119.

Mary M Moya and Don R Hush. 1996. Network constraints and multi-objective optimization for one-class classification. *Neural Networks*, 9(3):463–474.

Bo Pang, Lillian Lee, and Shivakumar Vaithyanathan. 2002. Thumbs up?: sentiment classification using machine learning techniques. In *Proceedings of the ACL-02 conference on Empirical methods in natural language processing-Volume 10*, pages 79–86. Association for Computational Linguistics.

Jeffrey Pennington, Richard Socher, and Christopher D Manning. 2014. Glove: Global vectors for word representation. In *EMNLP*, volume 14, pages 1532–1543.

Robert E Schapire, Marie Rochery, Mazin Rahim, and Narendra Gupta. 2002. Incorporating prior knowledge into boosting. In *ICML*, volume 2, pages 538–545.

Bernhard Schölkopf, John C Platt, John Shawe-Taylor, Alex J Smola, and Robert C Williamson. 2001. Estimating the support of a high-dimensional distribution. *Neural computation*, 13(7):1443–1471.

Burr Settles. 2011. Closing the loop: Fast, interactive semi-supervised annotation with queries on features and instances. In *Proceedings of the conference on empirical methods in natural language processing*, pages 1467–1478. Association for Computational Linguistics.

Duyu Tang, Furu Wei, Nan Yang, Ming Zhou, Ting Liu, and Bing Qin. 2014. Learning sentiment-specific word embedding for twitter sentiment classification. In *ACL (1)*, pages 1555–1565.

Shuai Wang, Zhiyuan Chen, Geli Fei, Bing Liu, and Sherry Emery. 2016. Targeted Topic Modeling for Focused Analysis. *Proceedings of the 22nd ACM SIGKDD International Conference on Knowledge Discovery and Data Mining - KDD '16*, pages 1235–1244.

Sida Wang and Christopher D Manning. 2012. Baselines and bigrams: Simple, good sentiment and topic classification. In *Proceedings of the 50th Annual Meeting of the Association for Computational Linguistics: Short Papers-Volume 2*, pages 90–94. Association for Computational Linguistics.

Hwanjo Yu, Jiawei Han, and Kevin Chen-Chuan Chang. 2002. Pebl: positive example based learning for web page classification using svm. In *Proceedings of the eighth ACM SIGKDD international conference on Knowledge discovery and data mining*, pages 239–248. ACM.

Li Zhao, Minlie Huang, Ziyu Yao, Rongwei Su, Yingying Jiang, and Xiaoyan Zhu. 2016. Semi-supervised multinomial naive bayes for text classification by leveraging word-level statistical constraint. In *Proceedings of the Thirtieth AAAI Conference on Artificial Intelligence*, pages 2877–2883. AAAI Press.

Capturing Long-range Contextual Dependencies with Memory-enhanced Conditional Random Fields

Fei Liu   **Timothy Baldwin**   **Trevor Cohn**
School of Computing and Information Systems
The University of Melbourne
Victoria, Australia
`fliu3@student.unimelb.edu.au`
`tb@ldwin.net  t.cohn@unimelb.edu.au`

Abstract

Despite successful applications across a broad range of NLP tasks, conditional random fields ("CRFs"), in particular the linear-chain variant, are only able to model local features. While this has important benefits in terms of inference tractability, it limits the ability of the model to capture long-range dependencies between items. Attempts to extend CRFs to capture long-range dependencies have largely come at the cost of computational complexity and approximate inference. In this work, we propose an extension to CRFs by integrating external memory, taking inspiration from memory networks, thereby allowing CRFs to incorporate information far beyond neighbouring steps. Experiments across two tasks show substantial improvements over strong CRF and LSTM baselines.

1 Introduction

While long-range contextual dependencies are prevalent in natural language, for tractability reasons, most statistical models capture only local features (Finkel et al., 2005). Take the sentence in Figure 1, for example. Here, while it is easy to determine that *Interfax* in the second sentence is a named entity, it is hard to determine its semantic class, as there is little context information. The usage in the first sentence, on the other hand, can be reliably disambiguated due to the post-modifying phase *news agency*. Ideally we would like to be able to share such contexts across all usages (and variants) of a given named entity for reliable and consistent identification and disambiguation.

A related example is forum thread discourse analysis. Previous work has largely focused on

linear-chain Conditional Random Fields (CRFs) (Wang et al., 2011; Zhang et al., 2017), framing the task as one of sequence tagging. Although CRFs are adept at capturing local structure, the problem does not naturally suit a linear sequential structure, i.e. , a post may be a reply to either a neighbouring post or one posted far earlier within the same thread. In both cases, contextual dependencies can be long-range, necessitating the ability to capture dependencies between arbitrarily distant items. Identifying this key limitation, Sutton and McCallum (2004) and Finkel et al. (2005) proposed the use of CRFs with skip connections to incorporate long-range dependencies. In both cases the graph structure must be supplied a priori, rather than learned, and both techniques incur the need for costly approximate inference.

Recurrent neural networks (RNNs) have been proposed as an alternative technique for encoding sequential inputs, however plain RNNs are unable to capture long-range dependencies (Bengio et al., 1994; Hochreiter et al., 2001) and variants such as LSTMs (Hochreiter and Schmidhuber, 1997), although more capable of capturing non-local patterns, still exhibit a significant locality bias in practice (Lai et al., 2015; Linzen et al., 2016).

In this paper, taking inspiration from the work of Weston et al. (2015) on memory networks (MEMNETs), we propose to extend CRFs by integrating external memory mechanisms, thereby enabling the model to look beyond localised features and have access to the entire sequence. This is achieved with attention over every entry in the memory. Experiments on named entity recognition and forum thread parsing, both of which involve long-range contextual dependencies, demonstrate the effectiveness of the proposed model, achieving state-of-the-art performance on the former, and outperforming a number of strong baselines in the case of the latter. A full imple-

Proceedings of the The 8th International Joint Conference on Natural Language Processing, pages 555–565,
Taipei, Taiwan, November 27 – December 1, 2017 ©2017 AFNLP

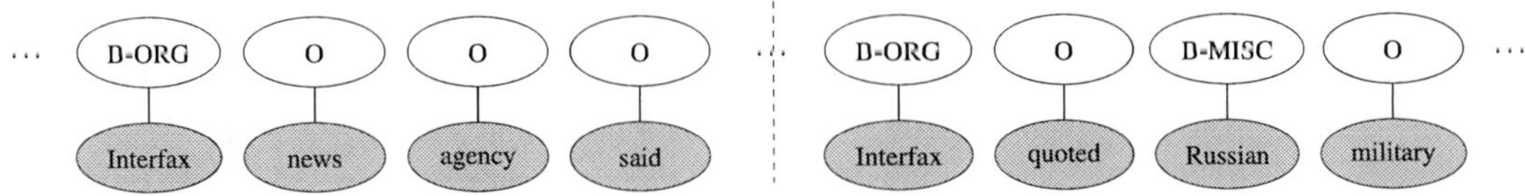

Figure 1: A NER example with long-range contextual dependencies. The vertical dash line indicates a sentence boundary.

mentation of the model is available at: `https://github.com/liufly/mecrf`.

The paper is organised as follows: after reviewing previous studies on capturing long range contextual dependencies and related models in Section 2, we detail the elements of the proposed model in Section 3. Section 4 and 5 present the experimental results on two different datasets: one for thread discourse structure prediction and the other named entity recognition (NER), with analyses and visualisation in their respective sections. Lastly, Section 6 concludes the paper.

2 Related Work

In this section, we review the different families of models that are relevant to this work, in capturing long-range contextual dependencies in different ways.

Conditional Random Fields (CRFs). CRFs (Lafferty et al., 2001), in particular linear-chain CRFs, have been widely adopted and applied to sequence labelling tasks in NLP, but have the critical limitation that they only capture local structure (Sutton and McCallum, 2004; Finkel et al., 2005), despite non-local structure being common in structured language classification tasks. In the context of named entity recognition ("NER"), Sutton and McCallum (2004) proposed skip-chain CRFs as a means of alleviating this shortcoming, wherein distant items are connected in a sequence based on a heuristic such as string identity (to achieve label consistency across all instances of the same string). The idea of label consistency and exploiting non-local features has also been explored in the work of Finkel et al. (2005), who take long-range structure into account while maintaining tractable inference with Gibbs sampling (Geman and Geman, 1984), by performing approximate inference over factored probabilistic models. While both of these lines of work report impressive results on information extraction tasks, they come at the price of high computational cost and incompatibility with exact inference.

Similar ideas have also been explored by Krishnan and Manning (2006) for NER, where they apply two CRFs, the first of which makes predictions based on local information, and the second combines named entities identified by the first CRF in a single cluster, thereby enforcing label consistency and enabling the use of a richer set of features to capture non-local dependencies. Liao and Grishman (2010) make a strong case for going beyond sentence boundaries and leveraging document-level information for event extraction.

While we take inspiration from these earlier studies, we do not enforce label consistency as a hard constraint, and additionally do not sacrifice inference tractability: our model is capable of incorporating non-local features, and is compatible with exact inference methods.

Recurrent Neural Networks (RNNs). Recently, the broad adoption of deep learning methods in NLP has given rise to the prevalent use of RNNs. Long short-term memories ("LSTMs": Hochreiter and Schmidhuber (1997)), a particular variant of RNN, have become particularly popular, and been successfully applied to a large number of tasks: speech recognition (Graves et al., 2013), sequence tagging (Huang et al., 2015), document categorisation (Yang et al., 2016), and machine translation (Cho et al., 2014; Bahdanau et al., 2014). However, as pointed out by Lai et al. (2015) and Linzen et al. (2016), RNNs — including LSTMs — are biased towards immediately preceding (or neighbouring, in the case of bi-directional RNNs) items, and perform poorly in contexts which involve long-range contextual dependencies, despite the inclusion of memory cells. This is further evidenced by the work of Cho et al. (2014), who show that the performance of a basic encoder–decoder deteriorates as the length of the input sentence increases.

Memory networks (MEMNETs). More recently, Weston et al. (2015) proposed memory networks and showed that the augmentation of memory is crucial to performing inference requiring long-range dependencies, especially when document-level reasoning between multiple supporting facts is required. Of particular interest to our work are so-called "memory hops" in memory networks, which are guided by an attention mechanism based on the relevance between a question and each supporting context sentence in the memory hop. Governed by the attention mechanism, the ability to access the entire sequence is similar to the soft alignment idea proposed by Bahdanau et al. (2014) for neural machine translation. In this work, we borrow the concept of memory hops and integrate it into CRFs, thereby enabling the model to look beyond localised features and have access to the whole sequence via an attention mechanism.

3 Methodology

In the context of sequential tagging, we assume the input is in the form of sequence pairs: $\mathcal{D} = \{\mathbf{x}^{(n)}, \mathbf{y}^{(n)}\}_{n=1}^{N}$ where $\mathbf{x}^{(n)}$ is the input of the n-th example in dataset $\mathcal{D}$ and consists of a sequence: $\{x_1^{(n)}, x_2^{(n)}, \ldots, x_T^{(n)}\}$. Similarly, $\mathbf{y}^{(n)}$ is of the same length as $\mathbf{x}^{(n)}$ and consists of the corresponding labels $\{y_1^{(n)}, y_2^{(n)}, \ldots, y_T^{(n)}\}$. For notational convenience, hereinafter we omit the superscript denoting the n-th example.

In the case of NER, each x_t is a word in a sentence with y_t being the corresponding NER label. For forum thread discourse analysis, x_t represents the text of an entire post whereas y_t is the dialogue act label for the t-th post.

The proposed model extends CRFs by integrating external memory and is therefore named a **Memory-Enhanced Conditional Random Field** ("ME-CRF"). We take inspiration from Memory Networks ("MEMNETs": Weston et al. (2015)) and incorporate so-called memory hops into CRFs, thereby allowing the model to have unrestricted access to the whole sequence rather than localised features as in RNNs (Lai et al., 2015; Linzen et al., 2016).

As illustrated in Figure 2, ME-CRF can be divided into two major parts: (1) the memory layer; and (2) the CRF layer. The memory layer can be further broken down into three main components: (a) the input memory $m_{1:t}$; (b) the output memory $c_{1:t}$; and (c) the current input u_t, which represents the current step (also known as the "question" in the context of MEMNET). The input and

output memory representations are connected via an attention mechanism whose weights are determined by measuring the similarity between the input memory and the current input. The CRF layer, on the other hand, takes the output of the memory layer as input. In the remainder of this section, we detail the elements of ME-CRF.

3.1 Memory Layer

3.1.1 Input memory

Every element (word/post) in a sequence $\mathbf{x}$ is encoded with $x_t = \Phi(x_t)$, where $\Phi(\cdot)$ can be any encoding function mapping the input x_t into a vector $x_t \in \mathbb{R}^d$. This results in the sequence $\{x_1, \ldots, x_T\}$. While this new sequence can be seen as the memory in the context of MEMNETs, one major drawback of this approach, as pointed out by Seo et al. (2017), is the insensitivity to temporal information between memory cells. We therefore follow Xiong et al. (2016) in injecting temporal signal into the memory using a bidirectional GRU encoding (Cho et al., 2014):

$$\overrightarrow{m}_t = \overrightarrow{\mathrm{GRU}}(x_t, \overrightarrow{m}_{t-1}) \tag{1}$$

$$\overleftarrow{m}_t = \overleftarrow{\mathrm{GRU}}(x_t, \overleftarrow{m}_{t+1}) \tag{2}$$

$$m_t = \tanh(\overrightarrow{W}_m \overrightarrow{m}_t + \overleftarrow{W}_m \overleftarrow{m}_t + b_m) \tag{3}$$

where $\overrightarrow{W}_m$, $\overleftarrow{W}_m$ and b_m are learnable parameters.

3.1.2 Current input

This is used to represent the current step x_t, be it a word or a post. As in MEMNETs, we want to enforce the current input to be in the same space as the input memory so that we can determine the attention weight of each element in the memory by measuring the relevance between the two. We denote the current input by $u_t = m_t$.

3.1.3 Attention

To determine the attention value of each element in the memory, we measure the relevance between the current step u_t and m_i for $i \in [1, t]$ with a softmax function:

$$p_{t,i} = \mathrm{softmax}(u_t^\top m_i) \tag{4}$$

where $\mathrm{softmax}(a_i) = \dfrac{e^{a_i}}{\sum_j e^{a_j}}$.

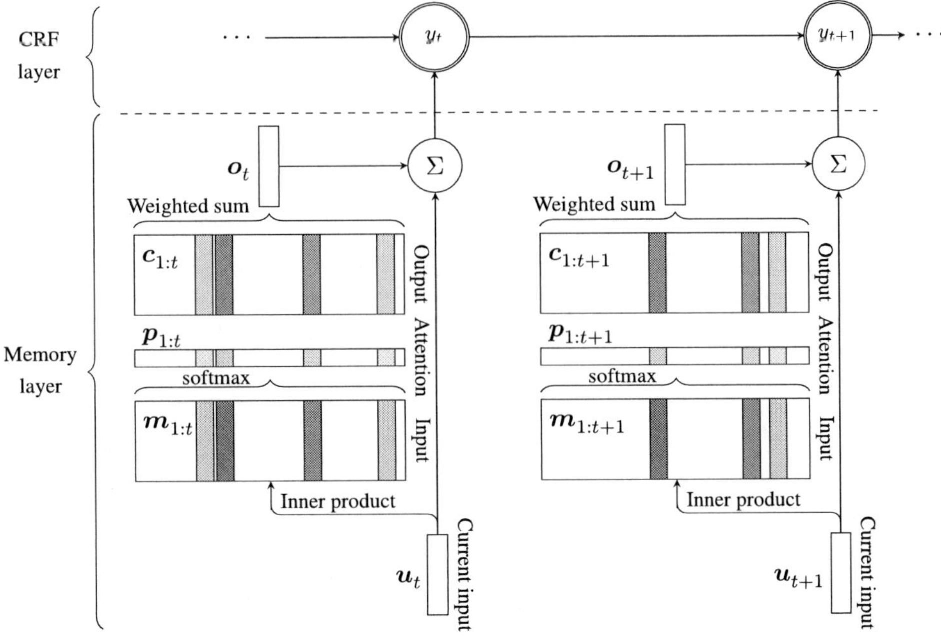

Figure 2: Illustration of ME-CRFs with a single memory hop, showing the network architecture at time step t and $t + 1$.

3.1.4 Output memory

Similar to m_t, c_t is the output memory, and is calculated analogously but with a different set of parameters in the GRUs and tanh layers of Equations (1), (2) and (3). The output memory is used to generate the final output of the memory layer and fed as input to the CRF layer.

3.1.5 Memory layer output

Once the attention weights have been computed, the memory access controller receives the response o in the form of a weighted sum over the output memory representations:

$$o_t = \sum_i p_{t,i} c_i \qquad (5)$$

This allows the model to have unrestricted access to elements in previous steps as opposed to a single vector h_t in RNNs, thereby enabling ME-CRFs to detect and effectively incorporate long-range dependencies.

3.1.6 Extension

For more challenging tasks requiring complex reasoning capabilities with multiple supporting facts from the memory, the model can be further extended by stacking multiple memory hops, in

which case the output of the k-th hop is taken as input to the $(k + 1)$-th hop:

$$u_t^{k+1} = o_t^k + u_t^k \qquad (6)$$

where u_t^{k+1} encodes not only information at the current step (u_t^k) but also relevant knowledge from the memory (o_t^k). In the scope of this work, we limit the number of hops to 1.

3.2 CRF Layer

Once the representation of the current step u_t^{K+1} is computed — incorporating relevant information from the memory (assuming the total number of memory hops is K) — it is then fed into a CRF layer:

$$s(\mathbf{x}, \mathbf{y}) = \sum_{t=0}^{T} A_{y_t, y_{t+1}} + \sum_{t=1}^{T} P_{t, y_t} \qquad (7)$$

where $A \in \mathbb{R}^{|\mathcal{Y}| \times |\mathcal{Y}|}$ is the CRF transition matrix, $|\mathcal{Y}|$ is the size of the label set, and $P \in \mathbb{R}^{T \times |\mathcal{Y}|}$ is a linearly transformed matrix from u_t^{K+1} such that $P_{t,:}^{\top} = W_s u_t^{K+1}$ where $W_s \in \mathbb{R}^{|\mathcal{Y}| \times h}$ with h being the size of m_t. Here, $A_{i,j}$ represents the score of the transition from the i-th tag to the j-th tag whereas $P_{i,j}$ is the score of the j-th tag at time i.

Using the scoring function in Equation (7), we calculate the score of the sequence $\mathbf{y}$ normalised by the sum of scores of all possible sequences $\tilde{\mathbf{y}}$, and this becomes the probability of the true sequence:

$$p(\mathbf{y}|\mathbf{x}) = \frac{\exp(s(\mathbf{x}, \mathbf{y}))}{\sum_{\tilde{\mathbf{y}} \in \mathbf{Y_x}} \exp(s(\mathbf{x}, \tilde{\mathbf{y}}))} \quad (8)$$

We train the model to maximise the probability of the gold label sequence with the following loss function:

$$\mathcal{L} = \sum_{n=1}^{N} \log p(\mathbf{y}^{(n)}|\mathbf{x}^{(n)}) \quad (9)$$

where $p(\mathbf{y}^{(n)}|\mathbf{x}^{(n)})$ is calculated using the forward–backward algorithm. Note that the model is fully end-to-end differentiable.

At test time, the model predicts the output sequence with maximum a posteriori probability:

$$\mathbf{y}^* = \arg\max_{\tilde{\mathbf{y}} \in \mathbf{Y_x}} p(\tilde{\mathbf{y}}|\mathbf{x}) \quad (10)$$

Since we are only modelling bigram interactions, we adopt the Viterbi algorithm for decoding.

4 Thread Discourse Structure Prediction

In this section, we describe how ME-CRFs can be applied to the task of thread discourse structure prediction, wherein we attempt to predict which post(s) a given post directly responds to, and in what way(s) (as captured by dialogue acts). This is a novel approach to this problem and capable of natively handling both tasks within the same network architecture.

4.1 Dataset and Task

In this work, we adopt the dataset of Kim et al. (2010),[1] which consists of 315 threads and 1,332 posts, collected from the Operating System, Software, Hardware and Web Development subforums of CNET.[2] Every post has been manually linked to preceding post(s) in the thread that it is a direct response to (in the form of "links"), and the nature of the response for each link (in the form of "dialogue acts", or "DAs"). In this dataset, it is not uncommon to see messages respond to posts which occur much earlier in the thread (based on the chronological ordering of posts). In fact, 18%

of the posts link to posts other than their immediately preceding post.

The task is defined as follows: given a list of preceding posts $x_1, \ldots, x_{t-1}$ and the current post x_t, to classify which posts it links to (l_t) and the dialogue act (y_t) of each such link. In the scope of this work, ME-CRFs are capable of modelling both tasks natively, and therefore a natural fit for this problem.

4.2 Experimental Setup

In this dataset, in addition to the body of text, each post is also associated with a title. We therefore use two encoders, $\Phi_{title}(\cdot)$ and $\Phi_{text}(\cdot)$, to process them separately and then concatenate $\boldsymbol{x}_t = [\Phi_{title}(x_t); \Phi_{text}(x_t)]^\top$. Here, $\Phi_{title}(\cdot)$ and $\Phi_{text}(\cdot)$ take word embeddings as input, processing each post at the word level, as opposed to the post-level bi-directional GRU in Equations (1) and (2), and the representation of a post $\boldsymbol{x}_t$ (either title or text) is obtained by transforming the last and first hidden states of the forward and backward word-level GRU, similar to Equation (3). Note that $\Phi_{title}(\cdot)$ and $\Phi_{text}(\cdot)$ do not share parameters. As in Tang et al. (2016), we further restrict $\boldsymbol{m}_i^k = \boldsymbol{c}_i^k$ to curb overfitting.

In keeping with Wang (2014), we complement the textual representations with hand-crafted structural features $\Phi_s(x_t) \in \mathbb{R}^2$:

- initiator: a binary feature indicating whether the author of the current post is the same as the initiator of the thread,
- position: the relative position of the current post, as a ratio over the total number of posts in the thread;

Also drawing on Wang (2014), we incorporate punctuation-based features $\Phi_p(x_t) \in \mathbb{R}^3$: the number of question marks, exclamation marks and URLs in the current post. The resultant feature vectors are projected into an embedding space by $\boldsymbol{W}_s$ and $\boldsymbol{W}_p$ and concatenated with $\boldsymbol{x}_i$, resulting in the new $\boldsymbol{x}_i'$. Subsequently, $\boldsymbol{x}_i'$ is fed into the bi-directional GRUs to obtain $\boldsymbol{m}_i$.

For link prediction, we generate a supervision signal from the annotated links, guiding the attention to focus on the correct memory position:

$$\mathcal{L}_{\text{LNK}} = \sum_{n=1}^{N} \sum_{t=1}^{T} \text{CrossEntropy}(\boldsymbol{l}_t^{(n)}, \boldsymbol{p}_t^{(n)}) \quad (11)$$

where $\boldsymbol{l}_t^{(n)}$ is a one-hot vector indicating where the link points to for the t-th post in the n-th thread,

---

[1] http://people.eng.unimelb.edu.au/tbaldwin/resources/conll2010-thread/

[2] http://forums.cnet.com/

and $\boldsymbol{p}_t^{(n)} = \{p_{t,1}, \ldots, p_{t,t}\}$ is the predicted distribution of attention over the t posts in the memory. To accommodate the first post in a thread, as it points to a virtual "head" post, we set a dummy post, $\boldsymbol{m}_0 = \boldsymbol{0}$, of the same size as $\boldsymbol{m}_i$. While the dataset contains multi-headed posts (posts with more than one outgoing link), following Wang (2014), we only include the most recent linked post during training, but evaluate over the full set of labelled links.

For this task, ME-CRF is jointly trained to predict both the link and dialogue act with the following loss function:

$$\mathcal{L}' = \alpha \mathcal{L}_{\text{DA}} + (1 - \alpha)\mathcal{L}_{\text{LNK}} \qquad (12)$$

where $\mathcal{L}_{\text{DA}}$ is the CRF likelihood defined in Equation (9), and α is a hyper-parameter for balancing the emphasis between the two tasks.

Training is carried out with Adam (Kingma and Ba, 2015) over 50 epochs with a batch size of 32. We use the following hyper-parameter settings: word embedding size of 20, $\boldsymbol{W}_p \in \mathbb{R}^{100 \times 3}$, $\boldsymbol{W}_s \in \mathbb{R}^{50 \times 2}$, $\alpha = 0.5$, hidden size of Φ_{title} and Φ_{text} is 20, hidden size of $\overrightarrow{\text{GRU}}$ and $\overleftarrow{\text{GRU}}$ is 50. Dropout is applied to all GRU recurrent units on the input and output connections with a keep rate of 0.7.

Lastly, we also explore the idea of curriculum learning (Bengio et al., 2009), by fixing the CRF transition matrix $\boldsymbol{A} = \boldsymbol{0}$ for the first $e = 20$ epochs, after which we train the parameters for the remainder of the run. This allows the ME-CRF to learn a good strategy for DA and link prediction, as independent "maxent" type classifier, before attempting to learn sequence dynamics. We refer to this variant as "ME-CRF+".

4.3 Evaluation

Following Wang (2014), we evaluate based on post-level micro-averaged F-score. All experiments were carried out with 10-fold cross validation, stratifying at the thread level.

We benchmark against the following previous work: the feature-rich CRF-based approach of Kim et al. (2010), where the authors trained independent models for each of link and DA classification ("CRF$_{\text{KIM}}$"); the feature-rich CRF-based approach of Wang (2014), where the author further extended the feature set of Kim et al. (2010) and jointly trained a CRF over the link and DA prediction tasks ("CRF$_{\text{WANG}}$"); and the dependency

Model	Link	DA	Joint
CRF$_{\text{KIM}}$	86.3	75.1	—
CRF$_{\text{WANG}}$	82.3	73.4	66.5
DEPPARSER	85.0	75.7	70.6
MEMNET	85.8	76.0	69.5
ME-CRF	**86.4**	**77.5**	70.9
ME-CRF+	86.3	77.4	**71.2**

Table 1: Post-level Link and DA F-scores. Performance for ME-CRF and ME-CRF+ is marco-averaged over 5 runs.

parser-based approach of Wang (2014), where the author treated the discourse structure prediction task as a constrained dependency parsing problem, with posts as nodes in the dependency graph, and the constraint that links must connect to preceding posts in the thread ("DEPPARSER").[3] In addition to the CRF/parser-based systems, we also build a MEMNET-based baseline (named MEMNET) where MEMNET shares the architecture of the memory layer in ME-CRF but excludes the use of the CRF layer. Instead, MEMNET, following the work of Sukhbaatar et al. (2015), predicts the final answer by:

$$\hat{\boldsymbol{y}} = \text{softmax}(\boldsymbol{W}_{\text{DA}}(\boldsymbol{u}^{K+1})) \qquad (13)$$

where $\hat{\boldsymbol{y}}$ is the predicted DA distribution, $\boldsymbol{W}_{\text{DA}} \in \mathbb{R}^{|\mathcal{Y}| \times d}$ is a parameter matrix for the model to learn, and $K = 1$ is the total number of hops. This is equivalent to classifying link and DA independently at each time step t without taking transitions between DA labels into account.

4.4 Results

The experimental results are presented in Table 1, wherein the first three rows are the three baseline systems.

State-of-the-art post-level results. ME-CRFs achieve state of the art results in terms of joint post-level F-score, substantially better than the baselines. While ME-CRF slightly outperforms the current state-of-the-art (DEPPARSER), ME-CRF+ improves the performance and achieves a further 0.3% absolute gain.

---

[3]Note that a mistake was found in the results in the original paper (Wang et al., 2011), and we use the corrected results from Wang (2014).

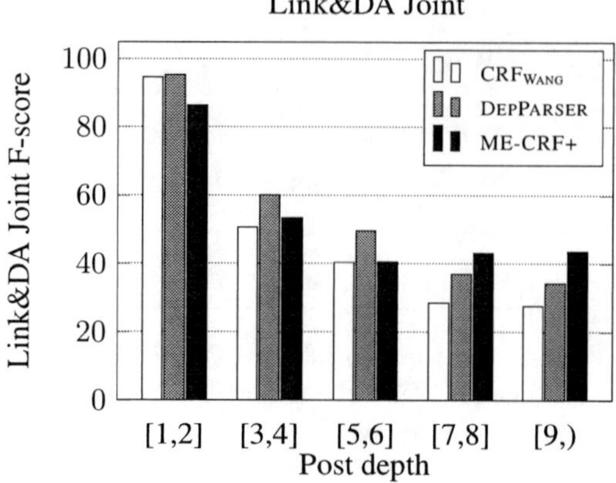

Figure 3: Breakdown of post-level Joint F-scores by post depth, where e.g. "[1, 2]" is the joint F-score over posts of depth 1–2, i.e. the first or second post in the thread. Note that we take the reported performance of CRF_WANG and DEP-PARSER from Wang (2014).

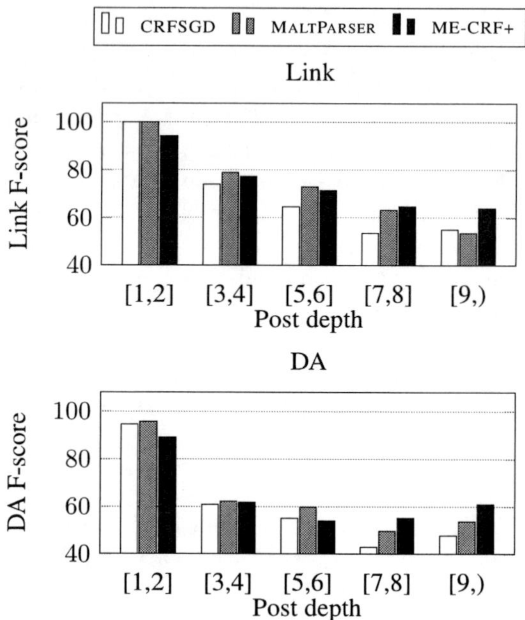

Figure 4: Breakdown of post-level Link and DA F-scores by post depth.

Curriculum learning improves joint prediction. Despite the slight performance drop on the DA and link prediction tasks, ME-CRF+, with the CRF transition matrix frozen for the first 20 epochs, achieves a $\sim$0.3% absolute gain in joint F-score over ME-CRF. This suggests that the sequence dynamics between posts, while difficult to capture, are beneficial to the overall task (resulting in more coherent DA and link predictions) if trained with proper initialisation.

MEMNET vs. ME-CRFs. We see consistent gains across all three tasks when the CRF layer is added. Although not presented in Table 1, the difference is most notable at the thread-level (i.e. a thread is correct iff all posts are tagged correctly), highlighting the importance of sequential transitional information between posts.

CRF vs. ME-CRFs. Note that CRF_{KIM} is not trained jointly on the two component tasks, but individually on each task. Without additional data, jointly training on the two tasks generates results that are comparable or substantially better over the individual tasks. This highlights the effectiveness of ME-CRF, especially with the link prediction performance comparable to that of a single-task model CRF, and surpassing it in the case of DA.

4.5 Analysis

We break the performance down by the depth of each post in a given thread, and present the results in Figure 3. Although below the baselines for the interval [1, 2], ME-CRF+ consistently outperforms CRF_{WANG} from depth 3 onwards, and is superior to DEPPARSER for depths [7,). Breaking down the performance further to the individual tasks of Link and DA prediction, as displayed in Figure 4, we observe a similar trend. In line with the findings in the work of Wang (2014), this confirms that prediction becomes progressively more difficult as threads grow longer, which is largely due to the increased variability in discourse structure. Despite the escalated difficulty, ME-CRF+ is substantially superior to the baselines when classifying deeper posts.

Between the CRF-based models, it is worth noting that despite the lower performance for [1, 2], ME-CRF+ benefits from having global access to the entire sequence, and consistently outperforms CRF_{WANG} for depths [3,), highlighting the effectiveness of the memory mechanism. Overall, these results validate our hypothesis that having unrestricted access to the whole sequence is beneficial, especially for long-range dependencies, offering further evidence of the power of

ME-CRFs.

5 Named Entity Recognition

In this section, we present experiments in a second setting: named entity recognition, over the CoNLL 2003 English NER shared task dataset (Tjong Kim Sang and De Meulder, 2003). Our interest here is in evaluating the ability of ME-CRF to capture document context, to aid in the identification and disambiguation of NEs.

5.1 Dataset and Task

The CoNLL 2003 NER shared task dataset consists of $14,041/3,250/3,453$ sentences in the training/development/test set, resp., extracted from $946/216/231$ Reuters news articles from the period 1996–97. The goal is to identify individual token occurrences of NEs, and tag each with its class (e.g. LOCATION or ORGANISATION). Here, we use the IOB tagging scheme. In terms of tagging schemes, while some have shown improvements with a more expressive IOBES marginally (Ratinov and Roth, 2009; Dai et al., 2015), we stick to the BIO scheme for simplicity and the observation of little improvement between these schemes by Lample et al. (2016).

5.2 Experimental Setup

We choose $\Phi(x_t)$ to be a lookup function, returning the corresponding embedding x_t of the word x_t. In addition to the word features, we employ a subset of the lexical features described in Huang et al. (2015), based on whether the word:

- starts with a capital letter;
- is composed of all capital letters;
- is composed of all lower case letters;
- contains non initial capital letters;
- contains both letters and digits;
- contains punctuation.

These features are all binary and refered to as $\Phi_l(x_t)$. Similar to the thread structure prediction experiments, we concatenate $\Phi_l(x_t)$ with x_t to generate the new input x' to the bi-directional GRUs in Equations (1) and (2).

In order to incorporate information in the document beyond sentence boundaries, we encode every word sequentially in a document with Φ and $\overrightarrow{\text{GRU}}$ and $\overleftarrow{\text{GRU}}$, and store them in the memory m_i and c_i for $i \in [1, t']$, where t' is the index of the current word t in the document.

Training is carried out with Adam, over 100 epochs with a batch size of 32. We use the following hyper-parameter settings: word embedding size $= 50$; hidden size of $\overrightarrow{\text{GRU}}$ and $\overleftarrow{\text{GRU}} = 50$; $\overrightarrow{W}_m$ and $\overleftarrow{W}_m \in \mathbb{R}^{50\times50}$; and $b_m \in \mathbb{R}^{50}$. Dropout is applied to all GRU recurrent units on the input and output connections, with a keep rate of 0.8. We initialise ME-CRF with pre-trained word embeddings and keep them fixed during training. While we report results only on the test set, we use early stopping based on the development set.

5.3 Evaluation

Evaluation is based on span-level NE F-score, based on the official CoNLL evaluation script.[4]

We compare against the following baselines:

1. a CRF over hand-tuned lexical features ("CRF": Huang et al. (2015))
2. an LSTM and bi-directional LSTM ("LSTM" and "BI-LSTM", resp.: Huang et al. (2015))
3. a CRF taking features from a convolutional neural network as input ("CONV-CRF": Collobert et al. (2011))
4. a CRF over the output of either a simple LSTM or bidirectional LSTM ("LSTM-CRF" and "BI-LSTM-CRF", resp.: Huang et al. (2015))

Note that for our word embeddings, while we observe better performance with GLOVE (Pennington et al., 2014), for fair comparison purposes, we adopt the same SENNA embeddings (Collobert et al., 2011) as are used in the baseline methods.[5]

5.4 Results

The experimental results are presented in Table 2. Results for the baseline methods are based on the published results of Huang et al. (2015) and Collobert et al. (2011). Note that none of the systems in Table 2 use external gazetteers, to make the comparison fair. As can be observed, ME-CRF achieves the best performance, beating all the baselines.

To gain a better understanding of what the model has learned, Table 3 presents two examples

---

[4] http://www.cnts.ua.ac.be/conll2000/ chunking/conlleval.txt

[5] Lample et al. (2016) report a higher result of 90.9 using a BI-LSTM-CRF architecture, but augmented with skip n-grams (Ling et al., 2015) and character embeddings. Due to the differing underlying representation, we exclude it from the comparison.

Model	F-score
CRF	86.1
LSTM	83.7
BI-LSTM	85.2
CONV-CRF	88.7
LSTM-CRF	88.4
BI-LSTM-CRF	88.8
ME-CRF	**89.5**

Table 2: NER performance on the CoNLL 2003 English NER shared task dataset.

where ME-CRF focuses on words beyond the current sentence boundaries. In the example on the left, where the target word is *Juventus* (an Italian soccer team), ME-CRF directs the attention mainly to the occurrence of the same word in a previous sentence and a small fraction to *Manchester* (a UK soccer team, in this context). Note that it does not attend to the other NE (*Europe*) in that sentence, which is of a different NE class. In the example on the right, on the other hand, ME-CRF allocates attention to the same words as the target word in the current sentence. Note that the second occurrence of *Interfax* in the memory is the same occurrence as the first word in the current sentence. While more weight is placed on the second *Interfax*, close to one third of the attention is also asigned to the first occurrence. Given that the memory, m_i and c_i, is encoded with bi-directional GRUs, the first *Interfax* should, to some degree, capture the succeeding neighbouring elements: *news agency*.

This is reminiscent of label consistency in the works of Sutton and McCallum (2004) and Finkel et al. (2005), but differs in that the consistency constraint is soft as opposed to hard in previous studies, and automatically learned without the use of heuristics.

6 Conclusion

In this paper, we have presented ME-CRF, a model extending linear-chain CRFs by including external memory. This allows the model to look beyond neighbouring items and access long-range context. Experimental results demonstrate the effectiveness of the proposed method over two tasks: forum thread discourse analysis, and named entity recognition.

Memory	$p_{t,i}$	Memory	$p_{t,i}$
...		...	
Manchester	0.23	,	0.00
United	0.00	Interfax	0.32
face	0.00	news	0.00
Juventus	0.65	agency	0.00
in	0.00	said	0.00
Europe	0.00	.	0.00
...		Interfax	0.68
European champions Juventus ...		Interfax quoted Russian ...	

Table 3: An NER example showing learned attention to long-range contextual dependencies. The last row is the current sentence. The underlined words indicate the target word x_t, and the dashed line indicates a sentence boundary.

Acknowledgments

We thank the anonymous reviewers for their valuable feedback, and gratefully acknowledge the support of Australian Government Research Training Program Scholarship and National Computational Infrastructure (NCI Australia). This work was also supported in part by the Australian Research Council.

References

Dzmitry Bahdanau, Kyunghyun Cho, and Yoshua Bengio. 2014. Neural machine translation by jointly learning to align and translate. In *Proceedings of the 3rd International Conference on Learning Representations (ICLR 2015)*. San Diego, USA.

Yoshua Bengio, Jérôme Louradour, Ronan Collobert, and Jason Weston. 2009. Curriculum learning. In *Proceedings of the 26th Annual International Conference on Machine Learning (ICML 2009)*. Montreal, Canada, pages 41–48.

Yoshua Bengio, Patrice Simard, and Paolo Frasconi. 1994. Learning long-term dependencies with gradient descent is difficult. *IEEE Transactions on Neural Networks* 5(2):157–166.

Kyunghyun Cho, Bart Van Merriënboer, Dzmitry Bahdanau, and Yoshua Bengio. 2014. On the properties of neural machine translation: Encoder-decoder approaches. In *Proceedings of SSST-8, Eighth Workshop on Syntax, Semantics and Structure in Statistical Translation*. Doha, Qatar, pages 103–111.

Ronan Collobert, Jason Weston, Léon Bottou, Michael Karlen, Koray Kavukcuoglu, and Pavel Kuksa. 2011. Natural language processing (almost) from scratch. *Journal of Machine Learning Research* 12:2493–2537.

Hong-Jie Dai, Po-Ting Lai, Yung-Chun Chang, and Richard Tzong-Han Tsai. 2015. Enhancing of chemical compound and drug name recognition using representative tag scheme and fine-grained tokenization. *Journal of Cheminformatics* 7(1):S14.

Jenny Rose Finkel, Trond Grenager, and Christopher Manning. 2005. Incorporating non-local information into information extraction systems by gibbs sampling. In *Proceedings of the 43rd Annual Meeting of the Association for Computational Linguistics (ACL 2005)*. Ann Arbor, USA, pages 363–370.

Stuart Geman and Donald Geman. 1984. Stochastic relaxation, Gibbs distributions, and the Bayesian restoration of images. *IEEE Transactions on Pattern Analysis and Machine Intelligence* 6:721–741.

Alex Graves, Abdel-rahman Mohamed, and Geoffrey Hinton. 2013. Speech recognition with deep recurrent neural networks. In *2013 IEEE International Conference on Acoustics, Speech and Signal Processing (ICASSP 2013)*. Vancouver, Canada, pages 6645–6649.

Sepp Hochreiter, Yoshua Bengio, Paolo Frasconi, and Jürgen Schmidhuber. 2001. Gradient flow in recurrent nets: the difficulty of learning long-term dependencies.

Sepp Hochreiter and Jürgen Schmidhuber. 1997. Long short-term memory. *Neural computation* 9(8):1735–1780.

Zhiheng Huang, Wei Xu, and Kai Yu. 2015. Bidirectional lstm-crf models for sequence tagging. *arXiv preprint arXiv:1508.01991* .

Su Nam Kim, Li Wang, and Timothy Baldwin. 2010. Tagging and linking web forum posts. In *Proceedings of the Fourteenth Conference on Computational Natural Language Learning (CoNLL 2010)*. Association for Computational Linguistics, Uppsala, Sweden, pages 192–202.

Diederik Kingma and Jimmy Ba. 2015. Adam: A method for stochastic optimization. In *Proceedings of the 3th International Conference on Learning Representations (ICLR 2015)*. San Diego, USA.

Vijay Krishnan and Christopher D. Manning. 2006. An effective two-stage model for exploiting non-local dependencies in named entity recognition. In *Proceedings of the 21st International Conference on Computational Linguistics and 44th Annual Meeting of the Association for Computational Linguistics (ACL 2006)*. Sydney, Australia, pages 1121–1128.

John D. Lafferty, Andrew McCallum, and Fernando C. N. Pereira. 2001. Conditional random fields: Probabilistic models for segmenting and labeling sequence data. In *Proceedings of the Eighteenth International Conference on Machine Learning (ICML 2001)*. San Francisco, USA, pages 282–289.

Siwei Lai, Liheng Xu, Kang Liu, and Jun Zhao. 2015. Recurrent convolutional neural networks for text classification. In *Proceedings of the 29th AAAI Conference on Artificial Intelligence (AAAI 2015)*. Austin, USA, volume 333, pages 2267–2273.

Guillaume Lample, Miguel Ballesteros, Sandeep Subramanian, Kazuya Kawakami, and Chris Dyer. 2016. Neural architectures for named entity recognition. In *Proceedings of the 2016 Conference of the North American Chapter of the Association for Computational Linguistics: Human Language Technologies (NAACL 2016)*. San Diego, USA, pages 260–270.

Shasha Liao and Ralph Grishman. 2010. Using document level cross-event inference to improve event extraction. In *Proceedings of the 48th Annual Meeting of the Association for Computational Linguistics (ACL 2010)*. Uppsala, Sweden, pages 789–797.

Wang Ling, Yulia Tsvetkov, Silvio Amir, Ramon Fermandez, Chris Dyer, Alan W Black, Isabel Trancoso, and Chu-Cheng Lin. 2015. Not all contexts are created equal: Better word representations with variable attention. In *Proceedings of the 2015 Conference on Empirical Methods in Natural Language Processing (EMNLP 2015)*. Lisbon, Portugal, pages 1367–1372.

Tal Linzen, Emmanuel Dupoux, and Yoav Goldberg. 2016. Assessing the ability of lstms to learn syntax-sensitive dependencies. *Transactions of the Association for Computational Linguistics (TACL 2016)* 4:521–535.

Jeffrey Pennington, Richard Socher, and Christopher Manning. 2014. GloVe: Global vectors for word representation. In *Proceedings of the 2014 Conference on Empirical Methods in Natural Language Processing (EMNLP 2014)*. Doha, Qatar, pages 1532–1543.

Lev Ratinov and Dan Roth. 2009. Design challenges and misconceptions in named entity recognition. In *Proceedings of the Thirteenth Conference on Computational Natural Language Learning (CoNLL 2009)*. Boulder, USA, pages 147–155.

Minjoon Seo, Sewon Min, Ali Farhadi, and Hannaneh Hajishirzi. 2017. Query-reduction networks for question answering. In *Proceedings of the 5th International Conference on Learning Representations (ICLR 2017)*. Toulon, France.

Sainbayar Sukhbaatar, Arthur Szlam, Jason Weston, and Rob Fergus. 2015. End-to-end memory networks. In *Proceedings of Advances in Neural Information Processing Systems (NIPS 2015)*. Montréal, Canada, pages 2440–2448.

Charles Sutton and Andrew McCallum. 2004. Collective segmentation and labeling of distant entities in information extraction. Technical report, Massachusetts Univ Amherst Dept of Computer Science.

Duyu Tang, Bing Qin, and Ting Liu. 2016. Aspect level sentiment classification with deep memory network. In *Proceedings of the 2016 Conference on Empirical Methods in Natural Language Processing (EMNLP 2016)*. Austin, USA, pages 214–224.

Erik F Tjong Kim Sang and Fien De Meulder. 2003. Introduction to the conll-2003 shared task: Language-independent named entity recognition. In *Proceedings of the seventh conference on North American Chapter of the Association for Computational Linguistics (NAACL 2003)*. Edmonton, Canada, pages 142–147.

Li Wang. 2014. *Knowledge discovery and extraction of domain-specific web data*. Ph.D. thesis, The University of Melbourne.

Li Wang, Marco Lui, Su Nam Kim, Joakim Nivre, and Timothy Baldwin. 2011. Predicting thread discourse structure over technical web forums. In *Proceedings of the 2011 Conference on Empirical Methods in Natural Language Processing (EMNLP 2011)*. Edinburgh, UK, pages 13–25.

Jason Weston, Sumit Chopra, and Antoine Bordes. 2015. Memory networks. In *Proceedings of the 3rd International Conference on Learning Representations (ICLR 2015)*. San Diego, USA.

Caiming Xiong, Stephen Merity, and Richard Socher. 2016. Dynamic memory networks for visual and textual question answering. In *Proceedings of the 33rd International Conference on Machine Learning (ICML 2016)*. New York, USA, pages 2397–2406.

Zichao Yang, Diyi Yang, Chris Dyer, Xiaodong He, Alex Smola, and Eduard Hovy. 2016. Hierarchical attention networks for document classification. In *Proceedings of the 2016 Conference of the North American Chapter of the Association for Computational Linguistics — Human Language Technologies (NAACL HLT 2016)*. San Diego, USA, pages 1480–1489.

Amy Zhang, Bryan Culbertson, and Praveen Paritosh. 2017. Characterizing online discussion using coarse discourse sequences. In *Proceedings of the 11th AAAI International Conference on Web and Social Media (ICWSM 2017)*. Palo Alto, USA, pages 357–366.

Named Entity Recognition with Stack Residual LSTM and Trainable Bias Decoding

Quan Tran, Andrew MacKinlay and **Antonio Jimeno Yepes**

IBM Research Australia

`hung.tran@monash.edu, admackin@au1.ibm.com, ayepes@au1.ibm.com`

Abstract

Recurrent Neural Network models are the state-of-the-art for Named Entity Recognition (NER). We present two innovations to improve the performance of these models. The first innovation is the introduction of residual connections between the Stacked Recurrent Neural Network model to address the degradation problem of deep neural networks. The second innovation is a bias decoding mechanism that allows the trained system to adapt to non-differentiable and externally computed objectives, such as the entity-based F-measure. Our work improves the state-of-the-art results for both Spanish and English languages on the standard train/development/test split of the CoNLL 2003 Shared Task NER dataset.

1 Introduction

In Natural Language Processing, the term "Named Entity" refers to special information units such as people, organizations, location names, numerical expression (Nadeau and Sekine, 2007). Identifying the references to these special entities in text is a crucial step toward Language Understanding. Thus, there have been many works on these areas.

Some of the early systems employed hand-crafted rules (Rau, 1991; Sekine and Nobata, 2004), however, the vast majority of current systems rely on machine learning models (Nadeau and Sekine, 2007) such as Conditional Random Field (CRF) (McCallum and Li, 2003), Hidden Markov Model (HMM) (Bikel et al., 1997) and Support Vector Machine (SVM) (Asahara and Matsumoto, 2003). Although the traditional machine learning models do not rely on manual rules, they require a manual feature engineering process, which is rather expensive and dependent on the domain and language.

In recent years, Recurrent Neural Network (RNN) models such as Long-Short-Term-Memory (LSTM) (Hochreiter and Schmidhuber, 1997) and Gated Recurrent Unit (GRU) (Chung et al., 2014) have been very successful in sequence modeling tasks, for example, Language Modeling (Mikolov et al., 2010; Sundermeyer et al., 2012), Machine Translation (Bahdanau et al., 2014) and Dialog Act Classification (Kalchbrenner and Blunsom, 2013; Tran et al., 2017). RNN models can learn from basic components of text (i.e. words and characters). This generalization capability facilitates the construction of Language Independent NER models (Ma and Hovy, 2016; Lample et al., 2016) that rely on unsupervised feature learning and a small annotated corpus.

One simple way of adding representational power to a neural network is layer stacking. A traditional feed forward neural network usually has three fully connected layers: an input layer, a hidden layer, and an output layer. For a Convolutional Neural Network (CNN) or Recurrent Neural Network, the number of stacked layers might be much larger (Amodei et al., 2016). One problem with this stacking scenario is the degraded representation problem (He et al., 2016). The proposed solution for this problem is the residual-identity connection (He et al., 2016). With the information from the lower-level inputs, the upper neural network layers can learn to compensate for the representation errors of lower layers. We adopt this idea for Stacking RNN, however, with a different implementation.

Most of the RNN-based models for NER and machine translation are trained with some form of maximum log-likelihood loss. However, it is often desirable to optimize task-specific metrics (Xu et al., 2016), for example, F-measure

Proceedings of the The 8th International Joint Conference on Natural Language Processing, pages 566–575,
Taipei, Taiwan, November 27 – December 1, 2017 ©2017 AFNLP

in NER, but optimizing the F-measure directly is not trivial (Busa-Fekete et al., 2015), especially in the case of complex Deep Neural Network models. It is even more difficult considering the way the F-measure is calculated in Named Entity Recognition in the CoNLL-2003 shared task[1] , where it depends on the actual/predicted entities and *not* on each token-prediction for which the system is trained for. Inspired by the idea of trainable decoding recently proposed in machine translation (Gu et al., 2017), we introduce a trainable *percentage bias decoding* system that manipulates the outputs of a base system trained with normal loss to adapt to a new objective. Our trainable bias decoding system also bears similarity to the thresholding technique (Lipton et al., 2014), traditionally used to maximize F-measures given a classifier. The proposed decoding system is trained directly on the externally computed F-measures (which relies on the the CoNLL evaluation script) using finite different gradient.

In the next sections, we describe the proposed innovations with detailed motivations and discussions. Results show that our proposed innovations improve the NER state-of-the-art for the English and Spanish languages in the CoNLL-2003 shared task data set.

2 Models

We describe first our RNN-CRF base architecture and then we describe our two modelling innovations: the Stack Residual RNN and the bias decoding.

2.1 The base RNN-CRF architecture

Our system is built upon the RNN-CRF architecture for Named Entity Recognition. Let us denote the input sequence of words as $w_0, ..., w_n$. In general, the RNN component encodes the words into a sequence of hidden vectors $h_0, ..., h_n$. This sequence of hidden vectors is then treated as features for a linear-chain CRF layer. The training objective will then be the log-likelihood of the correct sequence.

Following Lample et al. (2016); Ma and Hovy (2016); Yang et al. (2016), we employ the character level information and word-embeddings as features in NER. Similar to Lample et al. (2016), in our system, character information is encoded us-

ing a bi-directional RNN (biRNN) over characters. Given a word $w_k \in w_0, ..., w_n$ with m characters, let us denote the character-embedding sequence of this word as $\mathbf{c}_0, ..., \mathbf{c}_m$, the biRNN function as ρ and the concat function as ψ. The character embedding representation $\mathbf{h}_k^c$ of word w_k is calculated using a biRNN as in Equation 1, in which $\mathbf{f}_0, ..., \mathbf{f}_m$ and $\mathbf{b}_0, ..., \mathbf{b}_m$ denote the hidden units in the forward and backward RNNs respectively.

$$\mathbf{f}_0, ..., \mathbf{f}_m = \rho(\mathbf{c}_0, ..., \mathbf{c}_m)$$
$$\mathbf{b}_0, ..., \mathbf{b}_m = \rho(\mathbf{c}_m, ..., \mathbf{c}_0) \qquad (1)$$
$$\mathbf{h}_k^c = \psi([\mathbf{f}_m, \mathbf{b}_m])$$

The feature vector $\mathbf{x}_k$ of word w_k is then the concatenation of $\mathbf{h}_k^c$ and the traditional word-embedding $\mathbf{e}_k$ as shown in Equation 2. Figure 1 shows the feature extraction procedures. All the parameters of the biRNN as well as the embedding tables are jointly trained with other component of the model. The word embedding table is initialized with a pre-trained embedding table.

$$\mathbf{x}_k = \psi([\mathbf{h}_k^c, \mathbf{e}_k]) \qquad (2)$$

The most simple architecture would be a one-directional RNN over the word features: $h_0, ..., h_n = RNN(x_0, ..., x_n)$. However, it has been shown to be beneficial to have a bidirectional RNN over the input layer, as a bidirectional RNN captures both the left and the right context of a word: $h_0, ..., h_n = \rho(x_0, ..., x_n)$.

The final sequence of hidden vectors $\mathbf{h}_0, ..., \mathbf{h}_n$ is treated as the features for a linear-chained CRF layer. Similar to Lample et al. (2016), the observation scores λ are calculated with a linear transformation from the hidden vectors, as show in Equation 3, where λ_i is the vector observation scores for all the labels in ith time-step, $\mathbf{W}_p$ is an $l \times d$ weight matrix, and $\mathbf{b}_p$ is a bias vector of size l (with d is the size of vector $\mathbf{h}_i$), and l is the size of the label set $\mathbb{Y}$ (including the special sequence begin and end labels).

$$\lambda_i = \mathbf{W}_p \mathbf{h}_i + \mathbf{b}_p \qquad (3)$$

Given a sequence of input words $S = w_0, ..., w_n$, the score of a particular sequence of labels $Y = Y[0], ..., Y[n]$ is calculated using the observation scores λ and the transition scores δ as in Equation 4, where δ is a square matrix of dimension $l \times l$, $\delta(Y[j], Y[j+1])$ denotes the transition

---

[1] https://www.aclweb.org/aclwiki/index.php?title=CONLL-2003_(State_of_the_art)

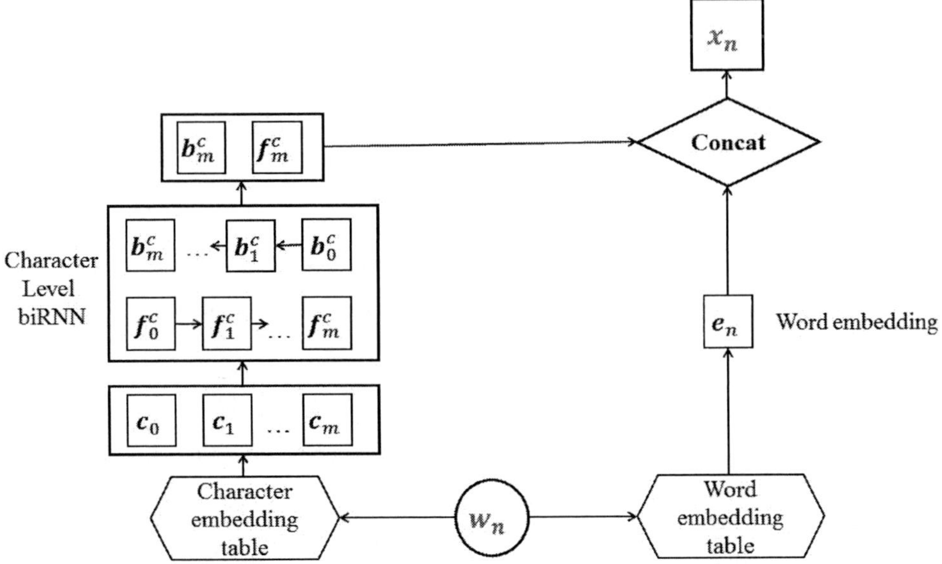

Figure 1: Extracting word features with word embeddings and character level biRNN

score between the label in position j and the label in position $j + 1$ in sequence Y, and $\lambda_i(Y[i])$ is the observation score of i-th label $Y[i]$.

$$\zeta(Y, S) = \sum_{i:[0..n]} \lambda_i(Y[i]),$$
$$+ \sum_{j:[0..n-1]} \delta(Y[j], Y[j+1]) \tag{4}$$

The probability of a sequence Y is calculated using a softmax over all the possible sequences $\mathbb{Y}$ (Equation 5).

$$Pr(Y|S) = \frac{e^{\zeta(Y,S)}}{\sum_{\bar{Y} \in \mathbb{Y}} e^{\zeta(\bar{Y},S)}} \tag{5}$$

During training, we maximize the log-likelihood of the correct sequence Y_c. The loss function $\mathbb{L}$ is defined in Equation 6. Because we employ a linear-chain CRF, the term $log(\sum_{\bar{Y} \in \mathbb{Y}} e^{\zeta(\bar{Y},S)})$ in Equation 6 can be efficiently calculated with dynamic programming.

$$\mathbb{L}(Y_c) = \zeta(Y_c, S) - log(\sum_{\bar{Y} \in \mathbb{Y}} e^{\zeta(\bar{Y},S)}) \tag{6}$$

During decoding, the best sequence can be found using the Viterbi algorithm. The original Viterbi decoding algorithm builds an $l \times n$ score

table ξ in which l is the size of the label set (including the beginning and end labels) and n is the length of the sequence. $\xi_j(y_i)$ denotes the score of the most probable partial path (up to position j) with position j having the label y_i. $\xi_j(y_i)$ is calculated using dynamic programming as in Equation 7.

$$\xi_j(y_i) = \sum_{y_k \in \mathbb{Y}} (\xi_{j-1}(y_k) + \delta(y_k, y_i)) + \lambda_j(y_i) \tag{7}$$

At the end of the decoding process, sequence $\hat{Y}$ is predicted by selecting the best score at the end of the sequence $j = n$ and then completing the sequence with a backward pointer (Equation 8). Figure 3 depicts the whole RNN-CRF architecture

$$\hat{Y}[n] = \arg\max_{y_i} \xi_n(y_i)$$
$$\hat{Y}[n-1] = \arg\max_{y_k}(\xi_{j-1}(y_k) + \delta(y_k, \hat{Y}[n]))$$
$$\tag{8}$$

2.2 Stacked Residual RNN

A traditional way of adding more representational power to a neural network is layer stacking. RNN stacking has been successfully used in a lot of works (Amodei et al., 2016). However, stacking

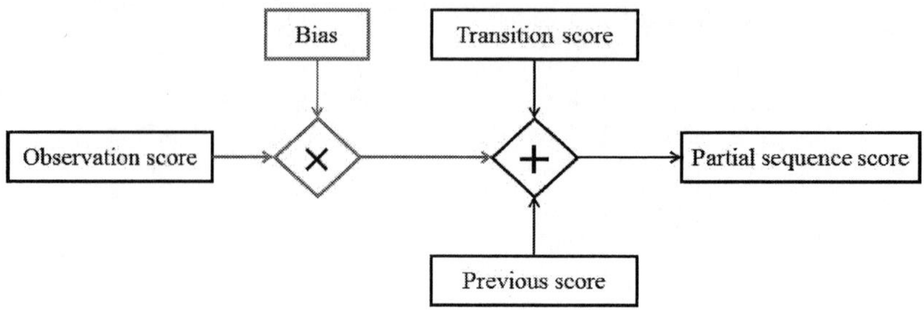

Figure 2: The application of percentage bias to Viterbi decoding

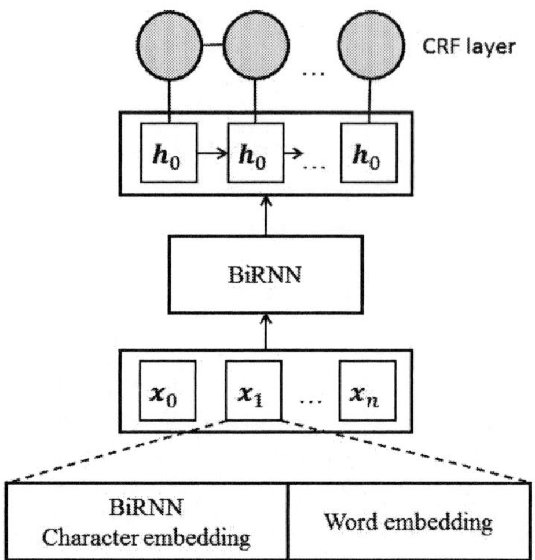

Figure 3: The RNN-CRF architecture

layers of neural networks suffers from the *degradation problem* (He et al., 2016). This is due to the difficulty in training a lot of stacked layers and fit these layers to desired underlying mappings, which leads to representational degradation.

The solution proposed to this problem, the *residual connection* (He et al., 2016; Prakash et al., 2016) tries to create shortcuts between non-consecutive layers. However, the original additional residual connection (adding the input vector to the hidden representation) adds several constraints on the dimensionality of the hidden and input layers, which might require vector clipping (Prakash et al., 2016), and it might lead to a loss of information.

In the original residual connection proposed for image recognition, the residual information is summed to the output of the upper layers ($\mathbb{F}(x) + x$). In our proposal, we want the upper layer of a neural network to have direct access to the original input, thus, the original input is now appended to the output of the lower layers instead of being

summed. With this formulation, there is no dimensionality restriction, and furthermore, we argue that our proposed residual connection can be used to mix feature learners of different complexity (Figure 4). For example, when equipped with our proposed residual connection, the top neural network layer can act like a shallow one-layer feature learner. The two top layers can act like a deeper two-layer feature learner. Equation set 9 shows the exact formulation of our proposed residual connection within the Stack RNN. Similar to the Equation 1, we denote the biRNN function as ρ and the concat function as ψ. This modelling procedure is depicted in Figure 4.

$$
\begin{aligned}
\mathbf{h}_0^0, ..., \mathbf{h}_n^0 &= \rho(\mathbf{x}_0, ..., \mathbf{x}_n) \\
\hat{\mathbf{h}}_0^0, ..., \hat{\mathbf{h}}_n^0 &= \psi([\mathbf{x}_0, \mathbf{h}_0^0]), ..., \psi([\mathbf{h}_n^0, \mathbf{x}_n]) \\
\mathbf{h}_0^1, ..., \mathbf{h}_n^1 &= \rho(\hat{\mathbf{h}}_0^0, ..., \hat{\mathbf{h}}_n^0) \\
\mathbf{h}_0^M, ..., \mathbf{h}_n^M &= \rho(\hat{\mathbf{h}}_0^{M-1}, ..., \hat{\mathbf{h}}_n^{M-1})
\end{aligned}
\tag{9}
$$

2.3 The bias decoding

Usually NER systems are evaluated with some form of F-measure. For example, for the CoNLL 2013 Shared Task NER dataset, the evaluation is performed by an external script using entity-based F1-measure. Although it has been noted that training on the evaluation metric is beneficial (Xu et al., 2016), most of the deep models for NER are trained with log-likelihood. The main reason for this discrepancy is the difficulty in training with F-measures. Instead of trying to train on F-measure directly, we look into a hybrid solution where we train a model on log-likelihood first, and then use a simpler "adaptation model" to manipulate the output of the base model to fit it to the F-measure.

Inspired by Machine Translation research on decoding with trainable noise (Gu et al., 2017), we

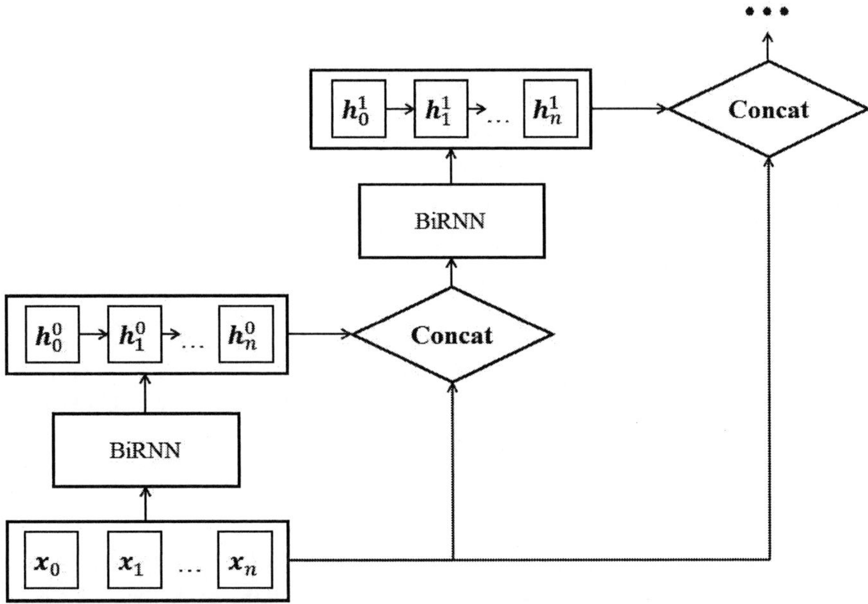

Figure 4: Feature learner mixture with residual connection

explore the possibility of adding trainable noise to the Viterbi decoding process. Analogously to the traditional threshold technique for maximizing the F1 score in binary classification, we introduce a simple *percentage noise* to the decoding process. That is, during the construction of the score table ξ (Equation 7), a label-specific percentage bias is added to the calculation as in Equation 10. Figure 2 shows the application of this bias to the Viterbi decoding.

$$\xi_j(y_i) = \sum_{y_k \in \mathbb{Y}} \left(\xi_{j-1}(y_k) + \delta(y_k, y_i) \right) + b_y \lambda_j(y_i)$$

(10)

To test this new percentage bias idea, we perform a quick experiment, where we limit the use of bias to the most numerous class in the CoNLL tag set, class O (words that do not belong to any entity). We search for the best bias b_O from the range of $[0.5, 1.5]$ using a value loop with step of 0.1. For each value of b_O, we calculate the F1-measure on the validation set, and choose the value with the highest F1. We use our trained model based on the Stack Residual architecture above as the base probabilistic model. We find that the best b_O value is 1.1 (a value of 1.0 means without any bias). Using this b_O bias for the test data yields

the F1-measures of 91.22 compared to the original score of 91.07 in the test set. This experiment supports our claim that the base model trained with log-likelihood might not optimize well on a different performance measure, and adding this percentage bias noise is really beneficial.

We extended this idea treating the biases as parameters. Thus the trainable bias decoding system has the number of parameters equal to the number of classes. Training with gradient descent with CoNLL's entity-based F1 loss is rather difficult, as it is hard to calculate the exact gradient. This is solved using the numerical gradient methods as an approximation, which is shown in Equation 11.

$$f_b' \sim \frac{f(b + \epsilon) - f(b - \epsilon)}{2\epsilon}$$

(11)

The training procedure is then very similar to stochastic gradient descent. Details on the choice of hyper parameters and other experimental settings are presented in the Experiment section.

3 Experiments

3.1 Dataset and Experimental settings

We have prepared and evaluated the proposed methods on the English and Spanish sets of the CoNLL 2003 NER data set[2] (Tjong Kim Sang and De Meulder, 2003). We have reused the training, development and test set configuration of the CoNLL-2003 Shared Task in our study.

The training set has been used to train the system using several hyperparameter configurations, the development set has been used to select the best configuration and the reported performance of the final system is based on the test set. The Spanish dataset has 8323/1915/1517 sentences in train/dev/test sets respectively. The English dataset is almost twice as large with 14041/3250/3453 sentences in train/dev/test set. For all of our models, the word-embedding size is set to 100 for English and 64 for Spanish. The hidden vector size is 100 for both English and Spanish sets without the LM embeddings. With the LM embeddings, the hidden vector size is changed to 300 for English. We trained the model with Stochastic Gradient Descent (SGD) with momentum, using the learning rate of 0.005. For the bias decoding, the ϵ hyperparameter for each update is randomly chosen from a range of $[0.01, ..., 0.1]$ with step-size of 0.01. Because the base model trained with sequence level log-likelihood fits very well on the training set, the gradient calculated with Equation 11 might be every small, thus we opt to calculate the finite difference with respect to the loss: $log2(1 - F1/100)$ instead of the $F1$ to boost the gradient information in the points where F1 is very close to 100 (perfect classification). The learning rate for bias training is also set to 0.005. Statistical significance has been determined using a randomization version of the paired sample t-test (Cohen, 1996).

We first conduct several series of experiments to confirm the effectiveness of our two proposed ideas: the Stack Residual RNN and the bias decoding, and the new Language Model embedding in sub-section 3.2. The second sub-section: 3.4 compares our method with state-of-the-art results.

3.2 Component Analysis

Adding stack Residual RNN

Due to computational complexity, there is a practical limit on how many RNN layers we can stack. In this series of experiment, we tested our model without Stacked Residual RNN, and with 2, 3 and 4 Stacked layers. The word embeddings are initialized using the pre-trained word vectors de-

scribed below. The result of this series of experiements is presented in Table 1.

From the result, we can see that the performance seems to increase as we add more stacked layers, and peak at three before dropping. We continue to analyze other components using 3 Stacked Residual Layers of CRF-RNN as the base model, we call this model *3 Res-RNN* for short.

For English, the 3 and 4 stacked layer improvements are significant ($p < 0.025$) compared to the baseline model and between the stacked layer models, the improvement between 2 and 3 layers is significant ($p < 0.035$).

For Spanish, the 3 stacked layer improvement is significant ($p < 0.03$), with respect to the baseline model. Improvement between the 3 stacked layer and the 4 stacked layer models is significant ($p < 0.03$).

Adding Language Model Embedding

Pre-trained word embeddings have shown useful in Natural Language Processing tasks, but provide information about the word but not about its context. Previous work has explored using language models in addition to word embeddings (Peters et al., 2017) with positive results. We have evaluated our system using pre-trained language models using the 3 Stacked Residual Layer configuration. First, we test the models with forward-only LM embeddings (foreLM), then we test the model with both forward and backLM (backLM). The result of this series of experiments is presented in Table 2.

The gain from the LM embedding is not consistent. It seems to work very well with English, where it improves performance substantially even though this improvement is not specially significant. However, the LM does not improve the performance at all in Spanish. Adding the foreLM and backLM significantly decreases performance.

Adding Bias Decoding

We test the bias decoding on models with and without LM embeddings, with results shown in Table 3. The bias-decoding increases the performance across the board, however the performance increases are not consistent. The increases are notable on some cases (3 Res-RNN + bias on both English and Spanish, 3 Res-RNN + foreLM + backLM + bias for Spanish), while in some cases the increases are minimal (3 Res-RNN + foreLM + bias on both English and Spanish, 3 Res-RNN + foreLM + backLM + bias on English).

---

[2]http://www.cnts.ua.ac.be/conll2003/ner

System	F1 English	F1 Spanish
CRF-RNN no Stack Residual	90.43	85.41
CRF-RNN 2 Stack Residual	90.72	85.88
CRF-RNN 3 Stack Residual	**91.07** $\star$	**86.24** $\star$
CRF-RNN 4 Stack Residual	91.02 $\star$	85.51

Table 1: Analysis of the Stack Residual Component. $\star$ indicates significance ($p < 0.05$) versus CRF-RNN no Stack Residual.

System	F1 English	F1 Spanish
3 Res-RNN	91.07 $\star$	**86.24** $\star$
3 Res-RNN+foreLM	91.43 $\star$	86.13 $\star$
3 Res-RNN+foreLM +backLM	**91.66** $\star$	85.83

Table 2: Analysis of the Language Model Embedding. $\star$ indicates significance ($p < 0.05$) versus CRF-RNN no Stack Residual in Table 1.

For English, adding bias to the 3 Res-RNN without LM yields a significant improvement ($p < 0.013$), while for Spanish, the boost from adding bias to the 3 Res-RNN + foreLM + backLM model is significant ($p < 0.011$).

3.3 External Knowledge Learning

3.3.1 Word embedding

English word embedding was obtained from Word2vec-api[3]. The embedding dimension is 100 and it was trained using GloVe with AdaGrad. For the generation of Spanish word embeddings we followed Lample et al. (2016), using Spanish Gigaword Third Edition[4] as corpus with an embedding dimension of 64, a minimum word frequency cutoff of 4 and a window size of 8.

3.3.2 Language Modeling

In some experiments, we used both forward and backward language models. The English forward language model was obtained from TensorFlow[5] using the One Billion Word Benchmark[6] (Chelba et al., 2013) and has a perplexity of 30. As the code generating this pre-trained model is not available, we made use of a substitute which produces a higher perplexity language model. For the backward English language model and the Spanish forward and backward ones, they were generated using an LSTM based baseline[7] (Jozefowicz

et al., 2016). This code estimates a forward language model and was adapted to estimate a backward language model. Language models were estimated using the One Billion Word benchmark. The vocabulary for the backward English model is the same as the pre-generated forward model. The perplexity for estimated backward English language model is 46; despite the discrepancy in perplexity with the forward language model the performance using this language model still improves the named entity recognition task. The vocabulary for the Spanish language models was generated using tokens with frequency > 2. The perplexity for the forward and backward Spanish language models are 56 and 57 respectively.

3.4 Comparative performance

Table 4 shows the performance of our best systems compared to the state-of-the-art results on ConLL dataset. We focus our comparison to the systems with the same experimental setups (standard train/val/test split, without the use of external label data). The best previous systems (Ma and Hovy, 2016; Lample et al., 2016) are based upon a similar architecture (CRF-RNN) to ours. Lample et al. (2016) employed LSTM for character-based embedding, while Ma and Hovy (2016) employed CNN for character-based embedding[8]. Overall, we achieve state-of-the-art results on both English and Spanish.

---

[3]https://github.com/3Top/word2vec-api/blob/master/README.md

[4]https://catalog.ldc.upenn.edu/ldc2011t12

[5]https://github.com/tensorflow/models/tree/master/lm_1b

[6]https://github.com/ciprian-chelba/1-billion-word-language-modeling-benchmark

[7]https://github.com/rafaljozefowicz/lm

[8]There are several other works reporting very strong result on English NER: Chiu et al. (91.62) (2015), Yang et al. (91.20) (2016) and Peter et al.(91.93) (2017), however, these results are not comparable to ours due to the difference in experimental setup (Ma and Hovy, 2016).

System	F1 on English	F1 on Spanish
3 Res-RNN	91.07 $\star$	86.24$\star$
3 Res-RNN + foreLM	91.43 $\star$	86.13$\star$
3 Res-RNN + foreLM + backLM	91.66 $\star$	85.83
3 Res-RNN + bias	91.23 $\star\dagger$	**86.31** $\star$
3 Res-RNN + foreLM + bias	91.45 $\star$	86.14 $\star$
3 Res-RNN + foreLM + backLM + bias	**91.69** $\star$	86.00 $\star\dagger$

Table 3: Analysis of the bias decoding. $\star$ indicates significance ($p < 0.05$) versus CRF-RNN no Stack Residual in Table 1. $\dagger$ indicates significance versus the configuration with no bias.

System	F1 on English	F1 on Spanish
CRF-RNN no Stack Residual	90.43	85.41
(Passos et al., 2014)	90.05	–
(dos Santos and Guimarães, 2015)	–	82.21
(Gillick et al., 2016)	84.57	81.83
(Lample et al., 2016)	90.94	85.75
(Ma and Hovy, 2016)	91.21	–
3 Res-RNN + bias	91.23	**86.31**
3 Res-RNN + foreLM + bias	91.45	86.14
3 Res-RNN + foreLM + backLM + bias	**91.69**	86.00

Table 4: Compare our model with systems with comparable experimental settings

4 Discussion

Overall, our model achieves the state-of-the-arts for both English and Spanish Named Entity Recognition. For Spanish, our base model with three layers of Stacked Residual RNN already outperforms the current state-of-the-art.

From the results above, we can see that our innovations, the Stacked Residual connection and bias decoding consistently improve the performance across both data sets. However, the improvements from bias decoding is somewhat small in some models. The numerical gradient for training is noisy, and sometimes the SGD process might take several epochs to find an improvement on the development set. This happens especially on the English dataset because the base model trained with sequence level log-likelihood fits very well on the training set. Even with the boosting trick presented during the Experiments section, the training is still very slow. At first, we expected that the biases might give us some ideas about the trade-off between precision and recall similar to the thresholding technique for binary classification, i.e. the based log-likelihood model might favors precision or recall. However, from the analysis of the biases, we found no obvious trends favoring precision or recall.

Interestingly, the Language Model embeddings seem to have opposite effects on Spanish and English. While it is very helpful in English, it only degrades the performance for Spanish. The English LMs also improve convergence rate, while it is the opposite for Spanish. We attribute this difference in the quality of the Language Model involved. For English, the LMs are arguably better, with much lower perplexities than the LMs for Spanish. The Spanish models also have less data to train with, and it might affect the performance.

5 Conclusions and Future Work

We have explored two innovations over the baseline CRF-RNN model for sequence classification: the Stacked Residual Connection, and bias decoding. With these two improvements, it is possible to achieve state-of-the-art performance in Named Entity Recognition for both English and Spanish.

As future work, we will further investigate trainable bias decoding, and try to solve the problems presented. As the methods presented are general and language/domain independent, we plan to apply it to other domains such as health-care and expand the applications beyond NER.

References

Dario Amodei, Sundaram Ananthanarayanan, Rishita Anubhai, Jingliang Bai, Eric Battenberg, Carl Case, Jared Casper, Bryan Catanzaro, Qiang Cheng, Guoliang Chen, et al. 2016. Deep speech 2: End-to-end speech recognition in english and mandarin. In *International Conference on Machine Learning*. pages 173–182.

Masayuki Asahara and Yuji Matsumoto. 2003. Japanese named entity extraction with redundant morphological analysis. In *Proceedings of the 2003 Conference of the North American Chapter of the Association for Computational Linguistics on Human Language Technology-Volume 1*. Association for Computational Linguistics, pages 8–15.

Dzmitry Bahdanau, Kyunghyun Cho, and Yoshua Bengio. 2014. Neural machine translation by jointly learning to align and translate. *arXiv preprint arXiv:1409.0473* .

Daniel M Bikel, Scott Miller, Richard Schwartz, and Ralph Weischedel. 1997. Nymble: a high-performance learning name-finder. In *Proceedings of the fifth conference on Applied natural language processing*. Association for Computational Linguistics, pages 194–201.

Robert Busa-Fekete, Baiázs Szörényi, Krzysztof Dembczyński, and Eyke Hüllermeier. 2015. Online f-measure optimization. In *Proceedings of the 28th International Conference on Neural Information Processing Systems*. MIT Press, Cambridge, MA, USA, NIPS'15, pages 595–603.

Ciprian Chelba, Tomas Mikolov, Mike Schuster, Qi Ge, Thorsten Brants, Phillipp Koehn, and Tony Robinson. 2013. One billion word benchmark for measuring progress in statistical language modeling. *arXiv preprint arXiv:1312.3005* .

Jason PC Chiu and Eric Nichols. 2015. Named entity recognition with bidirectional lstm-cnns. *arXiv preprint arXiv:1511.08308* .

Junyoung Chung, Caglar Gulcehre, KyungHyun Cho, and Yoshua Bengio. 2014. Empirical evaluation of gated recurrent neural networks on sequence modeling. *arXiv preprint arXiv:1412.3555* .

Paul R Cohen. 1996. Empirical methods for artificial intelligence. *IEEE Intelligent Systems* (6):88.

Cícero Nogueira dos Santos and Victor Guimarães. 2015. Boosting named entity recognition with neural character embeddings. *CoRR* abs/1505.05008.

Dan Gillick, Cliff Brunk, Oriol Vinyals, and Amarnag Subramanya. 2016. Multilingual language processing from bytes. In *Proceedings of the 2016 Conference of the North American Chapter of the Association for Computational Linguistics: Human Language Technologies*. Association for Computational Linguistics, San Diego, California, pages 1296–1306.

Jiatao Gu, Kyunghyun Cho, and Victor OK Li. 2017. Trainable greedy decoding for neural machine translation. *arXiv preprint arXiv:1702.02429* .

Kaiming He, Xiangyu Zhang, Shaoqing Ren, and Jian Sun. 2016. Deep residual learning for image recognition. In *Proceedings of the IEEE Conference on Computer Vision and Pattern Recognition*. pages 770–778.

Sepp Hochreiter and Jürgen Schmidhuber. 1997. Long short-term memory. *Neural computation* 9(8):1735–1780.

Rafal Jozefowicz, Oriol Vinyals, Mike Schuster, Noam Shazeer, and Yonghui Wu. 2016. Exploring the limits of language modeling. *arXiv preprint arXiv:1602.02410* .

Nal Kalchbrenner and Phil Blunsom. 2013. Recurrent convolutional neural networks for discourse compositionality. *arXiv preprint arXiv:1306.3584* .

Guillaume Lample, Miguel Ballesteros, Sandeep Subramanian, Kazuya Kawakami, and Chris Dyer. 2016. Neural architectures for named entity recognition. In *Proceedings of the 2016 Conference of the North American Chapter of the Association for Computational Linguistics: Human Language Technologies*. Association for Computational Linguistics, San Diego, California, pages 260–270.

Zachary C Lipton, Charles Elkan, and Balakrishnan Naryanaswamy. 2014. Optimal thresholding of classifiers to maximize f1 measure. In *Joint European Conference on Machine Learning and Knowledge Discovery in Databases*. Springer, pages 225–239.

Xuezhe Ma and Eduard Hovy. 2016. End-to-end sequence labeling via bi-directional lstm-cnns-crf. *arXiv preprint arXiv:1603.01354* .

Andrew McCallum and Wei Li. 2003. Early results for named entity recognition with conditional random fields, feature induction and web-enhanced lexicons. In *Proceedings of the seventh conference on Natural language learning at HLT-NAACL 2003-Volume 4*. Association for Computational Linguistics, pages 188–191.

Tomas Mikolov, Martin Karafiát, Lukas Burget, Jan Cernocký, and Sanjeev Khudanpur. 2010. Recurrent neural network based language model. In *Interspeech*. volume 2, page 3.

David Nadeau and Satoshi Sekine. 2007. A survey of named entity recognition and classification. *Lingvisticae Investigationes* 30(1):3–26.

Alexandre Passos, Vineet Kumar, and Andrew McCallum. 2014. Lexicon infused phrase embeddings for named entity resolution. *arXiv preprint arXiv:1404.5367* .

Matthew E Peters, Waleed Ammar, Chandra Bhagavatula, and Russell Power. 2017. Semi-supervised sequence tagging with bidirectional language models. *arXiv preprint arXiv:1705.00108* .

Aaditya Prakash, Sadid A Hasan, Kathy Lee, Vivek Datla, Ashequl Qadir, Joey Liu, and Oladimeji Farri. 2016. Neural paraphrase generation with stacked residual lstm networks. *arXiv preprint arXiv:1610.03098* .

Lisa F Rau. 1991. Extracting company names from text. In *Artificial Intelligence Applications, 1991. Proceedings., Seventh IEEE Conference on*. IEEE, volume 1, pages 29–32.

Satoshi Sekine and Chikashi Nobata. 2004. Definition, dictionaries and tagger for extended named entity hierarchy. In *LREC*. pages 1977–1980.

Martin Sundermeyer, Ralf Schlüter, and Hermann Ney. 2012. Lstm neural networks for language modeling. In *Interspeech*. pages 194–197.

Erik F Tjong Kim Sang and Fien De Meulder. 2003. Introduction to the conll-2003 shared task: Language-independent named entity recognition. In *Proceedings of the seventh conference on Natural language learning at HLT-NAACL 2003-Volume 4*. Association for Computational Linguistics, pages 142–147.

Quan Hung Tran, Ingrid Zukerman, and Gholamreza Haffari. 2017. A hierarchical neural model for learning sequences of dialogue acts. In *Proceedings of the 15th Conference of the European Chapter of the Association for Computational Linguistics: Volume 1, Long Papers*. Association for Computational Linguistics, Valencia, Spain, pages 428–437.

Wenduan Xu, Michael Auli, and Stephen Clark. 2016. Expected f-measure training for shift-reduce parsing with recurrent neural networks. In *Proceedings of the 2016 Conference of the North American Chapter of the Association for Computational Linguistics: Human Language Technologies*. Association for Computational Linguistics, San Diego, California, pages 210–220.

Zhilin Yang, Ruslan Salakhutdinov, and William Cohen. 2016. Multi-task cross-lingual sequence tagging from scratch. *arXiv preprint arXiv:1603.06270* .

Neuramanteau: A Neural Network Ensemble Model for Lexical Blends

Kollol Das
kolloldas@gmail.com
Independent Researcher
Bangalore, India

Shaona Ghosh
sg811@cam.ac.uk
University of Cambridge
Department of Engineering,
Cambridge, UK

Abstract

The problem of blend formation in generative linguistics is interesting in the context of neologism, their quick adoption in modern life and the creative generative process guiding their formation. Blend quality depends on multitude of factors with high degrees of uncertainty. In this work, we investigate if the modern neural network models can sufficiently capture and recognize the creative blend composition process. We propose recurrent neural network sequence-to-sequence models, that are evaluated on multiple blend datasets available in the literature. We propose an ensemble neural and hybrid model that outperforms most of the baselines and heuristic models upon evaluation on test data.

1 Introduction

Blending is the formation and intentional coinage of new words from existing two or more words (Gries, 2004). These are called neologisms. Neologisms effectively trace changing cultures and addition of new technologies. Blending is one way to create a neologism. A lexical blend is formed by combining parts of two or more words. Predicting a high quality lexical blend is often unpredictable due to the uncertainty in the formal structure of blends (Beliaeva, 2014). Merging source words `digital` and `camera`, the common expectation is the blend `digamera`, although, in practice, `digicam` is more common (Beliaeva, 2014). There are multiple unknown factors such as phonology, semantics, familiarity, recognizability and lexical creativity that contribute to blend formation. Some downstream applications that can leverage such

Word$_1$	Word$_2$	Blend	Structure	Category	Coverage
aviation	electronics	avionics	avi-onics	Prefix + Suffix	16.74%
communicate	fake	communifake	communi-fake	Prefix + Word	10.78%
speak	typo	speako	speak-o	Word + Letter	0.14%
west	indiea	windies	w-indies	Letter + Word	0.89%
point	broadcast	pointcast	point-cast	Word + Suffix	22.56%
scientific	fiction	scientifiction	scienti-fic-tion	Word + Word overlap	22.56%
affluence	influenza	affluenza	af-fluen-za	Prefix + Suffix overlap	13.98%
brad	angelina	brangelina	br-a-ngelina	Prefix + Word overlap	11.39%
subvert	advertising	subvertising	sub-vert-ising	Word + Suffix overlap	16.31%

Table 1: Sample blends in our dataset along with the type and coverage. There are other types of rare blends that is beyond the scope of this work.

blending systems include generating names of products, brands, businesses and advertisements to name a few especially if coupled with contextual information about the business or sector.

1.1 Related Work

Blends are compositional words consisting of whole word and a splinter (part of morpheme) or two splinters (Lehrer, 2007). The creative neologism of blend formation has been studied by linguists in an attempt to recognize patterns in the process that model human lexical creativity or to identify source words and blend meaning, context and influence. With the popularity of deep neural networks (DNN)s (LeCun et al., 2015), we are interested in the question if neural network models of learning can be leveraged in a generative capacity, that can sufficiently explore or formalize the process of blend formation. Blends can be formed in several closely related morphologically productive ways as shown in Table 1. Our work targets blends that are ordered combinations of prefixes of first word and suffixes of the second word. Examples include, `avionics` (prefix + suffix), `vaporware` (word + suffix), `robocop` (prefix + word), `carmageddon` (overlap). Several theories have been forwarded as to the structure and mechanism of blending (Gries, 2012), without much consensus (Shaw et al., 2014). Most

Proceedings of the The 8th International Joint Conference on Natural Language Processing, pages 576–583,
Taipei, Taiwan, November 27 – December 1, 2017 ©2017 AFNLP

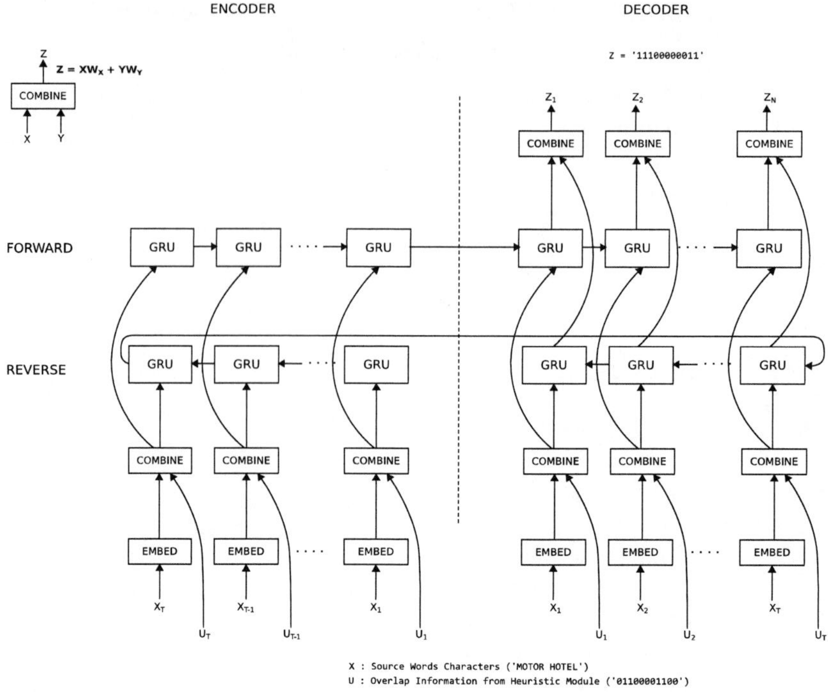

Figure 1: Architectural diagram of the bidirectional hybrid encoder decoder model.

implementation work in blenders and generators is quite sparse in the literature and mainly concern explicit blending of vector embeddings.

Naive implementations of generators exist on the internet [1][2][3], that are simply lists of all possible blend combinations. Some other work is based on greedy heuristics for better results [4][5]. Andrew et. Al (2014) built a statistical word blender as a part of a password generator. Ozbal (2012) uses a combination of edit distances and phonetic metrics and Pilichowski (2013) also uses a similar technique. Our work empirically captures some of these mechanisms from blend datasets used in the literature using neural networks. Numerous studies on deterministic rules for blend formation (Kelly, 1998; Gries, 2004, 2006, 2012; Bauer, 2012) do not find consensus on the blending process mainly due to the 'human factor' involved in designing rules.

The closest work of using novel multitape Finite State Transducers (FST) for blend creation is in work by Deri et. al. (2015). Our model is a neural model, different from the multitape FST model. The multitape FST model is similar to our baseline heuristic model with which we compare our neural model proposed in this paper. The primary benefit of our model is that it attempts to arrive at a consensus among various neural experts in the generative process of new blend creation.

1.2 Contributions

We summarize the main contributions of our work as follows:

1. We propose an ensemble neural network model to learn the compositional lexical blends from two given source words.

2. We generalize the problem of lexical blending by leveraging the character based sequence-to-sequence hybrid bidirectional models in order to predict the blends.

3. We release a blending dataset and demo of our neural blend generator along with open

---

[1] http://www.dcode.fr/word-contraction-generator

[2] http://werdmerge.com/

[3] http://www.portmanteaur.com/

[4] https://www.namerobot.com/namerobot/name-generators/name-factory/merger.html

[5] http://www.namemesh.com/company-name-generator

source software

2 Neural Lexical Blending Model

2.1 Sequence-to-sequence Models

Sequence-to-Sequence (Seq2Seq) neural network models (Sutskever et al., 2014), are a generalization of the recurrent neural network (RNN) sequence learning (Cho et al., 2014) paradigm, where a source sequence $x_1, \ldots, x_n$ is mapped to a fixed sized vector using a RNN often serving as the encoder, and another RNN is used to map the vector to the target sequence $y_1, \ldots, y_n$, functioning as the decoder. However, RNNs struggle to train on long term dependencies sufficiently; and therefore, Long Short Term Memory Models (LSTM) and Gated Recurrent Units (GRUs)(Cho et al., 2014) are more common for such sequence to sequence learning.

2.2 Bidirectional Seq2Seq Model

We propose a bidirectional forward and reverse GRU encoder-decoder model for our lexical blends. To this end, both the encoder and the decoder are bidirectional, i.e. they see the ordered input source words both in the forward direction and the backward direction. The motivation here is that in order to sufficiently capture the splinter point, there should be dependency on the neighbouring characters in both directions. Figure 1 shows the bidirectional Seq2Seq model that we propose. Since we have two source words for every blend, that is a sequence of characters, the input to our model has the source words concatenated with a space and padding to align to the longest concatenated example. For example in Figure 1, the source words `work` and `alcoholic` are concatenated as `cilohocla krow` and `work alcoholic` for the encoder and decoder respectively, which subsequently gets reversed to `work alcoholic` and `cilohocla krow` for the reverse encoder and decoder units. The representation of a sequence of characters in the input pair of source words is the concatenation of the fixed dimensional character to vector representations. The model's prediction corresponding to the two source words in the input, is the order preserving binary output $\{\hat{y}_t = \{0,1\}|x_t \in y_t\}$ for model prediction $\hat{y}$, ground truth target y and concatenated source input pair $x = (x_1, ..., x_T)$. For example, if x is `work alcoholic` with-

out padding, the prediction on the blended word is 11110000111111 for the target `workoholic`. The order is enforced implicitly in the concatenated inputs. The indices that are predicted 1 are for the characters in the concatenated input that are included in the blend.

The forward and reverse hidden states h_t^f and h_t^r of the encoder at time t is given by:

$$h_t^f = GRU_{enc}^f \left(h_{t-1}^f, x_{t_r} \right) \tag{1}$$

$$h_t^r = GRU_{enc}^r \left(h_{t+1}^r, x_{t_r} \right) \tag{2}$$

where GRU_{enc}^f and GRU_{enc}^r stand for forward and reverse GRU encoder units described by (Cho et al., 2014) and $t_r = T - t + 1$. Similarly, the forward y^f and reverse y^r intermediate outputs of the decoder are given by:

$$y_t^f = GRU_{dec}^f \left(y_{t-1}^f, x_t \right) \tag{3}$$

$$y_t^r = GRU_{dec}^r \left(y_{t+1}^r, x_t \right) \tag{4}$$

where $y_0^f = h_T^f$ and $y_{T+1}^r = h_1^r$. The final decoder output is the result of applying smooth non-linear sigmoid transformation to the GRU outputs

$$z_t^j = \sigma \left(W_f y_t^f + U_r y_t^r \right) \tag{5}$$

z is character wise probability of inclusion in the blend. We apply sigmoid loss on z for training.

2.3 Ensemble Hybrid Bidirectional Seq2Seq Model

We propose an ensemble model of our vanilla bidirectional encoder decoder model discussed in Section 2.2 in order to capture different representations of the source word, hidden state and a variety of blends. Blends can be inherently varying in structure of the blend formation resulting in multiple possible blend candidates. Each member or an expert in our ensemble model has the same underlying architecture as described in Section 2.2 and in Figure 1. However, the experts in the ensemble do not share the model parameters, the motivation being able to capture a wider range of parameter values thus tackling the variations and multiplicity in the blending process adequately. Further, there is a subjective and qualitative nature of the blend formation process that leads to naturally consider ensemble predictions with the notion that

578

Dataset	No. of Examples	No. of Overlaps
Wiktionary	2854	1379
Train	2140 (75%)	
Validation	428 (15%)	
Test	286 (10%)	
Test + Validation with overlaps	319	319
Test + Validation no overlaps	395	0
Cook	230	90
Thurner	482	320
Believa	335	168

Table 2: Datasets for experiments. Blends need not be overlapping even if the source words share common substrings. E.g. puny + unicode = punycode.

Figure 2: Attention Mask while predicting in attention baseline model.

Model	Character Accuracy			Word Accuracy		
	Test	*With Over-laps*	*No Over-laps*	*Test*	*With Over-laps*	*No Over-laps*
Baselines						
Conditional	-	-	-	0.192	0.185	0.203
Heuristic Conditional	-	-	-	0.420	**0.806**	0.063
char-to-char						
Vanilla	0.865	0.882	0.850	0.110	0.123	0.077
Split Encoder	0.856	0.871	0.832	0.085	0.120	0.053
Attention	0.912	0.925	0.886	0.280	0.367	0.133
Index based						
Pointer feedforward	-	-	-	0.185	0.197	0.195
Pointer decoder	-	-	-	0.245	0.220	0.250
char-to-binary						
Binary decoder	0.951	0.951	0.949	0.320	0.367	0.330
Bidirectional binary decoder	0.951	0.949	0.948	0.360	0.350	**0.353**
Hybrid binary decoder	0.954	0.964	0.940	**0.430**	0.520	0.313

Table 3: Single instance model results on the Wiktionary Test set. Accuracies are reported at the character and word level. To show fine grained performances the models are additionally tested on two mutually exclusive datasets, one with overlapping blends and the other without. We have run paired t-tests with the baseline heuristic model with p-value of 0.012.

the collective consensus should be more smooth than capturing individual preferences or specialization in the experts where each expert predicts differently. Each expert is independently initialized and parameterized by a GRU based encoder decoder neural network and trained end-to-end simultaneously.

The model makes the final prediction by using a method of combining the expert predictions known as *confidence measure*. Each expert predicts the blended target $z_t^i = [0, 1]$ using Equation 5, for the ith expert such that $i \in K$, where there are K experts. *Confidence* of each expert i with respect to a pre-defined threshold γ is given by:

$$Cf^i = \frac{\sum_{t=1}^{n} |z_t^i - \gamma|}{n} \quad (6)$$

For the purposes of evaluating the quality of the ensemble model prediction, we perform a confidence weighted voting on the blended words (at a word level instead of character level) predicted by the individual expert and report the top voted blend predictions by the ensemble by selecting the prediction of the expert(s) that has the highest weighted confidence. The accuracy with respect to the ground truth is then evaluated on the test set and reported in the Section on experiments.

We would like to introduce the two baseline models here, as they naturally lead to the hy-

brid aspect of our model which we discuss later. The conditional baseline model builds a conditional probability distribution of the splice points from source word lengths, i.e. $P(i_1|l_1)$ and $P(i_2|l_2)$, where i_1, i_2 are the splice indices and l_1, l_2 are the lengths of source word 1 and 2 respectively. The model predicts using argmax from the distributions and combines the prefix and suffix. The heuristic model greedily looks for common substrings in the two source words and joins them with the overlap e.g. group + coupon = groupon and group + coupon = gron. Then from the set of combinations, it picks the one that has the longest overlap. If no common substring is found, it reverts to plain conditional model.

The bidirectional binary encoder-decoder that we discussed before does poorly on overlapping blends because it struggles to determine the blends with overlaps. We propose a further enhancement to the ensemble model whereby we introduce extra information about the overlap and common substrings between the source words. This is a hybrid between the heuristic and neural model. Consider the overlap type blend group + coupon = groupon. A mapping is induced from the source words that indicates to the neural network that oup is the overlapping segment. This mapping is provided to the hybrid model as additional information in the form of a binary sequence indicating overlaps between the 2 source words so group + coupon gets mapped to 001110011100 and is fed into the encoder just after the embedding layer as shown in Figure 1. The motivation is that the extra information should take the burden off the model in finding common overlaps.

Effect of dominance To study the effect of dominance of either of the source words we add binary tags to the characters of each source word proportional to the portion of source word in the blend. If the proportion is greater than or equal to 50 percent, then the dominance is set to 1 else 0. Note that both words can have dominance set to 1. Additionally, we set dominance of both the words to 1 if the proportions differ by less than 0.1 percent.

3 Experiments

3.1 Dataset Details

We use modern collection of english blend words curated by Wiktionary[6] with a total of 3250 blends. Each example consists of two source words and a target blend word. We restrict the dataset to only prefixes of first source word and suffixes of second source word leading to a total of 2854 blends. As held out datasets we use the dataset created by Cook et al. (Cook and Stevenson, 2010) from `wordspy.com`, and collected in 2008. It has 179 samples distinct from our training set and 230 unique blends in total with a good balance among different types of blends.

[7] The Thurner dataset that we use has 482 unique blends which are a subset of the full Thurner dictionary (1993) of around 2300 words collected from 85 sources. The structure of the blends is skewed towards overlapping blends constituting roughly about 66 percentage of all the blends. The Believa dataset (2014) has 235 unique blends collected from multiple sources from year 2000 until recent. The dataset has upto 4 source words but we pick only ones with 2. The blends are well balanced with distributions very similar to Cook (2010).

3.2 Network and Training Details

In this section, we discuss the network structure and training details. All the code is written using Tensorflow (Abadi et al., 2016).

Network Layout: As discussed before we use GRU RNN network as our encoder decoder

Model	Top-1 Word Accuracy					
	Test	*OL*	*No OL*	*Cook*	*Thurner*	*Believa*
Bidirectional Binary (K=60)	0.470	0.495	**0.435**	0.487	0.320	0.373
Hybrid Bidirectional Binary (K=30)	**0.540**	0.677	0.400	**0.578**	0.465	**0.430**
Heuristic Conditional	0.420	**0.806**	0.063	0.375	**0.571**	0.409
Mixture of Experts (K=6)	0.365	0.347	0.363	0.370	0.228	0.277

Table 4: Results of the ensemble models (top-1 accuracy) on various datasets along with the heuristic model. The accuracies reported are based on weighted voting of the experts. K indicates number of experts. OL indicates overlap.

Model	Top-2 Words Accuracy					
	Test	*OL*	*No OL*	*Cook*	*Thurner*	*Believa*
Bidirectional Binary (K=60)	0.635	0.677	**0.570**	0.613	0.504	0.575
Hybrid Bidirectional Binary (K=30)	**0.677**	0.784	0.527	**0.674**	0.612	**0.597**
Heuristic Conditional	0.434	**0.909**	0.068	0.401	**0.641**	0.481

Table 5: Results of the ensemble models (top-2 accuracy) on various datasets along with the heuristic model.

Seq2Seq model. Our proposed model has single layer GRU units with 128 neurons. The character vocabulary has a size of 40. Our dataset contains blends with numbers, hyphens and also capitals. Larger, multiple layers or more number of experts in the ensemble networks did not improve performance drastically.

Training The ensemble model of experts is trained end-to-end on mini-batches using Adam Optimization (Kinga and Adam, 2015) over the Wiktionary dataset. The mini batch size is 100 and maximum length of the concatenated source word pair is 29. The learning rate is initialized to 0.006. The fixed sized vector embedding representation of the inputs to our model is set at 128 as well. We allow a dropout rate of 0.25 to prevent over-fitting. The parameters of the model are randomly initialized from a normal disribution with zero mean and standard deviation of 0.1. Training is run for 16 epochs. We tuned hyper-parameters based on our models performance over a range on the validation sets.

3.3 Baseline Heuristic, Neural and Hybrid Models

We compare the performance of our proposed model with other models. The baselines are the conditional probability distribution based model and the heuristic model described previously.

---

[6] `https://en.wiktionary.org/wiki/Category:English_blends` Note: Last accessed $14^{th} March, 2017$

[7] We are grateful to the authors for sharing with us their dataset.

We also compared our model with several types of Seq2Seq models. These include the vanilla char-to-char where the encoder takes source words concatenated and the decoder outputs target blend as characters, Attention char-to-char with added attention mechanism (Bahdanau et al., 2014) to the vanilla char-to-char and Split encoder where two encoders each takes one source word and the decoder takes concatenated encoder states as input. Index based target prediction models that we compared against are the Pointer feedforward model that has an encoder like the vanilla Seq2Seq but the decoder is replaced with feed forward network that outputs a distribution over two indices or pointers that indicate splice points. Pointer decoder is another variant where the decoder is unrolled for two time steps always, each providing a distribution over indices of the concatenated source words. Binary target prediction models including our proposed ensemble model outputs a probability of including the character from the source concatenation at each time step. Attention mechanisms were attempted for the other models but showed no meaningful improvement in performance; the attention mask results were blurred in most cases. We suspect this is due to the mismatch in the encoder and decoder representations (characters versus binary or indices).

3.4 Results and Analysis

The demo of our model is available online[8]. Dataset and source code[9] is also provided. In all the results reported, character level accuracy indicates the generalized accuracy over number of characters that were predicted correctly in the blend word. Word level accuracy indicates the generalized accuracy over the number of correct blend word predictions over all the source word pair instances.

Table 3 shows the results of all our single instance models as discussed in the previous section. The heuristic conditional model achieves high accuracy in correctly predicting overlapping blends. Its outperforms all the other models in the overlapping blends subset dataset. Overlapping blends account to about fifty percent of the total blends in general. The heuristic conditional model however does poorly in the non overlapping blends as it defaults to a greedy search in order to find the sin-

gle character overlaps, such that its performance is worse than the plain conditional model in this subset.

In the char-to-char models, the attention based model performs best as it is able to observe the input words in their entirety at every time step. Figure 2 shows the attention mask for this model while predicting the blend `infotopia`. We can clearly see where it jumps to the second word. The two other char-to-char models perform poorly as they have to additionally track the current character to output. The index based models perform slightly better as the problem is now about predicting the correct splice points. Their performance is relatively unaffected by the blend types - overlapping or non-overlapping. The char-to-binary models outperforms the rest as the solution space is restricted to predicting the binary vector indicating the characters that are present in the blend. The bidirectional model is further able to improve its performance due to its ability to scan the character sequence in both directions for exploiting neighbourhood structure. It can make a better decision on the splinters with this extra information. The vanilla binary model is able to perform better on the overlapping blends data than the bidirectional model but loses out on the non-overlapping case. The bidirectional model essentially is able to generalize to both overlapping and non-overlapping subsets. Finally the hybrid model between heuristic and neural performs the best by including extra information on the overlaps when available. Although it is unable to beat the heuristic model in the overlapping blends subset, it does better overall.

In Tables 4 and 5, we report the performance of our proposed bidirectional ensemble model. The ensemble models are able to bring in significant gains as compared to the single instance models. The hybrid model is able to get the best of both world: heuristic and neural models to get the best overall accuracy. However, its performance is skewed towards the overlapping blends resulting in lower performance on the no overlap data subset in comparison to the plain bidirectional model. The heuristic model performs well on the Thurner (1993) dataset due to the majority of the words in the Thurner data comprising overlapping blends. The Cook (2010) and Believa datasets (2014) are more balanced in which the hybrid model outperforms the rest. The Mix-

---

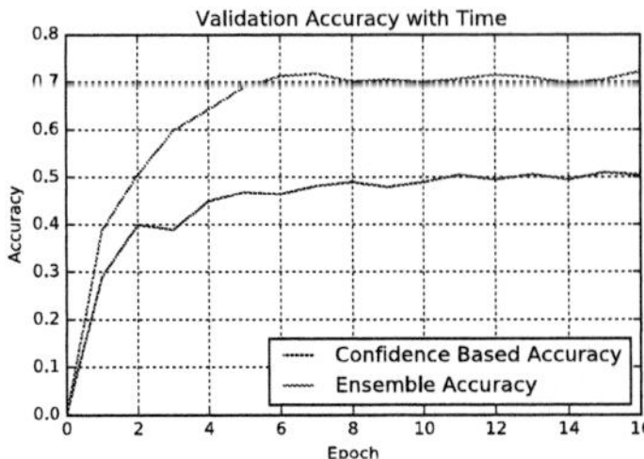

Figure 3: Performance Plot of the Bidirectional Encoder Decoder SeqToSeq model.

Word$_1$	Word$_2$	Hybrid Prediction	Heuristic Prediction	Ground Truth
work	alcoholic	workoholic, workholic	woholic, wolic	workoholic
snow	apocalypse	snowocalpyse, snowpocalypse	snocalypse	snowpocalypse
book	bootlegger	booklegger	boootlegger, bookbootlegger	booklegger
family	honeymoon	famimoon, familmoon	famoon, familymoon	familymoon
edge	pixel	edgixel, edxel	edgel	edgel

Table 6: Comparison of predictions from heuristic and ensemble hybrid models on sample inputs.

ture of Experts (MoE) ensemble causes experts to specialize individually to the examples early on, most often converging to a subset of experts. This led to reduced accuracies for MoE throughout. It was difficult to train the model as it preferred to converge (specialize) to a few experts even when enforcing a variance loss to encourage diversity. In contrast, the bidirectional ensemble model did not specialize as each expert is trained separately. That independence helps the ensemble to generalize in capturing the wider variations in the blends. In Table 6, we compare the predictions from the hybrid ensemble model and the heuristic single instance models. On observing the failure modes, due to the qualitative and subjective nature of blends, we find that some of the predicted blends are still quite plausible. We would hazard to say that some of these predictions actually look more natural than the dataset values.

Figure 3 shows the performance plot of the

Model	Top-1 Word Accuracy					
	Test	OL	No OL	Cook	Thurner	Believa
Bidirectional Binary with Dominance(K=15)	0.491	0.505	0.491	0.517	0.378	0.415
Hybrid Bidirectional Binary with Dominance (K=15)	0.572	0.721	0.453	0.643	0.525	0.487

Table 7: Results of dominance based models. K indicates number of experts. OL indicates overlaps.

Word$_1$	Word$_2$	Blend Predictions		
		Word$_1$ Dominant	Word$_2$ Dominant	Equal Dominance
breakfast	lunch	breaklunch	brunch	breaklunch
phone	tablet	phonelet	phablet	phonlet
aviation	electronics	aviationics	avionics	aviatonics
bombay	hollywood	bombaywood	bollywood	bombwood
republican	democrat	republicrat	repumocrat	repubocrat

Table 8: Sample predictions from hybrid ensemble with variation in dominance.

validation accuracy of any expert predicting correctly in comparison to the weighted voting prediction. The weaker metric of evaluating the accuracy based on any expert, outperforms the weighted voting prediction over the training duration. Tables 8 and 7 shows some sample predictions and accuracy by the dominance enhanced hybrid model on sample inputs. With the famous `brunch` blend, our model predicts that the blend would have been `breaklunch` if `breakfast` had been given more importance by the coiner. Similarly our model predicts `phone` and `tablet` gives `phonlet` when dominance of the source words are same. But when the word `tablet` is set to be dominant the model predicts `phablet`, the form of the blend which is in popular use now. We can hypothesize that the creator of this blend perhaps wanted more emphasis on tablets when marketing `phablet` form factor mobile devices.

Comparison with Deri et al. (2015) The main working example in their published paper: stay + vacation predicted `stacation` on their demo website, instead of `staycation` as claimed, whereas our model demo predicted `staycation`. Further, on their dataset (with common words with the Wiktionary dataset that we used removed), our baseline heuristic beat their model with accuracy of 47.7% in comparison to their models 45.3%, while our primary model achieved 48.3%. Their dataset consists of 400 examples in contrast to our dataset of 2854 examples. Their system is unable to generalize to non-overlapping blends like `staycation`, `workholic` correctly which our system can.

4 Future Work and Conclusions

In this work, we show that neural networks are well suited to modelling uncertainties in the blending process. The ensemble RNN neural and ensemble RNN neural-hybrid encoder-decoder systems that we propose generalized very well to overlapping and non-overlapping blended English words from two source words. They outperform statistical, heuristic, neural single instance and mixture of experts ensemble models over multiple datasets. However, these ensemble models are unable to capture the stringent rules and restrictions that disallow certain character combinations like `bxy, ii, gls`. An attempt to tag inputs with phonetic or articulatory information failed to correct these mistakes. One possibility is to use reinforcement learning (Sutton and Barto, 1998) to apply specific rules of word formation. Other types of errors are recognizability errors which causes loss of recognition of one or both source words and over-representation errors which adds extra (and unnecessary) characters from the source words. Some of these examples are provided in the Appendix. We believe these errors occur due to the sparsity in the training data.

References

Martín Abadi, Ashish Agarwal, Paul Barham, Eugene Brevdo, Zhifeng Chen, Craig Citro, Greg S Corrado, Andy Davis, Jeffrey Dean, Matthieu Devin, et al. 2016. Tensorflow: Large-scale machine learning on heterogeneous distributed systems. *arXiv preprint arXiv:1603.04467*.

Dzmitry Bahdanau, Kyunghyun Cho, and Yoshua Bengio. 2014. Neural machine translation by jointly learning to align and translate. *arXiv preprint arXiv:1409.0473*.

Laurie Bauer. 2012. Blends: Core and periphery. *Cross-disciplinary perspectives on lexical blending*, pages 11–22.

Natalia Beliaeva. 2014. A study of english blends: From structure to meaning and back again. *Word Structure*, 7(1):29–54.

Kyunghyun Cho, Bart Van Merriënboer, Caglar Gulcehre, Dzmitry Bahdanau, Fethi Bougares, Holger Schwenk, and Yoshua Bengio. 2014. Learning phrase representations using rnn encoder-decoder for statistical machine translation. *arXiv preprint arXiv:1406.1078*.

Paul Cook and Suzanne Stevenson. 2010. Automatically identifying the source words of lexical blends in english. *Computational Linguistics*, 36(1):129–149.

Aliya Deri and Kevin Knight. 2015. How to make a frenemy: Multitape fsts for portmanteau generation. In *HLT-NAACL*, pages 206–210.

Stefan Th Gries. 2004. Isnt that fantabulous? how similarity motivates intentional morphological blends in english. *Language, culture, and mind*, pages 415–428.

Stefan Th Gries. 2006. Cognitive determinants of subtractive word formation: A corpus-based perspective.

Stefan Th Gries. 2012. Quantitative corpus data on blend formation: psycho-and cognitive-linguistic perspectives. *Cross-disciplinary perspectives on lexical blending*, pages 145–167.

Michael H Kelly. 1998. To brunch or to brench: Some aspects of blend structure.

D Kinga and J Ba Adam. 2015. A method for stochastic optimization. In *International Conference on Learning Representations (ICLR)*.

Yann LeCun, Yoshua Bengio, and Geoffrey Hinton. 2015. Deep learning. *Nature*, 521(7553):436–444.

Adrienne Lehrer. 2007. Blendalicious. *Lexical creativity, texts and contexts*, pages 115–133.

Gözde Özbal and Carlo Strapparava. 2012. A computational approach to the automation of creative naming. In *Proceedings of the 50th Annual Meeting of the Association for Computational Linguistics: Long Papers-Volume 1*, pages 703–711. Association for Computational Linguistics.

Maciej Pilichowski and Włodzisław Duch. 2013. Braingene: computational creativity algorithm that invents novel interesting names. In *Computational Intelligence for Human-like Intelligence (CIHLI), 2013 IEEE Symposium on*, pages 92–99. IEEE.

Katherine E Shaw, Andrew M White, Elliott Moreton, and Fabian Monrose. 2014. Emergent faithfulness to morphological and semantic heads in lexical blends. In *Proceedings of the Annual Meetings on Phonology*, volume 1.

Ilya Sutskever, Oriol Vinyals, and Quoc V Le. 2014. Sequence to sequence learning with neural networks. In *Advances in neural information processing systems*, pages 3104–3112.

Richard S Sutton and Andrew G Barto. 1998. *Reinforcement learning: An introduction*, volume 1. MIT press Cambridge.

Dick Thurner. 1993. *Portmanteau dictionary: blend words in the English language, including trademarks and brand es*. McFarland & Company.

Andrew M White, Katherine Shaw, Fabian Monrose, and Elliott Moreton. 2014. Isn't that fantabulous: Security, linguistic and usability challenges of pronounceable tokens. In *Proceedings of the 2014 workshop on New Security Paradigms Workshop*, pages 25–38. ACM.

Leveraging Discourse Information Effectively for Authorship Attribution[*]

Elisa Ferracane[1], Su Wang[1,2] and Raymond J. Mooney[3]

[1]Department of Linguistics, The University of Texas at Austin
[2]Department of Statistics and Data Science, The University of Texas at Austin
[3]Department of Computer Science, The University of Texas at Austin
elisa@ferracane.com, shrekwang@utexas.edu, mooney@cs.utexas.edu

Abstract

We explore techniques to maximize the effectiveness of discourse information in the task of authorship attribution. We present a novel method to embed discourse features in a Convolutional Neural Network text classifier, which achieves a state-of-the-art result by a significant margin. We empirically investigate several featurization methods to understand the conditions under which discourse features contribute non-trivial performance gains, and analyze discourse embeddings.[1]

1 Introduction

Authorship attribution (AA) is the task of identifying the author of a text, given a set of author-labeled training texts. This task typically makes use of stylometric cues at the surface lexical and syntactic level (Stamatatos et al., 2015), although Feng and Hirst (2014) and Feng (2015) go beyond the sentence level, showing that discourse information can help. However, they achieve limited performance gains and lack an in-depth analysis of discourse featurization techniques. More recently, convolutional neural networks (CNNs) have demonstrated considerable success on AA relying only on character-level n-grams (Ruder et al., 2016; Shrestha et al., 2017). The strength of these models is evidenced by findings that traditional stylometric features such as word n-grams and POS-tags do not improve, and can sometimes even hurt performance (Ruder et al., 2016; Sari et al., 2017). However, none of these CNN models make use of discourse.

Our work builds upon these prior studies by exploring an effective method to (i) featurize the discourse information, and (ii) integrate discourse features into the best text classifier (i.e., CNN-based models), in the expectation of achieving state-of-the-art results in AA.

Feng and Hirst (2014) (henceforth F&H14) made the first comprehensive attempt at using discourse information for AA. They employ an entity-grid model, an approach introduced by Barzilay and Lapata (2008) for the task of ordering sentences. This model tracks how the grammatical relations of salient entities (e.g., `subj`, `obj`, etc.) change between pairs of sentences in a document, thus capturing a form of discourse coherence. The grid is summarized into a vector of transition probabilities. However, because the model only records the transition between two consecutive sentences at a time, the coherence is *local*. Feng (2015) (henceforth F15) further extends the entity-grid model by replacing grammatical relations with discourse relations from Rhetorical Structure Theory (Mann and Thompson, 1988, RST). Their study uses a linear-kernel SVM to perform pairwise author classifications, where a non-discourse model captures lexical and syntactic features. They find that adding the entity-grid with grammatical relations enhances the non-discourse model by almost 1% in accuracy, and using RST relations provides an improvement of 3%. The study, however, works with only one small dataset and their models produce overall unremarkable performance ($\sim$85%). Ji and Smith (2017) propose an advanced Recursive Neural Network (RecNN) architecture to work with RST in the more general area of text categorization and present impressive results. However, we suspect that the massive number of parameters of RecNNs would likely cause overfitting when working with smaller datasets, as is often the case in AA tasks.

[*]The first two authors contributed equally to this work.
[1]https://github.com/elisaF/authorship-attribution-discourse

Proceedings of the The 8th International Joint Conference on Natural Language Processing, pages 584–593,
Taipei, Taiwan, November 27 – December 1, 2017 ©2017 AFNLP

(1) [My father]$_S$ was a clergyman of the north of England, [who]$_O$ was deservedly respected by all who knew [him]$_O$; and, in his younger days, lived pretty comfortably on the joint income of a small incumbency and a snug little property of his own.

(2) [My mother]$_S$, who married [him]$_O$ against the wishes of her friends, was a squire's daughter, and a woman of spirit.

(3) In vain it was represented to [her]$_X$, that if [she]$_S$ became [the poor parson's]$_X$ wife, [she]$_S$ must relinquish her carriage and her lady's-maid, and all the luxuries and elegancies of affluence; which to [her]$_X$ were little less than the necessaries of life.

Table 1: Excerpt of 19th-century novel where sentences are labeled with the salient entities and their grammatical relations (subject **s**, object **o**, other relation **x**). A salient entity is a noun phrase coreferred to at least two times in a document.

	ss	so	sx	s-	os	oo	ox	o-	xs	xo	xx	x-	-s	-o	-x	-
d_1	0.25	0.25	0	0	0	0	0.25	0	0	0	0	0	0.25	0	0	0

Table 2: The probability vector for the excerpt in Table 1 capturing transition probabilities of length 2.

In our paper, we opt for a state-of-the-art character-bigram CNN classifier (Shrestha et al., 2017). We choose to use the entity-grid model because we find it helps avoid overfitting[2] (adding typical stylometric features such as word n-grams and POS tags results in overfitting) and further captures coreference chains, which we show are critical to improving performance on this task (see Section 5). We investigate various ways in which the discourse information can be featurized and integrated into the CNN. Specifically,

- *Featurization.* We attempt to capture a more *global* discourse coherence by modeling the entire sequence of relations in a document for every salient entity, instead of only the relations between pairs of sentences.

- *Feature integration.* Using a neural network architecture allows us to explore embedding the relations from the entity-grid model,[3] rather than only exploiting a vector of relation probabilities.

We explore these questions using two approaches to represent salient entities: grammatical relations, and RST discourse relations. We apply these models to datasets of varying sizes and genres, and find that adding any discourse information improves AA consistently on longer documents,

but has mixed results on shorter documents. Further, embedding the discourse features in a parallel CNN at the input end yields better performance than concatenating them to the output layer as a feature vector (Section 3). The global featurization is more effective than the local one. We also show that SVMs, which can only use discourse probability vectors, neither produce a competitive performance (even with fine-tuning), nor generalize in using the discourse information effectively.

2 Background

Entity-grid model. Typical lexical features for AA are relatively superficial and restricted to within the same sentence. F&H14 hypothesize that discourse features beyond the sentence level also help authorship attribution. In particular, they propose an author has a particular style for representing entities across a discourse. Their work is based on the entity-grid model of Barzilay and Lapata (2008) (henceforth B&L).

The entity-grid model tracks the grammatical relation (`subj`, `obj`, etc.) that salient entities take on throughout a document as a way to capture local coherence . A salient entity is defined as a noun phrase that co-occurs at least twice in a document. Extensive literature has shown that subject and object relations are a strong signal for salience and it follows from Centering Theory that you want to avoid rough shifts in the center (Grosz et al., 1995; Strube and Hahn, 1999). B&L thus focus on whether a salient entity is a subject (**s**), object (**o**), other (**x**), or is not present (**-**) in a given sentence, as illustrated in Table 1. Every sentence in a document is encoded with the grammatical relation of all the salient entities, resulting in a grid

---

[2]Primarily compared to previous work where discourse trees are modeled with Recursive Neural Nets (Ji and Smith, 2017).

[3]Tien Nguyen and Joty (2017) are the first to propose applying embeddings in modeling local coherence (for the coherence judgment task). Our methods roughly subsume theirs, which correspond to our GR CNN2-DE (global) model (Section 3). This scheme did not come out on top in our AA tasks.

similar to Table 3.

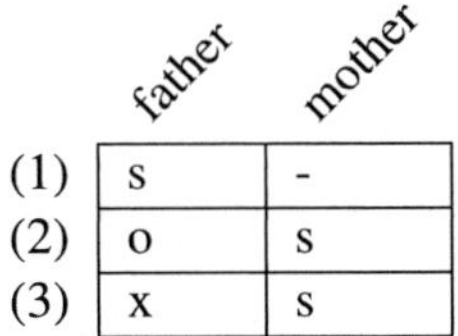

	father	mother
(1)	s	-
(2)	o	s
(3)	x	s

Table 3: The entity grid for the excerpt in Table 1, where columns are salient entities and rows are sentences. Each cell contains the grammatical relation of the given entity for the given sentence (subject **s**, object **o**, another grammatical relation **x**, or not present **-**). If an entity occurs multiple times in a sentence, only the highest-ranking relation is recorded.

The local coherence of a document is then defined on the basis of local entity transitions. A local entity transition is the sequence of grammatical relations that an entity can assume across n consecutive sentences, resulting in $\{s,o,x,-\}^n$ possible transitions. Following B&L, F&H14 consider sequences of length $n=2$, that is, transitions between two consecutive sentences, resulting in $4^2=16$ possible transitions. The probability for each transition is then calculated as the frequency of the transition divided by the total number of transitions. This step results in a single probability vector for every document, as illustrated in Table 2.

B&L apply this model to a sentence ordering task, where the more coherent option, as evidenced by its transition probabilities, was chosen. In authorship attribution, texts are however assumed to already be coherent. F&H14 instead hypothesize that an author unconsciously employs the same methods for describing entities as the discourse unfolds, resulting in discernible transition probability patterns across multiple of their texts. Indeed, F&H14 find that adding the B&L vectors increases the accuracy of AA by almost 1% over a baseline lexico-syntactic model.

RST discourse relations. F15 extends the notion of tracking salient entities to RST. Instead of using grammatical relations in the grid, RST discourse relations are specified. An RST discourse relation defines the relationship between two or more elementary discourse units (EDUs), which are spans of text that typically correspond to syntactic clauses. In a relation, an EDU can function as a nucleus (e.g., `result.N`) or as a satellite (e.g., `summary.S`). All the relations in a document then form a tree as in Figure 1.[4]

---

[4]For reasons of space, only the first sentence of the excerpt is illustrated.

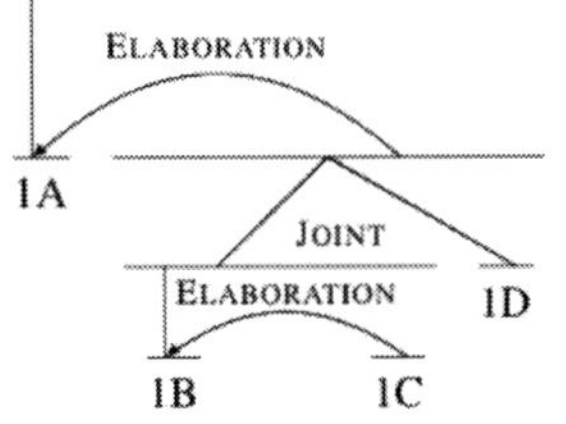

[My father was a clergyman of the north of England,][1A] [who was deservedly respected by all][1B] [who knew him;][1C] [and, in his younger days, lived pretty comfortably on a joint of a small incumbency and a snug little property of his own.][1D]

Figure 1: RST tree for the first sentence of the excerpt in Table 1.

F15 finds that RST relations are more effective for AA than grammatical relations. In our paper, we populate the entity-grid in the same way as F15's "Shallow RST-style" encoding, but use fine-grained instead of coarse-grained RST relations, and do not distinguish between intra-sentential and multi-sentential RST relations, or salient and non-salient entities. We explore various featurization techniques using the coding scheme.

CNN model. Shrestha et al. (2017) propose a convolutional neural network formulation for AA tasks (detailed in Section 3). They report state-of-the-art performance on a corpus of Twitter data (Schwartz et al., 2013), and compare their models with alternative architectures proposed in the literature: (i) SCH: an SVM that also uses character n-grams, among other stylometric features (Schwartz et al., 2013); (ii) LSTM-2: an LSTM trained on bigrams (Tai et al., 2015); (iii) CHAR: a *Logistic Regression* model that takes character n-grams (Stamatatos, 2009); (iv) CNN-W: a CNN trained on word embeddings (Kalchbrenner et al., 2014). The authors show that the model CNN2[5] produces the best performance overall. Ruder et al. (2016) apply character n-gram CNNs to a wide range of datasets, providing strong empirical evidence that the architecture generalizes well. Further, they find that including word n-grams in addition to character n-grams reduces performance, which is in agreement with Sari et al. (2017)'s findings.

---

[5]Shrestha et al. (2017) test two variants of CNN models: **CNN1/CNN2** for unigram/bigram character CNNs respectively.

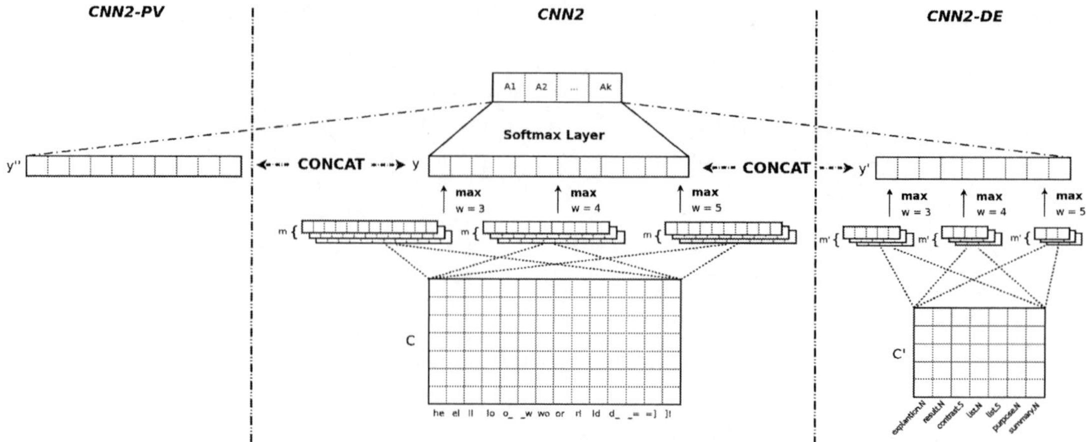

Figure 2: The bigram character CNN models

3 Models

Building on Shrestha et al. (2017)'s work, we employ their character-bigram CNN (**CNN2**)[6], and propose two extensions which utilize discourse information: (i) CNN2 enhanced with relation *probability vectors* (**CNN2-PV**), and (ii) CNN2 enhanced with *discourse embeddings* (**CNN2-DE**). The CNN2-PV allows us to conduct a comparison with F&H14 and F15, which also use relation probability vectors.

CNN2. CNN2 is the baseline model with no discourse features. Illustrated in Figure 2 (center), it consists of (i) an embedding layer, (ii) a convolution layer, (iii) a max-pooling layer, and (iv) a softmax layer. We briefly sketch the processing procedure and refer the reader to (Shrestha et al., 2017, Section 2) for mathematical details.

The network takes a sequence of character bigrams $x = \langle x_1, \ldots, x_l \rangle$ as input, and outputs a multinomial ϕ over class labels as the prediction. The model first looks up the embedding matrix to produce a sequence of embeddings for x (i.e., the matrix C), then pushes the embedding sequence through convolutional filters of three bigram-window sizes $w = 3, 4, 5$, each yielding m feature maps. We then apply the *max-over-time* pooling (Collobert et al., 2011) to the feature maps from each filter, and concatenate the resulting vectors to obtain a single vector y, which then goes through the softmax layer to produce predictions.

CNN2-PV. This model (Figure 2, left+center) fea-

turizes discourse information into a probability vector (PV). The discourse features come in two flavors: (i) grammatical relations (GR), and (ii) RST discourse relations (RST)[7]. For both types of discourse features, an entity grid is first constructed to identify salient entities[8]. Recall each row in the grid is a sentence, and each column is a salient entity. The values of each cell in the grid are then populated differently, depending on which flavor of discourse feature is used.

For GR features, the entity grid is populated with the grammatical relation of each entity in each sentence. The entity grid is then collapsed into a single probability vector as shown in Table 2. The GR feature vector thus consists of a sequence of *grammatical relation transitions* derived from the entity grid, e.g., $\langle \texttt{sx}, \texttt{xs}, \texttt{ss}, \ldots \rangle$. The vector is a distribution over all the grammatical role transitions, i.e., $\langle p(\texttt{sx}), p(\texttt{xs}), p(\texttt{ss}), \ldots \rangle$.

For RST features, the entity grid is populated with the RST relation and nulcearity of the entity, and additionally the relations and nuclearity of the main EDUs in the current and previous sentence (as in Feng (2015)). We do not encode the entire RST tree since prior work has shown better performance with underspecified trees (Ji and Smith, 2017; Hogenboom et al., 2015). The RST features are represented as *RST discourse relations* with their nuclearity, e.g., $\langle \texttt{definition.N}, \texttt{attribution.S}, \ldots \rangle$. The probability vector is a distribution

---

[6]Our preliminary experiments found that using character n-gram orders higher than 2 performed worse, likely due to the increased number of features and overfitting.

[7]Using RST Parser from Ji and Eisenstein (2014).

[8]Using neural coreference resolver, dependency parser in Stanford Core NLP (Clark and Manning, 2016).

Dataset	# authors	mean words/auth	range words/auth
NOVEL-9	9	376,242	124K-1M
NOVEL-50	50	709,880	184K-2.1M
IMDB62	62	349,004	9.8K-75K

Table 4: Statistics for datasets.

over all the RST discourse relations, i.e., $\langle p(\texttt{definition.N}), p(\texttt{attribution.S}), \ldots \rangle$

Denoting the discourse feature vector with y'', we construct the pooling vector y for the char-bigrams, and concatenate y'' to y before feeding the resulting vector to the softmax layer.

CNN2-DE. In this model (Figure 2, center+right), we embed discourse features in high-dimensional space (similar to char-bigram embeddings). Let $z = \langle z_1, \ldots, z_{l'} \rangle$ be a sequence of discourse features[9], we treat it in a similar fashion to the char-bigram sequence x, i.e. feeding it through a "parallel" convolutional net (Figure 2 right). We set the embedding size to the average number of relations, then either pad or truncate. The operation results in a pooling vector y'. We concatenate y' to the pooling vector y (which is constructed from x) then feed $[y; y']$ to the softmax layer for the final prediction.

4 Experiments and Results

We begin by introducing the datasets (Section 4.1), followed by detailing the featurization methods (Section 4.2), the experiments (Section 4.3), and finally reporting results (Section 4.4).

4.1 Datasets

The statistics for the three datasets used in the experiments are summarized in Table 4.

novel-9. This dataset was compiled by F&H14: a collection of 19 novels by 9 nineteenth century British and American authors in the Project Gutenberg. To compare to F&H14, we apply the same resampling method (F&H14, Section 4.2) to correct the imbalance in authors by oversampling the texts of less-represented authors.

novel-50. This dataset extends novel-9, compiling the works of 50 randomly selected authors of the

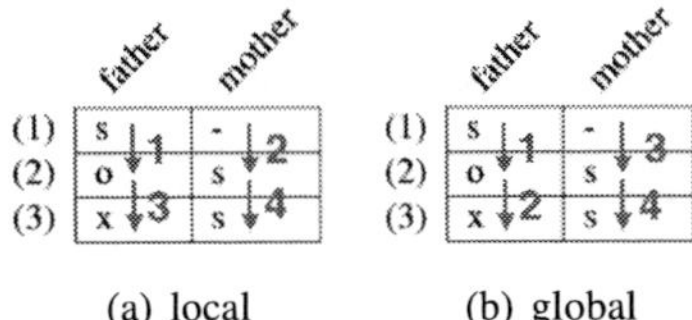

Figure 3: Two variants for creating sequences of grammatical relation transitions in an entity grid.

same period. For each author, we randomly select 5 novels for a total 250 novels.

IMDB62. IMDB62 consists of 62K movie reviews from 62 users (1,000 each) from the Internet Movie dataset, compiled by Seroussi et al. (2011). Unlike the novel datasets, the reviews are considerably shorter, with a mean of 349 words per text.

4.2 Featurization

As described in Section 2, in both the GR and RST variants, from each input entry we start by obtaining an entity grid.

CNN2-PV. We collect the probabilities of entity role transitions (in GR) or discourse relations (in RST) for the entries. Each entry corresponds to a probability distribution vector.

CNN2-DE. We employ two schemes for creating discourse feature sequences from an entity grid. While we always read the grid by column (by a salient entity), we vary whether we track the entity across a number of sentences (n rows at a time) or across the entire document (one entire column at a time), denoted as *local* and *global* readings respectively.

For the GR discourse features, in the case of local reading, we process the entity roles one sentence pair at a time (Figure 3, left). For example, in processing the pair (s_1, s_2), we find the first non-empty role r_{11} for entity $E1$ in s_1. If $E1$ also has a non-empty role r_{21} in the s_2, we collect the entity role transition $r_{11}r_{21}$. We then proceed to the following entity $E2$, until we process all the entities in the grid and move to the next sentence pair. For the global reading, we instead read the entity roles by traversing one column of the entire document at a time (Figure 3, right). The entity roles in all the sentences are read for one entity: we collect transitions for all the non-empty roles (e.g., $\texttt{so}$, but not $\texttt{s-}$).

For the RST discourse features, we process non-empty discourse relations also through either local or global reading. In the local reading, we read all the discourse relations in a sentence (a row) then

---

[9]The sequence comes in two variants, depending on the featurization technique, see Section 4.2.

move on to the next sentence.[10] In the global reading, we read in discourse relations for one entity at a time. This results in sequences of discourse relations for the input entries.

4.3 Experiments

Baseline-dataset experiments. All the baseline-dataset experiments are evaluated on novel-9. As a comparison to previous work (F15), we evaluate our models using a pairwise classification task with GR discourse features. In her model, each novel is partitioned into 1000-word chunks, and the model is evaluated with accuracy.[11] Surpassing F15's SVM model by a large margin, we then further evaluate the more difficult multi-class task, i.e., all-class prediction simultaneously, with both GR and RST discourse features and the more robust F1 evaluation. In this multi-class task, we implement two SVMs to extend F15's SVM models: (i) SVM2: a linear-kernel SVM which takes char-bigrams as input, as our CNNs, and (ii) SVM2-PV: an updated SVM2 which takes also probability vector features.

Further, we are interested in finding a performance threshold on the minimally-required input text length for discourse information to "kick in". To this end, we chunk each novel into different sizes: 200-2000 words, at 200-word intervals, and evaluate our CNNs in the multi-class condition.

Generalization-dataset experiments. To confirm that our models generalize, we pick the best models from the baseline-dataset experiments and evaluate on the novel-50 and IMDB62 datasets. For novel-50, the chunking size applied is 2000-word as per the baseline-dataset experiment results, and for IMDB62, texts are not chunked (i.e., we feed the models with the original reviews directly). For model comparison, we also run the SVMs (i.e., SVM2 and SVM2-PV) used in the baseline-dataset experiment. All the experiments conducted here are multi-class classification with macro-averaged F1 evaluation.

Model configurations. Following F15, we perform 5-fold cross-validation. The embedding sizes are tuned on novel-9 (multi-class condition): 50 for char-bigrams; 20 for discourse features. The learning rate is 0.001 using the Adam Optimizer

---

MODEL	AVG. ACCURACY
Baseline	49.8
SVM (LexSyn)	85.5
SVM (LexSyn-PV)	86.4
CNN2	99.5
CNN2-PV	**99.8**

Table 5: Accuracy for pairwise author classification on the novel-9 dataset, using either a dumb baseline, an SVM with and without discourse to replicate F15, or a bigram-character CNN (CNN2) with and without discourse.

DISC. TYPE	MODEL	F1
None	SVM2	84.9
	CNN2	95.9
GR	SVM2-PV	85.7
	CNN2-PV	96.1
	CNN2-DE (local)	97.0
	CNN2-DE (global)	96.9
RST	SVM2-PV	85.9
	CNN2-PV	96.3
	CNN2-DE (local)	97.4
	CNN2-DE (global)	**98.5**

Table 6: Macro-averaged F1 score for multi-class author classification on the novel-9 dataset, using either no discourse (None), grammatical relations (GR), or RST relations (RST). These experiments additionally include the Discourse Embedding (DE) models for GR and RST.

(Kingma and Ba, 2014). For all models, we apply dropout regularization of 0.75 (Srivastava et al., 2014), and run 50 epochs (batch size 32). The SVMs in the baseline-dataset experiments use default settings, following F15. For the SVMs in the generalization-dataset experiments, we tuned the hyperparameters on novel-9 with a grid search, and found the optimal setting as: stopping condition `tol` is 1e-5, at a max-iteration of 1,500.

4.4 Results

Baseline-dataset experiments. The results of the baseline-dataset experiments are reported in Table 5, 6 and Figure 4. In Table 5, Baseline denotes the dumb baseline model which always predicts the more-represented author of the pair. Both SVMs are from F15, and we report her results. SVM (LexSyn) takes character and word bi/trigrams and POS tags. SVM (LexSyn-PV) additionally includes probability vectors, similar to our CNN2-PV. In this part of the experiment, while the CNNs clear a large margin over SVMs (all differences

---

[10]We do not check the next sentences as in GR, because the discourse relations in one cell of the entity grid typically already capture relations beyond the sentence level.

[11]Averaged over all the author-author pair experiments.

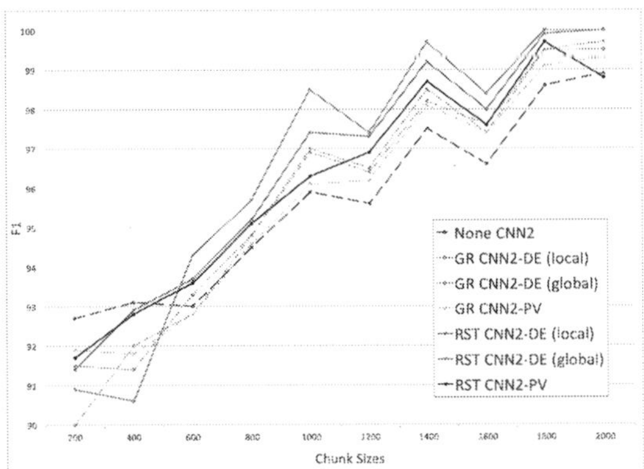

Figure 4: Macro-averaged F1 score for multi-class author classification on the novel-9 dataset in varied chunk sizes.

DISC. TYPE	MODEL	NOVEL-50	IMDB62
None	SVM2	92.9	90.4
	CNN2	95.3	91.5
GR	SVM2-PV	93.3	90.4
	CNN2-PV	95.1	90.5
	CNN2-DE (local)	96.9	90.8
	CNN2-DE (global)	97.5	90.9
RST	SVM2-PV	93.8	90.9
	CNN2-PV	95.5	90.7
	CNN2-DE (local)	97.7	91.4
	CNN2-DE (global)	**98.8**	**92.0**

Table 7: Macro-averaged F1 score for multi-class author classification on the large datasets, using either no discourse (None), grammatical relations (GR), or RST relations (RST).

are statistically significant at p<0.005), adding discourse in CNN2-PV brings only a small performance gain.

Table 6 reports the results from the multi-class classification task, the more difficult task. Here, probability vector features (i.e., PV) again fail to contribute much. The discourse embedding features, on the other hand, manage to increase the F1 score by a noticeable amount, with the maximal improvement seen in the CNN2-DE (global) model with RST features (by 2.6 points). In contrast, the discourse-enhanced SVM2-PVs increase F1 by about 1 point, with overall much lower scores in comparison to the CNNs. In general, RST features work better than GR features.

The results of the varying-sizes experiments are plotted in Figure 4. Again, we observe the overall pattern that discourse features improve the F1 score, and RST features procure superior performance. Crucially, however, we note there is no performance boost below the chunk size of 1000 for GR features, and below 600 for RST features. Where discourse features do help, the GR-based models achieve, on average, 1 extra point on F1, and the RST-based models around 2.

Generalization-dataset experiments. Table 7 summarizes the results of the generalization-dataset experiments. All reported statistical tests are t-test with a significance level of 0.05. First, we note that CNNs show a clear advantage over SVMs for all model variants on both datasets (confirmed significant for SVM2 vs. CNN2 with no discourse, SVM2-PV vs. CNN2-DE with GR and RST). On novel-50, most discourse-enhanced models significantly improve the performance of the baseline non-discourse CNN2 to varying de-

grees (significant for CNN2 with no discourse vs. CNN2-DE with GR and RST). The clear pattern again emerges that RST features work better, with the best F1 score evidenced in the CNN2-DE (global) model (3.5 improvement in F1) (significant for CNN2-DE with GR vs. CNN2-DE with RST). On IMDB62, as expected with short text inputs (mean=349 words/review), the discourse features in general do not add further contribution. Even the best model, CNN2-DE, brings only marginal improvement (not statistically significant), confirming our findings from varying the chunk size on novel-9, where discourse features did not help at this input size. However, the difference between the GR and RST variants for the IMDB CNN models are statistically significant. For the SVM models on both datasets, we note discourse features do not make noticeable improvements. On novel-50, SVM2-PV performs slightly better than the no-discourse SVM2 (by 0.4 with GR, 0.9 with RST features). On IMDB62, the same pattern persists with no gains for GR and 0.5 for RST features.

5   Analysis

General analysis. Overall, we have shown that discourse information can improve authorship attribution, but only when properly encoded. This result is critical in demonstrating the particular value of discourse information, because typical stylometric features such as word n-grams and POS tags do *not* add additional performance improvements (Ruder et al., 2016; Sari et al., 2017).

In addition, the type of discourse information and the way in which it is featurized are crucial to this performance improvement: RST features provide overall stronger improvement, and the global

TARGET EMBEDDING	TOP NEIGHBORS
`explanation.N`	`interpretation.N, explanation.S, example.N, purpose.S, reason.N`
`background.N`	`circumstances.S, contrast.N, comparison.N, antithesis.S, elaboration.N`
`consequence.N`	`result.N, list.N, result.S, comment.N, summary.N`

Table 8: Nearest neighbors of example embeddings with t-SNE clustering (top 5)

reading scheme for discourse embedding works better than the local one. The discourse embedding proves to be a superior featurization technique, as evidenced by the generally higher performance of CNN2-DE models over CNN2-PV models. With an SVM, where the option is not available, we are only able to use relation probability vectors to obtain a very modest performance improvement.

Further, we found an input-length threshold for utilizing discourse features is helpful (Section 4.4). Not surprisingly, discourse does not contribute on shorter texts. Many of the feature grids are empty for these shorter texts– either there are no coreference chains or they are not correctly resolved. Currently we only have empirical results on short novel chunks and movie reviews, but believe the finding would generalize to Twitter or blog posts.

Discourse embeddings. It does not come as a surprise that discourse-embedding-based models perform better than their relation-probability-based peers. The former (i) leverages the weight learning of the entire computational graph of the CNN rather than only the softmax layer, as the PV models do, and (ii) provides a more fine-grained featurization of the discourse information. Rather than merely taking a probability over grammatical relation transitions (in GR) or discourse relation types (in RST), in DE-based models we learn the dependency between grammatical relation transitions/discourse relations through the w-sized filter sweeps.

To further study the information encoded in the discourse embeddings, we performed `t-SNE` clustering (van der Maaten and Hinton, 2008) on them, using the best performing model CNN2-DE (global). We examined the closest neighbors of each embedding, and observed that similar discourse relations tend to go together (e.g., `explanation` and `interpretation`;

`consequence` and `result`). Some examples are given in Table 8. However, it is unclear how this pattern helps improve classification performance. We intend to investigate this question in future work.

Global vs. Local featurization. As described in Section 4.2, the global reading processes all the discourse features for one entity at a time, while the local approach reads one sentence (or one sentence pair) at a time. In all the relevant experiments, global featurization showed a clear performance advantage (on average 1 point gain in F1). Recall that the creation of the grids (both GR and RST) depend on coreference chains of entities (Section 2), and only the global reading scheme takes advantage of the coreference pattern whereas the local reading breaks the chains. To find out whether coreference pattern is the key to the performance difference, we further ran a probe experiment where we read RST discourse relations in the order in which EDUs are arranged in the RST tree (i.e., left-to-right), and evaluated this model on novel-50 and IMDB62 with the same hyperparameter setting. The F1 scores turned out to be very close to the CNN2-DE (local) model, at 97.5 and 90.9. Based on this finding, we tentatively confirm the importance of the coreference pattern, and intend to further investigate how exactly it matters for the classification performance.

GR vs. RST. RST features in general give higher performance gains than GR features (Table 7). The RST parser produces a tree of discourse relations for the input text, thus introducing a "global view." The GR features, on the other hand, are more restricted to a "local view" on entities between consecutive sentences. While a deeper empirical investigation is needed, one can intuitively imagine that identifying authorship by focusing on the local transitions between grammatical relations (as in GR) is more difficult than observing how the entire text is organized (as in RST).[12]

Error analysis. We conducted a brief error analysis in an effort to understand why discourse helps. Comparing performance by author, we found the least-represented author (Ambrose Bierce) obtains the biggest improvement from discourse. We speculate that although the document must be a certain length for discourse to "kick in", these features are effective even with few training examples. On the other hand, inspecting the gradients of the character bigrams for these cases reveals a higher incidence of 0s, suggesting the bigram feature is not as robust in the smaller sample space. We further note that two other authors who gained large improvements from the discourse features wrote a variety of genres (e.g., both supernatural/horror fiction and love stories), which we speculate manifests itself in different vocabularies that don't generalize well in character bigrams, but do have similar rhetorical styles which the discourse features can exploit.

6 Conclusion

We have conducted an in-depth investigation of techniques that (i) featurize discourse information, and (ii) effectively integrate discourse features into the state-of-the-art character-bigram CNN classifier for AA. Beyond confirming the overall superiority of RST features over GR features in larger and more difficult datasets, we present a discourse embedding technique that is unavailable for previously proposed discourse-enhanced models. The new technique enabled us to push the envelope of the current performance ceiling by a large margin.

Admittedly, in using the RST features with entity-grids, we lose the valuable RST tree structure. In future work, we intend to adopt more sophisticated methods such as RecNN, as per Ji and Smith (2017), to retain more information from the RST trees while reducing the parameter size. Further, we aim to understand how discourse embeddings contribute to AA tasks, and find alternatives to coreference chains for shorter texts.

---

[12]Note that, however, it is simpler to extract GR features, as we rely solely on a high-performance dependency parser, which is widely available, whereas for RST features, we need gold RST-labeled training data, which incurs higher cost and potentially relatively limited generalizability.

Acknowledgments

We thank Stephen Roller and three anonymous reviewers for their valuable feedback. Thanks to Sebastian Ruder for kindly offering his datasets in the exploratory stage of the project, and to Prasha Shrestha for sharing the code from her paper. The first author was supported by an NSF-GRFP fellowship.

References

Regina Barzilay and Mirella Lapata. 2008. Modeling local coherence: An entity-based approach. *Computational Linguistics*, 34(1).

Kevin Clark and Christopher D. Manning. 2016. Deep reinforcement learning for mention-ranking coreference models. In *Proceedings of the 2016 Conference on Empirical Methods in Natural Language Processing*, pages 2256–2262. Association for Computational Linguistics.

Ronan Collobert, Jason Weston, Léon Bottou, Michael Karlen, Koray Kavukcuoglu, and Pavel Kuksa. 2011. Natural language processing (almost) from scratch. *Journal of Machine Learning Research*, 12:2493–2537.

Vanessa Wei Feng. 2015. *RST-style discourse parsing and its applications in discourse analysis*. Ph.D. thesis, University of Toronto.

Vanessa Wei Feng and Graeme Hirst. 2014. Patterns of local discourse coherence as a feature for authorship attribution. *Literary and Linguistic Computing*, 29(2):191–198.

Barbara J. Grosz, Scott Weinstein, and Aravind K. Joshi. 1995. Centering: A framework for modeling the local coherence of discourse. *Computational Linguistics*, 21(2).

Alexander Hogenboom, Flavius Frasincar, Franciska De Jong, and Uzay Kaymak. 2015. Using rhetorical structure in sentiment analysis. *Communications of the ACM*, 58(7):69–77.

Yangfeng Ji and Jacob Eisenstein. 2014. Representation learning for text-level discourse parsing. In *Proceedings of the 52nd Annual Meeting of the Association for Computational Linguistics (Volume 1: Long Papers)*, pages 13–24. Association for Computational Linguistics.

Yangfeng Ji and Noah A. Smith. 2017. Neural discourse structure for text categorization. In *Proceedings of the 55th Annual Meeting of the Association for Computational Linguistics (Volume 1: Long Papers)*, pages 996–1005. Association for Computational Linguistics.

Nal Kalchbrenner, Edward Grefenstette, and Phil Blunsom. 2014. A convolutional neural network for modelling sentences. In *Proceedings of the 52nd Annual Meeting of the Association for Computational Linguistics (Volume 1: Long Papers)*, pages 655–665. Association for Computational Linguistics.

Diederik Kingma and Jimmy Ba. 2014. Adam: a method for stochastic optimization. In *CoRR: arXiv1412.6980*.

L.J.P. van der Maaten and G.E. Hinton. 2008. Visualizing high-dimensional data using t-SNE. *Journal of Machine Learning Research*, 9.

William Mann and Sandra Thompson. 1988. Rhetorical structure theory: Toward a functional theory of text organization. *Text*, 8(3):243–281.

Sebastian Ruder, Parsa Ghaffari, and John Breslin. 2016. Character-level and multi-channel convolutional neural networks for large-scale authorship attribution. *CoRR, arXiv:1609.06686*.

Yunita Sari, Andreas Vlachos, and Mark Stevenson. 2017. Continuous n-gram representations for authorship attribution. In *Proceedings of the 15th Conference of the European Chapter of the Association for Computational Linguistics: Volume 2, Short Papers*, pages 267–273. Association for Computational Linguistics.

Roy Schwartz, Oren Tsur, Ari Rappoport, and Moshe Koppel. 2013. Authorship attribution of micromessages. In *Proceedings of the 2013 Conference on Empirical Methods in Natural Language Processing*, pages 1880–1891. Association for Computational Linguistics.

Yanir Seroussi, Ingrid Zukerman, and Fabian Bohnert. 2011. Authorship attribution with latent dirichlet allocation.

Prasha Shrestha, Sebastian Sierra, Fabio Gonzalez, Manuel Montes, Paolo Rosso, and Thamar Solorio. 2017. Convolutional neural networks for authorship attribution of short texts. In *Proceedings of the 15th Conference of the European Chapter of the Association for Computational Linguistics: Volume 2, Short Papers*, pages 669–674. Association for Computational Linguistics.

Nitish Srivastava, Geoffrey Hinton, Alex Krizhevsky, Ilya Sutskever, and Ruslan Salakhutdinov. 2014. Dropout: a simple way to prevent neural networks from overfitting. *Journal of Machine Learning Research*, 15.

Efstathios Stamatatos. 2009. A survey of modern authorship attribution methods. *Journal of the Americal Society for Information Science and Technology*, pages 155–159.

Efstathios Stamatatos, Walter Daelemans, Ben Verhoeven, Patrick Juola, Aurelio López-López, Martin Potthast, and Benno Stein. 2015. *Overview of the Author Identification Task at PAN 2015*. Linda Cappellato and Nicola Ferro and Gareth Jones and Eric San Juan (eds.), CLEF 2015 Labs and Workshops, Toulouse, France.

Michael Strube and Udo Hahn. 1999. Functional centering grounding referential coherence in information structure. *Computational Linguistics*, 25(3).

Kai Sheng Tai, Richard Socher, and Christopher D. Manning. 2015. Improved semantic representations from tree-structured long short-term memory networks. In *Proceedings of the 53rd Annual Meeting of the Association for Computational Linguistics and the 7th International Joint Conference on Natural Language Processing (Volume 1: Long Papers)*, pages 1556–1566. Association for Computational Linguistics.

Dat Tien Nguyen and Shafiq Joty. 2017. A neural local coherence model. In *Proceedings of the 55th Annual Meeting of the Association for Computational Linguistics (Volume 1: Long Papers)*, pages 1320–1330. Association for Computational Linguistics.

Lightly-Supervised Modeling of Argument Persuasiveness

Isaac Persing and **Vincent Ng**
Human Language Technology Research Institute
University of Texas at Dallas
Richardson, TX 75083-0688
{persingq,vince}@hlt.utdallas.edu

Abstract

We propose the first lightly-supervised approach to scoring an argument's persuasiveness. Key to our approach is the novel hypothesis that lightly-supervised persuasiveness scoring is possible by explicitly modeling the major errors that negatively impact persuasiveness. In an evaluation on a new annotated corpus of online debate arguments, our approach rivals its fully-supervised counterparts in performance by four scoring metrics when using only 10% of the available training instances.

1 Introduction

Argumentation mining is a relatively new and active area of research in the natural language processing (NLP) community, focusing on extracting argument components (e.g., claims, premises) and determining the relationships (e.g., support, attack) between them. Recently, researchers have begun work on modeling an intriguing linguistic phenomenon, the *persuasiveness* of arguments.

In this paper, we examine argument persuasiveness in the context of an under-investigated task in argument mining, *argument persuasiveness scoring*. Given a text consisting of an argument written for a particular topic, the goal of argument persuasiveness scoring is to assign a score to the text that indicates how persuasive the argument is. An argument persuasiveness scoring system can be used in a variety of situations. In an online debate, for instance, an author's primary goal is to convince others of the argument expressed in her comment(s). Similarly, in persuasive essay writing, an author should establish convincing arguments. In both situations, a persuasiveness scoring system could provide useful feedback to these authors on how persuasive their arguments are.

Being a *discourse-level* task, argument persuasiveness scoring is potentially more challenging than many NLP tasks. Oftentimes, argument persuasiveness can only be determined by understanding the discourse, not by the presence or absence of lexical cues. As an example, consider the debate argument shown in Table 1, which is composed of the author's assertion and her justification of the assertion written in response to a debate motion. It is fairly easy for a human to determine that this argument should be assigned a low persuasiveness score because the argument could be more clear. However, the same is not true for a machine, primarily because it is not possible to determine the persuasiveness of this argument merely by considering the words or phrases appearing in it.

Given the difficulty of the task, it is conceivable that *unsupervised* argument persuasiveness scoring is very challenging. Nevertheless, a solution to unsupervised argument persuasiveness scoring is of practical significance. This is because of the high cost associated with manually creating persuasiveness-annotated data needed to train classifiers in a supervised manner. This contrasts with tasks such as polarity classification and stance classification. In these tasks, large amounts of annotated data can be harvested from the Web, as it is typical for a user to explicitly indicate her polarity/stance while writing her comments in a discussion/debate forum.

We propose a *lightly-supervised* approach to argument persuasiveness scoring. To our knowledge, this is the first lightly-supervised approach to the task: virtually all previous work involving argument persuasiveness has adopted supervised approaches, training models with a large number of surface features that encode lexico-syntactic information. Note that learning from a large number of lexico-syntactic features is difficult, if not im-

Proceedings of the The 8th International Joint Conference on Natural Language Processing, pages 594–604,
Taipei, Taiwan, November 27 – December 1, 2017 ©2017 AFNLP

Motion	This House would ban teachers from interacting with students via social networking websites.
Assertion	Acting as a warning signal for children at risk.
Justification	It is very difficult for a child to realize that he is being groomed; they are unlikely to know the risk. After all, a teacher is regarded as a trusted adult. But, if the child is aware that private electronic contact between teachers and students is prohibited by law, the child will immediately know the teacher is doing something he is not supposed to if he initiates private electronic contact. This will therefore act as an effective warning sign to the child and might prompt the child to tell a parent or another adult about what is going on.

Table 1: The motion, assertion, and justification text of a debate argument.

possible, when annotated data is scarce. Hence, we explore a different idea, addressing lightly-supervised argument persuasiveness scoring via an *error-modeling* approach. Specifically, guided by theoretical work on persuasiveness, we begin by defining a set of *errors* that could negatively impact an argument's persuasiveness. The key step, then, is to model an argument's errors: given an argument, we predict the presence and severity of the errors it possesses in an unsupervised manner by bootstrapping from a set of heuristically labeled seeds. Finally, we learn a persuasiveness predictor for each error-labeled argument from a small amount of persuasiveness-annotated data.

Our contributions are two-fold. First, we propose the first lightly-supervised approach to persuasiveness scoring that rivals its supervised counterparts in performance on a new dataset consisting of 1,208 online debate arguments. Second, we make our annotated dataset publicly available.[1] Given the difficulty of obtaining annotated data for this task, we believe that our dataset will be a valuable resource to the NLP community.

2   Related Work

There have been several recent attempts to address tasks related to argument persuasiveness. Habernal and Gurevych (2016a,b) *rank* a pair of arguments w.r.t. persuasiveness, but ranking alone cannot tell us *how* persuasive an argument is. Persing and Ng (2015) score a student essay based on whether it makes a (un)convincing argument for its thesis. Using the conversations in the Change-MyView subreddit, Tan et al. (2016) study factors affecting whether a challenger can successfully persuade a commenter to change the view she expressed in her original post.

While Wei et al. (2016) also predict the persuasiveness of debate posts, their work differs from ours in several aspects. First, many of their de-

bate posts are written in response to a preceding comment in the conversation. Hence, it is not uncommon to see emotional rather than logical arguments or even insults and personal attacks. In addition, it may not always be possible to understand what the argument is and why the author made a particular argument without understanding the (preceding) context. In contrast, the debate comments in our corpus are written in response to a given debate topic. In other words, each comment is written independently of the other comments and therefore can be understood without them.

In a broader sense, our error-modeling approach is related to work on holistically scoring an essay via detecting and totaling up specific errors in it. For details, we refer the reader to Shermis et al. (2010) and Leacock et al. (2014).

3   Corpus and Annotation

We use as our corpus a randomly selected subset of 165 debates obtained from the International Debate Education Association (IDEA) website[2]. These debates cover a wide range of topics including politics, economics, religion, and science. Each debate consists of a *Motion*, which expresses a stance on the debate's topic, and an average of 7.3 arguments, each of which either agrees or disagrees with the motion's stance. Each of the 1,208 arguments consists of an *Assertion*, which expresses in one sentence why the author agrees or disagrees with the motion, and a *Justification*, which explains in an average of 6.9 sentences why the author believes her assertion.

We ask two native speakers of English to annotate each of the 1,208 arguments with a persuasiveness score after familiarizing them with the (topic- and domain-independent) scoring rubric (see Table 2). Specifically, we ask our annotators to score each argument's persuasiveness on a scale of $1-6$. The example argument in Table 1 gets a persuasiveness score of 2 because it could be expressed more clearly.

---

[1]See   http://www.hlt.utdallas.edu/ ~persingq/Debate/ for a complete list of our annotations.

[2]http://idebate.org/

Score	Description of Argument Persuasiveness
6	A **very persuasive**, **clear** argument. It would persuade most previously uncommitted readers and is devoid of problems that might detract from its persuasiveness or make it difficult to understand.
5	A **persuasive**, or only **pretty clear** argument. It would persuade most previously uncommitted readers, but may contain some minor problems that detract from its persuasiveness or understandability.
4	A **decent**, or only **fairly clear** argument. It could persuade some previously uncommitted readers, but problems detract from its persuasiveness or understandability.
3	A **poor**, or only **mostly understandable** argument. It might persuade readers who are already inclined to agree with it, but contains severe problems that detract from its persuasiveness or understandability.
2	A **very unpersuasive** or **very unclear** argument. It is unclear what the author is trying to argue or the argument is just so riddled with problems as to be completely unpersuasive.
1	The author **does not make an argument** or it is **unclear what the argument is**. It could not persuade any readers because there is nothing to be persuaded of.

Table 2: Descriptions of argument persuasiveness scores.

	1	2	3	4	5	6
AP	3	12	20	21	20	24

Table 3: Distribution of error/argument persuasiveness scores as percentages.

Table 3 shows the distribution of scores for argument persuasiveness. To measure inter-annotator agreement, we select a subset of 69 arguments and ask both annotators to score them w.r.t. argument persuasiveness. The average difference between the annotator-assigned scores is 0.899. For the sake of our experiments, when annotators disagree on a score, we average their annotations together, rounding up to the nearest whole number to obtain the gold score.

4 Error Types

Key to our approach to persuasiveness scoring is the unsupervised modeling of the errors that could negatively impact persuasiveness. In this section, we define five such error classes, which are motivated by theoretical work on persuasiveness.[3]

Grammar Error (GE) Connor and Lauer (1985) note that grammar and/or mechanical errors can interrupt the flow of discourse in persuasive essays, so we give arguments a GE score of 1 if they contain GEs severe enough to make the argument hard to understand, and 0 otherwise. The argument in Table 1 gets a GE score of 0 because it contains no severe GEs.

Lack of Objectivity (LO) Oktavia et al. (2014) consider the use of personal opinions as evidence in argumentative writing a fallacy, so we give arguments a LO score of 1 if they display an in-appropriate lack of objectivity, and 0 otherwise.[4] The argument in Table 1 receives a LO score of 1 because the author weaves a scenario in which she repeatedly speculates on what a child thinks or will do.

Inadequate Support (IS) Petty and Cacioppo (1984) find that arguments with more support are more persuasive, so we give arguments an IS score of 0 if they offer adequate support to justify their assertion, 1 if they do not offer enough support, or 2 if they offer almost no support. The example argument gets an IS score of 2 because the author's scenario is completely unsupported.

Unclear Assertion (UA) In Connor's (1990) criteria for judging assertions in persuasive writing, the lowest score is assigned to essays which did not clearly assert the problem they address. So we give an argument an UA score of 1 if it is not clear how the assertion is related to the motion without reading the justification, or 2 if the assertion is incomprehensible without reading the justification. It receives a score of 0 otherwise. The example argument gets a UA score of 1 because it is not clear how the assertion is related to the motion.

Unclear Justification (UJ) Because a smooth flow of ideas throughout an argument is important to its persuasiveness, Connor (1990) also evaluates persuasive essays' coherence. Since it is not clear what an incoherent argument is arguing for, we give an argument an UJ score of 2 if the justification appears unrelated to the assertion, 1 if it does not concisely justify the assertion, or 0 if the justification is clear. The example argument gets

---

[3]We also annotated the 1,208 arguments in our corpus with these five errors even though they were not used in the experiments in this paper. See Persing and Ng (2017) for details on the error annotations.

[4]Note, however, that other forums may try to craft emotional debates on purpose for their effectiveness. For instance, Lukin et al. (2017) show that emotional arguments can indeed be very persuasive and that they resonate with different audiences due to audience/reader preset biases and their own personality traits.

an UJ score of 0 as it is easy to understand the author's point in the justification.

5 Approach

In this section, we present our approach to persuasiveness scoring. Broadly, it first predicts the *presence* and *severity* of the aforementioned errors (Section 5.1), then uses these predictions to assign persuasiveness scores (Section 5.2).

5.1 Prediction of Error Types

Our process for predicting error types consists of two steps. First, for each error type, we heuristically apply error severity values to a set of training arguments that can be confidently error-labeled (Section 5.1.1). Using these error-labeled arguments as seeds, we then apply the expectation maximization (EM) algorithm (Dempster et al., 1977) to predict the error severity values of the remaining training arguments (Section 5.1.2).

5.1.1 Heuristics

In this subsection, we describe our heuristics.

Grammar Error (GE) To detect GEs, we use the LanguageTool proofreading program[5] to detect all GEs (e.g., redundant phrases and typos) in all training set justifications. We then calculate the frequency with which GEs occur per sentence in each justification, clustering these values using k-means clustering[6]. Finally, we label the training set arguments in the highest cluster with a GEs value of 1, and training set arguments in the lowest cluster with a GEs value of 0. This makes intuitive sense because GEs can hinder persuasiveness if they occur very frequently, and cannot hinder persuasiveness if they never occur.

Lack of Objectivity (LO) We count how frequently the word "morally" appears in justifications per token. We employ k-means clustering on these frequencies to help us identify which justifications use it most. The justifications falling in the highest cluster's arguments are heuristically labeled with a LO severity of 1. We do the same with the word "certain". Finally, if an author uses less than five definite articles in her justification, we heuristically label her argument with a severity of 1. These rules make sense because arguments that are too concerned with the author's morality or in which the author seems too certain, or in which

the author is rarely specific are likely to display a LO.[7]

To find arguments not displaying a LO (severity = 0), we count and k-means cluster the frequency of first person plural pronouns in the justifications. Arguments whose justifications are in the lowest cluster are labeled with a LO severity of 0. This makes sense because justifications that lack objectivity often rely on stories about the writer's personal experiences. We use plural pronouns to capture this rather than singular ones because thesis statements (which are not inherently subjective) often begin with "I believe" or "I think".[8]

Inadequate Support (IS) To assign IS severities, we first need to know how many sources an argument cites.[9] An argument that cites no references is assigned an IS severity of 2. If the argument cites only one reference, it gets a score of 1. Finally, we cluster arguments by the number of sources they cite. Arguments in the highest cluster are assigned an IS severity of 0. These rules make sense because arguments that cite a lot of sources are probably adequately supported.

Unclear Assertion (UA) UAs typically consist of very short sentence fragments (e.g. "Europe"). For this reason, we heuristically assign an argument an unclear assertion severity of 2 if they are less than four words long.

To identify arguments with an UA severity of 1, we first identify all content lemmas (nouns, pronouns, verbs, adjectives, adverbs) in the assertion. If none of these lemmas are mentioned in the justification, the argument gets a severity of 1. Since this heuristic necessarily conflicts with the previous one, when applying UA heuristics, rules with greater severity take precedence.

Finally, we k-means cluster the counts of assertion content lemmas appearing in the justification and assertion lengths.[10] If an argument is not in the lowest cluster in either of these, it gets labeled

---

[7] We note that these lexical features are potentially specific to this particular domain. There have been a number of works examining objectivity and subjectivity that go beyond lexical features and use syntactic structures (Riloff and Wiebe, 2003; Wilson et al., 2005) and emotional and factual arguments (Oraby et al., 2015).

[8] Since more than one heuristic might apply to a given argument, we leave an argument unlabeled if the heuristics tell us to apply inconsistent labels to it. This is also how we handle contradictory heuristics for the remaining errors.

[9] We develop heuristics for extracting references from the justification. See the Appendix for these heuristics.

[10] We use $k = 6$ for assertion length clustering because assertions vary greatly in length.

---

[5] https://languagetool.org/

[6] Unless otherwise noted, $k = 4$ in k-means clustering.

1	# of grammar errors per sentence in justification (GE)
2	# of times the word "morally" appears in justification (LO)
3	# of times the word "certain" appears in justification (LO)
4	# of definite articles in justification (LO)
5	# of first person plural pronouns in justification (LO)
6	# of references cited in justification (IS)
7	# of words in assertion (UA)
8	# of content lemmas in assertion that also appear in justification (UA)
9	# of sentences in justification (UJ)
10	# of times words that lemmatically match the assertion's subject appear in the first argument of a contingency-cause discourse relation in justification (UJ)

Table 4: Features used by the generative model. The error type for which each feature is originally developed is shown in parentheses.

with an UA severity of 0.

Unclear Justification (UJ)   As with UAs, UJs are often very short. For this reason, we k-means cluster the sentence counts in our training set justifications, and label arguments whose justifications fall into the lowest cluster with an UJ severity of 2. As in the previous error, this rule takes precedence over other rules.

To identify arguments with UJ severities of 1 or 0, we first dependency and discourse parse our assertions and justifications using Stanford CoreNLP (Manning et al., 2014) and Lin et al.'s (2014) PDTB-style discourse parser, respectively. Using the dependency parse, we identify the assertion's main subject, which we assume is the first word that is a child in an nsubj or nsubjpass relationship. Next, we count the number of times words that lemmatically match the subject appear in the first argument of a contingency-cause discourse relation in the justification. Finally, we k-means cluster these counts, assigning arguments with justifications in the highest cluster an UJ severity of 0, and those in the lowest cluster a severity of 1. These rules make sense because a justification that discusses its assertion's topic's effects frequently is likely to be very topically coherent, thus having a clear justification.

5.1.2   Bootstrapping using EM

Recall that for each error type t, our heuristics only label a subset of the training arguments with error severity values for t.[11] To label the remain-

ing training arguments, we apply EM to bootstrap from the heuristically labeled seeds for t.

Specifically, we initialize the model parameters using only the seeds for t. After that, we iterate the E-step and the M-step until convergence. In the E-step, we probabilistically (re)label each unlabeled training argument with its error severity value for t using the current model parameter values. Then, in the M-step, we re-estimate the model parameters using both the seeds and the training arguments probabilistically (re)labeled in the E-step.

To understand what the model parameters are, we need to specify the generative model. In our experiments, we employ Naive Bayes as the underlying generative model, effectively assuming that each feature value is conditionally independent of other feature values given the class value (which in this case is the severity value for t).

To fully specify the model parameters, we need to specify the features used to represent each argument. Specifically, we employ the 10 features used in the heuristics described in the previous subsection. For the sake of clarity, we list them again in Table 4. Note that all of them have numerical values. Hence, to reduce data sparseness, we k-means cluster the values, and use the 10 k-valued features in the EM-based bootstrapping process.

Regardless of which error type we train the model for, the same set of 10 k-valued features will be used. In other words, the generative models for the five error classes differ only w.r.t. the set of seeds used to initialize the model parameters. After learning, we employ the model learned for each error type to error-label the test arguments.

5.2   Persuasiveness Prediction

Like many other unsupervised and weakly-supervised models, we make a modeling assumption in our approach in order to facilitate learning in an environment where annotated data is scarce. Specifically, we assume that the persuasiveness score of an argument inversely correlates with the sum of its severity scores over all errors.[12] This assumption intuitively makes sense: as the number and severity of the errors increase, the corresponding argument becomes less persuasive.

Given this assumption, we train a lightly supervised persuasiveness predictor as follows. First, we cluster the training arguments by the sum of

---

[11]The heuristics for GE, LO, IS, UA, and UJ can label 39%, 66.%, 86%, 50%, and 87% of the training arguments,

respectively.

[12]For instance, if an argument has an IS severity of 2 and a LO severity of 1, the sum of its severity scores will be 3.

severity scores over all errors.[13] Then, we randomly select n arguments from each cluster c (where $1 \leq n \leq 12$ in most of our experiments), and manually label them with their persuasiveness scores. Finally, we assign to each c a persuasiveness score that is the average of the persuasiveness scores of the n manually labeled arguments in c.

During testing, we compute the sum of severity scores over all errors for each test argument, assign it to the corresponding cluster, and predict its persuasiveness score as the score of the cluster it is assigned to. Since our system assigns the Average persuasiveness of training arguments having the same Error Severity count, we call it ASE.

6 Evaluation

In this section, we evaluate our approach to persuasiveness prediction. Since there is an element of randomness in our algorithm and the baselines (in which arguments get labeled), we report results using 5 repetitions of 5-fold cross validation.

6.1 Scoring Metrics

We employ four evaluation metrics for persuasiveness scoring, namely E, ME, MSE, and PC.

The simplest metric, E, measures the frequency at which a system predicts the wrong score. ME and MSE measure the mean error and mean squared error of our persuasiveness predictions, respectively. The formulas below illustrate how we calculate E, ME, and MSE, respectively:

$$\frac{1}{N}\sum_{A_j \neq E'_j} 1, \quad \frac{1}{N}\sum_{j=1}^{N} |A_j - E_j|, \quad \frac{1}{N}\sum_{j=1}^{N} (A_j - E_j)^2$$

where A_j, E_j, and E'_j are the annotator assigned, system predicted, and rounded system predicted persuasiveness scores[14] respectively for argument j, and N is the number of arguments.

The last metric, PC, computes Pearson's correlation coefficient between a system's predicted scores and the annotator-assigned scores. A positive (negative) PC implies that the two sets of predictions are positively (negatively) correlated.

Note that E, ME, and MSE are *error* metrics, so lower scores on them imply better performance. In contrast, PC is a *correlation* metric, so higher correlation implies better performance.

6.2 Baseline Systems

We employ six baseline systems. All baselines are support vector regressors (Drucker et al., 1997) trained using LibSVM (Chang and Lin, 2001) with default parameters, differing only in terms of the features used by the learner.

Bag of words (BOW) In the first baseline, we use as features the bag of words extracted from the argument's assertion and justification.

Word n-grams (WNG) The second baseline uses word n-grams (n=1,2,3) extracted from the argument's assertion and justification as features.

Bag of part-of-speech tags (BOPOS) Our third baseline employs as features the bag of POS tags in the argument's assertion and justification.

Style Our fourth baseline captures aspects of an argument's style. Specifically, it employs four types of features that are motivated by Tan et al.'s (2016) Style baseline, namely:

Length-based features: As longer arguments can be more detailed, we encode as a feature the length in tokens and sentences of an argument's assertion and justification.

Word category-based features: For each of the following categories of words/tokens, we employ as features the absolute count and frequency per token in an argument's justification: (1) definite and indefinite articles and first and second person pronouns, both of which we learned in Section 5.1 can be useful for detecting lack of objectivity; (2) question marks and quotations, which indicate how an argument is structured; (3) positive and negative sentiment words as determined by Mohammad and Yang (2011) since excessive emotion can also signal a lack of objectivity; (4) URLs, since these may be another way of citing evidence; (5) hedge words[15], which can be used to express argument uncertainty; and (6) phrases that indicate the author is giving an example ("e.g.", "for instance", "for example").

---

[13]While the highest possible error severity count is 8, there is no argument in our corpus for which we predict that count. Hence, we only end up with 8 clusters, one for each error severity count (0−7).

[14]Since a regressor assigns each argument a real value rather than an actual valid score, it would be difficult to obtain a reasonable E score without rounding the system estimated score to one of the possible values. For that reason, we round the estimated score to the nearest valid persuasiveness score (1−6 at one-point increments) when calculating E. For other scoring metrics, we round the predictions to 1.0 or 6.0 if they fall outside the 1.0−6.0 range.

[15]The hedge words are taken from http://english-language-skills.com/item/177writing-skills-hedge-words.html.

Word complexity features: These features capture the justification's complexity of word choice, namely the justification's word entropy, type-token ratio, and grade level (Kincaid et al., 1975).

Word score-based features: Warriner et al. (2013) and Brysbaert et al. (2014) associate each word in a lexicon with four real-valued numbers describing how abstract, intensely emotional, pleasant, and vulnerability-evoking the word is. We extract as features the average value of the words in an argument for each of these qualities.

Duplicated Tan et al. (Tan)   As our fifth baseline, we employ our re-implementation of Tan et al.'s (2016) system. Their feature set comprises all the features described in the *Style*, *BOW*, and *BOPOS* baselines, as well as a set of word score-based features exactly like those described above, except that they involve first quartering the justification, then calculating the word scores on each quarter of the text. These are useful because, for example, successful arguments begin by using calmer words.

Persing and Ng (P&N)   The sixth baseline is the system we previously designed and implemented for scoring argument persuasiveness in student essays (Persing and Ng, 2015). This system employs five types of features: (1) POS unigrams, bigrams and trigrams, which capture the syntactic generalizations of an argument's justification; (2) frame-semantic features, which capture the semantic generalizations of the justification; (3) features computed based on the frequency of occurrence of transitional phrases in the justification, which encode its degree of coherence; (4) topic relevance features, which capture the relevance of the justification to its motion based on the number of overlapping entities; and (5) argument label features, which are n-grams of sentence-based argument labels (e.g., CLAIM, SUPPORT) derived from the justification.

6.3   Results and Discussion

Five-fold cross-validation results of the six baselines when trained on 100% of the training data (966 arguments) are shown in the first six rows of Table 5. While BOW and WNG serve as strong baselines for many NLP tasks, the same is not true for persuasiveness scoring: they are among the worst baselines. This is perhaps not surprising given the discussion in the introduction: since persuasiveness scoring is a discourse-level task, in

System	E	ME	MSE	PC
BOW	0.786	1.218	2.087	0.073
WNG	0.786	1.218	2.088	0.063
BOPOS	0.786	1.217	2.084	0.089
Style	0.748	1.102	1.776	0.408
Tan	0.744	1.109	1.799	0.398
P&N	0.785	1.198	2.045	0.252
ASE	0.744	**1.097**	**1.753**	**0.422**

Table 5: Five-fold cross-validation results for persuasiveness scoring. Each baseline is trained on 100% of the training data (966 arguments), while ASE is trained on 96 arguments (10% of the available training data).

many cases an argument's persuasiveness cannot be determined solely from its words and phrases. The best baselines are Style and Tan, a system that builds upon Style. These systems offer considerably better performance than BOW, WNG, BOPOS, and P&N w.r.t. all four scoring metrics.

Results of our system, ASE, are shown in the last row of Table 5. These results are obtained when n is set to 12. Recall that n is a parameter of ASE that specifies the number of persuasiveness-labeled training arguments used to compute each cluster's persuasiveness score. Since we have eight clusters, these results are obtained when ASE is trained on 96 persuasiveness-labeled arguments (10% of the training data). Although ASE is lightly-supervised, it outperforms all the baseline systems by all four metrics. The improvements it yields are highly significant w.r.t. three of the four scoring metrics.[16] These results provide suggestive evidence for the efficacy of our error-modeling approach to persuasiveness scoring.

6.4   Additional Experiments

To gain additional insights into ASE, we perform additional experiments.

Lightly-supervised baselines.   To be fair in our comparison with the baselines, we retrain them on 10% of the arguments randomly sampled from the training data and compare their performances against ASE. Results are shown in Table 6. In comparison to the results in Table 5, almost all baselines suffer from performance deterioration, particularly w.r.t. ME, MSE, and PC. ASE continues to significantly outperform all baselines

---

[16]Unless otherwise stated, boldfaced results are highly significant compared to the best baseline ($p < .01$, paired t-test).

System	E	ME	MSE	PC
BOW	0.788	1.245	2.216	0.011
WNG	0.789	1.245	2.217	0.013
BOPOS	0.789	1.245	2.213	0.044
Style	0.755	1.239	2.343	0.261
Tan	0.755	1.238	2.340	0.267
P&N	0.791	1.291	2.432	0.147
ASE	0.744	**1.097**	**1.753**	**0.422**

Table 6: Results for persuasiveness scoring when all systems are trained on 10% of the training instances.

F #	E	ME	MSE	PC
1	0.749	1.112	1.795	0.415
2	0.751	1.112	1.803	0.405†
3	0.745	1.096	1.764	0.415
4	0.752	1.104	1.759	0.416
5	0.752†	1.114	1.802†	0.401†
6	0.748	1.109	1.798	0.407
7	0.744	1.11	1.811	0.413
8	0.753	1.105†	1.772	0.412
9	0.753	1.113	1.817†	0.400†
10	0.755	1.118	1.811	0.398

Table 7: Results for persuasiveness scoring when one feature is removed from ASE's generative model. F # indicates which feature is being referred to (as indexed in Table 4).

w.r.t. these three scoring metrics.

Feature ablation. In order to determine each feature's contribution to ASE's generative model, we perform ablation experiments wherein we retrain the model using all but one of the features. Table 7 shows how ASE performs after each feature is removed.[17]

From these results, we gather that no feature makes a negative contribution to the model, as no feature's removal significantly improves performance on any metric. Occurrences of "morally", first person plural pronouns, the number of content lemmas appearing in both the assertion and the justification, and justification length (features 2, 5, 8 and 9) make significant contributions to performance according to at least one metric.

Error ablation. Recall that ASE predicts persuasiveness based on a summation of the predicted severity scores over all errors. To determine the

Error	E	ME	MSE	PC
GE	0.745	1.082	1.71	0.443
LO	0.746	1.098	1.758	0.416
IS	0.766	1.171†	1.954†	0.317†
UA	0.743	1.106†	1.789†	0.409†
UJ	0.763†	1.132†	1.862†	0.367†

Table 8: Results for persuasiveness scoring when ASE predicts persuasiveness based on a summation of severity scores over all but one error. The error shown in each row is the ablated error.

n	E	ME	MSE	PC
1	0.771	1.430	3.393	0.240
2	0.750	1.304	2.688	0.299
3	0.758	1.221	2.302	0.320
4	0.746	1.177	2.113	0.348
5	0.747	1.153	1.980	0.361
6	0.749	1.151	1.969	0.374
7	0.752	1.143	1.918	0.379
8	0.747	1.119	1.842	0.386
9	0.754	1.104	1.790	0.407
10	0.754	1.112	1.808	0.413

Table 9: Learning curve results.

importance of each error's contribution, we perform five ablation experiments wherein we exclude each one of the errors from this summation.

Table 8 shows that the IS, UA, and UJ errors make the most important contributions to persuasiveness scoring since removing them from consideration significantly harms performance compared to ASE. Removing GE and LO, by contrast, harms performance the least since these are likely the two least frequent errors and therefore have less impact on performance.

Learning curve. Table 9 shows how our ASE system performs when n increases from 1 to 10. As we can see, the scores for all metrics with the exception of E follow the expected trajectory of a learning curve, with worse scores for $n = 1$ progressively becoming better as n approaches 10.

Fully-supervised results. Can ASE perform better given more training data? Table 10 shows the results of ASE when it is trained on 10% (ASE(10)) and 100% (ASE(100)) of the training data. As we can see, the answer is yes: ASE(100) significantly outperforms ASE(10) w.r.t. all but the E metric. While it is not surprising to see diminishing returns, what is perhaps surprising is the relative small performance gap between ASE(10)

---

[17]Unless otherwise stated, results that are significantly worse than that of the original model ($p < .01$, paired t-test) are marked with a dagger.

System	E	ME	MSE	PC
ASE(10)	0.744	1.097	1.753	0.422
ASE(100)	0.745	**1.078**	**1.678**	**0.441**

Table 10: Results for persuasiveness scoring when ASE is trained on 10% (row 1) and 100% (row 2) of the training data.

Train data	E	ME	MSE	PC
10%	0.739	1.110	1.901	0.408
100%	0.731	1.053	1.724	0.454

Table 11: Results for persuasiveness scoring when ASE predicts persuasiveness by means of a support vector regressor that is trained on 10% (row 1) and 100% (row 2) of the training data using only the error severity values as features.

and ASE(100): it suggests that ASE learns very fast from a small amount of labeled data.

Training a persuasiveness predictor with errors as features. Recall that ASE predicts persuasiveness based on the sum of severity scores. Can we instead predict persuasiveness by training a regressor using only the errors as features? To answer this question, we train a support vector regressor using the 13 binary features that correspond to the 13 severity values of the five errors. The value of a feature is 1 if and only if the argument is assigned the corresponding severity value.

Results of the regressor are shown in Table 11. When the regressor is trained on 10% of the training data, its results are worse than the ASE(10) results in Table 10 w.r.t. all but the E metric. However, when it is trained on 100% of the training data, its results are slightly better than the ASE(100) results in Table 10 w.r.t. all but the MSE metric. We speculate that being discriminatively trained, the support vector regressor can yield better results than the simplistic modeling assumption made by ASE only when training data is plentiful. Additional experiments are needed to determine the reason, however.

Correlation. Recall that ASE assumes that the persuasiveness score of an argument correlates with the sum of its severity scores over all errors. To better understand the extent to which this assumption is true, we cluster *all* 1,208 arguments by the sum of severity scores. For each of the eight resulting clusters, we average the gold persuasiveness scores of the arguments in the cluster.

Results are shown in Table 12. As we can see,

SS	Average	SD	SS	Average	SD
0	5.138	1.050	4	3.111	1.331
1	4.886	1.190	5	3.245	1.392
2	4.194	1.338	6	2.909	1.446
3	3.763	1.306	7	3.000	0.000

Table 12: Average persuasiveness score and its standard deviation (SD) against the sum of severity score (SS).

the data satisfies our assumption: average persuasiveness decreases as the sum of severity scores increases. The only exception occurs when SS=7, presumably due to the small sample size.

6.5 Error Analysis

Next, we conduct a qualitative error analysis.

While there is a definite correlation between error severity count and persuasiveness, error severity count is likely not the only factor that impacts persuasiveness. An examination of some essays whose persuasiveness scores are far from their ASE predicted scores shows that factors that are harder to analyze such as logical soundness and the presence of claims that seem to contradict the assertion also play a role in persuasiveness.

In other arguments, persuasiveness prediction error can be attributed to our system's misprediction of the presence/absence/severity of an error. Error annotated data might help address this problem by allowing us to tune our error severity heuristics.

Finally, our error severity scales are pretty coarse-grained. It is reasonable to expect, for example, that a real argument could have an unclear justification error whose severity is halfway between 2 and 1, but our EM algorithm for predicting error severities does not allow this. The introduction of a regression system into our algorithm might address this problem.

7 Conclusion

We proposed a lightly-supervised approach to the under-studied problem of predicting argument persuasiveness scores on debate arguments. Experimental results on 1,208 arguments demonstrated that our approach significantly outperformed six fully-supervised baselines by three out of four scoring metrics when using only 10% of the training data. To stimulate research on this task, we make our annotated data publicly available.

Acknowledgments

We thank the three anonymous reviewers for their detailed comments. We also thank our annotators, Dino Occhialini and Christopher Knoll. This work was supported in part by NSF Grants IIS-1219142 and IIS-1528037. Any opinions, findings, conclusions or recommendations expressed in this paper are those of the authors and do not necessarily reflect the views or official policies, either expressed or implied, of NSF.

References

Marc Brysbaert, Amy Beth Warriner, and Victor Kuperman. 2014. Concreteness ratings for 40 thousand generally known English word lemmas. *Behavior Research Methods* 46(3):904–911.

Chih-Chung Chang and Chih-Jen Lin. 2001. *LIBSVM: A library for Support Vector Machines.* Software available at http://www.csie.ntu.edu.tw/~cjlin/libsvm.

Ulla Connor. 1990. Linguistic/rhetorical measures for international persuasive student writing. *Research in the Teaching of English* pages 67–87.

Ulla Connor and Janice Lauer. 1985. Understanding persuasive essay writing: Linguistic/Rhetorical approach. *Text-Interdisciplinary Journal for the Study of Discourse* 5(4):309–326.

Arthur P. Dempster, Nan M. Laird, and Donald B. Rubin. 1977. Maximum likelihood from incomplete data via the EM algorithm. *Journal of the Royal Statistical Society. Series B (Methodological)* 39:1–38.

Harris Drucker, Christopher J. C. Burges, Linda Kaufman, Alex Smola, and Vladimir Vapnik. 1997. Support vector regression machines. In *Advances in Neural Information Processing Systems* 9, pages 155–161.

Ivan Habernal and Iryna Gurevych. 2016a. What makes a convincing argument? Empirical analysis and detecting attributes of convincingness in Web argumentation. In *Proceedings of the 2016 Conference on Empirical Methods in Natural Language Processing*, pages 1214–1223.

Ivan Habernal and Iryna Gurevych. 2016b. Which argument is more convincing? Analyzing and predicting convincingness of Web arguments using bidirectional LSTM. In *Proceedings of the 54th Annual Meeting of the Association for Computational Linguistics (Volume 1: Long Papers)*, pages 1589–1599.

J. Peter Kincaid, Robert P. Fishburne Jr., Richard L. Rogers, and Brad S. Chissom. 1975. Derivation of new readability formulas (automated readability index, fog count and flesch reading ease formula) for Navy enlisted personnel. Technical report, DTIC Document.

Claudia Leacock, Martin Chodorow, Michael Gamon, and Joel R. Tetreault. 2014. *Automated Grammatical Error Detection for Language Learners.* Synthesis Lectures on Human Language Technologies. Morgan & Claypool Publishers, second edition.

Ziheng Lin, Hwee Tou Ng, and Min-Yen Kan. 2014. A PDTB-styled end-to-end discourse parser. *Natural Language Engineering*, 20(2):151–184, 2014.

Stephanie Lukin, Pranav Anand, Marilyn Walker, and Steve Whittaker. 2017. Argument strength is in the eye of the beholder: Audience effects in persuasion. In *Proceedings of the 15th Conference of the European Chapter of the Association for Computational Linguistics: Volume 1, Long Papers.* pages 742–753.

Christopher D. Manning, Mihai Surdeanu, John Bauer, Jenny Finkel, Steven J. Bethard, and David McClosky. 2014. The Stanford CoreNLP natural language processing toolkit. In *Proceedings of 52nd Annual Meeting of the Association for Computational Linguistics: System Demonstrations.* pages 55–60.

Saif Mohammad and Tony Yang. 2011. Tracking sentiment in mail: How genders differ on emotional axes. In *Proceedings of the 2nd Workshop on Computational Approaches to Subjectivity and Sentiment Analysis*, pages 70–79.

Witri Oktavia, Anas Yasin, et al. 2014. An analysis of students' argumentative elements and fallacies in students' discussion essays. *English Language Teaching* 2(3).

Shereen Oraby, Lena Reed, Ryan Compton, Ellen Riloff, Marilyn Walker, and Steve Whittaker. 2015. And that's a fact: Distinguishing factual and emotional argumentation in online dialogue. In *Proceedings of the 2nd Workshop on Argumentation Mining.* pages 116–126.

Isaac Persing and Vincent Ng. 2015. Modeling argument strength in student essays. In *Proceedings of the 53rd Annual Meeting of the Association for Computational Linguistics and the 7th International Joint Conference on Natural Language Processing (Volume 1: Long Papers)*, pages 543–552.

Isaac Persing and Vincent Ng. 2017. Why can't you convince me? Modeling weaknesses in unpersuasive arguments. In *Proceedings of the 26th International Joint Conference on Artificial Intelligence.* pages 4082–4088.

Richard E. Petty and John T. Cacioppo. 1984. The effects of involvement on responses to argument quantity and quality: Central and peripheral routes to persuasion. *Journal of Personality and Social Psychology* 46(1):69.

Ellen Riloff and Janyce Wiebe. 2003. Learning extraction patterns for subjective expressions. In *Proceedings of the 2003 Conference on Empirical Methods in Natural Language Processing*. pages 105–112.

Mark D. Shermis, Jill Burstein, Derrick Higgins, and Klaus Zechner. 2010. Automated essay scoring: Writing assessment and instruction. In *International Encyclopedia of Education (3rd edition)*, Elsevier, Oxford, UK.

Chenhao Tan, Vlad Niculae, Cristian Danescu-Niculescu-Mizil, and Lillian Lee. 2016. Winning arguments: Interaction dynamics and persuasion strategies in good-faith online discussions. In *Proceedings of the 25th International World Wide Web Conference*, pages 613–624.

Amy Beth Warriner, Victor Kuperman, and Marc Brysbaert. 2013. Norms of valence, arousal, and dominance for 13,915 English lemmas. *Behavior Research Methods* 45(4):1191–1207.

Zhongyu Wei, Yang Liu, and Yi Li. 2016. Is this post persuasive? Ranking argumentative comments in online forum. In *Proceedings of the 54th Annual Meeting of the Association for Computational Linguistics (Volume 2: Short Papers)*, pages 195–200.

Theresa Wilson, Paul Hoffmann, Swapna Somasundaran, Jason Kessler, Janyce Wiebe, Yejin Choi, Claire Cardie, Ellen Riloff, and Siddharth Patwardhan. 2005. Opinionfinder: A system for subjectivity analysis. In *Proceedings of HLT/EMNLP 2005 Interactive Demonstrations*. pages 34–35.

Appendix: Reference Extraction and Internal Citation Cleanup

Given an argument, we employ the following steps to extract references and clean up internal citations.

1. We identify digits and locations in the justification that appear to refer to references. Particularly, we identify each digit in the text that satisfies all the following conditions: (a) it appears next to a punctuation (because the digits usually occur right before or after a sentence's end punctuation); (b) it does not appear next to another digit (because these are short arguments, a digit next to another digit is probably not a citation); (c) if we take the string consisting of the digit, the punctuation, the character next to the digit other than the punctuation, and the character on the other side of the punctuation, this string is not parsable as a floating point number (if it is part of a floating point number, it is probably not a citation); (d) a '$' does not appear before it; (e) a '%' does not appear after it; (f)

a '/' does not appear before it; and (g) a '/' does not appear after it.

2. We make a list of all digits identified in step 1 that occur at least twice in the text. (A digit needs to occur twice in order to be a citation because the first time it occurs in the justification text and the last time it occurs right before the reference.)

3. We sort the digits from step 2 in numerical order. We remove 0 from the list if it is present. If there are any gaps in the list (e.g., if '1', '2', and '4' appear in the list), we discard any digits after the gap. (People do not use 0 to make references. And if there are gaps, it usually means that whatever number appears after the gap was erroneously identified as a citation because people do not skip digits when numbering their references.)

4. We sequentially scan the list from step 3. If, at any point in the list, the last location (in the justification) of the digit we are examining occurs before the last location (in the justification) of the previous digit in the list, we discard the digit and all the digits after it in the list. (We expect references to begin with the last occurrences of their corresponding numbers. If one of the digits' last occurrences seems out of order, that means there is a problem with the list so we cannot rely on it beyond this point.)

5. We split the text according to the locations in the justification of the digits that remain in the list from step 4. The first text segment is the justification's text, and all the remaining segments are individual references.

6. Finally, we do some cleanup of the text. We remove all the digits identified in step 1 occurring in the justification's text. (This should help with parsing because the digits make sentences grammatically incorrect.) We also remove all occurrences of '[' or ']' in the text (because some people surround their citation digits with them). Finally we replace any urls (starting with "http:") with "url".

Multi-Task Learning for Speaker-Role Adaptation in Neural Conversation Models

Yi Luan[†*]   **Chris Brockett**[‡]   **Bill Dolan**[‡]   **Jianfeng Gao**[‡]   **Michel Galley**[‡]

[†]Department of Electrical Engineering, University of Washington
[‡]Microsoft Research

luanyi@uw.edu, {chrisbkt,billdol,jfgao,mgalley}@microsoft.com

Abstract

Building a persona-based conversation agent is challenging owing to the lack of large amounts of speaker-specific conversation data for model training. This paper addresses the problem by proposing a multi-task learning approach to training neural conversation models that leverages both conversation data across speakers and other types of data pertaining to the speaker and speaker roles to be modeled. Experiments show that our approach leads to significant improvements over baseline model quality, generating responses that capture more precisely speakers' traits and speaking styles. The model offers the benefits of being algorithmically simple and easy to implement, and not relying on large quantities of data representing specific individual speakers.

1 Introduction

Conversational engines are key components of intelligent "personal assistants" such as Apple's Siri and Amazon's Alexa. These assistants can perform simple tasks, answer questions, provide recommendations, and even engage in chitchats (De Mori et al., 2008; Chen et al., 2015, 2016). The emergence of these agents has been paralleled by burgeoning interest in training natural-sounding dialog systems from conversational exchanges between humans (Ritter et al., 2011; Sordoni et al., 2015; Luan et al., 2014, 2015; Vinyals and Le, 2015). A major challenge for data-driven systems is how to generate output that corresponds to specific traits that the agent needs to adopt, as they tend to generate "consensus" re-

---

* This work was performed at Microsoft.

> **User input:** *I am getting a loop back to login page.*
> **Baseline model:** Ah, ok. Thanks for the info.
> **Our model:** I'm sorry to hear that. Have you tried clearing your cache and cookies?

Figure 1: Existing neural conversational models (baseline) tend to produce generic responses. The system presented in this paper better represents the speaker role (support person), domain of expertise (technical), and speaking style (courteous).

sponses that are often commonplace and uninteresting (Li et al., 2016a; Shao et al., 2017).

This is illustrated in Fig. 1, where the output of a standard Sequence-to-Sequence conversation model is contrasted with that of the best system presented in this work. The baseline system generates a desultory answer that offers no useful information and is unlikely to inspire user confidence. The output of the second system, however, strongly reflects the agent's role in providing technical support. It not only evidences domain knowledge, but also manifests the professional politeness associated with a speaker in that role.

The challenge for neural conversation systems, then, is that an agent needs to exhibit identifiable role-specific characteristics (a 'persona'). In practice, however, the conversational data needed to train such systems may be scarce or unavailable in many domains. This may make it difficult to train a system represent a doctor or nurse, or a travel agent. Meanwhile, appropriate nonconversational data (e.g., blog and micro-blog posts, diaries, and email) are often abundant and may contain much richer information about the characteristics of a speaker, including expressive style and the role they play. Yet such data is difficult to exploit directly, since, not being in conversational format, it does not mesh easily with existing source-target conversational models.

Proceedings of the The 8th International Joint Conference on Natural Language Processing, pages 605–614,
Taipei, Taiwan, November 27 – December 1, 2017 ©2017 AFNLP

In this paper we address the joint problems of blandness and data scarcity with multi-task learning (Caruana, 1998; Liu et al., 2015; Luan et al., 2016a). This is a technique that has seen success in machine translation, where large monolingual data sets have been used to improve translation models (Sennrich et al., 2016). The intuition is that if two tasks are related, then joint training and parameter sharing can enable one task to benefit the other. In our case, this sharing is between two models: On one hand, a standard Sequence-to-Sequence conversational models is trained to predict the current response given the previous context. On the other hand, using the non-conversational data, we introduce an autoencoder multi-task learning strategy that predicts the response given the same sequence, but with the target parameters tied with the general conversational model.

Our experiments with 4M conversation triples show that multi-task adaptation is effective in that the generated responses capture speaker-role characteristics more precisely than the baseline. Experiments on a corpus of Twitter conversations demonstrate that multi-task learning can boost performance up to 46.2% in BLEU score and 23.0% in perplexity, with a commensurate consistency gains in human evaluation.

2 Related Work

2.1 Conversational Models

In contrast with much earlier work in dialog, our approach to conversation is wholly data-driven and end-to-end. In this respect, it follows a line of investigation begun by (Ritter et al., 2011), who present a statistical machine translation based conversation system. End-to-end conversation models have been explored within the framework of neural networks (Sordoni et al., 2015; Vinyals and Le, 2015; Li et al., 2016a,b; Luan et al., 2017). The flexibility of these Sequence-to-Sequence (SEQ2SEQ) encoder-decoder neural models opens the possibility of integrating different kinds of information beyond the single previous turn of the conversation. For example, (Sordoni et al., 2015) integrate additional contextual information via feed-forward neural networks. (Li et al., 2016a) use Maximum Mutual Information (MMI) as the objective function in order to produce more diverse and interesting responses. (Mei et al., 2017) introduce an attention mechanism into an encoder-decoder network for a conversation model.

(Wen et al., 2015) introduced a Dialog-Act component into the LSTM cell to guide generated content. (Luan et al., 2016b) use a multiplicative matrix on word embeddings to bias the word distribution of different speaker roles. That work, however, assumes only two roles (questioner and answerer) and is less generalizable than the model proposed here.

Most relevant to the present work, (Li et al., 2016b) propose employing speaker embeddings to encode persona information and allow conversation data of similar users on social media to be shared for model training. That work focused on individuals, rather than classes of people. The approach, moreover, is crucially dependent on the availability of large-scale conversational corpora that closely match the persona being modeled—data that, as we have already observed, may not be readily available in many domains. In this work, we circumvent these limitations by bringing non-conversation corpora (analogous to the use of monolingual data in machine translation) to bear on a general model of conversation. Doing so allows us to benefit in terms of representing both the role of the agent and domain content.

2.2 Multi-Task Learning

Multi-task learning has been successfully used to improve performance in various tasks, including machine translation (Sennrich et al., 2016) and image captioning (Luong et al., 2016). (Sennrich et al., 2016) report methods of exploiting monolingual data—usually available in much larger quantities—to improve the performance of machine translation, including multi-task learning of a language model for the decoder. Autoencoders are widely used to initialize neural networks (Dai and Le, 2015). (Luong et al., 2016) show that an autoencoder of monolingual data can help improve the performance of bilingual machine translation in the form of multi-task learning. In our models, we share the decoder parameters of a SEQ2SEQ model and autoencoder to incorporate textual information through multi-task learning.

3 Background

3.1 Task definition

The task of response generation is to generate a response given a context. In this paper, following (Sordoni et al., 2015), each data sample is represented as a *(context,message,response)* triple, where context is the response of the previous turn, and the message is the input string of the current turn. The response, then, is the sequence to be predicted given these two strings of information. In addition to the triple, large-scale non-conversational data from the responder is provided as side information.

3.2 Sequence-to-Sequence Conversational Models

Given a sequence of inputs $X = \{x_1, x_2, \ldots, x_{n_X}\}$ and the corresponding output $Y = \{y_1, y_2, \ldots, y_{n_Y}\}$, Sequence-to-Sequence (SEQ2SEQ) models use a Long Short-Term Memories (LSTM) (Hochreiter and Schmidhuber, 1997) to encode the input sequence, taking the last hidden state of encoder h_{n_X} to represent output sequence. The decoder is initialized by h_{n_X}, and predict output y_t given h_{n_X} and y_{t-1}.

Our input is context followed by message, delimited by an *EOS* token. The LSTM cell includes an input gate, a memory gate and an output gate, respectively denoted as i_t, f_t and o_t.

3.3 Persona-based conversational model

The persona-based conversational model is a variant of standard SEQ2SEQ models, with user information encoded at decoder. As in standard SEQ2SEQ models, the persona-based conversational model presented in (Li et al., 2016b) first encodes the source message into a vector representation using the source LSTM. Then, for each element in the target side, hidden units are obtained by combining the representation produced by the target LSTM at the previous time step h_{t-1}, the word representations e_t at the current time step, and the embedding s_i for user i.

$$\begin{bmatrix} i_t \\ f_t \\ o_t \\ l_t \end{bmatrix} = \begin{bmatrix} \sigma \\ \sigma \\ \sigma \\ \tanh \end{bmatrix} W \cdot \begin{bmatrix} h_{t-1} \\ e_t \\ s_i \end{bmatrix} \quad (1)$$

$$c_t = f_t \cdot c_{t-1} + i_t \cdot l_t \quad (2)$$

$$h_t = o_t \cdot \tanh(c_t) \quad (3)$$

where $W \in \mathbb{R}^{4K \times 3K}$. This model assigns one K dimensional vector representation to each of the speakers in the corpus. It thus relies on the availability of sufficient conversational training data

of each speaker to learn meaningful speaker embeddings. Since this type of data is usually hard to obtain in real application scenarios, we need a method that can leverage easier-to-obtain non-conversational personal data in order to incorporate richer personal information into conversational models.

4 A Multi-task Learning Approach

Given the limitations of previous methods, we propose the following multi-task learning approach in order to simultaneously leverage conversational data across many users on the one hand, and personal but non-conversation data (written text) of a specific user on the other. We define the following two tasks:

- A SEQ2SEQ task that learns conversational models described in Section 3 using conversation data of a large general population of speakers.
- An AUTOENCODER task that utilizes large volumes of non-conversational personal data from target speakers.

AUTOENCODER: An AUTOENCODER is an unsupervised method of obtaining sequence embeddings based on the SEQ2SEQ framework. Like a SEQ2SEQ model, it comprises encoding and decoding components built by an LSTM sequential model as in Section 3.2. Instead of mapping source to target as in a SEQ2SEQ model, the AUTOENCODER predicts the input sequence itself.

Parameter sharing: Given the same context, we want to generate a response that can mimic a particular target speaker. Therefore, we share only the decoder parameters of SEQ2SEQ and AUTOENCODER while performing multi-task learning, so that the language model for generation can be adapted to the target-speaker. Since the context is not constrained and can be from any speaker, the encoder parameters are not tied and are learned separately by each task. (See Fig. 2.)

Training Procedure The training procedure is shown in Fig. 3. In each iteration, the gradient of each task is calculated according to the task-specific objective. The training process finishes when perplexity performance converges in dev set and the best model is selected according to SEQ2SEQ perplexity performance.

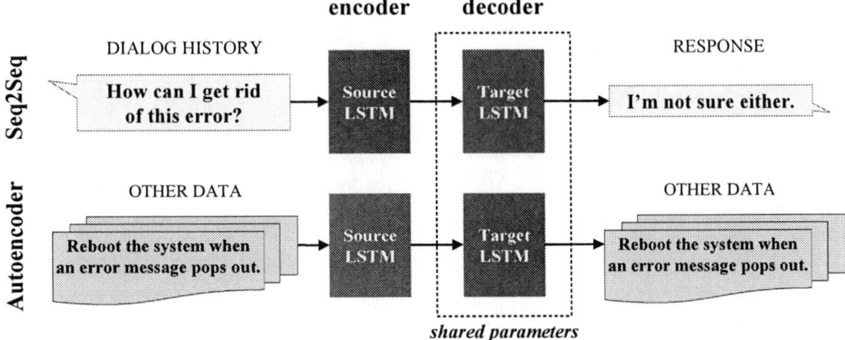

Figure 2: Framework of Multi-task learning. The parameters of decoder are shared across the two tasks.

Training procedure of Multi-task learning:
1. Randomly initialize SEQ2SEQ and AUTOEN-CODER encoder parameters.
2. Train SEQ2SEQ model until dev set performance converges in perplexity.
3. **While** not dev set performance converged in perplexity **do:**
   (a) Randomly pick a batch of samples from general conversational data.
   (b) Compute loss and gradient for SEQ2SEQ task and update parameters.
   (c) Randomly pick a batch of samples from non-conversational data of the target user.
   (d) Compute loss and gradient for AUTOEN-CODER task and update parameters.
4. Choose the best model based on SEQ2SEQ perplexity performance on dev set.

Figure 3: Training Procedure

5 Single v.s. Multiple speaker Settings

Two variants of SEQ2SEQ task are explored:

- **MTASK-S** Personalized response generation for a **single** user, which uses the basic SEQ2SEQ conversational model as described in Section 3.2.
- **MTASK-M** Response generation for **multiple** users, which uses the persona-based SEQ2SEQ model described in Section 3.3.

MTASK-S: We train a personalized conversational model for one speaker at a time. For each target user, we need to perform separate multi-task training which results in N models for N users. This is inefficient in both memory and computational cost.

MTASK-M: In order to address the memory and computation issue of MTASK-S, we introduce user embeddings to SEQ2SEQ model as in Eq. 1. We first train a persona-based conversational model using conversational data for a general population of speakers. This model differs MTASK-S in that it introduces two parameter matrices into the decoder: a speaker embedding s_i and its corresponding weight matrix that can decouple speaker dependent information from general language information. In the multi-task stage, since the target users have never appeared in the training data, we randomly initialize the user embeddings for those users and follow the training procedure as in Figure 3.[1] The embedding of the unseen user is updated by AUTOENCODER training together with the decoder LSTM parameters.

6 Experimental Setup

6.1 Datasets

As training data, we use a collection of 3-turn conversations extracted from the Twitter FireHose. The dataset covers the six-month period beginning January 1, 2012, and was limited to conversations where the responders had engaged in at least 60 3-turn conversational Twitter interactions during the period. In other words, these are people who reasonably frequently engaged in conversation, and might be experienced "conversationalists."

We selected the top 7k Twitter users who had most conversational data from that period (at least 480 turns, average: 571). This yielded a total of approximately 4M conversational interactions. In addition to these 7k general Twitter users, we also selected the 20 most frequent users, employing all of their conversation data for development and test. Twitter users typically have many more single posts than posts that interact with other people.

---

[1]The model can also be learned without pre-training (omitting step 2), but we found that pre-training usually helps.

We therefore treat single posts as non-conversation data. All single posts of the 20 top users (at least 9k per user, average 10.3k) were extracted for multi-task learning. The 20 users were of diverse backgrounds, including technical support personnel, novelists, and sports fans.

6.2 Evaluation

As in previous work (Sordoni et al., 2015), we use BLEU and human evaluation for evaluation. BLEU (Papineni et al., 2002) has been shown to correlate fairly well with human judgment at a document- and corpus-level, including on the response generation task.[2] We also report perplexity as an indicator of model capability.

We additionally report degree of diversity by calculating the number of distinct unigrams and bigrams in generated responses. The value is scaled by total number of generated tokens to avoid favoring long sentences (shown as distinct-1 and distinct-2). Finally, we present a human evaluation that validates our main findings.

6.3 Baseline

Our baseline is our implementation of the LSTM-MMI of (Li et al., 2016a). The MMI algorithm reduced the blandness of SEQ2SEQ models by scoring the generated N-best list with a function that linearly combines a length penalty and the log likelihood of source given target:

$$\log p(R|M, v) + \lambda \log p(M|R) + \gamma |R| \quad (4)$$

where $p(R|M, v)$ is the probability of the generated response given message M and the respondents user ID. $|R|$ is the length of the target and γ is the associated penalty weight. We use MERT (Och, 2003) to optimize γ and λ on BLEU using N-best lists of response candidates generated from the development set. To compute $p(M|R)$, we train an inverse SEQ2SEQ model by swapping messages and responses. The reverse SEQ2SEQ models $p(M|R)$ is trained with no user information considered.

6.4 Training and Decoding

We trained two-layer SEQ2SEQ models on the Twitter corpus, using the following settings:

[2](Liu et al., 2016) suggest that BLEU doesn't correlate well with human judgment at the sentence level. Other work, however, has shown that correlation increases substantially with larger units of analysis (e.g., document or corpus) (Galley et al., 2015; Przybocki et al., 2009).

	Baseline	MTASK-S	MTASK-M
Perplexity (dev)	56.33	**32.27** (-42.7%)	44.96 (-20.2%)
Perplexity (test)	61.17	**39.83** (-34.9%)	43.21 (-29.4%)

Table 1: Perplexity for standard SEQ2SEQ and the user model on the Twitter Persona dev set.

	Baseline	MTASK-S	MTASK-M
BLEU (dev)	1.32	1.76 (+33.3%)	**2.52** (+90.1%)
BLEU (test)	1.31	1.69 (+29.0%)	**2.25** (+71.7%)
distinct-1	1.69%	2.43%	**2.44%**
distinct-2	6.53%	**10.2%**	9.79%

Table 2: Performance on the Twitter dataset of 2-layer SEQ2SEQ models and MMI models. Distinct-1 and distinct-2 are respectively the number of distinct unigrams and bigrams divided by total number of generated words.

- 2 layer LSTM models with 500 hidden cells for each layer.
- Batch size is set to 128.
- Optimization method is Adam (Kingma and Ba, 2015).
- Parameters for SEQ2SEQ models are initialized by sampling from uniform distribution $[-0.1, 0.1]$.
- Vocabulary size is limited to 50k.
- Parameters are tuned based on perplexity.

For decoding, the N-best lists are generated with beam size $B = 50$. The maximum length of the generated candidates was set at 20 tokens. At each time step, we first examine all $B \times B$ possible next-word candidates, and add all hypotheses ending with an EOS token to the N-best list. We then preserve the top-B unfinished hypotheses and move to the next word position. We then use LSTM-MMI to rerank the N-best list and use the 1-best result of the re-ranked list in all evaluation.

7 Experimental Results

The perplexity and BLEU score results for three models are shown in Tables 1 and 2. Compared with the baseline model LSTM-MMI, we obtain a 34.9% decrease in perplexity for the MTASK-S model and a 29.4% decrease in perplexity for the MTASK-M model. Significant gains are obtained in BLEU score as well: MTASK-S gains

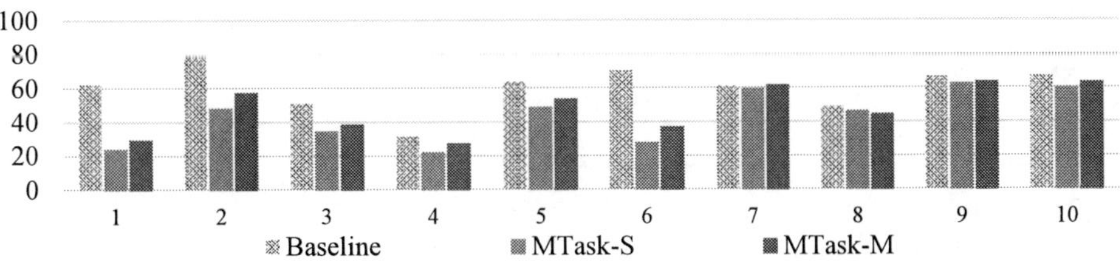

Figure 4: Perplexity scores for the top 10 users with most (non-conversational) training data. Users with obvious speaking styles or stronger user role characteristics (e.g., 1, 2, and 6) show much greater perplexity reduction than the other ones.

29.0% relative increase compared with the baseline and MTASK-M gains 71.7%. MTASK-S performance is better than MTASK-M in perplexity, but worse on BLEU score. Apart from the fact that BLEU does not necessarily correlate with perplexity, this result also indicates that MTASK-S has more parameters (each user has a unique model for MTASK-S) but tends to overfit on development set perplexity. Another possible reason that MTASK-M performs better than MTASK-S is the introduction of user embeddings. The persona-based conversational model can decouple the personalized information from general language patterns and can therefore encode user characteristic better. We further report degree of diversity by calculating the number of distinct unigrams (distinct-1) and bigrams (distinct-2) in generated responses as in Table 2. To avoid biasing toward longer sentences, this value is scaled by the total number of tokens generated. Both MTASK-S and MTASK-M models perform better than baseline in terms of distinct-1 and distinct-2, which we interpret to mean that our approach can help the system generate responses that are more diverse yet better approximate the targeted speaker or speaker type.

Fig. 4 shows the perplexities for the 10 individual users most represented in the non-conversational training data. Our multi-task approaches consistently outperform baseline on perplexity. However, the performance between individual target users can vary substantially.[3]

After inspecting dev set outputs, we observe that users with obvious speaking styles or stronger user role characteristics show much greater gain than the others. For example, User 1 is a technical support worker who answers web questions for Twitter users, while User 2 always expresses strong feelings and uses exclamation marks frequently. Conversely, tweets from users that did not show significant gain appear to be more about daily life and chitchat, with no strong role characteristics (e.g., Users 3 and 4). We present example outputs for User 1 and 2 in Section 8.

7.1 Human Evaluation

Human evaluation of the outputs was performed using crowdsourcing.[4] Evaluation took the form of a preference test in which judges were presented with a random sample of 5 tweets written by the targeted user as example texts, and asked which system output appeared most likely to have been produced by the same person. A 5-point scale that permitted ties was used, and system pairs were presented in random order. A short input message (the input that was used to generate the outputs) was also provided. We used 7 judges for each comparison; those judges whose variances differed by more than two standard deviations from the mean variance were discarded. Table 3 shows the results of pairwise evaluation, along with 95% confidence intervals of the means. MTASK-S and MTASK-M both perform better on average than LSTM-MMI, consistent with the BLEU results. MTASK-M's gain over the LSTM-MMI baseline is significant at the level of $\alpha = 0.05$ (p = 0.026), indicating that judges were better able to associate the output of that model with the target author.

In Table 3 the strength of the trends is obscured by averaging. We therefore converted the scores for each output into the ratio of judges who selected that system for each output (Figs. 5 and 6). To read the charts, bin 7 on the left represents

---

[3]We do not report BLEU scores for individual users, as the dev and test set for each specific user tends to be small (less than 500 samples) and BLEU is known to be unreliable when evaluated on small datasets (Graham et al., 2015; Liu et al., 2016).

[4]Two outputs were removed from the datasets owing to offensive content in the examples.

	Baseline	System
MTASK-S	0.491 ±0.011	0.504 ±0.011
MTASK-M	0.486 ±0.012	0.514 ±0.012

Table 3: Results of human evaluation, showing relative gain of MTASK-S and MTASK-M systems over the LSTM-MMI baseline in pairwise comparison, together with 95% confidence intervals of the means.

the case where all 7 judges "voted" for the system, bin 6 the case where 6 out of 7 judges "voted" for the system, and so forth.[5] Bins 3 through 0 are not shown since these are a mirror image of bins 7 through 4. It can be seen that judge support for MTASK-M (Figure 6) tends to be stronger than for MTASK-S (Figure 5).

These differences are statistically significant, but they also suggest that this was a challenging task for crowd workers. In many cases, the 5 random examples may not have been sufficed to distinguish individual styles,[6] and even when distinctive, similar outputs from arbitrary inputs may not be undesirable—indeed, different individuals may legitimately respond similarly to the same input, particularly when the input itself is bland or commonplace.

8 Discussion

Fig. 7 presents responses generated by baseline and multi-task (MTASK-M) response generation systems. Both systems are presented with a conversation history of up to two dialog turns (context and input message), and this larger context helps produce responses that are more in line with the conversation flow (Sordoni et al., 2015). The first six response examples are generated for the same underlying speaker (a technical support person, User 1 in Fig. 4). The two last multi-task responses are generated for User 2.

We notice striking differences between the baseline and the multi-task model. The six first responses of **Multitask** in Fig. 7 represent a very consistent register in three different aspects. First, it is relatively clear from these responses that the underlying speaker represented by the model is

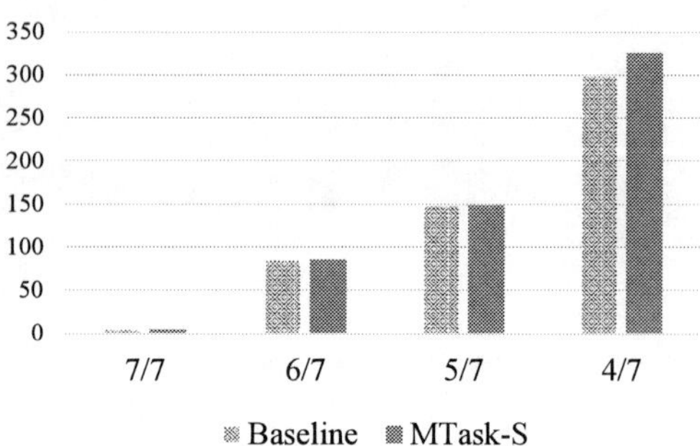

Figure 5: Judge agreement counts for MTASK-S versus Baseline. The difference between the two systems is statistically significant.

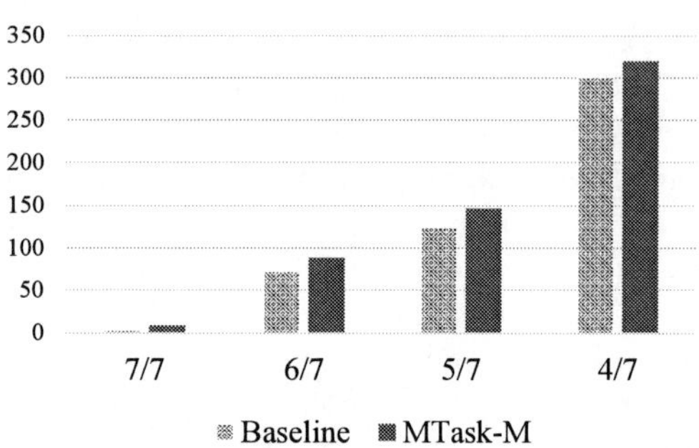

Figure 6: Judge agreement counts for MTASK-M versus Baseline. The difference between the two systems is statistically significant, and the preference for MTASK-M is more evident.

a tech support employee. Interestingly, this employee appears to give help with fitness-related software, and responds that the customer will be *"able to run a marathon"*. On the other hand, the output of the baseline system is relatively bland and deflective. More crucially the baseline does a relatively poor job producing content words that are relevant to the speaker's domain of expertise. Finally, the tone of the baseline system is often incongruous, e.g., when it responds *"I don't know what to do with it"*, which is unlikely to be a desirable response to offer a customer. In another case, the baseline responds *"thanks for the info"*. While this kind of response is appropriate for many speaker roles, it is less appropriate here, as the support employee is the one to give information and helpful advice.

The figure also illustrates current limitations of our speaker role model. For example, our response in the fourth example shows that such systems can be deflective (e.g., not giving any suggestion in response to *"any idea"*), but at least the system

---

[5]Partial scores were rounded up. This affects both systems equally.

[6]We limited the number to 5 with the intention of not overwhelming judges with too much information, which may have exacerbated the difficulty.

Context: have you tried uninstalling nike+ connec? how about docking it to a different computer?   *Input: Tried both of those techniques. But nothing works. I can try the other computer again.*   **Baseline:** Let me know if there's anything else I can help you with. Thanks for the help.   **Multitask:** Have you tried using a different browser? Let us know if you have any other questions.
Context: What do you see when you have a failed login attempt? Never ending spinner? Loop you back to login page?   *Input: I am getting a loop back to login page, windows.*   **Baseline:** Ah, ok. Thanks for the info. I'll check it out. Thanks for the feedback.   **Multitask:** I'm sorry to hear that. Have you tried clearing your cache and cookies?
Context: To clarify: your first run after resetting your connection will not post to Facebook. Does this help? Let us know.   *Input: That's correct. I reset it twice! It still doesn't work.*   **Baseline:** Let me know if there's anything else I can help you with. Thanks for the update.   **Multitask:** I'm sorry to hear that. Are you receiving any error messages? Let us know.
Context: To link your sensor to your iPod, from home screen go to settings>Nike+ iPod>sensor>link new. Any luck?   *Input: not work.. Any idea?*   **Baseline:** I'm not sure, I'll check it out when i get home. Thanks for the update   **Multitask:** Let me know if you have any other questions. Let us know if the issue persists.
Context: You're welcome. What generation of the iPod Nano are you using?   *Input: 5 years old and bought the kit then but my new Nano touch also not detecting sensor maybe receiver broken*   **Baseline:** Ah , I see. I'll have to check it out. Thanks for the update.   **Multitask:** Ah, I see. I see. Have you been able to try a different network?
Context: Unfortunately you can't transfer your Nike+ training program to your iPod at this time. Let us know if this helps!   *Input: Oh! That's a pity I bet I'd be able to run a couple more if this nice voice, told me to speed up in-between*   **Baseline:** That's what I'm hoping for, but I don't know what to do with it.   **Multitask:** I'm sure you will be able to run a marathon at least once a week or so.
Context: So when are you going to post more n/d stuff?   *Input: Soon I guess I have a chapter written, but it's way too short and not good enough to post just yet.*   **Baseline:** Let me know how you get on with it. I don't know what to write.   **Multitask:** Ah, I see. Well, I'm sure it'll be interesting to see what happens!
Context: Ah, no. Had kind of a crazy day, and I've been writing a lot tonight. I have a new one-shot almost finished!   *Input: Alright. I'm sure you'll read it eventually*   **Baseline:** I don't think I'll be able to sleep tonight, but I'm going to sleep.   **Multitask:** I hope so! I can't wait to read it, hehe.

Figure 7: Responses produced by our baseline and multi-task neural response generation system (Multi-S), given a conversation history (context and input message.) The first 6 examples and last 2 examples correspond respectively to Users 1 (tech support) and 2.

does respond in a customer-support register. In the fifth example, response of the system seems relatively irrelevant, but this kind of natural language comprehension problem seems almost unavoidable. Semantic congruity aside, the response strikes the right tone—it is pragmatically and socially appropriate, which is the primary purpose of this investigation. The final two examples of Fig. 7 show that the model is also able to learn a voice or register for a completely different kind of character. The underlying person is highly assertive—reflected in their use of exclamation marks—and speaks informally (e.g., "hehe"), in a way the tech support person would typically not.

9 Conclusion

This paper introduces a multi-task learning approach to incorporate speaker role character-istics into conversational models using non-conversational data. Both models presented here are relatively simple to implement, and show significant improvement in perplexity and BLEU score over a baseline system. Overall, MTASK-M is more computationally efficient, and effective in generating speaker-role-specific information, as reflected in human evaluation. Responses generated by these models exhibit a marked ability to capture speaker roles, expressive styles and domain expertise characteristic of the targeted user, without heavy recourse to an individual speaker's conversational data.

Acknowledgements

We thank Marjan Ghazvininejad, John Wieting, Vighnesh Shiv, Mari Ostendorf and Hannaneh Hajishirzi for helpful suggestions and discussions.

References

Rich Caruana. 1998. Multitask learning. In *Learning to learn*, Springer, pages 95–133.

Yun-Nung Chen, Dilek Hakkani-Tür, Gokhan Tur, Jianfeng Gao, and Li Deng. 2016. End-to-end memory networks with knowledge carryover for multi-turn spoken language understanding. In *Proc. Interspeech*.

Yun-Nung Chen, Ming Sun, Alexander I Rudnicky, and Anatole Gershman. 2015. Leveraging behavioral patterns of mobile applications for personalized spoken language understanding. In *Proceedings of the 2015 ACM on International Conference on Multimodal Interaction*. ACM, pages 83–86.

Andrew M Dai and Quoc V Le. 2015. Semi-supervised sequence learning. In *NIPS*.

Renato De Mori, Frédéric Bechet, Dilek Hakkani-Tur, Michael McTear, Giuseppe Riccardi, and Gokhan Tur. 2008. Spoken language understanding. *IEEE Signal Processing Magazine* 25(3).

Michel Galley, Chris Brockett, Alessandro Sordoni, Yangfeng Ji, Michael Auli, Chris Quirk, Margaret Mitchell, Jianfeng Gao, and Bill Dolan. 2015. deltaBLEU: A discriminative metric for generation tasks with intrinsically diverse targets. In *Proc. ACL-IJCNLP*.

Yvette Graham, Timothy Baldwin, and Nitika Mathur. 2015. Accurate evaluation of segment-level machine translation metrics. In *Proc. NAACL-HLT*.

Sepp Hochreiter and Jürgen Schmidhuber. 1997. Long short-term memory. *Neural computation* 9(8):1735–1780.

Diederik Kingma and Jimmy Ba. 2015. Adam: A method for stochastic optimization. In *Proc. ICLR*.

Jiwei Li, Michel Galley, Chris Brockett, Jianfeng Gao, and Bill Dolan. 2016a. A diversity-promoting objective function for neural conversation models. In *Proc. NAACL-HLT*.

Jiwei Li, Michel Galley, Chris Brockett, Georgios Spithourakis, Jianfeng Gao, and Bill Dolan. 2016b. A persona-based neural conversation model. In *Proc. ACL*.

Chia-Wei Liu, Ryan Lowe, Iulian Serban, Mike Noseworthy, Laurent Charlin, and Joelle Pineau. 2016. How NOT to evaluate your dialogue system: An empirical study of unsupervised evaluation metrics for dialogue response generation. In *Proc. EMNLP*.

Xiaodong Liu, Jianfeng Gao, Xiaodong He, Li Deng, Kevin Duh, and Ye-Yi Wang. 2015. Representation learning using multi-task deep neural networks for semantic classification and information retrieval. In *Proc. HLT-NAACL*.

Yi Luan, Yangfeng Ji, Hannaneh Hajishirzi, and Boyang Li. 2016a. Multiplicative representations for unsupervised semantic role induction. In *Proc. ACL*.

Yi Luan, Yangfeng Ji, and Mari Ostendorf. 2016b. LSTM based conversation models. *arXiv preprint arXiv:1603.09457* .

Yi Luan, Mari Ostendorf, and Hannaneh Hajishirzi. 2017. Scientific information extraction with semi-supervised neural tagging. *arXiv preprint arXiv:1708.06075* .

Yi Luan, Shinji Watanabe, and Bret Harsham. 2015. Efficient learning for spoken language understanding tasks with word embedding based pre-training. In *Proc. Interspeech*.

Yi Luan, Richard Wright, Mari Ostendorf, and Gina-Anne Levow. 2014. Relating automatic vowel space estimates to talker intelligibility. In *Proc. Interspeech*.

Minh-Thang Luong, Quoc V Le, Ilya Sutskever, Oriol Vinyals, and Lukasz Kaiser. 2016. Multi-task sequence to sequence learning. In *ICLR*.

Hongyuan Mei, Mohit Bansal, and Matthew R Walter. 2017. Coherent dialogue with attention-based language models. In *Proc. AAAI*.

Franz Josef Och. 2003. Minimum error rate training in statistical machine translation. In *Proc. ACL*.

Kishore Papineni, Salim Roukos, Todd Ward, and Wei-Jing Zhu. 2002. BLEU: a method for automatic evaluation of machine translation. In *Proc. ACL*.

Mark Przybocki, Kay Peterson, Sébastien Bronsart, and Gregory Sanders. 2009. The NIST 2008 metrics for machine translation challenge—overview, methodology, metrics, and results. *Machine Translation* 23(2):71–103.

Alan Ritter, Colin Cherry, and William B Dolan. 2011. Data-driven response generation in social media. In *Proc. EMNLP*.

Rico Sennrich, Barry Haddow, and Alexandra Birch. 2016. Improving neural machine translation models with monolingual data. In *Proc. ACL*.

Yuanlong Shao, Stephan Gouws, Denny Britz, Anna Goldie, Brian Strope, and Ray Kurzweil. 2017. Generating high-quality and informative conversation responses with sequence-to-sequence models. In *Proc. EMNLP*.

Alessandro Sordoni, Michel Galley, Michael Auli, Chris Brockett, Yangfeng Ji, Meg Mitchell, Jian-Yun Nie, Jianfeng Gao, and Bill Dolan. 2015. A neural network approach to context-sensitive generation of conversational responses. In *Proc. NAACL-HLT*.

Oriol Vinyals and Quoc Le. 2015. A neural conversational model. In *Proc. ICML Deep Learning Workshop*.

Tsung-Hsien Wen, Milica Gasic, Nikola Mrkšić, Pei-Hao Su, David Vandyke, and Steve Young. 2015. Semantically conditioned LSTM-based natural language generation for spoken dialogue systems. In *Proc. EMNLP*.

Chat Disentanglement: Identifying Semantic Reply Relationships with Random Forests and Recurrent Neural Networks

Shikib Mehri
Department of Computer Science
University of British Columbia
Vancouver, Canada
mehrishikib@gmail.com

Giuseppe Carenini
Department of Computer Science
University of British Columbia
Vancouver, Canada
carenini@cs.ubc.ca

Abstract

Thread disentanglement is a precursor to any high-level analysis of multiparticipant chats. Existing research approaches the problem by calculating the likelihood of two messages belonging in the same thread. Our approach leverages a newly annotated dataset to identify reply relationships. Furthermore, we explore the usage of an RNN, along with large quantities of unlabeled data, to learn semantic relationships between messages. Our proposed pipeline, which utilizes a reply classifier and an RNN to generate a set of disentangled threads, is novel and performs well against previous work.

1 Introduction

The problem of thread disentanglement is a precursor to high-level analysis of multiparticipant chats (Carenini et al., 2011). A typical chat consists of multiple simultaneous and distinct conversations, with Elsner and Charniak (2010) observing an average of 2.75 simultaneous threads of dialogue. Since a conversation does not necessarily entail a contiguous sequence of messages, the interwoven threads must be identified and segmented prior to any high-level analysis of the chat.

To further illustrate the need for thread disentanglement, consider the chat log in *Figure 1*. It should be clear to a reader that there are two independent threads of dialogue occurring within this sequence of messages, the first between John, Jack and Brian and the second between Jenny and Katie. Humans are adept at mentally disentangling conversations and even go as far as to adjust their behavior in order to ease the process of disentanglement which O'Neill and Martin (2003) observed in the form of name mentioning.

John:	i need a new tv show to watch
Jack:	psych/house of cards/breaking bad
	sound like things you might enjoy
Brian:	oh I should probably renew my
	Netflix
Katie:	I forgot my laprop at home D:
Jenny:	Katie, that sucks...
Jenny:	Are you going to go back home to
	get it?
Katie:	laptop*
Brian:	try Black Mirror

Figure 1. An example of a multiparticipant chat with two threads of dialogue.

Our work is novel because it approaches the problem of thread disentanglement by attempting to predict immediate reply relationships between messages. The potential benefits of this idea were discussed by Elsner and Charniak (2010) and Uthus and Aha (2013), but the idea has not yet been explored. Furthermore, Elsner and Charniak (2010) suggest that this approach "might yield more reliable annotations".

Additionally, we explore the usage of unlabeled data for the purpose of identifying semantic relationships between messages. Previous attempts at semantic modeling by Elsner and Charniak (2010) and Adams and Martel (2010) have not been very effective, however recent accomplishments in next utterance prediction (Lowe et al., 2015) can be leveraged for the purpose of thread disentanglement.

The main contributions of this paper are as follows.

1. We create an annotated dataset[1] which labels direct reply relationships between pairs

---

[1] The dataset is publicly available and can be found at http://shikib.com/td_annotations.

Proceedings of the The 8th International Joint Conference on Natural Language Processing, pages 615–623,
Taipei, Taiwan, November 27 – December 1, 2017 ©2017 AFNLP

of messages in a transcript.

2. We create and open-source a tool[2] for the efficient reply annotation of a dataset.

3. We propose a pipeline for the task of thread disentanglement, consisting of:

   (a) A classifier, trained on the aforementioned dataset, that predicts reply relationships,

   (b) A recurrent neural network that models semantic relationships between messages,

   (c) A thread partitioning algorithm that utilizes a variety of features, including the previous stages of the pipeline, to ultimately partition a transcript into threads.

4. We evaluate our algorithm against all comparable previous approaches and explore potential improvements to the pipeline.

As a preview of the paper, *Section 2* further describes related work. *Section 3* introduces the proposed pipeline, with the subsections detailing the distinct stages of the pipeline. *Section 4* presents the metrics used for evaluating the agreement between a pair of disentanglements. *Section 5* discusses the datasets used by the pipeline, with specific attention to our newly annotated dataset. *Section 6* describes our experiments and presents the results. Finally, *Section 7* discusses our results and suggests potential future improvements upon our work.

2   Related Work

There have been a number of approaches to thread disentanglement, the majority of which contain a clustering/partitioning algorithm using a measure of message relatedness to segment a chat transcript into distinct threads.

Shen et al. (2006) introduce the problem of thread disentanglement, and approach it by using the cosine-similarity of messages to compute the distance between a message and a thread.

Elsner and Charniak (2010) present comprehensive metrics for evaluation along with a corpus to aid with disentanglement. They train a classifier on their corpus, to predict whether two messages belong in the same thread.

Wang and Oard (2003) construct expanded messages using temporal, author and conversational context. By expanding messages using this contextual information, they have more signal to use when assigning a message to a thread.

We build on this work by using our newly annotated dataset to train a classifier which predicts immediate reply relationships. This is a supervised alternative to heuristics used by previous research. Additionally, it is an improvement over the classifier trained by Elsner and Charniak (2010) since the nature of the annotation leads to stronger relationships between message pairs in the training data.

Previous work has explored modeling semantic relationships between messages using a predefined list of technical words (Elsner and Charniak, 2010) and applying Latent Dirichlet Allocation (Adams and Martel, 2010). In contrast, we apply the research done by Lowe et al. (2015) by utilizing a Recurrent Neural Network to predict the probability of a message occurring in a given thread.

3   Proposed Pipeline

We propose a novel pipeline to approach the problem of thread disentanglement. This pipeline consists of four stages, as visualized in *Figure 2*.

The first stage, as described in *Section 3.1*, is a classifier to detect reply relationships between pairs of messages.

The second stage is a classifier that predicts whether two messages belong in the same thread. This classifier, described in *Section 3.2*, is similar to the one trained by Elsner and Charniak (2010).

The third stage, described in *Section 3.3*, is a recurrent neural network that uses the content of the messages to predict the probability of a message following a sequence of messages.

The fourth and final stage is a thread partitioning algorithm that uses the information outputted from the previous stages to generate threads. This stage is described in *Section 3.4*.

3.1   Reply Classifier

Given two input messages, the reply classifier outputs the likelihood of the first message being a reply to the second. Given a child and a parent message, a feature vector is generated in order to describe the relationship between the two messages. The features utilizes are described in *Table 1*.

---

[2] The open-sourced annotation interface can be found at https://github.com/Shikib/react-chat-reply-annotation.

Table 1: Description of features utilized for the reply classifier.

Time	The time difference in seconds.
Mention Parent	Whether the child message mentions the author of the parent message.
Mention Child	Whether the parent message mentions the author of the child message.
Same author	Whether the author of the two messages is the same.
Distance	The number of messages separating the two messages.
RNN Output	The probability outputted by the RNN.

These feature vectors are then used to train a random forest (Breiman, 2001) classifier with 250 trees. We performed comparisons to other classifiers, namely a logistic regression classifier, a support vector classifier and a multilayer perceptron classifier, however cross-validation proved random forests to have the highest accuracy. The models were trained and evaluated using scikit-learn (Pedregosa et al., 2011).

The pairs of input messages in the training data were specifically annotated as consisting of a reply relationship. This suggests that each pair of messages is directly related, leading to the classifier learning to identify strong, immediate relationships between messages.

3.2 Same-Thread Classification

Elsner and Charniak (2010) trained a classifier that predicted whether two input messages belonged to the same thread. We implemented a similar classifier through utilization of the features described in *Section 3.1* and a dataset that they provided.

Given a pair of messages, the same-thread classifier outputs the probability of the messages belonging to the same thread. The classifier trained was a random forest (Breiman, 2001) with 250 trees, using scikit-learn (Pedregosa et al., 2011).

Unlike the reply classifier, the same-thread classifier was trained on data with weak relationships. Instead of specifically annotated relationships, the pairs of messages used to train the same-thread classifier were labeled as belonging to the same thread. Because the same-thread pairs are a super-set of the reply pairs, this leads to the classifier learning to identify broader relationships between messages, rather than strictly immediate reply relationships.

As a result of the same-thread classifier being trained on a different set of data than the reply classifier, the learned relationships are different in nature, which suggests that the two classifiers can strongly complement each other.

3.3 RNN for Next Utterance Classification

The third stage of the pipeline attempts to leverage large amounts of unlabeled data for the purpose of modeling semantic relationships between messages. We train a recurrent neural network with LSTM (Hochreiter and Schmidhuber, 1997) hidden units to predict the probability of a message following a sequence of messages (Lowe et al., 2015).

The reasoning behind utilizing an LSTM is for the purposes of identifying dependencies between non-adjacent messages. LSTM units are best able to capture long-term dependencies through the use of a series of gates which control whether an input is remembered, forgotten or used as output. Formally, at every time step an LSTM unit updates the internal state C_t as a function of the observed variable x_t and the previous internal state C_{t-1} and h_{t-1}.

Both the context (the previous sequence of messages) and the message are passed through the LSTM units one word at a time, in the form of learned word embeddings. Let us use c and r to denote the final hidden state representations of the context and reply respectively. We can use these hidden states, along with a learned matrix M, to compute the probability of a reply, as:

$$P(reply \mid context) = \sigma(c^T M r) \qquad (1)$$

The model, implemented in PyTorch (A. Paszke, 2017), was trained using hyperparameters recommended by Lowe et al. (2015).

This RNN-based next utterance classification is useful as it supplements the aforementioned classifiers by leveraging unlabeled data to semantically model message relationships.

Additionally, the output of this classifier is added as a feature to the previous two classifiers as well. This allows the reply classifier and the same-thread classifier to use the semantic relatedness of the input messages during classification.

Table 2: Description of the features utilized by the in-thread classifier.

Same-Thread Mean	Mean output of the same-thread classifier.
Same-Thread STD	Standard deviation of the output of the same-thread classifier.
Reply Mean	Mean output of the reply classifier.
Reply STD	Standard deviation of the output of the reply classifier.
Thread Length	Current length of the thread.
Author count	Number of author's messages already in the thread.
Author total	Number of author's messages in the chat.
In-thread proportion	Author count divided by Author total.
Author proportion	Author count divided by Thread Length.
Author mentions	Number of times the author's name was mentioned in the thread.
Time	The time difference between the message and the last message in the thread.
RNN Prediction	The prediction outputted by the RNN.

3.4 Thread Partitioning

Our ultimate goal is to generate a set of disentangled threads, suggesting the usage of a thread partitioning algorithm as the next stage in the pipeline. Using the previously described classifiers, we must identify an optimal segmentation of an input transcript.

3.4.1 In-Thread Classifier

We construct a classifier, referred to as the in-thread classifier, which leverages the output of all previous stages of the pipeline to predict the probability of a message belonging to a thread.

Given a message and a thread, we generate a feature vector using the features described in *Table 2*.

The model used for classification, built in scikit-learn (Pedregosa et al., 2011), is a random forest classifier with 300 trees.

3.4.2 Thread Partitioning

Given the in-thread classifier, we can compute the probability that a message belongs in a given thread of conversation. This is used by our thread partitioning algorithm to generate threads.

This algorithm processes the messages in chronological order. For every message, m_i, the algorithm considers every existing thread, t_j, and passed m_i and t_j into the in-thread classifier.

Ultimately m_i is assigned to the thread which maximizes the probability outputted by the classifier, provided that the best probability output is above a threshold. If the best probability is below the threshold, a new thread is created for the message. This threshold was fine-tuned on the validation dataset.

After sequentially iterating over all of the messages in the transcript, the thread partitioning algorithm will output the disentangled threads.

3.5 Pipeline Overview

Figure 2 provides an overview of the proposed pipeline. The thread partitioning algorithm generates a feature vector to represent the relationship between a thread and a message. The features, as listed in *Table 2*, include the values outputted by the previous stages of the pipeline.

The in-thread classifier, trained on the pilot dataset provided by Elsner and Charniak (2010), uses this generated feature vector to predict the probability of the message belonging to the given thread. Using the outputted probabilities, the thread partitioning algorithm either assigns the message to the most probable existing thread or generates a new thread.

4 Metrics

A number of metrics are used throughout this paper to evaluate the agreement of two disentanglements. It is a non-trivial task to compare two disentanglements which have a different number of threads.

To measure the global similarity between annotations, we utilize **one-to-one accuracy**. This is computed by using optimal bipartite matching to pair up threads between the two annotations and computing the overlap between every pair of matched threads. This metric measures "how well

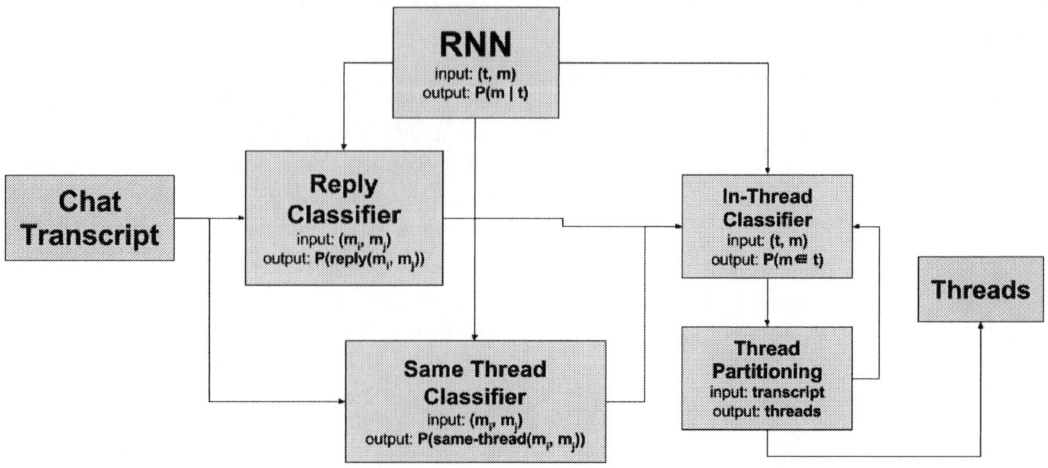

Figure 2. The proposed pipeline for disentangling a chat transcript into threads. Throughout the diagram, t represents a thread and m denotes a message.

we extract whole conversations intact" (Wang and Oard, 2009).

We also use the loc_k score to measure **local agreement**. For a particular message, the previous k messages are either in the **same** or a **different** thread. The loc_k score is computed by considering, for each message, the previous k messages and counting the matches in the same/different thread assignments across annotations.

The third and final metric used to score annotation agreement is the **Shen-F score**, as defined by Shen et al. (2006) which measures how well related messages are grouped. The Shen-F score is defined as:

$$F = \sum_i \frac{n_i}{n} max_j(F(i,j)) \qquad (2)$$

where i is a ground truth thread with a length of n_i, n is the total length of the transcript and $F(i,j)$ is the harmonic mean of the precision and the recall. If the thread overlap is n_{ij}, the length of the gold-standard thread is n_i and the length of the proposed thread is n_j, then $F(i,j)$ is defined as follows:

$$P = \frac{n_{ij}}{n_j} \quad R = \frac{n_{ij}}{n_i} \quad F(i,j) = \frac{2PR}{P+R} \qquad (3)$$

The max_j operation is taken over all detected threads. Since the matching is multiway (i.e., the same j can be chosen for different values of i), the score is not symmetric. When comparing human annotations, this lack of symmetry is addressed by

treating the annotation with higher entropy as the gold standard.

Given a transcript of length n, with thread i having a size of n_i, the entropy of the annotation can be computed as:

$$H(c) = \sum_i \frac{n_i}{n} log_2 \frac{n}{n_i} \qquad (4)$$

These metrics are utilized by both Elsner and Charniak (2010) and Wang and Oard (2009).

To account for differences in annotation specificity, Elsner and Charniak (2010) introduce **many-to-one accuracy**. This metric maps each of the threads of the source annotation to the single thread in the target with which it has the greatest overlap and counts the total percentage of overlap. Similarly to **Shen-F**, the higher entropy annotation is mapped to the lower one.

5 Datasets

We utilize a number of datasets to train various algorithms in our thread disentanglement pipeline. Two of these datasets are external datasets provided by previous research. The reply dataset[1] was annotated as part of this study as described in *Section 5.1*.

Since our classifier aims to learn immediate reply relationships between pairs of messages, there is a need for a newly annotated dataset. This section details the process of data acquisition and provides some preliminary analysis of the data.

Table 3: Single annotation statistics describing three annotations of a 524 message transcript. All of these metrics describe a single annotation. Thread density refers to the number of active threads at any given time.

	Mean	Max	Min
Threads	55.33	62	49
Avg. Thread Length	9.6	10.7	8.5
Avg. Thread Density	1.79	1.82	1.73
Entropy	3.99	4.42	3.64

Table 4: Pair annotation statistics describing three annotations of a 524 message transcript. These metrics are all computed on a pair of threads and therefore describe inter-annotator agreement.

	Mean	Max	Min
one-to-one	81.49	87.79	74.81
loc_3	90.36	91.81	88.61
many-to-one	97.39	98.28	95.80
Shen F	87.70	100.0	75.00

5.1 Data Acquisition

For the acquisition of our annotated reply dataset a subset of the #linux IRC log data provided by Elsner and Charniak (2010) was used.

An interface was built and open-sourced to allow volunteers to manually annotate the data for the purpose of identifying direct reply relationships between messages. Users were instructed to proceed through the messages in the chat and select the immediate parents for every message.

Three volunteers, familiar with Linux terminology, independently annotated a set of 524 messages from the development dataset provided by Elsner and Charniak (2010). For every message in the dataset, annotators identified the potential immediate parents of the message, where $parent(m)$ is identified as the messages to which m is a direct reply. It is possible for a message to have no parents (e.g., starting a new thread of conversation) and multiple parents (e.g., following up on a multi-participant conversation).

5.2 Data Analysis

On average, we find that a message has 1.22 direct parents and 1.70 direct children. The relatively high number of children suggests that typically a message receives more than one reply. On the other hand, the lower number of direct parents suggests that a message is typically replying to a single parent message.

We can use the reply annotations to retrieve a thread annotation which resembles the structure of the annotated data by Elsner and Charniak (2010). This is done by identifying a disjoint set of messages such that no two messages in different sets share a reply relationship. This allows us to apply the read-based metrics described in *Section 4* to evaluate the annotation quality.

As is demonstrated in *Table 4*, our annotations

have high inter-annotator agreement. While our agreement is not directly comparable to that of Elsner and Charniak (2010) due to our annotations being done on a subset of the data, our agreement is evidently much greater. This suggests that a reply-based annotation approach removes ambiguity and by extension removes noise from the data.

5.3 External Datasets

In addition to the aforementioned annotated dataset, we utilized the corpus provided by Elsner and Charniak (2010) to train the same-thread classifier described in *Section 3.2*. This corpus consists of a pilot set, a development set and a testing set.

We also utilize the Ubuntu Dialogue Corpus (Lowe et al., 2015) to train a recurrent neural network to output the probability of a message occurring after a sequence of messages, as described in *Section 3.3*.

It is reasonable to utilize both of these datasets, as both are IRC chat logs from channels concerned with Linux related content. The corpora provided by Elsner and Charniak (2010) is from the ##LINUX channel, whereas the Ubuntu Dialogue Corpus (Lowe et al., 2015) consists of data from the ##UBUNTU channel.

6 Experiments and Evaluation Results

6.1 Reply Classifier

We use our annotated data, described in *Section 5.1*, to generate a set of positive examples (i.e., labeled replies) and a set of negative examples (i.e., the complement of the annotated replies). This data is used to train and validate the reply classifier described in *Section 3.1*.

The data is very imbalanced, with most pairs being non-replies which naturally leads to a large number of false positives (i.e., non-replies classified as replies). This issue was addressed by adjusting the class weights in order to stronger penalize false positives when training the random forest model. Specifically, the class weight of the negative class was set to be $\frac{num\_non\_replies}{num\_replies}$ while the class of the positive class was 1.

To further address the problem of imbalanced data, we employ a strategy used by Elsner and Charniak (2010) by only having our classifier consider messages within 129 seconds of each other. This brings the ratio of the two classes much closer and is useful for speeding up inference as well.

Using 10-fold cross-validation, we obtain an average precision of 0.91 and average recall of 0.92. Most message pairs are non-replies and as such these scores are non-representative. For the reply class, we have a precision of 0.83 and a recall of 0.49.

Using Gini feature importance (Breiman, 2001), we find the most important feature to be the probability outputted by the RNN, followed by the time difference and the message distance. This confirms that semantic relatedness is vital for detecting reply relationships. The time difference and message distance are both temporal measurements which represent the fact that new messages are typically a reply to recently sent messages.

6.2 Same-Thread Classifier

The same-thread classifier, described in *Section 3.2*, was trained on the development set provided by Elsner and Charniak (2010) which was described in *Section 5.3*. This classifier obtains a precision and recall of 0.7, which is similar to the result obtained by Elsner and Charniak (2010).

The Gini feature importances (Breiman, 2001) indicate that for the same-thread classifier, the most important features are the output of the RNN, the time difference and the 'same author' feature. The relatively high importance of the 'same author' feature can be explained by the fact that an author typically responds numerous times within a conversation. This reaffirms the idea that the two classifiers learn to identify different relationships between messages, and therefore complement each other.

6.3 RNN

The recurrent neural network was trained with the hyperparameters described by Lowe et al. (2015) on the Ubuntu Dialogue corpus, described in *Section 5.3*. The final model performs within a few percentage points of the result they reported.

6.4 In-Thread Classifier

This classifier was trained and tuned on the pilot dataset provided by Elsner and Charniak (2010) as described in *Section 5.3*.

To handle the imbalance of the data, we adjust the class weight when training and only consider thread-message pairs within 129 seconds of each other.

With 10-fold cross-validation, we obtain an average precision of 0.91 and an average recall of 0.92. For the positive class, we have a precision of 0.89 and a recall of 0.69.

Using the Gini feature importances (Breiman, 2001), we find that the most important features for the in-thread classifier are the time difference, the proportion of the author's previous messages which belong to the thread, the mean output of the reply classifier and the mean output of the same-thread classifier.

The in-thread proportion of the author's messages is likely a strong feature because high activity within a particular conversation indicates a high likelihood of continued activity.

It is plausible that the output of the RNN is not a strongly used feature because it is already present in the output of the reply and same-thread classifiers.

6.5 Disentanglement Evaluation

We compare the performance of our thread partitioning pipeline to the results reported by Elsner and Charniak (2010) and Wang and Oard (2009). Both of these papers evaluated their disentanglement models on the same dataset, consisting of six annotations of the same transcript of 1000 messages, provided by Elsner and Charniak (2010). The comparison is shown in *Table 5*, where our approach is shown to outperform the other methods with respect to loc_3 and outperforms Elsner and Charniak (2010) in all metrics.

However, we suspect that the results reported by Wang and Oard (2009) were boosted by the inclusion of *system messages* when computing all of their metrics. In contrast, Elsner and Charniak (2010) only include them for the computation of loc_3.

System messages are classified into thread -1 by all of the annotators and are extremely easy to classify as they always appear in the form *"X joined the room"* or *"X left the room"*. We compare the performance of our pipeline, provided

Table 5: The results obtained by our pipeline compared to annotators, Elsner and Charniak (2010) and Wang and Oard (2009).

	Annotators	Elsner & Charniak	Wang & Oard	Proposed Pipeline
Mean one-to-one	52.98	41.23	47.00	44.02
Max one-to-one	63.50	52.12	-	52.75
Min one-to-one	35.63	31.62	-	36.75
Mean loc_3	81.09	72.94	75.13	78.64
Max loc_3	86.53	74.70	-	80.27
Min loc_3	74.75	70.77	-	77.23
Mean Shen F	53.87	43.47	52.79	45.86
Max Shen F	66.08	57.57	-	52.22
Min Shen F	33.43	32.97	-	36.75

Table 6: Our results compared to Wang and Oard (2009), provided we include the system messages when computing the metrics.

	Wang & Oard	Pipeline
Mean one-to-one	47.00	55.22
Mean loc_3	75.13	78.64
Mean Shen F	52.79	56.62

Table 7: Demonstration of the significant quality drop observed when removing the RNN.

	Pipeline	Without RNN
Mean one-to-one	44.02	41.06
Mean loc_3	78.64	76.52
Mean Shen F	45.86	43.01

that we include all system messages, to the results obtained by Wang and Oard (2009) in *Table 6* where our approach outperforms in all metrics.

6.6 Pipeline Discussion

Our pipeline strongly outperforms previous research, likely due to the fact that we leverage different models and data sources to capture a variety of relationships between messages.

The reply classifier is trained on specifically annotated reply relationships, leading it to excel at identifying strong, local agreements between messages.

The same-thread classifier is trained on pairs of messages that belong to the same thread, resulting in a model which captures broad relationships between messages in the same thread. This is observed in the relatively high importance the model places on the 'same author' feature.

The RNN, trained on a large corpus of unlabeled data, is adept at identifying the strength of semantic relationships between messages. As a result, it is utilized as a feature in every classifier of the pipeline.

Removing the RNN entirely from the pipeline results in a significant quality drop, as shown in *Table 7*. This drop reaffirms that the pipeline's quality stems from its ability to model semantic relationships between messages.

The in-thread classifier is the final model that trains and evaluates on top of the output of the previous models. This model decides how to best utilize the previous models and combines their outputs to ultimately decide whether a message belongs to a thread.

7 Conclusions and Future Work

This work approaches the problem of thread disentanglement from the perspective of identifying reply relationships between messages. A corpus of annotated data for this task is provided, which should allow future research to expand on the work presented in this paper. From our high inter-annotator agreement, it is evident that detecting reply relationships has relatively little noise. We incorporate a combination of features in our disentanglement pipeline, using both meta-data and semantic relationships between messages. We further show that unlabeled data in combination with neural based approaches are effective in aiding with thread disentanglement. The model that we present outperforms all previous work when system messages are included.

In the near future, we plan to expand our reply

annotated corpus, using our open-sourced annotation software, particularly for the purpose of evaluation. We have shown that our reply-based annotation has higher inter-annotator agreement relative to the annotations provided by Elsner and Charniak (2010), therefore supplementing the reply corpus and using it for evaluation may lead to less noisy evaluations.

While we have shown that using an RNN is effective for detecting replies, it may prove useful to perform further experiments to determine if it can be applied more effectively. For example, adding an attention mechanism could be beneficial for the purposes of disentanglement. Additionally, in order to reduce noise in the data and therefore lead the model to converge faster, it is worth experimenting with training the RNN on a disentangled corpus. Other directions for future research could involve exploring these ideas.

References

S. Gross S. Chintala A. Paszke. 2017. Pytorch. github.com/pytorch/pytorch.

Paige Adams and Craig Martel. 2010. Conversational thread extraction and topic detection in text-based chat. *Semantic Computing* pages 87–113.

Leo Breiman. 2001. Random forests. *Machine learning* 45(1):5–32.

Giuseppe Carenini, Gabriel Murray, and Raymond Ng. 2011. Methods for mining and summarizing text conversations. *Synthesis Lectures on Data Management* 3(3):1–130.

Micha Elsner and Eugene Charniak. 2010. Disentangling chat. *Computational Linguistics* 36(3):389–409.

Sepp Hochreiter and Jürgen Schmidhuber. 1997. Long short-term memory. *Neural computation* 9(8):1735–1780.

Ryan Lowe, Nissan Pow, Iulian Serban, and Joelle Pineau. 2015. The ubuntu dialogue corpus: A large dataset for research in unstructured multi-turn dialogue systems. *arXiv preprint arXiv:1506.08909* .

Jacki O'Neill and David Martin. 2003. Text chat in action. In *Proceedings of the 2003 international ACM SIGGROUP conference on Supporting group work*. ACM, pages 40–49.

F. Pedregosa, G. Varoquaux, A. Gramfort, V. Michel, B. Thirion, O. Grisel, M. Blondel, P. Prettenhofer, R. Weiss, V. Dubourg, J. Vanderplas, A. Passos, D. Cournapeau, M. Brucher, M. Perrot, and E. Duchesnay. 2011. Scikit-learn: Machine learning in Python. *Journal of Machine Learning Research* 12:2825–2830.

Dou Shen, Qiang Yang, Jian-Tao Sun, and Zheng Chen. 2006. Thread detection in dynamic text message streams. In *Proceedings of the 29th annual international ACM SIGIR conference on Research and development in information retrieval*. ACM, pages 35–42.

David C Uthus and David W Aha. 2013. Multiparticipant chat analysis: A survey. *Artificial Intelligence* 199:106–121.

Lidan Wang and Douglas W Oard. 2009. Context-based message expansion for disentanglement of interleaved text conversations. In *Proceedings of human language technologies: The 2009 annual conference of the North American chapter of the association for computational linguistics*. Association for Computational Linguistics, pages 200–208.

Towards Bootstrapping a Polarity Shifter Lexicon
using Linguistic Features

Marc Schulder*, Michael Wiegand*, Josef Ruppenhofer†, Benjamin Roth‡

* Spoken Language Systems, Saarland University

† Institute for German Language, Mannheim

‡ Center for Information and Language Processing, LMU Munich

`marc.schulder@lsv.uni-saarland.de`

`michael.wiegand@lsv.uni-saarland.de`

`ruppenhofer@ids-mannheim.de`

`beroth@cis.uni-muenchen.de`

Abstract

We present a major step towards the creation of the first high-coverage lexicon of polarity shifters. In this work, we bootstrap a lexicon of verbs by exploiting various linguistic features. Polarity shifters, such as *abandon*, are similar to negations (e.g. *not*) in that they move the polarity of a phrase towards its inverse, as in *abandon all hope*. While there exist lists of negation words, creating comprehensive lists of polarity shifters is far more challenging due to their sheer number. On a sample of manually annotated verbs we examine a variety of linguistic features for this task. Then we build a supervised classifier to increase coverage. We show that this approach drastically reduces the annotation effort while ensuring a high-precision lexicon. We also show that our acquired knowledge of verbal polarity shifters improves phrase-level sentiment analysis.

1 Introduction

We present an approach towards bootstrapping a lexicon of **polarity shifters**. Polarity shifters are content words that have semantic properties similar to negation. For example, the negated statement in (1) involving the negation word *not* can also be expressed by the verbal shifter *fail* in (2).

(1) Peter did **not** pass the exam.
(2) Peter **failed**$_{shifter}$ to pass the exam.

Similarly, shifting is also caused by nouns (e.g. *downfall*) and adjectives (e.g. *devoid*).

Polarity shifters are important for various tasks in NLP, such as relation extraction (Sanchez-Graillet and Poesio, 2007), recognition of textual entailment (Harabagiu et al., 2006) and particularly sentiment analysis (Wiegand et al., 2010).

Similarly to negation words, they may cause the polarity of a statement to shift. Even though (3) contains the positive polar expression *scholarship*, the overall polarity of the sentence is negative. (4) conveys positive polarity despite the presence of the negative polar expression *pain*.

(3) She was [**denied**$_{shifter}$ the [scholarship]$^{+}$]$^{-}$.
(4) The new treatment has [**alleviated**$_{shifter}$ her [pain]$^{-}$]$^{+}$.

Although there has been significant research on polarity shifting in sentiment analysis (Wiegand et al., 2010), this work has focused on the presence of negation words. Negation words (*no*, *not*, *never*, etc.) are typically function words, so only a few exist. Polarity shifters are content words, of which there are a lot more. For instance, WordNet (Miller et al., 1990) contains over 10k verbal, 20K adjectival and 110K nominal lemmas. An exhaustive manual annotation would be far too costly.

To reduce cost, we introduce a bootstrapping approach for the acquisition of polarity shifters. In this work we focus exclusively on verbs. As the main predicates of phrases they tend to have larger scopes than nouns and adjectives, increasing the impact of their polarity shifting. Their vocabulary size is also smaller, allowing us to cover a reasonable share of it in our evaluation.

Existing resources barely cover any verbal shifters at all. Even the most complex negation lexicon for sentiment analysis (Wilson et al., 2005) includes a mere 12 verbal shifters. In contrast, our initial random sample of 2000 verb lemmas contained 300 shifters. The corpora on which negation can be learned, such as the Sentiment Treebank (Socher et al., 2013) or the BioScope corpus (Szarvas et al., 2008), only comprise contiguous sentences of fairly small datasets, so only the most frequently occurring negation words are considered. For example, only 6 verbal shifters are observed on the BioScope corpus (Morante, 2010).

Proceedings of the The 8th International Joint Conference on Natural Language Processing, pages 624–633,
Taipei, Taiwan, November 27 – December 1, 2017 ©2017 AFNLP

In this work, we address this knowledge gap by bootstrapping a lexicon of polarity shifters. On a sample of manually annotated verbs extracted from WordNet, we first examine a variety of linguistic features for this task. Then we build a supervised classifier to classify the remaining WordNet verbs. Thus we can drastically cut down on the number of verbs to be annotated manually.

Our **contributions** are as follows:

(i) we present the first high-coverage lexicon of verbal polarity shifters, going substantially beyond what can be extracted from existing phrase-level corpus annotations;

(ii) we develop methods for high-precision recognition of polarity shifters;

(iii) in addition to using resource-based generic features, we show that we can boost performance with novel task-specific features, many of which are derived from corpora; and

(iv) we show that compositional classification based on recognition of polarity shifters significantly outperforms polarity classifiers that lack explicit knowledge of verbal shifters.

The main focus of this paper is to find ways to automatically *extract* verbal shifters. The question of their respective scope is part of future research.[1] While our work focuses on English, the concepts applied are not language-specific. We have made all data that were manually labeled as part of this research **publicly available**.[2]

2   Data

To obtain a gold standard for verbal shifters, an expert annotator labeled a random sample of 2000 verbs taken from WordNet 3.1 *(see footnote 2)*. To measure interannotator agreement, 200 of these were annotated again by one of the authors. The achieved $\kappa = 0.66$ indicates substantial agreement (Landis and Koch, 1977).

Due to the lack of robust word-sense disambiguation, our annotation is on the lemma level. We follow a simple **binary classification**: each verb either can cause polarities to shift or not. In order to qualify as a shifter, the verb must allow polar expressions as dependents and the polarity of the proposition that embeds both the verb and

	Freq	Perc
shifter	304	15.20
no shifter	1696	84.80

Table 1: Distribution of verbal shifters in annotated sample of WordNet 3.1.

	Polar Verbs		Positive V.		Negative V.	
	Freq	Perc	Freq	Perc	Freq	Perc
shifter	53	18.8	4	5.5	49	25.9
no shifter	229	81.2	69	94.5	140	74.1

Table 2: Distribution of verbal shifters in the *Subjectivity Lexicon* (Wilson et al., 2005).

polar expression must move towards a polarity that is opposite of the polar expression.

Table 1 shows the distribution of shifters among the set of verbs. At approximately 15%, shifters represent a large enough proportion of verbs to be considered for automatic extraction. Table 2 shows the distribution of shifters among polar verbs. (Polar expressions are identified with the help of the *Subjectivity Lexicon* (Wilson et al., 2005).) While a large number of shifters are themselves negative polar expressions, not all are.

3   Task-Specific Features

In the following we present task-specific features for both verbal shifters (§3.1) and their counterpart, anti-shifters (§3.2). Each feature creates a verb ranking, indicating how likely each verb is to be considered a verbal (anti-)shifter.

Most of our features are corpus-based. As a corpus we use *Amazon Product Review Data* (Jindal and Liu, 2008), comprising over 5.8 million reviews. We chose this dataset for its size and its sentiment-related content. Some features also require knowledge of opinion words and their respective polarity. Such knowledge is obtained from the *Subjectivity Lexicon*. Whenever we use syntactic information (e.g. dependency relations), we obtain it from the Stanford Parser (Chen and Manning, 2014).

3.1   Features for Shifter Detection

As baseline features, we consider all verbs ranked by their frequency in our text corpus (**FREQ**), as well as all negative polar expressions[3] ranked by frequency (**NEGATIVE**).

---

[1]We assume that the scope of a verbal shifter is the set of its dependents (typically its subject or objects).

[2]https://github.com/marcschulder/ijcnlp2017

[3]We consider negative polar expressions since the proportion of shifters is greatest among these expressions (Table 2).

EffectWordNet (EFFECT): This feature uses the idea that events may have beneficial or harmful *effects* on their objects. Wiebe and colleagues (Deng et al., 2013; Choi et al., 2014; Choi and Wiebe, 2014) introduced this idea in the context of annotation and lexical acquisition work for opinion inference.[4] For example, in (5) the combined facts that *fall* has a negative effect (henceforth referred to as *–effect*) on its theme (i.e. *Chavez*) and that people are happy about Chavez' fall suggest that people have a negative attitude towards Chavez. As (5) shows, verbs with a –effect, such as *fall*, often coincide with verbal shifters. However, –effect words do not necessarily shift polarity. For instance, while *abuse* has a –effect, it does not shift, as shown by the fact that the verb phrase remains negative in (6).

(5) I think people are happy because $[[\text{Chavez}]^-$ has **fallen**$_{-\textit{effect}}]^+$.

(6) We don't want the public getting the idea that we $[\textbf{abuse}_{-\textit{effect}}$ our $[\text{prisoners}]^-]^-$.

While –effect and shifting are not equivalent, their large overlap warrants investigating. We use the related EffectWordNet resource (Choi and Wiebe, 2014), which provides effect labels for synsets. To generalize to lemmas, we label a word as –effect if at least one of its synsets has a –effect and none have a +effect. Analogous to negative polar expressions, we take all –effect words and sort them by word frequency (−EFFECT).

Distributional Similarity (SIM): As our aim is to identify verbs whose semantics resembles that of negation words, a straightforward method is to extract verbs that are distributionally similar to negation words. Using Word2Vec (Mikolov et al., 2013), we compute word embeddings for our text corpus.[5] All verbs are ranked by their cosine similarity to a given negation word. The highest ranking verbs are considered verbal shifters. As negation words we consider the intersection of two negation word lists: the *negation* category in the valence shifter lexicon by Wilson et al. (2005) and the negation signals from Morante and Daelemans (2009). The negation words are *neither, never, no, none, nor, not* and *without*.

Polarity Clash (CLASH): Some of our previous examples (e.g. (3)) suggest that shifting is mainly caused by a polar verb (e.g. *lose⁻, alleviate⁺, deny⁻*) modifying a polar expression with the opposite polarity (e.g. $[[\textit{lose}_{\textit{shifter}}]^- [\textit{hope}]^+]^-$, $[[\textit{alleviate}_{\textit{shifter}}]^+ [\textit{pain}]^-]^+$, or $[[\textit{deny}_{\textit{shifter}}]^- [\textit{scholarship}]^+]^-$). We expect that the more often a verb occurs within such constructions, the more likely it is to be a shifter. As we saw in the *Subjectivity Lexicon* that the majority of verbal shifters have negative polarity (Table 2), we look exclusively for negative polar verbs that have a positive polar noun as a direct object. We rank those verbs by the frequency of occurring with positive nouns (CLASH), normalized by the overall frequency of the verb (CLASH$_{\text{norm}}$).

Particle Verbs (PRT): With many particle verbs, the particles signal a particular aspectual property, typically the occurrence of a complete transition to an end state (Brinton, 1985). For instance, *dry (something) out* means *dry (something) completely*. Since shifting normally involves producing a new (negative) end state of some entity, we assume a significant number of shifters among particle verbs ((7) and (8)).

(7) This $[\textbf{tore\_down}_{\textit{shifter}}$ our great $[\text{dream}]^+]^-$.

(8) Please $[\textbf{lay\_aside}_{\textit{shifter}}$ all your $[\text{worries}]^-]^+$.

We only consider particles which typically indicate a complete transition to a negative end state: *aside, away, back, down, off* and *out*. To produce rankings, we sort the particle verbs by their absolute frequency in our text corpus.

Heuristic using 'any' (ANY): Our final shifter feature rests on the linguistic insight that *negative polarity items (NPIs)* (Giannakidou, 2008), such as English *any*, typically appear in the context of a negation, as in (9). Our assumption is that NPIs may similarly occur in the context of a verbal shifter, as in (10), since it similarly conveys a negation. The concept of NPIs is not specific to the English language and can be found in many other languages (Krifka, 1991).

(9) They did $[\textbf{not}$ give us $\underline{\text{any}}$ $[\text{help}_{\textit{dobj}}]^+]^-$.

(10) They $[\textbf{denied}_{\textit{shifter}}$ us $\underline{\text{any}}$ $[\text{help}_{\textit{dobj}}]^+]^-$.

The feature we design collects all verbs that take a direct object that is modified by the NPI *any*, as in (10). We sort the verbs by their frequency of co-occurrence with this particular textual pattern (ANY). We normalize that pattern frequency by the frequency of the respective verb

---

[4]Initially, events with positive/negative effects were referred to as *good-for/bad-for* events. We use the terminology Choi and Wiebe (2014) introduced for EffectWordNet.

[5]Following the work of Wiegand and Ruppenhofer (2015) in verb category induction for sentiment roles, a task similar to ours, we use continuous bag-of-words with 500 dimensions.

(ANY_{norm}). As a further constraint we demand that the direct object represents a polar expression ($\text{ANY}_{norm+polar}$). This constraint is fulfilled in (10) since *help* is a positive polar expression.

3.2 Anti-Shifter Feature (ANTI)

We also introduce a feature for automatically retrieving verbs that – semantically speaking – are the exact opposite of what shifters convey. This is, therefore, a negative feature indicating the absence of a shifter. Our anti-shifter feature determines verbs co-occurring with a very small set of specific adverbials. Using the log-likelihood collocation measure of *Sketch Engine*[6] we select adverbials that showed attraction to verbs of creation on the one hand, and being repelled by verbs of destruction on the other. Verbs of creation are expected to be anti-shifters, since they typically entail a positive end state (i.e. something is created), while verbs of destruction typically entail a negative end state (i.e. something is destroyed) We identified four different adverbials: *exclusively*, *first*, *newly* and *specially*. Some typical examples are given in (11)–(14). In order to produce a ranking for this feature, we sort the anti-shifter candidate verbs according to their frequency of co-occurrence with either of the respective adverbs, normalized by the respective verb frequency (ANTI).

(11) In winter, black bears exclusively **live**_{antiShifter} on fish.
(12) Full keyboards on cellphones were first **introduced**_{antiShifter} in 1997.
(13) These buildings have been newly **constructed**_{antiShifter}.
(14) They specially **prepared**_{antiShifter} vegan dishes for me.

4 Generic Features

In addition to the task-specific features presented in §3 we examine some generic features derived from common lexical resources. Unlike the features in §3, the generic features do not produce a ranking. Therefore, we will only be able to evaluate them in the context of a supervised classifier.

WordNet (WN): WordNet is the largest English ontology. It is organized in synsets. However, we want to assign categories to words, rather than senses. Due to the lack of robust word-sense disambiguation, we represent a word as the union of synsets containing it.

A common way to harness WordNet for lexicon induction tasks in sentiment analysis is by using its **glosses** (Esuli and Sebastiani, 2005; Gyamfi et al.,

2009; Choi and Wiebe, 2014; Kang et al., 2014). We assume that the explanatory texts of glosses are similar among shifters. We treat glosses as a bag-of-words feature.

We also use WordNet to assign semantic types. Our intuition is that verbal shifters share the same semantic types. We consider two types of information that have been previously found effective for sentiment analysis in general, namely the **hypernyms** of verbs (Breck et al., 2007) and their **supersenses** (Flekova and Gurevych, 2016).

FrameNet (FN): FrameNet (Baker et al., 1998) is a semantic resource used for various sentiment related tasks, such as opinion holder and target extraction (Kim and Hovy, 2006), stance classification (Hasan and Ng, 2013) or opinion spam analysis (Kim et al., 2015). It provides over 1200 semantic frames that comprise words with similar semantic behavior. We use the frame-memberships of a verb as its features, expecting that verbal shifters are grouped in the same frames. For instance, the frame AVOIDING exclusively comprises verbal shifters (e.g. *desist, dodge, evade, shun, shirk* etc.).

The latest version of FrameNet (v1.6) covers only 31.4% of verbs from our gold standard. To **extend coverage**, we use the semantic-parser SemaFor (Das et al., 2010), which can infer frames for verbs missing from FrameNet (Das and Smith, 2011). For each missing verb, we have SemaFor label 100 sentences from our corpus and use the frame most frequently assigned. In our exploratory experiments with supervised classification, this expansion caused a significant increase of 6% in F-score (paired t-test, $p < 0.05$).

5 Experiments

We will now experimentally evaluate the features introduced in §3 and §4. In §5.1 we analyse the high-precision potential of individual task-specific features (§3). In §5.2 we run a recall-oriented evaluation of our entire gold standard with classifiers using both task-specific and generic features. Using the best classifier from this evaluation, we bootstrap the remaining WordNet verbs into a larger list of shifters in §5.3. Finally, we evaluate the impact of verbal shifter knowledge on phrase-level sentiment analysis in §5.4.

---

[6]http://www.sketchengine.co.uk/

Feature	Retr.	Prec@n			
		20	50	100	250
FREQ	2000	10.0	18.0	22.0	22.0
NEGATIVE	189	30.0	30.0	29.0	*N/A*
$-$EFFECT	175	45.0	44.0	46.0	*N/A*
SIM_{nor}	1901	15.0	24.0	16.0	18.4
$SIM_{neither}$	1901	20.0	18.0	18.0	21.6
SIM_{none}	1901	25.0	24.0	22.0	21.6
SIM_{not}	1901	25.0	24.0	23.0	23.2
SIM_{never}	1901	20.0	30.0	30.0	32.8
SIM_{no}	1901	35.0	28.0	36.0	28.8
$SIM_{without}$	1901	40.0	36.0	34.0	27.6
$SIM_{centroid}$	1901	45.0	30.0	29.0	27.6
CLASH	107	40.0	52.0	39.0	*N/A*
$CLASH_{norm}$	107	45.0	46.0	37.0	*N/A*
PRT	165	60.0	64.0	58.0	*N/A*
ANY	539	30.0	28.0	29.0	34.0
ANY_{norm}	539	65.0	60.0	53.0	38.8
$ANY_{norm+polar}$	272	75.0	66.0	62.0	41.2
$ANY_{norm+polar+pageR}$	1901	**80.0**	**70.0**	**63.0**	**45.2**

Table 3: Analysis of shifter features (§3.1).

Feature	Retrieved	Prec@n			
		20	50	100	250
FREQ	2000	90.0	82.0	78.0	78.0
POSITIVE	73	90.0	94.0	*N/A*	*N/A*
+EFFECT	95	90.0	92.0	*N/A*	*N/A*
ANTI	725	**95.0**	**96.0**	**93.0**	**87.4**

Table 4: Analysis of anti-shifter feature (§3.2).

5.1 Analysis of Task-Specific Features

In Table 3 we analyze how useful the task-specific shifter features from §3.1 are as high-precision candidate lists. Each feature produces a ranking, which we evaluate in terms of precision at a certain rank (*Prec@n*). We also state the number of retrieved verbs. Embedding-based methods (e.g. SIM) could theoretically rank all verbs. However, the default configuration of Word2Vec discards every word which occurs less than 5 times, which is why only 1901 verbs are retrieved.

Table 3 shows that filtering verbs by effect ($-$EFFECT) brings improvements over the FREQ and NEGATIVE baselines. Regarding distributional similarity to negation words (SIM), most negation words perform no better than the baselines. The only notable exception is *without*, which provides gains at high ranks. We also examined a combination of all negation words by merging them in a centroid vector ($SIM_{centroid}$) but got mixed results. Polarity clashes (CLASH) show good performance. Particles (PRT) are the second best feature while ANY is the best feature. Normalization and polarity restriction are effective.

We try to further improve the best ranking

Classifier	Acc	Prec	Rec	F1
$Baseline_{majority}$	84.8	42.4	50.0	45.9
$kNN_{noAntiShifter}$	67.6*	54.9	56.4	55.6*
kNN	71.5*	58.3	59.6	58.9*
$LP_{noAntiShifter}$	79.1*	63.0	56.6	59.6*
LP	80.7*	68.6	56.7	62.0*
$SVM_{task\text{-}spec.\ features\ (\S3)}$	79.9*	65.5	69.7	67.5*
$SVM_{generic\ features\ (\S4)}$	89.0*	79.6	74.4	76.9*
$SVM_{all\ features}$	**89.7***	**80.7**	**77.6**	**79.1***

*: better than previous feature (paired t-test with $p < 0.05$)

Table 5: Evaluation of classification (§5.2) on the 2000 verbs from gold standard (Table 1).

(i.e. $ANY_{norm+polar}$) by applying **personalized PageRank** (Haveliwala, 2002; Agirre and Soroa, 2009). In traditional *PageRank* a ranking of nodes in a graph is produced where the highest ranked nodes are the ones most highly connected. In *personalized PageRank* prior information is added. A biased graph is constructed in which attention is drawn towards particular regions of interest (i.e. sets of nodes). This is achieved by assigning specific re-entrance weights to the individual nodes.[7] In our case, we build a word-similarity graph where our verbs are nodes and edges encode similarities between them. The similarities are computed in the same fashion as our distributional similarity features (SIM) (§3). As prior information, we set the nodes representing the verbs returned by $ANY_{norm+polar}$ with a uniform re-entrance weight probability while all other nodes receive a weight of 0. We consider a standard setting of $\alpha = 0.1$ (Manning et al., 2008, ch. 21.2). The resulting ranking indeed improves performance.

In Table 4 we analyze our anti-shifter feature (§3.2). As baseline we again consider all verbs ranked by frequency (FREQ). Complementary to NEGATIVE and $-$EFFECT from Table 3, we consider positive polar expressions (POSITIVE) and +effects (+EFFECT). Our anti-shifter feature (ANTI) clearly outperforms the other approaches.

5.2 Classifier Evaluation

In preparation to our bootstrapping task, we perform a recall-oriented evaluation to consider the classification of *all* verbs from our gold standard as opposed to the n-best rankings used in §5.1. We consider two types of classifiers (as well as a simple majority-class baseline): **graph-based classifiers** and **supervised classifiers**. As graph-based

---

[7] A non-uniform distribution causes some preferred nodes of interest to be visited more often during the random walk.

Conf. Rank	1-250	251-500	501-750	751-1043[†]
Precision	92.8	73.2	62.4	33.2

[†]: final interval covers all remaining predicted *shifters*

Table 6: Classification of WordNet verbs that were ***not*** part of gold standard (§2); verbs are ranked by confidence-score of classifier and evaluated at intervals by precision of *shifter* label.

classifiers, we use one based on label propagation (**LP**), as well as a k-nearest neighbor classifier (**kNN**). **LP and kNN do *not* employ any manually labeled training data**. We use seeds produced by our best task-specific features (§3.1 and §3.2). Then labels are propagated with the help of a word-similarity graph. We use the graph we already employed for our PageRank experiments in §5.1. As shifter seeds we use the top 250 items from $\text{ANY}_{\text{norm+polar+pageR}}$. We use twice as many seeds for anti-shifters[8] (using ANTI from §3.2) to reflect the general bias towards non-shifter verbs (Table 1). In order to examine whether anti-shifters are actually necessary to get negative seeds of sufficient quality, we also run an alternative setting (*noAntiShifter*) in which the same number of negative seeds is simply extracted from the ranking of frequent verbs. The reasoning behind this is that the proportion of frequent verbs not being shifters is already fairly high, as shown by FREQ in Table 4. For LP, we considered the Adsorption label propagation algorithm as implemented in `junto` (Talukdar et al., 2008). For kNN, we set $k = 10$.

Apart from the graph-based classifiers, we also consider a **supervised classifier**, namely Support Vector Machines (**SVM**) as implemented in `SVM`[light] (Joachims, 1999). This classifier uses manually labeled training data, but, unlike LP and kNN, we may combine arbitrary feature sets. We perform 10-fold cross validation and report on accuracy and macro-average precision, recall and F-score. For the task-specific features (§3) we use their most complex configurations from Table 3 (e.g. $\text{SIM}_{\text{centroid}}$ rather than SIM_{nor} or $\text{SIM}_{\text{without}}$).

Table 5 shows that among the graph-based classifiers, LP is notably better than kNN. Both classifiers benefit from anti-shifter seeds. Supervised classification outperforms graph-based classification, so using labeled training data is beneficial.

---

[8]This value is a first estimate and could be improved by fine tuning on a development set.

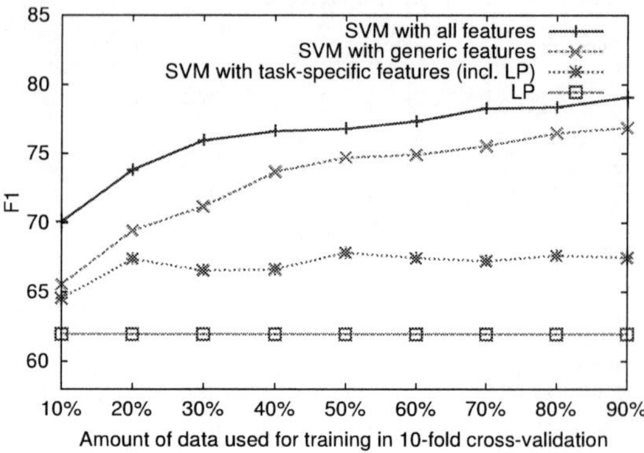

Figure 1: Learning curve on gold standard.

It also means that the *full* set of task-specific shifter features (§3.1) is more effective than just the strongest feature (which is used as seeds for graph-based classification). While the generic features outperform the task-specific features (in supervised classification), combining them results in another significant improvement, demonstrating the importance of the task-specific features.

Figure 1 displays the learning curve of the major feature sets using SVM. While the task-specific features on their own are always worse than the generic features, a classifier combining those feature groups always outperforms the classifier solely trained on the generic features. This improvement is particularly large when few labeled training data are available, which is a typical setting for lexicon bootstrapping tasks. Figure 1 also shows that the SVM classifier has reached roughly the point of saturation when using all features and the maximal amount of labeled training data. This amount should be sufficient for bootstrapping our gold standard lexicon on further unlabeled verbs (as will be shown in §5.3).

5.3 Bootstrapping the Lexicon

We now bootstrap a larger list of shifters from the remaining unlabeled 8581 WordNet verbs not included in our gold standard (§2). On this verb set we run an SVM trained on the gold standard (2000 verbs) with the best performing feature set (Table 5). The classifier predicts 1043 verbs as shifters. The remaining 7538 instances predicted as non-shifters will not be considered further. As our classifier reached a precision of 93.1% on non-shifters on our gold standard data, we are confident that the predicted non-shifters include few actual shifters. As our precision for shifters is lower, i.e.

Information	Example	Label
Sentence	Norah Jones' smooth voice could soothe any savage beast.	
Verb	soothe	
Polar Noun	beast	negative
Verb Phrase	soothe any savage beast	positive

Table 7: Annotation example for the contextual sentiment analysis task. The polarities of the polar noun and the verb phrase are annotated based on context given by the sentence.

Shifting Label	Noun Polarity $\Rightarrow$ VP Polarity		
shifted	$+ \Rightarrow -$ $+ \Rightarrow \sim$	$- \Rightarrow +$ $- \Rightarrow \sim$	$\sim \Rightarrow +$ $\sim \Rightarrow -$
not shifted	$+ \Rightarrow +$	$- \Rightarrow -$	$\sim \Rightarrow \sim$

Table 8: How the shifting label is derived from the polarities of the polar noun and the verb phrase (positive $(+)$; negative $(-)$; neutral $(\sim)$).

	Classifier	Acc	Prec	Rec	F1
Baseline	Majority	79.9	39.9	50.0	44.4
	RNTN	59.0	50.8	51.2	51.0
Proposed	LEX_{LP}	84.3	77.7	67.4	72.2
	LEX_{SVM}	87.1	80.0	79.4	79.7
	LEX_{gold}	90.8	88.9	81.2	84.8

Table 9: Evaluation of polarity classification.

68.3%, we manually check the predicted shifter instances. Using our classifier to pre-filter the data (Choi and Wiebe, 2014) reduced the amount to be annotated by 87.8% from 8581 to just 1043 instances. This is an enormous reduction in annotation effort. Table 6 shows the precision on different intervals ranked by confidence score of the SVM on the predicted 1043 shifters. Since the top 250 instances reach a very high precision, with hindsight, a manual annotation of at least these instances would not even have been necessary either.

Among the 1043 predicted shifters, manual annotation confirmed 676 actual shifters. In total we produced a novel list of 980 shifters (304 gold standard + 676 bootstrapping) in this paper *(all included in our public dataset (see footnote 2))*.

5.4 Impact on Sentiment Analysis

We now investigate whether knowledge of verbal shifters can be useful for the identification of contextual **phrase-level sentiment**. Apart from being an intermediate step in compositional sentence-level classification, phrase-level classification is also independently needed for applications such as knowledge base population (Mitchell, 2013), question answering (Dang, 2009) and summarization (Stoyanov and Cardie, 2011). For that reason and because we specifically study compositionality between verbs and their object, we exclusively consider polarity classification for verb phrases.

The experiment is treated as a binary classification task, where the polarity of a noun has either shifted in the context of a verb phrase (VP) or not. For example in (15), the VP *lack her usual passion* contains the positive polarity noun *passion* which is shifted by *lack*.

(15)   The book seemed to [**lack**$_\text{V}$ [her usual **passion**$_\text{N}^{+}$]$_\text{NP}$]$_\text{VP}^{-}$.

We compiled sentences from our text corpus (*Amazon Product Review Data*, §2) that contain

a VP headed by a verb that has a polar noun[9] as a dependent. We annotated 400 randomly sampled sentences in which the verb is a verbal shifter. We then annotated 2231 sentences with non-shifters to match the ratio of shifters and non-shifters in the gold standard (Table 1) *(see footnote 2)*.

To cover a variety of different verbs, rather than just the most frequent ones, each verbal shifter occurs only once. For each sentence, an annotator labeled the polarity of the polar noun and the polarity of the VP as either *positive*, *negative* or *neutral*. The annotator was also given the full sentence to establish context and the verb that is the head of the VP to avoid misunderstandings. Table 7 shows an example of the information provided, as well as the annotator's decision to label *beast* as negative and *soothe any savage beast* as positive.

Depending on whether the VP and its dependent noun have the same polarity or not, the polarity is considered to have *shifted* or *not shifted*, as detailed in Table 8. These are the class labels onto which the output of the systems (and the annotation) will be mapped. The quantitative evaluation happens on these labels. There is currently no consensus as to how shifting is to be modeled in terms of resulting polarities. For example, the shifting of *excellent* in (16) could either be interpreted as the resulting phrase *wasn't excellent* carrying negative or neutral polarity. The first interpretation simply flips the polarity (Choi and Cardie, 2008), while the second interpretation is driven by the fact that the negation of *excellent* is not synonymous with its antonym *atrocious* (Taboada et al., 2011; Kiritchenko and Mohammad, 2016). The polar in-

---

[9] Noun polarity is provided by the *Subjectivity Lexicon*.

tensity of *wasn't excellent* is certainly weaker than that of *atrocious* but it is a matter of interpretation whether to classify it as negative or neutral. To accommodate both legitimate interpretations, we count either of these behaviors as shifting (Table 8). We do this since our evaluation is concerned with whether shifting occurs, not with the exact polarities (or polar intensities) involved. Our own approach does not profit from this, as it is based on the knowledge of shifters, not polarities.

(16) Let's say, the movie [**wasn't** [excellent]$^+$]$^{-/\sim}$.

As baselines, we consider a majority class classifier (**Majority**) and the Recursive Neural Tensor Network tagger (**RNTN**) by Socher et al. (2013), which is considered the state-of-the-art for handling negation on the phrase level. RNTN is a compositional sentence-level polarity classifier providing polarity values for each tree node in the constituency parse of a sentence. This output allows us to extract polarity predictions for VPs and polar nouns in our data. Apart from achieving best performance on polarity classification datasets, a major highlight of RNTN is its capability of learning shifting directly from labeled training data without explicit knowledge of shifters and shifting rules. However, RNTN depends on manually labeled training data, i.e. sentences in which each node of the parse tree is labeled with polarity information. Such fine-grained manual annotation is currently only provided by the *Stanford Sentiment Treebank (SST)* (Socher et al., 2013). Resources like SST are not suitable for either training or testing a polarity classifier with respect to verbal shifters, since they do not contain each shifter with sufficient frequency. For example, SST contains instances for 16.9% of our verbal shifters, with less than half of these occurring more than once. We expect that RNTN, which has been trained on SST, may only be able to model shifting caused by frequently occurring negation words, but, unlike our own approach, will fail to account for shifting involving any but the most frequent verbal shifters.

Our own approach (**LEX**) is based on inferring the polarity of each VP from the polarity of the noun and whether the verb is a shifter. A VP with a shifter has a polarity moving to the opposite of the noun, a VP without shifter has the same polarity. We evaluate the shifter lexicons generated by our best graph-based classifier (**LEX$_{LP}$**) and best supervised classifier (**LEX$_{SVM}$**) from §5.2. Our

human annotated list of 980 shifters (§5.3) establishes an upper bound (**LEX$_{gold}$**).

Results in Table 9 show that all lexicons exceed the baselines. Even automatically induced shifter lexicons clearly outperform the prediction of existing sentiment analysis systems. Errors in LEX$_{gold}$ are mostly due to verbs that exhibit shifter behavior in some of their word senses, but not the one present in the phrase. In (17) *bring down* means *remove* and causes shifting, but in (18) its meaning of *inflict* does not cause shifting. The high scores produced by LEX$_{gold}$ also suggest that working on the lemma level instead of the sense level only means a moderate loss in performance.

(17) The revolution [[**brought down**]$_V$ the **tyrant$_N^-$**]$_{VP}^+$.
(18) She [[**brought down**]$_V$ a **curse$_N^-$**]$_{VP}^-$ on the village.

6 Related Work

Negation modeling is a central research issue in sentiment analysis, but only few works consider more than typical negation words. We refer the reader to the survey of Wiegand et al. (2010) for more information on negation modeling.

Approaches to learning negation from labeled corpora have been examined in the review domain (Ikeda et al., 2008; Kessler and Schütze, 2012; Socher et al., 2013; Yu et al., 2016), the biomedical domain (Huang and Lowe, 2007; Morante and Daelemans, 2009; Zou et al., 2013) and across domains (Fancellu et al., 2016). However, as outlined in §1, due to their small size the labeled datasets include few different verbal shifters. Moreover, these works mostly focus on scope detection rather than the identification of shifters.

The work most closely related to ours is Danescu-Niculescu-Mizil et al. (2009) who propose using NPIs for shifter extraction.[10] However, our work substantially extends that previous work. We show how the usage of NPIs can be further refined to improve the recognition of shifters (i.e. require the direct object to be a polar noun and subsequently apply PageRank). Moreover, we successfully combine this information with other features. Unlike Danescu-Niculescu-Mizil et al. (2009), we also carry out a recall-oriented evaluation and examine the impact of explicit knowledge of verbal shifters on contextual sentiment analysis.

---

[10]*Shifters* are referred to as *downward entailing operators*.

7 Conclusion

We took a major step toward producing a comprehensive lexicon of polarity shifters by bootstrapping a large list of verbal polarity shifters. Using a sample of 2000 manually annotated verbs extracted from WordNet, we built a supervised classifier to classify the remaining WordNet verbs. This reduced the number of verbs to be annotated manually by a large amount. We examined a variety of linguistic features and found that in addition to features derived from WordNet and FrameNet, the co-occurrence of the negative polarity item *any* with verbal shifters is particularly effective. We also showed that automatically learned knowledge of shifters improves the prediction of phrase-level sentiment.

Our approach should be largely transferable to other languages. This also applies to the features based on particular constructions such as the NPI *any*. The German NPI *jeglich*, Catalan *cap*, Japanese *dono mo* etc. can be expected to exhibit a very similar behavior (cf. Haspelmath (1997)).

Our goal is to build a complete lexicon of polarity shifters; to this end, future work will aim to add nouns and adjectives to our shifter lexicon.

Acknowledgements

The authors would like to thank Stephanie Köser for annotating the verb lexicon presented in this paper. For proofreading the paper, the authors would also like to thank Anna Schmidt, Meaghan Fowlie, Annemarie Friedrich, Andrea Fischer, David M. Howcroft, Clayton Greenberg, Ines Rehbein and Katja Markert. The authors were partially supported by the German Research Foundation (DFG) under grants RU 1873/2-1 and WI 4204/2-1.

References

E. Agirre and A. Soroa. 2009. Personalizing PageRank for Word Sense Disambiguation. In *Proceedings of EACL*.

C. F. Baker, C. J. Fillmore, and J. B. Lowe. 1998. The Berkeley FrameNet Project. In *Proceedings of COLING/ACL*.

E. Breck, Y. Choi, and C. Cardie. 2007. Identifying Expressions of Opinion in Context. In *Proceedings of IJCAI*.

L. Brinton. 1985. Verb Particles in English: Aspect or Aktionsart. *Studia Linguistica*, 39:157–68.

Danqi Chen and Christopher D Manning. 2014. A Fast and Accurate Dependency Parser using Neural Networks. In *Proceedings of EMNLP*.

Y. Choi and C. Cardie. 2008. Learning with Compositional Semantics as Structural Inference for Subsentential Sentiment Analysis. In *Proceedings of EMNLP*.

Y. Choi, L. Deng, and J. Wiebe. 2014. Lexical Acquisition for Opinion Inference: A Sense-Level Lexicon of Benefactive and Malefactive Events. In *Proceedings of WASSA*.

Y. Choi and J. Wiebe. 2014. +/-EffectWordNet: Sense-level Lexicon Acquisition for Opinion Inference. In *Proceedings of EMNLP*.

C. Danescu-Niculescu-Mizil, L. Lee, and R. Ducott. 2009. Without a 'doubt'? Unsupervised Discovery of Downward-Entailing Operators. In *Proceedings of HLT/NAACL*.

H. T. Dang. 2009. Overview of the TAC 2008 Opinion Question Answering and Summarization Tasks. In *Proceedings of TAC*.

D. Das, N. Schneider, D. Chen, and N. A. Smith. 2010. Probabilistic Frame-Semantic Parsing. In *Proceedings of HLT/NAACL*.

D. Das and N. A. Smith. 2011. Semi-Supervised Frame-Semantic Parsing for Unknown Predicates. In *Proceedings of ACL*.

L. Deng, Y. Choi, and J. Wiebe. 2013. Benefactive/Malefactive Event and Writer Attitude Annotation. In *Proceedings of ACL*.

A. Esuli and F. Sebastiani. 2005. Determining the Semantic Orientation of Terms through Gloss Classification. In *Proceedings of CIKM*.

F. Fancellu, A. Lopez, and B. Webber. 2016. Neural Networks for Negation Scope Detection. In *Proceedings of ACL*.

L. Flekova and I. Gurevych. 2016. Supersense Embeddings: A Unified Model for Supersense Interpretation, Prediction, Utilization. In *Proceedings of ACL*.

A. Giannakidou. 2008. Negative and Positive Polarity Items: Licensing, Compositionality and Variation. In C. Maienborn, K. von Heusinger, and P. Portner, editors, *Semantics: An International Handbook of Natural Language Meaning*, pages 1660–1712. Mouton de Gruyter.

Y. Gyamfi, J. Wiebe, R. Mihalcea, and C. Akkaya. 2009. Integrating Knowledge for Subjectivity Sense Labeling. In *Proceedings of HLT/NAACL*.

S. Harabagiu, A. Hickl, and F. Lacatusu. 2006. Negation, Contrast and Contradiction in Text Processing. In *Proceedings of AAAI*.

K. S. Hasan and V. Ng. 2013. Frame Semantics for Stance Classification. In *Proceedings of CoNLL*.

M. Haspelmath. 1997. *Indefinite Pronouns*. Clarendon Press Oxford.

T. H. Haveliwala. 2002. Topic-Sensitive PageRank. In *Proceedings of WWW*.

Y. Huang and H. J. Lowe. 2007. A Novel Hybrid Approach to Automated Negation Detection in Clinical Radiology Reports. *Journal of the American Medical Infomatics Association*, 14:304–311.

D. Ikeda, H. Takamura, L. Ratinov, and M. Okumura. 2008. Learning to Shift the Polarity of Words for Sentiment Classification. In *Proceedings of IJC-NLP*.

N. Jindal and B. Liu. 2008. Opinion Spam and Analysis. In *Proceedings of WSDM*.

T. Joachims. 1999. Making Large-Scale SVM Learning Practical. In B. Schölkopf, C. Burges, and A. Smola, editors, *Advances in Kernel Methods - Support Vector Learning*, pages 169–184. MIT Press.

J. S. Kang, S. Feng, L. Akoglu, and Y. Choi. 2014. ConnotationWordNet: Learning Connotation over the Word+Sense Network. In *Proceedings of ACL*.

W. Kessler and H. Schütze. 2012. Classification of Inconsistent Sentiment Words using Syntactic Constructions. In *Proceedings of COLING*.

S. Kim, H. Chang, S. Lee, M. Yu, and J. Kang. 2015. Deep Semantic Frame-Based Deceptive Opinion Spam Analysis. In *Proceedings of CIKM*.

S. Kim and E. Hovy. 2006. Extracting Opinions, Opinion Holders, and Topics Expressed in Online News Media Text. In *Proceedings of the ACL Workshop on Sentiment and Subjectivity in Text*.

S. Kiritchenko and S. M. Mohammad. 2016. The Effect of Negators, Modals, and Degree Adverbs on Sentiment Composition. In *Proceedings of WASSA*.

M. Krifka. 1991. Some Remarks on Polarity Items. In D. Zaefferer, editor, *Semantic Universals and Universal Semantics*, pages 150–189. Foris Publications.

J. R. Landis and G. G. Koch. 1977. The Measurement of Observer Agreement for Categorical Data. *Biometrics*, 33(1):159–174.

C. D. Manning, P. Raghavan, and H. Schütze. 2008. *Introduction to Information Retrieval*. Cambridge University Press.

T. Mikolov, K. Chen, G. Corrado, and J. Dean. 2013. Efficient Estimation of Word Representations in Vector Space. In *Proceedings of Workshop at ICLR*.

G. Miller, R. Beckwith, C. Fellbaum, D. Gross, and K. Miller. 1990. Introduction to WordNet: An Online Lexical Database. *International Journal of Lexicography*, 3:235–244.

M. Mitchell. 2013. Overview of the TAC2013 Knowledge Base Population Evaluation: English Sentiment Slot Filling. In *Proceedings of TAC*.

R. Morante. 2010. Descriptive Analysis of Negation Cues in Biomedical Texts. In *Proceedings of LREC*.

R. Morante and W. Daelemans. 2009. A Metalearning Approach to Processing the Scope of Negation. In *Proceedings of CoNLL*.

O. Sanchez-Graillet and M. Poesio. 2007. Negation of proteinprotein interactions: analysis and extraction. *Bioinformatics*, 23(13):i424–i432.

R. Socher, A. Perelygin, J. Y. Wu, J. Chuang, C. D. Manning, A. Y. Ng, and C. Potts. 2013. Recursive Deep Models for Semantic Compositionality over a Sentiment Treebank. In *Proceedings of EMNLP*.

V. Stoyanov and C. Cardie. 2011. Automatically Creating General-Purpose Opinion Summaries from Text. In *Proceedings of RANLP*.

G. Szarvas, V. Vincze, R. Farkas, and J. Csirik. 2008. The BioScope Corpus: Annotation for Negation, Uncertainty and their Scope in Biomedical Texts. In *Proceedings of BioNLP*.

M. Taboada, J. Brooke, M. Tofiloski, K. Voll, and M. Stede. 2011. Lexicon-Based Methods for Sentiment Analysis. *Computational Linguistics*, 37(2):267 – 307.

P. P. Talukdar, J. Reisinger, M. Pasca, D. Ravichandran, R. Bhagat, and F. Pereira. 2008. Weakly-Supervised Acquisition of Labeled Class Instances using Graph Random Walks. In *Proceedings of EMNLP*.

M. Wiegand, A. Balahur, B. Roth, D. Klakow, and A. Montoyo. 2010. A Survey on the Role of Negation in Sentiment Analysis. In *Proceedings of the Workshop on Negation and Speculation in Natural Language Processing*.

M. Wiegand and J. Ruppenhofer. 2015. Opinion Holder and Target Extraction based on the Induction of Verbal Categories. In *Proceedings of CoNLL*.

T. Wilson, J. Wiebe, and P. Hoffmann. 2005. Recognizing Contextual Polarity in Phrase-level Sentiment Analysis. In *Proceedings of HLT/EMNLP*.

H. Yu, J. Hsu, M. Castellanos, and J. Han. 2016. Data-driven Contextual Valence Shifter Quantification for Multi-Theme Sentiment Analysis. In *Proceedings of CIKM*.

B. Zou, G. Zhou, and Q. Zhu. 2013. Tree Kernel-based Negation and Speculation Scope Detection with Structured Syntactic Parse Features. In *Proceedings of EMNLP*.

Cascading Multiway Attention for Document-level Sentiment Classification

Dehong Ma, Sujian Li, Xiaodong Zhang, Houfeng Wang, Xu Sun
MOE Key Lab of Computational Linguistics, Peking University, Beijing 100871, China
{madehong, lisujian, zxdcs, wanghf, xusun}@pku.edu.cn

Abstract

Document-level sentiment classification aims to assign the user reviews a sentiment polarity. Previous methods either just utilized the document content without consideration of user and product information, or did not comprehensively consider what roles the three kinds of information play in text modeling. In this paper, to reasonably use all the information, we present the idea that user, product and their combination can all influence the generation of attention to words and sentences, when judging the sentiment of a document. With this idea, we propose a cascading multiway attention (CMA) model, where multiple ways of using user and product information are cascaded to influence the generation of attention on the word and sentence layers. Then, sentences and documents are well modeled by multiple representation vectors, which provide rich information for sentiment classification. Experiments on IMDB and Yelp datasets demonstrate the effectiveness of our model.

1 Introduction

Document-level sentiment classification aims to predict an overall sentiment polarity (e.g., 1-5 stars or 1-10 stars) for a user review document. This task recently draws increasing research concerns and is helpful to many downstream applications, such as user and product recommendation.

Early work focuses on traditional machine learning associated with handcraft text features for sentiment classification (Pang et al., 2002; Ding et al., 2008; Taboada et al., 2011). With the development of deep learning techniques, some researchers design neural networks to automatically learn features from document content and achieve comparable performance (Glorot et al., 2011; Kalchbrenner et al., 2014; Yang et al., 2016), though they ignore the use of user and product information. Almost at the same time, deep learning techniques exhibit another advantage that product and user information can be flexibly modeled with document content for sentiment classification (Tang et al., 2015a; Chen et al., 2016). Tang et al. (2015a) design user and product preference matrices to tune word representations, based on which convolutional neural networks (CNNs) are used to model the whole document. To avoid the high-cost preference matrix, Chen et al. (2016) develop the two-layer (i.e., word and sentence layers) model, where the combination of user and product information is used to generate attention to words and sentences respectively on each layer.

Though previous studies achieve improvements in synthesizing text, user and product for sentiment classification, they are somewhat limited to either of the following two aspects. First, when considering user and product information, previous work mostly models their combination which may cause adverse effects on sentiment classification. As we can see, user and product information also have their own influence on sentence and document representations. For example, a lenient user tends to focus on the good aspects, while a picky user is always concerned about unsatisfactory clues, no matter which product is reviewed. In another view, different products have their own concerns. For example, a car is closely related with fuel consumption while a hotel with bed or food, which are relatively independent of users. Second, in previous hierarchical modeling method, different layers are usually treated with similar means. In our opinion, different linguistic units (e.g., words and sentences) should be given

Proceedings of the The 8th International Joint Conference on Natural Language Processing, pages 634–643,
Taipei, Taiwan, November 27 – December 1, 2017 ©2017 AFNLP

different treatment to achieve good performance. As we can see, words are closely related with each other and sentences are relatively independent in reflecting their sentimental polarity. Take a restaurant review for example, the review *"Its dinner environment is good. But the pizza is not worth the money!"* is comprised of two sentences. For this review, a user who values environment may mark 5 stars, while a user who thinks highly of food may mark 1 star. Thus, we can not simply combine the two sentences together in judging its sentiment polarity. It is better to model each sentence independently before knowing the users' or products' attention.

To address the two issues above, we propose to comprehensively make use of the information of user, product, and their combination to generate attention on the word and sentence layers, and further cascade the multiple ways of attention on the generation of sentence and document representations. Here, we name our proposed model the cascading multiway attention (CMA) model. Specifically, each sentence is first represented with multiple representation vectors through using different ways of attention to focus on the important part. Next, the similar multiple ways of generating attention are applied on the sentence level and used to tune the generation of document representations. In such a case, document representation is not simply treated as a sequence of sentences, but considers more about the influence of user and product information. Finally, we can get a well modeled document representation for sentiment classification. Experiments on three real-world datasets demonstrate that CMA achieves state-of-the-art performance and fully considers the contributions from user and product information.

2 Cascading Multiway Attention Model for Sentiment Classification

In this section, we first give an overview of the cascading multiway attention (CMA) model for sentiment classification. Then, we focus on introducing how to design multiway attention for modeling sentences and documents through using user and product information. Next, we show the training details of CMA.

2.1 Model Overview

Figure 1(a) shows the overall architecture of our CMA model, which is mainly composed of four levels including word level, sentence level, document level, classification level. With word embeddings as input, we can employ convolutional neural networks or recurrent neural networks to obtain deeper semantic of words on the word level. On the sentence level, we design the multiway attention networks to generate attention to words from three different views and get three representation vectors to represent a sentence. On the document level, we keep generating multiple kinds of attention to sentences and get the document representation, which is fed into a softmax function for classification.

Specifically, let us first formalize the notation. We suppose that a document contains m sentences $\{S_1, S_2, ..., S_m\}$ whose lengths are set $n_1, n_2, ..., n_m$ respectively. For Sentence $S_t (1 \leq t \leq m)$, it is composed of a sequence of words $w_t^1, w_t^2, \cdots, w_t^{n_t}$ where w_t^j denotes a specific word. To represent a word, we embed each word into a low dimensional real-value vector, called word embedding (Bengio et al., 2003).

Then, we can get $w_t^j \in R^d$ from $M^{v \times d}$, where t is the sentence index in a document, j denotes the word index in sentence t, d means the embedding dimension and v gives the vocabulary size. Word embeddings can be regarded as parameters of neural networks or pre-trained from proper corpus via language model (Collobert and Weston, 2008; Mnih and Hinton, 2007; Mikolov et al., 2010; Huang et al., 2012). In our model, we choose the second strategy.

Next, deeper word semantics representations can be learned by using the neural network models, such as convolutional neural networks (CNN) or recurrent neural networks (RNN). In this paper, the LSTM model is employed to obtain the word representation, since it has the good performance of learning the long-term dependencies and can well model the dependence between words. Formally, for sentence S_t, we input its word embeddings $w_t^1, w_t^2, ..., w_t^{n_t}$ to the LSTM networks and get the final word representations $r_t^1, r_t^2, ..., r_t^{n_t}$.

With deeper word representations as input, we adopt the attention mechanism to model sentences. As Section 1 stated, we consider the influence from three views: user (δ^u), product (δ^p), and combination of user and product (δ^{up}), which can generate three kinds of attention to words. Then, we impose the three attention vectors on word representations respectively and get three represen-

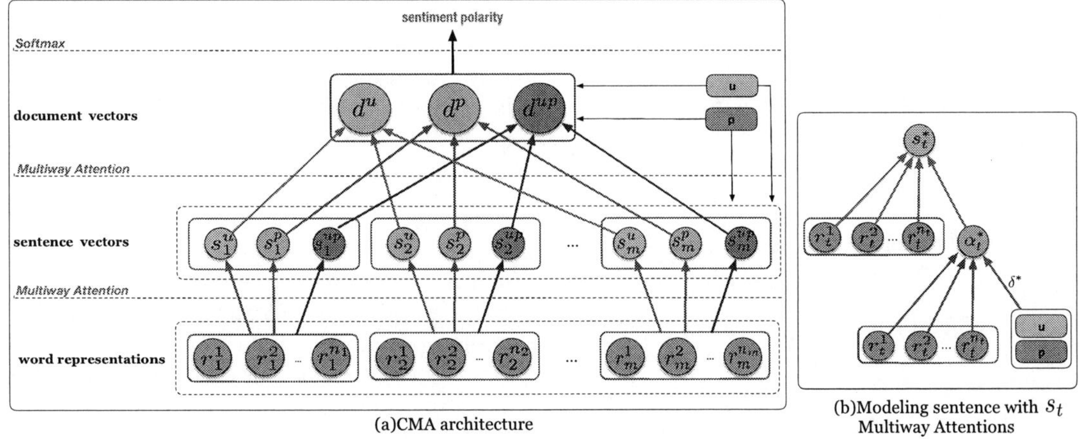

Figure 1: Overall Architecture of CMA.

tation vectors for each sentence. Formally, sentence S_t is represented by the concatenation of three vectors $\mathbf{s}_t^u, \mathbf{s}_t^p, \mathbf{s}_t^{up}$. On the document level, we still use δ^u, δ^p and δ^{up} respectively to generate attention to sentences and get three vectors $\mathbf{d}^u$, $\mathbf{d}^p$, $\mathbf{d}^{up}$ for representing the document. The concrete design is introduced in the next subsection.

Finally, the three vectors $\mathbf{d}^u$, $\mathbf{d}^p$, $\mathbf{d}^{up}$ are concatenated to a vector $\mathbf{d}$ for a classifier. Here, we use a non-linear layer to project $\mathbf{d}$ into the space of the targeted C classes. That is,

$$x = tanh(W_l \cdot \mathbf{d} + b_l) \tag{1}$$

where W_l and b_l are the weight matrix and bias respectively. The probability of labeling document with sentiment polarity $i(i \in [1, C])$ is computed by:

$$y_i = \frac{exp(x_i)}{\sum_{i=1}^{C} exp(x_i)} \tag{2}$$

The label with highest probability is set as the final result.

2.2 Cascading Multiway Attention

Now, we detail how to model user and product information and cascade their influence on representing sentences and documents.

As stated in Section 1, the meaning of a sentence has different interpretations from different views including user, product and their combination, under which words may be paid different attention on. With consideration of each view, only some specific parts are focused on. And different views have their own focuses which contribute

to sentiment classification. Thus, we propose the multiway attention mechanism to capture sentence focuses with repsect to different views.

Specifically, in our model, we represent each user and each product with a representation vector which is learned from the model, notated with $\mathbf{u}$ and $\mathbf{p}$ here. To consider the influence from user and product, we formalize user view, product view and their combination view respectively as:

$$\delta^u = W_u \cdot \mathbf{u} \tag{3}$$
$$\delta^p = W_p \cdot \mathbf{p} \tag{4}$$
$$\delta^{up} = W_u{}' \cdot \mathbf{u} + W_p{}' \cdot \mathbf{p} \tag{5}$$

where W_u, W_p, $W_u{}'$, and $W_p{}'$ are weight matrices for tuning the influence of $\mathbf{u}$ and $\mathbf{p}$.

We take sentence S_t for example to describe the sentence modeling process, as shown in Figure 1(b). With word representations $r_t^1, r_t^2, ..., r_t^{n_t}$, we can generate three attention vectors using δ^u, δ^p and δ^{up} respectively. For convenience we use δ^* to denote δ^u, δ^p or δ^{up}. Then, the attention mechanism generates the attention vector α_t^* with respect to δ^*. The jth dimension $[\alpha_t^*]^j$ denotes the attention weight of the jth word r_t^j.

$$[\alpha_t^*]^j = \frac{exp(\gamma(r_t^j, \delta^*))}{\sum_{j=1}^{n_t} exp(\gamma(r_t^j, \delta^*))} \tag{6}$$

where γ is a score function that measures the importance of r_t^j in the sentence. The score function γ is defined as:

$$\gamma(r_t^j, \delta^*) = tanh(W_H \cdot r_t^j + \delta^* + b_s) \cdot v^T \tag{7}$$

where W_H and b_s are weight matrix and bias respectively, and v^T is the transpose of the weight vector v.

After computing the word attention weights, we can get sentence representations $\mathbf{s}_t^*$ using different attention weights:

$$\mathbf{s}_t^* = \sum_{j=1}^{n_t} [\alpha_t^*]^j r_t^j. \tag{8}$$

Then, we get a multi-vector sentence representation: $[\mathbf{s}_t^u, \mathbf{s}_t^p, \mathbf{s}_t^{up}]$ for sentence S_t from three views.

On the sentence level, we apply the similar multiway attention strategy to get the document representation. Unlike the word level, each sentence is relatively independent of other sentences and takes its own part in determining the document sentiment. Thus, we ignore modeling the dependence between sentences and directly use the sentence representations derived from the word level. As we see, from different views each sentence plays a different role, and from a specific view all the sentences should be paid different attention, in document-level sentiment classification. Here, we still consider the influence from user, product and their combination, and get the corresponding document representation $\mathbf{d}^u, \mathbf{d}^p, \mathbf{d}^{up}$, where $\mathbf{d}^*$ ($* \in \{u, p, up\}$) is computed as follows:

$$\mathbf{d}^* = \sum_{t=1}^{m} \beta_t^* \mathbf{s}_t^* \tag{9}$$

$$\beta_t^* = \frac{exp(\gamma(\mathbf{s}_t^*, \delta^*))}{\sum_{t=1}^{m} exp(\gamma(\mathbf{s}_t^*, \delta^*))} \tag{10}$$

where $\mathbf{s}_t^*$ is the sentence representation of sentence S_t with respect to δ^*. β_t^* denotes the corresponding attention weight of S_t on the view of δ^*, and the γ function is the same as in Eq. (7).

2.3 Model Training

In CMA, we need to optimize all the parameters notated as Θ which are from all the user and product embedding vectors, LSTM networks, two multiway attention layers and the softmax layer.

We use cross entropy with L_2 regularization as the loss function, which is defined as:

$$J = -\sum_{i=1}^{C} g_i \log(y_i) + \lambda_r (\sum_{\theta \in \Theta} \theta^2) \tag{11}$$

where $g_i \in R^C$ denotes the ground truth, represented by one-hot vector. $y_i \in R^C$ is the estimated probability for each class, computed as in Eq. (2). λ_r is the coefficient for L_2 regularization.

After learning Θ, we test the instances by feeding their text with user and product information into CMA, and the label with the highest probability stands for the predicted sentiment polarity.

3 Experiments

In this section, we first introduce the datasets and metrics used in our experiments. Then, we show the hyperparameter setting of our model. Next, we present the results of our model and compare our model with other state-of-the-art methods. Finally, we use a case study to examine the experimental results of CMA.

Datasets

To validate the effectiveness of our model, we use three real-world datasets: IMDB, Yelp 2013 and Yelp 2014 collected by Tang et al. (2015b). For these data, we preprocess the text including using Stanford CoreNLP (Manning et al., 2014) to split the review documents into sentences and tokenizing all words. Table 1 shows the details of the three datasets including number of documents (#docs), average number of documents per user posts(#docs/user) etc. It is also noted that IMDB is rated with 10 sentiment labels (i.e., 1-10 stars) while Yelp has 5 labels (i.e., 1-5 stars). We also adopt the same data partition used in (Tang et al., 2015b) and (Chen et al., 2016) for training, developing and test.

Evaluation Metrics

To evaluate the performance of sentiment classification, we adopt the metrics of *Accuracy* and *RMSE*. *Accuracy* measures the overall performance. Given the number of correctly predicted samples T and the total number of samples N, *Accuracy* is defined as:

$$Acc = \frac{T}{N}. \tag{12}$$

RMSE evaluates the divergence between predicted labels and ground truth labels and is defined as:

$$RMSE = \sqrt{\frac{\sum_{k=1}^{N} (l_k - l_k')^2}{N}} \tag{13}$$

where l_k and l_k' denote the ground truth and predicted label of sample k respectively. Generally, a good system has a high accuracy and a low RMSE.

Dataset	#docs	#users	#products	#docs/user	#docs/product	#sents/doc	#words/doc	#labels
IMDB	84919	1310	1635	64.82	51.94	16.08	24.54	10
Yelp2013	78966	1631	1633	48.42	48.36	10.89	17.38	5
Yelp2014	231163	4818	4194	47.97	55.11	11.41	17.26	5

Table 1: Data Statistics of IMDB, Yelp2013 and Yelp 2014.

Hyperparameter Setting

Following (Chen et al., 2016) and (Tang et al., 2015b), we set the dimensions of word, user and product embeddings as 200 in our experiments. We train the word embeddings through using the training and developing sets of each dataset with word2vec tool (Mikolov et al., 2013). The user and product embeddings are initialized randomly. All the weight matrices are initialized by uniform distribution, and all biases are assigned as zero. We also set the dimensions of the LSTM hidden states and attention vectors as 200.

To train our model, we utilize AdaDelta (Zeiler, 2012), which adopts a self-adaptive learning rate, to optimize the parameters. The coefficient of penalty in the objective function is set to 10^{-5}.

3.1 Method Comparison

To comprehensively evaluate the performance of *CMA*, we list some baseline methods for comparison. The baselines are introduced as follows.

• **Majority** assigns the largest sentiment polarity occurred in the training set to each sample in the test set.

• **Trigram** uses the unigrams, bigrams and trigrams features to train a SVM classifier for sentiment classification.

• **TextFeature** extracts word/character ngrams, sentiment lexicon features, negation features, etc. for a SVM classifier.

• **UPF** extracts user-leniency features and product features from training data (Gao et al., 2013). There features can be concatenated with the features of *Trigram* and *TextFeature*.

• **AvgWordvec** averages the word embeddings in a document to generate the document representation as features for a SVM classifier.

• **SSWE** first learns the sentiment-specific word embeddings and then utilizes three kinds of pooling (i.e., max, min and average) to generate the document representation for a SVM classifier (Tang et al., 2014).

• **PV**(Paragraph Vector) is an unsupervised framework to learn distributed representations for text of any length (Le and Mikolov, 2014). (Tang et al., 2015a) implements the distributed memory model of paragraph vectors (PV-DM) to get document representations for sentiment classification.

• **RNTN+RNN** models sentences using recursive neural tensor networks (RNTN) (Socher et al., 2013). Then sentence representations are fed into the recurrent neural networks (RNN) and their hidden states are averaged to get the document representation.

• **UPNN** designs preference matrices for each user and product to modify word representations (Tang et al., 2015b). Word representations are then fed into the convolution neural networks (CNNs) and concatenated with the user/product representation to generate document representation before a softmax layer. Without considering user and product information, the *UPNN(noUP)* method just uses CNN to model the documents.

• **NSC+UPA** proposes the hierarchical neural networks which are composed of two LSTM models to generate word and sentence representations (Chen et al., 2016). The combination of user and product information is used to generate attention to words and sentences on the sentence and document levels. The document representation is fed into a softmax layer. The *NSC* model is similar to *NSC+UPA*, but ignores user and product information and directly applies two layers of LSTM and attention mechanism to model sentences and documents using only document content.

When comparing with our model, we directly use the results of the above baselines reported in (Chen et al., 2016), as we conduct the experiments on the same datasets.

• **CA-null** is a simplified version of our CMA model without consideration of user and product information. We use one LSTM with attention to model sentences. Based on the sentence representations, we directly use the attention mechanism to model documents for sentiment classification.

The performance comparison of CMA and all baselines are shown in Table 2. All the baseline methods are divided into two categories: the first category only uses document content and the second comprehensively considers document, user and

Model	IMDB		Yelp 2013		Yelp 2014	
	Acc.	RMSE	Acc.	RMSE	Acc.	RMSE
Majority	0.196	2.495	0.411	1.060	0.392	1.907
Trigram	0.399	1.783	0.569	0.841	0.577	0.804
TextFeature	0.402	1.793	0.556	0.814	0.572	0.800
AvgWordvec	0.304	1.985	0.526	0.898	0.530	0.893
SSWE	0.312	1.973	0.549	0.849	0.557	0.851
PV	0.341	1.814	0.554	0.832	0.564	0.802
RNTN+RNN	0.400	1.764	0.574	0.804	0.582	0.821
UPNN(noUP)	0.405	1.629	0.577	0.812	0.585	0.808
NSC+LA	0.487	**1.381**	0.631	0.706	0.630	0.715
CA-null	**0.491**	1.408	**0.635**	**0.689**	**0.640**	**0.690**
Trigram+UPF	0.404	1.764	0.570	0.803	0.579	0.789
TextFeature +UPF	0.402	1.774	0.561	0.822	0.579	0.791
UPNN	0.435	1.602	0.596	0.748	0.608	0.764
NSC+UPA	0.533	1.281	0.650	0.692	0.667	0.654
CMA	**0.540**	**1.191**	**0.664**	**0.677**	**0.676**	**0.637**

Table 2: Methods Comparison on IMDB, Yelp 2013 and Yelp 2014 Datasets.

Model	IMDB		Yelp 2013		Yelp 2014	
	Acc.	RMSE	Acc.	RMSE	Acc.	RMSE
CA-null	0.491	1.408	0.635	0.689	0.640	0.690
CA-δ^u	0.513	1.397	0.641	0.688	0.653	0.687
CA-δ^p	0.508	1.423	0.640	0.694	0.652	0.685
CA-δ^{up}	0.520	1.281	0.645	0.684	0.658	0.670
MA-max	0.528	1.314	0.654	0.680	0.663	0.667
MA-avg	0.521	1.341	0.651	0.678	0.662	0.672
CMA	**0.540**	**1.191**	**0.664**	**0.677**	**0.676**	**0.637**

Table 3: Analysis of Cascading and Multiway Attention.

product information.

In the first category of methods, the *Majority* method is the worst, meaning the majority sentiment polarity occupies 19.2%, 42.1% and 39.2% of all samples. All the other methods are better than the *Majority* method, showing that manual or automatic features can both bring performance improvement for sentiment classification. Though techniques of deep neural networks are widely used and have made a success in document modeling, its simple application (e.g., *AveWordvec*, *PV*) does not achieve better results than using manually selected features (e.g., *Trigram*, *TextFeature*) with respect to the accuracy metric. As for the three kinds of carefully designed neural networks, the *CA-null* and *NSC+LA* methods exhibit obvious advantages with high accuracy and low RMSR, compared to the *RNTN+RNN* and *UPNN(noUP)* methods. The main reason may be that *CA-null* and *NSC+LA* can learn the long-distance dependencies with LSTM networks and make full use of the important words and sentences with attention. We can also see that *CA-null* outperforms *NSC+LA* regarding the accuracy on the three datasets. This verifies that we may not consider sentence dependence when modeling documents for sentiment classification, as the main difference between *CA-null* and *NSC+LA* is that *CA-null* does not apply LSTM to model sentences.

From Table 2, we observe that user and product information can promote the performance of sentiment classification. Even the worst method (*TextFeature+UPF*) in the second category is comparable to the state-of-the-art system (RNTN+RNN) in the first category. For the methods with manually designed features, their performance improvement is smaller than those methods with deep learning methods. Both *Trigram-UPF* and *TextFeature-UPF* concatenate more user and product features, but have little improvement compared with *Trigram* and *TextFeature*. The reason may be that the text features are huge (1M trigram) enough and the newly added user and product features can not work well. Adding user and product information, *CMA* outperforms *CA-null* by about 5 percent with respect to the accuracy metric on IMDB dataset. At the same time, *CMA* performs stably better than NSC+UPA with higher accuracy and lower RMSE on three datasets, with cascading multiway attention on word and sentence levels and keeping independency between the sentences. This validates that only a combination of user and product information can not boost performance much and more ways of attention should be explored in text modeling. It is also noted that words need to be modeled with consideration of their dependence while sentences should be independently modeled.

3.2 Model Analysis

In this section, we design a series of models to verify the effectiveness of our model *CMA*. On one hand, we design three simplified models, i.e., CA-δ^u, CA-δ^p and CA-δ^{up}, which only consider one-way attention from user, product, combination of user and product respectively when modeling sentences and documents. On the other hand, we just keep the multiway attention on modeling sentences and directly adopt the maximization or average operation on sentence representations to model a document, which are named *MA-max* and *MA-avg* respectively. Table 3 shows the results of all the models.

From Table 3, we can see that *CA-null* gets the

worst result compared with other models utilizing user and product information, which indicates that both information is useful for document sentiment. The performance of CA-δ^u and CA-δ^p are worse than CA-δ^{up}, this is because CA-δ^u and CA-δ^p just uses one kind of information (user or product), but CA-δ^{up} uses both information. CMA achieves a much better result than the 'CA' models, which can verify the effectiveness of introducing multiway attention. We also observe that CA-δ^u is slightly better than CA-δ^p, verifying user information plays a more important role than product information as in (Chen et al., 2016).

As for *MA-max* and *MA-avg*, multiway attention on modeling sentences bring much performance improvement compared to *CA-null*, though the cascading structure is not adopted. *MA-avg* seems to treat each sentence equally while *MA-max* tries to seek the most represented sentences contributing to sentiment classification. We can see that *MA-max* performs better than *MA-avg*, verifying that sentences should not be treated equally and multiway attention are a good mechanism for computing the contributions of each sentence to representing a document.

We can also see that *CMA* achieves the best performance among all the models, since *CMA* fully considers the word importance to a sentence and sentence importance to a document via sentence-level and document-level multiway attention. Next, we give an example to illustrate the cascading multiway attention captured by CMA.

Case Study

Here, we use a five-star review document from Yelp as a case study, and the document is *"Biscuits made from scratch, not frozen. Homemade pancakes with real buttermilk, not from a mix or box. Homemade blueberry jam, no jam or can. True dinner coffee. A group of friendly, engaging staff. Five stars... need I say more."*. We apply *CMA* on the document and achieve the correct sentiment polarity. Figure 2 visualizes the multiway attention weights on the sentence and document levels computed by *CMA*. We represent three ways of attention, i.e., user(δ^u), product(δ^p), and combination of user and product (δ^{up}), with blue, red and green color series respectively. The deeper color means higher weight.

Figure 2(a)$\sim$(f) display the three ways of attention to words for sentence1 $\sim$ sentence6 respectively. We can see that different words are as-signed high weight values when using different ways of attention. For example, for sentence1, the word "biscuits" is paid more attention from the user view while "frozen" is focused on from the product view and "made" is emphasized considering the combination of user and product. At the same time, an interesting phenomenon is that all the three views pay little attention to some common words like "," and function words "a" "of". This conforms to our intuition: some function words and punctuation marks contribute little to sentiment classification, but different words are focused on from different views. Thus, multiple ways of using user and product information can well gather information which is helpful to representing a sentence.

Figure 2(g) shows the three ways of attention to sentences for the example document. We can see that the three ways are consistent with focusing on the sixth sentence, which gives high attention weights to the words "five" and "stars" reflecting the sentiment polarity. From the user view, high attention is also paid to sentence5, which includes the obvious sentiment word "friendly". Hence, we infer that the user may like to express his/her sentiment to a product with sentiment word. From the product view, we can see that the document representation is also closely related to many other sentences such as sentence2 (w.r.t food) and sentence5 (w.r.t. staff), which can show different attributes of a product.

This case study shows that cascading two layers of multiway attention are necessary to modeling a document in the sentiment classification task.

4   Related work

Document-level sentiment classification methods can be divided into two kinds of research lines, i.e., traditional machine learning methods and neural networks methods.

For the first kind of research line, Pang et al. (2002) validate the effectiveness of various machine learning methods with bag-of-words features on sentiment classification. Goldberg and Zhu (2006) use a graph-based semi-supervised learning algorithm with unlabeled data to predict the sentiment of reviews. There are also some work which focus on extracting effective features. Ganu et al. (2009) identify user experience information from free text. Qu et al. (2010) introduce a kind of bag-of-opinion representation.

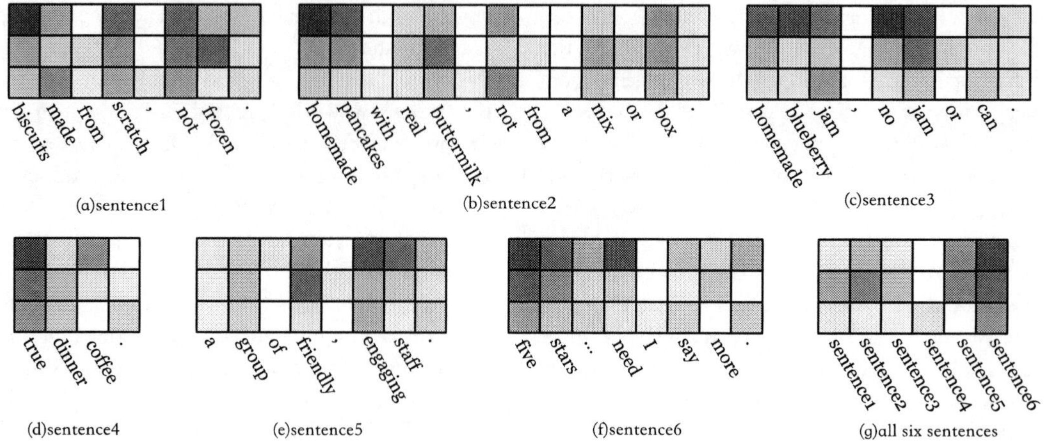

Figure 2: Case Study: Illustration of Attention Weights.

Kiritchenko et al. (2014) extract surface, semantic, and sentiment features from text. User information is also used in traditional methods. Tan et al. (2011) employ social relationships to improve user-level Twitter sentiment analysis. Gao et al. (2013) estimate the sentiment polarity by referring to the user leniency and product popularity computed during testing. Li et al. (2014) incorporate the user and product information into a topic model for sentiment analysis.

Recently, neural network approaches have achieved a comparable performance on document-level sentiment classification. Glorot et al. (2011) first propose a deep learning approach which learns to extract a meaningful representation for each review in an unsupervised fashion. Then, Socher et al. (2011, 2012, 2013) introduce recursive neural networks to document-level sentiment classification. Kim (2014) employ convolutional neural networks to model sentences with two kinds of embeddings for sentiment classification. Le and Mikolov (2014) introduce an unsupervised algorithm that learns fixed-length feature representations from variable-length pieces of texts. Tai et al. (2015) utilize tree-structured long-short memory networks to learn semantic representation for sentiment classification. In addition, user and product information are flexibly modeled for sentiment classification in the neural network methods (Tang et al., 2015b; Chen et al., 2016). Tang et al. (2015a) design preference matrices for each user and each product to tune word representations, based on which convolutional neural networks (CNNs) are used to model the whole document. Chen et al. (2016) employ two layers of long-short term memory (LSTM) with attention to model sentences and documents.

5 Conclusion

In this paper, we propose the cascading multiway attention networks for document-level sentiment classification. The main idea of CMA is to use multiway attention rather than one-way attention to learn representations for sentences and documents, as user, product and their combination can provide different views for modeling text and weaken the dependencies between sentences for better depicting the influence from user preference for document sentiment. On the sentence level, CMA uses three ways of exploiting user and product information to generate attention to words and get sentence representations. On the document level, CMA keeps using the multiway attention mechanism to generate attention to sentences. Experimental results on IMDB, Yelp 2013 and Yelp 2014 verify that CMA can learn efficient representations for sentences and documents and provide rich information for judging the document-level sentiment polarity.

Acknowledgments

We would like to thank the anonymous reviwers for thier insightful suggestions. Our work is supported by National High Technology Research and Development Program of China (863 Program) (No.2015AA015402) and National Natural Science Foundation of China (No.61370117 & No.61572049). The corresponding authors of this paper are Houfeng Wang & Sujian Li.

References

Yoshua Bengio, Réjean Ducharme, Pascal Vincent, and Christian Jauvin. 2003. A neural probabilistic language model. *journal of machine learning research*, 3(Feb):1137–1155.

Huimin Chen, Maosong Sun, Cunchao Tu, Yankai Lin, and Zhiyuan Liu. 2016. Neural sentiment classification with user and product attention. In *Proceedings of EMNLP*.

Ronan Collobert and Jason Weston. 2008. A unified architecture for natural language processing: Deep neural networks with multitask learning. In *Proceedings of the 25th international conference on Machine learning*, pages 160–167. ACM.

Xiaowen Ding, Bing Liu, and Philip S Yu. 2008. A holistic lexicon-based approach to opinion mining. In *Proceedings of the 2008 international conference on web search and data mining*, pages 231–240. ACM.

Gayatree Ganu, Noemie Elhadad, and Amélie Marian. 2009. Beyond the stars: Improving rating predictions using review text content. In *WebDB*, volume 9, pages 1–6. Citeseer.

Wenliang Gao, Naoki Yoshinaga, Nobuhiro Kaji, and Masaru Kitsuregawa. 2013. Modeling user leniency and product popularity for sentiment classification. In *IJCNLP*, pages 1107–1111.

Xavier Glorot, Antoine Bordes, and Yoshua Bengio. 2011. Domain adaptation for large-scale ssentiment classification: A deep learning approach. In *Proceedings of the 28th International Conference on Machine Learning (ICML-11)*, pages 513–520.

Andrew B Goldberg and Xiaojin Zhu. 2006. Seeing stars when there aren't many stars: graph-based semi-supervised learning for sentiment categorization. In *Proceedings of the First Workshop on Graph Based Methods for Natural Language Processing*, pages 45–52. Association for Computational Linguistics.

Eric H Huang, Richard Socher, Christopher D Manning, and Andrew Y Ng. 2012. Improving word representations via global context and multiple word prototypes. In *Proceedings of the 50th Annual Meeting of the Association for Computational Linguistics: Long Papers-Volume 1*, pages 873–882. Association for Computational Linguistics.

Nal Kalchbrenner, Edward Grefenstette, and Phil Blunsom. 2014. A convolutional neural network for modelling sentences. *arXiv preprint arXiv:1404.2188*.

Yoon Kim. 2014. Convolutional neural networks for sentence classification. *arXiv preprint arXiv:1408.5882*.

Svetlana Kiritchenko, Xiaodan Zhu, and Saif M Mohammad. 2014. Sentiment analysis of short informal texts. volume 50, pages 723–762.

Quoc V Le and Tomas Mikolov. 2014. Distributed representations of sentences and documents. In *ICML*, volume 14, pages 1188–1196.

Fangtao Li, Sheng Wang, Shenghua Liu, and Ming Zhang. 2014. Suit: A supervised user-item based topic model for sentiment analysis. In *AAAI*, pages 1636–1642.

Christopher D Manning, Mihai Surdeanu, John Bauer, Jenny Rose Finkel, Steven Bethard, and David McClosky. 2014. The stanford corenlp natural language processing toolkit. In *ACL (System Demonstrations)*, pages 55–60.

Tomas Mikolov, Martin Karafiát, Lukas Burget, Jan Cernocký, and Sanjeev Khudanpur. 2010. Recurrent neural network based language model. In *Interspeech*, volume 2, page 3.

Tomas Mikolov, Ilya Sutskever, Kai Chen, Greg S Corrado, and Jeff Dean. 2013. Distributed representations of words and phrases and their compositionality. In *Advances in neural information processing systems*, pages 3111–3119.

Andriy Mnih and Geoffrey Hinton. 2007. Three new graphical models for statistical language modelling. In *Proceedings of the 24th international conference on Machine learning*, pages 641–648. ACM.

Bo Pang, Lillian Lee, and Shivakumar Vaithyanathan. 2002. Thumbs up?: sentiment classification using machine learning techniques. In *Proceedings of the ACL-02 conference on Empirical methods in natural language processing-Volume 10*, pages 79–86. Association for Computational Linguistics.

Lizhen Qu, Georgiana Ifrim, and Gerhard Weikum. 2010. The bag-of-opinions method for review rating prediction from sparse text patterns. In *Proceedings of the 23rd International Conference on Computational Linguistics*, pages 913–921. Association for Computational Linguistics.

Richard Socher, Brody Huval, Christopher D Manning, and Andrew Y Ng. 2012. Semantic compositionality through recursive matrix-vector spaces. In *Proceedings of the 2012 Joint Conference on Empirical Methods in Natural Language Processing and Computational Natural Language Learning*, pages 1201–1211. Association for Computational Linguistics.

Richard Socher, Jeffrey Pennington, Eric H Huang, Andrew Y Ng, and Christopher D Manning. 2011. Semi-supervised recursive autoencoders for predicting sentiment distributions. In *Proceedings of the Conference on Empirical Methods in Natural Language Processing*, pages 151–161. Association for Computational Linguistics.

Richard Socher, Alex Perelygin, Jean Y Wu, Jason Chuang, Christopher D Manning, Andrew Y Ng, and Christopher Potts. 2013. Recursive deep models for semantic compositionality over a sentiment treebank. In *Proceedings of the conference on empirical methods in natural language processing (EMNLP)*, volume 1631, page 1642. Citeseer.

Maite Taboada, Julian Brooke, Milan Tofiloski, Kimberly Voll, and Manfred Stede. 2011. Lexicon-based methods for sentiment analysis. *Computational linguistics*, 37(2):267–307.

Kai Sheng Tai, Richard Socher, and Christopher D Manning. 2015. Improved semantic representations from tree-structured long short-term memory networks. *arXiv preprint arXiv:1503.00075*.

Chenhao Tan, Lillian Lee, Jie Tang, Long Jiang, Ming Zhou, and Ping Li. 2011. User-level sentiment analysis incorporating social networks. In *Proceedings of the 17th ACM SIGKDD international conference on Knowledge discovery and data mining*, pages 1397–1405. ACM.

Duyu Tang, Bing Qin, and Ting Liu. 2015a. Document modeling with gated recurrent neural network for sentiment classification. In *Proceedings of the 2015 Conference on Empirical Methods in Natural Language Processing*, pages 1422–1432.

Duyu Tang, Bing Qin, and Ting Liu. 2015b. Learning semantic representations of users and products for document level sentiment classification. In *Proc. ACL*.

Duyu Tang, Furu Wei, Nan Yang, Ming Zhou, Ting Liu, and Qin Bing. 2014. Learning sentiment specific word embedding for twitter sentiment classification. In *Proc. ACL*, pages 1555–1565. Association for Computational Linguistics.

Zichao Yang, Diyi Yang, Chris Dyer, Xiaodong He, Alex Smola, and Eduard Hovy. 2016. Hierarchical attention networks for document classification. In *Conference of the North American Chapter of the Association for Computational Linguistics: Human Language Technologies*, pages 1480–1489.

Matthew D Zeiler. 2012. Adadelta: an adaptive learning rate method. *arXiv preprint arXiv:1212.5701*.

An Ensemble Method with Sentiment Features and Clustering Support

Nguyen Huy Tien
Japan Advanced Institute of
Science and Technology (JAIST)
ntienhuy@jaist.ac.jp

Nguyen Minh Le
Japan Advanced Institute of
Science and Technology (JAIST)
nguyenml@jaist.ac.jp

Abstract

Deep learning models have recently been applied successfully in natural language processing, especially sentiment analysis. Each deep learning model has a particular advantage, but it is difficult to combine these advantages into one model, especially in the area of sentiment analysis. In our approach, Convolutional Neural Network (CNN) and Long Short Term Memory (LSTM) were utilized to learn sentiment-specific features in a freezing scheme. This scenario provides a novel and efficient way for integrating advantages of deep learning models. In addition, we also grouped documents into clusters by their similarity and applied the prediction score of Naive Bayes SVM (NB-SVM) method to boost the classification accuracy of each group. The experiments show that our method achieves the state-of-the-art performance on two well-known datasets: IMDB large movie reviews for document level and Pang & Lee movie reviews for sentence level.

1 Introduction

The emergence of web 2.0, which allows users to generate content, is causing the rapid increase in the amount of data. This platform, which enables millions of users to share information and comments, has a high demand for extracting knowledge from user-generated content. An important information to be analyzed from those comments is opinions/sentiments, which express subjective opinions of particular users. Sentiment analysis is a fundamental task and has attracted a huge amount of research in recent years (Pang and Lee, 2008; Liu, 2012). The task calls for identifying the sentiment polarity (positive, negative) of a comment or review.

Wang (2012) used a Support Vector Machine variant with Naive Bayes feature (NBSVM). Presenting a document or a sentence with Bag of bi-gram features, NBSVM consistently performs well across datasets of long and short reviews. Recently, the success of deep learning in natural language processing has led to many efficient methods for sentiment analysis such as Paragraph Vector (Le and Mikolov, 2014), CNN (Kalchbrenner et al., 2014; Kim, 2014; Zhang and Wallace, 2015), LSTM (Wang et al., 2015; Liu et al., 2015). In Paragraph Vector, Le and Mikolov employed the technique of Word embedding representation using neural networks (Bengio et al., 2003; Collobert and Weston, 2008; Mnih and Hinton, 2009; Turian et al., 2010; Mikolov et al., 2013) to represent a document or paragraph as a vector. This document modeling outperformed the Bag of Words model in sentiment analysis and information retrieval. Li (2015) has enhanced the architecture of Paragraph Vector by allowing the model to predict not only words but also n-gram features (DVngram). CNN is capable of capturing local relationships between neighbor words in a sentence but fails for long-distance dependencies. LSTM can handle CNN's limitation because it is able to memorize information for a long period of time. Our motivation is to build a combination approach taking the advantages of these methods.

In this paper, we separately designed CNN and LSTM models to encode sentiment information into feature vectors. To apply for sentiment classification, these sentiment-specific vectors and the semantic-specific DVngram vector were passed into the 3-layer neural network. In sentiment analysis, two sentences with a slight difference could provide opposite sentiments. Generative models, however, have a tendency to encode

Proceedings of the The 8th International Joint Conference on Natural Language Processing, pages 644–653,
Taipei, Taiwan, November 27 – December 1, 2017 ©2017 AFNLP

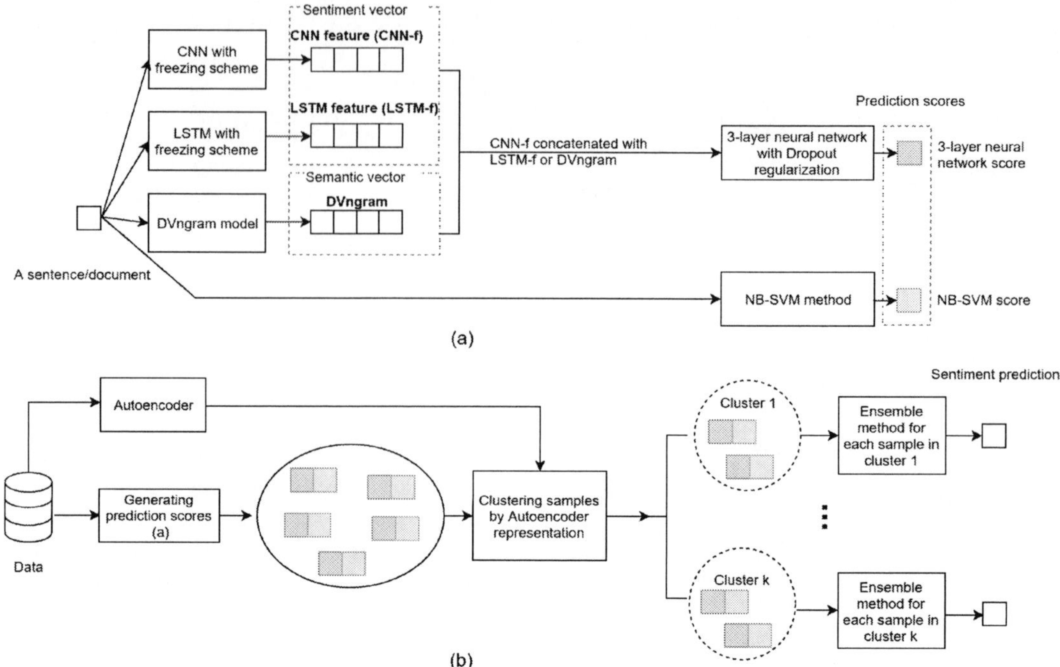

Figure 1: The proposed framework for sentiment analysis

similar sentences/documents into similar vectors. For that reason, we designed an autoencoder model to learn representation vectors for sentences/documents and used these vectors for clustering. The prediction score of NBSVM method is provided to enhance the sentiment prediction of each cluster. Figure 1 shows the architecture of our framework.

We compared our method with NBSVM, CNN, LSTM, Paragraph Vector, LinearEnsemble (Mesnil et al., 2014), DSCNN (Zhang et al., 2016) on three well-known datasets: IMDB large movie reviews (Maas et al., 2011) for document level, Pang & Lee (2005) movie reviews and Stanford Sentiment Treebank (Socher et al., 2013) for sentence level. The experimental results show that our method consistently performs well on both document and sentence level data. The main contributions of this work are as follows:

- We applied a freezing scheme to CNN and LSTM models for encoding sentiment information into vectors. These vectors provide a simple and efficient way to integrate the strong abilities of deep learning models.

- We proposed a scenario to divide data into groups of similar sentences/documents.

Then, each sentence/document in each group is represented by the prediction score of NB-SVM method and the prediction score of the proposed 3-layer neural network. We proposed an ensemble method to employ these scores.

2 Sentiment representation learning

In this section, we describe the freezing scheme to generate sentiment vectors from two models: (i) CNN, (ii) LSTM; and a method to employ these vectors. To feed into LSTM/CNN model, each word of a sentence/document is transformed into a word embedding vector using *Word2Vec*[1].

Le and Mikolov (2014) extended the word embedding learning model by incorporating paragraph information. Given a paragraph, Le's method captures and encodes semantics into a representation vector or a semantic feature.

This work inspired us to develop a document representation learning model to capture sentiment information. In our work, we proposed an approach to generating sentiment representation from CNN and LSTM models. Our idea is to train CNN and LSTM models under the sentiment classification task. In a deep learning network, we

---

[1]https://code.google.com/p/word2vec/

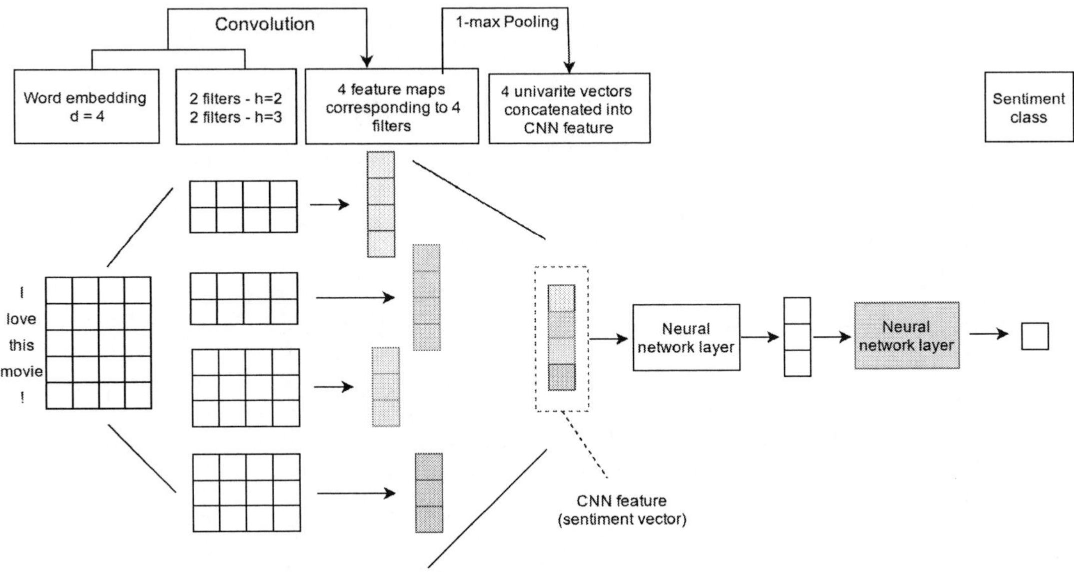

Figure 2: Illustration of our CNN framework to generate sentiment features. Given a sequence of d-dimension word embeddings ($d = 4$), the model applies 4 filters: 2 filters for region size $h = 2$ and 2 filters for region size $h = 3$ to generate 4 feature maps. During the training process, the parameters of the last neural network layer (blue one) are frozen (untrained)

could separate the model into two parts: (i) **Building target feature** - from input samples, the first part encodes target information into vectors, (ii) **Classifying layer** - the second part tries to learn a layer (or a boundary) for classifying these vectors into target labels. Sentiment vectors generated by a model, however, are much fitting to the classifying layer of this model. It is not efficient to combine two sentiment vectors generated from two models because each sentiment vector is fitting to its particular classifying layer. To address this problem, we proposed a freezing scheme. According to this scheme, the parameters of the classifying layer are initialized from the uniform distribution and in the training phase, these parameters are kept unchanged. This technique makes sentiment vectors not too fit to a particular classifying layer.

2.1 LSTM for sentiment feature engineering - LSTM feature

The LSTM architecture was introduced by Hochreiter (1997). By designing a memory cell preserving its state over a long period of time and non-linear gating units regulating information flow into and out of the cell, Hochreiter made LSTM able to capture efficiently long distance de-

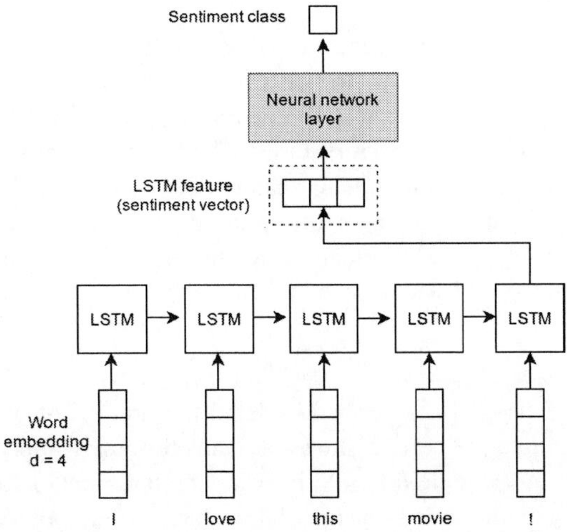

Figure 3: Illustration of our LSTM model to generate sentiment vectors. During the training process, the parameters of the neural network layer (blue one) are frozen (untrained)

pendencies of sequential data without suffering the exploding or vanishing gradient problem of Recurrent neural network (Goller and Kuchler, 1996).

Figure 3 explains how to employ the LSTM architecture for memorizing sentiment information over sequential data. The model contains two parts: (i) **Building sentiment feature** - the LSTM layer encodes sentiment information of input into a fixed-length vector; (ii) **Classifying layer** - this sentiment-specific representation vector will be classified by the last neural network (NN) layer (the blue layer in Figure 3). As applying the freezing scheme, this NN layer's parameters are unchanged during the training process.

2.2 CNN for sentiment feature engineering - CNN feature

We present a sentence of length s as a matrix $d \times s$, where each row is a d-dimension word embedding vector of each word. Given a sentence matrix $\mathbf{S}$, CNN performs convolution on this input via linear filters. A filter is denoted as a weight matrix W of length d and region size h. W will have $d \times h$ parameters to be estimated. For an input matrix $S \in \mathbb{R}^{d \times s}$, a feature map vector $O = [o_o, o_1, ..., o_{s-h}] \in \mathbb{R}^{s-h+1}$ of the convolution operator with a filter W is obtained by applying repeatedly W to sub-matrices of S:

$$o_i = W \cdot S_{i:i+h-1} \tag{1}$$

where $i = 0, 1, 2, ..., s - h$, $(\cdot)$ is dot product and $S_{i:j}$ is the sub-matrix of S from row i to j.

Each feature map O is fed to a pooling layer to generate potential features. The common strategy is 1-max pooling (Boureau et al., 2010). The idea of 1-max pooling is to capture the most important feature v corresponding to the particular feature map by selecting the highest value of that feature map:

$$v = \max_{0 \le i \le s-h} \{o_i\} \tag{2}$$

We have described in detail the process of one filter. Figure 2 shows an illustration of applying multiple filters with variant region sizes to obtain multiple 1-max pooling values. After pooling, these 1-max pooling values from feature maps are concatenated into a CNN feature carrying sentiment information. Intuitively, the CNN feature is a collection of maximum values from the feature maps. To make a connection to these values, we provide an NN layer to synthesize a high-level feature from the CNN feature. Finally, this high-level feature is passed to an NN layer with sigmoid activation to generate the probability distribution over sentiment labels.

In the training phase, similar to the strategy in our LSTM model, the last NN layer's parameters are kept untrained to make the sentiment vectors not too fit to a particular classifying layer.

2.3 Classifying with sentiment vectors

Figure 4 visualizes the results of encoding sentiments into vectors using our CNN model. As we can see in the development set, there are some unambiguous cases. Therefore, we add more information to CNN sentiment vectors by concatenating them with LSTM sentiment vectors or DVngram semantic vectors.

As CNN and LSTM sentiment vectors are, however, generated from models of sentiment classification, these vectors are easily separated in terms of sentimental categories by machine learning methods. In other words, a multi-layer NN sentiment classifier using both of these vectors as input reaches the state of perfect classification on the training set after a few epochs. In this case, the classifier's parameters are not efficiently optimized and the classifier's performance has no improvement on the testing set, compared with using LSTM or CNN for classification (or we call the model overfitting).

To address this problem, we employ a **3-layer NN** with Dropout regularization (Hinton et al., 2012) on the first and second layers. By randomly dropping out each hidden unit with a probability p on each presentation of each training case, Dropout prevents overfitting and provides a way to combine many variant NN architectures efficiently. By applying Dropout, our model has an ability to examine efficiently variant combination ways from feature vectors.

3 Ensemble with clustering support

As we discussed in Section 1, a slight difference between two sentences could lead to two opposite sentiments. However, similar sentences/documents have a tendency to be encoded into similar vectors by generative models. Therefore, it causes some difficulties in sentiment classification. To address this problem, we divided data into groups of similar sentences/documents and then provided an additional feature to boost the performance of classification in each group. For dividing data, we applied autoencoder models to encode word embedding representations of sentences/documents into fix-length vectors. These vectors then were used for clustering sentences/documents. For each sentence/document in

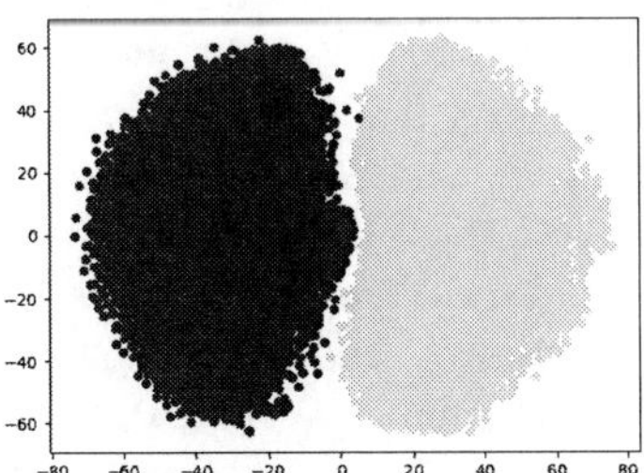

(a) Sentiment vectors in the train set

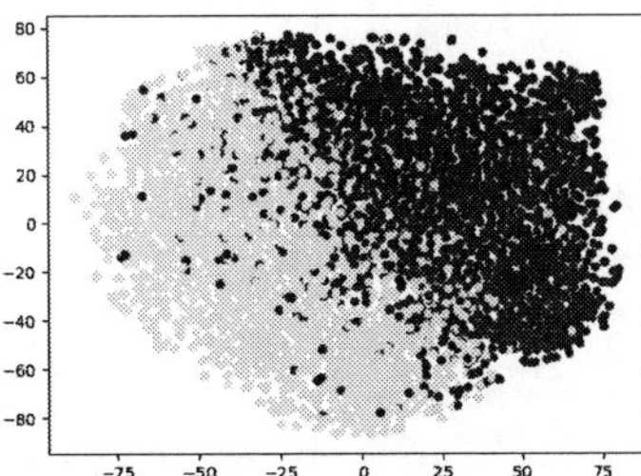

(b) Sentiment vectors in the development set

Figure 4: The t-SNE projection for IMDB dataset's sentiment vectors (positive and negative) generated from our CNN model.

each cluster, the prediction score of the method in section 2 are combined with the prediction score of NBSVM. The reason for choosing NBSVM is that NBSVM is an efficient method not based on neutral network architectures, and using Bag of Word model to represent sentences/documents, which is different from the word embedding representation. We consider NBSVM's score as an additional channel and expect it to support well for each group of similarity sentences/documents in terms of word embedding representation.

Given a sentence/document, we will have two prediction scores: one from the proposed method in section 2 and one from NBSVM. To employ these scores, we used a voting method. This scheme allows each classifier f_i to give a vote with a confident ratio r_i to the final probability score over classes distribution as follows:

$$p(c_i|x) = \frac{1}{N} \sum_{k=1}^{N} p_k(c_i|x) r_k \qquad (3)$$

where c_i is the ith sentiment class, N is the number of classifiers, $p_k(c_i|x)$ is the prediction score of the classifier k on the ith class for a sentence/document x.

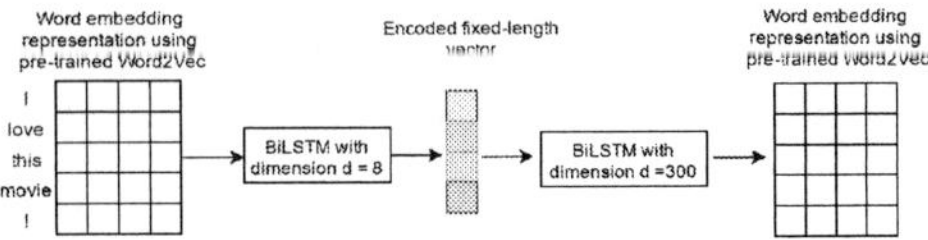

(a) BiLSTM model

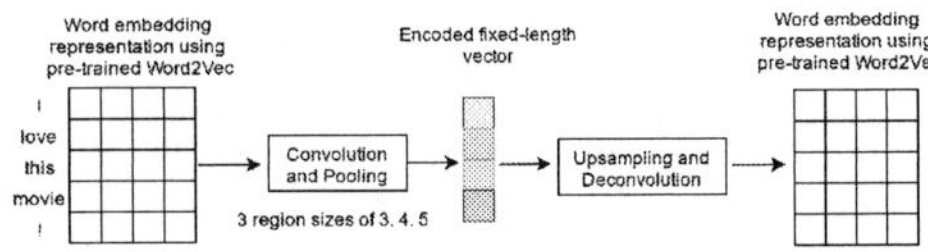

(b) CNN model. In MR-L dataset, each region size has 300 filters. In MR-S and SST dataset, each region size has 100 filters

Figure 5: Autoencoder models

The objective of this ensemble method is to select a suitable confident ratio for each classifier to optimize the performance of classification. In our approach, a 2-layer NN is employed to define a voting architecture. We consider a feedforward process in NN as a scheme of voting and the NN's weights as confident ratios. Adamax algorithm (Kingma and Ba, 2014) is applied to optimize the weights of the model.

Dataset	l	$train$	$test$	$|V|$
MR-L	300	25000	25000	169940
MR-S	20	10662	cv	18765
SST	19	9613	1821	16185

Table 1: Summary statistic of datasets. l denotes the average length of reviews, $train$ and $test$ are sizes of the training set and the test set respectively, cv is 10-fold cross validation, and $|V|$ is vocabulary size.

4 Dataset and Experiment setup

4.1 Dataset

We evaluated our models on three well-known datasets. Table 1 shows the statistic summary of datasets.

- For document level, IMDB large movie review dataset **MR-L** is used. Each review contains numerous sentences (Maas et al., 2011).

- For sentence level, Pang & Lee (2005) provided **MR-S** dataset having one sentence per movie review. In addition, we also did experiment on Stanford Sentiment Treebank **SST** (Socher et al., 2013) - an extension of MR-S with two labels (positive and negative). In SST, all sentences and phrases of the training set are used for training.

4.2 Experimental setup

To tune hyper-parameters of our models, we do a grid search on 30% of each dataset.

- For MR-L:
  - LSTM model has dimension $d = 32$.
  - CNN model: using 3 region sizes of $3, 4, 5$; the number of each region size is 300 and the dimension of penultimate NN layer is 100.
  - 3-layer NN model for classification with sentiment vectors: the first NN layer has the same dimension as the input feature, and the dropout ratio $p = 0.9$; the second NN layer has the dimension of 64 and the dropout ratio $p = 0.5$.
  - Autoencoder models: we examined two autoencoder models - CNN and BiLSTM. The details are in Figure 5.
  - Clustering: k-mean is applied. The number of clusters is $k = 2$.
  - Ensemble model: the first NN layer has the dimension of $3 \times$ the input's dimension or the number of classifiers.

- For MR-S and SST: the same configuration as MR-L, except the number of each region size is 100.

For word vectors, we obtained pre-trained word vectors *Word2Vec*. Its vectors have the dimension of 300. In our LSTM and CNN models, these pre-trained word vectors are optimized during the training process.

5 Results and Discussion

We compared our models against the other methods showed in table 2 on the binary sentiment classification task. In SST dataset, we could not reproduce the result 88.1% of CNN (Kim, 2014). According to the empirical results, our method of combining feature vectors *3-layer NN* outperforms the individual methods: LSTM, CNN, and DVngram. That proves the efficiency of the feature combination strategy. In addition, our ensemble method with clustering support outperforms the current state of the art method on MR-L and MR-S datasets. As we mentioned in Section 3, NBSVM uses a different way to present sentences/documents and a different approach to learning (a discriminative model), so it gives a significant support in our ensemble method. On document level, LSTM method produced a much lower performance than DVngram method. As a result, the feature vectors generated from LSTM model does not support as well as DVngram's vectors when combining with CNN feature vectors.

5.1 Freezing vs Unfreezing in the last NN layer of feature engineering phase

In the engineering phase, we freeze (untrain) the last NN layer's parameters to create efficient sentiment vectors. To evaluate the efficiency of this technique, we compared our vector's performance against the sentiment-specific vector from the unfreezing scheme. We passed these vectors to our 3-layer NN model to achieve the results (details in table 3). One interesting observation is that the performance of a feature vector in freezing mode is better than one in unfreezing mode for most of the cases. In addition, we combined a sentiment-specific vector with the semantic-specific vector - DVngram for evaluating the performance. In general, our freezing scheme provided a higher performance than the unfreezing scheme. The experimental results show that our freezing scheme works more efficiently on CNN model than LSTM model, especially in a case of combining a sentiment-specific vector and a semantic-specific vector.

5.2 Evaluation on combining features

In this section, we compared in performance our approach to combining features from variant models against **Merging scheme** which horizontally merges variant models (details in figure 6).

From the result showed in table 4, we found that our approach for feature vectors combination is applied more efficiently to CNN model than LSTM model. In the scheme of combining feature vectors, CNN feature vector provides a robust performance, while LSTM feature vector provides inconsistent results: better when combining with CNN feature vector, worse when combining with DVngram vector (compared with Merg-

Method	MR-S	MR-L	SST
LSTM	80.17	86.23	87.81
CNN (Kim, 2014)	81.31	91.18	86.33
DVngram (2015)	73.51	92.14	74.2
NBSVM (2012)	79.26	91.87	80.39
DV-Ensemble (2015)	-	93.05	-
DAN (2015)	80.3	89.4	86.3
SA-LSTM (2015)	80.7	92.8	-
DSCNN-Pretrain (2016)	82.2	90.7	**88.7**
Proposed methods			
3-layer NN (CNN-f+LSTM-f) (1)	81.59	91.16	88.41
3-layer NN (CNN-f+DVngram) (2)	81.11	92.98	86.66
Without clustering — Ensemble ((1) + NBSVM)	82.18	92.50	88.36
Without clustering — Ensemble ((2) + NBSVM)	81.1	93.25	87.31
CNN autoencoder — Ensemble ((1) + NBSVM)	82.2	92.55	88.46
CNN autoencoder — Ensemble ((2) + NBSVM)	81.74	93.29	86.87
BiLSTM autoencoder — Ensemble ((1) + NBSVM)	**82.22**	92.54	88.58
BiLSTM autoencoder — Ensemble ((2) + NBSVM)	81.8	**93.32**	87.09

Table 2: Accuracy results on the binary sentiment classification task. ***3-layer NN***$(F_1 + F_2)$ denotes using feature vector F_1 and F_2 as input; **CNN-f, LSTM-f** denote sentiment-specific feature vectors generated from the proposed CNN, LSTM respectively; ***Ensemble***$(p_1 + p_2)$ denotes applying the proposed Ensemble for the prediction scores of p_1 and p_2.

Feature	MR-S	MR-L	SST
CNNorg	80.61	91.22	86.05
CNN-f	**80.89**	**91.38**	**86.27**
LSTMorg	78.97	**85.5**	86.99
LSTM-f	**79.11**	85.14	**87.64**
CNNorg + LSTMorg	80.95	90.34	87.31
CNN-f + LSTM-f	**81.59**	**91.16**	**88.41**
CNNorg + DVngram	80.6	92.66	85.34
CNN-f + DVngram	**81.11**	**92.98**	**86.66**
LSTMorg + DVngram	79.38	**90.41**	87.2
LSTM-f + DVngram	**79.59**	88.04	**88.14**

Table 3: Accuracy results of 3-layer NN method on different features. **CNNorg, LSTMorg** denote sentiment-specific features engineering from the proposed CNN, LSTM without freezing the last NN layer respectively

Method	MR-S	MR-L	SST
3-layer NN (CNN-f + LSTM-f)	**81.59**	**91.16**	**88.41**
CNN-LSTM	81.07	91.07	86.49
3-layer NN (CNN-f + DVngram)	**81.11**	**92.98**	**86.66**
CNN-DVngram	80.79	92.12	85.39
3-layer NN (LSTM-f + DVngram)	79.59	88.04	**88.14**
LSTM-DVngram	**80.61**	**92.08**	86.49

Table 4: Accuracy results of features combining scheme and Merging scheme.

ing scheme). In most of the cases in Merging scheme, a composition model (i.e. CNN-LSTM) try to reproduce the result of its child models (e.g. CNN, LSTM) and does not provide a significant improvement.

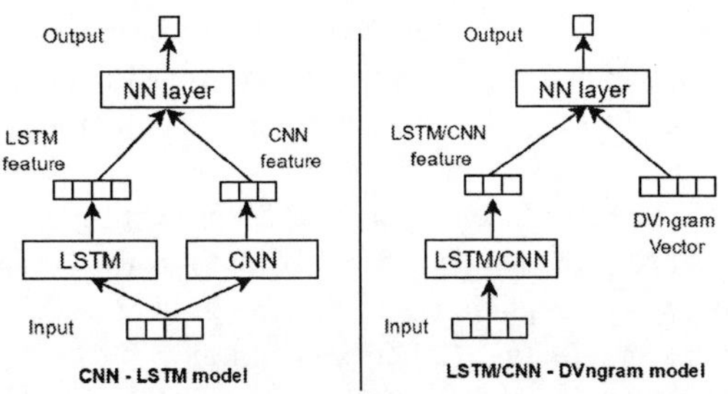

Figure 6: The architecture of merging models.

5.3 Error analysis

To get a better sense of the limitation of the proposed model, we manually inspect some cases of the wrong prediction, which are showed in table 5. These sentences are good examples of the proposed model's weakness.

The first source of false hits is the lack of syntactic information. The model tried to identify sentiment words in a sentence (i.g. not, bad, at all) but it failed to interpret the whole sentence.

The second reason of the wrong prediction comes from missing context information. A word (i.g. foul, freaky) carries a positive or negative sentiment depend on context or domains. We believe that the promising direction in future work will be to improve the model for capturing syntactic and context information.

id	Sentence	L
1	*Not a bad journey at all.*	1
2	*The best way to hope for any chance of enjoying this film is by lowering your expectations.*	0
3	*You've seen them a million times.*	0
4	*A whole lot foul, freaky and funny.*	1

Table 5: Examples of the wrong prediction. L denotes the true label with 0,1 for negative, positive sentiment labels respectively)

6 Related work

Sentiment analysis is a study of determining people's opinions, emotions toward to entities. Taboada (2011) assigned sentiment labels to text by extracting sentiment words. Liu (2012) formulated the sentiment analysis as a classification task and applied machine learning techniques for this problem. In this approach, dominant research concentrated on designing effective features such as word ngram (Wang and Manning, 2012), emoticon (Zhao et al., 2012), sentiment words (Kiritchenko et al., 2014). However, designing handcraft features requires an intensive effort.

Recently, the emergence of deep learning models has provided an efficient way to learn continuous representation vectors for sentiment classification. Bengio (2003) and Mikolov (2013) introduced learning techniques for semantic word representation. By using a neural network in the context of a word prediction task, the authors generated word embedding vectors carrying semantic meanings. Embedding vectors of words which share similar meanings are close to each other. Semantic information maybe provides opposite opinions in different contexts. Therefore, some research (Socher et al., 2011; Tang et al., 2014) worked on learning sentiment-specific word representation by employing sentiment text. For sentence and document level, composition approach attracted many studies. Yessenalina and Cardie (2011) modeled each word as a matrix and used iterated matrix multiplication to present a phrase. Deep recursive neural networks (DRNN) over tree structures were employed to learn sentence representation for sentiment classification such as DRNN with binary parse trees (Irsoy and Cardie, 2014), Recursive tensor neural network with sentiment treebank (Socher et al., 2013). CNN has recently been applied efficiently for semantic composition (Kim, 2014; Zhang and Wallace, 2015). This technique uses convolutional filters to capture local dependencies in term of context windows and applies a pooling layer to extract global features. Le and Mikolov (2014) applied paragraph information into the word embedding technique to learn semantic representation. Tang et al. (2015) used CNN or LSTM to learn sentence representation and encoded these semantic vectors in document representation by Gated recurrent neural network. Zhang (2016) proposed Dependency Sensitive CNN to build hierarchically textual representations by processing pretrained word embeddings. Wang (2016) used a regional CNN-LSTM to predict the valence arousal ratings of texts.

In our work, we designed a freezing approach for learning efficiently sentiment document representation from two variant deep-learning models: CNN and LSTM. Afterward, these sentiment-specific vectors and the semantic DVngram vector were employed for sentiment classification. This strategy captures the advantages of variant models by using vectors, which each model generated. We also used NBSVM in clustering mode to boost the performance of classification.

7 Conclusion

In this work, we introduced a novel approach to synthesize feature vectors for sentiment analysis from CNN, LSTM. These vectors provide a simple and efficient way to integrate the strong abilities of these models. For sentiment classification with CNN, LSTM vectors, we proposed a 3-layer neural network which efficiently takes advantages of these vectors. In addition, we proposed a strategy to cluster documents/sentences by their similarity. In each cluster, we applied an ensemble method of the 3-layer neural network and NB-SVM. It achieves the state of the art results in the datasets: MR-S and MR-L. In the current work, we just focused on individual models. Research on applying combination models for feature engineering maybe provides interesting results.

References

Yoshua Bengio, Réjean Ducharme, Pascal Vincent, and Christian Jauvin. 2003. A neural probabilistic language model. *journal of machine learning research*, 3(Feb):1137–1155.

Y-Lan Boureau, Jean Ponce, and Yann LeCun. 2010. A theoretical analysis of feature pooling in visual recognition. In *Proceedings of the 27th international conference on machine learning (ICML-10)*, pages 111–118.

Ronan Collobert and Jason Weston. 2008. A unified architecture for natural language processing: Deep neural networks with multitask learning. In *Proceedings of the 25th international conference on Machine learning*, pages 160–167. ACM.

Andrew M Dai and Quoc V Le. 2015. Semi-supervised sequence learning. In *Advances in Neural Information Processing Systems*, pages 3079–3087.

Christoph Goller and Andreas Kuchler. 1996. Learning task-dependent distributed representations by back-propagation through structure. In *Neural Networks, 1996., IEEE International Conference on*, volume 1, pages 347–352. IEEE.

Geoffrey E Hinton, Nitish Srivastava, Alex Krizhevsky, Ilya Sutskever, and Ruslan R Salakhutdinov. 2012. Improving neural networks by preventing co-adaptation of feature detectors. *arXiv preprint arXiv:1207.0580*.

Sepp Hochreiter and Jürgen Schmidhuber. 1997. Long short-term memory. *Neural computation*, 9(8):1735–1780.

Ozan Irsoy and Claire Cardie. 2014. Deep recursive neural networks for compositionality in language. In *Advances in Neural Information Processing Systems*, pages 2096–2104.

Mohit Iyyer, Varun Manjunatha, Jordan L Boyd-Graber, and Hal Daumé III. 2015. Deep unordered composition rivals syntactic methods for text classification. In *ACL (1)*, pages 1681–1691.

Nal Kalchbrenner, Edward Grefenstette, and Phil Blunsom. 2014. A convolutional neural network for modelling sentences. *arXiv preprint arXiv:1404.2188*.

Yoon Kim. 2014. Convolutional neural networks for sentence classification. *arXiv preprint arXiv:1408.5882*.

Diederik Kingma and Jimmy Ba. 2014. Adam: A method for stochastic optimization. *arXiv preprint arXiv:1412.6980*.

Svetlana Kiritchenko, Xiaodan Zhu, and Saif M Mohammad. 2014. Sentiment analysis of short informal texts. *Journal of Artificial Intelligence Research*, 50:723–762.

Quoc V Le and Tomas Mikolov. 2014. Distributed representations of sentences and documents. In *ICML*, volume 14, pages 1188–1196.

Bofang Li, Tao Liu, Xiaoyong Du, Deyuan Zhang, and Zhe Zhao. 2015. Learning document embeddings by predicting n-grams for sentiment classification of long movie reviews. *arXiv preprint arXiv:1512.08183*.

Bing Liu. 2012. Sentiment analysis and opinion mining. *Synthesis lectures on human language technologies*, 5(1):1–167.

Pengfei Liu, Shafiq Joty, and Helen Meng. 2015. Fine-grained opinion mining with recurrent neural networks and word embeddings. In *Conference on Empirical Methods in Natural Language Processing (EMNLP 2015)*.

Andrew L. Maas, Raymond E. Daly, Peter T. Pham, Dan Huang, Andrew Y. Ng, and Christopher Potts. 2011. Learning word vectors for sentiment analysis. In *Proceedings of the 49th Annual Meeting of the Association for Computational Linguistics: Human Language Technologies*, pages 142–150, Portland, Oregon, USA. Association for Computational Linguistics.

Grégoire Mesnil, Tomas Mikolov, Marc'Aurelio Ranzato, and Yoshua Bengio. 2014. Ensemble of generative and discriminative techniques for sentiment analysis of movie reviews. *arXiv preprint arXiv:1412.5335*.

Tomas Mikolov, Kai Chen, Greg Corrado, and Jeffrey Dean. 2013. Efficient estimation of word representations in vector space. *arXiv preprint arXiv:1301.3781*.

Andriy Mnih and Geoffrey E Hinton. 2009. A scalable hierarchical distributed language model. In *Advances in neural information processing systems*, pages 1081–1088.

Bo Pang and Lillian Lee. 2005. Seeing stars: Exploiting class relationships for sentiment categorization with respect to rating scales. In *Proceedings of the ACL*.

Bo Pang and Lillian Lee. 2008. Opinion mining and sentiment analysis. *Foundations and trends in information retrieval*, 2(1-2):1–135.

Richard Socher, Jeffrey Pennington, Eric H Huang, Andrew Y Ng, and Christopher D Manning. 2011. Semi-supervised recursive autoencoders for predicting sentiment distributions. In *Proceedings of the Conference on Empirical Methods in Natural Language Processing*, pages 151–161. Association for Computational Linguistics.

Richard Socher, Alex Perelygin, Jean Y Wu, Jason Chuang, Christopher D Manning, Andrew Y Ng, and Christopher Potts. 2013. Recursive deep models for semantic compositionality over a sentiment tree-bank. In *Proceedings of the conference on empirical methods in natural language processing (EMNLP)*, volume 1631, page 1642. Citeseer.

Maite Taboada, Julian Brooke, Milan Tofiloski, Kimberly Voll, and Manfred Stede. 2011. Lexicon-based methods for sentiment analysis. *Computational linguistics*, 37(2):267–307.

Duyu Tang, Bing Qin, and Ting Liu. 2015. Document modeling with gated recurrent neural network for sentiment classification. In *Proceedings of the 2015 Conference on Empirical Methods in Natural Language Processing*, pages 1422–1432.

Duyu Tang, Furu Wei, Nan Yang, Ming Zhou, Ting Liu, and Bing Qin. 2014. Learning sentiment-specific word embedding for twitter sentiment classification. In *ACL (1)*, pages 1555–1565.

Joseph Turian, Lev Ratinov, and Yoshua Bengio. 2010. Word representations: a simple and general method for semi-supervised learning. In *Proceedings of the 48th annual meeting of the association for computational linguistics*, pages 384–394. Association for Computational Linguistics.

Jin Wang, Liang-Chih Yu, K Robert Lai, and Xuejie Zhang. 2016. Dimensional sentiment analysis using a regional cnn-lstm model. In *The 54th Annual Meeting of the Association for Computational Linguistics*, volume 225.

Sida Wang and Christopher D Manning. 2012. Baselines and bigrams: Simple, good sentiment and topic classification. In *Proceedings of the 50th Annual Meeting of the Association for Computational Linguistics: Short Papers-Volume 2*, pages 90–94. Association for Computational Linguistics.

Xin Wang, Yuanchao Liu, Chengjie Sun, Baoxun Wang, and Xiaolong Wang. 2015. Predicting polarities of tweets by composing word embeddings with long short-term memory. In *Proceedings of the 53rd Annual Meeting of the Association for Computational Linguistics and the 7th International Joint Conference on Natural Language Processing*, volume 1, pages 1343–1353.

Ainur Yessenalina and Claire Cardie. 2011. Compositional matrix-space models for sentiment analysis. In *Proceedings of the Conference on Empirical Methods in Natural Language Processing*, pages 172–182. Association for Computational Linguistics.

Rui Zhang, Honglak Lee, and Dragomir Radev. 2016. Dependency sensitive convolutional neural networks for modeling sentences and documents. *arXiv preprint arXiv:1611.02361*.

Ye Zhang and Byron Wallace. 2015. A sensitivity analysis of (and practitioners' guide to) convolutional neural networks for sentence classification. *arXiv preprint arXiv:1510.03820*.

Jichang Zhao, Li Dong, Junjie Wu, and Ke Xu. 2012. Moodlens: an emoticon-based sentiment analysis system for chinese tweets. In *Proceedings of the 18th ACM SIGKDD international conference on Knowledge discovery and data mining*, pages 1528–1531. ACM.

Leveraging Auxiliary Tasks for Document-Level Cross-Domain Sentiment Classification

Jianfei Yu
School of Information Systems
Singapore Management University
jfyu.2014@phdis.smu.edu.sg

Jing Jiang
School of Information Systems
Singapore Management University
jingjiang@smu.edu.sg

Abstract

In this paper, we study domain adaptation with a state-of-the-art hierarchical neural network for document-level sentiment classification. We first design a new auxiliary task based on sentiment scores of domain-independent words. We then propose two neural network architectures to respectively induce document embeddings and sentence embeddings that work well for different domains. When these document and sentence embeddings are used for sentiment classification, we find that with both pseudo and external sentiment lexicons, our proposed methods can perform similarly to or better than several highly competitive domain adaptation methods on a benchmark dataset of product reviews.

1 Introduction

Sentiment classification is a fundamental task in opinion mining (Pang et al., 2002; Hu and Liu, 2004; Choi and Cardie, 2008; Nakagawa et al., 2010). Recently, with the advances of deep learning techniques for many NLP applications, various kinds of neural network (NN)-based models have been proposed for this task (Socher et al., 2013; Lei et al., 2015; Yang et al., 2016).

As with any supervised learning method, the NN-based models also suffer from the *domain adaptation* problem, where training data and test data come from different domains. The reason for this is that sentiments are often expressed with domain-specific words and expressions. For example, in the **Book** domain, expressions like *an insider's look* and *a must read* are usually positive, but they may not be useful for the **Kitchen** domain. Similarly, words such as *sharp* and *clean*, which are positive in the **Kitchen** domain, can rarely be seen in the **Book** domain. Due to the high cost of obtaining labeled data, it would be very attractive if we can adapt a model trained on a *source domain* to a *target domain*.

A number of different models have been proposed for cross-domain sentiment classification, and the core idea of them is to learn a shared latent representation that is general across domains. Most of these studies can be categorized into two lines. The first line of work focuses on carefully designing some auxiliary prediction tasks to induce a robust cross-domain representation (Blitzer et al., 2007; Pan et al., 2010; Bollegala et al., 2015, 2016). With the trend of deep learning, another line of work centers on employing denoising autoencoders to learn hidden representations across domains in a purely unsupervised learning manner (Glorot et al., 2011; Chen et al., 2012; Zhou et al., 2016).

However, most of the two lines of research are based on traditional discrete feature representations, and the induced shared representations are not necessarily specific to sentiment classification. In our recent work, we designed two simple auxiliary tasks, which are closely related to the actual end task, for sentence-level cross-domain sentiment classification (Yu and Jiang, 2016). Furthermore, we proposed to jointly learn domain-independent sentence embeddings based on the two auxiliary tasks together with the classifier for the end task in a unified NN framework. Although our joint learning model has been shown to outperform previous domain adaptation methods in sentence-level sentiment classification, it is unclear how to extend this to document-level sentiment classification since the two auxiliary tasks will become much less useful for documents.

In this paper, we aim to propose a domain adaptation method for document-level sentiment clas-

Proceedings of the The 8th International Joint Conference on Natural Language Processing, pages 654–663,
Taipei, Taiwan, November 27 – December 1, 2017 ©2017 AFNLP

sification based on our earlier joint model (Yu and Jiang, 2016). Specifically, instead of predicting the occurrence of pivot words as in previous work (Blitzer et al., 2007; Yu and Jiang, 2016), we introduce a new auxiliary task based on sentiment scores of pivot words. Moreover, we propose two different architectures to incorporate the auxiliary task into a state-of-the-art hierarchical NN model for document-level sentiment classification, in which we respectively induce a shared document embedding for each document in both domains and a shared sentence embedding for each sentence in all documents. Evaluation on a widely used dataset about product reviews from four different domains shows that our methods can significantly outperform a number of baselines and are able to achieve comparable or even better results compared with a strong baseline proposed by us.

2   Related Work

Domain Adaptation: Domain adaptation has been extensively studied in recent years (Pan and Yang, 2010). In NLP, it has also attracted much attention, where most domain adaptation methods can be categorized into two groups: instance re-weighting (Jiang and Zhai, 2007; Xia et al., 2014) and shared representation learning (Blitzer et al., 2006; Daumé III, 2007; Titov, 2011). In this work, we follow the latter line of work, and focus on inducing a domain-independent feature space based on a recently proposed NN architecture.

Neural Networks for Sentiment Classification: With the recent trend of deep learning, a large amount of NN models, including Convolutional Neural Network (Kim, 2014), Recursive Neural Network (Irsoy and Cardie, 2014) and Recurrent Neural Network (Tai et al., 2015), have been proposed for sentiment classification. Although these models have achieved highly competitive results on different benchmarks, most of them are targeted at sentence-level sentiment classification. Considering that the relations between sentences are important for predicting the sentiment polarity of any document, Tang et al. (2015) proposed a hieararchical NN model to encode the relations between sentences for document-level sentiment classification. Since it has been shown to significantly outperform standard non-hierarchical models on several benchmarks, we try to apply this model to domain adaptation settings in this work.

Cross-Domain Sentiment Classification: For sentiment classification, most existing domain adaptation methods focus on inducing shared representations across domains. One line of work tries to leverage the co-occurrences of domain-specific and domain-independent features to learn a general low-dimensional cross-domain representation (Blitzer et al., 2007; Pan et al., 2010; He et al., 2011; Bollegala et al., 2015; Bhatt et al., 2015). Another line of work is based on a purely unsupervised learning method, denoising auto-encoders, where the hidden layers in multi-layer neural networks are believed to be robust against domain shift (Glorot et al., 2011; Chen et al., 2012; Zhou et al., 2016). However, all these methods are still based on traditional discrete representations, and the shared representations are learned separately from the final classifier and therefore not directly related to sentiment classification. More recently, we proposed a unified neural model to jointly learn the shared sentence embeddings and the final classifier together for sentence-level sentiment domain adaptation (Yu and Jiang, 2016). But the auxiliary task in this earlier work is only designed for sentences; it will be less useful for documents. Moreover, the neural model is based on CNNs, which fail to achieve satisfactory results in document-level sentiment classification. Hence in this work, we focus on proposing a new auxiliary task for documents, followed by incorporating it into a state-of-the-art hierarchical NN model for document-level sentiment domain adaptation.

3   Methodology

In this section we present our domain adaptation method for document-level sentiment classification.

3.1   Problem Definition and Notation

Our task is sentiment classification at the document level. We assume that each input d is a document containing n sentences, and the ith sentence contains a sequence of m_i words. Let us use $w_{i,j} \in \mathcal{V}$ to denote the jth word of the ith sentence, where $\mathcal{V}$ is the vocabulary. Let $y \in \{+, -\}$ denote the sentiment label of input d, where $+$ and $-$ denote the positive sentiment and the negative sentiment, respectively.

We consider a cross-domain setting, in which we assume that we have a set of labeled training documents from a source domain, denoted by $\mathcal{D}^s$. In addition, we have a set of unlabeled documents from a target domain, denoted by $\mathcal{D}^{t,u}$. Our goal is to train a good document-level sentiment classifier using $\mathcal{D}^s$ and $\mathcal{D}^{t,u}$ so that the classifier can generally work well in the target domain. To evaluate the trained classifier, we test its performance on a set of labeled documents from the target domain, denoted by $\mathcal{D}^{t,l}$.

3.2 Method Overview

The core of our domain adaptation method is to use a domain-independent auxiliary task to help induce a cross-domain hidden representation that is useful for both source and target domains. The idea of learning cross-domain hidden representations by leveraging auxiliary tasks for domain adaptation is not new (Blitzer et al., 2006, 2007; Yu and Jiang, 2016; Ding et al., 2017). These previous studies essentially follow the multi-task learning framework (Ando and Zhang, 2005). The rationale behind them is that if there are some auxiliary tasks related to the actual prediction task and the labels of the auxiliary tasks can be easily obtained for both source and target domains, the induced low-dimensional feature space is a good representation for domain adaptation.

Our work follows this line of research and aims to extend our recently proposed domain adaptation method for sentence-level sentiment classification (Yu and Jiang, 2016). Our method is based on an existing hierarchical neural network (HNN) model for document-level sentiment classification proposed by Tang et al. (2015), which encodes each sentence in the input document into a sentence embedding vector through a CNN, followed by combining all sentence embeddings into a document embedding vector with a gated RNN. Different from Tang et al. (2015), however, we use the sentence embeddings or document embeddings for predicting not only the actual sentiment labels but also the labels of a carefully designed auxiliary task. Since the auxiliary task is domain-independent, we expect the sentence embeddings and document embeddings learned by our method to work well in both domains.

3.3 A Hierarchical Neural Network for Document-level Sentiment Classification

We first describe our baseline method for document-level sentiment classification. This is a HNN model proposed by Tang et al. (2015) that has been shown to significantly outperform simpler, non-hierarchical models. We re-implement this model with some minor modifications.

Recall that an input document d is represented by a sequence of sentences, each containing a sequence of words, and $w_{i,j} \in \mathcal{V}$ is the jth word of the ith sentence in d. We use $\mathbf{x}_{i,j} \in \mathbb{R}^l$ to denote an l-dimensional dense embedding vector for word $w_{i,j}$, which is retrieved from a lookup table $\mathbf{X} \in \mathbb{R}^{l \times |\mathcal{V}|}$ for all words. We first apply a one-layer CNN (Kim, 2014) to obtain an embedding vector $\mathbf{z}_i \in \mathbb{R}^p$ for the ith sentence: $\mathbf{z}_i = CNN_{\Theta_1}(\mathbf{x}_i)$, where Θ_1 denotes all the parameters in this CNN.

After obtaining the sentence embeddings for all the n sentences in d, we then apply an LSTM to sequentially combine all sentences together: $\mathbf{h}_i = LSTM_{\Theta_2}(\mathbf{h}_{i-1}, \mathbf{z}_i)$, where $\mathbf{h}_i \in \mathbb{R}^q$ is the ith hidden state, and Θ_2 denotes all the parameters in the LSTM[1]. Note that Tang et al. (2015) used bidirectional gated RNN to chain the sentences into a document embedding, but we did not observe any significant gain over LSTM based on our preliminary experiments.

Finally, a softmax classifier is learned to map the document representation $\mathbf{h}_n$ to a label y:

$$p(y \mid \mathbf{h}_n) = \text{softmax}(\mathbf{W}\mathbf{h}_n + \mathbf{b}),$$

where $\mathbf{W} \in \mathbb{R}^{2 \times q}$ is a weight matrix and $\mathbf{b} \in \mathbb{R}^2$ is a bias vector.

In the following sections, we will present two NN architectures built on top of the baseline method that leverages an auxiliary task for domain adaptation of document-level sentiment classification. The first architecture uses a document-level auxiliary task to help induce a document-level hidden representation, while the second architecture uses a sentence-level auxiliary task to help induce a sentence-level hidden representation.

3.4 Document-level Shared Representation Learning for Domain Adaptation

Document-level Auxiliary Task

We first introduce an auxiliary task that is closely related to the original task of document-level sentiment classification. Our auxiliary task is inspired by our recent work for sentence-level cross-domain sentiment classification (Yu and Jiang, 2016). In this recently proposed method, we used two auxiliary tasks to induce shared sentence embeddings across domains. Considering

---

[1] To simplify the discussion, we will not give the details of CNN and LSTM here. Interested readers can refer to Kim (2014) and Hochreiter and Schmidhuber (1997).

that an input sentence containing a positive (or negative) domain-independent sentiment word is more likely to express an overall positive (or negative) sentiment, the two auxiliary tasks are about whether an input sentence contains at least one positive or one negative domain-independent sentiment word, respectively.

Although the two auxiliary tasks have been shown to benefit sentence-level cross-domain sentiment classification, they may not work well in document-level sentiment classification. The reason is the following. In sentence-level sentiment classification, since sentences are short, a sentence is more likely about only one aspect of the topic being discussed, and it tends to express a consistent sentiment polarity towards that aspect. However, in document-level sentiment classification, a document may contain mixed opinions towards different aspects of the topic, and the sentiment polarities towards different aspects may differ. Moreover, at document level, there may also be comparison and contrast among different topics, and the sentiment polarities towards them could be different. In summary, it is highly possible for a document to contain both positive and negative domain-independent sentiment words. In this case, the two auxiliary tasks would not be of much use because most documents would have the same labels for both these two tasks[2].

To address this limitation, we propose an alternative auxiliary task based on sentiment scores of the domain-independent sentiment words. The intuition is as follows. Assume that we have an external sentiment lexicon, where each word is assigned a general sentiment score. For an input document, if it contains more domain-independent words with high positive sentiment scores, the document is more likely to express an overall positive sentiment, regardless of the domain the document is from. More importantly, the remainder of the document without domain-independent words may also contain domain-specific positive words or expressions.

Take the following review as an example.

> One of the *best*! You will go **wrong** if you read this as an intro to deep learning. *Truly* an insider's look. A must read for everyone who *loves* neural networks.

We can see that the document contains three words with high positive sentiment scores (shown in italic), and one word with a high negative sentiment score (shown in bold). But overall, its sentiment polarity is positive, which correlates with the sum of all the domain-independent words' sentiment scores. Then, if we hide all the domain-independent sentiment words and use the remaining domain-specific words to predict the overall sentiment score of the domain-independent sentiment words, it should be helpful for identifying some important domain-specific sentiment expressions such as *an insiders' look* and *a must read* in the example above.

Hence, we propose a new auxiliary task by predicting whether the sum of all the domain-independent sentiment words' sentiment scores is larger than, equal to or less than 0. It is worth noting that (1) given any sentiment lexicon, we can automatically derive the label of the auxiliary task[3], and (2) the auxiliary task is closely related to the main binary sentiment classification task.

Formally, let us assume that we have a sentiment lexicon, which can be either directly taken from an external resource or derived from the labeled source domain data. Details of how the sentiment lexicon is obtained will be given in Section 3.7.1. Following SCL (Blitzer et al., 2007), we choose the words which frequently occur in both domains and have a high (positive or negative) sentiment score as the domain-independent sentiment words, and refer to them as pivot words. For each input document d, we use a special token *UNK* to substitute these pivot words, which follows the practice in our earlier work (Yu and Jiang, 2016). To be consistent with the notation before, let us use d' to denote the new document with *UNK* tokens and $w'_{i,j}$ the jth token in the ith sentence in d'. Let $\mathbf{x}'_{i,j} \in \mathbb{R}^l$ denote the embedding vector of $w'_{i,j}$. $\mathbf{x}'_{i,j}$ is the same as $\mathbf{x}_{i,j}$ when $w'_{i,j}$ is not *UNK*. When $w'_{i,j}$ is *UNK*, $\mathbf{x}'_{i,j}$ is set to be a special embedding vector for *UNK*. We then introduce an auxiliary label y' for d', which indicates whether the sum of the sentiment scores of the pivot words in the original document d is larger than, equal to or less than 0. We further use $\mathcal{D}^{\text{a,d}}$ to denote documents with the document-level auxiliary labels derived from both $\mathcal{D}^{\text{s}}$ and $\mathcal{D}^{\text{t,u}}$.

---

[2]Based on our observation on a benchmark dataset collected by Blitzer et al. (2007), for almost all the 12 source/target pairs, over 90% of the reviews contained both positive and negative domain-independent sentiment words.

[3]For any sentiment lexicon, we can rescale its original sentiment scores to [-K, K], where K can be any positive integer, and -K and K respectively denote the most negative and the most positive sentiments. In this paper, we set K to 2.

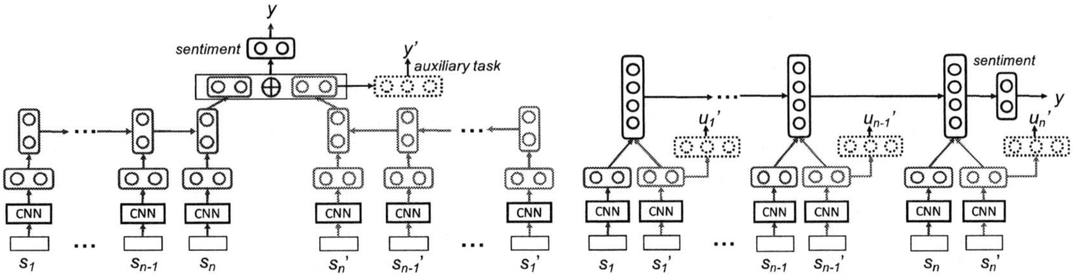

(a) Document-level Shared Representation   (b) Sentence-level Shared Representation

Figure 1: Overview of our proposed methods.

Document-level Shared Representation (DSR)

Now that we have defined the auxiliary task, we can present the NN architecture. Figure 1(a) gives the outline of this method, which essentially tries to directly learn an auxiliary hidden layer for each input document. For the ith sentence in d', we first use a CNN to obtain its auxiliary embedding vector $\mathbf{z}'_i = CNN_{\Theta'_1}(\mathbf{x}'_i)$. These sentence embeddings are further combined together with an LSTM parameterized by Θ'_2, and the final hidden state $\mathbf{h}'_n$ is fed to predict the auxiliary label y':

$$p(y' \mid \mathbf{h}'_n) = \text{softmax}(\mathbf{W}'\mathbf{h}'_n + \mathbf{b}').$$

Besides, we also apply another CNN and LSTM to obtain the standard document representation $\mathbf{h}_n$, and concatenate it with the auxiliary hidden vector $\mathbf{h}'_n$ to predict the sentiment label y:

$$p(y \mid \mathbf{h}_n, \mathbf{h}'_n) = \text{softmax}\Big(\mathbf{W}(\mathbf{h}_n \oplus \mathbf{h}'_n) + \mathbf{b}\Big).$$

3.5 Sentence-level Shared Representation Learning for Domain Adaptation

Unlike the first architecture, our second proposal focuses on learning an auxiliary hidden layer for each sentence in a given document. As illustrated in Figure 1(b), instead of using an overall auxiliary label for the whole document, we will have an auxiliary label for each sentence in the document.

Sentence-level Auxiliary Task

Although the auxiliary task in Section 3.4 is designed for documents, it is also suitable for sentences since if a sentence contains more domain-independent words with high positive sentiment scores, the rest of the sentence excluding these words may still express a positive sentiment.

To facilitate the discussion, let us use s_i to denote the ith sentence in the original document d

and s'_i the ith sentence in the modified document d'. We then introduce an auxiliary label u'_i for s'_i, which indicates whether the sum of the sentiment scores of the pivot words in s_i is larger than, equal to or less than 0. We further use $\mathbf{u}' \in \mathbb{R}^n$ to denote the auxiliary labels for all the n sentences in d'. Let $\mathcal{D}^{\text{a,s}}$ denote documents with the sentence-level auxiliary labels derived from both $\mathcal{D}^{\text{s}}$ and $\mathcal{D}^{\text{t,u}}$.

Sentence-level Shared Representation (SSR)

Based on the sentence-level auxiliary task, we use two CNNs to obtain sentence embeddings $\mathbf{z}_i$ and $\mathbf{z}'_i$, respectively for s_i and s'_i. Next, the auxiliary hidden layer $\mathbf{z}'_i$ will be used for predicting the auxiliary label u'_i:

$$p(u'_i \mid \mathbf{z}'_i) = \text{softmax}(\mathbf{W}'\mathbf{z}'_i + \mathbf{b}').$$

Besides, we also concatenate $\mathbf{z}_i$ and $\mathbf{z}'_i$ together as a combined sentence embedding for the i-th sentence. Then, all the n combined sentence embeddings are further combined together via an LSTM:

$$\mathbf{h}_i = LSTM_{\Theta_2}\Big(\mathbf{h}_{i-1}, (\mathbf{z}_i \oplus \mathbf{z}'_i)\Big).$$

Finally, we feed the last hidden representation $\mathbf{h}_n$ to predict the label of our main task:

$$p(y \mid \mathbf{h}_n) = \text{softmax}(\mathbf{W}\mathbf{h}_n + \mathbf{b}).$$

3.6 Parameter Learning

Since our two NN architectures consist of the main task and the auxiliary task, we jointly optimize them in a single loss function. For space limitation, here we only show the objective function for the first model, and the objective function for the latter one can be derived similarly. Using cross-entropy loss, we can learn Θ_1, Θ_2, Θ'_1, Θ'_2, $\mathbf{W}$, $\mathbf{b}$,

658

$\mathbf{W}'$ and $\mathbf{b}'$ by minimizing the following function:

$$J(\Theta_1, \Theta_2, \Theta'_1, \Theta'_2, \mathbf{W}, \mathbf{b}, \mathbf{W}', \mathbf{b}')$$
$$= -\Big(\sum_{(d,y)\in\mathcal{D}^s} \log p(y \mid d)$$
$$+ \sum_{(d',y')\in\mathcal{D}^{a,d}} \log p(y' \mid d') \Big).$$

3.7 Implementation Details

3.7.1 Sentiment Lexicons

We use two kinds of sentiment lexicons, which we refer to as WN and MI.

WN is extracted from a well-known sentiment lexicon called SentiWordNet (Baccianella et al., 2010). Since the original sentiment scores in SentiWordNet are probabilities for each word being positive or negative, we rescale them to $[-2, 2]$. Also, for the same words with different part-of-speech tags, we only keep the sentiment score with the highest absolute value.

To reduce the reliance on external resources, we also experiment with another method based on mutual information (MI) on the source labeled data $\mathcal{D}^s$ to automatically derive a pseudo sentiment lexicon. Specifically, we first extract only adjectives, adverbs and verbs from the documents in $\mathcal{D}^s$, and measure each remaining word's MI with the positive and the negative classes:

$$r(w_i, y) = \log \frac{\tilde{p}(w_i, y)}{\tilde{p}(w_i)\tilde{p}(y)},$$

where w_i denotes the ith word in $\mathcal{V}$, $y \in \{+, -\}$ is a sentiment label, and $\tilde{p}(w_i, y)$ is the empirical probability of observing w_i and y together. Then, we only keep those words with positive MI, i.e., $r(w_i, y) > 0$, and obtain two lists $\mathcal{R}_+$ and $\mathcal{R}_-$. Moreover, for each word $w \in \mathcal{R}_+$, we use its MI score as its sentiment score, while for each word $w \in \mathcal{R}_-$, we reverse its MI score as its sentiment score. Finally, we merge the two word lists to form the pseudo sentiment lexicon, and rescale the sentiment scores into $[-2, 2]$.

3.7.2 Pivot Words Selection

Recall that pivot words should frequently occur in both domains and be sentiment sensitive. Hence, we first choose those words occurring at least 10 times in $\mathcal{D}^s$ and at least 30 times in $\mathcal{D}^{t,u}$ as pivot candidates[4], and remove negation and stop words.

[4]The ratio between $|\mathcal{D}^s|$ and $|\mathcal{D}^{t,u}|$ is 1:3 in our dataset.

Then, we only keep those candidates with high sentiment scores ($[-2, -1]$ and $[1, 2]$ for WN or $[-2, -0.9]$ and $[0.9, 2]$ for MI) as the pivot words.

3.7.3 Training Details

In our domain adaptation setting, for the labeled data $\mathcal{D}^s$ from the source domain, we have labels for both the main task and the auxiliary task, while for the unlabeled data $\mathcal{D}^{t,u}$ from the target domain, we only have labels for the auxiliary task. Hence, we adopted an alternating training approach, where in each epoch we first optimize all the model parameters given $\mathcal{D}^s$, and then switch to only optimizing the parameters corresponding to the auxiliary task (including Θ'_1, Θ'_2, $\mathbf{W}'$ and $\mathbf{b}'$) given $\mathcal{D}^{t,u}$. During the training stage, we share the word embeddings of the actual task and our auxiliary task, and never update the word embedding of *UNK* by setting it as a zero vector.

4 Experiments

4.1 Experiment Settings

Datasets: To evaluate our proposed method, we conduct experiments on a benchmark dataset released by Blitzer et al. (2007). This dataset consists of Amazon product reviews from four different domains: Book, DVD, Electronics and Kitchen. Each domain has 1000 positive and 1000 negative reviews as well as 17547 unlabeled reviews on average. Since the number of unlabeled reviews in each domain is different, we randomly choose 6000 unlabeled reviews for each domain.

Following previous studies (Pan et al., 2010; Zhou et al., 2016), we consider 12 pairs of source-target domain pairs. For each pair, all the 2000 labeled reviews from the source domain are treated as training data. We randomly choose 200 positive and 200 negative reviews from the target domain as development data, and the remainder (i.e., 800 + 800 reviews) from the target domain as test data. Moreover, for domain adaptation methods, we also use the 6000 unlabeled reviews from the target domain during the training stage.

Methods for comparison:

- **Naive** is a non-domain-adaptive baseline based on traditional discrete representations.
- **SCL** is the Structural Correspondence Learning method, which uses all the non-pivot features to predict the occurrence of each pivot feature, and employs SVD on the learned weight vectors.

- **mDA** is one of the state-of-the-art methods, marginalized denoising auto-encoders (Chen et al., 2012), which learns a shared hidden representation by reconstructing pivot features.
- **HNN** is another non-domain-adaptive NN-based baseline as detailed in Section 3.3.
- **H-WN** simply combines **HNN** with our auxiliary task, which represents each label derived from our auxiliary task using WN as a three-dimensional one-hot vector and appends it to the document embedding $\mathbf{h}_n$ in **HNN**, followed by a softmax classifier.
- **H-SCL** is a naive combination of **SCL** with **HNN**, which appends the induced representation from **SCL** to the document embedding in **HNN**, followed by a softmax classifier.
- **H-mDA** is similar to **H-SCL** but uses the hidden representation from **mDA**, and this can be considered as a strong baseline.

Meanwhile, to show the effectiveness of the proposed auxiliary tasks, we also use the two auxiliary tasks in our earlier work as the auxiliary task of our two architectures for comparison, respectively denoted by **DSRE** and **SSRE** (Yu and Jiang, 2016).

Besides, we consider four variants of our proposed methods, where the auxiliary tasks in **DSR** and **SSR** are derived from the pseudo sentiment lexicon, while the auxiliary tasks in **DSRW** and **SSRW** are based on SentiWordNet.

- **DSRE**, **DSR** and **DSRW** are based on our first NN architecture to learn document-level shared representations, as introduced in 3.4.
- **SSRE**, **SSR** and **SSRW** are based on our second NN architecture to induce sentence-level shared representations, as introduced in 3.5.

Hyperparameters: For **Naive**, we train linear classifiers with LibLinear[5] by using unigrams and bigrams with a frequency of at least 5 as features. For **SCL** and **mDA**, we use mutual information to select pivot features, and the number of chosen pivots is tuned from $\{500, 1000, 1500, 2000\}$ on the development set. In **SCL**, we tune the number of induced features K in $\{25, 50, 100\}$, and also use normalization and rescaling. In **mDA**, we employ the dropout noise strategy used by Yang and Eisenstein (2014) without any parameter. In

all the neural network models, we set the dimension of word embeddings l to 300, and initialize the lookup table $\mathbf{X}$ with *word2vec*[6]. We set the non-linear activation function in CNN as ReLU, and set the sizes of hidden layers in both CNN and LSTM as 150, i.e., $p = q = 150$. All the models were trained using AdaGrad with a learning rate of 0.05 and a minibatch size of 5. Also, the dropout rate α equals 0.5, and all the model parameters are regularized with a L2 regularization strength of 10^{-4}.

4.2 Results

In Table 1, we report the results of all the methods. It is easy to see that the performance of **Naive** is very limited. **SCL** and **mDA** can outperform the baseline model respectively by 2.7 and 3.7 percentage points on average, which shows that these two methods are useful for domain adaptation based on discrete representations. However, we can also see that the performance of these domain adaptation methods is much lower than the hierarchical neural network model (**HNN**) based on continuous representations. This demonstrates that **HNN** is more robust against domain shift. But comparing the performance of **HNN** in standard in-domain and our cross-domain settings, we find that the in-domain performance still outperforms the cross-domain performance by 6.2 percentage points on average. This indicates that it will be more challenging and useful to develop domain adaptation methods based on such a competitive baseline.

Moreover, we can easily see that the performance of simply appending three-dimensional one-hot vector from the auxiliary task to **HNN** (i.e., **H-WN**) is close to the performance of **HNN** in most cases. In addition, although **SCL** can outperform **Naive** with a large margin on almost all the data set pairs, the performance of **H-SCL** is not satisfactory, which can only improve the baseline by 0.5 percentage point on average. But for **H-mDA**, although the shared hidden representations are also derived from discrete representations, it can improve the performance of **HNN** on all data set pairs except one. This implies that the derived shared hidden representations by **mDA** can generalize better across domains, and are generally useful for domain adaptation. Furthermore, it is easy to observe that by simply incorporating the

[5]http://www.csie.ntu.edu.tw/cjlin/liblinear/

[6]https://code.google.com/p/word2vec/

Task	In-D	Compared Methods (Cross-Domain)									Proposed Methods (Cross-Domain)			
	HNN	Naive	SCL	mDA	HNN	H-WN	H-SCL	H-mDA	DSRE	SSRE	DSR	SSR	DSRW	SSRW
E2D		0.680	0.700	0.727	0.805	0.806	0.820	0.811	0.798	0.814	0.810	**0.823**†	0.821	0.816
B2D	0.845	0.773	0.771	0.806	0.814	0.832	0.813	0.829	0.823	0.832	0.832	0.822	**0.840**†	0.837†
K2D		0.698	0.721	0.741	0.791	0.796	0.799	0.796	0.788	0.803	0.798	**0.808**†	0.805†	0.801
E2B		0.693	0.704	0.728	0.786	0.790	0.780	0.789	0.789	0.781	0.790	0.792	0.790	**0.794**†
D2B	0.843	0.751	0.780	0.802	0.805	0.810	0.796	0.818	0.809	0.826	**0.835**†	0.822	0.825†	0.822
K2B		0.690	0.740	0.725	0.766	0.773	0.772	0.774	0.781	0.773	0.774	**0.784**†	0.781	0.776†
B2E		0.701	0.746	0.753	0.755	0.751	0.751	**0.786**	0.758	0.758	0.760	0.773	0.771	**0.786**
D2E	0.858	0.706	0.743	0.746	0.772	0.768	0.771	0.786	0.774	0.782	0.787	0.790†	**0.810**†	0.799†
K2E		0.799	0.818	0.830	0.836	0.837	0.847	0.839	0.837	0.843	0.830	0.835	**0.850**†	0.846
E2K		0.828	0.829	0.833	0.852	0.848	0.865	0.859	0.864	0.862	0.859	**0.874**†	0.867	0.858
B2K	0.883	0.724	0.763	0.754	0.780	0.788	0.785	**0.798**	0.784	0.791	0.785	0.783	0.796	0.794
D2K		0.716	0.758	0.742	0.778	0.774	0.786	0.773	0.793	0.809	**0.809**†	0.806	0.800†	0.803
AVG	0.857	0.729	0.756	0.766	0.795	0.798	0.799	0.805	0.800	0.806	0.806	0.809	**0.813**	0.811

Table 1: Comparison of classification accuracies of different methods. † indicates that DSR and DSRW (or SSR and SSRW) are significantly better than HNN, H-WN, H-SCL and H-mDA, DSRE (or SSRE) with $p < 0.05$ based on McNemar's paired significance test. **In-D** denotes the in-domain setting by splitting each target domain's labeled reviews into 1400/200/400 as training, development and test sets.

two auxiliary tasks in our earlier work into our two architectures, the performance of **DSRE** is not satisfactory, but **SSRE** can perform the best on average among all the compared systems. This demonstrates that the two auxiliary tasks are more suitable in sentence level, but become less useful in document level, which agrees with the intuition behind our auxiliary task.

Finally, we observe that (1) all of our proposed methods can significantly outperform the baseline **HNN** in almost all the data set pairs, and perform better than **H-WN** and **H-SCL** in most cases, which shows that the idea of learning a hidden representation using our proposed auxiliary tasks is generally effective; (2) even compared with **H-mDA**, **DSR** can achieve comparable results while **SSR**, **DSRW** and **SSRW** can still achieve significantly better performance in most cases. We conjecture that the gains of our methods may come from the sharing between two word embedding lookup tables and joint learning of our auxiliary task and the actual task; (3) in comparison with **DSRE** and **SSRE**, **DSR** and **SSR** can bring improvements in both sentence level and document level on average, which shows the effectiveness of the proposed auxiliary task; (4) among our proposed models, we find that the performance of **DSR** and **SSR** is not stable: sometimes they can achieve the best result, but sometimes they perform even worse than or similar to the baseline **HNN**. In contrast, **DSRW** and **SSRW** can always outperform **HNN**, and perform better than **DSR** and **SSR** on average. This is intuitive since the sentiment scores in **MI**, derived from source la-

beled data, are specific to the source domain, while the sentiment scores in SentiWordNet are general across domains. Besides, we can also see that the gap between **SSR** and **SSRW** is much smaller than the gap between **DSR** and **DSRW**. This suggests that our document-level shared representation learning method is more sensitive to the quality of sentiment lexicons, and with a high quality sentiment lexicon, it can perform best on average.

4.3 Case Study

Finally, to explore how our proposed models help to improve the performance of **HNN** in the test data set, we conduct a case study on **B2D** to get a deeper insight of our model **DSR**.

Specifically, we sample several samples from the test data set, i.e., *DVD*. As shown in Table 2, **HNN** only correctly predicts the sentiment of the first document but gives wrong predictions on another two documents, since *worth watching* only occurs once in the source *Book* domain. However, our model **DSR** can make correct predictions for all of them. The reason is as follows. In Table 2, we can observe that in the unlabeled data from the the *DVD* domain, *worth watching* often co-occur with some general positive sentiment words like *good*, *great*, *wonderful* and *fantastic*. Based on these unlabeled documents, **DSR** can implicitly learn that *worth watching* are highly correlated with the positive sentiment via our auxiliary task, and ultimately make correct predictions for the two test samples. This further indicates that compared with **HNN**, our models can identify more domain-specific sentiment words, and there-

B2D	Review		HNN	DSR
Test	*Definitely a great movie, rules ...... It is a movie definitely* **worth watching** *...... Strongly recommended along with black hawk down, a few good men, and courage under fire .*		1	1
	If your not already hooked on the story of these interns you have some catching up to do. Its not your typical medical drama and certainly **worth watching**.		0	1
	This film gets 4 stars because the child actors shine so much in it. The plot is not very intriguing, and ...... So no wonder you can not compete with him. Anyway, this film is certainly **worth watching** *as a family entertainment!*		0	1
Unlabel	*Very good film with a great cast. Reese and wahlberg are wonderful in their roles and play them to perfection, walhberg especially. Very much* **worth watching** */ owning.*		-	-
	A great movie! What an all star cast! This movie is **worth watching** *over and over again.*		-	-
	I found this dvd to be well produced and engaging to go along with the powerful content. Fantastic. Loads of deleted scenes that are very **worth watching**.		-	-

Table 2: Examples drawn from **B2D** whose sentiment labels are incorrectly predicted by the baseline model (**HNN**) but correctly inferred by our model (**DSR**). The sentiment words specific to the target domain are in **bold** and *italic*, and the pivot sentiment words are only in **bold**. 0 and 1 denote the negative and positive sentiments respectively.

fore improve the performance.

5 Conclusions

We presented a domain adaptation method for document-level sentiment classification. We first devised a new auxiliary task based on sentiment scores of pivot words. Then, we proposed two neural network architectures to respectively induce shared document embeddings and sentence embeddings across domains. Experiment results show that with a pseudo sentiment lexicon, our methods can achieve comparable results compared with several highly competitive domain adaptation methods; and with an external sentiment lexicon, we can further boost the performance of both architectures to achieve the state-of-the-art result.

Acknowledgments

We would like to thank the anonymous reviewers for their constructive comments. This research is supported by the National Research Foundation, Prime Minister's Office, Singapore under its International Research Centres in Singapore Funding Initiative.

References

Rie Kubota Ando and Tong Zhang. 2005. A framework for learning predictive structures from multiple tasks and unlabeled data. *The Journal of Machine Learning Research* 6:1817–1853.

Stefano Baccianella, Andrea Esuli, and Fabrizio Sebastiani. 2010. Sentiwordnet 3.0: An enhanced lexical resource for sentiment analysis and opinion mining. In *Proceedings of the Seventh conference on International Language Resources and Evaluation.*

Himanshu Sharad Bhatt, Deepali Semwal, and Shourya Roy. 2015. An iterative similarity based adaptation technique for cross-domain text classification. In *Proceedings of the Nineteenth Conference on Computational Natural Language Learning.*

John Blitzer, Mark Dredze, and Fernando Pereira. 2007. Biographies, bollywood, boom-boxes and blenders: Domain adaptation for sentiment classification. In *Proceedings of the 45th Annual Meeting of the Association of Computational Linguistics.*

John Blitzer, Ryan McDonald, and Fernando Pereira. 2006. Domain adaptation with structural correspondence learning. In *Proceedings of the 2006 Conference on Empirical Methods in Natural Language Processing.*

Danushka Bollegala, Takanori Maehara, and Ken-ichi Kawarabayashi. 2015. Unsupervised cross-domain word representation learning. In *Proceedings of the 53rd Annual Meeting of the Association for Computational Linguistics.*

Danushka Bollegala, Tingting Mu, and John Goulermas. 2016. Cross-domain sentiment classification using sentiment sensitive embeddings. *IEEE TKDE* 6(2):398–410.

Minmin Chen, Zhixiang Eddie Xu, Kilian Q. Weinberger, and Fei Sha. 2012. Marginalized denoising autoencoders for domain adaptation. In *Proceedings of the 29th International Conference on Machine Learning.*

Yejin Choi and Claire Cardie. 2008. Learning with compositional semantics as structural inference for subsentential sentiment analysis. In *Proceedings of the Conference on Empirical Methods in Natural Language Processing*.

Hal Daumé III. 2007. Frustratingly easy domain adaptation. In *Proceedings of the 45th Annual Meeting of the Association of Computational Linguistics*.

Ying Ding, Jianfei Yu, and Jing Jiang. 2017. Recurrent neural networks with auxiliary labels for cross-domain opinion target extraction. In *Proceedings of the Thirty-First AAAI Conference on Artificial Intelligence*.

Xavier Glorot, Antoine Bordes, and Yoshua Bengio. 2011. Domain adaptation for large-scale sentiment classification: A deep learning approach. In *In Proceedings of the Twenty-eight International Conference on Machine Learning*.

Yulan He, Chenghua Lin, and Harith Alani. 2011. Automatically extracting polarity-bearing topics for cross-domain sentiment classification. In *Proceedings of the 49th Annual Meeting of the Association of Computational Linguistics*.

Sepp Hochreiter and Jürgen Schmidhuber. 1997. Long Short-Term Memory. *Neural Computation* pages 1735–1780.

Minqing Hu and Bing Liu. 2004. Mining and summarizing customer reviews. In *Proceedings of SIGKDD*.

Ozan Irsoy and Claire Cardie. 2014. Deep recursive neural networks for compositionality in language. In *Advances in Neural Information Processing Systems*.

Jing Jiang and ChengXiang Zhai. 2007. Instance weighting for domain adaptation in NLP. In *Proceedings of the 45th Annual Meeting of the Association of Computational Linguistics*.

Yoon Kim. 2014. Convolutional neural networks for sentence classification. In *Proceedings of the 2014 Conference on Empirical Methods in Natural Language Processing*.

Tao Lei, Regina Barzilay, and Tommi Jaakkola. 2015. Molding CNNs for text: non-linear, non-consecutive convolutions. In *Proceedings of the Conference on Empirical Methods in Natural Language Processing*.

Tetsuji Nakagawa, Kentaro Inui, and Sadao Kurohashi. 2010. Dependency tree-based sentiment classification using CRFs with hidden variables. In *Proceedings of the North American Chapter of the Association for Computational Linguistics*.

Sinno Jialin Pan, Xiaochuan Ni, Jian-Tao Sun, Qiang Yang, and Zheng Chen. 2010. Cross-domain sentiment classification via spectral feature alignment. In *Proceedings of of the 19th international conference on World Wide Web*.

Sinno Jialin Pan and Qiang Yang. 2010. A survey on transfer learning. *IEEE TKDE* 22(10):1345–1359.

Bo Pang, Lillian Lee, and Shivakumar Vaithyanathan. 2002. Thumbs up?: sentiment classification using machine learning techniques. In *Proceedings of the Conference on Empirical Methods in Natural Language Processing*.

Richard Socher, Alex Perelygin, Jean Wu, Jason Chuang, Christopher D. Manning, Andrew Ng, and Christopher Potts. 2013. Recursive deep models for semantic compositionality over a sentiment treebank. In *Proceedings of the Conference on Empirical Methods in Natural Language Processing*.

Kai Sheng Tai, Richard Socher, and Christopher D. Manning. 2015. Improved semantic representations from tree-structured long short-term memory networks. In *Proceedings of the 53rd Annual Meeting of the Association for Computational Linguistics*.

Duyu Tang, Bing Qin, and Ting Liu. 2015. Document modeling with gated recurrent neural network for sentiment classification. In *Proceedings of the Conference on Empirical Methods in Natural Language Processing*.

Ivan Titov. 2011. Domain adaptation by constraining inter-domain variability of latent feature representation. In *Proceedings of the 49th Annual Meeting of the Association for Computational Linguistics*.

Rui Xia, Jianfei Yu, Feng Xu, and Shumei Wang. 2014. Instance-based domain adaptation in NLP via in-target-domain logistic approximation. In *Proceedings of the Twenty-Eighth AAAI Conference on Artificial Intelligence*.

Yi Yang and Jacob Eisenstein. 2014. Fast easy unsupervised domain adaptation with marginalized structured dropout. In *Proceedings of the 52nd Annual Meeting of the Association for Computational Linguistics*.

Zichao Yang, Diyi Yang, Chris Dyer, Xiaodong He, Alex Smola, and Eduard Hovy. 2016. Hierarchical attention networks for document classification. In *Proceedings of the North American Chapter of the Association for Computational Linguistics*.

Jianfei Yu and Jing Jiang. 2016. Learning sentence embeddings with auxiliary tasks for cross-domain sentiment classification. In *Proceedings of the 2016 Conference on Empirical Methods in Natural Language Processing*.

Guangyou Zhou, Zhiwen Xie, Jimmy Xiangji Huang, and Tingting He. 2016. Bi-transferring deep neural networks for domain adaptation. In *Proceedings of the 54th Annual Meeting of the Association for Computational Linguistics*.

Measuring Semantic Relations between Human Activities

Steven R. Wilson and **Rada Mihalcea**
University of Michigan
{steverw|mihalcea}@umich.edu

Abstract

The things people do in their daily lives can provide valuable insights into their personality, values, and interests. Unstructured text data on social media platforms are rich in behavioral content, and automated systems can be deployed to learn about human activity on a broad scale if these systems are able to reason about the content of interest. In order to aid in the evaluation of such systems, we introduce a new phrase-level semantic textual similarity dataset comprised of human activity phrases, providing a testbed for automated systems that analyze relationships between phrasal descriptions of people's actions. Our set of 1,000 pairs of activities is annotated by human judges across four relational dimensions including similarity, relatedness, motivational alignment, and perceived actor congruence. We evaluate a set of strong baselines for the task of generating scores that correlate highly with human ratings, and we introduce several new approaches to the phrase-level similarity task in the domain of human activities.

1   Introduction

Our everyday behaviors say a lot about who we are. The things we do are related to our personality (Ajzen, 1987), values (Rokeach, 1973), interests (Goecks and Shavlik, 2000), and what we are going to do next (Ouellette and Wood, 1998). While we cannot always directly observe what people are doing on a day-to-day basis, we have access to a large number of unstructured text sources that describe real-world human activity, such as news outlets and social media sites. Fiction and non-fiction writings often revolve around the things that people do, and even encyclopedic texts can be rich in descriptions of human activities. Although many common sources of text contain human activities, reasoning about these activities and their relationships to one another is not a trivial task. Descriptions of human actions are fraught with ambiguity, subjectivity, and there are multitudinous lexically distinct ways to express highly similar events. If we want to gain useful insights from these data, it should be beneficial to develop effective systems that can successfully represent, compare, and ultimately understand human activity phrases.

In this paper, we consider the task of automatically determining the strength of a relationship between two human activities,[1] which can be helpful in reasoning about texts rich with activity-based content. The relationship between activities might be similarity in a strict sense, such as *watching a film* and *seeing a movie*, or a more general relatedness, such as the relationship between *turn on an oven* and *bake a pie*. Another way to categorize a pair of activities is by the degree to which they are typically done with a similar motivation, like *eating dinner with family* and *visiting relatives*. Or, in order to uncover which other behaviors a person is likely to exhibit, it might be useful to determine how likely a person might be to do an activity given some information about previous real-world actions that they have taken.

Success on our proposed task will be a valuable step forward for multiple lines of research, especially within the computational social sciences where human behavior and its relation to other variables (e.g., personality traits, personal values, or political orientation) is a key focus. Since the language human activities is so varied, it is not enough to store exact representations of activity

---

[1] Throughout this paper, we use the word "activity" to refer to what a person does or has done. Unlike the typical use of this term in the computer vision community, in this paper we use it in a broad sense, to also encompass non-visual activities such as "make vacation plans" or "have a dream".

Proceedings of the The 8th International Joint Conference on Natural Language Processing, pages 664–673,
Taipei, Taiwan, November 27 – December 1, 2017 ©2017 AFNLP

phrases that are unlikely to appear many times. It would be useful to instead have methods that can automatically find related phrases and group them based on one (or more) of several dimensions of interest. Moreover, the ability to automatically group related activities will also benefit research in video-based and multimodal human activity recognition where there is need for inference about activities based on their relationships to one another.

Reasoning about the relationships between activity phrases brings with it many of the difficulties often associated with phrase-level semantic similarity tasks. It is not enough to know that the two phrases share a root verb, as the semantic weight of verbs can vary, such as the word "go" in the phrases *go to a bar* and *go to a church*. While these phrases have high lexical overlap and are similar in that they both describe a traveling type of activity, they are usually done for different motivations and are associated with different sets of other activities. In this case, we could only consider the main nouns (i.e., "bar" and "church"), but that approach would cause difficulties when dealing with other phrases such as *sell a car* and *drive a car*, which both involve an automobile but describe dissimilar actions. Therefore, successful systems should be able to properly focus on the most semantically relevant tokens with a phrase. A final challenge when dealing with human activity phrase relations is evaluation. There should be a good way to determine the effectiveness of a system's ability to measure relations between these types of phrases, yet other commonly used semantic similarity testbeds (e.g., those presented in various Semeval tasks (Agirre et al., 2012, 2013; Marelli et al., 2014)) are not specifically focused on the domain of human activities. Currently, it is unclear whether or not the top-performing systems on general phrase similarity tasks will necessarily lead to the best results when looking specifically at human activity phrases.

To address these challenges, we introduce a new task in automatically identifying the strength of human activity phrase relations. We construct a dataset consisting of pairs of activities reportedly performed by actual people. The pairs that we have collected aim specifically to showcase diverse phenomena such as pairs containing the same verb, a range of degrees of similarity and relatedness, pairs unlikely to be done by the same type of person, and so forth. These pairs are each annotated by multiple human judges across the following four dimensions:

- **Similarity:** The degree to which the two activity phrases describe the same thing. Here we are seeking semantic similarity in a strict sense. Example of high similarity phrases: *to watch a film* and *to see a movie*.

- **Relatedness:** The degree to which the activities are related to one another. This relationship describes a general semantic association between two phrases. Example of strongly related phrases: *to give a gift* and *to receive a present*.

- **Motivational Alignment:** The degree to which the activities are (typically) done with similar motivations. Example of phrases with potentially similar motivations: *to eat dinner with family members* and *to visit relatives*.

- **Perceived Actor Congruence:** The degree to which the activities are often done by the same type of person. Put another way, does knowing that a person often performs an activity increase human judges' expectation that this person will also often do a second activity? Example of activities that might be expected to be done by the same person: *to pack a suitcase* and *to travel to another state*.

These relational dimensions were selected to cover a variety of types of relationships that may hold between two activity phrases. This way, automated methods that capture slightly different notions of similarity between phrases will potentially be able to perform well when evaluated on different scales. While the dimensions are correlated with one another, we show that they do in fact measure different things. We provide a set of benchmarks to show how well previously successful phrase-level similarity systems perform on this new task. Furthermore, we introduce several modifications and novel methods that lead to increased performance on the task.

2 Related Work

Semantic similarity tasks have been recently dominated by various methods that seek to embed segments of text as vectors into some high-dimensional space so that comparisons can be made between them using cosine similarity or other vector based metrics. While word embeddings have existed in various forms in the past (Church and Hanks, 1990; Bengio et al., 2003), many approaches used today draw inspiration directly from shallow neural network based models such as those described in (Mikolov et al., 2013).[2] In the common skip-gram variant of these neural embedding models, a neural network is trained to predict a word given its context within some fixed window size. (Levy and Goldberg, 2014a) and (Bansal et al., 2014) extended the idea of context to incorporate dependency structures into the training process, leading to vectors that were able to better capture certain types of long-distance syntactic relationships. One of the major strengths of neural word embedding methods is that they are able to learn useful representations from extremely large corpora that can then be leveraged as a source of semantic knowledge on other tasks of interest, such as predicting word analogies (Pennington et al., 2014) or the semantic similarity and relatedness of word pairs (Huang et al., 2012).

Researchers have taken the powerful semi-supervised ability of these word embedding methods to aid in tasks at the phrase-level, as well. The most straightforward way to accomplish a phrase-level representation is to use some binary vector-level operation to compose pre-trained vector representations of individual words that belong to a phrase (Mitchell and Lapata, 2010). Other methods have sought to directly find embeddings for larger sequences of words, such as (Le and Mikolov, 2014) and (Kiros et al., 2015).

Semantic textual similarity tasks are often evaluated by computing the correlation between human judgements of similarity and machine output. The wordsim353 (Finkelstein et al., 2001) and simlex999 (Hill et al., 2016) resources provide a set of human annotated pairs of words, labeled for similarity and/or general association. Simverb-3500 (Gerz et al., 2016) was introduced to provide researchers with a testbed for verb relations, a specific yet important class of words that was less common in earlier word-level similarity data sets. SemEval has released a series of semantic text similarity tasks at varying levels of granularity, ranging from words to entire documents, such as the SICK (Sentences Involving Compositional Knowledge) dataset (Marelli et al., 2014) which is specifically crafted to evaluate the ability of systems to effectively compose individual word semantics in order to achieve the overall meaning of a sentence. While many of these evaluation sets contain human activities to some degree, they also have contain other types of words or phrases due to the way in which they were created. For example, SICK contains actions done by animals such as *follow a fish*. Similarly, Simverb-3500 contains verbs that don't necessarily describe human activities, like *chirp* and *glow*, and does not contain phrase-level activities.

Several recent works have raised concerns over the standard evaluation approaches used in semantic textual similarity tasks. One potential issue is the use of inadequate metrics depending on the task that a practitioner is interested in tackling. While the Pearson correlation between human-judged similarity scores and predicted outputs is often used, this type of correlation can be misleading in the presence of outliers or nonlinear relationships (Reimers et al., 2016). Remiers et al. propose a framework for selecting a metric for semantic text similarity tasks, which we take into consideration when selecting our evaluation metric. Additionally, correlation with human judgments does not always give a good indication of success on some downstream applications, the human ratings themselves are somewhat subjective, and statistical significance is rarely reported in comparisons of word embedding methods (Faruqui et al., 2016). However, our goal in this work is not to evaluate the overall quality of distributional semantic models, but to find a method that has high utility in the domain of human activity relations, and so we do rely on comparisons with human judges as a means of assessment.

3 Data Collection and Annotation

One potential source of data containing people's self-reported descriptions of their activities is social media platforms, but these data are noisy and require preprocessing steps that, being imperfect, may propagate their own errors into the resulting data. In order to get a set of cleaner activities that people might actually talk about doing, we directly asked Amazon Mechanical Turk (AMT) workers to write short phrases describing five activities that they had done in the past week. We collected data from 1,000 people located in the United States for a total of 5,000 activities. The activity phrases were then normalized by converting them to their infinitive form (without a preceding "to"), correcting spelling errors, removing punctuation, and converting all characters to lowercase.

---

[2]It is worth noting that (Levy and Goldberg, 2014b) show that these embeddings are actually implicitly factorizing a shifted version of a more traditional PMI word-context matrix, which is similar to the word co-occurrence matrix factorization approach used in (Pennington et al., 2014)).

Activity	Prompt	User Selection
pay the phone bill	an activity that is EXTREMELY SIMILAR	pay one's student loan bill
play softball	an activity that is SOMEWHAT SIMILAR	go bowling
take a bath	an activity that uses the SAME VERB	take care of one's ill spouse
smoke	an activity that is RELATED, but not necessarily SIMILAR	get sick and go to the doctor
go out for ice cream	an activity that is NOT AT ALL SIMILAR	cash a check

Table 1: Examples of activity/prompt pairs and the corresponding activities that were selected by the annotators given the pair.

After removing duplicate entries (about 2,000) and any phrases referring specifically to doing work on AMT (e.g., those containing the tokens mTurk or Turking, about 150 cases), we were left with a set of 2,909 unique activity phrases.

We acknowledge that this methodology introduces some bias since the workers all come from the United States, and it is therefore likely that our set of activity phrases describe things that are more commonly done by Americans than people from other regions. Furthermore, primacy and recency effects (Murdock Jr, 1962) may bias the types of items listed toward things done in the morning or just before logging onto the AMT platform. Based on this, we expect that our set of activities is not necessarily a representative sample of everything that people might do, but they are still descriptions of actual activities that real humans have done and are useful for our task.

3.1 Forming Pairs of Activities

Next, we sought to create pairs of activities that showcase a variety of relationship types, including varying degrees of similarity and relatedness. To achieve this, we turned to another group to human annotators. After reading through a document which oriented them to the task, the annotators were given the full list of activities in addition to a subset of randomly selected activity phrases. Each of these phrases was randomly paired with one of several possible prompts (see Table 1 for examples) which instructed the annotators how they should select a second activity phrase from the complete list in order to form a pair. Each prompt was sampled an equal number of times in order to make sure that the final set of pairs exhibited various types of relationships to the same degree. All annotators had access to a searchable copy of the full list, but the order of the activities was shuffled each time in order to avoid potential bias from the annotators selecting phrases near the top of the list, and a new shuffled version of the list was given after every 25 pairs created. While a suitable second activity phrase was not always present (e.g.,

no phrase in our dataset matches "an activity that uses the SAME VERB" as *choreograph a dance*), it is not crucial that all of these pairs fit the prompts exactly since these are only intended to approximate various phenomena, and the final annotations will be done without the knowledge of the prompts used to generate the pairs. In total, 12 unique annotators created 1,000 pairs of phrases.

3.2 Annotating Activity Pairs

All of the activity phrase pairs were uploaded to AMT in order to be labeled. For each pair, ten workers were asked to rate the similarity, relatedness, motivational alignment, and perceived actor congruence on a 5-point Likert-type scales (a total of 40,000 annotated data points). The workers were given a set of instructions that included descriptions of the four types of relationships with examples, including cases in which a pair might be related but not similar, motivationally aligned but not similar, etc. By asking the same set of people to label all four relational dimensions for a given pair, we hoped to make them cognizant of the differences between the scales.

The first three relationships were prompted for using the form: "To what degree are the two activities similar/related/of the same motivation?" and were coded as 0 (e.g., for responses of "not at all similar") and the integers 1-4 with 4 representing the strongest relationship. Perceived actor congruence was solicited for using the form: "Person A often does *activity 1*, while person B rarely does *activity 1*. Who would you expect to do *activity 2* more often?" with choices ranging from "Most likely Person B" to "Most likely Person A." Perceived actor congruence ranges from -2 to 2 and has the lowest score when Person B is chosen and the highest when Person A is chosen. A score of 0 on this scale means that judges were unable to determine whether Person A or Person B would be more likely to perform the action being asked about (i.e., *activity 2*). Each individual Human Intelligence Task (HIT) posted to AMT required an annotator to label 25 pairs so that we could reliably

Activity 1	Activity 2	SIM	REL	MA	PAC
go jogging	lift weights	1.67	2.22	2.89	1.11
read to one's kids	go to a bar	0	0	0	-1.29
take transit to work	commute to work	3.38	3.5	3.38	0.5
make one's bed	organize one's desk	0.58	1.29	1.57	0.71

Table 2: Sample activity phrase pairs and average human annotation scores given for the four dimensions: Similarity (SIM), Relatedness (REL), Motivational Alignment (MA) and Perceived Actor Congruence (PAC). SIM, REL, and MA are on a 0-4 scale, while PAC scores can range from -2 to 2.

	SIM	REL	MA	PAC
SIM	1.000	.962	.928	.735
REL		1.000	.932	.776
MA			1.000	.738
PAC				1.000

Table 3: Spearman correlations between the four relational dimensions: Similarity (SIM), Relatedness (REL), Motivational Alignment (MA) and Perceived Actor Congruence (PAC).

compute agreement, and a worker could complete as many HITs as they desired.

To remove potential spammers (annotators seeking quick payment who do not follow the task instructions), we first eliminated all annotations by any AMT workers who left items blank or selected the same score for every item for any of the four relationships in any of their completed HITs. Then, inter-annotator agreement was computed by calculating the Spearman correlation coefficient ρ between each annotator's scores and the average scores of all other AMT workers who completed the HIT, excluding those already thrown out during spammer removal. We then removed any annotations from workers whose agreement scores were more than three standard deviations below the mean agreement score for the HIT under the assumption that these workers were not paying attention to the pairs when selecting scores.

The final scores for each pair were assigned by taking the average AMT worker score for each relationship type. Some sample activities and their ratings are shown in Table 2. Averaged across all four relationship types, there is a good level of inter-annotator agreement at $\rho = .720$ (recomputed after spammer removal). The highest levels of agreement were found for similarity and relatedness ($\rho = .768$ for both), which is to be expected as these are somewhat less subjective than motivational alignment ($\rho = .745$) and perceived actor congruence ($\rho = .620$). These agreement scores can be treated as an upper bound for performance on this task; achieving a score higher than

SIM	REL	Activity 1	Activity 2
↑	↑	call one's mom	call dad
↑	↓	-	-
↓	↑	rake leaves	mow the lawn
↓	↓	go for a run	shop at a thrift store

SIM	MA	Activity 1	Activity 2
↑	↑	check facebook	check twitter
↑	↓	drive to missouri	go on a road trip
↓	↑	write a romantic letter	kiss one's spouse
↓	↓	cut firewood	trim one's beard

SIM	PAC	Activity 1	Activity 2
↑	↑	make a cherry pie	bake a birthday cake
↑	↓	have dinner with friends	eat by oneself
↓	↑	go to the gym	take a shower
↓	↓	read a novel	go to a party

REL	MA	Activity 1	Activity 2
↑	↑	gamble	go to the casino
↑	↓	go swimming	clean the pool
↓	↑	clean out old email	vacuum the house
↓	↓	study abstract algebra	go to the state fair

REL	PAC	Activity 1	Activity 2
↑	↑	eat cereal	eat a lot of food
↑	↓	homeschool one's child	drive one's child to school
↓	↑	cut the grass	talk to neighbors
↓	↓	eat at a restaurant	cook beans from scratch

MA	PAC	Activity 1	Activity 2
↑	↑	go to the dentist	brush one's teeth
↑	↓	take the train to work	drive to work
↓	↑	walk one's dog	walk to the store
↓	↓	read	watch football all day

Table 4: Activity pairs from our dataset highlighting stark differences between the four relational dimensions. For each dimension, ↑ refers to phrases rated at least one full point above the middle value along the Likert scale, while ↓ indicates a score at least one full point below the middle value. No pairs with high similarity and low relatedness exist in the data.

these would mean that an automated system is as good at ranking activity phrases as the average human annotator.

3.3 Relationships Between Dimensions

While the four relationship types being measured are correlated with one another (Table 3.2), there were certainly cases in which humans gave different scores for each relationship type to the same pair which shed light on the nuanced differences between the dimensions. (Table 4). Therefore, it is not necessarily the case that the best method for capturing one dimension is also the most correlated with human judgements across all four dimensions. However, it appears that similarity, relatedness, and motivational alignment are more highly correlated with one another than perceived actor congruence.

4 Methods

To determine how well automated systems are able to model humans' judgements of similarity, relatedness, motivational alignment, and perceived actor congruence, we evaluate a group of semantic textual similarity systems that are either commonly used or have shown state-of-the-art results. Each method takes two texts of arbitrary length as input and produces a continuous valued score as output. All of the methods are trained on outside data sources and many have been proposed as generalized embeddings that can be successful across many tasks. The methods we assess fall into three different categories: Composed Word-level Embeddings, Graph-based Embeddings, and Phrase-level Embeddings.

Activity Phrase Pre-processing. For the first two classes of methods, we experiment with several variations in the set of words being passed to the model as input in order remove the influence of potentially less semantically important words. We do not apply these pre-processing approaches to the phrase-level embedding methods since those methods are designed specifically to operate on entire phrases (as opposed to the bag-of-words view that the other methods take). The five variations of each phrase we consider are:

Full: The original phrase in its entirety.

Simplified: Starting with the Full phrase, we remove several less semantically relevant edges from a dependency parse[3] of the phrase, including the removal of determiners, coordinating conjunctions, adjectival modifiers, adverbs, and particles. This step is somewhat similar to performing stopword removal. For example, this filtering step would result in the bag of words containing "clean", "living" and "room" for full phrase: *clean up the living room.*

Simplified - Light Verbs: Starting with the Simplified set of words, we remove the root verb of the activity if it is not the only word in the Simplified phrase and if it belongs to the following list of semantically light verbs (Kearns, 1988): "go", "make", "do", "have", "get", "give", "take", "let", "come", and "put". This means that we would

convert the phrase *go get a tattoo* to just *get a tattoo*, but *read a novel* would retain its verb and become *read novel* (i.e., it will remain equivalent to the Simplified variation).

Simplified - All Verbs: To compare against the effect of removing light verbs, this approach takes the Simplified phrase and removes the root verb unless the Simplified phrase only contains that one word. Performing this filtering step would convert the phrase *cook a sausage* to simply *sausage.*

Core: This method seeks to reduce the phrase to a single core concept. In many cases, this means simply using the root verb from the dependency parse. So, we might represent the phrase "clean up the living room" using only the word embedding for "clean". However, we acknowledge that semantically light verbs such as "go", "have", and "do" would not adequately represent an entire activity, and so in the case of light verbs we instead select either the direct object or a nominal modifier that is connected to the root verb. If the noun selected as the core concept has another noun attached by a compound relationship, we also include that noun. This means, for example, that we would represent the phrase "go to an amusement park" as just "amusement park" when we are considering just the core concept.

4.1 Composed Word-level Embeddings

The methods in this section are based on word-level embeddings trained on some outside data. Since they operate at a word level, we apply a composition function to the words in a given phrase in order to achieve an embedding for the phrase. We tested both the arithmetic mean and element-wise multiplication for composition functions, but the former gave better performance and thus we do not report results found when using the element-wise product. Given an aggregate embedding for a phrase, we generate a score for each pair of activity phrases by computing the cosine similarity between the embeddings for the two phrases. We consider the following word-level methods:

Wiki-BOW: Skip Gram with Negative Sampling Word Embeddings trained on Wikipedia data using a context window of size 2 (Wiki-BOW2) and size 5 (Wiki-BOW5). These vectors are the same ones used in (Levy and Goldberg, 2014a).

Wiki-DEP: Skip Gram with Negative Sampling Word Embeddings trained on Wikipedia data with dependency-based contexts (Wiki-DEP) from (Levy and Goldberg, 2014a).

GoogleNews: Skip Gram with Negative Sampling Word Embeddings trained on the Google News

---

[3]We use the dependency parser from Stanford CoreNLP (http://stanfordnlp.github.io/CoreNLP/).

corpus from (Mikolov et al., 2013).

Paragram: Embeddings trained on the Paraphrase Database (Ganitkevitch et al., 2013) by fitting the embeddings so that the difference between the cosine similarity of actual paraphrases and that of negative examples is maximized(Wieting et al., 2015). We use the Paragram-Phrase XXL embeddings combined with the Paragram-SL999 embeddings, the latter of which has been tuned on SimLex999 (Hill et al., 2016). We also use a variation of Paragram Embeddings that employs counter fitting (Paragram-CF). This method further tunes the Paragram embeddings to capture a more strict sense of similarity rather than general association between words. This is accomplished via optimization with the goal of increasing the vectorspace differences between known antonyms and altering synonym embeddings to make them more similar to one another (Mrkšić et al., 2016).

Nondistributional vectors: Highly sparse vectors that encode a huge number of binary variables that capture interesting features about the words such as part of speech, sentiment, and supersenses (Faruqui and Dyer, 2015).

4.1.1 Graph-Based Embeddings

We also experiment with approaches that seek to incorporate higher order relationships between activity phrases by building semantic graphs that can be exploited to discover relations that hold between the phrases. Each graph G is of the form $G = (V, E)$ where V is a set of human activity phrases and E is some measure of semantic similarity, which is computed differently depending on the graph type. We run Node2vec (Grover and Leskovec, 2016) using the default settings to generate an embedding for each node in the graph and then measure the cosine similarity between nodes (phrases) to get the final system output. The types of graphs that we use are:

Similarity Graph: We first generate a fully connected graph of all activities in our dataset using a high performing semantic similarity method (Paragram in this case) as a way to generate edge weights. Next, we prune all edges with a weight less than some threshold. The results reported here use a threshold of .5 (on a 0-1 continuous scale). We also tried threshold values of .3, .4, and .6., but found them to produce inferior results for all dimensions.

People Graph: For each activity, we know at least four other activities that were done by the same person because each person submitted five activities. We add an unweighted edge to the graph for each pair of activities that were done by the same person. On its own, this graph does not have enough information to be competitive, so we only report results for the combined graph.

Combined Graph: Here, we combine information from both the Similarity Graph and the People Graph. Since the People Graph is unweighted, we follow the approach used in (Tripodi and Pelillo, 2016) and compute the average weight of all edges in the Similarity Graph and assign this weight to all edges in the People Graph. We then add the edge weights of the two graphs, treating nonexistant edges as edges with weight 0.

4.1.2 Phrase-level Embeddings

The methods in this section are designed to create an embedding directly from phrases of arbitrary length. Since these approaches are tailored toward phrases in their entirety, we do not evaluate them on the pre-processed variations of the phrases in our dataset. The phrase-level approaches we consider are:

Skip-thoughts vectors: This encoder-decoder model induces sentence level vectors by learning to predict surrounding sentences of each sentence in a large corpus of books (Kiros et al., 2015). The encoder is a recurrent neural network (RNN) which creates a vector from the words in the input sentence, and the RNN decoder generates the neighboring sentences. The model also learns a linear mapping from word-level embeddings into the encoder space to handle rare words that may not appear in the training corpus.

Charagram embeddings: Embeddings that represent character sequences (i.e., words or phrases) based on an elementwise nonlinear transformation of embeddings of the character n-grams that comprise the sequence (Wieting et al., 2016). Here we use the pre-trained charagram-phrase model.

5 Results

Because human annotations should fall on an ordinal scale rather than a ratio scale, it would not be fair to directly compare the average values human judges gave to the systems' output. Rather, the systems should be evaluated based on their ability to rank the set of phrases in the same order as the ranking given by the average human annotations scores for each dimension. Therefore, we calculate the Spearman Rank correlation between scores given by the automated systems and the human judges our final score for each system. In a previous study of evaluation metrics for intrinsic semantic textual similarity tasks, this metric was

	Method	SIM	REL	MA	PAC
Full phrase	Wiki-BOW-2	.434	.395	.383	.230
	Wiki-BOW-5	.480	.446	.431	.268
	Wiki-DEP	.388	,346	,339	.191
	GoogleNews	.550	.528	.514	.343
	Paragram	.578	.554	.530	.363
	Paragram-CF	.487	.455	.434	.276
	Sim Graph	.508	.489	.460	.330
	+ People Graph	.520	.502	.467	.340
	Skip-thoughts	.435	.408	.411	.276
	Charagram	.566	.550	.520	.381*
Simplified	Wiki-BOW-2	.532	.501	.475	.316
	Wiki-BOW-5	.563	.537	.507	.342
	Wiki-DEP	.499	.463	.443	.284
	GoogleNews	.606*	.582*	.552*	.383*
	Paragram	.616*	.594*	.560*	.397*
	Paragram-CF	.617*	.592*	.556*	.394*
	Sim Graph	.533	.520	.478	.340
	+ People Graph	.543	.533	.492	.350
- Light Verbs	Wiki-BOW-2	.523	.500	.481	.315
	Wiki-BOW-5	.565	.545	.522	.350
	Wiki-DEP	.484	.457	.443	.280
	GoogleNews	.618*	.599*	.577*	.394*
	Paragram	**.639***	**.623***	**.595***	.418*
	Paragram-CF	.637*	.618*	.587*	.416*
	Sim Graph	.577	.572	.534	.360
	+ People Graph	.584	.576	.535	.375
- All Verbs	Wiki-BOW-2	.434	.436	.419	.334
	Wiki-BOW-5	.482	.492	.469	.381*
	Wiki-DEP	.395	.392	.379	.290
	GoogleNews	.529	.542	.515	.425*
	Paragram	.547	.566	.541	**.445***
	Paragram-CF	.522	.538	.510	.435*
	Sim Graph	.417	.452	.417	.363
	+ People Graph	.433	.468	.432	.379
Core Only	Wiki-BOW-2	.360	.321	.316	.153
	Wiki-BOW-5	.402	.364	.363	.184
	Wiki-DEP	.319	.276	.274	.108
	GoogleNews	.436	.394	.393	.209
	Paragram	.444	.401	.402	.223
	Paragram-CF	.438	.397	.397	.225
	Sim Graph	.330	.281	.291	.146
	+ People Graph	.334	.283	.293	.134
	Human Agree.	*.768*	*.768*	*.745*	*.620*

Table 5: Spearman correlation between phrase similarity methods and human annotations across four annotated relations: Similarity (SIM), Relatedness (REL), Motivational Alignment (MA) and Perceived Actor Congruence (PAC). Top performing methods for each dimension are in bold font. * indicates correlation coefficient is not statistically significantly lower than the best method for that relational dimension ($\alpha = .05$).

recommended for tasks in which the ranking of all items is important (Reimers et al., 2016). Results for all methods using all phrase variations are shown in Table (Table 5).

For our dataset, Paragram in the Simplified - Light Verbs setting gives the best results for similarity, relatedness, and motivational alignment. It is somewhat expected that the same method has the best performance for these three dimen-sions as they are strongly correlated with one another. Paragram in the Simplified - All Verbs setting gives the best result on perceived actor congruence. We can see that removing light verbs is a helpful step for most methods when trying to predict similarity, relatedness, and motivational alignment indicating that light verbs mostly add noise to the overall meaning of the phrases. Interestingly, the best results for pereceived actor congruence come when ignoring all root verbs in longer phrases. This was a filtering step that led to decreased performance when ranking across the other three dimensions. This suggests that for determining perceived actor congruence, the context of the action found within a phrase is more important than the action itself. Based on statistical significance testing (Z-test using Fisher r-z transformation, single-tailed), however, we cannot be confident that all of these results will hold for larger sets of human activity phrase pairs, as several other methods had scores that were not found to be significantly lower than the best methods.

6 Conclusion

In this paper, we addressed the task of measuring semantic relations between human activity phrases. We introduced a new dataset consisting of human activity pairs that have been annotated based on their similarity, relatedness, motivational alignment, and perceived actor congruence. Using this dataset, we evaluated a number of semantic textual similarity methods to automatically determine scores for each of the four dimensions, and found that similarity between averaged paragram embeddings of the simplified phrases with light verbs removed was most highly correlated with human judgements of similarity, relatedness, and motivational alignment. The method that yielded the best result for the perceived actor congruence dimension also used the paragram embeddings, but when averaged across the simplified phrases with all verbs removed.

We believe there is still plenty of room for improvement on this task, and we hope that the release of our data will encourage greater participation on this task. Future work should explore methods to handle more subtle semantic differences between activities that we noticed are often missed by the automated methods including the effects of function words and polysemy. It should also be helpful to learn better weight-based composition methods (e.g., those proposed in (Yu and Dredze, 2015)) rather than filtering out words in a rule-based fashion.

We make our dataset, including all activity pairs and averaged human ratings, publicly available at `http://lit.eecs.umich.edu/downloads.html`.

Acknowledgments

This material is based in part upon work supported by the Michigan Institute for Data Science, by the National Science Foundation (grant #1344257), and by the John Templeton Foundation (grant #48503). Any opinions, findings, and conclusions or recommendations expressed in this material are those of the author and do not necessarily reflect the views of the Michigan Institute for Data Science, the National Science Foundation, or the John Templeton Foundation. We would also like to thank members of the University of Michigan LIT lab for help with data annotation.

References

Eneko Agirre, Daniel Cer, Mona Diab, Aitor Gonzalez-Agirre, and Weiwei Guo. 2013. sem 2013 shared task: Semantic textual similarity, including a pilot on typed-similarity. In *SEM 2013: The Second Joint Conference on Lexical and Computational Semantics. Association for Computational Linguistics.* Citeseer.

Eneko Agirre, Mona Diab, Daniel Cer, and Aitor Gonzalez-Agirre. 2012. Semeval-2012 task 6: A pilot on semantic textual similarity. In *Proceedings of the First Joint Conference on Lexical and Computational Semantics-Volume 1: Proceedings of the main conference and the shared task, and Volume 2: Proceedings of the Sixth International Workshop on Semantic Evaluation*, pages 385–393. Association for Computational Linguistics.

Icek Ajzen. 1987. Attitudes, traits, and actions: Dispositional prediction of behavior in personality and social psychology. *Advances in experimental social psychology*, 20:1–63.

Mohit Bansal, Kevin Gimpel, and Karen Livescu. 2014. Tailoring continuous word representations for dependency parsing. Association for Computational Linguistics.

Yoshua Bengio, Réjean Ducharme, Pascal Vincent, and Christian Jauvin. 2003. A neural probabilistic language model. *Journal of machine learning research*, 3(Feb):1137–1155.

Kenneth Ward Church and Patrick Hanks. 1990. Word association norms, mutual information, and lexicography. *Computational linguistics*, 16(1):22–29.

Manaal Faruqui and Chris Dyer. 2015. Non-distributional word vector representations. *CoRR*, abs/1506.05230.

Manaal Faruqui, Yulia Tsvetkov, Pushpendre Rastogi, and Chris Dyer. 2016. Problems with evaluation of word embeddings using word similarity tasks. *arXiv preprint arXiv:1605.02276*.

Lev Finkelstein, Evgeniy Gabrilovich, Yossi Matias, Ehud Rivlin, Zach Solan, Gadi Wolfman, and Eytan Ruppin. 2001. Placing search in context: The concept revisited. In *Proceedings of the 10th international conference on World Wide Web*, pages 406–414. ACM.

Juri Ganitkevitch, Benjamin Van Durme, and Chris Callison-Burch. 2013. Ppdb: The paraphrase database. In *HLT-NAACL*, pages 758–764.

Daniela Gerz, Ivan Vulić, Felix Hill, Roi Reichart, and Anna Korhonen. 2016. SimVerb-3500: A Large-Scale Evaluation Set of Verb Similarity. In *EMNLP*.

Jeremy Goecks and Jude Shavlik. 2000. Learning users' interests by unobtrusively observing their normal behavior. In *Proceedings of the 5th international conference on Intelligent user interfaces*, pages 129–132. ACM.

Aditya Grover and Jure Leskovec. 2016. node2vec: Scalable feature learning for networks. In *Proceedings of the 22nd ACM SIGKDD International Conference on Knowledge Discovery and Data Mining*, pages 855–864. ACM.

Felix Hill, Roi Reichart, and Anna Korhonen. 2016. Simlex-999: Evaluating semantic models with (genuine) similarity estimation. *Computational Linguistics*.

Eric H Huang, Richard Socher, Christopher D Manning, and Andrew Y Ng. 2012. Improving word representations via global context and multiple word prototypes. In *Proceedings of the 50th Annual Meeting of the Association for Computational Linguistics: Long Papers-Volume 1*, pages 873–882. Association for Computational Linguistics.

Kate Kearns. 1988. Light verbs in english.

Ryan Kiros, Yukun Zhu, Ruslan R Salakhutdinov, Richard Zemel, Raquel Urtasun, Antonio Torralba, and Sanja Fidler. 2015. Skip-thought vectors. In *Advances in neural information processing systems*, pages 3294–3302.

Quoc V Le and Tomas Mikolov. 2014. Distributed representations of sentences and documents. In *ICML*, volume 14, pages 1188–1196.

Omer Levy and Yoav Goldberg. 2014a. Dependency-based word embeddings. In *ACL (2)*, pages 302–308. Citeseer.

Omer Levy and Yoav Goldberg. 2014b. Neural word embedding as implicit matrix factorization. In *Advances in neural information processing systems*, pages 2177–2185.

Marco Marelli, Stefano Menini, Marco Baroni, Luisa Bentivogli, Raffaella Bernardi, and Roberto Zamparelli. 2014. A sick cure for the evaluation of compositional distributional semantic models. In *LREC*, pages 216–223.

Tomas Mikolov, Ilya Sutskever, Kai Chen, Greg S Corrado, and Jeff Dean. 2013. Distributed representations of words and phrases and their compositionality. In *Advances in neural information processing systems*, pages 3111–3119.

Jeff Mitchell and Mirella Lapata. 2010. Composition in distributional models of semantics. *Cognitive science*, 34(8):1388–1429.

Nikola Mrkšić, Diarmuid O Séaghdha, Blaise Thomson, Milica Gašić, Lina Rojas-Barahona, Pei-Hao Su, David Vandyke, Tsung-Hsien Wen, and Steve Young. 2016. Counter-fitting word vectors to linguistic constraints. *arXiv preprint arXiv:1603.00892*.

Bennet B Murdock Jr. 1962. The serial position effect of free recall. *Journal of experimental psychology*, 64(5):482.

Judith A Ouellette and Wendy Wood. 1998. Habit and intention in everyday life: The multiple processes by which past behavior predicts future behavior. *Psychological bulletin*, 124(1):54.

Jeffrey Pennington, Richard Socher, and Christopher D Manning. 2014. Glove: Global vectors for word representation. In *EMNLP*, volume 14, pages 1532–1543.

Nils Reimers, Philip Beyer, and Iryna Gurevych. 2016. Task-oriented intrinsic evaluation of semantic textual similarity. In *COLING*, pages 87–96.

Milton Rokeach. 1973. *The nature of human values*. Free press.

Rocco Tripodi and Marcello Pelillo. 2016. A game-theoretic approach to word sense disambiguation. *Computational Linguistics*.

John Wieting, Mohit Bansal, Kevin Gimpel, and Karen Livescu. 2015. Towards universal paraphrastic sentence embeddings. *arXiv preprint arXiv:1511.08198*.

John Wieting, Mohit Bansal, Kevin Gimpel, and Karen Livescu. 2016. Charagram: Embedding words and sentences via character n-grams. *arXiv preprint arXiv:1607.02789*.

Mo Yu and Mark Dredze. 2015. Learning composition models for phrase embeddings. *Transactions of the Association for Computational Linguistics*, 3:227–242.

Learning Transferable Representation for Bilingual Relation Extraction via Convolutional Neural Networks

Bonan Min,[*] Zhuolin Jiang[*]
Raytheon BBN Technologies
10 Moulton St
Cambridge, MA 02138
{bonan.min,zhuolin.jiang}@raytheon.com

Marjorie Freedman,[†] Ralph Weischedel[†]
USC/Information Sciences Institute
4676 Admiralty Way
Marina del Rey, CA 90292
{mrf,weisched}@isi.edu

Abstract

Typically, relation extraction models are trained to extract instances of a relation ontology using only training data from a single language. However, the concepts represented by the relation ontology (e.g. *ResidesIn*, *EmployeeOf*) are language independent. The numbers of annotated examples available for a given ontology vary between languages. For example, there are far fewer annotated examples in Spanish and Japanese than English and Chinese. Furthermore, using only language-specific training data results in the need to manually annotate equivalently large amounts of training for each new language a system encounters. We propose a deep neural network to learn transferable, discriminative bilingual representation. Experiments on the ACE 2005 multilingual training corpus demonstrate that the joint training process results in significant improvement in relation classification performance over the monolingual counterparts. The learnt representation is discriminative and transferable between languages. When using 10% (25K English words, or 30K Chinese characters) of the training data, our approach results in doubling F1 compared to a monolingual baseline. We achieve comparable performance to the monolingual system trained with 250K English words (or 300K Chinese characters) With 50% of training data.

1 Introduction

Semantic relation extraction is critical to many applications including knowledge base population and question answering. The problem is well-studied when relation-specific annotations are available in a single target language. However, the same relations can be represented using a variety of languages. While the evidence of the relation in context is language specific (e.g. *John spent several years living in Beijing* vs 约翰在北京生活了几年), the definition of relation itself is often language independent (e.g. *ResidesIn*) and the meaning should be preserved across languages.

We hypothesize that common, shared representation can be learnt when annotations are available in multiple languages and propose a bilingual relation extraction algorithm for this purpose. Our basic building blocks are Convolutional Neural Networks (CNN) with cross-lingual word embeddings (Ammar et al., 2016). This allows the system to capture lexical similarities across languages as well as phrase-level semantics. Building on CNNs with cross-lingual embeddings, the algorithm is a joint training algorithm which trains a model from annotated datasets in a pair of languages. We require that the annotated classes be consistent across languages, but do not require annotations over parallel (or comparable) text. The base system combines two objectives: an objective that predicts the correct relation labels in each dataset in one of the languages, and another objective to separately learn a shared representation across languages as well as language-specific representations. To further force the learnt representation to be discriminative among classes regardless of language, a discriminative objective for learning the ideal representation (Section 3.3) is added onto the shared, bilingual representation.

674

Proceedings of the The 8th International Joint Conference on Natural Language Processing, pages 674–684,
Taipei, Taiwan, November 27 – December 1, 2017 ©2017 AFNLP

---

[*]indicates co-first authors. These two authors made equal contribution.

[†]This work was done while the author was at Raytheon BBN Technologies.

The final combined algorithm essentially learns two types of useful representations: a language-independent relation-specific representation with the shared neurons, and a language-dependent relation-specific representation with the language-specific neurons.

Our contributions are the following:

- Developing a bilingual transfer learning algorithm for relation extraction that can use independent multilingual corpora annotated with the same set of relations. Analysis shows that the representation is discriminative.
- Demonstrating that jointly training from two languages outperforms its monolingual counterparts significantly.
- Showing that knowledge can be transferred from resource-rich language to resource-poor languages: On the ACE multilingual training corpus, we achieve comparable performance with 50% of the target-language training data using our approach and are able to double performance with only 10% (250K words) of target language data. This provides a very cost effective way to develop relation extractors in new languages.

2 Related Work

Relation extraction is typically cast as a multi-class classification problem in which a supervised machine learning model is trained with labeled datasets for classifying relations. Traditional methods (Kambhatla, 2004; Zhou et al., 2005; Zhao and Grishman, 2005; Jiang and Zhai, 2007) either reply on a set of linguistic or semantic features, or use convolution tree kernels (Moschitti, 2006) with syntactic (Zhang et al., 2006), sub-sequence (Bunescu and Mooney, 2005b), or dependency trees (Bunescu and Mooney, 2005a) as means to represent input sentences. Recently, deep neural networks start to show promising results in relation extraction. In particular, Convolutional Neural Networks (Zeng et al., 2014a; dos Santos et al., 2015; Nguyen and Grishman, 2015), Reccurrent/Recursive Neural Networks such as bidirectional LSTMs (Zhang et al., 2015), LSTM along shortest dependency paths (Xu et al., 2015), bidirectional tree-structured LSTM-RNNs (Miwa and Bansal, 2016) are shown to be effective. Attention mechanism (Wang et al., 2016) is also effective in further improving performance. Our baseline monolingual model is similar to (Nguyen and Grishman, 2015) and we does not require

parsing or composing multiple models.

There is very little work on multilingual relation extraction. (Qian et al., 2014) proposed an active learning approach for bilingual relation extraction with pseudo parallel corpora. (Kim et al., 2010) and (Kim et al., 2014) proposed cross-lingual annotation projection approach for relation detection with parallel corpora. In contrast, our work don't require parallel corpora nor Machine Translation. More recently, (Faruqui and Kumar, 2015) applied cross-lingual projection for open-domain relation extraction in languages other than English. (Blessing and Schütze, 2012) and Compositional Universal Schema (Verga et al., 2016) performs cross-lingual relation extraction with distant supervision (Mintz et al., 2009; Riedel et al., 2010; Surdeanu et al., 2012; Hoffmann et al., 2011; Ritter et al., 2013). These works are significantly different from ours in that they either operates in the open-domain(Faruqui and Kumar, 2015) without a pre-defined relation schema, or in a distant supervision setting with a KB as source of supervision. POLY (Nakashole et al., 2012) mines relational paraphrases from multilingual sentences which can be useful for relation extraction.

Besides relation extraction, (Huang et al., 2013) performs cross-language knowledge transfer with deep neural networks for speech recognition. (Guo et al., 2016) proposed a distributed representation-based framework for cross-lingual transfer learning for dependency parsers.

3 Bilingual Relation Extraction

Given a pair of monolingual corpora in two different languages and each corpus having been annotated with sentence-level relations [1] of pre-defined types, the goal of bilingual relation extraction is to learn *discriminative* representations to identify the relation between a pair of mentions, regardless of which language the mention pair comes from (*transferable across languages*). We achieve the goal of learning discriminative representation by joint supervision of classification (softmax) loss and ideal representation loss. We achieve the additional cross-lingual transferring goal by learning shared representation across languages.

As shown in Figure 1, our CNN-based bilingual relation extraction model consists of 4 main parts: (1) an embedding layer to encode words (in bilingual space), word positions, entity types and

---

[1] A sentence with a pair of mentions will be annotated with a relation, if the relation holds between the pair of mentions.

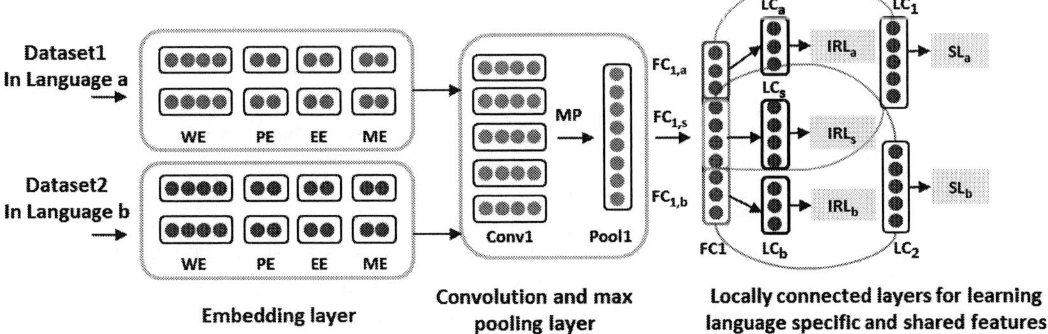

Figure 1: Bilingual relation extraction model trained with both softmax classification loss (SL) and ideal representation loss (IRL). IRL_a and IRL_b are language-specific ideal representation losses for language a and b respectively. IRL_s is the shared representation loss across 2 languages. $FC_{1,a}$ and $FC_{1,b}$ are 2 sets of language-specific neurons for language a and b, respectively. $FC_{1,s}$ is a set of shared neurons. SL_a and SL_b are the softmax classification losses for language a and b respectively.

mention levels by real-valued vectors; (2) a convolution and max pooling layer to generate a fixed-size feature vector for an input sentence; (3) 3 locally connected (LC) layers for learning language-specific and shared representations. These layers are learned to predict discriminative representation using proposed ideal representation loss (IRL) during training; (4) 2 LC layers for learning 2 relation classifiers with the softmax loss (SL). The 5 LC layers and the 5 prediction losses (3 IRLs and 2 SLs) are illustrated in Figure 1.

3.1 Embedding Layer

Word embeddings (WE) The inputs are sentences marked with pairs of mentions of interest. Given an input sentence $\mathbf{x}$ of length t, we firstly transform each word into a real-valued vector of dimension d_1 by looking up a word embedding matrix $W^1 \in \mathbb{R}^{d_1 \times |V|}$, where V is a fixed-sized vocabulary. To project similar words in a pair of languages into close proximity, we use cross-lingual embedding trained with multiCCA (Ammar et al., 2016) to initialize W^1. W^1 will also be finetuned during training.

MultiCCA only requires two monolingual corpora and a bilingual parallel dictionary. It first trains monolingual embeddings for each language independently from each monolingual corpus, capturing semantic similarity within each language. Then given the dictionary, it applies canonical correlation analysis (CCA) to estimate linear projections from the monolingual embeddings to bilingual embeddings. This makes translationally equivalent words in different languages to be embedded nearby each other.

Position embeddings (PE) The words close to the argument mentions are more informative to determine the relationship. Similar to (Santos et al., 2015), for each word, we map its relative distances to two argument mentions to two real-valued vectors of dimension d_2 by a embedding matrix $W^2 \in \mathbb{R}^{d_2 \times |D|}$, where D is the set of relative distances in a dataset. We obtain two vectors for each word with respect to the first and the second argument of the relation mention.

Entity type embeddings (EE) and mention level embeddings (ME) For each word, we map its entity type and mention level into real-valued vectors using embedding matrix $W^3 \in \mathbb{R}^{d_3 \times |E|}$ and $W^4 \in \mathbb{R}^{d_4 \times |M|}$ respectively. E is the set of entity types while M is the set of mention levels.

The final embedding dimension for each token is $n_1 = (d_1 + 2d_2 + d_3 + d_4)$. This layer will produce an embedding representation $\mathbf{x}^{(1)} \in \mathbb{R}^{n_1 \times t}$ when fed with an input sentence $\mathbf{x}^{(0)} = \mathbf{x}$. W^1, W^2, W^3, W^4 are parameters to be learnt via the end-to-end model.

3.2 Convolution and Max Pooling Layer

Relations can be expressed by words or their combinations. The model should utilize all local features extracted around each word in the sentence and predict the relation globally. Convolution operation is a natural approach to achieve this goal (Zeng et al., 2014b; Santos et al., 2015). Given a convolution filter i of window size k, the convolution operation on an input sentence $\mathbf{x}$ will produce a score vector $\mathbf{z} = (z_1, ..., z_{(t-k+1)})$, where $z_j = g_1(\mathbf{w}_i \mathbf{x}_j + b_i)$. $\mathbf{w}_i \in \mathbb{R}^{kn_1}$ are the linear transform parameters for filter i, $\mathbf{x}_j$ denotes the

j-th context window in $\mathbf{x}$, b_i is a bias scalar and g_1 is a non-linear function such as the rectified linear unit (ReLU). Then the max operation is applied to identify the most informative n-gram feature from this score vector: $m_i = \max(\mathbf{z})$. We replicate this process for a set of filters with different window sizes to capture important n-gram features from an input sentence. The matrix $W^{(2)} = [\mathbf{w}_1, ..., \mathbf{w}_{n_2}]$, where n_2 is the total number of filters, and vector $\mathbf{b}^{(2)} = [b_1, ..., b_{n_2}]$ are parameters to be learnt in this convolution layer. Finally we obtain a fixed-sized feature vector $\mathbf{x}^{(2)} = \mathbf{m} = [m_1, ..., m_{n_2}] \in \mathbb{R}^{n_2}$. The representation $\mathbf{x}^{(2)}$ is generated by taking max pooling over entire sentence with filters of multiple window sizes. To prevent these neurons that generate $\mathbf{m}$ from co-adapting and force them to learn individual useful features, a dropout layer is added after the pooling layer for regularization.

We added a fully connected layer to combine information captured by these filters: $\mathbf{x}^{(3)} = g_2(W^{(3)}\mathbf{x}^{(2)} + \mathbf{b}^{(3)}) \in \mathbb{R}^{n_3}$. $W^{(3)}$ and $\mathbf{b}^{(3)}$ are parameters learnt in this layer, and g_2 is a non-linear function.

3.3 Learning Transferable, Discriminative Bilingual Representation

Given two sets of training examples X^a and X^b in two languages a and b, we aim at learning transferable, discriminative bilingual representations. We achieve this by weight sharing at a high-level layer. We further improve the discriminative power of learnt representations using ideal representation loss. The bilingual representation learning model is shown in Figure 1.

Shared and Language-specific Neurons We aim at not only learning representation shared by both languages, but also learning representation specific to each language. We partition the neurons in the $FC1$ layer into three disjoint sets: two language-specific sets ($FC_{1,a}$ and $FC_{1,b}$) and a shared bilingual set $FC_{1,s}$ to represent shared features across languages. We expect that $FC_{1,a}$ and $FC_{1,b}$ can model language-specific features, while the common set $FC_{1,s}$ can model the share features.

Discriminative Representation Learning As described in (Zeiler and Fergus, 2014; Krizhevsky et al., 2012), the neurons from high-level layers of a CNN tend to extract more abstract and class-specific features. If each neuron in a high-level layer of our CNN activates only when a specific relation is presented, this will lead to a discrimi-

native representation for relations. Such representation, when learnt across language, would be extremely useful for transferring useful information across languages for relation extraction.

To achieve this, we partition the neurons in each high-level layer into subsets, and encourage each subset to only represent sentences of one of the relation types. This results in an explicit correspondence between blocks of neurons and relation types. Specifically, we partition the neurons in each sub-layer (*i.e.*, LC_a, LC_b and LC_s) into disjoint subsets and associate each subset with one specific relation label. For sentences of different relation types, we represent them using disjoint subsets of neurons. To do so, we integrate the ideal representation loss introduced in (Jiang et al., 2011) into our objective function during training. Let $(\mathbf{x}_i; y_i)$ denote training example $\mathbf{x}_i$. The ideal representation loss can be defined as:

$$L_r = \|\mathbf{q}_i - \mathbf{c}_i\| \tag{1}$$

where $\mathbf{c}_i = W^{(l_d)}\mathbf{x}_i^{(l_d-1)} + \mathbf{b}^{(l_d)}$ is the *predicted representation* for example $\mathbf{x}_i$ from locally connected layer $l_d = \{LC_a, LC_b, LC_s\}$. $\mathbf{x}_i^{(l_d-1)}$ is the representation of example $\mathbf{x}_i$ from $FC_{1,a}$, $FC_{1,b}$ or $FC_{1,s}$. $W^{(l_d)}$ and $\mathbf{b}^{(l_d)}$ are linear transform parameters and bias parameters learnt from these locally connected layers. We define $\mathbf{q}_i$ as the ideal representation corresponding to training sample $\mathbf{x}_i$ from locally connect layer l_d. The non-zero values of $\mathbf{q}_i$ occur at the indices where the training example $\mathbf{x}_i$ and neurons from layer l_d shared the same relation label. For example, suppose we have six training samples $\{\mathbf{x}_1, \ldots, \mathbf{x}_6\}$ and their relation labels $\mathbf{y} = [y_1, \ldots, y_6] = [1, 1, 2, 2, 3, 3]$. Further assume layer l_d has six neurons $\{p_1, \ldots, p_6\}$ with $\{p_1, p_2\}$ associated with label 1, $\{p_3, p_4\}$ label 2, and $\{p_6, p_7\}$ label 3. Then the ideal representations for these six samples are given by:

$$[\mathbf{q}_1, \ldots, \mathbf{q}_6] = \begin{bmatrix} 1 & 1 & 0 & 0 & 0 & 0 \\ 1 & 1 & 0 & 0 & 0 & 0 \\ 0 & 0 & 1 & 1 & 0 & 0 \\ 0 & 0 & 1 & 1 & 0 & 0 \\ 0 & 0 & 0 & 0 & 1 & 1 \\ 0 & 0 & 0 & 0 & 1 & 1 \end{bmatrix}, \tag{2}$$

where each column is an ideal discriminative representation corresponding to a training sample. Minimizing the ideal representation loss term ensure that the input sentence from the same type have similar representations while those from different types have dissimilar representations.

Relation Classification We trained a pair of softmax classifiers for relation classification for language a and b. The softmax classification loss $L_s^*, * = \{a, b\}$ can be defined as:

$$L_s^* = -\log(\frac{e^{o_{y_i}}}{\sum_j e^{o_j}}) \qquad (3)$$

where o_j is the j-th element of the predicted relation scoring vector from LC_1 or LC_2 layer in Figure 1. Let l_s denote these two locally connected layers, *i.e.*, $l_s = \{LC_1, LC_2\}$. We have $\mathbf{o} = W^{(l_s)}\mathbf{x}_i^{(l_s-1)} + \mathbf{b}^{(l_s)}$, where $W^{(l_s)}$ and $\mathbf{b}^{(l_s)}$ are learnt parameters from layer l_s. $\mathbf{x}_i^{(l_s-1)}$ is the representation of example $\mathbf{x}_i$ by concatenating the activations from $FC_{1,a}$ and $FC_{1,s}$, or $FC_{1,b}$ and $FC_{1,s}$.

We combine the ideal representation loss and softmax classification loss to obtain the final loss function for a training sample $(\mathbf{x}_i; y_i)$:

$$L(\mathbf{x}_i, y_i) = \begin{cases} L_s^a + \lambda(L_r^a + L_r^s) & \text{if } \mathbf{x}_i \text{ in lang. } a \\ L_s^b + \lambda(L_r^b + L_r^s) & \text{if } \mathbf{x}_i \text{ in lang. } b \end{cases} \qquad (4)$$

where L_s^a and L_s^b are the softmax loss for samples in language a and b, respectively. They are computed via equation 3. The terms L_r^a, L_r^b are the ideal representation losses for language a and b respectively, while L_r^s is shared by both languages. The term $L_r^*, * = \{a, b, s\}$ can be computed by equation 1. We minimized equation 4 using stochastic gradient descent.

4 Experiments

Parameter setting In the embedding layer, we used the pretrained 100-dimension bilingual word embeddings in (Ammar et al., 2016) to initialize W^1. We set the dimension of the other three embedding matrices W^2, W^3 and W^4 to 50 and initialize them randomly. In the convolution layer, we set the filter widths to $[2, 3, 4, 5]$, and use 150 filters per width. The number of neurons in the $FC1$ layer ($FC_{1,a} \cup FC_{1,s} \cup FC_{1,b}$) is 300. We use $tanh$ for g_1, g_2. All parameters are tuned with the ACE development set (described in next subsection). In bilingual experiments, we assigned 56 neurons [2] for each of $FC_{1,a}$ and $FC_{1,b}$ to learn

language-specific features and the remaining neurons for language-shared features. λ is fixed to be 0.5. Training is done via stochastic gradient descent with Adam (Kingma and Ba, 2014) optimizer with a learning rate of 0.001.

Benchmarking baseline monolingual models As we are not aware of prior work on bilingual relation extraction in similar settings, we first benchmark our baseline monolingual model on two popular monolingual datasets. We also use the ACE development dataset (described below) for tuning the parameters mentioned previously. The baseline monolingual model is similar to (Nguyen and Grishman, 2015) and only takes a English dataset as input. It is simplified from the model in Figure 1 by replacing the FC and LC layers with a fully-connected layer followed by a softmax loss. We evaluate it on two English datasets: the SemEval-2010 Task 8 dataset (Hendrickx et al., 2010) and the ACE 2005 dataset. The SemEval dataset contains 10,717 annotated examples (8,000 for training and 2,717 for testing). For ACE, to be comparable to state-of-the-art Neural Network models, we use the split in (Gormley et al., 2015; Nguyen and Grishman, 2015): find the ACE articles from news domains: broadcast conversation (*bc*), broadcast news (*bn*), newswire (*nw*), and uses news (*bn & nw*) as the training set, half of *bc* as the development set, the other half of *bc* as the test set. Table 1 and Table 2 [3] show that the performance of our monolingual baseline and various other systems. The monolingual model [4] achieves higher performance than state-the-art CNN methods with similar structure and no additional semantic features.

For the rest of the experiments, we focus on bilingual experiments. We evaluated our model on the ACE 2005 multilingual training corpus [5] which contains 596 English and 633 Chinese documents [6]. The ACE corpus consist of articles from weblogs, broadcast news, newsgroups, broadcast conversation, and is annotated exhaustively with

---

[3] The results reported in (Nguyen and Grishman, 2016) used a rich feature set (e.g., dependency parses). For fair comparison, we reported their results by running their code without those features.

[4] For fair comparison, we use the pre-trained word2vec word embeddings (Mikolov et al., 2013) with 300 dimensions for the monolingual experiments. For all other experiments, we use cross-lingual embeddings (Ammar et al., 2016).

[5] https://catalog.ldc.upenn.edu/LDC2006T06

[6] The English and Chinese documents are not translation of each other.

---

[2] We choose 56 to leave sufficient number of neurons for sharing across languages. We try 56, 63, 70 and no significant difference was observed.

Classifier	F1
SVM (Rink and Harabagiu, 2010)	77.6 (82.2)
CNN (Zeng et al., 2014a)	78.9 (82.7)
CNN (Nguyen and Grishman, 2015)	82.8
RNN (Socher et al., 2012)	74.8 (77.6)
MVRNN (Socher et al., 2012)	79.1 (82.4)
FCM (Yu et al., 2014)	80.6 (83.0)
Our English baseline	**83.23**

Table 1: Performance on SemEval-2010 Task 8 dataset (Hendrickx et al., 2010). The numbers inside parentheses are the systems using features such as WordNet (all systems), dependency parses (Yu et al., 2014) and Google n-grams (Rink and Harabagiu, 2010). Our approach does not use these features but still achieves the best result.

Classifier	P	R	F1
CNN (Nguyen and Grishman, 2016)	63.3	58.2	60.6
Our English baseline	62.1	60.1	**61.1**

Table 2: Performance on English ACE 2005 with the data split setting in (Gormley et al., 2015).

relations. For documents in English or Chinese, we collected all annotated relation mentions, and generated relation mentions for the *Other* class by sampling pairs of entity mentions within a sentence but is not annotated as having a relation. We refer to the resulted English dataset as *ACE05.ENG*, and refer to the Chinese ACE dataset as *ACE05.CHN* in the rest of this section. We divided relation mentions into 5 folds, performed cross-validation and averaged the results. As is standard (e.g. (Grishman et al., 2005)), we use the mention boundaries and types provided by the annotated data as input.

4.1 Comparing Bilingual Models to Alternative Approaches

To verify the effectiveness of our bilingual model, we compare four approaches:

- **Baseline**: We train two monolingual models on *ACE05.ENG* and *ACE05.CHN* respectively. These two models used bilingual word embedding and only used the softmax classification loss during training.
- **Bilingual-FT**: To see if having access to additional training data from another language helps, we pre-train each monolingual model with the other language(source)'s training dataset and then finetune it using the target language's training dataset [7]

---

[7]For example, we pre-train the Chinese model with ACE05.ENG, fine-tune with ACE05.CHN, then test with Chinese.

- **Bilingual-Joint** We train a bilingual model on the Chinese and English datasets jointly with the softmax loss. The model is similar to the bilingual model in Figure 1, but without the ideal representation losses [8].
- **Bilingual-Joint-IRL** We train the bilingual model on *ACE05.ENG* and *ACE05.CHN* jointly using the softmax and ideal representation loss (the complete model in Figure 1).

The results are summarized in Table 3. The pre-training approach (bilingual-FT), which pre-trains a model on the additional language's dataset and then finetune on the target language dataset, achieves better results than training the monolingual baseline. The bilingual-Joint approach can simultaneously learn language-specific and shared bilingual representations, therefore it is able to generalize across languages while still making use of language-specific information. Its performance exceeds that of baseline and bilingual-FT. The bilingual-Joint-IRL method achieves the best result: it encourages the learnt representation to be discriminative among relation types. In particular, the learnt cross-lingual representation is encouraged to differentiate relation types regardless of language. It captures both language-specific and cross-lingual relation semantics, and thus has the best of both worlds.

4.2 Transfer representations to lower-resource languages

For just a handful of languages, (e.g. English, Chinese) corpora of relation annotation are readily available. However, for most languages few (if any) such resources exist. We show that our approach yields large gains in F1 when a small amount of *target* training is combined with large amounts of existing *source* annotation.

We demonstrate our model's ability to use large amounts of *source* language data to supplement limited in-domain *target* language data with either Chinese and English as *target*. In each setting, we down-sample the *target* language dataset to 10%, 20%, 30%, 40% and 50% of its full training size and we report F1 in the test dataset in the *target* language. Figure 2 compares performance of *bilingual-Joint-IRL* with the performance of *baseline*. With access to existing, additional resources in the *source* through the bilingual model, performance on *target* doubles its F1 scores when only

---

[8]This performs bilingual representation learning by only sharing a subset of neurons in $FC1$

Approach	ACE05.ENG			ACE05.CHN		
	Precision	Recall	F1	Precision	Recall	F1
baseline	72.5	68.3	70.4	75.6	75	75.3
bilingual-FT	70.8	72.1	71.4	78.4	75.6	77.0
bilingual-Joint	72.6	73.3	72.9	77.7	76.4	77.1
bilingual-Joint-IRL	74.3	75.6	74.9	80.9	77.1	78.9

Table 3: Performances of the bilingual models on the ACE 2005 multilingual training corpus.

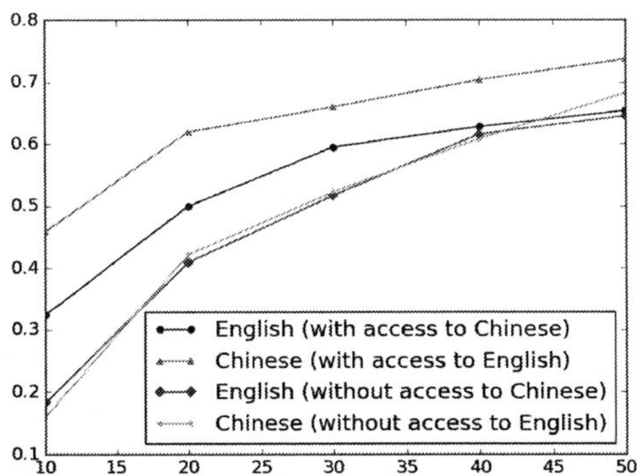

Figure 2: Performance of Chinese and English relation extraction by varying the size of in-domain training data. For the model with access to another language (*source*), we use the full dataset from the *source* but only a fraction of in-domain data in the *target* language. We sample each dataset from 10% to 50% with 10% as the incremental step size. x-axis is the percentage of training data in *target* is used, and y-axis shows F1 scores.

10% training data is available, and gains 30% to 66% relative improvement in F1 with 20% training data. The bilingual extractor trained with only 50% of the *target* training data achieves performance nearing ($< 5\%$ difference) that of the baseline approach using all of the *target* resources. This results provides a new and cost-effective way to perform relation extraction when resources are limited for a new language.

4.3 Analysis on learnt representation

Learning discriminative representations We use LC_a and LC_s to represent a sentence from language a, and use LC_b and LC_s to represent a sentence from language b. We visualize the predicted representations for testing examples in both English and Chinese in Figure 3. X-axis shows the 244 neurons [9] from locally connect layers LC_a-LC_s, and LC_b-LC_s. Y-axis shows all testing examples (each row represents an example). Each

---

[9] The number of neurons in layers LC_a and LC_b are both 56, while layer LC_s contains 188 neurons.

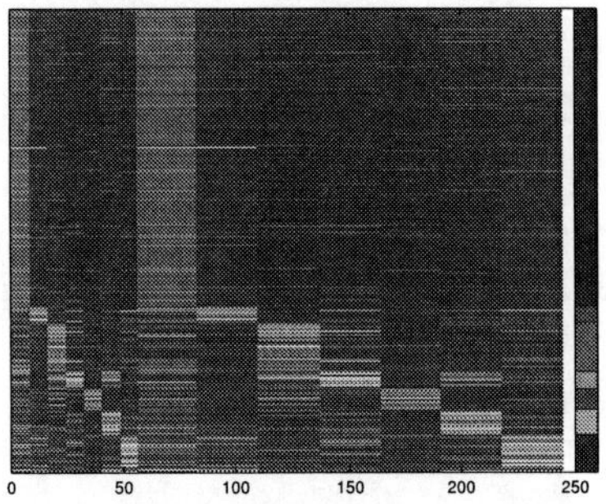

(a) ACE05.ENG set

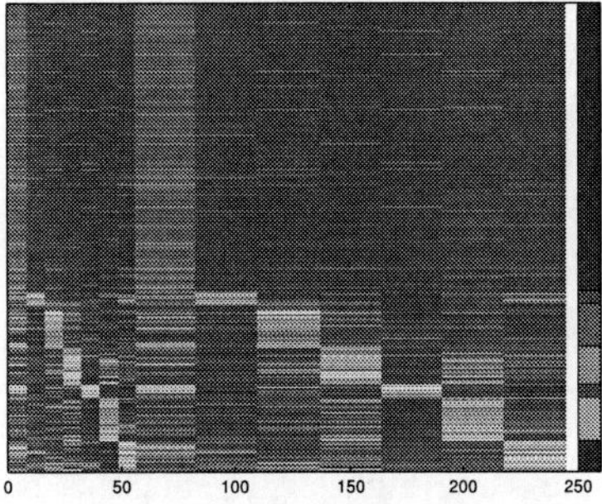

(b) ACE05.CHN set

Figure 3: Visualization of predicted presentation for test examples in both languages. X-axis indicates the 244 neurons from layers LC_a-LC_s (or LC_b-LC_s). Y-axis corresponds to the indices of test examples. The color shows strength of pairwise association between examples and neurons (the brighter the color, the stronger association). Each color in the color bar located at the right most of each subfigure represents one relation type for a subset of testing examples.

graph shows strong associations between testing examples from 7 types and 7 blocks of neurons in the hidden layer in 1) language-specific representations (the first 56 neurons as shows in x-axis [0, 55] in Figure 3 (a) and (b)) as well as 2) bilingual representation (the remaining 188 neurons as shown in x-axis [56,243] in each figure). The visualization is strongly block-diagonal. This shows that the learnt representation is discriminative in

Relation	English	Chinese
ORG-AFF	... while japanese officials ...	...应新加坡 总理吴作栋 的邀请...
PHYS	...which is ... outside the center of baghdad...	...前日在广州 被公安 寻回...
PART-WHOLE	...this is that city hall in orlando...	...亚齐省首府班达亚齐
PER-SOC	...you go to your grandma 's house	该名家长 起初以为孩子 撒谎...
GEN-AFF	joseph britt of kennesaw , ga , recently...	日本 历史上有过女天皇
ART	i 've decided i 'll take the train home later	我们 的军舰 在厂里...

Table 4: Examples of relation mentions that are found to be similar to its cross-lingual counterparts using our model. The two examples in each row is similar to each other.

predicting relation types.

Confusion matrix on bilingual relation extraction To further understand the discriminative power of the bilingual model with regard to predicting relation types, we plot the confusion matrix using the bilingual model over all examples in the ACE datasets. Figure 4 shows that our model performs well on differentiating the classes. It also shows that our algorithm performs slightly worse in differentiating *PHYS*, *PART-WHOLE* and *GEN-AFF* relations, in both English and Chinese. This is caused by the trumping rules in ACE relation definition. ACE annotation guideline defines a relation *Org-Location-Origin* (a subtype of *GEN-AFF*) for locations of ORG's, and defines another relation *Geographical* (a subtype of *PART-WHOLE*) for locations of facilities/locations/GPEs, and further defines a relation *Located* (as a subtype of *PHY*) to capture the physical location of a person. These relations share the same high-level semantics but are defined as different ACE types.

Examples of similar relation instances across languages We took the last-layer activations as a "relation embeddings" representation for each relation instance. To see how well the cross-lingual representation learning did, we calculated pairwise similarities [10] between all relation instances in Chinese and English. Table 4 shows examples in which each pair of instances in the same row in the two languages are very similar [11] to each other.

The model learns lexical similarity such as *japanese officials* and 新加坡 总理 *(Singapore prime minister)*. It also knows *city hall in orlando* is similar to 亚齐省首府班达亚齐 *(Aceh capital of Banda Aceh)*. It further learns complicated correspondence such as *you go to your grandma 's house* and 该名家长 起初以为孩子 撒谎*(The

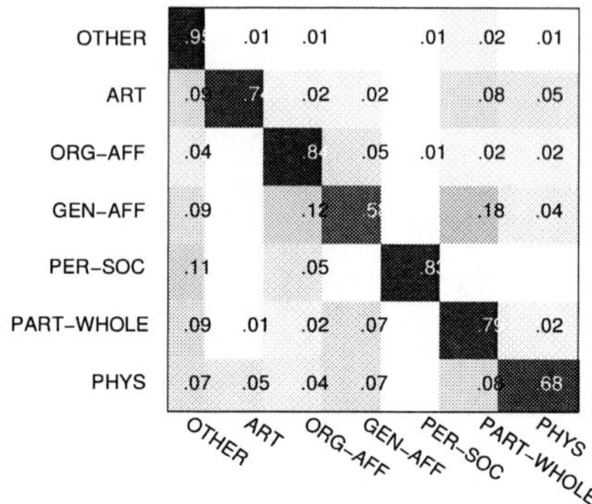

(a) ACE05.ENG set

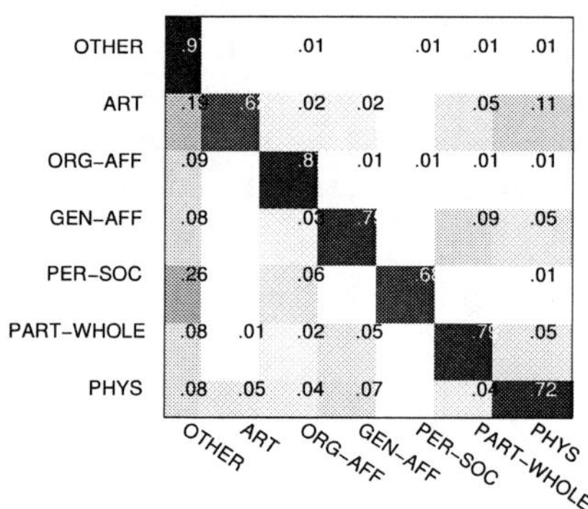

(b) ACE05.CHN set

Figure 4: Confusion matrices of *bilingual-Joint-IRL* on the ACE datasets.

parent previously thought the child was lying) The diverse range of examples in Table 4 shows that the model not only captures lexical similarity, but also syntactic and long-range semantic similarities across the pair of languages.

5 Conclusion

We present a bilingual relation extraction algorithm to learn discriminative and transferable representation across languages via a Convolutional Neural Network. Experiments show that it outperforms monolingual algorithms and the baseline algorithms significantly both when large amounts

---

[10]We use cosine distance as the similarity metric. The smaller cosine distance is, the more similar the pair.

[11]Here we define *very similar* as ranked within top-50 most similar instances in the entire dataset, with regard to the query instance from the other language.

of data are available in both languages and when only limited training data is available in the target language.

Acknowledgments

This work was supported by DARPA/I2O Contract No. FA8750-13-C-0008 under the DEFT program. The views, opinions, and/or findings contained in this article are those of the author and should not be interpreted as representing the official views or policies, either expressed or implied, of the Department of Defense or the U.S. Government. This document does not contain technology or technical data controlled under either the U.S. International Traffic in Arms Regulations or the U.S. Export Administration Regulations.

References

Waleed Ammar, George Mulcaire, Yulia Tsvetkov, Guillaume Lample, Chris Dyer, and Noah A. Smith. 2016. Massively multilingual word embeddings. *CoRR*, abs/1602.01925.

Andre Blessing and Hinrich Schütze. 2012. Crosslingual distant supervision for extracting relations of different complexity. In *Proceedings of the 21st ACM International Conference on Information and Knowledge Management*, CIKM '12, pages 1123–1132, New York, NY, USA. ACM.

Razvan Bunescu and Raymond Mooney. 2005a. A Shortest Path Dependency Kernel for Relation Extraction. In *Proceedings of Human Language Technology Conference and Conference on Empirical Methods in Natural Language Processing*, pages 724–731, Vancouver, British Columbia, Canada. Association for Computational Linguistics.

Razvan Bunescu and Raymond J Mooney. 2005b. Subsequence kernels for relation extraction. In *NIPS*, pages 171–178.

Manaal Faruqui and Shankar Kumar. 2015. Multilingual Open Relation Extraction Using Cross-lingual Projection. In *Proceedings of the 2015 Conference of the North American Chapter of the Association for Computational Linguistics: Human Language Technologies*, pages 1351–1356, Denver, Colorado. Association for Computational Linguistics.

Matthew R. Gormley, Mo Yu, and Mark Dredze. 2015. Improved relation extraction with feature-rich compositional embedding models. In *Proceedings of the 2015 Conference on Empirical Methods in Natural Language Processing*, pages 1774–1784, Lisbon, Portugal. Association for Computational Linguistics.

Ralph Grishman, David Westbrook, and Adam Meyers. 2005. Nyus english ace 2005 system description. In *ACE 2005 Evaluation Workshop*.

Jiang Guo, Wanxiang Che, David Yarowsky, Haifeng Wang, and Ting Liu. 2016. A Distributed Representation-based Framework for Cross-lingual Transfer Parsing. *J. Artif. Int. Res.*, 55(1):995–1023.

Iris Hendrickx, Su Nam Kim, Zornitsa Kozareva, Preslav Nakov, Diarmuid O Seaghdha, Sebastian Pado, Marco Pennacchiotti, Lorenza Romano, and Stan Szpakowicz. 2010. Semeval-2010 task 8: Multi-way classification of semantic relations between pairs of nominals. In *Proceedings of the 5th International Workshop on Semantic Evaluation*.

Raphael Hoffmann, Congle Zhang, Xiao Ling, Luke Zettlemoyer, and Daniel S Weld. 2011. Knowledge-Based Weak Supervision for Information Extraction of Overlapping Relations. In *Proceedings of the 49th Annual Meeting of the Association for Computational Linguistics: Human Language Technologies*, pages 541–550, Portland, Oregon, USA. Association for Computational Linguistics.

Jui-Ting Huang, Jinyu Li, Dong Yu, Li Deng, and Yifan Gong. 2013. Cross-language Knowledge Transfer using Multilingual Deep Neural Network with Shared Hidden Layers. In *IEEE International Conference on Acoustics, Speech, and Signal Processing (ICASSP)*.

Jing Jiang and ChengXiang Zhai. 2007. A systematic exploration of the feature space for relation extraction. In *Proceedings of NAACL HLT 2007*. Association for Computational Linguistics.

Zhuolin Jiang, Zhe Lin, and Larry Davis. 2011. Learning a discriminative dictionary for sparse coding via label consistent k-svd. In *Proceedings of CVPR*.

Nanda Kambhatla. 2004. Combining Lexical, Syntactic, and Semantic Features with Maximum Entropy Models for Information Extraction. In *The Companion Volume to the Proceedings of 42st Annual Meeting of the Association for Computational Linguistics*, pages 178–181, Barcelona, Spain. Association for Computational Linguistics.

Seokhwan Kim, Minwoo Jeong, Jonghoon Lee, and Gary Geunbae Lee. 2010. A Cross-lingual Annotation Projection Approach for Relation Detection. In *Proceedings of the 23rd International Conference on Computational Linguistics (Coling 2010)*, pages 564–571, Beijing, China. Coling 2010 Organizing Committee.

Seokhwan Kim, Minwoo Jeong, Jonghoon Lee, and Gary Geunbae Lee. 2014. Cross-lingual annotation projection for weakly-supervised relation extraction. *ACM Transactions on Asian Language Information Processing (TALIP)*, 13(1):3.

Diederik P. Kingma and Jimmy Ba. 2014. Adam: A method for stochastic optimization. *CoRR*, abs/1412.6980.

Alex Krizhevsky, Ilya Sutskever, and Geoffrey Hinton. 2012. Imagenet classification with deep convolutional neural networks. In *Proceedings of NIPS*.

Tomas Mikolov, Kai Chen, Greg Corrado, and Jeffrey Dean. 2013. Efficient estimation of word representations in vector space. *CoRR*, abs/1301.3781.

Mike Mintz, Steven Bills, Rion Snow, and Daniel Jurafsky. 2009. Distant supervision for relation extraction without labeled data. In *Proceedings of the Joint Conference of the 47th Annual Meeting of the ACL and the 4th International Joint Conference on Natural Language Processing of the AFNLP*, pages 1003–1011, Suntec, Singapore. Association for Computational Linguistics.

Makoto Miwa and Mohit Bansal. 2016. End-to-End Relation Extraction using LSTMs on Sequences and Tree Structures. In *Proceedings of the 54th Annual Meeting of the Association for Computational Linguistics (Volume 1: Long Papers)*, pages 1105–1116, Berlin, Germany. Association for Computational Linguistics.

Alessandro Moschitti. 2006. Efficient convolution kernels for dependency and constituent syntactic trees. In *ECML*, volume 4212, pages 318–329. Springer.

Ndapandula Nakashole, Gerhard Weikum, and Fabian Suchanek. 2012. Patty: A taxonomy of relational patterns with semantic types. In *Proceedings of the 2012 Joint Conference on Empirical Methods in Natural Language Processing and Computational Natural Language Learning*, pages 1135–1145, Jeju Island, Korea. Association for Computational Linguistics.

Thien Huu Nguyen and Ralph Grishman. 2015. Relation Extraction: Perspective from Convolutional Neural Networks. In *Proceedings of the 1st Workshop on Vector Space Modeling for Natural Language Processing*, pages 39–48, Denver, Colorado. Association for Computational Linguistics.

Thien Huu Nguyen and Ralph Grishman. 2016. Combining Neural Networks and Log-linear Models to Improve Relation Extraction. In *Proceedings of IJCAI Workshop on Deep Learning for Artificial Intelligence*, New York, USA.

Longhua Qian, Haotian Hui, Ya'nan Hu, Guodong Zhou, and Qiaoming Zhu. 2014. Bilingual Active Learning for Relation Classification via Pseudo Parallel Corpora. In *Proceedings of the 52nd Annual Meeting of the Association for Computational Linguistics (Volume 1: Long Papers)*, pages 582–592, Baltimore, Maryland. Association for Computational Linguistics.

Sebastian Riedel, Limin Yao, and Andrew McCallum. 2010. Modeling Relations and Their Mentions without Labeled Text. In *Joint European Conference on Machine Learning and Knowledge Discovery in Databases*, pages 148–163, Barcelona, Spain. Springer, Berlin, Heidelberg.

Bryan Rink and Sanda Harabagiu. 2010. Classifying semantic relations by combining lexical and semantic resources. In *Proceedings of the 5th International Workshop on Semantic Evaluation*.

Alan Ritter, Luke Zettlemoyer, Mausam, and Oren Etzioni. 2013. Modeling missing data in distant supervision. *Transactions of the Association for Computational Linguistics*.

Cicero dos Santos, Bing Xiang, and Bowen Zhou. 2015. Classifying Relations by Ranking with Convolutional Neural Networks. In *Proceedings of the 53rd Annual Meeting of the Association for Computational Linguistics and the 7th International Joint Conference on Natural Language Processing (Volume 1: Long Papers)*, pages 626–634, Beijing, China. Association for Computational Linguistics.

Cicero Nogueira Santos, Bing Xiang, and Bowen Zhou. 2015. Classifying relations by ranking with convolutional neural network. In *Proceedings of ACL*.

Richard Socher, Brody Huval, Christopher D. Manning, and Andrew Y. Ng. 2012. Semantic compositionality through recursive matrix-vector spaces. In *Proceedings of the 2012 Joint Conference on Empirical Methods in Natural Language Processing and Computational Natural Language Learning*, EMNLP-CoNLL '12, pages 1201–1211, Stroudsburg, PA, USA. Association for Computational Linguistics.

Mihai Surdeanu, Julie Tibshirani, Ramesh Nallapati, and Christopher D Manning. 2012. Multi-instance Multi-label Learning for Relation Extraction. In *Proceedings of the 2012 Joint Conference on Empirical Methods in Natural Language Processing and Computational Natural Language Learning*, pages 455–465, Jeju Island, Korea. Association for Computational Linguistics.

Patrick Verga, David Belanger, Emma Strubell, Benjamin Roth, and Andrew McCallum. 2016. Multilingual relation extraction using compositional universal schema. In *Proceedings of the 2016 Conference of the North American Chapter of the Association for Computational Linguistics: Human Language Technologies*, pages 886–896, San Diego, California. Association for Computational Linguistics.

Linlin Wang, Zhu Cao, Gerard de Melo, and Zhiyuan Liu. 2016. Relation Classification via Multi-Level Attention CNNs. In *Proceedings of the 54th Annual Meeting of the Association for Computational Linguistics (Volume 1: Long Papers)*, pages 1298–1307, Berlin, Germany. Association for Computational Linguistics.

Yan Xu, Lili Mou, Ge Li, Yunchuan Chen, Hao Peng, and Zhi Jin. 2015. Classifying Relations via Long Short Term Memory Networks along Shortest Dependency Paths. In *Proceedings of the 2015 Conference on Empirical Methods in Natural Language*

Processing, pages 1785–1794, Lisbon, Portugal. Association for Computational Linguistics.

Mo Yu, Matthew R. Gormley, and Mark Dredze. 2014. Factor-based compositional embedding models. In *Proceedings of the NIPS Learning Semantics Workshop*.

Matthew Zeiler and Rob Fergus. 2014. Visualizing and understanding convolutional networks. In *Proceedings of ECCV*.

Daojian Zeng, Kang Liu, Siwei Lai, Guangyou Zhou, and Jun Zhao. 2014a. Relation Classification via Convolutional Deep Neural Network. In *Proceedings of COLING 2014, the 25th International Conference on Computational Linguistics: Technical Papers*, pages 2335–2344, Dublin, Ireland. Dublin City University and Association for Computational Linguistics.

Daojian Zeng, Kang Liu, Siwei Lai, Guangyou Zhou, and Jun Zhao. 2014b. Relation classification via convolutional deep neural network. In *Proceedings of COLING*.

Min Zhang, Jie Zhang, and Jian Su. 2006. Exploring Syntactic Features for Relation Extraction using a Convolution Tree Kernel. In *Proceedings of the Human Language Technology Conference of the NAACL, Main Conference*, pages 288–295, New York City, USA. Association for Computational Linguistics.

Shu Zhang, Dequan Zheng, Xinchen Hu, and Ming Yang. 2015. Bidirectional Long Short-Term Memory Networks for Relation Classification. In *The 29th Pacific Asia Conference on Language, Information and Computation*, pages 73–78.

Shubin Zhao and Ralph Grishman. 2005. Extracting relations with integrated information using kernel methods. In *Proceedings of the 43rd Annual Meeting on Association for Computational Linguistics*, ACL '05, pages 419–426, Stroudsburg, PA, USA. Association for Computational Linguistics.

GuoDong Zhou, Jian Su, Jie Zhang, and Min Zhang. 2005. Exploring Various Knowledge in Relation Extraction. In *Proceedings of the 43rd Annual Meeting of the Association for Computational Linguistics (ACL'05)*, pages 427–434, Ann Arbor, Michigan. Association for Computational Linguistics.

Bilingual Word Embeddings for Bilingual Terminology Extraction from Specialized Comparable Corpora

Amir Hazem[1]   Emmanuel Morin[1]

[1] LS2N - UMR CNRS 6004, Université de Nantes, France
{amir.hazem,emmanuel.morin}@univ-nantes.fr

Abstract

Bilingual lexicon extraction from comparable corpora is constrained by the small amount of available data when dealing with specialized domains. This aspect penalizes the performance of distributional-based approaches, which is closely related to the reliability of word's cooccurrence counts extracted from comparable corpora. A solution to avoid this limitation is to associate external resources with the comparable corpus. Since bilingual word embeddings have recently shown efficient models for learning bilingual distributed representation of words, we explore different word embedding models and show how a general-domain comparable corpus can enrich a specialized comparable corpus via neural networks.

1 Introduction

Bilingual lexicon extraction from comparable corpora has shown substantial growth since the seminal work of Fung (1995) and Rapp (1995). Comparable corpora, which are comprised of texts sharing common features such as domain, genre, sampling period, etc. and without having a source text/target text relationship (McEnery and Xiao, 2007), are more abundant and reliable resources than parallel corpora. On the one hand, parallel corpora are difficult to obtain for language pairs not involving English. On the other hand, as parallel corpora are comprised of a pair of translated texts, the vocabulary appearing in the translated texts is highly influenced by the source texts. These problems are aggravated in specialized and technical domains.

Although it is easier to build large general-domain comparable corpora, specialized comparable corpora are often of modest size (around 1 million words) due to the difficulty to obtain many specialized documents in a language other than English. Consequently, word co-occurrence counts of the historical context-based projection approach, known as the *standard approach* (Fung, 1995; Rapp, 1995), dedicated to bilingual lexicon extraction from comparable corpora are unreliable in specialized domain. This problem persists with other paradigms such as Canonical Correlation Analysis (CCA) (Gaussier et al., 2004), Independent Component Analysis (ICA) (Hazem and Morin, 2012) and Bilingual Latent Dirichlet Allocation (BiLDA) (Vulić et al., 2011).

A solution to avoid this limitation and to increase the representativity of distributional representations is to associate external resources with the specialized comparable corpus. These resources can be lexical databases such as WordNet which allows the disambiguation of translations of polysemous words (Bouamor et al., 2013) or general-domain data to improve word cooccurrence counts of specialized comparable corpora (Hazem and Morin, 2016).

Our work is in this line and attempts to find out how a general-domain data can enrich a specialized comparable corpora to improve bilingual terminology extraction from specialized comparable corpora. Since bilingual word embeddings have recently provided efficient models for learning bilingual distributed representation of words from large general-domain data (Mikolov et al., 2013), we contrast different popular word embedding models for this task. In addition, we explore combinations of word embedding models as suggested by Garten et al. (2015) to improve distributed representations. We compare the results obtained with the state-of-the-art context-based projection approach. Our results show under which conditions the proposed model can compete with state-

Proceedings of the The 8th International Joint Conference on Natural Language Processing, pages 685–693,
Taipei, Taiwan, November 27 – December 1, 2017 ©2017 AFNLP

of-the art approaches. To the best of our knowledge, this is the first time that word embedding models have been used to extract bilingual lexicons from specialized comparable corpora.

The remainder of this paper is organized as follows. Section 2 presents the two state-of-the-art approaches used to extract bilingual lexicons from comparable corpora. Section 3 describes the two data combination approaches adapted to Skip-gram and CBOW models (Mikolov et al., 2013). Section 4 describes the different linguistic resources used in our experiments. Section 5 is then devoted to a large-scale evaluation of the different proposed methods. Finally, Section 6 presents our conclusion.

2 State-of-the-Art Approaches

In this section, we describe the two state-of-the-art approaches used to extract bilingual lexicons from comparable corpora.

These approaches are both based on monolingual lexical context analysis and relies on the distributional hypothesis (Harris, 1968) which postulates that a word and its translation tend to appear in the same lexical contexts. This is the hypothesis that tends to be reduced to the famous sentence of the British linguist J. R. Firth (1957, p. 11) who said: *"You shall know a word by the company it keeps."* even if the context was related to collocates.

The two approaches are known as distributional and distributed semantics (according to Hermann and Blunsom (2014)). The first one is based on vector space models while the second one is based on neural language models.

2.1 Context-Based Projection Approach

The historical context-based projection approach, known as the standard approach, has been studied by a number of researchers (Fung, 1998; Rapp, 1999; Chiao and Zweigenbaum, 2002; Morin et al., 2007; Prochasson and Fung, 2011; Bouamor et al., 2013; Morin and Hazem, 2016, among others). Its implementation can be carried out by applying the following steps:

1. For each word w of the source and the target languages, we build a context vector (resp. s and t for source and target languages) consisting in the measure of association of each word that appears in a short window of words around w. The association measures traditionally studied are Mutual Information, Log-likelihood, and the Discounted Odds-Ratio.

2. For a word i to be translated, its context vector $\mathbf{i}$ is projected from the source to the target language by translating each element of its context vector thanks to a bilingual seed lexicon.

3. The translated context vector $\bar{\mathbf{i}}$ is compared to each context vector $\mathbf{t}$ of the target language using a similarity measure such as Cosine or weighted Jaccard. The candidate translations are then ranked according to the scores of a given similarity measure.

This approach is very sensitive to the choice of parameters. We invite readers to consult the study of Laroche and Langlais (2010) in which the influence of parameters such as the size of the context, the choice of the association and similarity measures have been examined.

In order to improve the quality of bilingual terminology extraction from specialized comparable corpora, Hazem and Morin (2016) have proposed two ways to combine specialized comparable corpora with external resources. The hypothesis is that word co-occurrences learned from a large general-domain corpus for general words improve the characterisation of the specific vocabulary of the specialized corpus. The first adaptation called Global Standard Approach (GSA) is basic and consists in building the context vectors from a comparable corpus composed of the specialized and the general comparable corpora. The second adaptation called Selective Standard Approach (SSA) is more sophisticated and comprises: i) independently building context vectors of the specialized and general comparable corpus and then ii) merging under certain conditions, specialized and general context vectors of the words belonging to the specialized corpus when they appear in the general corpus.

2.2 Word Embedding Based Approach

Bilingual word embeddings has become a source of great interest in recent times (Mikolov et al., 2013; Vulić and Moens, 2013; Zou et al., 2013; Chandar et al., 2014; Gouws et al., 2014; Artetxe et al., 2016, among others). Mikolov et al. (2013) was the first to propose a method to learn a linear transformation from the source language to the target language to improve the task of lexicon extraction from bilingual corpora.

During the training time of Mikolov's method, for all $\{x_i, z_i\}_{i=1}^{n}$ bilingual word pairs of the seed lexicon, the word embedding $x_i \in \mathbb{R}^{d_1}$ of word i in the source language and the word embedding $z_i \in \mathbb{R}^{d_2}$ of its translation in the target language are computed. A transformation matrix W such as Wx_i approximates z_i is then learned by the objective function as follows:

$$\min_{W} \sum_{i=1}^{n} \|Wx_i - z_i\|^2 \tag{1}$$

At prediction time, we can transfer the word embedding x for a word to be translated in the target language using the translation matrix such as $z = Wx$. The candidate translations are obtained by ranking the closest target words to z according to a similarity measure such as the Cosine measure.

Recently, Artetxe et al. (2016) presented an approach for learning bilingual mappings of word embeddings that preserves monolingual invariance using several meaningful and intuitive constraints related to other proposed methods (Faruqui and Dyer, 2014; Xing et al., 2015). These constraints are orthogonality, vectors length normalization for maximum cosine and mean centering for maximum covariance. Monolingual invariance tends to preserve the dot products after mapping, in order to avoid performance drop in monolingual tasks, while dimension-wise mean centering tends to insure that two randomly taken words would not be semantically related. This approach has shown meaningful improvements for both monolingual and bilingual tasks.

Other work has focused on learning bilingual word representations without word-to-word alignments of comparable corpora. Chandar et al. (2014) and Gouws et al. (2014) use multilingual word embeddings based on sentence-aligned parallel data whereas Vulić and Moens (2015, 2016) propose a model to induce bilingual word embeddings directly from document-aligned non-parallel data. Theses works are based on sentence- or document-aligned of general-domain comparable corpora and are outside the scope of this study. It is unlikely, not to say impossible, to find this type of alignment in a specialized comparable corpus.

3 Data Combination Using Neural Networks

Recently, Hazem and Morin (2016) have shown that using external data drastically improves the performance of the traditional distributional-based approach for the task of bilingual lexicon extraction from specialized comparable corpora. Mikolov et al. (2013) have also shown that distributed vector representations over large corpora in a continuous space model capture many linguistic regularities and key aspects of words. Based on these findings, we pursue the preceding works and propose different ways to combine specialized and general domain data using neural network models. We adapt the two data combination approaches proposed in Hazem and Morin (2016) (see Section 2.1) using Skip-gram and CBOW models (Mikolov et al., 2013). Inspired by the work of Garten et al. (2015) which studied different combinations of distributed vector representations for word analogy task, we also propose different Skip-gram and CBOW models combinations over specialized and general domain data.

3.1 Global Data Combination Using Neural Network Models

This approach can be seen as similar to the GSA approach (Hazem and Morin, 2016), the difference is that instead of using the context-based projection approach to build context vectors, we use the distributed Skip-gram or Continuous Bag-of-Words (CBOW) models proposed in Mikolov et al. (2013). Given a specialized and a general domain corpus, we create a new corpus which is the combination of both. We then learn a Skip-gram model (respectively a CBOW model) using this new generated corpus. We denote this approach by GSG for the global[1] Skip-gram model and GCBOW for the global CBOW model.

After combining the two corpora, the steps for extracting bilingual lexicons are as follows:

1. We first build a CBOW (respectively a Skip-gram) model for source and target languages.

2. Then, we apply bilingual mapping (Artetxe et al., 2016) between the source and the target CBOW models (respectively the Skip-gram models). The mapping step needs a bilingual dictionary to compute the mapping ma-

---

[1]The term *global* refers to a global combination of data without any specific criterion.

trix. We used a dictionary subset of the 5,000 more frequent translation pairs. Different sizes of the seed dictionary have been studied and discussed in Jakubina and Langlais (2016). It should be noted that in our experiments, no great impact has been observed when varying the size of the dictionary subset.

3. For each word to be translated, we compute a Cosine similarity between its mapped embedding vector and the embedding vectors of all the target words.

4. Finally, we rank the candidates according to their similarity score.

3.2 Specific Data Combination Using Neural Network Models

This approach is in the line of the SSA (Hazem and Morin, 2016) approach but the idea is not exactly the same. Similarly to them we build two separate representations. One learned from a specialized domain corpus and the second learned from a general-domain corpus, but unlike them we concatenate the distributed models while they merge [2] distributional context vectors.

Our goal is to capture the two word characterisations thanks to CBOW/Skipgram models. One is issued from the specialized domain and the other one from the general domain, to finally combine both representations in the perspective of obtaining a better word representation. Our approach is as follows:

1. We first build a CBOW (respectively a Skipgram) model for both specialized and general domain source and target languages.

2. Then, we concatenate source CBOW vectors (respectively Skip-gram vectors) of the specialized and the general domain data. We apply the same process for specialized and general-domain target data.

3. We apply bilingual mapping (Artetxe et al., 2016) between the source and target concatenated vectors.

4. For each word to be translated, we compute a Cosine similarity between its mapped embedding vector and the embedding vectors of all the target words.

5. Finally, we rank the candidates according to their similarity score.

3.3 Combining Distributed Representations

We follow the findings of Garten et al. (2015) where they have shown substantial improvements on a standard word analogy task, combining distributed vector representations (more specifically, vectors concatenation). They compared their hybrid methods and have shown their advantages especially when training data is limited, which is the main problem in the task of extracting bilingual terminology from specialized comparable corpora.

In our case, word embedding models lead to three different ways of concatenation. The first one is a CBOW model concatenation between the specialized and the general domain data. The second one is a Skip-gram model concatenation and the third one is a concatenation of both CBOW and Skip-gram models.

If for instance we have a 100 dimension specialized CBOW model and a 200 dimension general domain CBOW model. The concatenation will lead to a resulting 300 dimension CBOW model. If we also have a 100 dimension specialized Skip-gram model and a 200 dimension general domain Skip-gram model. The concatenation will lead to a resulting 300 dimension Skip-gram model. Finally, if we concatenate the CBOW and Skip-gram models, this will result in a 600 dimension combined model. This final concatenation process allows to take advantage of both CBOW and Skip-gram models and to learn a mapping matrix of the combined models. To our knowledge this is the first attempt to first encode CBOW⌢CBOW[3], Skip-gram⌢Skip-gram and CBOW⌢Skip-gram models before learning a bilingual mapping matrix.

4 Data and Resources

In this section, we briefly outline the different textual resources used for our experiments: the comparable corpora, the bilingual dictionary and the terminology reference list. These textual resources are a subset of the data used in Hazem and Morin (2016).

---

[2] The merging process can be seen as a simple vector addition.

[3] CBOW⌢CBOW stands for the concatenation of two CBOW vectors issued from two different training datasets.

4.1 Comparable corpora

The specialized comparable corpus consists of scientific papers collected from the Elsevier website[4]. The scientific papers were taken from the medical domain within the sub-domain of "breast cancer". The breast cancer comparable corpus (BC) is composed of 103 English documents and 130 French documents.

The four general-domain comparable corpora are of different types and sizes often used in multiple evaluation campaigns such as WMT. News commentary corpus consists of political and economic commentary crawled from the web (NC), Europarl corpus is a parallel corpus extracted from the proceedings of the European Parliament (EP7), JRC acquis corpus is a collection of legislative European Union documents (JRC) and Common Crawl corpus (CC) which encompasses over petabytes of web crawled data collected over seven years. It should be noted that we do not take advantage of the parallel information encoded in the parallel corpora.

Table 1 shows the number of content words (# content words) for each corpus.

Comparable corpus	# content words	
	FR	EN
BC	8,221	79.07
NC	5.7M	4.7M
EP7	61.8M	55.7M
JRC	70.3M	64.2M
CC	91.3M	81.1M

Table 1: Characteristics of the specialized comparable corpus and the external data.

The documents were pre-processed through basic linguistic steps such as tokenization, part-of-speech tagging and lemmatization using the TTC TermSuite[5] tool that applies the same method to several languages including English and French. Finally, the function words were removed thanks to a stopword list and the hapax [6] were discarded.

4.2 Bilingual Dictionary

The bilingual dictionary is the French/English dictionary ELRA-M0033[7] (243,539 entries). This re-

source is a general language dictionary which contains only a few terms related to the medical domain.

4.3 Gold Standard

The bilingual terminology reference list required to evaluate the quality of bilingual terminology extraction from comparable corpora has been derived from the UMLS[8] meta-thesaurus. The terminology reference list is composed of 248 single word pairs for which each word appears at least 5 times in the comparable corpus. This list is of a standard size compared to other works such as Chiao and Zweigenbaum (2002): 95 single words, Morin et al. (2007): 100 single words and Bouamor et al. (2013): 125 and 79 single words.

5 Experiments and Results

The first piece of work comparing methods for identifying translation pairs in comparable corpora was presented in Jakubina and Langlais (2016). However the evaluation was conducted on Wikipedia, which is a general domain corpus. In our case, we are interested in specialized domains where there is a lack of specialized data. Our experiments aim at exploring word embeddings performance in specialized comparable corpora, which is to our knowledge, the first attempt at tackling this problem. Moreover, and as it has been pointed out in Mikolov et al. (2013), applications to low resource domains is a very interesting topic where there is still much to be explored.

In this section, we compare different word embedding representations for the extraction of bilingual terms from specialized comparable corpora. We contrast Skip-gram and CBOW models as well as different ways of combining them over specialized and general domain corpora.

5.1 Word2vec

For word2vec, we used as settings a window size of 10, negative sampling of 5, sampling of 1e-3 and training over 15 iterations. We applied both Skip-gram and CBOW models[9] to create vectors of 100 dimensions. We used hierarchical softmax for training the Skip-gram model. Other settings were assessed but on average the chosen ones tend to give the best results on our data.

---

[4] www.elsevier.com
[5] code.google.com/p/ttc-project
[6] Tokens that appear only once in the corpus.
[7] catalog.elra.info/product_info.php?products_id=666

[8] www.nlm.nih.gov/research/umls
[9] To train word embedding models we used the gensim toolkit (Rehurek and Sojka, 2010)

Corpus	CBOW	SG	Concat
BC	17.1	12.8	20.8
NC	33.9	31.2	33.6
EP7	42.3	40.8	43.1
JRC	40.3	40.5	43.4
CC	60.9	56.0	**61.0**
BC ∪ NC	42.9	37.7	46.3
BC ∪ EP7	47.2	49.0	53.3
BC ∪ JRC	49.9	46.5	53.0
BC ∪ CC	67.7	63.2	**68.4**
BC⌢(BC ∪ NC)	45.5	30.7	48.1
BC⌢(BC ∪ EP7)	51.6	35.7	53.8
BC⌢(BC ∪ JRC)	53.7	36.3	56.1
BC⌢(BC ∪ CC)	70.7	40.2	**70.9**

Table 2: Results (MAP %) of word2vec using the Skip-gram model (noted SG), the Continuous Bag of Words model (noted CBOW) and the concatenation of both models (noted Concat). The window size was set to 10 and the vector size to 100.

5.2 Bilingual Mappings of Word Embeddings

For mapping words of the source language to the target language we follow the method presented in Artetxe et al. (2016) where they presented an efficient exact method to learn the optimal linear transformation that gives the best results in translation induction. While we contrasted different configurations of there framework, we only present the best results. We used the orthogonal mapping with length normalization and mean centering of vectors[10].

5.3 Results

Table 2 shows the results of word2vec according to different configurations. The first column represents the corpora that have been used to train word2vec models. The first bloc lines compares the performance of word2vec models on the specialized breast cancer corpus (BC) and the four external data that are: news commentary (NC), EuroParl (EP7), JRC acquis (JRC) and common crawl (CC). The second bloc lines compares the models trained on the combination of BC with each external corpus. For instance BC ∪ EP7 consists of training word2vec on the combination of BC and EP7. Finally, the third bloc lines shows the concatenation of two models, the first one trained on the specialized corpus (BC) and the second one trained on the combination of BC with a given external corpus (BC ∪ EP7 for instance).

This is noted by BC⌢(BC∪EP7) for the concatenation (represented by ⌢) of vectors of BC with vectors of BC ∪ EP7. The first column of the second and third blocs shows CBOW concatenation while the second shows Skip-gram concatenation. The third column shows CBOW and Skip-gram concatenation. Concatenate BC with BC ∪ EP7 instead of BC with EP7 (noted BC⌢EP7) for instance, insures the presence of all specialized domain words in both models.

The first observation that can be seen from Table 2 is that the results are very low when using the specialized BC corpus only (the maximum obtained MAP is 20.8% for the Concat model). The second observation is that using external data only gives better results. The best obtained MAP score is 61.0% when using CC corpus. This is certainly due to the presence of medical terms in the general domain corpora which have been crawled from the web and can contain scientific pages. Over the first bloc lines results, we can see that CBOW model outperforms Skip-gram model in most cases which is not surprising in the sense that CBOW aims at characterising a word according to its context while Skip-gram characterises a context according to a given word. From this point CBOW is more appropriate for our task. However, combining both CBOW and Skip-gram as shown by the Concat model, always improves the MAP scores. This is an important finding that shows that both models are complementary.

According to the second bloc lines results, we

---

[10]These parameters have also shown the best results in Artetxe et al. (2016).

Word2vec + Mapping	BC_{concat}	CC_{concat}
Unconstrained + Original	11.4	48.0
Orthogonal + Original	19.5	69.9
Unconstrained + Unit	11.8	50.4
Orthogonal + Unit	19.0	70.1
Unconstrained + Unit + Center	12.3	54.0
Orthogonal + Unit + Center	**20.8**	**70.9**

Table 3: Results (MAP %) of word2vec using different mapping techniques.

	BC	NC	EP7	JRC	CC
SA	27.0	45.3	48.5	52.0	75.5
GSA	-	**58.9**	58.3	61.7	80.2
SSA	-	**58.9**	**60.8**	**66.6**	**82.3**
GCBOW	17.1	42.9	47.2	49.9	67.7
GSG	12.8	37.7	49.2	46.5	63.2
GCBOW + GSG	20.8	46.3	53.3	53.0	68.4
SCBOW	-	45.5	51.6	53.7	70.7
SSG	-	30.7	35.7	36.3	40.2
SCBOW + SSG	-	48.1	53.8	56.1	70.9

Table 4: Results (MAP %) of the *Standard Approach* (*SA*), the *Global Standard Approach* (*GSA*) and the *Selective Standard Approach* (*SSA*) for the breast cancer corpus (BC) using the different external data (the improvements indicate a significance at the 0.001 level using the Student t-test).

observe that combining the specialized bilingual corpus (BC) with external data always improves the results. This can be noticed for the BC ∪ CC corpus where we increase the MAP score for CBOW from 60.9% to 67.7%, the MAP score for Skip-gram from 56% to 63.2% and the MAP score for the Concat approach from 61% to 68.4%. These are also interesting results which coincide with the observations of Hazem and Morin (2016). Hence, combining specific and general domain corpora before applying any model always benefits the task of bilingual terminology extraction.

Finally, for the third bloc lines where we combine the model issued from the first bloc (the BC model) and models issued from the second bloc lines (BC∪EP7 for instance), two observations need to be pointed out. The first one is that for CBOW model concatenation we still get improvements as we can see for CC where we gain 3 points (from 67.7% to 70.7% of MAP score). The second surprising observation is that Skip-gram concatenation decreases the results. This drop may suggest that Skip-gram concatenation is not appropriate for this configuration. However the concatenation of CBOW and Skip-gram

models (the Concat approach) still improves the results as we can see for BC⌢(BC ∪ JRC) where we move from 53% to 56.1% of MAP score and for BC⌢(BC ∪ CC) where we increase the MAP score from 68.4% to 70.9%. For this last result the gain is not that important compared to the CBOW⌢CBOW model that obtains a MAP score of 70.7%.

In Table 3 we report a comparison of different mappings as studied in Artetxe et al. (2016). We contrast unconstrained and orthogonal mappings using original as well as length normalization (noted *unit*) and mean centering (noted *Center*). As we can see, the best results are those obtained using orthogonal mapping with length normalization and mean centering. We reach the same conclusions as Artetxe et al. (2016).

In Table 4 we present the results from Hazem and Morin (2016) of the standard approach (noted *SA*) using only specialized comparable corpora (BC) or using only external data (NC, EP7, JRC and CC), in addition to the two adapted standard approaches (noted *GSA* and *SSA*) using the combination of each specialized comparable corpus with each corpus of the external data. We also report the best results of each of the three word embedding methods that we introduced earlier in Table 2.

Even if we obtained improvements over our different embedding models, we are still below the standard approach as seen in Table 4. The lack of specialized data may partially explain these lower results as well as the multiple tuning parameters of CBOW and Skip-gram models.

6 Conclusion

In this paper, we have proposed and contrasted different data combinations using neural networks for bilingual terminology extraction from specialized comparable corpora. We have shown under which conditions external resources as well as Skip-gram and CBOW models can be jointly used to improve the performance of bilingual terms extraction. If the results are encouraging, we were unable to compete with the results of the historical context-based projection approach. However, our findings may suggest a starting point of applying word embeddings and the multiple proposed variants to specialized domains as well as to other tasks. We hope this work will help to lead the way in exploring low resource domains such as specialized comparable corpora.

Acknowledgments

The research leading to these results has received funding from the French National Research Agency under grant ANR-17-CE23-0001 ADDICTE (Distributional analysis in specialized domain).

References

Mikel Artetxe, Gorka Labaka, and Eneko Agirre. 2016. Learning principled bilingual mappings of word embeddings while preserving monolingual invariance. In *Proceedings of the 2016 Conference on Empirical Methods in Natural Language Processing (EMNLP'16)*, pages 2289–2294, Austin, TX, USA.

Dhouha Bouamor, Nasredine Semmar, and Pierre Zweigenbaum. 2013. Context vector disambiguation for bilingual lexicon extraction from comparable corpora. In *Proceedings of the 51st Annual Meeting of the Association for Computational Linguistics (ACL'13)*, pages 759–764, Sofia, Bulgaria.

A. P. Sarath Chandar, Stanislas Lauly, Hugo Larochelle, Mitesh M. Khapra, Balaraman Ravindran, Vikas C. Raykar, and Amrita Saha. 2014. An autoencoder approach to learning bilingual word representations. In *Proceedings of the Annual Conference on Neural Information Processing Systems (NIPS'14)*, pages 1853–1861, Montreal, Quebec, Canada.

Yun-Chuang Chiao and Pierre Zweigenbaum. 2002. Looking for candidate translational equivalents in specialized, comparable corpora. In *Proceedings of the 19th International Conference on Computational Linguistics (COLING'02)*, pages 1208–1212, Tapei, Taiwan.

Manaal Faruqui and Chris Dyer. 2014. Improving vector space word representations using multilingual correlation. In *Proceedings of the 14th Conference of the European Chapter of the Association for Computational Linguistics (EACL'14)*, pages 462–471, Gothenburg, Sweden.

John Rupert Firth. 1957. A synopsis of linguistic theory 1930–1955. In *Studies in Linguistic Analysis (special volume of the Philological Society)*, pages 1–32. Blackwell, Oxford.

Pascale Fung. 1995. Compiling bilingual lexicon entries from a non-parallel english-chinese corpus. In *Proceedings of the 3rd Annual Workshop on Very Large Corpora (VLC'95)*, pages 173–183, Cambridge, MA, USA.

Pascale Fung. 1998. A statistical view on bilingual lexicon extraction: From parallel corpora to nonparallel corpora. In *Proceedings of the 3rd Conference of the Association for Machine Translation in the Americas on Machine Translation and the Information Soup (AMTA'98)*, pages 1–17, Langhorne, PA, USA.

Justin Garten, Kenji Sagae, Volkan Ustun, and Morteza Dehghani. 2015. Combining distributed vector representations for words. In *Proceedings of the 1st Workshop on Vector Space Modeling for Natural Language Processing*, pages 95–101, Denver, CO, USA.

Eric. Gaussier, Jean-Michel Renders, Irena. Matveeva, Cyril. Goutte, and Hervé Déjean. 2004. A geometric view on bilingual lexicon extraction from comparable corpora. In *Proceedings of the 42nd Annual Meeting of the Association for Computational Linguistics (ACL'04)*, pages 526–533, Barcelona, Spain.

Stephan Gouws, Yoshua Bengio, and Greg Corrado. 2014. Bilbowa: Fast bilingual distributed representations without word alignments. *CoRR*, abs/1410.2455.

Z. S. Harris. 1968. *Mathematical Structures of Language*. Interscience Publishers.

Amir Hazem and Emmanuel Morin. 2012. Adaptive dictionary for bilingual lexicon extraction from comparable corpora. In *Proceedings of the Eight International Conference on Language Resources and Evaluation (LREC'12)*, pages 288–292, Istanbul, Turkey.

Amir Hazem and Emmanuel Morin. 2016. Efficient data selection for bilingual terminology extraction from comparable corpora. In *Proceedings of the 26th International Conference on Computational Linguistics (COLING'16)*, pages 3401–3411, Osaka, Japan.

Karl Moritz Hermann and Phil Blunsom. 2014. Multilingual models for compositional distributed semantics. In *Proceedings of the 52nd Annual Meeting of the Association for Computational Linguistics (ACL'14)*, pages 58–68, Baltimore, Maryland.

Laurent Jakubina and Phillippe Langlais. 2016. A comparison of methods for identifying the translation of words in a comparable corpus: Recipes and limits. *Computación y Sistemas*, 20(3):449–458.

Audrey Laroche and Philippe Langlais. 2010. Revisiting Context-based Projection Methods for Term-Translation Spotting in Comparable Corpora. In *Proceedings of the 23rd International Conference on Computational Linguistics (COLING'10)*, pages 617–625, Beijing, China.

Anthony McEnery and Zhonghua Xiao. 2007. Parallel and comparable corpora: What are they up to? In Gunilla Anderman and Margaret Rogers, editors, *Incorporating Corpora: Translation and the Linguist*, Multilingual Matters, chapter 2, pages 18–31. Clevedon, UK.

Tomas Mikolov, Quoc V. Le, and Ilya Sutskever. 2013. Exploiting similarities among languages for machine translation. *CoRR*, abs/1309.4168.

Emmanuel Morin, Béatrice Daille, Koichi Takeuchi, and Kyo Kageura. 2007. Bilingual Terminology Mining – Using Brain, not brawn comparable corpora. In *Proceedings of the 45th Annual Meeting of the Association for Computational Linguistics (ACL'07)*, pages 664–671, Prague, Czech Republic.

Emmanuel Morin and Amir Hazem. 2016. Exploiting unbalanced specialized comparable corpora for bilingual lexicon extraction. *Natural Language Engineering*, 22(4):575–601.

Emmanuel Prochasson and Pascale Fung. 2011. Rare Word Translation Extraction from Aligned Comparable Documents. In *Proceedings of the 49th Annual Meeting of the Association for Computational Linguistics (ACL'11)*, pages 1327–1335, Portland, OR, USA.

Reinhard Rapp. 1995. Identify Word Translations in Non-Parallel Texts. In *Proceedings of the 35th Annual Meeting of the Association for Computational Linguistics (ACL'95)*, pages 320–322, Boston, MA, USA.

Reinhard Rapp. 1999. Automatic Identification of Word Translations from Unrelated English and German Corpora. In *Proceedings of the 37th Annual Meeting of the Association for Computational Linguistics (ACL'99)*, pages 519–526, College Park, MD, USA.

Radim Rehurek and Petr Sojka. 2010. Software Framework for Topic Modelling with Large Corpora. In *Proceedings of the LREC 2010 Workshop on New Challenges for NLP Frameworks*, pages 45–50, Valletta, Malta. ELRA.

Ivan Vulić, Wim De Smet, and Marie-Francine Moens. 2011. Identifying word translations from comparable corpora using latent topic models. In *Proceedings of the 49th Annual Meeting of the Association for Computational Linguistics (ACL'11)*, pages 479–484, Portland, OR, USA.

Ivan Vulić and Marie-Francine Moens. 2013. A study on bootstrapping bilingual vector spaces from non-parallel data (and nothing else). In *Proceedings of the 2013 Conference on Empirical Methods in Natural Language Processing (EMNLP'13)*, pages 1613–1624, Seattle, WA, USA.

Ivan Vulić and Marie-Francine Moens. 2015. Bilingual word embeddings from non-parallel document-aligned data applied to bilingual lexicon induction. In *Proceedings of the 53rd Annual Meeting of the Association for Computational Linguistics (ACL'15)*, pages 719–725, Beijing, China.

Ivan Vulić and Marie-Francine Moens. 2016. Bilingual distributed word representations from document-aligned comparable data. *Journal of Artificial Intelligence Research (JAIR)*, 55(1):953–994.

Chao Xing, Dong Wang, Chao Liu, and Yiye Lin. 2015. Normalized word embedding and orthogonal transform for bilingual word translation. In *Proceedings of the 2015 Conference of the North American Chapter of the Association for Computational Linguistics: Human Language Technologies (NAACL'15)*, pages 1006–1011, Denver, CO, USA.

Will Y. Zou, Richard Socher, Daniel M. Cer, and Christopher D. Manning. 2013. Bilingual word embeddings for phrase-based machine translation. In *Proceedings of the 2013 Conference on Empirical Methods in Natural Language Processing (EMNLP'13)*, pages 1393–1398, Seattle, WA, USA.

A Bambara Tonalization System for Word Sense Disambiguation Using Differential Coding, Segmentation and Edit Operation Filtering

Luigi (Yu-Cheng) Liu
ER-TIM, INALCO, 2 rue de Lille, Paris, France
`luigi.liu@laposte.net`

Damien Nouvel
ER-TIM, INALCO, 2 rue de Lille, Paris, France
`damien.nouvel@inalco.fr`

Abstract

In many languages such as Bambara or Arabic, tone markers (diacritics) may be written but are actually often omitted. NLP applications are confronted to ambiguities and subsequent difficulties when processing texts. To circumvent this problem, tonalization may be used, as a word sense disambiguation task, relying on context to add diacritics that partially disambiguate words as well as senses. In this paper, we describe our implementation of a Bambara tonalizer that adds tone markers using machine learning (CRFs). To make our tool efficient, we used differential coding, word segmentation and edit operation filtering. We describe our approach that allows tractable machine learning and improves accuracy: our model may be learned within minutes on a 358K-word corpus and reaches 92.3% accuracy.

1 Introduction

Bambara (Bamana, Bamanankan, ISO-369 Bam) is the most widely spoken language of the Manding language group. It is spoken mainly in Mali (and among the considerable Malian diaspora) by 12 to 15 million people. It is not an official language; however it is the major language (besides French) on Malian radio and TV broadcasts, there are newspapers in Bambara, it is broadly used in humanities and in primary schools, and it is taught at several universities around the world. In the Mande language family, Bambara is among the best described: there are numerous works on Bambara language, such as dictionaries (Bailleul, 2007; Dumestre, 2011), description of its grammar (Dumestre, 2003; Vydrin, 1999b,a).

Bambara is a tonal language, with the important drawback that its official orthography does not represent tones. Because several tonalized forms can correspond to some unaccented tokens, it makes word sense more ambiguous in corpus and imposes important challenges to NLP applications. Our goal is to remedy this issue by implementing an automatic tonalizer for Bambara, to improve subsequent NLP processings and facilitate linguistic analysis for Bambara.

2 Bambara Reference Corpus

Our work relies on an annotated corpus, the Bambara Reference Corpus (BRC, in French *Corpus Bambara de Référence*), a linguistically annotated corpus suitable both for linguistic research and for NLP tools development. Building BRC started in 2010 as a project conducted by a small group of specialists in Manding linguistics and computer sciences in Russia. Later on, colleagues from other countries (France, Germany) joined the team to provide more texts, clean the corpus, and automatically preprocess it. The corpus is available online since April 2012, most relevant information about the project may be found online[1] or in publications (Vydrin, 2013, 2014).

Part \ Type	Words (dist.)	Punct.
Non-disamb.	2,160,155 (58,277)	358,659
Disamb.	358,794 (23,875)	61,847

Table 1: Corpus statistics

Table 1 and Figure 1 present overall corpus statistics and characteristics [2]. The corpus consists

---

[1] `http://cormand.huma-num.fr/index.html`
[2] Corpus is continuously growing and contains, as of June 2017, 4,113,006 raw words and 903,585 in the disambiguated part.

Proceedings of the The 8th International Joint Conference on Natural Language Processing, pages 694–703,
Taipei, Taiwan, November 27 – December 1, 2017 ©2017 AFNLP

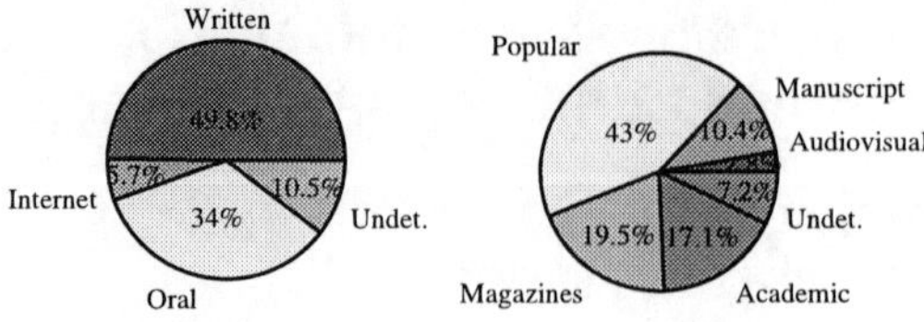

Figure 1: Corpus composition (medium, source)

of two parts: an automatically annotated subcorpus which contains ambiguous interpretations for each token (non-disambiguated), and a manually disambiguated subcorpus which serves as a gold-standard annotated dataset.

2.1 BRC Tools and Resources

The available data within the BRC project includes source text files and an electronic Bambara dictionary. Dedicated tools have been implemented to annotate the corpus. The collection of software tools developed for the BRC (parser, disambiguation interface, various auxiliary scripts) is called Daba (Maslinsky, 2014) and is available on-line[3]. Among them, a rule-based parser was built to bootstrap the annotation of the corpus.

Thanks to this data and these tools, a gold standard has been created by human annotators proficient in Bambara. This process is described in Figure 2: The parser's output is reviewed, and annotation is done by selecting or editing required information for each wordform.

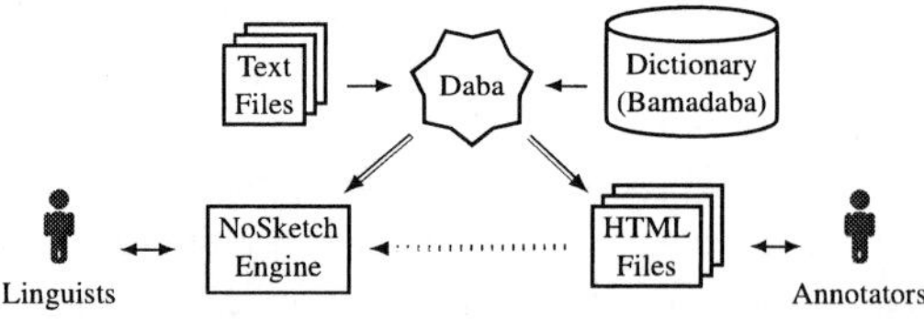

Figure 2: BRC data workflow

2.2 Main Goals for BRC

The project's goal is to disambiguate the whole corpus. Wordform annotation is done for each wordform and for three main features:

- POS Tagging

- Tone Marker Restoration

- Gloss Assignment

[3]https://github.com/maslinych/daba

We are currently working on these tasks by using sequential modeling with various additional techniques. For POS tagging, we use state of the art, Conditional random fields (CRFs; Lafferty et al. 2001) over 23 morpho-syntactic possible tags, our implementation reaches 94% accuracy, which is quite satisfying for such an under-resourced language.

For the tone marker restoration task, we considered using similar methods, but the tag set is much larger: 20,870 distinctive tonal forms are found, which prevents an efficient learning. We have to reduce training complexity by finding an adequate representation that will allow to model tone addition without listing every possible form.

2.3 Tone Markers in Bambara

The word-level tonal information is provided by tonal form or so-called diacritized form in the literature. The tone markers inserted in tonal form are mainly acute accent (´) for low tone, grave accent (`) for high tone, háček (ˇ) for phonetically rising tone and circumflex accent (^) for lexical rising tone. For instance, a non-tonalized token *tugu* can be tonalized as a noun *tùgu* (arms) or a verb *túgu* (to close) that we can find in its quasi-homonym list.

Ideally, the only difference between a tonalized token compared to its non-tonalized form is the presence of tone accents. In reality, annotators also often introduce other modifications, mainly typographic and orthographic correction. As we will see later, this fact makes it necessary to operate filtering on edit operations, in order to properly focus on tonalization operations.

To give an idea of tonal form variety, we propose to compare annotated tokens to their original forms. Related statistics are summarized in Table 2, showing that the probability for modifications other than tonalization during annotation is not negligible : 8.90% modification are related to other modification such as typographic or orthographic correction. We will have to take this into account for our system to focus on tonalization operations.

3 Problem Formulation

Our objective is to design a word sense disambiguation system for Bambara helping to choose the most correct interpretation from the quasi-homonym list provided for each token in the sub-

Operation	Ratio
Tonalization	38.73%
Other	**8.90%**
None	52.35%

Table 2: Distribution of edit operation to annotated forms receiving: only tone markers, other characters, or nothing (i.e., tonalized token is identical to its non-tonalized form)

corpus processed by Daba.

The drawback of modeling sequences of large-scale label set is the expensive computational cost needed to estimate CRF parameters. Indeed, the quasi-Newton method that CRF training employs for solving parameter estimation of CRF model has a computational cost proportional to M^2 where M is the size of label set (Sutton and McCallum, 2010). This makes CRF learning computationally expensive when labels are the set of possible tonalized words.

4 Related Works

4.1 Automatic Diacritization and Sub-word Level Modeling

Simard (1998) presented a method for accent insertion in French using a two-layers Hidden Markov Model (HMM) trained over a POS-tagged corpus while Tufiş and Chiţu (1999) adapted a trigram tagger to this task for Romanian. Focused on word-level modeling, their method requires lexical resources.

Elshafei et al. (2006) use a single-layer HHM for diacritization of Arabic text. Scannell (2011) extended diacritization to uni-codification in African languages by solving it using a Naive Bayes classifier. Their models, trained with trigram features on word and character levels, do not need other resources than an accented corpus, so it is compatible with resource-scarce languages.

Nguyen et al. (2012) implemented a system for accent restoration in Vietnamese based on two different models including the CRFs. The training corpus is preprocessed and annotated to indicate, both at syllable and character levels, the accents to insert to recover diacritic forms. Learning how to infer diacritic forms is indirectly reached by learning their differential representation.

Some hybrid approaches were also proposed for Arabic Diacritization : Said et al. (2013) com-

bined a CRF and a morphological analyzer to improve diacritization accuracy, while Metwally et al. (2016) proposed a three-layer processing composed of a CRF, a HMM and a morphological analyzer.

4.2 Category Decomposition

In the domain of CRF-based tagging, the idea to decompose label set in small pieces to train in order to gain learning performance can be found in (Tellier et al., 2010). They proposed to map total label set to a category tree and experiment to train on labels in a cascade manner or to train independently on each label components which correspond to a sub-category and then recombine them to obtain the total label. They concluded that their method, coined "category decomposition", improves greatly the time-wise efficiency of learning process.

5 Methodology

5.1 Fundamental Definitions

In the following, we will introduce essential elements to our methodology .

Let X, Y, Δ be three discrete random variables: non-tonalized token, tonalized token and code. X and Y take value from Ω (character set with or without diacritics) and Δ is either $\varnothing$ (no modification) or a concatenation of codewords, where a codeword is a triplet containing operation type (insertion or deletion), position for operation and character (if insertion) from Σ:

$$\Sigma \equiv \{+1, -1\} \times \mathbb{N}_{>0} \times \Omega \qquad (1)$$

We define E and D, respectively encoder and decoder functions, inverses of each other, such as:

$$\begin{aligned} \Delta &= E(Y; X) \\ Y &= D(\Delta; X) \end{aligned} \qquad (2)$$

5.1.1 Entropy Reduction Ratio

r_E is called entropy reduction ratio of E as defined:

$$r_E(\Delta, Y) \equiv \frac{\mathcal{H}(Y)}{\mathcal{H}(\Delta)} \ \ or \ \ \frac{\mathcal{H}(Y)}{\mathcal{H}(E(Y; X))} \qquad (3)$$

for any Δ satisfying $\mathcal{H}(\Delta) \neq 0$.

We need to predict tonalization for every non-tonalized token value $X = x$. Instead of predicting on Y, we can predict first on Δ and decode

Δ to obtain Y indirectly by using the second relation in (2). This will allow to greatly reduce the number of possible values of our model: we predict differential codes instead of tonalized words themselves.

In the next subsections, we try to design an efficient encoder E which maximizes r_E so that the resulting code Δ has a reduced set of possible values, it is more easy for a CRF-based modeler to learn on Δ than on Y as explained in the last paragraph of section 3.

5.2 Tonalization as Edit Operations

To maximize r_E (i.e. reduce Δ), we use an algorithm to represent the difference between Y and X by a minimal sequence of basic operations required for recovering Y from X. These basic operations are known as edit operations that we will present in the following.

By edit operation s, we mean a mapping from string a to string b, where a, b are sets of string drawn from the alphabet Ω such that if a is expressed as concatenation of characters as $a_1 a_2 \ldots a_{N-1} a_N$, then the mapping can be written as

$$b = s(a; \sigma) \tag{4}$$

where $\sigma = (m, p, c) \in \Sigma$ is a parameter tuple, m is an operation type indicator, p is a position parameter, c is a character involved by the operation.

And the mapping output b will be

$$b = \begin{cases} a_1 a_2 \ldots a_{p-1}\, c\, a_p \ldots a_N, & m = +1 \\ a_1 a_2 \ldots a_{p-1}\, a_{p+1} \ldots a_N, & m = -1 \end{cases} \tag{5}$$

We can see in (5), that when $m = +1$, s represents an insertion operation which consists in adding c just before the p-th character[4] in a, while in the case of $m = -1$, s denotes a deletion operation which removes the p-th character from a.

5.2.1 Use of Wagner-Fischer Algorithm

For any pair of strings (x, y), the Wagner-Fischer algorithm[5] in (Wagner and Fischer, 1974) allows to obtain a minimal sequence $S = (\sigma_1, \sigma_2, \ldots, \sigma_{M-1})$ such that:

$$\begin{aligned} A_{i+1} &= s(A_i; \sigma_i + (0, l_i, \varnothing)) \\ l_{i+1} &= l_i + m(\sigma_i) \\ A_0 &= x, A_M = y, l_0 = 0 \end{aligned} \tag{6}$$

---

[4] Or just after the $(p-1)$-th character, when $p = N$

[5] In this article, we apply Wagner-Fischer algorithm in its special case where there are only 2 available edit operations against 3 edit operations including the substitution as in its general case.

Where $0 \leq M, 1 \leq i \leq M-1$, position parameters p of σ_i denoted by $p(\sigma_i)$ form an increasing series with respect to index i:

$$p(\sigma_i) \leq p(\sigma_{i+1}) \tag{7}$$

For the edit operations acting on the same position p, insertions must precede[6] deletion as described below:

$$m(\sigma_i) \geq m(\sigma_{i+1}), \text{ if } p(\sigma_i) = p(\sigma_{i+1}) \tag{8}$$

Because it does not make sense to delete a character of a string twice, we assume that, for a given character position, only one deletion may occur:

Thus, $h(\sigma_i)$ below forms an increasing series

$$h(\sigma_i) \equiv 2 \cdot p(\sigma_i) + 0.5 \times [1 - m(\sigma_i)] \tag{9}$$

5.2.2 Encoder

If we set encoder $E(y; x)$ as an application of Wagner-Fischer algorithm on (x, y), and δ as the concatenation of elements of S like

$$\delta = \sigma_1 \sigma_2 \ldots \sigma_{M-1} \tag{10}$$

Then $E(y; x)$ is specified so that the first relation in (2) is satisfied.

5.2.3 Decoder

Moreover, if we choose $D(\delta; x)$ as an implementation of (6) applied on x with δ as parameter, this specifies a way to use x and the code δ to recovery y, and define a decoder.

To show that the entropy is effectively reduced, we will present experiments in section 8 for evaluation of entropy reduction ratio of r_E.

5.3 Segmentation

Segment decomposition of a string x is a mapping from a string x to strings called segments $x^{(1)} x^{(2)} x^{(3)} \ldots x^{(L)}$ so that the concatenation of the latter is equal to the original string x.

We can then divide the resulting code δ in L code segments $\delta^{(1)} \delta^{(2)} \ldots \delta^{(L)}$ described as:

$$\delta = \delta^{(1)} \delta^{(2)} \ldots \delta^{(L)} \tag{11}$$

$\delta^{(i)}$ is the code segment (i.e. a sub-sequence of code δ) associated with $x^{(i)}$:

$$\delta^{(i)} = \sigma_{\min(S_i)} \ldots \sigma_{\max(S_i)} \tag{12}$$

---

[6] Or we can also state that deletions precede insertions. In this case, the second relation of (6) will be different for that decoder to work properly. So this was our design choice.

where S_i is the set which contains the indices of all edit operations acting on segment $x^{(i)}$.

Furthermore, we define shifted version of $\delta^{(i)}$ as below

$$\delta'^{(i)} = \sigma'_{\min(S_i)}\cdots\sigma'_{\max(S_i)} \qquad (13)$$

where $\sigma'_{\min(S_i)} = \sigma_{\min(S_i)} + (0, -e_i, \varnothing)$, $e_i = \sum_{k=1}^{i-1}|x_k|$ position offset. It can be shown that y can be obtained by concatenation [7] of decoding results of D on shifted code segment $\delta'^{(i)}$ as below

$$y = D(\delta'^{(1)};x^{(1)})D(\delta'^{(2)};x^{(2)})...D(\delta'^{(L)};x^{(L)}) \quad (14)$$

Using the proposed segmentation allows to get the shifted code segment $\delta'^{(i)}$ associated with segment $x^{(i)}$. For obtaining y, it suffices to individually decode code segments $\delta'^{(i)}$ using the same decoder defined in (2). Hence, an encoder - decoder pair is indirectly specified as:

$$\begin{aligned} \delta'^{(i)} &= E'(y, x^{(i)}) \\ y^{(i)} &= D(\delta'^{(i)}, x^{(i)}) \end{aligned} \qquad (15)$$

The segmentation technique allows a CRF-based system to learn $\delta'^{(i)}$ individually instead of a total code δ at once. The relation in (14) can then be used to recover y from predicted code segments $\delta'^{(i)}$ produced by CRF taggers.

To show the effect of segmentation on entropy reduction ratio $r_{E'}$, we will evaluate experiments in section 8 with different segmentation settings such as syllabification and fixed-width segmentation.

5.4 Edit Operation Filtering

As previously explained, segmentation on x leads to splitting code δ in several code segments $\delta^{(i)}$ (or its shifted version $\delta'^{(i)}$) because it regroups edit operations $\sigma_j = (m_j, p_j, c_j)$ inside δ by position parameter p_j.

Edit operation filtering allows to split each code segment $\delta^{(i)}$ in some subgroups by operation type m_i and character involved by operation c_i. But as opposed to segmentation, in the filtering process, some edit operations are dropped because of their irrelevance regarding our tonalization goal for Bambara.

---

[7]Alternatively, it is also possible to obtain the integral code δ from $\delta'^{(i)}$ using relations (11), (12), (13) and to get the underlying tonalized token y by direct decoding on the integral code δ.

First, we recall that the order of edit operations called σ'_k inside the sequence $\delta'^{(i)}$ is partially determined by their elements. It can be shown, more generally that the order restriction in (7), (8) leads directly to

$$p'_k < p'_l \implies k < l \qquad (16)$$

$$m'_k > m'_l \wedge p'_k = p'_l \implies k < l \qquad (17)$$

where $m'_k \equiv m(\sigma'_k)$, $p'_k \equiv p(\sigma'_k)$, $k \neq l$.

Thus, the order between any two edit operations in $\delta'^{(i)}$, called σ'_k, σ'_l is free only in the case of multiple insertion acting on the same position of a string, i.e. $m'_k = m'_l = +1$, $p'_k = p'_l$.

5.4.1 Tone Marker Filtering

The aim of tone marker filtering is to remove edit operations irrelevant to tonalization. It consists in removing all insertions of characters which are not considered as tone markers, and keeping only the first of all insertions (also only the first one of all tone deletions) operating on the same position (because neither multiple insertions nor multiple deletions are supposed to be present in pure tonalization).

In addition, the filter contributes to reduce the code so that the order of edit operations in filter output becomes totally determined by edit operation arguments (i.e. p and m) via relations (16)(17). Therefore, the indexing function h defined in 9 forms a strictly increasing series.

5.4.2 Edit Operation Decomposition

We define an edit operation dispatcher F_m as a mapping from input code δ_{in} to its sub-sequence described as:

$$F_m(\delta_{in}; k) = \sigma_{\min(V_k(\delta_{in}))}\cdots\sigma_{\max(V_k(\delta_{in}))} \quad (18)$$

where $V_k(\delta)$ is the set which contains the indices of all edit operations in δ of type k, $k \in \{-1, +1\}$.

For recall, the tone marker filter produces a code result in which $h(\sigma_i), i > 0$ forms a strictly increasing sequence. This property implies that there exists an inverse mapping from $\{F_m(\delta_{in}; k)\}_{k\in\{-1,+1\}}$ to δ_{in} if δ_{in} is a filtered result. We call this underlying mapping edit operation assembler.

6 System Architecture

In this section, we present the architecture of our system for automatic tone marker insertion for Bambara text by detailing its functional blocks and internal data flow.

6.1 Training Stage

At training stage, as shown in Figure 3, the tonalization system uses an encoder to represent the difference of the tonalized token value y relative to its original non-tonalized token value x by the code δ. The code δ as well as the non-tonalized token x are then fed into the code segmenter which breaks down δ in small shifted code segments $\delta'^{(i)}$. The tone marker filter takes the shifted code segments, selects tone markers and sends its output to a dispatcher which distinguishes insertion and deletion operations.

In the following, two CRF models are trained individually on relation $(x, \delta'^{(i)}_+)$ and on relation $(x, \delta'^{(i)}_-)$ in the reference corpus.

6.2 Tonalization Stage

In tone recovery stage, the two trained CRF models are used to predict the two parts of shifted code segment $\delta'^{(i)}_+$, $\delta'^{(i)}_-$ from tonalized token x. Then they are fed to, as shown in Figure 4, an edit operation assembler to get predicted shifted code segment $\delta'^{(i)}$; at the same time, the non-tonalized token x is re-segmented to get $x^{(i)}$. Then, the non-tonalized segment $x^{(i)}$ as well as the shifted code segment $\delta'^{(i)}$ are sent to be decoded to obtain tonalized segment $y^{(i)}$ in decoder output. In the end, the decoded tonalized segments $y^{(i)}$ are re-united in the code assembler to give the estimated integral tonalized token value y.

7 Running examples

To illustrate more concretely how our system works at training stage, we propose in the following, two running examples: the first one shows how our system models a pure tonalization; the second one shows how the tone marker filter could be helpful when some typographic modifications are introduced in the tonalized form.

7.1 Example 1 (pure tonalization)

In this example, the system models the tonalization from *lakali* to *lákàlí*. Hence, x, y are set as

below:

$$x = lakali$$
$$y = lákàlí$$

The tone encoder compares x and y, then outputs the differential representation as tonal code δ below:

$$\delta = [(+1, 2, \acute{\ }), (+1, 4, \grave{\ }), (+1, 6, \acute{\ })]$$

In the above, the 3 codewords that δ contains represent the 3 tone markers inserted into x to model for this tonalization.

$$\delta^{(1)} = [(+1, 2, \acute{\ })]$$
$$\delta^{(2)} = [(+1, 4, \grave{\ })]$$
$$\delta^{(3)} = [(+1, 6, \acute{\ })]$$

The syllabification is examplified below on non-tonalized and tonalized form:

$$x^{(1)} = la, y^{(1)} = lá$$
$$x^{(2)} = ka, y^{(2)} = kà$$
$$x^{(3)} = li, y^{(3)} = lí$$

We observe that the 3 tone markers are all inserted after the second character for each of 3 syllables. Therefore, we got 3 shifted versions of code segments operating at position 2 as below.

$$\delta'^{(1)}_+ = \delta'^{(1)} = [(+1, 2, \acute{\ })]$$
$$\delta'^{(2)}_+ = \delta'^{(2)} = [(+1, 2, \grave{\ })]$$
$$\delta'^{(3)}_+ = \delta'^{(3)} = [(+1, 2, \acute{\ })]$$

As in this example, only the tone marker insertions are to be modeled, the tone marker filter, edit operation decomposition unit do not affect system result at training stage.

7.2 Example 2 (noisy tonalization)

The system models the tonalization from *taanikasegin* to *táa-ká-ségin*. Hence, x, y are set as below:

$$x = taanikasegin$$
$$y = táa - ká - ségin$$

In the following, we show the syllabification result of y presented with its related to non-tonalized

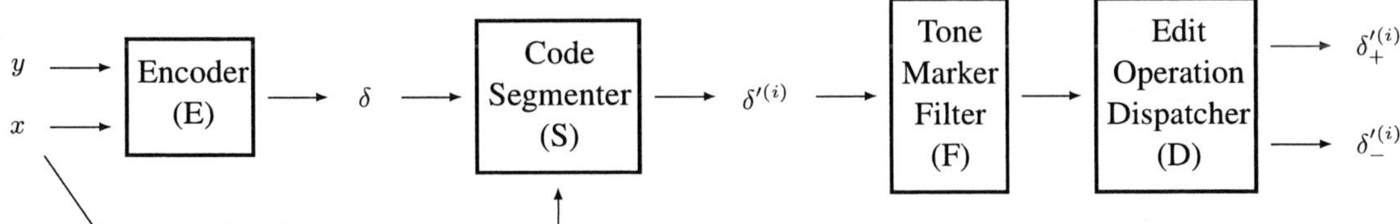

Figure 3: Block diagram for the proposed Bambara tonalization system at training stage

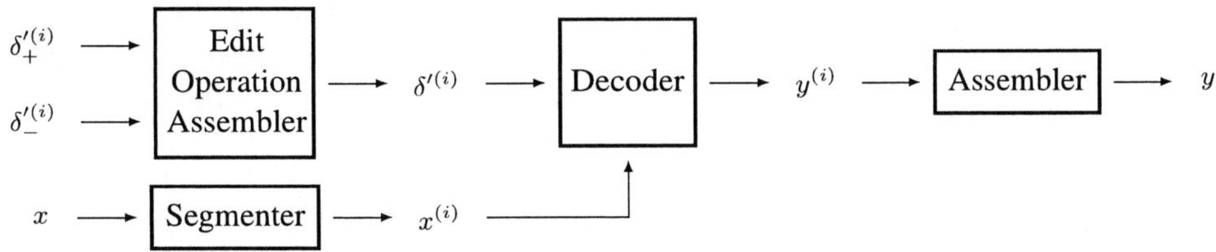

Figure 4: Block diagram for the proposed Bambara tonalization system at tonalization stage

form.

$$x^{(1)} = taani, y^{(1)} = táa-$$
$$x^{(2)} = ka, y^{(2)} = ká-$$
$$x^{(3)} = se, y^{(3)} = sé$$
$$x^{(4)} = y^{(4)} = gin$$

Subsequently, 7 codewords are obtained from differential tone encoding, then departed in 4 code segments corresponding to 4 syllables:

$$\delta^{(1)} = [(+1, 2, \prime),$$
$$(+1, 3, -), (-1, 4, n), (-1, 5, i)]$$
$$\delta^{(2)} = [(+1, 7, \prime), (+1, 7, -)]$$
$$\delta^{(3)} = [(+1, 9, \prime)]$$
$$\delta^{(4)} = \varnothing$$

As a remark, the first syllable in the above is the most concerned by noise : one dash symbol insertion and 2 character removals are observed. The tone marker filter removes all character deletions and insertions in code segments. Therefore, tonalization is modeled by only tone marker insertions as below:

$$\delta_+^{\prime(1)} = \delta^{\prime(1)} = [(+1, 2, \prime)]$$
$$\delta_+^{\prime(2)} = \delta^{\prime(2)} = [(+1, 2, \prime)]$$
$$\delta_+^{\prime(3)} = \delta^{\prime(3)} = [(+1, 2, \prime)]$$
$$\delta_+^{\prime(4)} = \delta^{\prime(4)} = \varnothing$$

Here, we found a tonalization representation similar to the one from the preceding example: insertion of a tone marker at position 2 for some syllables.

8 Experiment

8.1 Experiment Setup

The disambiguated corpus of BRC which contains tonalized tokens is chosen as training data. The train data then is split into training and evaluation data sets with ratio $p : (1 - p)$. By default, p is set to 50% for efficiency reason.

For CRF implementation, we use CRFSuite as open-source library with l-BFGS algorithm specified as training method, Viterbi algorithm as inference method (Okazaki, 2007) .

The segmentation mode is specified by the integer w described in the following : $w = -1$ indicates a syllabification (as obtained by BRC morphological parser), $w = 0$ for no segmentation and $w > 0$ signals a w-width regular segmentation[8].

We denote different configurations of our system by their functional layout at training stage. For specifying the functional layout, the following symbols D, F, S, E are used to indicate respectively four constituent blocks of the system : D for edit operation decomposition block, F for tone marker filter block, S for segmentation block, E for encoder block, and $\circ$ denotes an inter-block connection. For example, $S \circ E$ represents an encoder followed by a segmenter as system.

---

[8] A regular segmenter forms a segment of every w successive characters, from left to right (i.e. in direction of writing of Bambara), in its input string. By exception, the last segment at output contains the rest of the string which has not yet been segmented so that we allow it to be equal or shorter than a segment of w characters.

8.2 Feature Engineering

The feature patterns we created are the same for all CRF models. The features are generated for each segment[9] for tokens in the training data $x^{(i)}$.

For each segment, features indicate:

- At segment (sub-word) level

  - Previous, current and next segment
  - Substring containing all vowels for current segment
  - Position of current segment (integer) relative to beginning or ending of word
  - Typography of segment: all capital letters, presence of numbers or punctuation marks

- At word level

  - Previous, current and next words
  - Prefix and suffix for previous, current and next words
  - Position of current word (integer) relative to beginning or ending of sentence

8.3 Evaluation Measure

As shown by the example of the section 7.2, the tonalized token y can itself be noisy. On the other hand, we are particularly interested in errors introduced by CRF-based in predicting $\delta_+^{\prime(i)}, \delta_-^{\prime(i)}$ from x. Consequently, our accuracy evaluation is based on the comparison of two tokens described as below:

- A gold standard according to tonalization filtering (i.e. typographic modification are not expected)

- The token tonalized by our system, resulting from applying $\delta_+^{\prime(i)}, \delta_-^{\prime(i)}$ (predicted by the CRFs) to the segments $x^{(i)}$

8.4 Experiment Results

8.4.1 Coding and Segmentation

The entropy for the tonalized token Y that we calculated on the disambiguated part of BRC is 8.73 bits of entropy for 20,870 distinctive tonal forms. As shown in Table 3, the tonalization representation produced by tone encoder Δ has only 3.38 bits of entropy (1,273 distinctive codes). In other

---

word, the entropy is reduced by a factor of 2.58 by only using the differential tone encoder. If segmentation is also used, shorter segments lead to greater entropy reduction. The extreme case is to segment by character ($w = 1$), leading to an entropy reduction ratio of 4.82, and implies character-level processing.

8.4.2 Segmentation and Operation Filtering

Table 4 presents an experiment on the impact of system configuration (related to Figure 4) and segmentation mode on tonalization accuracy and training time of our system. For comparison, the accuracy of a baseline based on majority voting method is also provided in the last row.

We note first that segmentation improves accuracy. Syllabification as well as regular segmentation with a fixed width close to averaged syllable length (3.24 characters) gives the best result in accuracy (0.92). Regarding system configuration, accuracy is generally preserved over the four different configurations except of when applying operation decomposition without filtering. This can be explained by the fact that decomposition is not totally recoverable as mentioned in section 5.4.2 for data which is not processed by tone marker filter, it can introduce some errors within assembler at tonalization phase and degrades its accuracy.

Training time is dramatically reduced by segmentation and by edit operation decomposition. This may sometimes be at the cost of accuracy, but syllabification or fixed segmentation with width $w = 2$ is a nice trade-off, preserving accuracy and keeping training time acceptable.

Those experiments allow to state that segmentation is gainful both for accuracy and training time (see last column). Decomposition and filtering do not have a tremendous impact on accuracy, but are unavoidable to be able to train models on the whole dataset in reasonable time.

8.4.3 Effect of Train Size and Error Analysis

Figure 5 shows how the training set size influences the tonalization accuracy and training time. We can see the progress in accuracy with respect to training set size is less considerable when $p \geq 50\%$ than when $p < 50\%$. The training time increases dramatically with respect to training set size.

Table 5 shows distribution of errors which occur in automatic tone insertion (not in tone deletion). The error occurs due to a bad prediction in

Width w / Entropy	-1 (Syllabe)	1	2	3	4	5	6	0
$H(\delta'^{(i)})$	**2.67**	**1.81**	**2.56**	2.86	3.11	3.23	3.29	3.38
$r_E(\delta'^{(i)}, y^{(i)})$	**3.27**	**4.82**	**3.41**	3.05	2.80	2.70	2.65	2.58

Table 3: Encoder entropy $H(\Delta)$ and reduction ratio $r_E(\delta'^{(i)}, y^{(i)})$

Width w / Systems	-1 (Syll.)	1	2	3	4	5	6	0
$D \circ F \circ S \circ E$	**0.923**	0.912	**0.923**	**0.923**	0.918	0.911	0.904	0.893
time	19.88	17.62	13.17	15.67	19.62	32.40	44.25	261.83
$F \circ S \circ E$	**0.924**	0.916	**0.923**	**0.923**	0.918	0.911	0.905	0.894
time	57.68	19.42	20.72	35.70	62.85	121.08	168.27	2455.80
$D \circ S \circ E$	0.921	0.911	0.921	**0.922**	0.916	0.910	0.903	0.892
time	28.28	21.27	19.72	29.17	39.90	57.35	70.15	793.85
$S \circ E$	**0.923**	0.915	**0.922**	**0.922**	0.917	0.910	0.904	0.893
time	101.63	25.52	42.03	235.35	378.37	169.55	318.23	2683.72
Majority vote	**0.843**							

Table 4: Accuracy for our system trained with four different system configurations and eight segmentation modes (p = 50%)

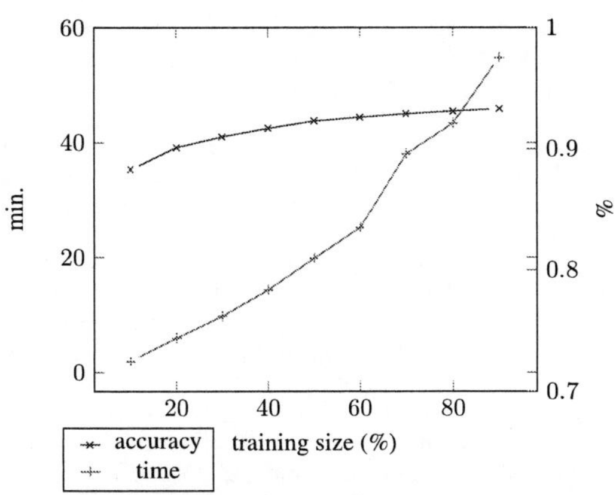

Figure 5: Accuracy and time of training (configured as $D \circ F \circ S \circ E$ using syllabification) with respect to different training size 90%-10%

Error Type	Ratio
Tone Only	**58.52%**
Position Only	1.17%
Tone and Position	0.023%
Silence	**40.08%**

Table 5: Error distribution by type for insertion operations with p = 50%, system = $D \circ F \circ S \circ E$

character to insert but correct prediction in character position is prevalent (58.52%) and the silence (40.08%) which is a false negative case is also very frequent. Prediction error only in character position is as weak (1.17%) as error rate (0.023%) for both character position and symbol error. This shows that our system correctly predicts positions (mainly at beginning of words) and that most of the errors are due to the difficulty to predict if a tone has to be added, and which one.

Actual \ Predicted	´	`	^	ˇ
´	0.9541	**0.0438**	0.0021	0.0000
`	**0.0841**	0.9141	0.0015	0.0003
^	0.0035	**0.0322**	0.9643	0.0000
ˇ	0.0000	**0.0952**	0.0000	0.9048

Table 6: Confusion matrix on prediction of tone markers

Table 6 presents the confusion matrix of the error occurring due to bad prediction in character mentioned previously in Table 5. It shows that these errors are mainly due to the confusion between low tone (´) and high tone (`), which are the two most frequent markers in BRC.

702

9 Conclusion

In this paper, we presented our Bambara tonalization system for automatic detection of tone markers in Bambara. Our experiments show that using segmentation both increases tonalization accuracy and greatly reduces training time. Our differential encoder reduces entropy of labels to be predicted, making CRF learning efficient and allowing to implement a tone marker filter and edit operation decomposition unit within the tonalization process. The tone marker filter plays the role of normalizator of tonalized token to learn in training phase and in normalizing the token, it leads to reduce training time. The edit operation decomposition unit which follows the filter split the tokens in insertion and deletion of tone markers, allows to accelerate furthermore the training time reduction without altering tonalization accuracy.

Acknowledgments

We thank National Institute for Oriental Languages and Civilizations which supports this work as part of its research project called MANTAL. We acknowledge, in this regard, Valentin Vydrin, Kirill Maslinsky, Davy Auffret, Elvis Mboning and Arthur Provenier for thier contributions, which make possible our work.

References

Charles Bailleul. 2007. *Dictionnaire Bambara-Franais (3e dition corrige)*. Bamako : Donniya.

Grard Dumestre. 2003. *Grammaire fondamentale du bambara*. Paris : Karthala.

Grard Dumestre. 2011. *Dictionnaire bambara-franais suivi dun index abrg franais-bambara*. Paris : Karthala.

Moustafa Elshafei, Husni Al-Muhtaseb, and Mansour Alghamdi. 2006. Statistical methods for automatic diacritization of arabic text. In *The Saudi 18th National Computer Conference. Riyadh*, volume 18, pages 301–306.

John Lafferty, Andrew McCallum, and Fernando CN Pereira. 2001. Conditional random fields: Probabilistic models for segmenting and labeling sequence data.

Kirill Maslinsky. 2014. Daba: a model and tools for manding corpora. In *TALN-RECITAL 2014 Workshop TALAf 2014 : Traitement Automatique des Langues Africaines (TALAf 2014: African Language Processing)*, pages 114–122. Association pour le Traitement Automatique des Langues.

Aya S Metwally, Mohsen A Rashwan, and Amir F Atiya. 2016. A multi-layered approach for arabic text diacritization. In *Cloud Computing and Big Data Analysis (ICCCBDA), 2016 IEEE International Conference on*, pages 389–393. IEEE.

Minh Trung Nguyen, Quoc Nhan Nguyen, and Hong Phuong Nguyen. 2012. Vietnamese diacritics restoration as sequential tagging. In *Computing and Communication Technologies, Research, Innovation, and Vision for the Future (RIVF), 2012 IEEE RIVF International Conference on*, pages 1–6. IEEE.

Naoaki Okazaki. 2007. Crfsuite: a fast implementation of conditional random fields (crfs).

Ahmed Said, Mohamed El-Sharqwi, Achraf Chalabi, and Eslam Kamal. 2013. A hybrid approach for arabic diacritization. In *International Conference on Application of Natural Language to Information Systems*, pages 53–64. Springer.

Kevin P Scannell. 2011. Statistical unicodification of african languages. *Language resources and evaluation*, 45(3):375–386.

Michel Simard. 1998. Automatic insertion of accents in french text. In *EMNLP*, pages 27–35.

Charles Sutton and Andrew McCallum. 2010. An introduction to conditional random fields. *arXiv preprint arXiv:1011.4088*.

Isabelle Tellier, Iris Eshkol, Samer Taalab, and Jean-Philippe Prost. 2010. Pos-tagging for oral texts with crf and category decomposition. *Research in Computing Science*, 46:79–90.

Dan Tufiş and Adrian Chiţu. 1999. Automatic diacritics insertion in romanian texts. In *Proceedings of COMPLEX99 International Conference on Computational Lexicography*.

Valentin Vydrin. 1999a. Les parties du discours en bambara : un essai de bilan. 35:73–93.

Valentin Vydrin. 1999b. Manding-english dictionary (maninka, bamana). In *St. Petersburg: Dmitry Bulanin Publishing House*, volume 1.

Valentin Vydrin. 2013. Bamana reference corpus (brc). *Procedia-Social and Behavioral Sciences*, 95:75–80.

Valentin Vydrin. 2014. Projet des corpus écrits des langues manding: le bambara, le maninka. In *Traitement Automatique du Langage Naturel 2014*.

Robert A Wagner and Michael J Fischer. 1974. The string-to-string correction problem. *Journal of the ACM (JACM)*, 21(1):168–173.

Joint Learning of Dialog Act Segmentation and Recognition in Spoken Dialog Using Neural Networks

Tianyu Zhao and **Tatsuya Kawahara**
{zhao, kawahara}@sap.ist.i.kyoto-u.ac.jp

Abstract

Dialog act segmentation and recognition are basic natural language understanding tasks in spoken dialog systems. This paper investigates a unified architecture for these two tasks, which aims to improve the model's performance on both of the tasks. Compared with past joint models, the proposed architecture can (1) incorporate contextual information in dialog act recognition, and (2) integrate models for tasks of different levels as a whole, i.e. dialog act segmentation on the word level and dialog act recognition on the segment level. Experimental results show that the joint training system outperforms the simple cascading system and the joint coding system on both dialog act segmentation and recognition tasks.

1 Introduction

Recently the burst of interactive assistants and chatbots leads to an increasing interest of dialog systems. Natural language understanding (NLU), as an important component of dialog system, is usually responsible for dialog act (DA) or dialog intent tagging, where text classification techniques are necessary. Dialog act (also speech act) is a representation of the meaning of a sentence at the level of illocutionary force (Stolcke et al., 2000). For instance, a sentence *"How is the weather?"* belongs to the dialog act class *Question*. For another sentence, *"The weather is quite good today."*, if it follows a previous *Question* sentence, it should be an *Answer* to the question. Otherwise it is likely to be a *Statement*. Therefore, DA recognition requires us to understand the sentence from semantic, pragmatic and syntactic aspects, and its context plays an important role as well.

Words	hi	my	name	is	Erica
Segment	E	I	I	I	E
DA	Greeting	Statement			

Table 1: DA segmentation and recognition.

The prerequisite for DA recognition is to split a sequence of words into segments, each of which corresponds to one DA unit. Especially for spoken dialog systems, NLU is based on Automatic Speech Recognition (ASR) hypotheses or transcripts, in which we cannot make any assumption of punctuation such as periods, commas and question marks for segmentation. Therefore DA segmentation becomes essential for spoken dialog systems. As the example given in Table 1 shows, a long utterance is firstly split into two segments *"hi"* and *"my name is Erica"*, to which DA tags *"Greeting"* and *"Statement"* are assigned afterwards. DA segmentation is a sequence labeling task and an "IE" tag coding scheme is adopted to describe segment boundaries, where "I" denotes "inside" of a segment and "E" denotes the "end". While the DA segmentation is a pre-process of DA recognition, recognition of DA in the sequence helps segmentation. Thus, DA segmentation and recognition are two highly related tasks. We can expect that joint learning of these two tasks can improve the performance of models. In this paper we investigate architectures of joint learning of DA segmentation and recognition, and analyze their performances. DA segmentation is a sequence labeling task on the word level and DA recognition is a classification task on the DA segment level. Our model is flexible and can be applied to tasks of different levels.

The rest of this paper is structured as follows. Section 2 gives a literature review. Section 3 describes a hierarchical neural network model for

Proceedings of the The 8th International Joint Conference on Natural Language Processing, pages 704–712,
Taipei, Taiwan, November 27 – December 1, 2017 ©2017 AFNLP

DA recognition and explains its ability to model sequential short texts. Section 4 focuses on joint learning of DA segmentation and recognition, and explores three models for joint tasks. Section 5 shows experimental results on three tasks using the proposed models. Lastly in Section 6 and 7 we discuss the results and give a conclusion.

2   Related Works

In the task of DA recognition, Shriberg et al. (1998) applied decision tree using rich features and emphasized the importance of prosodic features. Stolcke et al. (2000) used HMM to capture the intrinsic patterns of DA sequence. Variants of neural network have been recently used in this task. In (Lai et al., 2015), a recurrent convolutional neural network is applied to text classification, which consists of a RNN layer and a max-pooling layer over it. Ji et al. (2016) proposed a latent variable RNN for modeling discourse relations between sentences. Khanpour et al. (2016) investigated RNNs with different settings of hyperparameters. A hierarchical neural network was introduced by Lee and Dernoncourt (2016). It firstly uses a RNN layer or a CNN layer to generate vector representations of short texts. Then a two-layer feedforward ANN takes a sequence of these vector representations to predict the probability distribution of output labels. Li and Wu (2016) used gated RNN for both vector representation generation and classification in their hierarchical model. We base our work on hierarchical neural network for DA recognition and propose a unified architecture for joint DA segmentation and recognition, which is discussed in Section 4.

3   Hierarchical Neural Network

When we regard DA recognition as a text classification task, there are two difficulties in accurately recognizing a DA. In the first place, texts in DA recognition are often limited to a small number of words while tasks such as sentiment analysis and news topic categorization aim to classify fairly long documents and can exploit mainly n-gram models. Compared with long documents, dialog utterances have much fewer words and it is difficult to extract enough information from simple word co-occurrence features. Secondly, it is of great importance to consider contexts in DA recognition. For instance, a sentence *"the weather is quite good today"* is regarded as an *Answer* if

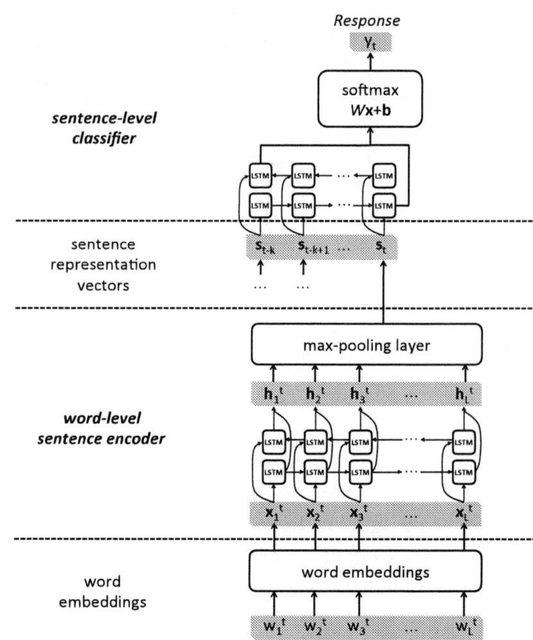

Figure 1: Hierarchical neural network: an example of input and output is given in the figure.

it appears after another speaker questioning the weather. Otherwise, it is a *Statement*.

In order to address aforementioned problems, we use a hierarchical neural network for DA recognition. The hierarchical model firstly takes distributed word representation as input, which contains richer semantic information than n-gram features do. Secondly, it exploits history information to recognize DA tags of ambiguous utterances such as *"the weather is quite good today"*. The general architecture of the hierarchical neural network consists of a sentence encoder and a classifier. A sentence encoder neural network encodes a sequence of words into a vector (sentence representation vector) of a fixed length, which will be explained in Section 3.1. A classifier neural network predicts the label given representation vectors of the corresponding sentence and its preceding sentences, which will be explained in Section 3.2. The architecture of hierarchical neural network used in our work is shown in Figure 1.

3.1   Sentence Representation

A sentence encoder encodes a sequence of words into a fixed-length vector. By training the encoder, it obtains the ability to mine useful task-related information from a word sequence. We choose Bidirectional Long Short-Term Memory (BiLSTM) - a variant of RNN. LSTM (Hochreiter and Schmidhuber, 1997) can better avoid the vanishing gradient problem compared with normal RNNs, thus it is suitable for processing information through many time steps.

Input words $\mathbf{w}_{1:L}^t$ are firstly converted to word embeddings through a lookup table in word embedding layer. Given word embeddings $\mathbf{x}_{1:L}^t$, BiLSTM outputs hidden states $\mathbf{h}_{1:L}^t$, where an output hidden state $\mathbf{h}_i$ is the concatenation of forward hidden state $\overrightarrow{\mathbf{h}}_i$ and backward hidden state $\overleftarrow{\mathbf{h}}_i$. We use a max pooling layer to extract the most informative features over time, and produce a single vector $\mathbf{s}_t$ as the encoding of word sequence $\mathbf{w}_{1:L}^t$.

3.2 Sequence Classification

Given sentence encoding vectors $\mathbf{s}_{t-k:t}$, we use the second neural network to predict the label of the t-th sentence. We use a history of length k instead of the whole history since dialog act usually depends on the very late history and it also accelerates training. Again we use BiLSTM and it works in a similar manner as the BiLSTM sentence encoder does but without max pooling layer, since the latest sentence provides the most information for DA recognition. Given the final hidden state, a fully-connected layer with a softmax function outputs the predicted label y_t.

4 Joint Learning

Joint learning (multi-task learning) is an approach to learn from several related tasks in parallel so that it improves the model's ability to generalize features, and promotes its performance on the different tasks. In natural language processing (NLP), many higher-level tasks usually depend on outputs from lower-level tasks, for example named entity recognition (NER) relies on part-of-speech (POS) tagging. Hence there are many cases where models can benefit from joint learning.

Collobert and Weston (2008) introduced a neural network-based joint architecture making minimal assumption of feature engineering, and also concluded three kinds of joint model, i.e. cascading features, shallow joint training, and deep joint training. A cascading model, however, does not include any joint learning procedure, and shallow joint training is actually to convert tags of different tasks into one tag. In the rest of this paper, we will name them cascading model, joint coding model, and joint training model for accuracy. Zheng et al. (2013) applied a joint coding method to Chinese word segmentation and POS tagging by changing POS labels using a "BIES" tag coding scheme. Peng and Dredze (2016) improved NER by word representation learnt in word segmentation task using a LSTM-CRF model. Yang et al. (2016) proposed a multi-task cross-lingual model for sequence labeling tasks using RNN-CRF structures. These approaches to joint learning mostly attempt to learn shared representation of words and characters from different tasks.

Unlike aforementioned NLP tasks, DA segmentation and recognition deal with units of different levels, i.e. word level and DA segment level. Joint learning of these two tasks does not naturally fit in the architectures above. Previous works usually use joint coding methods. Zimmermann 2006 (2006) used a hidden-event language model for sequence labeling of DA type and its boundary on word level. It also exploits prosodic features in classification. Zimmermann (2009) and Quarterono et al. (2011) applied conditional random field (CRF) and the former also investigated how different tag coding schemes affect the model's performance. Granell et al. (2009) incorporated syntactic features and used a combination of a HMM at the lexical level and a Language Model (LM) at the DA level. Hakkani-Tür et al. (2016) used a single sequence labeling LSTM model for joint semantic frame parsing, where sentence-level intent and domain tags are predicted at the last token of the sentence. An encoder-decoder-pointer framework was used for chunking in (Zhai et al., 2017), where segmentation was done by a pointer network and labeling was done by a decoder LSTM.

To our knowledge, there is no previous work on neural network based joint model applied to joint learning of DA segmentation and recognition. In this section, we investigate cascading model, joint coding model, and joint training model using neural networks. In the joint coding model, joint tag coding is used to combine segmentation and recognition tags and leads to a word-level sequence labeling task. For cascading and joint training models, the proposed architectures can deal with tasks of different unit levels and the hierarchical model introduced in Section 3 is integrated to make use of contextual information.

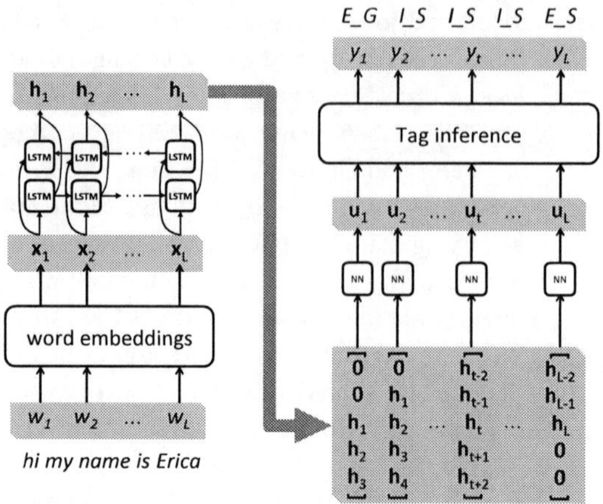

Figure 2: Joint coding model: an example of input and output is given in the figure.

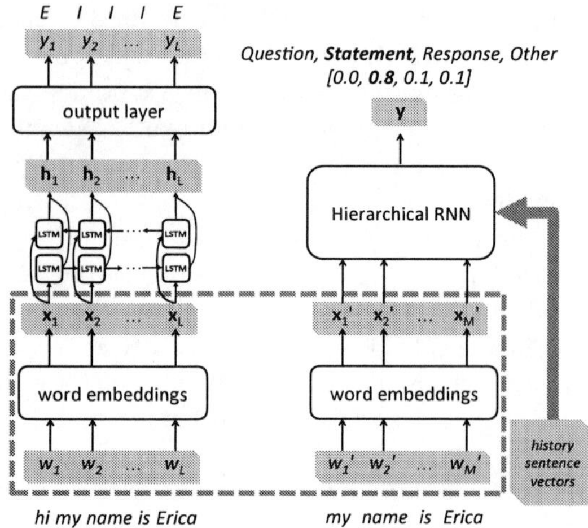

Figure 3: Cascading model and joint training model: in cascading model, part (a) on the left is a component for segmentation and part (b) on the right is for DA recognition. In joint training model, word embedding layers in dashed line rectangle are shared by both segmentation and recognition models. An example of input and output is given in the figure.

4.1 Joint Coding Model

4.1.1 Joint Coding

In the joint coding method, one single model predicts labels of DA segmentation and recognition at the same time, so that the units of these two tasks should keep consistency. We use a joint tag coding scheme to combine labels of segmentation and recognition and make them a word-level sequential labeling problem as shown in Table 2. This allows us to use one single sequential labeling model to solve two tasks simultaneously. The proposed joint coding model is given in Figure 2.

4.1.2 Tag Score

A sequence of words $\mathbf{w}_{1:L}$ is firstly mapped to word embeddings $\mathbf{x}_{1:L}$, then we feed them to the following RNN layer which produces hidden states $\mathbf{h}_{1:L}$. In order to provide contextual information explicitly, when we predict a label for the i-th step, we also make use of hidden states of preceding steps ($\mathbf{h}_{i-1}$, $\mathbf{h}_{i-2}$, etc.) and succeeding steps ($\mathbf{h}_{i+1}$, $\mathbf{h}_{i+2}$, etc.). The concatenated vector $[\mathbf{h}_{i-2}, \mathbf{h}_{i-1}, \mathbf{h}_i, \mathbf{h}_{i+1}, \mathbf{h}_{i+2}]$ is then fed to a neural network layer that computes a tag score $\mathbf{s}_i$, where $\mathbf{s}_i \in \mathbb{R}^{|C|}$, the t-th element in $\mathbf{s}_i$ indicates the score of choosing the t-th tag at the i-th step, and $|C|$ is the number of tag classes.

4.1.3 Tag Inference

Since there often exists invalid tag sequences such as an "E_S" following an "I_Q" and we would like to penalize such invalid tag transitions, we apply a post process to compute the optimal tag sequence considering the transition probabilities by using a transition score matrix A_{mn}, which indicates the score of jumping from m-th tag to the n-th tag. Let $\mathbf{s}_i^t$ denotes the t-th element of $\mathbf{s}_i$, the score of a tag sequence $\mathbf{t}_{1:L}$ is defined as:

$$score(\mathbf{t}_{1:L}) = \sum_{i=1}^{L} (A_{t_{i-1}t_i} + \mathbf{s}_i^t), \quad (1)$$

and we use the Viterbi algorithm to find the optimal tag sequence $\mathbf{t}_{1:L}^*$ that maximizes the sequence score:

$$\mathbf{t}_{1:L}^* = \underset{\forall \mathbf{t}_{1:L}}{\arg\max}\, score(\mathbf{t}_{1:L}). \quad (2)$$

4.2 Cascading Model and Joint Training Model

DA segmentation splits a sequence of words into segments, and DA recognition assigns a dialog act type to them. Thus, these two tasks are naturally conducted in a cascading manner. The proposed cascading model is shown in Figure 3.

The left part is a sequential labeling model for segmentation. Similar to the joint coding model, a word embedding layer and a layer of RNN are used to produce a sequence of hidden states $\mathbf{h}_{1:L}$.

Words	hi	my	name	is	Erica	nice	to	meet	you
Segmentation	E	I	I	I	E	I	I	I	E
DA	Greeting	Statement				Greeting			
Joint tag coding	E_G	I_S	I_S	I_S	E_S	I_G	I_G	I_G	E_G

Table 2: Joint "IE" tag coding scheme, where "I" and "E" refer to "inside" and "end" respectively. We concatenate segmentation tag with DA tag to produce coded tags. For example, "E_S" denotes the end of a *Statement* segment.

Then the top layer outputs predicted labels $\mathbf{y}_{1:L}$. The right part of Figure 3 uses the hierarchical neural network model introduced in Section 3. In order to provide contextual information, we also maintain a history of sentence representation vectors of previous sentences using the same hierarchical neural network.

Joint training model can be seen as a cascading model with shared components. As shown in Figure 3, the proposed model uses only one set of word embeddings compared with the cascading one, while other task-specific parts are still separated. By updating the shared word embeddings using errors from both tasks, the model is expected to learn features from DA segmentation and recognition and improve its ability of generalization.

5 Experimental Evaluations

In order to evaluate our models, we conducted three sets of experiments:

- **Segmentation task**: evaluate models' DA segmentation performance only.

- **Recognition task**: evaluate models' DA recognition performance given correct segments.

- **Joint segmentation and recognition task**: evaluate models' DA segmentation and recognition jointly, where predicted segments are given for DA recognition.

For each set of experiments, we also vary the length of history k for the cascading model and the joint training model.

5.1 Data Set

We use a one-to-one Japanese chatting corpus collected using a conversational android ERICA (Glas et al., 2016; Inoue et al., 2016). It is annotated with 4 DA tags (i.e. *Question*, *Statement*, *Response* and *Other*) following standards in (Bunt et al., 2010). Table 3 presents related statistics.

Corpus Statistics	
# of classes	4
avg. # of segments per session	165
avg. # of segments per turn	1.76
# of training sessions	30
# of test sessions	8

Table 3: Corpus statistics.

5.2 Implementation

We implemented the proposed models with *TensorFlow*[1]. Neural networks are trained using the Adam optimizer (Kingma and Ba, 2014). We use an initial learning rate of 0.0001 which decays in half when the objective loss does not decrease. A dropout layer of 0.25 dropout probability is added before every RNN layer for regularization. We choose 128 as the word embedding dimension since it works well in most NLP tasks. To find out how history length k affects the models, we experimented on k of 1, 3, 5, 10, 20. We also test CRFs implemented by *CRF++*[2] for comparison in our experiments.

5.3 Evaluation Metrics

For the segmentation task, we use the DA Segmentation Error Rate (DSER) in (Zimmermann et al., 2005). The DSER is the percentage of segments that are incorrectly segmented, i.e. its left or right boundary differs from the reference boundaries. Accuracy, Macro F1 measure, and Weighted F1 measure are used for evaluation of the recognition task since it is a text classification problem. For the joint task, we use the DA Error Rate (DER) which is the same as the DSER but also considers the DA type for correctness. Table 4 demonstrates the calculation of DSER and DER.

---

[1] https://www.tensorflow.org/
[2] https://taku910.github.io/crfpp/

Reference	E_G	L_S	L_S	E_S	L_Q	L_Q	E_Q	L_S	E_S
Prediction	E_G	L_S	L_S	L_S	E_S	L_Q	E_Q	L_R	E_R
DSER	√		×			×		√	
DER	√		×			×		×	

Table 4: An example of DSER and DER metrics. The DSER equals 0.5 (2/4) and the DER equals 0.75 (3/4).

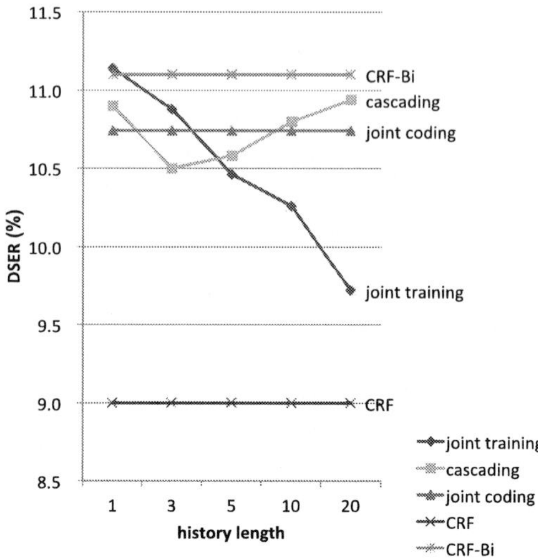

Figure 4: Results of the segmentation task.

5.4 Segmentation Result

In this task, a set of experiments are conducted to evaluate the model performances on DA segmentation specifically. We apply our models to segment every turn in dialogs, where one turn refers to a sequence of consecutive words uttered by one speaker without being interrupted by another speaker. We compare the cascading model, the joint coding model and the joint training model. Two CRFs are used for comparison. A simple CRF uses unigrams and bigrams of w_{t-2}, w_{t-1}, w_t, w_{t+1}, w_{t+2} as features, where w_t is the current word. Another CRF additionally uses the last tag as a feature and is named CRF-Bi in the following experiments.

Figure 4 shows the results of the segmentation task. The joint training model achieves 9.7% DSER at a history length of 20, which is comparable to CRF's 9.0% (without a significant difference), and it outperforms the cascading model's 10.5% at a history length of 3. The joint coding model lags behind slightly with the DSER of 10.7% and CRF-Bi gets a DSER of 11.1%.

5.5 Dialog Act Recognition Result

In the task of DA recognition, we evaluate the model performances of DA recognition. Therefore, we directly use ground-truth segments as inputs and predict a DA label for these segments. We only compare the cascading model and the joint training model in the recognition task because the joint coding model and CRFs are sequence labeling models and they do not naturally fit the text classification task.

As shown in Figure 5, the joint training model gets better results than the cascading model according to all three metrics. The joint training model achieves the best results of 78.0% accuracy, 77.4% Macro F1 measure and 78.1% Weighted F1 measure at the history length of 10, while the cascading model reaches 77.2%, 76.5% and 77.4% respectively. A significant improvement is obtained when we increase the history length from 1 to 3.

5.6 Joint Segmentation and Recognition Result

In the joint task, segmentation and recognition performances are evaluated jointly. We firstly segment each turn in dialogs into segments, then use the predicted segments as inputs of DA recognition. As in the segmentation task, we compare our proposed models and two CRFs.

Figure 6 shows the results of the joint task. The joint training model has the lowest error rate of 27.3% at the history length of 10, gaining an absolute improvement of 1.6% compared with the cascading model's 28.9%. CRF-Bi, CRF and the joint coding model got the DSER of 33.5%, 36.8% and 37.1% respectively.

6 Discussion

In the segmentation task, CRF using only n-gram features obtains a result of 9.0%, though there is not a statistically significant difference in performance between CRF and the joint training model, whose DSER is 9.7%. We conjecture that the re-

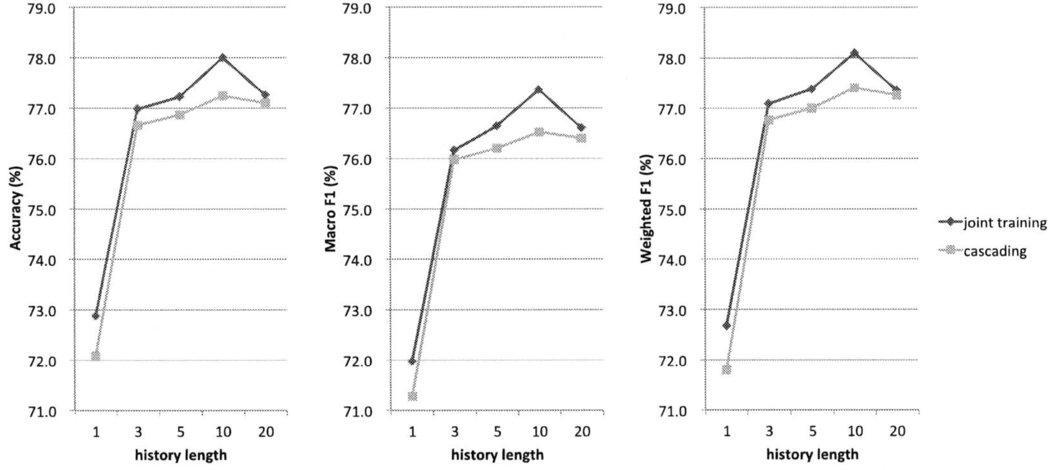

Figure 5: Recognition results evaluated using Accuracy, Macro F1 measure and Weighted F1 measure.

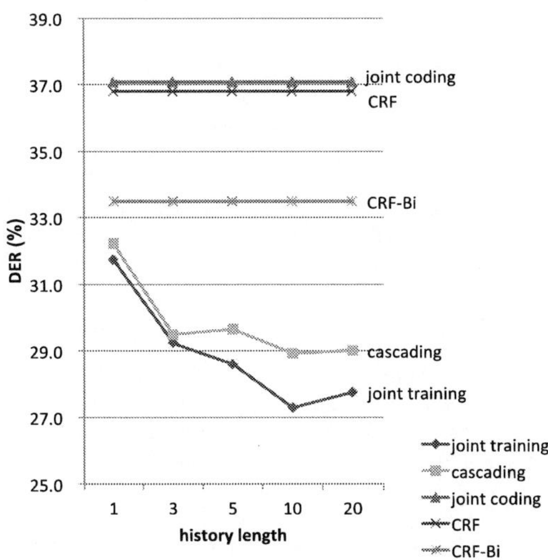

Figure 6: Results of the joint task.

sult is due to that the boundaries of DA segments in Japanese are usually marked with words such as *"masu"*, *"desu"*, *"kedo"*, and considering simple n-gram features can cover most of the cases in DA segmentation. CRF-Bi, which uses a previous tag as additional feature, has a higher error rate of 11.1% compared with CRF using n-grams. It implies that extra information (previous segmentation tag and dialog act tag) may hurt the model's performance in the sense of segmentation. However, by comparing the results of the cascading joint model and the joint training model (10.5% DSER of the cascading model and 9.7% DSER of

the joint training model), we can see that our joint training method is able to extract useful information from DA recognition task for segmentation and improve our models' ability of segmentation.

In the DA recognition task, we compare the best results of the cascading model and the joint training model at a history length of 10. Similar to aforementioned conclusion, joint training helps the joint training model outperform the cascading model by 0.8% in accuracy, 0.9% in Macro F1 measure and 0.7% in Weighted F1 measure. Thus we can conclude that joint training can also learn features from segmentation task to help recognize DA tags.

In the joint evaluation, we observe that even though CRFs obtain fairly good results in the segmentation task, they significantly lag behind the proposed cascading model and the joint training model. The hierarchical neural network introduced in Section 3 makes use of contexts and contributes to the improvement. Similarly, CRF-Bi gets a better result of 33.5% DER than CRF's 36.8%, which implies that contextual information (previous tag) plays an important role in DA recognition.

Finally the joint coding model has an acceptable result of segmentation but a very low performance in the joint task. There are three possible reasons: (1) The joint coding model only uses surrounding words as context instead of previous sentences, thus it fails to capture DA relations while the proposed hierarchical neural network is able to. (2) Failure in learning from the recognition task can degrade the model's performance on the segmentation task. (3) Lastly but the most important, DA recognition requires understanding of the whole segment. In the architecture of joint coding model, however, it has to predict the type of DA tag at the very beginning of a segment. Although a short context (i.e. 5 words in our experiments) is available, the model still cannot make use of complete information of the corresponding segment.

7 Conclusion

In this work, we explored joint learning of dialog act (DA) segmentation and recognition. To exploit contextual information in DA recognition, we introduced a hierarchical neural network architecture that incorporates history utterances. Based on the hierarchical neural network, we investigated three models for joint DA segmentation and recognition, i.e. cascading model, joint coding model, and joint training model. Our proposed models can (1) integrate the hierarchical neural network and (2) combine tasks of different levels (word level and DA segment level) in a unified architecture.

Three sets of experiments were carried out to evaluate the proposed models' performances on the segmentation task, the DA recognition task and the joint task. Experimental results showed that (1) contextual information plays an important role in DA recognition; (2) the cascading model and the joint training model outperform CRF baselines significantly (4.6% and 6.2% in DER respectively) in the joint task while having comparable performances in the segmentation task; (3) the joint training model outperforms the cascading model in all three tasks. The result demonstrates that joint training can learn useful generalized features.

Acknowledgments

This work was supported by JST ERATO Ishiguro Symbiotic Human-Robot Interaction program (Grant Number JPMJER1401), Japan.

References

Harry Bunt, Jan Alexandersson, Jean Carletta, Jae-Woong Choe, Alex Chengyu Fang, Kôiti Hasida, Kiyong Lee, Volha Petukhova, Andrei Popescu-Belis, Laurent Romary, Claudia Soria, and David R. Traum. 2010. Towards an ISO standard for dialogue act annotation. In Nicoletta Calzolari, Khalid Choukri, Bente Maegaard, Joseph Mariani, Jan Odijk, Stelios Piperidis, Mike Rosner, and Daniel Tapias, editors, *Proceedings of the International Conference on Language Resources and Evaluation, LREC 2010, 17-23 May 2010, Valletta, Malta.* European Language Resources Association.

Ronan Collobert and Jason Weston. 2008. A unified architecture for natural language processing: deep neural networks with multitask learning. In William W. Cohen, Andrew McCallum, and Sam T. Roweis, editors, *Machine Learning, Proceedings of the Twenty-Fifth International Conference (ICML 2008), Helsinki, Finland, June 5-9, 2008.* ACM, volume 307 of *ACM International Conference Proceeding Series*, pages 160–167.

Dylan F. Glas, Takashi Minato, Carlos Toshinori Ishi, Tatsuya Kawahara, and Hiroshi Ishiguro. 2016. ERICA: the ERATO intelligent conversational android. In *25th IEEE International Symposium on Robot and Human Interactive Communication, RO-MAN 2016, New York, NY, USA, August 26-31, 2016.* IEEE, pages 22–29.

Ramón Granell, Stephen G. Pulman, and Carlos D. Martínez-Hinarejos. 2009. Simultaneous dialogue act segmentation and labelling using lexical and syntactic features. In Patrick G. T. Healey, Roberto Pieraccini, Donna K. Byron, Steve J. Young, and Matthew Purver, editors, *Proceedings of the SIGDIAL 2009 Conference, The 10th Annual Meeting of the Special Interest Group on Discourse and Dialogue, 11-12 September 2009, London, UK.* The Association for Computer Linguistics, pages 333–336.

Dilek Hakkani-Tür, Gökhan Tür, Asli Çelikyilmaz, Yun-Nung Chen, Jianfeng Gao, Li Deng, and Ye-Yi Wang. 2016. Multi-domain joint semantic frame parsing using bi-directional RNN-LSTM. In Nelson Morgan, editor, *Interspeech 2016, 17th Annual Conference of the International Speech Communication Association, San Francisco, CA, USA, September 8-12, 2016.* ISCA, pages 715–719.

Sepp Hochreiter and Jürgen Schmidhuber. 1997. Long short-term memory. *Neural computation* 9(8):1735–1780.

Koji Inoue, Pierrick Milhorat, Divesh Lala, Tianyu Zhao, and Tatsuya Kawahara. 2016. Talking with erica, an autonomous android. In *Proceedings of the SIGDIAL 2016 Conference, The 17th Annual Meeting of the Special Interest Group on Discourse and Dialogue, 13-15 September 2016, Los Angeles, CA, USA.* The Association for Computer Linguistics, pages 212–215.

Yangfeng Ji, Gholamreza Haffari, and Jacob Eisenstein. 2016. A latent variable recurrent neural network for discourse relation language models. In *NAACL HLT 2016, The 2016 Conference of the North American Chapter of the Association for Computational Linguistics: Human Language Technologies, San Diego California, USA, June 12-17,*

2016. The Association for Computational Linguistics, pages 332–342.

Hamed Khanpour, Nishitha Guntakandla, and Rodney D. Nielsen. 2016. Dialogue act classification in domain-independent conversations using a deep recurrent neural network. In Nicoletta Calzolari, Yuji Matsumoto, and Rashmi Prasad, editors, *COLING 2016, 26th International Conference on Computational Linguistics, Proceedings of the Conference: Technical Papers, December 11-16, 2016, Osaka, Japan*. ACL, pages 2012–2021.

Diederik P. Kingma and Jimmy Ba. 2014. Adam: A method for stochastic optimization. *CoRR* abs/1412.6980.

Siwei Lai, Liheng Xu, Kang Liu, and Jun Zhao. 2015. Recurrent convolutional neural networks for text classification. In Blai Bonet and Sven Koenig, editors, *Proceedings of the Twenty-Ninth AAAI Conference on Artificial Intelligence, January 25-30, 2015, Austin, Texas, USA.*. AAAI Press, pages 2267–2273.

Ji Young Lee and Franck Dernoncourt. 2016. Sequential short-text classification with recurrent and convolutional neural networks. In Kevin Knight, Ani Nenkova, and Owen Rambow, editors, *NAACL HLT 2016, The 2016 Conference of the North American Chapter of the Association for Computational Linguistics: Human Language Technologies, San Diego California, USA, June 12-17, 2016*. The Association for Computational Linguistics, pages 515–520.

Wei Li and Yunfang Wu. 2016. Multi-level gated recurrent neural network for dialog act classification. In Nicoletta Calzolari, Yuji Matsumoto, and Rashmi Prasad, editors, *COLING 2016, 26th International Conference on Computational Linguistics, Proceedings of the Conference: Technical Papers, December 11-16, 2016, Osaka, Japan*. ACL, pages 1970–1979.

Nanyun Peng and Mark Dredze. 2016. Improving named entity recognition for chinese social media with word segmentation representation learning. In *Proceedings of the 54th Annual Meeting of the Association for Computational Linguistics, ACL 2016, August 7-12, 2016, Berlin, Germany, Volume 2: Short Papers*. The Association for Computer Linguistics.

Silvia Quarteroni, Alexei V. Ivanov, and Giuseppe Riccardi. 2011. Simultaneous dialog act segmentation and classification from human-human spoken conversations. In *Proceedings of the IEEE International Conference on Acoustics, Speech, and Signal Processing, ICASSP 2011, May 22-27, 2011, Prague Congress Center, Prague, Czech Republic*. IEEE, pages 5596–5599.

Elizabeth Shriberg, Andreas Stolcke, Daniel Jurafsky, Noah Coccaro, Marie Meteer, Rebecca Bates, Paul Taylor, Klaus Ries, Rachel Martin, and Carol Van Ess-Dykema. 1998. Can prosody aid the automatic classification of dialog acts in conversational speech? *Language and speech* 41(3-4):443–492.

Andreas Stolcke, Klaus Ries, Noah Coccaro, Elizabeth Shriberg, Rebecca Bates, Daniel Jurafsky, Paul Taylor, Rachel Martin, Carol Van Ess-Dykema, and Marie Meteer. 2000. Dialogue act modeling for automatic tagging and recognition of conversational speech. *Computational Linguistics* 26(3):339–373.

Zhilin Yang, Ruslan Salakhutdinov, and William W. Cohen. 2016. Multi-task cross-lingual sequence tagging from scratch. *CoRR* abs/1603.06270.

Feifei Zhai, Saloni Potdar, Bing Xiang, and Bowen Zhou. 2017. Neural models for sequence chunking. In Satinder P. Singh and Shaul Markovitch, editors, *Proceedings of the Thirty-First AAAI Conference on Artificial Intelligence, February 4-9, 2017, San Francisco, California, USA.*. AAAI Press, pages 3365–3371.

Xiaoqing Zheng, Hanyang Chen, and Tianyu Xu. 2013. Deep learning for chinese word segmentation and POS tagging. In *Proceedings of the 2013 Conference on Empirical Methods in Natural Language Processing, EMNLP 2013, 18-21 October 2013, Grand Hyatt Seattle, Seattle, Washington, USA, A meeting of SIGDAT, a Special Interest Group of the ACL*. ACL, pages 647–657.

Matthias Zimmermann. 2009. Joint segmentation and classification of dialog acts using conditional random fields. In *INTERSPEECH 2009, 10th Annual Conference of the International Speech Communication Association, Brighton, United Kingdom, September 6-10, 2009*. ISCA, pages 864–867.

Matthias Zimmermann, Yang Liu, Elizabeth Shriberg, and Andreas Stolcke. 2005. Toward joint segmentation and classification of dialog acts in multiparty meetings. In Steve Renals and Samy Bengio, editors, *Machine Learning for Multimodal Interaction, Second International Workshop, MLMI 2005, Edinburgh, UK, July 11-13, 2005, Revised Selected Papers*. Springer, volume 3869 of *Lecture Notes in Computer Science*, pages 187–193.

Matthias Zimmermann, Andreas Stolcke, and Elizabeth Shriberg. 2006. Joint segmentation and classification of dialog acts in multiparty meetings. In *2006 IEEE International Conference on Acoustics Speech and Signal Processing, ICASSP 2006, Toulouse, France, May 14-19, 2006*. IEEE, pages 581–584.

Predicting Users' Negative Feedbacks in Multi-Turn Human-Computer Dialogues *

Xin Wang[1], Jianan Wang[2], Yuanchao Liu[1], Xiaolong Wang[1],
Zhuoran Wang[3] and Baoxun Wang[3]
[1]Harbin Institute of Technology, Harbin, China
[2]Shanghai Jiao Tong University, Shanghai, China
[3]Tricorn (Beijing) Technology Co., Ltd, Beijing, China
[1]{xwang,lyc,wangxl}@insun.hit.edu.cn
[2]{wangjianan}@sjtu.edu.cn
[3]{wangzhuoran, wangbaoxun}@trio.ai

Abstract

User experience is essential for human-computer dialogue systems. However, it is impractical to ask users to provide explicit feedbacks when the agents' responses displease them. Therefore, in this paper, we explore to predict users' imminent dissatisfactions caused by intelligent agents by analysing the existing utterances in the dialogue sessions. To our knowledge, this is the first work focusing on this task. Several possible factors that trigger negative emotions are modelled. A relation sequence model (RSM) is proposed to encode the sequence of appropriateness of current response with respect to the earlier utterances. The experimental results show that the proposed structure is effective in modelling emotional risk (possibility of negative feedback) than existing conversation modelling approaches. Besides, strategies of obtaining distance supervision data for pre-training are also discussed in this work. Balanced sampling with respect to the last response in the distance supervision data are shown to be reliable for data augmentation.

1 Introduction

As an ideal interaction mode, the human-computer conversation technology has gradually been conducted into the practical systems, among which the automatic agents adopting the task-oriented conversation and open-domain chatting abilities have developed rapidly and even come to commercial application stage (see Duer[1] and XiaoIce[2]).

___
The work was done when the first author was an intern at Tricorn (Beijing) Technology Co., Ltd.

[1]http://duer.baidu.com/

[2]http://www.msxiaoice.com/

Figure 1: A example of multi-turn human-computer dialogue. The responses are readable and relevant to the corresponding queries, but the user in bad mood probably feel antipathy towards the computer's cheer.

Basically, the essence of such commercial dialogue agents is keeping user active, and for this purpose, it is critical to improve users' satisfaction in non-task oriented chatting services.

The reasons of users' displeasure lies in the sessions. As shown in Figure 1, the emotional conflict between the last agent's response and the user's mood leads to the dissatisfaction. Therefore, the negative feedback from user could be predicted according to the context utterances. Indeed, such prediction is of great necessity for improving users' satisfaction, since it is possible to address problems within systems only if there exist methodologies to locate problems and summarize reasons behind. Ideally, if a dialogue agent anticipates the occurrence of the user's negative feedback, it is able to avoid such situations by taking any possible actions, e.g., switching to an-

Proceedings of the The 8th International Joint Conference on Natural Language Processing, pages 713–722,
Taipei, Taiwan, November 27 – December 1, 2017 ©2017 AFNLP

other topic actively. Moreover, user satisfaction can be taken as a metric for evaluating the quality of a given dialogue session and the overall performance of a dialogue agent. In practice, user satisfaction could also be considered as the additional criterion for response selection or generation, which tend to intuitively take semantic relevance oriented features for model training. The adoption of user satisfaction is possible to provide a different view to optimize the models, so as to further improve user experience along the road beyond relevance, e.g., avoiding the responses that are relevant but lack of sociality (Higashinaka et al., 2015).

It is not a trivial task to predict negative feedbacks in the conversation flows between human being and dialogue agents. Generally, people tend to not express their dissatisfaction explicitly, thus, there are generally no clear signals before users turn angry and terminate dialogues, or people continue the conversations although they are not satisfied already. Apparently, it is unwise to introduce rating or other explicit feedback mechanisms into the dialogue flows considering the user experience issues. Meanwhile, this problem cannot be covered by classical sentiment analysis task because users' sentiment intention tends to be not obvious, and more importantly, the facts causing negative feedbacks are much more complicated than sentiment polarities as shown by Figure 1, in which the appropriateness of a certain response might be decided not only by itself, but also by the context.

In order to estimate the risk of dissatisfaction occurring in the human-computer dialogue sessions, in this work, we explore the feasibility of predicting users' emotional negative feedback caused by the dialogue agents' replies based on the dialogue contexts. To our knowledge, this is the first work attempting to discover the implicit factors causing users' dissatisfaction in dialogue agents' logs with deep learning models. Noticing that the occurrence of negative feedbacks depends on a complicated semantic mechanism and conversational contexts play an important role in this issue, this paper proposes to address the problem by learning to represent the possible determinant with different models. Especially, the proposed architecture based on Gated Convolutional Recurrent Neural Networks (GCRNN) is used to represent sequence of relations between the last response and the earlier utterances. Experimentally, it out-

performs existing conversational models, which indicates that the sequence of relation between utterances encodes the possibility of user's dissatisfaction. Besides, data augmentation with distance supervision method is also discussed in this work.

2 Related Work

2.1 Emotion prediction

Predicting sentiment category of text has been extensively studied. Most works focus on the sentiment orientations expressed by the writers in movie/product reviews or tweets (Pang et al., 2002; Hu and Liu, 2004; Go et al., 2009). However, the reader's emotion is not always consistent with that of the writer's (Yang et al., 2007). Thus, Lin et al. (2007) explore to predict the feelings that readers may have after reading particular articles. However, in this dissatisfaction prediction task, the user is not only the reader of the session text, but also the writer of some utterances. Therefore, some clues of the particular user's emotion may be contained in the context.

Modelling emotion in human-human conversation has been explored (Herzig et al., 2016; Tokuhisa and Terashima, 2006). However, triggers for negative emotion in human-computer dialogue might be different (e.g., low readability or relevance). The works of Tokuhisa et al. (2009) and Yu et al. (2016)'s analysed the emotion of a particular utterance in human-computer dialogue based on the textual features containing in the very sentence. Different from their studies analysing the explicit textual feedback, this work predicts the impending emotion based on the context because the cause of emotion of readers contains in the existing text (Li and Xu, 2014).

2.2 Conversation Modelling

Traditional conversation modelling mainly focuses on the one-turn conversations (aka. message-response pairs) (Banchs and Li, 2012; Ameixa et al., 2014; Ritter et al., 2011; Ji et al., 2014), while recent works show more interest in multi-turn dialogues.

The generation-based approaches model the context and generate the responses at the same time (Vinyals and Le, 2015), while the retrieval based studies model the sessions after knowing all utterances, which is more relevant to this work. Xu et al. (2016) represent sequence of utterances with recurrent neural networks (RNNs). The topic or intention in a dialogue session is relatively constant. In this perspective, all the utterances in the same session is homogenous and could be composed within RNNs. However, the influences of user's queries and the agent's responses are different in predicting user's emotion. Therefore, a targeted structure considering such heterogenicity is proposed in this work.

Wu et al. (2016) represent the relevance between utterances with CRNN architecture. Different from their work focusing on word-level matching with attention pooling on the convolutional result, we leverage a gate operation to simulate the sentence-level interaction.

3   Predicting Methodology

The task of predicting impending dissatisfaction could be formulated as: given the existing utterances (EU) that contain no agent-cause dissatisfaction, predicting the agent-cause dissatisfaction $D_1 \in \{0, 1\}$ of user at impending turn ($r = 1$), given the existing utterances (EU) that contain no agent-cause dissatisfaction.

$$EU = \{Q_{-n+1}, R_{-n+1}, ..., Q_{-1}, R_{-1}, Q_0, R_0\} \tag{1}$$

where Q_{-n} and R_{-n} respectively represent the user's query and computer response n round before current turn. For this work focusing on the agent-caused dissatisfaction, those queries Q_{-n} with negative emotion not related to the robot are not considered as negative feedback.

There are several possible factors influencing the emotion of the users, such as (1) the last response of the robot R_0, (2) the relation of Q_0 and R_0, (3) the sequence of context in the conversational sessions EU and (4) the sequence of relations between R_0 and the other utterances $UE - \{R_0\}$. In this session, we will discuss the factors above and learn the representation of them with deep neural network.

3.1   Utterance Modelling

The last response of the robot R_0 is the most straightforward factor that may cause the antipathy towards the agent. Predicting the negative emotions according to the latest response can be considered as reader-side emotion classification. In this work, such single sentence is modelled with convolutional neural network (CNN) with max pooling, and then classified in the full-connected

softmax layer (Kim, 2014). The illustration of the utterance model for R_0 is shown in Figure 2(b).

In this paper, all representations of utterances are attracted with CNN structure described in Figure 2(a). An n-word utterance can be represented as:

$$\mathbf{e}_{1:n} = \mathbf{e}_1 \oplus \mathbf{e}_2 \oplus ... \oplus \mathbf{e}_n \tag{2}$$

where $\mathbf{e}_n$ is the embedding of nth word in the utterance and $\oplus$ refers to concatenation operator. In the convolutional process, the word window starting with the ith word and scanned by a s-width filter j can be represented $\mathbf{e}_{i:i+s-1}$. And the activations corresponding with filter j in convolutional layer can be computed as:

$$c_i^j = f\left(\mathbf{w}^j \cdot \mathbf{e}_{i:i+s-1} + b^j\right) \tag{3}$$

where f is the non-linear activation function (ReLU is utilized in this work). And $\mathbf{w}^j$ and b^j represent the weight matrix and bias respectively. Finally, max-over-time pooling is leveraged. The activations corresponding with filter j in the pooling layer can be computed as:

$$\hat{c}^j = max\left\{c_1^j, c_1^j, ..., c_{n-s+1}^j\right\} \tag{4}$$

3.2   Utterance Pair Modelling

Recent works improve response ranking by model the semantic matching of query-response pairs (Qiu and Huang, 2015; Yin et al., 2015). The assumption implied in these works is that user experience is influenced by the relation of Q_0 and R_0. We model such relation with Architecture-I in Hu et al.'s (2014) work, where the representations of the query and the response are learned with two CNNs respectively and the concatenation of the representations is used as input of a multi-layer perceptron (MLP) classifier that measures the appropriateness.

3.3   Utterance Sequence Modelling

As shown in example in Figure 1, the latest response is active and related to the query, but may not appropriate in the context. Recent works encode the sequence of utterances with recurrent neural network based encoder-decoder to generate responses (Serban et al., 2016; Shang et al., 2015). However, in this work, the prediction is made with all existing utterances being known. The convolutional recurrent neural network has been proven to be effective in encoding the sequence of representations of text (Kalchbrenner and Blunsom, 2013;

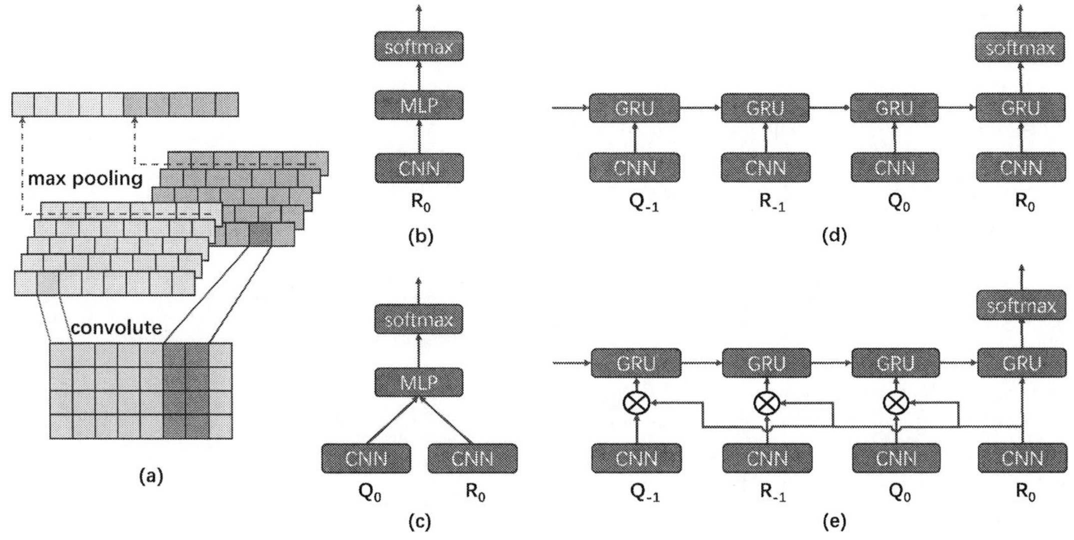

Figure 2: Structures for modelling different influential factors of negative feedbacks.

Li et al., 2016; Zhou et al., 2015). Thus, in this work, the sequence of existing utterances EU is modelled with CRNN, and the output of last time step R_0 is considered as the final representation of the sequence to be input to softmax classifier. The structure is shown in Figure 2(d), and Gated Recurrent Units (GRUs) are used in the structure.

A GRU stores context information in the internal memory structure. It performs comparably with long short-term memory (LSTM) and has lower complexity (Chung et al., 2014). There are two gates in the jth GRU structure, the update gate z_t^j and reset gate r_t^j, both gates are decided by the current input $\mathbf{x}_t$ and previous hidden activation $\mathbf{h}_{t-1}$:

$$z_t^j = \sigma \left(W_z \mathbf{x}_t + U_z \mathbf{h}_{t-1}\right)^j \qquad (5)$$

$$r_t^j = \sigma \left(W_r \mathbf{x}_t + U_r \mathbf{h}_{t-1}\right)^j \qquad (6)$$

where W and U is the weight matrices, while σ refers to the sigmoid function. The hidden activation h_t^j of the GRU at time t can be computed as:

$$h_t^j = \left(1 - z_t^j\right) h_{t-1}^j + z_t^j \tilde{h}_t^j \qquad (7)$$

where h_{t-1}^j refers to the hidden activation of previous time step and $\tilde{h}_t^j$ is the current candidate activation:

$$\tilde{h}_t^j = tanh \left(W \mathbf{x}_t + U \left(\mathbf{r}_t \odot \mathbf{h}_{t-1}\right)\right)^j \qquad (8)$$

GRUs compose the current and previous information with the gated units, and store the sequence representation in the memory.

3.4 Relation Sequence Modelling

Different from the intentions or topics of utterances being relatively constant in dialogue sessions, emotional influence of each utterance varies. For instance, the queries and responses are heterogeneous in a session. Queries are expressions of dissatisfaction, while responses are the reason of displeasure. The relations between particular response and context queries (or other responses) influence the user's emotion.

As shown in the example in Figure 1, the last response R_0 conveys conflicting emotion with the earlier utterances Q_{-2}, R_{-2} and Q_{-1}. The human user is probably unprepared for such rapid change in emotion and exhibits dissatisfaction. The consistency of mood is a kind of relation between sentences and the sequence of such consistency between sentence pairs can be treated as the emotional consistency of the whole conversation.

However, traditional RNNs are not adequate to represent such consistency. Therefore, we attempt to model the sequence of relation between utterances. As mentioned in the beginning of Section 3, the existing utterances EU contain no agent-cause dissatisfaction, which means Q_0 and the utterances before Q_0 are not the direct causes negative feedback. Thus, we only focus on the relation between the last response and the earlier utterances. The architecture is shown in Figure 2(e), the representation of earlier utterances $\mathbf{x}_t$ ($t \neq 0$)

are gated by representation of R_0:

$$\mathbf{x}_t = \mathbf{c}_t \odot \mathbf{m}_t \qquad (9)$$

where $\mathbf{c}_t$ is the output of convolutional neural network sentence model. And the matching gate $\mathbf{m}_t$ is influenced by the particular utterance $\mathbf{c}_t$ and the latest response $\mathbf{c}_0$.

$$\mathbf{m}_t = \sigma \left(W_m \mathbf{c}_t + U_m \mathbf{c}_0 \right) \qquad (10)$$

While the input of the last time step is the representation of R_0 itself ($\mathbf{x}_0 = \mathbf{c}_0$). Gating operation has been shown effective in further mapping abstract feature of convolutional result by involving additional information (Wang et al., 2015; Dauphin et al., 2016). With such structure, the emotional consistency of utterances could be extracted and the influence of latest response on negative feedback could be encoded.

4 Experiments

4.1 Dataset

The anonymized multi-turn dialogue session data is provided by a Chinese commercial intelligent agent service. There are 2 million sessions in the dataset, most of which contain task-oriented dialogues. However, we focus on those only including chat, and the amount of such pure chat sessions is 260,867.

As described in the introduction, the task is to predict the impending dissatisfaction given $n + 1$ round context. Thus, a sample in the dataset should contains utterances and label of following emotional polarity. In fact, the lengths of human-computer dialogue sessions vary within relatively wide range. To eliminate the influences from session length, n is set to 2 in this work. The appearance of dissatisfaction will be predicted based on 3 turns (0, 1 and 2) of dialogue (as shown in Figure 1). 40,000 of the non-task-oriented sessions are manual annotation to construct the data set. If a session has a negative feedback, the 3 turns of utterances before this feedback will be treated as positive (with dissatisfaction) sample. Otherwise, if there's no negative feedback, we randomly select continuous 3-turn utterances as a negative (without dissatisfaction) sample.

Two experienced annotators (long term employed for text annotation) are scheduled to label the sessions independently. If disagreement appears, a third senior annotator is invited to decide the final tag. Finally, 30,034 sessions meeting

Category	Amount
total sessions	2,000,000
pure char sessions	260,867
sessions for manually labelling	40,000
two annotators agreement	28,651
the third annotator decision	11,349
gold standard	30,039
negative in gold standard	17,618
positive in gold standard	12,421

Table 1: Statistical information of the dataset.

the requirements (non-negative sessions or negative sessions with 3 three turns or more utterances before the negative expressions) are used as gold-standard dataset. Some statistical information of the dataset is shown in Table 1.

4.2 Pre-training

4.2.1 Fragment Extraction

The manually labelled gold standard dataset might be insufficient for learning deep neural models. Thus, a distance supervision strategy is designed to obtain augmented data. We summarize 56 patterns of highly probable negative expressions as strict patterns (SP) and 86 patterns of possible or ambiguous negative feedbacks as uncertain patterns (UP). It is noted that the SP is a subset of UP. The sessions containing no utterances matching UP are considered as non-negative. While the utterances (1)containing any SP and (2)with no utterances in the above 3 turns match any UP are treated as negative feedbacks and the fragments are tagged as dissatisfaction ones. In this way, both positive and negative samples of dissatisfaction are automatically detected.

Besides the pure chat sessions, those task-oriented ones also contain multi-turn chat fragment. Therefore, the augmentation strategy is carried out on all available sessions and obtains 1,612,426 distance supervised labelled fragments. It is worthy to note that there may be multiple available fragments in a single session, those fragments (without overlap) are all extracted in the augmentation process.

4.2.2 Balanced Dataset Construction

In fact, the extraction strategy above may lead to a different distribution with the real-world data. Taking the cheerful response R_0 in Figure 1 as an example, most users in bad mood would be upset after the agents reply with such cheer. These users tend to express dissatisfaction towards the agents and the dissatisfactions are detected with designed patterns. While in the situations where the users are happy, the cheerful response result in a virtuous cycle and may not be selected as R_0 (may be selected as R_{-1} or R_{-2}). Therefore, such cheerful response is likely to closely related to the dissatisfaction.

To avoid such false association rules, we select the same number of positive and negative samples if R_0 is the same and obtain 335,314 fragments as balanced distance supervised labelled data.

4.3 Experimental Settings

All the neural network models are implemented with TensorFlow toolkit[3]. The max length of the input sentence is set to 10 and all sentences are padded to the max length with zero vectors. 32 filters are used for each filter size, while the sizes of word embeddings, hidden layer in RNN and full-connected layer are all set to 64.

The weights between full-connected layers are initialized with Xavier initializer (Glorot and Bengio, 2010), while the weights and biases in the convolutional layer are initialized with random numbers on uniform distribution $\mathcal{U}\{-0.2, 0.2\}$. Word embeddings are randomly initialized with uniform distribution $\mathcal{U}\{-0.1, 0.1\}$ and fine-tuned during training.

Batch learning is conducted with a batch size of 500. The learning rate of the training process is 0.001 while that of pre-training process is 0.005. 10-fold cross validation are implemented with 80% data as training set, and validation and test set divide equally the rest 20% samples. Early stopping is carried out on validation set during training. Training process stops when there's no better validation result within 5 epochs.

4.4 Competitor Models

SVM-R_0: Support vector machine (SVM) are wildly used as classifiers for sentiment analysis tasks (Pang et al., 2002). In this work, TF-IDF features based on uni-grams in R_0 are involved to build baseline model.

SVM-Q_0R_0 and SVM-EU: To make use of more context information, we involve Q_0-R_0 pair by connecting them into a whole and uni-gram TF-IDF features of the connection result are used as

input of a SVM classifier. In the same way, the all sentences in EU are also used in the SVM model. **UM-Q_0R_0 and UM-EU:** Similar to SVM, utterance model (UM) shown in Figure 2(b) is also designed to analyse a single sentence (or document). Thus, we leverage connection results of Q_0-R_0 pair and EU to introduce context utterance. **UPM-EU:** Besides Q_0-R_0 pair, the utterance pair model (UPM) could also be used to encode all sentences in EU. Each sentence is modelled by CNN respectively and the representations are concatenated in the hidden layer.

4.5 Experimental Results

4.5.1 Comparison with Baselines

We compare the models corresponding to the factor assumptions describe in section 3, including utterance model (UM), utterance pair model (UPM), utterance sequence model (USM) and relation sequence model (RSM) with the competitor systems. The numbers in Table 2 show the proportion of the particular model accurately predicting the emotional polarities. The neural models are pre-trained with balanced distance supervised labelled data, and tuned with the manually annotated samples.

Model	Accuracy
SVM-R_0	0.5486
SVM-Q_0R_0	0.5603
SVM-EU	0.5616
UM-R_0	0.5495
UM-Q_0R_0	0.5579
UM-EU	0.5638
UPM-Q_0R_0	0.5723
UPM-EU	0.5781
USM-EU	0.6022
RSM-EU	**0.6106**

Table 2: Accuracies of different models.

Firstly, the last computer's response R_0 is the basic feature that makes the prediction effective. Comparing the models involving Q_0-R_0 pair and EU with those only use R_0, we can easily find that the context provides more information about the trend of emotion.

SVM achieves comparable results with CNN based utterance model. We see that the convolutional process with a fixed-size filter encodes the similar information with n-gram features in SVM.

UPM outperforms UM with both Q_0-R_0 pair

---

[3] www.tensorflow.org/

and EU. UPM connects the abstract representation in the hidden layer, while UM connects the sentences into a whole as input. Although their structures are similar as shown in Figure 2, the logic depths of the two models are different. UM composes word embedding of all sentences in the convolutional process to learn an emotional representation, while UPM gets emotion features in two steps (composing word representation in convolutional layer and then adding mapped the sentence embedding after pooling). In practice, UPM works as a hierarchical compositional model. Such strategy makes the internal compositional process more flexible and expressive. In this way, the hidden layer simulates the relation between sentences in a more appropriate manner.

The CRNN based models (USM-EU and RSM-EU) achieve a significant improvement over other approaches including UPM (according to the two-sided paired t-test with a confidence level of $\alpha = 0.05$). UPM maps the representation of sentences to the same space and adds up the mapping result as the conversation representation. However, such process is less expressive than CRNN. In the test process, the weight matrix that mapping sentence representations in UPM is constant after training and the contribution of each sentence to the conversation is relatively fixed. While the GRUs in the CRNN could select the information resource flexibly through the reset gate r and update gate z, controlling the influence of particular sentence according to the context (Chung et al., 2014). Moreover, the gating process is a kind of multiplicative operation between sentence embeddings. Such multiplicative compositional functions are more expressive in simulating interaction between abstract features than additive ones (Socher et al., 2013; İrsoy and Cardie, 2015). Thus, CRNN based models handle the interaction between utterances in a more flexible way than UPM.

RSM is more effective than USM according to the results in Table 2. This is due to the fact that the gated operation makes it possible to adjust sentence representation according to R_0. Therefore, besides the interaction between adjacent utterances handled by the recurrent structure, the influence of interaction between R_0 and other utterances can be involved into the final representation and distance relation and consistency could be encoded.

4.5.2 Case Study

In order to illustrate the difference between USM and RSM in an intuitive way, we calculate the risk of negative feedback for each time step in these two recurrent models with the input of the session shown in Figure 1. The outputs of recurrent layer of each time step are used as inputs of the full-connection layer and the softmax regression results are considered as the probabilities of user's dissatisfaction.

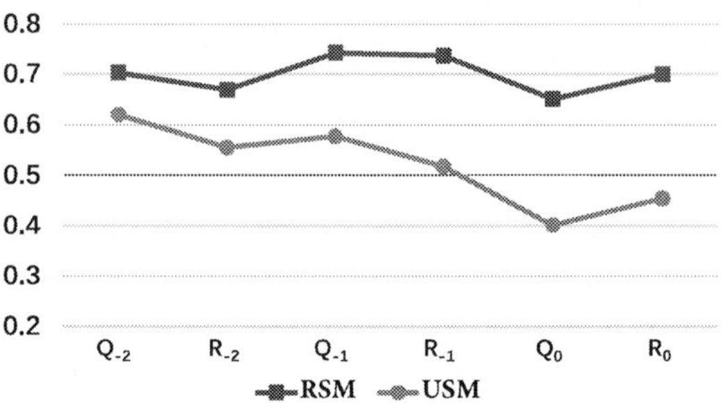

Figure 3: The probabilities of negative feedback for each utterance in sessions in Figure 1.

The line chart of the sequence of probabilities of the two models are shown in Figure 3. The tendencies of these two line are similar. It is due to the fact that the gates controlled by R_0 shrink the activations of recurrent layer and adjust the scales of values without changing the quadrant or feature space.

For the same utterance Q_{-2}, there's a difference between the probabilities of these two models, and the gap between the two line get more obvious after Q_{-1} is input. Both Q_{-2} and Q_{-1} contains negative emotions and possibly lead to dissatisfaction. Thus, the probabilities of negative feedback increase at the corresponding time step. However, the gated activations in RSM change more sharply. It indicates that the emotional inconsistency between R_0 and these two user messages lead to a further increasing of risk through the gated adjustment.

Finally, the RSM predicts that the negative feedback will occur in the next time step (with the probabilities larger than 0.5), which is true according to the corpus. However, the USM fails to make the correct prediction.

4.5.3 Comparison of Pre-training Strategies

As discussed in Subsection 4.2, different pre-training strategies are implemented during the

Models	NPT	UPT	BPT
UM-R_0	0.5365	0.5232	0.5495
UPM-Q_0R_0	0.5619	0.5547	0.5623
USM-EU	0.5865	**0.5808**	0.6022
RSM-EU	**0.5939**	0.5782	**0.6106**

Table 3: Comparison of accuracies with no pre-training (NPT), unbalanced pre-training (UPT) and balanced pre-training (BPT)

training process. The comparison of accuracy of these strategies are shown in Table 3.

Unbalanced pre-training strategy leads to a worse performance than only using manually labelled data. As discussed in 4.2.2, when a false rule is learned, a particular R_0 is associated with a wrong label, which hurts the performance obviously. Moreover, during the experimental process of unbalanced pre-training, it is observed that the models involving more context achieve better result than those only using R_0 as input. It is due to that the existence of the strong correlation between R_0 and the label itself is an inaccurate pattern, no matter whether the label is correct. The pre-training data encoding such strong correlation will makes the models ignore the context utterance and convergence to the local optimum only related to R_0.

However, the balanced pre-training dataset is effective in initializing the networks. The experimental results show that the balanced pre-training improves the performance of the networks. The underlying reason is that the pre-training process provides a better initialization for the networks, and the converging process of tuning continues based on an initial optimization.

4.5.4 Other Discussions

Directionality: Bi-directional and backward-directional recurrent networks are tested. Both structures lead to drop in accuracy (about 1%). We see that the last response R_0 is the essential determinant of emotion, the basic forward RNN structure has a bias on the last time steps for being free from the influence of small recurrent connection weight matrix. While adding backward-directional processing involving more parameters and weaken the influence of R_0 and Q_0-R_0 pair.

Filter Size: Inspired by the SVM baseline models performing not worse than the utterance model, we introduce 1×1 filters, working together with 2×1 ones, and such setting achieves an improve-

ment by about 1% than only using 2×1 ones (from 0.6019 to 0.6106 with RSM). In practice, the larger filter size (e.g. 3, 4 or 5) leads to instability in the prediction. It is due to the fact that the utterances conversations are relatively short. Features within a uni-gram or bi-gram window is eligible for representing the emotional information. Although covering some sparse features, involving more larger filters results in risk of over-fitting.

5 Conclusion and Future Work

In this paper, we propose the problem of predicting users impending negative feedbacks by modelling the context queries and replies in human-agent conversation. Four kinds of influencing factors, (1) the computer's last response R_0, (2) the relation of last turn dialogue pair Q_0-R_0, (3) the sequence of all utterance and (4) the sequence of relation between utterances, are modelled with deep neural networks. The experimental results show that these factors indeed influence the emotional trend. We have encoded the possibility of dissatisfaction by representing the sequence of relation between utterances with a gated convolutional recurrent neural network. Tested on the real-world human-agent dialogue dataset, the proposed architecture outperforms the existing conversation models. Besides, balanced sampling on distance supervision labelled data are shown to be reliable in network pre-training.

The accuracies of prediction is only about 60%, we see that different users show different emotional feedbacks towards the same context. Thus, there are a few potential explorations: (1) build corpus on fine-grained emotional categories and (2) predict the emotional distribution on these categories instead of classifying into a certain one. Moreover, we would like to apply the emotional risk to the response ranking to improve the user experience of dialogue system.

Acknowledgments

We thank the anonymous reviewers for their insightful comments. This research is partially supported by National Natural Science Foundation of China (No.61672192, No.61572151, No.61602131) and the National High Technology Research and Development Program ("863" Program) of China (No.2015AA015405).

References

David Ameixa, Luisa Coheur, Pedro Fialho, and Paulo Quaresma. 2014. *Luke, I am Your Father: Dealing with Out-of-Domain Requests by Using Movies Subtitles.*

Rafael E. Banchs and Haizhou Li. 2012. Iris: a chat-oriented dialogue system based on the vector space model. In *ACL 2012 System Demonstrations*, pages 37–42.

Junyoung Chung, Caglar Gulcehre, Kyung Hyun Cho, and Yoshua Bengio. 2014. Empirical evaluation of gated recurrent neural networks on sequence modeling. *Eprint Arxiv.*

Yann N. Dauphin, Angela Fan, Michael Auli, and David Grangier. 2016. Language modeling with gated convolutional networks.

Xavier Glorot and Yoshua Bengio. 2010. Understanding the difficulty of training deep feedforward neural networks. *Journal of Machine Learning Research*, 9:249–256.

Alec Go, Richa Bhayani, and Lei Huang. 2009. Twitter sentiment classification using distant supervision. *CS224N Project Report, Stanford*, pages 1–12.

Jonathan Herzig, Guy Feigenblat, Michal Shmueli-Scheuer, David Konopnicki, Anat Rafaeli, Daniel Altman, and David Spivak. 2016. Classifying emotions in customer support dialogues in social media. In *Meeting of the Special Interest Group on Discourse and Dialogue.*

Ryuichiro Higashinaka, Kotaro Funakoshi, Masahiro Araki, Hiroshi Tsukahara, Yuka Kobayashi, and Masahiro Mizukami. 2015. Towards taxonomy of errors in chat-oriented dialogue systems. In *Meeting of the Special Interest Group on Discourse and Dialogue*, pages 87–95.

Baotian Hu, Zhengdong Lu, Hang Li, and Qingcai Chen. 2014. Convolutional neural network architectures for matching natural language sentences. In *International Conference on Neural Information Processing Systems*, pages 2042–2050.

Minqing Hu and Bing Liu. 2004. Mining opinion features in customer reviews. In *AAAI*, volume 4, pages 755–760.

Ozan İrsoy and Claire Cardie. 2015. Modeling compositionality with multiplicative recurrent neural networks. In *International Conference on Learning Representations (ICLR).*

Zongcheng Ji, Zhengdong Lu, and Hang Li. 2014. An information retrieval approach to short text conversation. *Computer Science.*

Nal Kalchbrenner and Phil Blunsom. 2013. Recurrent convolutional neural networks for discourse compositionality. *Computer Science.*

Yoon Kim. 2014. Convolutional neural networks for sentence classification. *Eprint Arxiv.*

Linchuan Li, Zhiyong Wu, Mingxing Xu, Helen Meng, and Lianhong Cai. 2016. Combining cnn and blstm to extract textual and acoustic features for recognizing stances in mandarin ideological debate competition. In *INTERSPEECH*, pages 1392–1396.

Weiyuan Li and Hua Xu. 2014. Text-based emotion classification using emotion cause extraction. *Expert Systems with Applications An International Journal*, 41(4):1742–1749.

Hsin Yih Lin, Changhua Yang, and Hsin Hsi Chen. 2007. What emotions do news articles trigger in their readers? In *SIGIR 2007: Proceedings of the International ACM SIGIR Conference on Research and Development in Information Retrieval, Amsterdam, the Netherlands, July*, pages 733–734.

Bo Pang, Lillian Lee, and Shivakumar Vaithyanathan. 2002. Thumbs up?: sentiment classification using machine learning techniques. In *Acl-02 Conference on Empirical Methods in Natural Language Processing*, pages 79–86.

Xipeng Qiu and Xuanjing Huang. 2015. Convolutional neural tensor network architecture for community-based question answering. In *International Conference on Artificial Intelligence*, pages 1305–1311.

Alan Ritter, Colin Cherry, and William B Dolan. 2011. Data-driven response generation in social media. In *Conference on Empirical Methods in Natural Language Processing*, pages 583–593.

Iulian V. Serban, Alessandro Sordoni, Yoshua Bengio, Aaron Courville, and Joelle Pineau. 2016. Building end-to-end dialogue systems using generative hierarchical neural network models. *Computer Science*, (4).

Lifeng Shang, Zhengdong Lu, and Hang Li. 2015. Neural responding machine for short-text conversation. *Computer Science.*

Richard Socher, Alex Perelygin, Jean Y Wu, Jason Chuang, Christopher D Manning, Andrew Y Ng, and Christopher Potts. 2013. Recursive deep models for semantic compositionality over a sentiment treebank. In *Proceedings of the Conference on Empirical Methods in Natural Language Processing (EMNLP)*, pages 1631–1642.

Ryoko Tokuhisa, Kentaro Inui, and Yuji Matsumoto. 2009. Emotion classification using massive examples extracted from the web. In *COLING 2008, International Conference on Computational Linguistics, Proceedings of the Conference, 18-22 August 2008, Manchester, Uk*, pages 881–888.

Ryoko Tokuhisa and Ryuta Terashima. 2006. Relationship between utterances and "enthusiasm" in non-task-oriented. In *Meeting of the Special Interest Group on Discourse and Dialogue*, pages 161–167.

Oriol Vinyals and Quoc Le. 2015. A neural conversational model. *Computer Science*.

Mingxuan Wang, Zhengdong Lu, Hang Li, Wenbin Jiang, and Qun Liu. 2015. *gen*cnn: A convolutional architecture for word sequence prediction. *Computer Science*.

Bowen Wu, Baoxun Wang, and Hui Xue. 2016. Ranking responses oriented to conversational relevance in chat-bots.

Zhen Xu, Bingquan Liu, Baoxun Wang, Chengjie Sun, and Xiaolong Wang. 2016. Incorporating loose-structured knowledge into conversation modeling via recall-gate lstm.

Changhua Yang, Hsin Yih Lin, and Hsin Hsi Chen. 2007. Emotion classification using web blog corpora. In *Web Intelligence, IEEE/WIC/ACM International Conference on*, pages 275–278.

Wenpeng Yin, Hinrich Schtze, Bing Xiang, and Bowen Zhou. 2015. Abcnn: Attention-based convolutional neural network for modeling sentence pairs. *Computer Science*.

Zhou Yu, Leah Nicolich-Henkin, Alan W Black, and Alex I. Rudnicky. 2016. A wizard-of-oz study on a non-task-oriented dialog systems that reacts to user engagement. In *Meeting of the Special Interest Group on Discourse and Dialogue*, pages 55–63.

Chunting Zhou, Chonglin Sun, Zhiyuan Liu, and Francis C. M. Lau. 2015. A c-lstm neural network for text classification. *Computer Science*, 1(4):39–44.

Finding Dominant User Utterances And System Responses in Conversations

Dhiraj Madan and **Sachindra Joshi**
IBM Research Labs
New Delhi, India
{dhimadan,jsachind@in.ibm.com}

Abstract

There are several dialog frameworks which allow manual specification of intents and rule based dialog flow. The rule based framework provides good control to dialog designers at the expense of being more time consuming and laborious. The job of a dialog designer can be reduced if we could identify pairs of user intents and corresponding responses automatically from prior conversations between users and agents. In this paper we propose an approach to find these frequent user utterances (which serve as examples for intents) and corresponding agent responses. We propose a novel SimCluster algorithm that extends standard K-means algorithm to simultaneously cluster user utterances and agent utterances by taking their adjacency information into account. The method also aligns these clusters to provide pairs of intents and response groups. We compare our results with those produced by using simple K-means clustering on a real dataset and observe upto 10% absolute improvement in F1-scores. Through our experiments on synthetic dataset, we show that our algorithm gains more advantage over K-means algorithm when the data has large variance.

1 Introduction

There are several existing works that focus on modelling conversation using prior human to human conversational data (Gašić et al., 2013; Young et al., 2013; Henderson et al., 2014). (Higashinaka et al., 2011) models the conversation from pairs of consecutive tweets. Deep learning based approaches have also been used to model the dialog in an end to end manner (Vinyals and Le, 2015; Serban et al., 2015). Memory networks have been used by Bordes et al (2016) to model goal based dialog conversations. More recently, deep reinforcement learning models have been used for generating interactive and coherent dialogs (Li et al., 2016) and negotiation dialogs (Lewis et al., 2017).

Industry on the other hand has focused on building frameworks that allow manual specification of dialog models such as api.ai[1], Watson Conversational Services[2], and Microsoft Bot framework[3]. These frameworks provide ways to specify *intents*, and a *dialog flow*. The user utterances are mapped to intents that are passed to a dialog flow manager. The dialog manager generates a response and updates the dialog state. See Figure 1 for an example of some intents and a dialog flow in a technical support domain. The dialog flow shows that when a user expresses an intent of *# laptop_heat*, then the system should respond with an utterance *"Could you let me know the serial number of your machine "*. The designer needs to specify intents (for example *# laptop_heat, # email_not_opening*) and also provide corresponding system responses in the dialog flow. This way of specifying a dialog model using intents and corresponding system responses manually is more popular in industry than a data driven approach as it makes dialog model easy to interpret and debug as well as provides a better control to a dialog designer. However, this is very time consuming and laborious and thus involves huge costs.

One approach to reduce the task of a dialog designer is to provide her with frequent user intents and possible corresponding system responses in

---

[1]https://api.ai/
[2]https://www.ibm.com/watson/developercloud/conversation.html
[3]https://dev.botframework.com

Proceedings of the The 8th International Joint Conference on Natural Language Processing, pages 723–732,
Taipei, Taiwan, November 27 – December 1, 2017 ©2017 AFNLP

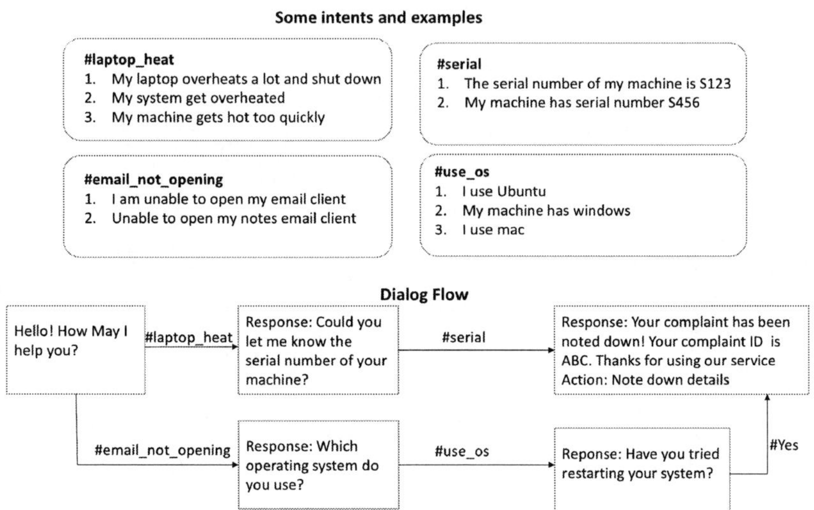

Figure 1: Some intents and dialog flow

a given domain. This can be done by analysing prior human to human conversations in the domain. Figure 2(a) provides some example conversations in the technical support domain between users and agents.

In order to identify frequent user intents, one can use existing clustering algorithms to group together all the utterances from the users. Here each cluster would correspond to a new intent and each utterance in the cluster would correspond to an example for the intent. Similarly the agents utterances can be clustered to identify system responses. However, we argue that rather than treating user utterances and agents responses in an isolated manner, there is merit in jointly clustering them. There is adjacency information of these utterances that can be utilized to identify better user intents and system responses. As an example, consider agent utterances A.2 in box A and A.2 in box C in Figure 2(a). The utterances "Which operating system do you use?" and "What OS is installed in your machine" have no syntactic similarity and therefore may not be grouped together. However the fact that these utterances are adjacent to the similar user utterances "I am unable to start notes email client" and "Unable to start my email client" provides some evidence that the agent utterances might be similar. Similarly the user utterances "My system keeps getting rebooted" and "Machine is booting time and again" (box B and D in Figure 2(a))- that are syntactically not similar - could be grouped together since the adjacent agent utterances, "Is your machine heating up?" and "Is the machine heating?" are similar.

Joint clustering of user utterances and agent utterances allow us to align the user utterance clusters with agent utterance clusters. Figure 2(b) shows some examples of user utterance clusters and agent utterance clusters along with their alignments. Note that the user utterance clusters can be used by a dialog designer to specify intents, the agent utterance clusters can be used to create system responses and their alignment can be used to create part of the dialog flow.

We propose two ways to take adjacency information into account. Firstly we propose a method called *SimCluster* for jointly or simultaneously clustering user utterances and agent utterances. SimCluster extends the K-means clustering method by incorporating additional penalty terms in the objective function that try to align the clusters together (described in Section 3). The algorithm creates initial user utterance clusters as well as agent utterance clusters and then use bi-partite matching to get the best alignment across these clusters. Minimizing the objective function pushes the cluster centroids to move towards the centroids of the aligned clusters. The process implicitly ensures that the similarity of adjacent agent utterances affect the grouping of user utterances and conversely similarity of adjacent user utterances affect the grouping of agent utterances. In our sec-

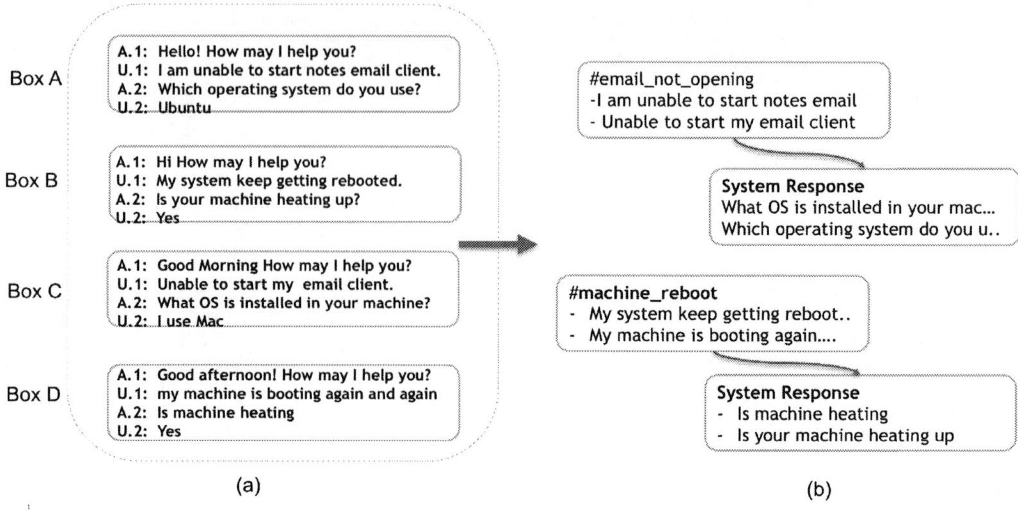

Figure 2: Some sample conversations and the obtained clusters

ond approach we use the information about neighbouring utterances for creating the vector representation of an utterance. For this we train a sequence to sequence model (Sutskever et al., 2014) to create the vectors (described in Section 5).

Our experiments described in section 5 show that we achieve upto 10% absolute improvement in F1 scores over standard K-means using SimCluster. Also we observe that clustering of customer utterances gains significantly by using the adjacency information of agent utterances whereas the gain in clustering quality of agent utterances is moderate. This is because the agent utterances typically follow similar syntactic constructs whereas customer utterances are more varied. Considering the agent utterances into account while clustering users utterances is thus helpful. The organization of the rest of the paper is as follows. In Section 2 we describe the related work. In Section 3 we describe our problem formulation for clustering and the associated algorithm. Finally in sections 4 and 5 we discuss our experiments on synthetic and real datasets respectively.

2   Related Work

The notion of adjacency pairs was introduced by Sacks et al (1974) to formalize the structure of a dialog. Adjacency pairs have been used to analyze the semantics of the dialog in computational linguistics community (Palomar and Martínez-Barco, 2000). Clustering has been used for different tasks related to conversation. (Ritter et al., 2010) considers the task of discovering dialog acts by clustering the raw utterances. We aim to obtain the frequent adjacency pairs through clustering. There have been several works regarding extensions of clustering to different scenarios such as:-

1. Co-clustering : Co-clustering considers the setting where data and features are clustered simultaneously. Dhillon (2001) considers a spectral graph theoretic approach to co-cluster documents and words simultaneously. Dhillon, Mallela and Modha (2003) consider an information theoretic formulation of co-clustering.

2. Multi task learning: Multi task learning considers task of learning from multiple domains simultaneously (Caruana, 1998). Gu and Zhou (2009) consider the problem of multi task clustering wherein they cluster multiple domains simultaneously and utilize the relation of the domains to enhance clustering performance. Their model consists a reduced subspace in which the projection of vectors from the two domains have similar distribution. They then try to learn this common subspace and the clusters simulta-

neously. Our scenario differs from multi task learning since here the distributions across the domains tend to be different. (The domains being the possible utterances of user and agent).

3. Transfer learning considers the task of transfering the knowledge across similar tasks (Danyluk et al., 2009). Bhattacharya et al (2012) consider the task of clustering in the target domain using the given clusters in a source domain. They formulate the problem of minimizing a weighted sum of the energy function in the clustering, along with the energy of aligning the clusters of the two domains. This setting differs from ours since again the utterances in the two domains can be very different. Moreover unlike the task of transfer learning we do not have clusters in any of the domains. However we do have information regarding the adjacency of utterances between the two domains.

3 The Proposed Approach

In this section we describe our approach SimCluster that performs clustering in the two domains simultaneously and ensures that the generated clusters can be aligned with each other. We will describe the model in section 3.1 and the algorithm in Section 3.2.

3.1 Model

We consider a problem setting where we are given a collection of pairs of consecutive utterances, with vector representations $\{x^{(i)}, y^{(i)}\}_{i=1}^m$ where $x^{(i)}$s are in speaker 1's domain and $y^{(i)}$s are in speaker 2's domain. We need to simultaneously cluster the utterances in their respective domains to minimize the variations within each domain and also ensure that the clusters for both domains are close together.

We denote the clusters for speaker 1's domain by $\{C_j^x\}_{j=1}^k$ with their respective means $\{\mu_j^x\}_{j=1}^k$. We denote the clusters assignments for $x^{(i)}$ by $ca^x(i) \in \{1, 2, ..., k\}$.

We denote the clusters for second speaker by $\{C_j^y\}_{j=1}^k$ with their respective means $\{\mu_j^y\}_{j=1}^k$. We denote the clusters assignments for $y^{(i)}$ by $Ca^y(i) \in \{1, 2, ...k\}$. The usual energy function has the terms for distance of points from their corresponding cluster centroids. To be able to ensure that the clusters in each domain are similar, we also consider an alignment between the centroids of the two domains. Since the semantic representations in the two domains are not comparable we consider a notion of **induced** centroids.

We define the induced centroids $\widetilde{\{\mu_j^x\}}_{j=1}^k$ as the arithmetic means of the points $\{x^{(i)}\}$s such that $y^{(i)}$'s have the same cluster assigned to them. Similarly, we define $\widetilde{\{\mu_j^y\}}_{j=1}^k$ as the arithmetic means of $\{y^{(i)}\}$s such that $x^{(i)}$s have the same cluster assigned to them. More formally, we define these induced centroids as:-

$$\widetilde{\{\mu_j^x\}} = \frac{\sum_{i:Ca^y(i)=j} x^{(i)}}{|\{i : Ca^y(i) = j\}|}$$

and

$$\widetilde{\{\mu_j^y\}} = \frac{\sum_{i:Ca^x(i)=j} y^{(i)}}{|\{i : Ca^x(i) = j\}|}$$

The alignment between these clusters given by the function $ma : [k] \mapsto [k]$, which is a bijective mapping from the cluster indices in speaker 1's domain to those in speaker 2's domain. Though there can be several choices for this alignment function, we consider this alignment to be a matching which **maximizes the sum of number of common indices** in the aligned clusters. More formally we define

$$N(j_1, j_2) = |\{i : x^{(i)} \in C_{j_1}^x \text{ and } y^{(i)} \in C_{j_2}^y\}|$$

Then the matching ma is defined to be the bijective function which maximizes $\sum_{j=1}^k N(j, ma(j))$. We consider a term in the cost function corresponding to the sum of distances between the original centroids and the matched induced centroids. Our overall cost function is now given by:-

$$J = \alpha(\sum_{i=1}^m \|x^{(i)} - \mu_{Ca^x(i)}^x\|^2$$

$$+ \sum_{i=1}^m \|y^{(i)} - \mu_{Ca^y(i)}^y\|^2)$$

$$+ (1-\alpha)(\sum_{j=1}^k \|\mu_j^x - \widetilde{\mu_{ma(j)}^x}\|^2 . |C_j^x|$$

$$+ \sum_{j=1}^k \|\mu_j^y - \widetilde{\mu_{ma^{-1}(j)}^y}\|^2 |C_j^y|)$$

We explain the above definition via an example. Consider the clusters shown in Figure 3. Here the ma would match C_1^x to C_1^y, C_2^x to C_3^y and C_3^x to C_2^y, giving a match score of 6. Since $y^{(1)}$, $y^{(2)}$ and $y^{(4)}$ are present in the cluster C_1^y, $\widetilde{\mu_1^x}$ is given by $\frac{x^{(1)}+x^{(2)}+x^{(4)}}{3}$. Similarly

$$\widetilde{\mu_2^x} = \frac{x^{(3)} + x^{(8)} + x^{(9)}}{3}$$
$$\widetilde{\mu_3^x} = \frac{x^{(5)} + x^{(6)} + x^{(7)}}{3}$$

In a similar manner, $\widetilde{\mu^y}$s can also be defined. Now the alignment terms are given by:-

$$\|\mu_1^x - \widetilde{\mu_1^x}\|^2|C_1^x| + \|\mu_2^x - \widetilde{\mu_3^x}\|^2|C_2^x| + \|\mu_3^x - \widetilde{\mu_2^x}\|^2|C_3^x| +$$
$$\|\mu_1^y - \widetilde{\mu_1^y}\|^2|C_1^y| + \|\mu_2^y - \widetilde{\mu_3^y}\|^2|C_2^y| + \|\mu_3^y - \widetilde{\mu_2^y}\|^2|C_3^y|$$

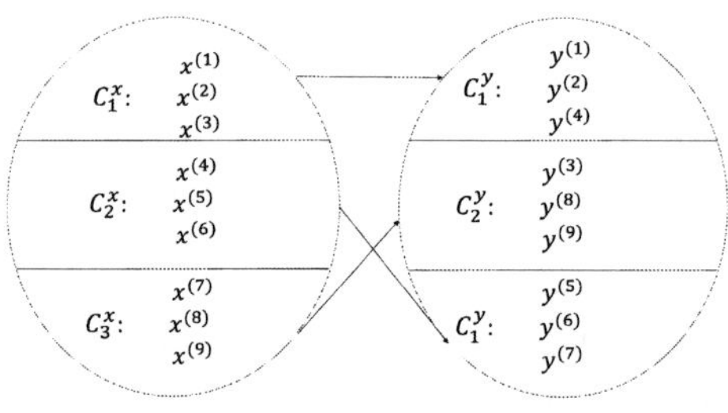

Figure 3: Sample clusters with matching

3.2 SimCluster Algorithm

To minimize the above energy term we adopt an approach similar to Lloyd's clustering algorithm (1982) . We assume that we are given a set of initial seeds for the cluster centroids $\{\mu_j^x\}_{j=1}^k$ and $\{\mu_j^y\}_{j=1}^k$. We **repeat** the following steps iteratively:-

1. Minimize the energy with respect to cluster assignment keeping centroids unchanged. As in standard K-means algorithm, this is achieved by updating the cluster assignment, Ca^x for each index i to be the cluster index j which minimizes $\|x^{(i)} - \mu_j^x\|^2$. Correspondingly for Ca^y, we pick the cluster index j' which minimizes $\|y^{(i)} - \mu_{j'}^y\|^2$.

2. Minimize the energy with respect to the centroids keeping cluster assignment unchanged. To achieve this step we need to minimize the energy function with respect to the centroids μ_j^x and μ_j^y. This is achieved by setting $\nabla_{\mu_j^x} J = 0$ for each j and $\nabla_{\mu_j^y} J = 0$ for each j.
Setting $\nabla_{\mu_j^x} J = 0$, we obtain

$$\mu_j^x = \alpha \left(\frac{\sum_{i:Ca^x(i)=j} x(i)}{|C_j^x|} \right) + (1-\alpha)\widetilde{\mu_{ma(j)}^x}$$

or equivalently

$$\mu_j^x = \alpha \left(\frac{\sum_{i:Ca^x(i)=j} x(i)}{|C_j^x|} \right)$$
$$+ (1-\alpha) \left(\frac{\sum_{i:Ca^y(i)=ma(j)} x(i)}{|C_j^y|} \right)$$

Similarly, setting $\nabla_{\mu_j^y} J = 0$, we obtain

$$\mu_j^y = \alpha \left(\frac{\sum_{i:Ca^y(i)=j} y(i)}{|C_j^y|} \right)$$
$$+ (1-\alpha) \left(\frac{\sum_{i:Ca^x(i)=ma^{-1}(j)} y(i)}{|C_j^x|} \right)$$

3. Finally we update the matching between the clusters. To do so, we need to find a bipartite matching match on the cluster indices so as to maximize $\sum_{j=1}^k N(j, ma(j))$. We use Hungarian algorithm (Kuhn, 1955) to perform the same i.e. we define a bipartite graph with vertices consisting of cluster indices in the two domains. There is an edge from vertex representing cluster indices j (in domain 1) and j' in domain 2, with weight N(j,j'). We find a maximum weight bipartite matching in this graph.

Similar to Lloyd's algorithm, each step of the above algorithm decreases the cost function. This ensures that the algorithm achieves a local minima of the cost function if it converges. See Algorithm 2 for a formal description of the approach. The centroid update step of the above algorithm also has an intuitive explanation i.e. we are slightly moving away the centroid towards the matched induced centroid. This is consistent with our goal of aligning the clusters together in the two domains.

3.3 Alignment

The algorithm above maintains a mapping between the clusters in each speaker's domain. This mapping serves to give us the alignment between the clusters required to provide a corresponding response for a given user intent.

Algorithm 1 SimCluster

1: **procedure** SIMCLUSTER(Input: $\{(x^{(i)}, y^{(i)})\}_{i=1}^{m}$,k (No. of cluster))
2:     Output: A cluster assignment Ca^x for $x^{(i)}$s and a cluster assignment Ca^y for $y^{(i)}$s
3:     Initialize a set of centroids $\{\mu_j^x\}_{j=1}^{k}$, and $\{\mu_j^y\}_{j=1}^{k}$
4:     Perform simple clustering for a few iterations
5:     **repeat**
6:         For each i, compute $Ca^x(i)$ as the index j among 1 to k which minimizes $\|x^{(i)} - \mu_j^x\|^2$.
7:         Similarly , compute $Ca^y(i)$ as the index j' among 1 to k which minimizes $\|y^{(i)} - \mu_{j'}^y\|^2$.
8:         Update the centroids, μ_j^x and μ_j^y as:-

$$\mu_j^x = \alpha \left(\frac{\sum_{i:Ca^x(i)=j} x(i)}{|C_j^x|} \right) + (1 - \alpha) \left(\frac{\sum_{i:Ca^y(i)=ma(j)} x(i)}{|C_j^y|} \right)$$

and

$$\mu_j^y = \alpha \left(\frac{\sum_{i:Ca^y(i)=j} y(i)}{|C_j^y|} \right) + (1 - \alpha) \left(\frac{\sum_{i:Ca^x(i)=ma^{-1}(j)} y(i)}{|C_j^x|} \right)$$

9:         Perform a Hungarian matching between the cluster indices in the two domains with weights
10:         N(j,j') on edges from index j to index j'.
11:     **until** convergence

	Domain 1		Domain 2	
	F1-score	ARI	F1-score	ARI
K-means	0.412	0.176	0.417	0.180
SimCluster	0.442	0.203	0.441	0.204

Table 1: Performance of SimCluster versus K-means clustering on synthetic dataset

4   Experiments on Synthetic Dataset

We performed experiments on synthetically generated dataset since it gives us a better control over the distribution of the data. Specifically we compared the gains obtained using our approach versus the variance of the distribution. We created dataset from the following generative process.

Algorithm 2 Generative Process

1: **procedure** GENERATE DATA
2:     Pick k points $\{\mu_x^{(i)}\}_{i=1}^{k}$ as domain -1 means and a corresponding set of k points $\{\mu_y^{(i)}\}_{i=1}^{k}$ as domain-2 means, and covariance matrices Σ_x and Σ_y
3:     **for** iter$\leftarrow$ 1 upto num_samples **do**
4:         Sample class $\sim U\{1, 2...k\}$
5:         Sample q $\sim \mathcal{N}(\mu_x^{class}, \Sigma_x)$
6:         Sample a $\sim \mathcal{N}(\mu_y^{class}, \Sigma_y)$
7:         Add q and a so sampled to the list of q,a pairs

We generated the dataset from the above sampling process with means selected on a 2 dimensional grid of size 3×3 with variance set as $\frac{1}{2}$ in each dimension.10000 sample points were gener-

ated. The parameter α of the above algorithm was set to 0.5 and k was set to 9 (since the points could be generated from one of the 9 gaussians with centroids on a 3×3 grid).

We compared the results with simple K-means clustering with k set to 9. For each of these, the initialization of means was done using D^2 sampling approach (Arthur and Vassilvitskii, 2007).

4.1   Evaluation and Results

To evaluate the clusters we computed the following metrics

1. ARI (Adjusted Rand Index): Standard Rand Index is a metric used to check the clustering quality against a given standard set of clusters by comparing the pairwise clustering decisions. It is defined as $\frac{a+b}{a+b+c+d}$, where a is the number of true positive pairs, b is the number of true negative pairs, c is the number of false positive pairs and d is the number of false negative pairs. Adjusted rand index corrects the standard rand index for chance and is defined as $\frac{\text{Index} - \text{Expected index}}{\text{Max Index} - \text{Expected index}}$ (Rand, 1971).

We compute ARI score for both the source clusters as well as the target clusters.

2. F1 scores: We also report F1 scores for the pairwise clustering decisions. In the above notation we considered the pair-precision as $\frac{a}{a+c}$ and recall as $\frac{a}{a+d}$. The F1 measure is the Harmonic mean given as $\frac{2PR}{P+R}$.

We used the gaussian index from which an utterance pair was generated as the ground truth label, which served to provide ground truth clusters for computation of the above evaluation metrics. Table 1 shows a comparison of the results on SimCluster versus K-means algorithm. Here our SimCluster algorithm improves the F1-scores from 0.412 and 0.417 in the two domains to 0.442 and 0.441. The ARI scores also improve from 0.176 and 0.180 to 0.203 and 0.204.

4.1.1 Variation with variance

We also performed experiments to see how the performance of SimCluster is affected by the variance in the cluster (controlled by the generative process in Algorithm 2). Intuitively we expect SimCluster to obtain an advantage over simple K-means when variance is larger. This is because at larger variance, the data points are more likely to be generated away from the centroid due to which they might be clustered incorrectly with the points from neighbouring cluster. However if the corresponding point from the other domain is generated closer to the centroid, it might help in clustering the given data point correctly. We performed these experiments with points generated from Algorithm 2 at differet values of variance. We generated the points with centroids located on a grid of size 3×3 in each domain. The value of k was set to 9. The experiment was repeated for each value of variance between 0.1 to 1.0 in the intervals of 0.1. Figures 4 and 5 show the percentage improvement on ARI score and F1 score respectively achieved by SimCluster (over K-means) versus variance.

5 Experiments on Real Dataset

5.1 Description and preprocessing of dataset

We have experimented on a dataset containing Twitter conversations between customers and Amazon help. The dataset consisted of 92130 conversations between customers and amazon help. We considered the conversations with exactly two speakers Amazon Help and a customer. Consecutive utterances by the same speaker were concatenated and considered as a single utterance. From these we extracted adjacency pairs of the form of a

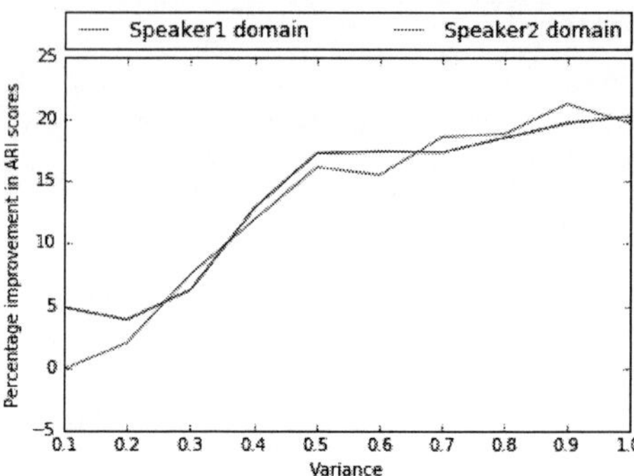

Figure 4: Improvement in ARI figures achieved by SimCluster versus variance

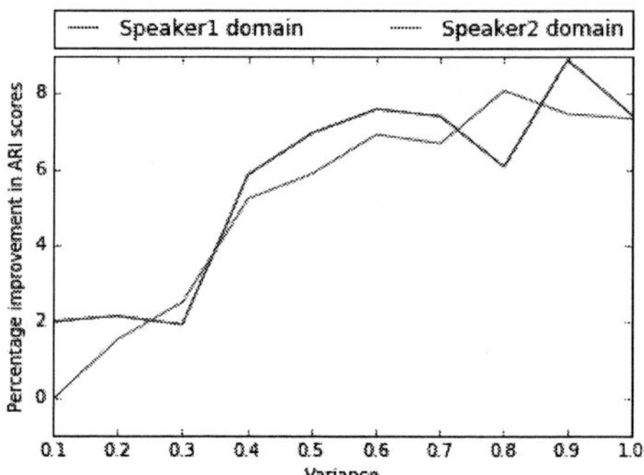

Figure 5: Variation of Improvement in F1 score figures achieved by SimCluster versus variance

customer utterance followed by an agent (Amazon Help) utterance. We then selected the utterance pairs from 8 different categories, like late delivery of item, refund, unable to sign into the account, replacement of item, claim of warranty, tracking delivery information etc. A total of 1944 utterance pairs were selected.

To create the vector representation we had used two distinct approaches:-

1. Paragraph to vector approach (Doc2Vec) by Le and Mikolov (2014). Here we trained the vectors using distributed memory algorithm and trained for 40 iterations. A window size of 4 was used.

2. We also trained the vectors using sequence to sequence approach (Sutskever et al., 2014), on the Twitter dataset where we considered the task of predicting the reply of Amazon Help for customer's query and vice versa. The encoded vector from the input sequence forms the corresponding vector representa-

	Customer		Agent	
	F1-score	ARI	F1-score	ARI
K-means (Doc2Vec)	0.787	0.150	0.783	0.136
SimCluster (Doc2Vec)	0.88	0.19	0.887	0.192
K-means (Seq2Seq)	0.830	0.159	0.900	0.218
SimCluster (Seq2Seq)	0.860	0.181	0.916	0.218

Table 2: Performance of SimCluster versus K-means clustering on both Doc2Vec as well as seq2seq based vectors

Clusters in user domain	Clusters in agent domain
no refund got for the refund request made on 12 ... 11 days & counting on a refund . was promised 3-5 days ... yes i contacted my bank 2 days ... there is no sign of an amazon refund processing . **@amazon refer screen shot ..When will i get my refund ?...** **... I have to wait 3-5 business days for Amazon to refund me money ...**	... You can view your order refund status here ... It can take up to 10 business days ... the refund has been processed **... if you have received the refund reference number then ... contact support team ...** **Refunds typically take 5-7 days to show on your account ...** **... As soon as the product reaches the shipper the refund will be initiated ...**
...my package is late so why did I get prime ? Paid $ 20 + in shipping for next day delivery yesterday but ... even tho I have prime **my order wasnt delivered yesterday ... why am I pay for prime ?** **do you bother to let anyone know ... What is the point of prime ?** **I'm a Amazon prime member . You promised me 2day delivery ...**	I'm sorry to see it's late ... I'm sorry it arrived late, but glad you did receive it . **I'm glad to hear it was delivered , but I'm sorry it was a day late ...** **I'm sorry your order is late ! When you contacted us...**

Table 3: Sample clusters in user and agent domains. Utterances in bold are those which were not in the given cluster using K-means, but could be correctly classified with the cluster using SimCluster

tion. For the task of generating the agent's response for customer utterance the encoding from the input sequence (in the trained model) forms the vector representation for the customer utterance. Similarly for the task of generating the previous customer utterance from the agent's response, the intermediate encoding forms the vector representation for the agent utterance. We used an LSTM based 3-layered sequence to sequence model with attention for this task.

We ran the K-means clustering algorithm for 5 iterations followed by our SimCluster algorithm for 30 iterations to form clusters in both the (customer and agent) domains. The hyper parameter(α) is chosen based on a validation set. We varied the value of α from 0.5 to 1.0 at intervals of 0.025. The initialization of centroids was performed using D^2 sampling approach (Arthur and Vassilvitskii, 2007).

5.2 Results

For the clusters so obtained we have computed F1 and ARI measures as before and compared with the K-means approach. We used the partitioning formed by the 8 categories (from which the utterance pairs were selected) as the ground truth clustering.

Table 2 summarizes the results. We observe that for K-means algorithm, the vectors generated from sequence to sequence model perform better than the vectors generated using paragraph to vector for both the domains. This is expected as the vectors generated from sequence to sequence model encode some adjacency information as well. We further observe that the SimCluster approach performs better than the K-means approach for both the vector representations. It improves the F1-scores for Doc2Vec representation from 0.787 and 0.783 to 0.88 and 0.887 in the two domains. Also the F1-scores on Seq2Seq based representation improve from 0.83 and 0.9 to 0.86 and 0.916 using SimCluster. However the gains are much more in case of Doc2Vec representations than Seq2Seq representations since Doc2Vec did not have any information from the other domain where as some amount of this information is already captured by Seq2Seq representation. Moreover it is the clustering of customer utterances which is likely to see an improvement. This is because agent utterances tends to follow a generic pattern while customer utterances tend to be more varied. Considering agent utterances while generating clusters in the user domain thus tends to be more helpful than the other way round.

Table 3 shows qualitative results on the same dataset. Column 1 and 2 consists of clusters of utterances in customer domain and agent domain respectively. The utterances with usual font are representative utterances from clusters obtained through K-means clustering. The utterances in bold face indicate the similar utterances which were incorrectly classified in different clusters using K-means but were correctly classified together with the utterances by SimCluster algorithm.

6 Conclusions

One of the first steps to automate the construction of conversational systems could be to identify the frequent user utterances and their corresponding system responses. In this paper we proposed an approach to compute these groups of utterances by clustering the utterances in both the domains using our novel SimCluster algorithm which seeks to simultaneously cluster the utterances and align the utterances in two domains. Through our experiments on synthetically generated datset we have shown that SimCluster has more advantage over K-means on datasets with larger variance. Our technique improves upon the ARI and F1 scores on a real dataset containing Twitter conversations.

Acknowledgments

We thank Dr. David Nahamoo (CTO, Speech Technology and Fellow IBM Research) for his valuable guidance and feedback. We also acknowledge the anonymous reviewers of IJCNLP 2017 for their comments.

References

David Arthur and Sergei Vassilvitskii. 2007. k-means++: The advantages of careful seeding. In *Proceedings of the eighteenth annual ACM-SIAM symposium on Discrete algorithms*, pages 1027–1035. Society for Industrial and Applied Mathematics.

Indrajit Bhattacharya, Shantanu Godbole, Sachindra Joshi, and Ashish Verma. 2012. Cross-guided clustering: Transfer of relevant supervision across tasks. *ACM Transactions on Knowledge Discovery from Data (TKDD)*, 6(2):9.

Antoine Bordes and Jason Weston. 2016. Learning end-to-end goal-oriented dialog. *arXiv preprint arXiv:1605.07683*.

Rich Caruana. 1998. Multitask learning. In *Learning to learn*, pages 95–133. Springer.

Andrea Pohoreckyj Danyluk, Léon Bottou, and Michael L. Littman, editors. 2009. *Proceedings of the 26th Annual International Conference on Machine Learning, ICML 2009, Montreal, Quebec, Canada, June 14-18, 2009*, volume 382 of *ACM International Conference Proceeding Series*. ACM.

Inderjit S Dhillon. 2001. Co-clustering documents and words using bipartite spectral graph partitioning. In *Proceedings of the seventh ACM SIGKDD international conference on Knowledge discovery and data mining*, pages 269–274. ACM.

Inderjit S Dhillon, Subramanyam Mallela, and Dharmendra S Modha. 2003. Information-theoretic co-clustering. In *Proceedings of the ninth ACM SIGKDD international conference on Knowledge discovery and data mining*, pages 89–98. ACM.

M Gašić, Catherine Breslin, Matthew Henderson, Dongho Kim, Martin Szummer, Blaise Thomson, Pirros Tsiakoulis, and Steve Young. 2013. Online policy optimisation of bayesian spoken dialogue systems via human interaction. In *Acoustics, Speech and Signal Processing (ICASSP), 2013 IEEE International Conference on*, pages 8367–8371. IEEE.

Quanquan Gu and Jie Zhou. 2009. Learning the shared subspace for multi-task clustering and transductive transfer classification. In *Data Mining, 2009. ICDM'09. Ninth IEEE International Conference on*, pages 159–168. IEEE.

Matthew Henderson, Blaise Thomson, and Steve Young. 2014. Word-based dialog state tracking with recurrent neural networks. In *Proceedings of the 15th Annual Meeting of the Special Interest Group on Discourse and Dialogue (SIGDIAL)*, pages 292–299.

Ryuichiro Higashinaka, Noriaki Kawamae, Kugatsu Sadamitsu, Yasuhiro Minami, Toyomi Meguro, Kohji Dohsaka, and Hirohito Inagaki. 2011. Building a conversational model from two-tweets. In *Automatic Speech Recognition and Understanding (ASRU), 2011 IEEE Workshop on*, pages 330–335. IEEE.

Harold W Kuhn. 1955. The hungarian method for the assignment problem. *Naval research logistics quarterly*, 2(1-2):83–97.

Quoc V Le and Tomas Mikolov. 2014. Distributed representations of sentences and documents. In *ICML*, volume 14, pages 1188–1196.

Mike Lewis, Denis Yarats, Yann N Dauphin, Devi Parikh, and Dhruv Batra. 2017. Deal or no deal? end-to-end learning for negotiation dialogues. *arXiv preprint arXiv:1706.05125*.

Jiwei Li, Will Monroe, Alan Ritter, Michel Galley, Jianfeng Gao, and Dan Jurafsky. 2016. Deep reinforcement learning for dialogue generation. *arXiv preprint arXiv:1606.01541*.

Stuart Lloyd. 1982. Least squares quantization in pcm. *IEEE transactions on information theory*, 28(2):129–137.

Manuel Palomar and Patricio Martínez-Barco. 2000. Anaphora resolution through dialogue adjacency pairs and topics. In *International Conference on Natural Language Processing*, pages 196–203. Springer.

William M Rand. 1971. Objective criteria for the evaluation of clustering methods. *Journal of the American Statistical association*, 66(336):846–850.

Alan Ritter, Colin Cherry, and Bill Dolan. 2010. Unsupervised modeling of twitter conversations. In *Human Language Technologies: The 2010 Annual Conference of the North American Chapter of the Association for Computational Linguistics*, pages 172–180. Association for Computational Linguistics.

Harvey Sacks, Emanuel A Schegloff, and Gail Jefferson. 1974. A simplest systematics for the organization of turn-taking for conversation. *language*, pages 696–735.

Iulian V Serban, Alessandro Sordoni, Yoshua Bengio, Aaron Courville, and Joelle Pineau. 2015. Building end-to-end dialogue systems using generative hierarchical neural network models. *arXiv preprint arXiv:1507.04808*.

Ilya Sutskever, Oriol Vinyals, and Quoc V Le. 2014. Sequence to sequence learning with neural networks. In *Advances in neural information processing systems*, pages 3104–3112.

Oriol Vinyals and Quoc Le. 2015. A neural conversational model. *arXiv preprint arXiv:1506.05869*.

Steve Young, Milica Gašić, Blaise Thomson, and Jason D Williams. 2013. Pomdp-based statistical spoken dialog systems: A review. *Proceedings of the IEEE*, 101(5):1160–1179.

End-to-End Task-Completion Neural Dialogue Systems

Xiujun Li[†]   **Yun-Nung Chen**[⋆]   **Lihong Li**[†]   **Jianfeng Gao**[†]   **Asli Celikyilmaz**[†]

[†]Microsoft Research, Redmond, WA, USA

[⋆]National Taiwan University, Taipei, Taiwan

[⋆]`y.v.chen@ieee.org`

[†]`{xiul,lihongli,jfgao,aslicel}@microsoft.com`

Abstract

One of the major drawbacks of modularized task-completion dialogue systems is that each module is trained individually, which presents several challenges. For example, downstream modules are affected by earlier modules, and the performance of the entire system is not robust to the accumulated errors. This paper presents a novel end-to-end learning framework for task-completion dialogue systems to tackle such issues. Our neural dialogue system can directly interact with a structured database to assist users in accessing information and accomplishing certain tasks. The reinforcement learning based dialogue manager offers robust capabilities to handle noises caused by other components of the dialogue system. Our experiments in a movie-ticket booking domain show that our end-to-end system not only outperforms modularized dialogue system baselines for both objective and subjective evaluation, but also is robust to noises as demonstrated by several systematic experiments with different error granularity and rates specific to the language understanding module[1].

1 Introduction

In the past decade, goal-oriented dialogue systems have been the most prominent component in today's virtual personal assistants, which allow users to speak naturally in order to accomplish tasks more efficiently. Traditional systems have a rather complex and modularized pipeline, consisting of a language understanding (LU) module, a dialogue

manager (DM), and a natural language generation (NLG) component (Rudnicky et al., 1999; Zue et al., 2000; Zue and Glass, 2000).

Recent advances of deep learning have inspired many applications of neural models to dialogue systems. Wen et al. (2017) and Bordes et al. (2017) introduced a network-based end-to-end trainable task-oriented dialogue system, which treated dialogue system learning as the problem of learning a mapping from dialogue histories to system responses, and applied an encoder-decoder model to train the whole system. However, the system is trained in a supervised fashion: not only does it require a lot of training data, but it may also fail to find a good policy robustly due to lack of exploration of dialogue control in the training data. Zhao and Eskenazi (2016) first presented an end-to-end reinforcement learning (RL) approach to dialogue state tracking and policy learning in the DM. This approach is shown to be promising when applied to the task-oriented dialogue problem of guessing the famous person a user thinks of. In the conversation, the agent asks the user a series of *Yes/No* questions to find the correct answer. However, this simplified task may not generalize to practical problems due to the following:

1. **Inflexible question types** — asking request questions is more natural and efficient than *Yes/No* questions. For example, it is more natural and efficient for the system to ask *"Where are you located?"* instead of *"Are you located in Palo Alto?"*, when there are a large number of possible values for the location slot.

2. **Poor robustness** — the user answers are too simple to be misunderstood, so the system lacks the robustness against noise in real user utterances.

3. **User requests during dialogues** — in a task-oriented dialogue, user may ask questions for

---

[1]The source code is available at: `https://github/com/MiuLab/TC-Bot`.

Proceedings of the The 8th International Joint Conference on Natural Language Processing, pages 733–743,
Taipei, Taiwan, November 27 – December 1, 2017 ©2017 AFNLP

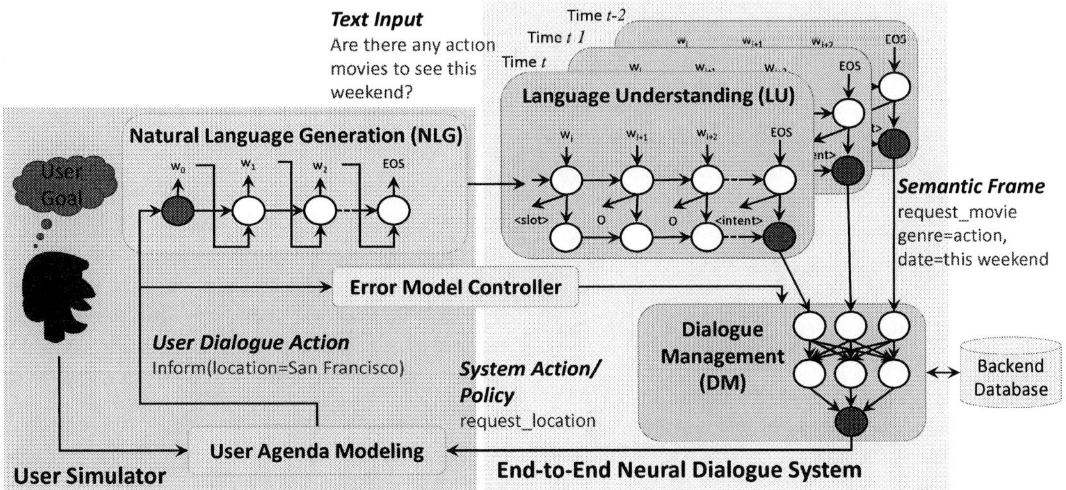

Figure 1: Illustration of the end-to-end neural dialogue system: given user utterances, reinforcement learning is used to train all components in an end-to-end fashion.

selecting the preferred slot values. In a flight-booking example, user might ask *"What flight is available tomorrow?"*.

For the second issue, Su et al. (2016) briefly investigated the effect of dialogue action level semantic error rates on the dialogue performance. Lemon and Liu (2007) compared policy transfer properties under different environments, showing that policies trained in high-noise conditions have better transfer properties than those trained in low-noise conditions. Recently, Dhingra et al. (2017) proposed an end-to-end differentiable KB-Infobot to provide the solutions to the first two issues, but the last one remained unsolved.

This paper addresses all three issues above by redefining the targeted system as a task-completion neural dialogue system. Our framework is more practical in that the information can be easily accessed by the user during the conversations, while the final goal of the system is to complete a task, such as movie-ticket booking. This paper is the first attempt of training a real-world task-completion dialogue system in an end-to-end fashion by leveraging supervised learning and reinforcement learning techniques. To further understand the robustness of reinforcement learning based dialogue systems, we conduct extensive experiments and quantitative analysis on a fine-grained level of LU errors, and provide meaningful insights on how the language understanding component impacts the overall performance of the

dialogue system.

Our contributions are three-fold:

- **Robustness** — We propose a neural dialogue system with greater robustness by automatically selecting actions based on uncertainty and confusion by reinforcement learning. We also provide the first systematic analysis to investigate the impact of different types of natural language understanding errors on dialogue system performance. We show that slot-level errors have a greater impact on the system performance than intent-level ones, and that slot value replacement degrades the performance most. Our findings shed some light on how to design multi-task natural language understanding models (intent classification and slot labeling) in the dialogue systems with consideration of error control.
- **Flexibility** — The system is the first neural dialogue system that allows user-initiated behaviors during conversations, where the users can interact with the system with higher flexibility that is important in realistic scenarios.
- **Reproducibility** — We demonstrate how to evaluate RL dialogue agents using crowd-sourced task-specific datasets and simulated users in an end-to-end fashion, guaranteeing reproducibility and consistent comparisons of competing methods in an identical setting.

W	find	action	movies	this	weekend
	↓	↓	↓	↓	↓
S	O	B-genre	O	B-date	I-date
I	find_movie				

Figure 2: An example utterance with annotations of semantic slots in IOB format (S) and intent (I), B-date and I-date denote the date slot.

2 Proposed Framework

The proposed framework[2] is illustrated in Figure 1. It includes a user simulator (left part) and a neural dialogue system (right part). In the user simulator, an agenda-based user modeling component based at the dialogue act level is applied to control the conversation exchange conditioned on the generated user goal, to ensure the user behaves in a consistent, goal-oriented manner. An NLG module is used to generate natural language texts corresponding to the user dialogue actions. In a neural dialogue system, an input sentence (recognized utterance or text input) passes through an LU module and becomes a corresponding semantic frame, and an DM, which includes a state tracker and policy learner, is to accumulate the semantics from each utterance, robustly track the dialogue states during the conversation, and generate the next system action.

2.1 Neural Dialogue System

Language Understanding (LU): A major task of LU is to automatically classify the domain of a user query along with domain specific intents and fill in a set of slots to form a semantic frame. The popular IOB (in-out-begin) format is used for representing the slot tags, as shown in Figure 2.

$$\vec{x} = w_1, ..., w_n, <\text{EOS}>$$
$$\vec{y} = s_1, ..., s_n, i_m$$

where $\vec{x}$ is the input word sequence and $\vec{y}$ contains the associated slots, s_k, and the sentence-level intent i_m. The LU component is implemented with a single LSTM, which performs intent prediction and slot filling simultaneously (Hakkani-Tür et al., 2016; Chen et al., 2016):

$$\vec{y} = \text{LSTM}(\vec{x}). \tag{1}$$

The LU objective is to maximize the conditional probability of the slots and the intent $\vec{y}$ given the

---

[2]The source code is available at: `https://github.com/MiuLab/TC-Bot`

word sequence $\vec{x}$:

$$p(\vec{y} \mid \vec{x}) = \left(\prod_i^n p(s_i \mid w_1, \ldots, w_i) \right) p(i_m \mid \vec{y}).$$

The weights of the LSTM model are trained using backpropagation to maximize the conditional likelihood of the training set labels. The predicted tag set is a concatenated set of IOB-format slot tags and intent tags; therefore, this model can be trained using all available dialogue actions and utterance pairs in our labeled dataset in a supervised manner.

Dialogue Management (DM): The symbolic LU output is passed to the DM in the dialogue act form (or semantic frame). The classic DM includes two stages, *dialogue state tracking* and *policy learning*.

- **Dialogue state tracking**: Given the LU symbolic output, such as request(moviename; genre=action; date=this weekend), three major functions are performed by the state tracker: a symbolic query is formed to interact with the database to retrieve the available results; the state tracker will be updated based on the available results from the database and the latest user dialogue action; and the state tracker will prepare the state representation s_t for policy learning.

- **Policy learning**: The state representation for the policy learning includes the latest user action (e.g., request(moviename; genre=action; date=this weekend)), the latest agent action (request(location)), the available database results, turn information, and history dialogue turns, etc. Conditioned on the state representation s_t from the state tracker, the policy π is to generate the next available system action a_t according to $\pi(s_t)$. Either supervised learning or reinforcement learning can be used to optimize π. Details about RL-based policy learning can be found in section 3.

Prior work used different implementation approaches summarized below. Dialogue state tracking is the process of constantly updating the state of the dialogue, and Lee (2014) showed that there is a positive correlation between state tracking performance and dialogue performance. Most production systems use manually designed heuristics, often based on rules, to update the dialogue states based on the highly confident output from LU. Williams et al. (2013) formalized the tracking problem as a supervised sequence labeling task, where the input is LU outputs and the output is the true slot values, and the state tracker's results can be translated into a dialogue policy. Zhao and Eskenazi (2016) proposed to jointly train the state tracker and the policy learner in order to optimize the system actions more robustly. Instead of explicitly incorporating the state tracking labels, this paper learns the system actions with implicit dialogue states, so that the proposed DM can be more flexible and robust to the noise propagated from the previous components (Su et al., 2016; Liu and Lane, 2017). A rule-based agent is employed to warm-start the system, via supervised learning on labels generated by the rules. The system is then further trained end-to-end with RL, as explained in section 3.

2.2 User Simulation

In order to perform end-to-end training for the proposed neural dialogue systems, a user simulator is required to automatically and naturally interact with the dialogue system. In the task-completion dialogue setting, the user simulator first generates a user goal. The agent does not know the user goal, but tries to help the user accomplish it in the course of conversations. Hence, the entire conversation exchange is around this goal implicitly. A user goal generally consists of two parts: *inform_slots* for slot-value pairs that serve as constraints from the user, and *request_slots* for slots whose value the user has no information about, but wants to get the values from the agent during the conversation. The user goals are generated using a set of labeled conversational data.

User Agenda Modeling: During the course of a dialogue, the user simulator maintains a compact, stack-like representation called *user agenda* (Schatzmann and Young, 2009), where the user state s_u is factored into an agenda A and a goal G. The goal consists of constraints C and request R. At each time-step t, the user simulator generates the next user action $a_{u,t}$ based on the current state $s_{u,t}$ and the last agent action $a_{m,t-1}$, and then updates the current status $s'_{u,t}$.

Natural Language Generation (NLG): Given the user's dialogue actions, the NLG module generates natural language texts. To control the quality of user simulation given limited labeled data, a hybrid approach including a template-based NLG and a model-based NLG is employed, where the model-based NLG is trained on the labeled dataset with a sequence-to-sequence model. It takes dialogue acts as input, and generates sentence sketch with slot placeholders via an LSTM decoder. Then a post-processing scan is performed to replace the slot placeholders with their actual values (Wen et al., 2015). In the LSTM decoder, we apply beam search, which iteratively considers the top k best sub-sentences when generating the next token.

In the hybrid model, if the user dialogue actions can be found in the predefined sentence templates, the template-based NLG is applied; otherwise, the utterance is generated by the model-based NLG. This hybrid approach allows a dialogue system developer to easily improve NLG by providing templates for sentences that the machine-learned model does not handle well.

2.3 Error Model Controller

When training or testing a policy based on semantic frames of user actions, an error model (Schatzmann et al., 2007) is introduced to simulate noises from the LU component, and noisy communication between the user and the agent in order to test the model robustness. Here, we introduce different levels of noises in the error model: one type of errors is at the *intent* level, another is at the *slot* level. For each level, there are more fine-grained noises.

Intent-Level Error: At the intent level, we categorize all intents into three groups:

- *Group 1*: general *greeting*, *thanks*, *closing*, etc.
- *Group 2*: users may *inform*, to tell the slot values (or constraints) to the agent, for example, inform(moviename='Titanic', starttime='7pm').
- *Group 3*: users may *request* information for specific slots. In a movie-booking scenario, users might ask "request(starttime; moviename='Titanic')".

In the specific task of movie-booking, for instance, there exist multiple *inform* and *request* intents, such as request_starttime, request_moviename, inform_starttime and inform_moviename, etc. Based on the above intent categories, there are three types of intent errors:

- *Random error (I0)*: the random noisy intent from the same category (*within group error*) or other categories (*between group error*).

- *Within-group error (I1)*: the noisy intent is from the same group of the real intent, for example, the real intent is request_theater, but the predicted intent from LU module might be request_moviename.
- *Between-group error (I2)*: the noisy intent is from the different group, for example, a real intent request_moviename might be predicted as the intent inform_moviename.

Slot-level Error: At the slot level, there are four error types:

- *Random error (S0)*: to simulate the noise that is randomly set to the following three types.
- *Slot deletion (S1)*: is to simulate the scenario where the slot is not recognized by the LU component.
- *Incorrect slot value (S2)*: is to simulate the scenario where the slot name is correctly recognized, but the slot value is wrong, e.g., wrong word segmentation.
- *Incorrect slot (S3)*: is to simulate the scenario where both the slot and its value are incorrectly recognized.

3 End-to-End Reinforcement Learning

To learn the interactive policy of our system, we apply reinforcement learning to the DM training in an end-to-end fashion, where each neural network component can be fine tuned. The policy is represented as a deep Q-network (DQN) (Mnih et al., 2015), which takes the state s_t from the state tracker as input, and outputs $Q(s_t, a; \theta)$ for all actions a. Two important DQN tricks, target network usage and experience replay are applied, where the experience replay strategy is changed for the dialogue setting.

During training, we use ϵ-greedy exploration and an experience replay buffer with dynamically changing buffer size. At each simulation epoch, we simulate N ($N = 100$) dialogues and add these state transition tuples (s_t, a_t, r_t, s_{t+1}) to the experience replay buffer for training. In one simulation epoch, the current DQN will be updated multiple times (depending on the batch size and the current size of experience replay buffer). At the last simulation epoch, the target network will be replaced by the current DQN, the target DQN network is only updated for once in one simulation epoch.

The experience replay strategy is critical for RL training (Schaul et al., 2015). In our buffer update strategy, we accumulate all experience tuples from the simulation and flush the pool till the current RL agent reaches a success rate threshold (i.e., a threshold which is equal to the performance of a rule-based agent), and then use the experience tuples from the current RL agent to re-fill the buffer. The intuition is that the initial performance of the DQN is not strong enough to generate good experience replay tuples, thus we do not flush the experience replay pool till the current RL agent can reach a certain success rate (for example, the success rate of a rule-based agent). In the rest of the training process, at every simulation epoch, we estimate the success rate of the current DQN agent (by running it multiple dialogues on simulated users). If the current DQN agent is better than the target network, the experience replay buffer will be flushed.

4 Experiments

We consider a task-completion dialogue system for helping users book movie tickets. Over the course of conversation, the dialogue system gathers information about the customer's desires and ultimately books the movie tickets. The environment then assesses a binary outcome (success or failure) at the end of the conversation, based on (1) whether a movie is booked, and (2) whether the movie satisfies the users constraints.

Dataset: The raw conversational data were collected via Amazon Mechanical Turk, with annotations provided by domain experts. In total, we have labeled 280 dialogues, and the average number of turns per dialogue is approximately 11. The annotated data includes 11 dialogue acts and 29 slots, most of the slots are *informable* slots, which users can use to constrain the search, and some are *requestable* slots, of which users can ask values from the agent. For example, *numberofpeople* cannot be a requestable slot, since arguably user knows how many tickets he or she wants to buy. The detailed annotations can be found in Appendix A.

4.1 Simulated User Evaluation

Two sets of experiments are conducted in the DM training, where two input formats are used for training the RL agents:

1. *frame-level semantics*: when training or testing a policy based on semantic frames of user

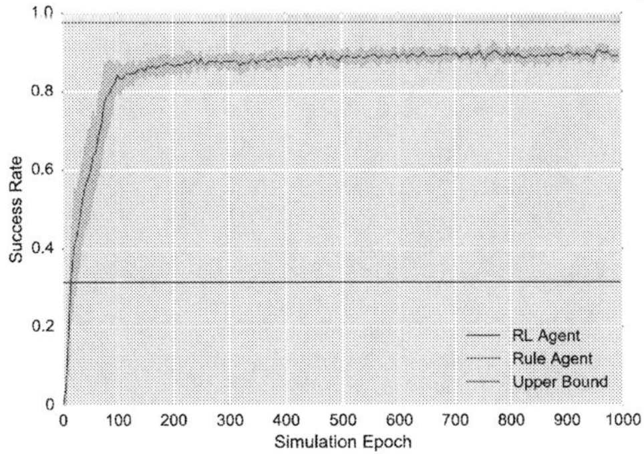

(a) Frame-level semantics for training

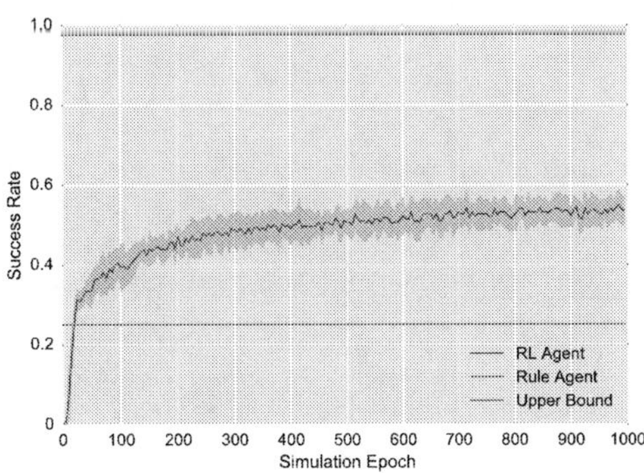

(b) Natural language for end-to-end training

Figure 3: Learning curves for policy training (average of 10 runs). The blue solid lines show the rule agent performance, where we employ to initialize the experience replay buffer pool; the orange dotted line is the optimal upper bound, which is the percentage of reachable user goals.

Setting		Intent Error		Slot Error	
		Type	Rate	Type	Rate
Basic	B1		0.00		0.00
	B2	0: random	0.10	0: random	0.10
	B3		0.20		0.20
Intent	I0	**0: random**	0.10		
	I1	**1: within group**	0.10		
	I2	**2: between group**	0.10	0: random	0.05
	I3	0: random	**0.00**		
	I4	0: random	**0.10**		
	I5	0: random	**0.20**		
Slot	S0			**0: random**	0.10
	S1			**1: deletion**	0.10
	S2			**2: value**	0.10
	S3	0: random	0.10	**3: slot**	0.10
	S4			0: random	**0.00**
	S5			0: random	**0.10**
	S6			0: random	**0.20**

Table 1: Experimental settings with different intent/slot error types described in section 2.3 and different error rates.

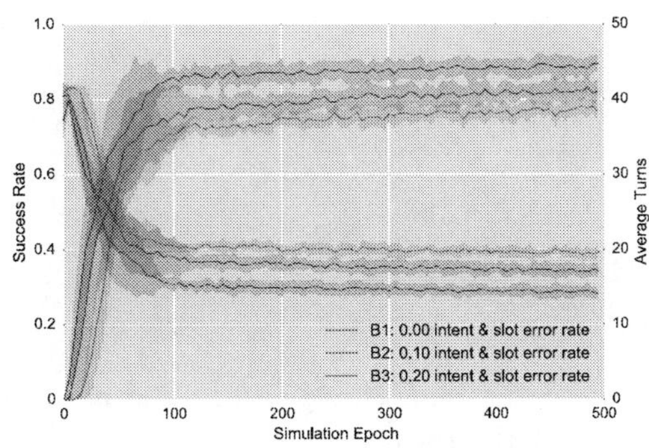

Figure 4: Learning curves for different LU error rates.

actions, a noise controller described in section 2.3 is used to simulate LU errors and noisy communications between the user and the agent.

2. *natural language*: when training or testing a policy on natural language level, in which LU and NLG may introduce noises. In our experiments, the NLG decoder uses *beam_size* $= 3$ to balance speed and performance.

Figure 3(a) shows a learning curve for the dialogue system performance trained with the frame-level information (user semantic frames and system actions), where the number is the average of 10 runs. Figure 3(b) is a learning curve for the system trained at the natural language level. In both settings, the RL agents significantly outperform the rule-based systems, showing the potential of a neural dialogue system that can perform real-world tasks and be improved autonomously through interactions with users. Also, the end-to-end system in Figure 3(b) takes longer for the RL agent to adapt to the noises from LU and NLG, indicating the difficulty of maintaining the system robustness. The consistently increasing trend of our proposed end-to-end system also suggests greater robustness in noisy, real-world scenarios. To further investigate and understand the real impact of the LU component to the robustness of RL agent in the dialogue system, we conduct a series of experiments under different error settings (intent and slot errors from LU) summarized in Table 1, where the learning curves are averaged over 10 runs.

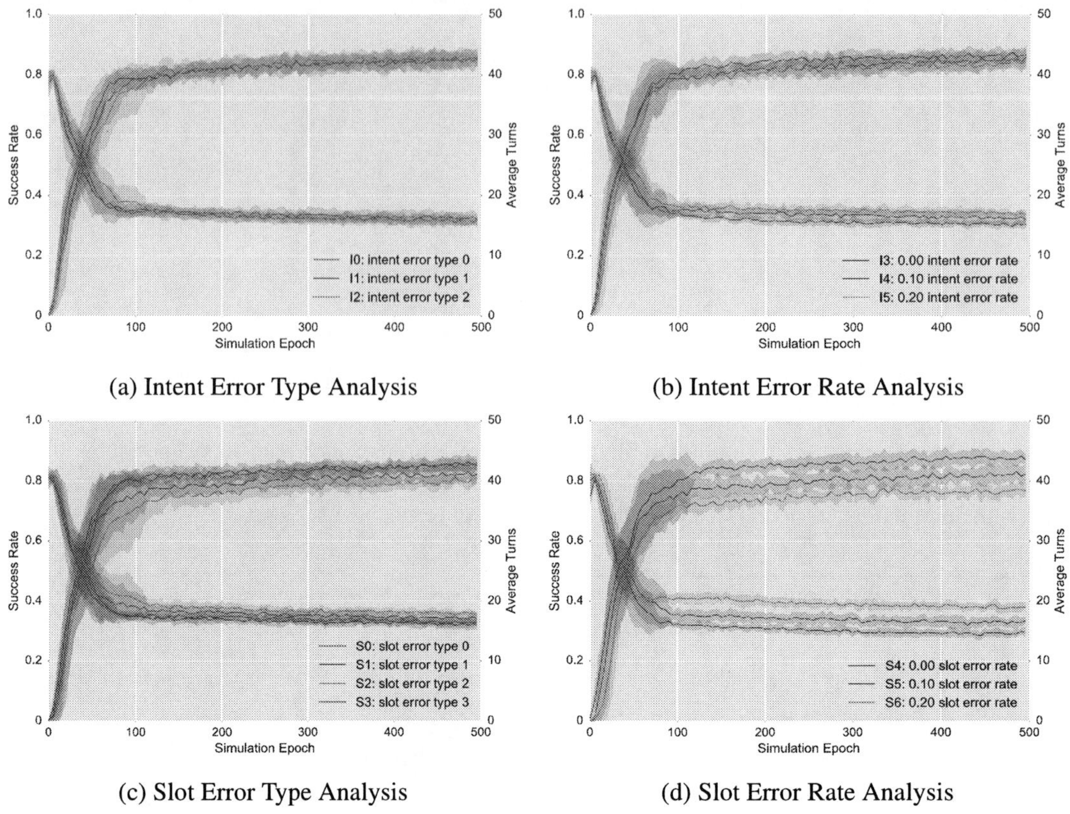

(a) Intent Error Type Analysis   (b) Intent Error Rate Analysis

(c) Slot Error Type Analysis   (d) Slot Error Rate Analysis

Figure 5: Learning curves of the different intent and slot errors in terms of success rate (left axis) and average turns (right axis).

4.2 Basic Error Analysis

The group of basic experiments (from B1 to B3) are in the settings that combine the noise from both intent and slot: 1) For both intent and slot, the error types are random, and the error rates are in $\{0.00, 0.10, 0.20\}$. The rule-based agent reports 41%, 21%, and 12% success rates under 0.00, 0.10, and 0.20 error rates respectively. In contrast, the RL-based agent achieves 90%, 79%, and 76% success rate under the same error rates, respectively. We compare the performance between two types of agents and find that the RL-based agent has greater robustness and is less sensitive to noisy inputs. Therefore, the following experiments are performed using a RL dialogue agent due to robustness consideration. From Fig. 4, the dialogue agents degrade remarkably when the error rate increases (leading to lower success rates and higher average turns).

4.3 Intent Error Analysis

To further understand the impact of intent-level noises to dialogue systems, two experimental groups are performed: the first group (I0–I2) focuses on the difference among all intent error types; the second group (I3–I5) focuses on the impact of intent error rates. Other factors are identical for the two groups, with the random slot error type and a 5% slot error rate.

4.3.1 Intent Error Type

Experiments with the settings of I0–I2 are under the same slot errors and same intent error rate (10%), but with different intent error types: I1 includes the noisy intents from the same categories, I2 includes the noisy intents from different categories, and I0 includes both via random selection. Fig. 5(a) shows the learning curves for all intent error types, where the difference among three curves is insignificant, indicating that the incorrect intents have similar impact no matter what categories they belong to.

4.3.2 Intent Error Rate

Experiments with the settings I3–I5 investigate the difference among different intent error rates. When the intent error rate increases, the dialogue agent performs slightly worse, but the difference is subtle. It suggests that the RL-based agent has better robustness to noisy intents. As shown in Fig. 5(a,b), all RL agents can converge to a similar success rate in both intent error type and intent error rate settings.

4.4 Slot Error Analysis

We further conducted two groups of experiments to investigate the impact of slot-level noises where other factors are fixed — with the random intent error type and a 10% intent error rate.

4.4.1 Slot Error Type

Experiments (S0 – S3) investigate the impact of different slot error types. Corresponding learning curves are given in Fig. 5(c). Among single error types (S1–S3), *incorrect slot value* (S2) performs worst, which means that the slot name is recognized correctly, but a wrong value is extracted with the slot (such as wrong word segmentation); in this case, the agent receives a wrong value for the slot, and eventually books a wrong ticket or fails to book it. The probable reason is that the dialogue agent has difficulty identifying the mistakes, and using the incorrect slot values for the following dialogue actions could significantly degrade the performance. Between *slot deletion* (S1) and *incorrect slot* (S3), the difference is limited, indicating that the RL agent has similar capability of handling these two kinds of slot-level noises.

4.4.2 Slot Error Rate

Experiments with the settings from S4 to S6 focus on different slot error rates (0%, 10%, and 20%) and report the results in Fig. 5(d). It is clear from Fig. 5(d) that the dialogue agent performs worse as the slot error rate increases (the curve of the success rate drops and the curve of average turns rises). Comparing with Fig. 5(b), the dialogue system performance is more sensitive to the slot error rate than the intent error rate.

4.5 Human Evaluation

We further evaluated the rule-based and DQN agents against real human users recruited from

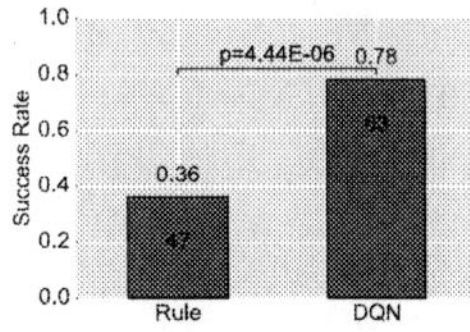

(a) Success Rate

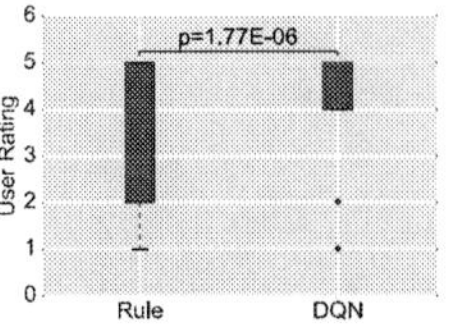

(b) User Rating Distribution

Figure 6: Performance of the rule-based agent versus DQN agent tested with real users: (a) success rate, number of tested dialogues and p-values are indicated on each bar; (b) Distribution of user ratings for two agents (difference in mean is significant with $p < 0.01$).

the authors affiliation, where the DQN agent was trained on the simulated user in the frame-level with 5% random slot errors. In each dialogue session, one of the agents was randomly picked to converse with a user, and the user was presented with a predefined user goal sampled from our corpus, and was instructed to converse with the agent to complete the presented task. At the end of each session, the user was asked to give a rating on a scale from 1 (worst) to 5 (best) based on both *naturalness* and *coherence* of the dialogue. We collected a total of 110 dialogue sessions from 8 human users. Figure 6(a) presents the performance of these agents against real users in terms of success rate. Figure 6(b) shows the subjective evaluation in terms of user rating. For all the cases, the RL agent significantly outperforms the rule-based agent for both objective (success rate) and subjective evaluation (user rating).

5 Discussion and Future Work

This paper presents an end-to-end learning framework for task-completion neural dialogue systems. Our experiments, both on simulated and real users, show that reinforcement learning systems outperform rule-based agents and have better robustness to allow natural interactions with users in real-world task-completion scenarios. Furthermore, we conduct a series of extensive experiments to understand the impact of natural language understanding errors on the performance of a reinforcement learning based, task-completion neural dialogue system. Our empirical results suggest several interesting findings: 1) slot-level errors have a greater impact than intent-level errors; A possible explanation is related to our dialogue action representation, *intent(slot-value pairs)*. If an intent is predicted wrong, for example, *inform* was predicted incorrectly as *request_ticket*, the dialogue agent can handle this unreliable situation and decide to make confirmation in order to keep the correct information for the following conversation. In contrast, if a slot *moviename* is predicted wrong, or a slot value is not identified correctly, this dialogue turn might directly pass the wrong information to the agent, which might lead the agent to book a wrong ticket. Another reason is that the dialogue agent can still maintain a correct intent based on slot information even though the predicted intent is wrong. In order to verify the hypotheses, further experiments are needed, which we leave as future work. 2) different slot error types have different impacts on the RL agents. 3) RL agents are more robust to certain types of slot-level errors — the agents can learn to double-check or confirm with users, at the cost of slightly longer conversations.

Finally, it should be noted that the experiments in this paper focus on task-completion dialogues. Another type of dialogues known as chit-chats has different optimization goals (Li et al., 2016). It would be interesting to extend our analysis from this paper to chit-chat dialogues to gain useful insights for impacts of LU errors.

Acknowledgments

We would like to thank Dilek Hakkani-Tür and reviewers for their insightful comments on the paper. Yun-Nung Chen is supported by the Ministry of Science and Technology of Taiwan and MediaTek Inc..

References

Antoine Bordes, Y-Lan Boureau, and Jason Weston. 2017. Learning end-to-end goal-oriented dialog. In *Proceedings of ICLR*.

Yun-Nung Chen, Dilek Hakanni-Tür, Gokhan Tur, Asli Celikyilmaz, Jianfeng Gao, and Li Deng. 2016. Syntax or semantics? knowledge-guided joint semantic frame parsing. In *Proceedings of the 6th IEEE Workshop on Spoken Language Technology*. pages 348–355.

Bhuwan Dhingra, Lihong Li, Xiujun Li, Jianfeng Gao, Yun-Nung Chen, Faisal Ahmed, and Li Deng. 2017. Towards end-to-end reinforcement learning of dialogue agents for information access. In *Proceedings of the 55th Annual Meeting of the Association for Computational Linguistics (Volume 1: Long Papers)*. pages 484–495.

Dilek Hakkani-Tür, Gokhan Tur, Asli Celikyilmaz, Yun-Nung Chen, Jianfeng Gao, Li Deng, and Ye-Yi Wang. 2016. Multi-domain joint semantic frame parsing using bi-directional rnn-lstm. In *Proceedings of Interspeech*. pages 715–719.

Sungjin Lee. 2014. Extrinsic evaluation of dialog state tracking and predictive metrics for dialog policy optimization. In *15th Annual Meeting of the Special Interest Group on Discourse and Dialogue*. page 310.

Oliver Lemon and Xingkun Liu. 2007. Dialogue policy learning for combinations of noise and user simulation: transfer results. In *Proc. SIGdial*.

Jiwei Li, Will Monroe, Alan Ritter, Michel Galley, Jianfeng Gao, and Dan Jurafsky. 2016. Deep reinforcement learning for dialogue generation .

Bing Liu and Ian Lane. 2017. An end-to-end trainable neural network model with belief tracking for task-oriented dialog. In *Proceedings of Interspeech*. pages 2506–2510.

Volodymyr Mnih, Koray Kavukcuoglu, David Silver, Andrei A. Rusu, Joel Veness, Marc G. Bellemare, Alex Graves, Martin Riedmiller, Andreas K. Fidjeland, Georg Ostrovski, Stig Petersen, Charles Beattie, Amir Sadik, Ioannis Antonoglou, Helen King, Dharshan Kumaran, Daan Wierstra, Shane Legg, and Demis Hassabis. 2015. Human-level control through deep reinforcement learning. *Nature* 518:529–533.

Alexander I Rudnicky, Eric H Thayer, Paul C Constantinides, Chris Tchou, R Shern, Kevin A Lenzo, Wei Xu, and Alice Oh. 1999. Creating natural dialogs in the carnegie mellon communicator system. In *Eurospeech*.

Jost Schatzmann, Blaise Thomson, and Steve Young. 2007. Error simulation for training statistical dialogue systems. In *IEEE Workshop on Automatic Speech Recognition & Understanding*.

Jost Schatzmann and Steve Young. 2009. The hidden agenda user simulation model. *IEEE transactions on audio, speech, and language processing* 17(4):733–747.

Tom Schaul, John Quan, Ioannis Antonoglou, and David Silver. 2015. Prioritized experience replay. *arXiv:1511.05952* .

Pei-Hao Su, Milica Gasic, Nikola Mrksic, Lina Rojas-Barahona, Stefan Ultes, David Vandyke, Tsung-Hsien Wen, and Steve Young. 2016. Continuously learning neural dialogue management. *arXiv:1606.02689* .

Tsung-Hsien Wen, Milica Gasic, Nikola Mrksic, Lina M Rojas-Barahona, Pei-Hao Su, Stefan Ultes, David Vandyke, and Steve Young. 2017. A network-based end-to-end trainable task-oriented dialogue system. pages 438–449.

Tsung-Hsien Wen, Milica Gasic, Nikola Mrksic, Pei-Hao Su, David Vandyke, and Steve Young. 2015. Semantically conditioned LSTM-based natural language generation for spoken dialogue systems. In *Proceedings of the 2015 Conference on Empirical Methods in Natural Language Processing*. pages 1711–1721.

Jason Williams, Antoine Raux, Deepak Ramachandran, and Alan Black. 2013. The dialog state tracking challenge. In *Proceedings of the SIGDIAL 2013 Conference*. pages 404–413.

Tiancheng Zhao and Maxine Eskenazi. 2016. Towards end-to-end learning for dialog state tracking and management using deep reinforcement learning. In *Proceedings of the 17th Annual Meeting of the Special Interest Group on Discourse and Dialogue*. pages 1–10.

Victor Zue, Stephanie Seneff, James R Glass, Joseph Polifroni, Christine Pao, Timothy J Hazen, and Lee Hetherington. 2000. JUPITER: a telephone-based conversational interface for weather information. *IEEE Transactions on speech and audio processing* 8(1):85–96.

Victor W Zue and James R Glass. 2000. Conversational interfaces: Advances and challenges. *Proceedings of the IEEE* 88(8):1166–1180.

A Dataset Annotation

Table 2 lists all annotated dialogue acts and slots in detail.

Annotations	
Intent	request, inform, deny, confirm_question, confirm_answer, greeting, closing, not_sure, multiple_choice, thanks, welcome
Slot	actor, actress, city, closing, critic_rating, date, description, distanceconstraints, greeting, implicit_value, movie_series, moviename, mpaa_rating, numberofpeople, numberofkids, taskcomplete, other, price, seating, starttime, state, theater, theater_chain, video_format, zip, result, ticket, mc_list

Table 2: The data annotation.

B Sample Dialogues

Table 3 shows one success and one failure dialogue examples generated by the rule-based agent and RL agent interacting with user simulator in the movie-booking domain. To be informative, we also explicitly show the user goal at the head of the dialogue, the purpose is to help the user to accomplish this goal and book the right movie tickets, but the agent knows nothing about the user goal.

New episode, user goal:	New episode, user goal:

{
   "request_slots": {
     "ticket": "UNK"
   },
   "inform_slots": {
     "city": "seattle",
     "numberofpeople": "2",
     "theater": "regal meridian 16",
     "starttime": "9:25 pm",
     "date": "tomorrow",
     "moviename": "zoolander 2"
   }
 }
	{
	   "request_slots": {
	     "ticket": "UNK"
	     "theater": "UNK"
	     "starttime": "UNK"
	   },
	   "inform_slots": {
	     "numberofpeople": "3",
	     "date": "tomorrow",
	     "moviename": "10 cloverfield lane"
	   }
	 }

Rule-based agent	**Rule-based Agent**
User: Can I get some tickets for zoolander 2? Agent: What movie are you interested in? User: I want to watch zoolander 2. Agent: What time would you like to see it? User: I want to watch at 9:25 pm. Agent: What city you would like? User: I want to watch at seattle. Agent: What date would you like to watch it? User: I want to set it up tomorrow. Agent: Which theater would you like? User: I want to watch at regal meridian 16. Agent: How many tickets do you need? User: I want 2 tickets please! Agent: Great - I was able to purchase 2 tickets for you to see zoolander 2 tomorrow at regal meridian 16 theater in seattle at 9:25 pm. User: Thank you. Agent: Thank you.	User: What is the start time for 10 cloverfield lane? Agent: What movie are you interested in? User: I want to watch at 10 cloverfield lane. Agent: What time would you like to see it? User: What time is it playing tomorrow? I need 3 tickets. Agent: What city you would like? User: I do not care. Agent: What date would you like to watch it? User: I want to set it up tomorrow. Agent: Which theater would you like? User: Which theater is available? Agent: How many tickets do you need? User: I want 3 tickets please! Agent: Okay, I have booked 3 tickets for 10 cloverfield lane tomorrow. User: Thank you. Agent: Thank you.
Success	**Failure:** Agent does not answer all the questions (starttime, theater) from user.
RL agent	**RL Agent**
User: Can I get tickets for zoolander 2 tomorrow? Agent: Which city would you like? User: I want to watch at seattle. Agent: How many tickets do you need? User: I want 2 tickets please! Agent: 9:25 pm is available. User: I want to watch at regal meridian 16. Agent: Great - I was able to purchase 2 tickets for you to see zoolander 2 tomorrow at regal meridian 16 theater in seattle at 9:25 pm. User: Thank you. Agent: Thank you.	User: Which theater can I book 3 tickets for 10 cloverfield lane? Agent: What time would you like to see it? User: Which theater and start time are available tomorrow? Agent: 11:45am is available. User: Which theater is available? Agent: regal la live stadium 14 is available. User: Could you help me to book the tickets? Agent: Okay - I was able to book 3 tickets for you to see 10 cloverfield lane at regal la live stadium 14 at 11:45am tomorrow. User:Thank you. Agent: Thank you.
Success	**Success**

Table 3: Two sample dialogues generated by rule-based and RL agents with user simulator: Left column shows both rule and RL agents succeed; Right column shows that rule-based agent fails, while RL agent succeeds.

End-to-end Network for Twitter Geolocation Prediction and Hashing

Jey Han Lau[1,2] **Lianhua Chi**[1] **Khoi-Nguyen Tran**[1] **Trevor Cohn**[2]

[1] IBM Research
[2] School of Computing and Information Systems,
The University of Melbourne

jeyhan.lau@gmail.com, lianhuac@au1.ibm.com,
khndtran@au1.ibm.com, t.cohn@unimelb.edu.au

Abstract

We propose an end-to-end neural network to predict the geolocation of a tweet. The network takes as input a number of raw Twitter metadata such as the tweet message and associated user account information. Our model is language independent, and despite minimal feature engineering, it is interpretable and capable of learning location indicative words and timing patterns. Compared to state-of-the-art systems, our model outperforms them by 2%-6%. Additionally, we propose extensions to the model to compress representation learnt by the network into binary codes. Experiments show that it produces compact codes compared to benchmark hashing algorithms. An implementation of the model is released publicly.[1]

1 Introduction

A number of applications benefit from geographical information in social data, from personalised advertising to event detection to public health studies. Sloan et al. (2013) estimate that less than 1% of tweets are geotagged with their locations, motivating the development of geolocation prediction systems.

Han et al. (2012) introduced the task of predicting the location based only the tweet message. A key difference to previous work is that the prediction is made at message or tweet level, while predecessor methods tend to focus on user-level prediction (Backstrom et al., 2010; Cheng et al., 2010). Since then, various methods have been proposed for the task (Han et al., 2014; Chi et al., 2016; Jayasinghe et al., 2016; Miura et al.,

2016), although most systems are engineered for a particular platform and language (e.g. website-specific parsers and language-specific tokenisers and gazetteers). Another strand of research leverages the social network structure to infer location; Jurgens et al. (2015) provided a standardised comparison of these systems. Our focus in this paper is on using only the tweets, although Rahimi et al. (2015) showed that the best approach maybe to combine both types of information.

In applications where fast retrieval of co-located tweets is necessary (e.g. disaster detection), efficient representation of large volume of tweets constitute an important issue. Traditionally, hashing techniques such as locality sensitive hashing (Indyk and Motwani, 1998) are used to compress data into binary codes for fast retrieval (e.g. with multi-index hash tables (Norouzi et al., 2012, 2014)), but it is not immediately clear how they can interact with raw Twitter metadata — as they often require a vector as input — and incorporate supervision.[2]

To this end, we propose an end-to-end neural network for tweet-level geolocation prediction. Our network is designed to be interpretable: we show it has the capacity to automatically learn location indicative words and activity patterns from different regions.

Our contribution in this paper is two-fold. First, our model outperforms state-of-the-art systems by 2-6%, even though it has minimal feature engineering and is completely language-independent, as it uses no gazetteers or language preprocessing tools such as tokenisers or parsers. Second, our network can further compress learnt representations into compact binary code that incorporates information about the tweet and its geolocation. To the best of our knowledge, this is the first end-to-end hashing method for tweets.

---

[1] https://github.com/jhlau/twitter-deepgeo

[2] In our case, the supervised information is the geolocation of tweets.

744

Proceedings of the The 8th International Joint Conference on Natural Language Processing, pages 744–753,
Taipei, Taiwan, November 27 – December 1, 2017 ©2017 AFNLP

2　Related Work

Early work in geolocation prediction operated at
the user-level. Backstrom et al. (2010) developed a methodology to predict the location of
a user on Facebook by measuring the relationship between geography and friendship networks,
and Cheng et al. (2010) proposed a content-based
prediction system to predict a Twitter user's location based purely on his/her tweet messages.
Han et al. (2012) introduced tweet-level prediction, where they first extract location indicative
words by leveraging the geotagged tweets and then
train a classifier for geolocation prediction using
the location indicative words as features. Extending on this, systems were developed to better rank
these location indicative or geospatial words by locality (Chang et al., 2012; Laere et al., 2014; Han
et al., 2014). More recently, Han et al. (2016) proposed a shared task for Twitter geolocation prediction, offering a benchmark dataset on the task.

Hashing is an effective method to compress data
for fast access and analysis. Broadly there are two
types of hashing techniques: data-independent
techniques which design arbitrary functions to
generate hashes, and data-dependent techniques
that leverage pairwise similarity in the training
data (Chi and Zhu, 2017). Locality-sensitive hashing (`lsh`: Indyk and Motwani (1998)) is a widely-
known data-independent hashing method that uses
randomised projections to generate hashcodes.
It preserves data characteristics and guarantees
the collision probability between data points.
`fasthash` (Lin et al., 2014), on the other hand, is
a supervised data-dependent hashing that incorporates label information to determine pairwise similarity. It uses decision tree based hash functions
and graph cut-based binary code inference to deal
with high dimensionality training data.

3　Geolocation Prediction

3.1　Dataset

We use the geolocation prediction shared task
dataset (Han et al., 2016) for our experiments.
There are 2 proposed tasks, predicting geolocation
given: (1) a tweet (tweet-level); and (2) a collection of tweets by a user (user-level). For each task,
there is a hard classification evaluation setting for
predicting a city class, and a soft evaluation setting
for predicting latitude and longitude coordinates.

We explore only the more challenging tweet-

Partition	#Tweets	#Characters
Training	8.9M	554M
Development	7.2K	439K
Test	10K	629K

Table 1: Dataset statistics.

level prediction task. In terms of evaluation setting, we experiment with the hard classification
setting, where the network is required to predict
one out of 3362 cities. Note that the metadata of
a tweet includes not only the message but a variety of information such as creation time and user
account data such as location and timezone.

Training, development and test partitions are
provided by the shared task organisers.[3] We pre-
process the data minimally, removing tweets that
have less than 5 characters in the training partition (development and testing data is untouched)
and keeping all character types that have occurred
5 times or more in training. Unseen character tokens are represented by <UNK>. Preprocessed
statistics of the dataset is given in Table 1.

3.2　Network Architecture

The overall architecture of our model (henceforth
`deepgeo`) is illustrated in Figure 1. `deepgeo`
uses 6 features from the metadata: (1) tweet message; (2) tweet creation time; (3) user UTC offset;
(4) user timezone; (5) user location; and (6) user
account creation time.[4]

Each feature from the metadata is processed by
a separate network to generate a feature vector $\mathbf{f}_j$.
These feature vectors are then concatenated (with
dropout applied) and connected to the penultimate
layer:

$$\hat{\mathbf{f}} = \mathbf{f}_1 \oplus \mathbf{f}_2 ... \oplus \mathbf{f}_N \qquad (1)$$

$$\mathbf{r} = \tanh(\mathbf{W}_r \hat{\mathbf{f}}) \qquad (2)$$

where N is the number of features (6 in total), $\mathbf{r} \in
\mathbb{R}^R$ is the hidden representation at the penultimate
layer and $\mathbf{W}_r$ is model parameter. For brevity, we
omit biases in equations.

$\mathbf{r}$ is fully connected to the output layer and ac-
tivated by softmax to generate a probability distribution over the classes. The model is trained with

---

[3]The organisers provide full metadata for the test partition but only the tweet IDs for training and development partitions. We collect metadata for training/development tweets
using the Twitter API.

[4]We also tested user description and username, but preliminary experiments found these features are not very useful.

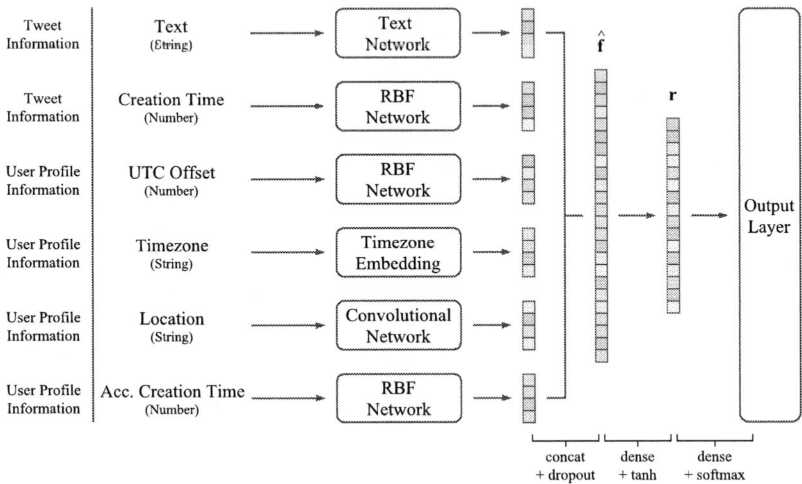

Figure 1: Overall architecture of deepgeo.

minibatches and optimised using Adam (Kingma and Ba, 2014) with standard cross-entropy loss.

We design several networks for the raw features. The first is a character-level recurrent convolutional network with a self-attention component for processing the tweet message (Section 3.2.1). The second is an RBF network[5] for processing numbers (Section 3.2.2). The third is a simple convolutional network for processing user location (Section 3.2.3), and the last is an embedding matrix for user timezone. We treat the timezone as a categorical feature, and learn embeddings for each timezone (309 unique timezones in total). Note that these feature-processing networks are disjointed and there is no parameter sharing between them.

3.2.1 Text Network

For the tweet message, we use a character-level recurrent convolutional network (Lai et al., 2015), followed by max-over-time pooling with a fixed window size and an attentional component to generate the feature vector, as illustrated in Figure 2.

Let $\mathbf{x}_t \in \mathbb{R}^E$ denote the character embedding of the t-th character, we run a bi-directional LSTM network (Hochreiter and Schmidhuber, 1997) to generate the forward and backward hidden states $\mathbf{h}_t^f$ and $\mathbf{h}_t^b$ respectively.[6] We then concatenate the left and right context's hidden states with $\mathbf{x}_t$ and

generate:

$$\hat{\mathbf{x}}_t = \mathbf{h}_{t-1}^f \oplus \mathbf{x}_t \oplus \mathbf{h}_{t+1}^b$$
$$\mathbf{g}_t = \text{ReLU}(\mathbf{W}_g \hat{\mathbf{x}}_t)$$

where $\hat{\mathbf{x}}_t \in \mathbb{R}^{3E}$, $\mathbf{W}_g \in \mathbb{R}^{O \times 3E}$ and $\mathbf{g}_t \in \mathbb{R}^O$. We iterate for each character to generate $\mathbf{g}_t$ for all time steps ($\mathbf{W}_g$ can be interpreted as O convolutional filters each with a window of $3 \times E$ striding 3 steps at a time). Next, we apply max-over-time (narrow) pooling with window size P over the vectors:

$$\hat{\mathbf{g}}_t = \max(\mathbf{g}_t, \mathbf{g}_{t+1}, ..., \mathbf{g}_{t+P-1})$$

where $\hat{\mathbf{g}}_t \in \mathbb{R}^O$ and max is a function that returns the element-wise maxima given a number of vectors of the same length. If there are T characters in the tweet, this yields $(T - P + 1)$ $\hat{\mathbf{g}}$ vectors, one for each span.

By setting $P = T$, we could generate one vector for the whole tweet. The idea of using a smaller window is that it enables a self-attention component, thereby allowing the network to discover the saliency of a character span — for our task this means attending to location indicative words (Section 3.4). We define the attention network as follows:

$$\alpha_t = \mathbf{v}^\top \tanh(\mathbf{W}_v \hat{\mathbf{g}}_t)$$
$$\mathbf{a} = \text{softmax}(\alpha_0, \alpha_1, ..., \alpha_{T-P})$$

where $\mathbf{W}_v \in \mathbb{R}^{V \times O}$, $\mathbf{v} \in \mathbb{R}^V$ and $\mathbf{a} \in \mathbb{R}^{T-P+1}$. Given the attention, we compute a weighted mean

---

[5] Also known as mixture density network.

[6] LSTM is implemented using one layer without any peephole connections and forget biases are initialised with 1.0.

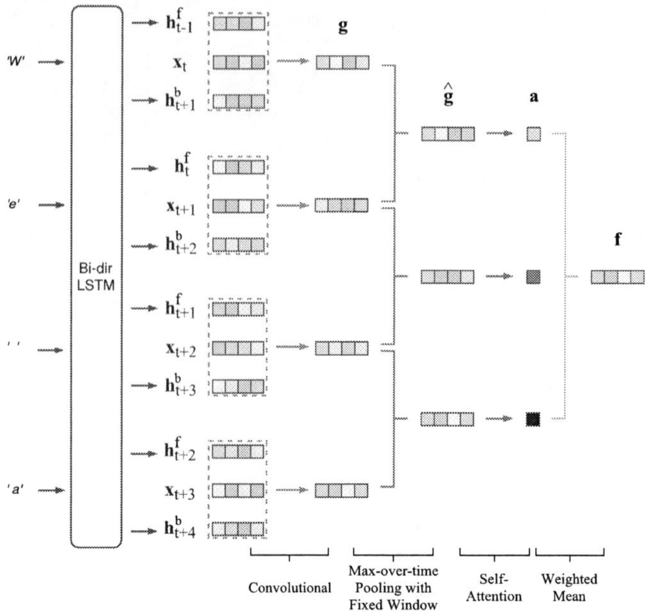

Figure 2: Text Network.

to generate the final feature vector:

$$\mathbf{f}_{\text{text}} = \sum_{t=0}^{T-P} \mathbf{a}_t \hat{\mathbf{g}}_t$$

where $\mathbf{a}_t$ denotes the t-th element in $\mathbf{a}$, and $\mathbf{f}_{\text{text}} \in \mathbb{R}^O$.

3.2.2 RBF Network

There are three time features in the metadata: tweet creation time, user account creation time and user UTC offset. The creation times are given in UTC time (i.e. not local time), e.g. *Thu Jul 29 17:25:38 +0000 2010* and the offset is an integer.

For the creation times, we use only time of the day information (e.g. *17:25*) and normalise it from 0 to 1.[7] UTC offset is converted to hours and normalised to the same range.[8]

The aim of the network is to split time into multiple bins. We can interpret each hour as one bin (24 bins in total) and tweets originated from a particular location (e.g. Europe) favour certain hours or bins. This preference of bins should be different to tweets from a distant location (e.g. East Asia). Assuming each bin follows a Gaussian distribution, then the goal of the network is to learn

the Gaussian means and standard deviations of the bins.

Formally, given an input value u, for bin i the network computes:

$$r_i = \exp\left(\frac{-(u - \mu_i)^2}{2\sigma_i^2}\right)$$

where r_i is the output value and μ_i and σ_i are the parameters for bin i. Let B be the total number of bins, the feature vector generated by a RBF network is given as follows:

$$\mathbf{f}_{\text{rbf}} = [r_0, r_1, ..., r_{B-1}]$$

where $\mathbf{f}_{\text{rbf}} \in \mathbb{R}^B$.

3.2.3 Convolutional Network

Location is a user self-declared field in the metadata. As it is free-form text, we use a standard character-level convolution neural network (Kim, 2014) to process it. The network architecture is simpler compared to the text network (Section 3.2.1): it has no recurrent and self-attention layers, and max-over-time pooling is performed over all spans.

Let $\mathbf{x}_t \in \mathbb{R}^E$ denote the character embedding of the t-th character in the tweet. A tweet of T characters is represented by a concatenation of its character vectors: $\mathbf{x}_{0:T-1} = \mathbf{x}_0 \oplus \mathbf{x}_1 \oplus ... \oplus \mathbf{x}_{T-1}$. We

---

[7]As an example, *17:25* is converted to 0.726.

[8]UTC offset minimum is assumed -12 and maximum +14 based on: `https://en.wikipedia.org/wiki/List_of_UTC_time_offsets`.

use convolutional filters and max-over-time (narrow) pooling to compute the feature vector:

$$\mathbf{g}_t = \mathrm{ReLU}(\mathbf{W}_g \mathbf{x}_{t:t+Q-1})$$
$$\mathbf{f}_{\mathrm{conv}} = \max(\mathbf{g}_0, \mathbf{g}_1, ..., \mathbf{g}_{T-Q})$$

where Q is the length of the character span, $\mathbf{W}_g \in \mathbb{R}^{O \times QE}$ ($\mathbf{W}_g$ can be interpreted as O convolutional filters each with a window of $Q \times E$) and $\mathbf{g}_t, \mathbf{f}_{\mathrm{conv}} \in \mathbb{R}^O$.

3.3 Experiments and Results

We explore two sets of features for predicting geolocation, using: (1) only the tweet message; and (2) both tweet and user metadata. For the latter approach, we have 6 features in total (see Figure 1). Classification accuracy is used as the metric for evaluation.

We tune network hyper-parameter values based on development accuracy; optimal hyper-parameter settings are presented in Table 2. The column "Message-Only" uses only the text content of tweets, while "Tweet+User" incorporates both tweet and user account metadata.

For tweet message and user location, the maximum character length is set to 300 and 20 characters respectively; strings longer than this threshold are truncated and shorter ones are padded.[9] Models are trained using 10 epochs without early stopping. In each iteration, we reset the model's parameters if its development accuracy is worse than that of previous iteration.

We compare deepgeo to 3 benchmark systems, all of which are systems submitted to the shared task (Han et al., 2016):

Chi et al. (2016) propose a geolocation prediction approach based on a multinomial naive Bayes classifier using a combination of automatically learnt location indicative words, city/country names, #hashtags and @mentions. A frequency-based feature selection strategy is used to select the optimal subset of word features.

Miura et al. (2016) experiment with a simple feedforward neural network for geolocation classification. The network draws inspiration from fastText (Joulin et al., 2016), where it uses mean word vectors to represent textual features and has only linear layers. To incorporate multiple

---

[9]Tweets can exceed the standard 140-character limit due to the use of non-ASCII characters.

Network	Hyper-Parameter	Message-Only	Tweet+User
Overall	Batch Size	512	
	Epoch No.	10	
	Dropout	0.2	
	Learning Rate	0.001	
	R	400	
Text	Max Length	300	300
	E	200	200
	P	10	10
	O	600	400
Time	B	–	50
UTC Offset	B	–	50
Timezone	Embedding Size	–	50
Location	Max Length	–	20
	E	–	300
	Q	–	3
	O	–	300
Account Time	B	–	10

Table 2: deepgeo hyper-parameters and values.

Accuracy	System	Features
0.146	Chi et al. (2016)	Message Only
0.212	deepgeo	Message Only
0.409	Miura et al. (2016)	Tweet + User Metadata
0.428	deepgeo	Tweet + User Metadata
0.436	Jayasinghe et al. (2016)	Tweet + User Metadata, Gazetteer, URL IP Lookup, Label Prop. Network

Table 3: Geolocation prediction test accuracy.

features — tweet message, user location, user description and user timezone — the network combines them via vector concatenation.

Jayasinghe et al. (2016) develop an ensemble of classifiers for the task. Individual classifiers are built using a number of features indepedently from the metadata. In addition to using information embedded in the metadata, the system relies on external knowledgebases such as gazetteer and IP look up system to resolve URL links in the message. They also build a label propagation network that links connected users, as users from a sub-network are likely to come from the same location. These classifiers are aggregated via voting, and weights are manually adjusted based on development performance.

We present test accuracy performance for all systems in Table 3. Using only tweet message as feature, deepgeo outperforms Chi et al. (2016) by a considerable margin (over 6% improvement), even though deepgeo has minimal feature en-

Tweet	True Label	Predicted Label	1st Span	2nd Span	3rd Span
Big thanks to @LouSnowPlow and all #CleanSidewalk participants today. You really make Louisville shine. To be happy, be compassionate!	louisville-ky111-us	louisville-ky111-us	'Louisville'	'ake Louisv'	' Louisvill'
McDonald's with aldha (@ Jalan A. P. Pettarani) http://t.co/HDVkhsKWBa	makassar-38-id	makassar-38-id	'Pettarani)'	' Pettarani'	'ettarani) '
Let's miss ALL the green lights on purpose! - every driver in Moncton this morning	moncton-04-ca	halifax-07-ca	'in Moncton'	'ncton this'	'Moncton th'
Harrys bar toilet selfie @sophiethielmann @ Carluccio's Newcastle https://t.co/rKT7RGe7Nd	newcastle upon tyne-engi7-gb	newcastle upon tyne-engi7-gb	's Newcastl'	'wcastle ht'	'castle htt'
Makan terosssssss wkwkwk (with Erwina and Indah at McDonald's Bintara) - https://t.co/T3KERFgap	bekasi-30-id	bekasi-30-id	' Bintara) '	'ntara) - h'	'intara) - '
@EileenOttawa For better or worse it's a revenue stream for Twitter made available to businesses. We all have to get used to it.	toronto-08-ca	ottawa-08-ca	'tawa For b'	'ttawa For '	'nOttawa Fo'
Hunt work!? (with @hadiseptiandani and @Febriantivivi at Jobforcareer Senayan) - https://t.co/u9myRDidtR	jakarta-04-id	jakarta-04-id	'nayan) - h'	' Senayan) '	'enayan) - '

Table 4: Examples of top character spans. Length of span is 10 characters. "1st Span" denotes the span that has the highest attention weight, "2nd Span" and "3rd Span" the second and third highest weight respectively.

Feature Set	Accuracy
All Features	0.428
−Text	0.342 (−0.086)
−Tweet Creation Time	0.419 (−0.009)
−UTC Offset	0.431 (+0.003)
−Timezone	0.422 (−0.006)
−Location	0.228 (−0.200)
−Account Creation Time	0.424 (−0.004)

Table 5: Feature ablation results.

gineering and is trained at character level. Next, we compare deepgeo to Miura et al. (2016). Both systems use a similar set of features from the tweet and user metadata. deepgeo sees an encouraging performance, with almost 2% improvement. The best system in the shared task, Jayasinghe et al. (2016), remains the top performer. Note, however, that their system depends on language-specific processing tools (e.g. tokenisers), website-specific parsers (e.g. for extracting location information from user profile page on Instagram and Facebook) and external knowledge sources (e.g. gazetteers and IP lookup) which were inaccessible by other systems.

To better understand the impact of each feature, we present ablation results where we remove one feature at a time in Table 5. We see that the two most important features are the user location and tweet message. These observations reveal that self-declared user location appears to be a reliable source of location, as task accuracy drops by almost half when this feature is excluded. For the other features, they generally have a small or negligible impact.

3.4 Qualitative Analyses

The self-attention component in the text network (Section 3.2.1) captures saliency of character spans. To demonstrate its effectiveness, we select a number of tweets from the test partition and present the top-3 spans that have the highest attention weights in Table 4.

Interestingly, we see that whenever a location word is in the message, deepgeo tends to focus around it (e.g. *Louisville* and *Newcastle*). Occasionally this can induce error in prediction, e.g. in the second last example the network focuses on *Ottawa* even though the word has little significance to the true location (*Toronto*). Focussing on the right span does not necessarily result in correct prediction as well; as we see in the third example the network focuses on *Moncton* but predicts a neighbouring city *Halifax* as the geolocation.

Next, we look at the Gaussian mixtures learnt by the RBF network. Using the gold-standard city labels, we collect bin weights ($\mathbf{f}_{rbf}$) for tweet creation times (from test data) for 6 cities and plot them in Figure 3. Each Gaussian distribution represents one bin, and its weight is computed as a mean weight over all tweets belonging to the city (line transparency indicates bin weight). Bins that have a mean weight < 0.075 are excluded.

For London (Figure 3c), we see that most tweets are created from 10:00–20:00 local time.[10] For Jakarta (Figure 3e), tweet activity mostly centers around 11:00–23:00 local time (04:00–16:00 UTC

---

[10]London's UTC offset is +00 so no adjustment is necessary to convert to local time.

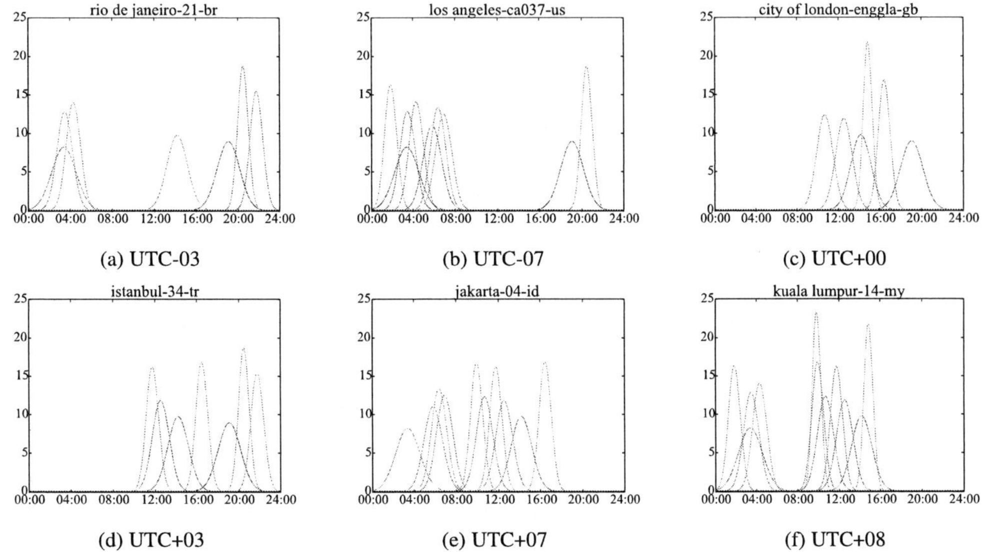

(a) UTC-03   (b) UTC-07   (c) UTC+00

(d) UTC+03   (e) UTC+07   (f) UTC+08

Figure 3: Tweet creation time distribution for 6 cities. Times in all plots are in UTC time. Sub-caption indicates a city's UTC offset.

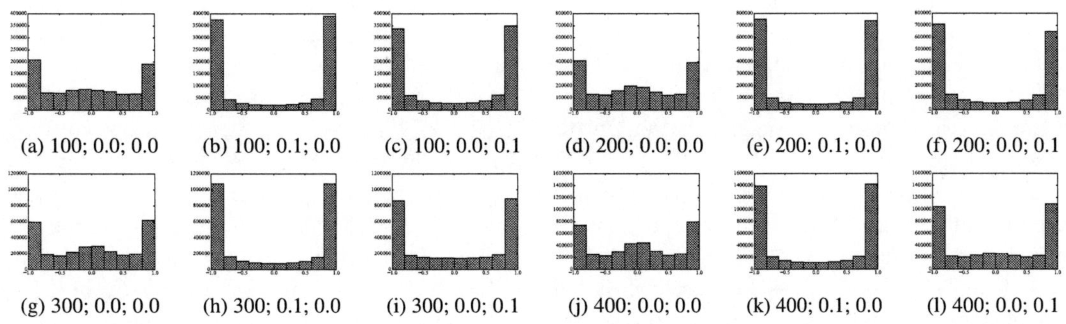

(a) 100; 0.0; 0.0   (b) 100; 0.1; 0.0   (c) 100; 0.0; 0.1   (d) 200; 0.0; 0.0   (e) 200; 0.1; 0.0   (f) 200; 0.0; 0.1

(g) 300; 0.0; 0.0   (h) 300; 0.1; 0.0   (i) 300; 0.0; 0.1   (j) 400; 0.0; 0.0   (k) 400; 0.1; 0.0   (l) 400; 0.0; 0.1

Figure 4: Histogram of **r** element values. Fields in the subcaptions denote vector dimension (R), corruption level (σ) and l scaling factor (α). Range of y-axis for the same vector dimension is standardised.

time). Most cities share a similar activity period, with the exception of Istanbul (Figure 3d): Turkish people seems to start their day much later, as tweets begin to appear from 15:00–01:00 local time (12:00 to 22:00 UTC time).

Another interesting trend we find is that for two cities (Los Angeles and Kuala Lumpur), there is a brief period of inactivity around noon (12:00) to evening (18:00) in local time. We hypothesise that most people are working during these times, and are thus too busy to use Twitter.

4 Hashing: Generating Binary Code For Tweets

`deepgeo` creates a low-dimensional dense vector representation (**r**) for a tweet in the penultimate layer. This representation captures the message, user timezone and other metadata (including the city label) that are incorporated to the network during training.

Storing the dense vector representation for a large volume of tweets can be costly.[11] If we can compress the dense vectors into compact binary codes, it would save storage space, as well as enabling more efficient retrieval of co-located tweets, e.g. using multi-index hash tables for K-nearest neighbour search (Norouzi et al., 2012, 2014).

Inspired by denoising autoencoders (Yu et al., 2016; Vincent et al., 2010), we *binarise* the dense

---

[11] If a tweet is represented by a vector of 400 32-bit floating point numbers, 1B tweets would take 1.6TiB of space.

750

Bits	deepgeo	deepgeo +noise	deepgeo +loss	lsh		fasthash	
				word2vec	deepgeo	word2vec	deepgeo
100	0.147	**0.149**	0.146	0.013	0.053	0.116	0.140
200	0.143	0.143	0.140	0.019	0.072	0.128	**0.160**
300	0.136	0.137	0.141	0.021	0.082	0.133	**0.165**
400	0.132	0.135	0.136	0.022	0.086	0.135	**0.170**

Table 6: Retrieval MAP performance.

R	deepgeo	deepgeo +noise	deepgeo +loss
100	**0.420**	0.396	0.410
200	**0.428**	0.417	0.414
300	**0.420**	0.416	0.422
400	**0.428**	0.419	0.418

Table 7: Classification performance for deepgeo with the addition of noise and loss term l.

vector generated by deepgeo by adding Gaussian noise. The intuition is that the addition of noise sharpens the activation values in order to counteract the random noise.

Equation (1) is thus modified to: $\hat{\mathbf{f}} = (\mathbf{f}_1 \oplus \mathbf{f}_2 ... \oplus \mathbf{f}_N) + \mathcal{N}(0, \sigma^2)$, where $\mathcal{N}(0, \sigma^2)$ is a zero-mean Gaussian noise with standard deviation (or corruption level) σ.[12] In the addition to the Gaussian noise, we also experiment with an additional loss term l to penalise elements that are not in the extrema: $l = \alpha \times \frac{1}{R} \sum_{i=0}^{R-1} |(\mathbf{r}_i - 1)(\mathbf{r}_i + 1)|$, where $\mathbf{r}_i$ is the i-th element in $\mathbf{r}$ and α is a scaling factor. We set $\sigma = \alpha = 0.1$, as both values were found to provide good performance.

To better understand the effectiveness of the noise and loss term l in binarising the vector values, we present a histogram plot of $\mathbf{r}$ element values from test data in Figure 4, for $R = 100, 200, 300, 400$. We see that the addition of noise and l helps in pushing the elements to the extrema. The noise term appears to work a little better than l, as the frequency for the -1.0 and $+1.0$ bins is higher. We also observe that there is a small increase in middle/zero values as R increases from 100 to 400, suggesting that there are more unused hidden units when number of parameters increases. We present classification accuracy performance when we add noise (deepgeo+noise) and l (deepgeo+loss) in Table 7. The performance drops a little, but generally stays within a gap of 1%. This suggests that both noise and l

works well in binarising $\mathbf{r}$ without trading off classification accuracy significantly.

Next we evaluate the retrieval performance using the binary codes. We binarise $\mathbf{r}$ for development and test tweets using the sign function. Given a test tweet, we retrieve the nearest development tweets based on hamming distance, and calculate average precision.[13] We aggregate the retrieval performance for all test tweets by computing mean average precision (MAP).

For comparison, we experiment with two hashing techniques: lsh (Indyk and Motwani, 1998) and fasthash (Lin et al., 2014) (see Section 2 for system descriptions). The input required for both lsh and fasthash is a vector. We test 2 types of input for these methods: (1) a word2vec baseline, where we concatenate mean word vectors of the tweet message, user account's time-zone and location, resulting in a 900-dimension vector;[14] and (2) deepgeo representation $\mathbf{r}$. The rationale for using deepgeo as input is to test whether its representation can be further compressed with these hashing techniques.[15]

We present MAP performance for all systems in Table 6. Looking at deepgeo systems (column 2–4), we see that adding noise and l helps, although the impact is greater when the bit size is large (300/400 bits). For lsh, which uses no label information, word2vec input produces poor binary code for retrieval. Changing the input to deepgeo improves retrieval considerably, implying that the representation produced by deepgeo captures geolocation information.

fasthash with word2vec input vector performs competitively. For smaller bit sizes (100 or 200), however, the gap in performance is substan-

---

[12]Dropout is applied to $\hat{\mathbf{f}}$, i.e. after the addition of noise.

[13]We remove 1328 test tweets that do not share city labels with any development tweets.

[14]300-dimension word2vec (skip-gram) vectors are trained on English Wikipedia.

[15]lsh and fasthash are trained using 400K tweets due to large memory requirement. We also tested these models using only 150K tweets, and found marginal performance improvement from 150K to 400K, suggesting that they are unlikely to improve even if it is trained with the full data.

tial. Pairing `fasthash` with `deepgeo` produces the best retrieval performance: for 200/300/400 bits it outperforms `deepgeo+noise` by 2–4%. Interestingly for 100 bits `fasthash` is unable to compress `deepgeo`'s representation any further, highlighting the compactness of `deepgeo` representation for smaller bit sizes.

5 Conclusion

We propose an end-to-end method for tweet-level geolocation prediction. We found strong performance, outperforming comparable systems by 2-6% depending on the feature setting. Our model is generic and has minimal feature engineering, and as such is highly portable to problems in other domains/languages (e.g. Weibo, a Chinese social platform, is one we intend to explore). We propose simple extensions to the model to compress the representation learnt by the network into binary codes. Experiments demonstrate its compression power compared to state-of-the-art hashing techniques.

References

L. Backstrom, E. Sun, and C. Marlow. 2010. Find me if you can: improving geographical prediction with social and spatial proximity. In *Proceedings of the 19th international conference on World wide web*, pages 61–70. ACM.

H. Chang, D. Lee, M. Eltaher, and J. Lee. 2012. @ phillies tweeting from philly? predicting twitter user locations with spatial word usage. In *Proceedings of the 2012 International Conference on Advances in Social Networks Analysis and Mining (ASONAM 2012)*, pages 111–118. IEEE Computer Society.

Z. Cheng, J. Caverlee, and K. Lee. 2010. You are where you tweet: a content-based approach to geolocating twitter users. In *Proceedings of the 19th ACM international conference on Information and knowledge management*, pages 759–768. ACM.

L. Chi, K.H. Lim, N. Alam, and C. Butler. 2016. Geolocation prediction in twitter using location indicative words and textual features. In *Proceedings of the 2nd Workshop on Noisy User-generated Text (WNUT)*, pages 227–234, Osaka, Japan.

L. Chi and X. Zhu. 2017. Hashing techniques: A survey and taxonomy. *ACM Computing Surveys (CSUR)*, 50(1):11.

B. Han, A. Rahimi, L. Derczynski, and T. Baldwin. 2016. Twitter geolocation prediction shared task of the 2016 workshop on noisy user-generated text. In *Proceedings of the 2nd Workshop on Noisy User-generated Text (WNUT)*, pages 213–217, Osaka, Japan.

Bo Han, Paul Cook, and Timothy Baldwin. 2012. Geolocation prediction in social media data by finding location indicative words. pages 1045–1062, Mumbai, India.

Bo Han, Paul Cook, and Timothy Baldwin. 2014. Text-based Twitter user geolocation prediction. 49:451–500.

S. Hochreiter and J. Schmidhuber. 1997. Long short-term memory. *Neural Computation*, 9:1735–1780.

P. Indyk and R. Motwani. 1998. Approximate nearest neighbors: towards removing the curse of dimensionality. In *Proceedings of the thirtieth annual ACM symposium on Theory of computing*, pages 604–613. ACM.

G. Jayasinghe, B. Jin, J. Mchugh, B. Robinson, and S. Wan. 2016. Csiro data61 at the wnut geo shared task. In *Proceedings of the 2nd Workshop on Noisy User-generated Text (WNUT)*, pages 218–226, Osaka, Japan.

A. Joulin, E. Grave, P. Bojanowski, and Mikolov T. 2016. Bag of tricks for efficient text classification. *CoRR*, abs/1607.01759.

D. Jurgens, T. Finethy, J. McCorriston, Y.T. Xu, and D. Ruths. 2015. Geolocation prediction in twitter using social networks: A critical analysis and review of current practice. In *Proceedings of the Ninth International Conference on Web and Social Media, ICWSM 2015*, pages 188–197, Oxford, UK.

Y. Kim. 2014. Convolutional neural networks for sentence classification. pages 1746–1751, Doha, Qatar.

Diederik P. Kingma and Jimmy Ba. 2014. Adam: A method for stochastic optimization. *CoRR*, abs/1412.6980.

Olivier Van Laere, Jonathan Quinn, Steven Schockaert, and Bart Dhoedt. 2014. Spatially-aware term selection for geotagging. *IEEE Transactions on Knowledge and Data Engineering*, 26(1):221–234.

S. Lai, L. Xu, K. Liu, and J. Zhao. 2015. Recurrent convolutional neural networks for text classification. pages 2267–2273, Austin, Texas.

G. Lin, C. Shen, Q. Shi, A. van den Hengel, and D. Suter. 2014. Fast supervised hashing with decision trees for high-dimensional data. In *Proceedings of the IEEE Conference on Computer Vision and Pattern Recognition*, pages 1963–1970.

Y. Miura, M. Taniguchi, T. Taniguchi, and T. Ohkuma. 2016. A simple scalable neural networks based model for geolocation prediction in twitter. In *Proceedings of the 2nd Workshop on Noisy User-generated Text (WNUT)*, pages 235–239, Osaka, Japan.

M. Norouzi, A. Punjani, and D.J. Fleet. 2012. Fast search in hamming space with multi-index hashing. In *Computer Vision and Pattern Recognition (CVPR), 2012 IEEE Conference on*, pages 3108–3115. IEEE.

M. Norouzi, A. Punjani, and D.J. Fleet. 2014. Fast exact search in hamming space with multi-index hashing. *IEEE transactions on pattern analysis and machine intelligence*, 36(6):1107–1119.

Afshin Rahimi, Duy Vu, Trevor Cohn, and Timothy Baldwin. 2015. Exploiting text and network context for geolocation of social media users. pages 1362–1367, Denver, USA.

L. Sloan, J. Morgan, W. Housley, M. Williams, A. Edwards, P. Burnap, and O. Rana. 2013. Knowing the tweeters: Deriving sociologically relevant demographics from twitter. *Sociological research online*, 18(3):7.

P. Vincent, H. Larochelle, I. Lajoie, Y. Bengio, and P. Manzagol. 2010. Stacked denoising autoencoders: Learning useful representations in a deep network with a local denoising criterion. *Journal of Machine Learning Research*, 11:3371–3408.

Z. Yu, H. Wang, X. Lin, and M. Wang. 2016. Understanding short texts through semantic enrichment and hashing. In *2016 IEEE 32nd International Conference on Data Engineering (ICDE)*, pages 1552–1553, Helsinki, Finland.

Assessing the Verifiability of Attributions in News Text

Edward Newell
McGill University
Computer Science

Ariane Schang
McGill University
Computer Science

Drew Margolin
Cornell University
Dept. of Communication

Derek Ruths
McGill University
Computer Science

{edward.newell, ariane.schang}@mail.mcgill.ca,
dm658@cornell.edu, derek.ruths@mcgill.ca

Abstract

When reporting the news, journalists rely on the statements of stakeholders, experts, and officials. The attribution of such a statement is *verifiable* if its fidelity to the source can be confirmed or denied. In this paper, we develop a new NLP task: determining the verifiability of an attribution based on linguistic cues. We operationalize the notion of verifiability as a score between 0 and 1 using human judgments in a comparison-based approach. Using crowdsourcing, we create a dataset of verifiability-scored attributions, and demonstrate a model that achieves an RMSE[1] of 0.057 and Spearman's rank correlation of 0.95 to human-generated scores. We discuss the application of this technique to the analysis of mass media.

1 Introduction

An attribution occurs when an author or speaker represents the discourse, attitude, or inner state of an external source (Piazza, 2009). Attributions are found in virtually every genre of discourse (Fairclough, 1995), but are fundamental to news reporting, where attribution to credible sources is a basic feature of objective, unbiased "hard news" (Esser and Umbricht, 2014). Recently news media have come under increasing scrutiny for spreading biased and even fabricated information[2]. This trend suggests the need for scalable, computational approaches to understanding attribution.

From a natural language processing perspective, attribution is a fundamental phenomenon that touches a broad set of applications, including summarization, question answering, information extraction, and discourse analysis. Once content is scoped under attribution, its contribution to the discourse can change substantially depending on the source of the attribution and their relationship to the statement. For instance, in 2001 U.S. President George W. Bush famously warned that in fighting terrorists, nations were either "with us or against us"[3]. This statement was threatening not only because it was made by the president, or because it was blunt, but because such blunt statements are not normally made by national leaders. If they are to reach human-level performance, systems for automated text understanding must not only accurately segment attribution in the flow of text, but also represent the many ways that attributions can differ rhetorically.

One important way in which attributions can differ, particularly with respect to news reporting, is in their *verifiability*, the ease with which an attribution's fidelity to the source can be checked. Consider the following hypothetical attributions:

> **Lindsay Walls**, CEO of Inovatron, <u>said</u> in a press release yesterday *that the "allegations of intentionally selling sub-par product are completely unfounded."*

> A **source** close to the issue <u>hinted</u> *that quality control standards had been on the decline.*

The former attribution is more verifiable insofar as it attributes a specific statement to a specific person who, in theory, could be asked to corroborate it. The latter is harder to verify. The source is not named, and even if it were known, it is not clear how it could be confirmed that such "hints"

---

[1] Root mean squared error

[2] theguardian.com/media/2016/dec/18/what-is-fake-news-pizzagate

[3] edition.cnn.com/2001/US/11/06/gen.attack.on.terror

Proceedings of the The 8th International Joint Conference on Natural Language Processing, pages 754–763,
Taipei, Taiwan, November 27 – December 1, 2017 ©2017 AFNLP

were given. Note that verifiability does not depend on the truth of a statement, nor its fidelity to the source, but rather on the *ability to confirm or deny* its fidelity.

The ability to confirm or deny an attribution's fidelity is not binary, but rather occupies a continuum of difficulty, which can depend on whether the source was precisely identified, and how definite the reported statement or content was. Therefore, we operationalize verifiability as a continuous variable between 0 and 1. Attributions are scored by having humans compare attributions and judge which are more verifiable.

We build a dataset[4] of verifiability-scored attributions on top of the Penn Attribution Relations Corpus, version 3 (PARC3) (Pareti, 2012, 2015). PARC3, derived from the Penn Discourse Tree-Bank, consists of Wall Street Journal news articles in which attributions have been manually annotated.

Prior work investigating sourcing typically relies on a binary concept of named versus anonymous sources (Wulfemeyer and McFadden, 1986). It is also common to distinguish between verbatim quotes, mixed quotes, and paraphrases (also known as reported speech) (Sundar, 1998). Therefore, we create a baseline model of verifiabilty based on these features. In reality, the sources of attributions span the range from completely obscured to named with credentials and affiliations, along with intermediate examples such as "Whitehouse official" or "company spokesperson". We compare the baseline model to a more sophisticated model that considers a large number of syntactic and semantic cues based on the source and other parts of the attribution[5]. Using ablation testing, we assess the contribution that these various features make to the regression of verifiability.

Before concluding the paper, we discuss the applications of automated verifiability scoring to the study of attribution in mass media. We explore the feasibility of an end-to-end system that extracts attributions from raw text and then scores the attribution's verifiability, by implementing an existing attribution extraction pipeline from prior work (Pareti et al., 2013). We analyze how errors cascade through the coupled extraction-regression pipeline, which illuminates the challenges to the

---

end-to-end version of the task for future work.

2 Related work

2.1 Computational approaches to attribution

The extraction of attributions from text requires (1) the detection of attributed content (e.g. a quotation), and (2) linking of that content to a source entity. Although detection of enquoted text is trivial, a great deal of attributed content is not found within quotes.

The earliest systems attempt to attribute quotations in children's stories to the correct speaker (Zhang et al., 2003; Mamede and Chaleira, 2004). These systems used rule-based approaches, and although they achieved high accuracy on extracting quotations, their accuracy in attributing them to the correct speaker was quite low. The performance of these systems was also highly dependant on the genre of material.

In news text, a substantial fraction of attributions are much harder to extract, being signaled by the discursive structure of the text instead of by explicit quotation marks (O'Keefe et al., 2012). Early systems for extracting and linking attributions in this domain assumed low recall to achieve higher precision (Pouliquen et al., 2007; de Morais et al., 2009). To perform well in such domains, a machine learning approach was needed. Elson and McKeown provided the first contribution in this direction (2010). However, their approach relied on gold-standard labels for attributions occurring earlier in the text as features to extract later attributions. In 2012, the first practical machine learning-based approach capable of extracting attributions from non-annotated news text was developed using a sequence labelling approach (O'Keefe et al., 2012).

Further efforts were spurred by the development of corpora with annotated attributions, including PARC3 (Pareti, 2012, 2015). In PARC3 an attribution consists of: (1) a source to whom content is being attributed, (2) the content being attributed, and (3) the cue phrase referring to the act of attribution (e.g. "said", "according to"). PARC3 enabled the development of an attribution extraction system that we replicate to investigate end-to-end attribution extraction and verifiability regression (Pareti et al., 2013). This multi-step extraction pipeline first identifies candidate reporting words (e.g. *said, lamented*), and uses these as features to extract the attribution content. Using the extracted content, candidate source entities are identified and correct links are found using a classifier. The source entity and cue word are then expanded deterministically into a source *span* and cue *span*, which collects informative modifiers such as the source's affiliation.

2.2 Attribution and verifiability in news

Attribution plays a fundamental yet complex role in news reporting. It is the "bread and butter" of hard news journalism (Sundar, 1998). However, attribution affords the author the opportunity to frame or interpret information by proxy. Attributions tend to have evaluative content, suggesting that "external voices are allowed to speak their minds much more loudly than journalists" (Jullian, 2011), yet the rhetorical use of attributions is often subtle (Fairclough, 1995).

The credibility of attributions is fundamental to trust in the media. As Burriss (1988) states, "one of the basic tenets of journalism is that news reports are supposed to deal with verifiable facts... Unfortunately the public who receive the news generally has no way to independently verify the accuracy of a news story and must thus depend upon (1) the reputation of the news organization, (2) the reputation of the reporter, or (3) information within the story itself, in order to determine the accuracy of a news report." Journalists do not always provide the information necessary to verify an attribution (Adams, 1962; Wulfemeyer, 1985; Wulfemeyer and McFadden, 1986). Anonymous sourcing has recently been criticized for distorting coverage of the 2016 presidential campaign (Silver, 2017), but the practice has been recognized and cautiously accepted by media researchers and practitioners for decades (Wulfemeyer, 1985; Boeyink, 1990; Duffy and Freeman, 2011). Anonymizing sources does tend to undermine the credibility of a story (Sternadori and Thorson, 2009; Pjesivac and Rui, 2014; Mackay and Bailey, 2012), though not in all cases (Sundar, 1998), and there is variation in the kinds of unnamed sources who are found credible (Adams, 1962; Riffe, 1980). A typical set of "code-words" are often applied to veil source identity (e.g. "official" or "spokesman") (Burriss, 1988), with the choice of terms having significant impact on the credibility of the report (Adams, 1962). Direct quotes also appear to enhance credibility compared with paraphrases (Sundar, 1998). Thus, re-

searchers have recently tracked the use of anonymous sources over time and across cultures (Esser and Umbricht, 2014; Lee and Wang, 2016).

2.3 Conceptualizing verifiability

Source anonymity is just one aspect of the problem of how attributions might be used to influence reader interpretations. Popper 2003 argued that any knowledge claim possesses a *degree of verifiability* [6]: the extent to which it is possible to test for evidence that could corroborate or contradict it. Claims with higher verifiability are more credible even prior to testing because authors have less incentive to be accurate when making unverifiable claims (Margolin and Monge, 2013). For example, since no one can know whether an anonymous source really made the statement attributed to them in a news article, the reporter could distort or even fabricate the attributed statement.

Source identification aside, we note that Popper emphasized the form of the proposition, for example, claims made with qualifiers or weak quantifiers. Additionally, physical and technical barriers also apply (Deutsch, 1997). Sources who are difficult to access or that lack a platform from which to correct mis-attribution are less verifiable. The language of attributed content may also matter: verbal categories can be vague or sharp (Hampton, 2007), modifying the extent to which claims made with them are verifiable.

3 Operationalizing verifiability

3.1 Task definition

As mentioned, the ability to confirm or deny the fidelity of an attribution occupies a sliding scale of difficulty, so we operationalize verifiability as a quantity between 0 and 1. Similar to credibility or relevancy, verifiability fundamentally reflects the perceptions on the part of readers. Although it is possible, at least in principle, to directly test the difficulty of verifying a given attribution, the psycholinguistic notion of verifiability is more relevant to characterizing mass media production and consumption.

To approximate the perceptions of the general public, we use crowdsourced human judgments in creating the ground truth verifiability-scored dataset. Crowdworkers were shown pairs of attributions, and asked to decide which is more ver-

---

[6]Popper technically refers to "falsifiability" which is the inverse of verifiability.

ifiable (we describe the details of the annotation setup below). Various methods exist to convert pairwise comparisons into a set of scores (e.g. (Kiritchenko and Mohammad, 2016)). We use the Bradley Terry model (Hunter, 2004) to assign verifiability scores, and then shift and scale the scores to fall into the $[0, 1]$ interval.

As discussed above, methods for extracting attributions from raw text have been developed in prior work. Therefore, this task focuses on the regression of perceived verifiability from text that has already been annotated with attributions in PARC3 annotation style.

3.2 Dataset annotation

Annotation was carried out using the Crowd-Flower platform[7]. Crowdworkers were shown pairs of attributions, and asked to consider the effort required to confirm or deny the fidelity of each. They were asked to select the attribution that was easiest to verify from each pair.

In judging verifiability, it is reasonable to expect that the precision with which a source is identified would be the major determinant in most cases. This creates a risk that crowdworkers will begin to rely only on source definiteness, rather than judging attribution verifiability holistically. Thus, we took steps to ensure that crowdworkers were vigilent to verifiability cues of various kinds. As part of general quality control, crowdworkers had to complete 7 out of 10 training / test examples correctly to ensure they understood the task, and then maintain this proportion of correct responses on test examples randomly dispersed throughout the annotation tasks. To address the specific concern that crowdworkers may become overly reliant on source definiteness, we selected training / test examples to which the correct answers depended on a variety of cues. Test examples were collected by performing a pilot round of annotation with 8 expert annotators, and selecting from the high-agreement examples.

Attributions were presented within the full sentence(s) that contained them. Limiting the context to the containing sentence(s) did not appear to interfere with annotation during the pilot round. Nevertheless, we took steps to mitigate effects from the loss of context. In the majority of cases where the definiteness of the source plays an important role in determining verifiability, the most

---

[7]crowdflower.com

useful context is likely to be how the source was first introduced in the article, e.g. whether the source's name and affiliation were given. To bring that context into the attribution, we used the CoreNLP coreference resolution software (Manning et al., 2014) to augment the source. Whenever a source was mentioned using a personal pronoun, we interpolated the pronoun using the representative coreferent mention, except where that mention already occured in the sentence. Thus, for example,

"I don't know," she said,

might become

"I don't know," Lindsay Walls, CEO of Inovatron said.

Spot checks of 100 pronoun-containing attributions in PARC3 showed that this produced reliable, grammatical interpolations. However, similarly interpolating non-personal pronouns and references such as "the company" was not reliable. We instructed workers to consider, when faced with such references, whether it appeared that the reference was to a specific named individual / entity. Thus, the worker should treat "a company" differently from "the company". We included many test examples in which workers had to act on that instruction to get the correct answer.

Attributions were presented with the source, cue, and content highlighted, to ensure that workers knew what specific attribution they they were annotating.

We solicited comparisons involving 2100 attributions, presented as 39930 unique pairs, with each pairing annotated by at least 3 workers (increased to 5 when the first judgments were non-unanimous), resulting in 140277 total pairwise comparisons. The data comprise annotations from 337 workers. These figures exclude the discarded data from 70 crowdworkers that had poor performance on training / test examples. Every attribution in the dataset was compared to at least 20 other attributions. After 20 pairings, we found that the verifiability scores and the model regression error (to be discussed below), had become relatively stable, as can be seen in **Fig. 1**.

Annotation proceeded in two phases (not including the pilot round). In the first phase, we randomly sampled 100 attributions from PARC3 and solicited an exhaustive set of annotations on all 4950 pairs. This gave highly accurate scores for a small subset of annotations. In the second

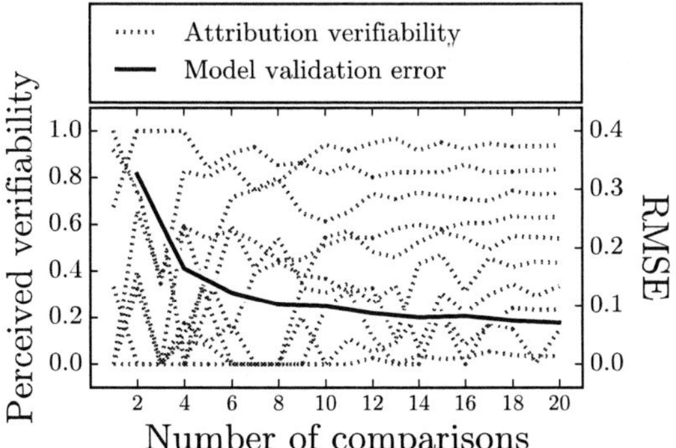

Figure 1: Estimated verifiability scores converged as a function of the number of comparisons per attribution increased, reducing error in the model.

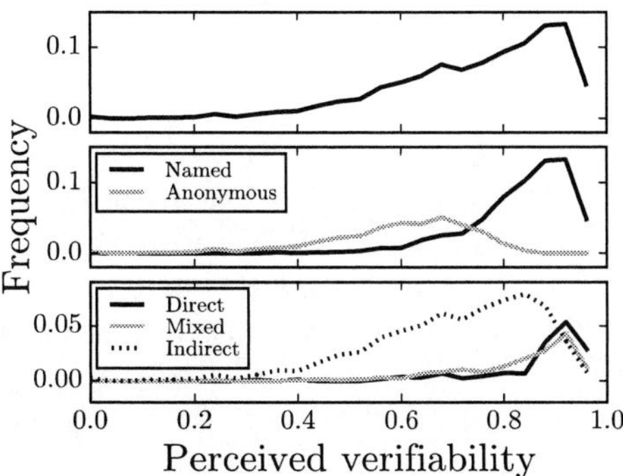

Figure 2: Distribution of crowdsourced verifiability scores for 2100 attributions (top), conditioned on the presence of ORG and PERS named entities (middle) and attribution directness (bottom).

phase, 2000 randomly sampled attributions were systematically compared to the attributions scored in phase 1. Each phase-2 attribution was paired with two phase-1 attributions randomly drawn from each decile of verifiability, giving twenty pairings each.

After the pairwise comparison data were collected we estimated the maximum-likelihood latent verifiability scores in a Bradley-Terry model using a majorization-minorization algorithm (Hunter, 2004), then linearly transformed the verifiability scores to fall in the range $[0, 1]$.

3.3 Annotation results

The resulting scores for the 2100 attributions produced a smooth unimodal distribution across a range of perceived verifiability (**Fig. 2**). In a plot of the latent scores inferred for a Bradley-Terry model, the distance between two scores is a direct

representation of the probability that the higher-scoring item would "win" in a comparison with the other[8]. The distribution has most of its mass near verifiability score 0.9, showing that most attributions adhere to a high standard of verifiability. In addition, we see heavy tail of low perceived verifiability. This distribution is, prima facie, consistent with the competing journalistic norms of transparent attribution and source protection.

It would be reasonable to have expected the distribution to be somewhat more clustered, with peaks in the data corresponding to discrete features such as named vs. anonymous sources (Wulfemeyer and McFadden, 1986) or direct vs. indirect quotes (Sundar, 1998). These features would have clear bearing on efforts to verify an attribution and should be fairly universally recognizable. The distribution instead suggests there is a diversity of factors that contribute to perceived verifiability and that focusing solely on one or two discrete, a priori obvious indicators to analyze attribution behavior conceals a great deal of variation. As shown in **Fig. 2** source anonymity and quote directness do have explanatory power, however they appear unable to explain the continuum of perceived verifiabilities.

3.4 Inter-annotator agreement

Inter-annotator agreement serves as a standard check to ensure that workers understood and reliably performed the task. In this case some care is needed in interpreting the inter-annotator agreement, however: we expect a certain amount of in-built disagreement due to comparisons made between attributions having very close verifiability scores. In fact, the Bradley-Terry model (and other methods for deriving scores from pairwise comparisons) is predicated on the notion that two items have similar latent score precisely when workers are unable to reliably decide which is to be preferred (i.e. which has higher verifiability).

For this reason, the agreement level for attributions having sufficiently similar scores will necessarily be low. To properly assess reliability for this kind of annotation, it is necessary to disaggregate the comparisons based on how far apart the compared attributions are in verifiability score.

To ensure that disaggregated agreement scores

---

[8]The probability of a worker judging a_1 to be more verifiable than a_2, given they have verifiability scores v_1 and v_2, is modeled as $\Pr(a_1 \succ a_2) = (1 + e^{\beta(v_2 - v_1)})^{-1}$, where β is the scale parameter used to transform scores to $[0, 1]$.

Separation	0	1	2	3	4
Agreement	.174	.363	.651	.825	.904

Table 1: Krippendorff's α for comparisons between attributions from quintiles of given separation. A separation of 0 means comparisons between attributions in the same quintile.

are unbiased, we use half of the pairings in the dataset to assign scores, and then assess agreement on the other half. Using the scores derived from half the data, we divide the attributions into quintiles. We then assess agreement on comparisons that are made between attributions from quintiles having a given separation.

For example, all comparisons made between attributions from the same quintile have separation 0, while comparisons made between attributions from adjacent quintiles have separation 1. The agreements associated to each level of separation are shown in **Table 1**. As the separation between attributions is increased, the level of agreement monotonically increases, becoming very high (Krippendorff's α 0.904) for comparisons between attributions from the highest and lowest quintiles. This indicates that once we factor out disagreement due to perceived similarity of attributions, workers were able to understand and perform the task with high reliability.

4 Modeling verifiability

In the PARC3 annotation style, an attribution consists of a *source*, the attributed *content*, and a *cue*, such as "said" or "according to", signalling the existence of an attribution. A priori, any of the three parts of an attribution (source, cue, content) could contribute to the perceived verifiability of an attribution. In addition to the baseline model based on source anonymity and whether the attribution is a direct, indirect, or mixed quote, we also test a "feature-rich" model based on a large number of features extracted from attributions' source, cue, and content, listed in **Table 2** (the baseline model is based on features S2 and C4). We test multiple regression algorithms for both the baseline and rich feature set, and we do feature ablation to optimize the feature-rich model. In the next subsection, we discuss the selection of features and ablation results, then in the following section, we describe the learning algorithms and the best results achieved for the baseline and feature-rich models.

		Feature set	RMSE$_i$	Δ_{-i}RMSE $\times 10^3$
source	S	All source features	.093	14.09
	S1	Length	.124	1.70
	S2	Anonymity	.110	1.34
	S3	Each of 7 NE types	.102	.79
	S4	Head's determiner	.164	.52
	S5	Head lemma	.115	.46
	S6	Head plural	.152	.15
	S7	Fuzzy quantifiers	.159	.04
	S8	Pronoun[9]	.163	.03
	S9	Date or numeric NEs	.164	-.04
	S10	Head's amod	.164	-.09
cue	Q	All cue features	.134	8.11
	Q1	LIWC dictionary counts	.137	.88
	Q2	Lemmatized BOW	.136	.39
	Q3	Length	.161	-.02
	Q4	Cue class	.142	-.33
content	C	All content features	.139	1.90
	C1	Date or numeric NEs	.163	.13
	C2	Fract. enquoted tokens	.149	.01
	C3	PERS or ORG NEs	.164	-.05
	C4	Direct, indirect, mixed	.149	-.11
	C5	Each of 7 NE types	.161	-.22
	C6	Length	.153	-.59

Table 2: Features for verifiability regression. RSME when using the feature on its own (RMSE$_i$), and drop in RMSE occurring when the feature is removed from a model built from all features (Δ_{-i}RMSE). Entries sorted in descending order of Δ_{-i}RMSE.

4.1 Feature design and selection

For the sake of continuity, as we describe features, we will also discuss the results of ablating them. Ablation results are based on the training-set performance of a Support Vector Regressor (SVR), optimizing for minimum root mean squared error (RMSE) between predicted verifiability scores and those derived from human annotations. The full set of features is listed in **Table 2**. For ablation testing, we assessed each feature in two contexts: (1) as the only feature used, and (2) as the only feature left out. While the first measures the straightforward predictiveness of the feature, the second measures the marginal improvement in the context of other features and is used for final feature selection in the feature-rich model.

Source features. Based on the CoreNLP named entity recognition (NER) software (Manning et al., 2014), we created features indicating whether any of the 7 types[10] of named entities (NEs) were present in the source (feature S3, **Ta-**

---

[9] Aside from "he", "she", and "they", which are interpolated.

[10] CoreNLP recognizes seven types of named entities: PERS, ORG, DATE, MONEY, DURATION, PERCENT, NUMBER.

ble 2). This feature was beneficial both alone and in the context of other features. We also included a feature encoding the anonymity of the source, based on whether either a PERS or ORG NE was present (this was one of the baseline features, S2). Although this may seem reduntant with S3, encoding the source anonymity in this way boosted performance even in the context of S3. Several of the other NEs are number-like: we also created a feature indicating whether any number-like NE was present (S9), but it hindered performance in the context of other features.

When not a NE, the head of the source span is often a title ("director"), occupation ("lawyer"), or collective designation ("homeowners"). Intuitively, pluralized designations seem more nebulous, so we introduced a feature indicating whether the head of the source span is pluralized (S6). Although less predictive on its own, this feature did provide a benefit to the model in the context of other features.

Similarly, the determiner of the head of the source can influence definiteness: consider "a lawyer" versus "the lawyer". We added feature S4 indicating the kind of determiner used, if any, which also made an important contribution to the overall model.

Quantifiers such as "most", "some", "many", and "several", can also render a source imprecise, so we included a feature indicating the presence of such quantifiers or the word "source(s)" (S7). In ablation testing this feature marginally improved the model's accuracy in the context of other features.

We included the lemma of the head (S5), which made a notable contribution. This feature subset likely suffered from sparsity, so its contribution might be more important given a larger training set.

Modifiers to the source could also influence verifiability, so we included features for the lemma of tokens under the `amod` dependency tree relation to the head (S10)[11]. This feature did not benefit the model, but again may perform better in larger datasets.

The source feature providing the greatest contribution in the context of other features was the length of the source (S1) (although on its own it is less predictive than source anonymity, S2). In-

tuitively, the longer the specification of the source, the more definite it is, and the more verifiable. The strong performance of this feature suggests additional features might account more specifically for language not accounted for by other features which contribute to verifiability.

Cue features. We derived four features from the cue, which were lemmatized bag-of-words (Q2), length (Q3), counts of words belonging to each of the LIWC dictionaries (Q1) (Tausczik and Pennebaker, 2010), and the presence of specific sets of reporting verbs (Q4). This last (Q4) was based on our observation that reporting verbs either indicate the statement neutrally ('said', 'reported'), qualify the statement as true ('confirmed', 'showed'), indicate an intention ('will', 'plans'), or call to question whether the statement is true ('believes', 'claimed'). The liwc dictionary counts (Q1) and lemmatized bag-of-words (Q2) both made substantial contributions to model accuracy.

Content features. A verbatim attribution seems inherently easier to verify than a paraphrase, so attribution directness was included (C4). Ablation testing showed that attribution directness was actually detrimental to the regression overall and was a poor predictor alone. However, we created a more nuanced representation of quote directness based on the fraction of enquoted words (C2), which was marginally beneficial.

Given that verifiability depends not on the truth of a statement, but on the ability to check the fidelity of the attribution to the source, one might expect that (aside from attribution directness) the content would have little effect on verifiability. However, it is inherently harder to verify the attribution of a vague paraphrase, which could be consistent with a wider range of original statements. Conversely, numerical quantities and the naming of people and organizations should increase the verifiability. As we did for the source, we included features representing the 7 types of named entities (C5), a feature indicating either PERS or ORG (C3), and a feature indicating numerical entities (C1). The numeric entities feature did indeed improved model accuracy although the other features derived from NEs in the content did not.

Finally, we included the length of the content (C6), but this feature was detrimental to the model.

Ablating feature blocks. Considering the role that they play in attribution, one would expect

---

[11]Based on the CoreNLP dependency parse (Manning et al., 2014)

Model	RMSE	ρ
baseline	0.102	0.833
feature-rich	0.057	0.951

Table 3: Test-set RMSE and Spearman's rank correlation (ρ) for each model.

that, overall, the source would be most informative due to its importance in being able to trace the attribution to a specific person, group, or artifact, followed by the cue, due to the fact that the cue describes the act of attribution and can indicate the certainty or degree of interpretive licence exercised by the author (e.g. if the cue is "hinted").

To test the importance of the source, cue, and content, we ablate each set of features as a whole, the results of which are indicated in **Table 2** by the rows that have feature symbols containing only an 'S', a 'Q', or a 'C' (with no number). These results confirm that the source is most informative, followed by the cue.

4.2 Models training and testing

We randomly separated the dataset of 2100 quotes into a testing and training set of 420 and 1680 attributions each. Using the training set, we used three learners to optimize the performance on models using the baseline set of features, and a rich set of features (those contributing positively to model accuracy in the context of other features, see third column of **Table 2**). The learners included linear regression with lasso regularization, a support vector classifier (SVC) that predicts the quintile from which an attribution was drawn (and returns the median score), and a support vector regressor (SVR). The support-vector-based models used linear, quadratic, and radial basis function as kernels. Using cross-validation on the training set, we optimized the learner selection, kernel selection, and learner hyperparameters, and performed ablation testing for the feature-rich model. Optimization was based on minimizing the RMSE. SVR performed best for both the baseline and ablation-optimized feature sets.

The optimized baseline and feature-rich model were then each run once on the test set, with the results summarized in **Table 3**.

RMSE gives a measure of error between the model's predicted scores, and the true verifiability scores. It's dimensionality and scale are equivalent to those of the variable predicted, so it can be

Verif.: quintile actual predicted	Attribution
1 0.316 0.482	<u>It is rumored</u> *to be bound for a new model in the luxury Acura line in the U.S.*
2 0.698 0.676	**Earlier U.S. trade reports** have complained of *videocassette piracy in Malaysia and disregard for U.S. pharmaceutical patents in Turkey*
3 0.802 0.766	**South Korea** <u>announced</u> *$450 million in loans to the financially strapped Warsaw government.*
4 0.884 0.887	*Mr. Paul has been characterised as "the Great Gatsby or something,"* <u>complains</u> **Karen E. Brinkman, an executive vice president of CenTrust**
5 0.960 0.959	*"It has an archival, almost nostalgic quality to it,"* <u>says</u> **Owen B. Butler, the chairman of the applied photography department at Rochester Institute of Technology.**

Table 4: Selected attributions from each quintile of the verifiability-scored subset of PARC3 along with model predictions.

compared to the range of values across which verifiability varies; the feature-rich RMSE was 5.7% of the prediction range. In many applications, the absolute verifiability may be less important than the relative verifiability. Both the baseline and the feature-rich model achieve relatively high Spearman's rank correlations ($p \ll 0.001$). The feature-rich model provides a substantial improvement in performance over the baseline, both in RMSE and rank correlation. This shows that a richer set of features, beyond source anonymity and quote directness, is needed to explain the perception of attribution verifiability.

A selection of attributions from each quintile, along with their human-judged and model-predicted verifiability scores are shown in **Table 4**. These examples demonstrate how the model has learned to consider various features in regressing verifiability. Aside from the first, each of the examples in **Table 4** contains a named entity, however, it would appear that the model has learned to attribute less verifiability to location names than names of individuals. Additionally, in the example from quintile 2, we can see that the head of the source is the word "reports", which is likely what has led to its appropriately lower predicted score: it would be quite difficult, though possible, to comb through a sufficient number of U.S. trade reports to reach a verdict about the fidelity of this attribution.

5 Application to the analysis of mass media

Journalists are frequently forced to decide whether given sources are sufficiently credible and relevant to cite, while balancing transparent attribution against the source's potential interest in remaining anonymous. It is reasonable to wonder what influences and biases exert themselves on such decisions.

If there are systematic influences at play, it should be possible to find evidence in the distribution of verifiability, and its correlation with publishers, topics, positions on given issues, and political alignments. To look for such patterns at scale, it will be necessary to create an end-to-end system for attribution extraction and verifiability regression.

Although prior work demonstrates good performance on attribution extraction, and we demonstrate accurate verifiability regression here, our initial investigations of an end-to-end extraction and regression system show that errors during extraction lead to large negative errors in verifiability (i.e. underestimates) during regression. This is especially true when there are errors in extracting the source span. Investigating verifiability at scale will require some combination of: (a) further improvements to extraction accuracy, (b) discarding poorly extracted attributions (with loss of recall), and (c) adjustment of the extraction / regression models to reduce error cascading, which we hope to investigate in future work.

6 Conclusion

Attribution is a critical feature of journalism, and a fundamental, challenging natural language phenomenon. We have introduced a new NLP task consisting of the prediction of attributions' perceived verifiability according to human judgments. We provide a dataset of verifiability-scored attributions based on a subset of PARC3.

Our models show that source anonymity and quote directness alone are insufficient to explain the continuum of perceived verifiability, but a richer set of linguistic features enables accurate verifiability regression. The source appears to be the dominant factor determining an attribution's verifiability, with an important contribution also coming from the cue, and a slight contribution from the content.

This new task, along with existing work in attribution extraction, creates a new opportunity to study attribution practices in mass media, at scale, and shed light on the shifting landscape of journalistic norms.

Acknowledgments

We thank Silvia Pareti for helpful discussions about PARC3 and attribution extraction.

References

John B Adams. 1962. The relative credibility of 20 unnamed news sources. *Journalism Quarterly* 39(1):79–82.

David E Boeyink. 1990. Anonymous sources in news stories: Justifying exceptions and limiting abuses. *Journal of Mass Media Ethics* 5(4):233–246.

Larry L Burriss. 1988. Attribution in Network Radio News A Cross-Network Analysis. *Journalism and Mass Communication Quarterly* 65(3):690.

Luís António Diniz Fernandes de Morais, Sérgio Sobral Nunes, et al. 2009. Automatic extraction of quotes and topics from news feeds. In *DSIE09-4th Doctoral Symposium on Informatics Engineering*.

D. Deutsch. 1997. *The Fabric of Reality: The science of parallel universes and its implications*. Allen Lane, New York.

Matt J. Duffy and Carrie P. Freeman. 2011. Unnamed Sources: A Utilitarian Exploration of their Justification and Guidelines for Limited Use. *Journal of Mass Media Ethics* 26(4):297–315.

David K Elson and Kathleen McKeown. 2010. Automatic attribution of quoted speech in literary narrative. In *Proceedings of the Twenty-Fourth AAAI Conference on Artificial Intelligence*.

Frank Esser and Andrea Umbricht. 2014. The evolution of objective and interpretative journalism in the Western press: Comparing six news systems since the 1960s. *Journalism & Mass Communication Quarterly* 91(2):229–249.

Norman Fairclough. 1995. *Critical discourse analysis*. Longman, New York.

J.A. Hampton. 2007. Typicality, graded membership, and vagueness. *Cognitive Science* 31:355–383.

David R Hunter. 2004. MM algorithms for generalized bradley-terry models. *Annals of Statistics* pages 384–406.

Paula M. Jullian. 2011. Appraising through someone elses words: The evaluative power of quotations in news reports. *Discourse & Society* 22(6):766–780.

Svetlana Kiritchenko and Saif M. Mohammad. 2016. Capturing reliable fine-grained sentiment associations by crowdsourcing and best–worst scaling. In *Proceedings of The 15th Annual Conference of the North American Chapter of the Association for Computational Linguistics: Human Language Technologies (NAACL)*. San Diego, California.

Seok Ho Lee and Qian Wang. 2016. A Comparative Investigation Into PressState Relations: Comparing Source Structures in Three News Agencies Coverage of the North Korean Missile Crisis. *International Journal of Communication* 10:22.

Jenn Burleson Mackay and Erica Bailey. 2012. Succulent Sins, Personalized Politics, and Mainstream Medias Tabloidization Temptation. *International Journal of Technoethics* 3(4):41–53.

Nuno Mamede and Pedro Chaleira. 2004. Character identification in children stories. In *Advances in natural language processing*, Springer, pages 82–90.

Christopher D. Manning, Mihai Surdeanu, John Bauer, Jenny Finkel, Steven J. Bethard, and David McClosky. 2014. The Stanford CoreNLP natural language processing toolkit. In *Association for Computational Linguistics (ACL) System Demonstrations*. pages 55–60.

Drew B. Margolin and Peter Monge. 2013. Conceptual retention in epistemic communities. In Patricia Moy, editor, *Communication and community*, Hampton Press, New York, pages 1–22.

Tim O'Keefe, Silvia Pareti, James R Curran, Irena Koprinska, and Matthew Honnibal. 2012. A sequence labelling approach to quote attribution. In *Proceedings of the 2012 Joint Conference on Empirical Methods in Natural Language Processing and Computational Natural Language Learning*. Association for Computational Linguistics, pages 790–799.

Silvia Pareti. 2012. A database of attribution relations. In *Language Resources and Evaluation Conference*. pages 3213–3217.

Silvia Pareti. 2015. Attribution: a computational approach .

Silvia Pareti, Timothy O'Keefe, Ioannis Konstas, James R Curran, and Irena Koprinska. 2013. Automatically detecting and attributing indirect quotations. In *Empirical Methods in Natural Language Processing*. pages 989–999.

Roberta Piazza. 2009. News is Reporting What was Said. Techniques and Patterns of Attribution. *Evaluation and Stance in War News* pages 170–194.

Ivanka Pjesivac and Rachel Rui. 2014. Anonymous sources hurt credibility of news stories across cultures: A comparative experiment in America and China. *International Communication Gazette* 76(8):641–660.

K.R. Popper. 2003. *The Logic of scientific discovery*. Routledge, New York.

Bruno Pouliquen, Ralf Steinberger, and Clive Best. 2007. Automatic detection of quotations in multilingual news. In *Proceedings of Recent Advances in Natural Language Processing*. pages 487–492.

Daniel Riffe. 1980. Relative credibility revisited: How 18 unnamed sources are rated. *Journalism Quarterly* 57(4):618–623.

Nate Silver. 2017. Why You Shouldnt Always Trust The Inside Scoop.

Miglena Mantcheva Sternadori and Esther Thorson. 2009. Anonymous sources harm credibility of all stories. *Newspaper Research Journal* 30(4):54–66.

S. Shyam Sundar. 1998. Effect of source attribution on perception of online news stories. *Journalism and Mass Communication Quarterly* 75(1):55–68.

Yla R Tausczik and James W Pennebaker. 2010. The psychological meaning of words: LIWC and computerized text analysis methods. *Journal of language and social psychology* 29(1):24–54.

K Tim Wulfemeyer. 1985. How and Why Anonymous Attribution Is Used by "Time" and "Newsweek". *Journalism and Mass Communication Quarterly* 62(1):81.

K. Tim Wulfemeyer and Lori L. McFadden. 1986. Anonymous attribution in network news. *Journalism and Mass Communication Quarterly* 63(3):468.

Jason Y Zhang, Alan W Black, and Richard Sproat. 2003. Identifying speakers in children's stories for speech synthesis. In *Interspeech*.

Domain Adaptation from User-level Facebook Models to County-level Twitter Predictions

Daniel Rieman
Positive Psychology Center
University of Pennsylvania
`rieman@seas.upenn.edu`

Kokil Jaidka
Positive Psychology Center
University of Pennsylvania
`jaidka@sas.upenn.edu`

H. Andrew Schwartz
Computer and Information Science
Stony Brook University
`has@cs.stonybrook.edu`

Lyle Ungar
Computer and Information Science
University of Pennsylvania
`ungar@cis.upenn.edu`

Abstract

Several studies have demonstrated how language models of user attributes, such as personality, can be built by using the Facebook language of social media users in conjunction with their responses to psychology questionnaires. It is challenging to apply these models to make general predictions about attributes of communities, such as personality distributions across US counties, because it requires 1. the potentially inavailability of the original training data because of privacy and ethical regulations, 2. adapting Facebook language models to Twitter language without retraining the model, and 3. adapting from users to county-level collections of tweets. We propose a two-step algorithm, *Target Side Domain Adaptation* (TSDA) for such domain adaptation when no labeled Twitter/county data is available. TSDA corrects for the different word distributions between Facebook and Twitter and for the varying word distributions across counties by adjusting *target side* word frequencies; no changes to the trained model are made. In the case of predicting the Big Five county-level personality traits, TSDA outperforms a state-of-the-art domain adaptation method, gives county-level predictions that have fewer extreme outliers, higher year-to-year stability, and higher correlation with county-level outcomes.

1 Introduction

Social media platforms offer an effective– and widely used– platform for administering surveys to individuals to measure their personality, socioeconomic status, mental and physical well-being, and political orientation, which can then be combined with user posts to build language-based predictive models of user attributes, traits and behaviors. As compared to surveys, language models can be used to assess personality and well-being across communities of the U.S, at a scale not easily achieved by surveys (Eichstaedt et al., 2015). In comparison, Twitter is a more effective tool to mine geographic trends from language, since tweets are publicly accessible, and one in five tweets can be mapped to the county from which they were sent (Schwartz et al., 2013b). However, to our knowledge, there are no tweet-based models of personality which are comparable in accuracy to the Facebook language models of personality.

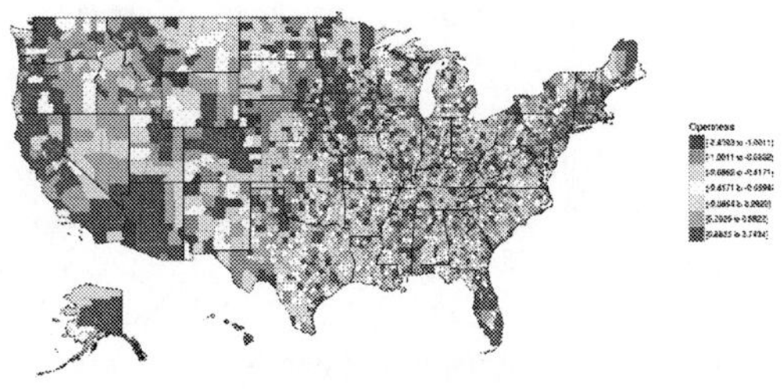

Figure 1: Predictions for county-level openness to experience created by applying a user-level Facebook model for openness on TSDA adjusted Twitter county data

Personality, as measured by the "Big Five" of *openness, conscientiousness, extraversion, agreeableness* and *neuroticism* is known to vary regionally worldwide (Rentfrow et al., 2013) and to cluster geographically in the United States (Rentfrow et al., 2013; Florida, 2002). In this paper, we wish to infer the regional variations of the Big Five Personality traits across the United States, through five language models trained on Facebook posts. We formulate our problem as one of domain adaptation - adapting Facebook models for Twitter's vocabulary, and adapting user-level models for county-level predictions. Figure 1 provides the county-level predictions for the psychological trait of *openness* to experience. At the individual level, *openness* has been found to be correlated with a higher education level and better academic performance (Poropat, 2009). At the regional level, we

Proceedings of the The 8th International Joint Conference on Natural Language Processing, pages 764–773,
Taipei, Taiwan, November 27 – December 1, 2017 ©2017 AFNLP

expect to replicate survey results from Rentfrow et al. (Rentfrow et al., 2013), which have demonstrated that regional variations in personality are stable over time, and correlate with key political, economic, social and health metrics.

We combine two forms of target side adaptation in this paper: first, we adapt from Facebook to Twitter; next, we compensate for the variation introduced by the fact that Tweets within each county have significant correlation, leading to spuriously high frequencies of various words in various counties, significantly reducing the predictive accuracy there of the source models. The remainder of the paper first motivates our domain adaptation problem and provides a background on the specific problem of personality prediction. We then situate our method within the field of domain adaptation. Next, we present the TSDA algorithm which, like other popular domain adaptation algorithms, is frustratingly easy (Daumé III, 2007). Finally, we demonstrate that TSDA improves the quality of county-level predictions by (a) removing extreme predictions, (b) improving year-to-year stability, (c) increasing average magnitude of correlations between predicted county-level personality and measured health and well-being metrics with which the personality constructs are known to correlate, and decreasing correlations where correlations are not expected.

1.1 The Need for Target Side Adaptation

Applying user-level language models learned on Facebook to make county-level predictions on Twitter poses three main challenges. The first challenge, typically addressed by traditional domain adaptation methods, is the difference in vocabulary between Facebook and Twitter, which motivates the need for domain transfer. For instance, "rt" is one of the most frequent Twitter 'words', but rare on Facebook. Secondly, although typical domain adaptation methods expect the availability of labeled training data, in this case there are new challenges due to the sensitivity of data. In cases where NLP is used to address social science problems, the training data is often unavailable when it comprises personally identifiable information, or when sharing would violate privacy and ethical regulations. Thus, an appropriate unsupervised domain adaptation approach would expect only a trained model – not the original data – to be available for predicting outcomes.

A third challenge is that there is a need to disambiguate words which have vastly different frequencies and often entirely different meanings in different counties. The implications of this artifact of the data are obvious when, on reviewing the relative ranking of counties by personality traits, it is observed that the most predictive features for the most- or least-scoring counties, often comprise words which are being used in a different local context (see Table 2). An appropriate domain adaptation approach should account for these local differences, and still generate a generic set of domain adapted features for all counties, rather than 3142 feature sets adapted to each of the counties individually.

We introduce *Target Side Domain Adaptation* (TSDA), an unsupervised method which adapts the target county-level data from Twitter to be more accurately predicted from the source user-level Facebook models *using no labels on the target Tweets or counties and without altering the source-side model*. We call it "Target Side" to emphasize that no retraining of the model is done during the domain adaptation. We assume no labels on the target side, and so only make use of the differences between the source and target distributions of the features. An important assumption in this paper is that differences in the frequencies for the same word among counties, reflects differences in its local meaning. TSDA works particularly well with words, since (a) words vary widely in frequency across domains, and (b) words vary widely in frequency and meaning across domains.

2 Background

2.1 Personality Traits

We take as our core case study extrapolating personality, as measured in individual level questionnaires, to the 'average' personality for a county. There is a rising research area of "Geographical Psychology" (Rentfrow and Jokela, 2016), which looks at region variations in different psychological traits such as personality, and their correlation with physical and mental well-being.

As a surrogate for large scale surveying, we propose using peoples' social media language to estimate their personality. Such language-based models based on Facebook posts have been built using data from roughly 70,000 people who took personality tests and shared their test results and Facebook posts with researchers (Schwartz et al.,

2013a). These models have proven to be as accurate at estimating personality as estimates from people's friends (Park et al., 2014). However at first blush, such use of Facebook only pushes the problem one level back, as even 70,000 Facebook users give poor coverage of 100 out of over 3,000 US counties. To get good coverage, we shift to a more open social media platform, Twitter.

Twitter is readily available and allows free access to its streaming API. Even though only a few percent of tweets come with latitude and longitude, roughly 20% of the Tweets from the US can still be mapped to their county of origin. Many language-based models of user traits including demographics (Rao et al., 2010; Burger et al., 2011), personality (Schwartz et al., 2013a), socioeconomic status (Preoţiuc-Pietro et al., 2015), popularity (Lampos et al., 2014) and political orientation (Pennacchiotti and Popescu, 2011) have been made from social media language. A number of these models are based on labels of individual tweets (e.g., using Amazon's Mechanical Turk); collecting questionnaire data and the Tweets from the same user is harder, in part due to restrictions on Amazon's terms of use for Mechanical Turk. Facebook requires consenting users to share their data, but while obtaining consent, it is easy to ask users questions to assess their personality, or to ask them to share other data such as their electronic medical records (Smith et al., 2017).

Thus, we face the technical question: How can we take a model trained to predict user attributes such as personality from Facebook language at the individual user level and use it to predict average personality from Twitter language at the county level? This requires a double domain adaptation: firstly from Facebook to Twitter, and secondly from users to counties. This domain adaptation is complicated by the fact that we have virtually no county-level personality measures to use to guide the domain adaptation; it must be unsupervised.

2.2 Domain Adaptation Background

Our task can be characterized as domain adaptation, or the closely related transfer learning (Pan and Yang, 2010), where we are adapting from a *source domain*: the words users use on their Facebook posts and associated user labels to a *target domain*: county-level Twitter language, where we want, but do not have, labels on the counties. Most prior work on domain adaptation has focused on the case where some labels are available on both the source and target domains, and is usually done by combining (often in some weighted fashion) training data sets or, less commonly, trained models from the source and target domains (Daume III and Marcu, 2006). Both of these approaches require at least some labeled target data, which we lack. Thus, methods such as EasyAdapt++ (Daumé III et al., 2010), which encourages source and target models to agree on unlabeled data cannot be used here.

In this paper, we have compared our proposed TSDA framework against the Correlation Alignment (CORAL) approach, an unsupervised approach which aims to minimizes domain shift by linearly transforming the covariance matrix of the target distribution to be as similar as possible (under the Frobenius norm) to the source distribution (Sun et al., 2015). It is similar in principle to the study by Daumé and Marcu, which applied Canonical Correlation Analysis (CCA) perform unsupervised machine translation by calculating the cosine similarity of projections in a lower dimensional space (Daumé III and Jagarlamudi, 2011). Transfer Component Analysis (TCA) is a more computationally expensive approach, which exploits the Maximum Mean Discrepancy Embedding (MMDE) metric for comparing the distributions between the source and target domain in the Reproducing Kernel Hilbert Space (RKHS) representation (Pan et al., 2011).

3 Target Side Domain Adaptation

Our Target Side Domain Adaptation (TSDA) is a two step process. The first step attempts to minimize the impact of spatially correlated word tokens in the county-level Twitter data by down-scaling the counts of words that are over-represented in some counties. The second step then removes words that have significantly different frequencies between Facebook and Twitter. Note that TSDA does not use any target-side labels. It is instead predicated on the assumption that any large differences in word frequencies between source and target will interfere with the correct generalization; we do not need to know anything about the model in order to do the domain adaptation, instead we use the observed distributions of words on the target side.

Our domain adaptation is motivated by the observation that word frequencies in counties may have multiple meanings, and that some counties will tend to use an alternative meaning more than others. More formally, we assume that word counts in each county are a mixture of the "true word frequencies" generated by the latent variable being estimated, such as personality combined with county-specific "noise" driven by different word meanings. For example, counties might use the word "jazz" proportionally to how open to experience they are, but a small number of counties (e.g. Salt Lake City) might also use it to refer to a sports team.

Because most words in most counties are generated based on the latent variables of interest (personality), we can compute the distribution of each word across counties (i.e. the distribution on the target side), identify the outliers (words in counties unlikely to come from the main meaning), and then replace them with an imputed value (e.g. the mean frequency for that word).

3.1 Step 1: Target-Side Adjustment

As the first step, we adjust the Twitter county-level word frequencies to help mitigate the influence of spatial variations and confounds in word use. This is done by identifying outlier feature values for a given county, and replacing them with the mean feature value across all counties. Extreme values can come from several sources. Common instances of such outliers are: (i) a concert or sports game in a small city, which can lead to disproportionately many mentions of e.g., Bieber or Cowboys. (ii) Some communities have unusually high concentrations of different ethnic groups, who may infuse their nominally English language tweets with Tagalog or Indonesian words. These words, present in small numbers on the source language training set, can significantly skew predictions.

We propose an extremely simple, robust method to address this problem: For each word w_j, for the 5% of counties with the largest word frequencies $w_{j,c}$, replace $w_{j,c}$ with the imputed $\bar{w}_j$ and then renormalize each county's word frequencies such that they sum to one.

We attempted using matrix imputation-based values from Singular Value Decomposition (SVD) as in (Troyanskaya et al., 2001) for imputation, as an alternative to using the mean frequency of words; however, we found that it did not make a significant difference on this data set. Also note that in each county, different words are replaced with their imputed values. No single adjustment to the source model is possible; each county effectively gets its own model - because, removing the same 5% of features from all counties would leave in too many harmful features, while removing a feature which is an "outlier" in any county from all other counties would remove too many features that are truly predictive, and also harm model accuracy.

3.2 Step 2: Source to Target Adjustment

The second step is to adjust frequencies for words that vary in usage between Facebook and Twitter. As in Step 1, our assumption is that differences in frequency correspond to differences in meaning. Accordingly, for each word in a county, we compute a ratio of its mean frequency for Facebook users, to the mean frequency for Twitter counties. Then, if the ratio for a word lies close to 1.0, word frequencies in the target Twitter counties are replaced with their corresponding means from the source data.

Specifically, we compute

$$\frac{|\bar{w}_j^F - \bar{w}_j^T|}{\bar{w}_j^F + \bar{w}_j^T} > \epsilon$$

Where $\bar{w}_j^F$ is the mean of word frequency j for Facebook users and $\bar{w}_j^T$ is the mean of word j for Twitter counties. In practice we used $\epsilon = 0.8$.

Note that the two domain adaptation steps, although superficially similar, are in fact qualitatively different. In the second step (Facebook to Twitter adaptation) the feature removal is "global", so one could easily remove the features that vary most between the source and target domains and then retrain the source Facebook model without those features. For the first step (cross-county regularization), no such simple retraining is possible.

4 Data and Model Description

Facebook user-level models were built using data consisting of 65,896 observations of statuses and personality questionnaire answers. Each user posted at least 1,000 words and answered a set of at least 20 questions to derive a score for each of the Big Five personality traits. Statuses for each of the Facebook users were tokenized, unigram word counts extracted, and converted to term frequencies by dividing the resulting word counts for each user by that user's total word count. An elastic net regularized linear regression model utilizing a feature selection pipeline described in (Park et al., 2014) was then trained on each of the personality traits.

We used Twitter data comprising the 10% random sample from years 2012-14. We mapped tweets to US counties using the method of Schwartz et al. (2013), which is based on latitude/longitude coordinates, and the self-reported location field when available . Roughly one fifth could be successfully mapped resulting over 150 million geolocated tweets. Only those counties with at least 40,000 words were kept, yielding 2,468 counties for 2012, 2,651 for 2013, and 2,197 for 2014.

5 Evaluation of TSDA for Known Outcomes

We first evaluate our predictions by comparing them to five state-level average personality scores (Rentfrow et al., 2013), where we have enough surveys to get a 'ground truth'. The results suggest that TSDA works well when the county-level scores are further aggregated to the state level (Rentfrow and Jokela, 2016). Table 1 shows Pearson r between average state personality predictions (population weighted average of the county predictions) and the 'ground truth'.

The baselines were calculated using predictions with no domain adaptation, with CORAL, and with retrained models on the TCA-transformed features both with and without the feature selection pipeline used in the other models. Recall that CORAL adjusts the source features to the target features using a transformation selected using an L_2 (Frobenius norm) loss; such methods work poorly when a small number of extreme values need to be removed.

Additionally, we used this state-level ground truth to test the sensitivity of our method to variation in the step 1 and step 2 parameters. Results showed a statistically significant increase in correlation using 0.8 over 0.9 in step 2 while the variation in the step 1 parameter is less clear. When step 2 uses 0.8, we see openness, conscientiousness and extraversion correlations strengthening with increasing step 1 parameter, agreeableness decreasing, and neuroticism remaining constant. The average increase in performance of TSDA with the range of parameters tested was also statistically significant above the no domain adaptation baseline.

Baselines	O	C	E	A	N
No domain adaptation	.47	.08	.49	.44	.53
CORAL	.14	.19	.20	-.16	.26
TCA no feature selection	.70	.26	-.06	.64	.47
TCA feature selection	.53	.28	-.16	.63	.48

TSDA						
Step 1	Step 2	O	C	E	A	N
1%	0.8	.61	.09	.50	.49	.57
2%	0.8	.63	.10	.50	.48	.57
5%	0.8	.69	.11	.52	.45	.58
10%	0.8	.71	.13	.52	.45	.57
1%	0.9	.59	.08	.49	.43	.56
2%	0.9	.61	.09	.48	.42	.56
5%	0.9	.69	.10	.49	.41	.57
10%	0.9	.71	.14	.48	.42	.56

Table 1: Pearson r between target side state-level predictions and 'ground truth' state personalities (Rentfrow et al., 2013). The first baseline uses the naive predictions, the second uses the CORAL method, and the third and fourth use the TCA method first without and then with the feature selection pipeline used in the other models. TSDA results are shown for a variety of parameters for steps 1 and 2, but in practice we use 5% and 0.8.

6 Unsupervised Validation Method

Validating unsupervised domain adaptation often presents a challenge, when no ground truth is available. We refer to the set of validity criteria developed by social scientists, such as testing *reliability*, the degree to which an assessment tool produces stable and consistent results e.g. over time and *external validity*, the degree to which the results generalize to other settings (ecological validity) and other people (population validity), as well as *predictive validity*, the ability of a stipulated theoretical construct (like Openness to Experience) to predict (correlate with) behavioral or other *criterion*, outcomes that it is theorized to relate to. In this paper, we demonstrate a three-pronged approach to validation, which relies on the fact that the predictions on the many targets (counties) should be (a) normally distributed as they capture natural phenomena, (b) consistent from year to year, (c) correlated with other state- and county-level outcomes such as education, income, health, and happiness which have been measured. Evaluating domain adaptation to a target domain which has no labeled ground truth presents a novel problem. We want, for example to predict the extraversion of different counties, but do not have sufficient data to know, for example, what the mean extraversion scores are of even hundreds of counties.

We propose a three-pronged approach to validating a domain adaptation method on a set of target observations (counties, here) where we have no ground truth:

1) Are the distributions of the predicted attributes reasonable? We know, for example, that personality scores are, by construction, Gaussian at the individual level, and that averaging these Gaussians should give a distribution of mean county-level personalities that are Gaussian. However, as shown below, we find our county-level predictions to be far from a normal distribution, with some predictions lying over 10 standard deviations from the mean. We use kurtosis as a concrete metric to assess the impact of domain adaptation on predictions.

2) Are the estimates stable? We know that personality at the level of individuals is relatively stable over time; average personality in a county level should be extremely stable from year to year. However, this wasn't the case for our county-level predictions. We use year to year Pearson correlation between predictions as the benchmark metric to measure stability; domain adaptation should increase these correlations.

3) Do estimates correlate as expected with other outcomes? We know that personality correlates with many measurable outcomes for which we *do* have county-level measurements such as health and subjective well-being. A good domain adaptation should produce personality predictions which correlate more highly with such outcomes, while reducing unexpected correlations.

7 Results

We now demonstrate the utility of TSDA by modeling how personality, as estimated using language on Facebook, can be used to predict county-level average personality from Twitter language.

We use the widely used Five Factor Model (or Big 5) of personality (thousands of papers have been written using it) (McCrae and John, 1992; Digman, 1990), which classifies personality traits into five dimensions: *extraversion* (outgoing, talkative, active), *agreeableness* (trusting, kind, generous), *conscientiousness* (self-controlled, responsible, thorough), *neuroticism* (anxious, depressive, touchy), and *openness* (intellectual, artistic, insightful) all measured using the revised neo personality inventory (Costa and McCrae, 2008).

7.1 Qualitative Analysis of TSDA

Recall that the first step of TSDA removes the most different 5% of each feature across counties, replacing them with imputed values, while step 2 removes the words that have the most different frequencies between Facebook and Twitter.

We first look at which words counts are being adjusted. Since step 1 imputes new frequencies for different words for each county, too many words are replaced to show them all. As representative examples, we show in Table 2 the 10 words with the largest change after TSDA step 1 for San Francisco, Salt Lake, and Philadelphia counties. These words, selected *without* looking at the labels, are removed from the model (replacing them with their mean values). We can also look, after the fact, and see which of the removed words had the most influence on the prediction. The 10 words which most affected the predicted openness when they were removed for each of the same three counties are shown in Table 3.

We can also see which words most affected the predicted openness when they were removed from Venango County, PA, one of two counties with extremely low predicted openness: 'yg, ini, sama, ada, lagi, yang, aku, hari, yaa, ga'. These words, lyrics from an Indonesian song, show what can go wrong when models are applied to different domains (counties and years here); a previously rare meme becomes common in one county, making predictions for it highly inaccurate.

Philadelphia	Salt Lake	San Francisco
ctfu	utah	-
philly	salt	)
philadelphia	lake	de
pa	city	que
ard	news	la
eagles	followers	TM
#philly	#jobs	,
instagram	ut	el
gm	#job	san
phillies	solutions	new

Table 2: Words with the largest change after TSDA step 1 for three cities. We see locations and sports teams, non-English terms, and abbreviations as some of the easily identifiable groups of words adjusted by step 1.

Step 2 imputes the same new word frequencies across all counties and, as shown below in Table 4, gives results that are intuitive. We run step 2 separately here for each of the 3 years of Twitter data, again giving top ranked words that differ slightly from year to year.

Philadelphia	Salt Lake	San Francisco
artist (-)	lake (+)	francisco (-)
corny (-)	jazz (-)	samsung (+)
jersey (+)	slc (-)	woww (+)
dickhead (+)	salt (-)	art (-)
sheesh (-)	projection (-)	itunes (+)
iggy (-)	international (-)	blog (-)
shore (+)	canvas (-)	content (-)
mic (-)	faucet (-)	vintage (-)
imu (+)	masturbation (-)	media (-)
eagles (+)	robert (-)	technology (-)

Table 3: Similar to Table 2, this table looks at features which changed the most, but weights the difference by the Openness model weight. The resulting table shows features whose alteration in TSDA step 1 changed the county-level openness prediction the most. The (+) and (-) indicate if the change had a positive or negative impact on each county's openness prediction respectively.

	Frequent on Facebook			Frequent on Twitter		
2012	2013	2014	2012	2013	2014
paste	=[	farmville	rt	rt	rt
^	paste	=]	tweets	2013	2014
8p	farmville	:[	#winning	tweets	http
%	=]	--	tf	tf	toned
repost	--	paste	tweeting	tweeting	waistline
--	^		tweet	<	2013
=[	finaly	http://	<<<<<	followers	sheds
maths	%	=(	<<<<	tweet	tf
ng	8p	=/	>>>>>	>>>>>	<
eid	mubarak	=p	>>>>>>	>>>>>>	tweets

Table 4: Features measured most different by TSDA Step 2 on three years of Twitter data. Reported both for features that occurred more on Facebook (the left) and those occurring more on Twitter (the right). All comparison were made with the same source Facebook data.

A consequence of readjusting frequencies of words that differ widely between source and target is that words representing years (e.g. '2015') have very different frequencies in the year that the post or tweet was written. Certain celebrity names behave similarly. Since we often predict on different years than we train, such time-correlated features are frequently dropped out.

7.2 Unsupervised Validation

As described above, we validate our model in three ways, measuring prediction 1) normality/kurtosis 2) year to year stability and 3) correlation to other county- and state-level outcomes.

Measuring Normality with kurtosis in Figure 2 shows that there were clear problems with the naive method. The personality measures were constructed to be normally distributed, therefore one should expect a sample of personality predictions to be approximately normally distributed with kurtosis near 3. This is clearly not the case with the original predictions, with a three year averaged kurtosis ranging between 8 and 36. The TCA and CORAL baseline predictions also had

Personality	Original	Step 1	Step 2	TSDA
O	35.33	3.01	27.63	2.99
C	22.22	4.10	8.47	3.60
E	24.99	6.41	16.43	3.90
A	8.95	2.68	10.84	2.75
N	10.56	2.61	17.97	2.71

Figure 2: Three year average of county prediction kurtosis

Personality	Original	Step 1	Step 2	TSDA
O	.83	.93	.82	.93
C	.76	.83	.82	.85
E	.49	.57	.51	.65
A	.84	.89	.82	.88
N	.81	.81	.78	.81

Figure 3: Pearson correlations between 2012 and 2013 predicted county-level personalities.

high kurtosis, with the TCA predictions ranging from 10 to 24 and CORAL from 6 to 69. TSDA however fixes this issue; all the predictions have kurtosis values between 2 and 4 when both steps of TSDA have been applied.

Year to Year Stability was assessed by correlating county-level predictions from one year to the following. Figure 3 shows that TSDA increased correlations for predictions that already appeared stable and those with lower correlations. When viewed in conjunction with Figure 2, one can see that the initially high correlations for openness and neuroticism, and to a lesser extent some other predictions, were due to high leverage points.

Spurious (county-specific) words that are stable from year to year can cause both high kurtosis and high year to year correlations. Spurious words that vary year to year, perhaps due to a local meme or news story, cause low year-to-year stability.

Correlations between Predicted Personality and County Health and Well-being were calculated. Successful domain adaptation should increase these correlations – or at least drive them towards what is expected from the previous literature. Figure 4 shows the average correlations across three years between observed county-level outcomes and personality predictions both original and post-TSDA word frequencies. We focus first on the overall results. TSDA yields an average increase in correlation magnitude of 11% above the original unadjusted correlations, when averaged over all the personality factors and outcomes listed in the table, as expected. However, some correlations increased due to domain adaptation, while some decreased. We asked a personality psychologist to frame hypotheses for the relationship of personality traits with other county-level outcomes, based on findings from the psychology literature and her considerable experience in the same domain. We tested our findings against these hypotheses, provided in Figure 4 and reflect the expected positive or negative relationship between the five personality traits and income, life satisfaction, mental health, education and income.

Hypothesis	O	C	E	A	N
Mentally Unhealthy Days		-	-	-	+
Life Satisfaction	+	+	+	+	-
Education	+	+			-
Income		+	+	-	-
No domain adaptation					
Mentally Unhealthy Days	-.03	-.04	-.04	-.06	.06
Life Satisfaction	.11	.20	.01	.13	-.17
Education	.32	.31	-.03	.22	-.30
Income	.18	.12	.01	.13	-.09
TSDA					
Mentally Unhealthy Days	.00	-.07	-.04	-.11	.10
Life Satisfaction	.12	.23	.00	.13	-.21
Education	.55	.35	-.25	.07	-.49
Income	.38	.11	-.15	-.01	-.25

Figure 4: **Top**: Individual-level correlation direction between personality traits and health, well-being, and socioeconomic status measures as predicted by a personality expert, supplemented by meta-analytic findings published in psychology where readily available (Roberts et al., 2007). **Middle**: Pearson r between original county-level personality predictions and externally measured metrics. **Bottom**: Pearson r between county-level predictions using TSDA and the same externally measured metrics.

We see that our predictions mostly accord with the personality literature, and that domain adaptation often strengthens the correlations that we expected and weakens the correlations that had been predicted from language, but were not expected. In particular, in the original data, there is a predicted strong correlation between agreeableness and education. Given the high kurtosis in agreeableness, this correlation is suspicious. TSDA reduces this correlation from 0.22 to 0.07, much more in line with what would be expected.

Several noteworthy correlations are found in our data, and strengthened by TSDA.

- Openness is known to correlate positively with higher educational attainment. This correlation increases 72% from 0.32 to 0.55 when TSDA is used.

- Conscientiousness is known to correlate positively with life satisfaction, education and income, and negatively with mentally unhealthy days. Our results are consistent with this.

7.3 TSDA: Contribution of the two steps

Both steps of TSDA contribute to its performance, as shown in Figures 2 and 3.

Step 1 (Between County normalization) appears mostly responsible for the final reduction in kurtosis from TSDA and on its own adds some increased year to year stability. It also significantly increased the county-level predictions' correlations with socioeconomic status, and health and well-being measures and removed the spurious correlation between agreeableness and education which was observed in both the naive application of the model and in results only relying on TSDA step 2.

Step 2 (Facebook to Twitter normalization) on its own gave mild improvements in kurtosis (Figure 2), but inconsistent performance in year-to-year stability and external county-level correlations. It is when step 2 is applied after step 1 that the method is truly able to find differing features that, when replaced with the source feature means, provide overall better predictions.

8 Conclusion

We have shown that the naive approach to applying Facebook user-level language models to county-level Twitter language has inherent problems due to two separate domain adaptation problems: the differences in Facebook to Twitter word token frequencies, and the spatially correlated terms introduced when aggregating tweets to counties. These problems were discovered when we constructed a list of counties with the most extreme predicted personalities (e.g., 'the 10 most agreeable counties in the US') and found our estimates to be many standard deviations outside what is plausible. We introduce Target Side Domain Adaptation (TSDA), which adjusts the observed word counts in the target (county-level Twitter) domain, leaving the source domain model unchanged, and we propose a set of validation methods based on assessing normality, year-to-year prediction stability, and the correlation of predictions with other outcomes measured on the target counties.

TSDA works particularly well with words, since words vary widely in frequency and meaning across domains and, critically, variations in frequency tend to be associated with differences in meaning. It has the further advantage that it does not require retraining the model; instead, the feature values passed to the model are readjusted. This could be particularly important when the original training data cannot be shared, for example when it contains personal health data or (as is the case here) private social media data, which are impossible to truly anonymize for sharing.

Acknowledgments

The authors acknowledge the support from Templeton Religion Trust, grant TRT-0048.

References

D. John Burger, John Henderson, George Kim, and Guido Zarrella. 2011. Discriminating Gender on Twitter. In *Proceedings of the 2011 Conference on Empirical Methods in Natural Language Processing*. EMNLP.

Paul T Costa and Robert R McCrae. 2008. The revised neo personality inventory (neo-pi-r). *The SAGE handbook of personality theory and assessment* 2:179–198.

Hal Daumé III. 2007. Frustratingly easy domain adaptation. *ACL 2007* page 256.

Hal Daumé III and Jagadeesh Jagarlamudi. 2011. Domain adaptation for machine translation by mining unseen words. In *Proceedings of the 49th Annual Meeting of the Association for Computational Linguistics: Human Language Technologies: short papers-Volume 2*. Association for Computational Linguistics, pages 407–412.

Hal Daumé III, Abhishek Kumar, and Avishek Saha. 2010. Frustratingly easy semi-supervised domain adaptation. In *Proceedings of the 2010 Workshop on Domain Adaptation for Natural Language Processing*. Association for Computational Linguistics, pages 53–59.

Hal Daume III and Daniel Marcu. 2006. Domain adaptation for statistical classifiers. *Journal of Artificial Intelligence Research* 26:101–126.

John M Digman. 1990. Personality structure: Emergence of the five-factor model. *Annual review of psychology* 41(1):417–440.

Johannes C Eichstaedt, Hansen Andrew Schwartz, Margaret L Kern, Gregory Park, Darwin R Labarthe, Raina M Merchant, Sneha Jha, Megha Agrawal, Lukasz A Dziurzynski, Maarten Sap, et al. 2015. Psychological language on twitter predicts county-level heart disease mortality. *Psychological science* 26(2):159–169.

Richard Florida. 2002. The rise of the creative class. *The Washington Monthly* 34(5):15–25.

Vasileios Lampos, Nikolaos Aletras, Daniel Preoţiuc-Pietro, and Trevor Cohn. 2014. Predicting and Characterising User Impact on Twitter. EACL.

Robert R McCrae and Oliver P John. 1992. An introduction to the five-factor model and its applications. *Journal of personality* 60(2):175–215.

Sinno Jialin Pan, Ivor W Tsang, James T Kwok, and Qiang Yang. 2011. Domain adaptation via transfer component analysis. *IEEE Transactions on Neural Networks* 22(2):199–210.

Sinno Jialin Pan and Qiang Yang. 2010. A survey on transfer learning. *IEEE Transactions on knowledge and data engineering* 22(10):1345–1359.

Gregory Park, H Andrew Schwartz, Johannes C Eichstaedt, Margaret L Kern, Michal Kosinski, David J Stillwell, Lyle H Ungar, and Martin EP Seligman. 2014. Automatic Personality Assessment through Social Media Language. *Journal of Personality and Social Psychology* 108(6):934–952.

Marco Pennacchiotti and Ana-Maria Popescu. 2011. A Machine Learning Approach to Twitter User Classification. ICWSM.

Arthur E Poropat. 2009. A meta-analysis of the five-factor model of personality and academic performance. *Psychological bulletin* 135(2):322.

Daniel Preoţiuc-Pietro, Vasileios Lampos, and Nikolaos Aletras. 2015. An Analysis of the User Occupational Class through Twitter Content. ACL.

Delip Rao, David Yarowsky, Abhishek Shreevats, and Manaswi Gupta. 2010. Classifying Latent User Attributes in Twitter. SMUC.

Peter J Rentfrow, Samuel D Gosling, Markus Jokela, David J Stillwell, Michal Kosinski, and Jeff Potter. 2013. Divided we stand: Three psychological regions of the united states and their political, economic, social, and health correlates. *Journal of Personality and Social Psychology* 105(6):996.

Peter J Rentfrow and Markus Jokela. 2016. Geographical psychology: The spatial organization of psychological phenomena. *Current Directions in Psychological Science* 25(6):393–398.

Brent W Roberts, Nathan R Kuncel, Rebecca Shiner, Avshalom Caspi, and Lewis R Goldberg. 2007. The power of personality: The comparative validity of personality traits, socioeconomic status, and cognitive ability for predicting important life outcomes. *Perspectives on Psychological Science* 2(4):313–345.

H Andrew Schwartz, Johannes C Eichstaedt, Margaret L Kern, Lukasz Dziurzynski, Stephanie M Ramones, Megha Agrawal, Achal Shah, Michal Kosinski, David Stillwell, Martin EP Seligman, and Lyle H Ungar. 2013a. Personality, Gender, and Age in the Language of Social Media: The Open-vocabulary Approach. *PLoS ONE* 8(9).

Hansen Andrew Schwartz, Johannes C Eichstaedt, Margaret L Kern, Lukasz Dziurzynski, Richard E Lucas, Megha Agrawal, Gregory J Park, Shrinidhi K Lakshmikanth, Sneha Jha, Martin EP Seligman, et al. 2013b. Characterizing geographic variation in well-being using tweets. In *ICWSM*.

Robert J Smith, Patrick Crutchley, H Andrew Schwartz, Lyle Ungar, Frances Shofer, Kevin A Padrez, and Raina M Merchant. 2017. Variations in facebook posting patterns across validated patient health conditions: A prospective cohort study. *Journal of Medical Internet Research* 19(1):e7.

Baochen Sun, Jiashi Feng, and Kate Saenko. 2015. Return of frustratingly easy domain adaptation. *arXiv preprint arXiv:1511.05547* .

Olga Troyanskaya, Michael Cantor, Gavin Sherlock, Pat Brown, Trevor Hastie, Robert Tibshirani, David Botstein, and Russ B Altman. 2001. Missing value estimation methods for dna microarrays. *Bioinformatics* 17(6):520–525.

Recognizing Explicit and Implicit Hate Speech Using a Weakly Supervised Two-path Bootstrapping Approach

Lei Gao
Texas A&M University
sjtuprog@tamu.edu

Alexis Kuppersmith
Stanford University
Lex54@stanford.edu

Ruihong Huang
Texas A&M University
huangrh@cse.tamu.edu

Abstract

In the wake of a polarizing election, social media is laden with hateful content. To address various limitations of supervised hate speech classification methods including corpus bias and huge cost of annotation, we propose a weakly supervised two-path bootstrapping approach for an online hate speech detection model leveraging large-scale unlabeled data. This system significantly outperforms hate speech detection systems that are trained in a supervised manner using manually annotated data. Applying this model on a large quantity of tweets collected before, after, and on election day reveals motivations and patterns of inflammatory language.

1 Introduction

Following a turbulent election season, 2016's digital footprint is awash with hate speech. Apart from censorship, the goals of enabling computers to understand inflammatory language are many. Sensing increased proliferation of hate speech can elucidate public opinion surrounding polarizing events. Identifying hateful declarations can bolster security in revealing individuals harboring malicious intentions towards specific groups.

Recent studies on supervised methods for online hate speech detection (Waseem and Hovy, 2016; Nobata et al., 2016) have relied on manually annotated data sets, which are not only costly to create but also likely to be insufficient to obtain wide-coverage hate speech detection systems. This is mainly because online hate speech is relatively infrequent (among large amounts of online contents) and tends to transform rapidly following a new trigger event. Our pilot annotation experiment with 5,000 randomly selected tweets shows that around 0.6% (31 tweets) of tweets are hateful. The mass-scale (Yahoo!Finance online comments) hate speech annotation effort from Yahoo! (Nobata et al., 2016) revealed that only 5.9% of online comments contained hate speech. Therefore, large amounts of online texts need to be annotated to adequately identify hate speech. In recent studies (Waseem and Hovy, 2016; Kwok and Wang, 2013), the data selection methods and annotations are often biased towards a specific type of hate speech or hate speech generated in certain scenarios in order to increase the ratio of hate speech content in the annotated data sets, which however made the resulting annotations too distorted to reflect the true distribution of hate speech. Furthermore, inflammatory language changes dramatically following new hate "trigger" events, which will significantly devalue annotated data.

To address the various limitations of supervised hate speech detection methods, we present a weakly supervised two-path bootstrapping approach for online hate speech detection that requires minimal human supervision and can be easily retrained and adapted to capture new types of inflammatory language. Our two-path bootstrapping architecture consists of two learning components, an explicit slur term learner and a neural net classifier (LSTMs (Hochreiter and Schmidhuber, 1997)), that can capture both explicit and implicit phrasings of online hate speech.

Specifically, our bootstrapping system starts with automatically labeled online hateful content that are identified by matching a large collection of unlabeled online content with several hateful

Proceedings of the The 8th International Joint Conference on Natural Language Processing, pages 774–782,
Taipei, Taiwan, November 27 – December 1, 2017 ©2017 AFNLP

slur terms. Then two learning components will be initiated simultaneously. A slur term learner will learn additional hateful slur terms from the automatically identified hateful content. Meanwhile, a neural net classifier will be trained using the automatically labeled hateful content as positive instances and randomly sampled online content as negative instances. Next, both string matching with the newly learned slur terms and the trained neural net classifier will be used to recognize new hateful content from the large unlabeled collection of online contents. Then the newly identified hateful content by each of the two learning components will be used to augment the initially identified hateful content, which will be used to learn more slur terms and retrain the classifier. The whole process iterates.

The design of the two-path bootstrapping system is mainly motivated to capture both explicit and implicit inflammatory language. Explicit hate speech is easily identifiable by recognizing a clearly hateful word or phrase. For example:

(1) *Don't talk to me from an anonymous account you faggot coward, whither up and die.*

(2) *And that's the kind of people who support Trump! Subhumans!*

In contrast, implicit hate speech employs circumlocution, metaphor, or stereotypes to convey hatred of a particular group, in which hatefulness can be captured by understanding its overall compositional meanings, For example:

(3) *Hillary's welfare army doesn't really want jobs. They want more freebies.*

(4) *Affirmative action means we get affirmatively second rate doctors and other professionals.*

Furthermore, our learning architecture has a flavor of co-training (Blum and Mitchell, 1998) in maintaining two learning components that concentrate on different properties of inflammatory language. By modeling distinct aspects of online hate speech, such a learning system is better equipped to combat semantic drift, which often occurs in self-learning where the learned model drifts away from the esteemed track. Moreover, training two complementary models simultaneously and utilizing both models to identify hate speech of different properties in each iteration of the learning process is important to maintain the learning momentum and to generate models with wide coverage. Indeed, our experimental results have shown that the

two-path bootstrapping system is able to jointly identify many more hate speech texts (214,997 v.s 52,958 v.s 112,535) with a significantly higher F-score (48.9% v.s 19.7% v.s 26.1%), when compared to the bootstrapping systems with only the slur term learner and only the neural net classifier. In addition, the evaluation shows that the two-path bootstrapping system identifies 4.4 times more hateful texts than hate speech detection systems that are trained using manually annotated data in a supervised manner.

2 Related Work

Previous studies on hate speech recognition mostly used supervised approaches. Due to the sparsity of hate speech overall in reality, the data selection methods and annotations are often biased towards a specific type of hate speech or hate speech generated in certain scenarios. For instance, Razavi et al. (2010) conducted their experiments on 1525 annotated sentences from a company's log file and a certain newsgroup. Warner and Hirschberg (2012) labeled around 9000 human labeled paragraphs from Yahoo!'s news group post and American Jewish Congress's website, and the labeling is restricted to anti-Semitic hate speech. Sood et al. (2012) studied use of profanity on a dataset of 6,500 labeled comments from Yahoo! Buzz. Kwok and Wang (2013) built a balanced corpus of 24582 tweets consisting of anti-black and non-anti black tweets. The tweets were manually selected from Twitter accounts that were believed to be racist based upon their reactions to anti-Obama articles. Burnap and Williams (2014) collected hateful tweets related to the murder of Drummer Lee Rigby in 2013. Waseem and Hovy (2016) collected tweets using hateful slurs, specific hashtags as well as suspicious user IDs. Consequently, all of the 1,972 racist tweets are by 9 users, and the majority of sexist tweets are related to an Australian TV show.

Djuric et al. (2015) is the first to study hate speech using a large-scale annotated data set. They have annotated 951,736 online comments from Yahoo!Finance, with 56,280 comments labeled as hateful. Nobata et al. (2016) followed Djuric et al. (2015)'s work. In addition to the Yahoo!Finance annotated comments, they also annotated 1,390,774 comments from Yahoo!News. Comments in both data sets were randomly sampled from their corresponding websites with a focus on comments by users who were reported to have posted hateful comments. We instead aim to detect hate speech w.r.t. its real distribution, using a weakly supervised method that does not rely on large amounts of annotations.

The commonly used classification methods in previous studies are logistic regression and Naive Bayes classifiers. Djuric et al. (2015) and Nobata et al. (2016) applied neural network models for training word embeddings, which were further used as features in a logistic regression model for classification. We will instead train a neural net classifier (Kim, 2014; Lai et al., 2015; Zhou et al., 2015) in a weakly supervised manner in order to capture implicit and compositional hate speech expressions.

Xiang et al. (2012) is related to our research because they also used a bootstrapping method to discover offensive language from a large-scale Twitter corpus. However, their bootstrapping model is driven by mining hateful Twitter users, instead of content analysis of tweets as in our approach. Furthermore, they recognize hateful Twitter users by detecting explicit hateful indicators (i.e., keywords) in their tweets while our bootstrapping system aim to detect both explicit and implicit expressions of online hate speech.

3 The Two-path Bootstrapping System for Online Hate Speech Detection

3.1 Overview

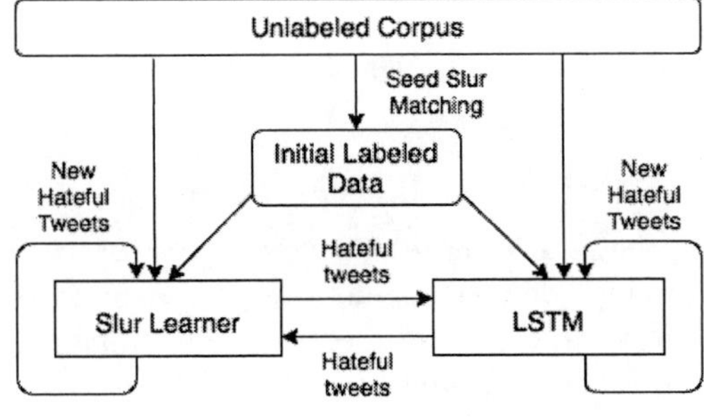

Figure 1: Diagram of co-training model

Figure 1 illustrates that our weakly supervised hate speech detection system starts with a few pre-identified slur terms as seeds and a large collection of unlabeled data instances. Specifically, we experiment with identifying hate speech from tweets. Hateful tweets will be automatically identified by matching the large collection of unlabeled tweets with slur term seeds. Tweets that contain one of the seed slur terms are labeled as hateful.

The two-path bootstrapping system consists of two learning components, an explicit slur term learner and a neural net classifier (LSTMs (Hochreiter and Schmidhuber, 1997)), that can capture both explicit and implicit descriptions of online hate speech. Using the initial seed slur term labeled hateful tweets, the two learning components will be initiated simultaneously. The slur term learner will continue to learn additional hateful slur terms. Meanwhile, the neural net classifier will be trained using the automatically labeled hateful tweets as positive instances and randomly sampled tweets as negative instances. Next, both the newly learned slur terms and the trained neural net classifier will be used to identify new hateful content from the unlabeled large collection of tweets. The newly labeled hateful tweets by each of the two learning components will be used to augment the initial slur term seed identified hateful tweet collection, which will be used to learn more slur terms and retrain the classifier in the next iteration. The whole process then iterates.

After each iteration, we have to determine if a stopping criterion is met and we should terminate the bootstrapping process. In general, a tuned threshold score is applied or a small annotated dataset is used to evaluate the learned classifiers. We adopt the latter method. Specifically, the bootstrapping system stops when the precision of the LSTM classifier is lower than 0.6 when evaluated using an existing small annotated tweet set (Waseem and Hovy, 2016).

3.2 Automatic Data Labeling of Initial Data

Seeing a hate slur term in a tweet strongly indicates that the tweet is hateful. Therefore, we use 20 manually selected slur terms to match with a large unlabeled tweet collection in order to quickly construct the initial small set of hateful tweets. Table 1 shows the 20 seed slurs we used.

bimbo	chink	commie	coon	cunt
fag	faggot	feminazi	honky	islamist
libtard	muzzie	negro	nigger	paki
skank	subhuman	tranny	twat	wanker

Table 1: Seed slurs

We obtained our initial list of slurs from Hatebase[1], the Racial Slurs Database [2], and a page of LGBT slang terms[3]. We ranked the slur terms by their frequencies in tweets, eliminating ambiguous and outdated terms. The slur "gypsy", for example, refers to derogatorily to people of Roma descent, but currently in popular usage is an idealization of a trendy bohemian lifestyle. The word "bitch" is ambiguous, sometimes a sexist slur but other times innocuously self-referential or even friendly.

For these reasons, we only selected the top 20 terms we considered reliable (shown in Table 1). We use both the singular and the plural form for each of these seed slur terms.

3.3 Slur Term Learner

The slur term learning component extracts individual words from a set of hateful tweets as new slurs. Intuitively, if a word occurs significantly more frequently in hateful tweets than in randomly selected tweets, this term is more likely to be a hateful slur term. Following this intuition, we assign a score to each unique unigram that appears 10 or more times in hateful tweets, and the score is calculated as the relative ratio of its frequency in the labeled hateful tweets over its frequency in the unlabeled set of tweets. Then the slur term learner recognizes a unigram with a score higher than a certain threshold as a new slur. Specifically, we use the threshold score of 100 in identifying individual word slur terms.

The newly identified slur terms will be used to match with unlabeled tweets in order to identify additional hateful tweets. A tweet that contains one of the slur terms is deemed to be a hateful tweet.

While we were aware of other more sophisticated machine learning models, one purpose of this research is to detect and learn new slur terms from constantly generated user data. Therefore, the simple and clean string matching based slur learner is designed to attentively look for specific words that alone can indicate hate speech. In addition, this is in contrast with the second learning component that uses a whole tweet and model its compositional meanings in order to recognize implicit hate speech. These two learners are complementary in the two-path bootstrapping system.

3.4 The LSTM Classifier

We aim to recognize implicit hate speech expressions and capture composite meanings of tweets using a sequence neural net classifier. Specifically, our LSTM classifier has a single layer of LSTM units. The output dimension size of the LSTM layer is 100. A sigmoid layer is built on the top of the LSTM layer to generate predictions. The input dropout rate and recurrent state dropout rate are both set to 0.2. In each iteration of the bootstrapping process, the training of the LSTM classifier runs for 10 epochs.

The input to our LSTM classifier is a sequence of words. We pre-process and normalize tokens in tweets following the steps suggested in (Pennington et al., 2014). In addition, we used the pre-processing of emoji and smiley described in a preprocess tool [4]. Then we retrieve word vector representations from the downloaded[5] pre-trained word2vec embeddings (Mikolov et al., 2013).

The LSTM classifier is trained using the automatically labeled hateful tweets as positive instances and randomly sampled tweets as negative instances, with the ratio of POS:NEG as 1:10. Then the classifier is used to identify additional hateful tweets from the large set of unlabeled tweets. The LSTM classifier will deem a tweet as hateful if the tweet receives a confidence score of 0.9 or higher. Both the low POS:NEG ratio and the high confidence score are applied to increase the precision of the classifier in labeling hateful tweets and control semantic drift in the bootstrapping learning process. To further combat semantic drift, we applied weighted binary cross-entropy as the loss function in LSTM.

3.5 One vs. Two Learning Paths

As shown in Figure 1, if we remove one of the two learning components, the two-path learning system will be reduced to a usual self-learning system with one single learning path. For instance, if we remove the LSTM classifier, the slur learner will learn new slur terms from initially seed labeled hateful tweets and then identify new hateful tweets by matching newly learned slurs with unlabeled tweets. The newly identified hateful tweets will be used to augment the initial hateful tweet collection and additional slur terms can be learned from the enlarged hateful tweet set. The process

---

[1] https://www.hatebase.org
[2] http://www.rsdb.org
[3] https://en.wikipedia.org/wiki/List_of_LGBT_slang_terms

[4] https://pypi.python.org/pypi/tweet-preprocessor/0.4.0
[5] https://code.google.com/archive/p/word2vec/

will iterates. However as shown later in the evaluation section, single-path variants of the proposed two-path learning system are unable to receive additional fresh hateful tweets identified by the other learning component and lose learning momentum quickly.

3.6 Tackling Semantic Drifts

Semantic drift is the most challenging problem in distant supervision and bootstrapping. First of all, we argue that the proposed two-path bootstrapping system with two significantly different learning components is designed to reduce semantic drift. According to the co-training theory (Blum and Mitchell, 1998), the more different the two components are, the better. In evaluation, we will show that such a system outperforms single-path bootstrapping systems. Furthermore, we have applied several strategies in controlling noise and imbalance of automatically labeled data, e.g., the high frequency and the high relative frequency thresholds enforced in selecting hate slur terms, as well as the low POS:NEG training sample ratio and the high confidence score of 0.9 used in selecting new data instances for the LSTM classifier.

4 Evaluations

4.1 Tweets Collection

We randomly sampled 10 million tweets from 67 million tweets collected from Oct. 1st to Oct. 24th using Twitter API. These 10 million tweets were used as the unlabeled tweet set in bootstrapping learning. Then we continued to collect 62 million tweets spanning from Oct.25th to Nov.15th, essentially two weeks before the US election day and one week after the election. The 62 million tweets will be used to evaluate the performance of the bootstrapped slur term learner and LSTM classifier. The timestamps of all these tweets are converted into EST. By using Twitter API, the collected tweets were randomly sampled to prevent a bias in the data set.

4.2 Supervised Baselines

We trained two supervised models using the 16 thousand annotated tweets that have been used in a recent study (Waseem and Hovy, 2016). The annotations distinguish two types of hateful tweets, sexism and racism, but we merge both categories and only distinguish hateful from non-hateful tweets.

First, we train a traditional feature-based classification model using logistic regression (LR). We apply the same set of features as mentioned in (Waseem and Hovy, 2016). The features include character-level bigrams, trigrams, and four-grams.

In addition, for direct comparisons, we train a LSTM model using the 16 thousand annotated tweets, using exactly the same settings as we use for the LSTM classifier in our two-path bootstrapping system.

4.3 Evaluation Methods

We apply both supervised classifiers and our weakly supervised hate speech detection systems to the 62 million tweets in order to identify hateful tweets that were posted before and after the US election day. We evaluate both precision and recall for both types of systems. Ideally, we can easily measure precision as well as recall for each system if we have ground truth labels for each tweet. However, it is impossible to obtain annotations for such a large set of tweets. The actual distribution of hateful tweets in the 62 million tweets is unknown.

Instead, to evaluate each system, we randomly sampled 1,000 tweets from the whole set of hateful tweets that *had been tagged as hateful* by the corresponding system. Then we annotate the sampled tweets and use them to estimate precision and recall of the system. In this case,

$$precision = \frac{n}{1000}$$

$$recall \propto precision \cdot N$$

Here, n refers to the number of hateful tweets that human annotators identified in the 1,000 sampled tweets, and N refers to the total number of hateful tweets the system tagged in the 62 million tweets. We further calculated system recall by normalizing the product, $precision \cdot N$, with an estimated total number of hateful tweets that exist in the 62 million tweets, which was obtained by multiplying the estimated hateful tweet rate of 0.6%[6] with the exact number of tweets in the test set. Finally, we calculate F-score using the calculated recall and precision.

Consistent across the statistical classifiers including both logistic regression classifiers and

---

[6]We annotated 5,000 tweets that were randomly sampled during election time and 31 of them were labeled as hateful, therefore the estimated hateful tweet rate is 0.6% (31/5,000).

LSTM models, only tweets that receive a confidence score over 0.9 were tagged as hateful tweets.

4.4 Human Annotations

When we annotate system predicted tweet samples, we essentially adopt the same definition of hate speech as used in (Waseem and Hovy, 2016), which considers tweets that explicitly or implicitly propagate stereotypes targeting a specific group whether it is the initial expression or a meta-expression discussing the hate speech itself (i.e. a paraphrase). In order to ensure our annotators have a complete understanding of online hate speech, we asked two annotators to first discuss over a very detailed annotation guideline of hate speech, then annotate separately. This went for several iterations.

Then we asked the two annotators to annotate the 1,000 tweets that were randomly sampled from all the tweets tagged as hateful by the supervised LSTM classifier. The two annotators reached an inter-agreement Kappa (Cohen, 1960) score of 85.5%. Because one of the annotators become unavailable later in the project, the other annotator annotated the remaining sampled tweets.

4.5 Experimental Results

Supervised Baselines

The first section of Table 2 shows the performance of the two supervised models when applied to 62 million tweets collected around election time. We can see that the logistic regression model suffers from an extremely low precision, which is less than 10%. While this classifier aggressively labeled a large number of tweets as hateful, only 121,512 tweets are estimated to be truly hateful. In contrast, the supervised LSTM classifier has a high precision of around 79%, however, this classifier is too conservative and only labeled a small set of tweets as hateful.

The Two-path Bootstrapping System

Next, we evaluate our weakly supervised classifiers which were obtained using only 20 seed slur terms and a large set of unlabeled tweets. The two-path weakly supervised bootstrapping system ran for four iterations. The second section of Table 2 shows the results for the two-path weakly supervised system. The first two rows show the evaluation results for each of the two learning components in the two-path system, the LSTM classifier and the slur learner, respectively. The third

row shows the results for the full system. We can see that the full system **Union** is significantly better than the supervised LSTM model in terms of recall and F-score. Furthermore, we can see that a significant portion of hateful tweets were identified by both components and the weakly supervised LSTM classifier is especially capable to identify a large number of hateful tweets. Then the slur matching component obtains an precision of around 56.5% and can identify roughly 3 times of hateful tweets compared with the supervised LSTM classifier. The last column of this section shows the performance of our model on a collection of human annotated tweets as introduced in the previous work (Waseem and Hovy, 2016). The recall is rather low because the data we used to train our model is quite different from this dataset which contains tweets related to a TV show (Waseem and Hovy, 2016). The precision is only slightly lower than previous supervised models that were trained using the same dataset.

Table 3 shows the number of hateful tweets our bootstrapping system identified in each iteration during training. Specifically, the columns **Slur Match** and **LSTMs** show the number of hateful tweets identified by the slur learning component and the weakly supervised LSTM classifier respectively. We can see that both learning components steadily label new hateful tweets in each iteration and the LSTM classifier often labels more tweets as hateful compared to slur matching.

Furthermore, we found that many tweets were labeled as hateful by both slur matching and the LSTM classifier. Table 4 shows the number of hateful tweets in each of the three segments, hateful tweets that have been labeled by both components as well as hateful tweets that were labeled by one component only. Note that the three segments of tweets are mutually exclusive from others. We can see that many tweets were labeled by both components and each component separately labeled some additional tweets as well. This demonstrates that hateful tweets often contain both explicit hate indicator phrases and implicit expressions. Therefore in our two-path bootstrapping system, the hateful tweets identified by slur matching are useful for improving the LSTM classifier, vice versa. This also explains why our two-path bootstrapping system learn well to identify varieties of hate speech expressions in practice.

One-path Bootstrapping System Variants

Classifier	Precision	Recall	F1	# of Predicted Tweets	# of Estimated Hateful
Supervised Baselines					
Logistic Regression	0.088	0.328	0.139	**1,380,825**	121,512
LSTMs	**0.791**	0.132	0.228	62,226	49,221
The Two-path Weakly Supervised Learning System					
LSTMs	0.419	0.546	0.474	483,298	202,521
Slur Matching	0.565	0.398	0.468	261,183	147,595
Union	0.422	**0.580**	**0.489**	509,897	**214,997**
Union*	0.626*	0.258*	0.365*	-	-
Variations of the Two-path Weakly Supervised Learning System					
Slur Matching Only	0.318	0.143	0.197	166,535	52,958
LSTMs Only	0.229	0.303	0.261	491,421	112,535

Table 2: Performance of Different Models

Its	Prev	Slur Match	LSTMs
1	8,866	422	3,490
2	12,776	4,890	13,970
3	27,274	6,299	21,579
4	50,721	9,895	22,768

Table 3: Number of Labeled Tweets in Each Iteration

Intersection	LSTM Only	Slur Only
234,584	248,714	26,599

Table 4: Number of Hateful Tweets in Each Segment

In order to understand how necessary it is to maintain two learning paths for online hate speech detection, we also ran two experiments with one learning component removed from the loop each time. Therefore, the reduced bootstrapping systems can only repeatedly learn explicit hate speech (with the slur learner) or implicit hateful expressions (with the LSTM classifier).

The third section of Table 2 shows the evaluation results of the two single-path variants of the weakly supervised system. We can see that both the estimated precision, recall, F score and the estimated number of truly hateful tweets by the two systems are significantly lower than the complete two-path bootstrapping system, which suggests that our two-path learning system can effectively capture diverse descriptions of online hate speech, maintain learning momentums as well as effectively combat with noise in online texts.

5 Analysis

5.1 Analysis of the Learned Hate Indicators

berk	chavs	degenerates	douches
facist	hag	heretics	jihadists
lesbo	pendejo	paedo	pinche
retards	satanist	scum	scumbag
slutty	tards	unamerican	wench

Table 5: New slurs learned by our model

We have learned 306 unigram phrases using the slur term learning component. Among them, only 45 phrases were seen in existing hate slur databases while the other terms, 261 phrases in total, were only identified in real-world tweets. Table 5 shows some of the newly discovered hate indicating phrases. Our analysis shows that 86 of the newly discovered hate indicators are strong hate slur terms and the remaining 175 indicators are related to discussions of identity and politics such as 'supremacist' and 'Zionism'.

5.2 Analysis of LSTM Identified Hateful Tweets

The LSTM labeled 483,298 tweets as hateful, and 172,137 of them do not contain any of the original seed slurs or our learned indicator phrases. The following are example hateful tweets that have no explicit hate indicator phrase:

(1) *@janh2h The issue is that internationalists keep telling outsiders that they're just as entitled to the privileges of the tribe as insiders.*

(2) *This is disgusting! Christians are very tolerant people but Muslims are looking to wipe us our and dominate us! Sen https://t.co/7DMTIrOLyw*

We can see that the hatefulness of these tweets is determined by their overall compositional meanings rather than a hate-indicating slur.

5.3 Error Analysis

The error of our model comes from semantic drift in bootstrapping learning, which partially results from the complexity and dynamics of language. Specifically, we found dynamic word sense of slurs and natural drifting of word semantic. Many slur terms are ambiguous and have multiple word senses. For instance, "Chink", an anti-Asian epithet, can also refer to a patch of light from a small aperture. Similarly, "Negro" is a toponym in addition to a racial slur. Further, certain communities have reclaimed slur words. Though the word "dyke" is derogatory towards lesbians, for example, some use it self-referentially to destigmatize it, a phenomenon we sometimes encountered.

5.4 Temporal Distributions of Tagged Hateful Tweets

By applying our co-training model on the 62 million tweets corpus, we found around 510 thousand tweets labeled as hateful in total.

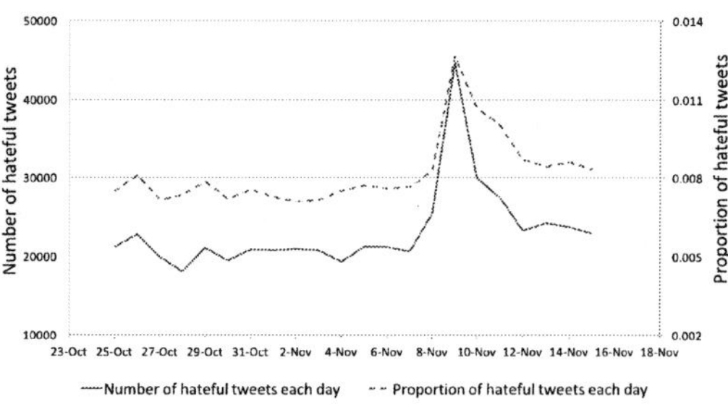

Figure 2: Temporal Distribution of Hateful Tweets

The figure 2 displays the temporal distribution of hateful tweets. There is a spike in hateful tweets from Nov.7th to Nov.12th in terms of both number of hateful tweets and ratio of hateful tweets to total tweets.

5.5 Most Frequent Mentions and Hashtags of Tagged Hateful Tweets

Table 6 and 7 show the top 30 most frequent mentions in hateful tweets. They are ranked by frequency from left to right and from top to bottom.

It is clear that the majority of mentions found in tweets tagged as hateful address polarizing political figures (i.e. @realDonaldTrump and @HillaryClinton), indicating that hate speech is often fueled by partisan warfare. Other common mentions include news sources, such as Politico and MSNBC, which further support that "trigger" events in the news can generate inflammatory responses among Twitter users. Certain individual Twitter users also received a sizable number of mentions. @mitchellvii is a conservative activist whose tweets lend unyielding support to Donald Trump. Meanwhile, Twitter user @purplhaze42 is a self-proclaimed anti-racist and anti-Zionist. Both figured among the most popular recipients of inflammatory language.

Table 7 shows that the majority of hashtags also indicate the political impetus behind hate speech with hashtags such as #Trump and #MAGA (Make America Great Again, Trump's campaign slogan) among the most frequent. The specific televised events also engender proportionally large amounts of hateful language as they can be commonly experienced by all television-owning Americans and therefore a widely available target for hateful messages.

@realDonaldTrump	@HillaryClinton	@megynkelly
@CNN	@FoxNews	@newtgingrich
@nytimes	@YouTube	@POTUS
@KellyannePolls	@MSNBC	@seanhannity
@washingtonpost	@narendramodi	@CNNPolitics
@PrisonPlanet	@guardian	@JoyAnnReid
@BarackObama	@thehill	@BreitbartNews
@politico	@ABC	@AnnCoulter
@jaketapper	@ArvindKejriwal	@FBI
@mitchellvii	@purplhaze42	@SpeakerRyan

Table 6: List of Top 30 Mentions in Hateful Tweets During Election Days

#Trump	#ElectionNight	#Election2016
#MAGA	#trndnl	#photo
#nowplaying	#Vocab	#NotMyPresident
#ElectionDay	#trump	#ImWithHer
#halloween	#cdnpoli	#Latin
#Hillary	#WorldSeries	#1
#Brexit	#Spanish	#auspol
#notmypresident	#C51	#NeverTrump
#hiring	#bbcqt	#USElection2016
#tcot	#TrumpProtest	#XFactor

Table 7: List of Top 30 Hashtags in Hateful Tweets During Election Days

6 Conclusions

Our work focuses on the need to capture both explicit and implicit hate speech from an unbiased corpus. To address these issues, we proposed a weakly supervised two-path bootstrapping model to identify hateful language in randomly sampled tweets. Starting from 20 seed rules, we found 210 thousand hateful tweets from 62 million tweets collected during the election. Our analysis shows a strong correlation between temporal distributions of hateful tweets and the election time, as well as the partisan impetus behind large amounts of inflammatory language. In the future, we will look into linguistic phenomena that often occur in hate speech, such as sarcasm and humor, to further improve hate speech detection performance.

References

Avrim Blum and Tom Mitchell. 1998. Combining labeled and unlabeled data with co-training. In *Proceedings of the eleventh annual conference on Computational learning theory*. ACM, pages 92–100.

Peter Burnap and Matthew Leighton Williams. 2014. Hate speech, machine classification and statistical modelling of information flows on twitter: Interpretation and communication for policy decision making. In *Proceedings of the Internet, Politics, and Policy conference*.

Jacob Cohen. 1960. A coefficient of agreement for nominal scales. *Educational and psychological measurement* 20(1):37–46.

Nemanja Djuric, Jing Zhou, Robin Morris, Mihajlo Grbovic, Vladan Radosavljevic, and Narayan Bhamidipati. 2015. Hate speech detection with comment embeddings. In *Proceedings of the 24th International Conference on World Wide Web*. ACM, pages 29–30.

Sepp Hochreiter and Jürgen Schmidhuber. 1997. Long short-term memory. *Neural computation* 9(8):1735–1780.

Yoon Kim. 2014. Convolutional neural networks for sentence classification. *arXiv preprint arXiv:1408.5882* .

Irene Kwok and Yuzhou Wang. 2013. Locate the hate: Detecting tweets against blacks. In *AAAI*.

Siwei Lai, Liheng Xu, Kang Liu, and Jun Zhao. 2015. Recurrent convolutional neural networks for text classification. In *AAAI*. volume 333, pages 2267–2273.

Tomas Mikolov, Ilya Sutskever, Kai Chen, Greg S Corrado, and Jeff Dean. 2013. Distributed representations of words and phrases and their compositionality. In *Advances in neural information processing systems*. pages 3111–3119.

Chikashi Nobata, Joel Tetreault, Achint Thomas, Yashar Mehdad, and Yi Chang. 2016. Abusive language detection in online user content. In *Proceedings of the 25th International Conference on World Wide Web*. International World Wide Web Conferences Steering Committee, pages 145–153.

Jeffrey Pennington, Richard Socher, and Christopher D Manning. 2014. Glove: Global vectors for word representation. In *EMNLP*. volume 14, pages 1532–1543.

Amir H Razavi, Diana Inkpen, Sasha Uritsky, and Stan Matwin. 2010. Offensive language detection using multi-level classification. In *Canadian Conference on Artificial Intelligence*. Springer, pages 16–27.

Sara Sood, Judd Antin, and Elizabeth Churchill. 2012. Profanity use in online communities. In *Proceedings of the SIGCHI Conference on Human Factors in Computing Systems*. ACM, pages 1481–1490.

William Warner and Julia Hirschberg. 2012. Detecting hate speech on the world wide web. In *Proceedings of the Second Workshop on Language in Social Media*. Association for Computational Linguistics, pages 19–26.

Zeerak Waseem and Dirk Hovy. 2016. Hateful symbols or hateful people? predictive features for hate speech detection on twitter. In *Proceedings of NAACL-HLT*. pages 88–93.

Guang Xiang, Bin Fan, Ling Wang, Jason Hong, and Carolyn Rose. 2012. Detecting offensive tweets via topical feature discovery over a large scale twitter corpus. In *Proceedings of the 21st ACM international conference on Information and knowledge management*. ACM, pages 1980–1984.

Chunting Zhou, Chonglin Sun, Zhiyuan Liu, and Francis Lau. 2015. A c-lstm neural network for text classification. *arXiv preprint arXiv:1511.08630* .

Estimating Reactions and Recommending Products with Generative Models of Reviews

Jianmo Ni and **Zachary C. Lipton** and **Sharad Vikram** and **Julian McAuley**
Department of Computer Science and Engineering
University of California San Diego
`jin018, zlipton, svikram, jmcauley@ucsd.edu`

Abstract

Traditional approaches to recommendation focus on learning from large volumes of historical feedback to estimate simple numerical quantities (Will a user click on a product? Make a purchase? etc.). Natural language approaches that model information like product reviews have proved to be incredibly useful in improving the performance of such methods, as reviews provide valuable auxiliary information that can be used to better estimate latent user preferences and item properties.

In this paper, rather than using reviews as an *inputs* to a recommender system, we focus on generating reviews as the model's *output*. This requires us to efficiently model text (at the character level) to capture the preferences of the user, the properties of the item being consumed, and the interaction between them (i.e., the user's preference). We show that this can model can be used to (a) generate plausible reviews and estimate nuanced reactions; (b) provide personalized rankings of existing reviews; and (c) recommend existing products more effectively.

1 Introduction

Review text has been extensively studied in modern recommender systems as a means of improving the performance on traditional recommendation tasks. Compared with conventional techniques that model simple numerical feedback (ratings, clicks, purchases, etc.), review text provides valuable information about user and item attributes, and more importantly the interaction between them. Recent systems have adapted ideas from topic modeling and sentiment analysis to leverage the side-information contained in reviews; in essence, these approaches use language models as a form of 'regularization,' such that the model should explain user preferences and review text simultaneously (McAuley and Leskovec, 2013; Bao et al., 2014; Ling et al., 2014).

In parallel, recent advances in generative text modeling have demonstrated the effectiveness of recurrent neural networks in capturing content, structure, and style in natural language. As a result, several recent works have focused on learning generative models of product reviews, either to generate reviews *per se*, or as a means of learning user and item attributes (Lipton et al., 2015; Radford et al., 2017; Dong et al., 2017; Hu et al., 2017). In this paper, we address the problem of how to leverage both review text and implicit feedback simultaneously in order to provide richer user experiences and more meaningful recommendations. In particular, we focus on estimating latent user preferences through implicit feedback while simultaneously predicting the contents of the reviews themselves. Thus, given an item that a user hasn't yet interacted with, our goals are to (a) generate a plausible review, in order to estimate the user's nuanced reaction to the product; (b) estimate whether the user would be likely to interact with the product, based on their learned latent attributes; and (c) rank existing reviews using the language model, in order to surface 'meaningful' reviews to the user.

To solve the above problems, we propose a model—CF-GGN—that combines Collaborative Filtering (CF) with Generative Concatenative Networks (GCN) (Lipton et al., 2015) to simultaneously perform item recommendation and review generation. Given a large dataset of implicit feedback (e.g. purchases vs. non-purchases), we start by modeling user and item latent factors through collaborative filtering; we also adapt ideas from

Proceedings of the The 8th International Joint Conference on Natural Language Processing, pages 783–791,
Taipei, Taiwan, November 27 – December 1, 2017 ©2017 AFNLP

text embeddings (e.g. word2vec), and use multi-layer perceptrons (MLP) to model complex interactions between embeddings and latent preference factors. Finally we build a generative concatenative model by stacking two LSTM layers; we adopt a simple replication strategy to concatenate latent factors with text input and jointly train the model in a supervised way. By sharing the same model parameters, the two tasks (recommendation and generation) mutually reinforce each other when all parameters are trained end-to-end.

To our knowledge, our work is the first to show that we can generate plausible reviews while simultaneously achieving substantial quantitative improvements on recommendation tasks. To summarize, our main contributions are as follows:

- We jointly perform recommendation and review generation by combining collaborative filtering with LSTM-based generative models. Our model captures latent information such as user preferences and item attributes, and learns to generate coherent, structured, and personalized reviews.

- We investigate the effect of sparsity in both reviews and implicit feedback data; a virtue of our joint training approach is that we can learn effective text models even for users with limited reviews at training time, i.e., we can learn to estimate likely reactions (in the form of reviews), on the basis of implicit feedback (e.g. purchases and clicks), even for users who write few reviews.

- We conduct extensive experiments on three real-word datasets in order to qualitatively and quantitatively demonstrate the effectiveness of our joint training approach.

2 Related Work

Review text provides valuable information about users' experiences and preferences toward the items they consume. Modeling the detailed information in reviews is especially important in sparse datasets, where a small amount of reviews carries substantially more information than is available in ratings alone. Several previous works have taken reviews into consideration to improve the performance of various recommendation tasks (McAuley and Leskovec, 2013; Ling et al., 2014; Bao et al., 2014; Wang et al., 2015).

Recently, neural-network-based models have been considered when modeling review text, in place of traditional topic modeling techniques. Zheng et al. (2017) leveraged Convolutional Neural Networks (CNN) to extract embeddings from reviews, which were used as features in a factorization machine (Rendle, 2010) to generate rating predictions. Catherine and Cohen (2017) proposed a model ('transNet') consisting of a source network and a target network; the former learns user and item embeddings from reviews while the latter performs sentiment analysis over the ground truth review. By minimizing the difference between the two networks' latent representation layers, the model learns more expressive latent factors. Wu et al. (2017) presented a neural network based model that jointly considers both ratings and reviews. Their approach models the temporal rating prediction task via a Recurrent Neural Network (RNN), and uses an additional LSTM network to model the review text as a regularization term in the loss function. Their experimental results show improvements on rating prediction tasks over state-of-the-art techniques, however they do not report results in terms of the model's ability to generate plausible reviews.

Given their expressive power when modeling sequential data, RNN-based methods have been widely studied for a variety of generation tasks (Graves, 2013; Zhang and LeCun, 2015; Sutskever et al., 2011). Recently, several works have focused on the task of learning language models to generate reviews. Generating coherent and personalized reviews still poses considerable challenges, due to their length, structure, and the sparsity of real datasets. Radford et al. (2017) trained a character-RNN language model based on the *Amazon* review dataset (McAuley et al., 2015); they consider a single multiplicative LSTM layer with 4096 hidden units and train the model for nearly a month. The authors find a sentiment unit among the hidden units which is highly correlated to review sentiment. They can then generate reviews by forcing this sentiment unit to be positive or negative. Lipton et al. (2015) proposed a generative concatenative network to supervise the training of a character-level language model; they concatenate auxiliary information in the form of one-hot representations of user/item IDs, categories and ratings. The model generates plausible reviews when conditioned on this auxiliary information, and demonstrates the potential for RNNs to capture subjective user information and generate personalized text, though they do not consider recommendation problems. Dong et al. (2017) studied attribute-to-sequence generative models with stacked LSTMs; they encode attributes such as user/item IDs and ratings and use the encoded information to initialize the hidden states of the LSTM layer. They also make use of an attention mechanism in the decoder to improve the accuracy of predictions. Their model is based on word-level LSTMs and struggles when generating long sequences. Moreover, their network does not have the ability to predict user preferences toward items, which limits performance when given unseen (user,item) pairs.

The most relevant work to ours is perhaps Li et al. (2017). They addressed the problem of jointly learning rating prediction and 'tip generation.' They employ a standard latent factor model with MLP layers to predict ratings, following which they use the latent factors to initialize the LSTM model for tip generation. Experimental results show quantitative improvements at rating prediction and their word-level generative model produces tips that are consistent with users' ratings. Compared with their task, we focus on review generation (rather than generating short tips), which requires the model to maintain generation quality over long sequences. Moreover, we consider review text as content during the training of our collaborative filtering model, which further enhances the prediction of user preferences.

3 Proposed Method

First we define our problem before introducing our CF-GCN model. Table 1 summarizes the notation used throughout this paper.

Given an implicit feedback dataset $\mathcal{R}$ (i.e., a set of 'positive' instances such as clicks or purchases), and the corresponding set of reviews $\mathcal{T}$, we focus on two tasks: item recommendation and review generation. We want to recommend a list of items to a user while also generating plausible reviews that the user might write.

3.1 Collaborative Filtering with Reviews

For the task of item recommendation with implicit feedback, our goal is to estimate pairwise preferences of a user u toward an item i via a scoring function $\hat{y}_{u,i}$. Many state-of-the-art techniques define their predictor in terms of matrix factorization

Table 1: Notation

Notation	Description
$\mathcal{R}, \mathcal{T}$	feedback set, review set
$\mathcal{U}, \mathcal{I}$	user set, item set
I^+, I^-	set of observed and unobserved entries
$\hat{y}_{ui}$	predicted 'score' for user u and item i
γ_u, γ_i	latent factors of user u and item i ($K \times 1$)
θ_u, θ_i	text factors for user u and item i ($K \times 1$)
f_u, f_i	word2vec embeddings of u and i ($D \times 1$)
E_u	$K \times D$ embedding matrix of user u
E_i	$K \times D$ embedding matrix of item i
Θ	set of neural network parameters
Φ	set of collaborative filtering parameters

(MF), i.e.,

$$\hat{y}_{ui} = \gamma_u^T \gamma_i, \tag{1}$$

where γ_u and γ_i represent K-dimensional user and item latent factors, whose inner product models the preference of u toward i.

There have been many extensions of standard MF methods by incorporating 'side information' such as categorical attributes, image features (He and McAuley, 2016), and text (Hu, 2017; Zheng et al., 2017). To fully take advantage of review text, we start by incorporating text embeddings from reviews into our predictor. Following this we use a single layer MLP to model the interactions between latent factors and text embeddings. The extended predicator is defined as

$$\hat{y}_{ui} = \sigma(\mathbf{W} \begin{bmatrix} \gamma_u^T \gamma_i \\ \theta_u^T E_i f_i \\ \theta_i^T E_u f_u \end{bmatrix} + \mathbf{b}), \tag{2}$$

where θ_u and θ_i are K-dimensional (latent) text factors that interact with the text embeddings of u and i. f_u and f_i are D-dimensional text features extracted from reviews written by user u or about item i. Only reviews in the training set are used (since reviews are not available at test time). Specifically, we first train a word2vec model on all reviews in the training set; then we aggregate reviews written by u or about i, and take an average over the representations. E_u and E_i are transform matrices that project D-dimensional text features into K-dimensional 'preference space.'

Given the preference predictor, we can learn the model by minimizing the point-wise classification loss (He et al., 2017):

$$\mathcal{L} = -\sum_{(u,i) \in \mathcal{I}^- \cup \mathcal{I}^+} y_{ui} \log \hat{y}_{ui} + (1 - y_{ui}) \log(1 - \hat{y}_{ui}), \tag{3}$$

where I^+ and I^- represent the set of observed and unobserved entries in $\mathcal{R}$. With (eq. 3), the item recommendation task becomes a classification problem of deciding whether i belongs to the positive or negative feedback set (I^+ or I^-).

3.2 Generative Concatenative Network

Recurrent neural networks with units such as long short term memory (LSTM) and gated recurrent units (GRU) have been widely used as generative models for tasks such as natural language generation, image captioning, dialogue generation, etc. (Józefowicz et al., 2016; Vinyals et al., 2015; Ghosh et al., 2017; Sutskever et al., 2014; Karpathy and Fei-Fei, 2017). In our model, we use a two-layer LSTM network to generate review text at the character level. We adopt the LSTM architecture from Zaremba et al. (2014). Updates of the LSTM layer are defined as:

$$
\begin{pmatrix} \mathbf{g} \\ \mathbf{i} \\ \mathbf{f} \\ \mathbf{o} \end{pmatrix} = \begin{pmatrix} \tanh \\ \text{sigmoid} \\ \text{sigmoid} \\ \text{sigmoid} \end{pmatrix} W_l \begin{pmatrix} \mathbf{h}_{l-1}^t \\ \mathbf{h}_l^{t-1} \end{pmatrix}
$$

$$
\mathbf{s}_l^t = \mathbf{g}_l^t \odot \mathbf{i}_l^t + \mathbf{s}_l^{t-1} \odot \mathbf{f}_l^t
$$

$$
\mathbf{h}_l^t = \tanh(\mathbf{s}_l^t) \odot \mathbf{o}_l^t, \tag{4}
$$

where $\mathbf{s}$ is the internal state of the cell; $\mathbf{g}$ represents the input node which has an activation function; $\mathbf{i}$, $\mathbf{o}$ and $\mathbf{f}$ are sigmoid gating units ('input,' 'output,' and 'forget,' respectively); and $\mathbf{h}$ is the hidden state of the cell. tanh and sigmoid are applied element-wise, as is the product $\odot$. W_l is the weight matrix for layer l.

Next we consider the text generation task using 'vanilla' LSTMs. For a character-LSTM model, each input x_t is a character of the original text. Given a text sequence $x^1 \dots x^T$, the LSTM-based network takes an input x^t for each step t and updates its hidden states $\mathbf{h}^t$ based on both the current input x^t and the previous step's hidden state $\mathbf{h}^{t-1}$. The network predicts the input x^{t+1} at the next step, given all inputs $x^{\leq t}$ before $t + 1$. The output layer is connected to a softmax layer:

$$
p(x^t|x^{<t}, \Theta) = \text{softmax}(W_s \mathbf{h}_L^t), \tag{5}
$$

where W_s is the weight matrix of the softmax layer, $\mathbf{h}_L^t$ is the hidden state at step t of the last hidden layer L, and Θ is the complete set of neural network parameters. Given the output probability distribution over all characters, we can predict the output by taking the character that maximizes the probability.

So far, the above method samples text from a 'background' distribution, but lacks the ability to generate personalized and item-specific text. We aim to address this by providing the network with auxiliary inputs x_{aux}. Here we hope that the same user and item latent factors γ_u and γ_i can also be effective as input to the generative model; this expectation is based on the notion that these factors describe the 'aspects' of user preferences and item properties that contribute to the user's overall opinion, and therefore the language in their review. Furthermore the use of low-dimensional latent factors means that the method can straightforwardly scale to large populations of users and items, which is not possible for methods based on one-hot encodings. Following Lipton et al. (2015) we adopt a simple replication strategy to concatenate the latent factors with the character input, So that the input to the model at each step becomes $x'^t = [x_{char}^t; \gamma_u; \gamma_i]$.

By concatenating the latent factors together with the character input, the auxiliary signal is preserved through hundreds of steps, allowing long and coherent sequences to be generated. If we were instead to treat latent factors as inputs to the hidden cell, the signal would quickly vanish or explode. In practice we found that a dimensionality of around $K = 8$ to 50 leads to acceptable performance when modeling users and items. This is a relatively small number compared with the hidden unit size (typically 256-1024), requiring only a modest computational overhead.

By sharing the same user and item latent factors, the tasks of item recommendation and review generation are learned jointly. The complete network structure is shown in Figure 1. We train the model in an end-to-end manner by optimizing the joint loss function:

$$
\mathcal{L} = - \sum_{(u,i) \in \mathcal{I}^- \cup \mathcal{I}^+} y_{ui} \log \hat{y}_{ui} + (1 - y_{ui}) \log(1 - \hat{y}_{ui})
$$

$$
- w \sum_{(u,i) \in \mathcal{T}} \sum_{t=1}^{T} \log p(x^t|x^{<t}, \Theta, \gamma_u, \gamma_i)
$$

$$
+ \lambda(\|\Theta\|_2^2 + \|\Phi\|_2^2), \tag{6}
$$

where w is a hyperparameter that trades off between the two tasks, $\Phi = \{\gamma_u, \gamma_i, \theta_u, \theta_i, \mathrm{E}_u, \mathrm{E}_i\}$ is the set of collaborative filtering parameters, and λ is a regularization hyperparameter.

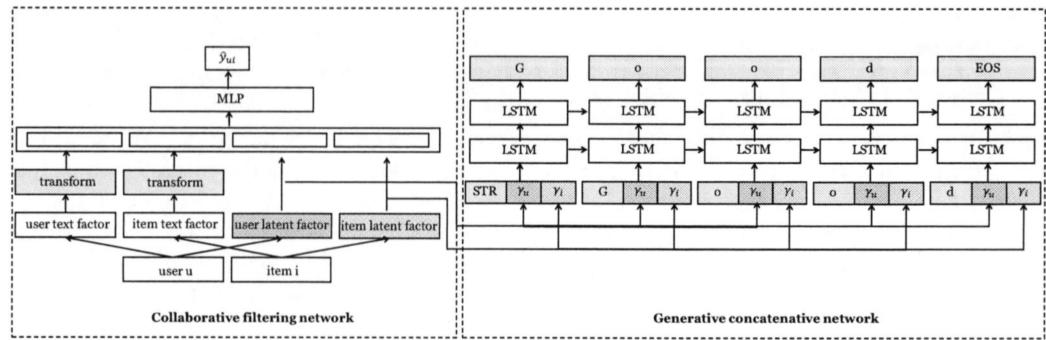

Figure 1: CF-GCN network structure

Table 2: Statistics after pre-processing.

Dataset	#users	#items	#reviews
BeerAdvocate	7,354	8,832	1,270,650
Electronics	20,247	11,589	306,899
Yelp	15,806	12,824	740,984

4 Experiments

We conduct experiments on multiple real-world datasets to investigate the following questions:

- **RQ1**: What can the model learn from review text? Does our joint training framework improve item recommendation performance?

- **RQ2**: What is the fidelity of the generative model? Does it successfully capture user/item attributes, sentiment, and writing style?

- **RQ3**: Can the model be used for personalized review ranking? How does performance improve as more reviews are available during training?

4.1 Datasets

We focus on three real-world datasets: BeerAdvocate,[1] Amazon Electronics,[2] and Yelp.[3] We discard users and items with few actions by extracting the k-core, with $k = 20$ for BeerAdvocate and Yelp, and $k = 10$ for Amazon Electronics (which is substantially sparser). The statistics of the datasets after pre-processing are shown in Table 2.

4.2 Experimental Setting

We consider two experimental settings for sampling implicit feedback instances and reviews. In one ('subset') we consider a subset of implicit feedback instances in $\mathcal{R}$ such that each is associated with exactly one review in $\mathcal{T}$; in the second ('wholeset') we consider *all* implicit feedback instances in $\mathcal{R}$, but only a subset of the reviews. In other words, the two settings have the same subset of reviews, but differ in the amount of implicit feedback used. Our reasons for considering the latter setting are twofold: First, training LSTM models with review data is time-consuming, but it is relatively inexpensive to add additional implicit feedback instances during training, meaning that we can achieve a boost in performance with only a modest increase in running time. And second, in real recommendation scenarios, most users do not write reviews, while all provide implicit feedback through their actions; thus this setup allows us to train on both types of feedback simultaneously, and even to model likely reviews for users who have written very few (or none!).

We randomly sample 10%/50%/20% of instances from BeerAdvocate/Electronics/Yelp, respectively. We use a different sample ratio so that the subset maintains around 100,000 reviews for each review model. Then we use a skip-gram model to train word2vec on the training set for each dataset so as to reduce noise and learn better representations for those words that are dataset-specific. We choose an embedding size of 64 and keep the most frequent 20,000 words in each training corpus.

We implemented the proposed method using Keras. For all datasets, we randomly withhold two

---

[1] https://snap.stanford.edu/data/
[2] http://jmcauley.ucsd.edu/data/amazon/
[3] https://www.yelp.com/dataset_challenge

Table 3: Comparisons of Hit Rate, NDCG and AUC on three datasets. CF-GCN improves all metrics over BPR and GMF for all settings (higher is better for all metrics).

Dataset	Setting	Hit Rate			NDCG			AUC		
		BPR	GMF	CF-GCN	BPR	GMF	CF-GCN	BPR	GMF	CF-GCN
BeerAdvocate	subset	0.583	0.584	**0.613**	0.351	0.334	**0.371**	0.826	0.847	**0.861**
	wholeset	0.752	0.763	**0.773**	0.476	0.487	**0.501**	0.925	0.925	**0.928**
Electronics	subset	0.375	0.428	**0.459**	0.224	0.254	**0.275**	0.690	0.746	**0.779**
	wholeset	0.494	0.521	**0.529**	0.295	0.317	**0.324**	0.665	0.824	**0.826**
Yelp	subset	0.641	0.660	**0.679**	0.378	0.392	**0.412**	0.899	0.895	**0.902**
	wholeset	0.811	0.830	**0.847**	0.514	0.530	**0.553**	0.946	0.946	**0.952**

interactions per user as our validation/test set, and use all other interactions for training, (i.e., leave-one-out evaluation (Rendle et al., 2009)). All results are reported on the test set, for the hyper-parameters resulting in the best performance on the validation set. The dimensionality of the latent factors is set to $K = 8$. Parameters of the user and item latent factors and text embeddings are initialized from a Gaussian distribution with $\mu = 0$ and $\sigma = 0.01$. For the review model, we stacked two LSTM layers with 256 hidden units per layer. We first train a conventional character-LSTM model then load the pre-trained parameters as initialization to speed up training. During training, we concatenate all reviews in the training set and add start and end tokens (e.g. STR, EOS) as delimiters. Then we split the concatenated string into sequences of length 200.

The model is trained in min-batches with batch-size 256. We adopt the Adam Optimizer (Kingma and Ba, 2014) to update weights. We consider learning rates in $\{0.01, 0.001, 0.0001\}$ and $\lambda \in \{0, 0.001, 0.0001, 0.00001, 0.000001\}$, selecting the optimal values on the validation set using grid search. We also tune the weight w between 0 to 1 to trade off item recommendation vs. review generation in (eq. 6).

4.3 Item Recommendation (RQ1)

We first demonstrate that our model can learn user preferences through both implicit feedback and review text. We focus on the item recommendation task and compare the proposed model with two state-of-the-art methods: Bayesian Personalized Ranking (BPR) (Rendle et al., 2009) and Generalized Matrix Factorization (GMF) (He et al., 2017). Both BPR and GMF use the predicator as eq. 1. We consider three metrics: Hit Rate, NDCG, and AUC. At test time, given a user and item pair from the held-out data, we return a truncated ranked list

of items with size 10. Then the Hit Rate at the top 10 (HR@10) represents the ratio of ground truth items existing in the ranked list, while the NDCG measures the position of the hits (He et al., 2017, 2016). The AUC (*Area Under the ROC curve*) is evaluated as:

$$\text{AUC} = \frac{1}{|\mathcal{U}|} \sum_u \frac{1}{|\mathcal{S}(u)|} \sum_{(i,j) \in \mathcal{S}(u)} \delta(\hat{y}_{ui} > \hat{y}_{uj}),$$

where δ is an indicator (1 iff its argument is true), and the set of pairs of u is defined as:

$$\mathcal{S}(u) = \{(i,j) | i \in \mathcal{I}_{test}^+(u) \\ \wedge j \notin \mathcal{I}_{train}^-(u) \cup \mathcal{I}_{valid}^-(u) \cup \mathcal{I}_{test}^-(u)\}.$$

As shown in Table 3, CF-GCN improves over BPR and GMF on the three metrics. Note that we only use a modest number of latent factors (8) and word2vec embedding dimensions (64). Moreover, we can see that CF-GCN achieves greater improvements in sparse settings, confirming the ability of review text to overcome the sparsity of implicit feedback datasets.

4.3.1 User Cold-Start

Real recommender systems often suffer from cold-start issues due to data sparsity. It is a critical task for the system to capture user preferences toward items given limited data. To explore the performance of CF-GCN, we further analyze the improvement on cold (or 'cool') users. Figure 2 shows the improvement (in Hit Rate and NDCG) for users with fewer than 5 reviews on BeerAdvocate. The largest improvement ratio happens for users with only a single review during training.

4.4 Review Generation Analysis (RQ2)

4.4.1 Perplexity

Perplexity is commonly used to measure the quality of generated text. It is defined as

$$\text{ppx} = e^{-\frac{1}{N} \sum_{(u,i)} \frac{1}{T} \sum_{c=1}^{T} \log p(c_t | c_{<t}, \Theta, \gamma_u, \gamma_i)},$$

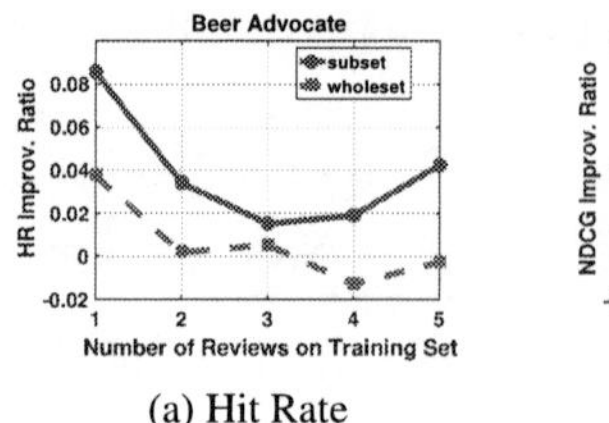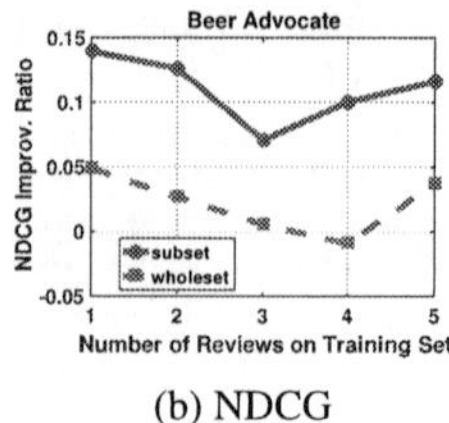

(a) Hit Rate   (b) NDCG

Figure 2: Improvement Ratio on Cold-Start Users

Table 4: Comparison of Perplexity on test set (lower is better).

Dataset	Character LSTM	CF-GCN (subset)	CF-GCN (wholeset)
BeerAdvocate	2.370	2.318	2.329
Electronics	3.033	2.998	2.959
Yelp	2.916	2.817	2.809

where (u, i) are pairs from the test set of reviews $\mathcal{T}_{test}$, N is the number of reviews on the test set, and T is the number of characters in each review.

We compare the test-set perplexity of CF-GCN to that of a standard character-LSTM. As shown in Table 4, CF-GCN achieves lower perplexity than an unsupervised character-LSTM, suggesting that the model is successfully able to leverage information encoded in the user and item representations.

4.4.2 Generated Examples

Figure 3 gives a representative example of a generated review, for a (user,item) pair that is not present in the training set. In other words, only the user and item IDs are provided to the model, from which it must synthesize a plausible review.

Qualitatively, CF-GCN appears to capture the user's writing style, the item's attributes, and the user's sentiment, and more importantly maintains the overall flow and structure of the review in spite of its length and complexity. For example, the synthetic review captures idiosyncrasies of the real review, including the user's tendency to use abbreviations to denote different sensory aspects ('A:' for Appearance, 'S:' for Smell, etc.) CF-GCN also provides descriptions of the item's color, taste and category ("Pours a very dark brown," "a slight sweetness," "bitter," "ale") which approximately match those of the real review. Moreover, the synthetic review shares the same overall sentiment with the real review (3 stars, 'not bad').

Figure 4 presents synthetic review examples conditioned on users who have not written *any* reviews in the training set. We include the ground-truth rating, which is a score between 1.0 and 5.0. The model appears to successfully generates plausible reviews that express sentiment matching the ground-truth rating.

Note here that we only use two LSTM layers with 256 hidden units. Performance could be further improved by increasing the number of hidden units and stacking more layers, at the cost of additional computational resources. For the current setting, it takes around 80 minutes to run 1 epoch for the BeerAdvocate dataset. Typically CF-GCN needs 5 to 10 epochs to converge.

4.5 Personalized review ranking (RQ3)

Besides synthesizing reviews, a more realistic application of our model is to recommend (or rank) existing reviews, by surfacing the review that is most consistent with a user's preferences or writing style. As with our previous experiments, this can be done even for users who have never written a review before: that is, based on their past behavior we can surface the types of reviews written by users who behave similarly.

Since CF-GCN captures both the sentiment and writing style of users, it can also be used in a discriminative way to identify which existing review of an item a particular user is most likely to have written. Given a target item and a list of users, the personalized review ranking problem can be quantitatively evaluated in terms of our ability to rank the 'true' review (i.e., the one the user actually wrote) higher than others. This target captures whether the model can recommend the most relevant existing review to a potential user.

For a review written by user u on item i, we first calculate the perplexity when the generative model is given the latent factors of u and i. We then estimate the AUC by randomly sampling reviews (of the same item) by other users u' and calculating their perplexity when the model is again given the latent factors of u and i. We can then evaluate the model in terms of its ability to associate a lower perplexity to the review u actually wrote. The model generates reasonable results given only a modest number of reviews, and can identify authors with almost perfect accuracy once sufficiently many reviews are provided during training.

Figure 5 shows AUC results for the personalized review ranking task. As the number of reviews available during training increases, the AUC

Real review	Synthetic review
12 oz. bottle, excited to see a new Victory product around, **A:** Pours a dark brown, much darker than I thought it would be, rich creamy head, with light lace. **S:** Dark cedar/pine nose with some dark bread/pumpernickel. **T:** This ale certainly has a lot of malt, bordering on Barleywine. Molasses, sweet maple with a clear bitter melon/white grapefruit hop flavour. Not a lot of complexity in the hops here for me. **M:** Full-bodied, creamy, resinous, nicely done. **D:** A good beer, it isn't exactly what I was expecting. In the end above average, though I found it monotonous at times, hence the 3. A sipper for sure.	**A:** Pours a very dark brown with a nice finger of tan head that produces a small bubble and leaves decent lacing on the glass. **S:** Smells like a nut brown ale. It has a slight sweetness and a bit of a woody note and a little cocoa. The nose is rather malty with some chocolate and coffee. The taste is strong but not overwhelmingly sweet. The sweetness is overpowering, but not overwhelming and is a pretty strong bitter finish. **M:** Medium bodied with a slightly thin feel. **D:** A good tasting beer. Not bad.

Figure 3: Real and synthetic reviews conditioned on the latent factor of user *Halcyondays* and item *Yakima Glory*. Colors added for emphasis. The model successfully captures the high-level structure of the review, as well as the fine-grained characteristics of their opinion.

Synthetic review: user *BeerShirts*, item *Black Albert*, sentiment *5.0*
A - Pours a brownish-copper color with a thick tan head. S - Strong and smoky aroma, fruity and sweet. The alcohol is not very prominent on the nose. Smells like a stout and enjoyable. It's almost like a hefeweizen and the smell is dominated by a slight burnt sugar character and a slight chocolate smell to it. The taste is sweet and malty. The mouthfeel is very light and watery. Overall a very nice beer that I'd have again.

Synthetic review: user *Morbo*, item *Avalon Spiced Ale*, sentiment *1.5*
I don't like this beer. I was not a big fan of this beer. The aroma was pretty accessible and the taste was a bit sweet and fruity. There was a hint of sweetness that was overwhelmed by the rice and malt also a bit of the hops in the finish. The mouthfeel was medium bodied with a medium carbonation. This was a good beer to drink but I would not be able to get more of this.

Figure 4: Synthetic reviews for users who have written *no* reviews in the training set. The model successfully predicts user preferences and generates plausible reviews.

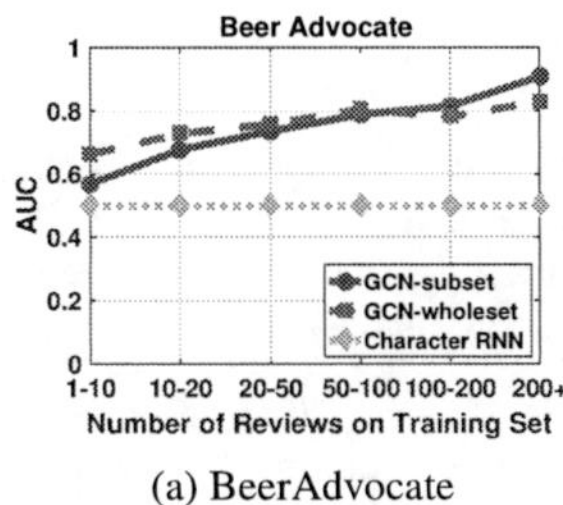

(a) BeerAdvocate

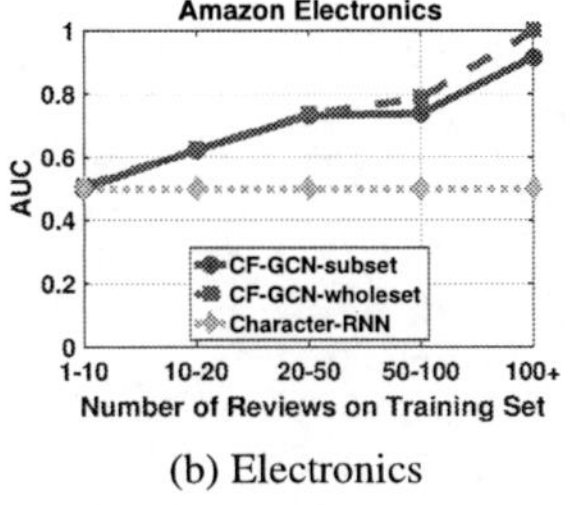

(b) Electronics

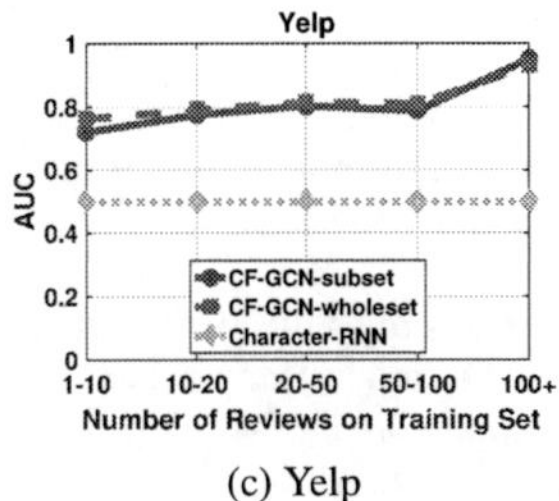

(c) Yelp

Figure 5: Comparisons of AUC for personalized review ranking for users with different number of reviews on the training set.

also increases, indicating that the method is better able to capture the characteristics of the user and item given more observations.

5 Conclusions

In this paper, we proposed to combine collaborative filtering with generative concatenative networks to jointly perform the tasks of item recommendation and review generation. We formulated the item recommendation task using matrix factorization, in order to capture low-dimensional user preferences and item properties, which we combined with a character-level LSTM model, so that the latent factors are simultaneously responsible for explaining both language and preferences. We adopted a simple input replication strategy to allow the LSTM model to 'remember' the input on which it is conditioned, so that it is able to generate long reviews that capture high-level structure as well as fine-grained sentiment. In addition to using the model generatively, we showed that it can also improve recommendation performance, both in terms of predicting products that a user is likely to interact with, as well as personalized review ranking.

References

Yang Bao, Hui Fang, and Jie Zhang. 2014. Topicmf: Simultaneously exploiting ratings and reviews for recommendation. In *AAAI Conference on Artificial Intelligence*.

Rose Catherine and William W. Cohen. 2017. Transnets: Learning to transform for recommendation. *CoRR*, abs/1704.02298.

Li Dong, Shaohan Huang, Furu Wei, Mirella Lapata, Ming Zhou, and Ke Xu. 2017. Learning to generate product reviews from attributes. In *Association for Computational Linguistics*.

Sayan Ghosh, Mathieu Chollet, Eugene Laksana, Louis-Philippe Morency, and Stefan Scherer. 2017. Affect-lm: A neural language model for customizable affective text generation. *CoRR*, abs/1704.06851.

Alex Graves. 2013. Generating sequences with recurrent neural networks. *CoRR*, abs/1308.0850.

Ruining He and Julian McAuley. 2016. Vbpr: Visual bayesian personalized ranking from implicit feedback. In *AAAI Conference on Artificial Intelligence*.

Xiangnan He, Lizi Liao, Hanwang Zhang, Liqiang Nie, Xia Hu, and Tat-Seng Chua. 2017. Neural collaborative filtering. In *World Wide Web*.

Xiangnan He, Hanwang Zhang, Min-Yen Kan, and Tat-Seng Chua. 2016. Fast matrix factorization for online recommendation with implicit feedback. In *SIGIR*.

Guang-Neng Hu. 2017. Integrating reviews into personalized ranking for cold start recommendation. In *Pacific-Asia Conference on Knowledge Discovery and Data Mining*.

Zhiting Hu, Zichao Yang, Xiaodan Liang, Ruslan Salakhutdinov, and Eric P. Xing. 2017. Controllable text generation. *CoRR*, abs/1703.00955.

Rafal Józefowicz, Oriol Vinyals, Mike Schuster, Noam Shazeer, and Yonghui Wu. 2016. Exploring the limits of language modeling. *CoRR*, abs/1602.02410.

Andrej Karpathy and Li Fei-Fei. 2017. Deep visual-semantic alignments for generating image descriptions. *IEEE Trans. Pattern Anal. Mach. Intell.*, 39(4):664–676.

Diederik P. Kingma and Jimmy Ba. 2014. Adam: A method for stochastic optimization. In *International Conference on Learning Representations*.

Piji Li, Zihao Wang, Zhaochun Ren, Lidong Bing, and Wai Lam. 2017. Neural rating regression with abstractive tips generation for recommendation. In *SIGIR*.

Guang Ling, Michael R. Lyu, and Irwin King. 2014. Ratings meet reviews, a combined approach to recommend. In *ACM Conference on Recommender Systems*.

Zachary Chase Lipton, Sharad Vikram, and Julian McAuley. 2015. Capturing meaning in product reviews with character-level generative text models. *CoRR*, abs/1511.03683.

Julian McAuley and Jure Leskovec. 2013. Hidden factors and hidden topics: understanding rating dimensions with review text. In *ACM Conference on Recommender Systems*.

Julian McAuley, Rahul Pandey, and Jure Leskovec. 2015. Inferring networks of substitutable and complementary products. In *Knowledge Discovery and Data Mining*.

Alec Radford, Rafal Józefowicz, and Ilya Sutskever. 2017. Learning to generate reviews and discovering sentiment. *CoRR*, abs/1704.01444.

Steffen Rendle. 2010. Factorization machines. In *International Conference on Data Mining*.

Steffen Rendle, Christoph Freudenthaler, Zeno Gantner, and Lars Schmidt-Thieme. 2009. Bpr: Bayesian personalized ranking from implicit feedback. In *Uncertainty in Artificial Intelligence*.

Ilya Sutskever, James Martens, and Geoffrey Hinton. 2011. Generating text with recurrent neural networks. In *International Conference on Machine Learning*.

Ilya Sutskever, Oriol Vinyals, and Quoc V. Le. 2014. Sequence to sequence learning with neural networks. In *International Conference on Neural Information Processing Systems*.

Oriol Vinyals, Alexander Toshev, Samy Bengio, and Dumitru Erhan. 2015. Show and tell: A neural image caption generator. In *IEEE Conference on Computer Vision and Pattern Recognition*.

Hao Wang, Naiyan Wang, and Dit-Yan Yeung. 2015. Collaborative deep learning for recommender systems. In *Knowledge Discovery and Data Mining*.

Chao-Yuan Wu, Amr Ahmed, and Alexander J. Smola Alex Beutel. 2017. Joint training of ratings and reviews with recurrent recommender networks. In *ICLR Workshops*.

Wojciech Zaremba, Ilya Sutskever, and Oriol Vinyals. 2014. Recurrent neural network regularization. *CoRR*, abs/1409.2329.

Xiang Zhang and Yann LeCun. 2015. Text understanding from scratch. *CoRR*, abs/1502.01710.

Lei Zheng, Vahid Noroozi, and Philip S. Yu. 2017. Joint deep modeling of users and items using reviews for recommendation. In *Web Search and Data Mining*.

Summarizing Lengthy Questions

Tatsuya Ishigaki   Hiroya Takamura   Manabu Okumura
Tokyo Institute of Technology
ishigaki@lr.pi.titech.ac.jp, {takamura, oku}@pi.titech.ac.jp

Abstract

In this research, we propose the task of *question summarization*. We first analyzed question-summary pairs extracted from a Community Question Answering (CQA) site, and found that a proportion of questions cannot be summarized by extractive approaches but requires abstractive approaches. We created a dataset by regarding the question-title pairs posted on the CQA site as question-summary pairs. By using the data, we trained extractive and abstractive summarization models, and compared them based on ROUGE scores and manual evaluations. Our experimental results show an abstractive method using an encoder-decoder model with a copying mechanism achieves better scores for both ROUGE-2 F-measure and the evaluations by human judges.

1 Introduction

Questions are asked in many situations, such as conference sessions and email communications. However, questions can sometimes be lengthy and hard to understand, because they often contain peripheral information in addition to the main focus of the question. To address this issue, we propose the task of *question summarization*; summarizing a lengthy question into a simple question that concisely represents the original content.

As an example of an excerpt from a Community Question Answering (CQA) site, Yahoo Answers[1], is shown in Table 1. In this example, the gist of the question is whether the chlorine will stripe the questioner's hair. However, the question also contains the additional information that the questioner swims five days a week and has black

---
[1] https://answers.yahoo.com/

Table 1: Example of question-summary pair

Question Text:
I'm a swimmer for my school swim team and I practice two hours a day, five days a week. I would like to dye my hair black (it is dark brown now) but I am wondering whether the chlorine will stripe it. Will it or will it not ?
Summary:
Will the chlorine stripe my hair ?

hair. Although such information can sometimes be important for finding the exact answer, it is often peripheral when we want to grasp what is being asked.

Summarizing a question, which can often be lengthy, helps respondents understand the question. The task of question summarization has not been studied yet and is worth being explored. In this work, we focus on a CQA site and examine the characteristics of the question summarization task with a CQA dataset as a case study. Specifically, we first examine CQA data consisting of pairs of a question text and its title, which we refer to as "question-title" pairs. We then propose a method for creating pairs of a question and its summary, which we refer to as "question-summary" pairs, out of the CQA data. We also propose methods for question summarization and describe an empirical evaluation we conducted.

Approaches used in generic summarization tasks are often classified into two different types: extractive and abstractive. Extractive approaches select and order units, which are usually sentences or words, from the input text. Abstractive approaches, rather than selecting units, generate a summary using words not found in the input text.

However, existing summarization approaches, whether extractive or abstractive, do not assume

Proceedings of the The 8th International Joint Conference on Natural Language Processing, pages 792–800,
Taipei, Taiwan, November 27 – December 1, 2017 ©2017 AFNLP

a question as an input. We therefore developed a number of methods designed for question summarization: extractive methods based on simple heuristic rules, extractive methods based on sentence classification/regression, and abstractive methods based on neural networks. We compared the performance of these methods through evaluations both by human judges and automatic scoring using Recall-Oriented Understudy for Gisting Evaluation (ROUGE) (Lin, 2004). The experimental results show that an abstractive approach using an encoder-decoder model with a copying mechanism achieves the highest score for both ROUGE and evaluations by human judges.

2 Related Work

Text summarization is one of the problems that have been studied for a long time in the field of natural language processing. In many of the existing summarization tasks including the shared tasks in Document Understanding Conference (DUC)[2], documents from newspapers or scientific articles are considered as an input. There are also other summarization tasks in which other types of input are assumed such as conversations or email threads (Duboue, 2012; Oya and Carenini, 2014; Oya et al., 2014). Unlike the researches, we assume a question as an input.

As a related attempt in Question Answering researches, Tamura et al. (2005) worked on classification of multiple-sentence questions into classes such as yes/no questions and definition questions, and attempted to extract the question sentence that was the most important in finding the correct class. However, the extracted question sentence is not always a summary of the question. Consider the last sentence "Wiil it or will it not?" for the aforementioned Table 1 question. This last sentence is important in finding the class of this question, which is a yes/no question, but is not appropriate as a summary, because it is impossible to understand what is being asked merely from "Will it or will it not?"

Many existing extractive approaches select the sentences to be included in the summary on the basis of calculated scores for each sentence. The scores are often calculated by the TF-IDF measure (Luhn, 1958), the similarity measure between sentences (Mihalcea and Tarau, 2004) and an approximation made by a regression model of the

ROUGE score or the bigram frequency included in a summary (Peyrard and Eckale-Kohler, 2016; Li et al., 2013). Other approaches consider summarization tasks as a classification problem. They adopt supervised machine learning techniques to solve them (Hirao et al., 2002; Shen et al., 2007).

Abstractive summarization approaches include methods based on syntactic transduction (Dorr et al., 2003; Zajic et al., 2004) or statistical machine translation models (Bank et al., 2010; Wubben et al., 2012; Cohn and Lapata, 2013) and templates (Oya et al., 2014). In addition, encoder-decoder approaches have been proposed in recent years. They were originally applied to machine translation tasks (Luong et al., 2015; Bahdanau et al., 2015; Cao et al., 2017), and have been actively applied to other sequence-to-sequence tasks including sentence summarization (Rush et al., 2015; Kikuchi et al., 2016; Gu et al., 2016).

3 Data Analysis

We first carried out an analysis on the dataset provided by Yahoo! Answers, "Yahoo! Answers Comprehensive Question and Answers version 1.0"[3]. The data contains 4,484,032 question-title pairs posted between June 28, 2005 and October 25, 2007. On the CQA site, users can freely write a question text and its title. Thus, some of the pairs in the data can be regarded as question-summary pairs, but some others cannot. To obtain a dataset that can be used for training, we need to filter out the pairs that are not suitable for our objective. Furthermore, it is not clear how questions are summarized, i.e., whether by extractive or abstractive methods. Therefore, in this study, we first analyzed the data to clarify the following issues:

1. What are the characteristics of the pairs that cannot be regarded as question-summary pairs?

2. Can an extractive approach generate a summary equivalent to the title, or are abstractive approaches required?

3.1 Question text length

To characterize the question-title pairs that could not be regarded as question-summary pairs, we first focus on the number of sentences in question text. We randomly extracted the question-title

---

[2]http://duc.nist.gov

[3]https://webscope.sandbox.yahoo.com/

Table 2: Number of sentences in question text and proportion of question-summary pairs

No. of sentences in question text	Proportion
1	3/20
2	8/20
3	14/20
4	15/20
5	15/20

Table 3: Number of titles generated by extractive and abstractive approaches

Not a question-summary pair	5/20
Extractive approach can summarize	8/20
Abstractive approach needed	7/20

pairs that contained 1-5 sentences in the question text, and manually classified them as to whether they could be regarded as a question-summary pair or not. Table 2 shows the number of question-title pairs that can be regarded as question-summary pairs for question text size measured by the number of sentences.

This analysis showed that if there are two or fewer sentences in the question text, the pairs are unlikely to be question-summary pairs because the question texts tend to contain only peripheral information to support the question presented in the title. In contrast, if there are three or more sentences, the proportion of the question-summary pairs becomes high and substantially constant. This suggests that the number of sentences in a question text is one of the clues to find question-summary pairs.

3.2 Nouns overlapping between question and title

We show here an example that cannot be regarded as a question-summary pair.

Title:

Why is there often a mirror in an

elevator?

Question text:

I just realized this when I was in an elevator. Does anybody know the reason? What is the history behind it?

This is not a question-summary pair because the question text does not express the content of the title. In such cases, people cannot grasp the gist of

the question text when only the title is presented. Here we focus on the words "mirror" and "elevator"; they appear in the title, but not in the question text. We actually observed many similar instances. This suggests that noun overlapping between a question and its title can be considered an important clue to determine whether the pair can be regarded as a question-summary pair or not.

3.3 Extractive vs. abstractive

We next analyzed question-summary pairs in terms of whether the summaries can be generated by an extractive method or an abstractive method is required. Specifically, we randomly selected pairs whose question text had 3-5 sentences and manually classified them into one of the following 3 categories: 1) The pair cannot be regarded as a question-summary pair, 2) An extractive method can generate a summary that is equivalent to the title, and 3) Others (i.e., an abstractive method might be needed to generate a summary that is equivalent to the title).

The manual classification results are shown in Table 3. We also show representative examples of question-summary pairs in Table 4.

Five out of 20 cases cannot be regarded as question-summary pairs. In Example 1 of Table 4, the questioner accidentally spilled buttered popcorn and needs to know how to remove it. However, the title "Please help!" does not contain enough information to grasp the gist of the question. In some cases, pronouns in the titles refer to nouns in the question text.

In eight of the 20 pairs, an extractive approach can generate a summary that is almost equivalent to the title. Example 2 in Table 4 is such a case. In this example, a summary can be generated by extracting the last sentence in the original content. However, if one takes the actual title into consideration, the idiom "get rid of" in the original question can be replaced by the word "remove". Even if a question text can be summarized by an extractive method, the actual titles are often generated by abstractive approaches.

In the remaining seven pairs, the question texts cannot be summarized by an extractive approach, and abstractive approaches might be required. The category is further split into two subcategories. In the first subcategory, pronoun resolution as well as sentence extraction is needed to generate a summary. In the second subcategory, a short question

Table 4: Representative examples of pairs in Yahoo! Answers dataset

Example 1 (The title does not express the content of the question text):
I accidentally spilled buttered popcorn on my leather hospital shoe.
It has dark spots on it now and I don't know how i can get them off.
...
Title: Please help!

Example 2 (Extractive approaches can be applied.):
I keep getting annoying Winfixer Pop Ups . I have tried all sorts of ad removal programs
to get rid of them but without success .
How can I get rid of them ?
Title:
How can one remove annoying pop ups ?

Example 3 (Abstractive approaches are required.):
"The Simpsons" is one of the funniest shows ever . It's one of my favorites . Do you like it ?
Title:
Do you like "The Simpsons" ?

Example 4 (Abstractive approaches are required.):
I want my chocolate chip cookies to be thicker and kind of gooey–crispy outside, chewy inside.
I've experimented with various recipes and various oven temperature, but my cookies always
turn out thin and flat. Why? What am I doing wrong? Title:
Why do my chocolate chip cookies always turn out thin and flat?

---

follows a lengthy explanation.

In Example 3 in Table 4, the pronoun "it" in the main question "Do you like it?" refers to the program name "the simpsons", which appeared previously. Therefore, the summary does not contain enough information to grasp the gist if we naively apply any extractive approaches. The short main question "why" in Example 4 follows the explanation about baking cookies. In examples such as these, we cannot naively use extractive approaches to generate an understandable summary, because the title is generated by picking up the information from multiple sentences.

4 Dataset and Methodology

In this section, we describe how we created a dataset consisting of question-summary pairs, and a number of methods for question summarization.

4.1 Dataset

As training data for extractive and abstractive models, we use question-title pairs posted to a CQA site, namely, "Yahoo! Answers Comprehensive Question and Answers version 1.0". The original data contains 4,485,032 question-title pairs. However, not all of them are question-summary pairs. To filter out the pairs that are not question-summary pairs, we removed the pairs that match

at least one of the following conditions:

Multiple sentences in the title Comprising two or more sentences

Long Title The title consists of over 16 words.

Short Title The title consists of three or less words.

Overlap of nouns
No nouns in the title appear in the question text.

Short Question Text
The question text consists of two or less sentences.

Long Question Text
The question text consists of over five sentences.

After applying the filtering, we obtained 251,420 pairs[4]. We use the pairs for training extractive and abstractive models, and also for evaluations.

---

[4]Note that the data still contains non-English question-title pairs, since the language recognition is not perfect.

4.2 Extractive approaches

As extractive approaches, we adopted rule-based approaches and machine learning based approaches.

4.2.1 Rule-based approaches

As rule-based approaches, we used three rules to compare: "Lead Sentence", "Lead Question", and "Last Question". The first sentence presented (Lead Sentence) is known as a strong baseline for generic summarization tasks. However, in the question summarization, the summaries should be also questions. Therefore, we adopted methods to select a question in the input by heuristic rules, choosing the first question (Lead Question) and the last question (Last Question). A sentence was determined to be a question if the last character is "?" or the first word is an interrogative word.

4.2.2 Machine learning-based approaches

We will here introduce two types of machine learning-based methods: a classification-based method and a regression-based method.

The regression-based model predicts the ROUGE-2 F-measure score for each sentence in the input question. After the prediction step finishes, the model outputs the sentence with the highest predicted ROUGE score. To train the regression model, we first calculated the ROUGE score for each sentence in the training set, regarding the title as a reference summary. After the calculation, we trained Support Vector Regression (SVR) (Basak et al., 2007).

The classification-based method predicts the sentence with the largest ROUGE-2 F-measure. In the training phase, we regarded the questions which had the highest ROUGE score and consisted of at least four words as positive instances. Other questions were used as negative instances. We adopted Support Vector Machine (SVM) (Suykens and Vandewalle, 1999) as a classifier. If the SVM classifies more than one sentence in a single input document as positive, then our method outputs the first question. In contrast, if the SVM classifies all questions in the input as negative, then the model outputs the first question. It outputs the first sentence if there is no question in the output. A sentence is regarded as a question if the last character is "?" or the first word is an interrogative word.

We trained the regression and classification models by using the following features:

- Word unigram

- Sentence length

- Whether the sentence is the initial sentence

- Whether the sentence is the first question

- Presence of other question sentences

All features are expressed as binary: i.e., 0 or 1. For unigram features, we adopted features that appeared at least five times in the training set. We used four sentence-lengthy features: the sentence had less than three, less than five, more than 10, and more than 15 unigrams.

4.3 Abstractive approaches

We adopted encoder-decoder based methods for abstractive approaches. Specifically, we trained three models: a vanilla encoder-decoder model, an encoder-decoder model with an attention mechanism and an encoder-decoder model with a copying mechanism.

Questions in the CQA site are usually composed of 3-5 sentences, which are longer than in the usual settings used in machine translations tasks. Therefore, in addition to the vanilla model, we trained a model with the attention mechanism (Luong et al., 2015). To reduce the model size, we replaced low-frequency words with the special token UNK, which is a well-known technique. After the preprocessing, the vocabulary size was reduced to approximately 136,000. In summarization tasks, the words in the input are often likely to appear in the summary. Therefore, we also adopted the encoder-decoder model with the copying mechanism (Gu et al., 2016), which can select words in the input as words in the output.

We briefly describe those models below.

4.3.1 Vanilla encoder-decoder

The encoder-decoder model is composed of two elements: an encoder and a decoder. The encoder receives the input question $x_1, ..., x_n$, and converts it into the fixed-length continuous value vector h_τ:

$$h_\tau = f(x_\tau, h_{\tau-1}), \qquad (1)$$

where f represents an activation function used in any Recurrent Neural Network (RNN). In this study, the vanilla encoder-decoder and the attention models use Long Short-Term Memory (Hochreiter and Schmidhuber, 1997), and Gated

Recurrent Unit (GRU) (Cho et al., 2014) is used in the model with the copying mechanism. All encoder-decoder models adopt bidirectional-RNNs as the encoder.

The decoder receives the last hidden state of the encoder and generates a sentence. Each node in the decoder receives the previously generated word and the hidden state generated in the previous time step to calculate the hidden state s_t and the $softmax$ function. The occurrence probability of y_t is calculated by using the hidden state s_t and a $softmax$ function:

$$s_t = f(y_{t-1}, s_{t-1}), \tag{2}$$

$$p(y_t|y_{<t}, \boldsymbol{x}) = softmax(g(\boldsymbol{s_t})). \tag{3}$$

The conditional probability given the input sequence $\boldsymbol{x}$ can be decomposed to the product of the probabilities of generating words as follows:

$$p(\boldsymbol{y}|\boldsymbol{x}) = \prod_{t=1}^{m} p(y_t|y_{<t}, \boldsymbol{x}). \tag{4}$$

In the training, we estimated the parameter values so that they maximize the log-likelihood of the training set:

$$\log p(\boldsymbol{y}|\boldsymbol{x}) = \log \sum_{j=1}^{m} p(y_t|y_{<t}, \boldsymbol{x}). \tag{5}$$

In the test phase, the model generates the output by beam-search.

4.3.2 Encoder-decoder with attention

In the vanilla encoder-decoder model, the input document is encoded into the hidden state $\boldsymbol{h_n}$. The decoder receives the hidden state as the initial state s_0 of the decoder ($s_0 = \boldsymbol{h_n}$). In contrast, the encoder-decoder model with the attention mechanism uses the context vector c_t represented as a weighted sum of the hidden states of the encoder:

$$\boldsymbol{c_t} = \sum_{\tau=1}^{n} \alpha_{t\tau} \boldsymbol{h_\tau}, \tag{6}$$

where $\alpha_{t\tau}$ is the weight of the t-th word of the input at time step τ and can be calculated as

$$\alpha_{t\tau} = \frac{exp(\boldsymbol{s_t} \cdot \boldsymbol{h_\tau})}{\sum_{h'} exp(\boldsymbol{s_t} \cdot \boldsymbol{h'})}. \tag{7}$$

Finally, the conditional probability of the word y_t is calculated by the $softmax$ function:

$$\tilde{h} = tanh(\boldsymbol{W_c}[\boldsymbol{c_t}; \boldsymbol{h_t}]), \tag{8}$$

$$p(y_t|y_{<t}, \boldsymbol{x}) = softmax(\boldsymbol{W_s}\tilde{h_t}). \tag{9}$$

Table 5: Evaluation on ROUGE-2

	Recall	F-measure
Lead	39.4	27.0
Last-Q	42.6	33.9
Lead-Q	45.3	34.5
Classification	44.3	35.1
Regression	44.7	29.7
EncDec	3.5	2.6
EncDec+Attn	38.5	38.5
CopyNet	47.4	42.2

4.3.3 Encoder-decoder with copying mechanism

As the encoder-decoder model with the copying mechanism, we used the model proposed by Gu et al. (2016). In the model, the decoder calculates the probability of generating y_t at time step t by using a mixed probabilistic model of two modes: the generate-mode and the copy-mode:

$$p(y_t|y_{<t}, \boldsymbol{x}) = p_{gen}(y_t|\boldsymbol{s_t}, y_{t-1}, \boldsymbol{c_t}, \boldsymbol{x}) + \\ p_{copy}(y_t|\boldsymbol{s_t}, y_{t-1}, \boldsymbol{c_t}, \boldsymbol{x}), \tag{10}$$

where p_{gen} is the probability calculated by the generate-mode using the same scoring function proposed by Bahdanau et al. (2015) and p_{copy} is the probability that the copy-mode will "copy" the word y_t from the input document if $y_t \in \boldsymbol{x}$. If $y_t \notin \boldsymbol{x}$, then p_{copy} is set to 0. Thus, the model increases the probability that words in the input will be generated. Refer to the original paper by Gu et al., (2016) for more detailed explanations.

5 Experiments and Evaluation

We adopted ROUGE-2 (Lin, 2004) as a metric for the automatic evaluation. Additionally, we carried out an evaluation on a 5-point scale scored by human judges. In this section, we will describe the details of model training, automatic and manual evaluations we conducted.

5.1 Experimental setting and training

The created dataset contained 251,420 pairs. We used 90% of the data for training. We separate the remaining equally for the development and the test set. Thus, we split the dataset into 18 (train):1 (development):1 (test).

As an implementation of SVM and SVR, we used Liblinear (Fan et al., 2008). The linear kernel was used as the kernel function for SVM and

SVR. We tuned the regularization parameter C on the development set.

For the encoder-decoder model, we adopted 256 dimensions for word embedding and hidden layers, setting the batch size to 64. The words that appeared at least twice in the training set were used in training, and other words were replaced by the special token UNK. The end of a sentence was represented by another special token, i.e., EOS. For testing, we used the model which achieves the minimum loss function in the development set. When the encoder-decoder model does not output the EOS token within 20 words in the decoding step, the model outputs the first question in the input text. If there is no question in the input, the first sentence is output.

5.2 Evaluation with ROUGE

In our task setting, the number of sentences in the output was limited to one. There was no length constraint in terms of the number of characters or words. However, we assumed that a better summary would contains more focused content in a shorter output. Therefore, as the evaluation metric, we adopted the ROUGE-2 F-measure in addition to Recall.

Table 5 shows ROUGE-2 scores for a number of methods. Lead method (Lead), Last Question (Last-Q) and Lead Question (Lead-Q) are rule-based methods. The classification-based model (Classification) and regression-based model (Regression) are non-neural machine-learning based methods. Vanilla encoder-decoder (EncDec), encoder-decoder with an attention mechanism (EncDec+Attn) and encoder-decoder with a copying mechanism (CopyNet) are neural-network based methods.

In rule-based extractive methods, the lead method, which simply outputs the first sentence, is known as a strong baseline. However, in question summarization, selecting questions such as Lead Question or Last Question increases the ROUGE score. Lead Question is a strong baseline in particular.

Classification was as good as Lead-Q, because most input texts contained only one to two question sentences; as a result, the two methods mostly output the same results. The encoder-decoder models with an attention and with a copying mechanism achieved a significantly higher ROUGE score than the extractive approaches. Note that the vanilla encoder-decoder model yielded significantly low ROUGE score, because it generated mostly the same question for all input texts. The input sequences in this task were longer than those in machine translation. As Loung et al. (2015) mentioned, encoder-decoders models without an attention do not work well for long sentences. Therefore, the model failed to decode the sequence. On average, outputs of extractive methods are longer than those of abstractive methods. This accounts for the relatively low F-measure and competitive recall obtained with extractive methods.

5.3 Manual evaluation

Since our work is the first attempt to address the task, no other annotated data exists. To make up for this, we adopted manual evaluation in addition to the evaluation using ROUGE scores. The manual evaluation was performed using the "Crowdflower", which is a crowdsoursing service[5].

The evaluators were presented with a question and four summaries from different models: Human, and the best model in each group, Lead-Q, Classification and CopyNet. They were asked to rate each summary on 1-5 scale: very poor(1), poor(2), acceptable(3), good(4) and very good(5). The evaluation criteria were "grammaticality" and "focus", which are based on the criteria used in DUC. We asked the evaluators to give a higher score for the aspect of "focus" if a summary expressed the main focus of the input text. We also asked them to give a high "grammaticality" score to a grammatical summary. To control the quality of the evaluation, we randomly presented clearly ungrammatical and non-focused summaries as test to all evaluators, and excluded the the evaluations by evaluators who failed the test questions. The data for the manual evaluation consists of 100 randomly selected instances from the test set for the automatic evaluation. Each instance was evaluated by 3 evaluators.

The results on "grammaticality" and "focus" are respectively shown in Tables 6 and 7. The tables show the number of times each method on a row was evaluated higher than another method on a column. Evaluations on both criteria showed a trend similar to that of the automatic evaluation: Human achieved the highest score, Lead-Q and Classification were competitive, and CopyNet got

---

[5]https://www.crowdflower.com

Table 6: Human Evaluation-Focus-

	Human	Lead-Q	Classification	CopyNet
Human	-	135	135	103
Lead-Q	69	-	11	72
Classification	70	10	-	68
CopyNet	89	107	103	-

Table 7: Human Evaluation - Grammaticality -

	Human	Lead-Q	Classification	CopyNet
Human	-	85	86	63
Lead-Q	51	-	10	54
Classification	54	10	-	53
CopyNet	69	79	82	-

Table 8: Example outputs from each model.

Question Text
The Simpsons is one of the funniest shows ever . its one of my favorites . do you like it ?
Human : Do you like The Simpsons?
Lead-Q : Do you like it?
Classification : Do you like it?
EncDec+Attn: Do you like UNK?
CopyNet : Do you like The Simpsons?

the better score than Lead-Q and Classification.

CopyNet was judged better than Human in terms of focus in 89 cases, and in terms of grammaticality in 69 cases, because Human sometimes removes specific information. For example, Copy-Net generated "How do you stop the itching after shaving?", while Human summary omits "after shaving". In terms of grammaticality, some Human summaries are not complete sentences such as "The best way to get money?". Therefore, Human was sometimes judged lower than CopyNet.

5.4 Qualitative analysis

In this section, we review the outputs of each model. Table 8 shows examples of each model.

The outputs of Lead-Q and Classification, which are generated by extraction, include the unresolved pronoun "it". This makes the summary not clearly focused. Such cases are often seen in lengthy questions that contain long supplementary explanations followed by a short question. These examples suggest that extractive approaches are intrinsically not suitable for cases where information needs to be picked up from multiple sentences in the input. In contrast to extractive approaches, the output of CopyNet properly resolves this; "it" is resolved by "The Simpsons" even if the model needed to use information across sentences. The EncDec+Attn model faces the difficulty in generating low frequency words such as "The Simpsons"; its output includes the special token UNK. This problem was also reported in other papers on encoder-decoder models (Bahdanau et al., 2015). Adding the copying mechanism effectively solved the problem.

6 Conclusion

We proposed a novel task of summarizing lengthy questions into simple questions that clearly express the focus of the original content. We created a dataset by filtering out inappropriate instances from a dataset provided by a CQA site, and developed extractive/abstractive models. Our results show that abstractive approaches outperform extractive approaches both in automatic and human evaluations. Since all the methods were inferior to the Human method in terms of performance, we believe there is still room for improvement. As a subject for future work, we will extend the approach to cover question summarization tasks that have multiple focuses. We are also interested in how existing analyzers such as coreference resolvers can improve the performance.

Acknowledgment

This work was supported by JST PRESTO (Grant Number JPMJPR1655).

References

Dzmitry Bahdanau, Kyunghyun Cho, and Yoshua Bengio. 2015. Neural machine translation by jointly learning to align and translate. In *Proceedings of ICLR2015*.

Michele Bank, Vibhu O. Mittal, and Michael J. Witbrock. 2010. Headline generation based on statistical translation. In *Proceedings of ACL2010*. pages 318–325.

Debasish Basak, Srimanta Pal, and Dipak Chandra Patranabis. 2007. Support vector regression. *Neural Information Processing-Letters and Reviews* 11(10):203–224.

Ziqiang Cao, Chuwei Luo, Wenjie Li, and Sujian Li. 2017. Joint copying and restricted generation for paraphrase. In *Proceedings of AAAI17*. pages 3152–3158.

Kyunghyun Cho, Bart van Merrienboer, Caglar Gulcehre, Dzmitry Bahdanau, Fethi Bougares, Holger Schwenk, and Yoshua Bengio. 2014. Learning phrase representations using rnn encoder-decoder for statistical machine translation. In *Proceedings of EMNLP2014*. pages 1724–1734.

Trevor Cohn and Mirella Lapata. 2013. An abstractive approach to sentence compression. *ACM Transactions on Intelligent Systems and Technology (TIST)* 4(3):41.

Bonnie Dorr, David Zajic, and Richard Schwartz. 2003. Hedge trimmer: A parse-and-trim approach to headline generation. In *Proceedings of HLT-NAACL03 Text Summarization Workshop*. pages 1–8.

Pablo Ariel Duboue. 2012. Extractive email thread summarization: Can we do better than he said she said? In *Proceedings of INLG2012*. pages 85–89.

Rong-En Fan, Kai-Wei Chang, Cho-Jui Hsieh, Xiang-Rui Wang, and Chih-Jen Lin. 2008. Liblinear: A library for large linear classification. *Journal of Machine Learning Research* .

Jiatao Gu, Zhengdong Lu, Hang Li, and Victor O.K Li. 2016. Incorporating copying mechanism in sequence-to-sequence learning. In *Proceedings of ACL2016*.

Tsutomu Hirao, Hideki Isozaki, Eisaku Maeda, and Yuji Matsumoto. 2002. Extracting important sentences with support vector machines. In *COLING 2002: The 19th International Conference on Computational Linguistics*.

Sepp Hochreiter and Jurgen Schmidhuber. 1997. Long short-term memory. *Neural Computation* 9(8):1735–1780.

Yuta Kikuchi, Graham Neubig, Ryohei Sasano, Hiroya Takamura, and Manabu Okumura. 2016. Controlling output length in neural encoder-decoders. In *Proceedings of EMNLP2016*. pages 1328–1338.

Chen Li, Xian Qian, and Yang Liu. 2013. Using supervised bigram-based ilp for extractive summarization. In *Proceedings of ACL2013*. pages 1004–1013.

Chin-Yew Lin. 2004. Rouge: A package for automatic evaluation of summaries. In *Proceedings of ACL2004 Workshop*. pages 74–81.

H. P. Luhn. 1958. The automatic creation of literature abstracts. *IBM J. Res. Dev.* 2(2):159–165.

Minh-Thang Luong, Hieu Pham, and Christopher D. Manning. 2015. Effective approaches to attention-based neural machine translation. In *Proceedings of EMNLP2015*. pages 1412–1421.

Rada Mihalcea and Paul Tarau. 2004. Textrank: Bridging order into texts. In *Proceedings of EMNLP2004*. pages 404–411.

Tatsuro Oya and Giuseppe Carenini. 2014. Extractive summarization and dialogue act modeling on email threads: An integrated probalistic approach. In *Proceedings of SIGDIAL2014*. pages 133–140.

Tatsuro Oya, Yashar Mehdad, Giuseppe Carenini, and Raymond Ng. 2014. A template-based abstractive meeting summarization: Leveraging summary and source text relationships. In *Proceedings of INLG2014*. pages 45–53.

Maxime Peyrard and Judith Eckale-Kohler. 2016. Optimizing an approximation of rouge- a problem-reduction approach to extractive multi-document summarization. In *Proceedings of ACL2016*. pages 1825–1836.

Alexander M. Rush, Sumit Chopra, and Jason Weston. 2015. A neural attention model for sentence summarization. In *Proceedings of EMNLP2015*. pages 379–389.

Dou Shen, Jian-Tao Sun, Hua Li, Qiang Yang, and Zheng Chen. 2007. Document summarization using conditional random fields. In *IJCAI-07*. pages 2862–2867.

Johan AK Suykens and Joos Vandewalle. 1999. Least squares support vector machine classifiers. *Neural processing letters* 9(3):293–300.

Akihiro Tamura, Hiroya Takamura, and Manabu Okumura. 2005. Classification of multiple-sentence questions. In *Proceedings of IJCNLP-05*. pages 426–437.

Sander Wubben, Yansong Feng, and Mirella Lapata. 2012. Title generation with quasi-synchronous grammar. In *Proceedings of ACL2012*.

David Zajic, Bonnie J Dorr, and Richard Schwartz. 2004. Bbn/umd at duc-2004. In *Proceedings of NAACL-HLT04 Document Understanding Workshop*. pages 112–119.

Concept-Map-Based Multi-Document Summarization using Concept Coreference Resolution and Global Importance Optimization

Tobias Falke, Christian M. Meyer, Iryna Gurevych

Research Training Group AIPHES and UKP Lab
Department of Computer Science, Technische Universität Darmstadt
`https://www.aiphes.tu-darmstadt.de`

Abstract

Concept-map-based multi-document summarization is a variant of traditional summarization that produces structured summaries in the form of concept maps. In this work, we propose a new model[1] for the task that addresses several issues in previous methods. It learns to identify and merge coreferent concepts to reduce redundancy, determines their importance with a strong supervised model and finds an optimal summary concept map via integer linear programming. It is also computationally more efficient than previous methods, allowing us to summarize larger document sets. We evaluate the model on two datasets, finding that it outperforms several approaches from previous work.

1 Introduction

Concept-map-based multi-document summarization (MDS) is a variant of traditional MDS that produces structured summaries in the form of a concept map instead of a coherent text (Falke and Gurevych, 2017a). A *concept map*, introduced by Novak and Gowin (1984), is a labeled graph showing *concepts* as nodes and *relations* between them as edges. As an example, consider a document collection discussing treatments for ADHD. A (very) small concept map would be

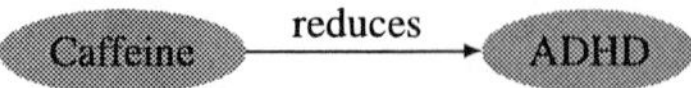

in which *Caffeine* and *ADHD* are concepts, while *reduces* is a relation, forming the *proposition "Caffeine – reduces – ADHD"*.

A summary in this form has interesting applications, as it provides a concise overview of a

document collection, structures it across document boundaries and can be used as a table-of-contents to navigate in the collection. Several studies report successful applications of concept maps in this direction (Carvalho et al., 2001; Briggs et al., 2004; Richardson and Fox, 2005; Villalon, 2012; Valerio et al., 2012; Falke and Gurevych, 2017b).

The task we consider in this work is defined as follows: *Given a set of documents on a certain topic, extract a concept map that represents the most important content on that topic, satisfies a specified size limit and is connected.*

Although work dealing with the automatic extraction of concept maps from text exists (§2), current methods have several limitations. First, most approaches do not attempt to detect coreferences between extracted concepts. For instance, if both *ADHD symptoms* and *symptoms of ADHD* are found, they treat them as separate concepts. In a concept map, such duplicate concepts are immediately visible to a user, waste valuable space and make it harder to look for relations of that concept, as they are spread among the duplicates.

Second, previous work mostly focused on the extraction of concepts and relations, largely ignoring the subsequent selection step necessary to produce a summary of manageable size. Existing studies suggested only a few unsupervised metrics to determine important elements, leaving it unclear whether the task can benefit from more sophisticated supervised approaches. In addition, no method has been suggested to find an optimal summary concept map under the constraints of the size limit and connectedness.

Third, most approaches for concept map extraction and also traditional summarization are typically evaluated on small document sets where the computational complexity of methods is less relevant. We work on a corpus with sets of around 40 documents that should be summarized, which,

---

[1]Source code available at `https://github.com/UKPLab/ijcnlp2017-cmaps`

Proceedings of the The 8th International Joint Conference on Natural Language Processing, pages 801–811,
Taipei, Taiwan, November 27 – December 1, 2017 ©2017 AFNLP

while being a realistic real-world application scenario, is 10 to 15 times larger than traditional DUC^2 and TAC^3 summarization corpora. This poses an additional challenge that requires the methods to scale to these sizes.

In this work, we propose a new model for concept-map-based MDS that overcomes the aforementioned issues. Building upon previous work in textual summarization, coreference resolution and semantic similarity, it learns to identify and merge coreferent concepts, scores them for importance and finds an optimal summary concept map via integer linear programming (ILP). We also present several optimizations that make it possible to apply our model to large document sets. Experiments on two datasets demonstrate the efficacy of the model, which outperforms several methods suggested in previous work.

2 Related Work

Previous approaches to construct concept maps from text, working with either single documents (Zubrinic et al., 2015; Villalon, 2012; Valerio and Leake, 2006; Kowata et al., 2010) or document clusters (Qasim et al., 2013; Zouaq and Nkambou, 2009; Rajaraman and Tan, 2002), all follow a similar pipeline: concept extraction, relation extraction, scoring and concept map construction.

During concept extraction, most approaches apply hand-written patterns to extract labels for concepts from syntactic representations, focusing on noun phrases-like structures. Similar approaches are used to extract relation labels for pairs of concepts. Alternatively, semantic representations have been suggested as a more easily accessible representation compared to syntax (Falke and Gurevych, 2017c; Olney et al., 2011).

Given these extractions, few attempts beyond string matching have been made to identify unique concepts. Valerio and Leake (2006) suggest to consider only certain part-of-speech during string matching, while the earlier approach of Rajaraman and Tan (2002) uses a clustering algorithm based on a vector space model. Our work proposes a more comprehensive approach, leveraging state-of-the-art semantic similarity measures and set partitioning to also detect coreferent concept labels that are paraphrases.

The selection of a summary-worthy subset of all extracted concepts and relations was largely ignored in previous work, as many studies did not have a focus on summarization. However, when dealing with larger document clusters, this step becomes inevitable. Zubrinic et al. (2015) suggest a tf-idf metric on the level of concept labels, Villalon (2012) uses Latent Semantic Analysis and Valerio and Leake (2006) suggest simple concept frequencies. Our model goes a step further and combines these with other features in a supervised model, which works well for textual summarization (Cao et al., 2016; Yang et al., 2017).

For building a summary concept map that is connected, does not exceed the target size and contains as many important concepts as possible, we are only aware of a heuristic approach suggested by Zubrinic et al. (2015). It iteratively removes low-scoring concepts from all extractions until a connected graph of the target size remains. However, it is not guaranteed that the optimal subset is found. Integer Linear Programming (ILP) has been successfully used to solve the knapsack problem that arises in sentence-level extractive summarization (McDonald, 2007). In our task, the knapsack problem is not present, as both the scoring and size restriction are defined on the level of concepts, but the connectedness requirement poses a similar constraint that restricts the subset selection. ILP formulations for such a problem have been proposed for graph-based abstractive summarization (Li et al., 2016; Liu et al., 2015). In our work, we transfer these ideas to concept maps and evaluate their efficacy. This is important, as the methods were originally proposed for different kinds of graphs (event networks and AMR graphs) and introduced to generate abstractive textual summaries, while we use our concept map graphs directly as the final summaries.

3 Model

Given a document set D, topic t and size limit L, our model applies the three stage approach that is illustrated in Figure 1 to create a summary concept map: (1) Concept and Relation Extraction, (2) Concept Graph Construction, (3) Graph Summarization. We describe these steps in the following sections in detail.

3.1 Concept and Relation Extraction

The goal of the first step is to identify spans in the documents that can be used as labels for concepts

---

[2] http://duc.nist.gov/
[3] https://tac.nist.gov/

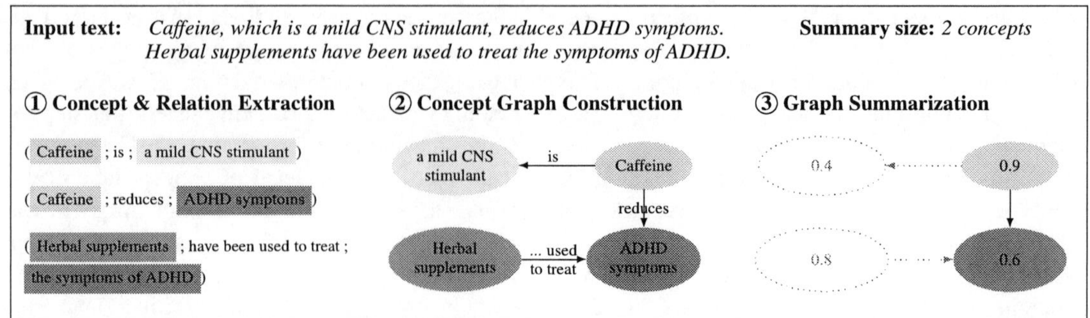

Figure 1: Conceptual illustration of the model: (1) Extracted propositions are (2) connected to a graph based on coreference and (3) the best subgraph, here of target size 2, is selected after scoring concepts.

and relations in the concept map.

Extraction For the extraction, we rely on Open Information Extraction (Banko et al., 2007), an approach that extracts binary *propositions* from text. Given a sentence such as

Caffeine, which is a mild CNS stimulant, reduces ADHD symptoms.

an Open IE system extracts the tuples:

(Caffeine ; is ; a mild CNS stimulant)
(Caffeine ; reduces ; ADHD symptoms)

This representation is particularly useful because it is very similar to propositions in a concept map, requiring only a few postprocessing steps. We use the extracted tuples (m_1, r, m_2), after applying the postprocessing steps discussed below, and use their arguments m_1, m_2 as *concept mentions* and predicates r as *relations*.

Filtering To ensure that the arguments of the extractions are meaningful concept mentions, we filter the candidate set with two simple constraints: First, an argument has to contain at least one noun token, and second, it cannot be longer than ten tokens. This removes overly long arguments that are clauses rather than suitable labels for concepts.

Post-Processing In addition, we apply three rule-based post-processing steps that refine the extractions in order to increase the recall of the candidate sets. First, using off-the-shelf coreference resolution, we try to resolve pronominal anaphora in arguments of the propositions.

Second, if an argument is a conjoining construction, as indicated by *conj*-edges in a dependency parse, we break it down into its conjuncts and in-troduce separate extractions for each of them:

(Caffeine ; works with ; young children and teens)

would be split into two extractions

(Caffeine ; works with ; young children)
(Caffeine ; works with ; teens)

And third, if the second argument starts with a verb, as in the following example,

(Herbal supplements ; have been used to ; treat the symptoms of ADHD)

we move that verb and subsequent prepositions to the predicate. In the example, the predicate is extended to *have been used to treat*, reducing the second argument to *the symptoms of ADHD*.

3.2 Concept Graph Construction

Given the concept mentions extracted in the previous step, several of these mentions may refer to the same concept. While this is obvious if the mentions are identical (e.g. *Caffeine* in the first two extractions of Figure 1), they could also differ slightly (e.g. *ADHD symptoms* and *the symptoms of ADHD*) or be synonyms or paraphrases without any lexical overlap. In this step, we connect all extracted propositions (m_1, r, m_2) to a concept graph by grouping coreferent mentions to a set of unique, non-redundant concepts (see Figure 1). As this special form of concept-specific and cross-document coreference goes beyond the capabilities of off-the-shelf coreference resolution systems, we propose a solution based on pairwise classification and set partitioning.

3.2.1 Pairwise Mention Classification

Given the set M of concept mentions, we want to determine whether a pair $(m_1, m_2) \in M^2$ refers to the same concept or not. We model this as a binary classification problem using a log-linear model

$$P(y = 1 | m_1, m_2, \theta) = \sigma(\theta^T \phi(m_1, m_2))$$

where a positive classification, $y = 1$, means that the mentions are coreferent, $\phi(m_1, m_2)$ are features for a pair of mentions, σ is the sigmoid function and θ are the learned parameters.

As features we use different similarity measures that indicate if both terms have the same meaning. Lexical features are normalized Levenshtein distance and the overlap (Jaccard coefficient) between stemmed content words. To capture similarity on a semantic level, we use cosine similarity between concept embeddings[4] and two measures using word-level similarity based on Latent Semantic Analysis (Deerwester et al., 1990) and WordNet (Resnik, 1995) together with a word alignment method, both implemented in Semilar (Rus et al., 2013). The selection of these features is driven by practical reasons: Since the number of pairs is in $\mathcal{O}(|M|^2)$, the feature set has to be small and restricted to fast-to-compute metrics to make the approach computationally feasible.

3.2.2 Mention Partitioning

The task of grouping mentions to concepts can be seen as finding a partition of M based on the pairwise classifications. However, this is non-trivial, as single predictions might conflict: Both (a, b) and (b, c) could be classified as coreferent, but not (a, c). Formally, the relation of all coreferent pairs $S \subseteq M^2$ has to be an equivalence relation, i.e. reflexive, symmetric and transitive, to represent a consistent partitioning.

For a similar problem, Barzilay and Lapata (2006) propose to use ILP to find a valid partitioning that maximally agrees with the pairwise classifications. Let $x_p \in \{0, 1\}$ indicate the coreference of mentions $p = (m_1, m_2)$ and be $c(p) = P(y = 1 | m_1, m_2)$. Then they optimize the assignments x_p to maximize

$$\sum_{p \in M^2} c(p)\, x_p + (1 - c(p))\, (1 - x_p) \qquad (1)$$

---

[4]Using the sum of vectors for all tokens; 300-dimensional word2vec Google News embeddings (Mikolov et al., 2013).

Algorithm 1 Greedy Local Partitioning Search

Input: pairwise predictions $c(p)$ for $p \in M^2$
Output: coreferent pairs $S \subseteq M^2$

```
 1: function SEARCH(x, y)
 2:     S ← { p | c(p) ≥ 0.5 }
 3:     b ← SCORE(S)
 4:     S_m ← SHUFFLE(TRANSREDUCTION(S))
 5:     for p ∈ S_m do
 6:         S' ← S \ {p}
 7:         if b < SCORE(S') then
 8:             b ← SCORE(S'), S ← S'
 9:     return TRANSCLOSURE(S)
10: function SCORE(S)
11:     S⁺ ← TRANSCLOSURE(S)
12:     return Compute Equation 1 for S⁺
```

---

under the transitivity constraints

$$x_{p_i} \geq x_{p_j} + x_{p_k} - 1 \qquad (2)$$

for all $p_i, p_j, p_k \in M^2$ where $i \neq j \neq k$. Unfortunately, this ILP needs $\mathcal{O}(|M|^2)$ variables and $\mathcal{O}(|M|^3)$ constraints, which makes it difficult to solve for our problem (where $|M|$ is up to 20k and we thus have up to 400 million variables and 8 trillion constraints). As an alternative approach, we use an approximate optimization algorithm.

Algorithm 1 shows our greedy local search algorithm. It creates the transitive closure over all positive classifications as the initial solution and computes the objective function (lines 2-3). This solution is a very aggressive grouping that joins as many mentions as possible, ignoring all negative classifications. The algorithm then tries to iteratively improve this solution by removing one positive classification at a time (line 6) if that improves the objective (lines 7-8). Removals are only tested for pairs in the transitive reduction of the initial solution (lines 4-5), as removing others would not change the partitioning. This approach still runs for several hours on large problem instances due to the expensive calculation of SCORE (lines 11-12), making more complete local searches, using best-first or beam search, impractical.

As a result, we obtain a relation S that partitions M into a set of sets $C = \{C_1, \ldots C_n\}$ where each C_i is a set of mentions representing a concept.

3.2.3 Graph Construction

Using the partitioning, we can now connect the extracted propositions to a graph $G = (C, R)$ in which the nodes are concepts C and an edge with label r exists for every proposition (m_1, r, m_2) between the nodes of the concepts of m_1 and m_2. For each concept C_i, we select one mention $m_l \in C_i$ as its label. We experimentally found that using the most frequent mention, breaking ties by choosing the shortest, is a good heuristic to choose the most generic and representative label.

3.3 Graph Summarization

With the concept graph $G = (C, R)$ built from the documents, we can cast the selection of a summary concept map as a subgraph selection problem:

Given G, find a subgraph $G' = (C', R')$ with $C' \subseteq C$ and $R' \subseteq R$ that maximizes

$$\sum_{C_i \in C'} s(C_i) \tag{3}$$

such that the subgraph is connected and satisfies the size constraint $|C'| \leq L$. With $s(C_i)$, we denote the importance of concept C_i.

3.3.1 Subgraph Selection

The selection of a subgraph that maximizes Equation 3 can be formulated as an ILP. Let x_i be a binary decision variable that represents whether concept C_i is part of the subgraph. Then, the objective can be written as

$$\max \sum_{i=1}^{|C|} x_i \, s(C_i) \tag{4}$$

subject to[5]

$$x_i \in \{0, 1\} \quad \forall i \in C \tag{5}$$

$$\sum_{i=1}^{|C|} x_i \leq L. \tag{6}$$

To ensure that the selected subgraph is connected, we introduce flow variables following previous work (Li et al., 2016; Liu et al., 2015). Let f_{ij} be a non-negative integer variable capturing the flow from concept C_i to C_j. We only introduce flow variables for concept pairs that have a relation in R. The constraints

$$f_{ij} \leq x_i \cdot |C| \quad \forall (i, j) \in R \tag{7}$$

$$f_{ij} \leq x_j \cdot |C| \quad \forall (i, j) \in R \tag{8}$$

$$\sum_i f_{ij} - \sum_k f_{jk} - x_j = 0 \quad \forall j \in C \tag{9}$$

$$f_{ij} \in \mathbb{N} \quad \forall (i, j) \in R \tag{10}$$

---

[5]To simplify the notation, we write $i \in C$ instead of $i \in \{1, \ldots, |C|\}$ and correspondingly for R.

enforce that flow can only move between concepts that are selected (7,8) and a selected concept consumes one unit of flow (9). Further, let $i = 0$ be a virtual root node and e_{0i} a virtual edge from the root to each concept. The additional constraints

$$|C| \cdot e_{0i} - f_{0i} \geq 0 \quad \forall i \in C \tag{11}$$

$$\sum_{i=1}^{|C|} e_{0i} = 1 \tag{12}$$

$$\sum_{i=1}^{|C|} f_{0i} - \sum_{i=1}^{|C|} x_i = 0 \tag{13}$$

$$e_{0i} \in \{0, 1\} \quad \forall i \in C \tag{14}$$

$$f_{0i} \in \mathbb{N}_0 \quad \forall i \in C \tag{15}$$

ensure that only one virtual edge can be active (12), that the virtual node can only send flow over this active edge (11) and that the total amount of flow sent from the root cannot exceed the size of the selected subgraph (13). As a consequence, if n concepts are selected, n units of flow are sent from the root over the edges of the graph and each selected concept consumes one of them. This is only possible if the subgraph is connected.

The above ILP formulation has the advantage that it only requires $\mathcal{O}(|C| + |R|)$ variables and constraints as opposed to $\mathcal{O}(|C|^2)$ with the flow constraints used by Li et al. (2016). For sparse graphs, where $|R| \ll |C|^2$, this leads to much smaller ILPs. We further leverage the fact that G is typically disconnected and solve separate ILPs for each connected component. Only with these measures, the ILP approach can be solved for the real-world problem sizes in our evaluation dataset.

3.3.2 Score Prediction

The subgraph selection introduced above relies on estimates $s(C_i)$ of a concept's importance. These scores are estimated with a linear model

$$s(C_i) = \vartheta^T \psi(C_i, t)$$

where $\psi(C_i, t)$ are features for a concept C_i in a document cluster on topic t. Parameters ϑ are learned with SVM^{rank} (Joachims, 2002). We use a rich set of features that are commonly used in summarization and keyphrase extraction and briefly describe them in the following section:

Frequency Concept frequency and document frequency based on the partitioned mentions. In addition, frequencies re-weighted with background inverse document frequencies from Google N-Grams (Klein and Nelson, 2009).

Position First, average and last position of a concept and the distance between first and last.

Topic Relatedness Relatedness of the concept to the topic, measured as the semantic similarity between the concept label and the document cluster's topic description t. As similarities, we use the measures introduced in Section 3.2.1.

Length Length of shortest, average and longest mention measured in tokens and in characters.

Label Several features describing the concept label, including the number of stopwords, capitalization, part-of-speech and named entities.

Word Categories As suggested in recent work by Yang et al. (2017), dictionary-based features that capture general properties of words such as concreteness, familiarity or imagery, using the MRC Psycholinguistic Database (Coltheart, 1981), the LIWC dictionary and an additional list of concreteness values (Brysbaert et al., 2014).

In addition, we derive several features from the concept's position in the concept graph G:

Centrality Measures Measures such as degree, closeness and betweenness centrality as well as PageRank scores that indicate the centrality of the node C_i in the graph G.

Concept Map HARD and CRD scores suggested by Reichherzer and Leake (2006) and their underlying metrics. They are slight variations or extensions of common graph metrics that were specifically developed to describe concept maps.

Graph Degeneracy Following Tixier et al. (2016) who show that graph degeneracy is helpful to identify keyphrases, we use the graph core number and core rank suggested by them.

All numeric features are discretized into bins, such that the final feature set has only binary features.

3.3.3 Finalization

After predicting scores for every concept and selecting the highest scoring subgraph with the ILP, we use this subgraph as the summary concept map. However, this graph might contain multiple edges between certain concepts. Because this is rare and the number of available relations is low, we use a simple heuristic and select the relation that was

	EDUC	WIKI
Topics	30	38
Documents	40.5	14.6
Tokens	97880	27066
Concepts	25.0	11.3
Relations	25.2	13.8
Compression	0.16%	0.33%

Table 1: Benchmark datasets used in experiments. Values are averages per topic. Compression = tokens in concept map / tokens in documents.

extracted with the highest confidence in the first step. The resulting graph is the final summary.

4 Experimental Setup

4.1 Data

We evaluate our approach using two benchmark datasets and compare the generated concept maps against reference maps. As the first dataset, we use a recently published corpus by Falke and Gurevych (2017a) that provides summary concept maps for document clusters on educational topics. They were manually created using crowdsourcing and expert annotators. As the second dataset, we use a corpus in which the introductions of featured Wikipedia articles are used as summaries for web documents (Zopf et al., 2016). This property allows us to make use of the links to other Wikipedia pages in the summaries as annotations of concepts. In combination with Open Information Extraction, we can therefore automatically derive concepts and relations from the Wikipedia summaries to obtain a second corpus of summary concept maps.

We refer to these datasets as EDUC and WIKI. Table 1 shows their characteristics. Note that in both datasets the summaries are much smaller than the document sets, posing a challenging summarization task. In addition, the document clusters of EDUC are very large, constituting a challenging but real-world evaluation setting regarding computational efficiency. We randomly split both datasets into equally sized training and test sets.

4.2 Evaluation Metrics

As input, our model receives the documents to summarize, the corresponding topic description and the number of concepts in the reference concept map as the size limit. To compare a system-generated concept map with a reference concept map we represent both as sets of propositions P, i.e. a set in which each element is the concatenation of a relation label with its two concept labels. We then calculate the overlap between the set P_S for the system map and the set P_R for the reference map. As the number of relations and thus propositions of the generated map can differ, we report precision, recall and F1-scores.

Our first metric based on **METEOR** (Denkowski and Lavie, 2014) has the advantage that it takes synonyms and paraphrases into account and does not solely rely on lexical matches. For each pair of propositions $p_s \in P_S$ and $p_r \in P_R$ we calculate the match score $meteor(p_s, p_r) \in [0, 1]$. Then, precision and recall per map are computed as:

$$Pr = \frac{1}{|P_S|} \sum_{p \in P_S} max\{meteor(p, p_r) \,|\, p_r \in P_R\}$$

$$Re = \frac{1}{|P_R|} \sum_{p \in P_R} max\{meteor(p, p_s) \,|\, p_s \in P_S\}$$

The F1-score is the equally weighted harmonic mean of precision and recall. Scores per map are macro-averaged over all topics.

As a second metric, we compute **ROUGE** (Lin, 2004), the standard metric for textual sumarization. We concatenate all propositions of a map into a single string, s_S and s_R, and separate propositions with a dot to ensure that no bigrams span across propositions and the metric is therefore order-independent. We run ROUGE 1.5.5[6] with s_S as the peer summary and s_R as a single model summary to compute ROUGE-2.

4.3 Implementation and Training

All source documents are preprocessed with Stanford CoreNLP 3.7.0 (Manning et al., 2014) to obtain tokenization, sentence splitting, part-of-speech tags, named entities, dependency parses and coreference chains. For Open Information Extraction, we use OpenIE-4[7], a system developed at the University of Washington that is currently state-of-the-art according to a recent comparison (Stanovsky and Dagan, 2016). ILPs are solved with the IBM CPLEX optimizer.[8]

The concept coreference model is implemented using the logistic regression model of Weka (Hall

et al., 2009). For EDUC, we trained it on 17,500 pairs of mentions, and for WIKI, on 4,500 pairs of mentions, which were in both cases derived from the reference concept maps of the training part of the respective dataset.

The SVM^{rank} model for importance scoring is trained with Dlib[9]. We use the set of all extracted concepts from all topics in the training set and assign binary labels if these concepts also occur in the reference concept maps. The SVM then learns weights for all features such that the positive instances per topic are ranked higher than the negative instances. We tuned the regularization parameter C of the SVM by testing values from 0.1 to 100 with leave-one-out cross-validation on the training topics. The final models are trained on the full training set with the best parameter. We did this separately for all ablations of our model that produce different training data, obtaining best parameters of $C = 10$ for *coref=lem* on EDUC and all models on WIKI as well as $C = 30$ for *coref=doc* and *our model* on EDUC (see Table 2).

5 Results and Analysis

5.1 Evaluation Results

We compare our model against several previously suggested methods. As unsupervised methods, we include concept selection based on frequency (Valerio and Leake, 2006), denoted as *Valerio 06*, selection with idf-corrected frequencies (Zubrinic et al., 2015), *Zubrinic 15*, and using the popular *PageRank* algorithm (Page et al., 1999). For a fair comparison, we run all methods on the same extracted concepts and relations and with our ILP-based subgraph selection. In addition, we include the baseline method *Falke 17* published along with the EDUC corpus (Falke and Gurevych, 2017a), which includes a supervised importance scoring model based on a binary classifier. To the best of our knowledge, this is all existing work for this task to which we can compare the proposed model.

Table 2 shows METEOR and ROUGE-2 scores for all methods on both datasets. Our model outperforms all three unsupervised approaches significantly on both datasets, demonstrating the superiority of the supervised scoring model. With regard to *Falke 17*, which is supervised to a similar extent, the results are twofold: While our model improves in ROUGE-2, it has a lower METEOR score. We looked into these results in de-

---

[6]Parameter: -n 2 -x -m -c 95 -r 1000 -f A -p 0.5 -t 0 -d -a
[7]https://github.com/knowitall/openie
[8]https://ibm.com/software/commerce/optimization/cplex-optimizer/
[9]http://dlib.net/ml.html

| | EDUC | | | | | | WIKI | | | | | |
| | METEOR | | | ROUGE-2 | | | METEOR | | | ROUGE-2 | | |
Approach	Pr	Re	F1	Pr	Re	F1	Pr	Re	F1	Pr	Re	F1
PageRank	11.78	16.21	†13.61	7.14	11.66	†8.66	13.27	14.13	†13.62	8.35	6.17	‡7.01
Valerio 06	11.89	16.12	†13.65	7.33	12.09	‡8.97	13.44	13.79	‡13.55	8.57	7.16	‡7.61
Zubrinic 15	12.48	16.44	†14.15	7.68	12.08	‡9.25	14.63	14.92	‡14.72	10.50	7.91	‡8.87
Falke 17	15.12	19.49	**17.00**	6.03	17.98	8.91	14.30	23.11	17.46	6.77	23.18	10.20
Our model	15.14	17.34	16.12	9.37	11.93	**10.38**	19.57	18.98	**19.18**	17.00	10.69	**12.91**
- coref=lem	13.93	15.42	†14.57	8.21	8.59	†8.25	18.32	17.24	17.59	13.99	9.53	11.07
- coref=doc	14.14	15.21	†14.54	7.99	6.78	†7.26	16.81	16.63	16.59	13.09	9.16	10.29
- w/o ILP	15.29	17.46	16.26	9.38	11.88	**10.38**	18.22	17.80	17.94	14.73	9.74	11.51
s, ILP*	23.32	27.52	25.16	26.09	23.93	24.74	29.04	26.76	27.73	29.08	18.79	22.54
s, w/o ILP*	18.28	25.15	†21.13	17.52	21.97	†19.34	24.45	24.46	†24.83	24.06	17.39	†19.57

Table 2: Results on test sections of both datasets for our model and previous work. (Improvements of our model are significant compared to approaches marked (for F1) with † ($p \leq 0.01$) or ‡ ($p \leq 0.05$)).[12]

tail and found that the high scores of *Falke 17* are due to heavy overgeneration during relation extraction, introducing many rather meaningless relations into the concept map.[10] Hence, the method only obtains higher scores by sacrificing the quality of the extracted propositions.

To verify this observation, we carried out an additional human evaluation between the two systems, capturing aspects beyond the content-oriented automatic metrics. For each topic, the concept maps generated by both approaches were shown to five crowdworkers on Mechanical Turk and they were asked for their preference with regard to different quality dimensions.[11] Table 3 shows that our concept maps tend to have more meaningful and topic-focused propositions and are especially more grammatical and less redundant.

5.2 Analysis

Concept Coreference To analyze the contribution of our concept coreference detection and partitioning (§3.2.1,§3.2.2), we replaced it with two simpler baselines: merging concepts based on string matches after lemmatization (*coref=lem*), as done in previous work, and using per-document coreference chains detected by CoreNLP and merging them across documents by lemmatized string matching (*coref=doc*). Both alternatives cause a drop in both metrics on EDUC and WIKI, showing that our approach is important for the model's performance. The baselines merge much less mentions than necessary but also tend to lump

Dimension	*Falke 2017*	*Our*
Meaning	44%	56%
Grammaticality	31%	69%
Focus	44%	56%
Non-Redundancy	21%	79%

Table 3: Human preference judgments between concept maps generated on EDUC ($n = 75$).

too many too different mentions together. In contrast, our model can make many more merges based on semantic similarity and at the same time manages to avoid lumping effects by relying on the global partitioning approach.

Subgraph Selection To analyze the effectiveness of the subgraph selection (§3.3.1), we replaced the ILP approach with a greedy heuristic similar to Zubrinic et al. (2015): Given the graph of scored concepts, start with the most important one and select the best neighbor (by score, breaking ties by node degree) until the size limit is reached. While the ILP will always find the optimal solution and hence the best subgraph, this heuristic approach does not have such a guarantee. In fact, it found the optimal subgraph for only 35% of the topics, selecting a subgraph with an on average 0.63% (EDUC) and 1.30% (WIKI) lower objective function score in the other cases.

Row *w/o ILP* in Table 2 shows the effect on the summary concept map. While it is rather small for EDUC, the differences on WIKI are bigger – in line with the observation that the selected subgraphs are less optimal. A problem for this analysis are errors in the preceding scoring step: The optimal

---

[10]Note that METEOR scores can be improved by incorrect relations if they are between a correct pair of concepts, leading to a partial match of the proposition.

[11]To control for the influence of graph layouting quality, we showed the concept maps as simple lists of propositions.

[12]Approximate randomization test with $N = 10000$.

Method	Var.	Const.	Time (s)
(Li et al., 2016)	37M	75M	2670.61
by component	26M	52M	999.25
Our ILP	22k	31k	7.31
by component	18k	26k	5.61

Table 4: Comparison of average ILP size and runtime per topic for subgraph selection on EDUC.

Step	EDUC		WIKI	
	Count	Recall	Count	Recall
Mentions	8630	73.87	2549	88.93
Concepts	4022	60.27	1315	82.38
Subgraph	25	16.53	11	30.71

Table 5: Average number of concepts and recall per topic at different steps in our model.

subgraph according to the estimated scores might not be the best with regard to the gold standard, explaining the slightly higher METEOR scores on EDUC without the ILP. To control for this effect, we also tested the selection using gold scores $s^*(C_i)$ for all concepts C_i, demonstrating that the optimal subgraphs selected by the ILP are clearly superior (last two rows in Table 2).

Score Prediction The contribution of our supervised scoring model based on ranking SVMs (§3.3.2) can be seen in Table 2 when comparing it to the unsupervised approaches *PageRank*, *Valerio 06* and *Zubrinic 15*. Note that all models use the same concepts and relations as input and the same ILP-based subgraph selection. Our model clearly outperforms all of them. Looking into the learned weights for our set of features, we observed that the most helpful features are frequencies, in particular document frequency and idf-weighted concept frequency, and topic relatedness as well as page rank. To identify unimportant concepts (i.e. assigning low scores), the model makes use of concreteness values and the label's length.

Runtime As mentioned earlier, the size of the document sets in EDUC resembles an interesting real-world setting that required us to pay special attention to complexity. Table 4 compares our subgraph selection ILP with the ILP formulation by Li et al. (2016). For the extracted graphs, with on average 4022 nodes and 5613 edges between them, our formulation leads to ILPs that are orders of magnitude smaller and can be solved in a fraction of the time.[13] For both formulations, solving separate ILPs for each connected component in the graph further improves the runtime.

Error Analysis Table 5 shows the number of concepts and their recall at different steps in our model, which is a good indicator of bottlenecks.

The recall of mentions shows that performance is already lost during extraction, suggesting that better approaches would be beneficial. We observed that the problem is mainly the identification of correct spans rather than missing some concepts completely. A custom extraction model instead of relying on Open IE could resolve this.

With regard to concept coreference, we found that even more coreferent mentions could be grouped together. However, while the current model only accidentally merged mentions of different gold concepts in two cases across all topics, a stronger grouping could introduce more of these errors. Please also note that the drop in recall in Table 5 is due to exact string matching of the recall metric used here, missing concepts for which the selected cluster label is not exactly the gold concept. As the METEOR and ROUGE evaluations show, this is not a problem for the final result.

Finally, Table 5 reveals that one of the main bottlenecks is to determine the important concepts. On both datasets, but especially on the bigger document sets of EDUC, a substantial amount of recall is lost during this challenging step.

6 Conclusion

We proposed a new model for concept-map-based MDS and showed that it outperforms several methods from previous work. All of our contributions, including concept coreference resolution, the supervised scoring model and the global optimization approach contribute to its efficacy. In addition, it is able to scale to large document sets, which makes it much faster than previous methods in realistic scenarios with such documents sets.

Acknowledgments

This work has been supported by the German Research Foundation as part of the Research Training Group "Adaptive Preparation of Information from Heterogeneous Sources" (AIPHES) under grant No. GRK 1994/1.

---

[13]Times for running CPLEX multi-threaded on 24 cores. Direct comparison with the same data on the same machine.

References

Michele Banko, Michael J. Cafarella, Stephen Soderland, Matt Broadhead, and Oren Etzioni. 2007. Open Information Extraction from the Web. In *Proceedings of the 20th International Joint Conference on Artifical Intelligence*, pages 2670–2676, Hyderabad, India.

Regina Barzilay and Mirella Lapata. 2006. Aggregation via set partitioning for natural language generation. In *Proceedings of the Human Language Technology Conference of the NAACL*, pages 359–366, New York, NY, USA.

Geoffrey Briggs, David A. Shamma, Alberto J. Cañas, Roger Carff, Jeffrey Scargle, and Joseph D. Novak. 2004. Concept Maps Applied to Mars Exploration Public Outreach. In *Concept Maps: Theory, Methodology, Technology. Proceedings of the First International Conference on Concept Mapping*, pages 109–116, Pamplona, Spain.

Marc Brysbaert, Amy Beth Warriner, and Victor Kuperman. 2014. Concreteness ratings for 40 thousand generally known English word lemmas. *Behavior Research Methods*, 46(3):904–911.

Ziqiang Cao, Furu Wei, Li Dong, Sujian Li, and Ming Zhou. 2016. Ranking with Recursive Neural Networks and Its Application to Multi-document Summarization. In *Proceedings of the Thirtieth AAAI Conference on Artificial Intelligence*, pages 2153–2159, Phoenix, AZ, USA.

Marco Carvalho, Rattikorn Hewett, and Alberto J. Cañas. 2001. Enhancing Web Searches from Concept Map-based Knowledge Models. In *Proceedings of the 5th World Multi-Conference on Systemics, Cybernetics and Informatics*, pages 69–73, Orlando, FL, USA.

Max Coltheart. 1981. The MRC psycholinguistic database. *The Quarterly Journal of Experimental Psychology Section A*, 33(4):497–505.

Scott Deerwester, Susan T. Dumais, George W. Furnas, Thomas K. Landauer, and Richard Harshman. 1990. Indexing by latent semantic analysis. *Journal of the American Society for Information Science*, 41(6):391–407.

Michael Denkowski and Alon Lavie. 2014. Meteor Universal: Language Specific Translation Evaluation for Any Target Language. In *Proceedings of the Ninth Workshop on Statistical Machine Translation*, pages 376–380, Baltimore, MD, USA.

Tobias Falke and Iryna Gurevych. 2017a. Bringing Structure into Summaries: Crowdsourcing a Benchmark Corpus of Concept Maps. In *Proceedings of the 2017 Conference on Empirical Methods in Natural Language Processing*, pages 2969–2979, Copenhagen, Denmark.

Tobias Falke and Iryna Gurevych. 2017b. GraphDocExplore: A Framework for the Experimental Comparison of Graph-based Document Exploration Techniques. In *Proceedings of the 2017 Conference on Empirical Methods in Natural Language Processing: System Demonstrations*, pages 19–24, Copenhagen, Denmark.

Tobias Falke and Iryna Gurevych. 2017c. Utilizing Automatic Predicate-Argument Analysis for Concept Map Mining. In *Proceedings of the 12th International Conference on Computational Semantics (IWCS)*, Montpellier, France.

Mark Hall, Eibe Frank, Geoffrey Holmes, Bernhard Pfahringer, Peter Reutemann, and Ian H. Witten. 2009. The WEKA Data Mining Software: An Update. *SIGKDD Explorations*, 11(1):10–18.

Thorsten Joachims. 2002. Optimizing search engines using clickthrough data. In *Proceedings of the Eighth ACM SIGKDD International Conference on Knowledge Discovery and Data Mining*, pages 133–142, Edmonton, Canada.

Martin Klein and Michael L. Nelson. 2009. Correlation of Term Count and Document Frequency for Google N-Grams. In *Advances in Information Retrieval*, volume 5478 of *Lecture Notes in Computer Science*, pages 620–627. Springer, Berlin, Heidelberg.

Juliana H. Kowata, Davidson Cury, and Maria Claudia Silva Boeres. 2010. Concept Maps Core Elements Candidates Recognition from Text. In *Concept Maps: Making Learning Meaningful. Proceedings of the 4th International Conference on Concept Mapping*, pages 120–127, Vina del Mar, Chile.

Wei Li, Lei He, and Hai Zhuge. 2016. Abstractive News Summarization based on Event Semantic Link Network. In *Proceedings of the 26th International Conference on Computational Linguistics (COLING)*, pages 236–246, Osaka, Japan.

Chin-Yew Lin. 2004. ROUGE: A Package for Automatic Evaluation of Summaries. In *Text Summarization Branches Out: Proceedings of the ACL-04 Workshop*, pages 74–81, Barcelona, Spain.

Fei Liu, Jeffrey Flanigan, Sam Thomson, Norman Sadeh, and Noah A. Smith. 2015. Toward Abstractive Summarization Using Semantic Representations. In *Proceedings of the 2015 Conference of the North American Chapter of the Association for Computational Linguistics: Human Language Technologies*, pages 1077–1086, Denver, Colorado.

Christopher D. Manning, Mihai Surdeanu, John Bauer, Jenny Finkel, Steven J. Bethard, and David McClosky. 2014. The Stanford CoreNLP Natural Language Processing Toolkit. In *Proceedings of the 52nd Annual Meeting of the Association for Computational Linguistics*, pages 55–60, Baltimore, MD, USA.

Ryan McDonald. 2007. A Study of Global Inference Algorithms in Multi-Document Summarization. In *Proceedings of the 29th European conference on IR research*, pages 557–564, Rome, Italy.

Tomas Mikolov, Ilya Sutskever, Kai Chen, Greg S. Corrado, and Jeffrey Dean. 2013. Distributed Representations of Words and Phrases and their Compositionality. In *Advances in Neural Information Processing Systems 26*, pages 3111–3119, Lake Tahoe, NV, USA.

Joseph D. Novak and D. Bob Gowin. 1984. *Learning How to Learn*. Cambridge University Press, Cambridge.

Andrew Olney, Whitney Cade, and Claire Williams. 2011. Generating Concept Map Exercises from Textbooks. In *Proceedings of the 6th Workshop on Innovative Use of NLP for Building Educational Applications*, pages 111–119, Portland, OR, USA.

Lawrence Page, Sergey Brin, Rajeev Motwani, and Terry Winograd. 1999. The PageRank Citation Ranking: Bringing Order to the Web: Technical Report.

Iqbal Qasim, Jin-Woo Jeong, Jee-Uk Heu, and Dong-Ho Lee. 2013. Concept map construction from text documents using affinity propagation. *Journal of Information Science*, 39(6):719–736.

Kanagasabai Rajaraman and Ah-Hwee Tan. 2002. Knowledge discovery from texts: A Concept Frame Graph Approach. In *Proceedings of the Eleventh International Conference on Information and Knowledge Management*, pages 669–671, McLean, VA, USA.

Thomas Reichherzer and David Leake. 2006. Understanding the Role of Structure in Concept Maps. In *Proceedings of the Twenty-Eighth Annual Conference of the Cognitive Science Society*, pages 2004–2009, Vancouver, Canada.

Philip Resnik. 1995. Using Information Content to Evaluate Semantic Similarity in a Taxonomy. In *Proceedings of the 14th International Joint Conference on Artificial Intelligence*, pages 448–453, Montreal, Canada.

Ryan Richardson and Edward A. Fox. 2005. Using concept maps as a cross-language resource discovery tool for large documents in digital libraries. In *Proceedings of the 5th ACM/IEEE-CS Joint Conference on Digital Libraries*, page 415, Denver, CO, USA.

Vasile Rus, Mihai Lintean, Rajendra Banjade, Nobal Niraula, and Dan Stefanescu. 2013. SEMILAR: The Semantic Similarity Toolkit. In *Proceedings of the 51st Annual Meeting of the Association for Computational Linguistics*, pages 163–168, Sofia, Bulgaria.

Gabriel Stanovsky and Ido Dagan. 2016. Creating a Large Benchmark for Open Information Extraction. In *Proceedings of the 2016 Conference on Empirical Methods in Natural Language Processing*, pages 2300–2305, Austin, TX, USA.

Antoine Tixier, Fragkiskos Malliaros, and Michaelis Vazirgiannis. 2016. A Graph Degeneracy-based Approach to Keyword Extraction. In *Proceedings of the 2016 Conference on Empirical Methods in Natural Language Processing*, pages 1860–1870, Austin, TX, USA.

Alejandro Valerio and David B. Leake. 2006. Jump-Starting Concept Map Construction with Knowledge Extracted from Documents. In *Proceedings of the 2nd International Conference on Concept Mapping*, pages 296–303, San José, Costa Rica.

Alejandro Valerio, David B. Leake, and Alberto J. Cañas. 2012. Using Automatically Generated Concept Maps for Document Understanding: A Human Subjects Experiment. In *Proceedings of the 5th International Conference on Concept Mapping*, pages 438–445, Valetta, Malta.

Jorge J. Villalon. 2012. *Automated Generation of Concept Maps to Support Writing*. PhD Thesis, University of Sydney, Australia.

Yinfei Yang, Forrest Bao, and Ani Nenkova. 2017. Detecting (Un)Important Content for Single-Document News Summarization. In *Proceedings of the 15th Conference of the European Chapter of the Association for Computational Linguistics*, pages 707–712, Valencia, Spain.

Markus Zopf, Maxime Peyrard, and Judith Eckle-Kohler. 2016. The Next Step for Multi-Document Summarization: A Heterogeneous Multi-Genre Corpus Built with a Novel Construction Approach. In *Proceedings of the 26th International Conference on Computational Linguistics (COLING)*, pages 1535–1545, Osaka, Japan.

Amal Zouaq and Roger Nkambou. 2009. Evaluating the Generation of Domain Ontologies in the Knowledge Puzzle Project. *IEEE Transactions on Knowledge and Data Engineering*, 21(11):1559–1572.

Krunoslav Zubrinic, Ines Obradovic, and Tomo Sjekavica. 2015. Implementation of method for generating concept map from unstructured text in the Croatian language. In *23rd International Conference on Software, Telecommunications and Computer Networks (SoftCOM)*, pages 220–223, Split, Croatia.

Abstractive Multi-document Summarization by Partial Tree Extraction, Recombination and Linearization

Litton J Kurisinkel
IIIT-H, Hyderabad
`litton.jKurisinkel@research.iiit.ac.in`

Yue Zhang
SUTD, Singapore
`yue_zhang@sutd.edu.sg`

Vasudeva Varma
IIIT-H, Hyderabad
`vv@iiit.ac.in`

Abstract

Existing work for abstractive multi-document summarization utilise existing phrase structures directly extracted from input documents to generate summary sentences. These methods can suffer from lack of consistence and coherence in merging phrases. We introduce a novel approach for abstractive multi-document summarization through partial dependency tree extraction, recombination and linearization. The method entrusts the summarizer to generate its own topically coherent sequential structures from scratch for effective communication. Results on TAC 2011, DUC- 2004 and 2005 show that our system gives competitive results compared with state-of-the-art abstractive summarization approaches in the literature. We also achieve competitive results in linguistic quality assessed by human evaluators.

1 Introduction

Multi-document summarization generates a textual summary from a corpus of documents dealing with a set of related topics. An optimum generated summary should encompass the most relevant and topically diverse content, which can represent the input corpus in stipulated summary space. Extractive multi-document summarization approaches pick out a subset of sentences to constitute the summary, which can be noisy and incoherent, as all the portions of a sentence may not be relevant for summary generation (Lin and Bilmes, 2011).

An abstractive multi-document summarizer, in contrast, infers the most relevant information and generates summary sentences exhibiting coherence and fluency. There has been relatively little existing work on abstractive multi-document summarization. Bing et al. (2015) merge phrases that are extracted from input documents into a coherent summary. Banerjee et al. (2015) utilize multi-sentence compression for summarization. Both of the above approaches rely on sequential arrangement of phrasal or subsentential structures existing in the input corpus to generate summary. However, an ideal abstractive multi-document summarizer should enjoy the freedom to exhibit its own writing style and to generate the sentences from scratch.

We build a model to this end by leveraging syntactic dependencies. Input for our model is the set of syntactic dependency trees obtained by parsing sentences in the corpus to be summarized. Relevant and noise pruned partial tree structures are extracted from the set of dependency trees and different subsets of maximally relevant partial dependency structures are identified. Partial trees in different subsets are linearized to generate individual summary sentences. In this work, we utilize transition-based syntactic linearization approach proposed by Puduppully et al. (2016) to linearize a combination of partial trees and to generate a noise free summary sentence. The combinability of a set of partial trees to form a full dependency tree of a valid sentence is estimated using a generative model of syntactic dependency trees (Zhang et al., 2016). As a result, the model is allowed to exhibit its own learnt writing style while generating summary sentences.

The summaries generated by our system are evaluated on the DUC 2004, DUC 2007 and TAC 2011 muti-document summarization data-sets. In addition, we relied on human evaluation to evaluate factual accuracy and linguistic quality of generated summary sentences. To our knowledge this is the first work on multi-document abstrac-

Proceedings of the The 8th International Joint Conference on Natural Language Processing, pages 812–821,
Taipei, Taiwan, November 27 – December 1, 2017 ©2017 AFNLP

tive summarization with syntactic dependency trees, which entrust the summarization model to generate summary sentences without exploiting any kind of subsentential or phrasal sequential structures originally present in the input corpus. Our code is released at `https://bitbucket.org/litton_kurisinkel/tree_sum`

2 Related Work

Text summarization can be achieved using extractive (Takamura and Okumura, 2009; Lin and Bilmes, 2011; Wang et al., 2008) and abstractive methods (Bing et al., 2015; Li, 2015). Extractive summarization has the advantage of output fluency due to direct use of human-written texts. However, extractive summarization cannot ensure a noise free and coherent summary. It can also result in a wrong inference to the reader due to out of context sentence usage. In contrast, abstractive summarization techniques can generate a noise-free summary out of most relevant information in the input corpus.

A subset of previous extractive summarization approaches utilized parsed sentence structures to execute noise pruning while extracting content for summary (Morita et al., 2013; Berg-Kirkpatrick et al., 2011). As a first step towards abstracting content for summary generation, sentence compression techniques were introduced (Lin, 2003; Zajic et al., 2006; Martins and Smith, 2009; Woodsend and Lapata, 2010; Almeida and Martins, 2013), but these techniques can merely prune noise, and cannot combine related facts from different sentences to generate new ones. (Banerjee et al., 2015) suggests a better way of doing sentence compression without harming linguistic quality.

Recent work attempts to solve the problem of abstractive multi-document summarization (Bing et al., 2015; Li, 2015), claiming that the method has the advantage of generating new sentences. Bing et al. (2015) extracts relevant noun phrases and verb phrases and recombines them to generate new sentences while Li (2015) system make use of semantic link network on basic semantic units (BSUs) to generate summary. Neither of these methods employ a learnt model to generate summary sentences. Instead, they make use sequential structures in the source text itself to construct the summary sentences. Cheng and Lapata (2016) propose a fully data driven approach using neu-

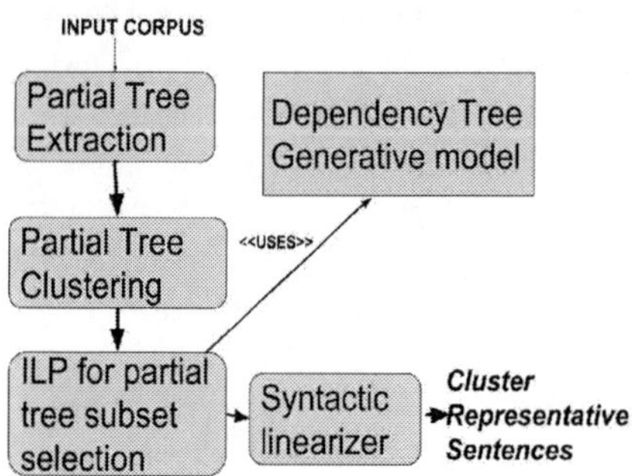

Figure 1: Overall approach

ral network for single document summarization by extracting words. They have treated highlighted text in news articles consisting of very short bulleted lines on the web as summary of the corresponding article.

A major challenge of using a fully data driven approach for multi-document abstractive summarization using neural network is the expensive task of creating dataset which can be used to jointly model extraction of relevant content and generation good quality summary sentences. But multi-document abstractive summarization becomes an achievable task, by disintegrating the extraction of knowledge granules from the input corpus and using a separate language generation model trained in a sophisticated dataset which can take a subset of extracted knowledge granules and generate a summary sentence of high linguistic quality. To this end, we leverage partial tree linearization (Zhang, 2013) synthesizing summaries from extracted treelets.

3 Approach

The overall approach (Figure 1) for abstractive multi-document summarization detailed in the current work starts with extracting the most relevant set of partial trees of varying sizes from the set of all syntactic dependency trees in the corpus using maximum density sub-graph cut algorithm (Su et al., 2008). In parallel, generative model for syntactic dependency trees is trained (Zhang et al., 2016) so that it can be leveraged for estimating the combinability of a set of partial trees for constructing a whole or part of a full dependency tree of a valid sentence during summary generation. Also, the transition based syntactic linearization model Puduppully et al. (2016) is trained using a dataset, consisting of dependency trees of sentences in Penn-tree bank and corresponding sentence.

The set of extracted partial dependency trees are clustered to ensure topical diversity. We identify a subset of partial trees from each cluster, which can be linearized to a single sentence which represents the cluster in the final summary. Integer linear programming is used for locating the most accurate subset of partial trees out of which representative sentence can be generated.

The objective function consists of linear components for maximising *total relevance* and *total combinability* of the subset of partial trees selected. *total combinability* is measured using the generative model Zhang et al. (2016). Here we try to jointly model the human summarizers method of collecting relevant knowledge granules and deciding the combinable set of information. Cluster representative sentence are generated using the linearization model of Puduppully et al. (2016) from the subset of partial trees identified earlier. The following sections explain how the system achieves each one of the tasks listed above in detail.

3.1 Extracting Relevant Partial Trees

For each dependency tree in the input corpus, there is a subtree rooted at every node. Each subtree do not necessarily contain extractable information to generate a summary. The method used to create a noise pruned subset of subtrees containing cognizable information from the set of all subtrees in the corpus can be split into two steps.

- Identify the roots of valid subtrees containing cognizable information in all the syntactic dependency trees in the input corpus.

- Prune the identified subtrees so that it contains nodes relevant for generating summary.

3.1.1 Identify Subtree Roots

The level of granularity at which syntactic elements chosen to generate summary sentence considerably decides factual accuracy of a generated sentence. As extracted set of subtrees are basic building units for summary sentence generation, the structure of subtrees extracted should be suitable for generating factually correct summary sentences with respect to the corpus to be summarized. We observe that a node containing *subject*

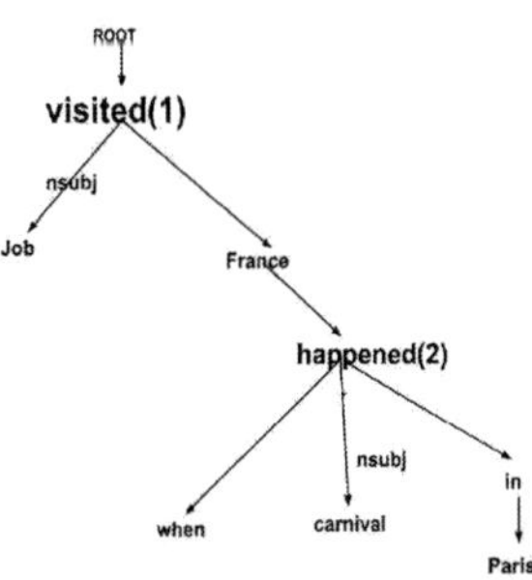

Figure 2: Marking relevant subtree roots

relationship with its child node is a valid candidate. Consequently any node in a dependency tree sharing dependency relations such as *nsubj, csubj, nsubjpass* or *xsubj* with any of its child node is treated as the root node of a subtree which contains extractable and cognizable information. In Figure 2, for example, subtrees rooted at words *visited* and *happened* are valid subtrees to contribute for summary generation as per the linguistic criteria discussed above.

3.1.2 Pruning Subtrees

Identified subtrees are dissected out from their original dependency trees after pruning away their noisy portions which are irrelevant for summary generation. Su et al. (2008) introduced a dynamic programming approach to find a length-constrained maximum-density subtree containing the root r, from a tree rooted at r for which weight and length is preset for all edges. The density of a tree T is defined as follows.

$$density = \frac{\sum_{e \epsilon E} W(e)}{\sum_{e \epsilon E} Len(e)} \quad (1)$$

where E is the set of all edges in T, $W(e)$ is the weight of edge e and $Len(e)$ is the length of edge e. The constraint on length implies that total length of all edges in the resultant maximum density subtree should be between lower bound L and upper bound U which are taken arguments by the algorithm. We leverage multi density subtree extraction algorithm for dissecting out a noise pruned subtree from an identified valid subtree in a dependency tree after setting values for edge weights, edge lengths, L and U.

The weight of an edge in a syntactic dependency in the input corpus should represent its topical relevance for summary generation. Consequently the weight depends on the frequency of *bigram* constituted by words on either side of the dependency edge(D_{bigram}). We set the weight of edge e as,

$$W(e) = \frac{\log(1 + fd_{bigram})}{depth(e)^2}, \qquad (2)$$

where fd_{bigram} is the frequency of the D_{bigram} of e in the corpus and *depth(e)* is the depth of dependent node of e in the tree. Summary should prefer general information over context specific information. The specificity of the information contained increases with depth in dependency tree and the denominator term in Equation 2 penalizes deeper edges.

The length of the edge is set as the size of the word in the dependent node in bytes so that length of all edges in the tree equals the total size of all words in the tree. Length constraint U is the total length of all edges in the tree and L is calculated as follows

$$L = \alpha * \tanh(\beta * twe - \sigma) * TL,$$

where *twe* is the total weight of all edges in the subtree, TL is the total length of all edges in the subtree and σ, α and β are constants optimized empirically. σ sets the universal upper bound for all subtrees minimum length while α and β set the slope and position of tanh curve. The value of L ensures that subtrees containing more relevant information are pruned lesser. We enforce a rule to retain the tree nodes to maintain grammaticality while pruning. If the grammatical relation pointing to a node from its parent is nsubj, csubj, nsubjpass, xsubj, aux, xcomp, pobj, acomp, dobj, case, det, poss, possessive, auxpass, ccomp, neg, expl, cop, prt, mwe, pcomp, iobj, number, quantmod, predet, dep or mark, then the node cannot be removed without also removing its parent to maintain grammatical and factual correctness.

For the rest of this paper, we refer to a noise-pruned subtree extracted out of a dependency tree as a *partial tree*. The partial trees pruned out of subtrees sharing anscestor-descendant relationship may contain overlapping information (eg: subtrees rooted at 'visited' and 'happened' in Figure 2). So ancestor-descendant relationship between corresponding partial trees is recorded to avoid redundant information during summary sentence generation.

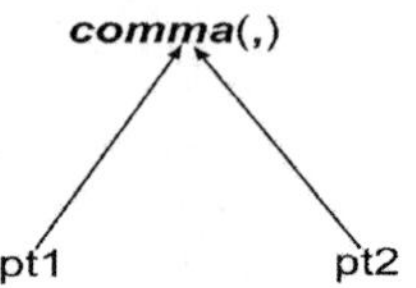

Figure 3: Combine(pt_1, pt_2)

3.2 Estimation of Combinability of Partial trees using Generative Model of Dependency Trees

During the final stage of summary sentence generation, each of the summary sentence is generated from a precisely identified subset of relevant partial trees. To arrive at such a precise subset, along with information regarding topical relevance, due consideration should be given to the combinability of partial trees in the subset to form a full dependency tree of a valid sentence w.r.t to the syntactic and semantic information contained in them. As a primitive measure upon which total combinability of a set of partial trees can be built upon, we estimate the combinability of any two partial trees to form whole or a part of a valid dependency tree as follows

$$DepTree \rightarrow Combine(pt_1, pt_2) \qquad (3)$$

$$C(pt_1, pt_2) \rightarrow P_{depgen}(DepTree), \qquad (4)$$

where $Combine(pt_1, pt_2)$ combines two partial trees pt_1 and pt_2 as represented in Figure 3 by adding a dummy root containing ',' with 'comma' as the dependency relation of edges and pt_1 comes before pt_2 in breadth first order. $C(pt_1, pt_2)$ is the *Combinability* of any two partial trees and P_{depgen} represents a generative distribution of syntactic dependency trees trained with a large set of dependency trees. $Combine(pt_1, pt_2)$ need not exactly represent a substep in the final process of combination and linearization of a set of selected partial trees to generate a summary sentence. But $P_{depgen}(DepTree)$ acts as an indicative measure on how much pt_1 and pt_2 can together participate in the construction of a full-dependency tree of a valid sentence with respect to the syntactic and semantic information contained in them.

3.2.1 Learning P_{depgen}

Zhang et al. (2016) introduced Tree Long Short-

Term Memory (TreeLSTM), a neural network model based on LSTM, which is designed to predict a tree rather than a linear sequence. They define probability of a sentence as the generation probability of its dependency tree. Under the assumption that each word w in a dependency tree is only conditioned on its dependency path, the probability of a sentence S given its dependency tree T is:

$$P(S|T) = \prod_{w \in BFS(T) \backslash ROOT} P(w|D(w)) \quad (5)$$

where D(w) is the dependency path of w and how dependency path for each node is identified is detailed in the paper Zhang et al. (2016) and each word w is visited according to its breadth-first search order (BFS(T)). $P(S|T)$ can be restated as a generative probability $P_{depgen}(T')$ where T' is a restricted syntactic dependency tree structure in which, for all nodes, left and right dependants and breadth first order of its children are fixed. As the above mentioned structural restrictions can be fixed in parameter for partial trees for *Combine* in Equation 3, we can directly use TreeLSTM network to estimate P_{depgen} in Equation 4.

The sentence dataset shared by Zhang et al. (2016) is parsed using Standford parser for training a TreeLSTM network. The negative log probability values produced by the network is normalized for partial tree pairs in the corpus.

3.3 Syntactic Linearization

We make use of the syntactic linearization model proposed by Puduppully et al. (2016) to linearize the input set of partial trees. Puduppully et al. (2016) and Liu et al. (2015) propose a transition-based word ordering model, which takes a bag of words, together with optional POS and dependency arcs on a subset of input words, yields a sentence together with its dependency parse tree that conforms to input syntactic constraints (Zhang, 2013). The system is flexible with respect to input constraints, performing abstract word ordering when no constraints are given, but gives increasingly confined outputs when more POS and dependency relations are specified. We retrain their model[1] using autoparsed data obtained using Stanford Dependency Parser.

---

[1] https://github.com/SUTDNLP/ZGen

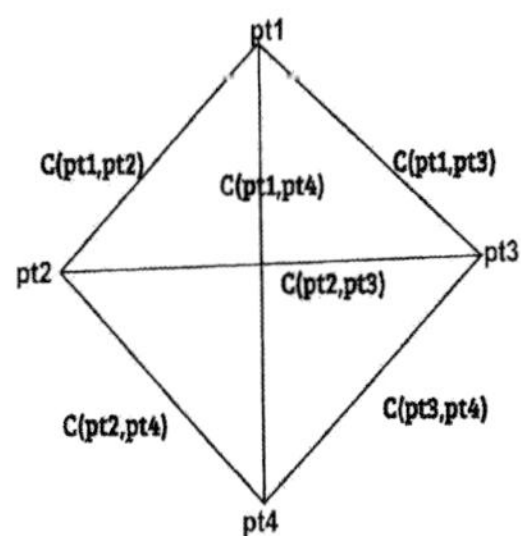

Figure 4: Cluster graph of partial trees

3.4 Clustering for Topical Diversity

To ensure topical diversity we apply K-means clustering in the set of partial trees with an aim of generating a sentence from each of the cluster as a topical representative of the respective cluster. Cosine similarity between D_{bigram} frequency vectors of partial trees is treated as the similarity metric during clustering. Number of clusters (K) is decided using the relation,

$$K = \lfloor q * ShannonEnt \rfloor \quad (6)$$

where *ShannonEnt* is the Shannon entropy of unigram distribution of the corpus and q is a constant.

3.5 Generating Cluster Representative Sentence

Our system generates a single sentence from each of the partial tree clusters identified as described in section 3.4 to represent the cluster in final summary. Here we search for a subset of partial trees from each cluster which maximise the *total relevance* and *total combinability* of the partial trees in the selected subset. Relevance of a partial tree is defined as the total weight of all dependency edges calculated using the Equation 2.

A data structure which searchably organizes the relevance and combination probabilities of partial trees belonging to a cluster is essential for formulating the partial tree subset selection as an integer linear programming problem. For this purpose we visualize the entire partial tree information organized in a *cluster graph (CG)* as shown in Figure 4 in which *nodes* represent partial trees, and *edge weights* represent the combination probability of partial trees represented by the edge nodes calculated using the Equation 4. An *edge exists* between two nodes if the partial trees at the nodes contain mention about same named entity.

From cluster graph we try to extract a *connected subgraph (SG)* which maximizes the objective function which takes a binary indicator vector representing a sub-graph of cluster graph as argument.

$$F(x_1, \ldots, x_n, e_{1,1}, \ldots, e_{n-1,n}) \rightarrow \sum_{i \epsilon Nodes} R(x_i) * x_i + \lambda * \sum_{\{i,j\} \epsilon Edges} W(\{i,j\}) * e_{ij} \qquad (7)$$

subject to constraints,

$$x_i + x_j - 2 * e_{ij} >= 0 \rightarrow C_1$$

$$x_i + x_j - 2 * e_{ij} <= 1 \rightarrow C_2$$

$$e_{i,j} <= I(x_i, x_j) \rightarrow C_3$$

$$\sum_i x_i * size(i) <= MaxLen \rightarrow C_4$$

$$x_i + ancestor(i) < 1 \rightarrow C_5$$

where λ is a constant, $R(i)$ is the relevance of partial tree at node i, $W(\{i,j\})$ is the weight of the edge $\{i,j\}$ in CG, *Nodes* is the set of all nodes in CG and *Edges* is the set of all edges in CG.

$$x_i = \begin{cases} 1 & \text{if node i is present in input SG} \\ 0 & \text{otherwise} \end{cases}$$

$$e_{ij} = \begin{cases} 1 & \text{if edge } \{i,j\} \text{ is present in input SG} \\ 0 & \text{otherwise} \end{cases}$$

$$I(x_i, x_j) = \begin{cases} 1 & \text{if edge } \{i,j\} \text{ is present in CG} \\ 0 & \text{otherwise} \end{cases}$$

ancestor(i) indicator variable that represents a partial tree that is extracted from a ancestor subtree of the subtree from which i is extracted (Explained in section 3.1). *size(i)* is the total size of all words in subtree i and *MaxLen* is the maximum size of a sentence in the input corpus.

The constraints C_1 and C_2 ensure that an edge will be present if and only if the corresponding edge nodes in CG are present in the input vector, while C_3 ensures that the input vector represents a subgraph of *CG*. The constraint C_4 keeps an upper bound on the size of sentence that is generated from a single cluster, while C_5 ensures that partial trees with overlapping information are not present together in the selected subset of partial trees in a cluster.

The set of partial trees represented by the nodes of the subgraph that maximizes the objective function in Equation 7 functions as the syntactic ingredients to generate the cluster's representative sentence. A selected subset of partial trees are linearized using the transition based syntactic linearization model detailed in Section 3.3 to generate cluster representative sentence.

4 Experiments

We evaluate our method using the test sets of DUC 2004, DUC-2007 and TAC-2011. In particular, the set of attributes of the summary including content coverage of summaries and linguistic quality and factuality of newly generated summary sentences are evaluated. The content coverage is evaluated using ROUGE (Lin, 2004) and we relied on human evaluation for evaluating linguistic quality and factuality.

4.1 Data

DUC 2004, DUC-2007 and TAC-2011 consist of several corpora, each of them consisting of 10 documents and four model summaries for those 10 documents. We have tuned our development parameters using DUC 2003 dataset.

4.2 Settings

The values of α, β, σ, q and λ are tuned on the development set for optimum content coverage and sentence quality. In order to objectively evaluate a summary sentence generated by linearizing a set of partial trees, we need a human written reference sentence of high linguistic quality which is written after carefully understanding the information contained in selected partial trees. As it is timeconsuming to create such reference sentences for each of the combination constituted by the possible values of α, β, σ, q and λ, we choose to separate parameter tuning for optimal content coverage and sentence quality. Optimal values of α, β, σ and q contributes prominently for better content coverage while that of λ contributes for better sentence quality as it weights combinability of partial trees. In Subsections 4.2.1 and 4.2.2 we explain how we tune different development parameters for optimal content coverage and sentence quality.

4.2.1 Tuning α, β, σ and q for maximum content coverage

The values α, β, σ and q are optimised for maximum content coverage where pruned partial trees are extracted to fill the allotted summary space without any combination to generate summary sentences. Content coverage is measured as the sum of ROUGE-1 and ROUGE-2 scores with reference summaries on the DUC-2003 dataset. The values of α, β, σ and q optimized using grid search to give maximum average ROUGE score for corpora in DUC-2003 are 0.5, 0.15, 0.5 and 1 respectively.

System	DUC 2004			DUC 2007			TAC 2011	
Metric	R-1	R-2	R-SU4	R-1	R-2	R-SU4	R-2	R-SU4
CompAbsum (Banerjee et al., 2015)	-	0.120	**0.148**	-	-	-	-	-
PhraseAbSum (Bing et al., 2015)	-	-	-	-	-	-	**0.117**	**0.147**
Semantic (Li, 2015)	-	-	-	0.421	**0.110**	**0.150**	-	-
WordCoverage(D_{bigram})	0.382	0.096	0.113	-	-	-	-	-
PartTreeAbSum(ours)	**0.439**	**0.120**	0.140	**0.431**	0.109	**0.150**	0.113	0.141

Table 1: Comparison with state of the art

λ	ROUGE	BLEU	NCS
0	0.431	0.41	17%
9	0.429	0.41	27%
27	0.410	0.48	61%
42	0.403	0.54	70%
48	**0.401**	**0.571**	70%
75	0.373	0.579	77%
105	0.361	0.570	79%

Table 2: Optimizing λ for better topical coverage sentence quality

4.2.2 Tuning λ for optimum content coverage and sentence quality

The values of α, β, σ and q are preset to the optimum values identified in the section above. The value of λ is varied from 0 to 100 with an increment of 3 and set partial trees to form each of the summary sentences for all corpora in DUC 2003 is identified. We asked a human annotator to write a linear sentence out of each of the selected partial trees sets without using new words which are not present in partial tree nodes in the set and the BLEU score of generated summary sentences with respect to the human written sentences is estimated. For each value of λ we estimate the average ROUGE-1 and BLEU for the generated summaries and summary sentences respectively. The value at which total value of average BLEU and ROUGE-1 scores is maximum is set as the value of λ during testing. Table 2 reports BLEU and ROUGE-1 for different values of λ. Column NCS in the Table 2 represents the percentage of complex sentences generated by linearizing more than one partial tree.

4.3 Final Results

4.3.1 Content coverage

While evaluating the relevant content coverage of abstractive summarization system, we also have to evidently substantiate the effectiveness of noise pruning done using multi density partial tree extraction algorithm. For this purpose we have created extractive summarizer using maximum weighted word coverage algorithm Takamura and Okumura (2009), which tries to extract sentences containing maximum weighted D_{bigram}s in their dependency trees.

Table 1 shows the results on DUC-2004, DUC-2007, TAC-2011 along with previous approaches. In the table R-1,R-2 and R-SU4 represents ROUGE-1, ROUGE-2 and ROUGE-SU4 (skip-bigrams with unigrams), respectively. *WordCoverage*(D_{bigram}) summarizer using maximum weighted word coverage algorithm represents the word coverage algorithm using D_{bigram} weights while *PartTreeAbSum* abstractive summarization approach detailed in the paper. Results on DUC-2004 shows that noise-pruning using maximum weighted partial tree extraction was effective in terms of better content coverage. Despite rephrasing content in many contexts, *PartTreeAbSum* shows results comparable with previous approaches. CompAbsum (Banerjee et al., 2015) demands high syntactic overlap between source sentences to recombine and generate new sentences, otherwise resembles an extractive summarization system. Our system shows better ROUGE-1 and equal ROUGE-2 values in DUC-2004 test set. PhraseAbSum (Bing et al., 2015) which extracts phrases from the corpus and phrases can enjoy lower granularity in terms of information content when compared to partial trees by compromising topical coherence in summary sentence generation. Still our results are comparable with that of PhraseAbSum in TAC 2011. Our results show competitiveness with Semantic (Li, 2015) which generate summary content from a corpus level semantic network utilizing linear structures smaller than a partial tree and does not employ explicit means to ensure gramaticality.

4.3.2 Linguistic quality and factual accuracy

In order to fully evaluate the effectiveness of an abstractive summarization approach it is also useful to evaluate the linguistic quality and factual accuracy of generated sentences. Here linguistic quality refers to the quality of sentences in terms

	Input Corpus Sentences
	Hun Sen's Cambodian People's Party won 64 of the 122 parliamentary seats in July's elections [1]
	Sam Rainsy and a number of opposition figures have been under court investigation for a grenade attack on Hun Sen's Phnom Penh residence on Sep. [2]
	Hun Sen was not home at the time of the attack. [3]
	Ranariddh and Sam Rainsy have charged that Hun Sen's victory in the elections was achieved through widespread fraud. [4]
	Sentence Generated by *PhraseAbSum* **(Bing et al., 2015)**
	Sam Rainsy and a number of opposition figures, have been under court investigation for a grenade attack on Hun Sen's Phnom Penh residence on Sep, charged that Hun Sen's victory in the elections was achieved through widespread fraud (*source sentences [2] and [4]*)
	Sentences Generated by *PartTreeSum* **(Current Work)**
	Sam Rainsy and a number of opposition figures have been under court investigation for attack on Hun Sen residence, at the time of the attack Hun Sen (He) was not home (*source sentences [2] and [3]*)
	Hun Sen's party won 64 of the 122 parliamentary seats in elections, victory in the elections was achieved through widespread fraud, Ranariddh and Sam Rainsy have charged (*source sentences [1] and [4]*)

Table 3: Tree Combination vs Phrase Combination

	LQ	FA
Human Summary	4.5	4.3
PartTreeSum(WC)	2.1	2.32
PartTreeSum	**3.15**	**3.09**

Table 4: Human Evaluation on sentence quality

of grammaticality and readability, and factual accuracy refers to how much the information conveyed by the generated summary sentences are true with respect to what is contained in the input corpus. For this purpose we employed 4 manual evaluators who are post-graduate students in English literature. 10 random corpora were chosen for manual evaluation and we asked the evaluators to read the documents in each corpus and rate corresponding summary sentences for their linguistic quality and factual accuracy.

For each corpus the summaries participated in manual evaluation include a randomly chosen human summary for corpus, current approach for abstractive summarization (PartTreeSum), the current approach without combinability measure by setting λ to 0 (PartTreeSum(WC)). Human evaluation results shown in Table 4 proves that linguistic quality and factual accuracy have considerably increased with the introduction of combinability measure.

4.4 Discussions

Tree combination vs phrase combination: Table 3 contains the fours input corpus sentences in one test example and sentences generated by

PhraseAbSum (Bing et al., 2015) and the current work (*PartTreeSum*), *PhraseAbSum* could generate only one sentence respectively, due to the hard constraint for verb phrases to coincidentally share same noun phrase in source sentences and the sentence exhibit poor topical coherence. In contrast, *PartTreeSum* is flexible to generate more sentences and the *Combinablity* component in Equation 7 ensures that generated summary sentence contain topically related content. The original content is rephrased when required as observed in the second half of generated sentences. In Table 3, the summary sentences generated by *PartTreeSum* are more topically coherent compared to those generated by *PhraseAbSum*.

Error analysis : We have analysed the low-rated sentences from human evaluators with their corresponding set of partial trees. Though the partial trees contained information which can be combined in a single complex sentence, text aggregation during linearization should be more effective to improve the quality of sentences. For future work we plan to construct a neural generation model, which can aggregate and generate a sentence from a set of partial trees while maintaining factual accuracy with respect to the input documents. Also there should be a means to treat quotes separately apart from normal sentences.

5   Conclusion

We built a model for abstractive multi-document summarization by extracting partial dependency trees to represent knowledge granules, and generating summary sentences using combinable granules utilizing syntactic linearization. Compared to existing methods for the task, our method has the advantages of generating new sequential sentential structures by rephrasing information if required as decided by the linearization model. On standard evaluation of using ROUGE metric and human evaluation for qualitative aspects of summary, this method showed competitive accuracies to the state-of-the-art methods for multi-document summarization.

Acknowledgements

We thank Ratish Puduppally, Zhiyang Teng and the three anonymous reviewers for conversations and feedback on earlier drafts. We thank Raghuram Vadapally and Faraaz Nadeem for their creative suggestions.

References

Miguel B Almeida and Andre FT Martins. 2013. Fast and robust compressive summarization with dual decomposition and multi-task learning. In *ACL (1)*. pages 196–206.

Siddhartha Banerjee, Prasenjit Mitra, and Kazunari Sugiyama. 2015. Multi-document abstractive summarization using ilp based multi-sentence compression. In *Proceedings of the 24th International Conference on Artificial Intelligence*. AAAI Press, pages 1208–1214.

Taylor Berg-Kirkpatrick, Dan Gillick, and Dan Klein. 2011. Jointly learning to extract and compress. In *Proceedings of the 49th Annual Meeting of the Association for Computational Linguistics: Human Language Technologies-Volume 1*. Association for Computational Linguistics, pages 481–490.

Lidong Bing, Piji Li, Yi Liao, Wai Lam, Weiwei Guo, and Rebecca J Passonneau. 2015. Abstractive multi-document summarization via phrase selection and merging. *arXiv preprint arXiv:1506.01597*.

Jianpeng Cheng and Mirella Lapata. 2016. Neural summarization by extracting sentences and words. *arXiv preprint arXiv:1603.07252*.

Wei Li. 2015. Abstractive multi-document summarization with semantic information extraction. In *Proceedings of the 2015 Conference on Empirical Methods in Natural Language Processing*. pages 1908–1913.

Chin-Yew Lin. 2003. Improving summarization performance by sentence compression: a pilot study. In *Proceedings of the sixth international workshop on Information retrieval with Asian languages-Volume 11*. Association for Computational Linguistics, pages 1–8.

Chin-Yew Lin. 2004. Rouge: A package for automatic evaluation of summaries. In *Text summarization branches out: Proceedings of the ACL-04 workshop*. Barcelona, Spain, volume 8.

Hui Lin and Jeff Bilmes. 2011. A class of submodular functions for document summarization. In *Proceedings of the 49th Annual Meeting of the Association for Computational Linguistics: Human Language Technologies-Volume 1*. Association for Computational Linguistics, pages 510–520.

Yijia Liu, Yue Zhang, Wanxiang Che, and Bing Qin. 2015. Transition-based syntactic linearization. In *NAACL HLT 2015, The 2015 Conference of the North American Chapter of the Association for Computational Linguistics: Human Language Technologies, Denver, Colorado, USA, May 31 - June 5, 2015*. pages 113–122. http://aclweb.org/anthology/N/N15/N15-1012.pdf.

André FT Martins and Noah A Smith. 2009. Summarization with a joint model for sentence extraction and compression. In *Proceedings of the Workshop on Integer Linear Programming for Natural Language Processing*. Association for Computational Linguistics, pages 1–9.

Hajime Morita, Ryohei Sasano, Hiroya Takamura, and Manabu Okumura. 2013. Subtree extractive summarization via submodular maximization. In *ACL (1)*. Citeseer, pages 1023–1032.

Ratish Puduppully, Yue Zhang, and Manish Shrivastava. 2016. Transition-based syntactic linearization with lookahead features. In *Proceedings of NAACL-HLT*. pages 488–493.

Hsin-Hao Su, Chin Lung Lu, and Chuan Yi Tang. 2008. An improved algorithm for finding a length-constrained maximum-density subtree in a tree. *Information Processing Letters* 109(2):161–164.

Hiroya Takamura and Manabu Okumura. 2009. Text summarization model based on maximum coverage problem and its variant. In *Proceedings of the 12th Conference of the European Chapter of the Association for Computational Linguistics*. Association for Computational Linguistics, pages 781–789.

Dingding Wang, Tao Li, Shenghuo Zhu, and Chris Ding. 2008. Multi-document summarization via sentence-level semantic analysis and symmetric matrix factorization. In *Proceedings of the 31st annual international ACM SIGIR conference on Research and development in information retrieval*. ACM, pages 307–314.

Kristian Woodsend and Mirella Lapata. 2010. Automatic generation of story highlights. In *Proceedings of the 48th Annual Meeting of the Association for

Computational Linguistics. Association for Computational Linguistics, pages 565–574.

David M Zajic, Bonnie Dorr, Jimmy Lin, and Richard Schwartz. 2006. Sentence compression as a component of a multi-document summarization system. In *Proceedings of the 2006 Document Understanding Workshop, New York*.

Xingxing Zhang, Liang Lu, and Mirella Lapata. 2016. Top-down tree long short-term memory networks. *arXiv preprint arXiv:1511.00060* pages 0–5.

Yue Zhang. 2013. Partial-tree linearization: Generalized word ordering for text synthesis.

Event Argument Identification on Dependency Graphs
with Bidirectional LSTMs

Alex Judea and **Michael Strube**
Heidelberg Institute for Theoretical Studies gGmbH
Schloss-Wolfsbrunnenweg 35
69118 Heidelberg, Germany
`(alex.judea|michael.strube)@h-its.org`

Abstract

In this paper we investigate the performance of event argument identification. We show that the performance is tied to syntactic complexity. Based on this finding, we propose a novel and effective system for event argument identification. Recurrent Neural Networks learn to produce meaningful representations of long and short dependency paths. Convolutional Neural Networks learn to decompose the lexical context of argument candidates. They are combined into a simple system which outperforms a feature-based, state-of-the-art event argument identifier without any manual feature engineering.

1 Introduction

Event extraction is a difficult information extraction task. The 2005 Automatic Content Extraction evaluation (ACE 2005) defines three challenging sub-tasks: *Entity mention detection*, the task of finding mentions of predefined entity types like persons and organizations; *event trigger detection*, the task of finding words, mostly verbs or nominalizations, indicating an event from a set of predefined event types; and *event argument identification*, the identification of entity mentions[1] playing a role in the events, as well as the identification of the roles they play.

When we look at the evaluations in three of the most influential recent event extraction papers (Li et al., 2013, 2014; Chen et al., 2015; Nguyen et al., 2016) we note that argument identification performance is low, ranging from 52.7 to 55.4 F_1. There are multiple reasons for the low performance. First, argument identification suffers from

---

[1] In this work we make no distinction between 'entity', 'time', and 'place' for the sake of simplicity.

error propagation. Missed or spurious event triggers or entity mentions may lead to missed or spurious event arguments. Second, event structure is complex. Multiple entities can play the same role in the same event. Additionally, one entity can play different roles across events (and thus cause multiple event arguments). Consider the following example.

> A Palestinian **boy** as well as his **brother**
> and a **sister** were *wounded* late Wednesday by Israeli *gunfire*.

Here, the three entity mentions (in bold) are all Victims of the INJURE event triggered by 'wounded' as well as Targets of the ATTACK event triggered by 'gunfire'. Such structures can become even more complex when more events and more entities are involved.

The third reason for low argument identification performance is syntactic complexity. Many arguments are syntactically far away from their triggers, making it hard to construct meaningful syntactic features. Section 3 shows that performance is tied to the length of the shortest dependency path connecting trigger and argument.

Error sources one and two were already targeted by systems which jointly infer triggers and their arguments. To the best of our knowledge, no previous work identified syntactic complexity as the third key problem for argument identification performance, and no previous system aimed to decompose syntactic structure in order to learn better classifiers for the task. The contributions of this paper are the following.

1. We observe that syntactic complexity is a crucial factor for argument identification. Argument identification performance highly correlates with dependency path length (Section 3.1).

Proceedings of the The 8th International Joint Conference on Natural Language Processing, pages 822–831,
Taipei, Taiwan, November 27 – December 1, 2017 ©2017 AFNLP

2. We propose to represent dependency paths
   with bidirectional Long Short-term Memory networks (biLSTMs) in order to account
   for their sequential and compositional nature. Using LSTMs to learn dependency path
   representations proved effective in other areas like relation extraction (Xu et al., 2015)
   and semantic role labeling (Roth and Lapata,
   2016). We investigate their use for argument
   identification.

3. We propose to represent lexical contexts of
   event arguments with Convolutional Neural
   Networks. Together with LSTMs, they form
   an effective and simple argument identifier
   which beats a state-of-the-art, feature-based
   system without any manual feature engineering, especially for long dependency paths.

2   Baseline

2.1   Baseline Argument Extraction

Our baseline is a re-implementation of Li et al.
(2013). It is a state-of-the-art event extractor that
predicts event triggers and arguments jointly. Because of this joint inference, it avoids error propagation and can draw features based on joint event
extraction decisions, e.g., how many arguments of
a specific type does a specific trigger have?

The system uses a structured perceptron with
beam search. It processes a sentence from left to
right and token by token. With each position it
advances, it constructs new hypotheses containing
event trigger and argument assignments. Then, it
prunes the hypotheses spaces to the n best alternatives and processes the next token position. After
the last token was processed, the hypothesis with
highest score is selected as the final prediction.
This hypothesis contains trigger and argument assignments for the entire sentence.

2.2   Baseline Argument Extraction Features

Our baseline system uses a rich, hand-engineered
feature set. Feature templates can be divided into
local templates and *global templates*. Local templates characterize single arguments, and they involve only the mentions and triggers of this argument. They capture, e.g., the trigger and entity
types, the mention context, and the dependency
path between trigger and mention.

Global templates on the other hand characterize
multiple arguments, either in terms of shared mentions, or in terms of shared roles. Global templates

Argument type	Support$_{train}$	$F_{1\,dev}$
Victim	578	79.0
Instrument	256	77.1
Artifact	605	75.6
Attacker	574	47.3
Target	438	42.6
Giver	94	32.9

Table 1: Training set support and development set
baseline F_1 for the three best and three worst performing argument types.

can be divided into *segment level templates* and
sentence level templates. Segment level templates
capture characteristics of the mentions within one
event, e.g., the words between two mentions sharing a role in one event, or the head and modifier of
nominal modifications like 'IBM CEO'. Sentence
level templates capture characteristics of events
sharing mentions, e.g., the roles such a mention
fills, or the dependency path connecting the two
triggers. The system uses two dozen feature templates, resulting in 150,000 features for argument
identification.

3   Performance Analysis

3.1   Analysis of Baseline Performance

We start the analysis of argument identification
performance with the observation that despite the
low overall performance, some argument types
perform reasonably well. Table 1 reports development set precision, recall, and F_1 of our baseline for the three best and the three worst performing argument types in the development set.[2] As
we can see, the difference between the best type
(Victim) and the worst type (Giver) is 46.1 F_1
points. What is the reason for this big difference?

Our first assumption is that the best performing types have more training samples. Indeed,
Victim has considerably more samples than
Giver. Attacker however has nearly the same
amount of training samples but a much lower
performance (-31.7 F_1). Instrument on the
other hand has only half the training samples of
Attacker, but a better performance (+29.8 F_1).

To further investigate this, Figure 1a plots training set support in decreasing magnitude against
development set F_1 for the 12 most frequent argument types. The plot is not conclusive: More

---

[2]We excluded types with less than 20 samples in the development set.

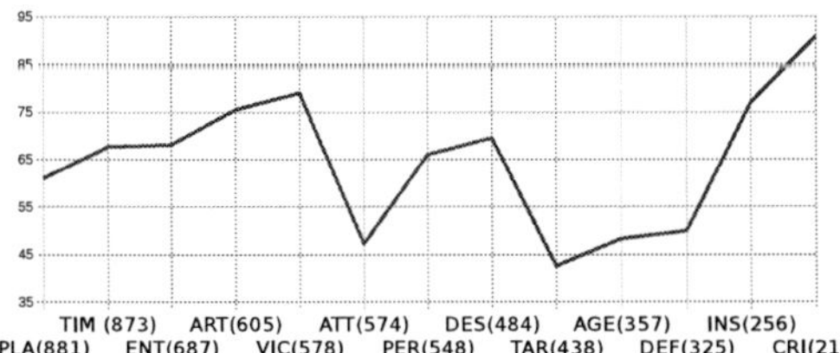
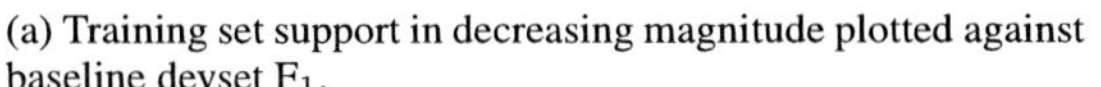

(a) Training set support in decreasing magnitude plotted against baseline devset F_1.

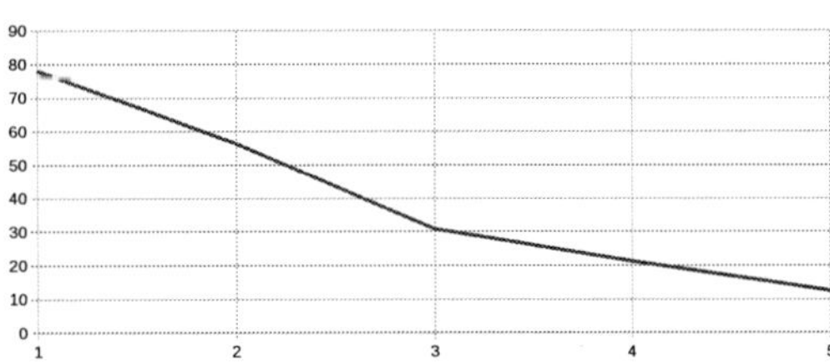

(b) Increasing dependency path length plotted against baseline devset F_1.

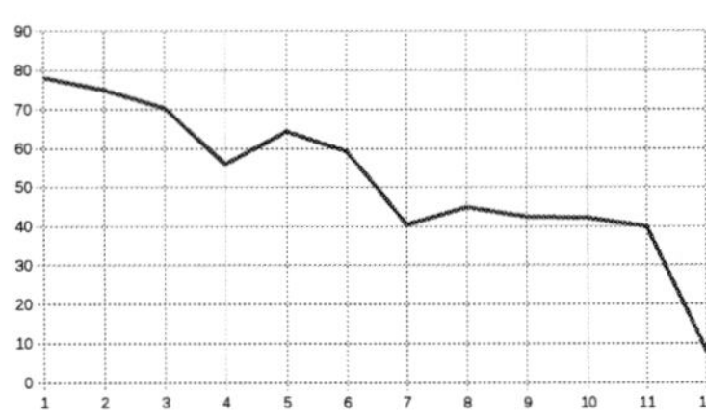

(c) Increasing lexical distance plotted against baseline devset F_1.

Figure 1: Training set support, lexical distance of trigger and argument, and dependency path length plotted against development set performance.

training data does not automatically lead to better performance. The most frequent argument type Place with 881 training samples has an F_1 of 61.1, whereas Victim with 34% less training samples has an F_1 of 79.0. Instrument has about 70% less training samples and an F_1 of 77.1. If the number of training samples is not an important factor for performance, what else could be?

One important factor is semantic variety: Some roles can only be filled by one or two entity types, and most of their mentions *are* role fillers. This is especially true for Instrument which can only be filled by vehicles and weapons in ACE 2005; in turn, most weapons are Instruments. This is reflected in the good performance of Instrument in Table 1 and Figure 1a.

However, most roles can be filled by more than two entity types, and their potential fillers are more frequent than vehicles and weapons: Entity for example can be filled by persons, organizations, and geopolitical entities. At the same time, most of the respective mentions are *not* Entities. Even if a role can only be filled by one entity type, it may be that most occurrences are not role fillers, making the task to correctly fill those roles harder. Consider Time for example, which can only be filled by *time* mentions, yet it has only a mediocre performance of 67.7 F_1 points on the development set. Semantic variety alone cannot explain the big performance differences between argument types.

Another important factor is syntactic complexity: How long and diverse are dependency paths connecting arguments and triggers? To investigate the effect of syntactic complexity, Figure 1b depicts length of dependency paths connecting triggers and arguments in decreasing magnitude against development set F_1. In this plot, we see a much clearer trend: Shorter syntactic distance leads to better performance. Length-1 paths (direct trigger-argument dependency) have an F_1 of 78.2. Length-2 path F_1 drops to 56.4, and to 30.8 for length-3 paths. Length-4 and length-5 paths have an F_1 of 21.3 and 12.5, respectively.

This trend is also reflected in the performance of individual argument types. The most frequent type Place has a high average path length of 2.2 and a low F_1 of 61.1. Victim on the other hand has considerably less training data, but an average path length of 1.5 and an F_1 of 79.0. For the three best performing types, the average path length is 1.7 vs. 2.3 for the three worst performing types.

Dependency path length is related to lexical distance – the longer a dependency path, the more words are usually between trigger and argument. To investigate the effect of lexical distance, Figure 1c depicts the number of words between trigger and argument against development set performance. Here, we see a somewhat less clearer trend: Increasing lexical distance leads to lower performance; however, with a considerable increase between distances 4 and 5, and a performance plateau between 8 and 11. Word sequences are much more diverse than dependency paths. A dependency path like returning $\xrightarrow{nmod:from}$ summit $\xrightarrow{nmod:in}$ Ireland abstracts from actual word sequences and ignores many words which are less relevant for argument identification, like adjectives and adverbs. This in turn alleviates data sparsity.

Syntactic complexity is a crucial factor for argument identification, both in terms of overall performance as well as and in terms of individual argument type performance. Therefore, it is inevitable to reduce or better handle syntactic complexity. Most systems incorporate dependency paths merely as strings, or rely on direct dependencies of triggers and arguments. They do not decompose or further analyze dependency paths in order to find relevant substructures, or to deal with data sparsity of long paths. In Section 4, we present a simple but efficient system which directly addresses syntactic complexity.

3.2 Dependency Paths

We now illustrate the benefits and difficulties of using dependency paths for argument identification. Our dependency paths are lexicalized; they always start with the trigger word and end with a mention word.[3] We say that a path has length 1 if trigger and argument are directly related, length 2 if the path includes one intermediate dependency, etc.

Often, short dependency paths directly reflect event argument structure:

$$killed \xrightarrow{nsubj} father\text{-}in\text{-}law$$
$$killed \xrightarrow{dobj} him$$

The trigger ('killed', a DIE event) has two dependencies, 'father-in-law' being the subject and 'him' being the object. Even without looking at more context we can say with confidence that the subject must be the Agent of the event and the object must be the Victim. Even longer paths may be quite clear:

$$returning \xrightarrow{nmod:from} summit \xrightarrow{nmod:in} Ireland$$

Here, 'returning' indicates a TRANSPORT event. The path conveys the information that some entity

---

[3]For multiword expressions, the path connects trigger and entity mention head.

returns from a summit in Ireland, making 'Ireland' the Origin of the event.

Of course, not all dependency paths are as easy to interpret. The following examples show the necessity to decompose dependency paths in order to catch similarities between them.

$$war \xleftarrow{dobj} fight \xrightarrow{nsubj} U.S.$$
$$war \xleftarrow{nmod:to} go \xrightarrow{nsubj} we$$

These paths are more complex than previous ones because trigger and argument are governed by other words, namely by 'fight' and 'go'. In both cases, 'war' triggers an ATTACK event and the subject is an Attacker argument. Humans can easily spot similarities in the two paths. The arguments are in both cases the subjects of the governing verbs: 'U.S.' is the entity fighting a war and 'we' is the entity going to war. However, the left sides of the paths look quite different: In one case, 'war' is the direct object of the governing verb, in the other it is the nominal modifier. Additionally, the governing verbs do not share meaning. In order to catch the similarities, a system needs the ability to decompose the paths and to learn the meaning of sequences of words and dependencies.

4 Approach

4.1 Problem Encoding

We cast argument identification as a classification task. For a trigger-mention pair (t, m) we make one instance for training/testing consisting of (a) event type, mention type, and text genre, (b) the shortest lexicalized dependency path $t \rightarrow m$ and (c) the sentence. Figure 2 depicts the pair ('returning', 'Ireland'). Event type (TRANSPORT), entity type (*loc*) and genre (newswire, not depicted) constitute the first information layer. The second Information layer is the lexicalized dependency path (returning $\xrightarrow{nmod:from}$ summit $\xrightarrow{nmod:in}$ Ireland). The third information layer is the sentence.

The three layers correspond to the most valuable information sources for the baseline. However, the baseline draws only simple categorical features from them. Most notably, it relies on having seen dependency paths during training because it cannot decompose them into meaningful subpaths, which is crucial for better identification performance (Section 3.1). The neural network architecture we present in Section 4.2 is able to automatically construct more meaningful features.

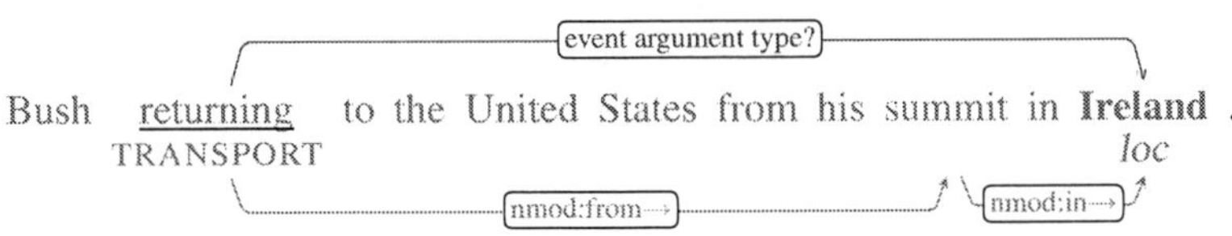

Figure 2: A training/test instance. Depicted in red is given information, depicted in blue is requested information. The trigger is underlined, the entity mention is bold.

4.2 biLSTM/CNN: Architecture

Input to our system (called biLSTM/CNN) are instances as described in Section 4.1. Each instance has three information layers, each layer is processed by a separate component. Figure 3 depicts the system architecture. The figure is split in four (bottom, middle left/right, and top), each part visualizing one component, plus the final classification. We will now describe each part. In the following, $\oplus$ means the concatenation of vectors.

Bias

The bias vector $\mathbf{b}$ provides a representation of the event type, entity type, and genre. The intuition behind the bias vector is that arguments are expressed differently across event types, entity types, and genres. $\mathbf{b}$ is input to the other two components and helps to learn better representations.

More formally, $\mathbf{b}$ is the last layer of a fully-connected three layer neural network whose input is defined as follows: $\mathbf{b}_1 = en \oplus ev \oplus ge$, where en, ev, and ge are representations of the entity type, event type, and genre. They are randomly initialized and will receive standard backpropagation updates during training.

biLSTMs

Representing dependency paths with Long Short-term Memory networks (LSTMs, Hochreiter and Schmidhuber 1997) shows good results in fields like relation extraction (Xu et al., 2015) and semantic role labeling (Roth and Lapata, 2016). We investigate their use for argument identification.

Our LSTMs produce a representation of lexicalized dependency paths, such that similar paths have similar representations. LSTMs automatically learn meaningful patterns in arbitrarily long paths. For example, they learn that the paths attacked$\xrightarrow{\text{nsubj}}$US and attacked$\xrightarrow{\text{nsubj}}$Iraq have similar representations given that both indicate an Attacker and only differ in two closely related words. They also learn that attacked$\xrightarrow{\text{dobj}}$Iraq has a different representation because the change from nsubj to dobj often distinguishes between Target and Attacker.

Input to our LSTM is a lexicalized dependency path $\mathbf{P} = (w_1, d^{1:2}, w_2, \ldots, d^{n-1:n}, w_n)$ where w_1 is the trigger word, w_n is the argument word, and $d^{a:b}$ is the dependency between w_a and w_b. The element at position i in $\mathbf{P}$ is resolved by a vector $\mathbf{v}_i = \mathbf{e}_i \oplus \text{dist}_{\text{trigger}} \oplus \text{dist}_{\text{mention}} \oplus \mathbf{b}$. $\mathbf{e}_i$ is either a pre-trained word embedding or a randomly-initialized dependency embedding, according to the element type at position i. $\text{dist}_{\text{trigger}}$ and $\text{dist}_{\text{mention}}$ refer to the lexical distance of a word to the trigger or the argument word, respectively.[4] Finally, $\mathbf{b}$ is our bias vector as defined above. We keep word embeddings fixed, but dependency embeddings receive backpropagation updates during training.

$\mathbf{P}$ is processed by a bidirectional LSTM (biLSTM). For a path element i, the biLSTM produces two (so-called) hidden states h_i^f (from the forward LSTM) and h_i^b (from the backward LSTM). These vectors contain information about the respective input, i.e., $\mathbf{v}_i$, as well as the hidden states of previously processed elements, i.e. elements to the left of i for h_i^f and elements to the right for h_i^b. We average the hidden states belonging to the same input vector: $\mathbf{a}_i = 1/2(\mathbf{h}_i^f + \mathbf{h}_{n-i+1}^b)$. Instead of averaging one could combine the vectors differently, e.g., by concatenating them. However, none of the other possibilities worked better in our case.

Using biLSTMs has the advantage that each $\mathbf{a}_i$ contains information from the entire sequence; using only a forward LSTM limits the representations at each position to the left context.

The middle-left part of Figure 3 depicts the biLSTM and its final output, the average vectors a.

Convolutional Neural Networks

In contrast to LSTMs, which are designed to capture the meaning of sequences, Convolutional Neural Networks (CNNs) are often used to pro-

---

[4]Dependencies have the same distance as their governor.

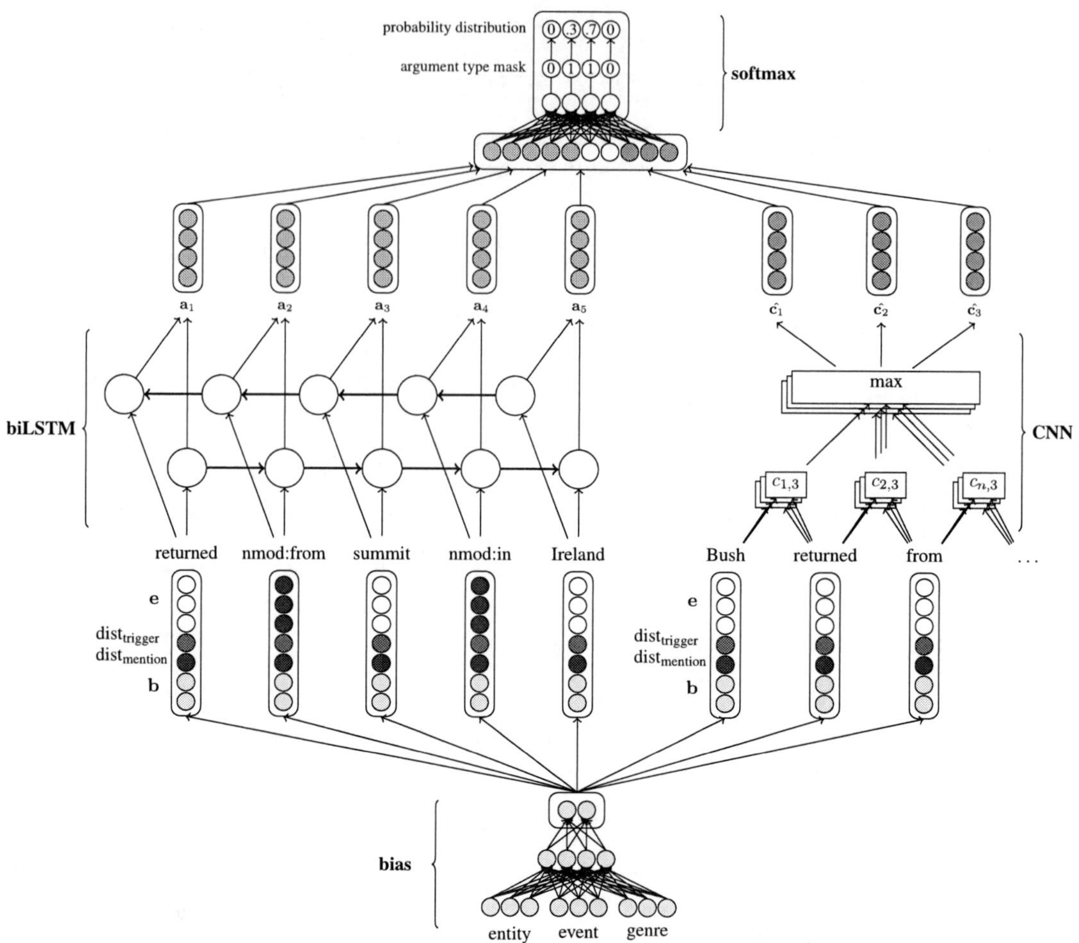

Figure 3: biLSTM/CNN architecture. Process flow is depicted from bottom to top. Embeddings e depicted in white are fixed, every other node receives backpropagation updates during training. Section 4.2 describes each component in detail.

duce bag-of-words-like representations. They were successfully applied to many NLP problems (Kim, 2014; Johnson and Zhang, 2015, inter alia).

Input to our CNN is a tokenized sentence where each word at position i is replaced by a vector $\mathbf{x}_i$ which is almost identical to the definition of $\mathbf{v}_i$ above. The only difference is that $\mathbf{x}_i$ contains only word embeddings.

CNNs apply filters (also called kernels) to a fixed number of consecutive input vectors. Filters are then moved by a certain offset (also called a stride) and re-applied. In our case, one filter produces one feature for one position i: $c_i = \sigma(\mathbf{W} \cdot \mathbf{x}_{i:i+h-1} + s)$ where σ is a non-linearity (tanh in our case), $\mathbf{W}$ is a weight matrix, $s \in \mathbb{R}$ is

a bias, and $\mathbf{x}_{i:i+h-1}$ is a concatenation of vectors $[\mathbf{x}_i \oplus \mathbf{x}_{i+1} \oplus \ldots \oplus \mathbf{x}_{i+h-1}]$. h is the filter width. $\mathbf{W}$ and s receive backpropagation updates during training, word embeddings are fixed.

We use CNNs to represent a sentence. The sentence is important because the lexical contexts of trigger and mention convey valuable information for argument identification. This means that in our case a filter of width h produces features for the entire sentence, $c = [c1, c2, \ldots, c_{n-h+1}]$. We apply max-pooling afterwards, i.e., the final output of one CNN filter is given by $\hat{c} = \max(c)$. Our CNN uses 20 filters for filter widths 2,3,4. The middle-right part of Figure 3 exemplifies a CNN with 3 filters and filter width 2.

Final Classification

Finally, the averaged biLSTM hidden vectors for the dependency path and the max values for all CNN filters applied to the entire sentence serve as input to a softmax layer which produces a probability distribution over all argument types. We pick the class with the highest probability as our final result. However, choosing between *all* classes is unnecessary because not all combinations of event type, entity type and argument type are possible. For example, the argument type `Vehicle` can only be assigned to TRANSPORT events, and only mentions with entity type *veh* can be possible fillers. We modify softmax to assign zero probability to classes which are disallowed:

$$y_i = \frac{m_i e^{x_i}}{\sum_j m_j e^{x_j}}$$

The above equation gives the probability for a particular argument type, y_i, where x is the input vector to softmax, and m is a binary vector indicating allowed types. Note that $y_i > 0$ only if the respective argument type is allowed.

The top part of Figure 3 visualizes the softmax component. The input vector is first reduced to 29 dimensions (28 argument types and one 'null' type), multiplied with the restriction mask, and forwarded to our modified softmax.

Parameter Averaging

Inspired by the Averaged Perceptron (Freund and Shapire, 1999; Collins, 2002) we do not use the learned parameters directly for prediction. Instead, in each epoch we keep a moving average of the parameters:

$$\theta^V = \alpha\theta^T + (1 - \alpha)\theta^{V-1}$$

Here, θ^T is the current weight vector after training epoch T, θ^{V-1} is the averaged weight vector before the new update, and α is the fraction of how much θ^T influences θ^V. We set $\alpha = 0.1$. θ^V is then used during testing. Note that this procedure does not change the training in any way.

With the formulation above, older weight vectors have less influence on θ^V than more recent vectors. After every training epoch, we evaluate θ^V on the development set and keep the version with highest F_1 for the final evaluation.

Parameter averaging leads to better generalization of our system. Furthermore, performance fluctuation for different training runs is reduced.

5 Experiments

5.1 Data, Evaluation Metrics and Parameters

We evaluate on ACE 2005 and use the same data split as most previous approaches (Ji and Grishman, 2008; Nguyen et al., 2016, inter alia). We follow standard evaluation procedures: An event argument is correct, if its span and role match a reference argument (Ji and Grishman, 2008). Section 1 gives an overview over the annotations provided in ACE 2005.

Because we want to measure argument identification performance by itself, we must ensure that compared systems use the same entity mention and trigger predictions; the best way to ensure this is to set both to gold. Using gold entity mentions is a common setting in event extraction (Li et al., 2013; Chen et al., 2015; Nguyen et al., 2016, inter alia). Since we have evaluation numbers only for biLSTM/CNN and our baseline in this setting, *there is no direct comparability* with previous work other than Li et al. (2013).

Both systems were trained on the same training set, and hyperparameters were optimized on the same development set. We trained both systems using `enhanced++` dependencies (Schuster and Manning, 2016).

We optimize hyper parameters for biLSTM/CNN using Random Search (Bergstra and Bengio, 2012). We use a batch size of 450, 20 CNN filters, 150 LSTM dimensions, and 130 bias dimensions. In order to deal with class imbalance, we set the weight of non-null training samples to 2; this value is used to scale the loss accordingly. We used Keras (Chollet et al., 2015) version 2.0.2 with the TensorFlow backend as the learning framework. Training the network on an NVIDIA P40 GPU takes about 20 seconds per epoch.

5.2 Experiments and Results

We report the results of four main experiments, namely measuring argument identification performance in general, grouped by argument type, grouped by dependency path length, and using only a dependency path biLSTM. We report precision, recall, and F_1.

Training neural networks is usually a non-deterministic process. In order to increase reliability, training was performed five times and the evaluation on the test set was averaged across five evaluation runs, one run per trained model.

		Baseline			biLSTM/CNN				
		P	**R**	**F_1**	**P**	**R**	**F_1**	**Support**	**ΔF_1**
1	**Micro**	**67.7**	**58.7**	**62.9**	**63.1**	**68.3**	**65.5†**	**916**	**2.6±0.5**
2	dep-path biLSTM	-	-		64.9	64.0	64.4	916	1.5
3	Time	69.9	70.9	70.4	70.9	80.1	75.2	134	4.8
4	Entity	63.7	56.7	60.0	57.7	65.2	61.2	127	1.2
5	Place	64.0	41.7	50.5	52.1	48.0	49.9	115	-0.6
6	Person	74.6	61.7	67.6	69.1	78.3	73.4	81	5.8
7	Artifact	78.5	71.8	75.0	70.3	77.2	73.5	71	-1.5
8	Destination	63.4	66.7	65.0	65.6	80.0	72.1	39	7.1
9	Crime	84.4	100.0	91.6	82.5	99.5	90.2	38	-1.4
10	Attacker	60.7	47.2	53.1	52.4	66.6	58.6	36	5.5
11	Defendant	70.0	63.6	66.7	67.6	75.2	71.1	33	4.4
12	Agent	64.7	34.3	44.9	55.9	40.6	46.8	32	1.9

Table 2: Test set precision, recall, and F_1 for the baseline and biLSTM/CNN, ordered by frequency. Reported are argument types with more than 30 instances. **Mirco** reports micro-averaged numbers, averaged across 5 training and testing rounds, 'dep-path biLSTM' reports numbers using only a dependency path biLSTM, the other rows report numbers per argument type. 'Support' reports the number of instances for the respective type. 'ΔF_1' reports the difference in F_1 between biLSTM/CNN and the baseline, as well as the standard deviation of biLSTM/CNN F_1. † means statistically significant for every training and testing round at the $p < 0.05$ level.

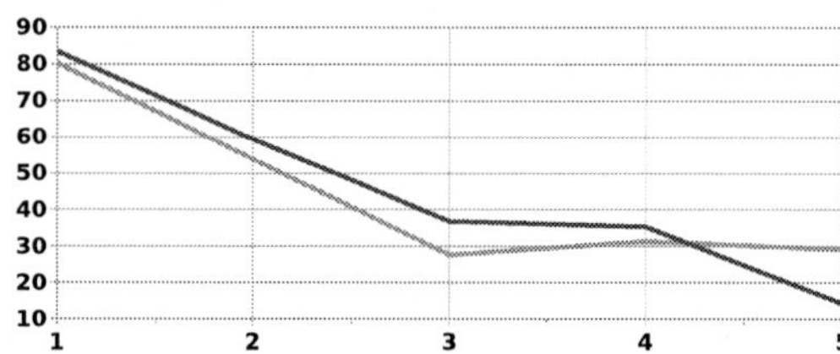

(a) Test set F_1 performance plotted against dependency path length. The red curve depicts baseline F_1, the blue curve depicts biLSTM/CNN F_1.

	Baseline	biLSTM/CNN		
Length	F_1	F_1	Support	ΔF_1
1	80.2	83.5	432	3.3
2	53.9	59.5	248	5.6
3	27.8	36.9	123	9.1
4	31.5	35.4	59	3.9
5	29.3	14.3	26	-15.0

(b) Test set F_1 by dependency path length for the baseline and biLSTM/CNN. 'Support' reports the number of instances, 'ΔF_1' reports the difference in F_1 between biLSTM/CNN and the baseline.

Figure 4: Test set F_1 by dependency path length for the baseline and biLSTM/CNN.

Table 2 reports micro-averaged evaluation numbers for the baseline and biLSTM/CNN (Line 1), a variant which uses only a dependency path biLSTM (without context CNNs, Line 2) as well as numbers per argument type (Lines 3-12). The column 'Support' gives the number of instances for the respective evaluation. Finally, the column 'ΔF_1' reports the difference in F_1 between biLSTM/CNN and the baseline, positive numbers meaning better biLSTM/CNN performance, as well as the standard deviation of the biLSTM/CNN F_1 score.

As we can see in Table 2, Line 1, biLSTM/CNN has a lower precision and a considerably higher recall than the baseline, resulting in an increase of 2.6 points in micro-averaged F_1 (with a standard deviation of 0.5 F_1 points). This is statistically significant at the $p < 0.05$ level.[5] Note

that biLSTM/CNN does not use any manually engineered features, whereas the baseline uses two dozen feature templates, resulting in 150,000 features. Furthermore, biLSTM/CNN is a simple trigger-argument-pair classifier, whereas the baseline jointly predicts all arguments of all triggers in a sentence.

When we compare the performance using dependency paths alone (Line 2), recall drops by 4.3 points, while increasing precision slightly by 1.8 points, resulting in a decrease of 1.1 F_1 points. The main advantage of the CNN is that it makes the lexical context outside of the shortest dependency path available to the system, which reflects itself in the increased recall.

When we look at individual argument types, we note that biLSTM/CNN improves performance for all but three types. Destination has the highest performance improvement (7.1 F_1 points), Artifact the highest loss (-1.5 F_1 points).

---

[5] We measured significance using approximate randomization (Noreen, 1989). Each of the 5 models we trained performed significantly better than the baseline.

`Time` as the most frequent type in the test data has a high improvement of 4.8 F_1 points.

Figure 4 reports micro-averaged numbers for the baseline and biLSTM/CNN per dependency path length. Figure 4a is a visualization of Table 4b. In total, 888 arguments (out of the 916 in the test set) were connected to their triggers by dependency paths of length 5 or less. biLSTM/CNN performs considerably better for lengths 1-4, especially for paths of length 2 (+5.6 F_1) and 4 (+9.1 F_1). Length-1 paths, which are nearly as frequent as all other path lenghts together, have an increased performance of 3.3 F_1 points. Only length-5 paths (with a test set support of 26) lose 15 F_1 points, mainly because biLSTM/CNN produced some false positives for this class.

Most of biLSTM/CNN's errors are either false positives (wrongly classified as an argument) or false negatives (missed an argument). When it confuses argument types, it usually confuses opposing types like `Seller` and `Buyer`.

6   Related Work

To the best of our knowledge, no other paper is targeting event argument identification directly. For this reason, we first summarize 'neural' event extractors, for which argument identification is one necessary step. Then, we report work on representing dependency paths with neural networks.

Chen et al. (2015) use a pipelined event extractor based on CNNs. The input is a sentence, and the output is, in phase one, all triggers in the sentence and, in phase two, a classification of the argument type of a trigger-argument candidate pair. The second phase is similar to the setting we analyze in this paper.

Nguyen et al. (2016) propose a joint and hybrid approach using a Gated Recurrent Unit network (Cho et al., 2014), a variant of an LSTM. Input to their network is the word embedding matrix of a sentence. In contrast to Chen et al. (2015), they predict triggers and arguments jointly. They concatenate a one-hot representation of dependencies to each word embedding. In contrast to this paper, they do not attempt to directly operate on syntactic structure. Instead, the GRU goes over the sentence and passes its hidden states on to higher levels of the network, which dynamically output triggers and arguments for the entire sentence. Their approach is hybrid because they additionally use the features from Li et al. (2013) We did not choose

this system as our baseline because it is considerably more complex and would heavily rely on the same features as our baseline in the setting we investigate in this paper.

Xu et al. (2015) use LSTMs for relation extraction. Similar to our work, they use LSTMs to compute a representation of the shortest dependency path connecting two related entities. While the general learning scheme is similar to our biLSTM component, they represent dependency paths differently. Instead of one lexicalized path, they construct four different representations, using only dependency labels, only words, only part-of-speech tags, and only WordNet categories. This results in four LSTMs whose output is concatenated.

Roth and Lapata (2016) use dependency path-encoding LSTMs for semantic role labeling (SRL). Event extraction and SRL are similar in terms of structures: SRL also involves finding 'triggers' and 'arguments'. They differ however in the nature of these structures. For example, potential arguments in SRL may be assigned to every verb in a sentence, while in event extraction, potential arguments must be assigned only to event triggers. Similar to our work, Roth and Lapata (2016) use an LSTM which processes a dependency path connecting predicate and argument. Their dependency paths mix words, part-of-speech tags and dependency relations.

7   Conclusions

In this paper, we show that argument identification performance is tied to the length of dependency paths connecting triggers and arguments. We propose a novel and efficient neural network that targets syntactic complexity. Without manual feature engineering, it learns to produce meaningful representations of dependency paths and to extract relevant lexical context of arguments. We show that our system outperforms a state-of-the-art baseline which uses manually engineered features and predicts arguments jointly.

Acknowledgments

This work has been funded by the Klaus Tschira Foundation, Heidelberg, Germany. The first author has been supported by a HITS PhD scholarship. We thank the anonymous reviewers for their helpful comments.

References

James Bergstra and Yoshua Bengio. 2012. Random search for hyper-parameter optimization. *Journal of Machine Learning Research*, 13(Feb):281–305.

Yubo Chen, Liheng Xu, Kang Liu, Daojian Zeng, and Jun Zhao. 2015. Event extraction via dynamic multi-pooling convolutional neural networks. In *Proceedings of the 53rd Annual Meeting of the Association for Computational Linguistics (Volume 1: Long Papers)*, Beijing, China, 26–31 July 2015, pages 167–176.

Kyunghyun Cho, Bart van Merriënboer Caglar Gulcehre, Dzmitry Bahdanau, Fethi Bougares Holger Schwenk, and Yoshua Bengio. 2014. Learning phrase representations using rnn encoder–decoder for statistical machine translation. In *Proceedings of the 2014 Conference on Empirical Methods in Natural Language Processing*, Doha, Qatar, 25–29 October 2014, pages 1724–1734.

François Chollet et al. 2015. Keras. `https://github.com/fchollet/keras`.

Michael Collins. 2002. Discriminative training methods for Hidden Markov Models: Theory and experiments with perceptron algorithms. In *Proceedings of the 2002 Conference on Empirical Methods in Natural Language Processing*, Philadelphia, Penn., 6–7 July 2002, pages 1–8.

Yoav Freund and Robert Shapire. 1999. A short introduction to boosting. *Journal of the Japanese Society for Artificial Intelligence*, 14:771–780.

Sepp Hochreiter and Jürgen Schmidhuber. 1997. Long short-term memory. *Neural computation*, 9(8):1735–1780.

Heng Ji and Ralph Grishman. 2008. Refining event extraction through cross-document inference. In *Proceedings of the 46th Annual Meeting of the Association for Computational Linguistics: Human Language Technologies*, Columbus, Ohio, 15–20 June 2008, pages 254–262.

Rie Johnson and Tong Zhang. 2015. Effective use of word order for text categorization with Convolutional Neural Networks. In *Proceedings of the 2015 Conference of the North American Chapter of the Association for Computational Linguistics: Human Language Technologies*, Denver, Col., 31 May – 5 June 2015, pages 103–112.

Yoon Kim. 2014. Convolutional Neural Networks for sentence classification. In *Proceedings of the 2014 Conference on Empirical Methods in Natural Language Processing*, Doha, Qatar, 25–29 October 2014, pages 1746–1751.

Qi Li, Heng Ji, Yu Heng, and Sujian Li. 2014. Constructing information networks using one single model. In *Proceedings of the 2014 Conference on Empirical Methods in Natural Language Processing*, Doha, Qatar, 25–29 October 2014, pages 1846–1851.

Qi Li, Heng Ji, and Liang Huang. 2013. Joint event extraction via structured prediction with global features. In *Proceedings of the 51st Annual Meeting of the Association for Computational Linguistics (Volume 1: Long Papers)*, Sofia, Bulgaria, 4–9 August 2013, pages 73–82.

Thien Huu Nguyen, Kyunghyun Cho, and Ralph Grishman. 2016. Joint event extraction via recurrent neural networks. In *Proceedings of the 2016 Conference of the North American Chapter of the Association for Computational Linguistics: Human Language Technologies*, San Diego, Cal., 12–17 June 2016, pages 300–309.

Eric W. Noreen. 1989. *Computer Intensive Methods for Hypothesis Testing: An Introduction*. Wiley, New York, N.Y.

Michael Roth and Mirella Lapata. 2016. Neural semantic role labeling with dependency path embeddings. In *Proceedings of the 54th Annual Meeting of the Association for Computational Linguistics (Volume 1: Long Papers)*, Berlin, Germany, 7–12 August 2016, pages 1192–1202.

Sebastian Schuster and Christopher D. Manning. 2016. Enhanced english universal dependencies: An improved representation for natural language understanding tasks. In *Proceedings of the 10th International Conference on Language Resources and Evaluation*, Portorož, Slovenia, 23–28 May 2016.

Yan Xu, Lili Mou, Ge Li, Yunchuan Chen, Hao Peng, and Zhi Jin. 2015. Classifying relations via Long Short Term Memory Networks along shortest dependency paths. In *Proceedings of the 2015 Conference on Empirical Methods in Natural Language Processing*, Lisbon, Portugal, 17–21 September 2015, pages 1785–1794.

Selective Decoding for Cross-lingual Open Information Extraction

Sheng Zhang
Johns Hopkins University
zsheng2@jhu.edu

Kevin Duh
Johns Hopkins University
kevinduh@cs.jhu.edu

Benjamin Van Durme
Johns Hopkins University
vandurme@cs.jhu.edu

Abstract

Cross-lingual open information extraction is the task of distilling facts from the source language into representations in the target language. We propose a novel encoder-decoder model for this problem. It employs a novel selective decoding mechanism, which explicitly models the sequence labeling process as well as the sequence generation process on the decoder side. Compared to a standard encoder-decoder model, selective decoding significantly increases the performance on a Chinese-English cross-lingual open IE dataset by 3.87-4.49 BLEU and 1.91-5.92 F_1. We also extend our approach to low-resource scenarios, and gain promising improvement.

1 Introduction

Cross-lingual open information extraction is defined as the task of extracting facts from the source language (e.g., Chinese text in Fig. 1(a)) and representing them in the target language (e.g. English predicate-argument information in Fig. 1(c))[1]. It is a challenging task and of great importance to solve the cross-lingual portability issues of various NLP systems which are in the support of open information extraction (Sudo et al., 2004). Additionally, there is often a great demand for rapid access to information across languages, especially when a large-scale incident occurs (Lu et al., 2016).

Conventional solutions decompose the task as a pipeline of machine translation followed by

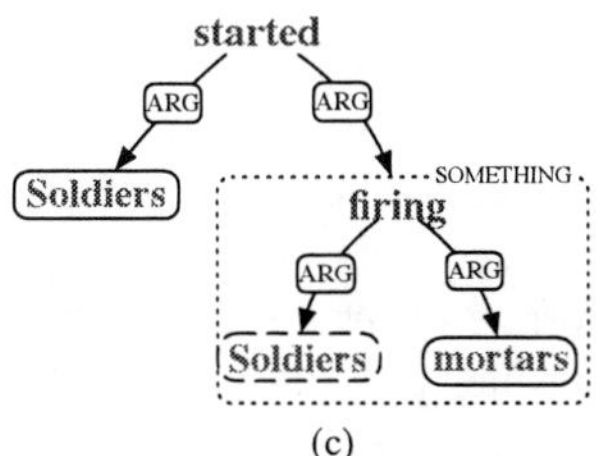

$[(\text{Soldiers}:a_h)\ \text{started}:p_h\ [(\text{Soldiers}:a_h)\ \text{firing}:p_h\ (\text{mortars}:a_h)]]$
(d)

[Soldiers started [Soldiers firing mortars]]
 P   A   P   P   A   P   A   P P
(e)

Figure 1: Example of cross-lingual open IE: Chinese input text (a), English translation (b), English predicate-argument information (c), linearized PredPatt output (d) and output with separated predicate and argument labels (e).

open information extraction (or vice versa), which causes a deviation since machine translation attaches equal importance to adequacy and fluency of the intermediate translation results (Snover et al., 2009), whereas the final goal focuses more on extracting correct predicates and arguments.

Recently Zhang et al. (2017a) proposes an end-to-end solution that outperforms the conventional pipeline solutions. They recast cross-lingual open IE as a sequence-to-sequence learning problem by converting the target facts in the tree structure (Fig. 1(c)) into a linear form called linearized PredPatt[2] (Fig. 1(d)), and employ a stan-

---

[1] The predicate-argument information is normally represented by relation tuples. Here, we use a richer representation (i.e., a tree structure) adopted by PredPatt (White et al., 2016), a lightweight tool for identifying predicate-argument information, available at https://github.com/hltcoe/PredPatt.

[2] Linearized PredPatt is converted from the PredPatt tree structure by taking an in-order traversal of every node in the tree. See Zhang et al. (2017a) for details.

Proceedings of the The 8th International Joint Conference on Natural Language Processing, pages 832–842,
Taipei, Taiwan, November 27 – December 1, 2017 ©2017 AFNLP

dard encoder-decoder model to address the problem (from (a) to (d) in Fig. 1). In the linearized PredPatt (Fig. 1(d)), special labels are appended to tokens as type indications. Brackets and parentheses have to be inserted to delimit predicate and argument spans. Such a workaround inevitably expands the vocabulary space and increases the burdens on the decoder, which is not ideal for sparse data scenarios and limits the overall performance.

In this paper, we reformulate cross-lingual open IE as a sequence generation and labeling problem (from (a) to (e) in Fig. 1) by separating the predicate and argument labels from the target linearized PredPatt, and removing unnecessary parentheses. We propose a novel encoder-decoder model which employs a selective decoding mechanism to explicitly model the sequence labeling as well as the sequence generation process. The new model substantially reduces the vocabulary space, eases the burden on the decoder, and leads to a significant gain of performance. And the natural of the selective decoding mechanism enables a joint training strategy that optimizes sequence generation and labeling simultaneously. In addition, we introduce an adapted beam search algorithm to further improve the prediction quality.

Experimental results demonstrate that our model employing the selective decoding mechanism significantly outperforms the previous end-to-end solution not only on a Chinese-English dataset, but also in low-resource cross-lingual open IE scenarios.

2 Problem Formulation

Our goal is to learn a model which directly maps a sentence input X in the source language into a sentence Y in the target language, and simultaneously labels each token in Y with type information T. For cross-lingual open IE, the types are *predicate* and *argument*. It is important to label types because they are used to annotate predicates and arguments in the generated tokens. Formally, we regard the input as a sequence $X = x_1, \cdots, x_{|X|}$, and the output as two sequences (Y, T): (1) the sentence in target language $Y = y_1, \cdots, y_{|Y|}$, and (2) the type information $T = t_1, \cdots, t_{|Y|}$, where $t_i \in \mathcal{T}$ is the label for the token y_i, and $|X|$ and $|Y|$ are the length of the sequence X and Y respectively. Our model maps X into (Y, T) using a conditional probability which is decomposed as:

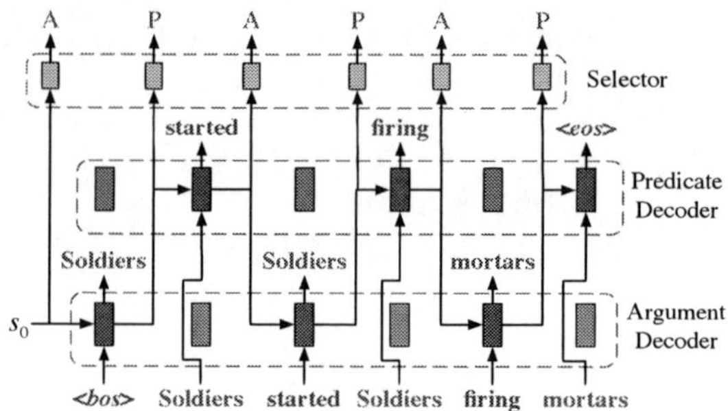

Figure 2: Selective decoding process. (Brackets and attention layers are omitted.)

$$P(Y, T \mid X) = \prod_{i=1}^{|Y|} P(y_i, t_i \mid y_{<i}, t_{<i}, X)$$

$$= \prod_{i=1}^{|Y|} P(y_i \mid y_{<i}, t_{\leq i}, X) P(t_i \mid y_{<i}, t_{<i}, X) \quad (1)$$

where $y_{<i} = y_1 \cdots y_{i-1}$ and $t_{\leq i} = t_1 \cdots t_i$.

Equation (1) can be interpreted as at each decoding time step, the model first decides which type (label) of tokens to generate, and then generates a token for that type.

3 Proposed Model

To learn the factored conditional probabilities as shown in Equation (1), we propose a novel encoder-decoder model with the selective decoding mechanism: on the encoder side, an input sentence X is encoded into vector representations; on the decoder side, the selective decoding mechanism employs multiple decoders each of which learns the conditional probability of decoding a specific type of token (i.e., $P(y_i \mid y_{<i}, t_{\leq i}, X)$), and a selector learning to decide which type of decoder to use (i.e., $P(t_i \mid y_{<i}, t_{<i}, X)$) at each decoding time step.

Fig. 2 illustrates the selective decoding process for the example shown in Fig. 1(e). s_0 is the initial decoder hidden state initialized by the last hidden state of the encoder. Special tokens $\langle bos \rangle$ and $\langle eos \rangle$ are added to the beginning and the end of the sequence to indicate the start and the finish of decoding. The connections at each decoding time step are dynamically changing according to the decision of the selector. Specifically, at the decoding time step i, firstly the selector on the top decides to use which type of decoder $D_{t_i} \in \{D_{\mathrm{P}}, D_{\mathrm{A}}\}^3$, and

---

[3] D_{P} stands for the predicate decoder, and D_{A} for the argument decoder.

then the decoder D_{t_i} decodes the token y_i which is naturally given the label t_i.

In addition to distinguish between labels, the multiple decoders used by the selective decoding mechanism has two prominent advantages over the single standard RNN decoder: (1) Multiple decoders learn different conditional probability distributions for predicate and argument generation respectively. For instance, given the same input token "*wanted*", the predicate decoder would like to next generate tokens such as "*to*" and "*by*" which starts a prepositional phrase, whereas the argument decoder would be in favor of tokens such as "*a*" and "*him*" which starts a direct object. (2) Multiple decoders reduce the decoder vocabulary size, which eases the burden of sequence generation. Moreover, we propose an efficient architecture that supports batch training of the model. The details of the architecture are described in the **Decoder with Selective Decoding** section.

3.1 Encoder

The encoder employs a bi-directional recurrent neural network (Schuster and Paliwal, 1997) to encode the input sequence $X = x_1, \cdots, x_{|X|}$ into a sequence of hidden states $\boldsymbol{h} = h_1, \cdots, h_{|X|}$. Each hidden state h_i in $\boldsymbol{h}$ is a concatenation of a left-to-right hidden state $\overrightarrow{h}_i \in \mathbb{R}^n$ and a right-to-left hidden state $\overleftarrow{h}_i \in \mathbb{R}^n$,

$$h_i = \begin{bmatrix} \overleftarrow{h}_i \\ \overrightarrow{h}_i \end{bmatrix} = \begin{bmatrix} \overleftarrow{f}(x_i, \overleftarrow{h}_{i+1}) \\ \overrightarrow{f}(x_i, \overrightarrow{h}_{i-1}) \end{bmatrix},$$

where $\overleftarrow{f}$ and $\overrightarrow{f}$ are two L-layer stacked LSTMs units (Hochreiter and Schmidhuber, 1997).

3.2 Decoder with Selective Decoding

Unlike the single standard RNN decoder (Bahdanau et al., 2014), which recurrently uses the same decoder to generate tokens, our model dynamically selects different decoders at each decoding time step to generate tokens (Fig. 2). However, since the decoding path may be different for each input sequence X, directly running the selective decoding process suffers from a key technical issue: it does not support batched computation, which makes them slow and unwieldy for large-scale NLP tasks (Bowman et al., 2016).

To address this issue, we introduce a general decoding architecture that is applicable to all selective decoding processes. The detailed connection

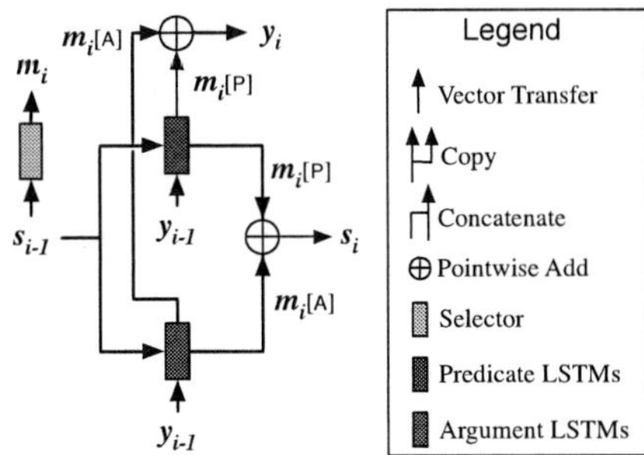

Figure 3: Detailed connection at a decoding step. (Attention layers are ommited.)

in the architecture is shown in Fig. 3. At each decoding time step, the model feeds the input token and the previous hidden state to all types of decoders, and use a mask vector created by the selector to select the decoder output to generate tokens and update the hidden state.

Formally, let $s_i \in \mathbb{R}^n$ denote the hidden state at decoding time step i. The last left-to-right hidden state $\overrightarrow{h}_{|X|}$ from the encoder is used to initialize the first hidden state s_0 in the decoder.

Selector: At the decoding time step i, given the sequence of encoder hidden states $\boldsymbol{h}$ and the previous decoder hidden state s_{i-1}, the selector computes the conditional probability of t_i (i.e., the type of decoder to use) as:

$$P(t_i \mid y_{<i}, t_{<i}, X) = g(t_i, s_{i-1}, \boldsymbol{h})$$
$$= \text{softmax}(U_o s_{i-1} + C_o c_{i-1} + b_o)[t_i], \quad (2)$$

where $U_o \in \mathbb{R}^{|\mathcal{T}| \times n}$, $C_o \in \mathbb{R}^{|\mathcal{T}| \times n}$ and $b_o \in \mathbb{R}^{|\mathcal{T}|}$ are weight matrices and bias.[4] $[t_i]$ indexes the element of a vector that corresponds to the type t_i.

Attention: The context vector c_{i-1} captures the attention to the encoder side (Bahdanau et al., 2014; Luong et al., 2015), computed as a weighted sum of encoder hidden states: $c_{i-1} = \sum_j^{|X|} a_{(i-1)j} h_j$. The weight $a_{(i-1)j}$ is computed by:

$$a_{(i-1)j} = \frac{\exp\left(\text{score}(s_{i-1}, h_j)\right)}{\sum_{j'=1}^{|X|} \exp\left(\text{score}(s_{i-1}, h_{j'})\right)}, \quad (3)$$

where $\text{score}(s_{i-1}, h_j) = s_{i-1}^{\mathsf{T}} W_a h_j$, and $W_a \in \mathbb{R}^{n \times 2n}$ is a transform matrix.

Hidden State Update: According to the conditional probability $P(t_i \mid y_{<i}, t_{<i}, X)$, a mask vector $\boldsymbol{m}_i$ is created, which is used to mask out the

---

[4] $|\mathcal{T}|$ is the number of token types. In the example shown in Fig. 3, $\mathcal{T} = \{\text{P}, \text{A}\}$, and $|\mathcal{T}| = 2$.

decoders' hidden states,

$$
\boldsymbol{m}_i[t_i] = \begin{cases} 1, \text{ if } t_i = \underset{t'_i \in \mathcal{T}}{\mathrm{argmax}} P(t'_i \,|\, y_{<i}, t_{<i}, X) \\[2ex] 0, \text{ otherwise} \end{cases}
$$

Then the hidden state s_i for the decoding time step i is computed by:

$$
s_i = \sum_{t_i \in \mathcal{T}} \boldsymbol{m}_i[t_i] f_{t_i}(y_{i-1}, s_{i-1}, c_i)
$$

where c_i is the context vector capturing the *attention*, computed in the same way as Equation (3). f_{t_i} is L-layer stacked LSTMs for the type t_i. In Fig. 3, there is an L-layer stacked LSTMs for generating predicate tokens f_P, and another L-layer stacked LSTMs for generating argument tokens f_A. They have untied parameters.

Token Generation: The conditional probability of the token y_i with the type t_i is defined as:

$$
P(y_i \mid y_{<i}, t_{\leq i}, X) = g'(y_{i-1}, s_{i-1}, \boldsymbol{h}, \boldsymbol{m}_i)
$$
$$
= \mathrm{softmax}(U'_o s_i + C'_o c_i + b'_o)[y_i], \qquad (4)
$$

where $U'_o \in \mathbb{R}^{|\mathcal{V}| \times n}$, $C'_o \in \mathbb{R}^{|\mathcal{V}| \times n}$ and $b_o \in \mathbb{R}^{|\mathcal{V}|}$ are weight matrices and bias.[5]

3.3 Training

In the training procedure, our optimization objective is to minimize the negative log-likelihood of the sequence Y and its type information T given the input sequence X over the training data, defined as:

$$
\text{minimize} - \sum_{(X,Y,T) \in \mathcal{D}} \log P(Y, T \mid X)
$$

According to Equation (1), the log-likelihood $\log P(Y, T \mid X)$ can be decomposed as:

$$
\sum_{i=1}^{|Y|} [\log P(y_i \,|\, y_{<i}, t_{\leq i}, X) + \log P(t_i \,|\, y_{<i}, t_{<i}, X)],
$$

where $P(y_i \,|\, y_{<i}, t_{\leq i}, X)$ models the sequence generation process, and $P(t_i \,|\, y_{<i}, t_{<i}, X)$ models the sequence labeling process. They are computed by Equations (4) and (2) respectively. The decomposition of the log-likelihood into these two parts enables a joint optimization for the sequence generation and labeling process simultaneously.

We use the Adam optimizer (Kingma and Ba, 2014) and mini-batch gradient to solve this optimization problem. To prevent overfitting, we apply dropout operators (Srivastava et al., 2014) to non-recurrent connections between LSTM layers.

---

[5] $|\mathcal{V}|$ is the vocabulary size of the target language.

3.4 Inference

In the inference procedure, we predict the sequence Y and its type information T for an input sequence X according to:

$$
(\hat{Y}, \hat{T}) = \underset{(Y',T') \in \mathcal{V}^{|Y'|} \times \mathcal{T}^{|Y'|}}{\mathrm{argmax}} P(Y', T' \mid X)
$$

$\mathcal{V}^{|Y'|} \times \mathcal{T}^{|Y'|}$ is the set of all possible (Y', T') pairs. And $(\hat{Y}, \hat{T})$ can be directly converted to the form of linearized PredPatt which is used for evaluation.

However, it is impractical to iterate over all these (Y', T') pairs during inference: here, we use beam search to generate tokens and labels as shown in Algorithm 1.

Algorithm 1 Beam search for selective decoding

Input: X - sequence in the source language
Output: (Y, T) - sequence in the target language
     and its type information
1:   $step \leftarrow 0$
2:   $b \leftarrow$ beam size
3:   $l \leftarrow$ max decoder length
4:   $fw\_hid \leftarrow$ Encoder(X)
5:   TERMINATED_STATES.$init(\varnothing)$
6:   $start\_state \leftarrow$ State$(\langle bos \rangle, fw_hid)$
7:   BEAM.$init(\{start\_state\})$
8:   **while** BEAM $\neq \varnothing$ and $step < l$ **do**
9:      $step \leftarrow step + 1$
10:     ACTIVE_STATES.$init(\varnothing)$
11:     **for** $state$ in BEAM **do**
12:        ▷ *Select the decoder.*
13:        $t \leftarrow$ Selector$(state)$
14:        ▷ *Generate the next token.*
15:        $states \leftarrow$ Decoder$_t(state)$
16:        ▷ *Update the active states.*
17:        ACTIVE_STATES.$update(states)$
18:     BEAM.$clean()$
19:     ▷ *Get the top-k candidates.*
20:     **for** $state$ in $top(b,$ ACTIVE_STATES$)$ **do**
21:        **if** $state.decoded\_token = \langle eos \rangle$ **then**
22:          $b \leftarrow b - 1$
23:          ▷ *Move out the terminated states.*
24:          TERMINATED_STATES.$add(state)$
25:        **else**
26:          ▷ *Update the beam.*
27:          BEAM.$add(state)$
28:   TERMINATED_STATES.$update($BEAM$)$
29:   $state \leftarrow top(1,$ TERMINATED_STATES$)$
30:   **return** $(state.Y, state.T)$

The beam is used to increase the search space for the sequence Y in the target language. At each decoding time step, we first greedily select the type of decoder, and then generate candidate tokens from the selected decoder to update the beam. When the special token $\langle eos \rangle$ is generated, we remove the candidate sequence from the beam.

4   Related Work

The model we propose in this paper is adapted from the RNN encoder-decoder architectures which have been successfully applied to a wide range of NLP tasks such as machine translation (Kalchbrenner and Blunsom, 2013; Cho et al., 2014; Bahdanau et al., 2014), image description generation (Karpathy and Fei-Fei, 2015; Vinyals et al., 2015b), syntactic parsing (Vinyals et al., 2015a), question answering (Hermann et al., 2015), summarization (Rush et al., 2015), and semantic parsing (Dong and Lapata, 2016).

As a novel variation of the encoder-decoder architecture, our model provides a general solution to tasks involving translation and labeling. cross-lingual open IE is an example of this kind of task. The end-to-end solution proposed by Zhang et al. (2017a) used a vanilla attention-based encoder-decoder model to achieve results which outperform the traditional pipeline solutions. Compared to the vanilla encoder-decoder model, our model splits the joint task into two concurrent tasks (i.e., labeling and translating), which are jointly learnt by a selector and multiple decoders. This eases the burden of the decoder by shifting the labeling task to the selector. As a result, our model requires a smaller vocabulary for the target language.

The selective decoding mechanism can be viewed as having different types of decoders stacking together and adding a hard gate to the RNN unit, through which the bit of information will be either totally kept or dropped. It may seem redundant since the RNN gated unit already has the sophisticated gating mechanism such as the GRU unit (Cho et al., 2014) and the LSTM unit (Hochreiter and Schmidhuber, 1997). However, we think that the selective decoding mechanism is a complement to the gated unit: rather than having a soft pointwise control, the selective decoding mechanism adopts a hard vectorwise control to explicitly select a certain type of information which corresponds to the predicate or the argument by keeping one and dropping the others,

whereas the GRU/LSTM gated unit itself learns to memorize long short-term dependencies. Similar mechanisms have been used in neural machine translating (Tu et al., 2016) and image caption generation (Xu et al., 2015) to explicitly control the influence from source or target contexts. The experiments in § 5 also confirms our point: our model using the selective decoding mechanism significantly improves the performance, compared to the standard encoder-decoder model.

Regarding to open IE systems for generating training data, PredPatt has shown promising performance on large-scale open IE benchmarks (Zhang et al., 2017c). Compared to other existing open IE systems (Banko et al., 2007; Fader et al., 2011; Angeli et al., 2015), PredPatt uses manual language-agnostic patterns on UD, which makes it a well-founded component across languages. Additionally, the underlying structure constructed by PredPatt has been shown to be a well-formed syntax-semantics interface (Zhang et al., 2017b).

5   Experiments

We describe the hyper-parameters setting for experiments, evaluate our approach in two kinds of scenarios, and compare the results of our approach and the other comparing approaches.

5.1   Hyper-parameters

On the encoder side, both the forward RNN and the backward RNN have 2-layer stacked LSTMs with 500 hidden units. On the decoder side, all types of decoders are 2-layer stacked LSTMs with 500 hidden units. All LSTM parameters are sampled from $\mathcal{U}(-0.1, 0.1)$. The dropout rate is set to 0.3. The word embedding size is 300 for input tokens on both the encoder side and the decoder side. We use open-source GloVe vectors (Pennington et al., 2014) trained on Common Crawl 840B with 300 dimensions[6] to initialize the word embeddings on the decoder side. The mini-batch size is set to 64 and the step size set to 50. Gradients are clipped when their norms are greater than 5 (Pascanu et al., 2013). For simplicity, we use vanilla softmax over the decoder vocabulary as opposed to more efficient alternatives such as sampled softmax (Jean et al., 2015). The vocabulary size is set to 40,000. The number of epochs

---

[6]https://nlp.stanford.edu/projects/glove/

is 20. Early stopping is used to avoid overfitting. The beam size is 5. Before feeding into the encoder, we reverse the input sentences (Sutskever et al., 2014).

5.2 Chinese-English

5.2.1 Dataset

We first evaluate our approach on the Chinese-English dataset (Zhang et al., 2017a), which contains pairs of Chinese sentences and English linearized PredPatt. Table 1 shows the number of data for training, validation and test.

#Train	#Valid	#Test
941,040	10,000	39,626

Table 1: Number of data used for Chinese-English cross-lingual open IE.

5.2.2 Comparisons

Our approach (**Selective Decoding**) is compared against four other approaches: (1) **Joint Seq2Seq**, which trains a standard encoder-decoder model on the Chinese-English dataset described in Table 1; (2) **Joint Moses**, which trains a phrase-based machine translation system, Moses (Koehn et al., 2007), directly on the same data; (3) **Pipeline-S** which consists of a Moses system that translates Chinese sentence to English *sentence*, followed by SyntaxNet Parser (Andor et al., 2016) for Universal Dependency parsing on English, and PredPatt (White et al., 2016) for predicate-argument identification; and (4) **Pipeline-N** is the same as Pipeline-S except that the Moses system is replaced by OpenNMT (Klein et al., 2017), a neural machine translation system.

5.2.3 Evaluation Metrics

For evaluation, we directly convert the output by our approach (e.g. Fig. 1(e)) to the form of linearized PredPatt (e.g., Fig. 1(d)), and follow the same manner in Zhang et al. (2017a), using the cased BLEU score and the token-level F_1 score to evaluate the results, since the generation of linearized PredPatt involves translation and information extraction. We also compute the recoverability: the number of outputs can not be recovered to the tree structure (e.g., Fig. 1(c)).

5.2.4 Evaluation using BLEU

Table 2 shows the cased BLEU scores of linearized PredPatt and linearized predicates[7] on the test set. Selective Decoding significantly improves the performance on both of them. Compared to the previous best approach (Joint Seq2Seq), Selective Decoding improves the BLEU score of linearized PredPatt to 23.88, and the score of linearized predicates to 25.42.

Approach	Linearized PredPatt	Linearized Predicate
Pipeline-S	17.19	17.24
Pipeline-N	18.03	18.59
Joint Moses	18.34	16.43
Joint Seq2Seq	18.94	21.55
Selective Decoding	**23.88**	24.81
- pretrained embeddings	23.67	**25.42**
- beam search	22.07	23.94

Table 2: Evaluation results (BLEU) of linearized PredPatt and linearized predicates on the test set.

We also report two ablation variants of Selective Decoding, i.e., without the pretrained word embeddings for parameter initialization (-pretrained embeddings), and without beam search, only using greedy search during inference (-beam search). As shown in Table 2, while the pretrained word embeddings moderately improve the BLEU score of linearized PredPatt, they have slightly negative impact on linearized predicates. Beam search helps improve the BLEU score of both.

Selective Decoding explicitly models sequence generation and sequence labeling, which enables a standalone evaluation of the sequence generation process (i.e., the final output without predicate and argument labels). To make a baseline comparison, we train an OpenNMT system (Klein et al., 2017) directly on the same data ignoring the labels.

OpenNMT	Selective Decoding
24.92	**25.16**

Table 3: Evaluation results (BLEU) of sequence generation on the test set.

Table 3 shows the BLEU score of sequence generation on the test set. Selective Decoding achieves higher BLEU than OpenNMT. It demonstrates that the selective decoding mechanism

---

[7]In linearized predicates, arguments are replaced by placeholders. For example, the linearized PredPatt in Fig. 1(d) becomes "[?arg started:p_h Sth:= [?arg firing:p_h ?arg]]" after replacement.

learning with extra labels helps improve the quality of sequence generation. We also notice that the BLEU score (25.16 in Table 2) of the final linearized PredPatt from Selective Decoding is even higher than OpenNMT (24.92 in Table 3). Hence, we can draw a conclusion that simply placing a labeler atop the OpenNMT system to tackle the cross-lingual open IE problem will not narrow the gap in BLEU between itself and our Selective Decoding approach.

5.2.5 Evaluation using F_1

Approach	Predicate	Argument
Pipeline-S	24.24	33.54
Pipeline-N	24.41	33.51
Joint Moses	25.11	38.90
Joint Seq2Seq	25.79	34.44
Selective Decoding	**31.71**	40.81
- pretrained embeddings	31.56	**40.81**
- beam search	30.06	39.06

Table 4: Evaluation results (F_1) of predicates and arguments on the test set.

We compute the token-level F_1 score (Liu et al., 2015) of predicates and arguments. As shown in Table 4, Selective Decoding substantially improves the F_1 score of both predicates and arguments. In the ablation test, pretrained word embeddings slightly improve F_1 of predicates, but have no improvement on F_1 of arguments. Beam search helps improve the score of both.

5.2.6 Recoverability

We compute the number of the linearized PredPatt outputs from which the tree structure representation can not be recovered, including the empty outputs and the outputs which have unmatched brackets, or have zero or multiple heads for an argument or a predicate. As shown in Table 5, compared to the previous best Joint Seq2Seq approach, Selective Decoding further reduces the number of unrecoverable outputs by one order of magnitude.

Pipeline-S	Pipeline-N	Joint Moses	Joint Seq2Seq	Selective Decoding
5,965	6,014	33,178	557	**53**

Table 5: Number of unrecoverable outputs.

5.2.7 Analysis

To analyze the difference between Selective Decoding and the previous best approach Joint

Seq2Seq, we plot the BLEU scores of the linearized PredPatt on the test set with respect to the lengths of the reference. As shown in Fig. 4, when the reference length is greater than 20, the linearized PredPatt generated by Selective Decoding gets notably better BLEU scores, especially for the reference length around 30. However, when the reference length is shorter than 11, the performance of Selective Decoding drops below the Joint Seq2Seq approach.

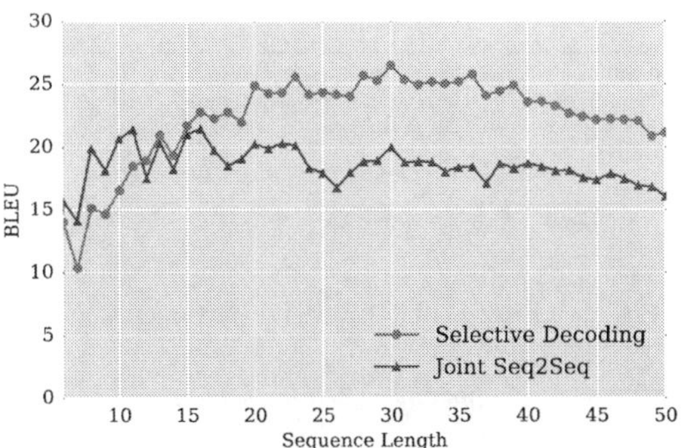

Figure 4: BLEU scores of the linearized PredPatt on the test set w.r.t. the lengths of the references.

To explain this performance drop, we randomly sample an example from the test set, where the reference length is shorter than 11, and the BLEU score of the linearized PredPatt generated by Joint Seq2Seq is higher than Selective Decoding. The example is shown in Table 6.

Input sentence and its English translation:

我 哪怕 有 千分之一 的 希望 呢 , 我 死
活 都 要 给 他 做 最后 的
(Even if there was only a one thousandth of a hope , er , live or die I would give him my all.)

Reference[8]:

  (1) (**I**) would **give** (**him**) (my **all**)

Selective Decoding:

  (1) Even if (**we**) **have** (a _UNK per cent **hope**)

  (2) uh , (**I**) would **have** SOMETHING[9]

  (3) SOMETHING := (**I**) **give** (**him**) (the final **thing**)

Joint Seq2Seq:

  (1) (**I**) **wish** (**everyone**) (last **hope**)

Table 6: Example outputs with the reference length shorter than 11.

In this example (Table 6), the Chinese input sentence has a grammatical error: the object modified by "最后 的" is missing. Additionally, the reference linearized PredPatt output in this example is incomplete: the fact related to the concessive clause is missing. Although here Joint Seq2Seq gets the better BLEU score against the incomplete reference, Selective Decoding is able to better generlize over the train data: the facts it generates are much closer to the original input sentence, and even better than the reference.

Input sentence and its English translation:
结果 , 民主党 失去 了 列举 布什 " 罪状 " 的 良机 ,
(*As a result, the Democratic party lost a good opportunity to list the ' charges ' against Bush.*)

Reference:

(1) As (a **result**) , (the Democratic **party**) **lost** (a good **opportunity**)

(2) (a good **opportunity**) **list** (the ' **charges** ` against Bush)

Selective Decoding:

(1) As (a **result**) , (the Democratic **Party**) **lost** (the good **opportunity**)

(2) (the good **opportunity**) **cite** (**Bush**)

Joint Seq2Seq:

(1) (The **result**) **is** SOMETHING

(2) SOMETHING := (the Democratic **Party**) **lost** (his **opportunity**)

(3) (his **opportunity**) **give** (**him**) (good **opportunity**)

Table 7: Example outputs with the reference length longer than 20.

Another example where the reference length is greater than 20 is shown in Table 7. In this example, Selective Decoding generates the same number of facts as the reference, and the meaning of the facts is closer to the reference than Joint Seq2Seq: though not perfect, Selective Decoding captures "列举 布什 ' 罪状 '" ("list the 'charges' against Bush") by generating "**cite** (**Bush**)", whereas Joint Seq2Seq fails to generate any thing related.

₈

5.3 Low-resource Scenarios

One of the goals of cross-lingual open IE is to extract facts from languages for which few NLP resources and tools are available, and represent the facts in the language for which plenties of resources and tools can be used. Therefore, we extend the experiments to cross-lingual open IE from 5 languages to English in a low-resource setting.

5.3.1 Datasets

Task	#Train	#Valid	#Test
uzb-eng	31,581	1,373	1,373
tur-eng	20,774	903	903
amh-eng	12,140	527	527
som-eng	10,702	465	465
yor-eng	5,787	251	251

Table 8: Number of data used for cross-lingual open IE in low-resource scenarios.

To prepare the experiment datasets, we first collect bitexts from DARPA LORELEI language packs (Strassel and Tracey, 2016). The source languages of the bitexts are Uzbek, Turkish, Amharic, Somali, and Yoruba.[10]

We then run a process similar to Zhang et al. (2017a) to generate pairs of source-language sentences and English linearized PredPatt: first, we employ SyntaxNet Parser (Andor et al., 2016) to generate Universal Dependency parses for the English sentences, and then run PredPatt (White et al., 2016) to generate English linearized PredPatt from the Universal Dependency parses. We remove empty sequences and very long sequences (length>50) in the pairs, and randomly split them into training, validation and test sets in the ratio of 23:1:1. The detailed number of pairs for each experiment is shown in Table 8.

5.3.2 Baseline

To compare with Selective Decoding, we implement the Joint Seq2Seq approach which uses a standard encoder-decoder model as the baseline.

5.3.3 Evaluation Results

We train the models of Selective Decoding and Joint Seq2Seq respectively using the same hyper-

---

⁸The predicate tokens are colored blue, and the argument tokens are colored purple. Head tokens are underlined in bold. Token labels and brackets are omitted.

⁹"SOMETHING" is a special argument used to indicate that the argument is a proposition.

¹⁰These bitexts are from LDC2016E29 (uzb-eng); LDC2014E115 (tur-eng); LDC2016E86 and LDC2016E87 (amh-eng); LDC2016E90 and LDC2016E91 (som-eng); LDC2016E104 and LDC2016E105 (yor-eng).

parameters setting described in § 5.1, and evaluate the results on the test set by computing the cased BLEU score of the linearized PredPatt, and the token-level F_1 scores.

Task	Joint S2S	Selective Decoding
uzb-eng	8.66	**10.76**
tur-eng	7.18	**7.47**
amh-eng	7.18	**8.37**
som-eng	10.61	**13.06**
yor-eng	11.31	**12.19**

Table 9: Evaluation results in low-resource cross-lingual open IE scenarios: BLEU of linearized PredPatt.

Table 9 shows the evaluation results using BBLEU. Selective Decoding outperforms the Joint Seq2Seq approach by 0.29-2.45, which is expected since Selective Decoding employs the decoder solely for sequence generation and the selector solely for sequence labeling.

Task	Predicate		Argument	
	Joint S2S	Selective Decoding	Joint S2S	Selective Decoding
uzb-eng	**12.50**	12.46	19.57	**24.08**
tur-eng	**9.89**	6.49	17.39	**17.76**
amh-eng	8.44	**8.82**	17.31	**18.58**
som-eng	13.64	**13.91**	22.81	**25.38**
yor-eng	**11.97**	10.74	22.61	**25.57**

Table 10: Evaluation results in low-resource cross-lingual open IE scenarios: the token-level F_1 of predicates and arguments.

The F_1 score measure is shown in Table 10 where both the F_1 scores of predicates and arguments are computed seperately. For predicates, Selective Decoding shows no advantage to the Joint Seq2Seq approach. In the tur-eng task, its F_1 score is obviously worse than the baseline. However, Selective Decoding in general shows promising results in the argument F_1 scores.

6 Conclusions

In this paper, we recast cross-lingual open IE as a more general problem, which involves sequence generation and sequence labeling. We propose a novel encoder-decoder model which employs the selective decoding mechanism to explicitly model the sequence generation and sequence labeling process. Experimental results show our approach achieves consistent and significant improvements in a variety of cross-lingual open IE scenarios.

Since the selective decoding mechanism is not limited to cross-lingual open IE, we believe that it will also benefit other NLP tasks which can be generalized as jointly doing sequence generation and sequence labeling. In the future, we plan to investigate its effectiveness to tasks such as cross-lingual information retrieval.

Acknowledgments

Thank you to the anonymous reviewers for their feedback. This work was supported in part by the JHU Human Language Technology Center of Excellence (HLTCOE), and DARPA LORELEI. The U.S. Government is authorized to reproduce and distribute reprints for Governmental purposes. The views and conclusions contained in this publication are those of the authors and should not be interpreted as representing official policies or endorsements of DARPA or the U.S. Government.

References

Daniel Andor, Chris Alberti, David Weiss, Aliaksei Severyn, Alessandro Presta, Kuzman Ganchev, Slav Petrov, and Michael Collins. 2016. Globally normalized transition-based neural networks. In *Proceedings of the 54th Annual Meeting of the Association for Computational Linguistics (Volume 1: Long Papers)*, pages 2442–2452, Berlin, Germany. Association for Computational Linguistics.

Gabor Angeli, Melvin Jose Johnson Premkumar, and Christopher D. Manning. 2015. Leveraging linguistic structure for open domain information extraction. In *Proceedings of the 53rd Annual Meeting of the Association for Computational Linguistics and the 7th International Joint Conference on Natural Language Processing (Volume 1: Long Papers)*, pages 344–354, Beijing, China. Association for Computational Linguistics.

Dzmitry Bahdanau, Kyunghyun Cho, and Yoshua Bengio. 2014. Neural machine translation by jointly learning to align and translate. *arXiv preprint arXiv:1409.0473*.

Michele Banko, Michael J. Cafarella, Stephen Soderland, Matt Broadhead, and Oren Etzioni. 2007. Open information extraction from the web. In *Proceedings of the 20th International Joint Conference on Artifical Intelligence*, IJCAI'07, pages 2670–2676, San Francisco, CA, USA. Morgan Kaufmann Publishers Inc.

Samuel R. Bowman, Jon Gauthier, Abhinav Rastogi, Raghav Gupta, Christopher D. Manning, and Christopher Potts. 2016. A fast unified model for parsing and sentence understanding. In *Proceedings of the 54th Annual Meeting of the Association* for Computational Linguistics (Volume 1: Long Papers), pages 1466–1477, Berlin, Germany. Association for Computational Linguistics.

Kyunghyun Cho, Bart van Merrienboer, Caglar Gulcehre, Dzmitry Bahdanau, Fethi Bougares, Holger Schwenk, and Yoshua Bengio. 2014. Learning phrase representations using rnn encoder–decoder for statistical machine translation. In *Proceedings of the 2014 Conference on Empirical Methods in Natural Language Processing (EMNLP)*, pages 1724–1734, Doha, Qatar. Association for Computational Linguistics.

Li Dong and Mirella Lapata. 2016. Language to logical form with neural attention. In *Proceedings of the 54th Annual Meeting of the Association for Computational Linguistics (Volume 1: Long Papers)*, pages 33–43, Berlin, Germany. Association for Computational Linguistics.

Anthony Fader, Stephen Soderland, and Oren Etzioni. 2011. Identifying relations for open information extraction. In *Proceedings of the 2011 Conference on Empirical Methods in Natural Language Processing*, pages 1535–1545, Edinburgh, Scotland, UK. Association for Computational Linguistics.

Karl Moritz Hermann, Tomas Kocisky, Edward Grefenstette, Lasse Espeholt, Will Kay, Mustafa Suleyman, and Phil Blunsom. 2015. Teaching machines to read and comprehend. In C. Cortes, N. D. Lawrence, D. D. Lee, M. Sugiyama, and R. Garnett, editors, *Advances in Neural Information Processing Systems 28*, pages 1693–1701. Curran Associates, Inc.

Sepp Hochreiter and Jürgen Schmidhuber. 1997. Long short-term memory. *Neural computation*, 9(8):1735–1780.

Sébastien Jean, Kyunghyun Cho, Roland Memisevic, and Yoshua Bengio. 2015. On using very large target vocabulary for neural machine translation. In *Proceedings of the 53rd Annual Meeting of the Association for Computational Linguistics and the 7th International Joint Conference on Natural Language Processing (Volume 1: Long Papers)*, pages 1–10, Beijing, China. Association for Computational Linguistics.

Nal Kalchbrenner and Phil Blunsom. 2013. Recurrent continuous translation models. In *Proceedings of the 2013 Conference on Empirical Methods in Natural Language Processing*, pages 1700–1709, Seattle, Washington, USA. Association for Computational Linguistics.

Andrej Karpathy and Li Fei-Fei. 2015. Deep visual-semantic alignments for generating image descriptions. In *Proceedings of the IEEE Conference on Computer Vision and Pattern Recognition*, pages 3128–3137.

Diederik Kingma and Jimmy Ba. 2014. Adam: A method for stochastic optimization. *arXiv preprint arXiv:1412.6980*.

G. Klein, Y. Kim, Y. Deng, J. Senellart, and A. M. Rush. 2017. OpenNMT: Open-Source Toolkit for Neural Machine Translation. *ArXiv e-prints*.

Philipp Koehn, Hieu Hoang, Alexandra Birch, Chris Callison-Burch, Marcello Federico, Nicola Bertoldi, Brooke Cowan, Wade Shen, Christine Moran, Richard Zens, et al. 2007. Moses: Open source toolkit for statistical machine translation. In *Proceedings of the 45th annual meeting of the ACL on interactive poster and demonstration sessions*, pages 177–180. Association for Computational Linguistics.

Zhengzhong Liu, Teruko Mitamura, and Eduard Hovy. 2015. Evaluation algorithms for event nugget detection: A pilot study. In *Proceedings of the 3rd Workshop on EVENTS at the NAACL-HLT*, pages 53–57.

Di Lu, Xiaoman Pan, Nima Pourdamghani, Shih-Fu Chang, Heng Ji, and Kevin Knight. 2016. A multimedia approach to cross-lingual entity knowledge transfer. In *Proceedings of the 54th Annual Meeting of the Association for Computational Linguistics (Volume 1: Long Papers)*, pages 54–65, Berlin, Germany. Association for Computational Linguistics.

Minh-Thang Luong, Hieu Pham, and Christopher D. Manning. 2015. Effective approaches to attention-based neural machine translation. In *Proceedings of the 2015 Conference on Empirical Methods in Natural Language Processing*, pages 1412–1421, Lisbon, Portugal. Association for Computational Linguistics.

Razvan Pascanu, Tomas Mikolov, and Yoshua Bengio. 2013. On the difficulty of training recurrent neural networks. In *Proceedings of The 30th International Conference on Machine Learning*, pages 1310–1318.

Jeffrey Pennington, Richard Socher, and Christopher D. Manning. 2014. Glove: Global vectors for word representation. In *Empirical Methods in Natural Language Processing (EMNLP)*, pages 1532–1543.

Alexander M. Rush, Sumit Chopra, and Jason Weston. 2015. A neural attention model for abstractive sentence summarization. In *Proceedings of the 2015 Conference on Empirical Methods in Natural Language Processing*, pages 379–389, Lisbon, Portugal. Association for Computational Linguistics.

Mike Schuster and Kuldip K Paliwal. 1997. Bidirectional recurrent neural networks. *IEEE Transactions on Signal Processing*, 45(11):2673–2681.

Matthew Snover, Nitin Madnani, Bonnie J Dorr, and Richard Schwartz. 2009. Fluency, adequacy, or hter?: exploring different human judgments with a tunable mt metric. In *Proceedings of the Fourth*

Workshop on Statistical Machine Translation, pages 259–268. Association for Computational Linguistics.

Nitish Srivastava, Geoffrey E Hinton, Alex Krizhevsky, Ilya Sutskever, and Ruslan Salakhutdinov. 2014. Dropout: a simple way to prevent neural networks from overfitting. *Journal of Machine Learning Research*, 15(1):1929–1958.

Stephanie Strassel and Jennifer Tracey. 2016. Lorelei language packs: Data, tools, and resources for technology development in low resource languages. In *Proceedings of the Tenth International Conference on Language Resources and Evaluation (LREC 2016)*, Paris, France. European Language Resources Association (ELRA).

Kiyoshi Sudo, Satoshi Sekine, and Ralph Grishman. 2004. Cross-lingual information extraction system evaluation. In *Proceedings of the 20th international Conference on Computational Linguistics*, page 882. Association for Computational Linguistics.

Ilya Sutskever, Oriol Vinyals, and Quoc V Le. 2014. Sequence to sequence learning with neural networks. In *Advances in neural information processing systems*, pages 3104–3112.

Zhaopeng Tu, Yang Liu, Zhengdong Lu, Xiaohua Liu, and Hang Li. 2016. Context gates for neural machine translation. *arXiv preprint arXiv:1608.06043*.

Oriol Vinyals, Łukasz Kaiser, Terry Koo, Slav Petrov, Ilya Sutskever, and Geoffrey Hinton. 2015a. Grammar as a foreign language. In *Advances in Neural Information Processing Systems*, pages 2773–2781.

Oriol Vinyals, Alexander Toshev, Samy Bengio, and Dumitru Erhan. 2015b. Show and tell: A neural image caption generator. In *Proceedings of the IEEE Conference on Computer Vision and Pattern Recognition*, pages 3156–3164.

Aaron Steven White, Drew Reisinger, Keisuke Sakaguchi, Tim Vieira, Sheng Zhang, Rachel Rudinger, Kyle Rawlins, and Benjamin Van Durme. 2016. Universal decompositional semantics on universal dependencies. In *Proceedings of the 2016 Conference on Empirical Methods in Natural Language Processing*, pages 1713–1723, Austin, Texas. Association for Computational Linguistics.

Kelvin Xu, Jimmy Ba, Ryan Kiros, Kyunghyun Cho, Aaron C Courville, Ruslan Salakhutdinov, Richard S Zemel, and Yoshua Bengio. 2015. Show, attend and tell: Neural image caption generation with visual attention. In *ICML*, volume 14, pages 77–81.

Sheng Zhang, Kevin Duh, and Benjamin Van Durme. 2017a. Mt/ie: Cross-lingual open information extraction with neural sequence-to-sequence models. In *Proceedings of the 15th Conference of the European Chapter of the Association for Computational Linguistics: Volume 2, Short Papers*, pages 64–70, Valencia, Spain. Association for Computational Linguistics.

Sheng Zhang, Rachel Rudinger, Kevin Duh, and Ben Van Durme. 2017b. Ordinal common-sense inference. *Transactions of the Association for Computational Linguistics*.

Sheng Zhang, Rachel Rudinger, and Ben Van Durme. 2017c. An evaluation of predpatt and open ie via stage 1 semantic role labeling. In *Proceedings of the 12th International Conference on Computational Semantics (IWCS)*, Montpellier, France.

Event Ordering with a Generalized Model for Sieve Prediction Ranking

Bill McDowell
The Pennsylvania State University
forkunited@gmail.com

Nathanael Chambers
United States Naval Academy
nchamber@usna.edu

Alexander G. Ororbia II
The Pennsylvania State University
ago109@psu.edu

David Reitter
The Pennsylvania State University
reitter@psu.edu

Abstract

This paper improves on several aspects of a sieve-based event ordering architecture, CAEVO (Chambers et al., 2014), which creates globally consistent temporal relations between events and time expressions. First, we examine the usage of word embeddings and semantic role features. With the incorporation of these new features, we demonstrate a 5% relative F1 gain over our replicated version of CAEVO. Second, we reformulate the architecture's sieve-based inference algorithm as a *prediction reranking* method that approximately optimizes a scoring function computed using classifier precisions. Within this prediction reranking framework, we propose an alternative scoring function, showing an 8.8% relative gain over the original CAEVO. We further include an in-depth analysis of one of the main datasets that is used to evaluate temporal classifiers, and we show that in spite of the density of this corpus, there is still a danger of overfitting. While this paper focuses on temporal ordering, its results are applicable to other areas that use sieve-based architectures.

1 Introduction

Narratives that describe a series of events rarely do so in order. Basic rules of journalism dictate that important information leads a news report, and accordingly, algorithms that re-order events chronologically need to combine a wealth of contextual, rhetorical, and commonsense information.

Most research on event ordering aims to produce only partial orderings of event mentions and time expressions (Bethard and Martin, 2007; Cheng et al., 2007; UzZaman and Allen, 2010; Llorens et al., 2010; Bethard, 2013). In the past, labeled corpora used for training and evaluation contained only small subsets of pairs of events and times. Some of these corpora, like *Timebank*, have annotations restricted to salient, easily labeled pairs within the same document. Other more recent data sets contain annotations that form timelines of events that involve common entities (Pustejovsky et al., 2003; Minard et al., 2015). Due to the lack of consistency of annotations across event pairs, it is difficult to use these corpora in accurately measuring the practical performance of event ordering algorithms.

Richer datasets are becoming available that provide more complete event orderings which include logically implied relations that are less evident from local text features. In particular, the *TimeBank-Dense* corpus provides a significantly more dense and complete set of annotations, allowing for the evaluation of methods that make use of broad contextual information across many event pairs (Cassidy et al., 2014). One method that has been developed to leverage such information is CAEVO—a sieve-based architecture that made the first effort toward dense event ordering (Chambers et al., 2014). This method maintains transitivity constraints across independent predictions from several specialized classifiers. More specifically, the architecture runs a series of "sieve" classifiers with their predictions ranked in order by precision using a held-out dataset. The higher precision classifiers are ranked more highly in the series, and predictions are expanded by transitivity rules (e.g. if event e_1 is before e_2, and e_2 is before e_3, then e_1 is before e_3) after each individual classifier generates its predictions. The high den-

Proceedings of the The 8th International Joint Conference on Natural Language Processing, pages 843–853,
Taipei, Taiwan, November 27 – December 1, 2017 ©2017 AFNLP

sity of the constructed prediction graph allows the transitivity rules to generate accurate predictions for links that would otherwise be difficult to predict from the text.

This paper proposes improvements to CAEVO with respect to (1) feature engineering within machine learned sieves, (2) generalization of the sieve-based architecture to facilitate higher performing sieve prediction rerankings, and (3) the leveraging of unlabeled data. First, for our feature engineering improvements, we are motivated by the fact that TimeBank-Dense contains a relatively small training sample, and so we extend the feature sets for the architecture's machine learned classifiers to include features that encode lexical information about events in relatively low dimensional spaces based on word embeddings (Mikolov et al., 2013) and semantic role labeling (SRL) annotations (Gildea and Jurafsky, 2002). Second, our generalization of the sieve-based architecture allows us to experiment with alternative methods for establishing the precedence ranking of sieve predictions. Furthermore, we identify an approximate upper bound on any ranking method's performance. Lastly, in our experiments with unlabeled data, we analyze the effect of changing the density of the architecture's prediction graph. Our hypothesis is that increasing the number of predictions on unlabeled data will increase performance on labeled data through the application of CAEVO's transitivity constraints.

Our extensions produce new state-of-the-art results on the original test split of TimeBank-Dense (8.8% F1 increase). Beyond this, we describe alternative evaluations on other splits of the data in order to analyze the effect of the common small sizes of temporal corpora like TimeBank-Dense. This analysis is critical for future work in temporal ordering, and sheds further light on previous work's results.

2 Related Work

Early work on event ordering focused on developing machine-learned classifiers that label the temporal relations between small subsets of pairs of events within documents using lexical and syntactical features (Bethard and Martin, 2007; Cheng et al., 2007; UzZaman and Allen, 2010; Llorens et al., 2010; Bethard, 2013). Later work leveraged information across pairwise predictions by imposing transitivity constraints using techniques

like integer linear programming and Markov logic networks (Bramsen et al., 2006; Chambers and Jurafsky, 2008; Tatu and Srikanth, 2008; Yoshikawa et al., 2009). CAEVO followed these and other hybrid rule-based approaches (D'Souza and Ng, 2013), but with the transitivity constraints yielding larger gains in performance for the more complete temporal graph constructed on the TimeBank-Dense corpus (Cassidy et al., 2014; Chambers et al., 2014).

The *TimeBank-Dense* corpus provides a significantly more dense and complete set of annotations compared to previous corpora.[1] TimeBank-Dense extends a subset of the original TimeBank corpus with annotations for (almost) *all* event-time, time-time, and event-time pairs across consecutive sentences, as well as relations to the document creation time. This dense corpus facilitated the evaluation of CAEVO—a sieve-based architecture which maintains transitivity constraints across independent predictions from several specialized classifiers.

Recent work has focused on the construction of timelines of related events, using SRL annotations to determine which events are related through common actors (Laparra et al., 2015). In addition, other work has outperformed the original CAEVO with a 2.2% relative F1 gain on TimeBank-Dense using word embedding features within a stacked ensemble of event-event, event-time, and event-creation-time logistic regression classifiers (Mirza and Tonelli, 2016). We draw inspiration from this recent work by incorporating SRL and word embedding features into the machine-learned CAEVO sieves.

The CAEVO architecture is itself inspired by the sieve-based architectures that have been successfully applied to event and entity coreference as well as spatial relation extraction tasks (Lee et al., 2012, 2013; D'Souza and Ng, 2015). Years since CAEVO's introduction, a coreference sieve architecture still achieves top performance (Lee et al., 2017). The key idea behind these architectures is to combine information from several classifiers by assigning precedence to predictions according to the reliability of the classifier from which they originate. A precision-ranked series of

---

[1]The new corpus is the result of several TempEval competitions (Verhagen et al., 2007, 2010; UzZaman et al., 2012) which prompted efforts to develop more complete event ordering annotations (Bramsen et al., 2006; Kolomiyets et al., 2012; Do et al., 2012).

"sieve" classifiers generate predictions, and predictions from the more reliable sieves earlier in the series inform the predictions of the less reliable sieves later in the series. Generally, the predictions from a highly-ranked sieve can inform a low-ranked sieve in several ways, but within CAEVO, predictions from early classifiers are coupled via transitive inference rules to generate an expanding set of predictions that override output from less reliable classifiers later on in the series. In the next section, we describe a more generic view of this architecture which will motivate alternative methods for assigning precedence to predictions from the collection of classifiers.

3 Generalizing Sieve Architectures

Sieve architectures are used in many areas such as entity coreference, relation extraction, and temporal ordering. A core contribution of this paper is a generalization of how these models score and rank their decisions. Like other sieve models, CAEVO uses a precision-ranked series of classifiers (i.e. "sieves") coupled with transitivity constraints to provide a solution to the event ordering task. However, prior work has not investigated alternatives to the coarse-grained precision-based rankings provided by the architecture. This section gives a generalized formal view on this precision-ranked setup, and Section 4.3.1 describes our experiments with new alternatives to traditional sieve architectures that are available within our generalized view.

Informally speaking, a sieve architecture applies a sequence of classifiers that each make their own independent labeling decisions, and the architecture resolves conflicts between these decisions by assigning precedence to those which have higher estimated precision. The architecture estimates the precision for each sieve on a development set of data, and associates all predictions from a given sieve with this precision estimate. These precision scores determine an overall ranking to predictions within the final system. When labeling a new test document, the architecture chooses predictions from all higher precision sieves over predictions from lower precision sieves. But this common ranking of predictions is coarse-grained, so this paper proposes other ways of ordering the classifier predictions. Figure 1 illustrates the difference between prediction rankings from traditional sieve architectures and our

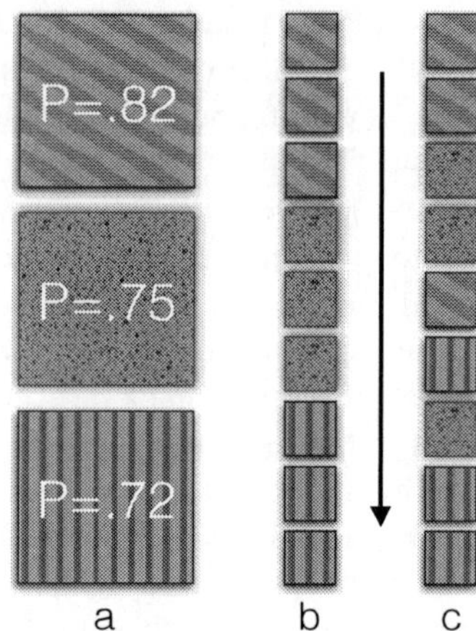

Figure 1: Sieve classifier decisions as ranked in a sieve architecture: (a) three sieves with their precisions, (b) each sieve's decisions ranked as in a traditional system, (c) a potential ranking influenced by precision, but not strictly bound to it.

alternatives. The middle column shows the strict prediction ordering given by traditional sieve systems, but the fuzzy ordering in the right column is possible within our proposed alternative architectures. Section 4.3.1 explores this in depth.

We now formally define a typical sieve architecture (in terms of the temporal ordering domain). Consider the set of event mentions E, time expressions T, and temporal relation types $L =$ {BEFORE, AFTER, INCLUDES, INCLUDED, SIMULTANEOUS, VAGUE}. We desire an architecture that encodes functions $f_{ee} : E \times E \rightarrow L$, $f_{et} : E \times T \rightarrow L$, and $f_{tt} : T \times T \rightarrow L$ which accurately classify relations between event-event, event-time, and time-time pairs, respectively. The gold-standard annotations within our corpora are logically consistent, so we can assume that the true event orderings induced by the functions f_{ee}, f_{et}, and f_{tt} conform to the transitivity constraints given in Table 1.

Algorithm 1 depicts a generalized view of the CAEVO architecture which encodes approximations to the desired f_{ee}, f_{et}, and f_{tt} labeling functions (and this view also applies to other typical sieve systems). The algorithm combines predictions from a set of sieve classifiers $\hat{F}$ that provide partial approximations to f_{ee}, f_{et}, and f_{tt} within restricted syntactic contexts. As described by Chambers et al. (2014), $\hat{F}$ contains both rule based and machine-learned classifiers. In this pa-

Constraints
BEFORE(o_1, o_2), BEFORE(o_2, o_3) $\rightarrow$ BEFORE(o_1, o_3)
BEFORE(o_1, o_2), INCLUDES(o_2, o_3) $\rightarrow$ BEFORE(o_1, o_3)
BEFORE(o_1, o_2), SIMULTAN(o_2, o_3) $\rightarrow$ BEFORE(o_1, o_3)
INCLUDED(o_1, o_2), BEFORE(o_2, o_3) $\rightarrow$ BEFORE(o_1, o_3)
INCLUDED(o_1, o_2), INCLUDED(o_2, o_3) $\rightarrow$ INCLUDED(o_1, o_3)
INCLUDED(o_1, o_2), SIMULTAN(o_2, o_3) $\rightarrow$ INCLUDED(o_1, o_3)
INCLUDED(o_1, o_2), AFTER(o_2, o_3) $\rightarrow$ AFTER(o_1, o_3)
INCLUDES(o_1, o_2), INCLUDES(o_2, o_3) $\rightarrow$ INCLUDES(o_1, o_3)
INCLUDES(o_1, o_2), SIMULTAN(o_2, o_3) $\rightarrow$ INCLUDES(o_1, o_3)
SIMULTAN(o_1, o_2), BEFORE(o_2, o_3) $\rightarrow$ BEFORE(o_1, o_3)
SIMULTAN(o_1, o_2), INCLUDED(o_2, o_3) $\rightarrow$ INCLUDED(o_1, o_3)
SIMULTAN(o_1, o_2), INCLUDES(o_2, o_3) $\rightarrow$ INCLUDES(o_1, o_3)
SIMULTAN(o_1, o_2), SIMULTAN(o_2, o_3) $\rightarrow$ SIMULTAN(o_1, o_3)
SIMULTAN(o_1, o_2), AFTER(o_2, o_3) $\rightarrow$ AFTER(o_1, o_3)
AFTER(o_1, o_2), INCLUDES(o_2, o_3) $\rightarrow$ AFTER(o_1, o_3)
AFTER(o_1, o_2), SIMULTAN(o_2, o_3) $\rightarrow$ AFTER(o_1, o_3)
AFTER(o_1, o_2), AFTER(o_2, o_3) $\rightarrow$ AFTER(o_1, o_3)
BEFORE(o_1, o_2) $\rightarrow$ AFTER(o_2, o_1)
AFTER(o_1, o_2) $\rightarrow$ BEFORE(o_2, o_1)
INCLUDES(o_1, o_2) $\rightarrow$ INCLUDED(o_2, o_1)
INCLUDED(o_1, o_2) $\rightarrow$ INCLUDES(o_2, o_1)
SIMULTAN(o_1, o_2) $\rightarrow$ SIMULTAN(o_2, o_1)
VAGUE(o_1, o_2) $\rightarrow$ VAGUE(o_2, o_1)

Table 1: Transitivity and symmetry constraints in C from Equation 1 and Algorithm 1. In this list, every constraint applies to events and/or times o_1, o_2 and o_3. We abbreviate "SIMULTANEOUS" with "SIMULTAN" due to space constraints.

per, our experiments focus on the machine learned sieves that give within-sentence event-event predictions (EEWS), within-sentence event-time predictions (ETWS), within-syntactic dominance relation event-event predictions (EED), and event to document creation time relations (EDCT).

Given a set of unlabeled data points $D \subseteq (E \cup T) \times (E \cup T)$, Algorithm 1 uses the sieves in $\hat{F}$ to construct a set of predictions $\hat{F}_D = \{(d, \hat{f}(d), \hat{f}) \mid d \in D, \hat{f} \in \hat{F}\}$ where each prediction is indexed with its associated sieve $\hat{f}$. The algorithm then sorts and partitions $\hat{F}_D$ according to a prediction scoring function $s : (D \times L \times \hat{F}) \rightarrow \mathbb{R}$. Finally, the returned set of predictions R is constructed by iteratively adding predictions from $\hat{F}_D$ in descending order (with respect to s) while applying constraints C. C consists of the transitive rules (depicted in Table 1) along with the constraint that prior predictions in R cannot be overwritten by later predictions. The rules C are applied at each iteration by extending the current predictions with those implied by transitivity.

Algorithm 1 Sieve Inference

1: **function** SIEVEINFERENCE
2:     Input $\hat{F}$:= learned and rule-based sieves
3:     Input D := data to classify
4:     Input s := prediction scoring function
5:     Input C := constraint application function
6:     $\hat{F}_D \leftarrow \{(d, \hat{f}(d), \hat{f}) \mid d \in D, \hat{f} \in \hat{F}\}$
7:     $P \leftarrow \hat{F}_D$ sorted and partitioned by s
8:     $R \leftarrow \{\}$
9:     **for** $i := 1$ to $|P|$ **do**
10:         $R \leftarrow C(P_i \cup R)$
    return R

One of the weaknesses of CAEVO (and other sieve-based systems) addressed in this paper is that its scoring function, $s(d, \hat{f}(d), \hat{f})$, is simply the precision of $\hat{f}$ as measured on held-out data. All predictions made by $\hat{f}$ must have the same ranking score (see Figure 1 again). This coarse-ranking is likely to be sub-optimal relative to rankings based on other scoring functions.

We can motivate improvements to Algorithm 1 by viewing it as a greedy approximation to the optimization problem which chooses a set of scored predictions according to:

$$R = \arg\max_{S \subseteq \hat{F}_D} \left(\sum_{p \in S} s(p) \right) \text{ subject to } C \quad (1)$$

Given the view that CAEVO is providing a solution to the objective in Equation 1 using Algorithm 1, it is straightforward to see possible directions for improvement. Namely, the architecture can be improved through changes to the sieves $\hat{F}$, the scoring methods s, the constraints C, the data D, and the underlying greedy approximation algorithm. Intuitively, if we want Equation 1 to give a highly accurate set of predictions, then we should pick an $\hat{F}$ to contain more accurate classifiers [2], an s which ranks correct predictions above incorrect predictions, and a large set D which enables C to propagate precise labels from easy-to-classify data samples onto hard-to-classify data samples. Notably, CAEVO's rigid choice of scoring function s to be the precision of $\hat{f}$ only allows s to give a coarse-grained scoring, which can score incorrect predictions higher than correct predictions.

---

[2]This includes possibility that one or more $\hat{f} \in \hat{F}$ could be parameterized by more complex function approximators, such as neural networks (LeCun et al., 2015).

Furthermore, CAEVO's sieve-inference in Algorithm 1 is greedy, and other methods like integer linear programming (ILP) which provide better solutions to Equation 1 might yield more accurate predictions. Lastly, CAEVO limits D to only contain *labeled* evaluation data without taking advantage of constraints imposed across *unlabeled* event pairs. These observations motivate several of the extensions we describe and experiment with below.

4 Models and Experiments

In our experiments, we replicate CAEVO, add new features to the sieves, modify the scoring function, and include larger amounts of related unlabeled data to further constrain the predictions. Unless otherwise noted, results are computed using the original train-dev-test split of the TimeBank-Dense and original CAEVO experiments (Chambers et al., 2014; Cassidy et al., 2014).

4.1 Replication

We replicate the CAEVO architecture within a more generic framework with the aim of substantiating and extending the CAEVO results from Chambers et al. (2014). The replication process allows us to validate the robustness of the originally published results while determining their sensitivity to various parameter settings.

We reconstruct features within an alternative feature engineering pipeline, and ensure that the feature matrices match those from the original system. During this process, we observed two issues in the original system. First, features based on gold-standard event "tense", "aspect", and "class" were not included in the machine-learned models that produced the reported results even though they were described in the original paper (they appear to have been inadvertently configured off). In light of this, we leave these features out of our replicated architecture, but add them into the revised architecture in our feature engineering experiments. Second, the EEWS, EED, and ETWS sieves in CAEVO used a minimum feature occurrence cutoff of 2 across training data whereas EDCT used a cutoff of 1. We experiment with different settings of these values in the next section. Other minor bugs and the details of replication are described in the appendix.

The **R** column of Table 2 gives micro-averaged accuracies[3] for the four machine-learned sieves and the full replicated architecture. These accuracies reproduce the original CAEVO results up to less than 1% discrepancy in accuracy due to version differences between the machine-learning libraries and minor bugs in the original system. [4]

4.2 Rich Feature Engineering

We extend our CAEVO replication with additional knowledge of event attributes, word embeddings, and SRL labels for each of the machine learned sieves.

4.2.1 Event Attributes

As noted above, the original CAEVO paper had reported the use of gold-standard TimeML tense, aspect, class, polarity, and modality event attribute features, but close inspection of the architecture suggests that these features had been left out when computing the final results. We experimented with adding features computed from these attributes into each of the machine-learned classifiers. For each event in a given event-event or event-time pair, we extend the feature vector with indicators for possible values of each event attribute. Also, for each event-event pair, we extend the feature vector with indicators of whether the event attributes are equal for the source and target (e.g. equal tense), as well as features representing the conjunction of each attribute across source and target (e.g. for the tense attribute, one of the indicators is *PAST-FUTURE*, which is for a pair containing a past tensed event and a future tensed event).

The F1 scores computed on the TimeBank-Dense test-set with the additional event attribute features are given in the **Ev** column of Table 2. Each machine-learned sieve increases in F1, but the overall architecture *decreases* slightly. This highlights the non-monotonic relationship between the performance of individual sieves and the performance of the overall architecture.

4.2.2 Semantic Role Labeling

We compute additional features from annotations generated using the *mate-tools* SRL system (Björkelund et al., 2009). Specifically, for a given pair, we compute features representing SRL predicates of the events as well as their conjunction.

---

[3] The micro-averaged accuracies are equivalent to micro-averaged F1 scores computed on data for which some label is output by a classifier.

[4] The results for the rule-based sieves are not shown, but they match the original system exactly.

Sieve	R	Ev	SRL	W2V	R+	F+
EDCT	.524	.547	.511	.524	.553	.553
ETWS	.414	.450	.414	.450	.443	.480
EEWS	.442	.466	.424	.450	.450	.456
EED	.428	.500	.435	.473	.488	.466
Full	**.502**	**.495**	**.493**	**.504**	**.520**	**.527**

Table 2: Micro-averaged accuracies on the TimeBank-Dense test-set for machine-learned sieves and the fully replicated architecture with various feature extensions. Results are given for our baseline CAEVO replication (**R**) and extensions with gold-standard event attribute features (**Ev**), SRL features (**SRL**), word embedding features (**W2V**), all new features (**R+**), and all new features with new feature count cutoffs (**F+**).

Also, we compute the shortest path between a pair within the undirected graph formed by the SRL predicates and arguments (i.e. where there are nodes for predicate spans and argument spans, and there is an edge between two spans if one is the argument of the other). As shown in Table 2 under the **SRL** column, these features only give a minor improvement in micro-averaged F1 for the EED sieve, but hurt performance of the other sieves and the architecture on the TimeBank-Dense test set. However, we believe this may be due to overfitting, as we observe 3% and 4% gains for the ETWS and EED sieves with these features on the development set.

4.2.3 Word Embeddings

Given that recent work has shown improvements using word embeddings (using log-linear neural language models such as the Skip-Gram architecture), we extend feature vectors with the word vectors representing events and their similarity. Following Mirza and Tonelli (2016), we use the three million 300-dimensional *word2vec* vectors [5] pre-trained on part of the Google News dataset (Mikolov et al., 2013). For each token span corresponding to either an event mention or time expression in a given pair datum, we extend the feature vector with normalized sums of word vectors computed from tokens of the span. In addition, we include the cosine similarity between the vectors for the events in a pair, as well as a vector representing the normalized difference between the pair's vectors. Micro-averaged F1 scores on the TimeBank-Dense test set with these word embed-

ding features are given in the **W2V** column of Table 2. The ETWS and EED sieves show improvements of more than 3%, and the EEWS shows a gain of about 1%. However, the F1 score for the overall architecture remains nearly the same.

4.2.4 Full Extension

We extend the machine learned sieves with the full set of event attributes, SRL, and word embedding features as described above. As shown under the **R+** column of Table 2, this yields a 2% gain in micro-averaged F1 for the overall architecture as well as gains for each individual sieve. Also, Section 4.1 mentioned that the feature count cutoffs in **R** and **R+** are set to 1 for EDCT and 2 for all remaining machine-learned sieves. For simplicity, we set the cutoff to 1 across all sieves in **F+**, yielding a 4% improvement in ETWS and minor gains in EEWS and the full system over **R+**. Overall, our feature engineering efforts give **F+** a 5% relative gain (2.5% absolute) over the replicated CAEVO architecture (**R**).

4.3 Modifying Sieve Inference

This section proposes new inference methods for sieve architectures by varying the scoring function s and adding unlabeled data to D from Algorithm 1 and Equation 1 in Section 3. This is a core contribution that can benefit not just temporal ordering, but also other sieve systems applied to other NLP tasks.

4.3.1 Alternative Scoring Methods

In the original CAEVO architecture's implementation of Algorithm 1 from Section 3, the score $s(d, \hat{f}(d), \hat{f})$ is computed as the precision of the sieve $\hat{f}$ on the development set. This greedy scorer s gives a coarse-grain ranking of sieve predictions, assigning equal precedence to all predictions from a given sieve $\hat{f}$. Intuitively, if we want to produce a higher accuracy architecture, then we should adjust the scoring function s to score all correct predictions more highly than all incorrect predictions[6]. CAEVO's use of $\hat{f}$ precision in computing s is a coarse-grained heuristic in line with this goal, but there are better choices.

Ideal Scorer In the best case, the **F+*** column of Table 3 shows the micro-averaged F1 (equivalent to accuracy) when s scores a prediction as

---

[5] Pre-trained word vectors can be retrieved from `https://code.google.com/archive/p/word2vec/`.

[6] Note that while such a choice of s should produce good performance, this performance is not necessarily optimal under the transitivity constraints.

Data	V	CAEVO (R)	F+	F+L	F+S	F+LU	F+*
Dev	.378	.481	.485	**.490**	.481	.491	.585
Test	.403	.502	.527	**.546**	.521	.541	.642

Table 3: Micro-averaged F1 scores on the original TimeBank-Dense train-dev-test split for several versions of the sieve architecture. Results are given for the VAGUE majority baseline (**V**), the CAEVO replication (**R**), the architecture with the extended feature set (**F+**), and varying inference methods under the extended feature set. The varying inference methods include an alternative prediction scoring function s computed by precision of each sieve on each relation label (**F+L**), s computed by precision multiplied by classifier probability estimates (**F+S**), s computed by precision on each label with extra unlabeled data (**F+LU**), and s computed to produce near-optimal ordering (**F+***).

$s(d, \hat{f}(d), \hat{f}) = 1$ if $\hat{f}(d)$ is the correct label for datum d, and 0 otherwise. This near-optimal choice of s in **F+*** gives a 10% gain over **F+**, suggesting a large room for improvement by reranking sieve predictions rather than improving the accuracy of the individual sieves. This suggests that architecture performance will increase by improving the estimates of the prediction *confidence* encoded by s, rather than improving the predictions themselves.

New Scorers We thus consider several alternatives for s. First, we attempted estimating s by training a reranking logistic regression model to predict whether $\hat{f}(d)$ is the correct label for d within prediction $(d, \hat{f}(d), \hat{f})$. This approach did not improve performance over other simpler approaches (possibly due to the small size of reranking training data), and so we only report results for the simpler approaches. In one approach, motivated by the observation that precision varies across relation labels, we compute $s(d, \hat{f}(d), \hat{f})$ as the precision of $\hat{f}$ for predictions with label $\hat{f}(d)$ on the dev data. This sieve-label precision approach improves F1 over **F+** as shown in the **F+L** column of Table 3. In a second approach, we compute $s(d, \hat{f}(d), \hat{f})$ as the precision of $\hat{f}$ multiplied by the probability assigned to $\hat{f}(d)$ by the logistic regression model employed by $\hat{f}$. According to the **F+S** column of Table 3, this approach does not show improvement over **F+**.

4.3.2 Leveraging Unlabeled Data

CAEVO uses Algorithm 1 to draw inferences about a data set D. In the original implementation, this set contained only the gold-standard labeled evaluation pairs within two sentence windows. However, if D were expanded with other unlabeled data points outside of two sentence windows (for which it is easy to predict labels with high precision), the transitivity constraints in C might generate further high precision predictions on the labeled data. Interestingly, this gives the architecture the property that making a larger number of predictions on a logically connected set of data can lead to higher overall performance on subsets of that data. Given this observation, we apply the **F+L** version of the architecture to all pairs of events and times within a document. The resulting F1 scores given this expansion of D with the unlabeled TimeBank-Dense pairs are shown under column **F+LU** of Table 3. Unfortunately, these scores show no improvement over the scores under column **F+L** which suggests that the architecture did not draw high precision inferences from the unlabeled data to labeled data. This may be due to the lack of sieves tuned specifically to make between-sentence unlabeled data predictions, or it may be due to an inherent difficulty in making these predictions over the labeled within-sentence and consecutive sentence predictions.

5 Deep Dive into the Data

One of the difficulties facing the temporal ordering community is sparse data. This has been an issue since the original TimeBank Corpus, and the TimeBank-Dense Corpus had data expansion as one of its core goals. However, we argue that data sparsity is still a problem, and previous work tends not to explore different test sets, potentially misidentifying positive and negative results specific to particular splits of the data. This issue seems especially relevant due to the small size of the TimeBank-Dense data (only 5 documents in dev and 9 documents in test for the original split (Chambers et al., 2014)).

The underlying question is whether new results present a significant improvement upon older ones. We consider multiple cross-validation splits of the data to get some sense about the answer to this question. We chose this approach over null-hypothesis significance testing due to limitations induced by small sample size in conjunction with the dependencies between predictions arising through the transitivity constraints. These two issues render it difficult to make a hard determination of significance in a way that does not violate hypothesis testing assumptions. Instead, our cross-validation splits give a weak qualitative sense of the generalizability of our methods.

Our cross validation setup consisted of four splits of the 36 documents with 5 documents per test set and 4 documents per development set for each split. Table 4 shows the micro-averaged F1 scores of the architectures described in the previous sections on each of these splits. Unsurprisingly, the results show that some architecture scores were boosted while others lessened on these alternative splits. Notably, the added features in **F+** still make consistent gains over the CAEVO replication **R**, and the ideal scorer **F+*** makes consistent large gains (as high as 18% on Fold 3, and a low of 6% on Fold 1). However, **F+L** performs well on the development sets but does not improve performance on the test sets. We hypothesize that **F+L** overfits to the development sets due to their small size and the small number of predictions available to compute sieve-label precisions. The consistently large gains of **F+L** on the dev sets suggest that the method will achieve high performance as long as the precision estimates in s are accurate, but the method requires more development data than **F+** to compute accurate estimates without overfitting due to the large number of sparsely distributed sieve-label combinations.

This extra analysis helps to highlight the potential for overfitting. We hope this encourages future work to bear this in mind, and to also present results across multiple tests. Extra evaluations like those in this section are often unexciting, but **we argue that it is of utmost importance that they are conducted**. This paper could have ended at the previous section's top test set results, but we hope the reader sees extra value in the deep analysis of one's results.

6 Discussion

In the above experiments, we successfully replicated the CAEVO system from Chambers et al. (2014), and then proposed a generalization of the sieve-based architecture that enabled several new extensions and improvements. With the injection of new features, we improve the overall system with a **5%** relative gain in F1. Furthermore, our generalized version of CAEVO's sieve architecture allowed us to score and rank predictions based on both label and sieve precision, raising the F1 results to an **8.8%** relative improvement over our replicated CAEVO (under **F+L** in Table 3). We consider these results a new state-of-the-art on the TimeBank-Dense corpus. In addition, the large gains using a near-optimal scoring function (under **F+*** in Table 3) suggest that future work might make substantial progress by building further alternative prediction scoring methods.

We also perform an in-depth analysis of our improvements on alternative splits of the data. Through this analysis, we find that our feature engineering results are robust. More interestingly, while the **F+L** scoring method gives increased F1 on the original TimeBank-Dense split and all cross-validation dev sets, it does not yield improved performance on our alternative cross-validation test sets. This analysis suggests significant improvement for **F+L** over the original architecture, but with possible overfitting label-specific precision estimates on our small amount of development data.

Finally, we presented the first experiments that leveraged unlabeled data. These experiments gave negative results, but we believe future research might see improvements through inference over unlabeled data by (1) improving the precision of unlabeled data predictions (through the incorporation of precise between-sentence prediction sieves), (2) increasing the density of the unlabeled data (e.g. by including easy-to-predict cross-document links between related events), (3) increasing the number of constraints across the data through the incorporation of sieves for additional tasks like event and entity coreference (coref), or (4) increasing the size of the data for more reliable evaluation and training. With respect to (4), we hypothesize that although Timebank-Dense contains more temporal relations than other temporal corpora, it is still small in size. Our hope for future work is to extend the data set with more dense annotations, but spread across a larger number of document contexts, such that different scoring and inference methods may be robustly trained and evaluated.

Split	Data	V	CAEVO (R)	F+	F+L	F+S	F+LU	F+*
Fold 0	Dev	.385	.574	.571	**.596**	.593	.596	.676
Fold 0	Test	.400	.503	**.535**	.534	.530	.534	.632
Fold 1	Dev	.435	.519	.537	**.592**	.543	.592	.663
Fold 1	Test	.312	.443	.503	.501	**.506**	.501	.558
Fold 2	Dev	.450	.522	.542	**.555**	.521	.516	.684
Fold 2	Test	.462	.528	.540	.507	**.541**	.506	.706
Fold 3	Dev	.436	.536	.562	**.575**	.535	.573	.664
Fold 3	Test	.470	.484	.497	**.500**	**.500**	.497	.682

Table 4: Micro-averaged F1 scores on four cross-fold validation train-dev-test splits of TimeBank-Dense for the sieve architectures defined in Table 3. The new features in **F+** make conistent gains across folds, and the ideal scorer **F+*** demonstrates consistently large room for improvement using alternative scoring methods. The **F+L** model still performs well on the dev sets, but it gives no performance gains on test sets. This suggests the danger of overfitting the scoring functions s within sieve architectures, as the sieve-label precision scores use in **F+L** were computed over a small, four document dev set in each fold.

In sum, we present a new state-of-the-art event ordering model. Furthermore, we propose a generalized approach to classifier ranking that is applicable to all sieve architectures (not just temporal ordering). Instead of producing coarse-grained ranking of classifier predictions, our proposal selects more fine-grained, higher performing prediction rerankings. In addition, we show temporal ordering gains using SRL and word embedding features. The code for our event-ordering architectures and experiments is publicly available[7]. We hope that this work will encourage further efforts in dense event ordering research.

Acknowledgments

We thank Jesse Dodge and Noah Smith for advising and support with preliminary experiments that gave several negative results prior to the work in this paper, helping to prune likely dead-end research directions. We also thank the RTW group at CMU for allowing us to use their library repositories. The work of authors BM and DR was funded under NSF grant SES-1528409. NC was partially supported by a grant from the Office of Naval Research.

References

Steven Bethard. 2013. Cleartk-timeml: A minimalist approach to tempeval 2013. In *Second Joint Conference on Lexical and Computational Semantics (* SEM)*. volume 2, pages 10–14.

Steven Bethard and James H Martin. 2007. Cu-tmp: Temporal relation classification using syntactic and semantic features. In *Proceedings of the 4th International Workshop on Semantic Evaluations*. Association for Computational Linguistics, pages 129–132.

Anders Björkelund, Love Hafdell, and Pierre Nugues. 2009. Multilingual semantic role labeling. In *Proceedings of the Thirteenth Conference on Computational Natural Language Learning: Shared Task*. Association for Computational Linguistics, pages 43–48.

Philip Bramsen, Pawan Deshpande, Yoong Keok Lee, and Regina Barzilay. 2006. Inducing temporal graphs. In *Proceedings of the 2006 Conference on Empirical Methods in Natural Language Processing*. Association for Computational Linguistics, pages 189–198.

Taylor Cassidy, Bill McDowell, Nathanel Chambers, and Steven Bethard. 2014. An annotation framework for dense event ordering. Technical report, DTIC Document.

Nathanael Chambers, Taylor Cassidy, Bill McDowell, and Steven Bethard. 2014. Dense event ordering with a multi-pass architecture. *Transactions of the Association for Computational Linguistics* 2:273–284.

Nathanael Chambers and Dan Jurafsky. 2008. Jointly combining implicit constraints improves temporal ordering. In *Proceedings of the Conference on Empirical Methods in Natural Language Processing*. Association for Computational Linguistics, pages 698–706.

Yuchang Cheng, Masayuki Asahara, and Yuji Matsumoto. 2007. Naist. japan: Temporal relation identification using dependency parsed tree. In *Proceedings of the 4th International Workshop on Seman-

---

[7] `https://github.com/forkunited/CAEVO-plus`

tic Evaluations. Association for Computational Linguistics, pages 245–248.

Quang Xuan Do, Wei Lu, and Dan Roth. 2012. Joint inference for event timeline construction. In *Proceedings of the 2012 Joint Conference on Empirical Methods in Natural Language Processing and Computational Natural Language Learning*. Association for Computational Linguistics, pages 677–687.

Jennifer D'Souza and Vincent Ng. 2013. Classifying temporal relations with rich linguistic knowledge. In *HLT-NAACL*. pages 918–927.

Jennifer D'Souza and Vincent Ng. 2015. Sieve-based spatial relation extraction with expanding parse trees. In *Proceedings of the 2015 Conference on Empirical Methods in Natural Language Processing*. pages 758–768.

Daniel Gildea and Daniel Jurafsky. 2002. Automatic labeling of semantic roles. *Computational linguistics* 28(3):245–288.

Oleksandr Kolomiyets, Steven Bethard, and Marie-Francine Moens. 2012. Extracting narrative timelines as temporal dependency structures. In *Proceedings of the 50th Annual Meeting of the Association for Computational Linguistics: Long Papers-Volume 1*. Association for Computational Linguistics, pages 88–97.

Egoitz Laparra, Itziar Aldabe, and German Rigau. 2015. Document level time-anchoring for timeline extraction. *Volume 2: Short Papers* page 358.

Yann LeCun, Yoshua Bengio, and Geoffrey Hinton. 2015. Deep learning. *Nature* 521(7553):436–444.

Heeyoung Lee, Angel Chang, Yves Peirsman, Nathanael Chambers, Mihai Surdeanu, and Dan Jurafsky. 2013. Deterministic coreference resolution based on entity-centric, precision-ranked rules. *Computational Linguistics* 39(4):885–916.

Heeyoung Lee, Marta Recasens, Angel Chang, Mihai Surdeanu, and Dan Jurafsky. 2012. Joint entity and event coreference resolution across documents. In *Proceedings of the 2012 Joint Conference on Empirical Methods in Natural Language Processing and Computational Natural Language Learning*. Association for Computational Linguistics, pages 489–500.

Heeyoung Lee, Mihai Surdeanu, and Dan Jurafsky. 2017. A scaffolding approach to coreference resolution integrating statistical and rule-based models. *Natural Language Engineering* pages 1–30.

Hector Llorens, Estela Saquete, and Borja Navarro. 2010. Tipsem (english and spanish): Evaluating crfs and semantic roles in tempeval-2. In *Proceedings of the 5th International Workshop on Semantic Evaluation*. Association for Computational Linguistics, pages 284–291.

Tomas Mikolov, Kai Chen, Greg Corrado, and Jeffrey Dean. 2013. Efficient estimation of word representations in vector space. *arXiv preprint arXiv:1301.3781* .

Anne-Lyse Minard, Manuela Speranza, Eneko Agirre, Itziar Aldabe, Marieke van Erp, Bernardo Magnini, German Rigau, Ruben Urizar, and Fondazione Bruno Kessler. 2015. Semeval-2015 task 4: Timeline: Cross-document event ordering. In *Proceedings of the 9th International Workshop on Semantic Evaluation (SemEval 2015)*. pages 778–786.

Paramita Mirza and Sara Tonelli. 2016. On the contribution of word embeddings to temporal relation classification. In *The 26th International Conference on Computational Linguistics*. pages 2818–2828.

James Pustejovsky, Patrick Hanks, Roser Sauri, Andrew See, Robert Gaizauskas, Andrea Setzer, Dragomir Radev, Beth Sundheim, David Day, Lisa Ferro, et al. 2003. The timebank corpus. In *Corpus linguistics*. volume 2003, page 40.

Marta Tatu and Munirathnam Srikanth. 2008. Experiments with reasoning for temporal relations between events. In *Proceedings of the 22nd International Conference on Computational Linguistics-Volume 1*. Association for Computational Linguistics, pages 857–864.

Naushad UzZaman and James F Allen. 2010. Trips and trios system for tempeval-2: Extracting temporal information from text. In *Proceedings of the 5th International Workshop on Semantic Evaluation*. Association for Computational Linguistics, pages 276–283.

Naushad UzZaman, Hector Llorens, James Allen, Leon Derczynski, Marc Verhagen, and James Pustejovsky. 2012. Tempeval-3: Evaluating events, time expressions, and temporal relations. *arXiv preprint arXiv:1206.5333* .

Marc Verhagen, Robert Gaizauskas, Frank Schilder, Mark Hepple, Graham Katz, and James Pustejovsky. 2007. Semeval-2007 task 15: Tempeval temporal relation identification. In *Proceedings of the 4th International Workshop on Semantic Evaluations*. Association for Computational Linguistics, pages 75–80.

Marc Verhagen, Roser Sauri, Tommaso Caselli, and James Pustejovsky. 2010. Semeval-2010 task 13: Tempeval-2. In *Proceedings of the 5th international workshop on semantic evaluation*. Association for Computational Linguistics, pages 57–62.

Katsumasa Yoshikawa, Sebastian Riedel, Masayuki Asahara, and Yuji Matsumoto. 2009. Jointly identifying temporal relations with markov logic. In *Proceedings of the Joint Conference of the 47th Annual Meeting of the ACL and the 4th International Joint Conference on Natural Language Processing of the AFNLP: Volume 1-Volume 1*. Association for Computational Linguistics, pages 405–413.

A   Replication Details

While replicating CAEVO, we did not find any major issues that significantly change the results reported in the original paper. However, we found the following minor bugs: (1) bias features are included in the EEWS, EED, and ETWS machine-learned sieves but not in EDCT, (2) the computation of dependency path features does not always compute the shortest paths, and (3) code that computes token paths is specified to only compute for paths with length less than 4, but does not do this correctly. In our replicated version, we remove each of these bugs.

We also noticed the following quirks in the original system:

- Features based on gold-standard event tense, aspect, and class were not included in the machine-learned models that produced the reported results even though they were described in the original CAEVO paper.

- The EEWS, EED, and ETWS sieves were trained using feature matrices with a minimum feature occurrence count of 2 across training data whereas EDCT has a minimum feature occurrence count of 1. We know of no motivation for setting this parameter differently for the EDCT sieve, but resetting it to 2 within EDCT drops its performance to below the "All Vague" baseline sieve, resulting it from it being effectively removed from the system, and yielding a 5% drop in performance. The sensitivity of the overall system's performance to this parameter setting highlights the importance of using enough data to acquire accurate precision estimates to determine the prediction scoring.

- The EED sieve had a lower precision estimate than EEWS, but EEWS makes predictions on a superset of the event pairs for which EED makes predictions. This means that EED has no functional relevance with respect to the performance of the original architecture.

The replication process also revealed the sensitivity of the results to the details of feature engineering and feature selection. Overall, the process confirmed that minor flaws and oddities will likely remain in complicated architectures like CAEVO after they have been documented, and it can be worthwhile to repeatedly inspect and replicate these systems to ensure that they function as specified.

Open Relation Extraction and Grounding

Dian Yu, Lifu Huang, Heng Ji
Computer Science Department
Rensselaer Polytechnic Institute
{yud2, huangl7, jih}@rpi.edu

Abstract

Previous open Relation Extraction (open RE) approaches mainly rely on linguistic patterns and constraints to extract important relational triples from large-scale corpora. However, they lack of abilities to cover diverse relation expressions or measure the relative importance of candidate triples within a sentence. It is also challenging to name the relation type of a relational triple merely based on context words, which could limit the usefulness of open RE in downstream applications. We propose a novel importance-based open RE approach by exploiting the global structure of a dependency tree to extract salient triples. We design an unsupervised method to name relation types by grounding relational triples to a large-scale Knowledge Base (KB) schema, leveraging KB triples and weighted context words associated with relational triples. Experiments on the English Slot Filling 2013 dataset demonstrate that our approach achieves 8.1% higher F-score over state-of-the-art open RE methods.

1 Introduction

Open Relation Extraction (open RE) (Banko and Etzioni, 2008) aims at extracting relational triples from an open-domain corpus. Each triple contains two arguments and a phrase which denotes the relation between them. In this paper, we focus on discovering relations between *entities*.

Most successful open RE approaches (Fader et al., 2011; Xu et al., 2013; Bovi et al., 2015; Bhutani et al., 2016) extract salient relational triples based on lexical or syntactic patterns. However, such handcrafted or automatically learned patterns are incapable of covering diverse relation expressions (Soderland et al., 2013). Subsequently, the shortest path between arguments derived from a dependency tree has been widely applied to generate patterns to capture long-distance and complex relations. However, additional heuristic rules are usually needed to filter out the resulting large number of meaningless patterns (Wu and Weld, 2010; Mausam et al., 2012; Bovi et al., 2015). Besides, such flat syntactic structures lack the ability to measure the relative importance of candidate triples in a sentence. For example, the sentence in $E1$ places particular emphasis on the relation between *"Lucille Clifton"* and *"1936"* which therefore should be retained.

$\boxed{\text{E1}}$ *"Lucille Clifton, whom he married in 1958, was born in 1936."*

We notice that a candidate relational triple is likely to be salient if its two arguments are strongly connected in a dependency tree. Instead of relying on patterns to capture important triples, we use an importance-based strategy by exploring the entire dependency tree structure to automatically measure the connection strength of candidate argument pairs. Specifically, we assume that a relational triple is important if there is a relatively short random walk-based distance between two relatively important arguments, measured against the entire dependency tree of a given sentence. For each argument pair, we apply an effective random-walk based method to assign weights to context words in the sentence (Section 2).

How to assign a meaningful relation type name to a relational triple is also a primary challenge for open RE. Previous methods use relevant context words in the associated sentence as relation phrases (type names) (Del Corro and Gemulla, 2013; Bhutani et al., 2016). However, there is still no generally accepted guideline for relation phrase extraction. Multiple relation phrases can corre-

854

Proceedings of the The 8th International Joint Conference on Natural Language Processing, pages 854–864,
Taipei, Taiwan, November 27 – December 1, 2017 ©2017 AFNLP

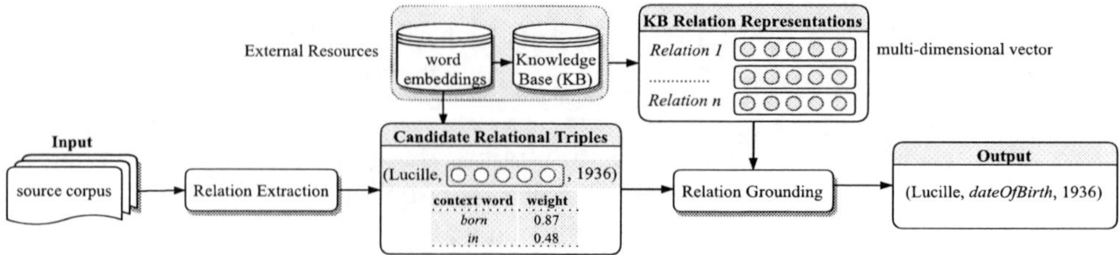

Figure 1: Framework overview.

spond to the same relation type. Besides, overly-specific or implicit relation phrases are incapable of providing adequate information for downstream applications. For example, the relation between *"Patricia"* and *"Gary Cooper"* cannot be clearly expressed by a set of words in the following sentence $E2$. Therefore, previous studies heavily rely on resources such as patterns (Soderland et al., 2013), training data (Weston et al., 2013), or distantly-labeled corpora (Angeli et al., 2015b) to map open RE triples to a known relation schema.

E2 *"Patricia later described her relation with Gary Cooper as one of the most beautiful things that ever happed to her in her life."*

Compared with a small number of predefined relation types such as those defined in Automatic Content Extraction (ACE) [1], the relation schema in a large-scale Knowledge Base (KB) such as DBpedia (Auer et al., 2007) covers a much wider range of informative relations along with their type signatures. Considering the open-domain nature shared by open RE and a large-scale KB, we propose an unsupervised grounding method to name the relation type between two arguments as either a KB relation or NONE, by leveraging KB triples and weighted context information associated with each argument pair based on pre-trained word embeddings (Section 3). Compared with previous methods (*e.g.*, (Riedel et al., 2013; Weston et al., 2013)), we regard intra-sentence context words as intermediate results for the subsequent grounding process, and we do not require any aligned training corpora or relation phrases for KB triples. The proposed framework is illustrated in Figure 1.

To the best of our knowledge, this is the first open RE method which exploits the global structure of a dependency tree to extract salient relational triples. This is also the first unsupervised relation grounding method to name relation

types for open RE based on KB triples and intra-sentence context information. Experiments on the English Slot Filling (SF) (Ji et al., 2010, 2011) 2013 dataset demonstrate that our approach outperforms state-of-the-art open RE approaches.

2 Relation Extraction

In this section, we introduce a graph-based method to extract argument pairs of salient relational triples. We first present the extended dependency tree construction for each sentence (Section 2.1). Then we show the computation of the relation strength between two arguments (Section 2.4) considering both their random-walk based distance (Section 2.2) and the relative importance of each argument in the tree (Section 2.3).

2.1 Extended Dependency Tree Construction

Given a sentence containing N words, we construct a weighted directed graph $G = (\mathcal{V}, \mathcal{E})$, where $\mathcal{V} = \{v_1, \ldots, v_N\}$ represents words, and $\mathcal{E}$ is a directed edge set, associated with each directed edge $v_i \rightarrow v_j$ representing a dependency relation originating from v_i to v_j. We assign a weight $w_{ij} = 1$ to $v_i \rightarrow v_j$ and add its reverse edge $v_j \rightarrow v_i$ with $w_{ji} = 0.5$. By adding lower-weighted reverse edges, we can analyze the relation between two nodes which are not connected by directed dependency links while maintaining our preferences toward the original directions.

We first apply a dependency parser to generate basic uncollapsed dependencies.[2] We annotate an entity or time mention node with its type. For example in $E1$, *"Lucille Clifton"* is annotated as a person, and *"1936"* is annotated as a date. Finally we perform coreference resolution which introduces coreference links between nodes that refer to the same entity within a document. We replace any nominal or pronominal entity mention with its coreferential name mention. For example, *"he"* is

---

[1] www.ldc.upenn.edu/collaborations/past-projects/ace.

[2] All the tools we used are introduced in Section 4.

replaced by *"Fred James Clifton"*. Formally, an extended dependency tree is an annotated tree of entity mentions and their links. By adding the reverse edges, we generate the final extended dependency tree in Figure 2. We regard any two entities as a candidate argument pair. $E1$ contains 4 entities and therefore we can extract $\binom{4}{2} = 6$ argument pairs (e.g., (*"Lucille Clifton"*, *"1936"*)).

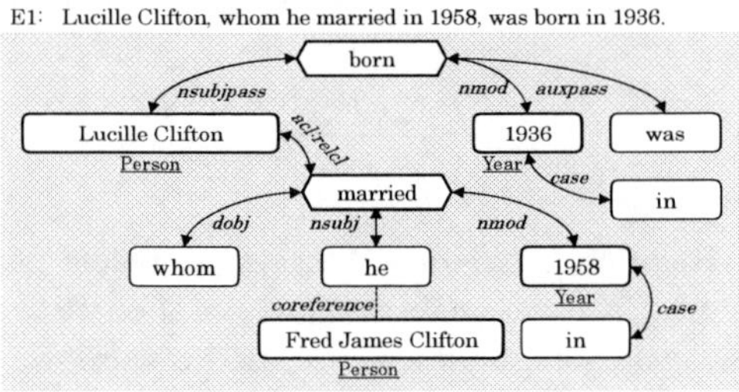

Figure 2: Extended dependency tree of E1.

2.2 Distance Computation

As mentioned previously, a shorter distance between two strongly connected nodes is more likely to indicate the existence of an important relation. We compute the distance between two nodes based on a Markov-chain model of random walk. We define a random walk through G by assigning a transition probability to each directed edge. Thus, a random walker can jump from node v_i to v_j and represent a state of the Markov chain. For a node v_i, we denote $\mathcal{N}(i)$ as the set of its neighbors. The probability of transitioning from node v_j to node v_i is defined as $p_{ji} = w_{ji}/\sum_{k \in \mathcal{N}(j)} w_{jk}$ for nodes v_i that have an edge from v_j to v_i, and 0 otherwise. We define the transition probability matrix of the Markov chain associated with random walks on G as P.

The ***mean first-passage time*** m_{ji} (Aldous and Fill, 2002) is the average number of steps needed by a random walker for reaching state i for the first time, when starting from state j. We call $c_{ij} = m_{ij} + m_{ji}$ as the ***average commute time*** (Lovász, 1993). The fact that c_{ij} can be regarded as a distance in G between nodes v_i and v_j is proven by Klein and Randić (1993). Compared with the shortest path between v_i and v_j, the value of c_{ij} will decrease when the number of paths connecting v_i and v_j increases and when the length of any path decreases (Fouss et al., 2007).

The fundamental matrix Z plays an essential role in computing various quantities related to random walks. For a weighted and directed graph, Li and Zhang (2010) demonstrate that Z can be computed directly using the following equation:

$$Z = (I - P + ED)^{-1} - ED \tag{1}$$

where I is the identity matrix, E is a matrix containing all 1s, and D is the diagonal matrix with elements $d_{kk} = \pi(k)$ where $\pi(k)$ is the stationary distribution of node v_k in the Markov chain.

We can directly compute a mean first-passage $|\mathcal{V}| \times |\mathcal{V}|$ matrix and a symmetric average commute time matrix C based on Z as follows:

$$m_{ij} = \frac{z_{jj} - z_{ij}}{\pi_j} \tag{2}$$

$$c_{ij} = \frac{z_{jj} - z_{ij}}{\pi_j} + \frac{z_{ii} - z_{ji}}{\pi_i} \tag{3}$$

Using the example in Figure 2, we can obtain a 10×10 matrix M based on the above steps (10 nodes in total). We list the result involving only entity nodes in Table 1.

$m(row, col)$	Lucille	1958	he	1936
Lucille	0.0	64.2	24.7	**74.7**
1958	24.3	0.0	17.3	90.2
he	22.6	32.1	0.0	87.7
1936	**20.2**	101.3	37.1	0.0

Table 1: Mean first-passage time matrix M for E1.

Argument Role Identification: We notice that argument roles can be identified based on the mean first-passage time. In a weighted directed graph, m_{ij} and m_{ji} are not necessarily similar. Actually in many cases nodes that lie on the boundaries have shorter mean first-passage time to the central nodes in the graph while there exists longer mean first-passage time from a central node to a node close to the boundary. A central node is more likely to be the central argument. We define the first argument as the more important argument. Therefore, we can regard v_i as the first argument of the argument pair (v_i, v_j) if m_{ij} is larger than m_{ji}. If m_{ij} and m_{ji} are equal, v_i and v_j have similar argument roles. For example, the boundary node *"1936"* in Figure 2 has shorter first-passage time to the central node *"Lucille Clifton"* (i.e., the first argument) compared with the reverse direction.

2.3 Node Importance Computation

As we mentioned earlier, a candidate relational triple is more likely to be salient if it involves important entities of the sentence. In this section, we illustrate the node importance computation based on the extended dependency tree of a sentence.

TextRank (Mihalcea and Tarau, 2004) can be used to compute the importance of each node within G. Similarly, suppose a random walker keeps visiting adjacent nodes in G at random. The expected percentage of walkers visiting each node converges to the TextRank score.

We define a set of preferred nodes $\mathcal{R}$ which correspond to entities in a sentence. We assign higher preferences toward these nodes when computing the importance scores since entities are more informative for relation extraction (Björkelund and Farkas, 2012). We extend TextRank by introducing a new measure called "back probability" $d \in [0,1]$ to determine how often walkers jump back to the nodes in $\mathcal{R}$ so that the converged score can be used to estimate the relative probability of visiting these preferred nodes. We define a preference vector $p_{\mathcal{R}} = \{p_1, ..., p_{|\mathcal{V}|}\}$ such that the probabilities sum to 1, and p_k denotes the relative importance attached to v_k. p_k is set to $1/|\mathcal{R}|$ for $v_k \in \mathcal{R}$, otherwise 0. Let I be the $1 \times |\mathcal{V}|$ importance vector to be computed over all nodes as follows.

$$I(i) = (1 - d) \sum_{j \in \mathcal{N}(i)} \frac{w_{ji}}{\sum_{k \in \mathcal{N}(j)} w_{jk}} I(j) + d \cdot p_i \quad (4)$$

ENTITY i	Lucille	he	1958	1936
$I(i)$	0.28	0.12	0.06	0.01

Table 2: Importance score of each entity in $E1$.

2.4 Combination and Filtering

Given the average commute time c_{ij} between nodes v_i and v_j (Section 2.2) and their relative importance scores $I(i)$ and $I(j)$ in G (Section 2.3), we will discuss how to combine them and generate the final score which can be used to measure the relation strength between two nodes. Intuitively, there exists a strong relation when there is a shorter distance between two relatively important nodes.

Previous approaches (Spagnola and Lagoze, 2011; Guo et al., 2011) consider the distance between two nodes and the influence of each node

modeled by its weighted frequency to measure the strength of links in networks. Similarly, in our setting we can regard c_{ij} as the distance between v_i and v_j and use the relative importance score to measure the influence of each node in G. Therefore, we obtain Equation 5 to compute the relation strength $F(i, j)$ between nodes v_i and v_j. We are more confident in predicting the existence of a salient relation with stronger relation strength.

$$F(i, j) = \frac{I(i) \times I(j)}{c_{ij}^2} \quad (5)$$

Relation Filtering: We get a complete entity graph since we analyze the connection between any two entities in a sentence. In this work, we focus on identifying the most significant structures among entities based on the connection strength we have obtained. Since the entity graph is undirected, we can simply apply the maximum spanning tree algorithm to keep those relatively important pairs. For $E1$, we obtain three argument pairs resulting after filtering: (*"Lucille"*, *"1936"*), (*"Fred"*, *"1958"*), and (*"Lucille"*, *"Fred"*). In comparison, the relations between argument pairs such as (*"1958"*, *"1936"*) and (*"he"*, *"1936"*) are less important.

3 Relation Grounding

We have presented how to extract candidate argument pairs in Section 2. In this section, we first introduce how to rank the context words given a pair of arguments (Section 3.1). Then we describe methods of learning KB relation representations from existing KB triples based on pretrained word embeddings. Finally we ground each relational triple to a KB relation or assign NONE (Section 3.2).

3.1 Context Word Selection and Weighting

In this section, we introduce how to extract informative context words and their associated weights given an argument pair (v_i, v_j) in a sentence based on the average commute time matrix $\mathbf{C}$ introduced in Section 2.2. Previous work (Yu and Ji, 2016) regards this problem as finding important nodes in G relative to given arguments. However, they need to run the algorithm repeatedly to analyze the same graph for each argument pair. Here we discuss an efficient method to extract weighted context words.

We only keep nouns, verbs, adjectives, prepositions, and particles as indicative context words $\mathcal{X}$. We assume that a context word $v_k \in \mathcal{X}$ is more important relative to (v_i, v_j) if $c_{ik} + c_{kj}$ is close to c_{ij}. Actually if the relation between v_i and v_j does not rely on any indicative words, c_{ij} will be much smaller than $c_{ik} + c_{kj}$ considering other nodes in the same sentence. We denote Λ as the weight set for all the context words of a given argument pair (v_i, v_j) as follows. The higher λ_k is, the more important the context word v_k is relative to (v_i, v_j).

$$\lambda_k = \frac{c_{ij}}{c_{ik} + c_{kj}} \qquad (6)$$

In $E1$, given the argument pair (*Lucille Clifton*, *Fred James Clifton*), we generate the following weighted context words: {*married* : 0.60, *in*^{1} : 0.36, *born* : 0.29, *in*^{2} : 0.24}.

3.2 Grounding

The associated weighted context words of each candidate argument pair are not sufficiently informative and flexible to clearly express the relation between two arguments. Thus, we aim to name the relation between a pair of arguments as one of the KB relations or NONE by comparing the semantic representations of context words and KB relations based on word embeddings. We also learn argument type signatures from KB triples.

For each word we obtain its pretrained word embedding $e \in \mathbb{R}^k$ where k is the embedding dimensionality. For a phrase which contains multiple words, we simply average the vectors of all the single words in the phrase as its embedding.

Given a KB triple (h, l, t) composed of two entities h, t and a KB relation $l \in \mathcal{L}$ (the set of KB relations), we leverage a large-scale KB to learn the representation for each KB relation motivated by the basic idea behind previous studies (Bordes et al., 2013; Mikolov et al., 2013) that relation patterns can be represented as linear translations. We use $\mathcal{S}_l = \{(h_i, l, t_i), i = 1, \ldots, |\mathcal{S}_l|\}$ to represent all the KB triples with the KB relation l.

KB relation type names can also provide important semantic information for relation representation and disambiguation especially when multiple relations co-occur in the same sentence, such as family relations (e.g., *spouse*, *parents*, and *other family*). We segment a compound name of a KB relation type into a set of words. For example, we

separate a DBpedia relation type name *political-Groups* into {*political, groups*}. Similarly, we average the vectors of all the words in a relation type name as its embedding $\widetilde{e}_l \in \mathbb{R}^k$. Incorporating both implicit semantics from KB tuples and explicit semantics from KB relation names, we represent the relation embedding of each KB relation l as follows.

$$e_l = \frac{1}{|\mathcal{S}_l|} \sum_{i=1}^{|\mathcal{S}_l|} (e_{h_i} - e_{t_i} + \widetilde{e}_l) \qquad (7)$$

Both of the involved embeddings are obtained from the linear combination of pretrained word embeddings, which guarantees that they are in the same space.

Given a single KB relation type l, an argument pair (v_i, v_j) and a single context word x, we can compute the cosine similarity between any candidate open RE triple and any KB relation. We calculate the absolute value since we have already captured the direction of arguments in Section 2.2. Therefore, we can regard similarity scores -1 and 1 equally and 0 as the lowest score.

$$S(l, (i, j, x)) = \frac{|e_x \cdot e_l|}{\|e_x\|\|e_l\|} \qquad (8)$$

When there are multiple context words $x \in \mathcal{X}$, we can compute the weighted cosine similarity between them as follows based on the squared weights of context words described in Section 3.1.

$$S(l, (i, j, \mathcal{X})) = \max_{x \in \mathcal{X}} S(l, (i, j, x)) \times \lambda_x^2 \qquad (9)$$

Since we have multiple KB relations $l \in \mathcal{L}$, we can ground a candidate relational triple $(i, j, \mathcal{X})$ and obtain its relation $\widehat{l}_{i,j,\mathcal{X}}$ considering all the possible relations. The predicted relation can either be assigned a valid KB relation or NONE. We use a marker to denote the relation between v_i and v_j which cannot be grounded to any KB relation.

$$\widehat{l}_{i,j,\mathcal{X}} = \arg\max_{l \in \mathcal{L}} S(l, (i, j, \mathcal{X})) \qquad (10)$$

Relation Argument Type Constraints

For each KB relation, we can obtain its type constraints for its two arguments. Take the relation *birthPlace* as an example: the entity types of two arguments should be person and location.

Given all the KB triples, we can estimate the probability of one of the arguments belonging to a certain entity type $z \in \mathcal{Z}$, where $\mathcal{Z}$ represents the set of all the KB concept types. For a given KB relation l, we define $c(k \rightsquigarrow z \mid l)$ to be the number of times the k_{th} argument is seen paired with the entity type z where $k \in \{1, 2\}$ since there are two arguments. Given the above definitions, the maximum likelihood estimate is as follows.

$$p(k, z \mid l) = \frac{c(k \rightsquigarrow z \mid l)}{\sum_{z \in \mathcal{Z}} c(k \rightsquigarrow z \mid l)} \quad (11)$$

Therefore, given a candidate argument pair (v_i, v_j) and their entity types z_i and z_j, we can compute the probability of its being labeled as the relation l by considering both $p(1, z_i \mid l)$ and $p(2, z_j \mid l)$. We set $S(l, (i, j, \mathcal{X}))$ to 0 if the harmonic mean of $p(1, z_i \mid l)$ and $p(2, z_j \mid l)$ is smaller than a given threshold which will be introduced later in Section 4.4. We will not consider a candidate KB relation for comparison if the argument type of i or j fails to satisfy its type constraints. In this way, we can filter out some candidate triples and reduce the number of similarity computations. For example, given a KB relation *placeOfBurial*, the concept type *Species* is less likely to be the correct second argument type compared with other entity types such as *City* and *Location*. Remind that the order of arguments in the candidate triple has been introduced in Section 2.2.

4 Experiments

4.1 Knowledge Base and Word Embeddings

We use the April 2016 dump of DBpedia as our KB which contains $2,060$ relation types and $30,024,093$ relation triples in total. We use the 300-dimensional GloVe vectors (Pennington et al., 2014) pretrained on 6 billion tokens from the English Gigaword Fifth Edition and a 2014 Wikipedia dump.

4.2 Evaluation based on Slot Filling

There are several benchmarks developed for open RE (*e.g.*, (Fader et al., 2011; Stanovsky and Dagan, 2016)). However, we mainly focus on relations between entities and therefore we cannot directly compare with state-of-the-art open RE methods on those datasets. To evaluate the effectiveness of our approach, we choose the TAC-KBP SF (McNamee and Dang, 2009; Ji et al.,

2010, 2011; Surdeanu and Ji, 2014) task as our evaluation platform which has been widely used by open RE methods (Soderland et al., 2013; Angeli et al., 2015b) since 2009. The goal of SF is to extract the values (***slot fillers***) of specific attributes (***slot types***) for a given entity (***query***) from a large-scale corpus which includes news documents, web blogs, and discussion forum posts. Justification sentences should be provided to support slot fillers. SF defines 25 slot types for person queries and 16 slots for organization queries.

We use the SF 2013 dataset for which we can compare with the ground truth and state-of-the-art open RE results reported in SF. We obtain $1,701$ relevant documents from the official evaluation assessment for 50 person queries and 50 organization queries. We manually map KB relations to slot types based on TAC-KBP slot descriptions.[3] Note that a single KB relation can be mapped to multiple slot types. For example, *birthPlace* can be mapped to *per:city_of_birth*, *per:stateofprovince_of_birth*, and *per:country_of_birth*. We assign a subtype (e.g., country, province, or city) to a location entity based on gazetteer matching.

DBpedia Relations	Slot Types
founder	org:founded_by
keyPeople	org:top_members_employees
education	per:schools_attended
workInstitution	per:employee_or_member_of
birthDate	per:date_of_birth

Table 3: Example Mappings from DBpedia relations to slot types.

We ignore all the slot types which require nominal phrases as fillers (*e.g.*, *per:cause_of_death*) and slot types *per/org:alternate_names* which depend on cross-document coreference resolution. We apply Stanford CoreNLP (Manning et al., 2014) for English part-of-speech tagging, name tagging, time expression extraction, dependency parsing, and coreference resolution. We use the official Slot Filling evaluation scoring metrics: Precision (P), Recall (R), and F-measure (F_1).

As shown in Table 4, our method outperforms the KBP2013 SF submission from the University of Washington (Soderland et al., 2013) which applies Open IE V4.0, which is an extension of SRL-based IE (Christensen et al., 2011) and noun

---

[3]The resource is publicly available for research purposes at: http://nlp.cs.rpi.edu/data/dbpedia2slot.zip.

Method	P	R	F$_1$
UW Official (Soderland et al., 2013)	**69.9**	12.2	20.8
UMass Official (Singh et al., 2013)	10.6	19.5	13.7
[1] KB Tuples	17.3	21.1	19.0
Our Approach [2] Relation Names	24.3	30.9	27.2
[1]+[2] Joint	26.2	**32.4**	**28.9**

Table 4: Performance (%) on KBP2013 English SF based on different relation representations.

phrase processing (Pal and Mausam, 2016), to generate relation triples. This is their latest published approach which uses Open IE for Regular Slot Filling. Their approach achieves very high precision but comparatively low recall (12.2%). In our experiments, we keep all the candidate triples which could be mapped to a slot type without tuning thresholds. On the same dataset, we also compare with an approach (Singh et al., 2013) which extracts relations with matrix factorization and *universal schemas* (Riedel et al., 2013) consisted of textual patterns and all the slot types. We do not directly compare with the work of Angeli et al. (2015b) because of the lack of access to their SF output.[4]

The importance-based strategy is effective at extracting more salient information. For example, previous methods only extract one argument pair (*"the top Egyptian cleric"*, *"Wednesday"*) from the sentence *"**Sheikh Tantawi**, the top **Egyptian cleric** who died on **Wednesday** on a visit to ..."* while omitting the person name. Our method extracts both (*"Sheikh Tantawi"*, *"Egyptian"*) and (*"Sheikh Tantawi"*, *"Wednesday"*) with their associated top-weighted context words *"cleric"* and *"died"* respectively, since the connection between *"Egyptian"* and *"Wednesday"* is much weaker.

Compared with relation phrases, the word embeddings of weighted context words are more flexible for comparison when we map relational triples to a known schema. For example, it is impossible for previous methods (e.g., (Soderland et al., 2013)) to summarize all the related mentions (e.g., *"appointed"* and *"CEO"*) and manually map them to the relation *employment*. Therefore previous approaches missed the slot filler *"Al-Azhar University"* of the query *"Mohammed Sayed Tantawi"* from the following sentence *"Tayeb, the president of **Al-Azhar University** since 2003, succeeds **Mohammed Sayed***

---

[4]The highest recall they achieve is around 13% on all the slot types including nominal relations on the same dataset.

Tantawi" as *"succeeds"* was not included into the related terms. Our approach extracts it based on their semantic representations.

In addition, we obtain more generalized relation type names based from the KB schema. For example, we ground the relation in $E2$ between *"Patricia"* and *"Gary"* to *influencedBy*. Similarly, in the sentence *"**Ginzburg** shared the Nobel Physics Prize with US physicists **Alexei Abrikosov** and Anthony Leggett for their contributions to the theory of superconductors ..."*, the relation phrase *"shared the Nobel Physics Prize with"* between *"Ginzburg"* and *"Alexei"* is too specific compared with the grounded KB relation *alongside* by our approach for subsequent applications.

4.3 Impact of Relation Representations

In Section 3.2, we use KB tuples and their relation type names to learn KB relation representations. As shown in Table 4, our approach can already achieve promising performance based on the relation representations learned from KB relation names. However, sometimes relations are implicitly expressed. It is likely that the context words of a relation triple and its corresponding KB relation name are not semantically similar. In this case, we need more general relation representations with the help of millions of KB tuples. For example, we can ground the relation *school* between *"McGregor"* and *"Colorado State University"* successfully by comparing the representation of context words *"tight"* and *"end"* with the joint relation representations from the following sentence: *"**McGregor** was a two-time All-America tight end at **Colorado State University**"* even though this relation is not explicitly described.

4.4 Impact of Argument Type Constraints

As mentioned in Section 3.2, we aim to filter out some candidate relation triples if the entity types of the arguments are not popular for a given KB relation. By tuning thresholds, there are no significant differences in performance when the threshold falls in the range 0.05–0.2. On the other hand, if the threshold is set too high (e.g., greater than 0.35%), we will mistakenly discard correct candidates which satisfy type constraints.

We implement Jenks optimization (Wikipedia, 2017) to automatically split the frequency values of all entity types into two tiers given a certain argument position and a KB relation. This is done by minimizing each tier's average deviation from the tier mean, while maximizing each tier's deviation from the means of other groups (McMaster and McMaster, 2002). We set the threshold automatically using the obtained natural breaks for two arguments respectively to compute the harmonic mean of them. This approach achieves 28.9% F_1 which is comparable to the highest F_1 (29.2%) obtained by threshold tuning.

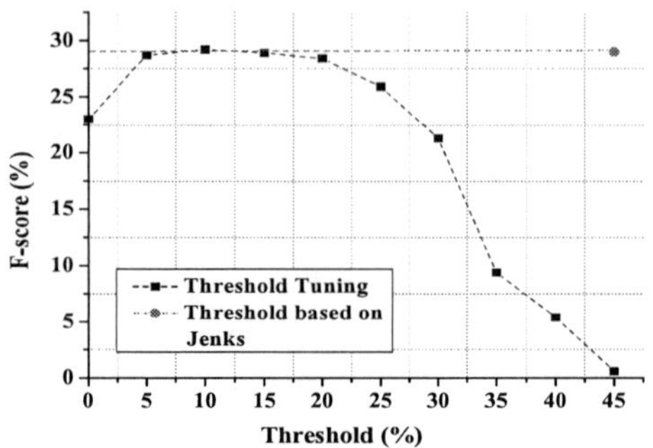

Figure 3: Performance (%) based on different thresholds for argument type constraints.

5   Related Work

5.1   Open Information Extraction

Lexical or syntactic features and patterns have been widely used to extract relational triples (Suchanek et al., 2009; Poon and Domingos, 2009; Wu and Weld, 2010; Nakashole et al., 2011; Fader et al., 2011; Nakashole et al., 2012; Mausam et al., 2012; Bovi et al., 2015; Angeli et al., 2015b; Grycner and Weikum, 2016). Our work explores the global structure of a dependency tree to identify salient triples within a sentence. Some open IE approaches have the capability to extract relations between concepts or phrases (Kok and Domingos, 2008; Min et al., 2012; Del Corro and Gemulla, 2013). Currently we focus on relations between two entities.

Given the SF schema, Soderland et al. (2013) manually design rules to map relational triples to slot types within hours. Researchers also use distantly labeled corpora to compute the PMI[2] value between open IE and SF relation pairs (Angeli et al., 2015b). Instead, we propose a novel grounding approach which facilitates building a mapping table between KB relations and slot types. We do not compare with RE methods specifically designed for SF (Sun et al., 2011; Li et al., 2012; Angeli et al., 2015a) since these methods actively search for candidate fillers of the given queries based on slot-specific training resources while ignoring the salient relations which are irrelevant to the queries or the predefined slot types.

5.2   Relation Grounding

Besides textual features, large-scale knowledge bases are widely used for distant supervised relation extraction (Mintz et al., 2009; Riedel et al., 2010) to deal with the challenges caused by insufficient training data. Weston et al. (2013) combine two relation representations trained from KB triples and context words independently for relation extraction. Recent studies such as (Toutanova et al., 2015) train relation representations of KB and textual relations jointly. Another kind of representations combining matrix factorization (Riedel et al., 2013) with first-order logic information is learned by Rocktäschel et al. (2015). Compared with these previous efforts, our unsupervised grounding method does not need the aligned training corpus or relation mentions for KB tuples. Wijaya and Mitchell (2016) introduce an approach to map words to KB relations based on web text, but they only focus on verb phrases.

5.3   Node Importance Computation

Graph-based algorithms such as PageRank (Page et al., 1999) and TextRank (Mihalcea and Tarau, 2004) are useful in keyword extraction. The way we rank nodes is most similar to the work of White and Smyth (2003) and Yu and Ji (2016) which generate the relative importance score of each node toward a set of preferred nodes. However, they only deal with unweighted undirected graphs.

6   Conclusions and Future Work

We propose an unsupervised open relation extraction method by exploring the global structure of dependency tree and show its effectiveness in extracting salient candidate relation triples. We also leverage the knowledge from the large-scale KB relation triples and weighted context words based on general embeddings to enhance the quality of our relation grounding technique. Experiments on English Slot Filling demonstrate that our approach outperforms state-of-the-art open RE approaches. In the future, we aim to extend our framework for multilingual open RE based on the KB schema.

Acknowledgments

This work was supported by the DARPA DEFT No. FA8750-13-2-0041, U.S. ARL NS-CTA No. W911NF-09-2-0053, and NSF IIS 1523198. The views and conclusions contained in this document are those of the authors and should not be interpreted as representing the official policies, either expressed or implied, of the U.S. Government. The U.S. Government is authorized to reproduce and distribute reprints for Government purposes notwithstanding any copyright notation here on.

References

David Aldous and Jim Fill. 2002. Reversible markov chains and random walks on graphs.

Gabor Angeli, Sonal Gupta, Melvin Johnson Premkumar, Christopher D Manning, Christopher Ré, Julie Tibshirani, Jean Y Wu, Sen Wu, and Ce Zhang. 2015a. Stanford's distantly supervised slot filling systems for kbp 2014. In *Proceedings of the TAC*, Gaithersburg, MD.

Gabor Angeli, Melvin Johnson Premkumar, and Christopher D Manning. 2015b. Leveraging linguistic structure for open domain information extraction. In *Proceedings of the ACL*, pages 344–354, Beijing, China.

Sören Auer, Christian Bizer, Georgi Kobilarov, Jens Lehmann, Richard Cyganiak, and Zachary Ives. 2007. Dbpedia: A nucleus for a web of open data. In *The semantic web*, pages 722–735, Busan, Korea.

Michele Banko and Oren Etzioni. 2008. The tradeoffs between open and traditional relation extraction. In *Proceedings of the ACL*, pages 28–36, Columbus, OH.

Nikita Bhutani, HV Jagadish, and Dragomir R Radev. 2016. Nested propositions in open information extraction. In *Proceedings of the EMNLP*, pages 55–64, Austin, TA.

Anders Björkelund and Richárd Farkas. 2012. Data-driven multilingual coreference resolution using resolver stacking. In *Proceedings of the EMNLP-CoNLL*, pages 49–55, Jeju, South Korea.

Antoine Bordes, Nicolas Usunier, Alberto Garcia-Duran, Jason Weston, and Oksana Yakhnenko. 2013. Translating embeddings for modeling multi-relational data. In *Proceedings of the NIPS*, pages 2787–2795, Lake Tahoe, NV.

Claudio Delli Bovi, Luca Telesca, and Roberto Navigli. 2015. Large-scale information extraction from textual definitions through deep syntactic and semantic analysis. *TACL*, 3:529–543.

Janara Christensen, Mausam, Stephen Soderland, and Oren Etzioni. 2011. An analysis of open information extraction based on semantic role labeling. In *Proceedings of the 6th International Conference on Knowledge Capture*, pages 113–120, Banff, Canada.

Luciano Del Corro and Rainer Gemulla. 2013. Clausie: clause-based open information extraction. In *Proceedings of the WWW*, pages 355–365, Rio de Janeiro, Brazil.

Anthony Fader, Stephen Soderland, and Oren Etzioni. 2011. Identifying relations for open information extraction. In *Proceedings of the EMNLP*, pages 1535–1545, Edinburgh, UK.

Francois Fouss, Alain Pirotte, Jean-Michel Renders, and Marco Saerens. 2007. Random-walk computation of similarities between nodes of a graph with application to collaborative recommendation. *IEEE TKDE*, 19:355–369.

Adam Grycner and Gerhard Weikum. 2016. Poly: Mining relational paraphrases from multilingual sentences. In *Proceedings of the EMNLP*, pages 2183–2192, Austin, TX.

Jun Guo, Hanliang Guo, and Zhanyi Wang. 2011. An activation force-based affinity measure for analyzing complex networks. *Scientific reports*, 1:113–122.

Heng Ji, Ralph Grishman, and Hoa T. Dang. 2011. An overview of the tac2011 knowledge base population track. In *Proceedings of the TAC*, Gaithersburg, MD.

Heng Ji, Ralph Grishman, Hoa T. Dang, Kira Griffitt, and Joe Ellis. 2010. An overview of the tac2010 knowledge base population track. In *Proceedings of the TAC*, Gaithersburg, MD.

Douglas J Klein and Milan Randić. 1993. Resistance distance. *J. Math. Chemistry*, 12:81–95.

Stanley Kok and Pedro Domingos. 2008. Extracting semantic networks from text via relational clustering. In *Proceeding of the Joint Conference on Machine Learning and Knowledge Discovery in Databases*, pages 624–639, Antwerp, Belgium.

Yan Li, Sijia Chen, Zhihua Zhou, Jie Yin, Hao Luo, Liyin Hong, Weiran Xu, Guang Chen, and Jun Guo. 2012. Pris at tac2012 kbp track. In *Proceedings of the TAC*, Gaithersburg, MD.

Yanhua Li and Zhi-Li Zhang. 2010. Random walks on digraphs, the generalized digraph laplacian and the degree of asymmetry. In *Proceedings of the WAW*, pages 74–85, Stanford, CA.

László Lovász. 1993. Random walks on graphs. *Combinatorics, Paul erdos is eighty*, 2:1–46.

Christopher D Manning, Mihai Surdeanu, John Bauer, Jenny Rose Finkel, Steven Bethard, and David McClosky. 2014. The Stanford CoreNLP natural language processing toolkit. In *Proceedings of the*

ACL: System Demonstrations, pages 55–60, Baltimore, MD.

Mausam, Michael Schmitz, Stephen Soderland, Robert Bart, and Oren Etzioni. 2012. Open language learning for information extraction. In *Proceedings of the Joint Conference on EMNLP and CONLLL*, pages 523–534, Jeju, South Korea.

Robert McMaster and Susanna McMaster. 2002. A history of twentieth-century american academic cartography. *Cartography and Geographic Inform. Sci.*, 29:305–321.

Paul McNamee and Hoa Trang Dang. 2009. Overview of the tac 2009 knowledge base population track. In *Proceeding of the TAC*, Gaithersburg, MD.

Rada Mihalcea and Paul Tarau. 2004. Textrank: Bringing order into texts. In *Proceedings of the EMNLP*, pages 404–411, Barcelona, Spain.

Tomas Mikolov, Ilya Sutskever, Kai Chen, Greg S Corrado, and Jeff Dean. 2013. Distributed representations of words and phrases and their compositionality. In *Advances in neural information processing systems*, pages 3111–3119, Lake Tahoe, NV.

Bonan Min, Shuming Shi, Ralph Grishman, and Chin-Yew Lin. 2012. Ensemble semantics for large-scale unsupervised relation extraction. In *Proceedings of the 2012 Joint Conference on EMNLP and CONLL*, pages 1027–1037, Jeju, South Korea.

Mike Mintz, Steven Bills, Rion Snow, and Dan Jurafsky. 2009. Distant supervision for relation extraction without labeled data. In *Proceedings of the ACL-IJCNLP*, pages 1003–1011, Suntec, Singapore.

Ndapandula Nakashole, Martin Theobald, and Gerhard Weikum. 2011. Scalable knowledge harvesting with high precision and high recall. In *Proceedings of the WSDM*, pages 227–236, Hong Kong, China.

Ndapandula Nakashole, Gerhard Weikum, and Fabian Suchanek. 2012. Patty: a taxonomy of relational patterns with semantic types. In *Proceedings of the Joint Conference on EMNLP and CoNLL*, pages 1135–1145, Jeju, South Korea.

Lawrence Page, Sergey Brin, Rajeev Motwani, and Terry Winograd. 1999. The pagerank citation ranking: Bringing order to the web. Technical Report 1999-66, Stanford InfoLab, Stanford, CA.

Harinder Pal and Mausam. 2016. Demonyms and compound relational nouns in nominal open IE. In *Proceedings of the 5th Workshop on AKBC*, pages 35–39, San Diego, CA.

Jeffrey Pennington, Richard Socher, and Christopher Manning. 2014. Glove: Global vectors for word representation. In *Proceedings of the EMNLP*, pages 1532–1543, Doha, Qatar.

Hoifung Poon and Pedro Domingos. 2009. Unsupervised semantic parsing. In *Proceedings of the EMNLP*, pages 1–10, Suntec, Singapore.

Sebastian Riedel, Limin Yao, and Andrew McCallum. 2010. Modeling relations and their mentions without labeled text. In *Proceedings of the Joint ECML and PAKDD*, pages 148–163, Barcelona, Spain.

Sebastian Riedel, Limin Yao, Andrew McCallum, and Benjamin M Marlin. 2013. Relation extraction with matrix factorization and universal schemas. In *Proceedings of the NAACL-HLT*, pages 74–84, Atlanta, GA.

Tim Rocktäschel, Sameer Singh, and Sebastian Riedel. 2015. Injecting logical background knowledge into embeddings for relation extraction. In *Proceeding of the NAACL-HLT*, pages 1119–1129, Denver, CO.

Sameer Singh, Limin Yao, David Belanger, Ari Kobren, Sam Anzaroot, Mike Wick, Alexandre Passos, Harshal Pandya, Jinho D Choi, Brian Martin, et al. 2013. Universal schema for slot filling and cold start: Umass iesl at tackbp 2013. In *Proceedings of the TAC*, Gaithersburg, MD.

Stephen Soderland, John Gilmer, Robert Bart, Oren Etzioni, and Daniel S Weld. 2013. Open information extraction to kbp relations in 3 hours. In *Proceedings of the TAC*, Gaithersburg, MD.

Steve Spagnola and Carl Lagoze. 2011. Edge dependent pathway scoring for calculating semantic similarity in conceptnet. In *Proceedings of IWCS*, pages 385–389, Oxford, UK.

Gabriel Stanovsky and Ido Dagan. 2016. Creating a large benchmark for open information extraction. In *Proceedings of the EMNLP*, pages 2300–2305, Austin, TX.

Fabian M Suchanek, Mauro Sozio, and Gerhard Weikum. 2009. Sofie: a self-organizing framework for information extraction. In *Proceedings of the International Conference on WWW*, pages 631–640, Madrid, Spain.

Ang Sun, Ralph Grishman, Wei Xu, and Bonan Min. 2011. Nyu 2011 system for kbp slot filling. In *Proceedings of the TAC*, Gaithersburg, MD.

Mihai Surdeanu and Heng Ji. 2014. Overview of the english slot filling track at the tac2014 knowledge base population evaluation. In *Proceedings of the TAC*, Gaithersburg, MD.

Kristina Toutanova, Danqi Chen, Patrick Pantel, Hoifung Poon, Pallavi Choudhury, and Michael Gamon. 2015. Representing text for joint embedding of text and knowledge bases. In *Proceedings of the EMNLP*, pages 1499–1509, Lisbon, Portugal.

Jason Weston, Antoine Bordes, Oksana Yakhnenko, and Nicolas Usunier. 2013. Connecting language and knowledge bases with embedding models for relation extraction. In *Proceedings of the EMNLP*, pages 1366–1371, Seattle, WA.

Scott White and Padhraic Smyth. 2003. Algorithms for estimating relative importance in networks. In *Proceedings of the 9th ACM SIGKDD international conference on Knowledge discovery and data mining*, pages 266–275, Washington, D.C.

Derry Tanti Wijaya and Tom M Mitchell. 2016. Mapping verbs in different languages to knowledge base relations using web text as interlingua. In *Proceedings of the NAACL-HLT*, pages 818–827, San Diego, CA.

Wikipedia. 2017. Jenks natural breaks optimization — wikipedia, the free encyclopedia.

Fei Wu and Daniel S Weld. 2010. Open information extraction using wikipedia. In *Proceedings of the ACL*, pages 118–127, Uppsala, Sweden.

Ying Xu, Mi-Young Kim, Kevin Quinn, Randy Goebel, and Denilson Barbosa. 2013. Open information extraction with tree kernels. In *Proceedings of the NAACL-HLT*, pages 868–877, Atlanta, GA.

Dian Yu and Heng Ji. 2016. Unsupervised person slot filling based on graph mining. In *Proceedings of the ACL*, pages 44–53, Berlin, Germany.

Extraction of Gene-Environment Interaction
from the Biomedical Literature

Jinseon You   Jin-Woo Chung   Wonsuk Yang   Jong C. Park[*]

School of Computing
Korea Advanced Institute of Science and Technology
{jsyou, jwchung, derrick0511, park}@nlp.kaist.ac.kr

Abstract

Genetic information in the literature has been extensively looked into for the purpose of discovering the etiology of a disease. As the gene-disease relation is sensitive to external factors, their identification is important to study a disease. Environmental influences, which are usually called Gene-Environment interaction (GxE), have been considered as important factors and have extensively been researched in biology. Nevertheless, there is still a lack of systems for automatic GxE extraction from the biomedical literature due to new challenges: (1) there are no preprocessing tools and corpora for GxE, (2) expressions of GxE are often quite implicit, and (3) document-level comprehension is usually required. We propose to overcome these challenges with neural network models and show that a modified sequence-to-sequence model with a static RNN decoder produces a good performance in GxE recognition.[1]

1   Introduction

Identifying genetic information related to a disease is an effective method for discovering the etiology of the disease. Many researchers in biology have attempted to identify the relationship between different types of genetic information, such as genes, gene mutations or other biological events, and diseases.

One of the difficult aspects in the research is that it is necessary to consider various external factors, because they can affect whether such biological relationships hold or not. For example, it has been shown that there is no association of NAT2 gene and breast cancer (Zgheib et al., 2013), but after three years, other researchers made a conflicting claim that NAT2 gene is associated with breast cancer (Kasajova et al., 2016). There may be many factors causing this difference, but investigating the environmental factors has been one of the important research topics. Kasajova et al. (2016) found that NAT2 gene is associated with breast cancer when women with NAT2 gene polymorphisms have been exposed to long-period active smoking. As a result, active smoking has been considered as a crucial factor that determines the relation between NAT2 gene and breast cancer, which biologists called gene and environment interaction (GxE).

Since the importance of studying GxE is recognized, the amount of related work has steadily been increasing (Hunter, 2005). Nonetheless, there is still a lack of systems and databases that deal with this information (Simonds et al., 2016). For the purpose of addressing this situation, we present an automatic system that extracts environment terms indicating a change of gene-disease relations from the biomedical literature.

There are three major challenges that make it difficult to perform GxE recognition using existing systems in the biomedical domain. First, in contrast to general biomedical natural language processing (BioNLP) tasks, there are no preprocessing tools and corpora for GxE, though there are some resources for chemical-disease relations, such as named entity recognition systems specialized for chemical and disease names and corpora that annotate chemical and disease relations in abstracts (Wei et al., 2015b). Second, research on discovering biomedical relations usually specifies environmental information in the literature in various ways, using not only expressions that explicitly refer to certain biomedical concepts such as

---

[*]Corresponding author
[1]Our source code and gold standard corpus are available at http://biopathway.org/GxE

pregnancy and smoking, but also statistical terms that refer to a comparison between two control groups, such as p-value and odds ratio, which are quite difficult to capture using conventional tools. Since the literature for GxE also tends to report experiment results in similar ways, the system needs to understand such implicit information to determine whether the result is meaningful or not. Third, information of this kind indicating GxE is usually not reported in a single sentence, requiring document-level comprehension of text.

To address this situation, we build an annotated corpus for GxE and develop an end-to-end system that recognizes environment information for gene-disease pairs given in single document. We exploit high-dimensional models based on neural networks to enable document-level understanding of text and to deal with the issues above. We also perform experiments with different neural network models to investigate which models are most suitable to GxE recognition.

2 Related work

One of the related areas that have been actively researched in BioNLP is biomedical event extraction. For example, a system was proposed in the recent shared tasks (Kim et al., 2013), attempting to extract ten biological events, with the best performance under a 0.6 F1-score. This score, however, was extremely skewed to particular event types. While all the systems showed good performance, with nearly a 0.8 F1-score, in extracting simple events such as gene expression and transcription, they showed quite poor performance for complex events such as binding and regulation. This is because, in contrast to simple events, complex events consist of more than two elements or another event. In particular, the task of extracting binding events is usually treated as finding ternary relations, where a system is supposed to recognize two biological entities together with a particular site where their binding takes place. This task is similar to our task as the relation between two entities can be changed according to the third entity. The best system for binding event extraction achieved a 0.49 F1-score.

Another recent work on dealing with complex relations in BioNLP is reading comprehension (RC), where the system is to find proper answers to given questions about a biological process within single document. For example, the

system in (Berant et al., 2014) attempts to find answers through comparisons between two graphs constructed from given documents and questions. Although the system explicitly combines biological events extracted from sentences to construct a long biological process, possibly leading to the propagation of errors, they reported fairly good performance and meaningful results, considering that it is the first attempt for document-level biological information extraction.

On the other hand, there are quite a few systems and corpora for document-level comprehension from a similar perspective in other domains, such as news articles (Hermann et al., 2015) and children's books (Hill et al., 2016). One of the recent studies, (Hermann et al., 2015), addresses the reading comprehension task for which proposed models infer missing entities. From the perspective of evaluating how well such models understand documents for answering given questions, the task is similar to the present work. In this task, neural network models were shown to be effective for processing document-level information. More specifically, they demonstrated that a variant of neural network, RNN with attention mechanism, achieved the state-of-the-art performance (Chen et al., 2016).

WikiReading is most similar to our task as it deals with inference over entities based on a sequence of tokens (Hewlett et al., 2016). The authors were inspired from the QA task, treating given properties as questions and developing models to find proper entities that could be answers to the questions. There are two types of properties in WikiReading: (1) the categorical property that requires selection among a relatively small number of possible answers and (2) the relational property that requires extraction of rare or unique answers from the document. The authors compared various types of models from simple word embedding models to sequence-to-sequence models and showed that the sequence-to-sequence model gives rise to outstanding performance in both types of properties.

3 Task definition

3.1 GxE extraction

We formulate the GxE recognition task as extracting terms indicating a particular environment that is involved in a change of gene-disease relations. Figure 1 illustrates an example abstract that con-

Melatonin pathway genes and breast cancer risk among Chinese women. [PMID: 22138747]

Previous studies suggest that melatonin may act on cancer growth through a variety of mechanisms, most notably by direct anti-proliferative effects on breast cancer cells and via interactions with the estrogen pathway. Three genes are largely responsible for mediating the downstream effects of melatonin: melatonin receptors 1a and 1b (MTNR1a and MTNR1b), and arylalkylamine N-acetyltransferase (AANAT). It is hypothesized that genetic variation in these genes may lead to altered protein production or function. To address this question, we conducted a comprehensive evaluation of the association between common single nucleotide polymorphisms (SNPs) in the MTNR1a, MTNR1b, and AANAT genes and breast cancer risk among 2,073 cases and 2,083 controls, using a two-stage analysis of genome-wide association data among women of the Shanghai Breast Cancer Study. Results demonstrate two SNPs were consistently associated with breast cancer risk across both study stages. Compared with MTNR1b rs10765576 major allele carriers (GG or GA), a decreased risk of breast cancer was associated with the AA genotype (OR = 0.78, 95% CI = 0.62-0.97, P = 0.0281). Although no overall association was seen in the combined analysis, the effect of MTNR1a rs7665392 was found to vary by **menopausal status** (P-value for interaction = 0.001). **Premenopausal women** with the GG genotype were at increased risk for breast cancer compared with major allele carriers (TT or TG) (OR = 1.57, 95% CI = 1.07-2.31, P = 0.020), while **postmenopausal women** were at decreased risk (OR = 0.58, 95% 0.36-0.95, P = 0.030). No significant breast cancer associations were found for variants in the AANAT gene. These results suggest that common genetic variation in the MTNR1a and 1b genes may contribute to breast cancer susceptibility, and that associations may vary by **menopausal status**. Given that multiple variants in high linkage disequilibrium with MTNR1b rs76653292 have been associated with altered function or expression of insulin and glucose family members, further research may focus on clarifying this relationship.

Figure 1: An illustrated abstract describing GxE for lung cancer. In this figure, gene and disease are shown in blue and red, respectively. Expressions in bold-face are targeted environment terms. Sentences highlighted in gray are the evidence supporting the claim that an association between MTNR1a and breast cancer is changed by menopausal status.

Environment type	Example
Energy balance	dietary factors, physical activity
Lifestyle	smoking, alcohol, breastfeeding
Exogenous hormones	HRT, OC use
Endogenous hormones	menopausal status, age of menarche
Chemical environment	grilled foods/meats, heterocyclic amines
Drugs/treatment	statin, NSAIDS
Infection and inflammation	helicobacter pylori, autoimmune disease
Physical environment	x-rays, sun exposure

Table 1: The list of biological environment types (Simonds et al., 2016)

tains information about GxE for breast cancer, where gene and disease names are shown in blue and red, respectively (Wei et al., 2015a; Lee et al., 2016). There are four types of genes (MTNR1a, MTNR1b, AANAT, insulin) and two types of diseases (breast cancer, cancer). Therefore, we consider twelve gene-disease combinations for which our system attempts to find environment terms from the abstract. As an example of environment terms, it is claimed in the abstract that the association between MTNR1a and 1b genes and breast cancer may vary to *menopausal status*. Sentences highlighted in gray are the evidence supporting the claim. Expressions in bold-face are targeted environment terms to be extracted by our system.

Our model is given the abstract marked with genes and diseases, and considers each unique gene-disease combination, one at a time, to find its environment terms. For example, if we want to consider the combination of MTNR1a and breast cancer, the input is the abstract marked only with these two entities, without other entities marked such as MTNR1b or AANAT. We used two state-of-the-art named entity recognizers (Wei et al., 2015a; Lee et al., 2016) to identify gene and disease names from a given abstract. For each combination, we consider the following four cases: (1) the combination consists of an unassociated gene-disease pair, not affected by an environment; (2) although the combination consists of a pair that is basically unassociated, it becomes associated due to a particular environment; (3) the combination consists of an associated pair but it is not affected by an environment; and (4) the combination consists of an associated pair and the degree of its association is changed by an environment. Our system is trained to choose the most proper environment term for a given combination in cases (2) and (4), but not to choose any term in cases (1) and (3).

3.2 Corpus

For experimental data, we collected 253 raw abstracts that are taken from review papers on GxE for diverse diseases (Simonds et al., 2016; Dunn et al., 2011; DiGangi et al., 2013; Iyegbe et al., 2014; Hunter, 2005). To establish the gold standard data to train and test the system, we manually annotated the biological environments that should be extracted. For the clear definition of an environment, we only annotated the terms that can be categorized into one of the types in Table 1 and that are clearly reported as associated with gene-disease relations in the abstract.

Annotation was conducted by two experts in bioinformatics, who were given abstracts marked with gene and disease names. They did not annotate combinations consisting of entities that are incorrectly recognized by the named entity recognizer (i.e., entities that are neither gene nor disease). For each abstract, one annotator read the entire body of its text and annotated terms referring to an environment that is involved in a given combination of gene and disease, and then another annotator validated its correctness, in a way similar to other annotation tasks in BioNLP (e.g., Berant et al. 2014). The agreement on annotated environment terms between the two annotators is 0.81. If they did not agree on a certain annotation, they had a discussion on the disagreement and resolved it afterwards. The corpus contains a total of 1,429 combinations of unique genes and diseases. Among them, 341 combinations are annotated as being affected by environment, i.e., they are linked to some environment terms annotated in the same abstract.

4 Method

We use two types of models, a feature-based model and an neural-based model, that could be applied to document-level understanding of relations between entities in order to investigate which models are suitable to GxE recognition and whether or not there are important issues particularly in this new task. There are three variants based on the neural-based model: (1) an attentive reader (Hermann et al., 2015), (2) a sequence-to-sequence model (Sutskever et al., 2014), and (3) a static RNN decoder. We envision that different characteristics of these models would lead to different performance, according to the types of task.

In our experiment, the three models relied neither on any prior knowledge nor on external tools for collecting candidate environment terms. Even though such words as 'smoking' or 'alcohol' can be considered to have a higher probability to be a biological environment than other words, we did not use such information to prevent error propaga-

tion and to investigate the possibility of handling newly introduced terms.

4.1 A feature-based model

We combined two models proposed by Chen et al. (2016) and Xu et al. (2016): a model that adapts an entity-centric approach to the RC task, and a feature-based model that extracts chemical-disease relations on a document level.

Inspired by these two models, we use the following feature sets that we expect are suitable to our task. We describe each feature in detail below, where g, d, and e indicate gene terms, disease terms, and candidate environment terms, respectively: (1) shortest distance from e to g and d in the abstract, (2) whether e and g pair in the same sentence, (3) whether e and d pair in the same sentence, (4) whether e, d, and g pair in the same sentence, (5) whether e is included in MeSH (Medical Subject Headings) terms, (6) the frequency of e in an abstract, (7) the frequency of e in all abstracts, (8) whether e and g are connected by the dependency parser (De Marneffe et al., 2006), and (9) whether e and d are connected by the dependency parser (De Marneffe et al., 2006).

Using these features, the model tried to classify all terms that are present in the abstract. If the model assigns 1 to a term, we regard it as an environment. If the model classifies all terms for a particular gene-disease combination as 0, we assume that there is no environment for this combination in the abstract.

4.2 An neural-based model

We propose three neural-based models; 1) an attentive reader, 2) a sequence-to-sequence model, and 3) a static RNN decoder. The three models comprise two parts: converting text to vector representation, called encoding, and predicting the vector to answer, called decoding. The encoding is the same in all the three models. We look over the encoding and then compare each decoding part of the three models.

4.2.1 Encoding

Our encoding with attention is based on the model proposed by Chen et al. (2016), which shows better performance than any other encoders. The model runs in two steps, **text encoding** and **attention**, described in detail as follows.

Text encoding: All words are mapped to d-dimensional vectors using the PubMed/PMC word embedding model (Pyysalo et al., 2013) with a limited dictionary size (V). We include special tokens, '<NOE>', that stands for no environment terms for the combination and '<UNK>', that stands for terms that are not included in the dictionary. The sequence of words in an abstract excluding stop words and special characters is encoded as $\mathbf{p}_1, ..., \mathbf{p}_m \in \mathbb{R}^d$ where m is the number of words in the abstract. Then, we pass the sequence $\mathbf{p}_1, ..., \mathbf{p}_m$ to bi-directional RNN:

$$\overrightarrow{\mathbf{h}_i} = RNN(\overrightarrow{\mathbf{h}}_{i-1}, \mathbf{p}_i) \in \mathbb{R}^h, i = 1, ..., m$$

$$\overleftarrow{\mathbf{h}_i} = RNN(\overleftarrow{\mathbf{h}}_{i+1}, \mathbf{p}_i) \in \mathbb{R}^h, i = m, ..., 1$$

$$\tilde{\mathbf{p}}_i = concat(\overrightarrow{\mathbf{h}_i}, \overleftarrow{\mathbf{h}_i}) = \begin{bmatrix} \overrightarrow{\mathbf{h}_i} \\ \overleftarrow{\mathbf{h}_i} \end{bmatrix} \in \mathbb{R}^{2h}, i = 1, ..., m$$

where h is the dimension of hidden units of RNN.

From $\mathbf{p}_1, ..., \mathbf{p}_m$, the model extracts marked gene and disease names. Let the set of gene names be $\{\mathbf{g}_1, ...\mathbf{g}_n\}$ where n is the number of gene names in the abstract. Let the set of disease names be $\{\mathbf{d}_1, ...\mathbf{d}_l\}$ where l is the number of disease names in the abstract. Then, we make the gene-disease combination vector $\mathbf{c}$ by element-wise summation of concatenated vectors:

$$\mathbf{c} = \mathbf{W}_c^T (\begin{bmatrix} \mathbf{g}_1 \\ \mathbf{d}_1 \end{bmatrix} \oplus \begin{bmatrix} \mathbf{g}_2 \\ \mathbf{d}_1 \end{bmatrix} ... \oplus \begin{bmatrix} \mathbf{g}_n \\ \mathbf{d}_l \end{bmatrix})$$

where $\mathbf{W}_c \in \mathbb{R}^{2d \times 2h}$ is the weight vector for gene and disease.

Attention: In order to enable the model to focus more on evidence for identifying environment terms in the abstract, we used the attention mechanism. In the QA task, the vector of questions is projected to a document for calculating the probability of relevance degree between a question and a document. Likewise, we project the gene-disease combination vector ($\mathbf{c}$) to the sequence of word vectors ($\tilde{\mathbf{p}}_1, ..., \tilde{\mathbf{p}}_m$). We applied a bilinear term, a variant of attention mechanism, to combine the combination vector and the sequence of vectors:

$$\mathbf{a} = softmax(\mathbf{c}^T \mathbf{W}_b \tilde{\mathbf{p}}_i), i = 1, ..., m$$

where $\mathbf{W}_b \in \mathbb{R}^{2h \times 2h}$.

And then, we generated an attention vector by summation of projecting the bilinear term to the sequence of vectors:

$$\tilde{\mathbf{a}} = \sum_i \mathbf{a} \tilde{\mathbf{p}}_i, i = 1, ..., m$$

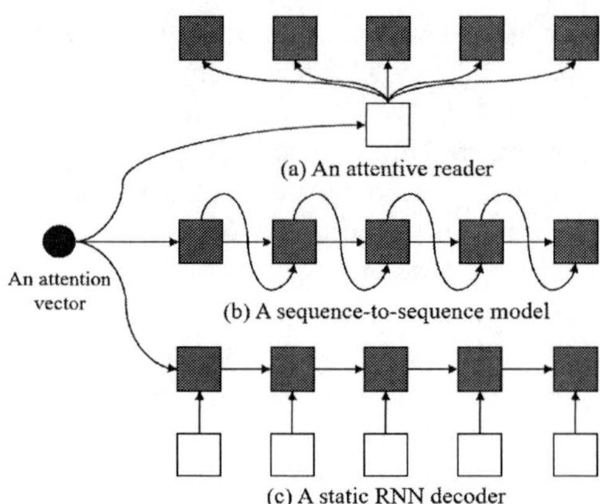

Figure 2: An overview of each decoding part in three models

4.2.2 Decoding

In this section, we describe each decoding of the three models. Figure 2 illustrates an overview of three models.

(a) An attentive reader

By mapping the attention vector ($\tilde{\mathbf{a}}$) to vocabulary, we compute output vector ($\mathbf{o}_a$) as follows,

$$\mathbf{o}_a = \mathbf{W}_a^T \tilde{\mathbf{a}}$$

where $\mathbf{W}_a \in \mathbb{R}^{2h \times V}$:

We choose terms that come from their conjunction showing the top values of the output vector and that are represented in the abstract, and consider them as environment. However, if the top value of the output vector indicates '<NOE>', we conclude that there is no environment.

(b) A sequence-to-sequence model

A decoder in the sequence-to-sequence model dynamically generates tokens from '<SOE>' (start of token) to '<EOE>' (end of token). The model is based on a previous hidden vector, a previous token vector and an encoding vector that is an output vector of the encoding. The previous token vector is computed by projecting a token generated in previous time step to an embedding layer. We try to set the attention vector ($\tilde{\mathbf{a}}$) to the encoding vector as we expect that the attention vector is more properly tuned to extract terms depending on the gene-disease combinations than the original encoding vector:

$$\mathbf{t}_{i-1} = \mathbf{W}_e^T o_{i-1}$$

$$\mathbf{y}_i = RNN(\overrightarrow{\mathbf{h}}_{i-1}, \mathbf{t}_{i-1}, \tilde{\mathbf{a}}) \in \mathbb{R}^{2h}, i = 1, ..., e$$

where e is the number of environment terms and $\mathbf{W}_e^T$ is an embedding layer.

$$o_i = argmax(\mathbf{W}_s^T \mathbf{y}_i), i = 1, ..., e$$

where $\mathbf{W}_s^T \in \mathbb{R}^{2h \times V}$. The o_i is the index of the vocabulary and a sequence of tokens, $(o_{1,...,e})$, is regarded as environment terms predicted by the model.

If the first decoding token indicates '<NOE>' in the output sequence, we assume that there is no environment.

(c) A static RNN decoder

As a modification to the sequence-to-sequence model, we suggest that the model uses a static RNN decoder, which does not use a previous token vector ($\mathbf{t}_{i-1}$). In particular, the model used randomly normalized token vectors. Because the model is needed to set the length of the decoder in advance, it seems to statically generate environment terms, which is an outstanding feature in comparison to the sequence-to-sequence model. Because our answer tokens are usually atomic and spread over the abstract, the previous output state, which is usually used when making a long sequence of tokens, is not useful for our task.

$$\mathbf{y}_i = RNN(\overrightarrow{\mathbf{h}}_{i-1}, \mathbf{t}'_i, \tilde{\mathbf{a}}) \in \mathbb{R}^{2h}, i = 1, ..., e'$$

where e' is the number of environment tokens that is set in advance.

$$o_i = argmax(\mathbf{W}_r^T \mathbf{y}_i), i = 1, ..., e'$$

where $\mathbf{W}_r^T \in \mathbb{R}^{2h \times V}$. The o_i is the index of the vocabulary and a sequence of tokens, $(o_{1,...,e'})$, is regarded as environment terms predicted by the model.

Similar to the sequence-to-sequence model, if the first decoding token indicates '<NOE>' in the output sequence, we assume that there is no environment.

5 Experiments

5.1 Corpus statistics

In the 253 abstracts that report the presence of GxE, 341 out of 1429 gene-disease combinations show a relationship and are considered affected by environment. Table 2 provides some statistics of the dataset. There are a total of 247 types of gene and 106 types of disease. In an abstract,

Category	#
Types of genes	267
Types of diseases	106
Avg. # of tokens	304.1
Avg. # of sentences	10.4
Avg. # of environment tokens	2.7
Min. # of environment tokens	1
Max. # of environment tokens	15
Avg. # of environments per combination	1.4
Min. # of environments per combination	1
Max. # of environments per combination	8

Table 2: Data statistics of the GxE dataset. All values are based on the statistics from the entire dataset.

there are about 304 tokens and 10 lines on average. Also, the average number of environment tokens is about 3 and the maximum number is 15. Assuming that the combination shows GxE in an abstract, the average number of unique environments per combination is 1.4. From the statistics, we see that the environment is made of just one or two words and that the combinations showing GxE appear rarely.

In order to balance positive and negative values, we randomly sampled 146 combinations from almost 1000 redundant combinations that do not show GxE, and abstracts with a total of 487 combinations were given as input to the system. The input is already marked with gene and disease, and the annotated gold standard environment term was used as the target answer. We randomly selected 80% of the dataset (389) and used them for training, 10% for validation (49), and 10% for test (49).

5.2 Setup

For training the proposed model, we set common parameters empirically as follows. According to a given embedding model, the dimension of word vectors is 200. We built a dictionary using the most frequent $2.5K$ words. And we split sentences using the tool (Kazama and Tsujii, 2003) and tokenized the sentences using the supporting tool in BioNLP Shared Task 2011[2], where both tools are specialized to BioNLP.

---

[2] `https://github.com/ninjin/bionlp_st_2011_supporting/blob/master/tools/GTB-tokenize.pl`

Model	P	R	F1
Baseline model (DT)	0.157	0.172	0.152
Baseline model (SVM)	0.279	0.274	0.275
Baseline model (RF)	0.204	0.196	0.196
Baseline model (GB)	0.1	0.123	0.095
Baseline model (AB)	0.168	0.155	0.153
RNN reader (top-5)	0.321	0.359	0.338
Attentive reader (top-5)	0.362	0.373	0.366
Attentive reader (top-10)	0.290	0.542	0.378
Attentive reader (top-15)	0.283	0.639	0.390
Attentive reader (top-20)	0.214	**0.670**	0.324
Seq2seq model (basic encoding)	0.305	0.298	0.301
Seq2seq model (attention encoding)	0.322	0.319	0.320
Static RNN decoder (basic encoding)	**0.484**	0.389	**0.426**
Static RNN decoder (attention encoding)	0.450	0.380	0.409

Table 3: The performances of different models on GxE recognition. P and R stand for precision and recall, respectively. DT, SVM, RF, GB and AB stand for Decision Tree, Support Vector Machine, Random Forest, Gradient Boosting, and AdaBoost, respectively. The RNN reader indicates attentive reader without attention encoding.

The baseline models followed the initial parameter setting of a machine learning framework, *sklearn*[3]. We tried to change the parameter setting, without any significant difference in performance.

In the attentive reader and the static RNN decoder, we used LSTM (Hochreiter and Schmidhuber, 1997), a variant of the RNN model, and set the hidden size and dropout rate of RNN to 64 and 0.5, respectively. On the other hand, the sequence-to-sequence model used GRU (Cho et al., 2014), another variant of the RNN model, and we set the hidden size of 64 and dropout rate of 0.5. In the case of the static RNN decoder, it is necessary to set the length of the model due to a static attribute. Therefore, we evaluated the performance of the model according to the length, and we found that the model with a length of 25 performs best.

All weights of three models are initialized from Gaussian distribution with 0 mean and 0.01 STD. At each update, we randomly sampled a mini-batch of 16, and the attentive reader, sequence-to-sequence model, and static RNN decoder used the Adam algorithm (Kingma and Ba, 2015) with 0.0001, 0.001, and 0.01 learning rates for optimization, respectively. Except for the attentive reader, we additionally used l2 regularizations. And we clipped the gradients when the norm of

the gradients exceeds 10. We ran all neural network models up to 100 epochs.

We implemented the proposed neural network models using *TensorFlow*[4].

5.3 Results

The overall performance of our proposed models is shown in Table 3. We ran each model 10 times independently, and reported average scores in the table. Among others, it shows that it is hard to detect environment terms with feature-based models and that it is necessary to use high-dimensional models such as deep neural network. It also shows that the static RNN decoders outperform other models. It is an interesting result because, contrary to our result, the sequence-to-sequence model showed outstanding performance in WikiReading, which is the most similar task to ours. The fact that the static RNN decoder shows best performance is probably due to the characteristics of our corpus where environment tokens are more widespread and atomic.

If the reader model and the sequence-to-sequence model use attention as demonstrated in other studies, it shows higher performance than the model without attention. On the other hand, the static RNN decoders show a different case, in that our proposed attention seems to hamper the model in exactly extracting the environment.

In order to monitor how performance varies to the choice of top-k values, we evaluated the attention model with different top-k values ($k = 5, 10, 15, 20$). When we increase k values, recall increases and precision decreases. Overall, precision of the static RNN decoder is found better than that of the other models. On the other hand, the attentive reader model shows outstanding performance in extracting all relevant environment tokens.

5.4 Analysis

The baseline models mainly show F1-scores under 30, which are worse than we expected. Among them, SVM outputs skewed results, failing to find any environment terms, and classifying all test data to '<NOE>'. As a result, its performance depends on the number of input data showing no environment terms, which explains why the model shows even precision and recall. In contrast to SVM, the other two models can detect environ-

[3]http://scikit-learn.org

[4]https://www.tensorflow.org/

Polymorphisms in CRHR1 and the serotonin transporter loci: gene x gene x environment interactions on depressive symptoms. [PMID: 20029939]		
... These data suggest that G x E interactions predictive of depressive symptoms may be differentially sensitive to **levels of childhood trauma**, ...		
attentive reader	**seq2seq**	**static RNN decoder**
high history low status <UNK> levels current hormone stress ...	<UNK>	<UNK> childhood levels high trauma
Peroxisome proliferator-activated receptor-alpha (PPARA) genetic polymorphisms and breast cancer risk: a Long Island ancillary study. [PMID: 18586686]		
... but there was some evidence of interaction between PPARA variants and **aspirin use**, defined as **use at least once per week for 6 months or longer**. ...		
attentive reader	**seq2seq**	**static RNN decoder**
use aspirin <UNK> women levels body mass cancer index ...	hcas	aspirin

Table 4: Results of experiment with four proposed models. Words in red and blue indicate disease and gene names, respectively, and the words in bold-face indicate environment terms.

ment terms, but they also identify irrelevant tokens as environment terms in most cases.

In order to analyze how differently the proposed models output, we select three proposed models showing the best performance, the attentive reader, the sequence-to-sequence model (attention encoding), and the static RNN decoder (basic encoding) among them, and show the result of experiments for two abstracts. In Table 4, the first row represents a partial content of the abstract and the second row represents the results. We show a sequence of tokens in the attentive reader as much as possible, and the sequence is ordered by scores. On the other hand, a sequence of tokens in the sequence-to-sequence model and static RNN decoder is ordered in which they were made in the decoding part.

The first example in Table 4 provides GxE for two genes, where we ask our models to extract environment tokens for *serotonin transport* and *depressive symptoms*. Although the three models failed to identify all answer tokens, the static RNN decoder shows better performance than the others. In tokens extracted by the attentive reader, there are not only answer tokens but also error tokens, which results in decreasing the performance. These weaknesses sometimes work as an advantage for the cases with many environment terms as shown in the abstract in the second example.

In the second example, the number of tokens is bigger than that in the first example. Interestingly, the performance of the attentive reader and that of the static RNN decoder are reversed. Although there are many answer tokens, the static RNN decoder seems to extract minimal tokens. On the other hand, the majority of tokens extracted by the

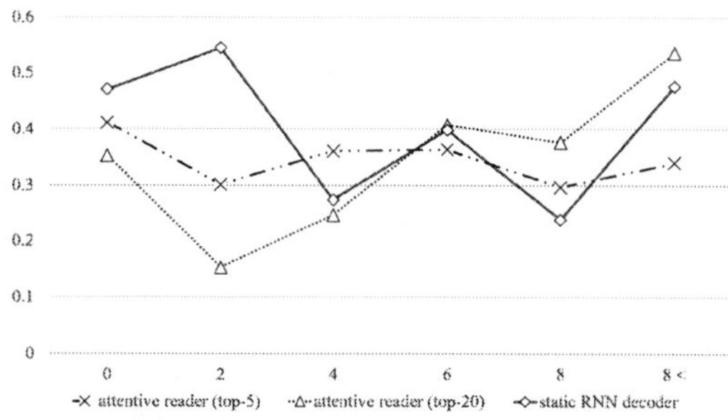

Figure 3: Performance of the two models, the attentive reader and the static RNN decoder model, according to the number of environment tokens. X-axis and Y-axis represent the number and F1 score, respectively.

attentive reader are included in answer tokens.

As shown in Table 4, the static RNN decoder models work better in extracting a small number of tokens. On the other hand, the attentive reader is suitable to the data with a large number of tokens. And the choice of k seems an important factor to affect the performance of the attentive reader. In order to see that the observations are common, we compared F1-scores of three models, the attentive reader (top-5 and top-20) and the static RNN decoder, according to the number of environment tokens.

Figure 3 presents the change of F1-score when the number of environment tokens varies. When the number is smaller than 2, the static RNN decoder works best. While the static RNN decoder is sensitive to the number, the attentive reader (top-5) shows stable performance. Therefore, the attentive reader (top-5) shows better performance than the static RNN reader at both 4 and 8 points. The per-

Serious obstetric complications interact with hypoxia-regulated/vascular-expression genes to influence schizophrenia risk. [PMID: 18195713]	
basic encoding	**attention encoding**
<NOE>	obstetric serious complications

Table 5: An example showing the benefits of using attention model: the words in bold-face indicate environment terms.

formance of the attentive reader (top-20), however, increases steadily according to the number. As a result, the attentive reader (top-20) works best at 6 points afterwards.

At 6 points, the performance of the static RNN decoder and that of attentive reader (top-20) are reversed, so it seems that there is not much performance difference among them in the graph. But, the overall difference in performance is much bigger because the average of the numbers in the corpus is nearly 5. As a result, the static RNN decoder outperforms other models. From this observation, we anticipate that if we address the GxE task focusing on the number by combining the two models, the performance will exceed the current best score, 0.426.

In the static RNN decoder, the attention encoding did not seem to work well, which is in contrast to our assumption that it would be better to consider combinations for our task. However, there is a special case showing the benefits of attention encoding as shown in Table 5. Table 5 shows part of an abstract where there are 39 combinations (13 genes and 3 diseases) and four genes associated with schizophrenia among them have the same environment terms (*serious obstetric complications*). Unless considering the combination, it seems hard to identify environment terms due to many negative examples. As a result, given a combination, (*RGS4* and *fetal hypoxia*), without an environment term such as the example in Table 5, the static RNN decoder using a basic encoding seems to regard the majority of combinations including the combination with environment as a negative example, as shown in the first column of Table 5. However, interestingly, the static RNN decoder using attention encoding identified three tokens that are correct environment terms when the four combinations with environment are given. This incor-

rect result may be due to the lack of training examples like this case. So, if we are given many cases as shown in Table 5, we envision that attention encoding will help improve performance.

6 Conclusion

In this paper, we proposed various methods for GxE recognition and showed that our models achieved good performance, despite the inherent difficulty of the task. Unlike general approaches, such as CNN, RNN, and attention mechanism, in order to extract targeted relations or infer the correct answer, we used an RNN decoder as a sequence-to-sequence model with a static decoder, and demonstrated that it is suitable to the task in extracting terms from documents. It is necessary to identify conditional information that creates the contradiction of gene-disease relations to develop advanced systems for understanding the full etiology of a disease or the full genetic network. We anticipate that the model will help researchers not only to identify correct gene-disease relations but also to apply them to other tasks, such as extracting location information that indicates where events occur.

Acknowledgments

This work was supported by the National Research Foundation of Korea (NRF) grant funded by the Korea government (MSIP) (No. NRF-2017R1A2B4012788).

References

Jonathan Berant, Vivek Srikumar, Pei-Chun Chen, Abby Vander Linden, Brittany Harding, Brad Huang, Peter Clark, and Christopher D Manning. 2014. Modeling Biological Processes for Reading Comprehension. In *Proceedings of the 2014 Conference on Empirical Methods in Natural Language Processing*, pages 1499–1510.

Danqi Chen, Jason Bolton, and Christopher D. Manning. 2016. A Thorough Examination of the CNN/Daily Mail Reading Comprehension Task. In *Proceedings of the 54th Annual Meeting of the Association for Computational Linguistics*, pages 2358–2367.

Kyunghyun Cho, Bart Van Merriënboer, Caglar Gulcehre, Dzmitry Bahdanau, Fethi Bougares, Holger Schwenk, and Yoshua Bengio. 2014. Learning phrase representations using RNN encoder-decoder for statistical machine translation. In *Proceedings of the 2014 Conference on Empirical Methods in Natural Language Processing*, pages 1724–1734.

Marie-Catherine De Marneffe, Bill MacCartney, Christopher D Manning, et al. 2006. Generating Typed Dependency Parses from Phrase Structure Parses. In *Proceedings of the Fifth International Conference on Language Resources and Evaluation*, volume 6, pages 449–454.

Julia DiGangi, Guia Guffanti, Katie A McLaughlin, and Karestan C Koenen. 2013. Considering trauma exposure in the context of genetics studies of posttraumatic stress disorder: a systematic review. *Biology of mood & anxiety disorders*, 3(1):2.

Erin C Dunn, Monica Uddin, SV Subramanian, Jordan W Smoller, Sandro Galea, and Karestan C Koenen. 2011. Research Review: Gene-environment interaction research in youth depression-a systematic review with recommendations for future research. *Journal of Child Psychology and Psychiatry*, 52(12):1223–1238.

Karl Moritz Hermann, Tomas Kocisky, Edward Grefenstette, Lasse Espeholt, Will Kay, Mustafa Suleyman, and Phil Blunsom. 2015. Teaching Machines to Read and Comprehend. In *Advances in Neural Information Processing Systems 28*, pages 1693–1701.

Daniel Hewlett, Alexandre Lacoste, Llion Jones, Illia Polosukhin, Andrew Fandrianto, Jay Han, Matthew Kelcey, and David Berthelot. 2016. WikiReading: A Novel Large-scale Language Understanding Task over wikipedia. In *Proceedings of the 54th Annual Meeting of the Association for Computational Linguistics*, pages 1535–1545.

Felix Hill, Antoine Bordes, Sumit Chopra, and Jason Weston. 2016. The Goldilocks Principle: Reading Children's Books with Explicit Memory Representations. In *International Conference on Learning Representations 2016*.

Sepp Hochreiter and Jürgen Schmidhuber. 1997. Long short-term memory. *Neural computation*, 9(8):1735–1780.

David J Hunter. 2005. Gene-environment interactions in human diseases. *Nature Reviews Genetics*, 6(4):287–298.

Conrad Iyegbe, Desmond Campbell, Amy Butler, Olesya Ajnakina, and Pak Sham. 2014. The emerging molecular architecture of schizophrenia, polygenic risk scores and the clinical implications for gxe research. *Social psychiatry and psychiatric epidemiology*, 49(2):169–182.

Petra Kasajova, Veronika Holubekova, Andrea Mendelova, Zora Lasabova, Pavol Zubor, Erik Kudela, Kristina Biskupska-Bodova, and Jan Danko. 2016. Active cigarette smoking and the risk of breast cancer at the level of N-acetyltransferase 2 (NAT2) gene polymorphisms. *Tumor Biology*, 37(6):7929.

Jun'ichi Kazama and Jun'ichi Tsujii. 2003. Evaluation and extension of maximum entropy models with inequality constraints. In *Proceedings of the 2003 conference on Empirical Methods in Natural Language Processing*, pages 137–144.

Jin-Dong Kim, Yue Wang, and Yamamoto Yasunori. 2013. The Genia Event Extraction Shared Task, 2013 Edition-Overview. In *Proceedings of the 3rd BioNLP Shared Task Workshop*, pages 8–15.

Diederik Kingma and Jimmy Ba. 2015. Adam: A Method for Stochastic Optimization. In *International Conference on Learning Representations 2015*.

Hsin-Chun Lee, Yi-Yu Hsu, and Hung-Yu Kao. 2016. AuDis: an automatic CRF-enhanced disease normalization in biomedical text. *Database*, 2016:baw091.

S. Pyysalo, F. Ginter, H. Moen, T. Salakoski, and S. Ananiadou. 2013. Distributional Semantics Resources for Biomedical Text Processing. In *Proceedings of the 5th International Symposium on Languages in Biology and Medicine*, pages 39–44.

Naoko I Simonds, Armen A Ghazarian, Camilla B Pimentel, Sheri D Schully, Gary L Ellison, Elizabeth M Gillanders, and Leah E Mechanic. 2016. Review of the Gene-Environment Interaction Literature in Cancer: What Do We Know? *Genetic epidemiology*, 40(5):356–365.

Ilya Sutskever, Oriol Vinyals, and Quoc V Le. 2014. Sequence to sequence learning with neural networks. In *Advances in Neural Information Processing Systems*, pages 3104–3112.

Chih-Hsuan Wei, Hung-Yu Kao, and Zhiyong Lu. 2015a. GNormPlus: An Integrative Approach for Tagging Genes, Gene Families, and Protein Domains. *BioMed research international*, 2015.

Chih-Hsuan Wei, Yifan Peng, Robert Leaman, Allan Peter Davis, Carolyn J Mattingly, Jiao Li, Thomas C Wiegers, and Zhiyong Lu. 2015b. Overview of the BioCreative V chemical disease relation (CDR) task. In *Proceedings of the fifth BioCreative challenge evaluation workshop*, pages 154–166. Sevilla Spain.

Jun Xu, Yonghui Wu, Yaoyun Zhang, Jingqi Wang, Hee-Jin Lee, and Hua Xu. 2016. CD-REST: a system for extracting chemical-induced disease relation in literature. *Database*, 2016:baw036.

Nathalie K Zgheib, Ashraf A Shamseddine, Eddy Geryess, Arafat Tfayli, Ali Bazarbachi, Ziad Salem, Ali Shamseddine, Ali Taher, and Nagi S El-Saghir. 2013. Genetic polymorphisms of CYP2E1, GST, and NAT2 enzymes are not associated with risk of breast cancer in a sample of Lebanese women. *Mutation Research/Fundamental and Molecular Mechanisms of Mutagenesis*, 747:40–47.

Course Concept Extraction in MOOCs via Embedding-Based Graph Propagation

Liangming Pan, Xiaochen Wang, Chengjiang Li, Juanzi Li and **Jie Tang**
Knowledge Engineering Laboratory
Department of Computer Science and Technology
Tsinghua University, Beijing 100084, China
{panlm14, wangxc15, licj17}@mails.tsinghua.edu.cn
{lijuanzi, tangjie}@tsinghua.edu.cn

Abstract

Massive Open Online Courses (MOOCs), offering a new way to study online, are revolutionizing education. One challenging issue in MOOCs is how to design effective and fine-grained course concepts such that students with different backgrounds can grasp the essence of the course. In this paper, we conduct a systematic investigation of the problem of course concept extraction for MOOCs. We propose to learn latent representations for candidate concepts via an embedding-based method. Moreover, we develop a graph-based propagation algorithm to rank the candidate concepts based on the learned representations. We evaluate the proposed method using different courses from XuetangX and Coursera. Experimental results show that our method significantly outperforms all the alternative methods (+0.013-0.318 in terms of R-precision; $p \ll 0.01$, t-test).

1 Introduction

In contrast with traditional courses that have limited numbers of students, each online course in a MOOC platform may draw more than 100,000 registrants (Seaton et al., 2014). The students have very diverse backgrounds; and knowledge presented in MOOCs is well understood by certain students, but might be difficult to others. In MOOCs, we use *course concepts* to refer to the knowledge concepts taught in the course videos, and related topics that help students better understand course videos. Identifying course concepts at a fine level is very important, as students with different backgrounds have totally different requirements. Figure 1 shows an example to illustrate the

You might learn how to write a **bubble sort** and learn why a **bubble sort** is not as good as a **heapsort**. Next. we are going to talk about the **quick sort** algorithm. Quicksort is an algorithm invented in the 1960s by doctor Tony Hoare. It is also called the **partition exchange sort**, and is a typical algorithm based on **divide-and-conquer**.
....
Now we have the first version of Q **sort**. After we make an analysis on its performance, performance, we will find that **quicksort** is an **unstable sorting algorithm**. Fortunately. the **quick sort** has an average **time complexity** of n log n, and in most cases, it can achieve its optimal performance. We first estimate its performance under **independent uniform distribution**.

Figure 1: Example of a video clip and its course concepts

problem addressed in this work. It is a clip (about ten minutes long) of video captions from the *data structure* course in XuetangX [1], one of the largest MOOCs in China. The related course concepts are marked in red and blue. We see that there are a dozen concepts mentioned in this clip. The major concept is "quick sort" (marked in red), but the content is related to many other prerequisite concepts such as "divide-and-conquer", "bubble sort", and "unstable sorting algorithm" (marked in blue). For students with a computer science background, those concepts would be easy; however, for students from other discipline areas, the concepts may be completely new. With the identified course concepts, we can build an interactive learning environment to help individual students better grasp the knowledge in a course. For example, for a non-science student, the system may display the definition of "unstable sorting" and "uniform distribution"; while for a science student, the system could recommend advanced concepts or potential applications of "quick sort".

Course concepts were previously provided by the teacher, but only at a coarse level—it is time-consuming and tedious to annotate all fine-grained concepts in all videos of a course. Our goal is to automatically identify all course concepts from each video clip. Despite quite a few studies on related research topics, including keyphrase extraction (Salton and Buckley, 1988; Mihalcea and Tarau, 2004; Liu et al., 2010) and term extrac-

---

[1]http://www.xuetangx.com/

Proceedings of the The 8th International Joint Conference on Natural Language Processing, pages 875–884,
Taipei, Taiwan, November 27 – December 1, 2017 ©2017 AFNLP

tion (Hisamitsu et al., 2000; Li et al., 2013), the problem of course concept extraction in MOOCs is far from solved. The most challenging issue in the MOOC context is the **low-frequency problem**. Course video captions often contain many course concepts with low frequency, primarily for three reasons: (1) course video captions are relatively short documents, containing small numbers of words; (2) many infrequent course concepts are from other prerequisite or related courses (e.g., "uniform distribution" is from mathematical courses and "divide-and-conquer" is from courses about algorithms); (3) a disambiguated course concept tends to be expressed in various ways, which produces many scattered infrequent terms. For example, "Q sort" is a colloquial expression referring to quick sort, and "partition exchange sort" is another name for quick sort. They both have infrequent presence in course videos.

Handling infrequency errors remains an open challenge for state-of-the-art keyphrase extractors (Hasan and Ng, 2014). In MOOCs, the low-frequency problem makes it difficult for video captions to provide reliable statistical information (e.g., *tf-idf*, *c-value*, and co-occurrence) for extracting and ranking terms, and results in the ignoring of many course-relevant yet infrequent concepts. For example, in Figure 1, we can correctly extract the frequent concept "quick sort" using *tf-idf*, but fail to extract "partition exchange sort" due to its infrequent presence, even if these two concepts have the same meaning. The above problem can be addressed if we know the semantic relationship between "quick sort" and "partition exchange sort". Such an "understanding" can be facilitated by the incorporation of background knowledge from external data sources. There exist quite a few attempts (Vivaldi and Rodr?uez, 2010; Rospocher et al., 2012) that utilize external knowledge sources such as Wikipedia categories and WordNet to incorporate semantic relations (e.g. synonymy, is-a) into keyphrase extraction. However, these methods are not suitable in the MOOC context, because many highly technical course concepts are not covered by generic semantic resources, including Wikipedia and WordNet.

Recently, distributed representations of words, namely word embeddings (Mikolov et al., 2013b,a), provides us with powerful tools to represent semantic relations between words. In our work, to address the low-frequency problem, we incorporate online encyclopedias to learn the latent representations for candidate course concepts. Moreover, we present a novel graph-based propagation algorithm to rank the candidates based on the learned representations. We evaluate the proposed method using real courses from XuetangX and Coursera [2] with different domains and different languages, and compare our method with state-of-the-art keyphrase extractors. In summary, our contributions include: a) the first attempt, to the best of our knowledge, to systematically investigate the problem of course concept extraction in MOOCs; b) proposal of an efficient model for course concept extraction via semantic representation learning, and ranking candidates through graph-based propagation; c) design of four novel datasets using real courses of different disciplines from XuetangX and Coursera to evaluate our proposed method.

2 Problem Formulation & Framework

In this section, we first give some necessary definitions and then formulate the problem of course concept extraction.

A **course corpus** is composed of n courses in the same subject area, denoted as $\mathcal{D} = \{\mathcal{C}_j\}_{j=1,\ldots,n}$, where $\mathcal{C}_j$ is one course. We assume that course $\mathcal{C}_j = \{v_{ij}\}_{i=1,\cdots,m_j}$ consists of m_j course videos, where v_{ij} stands for the i-th video. Each video v_{ij} is composed of its video title t_{ij} and its video texts (video subtitles or speech scripts) d_{ij}.

Course concepts are subjects taught in the course. Formally, a course concept c can be defined as a k-gram in $\mathcal{D}$ with the following properties: a) *phraseness*: c should be a semantically and syntactically correct phrase; b) *informativeness*: c should represent a scientific or technical concept related to courses in $\mathcal{D}$.

Course concept extraction is formally defined as follows. Given the course corpus $\mathcal{D}$, the objective is to extract candidate course concepts from $\mathcal{D}$, denoted as $\mathcal{T} = \{c_1, \ldots, c_M\}$, and output the confidence score s_i for each candidate $c_i \in \mathcal{T}$. s_i indicates the likelihood of c_i to be a course concept in $\mathcal{D}$.

The fundamental challenge for course concept extraction is how to capture the phraseness and informativeness of course concepts. The general

---

[2] https://www.coursera.org/

architecture of our model consists of three parts: (1) **candidate concepts extraction**, (2) **candidate concepts ranking**, and (3) **postprocessing**.

Candidate concepts extraction pre-processes the input corpus and extracts candidate course concepts. Considering that most concepts are noun phrases consisting of nouns, adjectives and some variants of verbs, and end with a noun word (Liu et al., 2010; Hulth, 2003; Li et al., 2013), we obtain candidate course concepts by extracting all noun phrases in the course corpus. The input text is first tokenized and annotated with part-of-speech (POS) tags. Next, we employ the linguistic pattern $((A|N)^+|(A|N)^*(NP)?(A|N)^*)N$, introduced by Justeson and Katz (1995), to extract all k-gram noun phrases as our candidates, where A, N, and P denote the adjectives, nouns, and prepositions, respectively.

Candidate concepts ranking, which is the most important part of our method, involves ranking the extracted candidates based on their phraseness and informativeness. In our model, we utilize local mutual frequencies to measure the phraseness of the extracted candidates. The informativeness of a candidate is largely dependent on its semantic meaning. Due to the low-frequency problem, local statistical features do not provide sufficient information for capturing the semantic meaning carried by each candidate concept. In our method, we propose an embedding-based method, which incorporates external knowledge from online encyclopedias, to provide semantic representations for candidate concepts. Based on the learned phraseness and informativeness information, we construct a weighted undirected graph, namely a *course concept graph* (CCG), where each vertex represents a candidate course concept. We then rank the vertexes in the graph via a novel iterative graph-based propagation algorithm, namely *course concept propagation* (CCP).

In the *postprocessing* step, by choosing an appropriate cut-off value for the ranking list, we can easily annotate course concepts in video texts via string matching.

3 Course Concept Graph

We combine the phraseness and informativeness information of candidate course concepts synergistically to construct the course concept graph, formally defined as follows.

The **course concept graph** (CCG) of $\mathcal{D}$ is a weighted undirected fully-connected graph denoted as $\mathcal{G} = (V, E)$, where V is the vertex set of $\mathcal{G}$ and E is the edge set of $\mathcal{G}$. Each vertex in V represents a candidate course concept $c_i \in \mathcal{T}$ and is associated with a *phraseness score* $ph(c_i)$, indicating the phraseness of c_i. For an edge $(c_i, c_j) \in E$, its edge weight $e(c_i, c_j) = SR(c_i, c_j)$, where $SR(c_i, c_j)$ indicates the *semantic relatedness* (SR) between c_i and c_j, i.e., the likeness of their meaning or semantic content.

A fully-connected CCG stores the SR between any candidate pair. But in practice, we introduce a parameter θ for pruning the graph. An edge (c_i, c_j) exists in a CCG only if $SR(c_i, c_j) > \theta$. The reason for pruning is: (1) the propagation on a fully connected CCG is computationally challenging, and (2) low-SR candidate pairs may introduce noise during propagation. In the following subsections, we introduce the essential building blocks of CCG, i.e., the calculation of phraseness and the representation of semantic relatedness.

3.1 Phraseness Measurement

Phraseness examines the likelihood of a multi-word term to be a semantically and syntactically correct phrase. There exists several mechanisms such as Log-likelihood (LL) (Dunning, 1993) and Pointwise Mutual Information (PMI) (Church and Hanks, 1990) to measure the phraseness of a term. These methods are mostly based on the assumption that if the constituents of a multi-word candidate term form a collocation, rather than co-occurring by chance, it is more likely to be considered as a phrase (Korkontzelos et al., 2008). In our paper, we propose a simple PMI-based approach, which utilizes local mutual frequencies in the course corpus, to calculate the phraseness score for each candidate. Specifically, for a k-gram candidate $c = \{w_1, \cdots, w_k\} \in \mathcal{T}$, where $k > 1$, we split c into $f_i = \{w_1, \cdots, w_i\}$ (prefix) and $b_i = \{w_{i+1}, \cdots, w_k\}$ (suffix), where $i = 1, \cdots, k-1$. Then, the phraseness score $ph(c)$ is defined as follows.

$$ph(c) = max\{pmi(f_i, b_i) \mid i = 1, \cdots, k - 1\} \quad (1)$$

where $pmi(f_i, b_i)$ is the PMI of the prefix f_i and the suffix b_i, defined as follows.

$$pmi(f_i, b_i) = \frac{2 \times freq(c)}{freq(f_i) + freq(b_i)} \quad (2)$$

where $freq(c)$, $freq(f_i)$, $freq(b_i)$ are the occurrence frequencies of terms c, f_i and b_i in the corpus, respectively. Due to the low-frequency problem in the MOOC corpus, the phraseness scores for infrequent candidates may be statistically unreliable. Thus, the final phraseness of a candidate is estimated on both the MOOC corpus and the online encyclopedia corpus as follows.

$$ph(c) = \alpha \cdot F[ph^D(c)] + (1 - \alpha) \cdot F[ph^E(c)] \quad (3)$$

where $ph^D(c)$ and $ph^E(c)$ are the phraseness calculated on the course corpus and the encyclopedia corpus, respectively. α ranges between 0 and 1, controlling the phraseness contribution of each corpus. $F[\cdot]$ is a filter for the value of $ph(c)$. If the frequency of c is lower than a pre-defined threshold $minc$, or c is an unigram, the filter simply assigns a priori value of 0.5 to the term, i.e., $F[ph(c)] = 0.5$.

3.2 Semantic Relatedness Learning

As mentioned in Section 2, statistical information in the course corpus cannot adequately capture the informativeness of concepts because of the low-frequency problem. In our method, we use word embeddings (Mikolov et al., 2013b,a) based on the online encyclopedia corpus to provide semantic representations for candidate concepts. Word embeddings represents each word as a low-dimensional, real-valued vector, and the semantic similarity between two words can be reflected by the cosine distance of their vectors. Our method for calculating semantic relatedness between candidate concepts consists of three steps: (1) corpus annotation, (2) representation learning, and (3) relatedness calculation.

Corpus Annotation. An online encyclopedia corpus is a set of articles, and can be represented as a sequence of words $\mathcal{W} = \langle w_1 \cdots w_i \cdots w_m \rangle$, where w_i denotes a word and m is the length of the word sequence. In $\mathcal{W}$, we replace any adjacent words which literally matches a candidate in $\mathcal{T}$ as an unique token. After this step, we obtain a concept-annotated corpus $\mathcal{W}' = \langle x_1 \cdots x_i \cdots x_{m'} \rangle$, where x_i corresponds to a word $w \in \mathcal{W}$ or a concept $c \in \mathcal{T}$. Note that the length m' of $\mathcal{W}'$ is less than the length m of $\mathcal{W}$ because multiple adjacent words are labeled as one token.

Representation Learning. We then learn word embeddings on $\mathcal{W}'$ to obtain vector representations for all annotated candidates and words in $\mathcal{W}'$. For any unannotated candidate concept in $\mathcal{T}$, we obtain its semantic representations via the vector addition of its individual word vectors.

Relatedness Calculation. When vector representations of candidate concepts are learned, we define the **semantic relatedness** between two candidates c_1 and c_2 as the cosine similarity of their vectors, denoted as $SR(c_1, c_2)$.

With this method, a candidate course concept has no corresponding vector only if any of its constituent word is absent in the whole encyclopedia corpus. This case is unusual because a large online encyclopedia corpus can easily cover almost all individual words of the vocabulary. Our experimental results verify that over 98% of the candidates have vector representations in this way.

4   Graph Propagation-Based Ranking

After the construction of a course concept graph, we propose an algorithm to rank the candidate course concepts, based on the following assumption about CCG. *In CCG, a course concept is likely to connect with other course concepts with high semantic relatedness.* We make this assumption based on two reasons. First, course concepts are usually scientific concepts. Scientific concepts in the same domain usually have strong semantic relations. Second, the main ideas of a document can be captured by a group or groups of words with strong semantic relationships. Course concepts are strongly related to the course corpus, which makes them more likely to connect with each other with high semantic relatedness.

For a vertex c in CCG, we denote $conf(c)$ as its **confidence score** of being a course concept. Following the above assumption, the confidence score of a candidate course concept is evidenced by its semantic relations with other course concepts. In other words, high-confidence course concepts in CCG could propagate their confidence scores to their neighbor nodes that have high semantic relatedness with them, to discover other potential course concepts. Therefore, we propose an iterative graph-based algorithm, namely course concept propagation (CCP), which first assigns each vertex of CCG an initial confidence score, and iteratively updates the score for each vertex through propagation. The initial confidence score of each candidate course concept is determined by a **seed set** S, which contains a list of known course concepts in $\mathcal{D}$. Specifically, let us denote the confidence score of the vertex c in the k-th iteration as

$conf^k(c)$, and the initial confidence score of c as $conf^0(c)$. We set $conf^0(c) = 1$ if $c \in S$ and $conf^0(c) = 0$, otherwise. In the following sub-sections, we first introduce the construction of a seed set, and then present the propagation process in detail.

4.1 Seed Set Construction

In our method, the seed set can be constructed either manually or automatically. For some courses, key course concepts may already be included in course materials; however, this is not the case for most MOOC courses. For those courses in which key course concepts are not explicitly provided, we propose to extract them automatically from course outlines. A course in a MOOC usually contains hundreds of videos, each of which is associated with a video title. These video titles serve as an outline of a course and become a potential good resource for providing high-quality course concepts. Specifically, for each course C_i, we first extract candidates from video titles of C_i, following the same pattern-based procedure in the candidate extraction step. Then, candidates are ranked based on their *tf-idf* in C_i. Finally, we select the top-N ranked candidates to form the seed set S.

4.2 Propagation Process

To design the propagation process, we need to answer two crucial questions. First, a vertex should receive confidence scores from which vertexes in each iteration? Second, how much score should a vertex receives from another vertex in each iteration? Based on the above questions, we define two general functions as follows: a) *voting score* $vs^k(c_j, c_i)$: determines the confidence score c_j propagates to c_i in the k-th iteration; b) *voters* $A(c_i)$: it specifies the vertex set from which c_i receives the voting scores in each iteration. Therefore, a general propagation process can be defined as follows.

$$conf^{k+1}(c_i) = \frac{1}{Z}\left(\frac{\sum_{c_j \in A(c_i)} vs^k(c_j, c_i)}{|A(c_i)|}\right) \quad (4)$$

where Z a the normalization factor. The main idea of Equation 4 can be explained as a voting process. During each iteration, each vertex in $A(c_i)$ will vote for c_i. The score of c_i in the next iteration is dependent on the average voting score of vertexes in $A(c_i)$. We implement the voting score function as follows.

$$vs^k(c_j, c_i) = ph(c_j) \cdot e(c_i, c_j) \cdot conf^k(c_j) \quad (5)$$

where $ph(c_j) \cdot e(c_i, c_j)$ determines the "authoritativeness" of the vote from c_j to c_i. If c_j has a higher phraseness (the voter is more credible) and c_j is more relevant to c_i (the voter knows more about the candidate), then c_j tends to propagate more of its score to c_i (the vote from c_j has a greater impact on determining whether c_i is a course concept than the votes from other voters). As for the implemention of $A(c_i)$, a natural way would be to set $A(c_i)$ as the neighbor vertexes of c_i in CCG. Because a course concept is likely to connect with other course concepts with high semantic relatedness, it tends to receive high voting scores from its course concept neighbors, compared with other vertexes, during propagation.

However, in practice, the propagation process is usually hampered by the **overlapping problem**. If two terms c_i and c_j contain one or more identical words, we say that c_i and c_j are *overlapping*. For example, "merge sort" and "bubble sort" are overlapping because they both have the word "sort." Overlapping frequently occurs among course concepts because scientific terms often have background words such as "function," "algorithm," and "culture". We find that $vs(c_j, c_i)$ is less reliable if c_j and c_i overlap. For example, the term "same algorithm" is not a course concept, but it contains the word "algorithm," which makes it to have a high SR with the course concepts including word "algorithm," as in "bfs algorithm" and "kmp algorithm". Therefore, the score of the term "same algorithm" tends to be blindly increased by votes from these course concept neighbors. To solve this problem, we generalize the voting score by introducing a **penalty function** opf, which restricts the propagation of voting scores among overlapping terms. The **generalized voting score** (gvs) is defined as follows.

$$gvs^k(c_j, c_i) = opf(c_i, c_j) \cdot ph(c_j) \cdot e(c_i, c_j) \cdot conf^k(c_j) \quad (6)$$

where $opf(c_i, c_j) = 1$ when c_i and c_j is not overlapping, and $opf(c_i, c_j) = \lambda$ otherwise, where λ ranges from 0 to 1.

Termination Condition. To determine when the iteration process stops, we introduce a **termination set** $\mathcal{F}$, including S course concepts. Let us denote the average ranking of concepts in $\mathcal{F}$ after the k-th iteration as $Ar^k(\mathcal{F})$. The propagation process terminates if $Ar^{k+1}(\mathcal{F}) > Ar^k(\mathcal{F})$.

Dataset	Domain	Language	#courses	#videos	#tokens	#candidates	#labeled	correlation
CSEN	Computer Science	English	8	690	1,242,156	59,050	4,096	0.734
EcoEN	Economics	English	5	381	401,192	27,571	3,652	0.696
CSZH	Computer Science	Chinese	18	2,849	2,291,258	79,009	5,309	0.721
EcoZH	Economics	Chinese	8	455	645,016	60,566	3,663	0.646

Table 1: Dataset Statistics

5 Experiments

5.1 Datasets

Because there is no publicly available dataset for course concept extraction in MOOCs, we construct four course corpuses with different domains and languages to evaluate our model. Specifically, we collect Computer Science and Economics courses from two famous MOOC platforms — Coursera and XuetangX — to construct our evaluation datasets.

Coursera is one of the first MOOC platforms in the world. We collect video captions from 8 Computer Science courses to form the **CSEN** dataset. Similarly, video captions from 5 Economics courses are picked to construct the **EcoEN** dataset. All video captions in CSEN and EcoEN are in English. XuetangX is one of the most popular MOOC websites in China. Video captions of 18 Computer Science courses and 8 Economics courses are collected to form the **CSZH** dataset and **EcoZH** dataset, respectively. All video captions in CSZH and EcoZH are in Chinese.

The statistics of the four datasets are listed in Table 1, where *#courses*, *#videos*, and *#tokens* are the total number of courses, videos, and tokens in each dataset. For each dataset, the video captions are preprocessed following the procedure of *Candidate concepts extraction* in Section 2. *#candidates* denotes the number of extracted candidates for each dataset. To create a gold standard for evaluation, candidates for each dataset are sent to two human annotators majoring in the corresponding domain. For each candidate, the annotator is asked to make a judgement about whether it is a course concept based on the course contents. Thus, each dataset is doubly annotated, and pearson correlation coefficient is applied to assess inter-annotator agreement. A candidate is labeled as a course concept only if the two annotators are in agreement. The column *#labeled* presents the ground-truth number for each dataset. In each dataset, we use 10% of ground truth to form the termination set and others for evaluation.

The datasets will be publicly available later.

As for the online encyclopedia corpus, we employ the Baidu encyclopedia[3], which is the largest web-based encyclopedia in China, for Chinese language. Our training corpus includes 6,223,649 web pages crawled from the latest Baidu encyclopedia. For the English language, we extract 9,834,664 articles from the latest publicly available Wikipedia dump.[4]

5.2 Evaluation Metrics

For our experiments, we select two evaluation metrics. The first metric is **R-precision** (R_p) (Zesch and Gurevych, 2009), which is an IR metric that focuses on ranking. Given a ranking list with n gold keyphrases, it computes the precision of a system over its n highest-ranked candidates. However, R-precision does not take the order of extracted keyphrases into account. To address the problem, we select the **Mean Average Precision** (MAP), which has been the preferred metric in information retrieval for evaluating ranked lists.

5.3 Influence of Parameters

We first investigate the parameters that may influence the performance including: (1) α in Equation 3, (2) the size of seed set N, and (3) the penalty factor λ.

The phraseness parameter α. The parameter α controls the contribution of a course corpus when calculating the phraseness score. If α is too large, the calculated phraseness may suffer from unreliable estimation; however, the calculated score may fail to reflect the real phraseness distribution in the course course when α is too small. We investigate the influence of α in Figure 2(a). This figure shows the R-precision of CCP when $\lambda = 0.3$, $N = 100$, and α ranges from 0 to 1. From this figure we find that, when α is set from 0.2 to 0.7, the performance is consistently good, and remains stable with the variations of α. When α is larger than 0.85, the R-precision drops in all

---

[3] http://baike.baidu.com/
[4] https://dumps.wikimedia.org/enwiki/20170120/

evaluation datasets. The results demonstrate that the large-scale encyclopedia data is conducive to making reliable estimations of the phraseness. In our experiment, α is set as 0.4 for all four datasets.

The size of seed set N. As mentioned in Section 4.1, we utilize the video titles to automatically construct the seed set for each dataset. We set the size of the seed set $N = 10, 50, 100, 200$ for each dataset and explore the influences of N on CCP. Figure 2(b) shows the R-precision of CCP with different N on CSEH ($\lambda = 0.3, \alpha = 0.4$). From the figures, we observe that the CCP reaches its best performance through 3 to 5 iterations. When N becomes larger, the algorithm tends to achieve the best performance faster, i.e., it terminates with fewer iterations. However, different settings of N all lead to a competitive best performance (around 0.43 on CSEN). We obtain similar observations on other datasets. In our experiments, we set $N = 100$ for all datasets.

The penalty factor λ. The parameter λ reconciles the influence of voting scores from overlapping terms. We demonstrate the influence of λ in Figure 2(c). This figure shows that the CCP achieves its best R-precision when λ ranges from 0.20 to 0.40 in all datasets. If we do not severely lower the voting scores from overlapping terms ($\lambda > 0.5$), or even have no penalty ($\lambda = 1.0$), the performance is consistently unsatisfactory. The experimental results verify that the voting score from a non-overlapping neighbor (e.g., "data mining" to "machine learning") is relatively more reliable than an overlapping one (e.g., "difficult learning" to "machine learning") in CCP. However, voting scores from overlapping terms still encode some useful semantics (e.g., "merge sort" to "quick sort"), ignoring them (λ close to 0.0) may cause a decline in performance. We set $\lambda = 0.3$ for all datasets.

5.4 Comparison with Baselines

After we explore the influences of parameters, we employ four baseline methods to compare with our proposed method, i.e., course concept propagation (CCP).

5.4.1 Baseline Approaches

First, we select two *statistics-based methods*, i.e., TF-IDF and PMI, as our baselines. **TF-IDF** ranks the candidate course concepts based on their *tf-idf* in the course corpus. For a candidate $c \in \mathcal{T}$, its tfidf $R(c) = tf_c \times log(idf_c)$, where tf_c is the fre-

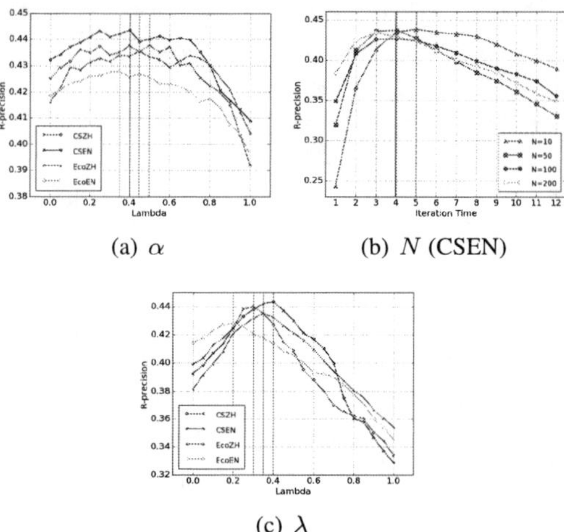

Figure 2: The Study of Parameter Influence on CCP

quency of c in $\mathcal{D}$, and idf_c is based on the number of videos in which c appears. In the **PMI** method, we directly rank candidates based on their phraseness, using the method described in Section 3.1. We use the same parameter α with CCP for a fair comparison. Second, we also employ two *graph-based methods*. **TextRank** (Mihalcea and Tarau, 2004) and **Topical PageRank** (TPR) (Liu et al., 2010) are two state-of-the-art graph-based keyphrase extraction approaches. They all construct a graph based on word co-occurrences within the corpus, and apply the PageRank algorithm (Brin and Page, 1998) to score the vertices. The score of a multi-word candidate is the average score of all words within the candidate. Different from TextRank, TPR decomposes traditional PageRank into multiple PageRanks specific to various topics using LDA (Blei et al., 2003). Topics in TPR are learned from external data sources, and we use the same encyclopedia corpus as ours to make a fair comparison.

5.4.2 Implementation Details

For pruning the CCG, we set $\theta = 0.3$ for all datasets. The $minc$ is heuristically set as 5 in our experiments. The skip-gram model (Mikolov et al., 2013b) is applied to train word embeddings using the Python library gensim [5] with default parameters. For TextRank and TPR, we use the THUTag[6], a state-of-the-art keyphrase extraction package, which provides the implementations of these methods.

---

[5] http://radimrehurek.com/gensim/
[6] https://github.com/YeDeming/THUTag

Method		CSEN	EcoEN	CSZH	EcoZH
TF-IDF	R_p	0.125	0.303	0.118	0.198
	MAP	0.105	0.232	0.109	0.145
PMI	R_p	0.239	0.222	0.246	0.179
	MAP	0.141	0.197	0.187	0.121
TextRank	R_p	0.151	0.290	0.142	0.161
	MAP	0.137	0.263	0.131	0.115
TPR	R_p	0.284	0.414	0.305	0.303
	MAP	0.255	**0.387**	0.267	0.288
CCP	R_p	**0.443**	**0.427**	**0.434**	**0.435**
	MAP	**0.432**	0.365	**0.416**	**0.423**

Table 2: Performance of Different Methods on Different Datasets

5.4.3 Performance Comparison

In Table 2 we summarize the results of different methods across different datasets. From the table, we find that the proposed methods outperform all baselines on all datasets, which indicates the robustness and effectiveness of CCP [7]. Specifically, we have the following observations.

First, TF-IDF performs competitively with TextRank, but they both perform worse than TPR and CCP. TF-IDF and TextRank only use statistical information within the course corpus and have a strong reliance on term frequency, which hampers their performances. For example, both TF-IDF and TextRank correctly extract the concept "IP", which appears 139 times in the Computer Network course, but failed to extract "Internet Protocol", the full name of "IP", due to its infrequent presence. Moreover, they also highly ranked many irrelevant yet frequent terms, such as "English language". These errors are significantly reduced in CCP with the incorporation of semantic relations.

Second, TPR performs better than TextRank across all datasets (an average of +0.141 in terms of R-precision), but is worse than CCP. In MOOCs, a course usually contain multiple topics, but TextRank often falls into a single topic, and fails to cover other substantial topics of a course. For example, in the Data Structure course, TextRank highly ranked phrases with "tree", but lower-ranked concepts related to "sort". TPR alleviates this problem by incorporating topic information from online encyclopedias. However, TPR also favors frequent course concepts, because frequent words tend to have high connectivity in the co-occurrence graph, and thus receive high rankings using PageRank.

---

[7] The improvements are all statistically significant tested with bootstrap re-sampling with 95% confidence.

6 Related Works

Our work is relevant to automatic keyphrase extraction, which concerns the automatic extraction of important and topical phrases from the body of a document" (Turney, 2000). Generally, keyphrase extraction techniques can be classified into two groups: supervised approaches and unsupervised approaches. In supervised machine-learning approaches, the training phase usually includes a classification task: each phrase in the document is either a keyphrase or not (You et al., 2013). Different learning algorithms have been employed to train the classifier, including naïve bayes (Frank et al., 1999; Witten et al., 1999), decision trees (Turney, 2000), maximum entropy (Yih et al., 2006; Kim and Kan, 2009) and support vector machines (Lopez and Romary, 2010; Kim and Kan, 2009). Unsupervised approaches usually involve assigning a saliency score to each candidate phrase, by considering various features (Wan and Xiao, 2008). Generally speaking, the information such as *tf-idf*, co-occurrence, or neighbor documents are frequently used in unsupervised keyphrase extraction. For example, TextRank (Mihalcea and Tarau, 2004) is a well-known method that ranks keywords based on the co-occurrence graph. Huang et al. (2006) utilize co-occurrence information to construct a semantic network for each document and derive the importance of phrases by analyzing the network. The ExpandRank (Wan and Xiao, 2008) model uses a set of neighborhood documents to enhance single-document keyphrase extraction. Recently, Liu et al., (2015) proposed a new framework that extracts quality phrases from text corpora integrated with phrasal segmentation. This model also rely on local statistical information and requires a relatively large corpus.

However, extracting low-frequency keyphrases remains an open challenge for all these methods. To address this problem, many related works consider not only the document level information but also knowledge from external data sources, to improve the effectiveness of automatic keyphrase extraction. Representative examples include the KEA++ system (Medelyan and Witten, 2006) that obtains candidate phrases from a domain-specific thesaurus. The work of Gazendam et al. (2010) also use the thesaurus as a background corpus. Besides the thesaurus, knowledge bases are widely used to calculate semantic relations between terms. For example, Rospocher et al. (2012) use the WordNet to detect synonym terms, and then rank a synonym term higher even if it is ranked lower by the statistical method. The work of Vivaldi and Rodríguez (2010) utilizes an ontology hierarchy extracted from Wikipedia categories to provide background knowledge. Similarly, Berend and Farkas (2010) invent features concerning the Wikipedia level to achieve enhancements in performance. All these methods make use of only the explicit semantic knowledge contained in the external source. Different from them, we use word embeddings to learn semantic representations for candidate concepts and rank them via a novel graph-based propagation process.

7 Conclusion and Future Work

In this paper, we study the problem of course concept extraction in MOOCs. We precisely define the problem and propose a graph-based propagation method to extract course concepts by incorporating external knowledge from online encyclopedias. Experimental results on evaluation datasets validate the effectiveness of the proposed method. Incorporating external knowledge of various kind to help extract course concepts is an intriguing direction for future research. A straightforward task is to incorporate structured information such as "is-a" relation into the proposed model.

References

Gábor Berend and Richárd Farkas. 2010. SZTERGAK : Feature engineering for keyphrase extraction. In *Proceedings of the 5th International Workshop on Semantic Evaluation, SemEval@ACL 2010, Uppsala University, Uppsala, Sweden, July 15-16, 2010*, pages 186–189.

David M. Blei, Andrew Y. Ng, and Michael I. Jordan. 2003. Latent dirichlet allocation. *International Journal of Machine Learning Research*, 3:993–1022.

Sergey Brin and Lawrence Page. 1998. The anatomy of a large-scale hypertextual web search engine. *International Journal of Computer Networks*, 30(1-7):107–117.

Kenneth Ward Church and Patrick Hanks. 1990. Word association norms, mutual information, and lexicography. *International Journal of Computational Linguistics*, 16(1):22–29.

Ted Dunning. 1993. Accurate methods for the statistics of surprise and coincidence. *International Journal of Computational Linguistics*, 19(1):61–74.

Eibe Frank, Gordon W. Paynter, Ian H. Witten, Carl Gutwin, and Craig G. Nevill-Manning. 1999. Domain-specific keyphrase extraction. In *Proceedings of IJCAI*, pages 668–673.

Luit Gazendam, Christian Wartena, and Rogier Brussee. 2010. Thesaurus based term ranking for keyword extraction. In *Database and Expert Systems Applications, Dexa, International Workshops, Bilbao, Spain, August 30 - September*, pages 49–53.

Kazi Saidul Hasan and Vincent Ng. 2014. Automatic keyphrase extraction: A survey of the state of the art. In *Proceedings of ACL*, pages 1262–1273.

Toru Hisamitsu, Yoshiki Niwa, and Jun'ichi Tsujii. 2000. A method of measuring term representativeness - baseline method using co-occurrence distribution. In *Proceedings of COLING*, pages 320–326.

Chong Huang, YongHong Tian, Zhi Zhou, Charles X. Ling, and Tiejun Huang. 2006. Keyphrase extraction using semantic networks structure analysis. In *Proceedings of ICDM*, pages 275–284.

Anette Hulth. 2003. Improved automatic keyword extraction given more linguistic knowledge. In *Proceedings of EMNLP*, pages 216–223.

John S. Justeson and Slava M. Katz. 1995. Technical terminology: some linguistic properties and an algorithm for identification in text. *Natural Language Engineering*, 1(1):9–27.

Su Nam Kim and Min-Yen Kan. 2009. Re-examining automatic keyphrase extraction approaches in scientific articles. In *Proceedings of the ACL-IJCNLP Workshop on Multiword Expressions*, pages 9–16.

Ioannis Korkontzelos, Ioannis P. Klapaftis, and Suresh Manandhar. 2008. Reviewing and evaluating automatic term recognition techniques. In *Proceedings of GoTAL*, pages 248–259.

Sujian Li, Jiwei Li, Tao Song, Wenjie Li, and Baobao Chang. 2013. A novel topic model for automatic term extraction. In *Proceedings of SIGIR*, pages 885–888.

Jialu Liu, Jingbo Shang, Chi Wang, Xiang Ren, and Jiawei Han. 2015. Mining quality phrases from massive text corpora. In *Proceedings of ACM SIGMOD*, pages 1729–1744.

Zhiyuan Liu, Wenyi Huang, Yabin Zheng, and Maosong Sun. 2010. Automatic keyphrase extraction via topic decomposition. In *Proceedings of EMNLP*, pages 366–376.

Patrice Lopez and Laurent Romary. 2010. Humb: Automatic key term extraction from scientific articles in grobid. In *Proceedings of the 5th International Workshop on Semantic Evaluation*, pages 248–251. Association for Computational Linguistics.

Olena Medelyan and Ian H. Witten. 2006. Thesaurus based automatic keyphrase indexing. In *Proceedings of JCDL*, pages 296–297.

Rada Mihalcea and Paul Tarau. 2004. Textrank: Bringing order into text. In *Proceedings of EMNLP*, pages 404–411.

Tomas Mikolov, Kai Chen, Greg Corrado, and Jeffrey Dean. 2013a. Efficient estimation of word representations in vector space. *International Journal of CoRR*, abs/1301.3781.

Tomas Mikolov, Ilya Sutskever, Kai Chen, Gregory S. Corrado, and Jeffrey Dean. 2013b. Distributed representations of words and phrases and their compositionality. In *Proceedings of NIPS*, pages 3111–3119.

Marco Rospocher, Sara Tonelli, Luciano Serafini, and Emanuele Pianta. 2012. Corpus-based terminological evaluation of ontologies. *Applied Ontology*, 7(4):429–448.

Gerard Salton and Chris Buckley. 1988. Term-weighting approaches in automatic text retrieval. *International Journal of Information Processing and Management*, 24(5):513–523.

Daniel T. Seaton, Yoav Bergner, Isaac L. Chuang, Piotr Mitros, and David E. Pritchard. 2014. Who does what in a massive open online course? *Commun. ACM*, 57(4):58–65.

Peter D. Turney. 2000. Learning algorithms for keyphrase extraction. *International Journal of Information Retrieval*, 2(4):303–336.

Jorge Vivaldi and Horacio Rodr?uez. 2010. Finding domain terms using wikipedia. In *Proceeding of L-REC 2010*.

Xiaojun Wan and Jianguo Xiao. 2008. Single document keyphrase extraction using neighborhood knowledge. In *Proceedings of AAAI*, pages 855–860.

Ian H. Witten, Gordon W. Paynter, Eibe Frank, Carl Gutwin, and Craig G. Nevill-Manning. 1999. Kea: practical automatic keyphrase extraction. In *ACM Conference on Digital Libraries*, pages 254–255.

Wen-tau Yih, Joshua Goodman, and Vitor R. Carvalho. 2006. Finding advertising keywords on web pages. In *Proceedings of WWW*, pages 213–222.

Wei You, Dominique Fontaine, and Jean-Paul A. Barthès. 2013. An automatic keyphrase extraction system for scientific documents. *Knowl. Inf. Syst.*, 34(3):691–724.

Torsten Zesch and Iryna Gurevych. 2009. Approximate matching for evaluating keyphrase extraction. In *Proceedings of RANLP*, pages 484–489.

Identity Deception Detection

**Verónica Pérez-Rosas[1], Quincy Davenport[1], Anna Mengdan Dai[1],
Mohamed Aboulenien[2]** and **Rada Mihalcea[1]**
[1]Computer Science and Electrical Engineering. University of Michigan
[2]Computer and Information Science. University of Michigan, Dearborn
{vrncapr,quincyd,annadai,zmohamed,mihalcea}@umich.edu

Abstract

This paper addresses the task of detecting identity deception in language. Using a novel identity deception dataset, consisting of real and portrayed identities from 600 individuals, we show that we can build accurate identity detectors targeting both age and gender, with accuracies of up to 88%. We also perform an analysis of the linguistic patterns used in identity deception, which lead to interesting insights into identity portrayers.

1 Introduction

With the ever growing usage of social media and other online interactions, cyber-crimes such as identity thief, fraud, and sexual predation have become increasingly common. The availability of a wide variety of social platforms and apps further facilitates these kind of crimes, which are often characterized by the ease of deception and concealment of one's real identity. Moreover, the increased sense of security due to the spatial and temporal "distanciation" involved with online communications leads to a growing number of occurrences of identity deception.

Identity deception is defined as "pretending to be someone you are not" (Rowe, 2009). The intentions of identity deceivers differ between achieving monetary benefits, committing fraud, sexual predating, appearing more attractive in online dating, and so on. The risk is further increased with the massive number of children and teens using social media as well as the elderly who get involved in online interactions that they assume to be trustworthy by default due to their lack of experience. Multiple stories of teenagers who became victims of these activities, as well as elderly who lost hundreds of thousands of dollars are now

often encountered in the news. For instance, a recent study reported that 92% of teens go online on daily basis including 24% who are online "almost constantly". [1] The study additionally reported that females tend to use social media more than males.

Hence, due to the financial, social, physical, and psychological damages associated with cyber-crimes, there is a growing need to learn more about the patterns and behaviors of identity deceivers, in order to develop computational approaches that can aid in preventing such crimes.

In this work, we seek to identify linguistic differences in individuals' self-presentation when engaging in identity deception behaviors. We target the two most common behaviors related with online identity deception i.e., individuals portraying themselves as either younger and older, and individuals lying about their gender –also known as gender switching (Macwan and inz. Grzegorz Filcek, 2017; Herring and Martinson, 2004) .

We perform a set of experiments to explore three main research questions. First, given a deceptive corpus consisting of written samples of gender switching, can we build fake identity detectors that predict gender deception? Second, given a deceptive corpus consisting of written samples of age deception, can we build fake identity detectors that predict age deception? Lastly, are there linguistic differences associated with individuals' gender and age in identity deception?

2 Related Work

Several approaches have been developed to detect and prevent identity deception (Tsikerdekis and Zeadally, 2015). Integration of latent textual features with spatial and temporal features has been suggested using probabilistic generative

---

[1]http://www.pewinternet.org/2015/04/09/teens-social-media-technology-2015/

Proceedings of the The 8th International Joint Conference on Natural Language Processing, pages 885–894,
Taipei, Taiwan, November 27 – December 1, 2017 ©2017 AFNLP

modelling to detect identity thieves (Wang et al., 2017). Another study analyzed the connection between time traces of stolen accounts and compared them to that of the original users using support vector machines (Villar-Rodrguez et al., 2016).

As linguistic patterns represent the main method for detecting identity theft, previous work used text mining techniques by extracting semi-structured information from online news stories and reports on the topic of identity theft, and identified behavioral and temporal patterns and resources used by identity thieves (Zaeem et al., 2017). An analysis of thieves' behavior in the Massive Multiuser Online Role Playing Game suggested a detection model based on specific sequences including item production, item sales, and acquisition of game money (Kim et al., 2015).

Focusing specifically on the patterns associated with impersonating the opposite gender, a research study using the Turing Game identified stereotypical content performed by the deceivers as well as stylistic cues to their real gender (Herring and Martinson, 2004). The study additionally suggested that linguistic cues referring to gender seem to be unconsciously generated.

One of the common practices of identity thieves is online sexual predation. To identify such behavior, word patterns and search engine query detection were suggested as means for detecting pedophilic activity (Macwan and inz. Grzegorz Filcek, 2017). Examples include the detection of predators using lexical and behavioral features and calculating the predator-hood score as a function of features weights (Dhouioui and Akaichi, 2016). A method was developed to identify sexual predation using phrase-matching and rule-based systems and reported the usefulness of statement lengths in chat lines for improving the identification process (Mcghee et al., 2011). A study (Bogdanova et al., 2012) analyzing a corpus of chats for detecting cyberpedophilia found that character n-grams are capable of discriminating pedophiles' chats. However, higher-level features that modeled behavior and emotion were required to detect conversations with cyberpedophiles from cybersex chat logs (Bogdanova et al., 2014).

An analysis of twenty chat rooms to detect sex offenders indicated eight recurrent themes, including 'implicit and explicit content of discourse', 'on-line solicitation', 'fixated discourse', 'use of colloquialisms', 'conscience', 'acknowledging illegal/immoral behavior', 'risk minimization', and 'preparing to meet offline' (Egan et al., 2011). Other work used automatic text categorization techniques with a support vector machine and distance weighted k-NN classifiers to distinguish between a sexual predator and a pseudo victim using data collected from volunteers posing as underage victims (Pendar, 2007). A language processing module was developed in order to successfully differentiate between porn titles and titles of encyclopedia articles using support vector machine and linear regression (Panchenko et al., 2012).

More recently, a conversational agent was developed by mimicking the behavior of a teenager and inferring its conversational rules from a real dialogue corpus in order to detect cyberpedophilia (Callejas-Rodríguez, 2016). The study reported a successful approach using a combination of the least frequent word and the most frequent bigram.

In summary, most of the previous work has focused on specific topics and in particular sexual predation and gaming, and relied primarily on limited text mining approaches. Instead, our approach uses a novel dataset where the participants are not restricted from discussing any topics, and hence we can identify general patterns of identity deception related to both gender and age. Moreover, an advantage of our dataset is the knowledge of the real identity and demographic information of the participants. Furthermore, we conduct multiple experiments using a wide variety of linguistic features in order to explore and analyze the textual clues that identify identity deceivers.

3   Data Collection

We seek to examine written samples of individuals presenting themselves with their real identity as well as a fake identity. To achieve this, we collect a corpus of writings from several participants, including responses to open-ended questions about their real identity, as well as about a pre-assigned fake identity. We target four fake identities: 1) 18-year-old female, 2) 18-year-old male, 3) 65-year-old female, 4) 65-year-old male. The choice of the fake identities was based on two practical considerations. First, the most prominent form of online identity deception is gender switching, thus we seek to collect samples of individuals portraying themselves as being from the opposite sex. Second, 18 and 65 years are extreme values on the age

Fake Identity	Real Identity
I'm Ashley, and I'm currently enrolled in a freshman in the nursing program at my university. My family is very important to me. I have two sisters, both of whom are younger than me. I do volunteer work in my free time through my church I enjoy hanging out with my friends, traveling (I get a lot of chances to do this through mission trips I go on). I want a husband and family, but my career comes first. I'm excited to see what new opportunities will appear on life's path.	I am a guy in his mid-30's. I have a cat and live with two roommates. I am self employed, selling various items on eBay as well as doing my Mechanical Turk work. I love music (alt and indie rock, electronica, and 80's especially), concerts, karaoke, video games, DC Comics, technology, reading, streaming TV and movies, camping and hiking, exploring the city, and good food and coffee. I'm currently involved in various projects to improve my life.
I am a male, aged 65 years old. I have a wife who is 59 years old and two grown children ages 30 and 32, both boys. I worked for Boeing making airplanes for thirty years before I was injured and needed shoulder surgery. I retired just recently and teach an after school class about airplanes and how they are built. I check the mail at 3 pm each day and go to the grocery store four times a week, my wife picks me up a 6 pack of Ice House nightly ...	I am a 35 year old female with bleached blonde hair and hazel eyes. I am a graduate in Public Admin and I enjoy bodybuilding. I have four children and a husband and we live in Seattle. I like to take hikes outside in the mountains but not when it is too hot outside. I am from Maine originally but lived in florida for ten years and hated it. The weather is too hot and there are too many snakes and lizards crawling all over your yard.

Table 1: Sample responses from our dataset. Top row: 35-year-old male acting as an 18-year-old female; bottom row: 35-year-old female acting as a 65-year-old male

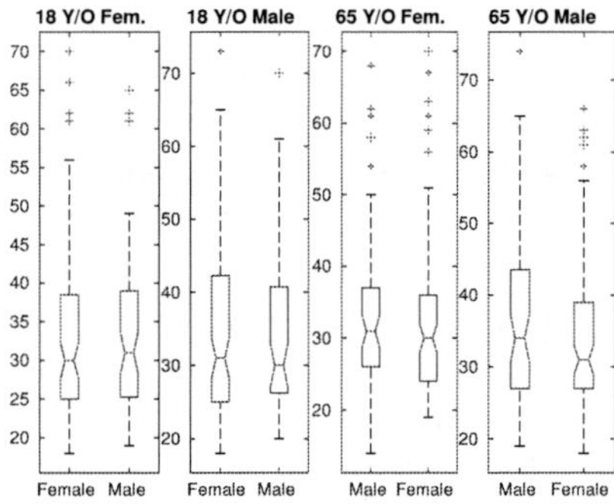

Figure 1: Participants' age clustered by gender when assuming four fake identities

distribution of Internet users, and this can allow us to explore deceptive behaviors in individuals portraying themselves as being younger or older than they actually are.

We designed four surveys using the Qualtrics survey software and distributed them via Mechanical Turk. In each survey, participants were asked to respond to the following prompt:

1. *Describe yourself.*

2. *Discuss any topic that comes to your mind.*

3. *Imagine you are trying to convince someone that you are a* 18 | 65 *year old male* | *female. Briefly describe yourself, pretending you are a* 18 | 65 *year old male* | *female.*

4. *Imagine you are trying to convince someone that you are a* 18 | 65 *year old male* | *female. Discuss any topic that comes to your mind as if pretending you are a* 18 | 65 *year old male* | *female.*

Note that the participants are asked to respond to two open-ended questions when presenting themselves with their real and fake identity: one asking for a self-description, and another one asking for an essay on a topic of choice. Our motivation for this setup is to avoid stereotypical responses for each target identity, i.e., descriptions focusing on physical appearance and activities frequently associated to the target gender and age. Two sample responses (self-description only) from individuals posing as female and male are shown in Table 1.

We also collect demographic data from participants, including their gender, age, education, primary language, ethnicity, country of origin, and country of residence. During the data collection, participants self-reported their gender, using the male/female options. In the future, with larger-scale data collections, we will be able to work with an extended set of gender options. Also, note that individual's true identity is self-reported so we assume workers to provide accurate information – previous studies analyzing Mechanical Turk as a participant's pool show that this is often the case (Paolacci and Chandler, 2014).

In order to obtain responses with a reasonable amount of text, we constrain the response's length to be at least 400 characters. Additionally, we

Fake Identity	Respondents	Male	Female	Age (M,SD)
18 Y/O Fem.	151	41.7%	58.3%	(33.24, 10.82)
18 Y/O Male	154	35.7%	64.3%	(34.24,11.62)
65 Y/O Fem.	150	38.0%	62.0%	(33.42, 12.03)
65 Y/O Male	149	42.3%	57.7%	(35.07,11.96)

Table 2: Gender distribution and age statistics for four fake identities.

manually check for coherence and relevance to the prompt. We reject contributions that failed to follow the provided guidelines and did not pass the manual verification.

After this filtering, we obtained a total of 604 completed surveys, each of them containing descriptions of participants' real and fake identities, as well as their corresponding demographic data. The data statistics are shown in Table 2.

Figure 1 shows the participants real age, clustered by gender, when assuming different fake identities. We observe that the average age of the respondents ranges between 33-35 year-old, thus suggesting a reasonable distance between their actual and fake age. In addition, the graph suggests differences in how deceivers portray themselves given their actual gender, which we further explore in section 5.

4 Features

In this section, we describe the sets of features extracted, which are used to build our classifiers.

Unigrams We extract unigrams and bigrams derived from the bag of words representation of each identity response.

POS These features consist of part-of-speech (POS) tags obtained with the Stanford Parser (Chen and Manning, 2014).

Semantic LIWC These features include the 74 semantic classes present in the LIWC lexicon 2015 (Pennebaker et al., 2015). Each feature represents the number of words in a response belonging to a specific semantic class, normalized with respect to the length of the response.

Semantic Word2Vec To obtain these features, we use the word2vec (Mikolov et al., 2013) implementation available in the Gensim toolkit (Řehůřek and Sojka, 2010) to obtain word vectors with dimension 300 for each word in the responses. The final identity vector is calculated by adding all the word vectors in the response.

Lexical diversity This set includes four lexical diversity metrics, including type/token ratio (McCarthy and Jarvis, 2010), mean word frequency, and the Yule's I and K indexes (Oakes, 2000).

Readability We also extract features that indicate text understandability. These include readability metrics such as the Flesch-Kincaid, Flesch Reading Ease, Gunning Fog, and the Automatic Readability Index (ARI) (Kincaid et al., 1975; Senter and Smith, 1967)

5 Experimental Results

We conduct several experiments to answer the research questions formulated at the beginning of this paper. During our experiments, we perform the evaluations at individual level, by merging the two open-ended questions asked during the survey (i.e., the self-description and topic-of-choice essay), for both the real and the fake identities. Also, given the contributors' age distribution shown in Figure 1, we opted to cluster the participants age into into two groups: young (≤ 30 years) and old (>30 years).

The classifiers are built using the SVM algorithm[2] and the different sets of features described in section 4. We perform leave-one-out cross-validation in all our experiments. In all cases, we use the majority class baseline as a reference value.

5.1 Classification of Real and Fake Identities

Before focusing on our main research questions, we seek to evaluate whether deception detection can be conducted using our fake identity dataset. Thus, we focus on two main classification tasks. First, using our entire dataset, we explore whether we can discriminate between the portrayed identities and the real identities. Second, we once again attempt to discriminate between real and fake identities, but this time filtering by either age or gender.

---

[2]As implemented in the LIBLINEAR library, using (L2) SVM classification.

Features	All Identities	Gender		Age	
		Female	Male	Young	Old
Baseline	50.12	49.93	50.21	49.90	50.14
Ngrams	86.67	86.59	84.25	85.35	84.31
POS	66.61	68.39	68.93	68.97	67.30
LIWC	63.28	64.70	64.89	60.69	66.56
Word2Vec	77.51	77.70	72.34	77.26	75.51
LexDiv	49.45	50.47	46.38	46.62	48.09
Readability	54.55	52.25	51.16	51.55	54.45
All features	85.76	87.50	85.10	85.74	85.48

Table 3: Classification results for deception detection regardless of gender or age (All Identities); for people with a certain gender, according to their real identity (Gender); and people with a certain age according to their real identity (Age).

		Identity		
		Fake	Real	Total
Gender	Male	234	236	470
	Female	355	366	721
Age	Old	340	342	682
	Young	259	260	519
All identities		599	602	1201

Table 4: Class distribution for all identities, filtered by gender, and filtered by age.

To perform these experiments, we start by creating five subsets from all the data. The first one consists of all the real and fake identities that we collected; the second and third one consist of responses filtered by the individuals' actual gender, i.e., male and female; and the last two consist of responses filtered by the individuals' actual age, i.e., old and young. During this process, we discard those instances where the fake identity overlaps with the actual identity. The class distribution of the resulting subsets is shown in Table 4.

We then build classification models that attempt to discriminate between the real and fake identities under the following scenarios: a) having no previous knowledge of the actual individual's age or gender, i.e., all data; b) knowing that the individual's actual gender is female; c) knowing that the individual's actual gender is male; d) knowing that the individual's actual age is 30 years and under; and e) knowing that the individual's actual age is over 30 years.

Classification results and the corresponding majority class baselines are shown in Table 3. For most of the prediction tasks, except for the first one, the best performing feature set is the combination of all features (*All features*), followed by *Ngrams*. The remaining sets of features achieve accuracy values ranging from 63% to 77%, which still represent a noticeable improvement over the majority class baseline (the only exception is the

Real Identity	Fake Identity	
	Male	Female
Male	185	181
Female	116	120
Total	301	301

Table 5: Class distribution for gender deceivers

lexical diversity feature set).

While the overall results are largely similar across the five experiments, note that the size of the datasets used in the gender and age-filtered experiments is much smaller than the one used in the All Identities experiment. This suggests that the gender (or age) of the writer plays an important role in this classification, and the gender (or age) characteristics can make up for the smaller data size.

5.2 Classification of Gender Deceivers

Motivated by our previous findings, we investigate our first research question. Can we build fake identity detectors that predict gender deception? This question focuses on the scenario in which we are interested in knowing if a text whose author claims to be of a certain gender is indeed authored by that particular gender. E.g., if the author claims to be a female, is the writer indeed a female or a male? This can be useful in the verification of user profiles in dating websites, where gender switching is a common form of deception.

For this classification task, we use only the data from the portrayed identities. That is, we use the responses from the 16 Y/O male, 65 Y/O male, 16 Y/O female, and 65 Y/O female identities. While we could have potentially also used the real identities, we chose to focus only on the portrayed ones so that we obtain a more consistent dataset. The distribution for this subsets is shown in Table 5.

For each portrayed gender, the classifier aims to

Features	Fake Identity		
	Female+Male	Female	Male
Baseline	50.00	60.00	61.00
Ngrams	86.20	82.72	87.04
LIWC	70.40	66.11	73.08
Word2Vec	75.90	63.78	65.11
POS	67.40	64.45	66.77
LexDiv	54.30	57.14	54.15
Readability	61.29	54.48	71.42
All features	86.04	83.05	87.70

Table 6: Classification results for gender deceivers, overall (Female+Male column) and broken down by portrayed gender.

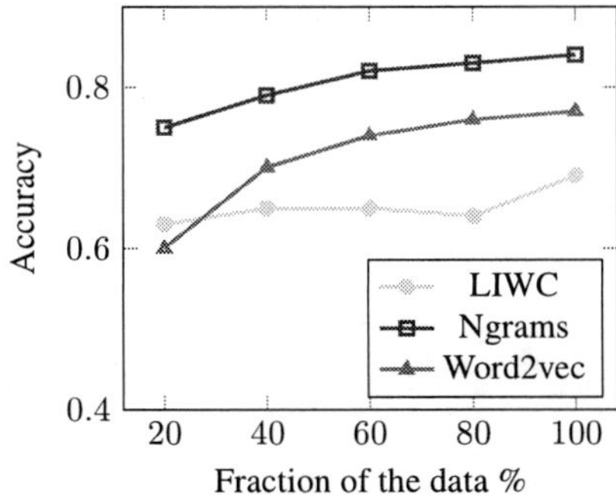

Figure 2: Learning curves on gender deceivers classification using three feature sets

Real Identity	Fake Identity	
	Young	Old
Young	168	174
Old	137	123
Total	305	297

Table 7: Class distribution for age deceivers

Features	Fake Identity		
	Young+Old	Young	Old
Baseline	51.00	55.00	58.00
Ngrams	83.38	86.22	83.83
LIWC	71.26	73.11	67.67
Word2Vec	77.24	73.77	65.99
POS	69.76	63.27	64.30
LexDiv	49.66	50.16	56.90
Readability	60.32	60.54	53.87
All features	82.72	87.21	81.81

Table 8: Classification results for age deceivers overall, and broken down by portrayed age.

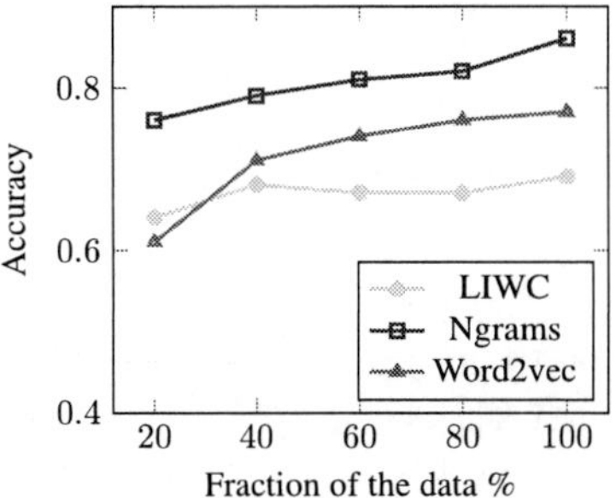

Figure 3: Learning curves on age deceivers classification using three feature sets

predict the real gender. Classification accuracies for the resulting models are shown in Table 6. This table also shows the results of the models built using the portrayed male and female responses separately. In these experiments, the *Ngrams* features outperform all the other feature sets. The second best performing features are the ones based on the LIWC lexicon, followed by the part-of-speech features *POS*. Overall, the results suggest that it is easier to identify females portraying themselves as males (*Male* identity column) than males portraying themselves as females (*Female* identity column).

As an additional experiment, we investigate whether larger amounts of training data can improve the identification of gender deceivers. We plot the learning curves of the best performing sets of features using incremental amounts of data as shown in Figure 2. In this graph, the learning trends for the *LIWC* and *Word2Vec* features suggest that larger amounts of training data could improve the classification performance.

5.3 Classification of Age Deceivers

Next, we focus our attention on identifying age deceivers to answer our second research question: can we build fake identity detectors that predict age deception? This time we focus on the scenario where the author of a text claims to be either young or old (using our earlier definition of young/old), and we want to determine if the real age of the writer is indeed corresponding to their claims. This can be particularly useful in the identification of sexual predators who target younger people, or scammers who target elderly people.

For this classification task, we once again use only the data from the portrayed identities, i.e., we use only the responses corresponding to the portrayed 16 Y/O male, 65 Y/O male, 16 Y/O female, and 65 Y/O female identities. The distribution for this dataset is shown in Table 7.

For each portrayed age range (young or old), the classifier aims to predict the real age range. Clas-

Female as a Male		Real Female		Male as a Female		Real Male	
SWEAR	2.35	SEXUAL	2.03	FILLER	4.07	ACHIEV	1.57
FILLER	2.35	ANX	1.48	FEMALE	3.16	MONEY	1.51
ASSENT	2.15	INGEST	1.44	SWEAR	2.29	WORK	1.50
FRIEND	1.96	BIO	1.36	FAMILY	1.96	SEXUAL	1.36
INFORMAL	1.81	RISK	1.31	BODY	1.94	DEATH	1.34
YOU	1.75	HEALTH	1.28	NETSPEAK	1.91	RISK	1.29
DEATH	1.70	NUMBER	1.20	FRIEND	1.81	RELIG	1.27
NETSPEAK	1.61	RELIG	1.19	YOU	1.67	CAUSE	1.24
MOTION	1.50	INSIGHT	1.18	MALE	1.63	INSIGHT	1.23
FOCUSFUTURE	1.43	ADJ	1.17	INFORMAL	1.60	IPRON	1.18

Table 9: Top ranked semantic classes from the LIWC lexicon associated to gender impersonators and actual gender.

Younger as Older		Real Young		Older as Younger		Real Old	
YOU	2.02	ASSENT	1.76	NETSPEAK	5.43	RELIG	2.71
FAMILY	2.00	ANX	1.63	FILLER	4.48	INGEST	1.92
DEATH	1.86	ACHIEV	1.56	SWEAR	4.05	HEALTH	1.84
FILLER	1.79	NETSPEAK	1.47	FRIEND	3.05	SEXUAL	1.75
FEMALE	1.72	WORK	1.34	INFORMAL	2.82	RISK	1.73
THEY	1.66	HEAR	1.34	ASSENT	2.32	NUMBER	1.59
FOCUSPAST	1.63	LEISURE	1.25	FOCUSFUTURE	1.84	DEATH	1.56
TIME	1.42	ANGER	1.25	YOU	1.62	SAD	1.48
SEXUAL	1.39	NEGEMO	1.23	MOTION	1.51	BIO	1.48
HEALTH	1.33	POSEMO	1.18	HEAR	1.42	ANX	1.26

Table 10: Top ranked semantic classes from the LIWC lexicon associated to age impersonators and actual age.

sification accuracies for the resulting models are shown in Table 8. This table also shows the results of models built using the portrayed young or portrayed old responses separately. In these experiments, the *Ngrams* features also outperform all the other feature sets. The second best performing features are the ones based on the semantic vector obtained with *Word2vec*, followed by *LIWC* and part-of-speech *POS* features. Overall, the results suggest that it is easier to identify older individuals portraying themselves as being younger (*Young* identity column) than younger individuals portraying themselves as being older (*Old* identity column).

To explore whether more training data would be beneficial to improve classifiers performance, we plot the learning curves of the bests sets of features using incremental amounts of data as shown in Figure 3. As observed, all feature sets show a positive learning trend suggesting that more training data might improve the performance in the age deception task.

5.4 Analysis of Linguistic Differences Associated to Gender and Age Deceivers

Seeking to answer our third research question: are there linguistic differences associated to individuals' gender and age in identity deception? we analyze differences in word usage that might reveal the real identity of age and gender impersonators.

From the gender-based analysis, we use responses from actual females writing as males and responses from actual males writing as females as well as their truthful self-descriptions. Similarly, in the age-based analysis, we consider the responses from younger respondents writing as older and older respondents writing as younger as well as their truthful self-descriptions.

Our analyses are based on the semantic word classes from the LIWC lexicon and the semantic word-class scoring by (Mihalcea and Pulman, 2009). Tables 9 and 10 show the top classes for each deception group and their real identities.

The analyses reveal interesting word usage patterns among gender impersonators. On the one hand, when females pose as males they use more 'swear', 'fillers', and 'informal talk' words. On the other hand, males that impersonate females use more 'fillers', 'female', and 'family' words. When looking at the word associations for actual genders, it would seem that there is no clear relation with how males and females portray each other when faking their gender. We believe that this could be attributed to gender-related stereotypes and biases. In the age deceiver case, the younger individuals who portray themselves as older use

	Real Female	Male as Female	Real Male	Female as Male
Real Female	1			
Male as Female	0.670**	1		
Real Male	0.663**	0.994**	1	
Female as Male	0.668**	0.999**	0.995**	1

Table 11: Correlation of LIWC classes across real and fake gender identities. ** Correlation is significant at 0.001 level (2-tailed)

	Real Young	Old as Young	Real Old	Young as Old
Real Young	1			
Old as Young	0.973**	1		
Real Old	0.975**	0.996**	1	
Young as Old	0.976**	0.997**	0.994**	1

Table 12: Correlation of LIWC clases across real and fake age identities. ** Correlation is significant at 0.001 level (2-tailed)

more 'you', 'family', 'death' and 'filler' words. In contrast, older individuals who portray themselves as younger use more internet slang 'netspeak', 'fillers', and 'swear' words. Similar to the gender findings, age deception seems to be affected by stereotypes.

For further insights into the linguistic differences between gender and age impersonators, we also calculate the Pearson correlation of the LIWC class counts across actual and corresponding fake identities. We use word class counts normalized by the number of words in the sentence.

The correlation between *Real Female and Real Male* shown in Table 5.3 present an estimate of how similar the actual male and female writings are. We observe a positive mid-strength correlation as compared with the other correlation pairs. The *Real Male vs Female as Male* correlation suggests that females are good at emulating males' writing. In contrast, the analysis shows that males are not as good emulating female language (see correlation of *Real Female vs Male*).

Surprisingly, the analysis of age deceivers in Table 5.3 shows a strong correlation trend between the different age-based identities. In particular, the correlation between *Real Old and Young* suggests high language similarity between the two groups. Furthermore, the correlation between the *Real Old vs Old as Young* and *Real Young vs Young as Old* indicates that in general, older people are good at imitating younger people and vice versa.

6 Conclusions

In this paper, we addressed the task of identity deception detection. We collected a novel identity deception dataset, consisting of individuals portraying themselves with four fake identities, targeting different ages and genders.

Through several experiments, we showed that we can build accurate identity detectors. Specifically, we focused on the prediction of gender and age impersonators. We were able to identify identity deceivers with accuracies up to 88%. Our main findings showed that it is easier to identity females posing as males and similarly, it is easier to identify older individuals posing as younger individuals.

Furthermore, we presented a statistical analysis of linguistic patterns that differentiate between fake and real identities based on age and gender.

The datasets introduced in this paper are publicly available under `http://lit.eecs.umich.edu/downloads.html`.

Acknowledgments

This material is based in part upon work supported by the Michigan Institute for Data Science, by the National Science Foundation (grant #1344257), by the Defense Advanced Research Projects Agency (DARPA-BAA-12-47 DEFT grant #12475008), and by the John Templeton Foundation (grant #48503). Any opinions, findings, and conclusions or recommendations expressed in this material are those of the author and do not necessarily reflect the views of the Michigan Institute for Data Science, the National Science Foundation, the Defense Advanced Research Projects Agency, or the John Templeton Foundation.

References

Dasha Bogdanova, Paolo Rosso, and Thamar Solorio. 2012. On the impact of sentiment and emotion based features in detecting online sexual predators. In *Proceedings of the 3rd Workshop in Computational Approaches to Subjectivity and Sentiment Analysis*. Association for Computational Linguistics, Stroudsburg, PA, USA, WASSA '12, pages 110–118.

Dasha Bogdanova, Paolo Rosso, and Thamar Solorio. 2014. Exploring high-level features for detecting cyberpedophilia. *Computer Speech & Language* 28(1):108 – 120.

Ángeland Villatoro-Tello Esaúand Meza Ivanand Ramírez-de-la-Rosa Gabriela Callejas-Rodríguez. 2016. *From Dialogue Corpora to Dialogue Systems: Generating a Chatbot with Teenager Personality for Preventing Cyber-Pedophilia*, Springer International Publishing, Cham, pages 531–539.

Danqi Chen and Christopher D Manning. 2014. A fast and accurate dependency parser using neural networks. In *Emnlp*. pages 740–750.

Zeineb Dhouioui and Jalel Akaichi. 2016. Privacy protection protocol in social networks based on sexual predators detection. In *Proceedings of the International Conference on Internet of Things and Cloud Computing*. ACM, New York, NY, USA, ICC '16, pages 63:1–63:6. https://doi.org/10.1145/2896387.2896448.

V. Egan, J. Hoskinson, and D. Shewan. 2011. *Perverted justice: a content analysis of the language used by offenders detected attempting to solicit children for sex*, Nova Science Publishers, Inc, pages 273–297.

Susan C. Herring and Anna Martinson. 2004. Assessing gender authenticity in computer-mediated language use. *Journal of Language and Social Psychology* 23(4):424–446. https://doi.org/10.1177/0261927X04269586.

Hana Kim, Byung Il Kwak, and Huy Kang Kim. 2015. A study on the identity theft detection model in mmorpgs. *Journal of the Korea Institute of Information Security and Cryptology* 25(3):627–637.

J Peter Kincaid, Robert P Fishburne Jr, Richard L Rogers, and Brad S Chissom. 1975. Derivation of new readability formulas (automated readability index, fog count and flesch reading ease formula) for navy enlisted personnel. Technical report, Naval Technical Training Command Millington TN Research Branch.

Shweta Macwan and Dr. inz. Grzegorz Filcek. 2017. Web mining against pedophilia. *International Education and Research Journal* 3(5).

Philip M McCarthy and Scott Jarvis. 2010. Mtld, vocd-d, and hd-d: A validation study of sophisticated approaches to lexical diversity assessment. *Behavior research methods* 42(2):381–392.

India Mcghee, Jennifer Bayzick, April Kontostathis, Lynne Edwards, Alexandra Mcbride, and Emma Jakubowski. 2011. Learning to identify internet sexual predation. *International Journal on Electronic Commerce* 15(3):103–122. https://doi.org/10.2753/JEC1086-4415150305.

Rada Mihalcea and Stephen Pulman. 2009. Linguistic ethnography: Identifying dominant word classes in text. In *Computational Linguistics and Intelligent Text Processing*, Springer, pages 594–602.

Tomas Mikolov, Kai Chen, Greg Corrado, and Jeffrey Dean. 2013. Efficient estimation of word representations in vector space. *arXiv preprint arXiv:1301.3781* .

Michael P. Oakes. 2000. Statistics for corpus linguistics. *International Journal of Applied Linguistics* 10(2):269–274.

Alexander Panchenko, Richard Beaufort, and Cédrick Fairon. 2012. Detection of Child Sexual Abuse Media on P2P Networks: Normalization and Classification of Associated Filenames. In Zygmunt Vetulani and Edouard Geoffrois, editors, *Proceedings of the Language Resources for Public Security Workshop 2012 (LRPS 2012) at LREC 2012*. Instanbul, Turkey, pages 27–31.

Gabriele Paolacci and Jesse Chandler. 2014. Inside the turk. *Current Directions in Psychological Science* 23(3):184–188. https://doi.org/10.1177/0963721414531598.

Nick Pendar. 2007. Toward spotting the pedophile telling victim from predator in text chats. In *Proceedings of the International Conference on Semantic Computing*. IEEE Computer Society, Washington, DC, USA, ICSC '07, pages 235–241. https://doi.org/10.1109/ICSC.2007.102.

James W Pennebaker, Ryan L Boyd, Kayla Jordan, and Kate Blackburn. 2015. The development and psychometric properties of liwc2015. Technical report.

Radim Řehůřek and Petr Sojka. 2010. Software Framework for Topic Modelling with Large Corpora. In *Proceedings of the LREC 2010 Workshop on New Challenges for NLP Frameworks*. ELRA, Valletta, Malta, pages 45–50.

Neil C Rowe. 2009. *The Ethics of Deception in Cyberspace*, IGI Global, pages 529–541.

RJ Senter and Edgar A Smith. 1967. Automated readability index. Technical report, CINCINNATI UNIV OH.

Michael Tsikerdekis and Sherali Zeadally. 2015. Detecting and preventing online identity deception in social networking services. *IEEE Internet Computing* 19(3):41–49. https://doi.org/10.1109/MIC.2015.21.

Esther Villar-Rodrguez, Javier Del Ser, Ana I. Torre-Bastida, Miren N. Bilbao, and Sancho Salcedo-Sanz. 2016. A novel machine learning approach to the detection of identity theft in social networks based on emulated attack instances and support vector machines. *Concurrency and Computation: Practice and Experience* 28(4):1385–1395. Cpe.3633. https://doi.org/10.1002/cpe.3633.

Chen Wang, Bo Yang, and Jing Luo. 2017. Identity theft detection in mobile social networks using behavioral semantics. In *2017 IEEE International Conference on Smart Computing (SMARTCOMP)*. pages 1–3.

Razieh Nokhbeh Zaeem, Monisha Manoharan, Yongpeng Yang, and K. Suzanne Barber. 2017. Modeling and analysis of identity threat behaviors through text mining of identity theft stories. *Computers & Security* 65:50–63.

Learning to Diagnose: Assimilating Clinical Narratives using Deep Reinforcement Learning

**Yuan Ling, Sadid A. Hasan, Vivek Datla, Ashequl Qadir,
Kathy Lee, Joey Liu,** and **Oladimeji Farri**
Artificial Intelligence Lab, Philips Research North America, Cambridge, MA, USA
{yuan.ling,sadid.hasan,vivek.datla,ashequl.qadir}@philips.com
{kathy.lee_1,joey.liu,dimeji.farri}@philips.com

Abstract

Clinical diagnosis is a critical and non-trivial aspect of patient care which often requires significant medical research and investigation based on an underlying clinical scenario. This paper proposes a novel approach by formulating clinical diagnosis as a reinforcement learning problem. During training, the reinforcement learning agent mimics the clinician's cognitive process and learns the optimal policy to obtain the most appropriate diagnoses for a clinical narrative. This is achieved through an iterative search for candidate diagnoses from external knowledge sources via a sentence-by-sentence analysis of the inherent clinical context. A deep Q-network architecture is trained to optimize a reward function that measures the accuracy of the candidate diagnoses. Experiments on the *TREC CDS* datasets demonstrate the effectiveness of our system over various non-reinforcement learning-based systems.

1 Introduction

Clinical diagnosis is a critical aspect of patient care requiring expert medical knowledge and intuition. Given a clinical case narrative such as a patient's past medical history and current condition, a clinician performs complex cognitive processes to infer the probable diagnosis based on his/her experience or up-to-date knowledge obtained from relevant external resources (Norman et al., 2007). Table 1 shows an example clinical narrative with relevant external knowledge, which suggests that *Pulmonary Embolism* is the diagnosis for this clinical scenario.[1]

Clinical Narrative:
An 87 yo woman with h/o osteoporosis, DM2, dementia, depression, and anxiety presents s/p fall with evidence of C2 fracture, chest pain, tachycardia, tachypnea, and low blood pressure.
External Knowledge (partially shown)
From Wikipedia page for Pulmonary Embolism - "Signs and symptoms" Section:
Symptoms of pulmonary embolism are typically sudden in onset and may include one or many of the following: dyspnea (shortness of breath), tachypnea (rapid breathing), chest pain of a "pleuritic" nature (worsened by breathing), cough and hemoptysis (coughing up blood).
From MayoClinic page for Pulmonary Embolism - "Symptoms" Section:
Pulmonary embolism symptoms can vary greatly, depending on how much of your lung is involved, the size of the clots, and whether you have underlying lung or heart disease.
Diagnosis:
Pulmonary Embolism

Table 1: An example clinical narrative with relevant external knowledge and diagnosis.

This paper considers the challenge of inferring the diagnoses of a patient condition based on available documentation in the Electronic Health Record (EHR), specifically free text clinical reports. Earlier work that builds Artificial Intelligence (AI) systems to support clinical decision making, mostly uses structured clinical data (e.g. physiological signals, vital signs, lab tests etc.) stored in the EHR (Lipton et al., 2015; Choi et al., 2015, 2016). They commonly formulate diagnosis inferencing as a supervised classification task.

The efficacy of these models largely depends on the size of the annotated datasets used for training, which requires expert-derived annotations that are expensive to obtain. These models also tend to lack the ability to capture the underlying uncertainties related to generating differential diagnoses (Richardson et al., 1999) and linguistic complex-

---

[1]The clinical narrative with corresponding diagnosis is obtained from the Text REtrieval Conference (TREC) Clinical Decision Support (CDS) track 2016 dataset (Roberts et al., 2016a).

Proceedings of the The 8th International Joint Conference on Natural Language Processing, pages 895–905,
Taipei, Taiwan, November 27 – December 1, 2017 ©2017 AFNLP

ities (Seidel et al., 2015) of a clinical scenario as they consider medical codes and a finite number of diagnoses for prediction labels.

By contrast, we explore the discriminatory capability of the unstructured clinical narratives to infer the possible diagnoses. To overcome the sparsity in annotated data and adequate representation of ambiguities, we formulate the problem as a sequential decision-making process using deep reinforcement learning while leveraging external knowledge to infer the differential diagnoses.

Our proposed approach is novel as, unlike previous approaches, it focuses on the clinician's cognitive process to infer the most probable diagnoses from clinical narratives. Given a clinical text scenario, a physician typically reviews the sentences sequentially, skipping those s/he deems irrelevant and focusing on those that would contribute to his/her understanding of the clinical scenario.

While assimilating the sentences (i.e. understanding partial information), s/he tries to recognize a logical pattern or clinical progression similar to one or more prior patient encounters towards arriving at a candidate diagnosis. Ultimately, the intuition of the clinician is guided by understanding of these sentences and s/he can make an overall assessment of the scenario based on the narrative and/or additional evidence obtained from relevant external knowledge sources.

Our system replicates this cognitive flow by using a deep reinforcement learning technique. During training, the agent learns the optimal policy to obtain the final diagnoses through iterative search for candidate diagnoses from external knowledge sources via a sentence-by-sentence analysis of the inherent clinical context.

A deep Q-network architecture (Mnih et al., 2015) is trained to optimize a reward function that measures the accuracy of the candidate diagnoses. Our model predicts the differential diagnoses by utilizing the optimum policy learned to maximize the overall possible reward for an action during training. Extensive experiments on the TREC CDS track (Roberts et al., 2015, 2016a) datasets demonstrate the effectiveness of our system over several non-reinforcement learning-based systems.

In recent TREC CDS tracks, clinical diagnosis inferencing from free text clinical narratives has been showcased as a significant milestone in clinical question answering and a path to improv-

ing the accuracy of relevant biomedical article retrieval (Roberts et al., 2015, 2016b; Goodwin and Harabagiu, 2016).

In addition to these established use cases, we envisage that our work can also lead to a busy clinician considering relevant differential diagnoses that could otherwise be ignored due to inadvertent diagnostic errors (Nendaz and Perrier, 2012; Graber et al., 2012; Berge and Mamede, 2013). Also, nurse practitioners can use the proposed system as a source of second opinion before contacting a physician towards accurately diagnosing and managing their patients.

2   Related Work

Addressing inference tasks generally requires significant contributions from domain experts and access to a variety of resources (Ferrucci et al., 2013; Lally et al., 2014) such as structured knowledge bases (KBs) (Yao and Van Durme, 2014; Bao et al., 2014; Dong et al., 2015). However, KBs are known to have limitations such as knowledge incompleteness, sparsity, and fixed schema (Socher et al., 2013; West et al., 2014; Bordes et al., 2014), which have motivated researchers to use unstructured textual resources like Wikipedia for various related tasks (Katz et al., 2005; Wu and Weld, 2010; Miller et al., 2016; Chen et al., 2017). In this paper, we also leverage the power of unstructured knowledge sources to address clinical diagnosis inferencing.

Previous clinical diagnosis inferencing works mostly utilized various bio-signals from patients (Lipton et al., 2015; Choi et al., 2015, 2016). EHRs typically store such structured clinical data (e.g. physiological signals, vital signs, lab tests etc.) along with unstructured text documents that contain a relatively more narrative picture of the associated clinical events.

Recently, diagnosis inferencing from unstructured clinical text has gained much attention among AI and Natural Language Processing researchers, with the advent of the *TREC CDS* tracks (Simpson et al., 2014; Roberts et al., 2015, 2016b; Goodwin and Harabagiu, 2016; Zheng and Wan, 2016; Balaneshin-kordan and Kotov, 2016; Prakash et al., 2017; Ling et al., 2017a). Although the main task in the CDS track was to retrieve relevant biomedical articles given a clinical scenario, researchers also explored diagnosis inferencing from clinical narratives as part of the pilot

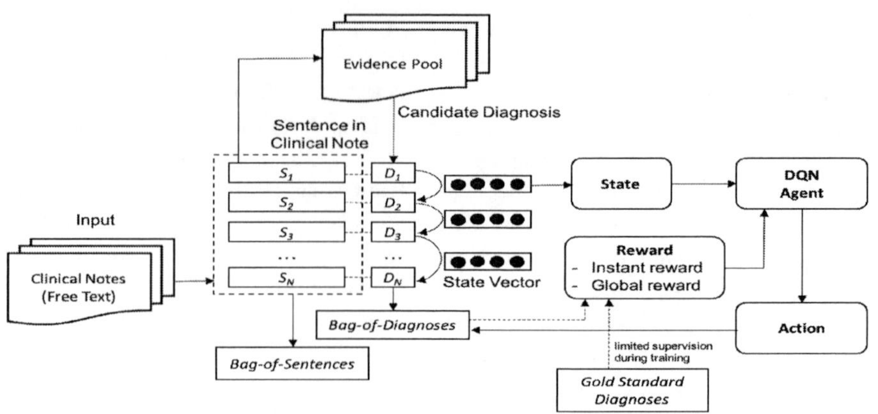

Figure 1: Overall architecture of the DBrain system.

task in 2015 that investigated the impact of diagnostic information on retrieving relevant biomedical articles (Roberts et al., 2015, 2016b).

Existing approaches for diagnosis inferencing mostly propose supervised classification models using various neural network architectures (Lipton et al., 2015; Choi et al., 2015; Prakash et al., 2017). However, such models heavily rely on large labeled data, and lack the ability to capture inherent ambiguities and complexities of a clinical scenario. Moreover, they are limited by the number of diagnosis labels and the use of medical codes to simplify the computational and linguistic difficulties of a clinical case. Other works have explored graph-based reasoning methods to incorporate relevant medical concepts and their associations (Shi et al., 2017; Geng and Zhang, 2014; Goodwin and Harabagiu, 2016; Zheng and Wan, 2016; Ling et al., 2017a).

These approaches do not focus on the intuitive and analytical processes of a clinician to infer the probable diagnoses from a clinical case narrative (Pelaccia et al., 2011; Kushniruk, 2001). By contrast, we propose a novel approach for clinical diagnosis inferencing that formulates the task as a reinforcement learning problem to mimic the clinician's cognitive process for clinical reasoning.

Prior works that use reinforcement learning for clinical decision support tasks focused on other modalities e.g. medical imaging (Netto et al., 2008) or specific domain-dependent use cases, and clinical trials (Poolla, 2003; Shortreed et al., 2011; Zhao et al., 2011), but not for inferencing diagnosis. Recent works have shown the utility of deep reinforcement learning techniques for chal-

lenging tasks like playing games and entity extraction via utilizing external evidence (Mnih et al., 2015; Narasimhan et al., 2015, 2016). To the best of our knowledge, we are the first to explore deep-reinforcement learning for clinical diagnosis inference using text data from EHR.

3 Inferencing Diagnoses with Deep Reinforcement Learning

Our proposed approach, DBrain, uses a reinforcement learning formulation that leverages evidence from external resources to mimic the clinician's complex reasoning. The overall architecture of our method is depicted in Figure 1.

DBrain takes free-text clinical narratives as input, and generates differential diagnoses as output. It scans the clinical narrative sentence-by-sentence and each sentence is used as a query to obtain a candidate diagnosis from external knowledge sources. We use a Markov Decision Process (MDP) to model this process. DBrain system creates two pools for each clinical narratives to keep the candidate sentences and the candidate diagnoses, namely: 1) bag-of-sentences, and 2) bag-of-diagnoses. Actions are taken at each step to decide which candidate sentence goes into the bag-of-sentences, and which candidate diagnosis goes into the bag-of-diagnoses.

3.1 MDP Framework

We model the integration of external knowledge sources for clinical diagnosis inferencing as a Markov Decision Process (MDP) (Bellman, 1957; Sutton and Barto, 1998). At each MDP step, the agent takes a sentence from the clinical narrative and uses it as a query to obtain an external article from the evidence pool so that the sentence can be mapped to a candidate diagnosis. The evidence pool contains external knowledge sources, such as Wikipedia articles (details in Section 4.1).

For each sentence and the corresponding candidate diagnosis, a state vector s is created to encode their information. The state vector comprises information on the importance of the current sentence and the current candidate diagnosis with respect to inferring the most probable diagnoses for a clinical narrative. In a state s, the agent takes an action a to get to the next state, $s' = s + a$. A reward function $r(s, a)$ is used to estimate the reward at each state s after taking an action a.

We estimate a state-action value function $Q(s, a)$, which determines the optimal action a to take in a state s using the Q-learning technique (Watkins and Dayan, 1992). The Q-function is approximated using a deep Q-network (DQN) architecture (Mnih et al., 2015). The trained DQN agent takes state s and reward r as input, and outputs an action a.

Once the training is complete, the sentences in the bag-of-sentences represent the most important sentences, and the diagnoses in the bag-of-diagnoses denote the final predicated diagnoses for the clinical narrative. The overall MDP framework for clinical diagnosis inferencing is presented in Algorithm 1.

Algorithm 1: MDP framework

Input : clinical narrative $C = s_1, s_2, ..., s_n$
Output: bag-of-diagnoses D, bag-of-sentences S
1   $D = \emptyset$ and $S = \emptyset$;
2   **for** *each sentence s_i in C* **do**
3   Use s_i as query, search in knowledge sources, get candidate diagnosis d;
4   Generate state vector v for sentence-diagnosis pair (s_i, d);
5   Calculate reward value r;
6   Send (v, r) to DQN agent, and get action value a_1 and a_2 from agent (where a_1 and a_2 denote actions for diagnoses and sentences, respectively);
7   **if** action == "stop" **then break**;
8   Update D according to a_1;
9   Update S according to a_2;
10   **end**
11   return D, S

For each clinical narrative, the output is a bag-of-diagnoses D and a bag-of-sentences S. For the training phase, the steps in Algorithm 1 for each clinical narrative are run for multiple epochs. During the testing stage, each clinical narrative is processed only once in a single epoch. The next subsections provide details on the state, actions, and the reward function of the MDP framework.

3.1.1   State

The state s in our MDP comprises DBrain system's confidence on the current sentence and the corresponding candidate diagnosis. We represent state s as a continuous real-valued vector containing the following information: 1) $S1$: similarity between the current sentence and the bag-of-sentences, 2) $S2$: similarity between the current sentence and the context of the clinical narrative, 3) $S3$: similarity between the current sentence and the source article context of a candidate diagnosis, 4) $S4$: similarity between the bag-of-sentences and the source article context of a candidate diagnosis, 5) $S5$: similarity between a candidate diagnosis and the bag-of-diagnoses, and 6) number of words in the current sentence.

We compute the aforementioned similarities in two ways: 1) string similarity, which includes n-gram (unigram/bigram/trigram), and Levenshtein distance, 2) similarity/distance measures using one-hot vector representations including Jaccard similarity, cosine similarity, Manhattan distance, Euclidean distance, and fractional distance.

In addition to the above similarities, words in the current sentence are encoded into the state vector using a Long Short Term Memory (LSTM) network and mean pooling. In particular, we take the sequence of words in the current sentence as input, pass their one-hot vector embeddings to the LSTM cells, and output a corresponding vector representation, which combined with the similarities (described above) produces a state vector to serve as the input for the DQN module.

3.1.2   Actions

At each step, there are two kinds of actions for the agent: a_1 for updating the bag-of-diagnoses and a_2 for updating the bag-of-sentences, where a_1 includes: 1) accept the candidate diagnosis, 2) reject the candidate diagnosis, 3) reject all candidate diagnoses, and 4) stop; and, a_2 includes: 1) accept the current sentence, and 2) reject the current sentence.

3.1.3   Reward Function

The agent receives limited supervision from the ground truth diagnoses via a reward function during training. The reward function is chosen in

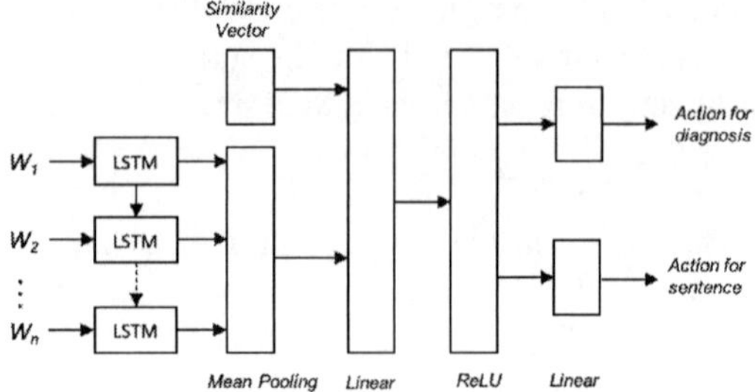

Figure 2: DQN architecture.

a way such that the accuracy of the final diagnoses prediction can be maximized. We consider two types of rewards: instant reward $r_{instant}$ and global reward r_{global}. The overall reward r is computed as:

$$r = r_{instant} + r_{global} \qquad (1)$$

where $r_{instant}$ is calculated based on the match of a candidate diagnosis with gold standard diagnoses as:

$$r_{instant} = \begin{cases} 1, & \text{if candidate diagnosis matches} \\ 0, & \text{otherwise} \end{cases} \qquad (2)$$

On the other hand, r_{global} is equal to the number of correct diagnoses minus the number of incorrect diagnoses in the bag-of-diagnoses.

3.2 DQN Architecture

In order to learn the Q-value, the iterative updates are derived from the Bellman equation(Sutton and Barto, 1998):

$$Q_{i+1}(s, a) = E[r + \gamma max_{a'}Q_i(s', a')|s, a], \qquad (3)$$

where γ is a discount factor for the future rewards and the expectation is over the whole training process.

It is impractical to maintain the Q-values for all possible state-action pairs. Mnih et al. (2015) proposed a deep Q-network (DQN) architecture, which approximates the Q-value function and predicts $Q(s, a)$ for all possible actions. We extended the DQN architecture in Narasimhan et al. (2015) to fit our problem formulation (Figure 2).

4 Experimental Setup

4.1 External Knowledge Sources

Our work relies on external knowledge sources to provide candidate diagnoses for the sentences from a clinical narrative. We use two external knowledge sources: Wikipedia pages and MayoClinic pages. We index Wikipedia and MayoClinic using Elasticsearch[2]. As an example, Wikipedia and MayoClinic pages for the diagnosis "pulmonary embolism" are partially displayed in Table 1.

4.1.1 Wikipedia

We select 37,245 Wikipedia pages under the "clinical medicine" category[3]. Each page title is used as the diagnosis name and the texts from the *Signs and symptoms* subsection are used as an evidence for mapping candidate diagnosis. As shown in Table 1, "*Sign and symptom*" section describes symptoms of "pulmonary embolism". These symptoms have a higher chance of appearing in a clinical narrative if the documented diagnosis is "pulmonary embolism".

4.1.2 MayoClinic

The MayoClinic[4] disease corpus contains 1,117 pages, which include sections of *Symptoms, Causes, Risk Factors, Treatments and Drugs, Prevention*, etc. Each MayoClinic page title is regarded as one diagnosis. We select sentences from the "*Symptoms*" section as the external source of evidence for mapping candidate diagnoses.

4.2 Candidate Diagnosis Mapping

Each sentence from a clinical narrative is used as a query to search in both Wikipedia and MayoClinic corpora. Each search returns top 10 results per corpus. If there is any common diagnoses, we return the top ranked diagnosis as the candidate diagnosis. Otherwise, we consider the top ranked diagnosis from Wikipedia as the candidate diagnosis since Wikipedia has a higher coverage for ground truth diagnoses in both training and testing dataset. Table 2 presents the diagnoses coverage for Wikipedia and MayoClinic in our training and test set, where the test set numbers essentially denote the maximum possible recall of our systems.

	Wikipedia	MayoClinic
Training Set	93.33%	80.00%
Test Set	96.67%	86.67%

Table 2: Diagnoses coverage.

---

[2]https://www.elastic.co/
[3]https://en.wikipedia.org/wiki/Category:Clinical_medicine
[4]http://www.mayoclinic.org/diseases-conditions

4.3 Datasets of Clinical Narratives

We use the 2015 and 2016 *TREC CDS* track datasets (Roberts et al., 2015, 2016a) for our experiments. Each dataset contains 30 topics, where each topic is a medical case narrative that describes a patient scenario. A topic example is partially shown as the clinical narrative in Table 1 (see accompanied dataset for all topics).

Each topic contains *"description"*, *"summary"*, and *"diagnosis"* fields. *"description"* includes a comprehensive description of the patient's situation, whereas *"summary"* contains an abridged version of the most important information. In addition, the *2016* dataset includes a *"note"* field for each topic, which resembles an actual clinical note in terms of linguistic complexity. We use *"description"*, *"summary"* and *"note"* fields separately to generate more samples with same/similar patient situations.

We use all fields from the *2016* dataset for training our systems, while *"description"* and *"summary"* fields from the *2015* dataset are used separately for testing (see dataset statistics in Table 3).

	Train	**Test-** *description*	**Test-** *summary*
# of Topics	30	30	30
# of Samples	90	30	30
Total # of Sent.	703	152	45
Avg. # of Sent.	7.8	5.1	1.5

Table 3: Dataset statistics.

4.4 Evaluation Metrics

We use precision, recall and F-score as the evaluation metrics. Precision is the fraction of correctly predicted diagnoses among all predicted diagnoses. Recall is the fraction of correctly predicted diagnoses among all gold standard diagnoses. F-score is calculated based on precision and recall as follows:

$$F = \frac{2 \times precision \times recall}{precision + recall} \qquad (4)$$

Instead of using an exact match for comparing predicted diagnosis and gold diagnosis, we use paraphrases and disease synonyms based on the human disease network (Schriml et al., 2012) to compare two diagnosis terms.

4.5 Systems for Comparison

We explore a supervised method using Support Vector Machines (SVM), an information retrieval-based method (*IR-based*), and two heuristic methods (*KG-based* and *Concept-based*) to systematically evaluate the performance of our DBrain system. In addition, we also compare the performance among different representational variations of the DQN architecture.

4.5.1 Supervised Method

We build a supervised method using SVM (Cortes and Vapnik, 1995). Each sentence s_i in a clinical narrative is used as a query to search in knowledge sources. We use the top retrieved Wiki page, p as the candidate diagnosis. For each sentence, we get a sentence-page pair (s_i, p). If the page title indicates the correct diagnosis for a clinical narrative, we label the sentence-page pair (s_i, p) as a positive example, otherwise, the pair is labeled as a negative example.

The feature space for SVM contains 13 features[5] denoting the similarity between a sentence from the clinical narrative and an external knowledge source page: cosine similarity, Damerau-Levenshtein distance, Jaccard similarity, JaroWinkler distance (Winkler, 1995), Levenshtein distance, weighted Levenshtein distance, longest common subsequence, metric longest common subsequence (Bakkelund, 2009), N-gram similarity (Kondrak, 2005), optimal string alignment, Q-gram distance (Ukkonen, 1992), Sorensen-Dice coefficient, and the relevance score returned from Elasticsearch. The similarity scores are concatenated to generate a vector. Finally, the similarity vector and positive/negative labels are used as input to train the SVM model. During testing, each clinical narrative generates multiple sentence-page pairs and the positive diagnoses predicted by the SVM model are considered as the final diagnoses.

4.5.2 *IR-based* Method

The IR-based method has the similar setting as the supervised method. Each sentence s_i is used as a query to obtain top 5 pages as candidate diagnoses. Each page is associated with a relevance score. We combine the results from each sentence in the narrative, and use the cumulative relevance scores to get top 5 ranked diagnoses pages per clinical narrative.

4.5.3 *KG-based* Method

We create a knowledge graph (KG)-based method, which uses Wikipedia pages under the "clinical

---

[5]https://github.com/tdebatty/java-string-similarity

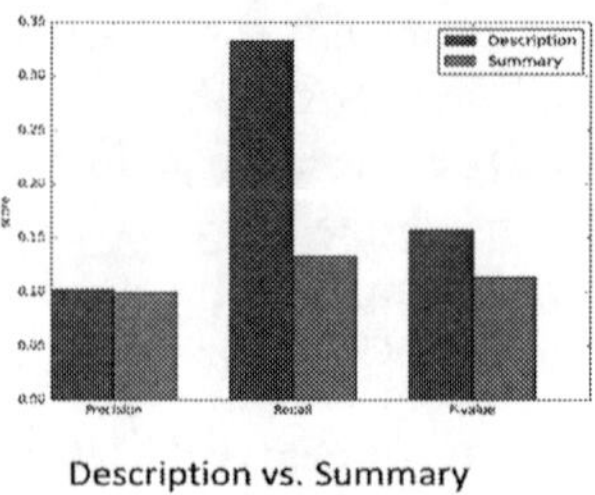
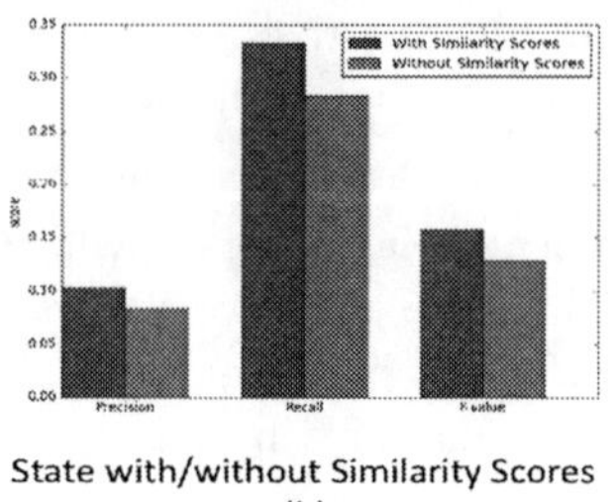

Description vs. Summary
(a)

State with/without Similarity Scores
(b)

Figure 3: **(a)** Description vs. Summary. **(b)** State vectors with or without similarity scores.

medicine" category to build a knowledge graph. The hierarchy of each Wikipedia page is preserved to encode its distinguishing characteristics with respect to other pages. Each page consists of several sections and is related to other medical conditions. We build a directed graph (digraph) by using these relations, where each node is a medical condition, diagnosis, test, procedure, medication or any other clinical concept, and each edge is a relation between two nodes.

The constructed knowledge graph contains $\sim 100K$ nodes and $\sim 1M$ edges, where leaf nodes represent medical symptoms and are connected to relevant diseases and medical conditions. Based on this graph, we infer the clinical diagnoses given a list of signs and symptoms extracted from a clinical narrative using a clinical information extraction engine. This method produces a ranked list of diagnoses. We take the top 5 ranked results as the diagnoses.

4.5.4 *Concept-based* Method

We compare our system with the concept graph-based method proposed by Ling et al. (2017a). This method builds a concept graph by integrating knowledge from structured and unstructured sources to infer top 5 ranked diagnoses from a clinical narrative.

4.5.5 Representational Variations of DQN

As discussed in Section 3.1.1, we use LSTM and mean pooling to encode words in a sentence. We compare the DQN-LSTM model with two variations (Figure 6) (Narasimhan et al., 2015): 1) DQN-BOW, which uses a bag-of-words approach to represent words in a sentence, and 2) DQN-Rand, where instead of using the DQN agent to choose actions, we randomly choose an action in each step.

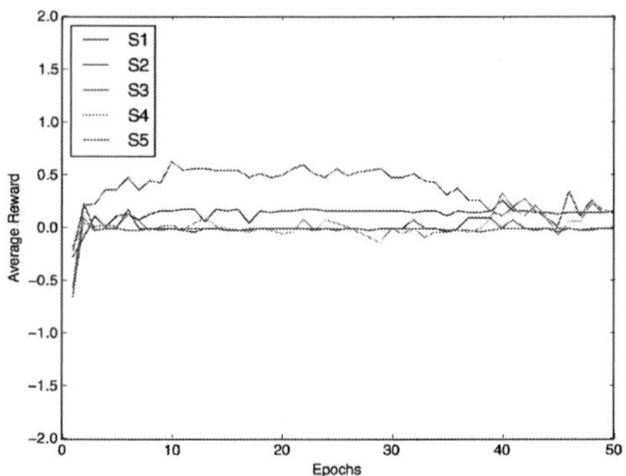

Figure 4: Evolution of reward with different similarities.

4.6 DQN Settings

For the DQN learning, we use a replay memory of size 50K, and a discount of 0.99. The embedding dimension is 300. All other settings are kept similar to Narasimhan et al. (2015).

5 Results and Discussion

5.1 Description vs. Summary

We use *Description* and *Summary* separately as clinical narratives for our experiments to evaluate their impact on the performance of our system. Figure 3 (a) shows Precision, Recall, and F-scores for *Description* and *Summary*. We can see that the results for *Description* is better than *Summary*. One reason is that *Description* has more average number of sentences than *Summary*. It is important for the reinforcement learning agent to infer candidate diagnoses from a sufficient number of sentences. Only one or two sentences may not be adequate for this purpose. Therefore, in the following experiments, we only use *Description* for system comparisons.

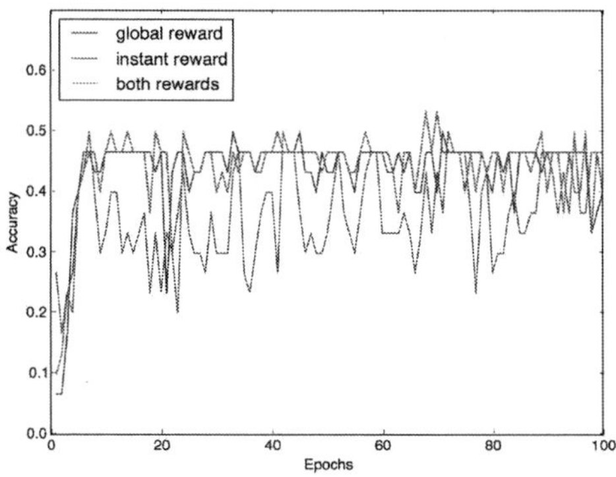

Figure 5: Evolution of accuracy.

	Precision	Recall	F-Value
Supervised Method			
SVM	4.44	33.33	7.84
IR Method			
IR-based	7.33	36.67	12.22
Heuristic Methods			
KG-based	7.33	36.67	12.22
Concept-based	8.96	**44.78**	14.93
Our System			
DQN-BOW	**11.94**	20.00	14.11
DQN-LSTM	10.28	33.33	**15.71**

Table 4: Evaluation results (%).

5.2 State Vector Variations

In Figure 3 (b), we compare results for similarity scores in state vector to omitting similarity scores on state vector. We see that the inclusion of similarity vectors with the mean pooling of the context of a current sentence inside the DQN architecture provides better results for our model.

In Figure 4, we display the evolution of rewards by comparing with different similarities (used separately) as listed in Section 3.1.1. We see that $S3$, the similarity between the current sentence and the source article context of a candidate diagnosis, has better performance compared to other similarities.

5.3 Reward Functions

Figure 5 shows the learning curve of our DBrain system by measuring accuracy over epochs for different rewards functions. By using instant reward only, the accuracy trend over epochs on training set is not stable. Global reward function becomes stable after $\sim$ 10 epochs. By combining instant reward with global reward, the accuracy is slightly better than just using global reward. Therefore, we use the combined reward function in other experiments.

5.4 System Comparison Results

Table 4 presents the evaluation results of our system in comparison to other considered systems.

From these results we can see that the DBrain system achieves the best precision and F-value scores over other methods demonstrating the effectiveness of our reinforcement learning formulation. The concept-based approach shows an impressive recall score although with a loss in preci-

sion. On the other hand, DQN-LSTM achieves the best F-Value, which is better than DQN-BOW, illustrating the importance of having a better representation of words as input. All the improvements of our system (DQN-LSTM) are statistically significant ($p < 0.05$) over SVM using the paired samples t-test (David and Gunnink, 1997) except for the methods that compute scores for the top 5 diagnoses as output (IR and heuristic-based).

Overall, the low F-measures demonstrate the difficulty of the task, as they are consistently low for all methods. We use exact sentences from a clinical narrative as queries to search for the diagnoses in the knowledge sources. Thus, sometimes our system is not able to identify the correct diagnosis due to noise in the query (see Table 6). This can be rectified with forming the query by extracting relevant clinical concepts from a sentence as shown in Ling et al. (2017b). Another reason for low F-scores is that some ground-truth diagnoses (from the training and test set) are missing in both MayoClinic and Wikipedia (Table 2). A knowledge source with a better coverage for diagnoses may offer additional room for improvements.

Figure 6 shows the evolution of average rewards for DQN-LSTM, DQN-BOW, and DQN-Rand. DQN-Rand performs poorly, which again demonstrates the importance of using a DQN agent to learn the best strategies for actions.

5.5 Example Outputs from DBrain System

We present two detailed examples to show how our DBrain system predicts the diagnoses for two test set topics. Table 5 shows that our system can correctly predict the diagnosis "Hypothyroidism" while Table 6 shows an example where the DBrain system failed to predict the correct diagnosis as the candidate diagnoses list mapped from the sentences of the clinical narrative did not contain the correct diagnosis.

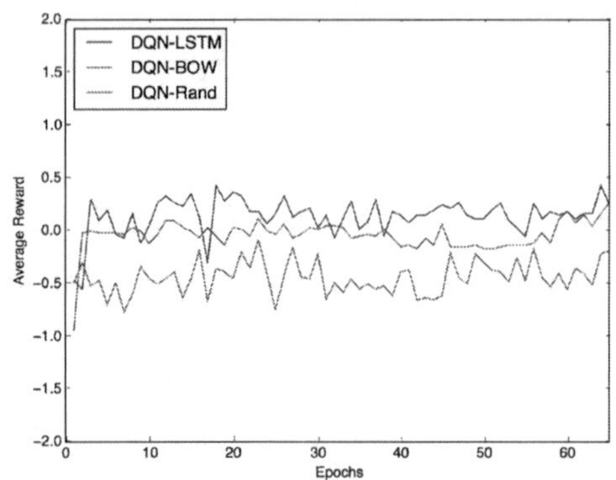

Figure 6: Evolution of reward with representational variations.

6 Conclusion

We present a novel approach for clinical diagnosis inferencing that mimics the cognitive process of clinicians using deep reinforcement learning via leveraging evidence from external resources. Our experiments on the *TREC CDS* datasets demonstrate that the DBrain system learns to diagnose by digesting clinical narratives sentence by sentence and achieves better results than supervised, IR-based, and heuristic-based methods. Furthermore, our experiments using different variations such as *Description vs. Summary* for clinical narratives, *Instant vs. Global vs. Combined* for reward functions, *State Vector with/without Similarity Scores* as input to the DQN module along with various representational variations for the DQN architecture reveal that *Description, Combined* reward function, *State Vector with Similarity Score*, and *DQN-LSTM* provide the best results to infer the probable diagnoses, respectively.

Example 1
Input:
Description: A 56-year old Caucasian female complains of being markedly more sensitive to the cold than most people. She also gets tired easily, has decreased appetite, and has recently tried home remedies for her constipation. Physical examination reveals hyporeflexia with delayed relaxation of knee and ankle reflexes, and very dry skin. She moves and talks slowly. *Ground-Truth Diagnosis:* Hypothyroidism
Stage 1:
Sentence 1: A 56-year old Caucasian female complains of being markedly more sensitive to the cold than most people. *Candidate Diagnosis:* Triple X syndrome *Action for the agent:* reject the candidate diagnosis
Stage 2:
Sentence 2: She also gets tired easily, has decreased appetite, and has recently tried home remedies for her constipation. *Candidate Diagnosis:* Colorectal cancer *Action for the agent:* reject the candidate diagnosis
Stage 3:
Sentence 3: Physical examination reveals hyporeflexia with delayed relaxation of knee and ankle reflexes, and very dry skin. *Candidate Diagnosis:* Hypothyroidism *Action for the agent:* accept the candidate diagnosis
Stage 4:
Sentence 4: She moves and talks slowly. *Candidate Diagnosis:* Conjugate gaze palsy *Action for the agent:* reject the candidate diagnosis
Output:
Bag-of-Diagnoses: {Hypothyroidism}

Table 5: DBrain predicts the correct diagnosis.

Example 2
Input:
Description: A 31-year-old woman with no previous medical problems comes to the emergency room with a history of 2 weeks of joint pain and fatigue. Initially she had right ankle swelling and difficulty standing up and walking, all of which resolved after a few days. For the past several days she has had pain, swelling and stiffness in her knees, hips and right elbow. She also reports intermittent fevers ranging from 38.2 to 39.4 degrees Celsius and chest pain. *Ground-Truth Diagnosis:* Rheumatic fever
Stage 1:
Sentence 1: A 31-year-old woman with no previous medical problems comes to the emergency room with a history of 2 weeks of joint pain and fatigue. *Candidate Diagnosis:* Premenstrual syndrome *Action for the agent:* reject the candidate diagnosis
Stage 2:
Sentence 2: Initially she had right ankle swelling and difficulty standing up and walking, all of which resolved after a few days. *Candidate Diagnosis:* Caput succedaneum *Action for the agent:* reject the candidate diagnosis
Stage 3:
Sentence 3: For the past several days she has had pain, swelling and stiffness in her knees, hips and right elbow. *Candidate Diagnosis:* Synovial osteochondromatosis *Action for the agent:* reject the candidate diagnosis
Stage 4:
Sentence 4: She also reports intermittent fevers ranging from 38.2 to 39.4 degrees Celsius and chest pain. *Candidate Diagnosis:* Dientamoebiasis *Action for the agent:* reject the candidate diagnosis
Output:
Bag-of-Diagnoses: {}

Table 6: DBrain fails to predict the correct diagnosis.

References

Daniel Bakkelund. 2009. An lcs-based string metric. *Olso, Norway: University of Oslo*.

Saeid Balaneshin-kordan and Alexander Kotov. 2016. Optimization method for weighting explicit and latent concepts in clinical decision support queries. In *ICTIR*, pages 241–250. ACM.

Junwei Bao, Nan Duan, Ming Zhou, and Tiejun Zhao. 2014. Knowledge-based question answering as machine translation. *Cell*, 2(6).

Richard Bellman. 1957. A Markovian Decision Process. *Journal of Mathematics and Mechanics*, 6:679–684.

K. Berge and S. Mamede. 2013. Cognitive diagnostic error in internal medicine. *European Journal of Internal Medicine*, 24.

Antoine Bordes, Sumit Chopra, and Jason Weston. 2014. Question answering with subgraph embeddings. *arXiv preprint arXiv:1406.3676*.

Danqi Chen, Adam Fisch, Jason Weston, and Antoine Bordes. 2017. Reading wikipedia to answer open-domain questions. *arXiv preprint arXiv:1704.00051*.

Edward Choi, Mohammad Taha Bahadori, Andy Schuetz, Walter F. Stewart, and Jimeng Sun. 2016. Retain: Interpretable predictive model in healthcare using reverse time attention mechanism. *CoRR*, abs/1608.05745.

Edward Choi, Mohammad Taha Bahadori, and Jimeng Sun. 2015. Doctor ai: Predicting clinical events via recurrent neural networks. *arXiv preprint arXiv:1511.05942*.

C. Cortes and V. N. Vapnik. 1995. Support Vector Networks. *Machine Learning*, 20:273–297.

Herbert A David and Jason L Gunnink. 1997. The paired t test under artificial pairing. *The American Statistician*, 51(1):9–12.

Li Dong, Furu Wei, Ming Zhou, and Ke Xu. 2015. Question answering over freebase with multi-column convolutional neural networks. In *ACL*, pages 260–269.

David Ferrucci, Anthony Levas, Sugato Bagchi, David Gondek, and Erik T Mueller. 2013. Watson: beyond jeopardy! *Artificial Intelligence*, 199:93–105.

Shichao Geng and Qin Zhang. 2014. Clinical diagnosis expert system based on dynamic uncertain causality graph. In *Information Technology and Artificial Intelligence Conference (ITAIC), 2014 IEEE 7th Joint International*, pages 233–237. IEEE.

Travis R Goodwin and Sanda M Harabagiu. 2016. Medical question answering for clinical decision support. In *CIKM*, pages 297–306. ACM.

M. L. Graber, S. Kissam, V. L. Payne, A. N. Meyer, A. Sorensen, and N. Lenfestey. 2012. Cognitive interventions to reduce diagnostic error: a narrative review. *BMJ Quality & Safety*, 21.

Boris Katz, Gregory Marton, Gary C Borchardt, Alexis Brownell, Sue Felshin, Daniel Loreto, Jesse Louis-Rosenberg, Ben Lu, Federico Mora, Stephan Stiller, et al. 2005. External knowledge sources for question answering. In *TREC*.

Grzegorz Kondrak. 2005. N-gram similarity and distance. In *String processing and information retrieval*, pages 115–126. Springer.

Andre W. Kushniruk. 2001. Analysis of complex decision-making processes in health care: Cognitive approaches to health informatics. *Journal of Biomedical Informatics*, 34:365–376.

Adam Lally, Sugato Bachi, Michael A Barborak, David W Buchanan, Jennifer Chu-Carroll, David A Ferrucci, Michael R Glass, Aditya Kalyanpur, Erik T Mueller, J William Murdock, et al. 2014. Watsonpaths: scenario-based question answering and inference over unstructured information. *Yorktown Heights: IBM Research*.

Yuan Ling, Yuan An, and Sadid A. Hasan. 2017a. Improving clinical diagnosis inference through integration of structured and unstructured knowledge. In *Proceedings of the 1st Workshop on Sense, Concept and Entity Representations and their Applications*, pages 31–36, Valencia, Spain. Association for Computational Linguistics.

Yuan Ling, Sadid A. Hasan, Vivek Datla, Ashequl Qadir, Kathy Lee, Joey Liu, and Oladimeji Farri. 2017b. Diagnostic inferencing via improving clinical concept extraction with deep reinforcement learning: A preliminary study. In *Proceedings of Machine Learning for Healthcare*.

Zachary C Lipton, David C Kale, Charles Elkan, and Randall Wetzell. 2015. Learning to diagnose with lstm recurrent neural networks. *arXiv preprint arXiv:1511.03677*.

Alexander Miller, Adam Fisch, Jesse Dodge, Amir-Hossein Karimi, Antoine Bordes, and Jason Weston. 2016. Key-value memory networks for directly reading documents. *CoRR*, abs/1606.03126.

Volodymyr Mnih, Koray Kavukcuoglu, David Silver, Andrei A Rusu, Joel Veness, Marc G Bellemare, Alex Graves, Martin Riedmiller, Andreas K Fidjeland, Georg Ostrovski, et al. 2015. Human-level control through deep reinforcement learning. *Nature*, 518(7540):529–533.

Karthik Narasimhan, Tejas D. Kulkarni, and Regina Barzilay. 2015. Language understanding for text-based games using deep reinforcement learning. In *EMNLP*, pages 1–11.

Karthik Narasimhan, Adam Yala, and Regina Barzilay. 2016. Improving information extraction by acquiring external evidence with reinforcement learning. *arXiv preprint arXiv:1603.07954*.

Mathieu Nendaz and Arnaud Perrier. 2012. Diagnostic errors and flaws in clinical reasoning: mechanisms and prevention in practice. *Swiss Medical Weekly*, 142.

Stelmo Magalhães Barros Netto, Anselmo Cardoso de Paiva, Areolino de Almeida Neto, Aristofanes Correa Silva, and Vanessa Rodrigues Coelho Leite. 2008. *Application on Reinforcement Learning for Diagnosis Based on Medical Image*. IN-TECH Open Access Publisher.

Geoff Norman, Meredith Young, and Lee Brooks. 2007. Non-analytical models of clinical reasoning: the role of experience. *Medical Education*, 41(12):1140–1145.

Thierry Pelaccia, Jacques Tardif, Emmanuel Triby, and Bernard Charlin. 2011. An analysis of clinical reasoning through a recent and comprehensive approach: the dual-process theory. *Medical Education Online*, 16(0).

Radhika Poolla. 2003. A reinforcement learning approach to obtain treatment strategies in sequential medical decision problems. *Graduate Theses and Dissertations, University of South Florida*.

Aaditya Prakash, Siyuan Zhao, Sadid A. Hasan, Vivek Datla, Kathy Lee, Ashequl Qadir, Joey Liu, and Oladimeji Farri. 2017. Condensed Memory Networks for Clinical Diagnostic Inferencing. In *AAAI*, pages 3274–3280.

W. S. Richardson, M. C. Wilson, G. H. Guyatt, D. J. Cook, and J. Nishikawa. 1999. Users' guides to the medical literature: XV. How to use an article about disease probability for differential diagnosis. Evidence-Based Medicine Working Group. *JAMA : The Journal of the American Medical Association*, 281(13):1214–1219.

Kirk Roberts, Dina Demner-Fushman, Ellen Voorhees, and William R Hersh. 2016a. Overview of the TREC 2016 Clinical Decision Support Track. In *TREC*.

Kirk Roberts, Matthew S. Simpson, Dina Demner-Fushman, Ellen M. Voorhees, and William R. Hersh. 2016b. State-of-the-art in biomedical literature retrieval for clinical cases: a survey of the TREC 2014 CDS track. *Information Retrieval Journal*, 19(1-2):113–148.

Kirk Roberts, Matthew S. Simpson, Ellen Voorhees, and William R Hersh. 2015. Overview of the TREC 2015 Clinical Decision Support Track. In *TREC*.

Lynn Marie Schriml, Cesar Arze, Suvarna Nadendla, Yu-Wei Wayne Chang, Mark Mazaitis, Victor Felix, Gang Feng, and Warren Alden Kibbe. 2012. Disease ontology: a backbone for disease semantic integration. *Nucleic acids research*, 40(D1):D940–D946.

Bastian M. Seidel, Steven Campbell, and Erica Bell. 2015. Evidence in clinical reasoning: a computational linguistics analysis of 789,712 medical case summaries 1983–2012. *BMC Medical Informatics and Decision Making*, 15(1).

Longxiang Shi, Shijian Li, Xiaoran Yang, Jiaheng Qi, Gang Pan, and Binbin Zhou. 2017. Semantic health knowledge graph: Semantic integration of heterogeneous medical knowledge and services. *BioMed Research International*, 2017.

Susan M. Shortreed, Eric Laber, Daniel J Lizotte, T Scott Stroup, Joelle Pineau, and Susan A Murphy. 2011. Informing sequential clinical decision-making through reinforcement learning: an empirical study. *Machine learning*, 84(1-2):109–136.

Matthew S Simpson, Ellen M Voorhees, and William Hersh. 2014. Overview of the TREC 2014 Clinical Decision Support Track. In *TREC*.

Richard Socher, Danqi Chen, Christopher D Manning, and Andrew Ng. 2013. Reasoning with neural tensor networks for knowledge base completion. In *NIPS*, pages 926–934.

Richard S. Sutton and Andrew G. Barto. 1998. *Reinforcement Learning: An Introduction* . The MIT Press, Cambridge, Massachusetts, London, England.

Esko Ukkonen. 1992. Approximate string-matching with q-grams and maximal matches. *Theoretical computer science*, 92(1):191–211.

Christopher J. C. H. Watkins and Peter Dayan. 1992. Q-learning. In *Machine Learning*, pages 279–292.

Robert West, Evgeniy Gabrilovich, Kevin Murphy, Shaohua Sun, Rahul Gupta, and Dekang Lin. 2014. Knowledge base completion via search-based question answering. In *WWW*, pages 515–526. ACM.

William E Winkler. 1995. Matching and record linkage. *Business survey methods*, 1:355–384.

Fei Wu and Daniel S. Weld. 2010. Open information extraction using wikipedia. In *ACL*, pages 118–127.

Xuchen Yao and Benjamin Van Durme. 2014. Information extraction over structured data: Question answering with freebase. In *ACL (1)*, pages 956–966. Citeseer.

Yufan Zhao, Donglin Zeng, Mark A Socinski, and Michael R Kosorok. 2011. Reinforcement learning strategies for clinical trials in nonsmall cell lung cancer. *Biometrics*, 67(4):1422–1433.

Ziwei Zheng and Xiaojun Wan. 2016. Graph-based multi-modality learning for clinical decision support. In *Proceedings of the 25th ACM International on Conference on Information and Knowledge Management*, pages 1945–1948. ACM.

Dataset for a Neural Natural Language Interface for Databases (NNLIDB)

Florin Brad[1], Radu Iacob[2], Ionel Hosu[2], and Traian Rebedea[2]

[1]Bitdefender Romania
fbrad@bitdefender.com
[2]University Politehnica of Bucharest
{radu.iacob23, ionel.hosu, traian.rebedea}@gmail.com

Abstract

Progress in natural language interfaces to databases (NLIDB) has been slow mainly due to linguistic issues (such as language ambiguity) and domain portability. Moreover, the lack of a large corpus to be used as a standard benchmark has made data-driven approaches difficult to develop and compare. In this paper, we revisit the problem of NLIDBs and recast it as a sequence translation problem. To this end, we introduce a large dataset extracted from the Stack Exchange Data Explorer website, which can be used for training neural natural language interfaces for databases. We also report encouraging baseline results on a smaller manually annotated test corpus, obtained using an attention-based sequence-to-sequence neural network.

1 Introduction

Natural language interfaces have received attention as tools for simplifying the interaction between users and computers. These interfaces often exclude or complement input devices, such as keyboard or touch screens, or even specific languages used for interacting with an application. A more focused area is composed of Natural Language Interface to Databases (NLIDB), which would allow a person to retrieve useful information from any database without knowledge of specific query languages such as structured query language (SQL) for relational databases.

Despite initial efforts into NLIDBs started decades ago, research has advanced slowly and at this moment there are no commercial solutions or widespread prototypes. The main difficulties in solving this problem stem from linguistic failures and the inability to develop general-purpose solutions that are portable to different databases and schemas.

Due to the recent success of deep neural approaches in natural language processing, our aim is twofold. First, we hope to rejuvenate interest in the NLIDB problem by proposing a large dataset, called the Stack Exchange Natural Language Interface to Database (SENLIDB) corpus, for developing data-driven machine learning models and for reporting progress. The training set consists of $24,890$ pairs (textual description, SQL snippet) crawled using the Stack Exchange API that we filtered and cleaned. A smaller test set consisting of 780 pairs that were manually created by two annotators is also available for comparing solutions.

Second, we report results on a neural baseline that uses an attention-enhanced sequence-to-sequence (SEQ2SEQ) architecture (Bahdanau et al., 2014) to model the conditional probability of an SQL query given a natural language description. This model is trained on the aforementioned dataset and its performance is computed both using cross-validation and on the manually labeled test set. Qualitative results reveal code that is syntactically correct most of the times and closely related to the user's intention. Moreover, we report results on two smaller tasks, which we call the tables and columns identification tasks. These results suggest that our dataset is indeed valuable for training end-to-end neural natural language interfaces for databases (NNLIDB).

The paper continues with a short overview of related work in natural language interfaces for databases and in similar tasks where deep networks have been successfully employed. Section 3 contains a detailed description of the large SENLIDB dataset created for training, together with the smaller dataset used for testing and comparing various NLIDB systems. Preliminary results using a SEQ2SEQ neural model with attention trained

Proceedings of the The 8th International Joint Conference on Natural Language Processing, pages 906–914,
Taipei, Taiwan, November 27 – December 1, 2017 ©2017 AFNLP

on the dataset proposed in this paper are presented in Section 4. We then propose alternative indicators for assessing the correctness of generated SQL queries in Section 5, while Section 6 concludes the paper by highlighting the key insights and future work.

2 Related Work

As all current NLIDB solutions are using mainly dependency and semantic parsing together with rule-based or constraint-based algorithms, we also present similar problems which inspired our approach, where deep networks have achieved state of the art results. In the last part of the section, we introduce the most frequently used corpora for evaluating the performance of NLIDB systems.

2.1 Current approaches for NLIDB

Natural language interfaces for databases have been studied for decades. Early solutions proposed using dictionaries, grammars and dialogue systems for guiding the user articulate the query in natural language on a step by step basis (Codd, 1974; Hendrix et al., 1978). Most systems developed until mid-90s used a mix of pattern matching, syntactic parsing, semantic grammar systems, and intermediate representation languages for generating the query from text (Androutsopoulos et al., 1995). The most important problems encountered by NLIDBs were related to ambiguity in semantics and pragmatics present in natural language: modifier attachment, understanding quantifiers, conjunction and disjunction, nominal compounds, anaphora, and elliptical sentences (Androutsopoulos et al., 1995).

In more recent studies, Popescu et al. (2004) combine syntactic parsing and semantic interpretation for natural language queries to change parse trees such that, by changing the order of some nodes in a tree, it will be correctly interpreted by the semantic analyzer. Then they use a maximum flow algorithm and dictionaries for semantic alignment between the text and several SQL candidates. One of their main contributions is that they introduce a subset of semantically tractable text queries, for which the proposed method generates correct SQL queries in most cases.

NaLIR (Li and Jagadish, 2014) uses dependency parse trees generated with CoreNLP (Manning et al., 2014) and several heuristics and rules to generate mappings from natural language to candidate SQL queries. Given the dependency tree, the database schema and associated semantic mappings, the system proceeds in building alternative query trees which can be easily translated to SQL. To determine the best query tree, the system combines a scoring mechanism and an interaction with the user to select the best choice (from a list of reformulations of the query tree into natural language). The scoring for each query tree takes into account the number of alterations performed on the dependency tree in order to generate it, the database similarity/proximity between nodes adjacent in the query tree, and the syntactic correctness of the generated SQL query.

The most promising results reported on several databases used for validating NLIDBs have been recently achieved by Sqlizer (Yaghmazadeh et al., 2017). Its main contributions are related to the fact that it uses a semantic parser to generate a query sketch, which is then completed using a rule based system, and iteratively refined and repaired using rules and heuristics until the score of the generated SQL query cannot be improved. Sqlizer is one of the few systems which employs machine learning and Word2Vec (Mikolov et al., 2013) for generating the query sketch - a general form of the query, including clauses, but which does not contain any specific database schema information (e.g. table and column names).

2.2 Deep learning solutions for NLIDB and related problems

Mou et al. (2015) introduced a case study for code generation from problem descriptions using recurrent neural networks (RNN). They trained a SEQ2SEQ architecture with a character-level decoder and produced program snippets that are syntactically correct most of the times and retain functionality. Moreover, they showed that the RNN generates novel code alternatives compared to the programs seen during training, thus ruling out the possibility that the network merely memorizes the input examples. Ling et al. (2016) combined the SEQ2SEQ approach with a pointing mechanism (Vinyals et al., 2015) in order to generate Python and Java code using textual descriptions automatically extracted from collectible trading card games.

More recently, Yin and Neubig (2017) proposed a syntax-aware neural model that generates Abstract Syntax Trees from natural language descriptions, which then get mapped deterministically to the target source code. The decoder is guided by a predefined grammar, so their solution is agnostic of the target programming language. Using this syntax aware decoding mechanism, they show to improve the SEQ2SEQ baseline for code generation.

Another related topic is semantic parsing using deep neural networks. Semantic parsing focuses on converting natural language into logical forms which are used for querying knowledge bases (Berant et al., 2013). Neural approaches for semantic parsing use a SEQ2SEQ network to map natural language text to logical forms (Dong and Lapata, 2016; Herzig and Berant, 2017). Other solutions bypass the need for ground truth logical forms and instead train a supervised neural model from query-answer pairs (Yin et al., 2015; Neelakantan et al., 2016). Iyer et al. (2017) are the first to use a SEQ2SEQ network to map natural language directly to SQL language. They leverage feedback-based learning to continuously improve the parser accuracy.

2.3 Existing corpora for NLIDB evaluation

Solutions to the NLIDB problem have been traditionally evaluated against databases with few tables and on validation datasets with a small number of entries.

One of the most complex databases for NLIDB evaluation is ATIS (Air Travel Information Corpus) (Hemphill et al., 1990), which stores information about data flights and features 27 tables. However, it only has 2,886 natural language queries and no corresponding SQL statements, making it unsuitable for a data-driven approach. Most recent systems have moved to validation datasets which contain both the natural language query and the corresponding SQL snippet, such as MAS (Microsoft Academic Search), IMDB, and Yelp. For example, Sqlizer (Yaghmazadeh et al., 2017) achieves 80% accuracy on MAS, while NaLIR (Li and Jagadish, 2014) obtains only 32% accuracy on the same data. There also exist some slightly larger corpora for querying geolocation databases, the largest being NLmaps (Haas and Riezler, 2016) which contains 2,380 text queries but with no corresponding SQL code (instead they use machine readable language - MRL for expressing queries).

The training set (SENLIDB Train) proposed in this paper is by far larger than any of the existing datasets, as can be seen from Table 1. This makes it extremely useful for training solutions using machine learning, including neural NLIDBs. More, the test set (SENLIDB Test), which has been manually annotated by two experts, is twice as large as current validation corpora and contains several text formulations for the same SQL query.

3   Dataset construction

A deep neural architecture, such as SEQ2SEQ, requires a large number of input-output pairs to produce qualitative results. The next subsections describe the steps taken to build the SENLIDB dataset, including our attempts to correct some of the problems inherent with crowdsourced data.

3.1   Data crawling and preprocessing

The Stack Exchange Data Explorer allows users to query the entire database of the well-known question-answering platform through a public API [1]. The database uses Microsoft SQL Server, therefore users query it using the SQL extension developed by Microsoft, called Transact-SQL (T-SQL). For each query to the Stack Exchange database issued by a user, the web interface enforces the user to add a title and also an optional longer description. The main rationale for these two fields is for users to provide an accurate textual description for each query they make. However, there is no method to ensure that the title or the description entered for a query are actually relevant in describing it.

The list of all user queries is available online [2] and Stack Exchange offers various sorting and filtering capabilities including most upvoted or viewed queries. An important characteristic is that all available queries are correct, meaning that they do not throw any errors when querying the Stack Exchange database. Moreover, some of them are "interactive" - users can input values in the web interface for temporary variables enclosed by '##' or '#' in the SQL query.

In order to build the proposed dataset, we started by crawling all user queries from Stack Exchange, as they appear in the section 'Everything' in descending order by creation date.

---

[1] http://data.stackexchange.com/ stackoverflow/query/new
[2] http://data.stackexchange.com/ stackoverflow/queries

Dataset	# Tables	# Columns	# Text queries	# SQL queries
ATIS	27	-	2,866	N/A
NLmaps	N/A	N/A	2,380	N/A
MAS	17	53	196	196
IMDB	16	65	131	131
Yelp	7	38	128	128
SENLIDB Train	29	204	24,890	24,890
SENLIDB Test	15	98	780	296

Table 1: Comparison of existing datasets and the SENLIDB corpora for NLIDB systems

First of all, we discarded SQL snippets longer than $2,000$ characters as we considered them to be too complex. This step resulted in about $2,000,000$ queries. The next step was to create pairs of textual description (which included the title and the actual description of a query) and corresponding SQL snippet. We then removed duplicate pairs (identical SQL code and description) and approximately 600,000 pairs were left. After this step, we removed items with SQL code in the description using simple empirical rules (descriptions starting with 'select' and containing 'from'). The remaining dataset was reduced to roughly 170,000 pairs.

Afterwards, we removed the comments from the SQL snippets and eliminated the entries that now had void snippets. Finally, we took away items with identical textual descriptions and different SQL snippets. For description d and corresponding SQL snippets $s_1, ..., s_n$, we kept the code snippet s_i of median length, as we consider that an average length description is probably better than very long and very short ones which are probably outliers. This resulted in a dataset with 24,890 items, each having an unique textual description and an associated SQL query.

Although descriptions in this dataset are unique, there are $2,225$ identical SQL queries with different descriptions.

3.2 Large dataset for training and validation

We consider that the previously described dataset can be used effectively for training machine learning models for NLIDB, including more data-hungry models such as neural NLIDBs. As this corpus was created by a large number of users from the Stack Exchange data portal, one might expect that the quality of the entries to be similar to other corpora created using various crowdsourcing mechanisms. To this extent, although this dataset can also be used for validation (using either cross-validation or a hold-out set), the results will be impacted by the inherent biases, noise and errors collected through crowdsourcing. Some of the particularities of these data are addressed next.

First, most of the SQL snippets are relatively simple, containing at most 10 distinct tokens, as can be easily seen in Table 2. In contrast, textual descriptions are more evenly distributed, based on the number of tokens, with $2,003$ of the entries in the dataset having more than 100 tokens. Thus although some queries might have an incomplete textual description, most of them are well explained.

Second, the Stack Exchange database schema available in the dataset contains 29 tables. Interestingly, their actual appearances in the dataset, judging by the number of occurrences in individual queries, follows Zipf's law (Zipf, 1949) as it can be observed in Table 3. We note that a large majority of queries refer to the 'Posts' and 'Users' tables, while other tables make almost no appearance in the dataset (e.g. 'PostNotices', 'PostNoticeTypes'). In Table 4 we present the most frequent SQL expressions in the datasets. Half of the queries contain ordering clauses and almost a third include multiple joined tables and group by clauses.

Third, the dataset contains samples of varied difficulty, from simple select operations to complex nested queries. We computed the Halstead complexity metrics (Halstead, 1977) to gain an insight into the difficulty of the SQL snippets in our datasets. To measure the difficulty of a snippet we used the formula (Halstead, 1977):

$$Difficulty = \frac{\eta_1}{2} \cdot \frac{N}{\eta_2} \tag{1}$$

where η_1 is the number of distinct operators, η_2 is the number of distinct operands and N is the total

# SQL query tokens \ # text tokens	1-10	11-25	26-50	51-100	100+	Total
2-4	2094	3321	2634	1536	605	10190
5-10	641	2547	3182	2306	742	9418
11-20	121	724	1150	876	318	3189
21-50	21	239	470	584	266	1580
51+	1	10	35	99	72	217
Total	2878	6841	7471	5401	2003	

(a) Length statistics for the training dataset

#SQL query tokens \ # text tokens	1-10	11-25	26-50	51-100	Total
2-4	88	1	0	0	89
5-10	270	69	8	4	351
11-20	77	181	23	4	285
21-50	1	34	18	2	55
Total	436	285	49	10	

(b) Length statistics for the test dataset

Table 2: Overview of the number of tokens from the SQL snippet and the textual description for the SENLIDB corpora

Table name	# occur. train	# occur. test
Posts	15159	383
Users	7672	229
Tags	4765	134
Posttags	3370	39
Votes	2476	22
Comments	1583	41
Posthistory	1214	2
Badges	625	16
Posttypes	616	4
Votetypes	336	6
Other tables	1080	16

Table 3: Most frequent table names in SENLIDB sorted descending by occurrences in training set

SQL expr.	# occur. train	# occur. test
select	22145	295
from	21982	295
where	18894	203
order	13114	77
count	8294	57
join	7943	29
group	7366	27

Table 4: Most frequent SQL expressions in SENLIDB

number of operands.

Finally, we used an off-the-shelf library [3] to detect the language of the query descriptions. More than 95% were classified as English, followed at a great distance by French and Russian with less than 100 entries each. We remarked that some of the descriptions contain table and column names, which could affect the language identification performance (with a small bias towards English).

3.3 Manually annotated test dataset

In order to have a reliable test and validation dataset for the Stack Exchange database, we also developed a smaller corpus which was manually annotated by two senior undergraduate students in Computer Science. The SQL queries included in the test dataset are a subset of the data collected from the Stack Exchange Data Explorer as previously described. Each query has been labelled by at least one annotator using between 1 and 3 different textual descriptions that describe the respective SQL snippet in natural language (English). The annotators then ran the query in the interface and verified that the returned results are correct and correspond to the description. The total number of distinct queries is 296, while the number of tex-

---

[3] https://pypi.python.org/pypi/polyglot

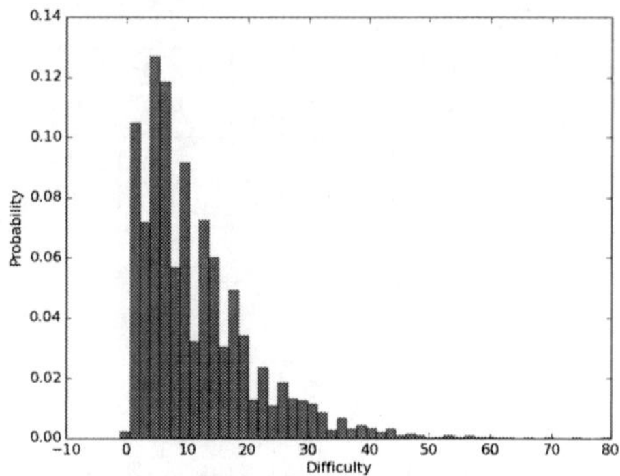

(a) Training dataset difficulty

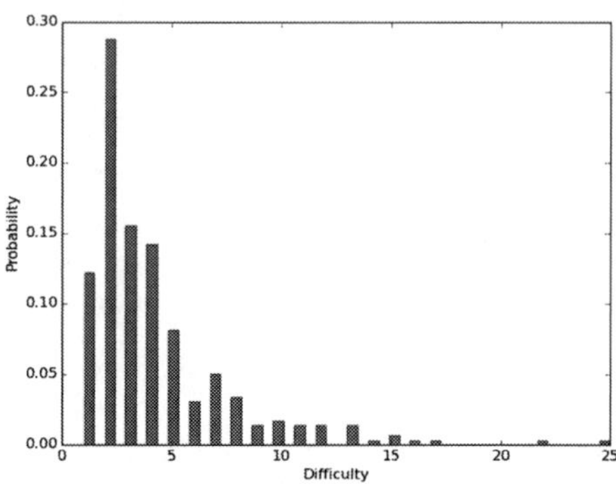

(b) Test dataset difficulty

Figure 1: Histograms of the Halstead difficulty measure for the training (a) and test (b) sets

tual annotations is 780, averaging to 2.63 textual reformulations per query.

In order to facilitate the annotation process, the annotators used an application which allowed the user to view a SQL query from the original dataset and add one or more possible descriptions. The SQL queries chosen for manual annotation were randomly selected from those with a very short textual description in the original corpus, consisting of only 1-2 tokens. These items were considered not informative enough to be included in the training set and were thus added to the human-annotated test set.

In order to achieve a better understanding of how similar or different the produced annotations are, for each sample we computed the BLEU score (Papineni et al., 2002), with the smoothing function proposed in Chen and Cherry (2014), between the descriptions of one annotator and those produced by the other annotator. The average of the scores obtained for each sample was 57.10, which

Dataset	Perplexity	BLEU
Validation	1.16	16.9
Test-original	1.24	13.5
Test-annotated	1.23	18.2

Table 5: Perplexity and BLEU score of the generated SQL statements on the validation set, original test set and annotated test set descriptions

is consistent with inter-translator BLEU scores observed in machine translation. It is important to notice that there are some differences between the train and test dataset. The most important one is highlighted in Figure 1 where the Halstead difficulty score for the test set is concentrated between 0-5 as opposed to the train dataset where the mode is at 8. This means that the queries in the test dataset are slightly less complex than the queries in the train dataset. There are also some other differences between the two datasets, such as the distribution of query and description sizes (see Table 2) and most frequent table names (see Table 3); these arise from how the test SQL queries were subsampled and annotated.

4 Model and experiments

We trained a SEQ2SEQ model with attention on the (description, SQL) pairs in the SENLIDB train set. We used the open-source neural machine translation toolkit OpenNMT (`http://opennmt.net/`) (Klein et al., 2017). This system implements a standard SEQ2SEQ model with global-general-attention (Luong et al., 2015). Both the encoder and the decoder are long short-term memory (LSTM) cells with two hidden layers and 500 neurons. The word embedding layer has 500 neurons. We used batches of maximum size 64. We trained the models with Stochastic Gradient Descent (SGD) for 25 epochs with a learning rate of 1.0 and a learning decay of 0.5 if perplexity did not decrease on the validation set. We generated SQL statement using a beam search of size 5.

Similarly to Ling et al. (2016), we report the BLEU score between the generated SQL queries and the ground truth SQL snippets in Table 5. While the BLEU score could penalize differently written, but otherwise correct, code snippets, it is still useful to measure the degree of token overlap. The results are reported for a validation set (holdout of 4,000 random samples from the train set)

Natural language description	Predicted SQL query
top 50 users from india	select top 50 id , displayname , reputation , websiteurl , location from users where location like india order by reputation desc
top 100 users with no of gold badge	select top 100 b . userid , u . displayname , count (*) as gold from badges b inner join users u on u . id = b . userid group by b . userid , u . displayname order by count (b . name) desc
user rep	select reputation , count (*) from users group by reputation order by reputation
text of highest - scored comment	select top 100 id as [comment link] , score , text from comments order by score desc
questions with most view	select top 500 id as [post link] , viewcount from posts order by viewcount desc

Table 6: Examples of SQL queries generated by the SEQ2SEQ model with attention

Dataset	Precision	Recall	F1 score
Validation	0.71	0.55	0.62
Test-original	0.51	0.41	0.45
Test-annotated	0.82	0.72	0.76

Table 7: Precision, recall and F1 score for the tables identification task

Dataset	Precision	Recall	F1 score
Validation	0.65	0.47	0.54
Test-original	0.35	0.29	0.31
Test-annotated	0.55	0.47	0.50

Table 8: Precision, recall and F1 score for the columns identification task

and for the test set, using both the original and the manually annotated texts. We notice similar perplexities for SQL code generated from the original test titles and from the manually annotated ones, which means that both generate likely code. This is to be expected as the decoder is trained on SQL select statement therefore it will probably generate some sort of select statement even for short input texts given to the encoder. However, the original titles are much shorter compared to the annotated titles, and so the more informative natural language descriptions yield a SQL query that resembles more closely the ground truth SQL under a BLEU score. Thus, although both shorter (incomplete) and longer (and more descriptive) texts generate likely SQL statements, the manually annotated texts generate queries significantly more similar to the ground truth (BLEU score 18.2 vs

13.5, as reported in Table 5) than the original descriptions.

The initial vocabulary for the encoder (text descriptions) had 6, 000 tokens, while the vocabulary of the decoder (SQL queries) consisted of 16, 000 tokens. This resulted in a very large embedding matrix, thus we decided to restrict the number of tokens for both encoder and decoder to 500 and 2, 000, respectively, by keeping only the most frequent tokens and replacing the others with the UNK token. Reducing the size of the vocabularies for both encoder and decoder resulted in a significant improvement for the performance of the model (BLEU score 18.2 vs 13.06 for the annotated test set).

From a qualitative perspective, Table 6 provides several examples of SQL queries generated for the validation set. The generated SQL statement are syntactically correct most of the time even when the textual description is incomplete or use abbreviations (e.g. "no" for "number). More, in the second example, we can also observe that the model learns to use table aliases correctly in complex queries with joined tables. On another hand, although the generated queries are syntactically correct, in most cases they fail to return the desired results when they are executed against the database. When the system fails to generate the correct SQL query for a description, it still generates a query related to the natural language description.

It is important to mention that, in order to correctly write an SQL statement, one needs to know the schema of the database. This is an aspect that we did not take into consideration when training the baseline model. Thus the model is not explicitly provided with the database schema, however it can infer it from the training set. However, we believe that more complex approaches that integrate schema information and are syntax-aware can produce better results than a SEQ2SEQ model.

5 Discussion

Generating SQL queries from natural language can be broken down to a number of independent sub-problems. For example, in order to retrieve the desired information from a database, the appropriate table columns need to be instantiated in the SELECT clauses, and the correct tables need to be instantiated in the FROM clause. Breaking down the complex task of automatically generating SQL in multiple simpler tasks and working on each task separately can, in our opinion, yield significant improvements faster.

Apart from the BLEU score, we propose two new tasks that are easier than the NLIDB problem. This approach stemmed from the difficulty of the problem and the need for a more structured grasp of the performance of a certain system on this task. Therefore, we chose to also evaluate the ability of the proposed NNLIDB to correctly instantiate tables and columns from the database schema. For these two tasks, the most important metrics are precision and recall. For example, given a sample from the dataset, we compare the SQL query generated by the neural network architecture with the correct SQL statement and count existing and missing table and column names.

In Tables 7 and 8 we evaluate the performance of our baseline on the tables and columns identification tasks. We observe that on the validation and annotated test set, precision and recall scores are significantly higher, due to the fact that these are more informative than the original test set descriptions. Given the fact that the database schema contains a total of 29 entities (table names) and 204 attributes (column names), the precision and recall scores prove that the baseline model delivers decent performance on these tasks and moreover, that both tasks are representative for measuring the performance of a system on the NLIDB problem. It is important to mention that, for the sake of simplicity, for the columns identification task we ignored the fact that in different tables there may be columns with the same name (e.g. "id").

Both the tables and columns identification tasks

can be made more difficult using stricter evaluation. For example, for the table task, one could consider only the entities that are instantiated strictly in the FROM clause and the attributes that are instantiated in the SELECT clause.

6 Conclusions

In this paper we have introduced new datasets for training and validating natural language interfaces to databases. The SENLIDB train dataset is the first large corpus designed to develop data-driven NLIDB systems and it has been successfully used to train an end-to-end neural NLIDB (NNLIDB) using a SEQ2SEQ model with attention. Although the generated SQL output may sometimes be syntactically invalid and is rarely the desired SQL statement for the given textual query, we hope the dataset will prove valuable for future research.

The pursuit of a successful NNLIDB is still at the beginning and we hope that the current research will provide the first steps needed to investigate more complex solutions. Future research will investigate whether using a stacked decoder - one for generating a query sketch (e.g. subclauses) and one for the elements related to the database schema - will provide a better solution.

In comparison with existing approaches for NLIDB systems, our solution does not use any rules, heuristics or information about the underlying database schema or SQL syntax. On the other hand, the generated SQL queries are more often than not inaccurate and thus we have not compared the accuracy of the NNLIDB with existing solutions. However, we have focused on verifying how similar the generated SQL queries are to the annotated ones using measures from machine translation (BLEU) and also precision and recall for simpler tasks, such as generating the correct table and column names in a SQL statement.

Acknowledgments

We would like to thank Laurenţiu Pantelimon and Alexandru-Robert Velcu for their help in annotating the test set. This work has been funded by the project Text2NeuralQL (PN-III-PTE-2016-0109).

References

I. Androutsopoulos, G.D. Ritchie, and P. Thanisch. 1995. Natural language interfaces to databases – an introduction. *Natural Language Engineering*, 1(1):29–81.

Dzmitry Bahdanau, Kyunghyun Cho, and Yoshua Bengio. 2014. Neural machine translation by jointly learning to align and translate. *CoRR*, abs/1409.0473.

Jonathan Berant, Andrew Chou, Roy Frostig, and Percy Liang. 2013. Semantic parsing on freebase from question-answer pairs. In *Proceedings of the 2013 Conference on Empirical Methods in Natural Language Processing, EMNLP 2013, 18-21 October 2013, Grand Hyatt Seattle, Seattle, Washington, USA, A meeting of SIGDAT, a Special Interest Group of the ACL*, pages 1533–1544.

Boxing Chen and Colin Cherry. 2014. A systematic comparison of smoothing techniques for sentence-level bleu. *ACL 2014*, page 362.

E. F. Codd. 1974. Seven steps to rendezvous with the casual user. In *IFIP Working Conference Data Base Management*, pages 179–200. IBM Research Report RJ 1333, San Jose, California.

Li Dong and Mirella Lapata. 2016. Language to logical form with neural attention. *CoRR*, abs/1601.01280.

Carolin Haas and Stefan Riezler. 2016. A corpus and semantic parser for multilingual natural language querying of openstreetmap. In *Proceedings of NAACL-HLT*, pages 740–750.

Maurice Howard Halstead. 1977. *Elements of software science*, volume 7. Elsevier New York.

Charles T Hemphill, John J Godfrey, George R Doddington, et al. 1990. The atis spoken language systems pilot corpus. In *Proceedings of the DARPA speech and natural language workshop*, pages 96–101.

Gary G. Hendrix, Earl D. Sacerdoti, Daniel Sagalowicz, and Jonathan Slocum. 1978. Developing a natural language interface to complex data. *ACM Trans. Database Syst.*, 3(2):105–147.

Jonathan Herzig and Jonathan Berant. 2017. Neural semantic parsing over multiple knowledge-bases. *CoRR*, abs/1702.01569.

Srinivasan Iyer, Ioannis Konstas, Alvin Cheung, Jayant Krishnamurthy, and Luke Zettlemoyer. 2017. Learning a neural semantic parser from user feedback.

Guillaume Klein, Yoon Kim, Yuntian Deng, Jean Senellart, and Alexander M. Rush. 2017. Opennmt: Open-source toolkit for neural machine translation. *CoRR*, abs/1701.02810.

Fei Li and H. V. Jagadish. 2014. Constructing an interactive natural language interface for relational databases. *VLDB*, 8(1):73–84.

Wang Ling, Edward Grefenstette, Karl Moritz Hermann, Tomas Kocisky, Andrew Senior, Fumin Wang, and Phil Blunsom. 2016. Latent predictor networks for code generation. *Acl*, pages 1–13.

Minh-Thang Luong, Hieu Pham, and Christopher D Manning. 2015. Effective approaches to attention-based neural machine translation. *arXiv preprint arXiv:1508.04025*.

Christopher D. Manning, Mihai Surdeanu, John Bauer, Jenny Finkel, Steven J. Bethard, and David McClosky. 2014. The stanford corenlp natural language processing toolkit. In *Association for Computational Linguistics (ACL) System Demonstrations*, pages 55–60.

Tomas Mikolov, Ilya Sutskever, Kai Chen, Greg Corrado, and Jeffrey Dean. 2013. Distributed representations of words and phrases and their compositionality. In *Proceedings of the 26th International Conference on Neural Information Processing Systems*, NIPS13, pages 3111–3119, USA. Curran Associates Inc.

Lili Mou, Rui Men, Ge Li, Lu Zhang, and Zhi Jin. 2015. On End-to-End Program Generation from User Intention by Deep Neural Networks. *Arxiv*, (March 2016).

Arvind Neelakantan, Quoc V. Le, Martin Abadi, Andrew McCallum, and Dario Amodei. 2016. Learning a natural language interface with neural programmer. *CoRR*, abs/1611.08945.

Kishore Papineni, Salim Roukos, Todd Ward, and Wei-Jing Zhu. 2002. Bleu: a method for automatic evaluation of machine translation. In *Proceedings of the 40th annual meeting on association for computational linguistics*, pages 311–318. Association for Computational Linguistics.

Ana-Maria Popescu, Alex Armanasu, Oren Etzioni, David Ko, and Alexander Yates. 2004. Modern natural language interfaces to databases: Composing statistical parsing with semantic tractability. In *Proceedings of the 20th International Conference on Computational Linguistics*, COLING '04, Stroudsburg, PA, USA. Association for Computational Linguistics.

Oriol Vinyals, Meire Fortunato, and Navdeep Jaitly. 2015. Pointer networks. pages 1–9.

Navid Yaghmazadeh, Yuepeng Wang, Isil Dillig, and Thomas Dillig. 2017. Type and content-driven synthesis of sql queries from natural language. *CoRR*, abs/1702.01168.

Pengcheng Yin, Zhengdong Lu, Hang Li, and Ben Kao. 2015. Neural enquirer: Learning to query tables. *arXiv preprint arXiv:1512.00965*.

Pengcheng Yin and Graham Neubig. 2017. A syntactic neural model for general-purpose code generation.

George Kingsley Zipf. 1949. *Human behavior and the principle of least effort: An introduction to human ecology*. Ravenio Books.

Acquisition and Assessment of Semantic Content for the Generation of Elaborateness and Indirectness in Spoken Dialogue Systems

Louisa Pragst[1], Koichiro Yoshino[2], Wolfgang Minker[1],
Satoshi Nakamura[2] and Stefan Ultes[3]
[1]Ulm University, Ulm, Germany
[2] Nara Institute of Science and Technology (NAIST), Nara, Japan
[3] University of Cambridge, Cambridge, UK
{louisa.pragst,wolfgang.minker}@uni-ulm.de
{koichiro,s-nakamura}@is.naist.jp, su259@cam.ac.uk

Abstract

In a dialogue system, the dialogue manager selects one of several system actions and thereby determines the system's behaviour. Defining all possible system actions in a dialogue system by hand is a tedious work. While efforts have been made to automatically generate such system actions, those approaches are mostly focused on providing functional system behaviour. Adapting the system behaviour to the user becomes a difficult task due to the limited amount of system actions available. We aim to increase the adaptability of a dialogue system by automatically generating variants of system actions. In this work, we introduce an approach to automatically generate action variants for elaborateness and indirectness. Our proposed algorithm extracts RDF triplets from a knowledge base and rates their relevance to the original system action to find suitable content. We show that the results of our algorithm are mostly perceived similarly to human generated elaborateness and indirectness and can be used to adapt a conversation to the current user and situation. We also discuss where the results of our algorithm are still lacking and how this could be improved: Taking into account the conversation topic as well as the culture of the user is likely to have beneficial effect on the user's perception.

1 Introduction

In a dialogue system (DS), the dialogue manager (DM) is responsible for choosing the system's contribution to a conversation. Several studies (e.g. (Ultes et al., 2015; Bertrand et al., 2011; Jaksic et al., 2006; Partala and Surakka, 2004)) show that adjusting the system's behaviour to the user can improve the user experience. To enable such adaptivity, the system needs several possible dialogue actions from which to choose. Often, those system actions are predefined manually. Hence, the amount of variants that the DM can choose from to adapt the system behaviour is limited by conversational skills, creativity and time of the person responsible for creating those actions. Foreseeing every possible situation the DS could find itself in and coming up with multiple viable system actions while considering possible types of users and their preferences in a conversation is demanding work. Approaches to the automatic generation of system actions, such as (Kadlec et al., 2015), have been presented to facilitate that process. However, those approaches often consider only system actions that are necessary from a functional point of view. There is no variety of system actions produced that would enable the DM to adapt to specific users characteristics or preferences. However, automatically generating variants of system actions can greatly increase the adaptability of a DM and thereby improve the user experience.

Studies (e.g. (Miehle et al., 2016; Pragst et al., 2017)) have shown that elaborateness and indirectness can be useful in adaptive DM. Here, elaborateness refers to the amount of additional information provided to the user and the level of indirectness describes how concretely information is addressed by a speaker. We have proposed the automatic generation of elaborateness and indirectness in (Pragst et al., 2016). In this work, we introduce an algorithm that, given a core statement on a semantic level, automatically creates more elaborated or indirect versions of that statement by retrieving semantic content from a knowledge base (KB) and assessing its relevance to the original

915

statement. Additionally, we ascertain that elaborateness and indirectness are suitable options for providing adaptability to the DM, and that our automatically generated system actions are mostly perceived similarly compared to human instances of elaborated and indirect statements. We further examine the circumstances under which the perception of automatically generated system actions deviates from human ones and discuss how to improve our algorithm based on those insights.

The remainder of the paper is structured as follows: In Section 2, we discuss related work. Section 3 gives an overview of the DS our approach is employed in. Our algorithm for the automatic generation of elaborateness and indirectness is presented in Section 4 and evaluated in Section 5. Finally, we draw a conclusion in Section 6.

2   Related Work

Adaptive DMs can be beneficial to the user experience (Ultes et al., 2015; Bertrand et al., 2011; Jaksic et al., 2006; Partala and Surakka, 2004) and has been implemented in a number of DMs (e.g. (Gnjatović and Rösner, 2008; Ultes and Minker, 2014; Rieser and Lemon, 2011)). Often, adaptive DMs consider user characteristics such as culture (Aylett and Paiva, 2012; Mascarenhas et al., 2013) or emotion (André et al., 2004; Gnjatović and Rösner, 2008; Pittermann and Pittermann, 2007). Komatani et al. (2005) use the amount of information presented as adaptation mechanism to the user's knowledge and the degree of urgency. Such architectures provide the decision making process necessary for choosing the best suited system action. However, they depend on the availability of suitable system actions to perform optimally.

To facilitate the process of defining system actions, efforts have been made to model dialogues automatically, e.g (Beveridge and Fox, 2006; Kadlec et al., 2015; Zhai and Williams, 2014; Niraula et al., 2014). Those approaches are mostly focused on functional system behaviour. Only system actions that are necessary to solve a task are defined, limiting the possibilities for adaptation. Our goal is to generate variants of system actions that address the same functionality, and thereby increase the adaptability.

Our efforts to generate variants of system actions is paralleled by a number of tasks in the area of natural language generation. Natural language generators produce human-readable sentences from a more structured representation.

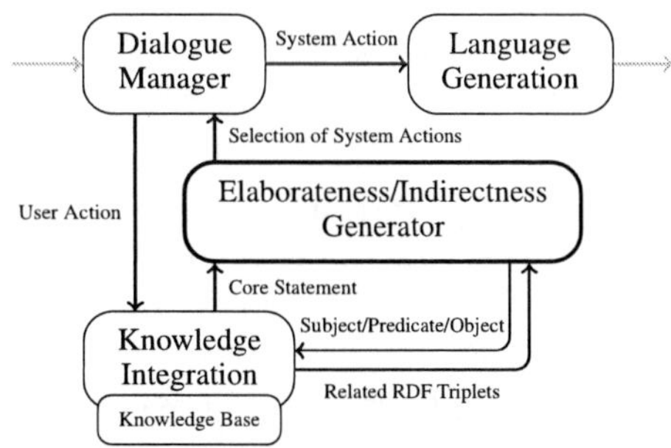

Figure 1: Partial architecture of the KRISTINA system, enhanced by the proposed algorithm.

With regard to surface realisation, one characteristic of good generators is their ability to provide variation in the generated sentences, which has been explored, among others, by Wen et al. (2015). With a similar goal, efforts towards the paraphrasing of sentences have been made (e.g. (Kozlowski et al., 2003; Langkilde and Knight, 1998)). Those approaches provide variation at the word level and preserve the semantic content of a sentence. They are complemented by our approach that focuses on variations of the semantic content of a system action. The content selection task is concerned with choosing relevant information that is to be communicated in the generated text, often with the goal of creating summaries (e.g. (Duboue and McKeown, 2003; Barzilay and Lapata, 2005)). While this research area certainly provides important insights to the generation of elaborateness, they need to be considered with respect to the peculiarities of dialogue. Instead of providing an overview over the most important information in a larger amount of data, the goal of our work is to augment an already determined piece of information with relevant further information. Hence, content selection is more concerned with filtering information, while our approach focuses on adding information.

3   System Architecture

We embed our approach to the generation of elaborateness and indirectness into an existing DS, the KRISTINA system (Wanner et al., 2016; Meditskos et al., 2016). It is employed in the healthcare domain, with the overarching goal to support immigrants with health-care related issues in a socially competent manner. To enable a deeper understanding of the workings of the proposed algorithm, this section presents the system architecture of KRISTINA. A graphic representation of the relevant parts can be found in Figure 1.

The KRISTINA system does not rely on predefined system actions. Instead, a knowledge integration component (KI) (Meditskos et al., 2017) is responsible for interpreting the user request and searching a KB for the required information. The information retrieved from the KB is represented as RDF triplets. RDF triplets consist of subject, predicate and object and are used to describe the relationship between objects, e.g *(s:mother, p:is_from, o:Berlin)*. As a result of this representation, system actions are given as a set of RDF triplets that represent the semantic content to be conveyed to the user. A language generation component (Bouayad-Agha et al., 2012) transfers those RDF triplets into sentences.

To enhance our system from a purely functionally oriented DS to a user oriented DS, our goal is to transform the RDF triplets retrieved by the KI in a way that makes them either more elaborated or more indirect, while preserving the original meaning. Thereby, the DM has more choices than just the functional answer to the user question. The KB employed by the KI is utilised to gather suitable RDF triplets for the new system action variants. Newly created system actions can be transformed to sentences by the language generation in the same manner as the output from the KI.

4   Generation of Elaborateness and Indirectness

The starting point for both the generation of elaborateness and indirectness is the set of RDF triplets that was selected to answer the user request by the KI. We call this set the *core statement*. To generate a more elaborated version of the core statement, further RDF triplets that are relevant to the core statement are added. To achieve a more indirect variant, the core statement is omitted from the system response and instead a set of RDF triplets that is closely related to it is used. This process is divided in two parts: the acquisition of relevant RDF triplets from the KB and the assessment of those triplets to find the ones most suitable with regard to the core statement. In the following, the procedure is described in more detail.

Algorithm 1: Pseudocode for the acquisition of RDF triplets from the KB.

Data: $coreStmt$, the set of RDF triplets selected by the KI
spo, a function that relates each triplet to the set of its subject, predicate and object
$maxDist$, the maximal number of iterations for the search of the KB
$minDist$, the minimal number of iterations after which triplets are included
$retrAll$, a function that retrieves all triplet containing the given resource or predicate from the KB
Result: $triplets$, the set of gathered triplets

$stmtSet \longleftarrow coreStmt$
$rmStmt \longleftarrow \emptyset$
if $minDist > 0$ **then**
$\quad \lfloor rmStmt \longleftarrow coreStmt$

for $dist = 1$ **to** $maxdist$ **do**
$\quad stmtSet \longleftarrow \bigcup_{x \in stmtSet} \bigcup_{y \in spo(x)} retrAll(y)$
$\quad$ **if** $dist < minDist$ **then**
$\quad\quad \lfloor rmStmt \longleftarrow stmtSet$

$triplets \longleftarrow stmtSet \setminus rmStmt$

4.1   Acquisition of Semantic Content

To avoid having to assess every RDF triplet stored in the KB with regard to its relevance to the core statement, triplets that are connected to the core statement are preselected. The pseudocode for this process is depicted in Algorithm 1. For every triplet in the core statement, the KB is searched for all further triplets that contain either its subject, predicate or object. Exemplary, if *(s:mother, p:is_from, o:Berlin)* is part of the core statement, the triplets *(s:Berlin, p:is_in, o:Germany)* and *(s:mother, p:has_age, o:42)* could be retrieved from the KB. This process is repeated for the newly gathered triplets to find further candidates. The number of iterations is determined by the desired level of elaborateness. The higher the targeted elaborateness, the more iterations are performed. A further parameter is used to adjust the level of indirectness. It determines the number of iterations that have to be performed before a triplet can be added to the final system action. If a triplet is encountered before sufficient iterations have been performed, it can be used to find further triplets, but is not allowed as part of the final system action. If an elaborated, but direct answer is desired, this parameter is set to 0. After gathering potential RDF triplets as candidates, the next step is to assess their relevance to the core statement.

Algorithm 2: Pseudocode for the assessment of semantic content.

> **Data:** $coreStmt$, the set of RDF triplets selected by the KI
> $triplets$, the set of gathered RDF triplets
> $nrTriplets$, the number of desired triplets, derived from the level of elaborateness
> f, a function to adjust the weight of the individual inputs to the rating
> **Result:** $addStmt$, the set of additional statements chosen
>
> $addStmt \longleftarrow \emptyset$
> **while** $|addStmt| < nrTriplets$ **do**
> > $allStmts \longleftarrow coreStmt \cup addStmt$
> > $p \longleftarrow getCondProb(t, allStmt)$
> > $d \longleftarrow getDistance(t, allStmt)$
> > $i \longleftarrow getInterrelation(t, allStmt)$
> > $best \longleftarrow \text{argmax}_{t \in triplets} f(p, d, i)$
> > $addStmt \longleftarrow addStmt \cup best$
> > $triplets \longleftarrow triplets \setminus best$

Algorithm 3: The function that estimates the conditioned probability of a triplet given the core statement.

> **Data:** p, the probability function
> spo, a function that relates each triplet to the set of its subject, predicate and object
>
> **Function** `getCondProb` $(t, coreStmt)$
> > **return**
> > $mean_{s \in coreStmt} mean_{x \in spo(s)} mean_{y \in spo(t)} \frac{p(x,y)}{p(x)}$

Algorithm 4: The function that calculates the mean distance between a triplet and the core statement.

> **Data:** spo, a function that relates each triplet to the set of its subject, predicate and object
> $maxDist$, the maximal number of iteration for the search of the KB
> $retrAll$, a function that retrieves all triplet containing the given resource or predicate from the KB
>
> **Function** `getDistance` $(t, coreStmt)$
> > $accDist \longleftarrow 0$
> > **for** $s \in coreStmt$ **do**
> > > $dist \longleftarrow 0$
> > > $stmtSet \longleftarrow \{s\}$
> > > **while** $t \notin stmtSet \wedge dist \leq maxDist$ **do**
> > > > $dist \longleftarrow dist + 1$
> > > > $stmtSet \longleftarrow \bigcup_{x \in stmtSet} \bigcup_{y \in spo(x)} retrAll(y)$
> > >
> > > **if** $t \notin stmtSet$ **then**
> > > > $meanDist \longleftarrow meanDist + 100$
> > >
> > > **else**
> > > > $meanDist \longleftarrow meanDist + dist$
> >
> > **return** $\frac{accDist}{|coreStmt|}$

4.2 Assessment of Semantic Content

The overall process to choose triplets for the final system action is depicted in Algorithm 2, with Algorithms 3, 4 and 5 contributing necessary functions. All gathered RDF triplets are ranked with regard to the core statement and those with the highest rank are included in the final system action. After the inclusion of each new RDF triplet, the ranking is repeated. It takes as reference the newly added triplets as well as the core statement. This improves the overall consistency. The number of triplets in the final system action is restricted by the targeted level of elaborateness.

The ranking function f takes into account several factors: p, the probability for the triplet to occur given the core statement, d, the mean distance between triplet and core statement in the KB, and i, the number of triplets in the core statement related to the triplet. It can be chosen freely to reflect the importance of the individual factors. In our experiments, we choose $f(p, d, i) = p + 2di$.

The probability for a triplet to occur given the core statement is derived from a corpus of dialogues between humans. An automated mapping of words to the semantic concepts that are used in the KB was performed and this data was used to calculate the probability that two concepts would appear in one dialogue turn as well as the overall probability that a concept would occur in a dialogue turn. From those probabilities, the conditioned probability that the concept of a new triplet will be in a turn if a concept of the core statement occurs in that turn can be calculated, as is shown in Algorithm 3. The mean of all conditioned probabilities between the concepts of the core statement and the triplet that is to be rated is used as input to the ranking.

Pseudocode for the calculation of the mean distance between a triplet and the core statement is given in Algorithm 4. The distance between two triplets in the KB refers to the number of iterations that have to be performed to find one triplet when starting from the other. If the triplet cannot be found due to the elaborateness restriction, a high number is assumed instead. The mean distance between a triplet and the core statement is used as a metric on how closely related they are.

The process to determine the number of triplets a triplet is related to can be found in Algorithm 5. A triplet is related to another triplet of the core statement if the triplet could be reached from it during the acquisition. It can be assumed that a

---

Algorithm 5: The function that calculates the number of relations between a triplet and the core statement.

Data: spo, a function that relates each triplet to the set of its subject, predicate and object
$maxDist$, the maximal number of iteration for the search of the KB
$retrAll$, a function that retrieves all triplet containing the given resource or predicate from the KB

Function getInterrelation(t, $coreStmt$)

$nrRel \longleftarrow 0$
for $s \in coreStmt$ **do**
    $stmtSet \longleftarrow \{s\}$
    for $dist = 1$ **to** $maxdist$ **do**
        $stmtSet \longleftarrow$
        $\bigcup_{x \in stmtSet} \bigcup_{y \in spo(x)} retrAll(y)$
    if $t \in stmtSet$ **then**
        $nrRel \longleftarrow nrRel + 1$

return $nrRel$

Statement 4
KRISTINA: Your mother is not originally from here? Does she miss Germany sometimes?
TOM (ORIG.): Yes, my mother misses Germany.
TOM (HG): I think my mother misses Germany because most of her relatives and friends are there and when she is there she is able to communicate much better.
TOM (CG): My mother misses Germany. She and my father married there. They immigrated, but they visit Germany. My father is happy.

Statement 6
TOM: Do you know how the weather is going to be?
KRISTINA (ORIG.): It is going to rain this afternoon.
KRISTINA (HG): It is going to rain this afternoon, but it's not going to be cold, still 20°C. But I would take an umbrella.
KRISTINA (CG): It is going to rain this afternoon. It is not going to be cold in the afternoon, 20°C by then. The temperature tomorrow is also going to be 20°C.

Figure 2: Examples for human and computer generated elaborated statements.

triplet that is related to the whole core statement is more relevant to the situation than one that is related to part of it.

5 Evaluation

Our approach has been evaluated in an online user study. Participants were asked to rate both human generated (HG) and computer generated (CG) variants of dialogue contributions with regard to the original statement. The research question of the study was twofold: First, to compare the variants produced by our algorithm to HG ones. Second, to show that elaborateness and indirectness have the potential to be used in adaptive DM. In the following, an overview of the participants of the user study, the study design as well as the results are presented. Finally, the findings and their implications for the proposed algorithm and adaptive DM in general are discussed.

5.1 Participants

The study included 21 Japanese and 21 German participants, most of which were between the age of 20 and 30. The 26 male participants slightly outweigh the female participants. The language of the study was English, so to identify potential influences of the individual English reading skill, participants were asked to rate their English skill using either the Common European Framework of Reference for Languages (CEFR), which is often used in Germany to assess language skills, or the Test of English for International Communication (TOEIC), which is more common in Japan. All of the participants reported English reading skills above the beginner level (CEFR: A1/TOEIC reading: 115), with the majority even reporting skills at or above the upper intermediate level (CEFR: B2/TOEIC reading: 385 or better).

5.2 Study Design

The proposed algorithm was evaluated by comparing its results to actual human generated examples of elaborateness and indirectness. To this end, ten elaborated and ten indirect statements were extracted from natural conversations. The conversations take place between caregivers, caretakers and their relatives, with topics ranging from biographical information, eating preferences, health issues to recreational activities. For the extracted statements, the concise/direct version of the statement was determined manually, taking into consideration both previous and following parts of the conversation. Those concise/direct statements are referred to as the *original statements* for the remainder of the paper. The original statements were transformed into semantic representations of their content and the proposed algorithm was used to produce an altered semantic representation, either aiming to be more elaborated or more indirect. As the performance of our content acquisition and rating component was to be tested, not that of a language generation component, a human transformed the semantic representation of the content into sentences. They were instructed to create simple sentences and only include the information provided by the RDF triplets. Examples

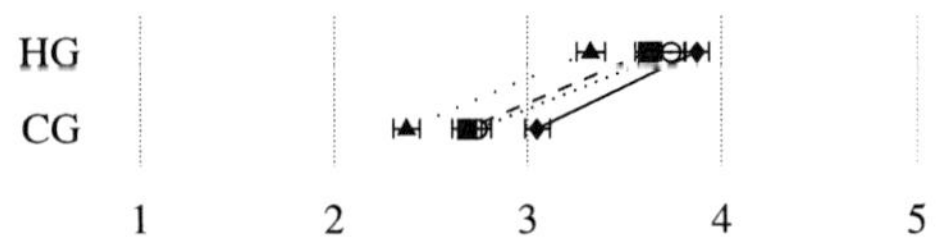

Figure 4: Comparison of the mean rating and standard error by the generation method used.

Statement 1
TOM: My mother doesn't speak English very well.
KRISTINA (ORIG.): Can you translate for the nurses?
KRISTINA (HG): If the nurses need someone for translation can they contact you?
KRISTINA (CG): Can the nurses contact you to give them information about your mother?

Statement 6
KRISTINA: How much support does your father need? Can he walk on his own?
TOM (ORIG.): My father needs support walking.
TOM (HG): My father is unsteady and shaky if he has nothing to hold onto. He can do two, three steps if someone holds him.
TOM (CG): My father can do two, three steps if someone holds him.

Figure 3: Examples for human and computer generated indirect statements.

of the resulting sentence pairs can be found in Figure 2 and 3. A full list of the sentences pairs is provided in the additional material.

The study consisted of an online questionnaire, presenting pairs of an original statement and a HG or CG variant of it to the participants. The participants were not made aware that some of the statements were computer generated. Furthermore, the exchanges were presented as human-human instead of human-computer interaction. All participants assessed all HG and CG variants, resulting in 20 evaluated statements pairs for elaborateness and indirectness each. For elaborated variants, the participants were asked how relevant the additional information is. This question was rated on a five point scale from 1 - 'not at all' to 5 - 'very relevant'. For indirect statements, participants rated how easily they could derive the meaning of the original statement from the indirect statement on a five point scale from 1 - 'it is impossible' to 5 - 'it is obvious'. For all sentence pairs, participants were asked to rate which statement they preferred on a 5 point scale from 1 - 'the original one' to 5 - 'the elaborated/indirect variant'.

Apart from the comparison of the generation methods, differences between the nationalities and the individual original statements were also considered. Differing ratings in those areas suggest possible adaptations that may be employed by a DM to cater to different cultures or different situations.

The results for each research question were obtained using a three-way mixed ANOVA.

Statement	Japanese		German	
	HG	CG	HG	CG
1	4.05	3.43	4.29	2.38
2	3.95	3.00	4.48	1.95
3	4.62	3.71	2.76	2.81
4	4.38	3.38	3.76	2.57
5	3.71	2.29	3.00	2.81
6	3.86	3.67	3.48	2.76
7	4.00	3.67	3.57	2.71
8	4.33	4.33	3.52	3.14
9	4.29	3.10	4.19	2.48
10	3.57	3.62	3.71	3.19

Table 1: Mean ratings for the question 'How relevant is the additional information?'.

5.3 Results

Figure 4 depicts the mean and standard error of the rating for each of our research questions. Statistical tests show that HG and CG statements yield mostly similar results. No significant differences between the generation methods can be found for a significance level of 0.05, except for the ease with which indirect statements can be interpreted. Here, CG statements are harder to understand than HG ones. However, this does not significantly influence the preference of participants for either direct or indirect statements. Additionally, we find that nationality and situation influence the rating, suggesting that adapting to them by changing the level of elaborateness and indirectness is viable. Apart from the main factors generation method, nationality and original statement, we also tested for influences of age, gender or proficiency in English on the results of our study but found no significant effects.

In the following, a more detailed description of the results is presented. A complete list of mean ratings for each research question can be found in Tables 1, 2, 3 and 4.

Statement	Japanese HG	Japanese CG	German HG	German CG
1	3.75	2.95	4.14	2.24
2	3.76	2.86	4.48	1.90
3	3.95	3.57	2.86	2.57
4	4.29	2.81	3.95	2.62
5	3.29	2.00	2.57	2.81
6	2.86	2.62	3.62	2.57
7	3.24	1.95	3.76	2.43
8	3.90	3.90	3.76	3.19
9	4.33	3.10	4.24	2.52
10	4.10	3.10	4.05	3.14

Table 2: Mean ratings for the question 'Which statement do you prefer?' (Elaborateness).

Statement	Japanese HG	Japanese CG	German HG	German CG
1	4.19	3.24	4.81	3.00
2	3.33	3.14	4.24	2.86
3	1.67	1.19	2.29	1.00
4	2.67	2.19	2.48	1.71
5	4.00	3.48	4.76	4.38
6	3.86	3.81	4.62	4.24
7	2.81	1.81	4.14	1.71
8	3.29	2.71	3.95	2.38
9	3.00	1.38	2.90	1.05
10	4.52	4.10	5.00	4.38

Table 3: Mean ratings for the question 'How easy is it to derive the original meaning?'.

5.3.1 Impact of Generation Method

The relevance of additional information as well as the user preference for either the original or the elaborated/indirect statement do not show significant differences regarding the generation method with a significance level of 0.05. Only the ease with which the meaning of an indirect statement can be derived is significantly influenced by the generation method ($F(1, 37) = 5.401, p = .026$). This indicates that overall participants perceived HG and CG statements to be similar, but had problems to interpret CG indirect statements. In addition to those results, several significant interaction effects can be found. Those interaction effects offer valuable information about potential improvements that can be made to the proposed algorithm. Hence, they are examined in closer detail in the following.

Significant interaction effects between generation method, nationality and original statement exist for both the relevance of additional information ($F(9, 333) = 2.731$, $p = .004$) as well as the user preference for either the original or the elaborated statement ($F(9, 333) = 2.486$, $p = .009$). For both question, several interaction patterns can be observed, depending on the original statement:

Statement	Japanese HG	Japanese CG	German HG	German CG
1	3.57	3.05	4.19	2.57
2	3.05	2.38	2.95	1.43
3	2.62	2.14	2.24	1.38
4	1.95	1.52	2.00	1.38
5	3.90	2.57	3.90	2.57
6	3.86	3.29	3.76	3.19
7	4.33	3.00	3.10	2.38
8	3.81	3.67	3.71	2.76
9	3.95	2.29	2.71	1.52
10	3.29	3.10	3.62	1.33

Table 4: Mean ratings for the question 'Which statement do you prefer?' (Indirectness).

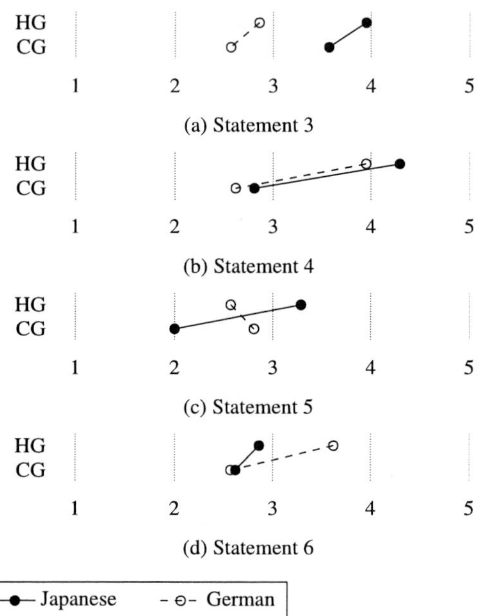

Figure 5: Interactions between nationality and generation method for the question 'Which statement do you prefer?' (Elaborateness). Different patterns can be found: Nearly no difference between HG and CG, a sharp decline for CG, a sharp decline only for Japanese and a sharp decline only for Germans.

The generation method can have almost no impact or lead to a declining rating from either Japanese, Germans or both, as can be seen exemplary in Figure 5. For some statements, one of the cultures rates the CG statement in a similar manner as the HG one, while the rating of the other culture shows a sharp decline for CG statements. As a consequence of the different perceptions across cultures, it might be beneficial to consider the target culture during the generation process and thereby improve its performance. Furthermore, a few original statements receive a worse rating for CG variants than for HG variants by both cultures. This suggests that while the generation of elaborateness often works well, potential for improvements still exists in those cases.

The ease with which the meaning of an indirect statement can be derived depends significantly on the interaction between generation method and nationality ($F(1, 37) = 10.469$, $p = .003$). The corresponding interaction pattern is depicted in Figure 6. If the indirect statement is HG, Germans seem to have an easier time to derive the original meaning than Japanese ($F(1, 37) = 5.547$, $p = .024$), who mostly rate this question neutrally. This difference between cultures disappears for CG statements. It is possible that Germans have an advantage with the HG statements, as those statements were extracted from German dialogues and the original statements were derived by a German. Hence, the implicit connections between original and indirect statement could be more obvious to Germans due to a similar cultural imprint. This advantage disappears when the implicit connection between original statement and indirect one is made automatically by an algorithm and therefore foreign to both cultures. This would suggest that an effort should be made to better capture the human approach to generating indirectness and thereby reduce the difficulty of interpreting it. In this endeavour, the target culture needs to be taken into account.

The preference for either the original or the indirect statement is influenced significantly by the interaction between generation method, nationality and original statement ($F(9, 333) = 3.124$, $p = .001$). Here, patterns similar to the ones found for the preference regarding elaborated statements can be observed: The generation method can have almost no impact or lead to a declining rating from either Japanese, Germans or both, depending on the original statement. This affirms the potential for improvements regarding the adjustment to the target culture as well as the overall performance.

5.3.2 Potential for Adaptation

To ascertain the ability of elaborateness and indirectness to contribute to the adaptability of a DM, we assess the impact of nationality and original statement on user preferences.

A significant interaction effect of nationality and original statement on the preference for ei-

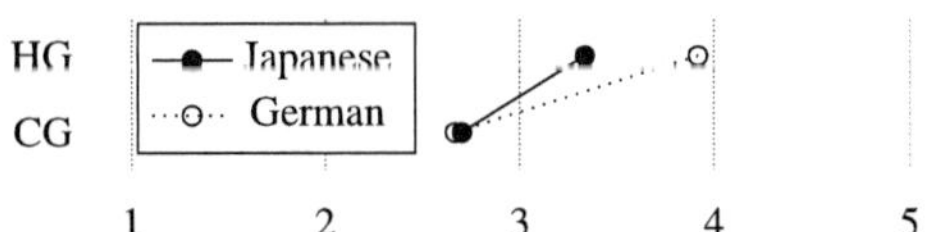

Figure 6: Interactions between nationality and generation method for the question 'How easy is it is to derive the original meaning?'.

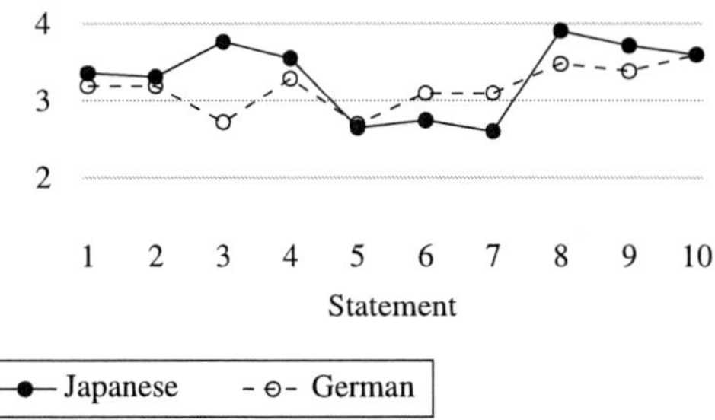

Figure 7: Interactions between nationality and original statement for the question 'Which statement do you prefer?' (Elaborateness).

ther the original or the elaborated statement can be found ($F(9, 333) = 2.578$, $p = .007$). As can be seen in Figure 7, Germans seem to be rather indifferent to the level of elaborateness. They mostly rate neutrally. In contrast, a clear distinction between topics can be found for Japanese. They tend to prefer concise statements if the topic of conversation is uncritical, such as the weather or day trips. This can be seen for Statements 5, 6 and 7. When talking about family members, more elaborated statements are preferred. Considering those findings, a culture and situation adaptive DM could utilise elaborateness as means to implement suitable adaptation.

As discussed in Section 5.3.1, there exist significant interactions of generation method, nationality and original statement on the preference of elaborateness/indirectness. If the generation methods are examined separately, the interaction of nationality and original statement still impacts the rating for both elaborateness (HG: $F(9, 333) = 2.197$, $p = .022$, CG: $F(9, 333) = 2.838$, $p = .003$) and indirectness (HG: $F(9, 333) = 2.143$, $p = .026$, CG: $F(9, 333) = 1.922$, $p = .048$). This implies that, while nationality and original statement always influence the user preference, the way they impact it is not the same for HG and CG statements. The different interac-

922

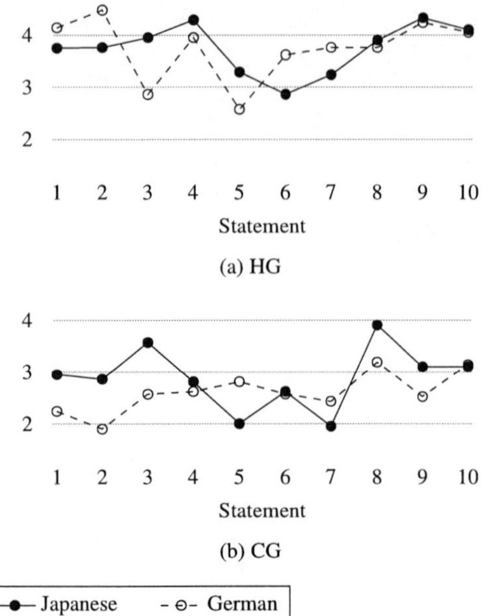

(a) HG

(b) CG

Figure 8: Comparison of the interaction pattern between nationality and original statement for the question 'Which statement do you prefer?' (Elaborateness) for HG and CG statements.

tion patterns are depicted exemplary in Figure 8. Those results suggests that an adaptive DM should not learn its dialogue strategy based on human-human dialogue containing examples of elaborateness/indirectness, as this can lead to wrong assumption about the user preferences. Instead, the dialogue strategy should be based on CG variants that reflect more accurately the elaborateness/indirectness variants that will be used.

5.4 Discussion

Overall, CG statements perform well compared to HG ones. However, there are cases when the rating of CG generated statements decreases for one or both of the considered cultures when compared to the HG statement. Therefore, it might be beneficial to consider both nationality as well as the topic of the original statement during the generation of system action variants. Another possibility would be to generate multiple elaborated/indirect variants and let the DM choose the most suitable with regard to the context and culture. Both approaches might improve the results of CG statements in cases where participants rated them worse than HG ones with the current approach.

In our study, the potential for adaptivity that is provided by system actions with different levels elaborateness and indirectness was investigated. For elaborateness, we could show that different preferences exist depending on the culture and original statement. Therefore, it is feasible for an adaptive DM to choose either the elaborated or the concise variant depending on both the culture of the user as well as the current context of the conversation to improve the user satisfaction. Furthermore, our results show that the interaction between generation method, nationality and original statement has an impact on the user's preference for elaborated/indirect statements. This implies that, while both elaborateness and indirectness can be used for adaptation, the DM should base its dialogue policy on experiences with CG statements instead of HG ones.

6 Conclusion

In this work, an approach to the automatic generation of more elaborated or indirect variants of a system action on the semantic level has been discussed. We proposed an algorithms for the acquisition of semantic data and the assessment of this data with regard to the dialogue contribution under consideration. Furthermore, a user study was performed to investigate the performance of our approach compared to humans and the applicability of elaborateness and indirectness for adaptiveness. The results show that, while the variants produced by the proposed algorithm are often perceived in a similar manner as human generated variants, complex interactions exist with both nationality and topic of the statement. Taking those into account can further improve the performance. Additionally, the study shows that differing preferences across cultures and statements exist and hence can be considered in adaptive DM.

In future work, the presented approach will be integrated into a fully functional DS, including the knowledge integration and language generation components that it relies on. Furthermore, the proposed algorithm will be further improved to better adjust to the user culture and the topic of the conversation.

Acknowledgements

This work is part of a project that has received funding from the *European Union's Horizon 2020 research and innovation programme* under grant agreement No 645012.

References

Elisabeth André, Matthias Rehm, Wolfgang Minker, and Dirk Bühler. 2004. Endowing spoken language dialogue systems with emotional intelligence. In *Affective Dialogue Systems*, pages 178–187. Springer.

Ruth Aylett and Ana Paiva. 2012. Computational modelling of culture and affect. *Emotion Review*, 4(3):253–263.

Regina Barzilay and Mirella Lapata. 2005. Collective content selection for concept-to-text generation. In *Proceedings of the conference on Human Language Technology and Empirical Methods in Natural Language Processing*, pages 331–338. Association for Computational Linguistics.

Gregor Bertrand, Florian Nothdurft, Wolfgang Minker, Harald Traue, and Steffen Walter. 2011. Adapting dialogue to user emotion-a wizard-of-oz study for adaptation strategies. *Proc. of IWSDS*, pages 285–294.

Martin Beveridge and John Fox. 2006. Automatic generation of spoken dialogue from medical plans and ontologies. *Journal of biomedical informatics*, 39(5):482–499.

Nadjet Bouayad-Agha, Gerard Casamayor, Simon Mille, Marco Rospocher, Horacio Saggion, Luciano Serafini, and Leo Wanner. 2012. From ontology to NL: generation of multilingual user-oriented environmental reports. In *Natural Language Processing and Information Systems - 17th International Conference on Applications of Natural Language to Information Systems, NLDB 2012, Groningen, The Netherlands, June 26-28, 2012. Proceedings*, pages 216–221.

Pablo A Duboue and Kathleen R McKeown. 2003. Statistical acquisition of content selection rules for natural language generation. In *Proceedings of the 2003 conference on Empirical methods in natural language processing*, pages 121–128. Association for Computational Linguistics.

Milan Gnjatović and Dietmar Rösner. 2008. Adaptive dialogue management in the NIMITEK prototype system. In *Perception in Multimodal Dialogue Systems*, pages 14–25. Springer.

Nada Jaksic, Pedro Branco, Peter Stephenson, and L Miguel Encarnação. 2006. The effectiveness of social agents in reducing user frustration. In *CHI'06 extended abstracts on Human factors in computing systems*, pages 917–922. ACM.

Rudolf Kadlec, Martin Schmid, and Jan Kleindienst. 2015. Improved deep learning baselines for ubuntu corpus dialogs. *arXiv preprint arXiv:1510.03753*.

Kazunori Komatani, Shinichi Ueno, Tatsuya Kawahara, and Hiroshi G Okuno. 2005. User modeling in spoken dialogue systems to generate flexible guidance. *User Modeling and User-Adapted Interaction*, 15(1):169–183.

Raymond Kozlowski, Kathleen F McCoy, and K Vijay-Shanker. 2003. Generation of single-sentence paraphrases from predicate/argument structure using lexico-grammatical resources. In *Proceedings of the second international workshop on Paraphrasing-Volume 16*, pages 1–8. Association for Computational Linguistics.

Irene Langkilde and Kevin Knight. 1998. Generation that exploits corpus-based statistical knowledge. In *Proceedings of the 36th Annual Meeting of the Association for Computational Linguistics and 17th International Conference on Computational Linguistics-Volume 1*, pages 704–710. Association for Computational Linguistics.

Samuel Mascarenhas, Rui Prada, Ana Paiva, and Gert Jan Hofstede. 2013. Social importance dynamics: a model for culturally-adaptive agents. In *Intelligent virtual agents*, pages 325–338. Springer.

Georgios Meditskos, Stamatia Dasiopoulou, Louisa Pragst, Stefan Ultes, Stefanos Vrochidis, Ioannis Kompatsiaris, and Leo Wanner. 2016. Towards an ontology-driven adaptive dialogue framework. In *Proceedings of the 1st International Workshop on Multimedia Analysis and Retrieval for Multimodal Interaction*, pages 15–20. ACM.

Georgios Meditskos, Stefanos Vrochidis, and Ioannis Kompatsiaris. 2017. *Description Logics and Rules for Multimodal Situational Awareness in Healthcare*. Springer International Publishing, Cham.

Juliana Miehle, Koichiro Yoshino, Louisa Pragst, Stefan Ultes, Satoshi Nakamura, and Wolfgang Minker. 2016. Cultural communication idiosyncrasies in human-computer interaction. In *Proceedings of the 17th Annual Meeting of the Special Interest Group on Discourse and Dialogue (SIGDIAL)*, Los Angeles, USA. Association for Computational Linguistics.

Nobal B Niraula, Amanda Stent, Hyuckchul Jung, Giuseppe Di Fabbrizio, I Dan Melamed, and Vasile Rus. 2014. Forms2dialog: Automatic dialog generation for web tasks. In *Spoken Language Technology Workshop (SLT), 2014 IEEE*, pages 608–613. IEEE.

Timo Partala and Veikko Surakka. 2004. The effects of affective interventions in human–computer interaction. *Interacting with computers*, 16(2):295–309.

Johannes Pittermann and Angela Pittermann. 2007. A data-oriented approach to integrate emotions in adaptive dialogue management. In *Proceedings of the 12th international conference on Intelligent user interfaces*, pages 270–273. ACM.

Louisa Pragst, Juliana Miehle, Stefan Ultes, and Wolfgang Minker. 2016. Automatic modification of communication style in dialogue management. In *Proceedings of the INLG 2016 Workshop on Computational Creativity in Natural Language Generation*, pages 36–40. Association for Computational Linguistics.

Louisa Pragst, Wolfgang Minker, and Stefan Ultes. 2017. Exploring the applicability of elaborateness and indirectness in dialogue management. In *Proceedings of the 8th International Workshop On Spoken Dialogue Systems (IWSDS)*.

Verena Rieser and Oliver Lemon. 2011. *Reinforcement learning for adaptive dialogue systems: a data-driven methodology for dialogue management and natural language generation*. Springer Science & Business Media.

Stefan Ultes, Matthias Kraus, Alexander Schmitt, and Wolfgang Minker. 2015. Quality-adaptive spoken dialogue initiative selection and implications on reward modelling. In *Proceedings of the 16th Annual Meeting of the Special Interest Group on Discourse and Dialogue (SIGDIAL)*, pages 374–383.

Stefan Ultes and Wolfgang Minker. 2014. Managing adaptive spoken dialogue for intelligent environments. *Journal of Ambient Intelligence and Smart Environments*, 6(5):523–539.

Leo Wanner, Josep Blat, Stamatia Dasiopoulou, Mónica Domínguez, Gerard Llorach, Simon Mille, Federico Sukno, Eleni Kamateri, Stefanos Vrochidis, Ioannis Kompatsiaris, et al. 2016. Towards a multimedia knowledge-based agent with social competence and human interaction capabilities. In *Proceedings of the 1st International Workshop on Multimedia Analysis and Retrieval for Multimodal Interaction*, pages 21–26. ACM.

Tsung-Hsien Wen, Milica Gasic, Nikola Mrksic, Pei-Hao Su, David Vandyke, and Steve Young. 2015. Semantically conditioned lstm-based natural language generation for spoken dialogue systems. *arXiv preprint arXiv:1508.01745*.

Ke Zhai and Jason D Williams. 2014. Discovering latent structure in task-oriented dialogues. In *ACL (1)*, pages 36–46.

Demographic Word Embeddings for Racism Detection on Twitter

Mohammed Hasanuzzaman
ADAPT Centre
Dublin City University
Ireland

Gaël Dias
GREYC UMR 6072
Université de Caen Normandie
France

Andy Way
ADAPT Centre
Dublin City University
Ireland

Abstract

Most social media platforms grant users freedom of speech by allowing them to freely express their thoughts, beliefs, and opinions. Although this represents incredible and unique communication opportunities, it also presents important challenges. Online racism is such an example. In this study, we present a supervised learning strategy to detect racist language on Twitter based on word embedding that incorporate demographic (Age, Gender, and Location) information. Our methodology achieves reasonable classification accuracy over a gold standard dataset (F_1=76.3%) and significantly improves over the classification performance of demographic-agnostic models.

1 Introduction

The advent of microblogging services has impacted the way people think, communicate, behave, learn, and conduct their daily activities. In particular, the lack of regulation has made social media an attractive tool for people to express online their thoughts, beliefs, emotions and opinions. However, this transformative potential goes with the challenge of maintaining a complex balance between freedom of expression and the defense of human dignity (Silva et al., 2016). Indeed, some users misuse the medium to promote offensive and hateful language, which mars the experience of regular users, affects the business of online companies, and may even have severe real-life consequences (Djuric et al., 2015). In the latter case, (Priest et al., 2013; Tynes et al., 2008; Paradies, 2006b; Darity Jr., 2003) evidenced strong correlations between experiences of racial discrimination and negative mental health outcomes such as depression, anxiety, and emotional stress as well as negative physical health outcomes such as high blood pressure and low infant birth weight.

As the information contained in social media often reflects the real-world experiences of their users, there is an increased expectation that the norms of society will also apply in social media settings. As such, there is an increasing demand for social media platforms to empower users with the tools to report offensive and hateful content (Oboler and Connelly, 2014).

Hateful content can be defined as "speech or expression which is capable of instilling or inciting hatred of, or prejudice towards, a person or group of people on a specified ground, including race, nationality, ethnicity, country of origin, ethno-religious identity, religion, sexuality, gender identity or gender" (Gelber and Stone, 2007). While there are many forms of hate speech, racism is the most general and prevalent form of hate speech in Twitter (Silva et al., 2016). Racist speech relates to a socially constructed idea about differences between social groups based on phenotype, ancestry, culture or religion (Paradies, 2006a) and covers the categories of race (e.g. black people), ethnicity (e.g. Chinese people), and religion (e.g. jewish people) introduced in Silva et al. (2016).

Racism is often expressed through negative and inaccurate stereotypes with one-word epithets (e.g. tiny), phrases (e.g. big nose), concepts (e.g. head bangers), metaphors (e.g. coin slot), and juxtapositions (e.g. yellow cab) that convey hateful intents (Warner and Hirschberg, 2012). As such, its automatic identification is a challenging task. Moreover, the racist language is not uniform. First, it highly depends on contextual features of the targeted community. For example, anti-african-american messages often refer to unemployment or single parent upbringing whereas anti-semitic language predominantly makes refer-

926

Proceedings of the The 8th International Joint Conference on Natural Language Processing, pages 926–936,
Taipei, Taiwan, November 27 – December 1, 2017 ©2017 AFNLP

ence to money, banking, and media (Warner and Hirschberg, 2012). Second, the demographic context of the speaker may greatly influence word choices, syntax, and even semantics (Hovy, 2015). For instance, a young female rapper from Australia may not use the exact same language as an elder male economist from South Africa to express her racists thoughts (Figure 1).

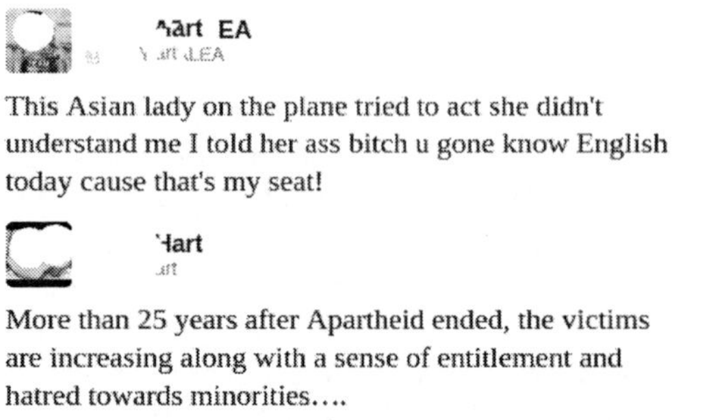

This Asian lady on the plane tried to act she didn't understand me I told her ass bitch u gone know English today cause that's my seat!

More than 25 years after Apartheid ended, the victims are increasing along with a sense of entitlement and hatred towards minorities....

Figure 1: (Top) Tweet from a 25 years-old Australian rapper. (Bottom) Tweet from a senior South African economist.

To address these issues, we propose to focus on demographic features (age, gender, and location) of Twitter users to learn demographic word embeddings following the ideas of Bamman et al. (2014) for geographically situated language. The distributed representations learned from a large corpus containing a great proportion of racist tweets are then used to represent tweets in a straightforward way and serve as input to build an accurate supervised classification model for racist tweet detection. Different evaluations over a gold-standard dataset show that the demographic (age, gender, location) word embeddings methodology achieves F_1 score of 76.3 and significantly improves over the classification performance of demographic-agnostic models.

2 Related Work

Despite the prevalence and large impact of online hateful speech, there has been a lack of published works addressing this problem. The first studies on hateful speech detection are proposed by (Xu and Zhu, 2010; Kwok and Wang, 2013; Warner and Hirschberg, 2012) but with very limited scope and basic supervised machine learning techniques.

One of the very first attempts to propose a computational model that deals with offensive language in online communities is proposed by Xu and Zhu (2010). The authors pro-pose a sentence-level rule-based semantic filtering approach, which utilizes grammatical relations among words to remove offensive contents in a sentence from Youtube comments. Although this may be a valuable work, its scope deviates from our specific goal, which aims at automatically detecting racist online messages.

The first identified studies that can directly match our objectives are proposed by Kwok and Wang (2013) and Warner and Hirschberg (2012). In Kwok and Wang (2013), the authors propose a naïve Bayes classifier based on unigram features to classify tweets as racist or non-racist. It is important to notice that the standard data sets of racist tweets were selected from Twitter accounts that were self-classified as racist or deemed racist through reputable news sources with regards to anti-Barack-Obama articles. Although this is the very first attempt to deal with Twitter posts, the final model is of very limited scope as it mainly deals with anti-black community racism. Similarly, (Warner and Hirschberg, 2012) propose a template-based strategy that exclusively focuses on the detection of anti-semitic posts from Yahoo!. In particular, some efforts were made to propose new feature sets, but with unsuccessful results.

In Warner and Hirschberg (2012), the authors propose a similar idea focusing on the specific manifestation of anti-semitic posts from Yahoo! and xenophobic urls identified by the American Jewish Congress. In particular, they use a template-based strategy to generate features from the part-of-speech tagged corpus augmented with Brown clusters. Then, a model is generated for each type of feature template strategy, resulting in six SVM classifiers. Surprisingly, the smallest feature set comprised of only positive unigrams performed better than bigram and trigram features. Similarly to Kwok and Wang (2013), this study focuses on a specific community and is of limited scope. However, efforts were made to propose new features, although with unsuccessful results.

Burnap and Williams (2016) is certainly the first study to propose a global understanding of hateful speech on Twitter including a wide range of protected characteristics such as race, disability, sexual orientation and religion. First, they build individual SVM classifiers for each of the four hateful-speech categories using combinations of feature types: ngrams (1 to 5), slur words and typed-dependencies. Overall, the highest F_1 scores are achieved by combining ngrams and hateful terms, although the inclusion of typed dependencies reduces false positive rates. In a second step, the authors build a data-driven blended model where more than one protected characteristic is taken at a time and show that hateful speech is a domain dependent problem. The important finding of this work is the relevance of the simple dictionary lookup feature of slur words.

In Waseem and Hovy (2016), the authors study the importance of demographic features (gender and location) for hateful speech (racism, sexism and others) classification from Twitter as well as proposed to deal with data sparseness by substituting word ngrams with character ngram (1 to 4) features. 10-fold cross validation results with a logistic regression show that the demographic features (individually or combined) do to not lead to any improvement, while character-based classification outperforms by at least 5 points the F_1 score of word-based classification. Although nonconclusive results are obtained with demographic features, we deeply believe that these contextual features can lead to improvements.

While all these efforts are of great importance, most works point at the drawbacks of discrete representations of words and texts. This especially holds in the context of the racist language where offenders often use simple yet effective tricks to obfuscate their comments and make them more difficult for automatic detection (such as replacing or removing characters of offensive words), while still keeping the intent clear to a human reader. For that purpose, including continuous distributed representations of words and texts may lead to improved classification results.

Following this assumption, two studies have been proposed with different strategies. Tulkens et al. (2016) present a dictionary-based approach to racism detection in Dutch social media comments following the findings of Burnap and Williams (2016). In particular, they broaden the coverage of the categories in their dictionaries by performing a dictionary expansion strategy that uses a word embedding (skip-gram model) obtained from a general-purpose 3.9 billion words Dutch corpus. For instance, they show that the entry "mohammed"[1] can be expanded with "mohamed", "mohammad" and "muhammed". The SVM classification results show that the auto-

mated expansion of the dictionary slightly boosts the performance, but with no statistical significance. To our point of view, this may be due to the non-specificity of the corpus used to produce the word embeddings.

Indeed, more successful results are obtained by Djuric et al. (2015), who propose to build a specific paragraph embeddings for hateful speech. In particular, they show a two-step method. First, paragraph2vec (Le and Mikolov, 2014) is used for joint modeling of comments and words from Yahoo! comments with the bag-of-words neural language model. Then, these embeddings are used to train a binary classifier to distinguish between hateful and clean comments. The results of the logistic regression for 5-fold cross-validation show improved performance of the continuous representation when compared to discrete ngram features.

In this paper, we propose to study further the initial "unsuccessful" idea of Waseem and Hovy (2016) of taking into account demographic factors for racism classification in Twitter. Indeed, recent linguistic studies have shown that the racist language can differ from place to place (Chaudhry, 2015). Moreover, we deeply think that the specificity of racist language can be better modeled by continuous spaces as shown in Djuric et al. (2015).

As a consequence, we propose to build demographic word embeddings following the initial findings of Bamman et al. (2014) (location) and Hovy (2015) (age and gender) for discrete features. These embeddings are computed on a corpus specifically built for racism detection and obtained by massive gathering of tweets containing slur words listed in different referenced sources such as the racial slur database.[2] Then, the low-space distributed continuous representations are used as direct input of binary (racist vs. non racist) SVM classifiers, which are compared to concurrent approaches over a gold standard data set.

3 Data Sets

In this section, we first detail the process that consists in gathering a huge quantity of potentially racist and non-racist tweets from which the demographic word embeddings are computed. Then, we present the manual annotation process defined to create a gold standard data set and used to evaluate the proposed classification strategy.

---

[1]The study specifically focuses on anti-Islamic racism.

[2]`http://www.rsdb.org/` Last accessed on 10-04-2017.

3.1 Unlabeled Data Set

The process starts by crawling English tweets using the Twitter streaming API[3] for a period of three months (05/02/2015 to 05/05/2015). From this set, potentially racist tweets are collected by selecting all those that contain at least one racist candidate keyword from (1) a collection of 3000 plus racial and ethnic slurs or (2) a set of racially motivated phrases. In particular, the first list of keywords is compiled from the Wikipedia list of ethnic slurs[4] and the racial slur database.[5] The second list of racist phrases is produced by combining a general purpose insult with the name of a given ethnicity, giving rise to slurs such as "dirty jew" or "russian pig". For that particular purpose, we collected 70 common insulting modifiers such as "dog", "filthy", "honky", "redneck", or "rat". This process allowed to gather about 17.2 million potentially racist tweets from 1.8 million users.

In parallel, a random sample ($\approx 1\%$ of all retrieved tweets) of potentially clean (i.e. that do not contain racial and ethnic slurs) tweets is collected resulting in 41.3 million tweets from 4.6 million users all over the world.

In addition to the message conveyed in a given tweet, some information is stored for all tweets, such as location, time and user's profile. However, this information is not accessible for most tweets. As a consequence, we propose different text processing methodologies to compute the three demographic variables: age, gender and location.

In particular, age and gender are predicted using the text-based models described in Sap et al. (2014). These models are trained on data from over 70,000 Facebook users and report an accuracy rate of 91.9% for gender (resp. 88.9% on Twitter data) and a Pearson correlation coefficient of 0.84 for age prediction. For location, we use the geo-coding scheme proposed in Chen and Neill (2014), which is based on three major rules with priorities.[6] For each tweet, (1) we search for a location mention from GeoNames[7] in the text message, then (2), we verify if the user enabled

the geo-coding function of his/her device, and (3) we look for location information from the stored user's profile. The first location information identified is then returned as the geographic location of the tweet. Note that the returned location information is at country-level.

Finally, similarly to Hovy (2015), we lowercase tweet texts, remove special characters, replace numbers with a 0, and join frequent bigrams with an underscore to form a single token.

Table 1 presents the distribution of the obtained corpus broken down by the contextual variables.

Country	Tweets	Users	Users Demographics			
			U. 35	O. 35	M	F
Potentially racist tweets						
USA	3.9M	124.2k	54.7k	69.5k	79.9k	44.3k
India	3.4M	132k	89.7k	42.3k	93.8k	38.2k
UK	2.8M	105k	55.8k	49.2k	61.3k	43.7k
Canada	1.3M	96k	44.7k	51.3k	52.8k	43.2k
Japan	1.1M	98.4k	50.6k	44.8k	49.8k	45.6k
Potentially clean tweets						
USA	11.8M	259.4k	121.6k	137.8k	137.4k	121.9k
UK	8.3M	184.5k	98.3k	86.2k	94.1k	90.4k
India	6.4M	218.4k	136.2k	82.2k	145.6k	72.8k
Japan	2.3M	102.5k	54.8k	47.7k	57.3k	45.2k
Indon.	2.1M	109.4k	63.2k	46.2k	71.9k	37.5k

Table 1: Top five countries with most tweets in the unlabeled data sets. Tweet users are broken down by age - (i) Under 35 (U. 35); (ii) Over 35 (O. 35) - and gender - (i) Male (M); (ii) Female (F).

3.2 Classification Data Set

It is anticipated that recognizing racist tweets can be difficult. Certainly, the use of ethnic and racial slurs has been clearly not always hateful. A number of studies have examined how the slur "nigger" has been appropriated by African Americans as a way of actively rejecting the connotations it carries, e.g. for comedic purposes, a status symbol, a shorthand term expressing familiarity among friends, or even forgetting what the term ever denoted in the first place (Anderson and Lepore, 2013). Therefore, tweets that merely contain these slurs may not be always offensive.

In order to build a gold-standard data set that allows the evaluation of classifiers learned to detect "true" racist tweets, we adopt an approach, which depends on the assessments made by users of a crowdsourcing platform. For that purpose, we randomly sample 4 sub-collections from the collection of potentially racist tweets gathered in section 3.1, namely two for gender (Male and Female), and two for age (Under 35 and Over 35). The same strategy is followed to select 4 sub-

---

[3] https://dev.twitter.com/streaming/overview. Last accessed on 10-04-2017.

[4] https://en.wikipedia.org/wiki/List_of_ethnic_slurs. Last accessed on 10-04-2017.

[5] http://www.rsdb.org/. Last accessed on 10-04-2017.

[6] This methodology is clearly prone to error. But, improving this pre-processing step is out of the scope of this paper.

[7] http://www.geonames.org/. Last accessed on 10-04-2017.

Tweet	R1	R2	R3	Maj.V
Dog, this nigga does not stop staring at me in the gym. Dickface got a staring problem!	Y	Y	Y	Y
The after effect of being a wigger. http:/***	N	N	N	N
@*** i told yo racist ass to stop callin me a niger. Dumb white boy!	Y	N	Y	Y
Who cares where they were born, camel breath, they call themselves Israelis and Jews.	Un	Y	Un	Un
Radical Islam on the rise in Indonesia. http://****.	N	Un	Un	Un
So I can see iphone emojis now, soooo coolie!!!!	N	N	Y	N

Table 2: Examples of tweets annotated for racism: Yes (Y), No (N), and Unsure (Un.). R1, R2, R3: judgements from each rater. Maj.V: choice from majority voting.

Country	Number of Tweets				
	Total	U. 35	O. 35	M	F
Racist tweets					
USA	1036	387	649	572	464
UK	728	346	382	382	346
India	587	413	174	445	142
Japan	485	268	217	289	196
Canada	431	198	233	256	175
Clean tweets					
India	1132	712	420	694	438
USA	956	438	518	534	422
UK	762	352	410	387	375
Canada	631	309	322	336	295
Japan	610	294	316	327	283

Table 3: Top five countries with most tweets in the classification data set. Tweets are broken down by age and gender.

collections from the set of potentially clean tweets.

The samples are equally distributed among male, female, and the two age groups, and the geographic distributions (at the country level) in the 8 sub-collections are in line with the distributions over the whole corpus of tweets.

Note that while the effect of age on language use is undisputed (Rickford and Price, 2013), providing a clear cut-off is hard. We therefore used age ranges that result in roughly equally sized data sets for both groups in the overall corpus.

Each sub-collection consists of 1000 tweets that are uploaded to the crowdsourcing service of the CrowdFlower platform[8] for annotation. In particular, each tweet is represented by its text, location information, user's age and gender, and a multiple choice question is asked to the annotators to decide whether the tweet has indeed a racist intent or not. The available answers are "Yes", "No", and "Unsure". Each tweet is annotated by at least 3 annotators. Each annotator requires to be an English speaker and preferably in the same country as the origin of the tweet.

Out of the 8000 tweets that were judged, 7358 received a majority of "Yes" or "No" votes. The

remainder were less determinant with the addition of "Unsure" votes. Of these 7358 tweets, 3267 (44%) had a majority of votes confirming they were racist, with the remaining 4091 (56%) considered as not racially motivated tweets. Table 2 shows some examples of tweets with their annotations and Table 3 summarizes the classification data set by demographic variable.

This data set can be thought as a hard test for classifiers as non racist tweets may contain slurs unlike most works so far, which assess their models based on the hypothesis that non racist tweets usually contain general vocabulary and do not exhibit any critical content. In parallel, we acknowledge that some racist tweets may not contain any slur such as illustrated in Figure 1. Future work will definitely have to deal with the integration of racist tweets that do not present any direct racist mention, in the classification data set.

4 Methodology

Following the self-taught learning paradigm (Raina et al., 2007), we first construct demographic word embeddings from the unlabeled data described in section 3.1. Then, we obtained context-aware high-level low-dimensional features form a succinct input representation for the specific task of racist tweet detection.

4.1 Demographic Word Embeddings

Djuric et al. (2015) were the first to propose a self-taught learning strategy in the context of hateful speech detection, where they simultaneously learn low-dimension representations of documents and words in a common vector space. However, contextual/demographic characteristics were not taken into account.

A simple way to take demographic variables into account when building word embeddings is to train individual models on each variable value (e.g. a "male" model is obtained by using data

---

[8] http://www.crowdflower.com/. Last accessed on 10-04-2017.

only from male users). This has been the strategy followed by Hovy (2015) for age and gender in the context of sentiment classification, topic identification, and author attributes identification.[9]

A more sophisticated model has been proposed in Bamman et al. (2014), which defines a joint parameterization over all variable values in the data. In this specific case, they study geographic variables. As such, information from data originating in some location can influence the representations learned for other locations. A joint model has three a priori advantages over independent models: (i) sharing data across variable values, encourages representations across those values to be similar; (ii) such sharing can mitigate data sparseness for less-witnessed variables; and (iii) all representations are guaranteed to be in the same vector space and can therefore be compared to each other.

In this work, we propose to follow the work of Bamman et al. (2014) and introduce a set of demographic features, namely Age (Under 35 and Over 35), Gender (Male and Female) and Location (top 20 countries in the unlabeled data set[10]).

This model corresponds to an extension of the skip-gram language model proposed in (Mikolov et al., 2013). Formally, given an input word w_i in a vocabulary V and a set of demographic variables A, the objective is to maximize the average data log-likelihood given in equation (1), where c is the length of the word context.

$$
\mathcal{L} \;=\; \frac{1}{|V|}\sum_{i=1}^{|V|}\sum_{c\in\{-1,1\}} \log\Pr(w_{i+c}|w_i) \;+ \tag{1}
$$

$$
\frac{1}{|A|}\sum_{a=1}^{|A|}\frac{1}{|V_a|}\sum_{i=1}^{|V_a|}\sum_{c\in\{-1,1\}} \log\Pr(w_{i+c}|w_i^a)
$$

So, while any word has a common low-dimension representation that is invoked for every instance of its use (regardless of its demographic context), the word embedding specific to a given demographic variable indicates how that common representation should shift in the k-dimension space when used in this special context.

In terms of implementation, back-propagation functions as in the standard skip-gram language model, with gradient updates for each training ex-

---

ample and computation is speeded up using the hierarchical softmax function.

4.2 Racist Tweet Classification

For the classification process, we use linear Support Vector Machines (SVM) models that take as input a feature representation of tweets based on demographic word embeddings.

On the one hand, each word of a given tweet is represented by its joint embedding, which is the concatenation of its common low-dimension representation of dimension k and each low-dimension representation of its specific demographic embeddings, each one also of dimension k. For example, if a given word appears in a tweet issued by a male user of 45 years-old in the USA, its representation will be the concatenation of its common embedding with its 3 specific embeddings computed from the active variables Age=Over 35, Gender=Male and Location=USA. In this particular case, each word will be represented by a vector of $4k$ continuous values.

On the other hand, we need to represent tweets with variable lengths based only upon the concatenated embeddings of the words they contain. For that purpose, we follow the same strategy as proposed in Hovy (2015). For each learning instance (i.e. tweet), we collect 5 N-dimensional statistics (i.e. minimum, maximum, mean representation, as well as one standard deviation above and below the mean) over a $N \times t$ input matrix, where N is the dimensionality of the concatenated embeddings (i.e. $N = |A^*| \times k$, where $|A^*|$ is the number of active variables and k is the dimension of each individual embedding), and t is the sentence length in words. We then concatenate those 5 N-dimension vectors to a $(5N)$-dimension vector to represent each learning instance in a single format and feed it to the SVM classifiers.

Note that taking the maximum and minimum across all embedding dimensions is equivalent to representing the exterior surface of the instance manifold (i.e. the volume in the embedding space within which all words in the instance reside). And adding the mean and standard deviation acts as the density per-dimension within the manifold.

We are aware that different tweet representations could have been tested, namely those based on neural sequence modeling. In particular, future work will aim to adapt models such as paragraph2vec (Le and Mikolov, 2014) or LSTM (Tai et al., 2015) to demographic embeddings.

5 Evaluation

5.1 Experimental Setups

The demographic word embeddings were computed based on the implementation provided by Bamman et al. (2014)[11] with $k = 100$ for the low representation dimension, while demographic-agnostic models were built using the word2vec[12] implementation for the same size of k. In particular, we built 8 different embeddings i.e. one demographic-agnostic embedding based on the unlabeled data set presented in section 3.1 without any demographic variable and 7 others with different demographic variables combinations such as Age, Gender, Location, Age+Gender, Age+Location, Gender+Location and Age+Gender+Location. With respect to the discrete representation of tweets, we proposed 6 different configurations using either word unigrams and/or bigrams, or character ngrams (n=1 to 4). In this context, the demographic information was included as binary variables for Gender and Age, and a n-ary variable for Location. One final model was proposed that joins demographic-agnostic word embeddings with demographic dicrete variables. As a consequence, 15 different input settings were tested for classification as shown in the first column of Table 4, using the linear SVM model implemented in the Weka[13] platform with standard parameters settings[14].

As for evaluation, we proposed to split the gold-standard data set of 7358 tweets described in section 3.2 into a training data set of 5149 tweets (70%) and a test data set of 2209 tweets (30%). In particular, the test data set is equally distributed among male, female, the two age groups, and the top 20 countries with most tweets in our collected unlabeled data set. In order to evaluate the capacity of the classification models to generalize over the original data distribution, we also performed 10-fold cross-validation for all the settings. Moreover, we analyzed the effect of the training data size for the classification purposes.

[11]https://github.com/dbamman/geoSGLM. Last accessed on 10-04-2017.

[12]https://code.google.com/archive/p/word2vec/. Last accessed on 03-10-2017.

[13]http://www.cs.waikato.ac.nz/ml/weka/. Last accessed on 10-04-2017.

[14]The magnitude of the improvements could be improved by tuning the parameters over a development set. But this remains out of the scope of this paper.

5.2 Quantitative Results

The classification results over the annotated gold standard test data presented in section 3.2 are given in Table 4 for all 15 different configurations.

Tweet Representation	Prec.	Rec.	F_1
Uni.	58.2	54.2	56.1
Uni. + Age + Loc. + Gen.	60.1	58.3	59.0
Uni. + Bi.	58.9	57.2	58.0
Uni. + Bi. + Age + Loc. + Gen.	61.8	60.2	60.9
Ch. ngrams	60.6	62.2	61.3
Ch. ngrams + Age + Loc. + Gen.	60.3	61.8	61.0
W.2V.	67.3	66.4	66.8
W.2V. + Age + Loc. + Gen.	70.3	70.7	70.5
Demo. W.2V. (Age)	72.3	71.5	71.9
Demo. W.2V. (Gen.)	68.7	67.5	68.0
Demo. W.2V. (Loc.)	73.6	73.1	73.4
Demo. W.2V. (Age + Gen.)	72.7	72.1	72.4
Demo. W.2V. (Age + Loc.)	75.3	**76.2**	75.8
Demo. W.2V. (Gen. + Loc.)	74.0	73.4	73.7
Demo. W.2V. (Age + Gen. + Loc.)	**76.4**	76.1	**76.3**

Table 4: Precision (Prec.), Recall (Rec.), and F_1 Score (F_1) for racist tweet detection over the test data set. Demographic variables Location and Gender are represented by Loc. and Gen., respectively. W.2V. stands for word2vec model learned over the racist data set.

The first finding is that demographic-aware models perform better than the demographic-agnostic ones across almost all configurations. This improvement raises at 5.3% of F_1 on average with a maximum increase of 9.5%. The only contradictory case is when character ngrams (n=1 to 4) are used as text representation. In that specific configuration, the inclusion of demographic variables has no impact on the results, confirming previous results of Waseem and Hovy (2016). However, using character ngrams improves over a word ngrams representation as noted by Waseem and Hovy (2016) but, it fails to benefit from the introduction of demographic variables, unlike the word ngrams representation which is boosted by the introduction of contextual variables. Note that this result was not reported in Waseem and Hovy (2016). Furthermore, we computed the exact same best configuration of Waseem and Hovy (2016), i.e. logistic regression over character ngrams with the Gender variable, and a F_1 score of 60.7% was achieved, which is comparable to our results with SVM reaching F_1 score of 61.0%.

The second important result is that the model learned over continuous feature representations of tweets from general embeddings in combination with features containing demographic information, namely Age, Gender, Location (row 8 in Table 4) outperforms all demographic-aware configurations based on discrete text representations (i.e. unigrams, bigrams or character ngrams) by a minimum (resp. maximum) margin of 9.5% (resp. 11.5%) of F_1 score. This result, particularly shows that word semantics is better captured by word embeddings than classical text representations.

The third result supports our initial hypothesis that demographic word embeddings can improve the task of racist tweet classification. Indeed, all demographic-aware embeddings improve over the demographic-agnostic embeddings, even boosted by discrete demographic variables, to the only exception of the gender-aware model (row 10 in Table 4). In particular, a maximum difference is obtained by the demographic word embedding that counts with Age, Gender and Location variables at levels of 9.5% of F_1 score, when compared to demographic-agnostic word embeddings.

Finally, although all demographic variables improve on classification, the Gender variable seems to have the smallest impact on the overall results. Indeed, at each inclusion it slightly improves results, while Location is the most productive variable, as hypothesized by Chaudhry (2015). In particular, note that the demographic-aware continuous model with the single Gender variable is outperformed by the model built on general word embeddings increased by discrete context variable (row 8 in Table 4).

Tweet Representation	Prec.	Rec.	F_1
Uni.	65.3	61.5	63.3
Uni. + Age + Loc. + Gen.	66.7	62.4	64.4
Uni. + Bi.	65.8	60.7	63.1
Uni. + Bi. + Age + Loc. + Gen.	66.2	62.3	64.1
Ch. ngrams	64.2	65.6	64.8
Ch. ngrams + Age + Loc. + Gen.	65.0	67.2	66.0
W.2V.	71.2	69.5	70.3
W.2V. + Age + Loc. + Gen.	73.5	72.8	73.1
Demo. W.2V. (Age)	75.3	74.5	74.8
Demo. W.2V. (Gen.)	72.3	71.2	71.7
Demo. W.2V. (Loc.)	75.4	76.3	75.8
Demo. W.2V. (Age + Gen.)	75.1	74.4	74.7
Demo. W.2V. (Age + Loc.)	78.2	**78.8**	78.5
Demo. W.2V. (Gen. + Loc.)	77.6	74.2	75.8
Demo. W.2V. (Age + Gen. + Loc.)	**79.0**	77.4	**77.1**

Table 5: Precision (Prec.), Recall (Rec.), and F_1 Score (F_1) for 10-fold cross-validation.

Results of the 10-fold cross-validation are presented in Table 5 and show similar conclusions, but following the original distribution of the learning data sets, oppositely to the first experiment, where we forced the test data to be balanced. The only small difference is that in these conditions the character ngrams representation seems to take advantage of the introduction of contextual variables reaching the best results in terms of discrete text representation.

Note that all improvements in Table 4 and Table 5 are statistically significant. In particular, we adopted a bootstrap-sampling test similarity to Hovy (2015) with a standard cutoff of $p < 0.05$.

Effect of Training Data Size: The size of the training data set is an important concern in supervised learning methods as lots of manual efforts are required to tag learning instances. Thus, we want to evaluate the impact of the training data set size on the performances of two different word embeddings configurations: (1) W.2V. + Age + Gen. + Loc. (Baseline) and (2) Demo. W.2V. (Age + Gen. + Loc.).

For that purpose, we randomly select $d\%$ (by steps of 20%) of the training data set to train the classifiers and test them on the test data set. Note that for each $d\%$, we generate the training set 20 times and the averaged performance is recorded. F_1 scores for both approaches over the test data are presented in Table 6.

Data size	Baseline	Demo. W.2V. (Age+Gen.+Loc.)
1k	63.4	68.3
2k	65.2	70.2
3k	68.5	73.8
4k	69.9	75.5
5.1k (all)	70.5	76.3

Table 6: Classification performances (F_1 score) with different sizes of training data.

Results show that our proposed framework performs consistently better than its counterpart. In particular, the results show that with 3k training examples better results can be obtained by our approach than relying on 5.1k training examples for the state-of-the-art supervised machine learning approach (Baseline) based on common word embeddings for racist tweet detection.

5.3 Qualitative Results

In order to better understand figures given in section 5.2, we examined different qualitative criteria.

Error Analysis We performed a manual error analysis of the instances where our best performing configuration and manual annotation differed. We noticed that some of the tweets were difficult to classify because of their ambiguity with respect to racism classification. For example, tweets such as *"adam 15 boy prob bi whitey is an irl egg"* or *"@... but the pakis are still trying to get across the border"* could be "racist" tweets, but without the context it is difficult to judge even for humans. Part of our future work will be to extract the context (e.g. previous tweets, threads) of tweets and use it for (i) annotation purposes and (2) classification issues.

Lexical Distribution. Table 7 represents the top ten most frequent racial slurs occurring in automatically tagged racist tweets broken down by Age and Gender. Results show that majority of racial slurs discuss about Islam. Considering that many tweets are issued from the USA or India rather than other countries, it is not surprising that several of the terms are in line with the Indian and American political discourses orientations.

Overall	U.35	O.35	M	F
islam	nigger	islam	islam	nigga
nigger	muslims	hebe	muslims	islam
muslims	paki	muslims	paki	nigger
white boy	islam	white boy	white boy	desi
mohammed	prophet	nigger	chinki	mohammed
pedophile	bihari	negro	mohammed	pedophile
paki	white boy	pedophile	nigger	whitey
prophet	pedophile	whitey	whitey	muslims
whitey	gook	paki	bihari	hebe
bihari	whitey	coon	mallu	coon

Table 7: Ten most frequently occurring racial slurs in racist tweets broken down by age and gender.

Demographic Distribution. The distributions by Age and Gender of the automatically tagged racist tweets are presented in Table 8. It can be seen that the Gender distribution is skewed towards men. This goes in line with an earlier study made by (Roberts et al., 2013) who found that the majority (more than 70%) of the offenders of hate crimes were men. The results also demonstrate that people under the age of 35 years-old seem to be more racist than people with the age over 35. Note that 40.2% of the Twitter users are less than 35 years old[15], which indicates a clear bias towards racism by youngers. We further analyzed the racist tweets and found that roughly 35% of total racist offenders are aged under 25. So, it seems

<hr>

[15]http://goo.gl/qHlIQq. Last Accessed on 6-06-2017.

that younger adults are more likely to be involved in racist offenses than older adults.

Variable	Value	% Racist tweets
Gender	Men	64.7%
	Women	35.3%
Age	Under 35	67.2%
	Over 35	32.8%

Table 8: Distribution of tweets by Gen. and Age.

Usage Patterns of Racial Slurs. Finally, we analyzed the set of automatically tagged racist tweets and categorized the patterns of usage of racial slurs into four main categories:

- *Group Demarcation:* The user's intention is to demarcate group boundaries (people as in or out) as in the following example *"Dirty Jews, Im Hitler, Ill kill the Jews."*.

- *Directed Attack:* Here, an attack is directed at an individual or group known personally to the sender. Tweets in this pattern use racial/ethnic slurs directly such as in *"@ *** why you rotten nigger bitch, how dare you."*.

- *Unnecessary Use:* In this case, the main discourse of the tweet may not be race or ethnicity, but rather the use of a given slur in an offhand or casual fashion, e.g. *"@: disgusting Indian shops that charge you for paying by card."* ;

- *Ideological:* Here, authors consciously use racial/ethnic slurs within a political statement that would justify an action in the real world, such as in *"Leftist have no right view. They have an agenda for Paki and muslim. Support BJP"*.

6 Conclusions

In this paper, we proposed to build demographic-aware word embeddings for the classification of racist tweets. We showed that such models outperform strategies based on discrete text representations and demographic-agnostic word embeddings. However, overall performance ($F_1 = 76.3\%$) is still insufficient confirming that hateful speech detection is a hard task. To improve initial results, future works will aim to (1) incorporate additional context (such as connected tweets) to leverage tweet ambiguity, (2) build demographic-aware sequence embeddings to better capture text semantics, (3) combine both discrete and continuous representations to build semi-supervised models, as weak detection of racist tweets in large amount is possible and (4) test new character-based word embeddings (Bojanowski et al., 2017).

Acknowledgments

The ADAPT Centre for Digital Content Technology is funded under the SFI Research Centres Programme (Grant 13/RC/2106) and is co-funded under the European Regional Development Fund.

References

Luvell Anderson and Ernie Lepore. 2013. Slurring words 1. *Noûs*, 47(1):25–48.

David Bamman, Chris Dyer, and Noah A. Smith. 2014. Distributed representations of geographically situated language. In *Proceedings of the Association for Computational Linguistics (ACL 2014)*, pages 828–834.

Piotr Bojanowski, Edouard Grave, Armand Joulin, and Tomas Mikolov. 2017. Enriching word vectors with subword information. *TACL*, 5:135–146.

Pete Burnap and Matthew L. Williams. 2016. Us and them: identifying cyber hate on twitter across multiple protected characteristics. *EPJ Data Science*, 5(1):11.

Irfan Chaudhry. 2015. hashtagging hate: Using twitter to track racism online. *First Monday*, 20(2).

Feng Chen and Daniel B. Neill. 2014. Non-parametric scan statistics for event detection and forecasting in heterogeneous social media graphs. In *Proceedings of the 20th ACM SIGKDD international conference on Knowledge discovery and data mining*, pages 1166–1175. ACM.

William A. Darity Jr. 2003. Employment discrimination, segregation, and health. *American Journal of Public Health*, 93(2):226–231.

Nemanja Djuric, Jing Zhou, Robin Morris, Mihajlo Grbovic, Vladan Radosavljevic, and Narayan Bhamidipati. 2015. Hate speech detection with comment embeddings. In *Proceedings of the 24th International Conference on World Wide Web (WWW 2015)*, pages 29–30.

Katharine Gelber and Adrienne Sarah Ackary Stone. 2007. *Hate Speech and Freedom of Speech in Australia*, volume 2118. Federation Press.

Dirk Hovy. 2015. Demographic factors improve classification performance. In *Proceedings of the Association for Computational Linguistics (ACL 2015)*, pages 752–762.

Irene Kwok and Yuzhou Wang. 2013. Locate the hate: Detecting tweets against blacks. In *Proceedings of the 27th AAAI Conference on Artificial Intelligence (AAAI 2013)*, pages 1621–1622.

Quoc Le and Tomas Mikolov. 2014. Distributed representations of sentences and documents. In *Proceedings of the 31st International Conference on Machine Learning (ICML 2014)*, pages 1188–1196.

Tomas Mikolov, Kai Chen, Greg Corrado, and Jeffrey Dean. 2013. Efficient estimation of word representations in vector space. *CoRR*, abs/1301.3781.

Andre Oboler and Karen Connelly. 2014. Hate speech: A quality of service challenge. In *Proceedings of IEEE Conference on E-Learning, E-Management and E-Services (IC3E 2014)*, pages 117–121.

Yin C. Paradies. 2006a. Defining, conceptualizing and characterizing racism in health research. *Critical Public Health*, 16(2):143–157.

Yin C. Paradies. 2006b. A systematic review of empirical research on self-reported racism and health. *International Journal of Epidemiology*, 35(4):888–901.

Naomi Priest, Yin C. Paradies, Brigid Trenerry, Mandy Truong, Saffron Karlsen, and Yvonne Kelly. 2013. A systematic review of studies examining the relationship between reported racism and health and well-being for children and young people. *Social Science & Medicine*, 95:115–127.

Rajat Raina, Alexis Battle, Honglak Lee, Benjamin Packer, and Andrew Y Ng. 2007. Self-taught learning: transfer learning from unlabeled data. In *Proceedings of the 24th International Conference on Machine Learning (ICML 2007)*, pages 759–766. ACM.

John Rickford and Mackenzie Price. 2013. Girlz ii women: Age-grading, language change and stylistic variation. *Journal of Sociolinguistics*, 17(2):143–179.

Colin Roberts, Martin Innes, Matthew Leighton Williams, Jasmin Tregidga, and David Gadd. 2013. *Understanding who commits hate crimes and why they do it*. Welsh Government.

Maarten Sap, Gregory J. Park, Johannes C. Eichstaedt, Margaret L. Kern, David Stillwell, Michal Kosinski, Lyle H. Ungar, and H. Andrew Schwartz. 2014. Developing age and gender predictive lexica over social media. In *Proceedings of the Conference on Empirical Methods in Natural Language Processing (EMNLP 2014)*, pages 1146–1151.

Leandro Silva, Mainack Modal, Denzil Correa, Fabricio Benevenuto, and Ingmar Weber. 2016. Analyzing the targets of hate in online social media. In *Proceedings of the International AAAI Conference on Web-Blogs and Social Media (ICWSM 2016)*.

Kai Sheng Tai, Richard Socher, and Christopher D. Manning. 2015. Improved semantic representations from tree-structured long short-term memory networks. In *Proceedings of the 53rd Annual Meeting of the Association for Computational Linguistics and the 7th International Joint Conference on Natural Language Processing of the Asian Federation of Natural Language Processing, (ACL/IJCNLP 2015)*, pages 1556–1566.

Stéphan Tulkens, Lisa Hilte, Elise Lodewyckx, Ben Verhoeven, and Walter Daelemans. 2016. A dictionary-based approach to racism detection in dutch social media. *CoRR*, abs/1608.08738.

Brendesha M. Tynes, Michael T. Giang, David R. Williams, and Geneene N. Thompson. 2008. Online racial discrimination and psychological adjustment among adolescents. *Journal of Adolescent Health*, 43(6):565–569.

William Warner and Julia Hirschberg. 2012. Detecting hate speech on the world wide web. In *Proceedings of the Second Workshop on Language in Social Media (LSM 2012) of the Association for Computational Linguistics (ACL 2012)*, pages 19–26.

Zeerak Waseem and Dirk Hovy. 2016. Hateful symbols or hateful people? predictive features for hate speech detection on twitter. In *Proceedings of the Student Research Workshop of the 2016 Conference of the North American Chapter of the Association for Computational Linguistics: Human Language Technologies (HLT-NAACL 2016)*, pages 88–93.

Zhi Xu and Sencun Zhu. 2010. Filtering offensive language in online communities using grammatical relations. In *Proceedings of the 7th Annual Collaboration, Electronic Messaging, Anti-Abuse and Spam Conference (CEAS 2010)*, pages 1–10.

Automatically Extracting Variant-Normalization Pairs
for Japanese Text Normalization

Itsumi Saito   Kyosuke Nishida   Kugatsu Sadamitsu[*]
Kuniko Saito   Junji Tomita
NTT Media Intelligence Laboratories
{saito.itsumi, nishida.kyosuke}@lab.ntt.co.jp
{saito.kuniko, tomita.junji}@lab.ntt.co.jp
k.sadamitsu.ic@future.co.jp

Abstract

Social media texts, such as tweets from Twitter, contain many types of non-standard tokens, and the number of normalization approaches for handling such noisy text has been increasing. We present a method for automatically extracting pairs of a variant word and its normal form from unsegmented text on the basis of a pair-wise similarity approach. We incorporated the acquired variant-normalization pairs into Japanese morphological analysis. The experimental results show that our method can extract widely covered variants from large Twitter data and improve the recall of normalization without degrading the overall accuracy of Japanese morphological analysis.

1 Introduction

Social media texts contain many non-standard tokens (lexical variants), e.g., by lengthening ("goooood" for "good") or abbreviating them ("tmrw" for "tomorrow"). Current language processing systems often fail to analyze such non-standard tokens, so normalizing them into standard tokens as a preprocess is promising for analyzing such noisy texts robustly (Cook and Stevenson, 2009; Han et al., 2012; Li and Liu, 2012, 2014). The normalization task mainly consists of two components. One is detecting variant words and generating normalization candidates. The other is constructing a word lattice from possible normalization candidates and decoding to select the best normalized word sequences. Early work on normalization focused on supervised approaches using labeled text, e.g., an approach based on a statistical machine translation

(Aw et al., 2006; Pennell and Liu, 2011). However, social network service (SNS) text has a dynamic nature, and large SNS text is costly to annotate. Recent work has been focused on unsupervised approaches. For example, Han et al. (2012) proposed generating variant-normalization pairs automatically on the basis of distributional similarity and string similarity. Hassan and Menezes (2013) developed the approach by using a graph-based approach. Yang and Eisenstein (2013) introduced a highly accurate unsupervised normalization model. As just described, unsupervised methods have been developed for English normalization tasks.

Japanese SNS text also contains variant words, and several normalization methods have been proposed (Sasano et al., 2013; Kaji and Kitsuregawa, 2014; Saito et al., 2014). The basic framework of Japanese normalization is quite similar to that of English normalization. However, the problem is more complicated in Japanese normalization because Japanese words are not segmented using explicit delimiters, so we have to estimate word segmentation simultaneously in the decoding step. Variant words are also more difficult to extract automatically in Japanese than in explicitly segmented languages such as English. Unlike English normalization, the approaches for generating normalization candidates in Japanese are based on manually created rules or supervised training using annotated text. Japanese normalization contains problems to which the English unsupervised approach is simply applied. Although the English unsupervised approach assumes that there are explicit word segmentations, conventional analyzers often fail to segment non-standard words in Japanese. Therefore, to extract variants in an unsupervised fashion, we have to introduce an idea to generate correct word segmentation of variant words.

Present affiliation: Future Architect,Inc.

Proceedings of the The 8th International Joint Conference on Natural Language Processing, pages 937–946,
Taipei, Taiwan, November 27 – December 1, 2017 ©2017 AFNLP

Our idea for this problem is to use short sentences and phrases in SNS text. SNS text, like tweets from Twitter, contains many short sentences and phrases consisting of a single word or several words. For Example, "おっはよーん！ (*ohayon*, Good Morning)" is a variant form of "おはよう！(*ohayou*)," and "ちょーさみー (*cho samii*, It is very cold)" is a variant form of "超 (*cho*, very)/寒い (*samui*, cold)." Since these short sentences often contain variant words, they can be used as efficient cues for extracting a variant word. Our idea is to not extract a variant-normalization pair in one step. Instead, we present a two-step normalization approach. In the first step, we extract coarse candidates for variant-normalization pairs from unlabeled text, and in the second step, we incorporate the extracted pairs into Japanese morphological analysis and normalization. The appropriate normalization candidates are selected in the second step. We use training data for morphological analysis in the second step but do not use annotated data in the first step. Therefore, we can efficiently extract many types of variant-normalization pairs that appear in real text.

The contributions of this study are summarized as follows.

- We developed a new method for extracting pairs of variant and normal forms from tweets, which have no explicit delimiters, by focusing on short phrases and sentences in Twitter.

- We incorporated the variant-normalization pairs extracted by our method from tweets into a Japanese morphological analysis method and statistically significantly improved the accuracy for variant words without degrading the overall accuracy for Japanese morphological analysis.

2 Background

2.1 Japanese Morphological Analysis

As we mentioned above, we have to consider Japanese normalization tasks with Japanese morphological analysis. In this section, we describe the basic idea of Japanese morphological analysis. Japanese Morphological analysis can be interpreted as ranking while using a word lattice and scores of each path (Kaji and Kitsuregawa, 2013). There are two points to consider in the analysis procedure: how to generate the

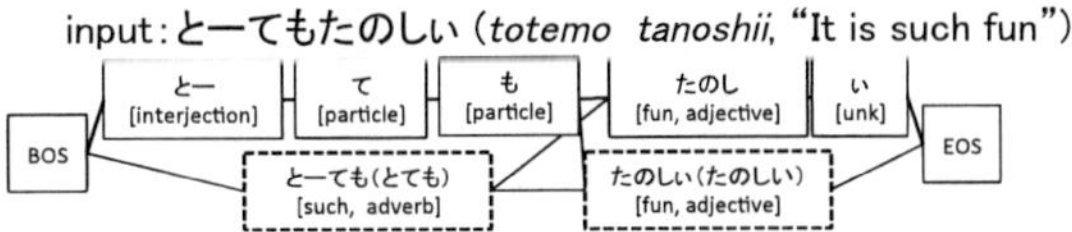

Figure 1: Example of Japanese morphological analysis and normalization

word lattice and how to formulate the score of each path. In Japanese morphological analysis, the dictionary-based approach has been widely used to generate word lattices (Kudo et al., 2004; Kaji and Kitsuregawa, 2013). To calculate the score of each path, two main scores are widely used: the score for a candidate word and the score for a pair of adjacent parts-of-speech (POSs). We can consider other various scores by using discriminative model (Kudo et al., 2004; Kaji and Kitsuregawa, 2013).

2.2 Related Work

Several studies have been conducted on Japanese morphological analysis and normalization. The approach proposed by Sasano et al. (2013) developed heuristics to flexibly search by using a simple, manually created derivational rule. Their system generates a normalized character sequence based on derivational rules and adds new nodes when generating the word lattice using dictionary lookup. Figure 1 presents an example of this approach. If the non-standard written sentence "とーてもたのしい (*totemo tanoshii*, It is such fun)" is input, the traditional dictionary-based system generates nodes that are described using solid lines, as shown in Figure 1. Since "とーても (*totemo*, such)" and "たのしい (*tanoshii*, fun)" are Out Of Vocabulary (OOVs), the traditional system cannot generate the correct word segments or POS tags. However, their system generates additional nodes for the OOVs, shown as broken line rectangles in Figure 1. In this case, derivational rules are used that substitute "ー" with "null" and "い (i)" with "い (i)", and the system can generate the standard forms "とても (*totemo*, such)" and "たのしい (*tanoshii*, fun)" and their POS tags. If we can generate sufficiently appropriate rules, these approaches seem to be effective. However, there are many types of derivational patterns in SNS text, and they are difficult to all cover manually. Moreover, how to set the path score for appropriately

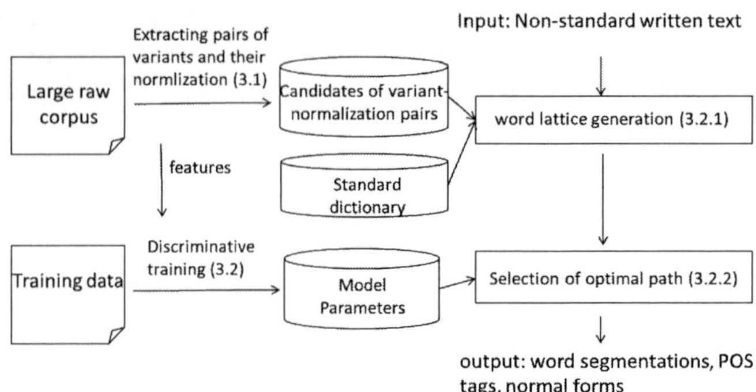

Figure 2: Overview of proposed system

ranking the word lattice when the number of candidates increases becomes a serious problem.

Saito et al. (2014) proposed supervised extraction of derivational patterns (we call them transformation patterns), incorporated these patterns into a word lattice, and formulated morphological analysis and normalization using a discriminate model. Although this approach can generate broad-coverage normalization candidates, it needs a large amount of annotation data of variant words and their normalization. Kaji and Kitsuregawa (2014) also proposed morphological analysis and normalization based on a discriminative model and created variant words on the basis of handmade rules. As far as we know, automatic extraction of variant-normalization pairs has not been researched. If we can extract variant-normalization pairs automatically, we can decrease the annotation cost and possibly increase accuracy by combining our method with other conventional methods.

Several studies have applied a character-based approach. For example, Sasaki et al. (2013) proposed a character-level sequential labeling method for normalization. However, it handles only one-to-one character transformations and does not take the word-level context into account. The proposed method can handle many-to-many character transformations and takes word-level context into account, so it has a wider scope for handling non-standard tokens.

Many studies have been done on text normalization for English; for example, Han and Baldwin (2011) classifies whether or not OOVs are non-standard tokens and estimates standard forms on the basis of contextual, string, and phonetic similarities. Han et al. (2012) and Hassan and Menezes (2013) developed the method of extracting variant-normalization pairs automatically for English. Yang and Eisenstein (2013) introduced a highly accurate unsupervised normalization model using log-linear model. In these studies, clear word segmentations were assumed to exist. However, since Japanese is unsegmented, the normalization problem needs to be treated as a joint normalization, word segmentation, and POS tagging problem.

Thus, we propose automatically extracting normalization candidates from unlabeled data and present a method for incorporating these candidates into Japanese morphological analysis and normalization. Our method can extract new variant patterns from real text.

3 Proposed Method

Our method consists of two parts. The first involves extracting normalization candidates and their normal forms from unlabeled data. The second involves a morphological analysis and normalization using extracted variants. Basically, we use a previously proposed dictionary based approach (Sasano et al., 2013; Saito et al., 2014; Kaji and Kitsuregawa, 2014), but the method for generating normalization candidates and some features used in a discriminative model are new. The proposed system is illustrated in Figure 2.

In the first part, we generate a coarsely segmented corpus and calculate the pairwise similarity of two arbitrary nodes that appear in the segmented corpus. In a previous study (Han and Baldwin, 2011), the nodes were assumed to be single words. On the other hand, our

939

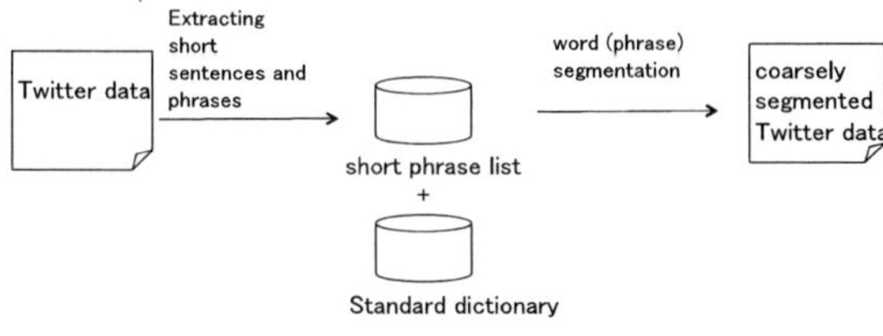

Figure 3: Flow of generating coarsely segmented corpus

method assigns a node to not only single words but also short phrases (See. 3.1). To calculate similarity between two nodes, we use semantic similarity and phonetic similarity. After calculating similarity, we filter the pairs that do not exceed a similarity threshold. We use word embeddings as a semantic similarity measure. We describe this more precisely in 3.1.2.

In the second part, the problem is how to incorporate extracted variants into Japanese morphological analysis. We use a discriminative model and Viterbi decoding for estimating word segmentation, POS tagging, and normalization. To prevent degradation induced by incorporating extracted variants, we introduce many types of features. We describe this more precisely in 3.2.

3.1 Extracting Candidates of Variant-Normalization Pairs from Twitter Texts

3.1.1 Preparation of Coarsely Segmented Corpus Using Short SNS Sentences and Phrases

We have to prepare a segmented corpus for generating normalization candidates and calculating similarity. The flow of generating coarsely segmented corpus is shown in Figure 3. As we mentioned above, we cannot determine the explicit word segmentation of unlabeled data, especially for variant words. However, we can assume that there are some explicit segmentations in text: the left and right ends of sentences and symbols such as punctuation, brackets, pictographs, emoticons, linefeed characters, commas, and spaces. SNS text contains many short sentences and phrases consisting of a word or several words. Our idea is to use the units of short sentences and short phrases delimited in symbols in SNS text as cues for extracting variant words.

More specifically, we first segment large Twitter

text with several predefined symbols, extract character sequences consisting of ten or fewer characters, and insert them into a standard dictionary. Then we segment the large twitter corpus using an expanded dictionary and conventional analyzer. An example of a segmented sentence using an expanded dictionary is "おっはよーう (*ohhayou*)/ ! (Good morning!)", whereas the result using a standard dictionary is "おっ(*o*)/は (*ha*)/よー (*yo*)/う (*u*)/ ! " Since this segmented text contains several segmentation errors and noise, we extract reliable candidates using a similarity threshold described in the next subsection.

3.1.2 Similarity Measures

To calculate the similarity between two nodes w_i and w_j appearing in a segmented corpus (3.1.1), we mainly use two similarity measures: semantic and phonetic.

Semantic Similarity We calculate semantic similarity between w_i and w_j by inducing dense real-valued low-dimensional embeddings from large unlabeled text (Mikolov et al., 2013). We use the tool word2vec [1] to calculate embeddings of each node. Semantic similarity is defined as

$$semsim(w_i, w_j) = cos(vec(w_i), vec(w_j)) \quad (1)$$

This semantic similarity is used as a feature of a normalization and morphological analysis model (3.2.3). We set the embedding size is 200.

Phonetic Similarity We first convert a surface string into pronunciations (Japanese Kanji to Hiragana) and calculate the edit distance. We use two types of edit distance: standard and modified. For calculating modified edit distance, we set the substitution cost of two strings 0.5 when two strings have the same vowels, two strings have the same consonant or two strings are vowels. We also set insertion and deletion cost of vowels 0.5, while the standard cost of substitution, insertion and deletion is 1.

We use standard edit distance and modified edit distance as a threshold of candidate filtering (3.1.3) and modified edit distance as an element of a feature of a normalization and morphological analysis model (3.2.3). For a feature and threshold, we set the phonetic similarity $psim(w_i, w_j)$ as follows:

$$psim(w_i, w_j) = \prod_{m_i, m_j} p(m_i, m_j) \quad (2)$$

---

[1] http://code.google.com/p/word2vec/

$$p(m_i, m_j) = 1 - MED(m_i, m_j)/OC(m_i, m_j)$$
$$(3)$$

Where $OC(m_i, m_j)$ indicates the total number of operations for calculating edit distance of m_i and m_j and $MED(m_i, m_j)$ indicates the modified edit distance. m_i and m_j indicate the morphemes in w_i and w_j, respectively.

To calculate morphological-level features, we analyzed w_j using conventional morphological analyzer and make morphological-level alignment using character-level alignment of w_i and w_j and morphological information of w_j. Here, w_j and w_i are regarded as a normal form and a variant form, respectively. Here is an example of w_i = "たんじょーび (birthday)" and w_j = "たんじょうび (birthday)". In this case, morphological-level alignment is (たんじょー/たんじょう, び/び) since character-level alignment is (た/た, ん/ん, じ/じ, ょ/ょ, ー/う, び/び) and word segmentation of w_j is (たんじょう, び).

3.1.3 Candidate Filtering using Similarity Measures

We calculate the pairwise similarity between two nodes appearing in a segmented corpus (3.1.1) and their filter using a similarity measure we defined (3.1.2). The set of nodes N consists of all tokens w that appear in the segmented corpus. Since there is a huge number of node pairs and most are irrelevant, we have to filter the pairs that have low similarities. Here, we set the threshold of *semsim* to 0.4, and the threshold of standard phonetic edit distance is 2. Moreover, we filter the pairs in which the consonants of the beginning phonetic symbols of each morphemes are different or morphological-level phonetic similarity $p(m_i, m_j)$ is lower than 0.6. We also filtered the candidates when the number of consonants and all characters in a variant form (except for "っ", "ん", and lower case letters) are larger than that of a normal form at morphological level. If a variant word is already exists in a standard dictionary, we filtered the candidate. Note that this filtering is not intended to exactly identify whether the pair has the relationship of variant and normalization. Since we use only two similarities, simple phonetic information and the coarsely segmented corpus in this phase, we only extract candidates of variants and their normal forms coarsely in the first step. Then, we exactly identify the word segmentation and normalization simultaneously in the

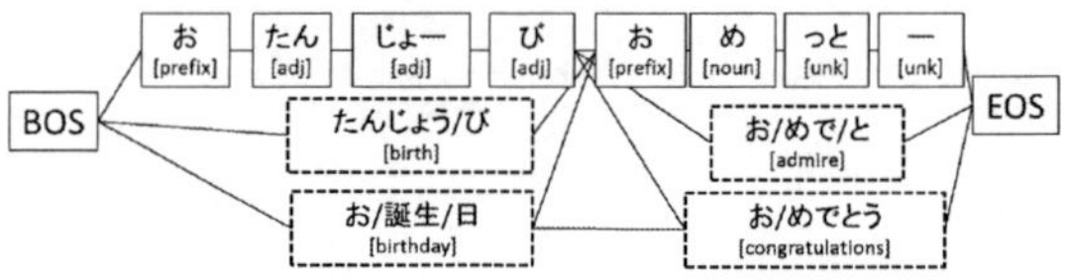

Figure 4: Example of proposed lattice

second step (3.2).

3.2 Normalization and Morphological Analysis

3.2.1 Incorporating Normalization Candidates in Japanese Morphological Analysis

We generate the word lattice using extracted candidate for variant-normalization pairs and dictionary lookup (See Figure 4). The broken line rectangles in Figure4 are nodes added by the proposed method. We exploit dictionary lookup by using the possible character sequence of the extracted normalized character sequences when variant character sequences match the input character sequences. For example, we exploit dictionary lookup for input character sequences such as "おたんじょーびおめっとー (happy birthday)" and add the possible normalized word sequences such as "お/誕生/日 (birthday) " and "お/めでとう (congratulations)" which are from extracted variant-normalization candidates. The proposed method is intended to generate normalized word sequences. In the first step, appropriateness of word segmentation is not taken into account, but in this phase, we can exactly evaluate whether the acquired pair is appropriate for normalization or not by considering the morphological connectivity.

3.2.2 Objective Function

We used a discriminative model for incorporating many features. The decoder selects the optimal sequence $\hat{y}$ from $L(s)$ when given the candidate set $L(s)$ for sentence s. This is formulated as follows (Jiang et al., 2008; Kaji and Kitsuregawa, 2013):

$$\hat{y} = \arg\max_{y \in L(s)} \mathbf{w} \cdot \mathbf{f}(y) \qquad (4)$$

Where $\hat{y}$ is the optimal path, $L(s)$ is the lattice created for s, $\mathbf{w} \cdot \mathbf{f}(y)$ is the dot product between

Name	Feature
Word unigram score	$f_{m_i p_i}$
POS bi-gram score	f_{p_{i-1}, p_i}
Character sequence score	$1/\log(p'_{t_i}/p'_s)$ if $p'_{t_i} > p'_s$ otherwise 0.
	where, $p'_x = p_x^{1/length(x)}$, $p_x = \prod_{j=1}^{k} p(c_j \mid c_{j-5}^{j-1})$, $x \in (s, t_i)$
Character similarity score	$\log(psim)$
Semantic similarity score	$\log(semsim)$
Character frequency score	$\log(freq_w + 1)$
Character and morph transformation score	$\log(freq_{ct} + 1), \log(freq_{mt} + 1), \phi_{ct}, \phi_{mt}$

Table 1: Feature list

weight vector $\mathbf{w}$ and feature vector $\mathbf{f}(y)$. The optimal path is selected in accordance with the $\mathbf{w} \cdot \mathbf{f}(y)$ value. For estimating parameters, we used the averaged perceptron, which is widely used (Collins, 2002).

3.2.3 Features

The proposed lattice generation method generates a lattice larger than that generated in traditional dictionary-based lattice generation. Therefore, we need to introduce appropriate normalization scores into the objective function to prevent degradation. Table 1 lists the features we used. Let m_i be the ith word candidate and p_i be the POS tag of m_i. p_{i-1} and m_{i-1} are adjacent POS tag and word, respectively. We used the word unigram score $f_{m_i p_i}$, the cost for a pair of adjacent POSs f_{p_{i-1}, p_i} that are estimated by MeCab [2], and additional scores.

The character sequence score reflects the character sequence probability of the normalization candidates (Saito et al., 2014). Here, s and t_i are input string and transformed string, respectively (e.g., in Figure 4, for the normalized node "お誕生日 (birthday)", s is "おたんじょーびおめっとー" and t_i is "お誕生日おめっとー". Then p_s and p_{t_i} are calculated by using the character 5-gram of a news corpus. c_j is the jth character of character sequence. We also used character sequence score as a candidate filter. We filtered the candidates that did not satisfy the pre-defined condition that $p'_s \leq p'_{t_i}$.

The character similarity score is calculated using $psim$ (see 3.1.2). The semantic similarity score is calculated using $semsim$ (see 3.1.2). The Character frequency score is a frequency of surface character sequences of variant nodes appeared in news data. Since vari-

ant words rarely appear in the news data, we use this feature to identify variant words and standard words. The character and morph transformation score is related to transformation patterns. $\log(freq_{ct} + 1)$ and $\log(freq_{mt} + 1)$ are the frequency of transformation patterns ct (character-level) and mt (morphological-level) that are extracted from variant-normalization candidates, respectively. ϕ_{ct} and ϕ_{mt} are 1 if a node contains transformation patterns ct and mt, otherwise 0, respectively. The scale of features were adjusted.

Since all those features can be factorized, the optimal path is searched by using the Viterbi algorithm.

3.2.4 Candidate Expansion

Although our method can extract many variants, we expand the variants to achieve higher recall. We use a simple rule for adding simple variation in the decoding step. For example, first, repetitions of more than one character of "ー", "〜" and "っ" are reduced to one character and repetitions of more than three characters of Japanese Hiragana and Katakana are reduced to three characters and one character. Moreover, we use the patterns of deletions of "ー", "〜", "っ" and lowercase characters (Saito et al., 2014).

4 Experiments

4.1 Data and Settings

We prepared the Balanced Corpus of Contemporary Written Japanese (BCCWJ) (Maekawa et al., 2014), which is a commonly used dataset in Japan and Twitter data. For unsupervised variant extraction, we used about 70 million unlabeled Twitter corpora. We used 2,000 sentences of BCCWJ text for training the decoder and Twitter data for the test. Twitter data contain manually annotated

---

variant forms	norm forms	translation	*semsim*
うれしーい (*ureshiii*)	うれしい (*ureshii*)	happy	0.655
うれしー (*ureshii*)	うれしい (*ureshii*)	happy	0.684
うれしぃ (*ureshii*)	うれしい (*ureshii*)	happy	0.575
うれすぃ (*uresui*)	うれしい (*ureshii*)	happy	0.568
うれちい (*uretii*)	うれしい (*ureshii*)	happy	0.649
うれしす (*ureshishu*)	うれしい (*ureshii*)	happy	0.715
かわええ (*kawaee*)	かわいい (*kawaii*)	cute	0.744
かんわいい (*kanwaii*)	かわいい (*kawaii*)	cute	0.683
きゃわいい (*kyawaii*)	かわいい (*kawaii*)	cute	0.770
お/ねげー/し/ます (*o/negee/shi/masu*)	お/ねがい/し/ます (*o/negai/shi/masu*)	please	0.657
お/ながい/し/ます (*o/nagai/si/masu*)	お/ねがい/し/ます (*o/negai/shi/masu*)	please	0.590
お/ねがい/し/まふ (*o/negai/shi/mahu*)	お/ねがい/し/ます (*o/negai/shi/masu*)	please	0.678
ちかれ/た (*tikare/ta*)	疲れ/た (*tukare/ta*)	I'm tired	0.742
お/めでとー (*o/medeto*)	お/めでとう (*o/medetou*)	congratulations	0.911
お/めでとぉ (*o/medeto*)	お/めでとう (*o/medetou*)	congratulations	0.796
お/めっとー (*o/metto*)	お/めでとう (*o/medetou*)	congratulations	0.753
お/めてとう (*o/meteto*)	お/めでとう (*o/medetou*)	congratulations	0.665

Table 2: Example of extracted pair of variants-normalization candidates

word segmentations, POS tags, and normal forms for variant words and consist of 7,213 sentences and 995 variant words. We used Unidic (unidic-mecab) [3] as a standard dictionary.

4.2 Baselines and Evaluation Metrics

We compared the three methods listed in Table 3 in our experiments. Conventional means a method that generates no normalization candidates and only uses the word cost and the cost for a pair of adjacent POSs, so we can consider it as a conventional Japanese morphological analysis. Rule-based means the conventional rule-based method proposed by Sasano et al. (2013). The rule-based method considers insertion of long sound symbols and lowercase characters and substitution with long sound symbols and lowercase characters. We basically use the transformation rule of Sasano et al. (2013) and use three features for the model of Rule-based method: the word score, score for a pair of adjacent POSs, and character transformation score. The character transformation score is constant for all transformation rules. Proposed is our method. We used extracted variant-normalization pairs and all features described in 3.2.3.

We evaluated each method on the basis of precision, recall, and the F-value for the overall system accuracy and the recall for normalization. Since Japanese morphological analysis simultaneously estimates the word segmentation and POS tagging, we have to assess whether or not adding the normalization candidates negatively affects a system.

4.3 Results

4.3.1 Results of Extracted Variant-Normalization Candidates

Table 2 lists examples of the extracted variant-normalization candidates. Our method automatically extracted well-known transformation patterns such as substitution of lowercase characters, insertion of lowercase characters, and insertion of "ー" and "っ" such as "うれしーい (*ureshii*)".

Our method also extracted more variant phonetic transformation patterns such as substitution of "shi" with "pi," "ji," or "hi" and these combinations such as "うれちい (*uretii*)". We also list examples of extracted multi-word variant-normalization pairs. The phrase "お/ねげー/し/ます (*o/nege/shi/masu*)" is a variant pattern of the original phrase "お/ねがい/します (*o/negai/shi/masu*)". Our method extracted these multi-word mappings.

Moreover, our method can extract typing errors such as "お/めでとう (*o/medetou*)" with "お/めてとう (*o/meteto*)" and slang such as "うれしす (*ureshisu*)" with "うれしい (*ureshii*)." Such relatively less frequent patterns were often excluded from normalization targets. Our method also extracts many paraphrases: semantically and phonetically similar pairs that are not variant-normalization

<hr>

[3]http://osdn.jp/projects/unidic/ (in Japanese)

943

method	word seg			word seg and POS tag			normalization
	prec	rec	F	prec	rec	F	rec
Conventional	0.865	0.949	0.905	0.837	0.919	0.876	-
Rule-based	0.879	0.952	0.914	0.848	0.918	0.881	0.294
Proposed	0.882	0.951	**0.915**	0.851	0.918	**0.883**	**0.340**

Table 3: Test data (Twitter) precision, recall, and F-value results

proposed	conventional	gold	*translation*
(1) おも (思っ) /た *omo* (omott) */ta*	おもた *omota*	おも (思っ) /た *omo* (omott) */ta*	I thought
(2) ばよりん (バイオリン) *bayorin* (*baiorin*)	ば/より/ん *ba/yo/rin*	ばよりん (バイオリン) *bayorin* (*baiorin*)	violin
(3) かんわいい (かわいい) *kanwaii* (*kawaii*)	かん/わ/いい *kan/wa /ii*	かんわいい (かわいい) *kanwaii* (*kawaii*)	cute
(4) さっむ (寒い) *samu* (*samui*)	さっ/む *sa/mu*	さっむ (寒い) *samu* (*samui*)	It is cold
(5) わろえる (笑える) *waroeru* (*waraeru*)	わろ/える *waro/eru*	わろえる (笑える) *waroeru* (*waraeru*)	It is funny
(6) おー/こく *oo/koku*	おー/こく *oo/koku*	おーこく (王国) *ookoku* (*oukoku*)	Kingdom
(7) ついった (ツイート) *tuitta* (*tuitta*)	つ/いっ/た *tu/i/ta*	ついった (ツイッター) *tuitta* (*tuitta*)	Twitter

"/" indicates the estimated word segmentation. Words in parentheses "()" are estimated normal forms. Underlined words are variant words.

Table 4: Example of morphological analysis and normalization outputs

pairs. This often degrades the results of morphological analysis. We use a discriminative model to prevent such paraphrase pairs appearing in the decoding step.

4.3.2 Morphological Analysis and Normalization Results

Tables 3 and 4 list the results for the Twitter text. The F-value of the proposed method is significantly higher than those of the conventional method and rule-based method. Our method was able to extract broad-coverage variant words, and these candidates also improve the recall of normalization without degrading the overall accuracy of morphological analysis.

Table 4 show examples of the system output. In the table, slashes indicate the positions of the estimated word segmentations, and the correctly analyzed words are written in bold. Examples (1) to (5) are examples improved by using the proposed method. Examples (6) and (7) are examples that were not improved.

Error Analysis There were roughly two types of errors. The first occurred as a result of a lack of variant-normalization candidates, and the second was search errors. Example (6) shows an example of a case in which our method could not generate the correct normalized form because we could not extract the correct normalized form. Because we extract normalization candidates by phrase level, some patterns are difficult to extract as a word unit. To increase recall, we need to extract character-level and morph-level transformation patterns that occur frequently from phrase-level patterns and add them into morphological analysis and normalization. Example (7) shows an example of a case in which a normalized candidate was generated but a search failed. We will need to develop a more complicated model or introduce other features into the current model to reduce the number of search errors.

Besides the above errors, there are some errors in which correct normalization candidates were filtered. In this study, we filtered many candidates to eliminate noise. Some normalization candidates are filtered, and the correct normalization candidates cannot be generated in the word lattice. To increase recall further, we have to filter functions or calculate similarity scores more precisely. Also, some errors are associated with unknown words. Twitter data contain many unknown words such as names, and our system sometimes treats these names as other nouns. Non-standard and standard words needs to be more precisely discriminated between for higher accuracy.

5 Conclusion and Future Work

We introduced a new idea for extracting variant words from an unsegmented corpus and incorporated it into morphological analysis. The proposed method can effectively analyze noisy words without manual annotation. The limitation of this work is that this method is based on phonetic similarity. Although our method can extract many variant patterns, it cannot extract a pair of words that have quite low phonetic similarity. In addition, our method is based on a heuristic segmentation method for extracting normalization candidates. Though it works well in practice, we want to extend this idea for a more general framework.

In future work, we would like to increase the coverage of variant-normalization pairs. For this, we have to extract the character- and morph-level transformation patterns from the acquired phrase level variant-normalization pairs.

References

AiTi Aw, Min Zhang, Juan Xiao, and Jian Su. 2006. A phrase-based statistical model for sms text normalization. *Proceedings of the COLING/ACL on Main Conference Poster Sessions*, pages 33–40.

Michael Collins. 2002. Discriminative training methods for hidden markov models: Theory and experiments with perceptron algorithms. In *Proceedings of the 2002 Joint Conference on Empirical Methods in Natural Language Processing*, pages 1–8.

Paul Cook and Suzanne Stevenson. 2009. An unsupervised model for text message normalization. *Proceedings of the Workshop on Computational Approaches to Linguistic Creativity*, pages 71–78.

Bo Han and Timothy Baldwin. 2011. Lexical normalisation of short text messages: Makn sens a #twitter. *Proceedings of the 49th Annual Meeting of the Association for Computational Linguistics: Human Language Technologies - Volume 1*, pages 368–378.

Bo Han, Paul Cook, and Timothy Baldwin. 2012. Automatically constructing a normalisation dictionary for microblogs. *Proceedings of the 2012 Joint Conference on Empirical Methods in Natural Language Processing and Computational Natural Language Learning*, pages 421–432.

Hany Hassan and Arul Menezes. 2013. Social text normalization using contextual graph random walks. *Proceedings of the 51st Annual Meeting of the Association for Computational Linguistics (Volume 1: Long Papers)*, pages 1577–1586.

Wenbin Jiang, Haitao Mi, and Qun Liu. 2008. Word lattice reranking for chinese word segmentation and part-of-speech tagging. *Proceedings of the 22Nd International Conference on Computational Linguistics - Volume 1*, pages 385–392.

Nobuhiro Kaji and Masaru Kitsuregawa. 2013. Efficient word lattice generation for joint word segmentation and pos tagging in japanese. *Proceedings of the Sixth International Joint Conference on Natural Language Processing*, pages 153–161.

Nobuhiro Kaji and Masaru Kitsuregawa. 2014. Accurate word segmentation and pos tagging for japanese microblogs: Corpus annotation and joint modeling with lexical normalization. In *Proceedings of the 2014 Conference on Empirical Methods in Natural Language Processing (EMNLP)*, pages 99–109, Doha, Qatar. Association for Computational Linguistics.

Taku Kudo, Kaoru Yamamoto, and Yuji Matsumoto. 2004. Applying conditional random fields to japanese morphological analysis. *In Proc. of EMNLP*, pages 230–237.

Chen Li and Yang Liu. 2012. Improving text normalization using character-blocks based models and system combination. *Proceedings of COLING 2012*, pages 1587–1602.

Chen Li and Yang Liu. 2014. Improving text normalization via unsupervised model and discriminative reranking. In *Proceedings of the ACL 2014 Student Research Workshop*, pages 86–93, Baltimore, Maryland, USA. Association for Computational Linguistics.

Kikuo Maekawa, Makoto Yamazaki, Toshinobu Ogiso, Takehiko Maruyama, Hideki Ogura, Wakako Kashino, Hanae Koiso, Masaya Yamaguchi, Makiro Tanaka, and Yasuharu Den. 2014. Balanced corpus of contemporary written japanese. *Language Resources and Evaluation*, pages 345–371.

Tomas Mikolov, Wen-tau Yih, and Geoffrey Zweig. 2013. Linguistic regularities in continuous space word representations. In *Proceedings of the 2013 Conference of the North American Chapter of the Association for Computational Linguistics: Human Language Technologies*, pages 746–751, Atlanta, Georgia. Association for Computational Linguistics.

Deana Pennell and Yang Liu. 2011. A character-level machine translation approach for normalization of sms abbreviations. *Proceedings of 5th International Joint Conference on Natural Language Processing*, pages 974–982.

Itsumi Saito, Kugatsu Sadamitsu, Hisako Asano, and Yoshihiro Matsuo. 2014. Morphological analysis for japanese noisy text based on character-level and word-level normalization. In *Proceedings of COL-ING 2014, the 25th International Conference on Computational Linguistics: Technical Papers*, pages 1773–1782, Dublin, Ireland. Dublin City University and Association for Computational Linguistics.

Akira Sasaki, Junta Mizuno, Naoaki Okazaki, and Kentaro Inui. 2013. Normalization of text in microblogging based on machine learning(in japanese) (in japanese). *In Proc. of The 27th Annual Conference of the Japanese Society for Articial Intelligence.*

Ryohei Sasano, Sadao Kurohashi, and Manabu Okumura. 2013. A simple approach to unknown word processing in japanese morphological analysis. *Proceedings of the Sixth International Joint Conference on Natural Language Processing*, pages 162–170.

Yi Yang and Jacob Eisenstein. 2013. A log-linear model for unsupervised text normalization. In *Proceedings of the 2013 Conference on Empirical Methods in Natural Language Processing*, pages 61–72, Seattle, Washington, USA. Association for Computational Linguistics.

Semantic Document Distance Measures and Unsupervised Document Revision Detection

Xiaofeng Zhu, Diego Klabjan
Northwestern University, USA
xiaofengzhu2013@u.northwestern.edu
d-klabjan@northwestern.edu

Patrick N Bless
Intel Corporation,
Chandler, AZ, USA
patrick.n.bless@intel.com

Abstract

In this paper, we model the document revision detection problem as a minimum cost branching problem that relies on computing document distances. Furthermore, we propose two new document distance measures, word vector-based Dynamic Time Warping (wDTW) and word vector-based Tree Edit Distance (wTED). Our revision detection system is designed for a large scale corpus and implemented in Apache Spark. We demonstrate that our system can more precisely detect revisions than state-of-the-art methods by utilizing the Wikipedia revision dumps [1] and simulated data sets.

1 Introduction

It is a common habit for people to keep several versions of documents, which creates duplicate data. A scholarly article is normally revised several times before being published. An academic paper may be listed on personal websites, digital conference libraries, Google Scholar, etc. In major corporations, a document typically goes through several revisions involving multiple editors and authors. Users would benefit from visualizing the entire history of a document. It is worthwhile to develop a system that is able to intelligently identify, manage and represent revisions. Given a collection of text documents, our study identifies revision relationships in a completely unsupervised way. For each document in a corpus we only use its content and the last modified timestamp. We assume that a document can be revised by many users, but that the documents are not merged together. We consider collaborative editing as revising documents one by one.

[1] https://snap.stanford.edu/data/wiki-meta.html

The two research problems that are most relevant to document revision detection are plagiarism detection and revision provenance. In a plagiarism detection system, every incoming document is compared with all registered non-plagiarized documents (Si et al., 1997; Oberreuter and VeláSquez, 2013; Hagen et al., 2015; Abdi et al., 2015). The system returns true if an original copy is found in the database; otherwise, the system returns false and adds the document to the database. Thus, it is a 1-to-n problem. Revision provenance is a 1-to-1 problem as it keeps track of detailed updates of one document (Buneman et al., 2001; Zhang and Jagadish, 2013). Real-world applications include GitHub, version control in Microsoft Word and Wikipedia version trees (Sabel, 2007). In contrast, our system solves an n-to-n problem on a large scale. Our potential target data sources, such as the entire web or internal corpora in corporations, contain numerous original documents and their revisions. The aim is to find all revision document pairs within a reasonable time.

Document revision detection, plagiarism detection and revision provenance all rely on comparing the content of two documents and assessing a distance/similarity score. The classic document similarity measure, especially for plagiarism detection, is fingerprinting (Hoad and Zobel, 2003; Charikar, 2002; Schleimer et al., 2003; Fujii and Ishikawa, 2001; Manku et al., 2007; Manber et al., 1994). Fixed-length fingerprints are created using hash functions to represent document features and are then used to measure document similarities. However, the main purpose of fingerprinting is to reduce computation instead of improving accuracy, and it cannot capture word semantics. Another widely used approach is computing the sentence-to-sentence Levenshtein distance and assigning an overall score for every document pair (Gustafson et al., 2008). Neverthe-

Proceedings of the The 8th International Joint Conference on Natural Language Processing, pages 947–956,
Taipei, Taiwan, November 27 – December 1, 2017 ©2017 AFNLP

less, due to the large number of existing documents, as well as the large number of sentences in each document, the Levenshtein distance is not computation-friendly. Although alternatives such as the vector space model (VSM) can largely reduce the computation time, their effectiveness is low. More importantly, none of the above approaches can capture semantic meanings of words, which heavily limits the performances of these approaches. For instance, from a semantic perspective, "*I went to the bank*" is expected to be similar to "*I withdrew some money*" rather than "*I went hiking.*" Our document distance measures are inspired by the weaknesses of current document distance/similarity measures and recently proposed models for word representations such as word2vec (Mikolov et al., 2013) and Paragraph Vector (PV) (Le and Mikolov, 2014). Replacing words with distributed vector embeddings makes it feasible to measure semantic distances using advanced algorithms, e.g., Dynamic Time Warping (DTW) (Sakurai et al., 2005; Müller, 2007; Matuschek et al., 2008) and Tree Edit Distance (TED) (Tai, 1979; Zhang and Shasha, 1989; Klein, 1998; Demaine et al., 2007; Pawlik and Augsten, 2011, 2014, 2015, 2016). Although calculating text distance using DTW (Liu et al., 2007), TED (Sidorov et al., 2015) or Word Mover's Distance (WMV) (Kusner et al., 2015) has been attempted in the past, these measures are not ideal for large-scale document distance calculation. The first two algorithms were designed for sentence distances instead of document distances. The third measure computes the distance of two documents by solving a transshipment problem between words in the two documents and uses word2vec embeddings to calculate semantic distances of words. The biggest limitation of WMV is its long computation time. We show in Section 5.3 that our wDTW and wTED measures yield more precise distance scores with much shorter running time than WMV.

We recast the problem of detecting document revisions as a network optimization problem (see Section 2) and consequently as a set of document distance problems (see Section 4). We use trained word vectors to represent words, concatenate the word vectors to represent documents and combine word2vec with DTW or TED. Meanwhile, in order to guarantee reasonable computation time in large data sets, we calculate document distances at the paragraph level with Apache Spark. A distance score is computed by feeding paragraph representations to DTW or TED. Our code and data are publicly available. [2]

The primary contributions of this work are as follows.

- We specify a model and algorithm to find the optimal document revision network from a large corpus.

- We propose two algorithms, wDTW and wTED, for measuring semantic document distances based on distributed representations of words. The wDTW algorithm calculates document distances based on DTW by sequentially comparing any two paragraphs of two documents. The wTED method represents the section and subsection structures of a document in a tree with paragraphs being leaves. Both algorithms hinge on the distance between two paragraphs.

The rest of this paper is organized in five parts. In Section 2, we clarify related terms and explain the methodology for document revision detection. In Section 3, we provide a brief background on existing document similarity measures and present our wDTW and wTED algorithms as well as the overall process flow. In Section 4, we demonstrate our revision detection results on Wikipedia revision dumps and six simulated data sets. Finally, in Section 5, we summarize some concluding remarks and discuss avenues for future work and improvements.

2 Revision Network

The two requirements for a document $\bar{D}$ being a revision of another document $\tilde{D}$ are that $\bar{D}$ has been created later than $\tilde{D}$ and that the content of $\bar{D}$ is similar to (has been modified from) that of $\tilde{D}$. More specifically, given a corpus $\mathscr{D}$, for any two documents $\bar{D}, \tilde{D} \in \mathscr{D}$, we want to find out the yes/no revision relationship of $\bar{D}$ and $\tilde{D}$, and then output all such revision pairs.

We assume that each document has a creation date (the last modified timestamp) which is readily available from the meta data of the document. In this section we also assume that we have a *Dist* method and a cut-off threshold τ. We represent a corpus as network $N^0 = (V^0, A)$, for example

---

[2]https://github.com/XiaofengZhu/wDTW-wTED

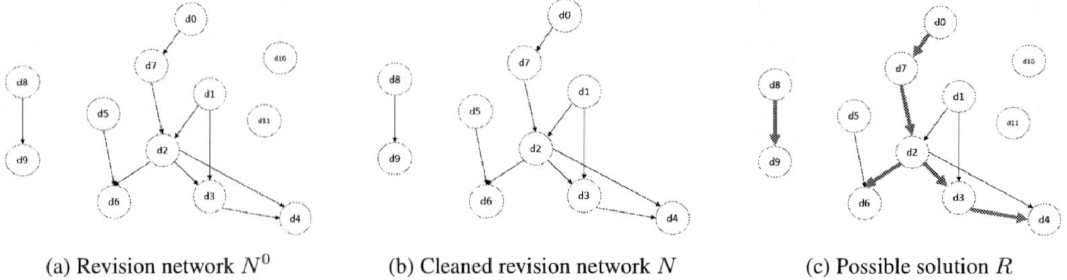

|(a) Revision network N^0|(b) Cleaned revision network N|(c) Possible solution R|

Figure 1: Revision network visualization

Figure 1a, in which a vertex corresponds to a document. There is an arc $a = (\bar{D}, \tilde{D})$ if and only if $Dist(\bar{D}, \tilde{D}) \leq \tau$ and the creation date of $\bar{D}$ is before the creation date of $\tilde{D}$. In other words, $\tilde{D}$ is a revision candidate for $\bar{D}$. By construction, N^0 is acyclic. For instance, d_2 is a revision candidate for d_7 and d_1. Note that we allow one document to be the original document of several revised documents. As we only need to focus on revision candidates, we reduce N^0 to $N = (V, A)$, shown in Figure 1b, by removing isolated vertices. We define the weight of an arc as the distance score between the two vertices. Recall the assumption that a document can be a revision of at most one document. In other words, documents cannot be merged. Due to this assumption, all revision pairs form a branching in N. (A branching is a subgraph where each vertex has an in-degree of at most 1.) The document revision problem is to find a minimum cost branching in N (see Fig 1c).

The minimum branching problem was earlier solved by Edmonds (1967) and Velardi et al. (2013). The details of his algorithm are as follows.

- For each node select the smallest weighted incoming arc. This yields a subgraph.

- If cycles are present in the selected subgraph, then recursively find the replacing arc that has the minimum weight among previously non-selected arcs to eliminate cycles.

In our case, N is acyclic and, therefore, the second step never occurs. For this reason, Algorithm 1 solves the document revision problem.

The essential part of determining the minimum branching R is extracting arcs with the lowest distance scores. This is equivalent to finding the most similar document from the revision candidates for every original document.

Algorithm 1 Find minimum branching R for network $N = (V, A)$

1: **Input:** N
2: $R = \emptyset$
3: **for** every vertex $v \in V$ **do**
4:     Set $\delta(u)$ to correspond to all arcs with head u.
5:     Select $a = (v, u) \in \delta(u)$ such that $Dist(v, u)$ is minimum
6:     $R = R \cup a$
7: **end for**
8: **Output:** R

---

3   Distance/similarity Measures

In this section, we first introduce the classic VSM model, the word2vec model, DTW and TED. We next demonstrate how to combine the above components to construct our semantic document distance measures: wDTW and wTED. We also discuss the implementation of our revision detection system.

3.1   Background

3.1.1   Vector Space Model

VSM represents a set of documents as vectors of identifiers. The identifier of a word used in this work is the tf-idf weight. We represent documents as tf-idf vectors, and thus the similarity of two documents can be described by the cosine distance between their vectors. VSM has low algorithm complexity but cannot represent the semantics of words since it is based on the bag-of-words assumption.

3.1.2   Word2vec

Word2vec produces semantic embeddings for words using a two-layer neural network. Specifically, word2vec relies on a skip-gram model that uses the current word to predict context words in a surrounding window to maximize the average log probability. Words with similar meanings tend to have similar embeddings.

3.1.3 Dynamic Time Warping

DTW was developed originally for speech recognition in time series analysis and has been widely used to measure the distance between two sequences of vectors.

Given two sequences of feature vectors: $A = a_1, a_2, ..., a_i, ..., a_m$ and $B = b_1, b_2, ..., b_j, ..., b_n$, DTW finds the optimal alignment for A and B by first constructing an $(m + 1) \times (n + 1)$ matrix in which the $(i, j)^{th}$ element is the alignment cost of $a_1...a_i$ and $b_1...b_j$, and then retrieving the path from one corner to the diagonal one through the matrix that has the minimal cumulative distance. This algorithm is described by the following formula.

$$DTW(i, j) = Dist(a_i, b_j) + min($$
$$DTW(i - 1, j), \quad //insertion$$
$$DTW(i, j - 1), \quad //deletion$$
$$DTW(i - 1, j - 1)) \ //substitution$$

3.1.4 Tree Edit Distance

TED was initially defined to calculate the minimal cost of node edit operations for transforming one labeled tree into another. The node edit operations are defined as follows.

- **Deletion** Delete a node and connect its children to its parent maintaining the order.

- **Insertion** Insert a node between an existing node and a subsequence of consecutive children of this node.

- **Substitution** Rename the label of a node.

Let L_1 and L_2 be two labeled trees, and $L_k[i]$ be the ith node in $L_k(k = 1, 2)$. M corresponds to a mapping from L_1 to L_2. TED finds mapping M with the minimal edit cost based on

$$c(M) = min\{ \sum_{(i,j) \in M} cost(L_1[i] \rightarrow L_2[j])$$
$$+ \sum_{i \in I} cost(L_1[i] \rightarrow \wedge)$$
$$+ \sum_{j \in J} cost(\wedge \rightarrow L_2[j])\}$$

where $L_1[i] \rightarrow L_2[j]$ means transferring $L_1[i]$ to $L_2[j]$ based on M, and $\wedge$ represents an empty node.

3.2 Semantic Distance between Paragraphs

According to the description of DTW in Section 3.1.3, the distance between two documents can be calculated using DTW by replacing each element in the feature vectors A and B with a word vector. However, computing the DTW distance between two documents at the word level is basically as expensive as calculating the Levenshtein distance. Thus in this section we propose an improved algorithm that is more appropriate for document distance calculation.

In order to receive semantic representations for documents and maintain a reasonable algorithm complexity, we use word2vec to train word vectors and represent each paragraph as a sequence of vectors. Note that in both wDTW and wTED we take document titles and section titles as paragraphs. Although a more recently proposed model PV can directly train vector representations for short texts such as movie reviews (Le and Mikolov, 2014), our experiments in Section 5.3 show that PV is not appropriate for standard paragraphs in general documents. Therefore, we use word2vec in our work. Algorithm 2 describes how we compute the distance between two paragraphs based on DTW and word vectors. The distance between one paragraph in a document and one paragraph in another document can be pre-calculated in parallel using Spark to provide faster computation for wDTW and wTED.

Algorithm 2 DistPara

Replace the words in paragraphs p and q with word2vec embeddings: $\{v_i\}_{i=1}^{e}$ and $\{w_j\}_{j=1}^{f}$
Input: $p = [v_1, .., v_e]$ and $q = [w_1, .., w_f]$
Initialize the first row and the first column of $(e + 1) \times (f + 1)$ matrix DTW_{para} $+\infty$
$DTW_{para}(0, 0) = 0$
for i in range $(1, e + 1)$ **do**
    for j in range $(1, f + 1)$ **do**
        $Dist(v_i, w_j) = ||v_i - w_j||$
        calculate $DTW_{para}(i, j)$
    end for
end for
Return: $DTW_{para}(e, f)$

---

4 wDTW and wTED Measures

4.1 Word Vector-based Dynamic Time Warping

As a document can be considered as a sequence of paragraphs, wDTW returns the distance between two documents by applying another DTW on top of paragraphs. The cost function is exactly the DistPara distance of two paragraphs given in Algorithm 2. Algorithm 3 and Figure 2 describe our wDTW measure. wDTW observes semantic information from word vectors, which is fundamentally different from the word distance calculated from hierarchies among words in the algorithm proposed by Liu et al. (2007). The shortcomings of their work are that it is difficult to learn semantic taxonomy of all words and that their DTW algorithm can only be applied to sentences not documents.

Algorithm 3 wDTW

> Represent documents d_1 and d_2 with vectors of paragraphs: $\{p_i\}_{i=1}^{m}$ and $\{q_j\}_{j=1}^{n}$
> **Input:** $d_1 = [p_1, .., p_m]$ and $d_2 = [q_1, .., q_n]$
> Initialize the first row and the first column of $(m+1) \times (n+1)$ matrix $DTW_{doc} + \infty$
> $DTW_{doc}(0,0) = 0$
> **for** i in range $(1, m+1)$ **do**
>   **for** j in range $(1, n+1)$ **do**
> $Dist(p_i, q_j) = \text{DistPara}(p_i, q_j)$
>   calculate $DTW_{doc}(i, j)$
>   **end for**
> **end for**
> **Return:** $DTW_{doc}(m, n)$

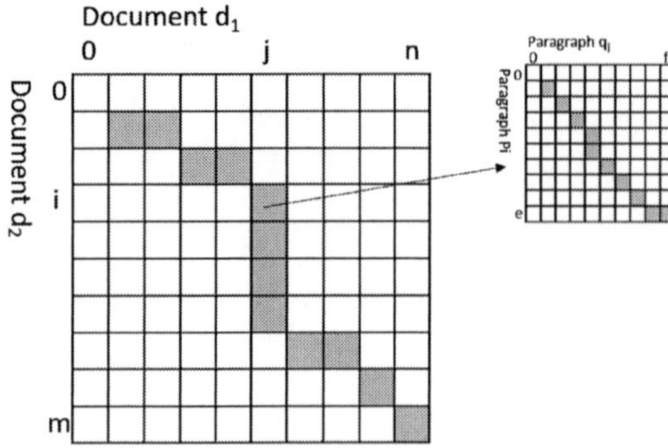

Figure 2: wDTW visualization

4.2 Word Vector-based Tree Edit Distance

TED is reasonable for measuring document distances as documents can be easily transformed to tree structures visualized in Figure 3. The document tree concept was originally proposed by Si et al. (1997). A document can be viewed at multiple abstraction levels that include the document title, its sections, subsections, etc. Thus for each document we can build a tree-like structure with title $\rightarrow$ sections $\rightarrow$ subsections $\rightarrow...\rightarrow$ paragraphs being paths from the root to leaves. Child nodes are ordered from left to right as they appear in the document.

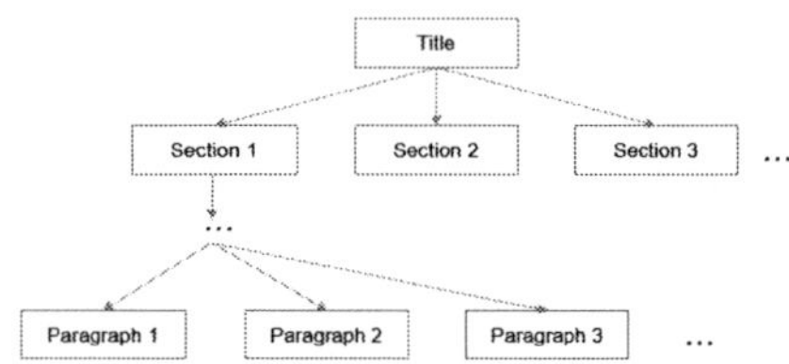

Figure 3: Document tree

We represent labels in a document tree as the vector sequences of titles, sections, subsections and paragraphs with word2vec embeddings. wTED converts documents to tree structures and then uses DistPara distances. More formally, the distance between two nodes is computed as follows.

- The cost of substitution is the DistPara value of the two nodes.

- The cost of insertion is the DistPara value of an empty sequence and the label of the inserted node. This essentially means that the cost is the sum of the L2-norms of the word vectors in that node.

- The cost of deletion is the same as the cost of insertion.

Compared to the algorithm proposed by Sidorov et al. (2015), wTED provides different edit cost functions and uses document tree structures instead of syntactic n-grams, and thus wTED yields more meaningful distance scores for long documents. Algorithm 4 and Figure 4 describe how we calculate the edit cost between two document trees.

Algorithm 4 wTED
1: Convert documents d_1 and d_2 to trees T_1 and T_2
2: **Input:** T_1 and T_2
3: Initialize tree edit distance $c = +\infty$
4: **for** node label $p \in T_1$ **do**
5:    **for** node label $q \in T_2$ **do**
6:       Update TED mapping cost c using
7:       $cost(p \rightarrow q) = \mathrm{DistPara}(p, q)$
8:       $cost(p \rightarrow \wedge) = \mathrm{DistPara}(p, \wedge)$
9:       $cost(\wedge \rightarrow q) = \mathrm{DistPara}(\wedge, q)$
10:   **end for**
11: **end for**
12: **Return:** c

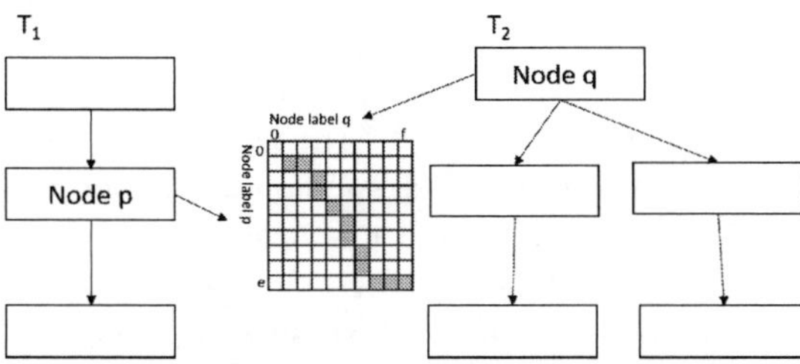

Figure 4: wTED visualization

4.3 Process Flow

Our system is a boosting learner that is composed of four modules: weak filter, strong filter, revision network and optimal subnetwork. First of all, we sort all documents by timestamps and pair up documents so that we only compare each document with documents that have been created earlier. In the first module, we calculate the VSM similarity scores for all pairs and eliminate those with scores that are lower than an empirical threshold ($\tilde{\tau} = 0.5$). This is what we call the weak filter. After that, we apply the strong filter wDTW or wTED on the available pairs and filter out document pairs having distances higher than a threshold τ. For VSM in Section 5.1, we directly filter out document pairs having similarity scores lower than a threshold τ. The cut-off threshold estimation is explained in Section 4.4. The remaining document pairs from the strong filter are then sent to the revision network module. In the end, we output the optimal revision pairs following the minimum branching strategy.

4.4 Estimating the Cut-off Threshold

Hyperprameter τ is calibrated by calculating the absolute extreme based on an initial set of documents, i.e., all processed documents since the moment the system was put in use. Based on this set, we calculate all distance/similarity scores and create a histogram, see Figure 5. The figure shows the correlation between the number of document pairs and the similarity scores in the training process of one simulated corpus using VSM. The optimal τ in this example is around 0.6 where the number of document pairs noticeably drops.

As the system continues running, new documents become available and τ can be periodically updated by using the same method.

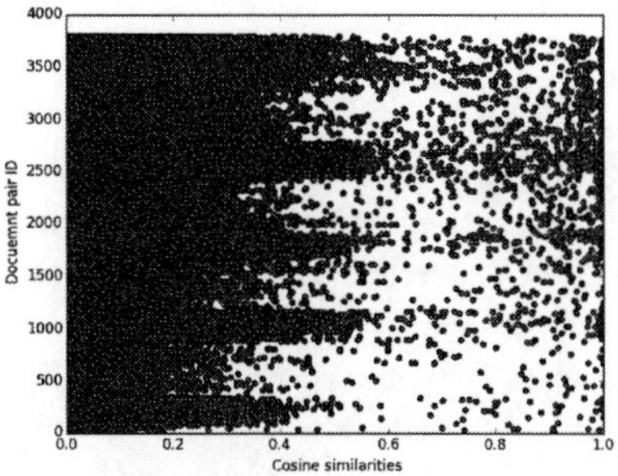

Figure 5: Setting τ

5 Numerical Experiments

This section reports the results of the experiments conducted on two data sets for evaluating the performances of wDTW and wTED against other baseline methods.

5.1 Distance/Similarity Measures

We denote the following distance/similarity measures.

- wDTW: Our semantic distance measure explained in Section 4.1.

- wTED: Our semantic distance measure explained in Section 4.2.

- WMD: The Word Mover's Distance introduced in Section 1. WMD adapts the earth mover's distance to the space of documents.

- VSM: The similarity measure introduced in Section 3.1.1.

– PV-DTW: PV-DTW is the same as Algorithm 3 except that the distance between two paragraphs is not based on Algorithm 2 but rather computed as $\|PV(p_1) - PV(p_2)\|$ where $PV(p)$ is the PV embedding of paragraph p.

– PV-TED: PV-TED is the same as Algorithm 4 except that the distance between two paragraphs is not based on Algorithm 2 but rather computed as $\|PV(p_1) - PV(p_2)\|$.

Our experiments were conducted on an Apache Spark cluster with 32 cores and 320 GB total memory. We implemented wDTW, wTED, WMD, VSM, PV-DTW and PV-TED in Java Spark. The paragraph vectors for PV-DTW and PV-TED were trained by gensim. [3]

5.2 Data Sets

In this section, we introduce the two data sets we used for our revision detection experiments: Wikipedia revision dumps and a document revision data set generated by a computer simulation. The two data sets differ in that the Wikipedia revision dumps only contain linear revision chains, while the simulated data sets also contains tree-structured revision chains, which can be very common in real-world data.

5.2.1 Wikipedia Revision Dumps

The Wikipedia revision dumps that were previously introduced by Leskovec et al. (2010) contain eight GB (compressed size) revision edits with meta data.

We pre-processed the Wikipedia revision dumps using the JWPL Revision Machine (Ferschke et al., 2011) and produced a data set that contains 62,234 documents with 46,354 revisions. As we noticed that short documents just contributed to noise (graffiti) in the data, we eliminated documents that have fewer than three paragraphs and fewer than 300 words. We removed empty lines in the documents and trained word2vec embeddings on the entire corpus. We used the documents occurring in the first 80% of the revision period for τ calibration, and the remaining documents for test.

5.2.2 Simulated Data Sets

The generation process of the simulated data sets is designed to mimic the real world. Users open

[3]https://radimrehurek.com/gensim/models/doc2vec.html

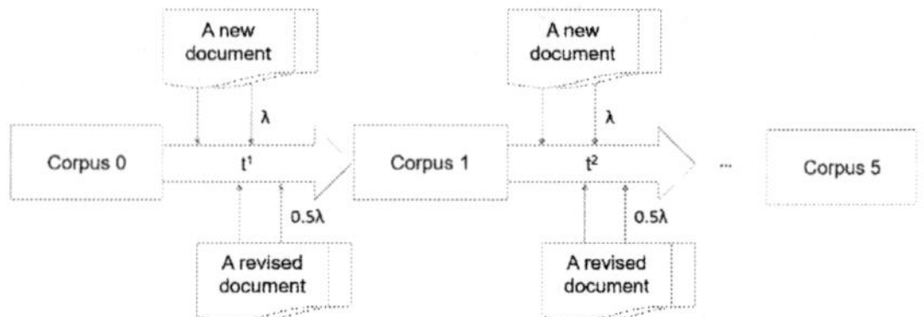

Figure 6: Corpora simulation

some existing documents in a file system, make some changes (e.g. *addition, deletion* or *replacement*), and save them as separate documents. These documents become revisions of the original documents. We started from an initial corpus that did not have revisions, and kept adding new documents and revising existing documents. Similar to a file system, at any moment new documents could be added and/or some of the current documents could be revised. The revision operations we used were *deletion, addition* and *replacement* of words, sentences, paragraphs, section names and document titles. The *addition* of words, ..., section names, and new documents were pulled from the Wikipedia abstracts. This corpus generation process had five time periods $\{t^1, t^2, ..., t^5\}$. Figure 6 illustrates this simulation. We set a Poisson distribution with rate $\lambda = 550$ (the number of documents in the initial corpus) to control the number of new documents added in each time period, and a Poisson distribution with rate 0.5λ to control the number of documents revised in each time period.

We generated six data sets using different random seeds, and each data set contained six corpora (Corpus 0 - 5). Table 1 summarizes the first data set. In each data set, we name the initial corpus Corpus 0, and define T_0 as the timestamp when we started this simulation process. We set $T_j = T_{j-1} + t^j$, $j \in [1, 5]$. Corpus j corresponds to documents generated before timestamp T_j. We extracted document revisions from Corpus $k \in [2, 5]$ and compared the revisions generated in (Corpus k - Corpus $(k - 1)$) with the ground truths in Table 1. Hence, we ran four experiments on this data set in total. In every experiment, τ^k is calibrated based on Corpus $(k - 1)$. For instance, the training set of the first experiment was Corpus 1. We trained τ^1 from Corpus 1. We extracted all revisions in Corpus 2, and compared revisions generated in the test set (Corpus 2 - Corpus 1) with the ground truth: 258 revised documents. The word2vec model shared in the four experiments was trained on Corpus 5.

Table 1: A simulated data set

Corpus	Number of documents	Number of new documents	Number of revision pairs
0	550	0	0
1	1347	542	255
2	2125	520	258
3	2912	528	259
4	3777	580	285
5	4582	547	258

5.3 Results

We use precision, recall and F-measure to evaluate the detected revisions. A true positive case is a correctly identified revision. A false positive case is an incorrectly identified revision. A false negative case is a missed revision record.

We illustrate the performances of wDTW, wTED, WMD, VSM, PV-DTW and PV-TED on the Wikipedia revision dumps in Figure 7. wDTW and wTED have the highest F-measure scores compared to the rest of four measures, and wDTW also have the highest precision and recall scores. Figure 8 shows the average evaluation results on the simulated data sets. From left to right, the corpus size increases and the revision chains become longer, thus it becomes more challenging to detect document revisions. Overall, wDTW consistently performs the best. WMD is slightly better than wTED. In particular, when the corpus size increases, the performances of WMD, VSM, PV-DTW and PV-TED drop faster than wDTW and wTED. Because the revision operations were randomly selected in each corpus, it is possible that there are non-monotone points in the series.

wDTW and wTED perform better than WMD especially when the corpus is large, because they use dynamic programming to find the global optimal alignment for documents. In contrast, WMD relies on a greedy algorithm that sums up the minimal cost for every word. wDTW and wTED perform better than PV-DTW and PV-TED, which indicates that our DistPara distance in Algorithm 2 is more accurate than the Euclidian distance between paragraph vectors trained by PV.

We show in Table 2 the average running time of the six distance/similarity measures. In all the experiments, VSM is the fastest, wTED is faster than wDTW, and WMD is the slowest. Running WMD is extremely expensive because WMD needs to solve an x^2 sequential transshipment problem for every two documents where x is the average number of words in a document. In contrast, by splitting this heavy computation into several smaller problems (finding the distance between any two paragraphs), which can be run in parallel, wDTW and wTED scale much better.

Combining Figure 7, Figure 8 and Table 2 we conclude that wDTW yields the most accurate results using marginally more time than VSM, PV-TED and PV-DTW, but much less running time than WMD. wTED returns satisfactory results using shorter time than wDTW.

6 Conclusion

This paper has explored how DTW and TED can be extended with word2vec to construct semantic document distance measures: wDTW and wTED. By representing paragraphs with concatenations of word vectors, wDTW and wTED are able to capture the semantics of the words and thus give more accurate distance scores. In order to detect revisions, we have used minimum branching on an appropriately developed network with document distance scores serving as arc weights. We have also assessed the efficiency of the method of retrieving an optimal revision subnetwork by finding the minimum branching.

Furthermore, we have compared wDTW and

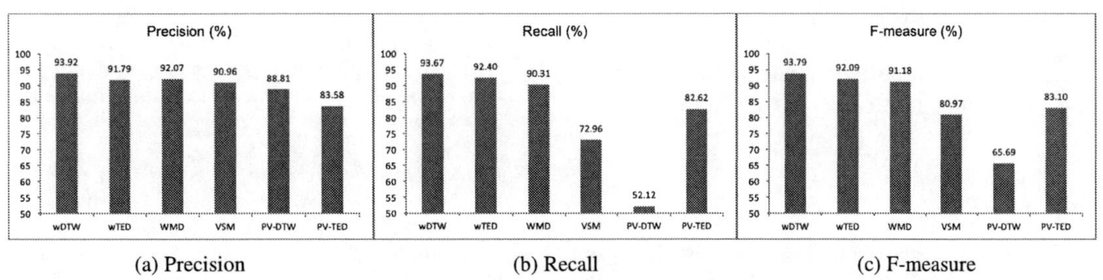

(a) Precision   (b) Recall   (c) F-measure

Figure 7: Precision, recall and F-measure on the Wikipedia revision dumps

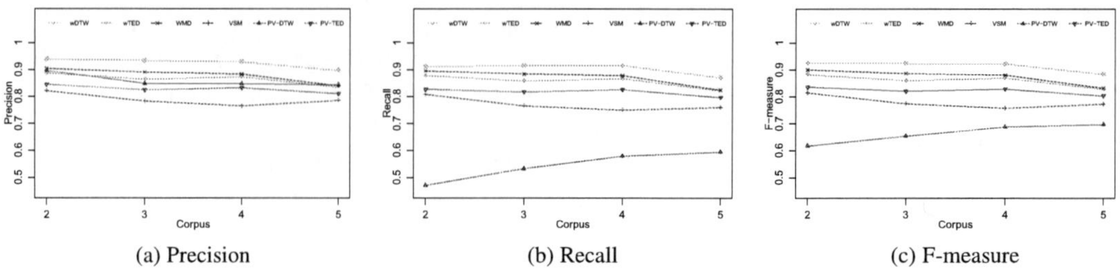

(a) Precision   (b) Recall   (c) F-measure

Figure 8: Average precision, recall and F-measure on the simulated data sets

Table 2: Running time of VSM, PV-TED, PV-DTW, wTED, wDTW and WMD

	VSM	PV-TED	PV-DTW	wTED	wDTW	WMD
Wikipedia revision dumps	1h 38min	3h 2min	3h 18min	5h 13min	13h 27min	515h 9min
corpus 2	2 min	3 min	3 min	7 min	8 min	8 h 53 min
corpus 3	3 min	4 min	5 min	9 min	11 min	12 h 45 min
corpus 4	4 min	6 min	6 min	11 min	12 min	14 h 34 min
corpus 5	7 min	9 min	9 min	14 min	16 min	17 h 31 min

wTED with several distance measures for revision detection tasks. Our results demonstrate the effectiveness and robustness of wDTW and wTED in the Wikipedia revision dumps and our simulated data sets. In order to reduce the computation time, we have computed document distances at the paragraph level and implemented a boosting learning system using Apache Spark. Although we have demonstrated the superiority of our semantic measures only in the revision detection experiments, wDTW and wTED can also be used as semantic distance measures in many clustering, classification tasks.

Our revision detection system can be enhanced with richer features such as author information and writing styles, and exact changes in revision pairs. Another interesting aspect we would like to explore in the future is reducing the complexities of calculating the distance between two paragraphs.

Acknowledgments

This work was supported in part by Intel Corporation, Semiconductor Research Corporation (SRC).

References

Asad Abdi, Norisma Idris, Rasim M Alguliyev, and Ramiz M Aliguliyev. 2015. Pdlk: Plagiarism detection using linguistic knowledge. *Expert Systems with Applications*, 42(22):8936–8946.

Peter Buneman, Sanjeev Khanna, and Tan Wang-Chiew. 2001. Why and where: A characterization of data provenance. In *Database Theory ICDT 2001*, pages 316–330. Springer.

Moses S Charikar. 2002. Similarity estimation techniques from rounding algorithms. In *Proceedings of the thiry-fourth annual ACM symposium on Theory of computing*, pages 380–388. ACM.

Erik D Demaine, Shay Mozes, Benjamin Rossman, and Oren Weimann. 2007. An optimal decomposition algorithm for tree edit distance. In *Automata, Languages and Programming*, pages 146–157. Springer.

Jack Edmonds. 1967. Optimum branchings. *Journal of Research of the National Bureau of Standards B*, 71(4):233–240.

Oliver Ferschke, Torsten Zesch, and Iryna Gurevych. 2011. Wikipedia revision toolkit: Efficiently accessing wikipedias edit history. In *Proceedings of the ACL-HLT 2011 System Demonstrations*, pages 97–102. ACL.

Atsushi Fujii and Tetsuya Ishikawa. 2001. Japanese/english cross-language information retrieval: Exploration of query translation and transliteration. *Computers and the Humanities*, 35(4):389–420.

Nathaniel Gustafson, Maria Soledad Pera, and Yiu-Kai Ng. 2008. Nowhere to hide: Finding plagiarized documents based on sentence similarity. In *Proceedings of the 2008 IEEE/WIC/ACM International Conference on Web Intelligence and Intelligent Agent Technology - Volume 01*, pages 690–696. IEEE.

Matthias Hagen, Martin Potthast, and Benno Stein. 2015. Source retrieval for plagiarism detection from large web corpora: recent approaches. *Working Notes Papers of the CLEF*, pages 1613–0073.

Timothy C. Hoad and Justin Zobel. 2003. Methods for identifying versioned and plagiarized documents. *Journal of the American Society for Information Science Technology*, 54(3):203–215.

Philip N Klein. 1998. Computing the edit-distance between unrooted ordered trees. In *European Symposium on Algorithms*, pages 91–102. Springer.

Matt J Kusner, Yu Sun, Nicholas I Kolkin, and Kilian Q Weinberger. 2015. From word embeddings to document distances. In *Proceedings of the 32nd International Conference on Machine Learning*, pages 957–966.

Quoc V Le and Tomas Mikolov. 2014. Distributed representations of sentences and documents. *arXiv preprint arXiv:1405.4053*.

Jure Leskovec, Daniel P Huttenlocher, and Jon M Kleinberg. 2010. Governance in social media: A case study of the wikipedia promotion process. In *International Conference on Weblogs and Social Media*.

Xiaoying Liu, Yiming Zhou, and Ruoshi Zheng. 2007. Sentence similarity based on dynamic time warping. In *International Conference on Semantic Computing*, pages 250–256. IEEE.

Udi Manber et al. 1994. Finding similar files in a large file system. In *Usenix Winter*, volume 94, pages 1–10.

Gurmeet Singh Manku, Arvind Jain, and Anish Das Sarma. 2007. Detecting near-duplicates for web crawling. In *Proceedings of the 16th international conference on World Wide Web*, pages 141–150. ACM.

Michael Matuschek, Tim Schlüter, and Stefan Conrad. 2008. Measuring text similarity with dynamic time warping. In *Proceedings of the 2008 international symposium on Database engineering & applications*, pages 263–267. ACM.

Tomas Mikolov, Ilya Sutskever, Kai Chen, Greg S Corrado, and Jeff Dean. 2013. Distributed representations of words and phrases and their compositionality. In *Advances in Neural Information Processing Systems*, pages 3111–3119.

Meinard Müller. 2007. Dynamic time warping. *Information Retrieval for Music and Motion*, pages 69–84.

Gabriel Oberreuter and Juan D VeláSquez. 2013. Text mining applied to plagiarism detection: The use of words for detecting deviations in the writing style. *Expert Systems with Applications*, 40(9):3756–3763.

Mateusz Pawlik and Nikolaus Augsten. 2011. Rted: a robust algorithm for the tree edit distance. *Proceedings of the VLDB Endowment*, 5(4):334–345.

Mateusz Pawlik and Nikolaus Augsten. 2014. A memory-efficient tree edit distance algorithm. In *Database and Expert Systems Applications*, pages 196–210. Springer.

Mateusz Pawlik and Nikolaus Augsten. 2015. Efficient computation of the tree edit distance. *ACM Transactions on Database Systems*, 40(1):3.

Mateusz Pawlik and Nikolaus Augsten. 2016. Tree edit distance: Robust and memory-efficient. *Information Systems*, 56:157–173.

Mikalai Sabel. 2007. Structuring wiki revision history. In *Proceedings of the 2007 International Symposium on Wikis*, pages 125–130. ACM.

Yasushi Sakurai, Masatoshi Yoshikawa, and Christos Faloutsos. 2005. Ftw: fast similarity search under the time warping distance. In *Proceedings of the twenty-fourth ACM SIGMOD-SIGACT-SIGART Symposium on Principles of Database Systems*, pages 326–337. ACM.

Saul Schleimer, Daniel S Wilkerson, and Alex Aiken. 2003. Winnowing: local algorithms for document fingerprinting. In *Proceedings of the 2003 ACM SIGMOD International Conference on Management of Data*, pages 76–85. ACM.

Antonio Si, Hong Va Leong, and Rynson WH Lau. 1997. Check: a document plagiarism detection system. In *Proceedings of the 1997 ACM Symposium on Applied Computing*, pages 70–77. ACM.

Grigori Sidorov, Helena Gómez-Adorno, Ilia Markov, David Pinto, and Nahun Loya. 2015. Computing text similarity using tree edit distance. In *Fuzzy Information Processing Society (NAFIPS) held jointly with 2015 5th World Conference on Soft Computing, 2015 Annual Conference of the North American*, pages 1–4. IEEE.

Kuo-Chung Tai. 1979. The tree-to-tree correction problem. *Journal of the ACM*, 26(3):422–433.

Paola Velardi, Stefano Faralli, and Roberto Navigli. 2013. Ontolearn reloaded: A graph-based algorithm for taxonomy induction. *Computational Linguistics*, 39(3):665–707.

Jing Zhang and HV Jagadish. 2013. Revision provenance in text documents of asynchronous collaboration. In *2013 IEEE 29th International Conference on Data Engineering*, pages 889–900. IEEE.

Kaizhong Zhang and Dennis Shasha. 1989. Simple fast algorithms for the editing distance between trees and related problems. *SIAM Journal on Computing*, 18(6):1245–1262.

An Empirical Analysis of Multiple-Turn Reasoning Strategies in Reading Comprehension Tasks

Yelong Shen[†], Xiaodong Liu[†], Kevin Duh[‡], Jianfeng Gao[†]
[†] Microsoft Research, Redmond, WA, USA
[‡] Johns Hopkins University, Baltimore, MD, USA
[†]{yeshen,xiaodl,jfgao}@microsoft.com [‡]kevinduh@cs.jhu.edu

Abstract

Reading comprehension (RC) is a challenging task that requires synthesis of information across sentences and multiple turns of reasoning. Using a state-of-the-art RC model, we empirically investigate the performance of single-turn and multiple-turn reasoning on the SQuAD and MS MARCO datasets. The RC model is an end-to-end neural network with iterative attention, and uses reinforcement learning to dynamically control the number of turns. We find that multiple-turn reasoning outperforms single-turn reasoning for all question and answer types; further, we observe that enabling a flexible number of turns generally improves upon a fixed multiple-turn strategy. We achieve results competitive to the state-of-the-art on these two datasets.

1 Introduction

There is an old Chinese proverb that says: *"Read a hundred times and the meaning will appear."* Several recent reading comprehension (RC) models have embraced this kind of multiple-turn strategy; they generate predictions by making multiple passes through the same text and integrating intermediate information in the process (Hill et al., 2016; Dhingra et al., 2016; Sordoni et al., 2016; Shen et al., 2016). While state-of-the-art results have been achieved by these models, there has yet to be an in-depth analysis of the impact of the multiple-turn strategy to reasoning. This paper attempts to fill this gap.

We provide empirical results and analysis on two challenging RC datasets: the Stanford Question Answering Dataset (SQuAD) (Rajpurkar et al., 2016), and the Microsoft Machine Reading Comprehension Dataset (MS MARCO) (Nguyen et al., 2016). Given a question Q, the RC model is to read passages P and produce an answer A, which could be free-form text or one of the possible candidate spans in the passage.

The following example from SQuAD illustrates the need for synthesis of information across sentences and multiple turns of reasoning:

Q: What collection does **the V&A Theator & Performance galleries** hold?

P: **The V&A Theator & Performance galleries** opened in March 2009.   ...   **They** hold the UK's biggest national collection of <u>material about live performance.</u>

To infer the answer (the underlined portion of the passage P), the model needs to first perform coreference resolution so that it knows "**They**" refers "**V&A Theator**", then extract the subspan in the direct object corresponding to the answer. This process can be modeled by the repeated processing of intermediate states and input in a neural net.

To perform the analysis, we adopt the ReasoNet model of Shen et al. (2016). This is an end-to-end neural network that uses an iterative attention mechanism to simulate multiple-turn reasoning in RC. It has achieved strong results on cloze-style RC tasks like CNN/DailyMail (Hermann et al., 2015) and we extend it to SQuAD and MS MARCO tasks. The advantage of using ReasoNet for our purpose is that it uses reinforcement learning to dynamically determine the number of turns for each question-passage pair. This enables us to analyze the behavior of multiple-turn reasoning in neural network models.

We find that multiple-turn reasoning outperforms single-turn reasoning across the board for various types of question and answer types. Furthermore, the flexibility to dynamically decide the

Proceedings of the The 8th International Joint Conference on Natural Language Processing, pages 957–966,
Taipei, Taiwan, November 27 – December 1, 2017 ©2017 AFNLP

	SQuAD	MS MARCO
query source	crowdsourced	user logs
answer (A)	span of words	free-form text
#questions (Q)	100K questions	100K queries
#passages (P)	23K paragraphs	1M paragraphs

Table 1: Dataset characteristics

number of turns generally improves over a fixed multiple-turn strategy, where the number of turns are set a priori. As an additional contribution, our extension to the ReasoNet model achieves results competitive with the state-of-the-art on SQuAD and MS MARCO.

In the following, Section 2 describes our two RC tasks, Section 3 explains the model we used for analysis, and Section 4 discusses results.

2 Reading Comprehension Tasks

We focus this study on two RC tasks which we believe require sophisticated reasoning.

SQuAD: SQuAD is a machine comprehension dataset constructed on 536 Wikipedia articles (23K paragraphs), with more than 100,000 questions. In contrast to prior datasets such as (Richardson et al., 2013; Hermann et al., 2015), SQuAD does not provide a multiple choice list of answer candidates. Instead, the RC model must select the answer from all possible spans in the passage. Crowdsourced workers are asked to read each passage (a paragraph), come up with questions, and then mark the answer spans.

There is a variety of questions and answers. The authors of SQuAD described several types of reasoning required to answer questions: (a) lexical variation between question (Q) and answer (A) that can be solved by understanding synonyms, (b) lexical variation that could be solved by world knowledge, (c) syntactic variation between Q and A sentence, and (d) multiple sentence reasoning that require anaphora or higher-level fusion.

The 100K (question, passage, answer) tuples is randomly partitioned into a training (80%), a development (10%) and test set splits (10%). Two evaluation metrics are used: Exact Match (EM), which measures the percentage of span predictions that matched any one of the ground truth answer exactly, and Macro-averaged F1 score, which measures the average overlap between the prediction and the ground truth answer. Human performance on the test set is 82.3% EM and 91.2% F1.

MS MARCO: MS MARCO is a large scale real-world RC dataset that contains 100,000 queries collected from anonymized user logs from the Bing search engine. The characteristic of MS MARCO is that all the questions are real user queries and passages are extracted from real web documents. The data is constructed as follows: for each question/query Q, up to approximately 10 passages P are extracted from public web documents and presented to human judges. These passages might potentially have the answer to the question, and are selected through a separate information retrieval system. The judges write down answers in free-form text, and according to the authors of MS MARCO, the complexity of answer varies from a single "yes/no" or entity name (e.g. Q: "What is the capital of Italy"; A: Rome), to long textual answers (e.g. Q: "What is the agenda for Hollande's state visit to Washington?"). Long textual answers may need to be derived through reasoning across multiple pieces of text.

The dataset is partitioned into a 82,430 training, a 10,047 development, and 9,650 test tuples. Since the answer is free-form text, the evaluation metrics of choice are BLEU (Papineni et al., 2002) and ROUGE-L (Lin, 2004). To apply the same RC model to both SQuAD (where answers are text spans in P) and MS MARCO (where answer are free-form text), we search for spans in MS MARCO's passages that maximizes the ROUGE-L score with the raw free-form answers. Our training data uses these spans as labels, but we evaluate our model with respect to the raw free-form answers; this has an upper bound of 94.23 BLEU and 87.53 ROUGE-L on the dev set. By this construction, there are multiple number of passages to read for each question, but the answer span might only involve a few passages (i.e. the ones that include the max ROUGE substring). We describe techniques to handle this case in Section 3.2.

3 Model: ReasoNet++

The reading comprehension task involves a question/query $Q = \{q_0, q_1, ..., q_{m-1}\}$ and a passage $P = \{p_0, p_1, p_{n-1}\}$ and aims to find an answer span $A = \langle a_{start}, a_{end} \rangle$ in P. Here, m and n denote the number of tokens in Q and P, respectively, while a_{start} and a_{end} indicate the indices of tokens in P. The learning process for reading comprehension is to learn a function $f(Q, P) \rightarrow A$ trained on a set of tuples $\langle Q, P, A \rangle$.

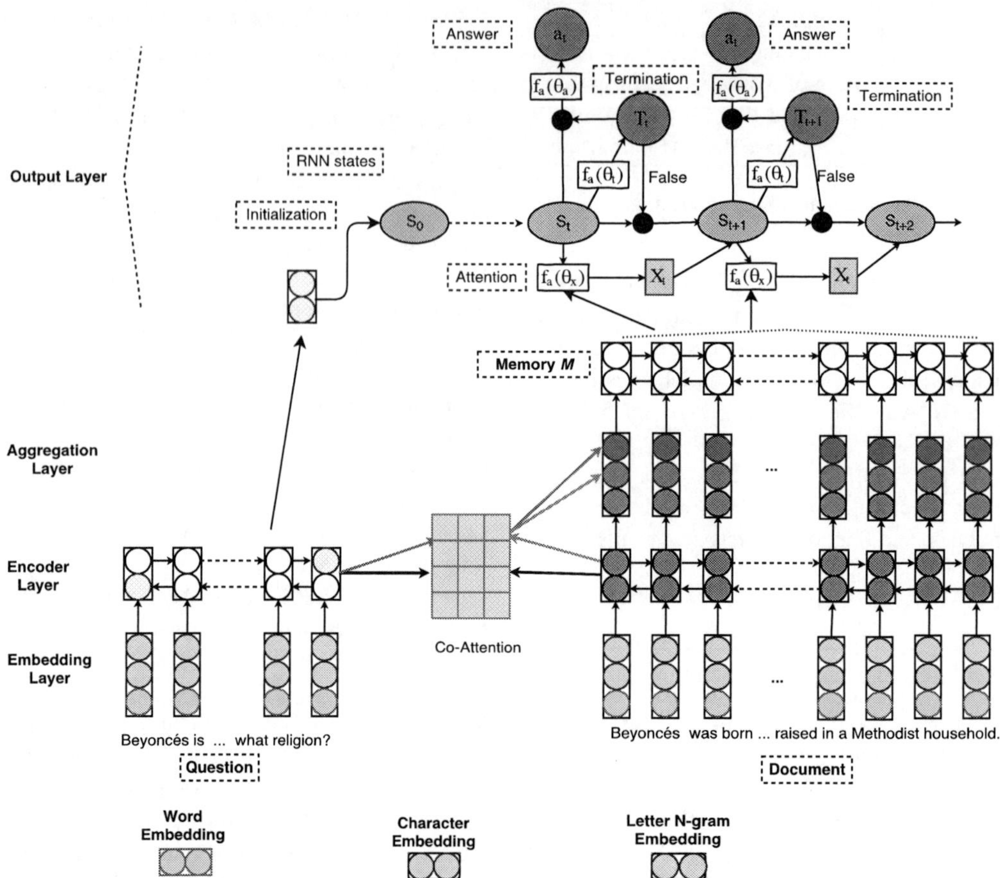

Figure 1: **Architecture of ReasoNet++**: The embedding/encoder layers compute representations for the question Q and the passage document P. The aggregation layer uses co-attention to compute question-aware passage information and passage-aware question information. Then a GRU combines these information into memory cells and feeds them to the output layer. The output layer models the multiple-turn reasoning mechanism, where intermediate results are stored in S_t and the answer is generated only when the termination signal is triggered. Each S_t is a recurrent network state and models one turn of reasoning.

Our model **ReasoNet++**, is an extension of ReasoNet (Shen et al., 2016) with three enhancements: (1) In the input layer, we added character and letter 3-gram embeddings to improve robustness to rare words. (2) We implemented co-attention (Seo et al., 2016) in the aggregation layer to focus on relevant words in both Q and P. (3) For the MS MARCO task, which needs to handle multiple passages, we incorporated an extra passage ranker component. The architecture is shown in Figure 1. In brief, the embedding/encoder layers first build representations of Q and P. The aggregation layer uses co-attention to fuse information from the Q-P pair. The output layer is a recurrent net that maintains intermediate state and dynamically decides at which turn to generate the answer.

3.1 Detailed description of ReasoNet++

Embedding Layer: We adopt three types of embeddings to represent input word tokens in Q and P. For word embeddings, we use pre-trained GloVe vectors (Pennington et al., 2014). To address the out-of-vocabulary problem, we also include character and letter 3-gram embeddings. Character embeddings are fed into a convolutional neural network (CNN) as in (Kim, 2014), then max-pooled to form a fixed-size vector for each token. For letter 3-gram embeddings, we follow Huang et al. (2013) by first *hashing* each word as a bag of letter 3-gram, then feeding them into another CNN. The concatenation of all embeddings are then fed to a two-layer Highway Network (Srivastava et al., 2015). Therefore, we obtain the final embedding for the words in Q as a matrix $E^q \in \mathbb{R}^{d \times m}$, and words in P as $E^p \in \mathbb{R}^{d \times n}$, where d is the dimension of the embedding.

Encoding Layer: On the top of embedding layer, we utilize a bidirectional Gated Recurrent Unit (GRU), a variety of the Long Short-Term Memory Network (LSTM) (Hochreiter and Schmidhuber, 1997), to encode the words in context. We obtain $H^q \in \mathbb{R}^{2d \times m}$ as the representation of Q and $H^p \in \mathbb{R}^{2d \times n}$ as the representation of P.

Aggregation Layer: In this layer, we construct the memory, a summary of information from both the Q and P, for each word in P. A co-attention mechanism (Seo et al., 2016), which attends to Q and P simultaneously, is applied by first computing an alignment matrix in two directions: from Q to P and from P to Q. The alignment matrix C measures the similarity between Q and P:

$$C = f_{match}(H^q, H^p) \in \mathbb{R}^{m \times n} \qquad (1)$$

The element at i-th row and j-th of the alignment matrix, C_{ij}, indicates the similarity between i-th word in the question and j-th word in the passage. In detail, $C_{ij} = f_{match}(H^q_{:i}, H^p_{:j})$ is a trainable scalar function that measures the similarity between two input vectors, $H^q_{:i}$, which is the i-th column vector of H^q, and $H^p_{:j}$, which is the j-th column vector of H^p. We parameterize $f_{match}(a, b) = w^T_C[a; b; a \circ b]$, where $\circ$ denotes the Hadmard product, $[;]$ indicates vector concatenation across rows, and $w_C \in \mathbb{R}^{6d}$ is a trainable weight vector. We normalize C row-wise to produce the attention weight across the passage for each word of the question:

$$C^q = softmax(C) \in \mathbb{R}^{m \times n}. \qquad (2)$$

To measure which context words in the P have the closest similarity to the words in the Q, we define an attention weight on the words in passage as:

$$c^p = softmax(max_{col}(C))^T \in \mathbb{R}^n. \qquad (3)$$

The final context representation of the P is:

$$U = f_{agg}(H^p, H^q C^q, \sum_{i=0}^{i=m-1} H^p_{:i} c^p) \in \mathbb{R}^{8d \times n}. \qquad (4)$$

In our experiment, we define $f_{agg}(B, C, D) = [B; C; B \circ C; B \circ D]$. Note that B, C, D are matrices with the same dimension, $\circ$ denotes the Hadmard product and ; indicates matrix concatenation across columns. Note that since

$H^p, H^q C^q, \sum_{i=0}^{i=m-1} H^p_{:i} c^p$ are all $2d$ by n matrices, U is a $8d$ by n matrix. Finally, to incorporate the full context, the "memory cells" of the passage are computed by a bidirectional GRU on top of U:

$$M^p = BiGRU(U) \in \mathbb{R}^{2d \times n} \qquad (5)$$

Output Layer: This layer dynamically decides when to stop reasoning and output the answer. A recurrent neural network (Rumelhart et al., 1986; Elman, 1990) is adopted to maintain the states of the reasoning process. Formally, the t-th time step of inference state is denoted as S_t, and the next state is defined by $S_{t+1} = GRU(S_t, X_t)$. Note that the X_t is an attention vector generated based on the current state and the memory of the passage: $X_t = f_a(S_t, M^p)$ as in (Shen et al., 2016). Specifically, the attention score $a_{t,i}$ on a memory vector $m_i \in M^p$ given a state S_t is computed as $a_{t,i} = softmax_{i=1,...,|M^p|} \lambda cosine(w_1 m_i, w_2 S_t)$, where λ is set to 10 in our experiments and the projection matrices w_1 and w_2 map the memory vector and state into the same space, they are learned during training. The attention vector X_t can be written as $X_t = \sum_i^{|M|} a_{t,i} m_i$. The initial state S_0 of the inference is from the encoding representation of the question (we pick the last state of the forward GRU and the backward GRU in the H^q).

The *termination gate* will produce a stochastic random variable according to the current inference state: $T_t \sim p(\cdot | f_t(S_t))$, where f_t is modeled by a $2d \times 10 \times 10 \times 10 \times 1$ feed-forward neural network. Note T_t is a binary random variable: if T_t is true, the recurrent net will stop and the answer model will execute; otherwise it will generate an attention vector X_{t+1} and update the next state S_{t+1}.

The answer module needs to output a span in passage. We do this with two feedforward networks, one predicting the start point of the span and the other predicting the end point, so predicted answer at turn t is $a_t = (y_s^t, y_e^t)$:

$$y_s^t = softmax(w_s^T[M^p, (w_{ps}^T M^p) \circ S_t]) \qquad (6)$$

$$y_e^t = softmax(w_e^T[M^p, (w_{pe}^T M^p) \circ S_t]). \qquad (7)$$

where w_s, w_e, w_{ps} and w_{pe} are trainable model parameters. Since the termination state is discrete and is not connected to the final output directly, we use the Contrastive Reward method (Shen et al., 2016) inspired by deep reinforcement learning (Weissenborn, 2016; Mnih et al., 2014) for training.

3.2 Passage ranking extension

The MS MARCO dataset provides multiple passages per question/query. Our architecture in Figure 1 is built for a single passage-question pair, so we need to extend it to handle multiple passages. We propose a solution using passage ranking. Assume there are J passages, $P^{(1)}, \ldots, P^{(J)}$. First, our model runs independently on every $(P^{(j)}, Q)_{j=1,\ldots,J}$ pair, generating J different answer spans (empty spans are possible). Then, we multiply the probability of each answer span with a score $r(P^{(j)}, Q)$ provided by a passage ranker, and output the answer with the maximum combined score, similar to EpiReader (Trischler et al., 2016). The passage ranker is a information retrieval model (Shen et al., 2014).[1] It can be trained on the same RC data, where documents with answers are considered relevant and those that do not are considered irrelevant.

All our MS MARCO results use the passage ranking extension, unless otherwise mentioned.

4 Experiments

We seek to answer the following questions:

1. Is multiple-turn reasoning beneficial for RC? (Section 4.1)

2. What types of questions/answers benefit most from multiple-turn reasoning? (Section 4.2)

3. How many turns are employed in practice by ReasoNet++, and what are the implications for dynamic versus fixed strategies in multiple-turn reasoning? (Section 4.3)

In addition to the above analyses, we also demonstrate that our ReasoNet++ achieves state-of-the-art results (Section 4.4) and discuss some ablation studies on model variants (Section 4.5).[2]

---

[1] Our implementation first hashes words into letter 3-gram (50K dimension), then use a CNN with 256 hidden nodes and the size of window 5, and lastly optimizes the similarity between the vector representations of P and Q.

[2] A note on hyperparameters: Throughout all experiments, we use NLTK to tokenize P and Q, and employ pre-trained case-sensitive 300 dimension GloVe embeddings[3]. A one layer CNN with 100 dimensions and window size of 5 is used to compute the character embeddings; a one layer CNN with 100 dimension and window size of 1 is used for letter 3-gram embeddings. The size of hidden nodes of all GRU's is set to 128. A five layers feedforward network $(2d(256) \times 10 \times 10 \times 10 \times 1)$ is used for the terminate network and the maximum number of reasoning turns in the recurrent net is capped at 5. To avoid overfitting, we adopt 0.15 dropout rate over the letter 3-gram and character embeddings,

Single model	SQuAD EM/F1 Score	MS MARCO BLEU/ROUGE-L
Single turn	67.8/76.7	33.65/36.54
Fixed 5-turn	70.1/78.9	34.93/36.67
ReasoNet++	**70.8/79.4**	**38.62/38.01**

Table 2: **Main results**—Comparison of single turn to multiple turn reasoning strategies on SQuAD and MS MARCO dev sets. Both multiple turn strategies (fixed at 5, or dynamically decided based on ReasoNet++) outperform Single turn in all metrics. The dynamic strategy further improves upon the fixed multiple 5-turn strategy.

Figure 2: Case study from SQuAD of answers from multiple turns. In Turn 1, the model identifies a span similar to the question. This is refined and at Turn 3 a better answer becomes attainable.

4.1 Is multiple-turn reasoning beneficial?

In summary, yes. We compare three systems:

Single turn: the RC model only has one turn of reasoning. This corresponds to a model like Figure 1 without termination nodes, where the output layer always stops at $S_{t=1}$.

Fixed 5-turn: the RC model runs 5 turns of iterative attention. This is Figure 1 without termination nodes, where output layer always stops at $S_{t=5}$.

ReasoNet++ (Dynamic multiple-turn reasoning): this is the RC model in Figure 1, which can decide from 1 to T turns based on the termination probability on each Q-P pair at test time. We set $T = 5$ to compare with the Fixed 5-turn system.

The main results are shown in Table 2. We observe that both multiple turn strategies (either fixed at 5 turns, or dynamically decided based on ReasoNet++) outperform the single turn system in all metrics. The dynamic strategy further improves upon the fixed multiple 5-turn strategy. For ex-

---

and 0.25 dropout rate (Srivastava et al., 2014) over GRU network. The model is optimized with AdaDelta (Zeiler, 2012) with an initial learning rate 0.5.

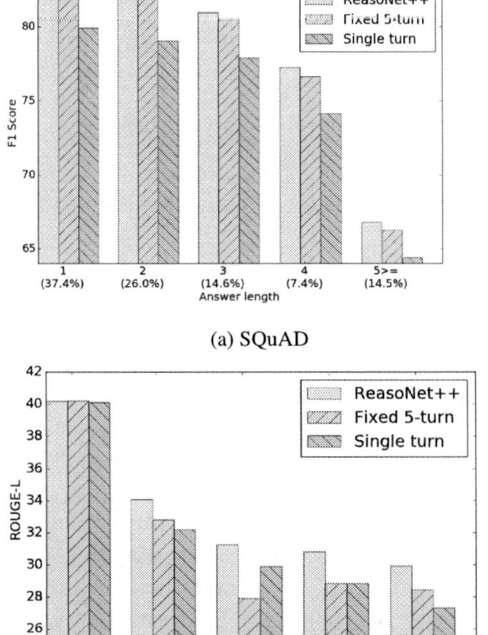

(a) SQuAD

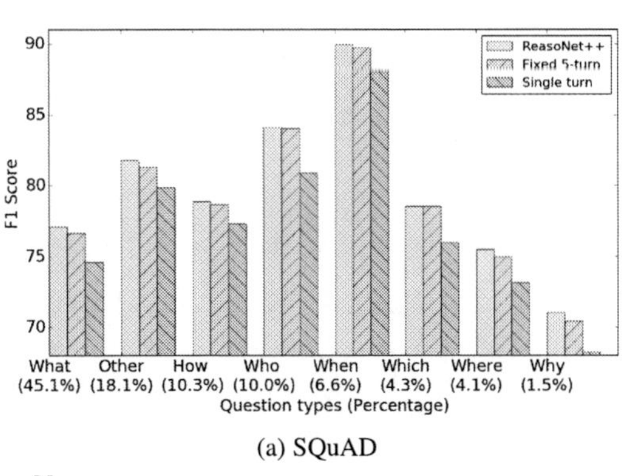

(a) SQuAD

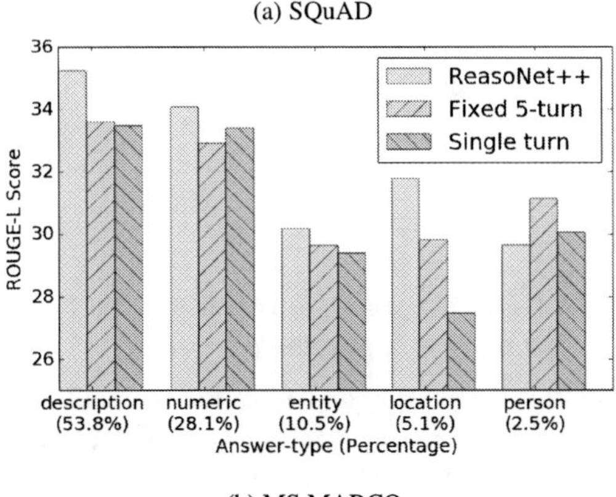

(b) MS MARCO

(b) MS MARCO

Figure 3: Score breakdown by answer length

Figure 4: Score breakdown by query/answer type

ample, the F1 score on SQuAD improves from 76.7 to 78.9 when increasing the number of turns from 1 to 5, and further improves to 79.4 with dynamic multiple turns. On MS MARCO, we see a ROUGE improvement from 36.54 (1-turn) to 36.67(5-turn) and 38.62 (dynamic multi-turn). These results convincingly show that multiple-turn reasoning is helpful for SQuAD and MS MARCO tasks. Figure 2 shows a case study of how answers improve with each turn.

4.2 What types of questions/answers benefit most from multiple-turn reasoning?

We find that improvements from multiple-turn reasoning is generally seen across the board, but particularly helps questions with longer answers. Figure 3 shows the score breakdown of Table 2 according to answer length (# of words). For SQuAD, both ReasoNet++ and Fixed 5-turn outperform Single turn for all answer lengths, and ReasoNet++ outperforms Fixed 5-turn for answer lengths > 3. For MS MARCO, ReasoNet++ outperforms Fixed 5-turn for answer lengths > 5; on the other hand, there is almost no difference among systems for short answers (0-4). We hy-

pothesize there is a correlation between answer length and the difficulty of the question; for difficult questions there may be more potential for multiple-turn reasoning to improve results.

We also visualize the score breakdown according to question/answer type (Figure 4). For MS MARCO, the questions are annotated by the type of the correct answer: description (e.g. Q: "How to cook a turkey"), numeric (e.g. Q: "Xbox one release data"), entity, location, person. There is no such annotation for the entire SQuAD dev data, but we can classify questions by their first word: What, Who, When, Which, etc. Similar to the answer length results, we observe that multiple-turn reasoning outperforms single turn for SQuAD across the board, regardless of question type. For MS MARCO, ReasoNet++ gave large improvements over single turn in particular for description and location types. Descriptions tend to be lengthy, so this again corroborates our hypothesis that there may be more potential gains for questions requiring long answers.

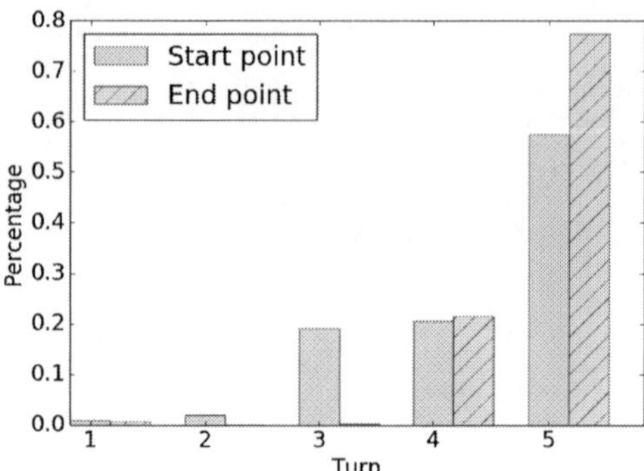

Figure 5: Distribution on the number of turns by ReasoNet++on the SQuAD dev set. Note that start points are often decided before end points, and most answer spans are generated after 3 turns.

4.3 How many turns of reasoning are employed in practice?

We are interested in understanding the number of turns determined by ReasoNet++. When does it decide to terminate? In Figure 5, we plot the distribution of turns until the model decides on start points and end points (of the answer span).

First, note the start point is often decided before the end point, e.g. the start is already determined at turn 3 for approximately 20% of the questions , but the end does not get predicted until turn 4 or 5. Intuitively, we think it is easier to first identify the start of an answer, then use that signal as intermediate state S_t to identify the end point.

Second, there is almost no termination at turns 1 or 2, implying the model prefers more iterations of reasoning. Most terminations are done at step 4 or 5, which explains the relatively close performance results between Fixed 5-turn and ReasoNet++.

4.4 Comparison with state-of-the-art

Our ReasoNet++ model, which is an extension of ReasoNet (Shen et al., 2016), achieves scores competitive with state-of-the-art results. The official leaderboard results are shown in Table 3 (MS MARCO) and Table 4 (SQuAD) Results are divided by whether we use an individual model or an ensemble of models. For SQuAD, the ReasoNet++ ensemble model achieves the best EM and F1 test score among all published works, and places second if we include r-net. Similarly, the ReasoNet++ individual model results are in the top 1 or 2 ranks, competitive with published works like Zhang et al. (2017) and Weis-

System	BLEU/ROUGE-L	
	Dev Set	Test Set
ReasoNet++ *Individual*	38.62/38.01	39.86/38.81
Match-LSTM	-/-	40.72/37.33
FastQA_Ext	35.0/34.4	33.93/33.67
FastQA	34.9/33.0	33.99/32.09
Human Performance	-/-	46/47

Table 3: Official MS MARCO leaderboard performance on April 5, 2017.

senborn et al. (2017). For MS MARCO (Table 3), ReasoNet++ ranks first in test ROUGE and second in test BLEU (after Match-LSTM (Wang and Jiang, 2016)). Note that some of the models on the leaderboard use multiple-turn reasoning, while others do not. But we refrain from drawing conclusions about multiple-turn reasoning by comparing across models, due to other confounding variables, e.g. different embeddings and network architectures.

4.5 Ablation studies and model variants

We now present some ablation studies to demonstrate the differences between our ReasoNet++ and the original ReasoNet (Shen et al., 2016) in which we are based on.[4]

First, Table 5 shows the improvement from adding sub-word level modeling to ReasoNet, which only used word embeddings. We observe marked improvements of update number +1.1 F1 in SQuAD and +0.9 ROUGE in MS MARCO. Although these improvements are not as large as those we achieved with multiple-turn reasoning, they are are still considerable and imply that robust representations of words is an important building block to strong RC models.

Secondly, Table 6 shows the impact of passage ranking—this is only relevant for MS MARCO, which contains multiple passages for each question/query. Recall that the RC model needs to read approximately 10 passages to answer each query, and on average only one or two passage contain answer spans. ReasoNet++ extracts answer spans from each passage independently, then combines with an IR model to output the final answer. If we assume oracle ranking from the IR model, we can achieve 62 BLEU / 63 ROUGE, suggesting that

---

[4]Due to time constraints, we only perform ablation studies on the embedding and passage ranking enhancements, and leave the study of the impact of co-attention to future work.

Ensemble model results:	Dev Set (EM/F1)	Test Set (EM/F1)
r-net*	-/-	76.9/84.0
ReasoNet++ (Ensemble model)	75.4/82.9	75.0/82.6
BiDAF (Seo et al., 2016)	73.3/81.1	73.7/81.5
Multi-Perspective Matching (Wang et al., 2016)	69.4/78.6	73.8/81.3
Dynamic Coattention Networks (Xiong et al., 2016)	70.3/79.4	71.6/80.4
Match-LSTM with Ans-Ptr (Wang and Jiang, 2016)	67.6/76.8	67.9/77.0
Fine-Grained Gating(Yang et al., 2017)	62.4/73.4	62.4/73.3
Individual model results:		
r-net*	-/-	72.3/80.7
jNet (Zhang et al., 2017)	-/-	70.6/79.8
Ruminate Reader*	-/-	70.6/79.5
ReasoNet++ (Individual model)	70.8/79.4	70.6/79.36
Document Reader*	-/-	70.7/79.35
FastQAExt (Weissenborn et al., 2017)	70.3/78.5	70.8/78.9
RaSoR (Lee et al., 2016)	66.4/74.9	70.0/77.7
BiDAF (Seo et al., 2016)	67.7/77.3	68.0/77.3
Iterative Co-attention Network*	-/-	67.5/76.8
Dynamic Coattention Networks (Xiong et al., 2016)	65.4/75.6	66.2/75.9
Match-LSTM with Bi-Ans-Ptr (Wang and Jiang, 2016)	64.1/73.9	64.7/73.7
Attentive CNN context with LSTM*	-/-	63.3/73.5
Dynamic Chunk Reader (Wang and Jiang, 2016)	62.5/71.2	62.5/71.0
LR baseline (Rajpurkar et al., 2016)	40.0/51.0	40.4/51.0
Human Performance	80.3/90.5	82.3/91.2

Table 4: Official SQuAD leaderboard performance on April 5, 2017. Asterisk * denotes unpublished works. Results are sorted by Test F1.

System	SQuAD	MS MARCO
	EM/F1 Score	BLEU/ROUGE
word+char+3gram	70.8/79.4	38.62/38.01
word+char	70.4/79.1	38.37/37.91
word	69.9/78.3	37.77/37.14

Table 5: Comparison of input embeddings: the addition of character (char) and letter trigram (3gram) embeddings to word embeddings (word) clearly improve results on SQuAD and MS MARCO development sets.

	BLEU/ROUGE-L
Oracle passage selection	62.83/63.17
Passage ranking	38.62/38.01

Table 6: Effect of multiple passages per query in MS MARCO.

better passage ranking models (e.g. via joint training with RC models) is fruitful as future work.

5 Conclusion

This paper empirically investigates the performance of single-turn and multiple-turn reasoning on two challenging reading comprehension tasks: SQuAD and MS MARCO. To perform the analysis, we adopt the neural network model of Shen et al. (2016), which employs iterative attention and uses reinforcement learning to dynamically control the number of turns. We find that multiple-turn reasoning outperforms single-turn reasoning for all question and answer types; further, we observe that enabling a flexible number of turns generally improves upon a fixed multiple-turn strategy. While our analysis is based on a single model, we believe the conclusions will be valuable for most RC methods using attention-based neural network. Our model extension to (Shen et al., 2016) achieves results competitive to the state-of-the-art on both tasks. As future work, we plan to investigate the impact of even deeper layers of reasoning and explore fast training methods to make such methods practical for large-scale datasets.

References

Bhuwan Dhingra, Hanxiao Liu, William W Cohen, and Ruslan Salakhutdinov. 2016. Gated-attention readers for text comprehension. *arXiv preprint arXiv:1606.01549* .

Jeffrey L Elman. 1990. Finding structure in time. *Cognitive science* 14(2):179–211.

Karl Moritz Hermann, Tomas Kocisky, Edward Grefenstette, Lasse Espeholt, Will Kay, Mustafa Suleyman, and Phil Blunsom. 2015. Teaching machines to read and comprehend. In *Advances in Neural Information Processing Systems*. pages 1693–1701.

Felix Hill, Antoine Bordes, Sumit Chopra, and Jason Weston. 2016. The goldilocks principle: Reading children's books with explicit memory representations. *ICLR* .

Sepp Hochreiter and Jürgen Schmidhuber. 1997. Long short-term memory. *Neural computation* 9(8):1735–1780.

Po-Sen Huang, Xiaodong He, Jianfeng Gao, Li Deng, Alex Acero, and Larry Heck. 2013. Learning deep structured semantic models for web search using clickthrough data. In *Proceedings of the 22nd ACM international conference on Conference on information & knowledge management*. ACM, pages 2333–2338.

Yoon Kim. 2014. Convolutional neural networks for sentence classification. In *Proceedings of the 2014 Conference on Empirical Methods in Natural Language Processing (EMNLP)*. Association for Computational Linguistics, Doha, Qatar, pages 1746–1751. http://www.aclweb.org/anthology/D14-1181.

Kenton Lee, Tom Kwiatkowski, Ankur Parikh, and Dipanjan Das. 2016. Learning recurrent span representations for extractive question answering. *arXiv preprint arXiv:1611.01436* .

Chin-Yew Lin. 2004. Rouge: A package for automatic evaluation of summaries.

Volodymyr Mnih, Nicolas Heess, Alex Graves, et al. 2014. Recurrent models of visual attention. In *Advances in neural information processing systems*. pages 2204–2212.

Tri Nguyen, Mir Rosenberg, Xia Song, Jianfeng Gao, Saurabh Tiwary, Rangan Majumder, and Li Deng. 2016. Ms marco: A human generated machine reading comprehension dataset. *arXiv preprint arXiv:1611.09268* .

Kishore Papineni, Salim Roukos, Todd Ward, and Wei-Jing Zhu. 2002. Bleu: a method for automatic evaluation of machine translation. In *Proceedings of the 40th annual meeting on association for computational linguistics*. Association for Computational Linguistics, pages 311–318.

Jeffrey Pennington, Richard Socher, and Christopher Manning. 2014. Glove: Global vectors for word representation. In *Proceedings of the 2014 Conference on Empirical Methods in Natural Language Processing (EMNLP)*. Association for Computational Linguistics, Doha, Qatar, pages 1532–1543. http://www.aclweb.org/anthology/D14-1162.

Pranav Rajpurkar, Jian Zhang, Konstantin Lopyrev, and Percy Liang. 2016. Squad: 100,000+ questions for machine comprehension of text pages 2383–2392. https://aclweb.org/anthology/D16-1264.

Matthew Richardson, Christopher J.C. Burges, and Erin Renshaw. 2013. MCTest: A challenge dataset for the open-domain machine comprehension of text. In *Proceedings of the 2013 Conference on Empirical Methods in Natural Language Processing*. Association for Computational Linguistics, Seattle, Washington, USA, pages 193–203.

David E Rumelhart, Geoffrey E Hinton, and Ronald J Williams. 1986. Learning representations by back-propagating errors. *Cognitive modeling* 5(3):1.

Minjoon Seo, Aniruddha Kembhavi, Ali Farhadi, and Hannaneh Hajishirzi. 2016. Bidirectional attention flow for machine comprehension. *arXiv preprint arXiv:1611.01603* .

Yelong Shen, Xiaodong He, Jianfeng Gao, Li Deng, and Grégoire Mesnil. 2014. A latent semantic model with convolutional-pooling structure for information retrieval. In *Proceedings of the 23rd ACM International Conference on Conference on Information and Knowledge Management*. ACM, pages 101–110.

Yelong Shen, Po-Sen Huang, Jianfeng Gao, and Weizhu Chen. 2016. Reasonet: Learning to stop reading in machine comprehension. *arXiv preprint arXiv:1609.05284* .

Alessandro Sordoni, Philip Bachman, Adam Trischler, and Yoshua Bengio. 2016. Iterative alternating neural attention for machine reading. *arXiv preprint arXiv:1606.02245* .

Nitish Srivastava, Geoffrey E Hinton, Alex Krizhevsky, Ilya Sutskever, and Ruslan Salakhutdinov. 2014. Dropout: a simple way to prevent neural networks from overfitting. *Journal of Machine Learning Research* 15(1):1929–1958.

Rupesh Kumar Srivastava, Klaus Greff, and Jürgen Schmidhuber. 2015. Highway networks. *arXiv preprint arXiv:1505.00387* .

Adam Trischler, Zheng Ye, Xingdi Yuan, Philip Bachman, Alessandro Sordoni, and Kaheer Suleman. 2016. Natural language comprehension with the epireader. In *Proceedings of the 2016 Conference on Empirical Methods in Natural Language Processing*. Association for Computational Linguistics, Austin, Texas, pages 128–137. https://aclweb.org/anthology/D16-1013.

Shuohang Wang and Jing Jiang. 2016. Machine comprehension using match-lstm and answer pointer. *arXiv preprint arXiv:1608.07905* .

Zhiguo Wang, Haitao Mi, Wael Hamza, and Radu Florian. 2016. Multi-perspective context matching for machine comprehension. *arXiv preprint arXiv:1612.04211* .

Dirk Weissenborn. 2016. Separating answers from queries for neural reading comprehension. *arXiv preprint arXiv:1607.03316* .

Dirk Weissenborn, Georg Wiese, and Laura Seiffe. 2017. Fastqa: A simple and efficient neural architecture for question answering. *arXiv preprint arXiv:1703.04816* .

Caiming Xiong, Victor Zhong, and Richard Socher. 2016. Dynamic coattention networks for question answering. *arXiv preprint arXiv:1611.01604* .

Fan Yang, Zhilin Yang, and William W Cohen. 2017. Differentiable learning of logical rules for knowledge base completion. *arXiv preprint arXiv:1702.08367* .

Matthew D Zeiler. 2012. Adadelta: an adaptive learning rate method. *arXiv preprint arXiv:1212.5701* .

Junbei Zhang, Xiaodan Zhu, Qian Chen, Lirong Dai, and Hui Jiang. 2017. Exploring question understanding and adaptation in neural-network-based question answering. *arXiv preprint arXiv:1703.04617* .

Automated Historical Fact-Checking by Passage Retrieval, Word Statistics, and Virtual Question-Answering

Mio Kobayashi[1]   **Ai Ishii**[1]   **Chikara Hoshino**[1]   **Hiroshi Miyashita**[1]

Takuya Matsuzaki[2]

[1]Nihon Unisys Ltd., Japan
{mio.kobayashi, ai.ishii, chikara.hoshino,
hiroshi.miyashita}@unisys.co.jp
[2]Nagoya University, Japan
matuzaki@nuee.nagoya-u.ac.jp

Abstract

This paper presents a hybrid approach to the verification of statements about historical facts. The test data was collected from the world history examinations in a standardized achievement test for high school students. The data includes various kinds of false statements that were carefully written so as to *deceive* the students while they can be disproven on the basis of the teaching materials. Our system predicts the truth or falsehood of a statement based on text search, word cooccurrence statistics, factoid-style question answering, and temporal relation recognition. These features contribute to the judgement complementarily and achieved the state-of-the-art accuracy.

1 Introduction

The proliferation of social media in the Internet drastically changed the status of traditional journalism, which has been an indispensable building block of modern democracy. News are now produced, propagated, and consumed by people in quite a different way than twenty years ago (Pew Research Center, 2016). The downside is that fake news and hoaxes spread through the social network as quickly as those from trustable sources. A mechanism for *fact-checking*, i.e., finding a support or disproof of a claim in a credible information source, is thus needed as a new social infrastructure.

The sheer amount of the information flow as well as the decentralized nature of the social media calls for support to the fact-checking by information technology (Cohen et al., 2011a,b). Although its full automation seems to be beyond current technology (Vlachos and Riedel, 2014; Has-

---

> **Context:** ... During the period of the Carolingian dynasty of Francia, the Roman Catholic Church preached that the religious cleansing of sins was necessary in order to achieve salvation after death. ...
>
> **Instruction:** From (1)-(4) below, choose the one correct sentence concerning events during the 8th century when the kingdom referred to in the underlined portion was established.
>
> **Choices:**
>
> (1) Pepin destroyed the Kingdom of the Lombards.
> (2) Charlemagne repelled the Magyars.
> (3) The reign of Emperor Taizong of Tang was called the Kaiyuan era.
> (4) The reign of Harun al-Rashid began.

Figure 1: Example of a True-or-False question

---

san et al., 2015), even its partial automation would greatly enhance the power of the current fact-checking services.

As a step towards this direction, we take up the automatic verification of a statement about historical facts against credible information sources. The test statements are collected from the world history examinations in a standardized achievement test for high school students in Japan (the National Center Test for University Admissions, NTCUA). Approximately 60% of the NCTUA world history exams are "True-or-False" questions. A question in this format consists of a paragraph of text that provides the context of the question, an instruction sentence, and four choices (Fig. 1)[1]. One has to choose a correct or incorrect statement from the four choices according to the instruction.

The test statements in the True-or-False questions are thoroughly tuned and checked by the examining board so that they are not too easy nor too difficult for human, and their truth or falsehood can be objectively determined on the basis

---

[1]The questions are posed in Japanese but we use English in the examples for the sake of readability.

Proceedings of the The 8th International Joint Conference on Natural Language Processing, pages 967–975,
Taipei, Taiwan, November 27 – December 1, 2017 ©2017 AFNLP

of the teaching materials written according to the official curriculum guidelines. The automatic verification of these statements hence serves as an idealized but still difficult test-bed for the basic fact-checking technologies.

In previous studies, three main approaches for answering True-or-False questions were presented: passage retrieval (Kano, 2014), conversion to factoid-style question answering (Kanayama et al., 2012), and textual entailment recognition (Tian and Miyao, 2014). In these approaches, the fact-checking task is directly converted to another, existing problem setting. We however show that the test statements in the True-or-False questions have compound characteristics through an analysis of past exams (§3). Thus, direct conversion alone does not suffice for solving this task satisfactorily, because each method is built on its own problem setting, which does not fully cover the variety of the test statements, especially the false ones. In this work, to overcome this difficulty, we attempt to decompose the problems according to our observations of past exams and design a solver that integrates the ideas behind the existing methods as the features of a statistical classifier (§4). Experimental results show that our decomposition of the task of historical fact-checking is successful in that the features work complementarily and the solver achieved the state-of-the-art accuracy (§6). An analysis of the remaining errors indicates a room for further improvement by the incorporation of linguistic and domain-specific knowledge into the system (§7).

Our essential contributions to this problem are as follows.

- Careful observations of past exams were conducted, based on which hypothetical characterizations of the task were formulated. Evidences were then collected to support these hypotheses.

- According to the observed evidences, five features that range over text search, statistics, and logical entailment were designed. They were combined as the features of a classifier and yielded state-of-the-art results on the task.

2 Related Work

Fact-checking can be framed as a question-answering (QA) task in a broad sense. However, it has not been studied as intensively as other QA tasks such as factoid-style question-answering (Ravichandran and Hovy, 2002; Bian et al., 2008; Ferrucci, 2012). Kanayama et al. (2012) proposed to convert a fact-checking question into a set of factoid-style questions. In the conversion, the named entities in a test statement are in turn replaced with an empty slot. The answer, i.e., the most appropriate word that fills the slot, was obtained by an open-domain factoid QA system. They define a confidence score that decreases when the QA system's answer differs from the hidden named entity (i.e., the one replaced with the empty slot). They experimented the idea by *manually* converting the test statements to factoid questions. We follow their idea in designing one of the features. We however fully automatized the conversion and defined another confidence score based on a simple document retrieval system instead of a full-fledged factoid QA system (§4.2.2).

Textual entailment recognition (RTE) (Dagan et al., 2013) has been extensively studied in the field of language processing. RTE can be seen as a quite restricted form of fact-checking where two sentences t and h are given and a system judges whether t is an evidence of (i.e., it entails) h or not. Tian and Miyao (2014) showed the effectiveness of their logic-based RTE system on the True-or-False questions of NCTUA history exams cast in the form of RTE (i.e., a test statement *and* an evidence sentence are given to the system).

Recent effort pursued a more realistic task setting for RTE, in which a system is given a sentence h and a large number of candidates of its evidence $\{t_i\}$ that are drawn from a document collection in advance. The system tests the entailment relation between each of t_is and h (Bentivogli et al., 2010, 2011). In the RITE-VAL shared task in NTCIR-2014 conference (Matsuyoshi et al., 2014), the participating RTE systems were evaluated both in the traditional RTE task setting and one that fully integrates the document retrieval and entailment recognition (i.e., only h and a document collection are given to the systems). The test sentences (i.e., hs) included those taken from NCTUA world history exams and hence the latter task setting is close to ours. The performance degradation between the two task settings was around 14% (absolute) for the case of the best-performing system. It indicates the difficulty of our task setting of historical fact-checking.

In a series of recent papers, elementary science

questions are used as a benchmark of AI systems (Khot et al., 2015; Jansen et al., 2016; Clark et al., 2016; Khashabi et al., 2016). The questions, all in the form of multiple-choice questions, were collected from 4th grade science tests. In the majority of the questions, the choices are nouns rather than sentences as in the following example taken from (Khashabi et al., 2016):

> Q. In New York State, the longest period of daylight occurs during which month? (A) December (B) June (C) March (D) September

The majority of them can hence be regarded as a factoid-style question with hints (i.e., the answer is one of the four). Clark et al. (2016) and Khashabi et al. (2016) demonstrated that the system performance was boosted by multi-step inference that combines, e.g., taxonomic knowledge ("N.Y. is in the northern hemisphere") and general law ("The summer solstice in the northern hemisphere is in June"). A special kind of logical relation, temporal inclusion, is considered in our system (§4.3). The intention is however on the detection of the falsity of a statement that is not in a temporal inclusion relation with an evidence sentence. The feature based on the conversion to factoid questions is also designed for the detection of falsehood by finding a counter-evidence. The different orientations, i.e., proof of a scientific fact vs. disproof of a historical non-fact, reflect the different natures of the problems.

3 Observation of Task

We examined past True-or-False questions prior to implementing the solver. The observation targets were the NCTUA world history exams 2005, 2007, 2009, 2011, and 2013s (supplementary exam). We used four sets of high school textbooks of world history and Wikipedia as knowledge resources.

From the observations, we formulated three hypotheses as follows. First, to verify most of the test statements (i.e., the choices), it is not necessary to gather several evidence sentences across different paragraphs in the resources; usually there is sufficient information in a local portion, such as a paragraph or a sentence in a knowledge resource. This is a natural consequence of the fact that most of the test statements describe a single historical event. Second, the knowledge resources include a

Knowledge resource	Count (ratio)
Textbook	111/137 (0.81)
Wikipedia	118/137 (0.86)
Textbook + Wikipedia	129/137 (0.94)

Table 1: Ratio of correct statements that can be evidenced by a single paragraph in the knowledge resource

	Count (ratio)
NE change	163 / 275 (0.59)
Time change	47 / 275 (0.17)
NE or Time change	210 / 275 (0.76)

Table 2: Ratio of incorrect statements in which one named entity or time expression is the reason of the falsity

more detailed time expression than the questions, e.g., "1453" as compared to "15th Century," and "1945" as compared to "1940s." Third, the falsity of many incorrect statements is attributed to a single named entity (NE) or time expression in them. For example, Choice (2) in Fig. 1, "Charlemagne repelled the Magyars." is an incorrect statement created by changing "Avars" to "Magyars" in a correct sentence "Charlemagne repelled the Avars."

To support these hypotheses, we gathered evidences from past exams. First, we examined the correct statements (137 in total) to determine whether: (1) a single paragraph in the knowledge resources includes all the NEs in the statement and (2) the knowledge resources include a more detailed time expression than the statement. Table 1 shows that, in most cases, a single paragraph includes sufficient information to allow the solver to verify the truth of a statement. Among the 137 correct statements, 48 of them included a time expression. The knowledge resources provided a more detailed time for 45 out of these 48 statements (94%). It is thus important to resolve the level of detail of the time expressions. Next, we counted the incorrect statements (275 in total) which can be turned into a correct one by changing one NE or time expression in it. Table 2 shows that to detect the falsity of an incorrect statement, detection of the changed NE is crucial.

4 Features and their Combination

Based on the above observations, we designed the following five features to score the confidence of truth. This section describes them in turn and explains how they are combined as the features of a statistical classifier.

These features are defined using several statistics collected on a set of documents. We created three document sets, D_s, D_p, and D_m, all from Wikipedia and four high school textbooks of world history, as follows. We first segmented the Wikipedia pages and the textbooks in two ways: one into a set of sentences D_s and the other into a set of paragraphs D_p. D_m is the union of D_s and D_p.

4.1 Text Search Feature

The observations revealed that, in most cases, the NEs in a correct statement are fully included in one paragraph or one sentence in the knowledge resources. The text search feature of the statement S is defined as the number of documents in D_m which include all NEs and content nouns in S. The solver expects that the greater the number is, the more likely the statement is true.

4.2 Statistical Features

The observations showed that an incorrect statement is created mainly by changing one NE in a correct sentence. To detect such a conversion, the solver estimates the strength of relatedness among the NEs in the statement. The solver uses two statistical features, which are respectively defined using global and local statistics collected on the document set.

4.2.1 Pointwise Mutual Information (PMI) Feature

The first statistical feature is PMI (Church and Hanks, 1989), which is defined for a pair of words as,

$$pmi(w_1, w_2) \equiv \log \frac{p(w_1, w_2 | D_s)}{p(w_1 | D_s) p(w_2 | D_s)},$$

where $p(w_i | D_s)$ denotes the probability of observing the word w_i in a sentence that is randomly chosen from D_s and $p(w_1, w_2 | D_s)$ denotes the probability of observing both w_1 and w_2 in a randomly chosen sentence. A low PMI score indicates the independence of the two words. The solver expects that a low PMI score indicates that two NEs are not related to each other and suggests that the statement is incorrect.

The solver calculates PMI for the pairs of an NE and the subsequent NE or a content word that appears before the subsequent NE in the statement, because the two words positioned close to

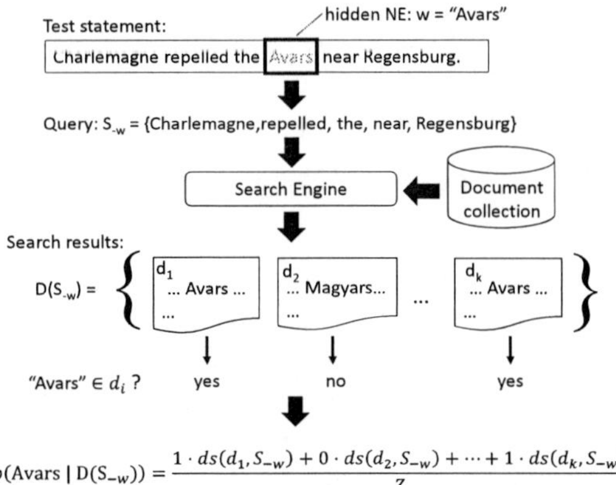

$$p(\text{Avars} \mid D(S_{-w})) = \frac{1 \cdot ds(d_1, S_{-w}) + 0 \cdot ds(d_2, S_{-w}) + \cdots + 1 \cdot ds(d_k, S_{-w})}{Z}$$

Figure 2: Calculation of the probability $p(w|D(S_{-w}))$ of finding w in the search results $D(S_{-w})$

each other tend to have strong relation. We write $WP(S)$ for the set of such pairs of words in S excluding the pairs of synonymous words. The final PMI feature of the statement S is defined by the average of $pmi(w_i, w_j)$.

$$\overline{pmi}(S) = \frac{1}{|WP(S)|} \sum_{(w_i, w_j) \in WP(S)} pmi(w_i, w_j).$$

4.2.2 Virtual Question Answering (VQA) Feature

The second feature is based on the result of a search that approximates the process of factoid QA. It directly attempts to detect the changed word in an incorrect statement (Fig. 2). The solver hides each NE w in a statement S in order and makes a VQA query S_{-w}, which is the set of words in S excluding w. If the statement is correct, the hidden word is expected to be found in the search results of the query S_{-w} at high probability.

For a hidden NE w, we first calculate the ratio $vqa(w)$ of the probabilities of finding w in the search results $D(S_{-w})$ of the query S_{-w} and in a randomly chosen document in the collection D_m:

$$vqa(w) = \log \frac{p(w|D(S_{-w}))}{p(w|D_m)}.$$

In the numerator, we consider the probability of finding w in a document $d \in D(S_{-w})$ that is sampled according to the confidence on the search result d against the query S_{-w}, rather than assuming a uniform distribution on $D(S_{-w})$:

$$p(w|D(S_{-w})) =$$
$$\sum_{d \in D(S_{-w})} [w \in d] \cdot p(d|D(S_{-w})), \quad (1)$$

where $[w \in d]$ is the binary indicator function that takes value 1 if d includes w, and 0 otherwise. The confidence factor $p(d|D(S_{-w}))$ is assumed to be proportional to a document score $ds(d, S_{-w})$ and we only consider top-k search results. That is, letting d_i denote the document ranked i-th in the search results according to $ds(d, S_{-w})$, we assume

$$p(d_i|D(S_{-w})) =$$
$$\begin{cases} ds(d_i, S_{-w}) \cdot Z^{-1} & (1 \leq i \leq k) \\ 0 & (k < i) \end{cases} \quad (2)$$

where $Z = \sum_{j=1}^{k} ds(d_j, S_{-w})$ is the normalization factor. From (1) and (2), we have

$$p(w|D(S_{-w})) = \sum_{\substack{i=1 \\ w \in d_i}}^{k} \frac{ds(d_i, S_{-w})}{\sum_{j=1}^{k} ds(d_j, S_{-w})}.$$

We set $k = 30$ in our experiments.

The document score ds is defined by Term Frequency-Inverse Document Frequency (TF-IDF), which is written as

$$ds(d, S_{-w}) = \frac{1}{\ell(d)} \sum_{w' \in S_{-w}} tf(w', d) \cdot idf(w'),$$

where $tf(w', d)$ is the frequency of the word w' in the document d, $idf(w')$ is the inverse document frequency of the word w', and $\ell(d)$ is the length of d.

The VQA feature uses document-local statistics (except for IDF) and counts only in the top-k search results. However, in this feature, all the query words jointly contribute through the document score ds, in contrast to the case of PMI where only the pairwise relations are considered. The final VQA feature is defined as the average of $vqa(w)$.

$$\overline{vqa}(S) = \frac{1}{|\text{NE}(S)|} \sum_{w \in \text{NE}(S)} vqa(w),$$

where $\text{NE}(S)$ is the set of NEs in the statement S.

4.2.3 Length Feature

We also use the length of the statement (number of words) as a feature. PMI and VQA features of a long statement tend to have low values regardless of the correctness of the statement. The length feature adjusts this bias.

4.3 Time Feature (Logical Entailment)

The observations revealed that the level of detail of the time expressions in the choice sentences differs from that in the knowledge resources. The time information is a key factor of historical events. Therefore, the solver needs a more rigorous inference about temporal relations than about the matching of other NEs. We implemented a module that logically determines the inclusion relation between two time expressions. The time expressions in the statements and the knowledge resources are extracted and converted to ranges of date (e.g., "19th century" → 1801-01-01 ... 1900-12-31) by NormalizedNumexp[2]. If the range of a time expression in a statement includes one in the knowledge resources, they are judged as "matched". The solver hides the time expression t from the statement S and makes the VQA query S_{-t}. The time feature of the statement S is defined as the number of documents in the top-k search results of query S_{-t} ($k = 30$) that include a time expression that matches the hidden time expression t.

4.4 Combination of Features (Machine Learning)

The solver combines the above five features using statistical binary classifiers. In our settings, N training samples $\{(x_1, y_1), \ldots, (x_N, y_N)\}$ are given, where x_i is a five-dimensional feature vector and $y_i \in \{1, 0\}$ indicates the truth or falsehood of the sample. We used the "scikit-learn" toolkit[3] and created an ensemble of three classifiers, by simply averaging their [0, 1] probabilistic outputs to reduce variance of each classifier (Pedro, 2012). As the classifiers, we used logistic regression, gradient boosting classifier, and support vector machine. The hyperparameters of each classifier are determined by cross validation.

5 Resources and Common Modules

This section describes additional modules that were used in the experiments described in §6.

Dataset	# test statements	%correct	%incorrect
DEV	412	33.3%	66.7%
TEST	1112	35.3%	64.7%

Table 3: Size of development and test data

5.1 Custom Dictionary

We use a named entity dictionary and a synonym dictionary, both of which were manually compiled based on textbooks and Wikipedia. The named entity dictionary was created by mainly using the index of textbooks. In the dictionary, approximately 20,000 NEs are categorized into various classes (time, person, etc.) by human experts. The synonym dictionary was created based on Wikipedia redirect and bracketed expressions after NEs (e.g., "Charlemagne (Charles I)"). Additionally, the solver uses Nihongo Goi-Taikei[4], a Japanese thesaurus, to discriminate NEs from common nouns.

5.2 Retrieval Module

The retrieval module of the solver is based on Apache Solr[5]. We used the Solr defaults (TFIDF-weighted cosine similarity) and the Kuromoji Japanese morphological analyzer[6] to tokenize Japanese sentences. As mentioned in §4, all knowledge resources are indexed at overlapping levels of the sentence and the paragraph, and retrieval is executed across fields of both levels by means of the ExtendedDisMax Query Parser[7].

5.3 Matching of Words

When two words are compared in the solver, some suffixes are ignored to absorb orthographical variants (e.g., "Japan" and "Japanese" are considered to be the same). The suffix list is made from high frequency morphemes (Okita and Liu, 2014). We examined the frequency of morphemes in the textbooks, and then from the top, if the morpheme is a suffix of NE, we added to the list.

Additionally, if a word w in a question has a synonym in a document retrieved from the knowledge resources, the word w is considered to be included in the document.

5.4 Complementing the Lack of Information

The truth or falsehood of a choice sentence is often indeterminable without the information pro-

---

Context: Coexistence between Christians and Muslims was seen on the <u>Iberian Peninsula</u> in the Middle Ages, ...

Instruction: From (1)-(4) below, choose the most appropriate sentence that describes the history of Spain in the 20th century related to the underlined portion.

Choices:

(1) The French army suffered in guerrilla warfare in Spain.
(2) In the Spanish Civil War, Germany and Italy maintained a policy of non-intervention.
(3) Franco established a dictatorial regime.
(4) The Philippines were seized from it by the U.S.A.

Figure 3: Question 31 in the 2011 data set

vided in the context and the instruction. For instance, (1), (3), and (4) in Fig. 3 all describe historical facts but the condition in the instruction, "in the 20th century," turns (1) and (4) to false since they happened in the 19th century. Meanwhile, the context and the instruction also include irrelevant information that does not affect the truth of the choices. For instance, the underlined portion, "Iberian Peninsula," is redundant since the instruction asks more restrictively about "Spain." Furthermore, "the Middle Ages" in the context is not relevant to any of the choices.

The instruction tends to include a condition that applies to all choices, such as the location and the time of the historical events described in them. The context usually provides relevant condition only when it is explicitly indicated so.

We utilize these observations as well as the category of the NEs to extract only relevant keywords from the instruction and the context. First, the location names and time expressions are extracted from the instruction if a choice includes no such phrases. The NEs in the underlined portion of the context are then extracted if the instruction includes none of the phrases in a pre-defined set of cue phrases, such as "related to," that indicate the context is not so relevant to the determination of the truth of the choices. Finally, among the NEs extracted from the context, we discard those categorized as an abstract concept in the NE dictionary, such as "social phenomena" and "social role." For the choice (1) in Fig. 3, "the 20th century" in the instruction is extracted since (1) does not include a time expression but "Iberian Peninsula" in the context is not extracted since the instruction refers to the underlined portion using the cue phrase "related to."

---

[4] http://www.iwanami.co.jp/hotnews/GoiTaikei/

[5] http://lucene.apache.org/solr/

[6] http://www.atilika.org/

[7] https://cwiki.apache.org/confluence/display/solr/The+Extended+DisMax+Query+Parser

Features	DEV		TEST	
	Binary T/F	4-way	Binary T/F	4-way
All	80.8%	75.7%	74.2%	68.0%
-Text search	77.7%	66.0%	70.5%	60.1%
-PMI	79.6%	74.8%	73.7%	66.2%
-VQA	74.0%	64.1%	71.2%	60.8%
-Time	79.6%	75.7%	73.4%	66.9%
-Length	80.6%	75.7%	73.8%	67.3%

Table 4: Feature ablation study

Features	DEV		TEST	
	Binary T/F	4-way	Binary T/F	4-way
Text search	73.8%	58.3%	71.0%	52.5%
PMI	67.7%	53.4%	66.3%	45.7%
VQA	74.8%	58.3%	70.8%	53.2%
Time	68.2%	35.0%	65.3%	28.4%
Length	66.5%	33.0%	65.3%	23.7%

Table 5: Accuracy with only one feature

6 Experiments

6.1 Experimental Setup

We exhaustively extracted the True-or-False questions from past NCTUA world history exams held from 2005 to 2015 and evaluated the accuracy of the true-or-false (T/F) binary predictions individually made on each of the choice sentences[8]. The data was divided into two disjoint subsets, DEV and TEST. DEV consists of the questions used in the preliminary analysis described in §3. TEST consists of the rest of the questions. Table 3 provides the number of the test statements (i.e., the choice sentences) and the distributions of the correct and incorrect statements. Approximately 20% of the questions ask to choose a false statement in four choices, which include three correct statements. For reference, we also report the accuracy on the 4-way multiple-choice questions. The answer to a multiple-choice question is the choice on which the ensemble of the classifiers yielded the maximum or minimum score.

For the evaluation, we adopted cross validation. DEV and TEST were divided into 20 subsets, each of which was taken from the questions in the same exam. We applied 20-fold cross validation on the subsets. We summarized the results with DEV and TEST respectively.

6.2 Experimental Results

To evaluate the importance of each feature, we tested two feature combination patterns. In the

---

[8] Although the instruction sentences indicate either (i) only one of the choices is correct ("choose the correct one") or (ii) only one of them is incorrect ("choose the incorrect one"), our solver does not utilize this information in any form when it makes binary T/F prediction.

System	T/F binary acc.	4-way acc.
Kanayama et al. (2012)	79% (73/92)	65% (15/23)
This paper (VQA only)	73% (67/92)	52% (12/23)
This paper (all features)	84% (77/92)	83% (19/23)

Table 6: Comparison with manual question conversion on NCTUA 2007 questions

first pattern, the classifiers were trained excluding one feature (Table 4) and in the second one the classifiers were trained with only one feature (Table 5). These results show that the VQA and Text search features are more important than the others. The highest T/F judgement accuracy, 80.8% on DEV and 74.2% on TEST, was obtained using all the features. On the DEV set, the ablation of one of the five features resulted in a loss of 0.2-6.8 points in the T/F judgement accuracy and 0.0-11.6 points in the 4-way multiple-choice accuracy (Table 4). It suggests that the combination of the features is more effective for comparing the confidence on the truth of four statements rather than for the T/F judgement on a single statement. Comparison of the results in Table 5 with 'All' in Table 4 further supports it; the effect of combining the five features compared with the result by a single feature is far more evident in the accuracy on the multiple-choice format. These results show the five features worked complementarily and validates our decomposition of the task into the five features.

Table 6 presents a comparison with Kanayama et al. (2012)'s result based on the conversion of T/F judgement to factoid-style questions. The test questions were taken from NCTUA 2007 exam. This comparison is not strict in a few regards. First, Kanayama et al. used English translations of the questions while we used the original questions in Japanese. Second, they manually supplied the choice sentences with necessary information extracted from the instruction and the context. Finally, they converted the choice sentences to factoid-style questions also manually, while our system is fully automated. The results of VQA feature are slightly worse than Kanayama et al.'s which is based on a similar idea. The addition of the other four features boosted the accuracy and it surpassed their result.

Finally, Table 7 presents the accuracy of our system in comparison with previously reported results by fully automatic systems (Shibuki et al., 2014, 2016). We compared the accuracy on the

System	4-way acc. NCTUA 2007
This paper	83% (19/23)
Okita and Liu (2014)	74% (17/23)
Kano (2014)	57% (13/23)
Sakamoto et al. (2014)	52% (12/23)

System	4-way acc. NCTUA 2011
This paper	90% (18/20)
Kobayashi et al. (2016)	80% (16/20)
Takada et al. (2016)	60% (12/20)
Sakamoto et al. (2016)	60% (12/20)

Table 7: Comparison with previous automatic systems

True-or-False questions in the 4-way multiple-choice format. Our system achieved a higher accuracy than the best previous results on NTCUA 2007 and 2011 exams.

7 Error Analysis

We now show some examples that cannot be solved by our current approach and describe the cause of the errors.

Antonym of Verbs (10 sentences) Some incorrect statements in the choices are created by changing a verb to its antonym. For example, in Question 8 in the 2009 exam, the falsity of the sentence "The Agricultural Adjustment Act (AAA) resulted in the prices of agricultural produce being lowered," is attributed to the verb "lowered" because the sentence becomes correct if we replace "lowered" with "raised." To properly recognize such false sentences, we need to utilize lexical knowledge about the antonymy and synonymy relations among verbs.

Semantic Roles (five sentences) Many historical events involve two or more participants. For example, in Question 3 in the 2007 exam, the sentence "The Almohad Caliphate, which advanced into the Iberian Peninsula, was overthrown by the Almoravid dynasty." includes the two participants, "The Almohad Caliphate" and "the Almoravid dynasty." The sentence is incorrect because the truth was "The Almoravid dynasty was overthrown by the Almohad Caliphate." To detect this kind of falsity, we need to recognize the semantic roles (e.g., agent and patient) of the participants in the event denoted by the verb. It is beyond the expressiveness of the VQA and PMI features that are largely based on word cooccurrence.

Indirect Description of Time (four sentences) In Question 15 in the 2007 exam, the instruction includes the following phrase: "choose the one term that correctly describes the religion that was established after the time of Genghis Khan." The current system cannot extract any temporal information from "after the time of Genghis Khan," which is equivalent to "after the *death* of Genghis Khan" and thus to "after 1227." To this end, we need to analyze the combination of the temporal expression (e.g., the time before/after/during of X) and the entity type (e.g., X: Person) and utilize domain-knowledge such as birth/death or establishment/abolishment years of historical entities.

8 Conclusion and Future Work

As a step towards the goal of automated fact-checking, we have worked on the task of true-or-false judgement on the statements about historical facts. We scrutinized the characteristics of the task and designed five confidence metrics according to the observations, which are integrated as the features in a statistical classifier. Experimental results showed that the five features complementarily contributed to the discrimination between a true statement and a false one. Our system achieved the state-of-the-art accuracy on a few datasets. An analysis of the remaining errors indicated a room for improvement by the incorporation of linguistic knowledge such as antonymy of verbs and semantic roles of the events, and extraction of temporal information based on linguistic patterns and domain-knowledge.

Acknowledgments

This research was supported by Todai Robot Project at National Institute of Informatics. We are gratefully acknowledge Tokyo Shoseki Co., Ltd. and Yamakawa Shuppansha Ltd. for providing the textbook data.

References

Luisa Bentivogli, Peter Clark, Ido Dagan, and Danilo Giampiccolo. 2010. The sixth PASCAL recognizing textual entailment challenge. In *TAC*.

Luisa Bentivogli, Peter Clark, Ido Dagan, and Danilo Giampiccolo. 2011. The seventh PASCAL recognizing textual entailment challenge. In *TAC*.

Jiang Bian, Yandong Liu, Eugene Agichtein, and Hongyuan Zha. 2008. Finding the right facts in the crowd: factoid question answering over social media. In *WWW*. pages 467–476.

K. Church and P. Hanks. 1989. Word association norms, mutual information, and lexicography. In *ACL-89*. pages 76–83.

Peter Clark, Oren Etzioni, Tushar Khot, Ashish Sabharwal, Oyvind Tafjord, Peter D. Turney, and Daniel Khashabi. 2016. Combining retrieval, statistics, and inference to answer elementary science questions. In *AAAI-2016*. pages 2580–2586.

Sarah Cohen, James T. Hamilton, and Fred Turner. 2011a. Computational journalism. *Commun. ACM* 54(10):66–71.

Sarah Cohen, Chengkai Li, Jun Yang, and Cong Yu. 2011b. Computational journalism: A call to arms to database researchers. In *CIDR*. pages 148–151.

Ido Dagan, Dan Roth, Mark Sammons, and Fabio Massimo Zanzotto. 2013. *Recognizing Textual Entailment: Models and Applications*. Morgan & Claypool Publishers.

David A. Ferrucci. 2012. Introduction to "this is watson". *IBM Journal of Research and Development* 56(3.4):1:1–1:15.

Naeemul Hassan, Bill Adair, James T. Hamilton, Chengkai Li, Mark Tremayne, Jun Yang, and Cong Yu. 2015. The quest to automate fact-checking. In *Proc. of the 2015 Computation+Journalism Symposium*.

Peter Jansen, Niranjan Balasubramanian, Mihai Surdeanu, and Peter Clark. 2016. What's in an explanation? characterizing knowledge and inference requirements for elementary science exams. In *COLING*. pages 2956–2965.

Hiroshi Kanayama, Yusuke Miyao, and John Prager. 2012. Answering yes/no questions via question inversion. In *COLING-2012*. pages 1377–1392.

Yoshinobu Kano. 2014. Solving history exam by keyword distribution: KJP. In *NTCIR-11*.

Daniel Khashabi, Tushar Khot, Ashish Sabharwal, Peter Clark, Oren Etzioni, and Dan Roth. 2016. Question answering via integer programming over semi-structured knowledge. In *IJCAI*. pages 1145–1152.

Tushar Khot, Niranjan Balasubramanian, Eric Gribkoff, Ashish Sabharwal, Peter Clark, and Oren Etzioni. 2015. Exploring markov logic networks for question answering. In *EMNLP*. pages 685–694.

Mio Kobayashi, Hiroshi Miyashita, Ai Ishii, and Chikara Hoshino. 2016. NUL system at QA Lab-2 task. In *NTCIR-12*.

Suguru Matsuyoshi, Yusuke Miyao, Tomohide Shibata, Chuan-Jie Lin, Cheng-Wei Shih, Yotaro Watanabe, and Teruko Mitamura. 2014. Overview of the NTCIR-11 recognizing inference in text and validation (RITE-VAL) task. In *NTCIR-11*.

Tsuyoshi Okita and Qun Liu. 2014. The question answering system of DCUMT in NTCIR-11 QA Lab. In *NTCIR-11*.

Domingos Pedro. 2012. A few useful things to know about machine learning. In *Commun. of the ACM*. volume 55(10), pages 78–87.

Pew Research Center. 2016. News use across social media platforms 2016.

Deepak Ravichandran and Eduard Hovy. 2002. Learning surface text patterns for a question answering system. In *ACL-2002*. pages 41–47.

Kotaro Sakamoto, Madoka Ishioroshi, Hyogo Matsui, Takahisa Jin, Fuyuki Wada, Shu Nakayama, Hideyuki Shibuki, Tatsunori Mori, and Noriko Kando. 2016. Forst: Question answering system for second-stage examinations at NTCIR-12 QA Lab-2 task. In *NTCIR-12*.

Kotaro Sakamoto, Hyogo Matsui, Eisuke Matsunaga, Takahisa Jin, Hideyuki Shibuki, Tatsunori Mori, Madoka Ishioroshi, and Noriko Kando. 2014. Forst: Question answering system using basic element at NTCIR-11 QA-Lab task. In *NTCIR-11*.

Hideyuki Shibuki, Kotaro Sakamoto, Madoka Ishioroshi, Akira Fujita, Yoshinobu Kano, Teruko Mitamura, Tatsunori Mori, and Noriko Kando. 2016. Task overview for NTCIR-12 QA Lab-2. In *NTCIR-12*.

Hideyuki Shibuki, Kotaro Sakamoto, Yoshinobu Kano, Teruko Mitamura, Madoka Ishioroshi, Kelly Y. Itakura, Di Wang, Tatsunori Mori, and Noriko Kando. 2014. Overview of the NTCIR-11 QA-Lab task. In *NTCIR-11*.

Takuma Takada, Takuya Imagawa, Takuya Matsuzaki, and Satoshi Sato. 2016. SML question-answering system for world history essay and multiple-choice exams at NTCIR-12 QA Lab-2. In *NTCIR-12*.

Ran Tian and Yusuke Miyao. 2014. Answering center-exam questions on history by textual inference. In *Proceedings of the 28th Annual Conference of the Japanese Society for Artificial Intelligence*.

Andreas Vlachos and Sebastian Riedel. 2014. Fact checking: Task definition and dataset construction. In *Proc. ACL 2014 Workshop on Language Technologies and Computational Social Science*. pages 18–22.

Integrating Subject, Type, and Property Identification for Simple Question Answering over Knowledge Base

Wei-Chuan Hsiao, Hen-Hsen Huang and **Hsin-Hsi Chen**
Department of Computer Science and Information Engineering
National Taiwan University, Taipei, Taiwan
weichuanhsiao@gmail.com; hhhuang@nlg.csie.ntu.edu.tw; hhchen@ntu.edu.tw

Abstract

This paper presents an approach to identify subject, type and property from knowledge base for answering simple questions. We propose new features to rank entity candidates in KB. Besides, we split a relation in KB into type and property. Each of them is modeled by a bi-directional LSTM. Experimental results show that our model achieves the state-of-the-art performance on the SimpleQuestions dataset. The hard questions in the experiments are also analyzed in detail.

1 Introduction

With the popularity of the Internet, more and more new information is generated every day. The information may be stored in unstructured data, such as Wikipedia, which is presented as an article or web page, or in the form of structured data. Knowledge base (KB), such as Freebase (Bollacker et al., 2008) and DBpedia (Lehmann et al., 2015), is very popular. The information in the KB is a description of the relationship between two entities and is stored in the form of (subject, relation, object) triple. In KB, each entity is represented by a unique id, for example, J.K. Rowling's mid (Machine ID) in Freebase is "m.042xh".

With these large-scale open-domain KBs, it is important to access the knowledge efficiently and effectively to meet what users need. The most direct and close to people's life is question answering (QA) system in natural language. People can ask any questions in their familiar languages, and then use the QA system to get answers from the web resources. Current QA research is often based on KB to find appropriate triples for answering question, which is called QA over KB.

QA systems can be classified by the form of the question. There are two categories of questions in QA system, i.e., simple questions and complex questions. Simple questions can be answered by exactly one triple in the KB. For example, the question "Who is the author of Harry Potter?" can be answered by triple "(Harry Potter, author, J.K. Rowling)". Although this category is "simple" question, retrieving a triple from the KB is not a trivial task due to the billions of facts in the KB. Complex questions contain more restrictions. These questions may involve two or more triples in the KB, or have other semantic constraints to restrict the answers to a smaller set. For example, "the first" in the question "What is the name of the first Harry Potter novel?" restricts that there is only one answer. Previous researches showed that simple questions are the more common category in community QA websites (Fader et al., 2013). This paper focuses on factoid simple question-answering over Freebase.

Simple question can be answered with the object of one KB triple. Thus, the systems only need to find the subject and relation of the triple which can describe the question properly. The issues of simple QA are the identification of the subject entity in a question, and the resolution of the gap between the natural language expression in the question and the relation description in the KB. After a QA system receives users' questions, it needs to transform a question into a KB query, e.g. SPARQL. The question can then be transformed into the KB query, which can access KB to get the answer.

Proceedings of the The 8th International Joint Conference on Natural Language Processing, pages 976–985,
Taipei, Taiwan, November 27 – December 1, 2017 ©2017 AFNLP

Previous simple QA model often adopts a two-step paradigm. Entity-linking step identifies the subject entities in questions, and forms the candidate entity set and relation set. The candidate relation set is formed by all the relations which have connections with any entity in candidate entity set. Relation-finding step further identifies a proper relation from the candidate relation set. Dai et al. (2016) propose a neural-network based two-step approach to simple QA over Freebase, and formulate the task into a probabilistic form. Given a question q, the first step is to find the candidate relation r with high probability $P(r|q)$. The second step is to find the subject s with high $P(s|r,q)$. As a result, the object in the KB triple which contains the subject s and the relation r with the highest $P(s,r|q)$ is the answer.

The relation in KB triple has hierarchical structure: domain-type-property. For example, in "people.person.place_of_birth", "place_of_birth" is the property used to present the birth place of a person. The type of this relation is "person", and the domain is "people". In Freebase, many relations have the same property, but are in different types. For example, both "film.film.genre" and "music.artist.genre" have the property "genre", but they are under different domains and types. These two relations are regarded as the same if we only consider the property. The major issue is: they are different relations although they have the same meaning. On the other hand, if the whole relation is considered as a class, the distribution of relations is getting sparser. The past two-step approaches cannot distinguish the subtlety in the structured relation.

In this paper, we will propose a novel three-step approach, including subject, type and property identification steps, to deal with the hierarchical structure of the relation. Our approach introduces new features in subject identification to distinguish similar entities from different aspects. Moreover, splitting relation into type and property predicts relation more precisely. Experimental results show our model outperforms the existing models and achieves a state-of-the-art accuracy of 76.7%.

This paper is organized as follows. Section 2 introduces related works of QA system. Section 3 presents our three-step paradigm. Section 4 shows the experiments on the SimpleQuestions dataset (Bordes et al., 2015) and compares ours with previous works. We also discuss the importance of each component of our system. Section 5 analyzes the errors in the experiments. Section 6 concludes the remarks.

2   Related Works

Previous simple QA models can be divided into two categories. The first one is based on semantic parsing, which maps a question to its logical form. Then, the logical form can be transformed to SPARQL for KB retrieval.

Berant et al. (2013) present a semantic parser that does not need to be trained through the annotated logical form. They construct a lexicon that maps natural language phrases to KB relations by aligning large text corpus with Freebase. Candidate logical forms can be obtained by this lexicon and the other bridging operations.

Berant and Liang (2014) propose a semantic parser via paraphrasing. They use the intermediate question to deal with the problem of the mismatch between input question and its logical forms.

Yih et al. (2015) treat a question as a query graph, which can be directly mapped to its logical form. Semantic parsing is then equivalent to finding a sub-graph of the KB which can represent the question.

The semantic parsing approach which often requires the human annotated logical form may increase the cost of obtaining training data. Although the use of rule-based method to generate logical forms can reduce the use of annotated data, it limits the application domain. The second approach is information extraction, which needs only question-answer pairs for training. This method retrieves some candidate answers from KB for each question, and ranks the candidates through several features. Deep neural network models are often employed for deriving the vector representations of questions and the KB elements.

The Memory Network based QA system is proposed by Bordes et al. (2015). By embedding all of the KB elements and questions in the same vector space, the system can deal with the relationship between input language and the KB language.

Glob and He (2016) propose a character-level, attention-based encoder-decoder QA model. Their model embeds the questions and KB elements by a long short-term memory (LSTM) (Hochreiter and Schmidhuber, 1997) encoder and a CNN-based encoder, respectively. And a LSTM decoder with attention mechanism is used to predict the appropriate answer entity and relation.

Dai et al. (2016) formulate the QA problem into a probabilistic form. Given a question, the answer is the triple in KB containing the subject and relation with the highest conditional probability. They first use a focused pruning method to tag the span in question which is most probable to be the subject entity and gets the candidate answer triples. Then they use a relation network and a subject network, both are a two-layer bidirectional-GRU model, to get the similarity scores between candidate triples and question. We modify their probabilistic form with the splitting of the relation part r into type t and property p.

Dong et al. (2015) introduce a multi-column CNNs (MCCNNs) to analyze the question in three different aspects: answer path, answer context and answer type. The system represents the question in three low-dimensional vectors, each of them then matches to one of the answer aspect to derive the scores of candidates.

Yin et al. (2016) also use the CNN-based approach to implement the QA system. They use a word-level CNN with attentive max-pooling to model the relationship between KB relations and question pattern. They also add an active linker, which is similar to the focused pruning method in Dai et al. (2016), to reduce the number of candidates and improve the performance significantly.

3 Methodology

Our method includes subject identification, type identification, and property identification steps, as shown in Figure 1. We first give an overall picture and then describe each of them in deep in the following sections.

3.1 A Three-Step Paradigm

The relation in a Freebase triple has a hierarchical structure in three levels: domain, type, and property. Many relations have the same property but they are in different types and domains. For example, both

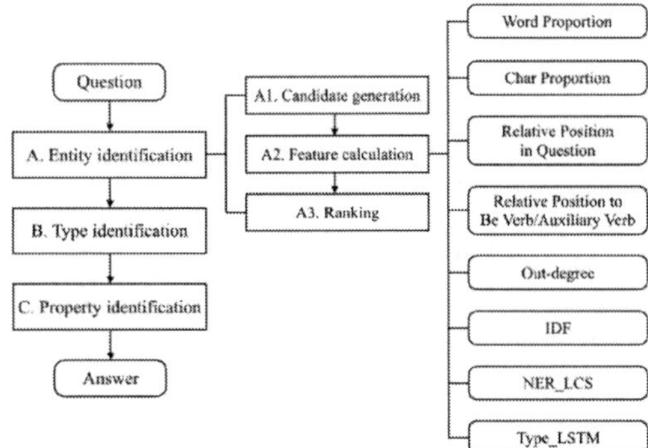

Figure 1: System Overview.

the relations "wine.wine.color" and "roses.roses.color" are used to describe the color of things, but they are in type "wine" and "roses", respectively. We separate a relation into type and property parts to understand the question meaning more precisely.

Given a KB $\mathcal{K}$ and a question q, the three-step paradigm aims at finding a KB triple containing s, t, and p with the highest probability $P(s, t, p|q)$, where s is a subject, and t and p are type and property of a structured relation, respectively. The process is formulated by Equations (1) and (2). The answer of the question is the object o of the triple (s, r, o) in $\mathcal{K}$.

$$P(s, t, p|q) = P(s|q) \cdot P(t|s, q) \\ \cdot P(p|s, t, q) \tag{1}$$

$$s^*, t^*, p^* = \operatorname*{argmax}_{s,t,p \in \mathcal{K}} P(s, t, p|q) \tag{2}$$

3.2 Entity Identification

The first step is to find potential entities in the question, and link them to KB. We use the Freebase subset FB5M in the SimpleQuestions dataset as the KB. We retrieve all candidate subject entities in question from the KB and calculate their entity linking scores on account of eight features, as in steps A1-A3 of Figure 1.

To find candidate entities for a question, we extract mentions in the question by maximum string matching. A mention that matches an entity name or an entity alias is extracted. When multiple matches are found in an overlapped span, the longest one is taken. And the mention is filtered if it is a stop word or a number that contains less than four digits. All the entities in $\mathcal{K}$ that have the same names or aliases as the mentions form the candidate entity set.

After obtaining all the candidate entities, we assign each of the candidates a linking score. The score is measured by a learning-to-rank model with eight features in different aspects. The eight features are described as follows.

Word Proportion (Yin et al., 2016): We compute the proportion as the length of candidate entity divided by the length of the question. The length is measured by the number of words. The longer the matched entity name is, the more likely it is a subject.

Char Proportion: Similar to word proportion, the length is computed by the number of characters instead.

Relative Position in Question (Yin et al., 2016): The relative position of a candidate entity is the position of its last token divided by the length of the question (in words). That models an observation: most entity is far from the beginning of the question.

Relative Position to Be Verb/Auxiliary Verb: Subject entity tends to be close to and behind Be verb/auxiliary verb in a question. We take the subtraction of the Be verb/auxiliary verb position and the first token of candidate entity position as α. If the candidate entity position is before the Be verb/auxiliary verb, this feature is α, which is a negative number. Otherwise, this feature is $1/\alpha$, which is a positive number. If no such verbs exist, this feature is set to 0

Out-degree: The number of out-going links of the entity in the KB is taken as Out-degree feature. The more the number of links the entity has, the higher the feature value is and the entity in the KB is more informative. The direction of links from subject to object represents the impact of the entity.

IDF: We take each question in SimpleQuesions training set as a document, and compute the inverse document frequency of the entity. The higher the value is, the more specific the entity is.

NER_LCS: We use the LSTM-CRF named entity recognition (NER) tagger[1] (Lample et al., 2016) to find the span from the question that is most

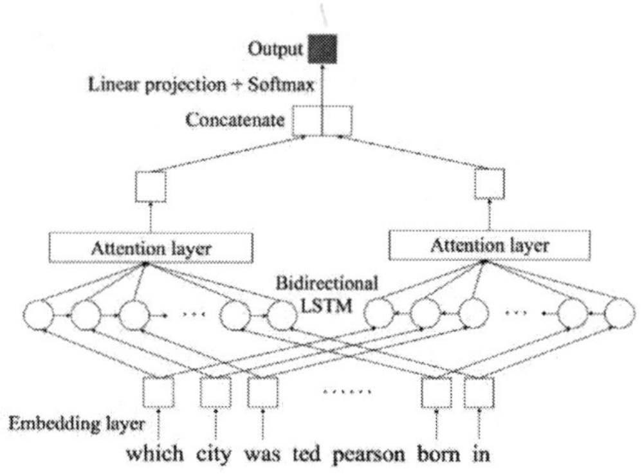

Figure 2: Structure of Type_LSTM in entity identification.

likely to be a subject entity, and compute the length of the longest common subsequence (in characters) between the candidate entity and the words in the tagged span. The tagger consists of an embedding layer, a bidirectional-LSTM layer, and a conditional random field layer to predict the label for each word. The higher the NER_LCS value is, the more possible the candidate is a subject entity.

Type_LSTM: Each entity has entity types in Freebase to describe its characteristics, e.g., entity "Alex Golfis" belongs to types "person", "actor", and "deceased_person". There are total 500 types for entities in FB5M. For a question, we estimate the types of its subject. A bidirectional-LSTM with attention is trained to derive the probability distribution of each question over the 500 types. The structure of the network is shown in Figure 2. The training input of the LSTM is the whole questions and the types of their ground truth entities, and the training objective is categorical cross entropy. The test input is a question, and the output is a probability distribution of the question over the 500 types. We can get the type information of the candidate entity from Freebase, and sum over all dimensions corresponding to the types to get this feature. It means how probable the question is in some types.

With the above eight features, support vector machine for ranking (SVM[rank]) (Joachims, 2006) is trained to combine these features and derive a score $u_1(s, q)$ for each candidate entity s in the question q. Then each entity has the probability $P(s|q)$:

---

[1] https://github.com/glample/tagger .

$$P(s|q) = \frac{\exp(u_1(s, q))}{\sum_{s'} \exp(u_1(s', q))} \tag{3}$$

where s' is an entity in the candidate entity set. For the entities in the KB but not in the candidate entity set, their $P(s|q) = 0$.

3.3 Type Identification

Given a question q, the type network determines the type of the relation most likely to be answered. We use $E(t)$ to represent the embedding of the type t, and use $g_1(q)$ to represent the vector of question q. Our goal is to make the cosine similarity between $g_1(q)$ and the correct type embedding $E(t^*)$ higher than the cosine similarities between $g_1(q)$ and the other types.

The network structure is shown in Figure 3. First, the question vector $g_1(q)$ is generated by a bidirectional-LSTM model. We change the words in q to lowercase and remove the punctuation. Then we put the words into the embedding layer. After the bidirectional-LSTM layer, the two vectors in left and right directions are concatenated together. The concatenated vector is put into a linear projection layer with sigmoid, and the question vector $g_1(q)$ is generated. After that, we calculate the similarity between $g_1(q)$ and different type embeddings $E(t)$. The embedding $E(t)$ is trained with the bidirectional-LSTM model, and has the same dimension as $g_1(q)$. $E(t)$ and $g_1(q)$ are in the same space so that the cosine similarity $u_2(t, q)$ can be computed by Equation (4).

$$u_2(t, q) = \cos(g_1(q), E(t)) \tag{4}$$

The probability of type t given the question q and the candidate entity set is defined as follows:

$$P(t|s, q) = \begin{cases} \frac{\exp(u_2(t, q))}{\sum_{t'} \exp(u_2(t', q))}, & \text{if } t \text{ has link with } s \\ 0 & , \text{otherwise} \end{cases} \tag{5}$$

where t' is a type in the candidate type set. To reduce the computation and the number of candidate types, only those types which have links with an entity in the candidate entity set is chosen into the candidate type set. $P(t|s, q)$ is set to 0 for those types which are impossible to be the correct answer due to the lack of links with any candidate entity.

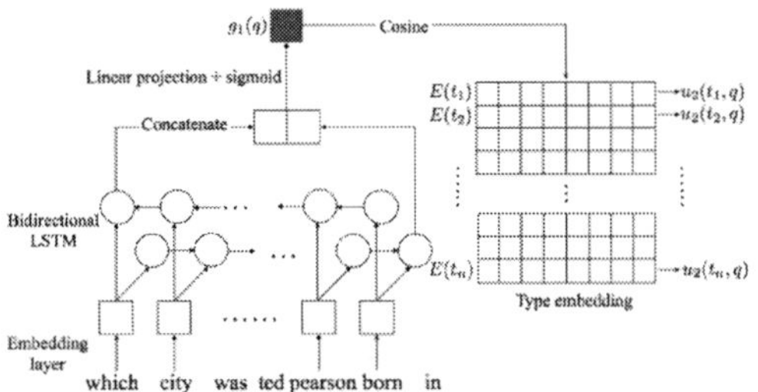

Figure 3: Type identification network.

For training the type network, the hinge loss with negative samples is the objective function to be minimized.

$$\ell(\theta_t) = \sum_{i=1}^{N_t} \max(0, m_t - u_2(t^*, q) + u_2(t_i, q)) \tag{6}$$

where θ_t is the parameters to learn, N_t is the number of negative samples, m_t is the margin, t^* is the correct type, and t_i is the type randomly sampled from all types except t^*.

3.4 Property Identification

Given a question q, property identification determines the property of the relation most likely to be answered. We use $E(p)$ to represent the embedding of the property p, and $g_2(q)$ to represent the vector of question q. Similar to the type network, our goal is to make the cosine similarity between $g_2(q)$ and the correct property embedding $E(p^*)$ higher than the cosine similarities between $g_2(q)$ and the other properties.

The structure of the property network is the same as that of the type network, which is shown in Figure 3, but all the weights and embedding matrixes are not shared with the type network. After deriving $g_2(q)$ and $E(p)$, we compute the cosine similarity $u_3(p, q)$:

$$u_3(p, q) = \cos(g_2(q), E(p)) \tag{7}$$

The probability of property p given question q, candidate entity s, and candidate type t is defined as follows:

$$P(p|s, t, q) = \begin{cases} \frac{\exp(u_3(p, q))}{\sum_{p'} \exp(u_3(p', q))}, & \text{if } p \text{ has link with } s, t \\ 0 & , \text{otherwise} \end{cases} \tag{8}$$

where p' is a property in the candidate property set. To reduce the computation and the number of candidate properties, only the properties which have links with an entity in the candidate entity set and

Method	Accuracy (%)
(Bordes et al., 2015)	63.9
(Dai et al., 2016)	75.7
(Yin et al., 2016)	75.9
(Golub and He, 2016)	70.3
Our approach (probability)	76.1
Our approach (sum)	**76.7**

Table 1: Results on the SimpleQuestions test data.

N	(Yin et al., 2016)		Our approach
	Passive	Active	
1	56.6	73.6	80.9
5	71.1	85.0	90.2
10	75.2	87.4	92.2
20	81.0	88.8	93.7
50	85.7	90.4	95.1
100	87.9	91.6	96.0

Table 2: Hit rates of the ground-truth entity.

belongs to a type in the candidate type set are chosen into the candidate property set. $P(p|s, t, q)$ is set to 0 for those properties which are impossible to be the correct answer due to the lack of links with any candidate entity and type.

For training property network, the hinge loss with negative samples is the objective function to be minimized.

$$\ell(\theta_p) = \sum_{i=1}^{N_p} \max(0, m_p - u_3(p^*, q) + u_3(p_i, q)) \quad (9)$$

where θ_p is the parameters to learn, N_p is the number of negative samples, m_p is the margin, p^* is the correct property, and p_i is the property randomly sampled from all properties except p^*.

4 Experiments

The SimpleQuestions[2] dataset (Bordes et al., 2015), which contains 75,910 training data, 10,845 validation data, and 21,687 test data, is adopted in the experiments. The evaluation is the same as in Bordes et al. (2015). The predicted answer is correct when the subject-relation pair is the same as the correct answer. We train our model on the training set. The validation set is used for early stop and parameter tuning. The test set is used for evaluation.

4.1 Experimental Setup

The number of negative samples used in SVM[rank] is set to 5. Other parameters for SVM[rank] are C = 0.1, epsilon = 0.01, and loss function option = 2. The word embeddings used in each neural network is initialized with the pre-trained GloVe (Pennington et al., 2014) with the dimension of 300. All the networks are optimized by mini-batch and Adam (Kingma et al., 2014) with the learning rate 0.001.

The TYPE_LSTM in entity identification step has a drop rate of 0.2. The hidden size of LSTM is

500. Batch size is 128. The parameters of type network and property network are the same. Maximal question length is 25. Mini-batch size is 100. The type and property embeddings are 500-dimensional with randomly initialized. The hidden size of LSTM is 500. Both hinge loss margins m_t and m_p are 0.4. The numbers of negative samples N_t and N_p are 65.

4.2 Overall Results

Table 1 shows the performances of our model compared with the other four methods. Bordes et al. (2015) use a memory network. Dai et al. (2016) employ a conditional focused neural-network based approach. Yin et al. (2016) apply attentive convolutional neural network with the passive or active linker. Golub and He (2016) use the character-level encoder-decoder framework. In our approach, "probability" means the outcome is the triple with the highest probability computed by Equation (1). We find that the subject entity and the property are more important than the type. The approach "sum" combines the scores $u_1(s, q)$, $u_2(t, q)$, and $u_3(p, q)$ by weighted summation, and selects the triple with the highest weighted sum. The weights are entity:type:property = 4:1:3, which are tuned on the validation data.

Our "probability" approach outperforms all previous models on FB5M, including the previous best model by Yin et al. (2016). The "sum" approach even significantly outperforms the "probability" approach on McNemar's test (p < 0.01).

4.3 Entity Identification Results

This section discusses the performance of the entity identification step. The hit rates of the top N entities are shown, which means the coverage of

---

[2] https://research.fb.com/downloads/babi/ .

the ground truth entity by top-N results. $N \in$ {1,10,20,50,100}. Entity linker proposed by Yin et al. (2016) has two versions, passive and active linker. The difference between them is that they use the longest consecutive common subsequence between question and KB entity names to get candidates in the passive linker. On the other hand, the active linker first gets the span from the question that is most likely to be a subject entity by sequential labeling, and the linker uses the labeled span to search the candidate entity from KB. The number of the candidates in the active linker is less than the passive linker, because the active linker uses specific span in question to search candidates, and entities not in this span are filtered out.

Table 2 shows our performance in entity identification compares to Yin et al. (2016). Our entity linker outperforms their approach by over 7% in top-1 result using FB5M as background KB. We have six new features to score the entities in different aspects. The features "Char Proportion" and "Relative Position to Be Verb/Auxiliary Verb" can analyze the entities by their surface form in question, e.g., name and relative position. The features "Out-degree" and "Type_LSTM" can distinguish entities even if they have the same name. The "IDF" feature can kick out common entities and keep the more important ones. And "NER_LCS" feature has the similar effect to the active linker of Yin et al. (2016), but our feature can withstand the wrong subject entity prediction in sequential labeling, because we do not filter out any candidates, we give them the lower score instead.

4.4 Importance of Entity Identification Features

In this section, we discuss the importance of each feature in entity identification in three ways. We first show the performances with a single feature. And then, we consider the performances with one feature or a group of features being removed.

Performance with Single Feature

Table 3 shows the hit rates of the top N entities generated by a single feature. The feature "NER_LCS" has the best performance because this feature contains a part of information from the four surface

N Fetures	Hit rates @ N					
	1	5	10	20	50	100
Word Prop.	41.0	62.7	70.5	77.6	85.8	90.3
Char Prop.	55.5	73.7	78.9	83.4	88.9	91.7
Rel. Position in Q	16.7	36.5	47.7	60.9	77.0	86.4
Rel. Position to BeV./AuxV.	30.2	44.2	52.6	61.4	75.7	84.2
Out-degree	15.0	39.6	52.5	67.2	82.6	89.5
IDF	43.4	68.9	76.4	82.5	88.5	91.6
NER_LCS	59.5	77.0	81.5	85.5	90.1	92.6
Type_LSTM	44.1	68.8	77.0	85.3	91.6	94.4

Table 3: Hit rates generated by a single feature in entity linker.

form features: "Word Proportion", "Char Proportion", "Relative Position in Question", and "Relative Position to Be Verb/Auxiliary Verb". The NER tagger labels the span of possible position of the subject entity in a question, and thus "NER_LCS" contains the position information. Moreover, the length of the longest common subsequence between the candidate entity and the words in the span gives the length proportion information.

The feature "Out-degree" has the lowest performance in $N=1$ hit rate, because the entities with many out-going links sometimes represent that they are general entities. For example, the entity "album (m.02lx2r)" in question "Which genre of album is harder......faster?" has 323,467 out-going links in FB5M, but the subject entity "harder......faster (m.01jp8ww)" has only 5 links. Although this feature sometimes highlights the general entities, it can distinguish entities that have the same names with the help of other features.

Table 3 also shows that the performance of "Relative Position to Be Verb/Auxiliary Verb" is almost twice the performance of "Relative Position in Question". It shows that the observation about position "subject entity tends to be close to and behind Be verb/auxiliary verb in a question" is more appropriate, and the Be verb/auxiliary verb plays an important role in identifying entities.

Performance without One of the Features

Table 4 shows the hit rates of the top N entities generated by removing one of the eight features from the entity linker. First, we can see that the performances without one of the first four features are only reduced by about 1%, because the feature "NER_LCS" contains a part of the information from them, and it can make up for the removal of them. And then, we can find that although the performance of the feature "Out-degree" has the lowest accuracy in Table 3, its removal affects the performance by more than 2%.

The removal of "Type_LSTM" has the greatest impact. The result with this feature outperforms the result without it by 6%. The comparison shows the importance of the entity types which can help us get deeper meanings of an entity. And the "Type_LSTM" is difficult to make up by other features.

Performance without a Group of Features

Table 5 shows the hit rates and overall accuracy of our "probability" approach generated by removing a group of features from the entity linker. We group the features with similar effect together. The first four features in Table 3 are about surface forms of entities, and thus they are put together. The "Individual features" group contains features "Out-degree" and "Type_LSTM", which can distinguish entities with the same name. The features "IDF" and "NER_LCS" are grouped into "features of specificity", which can identify the more likely subject entities in the question and kick out common entities.

The removal of individual features reduces the performance of entity identification by more than 20%. This result shows the importance of identifying entities with the same name. Otherwise, these entities would have the same score. However, the removal of these features only reduces the overall accuracy of 0.7%, because type identification step can make up a part of the removed "Type_LSTM" information. For example, the entity with name "Estonia" can be a country or a book, if one "Estonia" is a "book", it may not have a property in type "location", and thus we can distinguish these two types of "Estonia" a bit.

The removal of features of specificity affects the overall accuracy by 2.7%. These two features focus on more specific words and make the scores of the general entities, such as "album" or "movie", become lower. This behavior is important and cannot be replaced by the rest of the system.

4.5 Importance of Type Identification

Table 6 shows the importance of our type identification step. The models with type identification significantly outperform the models without type network on McNemar's test ($p < 0.01$), and increases the accuracies by at least 1%, no matter the final score is by probability or weighted sum. This shows that the type identification step can effectively handle the hierarchical structure of Freebase relations, and can better understand the semantics of the question.

Features \ N	Hit rates @ N					
	1	5	10	20	50	100
All features	80.9	90.2	92.2	93.7	95.1	96.0
w/o Word Prop.	79.8	89.6	91.7	93.3	95.0	96.0
w/o Char Prop.	79.4	89.3	91.4	93.2	94.9	95.9
w/o Rel. Position	79.6	89.6	91.8	93.4	95.0	96.0
w/o Rel. Position to BeV./AuxV.	79.7	89.6	91.7	93.3	95.0	96.0
w/o Out-degree	78.8	88.6	90.9	92.8	94.6	95.7
w/o IDF	79.1	89.3	91.4	93.1	94.9	95.9
w/o NER_LCS	78.4	88.8	91.1	92.9	94.8	95.8
w/o Type_LSTM	74.9	88.0	90.7	92.7	94.4	95.6

Table 4: Hit rates generated by removing one feature from entity linker. "w/o" means the removal of the feature.

Feature \ N	Entity identification (Hit rates @ N)				Overall (prob.)
	1	5	10	100	Acc.
All features	80.9	90.2	92.2	96.0	76.2
w/o Surface form features	78.8	89.1	91.4	96.0	75.1
w/o Individual features	60.7	77.9	82.5	92.8	75.5
w/o Features of specificity	75.8	87.1	89.9	95.6	73.5

Table 5: Hit rates generated by removing group of features from entity linker.

Settings	Accuracy (%)
Probability w/ type identification	76.1
Probability w/o type identification	75.1
Sum w/ type identification	76.7
Sum w/o type identification	75.2

Table 6: Gain by the addition of the type identification step.

5   Error Analysis

We categorize some errors into the following types.

- **Entities with the same name**: The subject entity of the question "What is the place of birth of Sam Edwards?" is "Sam Edwards". Both entities "m.03kt3y" (an actress) and "m.042gjt" (a physicist) have the same name. This question does not have enough information to distinguish the two entities.
- **Deleted entity in Freebase**: Some questions' subject entities are deleted in the Freebase dump.
- **Similar properties**: Some relations are very similar, e.g., both "music.release.track" and "music.release.track_list" indicate tracks in an album.
- **Incomplete question**: Some questions in the dataset are not complete. For example, the question "What production company produced?" does not provide any entities.
- **Question from object-relation pair**: There are some questions formed by object-relation pairs of the triple. E.g., the question "Name a lawyer." is from triple (Charlie Herschel, people.person.profession, lawyer). We cannot find the subject of the triple from the question.
- **Typo**: Some questions contain typo. For example, the question "What is Roger Molliens gender?" should be "What is Roger Mollien's gender?"
- **Wrong answer**: Some answers are wrong. For example, the answer of the question "Where was David Armstrong born?" is the triple (Undisputed Comedy Series: Lil Rel, film.film.language, English). Obviously, it is not a correct answer to the question.
- **Controversial answer**: E.g., the relation of the question "Leo Bertos was born in what country?" is "people.person.nationality", but the more appropriate relation should be "people.person.place_of_birth", because people can have the naturalized citizenship.

6   Conclusion

We propose a three-step approach to identify subject, type and property from knowledge base (KB) for answering simple questions. Our ranking model with additional features outperforms the previous models in subject entity identification. The experiments also show that all entity features are important. Besides, by splitting the structured relation into type and property, our model benefits from understanding the question meaning more precisely. Our model achieves the state-of-the-art performance on the SimpleQuestions dataset. Error analysis shows that most errors come from the problematic questions in the dataset. Extension to complex questions will be explored.

Acknowledgments

This research was partially supported by Ministry of Science and Technology, Taiwan, under grants MOST-104-2221-E-002-061-MY3, MOST-105-2221-E-002-154-MY3 and MOST-106-2923-E-002-012-MY3, and National Taiwan University under grant NTUCCP-106R891305.

References

Jonathan Berant, Andrew Chou, Roy Frostig, and Percy Liang. 2013. Semantic parsing on freebase from question-answer pairs. In *Proceedings of the 2013 Conference on Empirical Methods in Natural Language Processing (EMNLP 2013)*, pages 1533–1544, Seattle, Washington, USA.

Kurt Bollacker, Colin Evans, Praveen Paritosh, Tim Sturge, and Jamie Taylor. 2008. Freebase: a collaboratively created graph database for structuring human knowledge. In *Proceedings of the 2008 ACM SIGMOD international conference on Management of data (SIGMOD 2008)*, pages 1247–1249, Vancouver, BC, Canada.

Jonathan Berant and Percy Liang. 2014. Semantic parsing via paraphrasing. In *Association for Computational Linguistics (ACL 2014)*, volume 7, page 92–102, Baltimore, USA.

Antoine Bordes, Nicolas Usunier, Sumit Chopra, and Jason Weston. 2015. Large-scale simple question answering with memory networks. arXiv preprint arXiv:1506.02075.

Zihang Dai, Lei Li, and Wei Xu. 2016. CFO: Conditional focused neural question answering with large-scale knowledge bases. In *Association for Computational Linguistics (ACL 2016)*, pages 800–810, Berlin, Germany.

Li Dong, Furu Wei, Ming Zhou, and Ke Xu. 2015. Question answering over freebase with multi-column convolutional neural networks. In *Proceedings of ACL-IJCNLP*, volume 1, pages 260–269, Beijing, China.

Anthony Fader, Luke Zettlemoyer, and Oren Etzioni. 2013. Paraphrase-driven learning for open question answering. In *Association for Computational Linguistics (ACL 2013)*, pages 1608–1618. Sofia, Bulgaria.

David Golub and Xiaodong He. 2016. Character-level question answering with attention. In *Proceedings of the 2016 Conference on Empirical Methods in Natural Language Processing (EMNLP 2016)*, pages 1598–1607, Austin, Texas.

Sepp Hochreiter and Jürgen Schmidhuber. 1997. Long short-term memory. *Neural computation*, 9(8):1735–1780.

Thorsten Joachims. 2006. Training Linear SVMs in Linear Time. In *Proceedings of the ACM Conference on Knowledge Discovery and Data Mining (KDD 2006)*, Philadelphia, Pennsylvania, USA.

Diederik P. Kingma and Jimmy Lei Ba. 2014. Adam: A method for stochastic optimization. arXiv preprint arXiv:1412.6980, 2014.

Guillaume Lample, Miguel Ballesteros, Sandeep Subramanian, Kazuya Kawakami, and Chris Dyer. 2016. Neural architectures for named entity recognition. In *Proceedings of NAACL-HLT 2016*, pages 260–270, San Diego, California.

Jens Lehmann, Robert Isele, Max Jakob, Anja Jentzsch, Dimitris Kontokostas, Pablo N. Mendes, Sebastian Hellmann, Mohamed Morsey, Patrick van Kleef, Sören Auer, and Christian Bizer. 2015. Dbpedia-a large-scale, multilingual knowledge base extracted from wikipedia. Semantic Web Journal, 6(2):167–195.

Jeffrey Pennington, Richard Socher, and Christopher D. Manning. 2014. Glove: Global vectors for word representation. In *Proceedings of the 2014 Conference on Empirical Methods in Natural Language Processing (EMNLP 2014)*, pages 1532–1543, Doha, Qatar.

Wen-tau Yih, Ming-Wei Chang, Xiaodong He, and Jianfeng Gao. 2015. Semantic parsing via staged query graph generation: Question answering with knowledge base. In *Association for Computational Linguistics (ACL 2015)*, pages 1321–1331, Beijing, China.

Wenpeng Yin, MoYu, Bing Xiang, Bowen Zhou, and Hinrich Schütze. 2016. Simple question answering by attentive convolutional neural network. In *Proceedings of COLING*, pages 1746–1756, Osaka, Japan.

DailyDialog: A Manually Labelled Multi-turn Dialogue Dataset

†Yanran Li,* †,§Hui Su,* ‡Xiaoyu Shen, †Wenjie Li, †Ziqiang Cao, §Shuzi Niu
†Department of Computing, The Hong Kong Polytechnic University, Hong Kong
§Institute of Software, Chinese Academy of Science, China
‡Spoken Language Systems (LSV), Saarland University, Germany

Abstract

We develop a high-quality multi-turn dialog dataset, **DailyDialog**, which is intriguing in several aspects. The language is human-written and less noisy. The dialogues in the dataset reflect our daily communication way and cover various topics about our daily life. We also manually label the developed dataset with communication intention and emotion information. Then, we evaluate existing approaches on DailyDialog dataset and hope it benefit the research field of dialog systems[1].

1 Introduction

Developing intelligent chatbots and dialog systems is of great significance to both commercial and academic camps. A good conversational agent enables enterprises to provide automatic customer services and thus reduce human labor costs. For academia, it is challenging yet appealing to build up such an intelligent chatbot which involves a series of high-level natural language processing techniques, such as understanding the underlying semantics of user input utterance, and generating coherent and meaningful responses.

However, the training datasets for this research area are still deficient. Traditional dialogue systems are often trained with domain-specific spoken dialogue datasets (Ringger et al., 1996; Petukhova et al., 2014), which are often small-scale and oriented to complete a specific task. More recent work feed their conversational models with open-domain datasets. Switchboard (Godfrey et al., 1992) and OpenSubtitles (Jörg Tiedemann, 2009) datasets

A: I'm <u>worried</u> about something.

B: What's that?

A: Well, I have to drive to school for a meeting this morning, and I'm going to end up getting stuck in rush-hour traffic.

B: That's <u>annoying</u>, but nothing to worry about. *Just breathe deeply when you feel yourself getting upset.*

A: Ok, I'll try that.

B: Is there anything else <u>bothering</u> you?

A: Just one more thing. A school called me this morning to see if I could teach a few classes this weekend and I don't know what to do.

B: Do you have any other plans this weekend?

A: I'm supposed to work on a paper that'd due on Monday.

B: *Try not to take on more than you can handle.*

A: You're right. I probably should just work on my paper. <u>Thanks</u>!

Figure 1: An example in **DailyDialog** dataset. Some text is shortened for space. Best viewed in color.

comprise approximately 150 turns in a "conversation" and thus are too disperse to capture the main topic. Twitter Dialog Corpus (Ritter et al., 2011) and Chinese Weibo dataset (Wang et al., 2013) are comprised of posts and replies on social networks, which are noisy, informal and different from real conversations.

In this work, we develop a high-quality multi-turn dialogue dataset, which contains conversations about our daily life. We refer to it as **DailyDialog**. In our daily life, we communicate with others by two main reasons: *exchanging information* and *enhancing social bonding*. To exchange and share ideas, we often communicate with others following certain dialog flow. Typically, we do not rigidly answer others' questions and wait for the next ques-

---

*Authors contributed equally. Correspondence should be sent to Y. Li (csyli@comp.polyu.edu.hk).

[1]The dataset is available on `http://yanran.li/dailydialog`

Proceedings of the The 8th International Joint Conference on Natural Language Processing, pages 986–995,
Taipei, Taiwan, November 27 – December 1, 2017 ©2017 AFNLP

tion. Instead, humans often first respond to previous context and then propose their own questions and suggestions. In this way, people show their attention others' words and are willing to continue the conversation. Another reason why people communicate is to strengthen their social bonding with others. Therefore, daily conversations are rich in emotion. By expressing emotions, people show their mutual respect, empathy and understanding to each other, and thus improve the relationship between them.

We demonstrate the above two phenomena by an example conversation as in Figure 1. The *words in Italic* are speaker B's own ideas that are new for the other speaker A. The underlined words in purple explicitly indicate the emotions. In the fourth speaker turn, speaker B first expresses his/her feeling on what he/she has heared from speaker A, which reveals his/her understanding. Then, speaker B suggests by saying *Just breathe deeply when you feel yourself getting upset*. Following the direct response towards A, B's suggestion is original yet context-dependent. It shows that B builds up a connection link by responding to forgoing context and proposing new suggestions.

We describe the dataset construction process and annotation criteria in Section 2, present and analyze the detailed characteristics in Section 3. We then evaluate existing mainstream approaches, including retrieval-based and generation-based approaches on the developed datasets in Section 4.

2 Dataset Construction

2.1 Basic Features and Statistics

To construct a multi-turn dialog dataset, we crawl the raw data from various websites which serve for English learner to practice English dialog in daily life. That's why we refer it as **DailyDialog** dataset. The dialogues in the dataset preserve the following three appealing properties.

First, the language in DailyDialog is human-written and thus is more formal than those datasets like Twitter Dialog Corpus (Ritter et al., 2011) and Chinese Weibo dataset (Wang et al., 2013). The latters are constructed by posts and replies on social networks, which are noisy, short and different from real conversations.

Second, the conversations in DailyDialog often focus on a certain topic and under a certain physical context. For example, a conversation happens in a shop is often between a customer looking for

suitable goods and a salesman who is willing to help for purchasing. Another typical conversation happens between two students talking about their summer vacation trips.

The third desirable feature is that the crawled dialogues usually end after reasonable speaker turns. This makes DailyDialog distinguished from existing dialog datasets such as Switchboard (Godfrey et al., 1992) and OpenSubtitles (Jörg Tiedemann, 2009), which often have 150+ and 1,000+ speaker turns in one "conversation". By examining some examples, we find that in such a conversation, people often talk about three or more topics (or scenes). Compared with them, our dataset has in average approximate 8 turns, which is more suitable to train compact conversational models.

After crawling, we de-duplicate the raw data, filter out those dialogues involving more than two parties (three or more speakers) and automatically correct the misspelling using autocorrect package[2]. Finally, the DailyDialog datasets contain 13,118 multi-turn dialogues. We also count the average speaker turns and tokens to give a brief view of the dataset. The resulting statistics are given in Table 1. From the statistics we can see, the speaker turns are roughly 8, and the average tokens per utterance is about 15.

Total Dialogues	13,118
Average Speaker Turns Per Dialogue	7.9
Average Tokens Per Dialogue	114.7
Average Tokens Per Utterance	14.6

Table 1: Basic Statistics of DailyDialog.

2.2 Annotation Criteria and Procedure

Because the dialogues in DailyDialog datasets are written to reflect our daily conversations, they mainly conform certain communication ways. As stated before, the purpose of the dialogues are *exchanging information* and *enhancing social bonding*. To allow further research on our daily communication behaviors, we manually label the DailyDialog dataset to reflect the two purposes.

The communication purpose of exchanging information is related to the communication intentions. This factor has been extensively explored under the name of dialog act and speech act. In general, dialog acts represent the communication

---

[2] https://github.com/phatpiglet/autocorrect/

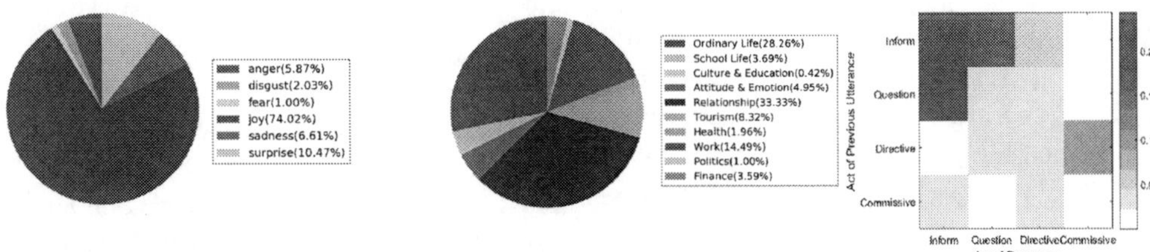

(a) Emotion distributions in DailyDialog. (b) Topic distributions in DailyDialog. (c) Interactions of dialog acts in each utterance pairs.

Figure 2: Statistics in DailyDialog.

functions when people saying something. To label the dialog acts in DailyDialog, we follow the criteria in Amanova et al. (2016) because it is adaptive to mainstream annotation criteria ISO 24617-2 (Petukhova, 2011) and consistent with existing annotated dataset such as Trains (Ringger et al., 1996) and DBox (Petukhova et al., 2014). Following Amanova et al. (2016), we label each utterance as one of four dialog act classes: {Inform, Questions, Directives, Commissive}. The **Inform** class contains all statements and questions by which the speaker is providing information. The **Questions** class is labeled when the speaker wants to know something and seeks for some information. The **Directives** class contains dialog acts like request, instruct, suggest and accept/reject offer. The **Commissive** class is about accept/reject request or suggestion and offer. The former two classes are information transfer acts, while the latter two are action discussion acts. Detailed explanations can be found in Amanova et al. (2016). Thereafter, in the DailyDialog dataset, we have four intention classes.

The second communication purpose, enhancing social bonding, is highly correlated with human emotion. Following (Wang et al., 2013), we adopt the "BigSix Theory" (Ekman, 1992) to label each utterance in DailyDialog. Ekman (1992) thinks that there are six primary and universal emotions in human beings: {Anger, Disgust, Fear, Happiness, Sadness, Surprise}. Besides the main six categories of emotions, we find it necessary to add additional category to represent other emotions. Hence, we have seven emotion categories in DailyDialog.

To guarantee the annotation quality, we recruit three experts who have good knowledge in dialog and communication theory. After teaching them the criteria, we sample 100 dialogues for them to annotate and reduce the discrepancy by discussion among them. Then, they independently annotate the whole dataset and achieve the inter annotator agreement of 78.9%. When the disagreement happens, we follow the majority rule or let them reannotate to find a "common" annotation. The detailed statistics of the final annotation information are given in the following section.

3 Characteristics

In this section, we delve deeply into DailyDialog datasets, and show our datasets are beneficial in several aspects:

- *Daily Topics*: It covers ten categories ranging from ordinary life to financial topics, which is different from domain-specific datasets.

- *Bi-turn Dialog Flow*: It conforms basic dialog act flows, such as Questions-Inform and Directives-Commissives bi-turn flows, making it different from question answering (QA) datasets and post-reply datasets.

- *Certain Communication Pattern*: It follows unique multi-turn dialog flow patterns reflecting human communication style, which are rarely seen in task-oriented datasets.

- *Rich Emotion*: It contains rich emotions and is labeled manually to keep high-quality, which is distinguished from most existing dialog datasets.

3.1 Daily Topics

The dialogues in the developed dataset happens in our everyday life, and that's why we name it **DailyDialog**. They cover a wide range of daily scenarios: chit-chats about holidays and tourisms, service-dialog in shops and restaurants, and so on. After looking into its topics, we cluster them into ten categories. The statistics for each category is summarized in Figure 2(b).

The largest three categories are: Relationship (33.33%), Ordinary Life (28.26%) and Work (14.49%). This is also consistent with our real experience that we often invite people for social activities (Relationship), talk about what happened recently (Ordinary Life) and what happened at work (Work).

3.2 Bi-turn Dialog Flow

Because the dialogues are assumed to happen in daily life, they follow natural dialog flow. It makes DailyDialog dataset quite different from existing QA datasets such as SubTle dataset (Dodge et al., 2015)which are improperly used for training dialog systems. DailyDialog dataset also distinguishes from those post-reply datasets such as Reddit comment (Al-Rfou' et al., 2016), Sina Weibo (Shang et al., 2015) and Twitter (Ritter et al., 2011) datasets. The latter datasets comprise post-reply pairs on social networks where people interact with others more freely (often more than two speakers) and results in ambiguous dialog flows.

Instead, the dialog act flows in Dailydialog are more consistent with our daily communication. For example, we usually do not leave alone others' question and just tersely change the topic. Instead, we will answer others' questions politely. By the definitions we introduce in Section 2.2, this reflects a *Questions-Inform* bi-turn dialog flow. This is a frequent circle phenomena because it represents a information transfer between the two speakers in the dialog. Another example is that when someone proposes a idea, such as going out for dinner, the other speaker in the dialog usually responds to this proposal. This reflects a *Directives-Commissives* dialog flow and captures the speakers' suggestions and commitments to conduct certain acts. By labeling each utterances in dialogues, Dailydialog datasets contain more than ten thousands examples of approximately 8-turn dialog act flows. We hope this is beneficial for the research in dialog management. The distributions of these four dialog acts are given in Table 2. We also demonstrate the interactions between each four dialog acts in Figure 2(c).

Inform	Questions	Directives	Commissive
46,532	29,428	17,295	9,724
45.2%	28.6%	16.8%	9.4%

Table 2: Intention Statistics in DailyDialog.

3.3 Certain Communication Pattern

Besides the basic *Questions-Inform* and *Directives-Commissives* bi-turn dialog flows, we also find two unique multi-turn flow patterns in DailyDialog dataset.

Pattern 1: In human-to-human communication, people are inclined to both answer the questions and then initiate a new question to let the dialog last. In other words, a speaker can change from information-provider to information-seeker in a single speaker turn. We find 2,398 (18.3%) dialogues in DailyDialog exhibits this patterns, which is quite frequent.

Pattern 2: When someone is proposing an activity or offering a suggestion, the other speaker usually comes up with another idea. This is sensible because the two speakers often have different views about a topic and by exchanging different proposals, they persuade and influence the other. This results in a *Directives-Directives-Commissives*-like pattern in dialog flows, which happens totally 1,203 times (9.2%) in our dataset.

The two patterns shed light on our daily communications style, which are merely found in single-turn datasets or task-oriented datasets like Ubuntu (Lowe et al., 2015) and restaurant reservation datasets (Bordes and Weston, 2016).

3.4 Rich Emotion

As discussed before, the other main purpose of our daily communication is *enhancing social bonding*. Hence, people tend to express their emotions during communication. When hearing from others' miseries, we often say "I'm sorry to hear that" or "What a poor guy". And when we appease others, the listener often feels better. Such emotional words are rich in DailyDialog dataset. Because automatic emotion classification is difficult (Zhou et al., 2017), we manually label the emotion for each utterance to make them as accurate as possible. This distinguishes DailyDialog datasets from most existing dialog datasets. Similarly, we summarize the basic statistics on labelled emotion in Table 3.[3]

Additionally, we observe in our daily life, a healthy and pleasant conversation often ends with positive emotions. Therefore we examine our Dai-

---

[3]The imbalanced emotion categories suggest that it might be improper to label the emotion following "BigSix" Theory (Ekman, 1992). However, we keep it in this work to follow previous work (Wang et al., 2013). To propose a novel emotion theory is beyond this work.

	Count	of EU	of Total
Anger	1022	5.87	0.99
Disgust	353	2.03	0.34
Fear	74	1.00	0.17
Happiness	12885	74.02	12.51
Sadness	1150	6.61	1.12
Surpise	1823	10.47	1.77
Other	85572	-	83.10

Table 3: Emotion Statistics in DailyDialog. EU denotes for utterances that contain the main six categories of emotion, while Total denotes for all utterances in the dataset. Numbers are multiplied by 100%.

lyDialog dataset by how many conversations are ending or positive emotions (i.e., happy), and find 3,675 (28.0%) "happy" dialogues. We also count how many conversations have changed to positive emotions even though they begin with negative emotions (e.g., sad, disgust, anger) and find 113 (0.8%) such examples. We hope our dataset facilitates future research on developing conversational agents able to regulate the conversation towards a happy ending.

4 Evaluating Existing Approaches

In this section, we evaluate existing mainstream approaches on the proposed DailyDialog. We mainly compare five categories of approaches: (1) Embedding-based Similarity for Response Retrieval (Luo and Li, 2016); (2) Feature-based Similarity for Response Retrieval (Jafarpour et al., 2010); (3) Feature-based Similarity for Response Retrieval and Reranking (Luo and Li, 2016; Otsuka et al., 2017); (4) Neural network-based for Response Generation (Shang et al., 2015; Sordoni et al., 2015); (5) Neural network-based for Response Generation with Labeling Information (Zhou et al., 2017). All the evaluated approaches are implemented by TensorFlow (Abadi et al., 2015).

4.1 Experimental Setup

We randomly separate the DailyDialog datasets into training/validation/test sets with 11,118/1,000/1,000 conversations. We tune the parameters on validation set and report the performance on test sets. In all experiments, the vocabulary size is set as 25,000 and all the OOV words are mapped to a special token UNK. We

set word embeddings to size of 300 and initialize them with Word2Vec embeddings trained on the Google News Corpus[4]. The encoder and decoder RNN in the following experiments are 1-layer GRU with 512 hidden neurons (Cho et al., 2014). All the trained model parameters are then used as an initialization point. We set the batch size as 128 and fix the learning rate as 0.0002. Models are trained to minimize the cross entropy using Adam optimizer (Kingma and Ba, 2014).

4.2 Retrieval-based Approaches

4.2.1 Compared Approaches

First, we choose three categories of four retrieval-based approaches, i.e., (1) Embedding-based Similarity (Luo and Li, 2016); (2) Feature-based Similarity (Jafarpour et al., 2010; Yan et al., 2016); (3)(4) Feature-based Similarity with Intention and Emotion Reranking (Luo and Li, 2016; Otsuka et al., 2017). We aim to see whether classical embeddings-based, feature-based and reranking-enhanced approaches are effective on DailyDialog.

Embedding-based The embedding-based approach is using basic neural networks as described in Section 4.1 and denoted as {Embedding} below. We measure the distance between embeddings as the average of cosine similarity, Jaccard distance and Euclidean distance. At test time, candidates whose context embedding is closer to the test context embedding are ranked higher. Similar approaches have been adopted extensively on response retrieval task, such as Luo and Li (2016).

Feature-based We then evaluate the performance of feature-based retrieval approach. We adopt several linguistic features: TF-IDF and three fuzzy string matching features, i.e., QRatio, WRatio, and Partial ratio. We first use TF-IDF to select 1,000 candidates and rank them with the fuzzy features. These fuzzy features is implemented with fuzzywuzzy package[5]. We denote this feature engineering approach as {Feature}. Similar approaches have been demonstrated effectively on response retrieval task and duplicate question detection task[6], such as Yan et al. (2016); Luo and Li (2016).

Reranking By Intention We also examine reranking-enhanced retrieval approaches, which

---

[4] ttps://code.google.com/archive/p/word2vec/

[5] https://github.com/seatgeek/fuzzywuzzy

[6] https://github.com/abhishekkrthakur/is_that_a_duplicate_quora_question

	Epoch	Test Loss	PPL	BLEU-1	BLEU-2	BLEU-3	BLEU-4
Seq2Seq	30	4.024	55.94	0.352	0.146	0.017	0.006
Attn-Seq2Seq	60	4.036	56.59	0.335	0.134	0.013	0.006
HRED	44	4.082	59.24	0.396	0.174	0.019	0.009
L+Seq2Seq	21	3.911	49.96	0.379	0.156	0.018	0.006
L+Attn-Seq2Seq	37	3.913	50.03	0.464	0.220	0.016	0.009
L+HRED	27	3.990	54.05	0.431	0.193	0.016	0.009
Pre+Seq2Seq	18	3.556	35.01	0.312	0.120	0.0136	0.005
Pre+Attn-Seq2Seq	15	3.567	35.42	0.354	0.136	0.013	0.004
Pre+HRED	10	3.628	37.65	0.153	0.026	0.001	0.000

Table 4: Experiments Results of generation-based approaches.

	BLEU-2	BLEU-3	BLEU-4
Embedding	0.207	0.162	0.150
Feature	**0.258**	**0.204**	**0.194**
+ I-Rerank	0.204	0.189	0.181
+ I-E-Rerank	0.190	0.174	0.164

Table 5: BLEU scores of retrieval-based approaches.

encourages the retrieved response to follow a certain rules. Luo and Li (2016) provides a simplest way to realize it. Because intention has shown as a beneficial factor in response selection (Otsuka et al., 2017), we first examine reranking-enhanced retrieval approach based on the intention (dialog act) label in DailyDialog dataset. We compare the intention history of the test example with that of the candidate example, and use the compared similarity as reranking feature. For example, if the test intention history is {2,1,3}, then the candidate response whose intention history is also {2,1,3} will be reranked higher. Based on the feature-based retrieval approach, we denote the reranking by intention as {+I-Rerank}.

Reranking By Intention & Emotion The last retrieved-based approach we evaluate is similar with {+I-Rerank}, with the only difference that the candidate responses are reranked by both intention and emotion labels. We denote it as {+I-E-Rerank}.

Because the groundtruth responses in the test set are not seen in the training set, we can not evaluate the performance using ranking-like metrics such as Recall-k. We instead report the BLEU scores achieved by retrieval-based approaches in Table 5.

We also evaluate them by calculating the "Equivalence" percentage between the labels (i.e., intention, emotion) of the retrieved responses and those of the groundtruth responses. The results are reported in Table 6. Though subtle improvements can be seen when using labels, we speculate it as not a very strong evaluation metric. It is unsafe to conclude that the higher the "equivalence" percentage is, the better (more coherent, more suitable) the retrieved response will be.

	Feature	+I-Rerank	+I-E-Rerank
Intention	46.3	**47.3**	46.7
Emotion	73.7	72.3	**74.3**

Table 6: "Equivalence" percentage (%) of retrieval-based approaches.

4.2.2 Intention And Emotion Matters

In dialog response generation, word-level overlap metrics such as BLEU are inadequate (Liu et al., 2016). To provide insights on whether intention and emotion are beneficial, and how they works, we conduct several case studies in Table 7.

In the first block, we give an example of how intention helps to find more proper response. The intentions in the test context (U1 & U2) are {3, 3}, meaning {Directives, Directives}. The gold answer (GA) in the test set is "Thanks." Although both three retrieved responses are not exactly same with GA, the approaches that reranking by intention (+I) and reranking by intention and emotion (+I-E) find more suitable response than the feature-based approach without reranking (F). It is because, the context corresponding to the retrieved response "About how long will it take me to get there?" is "Excuse me, but can you tell me the way... Just go straight... You can t miss it", whose dialog act flow {3, 3} is consistent with the context test. On the contrary, the response found by feature-based approach has the context "Can you direct me to

Test Context	Retrieved Response
U1: *Can you direct me to Holiday inn ?* (3) U2: *Cross the street... You can't miss it.* (3) GA: **Thanks.**	F: *Well, we've got some great mangoes on sale.* +I: *About how long will it take me to get there?* +I-E: *About how long will it take me to get there?*
U1: *No way... You can't keep it here.* (1) U2: *Please...it's so cute and tame.* (0) U3: *All right. But you have to...* (0) GA: **I will. Thank you, Mummy.**	F: *Is there somewhere you wanted to go eat at?* +I: *Sprite with ice, please.* +I-E: *Now we get along very well. It makes me feel...*

Table 7: Case Study of Reranking-enhanced Retrieve Approaches. Context words are shortened for space.

Test Context	Generated Response
U1: *I have to check out today.* *I'd like my bill ready by 10 in morning.* U2: *You can be sure of that, sir .* GA: **Thank you.**	Attn: *all right, sir.* Pre+Attn: *how long will it take to get there?* HRED: *here you are.* Pre+HRED: *how long will it take to get there?*

Table 8: Case Study of Generation-based Approaches.

some fresh produce that's on sale?", which should be attributed to the poor result.

Similar cases are given in the second block where emotion history information benefits. The emotions in the test context (U1, U2 & U3) are {1, 0, 0}, meaning {Anger, Others, Others}. The most proper retrieved responses are from the reranking approach by intention and emotion (+I-E) that finds "Now we get along very well. It makes me feel that I'm someone special. It makes me feel that I'm someone special." The context history for this response is "oh, really? so you just took home a stray cat? // Yes. It was starving and looking for something to eat when I saw it. // Poor cat." whose emotion history is {6, 0, 0}.

4.3 Generation-based Approaches

4.3.1 Compared Approaches

Seq2Seq The simplest generation-based approach we adopt is a vanilla Seq2Seq with GRU as basic cell, as described in Section 4.1. Such approach is widely selected as baseline models in dialog generation Shang et al. (2015); Lowe et al. (2015); Al-Rfou' et al. (2016).

Attention-based Seq2Seq We then evaluate the Seq2Seq approach with attention mechanism (Bahdanau et al., 2014) which has shown its effectiveness on various NLP tasks including dialog response (Hermann et al., 2015; Luong et al., 2015; Mei et al., 2017). We denote this approach as {Attn-Seq2Seq}.

HRED The third generation-based approach

we evaluate is hierarchical encoder-decoder (HRED) (Sordoni et al., 2015). Due to its context-aware modeling ability, HRED has shown better performances in previous work (Sordoni et al., 2015).

Intention and Emotion-enhanced To utilize the intention and emotion labels, we follow Zhou et al. (2017) to incorporate the label information during decoding. The intention and emotion labels are characterized as one-hot vectors. We denote the label-enhanced approaches as {L+} and the performances are given in the second box in Table 4.

Pretrained We also examine whether pre-training with other dataset will boost the performance of the first three generation-based approaches. Following Li et al. (2016, 2017), we use the OpenSubtitle dataset (Jörg Tiedemann, 2009)[7]. Because it has no clear and concise segmentation for each conversation, we treat each of three consecutive utterances as context, and the foregoing one as response. Finally, 3,000,000 three-turn dialogs are randomly sampled and used to pre-train the compared models for 12 epochs. We denote the approaches using pre-training as {Pre+}.

According to BLEU scores from Table 4 (last four columns), we can see that in general attention-based approaches are better than vanilla Seq2Seq model. Among the three compared approaches, HREDs achieve highest BLEU scores because they take history information into consideration.

---

[7]`https://github.com/jiweil/Neural-Dialogue-Generation`

Furthermore, label information is effective even though we utilize them in the simplest way. These findings are consistent with previous work (Sordoni et al., 2015; Serban et al., 2016b).

On the other hand, the first three columns in Table 4 show that models pretrained by OpenSubtitle converge faster, achieving lower Perplexity (PPL) but poorer BLEU scores. We conjecture it as a result of domain difference. OpenSubtitle dataset is constructed by movie lines, whereas our datasets are daily dialogues. Moreover, OpenSubtitles has approximately 1000+ speaker turns in one conversation, while our dataset has in average 8 turns. To pretrain a model by corpus from different domain will harm its performance on the target domain. Hence, it is less optimal to simply pretrain models with large-scale datasets such as OpenSubtitle, which is domain different from the evaluation datasets. We further examine this issue by comparing the generated answers by models trained solely on DailyDialog with and without pre-training.

4.3.2 Case Study

We give a case study in Table 8. It can be seen the two pre-trained models (the second and the fourth row) generate responses that are irrelevant with the context. In contrast, the corresponding model without pre-training produce more reasonable responses.

5 Related Work

5.1 Domain-Specific Datasets

The research on chatbots and dialog systems is still new and developing. Literature on traditional dialog system primarily relies on template-based and retrieval-based approaches and applies to specific-domain of data.

Popular datasets for this research area include TRAINS (Ringger et al., 1996), DBOX (Petukhova et al., 2014), bAbI synthetic dialog (Bordes and Weston, 2016) and Movie Dialog datasets (Dodge et al., 2015). These datasets feature different types of dialogues happening in different physical contexts. For example, the TRAINS corpus contains problem-solving dialogues and the dialog systems trained with TRAINS are performing as task-oriented assistants. The tasks are often about the shipping of railroad goods and thereafter it is called TRAINS. The bAbI (Bordes and Weston, 2016) and Movie Dialog dataset (Dodge et al., 2015) contain dialogues about movies and the tasks

in these datasets are movie question answering, movie recommendation and so on. Another popular dataset is Ubuntu dataset (Lowe et al., 2015) which extracts the user posts and replies in Ubuntu forums and the task is to answer users' computer-related questions.

5.2 Open-Domain Datasets

More recent work concentrates on generation-based approaches, which are mainly based on the sequence-to-sequence encoder-decoder architecture (Sordoni et al., 2015; Serban et al., 2016b). These generation-based approaches are often trained with large-scale open-domain datasets.

In Shang et al. (2015), the authors propose a neural responding machine (NRM) and examine their approach on Sina Weibo dataset (Wang et al., 2013). The Sina Weibo dataset is constructed by crawling users' posts and replies on a Chinese social network. Similar dataset is constructed by Ritter et al. (2011) who provides a Twitter dataset. Besides social network, Al-Rfou' et al. (2016) constructs a dialog training dataset with Reddit Forum posts. Existing work based on neural networks has examined their approaches on these datasets (Zhou et al., 2017; Wang et al., 2013; Sordoni et al., 2015; Serban et al., 2016b). Although these datasets are large-scale, the dialogues in them are often noisy and short. Even worse, the artificially constructed post-reply pairs are different from our real conversations.

To train neural network based conversational models, researchers often pre-train their models by using movie subtitles which are large-scale and conversation-like. The most widely adopted dataset is OpenSubtitle (Jörg Tiedemann, 2009) which is used in Li et al. (2016, 2017). Other similar datasets are SubTle dataset (Bordes and Weston, 2016) which is then used to build up MovieQA sub-dataset and MovieTriples (Serban et al., 2016a).

6 Conclusions and Future Work

In this work, we develop the dataset DailyDialog which is high-quality, multi-turn and manually labeled. We show the proposed dataset is appealing in four main aspects. The dialogues in the dataset cover totally ten topics and conform common dialog flows such as Questions-Inform and Directives-Commissives bi-turn flows. In addition, DailyDialog contains unique multi-turn dialog flow patterns, which reflect our realistic communication ways. And it is rich in emotion. The evaluation results in Section 4 are initial but indicative.

In the future we plan to design advanced mechanisms to explore the unique multi-turn dialog flows described in Section 3. It is also promising to utilize the topic information in our dataset by domain adaptation and transfer learning. Our dataset is available on `http://yanran.li/dailydialog`, and we hope it is beneficial for future research in this field.

Acknowledgements

We appreciate for the valuable suggestions and comments from the anonymous reviewers. The work described in this paper was supported by Research Grants Council of Hong Kong (PolyU 152094/14E, 152036/17E), National Natural Science Foundation of China (61672445, 61272291 and 61602451) and The Hong Kong Polytechnic University (GYBP6, 4-BCB5, B-Q46C).

References

Martín Abadi, Ashish Agarwal, Paul Barham, Eugene Brevdo, Zhifeng Chen, Craig Citro, Gregory S. Corrado, Andy Davis, Jeffrey Dean, Matthieu Devin, Sanjay Ghemawat, Ian J. Goodfellow, Andrew Harp, Geoffrey Irving, Michael Isard, Yangqing Jia, Rafal Józefowicz, Lukasz Kaiser, Manjunath Kudlur, Josh Levenberg, Dan Mané, Rajat Monga, Sherry Moore, Derek Gordon Murray, Chris Olah, Mike Schuster, Jonathon Shlens, Benoit Steiner, Ilya Sutskever, Kunal Talwar, Paul A. Tucker, Vincent Vanhoucke, Vijay Vasudevan, Fernanda B. Viégas, Oriol Vinyals, Pete Warden, Martin Wattenberg, Martin Wicke, Yuan Yu, and Xiaoqiang Zheng. 2015. Tensorflow: Large-scale machine learning on heterogeneous distributed systems. *CoRR*, abs/1603.04467.

Rami Al-Rfou', Marc Pickett, Javier Snaider, Yun-Hsuan Sung, Brian Strope, and Ray Kurzweil. 2016. Conversational contextual cues: The case of personalization and history for response ranking. *CoRR*, abs/1606.00372.

Dilafruz Amanova, Volha Petukhova, and Dietrich Klakow. 2016. Creating annotated dialogue resources: Cross-domain dialogue act classification. In *LREC*.

Dzmitry Bahdanau, Kyunghyun Cho, and Yoshua Bengio. 2014. Neural machine translation by jointly learning to align and translate. *CoRR*, abs/1409.0473.

Antoine Bordes and Jason Weston. 2016. Learning end-to-end goal-oriented dialog. *CoRR*, abs/1605.07683.

Kyunghyun Cho, Bart Van Merriënboer, Dzmitry Bahdanau, and Yoshua Bengio. 2014. On the properties of neural machine translation: Encoder-decoder approaches. *arXiv preprint arXiv:1409.1259*.

Jesse Dodge, Andreea Gane, Xiang Zhang, Antoine Bordes, Sumit Chopra, Alexander H. Miller, Arthur Szlam, and Jason Weston. 2015. Evaluating prerequisite qualities for learning end-to-end dialog systems. *CoRR*, abs/1511.06931.

Paul Ekman. 1992. An argument for basic emotions. *Cognition & emotion*, 6(3-4):169–200.

John J Godfrey, Edward C Holliman, and Jane McDaniel. 1992. Switchboard: Telephone speech corpus for research and development. In *Acoustics, Speech, and Signal Processing, 1992. ICASSP-92., 1992 IEEE International Conference on*, volume 1, pages 517–520. IEEE.

Karl Moritz Hermann, Tomás Kocisky, Edward Grefenstette, Lasse Espeholt, Will Kay, Mustafa Suleyman, and Phil Blunsom. 2015. Teaching machines to read and comprehend. In *NIPS*.

Sina Jafarpour, Christopher JC Burges, and Alan Ritter. 2010. Filter, rank, and transfer the knowledge: Learning to chat. *Advances in Ranking*, 10.

Jörg Tiedemann. 2009. *News from OPUS A Collection of Multilingual Parallel Corpora with Tools and Interfaces*.

Diederik Kingma and Jimmy Ba. 2014. Adam: A method for stochastic optimization. *International Conference for Learning Representations*.

Jiwei Li, Will Monroe, Alan Ritter, Daniel Jurafsky, Michel Galley, and Jianfeng Gao. 2016. Deep reinforcement learning for dialogue generation. In *EMNLP*.

Jiwei Li, Will Monroe, Tianlin Shi, Alan Ritter, and Dan Jurafsky. 2017. Adversarial learning for neural dialogue generation. *arXiv preprint arXiv:1701.06547*.

Chia-Wei Liu, Ryan Lowe, Iulian V Serban, Michael Noseworthy, Laurent Charlin, and Joelle Pineau. 2016. How not to evaluate your dialogue system: An empirical study of unsupervised evaluation metrics for dialogue response generation. In *EMNLP*.

Ryan Lowe, Nissan Pow, Iulian Serban, and Joelle Pineau. 2015. The ubuntu dialogue corpus: A large dataset for research in unstructured multi-turn dialogue systems. In *SIGDIAL Conference*.

Chuwei Luo and Wenjie Li. 2016. A combination of similarity and rule-based method of polyu for ntcir-12 stc task. In *Proceedings of the 12th NTCIR Conference on Evaluation of Information Access Technologies*.

Thang Luong, Hieu Pham, and Christopher D. Manning. 2015. Effective approaches to attention-based neural machine translation. In *EMNLP*.

Hongyuan Mei, Mohit Bansal, and Matthew R. Walter. 2017. Coherent dialogue with attention-based language models. In *AAAI*.

Atsushi Otsuka, Toru Hirano, Chiaki Miyazaki, Ryuichiro Higashinaka, Toshiro Makino, and Yoshihiro Matsuo. 2017. Utterance selection using discourse relation filter for chat-oriented dialogue systems. In *Dialogues with Social Robots*, pages 355–365. Springer.

Volha Petukhova. 2011. Emultidimensional dialogue modelling. phd dissertation. *Tilburg University, The Netherlands*.

Volha Petukhova, Martin Gropp, Dietrich Klakow, Anna Schmidt, Gregor Eigner, Mario Topf, Stefan Srb, Petr Motlicek, Blaise Potard, John Dines, et al. 2014. The dbox corpus collection of spoken human-human and human-machine dialogues. In *Proceedings of the Ninth International Conference on Language Resources and Evaluation (LREC" 14)*, EPFL-CONF-201766. European Language Resources Association (ELRA).

Eric K Ringger, James F Allen, Bradford W Miller, and Teresa Sikorski. 1996. A robust system for natural spoken dialogue.

Alan Ritter, Colin Cherry, and William B Dolan. 2011. Data-driven response generation in social media. In *Proceedings of the conference on empirical methods in natural language processing*, pages 583–593. Association for Computational Linguistics.

Iulian Serban, Alessandro Sordoni, Yoshua Bengio, Aaron C. Courville, and Joelle Pineau. 2016a. Building end-to-end dialogue systems using generative hierarchical neural network models. In *AAAI*.

Iulian Vlad Serban, Alessandro Sordoni, Ryan Lowe, Laurent Charlin, Joelle Pineau, Aaron Courville, and Yoshua Bengio. 2016b. A hierarchical latent variable encoder-decoder model for generating dialogues. *arXiv preprint arXiv:1605.06069*.

Lifeng Shang, Zhengdong Lu, and Hang Li. 2015. Neural responding machine for short-text conversation. In *ACL*.

Alessandro Sordoni, Yoshua Bengio, Hossein Vahabi, Christina Lioma, Jakob Grue Simonsen, and Jian-Yun Nie. 2015. A hierarchical recurrent encoder-decoder for generative context-aware query suggestion. In *Cikm'15 Proceedings of the 24th Acm International on Conference on Information and Knowledge Management*. Association for Computing Machinery.

Hao Wang, Zhengdong Lu, Hang Li, and Enhong Chen. 2013. A dataset for research on short-text conversations. In *EMNLP*, pages 935–945.

Zhao Yan, Nan Duan, Junwei Bao, Peng Chen, Ming Zhou, Zhoujun Li, and Jianshe Zhou. 2016. Docchat: an information retrieval approach for chatbot engines using unstructured documents. In *ACL*.

Hao Zhou, Minlie Huang, Tianyang Zhang, Xiaoyan Zhu, and Bing Liu. 2017. Emotional chatting machine: Emotional conversation generation with internal and external memory. *arXiv preprint arXiv:1704.01074*.

Inference is Everything: Recasting Semantic Resources into a Unified Evaluation Framework

Aaron Steven White
University of Rochester

Pushpendre Rastogi
Johns Hopkins University

Kevin Duh
Johns Hopkins University

Benjamin Van Durme
Johns Hopkins University

Abstract

We propose to unify a variety of existing semantic classification tasks, such as semantic role labeling, anaphora resolution, and paraphrase detection, under the heading of Recognizing Textual Entailment (RTE). We present a general strategy to automatically generate one or more sentential hypotheses based on an input sentence and pre-existing manual semantic annotations. The resulting suite of datasets enables us to probe a statistical RTE model's performance on different aspects of semantics. We demonstrate the value of this approach by investigating the behavior of a popular neural network RTE model.

1 Introduction

The Recognizing Textual Entailment (RTE) task aims to assess a system's ability to do textual inference—i.e. derive valid conclusions from textual clues (Dagan et al., 2006, 2013; Bar-Haim et al., 2006; Giampiccolo et al., 2007, 2009; Bentivogli et al., 2009, 2010, 2011). In this task, a system judges whether "typically, a human reading [the sentential context, or *text*] T would infer that [the sentential hypothesis] H is most likely true" (Dagan et al., 2006).

Recent efforts in textual inference have focused on the Stanford Natural Language Inference (SNLI) dataset. SNLI is made up of hundreds of thousands of text-hypothesis pairs, wherein the texts are image captions drawn from the Flickr30k corpus (Young et al., 2014) and the hypotheses are elicited from crowdsourcing workers based on those captions (but not the corresponding image). While SNLI has led to significant methodological improvements, its collection protocol does not lend itself to understanding the types of semantic knowl-

edge necessary for properly understanding a particular example. Researchers compete on which system achieves the highest score on a test set, but this itself does not lead to an understanding of which linguistic properties are better captured by a quantitatively superior system.

In contrast, datasets such as FraCaS (Cooper et al., 1996) are precisely designed to illustrate a range of semantic phenomenon that a text understanding system should handle. But though this careful design enables fine-grained probes into a system's semantic capabilities, FraCaS-like datasets tend not to be large-scale enough for recent work in data-driven computational semantics. Asking experts, such as those who constructed FraCaS, to author hundreds of thousands of examples is not practical, just as the existing elicitation protocol behind SNLI will not lead to cleanly partitioned sets of examples that focus specifically on certain kinds of semantic inference.

Our proposal is to leverage existing large-scale semantic annotation collections as a source of targeted textual inference examples. This strategy requires only minor effort in developing dataset-specific generation capabilities to recast annotations into a shared universal representation: natural language sentences.

We demonstrate the use of this strategy in two steps. First, we construct three recasted datasets from three existing semantic resources that target three distinct semantic phenomena:[1] (i) the Semantic Proto-Roles v1 (SPR) dataset (Reisinger et al., 2015), which contains likelihood judgments about the semantic *proto-role* properties (Dowty, 1991) of verbal arguments found in PropBank (Palmer et al., 2005), (ii) the FrameNet Plus (FN+) dataset, which contains likelihood judgments about the paraphrase validity of *frame triggers* (Pavlick et al., 2015), and

---

[1]These recasted datasets are made publicly available at `http://decomp.net`.

996

(iii) the Definite Pronoun Resolution (DPR) dataset, which contains annotations relevant to complex anaphora resolution (Rahman and Ng, 2012). We use these recast datasets to train a recent neural RTE model (Bowman et al., 2015) and measure its performance. We show that complex anaphora is the most difficult semantic phenomenon for neural RTE models to capture, followed by predicting thematic proto-role properties. Perhaps unsurprisingly, given the nature of the RTE task, paraphrasing seems to be the easiest phenomenon to model.

In the next section (§2), we discuss previous work in RTE, focusing in particular on the development of RTE datasets. We then discuss our data creation process (§3) as well as the results of a small validation (§4). Finally, we report on the setup and results of our three experiments (§5) and then conclude (§6).

2 Background and Prior Work

The current paper touches on both the broad theme of understanding continuous approaches to natural language understanding as well as the more narrow focus on textual entailment. We begin by discussing how the current paper fits within the broader context and then specify its place within textual entailment.

2.1 Approaches to logical form

All approaches to natural language understanding utilize intermediate logical forms that are interpretable to varying degrees. On one end of the spectrum are approaches that utilize declarative logical forms. In such approaches, semantic parsers first convert a sequence into a meaning representation that expresses the semantics needed for inference. In this case, each individual component of the logical form is clearly interpretable. Tremendous energies within computational linguistics have been spent on building declarative, component-wise-interpretable logical forms such as Hobbsian Logic (Hobbs, 1985), Discourse Representation Theory (Kamp et al., 2011), the Rochester Interactive Planning System (Allen et al., 2007), Minimal Recursion Semantics (Copestake et al., 2005), Episodic Logic (Schubert and Hwang, 2000), Combinatory Categorical Grammar (Steedman, 2000), Semantic Role Labeling (Gildea and Jurafsky, 2002), Framenet Parsing (Fillmore et al., 2003) and Abstract Meaning Representation (Banarescu et al., 2013).

Opposite the above approaches are methods that utilize vector space-based logical forms. Recent work on word and string embeddings (Mikolov et al., 2013; Pennington et al., 2014) has produced vector space representations that can be induced from large corpora in an unsupervised manner that have been used to initialize the training of neural networks for tasks as complex as English-to-French machine translation (Sutskever et al., 2014). Vector space-based intermediate forms are not commonly recognized as logical forms but in light of recent work (Bouchard et al., 2015) it seems worthwhile to reconsider this view.

An argument in favor of declarative, interpretable logical forms is that one can directly observe the specific mistakes made by a system in the interpretive process of mapping natural language strings to logical forms—e.g., it is possible to find out whether a prepositional phrase was attached incorrectly, or the wrong sense of a particular word was selected, causing a cascade of downstream errors. Neural systems that use vector space representations for textual inference, instead of logical forms, lack such modularity and interpretability, and therefore it is very difficult to figure out the cause of a particular error in a neural network.

Much prior work has aimed to improve the interpretability of neural networks, focusing in particular on extracting rules from the activations of feed forward networks (Towell and Shavlik, 1993; Thrun, 1993; Fu, 1994; Thrun, 1995). In recent years, this focus has shifted to understanding and visualizing other architectures such as Convolutional Neural Networks and Recurrent Neural Networks (Zeiler and Fergus, 2014; Karpathy et al., 2015), though the guiding principle remains the same: understanding the behavior of neural networks in terms of its activations.

The current paper also presents a strategy for understanding the behavior of neural RTE systems used for solving the task of RTE, but we take a different route. Instead of explaining the behavior of neural networks in terms of its parameters and activations, we benchmark their performance on datasets that each require distinct types of semantic reasoning for high performance. In this sense, our motivation and strategy is similar to the reasoning behind the bAbI dataset for question answering (Weston et al., 2016). Weston et al. argue that, in order to measure the progress towards building dialogue agents, it can be useful to evaluate the

ID	Dataset	Label	Text	Hypothesis
1	SPR	entailed	The network must refund money to the advertisers and loses considerable revenue and prestige.	The network was altered or somehow changed during or by the end of the losing.
2	SPR	entailed	He turned himself in to authorities in New York earlier this year.	He changes location during the turning.
3	SPR	not-entailed	Later, he marketed glue.	He changes location during the marketing.
4	SPR	not-entailed	So he asked the IRS if the plan would work.	The asking caused a change in the IRS.
5	FN+	entailed	An agreement is to be signed in late 10/92.	An agreement is to be inked in late 10/92.
6	FN+	entailed	So our work must continue.	So our labor must continue.
7	FN+	not-entailed	Friday had beautiful weather.	Friday had beautiful forecast.
8	FN+	not-entailed	Your support will help them go to work.	Your support will allow them go to work.
9	DPR	entailed	The bird ate the pie and it died.	The bird ate the pie and the bird died.
10	DPR	not-entailed	The bird ate the pie and it died.	The bird ate the pie and the pie died.
11	DPR	entailed	The bird ate the pie and it was ruined.	The bird ate the pie and the pie was ruined.
12	DPR	not-entailed	The bird ate the pie and it was ruined.	The bird ate the pie and the bird was ruined.

Table 1: Examples of *text-hypothesis* pairs generated from the SPR, FN+, and DPR datasets.

ability of systems to perform different kinds of question answering tasks that require specific types of reasoning. Our strategy for building specific datasets that can probe the ability of machine learning systems to perform specific types of reasoning is similar to theirs; however, instead of constructing completely artificial datasets, we *recast* datasets constructed on top of natural text.

2.2 Approaches to textual entailment

Research in textual entailment, at least in its most recent form, was catalyzed by the RTE shared task (Dagan et al., 2006; Bar-Haim et al., 2006; Giampiccolo et al., 2007, 2009; Bentivogli et al., 2009, 2010, 2011). With each iteration of this shared task, manually annotated examples were created for testing competing systems. But even after multiple iterations, the amount of available data for RTE was still small. The Sentences Involving Compositional Knowledge (SICK) corpus was released with the goal of alleviating this problem (Marelli et al., 2014).

A significant further contribution was made with the Stanford Natural Language Inference (SNLI) corpus, which uses crowdsourcing to gather two orders of magnitude more examples than all previous datasets (Bowman et al., 2015). SNLI enabled fully supervised training of powerful machine learning models like neural networks. A number of researchers have pursued this direction by applying completely supervised neural models for sequential data to the problem of textual entailment (Rocktäschel et al., 2015; Mou et al., 2015; Shuohang and Jing, 2015; Liu et al., 2016; Cheng et al., 2016; Parikh et al., 2016; Munkhdalai and Yu, 2016).

But though the state of the art performance of neural sequential models has steadily increased over the past year, it appears that this area has reached a point where the paradigm of training and evaluating on a single general-purpose RTE dataset has become insufficient for reaching the next level of improvements. It is still informative to measure the performance of a new RTE model on the SNLI dataset, but this black-box evaluation does not help us understand the fine-grained aspects of a model's capability in performing particular types of natural language inference, such as its ability to handle coreference, paraphrasing, or its ability to judge thematic properties of a named entity. The issue of lack of understandability is especially important for neural models, which are notoriously difficult to interpret.

To address this issue, we take inspiration from the FraCaS dataset (Cooper et al., 1996) and construct a suite of targeted datasets that separately test a system's ability to perform individual bits of interpretation such as paraphrasing, semantic role labeling, and coreference. In contrast to the original FraCaS data set, which is relatively small and which could not support the training of purely lexical neural RTE classifiers, we pursue the strategy of automatically converting *semantic classifications*—i.e., human judgments about semantic properties—into labeled examples for textual entailment. This strategy allows us to construct textual entailment datasets that are of the same order of magnitude as SNLI—and hence support data-driven training of large neural networks—but that are also focused on specific semantic properties.

With our strategy we can also quantify the types of semantic phenomenon that an existing *semanti-*

cally undifferentiated dataset contains. For example, if a neural model trained on the SNLI dataset performs poorly on a test set from another domain that exercises the trained model's ability to perform anaphora resolution, then it can be inferred that either the original dataset did not contain enough examples of anaphora resolution, or that the statistical model failed to capture that phenomenon.

Finally, we note that the idea of converting question-answer pairs into text-hypothesis pairs is not novel: the RTE dataset for the second RTE Shared task was created by manually converting existing Information Extraction, Information Retrieval and QA pairs from manually curated datasets such as ACE, MUC, TREC and CLEF (Bar-Haim et al., 2006). The main contribution of the current work is to show that such conversion need not be done manually; automatic conversion of some semantic datasets can be done with a high enough quality to create large-scale RTE datasets.

3 Data Creation Process

In order to create annotated RTE datasets that can probe specific aspects of understanding, our strategy is to rewrite semantic classifications into the form of textual entailment pairs. As mentioned above, we define a semantic classification dataset to be a text corpus, along with manual annotations of a particular meaning-related aspect of the data. Here, we describe how to apply this strategy to the SPR, FN+, and DPR datasets, but there exist many further datasets to which this strategy can be applied.

The SPR dataset Semantic Proto-Role Labeling (SPRL) is the problem of assigning a likelihood value for a particular *proto-role property* holding of a particular argument of a particular predicate (Reisinger et al., 2015; White et al., 2016; Teichert et al., 2017). These proto-role properties are inspired by the *thematic proto-role* theory proposed by Dowty (1991), who argued that, for the purpose of determining the mapping from predicates' semantic roles to its syntactic arguments, semantic roles should be viewed not as categories, but rather as sets of entailments that arguments must satisfy in the context of an event kind.

For purposes of recasting, we use the SPR1 dataset, which was collected by Reisinger et al. (2015) and contains likelihood judgments for the twelve *proto-role properties* listed in Table 2.

Role property	How likely or unlikely is it that...
instigation	ARG caused the PRED to happen?
volition	ARG chose to be involved in the PRED?
awareness	ARG was/were aware of being involved in the PRED?
sentient	ARG was/were sentient?
change of location	ARG changed location during the PRED?
exists as physical	ARG existed as a physical object?
existed before	ARG existed before the PRED began?
existed during	ARG existed during the PRED?
existed after	ARG existed after the PRED stopped?
change of possession	ARG changed possession during the PRED?
change of state	ARG was/were altered or somehow changed during or by the end of the PRED?
stationary	ARG was/were stationary during the PRED?
location of event	ARG described the location of the PRED?
physical contact	ARG made physical contact with someone or something else involved in the PRED?
was used	ARG was/were used in carrying out the PRED?
pred changed arg	The PRED caused a change in ARG?

Table 2: Questions posed to SPR annotators.

These judgments were collected by providing the annotator with a sentence in which a predicate and an argument of that predicate were highlighted and asking them to answer, on a five-point scale from 1 (very unlikely) to 5 (very likely), how likely or unlikely each property was to hold of the argument in the context of the predicate.[2]

For example, given (1), with *the antibody* as the highlighted argument and *killed* as the highlighted predicate, the annotator's job was to answer questions like the one in (2).

(1) The antibody killed the virus.

(2) How likely or unlikely is it that the antibody caused the killing to happen?

For the purposes of SPRL task, Teichert et al. (2017) propose to collapse the five-point scale to a binary variable by mapping response 1–3 to *not-entailed* and 4–5 to *entailed* and predicting the resulting binary variable. Collapsing across properties, the current state-of-the-art F1 for the resulting task of predicting this binary variable is reported by Teichert et al. (2017) at 81.7.

Binarized proto-role property judgments can be readily converted to text-hypothesis pairs by simply treating the original sentence as the text and converting the questions listed in Table 2 to statements for use as hypotheses. For example, (1) would be treated as a text, and (3) would be treated as a hypothesis generated from (2).

(3) The antibody caused the killing to happen.

In this case, the annotator gave a 5 (very likely) response to (2), and so in our recasted dataset, the resulting pair is labeled *entailed*.

---

[2]Annotators were also given the option of saying that the question was *not applicable* (*NA*). We filter these these responses from our dataset.

►	Three women enjoying a balloon joyride.
	Three women are on a balloon ride.
►	A woman sings into a microphone indoors.
	a women sings
►	The kid is sliding down a tan plastic slide.
	The kid is sliding.
►	A black dog is playing in water with a green toy.
	the dog has a toy
►	A woman with glasses and a pink hat rides her bike.
	A woman with glasses and a pink hat rides her bike

Table 3: Examples of artifacts in the SNLI dataset that promote hypothesis sentences to be substrings of the evidence sentences, specially in case of entailments. The bullet marked sentences are the *evidence* sentences and the *hypothesis* sentences below them.

This is a simple and inexpensive way of creating entailment pairs, with the benefit that this annotation scheme probes for fundamental semantic information from an annotator. Also, note that, since Reisinger et al. collect annotations for the twelve types of proto-role properties mentioned above, the errors made by a neural RTE model can be automatically subcategorized into these 12 categories, further aiding in interpretation.

One potential criticism of our method is that, because our hypothesis sentences are constructed by filling in templates, they do not have the same syntactic diversity as the free elicitation method used by Bowman et al.. We suggest that this is not a problem for two reasons.

First, since our goal is to distinguish between the kinds of semantic phenomenon that can be accurately modeled by statistical RTE models, the lack of diversity is not an obstacle as long as the particular phenomenon that we wish to probe is being covered properly. Second, even the method used by Bowman et al. of enlisting workers on the Amazon Mechanical Turk (AMT) Platform to write hypotheses sentences in response to an image caption is not without its drawbacks since their method introduces artifacts such as the fact that the *hypotheses* sentences in SNLI are on average half the length of the *text* prompts. We believe that this happens because workers on AMT have an incentive to spend the least amount of time possible in constructing their responses. In Table 3, we list a few such examples.

The FN+ dataset In Frame Semantics (Fillmore et al., 2003), the primary unit of lexical analysis is the *frame*, which captures the central properties of a concept, situation, or event. The largest resource for frame annotated sentences with information about evoked frames, their *trigger* phrases,

Dataset	Sentences	Label Percentage	
		Entailed	*Not-Entailed*
FN+	154,605	43.45	56.55
SPR	154,607	34.80	65.20
DPR	3,661	49.99	50.01
Total	312,873	39.13	60.87
SNLI[†]	569,033	33.41	66.59

Table 4: Number of *text-hypothesis* pairs generated from each dataset along with percentage of entailing v. non-entailing sentences. SNLI included for comparison.

and frame arguments is the FrameNet dataset (Fillmore and Baker, 2001), which despite its scale, still suffers from lexical sparsity.

In order to alleviate this problem of lexical sparsity Rastogi and Van Durme (2014) use the Paraphrase Database (Ganitkevitch et al., 2013) to automatically paraphrase *trigger* tokens that evoke frames inside sentences from the FrameNet dataset. These paraphrases are noisy, and their quality is not high enough for our use. However, these paraphrases were subsequently manually rated by Pavlick et al., who asked annotators to "judge each paraphrase in terms of how well it preserved the meaning of the original sentence" (Pavlick et al., 2015). These ratings were collected on a scale from 1 to 5, where 5 meant that the paraphrase retained all of the meaning of the original sentence and 1 meant that paraphrase did not mean anything close to the original phrase. We generate our *text–hypothesis* pairs using the manual judgments of meaning retention on these *sentence–paraphrase* pairs collected by Pavlick et al..

While the *sentence–paraphrase* pairs that are labeled *entailed* and rated 3.0 and above are usually grammatically correct, the sentences with an average rating below 3 and labeled *entailed* sometimes contain a grammatical errors, and some are rated *neutral* or contradictory. Therefore, we remove sentences with an average rating less than or equal to 3.0 and greater than 2.5. All of the sentence pairs that were rated less than 2.5 were not valid entailments and they were labeled as *not-entailed*.

As an example, consider (4), which is a sentence from FrameNet.

(4) So our work must continue.

The word *work* triggers a frame and is replaced by its paraphrase *labor* by Pavlick et al. to create (5).

(5) So our labor must continue.

We consider the first sentence to be the text and the second sentence to be the hypothesis. The annota-

Dataset	Accuracy	Grammaticality
FN+	85	77
SPR	94	92
DPR	98	96
SNLI	91	96

Table 5: Accuracy of the labels assigned to the RTE pairs and the grammaticality of the hypothesis sentences. 100 random RTE pairs from each dataset were selected and each pair was assigned a value of 1 if it was correctly labeled/grammatical and 0 otherwise. We report the average score as a percentage in two separate columns for each dataset.

Dataset	Sentence
FN+	12:06 a.m. hrh: i was per the berkeley main library when it hit.
SPR	Me existed as a physical object.
DPR	John could not understand his waiter, because the his waiter spoke Spanish.
SNLI	A person in on concrete.

Table 6: Examples of ungrammatical hypothesis sentences from each of our datasets and SNLI.

tors on Mechanical Turk gave this pair of sentences an average rating of around 4, and so we consider this pair of sentences as an instance of the *entailed* relation.

The DPR dataset Definite Pronoun Resolution is the problem of identifying the correct antecedent for a definite pronoun—e.g. *he/him, she/her, it,* etc.—in one clause, given two potential antecedents in a preceding clause. Data generation for this task is done manually and relies on the concept of *twin sentences.* Twin sentences are (minimally) biclausal sentences that share a (linearly) initial clause containing at least two non-pronominal referring expressions but differ on a non-initial clause containing a pronoun that could corefer with either of the two referring expressions in the initial clause but which is biased to corefer with only one.

This concept is exemplified in (6), where *the bee* and *the flower* are the two referring expressions in the initial clause for both (6a) and (6b), and *it* is the pronoun.

(6) The bee landed on the flower because...

    a. ...it wanted pollen.

    b. ...it had pollen.

In (6a), *it* is biased to corefer with *the bee*, and in (6b), *it* is biased to corefer with *the flower*.

In order to assign the correct antecedent of *it* in both sentences, a computational system would presumably need world-knowledge about bees and flowers. The DPR dataset is a collection of such problems and their solutions, collected by Rahman and Ng (2012) as a step towards solving the Winograd Schema Challenge (Hector et al., 2012). The ranking-based system that Rahman and Ng present obtains an accuracy of 73.1% on their dataset. This result—which, to our knowledge, remains the best posted on this dataset—outperforms a random baseline as well as various systems based on the Stanford resolver (Lee et al., 2011).

Each DPR coreference problem-solution pair can be converted to two annotated entailment problems by substituting the target pronoun with the two expressions that it could corefer with. Thus, two RTE pairs are generated for each DPR pair: one that is entailed and one that is not entailed.

For example, (6a) is rewritten to (7a) and (7b).

(7) a. The bee landed on the flower because the bee wanted pollen.

    b. The bee landed on the flower because the flower wanted pollen.

The two RTE pairs are then (7a)–(8a), which is paired with the output *entailed*, and (7a)–(8b), which is paired with the output *not-entailed*.

Statistics Table 4 summarizes the constructed datasets as well as number of sentences and the class category breakdown of the SNLI dataset.[3]

4   Data Validation

Since our data is automatically generated, we performed manual validation to ensure that the generated data was high quality. To conduct this validation, we assessed a small subset of our recasted datasets as well as the SNLI dataset.

We randomly sampled 100 RTE pairs from each of the four datasets, and then a single annotator rated those 400 RTE pairs on two criteria of grammaticality and correctness. The results of the manual validation presented in Table 5 show that the data quality of the DPR and SPR datasets is on par with the quality of the RTE pairs in the SNLI datasets. The grammaticality of the hypothesis sentences in the FN+ dataset is worse than the other three datasets, but its accuracy is reasonably high.

Tables 6 and 7 show examples of ungrammatical hypothesis sentences and incorrectly labeled

---

[3]For the SNLI statistics, we map the two categories of *contradiction* and *neutral* to *not-entailed.*

Assigned Category	Text and Hypothesis
(FN+) Not Entailed	► The steps passed along the path on the other side of the wall under which i crouched. the steps passed along the path on the other outboard of the wall under which i crouched.
(SPR) Not Entailed	► The machine employs reduced instruction-set computing, or RISC, technology. Reduced instruction-set computing, or RISC, technology existed after the employing stopped.
(DPR) Entailed	► A series of injections are used to battle a type of cancer in patients because they have a special type of drug which counteracts this sickness. A series of injections are used to battle a type of cancer in patients because patients have a special type of drug which counteracts this sickness.
(SNLI) Neural	► two guys playing music with a band The guys play music

Table 7: Examples of incorrectly labeled RTE pairs from each of our datasets and SNLI.

RTE sentence pairs to illustrate the types of errors that we make in comparison to the errors made by mechanical turkers.

5   Experiments and Results

We now conduct experiments to measure the variation in performance of neural RTE models trained using the datasets described above. The driving idea is that, by analyzing the variation in accuracy of a neural RTE model trained on different datasets on the same test set, such as the SNLI dataset, we can gain insights into the behavior of the model and potentially reveal interesting information about the SNLI dataset itself.

We first split our three datasets into train, validation, and test sets in the proportion of 80:10:10. Prior to training we convert the SNLI test set to a binary scheme by replacing both *neutral* and *contradiction* class labels with *not-entailed*.

For our model, we use the LSTM-based neural RTE model described by Bowman et al. (2015) which was their best performing individual neural model. This model first embeds the words using 300 dimensional word embeddings created using the Glove method (Pennington et al., 2014). Then, two LSTM neural networks (Hochreiter and Schmidhuber, 1997) independently encode the text and hypothesis sentences into 100 dimensional vectors. These representations are concatenated and input to a 3-layer deep 200 dimensional neural network classifier. The entire network is trained by maximizing the cross-entropy of the input-output pairs over the entire dataset using the AdaDelta (Zeiler, 2012) update rule with L2-regularization and Dropout. We evaluated each of our models on all the test sets to obtain the results in Table 8.

These results show that when the neural RTE model is trained and tested on the same dataset, the performance on the test set is high (above 80%) for FN+, SPR, and SNLI. This suggests that these three tasks are relatively amenable to the application of neural sequence models, with the FN+ and SPR dataset being comparable in their difficulty.

Moreover, we see that the performance of the model trained on all four datasets is equal to chance performance on the DPR dataset. Further, it is consistently lower than other cross-evaluation results shown on the off-diagonals of Table 8. This suggests that complex anaphora resolution is difficult for our model to capture, especially when its training data are not focused on demonstrating correct coreference resolution. And since the performance of the SNLI trained model is the least on the DPR dataset, this may suggest that the phenomenon of anaphora resolution occurs less often than paraphrasing or proto-role resolution in the SNLI dataset.

This is corroborated by a small manual analysis. In our random sample of 100 sentences from the SNLI dataset, we did not find a single example where pronoun coreference resolution was required to predict the label correctly. In fact, in this analysis, we found that the only text that might plausibly have been rewritten as a pronoun resolution problem (8a) was not; the hypothesis for (8a) is (8b).

(8)   a.   A man speaking to a woman in a grocery store as he selects a carton of juice.

b.   A man is complimenting a woman on her jacket.

Finally, we can see that the SNLI trained model achieves 62.0% on the FN+ test set. While better than a most frequent label baseline (56%), this is still considerably worse than the FN+ model (80.5%), optimized for paraphrastic inference under single word replacement. We believe this is because the sentences in FN+ contain language that is rarely seen. Thus, they contain more subtle

Train Set	FN+	SPR	DPR	SNLI
FN+	80.5	60.0	49.5	62.0
SPR	65.8	80.6	50.7	52.3
DPR	19.2	65.2	49.5	65.7
SNLI	62.0	57.6	48.8	85.3

Table 8: Accuracy under 0-1 loss of predicting the entailment relation. Each cell describes the accuracy of a model trained on the corresponding row's training set and tested on the corresponding column's test set

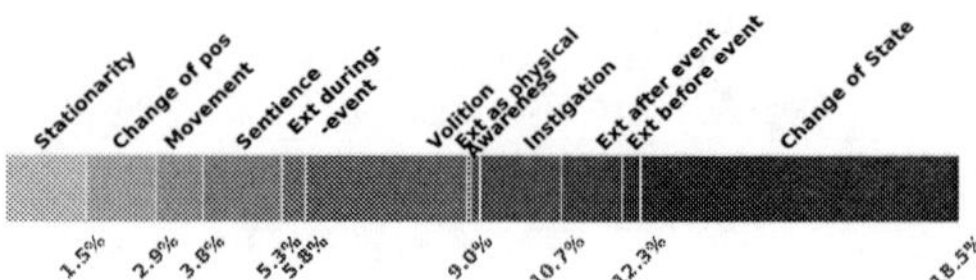

Figure 1: Percentage of errors of RTE model by *proto-role* properties on the SPR test set. The percentage numbers at the bottom are the contribution of the category above to the total errors. Error percentages that are close to each other are omitted for clarity.

differences compared to the differences between the text and the hypothesis in the SNLI dataset. This may also be why the model trained on SNLI does not perform well on any of the other datasets.

As a second illustration, we analyzed the SNLI trained RTE model's performance on the SPR test set by dissecting the overall performance of the model by the proto-role properties that the entailment pairs were generated from. Note that all the categories appear equally in the test data. The results, shown in Figure 1, show that entailments belonging to the *change of State* category caused the highest number of errors. Based on manual inspection of examples, such as sentence 4 in Table 1, we believe that this happens because such entailments are not easily captured using lexical patterns. On the other hand information about *stationarity* and *change of possession* may be captured by neural models because the entailments are tightly coupled to the argument tokens.

6 Conclusion

We argue for constructing a suite of large-scale textual inference datasets that probe specific aspects of semantics, in order to analyze a statistical RTE model's ability of "understanding" distinct semantic phenomena. To construct such datasets we presented a general strategy of converting semantic classification examples to annotated textual inference pairs that can be used to create large datasets for free on which even neural models for RTE can be trained. Further we used these datasets to gain insights into the behavior of a popular neural RTE model and the SNLI dataset itself. The variation in the performance of that model on the three datasets showed that neural models for natural language understanding recognise lexical variations or paraphrasing much better than anaphora resolution. Recently (Chen et al., 2016) also presented a similar conclusion after manually analyzing the errors made by neural systems on a reading comprehen-

sion task. Our approach can be thought of as an automatic way of automating the manual error analysis so that it can be used iteratively in a larger system and it can remove the requirement of a human in the loop. Our results also strongly suggested that the SNLI dataset does not contain examples of anaphora resolution which we validated manually. Our datasets and annotations are available at http://decomp.net.

In future work, we plan to execute our strategy on labeled data for Word Sense Disambiguation and Prepositional Phrase attachment resolution, among other semantic resources, because we believe that such diverse datasets will require sophisticated RTE models that combine world knowledge with the pattern recognition abilities of neural networks. For example, given the sentence *The dog wagged its tail* and a known sense of the dog the following hypotheses sentences can be generated: *The dog is a domestic dog* and *The dog is a wiener*. The former hypothesis is *entailed* but the latter is not. Disambiguating between word senses and deciding the correct governor of a prepositional phrase requires world knowledge and RTE examples generated from such sources, even though they are generated automatically unlike the FraCaS dataset, will help researchers build robust statistical models for RTE since each semantic classification dataset highlights a particular type of semantic phenomenon that a robust system for RTE must model.

Acknowledgments

This research was supported by the JHU HLT-COE, DARPA DEFT, DARPA LORELEI, and the JHU Science of Learning Institute. The U.S. Government is authorized to reproduce and distribute reprints for Governmental purposes. The views and conclusions contained in this publication are those of the authors and should not be interpreted as representing official policies or endorsements of DARPA or the U.S. Government.

References

James Allen, Mehdi Manshadi, Myroslava Dzikovska, and Mary Swift. 2007. Deep linguistic processing for spoken dialogue systems. In *Workshop on Deep Linguistic Processing*. ACL, pages 49–56.

Laura Banarescu et al. 2013. Abstract meaning representation for sembanking. In *7th Linguistic Annotation Workshop and Interoperability with Discourse*. ACL, Sofia, Bulgaria, pages 178–186. http://www.aclweb.org/anthology/W13-2322.

Roy Bar-Haim, Ido Dagan, Bill Dolan, Lisa Ferro, Danilo Giampiccolo, Bernardo Magnini, and Idan Szpektor. 2006. The second PASCAL recognising textual entailment challenge. In *Second PASCAL challenges workshop on RTE*. volume 6, pages 6–4.

Luisa Bentivogli, Peter Clark, Ido Dagan, Hoa T. Dang, and Danilo Giampiccolo. 2010. The sixth PASCAL recognizing textual entailment challenge. In *TAC*.

Luisa Bentivogli, Peter Clark, Ido Dagan, and Danilo Giampiccolo. 2011. The seventh PASCAL recognizing textual entailment challenge. In *TAC*.

Luisa Bentivogli, Ido Dagan, Hoa Trang Dang, Danilo Giampiccolo, and Bernardo Magnini. 2009. The fifth PASCAL recognizing textual entailment challenge. In *TAC*. volume 9, pages 14–24.

Guillaume Bouchard, Sameer Singh, and Théo Trouillon. 2015. On approximate reasoning capabilities of low-rank vector spaces. In *2015 AAAI Spring Symposium Series*.

Samuel R Bowman, Gabor Angeli, Christopher Potts, and Christopher D. Manning. 2015. A large annotated corpus for learning natural language inference. *arXiv preprint arXiv:1508.05326* .

Danqi Chen, Jason Bolton, and Christopher D. Manning. 2016. A thorough examination of the cnn/daily mail reading comprehension task. In *Proceedings of the ACL*. ACL.

Jianpeng Cheng, Li Dong, and Mirella Lapata. 2016. Long short-term memory-networks for machine reading http://arxiv.org/abs/1601.06733v6.

Robin Cooper et al. 1996. Using the framework FRACAS a framework for computational semantics. Technical report, The FRACAS consortium.

Ann Copestake, Dan Flickinger, Carl Pollard, and Ivan A. Sag. 2005. Minimal recursion semantics: An introduction. *Research on Language and Computation* 3(2-3):281–332.

Ido Dagan, Oren Glickman, and Bernardo Magnini. 2006. The pascal recognising textual entailment challenge. In *Machine learning challenges. Evaluating Predictive Uncertainty, Visual Object Classification, and Recognising textual Entailment*, Springer, pages 177–190.

Ido Dagan, Dan Roth, Mark Sammons, and Fabio Massimo Zanzotto. 2013. Recognizing textual entailment: Models and applications. *Synthesis Lectures on HLT* 6(4):1–220.

David Dowty. 1991. Thematic proto-roles and argument selection. *language* pages 547–619.

Charles Fillmore, Christopher Johnson, and Miriam R.L. Petruck. 2003. Background to framenet. *International Journal to Lexicography* 16(3).

Charles J. Fillmore and Collin F. Baker. 2001. Frame semantics for text understanding. In *WordNet and Other Lexical Resources Workshop*. NAACL.

LiMin Fu. 1994. Rule generation from neural networks. *IEEE Transactions on Systems, Man, and Cybernetics* 24(8):1114–1124. https://doi.org/10.1109/21.299696.

Juri Ganitkevitch, Benjamin Van Durme, and Chris Callison-Burch. 2013. Ppdb: The paraphrase database. In *NAACL-HLT*.

Danilo Giampiccolo, Hoa Trang Dang, Bernardo Magnini, Ido Dagan, Elena Cabrio, and Bill Dolan. 2009. The fourth PASCAL recognizing textual entailment challenge. In *TAC*.

Danilo Giampiccolo, Bernardo Magnini, Ido Dagan, and Bill Dolan. 2007. The third PASCAL recognizing textual entailment challenge. In *ACL-PASCAL workshop on textual entailment and paraphrasing*. ACL, pages 1–9.

Daniel Gildea and Daniel Jurafsky. 2002. Automatic labeling of semantic roles. *Computational linguistics* 28(3):245–288.

Levesque Hector, Davis Ernest, and Morgenstern Leora. 2012. The winograd schema challenge. In *Knowledge Representation and Reasoning Conference*.

Jerry R. Hobbs. 1985. Ontological promiscuity. In *Proceedings of the ACL*. ACL, pages 60–69.

Sepp Hochreiter and Jürgen Schmidhuber. 1997. Long short-term memory. *Neural computation* 9(8):1735–1780.

Hans Kamp, Josef Van Genabith, and Uwe Reyle. 2011. Discourse representation theory. In *Handbook of philosophical logic*, Springer, pages 125–394.

Andrej Karpathy, Justin Johnson, and Li Fei-Fei. 2015. Visualizing and understanding recurrent networks. *arXiv preprint arXiv:1506.02078* .

Heeyoung Lee, Yves Peirsman, Angel Chang, Nathanael Chambers, Mihai Surdeanu, and Dan Jurafsky. 2011. Stanford's multi-pass sieve coreference resolution system at the conll-2011 shared task. In *Proceedings of the fifteenth conference on computational natural language learning: Shared task*. Association for Computational Linguistics, pages 28–34.

Yang Liu, Chengjie Sun, Lei Lin, and Xiaolong Wang. 2016. Learning natural language inference using bidirectional lstm model and inner-attention http://arxiv.org/abs/1605.09090v1.

Marco Marelli, Stefano Menini, Marco Baroni, Luisa Bentivogli, Raffaella Bernardi, and Roberto Zamparelli. 2014. A sick cure for the evaluation of compositional distributional semantic models. In *LREC*. pages 216–223.

Tomas Mikolov, Wen Tau Yih, and Geoffrey Zweig. 2013. Linguistic regularities in continuous space word representations. In *NAACL-HLT*. pages 746–751.

Lili Mou, Rui Men, Ge Li, Yan Xu, Lu Zhang, Rui Yan, and Zhi Jin. 2015. Natural language inference by tree-based convolution and heuristic matching http://arxiv.org/abs/1512.08422v3.

Tsendsuren Munkhdalai and Hong Yu. 2016. Neural tree indexers for text understanding http://arxiv.org/abs/1607.04492v1.

Martha Palmer, Dan Gildea, and Paul Kingsbury. 2005. The proposition bank: A corpus annotated with semantic roles. *Computational Linguistics* 31:1.

Ankur P. Parikh, Oscar Täckström, Dipanjan Das, and Jakob Uszkoreit. 2016. A decomposable attention model for natural language inference http://arxiv.org/abs/1606.01933v1.

Ellie Pavlick, Travis Wolfe, Pushpendre Rastogi, Chris Callison-Burch, Mark Drezde, and Benjamin Van Durme. 2015. Framenet+: Fast paraphrastic tripling of framenet. In *ACL*. ACL, Beijing, China.

Jeffrey Pennington, Richard Socher, and Christopher D. Manning. 2014. Glove: Global vectors for word representation. In *EMNLP*. ACL.

Altaf Rahman and Vincent Ng. 2012. Resolving complex cases of definite pronouns: The winograd schema challenge. In *Joint Conference on EMNLP and CoNLL*. ACL, pages 777–789.

Pushpendre Rastogi and Benjamin Van Durme. 2014. Augmenting framenet via PPDB. In *Second Workshop on EVENTS: Definition, Detection, Coreference, and Representation*. ACL. http://www.aclweb.org/anthology/W14-2901.

Drew Reisinger, Rachel Rudinger, Francis Ferraro, Craig Harman, Kyle Rawlins, and Benjamin Van Durme. 2015. Semantic proto-roles. *Transactions of the ACL* 3:475–488.

Tim Rocktäschel, Edward Grefenstette, Karl Moritz Hermann, Tomáš Kočiský, and Phil Blunsom. 2015. Reasoning about entailment with neural attention. *arXiv preprint arXiv:1509.06664* .

Lenhart K. Schubert and Chung Hee Hwang. 2000. Episodic logic meets little red riding hood: A comprehensive, natural representation for language understanding. *NLP And Knowledge Representation* pages 111–174.

Wang Shuohang and Jiang Jing. 2015. Learning natural language inference with lstm http://arxiv.org/abs/1512.08849v1.

Mark Steedman. 2000. *The Syntactic Process*, volume 24. MIT Press.

Ilya Sutskever, Oriol Vinyals, and Quoc Le. 2014. Sequence to sequence learning with neural networks. In *Advances in Neural Information Processing Systems*. pages 3104–3112.

Adam R Teichert, Adam Poliak, Benjamin Van Durme, and Matthew R Gormley. 2017. Semantic proto-role labeling. In *AAAI*. pages 4459–4466.

Sebastian B. Thrun. 1993. Extracting provably correct rules from artificial neural networks. Technical report, University of Bonn.

Sebastian B. Thrun. 1995. Extracting rules from artificial neural networks with distributed representations. In *Advances in Neural Information Processing Systems*, pages 505–512. http://papers.nips.cc/paper/3869-conditional-neural-fields.pdf.

Geoffrey G. Towell and Jude W. Shavlik. 1993. Extracting refined rules from knowledge-based neural networks. *Machine Learning* 13(1):71–101. https://doi.org/10.1007/BF00993103.

Jason Weston, Antoine Bordes, Sumit Chopra, Sasha Rush, Bart van Merrienboer, Armand Joulin, and Tomas Mikolov. 2016. Towards ai-complete question answering: A set of prerequisite toy tasks. In *ICLR*.

Aaron Steven White, Drew Reisinger, Keisuke Sakaguchi, Tim Vieira, Sheng Zhang, Rachel Rudinger, Kyle Rawlins, and Benjamin Van Durme. 2016. Universal decompositional semantics on universal dependencies. In *Proceedings of the 2016 Conference on Empirical Methods in Natural Language Processing*. Association for Computational Linguistics, Austin, TX, pages 1713–1723.

Peter Young, Alice Lai, Micah Hodosh, and Julia Hockenmaier. 2014. From image descriptions to visual denotations: New similarity metrics for semantic inference over event descriptions. *Transactions of the Association for Computational Linguistics* 2:67–78.

Matthew Zeiler and Rob Fergus. 2014. Visualizing and understanding convolutional networks. In *ECCV*. Springer, pages 818–833.

Matthew D. Zeiler. 2012. Adadelta: An adaptive learning rate method. *arXiv preprint arXiv:1212.5701* .

Generating a Training Corpus for OCR Post-Correction Using Encoder-Decoder Model

Eva D'hondt

LIMSI, CNRS, Univ. Paris-Saclay

F-91405 Orsay

`eva.dhondt@gmail.com`

Cyril Grouin

LIMSI, CNRS, Univ. Paris-Saclay

F-91405 Orsay

`cyril.grouin@limsi.fr`

Brigitte Grau

LIMSI, CNRS, ENSIIE, Univ. Paris-Saclay

F-91405 Orsay

`bg@limsi.fr`

Abstract

In this paper we present a novel approach to the automatic correction of OCR-induced orthographic errors in a given text. While current systems depend heavily on large training corpora or external information, such as domain-specific lexicons or confidence scores from the OCR process, our system only requires a small amount of relatively clean training data from a representative corpus to learn a character-based statistical language model using Bidirectional Long Short-Term Memory Networks (biLSTMs). We demonstrate the versatility and adaptability of our system on different text corpora with varying degrees of textual noise, including a real-life OCR corpus in the medical domain.

1 Introduction

Recently, Optical Character Recognition (OCR) technology has improved substantially, which has allowed for a large-scale digitization of textual resources such as books, old newspapers, ancient hand-written documents, etc. (Romero et al., 2011). The quality of the subsequent digital corpora can vary substantially, depending on factors such as quality of the original paper, ink quality, differences in fonts, etc. The amount of noise in digital collections can have a severe negative impact on the accuracy of subsequent text mining processes (e.g., Named Entity Recognition, Information Extraction, etc.).

OCR post-correction techniques are used to improve the text quality of OCR output. Traditionally, they rely on domain-specific lexicons (de Does and Depuydt, 2013) and character-based errors statistics obtained from a corrected

training set (Kumar and Lehal, 2016). However, they have some drawbacks that limit their usefulness for specific, low-resource domains. Such resources are expensive to create and for highly specialized texts (e.g., medical domain) not always possible to obtain. The recent advances in neural network models, based on textual context and needing no external resources, provide new opportunities for OCR post-correction. Character-level sequence modeling architectures are especially suited for this task (Chrupała, 2014; Schmaltz et al., 2016), as they reduce the complexity at output time. Moreover, current systems are often limited to processing texts with a limited degree of OCR corruption, i.e., so-called single-error word corrections (Kissos and Dershowitz, 2016) and correction of OCRed corpora that have been generated by older OCR engines can prove too challenging. The correct recognition of historical texts remains an open challenge (Kluzner et al., 2009). A general-purpose OCR post-correction tool should be adaptable to the ratio of error that is present in the OCR output in order to deal with both types of errors.

In this paper, we propose a novel approach to OCR post-correction using bidirectional recurrent neural networks for learning a robust character-based language model that (i) captures the domain-specific vocabulary of a text and (ii) which is able to detect and correct noise in corrupted text in the same time. In order to overcome the problem of producing manually annotated data, our system requires zero pre-annotated training material. Rather than using a large corrected training corpus to learn an error model, we propose a method of generating our own training material from clean text. This has multiple advantages: it allows us complete control over the learning process, and we can train on larger and more diverse corpora.

Proceedings of the The 8th International Joint Conference on Natural Language Processing, pages 1006–1014,
Taipei, Taiwan, November 27 – December 1, 2017 ©2017 AFNLP

First, we demonstrate the flexibility of the proposed model by evaluating it on artificially created test sets with varying degrees of noise. We also show how variation inherent in the texts influences training rates. Second, we explore a more realistic setting in which very little clean training data is available to learn a language model. We test our method on a real-life OCRed corpus of French medical reports. Our method outperforms the baseline by 14.3% on domain-specific noisy data, even when the latter is supplemented with a domain-specific lexicon.

2   Background

The problem of OCR post-correction has been studied since the seventies (Kukich, 1992). While traditional OCR error detection systems focused on constructing 'confusion matrices' of likely character (pairs) to detect corruptions of existing words into non-words, recent systems improve accuracy using information on the language context in which the error appears (Evershed and Fitch, 2014), using bigrams (Kissos and Dershowitz, 2016), large-scale word n-grams and character n-grams from the web (Bassil and Alwani, 2012) or associating confusion scores into a Bayesian model (Tong and Evans, 1996) or a HMM model (Borovikov et al., 2004) to select the optimal word candidate. These systems are explicitly or implicitly limited to cases in which an erroneous word appears in an otherwise clean context. For serious degrees of corruption (e.g., historical texts), the common approach aims to optimally combine an ensemble of multiple OCR engines (Nakano et al., 2004; Lund and Ringger, 2009).

'Noisy channel paradigm' aims to learn error models describing the OCR output generation from the reference text, and as such combine error and language models. Kolak and Resnik (2005) used finite state machines on a small set of training material while Llobet et al. (2010) combined all OCR process hypotheses for each recognized character. Such models need a large amount of training material which is costly and not always easily available. In response, the Text-Induced Corpus Clean-up (TICCL) system (Reynaert, 2011) was developed to run with no annotated training data. It takes noisy texts and extracts the high-frequency word variants through statistical analysis and clusters typographical word variants within a user-defined Levenshtein distance.

Recently, Neural Network Language Models have proven to be extremely effective in complex NLP tasks. For spelling errors correction, systems either include auto-encoders to detect nearest neighbor matches of spelling errors with correct words (Raaijmakers, 2013) or learn edit operations from labeled data while incorporating features induced from unlabelled data via character-level neural text embeddings (Chrupała, 2014). Contrary to Azawi (2015) which makes use of LSTM based on character-aligned strings, our method does not require annotated training data (gold standard) to learn the character-based language model. Moreover, our method does not capitalize on learning character transformation rules based on frequently occurring errors, as done in Azawi (2015), but learns a robust character-based language model.

3   Method

The model we proposed consists of a many-to-many character sequence learning network using long short term memory (LSTM) nodes.

3.1   Definition

LSTM are a special type of Recurrent Neural Network (RNN), a neural network hierarchy designed to model times series or other sequences. Standard RNNs have trouble capturing long-distance sequential dependencies, as the error signal during back propagation tends to disperse or blow up over time, which is known as the problem of vanishing or exploding gradients (Hochreiter, 1991; Bengio et al., 1994). This problem is typically addressed by replacing the standard RNN cell with a long short-term memory cell, which allows for a constant error flow along the input sequence (Hochreiter and Schmidhuber, 1997).

Technically, the LSTM architecture is given by the following equations,

$$
\begin{aligned}
i^{(t)} &= \sigma(W^{ix}.x^{(t)}) + W^{ih}.h^{(t-1)} + b_i) \\
f^{(t)} &= \sigma(W^{fx}.x^{(t)}) + W^{fh}.h^{(t-1)} + b_f) \\
o^{(t)} &= \sigma(W^{ox}.x^{(t)} + W^{oh}.h^{(t-1)} + b_o) \\
g^{(t)} &= tanh(W^{gx}.x^{(t)} + W^{gh}.h^{(t-1)} + b_g) \\
c^{(t)} &= f^{(t)} \odot c^{(t-1)} + i^{(t)} \odot g^{(t)} \\
h^{(t)} &= tanh(c^{(t)}) \odot o^{(t)}
\end{aligned}
$$

in which σ is the sigmoid function, i stands for the input gate (a selection of information coming from a previous cell state, given the new information contained in x); f stands for the forget gate, which select which parts of the information to forget and which to retain; g creates a vector of new candidate values that are used to update the cell state; o stands for the output gate which decides what parts of the cell state should be outputted.

A bidirectional LSTM (biLSTM) is a combination of two unidirectional LSTM layers, the first of which encodes the input string from left-to-right, the second from right-to-left. This ensures that errors that occur at the beginning of the input string have enough context (on the right-hand side) to be corrected.

3.2 Encoder-Decoder Model: biLSTM model

We stack two bidirectional LSTM layers on top of each other: the first hidden level is an encoder that reads the source character sequence and the other is a decoder that functions as a language model and generates the output. Figure 1 shows the layers in their unrolled forms as they read in the input.

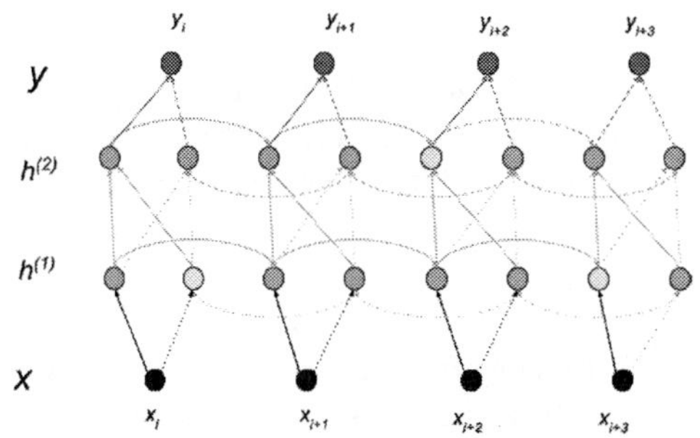

Figure 1: Hierarchy of bidirectional 2-layer many-to-many sequence learning network; lighter nodes in the hidden layers refer to disconnected nodes due to dropout

Architecture We first define a character vocabulary $V = \{v_1, v_2, ..., v_{|V|}\}$ which contains all the characters that are present in the training corpus. Each input string of 20 characters is padded on the right-hand side to a maximum length of 23, which allows for differences in string length due to insertions in the training phase (see Section 3.3). For an input string we define a 23-dimensional vector x in which each element corresponds to the index of the corresponding character in vocabulary V, thus preserving the order. The input x is then passed to an embedding layer that returns the sequence $S = \{c_j | j = x_1, x_2 ..., x_{23}\}$ where c_j is the character embedding (by a hyperparameter $d = 64$) for the characters in the initial string. This sequence is then passed to the first biLSTM, which combines two unidirectional LSTM layers that process the input from the left-to-right and right-to-left hand side, respectively. Each LSTM layer H consists of k LSTM memory units, and its output is a matrix $H = \{h_t \epsilon \mathbb{R}_k \mid t = 1, 2, ..., 23\}$. We set k at 512. The output of the individual LSTM layers is concatenated and given as input for the second biLSTM layer. The last hidden layer then projects unto a $|V|$-dimensional output layer. Finally, we apply the softmax function to select the character with the highest probability for a given timestep and obtain a 23-dimensional vector y with the characters indices for the corrected string.

We also added two drop-out layers to the hidden layers, each set at 0.5, since this has been shown to improve performance (Srivastava et al., 2014). The model was implemented in Keras, a python library for deep learning.

3.3 Training strategy

During training, the neural network is fed corrupted input strings and provided the original non-corrupted string as output labels. In this way, the network learns the domain-specific character-based language model that underlies the text in the training documents, while at the same time it learns to detect and eliminate noise introduced by OCR errors. Following the observations that OCR-induced variation is generally much less systematic than spelling errors (Reynaert, 2008), we generate corrupted strings by randomly deleting, inserting and substituting one or two characters for a given string (cf. algorithm 3.1).

We used a random number generator to determine if and which edit operations were selected. Character substitutions were performed at random with characters from the character set. Since a string could be submitted to multiple corrupting edits, this results in both single-error as well as multi-error words and environments in the corrupted string. Since the if-statements are independent, multiple edits on one string are possible, which can result in longer consecutive errors (three or more consecutive characters can be corrupted for a given string). In our script, the ratio of noise is set by the user, which corresponds to a fixed level of corruption in the training data.

Algorithm 3.1: CORRUPTSTRING(str, $noiseRatio$)

$len = len(str)$
$chars = set\ of\ characters\ in\ corpus$

comment: Randomly delete a character

if $rand() < (noiseRatio * len)$:
  then $\begin{cases} pos = randInt(len) \\ str = str[: pos] + str[pos + 1 :] \end{cases}$

comment: Randomly insert a character

if $rand() < (noiseRatio * len)$:
  then $\begin{cases} pos = randInt(len) \\ str = str[: pos] + randChoice(chars) \\ \quad + str[pos :] \end{cases}$

comment: Randomly replace 1 or 2 characters

if $rand() < (noiseRatio * len)$:
  then $\begin{cases} numChars = randChoice([1, 2]) \\ pos = randInt(len) \\ do\ numChars\ time \begin{cases} str = str[: pos] \\ \quad + (randChoice(chars)) \\ \quad + str[pos + 1 :] \\ pos + + \end{cases} \end{cases}$

Table 1 shows the generated input strings for a given string for the different noise ratios we used. In this table, the second row shows the percentage of strings with at least one OCR error in the real-life test set. We split the initial text into windows of 20 characters with an overlap per 3 characters. This length was empirically determined on training experiments w.r.t. accuracy and training speed.

Table 1: Percentage and examples of corrupted strings w.r.t. the noise ratio on the clean corpus. Bold highlights generated errors

noise ratio	corrupted strings	strings (20 characters length) original: n oven for 15 minute
0.001	5%	
0.003	17%	
0.005	30%	
0.01	48%	n o**5**en for 15 minute
0.02	76%	
0.03	92%	**n**oven f**Q**r 15 minute**#**
0.04	99%	n o**ee**n for 1**%** min**ü**te

4 Corpora

In our experiments, we used a few corpora, both 'clean' (digital corpora that contain no OCR or orthographic errors) and 'real-life' corpora (that contain varying degrees of OCR errors). They were selected according to two criteria: (i) text genre, either 'structured text' or 'free text', and (ii) domain, 'general domain' or 'specialized domain', more particularly the medical domain.

Table 2 gives an overview of the different corpora and their attributes. We give the sizes of the corpora in number of characters, rather than words since the varying degrees of OCR errors make the latter an unreliable metric.

Table 2: Overview of used corpora

	text style & language	domain	size train/test
CURD	structured English	general	150K 44K
LM	free text French	general	2M 100K
Handbook	free text French	foetopath	1M -
medical reports	structured French	other medical	1M -
foetopath reports	structured French	foetopath	500K 57K

We generate several artificial test sets for two clean corpora. Artificially corrupted strings are created using the same methodology as used for training. We generated two types of artificial test sets:

- test sets with a set noise ratio, which contain both corrupted and uncorrupted strings

- and test sets that contain only corrupted strings of a set Levenshtein Distance (LD)

4.1 Clean corpora

CURD corpus The Carnegie Mellon University Recipe Database corpus (Tasse and Smith, 2008) contains 260 structured cooking recipes in English: a list of ingredients followed by short descriptive sentences. This corpus closely resembles the real-life OCRed corpus of medical reports presented in the next section. Unlike medical reports, we consider it to be 'general domain'. We did not use the semantic annotations in the original CURD corpus but extracted only the plain text.

LM corpus We used documents from the *Le Monde* newspaper from 2000 to 2005 on as training material, and created test sets on a subset of articles from 2006.

Handbook on foetopathology We used an electronic copy of a comprehensive French handbook of foetopathology (Bouvier et al., 2008) to train a domain-specific language model of free text for the foetopathological domain.

Medical reports This set of in-house French medical reports were written in the same reporting style as the real-life OCRed foetopathological reports presented in Section 4.2. While medical, they do not treat the foetopathological domain but rather cancer and gastro-internal illnesses.

4.2 Real-life OCR corpora

The foetopathological reports corpus is a data set of French patient notes from the domain of foetopathology, spanning 22 years. In total, the corpus contains the files from 2476 individual patients. The files were processed with a custom-trained commercial OCR engine, and later de-identified with an in-house de-identification tool (Grouin and Zweigenbaum, 2013).

Since the model of the OCR engine used to convert the entire corpus was trained on a subset of documents of more recent years (implying good paper quality, clear font, etc.), the OCR quality of the OCRed documents decreases substantially for the older documents (D'hondt et al., 2016).

All evaluations in this paper were carried out on an annotated set of 53 files, for which reference texts have been created manually by one annotator in two passes.[1] We extracted two sets of training material from the corpus. One set has a reasonable OCR quality,[2] the second set is taken randomly from the corpus and contains texts with varying degrees of OCR quality. Both training sets have the same size.

5 Evaluation

5.1 Evaluation metrics

For evaluation, we use the CER metric (formula 1), as defined in OCR post-correction evaluations:

$$CER = \frac{S + D + I}{S + D + C} \quad (1)$$

where S refers to the number of substituted characters in the OCR text (w.r.t. the reference

texts), D to the number of deleted characters, I to the number of inserted characters and C to the number of 'correct' characters. We use the CER metric when comparing to the baseline system (see Section 6.4), using the `ocrevalUAtion`[3] package (Carrasco, 2014).

Since our models use overlapping[4] windows of 20 characters, a purely character-based metric is not ideal to evaluate. We want to measure the systems performance per input, rather than per character. We therefore introduce two complementary accuracy-based evaluation metrics, which evaluate on the level of the character window:

- detection accuracy (detAcc) shows the proportion of correctly detected errors and non-errors in the evaluated set of 20-character strings

- correction accuracy (corrAcc) reflects the ability of the language model to accurately correct corrupted strings without overgenerating and editing non-corrupted strings

These metrics are calculated as follows:

$$detAcc = \frac{(TP + TN + incorrectEdit)}{(TP + TN + FP + FN + incorrectEdit)}$$

$$corrAcc = \frac{(TP + TN)}{(TP + TN + FP + FN + incorrectEdit)}$$

Table 3 illustrates the different elements of the formulae.

5.2 Baseline model

We compare our system against the only other approach which requires zero annotated training material and no external resources, the TICCL system (Reynaert, 2011). As explained in Section 2, this system is word-based and uses anagram hashing to handle lexical variation in a large, noisy text collection. The system analyses a corpus to select high-frequency word variants, and then aims to map near-neighbours (in terms of edit distance) to those forms in order to reduce global variation in the corpus.

---

[1] These reference texts were later verified by a second annotator. The role of the second annotator was to check that the existing annotations were correct and consistent. Ergo the annotations were not done independently.

[2] Based on the proportion of out-of-vocabulary words present in a document for a given lexicon.

[3] `https://github.com/impactcentre/ocrevalUAtion`

[4] Allowing this overlap is a deliberate choice to maximize the ability to learn language models over a small corpus.

Table 3: Example of evaluation categories for the detection accuracy (detAcc) and correction accuracy (corrAcc) metrics, given the reference string `'n oven for 15 minute'`

	input string	output string
True Positive (TP)	n o**5**en for 15 minute	n o**ve**n for 15 minute
incorrectEdit	n o**5**en for 15 minute	n o**ve**n for 15 m**1**nute
True Negative (TN)	n o**ve**n for 15 minute	n o**ve**n for 15 minute
False Positive (FP)	n o**ve**n for 15 minute	n o**ve**n for 15 m**1**nute
False Negative (FN)	n o**5**en for 15 minute	n o**5**en for 15 minute

We used the system available for French with pretrained character confusion models with its default settings.[5] For the foetopathological reports test corpora, we provided TICCL with the full available corpora to extract word variants but calculated CER only on the test sets. TICCL performs specific preprocessing to limit the size of its character vocabulary (all numbers and digits are mapped unto the character '3').

6 Experiments and Discussion

Since our system does not use annotated data, the language and error models learned from the training data are approximations of what will be encountered in the test set. In Sections 6.1 and 6.2, we examine how the error model (the prior probability of encountering an error in a given input string) learned during training corresponds to the (expected) noise ratio in the test set, and how the text genre and size of the training corpus influence performance. Section 6.3 presents how Language Models can be learned when no clean training material is available for a given test set. Section 6.4 shows a comparison with the word-based baseline.

[5]Online TICCL interface for French with default settings: `http://ticclops.clarin.inl.nl/ticclops/`

6.1 Adaptability to different degrees of noise

One of the advantages of our approach is its adaptability to different levels of expected noise. It suffices to train the model with a noise ratio that corresponds to the noise found in the test set.

The upper subfigure in Figure 2 shows the detection accuracy (full line) and correction accuracy (dotted line) on a test set with a 0.005 noise ratio for three different models which were trained in 30 iterations on the CURD training data with 0.003, 0.01 and 0.03 noise ratio, respectively.

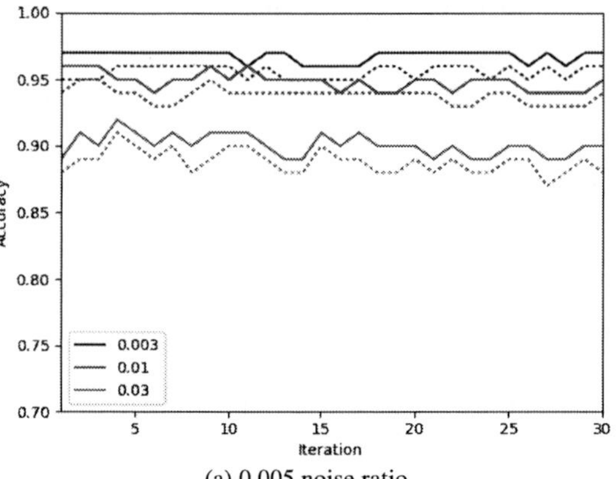

(a) 0.005 noise ratio

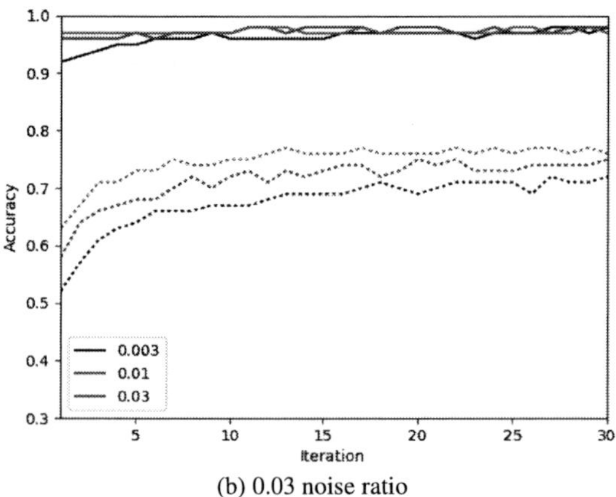

(b) 0.03 noise ratio

Figure 2: Performance of models trained with different noise ratios on the CURD corpus for the 0.005 noise ratio test (upper) and 0.03 noise ratio test (lower), in terms of detection accuracy (full line) and correction accuracy (dotted line)

A 0.005 noise ratio is a fairly easy test set, with few errors, as is evidenced by the overall high scores. We do see that the model which was trained to expect a lot of noise (0.03) underperforms compared to its more conservative counterparts. For the same models on the 0.03 test set, however, the more aggressively trained model performs the best. The high detection accuracy scores in both figures (full lines) show that the models are correctly identifying errors (i.e., unlikely character sequences) and have little tendency to ignore errors (FN) or incorrectly edit a correct string (FP). The difference between the detection accuracy (full lines) and correction accuracy (dotted lines) in Figure 2 shows the increased difficulty for the language models to make correct edits when the input strings have multiple corruptions.

Figure 3 examines this more closely. Here, the training model has been fixed (trained with noise ratio 0.03) and we examine its performance on test sets were each corrupted string has the same Levenshtein distances to its reference string. Here as well, overall detection accuracy is quite high, but the increasingly lower correction accuracy scores show the increased difficulties of the language model to propose correct edits for a given corrupted string. Since the 0.03 model is trained to expect moderate corruption, it performs best on corrupted strings with a Levenshtein distance of 2.

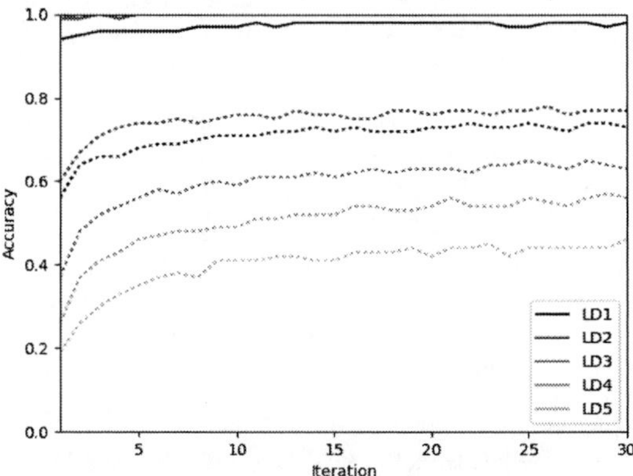

Figure 3: Performance of best model (ratio 0.03) on test sets which contain only corrupted substrings, with a fixed Levenshtein Distance (LD), in terms of detection accuracy (full line) and correction accuracy (dotted line)

6.2 Impact of text variability on training

The previous experiments were carried out on the CURD corpus, a small corpus with relatively fixed vocabulary and structured text, which makes it easy to learn a comprehensive model. Figure 4 shows the performance of a corpus with more inherent variation, the journalistic LM corpus.

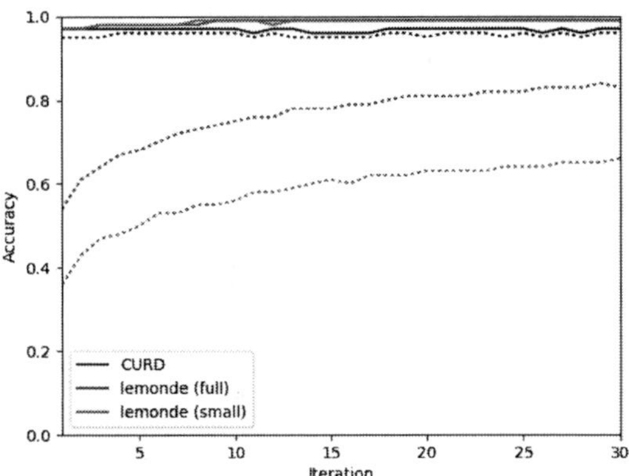

Figure 4: Performance of best-performing models on the CURD and LM 0.005 test set, in terms of detection accuracy (full line) and correction accuracy (dotted line)

As expected, the language model of a more variable corpus has a slower learning rate and needs more training data to achieve good performance. The green lines (lemonde (small)) refer to a subset of the LM corpus of exactly the same size as the CURD corpus (150K characters), which is clearly not enough training material to learn a language model on free text.

6.3 Adaptation to a real-life corpus

While the previous experiments only used artificial test sets, a more realistic setting is that in which an OCRed test set needs to be corrected but no clean data is available to train the system on.

Table 4 presents the results we achieved on the real life test set while training our model on different types of text that are either similar to the test set w.r.t. text genre or domain. We also compared these to the performance of models that were trained on noisy training data from the same corpus as the test set. For the foetopathological reports, we trained models on two test sets of similar size, one which contained data with relatively few OCR errors, and one whose text quality was mixed.

Overall, we find that the language model of the structured foetopathological reports is fairly easy to learn, as evidenced by the high correction scores. The scores in the first two rows of Table 4 show the impact of noisy training data. While relatively clean training data pose little problem, training on the mixed set leads to a more corrupted language model. Interestingly, we find that training

Table 4: Performance of different models trained on different training data (with 0.003 noise ratio) on real-life test set of foetopathological reports

	detAcc	corrAcc
foet. reports (fairly clean)	0.87	0.82
foet. reports (mixed)	0.86	0.76
medical reports (clean)	0.85	0.79
foet. handbook (clean)	0.87	0.81
LM corpus (clean)	0.60	0.52

on similar corpora, both in text genre (medical reports) and domain (Handbook) leads to almost as good correction accuracy as training on the original corpus. The language model trained on the LM corpus, whilst having seen the most training data, has the worst performance since the text in this corpus is too far removed from foetopathological reports, both in domain and text genre.

6.4 Comparison with baseline

To compare against our baseline system, we transformed the output of the two best performing systems from the experiments in Section 6.3 to a single final output string. Where two characters differed in the overlapping output strings from our system, we used majority vote to construct the final output string.

Table 5 shows the results against the TICCL baseline system, using the CER metric. TICCL-lex refers to a setting in which it was provided with a French, domain-specific lexicon of frequent terms in the foetopathology domain. We find that our system significantly outperforms the baseline on the structured, domain-specific data, by 14.3%.

Table 5: Comparison of baseline system (TICCL) with best performing systems on the foetopathological real-life test set

	Character Error Rate (CER)
original text	34.3
biLSTM	7.1
TICCL	34
TICCL-lex	21.4

7 Conclusion

In this paper we proposed a novel zero-annotated data approach to OCR post-correction. We used biLSTMs to build an encoder-decoder model.

Rather than learning from annotated data, we developed a method to generate our own training material. Our model is trained on clean or moderately clean data in order to produce a robust character-based language model.

We have evaluated our method on different text genres and domains. We found that our method is especially suited to correct domain-specific, structured text, even when no training text from the same corpus is available.

Acknowledgments

This work was partially supported by the French National Agency for Research under the grant Accordys[6] ANR-12-CORD-0007.

References

Mayce Ibrahim Ali Al Azawi. 2015. *Statistical Language Modeling for Historical Documents using Weighted Finite-State Transducers and Long Short-Term Memory*. Ph.D. thesis, University of Kaiserslautern.

Youssef Bassil and Mohammad Alwani. 2012. OCR context-sensitive error correction based on Google web 1t 5-gram data set. *American Journal of Scientific Research*.

Yoshua Bengio, Patrice Simard, and Paolo Frasconi. 1994. Learning long-term dependencies with gradient descent is difficult. *IEEE transactions on neural networks*, 5(2):157–166.

Eugene Borovikov, Ilya Zavorin, and Mark Turner. 2004. A filter based post-OCR accuracy boost system. In *Proc of ACM Work. on Hardcopy document processing*, pages 23–28.

Raymonde Bouvier, Dominique Carles, Marie-Christine Dauge, Pierre Déchelotte, Anne-Lise Delézoide, Bernard Foliguet, Dominique Gaillard, Bernard Gasser, Marie Gonzalès, and Férechté Encha-Razavi. 2008. *Pathologie fœtale et placentaire pratique*. Sauramps Médical.

Rafael C Carrasco. 2014. An open-source OCR evaluation tool. In *Proc of Digital Access to Textual Cultural Heritage*, pages 179–184.

Grzegorz Chrupała. 2014. Normalizing tweets with edit scripts and recurrent neural embeddings. In *Proc of ACL*, volume 2, pages 680–686.

Eva D'hondt, Cyril Grouin, and Brigitte Grau. 2016. Low-resource OCR error detection and correction in French Clinical Texts. In *Proc of LOUHI*, pages 61–68, Lisbon, Portugal.

---

[6]Agrégation de Contenus et de COnnaissances pour Raisonner à partir de cas dans la DYSmorphologie foetale

Jesse de Does and Katrien Depuydt. 2013. Lexicon-supported OCR of eighteenth century Dutch books: a case study. In *Proc. of SPIE*, volume 8658 of *Document Recognition and Retrieval*.

John Evershed and Kent Fitch. 2014. Correcting noisy OCR: Context beats confusion. In *Proc of ICDAR*, pages 45–51.

Cyril Grouin and Pierre Zweigenbaum. 2013. Automatic de-identification of French clinical records: Comparison of rule-based and machine-learning approches. In *Stud Health Technol Inform*, volume 192, pages 476–80, Copenhagen, Denmark.

Sepp Hochreiter. 1991. *Untersuchungen zu dynamischen neuronalen Netzen*. Ph.D. thesis, Technische Universität München.

Sepp Hochreiter and Jürgen Schmidhuber. 1997. Long short-term memory. *Neural computation*, 9(8):1735–1780.

Ido Kissos and Nachum Dershowitz. 2016. OCR error correction using character correction and feature-based word classification. In *Proc of Document Analysis Systems Work*, Santorini, Greece.

Vladimir Kluzner, Asaf Tzadok, Yuval Shimony, Eugene Walach, and Apostolos Antonacopoulos. 2009. Word-based adaptive OCR for historical books. In *Proc of ICDAR*, pages 501–505.

Okan Kolak and Philip Resnik. 2005. OCR post-processing for low density languages. In *Proc of EMNLP*, pages 867–874.

Karen Kukich. 1992. Techniques for automatically correcting words in text. *ACM Computing Surveys (CSUR)*, 24(4):377–439.

Atul Kumar and Gurpreet Singh Lehal. 2016. Automatic text correction for Devanagari OCR. *Indian Journal of Science and Technology*, 9(45).

Rafael Llobet, Jose-Ramon Cerdan-Navarro, Juan-Carlos Perez-Cortes, and Joaquim Arlandis. 2010. OCR post-processing using weighted finite-state transducers. In *Proc of ICPR*, pages 2021–2024.

William B Lund and Eric K Ringger. 2009. Improving optical character recognition through efficient multiple system alignment. In *Proc of Digital libraries*, pages 231–240.

Yasuaki Nakano, Toshihiro Hananoi, Hidetoshi Miyao, Minoru Maruyama, and Kenichi Maruyama. 2004. A document analysis system based on text line matching of multiple OCR outputs. *Lecture Notes in Computer Science*, pages 463–471.

Stephan Raaijmakers. 2013. A deep graphical model for spelling correction. In *Proc of Benelux Conference on Artificial Intelligence*, Delft, The Netherlands.

Martin Reynaert. 2008. Non-interactive OCR post-correction for giga-scale digitization projects. In *Proceedings of the 9th International Conference on Computational Linguistics and Intelligent Text Processing*, CICLing'08, pages 617–630, Berlin, Heidelberg. Springer-Verlag.

Martin WC Reynaert. 2011. Character confusion versus focus word-based correction of spelling and OCR variants in corpora. *International Journal on Document Analysis and Recognition*, 14(2):173–187.

Verónica Romero, Nicolás Serrano, Alejandro H. Toselli, Joan Andreu Sánchez, and Enrique Vidal. 2011. Handwritten text recognition for historical documents. In *Proceedings of the Language Technologies for Digital Humanities and Cultural Heritage Workshop*, pages 90–96, Hissar, Bulgaria.

Allen Schmaltz, Yoon Kim, Alexander M Rush, and Stuart M Shieber. 2016. Sentence-level grammatical error identification as sequence-to-sequence correction. *arXiv preprint arXiv:1604.04677*.

Nitish Srivastava, Geoffrey E Hinton, Alex Krizhevsky, Ilya Sutskever, and Ruslan Salakhutdinov. 2014. Dropout: a simple way to prevent neural networks from overfitting. *Journal of Machine Learning Research*, 15(1):1929–1958.

Dan Tasse and Noah A Smith. 2008. SOUR CREAM: Toward semantic processing of recipes. *Carnegie Mellon University, Pittsburgh, Tech. Rep. CMU-LTI-08-005*.

Xiang Tong and David A Evans. 1996. A statistical approach to automatic OCR error correction in context. In *Proc of Very Large Corpora Work*, pages 88–100.

Multilingual Hierarchical Attention Networks for Document Classification

Nikolaos Pappas
Idiap Research Institute
Rue Marconi 19
CH-1920 Martigny, Switzerland
nikolaos.pappas@idiap.ch

Andrei Popescu-Belis
HEIG-VD / HES-SO
Route de Cheseaux 1
CH-1401 Yverdon, Switzerland
andrei.popescu-belis@heig-vd.ch

Abstract

Hierarchical attention networks have recently achieved remarkable performance for document classification in a given language. However, when multilingual document collections are considered, training such models separately for each language entails linear parameter growth and lack of cross-language transfer. Learning a single multilingual model with fewer parameters is therefore a challenging but potentially beneficial objective. To this end, we propose multilingual hierarchical attention networks for learning document structures, with shared encoders and/or shared attention mechanisms across languages, using multi-task learning and an aligned semantic space as input. We evaluate the proposed models on multilingual document classification with disjoint label sets, on a large dataset which we provide, with 600k news documents in 8 languages, and 5k labels. The multilingual models outperform monolingual ones in low-resource as well as full-resource settings, and use fewer parameters, thus confirming their computational efficiency and the utility of cross-language transfer.

1 Introduction

Learning word sequence representations has become increasingly useful for a variety of NLP tasks such as document classification (Tang et al., 2015; Yang et al., 2016), neural machine translation (NMT) (Cho et al., 2014; Luong et al., 2015), question answering (Chen et al., 2015; Kumar et al., 2015) and summarization (Rush et al., 2015). However, when data are available in multiple languages, representation learning must ad-

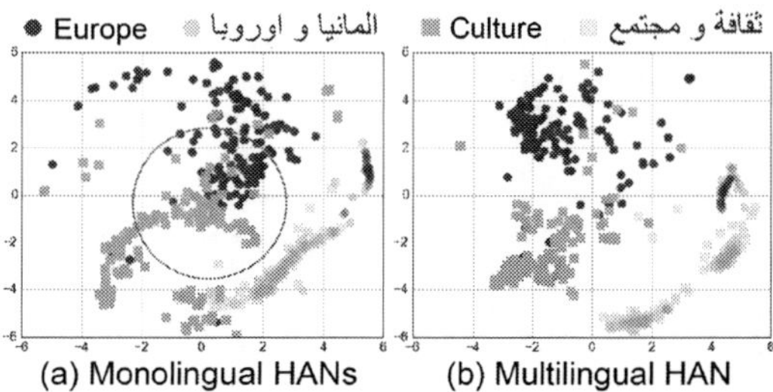

Figure 1: Vectors of documents labeled with *'Europe'*, *'Culture'* and their Arabic counterparts. The multilingual hierarchical attention network separates topics better than monolingual ones.

dress two main challenges. Firstly, the computational cost of training separate models for each language, which grows linearly with their number, or even quadratically in the case of multi-way multilingual NMT (Firat et al., 2016a). Secondly, the models should be capable of cross-language transfer, which is an important component in human language learning (Ringbom, 2007). For instance, Johnson et al. (2016) attempted to use a single sequence-to-sequence neural network model for NMT across multiple language pairs.

Previous studies in document classification attempted to address these issues by employing multilingual word embeddings, which allow direct comparisons and groupings across languages (Klementiev et al., 2012; Hermann and Blunsom, 2014; Ferreira et al., 2016). However, they are only applicable when common label sets are available across languages which is often not the case (e.g. Wikipedia or news). Moreover, despite recent advances in monolingual document modeling (Tang et al., 2015; Yang et al., 2016), multilingual models are still based on shallow approaches.

In this paper, we propose *Multilingual Hierarchical Attention Networks* to learn shared doc-

Proceedings of the The 8th International Joint Conference on Natural Language Processing, pages 1015–1025,
Taipei, Taiwan, November 27 – December 1, 2017 ©2017 AFNLP

ument structures across languages for document classification with disjoint label sets, as opposed to training language-specific training of hierarchical attention networks (HANs) (Yang et al., 2016). Our networks have a hierarchical structure with word and sentence encoders, along with attention mechanisms. Each of these can either be shared across languages or kept language-specific. To enable cross-language transfer, the networks are trained with multi-task learning across languages using an aligned semantic space as input. Fig. 1 displays document vectors, projected with t-SNE (van der Maaten, 2009), for two topics and two languages, either learned by monolingual HANs (a) or by our multilingual HAN (b). The multilingual HAN achieves better separation between 'Europe' and 'Culture' topics in English as a result of the knowledge transfer from Arabic.

We evaluate our model against strong monolingual baselines, in low-resource and full-resource scenarios, on a large multilingual document collection with 600k documents, labeled with general (1.2k) and specific topics (4.4k), in 8 languages from Deutsche Welle's news website.[1] Our multilingual models outperform monolingual ones in both scenarios, thus confirming the utility of cross-language transfer and the computational efficiency of the proposed architecture. To encourage further research in multilingual representation learning our code and dataset are made available at `https://github.com/idiap/mhan`.

2 Related Work

Research on *learning multilingual word representations* is based on early work on word embeddings (Turian et al., 2010; Mikolov et al., 2013; Pennington et al., 2014). The goal is to learn an aligned word embedding space for multiple languages by leveraging bilingual dictionaries (Faruqui and Dyer, 2014; Ammar et al., 2016), parallel sentences (Gouws et al., 2015) or comparable documents such as Wikipedia pages (Yih et al., 2011; Al-Rfou et al., 2013). Bilingual embeddings were learned from word alignments using neural language models (Klementiev et al., 2012; Zou et al., 2013), including auto-encoders (Chandar et al., 2014). Despite progress at the word level, the document level remains comparatively less explored. The approaches proposed by Hermann and Blunsom (2014) or Ferreira et al.

(2016) are based on shallow modeling and are applicable only to classification tasks with label sets shared across languages, which are costly to produce and are often unavailable. Here, we remove this constraint, and develop deeper multilingual document models with hierarchical structure based on prior art at the word level.

Early work on *neural document classification* was based on shallow feed-forward networks, which required unsupervised pre-training (Le and Mikolov, 2014). Later studies focused on neural networks with hierarchical structure. Kim (2014) proposed a convolutional neural network (CNN) for sentence classification. Johnson and Zhang (2015) proposed a CNN for high-dimensional data classification, while Zhang et al. (2015) adopted a character-level CNN for text classification. Lai et al. (2015) proposed a recurrent CNN to capture sequential information, which outperformed simpler CNNs. Lin et al. (2015) and Tang et al. (2015) proposed hierarchical recurrent NNs and showed that they were superior to CNN-based models. Recently, Yang et al. (2016) proposed a hierarchical attention network (HAN) with bi-directional gated encoders which outperforms traditional and neural baselines. Using such networks in multilingual settings has two drawbacks: the computational complexity increases linearly with the number of languages, and knowledge is acquired separately for each language. We address these issues by proposing a new multilingual model based on HANs, which learns shared document structures and to transfer knowledge across languages.

Early examples of *attention mechanisms* appeared in computer vision, e.g. for optical character recognition (Larochelle and Hinton, 2010), image tracking (Denil et al., 2012), or image classification (Mnih et al., 2014). For text classification, studies which aimed to learn the importance of sentences included those by Yessenalina et al. (2010); Pappas and Popescu-Belis (2014); Yang et al. (2016) and more recently those by Pappas and Popescu-Belis (2017); Ji and Smith (2017). For NMT, Bahdanau et al. (2015) proposed an attention-based encoder-decoder network, while Luong et al. (2015) proposed a local and ensemble attention model. Firat et al. (2016a) proposed a single encoder-decoder model with shared attention across language pairs for multi-way, multilingual NMT. Hermann et al. (2015) developed attention-based document readers for question an-

---

[1] Germany's news broadcaster: `http://dw.com`.

swering. Chen et al. (2015) proposed a recurrent attention model over an external memory. Similarly, Kumar et al. (2015) introduced a dynamic memory network for question answering and other tasks. We propose here to share attention across languages, at one or more levels of hierarchical document models, which, to our knowledge, has not been attempted before.

3 Background: Hierarchical Attention Networks for Document Classification

We adopt a general hierarchical attention architecture for document representation, displayed in Figure 2, which is derived from the one proposed by Yang et al. (2016). Our architecture is general in the sense that it defines only the hierarchical structure, but accommodates different types of individual components, i.e. encoders and attention models. We consider a dataset $D = \{(x_i, y_i), i = 1, \ldots, N\}$ made of N documents x_i with labels $y_i \in \{0, 1\}^k$. Each document is represented by the sequence of d-dimensional embeddings of their words grouped into sentences, $x_i = \{w_{11}, w_{12}, \ldots, w_{KT}\}$, T being the maximum number of words in a sentence, and K the maximum number of sentences in a document.

The network takes as input a document x_i and outputs a document vector u_i. In particular, it has two levels of abstraction, word vs. sentence. The word level is made of an encoder g_w with parameters H_w and an attention model a_w with parameters A_w, while the sentence level similarly includes an encoder and an attention model (g_s, H_s and a_s, A_s). The output u_i is used by the classification layer to determine y_i.

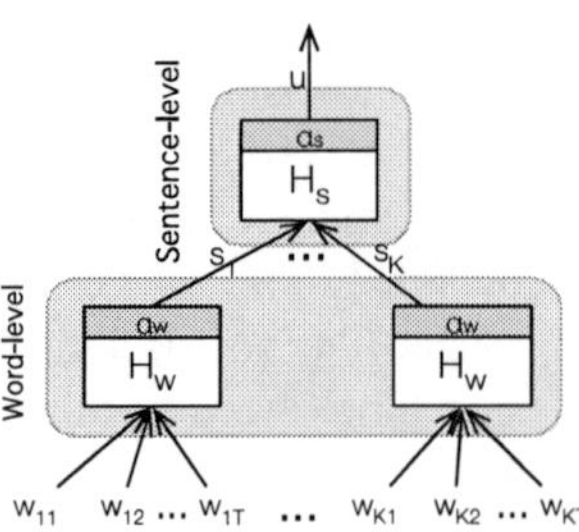

Figure 2: General architecture of hierarchical attention neural networks for modeling documents.

3.1 Encoder Layers

At the word level, the function g_w encodes the sequence of input words $\{w_{it} \mid t = 1, \ldots, KT\}$ for each sentence i of the document, noted as:

$$h_w^{(it)} = \{g_w(w_{it}) \mid t = 1, \ldots, K\} \qquad (1)$$

At the sentence level, after combining the intermediate word vectors $\{h_w^{(it)} \mid t = 1, \ldots, T\}$ to a sentence vector s_i (as explained in 3.2), the function g_s encodes the sequence of sentence vectors $\{s_i \mid i = 1, \ldots, K\}$, noted as $h_s^{(i)}$.

The g_w and g_s functions can be any feedforward or recurrent networks with parameters H_w and H_s respectively. We consider the following networks: a fully-connected one, noted as DENSE, a Gated Recurrent Unit network (Cho et al., 2014) noted as GRU[2], and a bi-directional GRU which captures temporal information forward or backward in time, noted as biGRU. The latter is defined as a concatenation of the hidden states for each input vector obtained from the forward GRU, $\vec{g_w}$, and the backward GRU, $\overleftarrow{g_w}$:

$$h_w^{(it)} = \left[\vec{g_w}(h_w^{(it)}); \overleftarrow{g_w}(h_w^{(it)})\right]. \qquad (2)$$

The same concatenation is applied for the hidden-state representation of a sentence $h_s^{(i)}$.

3.2 Attention Layers

A typical way to obtain a representation for a given word sequence at each level is by taking the last hidden-state vector that is output by the encoder. However, it is hard to encode all the relevant input information needed in a fixed-length vector. This problem is addressed by introducing an attention mechanism at each level (noted α_w and α_s) that estimates the importance of each hidden state vector to the representation of the sentence or document meaning respectively. The sentence vector $s_i \in R^{d_w}$, where d_w is the dimension of the word encoder, is thus obtained as follows:

$$\frac{1}{T}\sum_{t=1}^{T} \alpha_w^{(it)} h_w^{(it)} = \frac{1}{T}\sum_{t=1}^{T} \frac{\exp(v_{it}^{\top} u_w)}{\sum_j \exp(v_{ij}^{\top} u_w)} h_w^{(it)}$$
$$(3)$$

where $v_{it} = f_w(h_w^{(it)})$ is a fully-connected neural network with W_w parameters. Similarly, the document vector $u \in R^{d_s}$, where d_s is the dimension of the sentence encoder, is obtained as follows:

$$\frac{1}{K}\sum_{i=1}^{K} \alpha_s^{(i)} h_s^{(i)} = \frac{1}{K}\sum_{i=1}^{K} \frac{\exp(v_i^{\top} u_s)}{\sum_j \exp(v_j^{\top} u_s)} h_s^{(i)}$$
$$(4)$$

---

[2]GRU is a simplified version of Long-Short Term Memory, LSTM (Hochreiter and Schmidhuber, 1997).

where $v_i = f_s(h_s^{(i)})$ is a fully-connected neural network with W_s parameters. The vectors u_w and u_s are parameters which encode the word context and sentence context respectively, and are learned jointly with the rest of the parameters. The total set of parameters for a_w is $A_w = \{W_w, u_w\}$ and for a_s is $A_s = \{W_s, u_s\}$.

3.3 Classification Layers

The output of such a network is typically fed to a softmax layer for classification, with a loss based on the cross-entropy between gold and predicted labels (Tang et al., 2015) or on the negative log-likelihood of the correct labels (Yang et al., 2016). However, softmax overemphasizes the probability of the most likely label, which may not be ideal for multi-label classification because each document should have more than one likely labels independent of each other, as we verified empirically in our preliminary experiments. Hence, we replace the softmax with a sigmoid function, so that for each document i represented by the vector u_i we model the probability of the k labels as follows:

$$\hat{y}_i = p(y|u_i) = \frac{1}{1 + e^{-(W_c u_i + b_c)}} \in [0, 1]^k \quad (5)$$

where W_c is a $d_s \times k$ matrix and b_c is the bias term for the classification layer. The training loss based on cross-entropy is computed as follows:

$$\mathcal{L}(\theta) = -\frac{1}{N} \sum_{i=1}^{N} \mathcal{H}(y_i, \hat{y}_i) \quad (6)$$

where θ is a notation for all the parameters of the model (i.e. H_w, A_w, H_s, A_s, W_c), and $\mathcal{H}$ is the binary cross-entropy of the gold labels y_i and predicted labels $\hat{y}_i$ for a document i. The above objective is differentiable and can be minimized with stochastic gradient descent (SGD) (Bottou, 1998) or variants such as Adam (Kingma and Ba, 2014), to maximize classification performance.

4 Multilingual Hierarchical Attention Networks: MHANs

When multilingual data is available, the above network can be trained on each language separately, but in this case the needed parameters grow linearly with the number of languages. Moreover, this does not exploit common knowledge across languages or to transfer it from one to another. We propose here a HAN with shared components across languages, which has slower

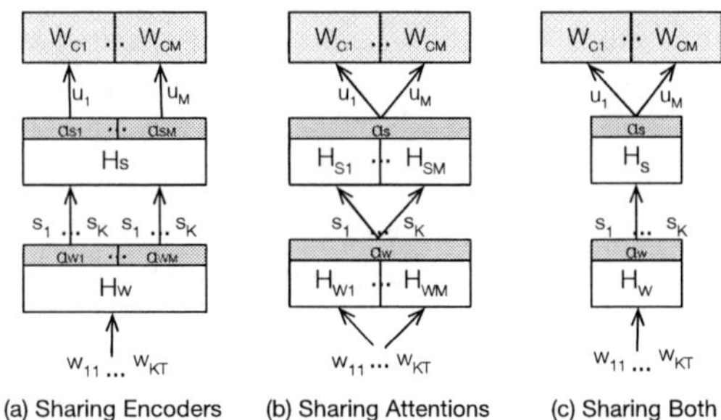

Figure 3: Multilingual hierarchical attention networks for modeling documents and classifying them over disjoint label sets.

parameter growth (hence sublinear) compared to monolingual ones and enables knowledge transfer across languages. We now consider M languages noted $L = \{L_l \mid l = 1, \ldots, M\}$, and a multilingual set of topic-labeled documents $D_l = \{(x_i^{(l)}, y_i^{(l)}) \mid i = 1, \ldots, N_l, l = 1, ..., M\}$ defined as above (Section 3).

4.1 Sharing Components across Languages

To enable multilingual learning, we propose three distinct ways for sharing components between networks in a multi-task learning setting, depicted in Figure 3, namely: (a) sharing the parameters of word and sentence encoders, noted $\theta_{enc} = \{H_w, W_w^{(l)}, H_s, W_s^{(l)}, W_c^{(l)}\}$; (b) sharing the parameters of word and sentence attention models, noted $\theta_{att} = \{H_w^{(l)}, W_w, H_s^{(l)}, W_s, W_c^{(l)}\}$; and (c) sharing both previous sets of parameters, noted $\theta_{both} = \{H_w, W_w, H_s, W_s, W_c^{(l)}\}$. For instance, the document representation of a text for language l based on a shared sentence-level attention would be computed based on Eq. 4 by using the same parameters W_s and u_s across languages.

Let $\theta_{mono} = \{H_w^{(l)}, W_w^{(l)}, H_s^{(l)}, W_s^{(l)}, W_c^{(l)}\}$ be the parameters of multiple independent monolingual models with DENSE encoders, then we have:

$$|\theta_{mono}| > |\theta_{enc}| > |\theta_{att}| > |\theta_{both}| \quad (7)$$

where $|\cdot|$ is the number of parameters in a set. For GRU and biGRU encoders, the inequalities still hold, but swapping $|\theta_{enc}|$ and $|\theta_{att}|$. Excluding the classification layer which is necessarily language-specific, the (a) and (b) networks have sublinear numbers of parameters and the (c) network has a constant number of parameters with respect to the number of languages. The word embeddings are not considered as parameters in our setup because they are fixed during training. For learned word embeddings, the argument still holds if we consider their parameters as part of the word-level encoder.

Depending on the label sets, several types of document classification problems can be solved with such architectures. First, label sets can be common or disjoint across languages. Second, considering labels as k-hot vectors, $k = 1$ corresponds to a multi-class task, while $k > 1$ is a multi-label task. We focus here on the multi-label problem with disjoint label sets. Moreover, we assume an aligned input space i.e. with multilingual word embeddings that have aligned meanings across languages (Ammar et al., 2016). With non-aligned word embeddings, the multilingual transfer is harder due to the lack of parallel information, as we show in Section 6.2, Table 4.

4.2 Training over Disjoint Label Sets

For training, we replace the monolingual training objective (Eq. 6) with a joint multilingual objective that facilitates the sharing of components, i.e. a subset of parameters for each language $\theta_1, \ldots, \theta_M$, across different language networks:

$$\mathcal{L}(\theta_1, \ldots, \theta_M) = -\frac{1}{Z} \sum_i^{N_e} \sum_l^M \mathcal{H}(y_i^{(l)}, \hat{y}_i^{(l)}) \quad (8)$$

where $Z = M \times N_e$ and N_e is the epoch size.[3]

The joint objective $\mathcal{L}$ can be minimized with respect to the parameters $\theta_1, \ldots, \theta_M$ using SGD as before. However, when training on examples from different languages consecutively it is difficult to learn a shared space that works well across languages. This is because updates for each language apply only on a subset of parameters and may bias the model away from other languages. To address this issue, we employ the training strategy proposed by (Firat et al., 2016a), who sampled parallel sentences for multi-way machine translation from different language pairs in a cyclic fashion at each iteration.[4] Here, we sample a document-label pair from each language at iteration. For mini-batch SGD, the number of samples per language is equal to the batch size divided by M.

---

[3] In the future, it may also be beneficial to add a γ_l term for each language objective, which encodes prior knowledge about its importance.

[4] We verified this empirically in our preliminary experiments and found that mixing languages in a single batch performed better than keeping them in separate batches.

Languages	Documents			Labels	
L	$\|X\|$	$\bar{s}$	$\bar{w}$	$\|Y_g\|$	$\|Y_s\|$
English	112,816	17.9	516.2	327	1,058
German	132,709	22.3	424.1	367	809
Spanish	75,827	13.8	412.9	159	684
Portuguese	39,474	20.2	571.9	95	301
Ukrainian	35,423	17.6	342.9	28	260
Russian	108,076	16.4	330.1	102	814
Arabic	57,697	13.3	357.7	91	344
Persian	36,282	18.7	538.4	71	127
All	598,304	17.52	436.7	1,240	4,397

Table 2: Statistics of the Deutsche Welle corpus: $\bar{s}$ and $\bar{w}$ are the average numbers of sentences and words per document.

5   A New Corpus for Multilingual Document Classification: DW

Multilingual document classification datasets are usually limited in size, have target categories aligned across languages, and assign documents to only one category. However, classification is often necessary in cases where the categories are not strictly aligned, and multiple categories may apply to each document. For instance, this is the case for online multilingual news agencies, which must keep track of news topics across languages.

Two datasets for multilingual document classification have been used in previous studies: Reuters RCV1/RCV2 (6,000 documents, 2 languages and 4 labels), introduced by (Klementiev et al., 2012), and TED talk transcripts (12,078 documents, 12 languages and 15 labels), introduced by Hermann and Blunsom (2014). The former is tailored for evaluating word embeddings aligned across languages, rather than complex multilingual document models. The latter is twice as large and covers more languages, in a multi-label setting, but biases evaluation by including translations of talks in all languages.

Here, we present and use a much larger dataset collected from Deutsche Welle, Germany's public international broadcaster, shown in Table 2. The DW dataset contains nearly 600,000 documents, in 8 languages, annotated by journalists with several topic labels. Documents are on average 2.6 times longer than in Yang et al.'s (2016) monolingual dataset (436 vs. 163 words). There are two types of labels, namely *general topics* (Y_g) and *specific* ones (Y_s) both described by one or more words. We consider (and count in Table 2) only those specific labels that appear at least 100 times, to avoid sparsity issues.

The number of labels varies greatly across the

			English + Auxiliary → English							English + Auxiliary → Auxiliary						
		Models	de	es	pt	uk	ru	ar	fa	de	es	pt	uk	ru	ar	fa
$Y_{general}$	Mono	NN (Avg)				50.7				53.1	70.0	57.2	80.9	59.3	64.4	66.6
		HNN (Avg)				70.0				67.9	82.5	70.5	86.8	77.4	79.0	76.6
		HAN (Att)				71.2				71.8	82.8	71.3	85.3	79.8	80.5	76.6
	Multi	MHAN-Enc	71.0	69.9	69.2	70.8	71.5	70.0	71.3	69.7	**82.9**	69.7	86.8	80.3	79.0	76.0
		MHAN-Att	**74.0**	**74.2**	**74.1**	**72.9**	**73.9**	**73.8**	**73.3**	**72.5**	82.5	70.8	**87.7**	80.5	**82.1**	76.3
		MHAN-Both	72.8	71.2	70.5	65.6	71.1	68.9	69.2	70.4	82.8	**71.6**	87.5	**80.8**	79.1	**77.1**
$Y_{specific}$	Mono	NN (Avg)				24.4				21.8	22.1	24.3	33.0	26.0	24.1	32.1
		HNN (Avg)				39.3				39.6	37.9	33.6	42.2	39.3	34.6	43.1
		HAN (Att)				43.4				44.8	46.3	41.9	46.4	45.8	41.2	49.4
	Multi	MHAN-Enc	45.4	45.9	44.3	41.1	42.1	44.9	41.0	43.9	46.2	39.3	47.4	45.0	37.9	48.6
		MHAN-Att	**46.3**	**46.0**	**45.9**	**45.6**	**46.4**	**46.4**	**46.1**	**46.5**	**46.7**	**43.3**	**47.9**	45.8	**41.3**	48.0
		MHAN-Both	45.7	45.6	41.5	41.2	45.6	44.6	43.0	45.9	46.4	40.3	46.3	**46.1**	40.7	**50.3**

Table 1: Full-resource classification performance (F_1) on general (top) and specific (bottom) topic categories using bilingual training with English as target (left) and the auxiliary language as target (right).

8 languages. Moreover, we found for instance that only 25-30% of the labels could be manually aligned between English and German. The commonalities are mainly concentrated on the most frequent labels, reflecting a shared top-level division of the news domain, but the long tail exhibits significant independence across languages.

6 Evaluation

6.1 Settings

We evaluate our multilingual models on full-resource and low-resource scenarios of multilingual document classification on the Deutsche Welle corpus. Following the typical evaluation protocol in the field, the corpus is split per language into 80% for training, 10% for validation and 10% for testing. We evaluate both type of labels (Y_g, Y_s) on a *full-resource scenario* and only the general topic labels (Y_g) on a *low-resource scenario*. We report the micro-averaged F1 scores for each test set, as in previous work (e.g., Hermann and Blunsom, 2014).

Model configuration. For all models, we use the aligned 40-dimensional multilingual embeddings pre-trained on the Leipzig corpus using multi-CCA from Ammar et al. (2016). The non-aligned embeddings used for comparison purposes are trained with the same method and data. We zero-pad documents up to a maximum of 30 words per sentence and 30 sentences per document. The hyper-parameters were selected on the validation sets. We made the following settings: 100-dimensional encoder and attention embeddings (at every level), relu activation function for all intermediate layers, batch size of 16, epoch size of 25k, and optimization using SGD with Adam until convergence.

All the hierarchical models have DENSE encoders in both scenarios (Tables 1, 4, and 5), and GRU and biGRU in the full-resource scenario for English+Arabic (Table 3). For the low-resource scenario, we define three levels of data availability: *tiny* from 0.1% to 0.5%, *small* from 1% to 5% and *medium* from 10% to 50% of the original training set. We report the average F_1 scores on the test set for each level based on discrete increments of 0.1, 1 and 10 percentage points respectively. The decision threshold for the value of p in Eq. 5 for the full-resource scenario is set to 0.4 for labels such that $|Y_s| < 400$ and 0.2 for $|Y_s| \geq 400$, and for the low-resource scenario it is 0.3 for all sets. For the *ensemble* in the low-resource setting, we train the three proposed multilingual models and choose the optimal one based on the validation data for each language respectively (see Fig. 4).

Baselines. We compare against the following monolingual neural networks, with shallow or hierarchical structures. These networks are based on the state of the art in the field, reviewed in Section 2, and thus represent strong baselines.

- **NN** : A neural network which feeds the average vector of the input words directly to a classification layer, as the common baseline for multilingual document classification (Klementiev et al., 2012).

- **HNN** : A hierarchical network with encoders and average pooling at every level, followed by a classification layer.

- **HAN**: A hierarchical network with encoders and attention, followed by a classification layer. This model is the one proposed by Yang et al. (2016) adapted to our task.

Our multilingual models with the three sharing

configurations from Section 4.1, are noted as *Enc*, *Att* and *Both*. Their implementation amounts to, first, creating a HAN model for each language, second, sharing components across multiple languages as illustrated in Fig. 3, and, third, training them with the objective of Eq. 8.

6.2 Results

Full-resource scenario. Table 1 displays the results of full-resource document classification using DENSE encoders for general and specific labels. On the left side, the performance on the English sub-corpus is shown when English and an auxiliary sub-corpus are used for training, and on the right side, the performance on the auxiliary sub-corpus is shown when that sub-corpus and the English sub-corpus are used for training.

The multilingual model trained on pairs of languages outperforms on average all the examined monolingual models, namely a bag-of-word neural model and two hierarchical neural models which use average pooling and attention respectively. The best-performing multilingual model bilingually on average is the one with shared attention across languages, especially when tested on English. The consistent gain for English as target could be attributed to the alignment of the word embeddings to English and to the many English labels, which makes it easier to find multilingual labels from which to transfer knowledge. Interestingly, this reveals that the transfer of knowledge across languages in a full-resource setting is maximized with language-specific word and sentence encoders, but language-independent (i.e. shared) attention for both words and sentences.

However, when transferring from English to Portuguese (en→pt), Russian (en→ru) and Persian (en→fa) on general categories, it is more effective to have only language-independent components. We hypothesize that this is due to the underlying commonness between the label sets rather than to a relationship between languages, which is hard to identify on linguistic grounds.

We will now quantify the impact of three important model choices on the performance: encoder type, word embeddings, and number of languages used for training. In Table 3, we observe that when we replace the DENSE encoder layers with GRU or biGRU layers, the improvement from the multilingual training is still present. In particular, the multilingual models with shared atten-

	Encoders	Mono	Multi		
	$Y_{general}$	HAN	Enc	Att	Both
ar→en	DENSE	71.2	70.0	**73.8**	68.9
ar→en	GRU	77.0	74.8	**77.5**	75.4
ar→en	biGRU	**77.7**	77.1	77.5	76.7
en→ar	DENSE	80.5	79.0	**82.1**	79.1
en→ar	GRU	81.5	81.2	**83.4**	83.1
en→ar	biGRU	82.2	82.7	**84.0**	83.0

Table 3: Full-resource classification performance (F_1) for English-Arabic with various encoders.

Word embeddings	$\|L\|$	$Y_{general}$		$Y_{specific}$	
		n_l	f_l	n_l	f_l
Aligned	1	50K –	77.41 –	90K –	44.90 –
Aligned	2	40K ↓	78.30 ↑	80K ↓	45.72 ↑
Aligned	8	32K ↓	77.91 ↑	72K↓	45.82 ↑
Non-aligned	8	32K ↓	71.23 ↓	72K ↓	33.41 ↓

Table 4: Average number of parameters per language (n_l), average F_1 per language (f_l), and their variation (arrows) with the number of languages $|L|$ and the word embeddings used for training.

tion are superior to alternatives, regardless of the employed encoders. For reference, using simply logistic regression with bag-of-words (counts) for classification leads to F_1 scores of 75.8% in English and 81.9% in Arabic, using many more parameters than biGRU: 56.5M vs. 410k in English and 5.8M vs. 364k in Arabic.

In Table 4, when we train our multilingual model (MHAN-att) on eight languages at the same time, the F_1 score improves on average across languages – for both types of labels, general or specific – while the number of parameters per language decrease, by 36% for $Y_{general}$ and 20% for $Y_{specific}$. Lastly, when we train the same model with word embeddings that are not aligned across languages, the performance of the multilingual model drops significantly. An input space that is aligned across languages is thus crucial.

Low-resource scenario. We assess the ability of the multilingual attention networks to transfer knowledge across languages in a low-resource scenario, i.e. training on a fraction of the available data, as defined in 6.1 above. The results for seven languages when trained jointly with English are displayed in detail in Table 5 and summarized in Figure 4. In all cases, at least one of the multilingual models outperforms the monolingual one, which demonstrates the usefulness of multilingual training for low-resource document classification.

Moreover, the improvements obtained from our multilingual models for lower levels of availabil-

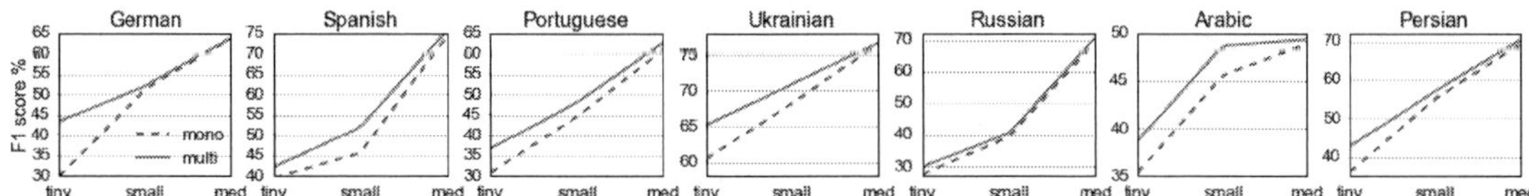

Figure 4: Low-resource document classification performance (F_1) of our *multilingual* attention network ensemble (blue lines) vs. a *monolingual* attention network (purple dashed lines) on the DW corpus.

	Size	Mono	Multi			
	$Y_{general}$	HAN	Enc	Att	Both	$\Delta\%$
en→de	0.1-0.5%	29.9	**41.0**	37.0	39.4	+37.2
	1-5%	51.3	51.7	49.7	**52.6**	+2.6
	10-50%	63.5	63.0	63.8	**63.8**	+0.5
en→es	0.1-0.5%	39.5	38.7	33.3	**41.5**	+4.9
	1-5%	45.6	45.5	**50.8**	50.1	+11.6
	10-50%	74.2	**75.7**	74.2	75.2	+2.0
en→pt	0.1-0.5%	30.9	25.3	31.6	**33.8**	+9.6
	1-5%	44.6	44.3	37.5	**47.3**	+6.0
	10-50%	60.9	61.9	62.1	**62.1**	+1.9
en→uk	0.1-0.5%	60.4	**62.4**	59.8	60.9	+3.1
	1-5%	68.2	67.7	**70.6**	69.0	+3.4
	10-50%	76.4	76.2	76.3	**76.7**	+0.3
en→ru	0.1-0.5%	27.6	26.6	27.0	**29.1**	+5.4
	1-5%	39.3	38.2	39.6	**40.2**	+2.2
	10-50%	69.2	**70.5**	70.4	69.4	+1.9
en→ar	0.1-0.5%	35.4	35.5	**39.5**	36.6	+11.7
	1-5%	45.6	**48.7**	47.2	46.6	+6.9
	10-50%	48.9	**52.2**	46.8	47.8	+6.8
en→fa	0.1-0.5%	36.0	35.6	33.6	**41.3**	+14.6
	1-5%	55.0	**55.6**	51.9	55.5	+1.0
	10-50%	69.2	**70.3**	70.1	70.0	+1.5

Table 5: Low-resource classification performance (F_1) with various sizes of training data.

ity (*tiny* and *small*) are larger than in higher levels (*medium*). This is also clearly observed in Figure 4 with our multilingual attention network ensemble, i.e. when we do model selection among the three multilingual variants on the development set. The best performing architecture in a majority of cases is the one which shares both the encoders and the attention mechanisms across languages. Moreover, this architecture also has the fewest number of parameters.

This promising finding for the low-resource scenario means that the classification performance can greatly benefit from the multilingual training (sharing encoders and attention) without increasing the number of parameters beyond that of a single monolingual document model. Nevertheless, in a few cases, we observe that the other architectures with increased complexity perform better than the "shared both" model. For instance, sharing encoders is superior to alternatives for Arabic language, i.e. the knowledge transfer benefits from shared word and sentence representations. Hence, to generalize to a large number of languages, we

may need to consider more dynamic models which are able to choose for each language individually which sharing scheme is the most appropriate for transferring from another language. Lastly, we did not generally observe a negative (or positive) correlation of the similarity between languages with the performance in the low-resource scenario, although the largest improvements were observed on languages more related to English (German, Spanish, Portuguese) than others (Arabic).

Overall, the above experiments pinpointed the most suitable multilingual sharing scheme (Figure 3) for each setting independently of the encoder type, rather than the optimal combination of sharing scheme and encoder. Therefore, as shown in Table 3, increasing the sophistication of the encoders (from DENSE to GRU to biGRU) is expected to further improve accuracy.

6.3 Qualitative Analysis

We analyze the performance of the multilingual model over the full range of labels, to observe on which type of labels it performs better than the monolingual model, and provide some qualitative examples. Figure 5 shows the cumulative true positive (TP) difference between the monolingual and multilingual models on the Arabic, German, Portuguese and Russian test sets, ordered by label frequency. We can observe that the cumulative TP difference of the multilingual model consistently increases as the frequencies of the labels decrease. This shows that labels across the entire range of frequencies benefit from joint training with English and not only a subset, for example only the highly frequent labels.

For example, the top 5 labels on which the multilingual model performed better than the monolingual one for en→de were: *russland* (21), *berlin* (19), *irak* (14), *wahlen* (13) and *nato* (13), while for the opposite direction those were: *germany* (259), *german* (97), *soccer* (73), *football* (47) and *merkel* (25). These topics are likely better covered in the respective auxiliary language which helps

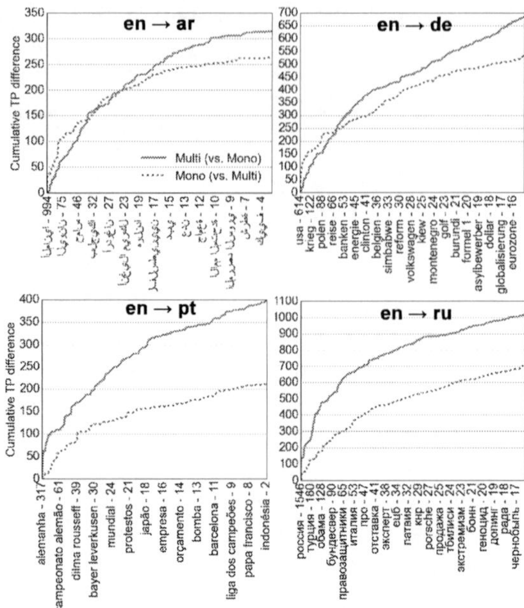

Figure 5: Cumulative true positive (TP) difference between *monolingual* and *multilingual* (ensemble) models for topic classification with *specific* labels, in the full resource scenario.

the multilingual model to better distinguish them in the target language as well. This is also observed in Figure 1 presented in the introduction, through an improved separation of topics using multilingual model vs. monolingual ones.

7 Conclusion

We proposed multilingual hierarchical attention networks for document classification and showed that they can benefit both full-resource and low-resource settings, while using fewer parameters than monolingual networks. In the former setting, the best option was to share only the attention mechanisms, while in the latter one, it was sharing the encoders along with the attention mechanisms. These results confirm the merits of language transfer, which is also an important component of human language learning (Odlin, 1989; Ringbom, 2007). Moreover, our study broadens the applicability of multilingual document classification, since our framework is not restricted to common label sets.

There are several future directions for this study. In their current form, our models cannot generalize to languages without any example, as attempted by Firat et al. (2016b) for neural machine

translation. This could be achieved by a classification layer independent of the size of the label set as in zero-shot classification (Qiao et al., 2016; Nam et al., 2016). Moreover, although we explored three distinct architectures, other configurations could be examined to improve document modeling, for example by sharing the attention mechanism at the sentence-level only. Lastly, the learning objective could be further constrained with sentence-level parallel information, to embed multilingual vectors of similar topics more closely together in the learned space.

Acknowledgments

We are grateful for the support from the European Union through its Horizon 2020 program in the SUMMA project n. 688139, see `http://www.summa-project.eu`. We would also like to thank Sebastião Miranda at Priberam for gathering the news articles from Deutsche Welle and the anonymous reviewers for their helpful suggestions. The second author contributed to the paper while at the Idiap Research Institute.

References

Rami Al-Rfou, Bryan Perozzi, and Steven Skiena. 2013. Polyglot: Distributed word representations for multilingual NLP. In *Proc. of the Seventeenth Conference on Computational Natural Language Learning*, Sofia, Bulgaria.

Waleed Ammar, George Mulcaire, Yulia Tsvetkov, Guillaume Lample, Chris Dyer, and Noah A. Smith. 2016. Massively multilingual word embeddings. *CoRR*, abs/1602.01925.

Dzmitry Bahdanau, Kyunghyun Cho, and Yoshua Bengio. 2015. Neural machine translation by jointly learning to align and translate. In *Proc. of the 5th International Conference on Learning Representations*, San Diego, CA, USA.

Léon Bottou. 1998. On-line learning and stochastic approximations. In David Saad, editor, *On-line Learning in Neural Networks*, pages 9–42. Cambridge University Press.

Sarath Chandar, Stanislas Lauly, Hugo Larochelle, Mitesh Khapra, Balaraman Ravindran, Vikas C. Raykar, and Amrita Saha. 2014. An autoencoder approach to learning bilingual word representations. In *Advances in Neural Information Processing Systems 27*, pages 1853–1861.

Jianshu Chen, Ji He, Yelong Shen, Lin Xiao, Xiaodong He, Jianfeng Gao, Xinying Song, and Li Deng.

2015. End-to-end learning of LDA by mirror-descent back propagation over a deep architecture. In *Advances in Neural Information Processing Systems 28*, pages 1765–1773, Montreal, Canada.

Kyunghyun Cho, Bart van Merrienboer, Caglar Gulcehre, Dzmitry Bahdanau, Fethi Bougares, Holger Schwenk, and Yoshua Bengio. 2014. Learning phrase representations using RNN encoder–decoder for statistical machine translation. In *Proc. of the Conference on Empirical Methods in Natural Language Processing*, pages 1724–1734, Doha, Qatar.

Misha Denil, Loris Bazzani, Hugo Larochelle, and Nando de Freitas. 2012. Learning where to attend with deep architectures for image tracking. *Neural Computation*, 24(8):2151–2184.

Manaal Faruqui and Chris Dyer. 2014. Improving vector space word representations using multilingual correlation. In *Proc. of the 14th Conference of the European Chapter of the Association for Computational Linguistics*, pages 462–471, Gothenburg, Sweden.

Daniel C. Ferreira, André F. T. Martins, and Mariana S. C. Almeida. 2016. Jointly learning to embed and predict with multiple languages. In *Proc. of the 54th Annual Meeting of the Association for Computational Linguistics (Volume 1: Long Papers)*, pages 2019–2028, Berlin, Germany.

Orhan Firat, Kyunghyun Cho, and Yoshua Bengio. 2016a. Multi-way, multilingual neural machine translation with a shared attention mechanism. In *Proc. of the 2016 Conference of the North American Chapter of the Association for Computational Linguistics: Human Language Technologies*, pages 866–875, San Diego, CA, USA.

Orhan Firat, Baskaran Sankaran, Yaser Al-Onaizan, Fatos T. Yarman Vural, and Kyunghyun Cho. 2016b. Zero-resource translation with multi-lingual neural machine translation. In *Proc. of the Conference on Empirical Methods in Natural Language Processing*, pages 268–277, Austin, Texas.

Stephan Gouws, Yoshua Bengio, and Gregory S. Corrado. 2015. BilBOWA: Fast bilingual distributed representations without word alignments. In *Proc. of the 32nd International Conference on Machine Learning*, pages 748–756, Lille, France.

Karl Moritz Hermann and Phil Blunsom. 2014. Multilingual models for compositional distributed semantics. In *Proc. of the 52nd Annual Meeting of the Association for Computational Linguistics*, pages 58–68, Baltimore, Maryland.

Karl Moritz Hermann, Tomáš Kočiský, Edward Grefenstette, Lasse Espeholt, Will Kay, Mustafa Suleyman, and Phil Blunsom. 2015. Teaching machines to read and comprehend. In *Proc. of the 28th International Conference on Neural Information Processing Systems*, NIPS'15, pages 1693–1701, Montreal, Canada.

Sepp Hochreiter and Jürgen Schmidhuber. 1997. Long short-term memory. In *Neural Computation*, volume 9 (8), pages 1735–1780. MIT Press.

Yangfeng Ji and Noah Smith. 2017. Neural discourse structure for text categorization. *CoRR*, abs/1702.01829.

Melvin Johnson, Mike Schuster, Quoc V. Le, Maxim Krikun, Yonghui Wu, Zhifeng Chen, Nikhil Thorat, Fernanda B. Viégas, Martin Wattenberg, Greg Corrado, Macduff Hughes, and Jeffrey Dean. 2016. Google's multilingual neural machine translation system: Enabling zero-shot translation. *CoRR*, abs/1611.04558.

Rie Johnson and Tong Zhang. 2015. Effective use of word order for text categorization with convolutional neural networks. In *Proc. of the 2015 Conference of the North American Chapter of the Association for Computational Linguistics: Human Language Technologies*, pages 103–112, Denver, Colorado.

Yoon Kim. 2014. Convolutional neural networks for sentence classification. In *Proc. of the Conference on Empirical Methods in Natural Language Processing*, pages 1746–1751, Doha, Qatar.

Diederik P. Kingma and Jimmy Lei Ba. 2014. Adam: A method for stochastic optimization. In *Proc. of the International Conference on Learning Representations*, Banff, Canada.

Alexandre Klementiev, Ivan Titov, and Binod Bhattarai. 2012. Inducing crosslingual distributed representations of words. In *Proc. of the International Conference on Computational Linguistics*, Bombay, India.

Ankit Kumar, Ozan Irsoy, Jonathan Su, James Bradbury, Robert English, Brian Pierce, Peter Ondruska, Ishaan Gulrajani, and Richard Socher. 2015. Ask me anything: Dynamic memory networks for natural language processing. In *Proc. of the 33rd International Conference on Machine Learning*, pages 334–343, New York City, NY, USA.

Siwei Lai, Liheng Xu, Kang Liu, and Jun Zhao. 2015. Recurrent convolutional neural networks for text classification. In *Proc. of the 29th AAAI Conference on Artificial Intelligence*, pages 2267–2273, Austin, Texas.

Hugo Larochelle and Geoffrey Hinton. 2010. Learning to combine foveal glimpses with a third-order Boltzmann machine. In *Proc. of the 23rd International Conference on Neural Information Processing Systems*, pages 1243–1251, Vancouver, Canada.

Quoc V. Le and Tomas Mikolov. 2014. Distributed representations of sentences and documents. In *Proc. of the 31st International Conference on Machine Learning*, pages 1188–1196, Beijing, China.

Rui Lin, Shujie Liu, Muyun Yang, Mu Li, Ming Zhou, and Sheng Li. 2015. Hierarchical recurrent neural network for document modeling. In *Proc. of the Conference on Empirical Methods in Natural Language Processing*, pages 899–907, Lisbon, Portugal.

Thang Luong, Hieu Pham, and Christopher D. Manning. 2015. Effective approaches to attention-based neural machine translation. In *Proc. of the Conference on Empirical Methods in Natural Language Processing*, pages 1412–1421, Lisbon, Portugal.

Laurens van der Maaten. 2009. Learning a parametric embedding by preserving local structure. In *Proc. of the 12th International Conference on Artificial Intelligence and Statistics*, pages 384–391, Clearwater Beach, FL, USA.

Tomas Mikolov, Kai Chen, Greg Corrado, and Jeffrey Dean. 2013. Efficient estimation of word representations in vector space. In *Proc. of the International Conference on Learning Representations*, Scottsdale, AZ, USA.

Volodymyr Mnih, Nicolas Heess, Alex Graves, and Koray Kavukcuoglu. 2014. Recurrent models of visual attention. *CoRR*, abs/1406.6247.

Jinseok Nam, Eneldo Loza Mencía, and Johannes Fürnkranz. 2016. All-in text: Learning document, label, and word representations jointly. In *Proc. of the 30th AAAI Conference on Artificial Intelligence*, pages 1948–1954, Phoenix, AR, USA.

Terence Odlin. 1989. Language transfer: Cross-linguistic influence in language learning. In *Cambridge Applied Linguistics*. Cambridge University Press.

Nikolaos Pappas and Andrei Popescu-Belis. 2014. Explaining the stars: Weighted multiple-instance learning for aspect-based sentiment analysis. In *Proc. of the Conference on Empirical Methods in Natural Language Processing*, pages 455–466, Doha, Qatar.

Nikolaos Pappas and Andrei Popescu-Belis. 2017. Explicit document modeling through weighted multiple-instance learning. *Journal of Artificial Intelligence Research*, pages 591–626.

Jeffrey Pennington, Richard Socher, and Christopher Manning. 2014. GloVe: Global vectors for word representation. In *Proc. of the Conference on Empirical Methods in Natural Language Processing*, pages 1532–1543, Doha, Qatar.

Ruizhi Qiao, Lingqiao Liu, Chunhua Shen, and Anton van den Hengel. 2016. Less is more: Zero-shot learning from online textual documents with noise suppression. In *Proc. of the IEEE Conference on Computer Vision and Pattern Recognition*, pages 2249–2257, Las Vegas, NV, USA.

Hakan Ringbom. 2007. *Cross-linguistic Similarity in Foreign Language Learning*. Second language acquisition series, vol. 21. Multilingual Matters, Clevedon, UK.

Alexander M. Rush, Sumit Chopra, and Jason Weston. 2015. A neural attention model for abstractive sentence summarization. In *Proc. of the Conference on Empirical Methods in Natural Language Processing*, pages 379–389, Lisbon, Portugal.

Duyu Tang, Bing Qin, and Ting Liu. 2015. Document modeling with gated recurrent neural network for sentiment classification. In *Empirical Methods on Natural Language Processing*, pages 1422–1432, Lisbon, Portugal.

Joseph Turian, Lev Ratinov, and Yoshua Bengio. 2010. Word representations: A simple and general method for semi-supervised learning. In *Proc. of the 48th Annual Meeting of the Association for Computational Linguistics*, pages 384–394, Uppsala, Sweden.

Zichao Yang, Diyi Yang, Chris Dyer, Xiaodong He, Alex Smola, and Eduard Hovy. 2016. Hierarchical attention networks for document classification. In *Proc. of the 2016 Conference of the North American Chapter of the Association for Computational Linguistics: Human Language Technologies*, pages 1480–1489, San Diego, CA, USA.

Ainur Yessenalina, Yisong Yue, and Claire Cardie. 2010. Multi-level structured models for document-level sentiment classification. In *Proc. of the Conference on Empirical Methods in Natural Language Processing*, pages 1046–1056, Cambridge, MA.

Wen-tau Yih, Kristina Toutanova, John C. Platt, and Christopher Meek. 2011. Learning discriminative projections for text similarity measures. In *Proc. of the 15th Conference on Computational Natural Language Learning*, pages 247–256, Portland, OR, USA.

Xiang Zhang, Junbo Zhao, and Yann LeCun. 2015. Character-level convolutional networks for text classification. In *Advances in Neural Information Processing Systems 28*, pages 649–657, Montreal, Canada.

Will Y. Zou, Richard Socher, Daniel Cer, and Christopher D. Manning. 2013. Bilingual word embeddings for phrase-based machine translation. In *Proc. of the Conference on Empirical Methods in Natural Language Processing*, pages 1393–1398, Seattle, WA, USA.

Roles and Success in Wikipedia Talk Pages:
Identifying Latent Patterns of Behavior

Keith Maki,   Michael Miller Yoder,   Yohan Jo and **Carolyn Penstein Rosé**
Language Technologies Institute
Carnegie Mellon University
Pittsburgh, PA, USA
`{kmaki,yoder,yohanj,cprose}@cs.cmu.edu`

Abstract

In this work we investigate how role-based behavior profiles of a Wikipedia editor, considered against the backdrop of roles taken up by other editors in discussions, predict the success of the editor at achieving an impact on the associated article. We first contribute a new public dataset including a task predicting the success of Wikipedia editors involved in discussion, measured by an operationalization of the lasting impact of their edits in the article. We then propose a probabilistic graphical model that advances earlier work inducing latent discussion roles using the light supervision of success in the negotiation task. We evaluate the performance of the model and interpret findings of roles and group configurations that lead to certain outcomes on Wikipedia.

1   Introduction

In this paper we explore the discussion strategies and configurations of conversational roles that allow Wikipedia editors to influence the content of articles. In so doing, we contribute both a new public dataset and proposed model that advance work towards induction of latent conversational roles using light supervision.

Online production communities like Wikipedia, an online encyclopedia which anyone can edit, have the potential to bring disparate perspectives together in producing a valuable public resource. Individual Wikipedia editors unavoidably carry their own perspectives; these voices can explicitly or subtly influence the jointly produced article content even when editors strive for neutrality[1].

This work explores the interaction between individual editors and the collaborative process that supervises the development of a Wikipedia article.

Wikipedia editors discuss article improvements, coordinate work and resolve disagreements on talk pages associated with each article (Ferschke, 2014). Pairing talk page discussions with simultaneous edits in shared content, we introduce a task predicting the success of a particular editor's article edits based on the corresponding discussion.

We propose a lightly supervised probabilistic graphical model of discussion roles and behaviors that offers advances over the prior discussion role modeling work of Yang et al. (2015), which employs a more restricted conceptualization of role taking. While the earlier model only allowed each role to be played by one editor, our extended model learns a distribution over roles for each editor. Furthermore, it can assign roles to an arbitrary number of editors rather than being restricted to a specific number.

This model allows the interpretation of configurations of roles that are conducive or detrimental to the success of individual editors. We find that the greatest success is achieved by detail-oriented editors working in cooperation with editors who play more abstract organizational roles.

2   Related Work

This work investigates influence in discussion as part of the collaborative editing process of Wikipedia, but achieving influence through discussion has also been studied in online environments other than Wikipedia. For example, other work in language technologies has studied the effectiveness of argumentative speech in changing others' minds (Tan et al., 2016) and revealing subgroups of users with similar attitudes (Hassan et al., 2012).

---

[1] `https://en.wikipedia.org/wiki/`
`Wikipedia:Neutral_point_of_view`

Proceedings of the The 8th International Joint Conference on Natural Language Processing, pages 1026–1035,
Taipei, Taiwan, November 27 – December 1, 2017 ©2017 AFNLP

Our work fits with research on editor behavior on Wikipedia, which is relatively well-studied on article pages and somewhat less studied on talk pages. Wikipedia has been a popular source of data for modeling social interaction and other issues of language behavior from multiple perspectives including collaboration (Ferschke et al., 2012), authority (Bender et al., 2011), influence (Bracewell et al., 2012; Swayamdipta and Rambow, 2012), and collegiality and adversity (Bracewell et al., 2012).

Much work analyzing behavior in Wikipedia has focused on types of edit behavior. Yang et al. (2016) use an LDA-based model to derive editor roles from edit behaviors. They then find correlations between certain editor roles and article quality improvements. Their approach differs from ours in that our model is supervised with an outcome measure and that we define editor roles based on talk page behavior.

Behavior in discussion can be characterized at multiple levels of granularity. Viégas et al. (2007) categorize talk page contributions into 11 classes, and find that the most common function of talk page behavior is to discuss edits to the corresponding article, but that requests for information, references to Wikipedia policies, and off-topic remarks are also commonly found. Bender et al. (2011) annotate authority claims and agreement in Wikipedia talk pages.

Above the level of individual contributions to discussion, the notion of a conversational role is relevant both for characterizing the rights and responsibilities an individual has within an interaction as well as the configuration of conversational behaviors the person is likely to engage in. Therefore, it is not surprising that prior work has revealed that the process of becoming a Wikipedia moderator is associated both with changes in language use and in the roles editors play on the talk pages (Danescu-Niculescu-Mizil et al., 2012).

Attempts have been made to understand roles Wikipedia editors play. Arazy et al. (2017) find self-organizing roles based on the edit behavior of thousands of editors. Editors frequently move in and out of those roles, but on the aggregate the proportions of these roles are relatively stable.

Our work is similar to that of Ferschke et al. (2015), who apply the role identification model of Yang et al. (2015) to Wikipedia talk page contributions. This model learns a predefined number of user roles, each of which is represented as weights on a set of user behaviors, and assigns the roles to the participants in each discussion. The roles are induced by rewarding latent role representations with high utility in selecting users whose behavior was highly predictive of the task outcome of article quality. We extend this work by predicting an outcome that is specific to one discussion participant, i.e. the editing success of a particular editor within an interaction. We also relax the constraint that every role must be assigned to a single participant and that each participant can take at most one role. Our model is thus more flexible in capturing more nuanced configurations of roles.

3 Data and Task

One of the contributions of this work is the creation of a new public dataset[2] and task for predicting the influence of editors in Wikipedia discussions. The dataset comprises 53,175 instances in which an editor interacts with one or more other editors in a talk page discussion and achieves a measured influence on the associated article page. In this section we detail the motivation for the conceptualization of the task as an influence prediction task, and the details for the construction of the dataset.

3.1 Task Conceptualization

Wikipedia talk pages are not stand-alone discussion forums. They are explicitly designed to support coordination in editing of their associated article pages. In order to extract task instances, we pair discussions with the record of concurrent edits to the associated article page.

Once a discussion has been paired with a sequence of edits, an assessment can be made for each editor who participated both in the discussion and in article edits of how successful that editor was in making changes to the article page. It is this assessment that forms the class value of our predictive task. In this study we explore negotiation strategies and role configurations that affect article editing; each data point in our task provides both discussion and an article edit success value for each editor involved.

---

[2]This dataset is available at `http://github.com/michaelmilleryoder/wikipedia-talk-scores`

3.2 Data Acquisition

To form our dataset, we extracted all versions (*revisions*) of English Wikipedia articles from 2004 to 2014 and removed much of the Mediawiki markup using the Java Wikipedia Library (JWPL) (Ferschke et al., 2011). The most recent revisions of talk pages corresponding to the articles were split into turns using paragraph boundaries and edit history. We grouped discussion posts under the same section headings as *discussion threads*.

We sampled 100,000 articles with talk page discussions and filtered to include discussion threads with 2 or more participants who made edits to the article page from 24 hours before the discussion began to 24 hours after the discussion ended. Discussion thread beginnings and endings are defined as the time of the first post and last post, respectively. Statistics on our discussion dataset can be seen in Table 1.

number of articles	7,211
number of discussion threads	21,108
number of editor-discussion pairs	53,175
average #editors/discussion	2.52

Table 1: Dataset statistics

3.3 Editor Success Scores

Editors frequently enter into talk page discussions to modify the article page in a particular way or challenge others' edits. We wish to quantify the success of editors on the article page as related to these goals on the talk page. In prior work, editor success has been measured with respect to the longevity of edits made to a page (Priedhorsky et al., 2007), and we take a similar approach. We define a success score y for each editor in a specific discussion. Intuitively, this measure is computed as the change in word frequency distribution associated with an editor's edits between the article revision prior to discussion and the article revision when the discussion ends. In particular, this score is the proportion of an editor's edits–words deleted and words added–that remain 1 day after the discussion ends. Note that this score only reflects changes in word frequencies and does not take word re-ordering into account.

Formally, we consider each edit e as a vector of word frequency changes, both positive (additions) and negative (deletions) for each word type, stopwords removed. For an example in English, an edit that changed one instance of *suggested* to *insinuated*, as well as adding *old* might be represented as {'suggested': -1, 'insinuated': +1, 'old': +1'}. For each edit e_i, let vector c_i be the changes in word frequencies from that edit to the final revision after the discussion. This change vector represents how many tokens that an editor deleted were put back and how many tokens the editor added were afterward deleted. Let $|e|$ be the number of tokens changed in that edit and $|c|$ be the total word frequency changes (deletions if tokens of the word were added in the edit, or vice versa) in those specific word types from the edit to the final revision. The score y of a particular Wikipedia editor u in thread t across edits $\{e_1, e_2, ..., e_n\}$ made by u in t is:

$$y(u, t) = 1 - \frac{\sum_{i=1}^{n} |c_i|}{\sum_{i=1}^{n} |e_i|}$$

Each editor's score is the proportion of tokens they changed that remain changed, so $s \in [0, 1]$.

The goal of this editor score is to capture the "ground truth" of an editor's influence on the article page. To validate this editor success measure, we sampled 20 conversations, read through the corresponding article edits by those editors, and made sure our automated editor success scores were reasonable compared with the success that editors seemed to achieve.

In our experiments, we aim to predict this editor success measure calculated from article revisions with behaviors and interactions simultaneously occurring on the talk page. This assumes that talk page discussions in our data are related to the simultaneous article edits that those same editors are doing. To validate that editors who were editing the article while having a discussion on the talk page simultaneously were talking about those simultaneous article edits, and not something else, we manually went through 20 conversations and simultaneous edits. Nineteen out of the 20 conversations directly related to simultaneous edits, and the only one not specifically about simultaneous edits related to similar content on the article page.

4 Model

We present a model which attempts to learn both discussion behaviors of the target editor (editor we are predicting the success of) and roles of other discussion participants that influence the success of a particular editor.

4.1 Role Modeling Task

The task of role modeling as described is to identify latent patterns of behavior in discourse which explain some conversational outcome measure. The learned roles can then be intuitively interpreted to better understand the nature of the discourse and the interactions between the participants with respect to the chosen outcome measure.

4.2 Prior Approach: Role Identification Model (RIM)

A similar task was explored by (Ferschke et al., 2015) and (Yang et al., 2015), who represented role modeling as a bipartite matching problem between participants and roles. More specifically, RIM learns conversational roles from discussion behaviors, supervised by discussion outcome. A role is defined as a weight vector over discussion behaviors, where the weights represent the positive or negative contribution of the behaviors toward outcome measures.

However, this approach suffers from several simplifying assumptions which reduce its applicability to realistic conversation settings:

1. All roles are present in every conversation.

2. Each role is played by exactly one editor.

3. Each editor plays exactly zero or one roles.

4. All behaviors from editors with a role contribute to the outcome metric under that role.

5. No behaviors from editors without a role contribute to the outcome metric.

The proposed approach addresses these limitations by using a probabilistic graphical model that encodes a more appropriate hierarchical structure for the task.

4.3 Probabilistic Role Profiling Model (PRPM)

For modeling roles in discourse, we propose a generative model shown in Figure 1, whose generative story is shown in Figure 2.

4.3.1 Inference

Appropriate values for the parameters η, β, and τ may be inferred from data, and represent the settings with which the data is best explained (i.e. has the highest likelihood) under the generative story.

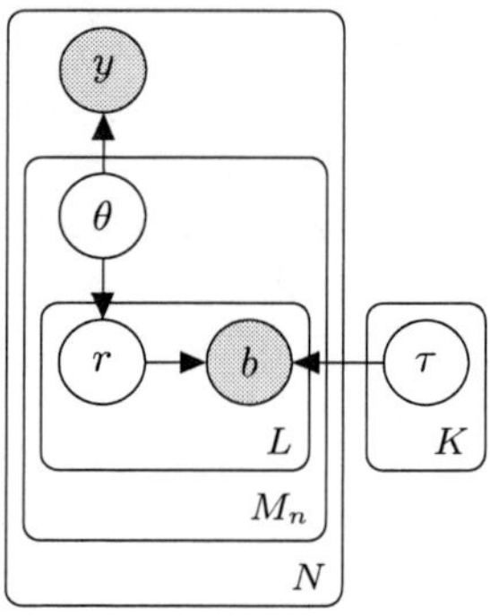

Figure 1: PRPM plate diagram relating for each conversation N the outcome measure y and each user M's L behaviors b.

- For each role $k \in \{1, \ldots, K\}$,
    - Draw behavior distribution $\tau_k \sim \mathrm{Dir}(\alpha)$.
- For each conversation $n \in \{1, \ldots, N\}$,
    - For each user $m \in \{1, \ldots, M\}$,
        * Observe user participation z_{nm}.
    - For each user $m \in M_n$, where $M_n = \{m | z_{nm} = 1\}$,
        * Draw role distribution $\theta_{nm} \sim \mathrm{Dir}(\gamma)$.
        * For each behavior $l \in \{1, \ldots, L\}$,
            · Draw role $r_{nml} \sim \mathrm{Multi}(\theta_{nm})$.
            · Draw behavior $b_{nml} \sim \mathrm{Multi}(\tau_{r_{nml}})$.
    - Draw outcome $y_n \sim \mathcal{N}(\mu_n, \sigma)$, where $\mu_n = \sum_m z_{nm} \theta_{nm} \cdot \beta$.

Figure 2: PRPM generative story

Computationally efficient methods for exact inference will not work for the proposed model due to the model structure, so approximate inference is used to estimate the parameter values.

We implement the model sampler using the JAGS framework (Plummer, 2003), which uses Gibbs sampling to generate dependent samples from the posterior distribution. These samples are used to obtain posterior mean estimates of the model parameters.

5 Features

5.1 Dialogue Act Features

We are interested in linguistic moves that characterize editors in conversation, and so we extract features that represent conversational acts. In particular, we extract dialogue act features from the model of Jo et al. (2017), an HMM-based unsupervised dialogue act identification method that has been found to usefully separate between content-related words that are relatively static across conversations and words more related to dialogue acts, which change over the course of discussion. These features were found to yield better performance with our model than unigrams with tf-idf selection.

The model of Jo et al. (2017) learns separate language models for dialogue acts (DA LMs) and topical content (content LMs), where each word can be generated from either type of language model. This structure helps the model identify content words that are consistent throughout a conversation and separate them out from language models for dialogue acts.

To identify dialogue acts on talk pages that may be related to conversational roles of interest, we ignore content-specific words by providing pre-trained content LMs trained using LDA over the content pages. Each conversation is provided with the topic distribution of the content page of the same article, and in the modified model, each word may come from a different content LM independently chosen from the provided distribution over content LMs.

5.2 Behavior Features

To be used in combination with roles, we extract general discussion features motivated by relevance in other work.

Along with a simple bag of words of each editor's talk contributions and the contributions of all other editors, we consider the following discussion features.

5.2.1 Position of the editor in a discussion.
- Number of editor turns
- Number of other editors' turns
- Whether the editor takes the first turn
- Whether the editor takes the last turn

5.2.2 Style characteristics.
Drawn from (Tan et al., 2016), these may reflect the style and state of editors.

- Number of definite/indefinite articles
- Number of singular/plural personal pronouns
- Examples: number of occurrences of "for example", "for instance", and "e.g."
- URLs: number of URLs that end with ".com", ".net", ".org", or ".edu"

- Questions: number of question marks that follow an alphabetic character

5.2.3 Authority claims.
Bender et al. (2011) define these authority claim categories annotate them in Wikipedia talk pages. For each word type in their annotated data, we calculated the pointwise mutual information for each category. In our data, we scored each sentence with the log sum of the word scores for each category.

The categories used are:

- Credentials: education or occupation
- Experiential: personal involvement
- Forum: policy or community norms
- External: outside authority, such as a book
- Social expectations: expected behavior of groups

5.2.4 Emotion expressed by editors.
For a simple measure of emotion, we use LIWC (Tausczik and Pennebaker, 2010).

- Counts of positive/negative emotion words

6 Experiments

We frame our task as a regression problem, predicting editor scores based on discussion behaviors of the target editor and the other editors. Our outcome measure is the editor success score of a single editor. Since there are multiple editors in a discussion, we have multiple instances per discussion.

We use root mean squared error (RMSE) between the true scores and the predicted scores as an evaluation metric. We hypothesize that in specifying our model with latent roles as mediators between the raw discussion data and the predictive task we can achieve a lower RMSE than from a baseline that takes only the behaviors into account, especially for conversations with a greater number of participants, for which there can be more interaction.

Furthermore, to the extent to which the proposed graphical model better captures a valid conceptualization of roles, we hypothesize that we can achieve a lower RMSE than the model of Yang et al. (2015). In this section we first specify the baselines used for comparison in our experiments, and then explain the testing process with our own model and experimental design.

6.1 Baselines

These two hypotheses suggests different baseline models. Our first hypothesis is that introducing a model with latent roles improves over simply using discussion features, and the second is that PRPM better captures interaction than the prior RIM model.

6.1.1 Linear Regression

The simplest baseline model allows us to evaluate the first hypothesis. This model assumes that the whole is not greater than its parts. In other words, it assumes that the sum total of positive impact the features can achieve on performance is just through their inclusion as separate features. For this baseline, we use a simple linear regression model. We bound the linear regression predictions to be between 0 and 1, the range of the editor scores. The full set of features in this model are included twice, once from the target editor in the discussion, and once from an aggregation across all non-target editors in the discussion.

6.1.2 RIM

We evaluate our model against RIM, introduced by Yang et al. (2015). RIM was originally applied to Wikipedia talk page discussions in Ferschke et al. (2015), who assigned a single success score to each page. In our work, for each discussion, we evaluate the success of each editor in each discussion thread separately. Since there is differential success between editors in the same interaction, the same interaction is associated with multiple different success measures. We handle this by slightly tweaking the original RIM model such that the first role is reserved exclusively for target editors, i.e., editors whose success measure is being evaluated. The other roles represent the roles of other editors in terms of their influence on the success of the target editor. Additionally, for conversations having fewer editors than the number of roles, we leave some of the roles unassigned by adding dummy editors whose behavior values are zero.

To predict the success measure of an editor for a test instance, RIM first assigns the learned roles to the editors. This process is identical to the training process, except that there is only the role assignment step without the weight adjustment step. Specifically, the first role is assigned to the target editor as in training, and the other roles are assigned according to the original model. Once the

roles are assigned, the predicted score is simply the sum over roles of the inner product of a role's weight vector and the behavior vector of the editor who is assigned the role.

6.2 PRPM

To infer role distributions for each editor in a test instance conversation, we first fix the model parameters to the estimates learned during the training phase. Gibbs sampling is then used to infer the non-target users' role distributions θ_m and the conversation outcome measure y over the unseen data. The role distributions for each non-target editor are then averaged together and concatenated with the target editor role distribution. Finally, a linear regressor is used analogously to the above baseline to evaluate the predictive power of the PRPM roles in aggregating the information from editor behavior features.

6.3 Experimental Design

In order to evaluate our approach and model, we split our data into a training set of 60%, a development set of 20% to train regression weights on the roles learned from the training set, and a test set of 20%.

For the original and proposed role identification models, we manipulated the number of latent roles the learned models were allowed to include.

7 Results and Discussion

Results from baselines and PRPM are presented in Table 2. We do not include scores with unigram tf-idf counts as features, as this decreases the performance of all models. The pattern of results is consistent with the hypotheses, i.e., role information and our model's configuration improves performance over both baselines.

First, the relatively high RMSE values indicate the challenging nature of this task. Talk page discussion is only one factor in editor success, and undoubtedly much interaction between editors comes from edit behavior, past interactions between editors, and even the short edit comments that editors leave about their edits. We were not able to find a comprehensive study of the effect of Wikipedia talk pages on article pages, but links from discussion features to outcomes in collaborative editing are often tenuous (Wen et al., 2016).

Our model performs slightly better than the linear regression baseline, though it performs

Model	Setting	2	3	4	5+	All
LinReg	tgt editor	**0.286**	**0.302**	**0.287**	0.302	0.292
LinReg	all	0.287	**0.302**	0.289	0.301	0.292
RIM	K=2	0.316	0.317	0.308	0.342	0.318
RIM	K=3	0.307	0.320	0.310	0.337	0.314
RIM	K=4	0.307	0.314	0.311	0.327	0.311
RIM	K=5	0.309	0.315	0.308	0.321	0.312
PRPM	K=2	**0.286**	**0.302**	0.288	0.297	0.292
PRPM	K=3	**0.286**	**0.302**	0.288	**0.295**	**0.291**
PRPM	K=4	**0.286**	**0.302**	0.289	**0.295**	**0.291**
PRPM	K=5	**0.286**	**0.302**	0.288	**0.295**	**0.291**

Table 2: RMSE for baselines and models. Rows are model settings. Scores are reported for different numbers of participants, which are the columns headings. (LinReg: editor uses only the target editor's features, and all uses all participants' features. RIM and PRPM: K is the number of roles.)

substantially better than the previously proposed RIM model. One advantage of our role-based model above the linear regression baseline is clear when looking at conversations with more editors (columns in Table 2 denote the number of discussion participants in analyzed conversations). This points to the utility of using role information with larger groups, when roles are likely more relevant.

Another advantage of PRPM over the linear regression baseline is that it allows interpretation of both target editor strategies and group dynamics that characterize the success or failure of a target editor. Where linear regression allows only the characterization of behaviors that make individual editors successful, PRPM captures roles in interaction with other roles in group conversation. In this way, PRPM allows a more full interpretation of group interaction.

7.1 PRPM Role Analysis

Our best-performing model classified editors into 5 different roles. We identified the combinations of roles that are predictive of editor success (or failure).

To assess roles, we examined the text and discussion features of editors who scored highly, as well as considered the weights assigned to each feature for each role. The relative frequencies of each behavior for each role are shown in Figure 3. A characteristic example discussion post for each role is given in Table 3. Each role is named and described qualitatively below.

Moderator. This role primarily helps discussion flow without getting too involved, perform-

ing and summarizing the results of administrative tasks. High probability dialogue act features for this role include asking questions of other editors and discussing itemized content. The moderator role is less likely than other roles to have success as a target editor and has the lowest target editor success when paired with other editors playing the moderator role.

Architect: This role is predominantly focused on page hierarchy, with the bulk of its probability focused on the page_format dialogue act, which is relevant to discussions of adding new page sections, merging, archiving, and creating new pages. The architect role is moderately likely to have success as a target editor.

Policy Wonk: This role is an knowledgeable Wikipedia user, frequently mentioning source accountability, fair use or copyright policy for images. Dialogue act features which have high probability for the policy wonk include appealing to Wikipedia policy and discussing engagement with other users on user talk pages. The policy wonk role is moderately unlikely to have success as a target editor.

Wordsmith: This role is predominantly concerned with the naming, creation, and wording of pages. Dialogue act features which have high probability for the wordsmith include discussing the spelling, pronunciation, or translation of words and phrases, as well as discussing the (re-)naming of new or existing pages or sections. The wordsmith role is strongly correlated with target editor success, especially when combined with the moderator or architect.

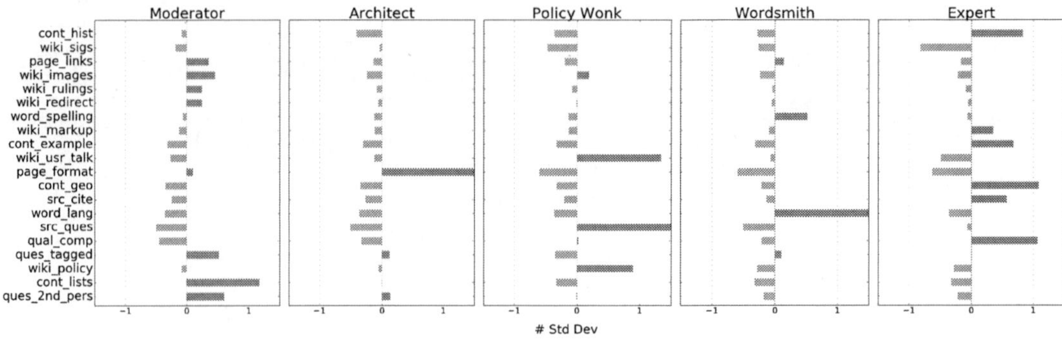

Figure 3: Behavior distributions for each role, expressed for each behavior as the number of standard deviations above the mean.

Role	Example post
Moderator	It was requested that this article be renamed but there was no consensus for it be moved.
Architect	I think a section in the article should be added about this.
Policy Wonk	The article needs more WP:RELIABLE sources.
Wordsmith	The name of the article should be ""Province of Toronto"" because that is the topic of the article.
Expert	There actually was no serious Entnazifizierung in East Germany.

Table 3: Examples of discussion posts from users in certain learned roles

Expert: This role is the most content-oriented role learned by our model. Dialogue act features which have high probability for the expert include making comparisons, discussing historical and geopolitical content, giving examples, and citing sources. The expert role is most strongly correlated with target editor success when combined with other users playing the expert role.

We find that the roles that lend themselves most strongly to target editor success (the Wordsmith and Expert) are more concrete edit-focused roles, while the roles associated with lower target editor success (the Moderator, Architect, and Policy Wonk) are more conceptual organizational roles. Note that it is not necessarily the case that editors that edit more frequently have higher scores. We find frequent editors across all roles.

Additionally, we find that configurations with multiple conceptual organizational roles lead to diminished outcomes for individual editors, suggesting that individual conceptual editors are unlikely to have their edits universally accepted. This could mean that talk page conversations that have multiple conceptual voices (which could be a measure of interesting discussion) are more likely to result in compromises or failure for a target editor. It is important to recognize that we are focusing on strategies and configurations of roles always in relation to the success of one editor; this editor score does not necessarily refer to a good, well-rounded discussion.

8 Conclusion and Future Work

The nature of collaboration on Wikipedia is still not fully understood, and we present a computational approach that models roles of talk page users with relation to success on article pages. We contribute both a new task with corresponding public dataset and a lightly-supervised graphical model for inducing role-based behavior profiles to predict the success of Wikipedia editors.

The proposed probabilistic graphical role model is unique in its structure of roles in relation to the outcome of one particular participant instead of group performance, and allows flexible mappings between roles and participants, assigning each participant a distribution over roles. The model we present retains one limitation of the RIM model, the assumption that editors in one conversation exist independently from those same editors in other conversations. Future work should address this.

Our model lends interpretability to combinations of talk page discussion roles. We find that detail-oriented roles are associated with success in combination with organizational roles, but that multiple participants taking organizational roles can lessen individual editing success.

We hope that this exploration into role-based discourse analysis will further enable systems to understand group interaction in text.

Acknowledgments

This work is supported in part by NSF GRFP Grant No. DGE1745016, NSF IIS STEM+C 1546393, NIH R01HL12263903, and by seedling funding from the Naval Research Lab.

References

Ofer Arazy, Johannes Daxenberger, Hila Lifshitz-Assaf, Oded Nov, and Iryna Gurevych. 2017. Turbulent Stability of Emergent Roles: The Dualistic Nature of Self-Organizing Knowledge Co-Production. *Information Systems Research*, page Forthcoming.

E.M. Bender, J.T. Morgan, Meghan Oxley, Mark Zachry, Brian Hutchinson, Alex Marin, Bin Zhang, and Mari Ostendorf. 2011. Annotating social acts: Authority claims and alignment moves in wikipedia talk pages. *Proceedings of the Workshop on Language in Social Media (LSM 2011)*, (June):48–57.

David B Bracewell, Marc T Tomlinson, Mary Brunson, Jesse Plymale, Jiajun Bracewell, and Daniel Boerger. 2012. Annotation of Adversarial and Collegial Social Actions in Discourse. *6th Linguistic Annotation Workshop*, (July):184–192.

C. Danescu-Niculescu-Mizil, L. Lee, B. Pang, and J. Kleinberg. 2012. Echoes of power: Language effects and power differences in social interaction. In *Proceedings of the 21st International Conference on World Wide Web*, pages 699–708, Lyon, France. ACM.

Oliver Ferschke. 2014. *The Quality of Content in Open Online Collaboration Platforms: Approaches to NLP-supported Information Quality Management in Wikipedia*. Ph.D. thesis, Technische Universität, Darmstadt.

Oliver Ferschke, Iryna Gurevych, and Yevgen Chebotar. 2012. Behind the Article: Recognizing Dialog Acts in Wikipedia Talk Pages. *Proceedings of the 13th Conference of the European Chapter of the Association for Computational Linguistics EACL 2012*.

Oliver Ferschke, Diyi Yang, and Carolyn P. Rosé. 2015. A Lightly Supervised Approach to Role Identification in Wikipedia Talk Page Discussions. (2009):43–47.

Oliver Ferschke, Torsten Zesch, and Iryna Gurevych. 2011. Wikipedia revision toolkit: Efficiently accessing wikipedia's edit history. In *Proceedings of the ACL-HLT 2011 System Demonstrations*, pages 97–102, Portland, Oregon. Association for Computational Linguistics.

Ahmed Hassan, A Abu-Jbara, and D Radev. 2012. Detecting subgroups in online discussions by modeling positive and negative relations among participants. In *Proceedings of the 2012 Joint Conference on Empirical Methods in Natural Language Processing and Computational Natural Language Learning*, July, pages 59–70.

Yohan Jo, Michael Miller Yoder, Hyeju Jang, and Carolyn P Rosé. 2017. Modeling Dialogue Acts with Content Word Filtering and Speaker Preferences. In *Proceedings of the 2017 Conference on Empirical Methods in Natural Language Processing*, September, pages 2169–2179.

Martyn Plummer. 2003. Jags: A program for analysis of bayesian graphical models using gibbs sampling.

Reid Priedhorsky, Jilin Chen, Shyong Tony K Lam, Katherine Panciera, Loren Terveen, and John Riedl. 2007. Creating, destroying, and restoring value in wikipedia. *Proceedings of the 2007 international ACM conference on Conference on supporting group work - GROUP '07*, page 259.

Swabha Swayamdipta and Owen Rambow. 2012. The pursuit of power and its manifestation in written dialog. *Proceedings - IEEE 6th International Conference on Semantic Computing, ICSC 2012*, pages 22–29.

Chenhao Tan, Vlad Niculae, Cristian Danescu-Niculescu-Mizil, and Lillian Lee. 2016. Winning Arguments: Interaction Dynamics and Persuasion Strategies in Good-faith Online Discussions. *Proceedings of WWW 2016*, pages 613–624.

Y. R. Tausczik and J. W. Pennebaker. 2010. The Psychological Meaning of Words: LIWC and Computerized Text Analysis Methods. *Journal of Language and Social Psychology*, 29(1):24–54.

Fernanda B. Viégas, Martin Wattenberg, Jesse Kriss, and Frank van Ham. 2007. Talk before you type: coordination in Wikipedia. *40th Hawaii International Conference on System Sciences*, 1:1–10.

Miaomiao Wen, Keith Maki, Xu Wang, Steven P Dow, James Herbsleb, and Carolyn Rose. 2016. Transactivity as a predictor of future collaborative knowledge integration in team-based learning in online courses. *Proceedings of the 9th International Conference on Educational Data Mining*.

Diyi Yang, Aaron Halfaker, Robert Kraut, and Eduard Hovy. 2016. Who Did What: Editor Role Identification in Wikipedia. *Proc. ICWSM*, pages 446–455.

Diyi Yang, Miaomiao Wen, and Carolyn Rosé. 2015.
Weakly Supervised Role Identification in Teamwork
Interactions. *Proceedings of the 53rd Annual Meeting of the Association for Computational Linguistics
and the 7th International Joint Conference on Natural Language Processing (Volume 1: Long Papers)*,
pages 1671–1680.

Author Index

Abdalla, Mohamed, 506
Abouelenien, Mohamed, 885
Abudukelimu, Halidanmu, 362
Allahyari, Mehdi, 316
Alva-Manchego, Fernando, 295
Arabnia, Hamid Reza, 316
Asahara, Masayuki, 404

Baldwin, Timothy, 555
Belinkov, Yonatan, 1, 142
Bethard, Steven, 90
Bhattacharya, Robin, 342
Bingel, Joachim, 295
Biran, Or, 306
Bisk, Yonatan, 100
Bless, Patrick, 947
Brad, Florin, 906
Brockett, Chris, 462, 605
Brychcín, Tomáš, 224

Cao, Yixin, 233
Cao, Ziqiang, 986
Carenini, Giuseppe, 615
Celikyilmaz, Asli, 733
Chambers, Nathanael, 843
Chen, Hsin-Hsi, 976
Chen, Kehai, 11
Chen, Yun-Nung, 733
Cheng, Gong, 316
Chi, Lianhua, 744
Chung, Jin-Woo, 865
Cohn, Trevor, 555, 744

D'hondt, Eva, 1006
Dai, Anna Mengdan, 885
Dalvi, Fahim, 1, 142
Das, Kollol, 576
Datla, Vivek, 895
Davenport, Quincy, 885
Demberg, Vera, 484
Dey, Kuntal, 525
Dias, Gaël, 926
Do, Quynh Ngoc Thi, 90
Dolan, Bill, 462, 605
Duan, Shaoyang, 352

Duh, Kevin, 832, 957, 996
Durrani, Nadir, 1, 142

Elliott, Desmond, 130
Erk, Katrin, 204

Falke, Tobias, 801
Farri, Oladimeji, 895
Ferracane, Elisa, 584
Ferret, Olivier, 273
Freedman, Marjorie, 674

Galley, Michel, 462, 605
Gan, Ling, 336
Gao, Jianfeng, 462, 605, 733, 957
Gao, Lei, 774
Gao, Yuze, 516
Ghaddar, Abbas, 413
Ghader, Hamidreza, 30
Ghosh, Shaona, 576
Glass, James, 1
Gong, Houyu, 336
Grau, Brigitte, 1006
Grouin, Cyril, 1006
Grundkiewicz, Roman, 120
Gurevych, Iryna, 801

Hardmeier, Christian, 173
Hasan, Sadid A., 895
Hasanuzzaman, Mohammed, 926
Hashimoto, Atsushi, 326
Hashimoto, Hayato, 326
Hazem, Amir, 685
He, Ruifang, 352
Hercig, Tomáš, 224
Hirst, Graeme, 506
Hockenmaier, Julia, 100
Hoshino, Chikara, 967
Hosu, Ionel Alexandru, 906
Hovy, Eduard, 59
Hsiao, Wei-Chuan, 976
Huang, Hen-Hsen, 976
Huang, Lifu, 854
Huang, Ruihong, 774
Huang, Shen, 184

Huy Tien, Nguyen, 644

Iacob, Radu Cristian Alexandru, 906
Inui, Kentaro, 473
Ishigaki, Tatsuya, 792
Ishii, Ai, 967

J Kurisinkel, Litton, 812
Jaidka, Kokil, 764
Ji, Heng, 362, 854
Jiang, Jing, 654
Jiang, Zhuolin, 674
Jimeno Yepes, Antonio, 566
Jin, Yiping, 545
Jo, Yohan, 1026
Johansson, Richard, 284
Joshi, Sachindra, 723
Judea, Alex, 822
Junczys-Dowmunt, Marcin, 120

Kádár, Ákos, 130
Kajiwara, Tomoyuki, 80
Kaneko, Masahiro, 40
Kato, Sachi, 404
Kawahara, Tatsuya, 704
Kelleher, John, 441
Klabjan, Diego, 947
Knight, Kevin, 362
Kobayashi, Mio, 967
Kobayashi, Sosuke, 473
Kochut, Krzysztof, 316
Komachi, Mamoru, 40, 80
Komatani, Kazunori, 243
Konkol, Michal, 224
Ku, Lun-Wei, 110
Kuppersmith, Alexis, 774

Lahiri, Shibamouli, 394
Lai, Alice, 100
Lakomkin, Egor, 423
Lang, Jun, 49
Langlais, Phillippe, 413
Lau, Jey Han, 744
Le, Phu, 545
Lee, Kathy, 895
Li, Chengjiang, 233, 875
Li, Juanzi, 233, 875
Li, Lihong, 733
Li, Sujian, 496, 634
Li, Wenjie, 986
Li, Xiujun, 733
Li, Yanran, 986
Li, Zhenghua, 49

Lin, Ying, 362
Ling, Yuan, 895
Lipton, Zachary C., 783
Liu, Fei, 555
Liu, Joey, 895
Liu, Luigi (Yu-Cheng), 694
Liu, Xiaodong, 957
Liu, Yuanchao, 713
Liu, Zhiyuan, 233
Lu, Di, 362
Luan, Yi, 605

Ma, Dehong, 634
Ma, Xuezhe, 59
MacKinlay, Andrew, 566
Madan, Dhiraj, 723
Magg, Sven, 423
Maki, Keith, 1026
Margolin, Drew, 754
Màrquez, Lluís, 1
Martinez, Ander, 21
Matsumoto, Yuji, 21, 264
Matsuzaki, Takuya, 967
McAuley, Julian, 783
McDowell, Bill, 843
McKeown, Kathleen, 306
Mehri, Shikib, 615
Meyer, Christian M., 801
Mihalcea, Rada, 394, 664, 885
Min, Bonan, 674
Minh Le, Nguyen, 644
Minker, Wolfgang, 915
Mishra, Abhijit, 525
Miyashita, Hiroshi, 967
Mochihashi, Daichi, 80
Moens, Marie-Francine, 90
Monz, Christof, 30
Mooney, Raymond, 584
Mori, Shinsuke, 326
Morin, Emmanuel, 685
Mostafazadeh, Nasrin, 462
Murawaki, Yugo, 451
Myaeng, Sung-Hyon, 214

Nagar, Seema, 525
Nakamura, Satoshi, 152, 431, 915
Nakayama, Hideki, 70
Neubig, Graham, 152
Newell, Edward, 754
Ng, Vincent, 594
Nguyen Le, An, 21
Nguyen, Huy-Thanh, 536

Nguyen, Minh-Le, 536
Ni, Jianmo, 783
Nieto Piña, Luis, 284
Nishida, Kyosuke, 937
Nishida, Noriki, 70
Niu, Shuzi, 986
Nivre, Joakim, 173
Nouvel, Damien, 694
Nykl, Michal, 224

Okazaki, Naoaki, 473
Okumura, Manabu, 792
Ororbia II, Alexander, 843

Paetzold, Gustavo, 295
Pan, Liangming, 875
Pan, Xiaoman, 362
Pappas, Nikolaos, 1015
Park, Jong C., 865
Park, Joohee, 214
Pérez-Rosas, Verónica, 885
Persing, Isaac, 594
Pinnis, Mārcis, 373
Popescu-Belis, Andrei, 1015
Potash, Peter, 342
Pouriyeh, Seyedamin, 316
Pragst, Louisa, 915

Qadir, Ashequl, 895

Rastogi, Pushpendre, 996
Rebedea, Traian, 906
Reitter, David, 843
Rieman, Daniel, 764
Roller, Stephen, 204
Rosé, Carolyn, 1026
Ross, Robert, 441
Roth, Benjamin, 624
Rubino, Raphael, 484
Rumshisky, Anna, 342
Ruppenhofer, Josef, 624
Ruths, Derek, 754

Sadamitsu, Kugatsu, 937
Saito, Itsumi, 937
Saito, Kuniko, 937
Sajjad, Hassan, 1, 142
Sakaizawa, Yuya, 40
Sakti, Sakriani, 431
Salton, Giancarlo, 441
Scarton, Carolina, 295
Schang, Ariane, 754
Schulder, Marc, 624

Schwartz, H. Andrew, 764
Shao, Yan, 173
Shen, Xiaoyu, 986
Shen, Yelong, 957
Shi, Jiaxin, 233
Shi, Wei, 484
Shindo, Hiroyuki, 264
Shroff, Gautam, 194
Skadina, Inguna, 373
Specia, Lucia, 295
Spithourakis, Georgios, 462
Strube, Michael, 822
Su, Hui, 986
Sumita, Eiichiro, 11
Sumita, Eiichro, 152
Sun, Xu, 184, 496, 634

Takamura, Hiroya, 792
Takeda, Ryu, 243
Tamilselvam, Srikanth, 525
Tang, Jie, 875
Teranishi, Hiroki, 264
Tiedemann, Jörg, 173
Tjandra, Andros, 431
Tomita, Junji, 937
Tran, Khoi-Nguyen, 744
Tran, Quan, 566

Ultes, Stefan, 915
Ungar, Lyle, 764
Ushiku, Atsushi, 326
Utiyama, Masao, 11, 152

Van Durme, Benjamin, 832, 996
Vanderwende, Lucy, 462
Varma, Vasudeva, 812
Vig, Lovekesh, 194
Vikram, Sharad, 783
Vishal, S, 194
Vogel, Stephan, 142
Vydiswaran, V.G.Vinod, 394

Wallace, Byron, 253
Wang, Baoxun, 713
Wang, Chunqi, 163
Wang, Houfeng, 184, 496, 634
Wang, Jianan, 713
Wang, Rui, 11
Wang, Su, 204, 584
Wang, Wei-Chung, 110
Wang, Xiaochen, 875
Wang, Xiaolong, 713
Wang, Xin, 713

Wang, Yining, 384
Wang, Yizhong, 496
Wang, Zhuoran, 713
Wanvarie, Dittaya, 545
Way, Andy, 926
Weber, Cornelius, 423
Weischedel, Ralph, 674
Wermter, Stefan, 423
White, Aaron Steven, 996
Wiegand, Michael, 624
Wilson, Steven, 664

Xia, Qingrong, 49
Xiao, Tong, 516
Xu, Bo, 163
Xue, Zhengshan, 384

Yadav, Mohit, 194
Yang, Jingfeng, 496
Yang, Wonsuk, 865
Yoder, Michael, 1026
Yoshimoto, Akifumi, 21
Yoshino, Koichiro, 915
You, Jinseon, 865
Yu, Dian, 854
Yu, Jianfei, 654
Yung, Frances, 484

Zhang, Boliang, 362
Zhang, Jiajun, 384
Zhang, Jingyi, 152
Zhang, Min, 49
Zhang, Sheng, 832
Zhang, Xiaodong, 634
Zhang, Ye, 253
Zhang, Yue, 49, 516, 812
Zhao, Tianyu, 704
Zhao, Tiejun, 11
Zhao, Wenli, 352
Zhao, Yang, 384
Zhu, Xiaofeng, 947
Zong, Chengqing, 384

Association for Computational Linguistics
209 N. Eighth Street
Stroudsburg, Pennsylvania 18360

ISBN 978-1-5108-5292-1